HBR'S 10 MUST READS

On Communication

HBR's 10 Must Reads series is the definitive collection of ideas and best practices for aspiring and experienced leaders alike. These books offer essential reading selected from the pages of *Harvard Business Review* on topics critical to the success of every manager.

Titles include:

HBR's 10 Must Reads on Change Management
HBR's 10 Must Reads on Collaboration
HBR's 10 Must Reads on Communication
HBR's 10 Must Reads on Innovation
HBR's 10 Must Reads on Leadership
HBR's 10 Must Reads on Making Smart Decisions
HBR's 10 Must Reads on Managing People
HBR's 10 Must Reads on Managing Yourself
HBR's 10 Must Reads on Strategic Marketing
HBR's 10 Must Reads on Strategy
HBR's 10 Must Reads on Teams
HBR's 10 Must Reads: The Essentials

HBR'S 10 MUST READS

On Communication

HARVARD BUSINESS REVIEW PRESS
Boston, Massachusetts

Printed in the United States of America
28 27 26 25 24 23 22

The web addresses referenced in this book were live and correct at the time of the book's publication but may be subject to change.

Library of Congress Cataloging-in-Publication Data

HBR's 10 must reads on communication.
p. cm.
Includes index.
ISBN 978-1-4221-8986-3 (alk. paper)
1. Business communication. 2. Communication in management. 3. Interpersonal communication. I. Harvard business review. II. Title: HBR's ten must reads on communication. III. Title: Harvard business review's 10 must reads on communication.

HF5718.H34 2013
658.4'5—dc23 2012037908

ISBN: 9781422189863
eISBN: 9781422191514

The paper used in this publication meets the requirements of the American National Standard for Permanence of Paper for Publications and Documents in Libraries and Archives z39.48-1992.

Contents

HBR'S 10 MUST READS

On Communication

Change the Way You Persuade

by Gary A. Williams and Robert B. Miller

IT'S HAPPENED TO YOU BEFORE. You call a meeting to try to convince your boss and peers that your company needs to make an important move—for instance, funding a risky but promising venture. Your argument is impassioned, your logic unassailable, your data bulletproof. Two weeks later, though, you learn that your brilliant proposal has been tabled. What went wrong?

All too often, people make the mistake of focusing too much on the content of their argument and not enough on how they deliver that message. Indeed, far too many decisions go the wrong way because information is presented ineffectively. In our experience, people can vastly improve their chances of having their proposals succeed by determining who the chief decision maker is among the executives they are trying to persuade and then tailoring their arguments to that business leader's decision-making style.

Specifically, we have found that executives typically fall into one of five decision-making categories: *Charismatics* can be initially exuberant about a new idea or proposal but will yield a final decision based on a balanced set of information. *Thinkers* can exhibit contradictory points of view within a single meeting and need to cautiously work through all the options before coming to a decision. *Skeptics* remain highly suspicious of data that don't fit with their worldview and make decisions based on their gut feelings. *Followers* make decisions based on how other trusted executives, or they themselves, have made similar decisions in the past. And *controllers* focus on the pure facts and analytics of a decision because of their own fears and uncertainties.

The five styles span a wide range of behaviors and characteristics. Controllers, for instance, have a strong aversion to risk; charismatics tend to seek it out. Despite such differences, people frequently use a one-size-fits-all approach when trying to convince their bosses, peers, and staff. They argue their case to a thinker the same way they would to a skeptic. Instead, managers should tailor their presentations to the executives they are trying to persuade, using the right buzzwords to deliver the appropriate information in the most effective sequence and format. After all, Bill Gates does not make decisions in the same way that Larry Ellison does. And knowing that can make a huge difference.

Five Approaches

Executives make it to the senior level largely because they are effective decision makers. Learning mostly from experience, they build a set of criteria that guides them. Each decision is influenced by both reason and emotion, but the weight given to each of these elements during the decision-making process can vary widely depending on the person.

In a two-year project, we studied the decision-making styles of more than 1,600 executives across a wide range of industries. Our work focused on how those people made purchasing decisions, but we contend that the results have broader applicability to decision making in general. We interviewed participants about various facets of their decision-making processes. For instance, how strong was their desire to have others educate them about the issues involved in a particular decision? How willing were they to move beyond the status quo? How much risk were they comfortable with in making the decision? These characteristics and preferences are often set early in a businessperson's career and evolve based on experience. In other words, people have a natural tendency toward a certain style of decision making that gets reinforced through successes—or that changes after repeated failures.

Idea in Brief

You call a meeting to try to convince your boss that your company needs to make an important move. Your argument is impassioned, your logic unassailable, your data bulletproof. Two weeks later, though, you learn that your brilliant proposal has been tabled. What went wrong? It's likely the proposal wasn't appropriately geared toward your boss's decision-making style, say consultants Gary Williams and Robert Miller. Over the course of several years' research, the authors have found that executives have a default style of decision making developed early in their careers. That style is reinforced through repeated successes or changed after several failures. Typically, the authors say, executives fall into one of five categories of decision-making styles: Charismatics are intrigued by new ideas, but experience has taught them to make decisions based on balanced information, not just on emotions. Thinkers are risk-averse and need as much data as possible before coming to decisions. Skeptics are suspicious of data that don't fit their worldview and, thus, make decisions based on their gut feelings. Followers make decisions based on how other trusted executives, or they themselves, have made similar decisions in the past. And controllers focus on the facts and analytics of decisions because of their own fears and uncertainties. But most business presentations aren't designed to acknowledge these different styles—to their detriment. In this article, the authors describe the various subtleties of the five decision-making styles and how best to persuade executives from each group. Knowing executives' preferences for hearing or seeing certain types of information at specific stages in their decision-making process can substantially improve your ability to tip the outcome in your favor, the authors conclude.

Our research should not be confused with standard personality tests and indicators like Myers-Briggs. Our framework is simply a categorization of how people tend to make decisions. Of course, people do not always make decisions in the same way; much depends on the situation they're in. But our research has shown that when it comes to making tough, high-stakes choices that involve many complex considerations and serious consequences, people tend to resort to a single, dominant style. Call it a default mode of decision making.

The Idea in Practice

Five Decision-Making Styles

Consider this fictional scenario: Sales and Marketing VP Mary Flood knows her company must become more customer focused. She recommends decentralizing her operations into regional account teams—but needs her CEO's support. Here's how she'd argue her case, *depending* on her CEO's decision-making style.

Style	Decision-Maker's Characteristics	Persuader's Strategy	Examples
CHARISMATIC Lee Iacocca, Herb Kelleher	Easily enthralled, but bases final decisions on balanced information Emphasizes bottom-line results	Focus on results. Make straight-forward arguments. Stress proposal's benefits with visual aids. Use buzzwords: **proven, actions, easy, clear.**	Diagrams current organization and problems, proposed restructuring and benefits—especially improved competitiveness. Explains potential challenges (resistance to staff relocation) and risk of inaction (losing largest customers). Provides detailed reports for CEO to review post-presentation.
THINKER Michael Dell, Bill Gates	Toughest to persuade Cerebral, logical Risk-averse Needs extensive detail	Present market research, customer surveys, case studies, cost/benefit analyses. Use buzzwords: **quality, numbers, expert, proof.**	Presents three different options in detail in first meeting. Explains data-gathering methods. Presents case studies of similar restructurings. Uses second meeting to fill argument gaps and recommend optimum plan. Waits weeks, months for CEO's decision.

In this article, we describe each of the five decision-making styles in detail. This information is intended to be neither exhaustive nor definitive, and most executives will exhibit only some of the traits we list. Nevertheless, knowing the general characteristics of the different styles can help you better tailor your presentations and arguments to your audience. Unfortunately, many people fail in this regard. In our experience, more than half of all sales presentations are mismatched to the decision maker's style. Specifically, close to

SKEPTIC Larry Ellison, Tom Siebel	Challenges every data point Decides based on gut feelings	Establish credibility with endorsements from someone the CEO trusts. Use buzzwords: **grasp, power, suspect, trust.**	Co-presents with trusted COO. Emphasizes information sources' credibility. Strokes CEO's ego ("You've probably seen this case study . . . "). Grounds arguments in real world.
FOLLOWER Peter Coors, Carly Fiorina	Relies on own or others' past decisions to make current choices Late adopter	Use testimonials to prove low risk. Present innovative, yet proven, solutions. Use buzzwords: **expertise, similar to, innovate, previous.**	Highlights case studies from other industries, but notes, "We could be the first in our industry to do this." Omits failed restructurings (though retains information in case CEO requests it). Presents three restructuring options. Uses multiple references to steer CEO toward her preferred choice; emphasizes option's affordability.
CONTROLLER Ross Perot, Martha Stewart	Unemotional, analytical Abhors uncertainty Only implements own ideas	Present highly structured arguments. Make listener "own" the idea. Avoid aggressive advocacy. Use buzzwords: **facts, reason, power, just do it.**	Over several months, continually sends CEO customer reports, marketing studies, financial projections. Emphasizes data highlighting company's problems. Identifies data contradictions, letting CEO analyze them. Waits for CEO to request meeting after large customer defects.

80% of all sales presentations focus on skeptics and controllers, but those two groups accounted for just 28% of the executives we surveyed.

To investigate the various subtleties of the five decision-making styles, we present the following hypothetical situation. In each of the subsequent sections devoted to explaining the categories, we will use this tale to demonstrate how our fictional protagonist should best argue her case to her CEO.

Five Styles of Decision Making—and the Ways to Influence Each

***IN OUR RESEARCH, WE FOUND** that executives typically have a default style of decision making that lands them in one of five distinct categories: charismatics, thinkers, skeptics, followers, and controllers.*

From January 1999 to June 2001, we and our colleagues at Miller-Williams surveyed 1,684 executives to study their decision-making processes. The participants were from a range of industries (including automotive, retail, and high tech) and were interviewed by e-mail, in person, or over the telephone. The participants described their decision-making tendencies for our researchers—for instance, how long it took them to make a decision; their willingness to make a choice that might have negative consequences; their desire for others to educate them about the issues involved; and so on.

We performed a cluster analysis of these data and found that the executives' behaviors fell into the five groupings described below. The accuracy of the survey results reported in this article—for example, that 25% of the executives we interviewed were charismatics—is plus or minus 2.9%. For many of the prominent CEO examples cited, the categorizations are based on our firsthand observations and experiences with those executives; other categorizations are based on secondary sources, including media accounts.

	Charismatics	Thinkers	Skeptics	Followers	Controllers
Description	Charismatics account for 25% of all the executives we polled. They are easily intrigued and enthralled by new ideas, but experience has taught them to make final decisions based on balanced information, not just emotions.	Thinkers account for 11% of the executives we surveyed and can be the toughest executives to persuade. They are impressed with arguments that are supported by data. They tend to have a strong aversion to risk and can be slow to make a decision.	Skeptics account for 19% of the executives we polled. They tend to be highly suspicious of every data point presented, especially any information that challenges their worldview. They often have an aggressive, almost combative style and are usually described as take-charge people.	Followers account for 36% of all the executives we surveyed. They make decisions based on how they've made similar choices in the past or on how other trusted executives have made them. They tend to be risk-averse.	Controllers account for 9% of the executives we interviewed. They abhor uncertainty and ambiguity, and they will focus on the pure facts and analytics of an argument.

Typical Characteristics	enthusiastic, captivating, talkative, dominant	cerebral, intelligent, logical, academic	demanding, disruptive, disagreeable, rebellious	responsible, cautious, brand-driven, bargain-conscious	logical, unemotional, sensible, detail-oriented, accurate, analytical
Prominent Examples	Richard Branson, Lee Iacocca, Herb Kelleher	Michael Dell, Bill Gates, Katharine Graham	Steve Case, Larry Ellison, Tom Siebel	Peter Coors, Douglas Daft, Carly Fiorina	Jacques Nasser, Ross Perot, Martha Stewart
Buzzwords to Use	results, proven, actions, show, watch, easy, clear, focus	quality, academic, think, numbers, intelligent, plan, expert, proof	feel, grasp, power, action, suspect, trust, demand, disrupt	innovate, expedite, expertise, similar to, previous	details, facts, reason, logic, power, handle, physical, grab, just do it
Bottom Line	When trying to persuade a charismatic, fight the urge to join in his excitement. Focus the discussion on results. Make simple and straightforward arguments, and use visual aids to stress the features and benefits of your proposal.	Have lots of data ready. Thinkers need as much information as possible, including all pertinent market research, customer surveys, case studies, cost-benefit analyses, and so on. They want to understand all perspectives of a given situation.	You need as much credibility as you can garner. If you haven't established enough clout with a skeptic, you need to find a way to have it transferred to you prior to or during the meeting—for example, by gaining an endorsement from someone the skeptic trusts.	Followers tend to focus on proven methods; references and testimonials are big persuading factors. They need to feel certain that they are making the right decision—specifically, that others have succeeded in similar initiatives.	Your argument needs to be structured and credible. The controller wants details, but only if presented by an expert. Don't be too aggressive in pushing your proposal. Often, your best bet is to simply give him the information he needs and hope that he will convince himself.

MaxPro is a leading manufacturer of office equipment, including printers, photocopiers, and fax machines. The company has a centralized structure, with the bulk of its marketing and sales operations located at corporate headquarters. Mary Flood, the executive vice president of sales and marketing, knows she must restructure her operations to become more customer focused. Specifically, she needs to form major-account teams at the regional level instead of at the corporate level. All national accounts and targeted marketing would be based in one of five regions (Northeast, Southeast, Midwest, Southwest, and West), each run by a different vice president. In Flood's plan, account executives for MaxPro's major customers (clients with revenues over $50 million) would relocate near the headquarters of those companies and would report directly to their respective regional VP. Each region would have its own marketing team and distribution channels, leaving corporate marketing responsible just for brand development. Flood needs to persuade George Nolan, MaxPro's CEO, to approve these changes.

1. Charismatics

Charismatics (25% of all the executives we interviewed) are easily enthralled by new ideas. They can absorb large amounts of information rapidly, and they tend to process the world visually.

They want to move quickly from the big idea to the specifics—especially those details regarding implementation. Charismatics are often described as enthusiastic, captivating, talkative, dominant, and persistent. They are risk-seeking yet responsible individuals. They are impressed with intelligence and facts and not usually given to self-absorption and compulsiveness. Prominent examples of charismatics include Richard Branson, Lee Iacocca, Herb Kelleher, and Oprah Winfrey. (Note that many of the categorizations of the executives we cite in this article are based on our firsthand observations and experiences with them. Some are based on secondary sources, including media accounts.)

Although charismatics may show great exuberance for a new idea, getting a final commitment from them can be difficult. They've learned from experience—particularly from the bad decisions they've made—to temper their initial enthusiasm with a good dose of reality. They seek out facts to support their emotions, and if such data can't be found, they will quickly lose their enthusiasm for an idea. Furthermore, charismatics prefer arguments that are tied directly to bottom-line results and are particularly keen on proposals that will make their company more competitive. They are rarely convinced by one-sided arguments that lack a strong orientation toward results. At the end of the day, charismatics make their final decisions very methodically, and the decisions are based on balanced information.

When trying to persuade a charismatic, you need to fight the urge to join in his excitement. One approach is to slightly undersell the parts of your proposal that pique his interest. In other words, you should be prepared to merely acknowledge the items that he greets with enthusiasm and discuss the risks of each of those things. This will ground your proposal in reality and strengthen his confidence and trust in you. You also need to keep the discussion focused on results. Your arguments must be simple and straightforward, and you should use visual aids to stress the features and benefits of your proposal. If you don't provide this results-oriented information (even when it's not asked for), you risk that the charismatic will not have it later when he needs it. Furthermore, you should be very honest and up-front about the risks involved with accepting your proposal, while also delineating the measures that can help minimize those risks. If you try to conceal any potential downsides, you can be sure that the charismatic will discover them later—when you're not available to address any concerns he may have.

All executives are busy people, but the attention span of a charismatic can be particularly short. In a meeting, you need to start with the most critical information. Otherwise, you risk losing his attention if you take your time leading up to a crucial point. Even if you have a two-hour meeting scheduled, you might not get through your entire presentation. Charismatics disdain canned arguments and will often interrupt you to get to the bottom line. Indeed, charismatics prefer highly interactive meetings; at times, they will want to move around the room and take control of the discussion.

Although charismatics might appear to be independent thinkers, they often rely on other high-profile executives in the company when making major decisions. Addressing this tendency will help increase your chances of success. Also critical will be your quiet perseverance: Charismatics expect you to wait patiently for them to make a decision, which could take some time, even though their initial enthusiasm may have led you to believe otherwise. Buzzwords that can help hold a charismatic's interest include: results, proven, actions, show, watch, look, bright, easy, clear, and focus.

Persuasion in practice: Nolan the charismatic

Flood has scheduled an hour-long meeting with Nolan and the other members of the senior executive committee to discuss her proposed reorganization. Before that day, she previews her recommendations with COO Jack Warniers, Nolan's most trusted lieutenant. Warniers has several concerns about the restructuring, which Flood addresses and resolves through follow-up memos and e-mails.

Flood has prepared a few charts for the meeting, but these are merely for her own reference. Because she wants Nolan to feel like he can steer the discussion any which way, she will modify the charts in her head as necessary and redraw the information on a white board. Flood also knows that Nolan will at some point need all the details of the implementation—most of this information won't be discussed in the meeting—so she prepares a full report that she will give him afterward.

Flood starts her presentation by drawing a diagram that shows the current organization and its problems. Then she immediately jumps into her recommendations with a chart that outlines the new structure and how it will solve those problems.

She emphasizes how the reorganization will increase MaxPro's overall competitiveness. "The restructuring," she says, "will help us to better focus on our customers, and the result will be fewer defections, particularly among our important accounts." She delineates how the reorganization will help propel MaxPro ahead of the competition.

Flood's ideas initially appeal to Nolan, who likes bold, out-of-the-box solutions, and he starts talking about the new restructuring as if it's already been accomplished. To keep him grounded, Flood outlines the potential impact of the new structure. Specifically, she notes the cost of relocating staff and the strong possibility that the change will meet fierce resistance from several groups, including the IT division, which would be responsible for supporting a large number of employees in remote locations.

Next, Flood presents a detailed risk assessment of the implementation—what will happen if the reorganization fails and the steps the company can take to minimize those risks. This information is as much for Nolan as it is for the others in the company who will be charged with implementing the plan. She then talks about the risk of doing nothing by highlighting evidence that at least three of MaxPro's major customers are already considering switching to a competitor because they are dissatisfied with MaxPro's customer service.

Knowing that the charismatic Nolan will want to move forward quickly, Flood ends her presentation by asking what their next steps should be. Nolan requests a detailed schedule, with milestone dates, of how the reorganization might progress. "I thought you might be interested in that information," she says, "so I've included it in this report, along with supporting data from the research we've conducted so far, case studies of similar reorganizations at other companies, and other pertinent facts. In particular, you might want to look at the section on risk assessment." Flood also tells Nolan that there are two versions of the report: an executive summary and an in-depth analysis. That night, on a red-eye flight to the East Coast, Nolan starts thinking about Flood's proposal and begins wondering how the restructuring will affect MaxPro's biggest customers. He turns to her report and finds that information in the table "Impact on Our Ten Largest Customers."

2. Thinkers

Thinkers (11% of the executives we interviewed) are the most difficult decision makers to understand and consequently the toughest to persuade.

They are often described as cerebral, intelligent, logical, and academic. Typically, they are voracious readers and selective about the words they use. They are impressed with arguments that are quantitative and supported by data. Not usually known for their social skills, thinkers tend to guard their emotions. They have two strong visceral desires in business—to anticipate change and to win—and they often pride themselves on their ability to outthink and outmaneuver the competition. They are driven more by the need to retain control than by the need to innovate. Prominent examples include Michael Dell, Bill Gates, Katharine Graham, and Alan Greenspan.

Thinkers have a strong desire for comparative data, which can make it difficult to persuade them. To make a decision, they need as much information as possible, including all pertinent market research, customer surveys, case studies, cost-benefit analyses, and so on. Perhaps the single-most important piece of information thinkers need is the presenter's methodology for getting from point A to point B. They strive to understand all perspectives of a given situation. And, unlike charismatics, thinkers have a strong aversion to risk.

When trying to persuade thinkers, your best approach is to openly communicate your worries and concerns about your proposal, because thinkers work best when they know the risks up front. Often they will ask a battery of questions to explore and understand all the risks associated with an option. Thinkers can be swayed when the arguments and presentation appeal directly to their intelligence. Interestingly, their thought process is very selective but not always completely methodical. They will, for instance, sometimes circumvent their own decision-making processes if they feel a bargain—a relatively low-risk opportunity to save time or money—is in their best interest.

Thinkers will never forget a bad experience, so you need to make sure that your recommendations to them are truly the best options. (Of course, you should do this for any of the five types of decision makers, but particularly so with thinkers.) And anyway, thinkers will eventually figure out for themselves whether something was truly the best alternative, so you might be better off refraining from drawing conclusions for them. Otherwise you'll risk being seen as too helpful and potentially not credible. One effective strategy for persuading thinkers is to give them ample time and space to come to their own conclusions.

In a meeting, thinkers will often take contradictory points of view. This can be extremely confusing, but remember that thinkers do not like to show their cards up front, so expect that you may not be able to discern how they feel about any of the options you present. In fact, thinkers often do not reveal their intentions until they render their final decisions. Furthermore, they can be self-absorbed, so be prepared for silence as they digest the information you've given them. Buzzwords and phrases that will capture a thinker's attention include: quality, academic, think, numbers, makes sense, intelligent, plan, expert, competition, and proof.

Persuasion in practice: Nolan the thinker

To convince Nolan, Flood knows she must present as many data, facts, and figures as possible, so her strategy is to deliver that information in huge chunks over a long-enough period of time for him to absorb and make sense of everything. Consequently, she decides that her best approach is to present her argument over the course of two meetings.

In the first, she begins by making her best case for why MaxPro needs to restructure. She emphasizes that if things stay the same,

MaxPro will likely lose customers to competitors. (Interestingly, this piece of information—the risk of doing nothing—would be one of the last things she would present to Nolan if he were a charismatic. In fact, the order of presentation to a thinker is almost exactly the reverse order of presentation to a charismatic.)

Flood then explains how she arrived at the three options she has proposed for the restructuring. She details the methodology she used to gather and assess the data, and Nolan is quick to point out where she may have missed certain steps or made incorrect assumptions. This will benefit Flood in the long run, because Nolan is now taking ownership of her methodology.

Next, Flood highlights the pros and cons of each option, and she presents case studies of similar restructurings, including those from other industries and from different time periods. The case studies represent roughly an equal number of successes and failures. Flood points out why each was successful or why each failed, and from that she begins to write on a white board a list of reorganizing dos and don'ts, to which Nolan is quick to add his input.

Throughout her presentation, Flood is undaunted by Nolan's barrage of questions. She knows it's not a personal attack; it's an attack on her process or data. Flood is very up-front about where her data might be inconclusive or conflicting, where she's made assumptions using just her intuition, and areas where her argument is weak. Together, she and Nolan pick through the presentation. For one risk assessment that Flood has weighted as 60-40, for example, Nolan says it should be 50–50.

At the end of the first meeting, Flood draws up a to-do list that indicates where she needs to plug in more data or fill in gaps in her argument before the next meeting; Nolan helps her prioritize the list. In several instances, however, he says, "Well, I don't think we can get good data here, so let's just go by gut feel."

During the second meeting, Flood briefly summarizes what they discussed previously—with all the corrections and adjustments that Nolan has requested. Knowing that he hates surprises, she clearly points out anything new and different from the first presentation—for example, revised data. Next, using the updated information, she explains how she arrived at the optimum restructuring that maximizes the probability of success while keeping risks to an acceptable level. In conclusion, she shows the projected financial costs and additional revenues that the change will likely generate. After the meeting, Flood is prepared to wait weeks, if not months, for Nolan's decision.

3. Skeptics

Skeptics (19% of the executives we polled) are highly suspicious of every single data point, especially any information that challenges their worldview.

Perhaps the most defining trait of skeptics is that they tend to have very strong personalities. They can be demanding, disruptive, disagreeable, rebellious, and even antisocial. They may have an aggressive, almost combative style and are usually described as take-charge people. They tend to be self-absorbed and act primarily on their feelings. Prominent examples include Steve Case, Larry Ellison, and Tom Siebel.

During your presentation, a skeptic may get up and leave temporarily, take a phone call, or even carry on a side conversation for an extended period of time. He will be demanding of both your time and energy, locking horns with you whenever the opportunity arises. The thinker launches a volley of questions, and it is not personal; with a skeptic, it is. Do not let it get to you; just go through your presentation coolly and logically. The good news is that you will know almost immediately where you stand with skeptics. You can almost always depend on them to tell you what they are thinking because of their strong personalities.

To persuade a skeptic, you need as much credibility as you can garner. Skeptics tend to trust people who are similar to them—for instance, people who went to the same college or worked for the same companies. If you haven't established credibility with a skeptic, you need to find a way to have it transferred to you prior to or during the meeting—for example, by gaining an endorsement from someone the skeptic trusts. Doing this will let the skeptic maintain his superior position while allowing you to openly discuss issues on his level. Credibility can be transferred (from a colleague, for instance), but ultimately it must be earned, and you may have to go through some very aggressive questioning to establish it.

Challenging a skeptic is risky and must be handled delicately. Sometimes, to make your case, you will need to correct bad information that the skeptic is relying on. If, for instance, the skeptic states incorrectly that your company's R&D costs have been spiraling out of control recently, you might reply, "Are you testing me? Because I remember you telling me a couple months ago that we need to spend more to regain our leadership in developing innovative products. But maybe that's changed?" In other words, when you need to correct a skeptic, give him room to save face. For him to trust you, he needs to maintain his reputation and ego. And remember that skeptics do not like being helped; they prefer having people think they know something already.

Although persuading a skeptic might sound daunting, the process is actually very straightforward. Skeptics want to move forward with groundbreaking ideas, but they first need to make sure that those ideas are from people they fully trust. Skeptics usually make decisions quickly—within days, if not right on the spot. Buzzwords to use with a skeptic include: feel, grasp, power, action, suspect, trust, agreeable, demand, and disrupt.

Persuasion in practice: Nolan the skeptic

Flood knows that she lacks the necessary clout to make her pitch directly to Nolan. So she enlists the aid of COO Jack Warniers, whom Nolan trusts. After she obtains Warniers's buy-in, she asks him to copresent the idea with her, hoping that his credibility will add to hers. They agree beforehand that Warniers will deliver all key messages, including the proposed restructuring and any data that might be controversial.

At the meeting, Flood and Warniers make their arguments in roughly the same order they would if Nolan were a thinker instead of a skeptic, but they emphasize the credibility of all their information sources. Flood knows that Nolan needs to hear things from multiple reputable sources—the more the better. So when discussing a recent marketing survey, she says, "I took the liberty of arranging a call between you and several other local market-research experts to discuss these results in greater detail." Whenever Nolan challenges anything, Flood and Warniers work quickly to ease his discomfort. Knowing that Nolan respects Bill Gates, for example, Flood softens one of Nolan's attacks by saying, "I see your point, but you probably remember that Microsoft made a similar move about two years ago."

At every turn, Flood and Warniers are careful to tread lightly around Nolan's ego. When discussing the case studies, for instance, they introduce each one by saying, "You've probably seen this before . . ." or "As you know, Hewlett-Packard failed in a similar restructuring because. . . ." For each example, Flood and Warniers are quick to point out whether the company's image and reputation were enhanced or degraded as a result of the restructuring.

Because Nolan is particularly skeptical of anything abstract, Flood and Warniers are careful to make their arguments as concrete as possible, usually by grounding them in the real world. When they talk about relocating 200 employees, for example, they try to include the specifics: "We would need to close our building here on Hunter Avenue and sublease the space, including the adjacent parking lot. Because the building has a modular, funky layout, we might consider turning it into a business incubator."

At the end of their presentation, Flood and Warniers appeal to Nolan's rebellious streak by stating how the proposed reorganization would buck the trend in their industry. They also are quick to credit Nolan for inspiring the idea. "At the last meeting of the senior executive committee," Warniers says, "you talked about how we needed to ensure that we didn't lose touch with our customers. Your comment started us thinking about this restructuring." Flood and Warniers end their presentation with their proposed action plan for the reorganization, complete with a schedule of milestones. At that point, Nolan takes charge of the discussion.

4. Followers

Followers (36% of the executives we interviewed) make decisions based on how they've made similar choices in the past or on how other trusted executives have made them.

Because they are afraid of making the wrong choice, followers will seldom be early adopters. Instead, they trust in known brands and in bargains, both of which represent less risk. They are also very good at seeing the world through other people's eyes. Interestingly, despite their cautiousness, followers can be spontaneous at times. Above all, though, they are responsible decision makers, which is why they are most often found in large corporations. In fact, followers account for more than a third of all the executives we surveyed, representing the largest group among the five types of decision makers. Prominent examples include Peter Coors, Douglas Daft, and Carly Fiorina.

Followers may engage you in long lists of issues and repeatedly challenge your position (similar to what a skeptic does), but don't be fooled. In the end, they will agree to something only if they've seen it done elsewhere. But followers won't admit this. In fact, they will seldom concede that they are followers; they would much rather have you believe that they are innovative and forward thinking. Frequently, followers are mistaken for skeptics. However, followers are not inherently suspicious; they prefer that you help them gain a better grasp of what they don't understand. And although followers may exhibit a take-charge approach, they will yield when challenged. (As a general rule, people who are difficult to classify into a decision-making style are usually followers, because people in the other four groups tend to show their characteristics more definitively.)

Although followers are often the most difficult to identify, they can be the easiest to persuade—if you know which buttons to push. To obtain buy-in from a follower, you need to make him feel confident about deciding to move in a certain direction by proving that others have succeeded on that path. Not surprisingly, followers tend to focus on proven methods, and references and testimonials are big persuading factors.

With a follower, don't try to sell yourself unless you have a strong track record of success. Instead, look for past decisions by the follower that support your views or find similar decisions by other executives the follower trusts. Ideally, followers want solutions that are innovative yet proven, new but trusted, leading-edge yet somewhat safe. At the end of the day, though, what followers need most is to know that they won't lose their jobs. This is why they rarely make out-of-the-box decisions. In fact, for some followers, the only way to persuade them to adopt a truly bold strategy is to get someone else to do it successfully first. Buzzwords and phrases to use with a follower include: innovate, expedite, swift, bright, just like before, expertise, similar to, previous, what works, and old way.

Persuasion in practice: Nolan the follower

Flood knows that her mission is simple: She must make Nolan feel comfortable that the decision to restructure has minimal risk. And to seal the deal, she must somehow also make him feel that he is being innovative.

In the meeting, Flood presents her arguments in roughly the same order that she would if Nolan were a thinker or skeptic. But because Nolan is a follower, Flood emphasizes the case studies—eight of them in all. This discussion resonates with Nolan because, like all followers, he is particularly adept at placing himself in others' shoes. As part of her strategy, Flood has decided to omit any examples of failed restructurings—but she has that information on hand, just in case Nolan asks for it. The eight case studies are from industries outside of MaxPro's business so that Flood can appeal to Nolan's desire to be innovative by saying, "We could be the first in our industry to do this kind of restructuring."

Next, Flood presents three options for the proposed restructuring, and she links each of her case studies to one of those options. To steer Nolan toward option three, which she prefers, she has linked four of the cases to that option; by contrast, she has provided Nolan with only two case study references for each of the other two options. When Nolan notes that option one is the cheapest, Flood is ready to address that issue head-on because she knows how bargain conscious he is: Her detailed analysis shows that, on a risk-adjusted basis, option three is actually the least expensive because it is more proven.

Presenting three options to Nolan does more than just give him the opportunity to make a choice; it also affords him the chance to be creative. He begins to combine aspects of options one and three—something Flood had anticipated he would do. In fact, she has even encouraged him to do so by presenting certain minor components of the different options individually. For Nolan, the ability to mix and match different parts of proven strategies is perfect: It makes him feel innovative without having to incur any major risk.

At the conclusion of the meeting, Flood further plays on Nolan's desire for both innovation and security by saying, "Yes, other companies have done this type of restructuring, but we will have more expertise implementing it, so we will do it faster and more cheaply. And because we already know what works and what doesn't, we'll be able to take the appropriate steps to avoid potential problems."

Flood understands that followers will maintain the status quo unless they're presented with information they can't afford to ignore. Because Nolan seems genuinely engrossed in hearing how the other companies have successfully reorganized, Flood expects she will hear from him within days. (Followers tend to act quickly once they see big potential for success with minimal risk.)

5. Controllers

Controllers (9% of the executives we surveyed) abhor uncertainty and ambiguity, and they will focus on the pure facts and analytics of an argument. They are both constrained and driven by their own fears and insecurities.

They are usually described as logical, unemotional, sensible, detail oriented, accurate, analytical, and objective. Like skeptics, controllers often have strong personalities and can even be overbearing. In their minds, they are the best salespeople, the best marketing experts, the best strategists, and so on. Whereas followers are good at putting themselves in others' shoes, controllers see things only from their own perspectives and will frequently make snap judgments and remarks that alienate others. Controllers can be loners and are often self-absorbed, traits that lead them to make unilateral decisions. Indeed, although a controller may talk to others about a decision, he will seldom genuinely listen to them or consider their input. Prominent examples include Jacques Nasser, Ross Perot, and Martha Stewart.

When dealing with controllers, you need to overcome their internal fears, which they will pretend they don't have. In fact, they will cover them up by paying an inordinate amount of attention to the intricate details of processes and methods. Dealing with controllers can be like playing a game of cat and mouse—you will always be chasing down some information at their request.

In a meeting, remember that controllers can be self-absorbed, so be prepared for long silences during your interactions. It is also crucial to remember that when cornered, controllers rarely capitulate. Furthermore, even though controllers seek accuracy and facts, that does not necessarily mean they will make intelligent, rational decisions. Often, a controller will jump to illogical conclusions. And unlike charismatics, who are willing to take responsibility for their decisions, controllers try to avoid being held accountable. When something goes wrong, they assume others are at fault.

To persuade controllers, your argument needs to be structured, linear, and credible. They want details, but only if presented by an expert. In practice, the only way to sell an idea to controllers is not to sell it; instead, let them make the choice to buy. Your best bet is to simply supply them with the information they need and hope they will convince themselves.

Although controllers and skeptics share several characteristics, a key difference is that controllers need ample time to make decisions (they hate to be rushed). By contrast, skeptics are much quicker on the draw. One of the worst things you can do with a controller is to push your proposal too aggressively. When that happens, controllers are likely to see you as part of the problem and not the solution. Buzzwords and phrases to use with a controller include: details, facts, reason, logic, power, handle, physical, grab, keep them honest, make them pay, and just do it.

Persuasion in practice: Nolan the controller

Nolan is notorious for implementing only his own ideas, so Flood knows she must somehow make him take ownership of her proposed restructuring plan. To do that, she gears herself up for the long journey ahead. Over the course of several months, she continually sends him information—customer reports, marketing studies, financial projections, and so on—through all types of media (including print, video, and the Web) and in person. She needs to gently wear down his defenses by steadily supplying him with so much information that he simply has to make a decision.

First, Flood focuses on data that highlight MaxPro's problems because she knows that case studies and other information won't be as important to him. Her memos often prompt Nolan to request other information, sometimes arcane and irrelevant data. She gets this for him, knowing full well that he may not even look at it.

After four months she is tempted to schedule a formal presentation, but she resists the urge. Nolan himself must request that meeting. Until that time, she will have to be content with sending him still more information. When she does, she always provides the information in a structured, linear format. In a typical memo, she begins by writing, "Attached, please find the results from a recent customer survey, and here's how they fit in with the other material we have." Flood is also quick to point out (but not resolve) apparent contradictions in the data, knowing that Nolan prides himself in uncovering those kinds of inconsistencies. In one memo, she writes, "Here's some new research from Walker Consulting. It seems to contradict the study we commissioned last year. I'm not sure which to trust."

Finally, an event—the defection of one of MaxPro's largest customers—triggers action. Thanks to Flood's patient but incessant prodding, Nolan is sensitized to this latest development. He calls a meeting of the senior staff to discuss what MaxPro should do. Included will be a discussion of a possible reorganization.

Critics might view some of our categorizations as derogatory—after all, few executives would like being classified as followers or controllers. We do not intend to imply that any decision-making style is superior to another; our labels are merely brief descriptors of the primary behavior of each group. In fact, each style can be highly effective in certain environments. Followers, for instance, have a high sense of responsibility and can be excellent leaders at large, established corporations. And controllers can be extremely effective business leaders; Martha Stewart is a case in point.

Furthermore, we do not mean to oversimplify the complex and often mysterious ways in which people reach conclusions. To be sure, decision making is a complicated, multifaceted process that researchers may never fully unpick. That said, we strongly believe that executives tend to make important decisions in predictable ways. And knowing their preferences for hearing or seeing certain types of information at specific stages in their decision-making process can substantially improve your ability to tip the outcome your way.

Originally published in May 2002. Reprint R0205D

Harnessing the Science of Persuasion

by Robert B. Cialdini

A LUCKY FEW HAVE IT; most of us do not. A handful of gifted "naturals" simply know how to capture an audience, sway the undecided, and convert the opposition. Watching these masters of persuasion work their magic is at once impressive and frustrating. What's impressive is not just the easy way they use charisma and eloquence to convince others to do as they ask. It's also how eager those others are to do what's requested of them, as if the persuasion itself were a favor they couldn't wait to repay.

The frustrating part of the experience is that these born persuaders are often unable to account for their remarkable skill or pass it on to others. Their way with people is an art, and artists as a rule are far better at doing than at explaining. Most of them can't offer much help to those of us who possess no more than the ordinary quotient of charisma and eloquence but who still have to wrestle with leadership's fundamental challenge: getting things done through others. That challenge is painfully familiar to corporate executives, who every day have to figure out how to motivate and direct a highly individualistic work force. Playing the "Because I'm the boss" card is out. Even if it weren't demeaning and demoralizing for all concerned, it would be out of place in a world where cross-functional teams, joint ventures, and intercompany partnerships have blurred the lines of authority. In such an environment, persuasion skills exert far greater influence over others' behavior than formal power structures do.

Which brings us back to where we started. Persuasion skills may be more necessary than ever, but how can executives acquire them if the most talented practitioners can't pass them along? By looking to science. For the past five decades, behavioral scientists have conducted experiments that shed considerable light on the way certain interactions lead people to concede, comply, or change. This research shows that persuasion works by appealing to a limited set of deeply rooted human drives and needs, and it does so in predictable ways. Persuasion, in other words, is governed by basic principles that can be taught, learned, and applied. By mastering these principles, executives can bring scientific rigor to the business of securing consensus, cutting deals, and winning concessions. In the pages that follow, I describe six fundamental principles of persuasion and suggest a few ways that executives can apply them in their own organizations.

The Principle of Liking

People like those who like them.

The application

Uncover real similarities and offer genuine praise.

The retailing phenomenon known as the Tupperware party is a vivid illustration of this principle in action. The demonstration party for Tupperware products is hosted by an individual, almost always a woman, who invites to her home an array of friends, neighbors, and relatives. The guests' affection for their hostess predisposes them to buy from her, a dynamic that was confirmed by a 1990 study of purchase decisions made at demonstration parties. The researchers, Jonathan Frenzen and Harry Davis, writing in the *Journal of Consumer Research,* found that the guests' fondness for their hostess weighed twice as heavily in their purchase decisions as their regard for the products they bought. So when guests at a Tupperware party

Idea in Brief

If leadership, at its most basic, consists of getting things done through others, then persuasion is one of the leader's essential tools. Many executives have assumed that this tool is beyond their grasp, available only to the charismatic and the eloquent. Over the past several decades, though, experimental psychologists have learned which methods reliably lead people to concede, comply, or change. Their research shows that persuasion is governed by several principles that can be taught and applied. The first principle is that people are more likely to follow someone who is similar to them than someone who is not. Wise managers, then, enlist peers to help make their cases. Second, people are more willing to cooperate with those who are not only like them but who like them, as well. So it's worth the time to uncover real similarities and offer genuine praise. Third, experiments confirm the intuitive truth that people tend to treat you the way you treat them. It's sound policy to do a favor before seeking one. Fourth, individuals are more likely to keep promises they make voluntarily and explicitly. The message for managers here is to get commitments in writing. Fifth, studies show that people really do defer to experts. So before they attempt to exert influence, executives should take pains to establish their own expertise and not assume that it's self-evident. Finally, people want more of a commodity when it's scarce; it follows, then, that exclusive information is more persuasive than widely available data. By mastering these principles—and, the author stresses, using them judiciously and ethically—executives can learn the elusive art of capturing an audience, swaying the undecided, and converting the opposition.

buy something, they aren't just buying to please themselves. They're buying to please their hostess as well.

What's true at Tupperware parties is true for business in general: If you want to influence people, win friends. How? Controlled research has identified several factors that reliably increase liking, but two stand out as especially compelling—similarity and praise. Similarity literally draws people together. In one experiment, reported in a 1968 article in the *Journal of Personality,* participants stood physically closer to one another after learning that they shared political beliefs and social values. And in a 1963 article in *American Behavioral Scientists,* researcher F. B. Evans used demographic data from insurance

The Idea in Practice

Persuasion Principles

Principle	Example	Business Application
LIKING: People like those like them, who like them.	At Tupperware parties, guests' fondness for their host influences purchase decisions twice as much as regard for the products.	**To influence people, win friends,** through: *Similarity*: Create *early* bonds with new peers, bosses, and direct reports by informally discovering common interests—you'll establish goodwill and trustworthiness. *Praise*: Charm *and* disarm. Make positive remarks about others—you'll generate more willing compliance.
RECIPROCITY: People repay in kind.	When the Disabled American Veterans enclosed free personalized address labels in donation-request envelops, response rate doubled.	**Give what you want to receive.** Lend a staff member to a colleague who needs help; you'll get *his* help later.
SOCIAL PROOF: People follow the lead of similar others.	More New York City residents tried returning a lost wallet after learning that other New Yorkers had tried.	**Use peer power** to influence horizontally, not vertically; e.g., ask an esteemed "old timer" to support your new initiative if other veterans resist.

company records to demonstrate that prospects were more willing to purchase a policy from a salesperson who was akin to them in age, religion, politics, or even cigarette-smoking habits.

Managers can use similarities to create bonds with a recent hire, the head of another department, or even a new boss. Informal conversations during the workday create an ideal opportunity to discover at least one common area of enjoyment, be it a hobby, a college basketball team, or reruns of *Seinfeld*. The important thing is to establish the bond early because it creates a presumption of goodwill and trustworthiness in every subsequent encounter. It's much easier

CONSISTENCY: People fulfill written, public, and voluntary commitments.	92% of residents of an apartment complex who signed a petition supporting a new recreation center later donated money to the cause.	**Make others' commitments active, public, and voluntary.** If you supervise an employee who should submit reports on time, get that understanding in writing (a memo); make the commitment public (note colleagues' agreement with the memo); and link the commitment to the employee's values (the impact of timely reports on team spirit).
AUTHORITY: People defer to experts who provide shortcuts to decisions requiring specialized information.	A single *New York Times* expert-opinion news story aired on TV generates a 4% shift in U.S. public opinion.	**Don't assume your expertise is self-evident.** Instead, establish your expertise *before* doing business with new colleagues or partners; e.g., in conversations before an important meeting, describe how you solved a problem similar to the one on the agenda.
SCARCITY: People value what's scarce.	Wholesale beef buyers' orders jumped 600% when they alone received information on a possible beef shortage.	**Use exclusive information to persuade.** Influence and rivet key players' attention by saying, for example: ". . . Just got this information today. It won't be distributed until next week."

to build support for a new project when the people you're trying to persuade are already inclined in your favor.

Praise, the other reliable generator of affection, both charms and disarms. Sometimes the praise doesn't even have to be merited. Researchers at the University of North Carolina writing in the *Journal of Experimental Social Psychology* found that men felt the greatest regard for an individual who flattered them unstintingly even if the comments were untrue. And in their book *Interpersonal Attraction* (Addison-Wesley, 1978), Ellen Berscheid and Elaine Hatfield Walster presented experimental data showing that positive remarks about another person's traits, attitude, or performance reliably generates liking in return, as well as willing compliance with the wishes of the person offering the praise.

Along with cultivating a fruitful relationship, adroit managers can also use praise to repair one that's damaged or unproductive. Imagine you're the manager of a good-sized unit within your organization. Your work frequently brings you into contact with another manager—call him Dan—whom you have come to dislike. No matter how much you do for him, it's not enough. Worse, he never seems to believe that you're doing the best you can for him. Resenting his attitude and his obvious lack of trust in your abilities and in your good faith, you don't spend as much time with him as you know you should; in consequence, the performance of both his unit and yours is deteriorating.

The research on praise points toward a strategy for fixing the relationship. It may be hard to find, but there has to be something about Dan you can sincerely admire, whether it's his concern for the people in his department, his devotion to his family, or simply his work ethic. In your next encounter with him, make an appreciative comment about that trait. Make it clear that in this case at least, you value what he values. I predict that Dan will relax his relentless negativity and give you an opening to convince him of your competence and good intentions.

The Principle of Reciprocity

People repay in kind.

The application

Give what you want to receive.

Praise is likely to have a warming and softening effect on Dan because, ornery as he is, he is still human and subject to the universal human tendency to treat people the way they treat him. If you have ever caught yourself smiling at a coworker just because he or she smiled first, you know how this principle works.

Charities rely on reciprocity to help them raise funds. For years, for instance, the Disabled American Veterans organization, using only a well-crafted fund-raising letter, garnered a very respectable 18% rate of response to its appeals. But when the group started enclosing a small gift in the envelope, the response rate nearly doubled to 35%. The gift—personalized address labels—was extremely modest, but it wasn't what prospective donors received that made the difference. It was that they had gotten anything at all.

What works in that letter works at the office, too. It's more than an effusion of seasonal spirit, of course, that impels suppliers to shower gifts on purchasing departments at holiday time. In 1996, purchasing managers admitted to an interviewer from *Inc.* magazine that after having accepted a gift from a supplier, they were willing to purchase products and services they would have otherwise declined. Gifts also have a startling effect on retention. I have encouraged readers of my book to send me examples of the principles of influence at work in their own lives. One reader, an employee of the State of Oregon, sent a letter in which she offered these reasons for her commitment to her supervisor:

> He gives me and my son gifts for Christmas and gives me presents on my birthday. There is no promotion for the type of job I have, and my only choice for one is to move to another department. But I find myself resisting trying to move. My boss is reaching retirement age, and I am thinking I will be able to move out after he retires. . . . [F]or now, I feel obligated to stay since he has been so nice to me.

Ultimately, though, gift giving is one of the cruder applications of the rule of reciprocity. In its more sophisticated uses, it confers a genuine first-mover advantage on any manager who is trying to foster positive attitudes and productive personal relationships in the office: Managers can elicit the desired behavior from coworkers and employees by displaying it first. Whether it's a sense of trust, a spirit of cooperation, or a pleasant demeanor, leaders should model the behavior they want to see from others.

The same holds true for managers faced with issues of information delivery and resource allocation. If you lend a member of your staff to a colleague who is shorthanded and staring at a fast-approaching deadline, you will significantly increase your chances of getting help when you need it. Your odds will improve even more if you say, when your colleague thanks you for the assistance, something like, "Sure, glad to help. I know how important it is for me to count on your help when I need it."

The Principle of Social Proof

People follow the lead of similar others.

The application

Use peer power whenever it's available.

Social creatures that they are, human beings rely heavily on the people around them for cues on how to think, feel, and act. We know this intuitively, but intuition has also been confirmed by experiments, such as the one first described in 1982 in the *Journal of Applied Psychology.* A group of researchers went door-to-door in Columbia, South Carolina, soliciting donations for a charity campaign and displaying a list of neighborhood residents who had already donated to the cause. The researchers found that the longer the donor list was, the more likely those solicited would be to donate as well.

To the people being solicited, the friends' and neighbors' names on the list were a form of social evidence about how they should respond. But the evidence would not have been nearly as compelling had the names been those of random strangers. In an experiment from the 1960s, first described in the *Journal of Personality and Social Psychology,* residents of New York City were asked to return a lost wallet to its owner. They were highly likely to attempt to return the wallet when they learned that another New Yorker had previously attempted to do so. But learning that someone from a foreign country had tried to return the wallet didn't sway their decision one way or the other.

The lesson for executives from these two experiments is that persuasion can be extremely effective when it comes from peers. The science supports what most sales professionals already know: Testimonials from satisfied customers work best when the satisfied customer and the prospective customer share similar circumstances. That lesson can help a manager faced with the task of selling a new corporate initiative. Imagine that you're trying to streamline your department's work processes. A group of veteran employees is resisting. Rather than try to convince the employees of the move's merits yourself, ask an old-timer who supports the initiative to speak up for it at a team meeting. The compatriot's testimony stands a much better chance of convincing the group than yet another speech from the boss. Stated simply, influence is often best exerted horizontally rather than vertically.

The Principle of Consistency

People align with their clear commitments.

The application

Make their commitments active, public, and voluntary.

Liking is a powerful force, but the work of persuasion involves more than simply making people feel warmly toward you, your idea, or your product. People need not only to like you but to feel committed to what you want them to do. Good turns are one reliable way to make people feel obligated to you. Another is to win a public commitment from them.

My own research has demonstrated that most people, once they take a stand or go on record in favor of a position, prefer to stick to it. Other studies reinforce that finding and go on to show how even a small, seemingly trivial commitment can have a powerful effect on future actions. Israeli researchers writing in 1983 in the *Personality and Social Psychology Bulletin* recounted how they asked half the residents of a large apartment complex to sign a petition favoring the establishment of a recreation center for the handicapped. The cause was good and the request was small, so almost everyone who was asked agreed to sign. Two weeks later, on National Collection Day for the Handicapped, all residents of the complex were approached at home and asked to give to the cause. A little more than half of those who were not asked to sign the petition made a contribution. But an astounding 92% of those who did sign donated money. The residents of the apartment complex felt obligated to live up to their commitments because those commitments were active, public, and voluntary. These three features are worth considering separately.

There's strong empirical evidence to show that a choice made actively—one that's spoken out loud or written down or otherwise made explicit—is considerably more likely to direct someone's future conduct than the same choice left unspoken. Writing in 1996 in the *Personality and Social Psychology Bulletin,* Delia Cioffi and Randy Garner described an experiment in which college students in one group were asked to fill out a printed form saying they wished to volunteer for an AIDS education project in the public schools. Students in another group volunteered for the same project by leaving blank a form stating that they didn't want to participate. A few days later, when the volunteers reported for duty, 74% of those who showed up were students from the group that signaled their commitment by filling out the form.

The implications are clear for a manager who wants to persuade a subordinate to follow some particular course of action: Get it in writing. Let's suppose you want your employee to submit reports in a more timely fashion. Once you believe you've won agreement, ask him to summarize the decision in a memo and send it to you. By doing so, you'll have greatly increased the odds that he'll fulfill the commitment because, as a rule, people live up to what they have written down.

Research into the social dimensions of commitment suggests that written statements become even more powerful when they're made public. In a classic experiment, described in 1955 in the *Journal of Abnormal and Social Psychology,* college students were asked to estimate the length of lines projected on a screen. Some students were asked to write down their choices on a piece of paper, sign it, and hand the paper to the experimenter. Others wrote their choices on an erasable slate, then erased the slate immediately. Still others were instructed to keep their decisions to themselves.

The experimenters then presented all three groups with evidence that their initial choices may have been wrong. Those who had merely kept their decisions in their heads were the most likely to reconsider their original estimates. More loyal to their first guesses were the students in the group that had written them down and immediately erased them. But by a wide margin, the ones most reluctant to shift from their original choices were those who had signed and handed them to the researcher.

This experiment highlights how much most people wish to appear consistent to others. Consider again the matter of the employee who has been submitting late reports. Recognizing the power of this desire, you should, once you've successfully convinced him of the need to be more timely, reinforce the commitment by making sure it gets a public airing. One way to do that would be to send the employee an e-mail that reads, "I think your plan is just what we need. I showed it to Diane in manufacturing and Phil in shipping, and they thought it was right on target, too." Whatever way such commitments are formalized, they should never be like the New Year's resolutions people privately make and then abandon with no one the wiser. They should be publicly made and visibly posted.

More than 300 years ago, Samuel Butler wrote a couplet that explains succinctly why commitments must be voluntary to be lasting and effective: "He that complies against his will/Is of his own opinion still." If an undertaking is forced, coerced, or imposed from the outside, it's not a commitment; it's an unwelcome burden. Think how you would react if your boss pressured you to donate to the campaign of a political candidate. Would that make you more apt to opt for that candidate in the privacy of a voting booth? Not likely. In fact, in their 1981 book *Psychological Reactance* (Academic Press), Sharon S. Brehm and Jack W. Brehm present data that suggest you'd vote the opposite way just to express your resentment of the boss's coercion.

This kind of backlash can occur in the office, too. Let's return again to that tardy employee. If you want to produce an enduring change in his behavior, you should avoid using threats or pressure tactics to gain

Persuasion Experts, Safe at Last

THANKS TO SEVERAL DECADES OF rigorous empirical research by behavioral scientists, our understanding of the how and why of persuasion has never been broader, deeper, or more detailed. But these scientists aren't the first students of the subject. The history of persuasion studies is an ancient and honorable one, and it has generated a long roster of heroes and martyrs.

A renowned student of social influence, William McGuire, contends in a chapter of the *Handbook of Social Psychology*, 3rd ed. (Oxford University Press, 1985) that scattered among the more than four millennia of recorded Western history are four centuries in which the study of persuasion flourished as a craft. The first was the Periclean Age of ancient Athens, the second occurred during the years of the Roman Republic, the next appeared in the time of the European Renaissance, and the last extended over the hundred years that have just ended, which witnessed the advent of large-scale advertising, information, and mass media campaigns. Each of the three previous centuries of systematic persuasion study was marked by a flowering of human achievement that was suddenly cut short when political authorities had the masters

his compliance. He'd likely view any change in his behavior as the result of intimidation rather than a personal commitment to change. A better approach would be to identify something that the employee genuinely values in the workplace—high-quality workmanship, perhaps, or team spirit—and then describe how timely reports are consistent with those values. That gives the employee reasons for improvement that he can own. And because he owns them, they'll continue to guide his behavior even when you're not watching.

The Principle of Authority

People defer to experts.

The application

Expose your expertise; don't assume it's self-evident.

Two thousand years ago, the Roman poet Virgil offered this simple counsel to those seeking to choose correctly: "Believe an expert." That may or may not be good advice, but as a description of what

of persuasion killed. The philosopher Socrates is probably the best known of the persuasion experts to run afoul of the powers that be.

Information about the persuasion process is a threat because it creates a base of power entirely separate from the one controlled by political authorities. Faced with a rival source of influence, rulers in previous centuries had few qualms about eliminating those rare individuals who truly understood how to marshal forces that heads of state have never been able to monopolize, such as cleverly crafted language, strategically placed information, and, most important, psychological insight.

It would perhaps be expressing too much faith in human nature to claim that persuasion experts no longer face a threat from those who wield political power. But because the truth about persuasion is no longer the sole possession of a few brilliant, inspired individuals, experts in the field can presumably breathe a little easier. Indeed, since most people in power are interested in remaining in power, they're likely to be more interested in acquiring persuasion skills than abolishing them.

people actually do, it can't be beaten. For instance, when the news media present an acknowledged expert's views on a topic, the effect on public opinion is dramatic. A single expert-opinion news story in the *New York Times* is associated with a 2% shift in public opinion nationwide, according to a 1993 study described in the *Public Opinion Quarterly.* And researchers writing in the *American Political Science Review* in 1987 found that when the expert's view was aired on national television, public opinion shifted as much as 4%. A cynic might argue that these findings only illustrate the docile submissiveness of the public. But a fairer explanation is that, amid the teeming complexity of contemporary life, a well-selected expert offers a valuable and efficient shortcut to good decisions. Indeed, some questions, be they legal, financial, medical, or technological, require so much specialized knowledge to answer, we have no choice but to rely on experts.

Since there's good reason to defer to experts, executives should take pains to ensure that they establish their own expertise before they attempt to exert influence. Surprisingly often, people mistakenly assume that others recognize and appreciate their experience.

That's what happened at a hospital where some colleagues and I were consulting. The physical therapy staffers were frustrated because so many of their stroke patients abandoned their exercise routines as soon as they left the hospital. No matter how often the staff emphasized the importance of regular home exercise—it is, in fact, crucial to the process of regaining independent function—the message just didn't sink in.

Interviews with some of the patients helped us pinpoint the problem. They were familiar with the background and training of their physicians, but the patients knew little about the credentials of the physical therapists who were urging them to exercise. It was a simple matter to remedy that lack of information: We merely asked the therapy director to display all the awards, diplomas, and certifications of her staff on the walls of the therapy rooms. The result was startling: Exercise compliance jumped 34% and has never dropped since.

What we found immensely gratifying was not just how much we increased compliance, but how. We didn't fool or browbeat any of the patients. We *informed* them into compliance. Nothing had to be invented; no time or resources had to be spent in the process. The staff's expertise was real—all we had to do was make it more visible.

The task for managers who want to establish their claims to expertise is somewhat more difficult. They can't simply nail their diplomas to the wall and wait for everyone to notice. A little subtlety is called for. Outside the United States, it is customary for people to spend time interacting socially before getting down to business for the first time. Frequently they gather for dinner the night before their meeting or negotiation. These get-togethers can make discussions easier and help blunt disagreements—remember the findings about liking and similarity—and they can also provide an opportunity to establish expertise. Perhaps it's a matter of telling an anecdote about successfully solving a problem similar to the one that's on the agenda at the next day's meeting. Or perhaps dinner is the time to describe years spent mastering a complex discipline—not in a boastful way but as part of the ordinary give-and-take of conversation.

Granted, there's not always time for lengthy introductory sessions. But even in the course of the preliminary conversation that precedes most meetings, there is almost always an opportunity to touch lightly on your relevant background and experience as a natural part of a sociable exchange. This initial disclosure of personal information gives you a chance to establish expertise early in the game, so that when the discussion turns to the business at hand, what you have to say will be accorded the respect it deserves.

The Principle of Scarcity

People want more of what they can have less of.

The application

Highlight unique benefits and exclusive information.

Study after study shows that items and opportunities are seen to be more valuable as they become less available. That's a tremendously useful piece of information for managers. They can harness the scarcity principle with the organizational equivalents of limited-time, limited-supply, and one-of-a-kind offers. Honestly informing a coworker of a closing window of opportunity— the chance to get the boss's ear before she leaves for an extended vacation, perhaps—can mobilize action dramatically.

Managers can learn from retailers how to frame their offers not in terms of what people stand to gain but in terms of what they stand to lose if they don't act on the information. The power of "loss language" was demonstrated in a 1988 study of California home owners written up in the *Journal of Applied Psychology.* Half were told that if they fully insulated their homes, they would save a certain amount of money each day. The other half were told that if they failed to insulate, they would lose that amount each day. Significantly more people insulated their homes when exposed to the loss language. The same phenomenon occurs in business. According to a 1994 study in the journal *Organizational Behavior and Human Decision*

Processes, potential losses figure far more heavily in managers' decision making than potential gains.

In framing their offers, executives should also remember that exclusive information is more persuasive than widely available data. A doctoral student of mine, Amram Knishinsky, wrote his 1982 dissertation on the purchase decisions of wholesale beef buyers. He observed that they more than doubled their orders when they were told that, because of certain weather conditions overseas, there was likely to be a scarcity of foreign beef in the near future. But their orders increased 600% when they were informed that no one else had that information yet.

The persuasive power of exclusivity can be harnessed by any manager who comes into possession of information that's not broadly available and that supports an idea or initiative he or she would like the organization to adopt. The next time that kind of information crosses your desk, round up your organization's key players. The information itself may seem dull, but exclusivity will give it a special sheen. Push it across your desk and say, "I just got this report today. It won't be distributed until next week, but I want to give you an early look at what it shows." Then watch your listeners lean forward.

Allow me to stress here a point that should be obvious. No offer of exclusive information, no exhortation to act now or miss this opportunity forever should be made unless it is genuine. Deceiving colleagues into compliance is not only ethically objectionable, it's foolhardy. If the deception is detected—and it certainly will be—it will snuff out any enthusiasm the offer originally kindled. It will also invite dishonesty toward the deceiver. Remember the rule of reciprocity.

Putting It All Together

There's nothing abstruse or obscure about these six principles of persuasion. Indeed, they neatly codify our intuitive understanding of the ways people evaluate information and form decisions. As a result, the principles are easy for most people to grasp, even those with no formal education in psychology. But in the seminars and workshops I conduct, I have learned that two points bear repeated emphasis.

First, although the six principles and their applications can be discussed separately for the sake of clarity, they should be applied in combination to compound their impact. For instance, in discussing the importance of expertise, I suggested that managers use informal, social conversations to establish their credentials. But that conversation affords an opportunity to gain information as well as convey it. While you're showing your dinner companion that you have the skills and experience your business problem demands, you can also learn about your companion's background, likes, and dislikes—information that will help you locate genuine similarities and give sincere compliments. By letting your expertise surface and also establishing rapport, you double your persuasive power. And if you succeed in bringing your dinner partner on board, you may encourage other people to sign on as well, thanks to the persuasive power of social evidence.

The other point I wish to emphasize is that the rules of ethics apply to the science of social influence just as they do to any other technology. Not only is it ethically wrong to trick or trap others into assent, it's ill-advised in practical terms. Dishonest or high-pressure tactics work only in the short run, if at all. Their long-term effects are malignant, especially within an organization, which can't function properly without a bedrock level of trust and cooperation.

That point is made vividly in the following account, which a department head for a large textile manufacturer related at a training workshop I conducted. She described a vice president in her company who wrung public commitments from department heads in a highly manipulative manner. Instead of giving his subordinates time to talk or think through his proposals carefully, he would approach them individually at the busiest moment of their workday and describe the benefits of his plan in exhaustive, patience-straining detail. Then he would move in for the kill. "It's very important for me to see you as being on my team on this," he would say. "Can I count on your support?" Intimidated, frazzled, eager to chase the man from their offices so they could get back to work, the department heads would invariably go along with his request. But because the commitments never felt voluntary, the department heads never followed through, and as a result the vice president's initiatives all blew up or petered out.

This story had a deep impact on the other participants in the workshop. Some gulped in shock as they recognized their own manipulative behavior. But what stopped everyone cold was the expression on the department head's face as she recounted the damaging collapse of her superior's proposals. She was smiling.

Nothing I could say would more effectively make the point that the deceptive or coercive use of the principles of social influence is ethically wrong and pragmatically wrongheaded. Yet the same principles, if applied appropriately, can steer decisions correctly. Legitimate expertise, genuine obligations, authentic similarities, real social proof, exclusive news, and freely made commitments can produce choices that are likely to benefit both parties. And any approach that works to everyone's mutual benefit is good business, don't you think? Of course, I don't want to press you into it, but, if you agree, I would love it if you could just jot me a memo to that effect.

Originally published in September 2001. Reprint R0109D

The Power of Talk

Who Gets Heard and Why.

by Deborah Tannen

THE HEAD OF A LARGE division of a multinational corporation was running a meeting devoted to performance assessment. Each senior manager stood up, reviewed the individuals in his group, and evaluated them for promotion. Although there were women in every group, not one of them made the cut. One after another, each manager declared, in effect, that every woman in his group didn't have the self-confidence needed to be promoted. The division head began to doubt his ears. How could it be that all the talented women in the division suffered from a lack of self-confidence?

In all likelihood, they didn't. Consider the many women who have left large corporations to start their own businesses, obviously exhibiting enough confidence to succeed on their own. Judgments about confidence can be inferred only from the way people present themselves, and much of that presentation is in the form of talk.

The CEO of a major corporation told me that he often has to make decisions in five minutes about matters on which others may have worked five months. He said he uses this rule: If the person making the proposal seems confident, the CEO approves it. If not, he says no. This might seem like a reasonable approach. But my field of research, sociolinguistics, suggests otherwise. The CEO obviously thinks he knows what a confident person sounds like. But his judgment, which may be dead right for some people, may be dead wrong for others.

Communication isn't as simple as saying what you mean. How you say what you mean is crucial, and differs from one person to the next, because using language is learned social behavior: How we talk and listen are deeply influenced by cultural experience. Although we might think that our ways of saying what we mean are natural, we can run into trouble if we interpret and evaluate others as if they necessarily felt the same way we'd feel if we spoke the way they did.

Since 1974, I have been researching the influence of linguistic style on conversations and human relationships. In the past four years, I have extended that research to the workplace, where I have observed how ways of speaking learned in childhood affect judgments of competence and confidence, as well as who gets heard, who gets credit, and what gets done.

The division head who was dumbfounded to hear that all the talented women in his organization lacked confidence was probably right to be skeptical. The senior managers were judging the women in their groups by their own linguistic norms, but women—like people who have grown up in a different culture—have often learned different styles of speaking than men, which can make them seem less competent and self-assured than they are.

What Is Linguistic Style?

Everything that is said must be said in a certain way—in a certain tone of voice, at a certain rate of speed, and with a certain degree of loudness. Whereas often we consciously consider what to say before speaking, we rarely think about how to say it, unless the situation is obviously loaded—for example, a job interview or a tricky performance review. Linguistic style refers to a person's characteristic speaking pattern. It includes such features as directness or indirectness, pacing and pausing, word choice, and the use of such elements as jokes, figures of speech, stories, questions, and apologies. In other words, linguistic style is a set of culturally learned signals by which we not only communicate what we mean but also interpret others' meaning and evaluate one another as people.

Idea in Brief

Most managerial work happens through talk—discussions, meetings, presentations, negotiations. And it is through talk that managers evaluate others and are themselves judged. Using research carried out in a variety of workplace settings, linguist Deborah Tannen demonstrates how conversational style often overrides what we say, affecting who gets heard, who gets credit, and what gets done. Tannen's linguistic perspective provides managers with insight into why there is so much poor communication. Gender plays an important role. Tannen traces the ways in which women's styles can undermine them in the workplace, making them seem less competent, confident, and self-assured than they are. She analyzes the underlying social dynamic created through talk in common workplace interactions. She argues that a better understanding of linguistic style will make managers better listeners and more effective communicators, allowing them to develop more flexible approaches to a full range of managerial activities.

Consider turn taking, one element of linguistic style. Conversation is an enterprise in which people take turns: One person speaks, then the other responds. However, this apparently simple exchange requires a subtle negotiation of signals so that you know when the other person is finished and it's your turn to begin. Cultural factors such as country or region of origin and ethnic background influence how long a pause seems natural. When Bob, who is from Detroit, has a conversation with his colleague Joe, from New York City, it's hard for him to get a word in edgewise because he expects a slightly longer pause between turns than Joe does. A pause of that length never comes because, before it has a chance to, Joe senses an uncomfortable silence, which he fills with more talk of his own. Both men fail to realize that differences in conversational style are getting in their way. Bob thinks that Joe is pushy and uninterested in what he has to say, and Joe thinks that Bob doesn't have much to contribute. Similarly, when Sally relocated from Texas to Washington, D.C., she kept searching for the right time to break in during staff meetings—and never found it. Although in Texas she was considered outgoing and confident, in Washington she was perceived as shy and retiring. Her boss even suggested she take an assertiveness

The Idea in Practice

This table shows examples of styles of *talking* (including the *assumptions* behind each style) and *unintended consequences* a company may suffer because of misinterpreted stylistic differences.

	Style of Talking	**Unintended Consequences of Style**
Sharing Credit	Uses "we" rather than "I" to describe accomplishments. *Why?* Using "I" seems too self-promoting.	Speaker doesn't get credit for accomplishments and may hesitate to offer good ideas in the future.
Acting Modest	Downplays their certainty, rather than minimizing doubts, about future performance. *Why?* Confident behavior seems too boastful.	Speaker *appears* to lack confidence and, therefore, competence; others reject speaker's good ideas.
Asking Questions	Asks questions freely. *Why?* Questions generate needed knowledge.	Speaker *appears* ignorant to others; if organization discourages speaker from asking questions, valuable knowledge remains buried.

training course. Thus slight differences in conversational style—in these cases, a few seconds of pause—can have a surprising impact on who gets heard and on the judgments, including psychological ones, that are made about people and their abilities.

Every utterance functions on two levels. We're all familiar with the first one: Language communicates ideas. The second level is mostly invisible to us, but it plays a powerful role in communication. As a form of social behavior, language also negotiates relationships. Through ways of speaking, we signal—and create—the relative status of speakers and their level of rapport. If you say, "Sit down!" you

Apologizing	Apologizes freely. *Why?* Apologies express concern for others.	Speaker *appears* to lack authority.
Giving Feedback	Notes weaknesses only after *first* citing strengths. *Why?* Buffering criticism saves face for the individual receiving feedback.	Person receiving feedback concludes that areas needing improvement aren't important.
Avoiding Verbal Opposition	Avoids challenging others' ideas, and hedges when stating own ideas. *Why?* Verbal opposition signals destructive fighting.	Others conclude that speaker has weak ideas.
Managing Up	Avoids talking up achievements with higher-ups. *Why?* Emphasizing achievements to higher-ups constitutes boasting.	Managers conclude that speaker hasn't achieved much and doesn't deserve recognition or promotion.
Being Indirect	Speaks indirectly rather than bluntly when telling subordinates what to do. *Why?* Blatantly directing others is too bossy.	Subordinates conclude that manager lacks assertiveness and clear thinking, and judge manager's directives as unimportant.

are signaling that you have higher status than the person you are addressing, that you are so close to each other that you can drop all pleasantries, or that you are angry. If you say, "I would be honored if you would sit down," you are signaling great respect—or great sarcasm, depending on your tone of voice, the situation, and what you both know about how close you really are. If you say, "You must be so tired—why don't you sit down," you are communicating either closeness and concern or condescension. Each of these ways of saying "the same thing"—telling someone to sit down—can have a vastly different meaning.

In every community known to linguists, the patterns that constitute linguistic style are relatively different for men and women. What's "natural" for most men speaking a given language is, in some cases, different from what's "natural" for most women. That is because we learn ways of speaking as children growing up, especially from peers, and children tend to play with other children of the same sex. The research of sociologists, anthropologists, and psychologists observing American children at play has shown that, although both girls and boys find ways of creating rapport and negotiating status, girls tend to learn conversational rituals that focus on the rapport dimension of relationships whereas boys tend to learn rituals that focus on the status dimension.

Girls tend to play with a single best friend or in small groups, and they spend a lot of time talking. They use language to negotiate how close they are; for example, the girl you tell your secrets to becomes your best friend. Girls learn to downplay ways in which one is better than the others and to emphasize ways in which they are all the same. From childhood, most girls learn that sounding too sure of themselves will make them unpopular with their peers—although nobody really takes such modesty literally. A group of girls will ostracize a girl who calls attention to her own superiority and criticize her by saying, "She thinks she's something"; and a girl who tells others what to do is called "bossy." Thus girls learn to talk in ways that balance their own needs with those of others—to save face for one another in the broadest sense of the term.

Boys tend to play very differently. They usually play in larger groups in which more boys can be included, but not everyone is treated as an equal. Boys with high status in their group are expected to emphasize rather than downplay their status, and usually one or several boys will be seen as the leader or leaders. Boys generally don't accuse one another of being bossy, because the leader is expected to tell lower-status boys what to do. Boys learn to use language to negotiate their status in the group by displaying their abilities and knowledge, and by challenging others and resisting challenges. Giving orders is one way of getting and keeping the high-status role. Another is taking center stage by telling stories or jokes.

This is not to say that all boys and girls grow up this way or feel comfortable in these groups or are equally successful at negotiating within these norms. But, for the most part, these childhood play groups are where boys and girls learn their conversational styles. In this sense, they grow up in different worlds. The result is that women and men tend to have different habitual ways of saying what they mean, and conversations between them can be like cross-cultural communication: You can't assume that the other person means what you would mean if you said the same thing in the same way.

My research in companies across the United States shows that the lessons learned in childhood carry over into the workplace. Consider the following example: A focus group was organized at a major multinational company to evaluate a recently implemented flextime policy. The participants sat in a circle and discussed the new system. The group concluded that it was excellent, but they also agreed on ways to improve it. The meeting went well and was deemed a success by all, according to my own observations and everyone's comments to me. But the next day, I was in for a surprise.

I had left the meeting with the impression that Phil had been responsible for most of the suggestions adopted by the group. But as I typed up my notes, I noticed that Cheryl had made almost all those suggestions. I had thought that the key ideas came from Phil because he had picked up Cheryl's points and supported them, speaking at greater length in doing so than she had in raising them.

It would be easy to regard Phil as having stolen Cheryl's ideas—and her thunder. But that would be inaccurate. Phil never claimed Cheryl's ideas as his own. Cheryl herself told me later that she left the meeting confident that she had contributed significantly, and that she appreciated Phil's support. She volunteered, with a laugh, "It was not one of those times when a woman says something and it's ignored, then a man says it and it's picked up." In other words, Cheryl and Phil worked well as a team, the group fulfilled its charge, and the company got what it needed. So what was the problem?

I went back and asked all the participants who they thought had been the most influential group member, the one most responsible for the ideas that had been adopted. The pattern of answers was revealing. The two other women in the group named Cheryl. Two of the three men named Phil. Of the men, only Phil named Cheryl. In other words, in this instance, the women evaluated the contribution of another woman more accurately than the men did.

Meetings like this take place daily in companies around the country. Unless managers are unusually good at listening closely to how people say what they mean, the talents of someone like Cheryl may well be undervalued and underutilized.

One Up, One Down

Individual speakers vary in how sensitive they are to the social dynamics of language—in other words, to the subtle nuances of what others say to them. Men tend to be sensitive to the power dynamics of interaction, speaking in ways that position themselves as one up and resisting being put in a one-down position by others. Women tend to react more strongly to the rapport dynamic, speaking in ways that save face for others and buffering statements that could be seen as putting others in a one-down position. These linguistic patterns are pervasive; you can hear them in hundreds of exchanges in the workplace every day. And, as in the case of Cheryl and Phil, they affect who gets heard and who gets credit.

Getting credit. Even so small a linguistic strategy as the choice of pronoun can affect who gets credit. In my research in the workplace, I heard men say "I" in situations where I heard women say "we." For example, one publishing company executive said, "I'm hiring a new manager. I'm going to put him in charge of my marketing division," as if he owned the corporation. In stark contrast, I recorded women saying "we" when referring to work they alone had done. One woman explained that it would sound too self-promoting to claim credit in an obvious way by saying, "I did this." Yet she expected—sometimes vainly—that others would know it was her work and would give her the credit she did not claim for herself.

Managers might leap to the conclusion that women who do not take credit for what they've done should be taught to do so. But that solution is problematic because we associate ways of speaking with moral qualities: The way we speak is who we are and who we want to be.

Veronica, a senior researcher in a high-tech company, had an observant boss. He noticed that many of the ideas coming out of the group were hers but that often someone else trumpeted them around the office and got credit for them. He advised her to "own" her ideas and make sure she got the credit. But Veronica found she simply didn't enjoy her work if she had to approach it as what seemed to her an unattractive and unappealing "grabbing game." It was her dislike of such behavior that had led her to avoid it in the first place.

Whatever the motivation, women are less likely than men to have learned to blow their own horn. And they are more likely than men to believe that if they do so, they won't be liked.

Many have argued that the growing trend of assigning work to teams may be especially congenial to women, but it may also create complications for performance evaluation. When ideas are generated and work is accomplished in the privacy of the team, the outcome of the team's effort may become associated with the person most vocal about reporting results. There are many women and men—but probably relatively more women—who are reluctant to put themselves forward in this way and who consequently risk not getting credit for their contributions.

Confidence and boasting

The CEO who based his decisions on the confidence level of speakers was articulating a value that is widely shared in U.S. businesses: One way to judge confidence is by an individual's behavior, especially verbal behavior. Here again, many women are at a disadvantage.

Studies show that women are more likely to downplay their certainty and men are more likely to minimize their doubts. Psychologist Laurie Heatherington and her colleagues devised an ingenious experiment, which they reported in the journal *Sex Roles* (Volume 29, 1993). They asked hundreds of incoming college students to predict what grades they would get in their first year. Some subjects were asked to make their predictions privately by writing them down and placing them in an envelope; others were asked to make their predictions publicly, in the presence of a researcher. The results showed that more women than men predicted lower grades for themselves if they made their predictions publicly. If they made their predictions privately, the predictions were the same as those of the men—and the same as their actual grades. This study provides evidence that what comes across as lack of confidence—predicting lower grades for oneself—may reflect not one's actual level of confidence but the desire not to seem boastful.

These habits with regard to appearing humble or confident result from the socialization of boys and girls by their peers in childhood play. As adults, both women and men find these behaviors reinforced by the positive responses they get from friends and relatives who share the same norms. But the norms of behavior in the U.S. business world are based on the style of interaction that is more common among men—at least, among American men.

Asking questions

Although asking the right questions is one of the hallmarks of a good manager, how and when questions are asked can send unintended signals about competence and power. In a group, if only one person asks questions, he or she risks being seen as the only ignorant one. Furthermore, we judge others not only by how they speak but also by how they are spoken to. The person who asks questions may end up being lectured to and looking like a novice under a schoolmaster's tutelage. The way boys are socialized makes them more likely to be aware of the underlying power dynamic by which a question asker can be seen in a one-down position.

One practicing physician learned the hard way that any exchange of information can become the basis for judgments—or misjudgments—about competence. During her training, she received a negative evaluation that she thought was unfair, so she asked her supervising physician for an explanation. He said that she knew less than her peers. Amazed at his answer, she asked how he had reached that conclusion. He said, "You ask more questions."

Along with cultural influences and individual personality, gender seems to play a role in whether and when people ask questions. For example, of all the observations I've made in lectures and books, the one that sparks the most enthusiastic flash of recognition is that men are less likely than women to stop and ask for directions when they are lost. I explain that men often resist asking for directions because they are aware that it puts them in a one-down position and because they value the independence that comes with finding their way by themselves. Asking for directions while driving is only one instance—along with many others that researchers have examined—in which men seem less likely than women to ask questions. I believe this is because they are more attuned than women to the potential face-losing aspect of asking questions. And men who believe that asking questions might reflect negatively on them may, in turn, be likely to form a negative opinion of others who ask questions in situations where they would not.

Conversational Rituals

Conversation is fundamentally ritual in the sense that we speak in ways our culture has conventionalized and expect certain types of responses. Take greetings, for example. I have heard visitors to the United States complain that Americans are hypocritical because they ask how you are but aren't interested in the answer. To Americans, How are you? is obviously a ritualized way to start a conversation rather than a literal request for information. In other parts of the world, including the Philippines, people ask each other, "Where are you going?" when they meet. The question seems intrusive to Americans, who do not realize that it, too, is a ritual query to which the only expected reply is a vague "Over there."

It's easy and entertaining to observe different rituals in foreign countries. But we don't expect differences, and are far less likely to recognize the ritualized nature of our conversations, when we are with our compatriots at work. Our differing rituals can be even more problematic when we think we're all speaking the same language.

Apologies

Consider the simple phrase *I'm sorry.*

Catherine: How did that big presentation go?

Bob: Oh, not very well. I got a lot of flak from the VP for finance, and I didn't have the numbers at my fingertips.

Catherine: Oh, I'm sorry. I know how hard you worked on that.

In this case, *I'm sorry* probably means "I'm sorry that happened," not "I apologize," unless it was Catherine's responsibility to supply Bob with the numbers for the presentation. Women tend to say *I'm sorry* more frequently than men, and often they intend it in this way—as a ritualized means of expressing concern. It's one of many learned elements of conversational style that girls often use to establish rapport. Ritual apologies—like other conversational rituals—work well when both parties share the same assumptions about their use. But people who utter frequent ritual apologies may end up appearing weaker, less confident, and literally more blameworthy than people who don't.

Apologies tend to be regarded differently by men, who are more likely to focus on the status implications of exchanges. Many men avoid apologies because they see them as putting the speaker in a one-down position. I observed with some amazement an encounter among several lawyers engaged in a negotiation over a speakerphone. At one point, the lawyer in whose office I was sitting accidentally elbowed the telephone and cut off the call. When his secretary got the parties back on again, I expected him to say what I would have said: "Sorry about that. I knocked the phone with my elbow." Instead, he said, "Hey, what happened? One minute you were there; the next minute you were gone!" This lawyer seemed to have an automatic impulse not to admit fault if he didn't have to. For me, it was one of those pivotal moments when you realize that the world you live in is not the one everyone lives in and that the way you assume is the way to talk is really only one of many.

Those who caution managers not to undermine their authority by apologizing are approaching interaction from the perspective of the power dynamic. In many cases, this strategy is effective. On the other hand, when I asked people what frustrated them in their jobs, one frequently voiced complaint was working with or for someone who refuses to apologize or admit fault. In other words, accepting responsibility for errors and admitting mistakes may be an equally effective or superior strategy in some settings.

Feedback

Styles of giving feedback contain a ritual element that often is the cause for misunderstanding. Consider the following exchange: A manager had to tell her marketing director to rewrite a report. She began this potentially awkward task by citing the report's strengths and then moved to the main point: the weaknesses that needed to be remedied. The marketing director seemed to understand and accept his supervisor's comments, but his revision contained only minor changes and failed to address the major weaknesses. When the manager told him of her dissatisfaction, he accused her of misleading him: "You told me it was fine."

The impasse resulted from different linguistic styles. To the manager, it was natural to buffer the criticism by beginning with praise. Telling her subordinate that his report is inadequate and has to be rewritten puts him in a one-down position. Praising him for the parts that are good is a ritualized way of saving face for him. But the marketing director did not share his supervisor's assumption about how feedback should be given. Instead, he assumed that what she mentioned first was the main point and that what she brought up later was an afterthought.

Those who expect feedback to come in the way the manager presented it would appreciate her tact and would regard a more blunt approach as unnecessarily callous. But those who share the marketing director's assumptions would regard the blunt approach as honest and no-nonsense, and the manager's as obfuscating. Because each one's assumptions seemed self-evident, each blamed the other: The manager thought the marketing director was not listening, and he thought she had not communicated clearly or had changed her mind. This is significant because it illustrates that incidents labeled vaguely as "poor communication" may be the result of differing linguistic styles.

Compliments

Exchanging compliments is a common ritual, especially among women. A mismatch in expectations about this ritual left Susan, a manager in the human resources field, in a one-down position. She and her colleague Bill had both given presentations at a national conference. On the airplane home, Susan told Bill, "That was a great talk!" "Thank you," he said. Then she asked, "What did you think of mine?" He responded with a lengthy and detailed critique, as she listened uncomfortably. An unpleasant feeling of having been put down came over her. Somehow she had been positioned as the novice in need of his expert advice. Even worse, she had only herself to blame, since she had, after all, asked Bill what he thought of her talk.

But had Susan asked for the response she received? When she asked Bill what he thought about her talk, she expected to hear not a critique but a compliment. In fact, her question had been an attempt to repair a ritual gone awry. Susan's initial compliment to Bill was the kind of automatic recognition she felt was more or less required after a colleague gives a presentation, and she expected Bill to respond with a matching compliment. She was just talking automatically, but he either sincerely misunderstood the ritual or simply took the opportunity to bask in the one-up position of critic. Whatever his motivation, it was Susan's attempt to spark an exchange of compliments that gave him the opening.

Although this exchange could have occurred between two men, it does not seem coincidental that it happened between a man and a woman. Linguist Janet Holmes discovered that women pay more compliments than men (*Anthropological Linguistics,* Volume 28, 1986). And, as I have observed, fewer men are likely to ask, "What did you think of my talk?" precisely because the question might invite an unwanted critique.

In the social structure of the peer groups in which they grow up, boys are indeed looking for opportunities to put others down and take the one-up position for themselves. In contrast, one of the rituals girls learn is taking the one-down position but assuming that the other person will recognize the ritual nature of the self-denigration and pull them back up.

The exchange between Susan and Bill also suggests how women's and men's characteristic styles may put women at a disadvantage in the workplace. If one person is trying to minimize status differences, maintain an appearance that everyone is equal, and save face for the other, while another person is trying to maintain the one-up position and avoid being positioned as one down, the person seeking the one-up position is likely to get it. At the same time, the person who has not been expending any effort to avoid the one-down position is likely to end up in it. Because women are more likely to take (or accept) the role of advice seeker, men are more inclined to interpret a ritual question from a woman as a request for advice.

Ritual opposition

Apologizing, mitigating criticism with praise, and exchanging compliments are rituals common among women that men often take literally. A ritual common among men that women often take literally is ritual opposition.

A woman in communications told me she watched with distaste and distress as her office mate argued heatedly with another colleague about whose division should suffer budget cuts. She was even more surprised, however, that a short time later they were as friendly as ever. "How can you pretend that fight never happened?" she asked. "Who's pretending it never happened?" he responded, as puzzled by her question as she had been by his behavior. "It happened," he said, "and it's over." What she took as literal fighting to him was a routine part of daily negotiation: a ritual fight.

Many Americans expect the discussion of ideas to be a ritual fight—that is, an exploration through verbal opposition. They present their own ideas in the most certain and absolute form they can, and wait to see if they are challenged. Being forced to defend an idea provides an opportunity to test it. In the same spirit, they may play devil's advocate in challenging their colleagues' ideas—trying to poke holes and find weaknesses—as a way of helping them explore and test their ideas.

This style can work well if everyone shares it, but those unaccustomed to it are likely to miss its ritual nature. They may give up an idea that is challenged, taking the objections as an indication that the idea was a poor one. Worse, they may take the opposition as a personal attack and may find it impossible to do their best in a contentious environment. People unaccustomed to this style may hedge when stating their ideas in order to fend off potential attacks. Ironically, this posture makes their arguments appear weak and is more likely to invite attack from pugnacious colleagues than to fend it off.

Ritual opposition can even play a role in who gets hired. Some consulting firms that recruit graduates from the top business schools use a confrontational interviewing technique. They challenge the candidate to "crack a case" in real time. A partner at one firm told me, "Women tend to do less well in this kind of interaction, and it certainly affects who gets hired. But, in fact, many women who don't 'test well' turn out to be good consultants. They're often smarter than some of the men who looked like analytic powerhouses under pressure."

The level of verbal opposition varies from one company's culture to the next, but I saw instances of it in all the organizations I studied. Anyone who is uncomfortable with this linguistic style—and that includes some men as well as many women—risks appearing insecure about his or her ideas.

Negotiating Authority

In organizations, formal authority comes from the position one holds. But actual authority has to be negotiated day to day. The effectiveness of individual managers depends in part on their skill in negotiating authority and on whether others reinforce or undercut their efforts. The way linguistic style reflects status plays a subtle role in placing individuals within a hierarchy.

Managing up and down

In all the companies I researched, I heard from women who knew they were doing a superior job and knew that their co-workers (and sometimes their immediate bosses) knew it as well, but believed that the higher-ups did not. They frequently told me that something outside themselves was holding them back and found it frustrating because they thought that all that should be necessary for success was to do a great job, that superior performance should be recognized and rewarded. In contrast, men often told me that if women weren't promoted, it was because they simply weren't up to snuff. Looking around, however, I saw evidence that men more often than women behaved in ways likely to get them recognized by those with the power to determine their advancement.

In all the companies I visited, I observed what happened at lunchtime. I saw young men who regularly ate lunch with their boss, and senior men who ate with the big boss. I noticed far fewer women who sought out the highest-level person they could eat with. But one is more likely to get recognition for work done if one talks about it to those higher up, and it is easier to do so if the lines of communication are already open. Furthermore, given the opportunity for a conversation with superiors, men and women are likely to have different ways of talking about their accomplishments because of the different ways in which they were socialized as children. Boys are rewarded by their peers if they talk up their achievements, whereas girls are rewarded if they play theirs down. Linguistic styles common among men may tend to give them some advantages when it comes to managing up.

All speakers are aware of the status of the person they are talking to and adjust accordingly. Everyone speaks differently when talking to a boss than when talking to a subordinate. But, surprisingly, the ways in which they adjust their talk may be different and thus may project different images of themselves.

Communications researchers Karen Tracy and Eric Eisenberg studied how relative status affects the way people give criticism. They devised a business letter that contained some errors and asked

13 male and 11 female college students to role-play delivering criticism under two scenarios. In the first, the speaker was a boss talking to a subordinate; in the second, the speaker was a subordinate talking to his or her boss. The researchers measured how hard the speakers tried to avoid hurting the feelings of the person they were criticizing.

One might expect people to be more careful about how they deliver criticism when they are in a subordinate position. Tracy and Eisenberg found that hypothesis to be true for the men in their study but not for the women. As they reported in *Research on Language and Social Interaction* (Volume 24, 1990/1991), the women showed more concern about the other person's feelings when they were playing the role of superior. In other words, the women were more careful to save face for the other person when they were managing down than when they were managing up. This pattern recalls the way girls are socialized: Those who are in some way superior are expected to downplay rather than flaunt their superiority.

In my own recordings of workplace communication, I observed women talking in similar ways. For example, when a manager had to correct a mistake made by her secretary, she did so by acknowledging that there were mitigating circumstances. She said, laughing, "You know, it's hard to do things around here, isn't it, with all these people coming in!" The manager was saving face for her subordinate, just like the female students role-playing in the Tracy and Eisenberg study.

Is this an effective way to communicate? One must ask, effective for what? The manager in question established a positive environment in her group, and the work was done effectively. On the other hand, numerous women in many different fields told me that their bosses say they don't project the proper authority.

Indirectness

Another linguistic signal that varies with power and status is indirectness—the tendency to say what we mean without spelling it out in so many words. Despite the widespread belief in the United States that it's always best to say exactly what we mean, indirectness is a fundamental and pervasive element in human communication. It also is one of the elements that vary most from one culture to another, and it can cause enormous misunderstanding when speakers have different habits and expectations about how it is used. It's often said that American women are more indirect than American men, but in fact everyone tends to be indirect in some situations and in different ways. Allowing for cultural, ethnic, regional, and individual differences, women are especially likely to be indirect when it comes to telling others what to do, which is not surprising, considering girls' readiness to brand other girls as bossy. On the other hand, men are especially likely to be indirect when it comes to admitting fault or weakness, which also is not surprising, considering boys' readiness to push around boys who assume the one-down position.

At first glance, it would seem that only the powerful can get away with bald commands such as, "Have that report on my desk by noon." But power in an organization also can lead to requests so indirect that they don't sound like requests at all. A boss who says, "Do we have the sales data by product line for each region?" would be surprised and frustrated if a subordinate responded, "We probably do" rather than "I'll get it for you."

Examples such as these notwithstanding, many researchers have claimed that those in subordinate positions are more likely to speak indirectly, and that is surely accurate in some situations. For example, linguist Charlotte Linde, in a study published in *Language in Society* (Volume 17, 1988), examined the black-box conversations that took place between pilots and copilots before airplane crashes. In one particularly tragic instance, an Air Florida plane crashed into the Potomac River immediately after attempting takeoff from National Airport in Washington, D.C., killing all but 5 of the 74 people on board. The pilot, it turned out, had little experience flying in icy weather. The copilot had a bit more, and it became heartbreakingly clear on analysis that he had tried to warn the pilot but had done so indirectly. Alerted by Linde's observation, I examined the transcript of the conversations and found evidence of her hypothesis. The copilot repeatedly called attention to the bad weather and to ice buildup on other planes:

> *Copilot:* Look how the ice is just hanging on his, ah, back, back there, see that? See all those icicles on the back there and everything?
>
> *Pilot:* Yeah.
> [The copilot also expressed concern about the long waiting time since deicing.]
>
> *Copilot:* Boy, this is a, this is a losing battle here on trying to deice those things; it [gives] you a false feeling of security, that's all that does.
> [Just before they took off, the copilot expressed another concern—about abnormal instrument readings—but again he didn't press the matter when it wasn't picked up by the pilot.]
>
> *Copilot:* That don't seem right, does it? [3-second pause]. Ah, that's not right. Well—
>
> *Pilot:* Yes it is, there's 80.
>
> *Copilot:* Naw, I don't think that's right. [7-second pause] Ah, maybe it is.

Shortly thereafter, the plane took off, with tragic results. In other instances as well as this one, Linde observed that copilots, who are second in command, are more likely to express themselves indirectly or otherwise mitigate, or soften, their communication when they are suggesting courses of action to the pilot. In an effort to avert similar disasters, some airlines now offer training for copilots to express themselves in more assertive ways.

This solution seems self-evidently appropriate to most Americans. But when I assigned Linde's article in a graduate seminar I taught, a Japanese student pointed out that it would be just as effective to train pilots to pick up on hints. This approach reflects assumptions about communication that typify Japanese culture, which places great value on the ability of people to understand one another without putting everything into words. Either directness or indirectness can be a successful means of communication as long as the linguistic style is understood by the participants.

In the world of work, however, there is more at stake than whether the communication is understood. People in powerful positions are likely to reward styles similar to their own, because we all tend to take as self-evident the logic of our own styles. Accordingly, there is evidence that in the U.S. workplace, where instructions from a superior are expected to be voiced in a relatively direct manner, those who tend to be indirect when telling subordinates what to do may be perceived as lacking in confidence.

Consider the case of the manager at a national magazine who was responsible for giving assignments to reporters. She tended to phrase her assignments as questions. For example, she asked, "How would you like to do the X project with Y?" or said, "I was thinking of putting you on the X project. Is that okay?" This worked extremely well with her staff; they liked working for her, and the work got done in an efficient and orderly manner. But when she had her midyear evaluation with her own boss, he criticized her for not assuming the proper demeanor with her staff.

In any work environment, the higher-ranking person has the power to enforce his or her view of appropriate demeanor, created in part by linguistic style. In most U.S. contexts, that view is likely to assume that the person in authority has the right to be relatively direct rather than to mitigate orders. There also are cases, however, in which the higher-ranking person assumes a more indirect style. The owner of a retail operation told her subordinate, a store manager, to do something. He said he would do it, but a week later he still hadn't. They were able to trace the difficulty to the following conversation: She had said, "The bookkeeper needs help with the billing. How would you feel about helping her out?" He had said, "Fine." This conversation had seemed to be clear and flawless at the time, but it turned out that they had interpreted this simple exchange in very different ways. She thought he meant, "Fine, I'll help the bookkeeper out." He thought he meant, "Fine, I'll think about how I would feel about helping the bookkeeper out." He did think about it and came to the conclusion that he had more important things to do and couldn't spare the time.

To the owner, "How would you feel about helping the bookkeeper out?" was an obviously appropriate way to give the order "Help the bookkeeper out with the billing." Those who expect orders to be given as bald imperatives may find such locutions annoying or even misleading. But those for whom this style is natural do not think they are being indirect. They believe they are being clear in a polite or respectful way.

What is atypical in this example is that the person with the more indirect style was the boss, so the store manager was motivated to adapt to her style. She still gives orders the same way, but the store manager now understands how she means what she says. It's more common in U.S. business contexts for the highest-ranking people to take a more direct style, with the result that many women in authority risk being judged by their superiors as lacking the appropriate demeanor—and, consequently, lacking confidence.

What to Do?

I am often asked, What is the best way to give criticism? or What is the best way to give orders?—in other words, What is the best way to communicate? The answer is that there is no one best way. The results of a given way of speaking will vary depending on the situation, the culture of the company, the relative rank of speakers, their linguistic styles, and how those styles interact with one another. Because of all those influences, any way of speaking could be perfect for communicating with one person in one situation and disastrous with someone else in another. The critical skill for managers is to become aware of the workings and power of linguistic style, to make sure that people with something valuable to contribute get heard.

It may seem, for example, that running a meeting in an unstructured way gives equal opportunity to all. But awareness of the differences in conversational style makes it easy to see the potential for unequal access. Those who are comfortable speaking up in groups, who need little or no silence before raising their hands, or who speak out easily without waiting to be recognized are far more likely to get heard at meetings. Those who refrain from talking until it's clear that the previous speaker is finished, who wait to be recognized, and who are inclined to link their comments to those of others will do fine at a meeting where everyone else is following the same rules but will have a hard time getting heard in a meeting with people whose styles are more like the first pattern. Given the socialization typical of boys and girls, men are more likely to have learned the first style and women the second, making meetings more congenial for men than for women. It's common to observe women who participate actively in one-on-one discussions or in all-female groups but who are seldom heard in meetings with a large proportion of men. On the other hand, there are women who share the style more common among men, and they run a different risk—of being seen as too aggressive.

A manager aware of those dynamics might devise any number of ways of ensuring that everyone's ideas are heard and credited. Although no single solution will fit all contexts, managers who understand the dynamics of linguistic style can develop more adaptive and flexible approaches to running or participating in meetings, mentoring or advancing the careers of others, evaluating performance, and so on. Talk is the lifeblood of managerial work, and understanding that different people have different ways of saying what they mean will make it possible to take advantage of the talents of people with a broad range of linguistic styles. As the workplace becomes more culturally diverse and business becomes more global, managers will need to become even better at reading interactions and more flexible in adjusting their own styles to the people with whom they interact.

Originally published in September 1995. Reprint 95510

The Necessary Art of Persuasion

by Jay A. Conger

IF THERE EVER WAS A time for businesspeople to learn the fine art of persuasion, it is now. Gone are the command-and-control days of executives managing by decree. Today businesses are run largely by cross-functional teams of peers and populated by baby boomers and their Generation X offspring, who show little tolerance for unquestioned authority. Electronic communication and globalization have further eroded the traditional hierarchy, as ideas and people flow more freely than ever around organizations and as decisions get made closer to the markets. These fundamental changes, more than a decade in the making but now firmly part of the economic landscape, essentially come down to this: work today gets done in an environment where people don't just ask What should I do? but Why should I do it?

To answer this why question effectively is to persuade. Yet many businesspeople misunderstand persuasion, and more still underutilize it. The reason? Persuasion is widely perceived as a skill reserved for selling products and closing deals. It is also commonly seen as just another form of manipulation—devious and to be avoided. Certainly, persuasion can be used in selling and deal-clinching situations, and it can be misused to manipulate people. But exercised constructively and to its full potential, persuasion supersedes sales and is quite the opposite of deception. Effective persuasion becomes a negotiating and learning process through which a persuader leads colleagues to a problem's shared solution. Persuasion does indeed involve moving people to a position they don't currently hold, but not by begging or cajoling. Instead, it involves careful preparation, the proper framing of arguments, the presentation of vivid supporting evidence, and the effort to find the correct emotional match with your audience.

Effective persuasion is a difficult and time-consuming proposition, but it may also be more powerful than the command-and-control managerial model it succeeds. As AlliedSignal's CEO Lawrence Bossidy said recently, "The day when you could yell and scream and beat people into good performance is over. Today you have to appeal to them by helping them see how they can get from here to there, by establishing some credibility, and by giving them some reason and help to get there. Do all those things, and they'll knock down doors." In essence, he is describing persuasion—now more than ever, the language of business leadership.

Think for a moment of your definition of persuasion. If you are like most businesspeople I have encountered (see the sidebar "Twelve Years of Watching and Listening"), you see persuasion as a relatively straightforward process. First, you strongly state your position. Second, you outline the supporting arguments, followed by a highly assertive, data-based exposition. Finally, you enter the deal-making stage and work toward a "close." In other words, you use logic, persistence, and personal enthusiasm to get others to buy a good idea. The reality is that following this process is one surefire way to fail at persuasion. (See the sidebar "Four Ways Not to Persuade.")

What, then, constitutes effective persuasion? If persuasion is a learning and negotiating process, then in the most general terms it involves phases of discovery, preparation, and dialogue. Getting ready to persuade colleagues can take weeks or months of planning as you learn about your audience and the position you intend to argue. Before they even start to talk, effective persuaders have considered their positions from every angle. What investments in time and money will my position require from others? Is my supporting

Idea in Brief

This article defines and explains the four essential elements of persuasion. Business today is largely run by teams and populated by authority-averse baby boomers and Generation Xers. That makes persuasion more important than ever as a managerial tool. But contrary to popular belief, author Jay Conger (director of the University of Southern California's Marshall Business School's Leadership Institute) asserts, persuasion is not the same as selling an idea or convincing opponents to see things your way. It is instead a process of learning from others and negotiating a shared solution. To that end, persuasion consists of these essential elements: establishing credibility, framing to find common ground, providing vivid evidence, and connecting emotionally. Credibility grows, the author says, out of two sources: expertise and relationships. The former is a function of product or process knowledge and the latter a history of listening to and working in the best interest of others. But even if a persuader's credibility is high, his position must make sense—even more, it must appeal—to the audience. Therefore, a persuader must frame his position to illuminate its benefits to everyone who will feel its impact. Persuasion then becomes a matter of presenting evidence—but not just ordinary charts and spreadsheets. The author says the most effective persuaders use vivid—even over-the-top—stories, metaphors, and examples to make their positions come alive. Finally, good persuaders have the ability to accurately sense and respond to their audience's emotional state. Sometimes, that means they have to suppress their own emotions; at other times, they must intensify them. Persuasion can be a force for enormous good in an organization, but people must understand it for what it is: an often painstaking process that requires insight, planning, and compromise.

evidence weak in any way? Are there alternative positions I need to examine?

Dialogue happens before and during the persuasion process. Before the process begins, effective persuaders use dialogue to learn more about their audience's opinions, concerns, and perspectives. During the process, dialogue continues to be a form of learning, but it is also the beginning of the negotiation stage. You invite people to discuss, even debate, the merits of your position, and then to offer honest feedback and suggest alternative solutions. That may sound

The Idea in Practice

The process of persuasion has four steps:

1. **Establish credibility.** Your credibility grows out of two sources: **expertise** and **relationships.** If you have a history of well-informed, sound judgment, your colleagues will trust your expertise. If you've demonstrated that you can work in the best interest of others, your colleagues will have confidence in your relationships.

   If you are weak on the expertise side, bolster your position by

   - learning more through formal and informal education—for example, conversations with in-house experts
   - hiring recognized outside experts
   - launching pilot projects.

   To fill in the relationship gap, try

   - meeting one-on-one with key people
   - involving like-minded coworkers who have good support with your audience.

   Example: Two developers at Microsoft envisioned a controversial new software product, but both were technology novices. By working closely with technical experts and market testing a prototype, they persuaded management that the new product was ideally suited to the average computer user. It sold half a million units.

2. **Frame goals on common ground.** Tangibly describe the benefits of your position. The fastest way to get a child to the grocery store is to point out the lollipops by the cash register. That is not deception—it's

like a slow way to achieve your goal, but effective persuasion is about testing and revising ideas in concert with your colleagues' concerns and needs. In fact, the best persuaders not only listen to others but also incorporate their perspectives into a shared solution.

Persuasion, in other words, often involves—indeed, demands—compromise. Perhaps that is why the most effective persuaders seem to share a common trait: they are open-minded, never dogmatic. They enter the persuasion process prepared to adjust their viewpoints and incorporate others' ideas. That approach to persuasion. When no shared advantages are apparent, adjust your position.

Example: An ad agency executive persuaded skeptical fast-food franchisees to support headquarters' new price discounts. She cited reliable research showing how the pricing scheme improved franchisees' profits. They supported the new plan unanimously.

3. **Vividly reinforce your position.** Ordinary evidence won't do. Make numerical data more compelling with examples, stories, and metaphors that have an emotional impact.

Example: The founder of Mary Kay Cosmetics made a speech comparing sales people's weekly meetings to gatherings among Christians resisting Roman rule. This drove home the importance of a mutually supportive sales force and imbued the work with a sense of heroic mission.

4. **Connect emotionally.** Adjust your own emotional tone to match each audience's ability to receive your message. Learn how your colleagues have interpreted past events in the organization and sense how they will probably interpret your proposal. Test key individuals' possible reactions.

Example: A Chrysler team leader raised the morale of employees demoralized by foreign competition and persuaded management to bring a new car design in-house. He showed both audiences slides of his hometown, which had been devastated by foreign mining competition. His patriotic appeal reinvigorated his team, and the chairman approved the plan.

persuasion is, interestingly, highly persuasive in itself. When colleagues see that a persuader is eager to hear their views and willing to make changes in response to their needs and concerns, they respond very positively. They trust the persuader more and listen more attentively. They don't fear being bowled over or manipulated. They see the persuader as flexible and are thus more willing to make sacrifices themselves. Because that is such a powerful dynamic, good persuaders often enter the persuasion process with judicious compromises already prepared.

Twelve Years of Watching and Listening

THE IDEAS BEHIND THIS ARTICLE spring from three streams of research.

For the last 12 years as both an academic and as a consultant, I have been studying 23 senior business leaders who have shown themselves to be effective change agents. Specifically, I have investigated how these individuals use language to motivate their employees, articulate vision and strategy, and mobilize their organizations to adapt to challenging business environments.

Four years ago, I started a second stream of research exploring the capabilities and characteristics of successful cross-functional team leaders. The core of my database comprised interviews with and observations of 18 individuals working in a range of U.S. and Canadian companies. These were not senior leaders as in my earlier studies but low- and middle-level managers. Along with interviewing the colleagues of these people, I also compared their skills with those of other team leaders—in particular, with the leaders of less successful cross-functional teams engaged in similar initiatives within the same companies. Again, my focus was on language, but I also studied the influence of interpersonal skills.

The similarities in the persuasion skills possessed by both the change-agent leaders and effective team leaders prompted me to explore the academic literature on persuasion and rhetoric, as well as on the art of gospel preaching. Meanwhile, to learn how most managers approach the persuasion process, I observed several dozen managers in company meetings, and I employed simulations in company executive-education programs where groups of managers had to persuade one another on hypothetical business objectives. Finally, I selected a group of 14 managers known for their outstanding abilities in constructive persuasion. For several months, I interviewed them and their colleagues and observed them in actual work situations.

Four Essential Steps

Effective persuasion involves four distinct and essential steps. First, effective persuaders establish credibility. Second, they frame their goals in a way that identifies common ground with those they intend to persuade. Third, they reinforce their positions using vivid language and compelling evidence. And fourth, they connect emotionally with their audience. As one of the most effective executives in our research commented, "The most valuable lesson I've learned about persuasion over the years is that there's just as much strategy in how you present your position as in the position itself. In fact, I'd say the strategy of presentation is the more critical."

Establish credibility

The first hurdle persuaders must overcome is their own credibility. A persuader can't advocate a new or contrarian position without having people wonder, Can we trust this individual's perspectives and opinions? Such a reaction is understandable. After all, allowing oneself to be persuaded is risky, because any new initiative demands a commitment of time and resources. Yet even though persuaders must have high credibility, our research strongly suggests that most managers overestimate their own credibility—considerably.

In the workplace, credibility grows out of two sources: expertise and relationships. People are considered to have high levels of expertise if they have a history of sound judgment or have proven themselves knowledgeable and well informed about their proposals. For example, in proposing a new product idea, an effective persuader would need to be perceived as possessing a thorough understanding of the product—its specifications, target markets, customers, and competing products. A history of prior successes would further strengthen the persuader's perceived expertise. One extremely successful executive in our research had a track record of 14 years of devising highly effective advertising campaigns. Not surprisingly, he had an easy time winning colleagues over to his position. Another manager had a track record of seven successful new-product launches in a period of five years. He, too, had an advantage when it came to persuading his colleagues to support his next new idea.

On the relationship side, people with high credibility have demonstrated—again, usually over time—that they can be trusted to listen and to work in the best interests of others. They have also consistently shown strong emotional character and integrity; that is, they are not known for mood extremes or inconsistent performance. Indeed, people who are known to be honest, steady, and reliable have an edge when going into any persuasion situation. Because their relationships are robust, they are more apt to be given the benefit of the doubt. One effective persuader in our research was

Four Ways Not to Persuade

IN MY WORK WITH MANAGERS as a researcher and as a consultant, I have had the unfortunate opportunity to see executives fail miserably at persuasion. Here are the four most common mistakes people make:

1. **They attempt to make their case with an up-front, hard sell.** I call this the John Wayne approach. Managers strongly state their position at the outset, and then through a process of persistence, logic, and exuberance, they try to push the idea to a close. In reality, setting out a strong position at the start of a persuasion effort gives potential opponents something to grab onto—and fight against. It's far better to present your position with the finesse and reserve of a lion tamer, who engages his "partner" by showing him the legs of a chair. In other words, effective persuaders don't begin the process by giving their colleagues a clear target in which to set their jaws.
2. **They resist compromise.** Too many managers see compromise as surrender, but it is essential to constructive persuasion. Before people buy into a proposal, they want to see that the persuader is flexible enough to respond to their concerns. Compromises can often lead to better, more sustainable shared solutions.

   By not compromising, ineffective persuaders unconsciously send the message that they think persuasion is a one-way street. But persuasion

considered by colleagues to be remarkably trustworthy and fair; many people confided in her. In addition, she generously shared credit for good ideas and provided staff with exposure to the company's senior executives. This woman had built strong relationships, which meant her staff and peers were always willing to consider seriously what she proposed.

If expertise and relationships determine credibility, it is crucial that you undertake an honest assessment of where you stand on both criteria before beginning to persuade. To do so, first step back and ask yourself the following questions related to expertise: How will others perceive my knowledge about the strategy, product, or change I am proposing? Do I have a track record in this area that others know about and respect? Then, to assess the strength of your relationship credibility, ask yourself, Do those I am hoping to persuade see me as helpful, trustworthy, and supportive? Will they see

is a process of give-and-take. Kathleen Reardon, a professor of organizational behavior at the University of Southern California, points out that a persuader rarely changes another person's behavior or viewpoint without altering his or her own in the process. To persuade meaningfully, we must not only listen to others but also incorporate their perspectives into our own.

3. **They think the secret of persuasion lies in presenting great arguments.** In persuading people to change their minds, great arguments matter. No doubt about it. But arguments, per se, are only one part of the equation. Other factors matter just as much, such as the persuader's credibility and his or her ability to create a proper, mutually beneficial frame for a position, connect on the right emotional level with an audience, and communicate through vivid language that makes arguments come alive.
4. **They assume persuasion is a one-shot effort.** Persuasion is a process, not an event. Rarely, if ever, is it possible to arrive at a shared solution on the first try. More often than not, persuasion involves listening to people, testing a position, developing a new position that reflects input from the group, more testing, incorporating compromises, and then trying again. If this sounds like a slow and difficult process, that's because it is. But the results are worth the effort.

me as someone in sync with them—emotionally, intellectually, and politically—on issues like this one? Finally, it is important to note that it is not enough to get your own read on these matters. You must also test your answers with colleagues you trust to give you a reality check. Only then will you have a complete picture of your credibility.

In most cases, that exercise helps people discover that they have some measure of weakness, either on the expertise or on the relationship side of credibility. The challenge then becomes to fill in such gaps.

In general, if your area of weakness is on the expertise side, you have several options:

- First, you can learn more about the complexities of your position through either formal or informal education and through conversations with knowledgeable individuals. You might also get more relevant experience on the job by asking, for instance, to be assigned to a team that would increase your insight into particular markets or products.

- Another alternative is to hire someone to bolster your expertise—for example, an industry consultant or a recognized outside expert, such as a professor. Either one may have the knowledge and experience required to support your position effectively. Similarly, you may tap experts within your organization to advocate your position. Their credibility becomes a substitute for your own.
- You can also utilize other outside sources of information to support your position, such as respected business or trade periodicals, books, independently produced reports, and lectures by experts. In our research, one executive from the clothing industry successfully persuaded his company to reposition an entire product line to a more youthful market after bolstering his credibility with articles by a noted demographer in two highly regarded journals and with two independent market-research studies.
- Finally, you may launch pilot projects to demonstrate on a small scale your expertise and the value of your ideas.

As for filling in the relationship gap:

- You should make a concerted effort to meet one-on-one with all the key people you plan to persuade. This is not the time to outline your position but rather to get a range of perspectives on the issue at hand. If you have the time and resources, you should even offer to help these people with issues that concern them.
- Another option is to involve like-minded coworkers who already have strong relationships with your audience. Again, that is a matter of seeking out substitutes on your own behalf.

For an example of how these strategies can be put to work, consider the case of a chief operating officer of a large retail bank, whom we will call Tom Smith. Although he was new to his job, Smith ardently wanted to persuade the senior management team that the company was in serious trouble. He believed that the bank's overhead was excessive and would jeopardize its position as the industry entered a more competitive era. Most of his colleagues, however, did not see the potential seriousness of the situation. Because the bank had been enormously successful in recent years, they believed changes in the industry posed little danger. In addition to being newly appointed, Smith had another problem: his career had been in financial services, and he was considered an outsider in the world of retail banking. Thus he had few personal connections to draw on as he made his case, nor was he perceived to be particularly knowledgeable about marketplace exigencies.

As a first step in establishing credibility, Smith hired an external consultant with respected credentials in the industry who showed that the bank was indeed poorly positioned to be a low-cost producer. In a series of interactive presentations to the bank's top-level management, the consultant revealed how the company's leading competitors were taking aggressive actions to contain operating costs. He made it clear from these presentations that not cutting costs would soon cause the bank to fall drastically behind the competition. These findings were then distributed in written reports that circulated throughout the bank.

Next, Smith determined that the bank's branch managers were critical to his campaign. The buy-in of those respected and informed individuals would signal to others in the company that his concerns were valid. Moreover, Smith looked to the branch managers because he believed that they could increase his expertise about marketplace trends and also help him test his own assumptions. Thus, for the next three months, he visited every branch in his region of Ontario, Canada—135 in all. During each visit, he spent time with branch managers, listening to their perceptions of the bank's strengths and weaknesses. He learned firsthand about the competition's initiatives and customer trends, and he solicited ideas for improving the bank's services and minimizing costs. By the time he was through, Smith had a broad perspective on the bank's future that few people even in senior management possessed. And he had built dozens of relationships in the process.

Finally, Smith launched some small but highly visible initiatives to demonstrate his expertise and capabilities. For example, he was concerned about slow growth in the company's mortgage business and the loan officers' resulting slip in morale. So he devised a program in which new mortgage customers would make no payments for the first 90 days. The initiative proved remarkably successful, and in short order Smith appeared to be a far more savvy retail banker than anyone had assumed.

Another example of how to establish credibility comes from Microsoft. In 1990, two product-development managers, Karen Fries and Barry Linnett, came to believe that the market would greatly welcome software that featured a "social interface." They envisioned a package that would employ animated human and animal characters to show users how to go about their computing tasks.

Inside Microsoft, however, employees had immediate concerns about the concept. Software programmers ridiculed the cute characters. Animated characters had been used before only in software for children, making their use in adult environments hard to envision. But Fries and Linnett felt their proposed product had both dynamism and complexity, and they remained convinced that consumers would eagerly buy such programs. They also believed that the home-computer software market—largely untapped at the time and with fewer software standards—would be open to such innovation.

Within the company, Fries had gained quite a bit of relationship credibility. She had started out as a recruiter for the company in 1987 and had worked directly for many of Microsoft's senior executives. They trusted and liked her. In addition, she had been responsible for hiring the company's product and program managers. As a result, she knew all the senior people at Microsoft and had hired many of the people who would be deciding on her product.

Linnett's strength laid in his expertise. In particular, he knew the technology behind an innovative tutorial program called PC Works.

In addition, both Fries and Linnett had managed Publisher, a product with a unique help feature called Wizards, which Microsoft's CEO, Bill Gates, had liked. But those factors were sufficient only to get an initial hearing from Microsoft's senior management. To persuade the organization to move forward, the pair would need to improve perceptions of their expertise. It hurt them that this type of social-interface software had no proven track record of success and that they were both novices with such software. Their challenge became one of finding substitutes for their own expertise.

Their first step was a wise one. From within Microsoft, they hired respected technical guru Darrin Massena. With Massena, they developed a set of prototypes to demonstrate that they did indeed understand the software's technology and could make it work. They then tested the prototypes in market research, and users responded enthusiastically. Finally, and most important, they enlisted two Stanford University professors, Clifford Nass and Bryon Reeves, both experts in human-computer interaction. In several meetings with Microsoft senior managers and Gates himself, they presented a rigorously compiled and thorough body of research that demonstrated how and why social-interface software was ideally suited to the average computer user. In addition, Fries and Linnett asserted that considerable jumps in computing power would make more realistic cartoon characters an increasingly malleable technology. Their product, they said, was the leading edge of an incipient software revolution. Convinced, Gates approved a full product-development team, and in January 1995, the product called BOB was launched. BOB went on to sell more than half a million copies, and its concept and technology are being used within Microsoft as a platform for developing several Internet products.

Credibility is the cornerstone of effective persuading; without it, a persuader won't be given the time of day. In the best-case scenario, people enter into a persuasion situation with some measure of expertise and relationship credibility. But it is important to note that credibility along either lines can be built or bought. Indeed, it must be, or the next steps are an exercise in futility.

Frame for common ground

Even if your credibility is high, your position must still appeal strongly to the people you are trying to persuade. After all, few people will jump on board a train that will bring them to ruin or even mild discomfort. Effective persuaders must be adept at describing their positions in terms that illuminate their advantages. As any parent can tell you, the fastest way to get a child to come along willingly on a trip to the grocery store is to point out that there are lollipops by the cash register. That is not deception. It is just a persuasive way of framing the benefits of taking such a journey. In work situations, persuasive framing is obviously more complex, but the underlying principle is the same. It is a process of identifying shared benefits.

Monica Ruffo, an account executive for an advertising agency, offers a good example of persuasive framing. Her client, a fast-food chain, was instituting a promotional campaign in Canada; menu items such as a hamburger, fries, and cola were to be bundled together and sold at a low price. The strategy made sense to corporate headquarters. Its research showed that consumers thought the company's products were higher priced than the competition's, and the company was anxious to overcome this perception. The franchisees, on the other hand, were still experiencing strong sales and were far more concerned about the short-term impact that the new, low prices would have on their profit margins.

A less experienced persuader would have attempted to rationalize headquarters' perspective to the franchisees—to convince them of its validity. But Ruffo framed the change in pricing to demonstrate its benefits to the franchisees themselves. The new value campaign, she explained, would actually improve franchisees' profits. To back up this point, she drew on several sources. A pilot project in Tennessee, for instance, had demonstrated that under the new pricing scheme, the sales of french fries and drinks—the two most profitable items on the menu—had markedly increased. In addition, the company had rolled out medium-sized meal packages in 80% of its U.S. outlets, and franchisees' sales of fries and drinks had jumped 26%. Citing research from a respected business periodical, Ruffo also showed that when customers raised their estimate of the value they receive from a retail establishment by 10%, the establishment's sales rose by 1%. She had estimated that the new meal plan would increase value perceptions by 100%, with the result that franchisee sales could be expected to grow 10%.

Ruffo closed her presentation with a letter written many years before by the company's founder to the organization. It was an emotional letter extolling the values of the company and stressing the importance of the franchisees to the company's success. It also highlighted the importance of the company's position as the low-price leader in the industry. The beliefs and values contained in the letter had long been etched in the minds of Ruffo's audience. Hearing them again only confirmed the company's concern for the franchisees and the importance of their winning formula. They also won Ruffo a standing ovation. That day, the franchisees voted unanimously to support the new meal-pricing plan.

The Ruffo case illustrates why—in choosing appropriate positioning—it is critical first to identify your objective's tangible benefits to the people you are trying to persuade. Sometimes that is easy. Mutual benefits exist. In other situations, however, no shared advantages are readily apparent—or meaningful. In these cases, effective persuaders adjust their positions. They know it is impossible to engage people and gain commitment to ideas or plans without highlighting the advantages to all the parties involved.

At the heart of framing is a solid understanding of your audience. Even before starting to persuade, the best persuaders we have encountered closely study the issues that matter to their colleagues. They use conversations, meetings, and other forms of dialogue to collect essential information. They are good at listening. They test their ideas with trusted confidants, and they ask questions of the people they will later be persuading. Those steps help them think through the arguments, the evidence, and the perspectives they will present. Oftentimes, this process causes them to alter or compromise their own plans before they even start persuading. It is through this thoughtful, inquisitive approach they develop frames that appeal to their audience.

Consider the case of a manager who was in charge of process engineering for a jet engine manufacturer. He had redesigned the work flow for routine turbine maintenance for airline clients in a manner that would dramatically shorten the turnaround time for servicing. Before presenting his ideas to the company's president, he consulted a good friend in the company, the vice president of engineering, who knew the president well. This conversation revealed that the president's prime concern would not be speed or efficiency but profitability. To get the president's buy-in, the vice president explained, the new system would have to improve the company's profitability in the short run by lowering operating expenses.

At first this information had the manager stumped. He had planned to focus on efficiency and had even intended to request additional funding to make the process work. But his conversation with the vice president sparked him to change his position. Indeed, he went so far as to change the work-flow design itself so that it no longer required new investment but rather drove down costs. He then carefully documented the cost savings and profitability gains that his new plan would produce and presented this revised plan to the president. With his initiative positioned anew, the manager persuaded the president and got the project approved.

Provide evidence

With credibility established and a common frame identified, persuasion becomes a matter of presenting evidence. Ordinary evidence, however, won't do. We have found that the most effective persuaders use language in a particular way. They supplement numerical data with examples, stories, metaphors, and analogies to make their positions come alive. That use of language paints a vivid word picture and, in doing so, lends a compelling and tangible quality to the persuader's point of view.

Think about a typical persuasion situation. The persuader is often advocating a goal, strategy, or initiative with an uncertain outcome. Karen Fries and Barry Linnett, for instance, wanted Microsoft to invest millions of dollars in a software package with chancy technology and unknown market demand. The team could have supported its case solely with market research, financial projections, and the like. But that would have been a mistake, because research shows that most people perceive such reports as not entirely informative. They are too abstract to be completely meaningful or memorable. In essence, the numbers don't make an emotional impact.

By contrast, stories and vivid language do, particularly when they present comparable situations to the one under discussion. A marketing manager trying to persuade senior executives to invest in a new product, for example, might cite examples of similar investments that paid off handsomely. Indeed, we found that people readily draw lessons from such cases. More important, the research shows that listeners absorb information in proportion to its vividness. Thus it is no wonder that Fries and Linnett hit a home run when they presented their case for BOB with the following analogy:

> Imagine you want to cook dinner and you must first go to the supermarket. You have all the flexibility you want—you can cook anything in the world as long as you know how and have the time and desire to do it. When you arrive at the supermarket, you find all these overstuffed aisles with cryptic single-word headings like "sundries" and "ethnic food" and "condiments." These are the menus on typical computer interfaces. The question is whether salt is under condiments or ethnic food or near the potato chip section. There are surrounding racks and wall spaces, much as our software interfaces now have support buttons, tool bars, and lines around the perimeters. Now after you have collected everything, you still need to put it all together in the correct order to make a meal. If you're a good cook, your meal will probably be good. If you're a novice, it probably won't be.
>
> We [at Microsoft] have been selling under the supermarket category for years, and we think there is a big opportunity for restaurants. That's what we are trying to do now with BOB: pushing the next step with software that is more like going to a restaurant, so the user doesn't spend all of his time searching for the ingredients. We find and put the ingredients together. You sit down, you get comfortable. We bring you a menu. We do the

> work, you relax. It's an enjoyable experience. No walking around lost trying to find things, no cooking.

Had Fries and Linnett used a literal description of BOB's advantages, few of their highly computer-literate colleagues at Microsoft would have personally related to the menu-searching frustration that BOB was designed to eliminate. The analogy they selected, however, made BOB's purpose both concrete and memorable.

A master persuader, Mary Kay Ash, the founder of Mary Kay Cosmetics, regularly draws on analogies to illustrate and "sell" the business conduct she values. Consider this speech at the company's annual sales convention:

> Back in the days of the Roman Empire, the legions of the emperor conquered the known world. There was, however, one band of people that the Romans never conquered. Those people were the followers of the great teacher from Bethlehem. Historians have long since discovered that one of the reasons for the sturdiness of this folk was their habit of meeting together weekly. They shared their difficulties, and they stood side by side. Does this remind you of something? The way we stand side by side and share our knowledge and difficulties with each other in our weekly unit meetings? I have so often observed when a director or unit member is confronted with a personal problem that the unit stands together in helping that sister in distress. What a wonderful circle of friendships we have. Perhaps it's one of the greatest fringe benefits of our company.

Through her vivid analogy, Ash links collective support in the company to a courageous period in Christian history. In doing so, she accomplishes several objectives. First, she drives home her belief that collective support is crucial to the success of the organization. Most Mary Kay salespeople are independent operators who face the daily challenges of direct selling. An emotional support system of fellow salespeople is essential to ensure that self-esteem and confidence remain intact in the face of rejection. Next she suggests by her analogy that solidarity against the odds is the best way to stymie powerful oppressors—to wit, the competition. Finally, Ash's choice of analogy imbues a sense of a heroic mission to the work of her sales force.

You probably don't need to invoke the analogy of the Christian struggle to support your position, but effective persuaders are not afraid of unleashing the immense power of language. In fact, they use it to their utmost advantage.

Connect emotionally

In the business world, we like to think that our colleagues use reason to make their decisions, yet if we scratch below the surface we will always find emotions at play. Good persuaders are aware of the primacy of emotions and are responsive to them in two important ways. First, they show their own emotional commitment to the position they are advocating. Such expression is a delicate matter. If you act too emotional, people may doubt your clearheadedness. But you must also show that your commitment to a goal is not just in your mind but in your heart and gut as well. Without this demonstration of feeling, people may wonder if you actually believe in the position you're championing.

Perhaps more important, however, is that effective persuaders have a strong and accurate sense of their audience's emotional state, and they adjust the tone of their arguments accordingly. Sometimes that means coming on strong, with forceful points. Other times, a whisper may be all that is required. The idea is that whatever your position, you match your emotional fervor to your audience's ability to receive the message.

Effective persuaders seem to have a second sense about how their colleagues have interpreted past events in the organization and how they will probably interpret a proposal. The best persuaders in our study would usually canvass key individuals who had a good pulse on the mood and emotional expectations of those about to be persuaded. They would ask those individuals how various proposals might affect colleagues on an emotional level—in essence, testing possible reactions. They were also quite effective at gathering information through informal conversations in the hallways or at lunch. In the end, their aim was to ensure that the emotional appeal behind their persuasion matched what their audience was already feeling or expecting.

To illustrate the importance of emotional matchmaking in persuasion, consider this example. The president of an aeronautics manufacturing company strongly believed that the maintenance costs and turnaround time of the company's U.S. and foreign competitors were so much better than his own company's that it stood to lose customers and profits. He wanted to communicate his fear and his urgent desire for change to his senior managers. So one afternoon, he called them into the boardroom. On an overhead screen was the projected image of a smiling man flying an old-fashioned biplane with his scarf blowing in the wind. The right half of the transparency was covered. When everyone was seated, the president explained that he felt as this pilot did, given the company's recent good fortune. The organization, after all, had just finished its most successful year in history. But then with a deep sigh, he announced that his happiness was quickly vanishing. As the president lifted the remaining portion of the sheet, he revealed an image of the pilot flying directly into a wall. The president then faced his audience and in a heavy voice said, "This is what I see happening to us." He asserted that the company was headed for a crash if people didn't take action fast. He then went on to lecture the group about the steps needed to counter this threat.

The reaction from the group was immediate and negative. Directly after the meeting, managers gathered in small clusters in the hallways to talk about the president's "scare tactics." They resented what they perceived to be the president's overstatement of the case. As the managers saw it, they had exerted enormous effort that year to break the company's records in sales and profitability. They were proud of their achievements. In fact, they had entered the meeting expecting it would be the moment of recognition. But to their absolute surprise, they were scolded.

The president's mistake? First, he should have canvassed a few members of his senior team to ascertain the emotional state of the group. From that, he would have learned that they were in need of thanks and recognition. He should then have held a separate session devoted simply to praising the team's accomplishments. Later, in a second meeting, he could have expressed his own anxieties about the coming year. And rather than blame the team for ignoring the future, he could have calmly described what he saw as emerging threats to the company and then asked his management team to help him develop new initiatives.

Now let us look at someone who found the right emotional match with his audience: Robert Marcell, head of Chrysler's small-car design team. In the early 1990s, Chrysler was eager to produce a new subcompact—indeed, the company had not introduced a new model of this type since 1978. But senior managers at Chrysler did not want to go it alone. They thought an alliance with a foreign manufacturer would improve the car's design and protect Chrysler's cash stores.

Marcell was convinced otherwise. He believed that the company should bring the design and production of a new subcompact in-house. He knew that persuading senior managers would be difficult, but he also had his own team to contend with. Team members had lost their confidence that they would ever again have the opportunity to create a good car. They were also angry that the United States had once again given up its position to foreign competitors when it came to small cars.

Marcell decided that his persuasion tactics had to be built around emotional themes that would touch his audience. From innumerable conversations around the company, he learned that many people felt as he did—that to surrender the subcompact's design to a foreign manufacturer was to surrender the company's soul and, ultimately, its ability to provide jobs. In addition, he felt deeply that his organization was a talented group hungry for a challenge and an opportunity to restore its self-esteem and pride. He would need to demonstrate his faith in the team's abilities.

Marcell prepared a 15-minute talk built around slides of his hometown, Iron River, a now defunct mining town in Upper Michigan, devastated, in large part, by foreign mining companies. On the screen flashed recent photographs he had taken of his boarded-up high school, the shuttered homes of his childhood friends, the crumbling ruins of the town's ironworks, closed churches, and an abandoned railroad yard. After a description of each of these places, he said the phrase, "We couldn't compete"—like the refrain of a hymn. Marcell's point was that the same outcome awaited Detroit if the production of small cars was not brought back to the United States. Surrender was the enemy, he said, and devastation would follow if the group did not take immediate action.

Marcell ended his slide show on a hopeful note. He spoke of his pride in his design group and then challenged the team to build a "made-in-America" subcompact that would prove that the United States could still compete. The speech, which echoed the exact sentiments of the audience, rekindled the group's fighting spirit. Shortly after the speech, group members began drafting their ideas for a new car.

Marcell then took his slide show to the company's senior management and ultimately to Chrysler chairman Lee Iacocca. As Marcell showed his slides, he could see that Iacocca was touched. Iacocca, after all, was a fighter and a strongly patriotic man himself. In fact, Marcell's approach was not too different from Iacocca's earlier appeal to the United States Congress to save Chrysler. At the end of the show, Marcell stopped and said, "If we dare to be different, we could be the reason the U.S. auto industry survives. We could be the reason our kids and grandkids don't end up working at fast-food chains." Iacocca stayed on for two hours as Marcell explained in greater detail what his team was planning. Afterward, Iacocca changed his mind and gave Marcell's group approval to develop a car, the Neon.

With both groups, Marcell skillfully matched his emotional tenor to that of the group he was addressing. The ideas he conveyed resonated deeply with his largely Midwestern audience. And rather than leave them in a depressed state, he offered them hope, which was more persuasive than promising doom. Again, this played to the strong patriotic sentiments of his American-heartland audience.

No effort to persuade can succeed without emotion, but showing too much emotion can be as unproductive as showing too little. The important point to remember is that you must match your emotions to your audience's.

The Force of Persuasion

The concept of persuasion, like that of power, often confuses and even mystifies businesspeople. It is so complex—and so dangerous when mishandled—that many would rather just avoid it altogether. But like power, persuasion can be a force for enormous good in an organization. It can pull people together, move ideas forward, galvanize change, and forge constructive solutions. To do all that, however, people must understand persuasion for what it is—not convincing and selling but learning and negotiating. Furthermore, it must be seen as an art form that requires commitment and practice, especially as today's business contingencies make persuasion more necessary than ever.

Originally published in May 1998. Reprint 98304

Is Silence Killing Your Company?

by Leslie Perlow and Stephanie Williams

SILENCE IS ASSOCIATED WITH MANY virtues: modesty, respect for others, prudence, decorum. Thanks to deeply ingrained rules of etiquette, people silence themselves to avoid embarrassment, confrontation, and other perceived dangers. There's an old saying that sums up the virtues of silence: "Better to be quiet and thought a fool than to talk and be known as one."

The social virtues of silence are reinforced by our survival instincts. Many organizations send the message—verbally or nonverbally—that falling into line is the safest way to hold on to our jobs and further our careers. The need for quiet submission is exaggerated by today's difficult economy, where millions of people have lost their jobs and many more worry that they might. A Dilbert cartoon poignantly expresses how pointless—and perilous—many people feel it is to speak out. Dilbert, the everyman underling, recognizes that a senior executive is making a poor decision. "Shouldn't we tell her?" he asks his boss, who laughs cynically. "Yes," the boss replies. "Let's end our careers by challenging a decision that won't change. That's a great idea."

To be sure, people who speak out sometimes get their day in the sun: Sherron Watkins of Enron, Cynthia Cooper of WorldCom, and Coleen Rowley at the FBI all ended up on the cover of *Time* as "Persons of the Year." But public recognition of a few people does not mean that speaking out is necessarily viewed as courageous or praiseworthy.

Most individuals who go against their organizations or express their concerns publicly are severely punished. If they're not fired outright, they're usually marginalized and made to feel irrelevant.

But it is time to take the gilt off silence. Our research shows that silence is not only ubiquitous and expected in organizations but extremely costly to both the firm and the individual. Our interviews with senior executives and employees in organizations ranging from small businesses to *Fortune* 500 corporations to government bureaucracies reveal that silence can exact a high psychological price on individuals, generating feelings of humiliation, pernicious anger, resentment, and the like that, if unexpressed, contaminate every interaction, shut down creativity, and undermine productivity.

Take the case of Jeff, a team leader at a *Fortune* 100 company who was working on a large, long-term, high-pressure project. Each Tuesday, Jeff and his peers had a project management meeting (PMM) with Matt, their boss. Jeff would start writing his weekly update reports on Wednesday, continuing to work on them when he had time on Thursday and Friday, working even into the weekend. On Monday morning, he would hand in his document to Matt. Jeff figured that a weekly update was probably useful for Matt; all the same, he felt deeply frustrated at the time he was wasting writing the elaborate reports. Yet despite complaining endlessly to his peers, week after week Jeff said nothing to Matt. With each act of silence, Jeff's resentment grew and his respect for Matt disintegrated, even as Jeff became more and more uncomfortable with the idea of questioning Matt. And so the process continued, as the project fell further behind schedule. For his part, when Matt was asked about the value of the PMM, he was mystified: "Not to insult my team leaders, but in my mind, every Tuesday morning I have a Painfully Meaningless Meeting."

The fact that no one suggested an alternative to the PMM was fairly typical of our findings. Individuals are frequently convinced that keeping quiet is the best way to preserve relationships and get work done. In the following pages, we will examine what makes this sort of silence so prevalent in organizations. From there, we will discuss the personal and organizational costs of silence, which often

Idea in Brief

Many times, often with the best of intentions, people at work decide it's more productive to remain silent about their differences than to air them. There's no time, they think, or no point in going against what the boss says.

But as new research by the authors shows, silencing doesn't smooth things over or make people more productive. It merely pushes differences beneath the surface and can set in motion powerfully destructive forces. When people stay silent about important disagreements, they can begin to fill with anxiety, anger, and resentment. As long as the conflict is unresolved, their repressed feelings remain potent, making them increasingly distrustful, self-protective, and all the more fearful that if they speak up they will be embarrassed or rejected. Their sense of insecurity grows, leading to further acts of silence, more defensiveness, and more distrust, thereby setting into motion a destructive "spiral of silence." Sooner or later, they mentally opt out—sometimes merely doing what they're told but contributing nothing of their own, sometimes spreading discontent and frustration throughout the workplace that can lead them, and others, to leave without thinking it through.

These vicious spirals of silence can be replaced with virtuous spirals of communication, but that requires individuals to find the courage to act differently and executives to create the conditions in which people will value the expression of differences. All too often, behind failed products, broken processes, and mistaken career decisions are people who chose to hold their tongues. Breaking the silence can bring an outpouring of fresh ideas from all levels of an organization—ideas that might just raise the organization's performance to a whole new level.

remain hidden for long periods of time even as they grow exponentially with each additional act of silence. Finally, we will investigate several ways to break free from the insidious silent sink.

The Reign of Silence

Silence often starts when we choose not to confront a difference. Given the dissimilarities in our temperaments, backgrounds, and experiences, it's inevitable that we will have different opinions, beliefs, and tastes. Most of us recognize the value of such variety: Who really wants to go into a brainstorming session with people who all have the same views and ideas? But we're also aware of how terribly painful it can be to raise and work through differences. The French word *différend,* tellingly, means "quarrel." Not surprisingly, most people decide it's easier to cover up their differences than to try to discuss them.

Our research shows that this tendency to remain silent rather than express a difference exists both in individual relationships and in groups, where we fear a loss of status or even expulsion if we differ from the rest. Most of us can remember from our adolescence how compelling the desire was to conform. Even as adults, many people in organizations are willing to go to enormous lengths to get along with members of their work groups—at least superficially. We do what we believe other group members want us to do. We say what we think other people want us to say.

Consider what happened at one off-site meeting of top management at a Web-based education company. Concerned about the company's vision, the managers met to share and discuss different perspectives. But one speaker after another just echoed what the previous speaker had said. When any manager did dare to dissent, a colleague would quickly dismiss his idea. Having effectively tabled every discussion in which disagreement surfaced, the management team crowed about the level of "consensus" they had achieved. One by one, team members celebrated their achievement. The head of marketing went first. "We made some great progress today," he said, "I'm excited—passionate—committed to the future." The CFO continued, "I thought today was going to be a lot uglier. I expected battles. Yet things were remarkably consistent." Yet despite the outward expression of consensus, at the end of the day, many of the attendees privately despaired that the off-site had been a waste of time. By silencing themselves and one another, they failed to create a compelling vision, and the company continued with no clear direction.

This meeting shows how the pressure for unanimity can prevent employees of roughly equal grade and status—even top managers—from exploring their differences. More familiar to many is the pressure to keep silent that's created by differences in rank. How easy it is for a boss to send a powerful signal that a worker should be quiet. Take the case of Robert and Linda. Robert was an attorney in charge of his law firm's support staff. Linda, who was head of the library, came to Robert one day to complain about the performance evaluation process. She felt that many of the lawyers weren't being fair in their evaluations of the library staff and that they shouldn't have the automatic right to determine the librarians' raises and promotions. Robert disagreed. "If you think of the lawyers as your clients," he advised, "you can see why they have every expectation to be able to critique the quality of service." When Linda pressed again, Robert got irritated and said, "This is the way we do it around here, and this is the way it's going to continue!" Linda said nothing more and quietly left his office.

At least Linda tried to speak up. Many members of organizations silence themselves before the boss has the slightest inkling of what they're thinking. Often in these instances, employees use silence as a strategy to get ahead. Consider Don, a senior analyst at an investment bank who carefully keeps his opinions to himself when he's around his superiors. "It comes down to the hierarchical nature of the bank," he says. "Basically you're just trying to make the person above you love you so you'll get a big bonus. If you start raising uncomfortable questions and being holier-than-thou, you may be absolutely right, but you shoot yourself in the foot. What the managing director says goes."

And it's not just that subordinates feel pressure to keep silent with their bosses. Bosses also may feel uncomfortable expressing their differences with subordinates. It is frequently difficult for managers, for instance, to give negative performance feedback to subordinates—especially in organizations that place a high value on being polite and avoiding confrontation.

The Costs of Suffering in Silence

When we silence ourselves and others—even when we're convinced that it is the best way, the right way, or the only way to preserve the relationships we care about and get on with our work—we may be

When to Zip It

ALTHOUGH MOST PEOPLE TEND TO speak up too little rather than too much, there are times when it's better to stay quiet. Some issues are simply not worth raising, and you don't want to unnecessarily turn small differences of opinion into broad conflicts. There's no sense in spending time and effort getting bogged down dealing with every little difference, especially ones that are not likely to affect the quality of people's work or those you're not likely to remember in a week or a month. And if the conflict is in an unimportant relationship or one that won't continue much longer, speaking up may not be crucial. You will still lose out on the creativity and learning that stem from expressing differences, but you don't need to worry about the additional costs of unresolved differences lurking beneath the surface and destroying the relationship.

Even when a difference should be addressed, there is the question of timing. It may be fruitless, for example, to raise a tough issue with your boss when you face an impending deadline—unless speaking up is important for the task at hand and there really is enough time to work through the issue. Waiting until the deadline has passed and people can focus on what you have to say may be the best option. Moreover, initially keeping a lid on differences when your own or the other person's emotions are highly charged can be beneficial in the longer run. If you've just had a row with a colleague and either of you is very upset, arrange a time to talk in the future when both of you have had a chance to cool down and can discuss differences without venting or blaming. But if you defer a difficult conversation, make sure you do not postpone it indefinitely. Otherwise, the unresolved differences will come back to haunt you.

There are no hard-and-fast rules about what needs to be discussed or when it's best to do so. You must rely on your best judgment. What's important is that you shift your mind-set from asking whether this is one of those rare times when you should speak to asking instead whether this is one of those rare times when you should remain quiet.

---

fooling ourselves. Let's return for a moment to the law firm where Robert and Linda worked. After meeting with Linda, Robert simply forgot about their discussion. As a senior partner, he thought his view was a no-brainer, and he assumed that the issue would just go away. Linda, for her part, was acutely aware that she had been forced into silence, but, given that Robert was the boss, she thought the best course was to say nothing further to him.

Still, she was profoundly angry. In an attempt to release her negative feelings, she complained bitterly to her peers about what Robert had said and how he had shut her down. But gossiping only alleviated Linda's anger temporarily, and news of Robert's insensitivity quickly spread throughout the support staff, which came to view the incident as evidence that "management doesn't listen." Ultimately, Robert's strained relations with the support staff led to high turnover. As he later reflected, "My action that day was probably the single greatest mistake I ever made."

The damage wasn't just to Robert and the organization. Linda, in choosing to respond to Robert with silence, caused herself great damage as well, far more in fact than she may have realized. That's because silencing doesn't resolve anything; rather than erase differences, it merely pushes them beneath the surface. Every time we keep silent about our differences, we swell with negative emotions like anxiety, anger, and resentment. Of course, we can go on for a long time pretending to ourselves and others that nothing is wrong. But as long as the conflict is not resolved, our repressed feelings remain potent and color the way we relate to other people. We begin to feel a sense of disconnection in our relationships, which in turn causes us to become increasingly self-protective.

When we feel defensive in this way, we become all the more fearful that if we speak up we will be embarrassed or rejected. Our sense of insecurity grows. In relationships we care about preserving, more acts of silence follow, which only bring more defensiveness and more distrust. A destructive "spiral of silence" is set in motion.

Caught up in just such a spiral was Maria, a project manager we interviewed at a management consulting firm. At the beginning of her first project, her boss, Max, suggested to Maria ways her team should make its initial presentation to the client. Maria wasn't convinced that Max's approach was the best. But Max was the partner, so Maria kept her concerns to herself. Later, when Max discovered that the team had failed to collect some of the data he wanted, he lost his temper and ordered Maria to push the team harder. Maria thought that the data were irrelevant and that searching for them

Speed Trap

THERE'S NO DOUBT THAT PRESSURE to go fast can have its benefits. It can, for example, push us to find more efficient, less bureaucratic ways of working. But it also makes us even more likely to keep silent. How many times has a looming deadline caused you to bite your tongue and think to yourself, "We don't have time to worry about this now; we just need to get it done."

When we perpetually silence ourselves in the short-sighted belief that we are getting our tasks done as expeditiously as possible, we may interfere with creativity, learning, and decision making. If our work depends on divergent thinking, these less-effective processes may in turn result in problems that take time and attention to resolve. Then, in addition to all the work we are rushing to complete, we will also have to address these new problems. That can lead to a vicious cycle that makes us feel the need to go even faster. A little fable about a farmer with a wagon full of apples helps illustrate the point. The farmer stopped a man on the side of the road and asked how far it was to market. The man responded, "It is an hour away, if you go slow." He continued, "If you go fast, it will take you all day." There was a bump in the road, and if the farmer went too fast he would hit it, all his apples would fall out, and he'd

---

would just waste the team's time. But, inwardly clenching her fists and gritting her teeth, she deferred to her superior.

A few days later, Maria and her team received a lukewarm response when they presented their findings to the client. Maria later met with Max to discuss the next steps. Convinced that she understood the client's needs better than he did, she was intent on laying out her own point of view and explaining to him the error in his approach. But Maria had become very uncomfortable around Max, so when he launched into a critique of her team's performance, she lost her nerve. Again she stifled her resistance and opted to do as Max said. Maria's discomfort grew each time she chose to remain silent, and she descended down the spiral of silence. Ultimately, her desire and ability to work with Max were destroyed.

There's a cruel and all too common irony here, for the reason Maria had silenced herself in the first place was to preserve her relationship with Max. We don't speak up for fear of destroying our relationships, but in the end our silence creates an emotional distance that becomes an unbridgeable rift.

have to spend the day picking up the fruit. The farmer would then be in all the greater hurry to get to market.

The pressure to go fast ends up feeding on itself, perpetuating an internally generated and self-destructive, ever-increasing need for speed. Overstretched workers become more overstretched; managers already focused on crises become all the more so. In our daily lives, many of us face pressure to go fast, and we end up silencing our differences in response. We need to be careful, though, or we may end up in a self-made "speed trap."

In the end, whether our primary concern is to preserve our relationships or to get our tasks done as expeditiously as possible, we must speak up rather than withhold our differences. Otherwise, we risk undermining both our relationships and our ability to complete our work.[1]

1. For a more detailed discussion of how speed relates to silencing, see Leslie A. Perlow, Gerardo A. Okhuysen, and Nelson P. Repenning, "The Speed Trap: Exploring the Relationship Between Decision Making and the Temporal Context," *Academy of Management Journal* (October 2002).

That's what happened to Shoney, a research fellow in pulmonary and critical-care medicine. When we interviewed him, he had already discovered where the spiral leads. Praveen, a research associate one level higher, was supposed to oversee Shoney's work. In exchange, Praveen's name would appear on everything Shoney published. Eager to maximize Shoney's productivity, Praveen constantly issued him instructions. Shoney resented being bossed around but always did as he was told, never pushing back. Over time, however, Shoney's resentment grew as Praveen continued to treat him more like an unknowing assistant than a highly qualified peer. One day, when Praveen started to question Shoney about how he had spent his time in the lab the previous evening, something inside Shoney snapped. He still said nothing. But from that day forth, Shoney refused to collaborate with Praveen. On their next assignment, they divided the tasks and carried them out independently.

That just made things worse. By shutting himself off, Shoney lost the opportunity to brainstorm with an informed colleague. He also precluded the possibility of sharing anything he may have learned that could have helped Praveen. And he foreclosed on any potential for eliminating redundancy in the two researchers' work. Silencing was not only costly to Shoney, but it was a cost doubly borne, for the organization paid it as well. Each time workers remain silent in the face of conflict, they keep new ideas to themselves and leave alternative courses of action unexplored. And they withhold important information from colleagues that could enhance the quality of both their own and the organization's work.

Breaking the Spiral of Silence

How do we get ourselves and others to speak up? Can the vicious spirals of silence be replaced with virtuous spirals of communication? The answer is yes, but doing so requires that we find the courage to act differently and that we create the context in which people will value the expression of such difference. Managers with a lot of authority need to be especially careful not to punish people, explicitly or implicitly, for speaking out, particularly on issues that may be difficult for the organization to deal with. Harry's case illustrates how a leader can create such a context.

Harry was a battalion commander, whose unit of more than 500 soldiers had just been miserably defeated in a mock battle against another unit. "If this had been a real battle, two-thirds of us would be dead," Harry said to the unit in the debriefing that followed. But he continued, "I was at fault. I failed you." And he went on to explain exactly how, taking full responsibility for the failure.

At first, no one said a word. Then Nick, a very junior scout who was responsible for detecting and alerting the battalion to the enemy's movements, said, "No sir, it wasn't your fault. I fell asleep on duty."

Harry was shocked. But rather than focus on Nick's failure, great as it was, Harry immediately redirected the unit's attention to uncovering the underlying problem—the exhaustion his men were suffering. How many had also slept through the opening rounds of the attack, he asked his soldiers to think to themselves. "Nick is a good soldier," he said. "All of you are good soldiers. We need to focus on the bigger issue: How can we sustain our capabilities during continuous operations in such high-intensity situations?"

Harry set the tone for this discussion. Had he not started by exhibiting his own failures, it's highly unlikely that Nick would have had the courage to speak up. Moreover, Harry carefully framed the ensuing discussion to avoid blame and instead focus on the larger problem they all faced. In the end, this unit gained a rich appreciation for the importance of speaking up and admitting mistakes.

Keeping quiet is too big a problem to be left just to leaders, however. If an organization wants to escape the spiral of silence, everyone has to fight the urge to withdraw and has to work hard to speak up. That's a tough challenge, for all the reasons we've explored, but the following practices can help.

Recognize your power

We all have the power to express ourselves and to encourage others to speak freely, whether they're subordinates, peers, or even bosses. Of course, nobody likes to be the one to break the ice; in the face of personal conflict, passivity always feels safer than action. Who would not prefer to sit back, blame the other person, and wait for him to make the first move? Yet it's almost never the case that something is entirely another person's fault. Instead of waiting for the other person to apologize or to broach the subject, we need to be willing to take the first step ourselves—to bring differences out into the open so that they can be explored.

This can even be a good strategy for dealing with a boss who has overtly silenced a subordinate, like Robert, from the law firm. In that situation, Linda could have chosen to go back to Robert to try to turn the situation around. She could have met with him again and said something like, "I know that you don't think the issue with the performance evaluation process is important. But it is very important to the library staff, and we would like you to understand our point of view. I don't feel comfortable dropping the issue, as you suggested. I would like a chance to better explain my perspective."

When one person finds the courage to take a step like this and presents new information in a way that the other person can absorb, the two are likely to join in a process of mutual exploration of the differences that separate them. Indeed, we all have much more power than we think. Our superiors certainly have formal power over us, but it's also true that their performance depends on how well we are doing. Don't forget: Your boss needs you, too. And knowing that should empower you to speak up and help him appreciate your point of view.

Act deviantly

To break the walls of silence, sometimes we have to behave in ways that are not considered appropriate for our particular organization. Put differently, we must act deviantly—for example, by choosing to ask tough questions at a company meeting where employees normally just accept the decisions of top management. Although deviance often carries negative connotations, it is not synonymous with dysfunctionality. Deviance is, at heart, a creative act—a way of searching out and inventing new approaches to doing things. Acts of deviance can point to areas where organizations need to change and can result in fruitful alternatives. The chief thing to keep in mind here is that norms can have exceptions. By challenging a particular norm, we can play a role in changing it.

Build a coalition

Reaching out to others can give us the strength to break the hold of silence. Not only is it easier to speak up when we know we're not alone, but a coalition also carries more legitimacy and resources. Even though it may feel threatening to approach people to join forces with you, it is surprising how often you may find that many people feel the same way you do. That's what happened to Nancy Hopkins, a scientist at MIT.[1] Hopkins repeatedly found herself having to fight harder than her male colleagues for resources like lab space. After dealing with the same issues for years, she drafted a letter to the MIT administration. Before sending it, however, she showed it to a female colleague whom she regarded as politically savvy. To Hopkins's surprise, the other woman wanted to add her signature to the letter; the same type of things had happened to her, too. In the end, 14 of the 15 women Hopkins approached decided to sign as well. As a result, a committee was formed, and a pattern of discrimination was uncovered and addressed.

We've recently seen in the scandals at Enron, Tyco, and WorldCom, to name but a few, just how catastrophic situations can become when silence prevails. Yet silence does not have to be about fraud and malfeasance to do grave damage to a company. All too often, behind failed products, broken processes, and mistaken decisions are people who chose to hold their tongues rather than to speak up. Breaking the silence can bring an outpouring of fresh ideas from all levels of an organization—ideas that might just raise the organization's performance to a whole new level.

Originally published in May 2003. Reprint R0305C

Note

1. The account here is taken from material in both Nancy H. Hopkins, "Experience of Women at the Massachusetts Institute of Technology," *Women in the Chemical Workforce: A Workshop Report to the Chemical Sciences Roundtable* (CPSMA, 2000) and Lotte Bailyn, "Academic Careers and Gender Equity: Lessons Learned from MIT," *Gender, Work, and Organizations* (March 2003).

How to Become an Authentic Speaker

by Nick Morgan

AT A COMPANYWIDE SALES MEETING, Carol, a vice president of sales, strides energetically to the podium, pauses for a few seconds to look at the audience, and then tells a story from her days as a field rep. She deftly segues from her anecdote to a positive assessment of the company's sales outlook for the year, supplementing her speech with colorful slides showing strong growth and exciting new products in the pipeline. While describing those products, she accents her words with animated gestures.

Having rehearsed carefully in front of a small audience of trusted colleagues, all of whom liked her message and her energy, she now confidently delivers the closer: Walking to the edge of the stage, she scans the room and challenges her listeners to commit to a stretch sales goal that will put many of them in the annual winners' circle.

But Carol senses that something's amiss. The audience isn't exhibiting the kind of enthusiasm needed to get the year off to a great start. She begins to panic: What's happening? Is there anything she can do to salvage the situation?

We all know a Carol. (You may be one yourself.) We've all heard speeches like hers, presentations in which the speaker is apparently doing all the right things, yet something—something we can't quite identify—is wrong.

If asked about these speeches, we might describe them as "calculated," "insincere," "not real," or "phoned in." We probably wouldn't be able to say exactly why the performance wasn't compelling. The speaker just didn't seem *authentic*.

In today's difficult economy, and especially in the aftermath of numerous scandals involving individual executives, employees and shareholders are more skeptical than ever. Authenticity—including the ability to communicate authentically with others—has become an important leadership attribute. When leaders have it, they can inspire their followers to make extraordinary efforts on behalf of their organizations. When they don't, cynicism prevails and few employees do more than the minimum necessary to get by.

In my 22 years of working as a communications coach, I have seen again and again how hard it is for managers to come across in public communications as authentic—even when they passionately believe their message. Why is this kind of communication so difficult? Why can't people just stand up and tell the truth?

What Science Teaches Us

The answer lies in recent research into the ways our brains perceive and process communication. We all know by now the power of nonverbal communication—what I call the "second conversation." If your spoken message and your body language are mismatched, audiences will respond to the nonverbal message every time. Gestures speak louder than words. And that means you *can't* just stand up and tell the truth. You'll often hear someone say in advance of a speech, "I don't want to look over-rehearsed, so I'm going to wing it." But during the presentation his body language will undermine his credibility. Because he's in a stressful situation with no preparation, he'll appear off-kilter. Whatever the message of his words, he'll seem to be learning as he goes—not likely to engender confidence in a leader.

So preparation is important. But the traditional approach—careful rehearsal like Carol's—often doesn't work either. That's because it usually involves specific coaching on nonverbal elements—"maintain eye

Idea in Brief

You rehearsed your speech thoroughly—and mastered that all-important body language. But when you delivered the talk, you sensed little enthusiasm in your audience.

What's going on? You're probably coming across as artificial. The reason: When we rehearse specific body language elements, we use them incorrectly during the actual speech—slightly *after* speaking the associated words. Listeners feel something's wrong, because during natural conversation, body language emerges *before* the associated words.

To demonstrate your authenticity, don't rehearse your body language. Instead, imagine meeting four aims:

- Being open to your audience
- Connecting with your audience
- Being passionate about your topic
- Listening to your audience

When you rehearse this way, you'll genuinely experience these feelings when delivering your speech. Your body language will emerge at the right moment. And your listeners will know you're the real thing.

contact," "spread your arms," "walk out from behind the podium"—that can ultimately make the speaker seem artificial. The audience can see the wheels turning in her head as she goes through the motions.

Why does this calculated body language come off as inauthentic? Here's where the brain research comes in. We're learning that in human beings the second, nonverbal conversation actually starts *first,* in the instant after an emotion or an impulse fires deep within the brain but before it has been articulated. Indeed, research shows that people's natural and unstudied gestures are often indicators of what they will think and say next.

You might say that words are after-the-fact explanations of why we just gestured as we did. Think of something as simple as a hug: The impulse to embrace someone begins *before* the thought that you're glad to see him or her has fully formed, much less been expressed aloud. Or think about a typical conversation: Reinforcement, contradiction, and commentary arise first in gesture. We nod vigorously, shake our heads, roll our eyes, all of which express our reactions more immediately—and more powerfully—than words can.

Idea in Practice

Morgan recommends rehearsing your speeches with these four aims in mind.

Being Open to Your Audience

To rehearse being open, practice your speech by envisioning what it would be like to give your presentation to someone you're completely comfortable with. The person could be your spouse, a close friend, or your child. Notice especially what this feels like: This is the emotional state you want to be in when you deliver the speech.

This state leads to more natural body language, such as smiles and relaxed shoulders. And the behaviors in turn lead to more candid expression of your thoughts and feelings.

Connecting with Your Audience

As you practice your speech, think about wanting to engage with your listeners. Imagine that a young child you know well isn't heeding you. You want to capture—and keep—his attention however you can.

In such situations, you don't strategize; you simply do what feels natural and appropriate. For example, you increase the intensity or volume of your voice or move closer to your listener. During your actual speech, these behaviors will happen naturally and with the right timing.

If gesture precedes conscious thought and thought precedes words—even if by no more than a tiny fraction of a second—that changes our thinking about speech preparation. When coached in the traditional way, rehearsing specific gestures one by one, speakers end up employing those gestures at the same time that—or even slightly after—they speak the associated words. Although audiences are not consciously aware of this unnatural sequence, their innate ability to read body language leads them to feel that something's wrong—that the speaker is inauthentic.

"Rehearsing" Authenticity

So if neither casual spontaneity nor traditional rehearsal leads to compelling communication, how can you prepare for an important presentation? You have to tap into the basic impulses underlying your speech. These should include four powerful aims: to be open,

Being Passionate About Your Topic

While rehearsing, ask yourself what in your topic you feel deeply about: What's at stake? What results do you want your presentation to produce? Focus not on what you want to say but on why you're giving the speech and how you feel about it. Let the underlying emotion come out in every word you deliver during rehearsal. You'll infuse the actual speech with some of that passion and come across as more human and engaging.

"Listening" to Your Audience

To practice fulfilling this aim, think about what your listeners will likely be feeling when you step up to begin your presentation. Are they excited about the future? Worried about bad news? As you practice, imagine watching them closely, looking for signs of their response to you.

During your presentation, you'll be more prepared to identify the emotions your listeners are sending to you via nonverbal means. And you'll be able to respond to them appropriately; for example, by picking up the pace, varying your language, asking an impromptu question, or even eliminating or changing parts of your talk.

to connect, to be passionate, and to listen. Each of these aims informs nearly all successful presentations.

Rehearse your speech with them in mind. Try practicing it four ways, adopting the mind-set of each aim in turn, feeling it more than thinking about it. Forget about rehearsing specific gestures. If you are able to sincerely realize these feelings, your body language will take care of itself, emerging naturally and at the right moment. (The approach described here may also lead you to refine some of your verbal message, to make it accord with your nonverbal one.) When you actually deliver the speech, continue to focus on the four underlying aims.

Note the paradox here. This method is designed to achieve authenticity through the mastery of a calculated process. But authenticity arises from the four aims, or what I call "intents," that I have mentioned. If you can physically and emotionally embody all four, you'll achieve the perceived *and* real authenticity that creates a powerful bond with listeners.

What Underlies an Authentic Speech

Creating that bond isn't easy. Let me offer some advice for tapping into each of the four intents.

The intent to be open with your audience

This is the first and in some ways the most important thing to focus on in rehearsing a speech, because if you come across as closed, your listeners will perceive you as defensive—as if they somehow represent a threat. Not much chance for communication there.

How can you become more open? Try to imagine giving your presentation to someone with whom you're completely relaxed—your spouse, a close friend, your child. Notice what that mental picture looks like but particularly what it *feels* like. This is the state you need to be in if you are to have an authentic rapport with your audience.

If it's hard to create this mental image, try the real thing. Find a patient friend and push yourself to be open with him or her. Notice what that scene looks like and, again, how you feel. Don't overintellectualize: This is a bit like practicing a golf swing or a tennis serve. Although you might make tiny mental notes about what you're doing, they shouldn't get in the way of recognizing a feeling that you can try to replicate later.

Openness immediately feels risky to many people. I worked with a CEO who was passionate about his work, but his audiences didn't respond. He realized that he'd learned as a boy not to show emotion precisely about the things that meant the most to him. We had to replace this felt experience with one of talking to a close friend he was excited to see.

Let's go back to Carol (a composite of several clients). As she works on feeling more open in her presentations, her face begins to light up with a big smile when she speaks, and her shoulders relax. She realizes that without meaning to, she has come across as so serious that she has alienated her audiences.

A change in nonverbal behavior can affect the spoken message. Over and over, I've seen clients begin speaking more comfortably—

and more authentically—as the intent to be more open physically led to a more candid expression of their thoughts.

The intent to connect with your audience

Once you begin to feel open, and you've stored away the memory of what it looks and feels like, you're ready to practice the speech again, this time focusing on the audience. Think about wanting—*needing*—to engage your listeners. Imagine that a young child you know well isn't heeding you. You want to capture that child's attention however you can. You don't strategize—you simply do what feels natural and appropriate. You increase the intensity or volume of your voice or move closer.

You also want to *keep* your audience's attention. Don't let listeners slide away into their thoughts instead of following yours. Here, you might transform your young child into a teenager and imagine yearning to keep this easily distractible listener focused on your words.

If openness is the ante that lets you into the game, connection is what keeps the audience playing. Now that Carol is intent on being connected with her listeners, she realizes that she typically waits too long—in fact, until the very end of her speech—to make contact with them. She begins her next presentation by reaching out to audience members who have contributed significantly to the company's sales success, establishing a connection that continues throughout her speech.

The intent to be passionate about your topic

Ask yourself what it is that you feel deeply about. What's at stake? What results do you want your presentation to produce? Are you excited about the prospects of your company? Worried that they look bleak? Determined to improve them?

Focus not on what you want to say but on why you're giving the speech and how you feel about that. Let the underlying emotion come out (once you've identified it, you won't need to force it) in every word you deliver during this round of rehearsal. Then raise the stakes for yourself: Imagine that somebody in the audience has the power to take everything away from you unless you win him or her over with your passionate argument.

I worked with a senior partner at a consulting firm who was planning to talk to her colleagues about the things at the firm she valued and wanted to pass on to the next generation as she got ready to retire. Her speech, when she began practicing it, was a crystal-clear but dull commentary on the importance of commitment and hard work. As she began focusing on the emotion beneath the speech, she recalled how her mother, a dancer, had instilled in her the value of persisting no matter what the obstacles. She decided to acknowledge her mother in her talk. She said that her mother, then 92, had never let the pain and difficulties she had experienced during her career obscure her joy in performing. Although the speaker shed most of her tears during rehearsal, her passion transformed the talk into something memorable.

Somewhat more prosaically, Carol begins to think about what she's passionate about—her determination to beat a close competitor—and how that might inform her presentations. She realizes that this passion fuels her energy and excitement about her job. She infuses her next speech with some of that passion and immediately comes across as more human and engaging.

The intent to "listen" to your audience

Now begin thinking about what your listeners are likely to be feeling when you step up to begin your presentation. Are they excited about the future? Worried about bad sales news? Hopeful they can keep their jobs after the merger? As you practice, imagine yourself watching them very closely, looking for signs of their response to you.

Of course, your intent to discover the audience's emotional state will be most important during the actual presentation. Usually your listeners won't actually be talking to you, but they will be sending you nonverbal messages that you'll need to pick up and respond to.

This isn't as hard as it may sound. As a fellow member of the human race, you are as expert as your audience in reading body language—if you have an intent to do so. As you read the messages your listeners are sending with their bodies, you may want to pick up the pace, vary your language, even change or eliminate parts of your talk. If this leads you to involve the audience in a real dialogue—say, by asking an impromptu question—so much the better.

If time has been set aside for questions at the end of your presentation, you'll want to listen to the audience with your whole body, keeping yourself physically and psychologically still in the way you might when someone is telling you something so important that you dare not miss a word. Without thinking about it, you'll find yourself leaning forward or nodding your head—gestures that would appear unnatural if you were doing them because you'd been told to.

Of course, listening to and responding to an audience in the middle of your speech requires that you have your material down cold. But you can also take what your listeners tell you and use it to improve future presentations. I worked with a sales executive who had been so successful that she began touring the world in order to share her secrets with others. In listening to audiences, paying attention to their bodies as well as their words, she began to realize that they didn't just want to receive what she had to say; they wanted to give her something in return. The executive's speeches were inspiring, and her listeners wanted to thank her. So we designed a brief but meaningful ceremony near the end of her speech that allowed the audience members to get up, interact with one another, and give back to the speaker some of the inspiration she was giving them.

Consider Carol once again. Because of her intent to pick up on her listeners' emotions, Carol begins to realize over the course of several speeches that she has been wrongly assuming that her salespeople share her sense of urgency about their major competitor. She resolves to spend more time at the beginning of her next presentation explaining why stretch goals are important. This response to her listeners' state of mind, when combined with her own desire to be open, connected, and passionate, strengthens her growing ability to come across as—and be—an authentic speaker.

Originally published in November 2008. Reprint R0811H

Telling Tales

by Stephen Denning

IN 1998, I MADE A pilgrimage to the International Storytelling Center in Jonesborough, Tennessee, seeking some enlightenment. Several years earlier, as the program director of knowledge management at the World Bank, I had stumbled onto the power of storytelling. Despite a career of scoffing at such touchy-feely stuff—like most business executives, I knew that analytical was good, anecdotal was bad—I had changed my thinking because I'd seen stories help galvanize an organization around a defined business goal.

In the mid-1990s, that goal was to get people at the World Bank to support efforts at knowledge management—a pretty foreign notion within the organization at the time. I offered people cogent arguments about the need to gather the knowledge that was scattered throughout the organization. They didn't listen. I gave PowerPoint presentations that compellingly demonstrated the importance of sharing and leveraging this information. My audiences merely looked dazed. In desperation, I was ready to try almost anything.

Then in 1996 I began telling people a story:

> In June of 1995, a health worker in a tiny town in Zambia went to the Web site of the Centers for Disease Control and got the answer to a question about the treatment for malaria. Remember that this was in Zambia, one of the poorest countries in the world, and it happened in a tiny place 600 kilometers from the capital city. But the most striking thing about this picture, at least for us, is that the World Bank isn't in it. Despite our

> know-how on all kinds of poverty-related issues, that knowledge isn't available to the millions of people who could use it. Imagine if it were. Think what an organization we could become.

This simple story helped World Bank staff and managers envision a different kind of future for the organization. When knowledge management later became an official corporate priority, I used similar stories to maintain the momentum. So I began to wonder how the tool of narrative might be put to work even more effectively. Being a typically rational manager, I decided to consult the experts.

At the International Storytelling Center, I told the Zambia story to a professional storyteller, J.G. "Paw-Paw" Pinkerton, and asked the master what he thought. You can imagine my chagrin when he said he didn't hear a story at all. There was no real telling. There was no plot. There was no building up of the characters. Who was this health worker in Zambia? And what was her world like? What did it feel like to be in the exotic environment of Zambia, facing the problems she faced? My anecdote, he said, was a pathetic thing, not a story at all. I needed to start from scratch if I hoped to turn it into a "real story."

Was I surprised? Well, not exactly. The story *was* pretty bland. There was a problem with this advice from the expert, though. I knew in my heart it was wrong. And with that realization, I was on the brink of an important insight: Beware the well-told story!

The Power of Narrative

But let's back up a bit. Do stories really have a role to play in the business world? Believe me, I'm familiar with the skepticism about them. When you talk about "storytelling" to a group of hardheaded executives, you'd better be prepared for some eye rolling. If the group is polite as well as tough, don't be surprised if the eyes simply glaze over.

That's because most executives operate with a particular—and generally justified—mind-set. Analysis is what drives business thinking. It cuts through the fog of myth, gossip, and speculation to get to the hard facts. It goes wherever the observations and premises and conclusions

Idea in Brief

A carefully chosen story can help the leader of an organization translate an abstract concept into a meaningful mandate for employees. The key is to know which narrative strategies are right for what circumstances.

Knowledge management expert Stephen Denning explains that, for optimal effect, form should follow function. Challenging one professional storyteller's view that more is better, Denning points out that it's not always desirable (or practical) to launch into an epic that's jam-packed with complex characters, cleverly placed plot points, an intricate rising action, and a neatly resolved denouement. True, if listeners have time and interest, a narrative-savvy leader can use a vividly rendered tale to promote communication between management and staff, for instance, or even to foster collaboration—especially when the story is emotionally moving. However, if the aim is to motivate people to act when they might not be inclined to do so, it's best to take an approach that's light on detail. Otherwise, particulars can bog down listeners and prevent them from focusing on the message.

Drawing on his experiences at the World Bank and observations made elsewhere, the author provides several dos and don'ts for organizational storytellers, along with examples of narratives that get results. The sidebar "A Storytelling Catalog" presents seven distinct types of stories, the situations in which they should be told, and tips on how to tell them. Many of these aren't even stories in the "well-told" sense—they run the rhetorical gamut from one-liners to full-blown speeches—but they succeed because they're tailored to fit the situation. So even though it's common in business to favor the analytical over the anecdotal, leaders with the strength to push past some initial skepticism about the enterprise of storytelling will find that the creative effort pays off.

take it, undistorted by the hopes or fears of the analyst. Its strength lies in its objectivity, its impersonality, its heartlessness.

Yet this strength is also a weakness. Analysis might excite the mind, but it hardly offers a route to the heart. And that's where we must go if we are to motivate people not only to take action but to do so with energy and enthusiasm. At a time when corporate survival often requires disruptive change, leadership involves inspiring people to act in unfamiliar, and often unwelcome, ways. Mind-numbing cascades of numbers or daze-inducing PowerPoint slides won't achieve this goal. Even the most logical arguments usually won't do the trick.

But effective storytelling often does. In fact, in certain situations nothing else works. Although good business arguments are developed through the use of numbers, they are typically approved on the basis of a story—that is, a narrative that links a set of events in some kind of causal sequence. Storytelling can translate those dry and abstract numbers into compelling pictures of a leader's goals. I saw this happen at the World Bank—by 2000, we were increasingly recognized as leaders in the area of knowledge management—and have seen it in numerous other large organizations since then.

So why was I having problems with the advice I had received from the professional storyteller in Jonesborough?

A "Poorly Told" Story

The timing of my trip to Tennessee was fortunate. If I had sought expert advice two years earlier, I might have taken the master's recommendations without question. But I'd had some time to approach the idea of organizational storytelling with a beginner's mind, free of strictures about "the right way" to tell a story.

It wasn't that I couldn't follow Paw-Paw Pinkerton's recommendations. I saw immediately how to flesh out my modest anecdote about the health worker in Zambia: You'd dramatically depict her life, the scourge of malaria that she faced in her work, and perhaps the pain and suffering of the patient she was treating that day. You'd describe the extraordinary set of events that had led to her being seated in front of a computer screen deep in the hinterland of Zambia. You'd describe the false leads she had followed before she came across the CDC Web site. You'd build up to the moment of triumph when she found the answer to her question about malaria and vividly describe how that answer was about to transform the life of her patient. The story would be a veritable epic.

This "maximalist" account would be more engrossing than my relatively dry anecdote. But I had learned enough by then to realize that telling the story in this way to a corporate audience would not galvanize implementation of a strange new idea like knowledge management. I knew that in the modern workplace, people had neither the time nor the patience—remember executives' general skepticism about storytelling in the first place—to absorb a richly detailed narrative. If I was going to hold the attention of my audience, I had to make my point in seconds, not in minutes.

There was another problem. Even if my audience did take the time to listen to a fully developed tale, my telling it in that fashion would not allow listeners the mental space to relate the story to their own quite different worlds. Although I was describing a health worker in Zambia, I wanted everyone to focus not on Zambia but on their own situations. I hoped they would think, "If the CDC can reach a health worker in Zambia, why can't the World Bank? Why don't we put our knowledge on the Web and broaden our scope?" But if my listeners were immersed in a saga about that health worker and her patient, they might not have any attention left to ask themselves these questions—or to provide answers. In other words, I didn't want my audience too interested in Zambia. A minimalist narrative was effective, in fact, because it lacked detail and texture. The same characteristic that the professional storyteller saw as a flaw was, for my purposes, a strength.

On my return from Jonesborough, I educated myself about the principles of traditional storytelling. More than 2,000 years ago, Aristotle, in his *Poetics,* said stories should have a beginning, a middle, and an end. They should include complex characters as well as a plot that incorporates a reversal of fortune and a lesson learned. Furthermore, the storyteller should be so engaged with the story—visualizing the action, feeling what the characters feel—that the listeners become drawn into the narrative's world. Aristotle's formula has proved successful over the ages, from *The Arabian Nights* to *The Decameron* to *The Adventures of Tom Sawyer* and most Hollywood screenplays.

Despite the narrative power of the traditional story, I knew that it probably wouldn't spark action in an organization. In retrospect, though, I realize that my insight blinded me to something else. Believing that this wonderful and rich tradition had no place in the

A Storytelling Catalog

STORYTELLING IS AN INCREASINGLY ACCEPTED way to achieve management goals. But leaders need to use a variety of narrative patterns for different aims.

Sparking Action

Leadership is, above all, about getting people to change. To achieve that goal, you need to communicate the sometimes complex nature of the changes required and inspire an often skeptical organization to enthusiastically carry them out. This is the place for what I call a "springboard story," one that enables listeners to visualize the transformation needed in their circumstances and then to act on that realization.

Such a story is based on an actual event, preferably recent enough to seem relevant. It has a single protagonist with whom members of the target audience can identify. And there is an authentically happy ending, in which a change has at least in part been successfully implemented. (There is also an implicit alternate ending, an unhappy one that would have resulted had the change not occurred.)

The story has enough detail to be intelligible and credible but—and this is key—not so much texture that the audience becomes completely wrapped up in it. If that happens, people won't have the mental space to create an analogous scenario for change in their own organization. For example, if you want to get an organization to embrace a new technology, you might tell stories about individuals elsewhere who have successfully implemented it, without dwelling on the specifics.

Communicating Who You Are

You aren't likely to lead people through wrenching change if they don't trust you. And if they're to trust you, they have to know you: who you are, where you've come from, and why you hold the views you do. Ideally, they'll end up not only understanding you but also empathizing with you.

Stories for this purpose are usually based on a life event that reveals some strength or vulnerability and shows what the speaker took from the experience. For example, Jack Welch's success in making General Electric a winner was undoubtedly aided by his ability to tell his own story, which includes a tongue-lashing he once received from his mother after he hurled a hockey stick across the ice in response to a disappointing loss. "You punk!" she said, as Welch tells it in his memoir *Jack: Straight from the Gut*. "If you don't know how to lose, you'll never know how to win."

Unlike a story designed to spark action, this kind is typically well told, with colorful detail and context. So the speaker needs to ensure that the audience has enough time and interest to hear the story.

Transmitting Values

Stories can be effective tools for ingraining values within an organization, particularly those that help forestall problems by clearly establishing limits on destructive behavior. A story of this type ensures that the audience understands "how things are done around here."

These narratives often take the form of a parable. Religious leaders have used them for thousands of years to communicate values. The stories are usually set in some kind of generic past and have few context-setting details—though the context needs to seem relevant to the listeners. The "facts" of such tales can be hypothetical, but they must be believable. For example, a story might tell the sad fate of someone who failed to see the conflict of interest in not disclosing his or her financial interest in a company supplier.

Of course, narratives alone cannot establish values in an organization. Leaders need to live the values on a daily basis.

Fostering Collaboration

Every management textbook talks about the value of getting people to work together. But the only advice most of them offer on making that happen in real-life work environments is "Encourage conversations." Yes, but how?

One approach is to generate a common narrative around a group's concerns and goals, beginning with a story told by one member of the group. Ideally, that first story sparks another, which sparks another. If the process continues, group members develop a shared perspective, one that creates a sense of community. The first story must be emotionally moving enough to unleash the narrative impulse in others and to create a readiness to hear more stories. It could, for example, vividly describe how the speaker had grappled with a difficult work situation.

For this process to occur, it is best if the group has an open agenda that allows the stories to surface organically. It is also desirable to have a plan ready so that the energy generated by the positive experience of sharing stories can be immediately channeled into action.

Taming the Grapevine

Rumors flow incessantly through every organization. "Have you heard the latest?" is a refrain that's difficult for managers to deal with. Denying a rumor can give it credibility. Asking how it got started can ensure its spread. Ignoring it risks allowing it to spiral out of control. Rumors about issues central to the future of the organization—takeovers, reorganizations, major managerial changes—can be an enormous distraction (or worse) to employees. So as an executive, what can you do? One response is to harness the energy of the

(*continued*)

A Storytelling Catalog (continued)

If your objective is:	You will need a story that:	In telling it, you will need to:	Your story will inspire such responses as:
Sparking action	Describes how a successful change was implemented in the past, but allows listeners to imagine how it might work in their situation.	Avoid excessive detail that will take the audience's mind off its own challenge.	"Just imagine . . ." "What if . . ."
Communicating who you are	Provides audience-engaging drama and reveals some strength or vulnerability from your past.	Include meaningful details, but also make sure the audience has the time and inclination to hear your story.	"I didn't know that about him!" "Now I see what she's driving at."
Transmitting values	Feels familiar to the audience and will prompt discussion about the issues raised by the value being promoted.	Use believable (though perhaps hypothetical) characters and situations, and never forget that the story must be consistent with your own actions.	"That's so right!" "Why don't we do that all the time?"
Fostering collaboration	Movingly recounts a situation that listeners have also experienced and that prompts them to share their own stories about the topic.	Ensure that a set agenda doesn't squelch this swapping of stories—and that you have an action plan ready to tap the energy unleashed by this narrative chain reaction.	"That reminds me of the time that I . . ." "Hey, I've got a story like that."
Taming the grapevine	Highlights, often through the use of gentle humor, some aspect of a rumor that reveals it to be untrue or unlikely.	Avoid the temptation to be mean-spirited, and be sure that the rumor is indeed false.	"No kidding!" "I'd never thought about it like that before!"

Sharing knowledge	Focuses on mistakes made and shows in some detail how they were corrected, with an explanation of why the solution worked.	Solicit alternative—and possibly better—solutions.	"There but for the grace of God . . ." "Wow! We'd better watch that from now on."
Leading people into the future	Evokes the future you want to create without providing excessive detail that will only turn out to be wrong.	Be sure of your storytelling skills. (Otherwise, use a story in which the past can serve as a springboard to the future.)	"When do we start?" "Let's do it!"

grapevine to defuse the rumor, using a story to convince listeners that the gossip is either untrue or unreasonable. This kind of story highlights the incongruity between the rumor and reality. You could use gentle satire to mock the rumor, the rumor's author, or even yourself, in an effort to undermine the rumor's power. For example, you might deal with a false rumor of "imminent companywide reorganization" by jokingly recounting how the front office's current struggles involving the seating chart for executive committee meetings would have to be worked out first. Keep in mind, though, that humor can backfire. Mean-spirited teasing can generate a well-deserved backlash.

The trick is to work with, not against, the flow of the vast underground river of informal communication that exists in every organization. Of course, you can't ridicule a rumor into oblivion if it's true or at least reasonable. If that's the case, there is little you can do but admit the substance of the rumor, put it in perspective, and move on.

Sharing Knowledge

Much of the intellectual capital of an organization is not written down anywhere but resides in people's minds. Communicating this know-how across an organization and beyond typically occurs informally, through the sharing of stories.

Knowledge-sharing narratives are unusual in that they lack a hero or even a detectable plot. They are more about problems, and how and why they got—or, more likely, didn't get—resolved. They include a description of the

(*continued*)

A Storytelling Catalog (continued)

problem, the setting, and the solution. Because they highlight a problem—say, the challenge employees face in learning to use a new system—they tend to have a negative tone. And because they often focus in detail on why a particular solution worked, they may be of little interest outside a defined group of people. Though unashamedly unentertaining and lacking most elements of a conventional story, they are nonetheless the uncelebrated workhorse of organizational narrative.

They present a difficulty, however. In a corporate setting, stories about problems don't flow easily, not only because people fear the consequences of admitting mistakes, but also because, in the flush of success, people tend to forget what they learned along the way. As a result, the knowledge-sharing story cannot be compelled; it has to be teased out. That is, a discussion of successes may be needed in order to get people to talk about what has gone wrong and how it can be fixed.

Leading People into the Future

An important part of a leader's job is preparing others for what lies ahead, whether in the concrete terms of an actual scenario or the more conceptual

time-constrained world of modern business was as wrongheaded as thinking that all stories had to be full of detail and color. I would later see that the well-told story is relevant in a modern organization. Indeed, a number of surprises about the use of storytelling in organizations awaited me.

Tales of Success and Failure

In December 2000, I left the World Bank and began to consult with companies on their knowledge management and, by extension, their use of organizational stories. As part of this work, I once found myself in London with Dave Snowden, a director of IBM's Institute of Knowledge Management, teaching a master class on storytelling to around 70 executives from private- and public-sector organizations.

During the class's morning session, I spoke about my experience at the World Bank and how a positive orientation was essential if a narrative like the one about Zambia was to be effective. But in the

terms of a vision. A story can help take listeners from where they are now to where they need to be, by making them comfortable with an image of the future. The problem, of course, lies in crafting a credible narrative about the future when the future is unknowable.

Thus, if such stories are to serve their purpose, they should whet listeners' imaginative appetite about the future without providing detail that will likely turn out to be inaccurate. Listeners should be able to remold the story in their minds as the future unfolds with all its unexpected twists and turns. And clearly, the story should portray that state in a positive way: People are more likely to overcome uncertainty about change if they are shown what to aim for rather than what to avoid.

Note that telling an evocative narrative about the future requires a high degree of verbal skill, something not every leader possesses. But the springboard story, described above, provides an alternative. Hearing about a change that has already happened elsewhere can help listeners to imagine how it might play out for them in the future.

afternoon, to my dismay, my fellow presenter emphatically asserted the opposite. At IBM and elsewhere, Dave had found purely positive stories to be problematic. They were, he said, like the Janet and John children's stories in the United Kingdom or the Dick and Jane stories in the United States: The characters were so good they made you feel queasy. The naughtiest thing Janet and John would do was spill a bottle of water in the yard. Then they would go and tell their mother about it and promise never to do it again. Janet would volunteer to help out with the cleanup and John would offer to help wash the car. These stories for children reflected a desire to show things as they should be rather than as they are. In a corporate environment, Dave told his audience, listeners would respond to such rosy tales by conjuring up negative "antistories" about what must have actually happened. His message: Beware the positive story!

After the workshop, Dave and I discussed why his stories focused on the negative while mine accentuated the positive. I could see he had a point, that negative stories can be more powerful than positive ones. I'd used negative stories myself when trying to teach people the nitty-gritty of any subject. The fact is, people learn more from their mistakes than from their successes.

Eventually, however, it dawned on me that our points of view were complementary and that our stories served different purposes: My stories were crafted to motivate people, and Dave's were designed to share knowledge. His stories might describe how and why a team failed to accomplish an objective, with the aim of helping others avoid the same mistakes. (To elicit such stories, Dave often had to start by getting people to talk about their successes, even if these accounts were ultimately less useful vehicles for conveying knowledge.) It was then I began to realize that the purpose of telling a story might determine its form.

Granted, even optimistic stories have to be true and believable, since jaded corporate audiences know too well the experience of being presented with half-truths. Stories told in order to spur action need to make good on their promises and contain sufficient evidence of a positive outcome. But stories intended mainly to transfer knowledge must be more than true. Because their objective is to generate understanding and not action, they tend to highlight the pitfalls of ignorance; they are meant not to inspire people but to make them cautious. Just as the minimalist stories that I told to spark action were different from traditional entertainment stories, so effective knowledge-sharing stories would have negative rather than positive overtones.

A Collective Yawn

Once I saw that different narrative forms could further different business goals, I looked for other ways that managers could make stories work for them. A number of distinct story types began to emerge—ones that didn't necessarily follow Aristotelian guidelines but were nonetheless used to good effect in a variety of organizations. (For descriptions of some of them and the purposes for which they might be used, see the sidebar "A Storytelling Catalog.") I continued to come across unexpected insights about the nature of storytelling within organizations.

For instance, if negative stories have their place, so do "boring" ones. In his book *Talking about Machines,* Julian Orr recounts a number of stories that have circulated among Xerox repair technicians. While rich in detail, they are even less storylike than my little anecdote about the health care worker in Zambia. Most of these tales, which present solutions to technical problems, lack a plot and a distinct character. In fact, they are hardly stories at all, with little to hold the interest of anyone except those close to the often esoteric subject matter. Why are they compelling even to this limited audience? Because they are driven by a detailed explanation of the cause-and-effect relationship between an action and its consequence. For example:

> You've got a malfunctioning copy machine with an E053 error code, which is supposed to mean a problem in the 24-volt Interlock Power Supply. But you could chase the source of that 24-volt Interlock problem forever, and you'd never, ever find out what it is. If you're lucky enough, you'll eventually get an F066 error code, which indicates the true source of the malfunction—namely, a shorted dicorotron. Apparently, this is happening because the circuitry in the XER board has been changed to prevent the damage that would otherwise occur when a dicorotron shorted. Before the change in circuitry, a shorted dicorotron would have fried the whole XER board. Changing the circuitry has prevented damage to the XER board, but it's created a different issue. Now an E053 error message doesn't give you the true source of the machine's malfunction.

This story, slightly condensed here, doesn't just describe the technician's accurate diagnosis of a problem; it also relates why things happened as they did. So the account, negative in tone and almost unintelligible to an outsider, is both informative and interesting to its intended audience.

As I continued my investigation, one area of particular interest to me was the link between storytelling and leadership. I already knew from personal experience how stories could be used as a catalyst for organizational action. And I had read in two influential books about leadership—*Leading Minds* by Howard Gardner and *The Leadership Engine* by Noel Tichy—how stories could help leaders define their personality for their followers, boosting others' confidence in the leaders' integrity and providing some idea of how they might act in a given situation.

I also had seen leaders using narrative to inculcate a positive set of corporate values and beliefs in the hearts and minds of their employees. Think, for example, of Tyco's effort to repair its battered value system. The company began by creating a straightforward manual that outlined new rules in such areas as sexual harassment, conflicts of interest, and fraud. But Eric Pillmore, senior vice president of corporate governance, quickly figured out that, as written, the booklet would merely gather dust on people's shelves. So he threw out what he had done and started again in an attempt to bring the principles alive through narrative. The story below became part of the revised guide, as a sidebar in the section on sexual harassment and other forms of intimidating behavior in the workplace:

> The entire team jokes about Tom being gay. Tom has never complained and doesn't seem to mind, but when Mark is assigned to work with Tom, the jokes turn on Mark. Now that Mark receives the brunt of the jokes, he tells his supervisor he wants to be reassigned. His supervisor complies with Mark's request.

While the guide clearly lays out the company's policy on harassment, the simple narrative helps bring the policy to life and provides a starting point for thinking about and discussing the complex issues involved. Dozens of similar stories illustrate an array of company policies.

An Enticing but Hazy Future

Although these types of stories furthered leadership goals in a relatively predictable way, others I came across were more quirky—particularly ones used to communicate vision. Noel Tichy writes in

The Leadership Engine about the importance of preparing an organization for change. He notes that "the best way to get humans to venture into unknown terrain is to make that terrain familiar and desirable by taking them there first in their imaginations." Aha! I thought. Here is a place where storytelling, perhaps the most powerful route to people's imaginations, could prove indispensable.

But as I looked at examples of such stories in a number of arenas, I discovered that most of the successful ones were surprisingly sketchy about the details of the imagined future. Consider Winston Churchill's "We Shall Fight on the Beaches" speech and Martin Luther King, Jr.'s "I Have a Dream" speech. Neither of these famous addresses came close to describing the future in enough detail that it became, in listeners' minds, "familiar terrain."

Over time—and, in part, through my work in corporate scenario planning—I realized why. Specific predictions about the future are likely to be proved wrong. Because such predictions almost inevitably differ in major or minor ways from what eventually happens, leaders who proclaim them risk losing people's confidence. Consequently, a story designed to prepare people for change needs to evoke the future and conjure up a direction for getting there—but without being too precise. Think of the corporate future that was laid out in a famous mandate by Jack Welch: "General Electric will be either number one or number two in the field, or we will exit the sector." This is a clear, but general, description of where Welch wanted to take the company. Like my Zambia story, although for different reasons, this statement doesn't convey *too* much information.

I also came across stories used in somewhat unusual situations that called for reactive rather than proactive measures. These stories counteracted negative ones that circulated like a virus within an organization and threatened to infect the entire body. Dave Snowden of IBM first pointed out to me how stories could be used in this manner. His hypothesis was that you could attach a positive story to a negative one in order to defuse it, as an antibody would neutralize an antigen.

For example, at an IBM manufacturing site for laptop computers in the United Kingdom, stories circulated among the blue-collar workers about the facility's managers, who were accused of "not doing any real work," "being overpaid," and "having no idea what it's like on the manufacturing line." But an additional story was injected into the mix: One day, a new site director turned up in a white coat, unannounced and unaccompanied, and sat on the line making ThinkPads. He asked workers on the assembly line for help. In response, someone asked him, "Why do you earn so much more than I do?" His simple reply: "If you screw up badly, you lose your job. If I screw up badly, 3,000 people lose their jobs."

While not a story in the traditional sense, the manager's words—and actions—served as a seed for the story that eventually circulated in opposition to the one about managers' being lazy and overpaid. You can imagine the buzz: "Blimey, you should've seen how he fumbled with those circuit boards. I guess *he'll* never work on the line. But you know, he does have a point about his pay." The atmosphere at the facility began improving within weeks.

Much work remains to be done in developing a menu of narrative patterns that can be used for different purposes in an organizational setting. Although the handful of story types that I've identified is no more than a start, I hope it inspires leaders to consider the various ways storytelling might be used. Certainly, the ability to tell the right story at the right time is emerging as an essential leadership skill, one that can help managers cope with, and get business results in, the turbulent world of the twenty-first century.

Originally published in May 2004. Reprint R0405H

How to Pitch a Brilliant Idea

by Kimberly D. Elsbach

COMING UP WITH CREATIVE IDEAS is easy; selling them to strangers is hard. All too often, entrepreneurs, sales executives, and marketing managers go to great lengths to show how their new business plans or creative concepts are practical and high margin—only to be rejected by corporate decision makers who don't seem to understand the real value of the ideas. Why does this happen?

It turns out that the problem has as much to do with the seller's traits as with an idea's inherent quality. The person on the receiving end tends to gauge the pitcher's creativity as well as the proposal itself. And judgments about the pitcher's ability to come up with workable ideas can quickly and permanently overshadow perceptions of the idea's worth. We all like to think that people judge us carefully and objectively on our merits. But the fact is, they rush to place us into neat little categories—they stereotype us. So the first thing to realize when you're preparing to make a pitch to strangers is that your audience is going to put you into a box. And they're going to do it really fast. Research suggests that humans can categorize others in less than 150 milliseconds. Within 30 minutes, they've made lasting judgments about your character.

These insights emerged from my lengthy study of the $50 billion U.S. film and television industry. Specifically, I worked with 50 Hollywood executives involved in assessing pitches from screenwriters.

Over the course of six years, I observed dozens of 30-minute pitches in which the screenwriters encountered the "catchers" for the first time. In interviewing and observing the pitchers and catchers, I was able to discern just how quickly assessments of creative potential are made in these high-stakes exchanges. (The deals that arise as a result of successful screenplay pitches are often multimillion-dollar projects, rivaling in scope the development of new car models by Detroit's largest automakers and marketing campaigns by New York's most successful advertising agencies.) To determine whether my observations applied to business settings beyond Hollywood, I attended a variety of product-design, marketing, and venture-capital pitch sessions and conducted interviews with executives responsible for judging creative, high-stakes ideas from pitchers previously unknown to them. In those environments, the results were remarkably similar to what I had seen in the movie business.

People on the receiving end of pitches have no formal, verifiable, or objective measures for assessing that elusive trait, creativity. Catchers—even the expert ones—therefore apply a set of subjective and often inaccurate criteria very early in the encounter, and from that point on, the tone is set. If a catcher detects subtle cues indicating that the pitcher isn't creative, the proposal is toast. But that's not the whole story. I've discovered that catchers tend to respond well if they are made to feel that they are participating in an idea's development.

The pitchers who do this successfully are those who tend to be categorized by catchers into one of three prototypes. I call them the *showrunner,* the *artist,* and the *neophyte*. Showrunners come off as professionals who combine creative inspiration with production know-how. Artists appear to be quirky and unpolished and to prefer the world of creative ideas to quotidian reality. Neophytes tend to be—or act as if they were—young, inexperienced, and naive. To involve the audience in the creative process, showrunners deliberately level the power differential between themselves and their catchers; artists invert the differential; and neophytes exploit it. If you're a pitcher, the bottom-line implication is this: By successfully projecting yourself as one of the three creative types and getting your catcher to view himself or herself

Idea in Brief

Coming up with creative ideas is easy; selling them to strangers is hard. Entrepreneurs, sales executives, and marketing managers often go to great lengths to demonstrate how their new concepts are practical and profitable—only to be rejected by corporate decision makers who don't seem to understand the value of the ideas. Why does this happen?

Having studied Hollywood executives who assess screenplay pitches, the author says the person on the receiving end—the "catcher"—tends to gauge the pitcher's creativity as well as the proposal itself. An impression of the pitcher's ability to come up with workable ideas can quickly and permanently overshadow the catcher's feelings about an idea's worth. To determine whether these observations apply to business settings beyond Hollywood, the author attended product design, marketing, and venture-capital pitch sessions and conducted interviews with executives responsible for judging new ideas. The results in those environments were similar to her observations in Hollywood, she says.

Catchers subconsciously categorize successful pitchers as *showrunners* (smooth and professional), *artists* (quirky and unpolished), or *neophytes* (inexperienced and naive). The research also reveals that catchers tend to respond well when they believe they are participating in an idea's development. As Oscar-winning writer, director, and producer Oliver Stone puts it, screenwriters pitching an idea should "pull back and project what he needs onto your idea in order to make the story whole for him."

To become a successful pitcher, portray yourself as one of the three creative types and engage your catchers in the creative process. By finding ways to give your catchers a chance to shine, you sell yourself as a likable collaborator.

as a creative collaborator, you can improve your chances of selling an idea.

My research also has implications for those who buy ideas: Catchers should beware of relying on stereotypes. It's all too easy to be dazzled by pitchers who ultimately can't get their projects off the ground, and it's just as easy to overlook the creative individuals who can make good on their ideas. That's why it's important for the catcher to test every pitcher, a matter we'll return to in the following pages.

The Sorting Hat

In the late 1970s, psychologists Nancy Cantor and Walter Mischel, then at Stanford University, demonstrated that we all use sets of stereotypes—what they called "person prototypes"—to categorize strangers in the first moments of interaction. Though such instant typecasting is arguably unfair, pattern matching is so firmly hard-wired into human psychology that only conscious discipline can counteract it.

Yale University creativity researcher Robert Sternberg contends that the prototype matching we use to assess originality in others results from our implicit belief that creative people possess certain traits—unconventionality, for example, as well as intuitiveness, sensitivity, narcissism, passion, and perhaps youth. We develop these stereotypes through direct and indirect experiences with people known to be creative, from personally interacting with the 15-year-old guitar player next door to hearing stories about Pablo Picasso.

When a person we don't know pitches an idea to us, we search for visual and verbal matches with those implicit models, remembering only the characteristics that identify the pitcher as one type or another. We subconsciously award points to people we can easily identify as having creative traits; we subtract points from those who are hard to assess or who fit negative stereotypes.

In hurried business situations in which executives must evaluate dozens of ideas in a week, or even a day, catchers are rarely willing to expend the effort necessary to judge an idea more objectively. Like Harry Potter's Sorting Hat, they classify pitchers in a matter of seconds. They use negative stereotyping to rapidly identify the no-go ideas. All you have to do is fall into one of four common negative stereotypes, and the pitch session will be over before it has begun. (For more on these stereotypes, see the sidebar "How to Kill Your Own Pitch.") In fact, many such sessions are strictly a process of elimination; in my experience, only 1% of ideas make it beyond the initial pitch.

Unfortunately for pitchers, type-based elimination is easy, because negative impressions tend to be more salient and memorable than positive ones. To avoid fast elimination, successful pitchers—only

25% of those I have observed—turn the tables on the catchers by enrolling them in the creative process. These pitchers exude passion for their ideas and find ways to give catchers a chance to shine. By doing so, they induce the catchers to judge them as likable collaborators. Oscar-winning writer, director, and producer Oliver Stone told me that the invitation to collaborate on an idea is a "seduction." His advice to screenwriters pitching an idea to a producer is to "pull back and project what he needs onto your idea in order to make the story whole for him." The three types of successful pitchers have their own techniques for doing this, as we'll see.

The Showrunner

In the corporate world, as in Hollywood, showrunners combine creative thinking and passion with what Sternberg and Todd Lubart, authors of *Defying the Crowd: Cultivating Creativity in a Culture of Conformity,* call "practical intelligence"—a feel for which ideas are likely to contribute to the business. Showrunners tend to display charisma and wit in pitching, say, new design concepts to marketing, but they also demonstrate enough technical know-how to convince catchers that the ideas can be developed according to industry-standard practices and within resource constraints. Though they may not have the most or the best ideas, showrunners are those rare people in organizations who see the majority of their concepts fully implemented.

An example of a showrunner is the legendary kitchen-gadget inventor and pitchman Ron Popeil. Perfectly coiffed and handsome, Popeil is a combination design master and ringmaster. In his *New Yorker* account of Popeil's phenomenally successful Ronco Showtime Rotisserie & BBQ, Malcolm Gladwell described how Popeil fuses entertainment skills—he enthusiastically showcases the product as an innovation that will "change your life"—with business savvy. For his television spots, Popeil makes sure that the chickens are roasted to exactly the resplendent golden brown that looks best on camera. And he designed the rotisserie's glass front to reduce glare, so that to the home cook, the revolving, dripping chickens look just as they do on TV.

How to Kill Your Own Pitch

BEFORE YOU EVEN GET TO the stage in the pitch where the catcher categorizes you as a particular creative type, you have to avoid some dangerous pigeonholes: the four negative stereotypes that are guaranteed to kill a pitch. And take care, because negative cues carry more weight than positive ones.

The pushover would rather unload an idea than defend it. ("I could do one of these in red, or if you don't like that, I could do it in blue.") One venture capitalist I spoke with offered the example of an entrepreneur who was seeking funding for a computer networking start-up. When the VCs raised concerns about an aspect of the device, the pitcher simply offered to remove it from the design, leading the investors to suspect that the pitcher didn't really care about his idea.

The robot presents a proposal too formulaically, as if it had been memorized from a how-to book. Witness the entrepreneur who responds to prospective investors' questions about due diligence and other business details with canned answers from his PowerPoint talk.

The first Hollywood pitcher I observed was a showrunner. The minute he walked into the room, he scored points with the studio executive as a creative type, in part because of his new, pressed jeans, his fashionable black turtleneck, and his nice sport coat. The clean hair draping his shoulders showed no hint of gray. He had come to pitch a weekly television series based on the legend of Robin Hood. His experience as a marketer was apparent; he opened by mentioning an earlier TV series of his that had been based on a comic book. The pitcher remarked that the series had enjoyed some success as a marketing franchise, spawning lunch boxes, bath toys, and action figures.

Showrunners create a level playing field by engaging the catcher in a kind of knowledge duet. They typically begin by getting the catcher to respond to a memory or some other subject with which the showrunner is familiar. Consider this give-and-take:

Pitcher: Remember Errol Flynn's *Robin Hood*?

Catcher: Oh, yeah. One of my all-time favorites as a kid.

Pitcher: Yes, it was classic. Then, of course, came Costner's version.

The used-car salesman is that obnoxious, argumentative character too often deployed in consultancies and corporate sales departments. One vice president of marketing told me the story of an arrogant consultant who put in a proposal to her organization. The consultant's offer was vaguely intriguing, and she asked him to revise his bid slightly. Instead of working with her, he argued with her. Indeed, he tried selling the same package again and again, each time arguing why his proposal would produce the most astonishing bottom-line results the company had ever seen. In the end, she grew so tired of his wheedling insistence and inability to listen courteously to her feedback that she told him she wasn't interested in seeing any more bids from him.

The charity case is needy; all he or she wants is a job. I recall a freelance consultant who had developed a course for executives on how to work with independent screenwriters. He could be seen haunting the halls of production companies, knocking on every open door, giving the same pitch. As soon as he sensed he was being turned down, he began pleading with the catcher, saying he really, *really* needed to fill some slots to keep his workshop going.

Catcher: That was much darker. And it didn't evoke as much passion as the original.

Pitcher: But the special effects were great.

Catcher: Yes, they were.

Pitcher: That's the twist I want to include in this new series.

Catcher: Special effects?

Pitcher: We're talking a science fiction version of *Robin Hood*. Robin has a sorcerer in his band of merry men who can conjure up all kinds of scary and wonderful spells.

Catcher: I love it!

The pitcher sets up his opportunity by leading the catcher through a series of shared memories and viewpoints. Specifically, he engages the catcher by asking him to recall and comment on familiar movies. With each response, he senses and then builds on the catcher's knowledge and interest, eventually guiding the catcher to the core idea by using a word ("twist") that's common to the vocabularies of both producers and screenwriters.

Showrunners also display an ability to improvise, a quality that allows them to adapt if a pitch begins to go awry. Consider the dynamic between the creative director of an ad agency and a prospective client, a major television sports network. As Mallorre Dill reported in a 2001 *Adweek* article on award-winning advertising campaigns, the network's VP of marketing was seeking help with a new campaign for coverage of the upcoming professional basketball season, and the ad agency was invited to make a pitch. Prior to the meeting, the network executive stressed to the agency that the campaign would have to appeal to local markets across the United States while achieving "street credibility" with avid fans.

The agency's creative director and its art director pitched the idea of digitally inserting two average teenagers into video of an NBA game. Initially, the catcher frowned on the idea, wondering aloud if viewers would find it arrogant and aloof. So the agency duo ad-libbed a rap that one teen could recite after scoring on all-star Shaquille O'Neal: "I'm fresh like a can of picante. And I'm deeper than Dante in the circles of hell." The catcher was taken aback at first; then he laughed. Invited to participate in the impromptu rap session, the catcher began inserting his own lines. When the fun was over, the presenters repitched their idea with a slight variation—inserting the teenagers into videos of home-team games for local markets—and the account was sold to the tune of hundreds of thousands of dollars.

Real showrunners are rare—only 20% of the successful pitchers I observed would qualify. Consequently, they are in high demand, which is good news for pitchers who can demonstrate the right combination of talent and expertise.

The Artist

Artists, too, display single-minded passion and enthusiasm about their ideas, but they are less slick and conformist in their dress and mannerisms, and they tend to be shy or socially awkward. As one

Hollywood producer told me, "The more shy a writer seems, the better you think the writing is, because you assume they're living in their internal world." Unlike showrunners, artists appear to have little or no knowledge of, or even interest in, the details of implementation. Moreover, they invert the power differential by completely commanding the catcher's imagination. Instead of engaging the catcher in a duet, they put the audience in thrall to the content. Artists are particularly adept at conducting what physicists call "thought experiments," inviting the audience into imaginary worlds.

One young screenwriter I observed fit the artist type to perfection. He wore black leather pants and a torn T-shirt, several earrings in each ear, and a tattoo on his slender arm. His hair was rumpled, his expression was brooding: Van Gogh meets Tim Burton. He cared little about the production details for the dark, violent cartoon series he imagined; rather, he was utterly absorbed by the unfolding story. He opened his pitch like this: "Picture what happens when a bullet explodes inside someone's brain. Imagine it in slow motion. There is the shattering blast, the tidal wave of red, the acrid smell of gunpowder. That's the opening scene in this animated sci-fi flick." He then proceeded to lead his catchers through an exciting, detailed narrative of his film, as a master storyteller would. At the end, the executives sat back, smiling, and told the writer they'd like to go ahead with his idea.

In the business world, artists are similarly nonconformist. Consider Alan, a product designer at a major packaged-foods manufacturer. I observed Alan in a meeting with business-development executives he'd never met. He had come to pitch an idea based on the premise that children like to play with their food. The proposal was for a cereal with pieces that interlocked in such a way that children could use them for building things, Legos style. With his pocket-protected laboratory coat and horn-rimmed glasses, Alan looked very much the absent-minded professor. As he entered the conference room where the suited-and-tied executives at his company had assembled, he hung back, apparently uninterested in the PowerPoint slides or the marketing and revenue projections of the business-development experts. His appearance and reticence spoke volumes about him. His type was unmistakable.

When it was Alan's turn, he dumped four boxes of prototype cereal onto the mahogany conference table, to the stunned silence of the executives. Ignoring protocol, he began constructing an elaborate fort, all the while talking furiously about the qualities of the corn flour that kept the pieces and the structure together. Finally, he challenged the executives to see who could build the tallest tower. The executives so enjoyed the demonstration that they greenlighted Alan's project.

While artists—who constituted about 40% of the successful pitchers I observed—are not as polished as showrunners, they are the most creative of the three types. Unlike showrunners and neophytes, artists are fairly transparent. It's harder to fake the part. In other words, they don't play to type; they *are* the type. Indeed, it is very difficult for someone who is not an artist to pretend to be one, because genuineness is what makes the artist credible.

The Neophyte

Neophytes are the opposite of showrunners. Instead of displaying their expertise, they plead ignorance. Neophytes score points for daring to do the impossible, something catchers see as refreshing. Unencumbered by tradition or past successes, neophytes present themselves as eager learners. They consciously exploit the power differential between pitcher and catcher by asking directly and boldly for help—not in a desperate way, but with the confidence of a brilliant favorite, a talented student seeking sage advice from a beloved mentor.

Consider the case of one neophyte pitcher I observed, a young, ebullient screenwriter who had just returned from his first trip to Japan. He wanted to develop a show about an American kid (like himself) who travels to Japan to learn to play *taiko* drums, and he brought his drums and sticks into the pitch session. The fellow looked as though he had walked off the set of *Doogie Howser, M.D.* With his infectious smile, he confided to his catchers that he was not going to pitch them a typical show, "mainly because I've never done one. But I think my inexperience here might be a blessing."

He showed the catchers a variety of drumming moves, then asked one person in his audience to help him come up with potential camera angles—such as looking out from inside the drum or viewing it from overhead—inquiring how these might play on the screen. When the catcher got down on his hands and knees to show the neophyte a particularly "cool" camera angle, the pitch turned into a collaborative teaching session. Ignoring his lunch appointment, the catcher spent the next half hour offering suggestions for weaving the story of the young drummer into a series of taiko performances in which artistic camera angles and imaginative lighting and sound would be used to mirror the star's emotions.

Many entrepreneurs are natural neophytes. Lou and Sophie McDermott, two sisters from Australia, started the Savage Sisters sportswear line in the late 1990s. Former gymnasts with petite builds and spunky personalities, they cartwheeled into the clothing business with no formal training in fashion or finance. Instead, they relied heavily on their enthusiasm and optimism and a keen curiosity about the fine points of retailing to get a start in the highly competitive world of teen fashion. On their shopping outings at local stores, the McDermott sisters studied merchandising and product placement—all the while asking store owners how they got started, according to the short documentary film *Cutting Their Own Cloth*.

The McDermott sisters took advantage of their inexperience to learn all they could. They would ask a store owner to give them a tour of the store, and they would pose dozens of questions: "Why do you buy this line and not the other one? Why do you put this dress here and not there? What are your customers like? What do they ask for most?" Instead of being annoying, the McDermotts were charming, friendly, and fun, and the flattered retailers enjoyed being asked to share their knowledge. Once they had struck up a relationship with a retailer, the sisters would offer to bring in samples for the store to test. Eventually, the McDermotts parlayed what they had learned into enough knowledge to start their own retail line. By engaging the store owners as teachers, the McDermotts were able to build a network of expert mentors who wanted to see the neophytes win. Thus neophytes, who constitute about 40% of successful pitchers, achieve their gains largely by sheer force of personality.

Which of the three types is most likely to succeed? Overwhelmingly, catchers look for showrunners, though artists and neophytes can win the day through enchantment and charm. From the catcher's perspective, however, showrunners can also be the most dangerous of all pitchers, because they are the most likely to blind through glitz.

Catchers Beware

When business executives ask me for my insights about creativity in Hollywood, one of the first questions they put to me is, "Why is there so much bad television?" After hearing the stories I've told here, they know the answer: Hollywood executives too often let themselves be wooed by positive stereotypes—particularly that of the showrunner—rather than by the quality of the ideas. Indeed, individuals who become adept at conveying impressions of creative potential, while lacking the real thing, may gain entry into organizations and reach prominence there based on their social influence and impression-management skills, to the catchers' detriment.

Real creativity isn't so easily classified. Researchers such as Sternberg and Lubart have found that people's implicit theories regarding the attributes of creative individuals are off the mark. Furthermore, studies have identified numerous personal attributes that facilitate practical creative behavior. For example, cognitive flexibility, a penchant for diversity, and an orientation toward problem solving are signs of creativity; it simply isn't true that creative types can't be down-to-earth.

Those who buy ideas, then, need to be aware that relying too heavily on stereotypes can cause them to overlook creative individuals who can truly deliver the goods. In my interviews with studio executives and agents, I heard numerous tales of people who had developed reputations as great pitchers but who had trouble producing usable scripts. The same thing happens in business. One well-known example occurred in 1985, when Coca-Cola announced it was changing the Coke formula. Based on pitches from market researchers who had tested the sweeter, Pepsi-like "new Coke" in numerous focus groups, the company's top management decided that the new formula could effectively compete with Pepsi. The idea was a marketing disaster, of course. There was a huge backlash, and the company was forced to reintroduce the old Coke. In a later discussion of the case and the importance of relying on decision makers who are both good pitchers and industry experts, Roberto Goizueta, Coca-Cola's CEO at the time, said to a group of MBAs, in effect, that there's nothing so dangerous as a good pitcher with no real talent.

If a catcher senses that he or she is being swept away by a positive stereotype match, it's important to test the pitcher. Fortunately, assessing the various creative types is not difficult. In a meeting with a showrunner, for example, the catcher can test the pitcher's expertise and probe into past experiences, just as a skilled job interviewer would, and ask how the pitcher would react to various changes to his or her idea. As for artists and neophytes, the best way to judge their ability is to ask them to deliver a finished product. In Hollywood, smart catchers ask artists and neophytes for finished scripts before hiring them. These two types may be unable to deliver specifics about costs or implementation, but a prototype can allow the catcher to judge quality, and it can provide a concrete basis for further discussion. Finally, it's important to enlist the help of other people in vetting pitchers. Another judge or two can help a catcher weigh the pitcher's—and the idea's—pros and cons and help safeguard against hasty judgments.

One CEO of a Northern California design firm looks beyond the obvious earmarks of a creative type when hiring a new designer. She does this by asking not only about successful projects but also about work that failed and what the designer learned from the failures. That way, she can find out whether the prospect is capable of absorbing lessons well and rolling with the punches of an unpredictable work environment. The CEO also asks job prospects what they collect and read, as well as what inspires them. These kinds of clues tell her about the applicant's creative bent and thinking style. If an interviewee passes these initial tests, the CEO has the prospect work with the rest of her staff on a mock design project. These diverse interview tools give her a good indication about the prospect's ability to combine creativity and organizational skills, and they help her understand how well the applicant will fit into the group.

One question for pitchers, of course, might be, "How do I make a positive impression if I don't fit into one of the three creative stereotypes?" If you already have a reputation for delivering on creative promises, you probably don't need to disguise yourself as a showrunner, artist, or neophyte—a résumé full of successes is the best calling card of all. But if you can't rely on your reputation, you should at least make an attempt to match yourself to the type you feel most comfortable with, if only because it's necessary to get a foot in the catcher's door.

Another question might be, "What if I don't *want* the catcher's input into the development of my idea?" This aspect of the pitch is so important that you should make it a priority: Find a part of your proposal that you are willing to yield on and invite the catcher to come up with suggestions. In fact, my observations suggest that you should engage the catcher as soon as possible in the development of the idea. Once the catcher feels like a creative collaborator, the odds of rejection diminish.

Ultimately, the pitch will always remain an imperfect process for communicating creative ideas. But by being aware of stereotyping processes and the value of collaboration, both pitchers and catchers can understand the difference between a pitch and a hit.

Originally published in September 2003. Reprint R0309J

The Five Messages Leaders Must Manage

by John Hamm

IF YOU WANT TO KNOW why so many organizations sink into chaos, look no further than their leaders' mouths. Leadership, at any level, certainly isn't easy—but unclear, vague, roller-coaster pronouncements make many top managers' jobs infinitely more difficult than they need to be. Leaders frequently espouse dozens of cliché-infused declarations such as "Let's focus on the key priorities this quarter," "Customers come first," or "We need a full-court press in engineering this month." Over and over again, they present grand, overarching—yet fuzzy—notions of where they think the company is going. Too often, they assume everyone shares the same definitions of broad terms like vision, loyalty, accountability, customer relationships, teamwork, focus, priority, culture, frugality, decision making, results, and so on, virtually ad infinitum.

Even the most senior managers nod in polite agreement when the CEO uses inflated terms like these, but the executives may feel somewhat discomfited, wondering whether they've truly understood. Rather than asking for clarification—a request they fear would make them look stupid—they pass on vague marching orders to their own troops, all of whom develop their own interpretations of what their bosses mean. In the absence of clear communication that satisfies the urgent desire to know what the boss is really thinking, people imagine all kinds of motives. The result is often sloppy behavior and misalignment that can cost a company dearly. Precious time is wasted, rumors abound, talented people lose their focus, big projects fail.

By contrast, think of the way a high-reliability team—say, an emergency room staff or a SWAT team—works. Every member has a precise understanding of what things mean. Surgeons and nurses speak the same medical language. SWAT teams know exactly what weapons to use, and when and how and under what conditions to use them. In these professions, there is absolutely no room for sloppy communication. If team members don't speak to each other with precision, people die. People don't die in corporations, but without clear definitions and directions from the top, they work ineffectively and at cross-purposes.

For the past five years, I've worked with hundreds of CEOs as a leadership coach, a board member, a venture capital investor, and a strategy consultant. I've also been a president and CEO myself (my company, Whistle Communications, was acquired by IBM in 1999). The companies whose CEOs I've worked with—typically technology firms—range in size from about 100 to several thousand people. In observing CEOs, I've come to the conclusion that the real job of leadership is to inspire the organization to take responsibility for creating a better future. I believe effective communication is a leader's single most critical management tool for making this happen. When leaders take the time to explain what they mean, both explicitly (by carefully defining their visions, intentions, and directions) and implicitly (through their behavior), they assert much-needed influence over the vague but powerful notions that otherwise run away with employees' imaginations. By clarifying amorphous terms and commanding and managing the corporate vocabulary, leaders effectively align precious employee energy and commitment within their organizations.

In researching this topic, I have discovered that many leaders don't take the time to define specifically what they mean when they

Idea in Brief

If you want to know why so many organizations sink into chaos, look no further than their leaders' mouths. Over and over, leaders present grand, overarching—yet fuzzy—notions of where they think the company is going. They assume everyone shares their definitions of "vision," "accountability," and "results." The result is often sloppy behavior and misalignment that can cost a company dearly. Effective communication is a leader's most critical tool for doing the essential job of leadership: inspiring the organization to take responsibility for creating a better future. Five topics wield extraordinary influence within a company: organizational structure and hierarchy, financial results, the leader's sense of his or her job, time management, and corporate culture. Properly defined, disseminated, and controlled, these topics give the leader opportunities for increased accountability and substantially better performance.

For example, one CEO always keeps communications about hierarchy admirably brief and to the point. When he realized he needed to realign internal resources, he told the staff: "I'm changing the structure of resources so that we can execute more effectively." After unveiling a new organization chart, he said, "It's 10:45. You have until noon to be annoyed, should that be your reaction. At noon, pizza will be served. At one o'clock, we go to work in our new positions." The most effective leaders ask themselves, "What needs to happen today to get where we want to go? What vague belief or notion can I clarify or debunk?" A CEO who communicates precisely to 10 direct reports, each of whom communicates with equal precision to 40 other employees, aligns the organization's commitment and energy with a well-understood vision of the firm's real goals and opportunities.

use generalized terms or clichés. They don't want to feel that they are talking down to people by providing what seems like unnecessary detail or context. Leaders simply assume that the exact meaning of their words is obvious; they're surprised to learn not only that their message has been unclear but that their teams crave definitions so they aren't forced to guess what the boss has in mind.

If we accept that the leader's job, at its core, is to inspire and support the organization's collective responsibility to create a better future for the company, then what are the keys to effectiveness?

The Idea in Practice

To inspire your workforce to greatness, Hamm recommends crystal-clear communication about these five topics:

Organizational Hierarchy

When your company reorganizes, quickly frame the change as a way to optimize your company's resources—not to oust or devalue employees.

Example: The CEO of a small software company had to realign internal resources when a close rival began gaining an advantage. He called an all-hands meeting, explaining, "We're in a war for market share. I don't think we're properly configured to win the battle, so I'm restructuring resources so we can execute more effectively. Most of you will continue doing the same jobs, but you may have a different supervisor." He showed them the new organization chart, then asked them to begin working in their new positions after lunch.

Financial Results

Discuss disappointing results not as evidence of punishable failure but as useful diagnostic and learning tools that enable constant improvement.

Example: When a technology firm missed a quarterly goal, the CEO asked his team rigorous questions about what caused the shortfall, rather than placing blame. Instead of worrying about who would take the heat, team members uncovered the problem's root cause and identified ways to prevent a recurrence. From then on, the company's track record for quality was the envy of the industry.

What tools do leaders need at hand for this mission? What mental models must they have? I like to think of good leaders as comparable to skilled locomotive drivers. The train is controlled by a set of switches and levers. When the driver pulls one lever, the train goes forward; when he pulls another, it stops, and so on. When an organization is well aligned, all the managerial levers are easily and neatly moved. They function smoothly so that driver, passengers, and train gracefully move forward as one.

In my experience, five such topics control the train: organizational structure and hierarchy, financial results, the leader's sense of his or her job, time management, and corporate culture. Messages

Your Job

Let followers know that your job is not to provide all the answers but to invite their ideas.

> ***Example:*** When one CEO met with functional leaders to discuss the company's failure to increase market share, he listened to their viewpoints, posed questions, and challenged opinions rather than stating his own theory. He then assigned a task force to address the problem. The team generated numerous recovery plans, the most compelling of which was implemented. The plan produced the desired market-share gains in the next three quarters.

Time Management

Communicate the importance of using time strategically, rather than trying to get more things done faster. Ask where you can best focus your team's energy. By understanding that you have a choice about how limited time can be used, you can free up needed resources to focus on your most important goals.

Corporate Culture

Create a healthy culture by articulating the right goals and defining criteria for success.

> ***Example:*** The CEO of a telephony-software company runs his firm like a high-performing sports team. He displays metrics—sales, expenses, revenues—on a scoreboard for all to see. And he clearly defines what success looks like: "P/E ratio of 15, market share of 20%, 30% year-over-year revenue growth." Large goals—"$20 million by the third quarter"—are broken into strategic parts marked on the scoreboard.

on these subjects wield extraordinary influence within the firm. When leaders take it for granted that everyone in the organization shares their assumptions or knows their mental models regarding the five subject areas, they lose their grip on the managerial levers and soon have the proverbial runaway train on their hands. But properly defined, disseminated, and controlled, the five topics afford the leader opportunities for organizational alignment, increased accountability, and substantially better performance.

Before examining each one, I'd like to address a few possible objections head-on. First, why do these five particular topics matter so much—why would defining corporate culture be a higher priority than, say, defining customer relationships? Certainly, other terms carry a premium in some organizations, but I've found that these five are excellent places to start and are highly representative of the kind of difficulties that exist for leaders as they speak to their teams day to day. The topics not only present the sharpest examples of the dangers of imprecise communication, but, when mastered, they also produce the greatest leadership leverage.

I am hardly suggesting that in defining the five concepts precisely, leaders should become dictators or blowhards. On the contrary, I am suggesting that when a leader defines what he or she really means and sets a clear direction according to that definition, relationships and feedback improve, action is more efficient and on-strategy, and improved performance follows.

Message 1: Organizational Structure and Hierarchy

The organizational chart, because it represents individual power or influence, is an emotionally charged framework even during a company's most stable times. But when the corporate structure is changing, the org chart can truly become fearsome, particularly in companies where, because of the political culture, employees worry about risk to their personal status.

If a CEO fails to take definitional control of a reorganization, with its prospect of job losses, boss changes, and new modes of working, the whole company can grind to a halt. Consider what happened when one well-known former CEO allowed the default assumptions surrounding the term "reorganization" to take hold. A few years ago, Carly Fiorina decided that Hewlett-Packard needed a top-to-bottom reshuffling. She had a fixed idea that reorganizations must be managed with extreme care, and she implicitly communicated her belief by the cautious way she floated her ideas with senior managers. She worried that a reshuffling plan would open a Pandora's box of political sensitivities, especially among middle managers. For this reason, everyone assumed that "reorganization" was cause for fear and trembling.

For two months prior to Fiorina's official announcement, work slowed or stopped as employees, not knowing precisely what to expect or fear, shifted their focus to the upcoming changes. Managers, jostling for power and position, got lost in political battles. Motivation plummeted. Contractors were put off, since no one knew who would be managing which divisions after the reorganization. When the new organizational structure was finally communicated, still more time passed unproductively as employees settled into their new positions. A total of 12 weeks—a full quarter—were effectively lost. If you multiply that time by employee salaries, and factor in the inevitable lapses in customer service and product innovation during the period, you can conservatively estimate the damage to the company.

It may be unreasonable to blame Fiorina for failing to realize that she was communicating her trepidation, or to fault her for not divining the consequences of talking about her reorganization ideas months ahead of time. After all, leaders cannot be held to perfection in execution. But they *can* be held to a standard when communicating a vision and its rationale. If Fiorina had laid out the master plan behind the reorganization more clearly, made her decisions more quickly, and communicated more explicitly, the troops at HP would have gained a better understanding of the process, the reasons for the extended time frame, and their future places within the company.

A leader who quickly takes charge of the communication around a reorganization can prevent the discourse from engendering fear. The most productive way for a leader to think about organizational structure is as a flexible map of accountability for action and, thus, results—a guideline whose purpose is to define goals and optimize resources, not to oust or devalue employees. When a reorganization is presented as such, it loses its reputation as a proxy for personal power shifts, whether real or imagined.

The CEO of a 150-employee software company shows how a leader can prevent political fears from taking hold by keeping communications brief and to the point. Rather than viewing the org chart as a source of anxiety, and communicating that attitude to the company, the CEO chose to see it as simply a temporary structure for optimizing resources. When a new strategy or direction was called for, he enlisted people as active agents of change, so they wouldn't be left to wonder whether they were to become victims. For example, the CEO realized at one point that he needed to realign internal resources because a close competitor was gaining an advantage. He called an all-hands meeting for a Monday morning. "Team," he said, "we're in a war for market share. I get paid to win it, and so do you. But right now I don't think we're properly configured to win the particular battle we're fighting, so I'm changing the structure of resources so that we can execute more effectively. Most of you will continue to do the jobs you're doing now, but you may have a different supervisor." After showing everyone the new organization chart, he looked at his watch. "It's 10:45 now," he said. "You have until noon to be annoyed, should that be your reaction. At noon, pizza will be served. At one o'clock, we go to work in our new positions."

The CEO later explained what he did: "We had a competitor who was showing us a better way to win the business. We were both like captains of firefighting teams. We each had seven people and a full set of buckets and hoses. My team had five guys armed with buckets and two with hoses. His team had three guys with buckets and four with hoses. We just weren't organized to compete and win. I wasn't trying to shift power; I was just trying to optimize our resources. I wasn't willing to let this change be viewed as a political event. I wanted it to be seen as a business necessity to remain competitive."

Obviously, it's one thing to shift personnel in a 150-person company and quite another to do so in a giant corporation like HP. But I would argue that the value of clear, honest, explicit communication rises exponentially with the size of the organization. In fact, a large company can be reshuffled much more quickly when the CEO deliberately decides not to inflate the political balloon and won't tolerate others doing so.

Having gathered the data and made her decision, Fiorina was under no obligation to provide previews of coming attractions. Within 48 hours of the announcement, she might have held a companywide meeting, complete with a Webcast, to explain why the change was necessary. To keep people's minds off who was headed down and who was headed up, she could have asked everyone involved in the changes to identify and submit, in short order, explicit goals for the next 60 days. She thus would have communicated that the organization chart has nothing to do with politics and everything to do with organizational effectiveness.

Message 2: Financial Results

"Results" is another powerful concept that, left unmanaged, poses a risk to a company's long-term health. When a top executive tells employees they need to "focus on our promised results," senior managers often interpret that as meaning "Do whatever it takes to meet investors' expectations." By losing sight of the connection between employee behavior and results, and failing to take advantage of learning opportunities, leaders miss out on building long-term value for their firms.

One CEO I knew truly believed that the only purpose of his job was to make aggressive predictions and promises about quarterly results and then achieve the numbers by any means possible. By the ninth week of every quarter, when projections fell short, he put enormous pressure on his sales professionals and finance people. His implicit message was: "These are the results I need; I don't care how you get it done." He fully expected the company to thrive.

Quite the opposite occurred. Because the CEO defined "results" so narrowly and failed to properly motivate or compensate his selling team, the sales force had no compunction about stuffing the sales channel. Though the company never met with any punitive action, its poor practices forced recalculations of results and exposed it to huge write-downs. Revenues stalled at $10 million a quarter, and the company was eventually acquired at a discount to its annual revenues.

In the long term, consistently positive results spring from intelligent strategy and an incessant focus on quality of execution. Think of a golf pro like Tiger Woods, whose best bet for winning major championships is to master his aim, setup, and swing. Once the ball is in the air, there is no way to control it; it will land where it will. Similarly, effective leaders understand that there is more leverage in using quarterly results as a metric for long-term improvement than in worrying only about short-term market wins. By using results as a diagnostic tool in the service of improving future execution, and by asking employees to participate in the analysis, effective leaders encourage honesty and engage their troops in open dialogue. Employees are more likely to generate good ideas, and the firm is more likely to surpass financial expectations quarter after quarter.

I had the pleasure of working for six years under John Adler, former CEO of the technology firm Adaptec. During his 12 years at the helm, Adler drove the company's valuation from $100 million to over $5 billion because he had a very healthy attitude about business goals and financial results. For him, results were not a punitive weapon but a useful diagnostic and learning tool. When the firm, at one point, missed a quarterly goal, he and his management team analyzed all the factors contributing to the shortfall. They discovered that, as a result of an unusual quality-control issue, the company had been unable to make some end-of-quarter shipments. Instead of reacting emotionally and assigning blame, Adler asked rigorous questions of the senior management team, which was able to uncover the root cause of the problem. He communicated this information broadly to ensure organizational learning. By focusing on and taking responsibility for the truth, Adler made others in the company feel safe to discuss the issue without fear of an emotional response that might lead to arbitrary punishment.

Through his actions, Adler sent an implicit message that the past was over and tomorrow was another day. Rather than being immobilized by uncertainty and wondering who would be forced to take the heat, software engineers and quality assurance technicians worked together to improve their processes to minimize the probability of missing sales projections because of last-minute quality or manufacturing glitches. From that point forward, the company's track record for quality was the envy of the industry. By adjusting his "swing," Adler was able to achieve accurate, consistently excellent results for the duration of his tenure.

Message 3: The Leader's Sense of His or Her Job

CEOs wear many hats and play many roles in the service of leadership, but, surrounded by people who seek their feedback and approval, some fall into the trap of thinking that their responsibility is to be the person who has all the answers. (This is especially true of entrepreneurial CEOs who are also founders, because their identities are closely tied with their companies.) The "answer man" falsely believes himself to be the final arbiter of conflicts, decisions, and dilemmas. This puts him in a very lonely, isolated position where information becomes unreliable and useful input is stifled.

A CEO I'll call Jim, who ran a once blazingly successful and now defunct desktop-publishing software firm, had been told his whole life that he was brilliant—and he was. The recipient of an MBA from Stanford and a PhD from MIT and the holder of ten software patents, Jim was also a Midas: Everything he touched seemed to turn to gold. It wasn't much of a leap for him to assume that because he was so smart, he necessarily knew what was best for the company. Jim took great comfort in this assumption; indeed, since he was deeply insecure in other leadership areas, his identity rested on it.

Though Jim made a point of hiring the best and the brightest from top engineering and business schools, he didn't listen to his new team. Strategy, for example, was not Jim's strongest suit, but he believed he knew best how to combat competitive threats. When his managers made suggestions for staving off the competition, Jim ignored them, using his positional power to drown out discussion. He'd say of a rival company: "There's no way those guys could be close to our technology. I've met the CEO there and I know we can beat them. I will explain what we have to do." While forceful and somewhat persuasive, he was out of touch with market reality, and his team knew it. Frustrated, his managers soon grasped the implicit message that they were neither heard nor valued, and they began to flee the company, taking much intellectual capital with them. Jim, oblivious to perceptions of his own behavior, was baffled by the exodus, telling himself that the people who left didn't "get it."

Effective leaders, by contrast, understand that their role is to bring out the answers in others. They do this by very clearly and explicitly seeking contributions, challenges, and collaboration from the people who report to them, using their positional power not to dominate but rather to drive the decision-making process. The more collaborative and apolitical that process is, the less isolated the leader, and the greater the likelihood that the business strategy will be grounded in reality.

Contrast Jim's understanding and communication of his role to that of a CEO I'll call Chris, who ran a technology research firm. Chris, too, was brilliant and confident—top of his class at Harvard and a military hero in the Gulf War—but instead of expressing his intelligence arrogantly, he conveyed curiosity. In functional meetings, he communicated that for the duration of the session, he wouldn't wield his positional power as CEO but instead would be just another contributor of ideas. He listened to everyone's point of view before expressing his own. He posed questions and challenged opinions. In one meeting with his marketing team, he listened to presentations from public relations, marketing, and advertising managers. When he finally spoke, he noted that the company had outspent competitors in a bid to raise visibility for its flagship product but had yet to make a dent in competitors' market share. He asked that a smaller group convene within a week to find out why. Aware that the "boss's answer" would stifle the group's creativity and thus do more harm than good, he resisted the temptation to state his own theory.

In asking his team to be accountable for diagnosing the problem, Chris didn't accuse anyone or cast blame. He thereby conveyed that his role was to help the team process information. He made it clear to the people who worked for him that it was not his job to provide the answers, but rather to help find the best solutions. His authentically collaborative approach encouraged the smart people around him to contribute their ideas. The task force generated a half dozen thoughtful and feasible theories and several comprehensive recovery plans, the most compelling of which was put into action. It produced the hoped-for changes in market share in the next three quarters. In the

Change your mind-set

When executives assume that managerial topics are understood the same way by everyone, they surrender the opportunity to lead effectively. Leaders who explicitly say what they mean are better able to leverage the energy and commitment of their followers.

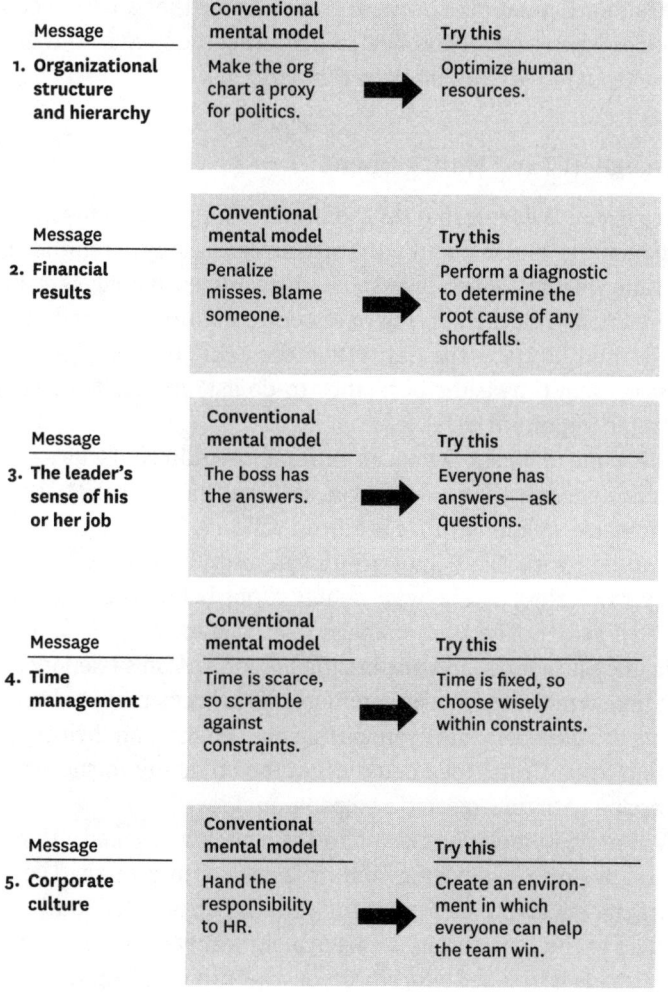

Message	Conventional mental model		Try this
1. Organizational structure and hierarchy	Make the org chart a proxy for politics.	→	Optimize human resources.
2. Financial results	Penalize misses. Blame someone.	→	Perform a diagnostic to determine the root cause of any shortfalls.
3. The leader's sense of his or her job	The boss has the answers.	→	Everyone has answers—ask questions.
4. Time management	Time is scarce, so scramble against constraints.	→	Time is fixed, so choose wisely within constraints.
5. Corporate culture	Hand the responsibility to HR.	→	Create an environment in which everyone can help the team win.

process, several ideas for other successful marketing campaigns were born. As a result of his leadership, Chris's firm established itself as a powerhouse of intellectual capital in the technology arena. His company is now regarded as a unique source of market information and is paid handsome fees to publish its findings.

Like the Level 5 leaders Jim Collins describes, Chris led by separating his ego from his job. Leaders like Chris understand that their role is to ask great questions, and they know that answers can be found as long as employees feel safe offering them. Accordingly, the entire team moves the company forward.

Message 4: Time Management

Every executive feels that time is in short supply. Organizers, time management classes, and administrative assistants remind us of the time we don't have. Obsessed with deadlines, managers struggle against constraints by trying to squeeze, manipulate, and control the limited hours in the day. When the CEO gives employees the message that time is the boss, the "to-do list" mentality can easily subsume important goals.

Allow me to illustrate with an extreme-sounding but true example of a CEO with whom I worked. Alan, as I'll call him, was the busy head of a midsize technology firm in Silicon Valley. A former engineer who was ruled by his Day-Timer, to-do list, and BlackBerry, he started every day feeling that he was "behind," long before the opening bell on Wall Street. The time management system was his scripture, efficiency his credo, and prioritizing his Job 1. Alan's fixed idea was that time was the enemy; he communicated this message to his team, telling the members that by managing time better than their counterparts at rival firms, they could drive the company to success. His obsession with time created a palpable anxiety.

When economic conditions in the valley worsened, Alan was forced to impose a moratorium on head-count growth. Then the company received a request for proposal from BellSouth. Alan jumped at the opportunity to make a big software sale and focused his already stretched workforce on the project. Implicitly, time management became the operational currency of the organization. Alan became even more conscious of employees' use of time, so he separated elements of the project into streams, telling his direct reports where and how to use their hours and minutes to produce the RFP. When he was giving feedback to his direct reports, his first question was about how they used the time they devoted to their work. Despite everyone's efforts, however, there weren't enough hours in the day to keep up.

The company submitted the RFP on time, all its i's dotted and t's crossed, then waited with bated breath for what Alan was certain would be a positive response from BellSouth. But the company lost to a firm with inferior technology. The problem had less to do with the content of the proposal than with the way it was delivered. Alan and his team had created a perfect RFP but failed to invest in any relationship building with anyone at BellSouth. The competitor, by contrast, had developed close relationships with the telecommunications firm. Simply put, Alan's people were so obsessed with meeting tasks on deadline that they had lost sight of the project as a whole, and the customer in particular. It was as if the cooks at Alan's firm had made an exquisite, five-course dinner but had forgotten the wine, the tablecloth, and the flowers and had served the food cold. They delivered what Alan said he expected.

A CEO can be more effective if she communicates to the company that the resource of time must not be squeezed for all it is worth but instead must be strategically utilized. It's a subtle but important distinction. A leader who harps on time constraints and breathes down managers' necks, trying to get them to do too much in the allotted period, can make the organization frantic and, ultimately, ineffective. A leader who communicates that when time is tight, it's better to do fewer things—but do them very well—gives managers the confidence to make the best use of this precious resource. That way, everyone involved works within the time parameters to do what needs to be done.

One leader who understands the importance of communicating properly about time is Mark King, the CEO of TaylorMade-adidas Golf. King desperately wanted to launch an industry-changing product to mark the company's 25th anniversary in the spring of 2004. The golf equipment business, like music, cars, and fashion, is trend driven; King knew that if his company could develop a breakthrough product and launch it at a very powerful point in the industry's history, the company would cement its status as golf's leading performance brand.

At first, King envisioned an entire new line of clubs based on the bold idea of movable weight, and he set all his best engineers working on development. They put in long hours, but as the six-month mark neared, he realized that his objective would be impossible to meet by the anniversary date. He could not ask for more time from the team, nor could he change the deadline. So he changed the goal. TaylorMade would develop a single golf club that would showcase the technology of movable weight, and the product would debut at the anniversary event in front of hundreds of reporters and industry influencers.

Instead of struggling against time, King shifted his choices within the time constraint. How, he asked himself, could his teams best use their hours? Instead of playing beat the clock by trying to do everything he wished, where could they best focus their energy? How could time be optimized? By understanding that he had a choice about how the limited time could best be used, he was able to free up needed technical and marketing resources and focus on quality and branding.

The new TaylorMade r7 quad driver, unveiled on the anniversary, garnered rave reviews. PGA and European Tour golfers snapped it up. By the time the 2004 PGA and European tours came to an end, half the professionals worldwide owned the new driver, guaranteeing its popularity among the golfing public. A dozen additional products followed, completing the team's vision for the line of clubs. The meal was well planned, cooked, and served. Today, TaylorMade is the fastest growing golf-equipment firm in the world, and its r7 driver is the flagship product in a multihundred-million-dollar product line.

Alan, the technology company CEO, sent the message that time was to be fought against, and he set unreasonable expectations.

84 Great Things

TO GET AN IDEA OF what can happen when a CEO manages time constraints by setting reasonable expectations, imagine that you have seven direct reports, each of whom commits to completing no more than three important, very doable initiatives each quarter. If these reports and their teams meet their goals, four quarters will yield 84 significant accomplishments. If your company were able to do anywhere near 84 significant things in a single year, the results would no doubt be astonishing. The real enemy to accomplishing 84 great things is the temptation to work on the 85th objective and beyond before, or at the expense of, the higher-priority goals. To keep people on track, a leader must communicate objectives very clearly and demand that action flow to the real priorities first.

Mark King's message was that time was not the enemy, just a fact of the situation, and there were other, more controllable levers that could be used to meet the challenges at hand. Alan saw time as a fearsome, inflexible monster, best overcome by brute force; King saw it as a neutral phenomenon, best handled with flexibility. Both men had a strong vision of what success would look like, but King was willing to make trade-offs in the service of quality. (See the sidebar "84 Great Things.")

Message 5: Corporate Culture

What is corporate culture, and why is communicating clearly and precisely about it important? Culture is not created by declaration; it derives from expectations focused on winning. You can only have a culture that encourages performance if you hire the right people, require them to behave in a way that is consistent with the values the company espouses, and implement processes that will allow the company to win in the marketplace.

CEOs who fail to define success and communicate their vision of it, and fail to make their expectations clear to employees, produce meaningless cultures. The silly cultural activity arising from the high-tech bubble of the late 1990s is a wonderful example. I remember one Silicon Valley CEO who opened the "culture cupboard" and fed employees with all kinds of treats—Friday beer bashes, foosball tables, and the like. He even hired a "chief culture officer," an HR executive whose job was making employees feel fleetingly happy, even when the company lost a client or had a bad quarter. The idea was that if people felt good, if they were "empowered" and were working together, then good results would follow naturally. It was all about employee morale and attitude and teamwork. But managers lost sight of core business metrics. In the end, people wanted to work for a firm that did more than cheerlead them—they wanted a share in a successful IPO. Eventually, the company was acquired for mere asset value because instead of developing a winning strategy, the CEO engaged in indulgent avoidance.

A healthy culture is created and maintained by focusing on the right goals and creating the experience of winning in the marketplace. A telephony-software company CEO I'll call Jeff runs his firm like a high-performing sports team. A big, football-style scoreboard on a conference room wall displays the company metrics—sales, expenses, revenues—for all to see. All personnel in the company, screened for their collaborative as well as their analytical skills, work on six-person teams (according to the U.S. Navy SEALs, six is the ideal number of participants on any high-intensity project). Individuals are only as effective as their teams; everyone in the firm adheres to a strict set of values and basic standards of conduct. Finally, everyone in the company knows what winning looks like: a P/E ratio of 15, a market share of 20%, and 30% year-over-year revenue growth. If the company's goal is to make $20 million by the third quarter, the goal is broken down into strategic parts marked on the scoreboard. The spirit of the company is a function of its collective commitment to success, not the most recent company outing. Successful companies are places where people want to come to work—not to be coddled but to make a difference.

In companies with healthy cultures, employees aren't kept in the dark; rather, they are supported in the belief that they are part of an exciting future. They come to work with a fire inside them, a result of clearly stated leadership and business practices that everyone explicitly understands. Every person in the company knows how to individually contribute to its future.

By recognizing the impact of clear and direct communication and seeking feedback from their teams, leaders leverage, rather than abuse, their positional power. The most effective leaders I know, CEOs who understand that the risks of miscommunication are very high, ask themselves the following questions on their way to work: What needs to happen today so that we can get where we want to go? Where is there confusion in my company? What vague belief or notion can I clarify or debunk today? What have I not communicated completely or clearly? What kinds of things are people taking for granted?

In the end, the power of clear communication is really a game of leverage. A CEO who communicates precisely to ten direct reports, each of whom communicates with equal precision to 40 other talented employees, effectively aligns the organization's commitment and energy around a clear, well-understood, shared vision of the company's real goals, priorities, and opportunities. He or she saves the company time, money, and resources and allows extraordinary things to happen.

Originally published in May 2006. Reprint R0605G

Taking the Stress Out of Stressful Conversations

by Holly Weeks

WE LIVE BY TALKING. That's just the kind of animal we are. We chatter and tattle and gossip and jest. But sometimes—more often than we'd like—we have stressful conversations, those sensitive exchanges that can hurt or haunt us in ways no other kind of talking does. Stressful conversations are unavoidable in life, and in business they can run the gamut from firing a subordinate to, curiously enough, receiving praise. But whatever the context, stressful conversations differ from other conversations because of the emotional loads they carry. These conversations call up embarrassment, confusion, anxiety, anger, pain, or fear—if not in us, then in our counterparts. Indeed, stressful conversations cause such anxiety that most people simply avoid them. This strategy is not necessarily wrong. One of the first rules of engagement, after all, is to pick your battles. Yet sometimes it can be extremely costly to dodge issues, appease difficult people, and smooth over antagonisms because the fact is that avoidance usually makes a problem or relationship worse.

Since stressful conversations are so common—and so painful—why don't we work harder to improve them? The reason is precisely because our feelings are so enmeshed. When we are not emotionally entangled in an issue, we know that conflict is normal, that it can be resolved—or at least managed. But when feelings get stirred up, most of us are thrown off balance. Like a quarterback who chokes in a tight play, we lose all hope of ever making it to the goal line.

For the past 20 years, I have been teaching classes and conducting workshops at some of the top corporations and universities in the United States on how to communicate during stressful conversations. With classrooms as my laboratory, I have learned that most people feel incapable of talking through sensitive issues. It's as though all our skills go out the window and we can't think usefully about what's happening or what we could do to get good results.

Stressful conversations, though, need not be this way. I have seen that managers can improve difficult conversations unilaterally if they approach them with greater self-awareness, rehearse them in advance, and apply just three proven communication techniques. Don't misunderstand me: There will never be a cookie-cutter approach to stressful conversations. There are too many variables and too much tension, and the interactions between people in difficult situations are always unique. Yet nearly every stressful conversation can be seen as an amalgam of a limited number of basic conversations, each with its own distinct set of problems. In the following pages, we'll explore how you can anticipate and handle those problems. But first, let's look at the three basic stressful conversations that we bump up against most often in the workplace.

"I Have Bad News for You"

Delivering unpleasant news is usually difficult for both parties. The speaker is often tense, and the listener is apprehensive about where the conversation is headed. Consider David, the director of a nonprofit institution. He was in the uncomfortable position of needing to talk with an ambitious researcher, Jeremy, who had a much higher opinion of his job performance than others in the organization did. The complication for David was that, in the past, Jeremy had received artificially high evaluations. There were several reasons for this. One had to do with the organization's culture: The nonprofit was not a confrontational kind of place. Additionally, Jeremy had tremendous confidence in both his own abilities and the quality of

Idea in Brief

Stressful conversations are unavoidable in life. In business, they can run the gamut from firing a subordinate to, curiously enough, receiving praise. But whatever the context, stressful conversations carry a heavy emotional load. Indeed, stressful conversations cause such anxiety that most people simply avoid them. Yet it can be extremely costly to dodge issues, appease difficult people, and smooth over antagonisms; avoidance usually only worsens a problem or a relationship. Using vivid examples of the three basic stressful conversations that people bump up against most often in the workplace, the author explains how managers can improve those interactions unilaterally. To begin with, they should approach the situations with greater self-awareness. Awareness building is not about endless self-analysis; much of it simply involves making tacit knowledge about oneself more explicit. Knowing how you react in a stressful situation will teach you a lot about your trouble areas and can help you master stressful situations. The author also recommends rehearsing difficult conversations in advance to fine-tune your phrasing and tone. We all know from past experience what kinds of conversations and people we handle badly. The trick is to have prepared conversational tactics to address those situations.

his academic background. Together with his defensive response to even the mildest criticism, this confidence led others—including David—to let slide discussions of weaknesses that were interfering with Jeremy's ability to deliver high-quality work. Jeremy had a cutting sense of humor, for instance, which had offended people inside and outside his unit. No one had ever said anything to him directly, but as time passed, more and more people were reluctant to work with him. Given that Jeremy had received almost no concrete criticism over the years, his biting style was now entrenched and the staff was restive.

In conversations like this, the main challenge is to get off to the right start. If the exchange starts off reasonably well, the rest of it has a good chance of going well. But if the opening goes badly, it threatens to bleed forward into the rest of the conversation. In an effort to be gentle, many people start these conversations on a light note.

The Idea in Practice

Types of Stressful Conversations

At work, stressful conversations take various forms:

- **"I have bad news for you."** For example, you have to criticize an employee's performance.
- **"What's going on here?"** Unexpectedly, a conversation becomes intensely charged.
- **"You are attacking me!"** Someone hits you with profanity, shouting, or other aggressive, accusatory moves.

Preparing for Stressful Conversations

1. Identify your weaknesses to particular people and situations. You'll avoid succumbing to your feelings and ignoring *your* needs during a stressful conversation.
2. Know *how* you react to feeling vulnerable. Do you bare your teeth when facing an overbearing competitor? Shut down when feeling excluded? Knowing your danger zones, you can anticipate your vulnerabilities and improve your responses.
3. With an honest, nonjudgmental friend, rehearse clear, neutral, and temperate responses. Get out everything you're thinking (emotions and all), then refine your phrasing until it expresses your message—in an honest but nonthreatening way. Eliminate emotionally charged behaviors. Write down your phrasing to remember it later.

Managing Stressful Conversations

Preparation isn't enough. *During* a stressful conversation, use these gambits:

And that was just what David did, opening with, "How about those Red Sox?"

Naturally Jeremy got the wrong idea about where David was heading; he remained his usual cocky, superior self. Sensing this, David felt he had to take off the velvet gloves. The conversation quickly became brutally honest, and David did almost all the talking. When the monologue was over, Jeremy stared icily at the floor. He got up in stiff silence and left. David was relieved. From his point of view, the interaction had been painful but swift. There was not too much blood on the floor, he observed wryly. But two days later,

Stressful Conversation	Gambit	Reason for Gambit	Example
"I have bad news for you"	**Honor thy partner:** Start by acknowledging your part in the problem.	You'll help your listener hear your difficult message, without provoking him.	David has to tell Jeremy his cruel humor alienates coworkers. David says, "I share responsibility because I've been reluctant to speak openly with you about these difficulties."
"What's going on here?"	**Disarm thy partner:** Grant your partner his perceptions, and restate your intentions.	You'll change confrontation into agreement without resorting to appeasement. No one loses face.	Elizabeth lists project tasks on a white board and says, "Is that it then?" Rafael snipes, "Who told *you* to assign work to me?" Elizabeth says, "I can see why you took what I said that way. That wasn't what I meant. Let's go over this list again."
"You are attacking me!"	**Fight tactics, not people:** Name the aggressive tactic your partner's using.	You neutralize the tactic without going on the offensive or being intimidated.	When Karen botches a presentation and senses her colleague Nick's disapproval, she lashes out. He says, "I don't know how to talk about what went wrong. Your take on what happened is so different from mine."

Jeremy handed in his resignation, taking a lot of institutional memory—and talent—with him.

"What's Going On Here?"

Often we have stressful conversations thrust upon us. Indeed, some of the worst conversations—especially for people who are conflict averse—are the altogether unexpected ones that break out like crackling summer storms. Suddenly the conversation becomes intensely charged emotionally, and electricity flies in all directions.

What's worse, nothing makes sense. We seem to have been drawn into a black cloud of twisted logic and altered sensibilities.

Consider the case of Elizabeth and Rafael. They were team leaders working together on a project for a major consulting firm. It seemed that everything that could have gone wrong on the project had, and the work was badly bogged down. The two consultants were meeting to revise their schedule, given the delays, and to divide up the discouraging tasks for the week ahead. As they talked, Elizabeth wrote and erased on the white board. When she had finished, she looked at Rafael and said matter-of-factly, "Is that it, then?"

Rafael clenched his teeth in frustration. "If you say so," he sniped.

Elizabeth recoiled. She instantly replayed the exchange in her mind but couldn't figure out what had provoked Rafael. His reaction seemed completely disconnected from her comment. The most common reaction of someone in Elizabeth's place is to guiltily defend herself by denying Rafael's unspoken accusation. But Elizabeth was uneasy with confrontation so she tried appeasement. "Rafael," she stammered, "I'm sorry. Is something wrong?"

"Who put you in charge?" he retorted. "Who told you to assign work to me?"

Clearly, Rafael and Elizabeth have just happened into a difficult conversation. Some transgression has occurred, but Elizabeth doesn't know exactly what it is. She feels blindsided—her attempt to expedite the task at hand has clearly been misconstrued. Rafael feels he's been put in a position of inferiority by what he sees as Elizabeth's controlling behavior. Inexplicably, there seem to be more than two people taking part in this conversation, and the invisible parties are creating lots of static. What childhood experience, we may wonder, is causing Elizabeth to assume that Rafael's tension is automatically her fault? And who is influencing Rafael's perception that Elizabeth is taking over? Could it be his father? His wife? It's impossible to tell. At the same time, it's hard for us to escape the feeling that Rafael is overreacting when he challenges Elizabeth about her alleged need to take control.

Elizabeth felt Rafael's resentment like a wave and she apologized again. "Sorry. How do you want the work divided?" Deferring to

Rafael in this way smoothed the strained atmosphere for the time being. But it set a precedent for unequal status that neither Elizabeth nor the company believed was correct. Worse, though Rafael and Elizabeth remained on the same team after their painful exchange, Elizabeth chafed under the status change and three months later transferred out of the project.

"You Are Attacking Me!"

Now let's turn our attention to aggressively stressful conversations, those in which people use all kinds of psychological and rhetorical mechanisms to throw their counterparts off balance, to undermine their positions, even to expose and belittle them. These "thwarting tactics" take many forms—profanity, manipulation, shouting—and not everyone is triggered or stumped by the same ones. The red zone is not the thwarting tactic alone but the pairing of the thwarting tactic with individual vulnerability.

Consider Nick and Karen, two senior managers working at the same level in an IT firm. Karen was leading a presentation to a client, and the information was weak and disorganized. She and the team had not been able to answer even basic questions. The client had been patient, then quiet, then clearly exasperated. When the presentation really started to fall apart, the client put the team on the spot with questions that made them look increasingly inadequate.

On this particular day, Nick was not part of the presenting team; he was simply observing. He was as surprised as the client at Karen's poor performance. After the client left, he asked Karen what happened. She lashed out at him defensively: "You're not my boss, so don't start patronizing me. You always undercut me no matter what I do." Karen continued to shout at Nick, her antagonism palpable. Each time he spoke, she interrupted him with accusations and threats: "I can't wait to see how you like it when people leave you flailing in the wind." Nick tried to remain reasonable, but Karen didn't wind down. "Karen," he said, "pull yourself together. You are twisting every word I say."

Here, Nick's problem is not that Karen is using a panoply of thwarting tactics, but that all her tactics—accusation, distortion, and digression—are aggressive. This raises the stakes considerably. Most of us are vulnerable to aggressive tactics because we don't know whether, or how far, the aggression will escalate. Nick wanted to avoid Karen's aggression, but his insistence on rationality in the face of emotionalism was not working. His cool approach was trumped by Karen's aggressive one. As a result, Nick found himself trapped in the snare of Karen's choosing. In particular, her threats that she would pay him back with the client rattled him. He couldn't tell whether she was just huffing or meant it. He finally turned to the managing director, who grew frustrated, and later angry, at Nick and Karen for their inability to resolve their problems. In the end, their lack of skill in handling their difficult conversations cost them dearly. Both were passed over for promotion after the company pinned the loss of the client directly on their persistent failure to communicate.

Preparing for a Stressful Conversation

So how can we prepare for these three basic stressful conversations before they occur? A good start is to become aware of your own weaknesses to people and situations. David, Elizabeth, and Nick were unable to control their counterparts, but their stressful conversations would have gone much better if they had been more usefully aware of their vulnerabilities. It is important for those who are vulnerable to hostility, for example, to know how they react to it. Do they withdraw or escalate—do they clam up or retaliate? While one reaction is not better than the other, knowing how you react in a stressful situation will teach you a lot about your vulnerabilities, and it can help you master stressful situations.

Recall Nick's problem. If he had been more self-aware, he would have known that he acts stubbornly rational in the face of aggressive outbursts such as Karen's. Nick's choice of a disengaged demeanor gave Karen control over the conversation, but he didn't have to allow Karen—or anyone else—to exploit his vulnerability. In moments of calm self-scrutiny, when he's not entangled in a live stressful conversation, Nick can take time to reflect on his inability to tolerate irrational aggressive outbursts. This self-awareness would free him to prepare himself—not for Karen's unexpected accusations but for his own predictable vulnerability to any sudden assault like hers.

Though it might sound like it, building awareness is not about endless self-analysis. Much of it simply involves making our tacit knowledge about ourselves more explicit. We all know from past experience, for instance, what kinds of conversations and people we handle badly. When you find yourself in a difficult conversation, ask yourself whether this is one of those situations and whether it involves one of those people. For instance, do you bare your teeth when faced with an overbearing competitor? Do you shut down when you feel excluded? Once you know what your danger zones are, you can anticipate your vulnerability and improve your response.

Explicit self-awareness will often help save you from engaging in a conversation in a way that panders to your feelings rather than one that serves your needs. Think back to David, the boss of the nonprofit institution, and Jeremy, his cocky subordinate. Given Jeremy's history, David's conversational game plan—easing in, then when that didn't work, the painful-but-quick bombshell—was doomed. A better approach would have been for David to split the conversation into two parts. In a first meeting, he could have raised the central issues of Jeremy's biting humor and disappointing performance. A second meeting could have been set up for the discussion itself. Handling the situation incrementally would have allowed time for both David and Jeremy to prepare for a two-way conversation instead of one of them delivering a monologue. After all, this wasn't an emergency; David didn't have to exhaust this topic immediately. Indeed, if David had been more self-aware, he might have recognized that the approach he chose was dictated less by Jeremy's character than by his own distaste for conflict.

An excellent way to anticipate specific problems that you may encounter in a stressful conversation is to rehearse with a neutral friend. Pick someone who doesn't have the same communication problems as you. Ideally, the friend should be a good listener, honest but nonjudgmental. Start with content. Just tell your friend what you want to say to your counterpart without worrying about tone or

The DNA of Conversation Management

THE TECHNIQUES I HAVE IDENTIFIED for handling stressful conversations all have tucked within them three deceptively simple ingredients that are needed to make stressful conversations succeed. These are clarity, neutrality, and temperance, and they are the building blocks of all good communication. Mastering them will multiply your chances of responding well to even the most strained conversation. Let's take a look at each of the components in turn.

Clarity means letting words do the work for us. Avoid euphemisms or talking in circles—tell people clearly what you mean: "Emily, from your family's point of view, the Somerset Valley Nursing Home would be the best placement for your father. His benefits don't cover it." Unfortunately, delivering clear content when the news is bad is particularly hard to do. Under strained circumstances, we all tend to shy away from clarity because we equate it with brutality. Instead, we often say things like: "Well, Dan, we're still not sure yet what's going to happen with this job, but in the future we'll keep our eyes open." This is a roundabout—and terribly misleading—way to inform someone that he didn't get the promotion he was seeking. Yet there's nothing inherently brutal about honesty. It is not the content but the delivery of the news that makes it brutal or humane. Ask a surgeon; ask a priest; ask a cop. If a message is given skillfully—even though the news is bad—the content may still be tolerable. When a senior executive, for example, directly tells a subordinate that "the promotion has gone to someone else," the news is likely to be highly unpleasant, and the appropriate reaction is sadness, anger, and anxiety. But if the content is clear, the listener can better begin to

---

phrasing. Be vicious, be timid, be sarcastically witty, jump around in your argument, but get it out. Now go over it again and think about what you would say if the situation weren't emotionally loaded. Your friend can help you because he or she is not in a flush of emotion over the situation. Write down what you come up with together because if you don't, you'll forget it later.

Now fine-tune the phrasing. When you imagine talking to the counterpart, your phrasing tends to be highly charged—and you can think of only one way to say anything. But when your friend says, "Tell me how you want to say this," an interesting thing happens: your phrasing is often much better, much more temperate, usable. Remember, you can say what you want to say, you just can't say it

process the information. Indeed, bringing clarity to the content eases the burden for the counterpart rather than increases it.

Tone is the nonverbal part of delivery in stressful conversations. It is intonation, facial expressions, conscious and unconscious body language. Although it's hard to have a neutral tone when overcome by strong feelings, neutrality is the desired norm in crisis communications, including stressful conversations. Consider the classic neutrality of NASA. Regardless of how dire the message, NASA communicates its content in uninflected tones: "Houston, we have a problem." It takes practice to acquire such neutrality. But a neutral tone is the best place to start when a conversation turns stressful.

Temperate phrasing is the final element in this triumvirate of skills. English is a huge language, and there are lots of different ways to say what you need to say. Some of these phrases are temperate, while others baldly provoke your counterpart to dismiss your words—and your content. In the United States, for example, some of the most intemperate phrasing revolves around threats of litigation: "If you don't get a check to me by April 23, I'll be forced to call my lawyer." Phrases like this turn up the heat in all conversations, particularly in strained ones. But remember, we're not in stressful conversations to score points or to create enemies. The goal is to advance the conversation, to hear and be heard accurately, and to have a functional exchange between two people. So next time you want to snap at someone—"Stop interrupting me!"—try this: "Can you hold on a minute? I want to finish before I lose my train of thought." Temperate phrasing will help you take the strain out of a stressful conversation.

like that. Also, work on your body language with your friend. You'll both soon be laughing because of the expressions that sneak out unawares—eyebrows skittering up and down, legs wrapped around each other like licorice twists, nervous snickers that will certainly be misinterpreted. (For more on preparing for stressful conversations, see the sidebar "The DNA of Conversation Management.")

Managing the Conversation

While it is important to build awareness and to practice before a stressful conversation, these steps are not enough. Let's look at what you can do as the conversation unfolds. Consider Elizabeth, the team leader whose colleague claimed she was usurping control. She couldn't think well on her feet in confrontational situations, and she knew it, so she needed a few hip-pocket phrases—phrases she could recall on the spot so that she wouldn't have to be silent or invent something on the spur of the moment. Though such a solution sounds simple, most of us don't have a tool kit of conversational tactics ready at hand. Rectifying this gap is an essential part of learning how to handle stressful conversations better. We need to learn communications skills, in the same way that we learn CPR: well in advance, knowing that when we need to use them, the situation will be critical and tense. Here are three proven conversational gambits. The particular wording may not suit your style, and that's fine. The important thing is to understand how the techniques work, and then choose phrasing that is comfortable for you.

Honor thy partner

When David gave negative feedback to Jeremy, it would have been refreshing if he had begun with an admission of regret and some responsibility for his contribution to their shared problem. "Jeremy," he might have said, "the quality of your work has been undercut—in part by the reluctance of your colleagues to risk the edge of your humor by talking problems through with you. I share responsibility for this because I have been reluctant to speak openly about these difficulties with you, whom I like and respect and with whom I have worked a long time." Acknowledging responsibility as a technique—particularly as an opening—can be effective because it immediately focuses attention, but without provocation, on the difficult things the speaker needs to say and the listener needs to hear.

Is this always a good technique in a difficult conversation? No, because there is never any one good technique. But in this case, it effectively sets the tone for David's discussion with Jeremy. It honors the problems, it honors Jeremy, it honors their relationship, and it honors David's responsibility. Any technique that communicates honor in a stressful conversation—particularly a conversation that will take the counterpart by surprise—is to be highly valued. Indeed, the ability to act with dignity can make or break a stressful conversation. More important, while Jeremy has left the company, he can still do harm by spreading gossip and using his insider's knowledge against the organization. The more intolerable the conversation with David has been, the more Jeremy is likely to make the organization pay.

Disarm by restating your intentions

Part of the difficulty in Rafael and Elizabeth's "What's Going On Here?" conversation is that Rafael's misinterpretation of Elizabeth's words and actions seems to be influenced by instant replays of other stressful conversations that he has had in the past. Elizabeth doesn't want to psychoanalyze Rafael; indeed, exploring Rafael's internal landscape would exacerbate this painful situation. So what can Elizabeth do to defuse the situation unilaterally?

Elizabeth needs a technique that doesn't require her to understand the underlying reasons for Rafael's strong reaction but helps her handle the situation effectively. "I can see how you took what I said the way you did, Rafael. That wasn't what I meant. Let's go over this list again." I call this the clarification technique, and it's a highly disarming one. Using it, Elizabeth can unilaterally change the confrontation into a point of agreement. Instead of arguing with Rafael about his perceptions, she grants him his perceptions—after all, they're his. Instead of arguing about her intentions, she keeps the responsibility for aligning her words with her intentions on her side. And she goes back into the conversation right where they left off. (For a fuller discussion of the disconnect between what we mean and what we say, see the sidebar "The Gap Between Communication and Intent.")

This technique will work for Elizabeth regardless of Rafael's motive. If Rafael innocently misunderstood what she was saying, she isn't fighting him. She accepts his take on what she said and did and corrects it. If his motive is hostile, Elizabeth doesn't concur just to appease him. She accepts and retries. No one loses face. No one scores points off the other. No one gets drawn off on a tangent.

The Gap Between Communication and Intent

ONE OF THE MOST COMMON OCCURRENCES in stressful conversations is that we all start relying far too much on our intentions. As the mercury in the emotional thermometer rises, we presume that other people automatically understand what we mean. We assume, for instance, that people know we mean well. Indeed, research shows that in stressful conversations, most speakers assume that the listener believes that they have good intentions, regardless of what they say. Intentions can never be that powerful in communications—and certainly not in stressful conversations.

To see what I mean, just think of the last time someone told you not to take something the wrong way. This may well have been uttered quite sincerely by the speaker; nevertheless, most people automatically react by stiffening inwardly, anticipating something at least mildly offensive or antagonistic. And that is exactly the reaction that phrase is always going to get. Because the simplest rule about stressful conversations is that people don't register intention despite words; we register intention through words. In stressful

Fight tactics, not people

Rafael may have baffled Elizabeth, but Karen was acting with outright malice toward Nick when she flew off the handle after a disastrous meeting with the client. Nick certainly can't prevent her from using the thwarting tactics with which she has been so successful in the past. But he can separate Karen's character from her behavior. For instance, it's much more useful for him to think of Karen's reactions as thwarting tactics rather than as personal characteristics. If he thinks of Karen as a distorting, hostile, threatening person, where does that lead? What can anyone ever do about another person's character? But if Nick sees Karen's behavior as a series of tactics that she is using with him because they have worked for her in the past, he can think about using countering techniques to neutralize them.

The best way to neutralize a tactic is to name it. It's much harder to use a tactic once it is openly identified. If Nick, for instance, had said, "Karen, we've worked together pretty well for a long time. I don't know how to talk about what went wrong in the meeting

conversations in particular, the emphasis is on what is actually said, not on what we intend or feel. This doesn't mean that participants in stressful conversations don't have feelings or intentions that are valid and valuable. They do. But when we talk about people in stressful communication, we're talking about communication between people—and not about intentions.

Of course, in difficult conversations we may all wish that we didn't have to be so explicit. We may want the other person to realize what we mean even if we don't spell it out. But that leads to the wrong division of labor—with the listener interpreting rather than the speaker communicating. In all conversations, but especially in stressful ones, we are all responsible for getting across to one another precisely what we want to say. In the end, it's far more dignified for an executive to come right out and tell an employee: "Corey, I've arranged a desk for you—and six weeks of outplacement service—because you won't be with us after the end of July." Forcing someone to guess your intentions only prolongs the agony of the inevitable.

when your take on what happened, and what's going on now, is so different from mine," he would have changed the game completely. He neither would have attacked Karen nor remained the pawn of her tactics. But he would have made Karen's tactics in the conversation the dominant problem.

Openly identifying a tactic, particularly an aggressive one, is disarming for another reason. Often we think of an aggressive counterpart as persistently, even endlessly, contentious, but that isn't true. People have definite levels of aggression that they're comfortable with—and they are reluctant to raise the bar. When Nick doesn't acknowledge Karen's tactics, she can use them unwittingly, or allegedly so. But if Nick speaks of them, it would require more aggression on Karen's part to continue using the same tactics. If she is at or near her aggression threshold, she won't continue because that would make her uncomfortable. Nick may not be able to stop Karen, but she may stop herself.

People think stressful conversations are inevitable. And they are. But that doesn't mean they have to have bad resolutions. Consider a client of mine, Jacqueline, the only woman on the board of an engineering company. She was sensitive to slighting remarks about women in business, and she found one board member deliberately insensitive. He repeatedly ribbed her about being a feminist and, on this occasion, he was telling a sexist joke.

This wasn't the first time that something like this had happened, and Jacqueline felt the usual internal cacophony of reactions. But because she was aware that this was a stressful situation for her, Jacqueline was prepared. First, she let the joke hang in the air for a minute and then went back to the issue they had been discussing. When Richard didn't let it go but escalated with a new poke—"Come on, Jackie, it was a *joke*"—Jacqueline stood her ground. "Richard," she said, "this kind of humor is frivolous to you, but it makes me feel pushed aside." Jacqueline didn't need to say more. If Richard had continued to escalate, he would have lost face. In fact, he backed down: "Well, I wouldn't want my wife to hear about my bad behavior a second time," he snickered. Jacqueline was silent. She had made her point; there was no need to embarrass him.

Stressful conversations are never easy, but we can all fare better if, like Jacqueline, we prepare for them by developing greater awareness of our vulnerabilities and better techniques for handling ourselves. The advice and tools described in this article can be helpful in unilaterally reducing the strain in stressful conversations. All you have to do is try them. If one technique doesn't work, try another. Find phrasing that feels natural. But keep practicing—you'll find what works best for you.

Originally published in July 2001. Reprint R0107H

About the Contributors

GARY A. WILLIAMS is the founder and CEO of wRatings Corporation.

ROBERT B. MILLER has more than 40 years of experience in sales, consulting, and executive management, and is a coauthor of several business books.

ROBERT B. CIALDINI is the president of Influence at Work and a professor emeritus of marketing at Arizona State University.

DEBORAH TANNEN is a professor of linguistics at Georgetown University.

JAY A. CONGER is the Henry R. Kravis Research Chair in Leadership Studies at Claremont McKenna College.

LESLIE PERLOW is the Konosuke Matsushita Professor of Leadership at Harvard Business School.

STEPHANIE WILLIAMS is a principal at North Star Consulting and a former Harvard Business School research associate.

NICK MORGAN is the CEO and founder of Public Words, a communications consulting firm.

STEPHEN DENNING, formerly the program director of knowledge management at the World Bank, works with organizations on leadership, management, innovation, and storytelling.

KIMBERLY D. ELSBACH is a professor of management at the University of California, Davis.

JOHN HAMM is a general partner at VSP Capital in San Francisco.

HOLLY WEEKS teaches and consults on communications issues. She is an adjunct lecturer in public policy and leadership at Harvard's Kennedy School of Government.

Index

HBR'S 10 MUST READS

On
Managing Yourself

HBR'S 10 MUST READS

On Managing Yourself

HARVARD BUSINESS REVIEW PRESS
Boston, Massachusetts

Printed in the United States of America
45 44

The web addresses referenced in this book were live and correct at the time of the book's publication but may be subject to change.

Library of Congress Cataloging-in-Publication Data

HBR's 10 must reads on managing yourself.
p. cm.
Includes index.
ISBN 978-1-4221-5799-2 (pbk. : alk paper)
1. Management. I. Harvard business review. II. Title: HBR's ten must reads on managing yourself. III. Title: Harvard business review's 10 must reads on managing yourself.
HD31.H3946 2010

ISBN: 9781422157992
eISBN: 9781422172032

The paper used in this publication meets the requirements of the American National Standard for Permanence of Paper for Publications and Documents in Libraries and Archives z39.48-1992.

Contents

HBR'S 10 MUST READS

On Managing Yourself

How Will You Measure Your Life?

by Clayton M. Christensen

BEFORE I PUBLISHED *The Innovator's Dilemma,* I got a call from Andrew Grove, then the chairman of Intel. He had read one of my early papers about disruptive technology, and he asked if I could talk to his direct reports and explain my research and what it implied for Intel. Excited, I flew to Silicon Valley and showed up at the appointed time, only to have Grove say, "Look, stuff has happened. We have only 10 minutes for you. Tell us what your model of disruption means for Intel." I said that I couldn't—that I needed a full 30 minutes to explain the model, because only with it as context would any comments about Intel make sense. Ten minutes into my explanation, Grove interrupted: "Look, I've got your model. Just tell us what it means for Intel."

I insisted that I needed 10 more minutes to describe how the process of disruption had worked its way through a very different industry, steel, so that he and his team could understand how disruption worked. I told the story of how Nucor and other steel minimills had begun by attacking the lowest end of the market—steel reinforcing bars, or rebar—and later moved up toward the high end, undercutting the traditional steel mills.

When I finished the minimill story, Grove said, "OK, I get it. What it means for Intel is ...," and then went on to articulate what would become the company's strategy for going to the bottom of the market to launch the Celeron processor.

I've thought about that a million times since. If I had been suckered into telling Andy Grove what he should think about the microprocessor business, I'd have been killed. But instead of telling him what to think, I taught him how to think—and then he reached what I felt was the correct decision on his own.

That experience had a profound influence on me. When people ask what I think they should do, I rarely answer their question directly. Instead, I run the question aloud through one of my models. I'll describe how the process in the model worked its way through an industry quite different from their own. And then, more often than not, they'll say, "OK, I get it." And they'll answer their own question more insightfully than I could have.

My class at HBS is structured to help my students understand what good management theory is and how it is built. To that backbone I attach different models or theories that help students think about the various dimensions of a general manager's job in stimulating innovation and growth. In each session we look at one company through the lenses of those theories—using them to explain how the company got into its situation and to examine what managerial actions will yield the needed results.

On the last day of class, I ask my students to turn those theoretical lenses on themselves, to find cogent answers to three questions: First, how can I be sure that I'll be happy in my career? Second, how can I be sure that my relationships with my spouse and my family become an enduring source of happiness? Third, how can I be sure I'll stay out of jail? Though the last question sounds lighthearted, it's not. Two of the 32 people in my Rhodes scholar class spent time in jail. Jeff Skilling of Enron fame was a classmate of mine at HBS. These were good guys—but something in their lives sent them off in the wrong direction.

Idea in Brief

Harvard Business School's Christensen teaches aspiring MBAs how to apply management and innovation theories to build stronger companies. But he also believes that these models can help people lead better lives. In this article, he explains how, exploring questions everyone needs to ask. How can I be happy in my career? How can I be sure that my relationship with my family is an enduring source of happiness? And how can I live my life with integrity? The answer to the first question comes from Frederick Herzberg's assertion that the most powerful motivator isn't money; it's the opportunity to learn, grow in responsibilities, contribute, and be recognized. That's why management, if practiced well, can be the noblest of occupations; no others offer as many ways to help people find those opportunities. It isn't about buying, selling, and investing in companies, as many think. The principles of resource allocation can help people attain happiness at home. If not managed masterfully, what emerges from a firm's resource allocation process can be very different from the strategy management intended to follow. That's true in life too: If you're not guided by a clear sense of purpose, you're likely to fritter away your time and energy on obtaining the most tangible, short-term signs of achievement, not what's really important to you. And just as a focus on marginal costs can cause bad corporate decisions, it can lead people astray. The marginal cost of doing something wrong "just this once" always seems alluringly low. You don't see the end result to which that path leads. The key is to define what you stand for and draw the line in a safe place.

As the students discuss the answers to these questions, I open my own life to them as a case study of sorts, to illustrate how they can use the theories from our course to guide their life decisions.

One of the theories that gives great insight on the first question—how to be sure we find happiness in our careers—is from Frederick Herzberg, who asserts that the powerful motivator in our lives isn't money; it's the opportunity to learn, grow in responsibilities, contribute to others, and be recognized for achievements. I tell the students about a vision of sorts I had while I was running the company I founded before becoming an academic. In my mind's eye I saw one of my managers leave for work one morning with a relatively strong level of self-esteem. Then I pictured her driving home to her family 10 hours later, feeling unappreciated, frustrated, underutilized, and demeaned. I imagined how profoundly her lowered self-esteem affected the way she interacted with her children. The vision in my mind then fast-forwarded to another day, when she drove home with greater self-esteem—feeling that she had learned a lot, been recognized for achieving valuable things, and played a significant role in the success of some important initiatives. I then imagined how positively that affected her as a spouse and a parent. My conclusion: Management is the most noble of professions if it's practiced well. No other occupation offers as many ways to help others learn and grow, take responsibility and be recognized for achievement, and contribute to the success of a team. More and more MBA students come to school thinking that a career in business means buying, selling, and investing in companies. That's unfortunate. Doing deals doesn't yield the deep rewards that come from building up people.

I want students to leave my classroom knowing that.

Create a Strategy for Your Life

A theory that is helpful in answering the second question—How can I ensure that my relationship with my family proves to be an enduring source of happiness?—concerns how strategy is defined and implemented. Its primary insight is that a company's strategy is determined by the types of initiatives that management invests in. If a company's resource allocation process is not managed masterfully, what emerges from it can be very different from what management intended. Because companies' decision-making systems are designed to steer investments to initiatives that offer the most tangible and immediate returns, companies shortchange investments in initiatives that are crucial to their long-term strategies.

Over the years I've watched the fates of my HBS classmates from 1979 unfold; I've seen more and more of them come to reunions unhappy, divorced, and alienated from their children. I can guarantee you that not a single one of them graduated with the deliberate strategy of getting divorced and raising children who would become estranged from them. And yet a shocking number of them implemented that strategy. The reason? They didn't keep the purpose of their lives front and center as they decided how to spend their time, talents, and energy.

It's quite startling that a significant fraction of the 900 students that HBS draws each year from the world's best have given little thought to the purpose of their lives. I tell the students that HBS might be one of their last chances to reflect deeply on that question. If they think that they'll have more time and energy to reflect later, they're nuts, because life only gets more demanding: You take on a mortgage; you're working 70 hours a week; you have a spouse and children.

For me, having a clear purpose in my life has been essential. But it was something I had to think long and hard about before I understood it. When I was a Rhodes scholar, I was in a very demanding academic program, trying to cram an extra year's worth of work into my time at Oxford. I decided to spend an hour every night reading, thinking, and praying about why God put me on this earth. That was a very challenging commitment to keep, because every hour I spent doing that, I wasn't studying applied econometrics. I was conflicted about whether I could really afford to take that time away from my studies, but I stuck with it—and ultimately figured out the purpose of my life.

Had I instead spent that hour each day learning the latest techniques for mastering the problems of autocorrelation in regression analysis, I would have badly misspent my life. I apply the tools of econometrics a few times a year, but I apply my knowledge of the purpose of my life every day. It's the single most useful thing I've ever learned. I promise my students that if they take the time to figure out their life purpose, they'll look back on it as the most important thing they discovered at HBS. If they don't figure it out, they will just sail off without a rudder and get buffeted in the very rough seas of life. Clarity about their purpose will trump knowledge of activity-based costing, balanced scorecards, core competence, disruptive innovation, the four Ps, and the five forces.

My purpose grew out of my religious faith, but faith isn't the only thing that gives people direction. For example, one of my former

The Class of 2010

"**I CAME TO BUSINESS SCHOOL** knowing exactly what I wanted to do—and I'm leaving choosing the exact opposite. I've worked in the private sector all my life, because everyone always told me that's where smart people are. But I've decided to try government and see if I can find more meaning there.

"I used to think that industry was very safe. The recession has shown us that nothing is safe."

Ruhana Hafiz, Harvard Business School, Class of 2010
Her Plans: To join the FBI as a special adviser (a management track position)

"You could see a shift happening at HBS. Money used to be number one in the job search. When you make a ton of money, you want more of it. Ironic thing. You start to forget what the drivers of happiness are and what things are really important. A lot of people on campus see money differently now. They think, 'What's the minimum I need to have, and what else drives my life?' instead of 'What's the place where I can get the maximum of both?'"

Patrick Chun, Harvard Business School, Class of 2010
His Plans: To join Bain Capital

"The financial crisis helped me realize that you have to do what you really love in life. My current vision of success is based on the impact I can have, the

students decided that his purpose was to bring honesty and economic prosperity to his country and to raise children who were as capably committed to this cause, and to each other, as he was. His purpose is focused on family and others—as mine is.

The choice and successful pursuit of a profession is but one tool for achieving your purpose. But without a purpose, life can become hollow.

Allocate Your Resources

Your decisions about allocating your personal time, energy, and talent ultimately shape your life's strategy.

I have a bunch of "businesses" that compete for these resources: I'm trying to have a rewarding relationship with my wife, raise great kids, contribute to my community, succeed in my career, contribute

experiences I can gain, and the happiness I can find personally, much more so than the pursuit of money or prestige. My main motivations are (1) to be with my family and people I care about; (2) to do something fun, exciting, and impactful; and (3) to pursue a long-term career in entrepreneurship, where I can build companies that change the way the world works."

Matt Salzberg, Harvard Business School, Class of 2010
His Plans: To work for Bessemer Venture Partners

"Because I'm returning to McKinsey, it probably seems like not all that much has changed for me. But while I was at HBS, I decided to do the dual degree at the Kennedy School. With the elections in 2008 and the economy looking shaky, it seemed more compelling for me to get a better understanding of the public and nonprofit sectors. In a way, that drove my return to McKinsey, where I'll have the ability to explore private, public, and nonprofit sectors.

"The recession has made us step back and take stock of how lucky we are. The crisis to us is 'Are we going to have a job by April?' Crisis to a lot of people is 'Are we going to stay in our home?'"

John Coleman, Harvard Business School, Class of 2010
His Plans: To return to McKinsey & Company

to my church, and so on. And I have exactly the same problem that a corporation does. I have a limited amount of time and energy and talent. How much do I devote to each of these pursuits?

Allocation choices can make your life turn out to be very different from what you intended. Sometimes that's good: Opportunities that you never planned for emerge. But if you misinvest your resources, the outcome can be bad. As I think about my former classmates who inadvertently invested for lives of hollow unhappiness, I can't help believing that their troubles relate right back to a short-term perspective.

When people who have a high need for achievement—and that includes all Harvard Business School graduates—have an extra half hour of time or an extra ounce of energy, they'll unconsciously allocate it to activities that yield the most tangible accomplishments. And our careers provide the most concrete evidence that we're moving forward. You ship a product, finish a design, complete a presentation, close a sale, teach a class, publish a paper, get paid, get promoted. In contrast, investing time and energy in your relationship with your spouse and children typically doesn't offer that same immediate sense of achievement. Kids misbehave every day. It's really not until 20 years down the road that you can put your hands on your hips and say, "I raised a good son or a good daughter." You can neglect your relationship with your spouse, and on a day-to-day basis, it doesn't seem as if things are deteriorating. People who are driven to excel have this unconscious propensity to underinvest in their families and overinvest in their careers—even though intimate and loving relationships with their families are the most powerful and enduring source of happiness.

If you study the root causes of business disasters, over and over you'll find this predisposition toward endeavors that offer immediate gratification. If you look at personal lives through that lens, you'll see the same stunning and sobering pattern: people allocating fewer and fewer resources to the things they would have once said mattered most.

Create a Culture

There's an important model in our class called the Tools of Cooperation, which basically says that being a visionary manager isn't all it's cracked up to be. It's one thing to see into the foggy future with acuity and chart the course corrections that the company must make. But it's quite another to persuade employees who might not see the changes ahead to line up and work cooperatively to take the company in that new direction. Knowing what tools to wield to elicit the needed cooperation is a critical managerial skill.

The theory arrays these tools along two dimensions—the extent to which members of the organization agree on what they want from their participation in the enterprise, and the extent to which they agree on what actions will produce the desired results. When there is little agreement on both axes, you have to use "power tools"—coercion, threats, punishment, and so on—to secure cooperation.

Many companies start in this quadrant, which is why the founding executive team must play such an assertive role in defining what must be done and how. If employees' ways of working together to address those tasks succeed over and over, consensus begins to form. MIT's Edgar Schein has described this process as the mechanism by which a culture is built. Ultimately, people don't even think about whether their way of doing things yields success. They embrace priorities and follow procedures by instinct and assumption rather than by explicit decision—which means that they've created a culture. Culture, in compelling but unspoken ways, dictates the proven, acceptable methods by which members of the group address recurrent problems. And culture defines the priority given to different types of problems. It can be a powerful management tool.

In using this model to address the question, How can I be sure that my family becomes an enduring source of happiness?, my students quickly see that the simplest tools that parents can wield to elicit cooperation from children are power tools. But there comes a point during the teen years when power tools no longer work. At that point parents start wishing that they had begun working with their children at a very young age to build a culture at home in which children instinctively behave respectfully toward one another, obey their parents, and choose the right thing to do. Families have cultures, just as companies do. Those cultures can be built consciously or evolve inadvertently.

If you want your kids to have strong self-esteem and confidence that they can solve hard problems, those qualities won't magically materialize in high school. You have to design them into your family's culture—and you have to think about this very early on. Like employees, children build self-esteem by doing things that are hard and learning what works.

Avoid the "Marginal Costs" Mistake

We're taught in finance and economics that in evaluating alternative investments, we should ignore sunk and fixed costs, and instead base decisions on the marginal costs and marginal revenues that each alternative entails. We learn in our course that this doctrine biases companies to leverage what they have put in place to succeed in the past, instead of guiding them to create the capabilities they'll need in the future. If we knew the future would be exactly the same as the past, that approach would be fine. But if the future's different—and it almost always is—then it's the wrong thing to do.

This theory addresses the third question I discuss with my students—how to live a life of integrity (stay out of jail). Unconsciously, we often employ the marginal cost doctrine in our personal lives when we choose between right and wrong. A voice in our head says, "Look, I know that as a general rule, most people shouldn't do this. But in this particular extenuating circumstance, just this once, it's OK." The marginal cost of doing something wrong "just this once" always seems alluringly low. It suckers you in, and you don't ever look at where that path ultimately is headed and at the full costs that the choice entails. Justification for infidelity and dishonesty in all their manifestations lies in the marginal cost economics of "just this once."

I'd like to share a story about how I came to understand the potential damage of "just this once" in my own life. I played on the Oxford University varsity basketball team. We worked our tails off and finished the season undefeated. The guys on the team were the best friends I've ever had in my life. We got to the British equivalent of the NCAA tournament—and made it to the final four. It turned out the championship game was scheduled to be played on a Sunday. I had made a personal commitment to God at age 16 that I would never play ball on Sunday. So I went to the coach and explained my problem. He was incredulous. My teammates were, too, because I was the starting center. Every one of the guys on the team came to me and said, "You've got to play. Can't you break the rule just this one time?"

I'm a deeply religious man, so I went away and prayed about what I should do. I got a very clear feeling that I shouldn't break my commitment—so I didn't play in the championship game.

In many ways that was a small decision—involving one of several thousand Sundays in my life. In theory, surely I could have crossed over the line just that one time and then not done it again. But looking back on it, resisting the temptation whose logic was "In this extenuating circumstance, just this once, it's OK" has proven to be one of the most important decisions of my life. Why? My life has been one unending stream of extenuating circumstances. Had I crossed the line that one time, I would have done it over and over in the years that followed.

The lesson I learned from this is that it's easier to hold to your principles 100% of the time than it is to hold to them 98% of the time. If you give in to "just this once," based on a marginal cost analysis, as some of my former classmates have done, you'll regret where you end up. You've got to define for yourself what you stand for and draw the line in a safe place.

Remember the Importance of Humility

I got this insight when I was asked to teach a class on humility at Harvard College. I asked all the students to describe the most humble person they knew. One characteristic of these humble people stood out: They had a high level of self-esteem. They knew who they were, and they felt good about who they were. We also decided that humility was defined not by self-deprecating behavior or attitudes but by the esteem with which you regard others. Good behavior flows naturally from that kind of humility. For example, you would never steal from someone, because you respect that person too much. You'd never lie to someone, either.

It's crucial to take a sense of humility into the world. By the time you make it to a top graduate school, almost all your learning has come from people who are smarter and more experienced than you: parents, teachers, bosses. But once you've finished at Harvard Business School or any other top academic institution, the vast majority of people you'll interact with on a day-to-day basis may not be smarter than you. And if your attitude is that only smarter people have something to teach you, your learning opportunities will be very limited. But if you have a humble eagerness to learn something from everybody, your learning opportunities will be unlimited.

Generally, you can be humble only if you feel really good about yourself—and you want to help those around you feel really good about themselves, too. When we see people acting in an abusive, arrogant, or demeaning manner toward others, their behavior almost always is a symptom of their lack of self-esteem. They need to put someone else down to feel good about themselves.

Choose the Right Yardstick

This past year I was diagnosed with cancer and faced the possibility that my life would end sooner than I'd planned. Thankfully, it now looks as if I'll be spared. But the experience has given me important insight into my life.

I have a pretty clear idea of how my ideas have generated enormous revenue for companies that have used my research; I know I've had a substantial impact. But as I've confronted this disease, it's been interesting to see how unimportant that impact is to me now. I've concluded that the metric by which God will assess my life isn't dollars but the individual people whose lives I've touched.

I think that's the way it will work for us all. Don't worry about the level of individual prominence you have achieved; worry about the individuals you have helped become better people. This is my final recommendation: Think about the metric by which your life will be judged, and make a resolution to live every day so that in the end, your life will be judged a success.

Originally published in July 2010. Reprint R1007B

Managing Oneself

by Peter F. Drucker

HISTORY'S GREAT ACHIEVERS—a Napoléon, a da Vinci, a Mozart—have always managed themselves. That, in large measure, is what makes them great achievers. But they are rare exceptions, so unusual both in their talents and their accomplishments as to be considered outside the boundaries of ordinary human existence. Now, most of us, even those of us with modest endowments, will have to learn to manage ourselves. We will have to learn to develop ourselves. We will have to place ourselves where we can make the greatest contribution. And we will have to stay mentally alert and engaged during a 50-year working life, which means knowing how and when to change the work we do.

What Are My Strengths?

Most people think they know what they are good at. They are usually wrong. More often, people know what they are not good at—and even then more people are wrong than right. And yet, a person can perform only from strength. One cannot build performance on weaknesses, let alone on something one cannot do at all.

Throughout history, people had little need to know their strengths. A person was born into a position and a line of work: The peasant's son would also be a peasant; the artisan's daughter, an artisan's wife; and so on. But now people have choices. We need to know our strengths in order to know where we belong.

The only way to discover your strengths is through feedback analysis. Whenever you make a key decision or take a key action, write down what you expect will happen. Nine or 12 months later, compare the actual results with your expectations. I have been practicing this method for 15 to 20 years now, and every time I do it, I am surprised. The feedback analysis showed me, for instance—and to my great surprise—that I have an intuitive understanding of technical people, whether they are engineers or accountants or market researchers. It also showed me that I don't really resonate with generalists.

Feedback analysis is by no means new. It was invented sometime in the fourteenth century by an otherwise totally obscure German theologian and picked up quite independently, some 150 years later, by John Calvin and Ignatius of Loyola, each of whom incorporated it into the practice of his followers. In fact, the steadfast focus on performance and results that this habit produces explains why the institutions these two men founded, the Calvinist church and the Jesuit order, came to dominate Europe within 30 years.

Practiced consistently, this simple method will show you within a fairly short period of time, maybe two or three years, where your strengths lie—and this is the most important thing to know. The method will show you what you are doing or failing to do that deprives you of the full benefits of your strengths. It will show you where you are not particularly competent. And finally, it will show you where you have no strengths and cannot perform.

Several implications for action follow from feedback analysis. First and foremost, concentrate on your strengths. Put yourself where your strengths can produce results.

Second, work on improving your strengths. Analysis will rapidly show where you need to improve skills or acquire new ones. It will also show the gaps in your knowledge—and those can usually be filled. Mathematicians are born, but everyone can learn trigonometry.

Third, discover where your intellectual arrogance is causing disabling ignorance and overcome it. Far too many people—especially

Idea in Brief

We live in an age of unprecedented opportunity: If you've got ambition, drive, and smarts, you can rise to the top of your chosen profession—regardless of where you started out. But with opportunity comes responsibility. Companies today aren't managing their knowledge workers' careers. Rather, we must each be our own chief executive officer.

Simply put, it's up to you to carve out your place in the work world and know when to change course. And it's up to you to keep yourself engaged and productive during a work life that may span some 50 years.

To do all of these things well, you'll need to cultivate a deep understanding of yourself. What are your most valuable strengths and most dangerous weaknesses? Equally important, how do you learn and work with others? What are your most deeply held values? And in what type of work environment can you make the greatest contribution?

The implication is clear: Only when you operate from a combination of your strengths and self-knowledge can you achieve true—and lasting—excellence.

people with great expertise in one area—are contemptuous of knowledge in other areas or believe that being bright is a substitute for knowledge. First-rate engineers, for instance, tend to take pride in not knowing anything about people. Human beings, they believe, are much too disorderly for the good engineering mind. Human resources professionals, by contrast, often pride themselves on their ignorance of elementary accounting or of quantitative methods altogether. But taking pride in such ignorance is self-defeating. Go to work on acquiring the skills and knowledge you need to fully realize your strengths.

It is equally essential to remedy your bad habits—the things you do or fail to do that inhibit your effectiveness and performance. Such habits will quickly show up in the feedback. For example, a planner may find that his beautiful plans fail because he does not follow through on them. Like so many brilliant people, he believes that ideas move mountains. But bulldozers move mountains; ideas show where the bulldozers should go to work. This planner will have to learn that the work does not stop when the plan is completed. He

Idea in Practice

To build a life of excellence, begin by asking yourself these questions:

"What are my strengths?"

To accurately identify your strengths, use **feedback analysis**. Every time you make a key decision, write down the outcome you expect. Several months later, compare the actual results with your expected results. Look for patterns in what you're seeing: What results are you skilled at generating? What abilities do you need to enhance in order to get the results you want? What unproductive habits are preventing you from creating the outcomes you desire? In identifying opportunities for improvement, don't waste time cultivating skill areas where you have little competence. Instead, concentrate on—and build on—your strengths.

"How do I work?"

In what ways do you work best? Do you process information most effectively by reading it, or by hearing others discuss it? Do you accomplish the most by working with other people, or by working alone? Do you perform best while making decisions, or while advising others on key matters? Are you in top form when things get stressful, or do you function optimally in a highly predictable environment?

"What are my values?"

What are your ethics? What do you see as your most important responsibilities for living a worthy, ethical life? Do your organization's ethics resonate with your own values? If not, your career will likely be marked by frustration and poor performance.

"Where do I belong?"

Consider your strengths, preferred work style, and values. Based on these qualities, in what kind of work environment would you fit in best? Find the perfect fit, and you'll transform yourself from a merely acceptable employee into a star performer.

"What can I contribute?"

In earlier eras, companies told businesspeople what their contribution should be. Today, you have choices. To decide how you can best enhance your organization's performance, first ask what the situation requires. Based on your strengths, work style, and values, how might you make the greatest contribution to your organization's efforts?

must find people to carry out the plan and explain it to them. He must adapt and change it as he puts it into action. And finally, he must decide when to stop pushing the plan.

At the same time, feedback will also reveal when the problem is a lack of manners. Manners are the lubricating oil of an organization. It is a law of nature that two moving bodies in contact with each other create friction. This is as true for human beings as it is for inanimate objects. Manners—simple things like saying "please" and "thank you" and knowing a person's name or asking after her family—enable two people to work together whether they like each other or not. Bright people, especially bright young people, often do not understand this. If analysis shows that someone's brilliant work fails again and again as soon as cooperation from others is required, it probably indicates a lack of courtesy—that is, a lack of manners.

Comparing your expectations with your results also indicates what not to do. We all have a vast number of areas in which we have no talent or skill and little chance of becoming even mediocre. In those areas a person—and especially a knowledge worker—should not take on work, jobs, and assignments. One should waste as little effort as possible on improving areas of low competence. It takes far more energy and work to improve from incompetence to mediocrity than it takes to improve from first-rate performance to excellence. And yet most people—especially most teachers and most organizations—concentrate on making incompetent performers into mediocre ones. Energy, resources, and time should go instead to making a competent person into a star performer.

How Do I Perform?

Amazingly few people know how they get things done. Indeed, most of us do not even know that different people work and perform differently. Too many people work in ways that are not their ways, and that almost guarantees nonperformance. For knowledge workers, How do I perform? may be an even more important question than What are my strengths?

Like one's strengths, how one performs is unique. It is a matter of personality. Whether personality be a matter of nature or nurture, it surely is formed long before a person goes to work. And *how* a person performs is a given, just as *what* a person is good at or not good at is a given. A person's way of performing can be slightly modified, but it is unlikely to be completely changed—and certainly not easily. Just as people achieve results by doing what they are good at, they also achieve results by working in ways that they best perform. A few common personality traits usually determine how a person performs.

Am I a reader or a listener?

The first thing to know is whether you are a reader or a listener. Far too few people even know that there are readers and listeners and that people are rarely both. Even fewer know which of the two they themselves are. But some examples will show how damaging such ignorance can be.

When Dwight Eisenhower was Supreme Commander of the Allied forces in Europe, he was the darling of the press. His press conferences were famous for their style—General Eisenhower showed total command of whatever question he was asked, and he was able to describe a situation and explain a policy in two or three beautifully polished and elegant sentences. Ten years later, the same journalists who had been his admirers held President Eisenhower in open contempt. He never addressed the questions, they complained, but rambled on endlessly about something else. And they constantly ridiculed him for butchering the King's English in incoherent and ungrammatical answers.

Eisenhower apparently did not know that he was a reader, not a listener. When he was Supreme Commander in Europe, his aides made sure that every question from the press was presented in writing at least half an hour before a conference was to begin. And then Eisenhower was in total command. When he became president, he succeeded two listeners, Franklin D. Roosevelt and Harry Truman. Both men knew themselves to be listeners and both enjoyed free-for-all press conferences. Eisenhower may have felt that he had to do what his two predecessors had done. As a result, he never even heard the questions journalists asked. And Eisenhower is not even an extreme case of a nonlistener.

A few years later, Lyndon Johnson destroyed his presidency, in large measure, by not knowing that he was a listener. His predecessor, John Kennedy, was a reader who had assembled a brilliant group of writers as his assistants, making sure that they wrote to him before discussing their memos in person. Johnson kept these people on his staff—and they kept on writing. He never, apparently, understood one word of what they wrote. Yet as a senator, Johnson had been superb; for parliamentarians have to be, above all, listeners.

Few listeners can be made, or can make themselves, into competent readers—and vice versa. The listener who tries to be a reader will, therefore, suffer the fate of Lyndon Johnson, whereas the reader who tries to be a listener will suffer the fate of Dwight Eisenhower. They will not perform or achieve.

How do I learn?

The second thing to know about how one performs is to know how one learns. Many first-class writers—Winston Churchill is but one example—do poorly in school. They tend to remember their schooling as pure torture. Yet few of their classmates remember it the same way. They may not have enjoyed the school very much, but the worst they suffered was boredom. The explanation is that writers do not, as a rule, learn by listening and reading. They learn by writing. Because schools do not allow them to learn this way, they get poor grades.

Schools everywhere are organized on the assumption that there is only one right way to learn and that it is the same way for everybody. But to be forced to learn the way a school teaches is sheer hell for students who learn differently. Indeed, there are probably half a dozen different ways to learn.

There are people, like Churchill, who learn by writing. Some people learn by taking copious notes. Beethoven, for example, left behind an enormous number of sketchbooks, yet he said he never actually looked at them when he composed. Asked why he kept them, he is reported to have replied, “If I don’t write it down immediately, I forget it right away. If I put it into a sketchbook, I never forget it and I never have to look it up again." Some people learn by doing. Others learn by hearing themselves talk.

A chief executive I know who converted a small and mediocre family business into the leading company in its industry was one of those people who learn by talking. He was in the habit of calling his entire senior staff into his office once a week and then talking at them for two or three hours. He would raise policy issues and argue three different positions on each one. He rarely asked his associates for comments or questions; he simply needed an audience to hear himself talk. That's how he learned. And although he is a fairly extreme case, learning through talking is by no means an unusual method. Successful trial lawyers learn the same way, as do many medical diagnosticians (and so do I).

Of all the important pieces of self-knowledge, understanding how you learn is the easiest to acquire. When I ask people, "How do you learn?" most of them know the answer. But when I ask, "Do you act on this knowledge?" few answer yes. And yet, acting on this knowledge is the key to performance; or rather, *not* acting on this knowledge condemns one to nonperformance.

Am I a reader or a listener? and How do I learn? are the first questions to ask. But they are by no means the only ones. To manage yourself effectively, you also have to ask, Do I work well with people, or am I a loner? And if you do work well with people, you then must ask, In what relationship?

Some people work best as subordinates. General George Patton, the great American military hero of World War II, is a prime example. Patton was America's top troop commander. Yet when he was proposed for an independent command, General George Marshall, the U.S. chief of staff—and probably the most successful picker of men in U.S. history—said, "Patton is the best subordinate the American army has ever produced, but he would be the worst commander."

Some people work best as team members. Others work best alone. Some are exceptionally talented as coaches and mentors; others are simply incompetent as mentors.

Another crucial question is, Do I produce results as a decision maker or as an adviser? A great many people perform best as advisers but cannot take the burden and pressure of making the decision. A good many other people, by contrast, need an adviser to force themselves to think; then they can make decisions and act on them with speed, self-confidence, and courage.

This is a reason, by the way, that the number two person in an organization often fails when promoted to the number one position. The top spot requires a decision maker. Strong decision makers often put somebody they trust into the number two spot as their adviser—and in that position the person is outstanding. But in the number one spot, the same person fails. He or she knows what the decision should be but cannot accept the responsibility of actually making it.

Other important questions to ask include, Do I perform well under stress, or do I need a highly structured and predictable environment? Do I work best in a big organization or a small one? Few people work well in all kinds of environments. Again and again, I have seen people who were very successful in large organizations flounder miserably when they moved into smaller ones. And the reverse is equally true.

The conclusion bears repeating: Do not try to change yourself—you are unlikely to succeed. But work hard to improve the way you perform. And try not to take on work you cannot perform or will only perform poorly.

What Are My Values?

To be able to manage yourself, you finally have to ask, What are my values? This is not a question of ethics. With respect to ethics, the rules are the same for everybody, and the test is a simple one. I call it the "mirror test."

In the early years of this century, the most highly respected diplomat of all the great powers was the German ambassador in London. He was clearly destined for great things—to become his country's foreign minister, at least, if not its federal chancellor. Yet in 1906 he abruptly resigned rather than preside over a dinner given by the diplomatic corps for Edward VII. The king was a notorious womanizer and made it clear what kind of dinner he wanted. The ambassador is reported to have said, "I refuse to see a pimp in the mirror in the morning when I shave."

That is the mirror test. Ethics requires that you ask yourself, What kind of person do I want to see in the mirror in the morning? What is ethical behavior in one kind of organization or situation is ethical behavior in another. But ethics is only part of a value system—especially of an organization's value system.

To work in an organization whose value system is unacceptable or incompatible with one's own condemns a person both to frustration and to nonperformance.

Consider the experience of a highly successful human resources executive whose company was acquired by a bigger organization. After the acquisition, she was promoted to do the kind of work she did best, which included selecting people for important positions. The executive deeply believed that a company should hire people for such positions from the outside only after exhausting all the inside possibilities. But her new company believed in first looking outside "to bring in fresh blood." There is something to be said for both approaches—in my experience, the proper one is to do some of both. They are, however, fundamentally incompatible—not as policies but as values. They bespeak different views of the relationship between organizations and people; different views of the responsibility of an organization to its people and their development; and different views of a person's most important contribution to an enterprise. After several years of frustration, the executive quit—at considerable financial loss. Her values and the values of the organization simply were not compatible.

Similarly, whether a pharmaceutical company tries to obtain results by making constant, small improvements or by achieving occasional, highly expensive, and risky "breakthroughs" is not primarily an economic question. The results of either strategy may be pretty much the same. At bottom, there is a conflict between a value system that sees the company's contribution in terms of helping physicians do better what they already do and a value system that is oriented toward making scientific discoveries.

Whether a business should be run for short-term results or with a focus on the long term is likewise a question of values. Financial analysts believe that businesses can be run for both simultaneously. Successful businesspeople know better. To be sure, every company has to produce short-term results. But in any conflict between short-term results and long-term growth, each company will determine its own priority. This is not primarily a disagreement about economics. It is fundamentally a value conflict regarding the function of a business and the responsibility of management.

Value conflicts are not limited to business organizations. One of the fastest-growing pastoral churches in the United States measures success by the number of new parishioners. Its leadership believes that what matters is how many newcomers join the congregation. The Good Lord will then minister to their spiritual needs or at least to the needs of a sufficient percentage. Another pastoral, evangelical church believes that what matters is people's spiritual growth. The church eases out newcomers who join but do not enter into its spiritual life.

Again, this is not a matter of numbers. At first glance, it appears that the second church grows more slowly. But it retains a far larger proportion of newcomers than the first one does. Its growth, in other words, is more solid. This is also not a theological problem, or only secondarily so. It is a problem about values. In a public debate, one pastor argued, "Unless you first come to church, you will never find the gate to the Kingdom of Heaven."

"No," answered the other. "Until you first look for the gate to the Kingdom of Heaven, you don't belong in church."

Organizations, like people, have values. To be effective in an organization, a person's values must be compatible with the organization's values. They do not need to be the same, but they must be close enough to coexist. Otherwise, the person will not only be frustrated but also will not produce results.

A person's strengths and the way that person performs rarely conflict; the two are complementary. But there is sometimes a conflict between a person's values and his or her strengths. What one does well—even very well and successfully—may not fit with one's value system. In that case, the work may not appear to be worth devoting one's life to (or even a substantial portion thereof).

If I may, allow me to interject a personal note. Many years ago, I too had to decide between my values and what I was doing successfully. I was doing very well as a young investment banker in London in the mid-1930s, and the work clearly fit my strengths. Yet I did not see myself making a contribution as an asset manager. People, I realized, were what I valued, and I saw no point in being the richest man in the cemetery. I had no money and no other job prospects. Despite the continuing Depression, I quit—and it was the right thing to do. Values, in other words, are and should be the ultimate test.

Where Do I Belong?

A small number of people know very early where they belong. Mathematicians, musicians, and cooks, for instance, are usually mathematicians, musicians, and cooks by the time they are four or five years old. Physicians usually decide on their careers in their teens, if not earlier. But most people, especially highly gifted people, do not really know where they belong until they are well past their mid-twenties. By that time, however, they should know the answers to the three questions: What are my strengths? How do I perform? and, What are my values? And then they can and should decide where they belong.

Or rather, they should be able to decide where they do *not* belong. The person who has learned that he or she does not perform well in a big organization should have learned to say no to a position in one. The person who has learned that he or she is not a decision maker should have learned to say no to a decision-making assignment. A General Patton (who probably never learned this himself) should have learned to say no to an independent command.

Equally important, knowing the answer to these questions enables a person to say to an opportunity, an offer, or an assignment, "Yes, I will do that. But this is the way I should be doing it. This is the way it should be structured. This is the way the relationships should be. These are the kind of results you should expect from me, and in this time frame, because this is who I am."

Successful careers are not planned. They develop when people are prepared for opportunities because they know their strengths, their method of work, and their values. Knowing where one belongs can transform an ordinary person—hardworking and competent but otherwise mediocre—into an outstanding performer.

What Should I Contribute?

Throughout history, the great majority of people never had to ask the question, What should I contribute? They were told what to contribute, and their tasks were dictated either by the work itself—as it was for the peasant or artisan—or by a master or a mistress—as it was for domestic servants. And until very recently, it was taken for granted that most people were subordinates who did as they were told. Even in the 1950s and 1960s, the new knowledge workers (the so-called organization men) looked to their company's personnel department to plan their careers.

Then in the late 1960s, no one wanted to be told what to do any longer. Young men and women began to ask, What do *I* want to do? And what they heard was that the way to contribute was to "do your own thing." But this solution was as wrong as the organization men's had been. Very few of the people who believed that doing one's own thing would lead to contribution, self-fulfillment, and success achieved any of the three.

But still, there is no return to the old answer of doing what you are told or assigned to do. Knowledge workers in particular have to learn to ask a question that has not been asked before: What *should* my contribution be? To answer it, they must address three distinct elements: What does the situation require? Given my strengths, my way of performing, and my values, how can I make the greatest contribution to what needs to be done? And finally, What results have to be achieved to make a difference?

Consider the experience of a newly appointed hospital administrator. The hospital was big and prestigious, but it had been coasting on its reputation for 30 years. The new administrator decided that his contribution should be to establish a standard of excellence in one important area within two years. He chose to focus on the emergency room, which was big, visible, and sloppy. He decided that every patient who came into the ER had to be seen by a qualified nurse within 60 seconds. Within 12 months, the hospital's emergency room had become a model for all hospitals in the United States, and within another two years, the whole hospital had been transformed.

As this example suggests, it is rarely possible—or even particularly fruitful—to look too far ahead. A plan can usually cover no more than 18 months and still be reasonably clear and specific. So the question in most cases should be, Where and how can I achieve results that will make a difference within the next year and a half? The answer must balance several things. First, the results should be hard to achieve—they should require "stretching," to use the current buzzword. But also, they should be within reach. To aim at results that cannot be achieved—or that can be only under the most unlikely circumstances—is not being ambitious; it is being foolish. Second, the results should be meaningful. They should make a difference. Finally, results should be visible and, if at all possible, measurable. From this will come a course of action: what to do, where and how to start, and what goals and deadlines to set.

Responsibility for Relationships

Very few people work by themselves and achieve results by themselves—a few great artists, a few great scientists, a few great athletes. Most people work with others and are effective with other people. That is true whether they are members of an organization or independently employed. Managing yourself requires taking responsibility for relationships. This has two parts.

The first is to accept the fact that other people are as much individuals as you yourself are. They perversely insist on behaving like human beings. This means that they too have their strengths; they too have their ways of getting things done; they too have their values. To be effective, therefore, you have to know the strengths, the performance modes, and the values of your coworkers.

That sounds obvious, but few people pay attention to it. Typical is the person who was trained to write reports in his or her first assignment because that boss was a reader. Even if the next boss is a listener, the person goes on writing reports that, invariably, produce no results. Invariably the boss will think the employee is stupid, incompetent, and lazy, and he or she will fail. But that could have been avoided if the employee had only looked at the new boss and analyzed how *this* boss performs.

Bosses are neither a title on the organization chart nor a "function." They are individuals and are entitled to do their work in the way they do it best. It is incumbent on the people who work with them to observe them, to find out how they work, and to adapt themselves to what makes their bosses most effective. This, in fact, is the secret of "managing" the boss.

The same holds true for all your coworkers. Each works his or her way, not your way. And each is entitled to work in his or her way. What matters is whether they perform and what their values are. As for how they perform—each is likely to do it differently. The first secret of effectiveness is to understand the people you work with and depend on so that you can make use of their strengths, their ways of working, and their values. Working relationships are as much based on the people as they are on the work.

The second part of relationship responsibility is taking responsibility for communication. Whenever I, or any other consultant, start to work with an organization, the first thing I hear about are all the personality conflicts. Most of these arise from the fact that people do not know what other people are doing and how they do their work, or what contribution the other people are concentrating on and what results they expect. And the reason they do not know is that they have not asked and therefore have not been told.

This failure to ask reflects human stupidity less than it reflects human history. Until recently, it was unnecessary to tell any of these things to anybody. In the medieval city, everyone in a district plied the same trade. In the countryside, everyone in a valley planted the same crop as soon as the frost was out of the ground. Even those few people who did things that were not "common" worked alone, so they did not have to tell anyone what they were doing.

Today the great majority of people work with others who have different tasks and responsibilities. The marketing vice president may have come out of sales and know everything about sales, but she knows nothing about the things she has never done—pricing, advertising, packaging, and the like. So the people who do these things must make sure that the marketing vice president understands what they are trying to do, why they are trying to do it, how they are going to do it, and what results to expect.

If the marketing vice president does not understand what these high-grade knowledge specialists are doing, it is primarily their fault, not hers. They have not educated her. Conversely, it is the marketing vice president's responsibility to make sure that all of her coworkers understand how she looks at marketing: what her goals are, how she works, and what she expects of herself and of each one of them.

Even people who understand the importance of taking responsibility for relationships often do not communicate sufficiently with their associates. They are afraid of being thought presumptuous or inquisitive or stupid. They are wrong. Whenever someone goes to his or her associates and says, "This is what I am good at. This is how I work. These are my values. This is the contribution I plan to concentrate on and the results I should be expected to deliver," the response is always, "This is most helpful. But why didn't you tell me earlier?"

And one gets the same reaction—without exception, in my experience—if one continues by asking, "And what do I need to know about your strengths, how you perform, your values, and your proposed contribution?" In fact, knowledge workers should request this of everyone with whom they work, whether as subordinate, superior, colleague, or team member. And again, whenever this is done, the reaction is always, "Thanks for asking me. But why didn't you ask me earlier?"

Organizations are no longer built on force but on trust. The existence of trust between people does not necessarily mean that they like one another. It means that they understand one another. Taking responsibility for relationships is therefore an absolute necessity. It is a duty. Whether one is a member of the organization, a consultant to it, a supplier, or a distributor, one owes that responsibility to all one's coworkers: those whose work one depends on as well as those who depend on one's own work.

The Second Half of Your Life

When work for most people meant manual labor, there was no need to worry about the second half of your life. You simply kept on doing what you had always done. And if you were lucky enough to survive 40 years of hard work in the mill or on the railroad, you were quite happy to spend the rest of your life doing nothing. Today, however, most work is knowledge work, and knowledge workers are not "finished" after 40 years on the job, they are merely bored.

We hear a great deal of talk about the midlife crisis of the executive. It is mostly boredom. At 45, most executives have reached the peak of their business careers, and they know it. After 20 years of doing very much the same kind of work, they are very good at their jobs. But they are not learning or contributing or deriving challenge and satisfaction from the job. And yet they are still likely to face another 20 if not 25 years of work. That is why managing oneself increasingly leads one to begin a second career.

There are three ways to develop a second career. The first is actually to start one. Often this takes nothing more than moving from one kind of organization to another: the divisional controller in a large corporation, for instance, becomes the controller of a medium-sized hospital. But there are also growing numbers of people who move into different lines of work altogether: the business executive or government official who enters the ministry at 45, for instance; or the midlevel manager who leaves corporate life after 20 years to attend law school and become a small-town attorney.

We will see many more second careers undertaken by people who have achieved modest success in their first jobs. Such people have substantial skills, and they know how to work. They need a community—the house is empty with the children gone—and they need income as well. But above all, they need challenge.

The second way to prepare for the second half of your life is to develop a parallel career. Many people who are very successful in their first careers stay in the work they have been doing, either on a full-time or part-time or consulting basis. But in addition, they create a parallel job, usually in a nonprofit organization, that takes another ten hours of work a week. They might take over the administration of their church, for instance, or the presidency of the local Girl Scouts council. They might run the battered women's shelter, work as a children's librarian for the local public library, sit on the school board, and so on.

Finally, there are the social entrepreneurs. These are usually people who have been very successful in their first careers. They love their work, but it no longer challenges them. In many cases they keep on doing what they have been doing all along but spend less and less of their time on it. They also start another activity, usually a nonprofit. My friend Bob Buford, for example, built a very successful television company that he still runs. But he has also founded and built a successful nonprofit organization that works with Protestant churches, and he is building another to teach social entrepreneurs how to manage their own nonprofit ventures while still running their original businesses.

People who manage the second half of their lives may always be a minority. The majority may "retire on the job" and count the years until their actual retirement. But it is this minority, the men and women who see a long working-life expectancy as an opportunity both for themselves and for society, who will become leaders and models.

There is one prerequisite for managing the second half of your life: You must begin long before you enter it. When it first became clear 30 years ago that working-life expectancies were lengthening very fast, many observers (including myself) believed that retired people would increasingly become volunteers for nonprofit institutions. That has not happened. If one does not begin to volunteer before one is 40 or so, one will not volunteer once past 60.

Similarly, all the social entrepreneurs I know began to work in their chosen second enterprise long before they reached their peak in their original business. Consider the example of a successful lawyer, the legal counsel to a large corporation, who has started a venture to establish model schools in his state. He began to do volunteer legal work for the schools when he was around 35. He was elected to the school board at age 40. At age 50, when he had amassed a fortune, he started his own enterprise to build and to run model schools. He is, however, still working nearly full-time as the lead counsel in the company he helped found as a young lawyer.

There is another reason to develop a second major interest, and to develop it early. No one can expect to live very long without experiencing a serious setback in his or her life or work. There is the competent engineer who is passed over for promotion at age 45. There is the competent college professor who realizes at age 42 that she will never get a professorship at a big university, even though she may be fully qualified for it. There are tragedies in one's family life: the breakup of one's marriage or the loss of a child. At such times, a second major interest—not just a hobby—may make all the difference. The engineer, for example, now knows that he has not been very successful in his job. But in his outside activity—as church treasurer, for example—he is a success. One's family may break up, but in that outside activity there is still a community.

In a society in which success has become so terribly important, having options will become increasingly vital. Historically, there was no such thing as "success." The overwhelming majority of people did not expect anything but to stay in their "proper station," as an old English prayer has it. The only mobility was downward mobility.

In a knowledge society, however, we expect everyone to be a success. This is clearly an impossibility. For a great many people, there is at best an absence of failure. Wherever there is success, there has to be failure. And then it is vitally important for the individual, and equally for the individual's family, to have an area in which he or she can contribute, make a difference, and be *somebody*. That means finding a second area—whether in a second career, a parallel career, or a social venture—that offers an opportunity for being a leader, for being respected, for being a success.

The challenges of managing oneself may seem obvious, if not elementary. And the answers may seem self-evident to the point of appearing naïve. But managing oneself requires new and unprecedented things from the individual, and especially from the knowledge worker. In effect, managing oneself demands that each knowledge worker think and behave like a chief executive officer. Further, the shift from manual workers who do as they are told to knowledge workers who have to manage themselves profoundly challenges social structure. Every existing society, even the most individualistic one, takes two things for granted, if only subconsciously: that organizations outlive workers, and that most people stay put.

But today the opposite is true. Knowledge workers outlive organizations, and they are mobile. The need to manage oneself is therefore creating a revolution in human affairs.

Originally published in January 1999. Reprint R0501K

Management Time: Who's Got the Monkey?

by William Oncken, Jr., and Donald L. Wass

W

WHY IS IT THAT MANAGERS are typically running out of time while their subordinates are typically running out of work? Here we shall explore the meaning of management time as it relates to the interaction between managers and their bosses, their peers, and their subordinates.

Specifically, we shall deal with three kinds of management time:

Boss-imposed time—used to accomplish those activities that the boss requires and that the manager cannot disregard without direct and swift penalty.

System-imposed time—used to accommodate requests from peers for active support. Neglecting these requests will also result in penalties, though not always as direct or swift.

Self-imposed time—used to do those things that the manager originates or agrees to do. A certain portion of this kind of time, however, will be taken by subordinates and is called *subordinate-imposed time*. The remaining portion will be the manager's own and is called *discretionary time*. Self-imposed time is not subject to penalty since neither the boss nor the system can discipline the manager for not doing what they didn't know he had intended to do in the first place.

To accommodate those demands, managers need to control the timing and the content of what they do. Since what their bosses and the system impose on them are subject to penalty, managers cannot tamper with those requirements. Thus their self-imposed time becomes their major area of concern.

Managers should try to increase the discretionary component of their self-imposed time by minimizing or doing away with the subordinate component. They will then use the added increment to get better control over their boss-imposed and system-imposed activities. Most managers spend much more time dealing with subordinates' problems than they even faintly realize. Hence we shall use the monkey-on-the-back metaphor to examine how subordinate-imposed time comes into being and what the superior can do about it.

Where Is the Monkey?

Let us imagine that a manager is walking down the hall and that he notices one of his subordinates, Jones, coming his way. When the two meet, Jones greets the manager with, "Good morning. By the way, we've got a problem. You see. . . ." As Jones continues, the manager recognizes in this problem the two characteristics common to all the problems his subordinates gratuitously bring to his attention. Namely, the manager knows (a) enough to get involved, but (b) not enough to make the on-the-spot decision expected of him. Eventually, the manager says, "So glad you brought this up. I'm in a rush right now. Meanwhile, let me think about it, and I'll let you know." Then he and Jones part company.

Let us analyze what just happened. Before the two of them met, on whose back was the "monkey"? The subordinate's. After they parted, on whose back was it? The manager's. Subordinate-imposed time begins the moment a monkey successfully leaps from the back of a subordinate to the back of his or her superior and does not end until the monkey is returned to its proper owner for care and feeding. In accepting the monkey, the manager has voluntarily assumed a position subordinate to his subordinate. That is, he has allowed

Idea in Brief

You're racing down the hall. An employee stops you and says, "We've got a problem." You assume you should get involved but can't make an on-the-spot decision. You say, "Let me think about it."

You've just allowed a "monkey" to leap from your subordinate's back to yours. *You're* now working for your *subordinate*. Take on enough monkeys, and you won't have time to handle your *real* job: fulfilling your own boss's mandates and helping peers generate business results.

How to avoid accumulating monkeys? Develop your subordinates' initiative, say Oncken and Wass. For example, when an employee tries to hand you a problem, clarify whether he should: recommend and implement a solution, take action then brief you immediately, or act and report the outcome at a regular update.

When you encourage employees to handle their own monkeys, they acquire new skills—and you liberate time to do your own job.

Jones to make him her subordinate by doing two things a subordinate is generally expected to do for a boss—the manager has accepted a responsibility from his subordinate, and the manager has promised her a progress report.

The subordinate, to make sure the manager does not miss this point, will later stick her head in the manager's office and cheerily query, "How's it coming?" (This is called supervision.)

Or let us imagine in concluding a conference with Johnson, another subordinate, the manager's parting words are, "Fine. Send me a memo on that."

Let us analyze this one. The monkey is now on the subordinate's back because the next move is his, but it is poised for a leap. Watch that monkey. Johnson dutifully writes the requested memo and drops it in his out-basket. Shortly thereafter, the manager plucks it from his in-basket and reads it. Whose move is it now? The manager's. If he does not make that move soon, he will get a follow-up memo from the subordinate. (This is another form of supervision.) The longer the manager delays, the more frustrated the subordinate will become (he'll be spinning his wheels) and the more guilty the

Idea in Practice

How to return monkeys to their proper owners? Oncken, Wass, and Steven Covey (in an afterword to this classic article) offer these suggestions.

Make Appointments to Deal with Monkeys

Avoid discussing any monkey on an ad hoc basis—for example, when you pass a subordinate in the hallway. You won't convey the proper seriousness. Instead, schedule an appointment to discuss the issue.

Specify Level of Initiative

Your employees can exercise five levels of initiative in handling on-the-job problems. From lowest to highest, the levels are:

1. Wait until told what to do.
2. Ask what to do.
3. Recommend an action, then with your approval, implement it.
4. Take independent action but advise you at once.
5. Take independent action and update you through routine procedure.

When an employee brings a problem to you, outlaw use of level 1 or 2. Agree on and assign level 3, 4, or 5 to the monkey. Take no more than 15 minutes to discuss the problem.

Agree on a Status Update

After deciding how to proceed, agree on a time and place when the employee will give you a progress report.

Examine Your Own Motives

Some managers secretly worry that if they encourage subordinates to take more initiative, they'll appear less strong, more vulnerable, and less useful. Instead, cultivate an inward sense of security that frees you to relinquish direct control and support employees' growth.

Develop Employees' Skills

Employees try to hand off monkeys when they lack the desire or ability to handle them. Help employees develop needed problem-solving skills. It's initially more time consuming than tackling problems yourself—but it saves time in the long run.

Foster Trust

Developing employees' initiative requires a trusting relationship between you and your subordinates. If they're afraid of failing, they'll keep bringing their monkeys to you rather than working to solve their own problems. To promote trust, reassure them it's safe to make mistakes.

manager will feel (his backlog of subordinate-imposed time will be mounting).

Or suppose once again that at a meeting with a third subordinate, Smith, the manager agrees to provide all the necessary backing for a public relations proposal he has just asked Smith to develop. The manager's parting words to her are, "Just let me know how I can help."

Now let us analyze this. Again the monkey is initially on the subordinate's back. But for how long? Smith realizes that she cannot let the manager "know" until her proposal has the manager's approval. And from experience, she also realizes that her proposal will likely be sitting in the manager's briefcase for weeks before he eventually gets to it. Who's really got the monkey? Who will be checking up on whom? Wheel spinning and bottlenecking are well on their way again.

A fourth subordinate, Reed, has just been transferred from another part of the company so that he can launch and eventually manage a newly created business venture. The manager has said they should get together soon to hammer out a set of objectives for the new job, adding, "I will draw up an initial draft for discussion with you."

Let us analyze this one, too. The subordinate has the new job (by formal assignment) and the full responsibility (by formal delegation), but the manager has the next move. Until he makes it, he will have the monkey, and the subordinate will be immobilized.

Why does all of this happen? Because in each instance the manager and the subordinate assume at the outset, wittingly or unwittingly, that the matter under consideration is a joint problem. The monkey in each case begins its career astride both their backs. All it has to do is move the wrong leg, and—presto!—the subordinate deftly disappears. The manager is thus left with another acquisition for his menagerie. Of course, monkeys can be trained not to move the wrong leg. But it is easier to prevent them from straddling backs in the first place.

Who Is Working for Whom?

Let us suppose that these same four subordinates are so thoughtful and considerate of their superior's time that they take pains to allow no more than three monkeys to leap from each of their backs to his in any one day. In a five-day week, the manager will have picked up 60 screaming monkeys—far too many to do anything about them individually. So he spends his subordinate-imposed time juggling his "priorities."

Late Friday afternoon, the manager is in his office with the door closed for privacy so he can contemplate the situation, while his subordinates are waiting outside to get their last chance before the weekend to remind him that he will have to "fish or cut bait." Imagine what they are saying to one another about the manager as they wait: "What a bottleneck. He just can't make up his mind. How anyone ever got that high up in our company without being able to make a decision we'll never know."

Worst of all, the reason the manager cannot make any of these "next moves" is that his time is almost entirely eaten up by meeting his own boss-imposed and system-imposed requirements. To control those tasks, he needs discretionary time that is in turn denied him when he is preoccupied with all these monkeys. The manager is caught in a vicious circle. But time is a-wasting (an understatement). The manager calls his secretary on the intercom and instructs her to tell his subordinates that he won't be able to see them until Monday morning. At 7 PM, he drives home, intending with firm resolve to return to the office tomorrow to get caught up over the weekend. He returns bright and early the next day only to see, on the nearest green of the golf course across from his office window, a foursome. Guess who?

That does it. He now knows who is really working for whom. Moreover, he now sees that if he actually accomplishes during this weekend what he came to accomplish, his subordinates' morale will go up so sharply that they will each raise the limit on the number of monkeys they will let jump from their backs to his. In short, he now sees, with the clarity of a revelation on a mountaintop, that the more he gets caught up, the more he will fall behind.

He leaves the office with the speed of a person running away from a plague. His plan? To get caught up on something else he hasn't had time for in years: a weekend with his family. (This is one of the many varieties of discretionary time.)

Sunday night he enjoys ten hours of sweet, untroubled slumber, because he has clear-cut plans for Monday. He is going to get rid of his subordinate-imposed time. In exchange, he will get an equal amount of discretionary time, part of which he will spend with his subordinates to make sure that they learn the difficult but rewarding managerial art called "The Care and Feeding of Monkeys."

The manager will also have plenty of discretionary time left over for getting control of the timing and the content not only of his boss-imposed time but also of his system-imposed time. It may take months, but compared with the way things have been, the rewards will be enormous. His ultimate objective is to manage his time.

Getting Rid of the Monkeys

The manager returns to the office Monday morning just late enough so that his four subordinates have collected outside his office waiting to see him about their monkeys. He calls them in one by one. The purpose of each interview is to take a monkey, place it on the desk between them, and figure out together how the next move might conceivably be the subordinate's. For certain monkeys, that will take some doing. The subordinate's next move may be so elusive that the manager may decide—just for now—merely to let the monkey sleep on the subordinate's back overnight and have him or her return with it at an appointed time the next morning to continue the joint quest for a more substantive move by the subordinate. (Monkeys sleep just as soundly overnight on subordinates' backs as they do on superiors'.)

As each subordinate leaves the office, the manager is rewarded by the sight of a monkey leaving his office on the subordinate's back. For the next 24 hours, the subordinate will not be waiting for the manager; instead, the manager will be waiting for the subordinate.

Later, as if to remind himself that there is no law against his engaging in a constructive exercise in the interim, the manager strolls by the subordinate's office, sticks his head in the door, and cheerily asks, "How's it coming?" (The time consumed in doing this is discretionary for the manager and boss imposed for the subordinate.)

Making Time for Gorillas

by Stephen R. Covey

WHEN BILL ONCKEN WROTE this article in 1974, managers were in a terrible bind. They were desperate for a way to free up their time, but command and control was the status quo. Managers felt they weren't allowed to empower their subordinates to make decisions. Too dangerous. Too risky. That's why Oncken's message—give the monkey back to its rightful owner—involved a critically important paradigm shift. Many managers working today owe him a debt of gratitude.

It is something of an understatement, however, to observe that much has changed since Oncken's radical recommendation. Command and control as a management philosophy is all but dead, and "empowerment" is the word of the day in most organizations trying to thrive in global, intensely competitive markets. But command and control stubbornly remains a common practice. Management thinkers and executives have discovered in the last decade that bosses cannot just give a monkey back to their subordinates and then merrily get on with their own business. Empowering subordinates is hard and complicated work.

The reason: when you give problems back to subordinates to solve themselves, you have to be sure that they have both the desire and the ability to do so. As every executive knows, that isn't always the case. Enter a whole new set of problems. Empowerment often means you have to develop people, which is initially much more time consuming than solving the problem on your own.

Just as important, empowerment can only thrive when the whole organization buys into it—when formal systems and the informal culture support it. Managers need to be rewarded for delegating decisions and developing people. Otherwise, the degree of real empowerment in an organization will vary according to the beliefs and practices of individual managers.

But perhaps the most important lesson about empowerment is that effective delegation—the kind Oncken advocated—depends on a trusting relationship between a manager and his subordinate. Oncken's message may have been ahead of his time, but what he suggested was still a fairly dictatorial solution. He basically told bosses, "Give the problem back!" Today, we know that this approach by itself is too authoritarian. To delegate effectively, executives need to establish a running dialogue with subordinates. They need to establish a partnership. After all, if subordinates are afraid of failing in front of their boss, they'll keep coming back for help rather than truly take initiative.

Oncken's article also doesn't address an aspect of delegation that has greatly interested me during the past two decades—that many managers are actually *eager* to take on their subordinates' monkeys. Nearly all the managers I talk with agree that their people are underutilized in their present jobs. But even some of the most successful, seemingly self-assured executives have talked about how hard it is to give up control to their subordinates.

I've come to attribute that eagerness for control to a common, deep-seated belief that rewards in life are scarce and fragile. Whether they learn it from their family, school, or athletics, many people establish an identity by comparing themselves with others. When they see others gain power, information, money, or recognition, for instance, they experience what the psychologist Abraham Maslow called "a feeling of deficiency"—a sense that something is being taken from them. That makes it hard for them to be genuinely happy about the success of others—even of their loved ones. Oncken implies that managers can easily give back or refuse monkeys, but many managers may subconsciously fear that a subordinate taking the initiative will make them appear a little less strong and a little more vulnerable.

How, then, do managers develop the inward security, the mentality of "abundance," that would enable them to relinquish control and seek the growth and development of those around them? The work I've done with numerous organizations suggests that managers who live with integrity according to a principle-based value system are most likely to sustain an empowering style of leadership.

Given the times in which he wrote, it was no wonder that Oncken's message resonated with managers. But it was reinforced by Oncken's wonderful gift for storytelling. I got to know Oncken on the speaker's circuit in the 1970s, and I was always impressed by how he dramatized his ideas in colorful detail. Like the Dilbert comic strip, Oncken had a tongue-in-cheek style that got to the core of managers' frustrations and made them want to take back control of their time. And the monkey on your back wasn't just a metaphor for Oncken—it was his personal symbol. I saw him several times walking through airports with a stuffed monkey on his shoulder.

I'm not surprised that his article is one of the two best-selling HBR articles ever. Even with all we know about empowerment, its vivid message is even more important and relevant now than it was 25 years ago. Indeed, Oncken's insight is a basis for my own work on time management, in which I have people categorize their activities according to urgency and importance. I've heard from executives again and again that half or more of their time is spent on matters that are urgent but not important. They're trapped in an endless

(continued)

cycle of dealing with other people's monkeys, yet they're reluctant to help those people take their own initiative. As a result, they're often too busy to spend the time they need on the real gorillas in their organization. Oncken's article remains a powerful wake-up call for managers who need to delegate effectively.

Stephen R. Covey is vice chairman of the Franklin Covey Company, a global provider of leadership development and productivity services and products.

When the subordinate (with the monkey on his or her back) and the manager meet at the appointed hour the next day, the manager explains the ground rules in words to this effect:

"At no time while I am helping you with this or any other problem will your problem become my problem. The instant your problem becomes mine, you no longer have a problem. I cannot help a person who hasn't got a problem.

"When this meeting is over, the problem will leave this office exactly the way it came in—on your back. You may ask my help at any appointed time, and we will make a joint determination of what the next move will be and which of us will make it.

"In those rare instances where the next move turns out to be mine, you and I will determine it together. I will not make any move alone."

The manager follows this same line of thought with each subordinate until about 11 AM, when he realizes that he doesn't have to close his door. His monkeys are gone. They will return—but by appointment only. His calendar will assure this.

Transferring the Initiative

What we have been driving at in this monkey-on-the-back analogy is that managers can transfer initiative back to their subordinates and keep it there. We have tried to highlight a truism as obvious as it is subtle: namely, before developing initiative in subordinates, the manager must see to it that they *have* the initiative. Once the manager takes it back, he will no longer have it and he can kiss his discretionary time good-bye. It will all revert to subordinate-imposed time.

Nor can the manager and the subordinate effectively have the same initiative at the same time. The opener, "Boss, we've got a problem," implies this duality and represents, as noted earlier, a monkey astride two backs, which is a very bad way to start a monkey on its career. Let us, therefore, take a few moments to examine what we call "The Anatomy of Managerial Initiative."

There are five degrees of initiative that the manager can exercise in relation to the boss and to the system:

1. wait until told (lowest initiative);
2. ask what to do;
3. recommend, then take resulting action;
4. act, but advise at once;
5. and act on own, then routinely report (highest initiative).

Clearly, the manager should be professional enough not to indulge in initiatives 1 and 2 in relation either to the boss or to the system. A manager who uses initiative 1 has no control over either the timing or the content of boss-imposed or system-imposed time and thereby forfeits any right to complain about what he or she is told to do or when. The manager who uses initiative 2 has control over the timing but not over the content. Initiatives 3, 4, and 5 leave the manager in control of both, with the greatest amount of control being exercised at level 5.

In relation to subordinates, the manager's job is twofold. First, to outlaw the use of initiatives 1 and 2, thus giving subordinates no choice but to learn and master "Completed Staff Work." Second, to see that for each problem leaving his or her office there is an agreed-upon level of initiative assigned to it, in addition to an agreed-upon time and place for the next manager-subordinate conference. The latter should be duly noted on the manager's calendar.

The Care and Feeding of Monkeys

To further clarify our analogy between the monkey on the back and the processes of assigning and controlling, we shall refer briefly to the manager's appointment schedule, which calls for five hard-and-fast rules governing the "Care and Feeding of Monkeys." (Violation of these rules will cost discretionary time.)

Rule 1

Monkeys should be fed or shot. Otherwise, they will starve to death, and the manager will waste valuable time on postmortems or attempted resurrections.

Rule 2

The monkey population should be kept below the maximum number the manager has time to feed. Subordinates will find time to work as many monkeys as he or she finds time to feed, but no more. It shouldn't take more than five to 15 minutes to feed a properly maintained monkey.

Rule 3

Monkeys should be fed by appointment only. The manager should not have to hunt down starving monkeys and feed them on a catch-as-catch-can basis.

Rule 4

Monkeys should be fed face-to-face or by telephone, but never by mail. (Remember—with mail, the next move will be the manager's.) Documentation may add to the feeding process, but it cannot take the place of feeding.

Rule 5

Every monkey should have an assigned next feeding time and degree of initiative. These may be revised at any time by mutual consent but never allowed to become vague or indefinite. Otherwise, the monkey will either starve to death or wind up on the manager's back.

"Get control over the timing and content of what you do" is appropriate advice for managing time. The first order of business is for the manager to enlarge his or her discretionary time by eliminating subordinate-imposed time. The second is for the manager to use a portion of this newfound discretionary time to see to it that each subordinate actually has the initiative and applies it. The third is for the manager to use another portion of the increased discretionary time to get and keep control of the timing and content of both boss-imposed and system-imposed time. All these steps will increase the manager's leverage and enable the value of each hour spent in managing management time to multiply without theoretical limit.

Originally published in November 1999. Reprint 99609

How Resilience Works

by Diane L. Coutu

WHEN I BEGAN MY CAREER IN JOURNALISM—I was a reporter at a national magazine in those days—there was a man I'll call Claus Schmidt. He was in his mid-fifties, and to my impressionable eyes, he was the quintessential newsman: cynical at times, but unrelentingly curious and full of life, and often hilariously funny in a sandpaper-dry kind of way. He churned out hard-hitting cover stories and features with a speed and elegance I could only dream of. It always astounded me that he was never promoted to managing editor.

But people who knew Claus better than I did thought of him not just as a great newsman but as a quintessential survivor, someone who had endured in an environment often hostile to talent. He had lived through at least three major changes in the magazine's leadership, losing most of his best friends and colleagues on the way. At home, two of his children succumbed to incurable illnesses, and a third was killed in a traffic accident. Despite all this—or maybe because of it—he milled around the newsroom day after day, mentoring the cub reporters, talking about the novels he was writing—always looking forward to what the future held for him.

Why do some people suffer real hardships and not falter? Claus Schmidt could have reacted very differently. We've all seen that happen: One person cannot seem to get the confidence back after a layoff; another, persistently depressed, takes a few years off from life after her divorce. The question we would all like answered is, Why? What exactly is that quality of resilience that carries people through life?

It's a question that has fascinated me ever since I first learned of the Holocaust survivors in elementary school. In college, and later in my studies as an affiliate scholar at the Boston Psychoanalytic Society and Institute, I returned to the subject. For the past several months, however, I have looked on it with a new urgency, for it seems to me that the terrorism, war, and recession of recent months have made understanding resilience more important than ever. I have considered both the nature of individual resilience and what makes some organizations as a whole more resilient than others. Why do some people and some companies buckle under pressure? And what makes others bend and ultimately bounce back?

My exploration has taught me much about resilience, although it's a subject none of us will ever understand fully. Indeed, resilience is one of the great puzzles of human nature, like creativity or the religious instinct. But in sifting through psychological research and in reflecting on the many stories of resilience I've heard, I have seen a little more deeply into the hearts and minds of people like Claus Schmidt and, in doing so, looked more deeply into the human psyche as well.

The Buzz About Resilience

Resilience is a hot topic in business these days. Not long ago, I was talking to a senior partner at a respected consulting firm about how to land the very best MBAs—the name of the game in that particular industry. The partner, Daniel Savageau (not his real name), ticked off a long list of qualities his firm sought in its hires: intelligence, ambition, integrity, analytic ability, and so on. "What about resilience?" I asked. "Well, that's very popular right now," he said. "It's the new buzzword. Candidates even tell us they're resilient; they volunteer the information. But frankly, they're just too young to know that about themselves. Resilience is something you realize you have *after* the fact."

Idea in Brief

These are dark days: people are losing jobs, taking pay cuts, suffering foreclosure on their homes. Some of them are snapping—sinking into depression or suffering a permanent loss of confidence.

But others are snapping back; for example, taking advantage of a layoff to build a new career. What carries them through tough times? Resilience.

Resilient people possess three defining characteristics: They coolly accept the harsh realities facing them. They find meaning in terrible times. And they have an uncanny ability to improvise, making do with whatever's at hand.

In deep recessions, resilience becomes more important than ever. Fortunately, you can learn to be resilient.

"But if you could, would you test for it?" I asked. "Does it matter in business?"

Savageau paused. He's a man in his late forties and a success personally and professionally. Yet it hadn't been a smooth ride to the top. He'd started his life as a poor French Canadian in Woonsocket, Rhode Island, and had lost his father at six. He lucked into a football scholarship but was kicked out of Boston University twice for drinking. He turned his life around in his twenties, married, divorced, remarried, and raised five children. Along the way, he made and lost two fortunes before helping to found the consulting firm he now runs. "Yes, it does matter," he said at last. "In fact, it probably matters more than any of the usual things we look for." In the course of reporting this article, I heard the same assertion time and again. As Dean Becker, the president and CEO of Adaptiv Learning Systems, a four-year-old company in King of Prussia, Pennsylvania, that develops and delivers programs about resilience training, puts it: "More than education, more than experience, more than training, a person's level of resilience will determine who succeeds and who fails. That's true in the cancer ward, it's true in the Olympics, and it's true in the boardroom."

Academic research into resilience started about 40 years ago with pioneering studies by Norman Garmezy, now a professor emeritus at the University of Minnesota in Minneapolis. After studying why

Idea in Practice

Resilience can help you survive and recover from even the most brutal experiences. To cultivate resilience, apply these practices.

Face Down Reality

Instead of slipping into denial to cope with hardship, take a sober, down-to-earth view of the reality of your situation. You'll prepare yourself to act in ways that enable you to endure—training yourself to survive before the fact.

Example: Admiral Jim Stockdale survived being held prisoner and tortured by the Vietcong in part by accepting he could be held for a long time. (He was held for eight years.) Those who didn't make it out of the camps kept optimistically assuming they'd be released on shorter timetables—by Christmas, by Easter, by the Fourth of July. "I think they all died of broken hearts," Stockdale said.

Search for Meaning

When hard times strike, resist any impulse to view yourself as a victim and to cry, "Why me?" Rather, devise constructs about your suffering to create meaning for yourself and others. You'll build bridges from your present-day ordeal to a fuller, better future. Those bridges will make the present manageable, by removing the sense that the present is overwhelming.

Example: Austrian psychiatrist and Auschwitz survivor Victor Frankl realized that to survive

many children of schizophrenic parents did not suffer psychological illness as a result of growing up with them, he concluded that a certain quality of resilience played a greater role in mental health than anyone had previously suspected.

Today, theories abound about what makes resilience. Looking at Holocaust victims, Maurice Vanderpol, a former president of the Boston Psychoanalytic Society and Institute, found that many of the healthy survivors of concentration camps had what he calls a "plastic shield." The shield was comprised of several factors, including a sense of humor. Often the humor was black, but nonetheless it provided a critical sense of perspective. Other core characteristics that helped included the ability to form attachments to others and the possession of an inner psychological space that protected the survivors from the intrusions of abusive others. Research about other

the camp, he had to find some purpose. He did so by imagining himself giving a lecture after the war on the psychology of the concentration camp to help outsiders understand what he had been through. By creating concrete goals for himself, he rose above the sufferings of the moment.

Continually Improvise

When disaster hits, be inventive. Make the most of what you have, putting resources to unfamiliar uses and imagining possibilities others don't see.

Example: Mike founded a business with his friend Paul, selling educational materials to schools, businesses, and consulting firms. When a recession hit, they lost many core clients. Paul went through a bitter divorce, suffered a depression, and couldn't work. When Mike offered to buy him out, Paul slapped him with a lawsuit claiming Mike was trying to steal the business.

Mike kept the company going any way he could—going into joint ventures to sell English-language training materials to Russian and Chinese competitors, publishing newsletters for clients, and even writing video scripts for competitors. The lawsuit was eventually settled in his favor, and he had a new and much more solid business than the one he started out with.

groups uncovered different qualities associated with resilience. The Search Institute, a Minneapolis-based nonprofit organization that focuses on resilience and youth, found that the more resilient kids have an uncanny ability to get adults to help them out. Still other research showed that resilient inner-city youth often have talents such as athletic abilities that attract others to them.

Many of the early theories about resilience stressed the role of genetics. Some people are just born resilient, so the arguments went. There's some truth to that, of course, but an increasing body of empirical evidence shows that resilience—whether in children, survivors of concentration camps, or businesses back from the brink—can be learned. For example, George Vaillant, the director of the Study of Adult Development at Harvard Medical School in Boston, observes that within various groups studied during a 60-year period, some people became markedly more resilient over their lifetimes. Other psychologists claim that unresilient people more easily develop resiliency skills than those with head starts.

Most of the resilience theories I encountered in my research make good common sense. But I also observed that almost all the theories overlap in three ways. Resilient people, they posit, possess three characteristics: a staunch acceptance of reality; a deep belief, often buttressed by strongly held values, that life is meaningful; and an uncanny ability to improvise. You can bounce back from hardship with just one or two of these qualities, but you will only be truly resilient with all three. These three characteristics hold true for resilient organizations as well. Let's take a look at each of them in turn.

Facing Down Reality

A common belief about resilience is that it stems from an optimistic nature. That's true but only as long as such optimism doesn't distort your sense of reality. In extremely adverse situations, rose-colored thinking can actually spell disaster. This point was made poignantly to me by management researcher and writer Jim Collins, who happened upon this concept while researching *Good to Great*, his book on how companies transform themselves out of mediocrity. Collins had a hunch (an exactly wrong hunch) that resilient companies were filled with optimistic people. He tried out that idea on Admiral Jim Stockdale, who was held prisoner and tortured by the Vietcong for eight years.

Collins recalls: "I asked Stockdale: 'Who didn't make it out of the camps?' And he said, 'Oh, that's easy. It was the optimists. They were the ones who said we were going to be out by Christmas. And then they said we'd be out by Easter and then out by Fourth of July and out by Thanksgiving, and then it was Christmas again.' Then Stockdale turned to me and said, 'You know, I think they all died of broken hearts.'"

In the business world, Collins found the same unblinking attitude shared by executives at all the most successful companies he studied.

Like Stockdale, resilient people have very sober and down-to-earth views of those parts of reality that matter for survival. That's not to say that optimism doesn't have its place: In turning around a demoralized sales force, for instance, conjuring a sense of possibility can be a very powerful tool. But for bigger challenges, a cool, almost pessimistic, sense of reality is far more important.

Perhaps you're asking yourself, "Do I truly understand—and accept—the reality of my situation? Does my organization?" Those are good questions, particularly because research suggests most people slip into denial as a coping mechanism. Facing reality, really facing it, is grueling work. Indeed, it can be unpleasant and often emotionally wrenching. Consider the following story of organizational resilience, and see what it means to confront reality.

Prior to September 11, 2001, Morgan Stanley, the famous investment bank, was the largest tenant in the World Trade Center. The company had some 2,700 employees working in the south tower on 22 floors between the 43rd and the 74th. On that horrible day, the first plane hit the north tower at 8:46 AM, and Morgan Stanley started evacuating just one minute later, at 8:47 AM. When the second plane crashed into the south tower 15 minutes after that, Morgan Stanley's offices were largely empty. All told, the company lost only seven employees despite receiving an almost direct hit.

Of course, the organization was just plain lucky to be in the second tower. Cantor Fitzgerald, whose offices were hit in the first attack, couldn't have done anything to save its employees. Still, it was Morgan Stanley's hard-nosed realism that enabled the company to benefit from its luck. Soon after the 1993 attack on the World Trade Center, senior management recognized that working in such a symbolic center of U.S. commercial power made the company vulnerable to attention from terrorists and possible attack.

With this grim realization, Morgan Stanley launched a program of preparedness at the micro level. Few companies take their fire drills seriously. Not so Morgan Stanley, whose VP of security for the Individual Investor Group, Rick Rescorla, brought a military discipline to the job. Rescorla, himself a highly resilient, decorated Vietnam vet, made sure that people were fully drilled about what to do in a catastrophe. When disaster struck on September 11, Rescorla was on a bullhorn telling Morgan Stanley employees to stay calm and follow their well-practiced drill, even though some building supervisors were telling occupants that all was well. Sadly, Rescorla himself, whose life story has been widely covered in recent months, was one of the seven who didn't make it out.

"When you're in financial services where so much depends on technology, contingency planning is a major part of your business," says President and COO Robert G. Scott. But Morgan Stanley was prepared for the very toughest reality. It had not just one, but three, recovery sites where employees could congregate and business could take place if work locales were ever disrupted. "Multiple backup sites seemed like an incredible extravagance on September 10," concedes Scott. "But on September 12, they seemed like genius."

Maybe it was genius; it was undoubtedly resilience at work. The fact is, when we truly stare down reality, we prepare ourselves to act in ways that allow us to endure and survive extraordinary hardship. We train ourselves how to survive before the fact.

The Search for Meaning

The ability to see reality is closely linked to the second building block of resilience, the propensity to make meaning of terrible times. We all know people who, under duress, throw up their hands and cry, "How can this be happening to me?" Such people see themselves as victims, and living through hardship carries no lessons for them. But resilient people devise constructs about their suffering to create some sort of meaning for themselves and others.

I have a friend I'll call Jackie Oiseaux who suffered repeated psychoses over a ten-year period due to an undiagnosed bipolar disorder. Today, she holds down a big job in one of the top publishing companies in the country, has a family, and is a prominent member of her church community. When people ask her how she bounced back from her crises, she runs her hands through her hair. "People sometimes say, 'Why me?' But I've always said, 'Why *not* me?' True, I lost many things during my illness," she says, "but I found many more—incredible friends who saw me through the bleakest times and who will give meaning to my life forever."

This dynamic of meaning making is, most researchers agree, the way resilient people build bridges from present-day hardships to a fuller, better constructed future. Those bridges make the present manageable, for lack of a better word, removing the sense that the present is overwhelming. This concept was beautifully articulated by Viktor E. Frankl, an Austrian psychiatrist and an Auschwitz survivor. In the midst of staggering suffering, Frankl invented "meaning therapy," a humanistic therapy technique that helps individuals make the kinds of decisions that will create significance in their lives.

In his book *Man's Search for Meaning*, Frankl described the pivotal moment in the camp when he developed meaning therapy. He was on his way to work one day, worrying whether he should trade his last cigarette for a bowl of soup. He wondered how he was going to work with a new foreman whom he knew to be particularly sadistic. Suddenly, he was disgusted by just how trivial and meaningless his life had become. He realized that to survive, he had to find some purpose. Frankl did so by imagining himself giving a lecture after the war on the psychology of the concentration camp, to help outsiders understand what he had been through. Although he wasn't even sure he would survive, Frankl created some concrete goals for himself. In doing so, he succeeded in rising above the sufferings of the moment. As he put it in his book: "We must never forget that we may also find meaning in life even when confronted with a hopeless situation, when facing a fate that cannot be changed."

Frankl's theory underlies most resilience coaching in business. Indeed, I was struck by how often businesspeople referred to his work. "Resilience training—what we call hardiness—is a way for us to help people construct meaning in their everyday lives," explains Salvatore R. Maddi, a University of California, Irvine psychology professor and the director of the Hardiness Institute in Newport Beach, California. "When people realize the power of resilience training, they often say, 'Doc, is this what psychotherapy is?' But psychotherapy is for people whose lives have fallen apart badly and need repair. We see our work as showing people life skills and attitudes. Maybe those things should be taught at home, maybe they should be taught in schools, but they're not. So we end up doing it in business."

Yet the challenge confronting resilience trainers is often more difficult than we might imagine. Meaning can be elusive, and just because you found it once doesn't mean you'll keep it or find it again. Consider Aleksandr Solzhenitsyn, who survived the war against the Nazis, imprisonment in the gulag, and cancer. Yet when he moved to a farm in peaceful, safe Vermont, he could not cope with the "infantile West." He was unable to discern any real meaning in what he felt to be the destructive and irresponsible freedom of the West. Upset by his critics, he withdrew into his farmhouse, behind a locked fence, seldom to be seen in public. In 1994, a bitter man, Solzhenitsyn moved back to Russia.

Since finding meaning in one's environment is such an important aspect of resilience, it should come as no surprise that the most successful organizations and people possess strong value systems. Strong values infuse an environment with meaning because they offer ways to interpret and shape events. While it's popular these days to ridicule values, it's surely no coincidence that the most resilient organization in the world has been the Catholic Church, which has survived wars, corruption, and schism for more than 2,000 years, thanks largely to its immutable set of values. Businesses that survive also have their creeds, which give them purposes beyond just making money. Strikingly, many companies describe their value systems in religious terms. Pharmaceutical giant Johnson & Johnson, for instance, calls its value system, set out in a document given to every new employee at orientation, the Credo. Parcel company UPS talks constantly about its Noble Purpose.

Value systems at resilient companies change very little over the years and are used as scaffolding in times of trouble. UPS Chairman and CEO Mike Eskew believes that the Noble Purpose helped the company to rally after the agonizing strike in 1997. Says Eskew: "It was a hugely difficult time, like a family feud. Everyone had close friends on both sides of the fence, and it was tough for us to pick sides. But what saved us was our Noble Purpose. Whatever side people were on, they all shared a common set of values. Those values are core to us and never change; they frame most of our important decisions. Our strategy and our mission may change, but our values never do."

The religious connotations of words like "credo," "values," and "noble purpose," however, should not be confused with the actual content of the values. Companies can hold ethically questionable values and still be very resilient. Consider Phillip Morris, which has demonstrated impressive resilience in the face of increasing unpopularity. As Jim Collins points out, Phillip Morris has very strong values, although we might not agree with them—for instance, the value of "adult choice." But there's no doubt that Phillip Morris executives believe strongly in its values, and the strength of their beliefs sets the company apart from most of the other tobacco companies. In this context, it is worth noting that resilience is neither ethically good nor bad. It is merely the skill and the capacity to be robust under conditions of enormous stress and change. As Viktor Frankl wrote: "On the average, only those prisoners could keep alive who, after years of trekking from camp to camp, had lost all scruples in their fight for existence; they were prepared to use every means, honest and otherwise, even brutal..., in order to save themselves. We who have come back... we know: The best of us did not return."

Values, positive or negative, are actually more important for organizational resilience than having resilient people on the payroll. If resilient employees are all interpreting reality in different ways, their decisions and actions may well conflict, calling into doubt the survival of their organization. And as the weakness of an organization becomes apparent, highly resilient individuals are more likely to jettison the organization than to imperil their own survival.

Ritualized Ingenuity

The third building block of resilience is the ability to make do with whatever is at hand. Psychologists follow the lead of French anthropologist Claude Levi-Strauss in calling this skill bricolage.[1] Intriguingly, the roots of that word are closely tied to the concept of resilience, which literally means "bouncing back." Says Levi-Strauss: "In its old sense, the verb *bricoler*... was always used with reference to some extraneous movement: a ball rebounding, a dog straying, or a horse swerving from its direct course to avoid an obstacle."

Bricolage in the modern sense can be defined as a kind of inventiveness, an ability to improvise a solution to a problem without proper or obvious tools or materials. *Bricoleurs* are always tinkering—building radios from household effects or fixing their own cars. They make the most of what they have, putting objects to unfamiliar uses. In the concentration camps, for example, resilient inmates knew to pocket pieces of string or wire whenever they found them. The string or wire might later become useful—to fix a pair of shoes, perhaps, which in freezing conditions might make the difference between life and death.

When situations unravel, bricoleurs muddle through, imagining possibilities where others are confounded. I have two friends, whom I'll call Paul Shields and Mike Andrews, who were roommates throughout their college years. To no one's surprise, when they graduated, they set up a business together, selling educational materials to schools, businesses, and consulting firms. At first, the company was a great success, making both founders paper millionaires. But the recession of the early 1990s hit the company hard, and many core clients fell away. At the same time, Paul experienced a bitter divorce and a depression that made it impossible for him to work. Mike offered to buy Paul out but was instead slapped with a lawsuit claiming that Mike was trying to steal the business. At this point, a less resilient person might have just walked away from the mess. Not Mike. As the case wound through the courts, he kept the company going any way he could—constantly morphing the business until he found a model that worked: going into joint ventures to sell English-language training materials to Russian and Chinese companies. Later, he branched off into publishing newsletters for clients. At one point, he was even writing video scripts for his competitors. Thanks to all this bricolage, by the time the lawsuit was settled in his favor, Mike had an entirely different, and much more solid, business than the one he had started with.

Bricolage can be practiced on a higher level as well. Richard Feynman, winner of the 1965 Nobel Prize in physics, exemplified what I like to think of as intellectual bricolage. Out of pure curiosity,

Feynman made himself an expert on cracking safes, not only looking at the mechanics of safecracking but also cobbling together psychological insights about people who used safes and set the locks. He cracked many of the safes at Los Alamos, for instance, because he guessed that theoretical physicists would not set the locks with random code numbers they might forget but would instead use a sequence with mathematical significance. It turned out that the three safes containing all the secrets to the atomic bomb were set to the same mathematical constant, *e,* whose first six digits are 2.71828.

Resilient organizations are stuffed with bricoleurs, though not all of them, of course, are Richard Feynmans. Indeed, companies that survive regard improvisation as a core skill. Consider UPS, which empowers its drivers to do whatever it takes to deliver packages on time. Says CEO Eskew: "We tell our employees to get the job done. If that means they need to improvise, they improvise. Otherwise we just couldn't do what we do every day. Just think what can go wrong: a busted traffic light, a flat tire, a bridge washed out. If a snowstorm hits Louisville tonight, a group of people will sit together and discuss how to handle the problem. Nobody tells them to do that. They come together because it's our tradition to do so."

That tradition meant that the company was delivering parcels in southeast Florida just one day after Hurricane Andrew devastated the region in 1992, causing billions of dollars in damage. Many people were living in their cars because their homes had been destroyed, yet UPS drivers and managers sorted packages at a diversion site and made deliveries even to those who were stranded in their cars. It was largely UPS's improvisational skills that enabled it to keep functioning after the catastrophic hit. And the fact that the company continued on gave others a sense of purpose or meaning amid the chaos.

Improvisation of the sort practiced by UPS, however, is a far cry from unbridled creativity. Indeed, much like the military, UPS lives on rules and regulations. As Eskew says: "Drivers always put their keys in the same place. They close the doors the same way. They wear their uniforms the same way. We are a company of precision." He believes that although they may seem stifling, UPS's rules were what allowed the company to bounce back immediately after Hurricane

Andrew, for they enabled people to focus on the one or two fixes they needed to make in order to keep going.

Eskew's opinion is echoed by Karl E. Weick, a professor of organizational behavior at the University of Michigan Business School in Ann Arbor and one of the most respected thinkers on organizational psychology. "There is good evidence that when people are put under pressure, they regress to their most habituated ways of responding," Weick has written. "What we do not expect under life-threatening pressure is creativity." In other words, the rules and regulations that make some companies appear less creative may actually make them more resilient in times of real turbulence.

Claus Schmidt, the newsman I mentioned earlier, died about five years ago, but I'm not sure I could have interviewed him about his own resilience even if he were alive. It would have felt strange, I think, to ask him, "Claus, did you really face down reality? Did you make meaning out of your hardships? Did you improvise your recovery after each professional and personal disaster?" He may not have been able to answer. In my experience, resilient people don't often describe themselves that way. They shrug off their survival stories and very often assign them to luck.

Obviously, luck does have a lot to do with surviving. It was luck that Morgan Stanley was situated in the south tower and could put its preparedness training to work. But being lucky is not the same as being resilient. Resilience is a reflex, a way of facing and understanding the world, that is deeply etched into a person's mind and soul. Resilient people and companies face reality with staunchness, make meaning of hardship instead of crying out in despair, and improvise solutions from thin air. Others do not. This is the nature of resilience, and we will never completely understand it.

Originally published in May 2002. Reprint R0205B

Note

1. See, e.g., Karl E. Weick, "The Collapse of Sense-making in Organizations: The Mann Gulch Disaster," *Administrative Science Quarterly*, December 1993.

Manage Your Energy, Not Your Time

by Tony Schwartz and Catherine McCarthy

STEVE WANNER IS A HIGHLY respected 37-year-old partner at Ernst & Young, married with four young children. When we met him a year ago, he was working 12- to 14-hour days, felt perpetually exhausted, and found it difficult to fully engage with his family in the evenings, which left him feeling guilty and dissatisfied. He slept poorly, made no time to exercise, and seldom ate healthy meals, instead grabbing a bite to eat on the run or while working at his desk.

Wanner's experience is not uncommon. Most of us respond to rising demands in the workplace by putting in longer hours, which inevitably take a toll on us physically, mentally, and emotionally. That leads to declining levels of engagement, increasing levels of distraction, high turnover rates, and soaring medical costs among employees. We at the Energy Project have worked with thousands of leaders and managers in the course of doing consulting and coaching at large organizations during the past five years. With remarkable consistency, these executives tell us they're pushing themselves harder than ever to keep up and increasingly feel they are at a breaking point.

The core problem with working longer hours is that time is a finite resource. Energy is a different story. Defined in physics as the capacity to work, energy comes from four main wellsprings in human beings: the body, emotions, mind, and spirit. In each, energy can be systematically expanded and regularly renewed by establishing specific rituals—behaviors that are intentionally practiced and precisely scheduled, with the goal of making them unconscious and automatic as quickly as possible.

To effectively reenergize their workforces, organizations need to shift their emphasis from getting more out of people to investing more in them, so they are motivated—and able—to bring more of themselves to work every day. To recharge themselves, individuals need to recognize the costs of energy-depleting behaviors and then take responsibility for changing them, regardless of the circumstances they're facing.

The rituals and behaviors Wanner established to better manage his energy transformed his life. He set an earlier bedtime and gave up drinking, which had disrupted his sleep. As a consequence, when he woke up he felt more rested and more motivated to exercise, which he now does almost every morning. In less than two months he lost 15 pounds. After working out he now sits down with his family for breakfast. Wanner still puts in long hours on the job, but he renews himself regularly along the way. He leaves his desk for lunch and usually takes a morning and an afternoon walk outside. When he arrives at home in the evening, he's more relaxed and better able to connect with his wife and children.

Establishing simple rituals like these can lead to striking results across organizations. At Wachovia Bank, we took a group of employees through a pilot energy management program and then measured their performance against that of a control group. The participants outperformed the controls on a series of financial metrics, such as the value of loans they generated. They also reported substantial improvements in their customer relationships, their engagement with work, and their personal satisfaction. In this article, we'll describe the Wachovia study in a little more detail. Then we'll explain what executives and managers can do to increase and regularly renew work capacity—the approach used by the Energy Project, which builds on, deepens, and extends several core concepts developed by Tony's former partner Jim Loehr in his seminal work with athletes.

Idea in Brief

Organizations are demanding ever-higher performance from their workforces. People are trying to comply, but the usual method—putting in longer hours—has backfired. They're getting exhausted, disengaged, and sick. And they're defecting to healthier job environments.

Longer days at the office don't work because time is a limited resource. But personal energy is renewable, say Schwartz and McCarthy. By fostering deceptively simple **rituals** that help employees regularly replenish their energy, organizations build workers' physical, emotional, and mental resilience. These rituals include taking brief breaks at specific intervals, expressing appreciation to others, reducing interruptions, and spending more time on activities people do best and enjoy most.

Help your employees systematically rejuvenate their personal energy, and the benefits go straight to your bottom line. Take Wachovia Bank: Participants in an energy renewal program produced 13 percentage points greater year-over-year in revenues from loans than a control group did. And they exceeded the control group's gains in revenues from deposits by 20 percentage points.

Linking Capacity and Performance at Wachovia

Most large organizations invest in developing employees' skills, knowledge, and competence. Very few help build and sustain their capacity—their energy—which is typically taken for granted. In fact, greater capacity makes it possible to get more done in less time at a higher level of engagement and with more sustainability. Our experience at Wachovia bore this out.

In early 2006 we took 106 employees at 12 regional banks in southern New Jersey through a curriculum of four modules, each of which focused on specific strategies for strengthening one of the four main dimensions of energy. We delivered it at one-month intervals to groups of approximately 20 to 25, ranging from senior leaders to lower-level managers. We also assigned each attendee a fellow employee as a source of support between sessions. Using Wachovia's own key performance metrics, we evaluated how the participant group performed compared with a group of employees at similar levels at a nearby set of Wachovia banks who did not go through the

Idea in Practice

Schwartz and McCarthy recommend these practices for renewing four dimensions of personal energy.

Physical Energy

- Enhance your sleep by setting an earlier bedtime and reducing alcohol use.
- Reduce stress by engaging in cardiovascular activity at least three times a week and strength training at least once.
- Eat small meals and light snacks every three hours.
- Learn to notice signs of imminent energy flagging, including restlessness, yawning, hunger, and difficulty concentrating.
- Take brief but regular breaks, away from your desk, at 90- to 120-minute intervals throughout the day.

Emotional Energy

- Defuse negative emotions—irritability, impatience, anxiety, insecurity—through deep abdominal breathing.
- Fuel positive emotions in yourself and others by regularly expressing appreciation to others in detailed, specific terms through notes, e-mails, calls, or conversations.
- Look at upsetting situations through new lenses. Adopt a "reverse lens" to ask, "What would the other person in this conflict say, and how might he be right?" Use a "long lens" to ask, "How will I likely view this situation in six months?" Employ a "wide lens" to ask, "How can I grow and learn from this situation?"

Mental Energy

- Reduce interruptions by performing high-concentration tasks away from phones and e-mail.
- Respond to voice mails and e-mails at designated times during the day.

training. To create a credible basis for comparison, we looked at year-over-year percentage changes in performance across several metrics.

On a measure called the "Big 3"—revenues from three kinds of loans—the participants showed a year-over-year increase that was 13 percentage points greater than the control group's in the first three months of our study. On revenues from deposits, the participants exceeded the control group's year-over-year gain by 20 percentage points during that same period. The precise gains varied month by month, but with only a handful of exceptions, the participants

- Every night, identify the most important challenge for the next day. Then make it your first priority when you arrive at work in the morning.

Spiritual Energy

- Identify your "sweet spot" activities—those that give you feelings of effectiveness, effortless absorption, and fulfillment. Find ways to do more of these. One executive who hated doing sales reports delegated them to someone who loved that activity.
- Allocate time and energy to what you consider most important. For example, spend the last 20 minutes of your evening commute relaxing, so you can connect with your family once you're home.
- Live your core values. For instance, if consideration is important to you but you're perpetually late for meetings, practice intentionally showing up five minutes early for meetings.

How Companies Can Help

To support energy renewal rituals in your firm:

- Build "renewal rooms" where people can go to relax and re-fuel.
- Subsidize gym memberships.
- Encourage managers to gather employees for midday workouts.
- Suggest that people stop checking e-mails during meetings.

continued to significantly outperform the control group for a full year after completing the program. Although other variables undoubtedly influenced these outcomes, the participants' superior performance was notable in its consistency. (See the exhibit "How Energy Renewal Programs Boosted Productivity at Wachovia.")

We also asked participants how the program influenced them personally. Sixty-eight percent reported that it had a positive impact on their relationships with clients and customers. Seventy-one percent said that it had a noticeable or substantial positive impact on their

How energy renewal programs boosted productivity at Wachovia

At Wachovia Bank, employees participating in an energy renewal program outperformed a control group of employees, demonstrating significantly greater improvements in year-over-year performance during the first quarter of 2006.

Percentage increase in loan revenues*

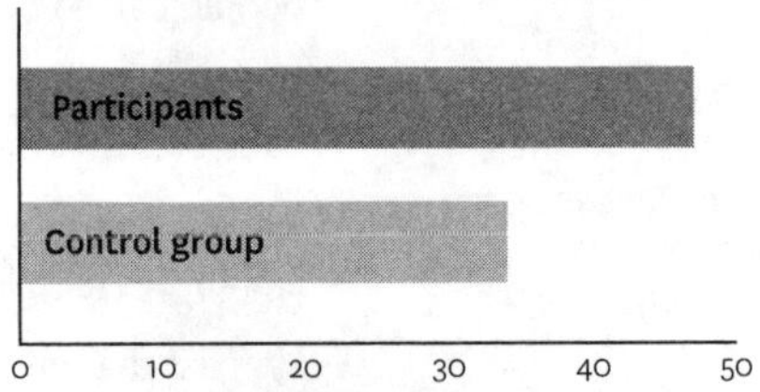

*From three critical kinds of loans

Percentage increase in deposit revenues

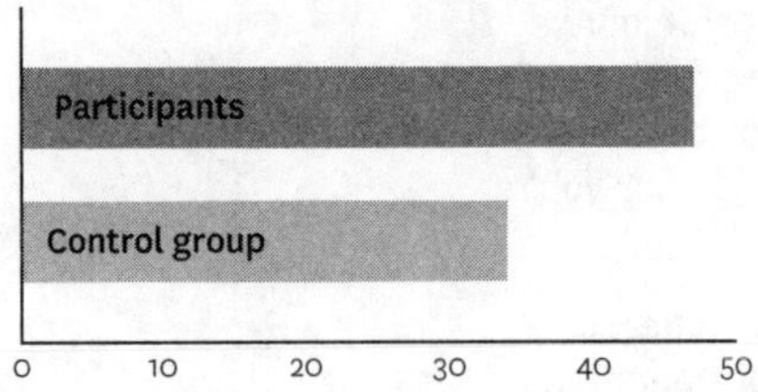

productivity and performance. These findings corroborated a raft of anecdotal evidence we've gathered about the effectiveness of this approach among leaders at other large companies such as Ernst & Young, Sony, Deutsche Bank, Nokia, ING Direct, Ford, and MasterCard.

The Body: Physical Energy

Our program begins by focusing on physical energy. It is scarcely news that inadequate nutrition, exercise, sleep, and rest diminish people's basic energy levels, as well as their ability to manage their emotions and focus their attention. Nonetheless, many executives don't find ways to practice consistently healthy behaviors, given all the other demands in their lives.

Before participants in our program begin to explore ways to increase their physical energy, they take an energy audit, which includes four questions in each energy dimension—body, emotions, mind, and spirit. (See the exhibit "Are You Headed for an Energy Crisis?") On average, participants get eight to ten of those 16 questions "wrong," meaning they're doing things such as skipping breakfast, failing to express appreciation to others, struggling to focus on one thing at a time, or spending too little time on activities that give them a sense of purpose. While most participants aren't surprised to learn these behaviors are counterproductive, having them all listed in one place is often uncomfortable, sobering, and galvanizing. The audit highlights employees' greatest energy deficits. Participants also fill out charts designed to raise their awareness about how their exercise, diet, and sleep practices influence their energy levels.

The next step is to identify rituals for building and renewing physical energy. When Gary Faro, a vice president at Wachovia, began the program, he was significantly overweight, ate poorly, lacked a regular exercise routine, worked long hours, and typically slept no more than five or six hours a night. That is not an unusual profile among the leaders and managers we see. Over the course of the program, Faro began regular cardiovascular and strength training. He started going to bed at a designated time and sleeping longer. He changed his eating habits from two big meals a day ("Where I usually gorged myself," he says) to smaller meals and light snacks every three hours. The aim was to help him stabilize his glucose levels over the course of the day, avoiding peaks and valleys. He lost 50 pounds in the process, and his energy levels soared. "I used to schedule tough projects for the morning, when I knew that I would be more focused," Faro says. "I don't have to do that anymore because I find that I'm just as focused now at 5 PM as I am at 8 AM."

Another key ritual Faro adopted was to take brief but regular breaks at specific intervals throughout the workday—always leaving his desk. The value of such breaks is grounded in our physiology.

Are you headed for an energy crisis?

Please check the statements below that are true for you.

Body

- ☐ I don't regularly get at least seven to eight hours of sleep, and I often wake up feeling tired.
- ☐ I frequently skip breakfast, or I settle for something that isn't nutritious.
- ☐ I don't work out enough (meaning cardiovascular training at least three times a week and strength training at least once a week).
- ☐ I don't take regular breaks during the day to truly renew and recharge, or I often eat lunch at my desk, if I eat it at all.

Emotions

- ☐ I frequently find myself feeling irritable, impatient, or anxious at work, especially when work is demanding.
- ☐ I don't have enough time with my family and loved ones, and when I'm with them, I'm not always really with them.
- ☐ I have too little time for the activities that I most deeply enjoy.
- ☐ I don't stop frequently enough to express my appreciation to others or to savor my accomplishments and blessings.

Mind

- ☐ I have difficulty focusing on one thing at a time, and I am easily distracted during the day, especially by e-mail.
- ☐ I spend much of my day reacting to immediate crises and demands rather than focusing on activities with longer-term value and high leverage.
- ☐ I don't take enough time for reflection, strategizing, and creative thinking.
- ☐ I work in the evenings or on weekends, and I almost never take an e-mail-free vacation.

Spirit

- ☐ I don't spend enough time at work doing what I do best and enjoy most.
- ☐ There are significant gaps between what I say is most important to me in my life and how I actually allocate my time and energy.
- ☐ My decisions at work are more often influenced by external demands than by a strong, clear sense of my own purpose.
- ☐ I don't invest enough time and energy in making a positive difference to others or to the world.

How is your overall energy?

Total number of statements checked: _

Guide to scores

0–3: Excellent energy management skills
4–6: Reasonable energy management skills

(continued)

7–10: Significant energy management deficits
11–16: A full-fledged energy management crisis

What do you need to work on?

Number of checks in each category:
Body __
Mind __
Emotions __
Spirit __

Guide to category scores

0: Excellent energy management skills
1: Strong energy management skills
2: Significant deficits
3: Poor energy management skills
4: A full-fledged energy crisis

"Ultradian rhythms" refer to 90- to 120-minute cycles during which our bodies slowly move from a high-energy state into a physiological trough. Toward the end of each cycle, the body begins to crave a period of recovery. The signals include physical restlessness, yawning, hunger, and difficulty concentrating, but many of us ignore them and keep working. The consequence is that our energy reservoir—our remaining capacity—burns down as the day wears on.

Intermittent breaks for renewal, we have found, result in higher and more sustainable performance. The length of renewal is less important than the quality. It is possible to get a great deal of recovery in a short time—as little as several minutes—if it involves a ritual that allows you to disengage from work and truly change channels. That could range from getting up to talk to a colleague about something other than work, to listening to music on an iPod, to walking up and down stairs in an office building. While breaks are countercultural in most organizations and counterintuitive for many high achievers, their value is multifaceted.

Matthew Lang is a managing director for Sony in South Africa. He adopted some of the same rituals that Faro did, including a

20-minute walk in the afternoons. Lang's walk not only gives him a mental and emotional breather and some exercise but also has become the time when he gets his best creative ideas. That's because when he walks he is not actively thinking, which allows the dominant left hemisphere of his brain to give way to the right hemisphere with its greater capacity to see the big picture and make imaginative leaps.

The Emotions: Quality of Energy

When people are able to take more control of their emotions, they can improve the quality of their energy, regardless of the external pressures they're facing. To do this, they first must become more aware of how they feel at various points during the workday and of the impact these emotions have on their effectiveness. Most people realize that they tend to perform best when they're feeling positive energy. What they find surprising is that they're not able to perform well or to lead effectively when they're feeling any other way.

Unfortunately, without intermittent recovery, we're not physiologically capable of sustaining highly positive emotions for long periods. Confronted with relentless demands and unexpected challenges, people tend to slip into negative emotions—the fight-or-flight mode—often multiple times in a day. They become irritable and impatient, or anxious and insecure. Such states of mind drain people's energy and cause friction in their relationships. Fight-or-flight emotions also make it impossible to think clearly, logically, and reflectively. When executives learn to recognize what kinds of events trigger their negative emotions, they gain greater capacity to take control of their reactions.

One simple but powerful ritual for defusing negative emotions is what we call "buying time." Deep abdominal breathing is one way to do that. Exhaling slowly for five or six seconds induces relaxation and recovery, and turns off the fight-or-flight response. When we began working with Fujio Nishida, president of Sony Europe, he had a habit of lighting up a cigarette each time something especially stressful occurred—at least two or three times a day. Otherwise, he didn't smoke. We taught him the breathing exercise as an alternative, and it worked immediately: Nishida found he no longer had the desire for a cigarette. It wasn't the smoking that had given him relief from the stress, we concluded, but the relaxation prompted by the deep inhalation and exhalation.

A powerful ritual that fuels positive emotions is expressing appreciation to others, a practice that seems to be as beneficial to the giver as to the receiver. It can take the form of a handwritten note, an e-mail, a call, or a conversation—and the more detailed and specific, the higher the impact. As with all rituals, setting aside a particular time to do it vastly increases the chances of success. Ben Jenkins, vice chairman and president of the General Bank at Wachovia in Charlotte, North Carolina, built his appreciation ritual into time set aside for mentoring. He began scheduling lunches or dinners regularly with people who worked for him. Previously, the only sit-downs he'd had with his direct reports were to hear monthly reports on their numbers or to give them yearly performance reviews. Now, over meals, he makes it a priority to recognize their accomplishments and also to talk with them about their lives and their aspirations rather than their immediate work responsibilities.

Finally, people can cultivate positive emotions by learning to change the stories they tell themselves about the events in their lives. Often, people in conflict cast themselves in the role of victim, blaming others or external circumstances for their problems. Becoming aware of the difference between the facts in a given situation and the way we interpret those facts can be powerful in itself. It's been a revelation for many of the people we work with to discover they have a choice about how to view a given event and to recognize how powerfully the story they tell influences the emotions they feel. We teach them to tell the most hopeful and personally empowering story possible in any given situation, without denying or minimizing the facts.

The most effective way people can change a story is to view it through any of three new lenses, which are all alternatives to seeing the world from the victim perspective. With the *reverse lens*, for example, people ask themselves, "What would the other person in this conflict say and in what ways might that be true?" With the *long lens* they ask, "How will I most likely view this situation in six months?"

With the *wide lens* they ask themselves, "Regardless of the outcome of this issue, how can I grow and learn from it?" Each of these lenses can help people intentionally cultivate more positive emotions.

Nicolas Babin, director of corporate communications for Sony Europe, was the point person for calls from reporters when Sony went through several recalls of its batteries in 2006. Over time he found his work increasingly exhausting and dispiriting. After practicing the lens exercises, he began finding ways to tell himself a more positive and empowering story about his role. "I realized," he explains, "that this was an opportunity for me to build stronger relationships with journalists by being accessible to them and to increase Sony's credibility by being straightforward and honest."

The Mind: Focus of Energy

Many executives view multitasking as a necessity in the face of all the demands they juggle, but it actually undermines productivity. Distractions are costly: A temporary shift in attention from one task to another—stopping to answer an e-mail or take a phone call, for instance—increases the amount of time necessary to finish the primary task by as much as 25%, a phenomenon known as "switching time." It's far more efficient to fully focus for 90 to 120 minutes, take a true break, and then fully focus on the next activity. We refer to these work periods as "ultradian sprints."

Once people see how much they struggle to concentrate, they can create rituals to reduce the relentless interruptions that technology has introduced in their lives. We start out with an exercise that forces them to face the impact of daily distractions. They attempt to complete a complex task and are regularly interrupted—an experience that, people report, ends up feeling much like everyday life.

Dan Cluna, a vice president at Wachovia, designed two rituals to better focus his attention. The first one is to leave his desk and go into a conference room, away from phones and e-mail, whenever he has a task that requires concentration. He now finishes reports in a third of the time they used to require. Cluna built his second ritual around meetings at branches with the financial specialists who report to him. Previously, he would answer his phone whenever it rang during these meetings. As a consequence, the meetings he scheduled for an hour often stretched to two, and he rarely gave anyone his full attention. Now Cluna lets his phone go to voice mail, so that he can focus completely on the person in front of him. He now answers the accumulated voice-mail messages when he has downtime between meetings.

E&Y's hard-charging Wanner used to answer e-mail constantly throughout the day—whenever he heard a "ping." Then he created a ritual of checking his e-mail just twice a day—at 10:15 AM and 2:30 PM. Whereas previously he couldn't keep up with all his messages, he discovered he could clear his in-box each time he opened it—the reward of fully focusing his attention on e-mail for 45 minutes at a time. Wanner has also reset the expectations of all the people he regularly communicates with by e-mail. "I've told them if it's an emergency and they need an instant response, they can call me and I'll always pick up," he says. Nine months later he has yet to receive such a call.

Michael Henke, a senior manager at E&Y, sat his team down at the start of the busy season last winter and told them that at certain points during the day he was going to turn off his Sametime (an in-house instant-message system). The result, he said, was that he would be less available to them for questions. Like Wanner, he told his team to call him if any emergency arose, but they rarely did. He also encouraged the group to take regular breaks throughout the day and to eat more regularly. They finished the busy season under budget and more profitable than other teams that hadn't followed the energy renewal program. "We got the same amount of work done in less time," says Henke. "It made for a win-win."

Another way to mobilize mental energy is to focus systematically on activities that have the most long-term leverage. Unless people intentionally schedule time for more challenging work, they tend not to get to it at all or rush through it at the last minute. Perhaps the most effective focus ritual the executives we work with have adopted is to identify each night the most important challenge for the next day and make it their very first priority when they arrive in the morning. Jean Luc Duquesne, a vice president for Sony Europe in

Paris, used to answer his e-mail as soon as he got to the office, just as many people do. He now tries to concentrate the first hour of every day on the most important topic. He finds that he often emerges at 10 AM feeling as if he's already had a productive day.

The Human Spirit: Energy of Meaning and Purpose

People tap into the energy of the human spirit when their everyday work and activities are consistent with what they value most and with what gives them a sense of meaning and purpose. If the work they're doing really matters to them, they typically feel more positive energy, focus better, and demonstrate greater perseverance. Regrettably, the high demands and fast pace of corporate life don't leave much time to pay attention to these issues, and many people don't even recognize meaning and purpose as potential sources of energy. Indeed, if we tried to begin our program by focusing on the human spirit, it would likely have minimal impact. Only when participants have experienced the value of the rituals they establish in the other dimensions do they start to see that being attentive to their own deeper needs dramatically influences their effectiveness and satisfaction at work.

For E&Y partner Jonathan Anspacher, simply having the opportunity to ask himself a series of questions about what really mattered to him was both illuminating and energizing. "I think it's important to be a little introspective and say, 'What do you want to be remembered for?'" he told us. "You don't want to be remembered as the crazy partner who worked these long hours and had his people be miserable. When my kids call me and ask, 'Can you come to my band concert?' I want to say, 'Yes, I'll be there and I'll be in the front row.' I don't want to be the father that comes in and sits in the back and is on his Blackberry and has to step out to take a phone call."

To access the energy of the human spirit, people need to clarify priorities and establish accompanying rituals in three categories: doing what they do best and enjoy most at work; consciously allocating time and energy to the areas of their lives—work, family, health, service to others—they deem most important; and living their core values in their daily behaviors.

When you're attempting to discover what you do best and what you enjoy most, it's important to realize that these two things aren't necessarily mutually inclusive. You may get lots of positive feedback about something you're very good at but not truly enjoy it. Conversely, you can love doing something but have no gift for it, so that achieving success requires much more energy than it makes sense to invest.

To help program participants discover their areas of strength, we ask them to recall at least two work experiences in the past several months during which they found themselves in their "sweet spot"—feeling effective, effortlessly absorbed, inspired, and fulfilled. Then we have them deconstruct those experiences to understand precisely what energized them so positively and what specific talents they were drawing on. If leading strategy feels like a sweet spot, for example, is it being in charge that's most invigorating or participating in a creative endeavor? Or is it using a skill that comes to you easily and so feels good to exercise? Finally, we have people establish a ritual that will encourage them to do more of exactly that kind of activity at work.

A senior leader we worked with realized that one of the activities he least liked was reading and summarizing detailed sales reports, whereas one of his favorites was brainstorming new strategies. The leader found a direct report who loved immersing himself in numbers and delegated the sales report task to him—happily settling for brief oral summaries from him each day. The leader also began scheduling a free-form 90-minute strategy session every other week with the most creative people in his group.

In the second category, devoting time and energy to what's important to you, there is often a similar divide between what people say is important and what they actually do. Rituals can help close this gap. When Jean Luc Duquesne, the Sony Europe vice president, thought hard about his personal priorities, he realized that spending time with his family was what mattered most to him, but it often got squeezed out of his day. So he instituted a ritual in which he switches off for at least three hours every evening when he gets home, so he can focus on his family. "I'm still not an expert on

PlayStation," he told us, "but according to my youngest son, I'm learning and I'm a good student." Steve Wanner, who used to talk on the cell phone all the way to his front door on his commute home, has chosen a specific spot 20 minutes from his house where he ends whatever call he's on and puts away the phone. He spends the rest of his commute relaxing so that when he does arrive home, he's less preoccupied with work and more available to his wife and children.

The third category, practicing your core values in your everyday behavior, is a challenge for many as well. Most people are living at such a furious pace that they rarely stop to ask themselves what they stand for and who they want to be. As a consequence, they let external demands dictate their actions.

We don't suggest that people explicitly define their values, because the results are usually too predictable. Instead, we seek to uncover them, in part by asking questions that are inadvertently revealing, such as, "What are the qualities that you find most off-putting when you see them in others?" By describing what they can't stand, people unintentionally divulge what they stand for. If you are very offended by stinginess, for example, generosity is probably one of your key values. If you are especially put off by rudeness in others, it's likely that consideration is a high value for you. As in the other categories, establishing rituals can help bridge the gap between the values you aspire to and how you currently behave. If you discover that consideration is a key value, but you are perpetually late for meetings, the ritual might be to end the meetings you run five minutes earlier than usual and intentionally show up five minutes early for the meeting that follows.

Addressing these three categories helps people go a long way toward achieving a greater sense of alignment, satisfaction, and well-being in their lives on and off the job. Those feelings are a source of positive energy in their own right and reinforce people's desire to persist at rituals in other energy dimensions as well.

This new way of working takes hold only to the degree that organizations support their people in adopting new behaviors. We have learned, sometimes painfully, that not all executives and companies are prepared to embrace the notion that personal renewal for employees will lead to better and more sustainable performance. To succeed, renewal efforts need solid support and commitment from senior management, beginning with the key decision maker.

At Wachovia, Susanne Svizeny, the president of the region in which we conducted our study, was the primary cheerleader for the program. She embraced the principles in her own life and made a series of personal changes, including a visible commitment to building more regular renewal rituals into her work life. Next, she took it upon herself to foster the excitement and commitment of her leadership team. Finally, she regularly reached out by e-mail to all participants in the project to encourage them in their rituals and seek their feedback. It was clear to everyone that she took the work seriously. Her enthusiasm was infectious, and the results spoke for themselves.

At Sony Europe, several hundred leaders have embraced the principles of energy management. Over the next year, more than 2,000 of their direct reports will go through the energy renewal program. From Fujio Nishida on down, it has become increasingly culturally acceptable at Sony to take intermittent breaks, work out at midday, answer e-mail only at designated times, and even ask colleagues who seem irritable or impatient what stories they're telling themselves.

Organizational support also entails shifts in policies, practices, and cultural messages. A number of firms we worked with have built "renewal rooms" where people can regularly go to relax and refuel. Others offer subsidized gym memberships. In some cases, leaders themselves gather groups of employees for midday workouts. One company instituted a no-meeting zone between 8 and 9 AM to ensure that people had at least one hour absolutely free of meetings. At several companies, including Sony, senior leaders collectively agreed to stop checking e-mail during meetings as a way to make the meetings more focused and efficient.

One factor that can get in the way of success is a crisis mentality. The optimal candidates for energy renewal programs are organizations that are feeling enough pain to be eager for new solutions but not so much that they're completely overwhelmed. At one organization where we had the active support of the CEO, the company was under intense pressure to grow rapidly, and the senior team couldn't tear themselves away from their focus on immediate survival—even though taking time out for renewal might have allowed them to be more productive at a more sustainable level.

By contrast, the group at Ernst & Young successfully went through the process at the height of tax season. With the permission of their leaders, they practiced defusing negative emotions by breathing or telling themselves different stories, and alternated highly focused periods of work with renewal breaks. Most people in the group reported that this busy season was the least stressful they'd ever experienced.

The implicit contract between organizations and their employees today is that each will try to get as much from the other as they can, as quickly as possible, and then move on without looking back. We believe that is mutually self-defeating. Both individuals and the organizations they work for end up depleted rather than enriched. Employees feel increasingly beleaguered and burned out. Organizations are forced to settle for employees who are less than fully engaged and to constantly hire and train new people to replace those who choose to leave. We envision a new and explicit contract that benefits all parties: Organizations invest in their people across all dimensions of their lives to help them build and sustain their value. Individuals respond by bringing all their multidimensional energy wholeheartedly to work every day. Both grow in value as a result.

Originally published in October 2007. Reprint R0710B

Overloaded Circuits

by Edward M. Hallowell

DAVID DRUMS HIS FINGERS on his desk as he scans the e-mail on his computer screen. At the same time, he's talking on the phone to an executive halfway around the world. His knee bounces up and down like a jackhammer. He intermittently bites his lip and reaches for his constant companion, the coffee cup. He's so deeply involved in multitasking that he has forgotten the appointment his Outlook calendar reminded him of 15 minutes ago.

Jane, a senior vice president, and Mike, her CEO, have adjoining offices so they can communicate quickly, yet communication never seems to happen. "Whenever I go into Mike's office, his phone lights up, my cell phone goes off, someone knocks on the door, he suddenly turns to his screen and writes an e-mail, or he tells me about a new issue he wants me to address," Jane complains. "We're working flat out just to stay afloat, and we're not getting anything important accomplished. It's driving me crazy."

David, Jane, and Mike aren't crazy, but they're certainly crazed. Their experience is becoming the norm for overworked managers who suffer—like many of your colleagues, and possibly like you—from a very real but unrecognized neurological phenomenon that I call attention deficit trait, or ADT. Caused by brain overload, ADT is now epidemic in organizations. The core symptoms are distractibility, inner frenzy, and impatience. People with ADT have difficulty staying organized, setting priorities, and managing time. These symptoms can undermine the work of an otherwise gifted executive. If

David, Jane, Mike, and the millions like them understood themselves in neurological terms, they could actively manage their lives instead of reacting to problems as they happen.

As a psychiatrist who has diagnosed and treated thousands of people over the past 25 years for a medical condition called attention deficit disorder, or ADD (now known clinically as attention-deficit/hyperactivity disorder), I have observed firsthand how a rapidly growing segment of the adult population is developing this new, related condition. The number of people with ADT coming into my clinical practice has mushroomed by a factor of ten in the past decade. Unfortunately, most of the remedies for chronic overload proposed by time-management consultants and executive coaches do not address the underlying causes of ADT.

Unlike ADD, a neurological disorder that has a genetic component and can be aggravated by environmental and physical factors, ADT springs entirely from the environment. Like the traffic jam, ADT is an artifact of modern life. It is brought on by the demands on our time and attention that have exploded over the past two decades. As our minds fill with noise—feckless synaptic events signifying nothing—the brain gradually loses its capacity to attend fully and thoroughly to anything.

The symptoms of ADT come upon a person gradually. The sufferer doesn't experience a single crisis but rather a series of minor emergencies while he or she tries harder and harder to keep up. Shouldering a responsibility to "suck it up" and not complain as the workload increases, executives with ADT do whatever they can to handle a load they simply cannot manage as well as they'd like. The ADT sufferer therefore feels a constant low level of panic and guilt. Facing a tidal wave of tasks, the executive becomes increasingly hurried, curt, peremptory, and unfocused, while pretending that everything is fine.

To control ADT, we first have to recognize it. And control it we must, if we as individuals and organizational leaders are to be effective. In the following pages, I'll offer an analysis of the origins of ADT and provide some suggestions that may help you manage it.

Idea in Brief

Frenzied executives who fidget through meetings, miss appointments, and jab at the elevator's "door close" button aren't crazy—just crazed. They're suffering from a newly recognized neurological phenomenon called **attention deficit trait (ADT)**. Marked by distractibility, inner frenzy, and impatience, ADT prevents managers from clarifying priorities, making smart decisions, and managing their time. This insidious condition turns otherwise talented performers into harried underachievers. And it's reaching epidemic proportions.

ADT isn't an illness or character defect. It's our brains' natural response to exploding demands on our time and attention. As data increasingly floods our brains, we lose our ability to solve problems and handle the unknown. Creativity shrivels; mistakes multiply. Some sufferers eventually melt down.

How to control ADT's ravaging impact on performance? *Foster positive emotions* by connecting face-to-face with people you like throughout the day. *Take physical care of your brain* by getting enough sleep, eating healthfully, and exercising regularly. *Organize for ADT,* designating part of each day for thinking and planning, and setting up your office to foster mental functioning (for example, keeping part of your desk clear at all times).

These strategies may seem like no-brainers. But they'll help you vanquish the ADT demon before it can strike.

Attention Deficit Cousins

To understand the nature and treatment of ADT, it's useful to know something of its cousin, ADD.

Usually seen as a learning disability in children, ADD also afflicts about 5% of the adult population. Researchers using MRI scans have found that people with ADD suffer a slightly diminished volume in four specific brain regions that have various functions such as modulating emotion (especially anger and frustration) and assisting in learning. One of the regions, made up of the frontal and prefrontal lobes, generates thoughts, makes decisions, sets priorities, and organizes activities. While the medications used to treat ADD don't change

Idea in Practice

How You Can Combat ADT

Promote positive emotions. Negative emotions—especially fear—can hamper productive brain functioning. To promote positive feelings, especially during highly stressful times, interact directly with someone you like at least every four to six hours. In environments where people are in physical contact with people they trust, brain functioning hums. By connecting comfortably with colleagues, you'll help your brain's "executive" center (responsible for decision making, planning, and information prioritizing) perform at its best.

Take physical care of your brain. Ample sleep, a good diet, and exercise are critical for staving off ADT. You're getting enough sleep if you can awake without an alarm clock. You're eating well if you're avoiding sugar and white flour and consuming more fruits, whole grains, vegetables, and protein instead. You're exercising enough if you're taking a brisk walk or going up and down a flight of stairs a few times a day.

Organize for ADT. Instead of getting sucked into the vortices of e-mail or voice mail first thing in the morning, attend to a critical task. With paperwork, apply the OHIO ("Only handle it once") rule: Whenever you touch a document, act on it, file it, or throw it away. Do crucial work during times of the day when you perform at your best. Use whatever small strategies help you function well mentally—whether it's listening to music or walking around while working, or doodling during meetings. And before you leave for the day, list three to five priority items you'll need to address tomorrow.

What Your Company Can Do. In firms that ignore ADT symptoms, employees underachieve, create clutter, and cut corners. Careless mistakes, illness, and turnover increase, as people squander their brainpower. To counteract ADT and harness employees' brainpower, invest in amenities that foster a positive, productive atmosphere.

> ***Example:*** Major software company SAS Institute creates a warm, connected, and relaxed work environment by offering employees perks such as a seven-hour workday that ends at 5:00; large on-site gym and day-care facility; and cafeteria that provides baby seats and high chairs so parents can eat lunch with their children. The payoff? Employees return the favors with high productivity. And SAS's turnover never exceeds 5%—saving the company millions on recruiting, training, and severance.

the anatomy of the brain, they alter brain chemistry, which in turn improves function in each of the four regions and so dramatically bolsters the performance of ADD sufferers.

ADD confers both disadvantages and advantages. The negative characteristics include a tendency to procrastinate and miss deadlines. People with ADD struggle with disorganization and tardiness; they can be forgetful and drift away mentally in the middle of a conversation or while reading. Their performance can be inconsistent: brilliant one moment and unsatisfactory the next. ADD sufferers also tend to demonstrate impatience and lose focus unless, oddly enough, they are under stress or handling multiple inputs. (This is because stress leads to the production of adrenaline, which is chemically similar to the medications we use to treat ADD.) Finally, people with ADD sometimes also self-medicate with excessive alcohol or other substances.

On the positive side, those with ADD usually possess rare talents and gifts. Those gifts often go unnoticed or undeveloped, however, because of the problems caused by the condition's negative symptoms. ADD sufferers can be remarkably creative and original. They are unusually persistent under certain circumstances and often possess an entrepreneurial flair. They display ingenuity and encourage that trait in others. They tend to improvise well under pressure. Because they have the ability to field multiple inputs simultaneously, they can be strong leaders during times of change. They also tend to rebound quickly after setbacks and bring fresh energy to the company every day.

Executives with ADD typically achieve inconsistent results. Sometimes they fail miserably because they're disorganized and make mistakes. At other times, they perform brilliantly, offering original ideas and strategies that lead to performance at the highest level.

David Neeleman, the CEO of JetBlue Airways, has ADD. School was torture; unable to focus, he hated to study and procrastinated endlessly. "I felt like I should be out doing things, moving things along, but here I was, stuck studying statistics, which I knew had no application to my life," Neeleman told me. "I knew I had to have an education, but at the first opportunity to start a business, I just blew out of college." He climbed quickly in the corporate world, making use of his strengths—original thinking, high energy, an ability to draw out the best in people—and getting help with organization and time management.

Like most people with ADD, Neeleman could sometimes offend with his blunt words, but his ideas were good enough to change the airline industry. For example, he invented the electronic ticket. "When I proposed that idea, people laughed at me, saying no one would go to the airport without a paper ticket," he says. "Now everyone does, and it has saved the industry millions of dollars." It seems fitting that someone with ADD would invent a way around having to remember to bring a paper ticket. Neeleman believes ADD is one of the keys to his success. Far from regretting having it, he celebrates it. But he understands that he must manage his ADD carefully.

Attention deficit trait is characterized by ADD's negative symptoms. Rather than being rooted in genetics, however, ADT is purely a response to the hyperkinetic environment in which we live. Indeed, modern culture all but requires many of us to develop ADT. Never in history has the human brain been asked to track so many data points. Everywhere, people rely on their cell phones, e-mail, and digital assistants in the race to gather and transmit data, plans, and ideas faster and faster. One could argue that the chief value of the modern era is speed, which the novelist Milan Kundera described as "the form of ecstasy that technology has bestowed upon modern man." Addicted to speed, we demand it even when we can't possibly go faster. James Gleick wryly noted in *Faster: The Acceleration of Just About Everything* that the "close door" button in elevators is often the one with the paint worn off. As the human brain struggles to keep up, it falters and then falls into the world of ADT.

This Is Your Brain

While brain scans cannot display anatomical differences between people with "normal" brains and people suffering from ADT, studies have shown that as the human brain is asked to process dizzying amounts of data, its ability to solve problems flexibly and creatively declines and the number of mistakes increases. To find out why, let's go on a brief neurological journey.

Blessed with the largest cortex in all of nature, owners of this trillion-celled organ today put singular pressure on the frontal and prefrontal lobes, which I'll refer to in this article as simply the frontal lobes. This region governs what is called, aptly enough, executive functioning (EF). EF guides decision making and planning; the organization and prioritization of information and ideas; time management; and various other sophisticated, uniquely human, managerial tasks. As long as our frontal lobes remain in charge, everything is fine.

Beneath the frontal lobes lie the parts of the brain devoted to survival. These deep centers govern basic functions like sleep, hunger, sexual desire, breathing, and heart rate, as well as crudely positive and negative emotions. When you are doing well and operating at peak level, the deep centers send up messages of excitement, satisfaction, and joy. They pump up your motivation, help you maintain attention, and don't interfere with working memory, the number of data points you can keep track of at once. But when you are confronted with the sixth decision after the fifth interruption in the midst of a search for the ninth missing piece of information on the day that the third deal has collapsed and the 12th impossible request has blipped unbidden across your computer screen, your brain begins to panic, reacting just as if that sixth decision were a bloodthirsty, man-eating tiger.

As a specialist in learning disabilities, I have found that the most dangerous disability is not any formally diagnosable condition like dyslexia or ADD. It is fear. Fear shifts us into survival mode and thus prevents fluid learning and nuanced understanding. Certainly, if a real tiger is about to attack you, survival is the mode you want to be in. But if you're trying to deal intelligently with a subtle task, survival mode is highly unpleasant and counterproductive.

When the frontal lobes approach capacity and we begin to fear that we can't keep up, the relationship between the higher and lower regions of the brain takes an ominous turn. Thousands of years of evolution have taught the higher brain not to ignore the lower brain's distress signals. In survival mode, the deep areas of the brain assume control and begin to direct the higher regions. As a result, the whole brain gets caught in a neurological catch-22. The deep regions interpret the messages of overload they receive from the frontal lobes in the same way they interpret everything: primitively. They furiously fire signals of fear, anxiety, impatience, irritability, anger, or panic. These alarm signals shanghai the attention of the frontal lobes, forcing them to forfeit much of their power. Because survival signals are irresistible, the frontal lobes get stuck sending messages back to the deep centers saying, "Message received. Trying to work on it but without success." These messages further perturb the deep centers, which send even more powerful messages of distress back up to the frontal lobes.

Meanwhile, in response to what's going on in the brain, the rest of the body—particularly the endocrine, respiratory, cardiovascular, musculoskeletal, and peripheral nervous systems—has shifted into crisis mode and changed its baseline physiology from peace and quiet to red alert. The brain and body are locked in a reverberating circuit while the frontal lobes lose their sophistication, as if vinegar were added to wine. In this state, EF reverts to simpleminded black-and-white thinking; perspective and shades of gray disappear. Intelligence dims. In a futile attempt to do more than is possible, the brain paradoxically reduces its ability to think clearly.

This neurological event occurs when a manager is desperately trying to deal with more input than he possibly can. In survival mode, the manager makes impulsive judgments, angrily rushing to bring closure to whatever matter is at hand. He feels compelled to get the problem under control immediately, to extinguish the perceived danger lest it destroy him. He is robbed of his flexibility, his sense of humor, his ability to deal with the unknown. He forgets the big picture and the goals and values he stands for. He loses his creativity and his ability to change plans. He desperately wants to kill the metaphorical tiger. At these moments he is prone to melting down, to throwing a tantrum, to blaming others, and to sabotaging himself. Or he may go in the opposite direction, falling into denial and total avoidance of the problems attacking him, only to be devoured. This is ADT at its worst.

Though ADT does not always reach such extreme proportions, it does wreak havoc among harried workers. Because no two brains are alike, some people deal with the condition better than others. Regardless of how well executives appear to function, however, no one has total control over his or her executive functioning.

Managing ADT

Unfortunately, top management has so far viewed the symptoms of ADT through the distorting lens of morality or character. Employees who seem unable to keep up the pace are seen as deficient or weak. Consider the case of an executive who came to see me when he was completely overloaded. I suggested he talk the situation over with his superior and ask for help. When my client did so, he was told that if he couldn't handle the work, he ought to think about resigning. Even though his performance assessments were stellar and he'd earned praise for being one of the most creative people in the organization, he was allowed to leave. Because the firm sought to preserve the myth that no straw would ever break its people's backs, it could not tolerate the manager's stating that his back was breaking. After he went out on his own, he flourished.

How can we control the rampaging effects of ADT, both in ourselves and in our organizations? While ADD often requires medication, the treatment of ADT certainly does not. ADT can be controlled only by creatively engineering one's environment and one's emotional and physical health. I have found that the following preventive measures go a long way toward helping executives control their symptoms of ADT.

Promote positive emotions

The most important step in controlling ADT is not to buy a superturbocharged BlackBerry and fill it up with to-dos but rather to create an environment in which the brain can function at its best. This means building a positive, fear-free emotional atmosphere, because emotion is the on/off switch for executive functioning.

There are neurological reasons why ADT occurs less in environments where people are in physical contact and where they trust and respect one another. When you comfortably connect with a colleague, even if you are dealing with an overwhelming problem, the deep centers of the brain send messages through the pleasure center to the area that assigns resources to the frontal lobes. Even when you're under extreme stress, this sense of human connection causes executive functioning to hum.

By contrast, people who work in physical isolation are more likely to suffer from ADT, for the more isolated we are, the more stressed we become. I witnessed a dramatic example of the danger of a disconnected environment and the healing power of a connected one when I consulted for one of the world's foremost university chemistry departments. In the department's formerly hard-driven culture, ADT was rampant, exacerbated by an ethic that forbade anyone to ask for help or even state that anything was wrong. People did not trust one another; they worked on projects alone, which led to more mistrust. Most people were in emotional pain, but implicit in the department's culture was the notion that great pain led to great gain.

In the late 1990s, one of the department's most gifted graduate students killed himself. His suicide note explicitly blamed the university for pushing him past his limit. The department's culture was literally lethal.

Instead of trying to sweep the tragedy under the rug, the chair of the department and his successor acted boldly and creatively. They immediately changed the structure of the supervisory system so that each graduate student and postdoc was assigned three supervisors, rather than a single one with a death grip on the trainee's career. The department set up informal biweekly buffets that allowed people to connect. (Even the most reclusive chemist came out of hiding for food, one of life's great connectors.) The department heads went as far as changing the architecture of the department's main building, taking down walls and adding common areas and an espresso bar complete with a grand piano. They provided lectures and written information to all students about the danger signs of mental wear and tear and offered confidential procedures for students who needed help. These steps, along with regular meetings that included senior faculty and university administrators, led to a more humane, productive culture in which the students and faculty felt fully engaged. The department's performance remained first-rate, and creative research blossomed.

The bottom line is this: Fostering connections and reducing fear promote brainpower. When you make time at least every four to six hours for a "human moment," a face-to-face exchange with a person you like, you are giving your brain what it needs.

Take physical care of your brain

Sleep, a good diet, and exercise are critical for staving off ADT. Though this sounds like a no-brainer, too many of us abuse our brains by neglecting obvious principles of care.

You may try to cope with ADT by sleeping less, in the vain hope that you can get more done. This is the opposite of what you need to do, for ADT sets in when you don't get enough sleep. There is ample documentation to suggest that sleep deprivation engenders a host of problems, from impaired decision making and reduced creativity to reckless behavior and paranoia. We vary in how much sleep we require; a good rule of thumb is that you're getting enough sleep if you can wake up without an alarm clock.

Diet also plays a crucial role in brain health. Many hardworking people habitually inhale carbohydrates, which cause blood glucose levels to yo-yo. This leads to a vicious cycle: Rapid fluctuations in insulin levels further increase the craving for carbohydrates. The brain, which relies on glucose for energy, is left either glutted or gasping, neither of which makes for optimal cognitive functioning.

The brain does much better if the blood glucose level can be held relatively stable. To do this, avoid simple carbohydrates containing sugar and white flour (pastries, white bread, and pasta, for example). Rely on the complex carbohydrates found in fruits, whole grains, and vegetables. Protein is important: Instead of starting your day with coffee and a Danish, try tea and an egg or a piece of smoked salmon on wheat toast. Take a multivitamin every day as well as supplementary omega-3 fatty acids, an excellent source of which is fish oil. The omega-3s and the E and B complex contained in multivitamins promote healthy brain function and may even stave off Alzheimer's disease and inflammatory ills (which can be the starting point for major killers like heart disease, stroke, diabetes, and cancer). Moderate your intake of alcohol, too, because too much kills brain cells and accelerates the development of memory loss and even dementia. As you change your diet to promote optimal brain function and good general health, your body will also shed excess pounds.

If you think you can't afford the time to exercise, think again. Sitting at a desk for hours on end decreases mental acuity, not only because of reduced blood flow to the brain but for other biochemical reasons as well. Physical exercise induces the body to produce an array of chemicals that the brain loves, including endorphins, serotonin, dopamine, epinephrine, and norepinephrine, as well as two recently discovered compounds, brain-derived neurotrophic factor (BDNF) and nerve growth factor (NGF). Both BDNF and NGF promote cell health and development in the brain, stave off the ravages of aging and stress, and keep the brain in tip-top condition. Nothing stimulates the production of BDNF and NGF as robustly as physical exercise, which explains why those who exercise regularly talk about the letdown and sluggishness they experience if they miss their exercise for a few days. You will more than compensate for the time you invest on the treadmill with improved productivity and efficiency. To fend off the symptoms of ADT while you're at work, get up from your desk and go up and down a flight of stairs a few times or walk briskly down a hallway. These quick, simple efforts will push your brain's reset button.

Organize for ADT

It's important to develop tactics for getting organized, but not in the sense of empty New Year's resolutions. Rather, your goal is to order your work in a way that suits you, so that disorganization does not keep you from reaching your goals.

First, devise strategies to help your frontal lobes stay in control. These might include breaking down large tasks into smaller ones and keeping a section of your work space or desk clear at all times. (You do not need to have a neat office, just a neat section of your office.) Similarly, you might try keeping a portion of your day free of appointments, e-mail, and other distractions so that you have time to think and plan. Because e-mail is a wonderful way to procrastinate and set yourself up for ADT at the same time, you might consider holding specific "e-mail hours," since it isn't necessary to reply to every e-mail right away.

When you start your day, don't allow yourself to get sucked into vortices of e-mail or voice mail or into attending to minor tasks that eat up your time but don't pack a punch. Attend to a critical task instead. Before you leave for the day, make a list of no more than five priority items that will require your attention tomorrow. Short lists force you to prioritize and complete your tasks. Additionally, keep torrents of documents at bay. One of my patients, an executive with ADD, uses the OHIO rule: Only handle it once. If he touches a document, he acts on it, files it, or throws it away. "I don't put it in a pile," he says. "Piles are like weeds. If you let them grow, they take over everything."

Pay attention to the times of day when you feel that you perform at your best; do your most important work then and save the rote work for other times. Set up your office in a way that helps mental functioning. If you focus better with music, have music (if need be, use earphones). If you think best on your feet, work standing up or walk around frequently. If doodling or drumming your fingers helps, figure out a way to do so without bothering anyone, or get a fidget toy to bring to meetings. These small strategies sound mundane, but they address the ADT devil that resides in distracting details.

Protect your frontal lobes

To stay out of survival mode and keep your lower brain from usurping control, slow down. Take the time you need to comprehend what is going on, to listen, to ask questions, and to digest what's been said so that you don't get confused and send your brain into panic. Empower an assistant to ride herd on you; insist that he or she tell you to stop e-mailing, get off the telephone, or leave the office.

Control Your ADT

In General

- Get adequate sleep.
- Watch what you eat. Avoid simple, sugary carbohydrates, moderate your intake of alcohol, add protein, stick to complex carbohydrates (vegetables, whole grains, fruit).
- Exercise at least 30 minutes at least every other day.
- Take a daily multivitamin and an omega-3 fatty acid supplement.

At Work

- Do all you can to create a trusting, connected work environment.
- Have a friendly, face-to-face talk with a person you like every four to six hours.
- Break large tasks into smaller ones.
- Keep a section of your work space or desk clear at all times.
- Each day, reserve some "think time" that's free from appointments, e-mail, and phone calls.
- Set aside e-mail until you've completed at least one or two more important tasks.

If you do begin to feel overwhelmed, try the following mind-clearing tricks. Do an easy rote task, such as resetting the calendar on your watch or writing a memo on a neutral topic. If you feel anxious about beginning a project, pull out a sheet of paper or fire up your word processor and write a paragraph about something unrelated to the project (a description of your house, your car, your shoes—anything you know well). You can also tackle the easiest part of the task; for example, write just the title of a memo about it. Open a dictionary and read a few definitions, or spend five minutes doing a crossword puzzle. Each of these little tasks quiets your lower brain by tricking it into shutting off alarmist messages and puts your frontal lobes back in full control.

- Before you leave work each day, create a short list of three to five items you will attend to the next day.
- Try to act on, file, or toss every document you touch.
- Don't let papers accumulate.
- Pay attention to the times of day when you feel that you are at your best; do your most important work then, and save the rote work for other times.
- Do whatever you need to do to work in a more focused way: Add background music, walk around, and so on.
- Ask a colleague or an assistant to help you stop talking on the telephone, e-mailing, or working too late.

When You Feel Overwhelmed

- Slow down.
- Do an easy rote task: Reset your watch, write a note about a neutral topic (such as a description of your house), read a few dictionary definitions, do a short crossword puzzle.
- Move around: Go up and down a flight of stairs or walk briskly.
- Ask for help, delegate a task, or brainstorm with a colleague. In short, do not worry alone.

Finally, be ready for the next attack of ADT by posting the sidebar "Control Your ADT" near your desk where you can see it. Knowing that you are prepared diminishes the likelihood of an attack, because you're not susceptible to panic.

What Leaders Can Do

All too often, companies induce and exacerbate ADT in their employees by demanding fast thinking rather than deep thinking. Firms also ask employees to work on multiple overlapping projects and initiatives, resulting in second-rate thinking. Worse, companies that ask their employees to do too much at once tend to reward those who say yes to overload while punishing those who choose to focus and say no.

Moreover, organizations make the mistake of forcing their employees to do more and more with less and less by eliminating support staff. Such companies end up losing money in the long run, for the more time a manager has to spend being his own administrative assistant and the less he is able to delegate, the less effective he will be in doing the important work of moving the organization forward. Additionally, firms that ignore the symptoms of ADT in their employees suffer its ill effects: Employees underachieve, create clutter, cut corners, make careless mistakes, and squander their brainpower. As demands continue to increase, a toxic, high-pressure environment leads to high rates of employee illness and turnover.

To counteract ADT and harness employee brainpower, firms should invest in amenities that contribute to a positive atmosphere. One company that has done an excellent job in this regard is SAS Institute, a major software company in North Carolina. The company famously offers its employees a long list of perks: a 36,000-square-foot, on-site gym; a seven-hour workday that ends at 5 PM; the largest on-site day care facility in North Carolina; a cafeteria that provides baby seats and high chairs so parents can eat lunch with their children; unlimited sick days; and much more. The atmosphere at SAS is warm, connected, and relaxed. The effect on the bottom line is profoundly positive; turnover is never higher than 5%. The company saves the millions other software companies spend on recruiting, training, and severance (estimated to be at least 1.5 times salary in the software industry). Employees return the favors with high productivity. The forces of ADT that shred other organizations never gain momentum at SAS.

Leaders can also help prevent ADT by matching employees' skills to tasks. When managers assign goals that stretch people too far or ask workers to focus on what they're not good at rather than what they do well, stress rises. By contrast, managers who understand the dangers of ADT can find ways of keeping themselves and their organizations on track. JetBlue's David Neeleman, for example, has shamelessly and publicly identified what he is not good at and found ways to deal with his shortcomings, either by delegating or by empowering his assistant to direct him. Neeleman also models this behavior for everyone else in the organization. His openness about the challenges of his ADD gives others permission to speak about their own attention deficit difficulties and to garner the support they need. He also encourages his managers to match people with tasks that fit their cognitive and emotional styles, knowing that no one style is best. Neeleman believes that helping people work to their strengths is not just a mark of sophisticated management; it's also an excellent way to boost worker productivity and morale.

ADT is a very real threat to all of us. If we do not manage it, it manages us. But an understanding of ADT and its ravages allows us to apply practical methods to improve our work and our lives. In the end, the most critical step an enlightened leader can take to address the problem of ADT is to name it. Bringing ADT out of the closet and describing its symptoms removes the stigma and eliminates the moral condemnation companies have for so long mistakenly leveled at overburdened employees. By giving people permission to ask for help and remaining vigilant for signs of stress, organizations will go a long way toward fostering more productive, well-balanced, and intelligent work environments.

Originally published in January 2005. Reprint R0501E

Be a Better Leader, Have a Richer Life

by Stewart D. Friedman

IN MY RESEARCH AND COACHING WORK over the past two decades, I have met many people who feel unfulfilled, overwhelmed, or stagnant because they are forsaking performance in one or more aspects of their lives. They aren't bringing their leadership abilities to bear in all of life's domains—work, home, community, and self (mind, body, and spirit). Of course, there will always be some tension among the different roles we play. But, contrary to the common wisdom, there's no reason to assume that it's a zero-sum game. It makes more sense to pursue excellent performance as a leader in all four domains—achieving what I call "four-way wins"—not trading off one for another but finding mutual value among them.

This is the main idea in a program called Total Leadership that I teach at the Wharton School and at companies and workshops around the world. "Total" because it's about the whole person and "Leadership" because it's about creating sustainable change to benefit not just you but the most important people around you.

Scoring four-way wins starts by taking a clear view of what you want from and can contribute to each domain of your life, now and in the future, with thoughtful consideration of the people who matter most to you and the expectations you have for one another. This is followed by systematically designing and implementing carefully crafted experiments—doing something new for a short period to see how it affects all four domains. If an experiment doesn't work out, you stop or adjust, and little is lost. If it does work out, it's a small win; over time these add up so that your overall efforts are focused increasingly on what and who matter most. Either way, you learn more about how to lead in all parts of your life.

This process doesn't require inordinate risk. On the contrary, it works because it entails realistic expectations, short-term changes that are in your control, and the explicit support of those around you. Take, for instance, Kenneth Chen, a manager I met at a workshop in 2005. (All names in this article are pseudonyms.) His professional goal was to become CEO, but he had other goals as well, which on the face of it might have appeared conflicting. He had recently moved to Philadelphia and wanted to get more involved with his community. He also wished to strengthen bonds with his family. To further all of these goals, he decided to join a city-based community board, which would not only allow him to hone his leadership skills (in support of his professional goal) but also have benefits in the family domain. It would give him more in common with his sister, a teacher who gave back to the community every day, and he hoped his fiancée would participate as well, enabling them to do something together for the greater good. He would feel more spiritually alive and this, in turn, would increase his self-confidence at work.

Now, about three years later, he reports that he is not only on a community board with his fiancée but also on the formal succession track for CEO. He's a better leader in all aspects of his life because he is acting in ways that are more consistent with his values. He is creatively enhancing his performance in all domains of his life and leading others to improve their performance by encouraging them to better integrate the different parts of their lives, too.

Kenneth is not alone. Workshop participants assess themselves at the beginning and the end of the program, and they consistently report improvements in their effectiveness, as well as a greater sense of harmony among the once-competing domains of their lives. In a study over a four-month period of more than 300 business professionals

Idea in Brief

Life's a zero-sum game, right? The more you strive to win in one dimension (e.g., your work), the more the other three dimensions (your self, your home, and your community) must lose. Not according to Friedman. You don't have to make trade-offs among life's domains. Nor should you: trading off can leave you feeling exhausted, unfulfilled, or isolated. And it hurts the people you care about most.

To excel in all dimensions of life, use Friedman's **Total Leadership** process. First, articulate who and what matters most in your life.

Then experiment with small changes that enhance your satisfaction and performance in *all four domains*. For example, exercising three mornings a week gives you more energy for work and improves your self-esteem and health, which makes you a better parent and friend.

Friedman's research suggests that people who focus on the concept of Total Leadership have a 20%–39% increase in satisfaction in all life domains, and a 9% improvement in job performance—even while working shorter weeks.

(whose average age was about 35), their *satisfaction* increased by an average of 20% in their work lives, 28% in their home lives, and 31% in their community lives. Perhaps most significant, their satisfaction in the domain of the self—their physical and emotional health and their intellectual and spiritual growth—increased by 39%. But they also reported that their *performance* improved: at work (by 9%), at home (15%), in the community (12%), and personally (25%). Paradoxically, these gains were made even as participants spent less time on work and more on other aspects of their lives. They're working smarter—and they're more focused, passionate, and committed to what they're doing.

While hundreds of leaders at all levels go through this program every year, you don't need a workshop to identify worthwhile experiments. The process is pretty straightforward, though not simple. In the sections that follow, I will give you an overview of the process and take you through the basics of designing and implementing experiments to produce four-way wins.

Idea in Practice

Total Leadership helps you mitigate a range of problems that stem from making trade-offs among the different dimensions of your life:

- Feeling **unfulfilled** because you're not doing what you love
- Feeling **inauthentic** because you're not acting according to your values
- Feeling **disconnected** from people who matter to you
- Feeling **exhausted** by trying to keep up with it all

To tackle such problems using Total Leadership, take these steps.

1. Reflect

For each of the four domains of your life—work, home, community, and self, reflect on how important each is to you, how much time and energy you devote to each, and how satisfied you are in each. Are there discrepancies between what is important to you and how you spend your time and energy? What is your overall life satisfaction?

2. Brainstorm Possibilities

Based on the insights you've achieved during your four-way reflection, brainstorm a long list of small experiments that may help you move closer to greater satisfaction in all four domains. These are new ways of doing things that would carry minimal risk and let you see results quickly. For example:

- Turning off cell phones during family dinners could help you sharpen your focus on the people who matter most to you.
- Exercising several times a week could give you more energy.
- Joining a club with coworkers could help you forge closer friendships with them.
- Preparing for the week ahead on Sunday evenings could help you sleep better and go into the new week refreshed.

3. Choose Experiments

Narrow the list of experiments you've brainstormed to the three most promising. They should:

The Total Leadership Process

The Total Leadership concept rests on three principles:

- Be real: Act with authenticity by clarifying what's important.
- Be whole: Act with integrity by respecting the whole person.

- Improve your satisfaction and performance in all four dimensions of your life.
- Have effects viewed as positive by the people who matter to you in every dimension of your life.
- Be the most costly—in regret and missed opportunities—if you *don't* do them.
- Position you to practice skills you most want to develop and do more of what you *want* to be doing.

4. Measure Progress

Develop a scorecard for each experiment you've chosen. For example:

Experiment: Exercise three mornings a week with spouse.

Life dimension	Experiment's goals	How I will measure success	Implementation steps
Work	Improved alertness and productivity	No caffeine to get through the day; more productive sales calls	• Get doctor's feedback on exercise plan. • Join gym. • Set alarm earlier on exercise days. • Tell coworkers, family, and friends about my plan, how I need their help, and how it will benefit them.
Home	Increased closeness with spouse	Fewer arguments with spouse	
Community	Greater strength to participate in athletic fundraising events with friends	Three 10K fundraising walks completed by end of year	
Self	Improved self-esteem	Greater confidence	

- Be innovative: Act with creativity by experimenting with how things get done.

You begin the process by thinking, writing, and talking with peer coaches to identify your core values, your leadership vision, and the current alignment of your actions and values—clarifying what's important. Peer coaching is enormously valuable, at this stage and throughout, because an outside perspective provides a sounding board for your ideas, challenges you, gives you a fresh way to see the possibilities for innovation, and helps hold you accountable to your commitments.

You then identify the most important people—"key stakeholders"—in all domains and the performance expectations you have of one another. Then you talk with them: If you're like most participants, you'll be surprised to find that what, and how much, your key stakeholders actually need from you is different from, and less than, what you thought beforehand.

These insights create opportunities for you to focus your attention more intelligently, spurring innovative action. Now, with a firmer grounding in what's most important, and a more complete picture of your inner circle, you begin to see new ways of making life better, not just for you but for the people around you.

The next step is to design experiments and then try them out during a controlled period of time. The best experiments are changes that your stakeholders wish for as much as, if not more than, you do.

Designing Experiments

To pursue a four-way win means to produce a change intended to fulfill multiple goals that benefit each and every domain of your life. In the domain of work, typical goals for an experiment can be captured under these broad headings: taking advantage of new opportunities for increasing productivity, reducing hidden costs, and improving the work environment. Goals for home and community tend to revolve around improving relationships and contributing more to society. For the self, it's usually about improving health and finding greater meaning in life.

As you think through the goals for your experiment, keep in mind the interests and opinions of your key stakeholders and anyone else who might be affected by the changes you are envisioning. In exploring the idea of joining a community board, for instance, Kenneth Chen sought advice from his boss, who had served on many boards, and also from the company's charitable director and the vice president of talent. In this way, he got their support. His employers could see how his participation on a board would benefit the company by developing Kenneth's leadership skills and his social network.

Some experiments benefit only a single domain directly while having indirect benefits in the others. For example, setting aside three mornings a week to exercise improves your health directly but may indirectly give you more energy for your work and raise your self-esteem, which in turn might make you a better father and friend. Other activities—such as running a half-marathon with your kids to raise funds for a charity sponsored by your company—occur in, and directly benefit, all four domains simultaneously. Whether the benefits are direct or indirect, achieving a four-way win is the goal. That's what makes the changes sustainable: Everyone benefits. The expected gains need not accrue until sometime in the future, so keep in mind that some benefits may not be obvious—far-off career advancements, for instance, or a contact who might ultimately offer valuable connections.

Identify possibilities

Open your mind to what's possible and try to think of as many potential experiments as you can, describing in a sentence or two what you would do in each. This is a time to let your imagination run free. Don't worry about all the potential obstacles at this point.

At first blush, conceiving of experiments that produce benefits for all the different realms may seem a formidable task. After all, if it were easy, people wouldn't be feeling so much tension between work and the rest of their lives. But I've found that most people realize it's not that hard once they approach the challenge systematically. And, like a puzzle, it can be fun, especially if you keep in mind that experiments must fit your particular circumstances. Experiments can and do take myriad forms. But having sifted through hundreds of experiment designs, my research team and I have found that they tend to fall into nine general types. Use the nine categories described in the exhibit "How Can I Design an Experiment to Improve All Domains of My Life?" to organize your thinking.

How can I design an experiment to improve all domains of my life?

Our research has revealed that most successful experiments combine components of nine general categories. Thinking about possibilities in this way will make it easier for you to conceive of the small changes you can make that will mutually benefit your work, your home, your community, and yourself. Most experiments are a hybrid of some combination of these categories.

Tracking and Reflecting

Keeping a record of activities, thoughts, and feelings (and perhaps distributing it to friends, family, and coworkers) to assess progress on personal and professional goals, thereby increasing self-awareness and maintaining priorities.

Examples

- Record visits to the gym along with changes in energy levels
- Track the times of day when you feel most engaged or most lethargic

Planning and Organizing

Taking actions designed to better use time and prepare and plan for the future.

Examples

- Use a PDA for all activities, not just work
- Share your schedule with someone else
- Prepare for the week on Sunday evening

Rejuvenating and Restoring

Attending to body, mind, and spirit so that the tasks of daily living and working are undertaken with renewed power, focus, and commitment.

Examples

- Quit unhealthy physical habits (smoking, drinking)
- Make time for reading a novel
- Engage in activities that improve emotional and spiritual health (yoga, meditation, etc.)

Appreciating and Caring

Having fun with people (typically, by doing things with coworkers outside work), caring for others, and appreciating relationships as a way of bonding at a basic human level to respect the whole person, which increases trust.

Examples

- Join a book group or health club with coworkers
- Help your son complete his homework
- Devote one day a month to community service

Focusing and Concentrating

Being physically present, psychologically present, or both when needed to pay attention to stakeholders who matter most. Sometimes this means saying no to opportunities or obligations. Includes attempts to show more respect to important people encountered in different domains and the need to be accessible to them.

Examples

- Turn off digital communication devices at a set time
- Set aside a specific time to focus on one thing or person
- Review e-mail at preset times during the day

Revealing and Engaging

Sharing more of yourself with others—and listening—so they can better support your values and the steps you want to take toward your leadership vision. By enhancing communication about different aspects of life, you demonstrate respect for the whole person.

Examples

- Have weekly conversations about religion with spouse
- Describe your vision to others
- Mentor a new employee

Time Shifting and "Re-Placing"

Working remotely or during different hours to increase flexibility and thus better fit in community, family, and personal activities while increasing efficiency; questioning traditional assumptions and trying new ways to get things done.

Examples

- Work from home
- Take music lessons during your lunch hour
- Do work during your commute

Delegating and Developing

Reallocating tasks in ways that increase trust, free up time, and develop skills in yourself and others; working smarter by reducing or eliminating low-priority activities.

(continued)

Examples

- Hire a personal assistant
- Have a subordinate take on some of your responsibilities

Exploring and Venturing

Taking steps toward a new job, career, or other activity that better aligns your work, home, community, and self with your core values and aspirations.

Examples

- Take on new roles at work, such as a cross-functional assignment
- Try a new coaching style
- Join the board of your child's day care center

One category of experiment involves changes in where and when work gets done. One workshop participant, a sales director for a global cement producer, tried working online from his local public library one day a week to free himself from his very long commute. This was a break from a company culture that didn't traditionally support employees working remotely, but the change benefited everyone. He had more time for outside interests, and he was more engaged and productive at work.

Another category has to do with regular self-reflection. As an example, you might keep a record of your activities, thoughts, and feelings over the course of a month to see how various actions influence your performance and quality of life. Still another category focuses on planning and organizing your time—such as trying out a new technology that coordinates commitments at work with those in the other domains.

Conversations about work and the rest of life tend to emphasize segmentation: How do I shut out the office when I am with my family? How can I eliminate distractions and concentrate purely on work? But, in some cases, it might be better to make boundaries between domains more permeable, not thicker. The very technologies that make it hard for us to maintain healthy boundaries among domains also enable us to blend them in ways—unfathomable even a decade ago—that can render us more productive and more fulfilled. These tools give us choices. The challenge we all face is learning how to use them wisely, and smart experiments give you an opportunity to increase your skill in doing so. The main point is to identify possibilities that will work well in your unique situation.

All effective experiments require that you question traditional assumptions about how things get done, as the sales director did. It's easier to feel free to do this, and to take innovative action, when you know that your goal is to improve performance in all domains and that you'll be gathering data about the impact of your experiment to determine if indeed it is working—for your key stakeholders and for you.

Whatever type you choose, the most useful experiments feel like something of a stretch: not too easy, not too daunting. It might be something quite mundane for someone else, but that doesn't matter. What's critical is that *you* see it as a moderately difficult challenge.

Choose a few, get started, and adapt

Coming up with possibilities is an exercise in unbounded imagination. But when it comes time to take action, it's not practical to try out more than three experiments at once. Typically, two turn out to be relatively successful and one goes haywire, so you will earn some small wins, and learn something useful about leadership, without biting off more than you can chew. Now the priority is to narrow the list to the three most-promising candidates by reviewing which will:

- Give you the best overall return on your investment
- Be the most costly in regret and missed opportunities if you don't do it
- Allow you to practice the leadership skills you most want to develop
- Be the most fun by involving more of what you want to be doing
- Move you furthest toward your vision of how you want to lead your life

Once you choose and begin to move down the road with your experiment, however, be prepared to adapt to the unforeseen. Don't become too wedded to the details of any one experiment's plan, because you will at some point be surprised and need to adjust. An executive I'll call Lim, for example, chose as one experiment to run the Chicago Marathon. He had been feeling out of shape, which in turn diminished his energy and focus both at work and at home. His wife, Joanne, was pregnant with their first child and initially supported the plan because she believed that the focus required by the training and the physical outlet it provided would make Lim a better father. The family also had a strong tradition of athleticism, and Joanne herself was an accomplished athlete. Lim was training with his boss and other colleagues, and all agreed that it would be a healthy endeavor that would improve professional communication (as they thought there would be plenty of time to bond during training).

But as her delivery date approached, Joanne became apprehensive, which she expressed to Lim as concern that he might get injured. Her real concern, though, was that he was spending so much time on an activity that might drain his energy at a point when the family needed him most. One adjustment that Lim made to reassure Joanne of his commitment to their family was to initiate another experiment in which he took the steps needed to allow him to work at home on Thursday afternoons. He had to set up some new technologies and agree to send a monthly memo to his boss summarizing what he was accomplishing on those afternoons. He also bought a baby sling, which would allow him to keep his new son with him while at home.

In the end, not only were Joanne and their baby on hand to cheer Lim on while he ran the marathon, but she ended up joining him for the second half of the race to give him a boost when she saw his energy flagging. His business unit's numbers improved during the period when he was training and working at home. So did the unit's morale—people began to see the company as more flexible, and they were encouraged to be more creative in how they got their own work done—and word got around. Executives throughout the firm began to come up with their own ideas for ways to pay more attention to other sides of their employees' lives and so build a stronger sense of community at work.

The investment in a well-designed experiment almost always pays off because you learn how to lead in new and creative ways in all parts of your life. And if your experiments turn out well—as they usually, but not always, do—it will benefit everyone: you, your business, your family, and your community.

Measuring Progress

The only way to fail with an experiment is to fail to learn from it, and this makes useful metrics essential. No doubt it's better to achieve the results you are after than to fall short, but hitting targets does not in itself advance you toward becoming the leader you want to be. Failed experiments give you, and those around you, information that helps create better ones in the future.

The exhibit "How Do I Know If My Experiment Is Working?" shows how Kenneth Chen measured his progress. He used this simple chart to spell out the intended benefits of his experiment in each of the four domains and how he would assess whether he had realized these benefits. To set up your own scorecard, use a separate sheet for each experiment; at the top of the page, write a brief description of it. Then record your goals for each domain in the first column. In the middle column, describe your results metrics: how you will measure whether the goals for each domain have been achieved. In the third column, describe your action metrics—the plan for the steps you will take to implement your experiment. As you begin to implement your plan, you may find that your initial indicators are too broad or too vague, so refine your scorecard as you go along to make it more useful for you. The main point is to have practical ways of measuring your outcomes and your progress toward them, and the approach you take only needs to work for you and your stakeholders.

Workshop participants have used all kinds of metrics: cost savings from reduced travel, number of e-mail misunderstandings averted, degree of satisfaction with family time, hours spent volunteering at a

How do I know if my experiment is working?

Using this tool, an executive I'll call Kenneth Chen systematically set out in detail his various goals, the metrics he would use to measure his progress, and the steps he would take in conducting an experiment that would further those goals—joining the board of a nonprofit organization. Kenneth's work sheet is merely an example: Every person's experiments, goals, and metrics are unique.

A Sample Scorecard

	EXPERIMENT'S GOALS	HOW I WILL MEASURE SUCCESS	IMPLEMENTATION STEPS
Work	▶ To fulfill the expectation that executives will give back to the local community ▶ To establish networks with other officers in my company and other professionals in the area ▶ To learn leadership skills from other board members and from the organization I join	▶ Collect business cards from everyone I meet on the board and during board meetings, and keep track of the number of professionals I meet ▶ After each meeting, regularly record the leadership skills of those I would like to emulate	☐ Meet with my manager, who has sat on many boards and can provide support and advice ☐ Meet with the director of my company's foundation to determine my real interests and to help assess what relationship our firm has with various community organizations
Home	▶ To join a board that can involve my fiancée, Celine ▶ To have something to discuss with my sister (a special-education instructor)	▶ See whether Celine gets involved in the board ▶ Record the number of conversations my sister and I have about community service for the next three months and see whether they have brought us closer	☐ Discuss my course of action with my fiancée and see whether joining a board interests her ☐ Sign up to attend the December 15 overview session of the Business on Board program ☐ Assess different opportunities within the community and then reach out to organizations I'm interested in

Community	▶ To provide my leadership skills to a nonprofit organization ▶ To get more involved in giving back to the community	▶ Record what I learn about each nonprofit organization I research ▶ Record the number of times I attend board meetings	☐ Apply for membership to a community board
Self	▶ To feel good about contributing to others' welfare ▶ To see others grow as a result of my efforts ▶ To become more compassionate	▶ Assess how I feel about myself in a daily journal ▶ Assess the effect I have on others in terms of potential number of people affected ▶ Ask for feedback from others about whether I've become more compassionate	

teen center, and so on. Metrics may be objective or subjective, qualitative or quantitative, reported by you or by others, and frequently or intermittently observed. When it comes to frequency, for instance, it helps to consider how long you'll be able to remember what you did. For example, if you were to go on a diet to get healthier, increase energy, and enhance key relationships, food intake would be an important metric. But would you be able to remember what you ate two days ago?

Small Wins for Big Change

Experiments shouldn't be massive, all-encompassing shifts in the way you live. Highly ambitious designs usually fail because they're too much to handle. The best experiments let you try something new while minimizing the inevitable risks associated with change. When the stakes are smaller, it's easier to overcome the fear of failure that inhibits innovation. You start to see results, and others take note, which both inspires you to go further and builds support from your key stakeholders.

Another benefit of the small-wins approach to experiments is that it opens doors that would otherwise be closed. You can say to people invested in the decision, "Let's just try this. If it doesn't work, we'll go back to the old way or try something different." By framing an experiment as a trial, you reduce resistance because people are more likely to try something new if they know it's not permanent and if they have control over deciding whether the experiment is working according to *their* performance expectations.

But "small" is a relative term—what might look like a small step for you could seem like a giant leap to me, and vice versa. So don't get hung up on the word. What's more, this isn't about the scope or importance of the changes you eventually make. Large-scale change is grounded in small steps toward a big idea. So while the steps in an experiment might be small, the goals are not. Ismail, a successful 50-year-old entrepreneur and CEO of an engineering services company, described the goal for his first experiment this way: "Restructure my company and my role in it." There's nothing small about that. He felt he was missing a sense of purpose.

Ismail designed practical steps that would allow him to move toward his large goal over time. His first experiments were small and achievable. He introduced a new method that both his colleagues and his wife could use to communicate with him. He began to hold sacrosanct time for his family and his church. As he looked for ways to free up more time, he initiated delegation experiments that had the effect of flattening his organization's structure. These small wins crossed over several domains, and eventually he did indeed transform his company and his own role in it. When I spoke with him 18 months after he'd started, he acknowledged that he'd had a hard time coping with the loss of control over tactical business matters, but he described his experiments as "a testament to the idea of winning the small battles and letting the war be won as a result." He and his leadership team both felt more confident about the firm's new organizational structure.

People try the Total Leadership program for a variety of reasons. Some feel unfulfilled because they're not doing what they love. Some don't feel genuine because they're not acting according to their values. Others feel disconnected, isolated from people who matter to them. They crave stronger relationships, built on trust, and yearn for enriched social networks. Still others are just in a rut. They want to tap into their creative energy but don't know how (and sometimes lack the courage) to do so. They feel out of control and unable to fit in all that's important to them.

My hunch is that there are more four-way wins available to you than you'd think. They are there for the taking. You have to know how to look for them and then find the support and zeal to pursue them. By providing a blueprint for how you can be real, be whole, and be innovative as a leader in all parts of your life, this program helps you perform better according to the standards of the most important people in your life; feel better in all the domains of your life;

and foster greater harmony among the domains by increasing the resources available to you to fit all the parts of your life together. No matter what your career stage or current position, you can be a better leader and have a richer life—if you are ready and willing to rise to the challenge.

Originally published in April 2008. Reprint R0804H

Reclaim Your Job

by Sumantra Ghoshal and Heike Bruch

ASK MOST MANAGERS WHAT GETS in the way of success at work, and you hear the familiar litany of complaints: Not enough time. Shrinking resources. Lack of opportunity. When you look more closely, you begin to see that these are, for the most part, excuses. What gets in the way of managers' success is something much more personal—a deep uncertainty about acting according to their own best judgment. Rather than doing what they really need to do to advance the company's fortunes—and their own careers—they spin their wheels doing what they presume everyone else wants them to do.

Over the past five years, we have studied hundreds of managers as they have gone about their daily work in a variety of settings, including a global airline and a large U.S. oil company. As we demonstrated in "Beware the Busy Manager" (HBR February 2002), fully 90% of the managers we observed wasted their time and frittered away their productivity, despite having well-defined projects, goals, and the knowledge necessary to get their jobs done. Such managers remain trapped in inefficiency because they simply assume that they do not have enough personal discretion or control. The ability to seize initiative is the most essential quality of any truly successful manager.

In most instances, the demands that managers accept as givens are actually discretionary in nature. We have repeatedly confronted in our research a curious but pervasive reality of corporate life: Most managers complain about having too little freedom in their jobs, while their bosses complain about managers' failure to grasp opportunities. The truly effective managers we've observed are purposeful, trust in their own judgment, and adopt long-term, big-picture views to fulfill personal goals that tally with those of the organization as a whole. They break out of their perceived boxes, take control of their jobs, and become more productive by learning to do the following:

Manage demands

Most managers feel overwhelmed by demands. They assume that the business will come to a crashing halt without them and so allow real or imagined day-to-day work demands to subsume their own judgment. Effective managers proactively control their tasks and the expectations of their major stakeholders, which allows them to meet strategic goals rather than fight fires.

Generate resources

By following what they believe are strict orders from the top, many typical managers tend to concentrate on working within budget and resource constraints—thereby developing a boxed-in, "can't do" mind-set. By contrast, effective managers develop inventive strategies for circumventing real or imagined limitations. They map out ways around constraints by developing and acting on long-term strategies, making trade-offs, and occasionally breaking rules to achieve their goals.

Recognize and exploit alternatives

Average managers don't have enough perspective on the company's overall business strategy to present an alternative view. Effective managers, by contrast, develop and use deep expertise about an individual area that dovetails with the company's strategy. This tactic allows them to come up with a variety of innovative approaches to a given situation.[1]

In short, truly effective managers don't operate in the context of individual tasks or jobs but in the much broader context of their organizations and careers. That approach sounds simple enough, but it is sometimes hard to act on because some organizational cultures that

Idea in Brief

90% of managers waste time and fritter away their productivity by grappling with an endless list of demands from others. Why? We assume—wrongly—that those demands are *requirements*, and that we lack personal discretion or control over our jobs. The consequence? We remain trapped in inefficiency.

But we can escape this trap—if we learn how to grasp opportunities, trust our own judgment, and methodically fulfill personal goals that tally with our organizations' objectives. The keys? Set priorities—then stick to them, focusing on efforts that support those priorities. Overcome resource constraints by attacking goals strategically, demonstrating success at every step. And develop a range of alternatives to exploit when plan A fails.

We all want to make a difference in our organizations, as well as build satisfying careers. By understanding how we inhibit ourselves and taking purposeful, strategic action, we can seize control of our jobs—rather than letting our jobs control us. The payoff? Impressive results for our companies and rewarding work lives for us.

tout "empowerment" actually discourage volition among their managers. Young, high-tech companies, for example, sometimes hold their managers hostage to frenzy, thus inhibiting the reflective and persistent pursuit of long-term goals. Other cultures—particularly those of old and established corporations with command-and-control hierarchies—can encourage people to go along with the status quo, regardless of the level of organizational dysfunction. In both kinds of environments, managers tend to fall into a reactive state of mind, assuming that any initiative they show will be either ignored or discouraged.

In most cases, however, it is not the environment that inhibits managers from taking purposeful action. Rather, it is managers themselves. We have found that managers can learn to act on their own potential and make a difference. Here's how.

Dealing with Demands

Almost everyone complains about not having enough time to deal with all the demands on them, but, in reality, a highly fragmented

Idea in Practice

To reclaim your job and better support your company's priorities, apply three strategies.

Prioritize Demands

To achieve personal and organizational goals quickly, *slow down* and focus your time and attention.

Example: McKinsey associate principal Jessica Spungin took on too many projects that had little connection to her skills and interests. Result? Her project teams rated her second from the bottom among her peers.

Realizing her desire to be indispensable sprang from lack of confidence, Spungin took steps to manage demands. She clarified her goal: to become a partner. Then she set long-term priorities supporting that goal. She began managing her own development; for example, choosing assignments that most interested her. And she started orchestrating her time, meeting only with people who really needed her and working on long-term projects during months when she traveled less.

Her reward? She scored second from the top in her peer group—and was named a McKinsey partner.

Liberate Resources

To relax resource constraints and win the backing you want, attack your goals strategically. Be patient. The process can take years.

Example: As the new head of HR development at airline Lufthansa, Thomas Sattelberger dreamed of launching Germany's first corporate business school. Knowing he needed several years to establish his credibility, he first overhauled inefficient HR processes. He then developed

day is also a very lazy day. It can seem easier to fight fires than to set priorities and stick to them. The truth is that managers who carefully set boundaries and priorities achieve far more than busy ones do.

To beat the busy habit, managers must overcome the psychological desire to be indispensable. Because their work is interactive and interdependent, most managers thrive on their sense of importance to others. When they are not worrying about meeting their superiors' (or their clients') expectations, they fret about their direct reports, often falling victim to the popular fallacy that good bosses

initiatives supporting the school, raising money for these projects by presenting compelling facts and arguments to his counterparts and CEO.

After four years of methodical work on Sattelberger's part, Lufthansa's CEO and board understood how his programs fit together. When he wrote a memo to directors requesting creation of the school before Daimler-Benz could beat Lufthansa to the punch, the board promptly approved the request.

Exploit Alternatives

Use your expertise to anticipate—and circumvent—possible obstacles to your goals. You'll expand the scope of opportunity for your company *and* yourself.

Example: Dan Andersson, a manager at oil refiner ConocoPhillips, was part of a team exploring Conoco's entrance into the Finnish market. Conoco decided to store petrol in tanks in Finland that Shell had abandoned. But Andersson developed contingency plans. Plan B, for instance, involved building a new facility.

His efforts paid off. When research revealed the abandoned tanks were unsuitable for petrol storage, Andersson activated Plan B. Though the new-facility target site was contaminated, Andersson discovered that Shell was responsible for cleaning the site. Once cleanup ended, Conoco built the tanks.

Conoco became the most efficient operator of automated self-service filling stations in Finland. Andersson now heads Conoco's retail development in Europe.

always make themselves available. At first, managers—particularly novices—seem to thrive on all this clamoring for their time; the busier they are, the more valuable they feel. Inevitably, however, things start to slip. Eventually, many managers simply burn out and fail, not only because they find little time to pursue their own agendas but also because, in trying to please everyone, they typically end up pleasing no one.

Jessica Spungin found herself caught in this trap when she was promoted to associate principal in McKinsey's London office. As an AP, a consultant is expected to take on more responsibilities of the partnership group, juggle multiple projects, serve as a team leader, and play an active role in office life. Spungin dove in to all these tasks headfirst. While she was handling two major client projects, she was asked to jointly lead recruitment for U.K. universities and business schools, participate in an internal research initiative, serve as a senior coach for six business analysts, run an office party for 750 people, get involved in internal training, and help out on a new project for a health care company.

In her first round of feedback from the three project teams she oversaw, she was rated second from the bottom among her peers. Spungin realized that her desire to be indispensable sprang from a lack of confidence. "I never said no to people in case they thought I couldn't cope. I never said no to a client who wanted me to be present at a meeting," she told us. "I did what I thought was expected—regardless of what I was good at, what was important, or what I could physically do."

The first step in Spungin's transformation from a busy to an effective manager was to develop a vision of what she really wanted to achieve at McKinsey: to be named a partner. In developing a clear mental picture of herself in that role, she traded in her habit of thinking in short time spans of three to six months to thinking in strategic time spans of one to five years.

This longer-term planning allowed Spungin to develop a set of long-term goals and priorities. Soon, she took control of her own development. For example, it became clear to Spungin that corporate banking—which her colleagues believed to be her area of expertise based on her past experience—did not hold any real interest for her, even though she had accepted one banking project after another. Instead, she decided to shift her focus to the organizational practice, something she really enjoyed. (McKinsey, like many companies, allows its consultants significant flexibility in terms of choosing assignments, but most managers do not avail themselves of this opportunity.) By claiming a personal agenda and integrating short-, medium-, and long-term responsibilities into her broader master plan, Spungin felt much more motivated and excited about her work than she had when she was merely responding to everyday demands.

Finally, Spungin took charge of her time. She realized that trying to be accessible to everyone made her inaccessible to those who really needed her. She began prioritizing the time she spent with clients and team members. With her personal assistant's help, she streamlined her work. Previously, her assistant would schedule meetings in an ad hoc manner. Now, Spungin drove the calendar, so she could make the calls about which meetings she needed to attend. She began to recognize patterns of work intensity according to the time of year; for example, she travelled less in the fall, so Spungin set aside half a day each week to work on her long-term projects then. In the end, Spungin realized the irony of effective management: To quickly achieve the goals that mattered, she had to slow down and take control. To her surprise, the people who reported to her, as well as her supervisors and clients, responded well to her saying no.

Spungin was better able to respond to and shape the demands she chose to meet once she stopped trying to please everyone. She became more proactive—presenting her own goals and ideas to influence what others expected of her. By focusing on the most important demands, she exceeded expectations. One year after having been rated second from the bottom in her peer group, she scored second from the top. In June 2003, Spungin was named a McKinsey partner.

Developing Resources

In addition to lack of time, many managers complain about a shortage of people, money, and equipment, and a surplus of rules and regulations. They struggle with limited resources. While some feel frustrated and keep beating their heads against a wall to no avail, others just give up. Managers who develop a long-term strategy and attack their goals slowly, steadily, and strategically, on the other hand, can eventually win the backing they want.

Thomas Sattelberger faced all kinds of impossible constraints in 1994 when he left Daimler-Benz to join Lufthansa as the head of corporate management and human resources development. At the time, Lufthansa was in the middle of a strategic cost-savings program that required every unit to reduce its total expenditures by 4% each year for the next five years. Employees generally interpreted the cost-cutting directive to mean that investing in anything other than what was necessary to keep the lights on was verboten. Additionally, Lufthansa's HR processes were a mess; responses to routine requests often took months, and contracts frequently contained typographical errors. These kinds of operational problems had existed in the department for years.

For most managers in Sattelberger's position, the goals would have been simple: Get the HR department to a functional level without increasing costs, make sure it doesn't backslide, and collect a paycheck. But Sattelberger had much higher aspirations. He had come to Lufthansa with the dream of building Germany's most progressive corporate human resources organization, which would help transform the formerly state-operated company into a world-class airline. Specifically, he envisioned starting Germany's first corporate university, the Lufthansa School of Business, which would extend far beyond traditional approaches to training and development. The university would tighten the links between strategy and organizational and individual development. Its curricula, including master's and nondegree management programs, would be designed, run, and evaluated by academics and leaders from global companies, so Lufthansa's managers would learn from the best.

In pursuing his dream, Sattelberger chose a methodical, clever, and patient mode of attack. First, he created an imaginary blueprint depicting his university as a kind of leadership development temple. The architectural conceit—the temple being built brick by brick and pillar by pillar—helped Sattelberger develop a long-term, strategic implementation plan. Cleaning up basic HR processes, he reasoned, was analogous to laying the foundation. With that accomplished, he would erect a series of development programs, each acting as a pillar that would hold up the "roof" of Lufthansa's overall corporate strategy. Seeing his plan as a blueprint also helped Sattelberger separate the "must-haves" from the "nice-to-haves" and the "can-live-withouts," which enabled him to focus on only the most vital and achievable elements.

Sattelberger understood that he had to be flexible and that building his temple would demand years of methodical work. He never spoke about his vision as a whole because its overall cost would have frightened most of the stakeholders. Instead, he secured their commitment for individual projects and programs and implemented the initiatives sequentially.

Step two was to lay the foundation that he had imagined. Over the course of two years, Sattelberger reorganized HR processes so that requests were met in a timely matter and operations made more efficient. Given the dismal state of Lufthansa's HR systems, no one anticipated that Sattelberger could possibly meet, much less exceed, expectations. He showed them wrong.

Capitalizing on his new credibility, he next set to work on step three: building the individual pillars. One project, Explorer 21, was a comprehensive development initiative in which managers would learn from one another. A separate program, ProTeam, was designed for management trainees. And another large-scale program focused on emulating best practices from companies such as General Electric, Citibank, Deutsche Bank, Daimler-Benz, and SAS.

The spending cap was a significant hurdle. Sattelberger had persuaded top management to allow him to rent out some training rooms to other companies to raise money for these projects, but he needed more. He understood that there was a limit to how far and how fast he could push: If he pressed too hard, a backlash would ensue. So in petitioning for funds, Sattelberger made sure he was better prepared than his counterparts with arguments and facts. When the controller failed to give him the green light, he made his case directly to Jürgen Weber, the CEO. Weber agreed in principle that the corporate university project was worthwhile, although the conversation was not an easy one. "For God's sake, do it," he ended up telling Sattelberger, "but do it right and stick to your budget."

Weber and the board eventually began to see how Sattelberger's development programs fit together. Then, in March 1998—when he learned that Daimler-Benz was about to beat Lufthansa to the punch with a corporate university of its own—Sattelberger made his final move. Determined not to let Daimler prevail, he wrote a memo requesting the creation of the Lufthansa School of Business to the board of directors. It approved the request without a moment's hesitation or debate, and Lufthansa opened Europe's first corporate university the following month.

The whole process took time, something purposeful managers, as we have shown previously, claim for themselves. Sattelberger coped with many setbacks and accepted significant delays and even cancellations of different aspects of his initiative. He delayed his plans for the corporate university for the first two years so he could focus solely on putting HR in order. Then, slowly and progressively, he worked to relax resource constraints. Although he started with much less than he expected, he never allowed his resolve to wither. Lufthansa has never measured the precise payback from its school of business, but the subjective judgment of top management is that the return has been much higher than the investment.

Exploiting Alternatives

When it comes to making decisions or pursuing initiatives, managers also fall victim to the trap of unexplored choices. Specifically, they either do not recognize that they have choices or do not take advantage of those they know they have. Because managers ignore their freedom to act, they surrender their options. Purposeful initiators, by contrast, hone their personal expertise, which confers confidence, a wide perspective of a particular arena, and greater credibility. These managers develop the ability to see, grasp, and fight for opportunities as they arise.

Dan Andersson was a midlevel manager who worked for the oil-refining company ConocoPhillips in Stockholm. As a native of Finland, he brought to Conoco a precious managerial commodity: deep knowledge of the Finnish market. This knowledge enabled him to convey information about specific regional conditions to senior managers, who did not speak the language or understand Finland's business issues. Because he had been mentored by the managing director of Conoco's Nordic operations, Andersson quickly grasped how the managerial invisibles—informal rules and norms, decision-making processes, interpersonal relationships, and social dynamics—influenced the reception of new ideas. He intuitively sensed the right way to present a proposal and the extent to which he could push at a particular point of time.

Andersson was assigned to a team charged with exploring Conoco's possible entrance into the Finnish market, which involved breaking a 50-year monopoly in the region. The first task was to set up storage facilities in Finland, an estimated $1 million project that would allow Conoco to import its own petrol. After several months of intense searching, the team eventually found an existing tank terminal, located in the city of Turku, that Shell had abandoned decades previously. Built in the 1920s, the old tanks appeared to be clean and usable. The Conoco team thought the solution had been found. In the back of his mind, however, Andersson was already at work on contingency plans. Plan B was to build a new facility, plan C was to create a joint venture with a competitor, and plan D was to find an investor for the tanks.

After months of negotiation, Turku's officials approved Conoco's lease of the old tanks. Then came the fateful phone call from Conoco's laboratory: There was too much carbon in the steel; the tanks were unsuitable for storing petrol. Without its own storage facility, Conoco could not enter the Finnish market. There was no other facility in the country that Conoco could buy. Abandoning the project seemed the only choice. Everyone on the team gave up except Andersson, who proposed putting plan B into action.

With the support of the local authorities, he persuaded the Conoco senior team to visit Finland for face-to-face discussions about the possibility of Conoco building its own tanks at the site. Once Andersson's boss saw the land and sensed the opportunity, he grew enthusiastic about a ground-up approach. As it happened, however, the land was contaminated; cleanup would have cost tens of millions of euros. Still, Andersson persisted. Working with city officials, he discovered the original contracts clearly showed that Shell was responsible for the cleanup of the land. Once the cleanup was complete, Conoco began work on the new tanks. When the first Conoco ship arrived at the harbor, three years after the project had begun, city representatives, hundreds of spectators, Finnish television crews, and Conoco's top management were present to celebrate. Today, Conoco is the most efficient operator of automated self-service filling stations in Finland.

As a manager, Andersson's allegiance was not merely to a job but to accomplishing, one way or another, the strategic goals of his company. By scanning the environment for possible obstacles and searching for ways around them, he was able to expand his company's, and his own, scope of opportunity. Today, he is responsible for ConocoPhillips' retail development in Europe.

A bias for action is not a special gift of a few. Most managers can develop this capacity. Spungin's story demonstrates how focusing on a clear, long-term goal widened her horizon. Sattelberger and Andersson countered limitations with plans of their own and showed their companies what was possible.

In our studies of managers, we have found that the difference between those who take the initiative and those who do not becomes particularly evident during phases of major change, when managerial work becomes relatively chaotic and unstructured. Managers who fret about conforming to the explicit or imagined expectations of others respond to lack of structure by becoming disoriented and paralyzed. Effective managers, by contrast, seize the opportunity to extend the scope of their jobs, expand their choices, and pursue ambitious goals.

Once managers command their agendas and sense their own freedom of choice, they come to relish their roles. They begin to search for situations that go beyond their scope and enjoy seizing opportunities as they arise. Above all, effective managers with a bias for action aren't managed by their jobs; rather, the reverse is true.

Originally published in March 2004. Reprint R0403B

Note

1. The framework of demands, constraints, and choices as a way to think about managerial jobs was first suggested by Rosemary Stewart in her book *Managers and Their Jobs* (Macmillan, 1967). See also Rosemary Stewart, *Choices for the Manager* (Prentice Hall, 1982).

Moments of Greatness

Entering the Fundamental State of Leadership.

by Robert E. Quinn

A

AS LEADERS, SOMETIMES we're truly "on," and sometimes we're not. Why is that? What separates the episodes of excellence from those of mere competence? In striving to tip the balance toward excellence, we try to identify great leaders' qualities and behaviors so we can develop them ourselves. Nearly all corporate training programs and books on leadership are grounded in the assumption that we should study the behaviors of those who have been successful and teach people to emulate them.

But my colleagues and I have found that when leaders do their best work, they don't copy anyone. Instead, they draw on their own fundamental values and capabilities—operating in a frame of mind that is true to them yet, paradoxically, not their normal state of being. I call it the *fundamental state of leadership*. It's the way we lead when we encounter a crisis and finally choose to move forward. Think back to a time when you faced a significant life challenge: a promotion opportunity, the risk of professional failure, a serious illness, a divorce, the death of a loved one, or any other major jolt. Most likely, if you made decisions not to meet others' expectations but to suit what you instinctively understood to be right—in other words, if you were at your very best—you rose to the task because you were being tested.

Is it possible to enter the fundamental state of leadership without crisis? In my work coaching business executives, I've found that if we ask ourselves—and honestly answer—just four questions, we can make the shift at any time. It's a temporary state. Fatigue and external resistance pull us out of it. But each time we reach it, we return to our everyday selves a bit more capable, and we usually elevate the performance of the people around us as well. Over time, we all can become more effective leaders by deliberately choosing to enter the fundamental state of leadership rather than waiting for crisis to force us there.

Defining the Fundamental State

Even those who are widely admired for their seemingly easy and natural leadership skills—presidents, prime ministers, CEOs—do not usually function in the fundamental state of leadership. Most of the time, they are in their normal state—a healthy and even necessary condition under many circumstances, but not one that's conducive to coping with crisis. In the normal state, people tend to stay within their comfort zones and allow external forces to direct their behaviors and decisions. They lose moral influence and often rely on rational argument and the exercise of authority to bring about change. Others comply with what these leaders ask, out of fear, but the result is usually unimaginative and incremental—and largely reproduces what already exists.

To elevate the performance of others, we must elevate ourselves into the fundamental state of leadership. Getting there requires a shift along four dimensions. (See the exhibit "There's Normal, and There's Fundamental.")

First, we move from being comfort centered to being results centered. The former feels safe but eventually leads to a sense of languishing and meaninglessness. In his book *The Path of Least Resistance,* Robert Fritz carefully explains how asking a single question can move us from the normal, reactive state to a much more generative condition. That question is this: What result do I want to

Idea in Brief

Like all leaders, sometimes you're "on," and sometimes you're not. How to tip the scale toward excellence and away from mere competence? Don't rely on imitating other leaders or poring over leadership manuals. Instead, enter the **fundamental state of leadership**: the way you lead when a crisis forces you to tap into your deepest values and instincts. In this state, you instinctively know what to do: You rise to the occasion and perform at your best.

Fortunately, you don't need a crisis to shift into the fundamental state of leadership. You can do so any time (before a crucial conversation, during a key meeting) by asking four questions:

- **"Am I results centered?"** Have you articulated the result you want to create?
- **"Am I internally directed?"** Are you willing to challenge others' expectations?
- **"Am I other focused?"** Have you put your organization's needs above your own?
- **"Am I externally open?"** Do you recognize signals suggesting the need for change?

No one can operate at the top of their game 24/7. But each time you enter the fundamental state of leadership, you make it easier to return to that state again. And you inspire others around you to higher levels of excellence.

create? Giving an honest answer pushes us off nature's path of least resistance. It leads us from problem solving to purpose finding.

Second, we move from being externally directed to being more internally directed. That means that we stop merely complying with others' expectations and conforming to the current culture. To become more internally directed is to clarify our core values and increase our integrity, confidence, and authenticity. As we become more confident and more authentic, we behave differently. Others must make sense of our new behavior. Some will be attracted to it, and some will be offended by it. That's not prohibitive, though: When we are true to our values, we are willing to initiate such conflict.

Third, we become less self-focused and more focused on others. We put the needs of the organization as a whole above our own. Few among us would admit that personal needs trump the collective

Idea in Practice

To enter the fundamental state of leadership, apply these steps:

1. **Recognize you've already been there.** You've faced great challenges before and, in surmounting them, you entered the fundamental state. By recalling these moments' lessons, you release positive emotions and see new possibilities for your current situation.
2. **Analyze your current state.** Compare your normal performance with what you've done at your very best. You'll fuel a desire to elevate what you're doing now and instill confidence that you can reenter the fundamental state.
3. **Ask the four questions shown in the following chart.**

BY ASKING . . .	YOU SHIFT FROM . . .	TO . . .
Am I results centered?	Remaining in your comfort zone and solving familiar problems	Moving toward possibilities that don't yet exist
Am I internally directed?	Complying with others' expectations and conforming to existing conditions	Clarifying your core values, acting with authenticity and confidence, and willingly initiating productive conflict
Am I other focused?	Allowing pursuit of your own self-interest to shape your relationships	Committing to the collective good in your organization—even at personal cost

good, but the impulse to control relationships in a way that feeds our own interests is natural and normal. That said, self-focus over time leads to feelings of isolation. When we put the collective good first, others reward us with their trust and respect. We form tighter, more sensitive bonds. Empathy increases, and cohesion follows. We create an enriched sense of community, and that helps us transcend the conflicts that are a necessary element in high-performing organizations.

Am I externally open?	Controlling your environment, making incremental changes, and relying on established routines	Learning from your environment, acknowledging the need for major change, and departing from routines

Example: John Jones, a successful change leader, had turned around two struggling divisions in his corporation. Promised the presidency of the largest division when the incumbent retired, he was told meanwhile to bide his time overseeing a dying division's "funeral." He determined to turn the division around. After nine months, though, he'd seen little improvement. Employees weren't engaged.

To enter the fundamental state, John asked:

- **"Am I results oriented?"** He suddenly envisioned a new strategy for his struggling division, along with a plan (including staff reassignments) for implementing it. With a clear, compelling strategy in mind, his energy soared.
- **"Am I internally directed?"** He realized that his focus on the promised plum job had prevented him from doing the hard work needed to motivate his division's people to give more.
- **"Am I other focused?"** He decided to turn down the presidency in favor of rescuing his failing division—a course truer to his leadership values. He thus traded personal security for a greater good.
- **"Am I externally open?"** He stopped deceiving himself into thinking he'd done all he could for his failing division and realized he had the capacity to improve things.

Fourth, we become more open to outside signals or stimuli, including those that require us to do things we are not comfortable doing. In the normal state, we pay attention to signals that we know to be relevant. If they suggest incremental adjustments, we respond. If, however, they call for more dramatic changes, we may adopt a posture of defensiveness and denial; this mode of self-protection and self-deception separates us from the ever-changing external world. We live according to an outdated, less valid, image of what is

There's normal, and there's fundamental

Under everyday circumstances, leaders can remain in their normal state of being and do what they need to do. But some challenges require a heightened perspective—what can be called the fundamental state of leadership. Here's how the two states differ.

In the normal state, I am . . .	In the fundamental state, I am . . .
COMFORT CENTERED I stick with what I know.	RESULTS CENTERED I venture beyond familiar territory to pursue ambitious new outcomes.
EXTERNALLY DIRECTED I comply with others' wishes in an effort to keep the peace.	INTERNALLY DIRECTED I behave according to my values.
SELF-FOCUSED I place my interests above those of the group.	OTHER FOCUSED I put the collective good first.
INTERNALLY CLOSED I block out external stimuli in order to stay on task and avoid risk.	EXTERNALLY OPEN I learn from my environment and recognize when there's a need for change.

real. But in the fundamental state of leadership, we are more aware of what is unfolding, and we generate new images all the time. We are adaptive, credible, and unique. In this externally open state, no two people are alike.

These four qualities—being results centered, internally directed, other focused, and externally open—are at the heart of positive human influence, which is generative and attractive. A person without these four characteristics can also be highly influential, but his or her influence tends to be predicated on some form of control or force, which does not usually give rise to committed followers. By entering the fundamental state of leadership, we increase the likelihood of attracting others to an elevated level of community, a high-performance state that may continue even when we are not present.

Preparing for the Fundamental State

Because people usually do not leave their comfort zones unless forced, many find it helpful to follow a process when they choose to enter the fundamental state of leadership. I teach a technique to executives and use it in my own work. It simply involves asking four awareness-raising questions designed to help us transcend our natural denial mechanisms. When people become aware of their hypocrisies, they are more likely to change. Those who are new to the "fundamental state" concept, however, need to take two preliminary steps before they can understand and employ it.

Step 1: Recognize that you have previously entered the fundamental state of leadership

Every reader of this publication has reached, at one time or another, the fundamental state of leadership. We've all faced a great personal or professional challenge and spent time in the dark night of the soul. In successfully working through such episodes, we inevitably enter the fundamental state of leadership.

When I introduce people to this concept, I ask them to identify two demanding experiences from their past and ponder what happened in terms of intention, integrity, trust, and adaptability. At first, they resist the exercise because I am asking them to revisit times of great personal pain. But as they recount their experiences, they begin to see that they are also returning to moments of greatness. Our painful experiences often bring out our best selves. Recalling the lessons of such moments releases positive emotions and makes it easier to see what's possible in the present. In this exercise, I ask people to consider their behavior during these episodes in relation to the characteristics of the fundamental state of leadership. (See the exhibit "You've Already Been There" for analyses of two actual episodes.)

Sometimes I also ask workshop participants to share their stories with one another. Naturally, they are reluctant to talk about such dark moments. To help people open up, I share my own moments of great challenge, the ones I would normally keep to myself. By exhibiting

You've already been there

Two participants in a leadership workshop at the University of Michigan's Ross School of Business used this self-assessment tool to figure out how they've transcended their greatest life challenges by entering the fundamental state of leadership. You can use the same approach in analyzing how you've conquered your most significant challenges.

	PARTICIPANT A	**PARTICIPANT B**
The pivotal crisis:	I was thrust into a job that was crucial to the organization but greatly exceeded my capabilities. I had to get people to do things they did not want to do.	I was driving myself hard at work, and things kept getting worse at home. Finally my wife told me she wanted a divorce.
How did you become more results centered?	I kept trying to escape doing what was required, but I could not stand the guilt. I finally decided I had to change. I envisioned what success might look like, and I committed to making whatever changes were necessary.	I felt I'd lost everything: family, wealth, and stature. I withdrew from relationships. I started drinking heavily. I finally sought professional help for my sorrow and, with guidance, clarified my values and made choices about my future.
How did you become more internally directed?	I stopped worrying so much about how other people would evaluate and judge me. I was starting to operate from my own values. I felt more self-empowered than ever and realized how fear driven I had been.	I engaged in a lot of self-reflection and journal writing. It became clear that I was not defined by marriage, wealth, or stature. I was more than that. I began to focus on how I could make a difference for other people. I got more involved in my community.
How did you become more focused on others?	I realized how much I needed people, and I became more concerned about them. I was better able to hear what they were saying. I talked not just from my head but also from my heart. My colleagues responded. Today, I am still close to those people.	As I started to grow and feel more self-confident, I became better at relating. At work, I now ask more of people than I ever did before, but I also give them far more support. I care about them, and they can tell.
How did you becom more externally open?	I experimented with new approaches. They often did not work, but they kept the brainstorming in motion. I paid attention to every kind of feedback. I was hungry to get it right. There was a lot of discovery. Each step forward was exhilarating.	I began to feel stronger. I was less intimidated when people gave me negative feedback. I think it was because I was less afraid of changing and growing.

vulnerability, I'm able to win the group's trust and embolden other people to exercise the same courage. I recently ran a workshop with a cynical group of executives. After I broke the testimonial ice, one of the participants told us of a time when he had accepted a new job that required him to relocate his family. Just before he was to start, his new boss called in a panic, asking him to cut his vacation short and begin work immediately. The entire New England engineering team had quit; clients in the region had no support whatsoever. The executive started his job early, and his family had to navigate the move without his help. He described the next few months as "the worst and best experience" of his life.

Another executive shared that he'd found out he had cancer the same week he was promoted and relocated to Paris, not knowing how to speak French. His voice cracked as he recalled these stressful events. But then he told us about the good that came out of them—how he conquered both the disease and the job while also becoming a more authentic and influential leader.

Others came forward with their own stories, and I saw a great change in the group. The initial resistance and cynicism began to disappear, and participants started exploring the fundamental state of leadership in a serious way. They saw the power in the concept and recognized that hiding behind their pride or reputation would only get in the way of future progress. In recounting their experiences, they came to realize that they had become more purposive, authentic, compassionate, and responsive.

Step 2: Analyze your current state

When we're in the fundamental state, we take on various positive characteristics, such as clarity of vision, self-empowerment, empathy, and creative thinking. (See the exhibit "Are You in the Fundamental State of Leadership?" for a checklist organized along the four dimensions.) Most of us would like to say we display these characteristics at all times, but we really do so only sporadically.

Comparing our normal performance with what we have done at our very best often creates a desire to elevate what we are doing now. Knowing we've operated at a higher level in the past instills

Are you in the fundamental state of leadership?

Think of a time when you reached the fundamental state of leadership—that is, when you were at your best as a leader—and use this checklist to identify the qualities you displayed. Then check off the items that describe your behavior today. Compare the past and present. If there's a significant difference, what changes do you need to make to get back to the fundamental state?

At my best I was ...	Today I am ...	
		RESULTS CENTERED
____	____	Knowing what result I'd like to create
____	____	Holding high standards
____	____	Initiating actions
____	____	Challenging people
____	____	Disrupting the status quo
____	____	Capturing people's attention
____	____	Feeling a sense of shared purpose
____	____	Engaging in urgent conversations
		INTERNALLY DIRECTED
____	____	Operating from my core values
____	____	Finding motivation from within
____	____	Feeling self-empowered
____	____	Leading courageously
____	____	Bringing hidden conflicts to the surface
____	____	Expressing what I really believe
____	____	Feeling a sense of shared reality
____	____	Engaging in authentic conversations
		OTHER FOCUSED
____	____	Sacrificing personal interests for the common good
____	____	Seeing the potential in everyone
____	____	Trusting others and fostering interdependence
____	____	Empathizing with people's needs
____	____	Expressing concern
____	____	Supporting people
____	____	Feeling a sense of shared identity
____	____	Engaging in participative conversations

		EXTERNALLY OPEN
___	___	Moving forward into uncertainty
___	___	Inviting feedback
___	___	Paying deep attention to what's unfolding
___	___	Learning exponentially
___	___	Watching for new opportunities
___	___	Growing continually
___	___	Feeling a sense of shared contribution
___	___	Engaging in creative conversations

confidence that we can do so again; it quells our fear of stepping into unknown and risky territory.

Asking Four Transformative Questions

Of course, understanding the fundamental state of leadership and recognizing its power are not the same as being there. Entering that state is where the real work comes in. To get started, we can ask ourselves four questions that correspond with the four qualities of the fundamental state.

To show how each of these qualities affects our behavior while we're in the fundamental state of leadership, I'll draw on stories from two executives. One is a company president; we'll call him John Jones. The other, Robert Yamamoto, is the executive director of the Los Angeles Junior Chamber of Commerce. Both once struggled with major challenges that changed the way they thought about their jobs and their lives.

I met John in an executive course I was teaching. He was a successful change leader who had turned around two companies in his corporation. Yet he was frustrated. He had been promised he'd become president of the largest company in the corporation as soon as the current president retired, which would happen in the near future. In the meantime, he had been told to bide his time with a company that everyone considered dead. His assignment was simply to oversee the funeral, yet he took it as a personal challenge to turn the company around. After he had been there nine months, however, there was little improvement, and the people were still not very engaged.

As for Robert, he had been getting what he considered to be acceptable (if not exceptional) results in his company. So when the new board president asked him to prepare a letter of resignation, Robert was stunned. He underwent a period of anguished introspection, during which he began to distrust others and question his own management skills and leadership ability. Concerned for his family and his future, he started to seek another job and wrote the requested letter.

As you will see, however, even though things looked grim for both Robert and John, they were on the threshold of positive change.

Am I results centered?

Most of the time, we are comfort centered. We try to continue doing what we know how to do. We may think we are pursuing new outcomes, but if achieving them means leaving our comfort zones, we subtly—even unconsciously—find ways to avoid doing so. We typically advocate ambitious outcomes while designing our work for maximum administrative convenience, which allows us to avoid conflict but frequently ends up reproducing what already exists. Often, others collude with us to act out this deception. Being comfort centered is hypocritical, self-deceptive, and normal.

Clarifying the result we want to create requires us to reorganize our lives. Instead of moving away from a problem, we move toward a possibility that does not yet exist. We become more proactive, intentional, optimistic, invested, and persistent. We also tend to become more energized, and our impact on others becomes energizing.

Consider what happened with John. When I first spoke with him, he sketched out his strategy with little enthusiasm. Sensing that lack of passion, I asked him a question designed to test his commitment to the end he claimed he wanted to obtain:

> What if you told your people the truth? Suppose you told them that nobody really expects you to succeed, that you were assigned to be a caretaker for 18 months, and that you

> have been promised a plum job once your assignment is through. And then you tell them that you have chosen instead to give up that plum job and bet your career on the people present. Then, from your newly acquired stance of optimism for the company's prospects, you issue some challenges beyond your employees' normal capacity.

To my surprise, John responded that he was beginning to think along similar lines. He grabbed a napkin and rapidly sketched out a new strategy along with a plan for carrying it out, including reassignments for his staff. It was clear and compelling, and he was suddenly full of energy.

What happened here? John was the president of his company and therefore had authority. And he'd turned around two other companies—evidence that he had the knowledge and competencies of a change leader. Yet he was *failing* as a change leader. That's because he had slipped into his comfort zone. He was going through the motions, doing what had worked elsewhere. He was imitating a great leader—in this case, John himself. But imitation is not the way to enter the fundamental state of leadership. If I had accused John of not being committed to a real vision, he would have been incensed. He would have argued heatedly in denial of the truth. All I had to do, though, was nudge him in the right direction. As soon as he envisioned the result he wanted to create and committed himself to it, a new strategy emerged and he was reenergized.

Then there was Robert, who went to what he assumed would be his last board meeting and found that he had more support than he'd been led to believe. Shockingly, at the end of the meeting, he still had his job. Even so, this fortuitous turn brought on further soul-searching. Robert started to pay more attention to what he was doing; he began to see his tendency to be tactical and to gravitate toward routine tasks. He concluded that he was managing, not leading. He was playing a role and abdicating leadership to the board president—not because that person had the knowledge and vision to lead but because the position came with the statutory right to lead.

"I suddenly decided to really lead my organization," Robert said. "It was as if a new person emerged. The decision was not about me. I needed to do it for the good of the organization."

In deciding to "really lead," Robert started identifying the strategic outcomes he wanted to create. As he did this, he found himself leaving his zone of comfort—behaving in new ways and generating new outcomes.

Am I internally directed?

In the normal state, we comply with social pressures in order to avoid conflict and remain connected with our coworkers. However, we end up feeling *less* connected because conflict avoidance results in political compromise. We begin to lose our uniqueness and our sense of integrity. The agenda gradually shifts from creating an external result to preserving political peace. As this problem intensifies, we begin to lose hope and energy.

This loss was readily apparent in the case of John. He was his corporation's shining star. But since he was at least partially focused on the future reward—the plum job—he was not fully focused on doing the hard work he needed to do at the moment. So he didn't ask enough of the people he was leading. To get more from them, John needed to be more internally directed.

Am I other focused?

It's hard to admit, but most of us, most of the time, put our own needs above those of the whole. Indeed, it is healthy to do so; it's a survival mechanism. But when the pursuit of our own interests controls our relationships, we erode others' trust in us. Although people may comply with our wishes, they no longer derive energy from their relationships with us. Over time we drive away the very social support we seek.

To become more focused on others is to commit to the collective good in relationships, groups, or organizations, even if it means incurring personal costs. When John made the shift into the fundamental state of leadership, he committed to an uncertain future for himself. He had been promised a coveted job. All he had to do was wait a few months. Still, he was unhappy, so he chose to turn down the opportunity in favor of a course that was truer to his leadership values. When he shifted gears, he sacrificed his personal security in favor of a greater good.

Remember Robert's words: "The decision was not about me. I needed to do it for the good of the organization." After entering the fundamental state of leadership, he proposed a new strategic direction to the board's president and said that if the board didn't like it, he would walk away with no regrets. He knew that the strategy would benefit the organization, regardless of how it would affect him personally. Robert put the good of the organization first. When a leader does this, people notice, and the leader gains respect and trust. Group members, in turn, become more likely to put the collective good first. When they do, tasks that previously seemed impossible become doable.

Am I externally open?

Being closed to external stimuli has the benefit of keeping us on task, but it also allows us to ignore signals that suggest a need for change. Such signals would force us to cede control and face risk, so denying them is self-protective, but it is also self-deceptive. John convinced himself he'd done all he could for his failing company when, deep down, he knew that he had the capacity to improve things. Robert was self-deceptive, too, until crisis and renewed opportunity caused him to open up and explore the fact that he was playing a role accorded him but not using his knowledge and emotional capacity to transcend that role and truly lead his people.

Asking ourselves whether we're externally open shifts our focus from controlling our environment to learning from it and helps us recognize the need for change. Two things happen as a result. First, we are forced to improvise in response to previously unrecognized cues—that is, to depart from established routines. And second, because trial-and-error survival requires an accurate picture of the results we're creating, we actively and genuinely seek honest feedback. Since people trust us more when we're in this state, they tend to offer more accurate feedback, understanding that we are likely to learn from the message rather than kill the messenger.

A cycle of learning and empowerment is created, allowing us to see things that people normally cannot see and to formulate transformational strategies.

Applying the Fundamental Principles

Just as I teach others about the fundamental state of leadership, I also try to apply the concept in my own life. I was a team leader on a project for the University of Michigan's Executive Education Center. Usually, the center runs weeklong courses that bring in 30 to 40 executives. It was proposed that we develop a new product, an integrated week of perspectives on leadership. C. K. Prahalad would begin with a strategic perspective, then Noel Tichy, Dave Ulrich, Karl Weick, and I would follow with our own presentations. The objective was to fill a 400-seat auditorium. Since each presenter had a reasonably large following in some domain of the executive world, we were confident we could fill the seats, so we scheduled the program for the month of July, when our facilities were typically underutilized.

In the early months of planning and organizing, everything went perfectly. A marketing consultant had said we could expect to secure half our enrollment three weeks prior to the event. When that time rolled around, slightly less than half of the target audience had signed up, so we thought all was well. But then a different consultant indicated that for our kind of event we would get few additional enrollments during the last three weeks. This stunning prediction meant that attendance would be half of what we expected and we would be lucky to break even.

As the team leader, I could envision the fallout. Our faculty members, accustomed to drawing a full house, would be offended by a half-empty room; the dean would want to know what went wrong; and the center's staff would probably point to the team leader as the problem. That night I spent several hours pacing the floor. I was filled with dread and shame. Finally I told myself that this kind of behavior was useless. I went to my desk and wrote down the four questions. As I considered them, I concluded that I was comfort centered, externally directed, self-focused, and internally closed.

So I asked myself, "What result do I want to create?" I wrote that I wanted the center to learn how to offer a new, world-class product that would be in demand over time. With that clarification came a freeing insight: Because this was our first offering of the product, turning a large profit was not essential. That would be nice, of course, but we'd be happy to learn how to do such an event properly, break even, and lay the groundwork for making a profit in the future.

I then asked myself, "How can I become other focused?" At that moment, I was totally self-focused—I was worried about my reputation—and my first inclination was to be angry with the staff. But in shifting my focus to what they might be thinking that night, I realized they were most likely worried that I'd come to work in the morning ready to assign blame. Suddenly, I saw a need to both challenge and support them.

Finally, I thought about how I could become externally open. It would mean moving forward and learning something new, even if that made me uncomfortable. I needed to engage in an exploratory dialogue rather than preside as the expert in charge.

I immediately began making a list of marketing strategies, though I expected many of them would prove foolish since I knew nothing about marketing. The next day, I brought the staff together—and they, naturally, were guarded. I asked them what result we wanted to create. What happened next is a good example of how contagious the fundamental state of leadership can be.

We talked about strategies for increasing attendance, and after a while, I told the staff that I had some silly marketing ideas and was embarrassed to share them but was willing to do anything to help. They laughed at many of my naive thoughts about how to increase publicity and create pricing incentives. Yet my proposals also sparked serious discussion, and the group began to brainstorm its way into a collective strategy. Because I was externally open, there was space and time for everyone to lead. People came up with better ways of approaching media outlets and creating incentives. In that meeting, the group developed a shared sense of purpose, reality, identity, and contribution. They left feeling reasonable optimism and went forward as a committed team.

In the end, we did not get 400 participants, but we filled more than enough seats to have a successful event. We more than broke even, and we developed the skills we needed to run such an event better in the future. The program was a success because something transformational occurred among the staff. Yet the transformation did not originate in the meeting. It began the night before, when I asked myself the four questions and moved from the normal, reactive state to the fundamental state of leadership. And my entry into the fundamental state encouraged the staff to enter as well.

While the fundamental state proves useful in times of crisis, it can also help us cope with more mundane challenges. If I am going to have an important conversation, attend a key meeting, participate in a significant event, or teach a class, part of my preparation is to try to reach the fundamental state of leadership. Whether I am working with an individual, a group, or an organization, I ask the same four questions. They often lead to high-performance outcomes, and the repetition of high-performance outcomes can eventually create a high-performance culture.

Inspiring Others to High Performance

When we enter the fundamental state of leadership, we immediately have new thoughts and engage in new behaviors. We can't remain in this state forever. It can last for hours, days, or sometimes months, but eventually we come back to our normal frame of mind. While the fundamental state is temporary, each time we are in it we learn more about people and our environment and increase the probability that we will be able to return to it. Moreover, we inspire those around us to higher levels of performance.

To this day, Robert marvels at the contrast between his organization's past and present. His transformation into a leader with positive energy and a willingness and ability to tackle challenges in new ways helped shape the L.A. Junior Chamber of Commerce into a high-functioning and creative enterprise. When I last spoke to Robert, here's what he had to say:

> I have a critical mass of individuals on both the staff and the board who are willing to look at our challenges in a new way and work on solutions together. At our meetings, new energy is present. What previously seemed unimaginable now seems to happen with ease.

Any CEO would be delighted to be able to say these things. But the truth is, it's not a typical situation. When Robert shifted into the fundamental state of leadership, his group (which started off in a normal state) came to life, infused with his renewed energy and vision. Even after he'd left the fundamental state, the group sustained a higher level of performance. It continues to flourish, without significant staff changes or restructuring.

All this didn't happen because Robert read a book or an article about the best practices of some great leader. It did not happen because he was imitating someone else. It happened because he was jolted out of his comfort zone and was forced to enter the fundamental state of leadership. He was driven to clarify the result he wanted to create, to act courageously from his core values, to surrender his self-interest to the collective good, and to open himself up to learning in real time. From Robert, and others like him, we can learn the value of challenging ourselves in this way—a painful process but one with great potential to make a positive impact on our own lives and on the people around us.

Originally published in July 2005. Reprint R0507F

What to Ask the Person in the Mirror

by Robert S. Kaplan

IF YOU'RE LIKE MOST successful leaders, you were, in the early stages of your career, given plenty of guidance and support. You were closely monitored, coached, and mentored. But as you moved up the ladder, the sources of honest and useful feedback became fewer, and after a certain point, you were pretty much on your own. Now, your boss—if you have one—is no longer giving much consideration to your day-to-day actions. By the time any mistakes come to light, it's probably too late to fix them—or your boss's perceptions of you. And by the time your management missteps negatively affect your business results, it's usually too late to make corrections that will get you back on course.

No matter how talented and successful you are, you will make mistakes. You will develop bad habits. The world will change subtly, without your even noticing, and behaviors that once worked will be rendered ineffective. Over a 22-year career at Goldman Sachs, I had the opportunity to run various businesses and to work with or coach numerous business leaders. I chaired the firm's senior leadership training efforts and cochaired its partnership committee, which focused on reviews, promotions, and development of managing directors. Through this experience and subsequent interviews with a large number of executives in a broad range of industries, I have observed that even outstanding leaders invariably struggle through stretches of their careers where they get off track for some period of time.

It's hard to see it when you're in the midst of it; changes in the environment, competitors, or even personal circumstances can quietly guide you off your game. I have learned that a key characteristic of highly successful leaders is not that they figure out how to always stay on course, but that they develop techniques to help them recognize a deteriorating situation and get back on track as quickly as possible. In my experience, the best way to do that is to step back regularly, say, every three to six months (and certainly whenever things feel as though they aren't going well), and honestly ask yourself some questions about how you're doing and what you may need to do differently. As simple as this process sounds, people are often shocked by their own answers to basic management and leadership questions.

One manager in a large financial services company who had been passed over for promotion told me he was quite surprised by his year-end performance review, which highlighted several management issues that had not been previously brought to his attention. His boss read several comments from the review that faulted him for poor communication, failure to effectively articulate a strategy for the business, and a tendency to isolate himself from his team. He believed that the review was unfair. After 15 years at the company, he began to feel confused and misunderstood and wondered whether he still had a future there. He decided to seek feedback directly from five of his key contributors and longtime collaborators. In one-on-one meetings, he asked them for blunt feedback and advice. He was shocked to hear that they were highly critical of several of his recent actions, were confused about the direction he wanted to take the business, and felt he no longer valued their input. Their feedback helped him see that he had been so immersed in the day-to-day business that he had failed to step back and think about what he was doing. This was a serious wake-up call. He immediately took steps to change his behavior and address these issues. His review the following year was dramatically better, he was finally promoted, and his business's performance improved. The manager was lucky to have received this feedback in time to get his career back on track, although he regretted that he had waited for a negative review to ask

Idea in Brief

If you're like most managers, the higher you go up the corporate ladder, the harder it is to get candid feedback on your performance. And without crucial input from bosses and colleagues, you can make mistakes that irreparably damage your organization—and your reputation.

How can you figure out how you're *really* doing and avoid business disasters? Kaplan recommends looking to *yourself* for answers. Regularly ask yourself questions like these: "Am I communicating a vision for my business to my employees?" "Am I spending my time in ways that enable me to achieve my priorities?" "Do I give people timely and direct feedback they can act on?" "How do I behave under pressure?"

It's far more important to ask the *right* questions than to have all the answers. By applying this process, you tackle the leadership challenges that inevitably arise during the course of your career—and craft new plans for staying on your game.

basic questions about his leadership activities. He promised himself he would not make that mistake again.

In this article, I outline seven types of questions that leaders should ask themselves on some periodic basis. I am not suggesting that there is a "right" answer to any of them or that they all will resonate with a given executive at any point in time. I am suggesting that successful executives can regularly improve their performance and preempt serious business problems by stepping back and taking the time to ask themselves certain key questions.

Vision and Priorities

It's surprising how often business leaders fail to ask themselves: *How frequently do I communicate a vision and priorities for my business? Would my employees, if asked, be able to articulate the vision and priorities?* Many leaders have, on paper, a wealth of leadership talents: interpersonal, strategic, and analytic skills; a knack for team building; and certainly the ability to develop a vision. Unfortunately, in the press of day-to-day activities, they often don't adequately communicate the vision to the organization, and in particular, they

Idea in Practice

Kaplan suggests periodically asking yourself questions related to seven leadership challenges.

To address this leadership challenge . . .	Ask ...	Because ...
Vision and priorities	How often do I communicate a vision and key priorities to achieve that vision?	Employees want to know where the business is going and what they need to focus on in order to help drive the business. As the world changes, they want to know how the vision and priorities might change.
Managing time	Does the way I spend my time match my key priorities?	Tracking your use of time can reveal startling—even horrifying—disconnects between your top priorities and your actions. Such disconnects send confusing messages to employees about your true priorities.
Feedback	Do I give people timely and direct feedback they can act on?	Employees want truthful, direct, and timely feedback. Retention and productivity improve when employees trust you to raise issues promptly and honestly.

don't convey it in a way that helps their people understand what they are supposed to be doing to drive the business. It is very difficult to lead people if they don't have a firm grasp of where they're heading and what's expected of them.

This was the problem at a large *Fortune* 200 company that had decided to invest in its 1,000 top managers by having them attend an intensive, two-day management-training program, 100 at a time. Before each session, the participants went through a 360-degree nonevaluative review in which critical elements of their individual performance were ranked by ten of their subordinates. The company's

Succession planning	Have I identified potential successors?	It's important to nurture future leaders who can grow the business. If you haven't identified possible successors, you're probably not delegating as much as you should, and you may even be a decision-making bottleneck.
Evaluation and alignment	Am I attuned to business changes that may require shifts in how we run the company?	All businesses encounter challenges posed by changes; for example, in customers' needs or the business's stage of maturity. To determine how best to evolve your business, regularly scan for changes, seek fresh perspectives from talented subordinates, and envision new organizational designs.
Leading under pressure	How do I behave under pressure?	During crises, employees watch you with a microscope—and mimic your behavior. By identifying your unproductive behaviors under pressure (such as blaming others or losing your temper), you can better manage those behaviors and avoid sending unintended messages to employees about how *they* should behave.
Staying true to yourself	Does my leadership style reflect who I truly am?	A business career is a marathon, not a sprint. If you've adopted a leadership style that doesn't suit your skills, values, and personality, you'll wear down.

senior management looked at the results, focusing on the top five and bottom five traits for each group. Despite this being an extremely well-managed firm, the ability to articulate a vision ranked in the bottom five for almost every group. Managers at that company did articulate a vision, but the feedback from their subordinates strongly indicated that they were not communicating it frequently or clearly enough to meet their people's tremendous hunger for guidance.

Employees want to know where the business is going and what they need to focus on. As the world changes, they want to know how the business vision and priorities might change along with it. While managers are taught to actively communicate, many either unintentionally undercommunicate or fail to articulate specific priorities that would give meaning to their vision. However often you think you discuss vision and strategy, you may not be doing it frequently enough or in sufficient detail to suit the needs of your people. Look at the CEO of an emerging biotechnology company, who was quite frustrated with what he saw as a lack of alignment within his top management team. He strongly believed that the company needed to do a substantial equity financing within the next 18 months, but his senior managers wanted to wait a few years until two or three of the company's key drugs were further along in the FDA approval process. They preferred to tell their story to investors when the company was closer to generating revenue. When I asked him about the vision for the company, the CEO sheepishly realized that he had never actually written down a vision statement. He had a well-articulated tactical plan relating to each of the company's specific product efforts but no fully formed vision that would give further context to these efforts. He decided to organize an off-site meeting for his senior management team to discuss and specifically articulate a vision for the company.

After a vigorous debate, the group quickly agreed on a vision and strategic priorities. They realized that in order to achieve their shared goals, the business would in fact require substantial financing sooner rather than later—or they would need to scale back some of the initiatives that were central to their vision for the company. Once they fully appreciated this trade-off, they understood what the CEO was trying to accomplish and left the meeting united about their financing strategy. The CEO was quite surprised at how easy it had been to bring the members of his leadership team together. Because they agreed on where they were going as a company, specific issues were much easier to resolve.

A common pitfall in articulating a vision is a failure to boil it down to a manageable list of initiatives. Culling the list involves thinking through and then making difficult choices and trade-off decisions. These choices communicate volumes to your people about how they should be spending their time. I spoke with the manager of a national sales force who felt frustrated that his direct reports were not focusing on the tasks necessary to achieve their respective regional sales goals. As a result, sales were growing at a slower rate than budgeted at the beginning of the year. When I asked him to enumerate the three to five key priorities he expected his salespeople to focus on, he paused and then explained that there were 15 and it would be very difficult to narrow the list down to five.

Even as he spoke, a light went on in his head. He realized why there might be a disconnect between him and his people: They didn't know precisely what he wanted because he had not told them in a prioritized, and therefore actionable, manner. He reflected on this issue for the next two weeks, thinking at length about his own experience as a regional manager and consulting with various colleagues. He then picked three priorities that he felt were crucial to achieving sales growth. The most important of these involved a major new-business targeting exercise followed by a substantial new-prospect calling effort. The regional managers immediately understood and began focusing on these initiatives. The fact is that having 15 priorities is the same as having none at all. Managers have a responsibility to translate their vision into a manageable number of priorities that their subordinates can understand and act on.

Failing to communicate your vision and priorities has direct costs to you in terms of time and business effectiveness. It's hard to delegate if your people don't have a good sense of the big picture; hence you end up doing more work yourself. This issue can cascade through the organization if your direct reports are, in turn, unable to communicate a vision and effectively leverage their own subordinates.

Managing Time

The second area to question is painfully simple and closely relates to the first: *How am I spending my time?* Once you know your priorities, you need to determine whether you're spending your time—your most precious asset—in a way that will allow you to achieve them. For example, if your two major priorities are senior talent development and global expansion but you're spending the majority of your

Testing Yourself

To assess your performance and stay on track, you should step back and ask yourself certain key questions.

Vision and Priorities

In the press of day-to-day activities, leaders often fail to adequately communicate their vision to the organization, and in particular, they don't communicate it in a way that helps their subordinates determine where to focus their own efforts.

How often do I communicate a vision for my business?

Have I identified and communicated three to five key priorities to achieve that vision?

If asked, would my employees be able to articulate the vision and priorities?

Managing Time

Leaders need to know how they're spending their time. They also need to ensure that their time allocation (and that of their subordinates) matches their key priorities.

How am I spending my time? Does it match my key priorities?

How are my subordinates spending their time? Does that match the key priorities for the business?

Feedback

Leaders often fail to coach employees in a direct and timely fashion and, instead, wait until the year-end review. This approach may lead to unpleasant surprises and can undermine effective professional development. Just as important, leaders need to cultivate subordinates who can give them advice and feedback during the year.

Do I give people timely and direct feedback that they can act on?

Do I have five or six junior subordinates who will tell me things I may not want to hear but need to hear?

Succession Planning

When leaders fail to actively plan for succession, they do not delegate sufficiently and may become decision-making bottlenecks. Key employees may leave if they are not actively groomed and challenged.

Have I, at least in my own mind, picked one or more potential successors?

Am I coaching them and giving them challenging assignments?

Am I delegating sufficiently? Have I become a decision-making bottleneck?

Evaluation and Alignment

The world is constantly changing, and leaders need to be able to adapt their businesses accordingly.

Is the design of my company still aligned with the key success factors for the business?

If I had to design my business with a clean sheet of paper, how would I design it? How would it differ from the current design?

Should I create a task force of subordinates to answer these questions and make recommendations to me?

Leading Under Pressure

A leader's actions in times of stress are watched closely by subordinates and have a profound impact on the culture of the firm and employees' behavior. Successful leaders need to be aware of their own stress triggers and consciously modulate their behavior during these periods to make sure they are acting in ways that are consistent with their beliefs and core values.

What types of events create pressure for me?

How do I behave under pressure?

What signals am I sending my subordinates? Are these signals helpful, or are they undermining the success of my business?

Staying True to Yourself

Successful executives develop leadership styles that fit the needs of their business but also fit their own beliefs and personality.

Is my leadership style comfortable? Does it reflect who I truly am?

Do I assert myself sufficiently, or have I become tentative?

Am I too politically correct?

Does worry about my next promotion or bonus cause me to pull punches or hesitate to express my views?

time on domestic operational and administrative matters that could be delegated, then you need to recognize there is a disconnect and you'd better make some changes.

It's such a simple question, yet many leaders, myself included, just can't accurately answer at times. When leaders finally do track their time, they're often surprised by what they find. Most of us go through periods where unexpected events and day-to-day chaos cause us to be reactive rather than acting on a proscribed plan. Crises, surprises, personnel issues, and interruptions make the workweek seem like a blur. I have recommended to many leaders that they track how they spend each hour of each day for one week, then categorize the hours into types of activities: business development, people management, and strategic planning, for example. For most executives, the results of this exercise are startling—even horrifying—with obvious disconnects between what their top priorities are and how they are spending their time.

For example, the CEO of a midsize manufacturing company was frustrated because he was working 70 hours a week and never seemed to catch up. His family life suffered, and, at work, he was constantly unavailable for his people and major customers. I suggested he step back and review how he was managing his time hour-by-hour over the course of a week. We sat down to examine the results and noticed that he was spending a substantial amount of time approving company expenditures, some for as little as $500—this in a business with $500 million in sales. Sitting in my office, he struggled to explain why he had not delegated some portion of this responsibility; it turned out that the activity was a holdover from a time when the company was much smaller. By delegating authority to approve recurring operating expenses below $25,000, he realized he could save as much as 15 hours per week. He was amazed that he had not recognized this issue and made this simple change much earlier.

How you spend your time is an important question not only for you but for your team. People tend to take their cues from the leader when it comes to time management—therefore, you want to make sure there's a match between your actions, your business priorities, and your team's activities. The CEO of a rapidly growing, 300-person professional services firm felt that, to build the business, senior managers needed to develop stronger and more substantive relationships with clients. This meant that senior professionals would need to spend significantly more time out of their offices in meetings with clients. When asked how his own time was being spent, the CEO was unable to answer. After tracking it for a week, he was shocked to find that he was devoting a tremendous amount of his time to administrative activities related to managing the firm. He realized that the amount of attention he was paying to these matters did not reflect the business's priorities and was sending a confusing message to his people. He immediately began pushing himself to delegate a number of these administrative tasks and increase the amount of time he spent on the road with customers, setting a powerful example for his people. He directed each of his senior managers to do a similar time-allocation exercise to ensure they were dedicating sufficient time to clients.

Of course, the way a leader spends his or her time must be tailored to the needs of the business, which may vary depending on time of year, personnel changes, and external factors. The key here is, whatever you decide, time allocation needs to be a conscious decision that fits your vision and priorities for the business. Given the pressure of running a business, it is easy to lose focus, so it's important to ask yourself this question periodically. Just as you would step back and review a major investment decision, you need to dispassionately review the manner in which you invest your time.

Feedback

When you think about the ways you approach feedback, you should first ask: *Do I give people timely, direct, and constructive feedback?* And second: *Do I have five or six junior people who will tell me things I don't want to hear but need to hear?*

If they're like most ambitious employees, your subordinates want to be coached and developed in a truthful and direct manner. They want to get feedback while there's still an opportunity to act on it; if you've waited until the year-end review, it's often too late. In my experience, well-intentioned managers typically fail to give blunt, direct, and timely feedback to their subordinates.

One reason for this failure is that managers are often afraid that constructive feedback and criticism will demoralize their employees. In addition, critiquing a professional in a frank and timely manner may be perceived as overly confrontational. Lastly, many managers fear that this type of feedback will cause employees not to like them. Consequently, leaders often wait until year-end performance reviews. The year-end review is evaluative (that is, the verdict on the year) and therefore is not conducive to constructive coaching. The subordinate is typically on the defensive and not as open to criticism. This approach creates surprises, often unpleasant ones, which undermine trust and dramatically reduce the confidence of the subordinate in the manager.

The reality is that managers who don't give immediate and direct feedback often are "liked" until year-end—at which time they wind up being strongly disliked. If employees have fallen short of expectations, the failing is reflected in bonuses, raises, and promotions. The feeling of injustice can be enormous. What's worse is the knowledge that if an employee had received feedback earlier in the year, it is likely that he or she would have made meaningful efforts to improve and address the issues.

While people do like to hear positive feedback, ultimately, they desperately want to know the truth, and I have rarely seen someone quit over hearing the truth or being challenged to do better—unless it's too late. On the contrary, I would argue that people are more likely to stay if they understand what issues they need to address and they trust you to bring those issues to their attention in a straightforward and prompt fashion. They gain confidence that you will work with them to develop their skills and that they won't be blindsided at the end of the year. Employees who don't land a hoped-for promotion will be much more likely to forgive you if you've told them all along what they need to do better, even if they haven't gotten there yet. They may well redouble their efforts to prove to you that they can overcome these issues.

During my career at Goldman Sachs, I consistently found that professional development was far more effective when coaching and direct feedback were given to employees throughout the year—well in advance of the annual performance review process. Internal surveys of managing directors showed that, in cases where feedback was confined to the year-end review, satisfaction with career development was dramatically lower than when it was offered throughout the year.

As hard as it is to give effective and timely feedback, many leaders find it much more challenging to get feedback from their employees. Once you reach a certain stage of your career, junior people are in a much better position than your boss to tell you how you're doing. They see you in your day-to-day activities, and they experience your decisions directly. Your boss, at this stage, is much more removed and, as a result, typically needs to talk to your subordinates to assess your performance at the end of the year. In order to avoid your own year-end surprises, you need to develop a network of junior professionals who are willing to give you constructive feedback. The problem is that, while your direct reports know what you are doing wrong, most of them are not dying to tell you. With good reason—there's very little upside and a tremendous amount of downside. The more senior and the more important you become, the less your subordinates will tell you the "awful truth"—things that are difficult to hear but that you need to know.

It takes a concerted effort to cultivate subordinates who will advise and coach you. It also takes patience and some relentlessness. When I ask subordinates for constructive feedback, they will typically and predictably tell me that I'm doing "very well." When I follow up and ask "What should I do differently?" they respond, "Nothing that I can think of." If I challenge them by saying, "There must be something!" still they say, "Nothing comes to mind." I then ask them to sit back and think—we have plenty of time. By this time, beads of sweat begin to become visible on their foreheads. After an awkward silence, they will eventually come up with something—and it's often devastating to hear. It's devastating because it's a damning criticism and because you know it's true.

What you do with this feedback is critical. If you act on it, you will improve your performance. Equally important, you will take a big step in building trust and laying the groundwork for a channel of honest feedback. When subordinates see that you respond positively to suggestions, they will often feel more ownership in the business and in your success. They'll learn to give you criticisms on their own initiative because they know you will actually appreciate it and do something with it. Developing a network of "coaching" subordinates will help you take action to identify your own leadership issues and meaningfully improve your performance.

Succession Planning

Another question that managers know is important yet struggle to answer affirmatively is: *Have I, at least in my own mind, picked one or more potential successors?* This issue is critical because if you aren't identifying potential successors, you are probably not delegating as extensively as you should and you may well be a decision-making bottleneck. Being a bottleneck invariably means that you are not spending enough time on vital leadership priorities and are failing to develop your key subordinates. Ironically, when leaders believe they are so talented that they can perform tasks far better than any of their subordinates and therefore insist on doing the tasks themselves, they will typically cause their businesses to underperform, and, ultimately, their careers will suffer as well.

The succession question also has significant implications that cascade through an organization: If leaders do not develop successors, then the organization may lack a sufficient number of leaders to successfully grow the business. Worse, if junior employees are not developed, they may leave the firm for better opportunities elsewhere. For these reasons, many well-managed companies will hesitate to promote executives who have failed to develop successors.

It is sufficient to identify possible successors without actually telling them you've done so—as long as this identification causes you to manage them differently. In particular, you will want to delegate more of your major responsibilities to these professionals. This will speed their maturation and prepare them to step up to the next level. By giving demanding assignments to these subordinates, you strongly signal an interest in their development and career progression—which will encourage them to turn down offers from competitors. Leaders who do this are much better able to keep their teams together and avoid losing up-and-coming stars to competitors.

A loss of talent is highly damaging to a company. It is particularly painful if you could have retained key employees by simply challenging them more intensively. I spoke with a division head of a large company who was concerned about what he perceived to be a talent deficit in his organization. He felt that he could not use his time to the fullest because he viewed his direct reports as incapable of assuming some of his major responsibilities. He believed this talent deficit was keeping him from launching several new product and market initiatives. In the midst of all this, he lost two essential subordinates over six months—each had left to take on increased responsibilities at major competitors. He had tried to persuade them to stay, emphasizing that he was actively considering them for significant new leadership assignments. Because they had not seen evidence of this previously, they were skeptical and left anyway. I asked him whether, prior to the defections, he had identified them (or anyone else) as potential successors, put increased responsibilities in their hands, or actively ratcheted up his coaching of these professionals. He answered that, in the chaos of daily events and in the effort to keep up with the business, he had not done so. He also admitted that he had underestimated the potential of these two employees and realized he was probably underestimating the abilities of several others in the company. He immediately sat down and made a list of potential stars and next to each name wrote out a career and responsibility game plan. He immediately got to work on this formative succession plan, although he suspected that he had probably waited too long already.

When you're challenging and testing people, you delegate to them more often, which frees you to focus on the most critical strategic matters facing the business. This will make you more successful and a more attractive candidate for your own future promotion.

Evaluation and Alignment

The world is constantly changing. Your customers' needs change; your business evolves (going, for instance, from high growth to mature); new products and distribution methods emerge as threats. When these changes happen, if you don't change along with them, you can get seriously out of alignment. The types of people you hire, the way you organize them, the economic incentives you offer them, and even the nature of the tasks you delegate no longer create the culture and outcomes that are critical to the success of your business. It's your job to make sure that the design of your organization is aligned with the key success factors for the business. Ask yourself: *Am I attuned to changes in the business environment that would require a change in the way we organize and run our business?*

Such clear-sightedness is, of course, hard to achieve. As a leader, you may be too close to the business to see subtle changes that are continually occurring. Because you probably played a central role in building and designing the business, it may be emotionally very difficult to make meaningful changes. You may have to fire certain employees—people you recruited and hired. You may also have to acknowledge that you made some mistakes and be open to changing your own operating style in a way that is uncomfortable for some period of time.

Because of the difficulty in facing these issues, it's sometimes wise to call on high-potential subordinates to take a fresh look at the business. This approach can be quite effective because junior employees are often not as emotionally invested as you are and can see more objectively what needs to be done. This approach is also a good way to challenge your future leaders and give them a valuable development experience. You'll give them a chance to exercise their strategic skills; you'll get a glimpse of their potential (which relates to the earlier discussion of succession planning), and you might just get some terrific new ideas for how to run the business.

This approach worked for the CEO of a high technology business in northern California, whose company had been one of the early innovators in its product space but, in recent years, had begun to falter and lose market share. In its early days, the company's primary success factors had been product innovation and satisfying customer needs. It had aggressively hired innovative engineers and marketing personnel. As new competitors emerged, customers began to focus more on cost and service (in the form of more sophisticated applications development). Stepping back, the CEO sensed that he needed to redesign the company with a different mix of people, a new organization, and a revised incentive structure. Rather than try to come up with a new model himself, he asked a more junior group of executives to formulate a new company design as if they had a "clean sheet of paper." Their study took a number of weeks, but upon completion, it led to several recommendations that the CEO immediately began to implement. For example, they suggested colocating the engineering and sales departments and creating integrated account coverage teams. They also recommended that the company push more of its engineers to interact with customers and focus on this skill in recruiting. The CEO regretted that he had not asked the question—and conducted this assignment—12 months earlier.

Even the most successful business is susceptible to new challenges posed by a changing world. Effective executives regularly look at their businesses with a clean sheet of paper—seeking advice and other perspectives from people who are less emotionally invested in the business—in order to determine whether key aspects of the way they run their organizations are still appropriate.

Leading Under Pressure

Pressure is a part of business. Changes in business conditions create urgent problems. New entrants in the market demand a competitive response. Valued employees quit, often at the most inopportune times. Leaders and their teams, no matter how smart they are, make mistakes.

The interesting thing about stressful events is that they affect each person differently—what causes you anxiety may not bother someone else, and vice versa. For some, extreme anxiety may be triggered by the prospect of a promotion; for others, by making a serious mistake; still others, by losing a piece of business to a competitor. Regardless of the source of stress, every leader experiences it, so a good question to ask yourself is: *How do I behave under pressure, and what signals am I sending my employees?*

As a leader, you're watched closely. During a crisis, your people watch you with a microscope, noting every move you make. In such times, your subordinates learn a great deal about you and what you really believe, as opposed to what you say. Do you accept responsibility for mistakes, or do you look for someone to blame? Do you support your employees, or do you turn on them? Are you cool and calm, or do you lose your temper? Do you stand up for what you believe, or do you take the expedient route and advocate what you think your seniors want to hear? You need to be self-aware enough to recognize the situations that create severe anxiety for you and manage your behavior to avoid sending unproductive messages to your people.

I've met a number of leaders who behave in a very composed and thoughtful manner the great majority of the time. Unfortunately, when they're under severe stress, they react in ways that set a very negative tone. They inadvertently train their employees to mimic that behavior and behave in a similar fashion. If your instinct is to shield yourself from blame, to take credit rather than sharing it with your subordinates, or to avoid admitting when you have made a mistake, you will give your employees license to do the same.

The CEO of a large asset-management firm was frustrated that he was unable to build a culture of accountability and teamwork in his growing business. At his request, I spoke to a number of his team members. I asked in particular about the actions of the CEO when investments they recommended declined in value. They recounted his frequent temper tantrums and accusatory diatribes, which led to an overwhelming atmosphere of blame and finger-pointing. The investment decisions had, in fact, been made jointly through a carefully constructed process involving portfolio managers, industry analysts, and the CEO. As a result of these episodes, employees learned that when investments went wrong it would be good to try to find someone else to blame. Hearing these stories, the CEO realized his actions under pressure were far more persuasive to employees than his speeches about teamwork and culture. He understood that he would have to learn to moderate his behavior under stress and, subsequently, took steps to avoid reacting so angrily to negative investment results. He also became more aware that subordinates typically felt quite regretful and demoralized when their investments declined and were more likely to need a pat on the back and coaching than a kick in the pants.

It's extremely difficult to expect employees to alert you to looming problems when they fear your reaction—and even more so when they think it's better to distance themselves from potential problems. This can create an atmosphere where surprises are, in fact, more likely as the company's natural early-warning system has been inadvertently disarmed. If you have created this kind of culture, it is quite unlikely that you will learn about problems from subordinates spontaneously—unless they want to commit career suicide.

Part of the process of maturing as a leader is learning to step back and think about what creates pressure for you, being self-aware in these situations, and disciplining your behavior to ensure that you act in a manner consistent with your core values.

Staying True to Yourself

Most business leaders ask themselves whether their leadership style fits the needs of their business. Fewer managers ask whether their style also fits their own beliefs and personality. The question here is: *Does my leadership style reflect who I truly am?*

A business career is a marathon, not a sprint, and if you aren't true to yourself, eventually you're going to wear down. As you are developing in your career, it is advisable to observe various leadership styles, and pick and choose elements that feel comfortable to you. Bear in mind, though, that observing and adopting aspects of other styles does not mean you should try to be someone else. During my career, I was fortunate to have had several superb bosses and colleagues with distinctive and unique leadership skills. While I tried to adopt some of their techniques, I also learned that I needed to develop an overall style that fit my unique skills and personality. Your style needs to fit you; even an unorthodox style can be enormously effective if it reflects your skills, values, and personality.

As you become more senior, you'll need to ask yourself an additional set of questions relating to style: *Do I assert myself sufficiently, or have I become tentative? Am I too politically correct? Does worry about my next promotion or my year-end bonus cause me to pull punches or hesitate to clearly express my views?* In many companies, ambitious executives may try to avoid confronting sensitive issues or making waves. Worse than that, they may spend an inordinate amount of energy trying to ascertain what their boss thinks and then act like they think the same thing. If they're very skilled at this, they may even get a chance to make their comments before the boss has a chance to express his opinion—and feel the warm glow of approval from the boss.

The problem is that confrontation and disagreement are crucial to effective decision making. Some of the worst decisions I've been involved in were made after a group of intelligent people had unanimously agreed to the course of action—though, later, several participants admitted that they had misgivings but were hesitant to diverge from the apparent group consensus. Conversely, it's hard for me to recall a poor decision I was involved in that was made after a thorough debate in which opposing views were vigorously expressed (even if I disagreed with the ultimate decision). Companies need their leaders to express strongly held views rather than mimic what they believe to be the party line. As a leader, therefore, you must ask yourself whether you are expressing your views or holding back and being too politic. At the same time, leaders must encourage their own subordinates to express their unvarnished opinions, make waves as appropriate, and stop tiptoeing around significant issues.

Successful leaders periodically struggle during stretches of their careers. To get back on track, they must devise techniques for stepping back, getting perspective, and developing a new game plan. In this process, having the answers is often far less important than taking time to ask yourself the right questions and gain key insights. The questions posed in this article are intended to spark your thinking. Only a subset of these may resonate with you, and you may find it more useful to come up with your own list. In either event, a self-questioning process conducted on a periodic basis will help you work through leadership challenges and issues that you invariably must tackle over the course of your career.

Originally published in January 2007. Reprint R0701H

Primal Leadership

The Hidden Driver of Great Performance. *by Daniel Goleman, Richard Boyatzis, and Annie McKee*

W

WHEN THE THEORY OF EMOTIONAL intelligence at work began to receive widespread attention, we frequently heard executives say—in the same breath, mind you—"That's incredible," and, "Well, I've known that all along." They were responding to our research that showed an incontrovertible link between an executive's emotional maturity, exemplified by such capabilities as self-awareness and empathy, and his or her financial performance. Simply put, the research showed that "good guys"—that is, emotionally intelligent men and women—finish first.

We've recently compiled two years of new research that, we suspect, will elicit the same kind of reaction. People will first exclaim, "No way," then quickly add, "But of course." We found that of all the elements affecting bottom-line performance, the importance of the leader's mood and its attendant behaviors are most surprising. That powerful pair set off a chain reaction: The leader's mood and behaviors drive the moods and behaviors of everyone else. A cranky and ruthless boss creates a toxic organization filled with negative underachievers who ignore opportunities; an inspirational, inclusive leader spawns acolytes for whom any challenge is surmountable. The final link in the chain is performance: profit or loss.

Our observation about the overwhelming impact of the leader's "emotional style," as we call it, is not a wholesale departure from our research into emotional intelligence. It does, however, represent a deeper analysis of our earlier assertion that a leader's emotional intelligence creates a certain culture or work environment. High levels of emotional intelligence, our research showed, create climates in which information sharing, trust, healthy risk-taking, and learning flourish. Low levels of emotional intelligence create climates rife with fear and anxiety. Because tense or terrified employees can be very productive in the short term, their organizations may post good results, but they never last.

Our investigation was designed in part to look at how emotional intelligence drives performance—in particular, at how it travels from the leader through the organization to bottom-line results. "What mechanism," we asked, "binds the chain together?" To answer that question, we turned to the latest neurological and psychological research. We also drew on our work with business leaders, observations by our colleagues of hundreds of leaders, and Hay Group data on the leadership styles of thousands of executives. From this body of research, we discovered that emotional intelligence is carried through an organization like electricity through wires. To be more specific, the leader's mood is quite literally contagious, spreading quickly and inexorably throughout the business.

We'll discuss the science of mood contagion in more depth later, but first let's turn to the key implications of our finding. If a leader's mood and accompanying behaviors are indeed such potent drivers of business success, then a leader's premier task—we would even say his primal task—is emotional leadership. A leader needs to make sure that not only is he regularly in an optimistic, authentic, high-energy mood, but also that, through his chosen actions, his followers feel and act that way, too. Managing for financial results, then, begins with the leader managing his inner life so that the right emotional and behavioral chain reaction occurs.

Managing one's inner life is not easy, of course. For many of us, it's our most difficult challenge. And accurately gauging how one's emotions affect others can be just as difficult. We know of one CEO, for example, who was certain that everyone saw him as upbeat and reliable; his direct reports told us they found his cheerfulness strained, even fake, and his decisions erratic. (We call this common

Idea in Brief

What *most* influences your company's bottom-line performance? The answer will surprise you—*and* make perfect sense: It's a leader's own mood.

Executives' emotional intelligence—their self-awareness, empathy, rapport with others—has clear links to their own performance. But new research shows that a leader's emotional style also drives everyone *else*'s moods and behaviors—through a neurological process called **mood contagion.** It's akin to "Smile and the whole world smiles with you."

Emotional intelligence travels through an organization like electricity over telephone wires. Depressed, ruthless bosses create toxic organizations filled with negative underachievers. But if you're an upbeat, inspirational leader, you cultivate positive employees who embrace and surmount even the toughest challenges.

Emotional leadership isn't just putting on a game face every day. It means understanding your impact on others—then adjusting your style accordingly. A difficult process of self-discovery—but essential *before* you can tackle your leadership responsibilities.

disconnect "CEO disease.") The implication is that primal leadership demands more than putting on a game face every day. It requires an executive to determine, through reflective analysis, how his emotional leadership drives the moods and actions of the organization, and then, with equal discipline, to adjust his behavior accordingly.

That's not to say that leaders can't have a bad day or week: Life happens. And our research doesn't suggest that good moods have to be high-pitched or nonstop—optimistic, sincere, and realistic will do. But there is no escaping the conclusion that a leader must first attend to the impact of his mood and behaviors before moving on to his wide panoply of other critical responsibilities. In this article, we introduce a process that executives can follow to assess how others experience their leadership, and we discuss ways to calibrate that impact. But first, we'll look at why moods aren't often discussed in the workplace, how the brain works to make moods contagious, and what you need to know about CEO disease.

Idea in Practice

Strengthening Your Emotional Leadership

Since few people have the guts to tell you the truth about your emotional impact, you must discover it on your own. The following process can help. It's based on brain science, as well as years of field research with executives. Use these steps to rewire your brain for greater emotional intelligence.

1. **Who do you want to be?** Imagine yourself as a highly effective leader. What do you see?

   Example: Sofia, a senior manager, often micromanaged others to ensure work was done "right." So she *imagined* herself in the future as an effective leader of her own company, enjoying trusting relationships with coworkers. She saw herself as relaxed, happy, and empowering. The exercise revealed gaps in her current emotional style.

2. **Who are you now?** To see your leadership style as others do, gather 360-degree feedback, especially from peers and subordinates. Identify your weaknesses *and* strengths.

3. **How do you get from here to there?** Devise a plan for closing the gap between who you are and who you want to be.

   Example: Juan, a marketing executive, was intimidating, impossible to please—a

No Way! Yes Way

When we said earlier that people will likely respond to our new finding by saying "No way," we weren't joking. The fact is, the emotional impact of a leader is almost never discussed in the workplace, let alone in the literature on leadership and performance. For most people, "mood" feels too personal. Even though Americans can be shockingly candid about personal matters—witness the *Jerry Springer Show* and its ilk—we are also the most legally bound. We can't even ask the age of a job applicant. Thus, a conversation about an executive's mood or the moods he creates in his employees might be construed as an invasion of privacy.

We also might avoid talking about a leader's emotional style and its impact because, frankly, the topic feels soft. When was the last time you evaluated a subordinate's mood as part of her performance

grouch. Charged with growing his company, he *needed* to be encouraging, optimistic—a coach with a vision. Setting out to understand others, he coached soccer, volunteered at a crisis center, and got to know subordinates by meeting outside of work. These new situations stimulated him to break old habits and try new responses.

4. **How do you make change stick?** Repeatedly rehearse new behaviors—physically *and* mentally—until they're automatic.

Example: Tom, an executive, wanted to learn how to coach rather than castigate struggling employees. Using his commuting time to visualize a difficult meeting with one employee, he envisioned asking questions and listening, and mentally rehearsed how he'd handle feeling impatient. This exercise prepared him to adopt new behaviors at the actual meeting.

5. **Who can help you?** Don't try to build your emotional skills alone—identify others who can help you navigate this difficult process. Managers at Unilever formed learning groups that helped them strengthen their leadership abilities by exchanging frank feedback and developing strong mutual trust.

appraisal? You may have alluded to it—"Your work is hindered by an often negative perspective," or "Your enthusiasm is terrific"—but it is unlikely you mentioned mood outright, let alone discussed its impact on the organization's results.

And yet our research undoubtedly will elicit a "But of course" reaction, too. Everyone knows how much a leader's emotional state drives performance because everyone has had, at one time or another, the inspirational experience of working for an upbeat manager or the crushing experience of toiling for a sour-spirited boss. The former made everything feel possible, and as a result, stretch goals were achieved, competitors beaten, and new customers won. The latter made work grueling. In the shadow of the boss's dark mood, other parts of the organization became "the enemy," colleagues became suspicious of one another, and customers slipped away.

Our research, and research by other social scientists, confirms the verity of these experiences. (There are, of course, rare cases when a brutal boss produces terrific results. We explore that dynamic in the sidebar "Those Wicked Bosses Who Win.") The studies are too numerous to mention here but, in aggregate, they show that when the leader is in a happy mood, the people around him view everything in a more positive light. That, in turn, makes them optimistic about achieving their goals, enhances their creativity and the efficiency of their decision making, and predisposes them to be helpful. Research conducted by Alice Isen at Cornell in 1999, for example, found that an upbeat environment fosters mental efficiency, making people better at taking in and understanding information, at using decision rules in complex judgments, and at being flexible in their thinking. Other research directly links mood and financial performance. In 1986, for instance, Martin Seligman and Peter Schulman of the University of Pennsylvania demonstrated that insurance agents who had a "glass half-full" outlook were far more able than their more pessimistic peers to persist despite rejections, and thus, they closed more sales. (For more information on these studies and a list of our research base, visit www.eiconsortium.org.)

Many leaders whose emotional styles create a dysfunctional environment are eventually fired. (Of course, that's rarely the stated reason; poor results are.) But it doesn't have to end that way. Just as a bad mood can be turned around, so can the spread of toxic feelings from an emotionally inept leader. A look inside the brain explains both why and how.

The Science of Moods

A growing body of research on the human brain proves that, for better or worse, leaders' moods affect the emotions of the people around them. The reason for that lies in what scientists call the open-loop nature of the brain's limbic system, our emotional center. A closed-loop system is self-regulating, whereas an open-loop system depends on external sources to manage itself. In other words, we rely on connections with other people to determine our moods. The

Those Wicked Bosses Who Win

Everyone knows of a rude and coercive CEO who, by all appearances, epitomizes the antithesis of emotional intelligence yet seems to reap great business results. If a leader's mood matters so much, how can we explain those mean-spirited, successful SOBs?

First, let's take a closer look at them. Just because a particular executive is the most visible, he may not actually lead the company. A CEO who heads a conglomerate may have no followers to speak of; it's his division heads who actively lead people and affect profitability.

Second, sometimes an SOB leader has strengths that counterbalance his caustic behavior, but they don't attract as much attention in the business press. In his early days at GE, Jack Welch exhibited a strong hand at the helm as he undertook a radical company turnaround. At that time and in that situation, Welch's firm, top-down style was appropriate. What got less press was how Welch subsequently settled into a more emotionally intelligent leadership style, especially when he articulated a new vision for the company and mobilized people to follow it.

Those caveats aside, let's get back to those infamous corporate leaders who seem to have achieved sterling business results despite their brutish approaches to leadership. Skeptics cite Bill Gates, for example, as a leader who gets away with a harsh style that should theoretically damage his company.

But our leadership model, which shows the effectiveness of specific leadership styles in specific situations, puts Gates's supposedly negative behaviors in a different light. (Our model is explained in detail in the HBR article "Leadership That Gets Results," which appeared in the March–April 2000 issue.) Gates is the achievement-driven leader par excellence, in an organization that has cherry-picked highly talented and motivated people. His apparently harsh leadership style—baldly challenging employees to surpass their past performance—can be quite effective when employees are competent, motivated, and need little direction—all characteristics of Microsoft's engineers.

In short, it's all too easy for a skeptic to argue against the importance of leaders who manage their moods by citing a "rough and tough" leader who achieved good business results despite his bad behavior. We contend that there are, of course, exceptions to the rule, and that in some specific business cases, an SOB boss resonates just fine. But in general, leaders who are jerks must reform or else their moods and actions will eventually catch up with them.

open-loop limbic system was a winning design in evolution because it let people come to one another's emotional rescue—enabling a mother, for example, to soothe her crying infant.

The open-loop design serves the same purpose today as it did thousands of years ago. Research in intensive care units has shown, for example, that the comforting presence of another person not only lowers the patient's blood pressure but also slows the secretion of fatty acids that block arteries. Another study found that three or more incidents of intense stress within a year (for example, serious financial trouble, being fired, or a divorce) triples the death rate in socially isolated middle-aged men, but it has no impact on the death rate of men with many close relationships.

Scientists describe the open loop as "interpersonal limbic regulation"; one person transmits signals that can alter hormone levels, cardiovascular functions, sleep rhythms, even immune functions, inside the body of another. That's how couples are able to trigger surges of oxytocin in each other's brains, creating a pleasant, affectionate feeling. But in all aspects of social life, our physiologies intermingle. Our limbic system's open-loop design lets other people change our very physiology and hence, our emotions.

Even though the open loop is so much a part of our lives, we usually don't notice the process. Scientists have captured the attunement of emotions in the laboratory by measuring the physiology—such as heart rate—of two people sharing a good conversation. As the interaction begins, their bodies operate at different rhythms. But after 15 minutes, the physiological profiles of their bodies look remarkably similar.

Researchers have seen again and again how emotions spread irresistibly in this way whenever people are near one another. As far back as 1981, psychologists Howard Friedman and Ronald Riggio found that even completely nonverbal expressiveness can affect other people. For example, when three strangers sit facing one another in silence for a minute or two, the most emotionally expressive of the three transmits his or her mood to the other two—without a single word being spoken.

Smile and the World Smiles with You

Remember that old cliché? It's not too far from the truth. As we've shown, mood contagion is a real neurological phenomenon, but not all emotions spread with the same ease. A 1999 study conducted by Sigal Barsade at the Yale School of Management showed that, among working groups, cheerfulness and warmth spread easily, while irritability caught on less so, and depression least of all.

It should come as no surprise that laughter is the most contagious of all emotions. Hearing laughter, we find it almost impossible not to laugh or smile, too. That's because some of our brain's open-loop circuits are designed to detect smiles and laughter, making us respond in kind. Scientists theorize that this dynamic was hardwired into our brains ages ago because smiles and laughter had a way of cementing alliances, thus helping the species survive.

The main implication here for leaders undertaking the primal task of managing their moods and the moods of others is this: Humor hastens the spread of an upbeat climate. But like the leader's mood in general, humor must resonate with the organization's culture and its reality. Smiles and laughter, we would posit, are only contagious when they're genuine.

The same holds true in the office, boardroom, or shop floor; group members inevitably "catch" feelings from one another. In 2000, Caroline Bartel at New York University and Richard Saavedra at the University of Michigan found that in 70 work teams across diverse industries, people in meetings together ended up sharing moods—both good and bad—within two hours. One study asked teams of nurses and accountants to monitor their moods over weeks; researchers discovered that their emotions tracked together, and they were largely independent of each team's shared hassles. Groups, therefore, like individuals, ride emotional roller coasters, sharing everything from jealousy to angst to euphoria. (A good mood, incidentally, spreads most swiftly by the judicious use of humor. For more on this, see the sidebar "Smile and the World Smiles with You.")

Moods that start at the top tend to move the fastest because everyone watches the boss. They take their emotional cues from him. Even when the boss isn't highly visible—for example, the CEO

Get Happy, Carefully

Good moods galvanize good performance, but it doesn't make sense for a leader to be as chipper as a blue jay at dawn if sales are tanking or the business is going under. The most effective executives display moods and behaviors that match the situation at hand, with a healthy dose of optimism mixed in. They respect how other people are feeling—even if it is glum or defeated—but they also model what it looks like to move forward with hope and humor.

This kind of performance, which we call resonance, is for all intents and purposes the four components of emotional intelligence in action.

Self-awareness, perhaps the most essential of the emotional intelligence competencies, is the ability to read your own emotions. It allows people to know their strengths and limitations and feel confident about their self-worth. Resonant leaders use self-awareness to gauge their own moods accurately, and they intuitively know how they are affecting others.

Self-management is the ability to control your emotions and act with honesty and integrity in reliable and adaptable ways. Resonant leaders don't let their occasional bad moods seize the day; they use self-management to leave it outside the office or to explain its source to people in a reasonable manner, so they know where it's coming from and how long it might last.

Social awareness includes the key capabilities of empathy and organizational intuition. Socially aware executives do more than sense other people's emotions, they show that they care. Further, they are experts at reading the currents of office politics. Thus, resonant leaders often keenly understand how their words and actions make others feel, and they are sensitive enough to change them when that impact is negative.

Relationship management, the last of the emotional intelligence competencies, includes the abilities to communicate clearly and convincingly, disarm

who works behind closed doors on an upper floor—his attitude affects the moods of his direct reports, and a domino effect ripples throughout the company.

Call That CEO a Doctor

If the leader's mood is so important, then he or she had better get into a good one, right? Yes, but the full answer is more complicated than that. A leader's mood has the greatest impact on performance

conflicts, and build strong personal bonds. Resonant leaders use these skills to spread their enthusiasm and solve disagreements, often with humor and kindness.

As effective as resonant leadership is, it is just as rare. Most people suffer through dissonant leaders whose toxic moods and upsetting behaviors wreak havoc before a hopeful and realistic leader repairs the situation.

Consider what happened recently at an experimental division of the BBC, the British media giant. Even though the group's 200 or so journalists and editors had given their best effort, management decided to close the division.

The shutdown itself was bad enough, but the brusque, contentious mood and manner of the executive sent to deliver the news to the assembled staff incited something beyond the expected frustration. People became enraged—at both the decision and the bearer of the news. The executive's cranky mood and delivery created an atmosphere so threatening that he had to call security to be ushered from the room.

The next day, another executive visited the same staff. His mood was somber and respectful, as was his behavior. He spoke about the importance of journalism to the vibrancy of a society and of the calling that had drawn them all to the field in the first place. He reminded them that no one goes into journalism to get rich—as a profession its finances have always been marginal, job security ebbing and flowing with the larger economic tides. He recalled a time in his own career when he had been let go and how he had struggled to find a new position—but how he had stayed dedicated to the profession. Finally, he wished them well in getting on with their careers.

The reaction from what had been an angry mob the day before? When this resonant leader finished speaking, the staff cheered.

when it is upbeat. But it must also be in tune with those around him. We call this dynamic *resonance*. (For more on this, see the sidebar "Get Happy, Carefully.")

We found that an alarming number of leaders do not really know if they have resonance with their organizations. Rather, they suffer from CEO disease; its one unpleasant symptom is the sufferer's near-total ignorance about how his mood and actions appear to the organization. It's not that leaders don't care how they are perceived; most do. But they incorrectly assume that they can decipher this information themselves. Worse, they think that if they are having a negative effect, someone will tell them. They're wrong.

As one CEO in our research explains, "I so often feel I'm not getting the truth. I can never put my finger on it, because no one is actually lying to me. But I can sense that people are hiding information or camouflaging key facts. They aren't lying, but neither are they telling me everything I need to know. I'm always second-guessing."

People don't tell leaders the whole truth about their emotional impact for many reasons. Sometimes they are scared of being the bearer of bad news—and getting shot. Others feel it isn't their place to comment on such a personal topic. Still others don't realize that what they really want to talk about is the effects of the leader's emotional style—that feels too vague. Whatever the reason, the CEO can't rely on his followers to spontaneously give him the full picture.

Taking Stock

The process we recommend for self-discovery and personal reinvention is neither newfangled nor born of pop psychology, like so many self-help programs offered to executives today. Rather, it is based on three streams of research into how executives can improve the emotional intelligence capabilities most closely linked to effective leadership. (Information on these research streams can also be found at www.eiconsortium.org.). In 1989, one of us (Richard Boyatzis) began drawing on this body of research to design the five-step process itself, and since then, thousands of executives have used it successfully.

Unlike more traditional forms of coaching, our process is based on brain science. A person's emotional skills—the attitude and abilities with which someone approaches life and work—are not genetically hardwired, like eye color and skin tone. But in some ways they might as well be, because they are so deeply embedded in our neurology.

A person's emotional skills do, in fact, have a genetic component. Scientists have discovered, for instance, the gene for shyness—which is not a mood, per se, but it can certainly drive a person toward a persistently quiet demeanor, which may be read as a "down" mood. Other people are preternaturally jolly—that is, their relentless cheerfulness seems preternatural until you meet their peppy parents. As one executive explains, "All I know is that ever since I was a baby, I have always been happy. It drives some people crazy, but I couldn't get blue if I tried. And my brother is the exact same way; he saw the bright side of life, even during his divorce."

Even though emotional skills are partly inborn, experience plays a major role in how the genes are expressed. A happy baby whose parents die or who endures physical abuse may grow into a melancholy adult. A cranky toddler may turn into a cheerful adult after discovering a fulfilling avocation. Still, research suggests that our range of emotional skills is relatively set by our mid-20s and that our accompanying behaviors are, by that time, deep-seated habits. And therein lies the rub: The more we act a certain way—be it happy, depressed, or cranky—the more the behavior becomes ingrained in our brain circuitry, and the more we will continue to feel and act that way.

That's why emotional intelligence matters so much for a leader. An emotionally intelligent leader can monitor his or her moods through self-awareness, change them for the better through self-management, understand their impact through empathy, and act in ways that boost others' moods through relationship management.

The following five-part process is designed to rewire the brain toward more emotionally intelligent behaviors. The process begins with imagining your ideal self and then coming to terms with your real self, as others experience you. The next step is creating a tactical plan to bridge the gap between ideal and real, and after that, to practice those activities. It concludes with creating a community of colleagues and family—call them change enforcers—to keep the process alive. Let's look at the steps in more detail.

"Who do I want to be?"

Sofia, a senior manager at a northern European telecommunications company, knew she needed to understand how her emotional leadership affected others. Whenever she felt stressed, she tended to communicate poorly and take over subordinates' work so that the job would be done "right." Attending leadership seminars hadn't changed her habits, and neither had reading management books or working with mentors.

When Sofia came to us, we asked her to imagine herself eight years from now as an effective leader and to write a description of a typical day. "What would she be doing?" we asked. "Where would she live? Who would be there? How would it feel?" We urged her to consider her deepest values and loftiest dreams and to explain how those ideals had become a part of her everyday life.

Sofia pictured herself leading her own tight-knit company staffed by ten colleagues. She was enjoying an open relationship with her daughter and had trusting relationships with her friends and coworkers. She saw herself as a relaxed and happy leader and parent, and as loving and empowering to all those around her.

In general, Sofia had a low level of self-awareness: She was rarely able to pinpoint why she was struggling at work and at home. All she could say was, "Nothing is working right." This exercise, which prompted her to picture what life would look like if everything were going right, opened her eyes to the missing elements in her emotional style. She was able to see the impact she had on people in her life.

"Who am I now?"

In the next step of the discovery process, you come to see your leadership style as others do. This is both difficult and dangerous. Difficult, because few people have the guts to tell the boss or a colleague what he's really like. And dangerous, because such information can sting or even paralyze. A small bit of ignorance about yourself isn't always a bad thing: Ego-defense mechanisms have their advantages. Research by Martin Seligman shows that high-functioning people generally feel more optimistic about their prospects and possibilities than average performers. Their rose-colored lenses, in fact, fuel the enthusiasm and energy that make the unexpected and the extraordinary achievable. Playwright Henrik Ibsen called such self-delusions "vital lies," soothing mistruths we let ourselves believe in order to face a daunting world.

But self-delusion should come in very small doses. Executives should relentlessly seek the truth about themselves, especially since it is sure to be somewhat diluted when they hear it anyway. One way to get the truth is to keep an extremely open attitude toward critiques. Another is to seek out negative feedback, even cultivating a colleague or two to play devil's advocate.

We also highly recommend gathering feedback from as many people as possible—including bosses, peers, and subordinates. Feedback from subordinates and peers is especially helpful because it most accurately predicts a leader's effectiveness, two, four, and even seven years out, according to research by Glenn McEvoy at Utah State and Richard Beatty at Rutgers University.

Of course, 360-degree feedback doesn't specifically ask people to evaluate your moods, actions, and their impact. But it does reveal how people experience you. For instance, when people rate how well you listen, they are really reporting how well they think you hear them. Similarly, when 360-degree feedback elicits ratings about coaching effectiveness, the answers show whether or not people feel you understand and care about them. When the feedback uncovers low scores on, say, openness to new ideas, it means that people experience you as inaccessible or unapproachable or both. In sum, all you need to know about your emotional impact is in 360-degree feedback, if you look for it.

One last note on this second step. It is, of course, crucial to identify your areas of weakness. But focusing only on your weaknesses can be dispiriting. That's why it is just as important, maybe even more so, to understand your strengths. Knowing where your real self overlaps with your ideal self will give you the positive energy you need to move forward to the next step in the process—bridging the gaps.

"How do I get from here to there?"

Once you know who you want to be and have compared it with how people see you, you need to devise an action plan. For Sofia, this meant planning for a real improvement in her level of self-awareness. So she asked each member of her team at work to give her feedback—weekly, anonymously, and in written form—about her mood and performance and their affect on people. She also committed herself to three tough but achievable tasks: spending an hour each day reflecting on her behavior in a journal, taking a class on group dynamics at a local college, and enlisting the help of a trusted colleague as an informal coach.

Consider, too, how Juan, a marketing executive for the Latin American division of a major integrated energy company, completed this step. Juan was charged with growing the company in his home country of Venezuela as well as in the entire region—a job that would require him to be a coach and a visionary and to have an encouraging, optimistic outlook. Yet 360-degree feedback revealed that Juan was seen as intimidating and internally focused. Many of his direct reports saw him as a grouch—impossible to please at his worst, and emotionally draining at his best.

Identifying this gap allowed Juan to craft a plan with manageable steps toward improvement. He knew he needed to hone his powers of empathy if he wanted to develop a coaching style, so he committed to various activities that would let him practice that skill. For instance, Juan decided to get to know each of his subordinates better; if he understood more about who they were, he thought, he'd be more able to help them reach their goals. He made plans with each employee to meet outside of work, where they might be more comfortable revealing their feelings.

Juan also looked for areas outside of his job to forge his missing links—for example, coaching his daughter's soccer team and volunteering at a local crisis center. Both activities helped him to experiment with how well he understood others and to try out new behaviors.

Again, let's look at the brain science at work. Juan was trying to overcome ingrained behaviors—his approach to work had taken hold over time, without his realizing it. Bringing them into awareness was a crucial step toward changing them. As he paid more attention, the situations that arose—while listening to a colleague, coaching soccer, or talking on the phone to someone who was distraught—all became cues that stimulated him to break old habits and try new responses.

Resonance in Times of Crisis

When talking about leaders' moods, the importance of resonance cannot be overstated. While our research suggests that leaders should generally be upbeat, their behavior must be rooted in realism, especially when faced with a crisis.

Consider the response of Bob Mulholland, senior VP and head of the client relations group at Merrill Lynch, to the terrorist attacks in New York. On September 11, 2001, Mulholland and his staff in Two World Financial Center felt the building rock, then watched as smoke poured out of a gaping hole in the building directly across from theirs. People started panicking: Some ran frantically from window to window. Others were paralyzed with fear. Those with relatives working in the World Trade Center were terrified for their safety. Mulholland knew he had to act: "When there's a crisis, you've got to show people the way, step by step, and make sure you're taking care of their concerns."

He started by getting people the information they needed to "unfreeze." He found out, for instance, which floors employees' relatives worked on and assured them that they'd have enough time to escape. Then he calmed the panic-stricken, one at a time. "We're getting out of here now," he said quietly, "and you're coming with me. Not the elevator, take the stairs." He remained calm and decisive, yet he didn't minimize people's emotional responses. Thanks to him, everyone escaped before the towers collapsed.

Mulholland's leadership didn't end there. Recognizing that this event would touch each client personally, he and his team devised a way for financial consultants to connect with their clients on an emotional level. They called every client to ask, "How are you? Are your loved ones okay? How are you feeling?" As Mulholland explains, "There was no way to pick up and do business as usual. The first order of 'business' was letting our clients know we really do care."

Bob Mulholland courageously performed one of the most crucial emotional tasks of leadership: He helped himself and his people find meaning in the face of chaos and madness. To do so, he first attuned to and expressed the shared emotional reality. That's why the direction he eventually articulated resonated at the gut level. His words and his actions reflected what people were feeling in their hearts.

This cueing for habit change is neural as well as perceptual. Researchers at the University of Pittsburgh and Carnegie Mellon University have shown that as we mentally prepare for a task, we activate the prefrontal cortex—the part of the brain that moves us into action. The greater the prior activation, the better we do at the task.

Such mental preparation becomes particularly important when we're trying to replace an old habit with a better one. As neuroscientist Cameron Carter at the University of Pittsburgh found, the prefrontal cortex becomes particularly active when a person prepares to overcome a habitual response. The aroused prefrontal cortex marks the brain's focus on what's about to happen. Without that arousal, a person will reenact tried-and-true but undesirable routines: The executive who just doesn't listen will once again cut off his subordinate, a ruthless leader will launch into yet another critical attack, and so on. That's why a learning agenda is so important. Without one, we literally do not have the brainpower to change.

"How do I make change stick?"

In short, making change last requires practice. The reason, again, lies in the brain. It takes doing and redoing, over and over, to break old neural habits. A leader must rehearse a new behavior until it becomes automatic—that is, until he's mastered it at the level of implicit learning. Only then will the new wiring replace the old.

While it is best to practice new behaviors, as Juan did, sometimes just envisioning them will do. Take the case of Tom, an executive who wanted to close the gap between his real self (perceived by colleagues and subordinates to be cold and hard driving) and his ideal self (a visionary and a coach).

Tom's learning plan involved finding opportunities to step back and coach his employees rather than jumping down their throats when he sensed they were wrong. Tom also began to spend idle moments during his commute thinking through how to handle encounters he would have that day. One morning, while en route to a breakfast meeting with an employee who seemed to be bungling a project, Tom ran through a positive scenario in his mind. He asked questions and listened to be sure he fully understood the situation before trying to solve the problem. He anticipated feeling impatient, and he rehearsed how he would handle these feelings.

Studies on the brain affirm the benefits of Tom's visualization technique: Imagining something in vivid detail can fire the same brain cells actually involved in doing that activity. The new brain circuitry appears to go through its paces, strengthening connections, even when we merely repeat the sequence in our minds. So to alleviate the fears associated with trying out riskier ways of leading, we should first visualize some likely scenarios. Doing so will make us feel less awkward when we actually put the new skills into practice.

Experimenting with new behaviors and seizing opportunities inside and outside of work to practice them—as well as using such methods as mental rehearsal—eventually triggers in our brains the neural connections necessary for genuine change to occur. Even so, lasting change doesn't happen through experimentation and brainpower alone. We need, as the song goes, a little help from our friends.

"Who can help me?"

The fifth step in the self-discovery and reinvention process is creating a community of supporters. Take, for example, managers at Unilever who formed learning groups as part of their executive development process. At first, they gathered to discuss their careers and how to provide leadership. But because they were also charged with discussing their dreams and their learning goals, they soon realized that they were discussing both their work and their personal lives. They developed a strong mutual trust and began relying on one another for frank feedback as they worked on strengthening their leadership abilities. When this happens, the business benefits through stronger performance. Many professionals today have created similar groups, and for good reason. People we trust let us try out unfamiliar parts of our leadership repertoire without risk.

We cannot improve our emotional intelligence or change our leadership style without help from others. We not only practice with other people but also rely on them to create a safe environment in which to experiment. We need to get feedback about how our actions affect others and to assess our progress on our learning agenda.

In fact, perhaps paradoxically, in the self-directed learning process we draw on others every step of the way—from articulating and refining our ideal self and comparing it with the reality to the final assessment that affirms our progress. Our relationships offer us the very context in which we understand our progress and comprehend the usefulness of what we're learning.

Mood over Matter

When we say that managing your mood and the moods of your followers is the task of primal leadership, we certainly don't mean to suggest that mood is all that matters. As we've noted, your actions are critical, and mood and actions together must resonate with the organization and with reality. Similarly, we acknowledge all the other challenges leaders must conquer—from strategy to hiring to new product development. It's all in a long day's work.

But taken as a whole, the message sent by neurological, psychological, and organizational research is startling in its clarity. Emotional leadership is the spark that ignites a company's performance, creating a bonfire of success or a landscape of ashes. Moods matter that much.

Originally published in December 2001. Reprint R0111C

About the Contributors

RICHARD BOYATZIS chairs the department of organizational behavior at the Weatherhead School of Management at Case Western Reserve University.

HEIKE BRUCH is a professor of leadership at the University of St. Gallen in Switzerland.

CLAYTON M. CHRISTENSEN is the Robert and Jane Cizik Professor of Business Administration at Harvard Business School.

DIANE L. COUTU is a former senior editor of *Harvard Business Review*.

STEPHEN R. COVEY is vice chairman of Franklin Covey, a global provider of leadership development and productivity services.

PETER F. DRUCKER was a professor of social science and management at Claremont Graduate University in California.

STEWART D. FRIEDMAN is the Practice Professor of Management at the University of Pennsylvania's Wharton School.

SUMANTRA GHOSHAL was a professor of strategy and international management at London Business School.

DANIEL GOLEMAN cochairs the Consortium for Research on Emotional Intelligence in Organizations at Rutgers University.

EDWARD M. HALLOWELL is a psychiatrist and the founder of the Hallowell Centers for Cognitive and Emotional Health.

ROBERT S. KAPLAN is a professor of management practice at Harvard Business School.

CATHERINE McCARTHY is a senior vice president at the Energy Project in New York.

ANNIE McKEE is on the faculty of the University of Pennsylvania's Graduate School of Education.

WILLIAM ONCKEN, JR., was chairman of the William Oncken Corporation, a management consulting company.

ROBERT E. QUINN is the Margaret Elliott Tracy Collegiate Professor in Business Administration at the University of Michigan's Ross School of Business.

TONY SCHWARTZ is the president and founder of the Energy Project in New York.

DONALD L. WASS heads the Dallas–Fort Worth region of The Executive Committee (TEC), an international organization for presidents and CEOs.

Index

Harvard
Business
Review
136 Marvel's
Blockbuster Machine
94 Digital Doesn't
Have to Be Disruptive
116 When a Colleague
Is Grieving
The AI-Powered
Organization
The main
challenge
isn't
technology.
It's culture.
62

VISUAL LIBRARY
The Good-Better-Best Approach to Pricing
Harvard
Business
Review
Are
METRICS
Undermining
Your
Business?
Too many leaders
confuse numbers
with strategy.
62

HBR'S 10 MUST READS

On Strategy

HBR'S 10 MUST READS

On Strategy

HARVARD BUSINESS REVIEW PRESS
Boston, Massachusetts

Printed in the United States of America
45 44 43 42 41

Library of Congress Cataloging-in-Publication Data
HBR's 10 must reads on strategy.
p. cm.
Includes index.
ISBN 978-1-4221-5798-5 (pbk. : alk. paper) 1. Strategic planning.
I. Harvard business review. II. Title: HBR's ten must reads on strategy.
III. Title: Harvard business review's 10 must reads on strategy.
HD30.28.H395 2010
658.4 '012—dc22
2010031619

The paper used in this publication meets the requirements of the American National Standard for Permanence of Paper for Publications and Documents in Libraries and Archives Z39.48-1992.

Contents

HBR'S 10 MUST READS

On Strategy

What Is Strategy?

by Michael E. Porter

I. Operational Effectiveness Is Not Strategy

For almost two decades, managers have been learning to play by a new set of rules. Companies must be flexible to respond rapidly to competitive and market changes. They must benchmark continuously to achieve best practice. They must outsource aggressively to gain efficiencies. And they must nurture a few core competencies in race to stay ahead of rivals.

Positioning—once the heart of strategy—is rejected as too static for today's dynamic markets and changing technologies. According to the new dogma, rivals can quickly copy any market position, and competitive advantage is, at best, temporary.

But those beliefs are dangerous half-truths, and they are leading more and more companies down the path of mutually destructive competition. True, some barriers to competition are falling as regulation eases and markets become global. True, companies have properly invested energy in becoming leaner and more nimble. In many industries, however, what some call *hypercompetition* is a self-inflicted wound, not the inevitable outcome of a changing paradigm of competition.

The root of the problem is the failure to distinguish between operational effectiveness and strategy. The quest for productivity, quality, and speed has spawned a remarkable number of management tools and techniques: total quality management, benchmarking, time-based competition, outsourcing, partnering, reengineering, change management. Although the resulting operational improvements have often been dramatic, many companies have been frustrated by their inability to translate those gains into sustainable profitability. And bit by bit, almost imperceptibly, management tools have taken the place of strategy. As managers push to improve on all fronts, they move farther away from viable competitive positions.

Operational effectiveness: necessary but not sufficient

Operational effectiveness and strategy are both essential to superior performance, which, after all, is the primary goal of any enterprise. But they work in very different ways.

A company can outperform rivals only if it can establish a difference that it can preserve. It must deliver greater value to customers or create comparable value at a lower cost, or do both. The arithmetic of superior profitability then follows: delivering greater value allows a company to charge higher average unit prices; greater efficiency results in lower average unit costs.

Ultimately, all differences between companies in cost or price derive from the hundreds of activities required to create, produce, sell, and deliver their products or services, such as calling on customers, assembling final products, and training employees. Cost is generated by performing activities, and cost advantage arises from performing particular activities more efficiently than competitors. Similarly, differentiation arises from both the choice of activities and how they are performed. Activities, then, are the basic units of competitive advantage. Overall advantage or disadvantage results from all a company's activities, not only a few.[1]

Operational effectiveness (OE) means performing similar activities *better* than rivals perform them. Operational effectiveness includes but is not limited to efficiency. It refers to any number of practices that allow a company to better utilize its inputs by, for example, reducing defects in products or developing better products faster. In contrast, strategic positioning means performing *different* activities from rivals' or performing similar activities in *different* ways.

Differences in operational effectiveness among companies are pervasive. Some companies are able to get more out of their inputs

Idea in Brief

The myriad activities that go into creating, producing, selling, and delivering a product or service are the basic units of competitive advantage. **Operational effectiveness** means performing these activities better—that is, faster, or with fewer inputs and defects—than rivals. Companies can reap enormous advantages from operational effectiveness, as Japanese firms demonstrated in the 1970s and 1980s with such practices as total quality management and continuous improvement. But from a competitive standpoint, the problem with operational effectiveness is that best practices are easily emulated. As all competitors in an industry adopt them, the **productivity frontier**—the maximum value a company can deliver at a given cost, given the best available technology, skills, and management techniques—shifts outward, lowering costs and improving value at the same time. Such competition produces absolute improvement in operational effectiveness, but relative improvement for no one. And the more benchmarking that companies do, the more **competitive convergence** you have—that is, the more indistinguishable companies are from one another.

Strategic positioning attempts to achieve sustainable competitive advantage by preserving what is distinctive about a company. It means performing *different* activities from rivals, or performing *similar* activities in different ways.

than others because they eliminate wasted effort, employ more advanced technology, motivate employees better, or have greater insight into managing particular activities or sets of activities. Such differences in operational effectiveness are an important source of differences in profitability among competitors because they directly affect relative cost positions and levels of differentiation.

Differences in operational effectiveness were at the heart of the Japanese challenge to Western companies in the 1980s. The Japanese were so far ahead of rivals in operational effectiveness that they could offer lower cost and superior quality at the same time. It is worth dwelling on this point, because so much recent thinking about competition depends on it. Imagine for a moment a *productivity frontier* that constitutes the sum of all existing best practices at any given time. Think of it as the maximum value that a

Idea in Practice

Three key principles underlie strategic positioning.

1. **Strategy is the creation of a unique and valuable position, involving a different set of activities.** Strategic position emerges from three distinct sources:
   - serving few needs of many customers (Jiffy Lube provides only auto lubricants)
   - serving broad needs of few customers (Bessemer Trust targets only very high-wealth clients)
   - serving broad needs of many customers in a narrow market (Carmike Cinemas operates only in cities with a population under 200,000)
2. **Strategy requires you to make trade-offs in competing—to choose what *not* to do.** Some competitive activities are incompatible; thus, gains in one area can be achieved only at the expense of another area. For example, Neutrogena soap is positioned more as a medicinal product than as a cleansing agent. The company says "no" to sales based on deodorizing, gives up large volume, and sacrifices manufacturing efficiencies. By contrast, Maytag's decision to extend its product line and acquire other brands represented a failure to make difficult trade-offs: the boost in revenues came at the expense of return on sales.
3. **Strategy involves creating "fit" among a company's activities.** Fit has to do with the ways a company's activities interact and reinforce one another. For example, Vanguard Group aligns all of its activities with a low-cost strategy; it distributes funds directly to consumers and minimizes portfolio turnover. Fit drives both competitive advantage and sustainability: when activities mutually reinforce each other, competitors can't easily imitate them. When Continental Lite tried to match a few of Southwest Airlines' activities, but not the whole interlocking system, the results were disastrous.

Employees need guidance about how to deepen a strategic position rather than broaden or compromise it. About how to extend the company's uniqueness while strengthening the fit among its activities. This work of deciding which target group of customers and needs to serve requires discipline, the ability to set limits, and forthright communication. Clearly, strategy and leadership are inextricably linked.

company delivering a particular product or service can create at a given cost, using the best available technologies, skills, management techniques, and purchased inputs. The productivity frontier can apply to individual activities, to groups of linked activities such as order processing and manufacturing, and to an entire company's activities. When a company improves its operational effectiveness, it moves toward the frontier. Doing so may require capital investment, different personnel, or simply new ways of managing.

The productivity frontier is constantly shifting outward as new technologies and management approaches are developed and as new inputs become available. Laptop computers, mobile communications, the Internet, and software such as Lotus Notes, for example, have redefined the productivity frontier for sales-force operations and created rich possibilities for linking sales with such activities as order processing and after-sales support. Similarly, lean production, which involves a family of activities, has allowed substantial improvements in manufacturing productivity and asset utilization.

Operational effectiveness versus strategic positioning

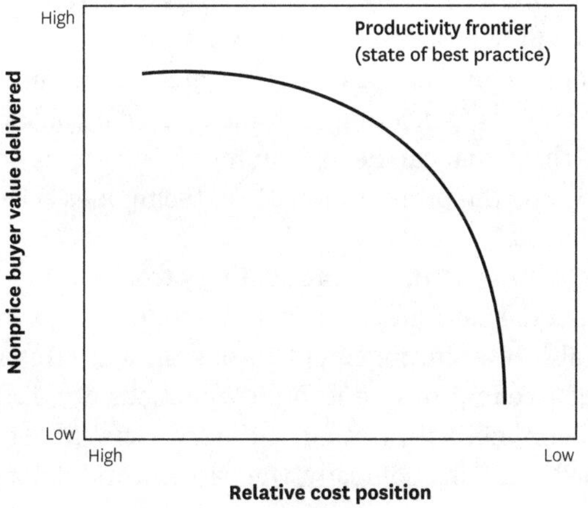

For at least the past decade, managers have been preoccupied with improving operational effectiveness. Through programs such as TQM, time-based competition, and benchmarking, they have changed how they perform activities in order to eliminate inefficiencies, improve customer satisfaction, and achieve best practice. Hoping to keep up with shifts in the productivity frontier, managers have embraced continuous improvement, empowerment, change management, and the so-called learning organization. The popularity of outsourcing and the virtual corporation reflect the growing recognition that it is difficult to perform all activities as productively as specialists.

As companies move to the frontier, they can often improve on multiple dimensions of performance at the same time. For example, manufacturers that adopted the Japanese practice of rapid changeovers in the 1980s were able to lower cost and improve differentiation simultaneously. What were once believed to be real trade-offs—between defects and costs, for example—turned out to be illusions created by poor operational effectiveness. Managers have learned to reject such false trade-offs.

Constant improvement in operational effectiveness is necessary to achieve superior profitability. However, it is not usually sufficient. Few companies have competed successfully on the basis of operational effectiveness over an extended period, and staying ahead of rivals gets harder every day. The most obvious reason for that is the rapid diffusion of best practices. Competitors can quickly imitate management techniques, new technologies, input improvements, and superior ways of meeting customers' needs. The most generic solutions—those that can be used in multiple settings—diffuse the fastest. Witness the proliferation of OE techniques accelerated by support from consultants.

OE competition shifts the productivity frontier outward, effectively raising the bar for everyone. But although such competition produces absolute improvement in operational effectiveness, it leads to relative improvement for no one. Consider the $5 billion-plus U.S. commercial-printing industry. The major players—R.R. Donnelley & Sons Company, Quebecor, World Color Press, and

Big Flower Press—are competing head to head, serving all types of customers, offering the same array of printing technologies (gravure and web offset), investing heavily in the same new equipment, running their presses faster, and reducing crew sizes. But the resulting major productivity gains are being captured by customers and equipment suppliers, not retained in superior profitability. Even industry-leader Donnelley's profit margin, consistently higher than 7% in the 1980s, fell to less than 4.6% in 1995. This pattern is playing itself out in industry after industry. Even the Japanese, pioneers of the new competition, suffer from persistently low profits. (See the sidebar "Japanese Companies Rarely Have Strategies.")

The second reason that improved operational effectiveness is insufficient—competitive convergence—is more subtle and insidious. The more benchmarking companies do, the more they look alike. The more that rivals outsource activities to efficient third parties, often the same ones, the more generic those activities become. As rivals imitate one another's improvements in quality, cycle times, or supplier partnerships, strategies converge and competition becomes a series of races down identical paths that no one can win. Competition based on operational effectiveness alone is mutually destructive, leading to wars of attrition that can be arrested only by limiting competition.

The recent wave of industry consolidation through mergers makes sense in the context of OE competition. Driven by performance pressures but lacking strategic vision, company after company has had no better idea than to buy up its rivals. The competitors left standing are often those that outlasted others, not companies with real advantage.

After a decade of impressive gains in operational effectiveness, many companies are facing diminishing returns. Continuous improvement has been etched on managers' brains. But its tools unwittingly draw companies toward imitation and homogeneity. Gradually, managers have let operational effectiveness supplant strategy. The result is zero-sum competition, static or declining prices, and pressures on costs that compromise companies' ability to invest in the business for the long term.

Japanese Companies Rarely Have Strategies

THE JAPANESE TRIGGERED A GLOBAL revolution in operational effectiveness in the 1970s and 1980s, pioneering practices such as total quality management and continuous improvement. As a result, Japanese manufacturers enjoyed substantial cost and quality advantages for many years.

But Japanese companies rarely developed distinct strategic positions of the kind discussed in this article. Those that did—Sony, Canon, and Sega, for example—were the exception rather than the rule. Most Japanese companies imitate and emulate one another. All rivals offer most if not all product varieties, features, and services; they employ all channels and match one anothers' plant configurations.

The dangers of Japanese-style competition are now becoming easier to recognize. In the 1980s, with rivals operating far from the productivity frontier, it seemed possible to win on both cost and quality indefinitely. Japanese companies were all able to grow in an expanding domestic economy and by penetrating global markets. They appeared unstoppable. But as the gap in operational effectiveness narrows, Japanese companies are increasingly caught in a trap of their own making. If they are to escape the mutually destructive battles now ravaging their performance, Japanese companies will have to learn strategy.

To do so, they may have to overcome strong cultural barriers. Japan is notoriously consensus oriented, and companies have a strong tendency to mediate differences among individuals rather than accentuate them. Strategy, on the other hand, requires hard choices. The Japanese also have a deeply ingrained service tradition that predisposes them to go to great lengths to satisfy any need a customer expresses. Companies that compete in that way end up blurring their distinct positioning, becoming all things to all customers.

This discussion of Japan is drawn from the author's research with Hirotaka Takeuchi, with help from Mariko Sakakibara.

II. Strategy Rests on Unique Activities

Competitive strategy is about being different. It means deliberately choosing a different set of activities to deliver a unique mix of value.

Southwest Airlines Company, for example, offers short-haul, low-cost, point-to-point service between midsize cities and secondary airports in large cities. Southwest avoids large airports and does not fly great distances. Its customers include business travelers, families, and students. Southwest's frequent departures and low fares attract price-sensitive customers who otherwise would travel by bus or car, and convenience-oriented travelers who would choose a full-service airline on other routes.

Most managers describe strategic positioning in terms of their customers: "Southwest Airlines serves price- and convenience-sensitive travelers," for example. But the essence of strategy is in the activities—choosing to perform activities differently or to perform different activities than rivals. Otherwise, a strategy is nothing more than a marketing slogan that will not withstand competition.

A full-service airline is configured to get passengers from almost any point A to any point B. To reach a large number of destinations and serve passengers with connecting flights, full-service airlines employ a hub-and-spoke system centered on major airports. To attract passengers who desire more comfort, they offer first-class or business-class service. To accommodate passengers who must change planes, they coordinate schedules and check and transfer baggage. Because some passengers will be traveling for many hours, full-service airlines serve meals.

Southwest, in contrast, tailors all its activities to deliver low-cost, convenient service on its particular type of route. Through fast turnarounds at the gate of only 15 minutes, Southwest is able to keep planes flying longer hours than rivals and provide frequent departures with fewer aircraft. Southwest does not offer meals, assigned seats, interline baggage checking, or premium classes of service. Automated ticketing at the gate encourages customers to bypass travel agents, allowing Southwest to avoid their commissions. A standardized fleet of 737 aircraft boosts the efficiency of maintenance.

Southwest has staked out a unique and valuable strategic position based on a tailored set of activities. On the routes served by Southwest, a full-service airline could never be as convenient or as low cost.

Ikea, the global furniture retailer based in Sweden, also has a clear strategic positioning. Ikea targets young furniture buyers who want style at low cost. What turns this marketing concept into a strategic

Finding New Positions: The Entrepreneurial Edge

STRATEGIC COMPETITION CAN BE THOUGHT of as the process of perceiving new positions that woo customers from established positions or draw new customers into the market. For example, superstores offering depth of merchandise in a single product category take market share from broad-line department stores offering a more limited selection in many categories. Mail-order catalogs pick off customers who crave convenience. In principle, incumbents and entrepreneurs face the same challenges in finding new strategic positions. In practice, new entrants often have the edge.

Strategic positionings are often not obvious, and finding them requires creativity and insight. New entrants often discover unique positions that have been available but simply overlooked by established competitors. Ikea, for example, recognized a customer group that had been ignored or served poorly. Circuit City Stores' entry into used cars, CarMax, is based on a new way of performing activities—extensive refurbishing of cars, product guarantees, no-haggle pricing, sophisticated use of in-house customer financing—that has long been open to incumbents.

New entrants can prosper by occupying a position that a competitor once held but has ceded through years of imitation and straddling. And entrants coming from other industries can create new positions because of distinctive activities drawn from their other businesses. CarMax borrows heavily from Circuit City's expertise in inventory management, credit, and other activities in consumer electronics retailing.

Most commonly, however, new positions open up because of change. New customer groups or purchase occasions arise; new needs emerge as societies evolve; new distribution channels appear; new technologies are developed; new machinery or information systems become available. When such changes happen, new entrants, unencumbered by a long history in the industry, can often more easily perceive the potential for a new way of competing. Unlike incumbents, newcomers can be more flexible because they face no trade-offs with their existing activities.

---

positioning is the tailored set of activities that make it work. Like Southwest, Ikea has chosen to perform activities differently from its rivals.

Consider the typical furniture store. Showrooms display samples of the merchandise. One area might contain 25 sofas; another will display five dining tables. But those items represent only a fraction of the choices available to customers. Dozens of books displaying fabric swatches or wood samples or alternate styles offer customers thousands of product varieties to choose from. Salespeople often escort customers through the store, answering questions and helping them navigate this maze of choices. Once a customer makes a selection, the order is relayed to a third-party manufacturer. With luck, the furniture will be delivered to the customer's home within six to eight weeks. This is a value chain that maximizes customization and service but does so at high cost.

In contrast, Ikea serves customers who are happy to trade off service for cost. Instead of having a sales associate trail customers around the store, Ikea uses a self-service model based on clear, in-store displays. Rather than rely solely on third-party manufacturers, Ikea designs its own low-cost, modular, ready-to-assemble furniture to fit its positioning. In huge stores, Ikea displays every product it sells in room-like settings, so customers don't need a decorator to help them imagine how to put the pieces together. Adjacent to the furnished showrooms is a warehouse section with the products in boxes on pallets. Customers are expected to do their own pickup and delivery, and Ikea will even sell you a roof rack for your car that you can return for a refund on your next visit.

Although much of its low-cost position comes from having customers "do it themselves," Ikea offers a number of extra services that its competitors do not. In-store child care is one. Extended hours are another. Those services are uniquely aligned with the needs of its customers, who are young, not wealthy, likely to have children (but no nanny), and, because they work for a living, have a need to shop at odd hours.

The origins of strategic positions

Strategic positions emerge from three distinct sources, which are not mutually exclusive and often overlap. First, positioning can be based on producing a subset of an industry's products or services. I call this *variety-based positioning* because it is based on the choice of product or service varieties rather than customer segments.

Variety-based positioning makes economic sense when a company can best produce particular products or services using distinctive sets of activities.

Jiffy Lube International, for instance, specializes in automotive lubricants and does not offer other car repair or maintenance services. Its value chain produces faster service at a lower cost than broader line repair shops, a combination so attractive that many customers subdivide their purchases, buying oil changes from the focused competitor, Jiffy Lube, and going to rivals for other services.

The Vanguard Group, a leader in the mutual fund industry, is another example of variety-based positioning. Vanguard provides an array of common stock, bond, and money market funds that offer predictable performance and rock-bottom expenses. The company's investment approach deliberately sacrifices the possibility of extraordinary performance in any one year for good relative performance in every year. Vanguard is known, for example, for its index funds. It avoids making bets on interest rates and steers clear of narrow stock groups. Fund managers keep trading levels low, which holds expenses down; in addition, the company discourages customers from rapid buying and selling because doing so drives up costs and can force a fund manager to trade in order to deploy new capital and raise cash for redemptions. Vanguard also takes a consistent low-cost approach to managing distribution, customer service, and marketing. Many investors include one or more Vanguard funds in their portfolio, while buying aggressively managed or specialized funds from competitors.

The people who use Vanguard or Jiffy Lube are responding to a superior value chain for a particular type of service. A variety-based positioning can serve a wide array of customers, but for most it will meet only a subset of their needs.

A second basis for positioning is that of serving most or all the needs of a particular group of customers. I call this *needs-based positioning,* which comes closer to traditional thinking about targeting a segment of customers. It arises when there are groups of customers with differing needs, and when a tailored set of activities can serve those needs best. Some groups of customers are more price sensitive

The Connection with Generic Strategies

IN COMPETITIVE STRATEGY (The Free Press, 1985), I introduced the concept of generic strategies—cost leadership, differentiation, and focus—to represent the alternative strategic positions in an industry. The generic strategies remain useful to characterize strategic positions at the simplest and broadest level. Vanguard, for instance, is an example of a cost leadership strategy, whereas Ikea, with its narrow customer group, is an example of cost-based focus. Neutrogena is a focused differentiator. The bases for positioning—varieties, needs, and access—carry the understanding of those generic strategies to a greater level of specificity. Ikea and Southwest are both cost-based focusers, for example, but Ikea's focus is based on the needs of a customer group, and Southwest's is based on offering a particular service variety.

The generic strategies framework introduced the need to choose in order to avoid becoming caught between what I then described as the inherent contradictions of different strategies. Trade-offs between the activities of incompatible positions explain those contradictions. Witness Continental Lite, which tried and failed to compete in two ways at once.

than others, demand different product features, and need varying amounts of information, support, and services. Ikea's customers are a good example of such a group. Ikea seeks to meet all the home furnishing needs of its target customers, not just a subset of them.

A variant of needs-based positioning arises when the same customer has different needs on different occasions or for different types of transactions. The same person, for example, may have different needs when traveling on business than when traveling for pleasure with the family. Buyers of cans—beverage companies, for example—will likely have different needs from their primary supplier than from their secondary source.

It is intuitive for most managers to conceive of their business in terms of the customers' needs they are meeting. But a critical element of needs-based positioning is not at all intuitive and is often overlooked. Differences in needs will not translate into meaningful positions unless the best set of activities to satisfy them *also* differs. If that were not the case, every competitor could meet those same needs, and there would be nothing unique or valuable about the positioning.

In private banking, for example, Bessemer Trust Company targets families with a minimum of $5 million in investable assets who want capital preservation combined with wealth accumulation. By assigning one sophisticated account officer for every 14 families, Bessemer has configured its activities for personalized service. Meetings, for example, are more likely to be held at a client's ranch or yacht than in the office. Bessemer offers a wide array of customized services, including investment management and estate administration, oversight of oil and gas investments, and accounting for racehorses and aircraft. Loans, a staple of most private banks, are rarely needed by Bessemer's clients and make up a tiny fraction of its client balances and income. Despite the most generous compensation of account officers and the highest personnel cost as a percentage of operating expenses, Bessemer's differentiation with its target families produces a return on equity estimated to be the highest of any private banking competitor.

Citibank's private bank, on the other hand, serves clients with minimum assets of about $250,000 who, in contrast to Bessemer's clients, want convenient access to loans—from jumbo mortgages to deal financing. Citibank's account managers are primarily lenders. When clients need other services, their account manager refers them to other Citibank specialists, each of whom handles prepackaged products. Citibank's system is less customized than Bessemer's and allows it to have a lower manager-to-client ratio of 1:125. Biannual office meetings are offered only for the largest clients. Both Bessemer and Citibank have tailored their activities to meet the needs of a different group of private banking customers. The same value chain cannot profitably meet the needs of both groups.

The third basis for positioning is that of segmenting customers who are accessible in different ways. Although their needs are similar to those of other customers, the best configuration of activities to reach them is different. I call this *access-based positioning*. Access can be a function of customer geography or customer scale—or of anything that requires a different set of activities to reach customers in the best way.

Segmenting by access is less common and less well understood than the other two bases. Carmike Cinemas, for example, operates movie theaters exclusively in cities and towns with populations under 200,000. How does Carmike make money in markets that are not only small but also won't support big-city ticket prices? It does so through a set of activities that result in a lean cost structure. Carmike's small-town customers can be served through standardized, low-cost theater complexes requiring fewer screens and less sophisticated projection technology than big-city theaters. The company's proprietary information system and management process eliminate the need for local administrative staff beyond a single theater manager. Carmike also reaps advantages from centralized purchasing, lower rent and payroll costs (because of its locations), and rock-bottom corporate overhead of 2% (the industry average is 5%). Operating in small communities also allows Carmike to practice a highly personal form of marketing in which the theater manager knows patrons and promotes attendance through personal contacts. By being the dominant if not the only theater in its markets—the main competition is often the high school football team—Carmike is also able to get its pick of films and negotiate better terms with distributors.

Rural versus urban-based customers are one example of access driving differences in activities. Serving small rather than large customers or densely rather than sparsely situated customers are other examples in which the best way to configure marketing, order processing, logistics, and after-sale service activities to meet the similar needs of distinct groups will often differ.

Positioning is not only about carving out a niche. A position emerging from any of the sources can be broad or narrow. A focused competitor, such as Ikea, targets the special needs of a subset of customers and designs its activities accordingly. Focused competitors thrive on groups of customers who are overserved (and hence overpriced) by more broadly targeted competitors, or underserved (and hence underpriced). A broadly targeted competitor—for example, Vanguard or Delta Air Lines—serves a wide array of customers, performing a set of activities designed to meet their common needs. It ignores or meets only partially the more idiosyncratic needs of particular customer customer groups.

Whatever the basis—variety, needs, access, or some combination of the three—positioning requires a tailored set of activities because it is always a function of differences on the supply side; that is, of differences in activities. However, positioning is not always a function of differences on the demand, or customer, side. Variety and access positionings, in particular, do not rely on *any* customer differences. In practice, however, variety or access differences often accompany needs differences. The tastes—that is, the needs—of Carmike's small-town customers, for instance, run more toward comedies, Westerns, action films, and family entertainment. Carmike does not run any films rated NC-17.

Having defined positioning, we can now begin to answer the question, "What is strategy?" Strategy is the creation of a unique and valuable position, involving a different set of activities. If there were only one ideal position, there would be no need for strategy. Companies would face a simple imperative—win the race to discover and preempt it. The essence of strategic positioning is to choose activities that are different from rivals'. If the same set of activities were best to produce all varieties, meet all needs, and access all customers, companies could easily shift among them and operational effectiveness would determine performance.

III. A Sustainable Strategic Position Requires Trade-offs

Choosing a unique position, however, is not enough to guarantee a sustainable advantage. A valuable position will attract imitation by incumbents, who are likely to copy it in one of two ways.

First, a competitor can reposition itself to match the superior performer. J.C. Penney, for instance, has been repositioning itself from a Sears clone to a more upscale, fashion-oriented, soft-goods retailer. A second and far more common type of imitation is straddling. The straddler seeks to match the benefits of a successful position while maintaining its existing position. It grafts new features, services, or technologies onto the activities it already performs.

For those who argue that competitors can copy any market position, the airline industry is a perfect test case. It would seem that nearly any competitor could imitate any other airline's activities. Any airline can buy the same planes, lease the gates, and match the menus and ticketing and baggage handling services offered by other airlines.

Continental Airlines saw how well Southwest was doing and decided to straddle. While maintaining its position as a full-service airline, Continental also set out to match Southwest on a number of point-to-point routes. The airline dubbed the new service Continental Lite. It eliminated meals and first-class service, increased departure frequency, lowered fares, and shortened turnaround time at the gate. Because Continental remained a full-service airline on other routes, it continued to use travel agents and its mixed fleet of planes and to provide baggage checking and seat assignments.

But a strategic position is not sustainable unless there are trade-offs with other positions. Trade-offs occur when activities are incompatible. Simply put, a trade-off means that more of one thing necessitates less of another. An airline can choose to serve meals—adding cost and slowing turnaround time at the gate—or it can choose not to, but it cannot do both without bearing major inefficiencies.

Trade-offs create the need for choice and protect against repositioners and straddlers. Consider Neutrogena soap. Neutrogena Corporation's variety-based positioning is built on a "kind to the skin," residue-free soap formulated for pH balance. With a large detail force calling on dermatologists, Neutrogena's marketing strategy looks more like a drug company's than a soap maker's. It advertises in medical journals, sends direct mail to doctors, attends medical conferences, and performs research at its own Skincare Institute. To reinforce its positioning, Neutrogena originally focused its distribution on drugstores and avoided price promotions. Neutrogena uses a slow, more expensive manufacturing process to mold its fragile soap.

In choosing this position, Neutrogena said no to the deodorants and skin softeners that many customers desire in their soap. It gave up the large-volume potential of selling through supermarkets and using price promotions. It sacrificed manufacturing efficiencies to achieve the soap's desired attributes. In its original positioning, Neutrogena made a whole raft of trade-offs like those, trade-offs that protected the company from imitators.

Trade-offs arise for three reasons. The first is inconsistencies in image or reputation. A company known for delivering one kind of value may lack credibility and confuse customers—or even undermine its reputation—if it delivers another kind of value or attempts to deliver two inconsistent things at the same time. For example, Ivory soap, with its position as a basic, inexpensive everyday soap, would have a hard time reshaping its image to match Neutrogena's premium "medical" reputation. Efforts to create a new image typically cost tens or even hundreds of millions of dollars in a major industry—a powerful barrier to imitation.

Second, and more important, trade-offs arise from activities themselves. Different positions (with their tailored activities) require different product configurations, different equipment, different employee behavior, different skills, and different management systems. Many trade-offs reflect inflexibilities in machinery, people, or systems. The more Ikea has configured its activities to lower costs by having its customers do their own assembly and delivery, the less able it is to satisfy customers who require higher levels of service.

However, trade-offs can be even more basic. In general, value is destroyed if an activity is overdesigned or underdesigned for its use. For example, even if a given salesperson were capable of providing a high level of assistance to one customer and none to another, the salesperson's talent (and some of his or her cost) would be wasted on the second customer. Moreover, productivity can improve when variation of an activity is limited. By providing a high level of assistance all the time, the salesperson and the entire sales activity can often achieve efficiencies of learning and scale.

Finally, trade-offs arise from limits on internal coordination and control. By clearly choosing to compete in one way and not another, senior management makes organizational priorities clear. Companies that try to be all things to all customers, in contrast, risk confusion in the trenches as employees attempt to make day-to-day operating decisions without a clear framework.

Positioning trade-offs are pervasive in competition and essential to strategy. They create the need for choice and purposefully limit what a company offers. They deter straddling or repositioning, because competitors that engage in those approaches undermine their strategies and degrade the value of their existing activities.

Trade-offs ultimately grounded Continental Lite. The airline lost hundreds of millions of dollars, and the CEO lost his job. Its planes were delayed leaving congested hub cities or slowed at the gate by baggage transfers. Late flights and cancellations generated a thousand complaints a day. Continental Lite could not afford to compete on price and still pay standard travel-agent commissions, but neither could it do without agents for its full-service business. The airline compromised by cutting commissions for all Continental flights across the board. Similarly, it could not afford to offer the same frequent-flier benefits to travelers paying the much lower ticket prices for Lite service. It compromised again by lowering the rewards of Continental's entire frequent-flier program. The results: angry travel agents and full-service customers.

Continental tried to compete in two ways at once. In trying to be low cost on some routes and full service on others, Continental paid an enormous straddling penalty. If there were no trade-offs between the two positions, Continental could have succeeded. But the absence of trade-offs is a dangerous half-truth that managers must unlearn. Quality is not always free. Southwest's convenience, one kind of high quality, happens to be consistent with low costs because its frequent departures are facilitated by a number of low-cost practices—fast gate turnarounds and automated ticketing, for example. However, other dimensions of airline quality—an assigned seat, a meal, or baggage transfer—require costs to provide.

In general, false trade-offs between cost and quality occur primarily when there is redundant or wasted effort, poor control or accuracy, or weak coordination. Simultaneous improvement of cost and differentiation is possible only when a company begins far behind the productivity frontier or when the frontier shifts outward. At the frontier, where companies have achieved current best practice, the trade-off between cost and differentiation is very real indeed.

After a decade of enjoying productivity advantages, Honda Motor Company and Toyota Motor Corporation recently bumped up against the frontier. In 1995, faced with increasing customer resistance to higher automobile prices, Honda found that the only way to produce a less-expensive car was to skimp on features. In the United States, it replaced the rear disk brakes on the Civic with lower-cost drum brakes and used cheaper fabric for the back seat, hoping customers would not notice. Toyota tried to sell a version of its best-selling Corolla in Japan with unpainted bumpers and cheaper seats. In Toyota's case, customers rebelled, and the company quickly dropped the new model.

For the past decade, as managers have improved operational effectiveness greatly, they have internalized the idea that eliminating trade-offs is a good thing. But if there are no trade-offs companies will never achieve a sustainable advantage. They will have to run faster and faster just to stay in place.

As we return to the question, What is strategy? we see that trade-offs add a new dimension to the answer. Strategy is making trade-offs in competing. The essence of strategy is choosing what *not* to do. Without trade-offs, there would be no need for choice and thus no need for strategy. Any good idea could and would be quickly imitated. Again, performance would once again depend wholly on operational effectiveness.

IV. Fit Drives Both Competitive Advantage and Sustainability

Positioning choices determine not only which activities a company will perform and how it will configure individual activities but also how activities relate to one another. While operational effectiveness is about achieving excellence in individual activities, or functions, strategy is about *combining* activities.

Southwest's rapid gate turnaround, which allows frequent departures and greater use of aircraft, is essential to its high-convenience, low-cost positioning. But how does Southwest achieve it? Part of the answer lies in the company's well-paid gate and ground crews, whose productivity in turnarounds is enhanced by flexible union rules. But the bigger part of the answer lies in how Southwest performs other activities. With no meals, no seat assignment, and no interline baggage transfers, Southwest avoids having to perform activities that slow down other airlines. It selects airports and routes to avoid congestion that introduces delays. Southwest's strict limits on the type and length of routes make standardized aircraft possible: every aircraft Southwest turns is a Boeing 737.

What is Southwest's core competence? Its key success factors? The correct answer is that everything matters. Southwest's strategy involves a whole system of activities, not a collection of parts. Its competitive advantage comes from the way its activities fit and reinforce one another.

Fit locks out imitators by creating a chain that is as strong as its *strongest* link. As in most companies with good strategies, Southwest's activities complement one another in ways that create real economic value. One activity's cost, for example, is lowered because of the way other activities are performed. Similarly, one activity's value to customers can be enhanced by a company's other activities. That is the way strategic fit creates competitive advantage and superior profitability.

Types of fit

The importance of fit among functional policies is one of the oldest ideas in strategy. Gradually, however, it has been supplanted on the management agenda. Rather than seeing the company as a whole, managers have turned to "core" competencies, "critical" resources, and "key" success factors. In fact, fit is a far more central component of competitive advantage than most realize.

Fit is important because discrete activities often affect one another. A sophisticated sales force, for example, confers a greater advantage when the company's product embodies premium technology and its marketing approach emphasizes customer assistance and support. A production line with high levels of model variety is more valuable when combined with an inventory and order processing system that minimizes the need for stocking finished goods, a sales process equipped to explain and encourage customization, and an advertising theme that stresses the benefits of product variations that meet a customer's special needs. Such complementarities are pervasive in strategy. Although some fit among activities is generic and applies to many companies, the most valuable fit is strategy-specific because it enhances a position's uniqueness and amplifies trade-offs.[2]

There are three types of fit, although they are not mutually exclusive. First-order fit is *simple consistency* between each activity (function) and the overall strategy. Vanguard, for example, aligns all activities with its low-cost strategy. It minimizes portfolio turnover and does not need highly compensated money managers. The company distributes its funds directly, avoiding commissions to brokers. It also limits advertising, relying instead on public relations and word-of-mouth recommendations. Vanguard ties its employees' bonuses to cost savings.

Consistency ensures that the competitive advantages of activities cumulate and do not erode or cancel themselves out. It makes the strategy easier to communicate to customers, employees, and shareholders, and improves implementation through single-mindedness in the corporation.

Second-order fit occurs when *activities are reinforcing*. Neutrogena, for example, markets to upscale hotels eager to offer their guests a soap recommended by dermatologists. Hotels grant Neutrogena the privilege of using its customary packaging while requiring other soaps to feature the hotel's name. Once guests have tried Neutrogena in a luxury hotel, they are more likely to purchase it at the drugstore or ask their doctor about it. Thus Neutrogena's medical and hotel marketing activities reinforce one another, lowering total marketing costs.

In another example, Bic Corporation sells a narrow line of standard, low-priced pens to virtually all major customer markets (retail, commercial, promotional, and giveaway) through virtually all available channels. As with any variety-based positioning serving a broad group of customers, Bic emphasizes a common need (low price for an acceptable pen) and uses marketing approaches with a broad reach

Mapping activity systems

Activity-system maps, such as this one for Ikea, show how a company's strategic position is contained in a set of tailored activities designed to deliver it. In companies with a clear strategic position, a number of higher-order strategic themes (in dark grey) can be identified and implemented through clusters of tightly linked activities (in light grey).

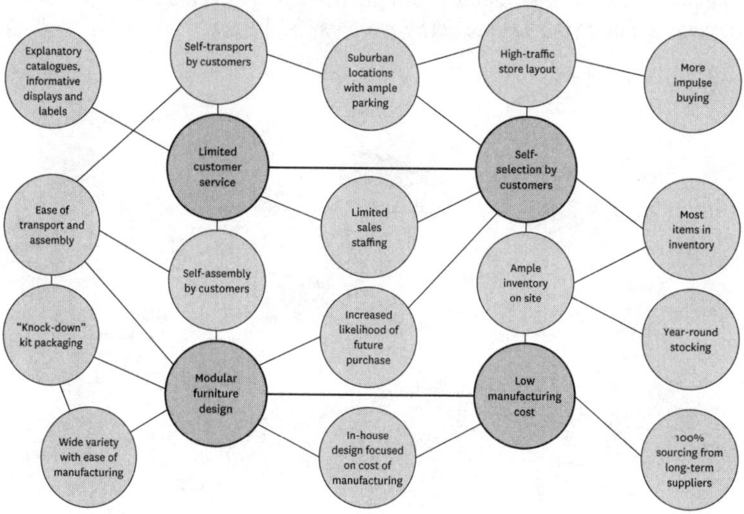

(a large sales force and heavy television advertising). Bic gains the benefits of consistency across nearly all activities, including product design that emphasizes ease of manufacturing, plants configured for low cost, aggressive purchasing to minimize material costs, and in-house parts production whenever the economics dictate.

Yet Bic goes beyond simple consistency because its activities are reinforcing. For example, the company uses point-of-sale displays and frequent packaging changes to stimulate impulse buying. To handle point-of-sale tasks, a company needs a large sales force. Bic's is the largest in its industry, and it handles point-of-sale activities better than its rivals do. Moreover, the combination of point-of-sale

Vanguard's activity system

Activity-system maps can be useful for examining and strengthening strategic fit. A set of basic questions should guide the process. First, is each activity consistent with the overall positioning—the varieties produced, the needs served, and the type of customers accessed? Ask those responsible for each activity to identify how other activities within the company improve or detract from their performance. Second, are there ways to strengthen how activities and groups of activities reinforce one another? Finally, could changes in one activity eliminate the need to perform others?

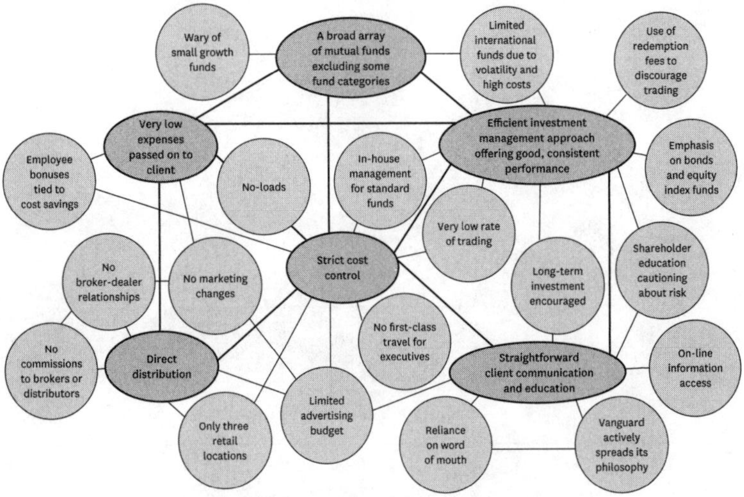

activity, heavy television advertising, and packaging changes yields far more impulse buying than any activity in isolation could.

Third-order fit goes beyond activity reinforcement to what I call *optimization of effort*. The Gap, a retailer of casual clothes, considers product availability in its stores a critical element of its strategy. The Gap could keep products either by holding store inventory or by restocking from warehouses. The Gap has optimized its effort across these activities by restocking its selection of basic clothing almost daily out of three warehouses, thereby minimizing the need to carry

Southwest Airlines' activity system

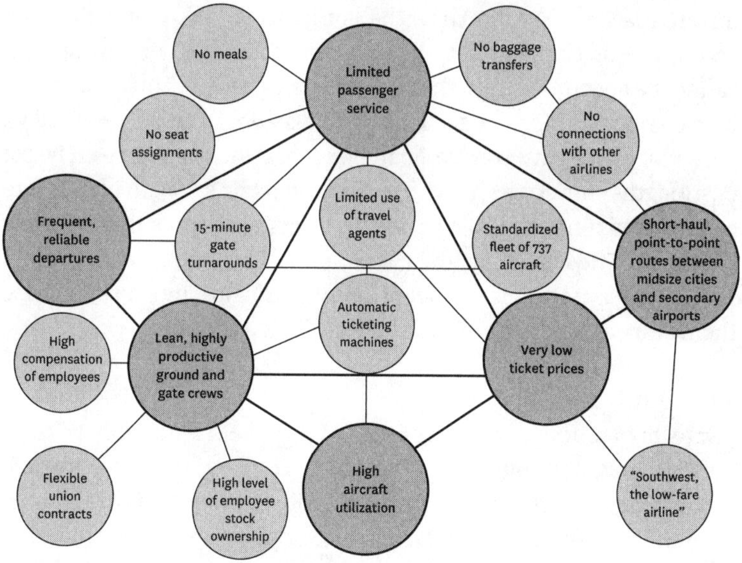

large in-store inventories. The emphasis is on restocking because the Gap's merchandising strategy sticks to basic items in relatively few colors. While comparable retailers achieve turns of three to four times per year, the Gap turns its inventory seven and a half times per year. Rapid restocking, moreover, reduces the cost of implementing the Gap's short model cycle, which is six to eight weeks long.[3]

Coordination and information exchange across activities to eliminate redundancy and minimize wasted effort are the most basic types of effort optimization. But there are higher levels as well. Product design choices, for example, can eliminate the need for after-sale service or make it possible for customers to perform service activities themselves. Similarly, coordination with suppliers or distribution channels can eliminate the need for some in-house activities, such as end-user training.

In all three types of fit, the whole matters more than any individual part. Competitive advantage grows out of the *entire system* of activities. The fit among activities substantially reduces cost or increases differentiation. Beyond that, the competitive value of individual activities—or the associated skills, competencies, or resources—cannot be decoupled from the system or the strategy. Thus in competitive companies it can be misleading to explain success by specifying individual strengths, core competencies, or critical resources. The list of strengths cuts across many functions, and one strength blends into others. It is more useful to think in terms of themes that pervade many activities, such as low cost, a particular notion of customer service, or a particular conception of the value delivered. These themes are embodied in nests of tightly linked activities.

Fit and sustainability

Strategic fit among many activities is fundamental not only to competitive advantage but also to the sustainability of that advantage. It is harder for a rival to match an array of interlocked activities than it is merely to imitate a particular sales-force approach, match a process technology, or replicate a set of product features. Positions built on systems of activities are far more sustainable than those built on individual activities.

Consider this simple exercise. The probability that competitors can match any activity is often less than one. The probabilities then quickly compound to make matching the entire system highly unlikely (.9 x .9 = .81; .9 x .9 x .9 x .9 = .66, and so on). Existing companies that try to reposition or straddle will be forced to reconfigure many activities. And even new entrants, though they do not confront the trade-offs facing established rivals, still face formidable barriers to imitation.

The more a company's positioning rests on activity systems with second- and third-order fit, the more sustainable its advantage will be. Such systems, by their very nature, are usually difficult to untangle from outside the company and therefore hard to imitate. And even if rivals can identify the relevant interconnections, they will have difficulty replicating them. Achieving fit is difficult because it requires the integration of decisions and actions across many independent subunits.

A competitor seeking to match an activity system gains little by imitating only some activities and not matching the whole. Performance does not improve; it can decline. Recall Continental Lite's disastrous attempt to imitate Southwest.

Finally, fit among a company's activities creates pressures and incentives to improve operational effectiveness, which makes imitation even harder. Fit means that poor performance in one activity will degrade the performance in others, so that weaknesses are exposed and more prone to get attention. Conversely, improvements in one activity will pay dividends in others. Companies with strong fit among their activities are rarely inviting targets. Their superiority in strategy and in execution only compounds their advantages and raises the hurdle for imitators.

When activities complement one another, rivals will get little benefit from imitation unless they successfully match the whole system. Such situations tend to promote winner-take-all competition. The company that builds the best activity system—Toys R Us, for instance—wins, while rivals with similar strategies—Child World and Lionel Leisure—fall behind. Thus finding a new strategic position is often preferable to being the second or third imitator of an occupied position.

The most viable positions are those whose activity systems are incompatible because of tradeoffs. Strategic positioning sets the trade-off rules that define how individual activities will be configured and integrated. Seeing strategy in terms of activity systems only makes it clearer why organizational structure, systems, and processes need to be strategy-specific. Tailoring organization to strategy, in turn, makes complementarities more achievable and contributes to sustainability.

One implication is that strategic positions should have a horizon of a decade or more, not of a single planning cycle. Continuity fosters improvements in individual activities and the fit across activities, allowing an organization to build unique capabilities and skills tailored to its strategy. Continuity also reinforces a company's identity.

Conversely, frequent shifts in positioning are costly. Not only must a company reconfigure individual activities, but it must also realign entire systems. Some activities may never catch up to the vacillating strategy. The inevitable result of frequent shifts in strategy, or of failure to choose a distinct position in the first place, is "me-too" or hedged activity configurations, inconsistencies across functions, and organizational dissonance.

What is strategy? We can now complete the answer to this question. Strategy is creating fit among a company's activities. The success of a strategy depends on doing many things well—not just a few—and integrating among them. If there is no fit among activities, there is no distinctive strategy and little sustainability. Management reverts to the simpler task of overseeing independent functions, and operational effectiveness determines an organization's relative performance.

V. Rediscovering Strategy

The failure to choose

Why do so many companies fail to have a strategy? Why do managers avoid making strategic choices? Or, having made them in the past, why do managers so often let strategies decay and blur?

Commonly, the threats to strategy are seen to emanate from outside a company because of changes in technology or the behavior of competitors. Although external changes can be the problem, the greater threat to strategy often comes from within. A sound strategy is undermined by a misguided view of competition, by organizational failures, and, especially, by the desire to grow.

Managers have become confused about the necessity of making choices. When many companies operate far from the productivity frontier, trade-offs appear unnecessary. It can seem that a well-run company should be able to beat its ineffective rivals on all dimensions simultaneously. Taught by popular management thinkers that they do not have to make trade-offs, managers have acquired a macho sense that to do so is a sign of weakness.

Unnerved by forecasts of hypercompetition, managers increase its likelihood by imitating everything about their competitors.

Alternative Views of Strategy

The Implicit Strategy Model of the Past Decade

- One ideal competitive position in the industry
- Benchmarking of all activities and achieving best practice
- Aggressive outsourcing and partnering to gain efficiencies
- Advantages rest on a few key success factors, critical resources, core competencies
- Flexibility and rapid responses to all competitive and market changes

Sustainable Competitive Advantage

- Unique competitive position for the company
- Activities tailored to strategy
- Clear trade-offs and choices vis-à-vis competitors
- Competitive advantage arises from fit across activities
- Sustainability comes from the activity system, not the parts
- Operational effectiveness a given

Exhorted to think in terms of revolution, managers chase every new technology for its own sake.

The pursuit of operational effectiveness is seductive because it is concrete and actionable. Over the past decade, managers have been under increasing pressure to deliver tangible, measurable performance improvements. Programs in operational effectiveness produce reassuring progress, although superior profitability may remain elusive. Business publications and consultants flood the market with information about what other companies are doing, reinforcing the best-practice mentality. Caught up in the race for operational effectiveness, many managers simply do not understand the need to have a strategy.

Companies avoid or blur strategic choices for other reasons as well. Conventional wisdom within an industry is often strong,

Reconnecting with Strategy

MOST COMPANIES OWE THEIR INITIAL success to a unique strategic position involving clear trade-offs. Activities once were aligned with that position. The passage of time and the pressures of growth, however, led to compromises that were, at first, almost imperceptible. Through a succession of incremental changes that each seemed sensible at the time, many established companies have compromised their way to homogeneity with their rivals.

The issue here is not with the companies whose historical position is no longer viable; their challenge is to start over, just as a new entrant would. At issue is a far more common phenomenon: the established company achieving mediocre returns and lacking a clear strategy. Through incremental additions of product varieties, incremental efforts to serve new customer groups, and emulation of rivals' activities, the existing company loses its clear competitive position. Typically, the company has matched many of its competitors' offerings and practices and attempts to sell to most customer groups.

A number of approaches can help a company reconnect with strategy. The first is a careful look at what it already does. Within most well-established companies is a core of uniqueness. It is identified by answering questions such as the following:

- Which of our product or service varieties are the most distinctive?
- Which of our product or service varieties are the most profitable?

---

homogenizing competition. Some managers mistake "customer focus" to mean they must serve all customer needs or respond to every request from distribution channels. Others cite the desire to preserve flexibility.

Organizational realities also work against strategy. Trade-offs are frightening, and making no choice is sometimes preferred to risking blame for a bad choice. Companies imitate one another in a type of herd behavior, each assuming rivals know something they do not. Newly empowered employees, who are urged to seek every possible source of improvement, often lack a vision of the whole and the perspective to recognize trade-offs. The failure to choose sometimes comes down to the reluctance to disappoint valued managers or employees.

- Which of our customers are the most satisfied?
- Which customers, channels, or purchase occasions are the most profitable?
- Which of the activities in our value chain are the most different and effective?

Around this core of uniqueness are encrustations added incrementally over time. Like barnacles, they must be removed to reveal the underlying strategic positioning. A small percentage of varieties or customers may well account for most of a company's sales and especially its profits. The challenge, then, is to refocus on the unique core and realign the company's activities with it. Customers and product varieties at the periphery can be sold or allowed through inattention or price increases to fade away.

A company's history can also be instructive. What was the vision of the founder? What were the products and customers that made the company? Looking backward, one can reexamine the original strategy to see if it is still valid. Can the historical positioning be implemented in a modern way, one consistent with today's technologies and practices? This sort of thinking may lead to a commitment to renew the strategy and may challenge the organization to recover its distinctiveness. Such a challenge can be galvanizing and can instill the confidence to make the needed trade-offs.

The growth trap

Among all other influences, the desire to grow has perhaps the most perverse effect on strategy. Trade-offs and limits appear to constrain growth. Serving one group of customers and excluding others, for instance, places a real or imagined limit on revenue growth. Broadly targeted strategies emphasizing low price result in lost sales with customers sensitive to features or service. Differentiators lose sales to price-sensitive customers.

Managers are constantly tempted to take incremental steps that surpass those limits but blur a company's strategic position. Eventually, pressures to grow or apparent saturation of the target market lead managers to broaden the position by extending product lines, adding new features, imitating competitors' popular services, matching processes, and even making acquisitions. For years, Maytag Corporation's success was based on its focus on reliable, durable washers and dryers, later extended to include dishwashers. However, conventional wisdom emerging within the industry supported the notion of selling a full line of products. Concerned with slow industry growth and competition from broad-line appliance makers, Maytag was pressured by dealers and encouraged by customers to extend its line. Maytag expanded into refrigerators and cooking products under the Maytag brand and acquired other brands—Jenn-Air, Hardwick Stove, Hoover, Admiral, and Magic Chef—with disparate positions. Maytag has grown substantially from $684 million in 1985 to a peak of $3.4 billion in 1994, but return on sales has declined from 8% to 12% in the 1970s and 1980s to an average of less than 1% between 1989 and 1995. Cost cutting will improve this performance, but laundry and dishwasher products still anchor Maytag's profitability.

Neutrogena may have fallen into the same trap. In the early 1990s, its U.S. distribution broadened to include mass merchandisers such as Wal-Mart Stores. Under the Neutrogena name, the company expanded into a wide variety of products—eye-makeup remover and shampoo, for example—in which it was not unique and which diluted its image, and it began turning to price promotions.

Compromises and inconsistencies in the pursuit of growth will erode the competitive advantage a company had with its original varieties or target customers. Attempts to compete in several ways at once create confusion and undermine organizational motivation and focus. Profits fall, but more revenue is seen as the answer. Managers are unable to make choices, so the company embarks on a new round of broadening and compromises. Often, rivals continue to match each other until desperation breaks the cycle, resulting in a merger or downsizing to the original positioning.

Profitable growth

Many companies, after a decade of restructuring and cost-cutting, are turning their attention to growth. Too often, efforts to grow blur uniqueness, create compromises, reduce fit, and ultimately

Emerging Industries and Technologies

DEVELOPING A STRATEGY IN A newly emerging industry or in a business undergoing revolutionary technological changes is a daunting proposition. In such cases, managers face a high level of uncertainty about the needs of customers, the products and services that will prove to be the most desired, and the best configuration of activities and technologies to deliver them. Because of all this uncertainty, imitation and hedging are rampant: unable to risk being wrong or left behind, companies match all features, offer all new services, and explore all technologies.

During such periods in an industry's development, its basic productivity frontier is being established or reestablished. Explosive growth can make such times profitable for many companies, but profits will be temporary because imitation and strategic convergence will ultimately destroy industry profitability. The companies that are enduringly successful will be those that begin as early as possible to define and embody in their activities a unique competitive position. A period of imitation may be inevitable in emerging industries, but that period reflects the level of uncertainty rather than a desired state of affairs.

In high-tech industries, this imitation phase often continues much longer than it should. Enraptured by technological change itself, companies pack more features—most of which are never used—into their products while slashing prices across the board. Rarely are trade-offs even considered. The drive for growth to satisfy market pressures leads companies into every product area. Although a few companies with fundamental advantages prosper, the majority are doomed to a rat race no one can win.

Ironically, the popular business press, focused on hot, emerging industries, is prone to presenting these special cases as proof that we have entered a new era of competition in which none of the old rules are valid. In fact, the opposite is true.

undermine competitive advantage. In fact, the growth imperative is hazardous to strategy.

What approaches to growth preserve and reinforce strategy? Broadly, the prescription is to concentrate on deepening a strategic position rather than broadening and compromising it. One approach is to look for extensions of the strategy that leverage the existing activity system by offering features or services that rivals would find impossible or costly to match on a stand-alone basis. In other words, managers can ask themselves which activities, features, or forms of competition are feasible or less costly to them because of complementary activities that their company performs.

Deepening a position involves making the company's activities more distinctive, strengthening fit, and communicating the strategy better to those customers who should value it. But many companies succumb to the temptation to chase "easy" growth by adding hot features, products, or services without screening them or adapting them to their strategy. Or they target new customers or markets in which the company has little special to offer. A company can often grow faster—and far more profitably—by better penetrating needs and varieties where it is distinctive than by slugging it out in potentially higher growth arenas in which the company lacks uniqueness. Carmike, now the largest theater chain in the United States, owes its rapid growth to its disciplined concentration on small markets. The company quickly sells any big-city theaters that come to it as part of an acquisition.

Globalization often allows growth that is consistent with strategy, opening up larger markets for a focused strategy. Unlike broadening domestically, expanding globally is likely to leverage and reinforce a company's unique position and identity.

Companies seeking growth through broadening within their industry can best contain the risks to strategy by creating stand-alone units, each with its own brand name and tailored activities. Maytag has clearly struggled with this issue. On the one hand, it has organized its premium and value brands into separate units with different strategic positions. On the other, it has created an umbrella appliance company for all its brands to gain critical mass. With shared design, manufacturing, distribution, and customer service, it will be hard to avoid homogenization. If a given business unit attempts to compete with different positions for different products or customers, avoiding compromise is nearly impossible.

The role of leadership

The challenge of developing or reestablishing a clear strategy is often primarily an organizational one and depends on leadership. With so many forces at work against making choices and tradeoffs in organizations, a clear intellectual framework to guide strategy is a necessary counterweight. Moreover, strong leaders willing to make choices are essential.

In many companies, leadership has degenerated into orchestrating operational improvements and making deals. But the leader's role is broader and far more important. General management is more than the stewardship of individual functions. Its core is strategy: defining and communicating the company's unique position, making trade-offs, and forging fit among activities. The leader must provide the discipline to decide which industry changes and customer needs the company will respond to, while avoiding organizational distractions and maintaining the company's distinctiveness. Managers at lower levels lack the perspective and the confidence to maintain a strategy. There will be constant pressures to compromise, relax trade-offs, and emulate rivals. One of the leader's jobs is to teach others in the organization about strategy—and to say no.

Strategy renders choices about what not to do as important as choices about what to do. Indeed, setting limits is another function of leadership. Deciding which target group of customers, varieties, and needs the company should serve is fundamental to developing a strategy. But so is deciding not to serve other customers or needs and not to offer certain features or services. Thus strategy requires constant discipline and clear communication. Indeed, one of the most important functions of an explicit, communicated strategy is to guide employees in making choices that arise because of trade-offs in their individual activities and in day-to-day decisions.

Improving operational effectiveness is a necessary part of management, but it is *not* strategy. In confusing the two, managers have unintentionally backed into a way of thinking about competition that is driving many industries toward competitive convergence, which is in no one's best interest and is not inevitable.

Managers must clearly distinguish operational effectiveness from strategy. Both are essential, but the two agendas are different.

The operational agenda involves continual improvement everywhere there are no trade-offs. Failure to do this creates vulnerability even for companies with a good strategy. The operational agenda is the proper place for constant change, flexibility, and relentless efforts to achieve best practice. In contrast, the strategic agenda is the right place for defining a unique position, making clear trade-offs, and tightening fit. It involves the continual search for ways to reinforce and extend the company's position. The strategic agenda demands discipline and continuity; its enemies are distraction and compromise.

Strategic continuity does not imply a static view of competition. A company must continually improve its operational effectiveness and actively try to shift the productivity frontier; at the same time, there needs to be ongoing effort to extend its uniqueness while strengthening the fit among its activities. Strategic continuity, in fact, should make an organization's continual improvement more effective.

A company may have to change its strategy if there are major structural changes in its industry. In fact, new strategic positions often arise because of industry changes, and new entrants unencumbered by history often can exploit them more easily. However, a company's choice of a new position must be driven by the ability to find new trade-offs and leverage a new system of complementary activities into a sustainable advantage.

Originally published in November 1996. Reprint 96608.

Notes

1. I first described the concept of activities and its use in understanding competitive advantage in *Competitive Advantage* (New York: The Free Press, 1985). The ideas in this article build on and extend that thinking.

2. Paul Milgrom and John Roberts have begun to explore the economics of systems of complementary functions, activities, and functions. Their focus is on the emergence of "modern manufacturing" as a new set of complementary activities, on the tendency of companies to react to external changes with coherent bundles of internal responses, and on the need for central coordination—a strategy—to align functional managers. In the latter case, they model what has long been a bedrock principle of strategy. See Paul Milgrom and John Roberts, "The Economics of Modern Manufacturing: Technology, Strategy, and Organization," *American Economic Review* 80 (1990): 511–528; Paul Milgrom, Yingyi Qian, and John Roberts, "Complementarities, Momentum, and Evolution of Modern Manufacturing," *American Economic Review* 81 (1991) 84–88; and Paul Milgrom and John Roberts,

"Complementarities and Fit: Strategy, Structure, and Organizational Changes in Manufacturing," *Journal of Accounting and Economics,* vol. 19 (March–May 1995): 179–208.

3. Material on retail strategies is drawn in part from Jan Rivkin, "The Rise of Retail Category Killers," unpublished working paper, January 1995. Nicolaj Siggelkow prepared the case study on the Gap.

The Five Competitive Forces That Shape Strategy

by Michael E. Porter

IN ESSENCE, THE JOB of the strategist is to understand and cope with competition. Often, however, managers define competition too narrowly, as if it occurred only among today's direct competitors. Yet competition for profits goes beyond established industry rivals to include four other competitive forces as well: customers, suppliers, potential entrants, and substitute products. The extended rivalry that results from all five forces defines an industry's structure and shapes the nature of competitive interaction within an industry.

As different from one another as industries might appear on the surface, the underlying drivers of profitability are the same. The global auto industry, for instance, appears to have nothing in common with the worldwide market for art masterpieces or the heavily regulated health-care delivery industry in Europe. But to understand industry competition and profitability in each of those three cases, one must analyze the industry's underlying structure in terms of the five forces. (See "The five forces that shape industry competition.")

If the forces are intense, as they are in such industries as airlines, textiles, and hotels, almost no company earns attractive returns on investment. If the forces are benign, as they are in industries such as software, soft drinks, and toiletries, many companies are profitable. Industry structure drives competition and profitability, not whether an industry produces a product or service, is emerging or mature, high tech or low tech, regulated or unregulated. While a myriad of factors can affect industry profitability in the short run—including the weather and the business cycle—industry structure, manifested in the competitive forces, sets industry profitability in the medium and long run. (See "Differences in Industry Profitability.")

Understanding the competitive forces, and their underlying causes, reveals the roots of an industry's current profitability while providing a framework for anticipating and influencing competition (and profitability) over time. A healthy industry structure should be as much a competitive concern to strategists as their company's own position. Understanding industry structure is also essential to effective strategic positioning. As we will see, defending against the competitive forces and shaping them in a company's favor are crucial to strategy.

Forces That Shape Competition

The configuration of the five forces differs by industry. In the market for commercial aircraft, fierce rivalry between dominant producers Airbus and Boeing and the bargaining power of the airlines that place huge orders for aircraft are strong, while the threat of entry, the threat of substitutes, and the power of suppliers are more benign. In the movie theater industry, the proliferation of substitute forms of entertainment and the power of the movie producers and distributors who supply movies, the critical input, are important.

The strongest competitive force or forces determine the profitability of an industry and become the most important to strategy formulation. The most salient force, however, is not always obvious.

For example, even though rivalry is often fierce in commodity industries, it may not be the factor limiting profitability. Low returns in the photographic film industry, for instance, are the result of a superior substitute product—as Kodak and Fuji, the world's leading producers of photographic film, learned with the advent of digital photography. In such a situation, coping with the substitute product becomes the number one strategic priority.

Idea in Brief

You know that to sustain long-term profitability you must respond strategically to competition. And you naturally keep tabs on your **established** rivals. But as you scan the competitive arena, are you also looking *beyond* your direct competitors? As Porter explains in this update of his revolutionary 1979 HBR article, four additional competitive forces can hurt your prospective profits:

- Savvy **customers** can force down prices by playing you and your rivals against one another.
- Powerful **suppliers** may constrain your profits if they charge higher prices.
- Aspiring **entrants,** armed with new capacity and hungry for market share, can ratchet up the investment required for you to stay in the game.
- **Substitute offerings** can lure customers away.

Consider commercial aviation: It's one of the least profitable industries because all five forces are strong. **Established rivals** compete intensely on price. **Customers** are fickle, searching for the best deal regardless of carrier. **Suppliers**—plane and engine manufacturers, along with unionized labor forces—bargain away the lion's share of airlines' profits. **New players** enter the industry in a constant stream. And **substitutes** are readily available—such as train or car travel.

By analyzing all five competitive forces, you gain a complete picture of what's influencing profitability in your industry. You identify game-changing trends early, so you can swiftly exploit them. And you spot ways to work around constraints on profitability—or even reshape the forces in your favor.

Industry structure grows out of a set of economic and technical characteristics that determine the strength of each competitive force. We will examine these drivers in the pages that follow, taking the perspective of an incumbent, or a company already present in the industry. The analysis can be readily extended to understand the challenges facing a potential entrant.

Threat of entry

New entrants to an industry bring new capacity and a desire to gain market share that puts pressure on prices, costs, and the rate of

Idea in Practice

By understanding how the five competitive forces influence profitability in your industry, you can develop a strategy for enhancing your company's long-term profits. Porter suggests the following:

Position Your Company Where the Forces Are Weakest

Example: In the heavy-truck industry, many buyers operate large fleets and are highly motivated to drive down truck prices. Trucks are built to regulated standards and offer similar features, so price competition is stiff; unions exercise considerable supplier power; and buyers can use substitutes such as cargo delivery by rail.

To create and sustain long-term profitability within this industry, heavy-truck maker Paccar chose to focus on one customer group where competitive forces are weakest: individual drivers who own their trucks and contract directly with suppliers. These operators have limited clout as buyers and are less price sensitive because of their emotional ties to and economic dependence on their own trucks.

For these customers, Paccar has developed such features as luxurious sleeper cabins, plush leather seats, and sleek exterior styling. Buyers can select from thousands of options to put their personal signature on these built-to-order trucks.

Customers pay Paccar a 10% premium, and the company has been profitable for 68 straight years and earned a long-run return on equity above 20%.

Exploit Changes in the Forces

Example: With the advent of the Internet and digital distribution of music, unauthorized downloading created an illegal but potent substitute for record companies' services. The record companies

investment necessary to compete. Particularly when new entrants are diversifying from other markets, they can leverage existing capabilities and cash flows to shake up competition, as Pepsi did when it entered the bottled water industry, Microsoft did when it began to offer internet browsers, and Apple did when it entered the music distribution business.

The threat of entry, therefore, puts a cap on the profit potential of an industry. When the threat is high, incumbents must hold down

tried to develop technical platforms for digital distribution themselves, but major labels didn't want to sell their music through a platform owned by a rival.

Into this vacuum stepped Apple, with its iTunes music store supporting its iPod music player. The birth of this powerful new gatekeeper has whittled down the number of major labels from six in 1997 to four today.

Reshape the Forces in Your Favor

Use tactics designed specifically to reduce the share of profits leaking to other players. For example:

- To neutralize **supplier power,** standardize specifications for parts so your company can switch more easily among vendors.
- To counter **customer power,** expand your services so it's harder for customers to leave you for a rival.
- To temper price wars initiated by **established rivals,** invest more heavily in products that differ significantly from competitors' offerings.
- To scare off **new entrants,** elevate the fixed costs of competing; for instance, by escalating your R&D expenditures.
- To limit the threat of **substitutes,** offer better value through wider product accessibility. Soft-drink producers did this by introducing vending machines and convenience store channels, which dramatically improved the availability of soft drinks relative to other beverages.

their prices or boost investment to deter new competitors. In specialty coffee retailing, for example, relatively low entry barriers mean that Starbucks must invest aggressively in modernizing stores and menus.

The threat of entry in an industry depends on the height of entry barriers that are present and on the reaction entrants can expect from incumbents. If entry barriers are low and newcomers expect little retaliation from the entrenched competitors, the threat of entry is high and industry profitability is moderated. It is the *threat* of entry, not whether entry actually occurs, that holds down profitability.

Barriers to entry. Entry barriers are advantages that incumbents have relative to new entrants. There are seven major sources:

1. *Supply-side economies of scale.* These economies arise when firms that produce at larger volumes enjoy lower costs per unit because they can spread fixed costs over more units, employ more efficient technology, or command better terms from suppliers. Supply-side scale economies deter entry by forcing the aspiring entrant either to come into the industry on a large scale, which requires dislodging entrenched competitors, or to accept a cost disadvantage.

Scale economies can be found in virtually every activity in the value chain; which ones are most important varies by industry.[1] In microprocessors, incumbents such as Intel are protected by scale economies in research, chip fabrication, and consumer marketing. For lawn care companies like Scotts Miracle-Gro, the most important scale economies are found in the supply chain and media advertising. In small-package delivery, economies of scale arise in national logistical systems and information technology.

2. *Demand-side benefits of scale.* These benefits, also known as network effects, arise in industries where a buyer's willingness to pay for a company's product increases with the number of other buyers who also patronize the company. Buyers may trust larger companies more for a crucial product: Recall the old adage that no one ever got fired for buying from IBM (when it was the dominant computer maker). Buyers may also value being in a "network" with a larger number of fellow customers. For instance, online auction participants are attracted to eBay because it offers the most potential trading partners. Demand-side benefits of scale discourage entry by limiting the willingness of customers to buy from a newcomer and by reducing the price the newcomer can command until it builds up a large base of customers.

3. *Customer switching costs.* Switching costs are fixed costs that buyers face when they change suppliers. Such costs may arise

because a buyer who switches vendors must, for example, alter product specifications, retrain employees to use a new product, or modify processes or information systems. The larger the switching costs, the harder it will be for an entrant to gain customers. Enterprise resource planning (ERP) software is an example of a product with very high switching costs. Once a company has installed SAP's ERP system, for example, the costs of moving to a new vendor are astronomical because of embedded data, the fact that internal processes have been adapted to SAP, major retraining needs, and the mission-critical nature of the applications.

4. *Capital requirements.* The need to invest large financial resources in order to compete can deter new entrants. Capital may be necessary not only for fixed facilities but also to extend customer credit, build inventories, and fund start-up losses. The barrier is particularly great if the capital is required for unrecoverable and therefore harder-to-finance expenditures, such as up-front advertising or research and development. While major corporations have the financial resources to invade almost any industry, the huge capital requirements in certain fields limit the pool of likely entrants. Conversely, in such fields as tax preparation services or short-haul trucking, capital requirements are minimal and potential entrants plentiful.

It is important not to overstate the degree to which capital requirements alone deter entry. If industry returns are attractive and are expected to remain so, and if capital markets are efficient, investors will provide entrants with the funds they need. For aspiring air carriers, for instance, financing is available to purchase expensive aircraft because of their high resale value, one reason why there have been numerous new airlines in almost every region.

5. *Incumbency advantages independent of size.* No matter what their size, incumbents may have cost or quality advantages not available to potential rivals. These advantages can stem from such sources as proprietary technology, preferential access to the best raw material sources, preemption of the most favorable geographic locations, established brand identities, or cumulative experience that has allowed incumbents to learn how to produce more efficiently.

The five forces that shape industry competition

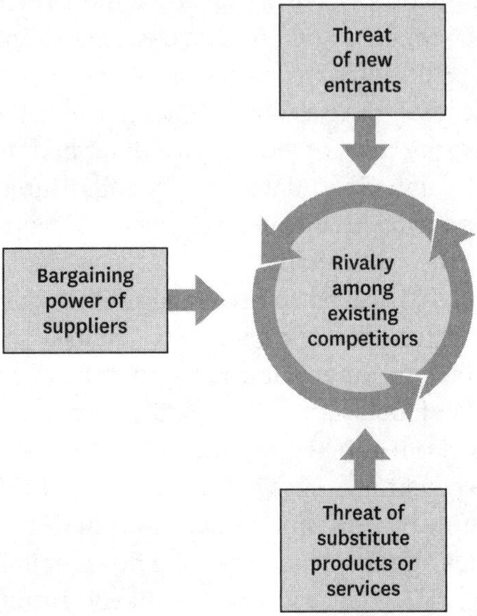

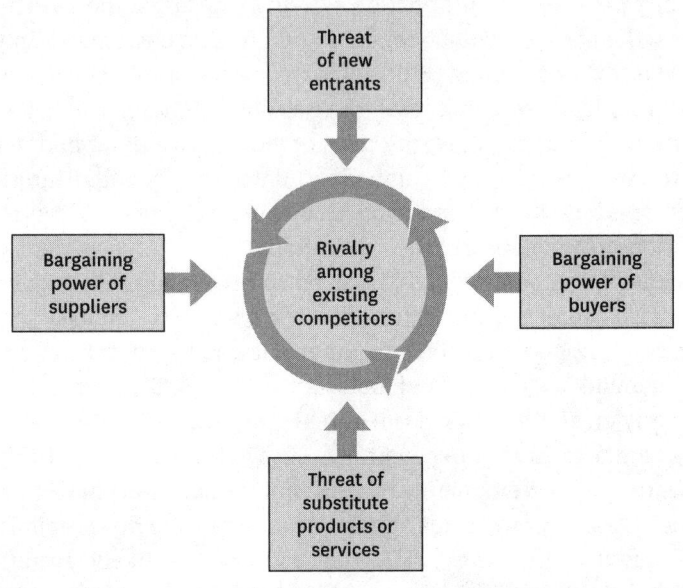

Entrants try to bypass such advantages. Upstart discounters such as Target and Wal-Mart, for example, have located stores in freestanding sites rather than regional shopping centers where established department stores were well entrenched.

6. *Unequal access to distribution channels.* The new entrant must, of course, secure distribution of its product or service. A new food item, for example, must displace others from the supermarket shelf via price breaks, promotions, intense selling efforts, or some other means. The more limited the wholesale or retail channels are and the more that existing competitors have tied them up, the tougher entry into an industry will be. Sometimes access to distribution is so high a barrier that new entrants must bypass distribution channels altogether or create their own. Thus, upstart low-cost airlines have avoided distribution through travel agents (who tend to favor

established higher-fare carriers) and have encouraged passengers to book their own flights on the internet.

7. *Restrictive government policy.* Government policy can hinder or aid new entry directly, as well as amplify (or nullify) the other entry barriers. Government directly limits or even forecloses entry into industries through, for instance, licensing requirements and restrictions on foreign investment. Regulated industries like liquor retailing, taxi services, and airlines are visible examples. Government policy can heighten other entry barriers through such means as expansive patenting rules that protect proprietary technology from imitation or environmental or safety regulations that raise scale economies facing newcomers. Of course, government policies may also make entry easier—directly through subsidies, for instance, or indirectly by funding basic research and making it available to all firms, new and old, reducing scale economies.

Entry barriers should be assessed relative to the capabilities of potential entrants, which may be start-ups, foreign firms, or companies in related industries. And, as some of our examples illustrate, the strategist must be mindful of the creative ways newcomers might find to circumvent apparent barriers.

Expected retaliation. How potential entrants believe incumbents may react will also influence their decision to enter or stay out of an industry. If reaction is vigorous and protracted enough, the profit potential of participating in the industry can fall below the cost of capital. Incumbents often use public statements and responses to one entrant to send a message to other prospective entrants about their commitment to defending market share.

Newcomers are likely to fear expected retaliation if:

- Incumbents have previously responded vigorously to new entrants.
- Incumbents possess substantial resources to fight back, including excess cash and unused borrowing power, available productive capacity, or clout with distribution channels and customers.

Differences in Industry Profitability

THE AVERAGE RETURN on invested capital varies markedly from industry to industry. Between 1992 and 2006, for example, average return on invested capital in U.S. industries ranged as low as zero or even negative to more than 50%. At the high end are industries like soft drinks and prepackaged software, which have been almost six times more profitable than the airline industry over the period.

Average return on invested capital in U.S. industries, 1992–2006

***Return on invested capital (ROIC)** is the appropriate measure of profitability for strategy formulation, not to mention for equity investors. Return on sales or the growth rate of profits fail to account for the capital required to compete in the industry. Here, we utilize earnings before interest and taxes divided by average invested capital less excess cash as the measure of ROIC. This measure controls for idiosyncratic differences in capital structure and tax rates across companies and industries.*

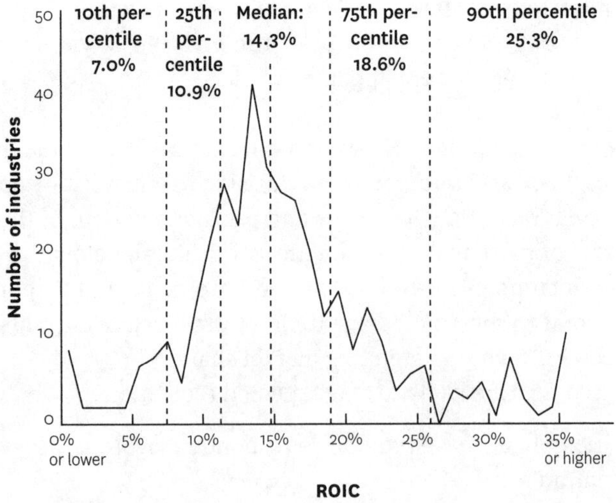

Source: Standard & Poor's, Compustat, and author's calculations

Profitability of selected U.S. industries

Average ROIC, 1992–2006

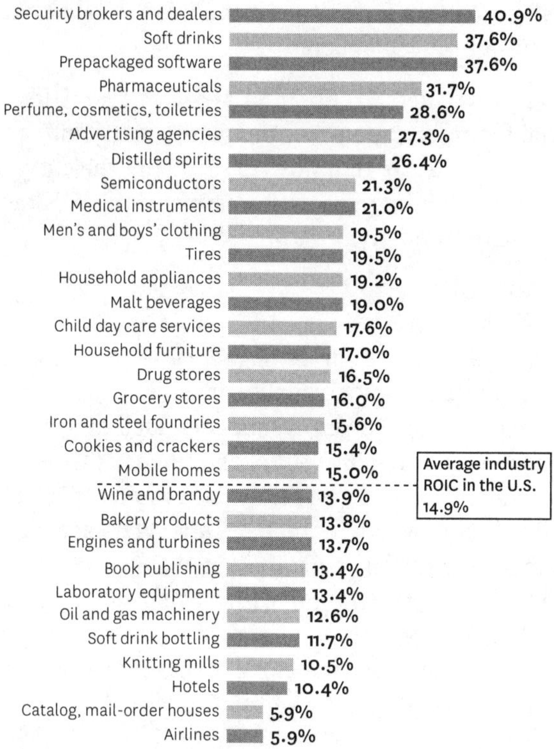
Security brokers and dealers 40.9%
Soft drinks 37.6%
Prepackaged software 37.6%
Pharmaceuticals 31.7%
Perfume, cosmetics, toiletries 28.6%
Advertising agencies 27.3%
Distilled spirits 26.4%
Semiconductors 21.3%
Medical instruments 21.0%
Men's and boys' clothing 19.5%
Tires 19.5%
Household appliances 19.2%
Malt beverages 19.0%
Child day care services 17.6%
Household furniture 17.0%
Drug stores 16.5%
Grocery stores 16.0%
Iron and steel foundries 15.6%
Cookies and crackers 15.4%
Mobile homes 15.0%
Wine and brandy 13.9%
Bakery products 13.8%
Engines and turbines 13.7%
Book publishing 13.4%
Laboratory equipment 13.4%
Oil and gas machinery 12.6%
Soft drink bottling 11.7%
Knitting mills 10.5%
Hotels 10.4%
Catalog, mail-order houses 5.9%
Airlines 5.9%
Average industry ROIC in the U.S. 14.9%

- Incumbents seem likely to cut prices because they are committed to retaining market share at all costs or because the industry has high fixed costs, which create a strong motivation to drop prices to fill excess capacity.

- Industry growth is slow so newcomers can gain volume only by taking it from incumbents.

An analysis of barriers to entry and expected retaliation is obviously crucial for any company contemplating entry into a new industry. The challenge is to find ways to surmount the entry barriers without nullifying, through heavy investment, the profitability of participating in the industry.

The power of suppliers

Powerful suppliers capture more of the value for themselves by charging higher prices, limiting quality or services, or shifting costs to industry participants. Powerful suppliers, including suppliers of labor, can squeeze profitability out of an industry that is unable to pass on cost increases in its own prices. Microsoft, for instance, has contributed to the erosion of profitability among personal computer makers by raising prices on operating systems. PC makers, competing fiercely for customers who can easily switch among them, have limited freedom to raise their prices accordingly.

Companies depend on a wide range of different supplier groups for inputs. A supplier group is powerful if:

- It is more concentrated than the industry it sells to. Microsoft's near monopoly in operating systems, coupled with the fragmentation of PC assemblers, exemplifies this situation.

- The supplier group does not depend heavily on the industry for its revenues. Suppliers serving many industries will not hesitate to extract maximum profits from each one. If a particular industry accounts for a large portion of a supplier group's volume or profit, however, suppliers will want to

Industry Analysis in Practice

Good industry analysis looks rigorously at the structural underpinnings of profitability. A first step is to understand the appropriate time horizon. One of the essential tasks in industry analysis is to distinguish temporary or cyclical changes from structural changes. A good guideline for the appropriate time horizon is the full business cycle for the particular industry. For most industries, a three-to-five-year horizon is appropriate, although in some industries with long lead times, such as mining, the appropriate horizon might be a decade or more. It is average profitability over this period, not profitability in any particular year, that should be the focus of analysis.

The point of industry analysis is not to declare the industry attractive or unattractive but to understand the underpinnings of competition and the root causes of profitability. As much as possible, analysts should look at industry structure quantitatively, rather than be satisfied with lists of qualitative factors. Many elements of the five forces can be quantified: the percentage of the buyer's total cost accounted for by the industry's product (to understand buyer price sensitivity); the percentage of industry sales required to fill a plant or operate a logistical network of efficient scale (to help assess barriers to entry); the buyer's switching cost (determining the inducement an entrant or rival must offer customers).

The strength of the competitive forces affects prices, costs, and the investment required to compete; thus the forces are directly tied to the income statements and balance sheets of industry participants. Industry structure defines the gap between revenues and costs. For example, intense rivalry drives down prices or elevates the costs of marketing, R&D, or customer service, reducing margins. How much? Strong suppliers drive up input costs. How much? Buyer power lowers prices or elevates the costs of meeting buyers' demands, such as the requirement to hold more inventory or provide financing. How much? Low barriers to entry or close substitutes limit the level of sustainable prices. How much? It is these economic relationships that sharpen the strategist's understanding of industry competition.

Finally, good industry analysis does not just list pluses and minuses but sees an industry in overall, systemic terms. Which forces are underpinning (or constraining) today's profitability? How might shifts in one competitive force trigger reactions in others? Answering such questions is often the source of true strategic insights.

protect the industry through reasonable pricing and assist in activities such as R&D and lobbying.

- Industry participants face switching costs in changing suppliers. For example, shifting suppliers is difficult if companies have invested heavily in specialized ancillary equipment or in learning how to operate a supplier's equipment (as with Bloomberg terminals used by financial professionals). Or firms may have located their production lines adjacent to a supplier's manufacturing facilities (as in the case of some beverage companies and container manufacturers). When switching costs are high, industry participants find it hard to play suppliers off against one another. (Note that suppliers may have switching costs as well. This limits their power.)
- Suppliers offer products that are differentiated. Pharmaceutical companies that offer patented drugs with distinctive medical benefits have more power over hospitals, health maintenance organizations, and other drug buyers, for example, than drug companies offering me-too or generic products.
- There is no substitute for what the supplier group provides. Pilots' unions, for example, exercise considerable supplier power over airlines partly because there is no good alternative to a well-trained pilot in the cockpit.
- The supplier group can credibly threaten to integrate forward into the industry. In that case, if industry participants make too much money relative to suppliers, they will induce suppliers to enter the market.

The power of buyers

Powerful customers—the flip side of powerful suppliers—can capture more value by forcing down prices, demanding better quality or more service (thereby driving up costs), and generally playing industry participants off against one another, all at the expense of industry profitability. Buyers are powerful if they have negotiating leverage relative to industry participants, especially if they are price sensitive, using their clout primarily to pressure price reductions.

As with suppliers, there may be distinct groups of customers who differ in bargaining power. A customer group has negotiating leverage if:

- There are few buyers, or each one purchases in volumes that are large relative to the size of a single vendor. Large-volume buyers are particularly powerful in industries with high fixed costs, such as telecommunications equipment, offshore drilling, and bulk chemicals. High fixed costs and low marginal costs amplify the pressure on rivals to keep capacity filled through discounting.
- The industry's products are standardized or undifferentiated. If buyers believe they can always find an equivalent product, they tend to play one vendor against another.
- Buyers face few switching costs in changing vendors.
- Buyers can credibly threaten to integrate backward and produce the industry's product themselves if vendors are too profitable. Producers of soft drinks and beer have long controlled the power of packaging manufacturers by threatening to make, and at times actually making, packaging materials themselves.

A buyer group is price sensitive if:

- The product it purchases from the industry represents a significant fraction of its cost structure or procurement budget. Here buyers are likely to shop around and bargain hard, as consumers do for home mortgages. Where the product sold by an industry is a small fraction of buyers' costs or expenditures, buyers are usually less price sensitive.
- The buyer group earns low profits, is strapped for cash, or is otherwise under pressure to trim its purchasing costs. Highly

profitable or cash-rich customers, in contrast, are generally less price sensitive (that is, of course, if the item does not represent a large fraction of their costs).

- The quality of buyers' products or services is little affected by the industry's product. Where quality is very much affected by the industry's product, buyers are generally less price sensitive. When purchasing or renting production quality cameras, for instance, makers of major motion pictures opt for highly reliable equipment with the latest features. They pay limited attention to price.
- The industry's product has little effect on the buyer's other costs. Here, buyers focus on price. Conversely, where an industry's product or service can pay for itself many times over by improving performance or reducing labor, material, or other costs, buyers are usually more interested in quality than in price. Examples include products and services like tax accounting or well logging (which measures below-ground conditions of oil wells) that can save or even make the buyer money. Similarly, buyers tend not to be price sensitive in services such as investment banking, where poor performance can be costly and embarrassing.

Most sources of buyer power apply equally to consumers and to business-to-business customers. Like industrial customers, consumers tend to be more price sensitive if they are purchasing products that are undifferentiated, expensive relative to their incomes, and of a sort where product performance has limited consequences. The major difference with consumers is that their needs can be more intangible and harder to quantify.

Intermediate customers, or customers who purchase the product but are not the end user (such as assemblers or distribution channels), can be analyzed the same way as other buyers, with one important addition. Intermediate customers gain significant bargaining power when they can influence the purchasing decisions of customers downstream. Consumer electronics retailers, jewelry retailers, and agricultural-equipment distributors are examples of distribution channels that exert a strong influence on end customers.

Producers often attempt to diminish channel clout through exclusive arrangements with particular distributors or retailers or by marketing directly to end users. Component manufacturers seek to develop power over assemblers by creating preferences for their components with downstream customers. Such is the case with bicycle parts and with sweeteners. DuPont has created enormous clout by advertising its Stainmaster brand of carpet fibers not only to the carpet manufacturers that actually buy them but also to downstream consumers. Many consumers request Stainmaster carpet even though DuPont is not a carpet manufacturer.

The threat of substitutes

A substitute performs the same or a similar function as an industry's product by a different means. Videoconferencing is a substitute for travel. Plastic is a substitute for aluminum. E-mail is a substitute for express mail. Sometimes, the threat of substitution is downstream or indirect, when a substitute replaces a buyer industry's product. For example, lawn-care products and services are threatened when multifamily homes in urban areas substitute for single-family homes in the suburbs. Software sold to agents is threatened when airline and travel websites substitute for travel agents.

Substitutes are always present, but they are easy to overlook because they may appear to be very different from the industry's product: To someone searching for a Father's Day gift, neckties and power tools may be substitutes. It is a substitute to do without, to purchase a used product rather than a new one, or to do it yourself (bring the service or product in-house).

When the threat of substitutes is high, industry profitability suffers. Substitute products or services limit an industry's profit potential by placing a ceiling on prices. If an industry does not distance itself from substitutes through product performance, marketing, or other means, it will suffer in terms of profitability—and often growth potential.

Substitutes not only limit profits in normal times, they also reduce the bonanza an industry can reap in good times. In emerging economies, for example, the surge in demand for wired telephone lines has been capped as many consumers opt to make a mobile telephone their first and only phone line.

The threat of a substitute is high if:

- It offers an attractive price-performance trade-off to the industry's product. The better the relative value of the substitute, the tighter is the lid on an industry's profit potential. For example, conventional providers of long-distance telephone service have suffered from the advent of inexpensive internet-based phone services such as Vonage and Skype. Similarly, video rental outlets are struggling with the emergence of cable and satellite video-on-demand services, online video rental services such as Netflix, and the rise of internet video sites like Google's YouTube.
- The buyer's cost of switching to the substitute is low. Switching from a proprietary, branded drug to a generic drug usually involves minimal costs, for example, which is why the shift to generics (and the fall in prices) is so substantial and rapid.

Strategists should be particularly alert to changes in other industries that may make them attractive substitutes when they were not before. Improvements in plastic materials, for example, allowed them to substitute for steel in many automobile components. In this way, technological changes or competitive discontinuities in seemingly unrelated businesses can have major impacts on industry profitability. Of course the substitution threat can also shift in favor of an industry, which bodes well for its future profitability and growth potential.

Rivalry among existing competitors

Rivalry among existing competitors takes many familiar forms, including price discounting, new product introductions, advertising campaigns, and service improvements. High rivalry limits the profitability of an industry. The degree to which rivalry drives down an industry's profit potential depends, first, on the *intensity* with which companies compete and, second, on the *basis* on which they compete.

The intensity of rivalry is greatest if:

- Competitors are numerous or are roughly equal in size and power. In such situations, rivals find it hard to avoid poaching business. Without an industry leader, practices desirable for the industry as a whole go unenforced.
- Industry growth is slow. Slow growth precipitates fights for market share.
- Exit barriers are high. Exit barriers, the flip side of entry barriers, arise because of such things as highly specialized assets or management's devotion to a particular business. These barriers keep companies in the market even though they may be earning low or negative returns. Excess capacity remains in use, and the profitability of healthy competitors suffers as the sick ones hang on.
- Rivals are highly committed to the business and have aspirations for leadership, especially if they have goals that go beyond economic performance in the particular industry. High commitment to a business arises for a variety of reasons. For example, state-owned competitors may have goals that include employment or prestige. Units of larger companies may participate in an industry for image reasons or to offer a full line. Clashes of personality and ego have sometimes exaggerated rivalry to the detriment of profitability in fields such as the media and high technology.
- Firms cannot read each other's signals well because of lack of familiarity with one another, diverse approaches to competing, or differing goals.

The strength of rivalry reflects not just the intensity of competition but also the basis of competition. The *dimensions* on which competition takes place, and whether rivals converge to compete on the *same dimensions,* have a major influence on profitability.

Rivalry is especially destructive to profitability if it gravitates solely to price because price competition transfers profits directly from an industry to its customers. Price cuts are usually easy for competitors to see and match, making successive rounds of retaliation likely. Sustained price competition also trains customers to pay less attention to product features and service.

Price competition is most liable to occur if:

- Products or services of rivals are nearly identical and there are few switching costs for buyers. This encourages competitors to cut prices to win new customers. Years of airline price wars reflect these circumstances in that industry.
- Fixed costs are high and marginal costs are low. This creates intense pressure for competitors to cut prices below their average costs, even close to their marginal costs, to steal incremental customers while still making some contribution to covering fixed costs. Many basic-materials businesses, such as paper and aluminum, suffer from this problem, especially if demand is not growing. So do delivery companies with fixed networks of routes that must be served regardless of volume.
- Capacity must be expanded in large increments to be efficient. The need for large capacity expansions, as in the polyvinyl chloride business, disrupts the industry's supply-demand balance and often leads to long and recurring periods of overcapacity and price cutting.
- The product is perishable. Perishability creates a strong temptation to cut prices and sell a product while it still has value. More products and services are perishable than is commonly thought. Just as tomatoes are perishable because they rot, models of computers are perishable because they soon become obsolete, and information may be perishable if it diffuses rapidly or becomes outdated, thereby losing its value.

Services such as hotel accommodations are perishable in the sense that unused capacity can never be recovered.

Competition on dimensions other than price—on product features, support services, delivery time, or brand image, for instance—is less likely to erode profitability because it improves customer value and can support higher prices. Also, rivalry focused on such dimensions can improve value relative to substitutes or raise the barriers facing new entrants. While nonprice rivalry sometimes escalates to levels that undermine industry profitability, this is less likely to occur than it is with price rivalry.

As important as the dimensions of rivalry is whether rivals compete on the *same* dimensions. When all or many competitors aim to meet the same needs or compete on the same attributes, the result is zero-sum competition. Here, one firm's gain is often another's loss, driving down profitability. While price competition runs a stronger risk than nonprice competition of becoming zero sum, this may not happen if companies take care to segment their markets, targeting their low-price offerings to different customers.

Rivalry can be positive sum, or actually increase the average profitability of an industry, when each competitor aims to serve the needs of different customer segments, with different mixes of price, products, services, features, or brand identities. Such competition can not only support higher average profitability but also expand the industry, as the needs of more customer groups are better met. The opportunity for positive-sum competition will be greater in industries serving diverse customer groups. With a clear understanding of the structural underpinnings of rivalry, strategists can sometimes take steps to shift the nature of competition in a more positive direction.

Factors, Not Forces

Industry structure, as manifested in the strength of the five competitive forces, determines the industry's long-run profit potential because it determines how the economic value created by the industry is divided—how much is retained by companies in the industry versus bargained away by customers and suppliers, limited by substitutes, or constrained by potential new entrants. By considering all five forces, a strategist keeps overall structure in mind instead of gravitating to any one element. In addition, the strategist's attention remains focused on structural conditions rather than on fleeting factors.

It is especially important to avoid the common pitfall of mistaking certain visible attributes of an industry for its underlying structure. Consider the following:

Industry growth rate

A common mistake is to assume that fast-growing industries are always attractive. Growth does tend to mute rivalry, because an expanding pie offers opportunities for all competitors. But fast growth can put suppliers in a powerful position, and high growth with low entry barriers will draw in entrants. Even without new entrants, a high growth rate will not guarantee profitability if customers are powerful or substitutes are attractive. Indeed, some fast-growth businesses, such as personal computers, have been among the least profitable industries in recent years. A narrow focus on growth is one of the major causes of bad strategy decisions.

Technology and innovation

Advanced technology or innovations are not by themselves enough to make an industry structurally attractive (or unattractive). Mundane, low-technology industries with price-insensitive buyers, high switching costs, or high entry barriers arising from scale economies are often far more profitable than sexy industries, such as software and internet technologies, that attract competitors.[2]

Government

Government is not best understood as a sixth force because government involvement is neither inherently good nor bad for industry profitability. The best way to understand the influence of government on competition is to analyze how specific government policies affect the five competitive forces. For instance, patents raise barriers to entry, boosting industry profit potential. Conversely, government policies favoring unions may raise supplier power and diminish profit potential. Bankruptcy rules that allow failing companies to reorganize rather than exit can lead to excess capacity and intense rivalry. Government operates at multiple levels and through many different policies, each of which will affect structure in different ways.

Complementary products and services

Complements are products or services used together with an industry's product. Complements arise when the customer benefit of two products combined is greater than the sum of each product's value in isolation. Computer hardware and software, for instance, are valuable together and worthless when separated.

In recent years, strategy researchers have highlighted the role of complements, especially in high-technology industries where they are most obvious.[3] By no means, however, do complements appear only there. The value of a car, for example, is greater when the driver also has access to gasoline stations, roadside assistance, and auto insurance.

Complements can be important when they affect the overall demand for an industry's product. However, like government policy, complements are not a sixth force determining industry profitability since the presence of strong complements is not necessarily bad (or good) for industry profitability. Complements affect profitability through the way they influence the five forces.

The strategist must trace the positive or negative influence of complements on all five forces to ascertain their impact on profitability. The presence of complements can raise or lower barriers to entry. In application software, for example, barriers to entry were lowered when producers of complementary operating system software, notably Microsoft, provided tool sets making it easier to write applications. Conversely, the need to attract producers of complements can raise barriers to entry, as it does in video game hardware.

The presence of complements can also affect the threat of substitutes. For instance, the need for appropriate fueling stations makes it difficult for cars using alternative fuels to substitute for conventional vehicles. But complements can also make substitution easier.

For example, Apple's iTunes hastened the substitution from CDs to digital music.

Complements can factor into industry rivalry either positively (as when they raise switching costs) or negatively (as when they neutralize product differentiation). Similar analyses can be done for buyer and supplier power. Sometimes companies compete by altering conditions in complementary industries in their favor, such as when videocassette-recorder producer JVC persuaded movie studios to favor its standard in issuing prerecorded tapes even though rival Sony's standard was probably superior from a technical standpoint.

Identifying complements is part of the analyst's work. As with government policies or important technologies, the strategic significance of complements will be best understood through the lens of the five forces.

Changes in Industry Structure

So far, we have discussed the competitive forces at a single point in time. Industry structure proves to be relatively stable, and industry profitability differences are remarkably persistent over time in practice. However, industry structure is constantly undergoing modest adjustment—and occasionally it can change abruptly.

Shifts in structure may emanate from outside an industry or from within. They can boost the industry's profit potential or reduce it. They may be caused by changes in technology, changes in customer needs, or other events. The five competitive forces provide a framework for identifying the most important industry developments and for anticipating their impact on industry attractiveness.

Shifting threat of new entry

Changes to any of the seven barriers described above can raise or lower the threat of new entry. The expiration of a patent, for instance, may unleash new entrants. On the day that Merck's patents for the cholesterol reducer Zocor expired, three pharmaceutical makers entered the market for the drug. Conversely, the proliferation of products in the ice cream industry has gradually filled up the limited freezer space in grocery stores, making it harder for new ice cream makers to gain access to distribution in North America and Europe.

Strategic decisions of leading competitors often have a major impact on the threat of entry. Starting in the 1970s, for example, retailers such as Wal-Mart, Kmart, and Toys "R" Us began to adopt new procurement, distribution, and inventory control technologies with large fixed costs, including automated distribution centers, bar coding, and point-of-sale terminals. These investments increased the economies of scale and made it more difficult for small retailers to enter the business (and for existing small players to survive).

Changing supplier or buyer power

As the factors underlying the power of suppliers and buyers change with time, their clout rises or declines. In the global appliance industry, for instance, competitors including Electrolux, General Electric, and Whirlpool have been squeezed by the consolidation of retail channels (the decline of appliance specialty stores, for instance, and the rise of big-box retailers like Best Buy and Home Depot in the United States). Another example is travel agents, who depend on airlines as a key supplier. When the internet allowed airlines to sell tickets directly to customers, this significantly increased their power to bargain down agents' commissions.

Shifting threat of substitution

The most common reason substitutes become more or less threatening over time is that advances in technology create new substitutes or shift price-performance comparisons in one direction or the other. The earliest microwave ovens, for example, were large and priced above $2,000, making them poor substitutes for conventional ovens. With technological advances, they became serious substitutes. Flash computer memory has improved enough recently to become a meaningful substitute for low-capacity hard-disk drives.

Trends in the availability or performance of complementary producers also shift the threat of substitutes.

New bases of rivalry

Rivalry often intensifies naturally over time. As an industry matures, growth slows. Competitors become more alike as industry conventions emerge, technology diffuses, and consumer tastes converge. Industry profitability falls, and weaker competitors are driven from the business. This story has played out in industry after industry; televisions, snowmobiles, and telecommunications equipment are just a few examples.

A trend toward intensifying price competition and other forms of rivalry, however, is by no means inevitable. For example, there has been enormous competitive activity in the U.S. casino industry in recent decades, but most of it has been positive-sum competition directed toward new niches and geographic segments (such as riverboats, trophy properties, Native American reservations, international expansion, and novel customer groups like families). Head-to-head rivalry that lowers prices or boosts the payouts to winners has been limited.

The nature of rivalry in an industry is altered by mergers and acquisitions that introduce new capabilities and ways of competing. Or, technological innovation can reshape rivalry. In the retail brokerage industry, the advent of the internet lowered marginal costs and reduced differentiation, triggering far more intense competition on commissions and fees than in the past.

In some industries, companies turn to mergers and consolidation not to improve cost and quality but to attempt to stop intense competition. Eliminating rivals is a risky strategy, however. The five competitive forces tell us that a profit windfall from removing today's competitors often attracts new competitors and backlash from customers and suppliers. In New York banking, for example, the 1980s and 1990s saw escalating consolidations of commercial and savings banks, including Manufacturers Hanover, Chemical, Chase, and Dime Savings. But today the retail-banking landscape of

Manhattan is as diverse as ever, as new entrants such as Wachovia, Bank of America, and Washington Mutual have entered the market.

Implications for Strategy

Understanding the forces that shape industry competition is the starting point for developing strategy. Every company should already know what the average profitability of its industry is and how that has been changing over time. The five forces reveal *why* industry profitability is what it is. Only then can a company incorporate industry conditions into strategy.

The forces reveal the most significant aspects of the competitive environment. They also provide a baseline for sizing up a company's strengths and weaknesses: Where does the company stand versus buyers, suppliers, entrants, rivals, and substitutes? Most importantly, an understanding of industry structure guides managers toward fruitful possibilities for strategic action, which may include any or all of the following: positioning the company to better cope with the current competitive forces; anticipating and exploiting shifts in the forces; and shaping the balance of forces to create a new industry structure that is more favorable to the company. The best strategies exploit more than one of these possibilities.

Positioning the company

Strategy can be viewed as building defenses against the competitive forces or finding a position in the industry where the forces are weakest. Consider, for instance, the position of Paccar in the market for heavy trucks. The heavy-truck industry is structurally challenging. Many buyers operate large fleets or are large leasing companies, with both the leverage and the motivation to drive down the price of one of their largest purchases. Most trucks are built to regulated standards and offer similar features, so price competition is rampant. Capital intensity causes rivalry to be fierce, especially during the recurring cyclical downturns. Unions exercise considerable supplier power. Though there are few direct substitutes for an

18-wheeler, truck buyers face important substitutes for their services, such as cargo delivery by rail.

In this setting, Paccar, a Bellevue, Washington-based company with about 20% of the North American heavy-truck market, has chosen to focus on one group of customers: owner-operators—drivers who own their trucks and contract directly with shippers or serve as subcontractors to larger trucking companies. Such small operators have limited clout as truck buyers. They are also less price sensitive because of their strong emotional ties to and economic dependence on the product. They take great pride in their trucks, in which they spend most of their time.

Paccar has invested heavily to develop an array of features with owner-operators in mind: luxurious sleeper cabins, plush leather seats, noise-insulated cabins, sleek exterior styling, and so on. At the company's extensive network of dealers, prospective buyers use software to select among thousands of options to put their personal signature on their trucks. These customized trucks are built to order, not to stock, and delivered in six to eight weeks. Paccar's trucks also have aerodynamic designs that reduce fuel consumption, and they maintain their resale value better than other trucks. Paccar's roadside assistance program and IT-supported system for distributing spare parts reduce the time a truck is out of service. All these are crucial considerations for an owner-operator. Customers pay Paccar a 10% premium, and its Kenworth and Peterbilt brands are considered status symbols at truck stops.

Paccar illustrates the principles of positioning a company within a given industry structure. The firm has found a portion of its industry where the competitive forces are weaker—where it can avoid buyer power and price-based rivalry. And it has tailored every single part of the value chain to cope well with the forces in its segment. As a result, Paccar has been profitable for 68 years straight and has earned a long-run return on equity above 20%.

In addition to revealing positioning opportunities within an existing industry, the five forces framework allows companies to rigorously analyze entry and exit. Both depend on answering the difficult question: "What is the potential of this business?" Exit is indicated when industry structure is poor or declining and the company has no prospect of a superior positioning. In considering entry into a new industry, creative strategists can use the framework to spot an industry with a good future before this good future is reflected in the prices of acquisition candidates. Five forces analysis may also reveal industries that are not necessarily attractive for the average entrant but in which a company has good reason to believe it can surmount entry barriers at lower cost than most firms or has a unique ability to cope with the industry's competitive forces.

Exploiting industry change

Industry changes bring the opportunity to spot and claim promising new strategic positions if the strategist has a sophisticated understanding of the competitive forces and their underpinnings. Consider, for instance, the evolution of the music industry during the past decade. With the advent of the internet and the digital distribution of music, some analysts predicted the birth of thousands of music labels (that is, record companies that develop artists and bring their music to market). This, the analysts argued, would break a pattern that had held since Edison invented the phonograph: Between three and six major record companies had always dominated the industry. The internet would, they predicted, remove distribution as a barrier to entry, unleashing a flood of new players into the music industry.

A careful analysis, however, would have revealed that physical distribution was not the crucial barrier to entry. Rather, entry was barred by other benefits that large music labels enjoyed. Large labels could pool the risks of developing new artists over many bets, cushioning the impact of inevitable failures. Even more important, they had advantages in breaking through the clutter and getting their new artists heard. To do so, they could promise radio stations and record stores access to well-known artists in exchange for promotion of new artists. New labels would find this nearly impossible to match. The major labels stayed the course, and new music labels have been rare.

This is not to say that the music industry is structurally unchanged by digital distribution. Unauthorized downloading created an illegal but potent substitute. The labels tried for years to develop technical platforms for digital distribution themselves, but major companies hesitated to sell their music through a platform owned by a rival. Into this vacuum stepped Apple with its iTunes music store, launched in 2003 to support its iPod music player. By permitting the creation of a powerful new gatekeeper, the major labels allowed industry structure to shift against them. The number of major record companies has actually declined—from six in 1997 to four today—as companies struggled to cope with the digital phenomenon.

When industry structure is in flux, new and promising competitive positions may appear. Structural changes open up new needs and new ways to serve existing needs. Established leaders may overlook these or be constrained by past strategies from pursuing them. Smaller competitors in the industry can capitalize on such changes, or the void may well be filled by new entrants.

Shaping industry structure

When a company exploits structural change, it is recognizing, and reacting to, the inevitable. However, companies also have the ability to shape industry structure. A firm can lead its industry toward new ways of competing that alter the five forces for the better. In reshaping structure, a company wants its competitors to follow so that the entire industry will be transformed. While many industry participants may benefit in the process, the innovator can benefit most if it can shift competition in directions where it can excel.

An industry's structure can be reshaped in two ways: by redividing profitability in favor of incumbents or by expanding the overall profit pool. Redividing the industry pie aims to increase the share of profits to industry competitors instead of to suppliers, buyers, substitutes, and keeping out potential entrants. Expanding the profit pool involves increasing the overall pool of economic value generated by the industry in which rivals, buyers, and suppliers can all share.

Redividing profitability. To capture more profits for industry rivals, the starting point is to determine which force or forces are currently constraining industry profitability and address them.

A company can potentially influence all of the competitive forces. The strategist's goal here is to reduce the share of profits that leak to suppliers, buyers, and substitutes or are sacrificed to deter entrants.

To neutralize supplier power, for example, a firm can standardize specifications for parts to make it easier to switch among suppliers. It can cultivate additional vendors, or alter technology to avoid a powerful supplier group altogether. To counter customer power, companies may expand services that raise buyers' switching costs or find alternative means of reaching customers to neutralize powerful channels. To temper profit-eroding price rivalry, companies can invest more heavily in unique products, as pharmaceutical firms have done, or expand support services to customers. To scare off entrants, incumbents can elevate the fixed cost of competing—for instance, by escalating their R&D or marketing expenditures. To limit the threat of substitutes, companies can offer better value through new features or wider product accessibility. When soft-drink producers introduced vending machines and convenience store channels, for example, they dramatically improved the availability of soft drinks relative to other beverages.

Sysco, the largest food-service distributor in North America, offers a revealing example of how an industry leader can change the structure of an industry for the better. Food-service distributors purchase food and related items from farmers and food processors. They then warehouse and deliver these items to restaurants, hospitals, employer cafeterias, schools, and other food-service institutions. Given low barriers to entry, the food-service distribution industry has historically been highly fragmented, with numerous local competitors. While rivals try to cultivate customer relationships, buyers are price sensitive because food represents a large share of their costs. Buyers can also choose the substitute approaches of purchasing directly from manufacturers or using retail sources, avoiding distributors altogether. Suppliers wield bargaining power: They are often large companies with strong brand names that food preparers and consumers recognize. Average profitability in the industry has been modest.

Defining the Relevant Industry

DEFINING THE INDUSTRY IN WHICH competition actually takes place is important for good industry analysis, not to mention for developing strategy and setting business unit boundaries. Many strategy errors emanate from mistaking the relevant industry, defining it too broadly or too narrowly. Defining the industry too broadly obscures differences among products, customers, or geographic regions that are important to competition, strategic positioning, and profitability. Defining the industry too narrowly overlooks commonalities and linkages across related products or geographic markets that are crucial to competitive advantage. Also, strategists must be sensitive to the possibility that industry boundaries can shift.

The boundaries of an industry consist of two primary dimensions. First is the *scope of products or services*. For example, is motor oil used in cars part of the same industry as motor oil used in heavy trucks and stationary engines, or are these different industries? The second dimension is *geographic scope*. Most industries are present in many parts of the world. However, is competition contained within each state, or is it national? Does competition take place within regions such as Europe or North America, or is there a single global industry?

The five forces are the basic tool to resolve these questions. If industry structure for two products is the same or very similar (that is, if they have the same buyers, suppliers, barriers to entry, and so forth), then the products are best treated as being part of the same industry. If industry structure differs markedly, however, the two products may be best understood as separate industries.

In lubricants, the oil used in cars is similar or even identical to the oil used in trucks, but the similarity largely ends there. Automotive motor oil is sold to fragmented, generally unsophisticated customers through numerous and often powerful channels, using extensive advertising. Products are packaged

Sysco recognized that, given its size and national reach, it might change this state of affairs. It led the move to introduce private-label distributor brands with specifications tailored to the food-service market, moderating supplier power. Sysco emphasized value-added services to buyers such as credit, menu planning, and inventory management to shift the basis of competition away from just price. These moves, together with stepped-up investments in information technology and regional distribution centers, substantially raised

in small containers and logistical costs are high, necessitating local production. Truck and power generation lubricants are sold to entirely different buyers in entirely different ways using a separate supply chain. Industry structure (buyer power, barriers to entry, and so forth) is substantially different. Automotive oil is thus a distinct industry from oil for truck and stationary engine uses. Industry profitability will differ in these two cases, and a lubricant company will need a separate strategy for competing in each area.

Differences in the five competitive forces also reveal the geographic scope of competition. If an industry has a similar structure in every country (rivals, buyers, and so on), the presumption is that competition is global, and the five forces analyzed from a global perspective will set average profitability. A single global strategy is needed. If an industry has quite different structures in different geographic regions, however, each region may well be a distinct industry. Otherwise, competition would have leveled the differences. The five forces analyzed for each region will set profitability there.

The extent of differences in the five forces for related products or across geographic areas is a matter of degree, making industry definition often a matter of judgment. A rule of thumb is that where the differences in any one force are large, and where the differences involve more than one force, distinct industries may well be present.

Fortunately, however, even if industry boundaries are drawn incorrectly, careful five forces analysis should reveal important competitive threats. A closely related product omitted from the industry definition will show up as a substitute, for example, or competitors overlooked as rivals will be recognized as potential entrants. At the same time, the five forces analysis should reveal major differences within overly broad industries that will indicate the need to adjust industry boundaries or strategies.

the bar for new entrants while making the substitutes less attractive. Not surprisingly, the industry has been consolidating, and industry profitability appears to be rising.

Industry leaders have a special responsibility for improving industry structure. Doing so often requires resources that only large players possess. Moreover, an improved industry structure is a public good because it benefits every firm in the industry, not just the company that initiated the improvement. Often, it is more in the

Typical Steps in Industry Analysis

Define the relevant industry:

- What products are in it? Which ones are part of another distinct industry?
- What is the geographic scope of competition?

Identify the participants and segment them into groups, if appropriate:

Who are

- the buyers and buyer groups?
- the suppliers and supplier groups?
- the competitors?
- the substitutes?
- the potential entrants?

Assess the underlying drivers of each competitive force to determine which forces are strong and which are weak and why.

Determine overall industry structure, and test the analysis for consistency:

- *Why* is the level of profitability what it is?
- Which are the *controlling* forces for profitability?
- Is the industry analysis consistent with actual long-run profitability?
- Are more-profitable players better positioned in relation to the five forces?

Analyze recent and likely future changes in each force, both positive and negative.

Identify aspects of industry structure that might be influenced by competitors, by new entrants, or by your company.

---

interests of an industry leader than any other participant to invest for the common good because leaders will usually benefit the most. Indeed, improving the industry may be a leader's most profitable strategic opportunity, in part because attempts to gain further market share can trigger strong reactions from rivals, customers, and even suppliers.

There is a dark side to shaping industry structure that is equally important to understand. Ill-advised changes in competitive positioning and operating practices can *undermine* industry structure. Faced with pressures to gain market share or enamored with innovation for its own sake, managers may trigger new kinds of competition that no incumbent can win. When taking actions to improve their own company's competitive advantage, then, strategists should ask whether they are setting in motion dynamics that will undermine industry structure in the long run. In the early days of the personal computer industry, for instance, IBM tried to make up for its late entry by offering an open architecture that would set industry standards and attract complementary makers of application software and peripherals. In the process, it ceded ownership of the critical components of the PC—the operating system and the microprocessor—to Microsoft and Intel. By standardizing PCs, it encouraged price-based rivalry and shifted power to suppliers. Consequently, IBM became the temporarily dominant firm in an industry with an enduringly unattractive structure.

Expanding the profit pool. When overall demand grows, the industry's quality level rises, intrinsic costs are reduced, or waste is eliminated, the pie expands. The total pool of value available to competitors, suppliers, and buyers grows. The total profit pool expands, for example, when channels become more competitive or when an industry discovers latent buyers for its product that are not currently being served. When soft-drink producers rationalized their independent bottler networks to make them more efficient and effective, both the soft-drink companies and the bottlers benefited. Overall value can also expand when firms work collaboratively with suppliers to improve coordination and limit unnecessary costs incurred in the supply chain. This lowers the inherent cost structure of the industry, allowing higher profit, greater demand through lower prices, or both. Or, agreeing on quality standards can bring up industrywide quality and service levels, and hence prices, benefiting rivals, suppliers, and customers.

Expanding the overall profit pool creates win-win opportunities for multiple industry participants. It can also reduce the risk of destructive rivalry that arises when incumbents attempt to shift bargaining power or capture more market share. However, expanding the pie does not reduce the importance of industry structure. How the expanded pie is divided will ultimately be determined by the five forces. The most successful companies are those that expand the industry profit pool in ways that allow them to share disproportionately in the benefits.

Defining the industry

The five competitive forces also hold the key to defining the relevant industry (or industries) in which a company competes. Drawing industry boundaries correctly, around the arena in which competition actually takes place, will clarify the causes of profitability and the appropriate unit for setting strategy. A company needs a separate strategy for each distinct industry. Mistakes in industry definition made by competitors present opportunities for staking out superior strategic positions. (See the sidebar "Defining the Relevant Industry.")

Competition and Value

The competitive forces reveal the drivers of industry competition. A company strategist who understands that competition extends well beyond existing rivals will detect wider competitive threats and be better equipped to address them. At the same time, thinking comprehensively about an industry's structure can uncover opportunities: differences in customers, suppliers, substitutes, potential entrants, and rivals that can become the basis for distinct strategies yielding superior performance. In a world of more open competition and relentless change, it is more important than ever to think structurally about competition.

Understanding industry structure is equally important for investors as for managers. The five competitive forces reveal whether

Common Pitfalls

In conducting the analysis avoid the following common mistakes:

- Defining the industry too broadly or too narrowly.
- Making lists instead of engaging in rigorous analysis.
- Paying equal attention to all of the forces rather than digging deeply into the most important ones.
- Confusing effect (price sensitivity) with cause (buyer economics).
- Using static analysis that ignores industry trends.
- Confusing cyclical or transient changes with true structural changes.
- Using the framework to declare an industry attractive or unattractive rather than using it to guide strategic choices.

an industry is truly attractive, and they help investors anticipate positive or negative shifts in industry structure before they are obvious. The five forces distinguish short-term blips from structural changes and allow investors to take advantage of undue pessimism or optimism. Those companies whose strategies have industry-transforming potential become far clearer. This deeper thinking about competition is a more powerful way to achieve genuine investment success than the financial projections and trend extrapolation that dominate today's investment analysis.

If both executives and investors looked at competition this way, capital markets would be a far more effective force for company success and economic prosperity. Executives and investors would both be focused on the same fundamentals that drive sustained profitability. The conversation between investors and executives would focus on the structural, not the transient. Imagine the improvement in company performance—and in the economy as a whole—if all the energy expended in "pleasing the Street" were redirected toward the factors that create true economic value.

Originally published in January 2008. Reprint R0801E.

Notes

1. For a discussion of the value chain framework, see Michael E. Porter, *Competitive Advantage: Creating and Sustaining Superior Performance* (The Free Press, 1998).

2. For a discussion of how internet technology improves the attractiveness of some industries while eroding the profitability of others, see Michael E. Porter, "Strategy and the Internet" (HBR, March 2001).

3. See, for instance, Adam M. Brandenburger and Barry J. Nalebuff, *Co-opetition* (Currency Doubleday, 1996).

Building Your Company's Vision

by James C. Collins and Jerry I. Porras

> *We shall not cease from exploration/And the end of all our exploring/Will be to arrive where we started/And know the place for the first time.*
>
> —T.S. Eliot, *Four Quartets*

COMPANIES THAT ENJOY ENDURING success have core values and a core purpose that remain fixed while their business strategies and practices endlessly adapt to a changing world. The dynamic of preserving the core while stimulating progress is the reason that companies such as Hewlett-Packard, 3M, Johnson & Johnson, Procter & Gamble, Merck, Sony, Motorola, and Nordstrom became elite institutions able to renew themselves and achieve superior long-term performance. Hewlett-Packard employees have long known that radical change in operating practices, cultural norms, and business strategies does not mean losing the spirit of the HP Way—the company's core principles. Johnson & Johnson continually questions its structure and revamps its processes while preserving the ideals embodied in its credo. In 1996, 3M sold off several of its large mature businesses—a dramatic move that surprised the business press—to refocus on its enduring core purpose of solving unsolved problems innovatively. We studied companies such as these in our research for *Built to Last: Successful Habits of Visionary Companies* and found that they have outperformed the general stock market by a factor of 12 since 1925.

Truly great companies understand the difference between what should never change and what should be open for change, between what is genuinely sacred and what is not. This rare ability to manage continuity and change—requiring a consciously practiced discipline—is closely linked to the ability to develop a vision. Vision provides guidance about what core to preserve and what future to stimulate progress toward. But *vision* has become one of the most overused and least understood words in the language, conjuring up different images for different people: of deeply held values, outstanding achievement, societal bonds, exhilarating goals, motivating forces, or raisons d'être. We recommend a conceptual framework to define vision, add clarity and rigor to the vague and fuzzy concepts swirling around that trendy term, and give practical guidance for articulating a coherent vision within an organization. It is a prescriptive framework rooted in six years of research and refined and tested by our ongoing work with executives from a great variety of organizations around the world.

A well-conceived vision consists of two major components: *core ideology* and *envisioned future*. (See the exhibit "Articulating a vision.") Core ideology, the yin in our scheme, defines what we stand for and why we exist. Yin is unchanging and complements yang, the envisioned future. The envisioned future is what we aspire to become, to achieve, to create—something that will require significant change and progress to attain.

Core Ideology

Core ideology defines the enduring character of an organization—a consistent identity that transcends product or market life cycles, technological breakthroughs, management fads, and individual leaders. In fact, the most lasting and significant contribution of those who build visionary companies is the core ideology. As Bill Hewlett said about his longtime friend and business partner David Packard upon Packard's death not long ago, "As far as the company is concerned, the greatest thing he left behind him was a code of ethics known as the HP Way." HP's core ideology, which has guided the company since its inception more than 50 years ago, includes a deep respect for the individual, a dedication to affordable quality and reliability, a commitment to community responsibility (Packard

Idea in Brief

Hewlett-Packard. 3M. Sony. Companies with exceptionally durable visions that are "built to last." What distinguishes their visions from most others, those empty muddles that get revised with every passing business fad, but never prompt anything more than a yawn? Enduring companies have clear plans for how they will advance into an uncertain future. But they are equally clear about how they will remain steadfast, about the values and purposes they will always stand for. This *Harvard Business Review* article describes the two components of any lasting vision: **core ideology** and an **envisioned future**.

himself bequeathed his $4.3 billion of Hewlett-Packard stock to a charitable foundation), and a view that the company exists to make technical contributions for the advancement and welfare of humanity. Company builders such as David Packard, Masaru Ibuka of Sony, George Merck of Merck, William McKnight of 3M, and Paul Galvin of Motorola understood that it is more important to know who you are than where you are going, for where you are going will change as the world around you changes. Leaders die, products become obsolete, markets change, new technologies emerge, and management fads come and go, but core ideology in a great company endures as a source of guidance and inspiration.

Core ideology provides the glue that holds an organization together as it grows, decentralizes, diversifies, expands globally, and develops workplace diversity. Think of it as analogous to the principles of Judaism that held the Jewish people together for centuries without a homeland, even as they spread throughout the Diaspora. Or think of the truths held to be self-evident in the Declaration of Independence, or the enduring ideals and principles of the scientific community that bond scientists from every nationality together in the common purpose of advancing human knowledge. Any effective vision must embody the core ideology of the organization, which in turn consists of two distinct parts: core values, a system of guiding principles and tenets; and core purpose, the organization's most fundamental reason for existence.

Idea in Practice

A company's practices and strategies should change continually; its core ideology should not. Core ideology defines a company's timeless character. It's the glue that holds the enterprise together even when everything else is up for grabs. Core ideology is something you *discover*—by looking inside. It's not something you can invent, much less fake.

A core ideology has two parts:

1. **Core values are the handful of guiding principles by which a company navigates.** They require no external justification. For example, Disney's core values of imagination and wholesomeness stem from the founder's belief that these should be nurtured for their own sake, not merely to capitalize on a business opportunity. Instead of changing its core values, a great company will change its markets—seek out different customers—in order to remain true to its core values.
2. **Core purpose is an organization's most fundamental reason for being.** It should not be confused with the company's current product lines or customer segments. Rather, it reflects people's idealistic motivations for doing the company's work. Disney's core purpose is to make people happy—not to build theme parks and make cartoons.

An envisioned future, the second component of an effective vision, has two elements:

1. **Big, Hairy, Audacious Goals (BHAGs) are ambitious plans that rev up the entire organization.** They typically require 10 to 30 years' work to complete.
2. **Vivid descriptions paint a picture of what it will be like to achieve the BHAGs.** They make the goals vibrant, engaging—and tangible.

Example: In the 1950s, Sony's goal was to "become the company most known for changing the worldwide poor-quality image of Japanese products." It made this BHAG vivid by adding, "Fifty years from now, our brand name will be as well known as any in the world . . . and will signify innovation and quality. . . . 'Made in Japan' will mean something fine, not something shoddy."

Don't confuse your company's core ideology with its envisioned future—in particular, don't confuse a BHAG with a core purpose. A BHAG is a clearly articulated goal that is reachable within 10 to 30 years. But your core purpose can never be completed.

Core values

Core values are the essential and enduring tenets of an organization. A small set of timeless guiding principles, core values require no external justification; they have *intrinsic* value and importance to those inside the organization. The Walt Disney Company's core values of imagination and wholesomeness stem not from market requirements but from the founder's inner belief that imagination and wholesomeness should be nurtured for their own sake. William Procter and James Gamble didn't instill in P&G's culture a focus on product excellence merely as a strategy for success but as an almost religious tenet. And that value has been passed down for more than 15 decades by P&G people. Service to the customer—even to the point of subservience—is a way of life at Nordstrom that traces its roots back to 1901, eight decades before customer service programs became stylish. For Bill Hewlett and David Packard, respect for the individual was first and foremost a deep personal value; they didn't get it from a book or hear it from a management guru. And Ralph S. Larsen, CEO of Johnson & Johnson, puts it this way: "The core values embodied in our credo might be a competitive advantage, but that is not *why* we have them. We have them because they define for us what we stand for, and we would hold them even if they became a competitive *dis*advantage in certain situations."

The point is that a great company decides for itself what values it holds to be core, largely independent of the current environment, competitive requirements, or management fads. Clearly, then, there is no universally right set of core values. A company need not have as its core value customer service (Sony doesn't) or respect for the individual (Disney doesn't) or quality (Wal-Mart Stores doesn't) or market focus (HP doesn't) or teamwork (Nordstrom doesn't). A company might have operating practices and business strategies around those qualities without having them at the essence of its being. Furthermore, great companies need not have likable or humanistic core values, although many do. The key is not *what* core values an organization has but that it has core values at all.

Companies tend to have only a few core values, usually between three and five. In fact, we found that none of the visionary companies we studied in our book had more than five: most had only three or four. (See the sidebar "Core Values Are a Company's Essential Tenets.") And, indeed, we should expect that. Only a few values can be truly *core*—that is, so fundamental and deeply held that they will change seldom, if ever.

To identify the core values of your own organization, push with relentless honesty to define what values are truly central. If you articulate more than five or six, chances are that you are confusing core values (which do not change) with operating practices, business strategies, or cultural norms (which should be open to change). Remember, the values must stand the test of time. After you've drafted a preliminary list of the core values, ask about each one, If the circumstances changed and *penalized* us for holding this core value, would we still keep it? If you can't honestly answer yes, then the value is not core and should be dropped from consideration.

A high-technology company wondered whether it should put quality on its list of core values. The CEO asked, "Suppose in ten years quality doesn't make a hoot of difference in our markets. Suppose the only thing that matters is sheer speed and horsepower but

Articulating a vision

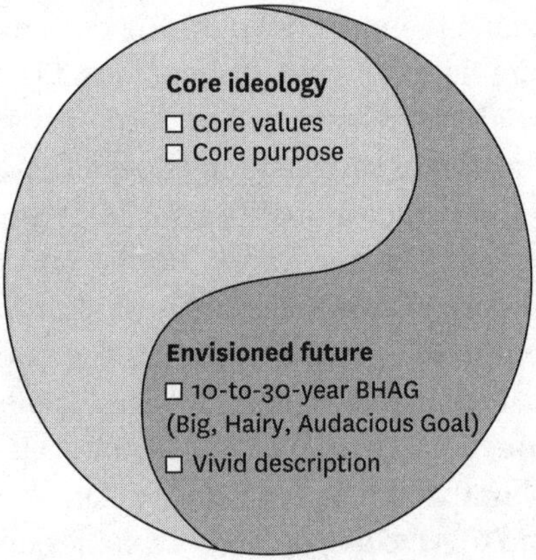

not quality. Would we still want to put quality on our list of core values?" The members of the management team looked around at one another and finally said no. Quality stayed in the *strategy* of the company, and quality-improvement programs remained in place as a mechanism for stimulating progress; but quality did not make the list of core values.

The same group of executives then wrestled with leading-edge innovation as a core value. The CEO asked, "Would we keep innovation on the list as a core value, no matter how the world around us changed?" This time, the management team gave a resounding yes. The managers' outlook might be summarized as, "We always want to do leading-edge innovation. That's who we are. It's really important to us and always will be. No matter what. And if our current markets don't value it, we will find markets that do." Leading-edge innovation went on the list and will stay there. A company should not change its core values in response to market changes; rather, it should change markets, if necessary, to remain true to its core values.

Who should be involved in articulating the core values varies with the size, age, and geographic dispersion of the company, but in many situations we have recommended what we call a *Mars Group*. It works like this: Imagine that you've been asked to re-create the very best attributes of your organization on another planet but you have seats on the rocket ship for only five to seven people. Whom should you send? Most likely, you'll choose the people who have a gut-level understanding of your core values, the highest level of credibility with their peers, and the highest levels of competence. We'll often ask people brought together to work on core values to nominate a Mars Group of five to seven individuals (not necessarily all from the assembled group). Invariably, they end up selecting highly credible representatives who do a super job of articulating the core values precisely because they are exemplars of those values—a representative slice of the company's genetic code.

Even global organizations composed of people from widely diverse cultures can identify a set of shared core values. The secret is to work from the individual to the organization. People involved in articulating the core values need to answer several questions: What

Core Values Are a Company's Essential Tenets

Merck

- Corporate social responsibility
- Unequivocal excellence in all aspects of the company
- Science-based innovation
- Honesty and integrity
- Profit, but profit from work that benefits humanity

Nordstrom

- Service to the customer above all else
- Hard work and individual productivity
- Never being satisfied
- Excellence in reputation; being part of something special

Philip Morris

- The right to freedom of choice
- Winning—beating others in a good fight
- Encouraging individual initiative
- Opportunity based on merit; no one is entitled to anything
- Hard work and continuous self-improvement

Sony

- Elevation of the Japanese culture and national status
- Being a pioneer—not following others; doing the impossible
- Encouraging individual ability and creativity

Walt Disney

- No cynicism
- Nurturing and promulgation of "wholesome American values"
- Creativity, dreams, and imagination
- Fanatical attention to consistency and detail
- Preservation and control of the Disney magic

core values do you personally bring to your work? (These should be so fundamental that you would hold them regardless of whether or not they were rewarded.) What would you tell your children are the core values that you hold at work and that you hope *they* will hold when they become working adults? If you awoke tomorrow morning with enough money to retire for the rest of your life, would you continue to live those core values? Can you envision them being as valid for you 100 years from now as they are today? Would you want to hold those core values, even if at some point one or more of them became a competitive *dis*advantage? If you were to start a new organization tomorrow in a different line of work, what core values would you build into the new organization regardless of its industry? The last three questions are particularly important because they make the crucial distinction between enduring core values that should not change and practices and strategies that should be changing all the time.

Core purpose

Core purpose, the second part of core ideology, is the organization's reason for being. An effective purpose reflects people's idealistic motivations for doing the company's work. It doesn't just describe the organization's output or target customers; it captures the soul of the organization. (See the sidebar "Core Purpose Is a Company's Reason for Being.") Purpose, as illustrated by a speech David Packard gave to HP employees in 1960, gets at the deeper reasons for an organization's existence beyond just making money. Packard said,

> I want to discuss why a company exists in the first place. In other words, why are we here? I think many people assume, wrongly, that a company exists simply to make money. While this is an important result of a company's existence, we have to go deeper and find the real reasons for our being. As we investigate this, we inevitably come to the conclusion that a group of people get together and exist as an institution that we call a company so they are able to accomplish something collectively that they could not accomplish separately—they make a contribution

> to society, a phrase which sounds trite but is fundamental . . . You can look around [in the general business world and] see people who are interested in money and nothing else, but the underlying drives come largely from a desire to do something else: to make a product, to give a service—generally to do something which is of value.[1]

Purpose (which should last at least 100 years) should not be confused with specific goals or business strategies (which should change many times in 100 years). Whereas you might achieve a goal or complete a strategy, you cannot fulfill a purpose; it is like a guiding star on the horizon—forever pursued but never reached. Yet although purpose itself does not change, it does inspire change. The very fact that purpose can never be fully realized means that an organization can never stop stimulating change and progress.

In identifying purpose, some companies make the mistake of simply describing their current product lines or customer segments. We do not consider the following statement to reflect an effective purpose: "We exist to fulfill our government charter and participate in the secondary mortgage market by packaging mortgages into investment securities." The statement is merely descriptive. A far more effective statement of purpose would be that expressed by the executives of the Federal National Mortgage Association, Fannie Mae: "To strengthen the social fabric by continually democratizing home ownership." The secondary mortgage market as we know it might not even exist in 100 years, but strengthening the social fabric by continually democratizing home ownership can be an enduring purpose, no matter how much the world changes. Guided and inspired by this purpose, Fannie Mae launched in the early 1990s a series of bold initiatives, including a program to develop new systems for reducing mortgage underwriting costs by 40% in five years; programs to eliminate discrimination in the lending process (backed by $5 billion in underwriting experiments); and an audacious goal to provide, by the year 2000, $1 trillion targeted at 10 million families that had traditionally been shut out of home ownership—minorities, immigrants, and low-income groups.

Similarly, 3M defines its purpose not in terms of adhesives and abrasives but as the perpetual quest to solve unsolved problems innovatively—a purpose that is always leading 3M into new fields. McKinsey & Company's purpose is not to do management consulting but to help corporations and governments be more successful: in 100 years, it might involve methods other than consulting. Hewlett-Packard doesn't exist to make electronic test and measurement equipment but to make technical contributions that improve people's lives—a purpose that has led the company far afield from its origins in electronic instruments. Imagine if Walt Disney had conceived of his company's purpose as to make cartoons, rather than to make people happy; we probably wouldn't have Mickey Mouse, Disneyland, EPCOT Center, or the Anaheim Mighty Ducks Hockey Team.

One powerful method for getting at purpose is the *five whys*. Start with the descriptive statement We make X products or We deliver X services, and then ask, Why is that important? five times. After a few whys, you'll find that you're getting down to the fundamental purpose of the organization.

We used this method to deepen and enrich a discussion about purpose when we worked with a certain market-research company. The executive team first met for several hours and generated the following statement of purpose for their organization: To provide the best market-research data available. We then asked the following question: Why is it important to provide the best market-research data available? After some discussion, the executives answered in a way that reflected a deeper sense of their organization's purpose: To provide the best market-research data available so that our customers will understand their markets better than they could otherwise. A further discussion let team members realize that their sense of self-worth came not just from helping customers understand their markets better but also from making a *contribution* to their customers' success. This introspection eventually led the company to identify its purpose as: To contribute to our customers' success by helping them understand their markets. With this purpose in mind, the company now frames its product decisions not with the

Core Purpose Is a Company's Reason for Being

3M: To solve unsolved problems innovatively

Cargill: To improve the standard of living around the world

Fannie Mae: To strengthen the social fabric by continually democratizing home ownership

Hewlett-Packard: To make technical contributions for the advancement and welfare of humanity

Lost Arrow Corporation: To be a role model and a tool for social change

Pacific Theatres: To provide a place for people to flourish and to enhance the community

Mary Kay Cosmetics: To give unlimited opportunity to women

McKinsey & Company: To help leading corporations and governments be more successful

Merck: To preserve and improve human life

Nike: To experience the emotion of competition, winning, and crushing competitors

Sony: To experience the joy of advancing and applying technology for the benefit of the public

Telecare Corporation: To help people with mental impairments realize their full potential

Wal-Mart: To give ordinary folk the chance to buy the same things as rich people

Walt Disney: To make people happy

---

question Will it sell? but with the question Will it make a contribution to our customers' success?

The five whys can help companies in any industry frame their work in a more meaningful way. An asphalt and gravel company might begin by saying, We make gravel and asphalt products. After a few whys, it could conclude that making asphalt and gravel is important because the quality of the infrastructure plays a vital role in people's safety and experience; because driving on a pitted road is annoying and dangerous; because 747s cannot land safely on runways built with poor workmanship or inferior concrete; because buildings with substandard materials weaken with time and crumble in earthquakes. From such introspection may emerge this purpose: To make people's lives better by improving the quality of man-made structures. With a sense of purpose very much along those lines, Granite Rock Company of Watsonville, California, won the Malcolm Baldrige National Quality Award—not an easy feat for a small rock quarry and asphalt company. And Granite Rock has gone on to be one of the most progressive and exciting companies we've encountered in *any* industry.

Notice that none of the core purposes fall into the category "maximize shareholder wealth." A primary role of core purpose is to guide and inspire. Maximizing shareholder wealth does not inspire people at all levels of an organization, and it provides precious little guidance. Maximizing shareholder wealth is the standard off-the-shelf purpose for those organizations that have not yet identified their true core purpose. It is a substitute—and a weak one at that.

When people in great organizations talk about their achievements, they say very little about earnings per share. Motorola people talk about impressive quality improvements and the effect of the products they create on the world. Hewlett-Packard people talk about their technical contributions to the marketplace. Nordstrom people talk about heroic customer service and remarkable individual performance by star salespeople. When a Boeing engineer talks about launching an exciting and revolutionary new aircraft, she does not say, "I put my heart and soul into this project because it would add 37 cents to our earnings per share."

One way to get at the purpose that lies beyond merely maximizing shareholder wealth is to play the "Random Corporate Serial Killer" game. It works like this: Suppose you could sell the company to someone who would pay a price that everyone inside and outside the company agrees is more than fair (even with a very generous set of assumptions about the expected future cash flows of the company). Suppose further that this buyer would guarantee stable employment for all employees at the same pay scale after the purchase but with no guarantee that those jobs would be in the same industry. Finally, suppose the buyer plans to kill the company after the purchase—its products or services would be discontinued, its operations would be shut down, its brand names would be shelved forever, and so on. The company would utterly and completely cease to exist. Would you accept the offer? Why or why not? What would be lost if the company ceased to exist? Why is it important that the company continue to exist? We've found this exercise to be very powerful for helping hard-nosed, financially focused executives reflect on their organization's deeper reasons for being.

Another approach is to ask each member of the Mars Group, How could we frame the purpose of this organization so that if you woke up tomorrow morning with enough money in the bank to retire, you would nevertheless keep working here? What deeper sense of purpose would motivate you to continue to dedicate your precious creative energies to this company's efforts?

As they move into the twenty-first century, companies will need to draw on the full creative energy and talent of their people. But why should people give full measure? As Peter Drucker has pointed out, the best and most dedicated people are ultimately volunteers, for they have the opportunity to do something else with their lives. Confronted with an increasingly mobile society, cynicism about corporate life, and an expanding entrepreneurial segment of the economy, companies more than ever need to have a clear understanding of their purpose in order to make work meaningful and thereby attract, motivate, and retain outstanding people.

Discovering Core Ideology

You do not create or set core ideology. You *discover* core ideology. You do not deduce it by looking at the external environment. You understand it by looking inside. Ideology has to be authentic. You cannot fake it. Discovering core ideology is not an intellectual exercise. Do not ask, What core values should we hold? Ask instead, What core values do we truly and passionately hold? You should not confuse values that you think the organization ought to have—but does not—with authentic core values. To do so would create cynicism throughout the organization. ("Who're they trying to kid? We all know that isn't a core value around here!") Aspirations are more appropriate as part of your envisioned future or as part of your strategy, not as part of the core ideology. However, authentic core values that have weakened over time can be considered a legitimate part of the core ideology—as long as you acknowledge to the organization that you must work hard to revive them.

Also be clear that the role of core ideology is to guide and inspire, not to differentiate. Two companies can have the same core values or purpose. Many companies could have the purpose to make technical contributions, but few live it as passionately as Hewlett-Packard. Many companies could have the purpose to preserve and improve human life, but few hold it as deeply as Merck. Many companies could have the core value of heroic customer service, but few create as intense a culture around that value as Nordstrom. Many companies could have the core value of innovation, but few create the powerful alignment mechanisms that stimulate the innovation we see at 3M. The authenticity, the discipline, and the consistency with which the ideology is lived—not the content of the ideology—differentiate visionary companies from the rest of the pack.

Core ideology needs to be meaningful and inspirational only to people inside the organization; it need not be exciting to outsiders. Why not? Because it is the people inside the organization who need to commit to the organizational ideology over the long term. Core ideology can also play a role in determining who *is* inside and who is not. A clear and well-articulated ideology attracts to the company people whose personal values are compatible with the company's core values; conversely, it repels those whose personal values are incompatible. You cannot impose new core values or purpose on people. Nor are core values and purpose things people can buy into. Executives often ask, How do we get people to share our core ideology? You don't. You can't. Instead, find people who are predisposed to share your core values and purpose; attract and retain those people; and let those who do not share your core values go elsewhere.

Indeed, the very process of articulating core ideology may cause some people to leave when they realize that they are not personally compatible with the organization's core. Welcome that outcome. It is certainly desirable to retain within the core ideology a diversity of people and viewpoints. People who share the same core values and purpose do not necessarily all think or look the same.

Don't confuse core ideology itself with core-ideology statements. A company can have a very strong core ideology without a formal statement. For example, Nike has not (to our knowledge) formally articulated a statement of its core purpose. Yet, according to our observations, Nike has a powerful core purpose that permeates the entire organization: to experience the emotion of competition, winning, and crushing competitors. Nike has a campus that seems more like a shrine to the competitive spirit than a corporate office complex. Giant photos of Nike heroes cover the walls, bronze plaques of Nike athletes hang along the Nike Walk of Fame, statues of Nike athletes stand alongside the running track that rings the campus, and buildings honor champions such as Olympic marathoner Joan Benoit, basketball superstar Michael Jordan, and tennis pro John McEnroe. Nike people who do not feel stimulated by the competitive spirit and the urge to be ferocious simply do not last long in the culture. Even the company's name reflects a sense of competition: Nike is the Greek goddess of victory. Thus, although Nike has not formally articulated its purpose, it clearly has a strong one.

Identifying core values and purpose is therefore not an exercise in wordsmithery. Indeed, an organization will generate a variety of statements over time to describe the core ideology. In Hewlett-Packard's archives, we found more than half a dozen distinct versions of the HP Way, drafted by David Packard between 1956 and 1972. All versions stated the same principles, but the words used varied depending on the era and the circumstances. Similarly, Sony's core ideology has been stated many different ways over the company's history. At its founding, Masaru Ibuka described two key elements of Sony's ideology: "We shall welcome technical difficulties and focus on highly sophisticated technical products that have great usefulness for society regardless of the quantity involved; we shall place our main emphasis on ability, performance, and personal character so that each individual can show the best in ability and skill."[2] Four decades later, this same concept appeared in a statement of core ideology called Sony Pioneer Spirit: "Sony is a pioneer and never intends to follow others. Through progress, Sony wants to serve the whole world. It shall be always a seeker of the unknown. . . . Sony has a principle of respecting and encouraging one's ability . . . and always tries to bring out the best in a person. This is the vital force of Sony."[3] Same core values, different words.

You should therefore focus on getting the content right—on capturing the essence of the core values and purpose. The point is not to create a perfect statement but to gain a deep understanding of your organization's core values and purpose, which can then be expressed in a multitude of ways. In fact, we often suggest that once the core has been identified, managers should generate their own statements of the core values and purpose to share with their groups.

Finally, don't confuse core ideology with the concept of core competence. Core competence is a strategic concept that defines your organization's capabilities—what you are particularly good at—whereas core ideology captures what you stand for and why you exist. Core competencies should be well aligned with a company's core ideology and are often rooted in it; but they are not the same thing. For example, Sony has a core competence of miniaturization—a strength that can be strategically applied to a wide array of products and markets. But it does not have a core *ideology* of miniaturization. Sony might not even have miniaturization as part of its strategy in 100 years, but to remain a great company, it will still have the same core values described in the Sony Pioneer Spirit and the same fundamental reason for being—namely, to advance technology for the benefit of the general public. In a visionary company like Sony, core competencies change over the decades, whereas core ideology does not.

Once you are clear about the core ideology, you should feel free to change absolutely *anything* that is not part of it. From then on, whenever someone says something should not change because "it's part of our culture" or "we've always done it that way" or any such excuse, mention this simple rule: If it's not core, it's up for change. The strong version of the rule is, *If it's not core, change it!* Articulating core ideology is just a starting point, however. You also must determine what type of progress you want to stimulate.

Envisioned Future

The second primary component of the vision framework is *envisioned future*. It consists of two parts: a 10-to-30-year audacious goal plus vivid descriptions of what it will be like to achieve the goal. We recognize that the phrase *envisioned future* is somewhat paradoxical. On the one hand, it conveys concreteness—something visible, vivid, and real. On the other hand, it involves a time yet unrealized—with its dreams, hopes, and aspirations.

Vision-level BHAG

We found in our research that visionary companies often use bold missions—or what we prefer to call *BHAGs* (pronounced BEE-hags and shorthand for Big, Hairy, Audacious Goals)—as a powerful way to stimulate progress. All companies have goals. But there is a difference between merely having a goal and becoming committed to a huge, daunting challenge—such as climbing Mount Everest. A true BHAG is clear and compelling, serves as a unifying focal point of effort, and acts as a catalyst for team spirit. It has a clear finish line, so the organization can know when it has achieved the goal; people like to shoot for finish lines. A BHAG engages people—it reaches out and grabs them. It is tangible, energizing, highly focused. People get it right away; it takes little or no explanation. For example, NASA's 1960s moon mission didn't need a committee of wordsmiths to spend endless hours turning the goal into a verbose, impossible-to-remember mission statement. The goal itself was so easy to grasp—so compelling in its own right—that it could be said 100 different ways yet be easily understood by everyone. Most corporate statements we've seen do little to spur forward movement because they do not contain the powerful mechanism of a BHAG.

Although organizations may have many BHAGs at different levels operating at the same time, vision requires a special type of BHAG—a vision-level BHAG that applies to the entire organization and requires 10 to 30 years of effort to complete. Setting the BHAG that far into the future requires thinking beyond the current capabilities of the organization and the current environment. Indeed, inventing such a goal forces an executive team to be visionary, rather than just strategic or tactical. A BHAG should not be a sure bet—it will have perhaps only a 50% to 70% probability of success—but the organization must believe that it can reach the goal anyway. A BHAG should require extraordinary effort and perhaps a little luck. We have helped companies create a vision-level BHAG by advising them to think in terms of four broad categories: target BHAGs, common-enemy BHAGs, role-model BHAGs, and internal-transformation BHAGs. (See the sidebar "Big, Hairy, Audacious Goals Aid Long-Term Vision.")

Vivid description

In addition to vision-level BHAGs, an envisioned future needs what we call vivid description—that is, a vibrant, engaging, and specific description of what it will be like to achieve the BHAG. Think of it as translating the vision from words into pictures, of creating an image that people can carry around in their heads. It is a question of painting a picture with your words. Picture painting is essential for making the 10-to-30-year BHAG tangible in people's minds.

For example, Henry Ford brought to life the goal of democratizing the automobile with this vivid description: "I will build a motor car for the great multitude. . . . It will be so low in price that no man making a good salary will be unable to own one and enjoy with his family the blessing of hours of pleasure in God's great open spaces. . . . When I'm through, everybody will be able to afford one, and everyone will have one. The horse will have disappeared from our highways, the automobile will be taken for granted . . . [and we will] give a large number of men employment at good wages."

The components-support division of a computer-products company had a general manager who was able to describe vividly the

Big, Hairy, Audacious Goals Aid Long-Term Vision

Target BHAGs can be quantitative or qualitative

- Become a $125 billion company by the year 2000 (Wal-Mart, 1990)
- Democratize the automobile (Ford Motor Company, early 1900s)
- Become the company most known for changing the worldwide poor-quality image of Japanese products (Sony, early 1950s)
- Become the most powerful, the most serviceable, the most far-reaching world financial institution that has ever been (City Bank, predecessor to Citicorp, 1915)
- Become the dominant player in commercial aircraft and bring the world into the jet age (Boeing, 1950)

Common-enemy BHAGs involve David-versus-Goliath thinking

- Knock off RJR as the number one tobacco company in the world (Philip Morris, 1950s)
- Crush Adidas (Nike, 1960s)
- *Yamaha wo tsubusu!* We will destroy Yamaha! (Honda, 1970s)

Role-model BHAGs suit up-and-coming organizations

- Become the Nike of the cycling industry (Giro Sport Design, 1986)
- Become as respected in 20 years as Hewlett-Packard is today (Watkins-Johnson, 1996)
- Become the Harvard of the West (Stanford University, 1940s)

Internal-transformation BHAGs suit large, established organizations

- Become number one or number two in every market we serve and revolutionize this company to have the strengths of a big company combined with the leanness and agility of a small company (General Electric Company, 1980s)
- Transform this company from a defense contractor into the best diversified high-technology company in the world (Rockwell, 1995)
- Transform this division from a poorly respected internal products supplier to one of the most respected, exciting, and sought-after divisions in the company (Components Support Division of a computer products company, 1989)

goal of becoming one of the most sought-after divisions in the company: "We will be respected and admired by our peers. . . . Our solutions will be actively sought by the end-product divisions, who will achieve significant product 'hits' in the marketplace largely because of our technical contribution. . . . We will have pride in ourselves. . . . The best up-and-coming people in the company will seek to work in our division. . . . People will give unsolicited feedback that they love what they are doing. . . . [Our own] people will walk on the balls of their feet. . . . [They] will willingly work hard because they want to. . . . Both employees and customers will feel that our division has contributed to their life in a positive way."

In the 1930s, Merck had the BHAG to transform itself from a chemical manufacturer into one of the preeminent drug-making companies in the world, with a research capability to rival any major university. In describing this envisioned future, George Merck said at the opening of Merck's research facility in 1933, "We believe that research work carried on with patience and persistence will bring to industry and commerce new life; and we have faith that in this new laboratory, with the tools we have supplied, science will be advanced, knowledge increased, and human life win ever a greater freedom from suffering and disease. . . . We pledge our every aid that this enterprise shall merit the faith we have in it. Let your light so shine—that those who seek the Truth, that those who toil that this world may be a better place to live in, that those who hold aloft that torch of science and knowledge through these social and economic dark ages, shall take new courage and feel their hands supported."

Passion, emotion, and conviction are essential parts of the vivid description. Some managers are uncomfortable expressing emotion about their dreams, but that's what motivates others. Churchill understood that when he described the BHAG facing Great Britain in 1940. He did not just say, "Beat Hitler." He said, "Hitler knows he will have to break us on this island or lose the war. If we can stand up to him, all Europe may be free, and the life of the world may move forward into broad, sunlit uplands. But if we fail, the whole world, including the United States, including all we have known and cared for, will sink into the abyss of a new Dark Age, made more sinister and perhaps more protracted by the lights of perverted science. Let us therefore brace ourselves to our duties and so bear ourselves that if the British Empire and its Commonwealth last for a thousand years, men will still say, 'This was their finest hour.'"

A few key points

Don't confuse core ideology and envisioned future. In particular, don't confuse core purpose and BHAGs. Managers often exchange one for the other, mixing the two together or failing to articulate both as distinct items. Core purpose—not some specific goal—is the reason why the organization exists. A BHAG is a clearly articulated goal. Core purpose can never be completed, whereas the BHAG is reachable in 10 to 30 years. Think of the core purpose as the star on the horizon to be chased forever; the BHAG is the mountain to be climbed. Once you have reached its summit, you move on to other mountains.

Identifying core ideology is a discovery process, but setting the envisioned future is a creative process. We find that executives often have a great deal of difficulty coming up with an exciting BHAG. They want to analyze their way into the future. We have found, therefore, that some executives make more progress by starting first with the vivid description and backing from there into the BHAG. This approach involves starting with questions such as, We're sitting here in 20 years; what would we love to see? What should this company look like? What should it feel like to employees? What should it have achieved? If someone writes an article for a major business magazine about this company in 20 years, what will it say? One biotechnology company we worked with had trouble envisioning its future. Said one member of the executive team, "Every time we come up with something for the entire company, it is just too generic to be exciting—something banal like 'advance biotechnology worldwide.'" Asked to paint a picture of the company in 20 years, the executives mentioned such things as "on the cover of *Business Week* as a model success story . . . the *Fortune* most admired top-ten list . . . the best science and business graduates want to work here . . . people on airplanes rave about one of our products to seatmates . . . 20

consecutive years of profitable growth . . . an entrepreneurial culture that has spawned half a dozen new divisions from within . . . management gurus use us as an example of excellent management and progressive thinking," and so on. From this, they were able to set the goal of becoming as well respected as Merck or as Johnson & Johnson in biotechnology.

It makes no sense to analyze whether an envisioned future is the right one. With a creation—and the task is creation of a future, not prediction—there can be no right answer. Did Beethoven create the right Ninth Symphony? Did Shakespeare create the right *Hamlet*? We can't answer these questions; they're nonsense. The envisioned future involves such essential questions as Does it get our juices flowing? Do we find it stimulating? Does it spur forward momentum? Does it get people going? The envisioned future should be so exciting in its own right that it would continue to keep the organization motivated even if the leaders who set the goal disappeared. City Bank, the predecessor of Citicorp, had the BHAG "to become the most powerful, the most serviceable, the most far-reaching world financial institution that has ever been"—a goal that generated excitement through multiple generations until it was achieved. Similarly, the NASA moon mission continued to galvanize people even though President John F. Kennedy (the leader associated with setting the goal) died years before its completion.

To create an effective envisioned future requires a certain level of unreasonable confidence and commitment. Keep in mind that a BHAG is not just a goal; it is a Big, Hairy, Audacious Goal. It's not reasonable for a small regional bank to set the goal of becoming "the most powerful, the most serviceable, the most far-reaching world financial institution that has ever been," as City Bank did in 1915. It's not a tepid claim that "we will democratize the automobile," as Henry Ford said. It was almost laughable for Philip Morris—as the sixth-place player with 9% market share in the 1950s—to take on the goal of defeating Goliath RJ Reynolds Tobacco Company and becoming number one. It was hardly modest for Sony, as a small, cash-strapped venture, to proclaim the goal of changing the poor-quality image of Japanese products around the world. (See the sidebar

"Putting It All Together: Sony in the 1950s.") Of course, it's not only the audacity of the goal but also the level of commitment to the goal that counts. Boeing didn't just envision a future dominated by its commercial jets; it bet the company on the 707 and, later, on the 747. Nike's people didn't just talk about the idea of crushing Adidas; they went on a crusade to fulfill the dream. Indeed, the envisioned future should produce a bit of the "gulp factor": when it dawns on people what it will take to achieve the goal, there should be an almost audible gulp.

But what about failure to realize the envisioned future? In our research, we found that the visionary companies displayed a remarkable ability to achieve even their most audacious goals. Ford did democratize the automobile; Citicorp did become the most far-reaching bank in the world; Philip Morris did rise from sixth to first and beat RJ Reynolds worldwide; Boeing did become the dominant commercial aircraft company; and it looks like Wal-Mart will achieve its $125 billion goal, even without Sam Walton. In contrast, the comparison companies in our research frequently did not achieve their BHAGs, if they set them at all. The difference does not lie in setting easier goals: the visionary companies tended to have even more audacious ambitions. The difference does not lie in charismatic, visionary leadership: the visionary companies often achieved their BHAGs without such larger-than-life leaders at the helm. Nor does the difference lie in better strategy: the visionary companies often realized their goals more by an organic process of "let's try a lot of stuff and keep what works" than by well-laid strategic plans. Rather, their success lies in building the strength of their organization as their primary way of creating the future.

Why did Merck become the preeminent drug-maker in the world? Because Merck's architects built the best pharmaceutical research and development organization in the world. Why did Boeing become the dominant commercial aircraft company in the world? Because of its superb engineering and marketing organization, which had the ability to make projects like the 747 a reality. When asked to name the most important decisions that have contributed to the growth and success of Hewlett-Packard, David Packard answered

Putting It All Together: Sony in the 1950s

Core Ideology

Core Values

- Elevation of the Japanese culture and national status
- Being a pioneer—not following others; doing the impossible
- Encouraging individual ability and creativity

Purpose

To experience the sheer joy of innovation and the application of technology for the benefit and pleasure of the general public

Envisioned Future

BHAG

Become the company most known for changing the worldwide poor-quality image of Japanese products

Vivid Description

We will create products that become pervasive around the world. . . . We will be the first Japanese company to go into the U.S. market and distribute directly. . . . We will succeed with innovations that U.S. companies have failed at—such as the transistor radio. . . . Fifty years from now, our brand name will be as well known as any in the world . . . and will signify innovation and quality that rival the most innovative companies anywhere. . . . "Made in Japan" will mean something fine, not something shoddy.

entirely in terms of decisions to build the strength of the organization and its people.

Finally, in thinking about the envisioned future, beware of the We've Arrived Syndrome—a complacent lethargy that arises once an organization has achieved one BHAG and fails to replace it with another. NASA suffered from that syndrome after the successful moon landings. After you've landed on the moon, what do you do for an encore? Ford suffered from the syndrome when, after it succeeded in democratizing the automobile, it failed to set a new goal of equal significance and gave General Motors the opportunity to jump ahead in the 1930s. Apple Computer suffered from the syndrome after achieving the goal of creating a computer that nontechies could use. Start-up companies frequently suffer from the We've Arrived Syndrome after going public or after reaching a stage in which survival no longer seems in question. An envisioned future helps an organization only as long as it hasn't yet been achieved. In our work with companies, we frequently hear executives say, "It's just not as exciting around here as it used to be; we seem to have lost our momentum." Usually, that kind of remark signals that the organization has climbed one mountain and not yet picked a new one to climb.

Many executives thrash about with mission statements and vision statements. Unfortunately, most of those statements turn out to be a muddled stew of values, goals, purposes, philosophies, beliefs, aspirations, norms, strategies, practices, and descriptions. They are usually a boring, confusing, structurally unsound stream of words that evoke the response "True, but who cares?" Even more problematic, seldom do these statements have a direct link to the fundamental dynamic of visionary companies: preserve the core and stimulate progress. That dynamic, not vision or mission statements, is the primary engine of enduring companies. Vision simply provides the context for bringing this dynamic to life. Building a visionary company requires 1% vision and 99% alignment. When you have superb alignment, a visitor could drop in from outer space and infer your vision from the operations and activities of the company without ever reading it on paper or meeting a single senior executive.

Creating alignment may be your most important work. But the first step will always be to recast your vision or mission into an effective context for building a visionary company. If you do it right, you shouldn't have to do it again for at least a decade.

Originally published in September 1996. Reprint 96501.

Notes

1. David Packard, speech given to Hewlett-Packard's training group on March 8, 1960; courtesy of Hewlett-Packard Archives.
2. See Nick Lyons, *The Sony Vision* (New York: Crown Publishers, 1976). We also used a translation by our Japanese student Tsuneto Ikeda.
3. Akio Morita, *Made in Japan* (New York: E.P. Dutton, 1986), p. 147.

Reinventing Your Business Model

by Mark W. Johnson, Clayton M. Christensen, and Henning Kagermann

IN 2003, APPLE INTRODUCED the iPod with the iTunes store, revolutionizing portable entertainment, creating a new market, and transforming the company. In just three years, the iPod/iTunes combination became a nearly $10 billion product, accounting for almost 50% of Apple's revenue. Apple's market capitalization catapulted from around $1 billion in early 2003 to over $150 billion by late 2007.

This success story is well known; what's less well known is that Apple was not the first to bring digital music players to market. A company called Diamond Multimedia introduced the Rio in 1998. Another firm, Best Data, introduced the Cabo 64 in 2000. Both products worked well and were portable and stylish. So why did the iPod, rather than the Rio or Cabo, succeed?

Apple did something far smarter than take a good technology and wrap it in a snazzy design. It took a good technology and wrapped it in a great business model. Apple's true innovation was to make downloading digital music easy and convenient. To do that, the company built a groundbreaking business model that combined hardware, software, and service. This approach worked like Gillette's famous blades-and-razor model in reverse: Apple essentially gave away the "blades" (low-margin iTunes music) to lock in purchase of the "razor" (the high-margin iPod). That model defined value in a new way and provided game-changing convenience to the consumer.

Business model innovations have reshaped entire industries and redistributed billions of dollars of value. Retail discounters such as Wal-Mart and Target, which entered the market with pioneering business models, now account for 75% of the total valuation of the retail sector. Low-cost U.S. airlines grew from a blip on the radar screen to 55% of the market value of all carriers. Fully 11 of the 27 companies born in the last quarter century that grew their way into the *Fortune* 500 in the past 10 years did so through business model innovation.

Stories of business model innovation from well-established companies like Apple, however, are rare. An analysis of major innovations within existing corporations in the past decade shows that precious few have been business-model related. And a recent American Management Association study determined that no more than 10% of innovation investment at global companies is focused on developing new business models.

Yet everyone's talking about it. A 2005 survey by the Economist Intelligence Unit reported that over 50% of executives believe business model innovation will become even more important for success than product or service innovation. A 2008 IBM survey of corporate CEOs echoed these results. Nearly all of the CEOs polled reported the need to adapt their business models; more than two-thirds said that extensive changes were required. And in these tough economic times, some CEOs are already looking to business model innovation to address permanent shifts in their market landscapes.

Senior managers at incumbent companies thus confront a frustrating question: Why is it so difficult to pull off the new growth that business model innovation can bring? Our research suggests two problems. The first is a lack of definition: Very little formal study has been done into the dynamics and processes of business model development. Second, few companies understand their existing business model well enough—the premise behind its development, its natural interdependencies, and its strengths and limitations. So they don't know when they can leverage their core business and when success requires a new business model.

Idea in Brief

When Apple introduced the iPod, it did something far smarter than wrap a good technology in a snazzy design. It wrapped a good technology in a **great business model.** Combining hardware, software, and service, the model provided game-changing convenience for consumers *and* record-breaking profits for Apple.

Great business models can reshape industries and drive spectacular growth. Yet many companies find business-model innovation difficult. Managers don't understand their existing model well enough to know when it needs changing—or how.

To determine whether your firm should alter its business model, Johnson, Christensen, and Kagermann advise these steps:

1. Articulate what makes your existing model successful. For example, what customer problem does it solve? How does it make money for your firm?
2. Watch for signals that your model needs changing, such as tough new competitors on the horizon.
3. Decide whether reinventing your model is worth the effort. The answer's yes only if the new model changes the industry or market.

After tackling these problems with dozens of companies, we have found that new business models often look unattractive to internal and external stakeholders—at the outset. To see past the borders of what is and into the land of the new, companies need a road map.

Ours consists of three simple steps. The first is to realize that success starts by not thinking about business models at all. It starts with thinking about the opportunity to satisfy a real customer who needs a job done. The second step is to construct a blueprint laying out how your company will fulfill that need at a profit. In our model, that plan has four elements. The third is to compare that model to your existing model to see how much you'd have to change it to capture the opportunity. Once you do, you will know if you can use your existing model and organization or need to separate out a new unit to execute a new model. Every successful company is already fulfilling a real customer need with an effective business model, whether that model is explicitly understood or not. Let's take a look at what that entails.

Idea in Practice

Understand Your Current Business Model

A successful model has these components:

- **Customer value proposition.** The model helps customers perform a specific "job" that alternative offerings don't address.

Example: MinuteClinics enable people to visit a doctor's office without appointments by making nurse practitioners available to treat minor health issues.

- **Profit formula**. The model generates value for your company through factors such as revenue model, cost structure, margins, and inventory turnover.

Example: The Tata Group's inexpensive car, the Nano, is profitable because the company has reduced many cost structure elements, accepted lower-than-standard gross margins, and sold the Nano in large volumes to its target market: first-time car buyers in emerging markets.

- **Key resources and processes**. Your company has the people, technology, products, facilities, equipment, and brand required to deliver the value proposition to your targeted customers. And it has processes (training, manufacturing, service) to leverage those resources.

Example: For Tata Motors to fulfill the requirements of the Nano's profit formula, it had to reconceive how a car is designed, manufactured, and distributed. It redefined its supplier strategy, choosing to outsource a remarkable 85% of the Nano's components and to use nearly 60% fewer vendors than normal to reduce transaction costs.

Identify When a New Model May Be Needed

These circumstances often require business model change:

Business Model: A Definition

A business model, from our point of view, consists of four interlocking elements that, taken together, create and deliver value. The most important to get right, by far, is the first.

Customer value proposition (CVP)

A successful company is one that has found a way to create value for customers—that is, a way to help customers get an important job

An *opportunity* to . . .	**Example**
Address needs of large groups who find existing solutions too expensive or complicated.	The Nano's goal is to open car ownership to low-income consumers in emerging markets.
Capitalize on new technology, or leverage existing technologies in new markets.	A company develops a commercial application for a technology originally developed for military use.
Bring a job-to-be-done focus where it doesn't exist.	FedEx focused on performing customers' unmet "job": Receive packages faster and more reliably than any other service could.
A *need* to . . .	**Example**
Fend off low-end disruptors.	Mini-mills threatened the integrated steel mills a generation ago by making steel at significantly lower prices.
Respond to shifts in competition.	Power-tool maker Hilti switched from selling to renting its tools in part because "good enough" low-end entrants had begun chipping away at the market for selling high-quality tools.

done. By "job" we mean a fundamental problem in a given situation that needs a solution. Once we understand the job and all its dimensions, including the full process for how to get it done, we can design the offering. The more important the job is to the customer, the lower the level of customer satisfaction with current options for getting the job done, and the better your solution is than existing alternatives at getting the job done (and, of course, the lower the price), the greater the CVP. Opportunities for creating a CVP are at their most potent, we have found, when alternative products and services have not been designed with the real job in mind and you can design an offering that gets that job—and only that job—done perfectly. We'll come back to that point later.

Profit formula

The profit formula is the blueprint that defines how the company creates value for itself while providing value to the customer. It consists of the following:

- *Revenue model:* price x volume
- *Cost structure:* direct costs, indirect costs, economies of scale. Cost structure will be predominantly driven by the cost of the key resources required by the business model.
- *Margin model:* given the expected volume and cost structure, the contribution needed from each transaction to achieve desired profits.
- *Resource velocity:* how fast we need to turn over inventory, fixed assets, and other assets—and, overall, how well we need to utilize resources—to support our expected volume and achieve our anticipated profits.

People often think the terms "profit formulas" and "business models" are interchangeable. But how you make a profit is only one piece of the model. We've found it most useful to start by setting the price required to deliver the CVP and then work backwards from there to determine what the variable costs and gross margins must be. This then determines what the scale and resource velocity needs to be to achieve the desired profits.

Key resources

The key resources are assets such as the people, technology, products, facilities, equipment, channels, and brand required to deliver the value proposition to the targeted customer. The focus here is on the *key* elements that create value for the customer and the company, and the way those elements interact. (Every company also has generic resources that do not create competitive differentiation.)

Key processes

Successful companies have operational and managerial processes that allow them to deliver value in a way they can successfully repeat and increase in scale. These may include such recurrent tasks as training, development, manufacturing, budgeting, planning, sales, and service. Key processes also include a company's rules, metrics, and norms.

These four elements form the building blocks of any business. The customer value proposition and the profit formula define value for the customer and the company, respectively; key resources and key processes describe how that value will be delivered to both the customer and the company.

As simple as this framework may seem, its power lies in the complex interdependencies of its parts. Major changes to any of these four elements affect the others and the whole. Successful businesses devise a more or less stable system in which these elements bond to one another in consistent and complementary ways.

How Great Models Are Built

To illustrate the elements of our business model framework, we will look at what's behind two companies' game-changing business model innovations.

Creating a customer value proposition

It's not possible to invent or reinvent a business model without first identifying a clear customer value proposition. Often, it starts as a quite simple realization. Imagine, for a moment, that you are standing on a Mumbai road on a rainy day. You notice the large number of motor scooters snaking precariously in and out around the cars. As you look more closely, you see that most bear whole families—both parents and several children. Your first thought might be "That's

The Elements of a Successful Business Model

EVERY SUCCESSFUL COMPANY ALREADY operates according to an effective business model. By systematically identifying all of its constituent parts, executives can understand how the model fulfills a potent value proposition in a profitable way using certain key resources and key processes. With that understanding, they can then judge how well the same model could be used to fulfill a radically different CVP—and what they'd need to do to construct a new one, if need be, to capitalize on that opportunity.

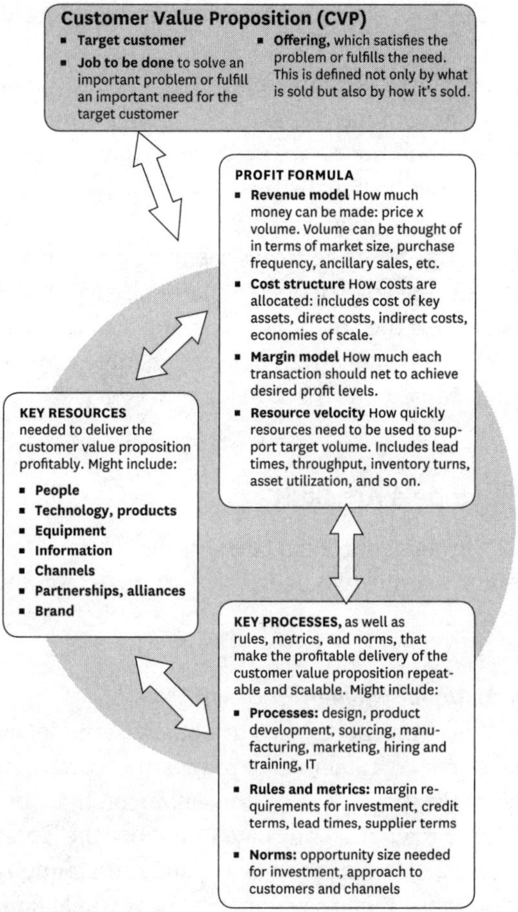
Customer Value Proposition (CVP)
Target customer
Job to be done to solve an important problem or fulfill an important need for the target customer
Offering, which satisfies the problem or fulfills the need. This is defined not only by what is sold but also by how it's sold.
PROFIT FORMULA
Revenue model How much money can be made: price x volume. Volume can be thought of in terms of market size, purchase frequency, ancillary sales, etc.
Cost structure How costs are allocated: includes cost of key assets, direct costs, indirect costs, economies of scale.
Margin model How much each transaction should net to achieve desired profit levels.
Resource velocity How quickly resources need to be used to support target volume. Includes lead times, throughput, inventory turns, asset utilization, and so on.
KEY RESOURCES needed to deliver the customer value proposition profitably. Might include:
People
Technology, products
Equipment
Information
Channels
Partnerships, alliances
Brand
KEY PROCESSES, as well as rules, metrics, and norms, that make the profitable delivery of the customer value proposition repeatable and scalable. Might include:
Processes: design, product development, sourcing, manufacturing, marketing, hiring and training, IT
Rules and metrics: margin requirements for investment, credit terms, lead times, supplier terms
Norms: opportunity size needed for investment, approach to customers and channels

crazy!" or "That's the way it is in developing countries—people get by as best they can."

When Ratan Tata of Tata Group looked out over this scene, he saw a critical job to be done: providing a safer alternative for scooter families. He understood that the cheapest car available in India cost easily five times what a scooter did and that many of these families could not afford one. Offering an affordable, safer, all-weather alternative for scooter families was a powerful value proposition, one with the potential to reach tens of millions of people who were not yet part of the car-buying market. Ratan Tata also recognized that Tata Motors' business model could not be used to develop such a product at the needed price point.

At the other end of the market spectrum, Hilti, a Liechtenstein-based manufacturer of high-end power tools for the construction industry, reconsidered the real job to be done for many of its current customers. A contractor makes money by finishing projects; if the required tools aren't available and functioning properly, the job doesn't get done. Contractors don't make money by *owning* tools; they make it by using them as efficiently as possible. Hilti could help contractors get the job done by selling tool *use* instead of the tools themselves—managing its customers' tool inventory by providing the best tool at the right time and quickly furnishing tool repairs, replacements, and upgrades, all for a monthly fee. To deliver on that value proposition, the company needed to create a fleet-management program for tools and in the process shift its focus from manufacturing and distribution to service. That meant Hilti had to construct a new profit formula and develop new resources and new processes.

The most important attribute of a customer value proposition is its precision: how perfectly it nails the customer job to be done—and nothing else. But such precision is often the most difficult thing to achieve. Companies trying to create the new often neglect to focus on *one* job; they dilute their efforts by attempting to do lots of things. In doing lots of things, they do nothing *really* well.

One way to generate a precise customer value proposition is to think about the four most common barriers keeping people from getting particular jobs done: insufficient wealth, access, skill, or time. Software maker Intuit devised QuickBooks to fulfill small-business owners' need to avoid running out of cash. By fulfilling that job with greatly simplified accounting software, Intuit broke the *skills barrier* that kept untrained small-business owners from using more-complicated accounting packages. MinuteClinic, the drugstore-based basic health care provider, broke the *time barrier* that kept people from visiting a doctor's office with minor health issues by making nurse practitioners available without appointments.

Designing a profit formula

Ratan Tata knew the only way to get families off their scooters and into cars would be to break the *wealth barrier* by drastically decreasing the price of the car. "What if I can change the game and make a car for one lakh?" Tata wondered, envisioning a price point of around US$2,500, less than half the price of the cheapest car available. This, of course, had dramatic ramifications for the profit formula: It required both a significant drop in gross margins and a radical reduction in many elements of the cost structure. He knew, however, he could still make money if he could increase sales volume dramatically, and he knew that his target base of consumers was potentially huge.

For Hilti, moving to a contract management program required shifting assets from customers' balance sheets to its own and generating revenue through a lease/subscription model. For a monthly fee, customers could have a full complement of tools at their fingertips, with repair and maintenance included. This would require a fundamental shift in all major components of the profit formula: the revenue stream (pricing, the staging of payments, and how to think about volume), the cost structure (including added sales development and contract management costs), and the supporting margins and transaction velocity.

Identifying key resources and processes

Having articulated the value proposition for both the customer and the business, companies must then consider the key resources and

Hilti Sidesteps Commoditization

HILTI IS CAPITALIZING ON a game-changing opportunity to increase profitability by turning products into a service. Rather than sell tools (at lower and lower prices), it's selling a "just-the-tool-you-need-when-you-need-it, no-repair-or-storage-hassles" service. Such a radical change in customer value proposition required a shift in all parts of its business model.

Traditional power tool company		**Hilti's tool fleet management service**
Sales of industrial and professional power tools and accessories	**Customer value proposition**	Leasing a comprehensive fleet of tools to increase contractors's on-site productivity
Low margins, high inventory turnover	**Profit formula**	Higher margins; asset heavy; monthly payments for tool maintenance, repair, and replacement
Distribution channel, low-cost manufacturing plants in developing countries, R&D	**Key resources and processes**	Strong direct-sales approach, contract management, IT systems for inventory management and repair, warehousing

processes needed to deliver that value. For a professional services firm, for example, the key resources are generally its people, and the key processes are naturally people related (training and development, for instance). For a packaged goods company, strong brands and well-selected channel retailers might be the key resources, and associated brand-building and channel-management processes among the critical processes.

Oftentimes, it's not the individual resources and processes that make the difference but their relationship to one another. Companies will almost always need to integrate their key resources and processes in a unique way to get a job done perfectly for a set of customers. When they do, they almost always create enduring competitive advantage. Focusing first on the value proposition and the profit formula makes clear how those resources and processes need to interrelate. For example, most general hospitals offer a value proposition that might be described as, "We'll do anything for anybody." Being all things to all people requires these hospitals to have a vast collection of resources (specialists, equipment, and so on) that can't be knit together in any proprietary way. The result is not just a lack of differentiation but dissatisfaction.

By contrast, a hospital that focuses on a specific value proposition can integrate its resources and processes in a unique way that delights customers. National Jewish Health in Denver, for example, is organized around a focused value proposition we'd characterize as, "If you have a disease of the pulmonary system, bring it here. We'll define its root cause and prescribe an effective therapy." Narrowing its focus has allowed National Jewish to develop processes that integrate the ways in which its specialists and specialized equipment work together.

For Tata Motors to fulfill the requirements of its customer value proposition and profit formula for the Nano, it had to reconceive how a car is designed, manufactured, and distributed. Tata built a small team of fairly young engineers who would not, like the company's more-experienced designers, be influenced and constrained in their thinking by the automaker's existing profit formulas. This team dramatically minimized the number of parts in the vehicle, resulting in a significant cost saving. Tata also reconceived its supplier strategy, choosing to outsource a remarkable 85% of the Nano's components and use nearly 60% fewer vendors than normal to reduce transaction costs and achieve better economies of scale.

At the other end of the manufacturing line, Tata is envisioning an entirely new way of assembling and distributing its cars. The ultimate plan is to ship the modular components of the vehicles to a combined network of company-owned and independent entrepreneur-owned assembly plants, which will build them to order. The Nano will be designed, built, distributed, and serviced in a radically new way—one that could not be accomplished without a new business model. And while the jury is still out, Ratan Tata may solve a traffic safety problem in the process.

For Hilti, the greatest challenge lay in training its sales representatives to do a thoroughly new task. Fleet management is not a half-hour sale; it takes days, weeks, even months of meetings to persuade customers to buy a program instead of a product. Suddenly, field reps accustomed to dealing with crew leaders and on-site purchasing managers in mobile trailers found themselves staring down CEOs and CFOs across conference tables.

Additionally, leasing required new resources—new people, more robust IT systems, and other new technologies—to design and develop the appropriate packages and then come to an agreement on monthly payments. Hilti needed a process for maintaining large arsenals of tools more inexpensively and effectively than its customers had. This required warehousing, an inventory management system, and a supply of replacement tools. On the customer management side, Hilti developed a website that enabled construction managers to view all the tools in their fleet and their usage rates. With that information readily available, the managers could easily handle the cost accounting associated with those assets.

Rules, norms, and metrics are often the last element to emerge in a developing business model. They may not be fully envisioned until the new product or service has been road tested. Nor should they be. Business models need to have the flexibility to change in their early years.

When a New Business Model Is Needed

Established companies should not undertake business-model innovation lightly. They can often create new products that disrupt competitors without fundamentally changing their own business model. Procter & Gamble, for example, developed a number of what it calls "disruptive market innovations" with such products as the Swiffer disposable mop and duster and Febreze, a new kind of air freshener. Both innovations built on P&G's existing business model and its established dominance in household consumables.

There are clearly times, however, when creating new growth requires venturing not only into unknown market territory but also into unknown business model territory. When? The short answer is "When significant changes are needed to all four elements of your existing model." But it's not always that simple. Management judgment is clearly required. That said, we have observed five strategic circumstances that often require business model change:

1. The opportunity to address through disruptive innovation the needs of large groups of potential customers who are shut out of a market entirely because existing solutions are too expensive or complicated for them. This includes the opportunity to democratize products in emerging markets (or reach the bottom of the pyramid), as Tata's Nano does.
2. The opportunity to capitalize on a brand-new technology by wrapping a new business model around it (Apple and MP3 players) or the opportunity to leverage a tested technology by bringing it to a whole new market (say, by offering military technologies in the commercial space or vice versa).
3. The opportunity to bring a job-to-be-done focus where one does not yet exist. That's common in industries where companies focus on products or customer segments, which leads them to refine existing products more and more, increasing commoditization over time. A jobs focus allows companies to redefine industry profitability. For example, when FedEx entered the package delivery market, it did not try to compete through lower prices or better marketing. Instead, it concentrated on fulfilling an entirely unmet customer need to receive packages far, far faster, and more reliably, than any service then could. To do so, it had to integrate its key processes and resources in a vastly more efficient way. The business model that resulted from this job-to-be-done emphasis gave FedEx a significant competitive advantage that took UPS many years to copy.
4. The need to fend off low-end disrupters. If the Nano is successful, it will threaten other automobile makers, much as minimills threatened the integrated steel mills a generation ago by making steel at significantly lower cost.
5. The need to respond to a shifting basis of competition. Inevitably, what defines an acceptable solution in a market will change over time, leading core market segments to

commoditize. Hilti needed to change its business model in part because of lower global manufacturing costs; "good enough" low-end entrants had begun chipping away at the market for high-quality power tools.

Of course, companies should not pursue business model reinvention unless they are confident that the opportunity is large enough to warrant the effort. And, there's really no point in instituting a new business model unless it's not only new to the company but in some way new or game-changing to the industry or market. To do otherwise would be a waste of time and money.

These questions will help you evaluate whether the challenge of business model innovation will yield acceptable results. Answering "yes" to all four greatly increases the odds of successful execution:

- Can you nail the job with a focused, compelling customer value proposition?
- Can you devise a model in which all the elements—the customer value proposition, the profit formula, the key resources, and the key processes—work together to get the job done in the most efficient way possible?
- Can you create a new business development process unfettered by the often negative influences of your core business?
- Will the new business model disrupt competitors?

Creating a new model for a new business does not mean the current model is threatened or should be changed. A new model often reinforces and complements the core business, as Dow Corning discovered.

How Dow Corning Got Out of Its Own Way

When business model innovation is clearly called for, success lies not only in getting the model right but also in making sure the incumbent business doesn't in some way prevent the new model from creating value or thriving. That was a problem for Dow Corning when it built a new business unit—with a new profit formula—from scratch.

Dow Corning Embraces the Low End

TRADITIONALLY HIGH-MARGIN DOW CORNING found new opportunities in low-margin offerings by setting up a separate business unit that operates in an entirely different way. By fundamentally differentiating its low-end and high-end offerings, the company avoided cannibalizing its traditional business even as it found new profits at the low end.

Established business		New business unit
Customized solutions, negotiated contracts	**Customer value proposition**	No frills, bulk prices, sold through the internet
High-margin, high-overhead retail prices pay for value-added services	**Profit formula**	Spot-market pricing, low overhead to accommodate lower margins, high throughput
R&D, sales, and services orientation	**Key resources and processes**	IT system, lowest-cost processes, maximum automation

For many years, Dow Corning had sold thousands of silicone-based products and provided sophisticated technical services to an array of industries. After years of profitable growth, however, a number of product areas were stagnating. A strategic review uncovered a critical insight: Its low-end product segment was commoditizing. Many customers experienced in silicone application no longer needed technical services; they needed basic products at low prices. This shift created an opportunity for growth, but to exploit that opportunity Dow Corning had to figure out a way to serve these customers with a lower-priced product. The problem was that both the business model and the culture were built on high-priced, innovative product and service packages. In 2002, in pursuit of what was essentially a commodity business for low-end customers, Dow Corning CEO Gary Anderson asked executive Don Sheets to form a team to start a new business.

The team began by formulating a customer value proposition that it believed would fulfill the job to be done for these price-driven customers. It determined that the price point had to drop 15% (which for a commoditizing material was a huge reduction). As the team analyzed what that new customer value proposition would require, it

When the Old Model Will Work

YOU DON'T ALWAYS NEED a new business model to capitalize on a game-changing opportunity. Sometimes, as P&G did with its Swiffer, a company finds that its current model is revolutionary in a new market. When will the old model do? When you can fulfill the new customer value proposition:

- With your current profit formula
- Using most, if not all, of your current key resources and processes
- Using the same core metrics, rules, and norms you now use to run your business

realized reaching that point was going to take a lot more than merely eliminating services. Dramatic price reduction would call for a different profit formula with a fundamentally lower cost structure, which depended heavily on developing a new IT system. To sell more products faster, the company would need to use the internet to automate processes and reduce overhead as much as possible.

Breaking the rules

As a mature and successful company, Dow Corning was full of highly trained employees used to delivering its high-touch, customized value proposition. To automate, the new business would have to be far more standardized, which meant instituting different and, overall, much stricter rules. For example, order sizes would be limited to a few, larger-volume options; order lead times would fall between two and four weeks (exceptions would cost extra); and credit terms would be fixed. There would be charges if a purchaser required customer service. The writing was on the wall: The new venture would be low-touch, self-service, and standardized. To succeed, Dow Corning would have to break the rules that had previously guided its success.

Sheets next had to determine whether this new venture, with its new rules, could succeed within the confines of Dow Corning's core enterprise. He set up an experimental war game to test how existing staff and systems would react to the requirements of the new customer value proposition. He got crushed as entrenched habits and existing processes thwarted any attempt to change the game. It became clear that the corporate antibodies would kill the initiative before it got off the ground. The way forward was clear: The new venture had to be free from existing rules and free to decide what rules would be appropriate in order for the new commodity line of business to thrive. To nurture the opportunity—and also protect the existing model—a new business unit with a new brand identity was needed. Xiameter was born.

Identifying new competencies

Following the articulation of the new customer value proposition and new profit formula, the Xiameter team focused on the new competencies it would need, its key resources and processes. Information technology, just a small part of Dow Corning's core competencies at that time, emerged as an essential part of the now web-enabled business. Xiameter also needed employees who could make smart decisions very quickly and who would thrive in a fast-changing environment, filled initially with lots of ambiguity. Clearly, new abilities would have to be brought into the business.

Although Xiameter would be established and run as a separate business unit, Don Sheets and the Xiameter team did not want to give up the incumbency advantage that deep knowledge of the industry and of their own products gave them. The challenge was to tap into the expertise without importing the old-rules mind-set. Sheets conducted a focused HR search within Dow Corning for risk takers. During the interview process, when he came across candidates with the right skills, he asked them to take the job on the spot, before they left the room. This approach allowed him to cherry-pick those who could make snap decisions and take big risks.

The secret sauce: patience

Successful new businesses typically revise their business models four times or so on the road to profitability. While a well-considered business-model-innovation process can often shorten this cycle, successful incumbents must tolerate initial failure and grasp the need for course correction. In effect, companies have to focus on learning and adjusting as much as on executing. We recommend companies with new business models be patient for growth (to allow

What Rules, Norms, and Metrics Are Standing in Your Way?

In any business, a fundamental understanding of the core model often fades into the mists of institutional memory, but it lives on in rules, norms, and metrics put in place to protect the status quo (for example, "Gross margins must be at 40%"). They are the first line of defense against any new model's taking root in an existing enterprise.

Financial

- Gross margins
- Opportunity size
- Unit pricing
- Unit margin
- Time to breakeven
- Net present value calculations
- Fixed cost investment
- Credit items

Operational

- End-product quality
- Supplier quality
- Owned versus outsourced manufacturing
- Customer service
- Channels
- Lead times
- Throughput

Other

- Pricing
- Performance demands
- Product-development life cycles
- Basis for individuals' rewards and incentives
- Brand parameters

the market opportunity to unfold) but impatient for profit (as an early validation that the model works). A profitable business is the best early indication of a viable model.

Accordingly, to allow for the trial and error that naturally accompanies the creation of the new while also constructing a development cycle that would produce results and demonstrate feasibility with minimal resource outlay, Dow Corning kept the scale of Xiameter's operation small but developed an aggressive timetable for launch and set the goal of becoming profitable by the end of year one.

Xiameter paid back Dow Corning's investment in just three months and went on to become a major, transformative success. Beforehand, Dow Corning had had no online sales component; now 30% of sales originate online, nearly three times the industry average. Most of these customers are new to the company. Far from cannibalizing existing customers, Xiameter has actually supported the main business, allowing Dow Corning's salespeople to more easily enforce premium pricing for their core offerings while providing a viable alternative for the price-conscious.

Established companies' attempts at transformative growth typically spring from product or technology innovations. Their efforts are often characterized by prolonged development cycles and fitful attempts to find a market. As the Apple iPod story that opened this article suggests, truly transformative businesses are never exclusively about the discovery and commercialization of a great technology. Their success comes from enveloping the new technology in an appropriate, powerful business model.

Bob Higgins, the founder and general partner of Highland Capital Partners, has seen his share of venture success and failure in his 20 years in the industry. He sums up the importance and power of business model innovation this way: "I think historically where we [venture capitalists] fail is when we back technology. Where we succeed is when we back new business models."

Originally published in December 2008. Reprint R0812C.

Blue Ocean Strategy

by W. Chan Kim and Renée Mauborgne

A ONETIME ACCORDION PLAYER, stilt walker, and fire-eater, Guy Laliberté is now CEO of one of Canada's largest cultural exports, Cirque du Soleil. Founded in 1984 by a group of street performers, Cirque has staged dozens of productions seen by some 40 million people in 90 cities around the world. In 20 years, Cirque has achieved revenues that Ringling Bros. and Barnum & Bailey—the world's leading circus—took more than a century to attain.

Cirque's rapid growth occurred in an unlikely setting. The circus business was (and still is) in long-term decline. Alternative forms of entertainment—sporting events, TV, and video games—were casting a growing shadow. Children, the mainstay of the circus audience, preferred PlayStations to circus acts. There was also rising sentiment, fueled by animal rights groups, against the use of animals, traditionally an integral part of the circus. On the supply side, the star performers that Ringling and the other circuses relied on to draw in the crowds could often name their own terms. As a result, the industry was hit by steadily decreasing audiences and increasing costs. What's more, any new entrant to this business would be competing against a formidable incumbent that for most of the last century had set the industry standard.

How did Cirque profitably increase revenues by a factor of 22 over the last ten years in such an unattractive environment? The tagline for one of the first Cirque productions is revealing: "We reinvent the circus." Cirque did not make its money by competing within the confines of the existing industry or by stealing customers from Ringling and the others. Instead it created uncontested market space that made the competition irrelevant. It pulled in a whole new group of customers who were traditionally noncustomers of the industry—adults and corporate clients who had turned to theater, opera, or ballet and were, therefore, prepared to pay several times more than the price of a conventional circus ticket for an unprecedented entertainment experience.

To understand the nature of Cirque's achievement, you have to realize that the business universe consists of two distinct kinds of space, which we think of as red and blue oceans. Red oceans represent all the industries in existence today—the known market space. In red oceans, industry boundaries are defined and accepted, and the competitive rules of the game are well understood. Here, companies try to outperform their rivals in order to grab a greater share of existing demand. As the space gets more and more crowded, prospects for profits and growth are reduced. Products turn into commodities, and increasing competition turns the water bloody.

Blue oceans denote all the industries *not* in existence today—the unknown market space, untainted by competition. In blue oceans, demand is created rather than fought over. There is ample opportunity for growth that is both profitable and rapid. There are two ways to create blue oceans. In a few cases, companies can give rise to completely new industries, as eBay did with the online auction industry. But in most cases, a blue ocean is created from within a red ocean when a company alters the boundaries of an existing industry. As will become evident later, this is what Cirque did. In breaking through the boundary traditionally separating circus and theater, it made a new and profitable blue ocean from within the red ocean of the circus industry.

Cirque is just one of more than 150 blue ocean creations that we have studied in over 30 industries, using data stretching back more than 100 years. We analyzed companies that created those blue oceans and their less successful competitors, which were caught in red oceans. In studying these data, we have observed a consistent pattern of strategic thinking behind the creation of new markets and

Idea in Brief

The best way to drive profitable growth? Stop competing in overcrowded industries. In those **red oceans,** companies try to outperform rivals to grab bigger slices of existing demand. As the space gets increasingly crowded, profit and growth prospects shrink. Products become commoditized. Ever-more-intense competition turns the water bloody.

How to avoid the fray? Kim and Mauborgne recommend creating **blue oceans**—uncontested market spaces where the competition is irrelevant. In blue oceans, you invent and capture new demand, and you offer customers a leap in value while also streamlining your costs. Results? Handsome profits, speedy growth—and brand equity that lasts for decades while rivals scramble to catch up.

Consider Cirque du Soleil—which invented a new industry that combined elements from traditional circus with elements drawn from sophisticated theater. In just 20 years, Cirque raked in revenues that Ringling Bros. and Barnum & Bailey—the world's leading circus—needed more than a century to attain.

industries, what we call blue ocean strategy. The logic behind blue ocean strategy parts with traditional models focused on competing in existing market space. Indeed, it can be argued that managers' failure to realize the differences between red and blue ocean strategy lies behind the difficulties many companies encounter as they try to break from the competition.

In this article, we present the concept of blue ocean strategy and describe its defining characteristics. We assess the profit and growth consequences of blue oceans and discuss why their creation is a rising imperative for companies in the future. We believe that an understanding of blue ocean strategy will help today's companies as they struggle to thrive in an accelerating and expanding business universe.

Blue and Red Oceans

Although the term may be new, blue oceans have always been with us. Look back 100 years and ask yourself which industries known

Idea in Practice

How to begin creating blue oceans? Kim and Mauborgne offer these suggestions:

Understand the Logic Behind Blue Ocean Strategy

The logic behind blue ocean strategy is counterintuitive:

- **It's not about technology innovation.** Blue oceans seldom result from technological innovation. Often, the underlying technology already exists—and blue ocean creators link it to what buyers value. Compaq, for example, used existing technologies to create its ProSignia server, which gave buyers twice the file and print capability of the minicomputer at one-third the price.
- **You don't have to venture into distant waters to create blue oceans.** Most blue oceans are created from within, not beyond, the red oceans of existing industries. Incumbents often create blue oceans within their core businesses. Consider the megaplexes introduced by AMC—an established player in the movie-theater industry. Megaplexes provided moviegoers spectacular viewing experiences in stadium-size theater complexes at lower costs to theater owners.

Apply Blue Ocean Strategic Moves

To apply blue ocean strategic moves:

- **Never use the competition as a benchmark.** Instead, make the competition irrelevant by creating a leap in value for both

today were then unknown. The answer: Industries as basic as automobiles, music recording, aviation, petrochemicals, pharmaceuticals, and management consulting were unheard-of or had just begun to emerge. Now turn the clock back only 30 years and ask yourself the same question. Again, a plethora of multibillion-dollar industries jump out: mutual funds, cellular telephones, biotechnology, discount retailing, express package delivery, snowboards, coffee bars, and home videos, to name a few. Just three decades ago, none of these industries existed in a meaningful way.

This time, put the clock forward 20 years. Ask yourself: How many industries that are unknown today will exist then? If history is any predictor of the future, the answer is many. Companies have a

yourself and your customers. Ford did this with the Model T. Ford could have tried besting the fashionable, customized cars that wealthy people bought for weekend jaunts in the countryside. Instead, it offered a car for everyday use that was far more affordable, durable, and easy to use and fix than rivals' offerings. Model T sales boomed, and Ford's market share surged from 9% in 1908 to 61% in 1921.

- **Reduce your costs while also offering customers more value.** Cirque du Soleil omitted costly elements of traditional circus, such as animal acts and aisle concessions. Its reduced cost structure enabled it to provide sophisticated elements from theater that appealed to adult audiences—such as themes, original scores, and enchanting sets, all of which change year to year. The added value lured adults who had not gone to a circus for years and enticed them to come back more frequently—thereby increasing revenues. By offering the best of circus and theater, Cirque created a market space that, as yet, has no name—and no equals.

huge capacity to create new industries and re-create existing ones, a fact that is reflected in the deep changes that have been necessary in the way industries are classified. The half-century-old Standard Industrial Classification (SIC) system was replaced in 1997 by the North American Industry Classification System (NAICS). The new system expanded the ten SIC industry sectors into 20 to reflect the emerging realities of new industry territories—blue oceans. The services sector under the old system, for example, is now seven sectors ranging from information to health care and social assistance. Given that these classification systems are designed for standardization and continuity, such a replacement shows how significant a source of economic growth the creation of blue oceans has been.

Looking forward, it seems clear to us that blue oceans will remain the engine of growth. Prospects in most established market spaces—red oceans—are shrinking steadily. Technological advances have substantially improved industrial productivity, permitting suppliers to produce an unprecedented array of products and services. And as trade barriers between nations and regions fall and information on products and prices becomes instantly and globally available, niche markets and monopoly havens are continuing to disappear. At the same time, there is little evidence of any increase in demand, at least in the developed markets, where recent United Nations statistics even point to declining populations. The result is that in more and more industries, supply is overtaking demand.

This situation has inevitably hastened the commoditization of products and services, stoked price wars, and shrunk profit margins. According to recent studies, major American brands in a variety of product and service categories have become more and more alike. And as brands become more similar, people increasingly base purchase choices on price. People no longer insist, as in the past, that their laundry detergent be Tide. Nor do they necessarily stick to Colgate when there is a special promotion for Crest, and vice versa. In overcrowded industries, differentiating brands becomes harder both in economic upturns and in downturns.

The Paradox of Strategy

Unfortunately, most companies seem becalmed in their red oceans. In a study of business launches in 108 companies, we found that 86% of those new ventures were line extensions—incremental improvements to existing industry offerings—and a mere 14% were aimed at creating new markets or industries. While line extensions did account for 62% of the total revenues, they delivered only 39% of the total profits. By contrast, the 14% invested in creating new markets and industries delivered 38% of total revenues and a startling 61% of total profits.

So why the dramatic imbalance in favor of red oceans? Part of the explanation is that corporate strategy is heavily influenced by its roots in military strategy. The very language of strategy is deeply imbued with military references—chief executive "officers" in "headquarters," "troops" on the "front lines." Described this way, strategy is all about red ocean competition. It is about confronting an opponent and driving him off a battlefield of limited territory. Blue ocean strategy, by contrast, is about doing business where there is no competitor. It is about creating new land, not dividing up existing land. Focusing on the red ocean therefore means accepting the key constraining factors of war—limited terrain and the need to beat an enemy to succeed. And it means denying the distinctive strength of the business world—the capacity to create new market space that is uncontested.

The tendency of corporate strategy to focus on winning against rivals was exacerbated by the meteoric rise of Japanese companies in the 1970s and 1980s. For the first time in corporate history, customers were deserting Western companies in droves. As competition mounted in the global marketplace, a slew of red ocean strategies emerged, all arguing that competition was at the core of corporate success and failure. Today, one hardly talks about strategy without using the language of competition. The term that best symbolizes this is "competitive advantage." In the competitive-advantage worldview, companies are often driven to outperform rivals and capture greater shares of existing market space.

Of course competition matters. But by focusing on competition, scholars, companies, and consultants have ignored two very important—and, we would argue, far more lucrative—aspects of strategy: One is to find and develop markets where there is little or no competition—blue oceans—and the other is to exploit and protect blue oceans. These challenges are very different from those to which strategists have devoted most of their attention.

Toward Blue Ocean Strategy

What kind of strategic logic is needed to guide the creation of blue oceans? To answer that question, we looked back over 100 years of data on blue ocean creation to see what patterns could be discerned. Some of our data are presented in "A snapshot of blue ocean creation." It shows an overview of key blue ocean creations in three

A snapshot of blue ocean creation

This table identifies the strategic elements that were common to blue ocean creations in three different industries in different eras. It is not intended to be comprehensive in coverage or exhaustive in content. We chose to show American industries because they represented the largest and least-regulated market during our study period. The pattern of blue ocean creations exemplified by these three industries is consistent with what we observed in the other industries in our study.

Key blue ocean creations	Was the blue ocean created by a new entrant or an incumbent?	Was it driven by technology pioneering or value pioneering?	At the time of the blue ocean creation, was the industry attractive or unattractive?
Automobiles			
Ford Model T Unveiled in 1908, the Model T was the first mass-produced car, priced so that many Americans could afford it.	New entrant	Value pioneering* (mostly existing technologies)	Unattractive
GM's "car for every purse and purpose" GM created a blue ocean in 1924 by injecting fun and fashion into the car.	Incumbent	Value pioneering (some new technologies)	Attractive
Japanese fuel-efficient autos Japanese automakers created a blue ocean in the mid-1970s with small, reliable lines of cars.	Incumbent	Value pioneering (some new technologies)	Unattractive
Chrysler minivan With its 1984 minivan, Chrysler created a new class of automobile that was as easy to use as a car but had the passenger space of a van.	Incumbent	Value pioneering (mostly existing technologies)	Unattractive

Key blue ocean creations	Was the blue ocean created by a new entrant or an incumbent?	Was it driven by technology pioneering or value pioneering?	At the time of the blue ocean creation, was the industry attractive or unattractive?
Computers			
CTR's tabulating machine In 1914, CTR created the business machine industry by simplifying, modularizing, and leasing tabulating machines. CTR later changed its name to IBM.	Incumbent	Value pioneering (some new technologies)	Unattractive
IBM 650 electronic computer and System/360 In 1952, IBM created the business computer industry by simplifying and reducing the power and price of existing technology. And it exploded the blue ocean created by the 650 when in 1964 it unveiled the System/360, the first modularized computer system.	Incumbent	Value pioneering (650: mostly existing technologies) Value and technology pioneering (System/360: new and existing technologies)	Nonexistent
Apple personal computer Although it was not the first home computer, the all-in-one, simple-to-use Apple II was a blue ocean creation when it appeared in 1978.	New entrant	Value pioneering (mostly existing technologies)	Unattractive
Compaq PC servers Compaq created a blue ocean in 1992 with its ProSignia server, which gave buyers twice the file and print capability of the minicomputer at one-third the price.	Incumbent	Value pioneering (mostly existing technologies)	Nonexistent

(continued)

Key blue ocean creations	Was the blue ocean created by a new entrant or an incumbent?	Was it driven by technology pioneering or value pioneering?	At the time of the blue ocean creation, was the industry attractive or unattractive?
Dell built-to-order computers In the mid-1990s, Dell created a blue ocean in a highly competitive industry by creating a new purchase and delivery experience for buyers.	New entrant	Value pioneering (mostly existing technologies)	Unattractive
Movie theaters			
Nickelodeon The first Nickelodeon opened its doors in 1905, showing short films around-the-clock to working-class audiences for five cents.	New entrant	Value pioneering (mostly existing technologies)	Nonexistent
Palace theaters Created by Roxy Rothapfel in 1914, these theaters provided an operalike environment for cinema viewing at an affordable price.	Incumbent	Value pioneering (mostly existing technologies)	Attractive
AMC multiplex In the 1960s, the number of multiplexes in America's suburban shopping malls mushroomed. The multiplex gave viewers greater choice while reducing owners' costs.	Incumbent	Value pioneering (mostly existing technologies)	Unattractive
AMC megaplex Megaplexes, introduced in 1995, offered every current blockbuster and provided spectacular viewing experiences in theater complexes as big as stadiums, at a lower cost to theater owners.	Incumbent	Value pioneering (mostly existing technologies)	Unattractive

*Driven by value pioneering does not mean that technologies were not involved. Rather, it means that the defining technologies used had largely been in existence, whether in that industry or elsewhere.

industries that closely touch people's lives: autos—how people get to work; computers—what people use at work; and movie theaters—where people go after work for enjoyment. We found that:

Blue oceans are not about technology innovation

Leading-edge technology is sometimes involved in the creation of blue oceans, but it is not a defining feature of them. This is often true even in industries that are technology intensive. As the exhibit reveals, across all three representative industries, blue oceans were seldom the result of technological innovation per se; the underlying technology was often already in existence. Even Ford's revolutionary assembly line can be traced to the meatpacking industry in America. Like those within the auto industry, the blue oceans within the computer industry did not come about through technology innovations alone but by linking technology to what buyers valued. As with the IBM 650 and the Compaq PC server, this often involved simplifying the technology.

Incumbents often create blue oceans—and usually within their core businesses

GM, the Japanese automakers, and Chrysler were established players when they created blue oceans in the auto industry. So were CTR and its later incarnation, IBM, and Compaq in the computer industry. And in the cinema industry, the same can be said of palace theaters and AMC. Of the companies listed here, only Ford, Apple, Dell, and Nickelodeon were new entrants in their industries; the first three were start-ups, and the fourth was an established player entering an industry that was new to it. This suggests that incumbents are not at a disadvantage in creating new market spaces. Moreover, the blue oceans made by incumbents were usually within their core businesses. In fact, as the exhibit shows, most blue oceans are created from within, not beyond, red oceans of existing industries. This challenges the view that new markets are in distant waters. Blue oceans are right next to you in every industry.

Company and industry are the wrong units of analysis

The traditional units of strategic analysis—company and industry—have little explanatory power when it comes to analyzing how and why blue oceans are created. There is no consistently excellent company; the same company can be brilliant at one time and wrong-headed at another. Every company rises and falls over time. Likewise, there is no perpetually excellent industry; relative attractiveness is driven largely by the creation of blue oceans from within them.

The most appropriate unit of analysis for explaining the creation of blue oceans is the strategic move—the set of managerial actions and decisions involved in making a major market-creating business offering. Compaq, for example, is considered by many people to be "unsuccessful" because it was acquired by Hewlett-Packard in 2001 and ceased to be a company. But the firm's ultimate fate does not invalidate the smart strategic move Compaq made that led to the creation of the multibillion-dollar market in PC servers, a move that was a key cause of the company's powerful comeback in the 1990s.

Creating blue oceans builds brands

So powerful is blue ocean strategy that a blue ocean strategic move can create brand equity that lasts for decades. Almost all of the companies listed in the exhibit are remembered in no small part for the blue oceans they created long ago. Very few people alive today were around when the first Model T rolled off Henry Ford's assembly line in 1908, but the company's brand still benefits from that blue ocean move. IBM, too, is often regarded as an "American institution" largely for the blue oceans it created in computing; the 360 series was its equivalent of the Model T.

Our findings are encouraging for executives at the large, established corporations that are traditionally seen as the victims of new market space creation. For what they reveal is that large R&D budgets are not the key to creating new market space. The key is making the right strategic moves. What's more, companies that understand what drives a good strategic move will be well placed to create multiple blue oceans over time, thereby continuing to deliver high growth and profits over a sustained period. The creation of blue oceans, in other words, is a product of strategy and as such is very much a product of managerial action.

The Defining Characteristics

Our research shows several common characteristics across strategic moves that create blue oceans. We found that the creators of blue oceans, in sharp contrast to companies playing by traditional rules, never use the competition as a benchmark. Instead they make it irrelevant by creating a leap in value for both buyers and the company itself. (The exhibit "Red ocean versus blue ocean strategy" compares the chief characteristics of these two strategy models.)

Perhaps the most important feature of blue ocean strategy is that it rejects the fundamental tenet of conventional strategy: that a trade-off exists between value and cost. According to this thesis, companies can either create greater value for customers at a higher cost or create reasonable value at a lower cost. In other words, strategy is essentially a choice between differentiation and low cost. But when it comes to creating blue oceans, the evidence shows that successful companies pursue differentiation and low cost simultaneously.

To see how this is done, let us go back to Cirque du Soleil. At the time of Cirque's debut, circuses focused on benchmarking one another and maximizing their shares of shrinking demand by tweaking traditional circus acts. This included trying to secure more and better-known clowns and lion tamers, efforts that raised circuses' cost structure without substantially altering the circus experience. The result was rising costs without rising revenues and a downward spiral in overall circus demand. Enter Cirque. Instead of following the conventional logic of outpacing the competition by offering a better solution to the given problem—creating a circus with even greater fun and thrills—it redefined the problem itself by offering people the fun and thrill of the circus *and* the intellectual sophistication and artistic richness of the theater.

In designing performances that landed both these punches, Cirque had to reevaluate the components of the traditional circus

Red ocean versus blue ocean strategy

The imperatives for red ocean and blue ocean strategies are starkly different.

Red ocean strategy	Blue ocean strategy
Compete in existing market space.	Create uncontested market space.
Beat the competition.	Make the competition irrelevant.
Exploit existing demand.	Create and capture new demand.
Make the value/cost trade-off.	Break the value/cost trade-off.
Align the whole system of a company's activities with its strategic choice of differentiation *or* low cost.	Align the whole system of a company's activities in pursuit of differentiation *and* low cost.

offering. What the company found was that many of the elements considered essential to the fun and thrill of the circus were unnecessary and in many cases costly. For instance, most circuses offer animal acts. These are a heavy economic burden, because circuses have to shell out not only for the animals but also for their training, medical care, housing, insurance, and transportation. Yet Cirque found that the appetite for animal shows was rapidly diminishing because of rising public concern about the treatment of circus animals and the ethics of exhibiting them.

Similarly, although traditional circuses promoted their performers as stars, Cirque realized that the public no longer thought of circus artists as stars, at least not in the movie star sense. Cirque did away with traditional three-ring shows, too. Not only did these create confusion among spectators forced to switch their attention from one ring to another, they also increased the number of performers needed, with obvious cost implications. And while aisle concession sales appeared to be a good way to generate revenue, the high prices discouraged parents from making purchases and made them feel they were being taken for a ride.

Cirque found that the lasting allure of the traditional circus came down to just three factors: the clowns, the tent, and the classic acrobatic acts. So Cirque kept the clowns, while shifting their humor away from slapstick to a more enchanting, sophisticated style. It glamorized the tent, which many circuses had abandoned in favor of rented venues. Realizing that the tent, more than anything else, captured the magic of the circus, Cirque designed this classic symbol with a glorious external finish and a high level of audience comfort. Gone were the sawdust and hard benches. Acrobats and other thrilling performers were retained, but Cirque reduced their roles and made their acts more elegant by adding artistic flair.

Even as Cirque stripped away some of the traditional circus offerings, it injected new elements drawn from the world of theater. For instance, unlike traditional circuses featuring a series of unrelated acts, each Cirque creation resembles a theater performance in that it has a theme and story line. Although the themes are intentionally vague, they bring harmony and an intellectual element to the acts. Cirque also borrows ideas from Broadway. For example, rather than putting on the traditional "once and for all" show, Cirque mounts multiple productions based on different themes and story lines. As with Broadway productions, too, each Cirque show has an original musical score, which drives the performance, lighting, and timing of the acts, rather than the other way around. The productions feature abstract and spiritual dance, an idea derived from theater and ballet. By introducing these factors, Cirque has created highly sophisticated entertainments. And by staging multiple productions, Cirque gives people reason to come to the circus more often, thereby increasing revenues.

Cirque offers the best of both circus and theater. And by eliminating many of the most expensive elements of the circus, it has been able to dramatically reduce its cost structure, achieving both differentiation and low cost. (For a depiction of the economics underpinning blue ocean strategy, see "The simultaneous pursuit of differentiation and low cost.")

By driving down costs while simultaneously driving up value for buyers, a company can achieve a leap in value for both itself and its customers. Since buyer value comes from the utility and price a company offers, and a company generates value for itself through cost structure and price, blue ocean strategy is achieved only when the whole system of a company's utility, price, and cost activities is properly aligned. It is this whole-system approach that makes the creation of blue oceans a sustainable strategy. Blue ocean strategy integrates the range of a firm's functional and operational activities.

A rejection of the trade-off between low cost and differentiation implies a fundamental change in strategic mind-set—we cannot emphasize enough how fundamental a shift it is. The red ocean assumption that industry structural conditions are a given and firms are forced to compete within them is based on an intellectual worldview that academics call the *structuralist* view, or *environmental determinism*. According to this view, companies and managers are largely at the mercy of economic forces greater than themselves. Blue ocean strategies, by contrast, are based on a worldview in which market boundaries and industries can be reconstructed by the actions and beliefs of industry players. We call this the *reconstructionist* view.

The founders of Cirque du Soleil clearly did not feel constrained to act within the confines of their industry. Indeed, is Cirque really a circus with all that it has eliminated, reduced, raised, and created? Or is it theater? If it is theater, then what genre—Broadway show, opera, ballet? The magic of Cirque was created through a reconstruction of elements drawn from all of these alternatives. In the end, Cirque is none of them and a little of all of them. From within the red oceans of theater and circus, Cirque has created a blue ocean of uncontested market space that has, as yet, no name.

Barriers to Imitation

Companies that create blue oceans usually reap the benefits without credible challenges for ten to 15 years, as was the case with Cirque du Soleil, Home Depot, Federal Express, Southwest Airlines, and CNN, to name just a few. The reason is that blue ocean strategy creates considerable economic and cognitive barriers to imitation.

The simultaneous pursuit of differentiation and low cost

A blue ocean is created in the region where a company's actions favorably affect both its cost structure and its value proposition to buyers. Cost savings are made from eliminating and reducing the factors an industry competes on. Buyer value is lifted by raising and creating elements the industry has never offered. Over time, costs are reduced further as scale economies kick in, due to the high sales volumes that superior value generates.

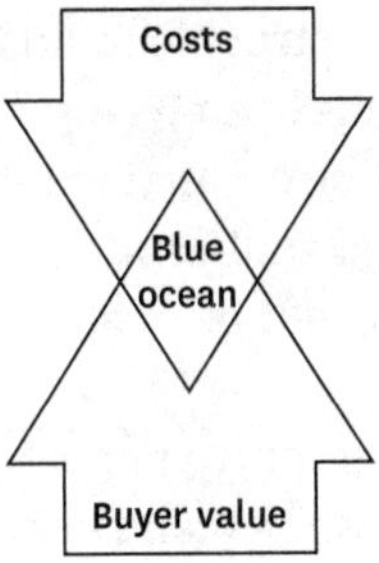

For a start, adopting a blue ocean creator's business model is easier to imagine than to do. Because blue ocean creators immediately attract customers in large volumes, they are able to generate scale economies very rapidly, putting would-be imitators at an immediate and continuing cost disadvantage. The huge economies of scale in purchasing that Wal-Mart enjoys, for example, have significantly discouraged other companies from imitating its business model. The immediate attraction of large numbers of customers can also create network externalities. The more customers eBay has online, the more attractive the auction site becomes for both sellers and buyers of wares, giving users few incentives to go elsewhere.

When imitation requires companies to make changes to their whole system of activities, organizational politics may impede a would-be competitor's ability to switch to the divergent business model of a blue ocean strategy. For instance, airlines trying to follow Southwest's example of offering the speed of air travel with the flexibility and cost of driving would have faced major revisions in routing, training, marketing, and pricing, not to mention culture. Few established airlines had the flexibility to make such extensive organizational and operating changes overnight. Imitating a whole-system approach is not an easy feat.

The cognitive barriers can be just as effective. When a company offers a leap in value, it rapidly earns brand buzz and a loyal following in the marketplace. Experience shows that even the most expensive marketing campaigns struggle to unseat a blue ocean creator. Microsoft, for example, has been trying for more than ten years to occupy the center of the blue ocean that Intuit created with its financial software product Quicken. Despite all of its efforts and all of its investment, Microsoft has not been able to unseat Intuit as the industry leader.

In other situations, attempts to imitate a blue ocean creator conflict with the imitator's existing brand image. The Body Shop, for example, shuns top models and makes no promises of eternal youth and beauty. For the established cosmetic brands like Estée Lauder and L'Oréal, imitation was very difficult, because it would have signaled a complete invalidation of their current images, which are based on promises of eternal youth and beauty.

A Consistent Pattern

While our conceptual articulation of the pattern may be new, blue ocean strategy has always existed, whether or not companies have been conscious of the fact. Just consider the striking parallels between the Cirque du Soleil theater-circus experience and Ford's creation of the Model T.

At the end of the nineteenth century, the automobile industry was small and unattractive. More than 500 automakers in America competed in turning out handmade luxury cars that cost around $1,500 and were enormously *un*popular with all but the very rich. Anticar activists tore up roads, ringed parked cars with barbed wire, and organized boycotts of car-driving businessmen and politicians. Woodrow Wilson caught the spirit of the times when he said in 1906 that "nothing has spread socialistic feeling more than the automobile." He called it "a picture of the arrogance of wealth."

Instead of trying to beat the competition and steal a share of existing demand from other automakers, Ford reconstructed the industry boundaries of cars and horse-drawn carriages to create a blue ocean. At the time, horse-drawn carriages were the primary means of local transportation across America. The carriage had two distinct advantages over cars. Horses could easily negotiate the bumps and mud that stymied cars—especially in rain and snow—on the nation's ubiquitous dirt roads. And horses and carriages were much easier to maintain than the luxurious autos of the time, which frequently broke down, requiring expert repairmen who were expensive and in short supply. It was Henry Ford's understanding of these advantages that showed him how he could break away from the competition and unlock enormous untapped demand.

Ford called the Model T the car "for the great multitude, constructed of the best materials." Like Cirque, the Ford Motor Company made the competition irrelevant. Instead of creating fashionable, customized cars for weekends in the countryside, a luxury few could justify, Ford built a car that, like the horse-drawn carriage, was for everyday use. The Model T came in just one color, black, and there were few optional extras. It was reliable and durable, designed to travel effortlessly over dirt roads in rain, snow, or sunshine. It was easy to use and fix. People could learn to drive it in a day. And like Cirque, Ford went outside the industry for a price point, looking at horse-drawn carriages ($400), not other autos. In 1908, the first Model T cost $850; in 1909, the price dropped to $609, and by 1924 it was down to $290. In this way, Ford converted buyers of horse-drawn carriages into car buyers—just as Cirque turned theatergoers into circusgoers. Sales of the Model T boomed. Ford's market share surged from 9% in 1908 to 61% in 1921, and by 1923, a majority of American households had a car.

Even as Ford offered the mass of buyers a leap in value, the company also achieved the lowest cost structure in the industry, much as Cirque did later. By keeping the cars highly standardized with limited options and interchangeable parts, Ford was able to scrap the prevailing manufacturing system in which cars were constructed by skilled craftsmen who swarmed around one workstation and built a car piece by piece from start to finish. Ford's revolutionary assembly line replaced craftsmen with unskilled laborers, each of whom worked quickly and efficiently on one small task. This allowed Ford to make a car in just four days—21 days was the industry norm—creating huge cost savings.

Blue and red oceans have always coexisted and always will. Practical reality, therefore, demands that companies understand the strategic logic of both types of oceans. At present, competing in red oceans dominates the field of strategy in theory and in practice, even as businesses' need to create blue oceans intensifies. It is time to even the scales in the field of strategy with a better balance of efforts across both oceans. For although blue ocean strategists have always existed, for the most part their strategies have been largely unconscious. But once corporations realize that the strategies for creating and capturing blue oceans have a different underlying logic from red ocean strategies, they will be able to create many more blue oceans in the future.

Originally published in October 2004. Reprint R0401D.

The Secrets to Successful Strategy Execution

by Gary L. Neilson, Karla L. Martin, and Elizabeth Powers

A BRILLIANT STRATEGY, blockbuster product, or breakthrough technology can put you on the competitive map, but only solid execution can keep you there. You have to be able to deliver on your intent. Unfortunately, the majority of companies aren't very good at it, by their own admission. Over the past five years, we have invited many thousands of employees (about 25% of whom came from executive ranks) to complete an online assessment of their organizations' capabilities, a process that's generated a database of 125,000 profiles representing more than 1,000 companies, government agencies, and not-for-profits in over 50 countries. Employees at three out of every five companies rated their organization weak at execution—that is, when asked if they agreed with the statement "Important strategic and operational decisions are quickly translated into action," the majority answered no.

Execution is the result of thousands of decisions made every day by employees acting according to the information they have and their own self-interest. In our work helping more than 250 companies learn to execute more effectively, we've identified four fundamental building blocks executives can use to influence those actions—clarifying decision rights, designing information flows, aligning motivators, and making changes to structure. (For simplicity's sake we refer to them as decision rights, information, motivators, and structure.)

In efforts to improve performance, most organizations go right to structural measures because moving lines around the org chart seems the most obvious solution and the changes are visible and concrete. Such steps generally reap some short-term efficiencies quickly, but in so doing address only the symptoms of dysfunction, not its root causes. Several years later, companies usually end up in the same place they started. Structural change can and should be part of the path to improved execution, but it's best to think of it as the capstone, not the cornerstone, of any organizational transformation. In fact, our research shows that actions having to do with decision rights and information are far more important—about twice as effective—as improvements made to the other two building blocks. (See "What matters most to strategy execution.")

Take, for example, the case of a global consumer packaged-goods company that lurched down the reorganization path in the early 1990s. (We have altered identifying details in this and other cases that follow.) Disappointed with company performance, senior management did what most companies were doing at that time: They restructured. They eliminated some layers of management and broadened spans of control. Management-staffing costs quickly fell by 18%. Eight years later, however, it was déjà vu. The layers had crept back in, and spans of control had once again narrowed. In addressing only structure, management had attacked the visible symptoms of poor performance but not the underlying cause—how people made decisions and how they were held accountable.

This time, management looked beyond lines and boxes to the mechanics of how work got done. Instead of searching for ways to strip out costs, they focused on improving execution—and in the process discovered the true reasons for the performance shortfall. Managers didn't have a clear sense of their respective roles and responsibilities. They did not intuitively understand which decisions were

Idea in Brief

A brilliant strategy may put you on the competitive map. But only solid execution keeps you there. Unfortunately, most companies struggle with implementation. That's because they overrely on structural changes, such as reorganization, to execute their strategy.

Though structural change has its place in execution, it produces only short-term gains. For example, one company reduced its management layers as part of a strategy to address disappointing performance. Costs plummeted initially, but the layers soon crept back in.

Research by Neilson, Martin, and Powers shows that execution exemplars focus their efforts on two levers far more powerful than structural change:

- **Clarifying decision rights**—for instance, specifying who "owns" each decision and who must provide input
- **Ensuring information flows where it's needed**—such as promoting managers laterally so they build networks needed for the cross-unit collaboration critical to a new strategy

Tackle decision rights and information flows first, and only then **alter organizational structures** and **realign incentives** to *support* those moves.

theirs to make. Moreover, the link between performance and rewards was weak. This was a company long on micromanaging and second-guessing, and short on accountability. Middle managers spent 40% of their time justifying and reporting upward or questioning the tactical decisions of their direct reports.

Armed with this understanding, the company designed a new management model that established who was accountable for what and made the connection between performance and reward. For instance, the norm at this company, not unusual in the industry, had been to promote people quickly, within 18 months to two years, before they had a chance to see their initiatives through. As a result, managers at every level kept doing their old jobs even after they had been promoted, peering over the shoulders of the direct reports who were now in charge of their projects and, all too frequently,

Idea in Practice

The following levers matter *most* for successful strategy execution:

Decision Rights

- Ensure that everyone in your company knows which decisions and actions they're responsible for.

  Example: In one global consumer-goods company, decisions made by divisional and geographic leaders were overridden by corporate functional leaders who controlled resource allocations. Decisions stalled. Overhead costs mounted as divisions added staff to create bulletproof cases for challenging corporate decisions. To support a new strategy hinging on sharper customer focus, the CEO designated accountability for profits unambiguously to the divisions.

- Encourage higher-level managers to delegate operational decisions.

  Example: At one global charitable organization, country-level managers' inability to delegate led to decision paralysis. So the leadership team encouraged country managers to delegate standard operational tasks. This freed these managers to focus on developing the strategies needed to fulfill the organization's mission.

Information Flow

- Make sure important information about the competitive environment flows quickly to corporate headquarters. That way, the top team can identify patterns and promulgate best practices throughout the company.

  Example: At one insurance company, accurate information about projects' viability was censored as it moved up the hierarchy. To improve information flow to senior levels of management, the company took steps

taking over. Today, people stay in their positions longer so they can follow through on their own initiatives, and they're still around when the fruits of their labors start to kick in. What's more, results from those initiatives continue to count in their performance reviews for some time after they've been promoted, forcing managers to live with the expectations they'd set in their previous jobs. As a consequence, forecasting has become more accurate and reliable. These actions did yield a structure with fewer layers and greater

to create a more open, informal culture. Top executives began mingling with unit leaders during management meetings and held regular brown-bag lunches where people discussed the company's most pressing issues.

- Facilitate information flow across organizational boundaries.

  Example: To better manage relationships with large, cross-product customers, a B2B company needed its units to talk with one another. It charged its newly created customer-focused marketing group with encouraging cross-company communication. The group issued regular reports showing performance against targets (by product and geography) and supplied root-cause analyses of performance gaps. Quarterly performance-management meetings further fostered the trust required for collaboration.

- Help field and line employees understand how their day-to-day choices affect your company's bottom line.

  Example: At a financial services firm, salespeople routinely crafted customized one-off deals with clients that cost the company more than it made in revenues. Sales didn't understand the cost and complexity implications of these transactions. Management addressed the information misalignment by adopting a "smart customization" approach to sales. For customized deals, it established standardized back-office processes (such as risk assessment). It also developed analytical support tools to arm salespeople with accurate information on the cost implications of their proposed transactions. Profitability improved.

spans of control, but that was a side effect, not the primary focus, of the changes.

The Elements of Strong Execution

Our conclusions arise out of decades of practical application and intensive research. Nearly five years ago, we and our colleagues set out to gather empirical data to identify the actions that were most effective in enabling an organization to implement strategy. What particular ways of restructuring, motivating, improving information flows, and clarifying decision rights mattered the most? We started by drawing up a list of 17 traits, each corresponding to one or more of the four building blocks we knew could enable effective execution—traits like the free flow of information across organizational boundaries or the degree to which senior leaders refrain from getting involved in operating decisions. With these factors in mind, we developed an online profiler that allows individuals to assess the execution capabilities of their organizations. Over the next four years or so, we collected data from many thousands of profiles, which in turn allowed us to more precisely calibrate the impact of each trait on an organization's ability to execute. That allowed us to rank all 17 traits in order of their relative influence. (See "The 17 fundamental traits of organizational effectiveness.")

Ranking the traits makes clear how important decision rights and information are to effective strategy execution. The first eight traits map directly to decision rights and information. Only three of the 17 traits relate to structure, and none of those ranks higher than 13th. We'll walk through the top five traits here.

1. Everyone has a good idea of the decisions and actions for which he or she is responsible

In companies strong on execution, 71% of individuals agree with this statement; that figure drops to 32% in organizations weak on execution.

Blurring of decision rights tends to occur as a company matures. Young organizations are generally too busy getting things done to define roles and responsibilities clearly at the outset. And why should they? In a small company, it's not so difficult to know what other people are up to. So for a time, things work out well enough. As the company grows, however, executives come and go, bringing in with them and taking away different expectations, and over time the approval process gets ever more convoluted and murky. It becomes increasingly unclear where one person's accountability begins and another's ends.

One global consumer-durables company found this out the hard way. It was so rife with people making competing and conflicting decisions that it was hard to find anyone below the CEO who felt truly accountable for profitability. The company was organized into 16 product divisions aggregated into three geographic groups—North America, Europe, and International. Each of the divisions was charged with reaching explicit performance targets, but functional staff at corporate headquarters controlled spending targets—how R&D dollars were allocated, for instance. Decisions made by divisional and geographic leaders were routinely overridden by functional leaders. Overhead costs began to mount as the divisions added staff to help them create bulletproof cases to challenge corporate decisions.

Decisions stalled while divisions negotiated with functions, each layer weighing in with questions. Functional staffers in the divisions (financial analysts, for example) often deferred to their higher-ups in corporate rather than their division vice president, since functional leaders were responsible for rewards and promotions. Only the CEO and his executive team had the discretion to resolve disputes. All of these symptoms fed on one another and collectively hampered execution—until a new CEO came in.

The new chief executive chose to focus less on cost control and more on profitable growth by redefining the divisions to focus on consumers. As part of the new organizational model, the CEO designated accountability for profits unambiguously to the divisions and also gave them the authority to draw on functional activities to support their goals (as well as more control of the budget). Corporate functional roles and decision rights were recast to better support the divisions' needs and also to build the cross-divisional links necessary for developing the global capabilities of the business as a whole. For the most part, the functional leaders understood the market realities—and that change entailed some adjustments to the operating model of the business. It helped that the CEO brought them into the organizational redesign process, so that the new model wasn't something imposed on them as much as it was something they engaged in and built together.

2. Important information about the competitive environment gets to headquarters quickly

On average, 77% of individuals in strong-execution organizations agree with this statement, whereas only 45% of those in weak-execution organizations do.

Headquarters can serve a powerful function in identifying patterns and promulgating best practices throughout business segments and geographic regions. But it can play this coordinating role only if it has accurate and up-to-date market intelligence. Otherwise, it will tend to impose its own agenda and policies rather than defer to operations that are much closer to the customer.

Consider the case of heavy-equipment manufacturer Caterpillar.[1] Today it is a highly successful $45 billion global company, but a generation ago, Caterpillar's organization was so badly misaligned that its very existence was threatened. Decision rights were hoarded at the top by functional general offices located at headquarters in Peoria, Illinois, while much of the information needed to make those decisions resided in the field with sales managers. "It just took a long time to get decisions going up and down the functional silos, and they really weren't good business decisions; they were more functional decisions," noted one field executive. Current CEO Jim Owens, then a managing director in Indonesia, told us that such information that did make it to the top had been "whitewashed and varnished several times over along the way." Cut off from information about the external market, senior executives focused on the organization's internal workings, overanalyzing issues and second-guessing decisions made at lower levels, costing the company opportunities in fast-moving markets.

Pricing, for example, was based on cost and determined not by market realities but by the pricing general office in Peoria. Sales representatives across the world lost sale after sale to Komatsu, whose competitive pricing consistently beat Caterpillar's. In 1982, the company posted the first annual loss in its almost-60-year history. In 1983 and 1984, it lost $1 million a day, seven days a week. By the end of 1984, Caterpillar had lost a billion dollars. By 1988, then-CEO George Schaefer stood atop an entrenched bureaucracy that was, in

What matters most to strategy execution

When a company fails to execute its strategy, the first thing managers often think to do is restructure. But our research shows that the fundamentals of good execution start with clarifying decision rights and making sure information flows where it needs to go. If you get those right, the correct structure and motivators often become obvious.

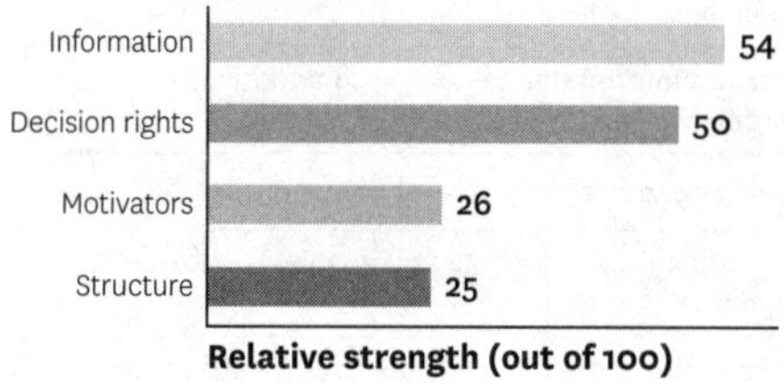

his words, "telling me what I wanted to hear, not what I needed to know." So, he convened a task force of "renegade" middle managers and tasked them with charting Caterpillar's future.

Ironically, the way to ensure that the right information flowed to headquarters was to make sure the right decisions were made much further down the organization. By delegating operational responsibility to the people closer to the action, top executives were free to focus on more global strategic issues. Accordingly, the company reorganized into business units, making each accountable for its own P&L statement. The functional general offices that had been all-powerful ceased to exist, literally overnight. Their talent and expertise, including engineering, pricing, and manufacturing, were parceled out to the new business units, which could now design their own products, develop their own manufacturing processes and schedules, and set their own prices. The move dramatically decentralized decision rights, giving the units control over market decisions. The business unit P&Ls were now measured consistently across the enterprise, as return on assets became the universal measure of success. With this accurate, up-to-date, and directly comparable information, senior decision makers at headquarters could make smart strategic choices and trade-offs rather than use

The 17 fundamental traits of organizational effectiveness

From our survey research drawn from more than 26,000 people in 31 companies, we have distilled the traits that make organizations effective at implementing strategy. Here they are, in order of importance.

Rank	Organization Trait	Strength Index (Out of 100)
1	Everyone has a good idea of the decisions and actions for which he or she is responsible.	81
2	Important information about the competitive environment gets to headquarters quickly.	68
3	Once made, decisions are rarely second-guessed.	58
4	Information flows freely across organizational boundaries.	58
5	Field and line employees usually have the information they need to understand the bottom-line impact of their day-to-day choices.	55
6	Line managers have access to the metrics they need to measure the key drivers of their business.	48
7	Managers up the line get involved in operating decisions.	32
8	Conflicting messages are rarely sent to the market.	32
9	The individual performance-appraisal process differentiates among high, adequate, and low performers.	32
10	The ability to deliver on performance commitments strongly influences career advancement and compensation.	32
11	It is more accurate to describe the culture of this organization as "persuade and cajole" than "command and control."	29
12	The primary role of corporate staff here is to support the business units rather than to audit them.	29
13	Promotions can be lateral moves (from one position to another on the same level in the hierarchy).	29
14	Fast-track employees here can expect promotions more frequently than every three years.	23
15	On average, middle managers here have five or more direct reports.	19
16	If the firm has a bad year, but a particular division has a good year, the division head would still get a bonus.	13
17	Besides pay, many other things motivate individuals to do a good job.	10

Building Blocks Decision rights · Information · Motivators · Structure

outdated sales data to make ineffective, tactical marketing decisions.

Within 18 months, the company was working in the new model. "This was a revolution that became a renaissance," Owens recalls, "a spectacular transformation of a kind of sluggish company into one that actually has entrepreneurial zeal. And that transition was very quick because it was decisive and it was complete; it was thorough; it was universal, worldwide, all at one time."

3. Once made, decisions are rarely second-guessed

Whether someone is second-guessing depends on your vantage point. A more senior and broader enterprise perspective can add value to a decision, but managers up the line may not be adding incremental value; instead, they may be stalling progress by redoing their subordinates' jobs while, in effect, shirking their own. In our research, 71% of respondents in weak-execution companies thought that decisions were being second-guessed, whereas only 45% of those from strong-execution organizations felt that way.

Recently, we worked with a global charitable organization dedicated to alleviating poverty. It had a problem others might envy: It was suffering from the strain brought on by a rapid growth in donations and a corresponding increase in the depth and breadth of its program offerings. As you might expect, this nonprofit was populated with people on a mission who took intense personal ownership of projects. It did not reward the delegation of even the most mundane administrative tasks. Country-level managers, for example, would personally oversee copier repairs. Managers' inability to delegate led to decision paralysis and a lack of accountability as the organization grew. Second-guessing was an art form. When there was doubt over who was empowered to make a decision, the default was often to have a series of meetings in which no decision was reached. When decisions were finally made, they had generally been vetted by so many parties that no one person could be held accountable. An effort to expedite decision-making through restructuring—by collocating key leaders with subject-matter experts in newly established central and regional centers of excellence—became instead another logjam. Key managers still weren't sure of their right to take advantage of these centers, so they didn't.

The nonprofit's management and directors went back to the drawing board. We worked with them to design a decision-making map, a tool to help identify where different types of decisions should be taken, and with it they clarified and enhanced decision rights at all levels of management. All managers were then actively encouraged to delegate standard operational tasks. Once people had a clear idea of what decisions they should and should not be making, holding them accountable for decisions felt fair. What's more, now they could focus their energies on the organization's mission. Clarifying decision rights and responsibilities also improved the organization's ability to track individual achievement, which helped it chart new and appealing career-advancement paths.

4. Information flows freely across organizational boundaries

When information does not flow horizontally across different parts of the company, units behave like silos, forfeiting economies of scale and the transfer of best practices. Moreover, the organization as a whole loses the opportunity to develop a cadre of up-and-coming managers well versed in all aspects of the company's operations. Our research indicates that only 21% of respondents from weak-execution companies thought information flowed freely across organizational boundaries whereas 55% of those from strong-execution firms did. Since scores for even the strong companies are pretty low, though, this is an issue that most companies can work on.

A cautionary tale comes from a business-to-business company whose customer and product teams failed to collaborate in serving a key segment: large, cross-product customers. To manage relationships with important clients, the company had established a customer-focused marketing group, which developed customer outreach programs, innovative pricing models, and tailored promotions and discounts. But this group issued no clear and consistent reports of its initiatives and progress to the product units and had difficulty securing time with the regular cross-unit management to discuss key performance issues. Each product unit communicated and planned in its own way, and it took tremendous energy for the customer group to understand the units' various priorities and tailor communications to each one. So the units were not aware, and had little faith, that this new division was making constructive inroads into a key customer segment. Conversely (and predictably), the customer team felt the units paid only perfunctory attention to its plans and couldn't get their cooperation on issues critical to multiproduct customers, such as potential trade-offs and volume discounts.

Historically, this lack of collaboration hadn't been a problem because the company had been the dominant player in a high-margin market. But as the market became more competitive, customers began to view the firm as unreliable and, generally, as a difficult supplier, and they became increasingly reluctant to enter into favorable relationships.

Once the issues became clear, though, the solution wasn't terribly complicated, involving little more than getting the groups to talk to one another. The customer division became responsible for issuing regular reports to the product units showing performance against targets, by product and geographic region, and for supplying a supporting root-cause analysis. A standing performance-management meeting was placed on the schedule every quarter, creating a forum for exchanging information face-to-face and discussing outstanding issues. These moves bred the broader organizational trust required for collaboration.

5. Field and line employees usually have the information they need to understand the bottom-line impact of their day-to-day choices

Rational decisions are necessarily bounded by the information available to employees. If managers don't understand what it will cost to capture an incremental dollar in revenue, they will always pursue the incremental revenue. They can hardly be faulted, even if their decision is—in the light of full information—wrong. Our research shows that 61% of individuals in strong-execution organizations agree that field and line employees have the information they need to understand the bottom-line impact of their decisions. This figure plummets to 28% in weak-execution organizations.

We saw this unhealthy dynamic play out at a large, diversified financial-services client, which had been built through a series of successful mergers of small regional banks. In combining operations, managers had chosen to separate front-office bankers who sold loans from back-office support groups who did risk assessments, placing each in a different reporting relationship and, in many cases, in different locations. Unfortunately, they failed to institute the necessary information and motivation links to ensure smooth operations. As a result, each pursued different, and often competing, goals.

For example, salespeople would routinely enter into highly customized one-off deals with clients that cost the company more than they made in revenues. Sales did not have a clear understanding of the cost and complexity implications of these transactions. Without sufficient information, sales staff believed that the back-end people were sabotaging their deals, while the support groups considered the front-end people to be cowboys. At year's end, when the data were finally reconciled, management would bemoan the sharp increase in operational costs, which often erased the profit from these transactions.

Executives addressed this information misalignment by adopting a "smart customization" approach to sales. They standardized the end-to-end processes used in the majority of deals and allowed for customization only in select circumstances. For these customized deals, they established clear back-office processes and analytical support tools to arm salespeople with accurate information on the cost implications of the proposed transactions. At the same time, they rolled out common reporting standards and tools for both the front- and back-office operations to ensure that each group had access to the same data and metrics when making decisions. Once each side understood the business realities confronted by the other, they cooperated more effectively, acting in the whole company's best interests—and there were no more year-end surprises.

About the Data

WE TESTED ORGANIZATIONAL effectiveness by having people fill out an online diagnostic, a tool comprising 19 questions (17 that describe organizational traits and two that describe outcomes).

To determine which of the 17 traits in our profiler are most strongly associated with excellence in execution, we looked at 31 companies in our database for which we had responses from at least 150 individual (anonymously completed) profiles, for a total of 26,743 responses. Applying regression analysis to each of the 31 data sets, we correlated the 17 traits with our measure of organizational effectiveness, which we defined as an affirmative response to the outcome statement, "Important strategic and operational decisions are quickly translated into action." Then we ranked the traits in order, according to the number of data sets in which the trait exhibited a significant correlation with our measure of success within a 90% confidence interval. Finally, we indexed the result to a 100-point scale. The top trait—"Everyone has a good idea of the decisions and actions for which he or she is responsible"—exhibited a significant positive correlation with our success indicator in 25 of the 31 data sets, for an index score of 81.

Creating a Transformation Program

The four building blocks that managers can use to improve strategy execution—decision rights, information, structure, and motivators—are inextricably linked. Unclear decision rights not only paralyze decision making but also impede information flow, divorce performance from rewards, and prompt workarounds that subvert formal reporting lines. Blocking information results in poor decisions, limited career development, and a reinforcement of structural silos. So what to do about it?

Since each organization is different and faces a unique set of internal and external variables, there is no universal answer to that question. The first step is to identify the sources of the problem. In our work, we often begin by having a company's employees take our profiling survey and consolidating the results. The more people in the organization who take the survey, the better.

Once executives understand their company's areas of weakness, they can take any number of actions. "Mapping improvements to the building blocks: Some sample tactics" shows 15 possible steps that can have an impact on performance. (The options listed represent only a sampling of the dozens of choices managers might make.) All of these actions are geared toward strengthening one or more of the 17 traits. For example, if you were to take steps to "clarify and streamline decision making" you could potentially strengthen two traits: "Everyone has a good idea of the decisions and actions for which he or she is responsible," and "Once made, decisions are rarely second-guessed."

You certainly wouldn't want to put 15 initiatives in a single transformation program. Most organizations don't have the managerial capacity or organizational appetite to take on more than five or six at a time. And as we've stressed, you should first take steps to address decision rights and information, and then design the necessary changes to motivators and structure to support the new design.

To help companies understand their shortcomings and construct the improvement program that will have the greatest impact, we have developed an organizational-change simulator. This interactive tool accompanies the profiler, allowing you to try out different elements of a change program virtually, to see which ones will best target your company's particular area of weakness. (For an overview of the simulation process, see the sidebar "Test Drive Your Organization's Transformation.")

To get a sense of the process from beginning to end—from taking the diagnostic profiler, to formulating your strategy, to launching your organizational transformation—consider the experience of a leading insurance company we'll call Goodward Insurance. Goodward was a successful company with strong capital reserves and steady revenue and customer growth. Still, its leadership wanted to further enhance execution to deliver on an ambitious five-year strategic agenda that included aggressive targets in customer growth, revenue increases, and cost reduction, which would require a new level of teamwork. While there were pockets of cross-unit collaboration within the company, it was far more common for each unit to focus on its own goals, making it difficult to spare resources to support another unit's goals. In many cases there was little

Mapping improvements to the building blocks: some sample tactics

Companies can take a host of steps to improve their ability to execute strategy. The 15 here are only some of the possible examples. Every one strengthens one or more of the building blocks executives can use to improve their strategy-execution capability: clarifying decision rights, improving information, establishing the right motivators, and restructuring the organization.

■ Focus corporate staff on supporting business-unit decision making.

■ Clarify and streamline decision making at each operating level.

■ Focus headquarters on important strategic questions.

■ ■ Create centers of excellence by consolidating similar functions into a single organizational unit.

■ ■ ■ Assign process owners to coordinate activities that span organizational functions.

■ ■ Establish individual performance measures.

■ Improve field-to-headquarters information flow.

■ Define and distribute daily operating metrics to the field or line.

■ ■ Create cross-functional teams.

■ Introduce differentiating performance awards.

■ Expand nonmonetary rewards to recognize exceptional performers.

■ ■ Increase position tenure.

■ ■ Institute lateral moves and rotations.

■ Broaden spans of control.

Building blocks ■ Decision rights ■ Information ■ Motivators ■ Structure

incentive to do so anyway: Unit A's goals might require the involvement of Unit B to succeed, but Unit B's goals might not include supporting Unit A's effort.

The company had initiated a number of enterprisewide projects over the years, which had been completed on time and on budget, but these often had to be reworked because stakeholder needs hadn't been sufficiently taken into account. After launching a shared-services center, for example, the company had to revisit its operating model and processes when units began hiring shadow staff to focus on priority work that the center wouldn't expedite. The center might decide what technology applications, for instance, to develop on its own rather than set priorities according to what was most important to the organization.

In a similar way, major product launches were hindered by insufficient coordination among departments. The marketing department would develop new coverage options without asking the claims-processing group whether it had the ability to process the claims. Since it didn't, processors had to create expensive manual work-arounds when the new kinds of claims started pouring in. Nor did marketing ask the actuarial department how these products would affect the risk profile and reimbursement expenses of the company, and for some of the new products, costs did indeed increase.

To identify the greatest barriers to building a stronger execution culture, Goodward Insurance gave the diagnostic survey to all of its 7,000-plus employees and compared the organization's scores on the 17 traits with those from strong-execution companies. Numerous previous surveys (employee-satisfaction, among others) had elicited qualitative comments identifying the barriers to execution excellence. But the diagnostic survey gave the company quantifiable data that it could analyze by group and by management level to determine which barriers were most hindering the people actually charged with execution. As it turned out, middle management was far more pessimistic than the top executives in their assessment of the organization's execution ability. Their input became especially critical to the change agenda ultimately adopted.

Through the survey, Goodward Insurance uncovered impediments to execution in three of the most influential organizational traits:

Information did not flow freely across organizational boundaries. Sharing information was never one of Goodward's hallmarks, but managers had always dismissed the mounting anecdotal evidence of poor cross-divisional information flow as "some other group's problem." The organizational diagnostic data, however, exposed such plausible deniability as an inadequate excuse. In fact, when the CEO reviewed the profiler results with his direct reports, he held up the chart on cross-group information flows and declared, "We've been discussing this problem for several years, and yet you always say that it's so-and-so's problem, not mine. Sixty-seven percent of [our] respondents said that they do not think information flows freely across divisions. This is not so-and-so's problem—it's our problem. You just don't get results that low [unless it comes] from everywhere. We are all on the hook for fixing this."

Contributing to this lack of horizontal information flow was a dearth of lateral promotions. Because Goodward had always promoted up rather than over and up, most middle and senior managers remained within a single group. They were not adequately apprised of the activities of the other groups, nor did they have a network of contacts across the organization.

Important information about the competitive environment did not get to headquarters quickly. The diagnostic data and subsequent surveys and interviews with middle management revealed that the wrong information was moving up the org chart. Mundane day-to-day decisions were escalated to the executive level—the top team had to approve midlevel hiring decisions, for instance, and bonuses of $1,000—limiting Goodward's agility in responding to competitors' moves, customers' needs, and changes in the broader marketplace. Meanwhile, more important information was so heavily filtered as it moved up the hierarchy that it was all but worthless for rendering key verdicts. Even if lower-level managers knew that a certain project could never work for highly valid reasons, they would not

Test-Drive Your Organization's Transformation

YOU KNOW YOUR ORGANIZATION could perform better. You are faced with dozens of levers you could conceivably pull if you had unlimited time and resources. But you don't. You operate in the real world.

How, then, do you make the most-educated and cost-efficient decisions about which change initiatives to implement? We've developed a way to test the efficacy of specific actions (such as clarifying decision rights, forming cross-functional teams, or expanding nonmonetary rewards) without risking significant amounts of time and money. You can go to www.simulator-orgeffectiveness.com to assemble and try out various five-step organizational-change programs and assess which would be the most effective and efficient in improving execution at your company.

You begin the simulation by selecting one of seven organizational profiles that most resembles the current state of your organization. If you're not sure, you can take a five-minute diagnostic survey. This online survey automatically generates an organizational profile and baseline execution-effectiveness score. (Although 100 is a perfect score, nobody is perfect; even the most effective companies often score in the 60s and 70s.)

Having established your baseline, you use the simulator to chart a possible course you'd like to take to improve your execution capabilities by selecting five out of a possible 28 actions. Ideally, these moves should directly address the weakest links in your organizational profile. To help you make the right choices, the simulator offers insights that shed further light on how a proposed action influences particular organizational elements.

Once you have made your selections, the simulator executes the steps you've elected and processes them through a web-based engine that evaluates them using empirical relationships identified from 31 companies representing more than 26,000 data observations. It then generates a bar chart indicating how much your organization's execution score has improved and where it now

communicate that dim view to the top team. Nonstarters not only started, they kept going. For instance, the company had a project under way to create new incentives for its brokers. Even though this approach had been previously tried without success, no one spoke up in meetings or stopped the project because it was a priority for one of the top-team members.

stands in relation to the highest-performing companies from our research and the scores of other people like you who have used the simulator starting from the same original profile you did. If you wish, you may then advance to the next round and pick another five actions. What you will see is illustrated below.

The beauty of the simulator is its ability to consider—consequence-free—the impact on execution of endless combinations of possible actions. Each simulation includes only two rounds, but you can run the simulation as many times as you like. The simulator has also been used for team competition within organizations, and we've found that it engenders very engaging and productive dialogue among senior executives.

While the simulator cannot capture all of the unique situations an organization might face, it is a useful tool for assessing and building a targeted and effective organization-transformation program. It serves as a vehicle to stimulate thinking about the impact of various changes, saving untold amounts of time and resources in the process.

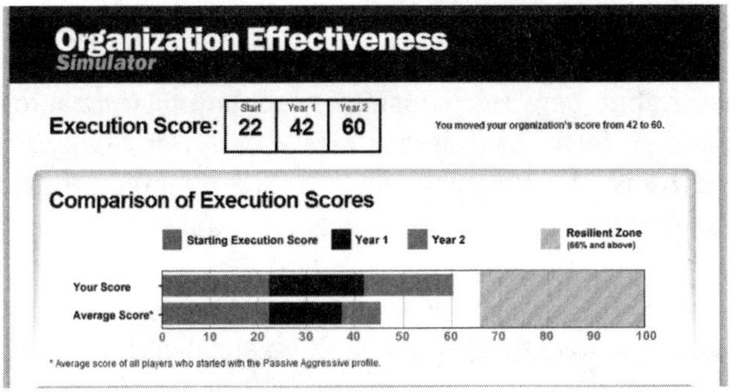

No one had a good idea of the decisions and actions for which he or she was responsible. The general lack of information flow extended to decision rights, as few managers understood where their authority ended and another's began. Accountability even for day-to-day decisions was unclear, and managers did not know whom to ask for clarification. Naturally, confusion over decision rights led to second-guessing. Fifty-five percent of respondents felt that decisions were regularly second-guessed at Goodward.

To Goodward's credit, its top executives immediately responded to the results of the diagnostic by launching a change program targeted at all three problem areas. The program integrated early, often symbolic, changes with longer-term initiatives, in an effort to build momentum and galvanize participation and ownership. Recognizing that a passive-aggressive attitude toward people perceived to be in power solely as a result of their position in the hierarchy was hindering information flow, they took immediate steps to signal their intention to create a more informal and open culture. One symbolic change: the seating at management meetings was rearranged. The top executives used to sit in a separate section, the physical space between them and the rest of the room fraught with symbolism. Now they intermingled, making themselves more accessible and encouraging people to share information informally. Regular brown-bag lunches were established with members of the C-suite, where people had a chance to discuss the overall culture-change initiative, decision rights, new mechanisms for communicating across the units, and so forth. Seating at these events was highly choreographed to ensure that a mix of units was represented at each table. Icebreaker activities were designed to encourage individuals to learn about other units' work.

Meanwhile, senior managers commenced the real work of remedying issues relating to information flows and decision rights. They assessed their own informal networks to understand how people making key decisions got their information, and they identified critical gaps. The outcome was a new framework for making important decisions that clearly specifies who owns each decision, who must provide input, who is ultimately accountable for the results, and how results are defined. Other longer-term initiatives include:

- Pushing certain decisions down into the organization to better align decision rights with the best available information. Most hiring and bonus decisions, for instance, have been delegated to immediate managers, so long as they are within preestablished boundaries relating to numbers hired and salary levels. Being clear about who needs what information is encouraging cross-group dialogue.

- Identifying and eliminating duplicative committees.
- Pushing metrics and scorecards down to the group level, so that rather than focus on solving the mystery of *who* caused a problem, management can get right to the root cause of *why* the problem occurred. A well-designed scorecard captures not only outcomes (like sales volume or revenue) but also leading indicators of those outcomes (such as the number of customer calls or completed customer plans). As a result, the focus of management conversations has shifted from trying to explain the past to charting the future—anticipating and preventing problems.
- Making the planning process more inclusive. Groups are explicitly mapping out the ways their initiatives depend on and affect one another; shared group goals are assigned accordingly.
- Enhancing the middle management career path to emphasize the importance of lateral moves to career advancement.

Goodward Insurance has just embarked on this journey. The insurer has distributed ownership of these initiatives among various groups and management levels so that these efforts don't become silos in themselves. Already, solid improvement in the company's execution is beginning to emerge. The early evidence of success has come from employee-satisfaction surveys: Middle management responses to the questions about levels of cross-unit collaboration and clarity of decision making have improved as much as 20 to 25 percentage points. And high performers are already reaching across boundaries to gain a broader understanding of the full business, even if it doesn't mean a better title right away.

Execution is a notorious and perennial challenge. Even at the companies that are best at it—what we call "resilient organizations"—just two-thirds of employees agree that important strategic and operational decisions are quickly translated into action. As long as companies continue to attack their execution problems primarily or solely with structural or motivational initiatives, they will continue to fail. As we've seen, they may enjoy short-term results, but they will inevitably slip back into old habits because they won't have addressed the root causes of failure. Such failures can almost always be fixed by ensuring that people truly understand what they are responsible for and who makes which decisions—and then giving them the information they need to fulfill their responsibilities. With these two building blocks in place, structural and motivational elements will follow.

Originally published in June 2008. Reprint R0806C.

Notes

1. The details for this example have been taken from Gary L. Neilson and Bruce A. Pasternack, *Results: Keep What's Good, Fix What's Wrong, and Unlock Great Performance* (Random House, 2005).

Using the Balanced Scorecard as a Strategic Management System

by Robert S. Kaplan and David P. Norton

AS COMPANIES AROUND the world transform themselves for competition that is based on information, their ability to exploit intangible assets has become far more decisive than their ability to invest in and manage physical assets. Several years ago, in recognition of this change, we introduced a concept we called the *balanced scorecard*. The balanced scorecard supplemented traditional financial measures with criteria that measured performance from three additional perspectives—those of customers, internal business processes, and learning and growth. (See "Translating vision and strategy: Four perspectives.") It therefore enabled companies to track financial results while simultaneously monitoring progress in building the capabilities and acquiring the intangible assets they would need for future growth. The scorecard wasn't a replacement for financial measures; it was their complement.

Recently, we have seen some companies move beyond our early vision for the scorecard to discover its value as the cornerstone of a new strategic management system. Used this way, the scorecard addresses a serious deficiency in traditional management systems: their inability to link a company's long-term strategy with its short-term actions.

Most companies' operational and management control systems are built around financial measures and targets, which bear little relation to the company's progress in achieving long-term strategic objectives. Thus the emphasis most companies place on short-term financial measures leaves a gap between the development of a strategy and its implementation.

Managers using the balanced scorecard do not have to rely on short-term financial measures as the sole indicators of the company's performance. The scorecard lets them introduce four new management processes that, separately and in combination, contribute to linking long-term strategic objectives with short-term actions. (See "Managing strategy: Four processes.")

The first new process—*translating the vision*—helps managers build a consensus around the organization's vision and strategy. Despite the best intentions of those at the top, lofty statements about becoming "best in class," "the number one supplier," or an "empowered organization" don't translate easily into operational terms that provide useful guides to action at the local level. For people to act on the words in vision and strategy statements, those statements must be expressed as an integrated set of objectives and measures, agreed upon by all senior executives, that describe the long-term drivers of success.

The second process—*communicating and linking*—lets managers communicate their strategy up and down the organization and link it to departmental and individual objectives. Traditionally, departments are evaluated by their financial performance, and individual incentives are tied to short-term financial goals. The scorecard gives managers a way of ensuring that all levels of the organization understand the long-term strategy and that both departmental and individual objectives are aligned with it.

The third process—*business planning*—enables companies to integrate their business and financial plans. Almost all organizations today are implementing a variety of change programs, each with its own champions, gurus, and consultants, and each competing for

Idea in Brief

Why do budgets often bear little direct relation to a company's long-term strategic objectives? Because they don't take enough into consideration. A balanced scorecard augments traditional financial measures with benchmarks for performance in three key nonfinancial areas:

- a company's relationship with its customers
- its key internal processes
- its learning and growth.

When performance measures for these areas are added to the financial metrics, the result is not only a broader perspective on the company's health and activities, it's also a powerful organizing framework. A sophisticated instrument panel for coordinating and fine-tuning a company's operations and businesses so that all activities are aligned with its strategy.

senior executives' time, energy, and resources. Managers find it difficult to integrate those diverse initiatives to achieve their strategic goals—a situation that leads to frequent disappointments with the programs' results. But when managers use the ambitious goals set for balanced scorecard measures as the basis for allocating resources and setting priorities, they can undertake and coordinate only those initiatives that move them toward their long-term strategic objectives.

The fourth process—*feedback and learning*—gives companies the capacity for what we call strategic learning. Existing feedback and review processes focus on whether the company, its departments, or its individual employees have met their budgeted financial goals. With the balanced scorecard at the center of its management systems, a company can monitor short-term results from the three additional perspectives—customers, internal business processes, and learning and growth—and evaluate strategy in the light of recent performance. The scorecard thus enables companies to modify strategies to reflect real-time learning.

Idea in Practice

The balanced scorecard relies on four processes to bind short-term activities to long-term objectives:

1. Translating the Vision

By relying on measurement, the scorecard forces managers to come to agreement on the metrics they will use to operationalize their lofty visions.

Example: A bank had articulated its strategy as providing "superior service to targeted customers." But the process of choosing operational measures for the four areas of the scorecard made executives realize that they first needed to reconcile divergent views of who the targeted customers were and what constituted superior service.

2. Communicating and Linking

When a scorecard is disseminated up and down the organizational chart, strategy becomes a tool available to everyone. As the high-level scorecard cascades down to individual business units, overarching strategic objectives and measures are translated into objectives and measures appropriate to each particular group. Tying these targets to individual performance and compensation systems yields "personal scorecards." Thus, individual employees understand how their own productivity supports the overall strategy.

None of the more than 100 organizations that we have studied or with which we have worked implemented their first balanced scorecard with the intention of developing a new strategic management system. But in each one, the senior executives discovered that the scorecard supplied a framework and thus a focus for many critical management processes: departmental and individual goal setting, business planning, capital allocations, strategic initiatives, and feedback and learning. Previously, those processes were uncoordinated and often directed at short-term operational goals. By building the scorecard, the senior executives started a process of change that has gone well beyond the original idea of simply broadening the company's performance measures.

For example, one insurance company—let's call it National Insurance—developed its first balanced scorecard to create a new vision for itself as an underwriting specialist. But once National started to

3. Business Planning

Most companies have separate procedures (and sometimes units) for strategic planning and budgeting. Little wonder, then, that typical long-term planning is, in the words of one executive, where "the rubber meets the sky." The discipline of creating a balanced scorecard forces companies to integrate the two functions, thereby ensuring that financial budgets do indeed support strategic goals. After agreeing on performance measures for the four scorecard perspectives, companies identify the most influential "drivers" of the desired outcomes and then set milestones for gauging the progress they make with these drivers.

4. Feedback and Learning

By supplying a mechanism for strategic feedback and review, the balanced scorecard helps an organization foster a kind of learning often missing in companies: the ability to reflect on inferences and adjust theories about cause-and-effect relationships.

Feedback about products and services. New learning about key internal processes. Technological discoveries. All this information can be fed into the scorecard, enabling strategic refinements to be made continually. Thus, at any point in the implementation, managers can know whether the strategy is working—and if not, why.

use it, the scorecard allowed the CEO and the senior management team not only to introduce a new strategy for the organization but also to overhaul the company's management system. The CEO subsequently told employees in a letter addressed to the whole organization that National would thenceforth use the balanced scorecard and the philosophy that it represented to manage the business.

National built its new strategic management system step-by-step over 30 months, with each step representing an incremental improvement. (See "How one company built a strategic management system . . .") The iterative sequence of actions enabled the company to reconsider each of the four new management processes two or three times before the system stabilized and became an established part of National's overall management system. Thus the CEO was able to transform the company so that everyone could focus on

Translation vision and strategy: four perspectives

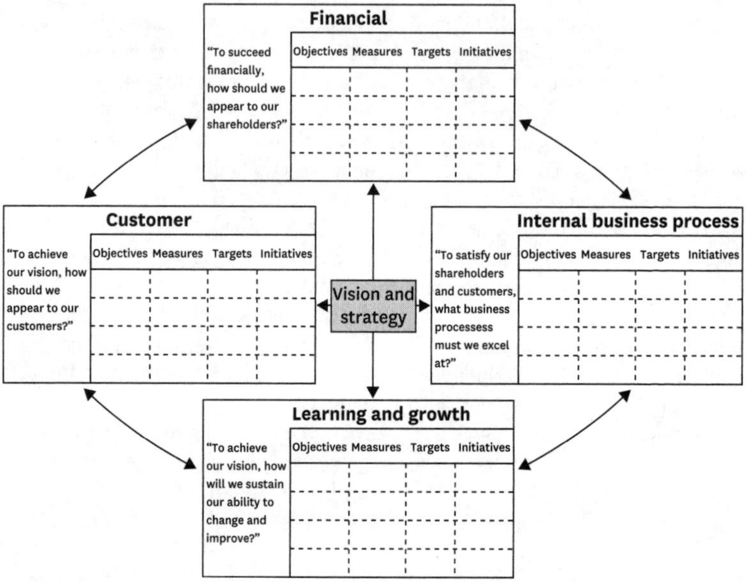

achieving long-term strategic objectives—something that no purely financial framework could do.

Translating the Vision

The CEO of an engineering construction company, after working with his senior management team for several months to develop a mission statement, got a phone call from a project manager in the field. "I want you to know," the distraught manager said, "that I believe in the mission statement. I want to act in accordance with the mission statement. I'm here with my customer. What am I supposed to do?"

Managing strategy: four processes

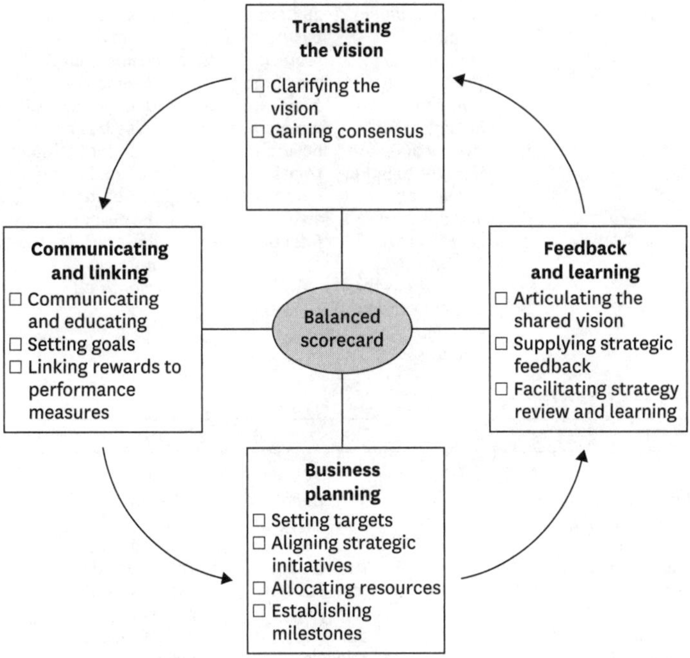

The mission statement, like those of many other organizations, had declared an intention to "use high-quality employees to provide services that surpass customers' needs." But the project manager in the field with his employees and his customer did not know how to translate those words into the appropriate actions. The phone call convinced the CEO that a large gap existed between the mission statement and employees' knowledge of how their day-to-day actions could contribute to realizing the company's vision.

Metro Bank (not its real name), the result of a merger of two competitors, encountered a similar gap while building its balanced scorecard. The senior executive group thought it had reached

How one company built a strategic management system . . .

Time frame *(in months)*

0	1	2	3	4	5	6	7	8	9	10	11	12

Actions:

1 *Clarify the vision.* Ten members of a newly formed executive team work together for three months. A balanced scorecard is developed to translate a generic vision into a strategy that is understood and can be communicated. The process helps build consensus and commitment to the strategy.

2A *Communicate to middle managers.* The top three layers of management (100 people) are brought together to learn about and discuss the new strategy. The balanced scorecard is the communication vehicle. *(months 4–5)*

2B *Develop business unit scorecards.* Using the corporate scorecard as a template, each business unit translates its strategy into its own scorecard. *(months 6–9)*

3A *Eliminate nonstrategic investments.* The corporate scorecard, by clarifying strategic priorities, identifies many active programs that are not contributing to the strategy. *(month 6)*

3B *Launch corporate change programs.* The corporate scorecard identifies the need for cross-business change programs. They are launched while the business units prepare their scorecards. *(month 6)*

4 *Review business unit scorecards.* The CEO and the executive team review the individual business units' scorecards. The review permits the CEO to participate knowledgeably in shaping business unit strategy. *(months 9–11)*

5 *Refine the vision.* The review of business unit scorecards identifies several cross-business issues not initially included in the corporate strategy. The corporate scorecard is updated. *(month 12)*

7 *Update long-range plan and budget*. Five-year goals are established for each measure. The investments required to meet those goals are identified and funded. The first year of the five-year plan becomes the annual budget. *(months 15–17)*

9 *Conduct annual strategy review*. At the start of the third year, the initial strategy has been achieved and the corporate strategy requires updating. The executive committee lists ten strategic issues. Each business unit is asked to develop a position on each issue as a prelude to updating its strategy and scorecard. *(months 25–26)*

13	14	15	16	17	18	19	20	21	22	23	24	25	26

6A *Communicate the balanced scorecard to the entire company*. At the end of one year, when the management teams are comfortable with the strategic approach, the scorecard is disseminated to the entire organization. *(month 12–ongoing)*

6B *Establish individual performance objectives*. The top three layers of management link their individual objectives and incentive compensation to their scorecards. *(months 13–14)*

8 *Conduct monthly and quarterly reviews*. After corporate approval of the business unit scorecards, a monthly review process, supplemented by quarterly reviews that focus more heavily on strategic issues, begins. *(month 18–ongoing)*

10 *Link everyone's performance to the balanced scorecard*. All employees are asked to link their individual objectives to the balanced scorecard. The entire organization's incentive compensation is linked to the scorecard. *(months 25–26)*

Note: Steps 7, 8, 9, and 10 are performed on a regular schedule. The balanced scorecard is now a routine part of the management process.

. . . around the balanced scorecard

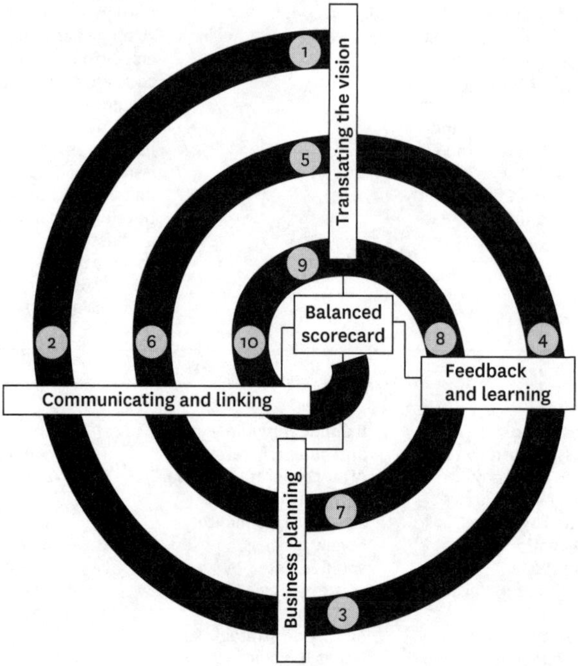

agreement on the new organization's overall strategy: "to provide superior service to targeted customers." Research had revealed five basic market segments among existing and potential customers, each with different needs. While formulating the measures for the customer-perspective portion of their balanced scorecard, however, it became apparent that although the 25 senior executives agreed on the words of the strategy, each one had a different definition of *superior service* and a different image of the *targeted customers*.

The exercise of developing operational measures for the four perspectives on the bank's scorecard forced the 25 executives to clarify the meaning of the strategy statement. Ultimately, they agreed to stimulate revenue growth through new products and services and also agreed on the three most desirable customer segments. They developed scorecard measures for the specific products and services that should be delivered to customers in the targeted segments as well as for the relationship the bank should build with customers in each segment. The scorecard also highlighted gaps in employees' skills and in information systems that the bank would have to close in order to deliver the selected value propositions to the targeted customers. Thus, creating a balanced scorecard forced the bank's senior managers to arrive at a consensus and then to translate their vision into terms that had meaning to the people who would realize the vision.

Communicating and Linking

"The top ten people in the business now understand the strategy better than ever before. It's too bad," a senior executive of a major oil company complained, "that we can't put this in a bottle so that everyone could share it." With the balanced scorecard, he can.

One company we have worked with deliberately involved three layers of management in the creation of its balanced scorecard. The senior executive group formulated the financial and customer objectives. It then mobilized the talent and information in the next two levels of managers by having them formulate the internal-business-process and learning-and-growth objectives that would drive the achievement of the financial and customer goals. For example, knowing the importance of satisfying customers' expectations of on-time delivery, the broader group identified several internal business processes—such as order processing, scheduling, and fulfillment—in which the company had to excel. To do so, the company would have to retrain frontline employees and improve the information systems available to them. The group developed performance measures for those critical processes and for staff and systems capabilities.

Broad participation in creating a scorecard takes longer, but it offers several advantages: Information from a larger number of managers is incorporated into the internal objectives; the managers gain a better understanding of the company's long-term strategic goals; and such broad participation builds a stronger commitment to achieving those goals. But getting managers to buy into the scorecard is only a first step in linking individual actions to corporate goals.

The balanced scorecard signals to everyone what the organization is trying to achieve for shareholders and customers alike. But to align employees' individual performances with the overall strategy, scorecard users generally engage in three activities: communicating and educating, setting goals, and linking rewards to performance measures.

Communicating and educating

Implementing a strategy begins with educating those who have to execute it. Whereas some organizations opt to hold their strategy close to the vest, most believe that they should disseminate it from top to bottom. A broad-based communication program shares with all employees the strategy and the critical objectives they have to meet if the strategy is to succeed. Onetime events such as the distribution of brochures or newsletters and the holding of "town meetings" might kick off the program. Some organizations post bulletin boards that illustrate and explain the balanced scorecard measures, then update them with monthly results. Others use groupware and electronic bulletin boards to distribute the scorecard to the desktops of all employees and to encourage dialogue about the measures. The same media allow employees to make suggestions for achieving or exceeding the targets.

The balanced scorecard, as the embodiment of business unit strategy, should also be communicated upward in the organization—to corporate headquarters and to the corporate board of directors. With the scorecard, business units can quantify and communicate their long-term strategies to senior executives using a comprehensive set of linked financial and nonfinancial measures. Such communication informs the executives and the board in specific terms that long-term strategies designed for competitive success are in place. The measures also provide the basis for feedback and accountability. Meeting short-term financial targets should not constitute satisfactory performance when other measures indicate that the long-term strategy is either not working or not being implemented well.

Should the balanced scorecard be communicated beyond the boardroom to external shareholders? We believe that as senior executives gain confidence in the ability of the scorecard measures to monitor strategic performance and predict future financial performance, they will find ways to inform outside investors about those measures without disclosing competitively sensitive information.

Skandia, an insurance and financial services company based in Sweden, issues a supplement to its annual report called "The Business Navigator"—"an instrument to help us navigate into the future and thereby stimulate renewal and development." The supplement describes Skandia's strategy and the strategic measures the company uses to communicate and evaluate the strategy. It also provides a report on the company's performance along those measures during the year. The measures are customized for each operating unit and include, for example, market share, customer satisfaction and retention, employee competence, employee empowerment, and technology deployment.

Communicating the balanced scorecard promotes commitment and accountability to the business's long-term strategy. As one executive at Metro Bank declared, "The balanced scorecard is both motivating and obligating."

Setting goals

Mere awareness of corporate goals, however, is not enough to change many people's behavior. Somehow, the organization's high-level strategic objectives and measures must be translated into objectives and measures for operating units and individuals.

The exploration group of a large oil company developed a technique to enable and encourage individuals to set goals for themselves that were consistent with the organization's. It created a small, fold-up, personal scorecard that people could carry in their shirt pockets or wallets. (See "The personal scorecard.") The scorecard contains three levels of information. The first describes corporate objectives, measures, and targets. The second leaves room for translating corporate targets into targets for each business unit. For the third level, the company asks both individuals and teams to articulate which of their own objectives would be consistent with the business unit and corporate objectives, as well as what initiatives they would take to achieve their objectives. It also asks them to define up to five performance measures for their objectives and to set targets for each measure. The personal scorecard helps to communicate corporate and business unit objectives to the people and teams performing the work, enabling them to translate the objectives into meaningful tasks and targets for themselves. It also lets them keep that information close at hand—in their pockets.

Linking rewards to performance measures

Should compensation systems be linked to balanced scorecard measures? Some companies, believing that tying financial compensation to performance is a powerful lever, have moved quickly to establish such a linkage. For example, an oil company that we'll call Pioneer Petroleum uses its scorecard as the sole basis for computing incentive compensation. The company ties 60% of its executives' bonuses to their achievement of ambitious targets for a weighted average of four financial indicators: return on capital, profitability, cash flow, and operating cost. It bases the remaining 40% on indicators of customer satisfaction, dealer satisfaction, employee satisfaction, and environmental responsibility (such as a percentage change in the level of emissions to water and air). Pioneer's CEO says that linking compensation to the scorecard has helped to align the company with its strategy. "I know of no competitor," he says, "who has this degree of alignment. It is producing results for us."

As attractive and as powerful as such linkage is, it nonetheless carries risks. For instance, does the company have the right measures on the scorecard? Does it have valid and reliable data for the selected

The personal scorecard

Corporate objectives

- ☐ Double our corporate value in seven years.
- ☐ Increase our earnings by an average of 20% per year.
- ☐ Achieve an internal rate of return 2% above the cost of capital.
- ☐ Increase both production and reserves by 20% in the next decade.

Corporate targets					Scorecard measures	Business unit targets					Team/individual objectives and initiatives
1995	1996	1997	1998	1999		1995	1996	1997	1998	1999	1.
					Financial						
100	120	160	180	250	Earnings (in $ millions)						
100	450	200	210	225	Net cash flow						
100	85	80	75	70	Overhead and operating expenses						2.
					Operating						
100	75	73	70	64	Production costs per barrel						
100	97	93	90	82	Development costs per barrel						
100	105	108	108	110	Total annual production						3.
Team/individual measures						**Targets**					
1.											
2.											
3.											4.
4.											
5.											
Name:											
Location:											5.

measures? Could unintended or unexpected consequences arise from the way the targets for the measures are achieved? Those are questions that companies should ask.

Furthermore, companies traditionally handle multiple objectives in a compensation formula by assigning weights to each objective and calculating incentive compensation by the extent to which each weighted objective was achieved. This practice permits substantial incentive compensation to be paid if the business unit overachieves on a few objectives even if it falls far short on others. A better approach would be to establish minimum threshold levels for a critical subset of the strategic measures. Individuals would earn no incentive compensation if performance in a given period fell short of any threshold. This requirement should motivate people to achieve a more balanced performance across short- and long-term objectives.

Some organizations, however, have reduced their emphasis on short-term, formula-based incentive systems as a result of introducing the balanced scorecard. They have discovered that dialogue among executives and managers about the scorecard—both the formulation of the measures and objectives and the explanation of actual versus targeted results—provides a better opportunity to observe managers' performance and abilities. Increased knowledge of their managers' abilities makes it easier for executives to set incentive rewards subjectively and to defend those subjective evaluations—a process that is less susceptible to the game playing and distortions associated with explicit, formula-based rules.

One company we have studied takes an intermediate position. It bases bonuses for business unit managers on two equally weighted criteria: their achievement of a financial objective—economic value added—over a three-year period and a subjective assessment of their performance on measures drawn from the customer, internal-business-process, and learning-and-growth perspectives of the balanced scorecard.

That the balanced scorecard has a role to play in the determination of incentive compensation is not in doubt. Precisely what that role should be will become clearer as more companies experiment with linking rewards to scorecard measures.

Business Planning

"Where the rubber meets the sky": That's how one senior executive describes his company's long-range-planning process. He might have said the same of many other companies because their financially based management systems fail to link change programs and resource allocation to long-term strategic priorities.

The problem is that most organizations have separate procedures and organizational units for strategic planning and for resource allocation and budgeting. To formulate their strategic plans, senior executives go off-site annually and engage for several days in active discussions facilitated by senior planning and development managers or external consultants. The outcome of this exercise is a strategic plan articulating where the company expects (or hopes or prays) to be in three, five, and ten years. Typically, such plans then sit on executives' bookshelves for the next 12 months.

Meanwhile, a separate resource-allocation and budgeting process run by the finance staff sets financial targets for revenues, expenses, profits, and investments for the next fiscal year. The budget it produces consists almost entirely of financial numbers that generally bear little relation to the targets in the strategic plan.

Which document do corporate managers discuss in their monthly and quarterly meetings during the following year? Usually only the budget, because the periodic reviews focus on a comparison of actual and budgeted results for every line item. When is the strategic plan next discussed? Probably during the next annual off-site meeting, when the senior managers draw up a new set of three-, five-, and ten-year plans.

The very exercise of creating a balanced scorecard forces companies to integrate their strategic planning and budgeting processes and therefore helps to ensure that their budgets support their strategies. Scorecard users select measures of progress from all four scorecard perspectives and set targets for each of them. Then they determine which actions will drive them toward their targets, identify the measures they will apply to those drivers from the four perspectives, and establish the short-term milestones that will mark their progress along the strategic paths they have selected. Building a scorecard thus enables a company to link its financial budgets with its strategic goals.

For example, one division of the Style Company (not its real name) committed to achieving a seemingly impossible goal articulated by the CEO: to double revenues in five years. The forecasts built into the organization's existing strategic plan fell $1 billion short of this objective. The division's managers, after considering various scenarios, agreed to specific increases in five different performance drivers: the number of new stores opened, the number of new customers attracted into new and existing stores, the percentage of shoppers in each store converted into actual purchasers, the portion of existing customers retained, and average sales per customer.

By helping to define the key drivers of revenue growth and by committing to targets for each of them, the division's managers eventually grew comfortable with the CEO's ambitious goal.

The process of building a balanced scorecard—clarifying the strategic objectives and then identifying the few critical drivers—also creates a framework for managing an organization's various change programs. These initiatives—reengineering, employee empowerment, time-based management, and total quality management, among others—promise to deliver results but also compete with one another for scarce resources, including the scarcest resource of all: senior managers' time and attention.

Shortly after the merger that created it, Metro Bank, for example, launched more than 70 different initiatives. The initiatives were intended to produce a more competitive and successful institution, but they were inadequately integrated into the overall strategy. After building their balanced scorecard, Metro Bank's managers dropped many of those programs—such as a marketing effort directed at individuals with very high net worth—and consolidated others into initiatives that were better aligned with the company's strategic objectives. For example, the managers replaced a program aimed at enhancing existing low-level selling skills with a major initiative aimed at retraining salespersons to become trusted financial advisers, capable of selling a broad range of newly introduced products to the three selected customer segments. The bank made both changes because the scorecard enabled it to gain a better understanding of the programs required to achieve its strategic objectives.

Once the strategy is defined and the drivers are identified, the scorecard influences managers to concentrate on improving or reengineering those processes most critical to the organization's strategic success. That is how the scorecard most clearly links and aligns action with strategy.

The final step in linking strategy to actions is to establish specific short-term targets, or milestones, for the balanced scorecard measures. Milestones are tangible expressions of managers' beliefs about when and to what degree their current programs will affect those measures.

In establishing milestones, managers are expanding the traditional budgeting process to incorporate strategic as well as financial goals. Detailed financial planning remains important, but financial goals taken by themselves ignore the three other balanced scorecard perspectives. In an integrated planning and budgeting process, executives continue to budget for short-term financial performance, but they also introduce short-term targets for measures in the customer, internal-business-process, and learning-and-growth perspectives. With those milestones established, managers can continually test both the theory underlying the strategy and the strategy's implementation.

At the end of the business-planning process, managers should have set targets for the long-term objectives they would like to achieve in all four scorecard perspectives; they should have identified the strategic initiatives required and allocated the necessary resources to those initiatives; and they should have established milestones for the measures that mark progress toward achieving their strategic goals.

Feedback and Learning

"With the balanced scorecard," a CEO of an engineering company told us, "I can continually test my strategy. It's like performing real-time research." That is exactly the capability that the scorecard should give senior managers: the ability to know at any point in its implementation whether the strategy they have formulated is, in fact, working, and if not, why.

The first three management processes—translating the vision, communicating and linking, and business planning—are vital for implementing strategy, but they are not sufficient in an unpredictable world. Together they form an important single-loop-learning process—single-loop in the sense that the objective remains constant, and any departure from the planned trajectory is seen as a defect to be remedied. This single-loop process does not require or even facilitate reexamination of either the strategy or the techniques used to implement it in light of current conditions.

Most companies today operate in a turbulent environment with complex strategies that, though valid when they were launched, may lose their validity as business conditions change. In this kind of environment, where new threats and opportunities arise constantly, companies must become capable of what Chris Argyris calls *double-loop learning*—learning that produces a change in people's assumptions and theories about cause-and-effect relationships. (See "Teaching Smart People How to Learn," HBR May–June 1991.)

Budget reviews and other financially based management tools cannot engage senior executives in double-loop learning—first, because these tools address performance from only one perspective, and second, because they don't involve strategic learning. Strategic learning consists of gathering feedback, testing the hypotheses on which strategy was based, and making the necessary adjustments.

The balanced scorecard supplies three elements that are essential to strategic learning. First, it articulates the company's shared vision, defining in clear and operational terms the results that the company, as a team, is trying to achieve. The scorecard communicates a holistic model that links individual efforts and accomplishments to business unit objectives.

Second, the scorecard supplies the essential strategic feedback system. A business strategy can be viewed as a set of hypotheses about cause-and-effect relationships. A strategic feedback system should be able to test, validate, and modify the hypotheses embedded in a business unit's strategy. By establishing short-term goals, or milestones, within the business-planning process, executives are forecasting the relationship between changes in performance drivers and the associated changes in one or more specified goals. For example, executives at Metro Bank estimated the amount of time it would take for improvements in training and in the availability of information systems before employees could sell multiple financial products effectively to existing and new customers. They also estimated how great the effect of that selling capability would be.

Another organization attempted to validate its hypothesized cause-and-effect relationships in the balanced scorecard by measuring the strength of the linkages among measures in the different perspectives. (See the exhibit "How one company linked measures from the four perspectives.") The company found significant correlations between employees' morale, a measure in the learning-and-growth perspective, and customer satisfaction, an important customer perspective measure. Customer satisfaction, in turn, was correlated with faster payment of invoices—a relationship that led to a substantial reduction in accounts receivable and hence a higher return on capital employed. The company also found correlations between employees' morale and the number of suggestions made by employees (two learning-and-growth measures) as well as between an increased number of suggestions and lower rework (an internal-business-process measure). Evidence of such strong correlations help to confirm the organization's business strategy. If, however, the expected correlations are not found over time, it should be an indication to executives that the theory underlying the unit's strategy may not be working as they had anticipated.

Especially in large organizations, accumulating sufficient data to document significant correlations and causation among balanced scorecard measures can take a long time—months or years. Over the short term, managers' assessment of strategic impact may have to rest on subjective and qualitative judgments. Eventually, however, as more evidence accumulates, organizations may be able to provide more objectively grounded estimates of cause-and-effect relationships. But just getting managers to think systematically about the

How one company linked measures from the four perspectives

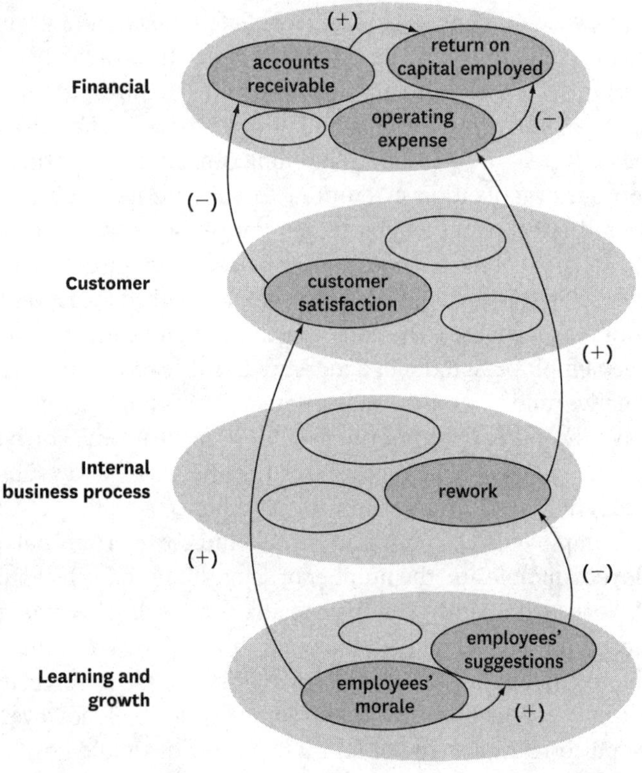

assumptions underlying their strategy is an improvement over the current practice of making decisions based on short-term operational results.

Third, the scorecard facilitates the strategy review that is essential to strategic learning. Traditionally, companies use the monthly or quarterly meetings between corporate and division executives to analyze the most recent period's financial results. Discussions focus on past performance and on explanations of why financial objectives were not achieved. The balanced scorecard, with its specification of the causal relationships between performance drivers and objectives, allows corporate and business unit executives to use their periodic review sessions to evaluate the validity of the unit's strategy and the quality of its execution. If the unit's employees and managers have delivered on the performance drivers (retraining of employees, availability of information systems, and new financial products and services, for instance), then their failure to achieve the expected outcomes (higher sales to targeted customers, for example) signals that the theory underlying the strategy may not be valid. The disappointing sales figures are an early warning.

Managers should take such disconfirming evidence seriously and reconsider their shared conclusions about market conditions, customer value propositions, competitors' behavior, and internal capabilities. The result of such a review may be a decision to reaffirm their belief in the current strategy but to adjust the quantitative relationship among the strategic measures on the balanced scorecard. But they also might conclude that the unit needs a different strategy (an example of double-loop learning) in light of new knowledge about market conditions and internal capabilities. In any case, the scorecard will have stimulated key executives to learn about the viability of their strategy. This capacity for enabling organizational learning at the executive level—strategic learning—is what distinguishes the balanced scorecard, making it invaluable for those who wish to create a strategic management system.

Toward a New Strategic Management System

Many companies adopted early balanced scorecard concepts to improve their performance measurement systems. They achieved tangible but narrow results. Adopting those concepts provided clarification, consensus, and focus on the desired improvements in performance. More recently, we have seen companies expand their use of the balanced scorecard, employing it as the foundation of an integrated and iterative strategic management system. Companies are using the scorecard to

- clarify and update strategy;
- communicate strategy throughout the company;
- align unit and individual goals with the strategy;
- link strategic objectives to long-term targets and annual budgets;
- identify and align strategic initiatives; and
- conduct periodic performance reviews to learn about and improve strategy.

The balanced scorecard enables a company to align its management processes and focuses the entire organization on implementing long-term strategy. At National Insurance, the scorecard provided the CEO and his managers with a central framework around which they could redesign each piece of the company's management system. And because of the cause-and-effect linkages inherent in the scorecard framework, changes in one component of the system reinforced earlier changes made elsewhere. Therefore, every change made over the 30-month period added to the momentum that kept the organization moving forward in the agreed-upon direction.

Without a balanced scorecard, most organizations are unable to achieve a similar consistency of vision and action as they attempt to change direction and introduce new strategies and processes. The balanced scorecard provides a framework for managing the implementation of strategy while also allowing the strategy itself to evolve in response to changes in the company's competitive, market, and technological environments.

Originally published in January 1996. Reprint R0707M.

Transforming Corner-Office Strategy into Frontline Action

by Orit Gadiesh and James L. Gilbert

WE ALL KNOW THE BENEFITS of pushing decision making from the CEO's office out to the far reaches of an organization. Fleeting business opportunities can be seized quickly. Products and services better reflect subtle shifts in customers' preferences. Empowered workers are motivated to innovate and take risks.

But while the value of such an approach is clear, particularly in a volatile business environment, there is also a built-in risk: an organization in which everyone is a decision maker has the potential to spin out of control. Within a single company, it's tricky to achieve both decentralized decision making and coherent strategic action. Still, some companies—think General Electric, America Online, Vanguard, Dell, Wal-Mart, Southwest Airlines, and eBay—have done just that.

These companies employ what we call a *strategic principle,* a memorable and actionable phrase that distills a company's corporate strategy into its unique essence and communicates it throughout the organization. (For a list of companies' strategic principles, see "It's all in a phrase.")

This tool—which we have observed in use at about a dozen companies, even though they don't label it as such—would always serve a company well. But it has become particularly useful in today's rapidly and constantly changing business environment. Indeed, in our conversations and work with more than 50 CEOs over the past two years, we have come to appreciate the strategic principle's power—its ability to help companies maintain strategic focus while fostering the flexibility among employees that permits innovation and a rapid response to opportunities. Strategic principles are likely to become even more crucial to corporate success in the years ahead.

Distillation and Communication

To better understand what a strategic principle is and how it can be used, it may be helpful to look at a military analogy: the rules of engagement for battle. For example, Admiral Lord Nelson's crews in Britain's eighteenth-century wars against the French were guided by a simple strategic principle: whatever you do, get alongside an enemy ship.

The Royal Navy's seamanship, training, and experience gave it the advantage every time it engaged one-on-one against any of Europe's lesser fleets. So Nelson rejected as impractical the common practice of an admiral attempting to control a fleet through the use of flag signals. Instead, he gave his captains strategic parameters—they knew they had to battle rival ships one-on-one—leaving them to determine exactly how to engage in such combat. By using a strategic principle instead of explicit signals to direct his forces, Nelson consistently defeated the French, including a great victory in the dark of night, when signals would have been useless. Nelson's rule of engagement was simple enough for every one of his officers and sailors to know by heart. And it was enduring, a valid directive that was good until the relative naval capabilities of Britain and its rivals changed.

The distillation of a company's strategy into a pithy, memorable, and prescriptive phrase is important because a brilliant business strategy, like an insightful approach to warfare, is of little use unless

Idea in Brief

Southwest Airlines keeps soaring. Its stock price rose a compounded 21,000% between 1972 and 1992 and leapt 300% between 1995 and 2000.

Why does Southwest succeed while so many other airlines fail? Because it sticks to its powerful **strategic principle**: "Meet customers' short-haul travel needs at fares competitive with the cost of automobile travel." This pithy, memorable, action-oriented phrase distills Southwest's unique strategy and communicates it throughout the company.

An effective **strategic principle** lets a company simultaneously:

- maintain strategic focus,
- empower workers to innovate and take risks,
- seize fleeting opportunities,
- create products and services that meet subtle shifts in customers' needs.

In today's rapidly changing world, companies must integrate decentralized decision making *with* coherent, strategic action. A well-crafted, skillfully implemented **strategic principle** lets them strike that delicate balance.

people understand it well enough to apply it—both to anticipated decisions and unforeseen opportunities. In our work, we often see evidence of what we call the 80-100 rule: you're better off with a strategy that is 80% right and 100% implemented than one that is 100% right but doesn't drive consistent action throughout the company. A strategic principle can help a company balance that ratio.

The beauty of having a corporate strategic principle—a company should have only one—is that everyone in an organization, the executives in the front office as well as people in the operating units, can knowingly work toward the same strategic objective without being rigid about how they do so. Decisions don't always have to make the slow trip to and from the executive suite. When a strategic principle is well crafted and effectively communicated, managers at all levels can be trusted to make decisions that advance rather than undermine company strategy.

Idea in Practice

Hallmarks of Powerful Strategic Principles

A successful strategic principle:

- Forces trade-offs between competing resources.

  Example: Southwest Airlines' 1983 expansion to the high-traffic Denver area *seemed* sensible. But unusually long delays there due to bad weather and taxi time would have forced Southwest to increase ticket prices—preventing it from adhering to its strategic principle of offering air fares competitive with the cost of auto travel. The company pulled out of Denver.

- Tests the strategic soundness of particular decisions by linking leaders' strategic insights with line operators' pragmatic sense.

  Example: AOL's strategic principle,"Consumer connectivity first—anytime, anywhere," tested the wisdom of a powerful business decision: expanding AOL's global network through alliances with local partners, rather than using its own technology everywhere. Partners' understanding of local culture greatly increased customers' connectivity.

- Sets clear boundaries within which employees operate and experiment.

  Example: At mutual-fund giant The Vanguard Group, frontline employees conceived a potent idea: Let customers access their accounts on-line, but limit on-line trading. This move kept Vanguard's costs low, enabling the company to

Given what we've said so far, a strategic principle might seem to be a mission statement by another name. But while both help employees understand a company's direction, the two are different tools that communicate different things. A mission statement informs a company's *culture*. A strategic principle drives a company's *strategy*. A mission statement is *aspirational:* it gives people something to strive for. A strategic principle is *action oriented:* it enables people to do something now. A mission statement is meant to *inspire* frontline workers. A strategic principle enables them to *act* quickly by giving them explicit guidance to make strategically consistent choices.

stick to its strategic principle: creating "unmatchable value for investors/owners."

Creating and Communicating Your Strategic Principle

Capturing and communicating the essence of your company's strategy in a simple, memorable, actionable phrase isn't easy. These steps can help:

1. **Draft a working strategic principle.** Summarize your *corporate strategy*—your plan to allocate scarce resources in order to create value that distinguishes you from competitors—in a brief phrase. That phrase becomes your working *strategic principle*.
2. **Test its endurance.** A good strategic principle endures. Ask: Does our working strategic principle capture the timeless essence of our company's unique competitive value?
3. **Test its communicative power.** Ask: Is the phrase clear, concise, memorable? Would you feel proud to paint it on the side of your firm's trucks, as Wal-Mart does?
4. **Test its ability to promote and guide action.** Ask: Does the principle exhibit the three essential attributes: forcing trade-offs, testing the wisdom of business moves, setting boundaries for employees' experimentation?
5. **Communicate it.** Communicate your strategic principle consistently, simply, and repeatedly. You'll know you've succeeded when employees—as well as business writers, MBA students, and competitors—all "chant the rant."

Consider the difference between GE's mission statement and its strategic principle. The company's mission statement exhorts GE's leaders—"always with unyielding integrity"—to be "passionately focused on driving customer success" and to "create an environment of 'stretch,' excitement, informality, and trust," among other things. The language is aspirational and emotional. By contrast, GE's well-known strategic principle—"Be number one or number two in every industry in which we compete, or get out"—is action oriented. The first part of the phrase is an explicit strategic challenge, and the second part leaves no question in line managers' minds about what they should do.

Three Defining Attributes

A strategic principle, as the distillation of a company's strategy, should guide a company's allocation of scarce resources—capital, time, management's attention, labor, and brand—in order to build a sustainable competitive advantage. It should tell a company what to do and, just as important, what not to do. More specifically, an effective strategic principle does the following:

- It forces trade-offs between competing resource demands;
- It tests the strategic soundness of a particular action;
- It sets clear boundaries within which employees must operate while granting them freedom to experiment within those constraints.

These three qualities can be seen in America Online's strategic principle. CEO Steve Case says personal interaction on-line is the soul of the Internet, and he has positioned AOL to create that interaction. Thus, AOL's strategic principle in the years leading up to its recent merger with Time Warner has been "Consumer connectivity first—anytime, anywhere."

This strategic principle has helped AOL make tough choices when allocating its resources. For example, in 1997, the company needed cash to grow, so it sold off its network infrastructure and outsourced that capability—a risky move at a time when it appeared that network ownership might be the key to success on the Internet. In keeping with its strategic principle, AOL instead spent its time and cash on improving connectivity at its Web site, focusing particularly on access, navigation, and interaction. As a result, it avoided investing capital in what turned out to be a relatively low-return business.

Its strategic principle has also helped AOL test whether a given business move makes strategic sense. For instance, the Internet company has chosen to expand its global network through alliances with local partners, even though that approach can take longer than simply transplanting AOL's own technology and know-how.

AOL acknowledges that a local partner better understands the native culture and community, which is essential for connecting with customers.

Finally, AOL's strategic principle has spurred focused experimentation in the field by clearly defining employees' latitude for making moves. For example, AOL's former vice president of marketing, Jan Brandt, mailed more than 250 million AOL diskettes to consumers nationwide. The innovative campaign turned the company into one of the best-known names in cyberspace—all because Brandt, now AOL's vice chair and chief marketing officer, guided by the principle of connecting consumers, put her resources into empowering AOL's target community rather than sinking time and money into slick advertising.

As AOL's experience illustrates, a strong strategic principle can inform high-level corporate decisions—those involving divestitures, for example—as well as decisions made by department heads or others further down in an organization. It also frees up CEOs from constant involvement in the implementation of their strategic mandates. "The genius of a great leader is to leave behind him a situation that common sense, without the grace of genius, can deal with successfully," said journalist and political thinker Walter Lippman. Scratch the surface of a number of high-performing companies, and you'll find that strategic principles are connecting the strategic insights—if not always the genius—of leaders with the pragmatic sense of line operators.

Now More Than Ever

In the past, a strategic principle was nice to have but was hardly required, unless a company found itself in a trying business situation. Today, many companies simultaneously face four situations that make a strategic principle crucial for success: decentralization, rapid growth, technological change, and institutional turmoil.

For the reasons mentioned above, *decentralization* is becoming common at companies of all stripes; thus, there is a corresponding need for a mechanism to ensure coherent strategic action. Especially in the case of diversified conglomerates, where strategy is formed in each of the business units, a strategic principle can help executives maintain consistency while giving unit managers the freedom to tailor their strategies to meet their own needs. It can also clarify the value of the center at such far-flung companies. For example, GE's long-standing strategic principle of always being number one or number two in an industry offers a powerful rationale for how a conglomerate can create value but still give individual units considerable strategic freedom.

A strategic principle is also crucial when a company is experiencing *rapid growth*. During such times, it's increasingly the case that less-experienced managers are forced to make decisions about nettlesome issues for which there may be no precedent. A clear and precise strategic principle can help counteract this shortage of experience. This is particularly true when a start-up company is growing rapidly in an established industry. For instance, as Southwest Airlines began to grow quickly, it might have been tempted to mimic its rivals' ultimately unsuccessful strategies if it hadn't had its own strategic principle to follow: "Meet customers' short-haul travel needs at fares competitive with the cost of automobile travel." Likewise, eBay, whose principle is "Focus on trading communities," might have been tempted, like many Internet marketplaces, to diversify into all sorts of services. But eBay has chosen to outsource certain services—for instance, management of the photos that sellers post on the site to illustrate the items they put up for bid—while it continues to invest in services like Billpoint, which lets sellers accept credit-card payments from bidders. EBay's strategic principle has ensured that the entire company stays focused on the core trading business.

The staggering pace of *technological change* over the past decade has been costly for companies that don't have a strategic principle. Never before in business has there been more uncertainty combined with so great an emphasis on speed. Managers in high-tech industries in particular must react immediately to sudden and unexpected developments. Often, the sum of the reactions across the

It's all in a phrase

A handful of companies have distilled their strategy into a phrase and have used it to drive consistent strategic action throughout their organizations.

Company	Strategic Principle
America Online	*Consumer connectivity first—anytime, anywhere*
Dell	*Be direct*
eBay	*Focus on trading communities*
General Electric	*Be number one or number two in every industry in which we compete, or get out*
Southwest Airlines	*Meet customers' short-haul travel needs at fares competitive with the cost of automobile travel*
Vanguard	*Unmatchable value for the investor-owner*
Wal-Mart	*Low prices, every day*

organization ends up defining the company's strategic course. A strategic principle—for example, Dell's mandate to sell direct to end users—helps ensure that the decisions made by frontline managers in such circumstances add up to a consistent, coherent strategy.

Finally, a strategic principle can help provide continuity during periods of *organizational turmoil*. An increasingly common example of turmoil in this era of short-term CEOs is leadership succession. A new CEO can bring with him or her a new strategy—but not necessarily a new strategic principle. For instance, when Jack Brennan took over as chairman and CEO at Vanguard five years ago, the strategic transition was seamless, despite some tension around the leadership transition. He maintained the mutual fund company's strategic principle—"Unmatchable value for the investor-owner"—thereby allowing managers to pursue their strategic objectives without many of the distractions so often associated with leadership changes. (For our own experience with organizational turmoil and strategic principles, see the sidebar "Bain & Company: Case Study of a Strategic Principle.")

Bain & Company: Case Study of a Strategic Principle

I LEARNED THE MOST ABOUT strategic principles in the trenches at Bain & Company when, a decade ago, we almost went bankrupt.

Bill Bain founded Bain & Company nearly 30 years ago on the basis of a simple but powerful notion: "The product of a consultant should be results for clients—not reports." Over time, this mandate to deliver results through strategy became Bain's strategic principle. It remains so today.

This directive fosters specific action, as an effective strategic principle should. It means that, from the very beginning of an assignment, you are constantly thinking about how a recommendation will get implemented. It also requires you to tell clients the truth, even if it's difficult, because you can't achieve results by whitewashing problems. And this strategic principle has teeth: Bain has always measured partners' performance according to the results they achieve for their clients, not just on billings to the firm.

That was the company I joined. And for many years it grew rapidly, all the time guided by its strategic principle. Then, just over a decade ago, the founding partners decided to get their money out and sold 30% of the firm to an employee stock-option plan. This saddled us with hundreds of millions of dollars of debt and tens of millions of dollars of interest payments. The move, whose details initially were not disclosed to the rest of us, was based on the assumption that the company would continue its historic growth rate of 50% a year, which couldn't be sustained at the size we had become. When growth slowed, the details came to light.

The nonfounding partners faced a critical choice. Everybody had attractive offers. Competitors and the press predicted we wouldn't survive. Recruits

Strategic Principles in Action

Strategic principles and their benefits can best be understood by seeing the results they create.

Forcing trade-offs at Southwest Airlines

Southwest Airlines is one of the air-travel industry's great success stories. It is the only airline that hasn't lost money in the past 25 years. Its stock price rose a compounded 21,000% between 1972 and 1992, and it is up 300% over the past five years, which have been

and clients were watchful. To make a long story short, we sat down around a conference table and resolved to turn the company around. The key to doing that, we decided, was to stick with our strategic principle.

What followed was a couple of years during which adhering to that goal was achingly difficult. But doing so forced important trade-offs. In one case, right in the middle of the crisis, we pulled out of a major assignment that was inconsistent with our principle. We believed the projects that the client was determined to undertake could not produce significant results for the company. Today, we all believe that had we veered from our principle in that instance, we would not be around.

More recently, our strategic principle has freed us to explore other ventures. Seven years ago, for instance, we became interested in private equity consulting, quite a different business from serving corporate clients. We initially struggled with the notion but quickly realized that it fit our strategic principle of delivering results through strategy, only to a new client segment. We knew that we could trust our colleagues forming the practice area to act consistently with the company's broader goals because the strategic principle was fundamental to their perspective. The strength of our shared principle permitted us to experiment and ultimately develop a successful new practice area.

Our principle continues to let partners develop new practices, markets, and interests quickly and without splintering the firm. It has given us the capacity to evolve and endure.

—Orit Gadiesh

difficult ones in the airline industry. For most companies, such rapid growth would cause problems: legions of frontline employees taking up the mantle of decision making from core executives and, inevitably, stumbling. But in Southwest's case, employees have consistently made trade-offs in keeping with the company's strategic principle.

The process for making important and complicated decisions about things like network design, service offerings, route selection and pricing, cabin design, and ticketing procedures is straightforward. That's because the trade-offs required by the strategic principle are clear. For instance, in 1983, Southwest initiated service to Denver, a potentially high-traffic destination and a seemingly sensible expansion of the company's presence in the Southwestern United States. However, the airline experienced longer and more consistent delays at Denver's Stapleton airport than it did anywhere else. These delays were caused not by slow turnaround at the gate but by increased taxi time on the runway and planes circling in the air because of bad weather. Southwest had to decide whether the potential growth from serving the Denver market was worth the higher costs associated with the delays, which would ultimately be reflected in higher ticket prices. The company turned to its strategic principle: would the airline be able to maintain fares competitive with the cost of automobile travel? Clearly, in Denver at least, it couldn't. Southwest pulled out of Stapleton three years after inaugurating the service there and has not returned.

Testing action at AOL

A large part of AOL's ability to move so far and so fast across untrod ground lies in its practice of testing potential moves against its strategic principle. Employees who see attractive opportunities can ask themselves whether seizing one or several will lead to deeper consumer connectivity or broader distribution. Take, for example, line manager Katherine Borescnik, now president of programming at AOL. Several years ago she noticed increased activity—call it consumer connectivity—around the bulletin-board folders created on the site by two irreverent stock analysts and AOL subscribers. She offered the analysts the chance to create their own financial site, which became Motley Fool, a point of connection and information for do-it-yourself investors.

And AOL's strategic principle reaches even deeper into the organization. The hundreds of acquisitions and deals that AOL has made in the past few years have involved numerous employees. While top officers make final decisions, employees on the ground first screen opportunities against the company's strategic principle.

Furthermore, the integration efforts following acquisitions, while choreographed at the top, are executed by a coterie of managers who ensure that the plans comply with the company's strategic principle. "We have succeeded, both in our deal making and in our integration, because our acquisitions have all been driven by our focus on how our customers communicate and connect," says Ken Novack, AOL Time Warner's vice chairman.

AOL's massive merger with Time Warner clearly furthers AOL's strategic principle of enabling consumer connections "anytime, anywhere" by adding TV and cable access to the Internet company's current dial-up access on the personal computer. But integrating this merger, which will involve hundreds of employees making and executing thousands of decisions, may be the ultimate test of AOL's strategic principle.

Experimenting within boundaries at Vanguard

The Vanguard Group, with $565 billion in assets under management, has quietly become a giant in the mutual fund industry. The company's strategy is a response to the inability of most mutual funds to beat the market, often because of the cost of their marketing activities, overhead, and frequent transactions. To counter this, Vanguard discourages investors from making frequent trades and keeps its own overhead and advertising costs far below the industry average. It passes the savings directly to investors, who, because Vanguard is a mutual rather than a public company, are the fund's owners.

While this was Vanguard's founding strategy, for years the company didn't communicate it widely to employees. As a result, they often suggested initiatives that were out of sync with the company's core strategy. "Midlevel managers would walk in holding the newspaper saying, 'Look at what Fidelity just did. How about if we do that?'" Jack Brennan says. It wasn't apparent to them that Vanguard's strategy was very different from that of its rival, which has higher costs and isn't mutually owned. Over the years, Vanguard has invested considerable energy in crafting a strategic principle and using it to disseminate the company's strategy. Now, because employees understand the strategy, top management trusts them to initiate moves on their own.

Consider Vanguard's response to a major trend in retail fund distribution: the emergence of the on-line channel. Industry surveys indicated that most investors wanted Internet access to their accounts and that on-line traders were more active than off-line traders. So Vanguard chose to integrate the Internet into its service in a way that furthered its strategy of keeping costs low: basically, it lets customers access their accounts on-line, but it limits Web-based trading. It should be noted that the original ideas for Vanguard's on-line initiatives, including early ventures with AOL, were conceived by frontline employees, not senior executives.

Brennan says the company's strategic principle affects the entire management process, including hiring, training, performance measurement, and incentives. He points to a hidden benefit of having a strong strategic principle: "You're more efficient and can run with a leaner management team because everyone is on the same page."

Creating a Strategic Principle

Many of the best and most conspicuous examples of strategic principles come from companies that were founded on them, companies such as eBay, Dell, Vanguard, Southwest Airlines, and Wal-Mart ("Low prices, every day"). The founders of those companies espoused a clear guiding principle that summarized the essence of what would become a full-blown business strategy. They attracted investors who believed it, hired employees who bought into it, and targeted customers who wanted it.

Leaders of long-standing multinationals, like GE, crafted their strategic principles at a critical juncture: when increasing corporate complexity threatened to confuse priorities on the front line and obscure the essence that truly differentiated their strategy from that of their rivals.

Companies in this second category, which represents most of the companies that are likely to contemplate creating a strategic principle, face a demanding exercise. It probably comes as no surprise that identifying the essence of your strategy so it can be translated into a simple, memorable phrase is no easy task. It's a bit like corporate genomics: the principle must isolate and capture the corporate equivalent of the genetic code that differentiates your company from its competitors. This is somewhat like identifying the 2% of DNA that separates man from monkey—or, even more difficult and more apt, the .1% of DNA that differentiates each human being.

There are different ways to identify the elements that must be captured in a strategic principle, but keep in mind that a corporate strategy represents a plan to effectively allocate scarce resources to achieve sustainable competitive advantage. Managers need to ask themselves: how does my company allocate those resources to create value in a unique way, one that differentiates my company from competitors? Try to summarize the answer in a brief phrase that captures the essence of your company's point of differentiation.

Once that idea has been expressed in a phrase, test the strategic principle for its enduring nature. Does it capture what you intend to do for only the next three to five years, or does it capture a more timeless essence: the genetic code of your company's competitive differentiation? Then test the strategic principle for its communicative power. Is it clear, concise, and memorable? Would you feel proud to paint it on the side of a truck, as Wal-Mart does?

Finally, test the principle for its ability to promote and guide action. In particular, assess whether it exhibits the three attributes of an effective strategic principle. Will it force trade-offs? Will it serve as a test for the wisdom of a particular business move, especially one that might promote short-term profits at the expense of long-term strategy? Does it set boundaries within which people will nonetheless be free to experiment?

Given the importance of getting your strategic principle right, it is wise to gather feedback on these questions from executives and other employees during an incubation period. Once you are satisfied that the statement is accurate and compelling, disseminate it throughout the organization.

Of course, just as a brilliant strategy is worthless unless it is implemented, a powerful strategic principle is of no use unless it is communicated effectively. When CEO Jack Welch talks about aligning employees around GE's strategy and values, he emphasizes the need for consistency, simplicity, and repetition. The approach is neither flashy nor complicated, but it takes enormous discipline and could scarcely be more important. Welch has so broadly evangelized GE's "Be number one or number two" strategic principle that employees are not the only ones to chant the rant. So can most business writers, MBA students, and managers at other companies.

When Rethinking Is Required

No strategy is eternal, nor is any strategic principle. But even if the elements of your strategy change, the very essence of it is likely to remain the same. Thus, your strategy may shift substantially as your customers' demographics and needs change. It may have to be modified in light of your company's changing costs and assets compared with those of competitors. Strategic half-lives are shortening, and, in general, strategy should be reviewed every quarter and updated every year. But while it's worth revisiting your strategic principle every time you reexamine your strategy, it is likely to change only when there is a significant shift in the basic economics and opportunities of your market caused by, say, legislation or a completely new technology or business model.

Even then, your strategic principle may need only refining or expanding. GE's strategic principle has been enhanced, but not replaced, since Welch articulated it in 1981. Similarly, AOL's strategic principle will need to be broadened, but not necessarily jettisoned, following its merger with Time Warner. Ultimately, the merged company's strategic principle will also need to embody the importance of high-quality and relevant content, Time Warner's hallmark.

Vanguard takes explicit steps to ensure that the direction provided by its strategic principle remains current. For example, as part of an internal "devil's advocacy" process, managers are divided into groups to critique and defend past decisions and current policies. Recently, the group reconsidered two major strategic policies: the prohibitions against opening branch offices and against acquiring money management firms. After considerable discussion, the policies remained in place. According to CEO Brennan, "Sometimes the greatest value [of revisiting our strategic principle] is reconfirming what we're already doing." At the same time, Vanguard has the process to identify when change is needed.

Fundamental Principles

Respondents to Bain's annual survey of executives on the usefulness of management tools repeatedly cite the key role a mission statement can play in a company's success. We agree that a mission statement is crucial for promulgating a company's values and building a robust corporate culture. But it still leaves a large gap in a company's management communications portfolio. At least as important as a mission statement is something that promulgates a company's strategy—that is, a strategic principle.

The ability of frontline employees to execute a company's strategy without close central oversight is vital as the pace of technological change accelerates and as companies grow rapidly and become increasingly decentralized. To drive such behavior, a company needs to give employees a mandate broad enough to encourage enterprising behavior but specific enough to align employees' initiatives with company strategy.

While not a perfect analogy, the U.S. Constitution is in some ways like a strategic principle. It articulates and embodies the essence of the country's "strategy"—to guarantee liberty and justice for all of its citizens—while providing direction to those drafting the laws and regulations that implement the strategy. While no corporate strategy has liberty and justice at its heart, the elements of an effective strategy are just as central to the success of a company as those concepts are to the prosperity of the United States. And in neither case will success be realized unless the core strategy is communicated broadly and effectively.

Bain consultant Coleman Mark assisted with this article.

Originally published in May 2001. Reprint R0105D.

Turning Great Strategy into Great Performance

by Michael C. Mankins and Richard Steele

THREE YEARS AGO, THE LEADERSHIP team at a major manufacturer spent months developing a new strategy for its European business. Over the prior half-decade, six new competitors had entered the market, each deploying the latest in low-cost manufacturing technology and slashing prices to gain market share. The performance of the European unit—once the crown jewel of the company's portfolio—had deteriorated to the point that top management was seriously considering divesting it.

To turn around the operation, the unit's leadership team had recommended a bold new "solutions strategy"—one that would leverage the business's installed base to fuel growth in after-market services and equipment financing. The financial forecasts were exciting—the strategy promised to restore the business's industry-leading returns and growth. Impressed, top management quickly approved the plan, agreeing to provide the unit with all the resources it needed to make the turnaround a reality.

Today, however, the unit's performance is nowhere near what its management team had projected. Returns, while better than before, remain well below the company's cost of capital. The revenues and profits that managers had expected from services and financing have not materialized, and the business's cost position still lags behind that of its major competitors.

At the conclusion of a recent half-day review of the business's strategy and performance, the unit's general manager remained steadfast and vowed to press on. "It's all about execution," she declared. "The strategy we're pursuing is the right one. We're just not delivering the numbers. All we need to do is work harder, work smarter."

The parent company's CEO was not so sure. He wondered: Could the unit's lackluster performance have more to do with a mistaken strategy than poor execution? More important, what should he do to get better performance out of the unit? Should he do as the general manager insisted and stay the course—focusing the organization more intensely on execution—or should he encourage the leadership team to investigate new strategy options? If execution was the issue, what should he do to help the business improve its game? Or should he just cut his losses and sell the business? He left the operating review frustrated and confused—not at all confident that the business would ever deliver the performance its managers had forecast in its strategic plan.

Talk to almost any CEO, and you're likely to hear similar frustrations. For despite the enormous time and energy that goes into strategy development at most companies, many have little to show for the effort. Our research suggests that companies on average deliver only 63% of the financial performance their strategies promise. Even worse, the causes of this strategy-to-performance gap are all but invisible to top management. Leaders then pull the wrong levers in their attempts to turn around performance—pressing for better execution when they actually need a better strategy, or opting to change direction when they really should focus the organization on execution. The result: wasted energy, lost time, and continued underperformance.

But, as our research also shows, a select group of high-performing companies have managed to close the strategy-to-performance gap through better planning *and* execution. These companies—Barclays, Cisco Systems, Dow Chemical, 3M, and Roche, to name a few—develop

Idea in Brief

Most companies' strategies deliver only 63% of their promised financial value. Why? Leaders press for better execution when they really need a sounder strategy. Or they craft a new strategy when execution is the true weak spot.

How to avoid these errors? View strategic planning and execution as inextricably linked—then raise the bar for both simultaneously. Start by applying seven deceptively straightforward rules, including: keeping your strategy simple and concrete, making resource-allocation decisions early in the planning process, and continuously monitoring performance as you roll out your strategic plan.

By following these rules, you reduce the likelihood of performance shortfalls. And even if your strategy still stumbles, you quickly determine whether the fault lies with the strategy itself, your plan for pursuing it, or the execution process. The payoff? You make the *right* midcourse corrections—promptly. And as high-performing companies like Cisco Systems, Dow Chemical, and 3M have discovered, you boost your company's financial performance 60% to 100%.

realistic plans that are solidly grounded in the underlying economics of their markets and then use the plans to drive execution. Their disciplined planning and execution processes make it far less likely that they will face a shortfall in actual performance. And, if they do fall short, their processes enable them to discern the cause quickly and take corrective action. While these companies' practices are broad in scope—ranging from unique forms of planning to integrated processes for deploying and tracking resources—our experience suggests that they can be applied by any business to help craft great plans and turn them into great performance.

The Strategy-to-Performance Gap

In the fall of 2004, our firm, Marakon Associates, in collaboration with the Economist Intelligence Unit, surveyed senior executives from 197 companies worldwide with sales exceeding $500 million. We wanted to see how successful companies are at translating their strategies into performance. Specifically, how effective are they at

Idea in Practice

Seven rules for successful strategy execution:

- **Keep it simple.** Avoid drawn-out descriptions of lofty goals. Instead, clearly describe what your company will and won't do.

  Example: Executives at European investment-banking giant Barclays Capital stated they wouldn't compete with large U.S. investment banks or in unprofitable equity-market segments. Instead, they'd position Barclays for investors' burgeoning need for fixed income.

- **Challenge assumptions.** Ensure that the assumptions underlying your long-term strategic plans reflect real market economics and your organization's actual performance relative to rivals'.

  Example: Struggling conglomerate Tyco commissioned cross-functional teams in each business unit to continuously analyze their markets' profitability and their offerings, costs, and price positioning relative to competitors'. Teams met with corporate executives biweekly to discuss their findings. The revamped process generated more realistic plans and contributed to Tyco's dramatic turnaround.

- **Speak the same language.** Unit leaders and corporate strategy, marketing, and finance teams must agree on a common framework for assessing performance. For example, some high-performing companies use benchmarking to estimate the size of the profit pool available in each market their company serves, the pool's

meeting the financial projections set forth in their strategic plans? And when they fall short, what are the most common causes, and what actions are most effective in closing the strategy-to-performance gap? Our findings were revealing—and troubling.

While the executives we surveyed compete in very different product markets and geographies, they share many concerns about planning and execution. Virtually all of them struggle to produce the financial performance forecasts in their long-range plans. Furthermore, the processes they use to develop plans and monitor potential growth, and the company's likely portion of that pool, given its market share and profitability. By using the shared approach, executives easily agree on financial projections.

- **Discuss resource deployments early.** Challenge business units about when they'll need new resources to execute their strategy. By asking questions such as, "How fast can you deploy the new sales force?" and "How quickly will competitors respond?" you create more feasible forecasts and plans.

- **Identify priorities.** Delivering planned performance requires a few key actions taken at the right time, in the right way. Make strategic priorities explicit, so everyone knows what to focus on.

- **Continuously monitor performance.** Track real-time results against your plan, resetting planning assumptions and reallocating resources as needed. You'll remedy flaws in your plan *and* its execution—and avoid confusing the two.

- **Develop execution ability.** No strategy can be better than the people who must implement it. Make selection and development of managers a priority.

Example: Barclays' top executive team takes responsibility for all hiring. Members vet each others' potential hires and reward talented newcomers for superior execution. And stars aren't penalized if their business enters new markets with lower initial returns.

performance make it difficult to discern whether the strategy-to-performance gap stems from poor planning, poor execution, both, or neither. Specifically, we discovered:

Companies rarely track performance against long-term plans

In our experience, less than 15% of companies make it a regular practice to go back and compare the business's results with the performance forecast for each unit in its prior years' strategic plans. As a result, top managers can't easily know whether the projections that underlie their

Where the performance goes

This chart shows the average performance loss implied by the importance ratings that managers in our survey gave to specific breakdowns in the planning and execution process.

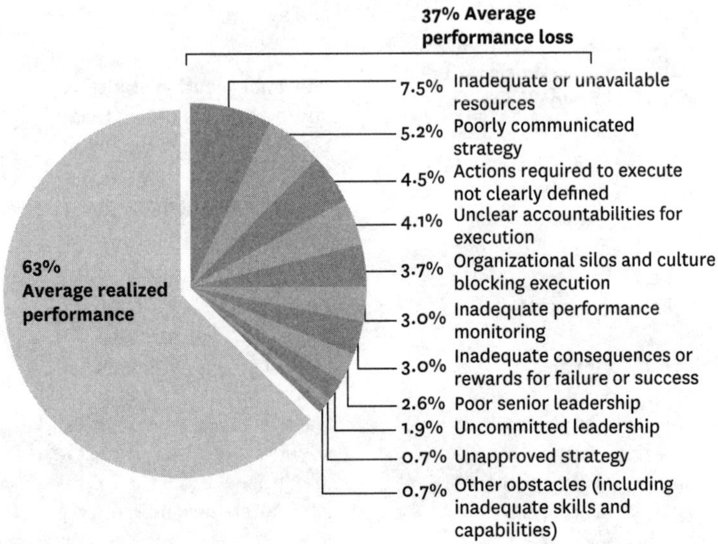

capital-investment and portfolio-strategy decisions are in any way predictive of actual performance. More important, they risk embedding the same disconnect between results and forecasts in their future investment decisions. Indeed, the fact that so few companies routinely monitor actual versus planned performance may help explain why so many companies seem to pour good money after bad—continuing to fund losing strategies rather than searching for new and better options.

Multiyear results rarely meet projections

When companies do track performance relative to projections over a number of years, what commonly emerges is a picture one of our clients recently described as a series of "diagonal venetian blinds," where each year's performance projections, when viewed side by side, resemble venetian blinds hung diagonally. (See "The venetian blinds of business.") If things are going reasonably well, the starting point for each year's new "blind" may be a bit higher than the prior year's starting point, but rarely does performance match the prior year's projection. The obvious implication: year after year of under-performance relative to plan.

The venetian blinds phenomenon creates a number of related problems. First, because the plan's financial forecasts are unreliable, senior management cannot confidently tie capital approval to strategic planning. Consequently, strategy development and resource allocation become decoupled, and the annual operating plan (or budget) ends up driving the company's long-term investments and strategy. Second, portfolio management gets derailed. Without credible financial forecasts, top management cannot know whether a particular business is worth more to the company and its shareholders than to potential buyers. As a result, businesses that destroy shareholder value stay in the portfolio too long (in the hope that their performance will eventually turn around), and value-creating businesses are starved for capital and other resources. Third, poor financial forecasts complicate communications with the investment community. Indeed, to avoid coming up short at the end of the quarter, the CFO and head of investor relations frequently impose a "contingency" or "safety margin" on top of the forecast produced by consolidating the business-unit plans. Because this top-down contingency is wrong just as often as it is right, poor financial forecasts run the risk of damaging a company's reputation with analysts and investors.

A lot of value is lost in translation

Given the poor quality of financial forecasts in most strategic plans, it is probably not surprising that most companies fail to realize their strategies' potential value. As we've mentioned, our survey indicates that, on average, most strategies deliver only 63% of their potential financial performance. And more than one-third of the

The venetian blinds of business

This figure illustrates a dynamic common to many companies. In January 2001, management approves a strategic plan (Plan 2001) that projects modest performance for the first year and a high rate of performance thereafter, as shown in the first solid line. For beating the first year's projection, the unit management is both commended and handsomely rewarded. A new plan is then prepared, projecting uninspiring results for the first year and once again promising a fast rate of performance improvement thereafter, as shown by the second solid line (Plan 2002). This, too, succeeds only partially, so another plan is drawn up, and so on. The actual rate of performance improvement can be seen by joining the start points of each plan (the dotted line).

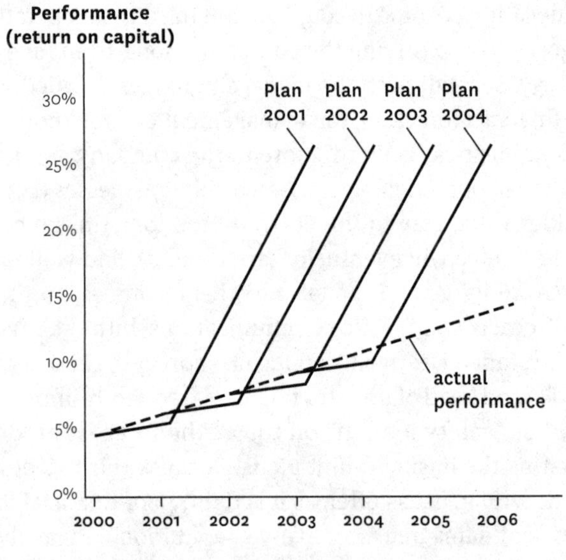

executives surveyed placed the figure at less than 50%. Put differently, if management were to realize the full potential of its current strategy, the increase in value could be as much as 60% to 100%!

As illustrated in "Where the performance goes," the strategy-to-performance gap can be attributed to a combination of factors, such as poorly formulated plans, misapplied resources, breakdowns in communication, and limited accountability for results. To elaborate, management starts with a strategy it believes will generate a certain level of financial performance and value over time (100%, as noted in the exhibit). But, according to the executives we surveyed, the failure to have the right resources in the right place at the right time strips away some 7.5% of the strategy's potential value. Some 5.2% is lost to poor communications, 4.5% to poor action planning, 4.1% to blurred accountabilities, and so on. Of course, these estimates reflect the average experience of the executives we surveyed and may not be representative of every company or every strategy. Nonetheless, they do highlight the issues managers need to focus on as they review their companies' processes for planning and executing strategies.

What emerges from our survey results is a sequence of events that goes something like this: Strategies are approved but poorly communicated. This, in turn, makes the translation of strategy into specific actions and resource plans all but impossible. Lower levels in the organization don't know what they need to do, when they need to do it, or what resources will be required to deliver the performance senior management expects. Consequently, the expected results never materialize. And because no one is held responsible for the shortfall, the cycle of underperformance gets repeated, often for many years.

Performance bottlenecks are frequently invisible to top management

The processes most companies use to develop plans, allocate resources, and track performance make it difficult for top management to discern whether the strategy-to-performance gap stems from poor planning, poor execution, both, or neither. Because so many plans incorporate overly ambitious projections, companies frequently write off performance shortfalls as "just another hockey-stick forecast." And when plans are realistic and performance falls short, executives have few early-warning signals. They often have no way of knowing whether critical actions were carried out as expected, resources were deployed on schedule, competitors responded as anticipated, and so on. Unfortunately, without clear information on how and why performance is falling short, it is virtually impossible for top management to take appropriate corrective action.

The strategy-to-performance gap fosters a culture of underperformance

In many companies, planning and execution breakdowns are reinforced—even magnified—by an insidious shift in culture. In our experience, this change occurs subtly but quickly, and once it has taken root it is very hard to reverse. First, unrealistic plans create the expectation throughout the organization that plans simply will not be fulfilled. Then, as the expectation becomes experience, it becomes the norm that performance commitments won't be kept. So commitments cease to be binding promises with real consequences. Rather than stretching to ensure that commitments are kept, managers, expecting failure, seek to protect themselves from the eventual fallout. They spend time covering their tracks rather than identifying actions to enhance performance. The organization becomes less self-critical and less intellectually honest about its shortcomings. Consequently, it loses its capacity to perform.

Closing the Strategy-to-Performance Gap

As significant as the strategy-to-performance gap is at most companies, management can close it. A number of high-performing companies have found ways to realize more of their strategies' potential. Rather than focus on improving their planning and execution processes separately to close the gap, these companies work both sides of the equation, raising standards for both planning and execution simultaneously and creating clear links between them.

Our research and experience in working with many of these companies suggests they follow seven rules that apply to planning and execution. Living by these rules enables them to objectively assess any performance shortfall and determine whether it stems from the strategy, the plan, the execution, or employees' capabilities. And the same rules that allow them to spot problems early also help them prevent performance shortfalls in the first place. These rules may seem simple—even obvious—but when strictly and collectively observed, they can transform both the quality of a company's strategy and its ability to deliver results.

Rule 1: Keep it simple, make it concrete

At most companies, strategy is a highly abstract concept—often confused with vision or aspiration—and is not something that can be easily communicated or translated into action. But without a clear sense of where the company is headed and why, lower levels in the organization cannot put in place executable plans. In short, the link between strategy and performance can't be drawn because the strategy itself is not sufficiently concrete.

To start off the planning and execution process on the right track, high-performing companies avoid long, drawn-out descriptions of lofty goals and instead stick to clear language describing their course of action. Bob Diamond, CEO of Barclays Capital, one of the fastest-growing and best-performing investment banking operations in Europe, puts it this way: "We've been very clear about what we will and will not do. We knew we weren't going to go head-to-head with U.S. bulge bracket firms. We communicated that we wouldn't compete in this way and that we wouldn't play in unprofitable segments within the equity markets but instead would invest to position ourselves for the euro, the burgeoning need for fixed income, and the end of Glass-Steigel. By ensuring everyone knew the strategy and how it was different, we've been able to spend more time on tasks that are key to executing this strategy."

By being clear about what the strategy is and isn't, companies like Barclays keep everyone headed in the same direction. More important, they safeguard the performance their counterparts lose to ineffective communications; their resource and action planning becomes more effective; and accountabilities are easier to specify.

Rule 2: Debate assumptions, not forecasts

At many companies, a business unit's strategic plan is little more than a negotiated settlement—the result of careful bargaining with the corporate center over performance targets and financial forecasts.

Planning, therefore, is largely a political process—with unit management arguing for lower near-term profit projections (to secure higher annual bonuses) and top management pressing for more long-term stretch (to satisfy the board of directors and other external constituents). Not surprisingly, the forecasts that emerge from these negotiations almost always understate what each business unit can deliver in the near term and overstate what can realistically be expected in the long-term—the hockey-stick charts with which CEOs are all too familiar.

Even at companies where the planning process is isolated from the political concerns of performance evaluation and compensation, the approach used to generate financial projections often has built-in biases. Indeed, financial forecasting frequently takes place in complete isolation from the marketing or strategy functions. A business unit's finance function prepares a highly detailed line-item forecast whose short-term assumptions may be realistic, if conservative, but whose long-term assumptions are largely uninformed. For example, revenue forecasts are typically based on crude estimates about average pricing, market growth, and market share. Projections of long-term costs and working capital requirements are based on an assumption about annual productivity gains—expediently tied, perhaps, to some companywide efficiency program. These forecasts are difficult for top management to pick apart. Each line item may be completely defensible, but the overall plan and projections embed a clear upward bias—rendering them useless for driving strategy execution.

High-performing companies view planning altogether differently. They want their forecasts to drive the work they actually do. To make this possible, they have to ensure that the assumptions underlying their long-term plans reflect both the real economics of their markets and the performance experience of the company relative to competitors. Tyco CEO Ed Breen, brought in to turn the company around in July 2002, credits a revamped plan-building process for contributing to Tyco's dramatic recovery. When Breen joined the company, Tyco was a labyrinth of 42 business units and several hundred profit centers, built up over many years through countless acquisitions. Few of Tyco's businesses had complete plans, and virtually none had reliable financial forecasts.

To get a grip on the conglomerate's complex operations, Breen assigned cross-functional teams at each unit, drawn from strategy, marketing, and finance, to develop detailed information on the profitability of Tyco's primary markets as well as the product or service offerings, costs, and price positioning relative to the competition. The teams met with corporate executives biweekly during Breen's first six months to review and discuss the findings. These discussions focused on the assumptions that would drive each unit's long-term financial performance, not on the financial forecasts themselves. In fact, once assumptions about market trends were agreed on, it was relatively easy for Tyco's central finance function to prepare externally oriented and internally consistent forecasts for each unit.

Separating the process of building assumptions from that of preparing financial projections helps to ground the business unit–corporate center dialogue in economic reality. Units can't hide behind specious details, and corporate center executives can't push for unrealistic goals. What's more, the fact-based discussion resulting from this kind of approach builds trust between the top team and each unit and removes barriers to fast and effective execution. "When you understand the fundamentals and performance drivers in a detailed way," says Bob Diamond, "you can then step back, and you don't have to manage the details. The team knows which issues it can get on with, which it needs to flag to me, and which issues we really need to work out together."

Rule 3: Use a rigorous framework, speak a common language

To be productive, the dialogue between the corporate center and the business units about market trends and assumptions must be conducted within a rigorous framework. Many of the companies we advise use the concept of profit pools, which draws on the competition theories of Michael Porter and others. In this framework, a business's long-term financial performance is tied to the total profit pool available in each of the markets it serves and its share of each profit pool—which, in turn, is tied to the business's market share and relative profitability versus competitors in each market.

In this approach, the first step is for the corporate center and the unit team to agree on the size and growth of each profit pool. Fiercely competitive markets, such as pulp and paper or commercial airlines, have small (or negative) total profit pools. Less competitive markets, like soft drinks or pharmaceuticals, have large total profit pools. We find it helpful to estimate the size of each profit pool directly—through detailed benchmarking—and then forecast changes in the pool's size and growth. Each business unit then assesses what share of the total profit pool it can realistically capture over time, given its business model and positioning. Competitively advantaged businesses can capture a large share of the profit pool—by gaining or sustaining a high market share, generating above-average profitability, or both. Competitively disadvantaged businesses, by contrast, typically capture a negligible share of the profit pool. Once the unit and the corporate center agree on the likely share of the pool the business will capture over time, the corporate center can easily create the financial projections that will serve as the unit's road map.

In our view, the specific framework a company uses to ground its strategic plans isn't all that important. What is critical is that the framework establish a common language for the dialogue between the corporate center and the units—one that the strategy, marketing, and finance teams all understand and use. Without a rigorous framework to link a business's performance in the product markets with its financial performance over time, it is very difficult for top management to ascertain whether the financial projections that accompany a business unit's strategic plan are reasonable and realistically achievable. As a result, management can't know with confidence whether a performance shortfall stems from poor execution or an unrealistic and ungrounded plan.

Rule 4: Discuss resource deployments early

Companies can create more realistic forecasts and more executable plans if they discuss up front the level and timing of critical resource deployments. At Cisco Systems, for example, a cross-functional team reviews the level and timing of resource deployments early in the planning stage. These teams regularly meet with John Chambers (CEO), Dennis Powell (CFO), Randy Pond (VP of operations), and the other members of Cisco's executive team to discuss their findings and make recommendations. Once agreement is reached on resource allocation and timing at the unit level, those elements are factored into the company's two-year plan. Cisco then monitors each unit's actual resource deployments on a monthly basis (as well as its performance) to make sure things are going according to plan and that the plan is generating the expected results.

Challenging business units about when new resources need to be in place focuses the planning dialogue on what actually needs to happen across the company in order to execute each unit's strategy. Critical questions invariably surface, such as: How long will it take us to change customers' purchase patterns? How fast can we deploy our new sales force? How quickly will competitors respond? These are tough questions. But answering them makes the forecasts and the plans they accompany more feasible.

What's more, an early assessment of resource needs also informs discussions about market trends and drivers, improving the quality of the strategic plan and making it far more executable. In the course of talking about the resources needed to expand in the rapidly growing cable market, for example, Cisco came to realize that additional growth would require more trained engineers to improve existing products and develop new features. So, rather than relying on the functions to provide these resources from the bottom up, corporate management earmarked a specific number of trained engineers to support growth in cable. Cisco's financial-planning organization carefully monitors the engineering head count, the pace of feature development, and revenues generated by the business to make sure the strategy stays on track.

Rule 5: Clearly identify priorities

To deliver any strategy successfully, managers must make thousands of tactical decisions and put them into action. But not all tactics are equally important. In most instances, a few key steps must be taken—at the right time and in the right way—to meet planned performance. Leading companies make these priorities explicit so that each executive has a clear sense of where to direct his or her efforts.

At Textron, a $10 billion multi-industrial conglomerate, each business unit identifies "improvement priorities" that it must act upon to realize the performance outlined in its strategic plan. Each improvement priority is translated into action items with clearly defined accountabilities, timetables, and key performance indicators (KPIs) that allow executives to tell how a unit is delivering on a priority. Improvement priorities and action items cascade to every level at the company—from the management committee (consisting of Textron's top five executives) down to the lowest levels in each of the company's ten business units. Lewis Campbell, Textron's CEO, summarizes the company's approach this way: "Everyone needs to know: 'If I have only one hour to work, here's what I'm going to focus on.' Our goal deployment process makes each individual's accountabilities and priorities clear."

The Swiss pharmaceutical giant Roche goes as far as to turn its business plans into detailed performance contracts that clearly specify the steps needed and the risks that must be managed to achieve the plans. These contracts all include a "delivery agenda" that lists the five to ten critical priorities with the greatest impact on performance. By maintaining a delivery agenda at each level of the company, Chairman and CEO Franz Humer and his leadership team make sure "everyone at Roche understands exactly what we have agreed to do at a strategic level and that our strategy gets translated into clear execution priorities. Our delivery agenda helps us stay the course with the strategy decisions we have made so that execution is actually allowed to happen. We cannot control implementation from HQ, but we can agree on the priorities, communicate relentlessly, and hold managers accountable for executing against their commitments."

Rule 6: Continuously monitor performance

Seasoned executives know almost instinctively whether a business has asked for too much, too little, or just enough resources to deliver the goods. They develop this capability over time—essentially through trial and error. High-performing companies use real-time performance tracking to help accelerate this trial-and-error process. They continuously monitor their resource deployment patterns and their results against plan, using continuous feedback to reset planning assumptions and reallocate resources. This real-time information allows management to spot and remedy flaws in the plan and shortfalls in execution—and to avoid confusing one with the other.

At Textron, for example, each KPI is carefully monitored, and regular operating reviews percolate performance shortfalls—or "red light" events—up through the management ranks. This provides CEO Lewis Campbell, CFO Ted French, and the other members of Textron's management committee with the information they need to spot and fix breakdowns in execution.

A similar approach has played an important role in the dramatic revival of Dow Chemical's fortunes. In December 2001, with performance in a free fall, Dow's board of directors asked Bill Stavropoulos (Dow's CEO from 1993 to 1999) to return to the helm. Stavropoulos and Andrew Liveris (the current CEO, then COO) immediately focused Dow's entire top leadership team on execution through a project they called the Performance Improvement Drive. They began by defining clear performance metrics for each of Dow's 79 business units. Performance on these key metrics was tracked against plans on a weekly basis, and the entire leadership team discussed any serious discrepancies first thing every Monday morning. As Liveris told us, the weekly monitoring sessions "forced everyone to live the details of execution" and let "the entire organization know how we were performing."

Continuous monitoring of performance is particularly important in highly volatile industries, where events outside anyone's control can render a plan irrelevant. Under CEO Alan Mulally, Boeing Commercial Airplanes' leadership team holds weekly business performance reviews to track the division's results against its multiyear plan. By tracking the deployment of resources as a leading indicator of whether a plan is being executed effectively, BCA's leadership team can make course corrections each week rather than waiting for quarterly results to roll in.

Furthermore, by proactively monitoring the primary drivers of performance (such as passenger traffic patterns, airline yields and load factors, and new aircraft orders), BCA is better able to develop and deploy effective countermeasures when events throw its plans off course. During the SARS epidemic in late 2002, for example, BCA's leadership team took action to mitigate the adverse consequences of the illness on the business's operating plan within a week of the initial outbreak. The abrupt decline in air traffic to Hong Kong, Singapore, and other Asian business centers signaled that the number of future aircraft deliveries to the region would fall—perhaps precipitously. Accordingly, BCA scaled back its medium-term production plans (delaying the scheduled ramp-up of some programs and accelerating the shutdown of others) and adjusted its multiyear operating plan to reflect the anticipated financial impact.

Rule 7: Reward and develop execution capabilities

No list of rules on this topic would be complete without a reminder that companies have to motivate and develop their staffs; at the end of the day, no process can be better than the people who have to make it work. Unsurprisingly, therefore, nearly all of the companies we studied insisted that the selection and development of management was an essential ingredient in their success. And while improving the capabilities of a company's workforce is no easy task—often taking many years—these capabilities, once built, can drive superior planning and execution for decades.

For Barclays' Bob Diamond, nothing is more important than "ensuring that [the company] hires only A players." In his view, "the hidden costs of bad hiring decisions are enormous, so despite the fact that we are doubling in size, we insist that as a top team we take responsibility for all hiring. The jury of your peers is the toughest judgment, so we vet each others' potential hires and challenge each other to keep raising the bar." It's equally important to make sure that talented hires are rewarded for superior execution. To reinforce its core values of "client," "meritocracy," "team," and "integrity," Barclays Capital has innovative pay schemes that "ring fence" rewards. Stars don't lose out just because the business is entering new markets with lower returns during the growth phase. Says Diamond: "It's so bad for the culture if you don't deliver what you promised to people who have delivered. . . . You've got to make sure you are consistent and fair, unless you want to lose your most productive people."

Companies that are strong on execution also emphasize development. Soon after he became CEO of 3M, Jim McNerney and his top team spent 18 months hashing out a new leadership model for the company. Challenging debates among members of the top team led to agreement on six "leadership attributes"—namely, the ability to "chart the course," "energize and inspire others," "demonstrate ethics, integrity, and compliance," "deliver results," "raise the bar," and "innovate resourcefully." 3M's leadership agreed that these six attributes were essential for the company to become skilled at execution and known for accountability. Today, the leaders credit this model with helping 3M to sustain and even improve its consistently strong performance.

The prize for closing the strategy-to-performance gap is huge—an increase in performance of anywhere from 60% to 100% for most companies. But this almost certainly understates the true benefits. Companies that create tight links between their strategies, their plans, and, ultimately, their performance often experience a cultural multiplier effect. Over time, as they turn their strategies into great performance, leaders in these organizations become much more confident in their own capabilities and much more willing to make the stretch commitments that inspire and transform large companies. In turn, individual managers who keep their commitments are rewarded—with faster progression and fatter paychecks—reinforcing the behaviors needed to drive any company forward.

Eventually, a culture of overperformance emerges. Investors start giving management the benefit of the doubt when it comes to bold moves and performance delivery. The result is a performance premium on the company's stock—one that further rewards stretch commitments and performance delivery. Before long, the company's reputation among potential recruits rises, and a virtuous circle is created in which talent begets performance, performance begets rewards, and rewards beget even more talent. In short, closing the strategy-to-performance gap is not only a source of immediate performance improvement but also an important driver of cultural change with a large and lasting impact on the organization's capabilities, strategies, and competitiveness.

Originally published in July 2005. Reprint R0507E.

Who Has the D?

How Clear Decision Roles Enhance Organizational Performance. *by Paul Rogers and Marcia Blenko*

DECISIONS ARE THE COIN of the realm in business. Every success, every mishap, every opportunity seized or missed is the result of a decision that someone made or failed to make. At many companies, decisions routinely get stuck inside the organization like loose change. But it's more than loose change that's at stake, of course; it's the performance of the entire organization. Never mind what industry you're in, how big and well known your company may be, or how clever your strategy is. If you can't make the right decisions quickly and effectively, and execute those decisions consistently, your business will lose ground.

Indeed, making good decisions and making them happen quickly are the hallmarks of high-performing organizations. When we surveyed executives at 350 global companies about their organizational effectiveness, only 15% said that they have an organization that helps the business outperform competitors. What sets those top performers apart is the quality, speed, and execution of their decision making. The most effective organizations score well on the major strategic decisions—which markets to enter or exit, which businesses to buy or sell, where to allocate capital and talent. But they truly shine when it comes to the critical operating decisions requiring consistency and speed—how to drive product innovation, the best way to position brands, how to manage channel partners.

Even in companies respected for their decisiveness, however, there can be ambiguity over who is accountable for which decisions.

As a result, the entire decision-making process can stall, usually at one of four bottlenecks: global versus local, center versus business unit, function versus function, and inside versus outside partners.

The first of these bottlenecks, *global versus local* decision making, can occur in nearly every major business process and function. Decisions about brand building and product development frequently get snared here, when companies wrestle over how much authority local businesses should have to tailor products for their markets. Marketing is another classic global versus local issue—should local markets have the power to determine pricing and advertising?

The second bottleneck, *center versus business unit* decision making, tends to afflict parent companies and their subsidiaries. Business units are on the front line, close to the customer; the center sees the big picture, sets broad goals, and keeps the organization focused on winning. Where should the decision-making power lie? Should a major capital investment, for example, depend on the approval of the business unit that will own it, or should headquarters make the final call?

Function versus function decision making is perhaps the most common bottleneck. Every manufacturer, for instance, faces a balancing act between product development and marketing during the design of a new product. Who should decide what? Cross-functional decisions too often result in ineffective compromise solutions, which frequently need to be revisited because the right people were not involved at the outset.

The fourth decision-making bottleneck, *inside versus outside partners,* has become familiar with the rise of outsourcing, joint ventures, strategic alliances, and franchising. In such arrangements, companies need to be absolutely clear about which decisions can be owned by the external partner (usually those about the execution of strategy) and which must continue to be made internally (decisions about the strategy itself). In the case of outsourcing, for instance, brand-name apparel and foot-wear marketers once assumed that overseas suppliers could be responsible for decisions about plant employees' wages and working conditions. Big mistake.

Idea in Brief

Decisions are the coin of the realm in business. Every success, every mishap, every opportunity seized or missed stems from a decision someone made—or failed to make. Yet in many firms, decisions routinely stall inside the organization—hurting the entire company's performance.

The culprit? Ambiguity over who's accountable for which decisions. In one auto manufacturer that was missing milestones for rolling out new models, marketers *and* product developers each thought they were responsible for deciding new models' standard features and colors. Result? Conflict over who had final say, endless revisiting of decisions—and missed deadlines that led to lost sales.

How to clarify decision accountability? Assign clear roles for the decisions that most affect your firm's performance—such as which markets to enter, where to allocate capital, and how to drive product innovation. Think "RAPID": Who should **r**ecommend a course of action on a key decision? Who must **a**gree to a recommendation before it can move forward? Who will **p**erform the actions needed to implement the decision? Whose **i**nput is needed to determine the proposal's feasibility? Who **d**ecides—brings the decision to closure and commits the organization to implement it?

When you clarify decision roles, you make the *right* choices—swiftly and effectively.

Clearing the Bottlenecks

The most important step in unclogging decision-making bottlenecks is assigning clear roles and responsibilities. Good decision makers recognize which decisions really matter to performance. They think through who should recommend a particular path, who needs to agree, who should have input, who has ultimate responsibility for making the decision, and who is accountable for follow-through. They make the process routine. The result: better coordination and quicker response times.

Companies have devised a number of methods to clarify decision roles and assign responsibilities. We have used an approach called RAPID, which has evolved over the years, to help hundreds of companies develop clear decision-making guidelines. It is, for sure, not a

Idea in Practice

The RAPID Decision Model

For every strategic decision, assign the following roles and responsibilities:

People Who . . .	Are Responsible For . . .
Recommend	• Making a proposal on a key decision, gathering input, and providing data and analysis to make a sensible choice in a timely fashion • Consulting with input providers—hearing and incorporating their views, and winning their buy-in
Agree	• Negotiating a modified proposal with the recommender if they have concerns about the original proposal • Escalating unresolved issues to the decider if the "A" and "R" can't resolve differences • If necessary, exercising veto power over the recommendation
Perform	• Executing a decision once it's made • Seeing that the decision is implemented promptly and effectively
Input	• Providing relevant facts to the recommender that shed light on the proposal's feasibility and practical implications
Decide	• Serving as the single point of accountability • Bringing the decision to closure by resolving any impasse in the decision-making process • Committing the organization to implementing the decision

panacea (an indecisive decision maker, for example, can ruin any good system), but it's an important start. The letters in RAPID stand for the primary roles in any decision-making process, although these roles are not performed exactly in this order: recommend, agree, perform, input, and decide—the "D." (See the sidebar "A Decision-Making Primer.")

Decision-Role Pitfalls

In assigning decision roles:

- Ensure that only one person "has the D." If two or more people think they're in charge of a particular decision, a tug-of-war results.
- Watch for a proliferation of "A's." Too many people with veto power can paralyze recommenders. If many people must agree, you probably haven't pushed decisions down far enough in your organization.
- Avoid assigning too many "I's." When many people give input, at least some of them aren't making meaningful contributions.

The RAPID Model in Action

Example: At British department-store chain John Lewis, company buyers wanted to increase sales and reduce complexity by offering fewer salt and pepper mill models. The company launched the streamlined product set without involving the sales staff. And sales fell. Upon visiting the stores, buyers saw that salespeople (not understanding the strategy behind the recommendation) had halved shelf space to match the reduction in product range, rather than maintaining the same space but stocking more of the products.

To fix the problem, the company "gave buyers the D" on how much space product categories would have. Sales staff "had the A": If space allocations didn't make sense to them, they could force additional negotiations. They also "had the P," implementing product layouts in stores.

Once decision roles were clarified, sales of salt and pepper mills exceeded original levels.

The people who *recommend* a course of action are responsible for making a proposal or offering alternatives. They need data and analysis to support their recommendations, as well as common sense about what's reasonable, practical, and effective.

The people who *agree* to a recommendation are those who need to sign off on it before it can move forward. If they veto a proposal, they must either work with the recommender to come up with an alternative or elevate the issue to the person with the D. For decision making to function smoothly, only a few people should have such veto power. They may be executives responsible for legal or regulatory compliance or the heads of units whose operations will be significantly affected by the decision.

People with *input* responsibilities are consulted about the recommendation. Their role is to provide the relevant facts that are the basis of any good decision: How practical is the proposal? Can manufacturing accommodate the design change? Where there's dissent or contrasting views, it's important to get these people to the table at the right time. The recommender has no obligation to act on the input he or she receives but is expected to take it into account—particularly since the people who provide input are generally among those who must implement a decision. Consensus is a worthy goal, but as a decision-making standard, it can be an obstacle to action or a recipe for lowest-common-denominator compromise. A more practical objective is to get everyone involved to buy in to the decision.

Eventually, one person will *decide*. The decision maker is the single point of accountability who must bring the decision to closure and commit the organization to act on it. To be strong and effective, the person with the D needs good business judgment, a grasp of the relevant trade-offs, a bias for action, and a keen awareness of the organization that will execute the decision.

The final role in the process involves the people who will *perform* the decision. They see to it that the decision is implemented promptly and effectively. It's a crucial role. Very often, a good decision executed quickly beats a brilliant decision implemented slowly or poorly.

RAPID can be used to help redesign the way an organization works or to target a single bottleneck. Some companies use the approach for the top ten to 20 decisions, or just for the CEO and his or her direct reports. Other companies use it throughout the organization—to improve customer service by clarifying decision roles on the front line, for instance. When people see an effective process for making decisions, they spread the word. For example, after senior managers at a major U.S. retailer used RAPID to sort out a particularly thorny set of corporate decisions, they promptly built the process into their own functional organizations.

To see the process in action, let's look at the way four companies have worked through their decision-making bottlenecks.

Global Versus Local

Every major company today operates in global markets, buying raw materials in one place, shipping them somewhere else, and selling finished products all over the world. Most are trying simultaneously to build local presence and expertise, and to achieve economies of scale. Decision making in this environment is far from straightforward. Frequently, decisions cut across the boundaries between global and local managers, and sometimes across a regional layer in between: What investments will streamline our supply chain? How far should we go in standardizing products or tailoring them for local markets?

The trick in decision making is to avoid becoming either mindlessly global or hopelessly local. If decision-making authority tilts too far toward global executives, local customers' preferences can easily be overlooked, undermining the efficiency and agility of local operations. But with too much local authority, a company is likely to miss out on crucial economies of scale or opportunities with global clients.

To strike the right balance, a company must recognize its most important sources of value and make sure that decision roles line up with them. This was the challenge facing Martin Broughton, the former CEO and chairman of British American Tobacco, the second-largest tobacco company in the world. In 1993, when Broughton was appointed chief executive, BAT was losing ground to its nearest competitor. Broughton knew that the company needed to take better advantage of its global scale, but decision roles and responsibilities were at odds with this goal. Four geographic operating units ran themselves autonomously, rarely collaborating and sometimes even competing. Achieving consistency across global brands proved difficult, and cost

A Decision-Making Primer

GOOD DECISION MAKING DEPENDS on assigning clear and specific roles. This sounds simple enough, but many companies struggle to make decisions because lots of people feel accountable—or no one does. RAPID and other tools used to analyze decision making give senior management teams a method for assigning roles and involving the relevant people. The key is to be clear who has input, who gets to decide, and who gets it done.

The five letters in RAPID correspond to the five critical decision-making roles: recommend, agree, perform, input, and decide. As you'll see, the roles are not carried out lockstep in this order—we took some liberties for the sake of creating a useful acronym.

Recommend

People in this role are responsible for making a proposal, gathering input, and providing the right data and analysis to make a sensible decision in a timely fashion. In the course of developing a proposal, recommenders consult with the people who provide input, not just hearing and incorporating their views but also building buy in along the way. Recommenders must have analytical skills, common sense, and organizational smarts.

Agree

Individuals in this role have veto power—yes or no—over the recommendation. Exercising the veto triggers a debate between themselves and the recommenders, which should lead to a modified proposal. If that takes too long, or if the two parties simply can't agree, they can escalate the issue to the person who has the D.

Input

These people are consulted on the decision. Because the people who provide input are typically involved in implementation, recommenders have a strong interest in taking their advice seriously. No input is binding, but this

synergies across the operating units were elusive. Industry insiders joked that "there are seven major tobacco companies in the world—and four of them are British American Tobacco." Broughton vowed to change the punch line.

The chief executive envisioned an organization that could take advantage of the opportunities a global business offers—global brands that could compete with established winners such as Altria Group's Marlboro; global purchasing of important raw materials,

shouldn't undermine its importance. If the right people are not involved and motivated, the decision is far more likely to falter during execution.

Decide

The person with the D is the formal decision maker. He or she is ultimately accountable for the decision, for better or worse, and has the authority to resolve any impasse in the decision-making process and to commit the organization to action.

Perform

Once a decision is made, a person or group of people will be responsible for executing it. In some instances, the people responsible for implementing a decision are the same people who recommended it.

Writing down the roles and assigning accountability are essential steps, but good decision making also requires the right process. Too many rules can cause the process to collapse under its own weight. The most effective process is grounded in specifics but simple enough to adapt if necessary.

When the process gets slowed down, the problem can often be traced back to one of three trouble spots. First is a lack of clarity about who has the D. If more than one person think they have it for a particular decision, that decision will get caught up in a tug-of-war. The flip side can be equally damaging: No one is accountable for crucial decisions, and the business suffers. Second, a proliferation of people who have veto power can make life tough for recommenders. If a company has too many people in the "agree" role, it usually means that decisions are not pushed down far enough in the organization. Third, if there are a lot of people giving input, it's a signal that at least some of them aren't making a meaningful contribution.

including tobacco; and more consistency in innovation and customer management. But Broughton didn't want the company to lose its nimbleness and competitive hunger in local markets by shifting too much decision-making power to global executives.

The first step was to clarify roles for the most important decisions. Procurement became a proving ground. Previously, each operating unit had identified its own suppliers and negotiated contracts for all materials. Under Broughton, a global procurement team was set up in headquarters and given authority to choose suppliers and negotiate pricing and quality for global materials, including bulk tobacco and certain types of packaging. Regional procurement teams were now given input into global materials strategies but ultimately had to implement the team's decision. As soon as the global team signed contracts with suppliers, responsibility shifted to the regional teams, who worked out the details of delivery and service with the suppliers in their regions. For materials that did not offer global economies of scale (mentholated filters for the North American market, for example), the regional teams retained their decision-making authority.

As the effort to revamp decision making in procurement gained momentum, the company set out to clarify roles in all its major decisions. The process wasn't easy. A company the size of British American Tobacco has a huge number of moving parts, and developing a practical system for making decisions requires sweating lots of details. What's more, decision-making authority is power, and people are often reluctant to give it up.

It's crucial for the people who will live with the new system to help design it. At BAT, Broughton created working groups led by people earmarked, implicitly or explicitly, for leadership roles in the future. For example, Paul Adams, who ultimately succeeded Broughton as chief executive, was asked to lead the group charged with redesigning decision making for brand and customer management. At the time, Adams was a regional head within one of the operating units. With other senior executives, including some of his own direct reports, Broughton specified that their role was to provide input, not to veto recommendations. Broughton didn't make the common mistake of seeking consensus, which is often an obstacle to action. Instead, he made it clear that the objective was not deciding whether to change the decision-making process but achieving buy in about how to do so as effectively as possible.

The new decision roles provided the foundation the company needed to operate successfully on a global basis while retaining flexibility at the local level. The focus and efficiency of its decision making were reflected in the company's results: After the decision-making overhaul, British American Tobacco experienced nearly ten years of growth well above the levels of its competitors in sales, profits, and market value. The company has gone on to have one of the best-performing stocks on the UK market and has reemerged as a major global player in the tobacco industry.

Center Versus Business Unit

The first rule for making good decisions is to involve the right people at the right level of the organization. For BAT, capturing economies of scale required its global team to appropriate some decision-making powers from regional divisions. For many companies, a similar balancing act takes place between executives at the center and managers in the business units. If too many decisions flow to the center, decision making can grind to a halt. The problem is different but no less critical if the decisions that are elevated to senior executives are the wrong ones.

Companies often grow into this type of problem. In small and midsize organizations, a single management team—sometimes a single leader—effectively handles every major decision. As a company grows and its operations become more complex, however, senior executives can no longer master the details required to make decisions in every business.

A change in management style, often triggered by the arrival of a new CEO, can create similar tensions. At a large British retailer, for example, the senior team was accustomed to the founder making all critical decisions. When his successor began seeking consensus on important issues, the team was suddenly unsure of its role, and many decisions stalled. It's a common scenario, yet most management teams and boards of directors don't specify how decision-making authority should change as the company does.

A growth opportunity highlighted that issue for Wyeth (then known as American Home Products) in late 2000. Through organic growth, acquisitions, and partnerships, Wyeth's pharmaceutical division had developed three sizable businesses: biotech, vaccines, and traditional pharmaceutical products. Even though each business had its own market dynamics, operating requirements, and research focus, most important decisions were pushed up to one group of senior executives. "We were using generalists across all issues," said Joseph M. Mahady, president of North American and global businesses for Wyeth Pharmaceuticals. "It was a signal that we weren't getting our best decision making."

The problem crystallized for Wyeth when managers in the biotech business saw a vital—but perishable—opportunity to establish a leading position with Enbrel, a promising rheumatoid arthritis drug. Competitors were working on the same class of drug, so Wyeth needed to move quickly. This meant expanding production capacity by building a new plant, which would be located at the Grange Castle Business Park in Dublin, Ireland.

The decision, by any standard, was a complex one. Once approved by regulators, the facility would be the biggest biotech plant in the world—and the largest capital investment Wyeth had ever undertaken. Yet peak demand for the drug was not easy to determine. What's more, Wyeth planned to market Enbrel in partnership with Immunex (now a part of Amgen). In its deliberations about the plant, therefore, Wyeth needed to factor in the requirements of building up its technical expertise, technology transfer issues, and an uncertain competitive environment.

Input on the decision filtered up slowly through a gauze of overlapping committees, leaving senior executives hungry for a more detailed grasp of the issues. Given the narrow window of opportunity, Wyeth acted quickly, moving from a first look at the Grange Castle project to implementation in six months. But in the midst of this process, Wyeth Pharmaceuticals' executives saw the larger issue: The company needed a system that would push more decisions down to the business units, where operational knowledge was greatest, and elevate the decisions that required the senior team's input, such as marketing strategy and manufacturing capacity.

In short order, Wyeth gave authority for many decisions to business unit managers, leaving senior executives with veto power over some of the more sensitive issues related to Grange Castle. But after that investment decision was made, the D for many subsequent decisions about the Enbrel business lay with Cavan Redmond, the executive vice president and general manager of Wyeth's biotech division, and his new management team. Redmond gathered input from managers in biotech manufacturing, marketing, forecasting, finance, and R&D, and quickly set up the complex schedules needed to collaborate with Immunex. Responsibility for execution rested firmly with the business unit, as always. But now Redmond, supported by his team, also had authority to make important decisions.

Grange Castle is paying off so far. Enbrel is among the leading brands for rheumatoid arthritis, with sales of $1.7 billion through the first half of 2005. And Wyeth's metabolism for making decisions has increased. Recently, when the U.S. Food and Drug Administration granted priority review status to another new drug, Tygacil, because of the antibiotic's efficacy against drug-resistant infections, Wyeth displayed its new reflexes. To keep Tygacil on a fast track, the company had to orchestrate a host of critical steps—refining the process technology, lining up supplies, ensuring quality control, allocating manufacturing capacity. The vital decisions were made one or two levels down in the biotech organization, where the expertise resided. "Instead of debating whether you can move your product into my shop, we had the decision systems in place to run it up and down the business units and move ahead rapidly with Tygacil," said Mahady. The drug was approved by the FDA in June 2005 and moved into volume production a mere three days later.

Function Versus Function

Decisions that cut across functions are some of the most important a company faces. Indeed, cross-functional collaboration has become an axiom of business, essential for arriving at the best answers for the company and its customers. But fluid decision making across functional teams remains a constant challenge, even for companies known for doing it well, like Toyota and Dell. For instance, a team that thinks it's more efficient to make a decision without consulting other functions may wind up missing out on relevant input or being overruled by another team that believes—rightly or wrongly—it

A Recipe for a Decision-Making Bottleneck

AT ONE AUTOMAKER WE STUDIED, marketers and product developers were confused about who was responsible for making decisions about new models.

When we asked, "Who has the right to decide which features will be standard?"

64% of product developers said, "We do."

83% of marketers said, "We do."

When we asked, "Who has the right to decide which colors will be offered?"

77% of product developers said, "We do."

61% of marketers said, "We do."

Not surprisingly, the new models were delayed.

should have been included in the process. Many of the most important cross-functional decisions are, by their very nature, the most difficult to orchestrate, and that can string out the process and lead to sparring between fiefdoms and costly indecision.

The theme here is a lack of clarity about who has the D. For example, at a global auto manufacturer that was missing its milestones for rolling out new models—and was paying the price in falling sales—it turned out that marketers and product developers were confused about which function was responsible for making decisions about standard features and color ranges for new models. When we asked the marketing team who had the D about which features should be standard, 83% said the marketers did. When we posed the same question to product developers, 64% said the responsibility rested with them. (See "A Recipe for a Decision-Making Bottleneck.")

The practical difficulty of connecting functions through smooth decision making crops up frequently at retailers. John Lewis, the leading department store chain in the United Kingdom, might reasonably expect to overcome this sort of challenge more readily than other retailers. Spedan Lewis, who built the business in the early twentieth century, was a pioneer in employee ownership. A strong connection between managers and employees permeated every aspect of the store's operations and remained vital to the company as it grew into the largest employee-owned business in the United Kingdom, with 59,600 employees and more than £5 billion in revenues in 2004.

Even at John Lewis, however, with its heritage of cooperation and teamwork, cross-functional decision making can be hard to sustain. Take salt and pepper mills, for instance. John Lewis, which prides itself on having great selection, stocked nearly 50 SKUs of salt and pepper mills, while most competitors stocked around 20. The company's buyers saw an opportunity to increase sales and reduce complexity by offering a smaller number of popular and well-chosen products in each price point and style.

When John Lewis launched the new range, sales fell. This made no sense to the buyers until they visited the stores and saw how the merchandise was displayed. The buyers had made their decision without fully involving the sales staff, who therefore did not understand the strategy behind the new selection. As a result, the sellers had cut shelf space in half to match the reduction in range, rather than devoting the same amount of shelf space to stocking more of each product.

To fix the communication problem, John Lewis needed to clarify decision roles. The buyers were given the D on how much space to allocate to each product category. If the space allocation didn't make sense to the sales staff, however, they had the authority to raise their concerns and force a new round of negotiations. They also had responsibility for implementing product layouts in the stores. When the communication was sorted out and shelf space was restored, sales of the salt and pepper mills climbed well above original levels.

Crafting a decision-making process that connected the buying and selling functions for salt and pepper mills was relatively easy; rolling it out across the entire business was more challenging. Salt and pepper mills are just one of several hundred product categories for John Lewis. This element of scale is one reason why cross-functional bottlenecks are not easy to unclog. Different functions have different incentives and goals, which are often in conflict. When it comes down to a struggle between two functions, there may be good reasons to locate the D in either place—buying or selling, marketing or product development.

Here, as elsewhere, someone needs to think objectively about where value is created and assign decision roles accordingly. Eliminating cross-functional bottlenecks actually has less to do with shifting decision-making responsibilities between departments and more to do with ensuring that the people with relevant information are allowed to share it. The decision maker is important, of course, but more important is designing a system that aligns decision making and makes it routine.

Inside Versus Outside Partners

Decision making within an organization is hard enough. Trying to make decisions between separate organizations on different continents adds layers of complexity that can scuttle the best strategy. Companies that outsource capabilities in pursuit of cost and quality advantages face this very challenge. Which decisions should be made internally? Which can be delegated to outsourcing partners?

These questions are also relevant for strategic partners—a global bank working with an IT contractor on a systems development project, for example, or a media company that acquires content from a studio—and for companies conducting part of their business through franchisees. There is no right answer to who should have the power to decide what. But the wrong approach is to assume that contractual arrangements can provide the answer.

An outdoor-equipment company based in the United States discovered this recently when it decided to scale up production of gas patio heaters for the lower end of the market. The company had some success manufacturing high-end products in China. But with the advent of superdiscounters like Wal-Mart, Target, and Home Depot, the company realized it needed to move more of its production overseas to feed these retailers with lower-cost offerings. The timetable left little margin for error: The company started tooling up factories in April and June of 2004, hoping to be ready for the Christmas season.

The Decision-Driven Organization

THE DEFINING CHARACTERISTIC of high-performing organizations is their ability to make good decisions and to make them happen quickly. The companies that succeed tend to follow a few clear principles.

Some decisions matter more than others

The decisions that are crucial to building value in the business are the ones that matter most. Some of them will be the big strategic decisions, but just as important are the critical operating decisions that drive the business day to day and are vital to effective execution.

Action is the goal

Good decision making doesn't end with a decision; it ends with implementation. The objective shouldn't be consensus, which often becomes an obstacle to action, but buy in.

Ambiguity is the enemy

Clear accountability is essential: Who contributes input, who makes the decision, and who carries it out? Without clarity, gridlock and delay are the most likely outcomes. Clarity doesn't necessarily mean concentrating authority in a few people; it means defining who has responsibility to make decisions, who has input, and who is charged with putting them into action.

Speed and adaptability are crucial

A company that makes good decisions quickly has a higher metabolism, which allows it to act on opportunities and overcome obstacles. The best decision makers create an environment where people can come together quickly and efficiently to make the most important decisions.

Decision roles trump the organizational chart

No decision-making structure will be perfect for every decision. The key is to involve the right people at the right level in the right part of the organization at the right time.

A well-aligned organization reinforces roles

Clear decision roles are critical, but they are not enough. If an organization does not reinforce the right approach to decision making through its measures and incentives, information flows, and culture, the behavior won't become routine.

Practicing beats preaching

Involve the people who will live with the new decision roles in designing them. The very process of thinking about new decision behaviors motivates people to adopt them.

A Decision Diagnostic

CONSIDER THE LAST THREE MEANINGFUL decisions you've been involved in and ask yourself the following questions.

1. Were the decisions right?
2. Were they made with appropriate speed?
3. Were they executed well?
4. Were the right people involved, in the right way?
5. Was it clear for each decision
    - who would recommend a solution?
    - who would provide input?
    - who had the final say?
    - who would be responsible for following through?
6. Were the decision roles, process, and time frame respected?
7. Were the decisions based on appropriate facts?
8. To the extent that there were divergent facts or opinions, was it clear who had the D?
9. Were the decision makers at the appropriate level in the company?
10. Did the organization's measures and incentives encourage the people involved to make the right decisions?

Right away, there were problems. Although the Chinese manufacturing partners understood costs, they had little idea what American consumers wanted. When expensive designs arrived from the head office in the United States, Chinese plant managers made compromises to meet contracted cost targets. They used a lower grade material, which discolored. They placed the power switch in a spot that was inconvenient for the user but easier to build. Instead of making certain parts from a single casting, they welded materials together, which looked terrible.

To fix these problems, the U.S. executives had to draw clear lines around which decisions should be made on which side of the ocean. The company broke down the design and manufacturing process into five steps and analyzed how decisions were made at each step. The company was also much more explicit about what the manufacturing specs would include and what the manufacturer was expected to do with them. The objective was not simply to clarify decision roles but to make sure those roles corresponded directly to the sources of value in the business. If a decision would affect the look and feel of the finished product, headquarters would have to sign off on it. But if a decision would not affect the customer's experience, it could be made in China. If, for example, Chinese engineers found a less expensive material that didn't compromise the product's look, feel, and functionality, they could make that change on their own.

To help with the transition to this system, the company put a team of engineers on-site in China to ensure a smooth handoff of the specs and to make decisions on issues that would become complex and time-consuming if elevated to the home office. Marketing executives in the home office insisted that it should take a customer ten minutes and no more than six steps to assemble the product at home. The company's engineers in China, along with the Chinese manufacturing team, had input into this assembly requirement and were responsible for execution. But the D resided with headquarters, and the requirement became a major design factor. Decisions about logistics, however, became the province of the engineering team in China: It would figure out how to package the heaters so that one-third more boxes would fit into a container, which reduced shipping costs substantially.

If managers suddenly realize that they're spending less time sitting through meetings wondering why they are there, that's an early signal that companies have become better at making decisions. When meetings start with a common understanding about who is responsible for providing valuable input and who has the D, an organization's decision-making metabolism will get a boost.

No single lever turns a decision-challenged organization into a decision-driven one, of course, and no blueprint can provide for all the contingencies and business shifts a company is bound to encounter. The most successful companies use simple tools that help them recognize potential bottlenecks and think through decision roles and responsibilities with each change in the business environment. That's difficult to do—and even more difficult for competitors to copy. But by taking some very practical steps, any company can become more effective, beginning with its next decision.

Originally published in January 2006. Reprint R0601D.

About the Contributors

MICHAEL E. PORTER is the Bishop William Lawrence University Professor at Harvard Business School.

JAMES C. COLLINS operates a management research laboratory in Boulder, Colorado.

JERRY I. PORRAS is the Lane Professor, Emeritus, at Stanford University's Graduate School of Business.

MARK W. JOHNSON is the chairman and a cofounder of Innosight, a strategic innovation and investing company based in Boston.

CLAYTON M. CHRISTENSEN is the Robert and Jane Cizik Professor of Business Administration at Harvard Business School.

HENNING KAGERMANN is a former CEO of SAP AG, a software corporation based in Germany.

W. CHAN KIM is the Boston Consulting Group Bruce D. Henderson Chaired Professor of Strategy and International Management at Insead in France.

RENÉE MAUBORGNE is the Insead Distinguished Fellow and a professor of strategy at Insead in France.

GARY L. NEILSON is a senior vice president in the Chicago office of Booz & Company, a management consulting firm.

KARLA L. MARTIN is a principal in Booz & Company's San Francisco office.

ELIZABETH POWERS is a principal in Booz & Company's New York office.

ROBERT S. KAPLAN is the Baker Foundation Professor at Harvard Business School and codeveloper, with David P. Norton, of the balanced scorecard.

DAVID P. NORTON is the founder and president of the Balanced Scorecard Collaborative, Palladium Group, in Massachusetts.

ORIT GADIESH is the chairman of Bain & Company, a management consulting firm based in Boston.

JAMES L. GILBERT, a former director of Bain & Company, is an executive vice president of strategy and business development at Boston Scientific.

MICHAEL C. MANKINS is a managing partner in the San Francisco office of Marakon Associates, an international strategy consulting firm.

RICHARD STEELE is a partner in the New York office of The Bridgespan Group, a nonprofit consulting firm.

PAUL ROGERS is managing partner for the United Kingdom at Bain & Company's London office.

MARCIA BLENKO is a partner at Bain & Company in Boston and leads Bain's Global Organization practice.

Index

HBR'S 10 MUST READS

On Change Management

HBR'S 10 MUST READS

On Change Management

HARVARD BUSINESS REVIEW PRESS
Boston, Massachusetts

Printed in the United States of America
39 38 37 36

Library of Congress Cataloging-in-Publication Data
HBR's 10 must reads on change management.
p. cm.
Includes index.
ISBN 978-1-4221-5800-5 (pbk. : alk. paper) 1. Organizational change
2. Leadership I. Harvard business review II. Title: HBR's ten must reads on change management III. Title: Harvard business review's 10 must reads on change management.
HD58.8.H394 2010
658.4'06—dc22

2010031616

The paper used in this publication meets the requirements of the American National Standard for Permanence of Paper for Publications and Documents in Libraries and Archives Z39.48-1992.

Contents

HBR'S 10 MUST READS

On Change Management

Leading Change

Why Transformation Efforts Fail. *by John P. Kotter*

OVER THE PAST DECADE, I have watched more than 100 companies try to remake themselves into significantly better competitors. They have included large organizations (Ford) and small ones (Landmark Communications), companies based in the United States (General Motors) and elsewhere (British Airways), corporations that were on their knees (Eastern Airlines), and companies that were earning good money (Bristol-Myers Squibb). These efforts have gone under many banners: total quality management, reengineering, rightsizing, restructuring, cultural change, and turnaround. But, in almost every case, the basic goal has been the same: to make fundamental changes in how business is conducted in order to help cope with a new, more challenging market environment.

A few of these corporate change efforts have been very successful. A few have been utter failures. Most fall somewhere in between, with a distinct tilt toward the lower end of the scale. The lessons that can be drawn are interesting and will probably be relevant to even more organizations in the increasingly competitive business environment of the coming decade.

The most general lesson to be learned from the more successful cases is that the change process goes through a series of phases that, in total, usually require a considerable length of time. Skipping steps creates only the illusion of speed and never produces a satisfying result. A second very general lesson is that critical mistakes in any of the phases can have a devastating impact, slowing momentum and

Eight steps to transforming your organization

1 **Establishing a sense of urgency**
- Examining market and competitive realities
- Identifying and discussing crises, potential crises, or major opportunities

2 **Forming a powerful guiding coalition**
- Assembling a group with enough power to lead the change effort
- Encouraging the group to work together as a team

3 **Creating a vision**
- Creating a vision to help direct the change effort
- Developing strategies for achieving that vision

4 **Communicating the vision**
- Using every vehicle possible to communicate the new vision and strategies
- Teaching new behaviors by the example of the guiding coalition

5 **Empowering others to act on the vision**
- Getting rid of obstacles to change
- Changing systems or structures that seriously undermine the vision
- Encouraging risk taking and nontraditional ideas, activities, and actions

6 **Planning for and creating short-term wins**
- Planning for visible performance improvements
- Creating those improvements
- Recognizing and rewarding employees involved in the improvements

7 **Consolidating improvements and producing still more change**
- Using increased credibility to change systems, structures, and policies that don't fit the vision
- Hiring, promoting, and developing employees who can implement the vision
- Reinvigorating the process with new projects, themes, and change agents

8 **Institutionalizing new approaches**
- Articulating the connections between the new behaviors and corporate success
- Developing the means to ensure leadership development and succession

Idea in Brief

Most major change initiatives—whether intended to boost quality, improve culture, or reverse a corporate death spiral—generate only lukewarm results. Many fail miserably.

Why? Kotter maintains that too many managers don't realize transformation is a *process*, not an event. It advances through stages that build on each other. And it takes years. Pressured to accelerate the process, managers skip stages. But shortcuts never work.

Equally troubling, even highly capable managers make critical mistakes—such as declaring victory too soon. Result? Loss of momentum, reversal of hard-won gains, and devastation of the entire transformation effort.

By understanding the stages of change—and the pitfalls unique to each stage—you boost your chances of a successful transformation. The payoff? Your organization flexes with tectonic shifts in competitors, markets, and technologies—leaving rivals far behind.

negating hard-won gains. Perhaps because we have relatively little experience in renewing organizations, even very capable people often make at least one big error.

Error 1: Not Establishing a Great Enough Sense of Urgency

Most successful change efforts begin when some individuals or some groups start to look hard at a company's competitive situation, market position, technological trends, and financial performance. They focus on the potential revenue drop when an important patent expires, the five-year trend in declining margins in a core business, or an emerging market that everyone seems to be ignoring. They then find ways to communicate this information broadly and dramatically, especially with respect to crises, potential crises, or great opportunities that are very timely. This first step is essential because just getting a transformation program started requires the aggressive cooperation of many individuals. Without motivation, people won't help, and the effort goes nowhere.

Compared with other steps in the change process, phase one can sound easy. It is not. Well over 50% of the companies I have watched

Idea in Practice

To give your transformation effort the best chance of succeeding, take the right actions at each stage—and avoid common pitfalls

Stage	**Actions needed**	**Pitfalls**
Establish a sense of urgency	• Examine market and competitive realities for potential crises and untapped opportunities. • Convince at least 75% of your managers that the status quo is more dangerous than the unknown.	• Underestimating the difficulty of driving people from their comfort zones • Becoming paralyzed by risks
Form a powerful guiding coalition	• Assemble a group with shared commitment and enough power to lead the change effort. • Encourage them to work as a team outside the normal hierarchy.	• No prior experience in teamwork at the top • Relegating team leadership to an HR, quality, or strategic-planning executive rather than a senior line manager
Create a vision	• Create a vision to direct the change effort. • Develop strategies for realizing that vision.	• Presenting a vision that's too complicated or vague to be communicated in five minutes
Communicate the vision	• Use every vehicle possible to communicate the new vision and strategies for achieving it. • Teach new behaviors by the example of the guiding coalition.	• Undercommunicating the vision • Behaving in ways antithetical to the vision

fail in this first phase. What are the reasons for that failure? Sometimes executives underestimate how hard it can be to drive people out of their comfort zones. Sometimes they grossly overestimate how successful they have already been in increasing urgency. Sometimes they lack patience: "Enough with the preliminaries; let's get on with it." In many cases, executives become paralyzed by the downside

Stage	Actions needed	Pitfalls
Empower others to act on the vision	• Remove or alter systems or structures undermining the vision. • Encourage risk taking and nontraditional ideas, activities, and actions.	• Failing to remove powerful individuals who resist the change effort
Plan for and create short-term wins	• Define and engineer visible performance improvements. • Recognize and reward employees contributing to those improvements.	• Leaving short-term successes up to chance • Failing to score successes early enough (12–24 months into the change effort)
Consolidate improvements and produce more change	• Use increased credibility from early wins to change systems, structures, and policies undermining the vision. • Hire, promote, and develop employees who can implement the vision. • Reinvigorate the change process with new projects and change agents.	• Declaring victory too soon—with the first performance improvement • Allowing resistors to convince "troops" that the war has been won
Institutionalize new approaches	• Articulate connections between new behaviors and corporate success. • Create leadership development and succession plans consistent with the new approach.	• Not creating new social norms and shared values consistent with changes • Promoting people into leadership positions who don't personify the new approach

possibilities. They worry that employees with seniority will become defensive, that morale will drop, that events will spin out of control, that short-term business results will be jeopardized, that the stock will sink, and that they will be blamed for creating a crisis.

A paralyzed senior management often comes from having too many managers and not enough leaders. Management's mandate is to minimize risk and to keep the current system operating. Change, by definition, requires creating a new system, which in turn always demands leadership. Phase one in a renewal process typically goes nowhere until enough real leaders are promoted or hired into senior-level jobs.

Transformations often begin, and begin well, when an organization has a new head who is a good leader and who sees the need for a major change. If the renewal target is the entire company, the CEO is key. If change is needed in a division, the division general manager is key. When these individuals are not new leaders, great leaders, or change champions, phase one can be a huge challenge.

Bad business results are both a blessing and a curse in the first phase. On the positive side, losing money does catch people's attention. But it also gives less maneuvering room. With good business results, the opposite is true: Convincing people of the need for change is much harder, but you have more resources to help make changes.

But whether the starting point is good performance or bad, in the more successful cases I have witnessed, an individual or a group always facilitates a frank discussion of potentially unpleasant facts about new competition, shrinking margins, decreasing market share, flat earnings, a lack of revenue growth, or other relevant indices of a declining competitive position. Because there seems to be an almost universal human tendency to shoot the bearer of bad news, especially if the head of the organization is not a change champion, executives in these companies often rely on outsiders to bring unwanted information. Wall Street analysts, customers, and consultants can all be helpful in this regard. The purpose of all this activity, in the words of one former CEO of a large European company, is "to make the status quo seem more dangerous than launching into the unknown."

In a few of the most successful cases, a group has manufactured a crisis. One CEO deliberately engineered the largest accounting loss in the company's history, creating huge pressures from Wall Street in the process. One division president commissioned first-ever customer satisfaction surveys, knowing full well that the results would be terrible. He then made these findings public. On the surface, such moves can look unduly risky. But there is also risk in playing it too safe: When the urgency rate is not pumped up enough, the transformation process cannot succeed, and the long-term future of the organization is put in jeopardy.

When is the urgency rate high enough? From what I have seen, the answer is when about 75% of a company's management is honestly convinced that business as usual is totally unacceptable. Anything less can produce very serious problems later on in the process.

Error 2: Not Creating a Powerful Enough Guiding Coalition

Major renewal programs often start with just one or two people. In cases of successful transformation efforts, the leadership coalition grows and grows over time. But whenever some minimum mass is not achieved early in the effort, nothing much worthwhile happens.

It is often said that major change is impossible unless the head of the organization is an active supporter. What I am talking about goes far beyond that. In successful transformations, the chairman or president or division general manager, plus another five or 15 or 50 people, come together and develop a shared commitment to excellent performance through renewal. In my experience, this group never includes all of the company's most senior executives because some people just won't buy in, at least not at first. But in the most successful cases, the coalition is always pretty powerful—in terms of titles, information and expertise, reputations, and relationships.

In both small and large organizations, a successful guiding team may consist of only three to five people during the first year of a renewal effort. But in big companies, the coalition needs to grow to the 20 to 50 range before much progress can be made in phase three and beyond. Senior managers always form the core of the group. But sometimes you find board members, a representative from a key customer, or even a powerful union leader.

Because the guiding coalition includes members who are not part of senior management, it tends to operate outside of the normal hierarchy by definition. This can be awkward, but it is clearly necessary. If the existing hierarchy were working well, there would be no need for a major transformation. But since the current system is not working, reform generally demands activity outside of formal boundaries, expectations, and protocol.

A high sense of urgency within the managerial ranks helps enormously in putting a guiding coalition together. But more is usually required. Someone needs to get these people together, help them develop a shared assessment of their company's problems and opportunities, and create a minimum level of trust and communication. Off-site retreats, for two or three days, are one popular vehicle for accomplishing this task. I have seen many groups of five to 35 executives attend a series of these retreats over a period of months.

Companies that fail in phase two usually underestimate the difficulties of producing change and thus the importance of a powerful guiding coalition. Sometimes they have no history of teamwork at the top and therefore undervalue the importance of this type of coalition. Sometimes they expect the team to be led by a staff executive from human resources, quality, or strategic planning instead of a key line manager. No matter how capable or dedicated the staff head, groups without strong line leadership never achieve the power that is required.

Efforts that don't have a powerful enough guiding coalition can make apparent progress for a while. But, sooner or later, the opposition gathers itself together and stops the change.

Error 3: Lacking a Vision

In every successful transformation effort that I have seen, the guiding coalition develops a picture of the future that is relatively easy to communicate and appeals to customers, stockholders, and employees. A vision always goes beyond the numbers that are typically found in five-year plans. A vision says something that helps clarify the direction in which an organization needs to move. Sometimes the first draft comes mostly from a single individual. It is usually a bit blurry, at least initially. But after the coalition works at it for three or five or even 12 months, something much better emerges through their tough analytical thinking and a little dreaming. Eventually, a strategy for achieving that vision is also developed.

In one midsize European company, the first pass at a vision contained two-thirds of the basic ideas that were in the final product. The concept of global reach was in the initial version from the beginning. So was the idea of becoming preeminent in certain businesses. But one central idea in the final version—getting out of low value-added activities—came only after a series of discussions over a period of several months.

Without a sensible vision, a transformation effort can easily dissolve into a list of confusing and incompatible projects that can take the organization in the wrong direction or nowhere at all. Without a sound vision, the reengineering project in the accounting department, the new 360-degree performance appraisal from the human resources department, the plant's quality program, the cultural change project in the sales force will not add up in a meaningful way.

In failed transformations, you often find plenty of plans, directives, and programs but no vision. In one case, a company gave out four-inch-thick notebooks describing its change effort. In mind-numbing detail, the books spelled out procedures, goals, methods, and deadlines. But nowhere was there a clear and compelling statement of where all this was leading. Not surprisingly, most of the employees with whom I talked were either confused or alienated. The big, thick books did not rally them together or inspire change. In fact, they probably had just the opposite effect.

In a few of the less successful cases that I have seen, management had a sense of direction, but it was too complicated or blurry to be useful. Recently, I asked an executive in a midsize company to describe his vision and received in return a barely comprehensible 30-minute lecture. Buried in his answer were the basic elements of a sound vision. But they were buried—deeply.

A useful rule of thumb: If you can't communicate the vision to someone in five minutes or less and get a reaction that signifies both understanding and interest, you are not yet done with this phase of the transformation process.

Error 4: Undercommunicating the Vision by a Factor of Ten

I've seen three patterns with respect to communication, all very common. In the first, a group actually does develop a pretty good transformation vision and then proceeds to communicate it by holding a single meeting or sending out a single communication. Having used about 0.0001% of the yearly intracompany communication, the group is startled when few people seem to understand the new approach. In the second pattern, the head of the organization spends a considerable amount of time making speeches to employee groups, but most people still don't get it (not surprising, since vision captures only 0.0005% of the total yearly communication). In the third pattern, much more effort goes into newsletters and speeches, but some very visible senior executives still behave in ways that are antithetical to the vision. The net result is that cynicism among the troops goes up, while belief in the communication goes down.

Transformation is impossible unless hundreds or thousands of people are willing to help, often to the point of making short-term sacrifices. Employees will not make sacrifices, even if they are unhappy with the status quo, unless they believe that useful change is possible. Without credible communication, and a lot of it, the hearts and minds of the troops are never captured.

This fourth phase is particularly challenging if the short-term sacrifices include job losses. Gaining understanding and support is tough when downsizing is a part of the vision. For this reason, successful visions usually include new growth possibilities and the commitment to treat fairly anyone who is laid off.

Executives who communicate well incorporate messages into their hour-by-hour activities. In a routine discussion about a business problem, they talk about how proposed solutions fit (or don't fit) into the bigger picture. In a regular performance appraisal, they talk about how the employee's behavior helps or undermines the vision. In a review of a division's quarterly performance, they talk not only about the numbers but also about how the division's executives are contributing to the transformation. In a routine Q&A with employees at a company facility, they tie their answers back to renewal goals.

In more successful transformation efforts, executives use all existing communication channels to broadcast the vision. They turn boring, unread company newsletters into lively articles about the vision. They take ritualistic, tedious quarterly management meetings and turn them into exciting discussions of the transformation. They throw out much of the company's generic management education and replace it with courses that focus on business problems and the new vision. The guiding principle is simple: Use every possible channel, especially those that are being wasted on nonessential information.

Perhaps even more important, most of the executives I have known in successful cases of major change learn to "walk the talk." They consciously attempt to become a living symbol of the new corporate culture. This is often not easy. A 60-year-old plant manager who has spent precious little time over 40 years thinking about customers will not suddenly behave in a customer-oriented way. But I have witnessed just such a person change, and change a great deal. In that case, a high level of urgency helped. The fact that the man was a part of the guiding coalition and the vision-creation team also helped. So did all the communication, which kept reminding him of the desired behavior, and all the feedback from his peers and subordinates, which helped him see when he was not engaging in that behavior.

Communication comes in both words and deeds, and the latter are often the most powerful form. Nothing undermines change more than behavior by important individuals that is inconsistent with their words.

Error 5: Not Removing Obstacles to the New Vision

Successful transformations begin to involve large numbers of people as the process progresses. Employees are emboldened to try new approaches, to develop new ideas, and to provide leadership. The only constraint is that the actions fit within the broad parameters of the overall vision. The more people involved, the better the outcome.

To some degree, a guiding coalition empowers others to take action simply by successfully communicating the new direction. But communication is never sufficient by itself. Renewal also requires the removal of obstacles. Too often, an employee understands the new vision and wants to help make it happen, but an elephant appears to be blocking the path. In some cases, the elephant is in the person's head, and the challenge is to convince the individual that no external obstacle exists. But in most cases, the blockers are very real.

Sometimes the obstacle is the organizational structure: Narrow job categories can seriously undermine efforts to increase productivity or make it very difficult even to think about customers. Sometimes compensation or performance-appraisal systems make people choose between the new vision and their own self-interest. Perhaps worst of all are bosses who refuse to change and who make demands that are inconsistent with the overall effort.

One company began its transformation process with much publicity and actually made good progress through the fourth phase. Then the change effort ground to a halt because the officer in charge of the company's largest division was allowed to undermine most of the new initiatives. He paid lip service to the process but did not change his behavior or encourage his managers to change. He did not reward the unconventional ideas called for in the vision. He allowed human resource systems to remain intact even when they were clearly inconsistent with the new ideals. I think the officer's motives were complex. To some degree, he did not believe the company needed major change. To some degree, he felt personally threatened by all the change. To some degree, he was afraid that he could not produce both change and the expected operating profit. But despite the fact that they backed the renewal effort, the other officers did virtually nothing to stop the one blocker. Again, the reasons were complex. The company had no history of confronting problems like this. Some people were afraid of the officer. The CEO was concerned that he might lose a talented executive. The net result was disastrous. Lower-level managers concluded that senior management had lied to them about their commitment to renewal, cynicism grew, and the whole effort collapsed.

In the first half of a transformation, no organization has the momentum, power, or time to get rid of all obstacles. But the big ones must be confronted and removed. If the blocker is a person, it is important that he or she be treated fairly and in a way that is consistent with the new vision. Action is essential, both to empower others and to maintain the credibility of the change effort as a whole.

Error 6: Not Systematically Planning for, and Creating, Short-Term Wins

Real transformation takes time, and a renewal effort risks losing momentum if there are no short-term goals to meet and celebrate. Most people won't go on the long march unless they see compelling evidence in 12 to 24 months that the journey is producing expected results. Without short-term wins, too many people give up or actively join the ranks of those people who have been resisting change.

One to two years into a successful transformation effort, you find quality beginning to go up on certain indices or the decline in net income stopping. You find some successful new product introductions or an upward shift in market share. You find an impressive productivity improvement or a statistically higher customer satisfaction rating. But whatever the case, the win is unambiguous. The result is not just a judgment call that can be discounted by those opposing change.

Creating short-term wins is different from hoping for short-term wins. The latter is passive, the former active. In a successful transformation, managers actively look for ways to obtain clear performance improvements, establish goals in the yearly planning system, achieve the objectives, and reward the people involved with recognition, promotions, and even money. For example, the guiding coalition at a U.S. manufacturing company produced a highly visible and successful new product introduction about 20 months after the start of its renewal effort. The new product was selected about six months into the effort because it met multiple criteria: It could be designed and launched in a relatively short period, it could be handled by a small team of people who were devoted to the new vision, it had upside potential, and the new product-development team could operate outside the established departmental structure without practical problems. Little was left to chance, and the win boosted the credibility of the renewal process.

Managers often complain about being forced to produce short-term wins, but I've found that pressure can be a useful element in a change effort. When it becomes clear to people that major change will take a long time, urgency levels can drop. Commitments to produce short-term wins help keep the urgency level up and force detailed analytical thinking that can clarify or revise visions.

Error 7: Declaring Victory Too Soon

After a few years of hard work, managers may be tempted to declare victory with the first clear performance improvement. While celebrating a win is fine, declaring the war won can be catastrophic. Until changes sink deeply into a company's culture, a process that can take five to ten years, new approaches are fragile and subject to regression.

In the recent past, I have watched a dozen change efforts operate under the reengineering theme. In all but two cases, victory was declared and the expensive consultants were paid and thanked when the first major project was completed after two to three years. Within two more years, the useful changes that had been introduced slowly disappeared. In two of the ten cases, it's hard to find any trace of the reengineering work today.

Over the past 20 years, I've seen the same sort of thing happen to huge quality projects, organizational development efforts, and more. Typically, the problems start early in the process: The urgency level is not intense enough, the guiding coalition is not powerful enough, and the vision is not clear enough. But it is the premature victory celebration that kills momentum. And then the powerful forces associated with tradition take over.

Ironically, it is often a combination of change initiators and change resistors that creates the premature victory celebration. In their enthusiasm over a clear sign of progress, the initiators go overboard. They are then joined by resistors, who are quick to spot any opportunity to stop change. After the celebration is over, the resistors point to the victory as a sign that the war has been won and the troops should be sent home. Weary troops allow themselves to be convinced that they won. Once home, the foot soldiers are reluctant to climb back on the ships. Soon thereafter, change comes to a halt, and tradition creeps back in.

Instead of declaring victory, leaders of successful efforts use the credibility afforded by short-term wins to tackle even bigger problems. They go after systems and structures that are not consistent with the transformation vision and have not been confronted before. They pay great attention to who is promoted, who is hired, and how people are developed. They include new reengineering projects that are even bigger in scope than the initial ones. They understand that renewal efforts take not months but years. In fact, in one of the most successful transformations that I have ever seen, we quantified the amount of change that occurred each year over a seven-year period. On a scale of one (low) to ten (high), year one received a two, year two a four, year three a three, year four a seven, year five an eight, year six a four, and year seven a two. The peak came in year five, fully 36 months after the first set of visible wins.

Error 8: Not Anchoring Changes in the Corporation's Culture

In the final analysis, change sticks when it becomes "the way we do things around here," when it seeps into the bloodstream of the corporate body. Until new behaviors are rooted in social norms and shared values, they are subject to degradation as soon as the pressure for change is removed.

Two factors are particularly important in institutionalizing change in corporate culture. The first is a conscious attempt to show people how the new approaches, behaviors, and attitudes have helped improve performance. When people are left on their own to make the connections, they sometimes create very inaccurate links. For example, because results improved while charismatic Harry was boss, the troops link his mostly idiosyncratic style with those results instead of seeing how their own improved customer service and productivity were instrumental. Helping people see the right connections requires communication. Indeed, one company was relentless, and it paid off enormously. Time was spent at every major management meeting to discuss why performance was increasing. The company newspaper ran article after article showing how changes had boosted earnings.

The second factor is taking sufficient time to make sure that the next generation of top management really does personify the new approach. If the requirements for promotion don't change, renewal rarely lasts. One bad succession decision at the top of an organization can undermine a decade of hard work. Poor succession decisions are possible when boards of directors are not an integral part of the renewal effort. In at least three instances I have seen, the champion for change was the retiring executive, and although his successor was not a resistor, he was not a change champion. Because the boards did not understand the transformations in any detail, they could not see that their choices were not good fits. The retiring executive in one case tried unsuccessfully to talk his board into a less seasoned candidate who better personified the transformation. In the other two cases, the CEOs did not resist the boards' choices, because they felt the transformation could not be undone by their successors. They were wrong. Within two years, signs of renewal began to disappear at both companies.

There are still more mistakes that people make, but these eight are the big ones. I realize that in a short article everything is made to sound a bit too simplistic. In reality, even successful change efforts are messy and full of surprises. But just as a relatively simple vision is needed to guide people through a major change, so a vision of the change process can reduce the error rate. And fewer errors can spell the difference between success and failure.

Originally published March 1995. Reprint R0701J

Change Through Persuasion

by David A. Garvin and Michael A. Roberto

FACED WITH THE NEED for massive change, most managers respond predictably. They revamp the organization's strategy, then round up the usual set of suspects—people, pay, and processes—shifting around staff, realigning incentives, and rooting out inefficiencies. They then wait patiently for performance to improve, only to be bitterly disappointed. For some reason, the right things still don't happen.

Why is change so hard? First of all, most people are reluctant to alter their habits. What worked in the past is good enough; in the absence of a dire threat, employees will keep doing what they've always done. And when an organization has had a succession of leaders, resistance to change is even stronger. A legacy of disappointment and distrust creates an environment in which employees automatically condemn the next turnaround champion to failure, assuming that he or she is "just like all the others." Calls for sacrifice and self-discipline are met with cynicism, skepticism, and knee-jerk resistance.

Our research into organizational transformation has involved settings as diverse as multinational corporations, government agencies, nonprofits, and high-performing teams like mountaineering expeditions and firefighting crews. We've found that for change to stick, leaders must design and run an effective persuasion campaign—one that begins weeks or months before the actual turnaround plan is set in concrete. Managers must perform significant work up front to ensure that employees will actually listen to tough messages, question old assumptions, and consider new ways of working. This means taking a series of deliberate but subtle steps to recast employees' prevailing views and create a new context for action. Such a shaping process must be actively managed during the first few months of a turnaround, when uncertainty is high and setbacks are inevitable. Otherwise, there is little hope for sustained improvement.

Like a political campaign, a persuasion campaign is largely one of differentiation from the past. To the typical change-averse employee, all restructuring plans look alike. The trick for turnaround leaders is to show employees precisely how their plans differ from their predecessors'. They must convince people that the organization is truly on its deathbed—or, at the very least, that radical changes are required if it is to survive and thrive. (This is a particularly difficult challenge when years of persistent problems have been accompanied by few changes in the status quo.) Turnaround leaders must also gain trust by demonstrating through word and deed that they are the right leaders for the job and must convince employees that theirs is the correct plan for moving forward.

Accomplishing all this calls for a four-part communications strategy. Prior to announcing a policy or issuing a set of instructions, leaders need to set the stage for acceptance. At the time of delivery, they must create the frame through which information and messages are interpreted. As time passes, they must manage the mood so that employees' emotional states support implementation and follow-through. And at critical intervals, they must provide reinforcement to ensure that the desired changes take hold without backsliding.

In this article, we describe this process in more detail, drawing on the example of the turnaround of Beth Israel Deaconess Medical Center (BIDMC) in Boston. Paul Levy, who became CEO in early 2002, managed to bring the failing hospital back from the brink of ruin. We had ringside seats during the first six months of the turnaround. Levy agreed to hold videotaped interviews with us every two to four weeks during that period as we prepared a case study describing his

Idea in Brief

When a company is teetering on the brink of ruin, most turnaround leaders revamp strategy, shift around staff, and root out inefficiencies. Then they wait patiently for the payoff—only to suffer bitter disappointment as the expected improvements fail to materialize.

How to make change stick? Conduct a four-stage persuasion campaign: 1) Prepare your organization's cultural "soil" months before setting your turnaround plan in concrete—by convincing employees that your company can survive only through radical change. 2) Present your plan—explaining in detail its purpose and expected impact. 3) After executing the plan, manage employees' emotions by acknowledging the pain of change—while keeping people focused on the hard work ahead. 4) As the turnaround starts generating results, reinforce desired behavioral changes to prevent backsliding.

Using this four-part process, the CEO of Beth Israel Deaconess Medical Center (BIDMC) brought the failing hospital back from near-certain death. Hemorrhaging $58 million in losses in 2001, BIDMC reported a $37.4 million net gain from operations in 2004. Revenues rose, while costs shrank. Morale soared—as reflected by a drop in nursing turnover from between 15% and 16% in 2002 to just 3% by 2004.

efforts. He also gave us access to his daily calendar, as well as to assorted e-mail correspondence and internal memorandums and reports. From this wealth of data, we were able to track the change process as it unfolded, without the usual biases and distortions that come from 20/20 hindsight. The story of how Levy tilled the soil for change provides lessons for any CEO in a turnaround situation.

Setting the Stage

Paul Levy was an unlikely candidate to run BIDMC. He was not a doctor and had never managed a hospital, though he had previously served as the executive dean for administration at Harvard Medical School. His claim to fame was his role as the architect of the Boston Harbor Cleanup, a multibillion-dollar pollution-control project that

Idea in Practice

Use these steps to persuade your workforce to embrace and execute needed change:

Set the Stage for Acceptance

Develop a bold message that provides compelling reasons to do things differently.

Example: On his first day as Beth Israel Deaconess Medical Center's CEO, Paul Levy publicized the possibility that BIDMC would be sold to a for-profit institution. He delivered an all-hands-on-deck e-mail to the staff citing the hospital's achievements while confirming that the threat of sale was real. The e-mail also signaled actions he would take, including layoffs, and described his open management style (hallway chats, lunches with staff). In addition, Levy circulated a third-party, warts-and-all report on BIDMC's plight on the hospital's intranet—so staff could no longer claim ignorance.

Frame the Turnaround Plan

Present your turnaround plan in a way that helps people interpret your ideas correctly.

Example: Levy augmented his several-hundred-page plan with an e-mail that evoked BIDMC's mission and uncompromising values and reaffirmed the importance of remaining an academic medical center. He provided further details about the plan, emphasizing needed tough measures based on the third-party report. He also explained past plans' deficiencies, contrasting earlier efforts'

he had led several years earlier. (Based on this experience, Levy identified a common yet insidiously destructive organizational dynamic that causes dedicated teams to operate in counterproductive ways, which he described in "The Nut Island Effect: When Good Teams Go Wrong," March 2001.) Six years after completing the Boston Harbor project, Levy approached the BIDMC board and applied for the job of cleaning up the troubled hospital.

Despite his lack of hospital management experience, Levy was appealing to the board. The Boston Harbor Cleanup was a difficult, highly visible change effort that required deft political and managerial skills. Levy had stood firm in the face of tough negotiations and often-heated public resistance and had instilled accountability in

top-down methods with his plan's collaborative approach. Employees thus felt the plan belonged to them.

Manage the Mood

Strike the right notes of optimism and realism to make employees feel cared for while also keeping them focused on your plan's execution.

Example: Levy acknowledged the pain of layoffs, then urged employees to look forward to "[setting] an example for what a unique academic medical center like ours means for this region." He also issued progress updates while reminding people that BIDMC still needed to control costs. As financial performance picked up, he lavishly praised the staff.

Prevent Backsliding

Provide opportunities for employees to practice desired behaviors repeatedly. If necessary, publicly criticize disruptive, divisive behaviors.

Example: Levy had established meeting rules requiring staff to state their objections to decisions and to "disagree without being disagreeable." When one medical chief e-mailed Levy complaining about a decision made during a meeting—and copied the other chiefs and board chairman—Levy took action. He responded with an e-mail to the same audience, publicly reprimanding the chief for his tone, lack of civility, and failure to follow the rule about speaking up during meetings.

city and state agencies. He was also a known quantity to the board, having served on a BIDMC steering committee formed by the board chairman in 2001.

Levy saw the prospective job as one of public service. BIDMC was the product of a difficult 1996 merger between two hospitals—Beth Israel and Deaconess—each of which had distinguished reputations, several best-in-the-world departments and specializations, and deeply devoted staffs. The problems began after the merger. A misguided focus on clinical practice rather than backroom integration, a failure to cut costs, and the repeated inability to execute plans and adapt to changing conditions in the health care marketplace all contributed to BIDMC's dismal performance.

By the time the board settled on Levy, affairs at BIDMC had reached the nadir. The hospital was losing $50 million a year. Relations between the administration and medical staff were strained, as were those between management and the board of directors. Employees felt demoralized, having witnessed the rapid decline in their institution's once-legendary status and the disappointing failure of its past leaders. A critical study was conducted by the Hunter Group, a leading health-care consulting firm. The report, detailing the dire conditions at the hospital and the changes needed to turn things around, had been completed but not yet released. Meanwhile, the state attorney general, who was responsible for overseeing charitable trusts, had put pressure on the board to sell the failing BIDMC to a for-profit institution.

Like many CEOs recruited to fix a difficult situation, Levy's first task was to gain a mandate for the changes ahead. He also recognized that crucial negotiations were best conducted before he took the job, when his leverage was greatest, rather than after taking the reins. In particular, he moved to secure the cooperation of the hospital board by flatly stating his conditions for employment. He told the directors, for example, that should they hire him, they could no longer interfere in day-to-day management decisions. In his second and third meetings with the board's search committee, Levy laid out his timetable and intentions. He insisted that the board decide on his appointment quickly so that he could be on the job before the release of the Hunter report. He told the committee that he intended to push for a smaller, more effective group of directors. Though the conditions were somewhat unusual, the board was convinced that Levy had the experience to lead a successful turnaround, and they accepted his terms. Levy went to work on January 7, 2002.

The next task was to set the stage with the hospital staff. Levy was convinced that the employees, hungry for a turnaround, would do their best to cooperate with him if he could emulate and embody the core values of the hospital culture, rather than impose his personal values. He chose to act as the managerial equivalent of a

The four phases of a persuasion campaign

A typical turnaround process consists of two stark phases: plan development, followed by an implementation that may or may not be welcomed by the organization. For the turnaround plan to be widely accepted and adopted, however, the CEO must develop a separate persuasion campaign, the goal of which is to create a continuously receptive environment for change. The campaign begins well before the CEO's first day on the job—or, if the CEO is long established, well before formal development work begins—and continues long after the final plan is announced.

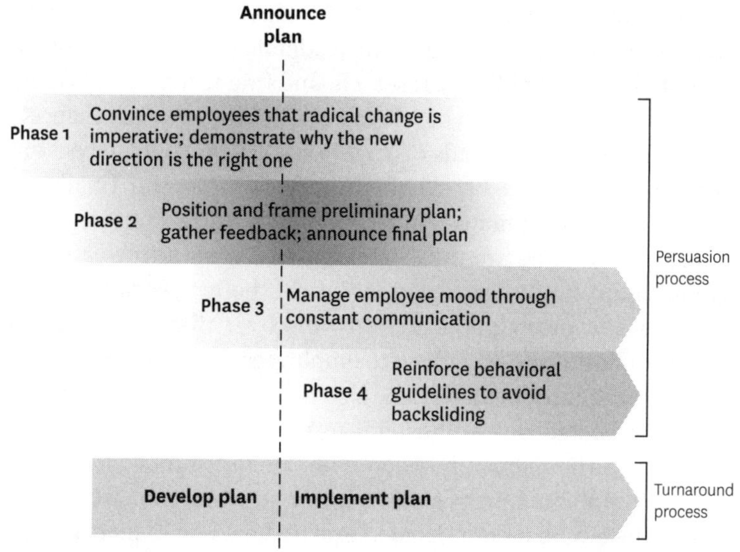

good doctor—that is, as one who, in dealing with a very ill patient, delivers both the bad news and the chances of success honestly and imparts a realistic sense of hope, without sugar coating.

Like any leader facing a turnaround, Levy also knew he had to develop a bold message that provided compelling reasons to do things differently and then cast that message in capital letters to signal the arrival of a new order. To give his message teeth, he linked it to an implicit threat. Taking his cue from his private discussions with the state attorney general, whom he had persuaded to keep the hospital open for the time being, Levy chose to publicize the very real possibility the hospital would be sold. While he realized he risked frightening the staff and the patients with this bad news, he believed that a strong wake-up call was necessary to get employees to face up to the situation.

During his first morning on the job, Levy delivered an all-hands-on-deck e-mail to the staff. The memo contained four broad messages. It opened with the good news, pointing out that the organization had much to be proud of ("This is a wonderful institution, representing the very best in academic medicine: exemplary patient care, extraordinary research, and fine teaching"). Second, Levy noted that the threat of sale was real ("This is our last chance"). Third, he signaled the kinds of actions employees could expect him to take ("There will be a reduction in staff"). And finally, he described the open management style he would adopt. He would manage by walking around—lunching with staff in the cafeteria, having impromptu conversations in the hallways, talking with employees at every opportunity to discover their concerns. He would communicate directly with employees through e-mail rather than through intermediaries. He also noted that the Hunter report would be posted on the hospital intranet, where all employees would have the opportunity to review its recommendations and submit comments for the final turnaround plan. The direct, open tone of the e-mail memo signaled exactly how Levy's management style would differ from that of his predecessors.

In the afternoon, he disclosed BIDMC's situation in interviews with the *Boston Globe* and the *Boston Herald,* the city's two major newspapers. He told reporters the same thing he had told the hospital's employees: that, in the absence of a turnaround, the hospital would be sold to a for-profit chain and would therefore lose its status as a Harvard teaching hospital. Staving off a sale would require tough measures, including the laying off of anywhere from 500 to 700 employees. Levy insisted that there would be no nursing layoffs, in keeping with the hospital's core values of high-quality patient care. The newspaper reports, together with the memo circulated that morning, served to immediately reset employee expectations while dramatically increasing staff cooperation and willingness to accept whatever new initiatives might prove necessary to the hospital's survival.

Two days later, the critical Hunter report came out and was circulated via the hospital's intranet. Because the report had been produced by an objective third party, employees were open to its unvarnished, warts-and-all view of the hospital's current predicament. The facts were stark, and the staff could no longer claim ignorance. Levy received, and personally responded to, more than 300 e-mail suggestions for improvement in response to the report, many of which he later included in the turnaround plan.

Creating the Frame

Once the stage has been set for acceptance, effective leaders need to help employees interpret proposals for change. Complex plans can be interpreted in any number of ways; not all of them ensure acceptance and favorable outcomes. Skilled leaders therefore use "frames" to provide context and shape perspective for new proposals and plans. By framing the issues, leaders help people digest ideas in particular ways. A frame can take many forms: It can be a companywide presentation that prepares employees before an unexpected change, for example, or a radio interview that provides context following an unsettling layoff.

Levy used one particularly effective framing device to help employees interpret a preliminary draft of the turnaround plan. This device took the form of a detailed e-mail memo accompanying the dense, several-hundred-page plan. The memo explained, in considerable detail, the plan's purpose and expected impact.

The first section of the memo sought to mollify critics and reduce the fears of doctors and nurses. Its tone was positive and uplifting; it discussed BIDMC's mission, strategy, and uncompromising values, emphasizing the hospital's "warm, caring environment." This section of the letter also reaffirmed the importance of remaining an academic medical center, as well as reminding employees of their shared mission and ideals. The second part of the letter told employees what to expect, providing further details about the turnaround plan. It emphasized that tough measures and goals would be required but noted that the specific recommendations were based, for the most part, on the advice in the Hunter report, which employees had already reviewed. The message to employees was, "You've already seen and endorsed the Hunter report. There are no future surprises."

The third part of the letter anticipated and responded to prospective concerns; this had the effect of circumventing objections. This section explicitly diagnosed past plans and explained their deficiencies, which were largely due to their having been imposed top-down, with little employee ownership, buy-in, or discussion. Levy then offered a direct interpretation of what had gone wrong. Past plans, he said, had underestimated the size of the financial problem, set unrealistic expectations for new revenue growth, and failed to test implementation proposals. This section of the letter also drove home the need for change at a deeper, more visceral level than employees had experienced in the past. It emphasized that this plan was a far more collective effort than past proposals had been, because it incorporated many employee suggestions.

By framing the turnaround proposal this way, Levy accomplished two things. First, he was able to convince employees that the plan belonged to them. Second, the letter served as the basis for an ongoing communication platform. Levy reiterated its points at every opportunity—not only with employees but also in public meetings and in discussions with the press.

Managing the Mood

Turnarounds are depressing events, especially when they involve restructuring and downsizing. Relationships are disrupted, friends move on, and jobs disappear. In such settings, managing the mood of the organization becomes an essential leadership skill. Leaders must pay close attention to employees' emotions—the ebb and flow of their feelings and moods—and work hard to preserve a receptive climate for change. Often, this requires a delicate balancing act between presenting good and bad news in just the right proportion. Employees need to feel that their sacrifices have not been in vain and that their accomplishments have been recognized and rewarded. At the same time, they must be reminded that complacency is not an option. The communication challenge is daunting. One must strike the right notes of optimism and realism and carefully calibrate the timing, tone, and positioning of every message.

Paul Levy's challenge was threefold: to give remaining employees time to grieve and recover from layoffs and other difficult measures; to make them feel that he cared for and supported them; and to ensure that the turnaround plan proceeded apace. The process depended on mutual trust and employees' desire to succeed. "I had to calibrate the push and pull of congratulations and pressure, but I also depended on the staff's underlying value system and sense of mission," he said. "They were highly motivated, caring individuals who had stuck with the place through five years of hell. They wanted to do good."

The first step was to acknowledge employees' feelings of depression while helping them look to the future. Immediately after the first round of layoffs, people were feeling listless and dejected; Levy knew that releasing the final version of the turnaround plan too soon after the layoffs could be seen as cold. In an e-mail he sent to all employees a few days later, Levy explicitly empathized with employees' feelings ("This week is a sad one . . . it is hard for those of us remaining . . . offices are emptier than usual"). He then urged employees to look forward and concluded on a strongly optimistic note (". . . our target is not just survival: It is to thrive and set an example for what a unique academic medical center like ours means for this region"). His upbeat words were reinforced by a piece of good luck that weekend when the underdog New England Patriots won their first Super Bowl championship in dramatic fashion in the last 90 seconds of the game. When Levy returned to work the following Monday, employees were saying, "If the Patriots can do it, we can, too."

Dysfunctional Routines

Six Ways to Stop Change in Its Tracks

Just as people are creatures of habit, organizations thrive on routines. Management teams, for example, routinely cut budgets after performance deviates from plan. Routines—predictable, virtually automatic behaviors—are unstated, self-reinforcing, and remarkably resilient. Because they lead to more efficient cognitive processing, they are, for the most part, functional and highly desirable.

A culture of "no"

In organizations dominated by cynics and critics, there is always a good reason not to do something. Piling on criticism is an easy way to avoid taking risks and claim false superiority. Lou Gerstner gets credit for naming this routine, which he found on his arrival at IBM, but it is common in many organizations. Another CEO described her team's response to new initiatives by likening it to a skeet shoot: "Someone would yell, 'Pull!' there would be a deafening blast, and the idea would be in pieces on the ground." This routine has two sources: a culture that overvalues criticism and analysis, and complex decision-making processes requiring multiple approvals, in which anybody can say "no" but nobody can say "yes." It is especially likely in organizations that are divided into large subunits or segments, led by local leaders with great power who are often unwilling to comply with directives from above.

The dog and pony show must go on

Some organizations put so much weight on process that they confuse ends and means, form and content. How you present a proposal becomes more important than what you propose. Managers construct presentations carefully and devote large amounts of time to obtaining sign-offs. The result is death by PowerPoint. Despite the appearance of progress, there's little real headway.

The grass is always greener

To avoid facing challenges in their core business, some managers look to new products, new services, and new lines of business. At times, such diversification is healthy. But all too often these efforts are merely an avoidance tactic that keeps tough problems at arm's length.

The next task was to keep employees focused on the continuing hard work ahead. On April 12, two months into the restructuring process, Levy sent out a "Frequently Asked Questions" e-mail giving a generally favorable view of progress to date. At the same time, he spoke plainly about the need to control costs and reminded employees that merit pay increases would remain on hold. This was hardly the rosy picture that most employees were hoping for, of course. But

Dysfunctional routines, by contrast, are barriers to action and change. Some are outdated behaviors that were appropriate once but are now unhelpful. Others manifest themselves in knee-jerk reactions, passivity, unproductive foot-dragging, and, sometimes, active resistance.

Dysfunctional routines are persistent, but they are not unchangeable. Novelty—the perception that current circumstances are truly different from those that previously prevailed—is one of the most potent forces for dislodging routines. To overcome them, leaders must clearly signal that the context has changed. They must work directly with employees to recognize and publicly examine dysfunctional routines and substitute desired behaviors.

After the meeting ends, debate begins
This routine is often hard to spot because so much of it takes place under cover. Cordial, apparently cooperative meetings are followed by resistance. Sometimes, resisters are covert; often, they end-run established forums entirely and take their concerns directly to the top. The result? Politics triumphs over substance, staff meetings become empty rituals, and meddling becomes the norm.

Ready, aim, aim. . .
Here, the problem is the organization's inability to settle on a definitive course of action. Staff members generate a continual stream of proposals and reports; managers repeatedly tinker with each one, fine tuning their choices without ever making a final decision. Often called "analysis paralysis," this pattern is common in perfectionist cultures where mistakes are career threatening and people who rock the boat drown.

This too shall pass
In organizations where prior leaders repeatedly proclaimed a state of crisis but then made few substantive changes, employees tend to be jaded. In such situations, they develop a heads-down, bunker mentality and a reluctance to respond to management directives. Most believe that the wisest course of action is to ignore new initiatives, work around them, or wait things out.

Levy believed sufficient time had passed that employees could accommodate a more realistic and tough tone on his part.

A month later, everything changed. Operational improvements that were put in place during the first phase of the turnaround had begun to take hold. Financial performance was well ahead of budget, with the best results since the merger. In another e-mail, Levy praised employees lavishly. He also convened a series of open question-and-answer forums, where employees heard more details about the hospital's tangible progress and received kudos for their accomplishments.

Reinforcing Good Habits

Without a doubt, the toughest challenge faced by leaders during a turnaround is to avoid backsliding into dysfunctional routines—habitual patterns of negative behavior by individuals and groups that are triggered automatically and unconsciously by familiar circumstances or stimuli. (For more on how such disruptive patterns work, see the sidebar "Dysfunctional Routines: Six Ways to Stop Change in Its Tracks.") Employees need help maintaining new behaviors, especially when their old ways of working are deeply ingrained and destructive. Effective change leaders provide opportunities for employees to practice desired behaviors repeatedly, while personally modeling new ways of working and providing coaching and support.

In our studies of successful turnarounds, we've found that effective leaders explicitly reinforce organizational values on a constant basis, using actions to back up their words. Their goal is to change behavior, not just ways of thinking. For example, a leader can talk about values such as openness, tolerance, civility, teamwork, delegation, and direct communication in meetings and e-mails. But the message takes hold only if he or she also signals a dislike of disruptive, divisive behaviors by pointedly—and, if necessary, publicly—criticizing them.

At Beth Israel Deaconess Medical Center, the chiefs of medicine, surgery, orthopedics, and other key functions presented Levy with special behavioral challenges, particularly because he was not a doctor. Each medical chief was in essence a "mini-dean," the head of a largely self-contained department with its own faculty, staff, and resources. As academic researchers, they were rewarded primarily for individual achievement. They had limited experience solving business or management problems.

In dealing with the chiefs, Levy chose an approach that blended with a strong dose of discipline with real-time, public reinforcement.

He developed guidelines for behavior and insisted that everyone in the hospital measure up to them. In one of his earliest meetings with the chiefs, Levy presented a simple set of "meeting rules," including such chestnuts as "state your objections" and "disagree without being disagreeable," and led a discussion about them, demonstrating the desired behaviors through his own leadership of the meeting. The purpose of these rules was to introduce new standards of interpersonal behavior and, in the process, to combat several dysfunctional routines.

One serious test of Levy's ability to reinforce these norms came a month and a half after he was named CEO. After a staff meeting at which all the department chairs were present, one chief—who had remained silent—sent an e-mail to Levy complaining about a decision made during the meeting. The e-mail copied the other chiefs as well as the chairman of the board. Many CEOs would choose to criticize such behavior privately. But Levy responded in an e-mail to the same audience, publicly denouncing the chief for his tone, his lack of civility, and his failure to speak up earlier in the process, as required by the new meeting rules. It was as close to a public hanging as anyone could get. Several of the chiefs privately expressed their support to Levy; they too had been offended by their peer's presumptuousness. More broadly, the open criticism served to powerfully reinforce new norms while curbing disruptive behavior.

Even as they must set expectations and reinforce behaviors, effective change leaders also recognize that many employees simply do not know how to make decisions as a group or work cooperatively. By delegating critical decisions and responsibilities, a leader can provide employees with ample opportunities to practice new ways of working; in such cases, employees' performance should be evaluated as much on their adherence to the new standards and processes as on their substantive choices. In this spirit, Levy chose to think of himself primarily as a kind of appeals court judge. When employees came to him seeking his intervention on an issue or situation, he explained, he would "review the process used by the 'lower court' to determine if it followed the rules. If so, the decision stands." He did not review cases de novo and substitute his judgment for that of the individual department or unit. He insisted that employees work through difficult issues themselves, even when they were not so inclined, rather than rely on him to tell them what to do. At other times, he intervened personally and coached employees when they lacked basic skills. When two members of his staff disagreed on a proposed course of action, Levy triggered an open, emotional debate, then worked with the participants and their bosses behind the scenes to resolve the differences. At the next staff meeting, he praised the participants' willingness to disagree publicly, reemphasizing that vigorous debate was healthy and desirable and that confrontation was not to be avoided. In this way, employees gained experience in working through their problems on their own.

Performance, of course, is the ultimate measure of a successful turnaround. On that score, BIDMC has done exceedingly well since Levy took the helm. The original restructuring plan called for a three-year improvement process, moving from a $58 million loss in 2001 to breakeven in 2004. At the end of the 2004 fiscal year, performance was far ahead of plan, with the hospital reporting a $37.4 million net gain from operations. Revenues were up, while costs were sharply reduced. Decision making was now crisper and more responsive, even though there was little change in the hospital's senior staff or medical leadership. Morale, not surprisingly, was up as well. To take just one indicator, annual nursing turnover, which was 15% to 16% when Levy became CEO, had dropped to 3% by mid-2004. Pleased with the hospital's performance, the board signed Levy to a new three-year contract.

Heads, Hearts, and Hands

It's clear that the key to Paul Levy's success at Beth Israel Deaconess Medical Center is that he understood the importance of making sure the cultural soil had been made ready before planting the seeds of change. In a receptive environment, employees not only understand why change is necessary; they're also emotionally committed to making it happen, and they faithfully execute the required steps.

On a cognitive level, employees in receptive environments are better able to let go of competing, unsubstantiated views of the nature and extent of the problems facing their organizations. They hold the same, objective views of the causes of poor performance. They acknowledge the seriousness of current financial, operational, and marketplace difficulties. And they take responsibility for their own contributions to those problems. Such a shared, fact-based diagnosis is crucial for moving forward.

On an emotional level, employees in receptive environments identify with the organization and its values and are committed to its continued existence. They believe that the organization stands for something more than profitability, market share, or stock performance and is therefore worth saving. Equally important, they trust the leader, believing that he or she shares their values and will fight to preserve them. Leaders earn considerable latitude from employees—and their proposals usually get the benefit of the doubt—when their hearts are thought to be in the right place.

Workers in such environments also have physical, hands-on experience with the new behaviors expected of them. They have seen the coming changes up close and understand what they are getting into. In such an atmosphere where it's acceptable for employees to wrestle with decisions on their own and practice unfamiliar ways of working, a leader can successfully allay irrational fears and undercut the myths that so often accompany major change efforts.

There is a powerful lesson in all this for leaders. To create a receptive environment, persuasion is the ultimate tool. Persuasion promotes understanding; understanding breeds acceptance; acceptance leads to action. Without persuasion, even the best of turnaround plans will fail to take root.

Originally published in February 2005. Reprint R0502F

Leading Change When Business Is Good

An Interview with *Samuel J. Palmisano.*

by Paul Hemp and Thomas A. Stewart

IN JULY 2003, *International Business Machines Corporation conducted a 72-hour experiment whose outcome was as uncertain as anything going on in its research labs. Six months into a top-to-bottom review of its management organization, IBM held a three-day discussion via the corporate intranet about the company's values. The forum, dubbed ValuesJam, joined thousands of employees in a debate about the very nature of the computer giant and what it stood for.*

Over the three days, an estimated 50,000 of IBM's employees—including CEO Sam Palmisano—checked out the discussion, posting nearly 10,000 comments about the proposed values. The jam had clearly struck a chord.

But it was a disturbingly dissonant one. Some comments were merely cynical. One had the subject line: "The only value in IBM today is the stock price." Another read, "Company values (ya right)." Others, though, addressed fundamental management issues. "I feel we talk a lot about trust and taking risks. But at the same time, we have endless audits, mistakes are punished and not seen as a welcome part of learning, and managers (and others) are consistently checked," wrote one employee. "There appears to be a great reluctance among our junior executive community to challenge the views of our senior execs," said another. "Many times I have heard expressions like, 'Would you tell Sam that his strategy is wrong!!?'" Twenty-four hours into the exercise, at least one senior executive wanted to pull the plug.

But Palmisano wouldn't hear of it. And then the mood began to shift. After a day marked by critics letting off steam, the countercritics began to weigh in. While acknowledging the company's shortcomings, they argued that much of IBM's culture and values was worth preserving. "Shortly after joining IBM 18 years ago," wrote one, "I was asked to serve on a jury. When I approached the bench and answered [the lawyers'] questions, I was surprised when the judge said, 'You guys can pick whoever else you want, but I want this IBMer *on that jury.' I have never felt so much pride. His statement said it all: integrity, excellence, and quality." Comments like these became more frequent, criticism became more constructive, and the ValuesJam conversation stabilized.*

The question of what was worth preserving and what needed to be changed was at the heart of ValuesJam. In 1914—when the company was making tabulating machines, scales for weighing meat, and cheese slicers—president Thomas Watson, Sr., decreed three corporate principles, called the Basic Beliefs: "respect for the individual," "the best customer service," and "the pursuit of excellence." They would inform IBM's culture, and help drive its success, for more than half a century.

By 2002, when Palmisano took over as CEO, much had happened to Big Blue. In the early 1990s, the company had suffered the worst reversal in its history and then, under Lou Gerstner, had fought its way back, transformed from a mainframe maker into a robust provider of integrated hardware, networking, and software solutions. Palmisano felt that the Basic Beliefs could still serve the company—but now as the foundation for a new set of corporate values that could energize employees even more than its near-death experience had. Looking for a modern-day equivalent, Palmisano first queried 300 of his senior executives, then quickly opened up the discussion, through a survey of over a thousand employees, to get a sense of how people at all levels, functions, and locations would articulate IBM's values and their

Idea in Brief

It's easy to fire up employees' passion for change when your business is about to go up in flames. Lou Gerstner knew this when he seized IBM's helm in 1993 and saved the faltering giant by transforming it from a mainframe maker into a provider of integrated solutions.

But how do you maintain people's commitment to change when business is *good*? *You* know your company must constantly adapt if it wants to maintain its competitive edge. Yet without an obvious threat on the horizon, your *employees* may grow complacent.

How to build a workforce of relentless change agents? Replace command-and-control with **values-based management:** Instead of galvanizing people through fear of failure, energize them through hope and aspiration. Inspire them to pursue a common purpose based on values *they* help to define. Ask them what's blocking them from living those values—and launch change initiatives to remove obstacles.

As enduring companies like IBM have discovered, values-based management enables your people to respond quickly, flexibly, and creatively to a never-ending stream of strategic challenges.

aspirations for the company. Out of this research grew the propositions that were debated in ValuesJam.

After—and even during—the jam, company analysts pored over the postings, mining the million-word text for key themes. Finally, a small team that included Palmisano came up with a revised set of corporate values. The CEO announced the new values to employees in an intranet broadcast in November 2003: "dedication to every client's success," "innovation that matters—for our company and for the world," "trust and personal responsibility in all relationships." Earthshaking? No, but imbued with legitimacy and packed with meaning and implications for IBM.

To prove that the new values were more than window dressing, Palmisano immediately made some changes. He called on the director of a major business unit—e-business hosting services for the U.S. industrial sector—and charged her with identifying gaps between the values and company practices. He bluntly told his 15 direct reports that they had better follow suit. Another online jam was held in Octo-

Idea in Practice

To create your values-based management system:

Gather Employees' Input on Values

Assess the strategic challenges facing your company. Propose values you believe will help your firm meet those challenges. Collect employees' feedback on your ideas.

> ***Example:*** IBM CEO Sam Palmisano knew that the IT industry was reintegrating: Customers wanted packages of computer products and services from single firms. Despite its far-flung, diverse 320,000-strong workforce, the company had to offer customized solutions at a single price. To achieve the required cooperation, IBM needed a shared set of values to guide people's decision making.

Using feedback from top managers and employees, Palmisano's team developed three working value statements—"Commitment to the customer," "Excellence through innovation," and "Integrity that earns trust." IBM posted these on its intranet and invited employees to debate them. Over three days, 50,000 debated the merits of the value statements.

Analyze Employees' Input

Examine employees' input for themes.

> ***Example:*** Many IBMers criticized the "integrity that earns trust" statement as vague, outdated, and inwardly focused. They wanted more specific guidance on how to behave with each other and with external stakeholders.

Revise Your Values

Based on the themes in employees' input, create a revised set of values. Gather employees' input again.

ber 2004 (this one informally dubbed a "logjam") in which employees were asked to identify organizational barriers to innovation and revenue growth.

Although Palmisano, by his own account, is building on a strategy laid down by Gerstner, the leadership styles of the two men are very different. Under Gerstner, there was little expansive talk about IBM's heritage. He was an outsider, a former CEO of RJR Nabisco and an ex-McKinsey consultant, who was faced with the daunting task of

Example: Palmisano's team revised the earlier value statements to read: "Dedication to every client's success," "Innovation that matters—for our company and for the world," and "Trust and personal responsibility in all relationships." The team published the revised statements on the intranet and once more invited feedback.

Identify Obstacles to Living the Values

Examine employees' responses to identify what's preventing your company from living its agreed-upon values.

Example: IBMers praised the revised value statements—often in highly emotional language—but wondered whether IBM was willing and able to live those values. They understood the need to reintegrate the company but lamented obstacles—such as frustrating financial controls—that prevented them from serving customers quickly.

Launch Change Initiatives to Remove Obstacles

Initiate change programs that enable people to live the values.

Example: IBM allocated $5,000 a year to individual managers to use, no questions asked, in order to generate business, develop client relationships, or respond to fellow IBMers' emergency needs. A pilot program run with 700 client-facing teams showed that they spent the money intelligently. The program was expanded to all 22,000 IBM first-line managers. The initiative demonstrated to employees that IBM lives by its values.

righting a sinking ship. In fact, he famously observed, shortly after taking over, that "the last thing IBM needs right now is a vision." Palmisano, by contrast, is a true-blue IBMer, who started at the company in 1973 as a salesman in Baltimore. Like many of his generation who felt such acute shame when IBM was brought to its knees in the early 1990s, he clearly has a visceral attachment to the firm—and to the hope that it may someday regain its former greatness. At the same time, the erstwhile salesman is, in the words of a colleague, "a results-driven, make-it-rain, close-the-deal sort of guy": not the first person you'd expect to hold forth on a subjective topic like "trust."

In this edited conversation with HBR senior editor Paul Hemp and HBR's editor, Thomas A. Stewart, Palmisano talks about the strategic importance of values to IBM. He begins by explaining why—and how—hard financial metrics and soft corporate values can coexist.

Corporate values generally are feel-good statements that have almost no effect on a company's operations. What made—what makes—you think they can be more than this?

Look at the portrait of Tom Watson, Sr., in our lobby. You've never seen such a stern man. The eyes in the painting stare right through you. This was *not* a soft individual. He was a capitalist. He wanted IBM to make money, lots of it. But he was perceptive enough to build the company in a way that would ensure its prosperity long after he left the scene. His three Basic Beliefs successfully steered this company through persistent change and repeated reinvention for more than 50 years.

An organic system, which is what a company is, needs to adapt. And we think values—that's what we call them today at IBM, but you can call them "beliefs" or "principles" or "precepts" or even "DNA"—are what enable you to do that. They let you change everything, from your products to your strategies to your business model, but remain true to your essence, your basic mission and identity.

Unfortunately, over the decades, Watson's Basic Beliefs became distorted and took on a life of their own. "Respect for the individual" became entitlement: not fair work for all, not a chance to speak out, but a guaranteed job and culture-dictated promotions. "The pursuit of excellence" became arrogance: We stopped listening to our markets, to our customers, to each other. We were so successful for so long that we could never see another point of view. And when the market shifted, we almost went out of business. We had to cut a workforce of more than 400,000 people in half. Over the course of several years, we wiped out the equivalent of a medium-sized northeastern city—say, Providence, Rhode Island.

If you lived through this, as I did, it was easy to see how the company's values had become part of the problem. But I believe values can once again help guide us through major change and meet some of the formidable challenges we face.

For instance, I feel that a strong value system is crucial to bringing together and motivating a workforce as large and diverse as ours has become. We have nearly one-third of a million employees serving clients in 170 countries. Forty percent of those people don't report daily to an IBM site; they work on the client's premises, from home, or they're mobile. And, perhaps most significant, given IBM's tradition of hiring and training young people for a lifetime of work, half of today's employees have been with the company for fewer than five years because of recent acquisitions and our relatively new practice of hiring seasoned professionals. In a modest hiring year, we now add 20,000 to 25,000 people.

In effect, gradually repopulating Providence, Rhode Island!

Exactly. So how do you channel this diverse and constantly changing array of talent and experience into a common purpose? How do you get people to *passionately* pursue that purpose?

You could employ all kinds of traditional, top-down management processes. But they wouldn't work at IBM—or, I would argue, at an increasing number of twenty-first-century companies. You just can't impose command-and-control mechanisms on a large, highly professional workforce. I'm not only talking about our scientists, engineers, and consultants. More than 200,000 of our employees have college degrees. The CEO can't say to them, "Get in line and follow me." Or "*I've* decided what *your* values are." They're too smart for that. And as you know, smarter people tend to be, well, a little more challenging; you might even say cynical.

But even if our people did accept this kind of traditional, hierarchical management system, our clients wouldn't. As we learned at IBM over the years, a top-down system can create a smothering bureaucracy that doesn't allow for the speed, the flexibility, the innovation that clients expect today.

So you're saying that values are about how employees behave when management isn't there, which it can't be—which it shouldn't be—given IBM's size and the need for people to make decisions quickly. You're basically talking about using values to manage.

Yes. A values-based management system. Let me cast the issue in a slightly different light. When you think about it, there's no optimal way to organize IBM. We traditionally were viewed as a large, successful, "well-managed" company. That was a compliment. But in today's fast-changing environment, it's a problem. You can easily end up with a bureaucracy of people overanalyzing problems and slowing down the decision-making process.

Think of our organizational matrix. Remember, we operate in 170 countries. To keep it simple, let's say we have 60 or 70 major product lines. We have more than a dozen customer segments. Well, if you mapped out the entire 3-D matrix, you'd get more than 100,000 cells—cells in which you have to close out P&Ls every day, make decisions, allocate resources, make trade-offs. You'll drive people crazy trying to centrally manage every one of those intersections.

So if there's no way to optimize IBM through organizational structure or by management dictate, you have to empower people while ensuring that they're making the right calls the right way. And by "right," I'm not talking about ethics and legal compliance alone; those are table stakes. I'm talking about decisions that support and give life to IBM's strategy and brand, decisions that shape a culture. That's why values, for us, aren't soft. They're the basis of what we do, our mission as a company. They're a touchstone for decentralized decision making. It used to be a rule of thumb that "people don't do what you expect; they do what you inspect." My point is that it's just not possible to inspect everyone anymore. But you also can't just let go of the reins and let people do what they want without guidance or context. You've got to create a management system that empowers people and provides a basis for decision making that is consistent with who we are at IBM.

How do the new values help further IBM's strategy?

In two main ways. Back some 12 years ago, three-fifths of our business was in computer hardware and roughly two-fifths was in software and services. Today, those numbers are more than reversed. Well, if three-fifths of your business is manufacturing, management is basically supervisory: "You do this. You do that." But that no longer works when your business is primarily based on knowledge. And your business model also changes dramatically.

For one thing, people—rather than products—become your brand. Just as our products have had to be consistent with the IBM brand promise, now more than ever, so do our people. One way to ensure that is to inform their behavior with a globally consistent set of values.

Second, the IT industry has continued to shift toward reintegration. We all know the story of how the industry fragmented in the 1980s and 1990s, with separate companies selling the processors, the storage devices, and the software that make up a computer system—almost killing IBM, the original vertically integrated computer company. Now customers are demanding a package of computer products and services from a single company, a company that can offer them an integrated solution to their business problems. This is a big opportunity for IBM. We probably have a wider array of computer products and services and know-how than anyone. But it's also a challenge. How can we get our people in far-flung business units with different financial targets and incentives working together in teams that can offer at a single price a comprehensive and customized solution—one that doesn't show the organizational seams?

Companies usually face the issue of workforce integration after a huge merger. We needed to integrate our existing workforce as a strategic response to the reintegration of the industry. It won't surprise you that I didn't think the answer lay in a new organizational structure or in more management oversight. What you need to foster this sort of cooperation is a common set of guidelines about how we make decisions, day in and day out. In other words, values.

And what happens when the strategy changes?

Ah, that's why the right set of values is so important. There's always going to be another strategy on the horizon as the market changes, as technologies come and go. So we wanted values that would foster an organization able to quickly execute a new strategy. At the same time, we wanted values that, like Watson's Basic Beliefs, would be enduring, that would guide the company through economic cycles and geopolitical shifts, that would transcend changes in products, technologies, employees, and leaders.

How did IBM distill new values from its past traditions and current employee feedback?

The last time IBM examined its values was nearly a century ago. Watson was an entrepreneur, leading what was, in today's lingo, a start-up. So in 1914, he simply said, "Here are our beliefs. Learn them. Live them." That was appropriate for his day, and there's no question it worked. But 90 years later, we couldn't have someone in headquarters sitting up in bed in the middle of the night and saying, "Here are our new values!" We couldn't be casual about tinkering with the DNA of a company like IBM. We had to come up with a way to get the employees to create the value system, to determine the company's principles. Watson's Basic Beliefs, however distorted they might have become over the years, had to be the starting point.

After getting input from IBM's top 300 executives and conducting focus groups with more than a thousand employees—a statistically representative cross-section—we came up with three perfectly sound values. [For a detailed description of how IBM got from the Basic Beliefs to its new set of values, see the sidebar "Continuity and Change."] But I knew we'd eventually throw out the statements to everyone in the company to debate. That's where ValuesJam came in—this live, companywide conversation on our intranet.

What was your own experience during the jam? Did you have the feeling you'd opened Pandora's box?

I logged in from China. I was pretty jet-lagged and couldn't sleep, so I jumped in with postings on a lot of stuff, particularly around client issues. [For a selection of Palmisano's postings during the ValuesJam, see the sidebar "Sam Joins the Fray."] And yes, the electronic argument was hot and contentious and messy. But you had to get comfortable with that. Understand, we had done three or four big online jams before this, so we had some idea of how lively they can be. Even so, none of those could have prepared us for the emotions unleashed by this topic.

You had to put your ego aside—not easy for a CEO to do—and realize that this was the best thing that could have happened. You could say, "Oh my God, I've unleashed this incredible negative energy." Or you could say, "Oh my God, I now have this incredible mandate to drive even more change in the company."

When Lou Gerstner came here in 1993, there was clearly a burning platform. In fact, the whole place was in flames. There was even talk of breaking up the company. And he responded brilliantly. Here's this outsider who managed to marshal the collective urgency of tens of thousands of people like me to save this company and turn it around: without a doubt one of the greatest saves in business history. But the trick then wasn't creating a sense of urgency—we had that. Maybe you needed to shake people out of being shell-shocked. But most IBMers were willing to do whatever it took to save the company, not to mention their own jobs. And there was a lot of pride at stake. Lou's task was mostly to convince people that he was making the right changes.

Once things got better, though, there was another kind of danger: that we would slip back into complacency. As our financial results improved dramatically and we began outperforming our competitors, people—already weary from nearly a decade of change—would say, "Well, why do I have to do things differently now? The leadership may be different, but the strategy is fundamentally sound. Why do I have to change?" This is, by the way, a problem that everyone running a successful company wrestles with.

So the challenge shifted. Instead of galvanizing people through fear of failure, you have to galvanize them through hope and aspiration. You lay out the opportunity to become a great company again—the greatest in the world, which is what IBM used to be. And you hope people feel the same need, the urgency you do, to get there. Well, I think IBMers today do feel that urgency. Maybe the jam's greatest contribution was to make that fact unambiguously clear to all of us, very visibly, in public.

Continuity and Change

IBM'S NEW VALUES GREW OUT OF A LONG TRADITION. In 1914, Thomas Watson, Sr., the founder of the modern International Business Machines Corporation, laid out three principles known as the *Basic Beliefs*:

- Respect for the individual
- The best customer service
- The pursuit of excellence

Although these beliefs played a significant role in driving IBM's success over most of the twentieth century, they eventually were subsumed—and, in effect, redefined—by a sense of entitlement and arrogance within the organization. That, according to CEO Sam Palmisano, contributed to the company's failure to respond to market changes in the early 1990s and to its near demise.

In February 2003, just under a year after taking over as CEO, at a meeting of IBM's top 300 managers, Palmisano raised the idea of reinventing the company's values as a way to manage and reintegrate the sprawling and diverse enterprise. He put forth *four concepts,* three of them drawn from Watson's Basic Beliefs, as possible bases for the new values:

- Respect
- Customer
- Excellence
- Innovation

These were "test marketed" through surveys and focus groups with more than 1,000 IBM employees. The notion of "respect" was thrown out because of its connotations of the past. It was also decided that statements rather than just words would be more compelling.

Out of this process grew the three *proposed values* discussed during the July 2003 online forum, ValuesJam:

- Commitment to the customer

What were the chief points of debate—or contention?

There was actually remarkable agreement on *what* we all value. The debate, as it turned out, wasn't over the values themselves so much. The debate was about whether IBM today is willing and able to live them.

For instance, people seemed to understand the need to reintegrate the company, but there were complaints—legitimate complaints—

- Excellence through innovation
- Integrity that earns trust

Using a specially tailored "jamalyzer" tool—based on IBM's e-classifier software, but turbocharged with additional capabilities designed to process constantly changing content—IBM analysts crunched the million-plus words posted during the ValuesJam. Some themes emerged. For example, many people said that a silo mentality pitted the business units against one another, to the detriment of IBM as a whole. Several people characterized this as a trust issue. But the proposed value "integrity that earns trust" was criticized as being too vague. Some thought it was just another way of saying "respect for the individual," one of the original Basic Beliefs that many now viewed as outdated. And the notion of trust was seen as being too inwardly focused—management trusting its employees—and not prescriptive enough in terms of how employees should behave with each other or with parties outside the company.

Drawing on this analysis, the results of pre- and post-jam surveys, and a full reading of the raw transcripts, a small team, with input from Palmisano, arrived at a revised set of *new corporate values*:

- **Dedication to every client's success**
- **Innovation that matters—for our company and for the world**
- **Trust and personal responsibility in all relationships**

These were published on the company intranet in November 2003.

about things that are getting in the way. People would describe extremely frustrating situations. They'd say something like: "I'm in Tokyo, prototyping software for a client, and I need a software engineer based in Austin *right now* to help in a blade server configuration. But I can't just say, 'Please come to Tokyo and help.' I need to get a charge code first so I can pay his department for his time!"

There's a collective impatience that we've been tapping into to drive the change needed to make IBM everything that all of us aspire for it to be. I'm convinced that we wouldn't have gotten to this point if we hadn't found a way to engage the entire IBM population in a genuine, candid conversation.

Sam Joins the Fray

IBM CEO SAM PALMISANO was in China on business during ValuesJam, and he logged on from there. Following are some of his comments (typos included) on a number of topics raised by employees during the online forum:

YES, values matter!!!!! (6 reply)

Samuel J. Palmisano 29 Jul 2003 20:00 GMT

Good discussion about the need for values/principles/belifes, etc. people can be very cynical and sarcastic about this kind of topic,but I appreciate the thoughtful constructive comments I'm seeing. Personaly, I believe "values" should embrace a company's broader role in the world —with customers, society, culture,etc. - as well as how its people work together.. I hope this Jam elevates IBMs ambitions about its mission inthe 21st century.. WE have a unique opprtunity for IBM to set the pace for ALL companies, not just the techs.

doing the right thing for customers . . . (21 reply)

Samuel J. Palmisano 29 Jul 2003 20:07 GMT

Early in my career when I was in the field in Baltimore,one of our systems failed for a healthcare customer. The customer went to manual processes,but said they would start losing patients within hours if the system couldnt be fixed. The branch mgr called one of our competitors and orderd another system. so two teams of IBMERS worked side by side.. one to fix the system, the others to bring up the new one. the mgr never asked Hq what to do.. it was a great lesson in how far this company will go to help a customer in time of need. btw, we fixed the system in time.

By the way, having a global, universally accessible intranet like ours certainly helps, but the technology isn't the point. I think we would've found a way to have this companywide dialogue if the Web didn't exist. [For an explanation of how the jam worked, see the sidebar "Managing ValuesJam."]

What happened after the jam?

Well, we got a mountain of employee comments. The team analyzed all of it, and it was clear that the proposed value statements needed to change to reflect some of the nuances and emotion people expressed. So, drawing on this analysis, along with other employee feedback, a small team settled on IBM's new corporate values.

integrity/trust in ALL our relationships matter!!!! (44 reply)

Samuel J. Palmisano 29 Jul 2003 20:12 GMT
very interesting discussion . . . one thing I'm noticing, and it was in the broadcast feedback too: not too many of you are talking about integrity and trust when it comes to our OTHER relationships that are key to IBMs success—customers, communities where we live, owners of the company etc. any thoghts on why thats so? maybe we're too inwardly focused?

a world without IBM???? (35 reply)

Samuel J. Palmisano 29 Jul 2003 20:20 GMT
No IBM? the industry would stop growing because no one would invent anything that ran for more than THREE MINUTES.. no IBM means no grownups . . . no IBM means no truly global company that brings economic growth, respect progress to societies everywhere . . . no iBM means no place to work for hundreds of thousands of people who want more than a job, they want to ,MAKE A DIFFERENCE in the world.

suggestion for Sam (9 reply)

Samuel J. Palmisano 29 Jul 2003 20:25 GMT
steve, you make good points about how/when we win . . . we can blow up more burecracy if we all behave like mature adutls and take into account ALL OF THE INTERESTS of IBm FIRST.. customers, employees, shareholders, doing whats right for the LONG TERM intersts of the company. mgrs have an important role to play in encouraing this kind of behavior . . . you have my support.

The first value is "dedication to every client's success." At one level, that's pretty straightforward: Bring together all of IBM's capability—in the laboratory, in the field, in the back office, wherever—to help solve difficult problems clients can't solve themselves. But this is also a lot more than the familiar claim of unstinting customer service. "Client success" isn't just "the customer is always right." It means maintaining a long-term relationship where what happens after the deal is more important than what happens before it's signed. It means a persistent focus on outcomes. It means having skin in the game of your client's success, up to and including how your contracts are structured and what triggers your getting paid.

The second is "innovation that matters—for our company and for the world." When employees talked about IBM making a difference in the world, they included more than our work of inventing and building great products. They talked about how their work touches people and society, how we can help save lives—say, through our cutting-edge work with the Mayo Clinic or by helping governments fight terrorism with our data technology. This kind of innovation is a major reason we are able to attract great scientists. They can do cool stuff and maybe make more money in Silicon Valley—for a while, anyway—but they can do work that actually changes business and society at IBM. And it's also about what I mentioned before: a continually experimental attitude toward IBM itself. Over most of our 90 years, with the exception of that one period when we became arrogant and complacent, this company never stopped questioning assumptions, trying out different models, testing the limits—whether in technology or business or in progressive workforce policies. Employees reminded us that those things are innovations that matter at least as much as new products.

The third value is "trust and personal responsibility in all relationships." There's a lot in that statement, too. Interestingly, the feedback from employees on this value has focused on relationships among people at IBM. But we're also talking about the company's relationships with suppliers, with investors, with governments, with communities.

We published the values in their final form—along with some elaboration on them and some direct employee postings from the jam—in November 2003. Over the next ten days, more than 200,000 people downloaded the online document. The responses just flooded in, both in the form of postings on the intranet and in more than a thousand e-mails sent directly to me, telling us in often sharp language just where IBM's operations fell short of, or clashed with, these ideals. Some of the comments were painful to read. But, again, they exhibited something every leader should welcome: People here aren't complacent about the company's future. And the comments were, by and large, extremely thoughtful.

Managing ValuesJam

IBM HAD EXPERIMENTED before with jam sessions—relatively unstructured employee discussions around broad topics—both on the corporate intranet and in face-to-face off-site brainstorming sessions. But the 72-hour ValuesJam, held in July 2003, was the most ambitious, focusing as it did on the very nature and future of IBM.

One thing was clear: You wouldn't be able to orchestrate a forum like this, the verbal equivalent of an improvisational jam session among jazz musicians. In the words of CEO Sam Palmisano, "It just took off." But, much like a musical jam, the dialogue was informed by a number of themes:

Forum 1. Company Values

Do company values exist? If so, what is involved in establishing them? Most companies today have values statements. But what would a company look and act like that truly lived its beliefs? Is it important for IBM to agree on a set of lasting values that drive everything it does?

Forum 2. A First Draft

What values are essential to what IBM needs to become? Consider this list: 1. Commitment to the customer. 2. Excellence through innovation. 3. Integrity that earns trust. How might these values change the way we act or the decisions we make? Is there some important aspect or nuance that is missing?

Forum 3. A Company's Impact

If our company disappeared tonight, how different would the world be tomorrow? Is there something about our company that makes a unique contribution to the world?

Forum 4. The Gold Standard

When is IBM at its best? When have you been proudest to be an IBMer? What happened, and what was uniquely meaningful about it? And what do we need to do—or change—to be the gold standard going forward?

What did you do with this feedback?

We collected and collated it. Then I printed all of it out—the stack of paper was about three feet high—and took it home to read over one weekend. On Monday morning, I walked into our executive committee meeting and threw it on the table. I said, "You guys ought to read every one of these comments, because if you think we've got this place plumbed correctly, think again."

Don't get me wrong. The passion in these e-mails was positive as well as negative. People would say, literally, "I'm weeping. These values describe the company I joined, the company I believe in. We can truly make this place great again. But we've got all these things in our way. . . ." The raw emotion of some of the e-mails was really something.

Now, if you've unleashed all this frustration and energy, if you've invited people to feel hope about something they really care about, you'd better be prepared to do something in response. So, in the months since we finalized the values, we've announced some initiatives that begin to close the gaps.

One I have dubbed our "$100 million bet on trust." We kept hearing about situations like our colleague in Tokyo who needed help from the engineer in Austin, cases in which employees were unable to respond quickly to client needs because of financial control processes that required several levels of management approval. The money would usually be approved, but too late. So we allocated managers up to $5,000 annually they could spend, no questions asked, to respond to extraordinary situations that would help generate business or develop client relationships or to respond to an IBMer's emergency need. We ran a pilot for a few months with our 700 client-facing teams, and they spent the money intelligently. There were lots of examples of teams winning deals and delighting clients with a small amount of "walk around money" to spend at their discretion. So, based on the success of that pilot, we expanded the program to all 22,000 IBM first-line managers.

You can do the math: $5,000 times 22,000 managers is a big number. I'm sure there were people in the company who said, "We need to get this under control." But they're not the CEO. Yes, you need financial controls. Yes, not every dollar spent from this Managers' Value Fund will yield some tangible return. But I'm confident that allowing line managers to take some reasonable risks, and trusting them with those decisions, will pay off over time. The program also makes a point: that we live by our values.

The value of "trust and personal responsibility in all relationships"—including those with IBM's shareholders—led to another initiative: a change in the way we grant top executive stock options. After getting a lot of outside experts to study this (and concluding that the complicated algorithms they recommended were wonderful, if you wanted to hire the outsiders as permanent consultants, but terrible if you wanted a simple formula that aligned executive behavior with shareholder interests), we settled on a straightforward idea. Senior executives will benefit from their options only after shareholders have realized at least 10% growth in their investments—that is, the strike price is 10% higher than the market price on the day the options are issued. Look at it this way: IBM's market value would have to increase by $17 billion from that date before any of the execs realize a penny of benefit. We think we are the first large company to take such a radical step—and it grew out of our values.

Let me give you one more example. It may not sound like a big deal, but for us, it was radical. We overhauled the way we set prices. We heard time and again from employees about how difficult it was to put together a client-friendly, cross-IBM solution, one involving a variety of products and services at a single, all-inclusive price. We couldn't do it. Every brand unit had its own P&L, and all the people who determine prices had been organized by brand. Remember those 100,000 cells in our 3-D matrix? Our people were pulling their cross-IBM bids apart, running them through our financial-accounting system as separate bids for individual products and services. This was nuts, because it's our ability to offer everything—hardware, software, services, and financing—that gives us a real advantage. When we bid on each of the parts separately, we go head-to-head against rivals by product: EMC in storage, say, or Accenture in services. This was tearing out the very heart of our strategy of integration, not to mention our unique kind of business-plus-technology innovation.

Let me give you a humorous (if somewhat discouraging) illustration. Every senior executive has responsibility for at least one major client—we call them "partnership accounts." Our former CFO John Joyce, who now heads IBM's services business, put together a deal for his account that involved some hardware, some software, and some services. He was told he couldn't price it as an integrated solution. And he's the CFO! So we figured out a way to set a single price for each integrated offering.

This sounds like a great business move. But what does it have to do with values? Wouldn't you ultimately have decided you had to do that in any case?

To be honest, we'd been debating the pricing issue at the executive level for a long time. But we hadn't done anything about it. The values initiative forced us to confront the issue, and it gave us the impetus to make the change. You know, there are always ingrained operations and habits of mind in any organization—I don't care whether it's a business or a university or a government. Well, the values and the jam were great inertia-busting vehicles. A small business in this place is $15 billion, and a big one is $40 billion. So you have senior vice presidents running Fortune 500-sized companies who aren't necessarily looking for bright ideas from the CEO or some task force every day. But when you hear from so many of our people on the front lines, you can't just ignore it. They're crying out: "We say we value 'client success,' and we want to grow our business. This one thing is getting in the way of both!" You've got to pay attention—if not to me, then to them.

So we took the pricers—the people who set the prices for client bids—and we said to them, "You work for IBM. When there's a cross-IBM bid with multiple products, you price it on the IBM income statement, not on the income statements of each product." Needless to say, this involved a series of very difficult meetings with senior executives. There was a huge debate among the finance people about all the reasons why we couldn't do it: "It will be too much work to reallocate all the costs and revenue of a project back to individual profit centers." And they're right: It isn't easy, especially when we now have to certify everything. But the CFO was with me on this: After all, he'd seen the problem firsthand! And we made the change, so that now when we make a truly cross-IBM bid, we can optimize it for the client and for us.

This brings us back to the tension between soft values and hard financial metrics. In the long run, they shouldn't conflict. But along the way, they're going to be jabbing at each other. After all, people still have to make their numbers.

Certainly, there's no getting around that in a commercial enterprise. But I think values inject balance in the company's culture and management system: balance between the short-term transaction and the long-term relationship, balance between the interests of shareholders, employees, and clients. In every case, you have to make a call. Values help you make those decisions, not on an ad hoc basis, but in a way that is consistent with your culture and brand, with who you are as a company.

Look at how we compensate our managing directors, who are responsible for our largest client relationships. We decided to take half their comp and calculate it not on an annual basis but on a rolling three-year basis. We ask clients to score the managing director's performance at the end of a project or engagement, which might last longer than a single year, and that plays a big part in his bonus. So a big piece of his compensation is based on a combination of the project's profitability—whether the manager made his annual numbers—and on the client's satisfaction over a longer-term horizon. The managing director can't trade off one for the other.

So we've tried to keep balance in the system, to make sure that things aren't completely oriented toward short-term financials. But you're absolutely right: There are times when people will argue, "Well, jeez, you guys are pushing us in both directions." It's a valid debate. I think, though, that the best place to have that debate is at the lowest level of your organization, because that's where these decisions are being made and having an impact. Thousands of these interactions go on every day that none of us at the top will ever, or should ever, know about. But you hope that the values are providing a counterweight to the drive for short-term profitability in all those interactions. In the long term, I think, whether or not you have a values-driven culture is what makes you a winner or a loser.

You've had the new values in place for just about a year now. They've already created strong emotions and high expectations. What's the prognosis?

We're just starting down the road on what is probably a ten- to 15-year process. I was back in Asia not long ago, and I did one of these town hall-style meetings with IBM employees and talked about the values. Probably two-thirds of the people clearly knew about them, had read about them. But a third of the people—you could look at their faces and see it—hadn't even heard of the values. Or at least the values hadn't resonated with them yet. So we have work to do. Not just in getting everyone to memorize three pithy statements. We need to do a heck of a lot to close the gaps between our stated values and the reality of IBM today. That's the point of it all.

I know that not everyone on my executive team is as enthusiastic about the values initiative as I am—though they'd never admit it! But people on the senior team who lived through IBM's near-death experience will do anything not to go back to that. The blow to everyone's pride when IBM became the laughingstock of the business world was almost too much to bear. I have zero resistance from the senior team to initiatives that can save us from a return to that. And our values work is one of the most important of those initiatives.

Then look at the employee response to ValuesJam. There is an unmistakable yearning for this to be a great company. I mean, why have people joined IBM over the years? There are a lot of places to make money, if that's what drives you. Why come here?

I believe it's because they want to be part of a progressive company that makes a difference in the world. They want to be in the kind of company that supports research that wins Nobel Prizes, that changes the way people think about business itself, that is willing to take firm positions on unpopular issues based on principle.

You know, back in the 1950s, Watson, Jr., wrote the governors of southern states that IBM would not adhere to separate-but-equal laws, and then the company codified an equal-opportunity policy years before it was mandated by law. I've got to believe that a company that conceives of itself that way, and that seriously manages itself accordingly, has strong appeal to a lot of people. We can't offer them the promise of instant wealth, which they may get at a start-up, or a job for life, as in the old days. But we can offer them something worth believing in and working toward.

If we get most people in this company excited about that, they're going to pull the rest of the company with them. If they become dedicated to these values and what we're trying to accomplish, I can go to sleep at night confident of our future.

Originally published in December 2004. Reprint R0412C

Radical Change, the Quiet Way

by Debra E. Meyerson

A

AT ONE POINT OR ANOTHER, many managers experience a spang of conscience—a yearning to confront the basic or hidden assumptions, interests, practices, or values within an organization that they feel are stodgy, unfair, even downright wrong. A vice president wishes that more people of color would be promoted. A partner at a consulting firm thinks new MBAs are being so overworked that their families are hurting. A senior manager suspects his company, with some extra cost, could be kinder to the environment. Yet many people who want to drive changes like these face an uncomfortable dilemma. If they speak out too loudly, resentment builds toward them; if they play by the rules and remain silent, resentment builds inside them. Is there any way, then, to rock the boat without falling out of it?

Over the past 15 years, I have studied hundreds of professionals who spend the better part of their work lives trying to answer this question. Each one of the people I've studied differs from the organizational status quo in some way—in values, race, gender, or sexual preference, perhaps (see the sidebar "How the Research Was Done"). They all see things a bit differently from the "norm." But despite feeling at odds with aspects of the prevailing culture, they genuinely like their jobs and want to continue to succeed in them, to effectively use their differences as the impetus for constructive change.

How the Research Was Done

THIS ARTICLE IS BASED ON a multipart research effort that I began in 1986 with Maureen Scully, a professor of management at the Center for Gender in Organizations at Simmons Graduate School of Management in Boston. We had observed a number of people in our own occupation—academia—who, for various reasons, felt at odds with the prevailing culture of their institutions. Initially, we set out to understand how these individuals sustained their sense of self amid pressure to conform and how they managed to uphold their values without jeopardizing their careers. Eventually, this research broadened to include interviews with individuals in a variety of organizations and occupations: business people, doctors, nurses, lawyers, architects, administrators, and engineers at various levels of seniority in their organizations.

Since 1986, I have observed and interviewed dozens of tempered radicals in many occupations and conducted focused research with 236 men and women, ranging from mid-level professionals to CEOs. The sample was diverse, including people of different races, nationalities, ages, religions, and sexual orientations, and people who hold a wide range of values and change agendas. Most of these people worked in one of three publicly traded corporations—a financial services organization, a high-growth computer components corporation, and a company that makes and sells consumer products. In this portion of the research, I set out to learn more about the challenges tempered radicals face and discover their strategies for surviving, thriving, and fomenting change. The sum of this research resulted in the spectrum of strategies described in this article.

They believe that direct, angry confrontation will get them nowhere, but they don't sit by and allow frustration to fester. Rather, they work quietly to challenge prevailing wisdom and gently provoke their organizational cultures to adapt. I call such change agents *tempered radicals* because they work to effect significant changes in moderate ways.

In so doing, they exercise a form of leadership within organizations that is more localized, more diffuse, more modest, and less visible than traditional forms—yet no less significant. In fact, top executives seeking to institute cultural or organizational change—who are, perhaps, moving tradition-bound organizations down new roads or who are concerned about reaping the full potential of marginalized employees—might do well to seek out these tempered

Idea in Brief

How do you rock your corporate boat—without falling out? You know your firm needs constructive change, but here's your dilemma: If you push your agenda too hard, resentment builds against you. If you remain silent, resentment builds inside you.

What's a manager to do? Become a **tempered radical**—an informal leader who quietly challenges prevailing wisdom and provokes cultural transformation. These radicals bear no banners and sound no trumpets. Their seemingly innocuous changes barely inspire notice. But like steady drops of water, they gradually erode granite.

Tempered radicals embody contrasts. Their commitments are firm, but their means flexible. They yearn for rapid change, but trust in patience. They often work alone, yet unite others. Rather than pressing their agendas, they start conversations. And instead of battling powerful foes, they seek powerful friends. The overall effect? Evolutionary—but relentless—change.

radicals, who may be hidden deep within their own organizations. Because such individuals are both dedicated to their companies and masters at changing organizations at the grassroots level, they can prove extremely valuable in helping top managers to identify fundamental causes of discord, recognize alternative perspectives, and adapt to changing needs and circumstances. In addition, tempered radicals, given support from above and a modicum of room to experiment, can prove to be excellent leaders. (For more on management's role in fostering tempered radicals, see the sidebar "Tempered Radicals as Everyday Leaders.")

Since the actions of tempered radicals are not, by design, dramatic, their leadership may be difficult to recognize. How, then, do people who run organizations, who want to nurture this diffuse source of cultural adaptation, find and develop these latent leaders? One way is to appreciate the variety of modes in which tempered radicals operate, learn from them, and support their efforts.

To navigate between their personal beliefs and the surrounding cultures, tempered radicals draw principally on a spectrum of incremental approaches, including four I describe here. I call these *disruptive self-expression, verbal jujitsu, variable-term opportunism,*

Idea in Practice

Tempered radicals use these tactics:

Disruptive Self-Expression

Demonstrate your values through your language, dress, office décor, or behavior. People notice and talk—often becoming brave enough to try the change themselves. The more people talk, the greater the impact.

> ***Example:*** Stressed-out manager John Ziwak began arriving at work earlier so he could leave by 6:00 p.m. to be with family. He also refused evening business calls. As his stress eased, his performance improved. Initially skeptical, colleagues soon accommodated, finding more efficient ways of working and achieving balance in their own lives.

Verbal Jujitsu

Redirect negative statements or actions into positive change.

> ***Example:*** Sales manager Brad Williams noticed that the new marketing director's peers ignored her during meetings. When one of them co-opted a thought she had already expressed, Williams said: "I'm glad George picked up on Sue's concerns. Sue, did George correctly capture what you were thinking?" No one ignored Sue again.

Variable-Term Opportunism

Be ready to capitalize on unexpected opportunities for short-term change, as well as orchestrate deliberate, longer term change.

and *strategic alliance building*. Disruptive self-expression, in which an individual simply acts in a way that feels personally right but that others notice, is the most inconspicuous way to initiate change. Verbal jujitsu turns an insensitive statement, action, or behavior back on itself. Variable-term opportunists spot, create, and capitalize on short- and long-term opportunities for change. And with the help of strategic alliances, an individual can push through change with more force.

Each of these approaches can be used in many ways, with plenty of room for creativity and wit. Self-expression can be done with a whisper; an employee who seeks more racial diversity in the ranks might wear her dashiki to company parties. Or it can be done with a roar; that same employee might wear her dashiki to the office every day. Similarly, a person seeking stricter environmental policies

Example: Senior executive Jane Adams joined a company with a dog-eat-dog culture. To insinuate her collaborative style, she shared power with direct reports, encouraged them to also delegate, praised them publicly, and invited them to give high-visibility presentations. Her division gained repute as an exceptional training ground for building experience, responsibility, and confidence.

Strategic Alliance Building

Gain clout by working with allies. Enhance your legitimacy and implement change more quickly and directly than you could alone. Don't make "opponents" enemies—they're often your best source of support and resources.

Example: Paul Wielgus started a revolution in his bureaucratic global spirits company—by persuading the opposition to join him. Others derided the training department Wielgus formed to boost employee creativity, and an auditor scrutinized the department for unnecessary expense. Rather than getting defensive, Paul treated the auditor as an equal and sold him on the program's value. The training spread, inspiring employees and enhancing productivity throughout the company.

might build an alliance by enlisting the help of one person, the more powerful the better. Or he might post his stance on the company intranet and actively seek a host of supporters. Taken together, the approaches form a continuum of choices from which tempered radicals draw at different times and in various circumstances.

But before looking at the approaches in detail, it's worth reconsidering, for a moment, the ways in which cultural change happens in the workplace.

How Organizations Change

Research has shown that organizations change primarily in two ways: through drastic action and through evolutionary adaptation. In the former case, change is discontinuous and often forced on the

MEYERSON

Tempered Radicals as Everyday Leaders

IN THE COURSE OF THEIR DAILY actions and interactions, tempered radicals teach important lessons and inspire change. In so doing, they exercise a form of leadership within organizations that is less visible than traditional forms—but just as important.

The trick for organizations is to locate and nurture this subtle form of leadership. Consider how Barry Coswell, a conservative, yet open-minded lawyer who headed up the securities division of a large, distinguished financial services firm, identified, protected, and promoted a tempered radical within his organization. Dana, a left-of-center, first-year attorney, came to his office on her first day of work after having been fingerprinted—a standard practice in the securities industry. The procedure had made Dana nervous: What would happen when her new employer discovered that she had done jail time for participating in a 1960s-era civil rights protest? Dana quickly understood that her only hope of survival was to be honest about her background and principles. Despite the difference in their political proclivities, she decided to give Barry the benefit of the doubt. She marched into his office and confessed to having gone to jail for sitting in front of a bus.

"I appreciate your honesty," Barry laughed, "but unless you've broken a securities law, you're probably okay." In return for her small confidence, Barry shared stories of his own about growing up in a poor county and about his life in the military. The story swapping allowed them to put aside ideological disagreements and to develop a deep respect for each other. Barry sensed a

organization or mandated by top management in the wake of major technological innovations, by a scarcity or abundance of critical resources, or by sudden changes in the regulatory, legal, competitive, or political landscape. Under such circumstances, change may happen quickly and often involves significant pain. Evolutionary change, by contrast, is gentle, incremental, decentralized, and over time produces a broad and lasting shift with less upheaval.

The power of evolutionary approaches to promote cultural change is the subject of frequent discussion. For instance, in "We Don't Need Another Hero" (HBR, September 2001), Joseph L. Badaracco, Jr., asserts that the most effective moral leaders often operate beneath the radar, achieving their reforms without widespread notice. Likewise, tempered radicals gently and continually

budding leader in Dana. Here was a woman who operated on the strength of her convictions and was honest about it but was capable of discussing her beliefs without self-righteousness. She didn't pound tables. She was a good conversationalist. She listened attentively. And she was able to elicit surprising confessions from him.

Barry began to accord Dana a level of protection, and he encouraged her to speak her mind, take risks, and most important, challenge his assumptions. In one instance, Dana spoke up to defend a female junior lawyer who was being evaluated harshly and, Dana believed, inequitably. Dana observed that different standards were being applied to male and female lawyers, but her colleagues dismissed her "liberal" concerns. Barry cast a glance at Dana, then said to the staff, "Let's look at this and see if we are being too quick to judge." After the meeting, Barry and Dana held a conversation about double standards and the pervasiveness of bias. In time, Barry initiated a policy to seek out minority legal counsel, both in-house and at outside legal firms. And Dana became a senior vice president.

In Barry's ability to recognize, mentor, and promote Dana there is a key lesson for executives who are anxious to foster leadership in their organizations. It suggests that leadership development may not rest with expensive external programs or even with the best intentions of the human resources department. Rather it may rest with the open-minded recognition that those who appear to rock the boat may turn out to be the most effective of captains.

push against prevailing norms, making a difference in small but steady ways and setting examples from which others can learn. The changes they inspire are so incremental that they barely merit notice—which is exactly why they work so well. Like drops of water, these approaches are innocuous enough in themselves. But over time and in accumulation, they can erode granite.

Consider, for example, how a single individual slowly—but radically—altered the face of his organization. Peter Grant[1] was a black senior executive who held some 18 positions as he moved up the ladder at a large West Coast bank. When he first joined the company as a manager, he was one of only a handful of people of color on the professional staff. Peter had a private, long-term goal: to bring more women and racial minorities into the fold and help them succeed. Throughout his 30-year career running the company's local banks, regional offices, and corporate operations, one of his chief responsibilities was to hire new talent. Each time he had the opportunity, Peter attempted to hire a highly qualified member of a minority. But he did more than that—every time he hired someone, he asked that person to do the same. He explained to the new recruits the importance of hiring women and people of color and why it was their obligation to do likewise.

Whenever minority employees felt frustrated by bias, Peter would act as a supportive mentor. If they threatened to quit, he would talk them out of it. "I know how you feel, but think about the bigger picture here," he'd say. "If you leave, nothing here will change." His example inspired viral behavior in others. Many stayed and hired other minorities; those who didn't carried a commitment to hire minorities into their new companies. By the time Peter retired, more than 3,500 talented minority and female employees had joined the bank.

Peter was the most tempered, yet the most effective, of radicals. For many years, he endured racial slurs and demeaning remarks from colleagues. He waited longer than his peers for promotions; each time he did move up he was told the job was too big for him and he was lucky to have gotten it. "I worked my rear end off to make them comfortable with me," he said, late in his career. "It wasn't *luck*." He was often angry, but lashing out would have been the path of least emotional resistance. So without attacking the system, advancing a bold vision, or wielding great power, Peter chipped away at the organization's demographic base using the full menu of change strategies described below.

Disruptive Self-Expression

At the most tempered end of the change continuum is the kind of self-expression that quietly disrupts others' expectations. Whether waged as a deliberate act of protest or merely as a personal demonstration of one's values, disruptive self-expression in language, dress, office decor, or behavior can slowly change the atmosphere at work. Once people take notice of the expression, they begin to talk about it. Eventually, they may feel brave enough to try the same thing themselves. The more people who talk about the transgressive act or repeat it, the greater the cultural impact.

Consider the case of John Ziwak, a manager in the business development group of a high-growth computer components company. As a hardworking business school graduate who'd landed a plum job, John had every intention of working 80-hour weeks on the fast track to the top. Within a few years, he married a woman who also held a demanding job; soon, he became the father of two. John found his life torn between the competing responsibilities of home and work. To balance the two, John shifted his work hours—coming into the office earlier in the morning so that he could leave by 6 pm. He rarely scheduled late-afternoon meetings and generally refused to take calls at home in the evening between 6:30 and 9. As a result, his family life improved, and he felt much less stress, which in turn improved his performance at work.

At first, John's schedule raised eyebrows; availability was, after all, an unspoken key indicator of commitment to the company. "If John is unwilling to stay past 6," his boss wondered, "is he really committed to his job? Why should I promote him when others are willing and able to work all the time?" But John always met his performance expectations, and his boss didn't want to lose him. Over time, John's colleagues adjusted to his schedule. No one set up conference calls or meetings involving him after 5. One by one, other employees began adopting John's "6 o' clock rule"; calls at home, particularly during dinner hour, took place only when absolutely necessary. Although the 6 o' clock rule was never formalized, it nonetheless became par for the course in John's department. Some of John's colleagues continued to work late, but they all appreciated these changes in work practice and easily accommodated them. Most people in the department felt more, not less, productive during the day as they adapted their work habits to get things done more efficiently—for example, running meetings on schedule and monitoring interruptions in their day. According to John's boss, the employees appreciated the newfound balance in their lives, and productivity in the department did not suffer in the least.

Tempered radicals know that even the smallest forms of disruptive self-expression can be exquisitely powerful. The story of Dr. Frances Conley offers a case in point. By 1987, Dr. Conley had already established herself as a leading researcher and neurosurgeon at Stanford Medical School and the Palo Alto Veteran's Administration hospital. But as one of very few women in the profession, she struggled daily to maintain her feminine identity in a macho profession and her integrity amid gender discrimination. She had to keep her cool when, for example, in the middle of directing a team of residents through complicated brain surgery, a male colleague would stride into the operating room to say, "Move over, honey." "Not only did that undermine my authority and expertise with the team," Dr. Conley recalled later, "but it was unwarranted—and even dangerous. That kind of thing would happen all the time."

Despite the frustration and anger she felt, Dr. Conley at that time had no intention of making a huge issue of her gender. She didn't want the fact that she was a woman to compromise her position, or vice versa. So she expressed herself in all sorts of subtle ways, including in what she wore. Along with her green surgical scrubs, she donned white lace ankle socks—an unequivocal expression of her femininity. In itself, wearing lace ankle socks could hardly be considered a Gandhian act of civil disobedience. The socks merely said, "I can be a neurosurgeon and be feminine." But they spoke loudly enough in the stolid masculinity of the surgical environment, and, along with other small actions on her part, they sparked conversation in the hospital. Nurses and female residents frequently commented on Dr. Conley's style. "She is as demanding as any man and is not afraid to take them on," they would say, in admiration. "But she is also a woman and not ashamed of it."

Ellen Thomas made a comparable statement with her hair. As a young African-American consultant in a technical services business, she navigated constantly between organizational pressures to fit in and her personal desire to challenge norms that made it difficult for her to be herself. So from the beginning of her employment, Ellen expressed herself by wearing her hair in neat cornrow braids.

For Ellen, the way she wore her hair was not just about style; it was a symbol of her racial identity.

Once, before making an important client presentation, a senior colleague advised Ellen to unbraid her hair "to appear more professional." Ellen was miffed, but she didn't respond. Instead, she simply did not comply. Once the presentation was over and the client had been signed, she pulled her colleague aside. "I want you to know why I wear my hair this way," she said calmly. "I'm a black woman, and I happen to like the style. And as you just saw," she smiled, "my hairstyle has nothing to do with my ability to do my job."

Does leaving work at 6 PM or wearing lacy socks or cornrows force immediate change in the culture? Of course not; such acts are too modest. But disruptive self-expression does do two important things. First, it reinforces the tempered radical's sense of the importance of his or her convictions. These acts are self-affirming. Second, it pushes the status quo door slightly ajar by introducing an alternative modus operandi. Whether they are subtle, unspoken, and recognizable by only a few or vocal, visible, and noteworthy to many, such acts, in aggregation, can provoke real reform.

Verbal Jujitsu

Like most martial arts, jujitsu involves taking a force coming at you and redirecting it to change the situation. Employees who practice verbal jujitsu react to undesirable, demeaning statements or actions by turning them into opportunities for change that others will notice.

One form of verbal jujitsu involves calling attention to the opposition's own rhetoric. I recall a story told by a man named Tom Novak, an openly gay executive who worked in the San Francisco offices of a large financial services institution. As Tom and his colleagues began seating themselves around a table for a meeting in a senior executive's large office, the conversation briefly turned to the topic of the upcoming Gay Freedom Day parade and to so-called gay lifestyles in general. Joe, a colleague, said loudly, "I can appreciate

A Spectrum of Tempered Change Strategies

THE TEMPERED RADICAL'S SPECTRUM of strategies is anchored on the left by *disruptive self-expression:* subtle acts of private, individual style. A slightly more public form of expression, *verbal jujitsu,* turns the opposition's negative expression or behavior into opportunities for change. Further along the spectrum, the tempered radical uses *variable-term opportunism* to recognize and act on short- and long-term chances to motivate others. And through *strategic alliance building,* the individual works directly with others to bring about more extensive change. The more conversations an individual's action inspires and the more people it engages, the stronger the impetus toward change becomes.

In reality, people don't apply the strategies in the spectrum sequentially or even necessarily separately. Rather, these tools blur and overlap. Tempered radicals remain flexible in their approach, "heating up" or "cooling off" each as conditions warrant.

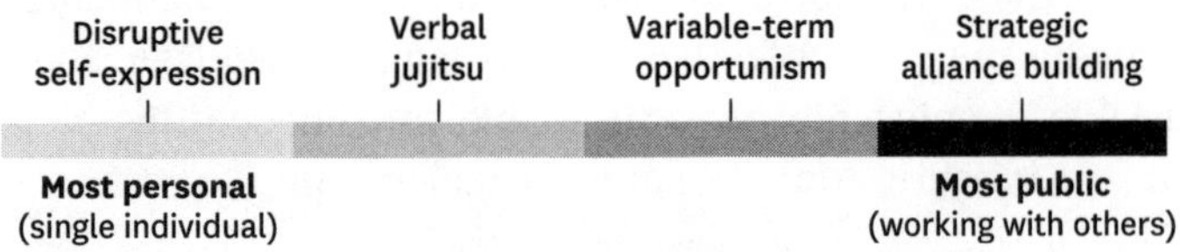

that some people choose a gay lifestyle. I just don't understand why they have to flaunt it in people's faces."

Stung, Tom was tempted to keep his mouth shut and absorb the injury, but that would have left him resentful and angry. He could have openly condemned Joe's bias, but that would have made him look defensive and self-righteous. Instead, he countered Joe with an altered version of Joe's own argument, saying calmly, "I know what you mean, Joe. I'm just wondering about that big picture of your wife on your desk. There's nothing wrong with being straight, but it seems that you are the one announcing your sexuality." Suddenly embarrassed, Joe responded with a simple, "Touché."

Managers can use verbal jujitsu to prevent talented employees, and their valuable contributions, from becoming inadvertently marginalized. That's what happened in the following story. Brad Williams was a sales manager at a high-technology company. During a meeting one day, Brad noticed that Sue, the new marketing director, had tried to interject a few comments, but everything she said was routinely ignored. Brad waited for the right moment to correct the situation. Later on in the meeting, Sue's colleague George raised similar concerns about distributing the new business's products outside the country. The intelligent remark stopped all conversation. During the pause, Brad jumped in: "That's an important idea," he said. "I'm glad George picked up on Sue's concerns. Sue, did George correctly capture what you were thinking?"

With this simple move, Brad accomplished a number of things. First, by indirectly showing how Sue had been silenced and her idea co-opted, he voiced an unspoken fact. Second, by raising Sue's visibility, he changed the power dynamic in the room. Third, his action taught his colleagues a lesson about the way they listened—and didn't. Sue said that after that incident she was no longer passed over in staff meetings.

In practicing verbal jujitsu, both Tom and Brad displayed considerable self-control and emotional intelligence. They listened to and studied the situation at hand, carefully calibrating their responses to disarm without harming. In addition, they identified the underlying issues (sexual bias, the silencing of newcomers) without sounding accusatory and relieved unconscious tensions by voicing them. In so doing, they initiated small but meaningful changes in their colleagues' assumptions and behavior.

Variable-Term Opportunism

Like jazz musicians, who build completely new musical experiences from old standards as they go along, tempered radicals must be creatively open to opportunity. In the short-term, that means being prepared to capitalize on serendipitous circumstances; in the long-term, it often means something more proactive. The first story that follows illustrates the former case; the second is an example of the latter.

Tempered radicals like Chris Morgan know that rich opportunities for reform can often appear suddenly, like a $20 bill found on a sidewalk. An investment manager in the audit department of a New York conglomerate, Chris made a habit of doing whatever he could to reduce waste. To save paper, for example, he would single-space his documents and put them in a smaller font before pressing the "Print" button, and he would use both sides of the paper. One day, Chris noticed that the company cafeteria packaged its sandwiches in Styrofoam boxes that people opened and immediately tossed. He pulled the cafeteria manager aside. "Mary," he said with a big smile, "those turkey-on-focaccia sandwiches look delicious today! I was wondering, though . . . would it be possible to wrap sandwiches only when people asked you to?" By making this very small change, Chris pointed out, the cafeteria would save substantially on packaging costs.

Chris gently rocked the boat by taking the following steps. First, he picked low-hanging fruit, focusing on something that could be done easily and without causing a lot of stir. Next, he attacked the problem not by criticizing Mary's judgment but by enrolling her in his agenda (praising her tempting sandwiches, then making a gentle suggestion). Third, he illuminated the advantages of the proposed change by pointing out the benefits to the cafeteria. And he started a conversation that, through Mary, spread to the rest of the cafeteria staff. Finally, he inspired others to action: Eventually, the cafeteria staff identified and eliminated 12 other wasteful practices.

Add up enough conversations and inspire enough people and, sooner or later, you get real change. A senior executive named Jane Adams offers a case in point. Jane was hired in 1995 to run a 100-person, mostly male software-development division in an extremely fast-growing, pre-IPO technology company. The CEO of the company was an autocrat who expected his employees to emulate his dog-eat-dog management style. Although Jane was new to the job and wanted very much to fit in and succeed, turf wars and command-and-control tactics were anathema to her. Her style was more collaborative; she believed in sharing power. Jane knew that she could not attack the company's culture by arguing with the CEO; rather, she took charge of her own division and ran it her own way. To that end, she took every opportunity to share power with subordinates. She instructed each of her direct reports to delegate responsibility as much as possible. Each time she heard about someone taking initiative in making a decision, she would praise that person openly before his or her manager. She encouraged people to take calculated risks and to challenge her.

When asked to give high-visibility presentations to the company's executive staff, she passed the opportunities to those who had worked directly on the project. At first, senior executives raised their eyebrows, but Jane assured them that the presenter would deliver. Thus, her subordinates gained experience and won credit that, had they worked for someone else, they would likely never have received.

Occasionally, people would tell Jane that they noticed a refreshing contrast between her approach and the company's prevailing one. "Thanks, I'm glad you noticed," she would say with a quiet smile. Within a year, she saw that several of her own direct reports began themselves to lead in a more collaborative manner. Soon, employees from other divisions, hearing that Jane's was one of the best to work for, began requesting transfers. More important, Jane's group became known as one of the best training grounds and Jane as one of the best teachers and mentors of new talent. Nowhere else did people get the experience, responsibility, and confidence that she cultivated in her employees.

For Chris Morgan, opportunity was short-term and serendipitous. For Jane Adams, opportunity was more long-term, something to be mined methodically. In both cases, though, remaining alert to such variable-term opportunities and being ready to capitalize on them were essential.

Strategic Alliance Building

So far, we have seen how tempered radicals, more or less working alone, can effect change. What happens when these individuals work with allies? Clearly, they gain a sense of legitimacy, access to resources and contacts, technical and task assistance, emotional support, and advice. But they gain much more—the power to move issues to the forefront more quickly and directly than they might by working alone.

When one enlists the help of like-minded, similarly tempered coworkers, the strategic alliance gains clout. That's what happened when a group of senior women at a large professional services firm worked with a group of men sympathetic to their cause. The firm's executive management asked the four-woman group to find out why it was so hard for the company to keep female consultants on staff. In the course of their investigation, the women discussed the demanding culture of the firm: a 70-hour work week was the norm, and most consultants spent most of their time on the road, visiting clients. The only people who escaped this demanding schedule were part-time consultants, nearly all of whom happened to be women with families. These part-timers were evaluated according to the same performance criteria—including the expectation of long hours—as full-time workers. Though many of the part-timers were talented contributors, they consistently failed to meet the time criterion and so left the company. To correct the problem, the senior women first gained the ear of several executive men who, they knew, regretted missing time with their own families. The men agreed that this was a problem and that the company could not continue to bleed valuable talent. They signed on to help address the issue and, in a matter of months, the evaluation system was adjusted to make success possible for all workers, regardless of their hours.

Tempered radicals don't allow preconceived notions about "the opposition" to get in their way. Indeed, they understand that those who represent the majority perspective are vitally important to gaining support for their cause. Paul Wielgus quietly started a revolution at his company by effectively persuading the opposition to join him. In 1991, Allied Domecq, the global spirits company whose brands include Courvoisier and Beefeater, hired Paul as a marketing director in its brewing and wholesaling division. Originally founded in 1961 as the result of a merger of three British brewing and pub-owning companies, the company had inherited a bureaucratic culture. Tony

Hales, the CEO, recognized the need for dramatic change inside the organization and appreciated Paul's talent and fresh perspective. He therefore allowed Paul to quit his marketing job, report directly to the CEO, and found a nine-person learning and training department that ran programs to help participants shake off stodgy thinking and boost their creativity. Yet despite the department's blessing from on high and a two-year record of success, some managers thought of it as fluff. In fact, when David, a senior executive from the internal audit department, was asked to review cases of unnecessary expense, he called Paul on the carpet.

Paul's strategy was to treat David not as a threat but as an equal, even a friend. Instead of being defensive during the meeting, Paul used the opportunity to sell his program. He explained that the trainers worked first with individuals to help unearth their personal values, then worked with them in teams to develop new sets of group values that they all believed in. Next, the trainers aligned these personal and departmental values with those of the company as a whole. "You wouldn't believe the changes, David," he said, enthusiastically. "People come out of these workshops feeling so much more excited about their work. They find more meaning and purpose in it, and as a consequence are happier and much more productive. They call in sick less often, they come to work earlier in the morning, and the ideas they produce are much stronger." Once David understood the value of Paul's program, the two began to talk about holding the training program in the internal audit department itself.

Paul's refusal to be frightened by the system, his belief in the importance of his work, his search for creative and collaborative solutions, his lack of defensiveness with an adversary, and his ability to connect with the auditor paved the way for further change at Allied Domecq. Eventually, the working relationship the two men had formed allowed the internal audit department to transform its image as a policing unit into something more positive. The new Audit Services department came to be known as a partner, rather than an enforcer, in the organization as a whole. And as head of the newly renamed department, David became a strong supporter of Paul's work.

Tempered radicals understand that people who represent the majority perspective can be important allies in more subtle ways as well. In navigating the course between their desire to undo the status quo and the organizational requirements to uphold it, tempered radicals benefit from the advice of insiders who know just how hard to push. When a feminist who wants to change the way her company treats women befriends a conservative Republican man, she knows he can warn her of political minefields. When a Latino manager wants his company to put a Spanish-language version of a manual up on the company's intranet, he knows that the white, monolingual executive who runs operations may turn out to be an excellent advocate.

Of course, tempered radicals know that not everyone is an ally, but they also know it's pointless to see those who represent the status quo as enemies. The senior women found fault with an inequitable evaluation system, not with their male colleagues. Paul won David's help by giving him the benefit of the doubt from the very beginning of their relationship. Indeed, tempered radicals constantly consider all possible courses of action: "Under what conditions, for what issues, and in what circumstances does it make sense to join forces with others?"; "How can I best use this alliance to support my efforts?"

Clearly, there is no one right way to effect change. What works for one individual under one set of circumstances may not work for others under different conditions. The examples above illustrate how tempered radicals use a spectrum of quiet approaches to change their organizations. Some actions are small, private, and muted; some are larger and more public. Their influence spreads as they recruit others and spawn conversations. Top managers can learn a lot from these people about the mechanics of evolutionary change.

Tempered radicals bear no banners; they sound no trumpets. Their ends are sweeping, but their means are mundane. They are firm in their commitments, yet flexible in the ways they fulfill them. Their actions may be small but can spread like a virus. They yearn for rapid change but trust in patience. They often work individually yet pull people together. Instead of stridently pressing their agendas, they start conversations. Rather than battling powerful foes, they seek powerful friends. And in the face of setbacks, they keep going. To do all this, tempered radicals understand revolutionary change for what it is—a phenomenon that can occur suddenly but more often than not requires time, commitment, and the patience to endure.

Originally published in October 2001. Reprint 7923

Notes

1. With the exception of those in the VA hospital and Allied Domecq cases, all the names used through this article are fictitious.

Tipping Point Leadership

by W. Chan Kim and Renée Mauborgne

IN FEBRUARY 1994, William Bratton was appointed police commissioner of New York City. The odds were against him. The New York Police Department, with a $2 billion budget and a workforce of 35,000 police officers, was notoriously difficult to manage. Turf wars over jurisdiction and funding were rife. Officers were underpaid relative to their counterparts in neighboring communities, and promotion seemed to bear little relationship to performance. Crime had gotten so far out of control that the press referred to the Big Apple as the Rotten Apple. Indeed, many social scientists had concluded, after three decades of increases, that New York City crime was impervious to police intervention. The best the police could do was react to crimes once they were committed.

Yet in less than two years, and without an increase in his budget, Bill Bratton turned New York into the safest large city in the nation. Between 1994 and 1996, felony crime fell 39%; murders, 50%; and theft, 35%. Gallup polls reported that public confidence in the NYPD jumped from 37% to 73%, even as internal surveys showed job satisfaction in the police department reaching an all-time high. Not surprisingly, Bratton's popularity soared, and in 1996, he was featured on the cover of *Time*. Perhaps most impressive, the changes have outlasted their instigator, implying a fundamental shift in the department's organizational culture and strategy. Crime rates have continued to fall: Statistics released in December 2002 revealed that New York's overall crime rate is the lowest among the 25 largest cities in the United States.

The NYPD turnaround would be impressive enough for any police chief. For Bratton, though, it is only the latest of no fewer than five successful turnarounds in a 20-year career in policing. In the hope that Bratton can repeat his New York and Boston successes, Los Angeles has recruited him to take on the challenge of turning around the LAPD. (For a summary of his achievements, see the table "Bratton in action.")

So what makes Bill Bratton tick? As management researchers, we have long been fascinated by what triggers high performance or suddenly brings an ailing organization back to life. In an effort to find the common elements underlying such leaps in performance, we have built a database of more than 125 business and nonbusiness organizations. Bratton first caught our attention in the early 1990s, when we heard about his turnaround of the New York Transit Police. Bratton was special for us because in all of his turnarounds, he succeeded in record time despite facing all four of the hurdles that managers consistently claim block high performance: an organization wedded to the status quo, limited resources, a demotivated staff, and opposition from powerful vested interests. If Bratton could succeed against these odds, other leaders, we reasoned, could learn a lot from him.

Over the years, through our professional and personal networks and the rich public information available on the police sector, we have systematically compared the strategic, managerial, and performance records of Bratton's turnarounds. We have followed up by interviewing the key players, including Bratton himself, as well as many other people who for professional—or sometimes personal—reasons tracked the events.

Our research led us to conclude that all of Bratton's turnarounds are textbook examples of what we call tipping point leadership. The theory of tipping points, which has its roots in epidemiology, is well known; it hinges on the insight that in any organization, once the beliefs and energies of a critical mass of people are engaged, conversion to a new idea will spread like an epidemic, bringing about

Idea in Brief

How can you overcome the hurdles facing any organization struggling to change: addiction to the status quo, limited resources, demotivated employees, and opposition from powerful vested interests?

Take lessons from police chief Bill Bratton, who's pulled the trick off five times. Most dramatically, he transformed the U.S.'s most dangerous city—New York—into its safest. Bratton used **tipping point leadership** to make unarguable calls for change, concentrate resources on what really mattered, mobilize key players' commitment, and silence naysayers.

Not every executive has Bratton's personality, but most have his potential—if they follow his success formula.

fundamental change very quickly. The theory suggests that such a movement can be unleashed only by agents who make unforgettable and unarguable calls for change, who concentrate their resources on what really matters, who mobilize the commitment of the organization's key players, and who succeed in silencing the most vocal naysayers. Bratton did all of these things in all of his turnarounds.

Most managers only dream of pulling off the kind of performance leaps Bratton delivered. Even Jack Welch needed some ten years and tens of millions of dollars of restructuring and training to turn GE into the powerhouse it is today. Few CEOs have the time and money that Welch had, and most—even those attempting relatively mild change—are soon daunted by the scale of the hurdles they face. Yet we have found that the dream can indeed become a reality. For what makes Bratton's turnarounds especially exciting to us is that his approach to overcoming the hurdles standing in the way of high performance has been remarkably consistent. His successes, therefore, are not just a matter of personality but also of method, which suggests that they can be replicated. Tipping point leadership is learnable.

In the following pages, we'll lay out the approach that has enabled Bratton to overcome the forces of inertia and reach the tipping point. We'll show first how Bratton overcame the cognitive hurdles that block companies from recognizing the need for radical

Idea in Practice

Four Steps to the Tipping Point

1. Break through the cognitive hurdle.

To make a compelling case for change, don't just point at the numbers and demand better ones. Your abstract message won't stick. Instead, make key managers *experience* your organization's problems.

> ***Example:*** New Yorkers once viewed subways as the most dangerous places in their city. But the New York Transit Police's senior staff pooh-poohed public fears—because none had ever ridden subways. To shatter their complacency, Bratton required all NYTP officers—himself included—to commute by subway. Seeing the jammed turnstiles, youth gangs, and derelicts, they grasped the need for change—and embraced responsibility for it.

2. Sidestep the resource hurdle.

Rather than trimming your ambitions (dooming your company to mediocrity) or fighting for more resources (draining attention from the underlying problems), concentrate *current* resources on areas *most* needing change.

> ***Example:*** Since the majority of subway crimes occurred at only a few stations, Bratton focused manpower there—instead of putting a cop on every subway line, entrance, and exit.

3. Jump the motivational hurdle.

To turn a mere strategy into a movement, people must recognize what needs to be done and yearn to do it themselves. But don't try reforming your whole organization; that's cumbersome and expensive. Instead, motivate *key influencers*—persuasive

change. Then we'll describe how he successfully managed around the public sector's endemic constraints on resources, which he even turned to his advantage. In the third section, we'll explain how Bratton overcame the motivational hurdles that had discouraged and demoralized even the most eager police officers. Finally, we'll describe how Bratton neatly closed off potentially fatal resistance from vocal and powerful opponents. (For a graphic summary of the ideas expressed in this article, see the figure "Tipping point leadership at a glance.")

people with multiple connections. Like bowling kingpins hit straight on, they topple all the other pins. Most organizations have several key influencers who share common problems and concerns—making it easy to identify and motivate them.

Example: Bratton put the NYPD's key influencers—precinct commanders—under a spotlight during semiweekly crime strategy review meetings, where peers and superiors grilled commanders about precinct performance. Results? A culture of performance, accountability, and learning that commanders replicated down the ranks.

Also make challenges attainable. Bratton exhorted staff to make NYC's streets safe "block by block, precinct by precinct, and borough by borough."

4. Knock over the political hurdle.

Even when organizations reach their tipping points, powerful vested interests resist change. Identify and silence key naysayers early by putting a respected senior insider on your top team.

Example: At the NYPD, Bratton appointed 20-year veteran cop John Timoney as his number two. Timoney knew the key players and how they played the political game. Early on, he identified likely saboteurs and resisters among top staff—prompting a changing of the guard.

Also, silence opposition with indisputable facts. When Bratton proved his proposed crime-reporting system required less than 18 minutes a day, time-crunched precinct commanders adopted it.

Break Through the Cognitive Hurdle

In many turnarounds, the hardest battle is simply getting people to agree on the causes of current problems and the need for change. Most CEOs try to make the case for change simply by pointing to the numbers and insisting that the company achieve better ones. But messages communicated through numbers seldom stick. To the line managers—the very people the CEO needs to win over—the case for change seems abstract and remote. Those whose units are doing well feel that the criticism is not directed at them, that the problem

Bratton in action

The New York Police Department was not Bill Bratton's first turnaround. The table describes his biggest challenges and achievements during his 20 years as a policy reformer.

Domain	Boston Police District 4	Massachusetts Bay Transit Authority (MBTA)	Boston Metropolitan Police ("The Mets")	New York Transit Police (NYTP)	New York Police Department (NYPD)
Years	1977–1982	1983–1986	1986–1990	1990–1992	1994–1996
Position	Sergeant, lieutenant	Superintendent	Superintendent	Chief of police	Commissioner
Setting	Assaults, drug dealing, prostitution, public drinking, and graffiti were endemic to the area. The Boston public shied away from attending baseball games and other events and from shopping in the Fenway neighborhood for fear of being robbed or attacked or having their cars stolen.	Subway crime had been on the rise for the past five years. The media dubbed the Boston subway the Terror Train. The *Boston Globe* published a series on police incompetence in the MBTA.	The Mets lacked modern equipment, procedures, and discipline. Physical facilities were crumbling. Accountability, discipline, and morale were low in the 600-person Mets workforce.	Crime had risen 25% per year in the past three years—twice the overall rate for the city. Subway use by the public had declined sharply; polls indicated that New Yorkers considered the subway the most dangerous place in the city. There were 170,000 fare evaders per day, costing the city $80 million annually. Aggressive panhandling and vandalism were endemic. More than 5,000 people were living in the subway system.	The middle class was fleeing to the suburbs in search of a better quality of life. There was public despair in the face of the high crime rate. Crime was seen as part of a breakdown of social norms. The budget for policing was shrinking. The NYPD budget (aside from personnel) was being cut by 35%. The staff was demoralized and relatively underpaid.

Domain	Boston Police District 4	Massachusetts Bay Transit Authority (MBTA)	Boston Metropolitan Police ("The Mets")	New York Transit Police (NYTP)	New York Police Department (NYPD)
Results	Crime throughout the Fenway area was dramatically reduced. Tourists, residents, and investment returned as an entire area of the city rebounded.	Crime on the MBTA decreased by 27%; arrests rose to 1,600 per year from 600. The MBTA police met more than 800 standards of excellence to be accredited by the National Commission on Accreditation for Police Agencies. It was only the 13th police department in the country to meet this standard. Equipment acquired during his tenure: 55 new midsize cars, new uniforms, and new logos. Ridership began to grow.	Employee morale rose as Bratton instilled accountability, protocol, and pride. In three years, the Metropolitan Police changed from a dispirited, do-nothing, reactive organization with a poor self-image and an even worse public image to a very proud, proactive department. Equipment acquired during his tenure: 100 new vehicles, a helicopter, and a state-of-the-art radio system.	In two years, Bratton reduced felony crime by 22%, with robberies down by 40%. Increased confidence in the subway led to increased ridership. Fare evasion was cut in half. Equipment acquired during his tenure: a state-of-the-art communication system, advanced handguns for officers, and new patrol cars (the number of cars doubled).	Overall crime fell by 17%. Felony crime fell by 39%. Murders fell by 50%. Theft fell by 35% (robberies were down by one-third, burglaries by one-quarter). There were 200,000 fewer victims a year than in 1990. By the end of Bratton's tenure, the NYPD had a 73% positive rating, up from 37% four years earlier.

is top management's. Managers of poorly performing units feel that they have been put on notice—and people worried about job security are more likely to be scanning the job market than trying to solve the company's problems.

For all these reasons, tipping point leaders like Bratton do not rely on numbers to break through the organization's cognitive hurdles.

Instead, they put their key managers face-to-face with the operational problems so that the managers cannot evade reality. Poor performance becomes something they witness rather than hear about. Communicating in this way means that the message—performance is poor and needs to be fixed—sticks with people, which is essential if they are to be convinced not only that a turnaround is necessary but that it is something they can achieve.

When Bratton first went to New York to head the transit police in April 1990, he discovered that none of the senior staff officers rode the subway. They commuted to work and traveled around in cars provided by the city. Comfortably removed from the facts of underground life—and reassured by statistics showing that only 3% of the city's major crimes were committed in the subway—the senior managers had little sensitivity to riders' widespread concern about safety. In order to shatter the staff's complacency, Bratton began requiring that all transit police officials—beginning with himself—ride the subway to work, to meetings, and at night. It was many staff officers' first occasion in years to share the ordinary citizen's subway experience and see the situation their subordinates were up against: jammed turnstiles, aggressive beggars, gangs of youths jumping turnstiles and jostling people on the platforms, winos and homeless people sprawled on benches. It was clear that even if few major crimes took place in the subway, the whole place reeked of fear and disorder. With that ugly reality staring them in the face, the transit force's senior managers could no longer deny the need for a change in their policing methods.

Bratton uses a similar approach to help sensitize his superiors to his problems. For instance, when he was running the police division of the Massachusetts Bay Transit Authority (MBTA), which runs the Boston-area subway and buses, the transit authority's board decided to purchase small squad cars that would be cheaper to buy and run. Instead of fighting the decision, Bratton invited the MBTA's general manager for a tour of the district. He picked him up in a small car just like the ones that were to be ordered. He jammed the seats forward to let the general manager feel how little legroom a six-foot cop would have, then drove him over every pothole he could find. Brat-

Tipping point leadership at a glance

Leaders like Bill Bratton use a four-step process to bring about rapid, dramatic, and lasting change with limited resources. The cognitive and resource hurdles shown here represent the obstacles that organizations face in reorienting and formulating strategy. The motivational and political hurdles prevent a strategy's rapid execution. Tipping all four hurdles leads to rapid strategy reorientation and execution. Overcoming these hurdles is, of course, a continuous process because the innovation of today soon becomes the conventional norm of tomorrow.

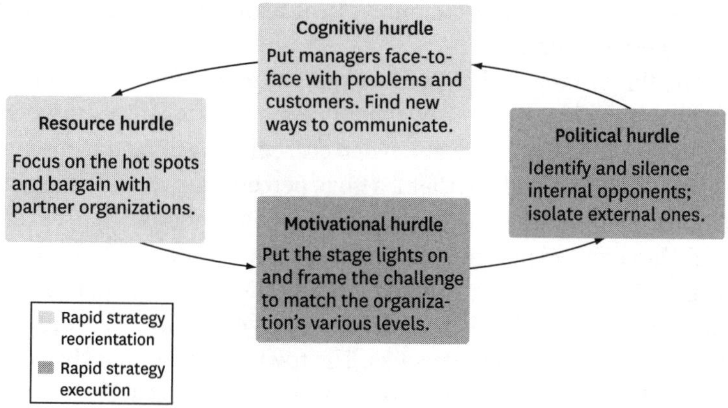

ton also put on his belt, cuffs, and gun for the trip so the general manager could see how little space there was for the tools of the officer's trade. After just two hours, the general manager wanted out. He said he didn't know how Bratton could stand being in such a cramped car for so long on his own—let alone if there were a criminal in the backseat. Bratton got the larger cars he wanted.

Bratton reinforces direct experiences by insisting that his officers meet the communities they are protecting. The feedback is often revealing. In the late 1970s, Boston's Police District 4, which included Symphony Hall, the Christian Science Mother Church, and other cultural institutions, was experiencing a surge in crime. The public was increasingly intimidated; residents were selling and leaving, pushing the community into a downward spiral. The Boston police performance statistics, however, did not reflect this reality. District 4 police, it seemed, were doing a splendid job of rapidly clearing 911 calls and tracking down perpetrators of serious crimes. To solve this paradox, Bratton had the unit organize community meetings in schoolrooms and civic centers so that citizens could voice their concerns to district sergeants and detectives. Obvious as the logic of this practice sounds, it was the first time in Boston's police history that anyone had attempted such an initiative—mainly because the practice up to that time had argued for detachment between police and the community in order to decrease the chances of police corruption.

The limitations of that practice quickly emerged. The meetings began with a show-and-tell by the officers: This is what we are working on and why. But afterward, when citizens were invited to discuss the issues that concerned them, a huge perception gap came to light. While the police officers took pride in solving serious offenses like grand larceny and murder, few citizens felt in any danger from these crimes. They were more troubled by constant minor irritants: prostitutes, panhandlers, broken-down cars left on the streets, drunks in the gutters, filth on the sidewalks. The town meetings quickly led to a complete overhaul of the police priorities for District 4. Bratton has used community meetings like this in every turnaround since.

Bratton's internal communications strategy also plays an important role in breaking through the cognitive hurdles. Traditionally, internal police communication is largely based on memos, staff bulletins, and other documents. Bratton knows that few police officers have the time or inclination to do more than throw these documents into the wastebasket. Officers rely instead on rumor and media stories for insights into what headquarters is up to. So Bratton typically calls on the help of expert communication outsiders. In New York, for instance, he recruited John Miller, an investigative television reporter known for his gutsy and innovative style, as his communication czar. Miller arranged for Bratton to communicate through video messages that were played at roll calls, which had the effect of bringing Bratton—and his opinions—closer to the people he had to win over. At the same time, Miller's journalistic savvy made it easier for the NYPD to ensure that press interviews and stories echoed the strong internal messages Bratton was sending.

Sidestep the Resource Hurdle

Once people in an organization accept the need for change and more or less agree on what needs to be done, leaders are often faced with the stark reality of limited resources. Do they have the money for the necessary changes? Most reformist CEOs do one of two things at this point. They trim their ambitions, dooming the company to mediocrity at best and demoralizing the workforce all over again, or they fight for more resources from their bankers and shareholders, a process that can take time and divert attention from the underlying problems.

That trap is completely avoidable. Leaders like Bratton know how to reach the organization's tipping point without extra resources. They can achieve a great deal with the resources they have. What they do is concentrate their resources on the places that are most in need of change and that have the biggest possible payoffs. This idea, in fact, is at the heart of Bratton's famous (and once hotly debated) philosophy of zero-tolerance policing.

Having won people over to the idea of change, Bratton must persuade them to take a cold look at what precisely is wrong with their operating practices. It is at this point that he turns to the numbers, which he is adept at using to force through major changes. Take the case of the New York narcotics unit. Bratton's predecessors had treated it as secondary in importance, partly because they assumed that responding to 911 calls was the top priority. As a result, less than 5% of the NYPD's manpower was dedicated to fighting narcotics crimes.

At an initial meeting with the NYPD's chiefs, Bratton's deputy commissioner of crime strategy, Jack Maple, asked people around the table for their estimates of the percentage of crimes attributable to narcotics use. Most said 50%; others, 70%; the lowest estimate was 30%. On that basis, a narcotics unit consisting of less than 5% of the police force was grossly understaffed, Maple pointed out. What's

The strategy canvas of transit:

How Bratton refocused resources

In comparing strategies across companies, we like to use a tool we call the strategy canvas, which highlights differences in strategies and resource allocation. The strategy canvas shown here compares the strategy and allocation of resources of the New York Transit Police before and after Bill Bratton's appointment as chief. The vertical axis shows the relative level of resource allocation. The horizontal axis shows the various elements of strategy in which the investments were made. Although a dramatic shift in resource allocation occurred and performance rose dramatically, overall investment of resources remained more or less constant. Bratton did this by de-emphasizing or virtually eliminating some traditional features of transit police work while increasing emphasis on others or creating new ones. For example, he was able to reduce the time police officers spent processing suspects by introducing mobile processing centers known as "bust buses."

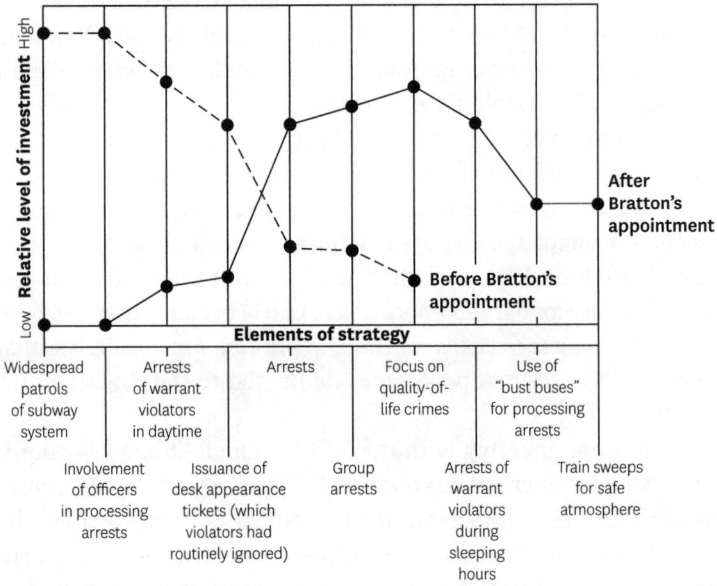

more, it turned out that the narcotics squad largely worked Monday through Friday, even though drugs were sold in large quantities—and drug-related crimes persistently occurred—on the weekends. Why the weekday schedule? Because it had always been done that way; it was an unquestioned modus operandi. Once these facts were presented, Bratton's call for a major reallocation of staff and resources within the NYPD was quickly accepted.

A careful examination of the facts can also reveal where changes in key policies can reduce the need for resources, as Bratton demonstrated during his tenure as chief of New York's transit police. His predecessors had lobbied hard for the money to increase the number of subway cops, arguing that the only way to stop muggers was to have officers ride every subway line and patrol each of the system's 700 exits and entrances. Bratton, by contrast, believed that subway crime could be resolved not by throwing more resources at the problem but by better targeting those resources. To prove the point, he had members of his staff analyze where subway crimes were being committed. They found that the vast majority occurred at only a few stations and on a couple of lines, which suggested that a targeted strategy would work well. At the same time, he shifted more of the force out of uniform and into plain clothes at the hot spots. Criminals soon realized that an absence of uniforms did not necessarily mean an absence of cops.

Distribution of officers was not the only problem. Bratton's analysis revealed that an inordinate amount of police time was wasted in processing arrests. It took an officer up to 16 hours per arrest to book the suspect and file papers on the incident. What's more, the officers so hated the bureaucratic process that they avoided making arrests in minor cases. Bratton realized that he could dramatically increase his available policing resources—not to mention the officers' motivation—if he could somehow improvise around this problem. His solution was to park "bust buses"—old buses converted into arrest-processing centers—around the corner from targeted subway stations. Processing time was cut from 16 hours to just one. Innovations like that enabled Bratton to dramatically reduce subway crime—even without an increase in the number of officers on duty at any given time. (The figure "The strategy canvas of transit: How Bratton refocused resources" illustrates how radically Bratton refocused the transit police's resources.)

Bratton's drive for data-driven policing solutions led to the creation of the famous Compstat crime database. The database, used to identify hot spots for intense police intervention, captures weekly crime and arrest activity—including times, locations, and associated enforcement activities—at the precinct, borough, and city levels. The Compstat reports allowed Bratton and the entire police department to easily discern established and emerging hot spots for efficient resource targeting and retargeting.

In addition to refocusing the resources he already controls, Bratton has proved adept at trading resources he doesn't need for those he does. The chiefs of public-sector organizations are reluctant to advertise excess resources, let alone lend them to other agencies, because acknowledged excess resources tend to get reallocated. So over time, some organizations end up well endowed with resources they don't need—even if they are short of others. When Bratton took over as chief of the transit police, for example, his general counsel and policy adviser, Dean Esserman, now police chief of Providence, Rhode Island, discovered that the transit unit had more unmarked cars than it needed but was starved of office space. The New York Division of Parole, on the other hand, was short of cars but had excess office space. Esserman and Bratton offered the obvious trade. It was gratefully accepted by the parole division, and transit officials were delighted to get the first floor of a prime downtown building. The deal stoked Bratton's credibility within the organization, which would make it easier for him to introduce more fundamental changes later, and it marked him, to his political bosses, as a man who could solve problems.

Jump the Motivational Hurdle

Alerting employees to the need for change and identifying how it can be achieved with limited resources are necessary for reaching an organization's tipping point. But if a new strategy is to become a movement, employees must not only recognize what needs to be done, they must also want to do it. Many CEOs recognize the importance of getting people motivated to make changes, but they make the mistake of trying to reform incentives throughout the whole organization. That process takes a long time to implement and can prove very expensive, given the wide variety of motivational needs in any large company.

One way Bratton solves the motivation problem is by singling out the key influencers—people inside or outside the organization with disproportionate power due to their connections with the organization, their ability to persuade, or their ability to block access to resources. Bratton recognizes that these influencers act like kingpins in bowling: When you hit them just right, all the pins topple over. Getting the key influencers motivated frees an organization from having to motivate everyone, yet everyone in the end is touched and changed. And because most organizations have relatively small numbers of key influencers, and those people tend to share common problems and concerns, it is relatively easy for CEOs to identify and motivate them.

Bratton's approach to motivating his key influencers is to put them under a spotlight. Perhaps his most significant reform of the NYPD's operating practices was instituting a semiweekly strategy review meeting that brought the top brass together with the city's 76 precinct commanders. Bratton had identified the commanders as key influential people in the NYPD, because each one directly managed 200 to 400 officers. Attendance was mandatory for all senior staff, including three-star chiefs, deputy commissioners, and borough chiefs. Bratton was there as often as possible.

At the meetings, which took place in an auditorium at the police command center, a selected precinct commander was called before a panel of the senior staff (the selected officer was given only two days' notice, in order to keep all the commanders on their toes). The commander in the spotlight was questioned by both the panel and other commanders about the precinct's performance. He or she was responsible for explaining projected maps and charts that showed, based on the Compstat data, the precinct's patterns of crimes and when and where the police responded. The commander would be required to provide a detailed explanation if police activity did not mirror crime spikes and would also be asked how officers were addressing the precinct's issues and why performance was improving or deteriorating. The meetings allowed Bratton and his senior staff to carefully monitor and assess how well commanders were motivating and managing their people and how well they were focusing on strategic hot spots.

The meetings changed the NYPD's culture in several ways. By making results and responsibilities clear to everyone, the meetings helped to introduce a culture of performance. Indeed, a photo of the commander who was about to be grilled appeared on the front page of the handout that each meeting participant received, emphasizing that the commander was accountable for the precinct's results. An incompetent commander could no longer cover up his failings by blaming his precinct's results on the shortcomings of neighboring precincts, because his neighbors were in the room and could respond. By the same token, the meetings gave high achievers a chance to be recognized both for making improvements in their own precincts and for helping other commanders. The meetings also allowed police leaders to compare notes on their experiences; before Bratton's arrival, precinct commanders hardly ever got together as a group. Over time, this management style filtered down through the ranks, as the precinct commanders tried out their own versions of Bratton's meetings. With the spotlight shining brightly on their performance, the commanders were highly motivated to get all the officers under their control marching to the new strategy.

The great challenges in applying this kind of motivational device, of course, are ensuring that people feel it is based on fair processes and seeing to it that they can draw lessons from both good and bad results. Doing so increases the organization's collective strength and everyone's chance of winning. Bratton addresses the issue of fair process by engaging all key influencers in the procedures, setting clear performance expectations, and explaining why these strategy meetings, for example, are essential for fast execution of policy.

He addresses the issue of learning by insisting that the team of top brass play an active role in meetings and by being an active moderator himself. Precinct commanders can talk about their achievements or failures without feeling that they are showing off or being shown up. Successful commanders aren't seen as bragging, because it's clear to everyone that they were asked by Bratton's top team to show, in detail, how they achieved their successes. And for commanders on the receiving end, the sting of having to be taught a lesson by a colleague is mitigated, at least, by their not having to suffer the indignity of asking for it. Bratton's popularity soared when he created a humorous video satirizing the grilling that precinct commanders were given; it showed the cops that he understood just how much he was asking of them.

Bratton also uses another motivational lever: framing the reform challenge itself. Framing the challenge is one of the most subtle and sensitive tasks of the tipping point leader; unless people believe that results are attainable, a turnaround is unlikely to succeed. On the face of it, Bratton's goal in New York was so ambitious as to be scarcely believable. Who would believe that the city could be made one of the safest in the country? And who would want to invest time and energy in chasing such an impossible dream?

To make the challenge seem manageable, Bratton framed it as a series of specific goals that officers at different levels could relate to. As he put it, the challenge the NYPD faced was to make the streets of New York safe "block by block, precinct by precinct, and borough by borough." Thus framed, the task was both all encompassing and doable. For the cops on the street, the challenge was making their beats or blocks safe—no more. For the commanders, the challenge was making their precincts safe—no more. Borough heads also had a concrete goal within their capabilities: making their boroughs safe—no more. No matter what their positions, officers couldn't say that what was being asked of them was too tough. Nor could they claim that achieving it was out of their hands. In this way, responsibility for the turnaround shifted from Bratton to each of the thousands of police officers on the force.

Knock Over the Political Hurdle

Organizational politics is an inescapable reality in public and corporate life, a lesson Bratton learned the hard way. In 1980, at age 34 one of the youngest lieutenants in Boston's police department, he had proudly put up a plaque in his office that said: "Youth and skill will win out every time over age and treachery." Within just a few months, having been shunted into a dead-end position due to a mixture of office politics and his own brashness, Bratton took the sign down. He never again forgot the importance of understanding the plotting, intrigue, and politics involved in pushing through change. Even if an organization has reached the tipping point, powerful vested interests will resist the impending reforms. The more likely change becomes, the more fiercely and vocally these negative influencers—both internal and external—will fight to protect their positions, and their resistance can seriously damage, even derail, the reform process.

Bratton anticipates these dangers by identifying and silencing powerful naysayers early on. To that end, he always ensures that he has a respected senior insider on the top team. At the NYPD, for instance, Bratton appointed John Timoney, now Miami's police commissioner, as his number two. Timoney was a cop's cop, respected and feared for his dedication to the NYPD and for the more than 60 decorations he had received. Twenty years in the ranks had taught him who all the key players were and how they played the political game. One of the first tasks Timoney carried out was to report to Bratton on the likely attitudes of the top staff toward Bratton's concept of zero-tolerance policing, identifying those who would fight or silently sabotage the new initiatives. This led to a dramatic changing of the guard.

Of course, not all naysayers should face the ultimate sanction—there might not be enough people left to man the barricades. In many cases, therefore, Bratton silences opposition by example and indisputable fact. For instance, when first asked to compile detailed crime maps and information packages for the strategy review meetings, most precinct commanders complained that the task would take too long and waste valuable police time that could be better spent fighting crime. Anticipating this argument, deputy commissioner Jack Maple set up a reporting system that covered the city's most crime-ridden areas. Operating the system required no more than 18 minutes a day, which worked out, as he told the precinct commanders, to less than 1% of the average precinct's workload. Try to argue with that.

Often the most serious opposition to reform comes from outside. In the public sector, as in business, an organization's change of strategy has an impact on other organizations—partners and competitors alike. The change is likely to be resisted by those players if they are happy with the status quo and powerful enough to protest the changes. Bratton's strategy for dealing with such opponents is to isolate them by building a broad coalition with the other independent powers in his realm. In New York, for example, one of the most serious threats to his reforms came from the city's courts, which were concerned that zero-tolerance policing would result in an enormous number of small-crimes cases clogging the court schedule.

To get past the opposition of the courts, Bratton solicited the support of no less a personage than the mayor, Rudolph Giuliani, who had considerable influence over the district attorneys, the courts, and the city jail on Rikers Island. Bratton's team demonstrated to the mayor that the court system had the capacity to handle minor "quality of life" crimes, even though doing so would presumably not be palatable for them.

The mayor decided to intervene. While conceding to the courts that a crackdown campaign would cause a short-term spike in court work, he also made clear that he and the NYPD believed it would eventually lead to a workload reduction for the courts. Working together in this way, Bratton and the mayor were able to maneuver the courts into processing quality-of-life crimes. Seeing that the mayor was aligned with Bratton, the courts appealed to the city's legislators, advocating legislation to exempt them from handling minor-crime cases on the grounds that such cases would clog the system and entail significant costs to the city. Bratton and the mayor, who were holding weekly strategy meetings, added another ally to their coalition by placing their case before the press, in particular the *New York Times*. Through a series of press conferences and articles and at every interview opportunity, the issue of zero tolerance was put at the front and center of public debate with a clear, simple message: If the courts did not help crack down on quality-of-life crimes, the city's crime rates would not improve. It was a matter not of saving dollars but of saving the city.

Bratton's alliance with the mayor's office and the city's leading media institution successfully isolated the courts. The courts could hardly be seen as publicly opposing an initiative that would not only make New York a more attractive place to live but would ultimately reduce the number of cases brought before them. With the mayor speaking aggressively in the press about the need to pursue quality-of-life crimes and the city's most respected—and liberal—newspaper giving credence to the policy, the costs of fighting Bratton's strategy were daunting. Thanks to this savvy politicking, one of Bratton's biggest battles was won, and the legislation was not enacted. The courts would handle quality-of-life crimes. In due course, the crime rates did indeed come tumbling down.

Of course, Bill Bratton, like any leader, must share the credit for his successes. Turning around an organization as large and as wedded to the status quo as the NYPD requires a collective effort. But the tipping point would not have been reached without him—or another leader like him. And while we recognize that not every executive has the personality to be a Bill Bratton, there are many who have that potential once they know the formula for success. It is that formula that we have tried to present, and we urge managers who wish to turn their companies around, but have limited time and resources, to take note. By addressing the hurdles to tipping point change described in these pages, they will stand a chance of achieving the same kind of results for their shareholders as Bratton has delivered to the citizens of New York.

Originally published in April 2003. Reprint R0304D

A Survival Guide for Leaders

by Ronald A. Heifetz and Marty Linsky

THINK OF THE MANY top executives in recent years who, sometimes after long periods of considerable success, have crashed and burned. Or think of individuals you have known in less prominent positions, perhaps people spearheading significant change initiatives in their organizations, who have suddenly found themselves out of a job. Think about yourself: In exercising leadership, have *you* ever been removed or pushed aside?

Let's face it, to lead is to live dangerously. While leadership is often depicted as an exciting and glamorous endeavor, one in which you inspire others to follow you through good times and bad, such a portrayal ignores leadership's dark side: the inevitable attempts to take you out of the game.

Those attempts are sometimes justified. People in top positions must often pay the price for a flawed strategy or a series of bad decisions. But frequently, something more is at work. We're not talking here about conventional office politics; we're talking about the high-stake risks you face whenever you try to lead an organization through difficult but necessary change. The risks during such times are especially high because change that truly transforms an organization, be it a multibillion-dollar company or a ten-person sales team, demands that people give up things they hold dear: daily habits, loyalties, ways of thinking. In return for these sacrifices, they may be offered nothing more than the possibility of a better future.

We refer to this kind of wrenching organizational transformation as "adaptive change," something very different from the "technical change" that occupies people in positions of authority on a regular basis. Technical problems, while often challenging, can be solved applying existing know-how and the organization's current problem-solving processes. Adaptive problems resist these kinds of solutions because they require individuals throughout the organization to alter their ways; as the people themselves are the problem, the solution lies with them. (See the sidebar "Adaptive Versus Technical Change: Whose Problem Is It?") Responding to an adaptive challenge with a technical fix may have some short-term appeal. But to make real progress, sooner or later those who lead must ask themselves and the people in the organization to face a set of deeper issues—and to accept a solution that may require turning part or all of the organization upside down.

It is at this point that danger lurks. And most people who lead in such a situation—swept up in the action, championing a cause they believe in—are caught unawares. Over and over again, we have seen courageous souls blissfully ignorant of an approaching threat until it was too late to respond.

The hazard can take numerous forms. You may be attacked directly in an attempt to shift the debate to your character and style and avoid discussion of your initiative. You may be marginalized, forced into the position of becoming so identified with one issue that your broad authority is undermined. You may be seduced by your supporters and, fearful of losing their approval and affection, fail to demand they make the sacrifices needed for the initiative to succeed. You may be diverted from your goal by people overwhelming you with the day-to-day details of carrying it out, keeping you busy and preoccupied.

Each one of these thwarting tactics—whether done consciously or not—grows out of people's aversion to the organizational disequilibrium created by your initiative. By attempting to undercut you, people strive to restore order, maintain what is familiar to them, and protect themselves from the pains of adaptive change. They want to be comfortable again, and you're in the way.

Idea in Brief

It's exciting—even glamorous—to lead others through good times and bad. But leadership also has its dark side: the inevitable attempts to take you out of the game when you're steering your organization through difficult change.

Leading change requires asking people to confront painful issues and give up habits and beliefs they hold dear. Result? Some people try to eliminate change's visible agent—you. Whether they attack you personally, undermine your authority, or seduce you into seeing things their way, their goal is the same: to derail you, easing *their* pain and restoring familiar order.

How to resist attempts to remove you—and continue to propel change forward? Manage your hostile *environment*—your organization and its people—and your own *vulnerabilities*.

So how do you protect yourself? Over a combined 50 years of teaching and consulting, we have asked ourselves that question time and again—usually while watching top-notch and well-intentioned folks get taken out of the game. On occasion, the question has become painfully personal; we as individuals have been knocked off course or out of the action more than once in our own leadership efforts. So we are offering what we hope are some pragmatic answers that grow out of these observations and experiences. We should note that while our advice clearly applies to senior executives, it also applies to people trying to lead change initiatives from positions of little or no formal organizational authority.

This "survival guide" has two main parts. The first looks outward, offering tactical advice about relating to your organization and the people in it. It is designed to protect you from those trying to push you aside before you complete your initiative. The second looks inward, focusing on your own human needs and vulnerabilities. It is designed to keep you from bringing yourself down.

A Hostile Environment

Leading major organizational change often involves radically reconfiguring a complex network of people, tasks, and institutions that

Idea in Practice

Managing Your Environment

To minimize threats to eliminate you:

Operate in and above the fray.

Observe what's happening to your initiative, *as* it's happening. Frequently move back and forth from the dance floor to the balcony, asking, "What's really going on here?" "Who's defending old habits?"

Court the uncommitted.

The uncommitted but wary are crucial to your success. Show your intentions are serious, for example, by dismissing individuals who can't make required changes. And practice what you preach.

> ***Example:*** The editor of the *St. Petersburg Times* wanted to create a harder-hitting newspaper. He knew that reporters—no longer sparing interviewees from warranted criticism—faced intense public pressure. He subjected *himself* to the same by insisting a story about his drunk-driving arrest appear on the paper's front page.

Cook the conflict.

Keep the heat high enough to motivate, but low enough to prevent explosions. *Raise the temperature* to make people confront hidden conflicts and other tough issues. Then *lower the heat* to reduce destructive turmoil. Slow the pace of change. Deliver humor, breaks, and images of a brighter future.

Place the work where it belongs.

Resist resolving conflicts yourself—people will blame *you* for whatever turmoil results. Mobilize *others* to solve problems.

have achieved a kind of modus vivendi, no matter how dysfunctional it appears to you. When the status quo is upset, people feel a sense of profound loss and dashed expectations. They may go through a period of feeling incompetent or disloyal. It's no wonder they resist the change or try to eliminate its visible agent. We offer here a number of techniques—relatively straightforward in concept but difficult to execute—for minimizing these external threats.

Operate in and above the fray

The ability to maintain perspective in the midst of action is critical to lowering resistance. Any military officer knows the importance of maintaining the capacity for reflection, especially in the "fog of

Example: When a star Chicago Bulls basketball player sat out a play, miffed because he wasn't tapped to take the game's final shot, the coach let the *team* handle the insubordination. An emotional conversation led by a team veteran reunited the players, who took the NBA series to a seventh game.

Managing Yourself

To avoid self-destructing during difficult change:

Restrain your desire for control and need for importance

Order for its own sake prevents organizations from handling contentious issues. And an inflated self-image fosters unhealthy dependence on you.

Example: Ken Olson, head of once-mighty Digital Equipment Corporation, encouraged such dependence that colleagues rarely challenged him. When he shunned the PC market (believing few people wanted PCs), top managers went along—initiating DEC's downfall.

Anchor yourself.

- Use a safe place (e.g., a friend's kitchen table) or routine (a daily walk) to repair psychological damage and recalibrate your moral compass.
- Acquire a confidant (*not* an ally from your organization) who supports you—not necessarily your initiative.
- Read attacks as reactions to your professional role, not to you personally. You'll remain calmer and keep people engaged.

war." Great athletes must simultaneously play the game and observe it as a whole. We call this skill "getting off the dance floor and going to the balcony," an image that captures the mental activity of stepping back from the action and asking, "What's really going on here?"

Leadership is an improvisational art. You may be guided by an overarching vision, clear values, and a strategic plan, but what you actually do from moment to moment cannot be scripted. You must respond as events unfold. To use our metaphor, you have to move back and forth from the balcony to the dance floor, over and over again throughout the days, weeks, months, and years. While today's plan may make sense now, tomorrow you'll discover the unanticipated effects of today's actions and have to adjust accordingly.

Sustaining good leadership, then, requires first and foremost the capacity to see what is happening to you and your initiative as it is happening and to understand how today's turns in the road will affect tomorrow's plans.

But taking a balcony perspective is extremely tough to do when you're fiercely engaged down below, being pushed and pulled by the events and people around you—and doing some pushing and pulling of your own. Even if you are able to break away, the practice of stepping back and seeing the big picture is complicated by several factors. For example, when you get some distance, you still must accurately interpret what you see and hear. This is easier said than done. In an attempt to avoid difficult change, people will naturally, even unconsciously, defend their habits and ways of thinking. As you seek input from a broad range of people, you'll constantly need to be aware of these hidden agendas. You'll also need to observe your own actions; seeing yourself objectively as you look down from the balcony is perhaps the hardest task of all.

Fortunately, you can learn to be both an observer and a participant at the same time. When you are sitting in a meeting, practice by watching what is happening while it is happening—even as you are part of what is happening. Observe the relationships and see how people's attention to one another can vary: supporting, thwarting, or listening. Watch people's body language. When you make a point, resist the instinct to stay perched on the edge of your seat, ready to defend what you said. A technique as simple as pushing your chair a few inches away from the table after you speak may provide the literal as well as metaphorical distance you need to become an observer.

Court the uncommitted

It's tempting to go it alone when leading a change initiative. There's no one to dilute your ideas or share the glory, and it's often just plain exciting. It's also foolish. You need to recruit partners, people who can help protect you from attacks and who can point out potentially fatal flaws in your strategy or initiative. Moreover, you are far less vulnerable when you are out on the point with a bunch of folks rather than alone. You also need to keep the opposition close. Knowing

Adaptive Versus Technical Change: Whose Problem Is It?

THE IMPORTANCE—AND DIFFICULTY—of distinguishing between adaptive and technical change can be illustrated with an analogy. When your car has problems, you go to a mechanic. Most of the time, the mechanic can fix the car. But if your car troubles stem from the way a family member drives, the problems are likely to recur. Treating the problems as purely technical ones—taking the car to the mechanic time and again to get it back on the road—masks the real issues. Maybe you need to get your mother to stop drinking and driving, get your grandfather to give up his driver's license, or get your teenager to be more cautious. Whatever the underlying problems, the mechanic can't solve them. Instead, changes in the family need to occur, and that won't be easy. People will resist the moves, even denying that such problems exist. That's because even those not directly affected by an adaptive change typically experience discomfort when someone upsets a group's or an organization's equilibrium.

Such resistance to adaptive change certainly happens in business. Indeed, it's the classic error: Companies treat adaptive challenges as if they were technical problems. For example, executives attempt to improve the bottom line by cutting costs across the board. Not only does this avoid the need to make tough choices about which areas should be trimmed, it also masks the fact that the company's real challenge lies in redesigning its strategy.

Treating adaptive challenges as technical ones permits executives to do what they have excelled at throughout their careers: solve other people's problems. And it allows others in the organization to enjoy the primordial peace of mind that comes from knowing that their commanding officer has a plan to maintain order and stability. After all, the executive doesn't have to instigate—and the people don't have to undergo—uncomfortable change. Most people would agree that, despite the selective pain of a cost-cutting exercise, it is less traumatic than reinventing a company.

what your opponents are thinking can help you challenge them more effectively and thwart their attempts to upset your agenda—or allow you to borrow ideas that will improve your initiative. Have coffee once a week with the person most dedicated to seeing you fail.

But while relationships with allies and opponents are essential, the people who will determine your success are often those in the middle, the uncommitted who nonetheless are wary of your plans.

They have no substantive stake in your initiative, but they do have a stake in the comfort, stability, and security of the status quo. They've seen change agents come and go, and they know that your initiative will disrupt their lives and make their futures uncertain. You want to be sure that this general uneasiness doesn't evolve into a move to push you aside.

These people will need to see that your intentions are serious—for example, that you are willing to let go of those who can't make the changes your initiative requires. But people must also see that you understand the loss you are asking them to accept. You need to name the loss, be it a change in time-honored work routines or an overhaul of the company's core values, and explicitly acknowledge the resulting pain. You might do this through a series of simple statements, but it often requires something more tangible and public—recall Franklin Roosevelt's radio "fireside chats" during the Great Depression—to convince people that you truly understand.

Beyond a willingness to accept casualties and acknowledge people's losses, two very personal types of action can defuse potential resistance to you and your initiatives. The first is practicing what you preach. In 1972, Gene Patterson took over as editor of the *St. Petersburg Times*. His mandate was to take the respected regional newspaper to a higher level, enhancing its reputation for fine writing while becoming a fearless and hard-hitting news source. This would require major changes not only in the way the community viewed the newspaper but also in the way *Times* reporters thought about themselves and their roles. Because prominent organizations and individuals would no longer be spared warranted criticism, reporters would sometimes be angrily rebuked by the subjects of articles.

Several years after Patterson arrived, he attended a party at the home of the paper's foreign editor. Driving home, he pulled up to a red light and scraped the car next to him. The police officer called to the scene charged Patterson with driving under the influence. Patterson phoned Bob Haiman, a veteran *Times* newsman who had just been appointed executive editor, and insisted that a story on his arrest be run. As Haiman recalls, he tried to talk Patterson out of it, arguing that DUI arrests that didn't involve injuries were rarely reported, even when prominent figures were involved. Patterson was adamant, however, and insisted that the story appear on page one.

Patterson, still viewed as somewhat of an outsider at the paper, knew that if he wanted his employees to follow the highest journalistic standards, he would have to display those standards, even when it hurt. Few leaders are called upon to disgrace themselves on the front page of a newspaper. But adopting the behavior you expect from others—whether it be taking a pay cut in tough times or spending a day working next to employees on a reconfigured production line—can be crucial in getting buy-in from people who might try to undermine your initiative.

The second thing you can do to neutralize potential opposition is to acknowledge your own responsibility for whatever problems the organization currently faces. If you have been with the company for some time, whether in a position of senior authority or not, you've likely contributed in some way to the current mess. Even if you are new, you need to identify areas of your own behavior that could stifle the change you hope to make.

In our teaching, training, and consulting, we often ask people to write or talk about a leadership challenge they currently face. Over the years, we have read and heard literally thousands of such challenges. Typically, in the first version of the story, the author is nowhere to be found. The underlying message: "If only other people would shape up, I could make progress here." But by too readily pointing your finger at others, you risk making yourself a target. Remember, you are asking people to move to a place where they are frightened to go. If at the same time you're blaming them for having to go there, they will undoubtedly turn against you.

In the early 1990s, Leslie Wexner, founder and CEO of the Limited, realized the need for major changes at the company, including a significant reduction in the workforce. But his consultant told him that something else had to change: long-standing habits that were at the heart of his self-image. In particular, he had to stop treating the company as if it were his family. The indulgent father had to become the chief personnel officer, putting the right people in the right jobs and holding them accountable for their work. "I was an athlete trained to be a baseball player," Wexner recalled during a recent speech at Harvard's Kennedy School. "And one day, someone tapped me on the shoulder and said, 'Football.' And I said, 'No, I'm a baseball player. 'And he said, 'Football.' And I said, 'I don't know how to play football. I'm not 6'4", and I don't weigh 300 pounds.' But if no one values baseball anymore, the baseball player will be out of business. So I looked into the mirror and said, 'Schlemiel, nobody wants to watch baseball. Make the transformation to football.'" His personal makeover—shedding the role of forgiving father to those widely viewed as not holding their own—helped sway other employees to back a corporate makeover. And his willingness to change helped protect him from attack during the company's long—and generally successful—turnaround period.

Cook the conflict

Managing conflict is one of the greatest challenges a leader of organizational change faces. The conflict may involve resistance to change, or it may involve clashing viewpoints about how the change should be carried out. Often, it will be latent rather than palpable. That's because most organizations are allergic to conflict, seeing it primarily as a source of danger, which it certainly can be. But conflict is a necessary part of the change process and, if handled properly, can serve as the engine of progress.

Thus, a key imperative for a leader trying to achieve significant change is to manage people's passionate differences in a way that diminishes their destructive potential and constructively harnesses their energy. Two techniques can help you achieve this. First, create a secure place where the conflicts can freely bubble up. Second, control the temperature to ensure that the conflict doesn't boil over—and burn you in the process.

The vessel in which a conflict is simmered—in which clashing points of view mix, lose some of their sharpness, and ideally blend into consensus—will look and feel quite different in different contexts. It may be a protected physical space, perhaps an off-site location where an outside facilitator helps a group work through its differences. It may be a clear set of rules and processes that give minority voices confidence that they will be heard without having to disrupt the proceedings to gain attention. It may be the shared language and history of an organization that binds people together through trying times. Whatever its form, it is a place or a means to contain the roiling forces unleashed by the threat of major change.

But a vessel can withstand only so much strain before it blows. A huge challenge you face as a leader is keeping your employees' stress at a productive level. The success of the change effort—as well as your own authority and even survival—requires you to monitor your organization's tolerance for heat and then regulate the temperature accordingly.

You first need to raise the heat enough that people sit up, pay attention, and deal with the real threats and challenges facing them. After all, without some distress, there's no incentive to change. You can constructively raise the temperature by focusing people's attention on the hard issues, by forcing them to take responsibility for tackling and solving those issues, and by bringing conflicts occurring behind closed doors out into the open.

But you have to lower the temperature when necessary to reduce what can be counterproductive turmoil. You can turn down the heat by slowing the pace of change or by tackling some relatively straightforward technical aspect of the problem, thereby reducing people's anxiety levels and allowing them to get warmed up for bigger challenges. You can provide structure to the problem-solving process, creating work groups with specific assignments, setting time parameters, establishing rules for decision making, and outlining reporting relationships. You can use humor or find an excuse for a break or a party to temporarily ease tensions. You can speak to people's fears and, more critically, to their hopes for a more promising future. By showing people how the future might look, you come to embody hope rather than fear, and you reduce the likelihood of becoming a lightning rod for the conflict.

The aim of both these tactics is to keep the heat high enough to motivate people but low enough to prevent a disastrous explosion—what we call a "productive range of distress." Remember, though, that most employees will reflexively want you to turn down the heat; their complaints may in fact indicate that the environment is just right for hard work to get done.

We've already mentioned a classic example of managing the distress of fundamental change: Franklin Roosevelt during the first few years of his presidency. When he took office in 1933, the chaos, tension, and anxiety brought on by the Depression ran extremely high. Demagogues stoked class, ethnic, and racial conflict that threatened to tear the nation apart. Individuals feared an uncertain future. So Roosevelt first did what he could to reduce the sense of disorder to a tolerable level. He took decisive and authoritative action—he pushed an extraordinary number of bills through Congress during his fabled first 100 days—and thereby gave Americans a sense of direction and safety, reassuring them that they were in capable hands. In his fireside chats, he spoke to people's anxiety and anger and laid out a positive vision for the future that made the stress of the current crisis bearable and seem a worthwhile price to pay for progress.

But he knew the problems facing the nation couldn't be solved from the White House. He needed to mobilize citizens and get them to dream up, try out, fight over, and ultimately own the sometimes painful solutions that would transform the country and move it forward. To do that, he needed to maintain a certain level of fermentation and distress. So, for example, he orchestrated conflicts over public priorities and programs among the large cast of creative people he brought into the government. By giving the same assignment to two different administrators and refusing to clearly define their roles, he got them to generate new and competing ideas. Roosevelt displayed both the acuity to recognize when the tension in the nation had risen too high and the emotional strength to take the heat and permit considerable anxiety to persist.

Place the work where it belongs

Because major change requires people across an entire organization to adapt, you as a leader need to resist the reflex reaction of providing people with the answers. Instead, force yourself to transfer, as Roosevelt did, much of the work and problem solving to others. If you don't, real and sustainable change won't occur. In addition, it's risky on a personal level to continue to hold on to the work that should be done by others.

As a successful executive, you have gained credibility and authority by demonstrating your capacity to solve other people's problems. This ability can be a virtue, until you find yourself faced with a situation in which you cannot deliver solutions. When this happens, all of your habits, pride, and sense of competence get thrown out of kilter because you must mobilize the work of others rather than find the way yourself. By trying to solve an adaptive challenge for people, at best you will reconfigure it as a technical problem and create some short-term relief. But the issue will not have gone away.

In the 1994 National Basketball Association Eastern Conference semifinals, the Chicago Bulls lost to the New York Knicks in the first two games of the best-of-seven series. Chicago was out to prove that it was more than just a one-man team, that it could win without Michael Jordan, who had retired at the end of the previous season.

In the third game, the score was tied at 102 with less than two seconds left. Chicago had the ball and a time-out to plan a final shot. Coach Phil Jackson called for Scottie Pippen, the Bulls' star since Jordan had retired, to make the inbound pass to Toni Kukoc for the final shot. As play was about to resume, Jackson noticed Pippen sitting at the far end of the bench. Jackson asked him whether he was in or out. "I'm out," said Pippen, miffed that he was not tapped to take the final shot. With only four players on the floor, Jackson quickly called another time-out and substituted an excellent passer, the reserve Pete Myers, for Pippen. Myers tossed a perfect pass to Kukoc, who spun around and sank a miraculous shot to win the game.

The Bulls made their way back to the locker room, their euphoria deflated by Pippen's extraordinary act of insubordination. Jackson recalls that as he entered a silent room, he was uncertain about what to do. Should he punish Pippen? Make him apologize? Pretend the whole thing never happened? All eyes were on him. The coach looked around, meeting the gaze of each player, and said, "What happened has hurt us. Now you have to work this out."

Jackson knew that if he took action to resolve the immediate crisis, he would have made Pippen's behavior a matter between coach and player. But he understood that a deeper issue was at the heart of the incident: Who were the Chicago Bulls without Michael Jordan? It wasn't about who was going to succeed Jordan, because no one was; it was about whether the players could jell as a team where no one person dominated and every player was willing to do whatever it took to help. The issue rested with the players, not him, and only they could resolve it. It did not matter what they decided at that moment; what mattered was that they, not Jackson, did the deciding. What followed was a discussion led by an emotional Bill Cartwright, a team veteran. According to Jackson, the conversation brought the team closer together. The Bulls took the series to a seventh game before succumbing to the Knicks.

Jackson gave the work of addressing both the Pippen and the Jordan issues back to the team for another reason: If he had taken ownership of the problem, he would have become the issue, at least for the moment. In his case, his position as coach probably wouldn't have been threatened. But in other situations, taking responsibility for resolving a conflict within the organization poses risks. You are likely to find yourself resented by the faction that you decide against and held responsible by nearly everyone for the turmoil your decision generates. In the eyes of many, the only way to neutralize the threat is to get rid of you.

Despite that risk, most executives can't resist the temptation to solve fundamental organizational problems by themselves. People expect you to get right in there and fix things, to take a stand and resolve the problem. After all, that is what top managers are paid to do. When you fulfill those expectations, people will call you admirable and courageous—even a "leader"—and that is flattering. But challenging your employees' expectations requires greater courage and leadership.

The Dangers Within

We have described a handful of leadership tactics you can use to interact with the people around you, particularly those who might undermine your initiatives. Those tactics can help advance your initiatives and, just as important, ensure that you remain in a position where you can bring them to fruition. But from our own observations and painful personal experiences, we know that one of the surest ways for an organization to bring you down is simply to let you precipitate your own demise.

In the heat of leadership, with the adrenaline pumping, it is easy to convince yourself that you are not subject to the normal human frailties that can defeat ordinary mortals. You begin to act as if you are indestructible. But the intellectual, physical, and emotional challenges of leadership are fierce. So, in addition to getting on the balcony, you need to regularly step into the inner chamber of your being and assess the tolls those challenges are taking. If you don't, your seemingly indestructible self can self-destruct. This, by the way, is an ideal outcome for your foes—and even friends who oppose your initiative—because no one has to feel responsible for your downfall.

Manage your hungers

We all have hungers, expressions of our normal human needs. But sometimes those hungers disrupt our capacity to act wisely or purposefully. Whether inherited or products of our upbringing, some of these hungers may be so strong that they render us constantly vulnerable. More typically, a stressful situation or setting can exaggerate a normal level of need, amplifying our desires and overwhelming our usual self-discipline. Two of the most common and dangerous hungers are the desire for control and the desire for importance.

Everyone wants to have some measure of control over his or her life. Yet some people's need for control is disproportionately high. They might have grown up in a household that was either tightly structured or unusually chaotic; in either case, the situation drove them to become masters at taming chaos not only in their own lives but also in their organizations.

That need for control can be a source of vulnerability. Initially, of course, the ability to turn disorder into order may be seen as an attribute. In an organization facing turmoil, you may seem like a godsend if you are able (and desperately want) to step in and take charge. By lowering the distress to a tolerable level, you keep the kettle from boiling over.

But in your desire for order, you can mistake the means for the end. Rather than ensuring that the distress level in an organization remains high enough to mobilize progress on the issues, you focus on maintaining order as an end in itself. Forcing people to make the difficult trade-offs required by fundamental change threatens a return to the disorder you loathe. Your ability to bring the situation under control also suits the people in the organization, who naturally prefer calm to chaos. Unfortunately, this desire for control makes you vulnerable to, and an agent of, the organization's wish to avoid working through contentious issues. While this may ensure your survival in the short term, ultimately you may find yourself accused, justifiably, of failing to deal with the tough challenges when there was still time to do so.

Most people also have some need to feel important and affirmed by others. The danger here is that you will let this affirmation give you an inflated view of yourself and your cause. A grandiose sense of self-importance often leads to self-deception. In particular, you tend to forget the creative role that doubt—which reveals parts of reality that you wouldn't otherwise see—plays in getting your organization to improve. The absence of doubt leads you to see only that which confirms your own competence, which will virtually guarantee disastrous missteps.

Another harmful side effect of an inflated sense of self-importance is that you will encourage people in the organization to become dependent on you. The higher the level of distress, the greater their hopes and expectations that you will provide deliverance. This relieves them of any responsibility for moving the organization forward. But their dependence can be detrimental not only to the group but to you personally. Dependence can quickly turn to contempt as your constituents discover your human shortcomings.

Two well-known stories from the computer industry illustrate the perils of dependency—and how to avoid them. Ken Olsen, the founder of Digital Equipment Corporation, built the company into a 120,000-person operation that, at its peak, was the chief rival of IBM.

A generous man, he treated his employees extraordinarily well and experimented with personnel policies designed to increase the creativity, teamwork, and satisfaction of his workforce. This, in tandem with the company's success over the years, led the company's top management to turn to him as the sole decision maker on all key issues. His decision to shun the personal computer market because of his belief that few people would ever want to own a PC, which seemed reasonable at the time, is generally viewed as the beginning of the end for the company. But that isn't the point; everyone in business makes bad decisions. The point is, Olsen had fostered such an atmosphere of dependence that his decisions were rarely challenged by colleagues—at least not until it was too late.

Contrast that decision with Bill Gates's decision some years later to keep Microsoft out of the Internet business. It didn't take long for him to reverse his stand and launch a corporate overhaul that had Microsoft's delivery of Internet services as its centerpiece. After watching the rapidly changing computer industry and listening carefully to colleagues, Gates changed his mind with no permanent damage to his sense of pride and an enhanced reputation due to his nimble change of course.

Anchor yourself

To survive the turbulent seas of a change initiative, you need to find ways to steady and stabilize yourself. First, you must establish a safe harbor where each day you can reflect on the previous day's journey, repair the psychological damage you have incurred, renew your stores of emotional resources, and recalibrate your moral compass. Your haven might be a physical place, such as the kitchen table of a friend's house, or a regular routine, such as a daily walk through the neighborhood. Whatever the sanctuary, you need to use and protect it. Unfortunately, seeking such respite is often seen as a luxury, making it one of the first things to go when life gets stressful and you become pressed for time.

Second, you need a confidant, someone you can talk to about what's in your heart and on your mind without fear of being judged or betrayed. Once the undigested mess is on the table, you can begin to separate, with your confidant's honest input, what is worthwhile from what is simply venting. The confidant, typically not a coworker, can also pump you up when you're down and pull you back to earth when you start taking praise too seriously. But don't confuse confidants with allies: Instead of supporting your current initiative, a confidant simply supports you. A common mistake is to seek a confidant among trusted allies, whose personal loyalty may evaporate when a new issue more important to them than you begins to emerge and take center stage.

Perhaps most important, you need to distinguish between your personal self, which can serve as an anchor in stormy weather, and your professional role, which never will. It is easy to mix up the two. And other people only increase the confusion: Colleagues, subordinates, and even bosses often act as if the role you play is the real you. But that is not the case, no matter how much of yourself—your passions, your values, your talents—you genuinely and laudably pour into your professional role. Ask anyone who has experienced the rude awakening that comes when they leave a position of authority and suddenly find that their phone calls aren't returned as quickly as they used to be.

That harsh lesson holds another important truth that is easily forgotten: When people attack someone in a position of authority, more often than not they are attacking the role, not the person. Even when attacks on you are highly personal, you need to read them primarily as reactions to how you, in your role, are affecting people's lives. Understanding the criticism for what it is prevents it from undermining your stability and sense of self-worth. And that's important because when you feel the sting of an attack, you are likely to become defensive and lash out at your critics, which can precipitate your downfall.

We hasten to add that criticism may contain legitimate points about how you are performing your role. For example, you may have been tactless in raising an issue with your organization, or you may have turned the heat up too quickly on a change initiative. But, at its heart, the criticism is usually about the issue, not you. Through the guise of attacking you personally, people often are simply trying to neutralize the threat they perceive in your point of view. Does anyone ever attack you when you hand out big checks or deliver good news? People attack your personality, style, or judgment when they don't like the message.

When you take "personal" attacks personally, you unwittingly conspire in one of the common ways you can be taken out of action—you make yourself the issue. Contrast the manner in which presidential candidates Gary Hart and Bill Clinton handled charges of philandering. Hart angrily counterattacked, criticizing the scruples of the reporters who had shadowed him. This defensive personal response kept the focus on his behavior. Clinton, on national television, essentially admitted he had strayed, acknowledging his piece of the mess. His strategic handling of the situation allowed him to return the campaign's focus to policy issues. Though both attacks were extremely personal, only Clinton understood that they were basically attacks on positions he represented and the role he was seeking to play.

Do not underestimate the difficulty of distinguishing self from role and responding coolly to what feels like a personal attack—particularly when the criticism comes, as it will, from people you care about. But disciplining yourself to do so can provide you with an anchor that will keep you from running aground and give you the stability to remain calm, focused, and persistent in engaging people with the tough issues.

Why Lead?

We will have failed if this "survival manual" for avoiding the perils of leadership causes you to become cynical or callous in your leadership effort or to shun the challenges of leadership altogether. We haven't touched on the thrill of inspiring people to come up with creative solutions that can transform an organization for the better. We hope we have shown that the essence of leadership lies in the capacity to deliver disturbing news and raise difficult questions in a way that moves people to take up the message rather than kill the messenger. But we haven't talked about the reasons that someone might want to take these risks.

Of course, many people who strive for high-authority positions are attracted to power. But in the end, that isn't enough to make the high stakes of the game worthwhile. We would argue that, when they look deep within themselves, people grapple with the challenges of leadership in order to make a positive difference in the lives of others.

When corporate presidents and vice presidents reach their late fifties, they often look back on careers devoted to winning in the marketplace. They may have succeeded remarkably, yet some people have difficulty making sense of their lives in light of what they have given up. For too many, their accomplishments seem empty. They question whether they should have been more aggressive in questioning corporate purposes or creating more ambitious visions for their companies.

Our underlying assumption in this article is that you can lead *and* stay alive—not just register a pulse, but really be alive. But the classic protective devices of a person in authority tend to insulate them from those qualities that foster an acute experience of living. Cynicism, often dressed up as realism, undermines creativity and daring. Arrogance, often posing as authoritative knowledge, snuffs out curiosity and the eagerness to question. Callousness, sometimes portrayed as the thick skin of experience, shuts out compassion for others.

The hard truth is that it is not possible to know the rewards and joys of leadership without experiencing the pain as well. But staying in the game and bearing that pain is worth it, not only for the positive changes you can make in the lives of others but also for the meaning it gives your own.

Originally published in June 2002. Reprint R0206C

The Real Reason People Won't Change

by Robert Kegan and Lisa Laskow Lahey

EVERY MANAGER IS FAMILIAR with the employee who just won't change. Sometimes it's easy to see why—the employee fears a shift in power, the need to learn new skills, the stress of having to join a new team. In other cases, such resistance is far more puzzling. An employee has the skills and smarts to make a change with ease, has shown a deep commitment to the company, genuinely supports the change—and yet, inexplicably, does nothing.

What's going on? As organizational psychologists, we have seen this dynamic literally hundreds of times, and our research and analysis have recently led us to a surprising yet deceptively simple conclusion. Resistance to change does not reflect opposition, nor is it merely a result of inertia. Instead, even as they hold a sincere commitment to change, many people are unwittingly applying productive energy toward a hidden *competing commitment*. The resulting dynamic equilibrium stalls the effort in what looks like resistance but is in fact a kind of personal immunity to change.

When you, as a manager, uncover an employee's competing commitment, behavior that has seemed irrational and ineffective suddenly becomes stunningly sensible and masterful—but unfortunately, on behalf of a goal that conflicts with what you and even the employee are trying to achieve. You find out that the project leader who's dragging his feet has an unrecognized competing commitment to avoid the even tougher assignment—one he fears he can't handle—that might come his way next if he delivers too successfully on the task at hand. Or you find that the person who won't collaborate despite a passionate and sincere commitment to teamwork is equally dedicated to avoiding the conflict that naturally attends any ambitious team activity.

In these pages, we'll look at competing commitments in detail and take you through a process to help your employees overcome their immunity to change. The process may sound straightforward, but it is by no means quick or easy. On the contrary, it challenges the very psychological foundations upon which people function. It asks people to call into question beliefs they've long held close, perhaps since childhood. And it requires people to admit to painful, even embarrassing, feelings that they would not ordinarily disclose to others or even to themselves. Indeed, some people will opt not to disrupt their immunity to change, choosing instead to continue their fruitless struggle against their competing commitments.

As a manager, you must guide people through this exercise with understanding and sensitivity. If your employees are to engage in honest introspection and candid disclosure, they must understand that their revelations won't be used against them. The goal of this exploration is solely to help them become more effective, not to find flaws in their work or character. As you support your employees in unearthing and challenging their innermost assumptions, you may at times feel you're playing the role of a psychologist. But in a sense, managers *are* psychologists. After all, helping people overcome their limitations to become more successful at work is at the very heart of effective management.

We'll describe this delicate process in detail, but first let's look at some examples of competing commitments in action.

Shoveling Sand Against the Tide

Competing commitments cause valued employees to behave in ways that seem inexplicable and irremediable, and this is enormously

Idea in Brief

Tearing out your managerial hair over employees who just won't change—especially the ones who are clearly smart, skilled, and deeply committed to your company and your plans for improvement?

Before you throw up your hands in frustration, listen to recent psychological research: These otherwise valued employees aren't *purposefully* subversive or resistant. Instead, they may be unwittingly caught in a **competing commitment** —a subconscious, hidden goal that conflicts with their *stated* commitments. For example: A project leader dragging his feet has an unrecognized competing commitment to avoid tougher assignments that may come his way if he delivers too successfully on the current project.

Competing commitments make people personally immune to change. Worse, they can undermine your best employees'—and your company's—success.

If the thought of tackling these hidden commitments strikes you as a psychological quagmire, you're not alone. However, you can help employees uncover and move beyond their competing commitments—*without* having to "put them on the couch." But take care: You'll be challenging employees' deepest psychological foundations and questioning their longest-held beliefs.

Why bother, you ask? Consider the rewards: You help talented employees become much more effective and make far more significant contributions to your company. And, you discover what's *really* going on when people who seem genuinely committed to change dig in their heels.

frustrating to managers. Take the case of John, a talented manager at a software company. (Like all examples in this article, John's experiences are real, although we have altered identifying features. In some cases, we've constructed composite examples.) John was a big believer in open communication and valued close working relationships, yet his caustic sense of humor consistently kept colleagues at a distance. And though he wanted to move up in the organization, his personal style was holding him back. Repeatedly, John was counseled on his behavior, and he readily agreed that he needed to change the way he interacted with others in the organization. But time after

Idea in Practice

Use these steps to break through an employee's immunity to change:

Diagnose the Competing Commitment

Take two to three hours to explore these questions with the employee:

"What would you like to see changed at work, so you could be more effective, or so work would be more satisfying?" Responses are usually complaints—e.g., Tom, a manager, grumbled, "My subordinates keep me out of the loop."

"What commitment does your complaint imply?" Complaints indicate what people care about most—e.g., Tom revealed, "I believe in open, candid communication."

"What are *you* doing, or not doing, to keep your commitment from being more fully realized?" Tom admitted, "When people bring bad news, I tend to shoot the messenger."

"Imagine doing the *opposite* of the undermining behavior. Do you feel any discomfort, worry, or vague fear?" Tom imagined listening calmly and openly to bad news and concluded, "I'm afraid I'll hear about a problem I can't fix."

"By engaging in this undermining behavior, what worrisome outcome are you committed to preventing?" The answer *is* the competing commitment—what causes them to dig in their heels against change. Tom conceded, *"I'm committed to not learning about problems I can't fix."*

Identify the Big Assumption

This is the worldview that colors everything we see and that generates our competing commitment.

People often form big assumptions early in life and then seldom, if

time, he reverted to his old patterns. Why, his boss wondered, did John continue to undermine his own advancement?

As it happened, John was a person of color working as part of an otherwise all-white executive team. When he went through an exercise designed to help him unearth his competing commitments, he made a surprising discovery about himself. Underneath it all, John believed that if he became too well integrated with the team, it would threaten his sense of loyalty to his own racial group. Moving too close to the mainstream made him feel very uncomfortable, as if he were

ever, examine them. They're woven into the very fabric of our lives. But only by bringing them into the light can people finally challenge their deepest beliefs and recognize why they're engaging in seemingly contradictory behavior.

To identify the big assumption, guide an employee through this exercise:

Create a sentence stem that inverts the competing commitment, then "fill in the blank." Tom turned his competing commitment to not hearing about problems he couldn't fix into this big assumption: "I assume that if I *did* hear about problems I can't fix, *people would discover I'm not qualified to do the job*."

Test—and Consider Replacing—the Big Assumption

By analyzing the circumstances leading up to and reinforcing their big assumptions, employees empower themselves to test those assumptions. They can now carefully and safely experiment with behaving differently than they usually do.

After running several such tests, employees may feel ready to reevaluate the big assumption itself—and possibly even replace it with a new worldview that more accurately reflects their abilities.

At the very least, they'll eventually find more effective ways to support their competing commitment *without* sabotaging other commitments. *They* achieve ever-greater accomplishments—and your *organization* benefits by finally gaining greater access to their talents.

becoming "one of them" and betraying his family and friends. So when people gathered around his ideas and suggestions, he'd tear down their support with sarcasm, inevitably (and effectively) returning himself to the margins, where he was more at ease. In short, while John was genuinely committed to working well with his colleagues, he had an equally powerful competing commitment to keeping his distance.

Consider, too, a manager we'll call Helen, a rising star at a large manufacturing company. Helen had been assigned responsibility for speeding up production of the company's most popular product, yet

Getting Groups to Change

ALTHOUGH COMPETING COMMITMENTS and big assumptions tend to be deeply personal, groups are just as susceptible as individuals to the dynamics of immunity to change. Face-to-face teams, departments, and even companies as a whole can fall prey to inner contradictions that "protect" them from significant changes they may genuinely strive for. The leadership team of a video production company, for instance, enjoyed a highly collaborative, largely flat organizational structure. A year before we met the group, team members had undertaken a planning process that led them to a commitment of which they were unanimously in favor: In order to ensure that the company would grow in the way the team wished, each of the principals would take responsibility for aggressively overseeing a distinct market segment.

The members of the leadership team told us they came out of this process with a great deal of momentum. They knew which markets to target, they had formed some concrete plans for moving forward, and they had clearly assigned accountability for each market. Yet a year later, the group had to admit it had accomplished very little, despite the enthusiasm. There were lots of rational explanations: "We were unrealistic; we thought we could do new things and still have time to keep meeting our present obligations." "We didn't pursue new clients aggressively enough." "We tried new things but gave up too quickly if they didn't immediately pay off."

Efforts to overcome these barriers—to pursue clients more aggressively, for instance—didn't work because they didn't get to the cause of the unproductive behavior. But by seeing the team's explanations as a potential window

she was spinning her wheels. When her boss, Andrew, realized that an important deadline was only two months away and she hadn't filed a single progress report, he called her into a meeting to discuss the project. Helen agreed that she was far behind schedule, acknowledging that she had been stalling in pulling together the team. But at the same time she showed a genuine commitment to making the project a success. The two developed a detailed plan for changing direction, and Andrew assumed the problem was resolved. But three weeks after the meeting, Helen still hadn't launched the team.

Why was Helen unable to change her behavior? After intense self-examination in a workshop with several of her colleagues, she came to an unexpected conclusion: Although she truly wanted the project to succeed, she had an accompanying, unacknowledged commitment

into the bigger competing commitment, we were able to help the group better understand its predicament. We asked, "Can you identify even the vaguest fear or worry about what might happen if you *did* more aggressively pursue the new markets? Or if you reduced some of your present activity on behalf of building the new business?" Before long, a different discourse began to emerge, and the other half of a striking groupwide contradiction came into view: The principals were worried that pursuing the plan would drive them apart functionally and emotionally.

"We now realize we are also committed to preserving the noncompetitive, intellectually rewarding, and cocreative spirit of our corporate enterprise," they concluded. On behalf of this commitment, the team members had to commend themselves on how "noncompetitively" and "cocreatively" they were finding ways to undermine the strategic plans they still believed were the best route to the company's future success. The team's big assumptions? "We assumed that pursuing the target-market strategy, with each of us taking aggressive responsibility for a given segment, would create the 'silos' we have long happily avoided and would leave us more isolated from one another. We also assumed the strategy would make us more competitively disposed toward one another." Whether or not the assumptions were true, they would have continued to block the group's efforts until they were brought to light. In fact, as the group came to discover, there were a variety of moves that would allow the leadership team to preserve a genuinely collaborative collegiality while pursuing the new corporate strategy.

to maintaining a subordinate position in relation to Andrew. At a deep level, Helen was concerned that if she succeeded in her new role—one she was excited about and eager to undertake—she would become more a peer than a subordinate. She was uncertain whether Andrew was prepared for the turn their relationship would take. Worse, a promotion would mean that she, not Andrew, would be ultimately accountable for the results of her work—and Helen feared she wouldn't be up to the task.

These stories shed some light on the nature of immunity to change. The inconsistencies between John's and Helen's stated goals and their actions reflect neither hypocrisy nor unspoken reluctance to change but the paralyzing effect of competing commitments. Any manager who seeks to help John communicate more effectively or

Helen move her project forward, without understanding that each is also struggling unconsciously toward an opposing agenda, is shoveling sand against the tide.

Diagnosing Immunity to Change

Competing commitments aren't distressing only to the boss; they're frustrating to employees as well. People with the most

A diagnostic test for immunity to change

The most important steps in diagnosing immunity to change are uncovering employees' competing commitments and unearthing their big assumptions. To do so, we ask a series of questions and record key responses in a simple grid. Below we've listed the responses for six people who went through this exercise, including the examples described in the text. The grid paints a picture of the change-immunity system, making sense of a previously puzzling dynamic.

	Stated commitment I am committed to . . .	What am I doing, or not doing, that is keeping my stated commitment from being fully realized?	Competing commitments	Big assumptions
John	**. . .high quality communication with my colleagues.**	Sometimes I use sarcastic humor to get my point across.	I am committed to maintaining a distance from my white colleagues.	I assume I will lose my authentic connection to my racial group if I get too integrated into the mainstream.
Helen	**. . .the new initiative.**	I don't push for top performance from my team members or myself; I accept mediocre products and thinking too often; I don't prioritize.	I am committed to not upsetting my relationship with my boss by leaving the mentee role.	I assume my boss will stop supporting me if I move toward becoming his peer; I assume that I don't have what it takes to successfully carry out a cutting-edge project.

Tom	**. . .hearing from my subordinates and maximizing the flow of information into my office.**	I don't ask questions or ask to be kept in the loop on sensitive or delicate matters; I shoot the messenger when I hear bad news.	I am committed to not learning about things I can't do anything about.	I assume as a leader I should be able to address all problems; I assume I will be seen as incompetent if I can't solve all problems that come up.
Mary	**. . .distributed leadership by enabling people to make decisions.**	I don't delegate enough; I don't pass on the necessary information to the people I distribute leadership to.	I am committed to having things go my way, to being in control, and to ensuring that the work is done to my high standards.	I assume that other people will waste my time and theirs if I don't step in; I assume others aren't as smart as I am.
Bill	**. . .being a team player.**	I don't collaborate enough; I make unilateral decisions too often; I don't really take people's input into account.	I am committed to being the one who gets the credit and to avoiding the frustration or conflict that comes with collaboration.	I assume that no one will appreciate me if I am not seen as the source of success; I assume nothing good will come of my being frustrated or in conflict.
Jane	**. . .turning around my department.**	Too often I let things slide; I'm not proactive enough in getting people to follow through with their tasks.	I am committed to not setting full sail until I have a clear map of how we get our department from here to there.	I assume that if I take my group out into deep waters and discover I am unable to get us to the other side, I will be seen as an incompetent leader who is undeserving of trust or responsibility.

sincere intentions often unwittingly create for themselves Sisyphean tasks. And they are almost always tremendously relieved when they discover just why they feel as if they are rolling a boulder up a hill only to have it roll back down again. Even though uncovering a competing commitment can open up a host of new concerns, the discovery offers hope for finally accomplishing the primary, stated commitment.

Based on the past 15 years of working with hundreds of managers in a variety of companies, we've developed a three-stage process to help organizations figure out what's getting in the way of change. First, managers guide employees through a set of questions designed to uncover competing commitments. Next, employees examine these commitments to determine the underlying assumptions at their core. And finally, employees start the process of changing their behavior.

We'll walk through the process fairly quickly below, but it's important to note that each step will take time. Just uncovering the competing commitment will require at least two or three hours, because people need to reflect on each question and the implications of their answers. The process of challenging competing commitments and making real progress toward overcoming immunity to change unfolds over a longer period—weeks or even months. But just getting the commitments on the table can have a noticeable effect on the decisions people make and the actions they take.

Uncovering Competing Commitments

Overcoming immunity to change starts with uncovering competing commitments. In our work, we've found that even though people keep their competing commitments well hidden, you can draw them out by asking a series of questions—as long as the employees believe that personal and potentially embarrassing disclosures won't be used inappropriately. It can be very powerful to guide people through this diagnostic exercise in a group—typically with several volunteers making their own discoveries public—so people can see that others, even the company's star performers, have competing commitments and inner contradictions of their own.

The first question we ask is, *What would you like to see changed at work, so that you could be more effective or so that work would be more satisfying?* Responses to this question are nearly always couched in a complaint—a form of communication that most managers bemoan because of its negative, unproductive tone. But complaints can be immensely useful. People complain only about the things they care about, and they complain the loudest about the things they care about most. With little effort, people can turn their familiar, uninspiring gripes into something that's more likely to energize and motivate them—a commitment, genuinely their own.

To get there, you need to ask a second question: *What commitments does your complaint imply?* A project leader we worked with, we'll call him Tom, had grumbled, "My subordinates keep me out of the loop on important developments in my project." This complaint yielded the statement, "I believe in open and candid communication." A line manager we'll call Mary lamented people's unwillingness to speak up at meetings; her complaint implied a commitment to shared decision making.

While undoubtedly sincere in voicing such commitments, people can nearly always identify some way in which they are in part responsible for preventing them from being fulfilled. Thus, the third question is: *What are* you *doing, or not doing, that is keeping your commitment from being more fully realized?* Invariably, in our experience, people can identify these undermining behaviors in just a couple of seconds. For example, Tom admitted: "When people bring me bad news, I tend to shoot the messenger." And Mary acknowledged that she didn't delegate much and that she sometimes didn't release all the information people needed in order to make good decisions.

In both cases, there may well have been other circumstances contributing to the shortfalls, but clearly both Tom and Mary were engaging in behavior that was affecting the people around them. Most people recognize this about themselves right away and are quick to say, "I need to stop doing that." Indeed, Tom had repeatedly vowed to listen more openly to potential problems that would slow his projects. However, the purpose of this exercise is not to make these behaviors disappear—at least not now. The purpose is to understand why people behave in ways that undermine their own success.

The next step, then, is to invite people to consider the consequences of forgoing the behavior. We do this by asking a fourth question: *If you imagine doing the opposite of the undermining behavior, do you detect in yourself any discomfort, worry, or vague fear?* Tom imagined himself listening calmly and openly to some bad news about a project and concluded, "I'm afraid I'll hear about a problem that I can't fix, something that I can't do anything about." And Mary? She considered allowing people more latitude and realized that, quite frankly, she feared people wouldn't make good decisions and she would be forced to carry out a strategy she thought would lead to an inferior result.

The final step is to transform that passive fear into a statement that reflects an active commitment to preventing certain outcomes. We ask, *By engaging in this undermining behavior, what worrisome outcome are you committed to preventing?* The resulting answer is the competing commitment, which lies at the very heart of a person's immunity to change. Tom admitted, "I am committed to not learning about problems I can't fix." By intimidating his staff, he prevented them from delivering bad news, protecting himself from the fear that he was not in control of the project. Mary, too, was protecting herself—in her case, against the consequences of bad decisions. "I am committed to making sure my group does not make decisions that I don't like."

Such revelations can feel embarrassing. While primary commitments nearly always reflect noble goals that people would be happy to shout from the rooftops, competing commitments are very personal, reflecting vulnerabilities that people fear will undermine how they are regarded both by others and themselves. Little wonder people keep them hidden and hasten to cover them up again once they're on the table.

But competing commitments should not be seen as weaknesses. They represent some version of self-protection, a perfectly natural and reasonable human impulse. The question is, if competing commitments are a form of self-protection, what are people protecting themselves from? The answers usually lie in what we call their *big assumptions*—deeply rooted beliefs about themselves and the world around them. These assumptions put an order to the world and at the same time suggest ways in which the world can go out of order. Competing commitments arise from these assumptions, driving behaviors unwittingly designed to keep the picture intact.

Examining the Big Assumption

People rarely realize they hold big assumptions because, quite simply, they accept them as reality. Often formed long ago and seldom, if ever, critically examined, big assumptions are woven into the very fabric of people's existence. (For more on the grip that big assumptions hold on people, see the sidebar "Big Assumptions: How Our Perceptions Shape Our Reality.") But with a little help, most people can call them up fairly easily, especially once they've identified their competing commitments. To do this, we first ask people to create the beginning of a sentence by inverting the competing commitment, and then we ask them to fill in the blank. For Tom ("I am committed to not hearing about problems I can't fix"), the big assumption turned out to be, "I assume that if I *did* hear about problems I can't fix, people would discover I'm not qualified to do my job." Mary's big assumption was that her teammates weren't as smart or experienced as she and that she'd be wasting her time and others' if she didn't maintain control. Returning to our earlier story, John's big assumption might be, "I assume that if I develop unambivalent relationships with my white coworkers, I will sacrifice my racial identity and alienate my own community."

This is a difficult process, and it doesn't happen all at once, because admitting to big assumptions makes people uncomfortable. The process can put names to very personal feelings people are reluctant to disclose, such as deep-seated fears or insecurities, highly discouraging or simplistic views of human nature, or perceptions of their own superior abilities or intellect. Unquestioning acceptance of a big assumption anchors and sustains an immune system: A competing commitment makes all the sense in the world, and the person continues to engage in behaviors that support it, albeit unconsciously, to the detriment of his or her "official," stated commitment. Only by bringing big assumptions to light can people

Big Assumptions: How Our Perceptions Shape Our Reality

BIG ASSUMPTIONS REFLECT the very human manner in which we invent or shape a picture of the world and then take our inventions for reality. This is easiest to see in children. The delight we take in their charming distortions is a kind of celebration that they are actively making sense of the world, even if a bit eccentrically. As one story goes, two youngsters had been learning about Hindu culture and were taken with a representation of the universe in which the world sits atop a giant elephant, and the elephant sits atop an even more giant turtle. "I wonder what the turtle sits on," says one of the children. "I think from then on," says the other, "it's turtles all the way down."

But deep within our amusement may lurk a note of condescension, an implication that this is what distinguishes children from grown-ups. Their meaning-making is subject to youthful distortions, we assume. Ours represents an accurate map of reality.

But does it? Are we really finished discovering, once we have reached adulthood, that our maps don't match the territory? The answer is clearly no. In our 20 years of longitudinal and cross-sectional research, we've discovered that adults must grow into and out of several qualitatively different views of

finally challenge their assumptions and recognize why they are engaging in seemingly contradictory behavior.

Questioning the Big Assumption

Once people have identified their competing commitments and the big assumptions that sustain them, most are prepared to take some immediate action to overcome their immunity. But the first part of the process involves observation, not action, which can be frustrating for high achievers accustomed to leaping into motion to solve problems. Let's take a look at the steps in more detail.

Step 1: Notice and record current behavior

Employees must first take notice of what does and doesn't happen as a consequence of holding big assumptions to be true. We specifically ask people *not* to try to make any changes in their thinking or the world if they are to master the challenges of their life experiences (see Robert Kegan, *In Over Our Heads,* Harvard University Press, 1994).

A woman we met from Australia told us about her experience living in the United States for a year. "Not only do you drive on the wrong side of the street over here," she said, "your steering wheels are on the wrong side, too. I would routinely pile into the right side of the car to drive off, only to discover I needed to get out and walk over to the other side.

"One day," she continued, "I was thinking about six different things, and I got into the right side of the car, took out my keys, and was prepared to drive off. I looked up and thought to myself, 'My God, here in the violent and lawless United States, they are even stealing *steering wheels!* '"

Of course, the countervailing evidence was just an arm's length to her left, but—and this is the main point—*why should she look?* Our big assumptions create a disarming and deluding sense of certainty. If we know where a steering wheel belongs, we are unlikely to look for it some place else. If we know what our company, department, boss, or subordinate can and can't do, why should we look for countervailing data—even if it is just an arm's length away?

behavior at this time but just to become more aware of their actions in relation to their big assumptions. This gives people the opportunity to develop a better appreciation for how and in what contexts big assumptions influence their lives. John, for example, who had assumed that working well with his white colleagues would estrange him from his ethnic group, saw that he had missed an opportunity to get involved in an exciting, high-profile initiative because he had mocked the idea when it first came up in a meeting.

Step 2: Look for contrary evidence

Next, employees must look actively for experiences that might cast doubt on the validity of their big assumptions. Because big assumptions are held as fact, they actually inform what people see, leading them to systematically (but unconsciously) attend to certain data and avoid or ignore other data. By asking people to search specifically for experiences that would cause them to question their assumptions, we help them see that they have filtering out certain types of information—information that could weaken the grip of the big assumptions.

When John looked around him, he considered for the first time that an African-American manager in another department had strong working relationships with her mostly white colleagues, yet seemed not to have compromised her personal identity. He also had to admit that when he had been thrown onto an urgent task force the year before, he had worked many hours alongside his white colleagues and found the experience satisfying; he had felt of his usual ambivalence.

Step 3: Explore the history

In this step, we people to become the "biographers" of their assumptions: How and when did the assumptions first take hold? How long have they been around? What have been some of their critical turning points?

Typically, this step leads people to earlier life experiences, almost always to times before their current jobs and relationships with current coworkers. This reflection usually makes people dissatisfied with the foundations of their big assumptions, especially when they see that these have accompanied them to their current positions and have been coloring their experiences for many years. Recently, a CEO expressed astonishment as she realized she'd been applying the same self-protective stance in her work that she'd developed during a difficult divorce years before. Just as commonly, as was the case for John, people trace their big assumptions to early experiences with parents, siblings, or friends. Understanding the circumstances that influenced the formation of the assumptions can free people to consider whether these beliefs apply to their present selves.

Step 4: Test the assumption

This step entails creating and running a modest test of the big assumption. This is the first time we ask people to consider making changes in their behavior. Each employee should come up with a scenario and run it by a partner who serves as a sounding board.

(Left to their own devices, people tend to create tests that are either too risky or so tentative that they don't actually challenge the assumption and in fact reaf-firm its validity.) After conferring with a partner, John, for instance, volunteered to join a short-term committee looking at his department's process for evaluating new product ideas. Because the team would dissolve after a month, he would be able to extricate himself fairly quickly if he grew too uncomfortable with the relationships. But the experience would force him to spend a significant amount of time with several of his white colleagues during that month and would provide him an opportunity to test his sense of the real costs of being a full team member.

Step 5: Evaluate the results

In the last step, employees evaluate the test results, evaluate the test itself, design and run new tests, and eventually question the big assumptions. For John, this meant signing up for other initiatives and making initial social overtures to white coworkers. At the same time, by engaging in volunteer efforts within his community outside of work, he made sure that his ties to his racial group were not compromised.

It is worth noting that revealing a big assumption doesn't necessarily mean it will be exposed as false. But even if a big assumption does contain an element of truth, an individual can often find more effective ways to operate once he or she has had a chance to challenge the assumption and its hold on his or her behavior. Indeed, John found a way to support the essence of his competing commitment—to maintain his bond with his racial group—while minimizing behavior that sabotaged his other stated commitments.

Uncovering Your Own Immunity

As you go through this process with your employees, remember that managers are every bit as susceptible to change immunity as employees are, and your competing commitments and big assumptions can have a significant impact on the people around you. Returning once more to Helen's story: When we went through this exercise with her boss, Andrew, it turned out that he was harboring some contradictions of his own. While he was committed to the success of his subordinates, Andrew at some level assumed that he alone could meet his high standards, and as a result he was laboring under a competing commitment to maintain absolute control over his projects. He was unintentionally communicating this lack of confidence to his subordinates—including Helen—in subtle ways. In the end, Andrew's and Helen's competing commitments were, without their knowledge, mutually reinforcing, keeping Helen dependent on Andrew and allowing Andrew to control her projects.

Helen and Andrew are still working through this process, but they've already gained invaluable insight into their behavior and the ways they are impeding their own progress. This may seem like a small step, but bringing these issues to the surface and confronting them head-on is challenging and painful—yet tremendously effective. It allows managers to see, at last, what's really going on when people who are genuinely committed to change nonetheless dig in their heels. It's not about identifying unproductive behavior and systematically making plans to correct it, as if treating symptoms would cure a disease. It's not about coaxing or cajoling or even giving poor performance reviews. It's about understanding the complexities of people's behavior, guiding them through a productive process to bring their competing commitments to the surface, and helping them cope with the inner conflict that is preventing them from achieving their goals.

Originally published in November 2001. Reprint R0110E

Cracking the Code of Change

by Michael Beer and Nitin Nohria

THE NEW ECONOMY HAS ushered in great business opportunities—and great turmoil. Not since the Industrial Revolution have the stakes of dealing with change been so high. Most traditional organizations have accepted, in theory at least, that they must either change or die. And even Internet companies such as eBay, Amazon.com, and America Online recognize that they need to manage the changes associated with rapid entrepreneurial growth. Despite some individual successes, however, change remains difficult to pull off, and few companies manage the process as well as they would like. Most of their initiatives—installing new technology, downsizing, restructuring, or trying to change corporate culture—have had low success rates. The brutal fact is that about 70% of all change initiatives fail.

In our experience, the reason for most of those failures is that in their rush to change their organizations, managers end up immersing themselves in an alphabet soup of initiatives. They lose focus and become mesmerized by all the advice available in print and online about why companies should change, what they should try to accomplish, and how they should do it. This proliferation of recommendations often leads to muddle when change is attempted. The result is that most change efforts exert a heavy toll, both human and economic. To improve the odds of success, and to reduce the human carnage, it is imperative that executives understand the nature and process of corporate change much better. But even that is not enough. Leaders need to crack the code of change.

For more than 40 years now, we've been studying the nature of corporate change. And although every business's change initiative is unique, our research suggests there are two archetypes, or theories, of change. These archetypes are based on very different and often unconscious assumptions by senior executives—and the consultants and academics who advise them—about why and how changes should be made. Theory E is change based on economic value. Theory O is change based on organizational capability. Both are valid models; each theory of change achieves some of management's goals, either explicitly or implicitly. But each theory also has its costs—often unexpected ones.

Theory E change strategies are the ones that make all the headlines. In this "hard" approach to change, shareholder value is the only legitimate measure of corporate success. Change usually involves heavy use of economic incentives, drastic layoffs, downsizing, and restructuring. E change strategies are more common than O change strategies among companies in the United States, where financial markets push corporate boards for rapid turnarounds. For instance, when William A. Anders was brought in as CEO of General Dynamics in 1991, his goal was to maximize economic value—however painful the remedies might be. Over the next three years, Anders reduced the workforce by 71,000 people—44,000 through the divestiture of seven businesses and 27,000 through layoffs and attrition. Anders employed common E strategies.

Managers who subscribe to Theory O believe that if they were to focus exclusively on the price of their stock, they might harm their organizations. In this "soft" approach to change, the goal is to develop corporate culture and human capability through individual and organizational learning—the process of changing, obtaining feedback, reflecting, and making further changes. U.S. companies that adopt O strategies, as Hewlett-Packard did when its performance flagged in the 1980s, typically have strong, long-held, commitment-based psychological contracts with their employees.

Idea in Brief

Here's the brutal fact: 70% of all change initiatives fail. Why? Managers flounder in an alphabet soup of change methods, drowning in conflicting advice. Change efforts exact a heavy toll—human *and* economic—as companies flail from one change method to another.

To effect successful change, first **grasp the two basic theories of change:**

1. **Theory E** change emphasizes economic value—as measured *only* by shareholder returns. This "hard" approach boosts returns through economic incentives, drastic layoffs, and restructuring. "Chainsaw Al" Dunlop's firing 11,000 Scott Paper employees and selling several businesses—tripling shareholder value to $9 billion—is a stunning example.
2. **Theory O** change—a "softer" approach—focuses on developing corporate culture and human capability, patiently building trust and emotional commitment to the company through teamwork and communication.

Then, carefully and simultaneously **balance these very different approaches.** It's not easy. Employees distrust leaders who alternate between nurturing and cutthroat behavior. But, done well, you'll boost profits and productivity, and achieve sustainable competitive advantage.

Managers at these companies are likely to see the risks in breaking those contracts. Because they place a high value on employee commitment, Asian and European businesses are also more likely to adopt an O strategy to change.

Few companies subscribe to just one theory. Most companies we have studied have used a mix of both. But all too often, managers try to apply theories E and O in tandem without resolving the inherent tensions between them. This impulse to combine the strategies is directionally correct, but theories E and O are so different that it's hard to manage them simultaneously—employees distrust leaders who alternate between nurturing and cutthroat corporate behavior. Our research suggests, however, that there is a way to resolve the tension so that businesses can satisfy their shareholders while building viable institutions. Companies that effectively combine hard and soft approaches to change can reap big payoffs in profitability and

Idea in Practice

The UK grocery chain, ASDA, teetered on bankruptcy in 1991. Here's how CEO Archie Norman combined change Theories E and O with spectacular results: a culture of trust and openness—*and* an eightfold increase in shareholder value.

Change dimension	How to combine theories E and O	Examples from ASDA
Goals	Embrace the paradox between economic value *and* organizational capability	Norman started his tenure by stating, "Our number one objective is to secure value for our shareholders" and "We need a culture built around common ideas . . . and listening, learning, and speed of response, from the stores upwards."
Leadership	Set direction from the top *and* engage people from below	Norman unilaterally set a new pricing strategy *and* shifted power from headquarters to stores. His forthright "Tell Archie" program encouraged dialogue with all employees. He hired warm, accessible Allan Leighton to complement his own Theory O leadership style and strengthened emotional commitment to the new ASDA.
Focus	Focus on both hard and soft sides of the organization	Norman set out to win both hearts *and* minds. He boosted economic value through hard, structural changes, e.g., removing top layers of hierarchy and freezing all wages. He paid equal attention to the soft side by spending 75% of his early months as HR director creating a more egalitarian and transparent organization—"a great place for everyone to work."

Change dimension	How to combine theories E and O	Examples from ASDA
Process	Plan for spontaneity	Norman encouraged experimentation, setting up three "risk-free" stores where employees could fail without penalty. Managers experimented with store layout, product range, employee roles. A cross-functional team redesigned ASDA's entire retail organization—and produced significant innovations.
Reward system	Use incentives to reinforce rather than drive change	ASDA applied Theory E incentives in an O-like way. It encouraged all employees to participate actively in changing ASDA. And it rewarded their commitment with stock ownership and variable pay based on corporate *and* store performance.

productivity. Those companies are more likely to achieve a sustainable competitive advantage. They can also reduce the anxiety that grips whole societies in the face of corporate restructuring.

In this article, we will explore how one company successfully resolved the tensions between E and O strategies. But before we do that, we need to look at just how different the two theories are.

A Tale of Two Theories

To understand how sharply theories E and O differ, we can compare them along several key dimensions of corporate change: goals, leadership, focus, process, reward system, and use of consultants. (For a side-by-side comparison, see the table "Comparing theories of change.") We'll look at two companies in similar businesses that adopted almost pure forms of each archetype. Scott Paper successfully used Theory E to enhance shareholder value, while Champion International used Theory O to achieve a complete cultural transformation that increased its productivity and employee commitment. But as we will soon observe, both paper producers also discovered the limitations of sticking with only one theory of change. Let's compare the two companies' initiatives.

Goals

When Al Dunlap assumed leadership of Scott Paper in May 1994, he immediately fired 11,000 employees and sold off several businesses. His determination to restructure the beleaguered company was almost monomaniacal. As he said in one of his speeches: "Shareholders are the number one constituency. Show me an annual report that lists six or seven constituencies, and I'll show you a mismanaged company." From a shareholder's perspective, the results of Dunlap's actions were stunning. In just 20 months, he managed to triple shareholder returns as Scott Paper's market value rose from about $3 billion in 1994 to about $9 billion by the end of 1995. The financial community applauded his efforts and hailed Scott Paper's approach to change as a model for improving shareholder returns.

Champion's reform effort couldn't have been more different. CEO Andrew Sigler acknowledged that enhanced economic value was an appropriate target for management, but he believed that goal would be best achieved by transforming the behaviors of management, unions, and workers alike. In 1981, Sigler and other managers launched a long-term effort to restructure corporate culture around a new vision called the Champion Way, a set of values and principles designed to build up the competencies of the workforce. By improving the organization's capabilities in areas such as teamwork and communication, Sigler believed he could best increase employee productivity and thereby improve the bottom line.

Leadership

Leaders who subscribe to Theory E manage change the old-fashioned way: from the top down. They set goals with little involvement from their management teams and certainly without input from lower levels or unions. Dunlap was clearly the commander in chief at Scott Paper. The executives who survived his purges, for example, had to agree with his philosophy that shareholder value was now the company's primary objective. Nothing made clear Dunlap's leadership style better than the nickname he gloried in: "Chainsaw Al."

By contrast, participation (a Theory O trait) was the hallmark of change at Champion. Every effort was made to get all its employees emotionally committed to improving the company's performance. Teams drafted value statements, and even the industry's unions were brought into the dialogue. Employees were encouraged to identify and solve problems themselves. Change at Champion sprouted from the bottom up.

Focus

In E-type change, leaders typically focus immediately on streamlining the "hardware" of the organization—the structures and systems. These are the elements that can most easily be changed from the top down, yielding swift financial results. For instance, Dunlap quickly decided to outsource many of Scott Paper's corporate functions—benefits and payroll administration, almost all of its management information systems, some of its technology research, medical services, telemarketing, and security functions. An executive manager of a global merger explained the E rationale: "I have a [profit] goal of $176 million this year, and there's no time to involve others or develop organizational capability."

By contrast, Theory O's initial focus is on building up the "software" of an organization—the culture, behavior, and attitudes of employees. Throughout a decade of reforms, no employees were laid off at Champion. Rather, managers and employees were encouraged to collectively reexamine their work practices and behaviors with a goal of increasing productivity and quality. Managers were replaced if they did not conform to the new philosophy, but the overall firing freeze helped to create a culture of trust and commitment. Structural change followed once the culture changed. Indeed, by the mid-1990s, Champion had completely reorganized all its

Comparing theories of change

Our research has shown that all corporate transformations can be compared along the six dimensions shown here. The table outlines the differences between the E and O archetypes and illustrates what an integrated approach might look like.

Dimensions of change	Theory E	Theory O	Theories E and O combined
Goals	Maximize share-holder value	Develop organiza-tional capabilities	Explicitly embrace the paradox between economic value and organizational capability
Leadership	Manage change from the top down	Encourage partici-pation from the bottom up	Set direction from the top and engage the people below
Focus	Emphasize structure and systems	Build up corporate culture: employ-ees' behavior and attitudes	Focus simultaneously on the hard (structures and systems) and the soft (corporate culture)
Process	Plan and establish programs	Experiment and evolve	Plan for spontaneity
Reward system	Motivate through financial incentives	Motivate through commitment—use pay as fair exchange	Use incentives to rein-force change but not to drive it
Use of consultants	Consultants analyze problems and shape solutions	Consultants sup-port management in shaping their own solutions	Consultants are expert resources who empower employees

corporate functions. Once a hierarchical, functionally organized company, Champion adopted a matrix structure that empowered employee teams to focus more on customers.

Process

Theory E is predicated on the view that no battle can be won without a clear, comprehensive, common plan of action that encourages internal coordination and inspires confidence among customers, suppliers, and investors. The plan lets leaders quickly motivate and mobilize their businesses; it compels them to take tough, decisive actions they presumably haven't taken in the past. The changes at Scott Paper unfolded like a military battle plan. Managers were instructed to achieve specific targets by specific dates. If they didn't adhere to Dunlap's tightly choreographed marching orders, they risked being fired.

Meanwhile, the changes at Champion were more evolutionary and emergent than planned and programmatic. When the company's decade-long reform began in 1981, there was no master blueprint. The idea was that innovative work processes, values, and culture changes in one plant would be adapted and used by other plants on their way through the corporate system. No single person, not even Sigler, was seen as the driver of change. Instead, local leaders took responsibility. Top management simply encouraged experimentation from the ground up, spread new ideas to other workers, and transferred managers of innovative units to lagging ones.

Reward System

The rewards for managers in E-type change programs are primarily financial. Employee compensation, for example, is linked with financial incentives, mainly stock options. Dunlap's own compensation package—which ultimately netted him more than $100 million—was tightly linked to shareholders' interests. Proponents of this system argue that financial incentives guarantee that employees' interests match stockholders' interests. Financial rewards also help top executives feel compensated for a difficult job—one in which they are often reviled by their onetime colleagues and the larger community.

The O-style compensation systems at Champion reinforced the goals of culture change, but they didn't drive those goals. A skills-based pay system and a corporatewide gains-sharing plan were installed to draw union workers and management into a community of purpose. Financial incentives were used only as a supplement to those systems and not to push particular reforms. While Champion did offer a companywide bonus to achieve business goals in two separate years, this came late in the change process and played a minor role in actually fulfilling those goals.

Use of Consultants

Theory E change strategies often rely heavily on external consultants. A SWAT team of Ivy League–educated MBAs, armed with an arsenal of state-of-the-art ideas, is brought in to find new ways to look at the business and manage it. The consultants can help CEOs get a fix on urgent issues and priorities. They also offer much-needed political and psychological support for CEOs who are under fire from financial markets. At Scott Paper, Dunlap engaged consultants to identify many of the painful cost-savings initiatives that he subsequently implemented.

Theory O change programs rely far less on consultants. The handful of consultants who were introduced at Champion helped managers and workers make their own business analyses and craft their own solutions. And while the consultants had their own ideas, they did not recommend any corporate program, dictate any solutions, or whip anyone into line. They simply led a process of discovery and learning that was intended to change the corporate culture in a way that could not be foreseen at the outset.

In their purest forms, both change theories clearly have their limitations. CEOs who must make difficult E-style choices understandably distance themselves from their employees to ease their own pain and guilt. Once removed from their people, these CEOs begin to see their employees as part of the problem. As time goes on, these leaders become less and less inclined to adopt O-style change strategies. They fail to invest in building the company's human resources, which inevitably hollows out the company and saps its capacity for sustained performance. At Scott Paper, for example, Dunlap trebled shareholder returns but failed to build the capabilities needed for sustained competitive advantage—commitment, coordination, communication, and creativity. In 1995, Dunlap sold Scott Paper to its longtime competitor Kimberly-Clark.

CEOs who embrace Theory O find that their loyalty and commitment to their employees can prevent them from making tough decisions. The temptation is to postpone the bitter medicine in the hopes that rising productivity will improve the business situation. But productivity gains aren't enough when fundamental structural change is required. That reality is underscored by today's global financial system, which makes corporate performance instantly transparent to large institutional shareholders whose fund managers are under enormous pressure to show good results. Consider Champion. By 1997, it had become one of the leaders in its industry based on most performance measures. Still, newly instated CEO Richard Olsen was forced to admit a tough reality: Champion shareholders had not seen a significant increase in the economic value of the company in more than a decade. Indeed, when Champion was sold recently to Finland-based UPM-Kymmene, it was acquired for a mere 1.5 times its original share value.

Managing the Contradictions

Clearly, if the objective is to build a company that can adapt, survive, and prosper over the years, Theory E strategies must somehow be combined with Theory O strategies. But unless they're carefully handled, melding E and O is likely to bring the worst of both theories and the benefits of neither. Indeed, the corporate changes we've studied that arbitrarily and haphazardly mixed E and O techniques proved destabilizing to the organizations in which they were imposed. Managers in those companies would certainly have been better off to pick either pure E or pure O strategies—with all their costs. At least one set of stakeholders would have benefited.

The obvious way to combine E and O is to sequence them. Some companies, notably General Electric, have done this quite successfully. At GE, CEO Jack Welch began his sequenced change by imposing an E-type restructuring. He demanded that all GE businesses be first or second in their industries. Any unit that failed that test would be fixed, sold off, or closed. Welch followed that up with a massive downsizing of the GE bureaucracy. Between 1981 and 1985, total employment at the corporation dropped from 412,000 to 299,000. Sixty percent of the corporate staff, mostly in planning and finance, was laid off. In this phase, GE people began to call Welch "Neutron Jack," after the fabled bomb that was designed to destroy people but leave buildings intact. Once he had wrung out the redundancies, however, Welch adopted an O strategy. In 1985, he started a series of organizational initiatives to change GE culture. He declared that the company had to become "boundaryless," and unit leaders across the corporation had to submit to being challenged by their subordinates in open forum. Feedback and open communication eventually eroded the hierarchy. Soon Welch applied the new order to GE's global businesses.

Unfortunately for companies like Champion, sequenced change is far easier if you begin, as Welch did, with Theory E. Indeed, it is highly unlikely that E would successfully follow O because of the sense of betrayal that would involve. It is hard to imagine how a draconian program of layoffs and downsizing can leave intact the psychological contract and culture a company has so patiently built up over the years. But whatever the order, one sure problem with sequencing is that it can take a very long time; at GE it has taken almost two decades. A sequenced change may also require two CEOs, carefully chosen for their contrasting styles and philosophies, which may create its own set of problems. Most turnaround managers don't survive restructuring—partly because of their own inflexibility and partly because they can't live down the distrust that their ruthlessness has earned them. In most cases, even the best-intentioned effort to rebuild trust and commitment rarely overcomes a bloody past. Welch is the exception that proves the rule.

So what should you do? How can you achieve rapid improvements in economic value while simultaneously developing an open, trusting corporate culture? Paradoxical as those goals may appear, our research shows that it is possible to apply theories E and O together. It requires great will, skill—and wisdom. But precisely because it is more difficult than mere sequencing, the simultaneous use of O and E strategies is more likely to be a source of sustainable competitive advantage.

One company that exemplifies the reconciliation of the hard and soft approaches is ASDA, the UK grocery chain that CEO Archie

Norman took over in December 1991, when the retailer was nearly bankrupt. Norman laid off employees, flattened the organization, and sold off losing businesses—acts that usually spawn distrust among employees and distance executives from their people. Yet during Norman's eight-year tenure as CEO, ASDA also became famous for its atmosphere of trust and openness. It has been described by executives at Wal-Mart—itself famous for its corporate culture—as being "more like Wal-Mart than we are." Let's look at how ASDA resolved the conflicts of E and O along the six main dimensions of change.

Explicitly confront the tension between E and O goals

With his opening speech to ASDA's executive team—none of whom he had met—Norman indicated clearly that he intended to apply both E and O strategies in his change effort. It is doubtful that any of his listeners fully understood him at the time, but it was important that he had no conflicts about recognizing the paradox between the two strategies for change. He said as much in his maiden speech: "Our number one objective is to secure value for our shareholders and secure the trading future of the business. I am not coming in with any magical solutions. I intend to spend the next few weeks listening and forming ideas for our precise direction. . . . We need a culture built around common ideas and goals that include listening, learning, and speed of response, from the stores upwards. [But] there will be management reorganization. My objective is to establish a clear focus on the stores, shorten lines of communication, and build one team." If there is a contradiction between building a high-involvement organization and restructuring to enhance shareholder value, Norman embraced it.

Set direction from the top and engage people below

From day one, Norman set strategy without expecting any participation from below. He said ASDA would adopt an everyday-low-pricing strategy, and Norman unilaterally determined that change would begin by having two experimental store formats up and running within six months. He decided to shift power from the headquarters to the stores, declaring: "I want everyone to be close to the stores.

We must love the stores to death; that is our business." But even from the start, there was an O quality to Norman's leadership style. As he put it in his first speech: "First, I am forthright, and I like to argue. Second, I want to discuss issues as colleagues. I am looking for your advice and your disagreement." Norman encouraged dialogue with employees and customers through colleague and customer circles. He set up a "Tell Archie" program so that people could voice their concerns and ideas.

Making way for opposite leadership styles was also an essential ingredient to Norman's—and ASDA's—success. This was most clear in Norman's willingness to hire Allan Leighton shortly after he took over. Leighton eventually became deputy chief executive. Norman and Leighton shared the same E and O values, but they had completely different personalities and styles. Norman, cool and reserved, impressed people with the power of his mind—his intelligence and business acumen. Leighton, who is warmer and more people oriented, worked on employees' emotions with the power of his personality. As one employee told us, "People respect Archie, but they love Allan." Norman was the first to credit Leighton with having helped to create emotional commitment to the new ASDA. While it might be possible for a single individual to embrace opposite leadership styles, accepting an equal partner with a very different personality makes it easier to capitalize on those styles. Leighton certainly helped Norman reach out to the organization. Together they held quarterly meetings with store managers to hear their ideas, and they supplemented those meetings with impromptu talks.

Focus simultaneously on the hard and soft sides of the organization

Norman's immediate actions followed both the E goal of increasing economic value and the O goal of transforming culture. On the E side, Norman focused on structure. He removed layers of hierarchy at the top of the organization, fired the financial officer who had been part of ASDA's disastrous policies, and decreed a wage freeze for everyone—management and workers alike. But from the start, the O strategy was an equal part of Norman's plan. He bought time for all this change by warning the markets that financial recovery would take three years. Norman later said that he spent 75% of his early months at ASDA as the company's human resource director, making the organization less hierarchical, more egalitarian, and more transparent. Both Norman and Leighton were keenly aware that they had to win hearts and minds. As Norman put it to workers: "We need to make ASDA a great place for everyone to work."

Plan for spontaneity

Training programs, total-quality programs, and top-driven culture change programs played little part in ASDA's transformation. From the start, the ASDA change effort was set up to encourage experimentation and evolution. To promote learning, for example, ASDA set up an experimental store that was later expanded to three stores. It was declared a risk-free zone, meaning there would be no penalties for failure. A cross-functional task force "renewed," or redesigned, ASDA's entire retail proposition, its organization, and its managerial structure. Store managers were encouraged to experiment with store layout, employee roles, ranges of products offered, and so on. The experiments produced significant innovations in all aspects of store operations. ASDA's managers learned, for example, that they couldn't renew a store unless that store's management team was ready for new ideas. This led to an innovation called the Driving Test, which assessed whether store managers' skills in leading the change process were aligned with the intended changes. The test perfectly illustrates how E and O can come together: it bubbled up O-style from the bottom of the company, yet it bound managers in an E-type contract. Managers who failed the test were replaced.

Let incentives reinforce change, not drive it

Any synthesis of E and O must recognize that compensation is a double-edged sword. Money can focus and motivate managers, but it can also hamper teamwork, commitment, and learning. The way to resolve this dilemma is to apply Theory E incentives in an O way. Employees' high involvement is encouraged to develop their commitment to change, and variable pay is used to reward that commitment.

ASDA's senior executives were compensated with stock options that were tied to the company's value. These helped attract key executives to ASDA. Unlike most E-strategy companies, however, ASDA had a stock-ownership plan for all employees. In addition, store-level employees got variable pay based on both corporate performance and their stores' records. In the end, compensation represented a fair exchange of value between the company and its individual employees. But Norman believed that compensation had not played a major role in motivating change at the company.

Use consultants as expert resources who empower employees
Consultants can provide specialized knowledge and technical skills that the company doesn't have, particularly in the early stages of organizational change. Management's task is figuring out how to use those resources without abdicating leadership of the change effort. ASDA followed the middle ground between Theory E and Theory O. It made limited use of four consulting firms in the early stages of its transformation. The consulting firms always worked alongside management and supported its leadership of change. However, their engagement was intentionally cut short by Norman to prevent ASDA and its managers from becoming dependent on the consultants. For example, an expert in store organization was hired to support the task force assigned to renew ASDA's first few experimental stores, but later stores were renewed without his involvement.

By embracing the paradox inherent in simultaneously employing E and O change theories, Norman and Leighton transformed ASDA to the advantage of its shareholders and employees. The organization went through personnel changes, unit sell-offs, and hierarchical upheaval. Yet these potentially destructive actions did not prevent ASDA's employees from committing to change and the new corporate culture because Norman and Leighton had won employees' trust by constantly listening, debating, and being willing to learn. Candid about their intentions from the outset, they balanced the tension between the two change theories.

By 1999, the company had multiplied shareholder value eightfold. The organizational capabilities built by Norman and Leighton

Change Theories in the New Economy

HISTORICALLY, THE STUDY of change has been restricted to mature, large companies that needed to reverse their competitive declines. But the arguments we have advanced in this article also apply to entrepreneurial companies that need to manage rapid growth. Here, too, we believe that the most successful strategy for change will be one that combines theories E and O.

Just as there are two ways of changing, so there are two kinds of entrepreneurs. One group subscribes to an ideology akin to Theory E. Their primary goal is to prepare for a cash-out, such as an IPO or an acquisition by an established player. Maximizing market value before the cash-out is their sole and abiding purpose. These entrepreneurs emphasize shaping the firm's strategy, structure, and systems to build a quick, strong market presence. Mercurial leaders who drive the company using a strong top-down style are typically at the helm of such companies. They lure others to join them using high-powered incentives such as stock options. The goal is to get rich quick.

Other entrepreneurs, however, are driven by an ideology more akin to Theory O—the building of an institution. Accumulating wealth is important, but it is secondary to creating a company that is based on a deeply held set of values and that has a strong culture. These entrepreneurs are likely to subscribe to an egalitarian style that invites everyone's participation. They look to attract others who share their passion about the cause—though they certainly provide generous stock options as well. The goal in this case is to make a difference, not just to make money.

Many people fault entrepreneurs who are driven by a Theory E view of the world. But we can think of other entrepreneurs who have destroyed businesses because they were overly wrapped up in the Theory O pursuit of a higher ideal and didn't pay attention to the pragmatics of the market. Steve Jobs's venture, Next, comes to mind. Both types of entrepreneurs have to find some way of tapping the qualities of theories E and O, just as large companies do.

---

also gave ASDA the sustainable competitive advantage that Dunlap had been unable to build at Scott Paper and that Sigler had been unable to build at Champion. While Dunlap was forced to sell a demoralized and ineffective organization to Kimberly-Clark, and while a languishing Champion was sold to UPM-Kymmene, Norman and Leighton in June 1999 found a friendly and culturally compatible suitor in Wal-Mart, which was willing to pay a substantial premium for the organizational capabilities that ASDA had so painstakingly developed.

In the end, the integration of theories E and O created major change—and major payoffs—for ASDA. Such payoffs are possible for other organizations that want to develop a sustained advantage in today's economy. But that advantage can come only from a constant willingness and ability to develop organizations for the long term combined with a constant monitoring of shareholder value—E dancing with O, in an unending minuet.

Originally published in May 2000. Reprint R00301

The Hard Side of Change Management

by Harold L. Sirkin, Perry Keenan, and Alan Jackson

WHEN FRENCH NOVELIST JEAN-BAPTISTE Alphonse Karr wrote *"Plus ça change, plus c'est la même chose,"* he could have been penning an epigram about change management. For over three decades, academics, managers, and consultants, realizing that transforming organizations is difficult, have dissected the subject. They've sung the praises of leaders who communicate vision and walk the talk in order to make change efforts succeed. They've sanctified the importance of changing organizational culture and employees' attitudes. They've teased out the tensions between top-down transformation efforts and participatory approaches to change. And they've exhorted companies to launch campaigns that appeal to people's hearts and minds. Still, studies show that in most organizations, two out of three transformation initiatives fail. The more things change, the more they stay the same.

Managing change *is* tough, but part of the problem is that there is little agreement on what factors most influence transformation initiatives. Ask five executives to name the one factor critical for the success of these programs, and you'll probably get five different answers. That's because each manager looks at an initiative from his or her viewpoint and, based on personal experience, focuses on different success factors. The experts, too, offer different perspectives. A recent search on Amazon.com for books on "change and management" turned up 6,153 titles, each with a distinct take on the topic. Those ideas have a lot to offer, but taken together, they force companies to tackle many priorities simultaneously, which spreads resources and skills thin. Moreover, executives use different approaches in different parts of the organization, which compounds the turmoil that usually accompanies change.

In recent years, many change management gurus have focused on soft issues, such as culture, leadership, and motivation. Such elements are important for success, but managing these aspects alone isn't sufficient to implement transformation projects. Soft factors don't directly influence the outcomes of many change programs. For instance, visionary leadership is often vital for transformation projects, but not always. The same can be said about communication with employees. Moreover, it isn't easy to change attitudes or relationships; they're deeply ingrained in organizations and people. And although changes in, say, culture or motivation levels can be indirectly gauged through surveys and interviews, it's tough to get reliable data on soft factors.

What's missing, we believe, is a focus on the not-so-fashionable aspects of change management: the hard factors. These factors bear three distinct characteristics. First, companies are able to measure them in direct or indirect ways. Second, companies can easily communicate their importance, both within and outside organizations. Third, and perhaps most important, businesses are capable of influencing those elements quickly. Some of the hard factors that affect a transformation initiative are the time necessary to complete it, the number of people required to execute it, and the financial results that intended actions are expected to achieve. Our research shows that change projects fail to get off the ground when companies neglect the hard factors. That doesn't mean that executives can ignore the soft elements; that would be a grave mistake. However, if companies don't pay attention to the hard issues first, transformation programs will break down before the soft elements come into play.

Idea in Brief

Two out of every three transformation programs fail. Why? Companies overemphasize the soft side of change: leadership style, corporate culture, employee motivation. Though these elements are critical for success, change projects can't get off the ground unless companies address harder elements first.

The essential hard elements? Think of them as DICE:

- ***D*uration:** time between milestone reviews—the shorter, the better
- ***I*ntegrity:** project teams' skill
- ***C*ommitment:** senior executives' and line managers' dedication to the program
- ***E*ffort:** the extra work employees must do to adopt new processes—the less, the better

By assessing each DICE element *before* you launch a major change initiative, you can identify potential problem areas and make the necessary adjustments (such as reconfiguring a project team's composition or reallocating resources) to ensure the program's success. You can also use DICE *after* launching a project—to make midcourse corrections if the initiative veers off track.

DICE helps companies lay the foundation for successful change. Using the DICE assessment technique, one global beverage company executed a multiproject organization-wide change program that generated hundreds of millions of dollars, breathed new life into its once-stagnant brands, and cracked open new markets.

That's a lesson we learned when we identified the common denominators of change. In 1992, we started with the contrarian hypothesis that organizations handle transformations in remarkably similar ways. We researched projects in a number of industries and countries to identify those common elements. Our initial 225-company study revealed a consistent correlation between the outcomes (success or failure) of change programs and four hard factors: project *duration,* particularly the time between project reviews; performance *integrity,* or the capabilities of project teams; the *commitment* of both senior executives and the staff whom the change will affect the most; and the additional *effort* that employees must make to cope with the change. We called these variables the DICE factors because we could load them in favor of projects' success.

Idea in Practice

Conducting a DICE Assessment

Your project has the greatest chance of success if the following hard elements are in place:

Duration

A long project reviewed frequently stands a far better chance of succeeding than a short project reviewed infrequently. Problems can be identified at the first sign of trouble, allowing for prompt corrective actions. Review complex projects every two weeks; more straightforward initiatives, every six to eight weeks.

Integrity

A change program's success hinges on a high-integrity, high-quality project team. To identify team candidates with the right portfolio of skills, solicit names from key colleagues, including top performers in functions other than your own. Recruit people who have problem-solving skills, are results oriented, and are methodical but tolerate ambiguity. Look also for organizational savvy, willingness to accept responsibility for decisions, and a disdain for the limelight.

Commitment

If employees don't see company leaders supporting a change initiative, they won't change. Visibly endorse the initiative—no amount of public support is too much. When you feel you're "talking up" a change effort at least three times more than you need to, you've hit it right.

Also continually communicate why the change is needed and what it

We completed our study in 1994, and in the 11 years since then, the Boston Consulting Group has used those four factors to predict the outcomes, and guide the execution, of more than 1,000 change management initiatives worldwide. Not only has the correlation held, but no other factors (or combination of factors) have predicted outcomes as well.

The Four Key Factors

If you think about it, the different ways in which organizations combine the four factors create a continuum—from projects that are set up to succeed to those that are set up to fail. At one extreme, a short

means for employees. Ensure that all messages about the change are consistent and clear. Reach out to managers and employees through one-on-one conversations to win them over.

Effort

If adopting a change burdens employees with too much additional effort, they'll resist. Calculate how much work employees will have to do beyond their existing responsibilities to implement the change. Ensure that no one's workload increases more than 10%. If necessary, remove nonessential regular work from employees with key roles in the transformation project. Use temporary workers or outsource some processes to accommodate additional workload.

Using the DICE Framework

Conducting a DICE assessment fosters successful change by sparking valuable senior leadership debate about project strategy It also improves change effectiveness by enabling companies to manage large portfolios of projects.

Example: A manufacturing company planned 40 projects as part of a profitability-improvement program. After conducting a DICE assessment for each project, leaders and project owners identified the five most important projects and asked, "How can we ensure these projects' success?" They moved people around on teams, reconfigured some projects, and identified initiatives senior managers should pay more attention to—setting up their most crucial projects for resounding success.

project led by a skilled, motivated, and cohesive team, championed by top management and implemented in a department that is receptive to the change and has to put in very little additional effort, is bound to succeed. At the other extreme, a long, drawn-out project executed by an inexpert, unenthusiastic, and disjointed team, without any top-level sponsors and targeted at a function that dislikes the change and has to do a lot of extra work, will fail. Businesses can easily identify change programs at either end of the spectrum, but most initiatives occupy the middle ground where the likelihood of success or failure is difficult to assess. Executives must study the four DICE factors carefully to figure out if their change programs will fly—or die.

The Four Factors

THESE FACTORS determine the outcome of any transformation initiative.

- **D.** The **duration** of time until the change program is completed if it has a short life span; if not short, the amount of time between reviews of milestones.
- **I.** The project team's performance **integrity**; that is, its ability to complete the initiative on time. That depends on members' skills and traits relative to the project's requirements.
- **C.** The **commitment** to change that top management (C1) and employees affected by the change (C2) display.
- **E.** The **effort** over and above the usual work that the change initiative demands of employees.

Duration

Companies make the mistake of worrying mostly about the time it will take to implement change programs. They assume that the longer an initiative carries on, the more likely it is to fail—the early impetus will peter out, windows of opportunity will close, objectives will be forgotten, key supporters will leave or lose their enthusiasm, and problems will accumulate. However, contrary to popular perception, our studies show that a long project that is reviewed frequently is more likely to succeed than a short project that isn't reviewed frequently. Thus, the time between reviews is more critical for success than a project's life span.

Companies should formally review transformation projects at least bimonthly since, in our experience, the probability that change initiatives will run into trouble rises exponentially when the time between reviews exceeds eight weeks. Whether reviews should be scheduled even more frequently depends on how long executives feel the project can carry on without going off track. Complex projects should be reviewed fortnightly; more familiar or straightforward initiatives can be assessed every six to eight weeks.

Scheduling milestones and assessing their impact are the best way by which executives can review the execution of projects, identify gaps, and spot new risks. The most effective milestones are those that describe major actions or achievements rather than day-to-day activities. They must enable senior executives and project sponsors to confirm that the project has made progress since the last review took place. Good milestones encompass a number of tasks that teams must complete. For example, describing a particular milestone as "Consultations with Stakeholders Completed" is more effective than "Consult Stakeholders" because it represents an achievement and shows that the project has made headway. Moreover, it suggests that several activities were completed—identifying stakeholders, assessing their needs, and talking to them about the project. When a milestone looks as though it won't be reached on time, the project team must try to understand why, take corrective actions, and learn from the experience to prevent problems from recurring.

Review of such a milestone—what we refer to as a "learning milestone"—isn't an impromptu assessment of the Monday-morning kind. It should be a formal occasion during which senior-management sponsors and the project team evaluate the latter's performance on all the dimensions that have a bearing on success and failure. The team must provide a concise report of its progress, and members and sponsors must check if the team is on track to complete, or has finished all the tasks to deliver, the milestone. They should also determine whether achieving the milestone has had the desired effect on the company; discuss the problems the team faced in reaching the milestone; and determine how that accomplishment will affect the next phase of the project. Sponsors and team members must have the power to address weaknesses. When necessary, they should alter processes, agree to push for more or different resources, or suggest a new direction. At these meetings, senior executives must pay special attention to the dynamics within teams, changes in the organization's perceptions about the initiative, and communications from the top.

Integrity

By performance integrity, we mean the extent to which companies can rely on teams of managers, supervisors, and staff to execute change projects successfully. In a perfect world, every team would be flawless, but no business has enough great people to ensure that. Besides, senior executives are often reluctant to allow star performers to join change efforts because regular work can suffer. But since the success of change programs depends on the quality of teams, companies must free up the best staff while making sure that day-to-day operations don't falter. In companies that have succeeded in implementing change programs, we find that employees go the extra mile to ensure their day-to-day work gets done.

Since project teams handle a wide range of activities, resources, pressures, external stimuli, and unforeseen obstacles, they must be cohesive and well led. It's not enough for senior executives to ask people at the watercooler if a project team is doing well; they must clarify members' roles, commitments, and accountability. They must choose the team leader and, most important, work out the team's composition.

Smart executive sponsors, we find, are very inclusive when picking teams. They identify talent by soliciting names from key colleagues, including human resource managers; by circulating criteria they have drawn up; and by looking for top performers in all functions. While they accept volunteers, they take care not to choose only supporters of the change initiative. Senior executives personally interview people so that they can construct the right portfolio of skills, knowledge, and social networks. They also decide if potential team members should commit all their time to the project; if not, they must ask them to allocate specific days or times of the day to the initiative. Top management makes public the parameters on which it will judge the team's performance and how that evaluation fits into the company's regular appraisal process. Once the project gets under way, sponsors must measure the cohesion of teams by administering confidential surveys to solicit members' opinions.

Executives often make the mistake of assuming that because someone is a good, well-liked manager, he or she will also make a decent team leader. That sounds reasonable, but effective managers of the status quo aren't necessarily good at changing organizations. Usually, good team leaders have problem-solving skills, are results oriented, are methodical in their approach but tolerate ambiguity, are organizationally savvy, are willing to accept responsibility for decisions, and while being highly motivated, don't crave the limelight. A CEO who successfully led two major transformation projects in the past ten years used these six criteria to quiz senior executives about the caliber of nominees for project teams. The top management team rejected one in three candidates, on average, before finalizing the teams.

Commitment

Companies must boost the commitment of two different groups of people if they want change projects to take root: They must get visible backing from the most influential executives (what we call C1), who are not necessarily those with the top titles. And they must take into account the enthusiasm—or often, lack thereof—of the people who must deal with the new systems, processes, or ways of working (C2).

Top-level commitment is vital to engendering commitment from those at the coal face. If employees don't see that the company's leadership is backing a project, they're unlikely to change. No amount of top-level support is too much. In 1999, when we were working with the CEO of a consumer products company, he told us that he was doing much more than necessary to display his support for a nettlesome project. When we talked to line managers, they said that the CEO had extended very little backing for the project. They felt that if he wanted the project to succeed, he would have to support it more visibly! A rule of thumb: When you feel that you are talking up a change initiative at least three times more than you need to, your managers will feel that you are backing the transformation.

Sometimes, senior executives are reluctant to back initiatives. That's understandable; they're often bringing about changes that may negatively affect employees' jobs and lives. However, if senior executives do not communicate the need for change, and what it means for employees, they endanger their projects' success. In one financial services firm, top management's commitment to a program that would improve cycle times, reduce errors, and slash costs was low because it entailed layoffs. Senior executives found it gut-wrenching to talk about layoffs in an organization that had prided itself on being a place where good people could find lifetime employment. However, the CEO realized that he needed to tackle the thorny issues around the layoffs to get the project implemented on schedule. He tapped a senior company veteran to organize a series of speeches and meetings in order to provide consistent explanations for the layoffs, the timing, the consequences for job security, and so on. He also appointed a well-respected general manager to lead the change program. Those actions reassured employees that the organization would tackle the layoffs in a professional and humane fashion.

Companies often underestimate the role that managers and staff play in transformation efforts. By communicating with them too late or inconsistently, senior executives end up alienating the people who are most affected by the changes. It's surprising how often something senior executives believe is a good thing is seen by staff as a bad thing, or a message that senior executives think is perfectly clear is misunderstood. That usually happens when senior executives articulate subtly different versions of critical messages. For instance, in one company that applied the DICE framework, scores for a project showed a low degree of staff commitment. It turned out that these employees had become confused, even distrustful, because one senior manager had said, "Layoffs will not occur," while another had said, "They are not expected to occur."

Organizations also underestimate their ability to build staff support. A simple effort to reach out to employees can turn them into champions of new ideas. For example, in the 1990s, a major American energy producer was unable to get the support of mid-level managers, supervisors, and workers for a productivity improvement program. After trying several times, the company's senior executives decided to hold a series of one-on-one conversations with mid-level managers in a last-ditch effort to win them over. The conversations focused on the program's objectives, its impact on employees, and why the organization might not be able to survive without the changes. Partly because of the straight talk, the initiative gained some momentum. This allowed a project team to demonstrate a series of quick wins, which gave the initiative a new lease on life.

Effort

When companies launch transformation efforts, they frequently don't realize, or know how to deal with the fact, that employees are already busy with their day-to-day responsibilities. According to staffing tables, people in many businesses work 80-plus-hour weeks. If, on top of existing responsibilities, line managers and staff have to deal with changes to their work or to the systems they use, they will resist.

Project teams must calculate how much work employees will have to do beyond their existing responsibilities to change over to new processes. Ideally, no one's workload should increase more than 10%. Go beyond that, and the initiative will probably run into trouble. Resources will become overstretched and compromise either the change program or normal operations. Employee morale will fall, and conflict may arise between teams and line staff. To minimize the dangers, project managers should use a simple metric like the percentage increase in effort the employees who must cope with the new ways feel they must contribute. They should also check if the additional effort they have demanded comes on top of heavy workloads and if employees are likely to resist the project because it will demand more of their scarce time.

Companies must decide whether to take away some of the regular work of employees who will play key roles in the transformation project. Companies can start by ridding these employees of discretionary or nonessential responsibilities. In addition, firms should review all the other projects in the operating plan and assess which ones are critical for the change effort. At one company, the project steering committee delayed or restructured 120 out of 250 subprojects so that some line managers could focus on top-priority projects. Another way to relieve pressure is for the company to bring in temporary workers, like retired managers, to carry out routine activities or to outsource current processes until the changeover is complete. Handing off routine work or delaying projects is costly and time-consuming, so companies need to think through such issues before kicking off transformation efforts.

Calculating DICE Scores

COMPANIES CAN DETERMINE if their change programs will succeed by asking executives to calculate scores for each of the four factors of the DICE framework—duration, integrity, commitment, and effort. They must grade each factor on a scale from 1 to 4 (using fractions, if necessary); the lower the score, the better. Thus, a score of 1 suggests that the factor is highly likely to contribute to the program's success, and a score of 4 means that it is highly unlikely to contribute to success. We find that the following questions and scoring guidelines allow executives to rate transformation initiatives effectively:

Duration [D]

Ask: Do formal project reviews occur regularly? If the project will take more than two months to complete, what is the average time between reviews?

Score: If the time between project reviews is less than two months, you should give the project 1 point. If the time is between two and four months, you should award the project 2 points; between four and eight months, 3 points; and if reviews are more than eight months apart, give the project 4 points.

Integrity of Performance [I]

Ask: Is the team leader capable? How strong are team members' skills and motivations? Do they have sufficient time to spend on the change initiative?

Score: If the project team is led by a highly capable leader who is respected by peers, if the members have the skills and motivation to complete the project in the stipulated time frame, and if the company has assigned at least 50% of the team members' time to the project, you can give the project 1 point. If the team is lacking on all those dimensions, you should award the project 4 points. If the team's capabilities are somewhere in between, assign the project 2 or 3 points.

Senior Management Commitment [C_1]

Ask: Do senior executives regularly communicate the reason for the change and the importance of its success? Is the message convincing? Is the message consistent, both across the top management team and over time? Has top management devoted enough resources to the change program?

Score: If senior management has, through actions and words, clearly communicated the need for change, you must give the project 1 point. If senior executives appear to be neutral, it gets 2 or 3 points. If managers perceive senior executives to be reluctant to support the change, award the project 4 points.

Local-Level Commitment [C_2]

Ask: Do the employees most affected by the change understand the reason for it and believe it's worthwhile? Are they enthusiastic and supportive or worried and obstructive?

Score: If employees are eager to take on the change initiative, you can give the project 1 point, and if they are just willing, 2 points. If they're reluctant or strongly reluctant, you should award the project 3 or 4 points.

[D]	[I]	[C_1]	[C_2]	[E]

Calculate

DICE score = $D + 2I + 2C_1 + C_2 + E$

Plot

Effort [E]

Ask: What is the percentage of increased effort that employees must make to implement the change effort? Does the incremental effort come on top of a heavy workload? Have people strongly resisted the increased demands on them?

Score: If the project requires less than 10% extra work by employees, you can give it 1 point. If it's 10% to 20% extra, it should get 2 points. If it's 20% to 40%, it must be 3 points. And if it's more than 40% additional work, you should give the project 4 points.

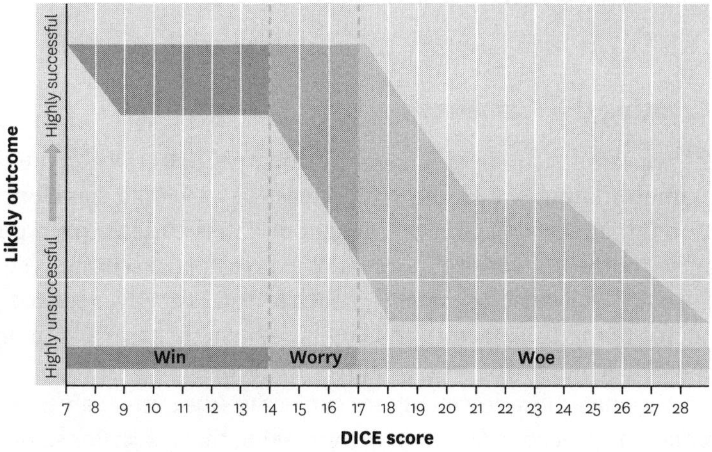

Calculating DICE Scores (continued)

Executives can combine the four elements into a project score. When we conducted a regression analysis of our database of change efforts, we found that the combination that correlates most closely with actual outcomes doubles the weight given to team performance (I) and senior management commitment (C1). That translates into the following formula:

DICE Score = $D + (2 \times I) + (2 \times C_1) + C_2 + E$

In the 1-to-4 scoring system, the formula generates overall scores that range from 7 to 28. Companies can compare a project's score with those of past projects and their outcomes to assess if the project is slated for success or failure. Our data show a clear distribution of scores:

Scores between 7 and 14: The project is very likely to succeed. We call this the Win Zone.

Scores higher than 14 but lower than 17: Risks to the project's success are rising, particularly as the score approaches 17. This is the Worry Zone.

Scores over 17: The project is extremely risky. If a project scores over 17 and under 19 points, the risks to success are very high. Beyond 19, the project is unlikely to succeed. That's why we call this the Woe Zone.

We have changed the boundaries of the zones over time. For instance, the Worry Zone was between 14 and 21 points at first, and the Woe Zone from 21 to 28 points. But we found that companies prefer to be alerted to trouble as soon as outcomes become unpredictable (17 to 20 points). We therefore compressed the Worry Zone and expanded the Woe Zone.

Creating the Framework

As we came to understand the four factors better, we created a framework that would help executives evaluate their transformation initiatives and shine a spotlight on interventions that would improve their chances of success. We developed a scoring system based on the variables that affect each factor. Executives can assign scores to the DICE factors and combine them to arrive at a project score. (See the sidebar "Calculating DICE Scores.")

Although the assessments are subjective, the system gives companies an objective framework for making those decisions. Moreover, the scoring mechanism ensures that executives are evaluating projects and making trade-offs more consistently across projects.

A company can compare its DICE score on the day it kicks off a project with the scores of previous projects, as well as their outcomes, to check if the initiative has been set up for success. When we calculated the scores of the 225 change projects in our database and compared them with the outcomes, the analysis was compelling. Projects clearly fell into three categories, or zones: *Win,* which means that any project with a score in that range is statistically likely to succeed; *worry,* which suggests that the project's outcome is hard to predict; and *woe,* which implies that the project is totally unpredictable or fated for mediocrity or failure. (See the figure "DICE scores predict project outcomes.")

Companies can track how change projects are faring by calculating scores over time or before and after they have made changes to a

DICE scores predict project outcomes

When we plotted the DICE scores of 225 change management initiatives on the horizontal axis, and the outcomes of those projects on the vertical axis, we found three sets of correlations. Projects with DICE scores between 7 and 14 were usually successful; those with scores over 14 and under 17 were unpredictable; and projects with scores over 17 were usually unsuccessful. We named the three zones Win, Worry, and Woe, respectively. (Each number plotted on the graph represents the number of projects, out of the 225 projects, having a particular DICE score.)

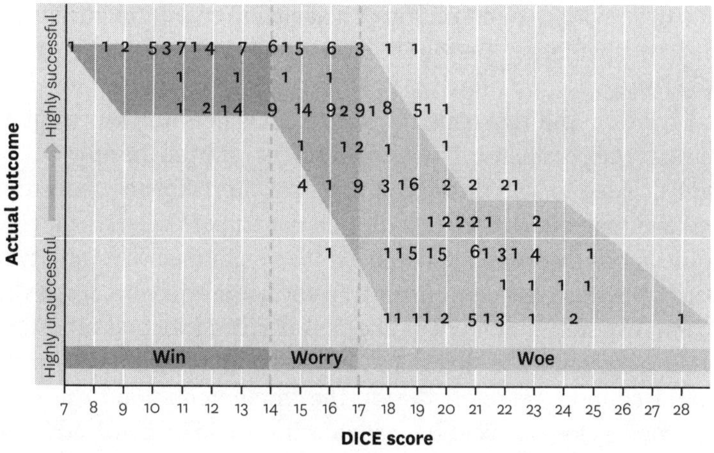

project's structure. The four factors offer a litmus test that executives can use to assess the probability of success for a given project or set of projects. Consider the case of a large Australian bank that in 1994 wanted to restructure its back-office operations. Senior executives agreed on the rationale for the change but differed on whether the bank could achieve its objectives, since the transformation required major changes in processes and organizational structures. Bringing the team and the senior executives together long enough to sort out their differences proved impossible; people were just too busy. That's when the project team decided to analyze the initiative using the DICE framework.

Doing so condensed what could have been a free-flowing two-day debate into a sharp two-hour discussion. The focus on just four elements generated a clear picture of the project's strengths and weaknesses. For instance, managers learned that the restructuring would take eight months to implement but that it had poorly defined milestones and reviews. Although the project team was capable and senior management showed reasonable commitment to the effort, there was room for improvement in both areas. The back-office workforce was hostile to the proposed changes since more than 20% of these people would lose their jobs. Managers and employees agreed that the back-office staff would need to muster 10% to 20% more effort on top of its existing commitments during the implementation. On the DICE scale, the project was deep in the Woe Zone.

However, the assessment also led managers to take steps to increase the possibility of success before they started the project. The bank decided to split the project time line into two—one short-term and one long-term. Doing so allowed the bank to schedule review points more frequently and to maximize team members' ability to learn from experience before the transformation grew in complexity. To improve staff commitment, the bank decided to devote more time to explaining why the change was necessary and how the institution would support the staff during the implementation. The bank also took a closer look at the people who would be involved in the project and changed some of the team leaders when it realized that they lacked the necessary skills. Finally, senior managers made a concerted effort to show their backing for the initiative by holding a traveling road show to explain the project to people at all levels of the organization. Taken together, the bank's actions and plans shifted the project into the Win Zone. Fourteen months later, the bank completed the project—on time and below budget.

Applying the DICE Framework

The simplicity of the DICE framework often proves to be its biggest problem; executives seem to desire more complex answers. By overlooking the obvious, however, they often end up making compromises that don't work. Smart companies try to ensure that they don't fall into that trap by using the DICE framework in one of three ways.

Track Projects

Some companies train managers in how to use the DICE framework before they start transformation programs. Executives use spreadsheet-based versions of the tool to calculate the DICE scores of the various components of the program and to compare them with past scores. Over time, every score must be balanced against the trajectory of scores and, as we shall see next, the portfolio of scores.

Senior executives often use DICE assessments as early warning indicators that transformation initiatives are in trouble. That's how Amgen, the $10.6 billion biotechnology company, used the DICE framework. In 2001, the company realigned its operations around some key processes, broadened its offerings, relaunched some mature products, allied with some firms and acquired others, and launched several innovations. To avoid implementation problems, Amgen's top management team used the DICE framework to gauge how effectively it had allocated people, senior management time, and other resources. As soon as projects reported troubling scores, designated executives paid attention to them. They reviewed the projects more often, reconfigured the teams, and allocated more resources to them. In one area of the change project, Amgen used DICE to track 300 initiatives and reconfigured 200 of them.

Both big and small organizations can put the tool to good use. Take the case of a hospital that kicked off six change projects in the late 1990s. Each initiative involved a lot of investment, had significant clinical implications, or both. The hospital's general manager felt that some projects were going well but was concerned about others. He wasn't able to attribute his concerns to anything other than a bad feeling. However, when the general manager used the DICE framework, he was able to confirm his suspicions. After a 45-minute discussion with project managers and other key people, he established that three projects were in the Win Zone but two were in the Woe Zone and one was in the Worry Zone.

The strongest projects, the general manager found, consumed more than their fair share of resources. Senior hospital staff sensed that those projects would succeed and spent more time promoting them, attending meetings about them, and making sure they had sufficient resources. By contrast, no one enjoyed attending meetings on projects that were performing poorly. So the general manager stopped attending meetings for the projects that were on track; he attended only sessions that related to the three underperforming ones. He pulled some managers from the projects that were progressing smoothly and moved them to the riskier efforts. He added more milestones to the struggling enterprises, delayed their completion, and pushed hard for improvement. Those steps helped ensure that all six projects met their objectives.

Manage portfolios of projects

When companies launch large transformation programs, they kick off many projects to attain their objectives. But if executives don't manage the portfolio properly, those tasks end up competing for attention and resources. For instance, senior executives may choose the best employees for projects they have sponsored or lavish attention on pet projects rather than on those that need attention. By deploying our framework before they start transformation initiatives, companies can identify problem projects in portfolios, focus execution expertise and senior management attention where it is most needed, and defuse political issues.

Take, for example, the case of an Australasian manufacturing company that had planned a set of 40 projects as part of a program to improve profitability. Since some had greater financial implications than others, the company's general manager called for a meeting with all the project owners and senior managers. The group went through each project, debating its DICE score and identifying the problem areas. After listing all the scores and issues, the general manager walked to a whiteboard and circled the five most important projects. "I'm prepared to accept that some projects will start off in the Worry Zone, though I won't accept anything outside the middle of this zone for more than a few weeks. For the top five, we're not going to start until these are well within the Win Zone. What do we have to do to achieve that?" he asked.

The group began thinking and acting right away. It moved people around on teams, reconfigured some projects, and identified those that senior managers should pay more attention to—all of which helped raise DICE scores before implementation began. The most important projects were set up for resounding success while most of the remaining ones managed to get into the Win Zone. The group left some projects in the Worry Zone, but it agreed to track them closely to ensure that their scores improved. In our experience, that's the right thing to do. When companies are trying to overhaul themselves, they shouldn't have all their projects in the Win Zone; if they do, they are not ambitious enough. Transformations should entail fundamental changes that stretch an organization.

Force conversation

When different executives calculate DICE scores for the same project, the results can vary widely. The difference in scores is particularly important in terms of the dialogue it triggers. It provokes participants and engages them in debate over questions like "Why do we see the project in these different ways?" and "What can we agree to do to ensure that the project will succeed?" That's critical, because even people within the same organization lack a common framework for discussing problems with change initiatives. Prejudices, differences in perspectives, and a reluctance or inability to speak up can block effective debates. By using the DICE framework, companies can create a common language and force the right discussions.

Sometimes, companies hold workshops to review floundering projects. At those two- to four-hour sessions, groups of eight to 15 senior and middle managers, along with the project team and the project sponsors, hold a candid dialogue. The debate usually moves beyond the project's scores to the underlying causes of problems and possible remedies. The workshops bring diverse opinions to light, which often can be combined into innovative solutions. Consider, for example, the manner in which DICE workshops helped a telecommunications service provider that had planned a major transformation effort. Consisting of five strategic initiatives and 50 subprojects that needed to be up and running quickly, the program confronted some serious obstacles. The projects' goals, time lines, and revenue objectives were unclear. There were delays in approving business cases, a dearth of rigor and focus in planning and identifying milestones, and a shortage of resources. There were leadership issues, too. For example, executive-level shortcomings had resulted in poor coordination of projects and a misjudgment of risks.

To put the transformation program on track, the telecom company incorporated DICE into project managers' tool kits. The Project Management Office arranged a series of workshops to analyze issues and decide future steps. One workshop, for example, was devoted to three new product development projects, two of which had landed in the Woe Zone and one in the Worry Zone. Participants traced the problems to tension between managers and technology experts, underfunding, lack of manpower, and poor definition of the projects' scopes. They eventually agreed on three remedial actions: holding a conflict-resolution meeting between the directors in charge of technology and those responsible for the core business; making sure senior leadership paid immediate attention to the resource issues; and bringing together the project team and the line-of-business head to formalize project objectives. With the project sponsor committed to those actions, the three projects had improved their DICE scores and thus their chances of success at the time this article went to press.

Conversations about DICE scores are particularly useful for large-scale transformations that cut across business units, functions, and locations. In such change efforts, it is critical to find the right balance between centralized oversight, which ensures that everyone in the organization takes the effort seriously and understands the goals, and the autonomy that various initiatives need. Teams must have the flexibility and incentive to produce customized solutions for their markets, functions, and competitive environments. The balance is difficult to achieve without an explicit consideration of the DICE variables.

Take the case of a leading global beverage company that needed to increase operational efficiency and focus on the most promising brands and markets. The company also sought to make key processes such as consumer demand development and customer fulfillment more innovative. The CEO's goals were ambitious and required investing significant resources across the company. Top management faced enormous challenges in structuring the effort and in spawning projects that focused on the right issues. Executives knew that this was a multiyear effort, yet without tight schedules and oversight of individual projects, there was a risk that projects would take far too long to be completed and the results would taper off.

To mitigate the risks, senior managers decided to analyze each project at several levels of the organization. Using the DICE framework, they reviewed each effort every month until they felt confident that it was on track. After that, reviews occurred when projects met major milestones. No more than two months elapsed between reviews, even in the later stages of the program. The time between reviews at the project-team level was even shorter: Team leaders reviewed progress biweekly throughout the transformation. Some of the best people joined the effort full time. The human resources department took an active role in recruiting team members, thereby creating a virtuous cycle in which the best people began to seek involvement in various initiatives. During the course of the transformation, the company promoted several team members to line- and functional leadership positions because of their performance.

The company's change program resulted in hundreds of millions of dollars of value creation. Its once-stagnant brands began to grow, it cracked open new markets such as China, and sales and promotion activities were aligned with the fastest-growing channels. There were many moments during the process when inertia in the organization threatened to derail the change efforts. However, senior management's belief in focusing on the four key variables helped move the company to a higher trajectory of performance.

By providing a common language for change, the DICE framework allows companies to tap into the insight and experience of their employees. A great deal has been said about middle managers who want to block change. We find that most middle managers are prepared to support change efforts even if doing so involves additional work and uncertainty and puts their jobs at risk. However, they resist change because they don't have sufficient input in shaping those initiatives. Too often, they lack the tools, the language, and the forums in which to express legitimate concerns about the design and implementation of change projects. That's where a standard, quantitative, and simple framework comes in. By enabling frank conversations at all levels within organizations, the DICE framework helps people do the right thing by change.

Originally published in October 2005. Reprint R0510G

Why Change Programs Don't Produce Change

by Michael Beer, Russell A. Eisenstat, and Bert Spector

IN THE MID-1980S, THE NEW CEO of a major international bank—call it U.S. Financial—announced a companywide change effort. Deregulation was posing serious competitive challenges—challenges to which the bank's traditional hierarchical organization was ill-suited to respond. The only solution was to change fundamentally how the company operated. And the place to begin was at the top.

The CEO held a retreat with his top 15 executives where they painstakingly reviewed the bank's purpose and culture. He published a mission statement and hired a new vice president for human resources from a company well-known for its excellence in managing people. And in a quick succession of moves, he established companywide programs to push change down through the organization: a new organizational structure, a performance appraisal system, a pay-for-performance compensation plan, training programs to turn managers into "change agents," and quarterly attitude surveys to chart the progress of the change effort.

As much as these steps sound like a textbook case in organizational transformation, there was one big problem: two years after the CEO launched the change program, virtually nothing in the way of actual changes in organizational behavior had occurred. What had gone wrong?

The answer is "everything." Every one of the assumptions the CEO made—about who should lead the change effort, what needed changing, and how to go about doing it—was wrong.

U.S. Financial's story reflects a common problem. Faced with changing markets and increased competition, more and more companies are struggling to reestablish their dominance, regain market share, and in some cases, ensure their survival. Many have come to understand that the key to competitive success is to transform the way they function. They are reducing reliance on managerial authority, formal rules and procedures, and narrow divisions of work. And they are creating teams, sharing information, and delegating responsibility and accountability far down the hierarchy. In effect, companies are moving from the hierarchical and bureaucratic model of organization that has characterized corporations since World War II to what we call the task-driven organization where what has to be done governs who works with whom and who leads.

But while senior managers understand the necessity of change to cope with new competitive realities, they often misunderstand what it takes to bring it about. They tend to share two assumptions with the CEO of U.S. Financial: that promulgating companywide programs—mission statements, "corporate culture" programs, training courses, quality circles, and new pay-for-performance systems—will transform organizations, and that employee behavior is changed by altering a company's formal structure and systems.

In a four-year study of organizational change at six large corporations (see the sidebar, "Tracking Corporate Change"; the names are fictitious), we found that exactly the opposite is true: the greatest obstacle to revitalization is the idea that it comes about through companywide change programs, particularly when a corporate staff group such as human resources sponsors them. We call this "the fallacy of programmatic change." Just as important, formal organization structure and systems cannot lead a corporate renewal process.

While in some companies, wave after wave of programs rolled across the landscape with little positive impact, in others, more successful transformations did take place. They usually started at the periphery of the corporation in a few plants and divisions far from

Idea in Brief

Two years after launching a change program to counter competitive threats, a bank CEO realized his effort had produced . . . no change. Surprising, since he and his top executives had reviewed the company's purpose and culture, published a mission statement, and launched programs (e.g., pay for-performance compensation) designed to push change throughout the organization.

But revitalization doesn't come from the top. It starts at an organization's periphery, led by unit managers creating ad hoc arrangements to solve concrete problems. Through **task alignment**—directing employees' responsibilities and relationships toward the company's central competitive task—these managers focus energy on *work,* not abstractions like "empowerment" or "culture."

Senior managers' role in this process? Specify the company's desired *general* direction, without dictating solutions. Then spread the lessons of revitalized units throughout the company.

corporate headquarters. And they were led by the general managers of those units, not by the CEO or corporate staff people.

The general managers did not focus on formal structures and systems; they created ad hoc organizational arrangements to solve concrete business problems. By aligning employee roles, responsibilities, and relationships to address the organization's most important competitive task—a process we call "task alignment"—they focused energy for change on the work itself, not on abstractions such as "participation" or "culture." Unlike the CEO at U.S. Financial, they didn't employ massive training programs or rely on speeches and mission statements. Instead, we saw that general managers carefully developed the change process through a sequence of six basic managerial interventions.

Once general managers understand the logic of this sequence, they don't have to wait for senior management to start a process of organizational revitalization. There is a lot they can do even without support from the top. Of course, having a CEO or other senior managers who are committed to change does make a difference—and when it comes to changing an entire organization, such support is

Idea in Practice

Successful change requires commitment, coordination, and competency.

1. Mobilize commitment to change through joint diagnosis of problems

Example: Navigation Devices had never made a profit or high-quality, cost-competitive product—because top-down decisions ignored cross-functional coordination.To change this,a new general manager had his *entire* team broadly assess the business. Then, his task force of engineers, production workers, managers, and union officials visited successful manufacturing organizations to identify improvement ideas. One plant's *team* approach impressed them, illuminated their own problem, and suggested a solution. Commitment to change intensified.

2. Develop a shared vision of how to organize for competitiveness

Remove functional and hierarchical barriers to information sharing and problem solving—by changing roles and responsibilities, not titles or compensation.

Example: Navigation's task force proposed developing products through cross-functional teams. A larger team refined this model and presented it to all employees—who supported it because it stemmed from their own analysis of their business problems.

3. Foster consensus for the new vision, competence to enact it, and cohesion to advance it

This requires the general manager's strong leadership.

essential. But top management's role in the change process is very different from that which the CEO played at U.S. Financial.

Grass-roots change presents senior managers with a paradox: directing a "nondirective" change process. The most effective senior managers in our study recognized their limited power to mandate corporate renewal from the top. Instead, they defined their roles as creating a climate for change, then spreading the lessons of both successes and failures. Put another way, they specified the general direction in which the company should move without insisting on specific solutions.

In the early phases of a companywide change process, any senior manager can play this role. Once grass-roots change reaches a critical mass, however, the CEO has to be ready to transform his or her

Example: Navigation's general manager fostered *consensus* by supporting those who were committed to change and offering outplacement and counseling to those who weren't; *competence* by providing requested training; and *cohesion* by redeploying managers who couldn't function in the new organization. Change accelerated.

4. Spread revitalization to all departments—without pushing from the top

Example: Navigation's new team structure required engineers to collaborate with production workers. Encouraged to develop their own approach to teamwork and coordination, the engineers selected matrix management. People willingly learned needed skills and attitudes, because the new structure was *their* choice.

5. Institutionalize revitalization through formal policies, systems, and structures . . . only *after* your new approach is up and running.

Example: Navigation boosted its profits—without changing reporting relationships, evaluation procedures, or compensation. Only then did the general manager alter formal structures; e.g., eliminating a VP so that engineering and manufacturing reported directly to him.

6. Monitor the revitalization process, adjusting in response to problems

Example: At Navigation, an oversight team of managers, a union leader, an engineer, and a financial analyst kept watch over the change process—continually learning, adapting, and strengthening the commitment to change.

own work unit as well—the top team composed of key business heads and corporate staff heads. At this point, the company's structure and systems must be put into alignment with the new management practices that have developed at the periphery. Otherwise, the tension between dynamic units and static top management will cause the change process to break down.

We believe that an approach to change based on task alignment, starting at the periphery and moving steadily toward the corporate core, is the most effective way to achieve enduring organizational change. This is not to say that change can never start at the top, but it is uncommon and too risky as a deliberate strategy. Change is about learning. It is a rare CEO who knows in advance the fine-grained details of organizational change that the many diverse units of a large corporation demand. Moreover, most of today's senior executives developed in an era in which top-down hierarchy was the primary means for organizing and managing. They must learn from innovative approaches coming from younger unit managers closer to the action.

The Fallacy of Programmatic Change

Most change programs don't work because they are guided by a theory of change that is fundamentally flawed. The common belief is that the place to begin is with the knowledge and attitudes of individuals. Changes in attitudes, the theory goes, lead to changes in individual behavior. And changes in individual behavior, repeated by many people, will result in organizational change. According to this model, change is like a conversion experience. Once people "get religion," changes in their behavior will surely follow.

This theory gets the change process exactly backward. In fact, individual behavior is powerfully shaped by the organizational roles that people play. The most effective way to change behavior, therefore, is to put people into a new organizational context, which imposes new roles, responsibilities, and relationships on them. This creates a situation that, in a sense, "forces" new attitudes and behaviors on people. (See the table, "Contrasting assumptions about change.")

One way to think about this challenge is in terms of three interrelated factors required for corporate revitalization. *Coordination* or teamwork is especially important if an organization is to discover and act on cost, quality, and product development opportunities. The production and sale of innovative, high-quality, low-cost products (or services) depend on close coordination among marketing, product design, and manufacturing departments, as well as between labor and management. High levels of *commitment* are essential for the effort, initiative, and cooperation that coordinated action demands. New *competencies* such as knowledge of the business as a whole, analytical skills, and interpersonal skills are necessary if people are to identify and solve problems as a team. If any of these elements are missing, the change process will break down.

Tracking Corporate Change

WHICH STRATEGIES FOR CORPORATE change work, and which do not? We sought the answers in a comprehensive study of 12 large companies where top management was attempting to revitalize the corporation. Based on preliminary research, we identified 6 for in-depth analysis: 5 manufacturing companies and 1 large international bank. All had revenues between $4 billion and $10 billion. We studied 26 plants and divisions in these 6 companies and conducted hundreds of interviews with human resource managers; line managers engaged in change efforts at plants, branches, or business units; workers and union leaders; and, finally, top management.

Based on this material, we ranked the 6 companies according to the success with which they had managed the revitalization effort. Were there significant improvements in interfunctional coordination, decision making, work organizations, and concern for people? Research has shown that in the long term, the quality of these 4 factors will influence performance. We did not define success in terms of improved financial performance because, in the short run, corporate financial performance is influenced by many situational factors unrelated to the change process.

To corroborate our rankings of the companies, we also administered a standardized questionnaire in each company to understand how employers viewed the unfolding change process. Respondents rated their companies on a scale of 1 to 5. A score of 3 meant that no change had taken place; a score below 3 meant that, in the employee's judgment, the organization had actually gotten worse. As the table suggests, with one exception—the company we call Livingston Electronics—employees' perceptions of how much their

Researchers and employees—similar conclusions

Extent of revitalization

Company	**Ranked by researchers**	**Rated by employees**	
		Average	*Standard deviation*
General Products	1	4.04	.35
Fairweather	2	3.58	.45
Livingston Electronics	3	3.61	.76
Scranton Steel	4	3.30	.65
Continental Glass	5	2.96	.83
U.S. Financial	6	2.78	1.07

Tracking Corporate Change (continued)

companies had changed were identical to ours. And Livingston's relatively high standard of deviation (which measures the degree of consensus among employees about the outcome of the change effort) indicates that within the company there was considerable disagreement as to just how successful revitalization had been.

The problem with most companywide change programs is that they address only one or, at best, two of these factors. Just because a company issues a philosophy statement about teamwork doesn't mean its employees necessarily know what teams to form or how to function within them to improve coordination. A corporate reorganization may change the boxes on a formal organization chart but not provide the necessary attitudes and skills to make the new structure work. A pay-for-performance system may force managers to differentiate better performers from poorer ones, but it doesn't help them internalize new standards by which to judge subordinates' performances. Nor does it teach them how to deal effectively with

Contrasting assumptions about change

Programmatic change	Task alignment
Problems in behavior are a function of individual knowledge, attitudes, and beliefs.	Individual knowledge, attitudes and beliefs are shaped by recurring patterns of behavioral interactions.
The primary target of renewal should be the content of attitudes and ideas; actual behavior should be secondary.	The primary target of renewal should be behavior; attitudes and ideas should be secondary.
Behavior can be isolated and changed individually.	Problems in behavior come from a circular pattern, but the effects of the organizational system on the individual are greater than those of the individual on the system.
The target for renewal should be at the individual level.	The target for renewal should be at the level of roles, responsibilities, and relationships.

performance problems. Such programs cannot provide the cultural context (role models from whom to learn) that people need to develop new competencies, so ultimately they fail to create organizational change.

Similarly, training programs may target competence, but rarely do they change a company's patterns of coordination. Indeed, the excitement engendered in a good corporate training program frequently leads to increased frustration when employees get back on the job only to see their new skills go unused in an organization in which nothing else has changed. People end up seeing training as a waste of time, which undermines whatever commitment to change a program may have roused in the first place.

When one program doesn't work, senior managers, like the CEO at U.S. Financial, often try another, instituting a rapid progression of programs. But this only exacerbates the problem. Because they are designed to cover everyone and everything, programs end up covering nobody and nothing particularly well. They are so general and standardized that they don't speak to the day-to-day realities of particular units. Buzzwords like "quality," "participation," "excellence," "empowerment," and "leadership" become a substitute for a detailed understanding of the business.

And all these change programs also undermine the credibility of the change effort. Even when managers accept the potential value of a particular program for others—quality circles, for example, to solve a manufacturing problem—they may be confronted with another, more pressing business problem such as new product development. One-size-fits-all change programs take energy *away* from efforts to solve key business problems—which explains why so many general managers don't support programs, even when they acknowledge that their underlying principles may be useful.

This is not to state that training, changes in pay systems or organizational structure, or a new corporate philosophy are always inappropriate. All can play valuable roles in supporting an integrated change effort. The problems come when such programs are used in isolation as a kind of "magic bullet" to spread organizational change rapidly through the entire corporation. At their best, change programs of this sort are irrelevant. At their worst, they actually inhibit change. By promoting skepticism and cynicism, programmatic change can inoculate companies against the real thing.

Six Steps to Effective Change

Companies avoid the shortcomings of programmatic change by concentrating on "task alignment"—reorganizing employee roles, responsibilities, and relationships to solve specific business problems. Task alignment is easiest in small units—a plant, department, or business unit—where goals and tasks are clearly defined. Thus the chief problem for corporate change is how to promote task-aligned change across many diverse units.

We saw that general managers at the business unit or plant level can achieve task alignment through a sequence of six overlapping but distinctive steps, which we call the *critical path*. This path develops a self-reinforcing cycle of commitment, coordination, and competence. The sequence of steps is important because activities appropriate at one time are often counterproductive if started too early. Timing is everything in the management of change.

1. Mobilize commitment to change through joint diagnosis of business problems. As the term task alignment suggests, the starting point of any effective change effort is a clearly defined business problem. By helping people develop a shared diagnosis of what is wrong in an organization and what can and must be improved, a general manager mobilizes the initial commitment that is necessary to begin the change process.

Consider the case of a division we call Navigation Devices, a business unit of about 600 people set up by a large corporation to commercialize a product originally designed for the military market. When the new general manager took over, the division had been in operation for several years without ever making a profit. It had never been able to design and produce a high-quality, cost-competitive product. This was due largely to an organization in which decisions were made at the top, without proper involvement of or coordination with other functions.

The first step the new general manager took was to initiate a broad review of the business. Where the previous general manager had set strategy with the unit's marketing director alone, the new general manager included his entire management team. He also brought in outside consultants to help him and his managers function more effectively as a group.

Next, he formed a 20-person task force representing all the stakeholders in the organization—managers, engineers, production workers, and union officials. The group visited a number of successful manufacturing organizations in an attempt to identify what Navigation Devices might do to organize more effectively. One high-performance manufacturing plant in the task force's own company made a particularly strong impression. Not only did it highlight the problems at Navigation Devices but it also offered an alternative organizational model, based on teams, that captured the group's imagination. Seeing a different way of working helped strengthen the group's commitment to change.

The Navigation Devices task force didn't learn new facts from this process of joint diagnosis; everyone already knew the unit was losing money. But the group came to see clearly the organizational roots of the unit's inability to compete and, even more important, came to share a common understanding of the problem. The group also identified a potential organizational solution: to redesign the way it worked, using ad hoc teams to integrate the organization around the competitive task.

2. Develop a shared vision of how to organize and manage for competitiveness. Once a core group of people is committed to a particular analysis of the problem, the general manager can lead employees toward a task-aligned vision of the organization that defines new roles and responsibilities. These new arrangements will coordinate the flow of information and work across interdependent functions at all levels of the organization. But since they do not change formal structures and systems like titles or compensation, they encounter less resistance.

At Navigation Devices, the 20-person task force became the vehicle for this second stage. The group came up with a model of the organization in which cross-functional teams would accomplish all work, particularly new product development. A business-management team composed of the general manager and his staff would set the unit's strategic direction and review the work of lower level teams. Business-area teams would develop plans for specific markets. Product-development teams would manage new products from initial design to production. Production-process teams composed of engineers and production workers would identify and solve quality and cost problems in the plant. Finally, engineering-process teams would examine engineering methods and equipment. The teams got to the root of the unit's problems—functional and hierarchical barriers to sharing information and solving problems.

To create a consensus around the new vision, the general manager commissioned a still larger task force of about 90 employees from different levels and functions, including union and management, to refine the vision and obtain everyone's commitment to it. On a retreat away from the workplace, the group further refined the new organizational model and drafted a values statement, which it presented later to the entire Navigation Devices work force. The vision and the values statement made sense to Navigation Devices employees in a way many corporate mission statements never do—because it grew out of the organization's own analysis of real business problems. And it was built on a model for solving those problems that key stakeholders believed would work.

3. Foster consensus for the new vision, competence to enact it, and cohesion to move it along. Simply letting employees help develop a new vision is not enough to overcome resistance to change—or to foster the skills needed to make the new organization work. Not everyone can help in the design, and even those who do participate often do not fully appreciate what renewal will require until the new organization is actually in place. This is when strong leadership from the general manager is crucial. Commitment to change is always uneven. Some managers are enthusiastic; others are neutral or even antagonistic. At Navigation Devices, the general manager used what his subordinates termed the "velvet glove." He made it clear that the division was going to encourage employee involvement and the team approach. To managers who wanted to help him, he offered support. To those who did not, he offered outplacement and counseling.

Once an organization has defined new roles and responsibilities, people need to develop the competencies to make the new setup work. Actually, the very existence of the teams with their new goals and accountabilities will force learning. The changes in roles, responsibilities, and relationships foster new skills and attitudes. Changed patterns of coordination will also increase employee participation, collaboration, and information sharing.

But management also has to provide the right supports. At Navigation Devices, six resource people—three from the unit's human resource department and three from corporate headquarters—worked on the change project. Each team was assigned one internal consultant, who attended every meeting, to help people be effective team members. Once employees could see exactly what kinds of new skills they needed, they asked for formal training programs to develop those skills further. Since these courses grew directly out of the employees' own experiences, they were far more focused and useful than traditional training programs.

Some people, of course, just cannot or will not change, despite all the direction and support in the world. Step three is the appropriate time to replace those managers who cannot function in the new organization—after they have had a chance to prove themselves. Such decisions are rarely easy, and sometimes those people who have difficulty working in a participatory organization have extremely valuable specialized skills. Replacing them early in the change process, before they have worked in the new organization, is not only unfair to individuals; it can be demoralizing to the entire organization and can disrupt the change process. People's understanding of what kind of manager and worker the new organization demands grows slowly and only from the experience of seeing some individuals succeed and others fail.

Once employees have bought into a vision of what's necessary and have some understanding of what the new organization requires, they can accept the necessity of replacing or moving people who don't make the transition to the new way of working. Sometimes people are transferred to other parts of the company where technical expertise rather than the new competencies is the main requirement. When no alternatives exist, sometimes they leave the company through early retirement programs, for example. The act of replacing people can actually reinforce the organization's commitment to change by visibly demonstrating the general manager's commitment to the new way.

Some of the managers replaced at Navigation Devices were high up in the organization—for example, the vice president of operations, who oversaw the engineering and manufacturing departments. The new head of manufacturing was far more committed to change and skilled in leading a critical path change process. The result was speedier change throughout the manufacturing function.

4. Spread revitalization to all departments without pushing it from the top. With the new ad hoc organization for the unit in place, it is time to turn to the functional and staff departments that must interact with it. Members of teams cannot be effective unless the department from which they come is organized and managed in a way that supports their roles as full-fledged participants in team decisions. What this often means is that these departments will have to rethink their roles and authority in the organization.

At Navigation Devices, this process was seen most clearly in the engineering department. Production department managers were the most enthusiastic about the change effort; engineering managers were more hesitant. Engineering had always been king at Navigation Devices; engineers designed products to the military's specifications without much concern about whether manufacturing could easily build them or not. Once the new team structure was in place, however, engineers had to participate on product-development teams with production workers. This required them to re-examine their roles and rethink their approaches to organizing and managing their own department.

The impulse of many general managers faced with such a situation would be to force the issue—to announce, for example, that now all parts of the organization must manage by teams. The temptation to force newfound insights on the rest of the organization can be great, particularly when rapid change is needed, but it would be the same mistake that senior managers make when they try to push programmatic change throughout a company. It short-circuits the change process.

It's better to let each department "reinvent the wheel"—that is, to find its own way to the new organization. At Navigation Devices, each department was allowed to take the general concepts of coordination and teamwork and apply them to its particular situation. Engineering spent nearly a year agonizing over how to implement the team concept. The department conducted two surveys, held off-site meetings, and proposed, rejected, then accepted a matrix management structure before it finally got on board. Engineering's decision to move to matrix management was not surprising, but because it was its own choice, people committed themselves to learning the necessary new skills and attitudes.

5. Institutionalize revitalization through formal policies, systems, and structures. There comes a point where general managers have to consider how to institutionalize change so that the process continues even after they've moved on to other responsibilities. Step five is the time: the new approach has become entrenched, the right people are in place, and the team organization is up and running. Enacting changes in structures and systems any earlier tends to backfire. Take information systems. Creating a team structure means new information requirements. Why not have the MIS department create new systems that cut across traditional functional and departmental lines early in the change process? The problem is that without a well-developed understanding of information requirements, which can best be obtained by placing people on task-aligned teams, managers are likely to resist new systems as an imposition by the MIS department. Newly formed teams can often pull together enough information to get their work done without fancy new systems. It's better to hold off until everyone understands what the team's information needs are.

What's true for information systems is even more true for other formal structures and systems. Any formal system is going to have some disadvantages; none is perfect. These imperfections can be minimized, however, once people have worked in an ad hoc team structure and learned what interdependencies are necessary. Then employees will commit to them too.

Again, Navigation Devices is a good example. The revitalization of the unit was highly successful. Employees changed how they saw their roles and responsibilities and became convinced that change could actually make a difference. As a result, there were dramatic improvements in value added per employee, scrap reduction, quality, customer service, gross inventory per employee, and profits. And all this happened with almost no formal changes in reporting relationships, information systems, evaluation procedures, compensation, or control systems.

When the opportunity arose, the general manager eventually did make some changes in the formal organization. For example, when he moved the vice president of operations out of the organization, he eliminated the position altogether. Engineering and manufacturing reported directly to him from that point on. For the most part, however, the changes in performance at Navigation Devices were sustained by the general manager's expectations and the new norms for behavior.

6. Monitor and adjust strategies in response to problems in the revitalization process. The purpose of change is to create an asset that did not exist before—a learning organization capable of adapting to a changing competitive environment. The organization has to know how to continually monitor its behavior—in effect, to learn how to learn.

Some might say that this is the general manager's responsibility. But monitoring the change process needs to be shared, just as analyzing the organization's key business problem does.

At Navigation Devices, the general manager introduced several mechanisms to allow key constituents to help monitor the revitalization. An oversight team—composed of some crucial managers, a union leader, a secretary, an engineer, and an analyst from finance—kept continual watch over the process. Regular employee attitude surveys monitored behavior patterns. Planning teams were formed and reformed in response to new challenges. All these mechanisms created a long-term capacity for continual adaptation and learning.

The six-step process provides a way to elicit renewal without imposing it. When stakeholders become committed to a vision, they are willing to accept a new pattern of management—here the ad hoc team structure—that demands changes in their behavior. And as the employees discover that the new approach is more effective (which will happen only if the vision aligns with the core task), they have to grapple with personal and organizational changes they might otherwise resist. Finally, as improved coordination helps solve relevant problems, it will reinforce team behavior and produce a desire to learn new skills. This learning enhances effectiveness even further and results in an even stronger commitment to change. This mutually reinforcing cycle of improvements in commitment, coordination, and competence creates a growing sense of efficacy. It can continue as long as the ad hoc team structure is allowed to expand its role in running the business.

The Role of Top Management

To change an entire corporation, the change process we have described must be applied over and over again in many plants, branches, departments, and divisions. Orchestrating this company-wide change process is the first responsibility of senior management. Doing so successfully requires a delicate balance. Without explicit efforts by top management to promote conditions for change in individual units, only a few plants or divisions will attempt change, and those that do will remain isolated. The best senior manager leaders we studied held their subordinates responsible for starting a change process without specifying a particular approach.

Create a market for change. The most effective approach is to set demanding standards for all operations and then hold managers accountable to them. At our best-practice company, which we call General Products, senior managers developed ambitious product and operating standards. General managers unable to meet these product standards by a certain date had to scrap their products and take a sharp hit to their bottom lines. As long as managers understand that high standards are not arbitrary but are dictated by competitive forces, standards can generate enormous pressure for better performance, a key ingredient in mobilizing energy for change.

But merely increasing demands is not enough. Under pressure, most managers will seek to improve business performance by doing more of what they have always done—overmanage—rather than alter the fundamental way they organize. So, while senior managers increase demands, they should also hold managers accountable for fundamental changes in the way they use human resources.

For example, when plant managers at General Products complained about the impossibility of meeting new business standards, senior managers pointed them to the corporate organization-development department within human resources and emphasized that the plant managers would be held accountable for moving revitalization along. Thus top management had created a demand system for help with the new way of managing, and the human resource staff could support change without appearing to push a program.

Use successfully revitalized units as organizational models for the entire company. Another important strategy is to focus the company's attention on plants and divisions that have already begun experimenting with management innovations. These units become developmental laboratories for further innovation.

There are two ground rules for identifying such models. First, innovative units need support. They need the best managers to lead them, and they need adequate resources—for instance, skilled human resource people and external consultants. In the most successful companies that we studied, senior managers saw it as their responsibility to make resources available to leading-edge units. They did not leave it to the human resource function.

Second, because resources are always limited and the costs of failure high, it is crucial to identify those units with the likeliest chance of success. Successful management innovations can appear to be failures when the bottom line is devastated by environmental factors beyond the unit's control. The best models are in healthy markets.

Obviously, organizational models can serve as catalysts for change only if others are aware of their existence and are encouraged to learn from them. Many of our worst-practice companies had plants and divisions that were making substantial changes. The problem was, nobody knew about them. Corporate management had never bothered to highlight them as examples to follow. In the leading companies, visits, conferences, and educational programs facilitated learning from model units.

Develop career paths that encourage leadership development. Without strong leaders, units cannot make the necessary organizational changes, yet the scarcest resource available for revitalizing corporations is leadership. Corporate renewal depends as much on developing effective change leaders as it does on developing effective organizations. The personal learning associated with leadership development—or the realization by higher management that a manager does not have this capacity—cannot occur in the classroom. It only happens in an organization where the teamwork, high commitment, and new competencies we have discussed are already the norm.

The only way to develop the kind of leaders a changing organization needs is to make leadership an important criterion for promotion, and then manage people's careers to develop it. At our best-practice companies, managers were moved from job to job and from organization to organization based on their learning needs, not on their position in the hierarchy. Successful leaders were assigned to units that had been targeted for change. People who needed to sharpen their leadership skills were moved into the company's model units where those skills would be demanded and therefore learned. In effect, top management used leading-edge units as hothouses to develop revitalization leaders.

But what about the top management team itself? How important is it for the CEO and his or her direct reports to practice what they preach? It is not surprising—indeed, it's predictable—that in the early years of a corporate change effort, top managers' actions are often not consistent with their words. Such inconsistencies don't pose a major barrier to corporate change in the beginning, though consistency is obviously desirable. Senior managers can create a climate for grass-roots change without paying much attention to how they themselves operate and manage. And unit managers will tolerate this inconsistency so long as they can freely make changes in their own units in order to compete more effectively.

There comes a point, however, when addressing the inconsistencies becomes crucial. As the change process spreads, general managers in the ever-growing circle of revitalized units eventually demand changes from corporate staff groups and top management. As they discover how to manage differently in their own units, they bump up against constraints of policies and practices that corporate staff and top management have created. They also begin to see opportunities for better coordination between themselves and other parts of the company over which they have little control. At this point, corporate organization must be aligned with corporate strategy, and coordination between related but hitherto independent businesses improved for the benefit of the whole corporation.

None of the companies we studied had reached this "moment of truth." Even when corporate leaders intellectually understood the direction of change, they were just beginning to struggle with how they would change themselves and the company as a whole for a total corporate revitalization.

This last step in the process of corporate renewal is probably the most important. If the CEO and his or her management team do not ultimately apply to themselves what they have been encouraging their general managers to do, then the whole process can break down. The time to tackle the tough challenge of transforming companywide systems and structures comes finally at the end of the corporate change process.

At this point, senior managers must make an effort to adopt the team behavior, attitudes, and skills that they have demanded of others in earlier phases of change. Their struggle with behavior change will help sustain corporate renewal in three ways. It will promote the attitudes and behavior needed to coordinate diverse activities in the company; it will lend credibility to top management's continued espousal of change; and it will help the CEO identify and develop a successor who is capable of learning the new behaviors. Only such a manager can lead a corporation that can renew itself continually as competitive forces change.

Companies need a particular mind-set for managing change: one that emphasizes process over specific content, recognizes organization change as a unit-by-unit learning process rather than a series of programs, and acknowledges the payoffs that result from persistence over a long period of time as opposed to quick fixes. This mindset is difficult to maintain in an environment that presses for quarterly earnings, but we believe it is the only approach that will bring about successful renewal.

Originally published in November 1990. Reprint 90601

About the Contributors

MICHAEL BEER is the Cahners-Rabb Professor of Business Administration, Emeritus, at Harvard Business School.

RUSSELL A. EISENSTAT is a partner at TruePoint, a management consulting firm in Massachusetts, and a former professor at Harvard Business School.

DAVID A. GARVIN is the C. Roland Christensen Professor of Business Administration at Harvard Business School.

RONALD A. HEIFETZ codirects the Center for Public Leadership at Harvard University's Kennedy School of Government.

PAUL HEMP, formerly a senior editor of *Harvard Business Review,* is the global director of brand transformation at HCL Technologies.

ALAN JACKSON is a senior partner at The Boston Consulting Group.

PERRY KEENAN is a partner and managing director in The Boston Consulting Group's Chicago office.

ROBERT KEGAN is the William and Miriam Meehan Professor in Adult Learning and Professional Development at Harvard's Graduate School of Education.

W. CHAN KIM is the Boston Consulting Group Bruce D. Henderson Chaired Professor of Strategy and International Management at Insead in France.

JOHN P. KOTTER is the Konosuke Matsushita Professor of Leadership, Emeritus, at Harvard Business School.

LISA LASKOW LAHEY is the associate director of the Change Leadership Group at Harvard's Graduate School of Education.

MARTY LINSKY is a cofounder and partner at Cambridge Leadership Associates, a consulting firm in Boston.

RENÉE MAUBORGNE is the Insead Distinguished Fellow and a professor of strategy at Insead in France.

DEBRA E. MEYERSON is an associate professor of organizational behavior at Stanford University's School of Education.

NITIN NOHRIA is the dean of Harvard Business School.

MICHAEL A. ROBERTO is a professor of management at Bryant University in Smithfield, Rhode Island.

HAROLD L. SIRKIN is a Chicago-based senior partner and managing director at The Boston Consulting Group, a global management consulting firm.

THOMAS A. STEWART, formerly the editor of *Harvard Business Review,* is the chief marketing and knowledge officer at Booz & Company in New York.

BERT SPECTOR is an associate professor of organizational behavior at Northeastern University in Boston.

Index

Harvard Business Review
136 Marvel's Blockbuster Machine
94 Digital Doesn't Have to Be Disruptive
116 When a Colleague is Grieving
The AI-Powered Organization
The main challenge isn't technology. It's culture.
62

HBR'S 10 MUST READS

On Making **Smart Decisions**

HBR's 10 Must Reads series is the definitive collection of ideas and best practices for aspiring and experienced leaders alike. These books offer essential reading selected from the pages of *Harvard Business Review* on topics critical to the success of every manager.

Titles include:

HBR's 10 Must Reads on Change Management
HBR's 10 Must Reads on Collaboration
HBR's 10 Must Reads on Communication
HBR's 10 Must Reads on Innovation
HBR's 10 Must Reads on Leadership
HBR's 10 Must Reads on Making Smart Decisions
HBR's 10 Must Reads on Managing People
HBR's 10 Must Reads on Managing Yourself
HBR's 10 Must Reads on Strategic Marketing
HBR's 10 Must Reads on Strategy
HBR's 10 Must Reads on Teams
HBR's 10 Must Reads: The Essentials

HBR'S 10 MUST READS

On Making Smart Decisions

HARVARD BUSINESS REVIEW PRESS
Boston, Massachusetts

Printed in the United States of America
20 19 18 17 16

The web addresses referenced in this book were live and correct at the time of book's publication but may be subject to change.

Library of Congress Cataloging-in-Publication Data

HBR's 10 must reads on making smart decisions.
pages cm.—(HBR's 10 must reads series)
ISBN 978-1-4221-8989-4 (alk. paper)
1. Decision making. I. Harvard business review. II. Title: HBR's ten must reads on making smart decisions.
HD30.23.H39 2013
658.4'03—dc23

2012045971

The paper used in this publication meets the requirements of the American National Standard for Permanence of Paper for Publications and Documents in Libraries and Archives Z39.48-1992.

Contents

HBR'S 10 MUST READS

On Making **Smart Decisions**

The Hidden Traps in Decision Making

by John S. Hammond, Ralph L. Keeney, and Howard Raiffa

MAKING DECISIONS IS THE MOST important job of any executive. It's also the toughest and the riskiest. Bad decisions can damage a business and a career, sometimes irreparably. So where do bad decisions come from? In many cases, they can be traced back to the way the decisions were made—the alternatives were not clearly defined, the right information was not collected, the costs and benefits were not accurately weighed. But sometimes the fault lies not in the decision-making process but rather in the mind of the decision maker. The way the human brain works can sabotage our decisions.

Researchers have been studying the way our minds function in making decisions for half a century. This research, in the laboratory and in the field, has revealed that we use unconscious routines to cope with the complexity inherent in most decisions. These routines, known as *heuristics,* serve us well in most situations. In judging distance, for example, our minds frequently rely on a heuristic that equates clarity with proximity. The clearer an object appears, the closer we judge it to be. The fuzzier it appears, the farther away we assume it must be. This simple mental shortcut helps us to make the continuous stream of distance judgments required to navigate the world.

Yet, like most heuristics, it is not foolproof. On days that are hazier than normal, our eyes will tend to trick our minds into thinking that things are more distant than they actually are. Because the resulting distortion poses few dangers for most of us, we can safely ignore it. For airline pilots, though, the distortion can be catastrophic. That's why pilots are trained to use objective measures of distance in addition to their vision.

Researchers have identified a whole series of such flaws in the way we think in making decisions. Some, like the heuristic for clarity, are sensory misperceptions. Others take the form of biases. Others appear simply as irrational anomalies in our thinking. What makes all these traps so dangerous is their invisibility. Because they are hardwired into our thinking process, we fail to recognize them—even as we fall right into them.

For executives, whose success hinges on the many day-to-day decisions they make or approve, the psychological traps are especially dangerous. They can undermine everything from new-product development to acquisition and divestiture strategy to succession planning. While no one can rid his or her mind of these ingrained flaws, anyone can follow the lead of airline pilots and learn to understand the traps and compensate for them.

In this article, we examine a number of well-documented psychological traps that are particularly likely to undermine business decisions. In addition to reviewing the causes and manifestations of these traps, we offer some specific ways managers can guard against them. It's important to remember, though, that the best defense is always awareness. Executives who attempt to familiarize themselves with these traps and the diverse forms they take will be better able to ensure that the decisions they make are sound and that the recommendations proposed by subordinates or associates are reliable.

The Anchoring Trap

How would you answer these two questions?

- Is the population of Turkey greater than 35 million?
- What's your best estimate of Turkey's population?

Idea in Brief

Bad decisions can often be traced back to the way the decisions were made—the alternatives were not clearly defined, the right information was not collected, the costs and benefits were not accurately weighed. But sometimes the fault lies not in the decision-making process but rather in the mind of the decision maker: The way the human brain works can sabotage the choices we make. In this article, first published in 1998, John S. Hammond, Ralph L. Keeney, and Howard Raiffa examine eight psychological traps that can affect the way we make business decisions. The anchoring trap leads us to give disproportionate weight to the first information we receive. The status-quo trap biases us toward maintaining the current situation—even when better alternatives exist. The sunk-cost trap inclines us to perpetuate the mistakes of the past. The confirming-evidence trap leads us to seek out information supporting an existing predilection and to discount opposing information. The framing trap occurs when we misstate a problem, undermining the entire decision-making process. The overconfidence trap makes us overestimate the accuracy of our forecasts. The prudence trap leads us to be overcautious when we make estimates about uncertain events. And the recallability trap prompts us to give undue weight to recent, dramatic events. The best way to avoid all the traps is awareness: forewarned is forearmed. But executives can also take other simple steps to protect themselves and their organizations from these mental lapses to ensure that their important business decisions are sound and reliable.

If you're like most people, the figure of 35 million cited in the first question (a figure we chose arbitrarily) influenced your answer to the second question. Over the years, we've posed those questions to many groups of people. In half the cases, we used 35 million in the first question; in the other half, we used 100 million. Without fail, the answers to the second question increase by many millions when the larger figure is used in the first question. This simple test illustrates the common and often pernicious mental phenomenon known as *anchoring*. When considering a decision, the mind gives disproportionate weight to the first information it receives. Initial impressions, estimates, or data anchor subsequent thoughts and judgments.

Anchors take many guises. They can be as simple and seemingly innocuous as a comment offered by a colleague or a statistic appearing in the morning newspaper. They can be as insidious as a stereotype about a person's skin color, accent, or dress. In business, one of the most common types of anchors is a past event or trend. A marketer attempting to project the sales of a product for the coming year often begins by looking at the sales volumes for past years. The old numbers become anchors, which the forecaster then adjusts based on other factors. This approach, while it may lead to a reasonably accurate estimate, tends to give too much weight to past events and not enough weight to other factors. In situations characterized by rapid changes in the marketplace, historical anchors can lead to poor forecasts and, in turn, misguided choices.

Because anchors can establish the terms on which a decision will be made, they are often used as a bargaining tactic by savvy negotiators. Consider the experience of a large consulting firm that was searching for new office space in San Francisco. Working with a commercial real-estate broker, the firm's partners identified a building that met all their criteria, and they set up a meeting with the building's owners. The owners opened the meeting by laying out the terms of a proposed contract: a ten-year lease; an initial monthly price of $2.50 per square foot; annual price increases at the prevailing inflation rate; all interior improvements to be the tenant's responsibility; an option for the tenant to extend the lease for ten additional years under the same terms. Although the price was at the high end of current market rates, the consultants made a relatively modest counteroffer. They proposed an initial price in the midrange of market rates and asked the owners to share in the renovation expenses, but they accepted all the other terms. The consultants could have been much more aggressive and creative in their counterproposal—reducing the initial price to the low end of market rates, adjusting rates biennially rather than annually, putting a cap on the increases, defining different terms for extending the lease, and so forth—but their thinking was guided by the owners' initial proposal. The consultants had fallen into the anchoring trap, and as a result, they ended up paying a lot more for the space than they had to.

What can you do about it?

The effect of anchors in decision making has been documented in thousands of experiments. Anchors influence the decisions not only of managers, but also of accountants and engineers, bankers and lawyers, consultants and stock analysts. No one can avoid their influence; they're just too widespread. But managers who are aware of the dangers of anchors can reduce their impact by using the following techniques:

- Always view a problem from different perspectives. Try using alternative starting points and approaches rather than sticking with the first line of thought that occurs to you.
- Think about the problem on your own before consulting others to avoid becoming anchored by their ideas.
- Be open-minded. Seek information and opinions from a variety of people to widen your frame of reference and to push your mind in fresh directions.
- Be careful to avoid anchoring your advisers, consultants, and others from whom you solicit information and counsel. Tell them as little as possible about your own ideas, estimates, and tentative decisions. If you reveal too much, your own preconceptions may simply come back to you.
- Be particularly wary of anchors in negotiations. Think through your position before any negotiation begins in order to avoid being anchored by the other party's initial proposal. At the same time, look for opportunities to use anchors to your own advantage—if you're the seller, for example, suggest a high, but defensible, price as an opening gambit.

The Status-Quo Trap

We all like to believe that we make decisions rationally and objectively. But the fact is, we all carry biases, and those biases influence the choices we make. Decision makers display, for example, a strong bias toward alternatives that perpetuate the status quo. On a broad scale, we can see this tendency whenever a radically new product is introduced. The first automobiles, revealingly called "horseless carriages," looked very much like the buggies they replaced. The first "electronic newspapers" appearing on the World Wide Web looked very much like their print precursors.

On a more familiar level, you may have succumbed to this bias in your personal financial decisions. People sometimes, for example, inherit shares of stock that they would never have bought themselves. Although it would be a straightforward, inexpensive proposition to sell those shares and put the money into a different investment, a surprising number of people don't sell. They find the status quo comfortable, and they avoid taking action that would upset it. "Maybe I'll rethink it later," they say. But "later" is usually never.

The source of the status-quo trap lies deep within our psyches, in our desire to protect our egos from damage. Breaking from the status quo means taking action, and when we take action, we take responsibility, thus opening ourselves to criticism and to regret. Not surprisingly, we naturally look for reasons to do nothing. Sticking with the status quo represents, in most cases, the safer course because it puts us at less psychological risk.

Many experiments have shown the magnetic attraction of the status quo. In one, a group of people were randomly given one of two gifts of approximately the same value—half received a mug, the other half a Swiss chocolate bar. They were then told that they could easily exchange the gift they received for the other gift. While you might expect that about half would have wanted to make the exchange, only one in ten actually did. The status quo exerted its power even though it had been arbitrarily established only minutes before.

Other experiments have shown that the more choices you are given, the more pull the status quo has. More people will, for instance, choose the status quo when there are two alternatives to it rather than one: A and B instead of just A. Why? Choosing between A and B requires additional effort; selecting the status quo avoids that effort.

In business, where sins of commission (doing something) tend to be punished much more severely than sins of omission (doing nothing), the status quo holds a particularly strong attraction. Many mergers, for example, founder because the acquiring company avoids taking swift action to impose a new, more appropriate management structure on the acquired company. "Let's not rock the boat right now," the typical reasoning goes. "Let's wait until the situation stabilizes." But as time passes, the existing structure becomes more entrenched, and altering it becomes harder, not easier. Having failed to seize the occasion when change would have been expected, management finds itself stuck with the status quo.

What can you do about it?

First of all, remember that in any given decision, maintaining the status quo may indeed be the best choice, but you don't want to choose it just because it is comfortable. Once you become aware of the status-quo trap, you can use these techniques to lessen its pull:

- Always remind yourself of your objectives and examine how they would be served by the status quo. You may find that elements of the current situation act as barriers to your goals.
- Never think of the status quo as your only alternative. Identify other options and use them as counterbalances, carefully evaluating all the pluses and minuses.
- Ask yourself whether you would choose the status-quo alternative if, in fact, it weren't the status quo.
- Avoid exaggerating the effort or cost involved in switching from the status quo.
- Remember that the desirability of the status quo will change over time. When comparing alternatives, always evaluate them in terms of the future as well as the present.
- If you have several alternatives that are superior to the status quo, don't default to the status quo just because you're having a hard time picking the best alternative. Force yourself to choose.

The Sunk-Cost Trap

Another of our deep-seated biases is to make choices in a way that justifies past choices, even when the past choices no longer seem valid. Most of us have fallen into this trap. We may have refused, for example, to sell a stock or a mutual fund at a loss, forgoing other, more attractive investments. Or we may have poured enormous effort into improving the performance of an employee whom we knew we shouldn't have hired in the first place. Our past decisions become what economists term *sunk costs*—old investments of time or money that are now irrecoverable. We know, rationally, that sunk costs are irrelevant to the present decision, but nevertheless they prey on our minds, leading us to make inappropriate decisions.

Why can't people free themselves from past decisions? Frequently, it's because they are unwilling, consciously or not, to admit to a mistake. Acknowledging a poor decision in one's personal life may be purely a private matter, involving only one's self-esteem, but in business, a bad decision is often a very public matter, inviting critical comments from colleagues or bosses. If you fire a poor performer whom you hired, you're making a public admission of poor judgment. It seems psychologically safer to let him or her stay on, even though that choice only compounds the error.

The sunk-cost bias shows up with disturbing regularity in banking, where it can have particularly dire consequences. When a borrower's business runs into trouble, a lender will often advance additional funds in hopes of providing the business with some breathing room to recover. If the business does have a good chance of coming back, that's a wise investment. Otherwise, it's just throwing good money after bad.

One of us helped a major U.S. bank recover after it made many bad loans to foreign businesses. We found that the bankers responsible for originating the problem loans were far more likely to advance additional funds—repeatedly, in many cases—than were bankers who took over the accounts after the original loans were made. Too often, the original bankers' strategy—and loans—ended in failure.

Having been trapped by an escalation of commitment, they had tried, consciously or unconsciously, to protect their earlier, flawed decisions. They had fallen victim to the sunk-cost bias. The bank finally solved the problem by instituting a policy requiring that a loan be immediately reassigned to another banker as soon as any problem arose. The new banker was able to take a fresh, unbiased look at the merit of offering more funds.

Sometimes a corporate culture reinforces the sunk-cost trap. If the penalties for making a decision that leads to an unfavorable outcome are overly severe, managers will be motivated to let failed projects drag on endlessly—in the vain hope that they'll somehow be able to transform them into successes. Executives should recognize that, in an uncertain world where unforeseeable events are common, good decisions can sometimes lead to bad outcomes. By acknowledging that some good ideas will end in failure, executives will encourage people to cut their losses rather than let them mount.

What can you do about it?

For all decisions with a history, you will need to make a conscious effort to set aside any sunk costs—whether psychological or economic—that will muddy your thinking about the choice at hand. Try these techniques:

- Seek out and listen carefully to the views of people who were uninvolved with the earlier decisions and who are hence unlikely to be committed to them.
- Examine why admitting to an earlier mistake distresses you. If the problem lies in your own wounded self-esteem, deal with it head-on. Remind yourself that even smart choices can have bad consequences, through no fault of the original decision maker, and that even the best and most experienced managers are not immune to errors in judgment. Remember the wise words of Warren Buffett: "When you find yourself in a hole, the best thing you can do is stop digging."

- Be on the lookout for the influence of sunk-cost biases in the decisions and recommendations made by your subordinates. Reassign responsibilities when necessary.
- Don't cultivate a failure-fearing culture that leads employees to perpetuate their mistakes. In rewarding people, look at the quality of their decision making (taking into account what was known at the time their decisions were made), not just the quality of the outcomes.

The Confirming-Evidence Trap

Imagine that you're the president of a successful midsize U.S. manufacturer considering whether to call off a planned plant expansion. For a while you've been concerned that your company won't be able to sustain the rapid pace of growth of its exports. You fear that the value of the U.S. dollar will strengthen in coming months, making your goods more costly for overseas consumers and dampening demand. But before you put the brakes on the plant expansion, you decide to call up an acquaintance, the chief executive of a similar company that recently mothballed a new factory, to check her reasoning. She presents a strong case that other currencies are about to weaken significantly against the dollar. What do you do?

You'd better not let that conversation be the clincher, because you've probably just fallen victim to the confirming-evidence bias. This bias leads us to seek out information that supports our existing instinct or point of view while avoiding information that contradicts it. What, after all, did you expect your acquaintance to give, other than a strong argument in favor of her own decision? The confirming-evidence bias not only affects where we go to collect evidence but also how we interpret the evidence we do receive, leading us to give too much weight to supporting information and too little to conflicting information.

In one psychological study of this phenomenon, two groups—one opposed to and one supporting capital punishment—each read two reports of carefully conducted research on the effectiveness of the death penalty as a deterrent to crime. One report concluded that the death penalty was effective; the other concluded it was not. Despite being exposed to solid scientific information supporting counterarguments, the members of both groups became even more convinced of the validity of their own position after reading both reports. They automatically accepted the supporting information and dismissed the conflicting information.

There are two fundamental psychological forces at work here. The first is our tendency to subconsciously decide what we want to do before we figure out why we want to do it. The second is our inclination to be more engaged by things we like than by things we dislike—a tendency well documented even in babies. Naturally, then, we are drawn to information that supports our subconscious leanings.

What can you do about it?

It's not that you shouldn't make the choice you're subconsciously drawn to. It's just that you want to be sure it's the smart choice. You need to put it to the test. Here's how:

- Always check to see whether you are examining all the evidence with equal rigor. Avoid the tendency to accept confirming evidence without question.
- Get someone you respect to play devil's advocate, to argue against the decision you're contemplating. Better yet, build the counterarguments yourself. What's the strongest reason to do something else? The second strongest reason? The third? Consider the position with an open mind.
- Be honest with yourself about your motives. Are you really gathering information to help you make a smart choice, or are you just looking for evidence confirming what you think you'd like to do?
- In seeking the advice of others, don't ask leading questions that invite confirming evidence. And if you find that an adviser always seems to support your point of view, find a new adviser. Don't surround yourself with yes-men.

The Framing Trap

The first step in making a decision is to frame the question. It's also one of the most dangerous steps. The way a problem is framed can profoundly influence the choices you make. In a case involving automobile insurance, for example, framing made a $200 million difference. To reduce insurance costs, two neighboring states, New Jersey and Pennsylvania, made similar changes in their laws. Each state gave drivers a new option: By accepting a limited right to sue, they could lower their premiums. But the two states framed the choice in very different ways: In New Jersey, you automatically got the limited right to sue unless you specified otherwise; in Pennsylvania, you got the full right to sue unless you specified otherwise. The different frames established different status quos, and, not surprisingly, most consumers defaulted to the status quo. As a result, in New Jersey about 80% of drivers chose the limited right to sue, but in Pennsylvania only 25% chose it. Because of the way it framed the choice, Pennsylvania failed to gain approximately $200 million in expected insurance and litigation savings.

The framing trap can take many forms, and as the insurance example shows, it is often closely related to other psychological traps. A frame can establish the status quo or introduce an anchor. It can highlight sunk costs or lead you toward confirming evidence. Decision researchers have documented two types of frames that distort decision making with particular frequency.

Frames as gains versus losses

In a study patterned after a classic experiment by decision researchers Daniel Kahneman and Amos Tversky, one of us posed the following problem to a group of insurance professionals:

> You are a marine property adjuster charged with minimizing the loss of cargo on three insured barges that sank yesterday off the coast of Alaska. Each barge holds $200,000 worth of cargo, which will be lost if not salvaged within 72 hours. The owner of a

local marine-salvage company gives you two options, both of which will cost the same:

Plan A: This plan will save the cargo of one of the three barges, worth $200,000.

Plan B: This plan has a one-third probability of saving the cargo on all three barges, worth $600,000, but has a two-thirds probability of saving nothing.

Which plan would you choose?

If you are like 71% of the respondents in the study, you chose the "less risky" Plan A, which will save one barge for sure. Another group in the study, however, was asked to choose between alternatives C and D:

Plan C: This plan will result in the loss of two of the three cargoes, worth $400,000.

Plan D: This plan has a two-thirds probability of resulting in the loss of all three cargoes and the entire $600,000 but has a one-third probability of losing no cargo.

Faced with this choice, 80% of these respondents preferred Plan D.

The pairs of alternatives are, of course, precisely equivalent—Plan A is the same as Plan C, and Plan B is the same as Plan D—they've just been framed in different ways. The strikingly different responses reveal that people are risk averse when a problem is posed in terms of gains (barges saved) but risk seeking when a problem is posed in terms of avoiding losses (barges lost). Furthermore, they tend to adopt the frame as it is presented to them rather than restating the problem in their own way.

Framing with different reference points

The same problem can also elicit very different responses when frames use different reference points. Let's say you have $2,000 in your checking account and you are asked the following question:

Would you accept a fifty-fifty chance of either losing $300 or winning $500?

Would you accept the chance? What if you were asked this question:

Would you prefer to keep your checking account balance of $2,000 or to accept a fifty-fifty chance of having either $1,700 or $2,500 in your account?

Once again, the two questions pose the same problem. While your answers to both questions should, rationally speaking, be the same, studies have shown that many people would refuse the fifty-fifty chance in the first question but accept it in the second. Their different reactions result from the different reference points presented in the two frames. The first frame, with its reference point of zero, emphasizes incremental gains and losses, and the thought of losing triggers a conservative response in many people's minds. The second frame, with its reference point of $2,000, puts things into perspective by emphasizing the real financial impact of the decision.

What can you do about it?

A poorly framed problem can undermine even the best-considered decision. But any adverse effect of framing can be limited by taking the following precautions:

- Don't automatically accept the initial frame, whether it was formulated by you or by someone else. Always try to reframe the problem in various ways. Look for distortions caused by the frames.
- Try posing problems in a neutral, redundant way that combines gains and losses or embraces different reference points. For example: Would you accept a fifty-fifty chance of either losing $300, resulting in a bank balance of $1,700, or winning $500, resulting in a bank balance of $2,500?
- Think hard throughout your decision-making process about the framing of the problem. At points throughout the process, particularly near the end, ask yourself how your thinking might change if the framing changed.

- When others recommend decisions, examine the way they framed the problem. Challenge them with different frames.

The Estimating and Forecasting Traps

Most of us are adept at making estimates about time, distance, weight, and volume. That's because we're constantly making judgments about these variables and getting quick feedback about the accuracy of those judgments. Through daily practice, our minds become finely calibrated.

Making estimates or forecasts about uncertain events, however, is a different matter. While managers continually make such estimates and forecasts, they rarely get clear feedback about their accuracy. If you judge, for example, that the likelihood of the price of oil falling to less than $15 a barrel one year hence is about 40% and the price does indeed fall to that level, you can't tell whether you were right or wrong about the probability you estimated. The only way to gauge your accuracy would be to keep track of many, many similar judgments to see if, after the fact, the events you thought had a 40% chance of occurring actually did occur 40% of the time. That would require a great deal of data, carefully tracked over a long period of time. Weather forecasters and bookmakers have the opportunities and incentives to maintain such records, but the rest of us don't. As a result, our minds never become calibrated for making estimates in the face of uncertainty.

All of the traps we've discussed so far can influence the way we make decisions when confronted with uncertainty. But there's another set of traps that can have a particularly distorting effect in uncertain situations because they cloud our ability to assess probabilities. Let's look at three of the most common of these uncertainty traps.

The overconfidence trap

Even though most of us are not very good at making estimates or forecasts, we actually tend to be overconfident about our accuracy. That can lead to errors in judgment and, in turn, bad decisions.

In one series of tests, people were asked to forecast the next week's closing value for the Dow Jones Industrial Average. To account for uncertainty, they were then asked to estimate a range within which the closing value would likely fall. In picking the top number of the range, they were asked to choose a high estimate they thought had only a 1% chance of being exceeded by the closing value. Similarly, for the bottom end, they were told to pick a low estimate for which they thought there would be only a 1% chance of the closing value falling below it. If they were good at judging their forecasting accuracy, you'd expect the participants to be wrong only about 2% of the time. But hundreds of tests have shown that the actual Dow Jones averages fell outside the forecast ranges 20% to 30% of the time. Overly confident about the accuracy of their predictions, most people set too narrow a range of possibilities.

Think of the implications for business decisions, in which major initiatives and investments often hinge on ranges of estimates. If managers underestimate the high end or overestimate the low end of a crucial variable, they may miss attractive opportunities or expose themselves to far greater risk than they realize. Much money has been wasted on ill-fated product-development projects because managers did not accurately account for the possibility of market failure.

The prudence trap

Another trap for forecasters takes the form of overcautiousness, or prudence. When faced with high-stakes decisions, we tend to adjust our estimates or forecasts "just to be on the safe side." Many years ago, for example, one of the Big Three U.S. automakers was deciding how many of a new-model car to produce in anticipation of its busiest sales season. The market-planning department, responsible for the decision, asked other departments to supply forecasts of key variables such as anticipated sales, dealer inventories, competitor actions, and costs. Knowing the purpose of the estimates, each department slanted its forecast to favor building more cars—"just to be safe." But the market planners took the numbers at face value and then made their own "just to be safe" adjustments. Not surprisingly, the number of cars produced far exceeded demand, and the company took six months to sell off the surplus, resorting in the end to promotional pricing.

Policy makers have gone so far as to codify overcautiousness in formal decision procedures. An extreme example is the methodology of "worst-case analysis," which was once popular in the design of weapons systems and is still used in certain engineering and regulatory settings. Using this approach, engineers designed weapons to operate under the worst possible combination of circumstances, even though the odds of those circumstances actually coming to pass were infinitesimal. Worst-case analysis added enormous costs with no practical benefit (in fact, it often backfired by touching off an arms race), proving that too much prudence can sometimes be as dangerous as too little.

The recallability trap

Even if we are neither overly confident nor unduly prudent, we can still fall into a trap when making estimates or forecasts. Because we frequently base our predictions about future events on our memory of past events, we can be overly influenced by dramatic events—those that leave a strong impression on our memory. We all, for example, exaggerate the probability of rare but catastrophic occurrences such as plane crashes because they get disproportionate attention in the media. A dramatic or traumatic event in your own life can also distort your thinking. You will assign a higher probability to traffic accidents if you have passed one on the way to work, and you will assign a higher chance of someday dying of cancer yourself if a close friend has died of the disease.

In fact, anything that distorts your ability to recall events in a balanced way will distort your probability assessments. In one experiment, lists of well-known men and women were read to different groups of people. Unbeknownst to the subjects, each list had an equal number of men and women, but on some lists the men were more famous than the women while on others the women were more famous. Afterward, the participants were asked to estimate the percentages of men and women on each list. Those who had heard the list with the more famous men thought there were more men on the list, while those who had heard the one with the more famous women thought there were more women.

Corporate lawyers often get caught in the recallability trap when defending liability suits. Their decisions about whether to settle a claim or take it to court usually hinge on their assessments of the possible outcomes of a trial. Because the media tend to aggressively publicize massive damage awards (while ignoring other, far more common trial outcomes), lawyers can overestimate the probability of a large award for the plaintiff. As a result, they offer larger settlements than are actually warranted.

What can you do about it?

The best way to avoid the estimating and forecasting traps is to take a very disciplined approach to making forecasts and judging probabilities. For each of the three traps, some additional precautions can be taken:

- To reduce the effects of overconfidence in making estimates, always start by considering the extremes, the low and high ends of the possible range of values. This will help you avoid being anchored by an initial estimate. Then challenge your estimates of the extremes. Try to imagine circumstances where the actual figure would fall below your low or above your high, and adjust your range accordingly. Challenge the estimates of your subordinates and advisers in a similar fashion. They're also susceptible to overconfidence.
- To avoid the prudence trap, always state your estimates honestly and explain to anyone who will be using them that they have not been adjusted. Emphasize the need for honest input to anyone who will be supplying you with estimates. Test estimates over a reasonable range to assess their impact. Take a second look at the more sensitive estimates.
- To minimize the distortion caused by variations in recallability, carefully examine all your assumptions to ensure they're not unduly influenced by your memory. Get actual statistics whenever possible. Try not to be guided by impressions.

Forewarned Is Forearmed

When it comes to business decisions, there's rarely such a thing as a no-brainer. Our brains are always at work, sometimes, unfortunately, in ways that hinder rather than help us. At every stage of the decision-making process, misperceptions, biases, and other tricks of the mind can influence the choices we make. Highly complex and important decisions are the most prone to distortion because they tend to involve the most assumptions, the most estimates, and the most inputs from the most people. The higher the stakes, the higher the risk of being caught in a psychological trap.

The traps we've reviewed can all work in isolation. But, even more dangerous, they can work in concert, amplifying one another. A dramatic first impression might anchor our thinking, and then we might selectively seek out confirming evidence to justify our initial inclination. We make a hasty decision, and that decision establishes a new status quo. As our sunk costs mount, we become trapped, unable to find a propitious time to seek out a new and possibly better course. The psychological miscues cascade, making it harder and harder to choose wisely.

As we said at the outset, the best protection against all psychological traps—in isolation or in combination—is awareness. Forewarned is forearmed. Even if you can't eradicate the distortions ingrained into the way your mind works, you can build tests and disciplines into your decision-making process that can uncover errors in thinking before they become errors in judgment. And taking action to understand and avoid psychological traps can have the added benefit of increasing your confidence in the choices you make.

Originally published in January 2006. Reprint R0601K

Before You Make That Big Decision . . .

by Daniel Kahneman, Dan Lovallo, and Olivier Sibony

THANKS TO A SLEW of popular new books, many executives today realize how biases can distort reasoning in business. *Confirmation bias,* for instance, leads people to ignore evidence that contradicts their preconceived notions. *Anchoring* causes them to weigh one piece of information too heavily in making decisions; *loss aversion* makes them too cautious. In our experience, however, awareness of the effects of biases has done little to improve the quality of business decisions at either the individual or the organizational level.

Though there may now be far more talk of biases among managers, talk alone will not eliminate them. But it is possible to take steps to counteract them. A recent McKinsey study of more than 1,000 major business investments showed that when organizations worked at reducing the effect of bias in their decision-making processes, they achieved returns up to seven percentage points higher. (For more on this study, see "The Case for Behavioral Strategy," *McKinsey Quarterly,* March 2010.) Reducing bias makes a difference. In this article, we will describe a straightforward way to detect bias and minimize its effects in the most common kind of decision that executives make: reviewing a recommendation from someone else and determining whether to accept it, reject it, or pass it on to the next level.

For most executives, these reviews seem simple enough. First, they need to quickly grasp the relevant facts (getting them from people who know more about the details than they do). Second, they need to figure out if the people making the recommendation are intentionally clouding the facts in some way. And finally, they need to apply their own experience, knowledge, and reasoning to decide whether the recommendation is right.

However, this process is fraught at every stage with the potential for distortions in judgment that result from cognitive biases. Executives can't do much about their own biases, as we shall see. But given the proper tools, they can recognize and neutralize those of their teams. Over time, by using these tools, they will build decision processes that reduce the effect of biases in their organizations. And in doing so, they'll help upgrade the quality of decisions their organizations make.

The Challenge of Avoiding Bias

Let's delve first into the question of why people are incapable of recognizing their own biases.

According to cognitive scientists, there are two modes of thinking, intuitive and reflective. (In recent decades a lot of psychological research has focused on distinctions between them. Richard Thaler and Cass Sunstein popularized it in their book, *Nudge*.) In intuitive, or System One, thinking, impressions, associations, feelings, intentions, and preparations for action flow effortlessly. System One produces a constant representation of the world around us and allows us to do things like walk, avoid obstacles, and contemplate something else all at the same time. We're usually in this mode when we brush our teeth, banter with friends, or play tennis. We're not consciously focusing on how to do those things; we just do them.

In contrast reflective, or System Two, thinking is slow, effortful, and deliberate. This mode is at work when we complete a tax form or learn to drive. Both modes are continuously active, but System Two is typically just monitoring things. It's mobilized when the stakes are

Idea in Brief

When an executive makes a big bet, he or she typically relies on the judgment of a team that has put together a proposal for a strategic course of action. After all, the team will have delved into the pros and cons much more deeply than the executive has time to do. The problem is, biases invariably creep into any team's reasoning—and often dangerously distort its thinking. A team that has fallen in love with its recommendation, for instance, may subconsciously dismiss evidence that contradicts its theories, give far too much weight to one piece of data, or make faulty comparisons to another business case. That's why, with important decisions, executives need to conduct a careful review not only of the content of recommendations but of the recommendation process. To that end, the authors—Kahneman, who won a Nobel Prize in economics for his work on cognitive biases; Lovallo of the University of Sydney; and Sibony of McKinsey—have put together a 12-question checklist intended to unearth and neutralize defects in teams' thinking. These questions help leaders examine whether a team has explored alternatives appropriately, gathered all the right information, and used well-grounded numbers to support its case. They also highlight considerations such as whether the team might be unduly influenced by self-interest, overconfidence, or attachment to past decisions. By using this practical tool, executives will build decision processes over time that reduce the effects of biases and upgrade the quality of decisions their organizations make. The payoffs can be significant: A recent McKinsey study of more than 1,000 business investments, for instance, showed that when companies worked to reduce the effects of bias, they raised their returns on investment by seven percentage points. Executives need to realize that the judgment of even highly experienced, superbly competent managers can be fallible. A disciplined decision-making process, not individual genius, is the key to good strategy.

high, when we detect an obvious error, or when rule-based reasoning is required. But most of the time, System One determines our thoughts.

Our visual system and associative memory (both important aspects of System One) are designed to produce a single coherent interpretation of what is going on around us. That sense making is highly sensitive to context. Consider the word "bank." For most

The Behavioral Economics of Decision Making

DANIEL KAHNEMAN (THE LEAD AUTHOR) and Amos Tversky introduced the idea of cognitive biases, and their impact on decision making, in 1974. Their research and ideas were recognized when Kahneman was awarded a Nobel Prize in economics in 2002. These biases, and behavioral psychology generally, have since captured the imagination of business experts. Below are some notable popular books on this topic:

> ***Nudge: Improving Decisions About Health, Wealth, and Happiness*** by Richard H. Thaler and Cass R. Sunstein (Caravan, 2008)
>
> ***Think Twice: Harnessing the Power of Counterintuition*** by Michael J. Mauboussin (Harvard Business Review Press, 2009)
>
> ***Think Again: Why Good Leaders Make Bad Decisions and How to Keep It from Happening to You*** by Sydney Finkelstein, Jo Whitehead, and Andrew Campbell (Harvard Business Review Press, 2009)
>
> ***Predictably Irrational: The Hidden Forces That Shape Our Decisions*** by Dan Ariely (HarperCollins, 2008)
>
> ***Thinking, Fast and Slow*** by Daniel Kahneman (Farrar, Straus and Giroux, 2011)

people reading HBR, it would signify a financial institution. But if the same readers encountered this word in *Field & Stream,* they would probably understand it differently. Context is complicated: In addition to visual cues, memories, and associations, it comprises goals, anxieties, and other inputs. As System One makes sense of those inputs and develops a narrative, it suppresses alternative stories.

Because System One is so good at making up contextual stories and we're not aware of its operations, it can lead us astray. The stories it creates are generally accurate, but there are exceptions. Cognitive biases are one major, well-documented example. An insidious feature of cognitive failures is that we have no way of knowing that they're happening: We almost never catch ourselves in the act of making intuitive errors. Experience doesn't help us recognize them. (By contrast, if we tackle a difficult problem using System Two thinking and fail to solve it, we're uncomfortably aware of that fact.)

Preliminary Questions

Ask yourself

1. **Check for self-interested biases**

   Is there any reason to suspect the team making the recommendation of errors motivated by self-interest?

   Review the proposal with extra care, especially for overoptimism.

2. **Check for the affect heuristic**

   Has the team fallen in love with its proposal?

   Rigorously apply all the quality controls on the checklist.

3. **Check for groupthink**

   Were there dissenting opinions within the team?

   Were they explored adequately?

   Solicit dissenting views, discreetly if necessary.

This inability to sense that we've made a mistake is the key to understanding why we generally accept our intuitive, effortless thinking at face value. It also explains why, even when we become aware of the existence of biases, we're not excited about eliminating them in ourselves. After all, it's difficult for us to fix errors we can't see.

By extension, this also explains why the management experts writing about cognitive biases have not provided much practical help. Their overarching theme is "forewarned is forearmed." But knowing you have biases is not enough to help you overcome them. You may accept that you have biases, but you cannot eliminate them in yourself.

There is reason for hope, however, when we move from the individual to the collective, from the decision maker to the decision-making process, and from the executive to the organization. As researchers have documented in the realm of operational management, the fact that individuals are not aware of their own biases does not mean that biases can't be neutralized—or at least reduced—at the organizational level.

Challenge Questions

Ask the recommenders

4. **Check for saliency bias**

   Could the diagnosis be overly influenced by an analogy to a memorable success?

   Ask for more analogies, and rigorously analyze their similarity to the current situation.

5. **Check for confirmation bias**

   Are credible alternatives included along with the recommendation?

   Request additional options.

6. **Check for availability bias**

   If you had to make this decision again in a year's time, what information would you want, and can you get more of it now?

   Use checklists of the data needed for each kind of decision.

7. **Check for anchoring bias**

   Do you know where the numbers came from? Can there be

   . . . unsubstantiated numbers?

   . . . extrapolation from history?

   . . . a motivation to use a certain anchor?

   Reanchor with figures generated by other models or benchmarks, and request new analysis.

8. **Check for halo effect**

   Is the team assuming that a person, organization, or approach that is successful in one area will be just as successful in another?

   Eliminate false inferences, and ask the team to seek additional comparable examples.

9. **Check for sunk-cost fallacy, endowment effect**

   Are the recommenders overly attached to a history of past decisions?

   Consider the issue as if you were a new CEO.

Evaluation Questions

Ask about the proposal

10. **Check for overconfidence, planning fallacy, optimistic biases, competitor neglect**

    Is the base case overly optimistic?

    Have the team build a case taking an outside view; use war games.

11. **Check for disaster neglect**

    Is the worst case bad enough?

    Have the team conduct a premortem: Imagine that the worst has happened, and develop a story about the causes.

12. **Check for loss aversion**

    Is the recommending team overly cautious?

    Realign incentives to share responsibility for the risk or to remove risk.

This is true because most decisions are influenced by many people, and because decision makers can turn their ability to spot biases in others' thinking to their own advantage. We may not be able to control our own intuition, but we can apply rational thought to detect others' faulty intuition and improve *their* judgment. (In other words, we can use our System Two thinking to spot System One errors in the recommendations given to us by others.)

This is precisely what executives are expected to do every time they review recommendations and make a final call. Often they apply a crude, unsystematic adjustment—such as adding a "safety margin" to a forecasted cost—to account for a perceived bias. For the most part, however, decision makers focus on *content* when they review and challenge recommendations. We propose adding a systematic review of the recommendation *process,* one aimed at identifying the biases that may have influenced the people putting forth proposals. The idea is to retrace their steps to determine where intuitive thinking may have steered them off-track.

In the following section, we'll walk you through how to do a process review, drawing on the actual experiences of three corporate executives—Bob, Lisa, and Devesh (not their real names)—who were asked to consider very different kinds of proposals:

A radical pricing change. Bob is the vice president of sales in a business services company. Recently, his senior regional VP and several colleagues recommended a total overhaul of the company's pricing structure. They argued that the company had lost a number of bids to competitors, as well as some of its best salespeople, because of unsustainable price levels. But making the wrong move could be very costly and perhaps even trigger a price war.

A large capital outlay. Lisa is the chief financial officer of a capital-intensive manufacturing company. The VP of manufacturing in one of the corporation's business units has proposed a substantial investment in one manufacturing site. The request has all the usual components—a revenue forecast, an analysis of return on investment under various scenarios, and so on. But the investment would be a very large one—in a business that has been losing money for some time.

A major acquisition. Devesh is the CEO of a diversified industrial company. His business development team has proposed purchasing a firm whose offerings would complement the product line in one of the company's core businesses. However, the potential deal comes on the heels of several successful but expensive takeovers, and the company's financial structure is stretched.

While we are intentionally describing this review from the perspective of the individual decision makers, organizations can also take steps to embed some of these practices in their broader decision-making processes. (For the best ways to approach that, see the sidebar "Improving Decisions Throughout the Organization.")

Decision Quality Control: A Checklist

To help executives vet decisions, we have developed a tool, based on a 12-question checklist, that is intended to unearth defects in thinking—in other words, the cognitive biases of the teams making recommendations. The questions fall into three categories: questions the decision makers should ask themselves, questions they should use to challenge the people proposing a course of action, and questions aimed at evaluating the proposal. It's important to note that, because you can't recognize your own biases, the individuals using this quality screen should be completely independent from the teams making the recommendations.

Questions that decision makers should ask themselves

1. Is there any reason to suspect *motivated errors,* or errors driven by the self-interest of the recommending team? Decision makers should never directly ask the people making the proposal this. After all, it's nearly impossible to do so without appearing to question their diligence and even their integrity, and that conversation cannot end well.

The issue here is not just intentional deception. People do sometimes lie deliberately, of course, but self-deception and rationalization are more common problems. Research has shown that professionals who sincerely believe that their decisions are "not for sale" (such as physicians) are still biased in the direction of their own interests.

Bob, for instance, should recognize that lowering prices to respond to competitive pressures will have a material impact on the commissions of his sales team (especially if bonuses are based on revenues, not margins). Devesh should wonder whether the team recommending the acquisition would expect to run the acquired company and therefore might be influenced by "empire building" motives.

Of course, a preference for a particular outcome is built into every recommendation. Decision makers need to assess not whether there's a risk of motivated error but whether it is significant. A proposal from a set of individuals who stand to gain more than usual from the outcome—either in financial terms or, more frequently, in terms of organizational power, reputation, or career options—needs especially careful quality control. Reviewers also should watch out for pernicious sets of options that include only one realistic alternative—the one that the recommending team prefers. In such cases, decision makers will have to pay even more attention to the remaining questions on this checklist, particularly those covering optimistic biases.

2. Have the people making the recommendation fallen in love with it? All of us are subject to the *affect heuristic:* When evaluating something we like, we tend to minimize its risks and costs and exaggerate its benefits; when assessing something we dislike, we do the opposite. Executives often observe this phenomenon in decisions with a strong emotional component, such as those concerning employees, brands, or locations.

This question is also best left unspoken but is usually easy to answer. It is likely that Devesh will easily sense whether the members of the deal team have maintained a neutral perspective regarding the acquisition. If they have become emotional about it, the remedy, again, is to examine with extra thoroughness all the components of the recommendation and all the biases that may have affected the people making it.

3. Were there dissenting opinions within the recommending team? If so, were they explored adequately? In many corporate cultures, a team presenting a recommendation to a higher echelon will claim to be unanimous. The unanimity is sometimes genuine, but it could be sham unity imposed by the team's leader or a case of groupthink—the tendency of groups to minimize conflict by converging on a decision because it appears to be gathering support. Groupthink is especially likely if there is little diversity of background and viewpoint within a team. Lisa, for instance, should worry if no one in the manufacturing team that is proposing the large investment has voiced any concerns or disagreement.

Regardless of its cause, an absence of dissent in a team addressing a complex problem should sound an alarm. In the long run, a senior executive should strive to create a climate where substantive disagreements are seen as a productive part of the decision process (and resolved objectively), rather than as a sign of conflict between individuals (and suppressed). In the short run, if faced with a recommendation in which dissent clearly was stifled, a decision maker has few options. Because asking another group of people to generate additional options is often impractical, the best choice may be to discreetly solicit dissenting views from members of the recommending team, perhaps through private meetings. And the opinions of those who braved the pressure for conformity in the decision-making process deserve special attention.

Questions that decision makers should ask the team making recommendations

4. Could the diagnosis of the situation be overly influenced by salient analogies? Many recommendations refer to a past success story, which the decision maker is encouraged to repeat by approving the proposal. The business development team advocating the acquisition to Devesh took this approach, using the example of a recent successful deal it had completed to bolster its case. The danger, of course, is that the analogy may be less relevant to the current deal than it appears. Furthermore, the use of just one or a few analogies almost always leads to faulty inferences.

The decision maker who suspects that an analogy to an especially memorable event has unduly influenced a team's judgment (a type of cognitive flaw known as *saliency bias*) will want the team to explore alternative diagnoses. This can be done by asking for more analogies and a rigorous analysis of how comparable examples really are. (For more details on the technique for doing this, called *reference class forecasting*, see "Delusions of Success: How Optimism Undermines Executives' Decisions," by Dan Lovallo and Daniel Kahneman, HBR July 2003.) More informally, a decision maker can simply prompt the team to use a broader set of comparisons. Devesh could ask for descriptions of five recent deals, other than the recently acquired company, that were somewhat similar to the one being considered.

5. Have credible alternatives been considered? In a good decision process, other alternatives are fully evaluated in an objective and fact-based way. Yet when trying to solve a problem, both individuals and groups are prone to generating one plausible hypothesis and then seeking only evidence that supports it.

A good practice is to insist that people submit at least one or two alternatives to the main recommendation and explain their pros and cons. A decision maker should ask: What alternatives did you consider? At what stage were they discarded? Did you actively look for information that would disprove your main hypothesis or only for the confirming evidence described in your final recommendation?

Some proposals feature a perfunctory list of "risks and mitigating actions" or a set of implausible alternatives that make the recommendation look appealing by contrast. The challenge is to encourage a *genuine* admission of uncertainty and a sincere recognition of multiple options.

In his review, Bob should encourage his sales colleagues to recognize the unknowns surrounding their proposal. The team may eventually admit that competitors' reactions to an across-the-board price cut are unpredictable. It should then be willing to evaluate other options, such as a targeted marketing program aimed at the customer segments in which Bob's company has a competitive advantage.

6. If you had to make this decision again in a year, what information would you want, and can you get more of it now? One challenge executives face when reviewing a recommendation is the WYSIATI assumption: What you see is all there is. Because our intuitive mind constructs a coherent narrative based on the evidence we have, making up for holes in it, we tend to overlook what is missing. Devesh, for instance, found the acquisition proposal compelling until he realized he had not seen a legal due diligence on the target company's patent portfolio—perhaps not a major issue if the acquisition were being made primarily to gain new customers but a critical question when the goal was to extend the product line.

To force yourself to examine the adequacy of the data, Harvard Business School professor Max Bazerman suggests asking the question above. In many cases, data are unavailable. But in some cases, useful information will be uncovered.

Checklists that specify what information is relevant to a certain type of decision are also helpful. Devesh, for his part, could tap his experience reviewing acquisition proposals and develop lists of data that should be collected for each different kind of deal his company does, such as acquiring new technology or buying access to new customers.

7. Do you know where the numbers came from? A focused examination of the key numbers underlying the proposal will help decision makers see through any anchoring bias. Questions to ask include: Which numbers in this plan are facts and which are estimates? Were these estimates developed by adjusting from another number? Who put the first number on the table?

Three different types of anchoring bias are common in business decisions. In the classic case, initial estimates, which are often best guesses, are used, and their accuracy is not challenged. The team making the proposal to Lisa, for instance, used a guesstimate on an important cost component of the capital investment project. More frequently, estimates are based on extrapolations from history, as they were when Devesh's team predicted the target company's sales by drawing a straight line. This, too, is a form of anchoring bias; one cannot always assume trends will continue. Finally, some anchors are clearly deliberate, such as when a buyer sets a low floor in a price negotiation. The trap of anchors is that people always believe they can disregard them, but in fact they cannot. Judges who are asked to roll a set of dice before making a (fortunately simulated) sentencing decision will of course deny that the dice influenced them, but analysis of their decisions shows that they did.

When a recommendation appears to be anchored by an initial reference and the number in question has a material impact, the decision maker should require the team behind the proposal to adjust its estimates after some reanchoring. If Lisa discovers that the investment budget she was asked to approve was derived from the costing of an earlier project, she can reanchor the team with a number she arrives at in a completely different way, such as a linear model based on investment projects carried out in other divisions, or competitive benchmarks. The aim is neither to arrive directly at a different number nor to slavishly "copy and paste" the practices of benchmarked competitors, but to force the team to consider its assumptions in another light.

8. Can you see a *halo effect*? This effect is at work when we see a story as simpler and more emotionally coherent than it really is. As Phil Rosenzweig shows in the book *The Halo Effect,* it causes us to attribute the successes and failures of firms to the personalities of their leaders. It may have led Devesh's team to link the success of the acquisition target to its senior management and assume that its recent outperformance would continue as long as those managers were still in place.

Companies deemed "excellent" are frequently circled by halos. Once an expert brands them in this way, people tend to assume that all their practices must be exemplary. In making its case for its capital investment, Lisa's team, for instance, pointed to a similar project undertaken by a highly admired company in another cyclical industry. According to the proposal, that company had "doubled down" on a moderately successful manufacturing investment, which paid off when the economy rebounded and the extra capacity was fully used.

Naturally, Lisa should ask whether the inference is justified. Does the team making the recommendation have specific information regarding the other company's decision, or is the team making assumptions based on the company's overall reputation? If the investment was indeed a success, how much of that success is attributable to chance events such as lucky timing? And is the situation of the other company truly similar to the situation of Lisa's company?

Such difficult questions are rarely asked, in part because it may seem off-base to take apart an outside comparison that is made in passing. Yet if Lisa simply tries to disregard the comparison, she will still be left with a vague, but hard to dispel, positive impression of the recommendation. A good and relatively simple practice is to first assess the relevance of the comparison ("What about this case is comparable with ours?") and then ask the people making it to propose other examples from less successful companies ("What other companies in our industry invested in a declining business, and how did it turn out for them?").

9. Are the people making the recommendation overly attached to past decisions? Companies do not start from scratch every day. Their history, and what they learn from it, matter. But history leads us astray when we evaluate options in reference to a past starting point instead of the future. The most visible consequence is the *sunk-cost fallacy*: When considering new investments, we should disregard past expenditures that don't affect future costs or revenues, but we don't. Note that Lisa's team was evaluating a capacity improvement in a product line that was struggling financially—partly because it was subscale, the team argued. Lisa should ask the team to look at this investment the way an incoming CEO might: If I personally hadn't decided to build the plant in the first place, would I invest in adding capacity?

Questions focused on evaluating the proposal

10. Is the base case overly optimistic? Most recommendations contain forecasts, which are notoriously prone to excessive optimism. One contributing factor is overconfidence, which could, say, lead Devesh's team to underestimate the challenge of integrating the acquired company and capturing synergies. Groups with a successful track record are more prone to this bias than others, so Devesh should be especially careful if the business development team has been on a winning streak.

Another factor frequently at work here is the *planning fallacy.* The planning fallacy arises from "inside view" thinking, which focuses exclusively on the case at hand and ignores the history of similar projects. This is like trying to divine the future of a company by considering only its plans and the obstacles it anticipates. An "outside view" of forecasting, in contrast, is statistical in nature and mainly uses the generalizable aspects of a broad set of problems to make predictions. Lisa should keep this in mind when reviewing her team's proposal. When drawing up a timeline for the completion of the proposed plant, did the team use a top-down (outside-view) comparison with similar projects, or did it estimate the time

Improving Decisions Throughout the Organization

To critique recommendations effectively and in a sustainable way, you need to make quality control more than an individual effort.

Organizations pursue this objective in various ways, but good approaches have three principles in common. First, they adopt the right mind-set. The goal is not to create bureaucratic procedures or turn decision quality control into another element of "compliance" that can be delegated to a risk assessment unit. It's to stimulate discussion and debate. To accomplish this, organizations must tolerate and even encourage disagreements (as long as they are based on facts and not personal).

Second, they rotate the people in charge, rather than rely on one executive to be the quality policeman. Many companies, at least in theory, expect a functional leader such as a CFO or a chief strategy officer to play the role of challenger. But an insider whose primary job is to critique others loses political capital quickly. The use of a quality checklist may reduce this downside, as the challenger will be seen as "only playing by the rules," but high-quality debate is still unlikely.

Third, they inject a diversity of views and a mix of skills into the process. Some firms form ad hoc critique teams, asking outsiders or employees rotating in from other divisions to review plans. One company calls them "provocateurs" and makes playing this role a stage of leadership development. Another, as part of its strategic planning, systematically organizes critiques and brings in outside experts to do them. Both companies have explicitly thought about their decision processes, particularly those involving strategic plans, and invested effort in honing them. They have made their decision processes a source of competitive advantage.

required for each step and add it up—a bottom-up (inside-view) approach that is likely to result in underestimates?

A third factor is the failure to anticipate how competitors will respond to a decision. For instance, in proposing price cuts, Bob's team did not account for the predictable reaction of the company's competitors: starting a price war.

All these biases are exacerbated in most organizations by the inevitable interplay (and frequent confusion) between forecasts and estimates on the one hand, and plans or targets on the other.

Forecasts should be accurate, whereas targets should be ambitious. The two sets of numbers should not be confused by senior leadership.

Correcting for optimistic biases is difficult, and asking teams to revise their estimates will not suffice. The decision maker must take the lead by adopting an outside view, as opposed to the inside view of the people making proposals.

Several techniques help promote an outside view. Lisa could construct a list of several similar investment projects and ask her team to look at how long those projects took to complete, thus removing from the equation all inside information on the project at hand. Sometimes, removing what appears to be valuable information yields better estimates. In some situations decision makers might also put themselves in the shoes of their competitors. The use of "war games" is a powerful antidote to the lack of thinking about competitors' reactions to proposed moves.

11. Is the worst case bad enough? Many companies, when making important decisions, ask strategy teams to propose a range of scenarios, or at least a best and a worst case. Unfortunately, the worst case is rarely bad enough. A decision maker should ask: Where did the worst case come from? How sensitive is it to our competitors' responses? What could happen that we have not thought of?

The acquisition proposal Devesh is reviewing hinges on the target's sales forecast, and like most sales forecasts in due diligence reports, it follows a steep, straight, upward line. Devesh may ask his team to prepare a range of scenarios reflecting the merger's risks, but the team is likely to miss risks it has not experienced yet.

A useful technique in such situations is the "premortem," pioneered by psychologist Gary Klein. Participants project themselves into the future, imagine the worst has already happened, and make up a story about how it happened. Devesh's team could consider such scenarios as the departure of key executives who do not fit into the acquiring company's culture, technical problems with the target's key product lines, and insufficient resources for integration. It would then be able to consider whether to mitigate those risks or reassess the proposal.

12. Is the recommending team overly cautious? On the flip side, excessive conservatism is a source of less visible but serious chronic underperformance in organizations. Many executives complain that their teams' plans aren't creative or ambitious enough.

This issue is hard to address for two reasons. First and most important, the people making recommendations are subject to loss aversion: When they contemplate risky decisions, their wish to avoid losses is stronger than their desire for gains. No individual or team wants to be responsible for a failed project. Second, the fact that very few companies make explicit choices about what level of risk they will assume only exacerbates individual managers' loss aversion.

This helps explain why Lisa's colleagues had ruled out a new technology providing an alternative to the proposed investment: They deemed it too risky. To get her team to explore this option, she could provide assurances or (perhaps more credibly) explicitly share responsibility for the risk. When launching new ventures, many companies tackle this problem by creating separate organizational units with different objectives and budgets. But dealing with excessive conservatism in "ordinary" operations remains a challenge.

Implementing Quality Control Over Decisions

These 12 questions should be helpful to anyone who relies substantially on others' evaluations to make a final decision. But there's a time and place to ask them, and there are ways to make them part and parcel of your organization's decision-making processes.

When to use the Checklist

This approach is not designed for routine decisions that an executive formally rubber-stamps. Lisa, the CFO, will want to use it for major capital expenditures but not her department's operating budget. The sweet spot for quality control is decisions that are both important and recurring, and so justify a formal process. Approving an R&D project, deciding on a large capital expenditure, and making a midsize acquisition of a company are all examples of "quality controllable" decisions.

Who should conduct the review

As we mentioned earlier, the very idea of quality control also assumes a real separation between the decision maker and the team making the recommendation. In many instances an executive will overtly or covertly influence a team's proposal, perhaps by picking team members whose opinions are already known, making his or her preferences clear in advance, or signaling opinions during the recommendation phase. If that is the case, the decision maker becomes a de facto member of the recommendation team and can no longer judge the quality of the proposal because his or her own biases have influenced it.

A clear and common sign that this has happened is overlap between the decision and action stages. If, at the time of a decision, steps have already been taken to implement it, the executive making the final call has probably communicated a preference for the outcome being recommended.

Enforcing discipline

Last, executives need to be prepared to be systematic—something that not all corporate cultures welcome. As Atul Gawande points out in *The Checklist Manifesto,* because each item on a checklist tends to seem sensible and unsurprising, it is tempting to use checklists partially and selectively. Doctors who adopted the World Health Organization's Surgical Safety Checklist knew that measures as simple as checking the patient's medication allergies made sense. But only by going through the checklist completely, systematically, and routinely did they achieve results—a spectacular reduction in complications and mortality. Using checklists is a matter of discipline, not genius. Partial adherence may be a recipe for total failure.

Costs and benefits

Is applying quality control to decisions a good investment of effort? Time-pressed executives do not want to delay action, and few corporations are prepared to devote special resources to a quality control exercise.

But in the end, Bob, Lisa, and Devesh all did, and averted serious problems as a result. Bob resisted the temptation to implement the price cut his team was clamoring for at the risk of destroying profitability and triggering a price war. Instead, he challenged the team to propose an alternative, and eventually successful, marketing plan. Lisa refused to approve an investment that, as she discovered, aimed to justify and prop up earlier sunk-cost investments in the same business. Her team later proposed an investment in a new technology that would leapfrog the competition. Finally, Devesh signed off on the deal his team was proposing, but not before additional due diligence had uncovered issues that led to a significant reduction in the acquisition price.

The real challenge for executives who want to implement decision quality control is not time or cost. It is the need to build awareness that even highly experienced, superbly competent, and well-intentioned managers are fallible. Organizations need to realize that a disciplined decision-making process, not individual genius, is the key to a sound strategy. And they will have to create a culture of open debate in which such processes can flourish.

Originally published in June 2011. Reprint R1106B

How to Avoid Catastrophe

Failures happen. But if you pay attention to near misses, you can predict and prevent crises.

by Catherine H. Tinsley, Robin L. Dillon, and Peter M. Madsen

MOST PEOPLE THINK OF "near misses" as harrowing close calls that could have been a lot worse—when a firefighter escapes a burning building moments before it collapses, or when a tornado miraculously veers away from a town in its path. Events like these are rare narrow escapes that leave us shaken and looking for lessons.

But there's another class of near misses, ones that are much more common and pernicious. These are the often unremarked small failures that permeate day-to-day business but cause no immediate harm. People are hardwired to misinterpret or ignore the warnings embedded in these failures, and so they often go unexamined or, perversely, are seen as signs that systems are resilient and things are going well. Yet these seemingly innocuous events are often harbingers; if conditions shift slightly, or if luck does not intervene, a crisis erupts.

Consider the BP Gulf oil rig disaster. As a case study in the anatomy of near misses and the consequences of misreading them, it's close to perfect. In April 2010, a gas blowout occurred during the cementing of the *Deepwater Horizon* well. The blowout ignited, killing 11 people, sinking the rig, and triggering a massive underwater spill that would take months to contain. Numerous poor decisions and dangerous conditions contributed to the disaster: Drillers had used too few centralizers to position the pipe, the lubricating "drilling mud" was removed too early, managers had misinterpreted vital test results that would have confirmed that hydrocarbons were seeping from the well. In addition, BP relied on an older version of a complex fail-safe device called a blowout preventer that had a notoriously spotty track record.

Why did Transocean (the rig's owner), BP executives, rig managers, and the drilling crew overlook the warning signs, even though the well had been plagued by technical problems all along (crew members called it "the well from hell")? We believe that the stakeholders were lulled into complacency by a catalog of previous near misses in the industry—successful outcomes in which luck played a key role in averting disaster. Increasing numbers of ultradeep wells were being drilled, but significant oil spills or fatalities were extremely rare. And many Gulf of Mexico wells had suffered minor blowouts during cementing (dozens of them in the past two decades); however, in each case chance factors—favorable wind direction, no one welding near the leak at the time, for instance—helped prevent an explosion. Each near miss, rather than raise alarms and prompt investigations, was taken as an indication that existing methods and safety procedures worked.

For the past seven years, we have studied near misses in dozens of companies across industries from telecommunications to automobiles, at NASA, and in lab simulations. Our research reveals a pattern: Multiple near misses preceded (and foreshadowed) every disaster and business crisis we studied, and most of the misses were ignored or misread. Our work also shows that cognitive biases conspire to blind managers to the near misses. Two in particular cloud our judgment. The first is "normalization of deviance," the tendency over time to accept anomalies—particularly risky ones—as normal. Think of the growing comfort a worker might feel with using a ladder with a broken rung; the more times he climbs the dangerous ladder without incident, the safer he feels it is. For an organization, such normalization can be catastrophic. Columbia University sociologist

Idea in Brief

Most business failures—such as engineering disasters, product malfunctions, and PR crises—are foreshadowed by near misses, close calls that, had luck not intervened, would have had far worse consequences. The space shuttle Columbia's fatal reentry, BP's Gulf oil rig disaster, Toyota's stuck accelerators, even the iPhone 4's antenna failures—all were preceded by near-miss events that should have tipped off managers to impending crises. The problem is that near misses are often overlooked—or, perversely, viewed as a sign that systems are resilient and working well. That's because managers are blinded by cognitive biases, argue Georgetown professors Tinsley and Dillon and Brigham Young University's Madsen. Seven strategies can help managers recognize and learn from near misses: They should be on increased alert when time or cost pressures are high; watch for deviations in operations from the norm and uncover their root causes; make decision makers accountable for near misses; envision worst-case scenarios; be on the lookout for near-misses masquerading as successes; and reward individuals for exposing near misses.

Diane Vaughan coined the phrase in her book *The Challenger Launch Decision* to describe the organizational behaviors that allowed a glaring mechanical anomaly on the space shuttle to gradually be viewed as a normal flight risk—dooming its crew. The second cognitive error is the so-called outcome bias. When people observe successful outcomes, they tend to focus on the results more than on the (often unseen) complex processes that led to them.

Recognizing and learning from near misses isn't simply a matter of paying attention; it actually runs contrary to human nature. In this article, we examine near misses and reveal how companies can detect and learn from them. By seeing them for what they are—instructive failures—managers can apply their lessons to improve operations and, potentially, ward off catastrophe.

Roots of Crises

Consider this revealing experiment: We asked business students, NASA personnel, and space-industry contractors to evaluate a fictional project manager, Chris, who was supervising the launch

Focus on failure

"Every strike brings me closer to the next home run."

Babe Ruth
Baseball player

of an unmanned spacecraft and had made a series of decisions, including skipping the investigation of a potential design flaw and forgoing a peer review, because of time pressure. Each participant was given one of three scenarios: The spacecraft launched without issue and was able to transmit data (success outcome); shortly after launch, the spacecraft had a problem caused by the design flaw, but because of the way the sun happened to be aligned with the vehicle it was still able to transmit data (near-miss outcome); or the craft had a problem caused by the flaw and, because of the sun's chance alignment, it failed to transmit data and was lost (failure outcome).

How did Chris fare? Participants were just as likely to praise his decision making, leadership abilities, and the overall mission in the success case as in the near-miss case—though the latter plainly succeeded only because of blind luck. When people observe a successful outcome, their natural tendency is to assume that the process that led to it was fundamentally sound, even when it demonstrably wasn't; hence the common phrase "you can't argue with success." In fact, you can—and should.

Organizational disasters, studies show, rarely have a single cause. Rather, they are initiated by the unexpected interaction of multiple small, often seemingly unimportant, human errors, technological failures, or bad business decisions. These latent errors combine with enabling conditions to produce a significant failure. A latent error on an oil rig might be a cementing procedure that allows gas to escape; enabling conditions might be a windless day and a welder working near the leak. Together, the latent error and enabling conditions ignite a deadly firestorm. Near misses arise from the same preconditions, but in the absence of enabling conditions, they produce only small failures and thus go undetected or are ignored.

Latent errors often exist for long periods of time before they combine with enabling conditions to produce a significant failure. Whether an enabling condition transforms a near miss into a crisis generally depends on chance; thus, it makes little sense to try to predict or control enabling conditions. Instead, companies should focus on identifying and fixing latent errors before circumstances allow them to create a crisis.

Oil rig explosions offer a dramatic case in point, but latent errors and enabling conditions in business often combine to produce less spectacular but still costly crises—corporate failures that attention to latent errors could have prevented. Let's look at three.

Bad Apple

Take Apple's experience following its launch of the iPhone 4, in June 2010. Almost immediately, customers began complaining about dropped calls and poor signal strength. Apple's initial response was to blame users for holding the phone the wrong way, thus covering

Focus on failure

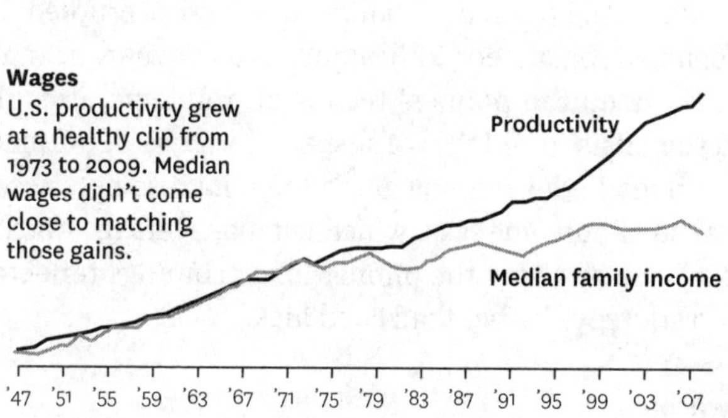

Source: Economic Policy Institute

the external antenna, and to advise them to "avoid gripping [the phone] in the lower left corner." When questioned about the problem by a user on a web forum, CEO Steve Jobs fired back an e-mail describing the dropped calls as a "non issue." Many customers found Apple's posture arrogant and insulting and made their displeasure known through social and mainstream media. Several filed class action lawsuits, including a suit that alleged "fraud by concealment, negligence, intentional misrepresentation and defective design." The reputation crisis reached a crescendo in mid-July, when *Consumer Reports* declined to recommend the iPhone 4 (it had recommended all previous versions). Ultimately Apple backpedaled, acknowledging software errors and offering owners software updates and iPhone cases to address the antenna problem.

The latent errors underlying the crisis had long been present. As Jobs demonstrated during a press conference, virtually all smartphones experience a drop in signal strength when users touch the external antenna. This flaw had existed in earlier iPhones, as well as in competitors' phones, for years. The phones' signal strength problem was also well known. Other latent errors emerged as the crisis gained momentum, notably an evasive PR strategy that invited a backlash.

That consumers had endured the performance issues for years without significant comment was not a sign of a successful strategy but of an ongoing near miss. When coupled with the right enabling conditions—*Consumer Reports'* withering and widely quoted review and the expanding reach of social media—a crisis erupted. If Apple had recognized consumers' forbearance as an ongoing near miss and proactively fixed the phones' technical problems, it could have avoided the crisis. It didn't, we suspect, because of normalization bias, which made the antenna glitch seem increasingly acceptable; and because of outcome bias, which led managers to conclude that the lack of outcry about the phones' shortcomings reflected their own good strategy—rather than good luck.

Speed warning

On August 28, 2009, California Highway Patrol officer Mark Saylor and three family members died in a fiery crash after the gas pedal of the Lexus sedan they were driving in stuck, accelerating the car to more than 120 miles per hour. A 911 call from the speeding car captured the horrifying moments before the crash and was replayed widely in the news and social media.

Up to this point, Toyota, which makes Lexus, had downplayed the more than 2,000 complaints of unintended acceleration among its cars it had received since 2001. The Saylor tragedy forced the company to seriously investigate the problem. Ultimately, Toyota recalled more than 6 million vehicles in late 2009 and early 2010 and temporarily halted production and sales of eight models, sustaining an estimated $2 billion loss in North American sales alone and immeasurable harm to its reputation.

Complaints about vehicle acceleration and speed control are common for all automakers, and in most cases, according to the National Highway Traffic Safety Administration, the problems are

Toyota pedal problems

Errors in process or product design are often ignored, even when the warning signs clearly call for action. The more times small failures occur without disaster, the more complacent managers become.

Percentage of customer complaints having to do with speed control

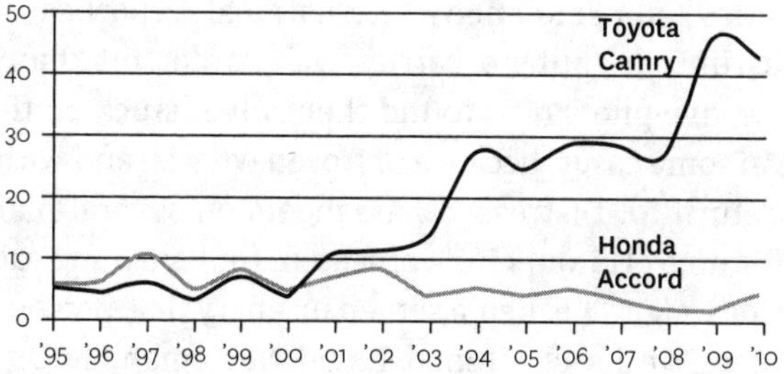

Source: National Highway Traffic Safety Administration

caused by driver error, not a vehicle defect. However, beginning in 2001, about the time that Toyota introduced a new accelerator design, complaints of acceleration problems in Toyotas increased sharply, whereas such complaints remained relatively constant for other automakers (see the exhibit "Toyota pedal problems"). Toyota could have averted the crisis if it had noted this deviation and acknowledged the thousands of complaints for what they were—near misses. Here, too, normalization of deviance and outcome bias, along with other factors, conspired to obscure the grave implications of the near misses. Only when an enabling condition occurred—the Saylor family tragedy and the ensuing media storm—did the latent error trigger a crisis.

Jet Black and Blue

Since it began operating, in 2000, JetBlue Airways has taken an aggressive approach to bad weather, canceling proportionately fewer flights than other airlines and directing its pilots to pull away from gates as soon as possible in severe weather so as to be near the front of the line when runways were cleared for takeoff—even if that meant loaded planes would sit for some time on the tarmac. For several years, this policy seemed to work. On-tarmac delays were not arduously long, and customers were by and large accepting of them. Nonetheless, it was a risky strategy, exposing the airline to the danger of stranding passengers for extended periods if conditions abruptly worsened.

The wake-up call came on February 14, 2007. A massive ice storm at New York's John F. Kennedy International Airport caused widespread disruption—but no carrier was harder hit than JetBlue, whose assertive pilots now found themselves stuck on the tarmac (literally, in some cases, because of frozen wheels) and with no open gates to return to. Distressed passengers on several planes were trapped for up to 11 hours in overheated, foul-smelling cabins with little food or water. The media served up angry first-person accounts of the ordeal, and a chastened David Neeleman, JetBlue's CEO, acknowledged on CNBC, "We did a horrible job, actually, of getting

JetBlue tarmac trouble

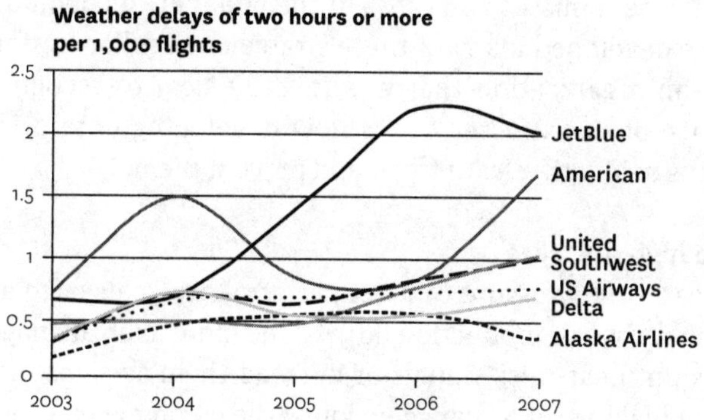

Source: Department of Transportation's Bureau of Transportation Statistics

our customers off those airplanes." The airline reported canceling more than 250 of its 505 flights that day—a much higher proportion than any other airline. It lost millions of dollars and squandered priceless consumer loyalty.

For JetBlue, each of the thousands of flights that took off before the competition during previous weather delays was a near miss. As the airline continued to get away with the risky strategy, managers who had expressed concern early on about the way the airline handled flight delays became complacent, even as long delays mounted. Indeed, the proportion of JetBlue weather-based delays of two hours or more roughly tripled between 2003 and 2007, whereas such delays remained fairly steady at other major U.S. airlines (see the exhibit "JetBlue tarmac trouble").

Rather than perceiving that a dramatic increase in delays represented a dramatic increase in risk, JetBlue managers saw only successfully launched flights. It took an enabling condition—the ferocious ice storm—to turn the latent error into a crisis.

Recognizing and Preventing Near Misses

Our research suggests seven strategies that can help organizations recognize near misses and root out the latent errors behind them. We have developed many of these strategies in collaboration with NASA—an organization that was initially slow to recognize the relevance of near misses but is now developing enterprisewide programs to identify, learn from, and prevent them.

1. Heed high pressure

The greater the pressure to meet performance goals such as tight schedules, cost, or production targets, the more likely managers are to discount near-miss signals or misread them as signs of sound decision making. BP's managers knew the company was incurring overrun costs of $1 million a day in rig lease and contractor fees, which surely contributed to their failure to recognize warning signs.

The high-pressure effect also contributed to the *Columbia* space shuttle disaster, in which insulation foam falling from the external fuel tank damaged the shuttle's wing during liftoff, causing the shuttle to break apart as it reentered the atmosphere. Managers had been aware of the foam issue since the start of the shuttle program and were concerned about it early on, but as dozens of flights proceeded without serious mishap, they began to classify foam strikes as maintenance issues—rather than as near misses. This classic case of normalization of deviance was exacerbated by the enormous political pressure the agency was under at the time to complete the International Space Station's main core. Delays on the shuttle, managers knew, would slow down the space station project.

Despite renewed concern about foam strikes caused by a particularly dramatic recent near miss, and with an investigation under way, the *Columbia* took off. According to the Columbia Accident Investigation Board, "The pressure of maintaining the flight schedule created a management atmosphere that increasingly accepted less-than-specification performance of various components and systems."

When people make decisions under pressure, psychological research shows, they tend to rely on heuristics, or rules of thumb, and thus are more easily influenced by biases. In high-pressure work environments, managers should expect people to be more easily swayed by outcome bias, more likely to normalize deviance, and more apt to believe that their decisions are sound. Organizations should encourage, or even require, employees to examine their decisions during pressure-filled periods and ask, "If I had more time and resources, would I make the same decision?"

2. Learn from deviations

As the Toyota and JetBlue crises suggest, managers' response when some aspect of operations skews from the norm is often to recalibrate what they consider acceptable risk. Our research shows that in such cases, decision makers may clearly understand the statistical risk represented by the deviation, but grow increasingly less concerned about it.

We've seen this effect clearly in a laboratory setting. Turning again to the space program for insight, we asked study participants to assume operational control of a Mars rover in a simulated mission. Each morning they received a weather report and had to decide whether or not to drive onward. On the second day, they learned that there was a 95% chance of a severe sandstorm, which had a 40% chance of causing catastrophic wheel failure. Half the participants were told that the rover had successfully driven through sandstorms in the past (that is, it had emerged unscathed in several prior near misses); the other half had no information about the rover's luck in past storms. When the time came to choose whether or not to risk the drive, three quarters of the near-miss group opted to continue driving; only 13% of the other group did. Both groups knew, and indeed stated that they knew, that the risk of failure was 40%—but the near-miss group was much more comfortable with that level of risk.

Managers should seek out operational deviations from the norm and examine whether their reasons for tolerating the associated risk have merit. Questions to ask might be: Have we always been comfortable with this level of risk? Has our policy toward this risk changed over time?

3. Uncover root causes

When managers identify deviations, their reflex is often to correct the symptom rather than its cause. Such was Apple's response when it at first suggested that customers address the antenna problem by changing the way they held the iPhone. NASA learned this lesson the hard way as well, during its 1998 Mars Climate Orbiter mission. As the spacecraft headed toward Mars it drifted slightly off course four times; each time, managers made small trajectory adjustments, but they didn't investigate the cause of the drifting. As the $200 million spacecraft approached Mars, instead of entering into orbit, it disintegrated in the atmosphere. Only then did NASA uncover the latent error—programmers had used English rather than metric units in their software coding. The course corrections addressed the symptom of the problem but not the underlying cause. Their apparent success lulled decision makers into thinking that the issue had been adequately resolved.

The health care industry has made great strides in learning from near misses and offers a model for others. Providers are increasingly encouraged to report mistakes and near misses so that the lessons can be teased out and applied. An article in *Today's Hospitalist,* for example, describes a near miss at Delnor-Community Hospital, in Geneva, Illinois. Two patients sharing a hospital room had similar last names and were prescribed drugs with similar-sounding names—Cytotec and Cytoxan. Confused by the similarities, a nurse nearly administered one of the drugs to the wrong patient. Luckily, she caught her mistake in time and filed a report detailing the close call. The hospital immediately separated the patients and created a policy to prevent patients with similar names from sharing rooms in the future.

4. Demand accountability

Even when people are aware of near misses, they tend to downgrade their importance. One way to limit this potentially dangerous effect is to require managers to justify their assessments of near misses.

Remember Chris, the fictional manager in our study who neglected some due diligence in his supervision of a space mission? Par-

Little Near Misses and Small-Scale Failures

We've used dramatic cases such as oil spills and shuttle disasters to illustrate how near misses can foreshadow huge calamities.

But near misses are relevant to managers at all levels in their day-to-day work, as they can also presage lesser but still consequential problems. Research on workplace safety, for example, estimates that for every 1,000 near misses, one accident results in a serious injury or fatality, at least 10 smaller accidents cause minor injuries, and 30 cause property damage but no injury. Identifying near misses and addressing the latent errors that give rise to them can head off the more mundane problems that distract organizations and sap their resources.

Imagine an associate who misses deadlines and is chronically late for client meetings but is otherwise a high performer. Each tardy project and late arrival is a near miss; but by addressing the symptoms of the problem—covering for the employee in a variety of ways—his manager is able to prevent clients from defecting. By doing this, however, she permits a small but significant erosion of client satisfaction, team cohesiveness, and organizational performance. And eventually, a client may jump ship—an outcome that could have been avoided by attending to the near misses. Your organization needn't face a threat as serious as an oil spill to benefit from exposing near misses of all types and addressing their root causes.

ticipants gave him equally good marks for the success scenario and the near-miss scenario. Chris's raters didn't seem to see that the near miss was in fact a near disaster. In a continuation of that study, we told a separate group of managers and contractors that they would have to justify their assessment of Chris to upper management. Knowing they'd have to explain their rating to the bosses, those evaluating the near-miss scenario judged Chris's performance just as harshly as did those who had learned the mission had failed—recognizing, it seems, that rather than managing well, he'd simply dodged a bullet.

5. Consider worst-case scenarios

Unless expressly advised to do so, people tend not to think through the possible negative consequences of near misses. Apple managers, for example, were aware of the iPhone's antenna problems but probably hadn't imagined how bad a consumer backlash could get. If they had considered a worst-case scenario, they might have headed off the crisis, our research suggests.

In one study, we told participants to suppose that an impending hurricane had a 30% chance of hitting their house and asked them if they would evacuate. Just as in our Mars rover study, people who were told that they'd escaped disaster in previous near misses were more likely to take a chance (in this case, opting to stay home). However, when we told participants to suppose that, although their house had survived previous hurricanes, a neighbor's house had been hit by a tree during one, they saw things differently; this group was far more likely to evacuate. Examining events closely helps people distinguish between near misses and successes, and they'll often adjust their decision making accordingly.

Managers in Walmart's business-continuity office clearly understand this. For several years prior to Hurricane Katrina, the office had carefully evaluated previous hurricane near misses of its stores and infrastructure and, based on them, planned for a direct hit to a metro area where it had a large presence. In the days before Katrina made landfall in Louisiana, the company expanded the staff of its emergency command center from the usual six to 10 people to more than 50, and stockpiled food, water, and emergency supplies in its local warehouses. Having learned from prior near misses, Walmart famously outperformed local and federal officials in responding to the disaster. Said Jefferson Parish sheriff Harry Lee, "If the American government had responded like Walmart has responded, we wouldn't be in this crisis."

6. Evaluate projects at every stage

When things go badly, managers commonly conduct postmortems to determine causes and prevent recurrences. When they go well, however, few do formal reviews of the success to capture its lessons. Because near misses can look like successes, they often escape scrutiny.

The chief knowledge officer at NASA's Goddard Space Flight Center, Edward Rogers, instituted a "pause and learn" process in which teams discuss at each project milestone what they have learned. They not only cover mishaps but also expressly examine perceived successes and the design decisions considered along the way. By critically examining projects while they're under way, teams avoid outcome bias and are more likely to see near misses for what they are. These sessions are followed by knowledge-sharing workshops involving a broader group of teams. Other NASA centers, including the Jet Propulsion Laboratory, which manages NASA's Mars program, are beginning similar experiments. According to Rogers, most projects that have used the pause-and-learn process have uncovered near misses—typically, design flaws that had gone undetected. "Almost every mishap at NASA can be traced to some series of small signals that went unnoticed at the critical moment," he says.

7. Reward owning up

Seeing and attending to near misses requires organizational alertness, but no amount of attention will avert failure if people aren't motivated to expose near misses—or, worse, are discouraged from doing so. In many organizations, employees have reason to keep quiet about failures, and in that type of environment they're likely to keep suspicions about near misses to themselves.

Political scientists Martin Landau and Donald Chisholm described one such case that, though it took place on the deck of a warship, is relevant to any organization. An enlisted seaman on an aircraft carrier discovered during a combat exercise that he'd lost a tool on the deck. He knew that an errant tool could cause a catastrophe if it were sucked into a jet engine, and he was also aware that admitting the mistake could bring a halt to the exercise—and potential punishment. As long as the tool was unaccounted for, each successful takeoff and landing would be a near miss, a lucky outcome. He reported the mistake, the exercise was stopped, and all aircraft aloft were redirected to bases on land, at a significant cost.

Rather than being punished for his error, the seaman was commended by his commanding officer in a formal ceremony for his bravery in reporting it. Leaders in any organization should publicly reward staff for uncovering near misses—including their own.

Two Forces conspire to make learning from near misses difficult: Cognitive biases make them hard to see, and, even when they are visible, leaders tend not to grasp their significance. Thus, organizations often fail to expose and correct latent errors even when the cost of doing so is small—and so they miss opportunities for organizational improvement before disaster strikes. This tendency is itself a type of organizational failure—a failure to learn from "cheap" data. Surfacing near misses and correcting root causes is one of the soundest investments an organization can make.

Originally published in April 2011. Reprint R1104G

Conquering a Culture of Indecision

by Ram Charan

DOES THIS SOUND FAMILIAR? You're sitting in the quarterly business review as a colleague plows through a two-inch-thick proposal for a big investment in a new product. When he finishes, the room falls quiet. People look left, right, or down, waiting for someone else to open the discussion. No one wants to comment—at least not until the boss shows which way he's leaning.

Finally, the CEO breaks the loud silence. He asks a few mildly skeptical questions to show he's done his due diligence. But it's clear that he has made up his mind to back the project. Before long, the other meeting attendees are chiming in dutifully, careful to keep their comments positive. Judging from the remarks, it appears that everyone in the room supports the project.

But appearances can be deceiving. The head of a related division worries that the new product will take resources away from his operation. The vice president of manufacturing thinks that the first-year sales forecasts are wildly optimistic and will leave him with a warehouse full of unsold goods. Others in the room are lukewarm because they don't see how they stand to gain from the project. But they keep their reservations to themselves, and the meeting breaks up inconclusively. Over the next few months, the project is slowly strangled to death in a series of strategy, budget, and operational reviews. It's not clear who's responsible for the killing, but it's plain that the true sentiment in the room was the opposite of the apparent consensus.

In my career as an adviser to large organizations and their leaders, I have witnessed many occasions even at the highest levels when silent lies and a lack of closure lead to false decisions. They are "false" because they eventually get undone by unspoken factors and inaction. And after a quarter century of first-hand observations, I have concluded that these instances of indecision share a family resemblance—a misfire in the personal interactions that are supposed to produce results. The people charged with reaching a decision and acting on it fail to connect and engage with one another. Intimidated by the group dynamics of hierarchy and constrained by formality and lack of trust, they speak their lines woodenly and without conviction. Lacking emotional commitment, the people who must carry out the plan don't act decisively.

These faulty interactions rarely occur in isolation. Far more often, they're typical of the way large and small decisions are made—or not made—throughout a company. The inability to take decisive action is rooted in the corporate culture and seems to employees to be impervious to change.

The key word here is "seems," because, in fact, leaders create a culture of indecisiveness, and leaders can break it. The primary instrument at their disposal is the human interactions—the dialogues—through which assumptions are challenged or go unchallenged, information is shared or not shared, disagreements are brought to the surface or papered over. Dialogue is the basic unit of work in an organization. The quality of the dialogue determines how people gather and process information, how they make decisions, and how they feel about one another and about the outcome of these decisions. Dialogue can lead to new ideas and speed as a competitive advantage. It is the single-most important factor underlying the productivity and growth of the knowledge worker. Indeed, the tone and content of dialogue shapes people's behaviors

Idea in Brief

The single greatest cause of corporate underperformance is the failure to execute. According to author Ram Charan, such failures usually result from misfires in personal interactions. And these faulty interactions rarely occur in isolation, Charan says in this article originally published in 2001. More often than not, they're typical of the way large and small decisions are made (or not made) throughout an organization. The inability to take decisive action is rooted in a company's culture. Leaders create this culture of indecisiveness, Charan says—and they can break it by doing three things: First, they must engender intellectual honesty in the connections between people. Second, they must see to it that the organization's social operating mechanisms—the meetings, reviews, and other situations through which people in the corporation transact business—have honest dialogue at their cores. And third, leaders must ensure that feedback and follow-through are used to reward high achievers, coach those who are struggling, and discourage those whose behaviors are blocking the organization's progress. By taking these three approaches and using every encounter as an opportunity to model open and honest dialogue, leaders can set the tone for an organization, moving it from paralysis to action.

and beliefs—that is, the corporate culture—faster and more permanently than any reward system, structural change, or vision statement I've seen.

Breaking a culture of indecision requires a leader who can engender intellectual honesty and trust in the connections between people. By using each encounter with his or her employees as an opportunity to model open, honest, and decisive dialogue, the leader sets the tone for the entire organization.

But setting the tone is only the first step. To transform a culture of indecision, leaders must also see to it that the organization's *social operating mechanisms*—that is, the executive committee meetings, budget and strategy reviews, and other situations through which the people of a corporation do business—have honest dialogue at their center. These mechanisms set the stage. Tightly linked and consistently practiced, they establish clear lines of accountability for reaching decisions and executing them.

Follow-through and feedback are the final steps in creating a decisive culture. Successful leaders use follow-through and honest feedback to reward high achievers, coach those who are struggling, and redirect the behaviors of those blocking the organization's progress.

In sum, leaders can create a culture of decisive behavior through attention to their own dialogue, the careful design of social operating mechanisms, and appropriate follow-through and feedback.

It All Begins with Dialogue

Studies of successful companies often focus on their products, business models, or operational strengths: Microsoft's world-conquering Windows operating system, Dell's mass customization, Wal-Mart's logistical prowess. Yet products and operational strengths aren't what really set the most successful organizations apart—they can all be rented or imitated. What can't be easily duplicated are the decisive dialogues and robust operating mechanisms and their links to feedback and follow-through. These factors constitute an organization's most enduring competitive advantage, and they are heavily dependent on the character of dialogue that a leader exhibits and thereby influences throughout the organization.

Decisive dialogue is easier to recognize than to define. It encourages incisiveness and creativity and brings coherence to seemingly fragmented and unrelated ideas. It allows tensions to surface and then resolves them by fully airing every relevant viewpoint. Because such dialogue is a process of intellectual inquiry rather than of advocacy, a search for truth rather than a contest, people feel emotionally committed to the outcome. The outcome seems "right" because people have helped shape it. They are energized and ready to act.

Not long ago, I observed the power of a leader's dialogue to shape a company's culture. The setting was the headquarters of a major U.S. multinational. The head of one of the company's largest business units was making a strategy presentation to the CEO and a few of his senior lieutenants. Sounding confident, almost cocky, the unit head laid out his strategy for taking his division from number three in Europe to number one. It was an ambitious plan that hinged on making rapid, sizable market-share gains in Germany, where the company's main competitor was locally based and four times his division's size. The CEO commended his unit head for the inspiring and visionary presentation, then initiated a dialogue to test whether the plan was realistic. "Just how are you going to make these gains?" he wondered aloud. "What other alternatives have you considered? What customers do you plan to acquire?" The unit manager hadn't thought that far ahead. "How have you defined the customers' needs in new and unique ways? How many salespeople do you have?" the CEO asked.

"Ten," answered the unit head.

"How many does your main competitor have?"

"Two hundred," came the sheepish reply.

The boss continued to press: "Who runs Germany for us? Wasn't he in another division up until about three months ago?"

Had the exchange stopped there, the CEO would have only humiliated and discouraged this unit head and sent a message to others in attendance that the risks of thinking big were unacceptably high. But the CEO wasn't interested in killing the strategy and demoralizing the business unit team. Coaching through questioning, he wanted to inject some realism into the dialogue. Speaking bluntly, but not angrily or unkindly, he told the unit manager that he would need more than bravado to take on a formidable German competitor on its home turf. Instead of making a frontal assault, the CEO suggested, why not look for the competition's weak spots and win on speed of execution? Where are the gaps in your competitor's product line? Can you innovate something that can fill those gaps? What customers are the most likely buyers of such a product? Why not zero in on them? Instead of aiming for overall market-share gains, try resegmenting the market. Suddenly, what had appeared to be a dead end opened into new insights, and by the end of the meeting, it was decided that the manager would rethink the strategy and return in 90 days with a more realistic alternative. A key player whose strategy proposal had been flatly rejected left the room feeling energized, challenged, and more sharply focused on the task at hand.

Think about what happened here. Although it might not have been obvious at first, the CEO was not trying to assert his authority or

Dialogue Killers

IS THE DIALOGUE IN YOUR meetings an energy drain? If it doesn't energize people and focus their work, watch for the following.

Dangling Dialogue

Symptom: Confusion prevails. The meeting ends without a clear next step. People create their own self-serving interpretations of the meeting, and no one can be held accountable later when goals aren't met.
Remedy: Give the meeting closure by ensuring that everyone knows who will do what, by when. Do it in writing if necessary, and be specific.

Information Clogs

Symptom: Failure to get all the relevant information into the open. An important fact or opinion comes to light after a decision has been reached, which reopens the decision. This pattern happens repeatedly.
Remedy: Ensure that the right people are in attendance in the first place. When missing information is discovered, disseminate it immediately. Make the expectation for openness and candor explicit by asking, "What's missing?" Use coaching and sanctions to correct information hoarding.

Piecemeal Perspectives

Symptom: People stick to narrow views and self-interests and fail to acknowledge that others have valid interests.

---

diminish the executive. He simply wanted to ensure that the competitive realities were not glossed over and to coach those in attendance on both business acumen and organizational capability as well as on the fine art of asking the right questions. He was challenging the proposed strategy not for personal reasons but for business reasons.

The dialogue affected people's attitudes and behavior in subtle and not so subtle ways: They walked away knowing that they should look for opportunities in unconventional ways and be prepared to answer the inevitable tough questions. They also knew that the CEO was on their side. They became more convinced that growth was possible and that action was necessary. And something else happened: They began to adopt the CEO's tone in subsequent meetings. When, for example, the head of the German unit met with his senior staff to brief them on the new approach to the German market, the questions he fired at his sales chief and product development head

Remedy: Draw people out until you're sure all sides of the issue have been represented. Restate the common purpose repeatedly to keep everyone focused on the big picture. Generate alternatives. Use coaching to show people how their work contributes to the overall mission of the enterprise.

Free-for-All

Symptom: By failing to direct the flow of the discussion, the leader allows negative behaviors to flourish. "Extortionists" hold the whole group for ransom until others see it their way; "sidetrackers" go off on tangents, recount history by saying "When I did this ten years ago . . .," or delve into unnecessary detail; "silent liars" do not express their true opinions, or they agree to things they have no intention of doing; and "dividers" create breaches within the group by seeking support for their viewpoint outside the social operating mechanism or have parallel discussions during the meeting.

Remedy: The leader must exercise inner strength by repeatedly signaling which behaviors are acceptable and by sanctioning those who persist in negative behavior. If less severe sanctions fail, the leader must be willing to remove the offending player from the group.

were pointed, precise, and aimed directly at putting the new strategy into action. He had picked up on his boss's style of relating to others as well as his way of eliciting, sifting, and analyzing information. The entire unit grew more determined and energized.

The chief executive didn't leave the matter there, though. He followed up with a one-page, handwritten letter to the unit head stating the essence of the dialogue and the actions to be executed. And in 90 days, they met again to discuss the revised strategy. (For more on fostering decisive dialogue, see the sidebar "Dialogue Killers.")

How Dialogue Becomes Action

The setting in which dialogue occurs is as important as the dialogue itself. The social operating mechanisms of decisive corporate cultures feature behaviors marked by four characteristics: openness, candor, informality, and closure. Openness means that the outcome is not predetermined. There's an honest search for alternatives and new discoveries. Questions like "What are we missing?" draw people in and signal the leader's willingness to hear all sides. Leaders create an atmosphere of safety that permits spirited discussion, group learning, and trust.

Candor is slightly different. It's a willingness to speak the unspeakable, to expose unfulfilled commitments, to air the conflicts that undermine apparent consensus. Candor means that people express their real opinions, not what they think team players are supposed to say. Candor helps wipe out the silent lies and pocket vetoes that occur when people agree to things they have no intention of acting on. It prevents the kind of unnecessary rework and revisiting of decisions that saps productivity.

Formality suppresses candor; informality encourages it. When presentations and comments are stiff and prepackaged, they signal that the whole meeting has been carefully scripted and orchestrated. Informality has the opposite effect. It reduces defensiveness. People feel more comfortable asking questions and reacting honestly, and the spontaneity is energizing.

If informality loosens the atmosphere, closure imposes discipline. Closure means that at the end of the meeting, people know exactly what they are expected to do. Closure produces decisiveness by assigning accountability and deadlines to people in an open forum. It tests a leader's inner strength and intellectual resources. Lack of closure, coupled with a lack of sanctions, is the primary reason for a culture of indecision.

A robust social operating mechanism consistently includes these four characteristics. Such a mechanism has the right people participating in it, and it occurs with the right frequency.

When Dick Brown arrived at Electronic Data Systems (EDS) in early 1999, he resolved to create a culture that did more than pay lip service to the ideals of collaboration, openness, and decisiveness. He had a big job ahead of him. EDS was known for its bright, aggressive people, but employees had a reputation for competing against one another at least as often as they pulled together. The organization was marked by a culture of lone heroes. Individual operating units had little or no incentive for sharing information or cooperating with one another to win business. There were few sanctions for "lone" behaviors and for failure to meet performance goals. And indecision was rife. As one company veteran puts it, "Meetings, meetings, and more meetings. People couldn't make decisions, wouldn't make decisions. They didn't have to. No accountability." EDS was losing business. Revenue was flat, earnings were on the decline, and the price of the company's stock was down sharply.

A central tenet of Brown's management philosophy is that "leaders get the behavior they tolerate." Shortly after he arrived at EDS, he installed six social operating mechanisms within one year that signaled he would not put up with the old culture of rampant individualism and information hoarding. One mechanism was the "performance call," as it is known around the company. Once a month, the top 100 or so EDS executives worldwide take part in a conference call where the past month's numbers and critical activities are reviewed in detail. Transparency and simultaneous information are the rules; information hoarding is no longer possible. Everyone knows who is on target for the year, who is ahead of projections, and who is behind. Those who are behind must explain the shortfall—and how they plan to get back on track. It's not enough for a manager to say she's assessing, reviewing, or analyzing a problem. Those aren't the words of someone who is acting, Brown says. Those are the words of someone getting ready to act. To use them in front of Brown is to invite two questions in response: When you've finished your analysis, what are you going to do? And how soon are you going to do it? The only way that Brown's people can answer those questions satisfactorily is to make a decision and execute it.

The performance calls are also a mechanism for airing and resolving the conflicts inevitable in a large organization, particularly when it comes to cross selling in order to accelerate revenue growth. Two units may be pursuing the same customer, for example, or a customer serviced by one unit may be acquired by a customer serviced by another. Which unit should lead the pursuit? Which unit should

GE's Secret Weapon

KNOWN FOR ITS STATE-OF-THE-ART management practices, General Electric has forged a system of ten tightly linked social operating mechanisms. Vital to GE's success, these mechanisms set goals and priorities for the whole company as well as for its individual business units and track each unit's progress toward those goals. CEO Jack Welch also uses the system to evaluate senior managers within each unit and reward or sanction them according to their performance.

Three of the most widely imitated of these mechanisms are the Corporate Executive Council (CEC), which meets four times a year; the annual leadership and organizational reviews, known as Session C; and the annual strategy reviews, known as S-1 and S-2. Most large organizations have similar mechanisms. GE's, however, are notable for their intensity and duration; tight links to one another; follow-through; and uninhibited candor, closure, and decisiveness.

At the CEC, the company's senior leaders gather for two-and-a-half days of intensive collaboration and information exchange. As these leaders share best practices, assess the external business environment, and identify the company's most promising opportunities and most pressing problems, Welch has a chance to coach managers and observe their styles of working, thinking, and collaborating. Among the ten initiatives to emerge from these meetings in the past 14 years are GE's Six Sigma quality-improvement drive and its companywide e-commerce effort. These sessions aren't for the faint-hearted—at times, the debates can resemble verbal combat. But by the time the CEC breaks up, everyone in attendance knows both what the corporate priorities are and what's expected of him or her.

At Session C meetings, Welch and GE's senior vice president for human resources, Bill Conaty, meet with the head of each business unit as well as his or her top HR executive to discuss leadership and organizational issues. In these intense 12- to 14-hour sessions, the attendees review the unit's prospective talent pool and its organizational priorities. Who needs to be promoted,

service the merged entity? It's vitally important to resolve these questions. Letting them fester doesn't just drain emotional energy, it shrinks the organization's capacity to act decisively. Lack of speed becomes a competitive disadvantage.

Brown encourages people to bring these conflicts to the surface, both because he views them as a sign of organizational health and because they provide an opportunity to demonstrate the style of

rewarded, and developed? How? Who isn't making the grade? Candor is mandatory, and so is execution. The dialogue goes back and forth and links with the strategy of the business unit. Welch follows up each session with a handwritten note reviewing the substance of the dialogue and action items. Through this mechanism, picking and evaluating people has become a core competence at GE. No wonder GE is known as "CEO University."

The unit head's progress in implementing that action plan is among the items on the agenda at the S-1 meeting, held about two months after Session C. Welch, his chief financial officer, and members of the office of the CEO meet individually with each unit head and his or her team to discuss strategy for the next three years. The strategy, which must incorporate the companywide themes and initiatives that emerged from the CEC meetings, is subjected to intensive scrutiny and reality testing by Welch and the senior staff. The dialogue in the sessions is informal, open, decisive, and full of valuable coaching from Welch on both business and human resources issues. As in Session C, the dialogue about strategy links with people and organizational issues. Again, Welch follows up with a handwritten note in which he sets out what he expects of the unit head as a result of the dialogue.

S-2 meetings, normally held in November, follow a similar agenda to the S-1 meeting, except that they are focused on a shorter time horizon, usually 12 to 15 months. Here, operational priorities and resource allocations are linked.

Taken together, the meetings link feedback, decision making, and assessment of the organization's capabilities and key people. The mechanism explicitly ties the goals and performance of each unit to the overall strategy of the corporation and places a premium on the development of the next generation of leaders. The process is unrelenting in its demand for managerial accountability. At the same time, Welch takes the opportunity to engage in follow-through and feedback that is candid, on point, and focused on decisiveness and execution. This operating system may be GE's most enduring competitive advantage.

dialogue he advocates. He tries to create a safe environment for disagreement by reminding employees that the conflict isn't personal.

Conflict in any global organization is built in. And, Brown believes, it's essential if everyone is going to think in terms of the entire organization, not just one little corner of it. Instead of seeking the solution favorable to their unit, they'll look for the solution that's best for EDS and its shareholders. It sounds simple, even obvious. But in an organization once characterized by lone heroes and self-interest, highly visible exercises in conflict resolution remind people to align their interests with the company as a whole. It's not enough to state the message once and assume it will sink in. Behavior is changed through repetition. Stressing the message over and over in social operating mechanisms like the monthly performance calls—and rewarding or sanctioning people based on their adherence to it—is one of Brown's most powerful tools for producing the behavioral changes that usher in genuine cultural change.

Of course, no leader can or should attend every meeting, resolve every conflict, or make every decision. But by designing social operating mechanisms that promote free-flowing yet productive dialogue, leaders strongly influence how others perform these tasks. Indeed, it is through these mechanisms that the work of shaping a decisive culture gets done.

Another corporation that employs social operating mechanisms to create a decisive culture is multinational pharmaceutical giant Pharmacia. The company's approach illustrates a point I stress repeatedly to my clients: Structure divides; social operating mechanisms integrate. I hasten to add that structure is essential. If an organization didn't divide tasks, functions, and responsibilities, it would never get anything done. But social operating mechanisms are required to direct the various activities contained within a structure toward an objective. Well-designed mechanisms perform this integrating function. But no matter how well designed, the mechanisms also need decisive dialogue to work properly.

Two years after its 1995 merger with Upjohn, Pharmacia's CEO Fred Hassan set out to create an entirely new culture for the combined entity. The organization he envisioned would be collaborative, customer focused, and speedy. It would meld the disparate talents of a global enterprise to develop market-leading drugs—and do so faster than the competition. The primary mechanism for fostering collaboration: Leaders from several units and functions would engage in frequent, constructive dialogue.

The company's race to develop a new generation of antibiotics to treat drug-resistant infections afforded Pharmacia's management an opportunity to test the success of its culture-building efforts. Dr. Göran Ando, the chief of research and development, and Carrie Cox, the head of global business management, jointly created a social operating mechanism comprising some of the company's leading scientists, clinicians, and marketers. Just getting the three functions together regularly was a bold step. Typically, drug development proceeds by a series of handoffs. One group of scientists does the basic work of drug discovery, then hands off its results to a second group, which steers the drug through a year or more of clinical trials. If and when it receives the Food and Drug Administration's stamp of approval, it's handed off to the marketing people, who devise a marketing plan. Only then is the drug handed off to the sales department, which pitches it to doctors and hospitals. By supplanting this daisy-chain approach with one that made scientists, clinicians, and marketers jointly responsible for the entire flow of development and marketing, the two leaders aimed to develop a drug that better met the needs of patients, had higher revenue potential, and gained speed as a competitive advantage. And they wanted to create a template for future collaborative efforts.

The company's reward system reinforced this collaborative model by explicitly linking compensation to the actions of the group. Every member's compensation would be based on the time to bring the drug to market, the time for the drug to reach peak profitable share, and total sales. The system gave group members a strong incentive to talk openly with one another and to share information freely. But the creative spark was missing. The first few times the drug development group met, it focused almost exclusively on their differences, which were considerable. Without trafficking in clichés, it is safe to say that scientists, clinicians, and marketers tend to have different ways of speaking, thinking, and relating. And each tended to defend what it viewed as its interests rather than the interests of shareholders and customers. It was at this point that Ando and Cox took charge of the dialogue, reminding the group that it was important to play well with others but even more important to produce a drug that met patients' needs and to beat the competition.

Acting together, the two leaders channeled conversation into productive dialogue focused on a common task. They shared what they knew about developing and marketing pharmaceuticals and demonstrated how scientists could learn to think a little like marketers, and marketers a little like scientists. They tackled the emotional challenge of resolving conflicts in the open in order to demonstrate how to disagree, sometimes strongly, without animosity and without losing sight of their common purpose.

Indeed, consider how one dialogue helped the group make a decision that turned a promising drug into a success story. To simplify the research and testing process, the group's scientists had begun to search for an antibiotic that would be effective against a limited number of infections and would be used only as "salvage therapy" in acute cases, when conventional antibiotic therapies had failed. But intensive dialogue with the marketers yielded the information that doctors were receptive to a drug that would work against a wide spectrum of infections. They wanted a drug that could treat acute infections completely by starting treatment earlier in the course of the disease, either in large doses through an intravenous drip or in smaller doses with a pill. The scientists shifted their focus, and the result was Zyvox, one of the major pharmaceutical success stories of recent years. It has become the poster drug in Pharmacia's campaign for a culture characterized by cross-functional collaboration and speedy execution. Through dialogue, the group created a product that neither the scientists, clinicians, nor marketers acting by themselves could have envisioned or executed. And the mechanism that created this open dialogue is now standard practice at Pharmacia.

Follow-Through and Feedback

Follow-through is in the DNA of decisive cultures and takes place either in person, on the telephone, or in the routine conduct of a social operating mechanism. Lack of follow-through destroys the discipline of execution and encourages indecision.

A culture of indecision changes when groups of people are compelled to always be direct. And few mechanisms encourage directness more effectively than performance and compensation reviews, especially if they are explicitly linked to social operating mechanisms. Yet all too often, the performance review process is as ritualized and empty as the business meeting I described at the beginning of this article. Both the employee and his manager want to get the thing over with as quickly as possible. Check the appropriate box, keep up the good work, here's your raise, and let's be sure to do this again next year. Sorry—gotta run. There's no genuine conversation, no feedback, and worst of all, no chance for the employee to learn the sometimes painful truths that will help her grow and develop. Great compensation systems die for lack of candid dialogue and leaders' emotional fortitude.

At EDS, Dick Brown has devised an evaluation and review process that virtually forces managers to engage in candid dialogue with their subordinates. Everyone at the company is ranked in quintiles and rewarded according to how well they perform compared with their peers. It has proved to be one of the most controversial features of Dick Brown's leadership—some employees view it as a Darwinian means of dividing winners from losers and pitting colleagues against one another.

That isn't the objective of the ranking system, Brown insists. He views the ranking process as the most effective way to reward the company's best performers and show laggards where they need to improve. But the system needs the right sort of dialogue to make it work as intended and serve its purpose of growing the talent pool. Leaders must give honest feedback to their direct reports, especially to those who find themselves at the bottom of the rankings.

Brown recalls one encounter he had shortly after the first set of rankings was issued. An employee who had considered himself one of EDS's best performers was shocked to find himself closer to the bottom of the roster than the top. "How could this be?" the employee asked. "I performed as well this year as I did last year, and last year my boss gave me a stellar review." Brown replied that he could think of two possible explanations. The first was that the employee wasn't as good at his job as he thought he was. The second possibility was that even if the employee was doing as good a job as he did the previous year, his peers were doing better. "If you're staying the same," Brown concluded, "you're falling behind."

That exchange revealed the possibility—the likelihood, even—that the employee's immediate superior had given him a less-than-honest review the year before rather than tackle the unpleasant task of telling him where he was coming up short. Brown understands why a manager might be tempted to duck such a painful conversation. Delivering negative feedback tests the strength of a leader. But critical feedback is part of what Brown calls "the heavy lifting of leadership." Avoiding it, he says, "sentences the organization to mediocrity." What's more, by failing to provide honest feedback, leaders cheat their people by depriving them of the information they need to improve.

Feedback should be many things—candid; constructive; relentlessly focused on behavioral performance, accountability, and execution. One thing it shouldn't be is surprising. "A leader should be constructing his appraisal all year long," Brown says, "and giving his appraisal all year long. You have 20, 30, 60 opportunities a year to share your observations. Don't let those opportunities pass. If, at the end of the year, someone is truly surprised by what you have to say, that's a failure of leadership."

Ultimately, changing a culture of indecision is a matter of leadership. It's a matter of asking hard questions: How robust and effective are our social operating mechanisms? How well are they linked? Do they have the right people and the right frequency? Do they have a rhythm and operate consistently? Is follow-through built in? Are rewards and sanctions linked to the outcomes of the decisive dialogue? Most important, how productive is the dialogue within these mechanisms? Is our dialogue marked by openness, candor, informality, and closure?

Transforming a culture of indecision is an enormous and demanding task. It takes all the listening skills, business acumen, and operational experience that a corporate leader can summon. But just as important, the job demands emotional fortitude, follow-through, and inner strength. Asking the right questions; identifying and resolving conflicts; providing candid, constructive feedback; and differentiating people with sanctions and rewards is never easy. Frequently, it's downright unpleasant. No wonder many senior executives avoid the task. In the short term, they spare themselves considerable emotional wear and tear. But their evasion sets the tone for an organization that can't share intelligence, make decisions, or face conflicts, much less resolve them. Those who evade miss the very point of effective leadership. Leaders with the strength to insist on honest dialogue and follow-through will be rewarded not only with a decisive organization but also with a workforce that is energized, empowered, and engaged.

Originally published in April 2001. Reprint R0601J

What You Don't Know About Making Decisions

by David A. Garvin and Michael A. Roberto

LEADERS SHOW THEIR METTLE IN many ways—setting strategy and motivating people, just to mention two—but above all else leaders are made or broken by the quality of their decisions. That's a given, right? If you answered yes, then you would probably be surprised by how many executives approach decision making in a way that neither puts enough options on the table nor permits sufficient evaluation to ensure that they can make the best choice. Indeed, our research over the past several years strongly suggests that, simply put, most leaders get decision making all wrong.

The reason: Most businesspeople treat decision making as an event—a discrete choice that takes place at a single point in time, whether they're sitting at a desk, moderating a meeting, or staring at a spreadsheet. This classic view of decision making has a pronouncement popping out of a leader's head, based on experience, gut, research, or all three. Say the matter at hand is whether to pull a product with weak sales off the market. An "event" leader would mull in solitude, ask for advice, read reports, mull some more, then say yea or nay and send the organization off to make it happen. But to look at decision making that way is to overlook larger social and organizational contexts, which ultimately determine the success of any decision.

The fact is, decision making is not an event. It's a process, one that unfolds over weeks, months, or even years; one that's fraught with power plays and politics and is replete with personal nuances and institutional history; one that's rife with discussion and debate; and one that requires support at all levels of the organization when it comes time for execution. Our research shows that the difference between leaders who make good decisions and those who make bad ones is striking. The former recognize that all decisions are processes, and they explicitly design and manage them as such. The latter persevere in the fantasy that decisions are events they alone control.

In the following pages, we'll explore how leaders can design and manage a sound, effective decision-making process—an approach we call inquiry—and outline a set of criteria for assessing the quality of the decision-making process. First, a look at the process itself.

Decisions as Process: Inquiry Versus Advocacy

Not all decision-making processes are equally effective, particularly in the degree to which they allow a group to identify and consider a wide range of ideas. In our research, we've seen two broad approaches. *Inquiry*, which we prefer, is a very open process designed to generate multiple alternatives, foster the exchange of ideas, and produce a well-tested solution. Unfortunately, this approach doesn't come easily or naturally to most people. Instead, groups charged with making a decision tend to default to the second mode, one we call *advocacy*. The two look deceptively similar on the surface: groups of people, immersed in discussion and debate, trying to select a course of action by drawing on what they believe is the best available evidence. But despite their similarities, inquiry and advocacy produce dramatically different results.

When a group takes an advocacy perspective, participants approach decision making as a contest, although they don't necessarily compete openly or even consciously. Well-defined groups with special interests—dueling divisions in search of budget increases, for example—advocate for particular positions. Participants are

Idea in Brief

The quality of a leader's decisions can make or break him. Yet most of us get decision making all wrong. Why? We take the least productive approach: **advocacy**. We argue our position with a passion that prevents us from weighing opposing views. We downplay our position's weaknesses to boost our chances of "winning." And we march into decision-making discussions armed for a battle of wills. The consequences? Fractious exchanges that discourage innovative thinking and stifle diverse, valuable viewpoints.

Contrast advocacy with **inquiry**—a much more productive decision-making approach. With inquiry, you carefully consider a variety of options, work with others to discover the best solutions, and stimulate creative thinking rather than suppressing dissension. The payoff? High-quality decisions that advance your company's objectives, and that you reach in a timely manner and implement effectively.

Inquiry isn't easy. You must promote constructive conflict and accept ambiguity. You also must balance *divergence* during early discussions with *unity* during implementation.

How to accomplish this feat? Master the "three C's" of decision making: **conflict, consideration,** and **closure**.

passionate about their preferred solutions and therefore stand firm in the face of disagreement. That level of passion makes it nearly impossible to remain objective, limiting people's ability to pay attention to opposing arguments. Advocates often present information selectively, buttressing their arguments while withholding relevant conflicting data. Their goal, after all, is to make a compelling case, not to convey an evenhanded or balanced view. Two different plant managers pushing their own improvement programs, for example, may be wary of reporting potential weak points for fear that full disclosure will jeopardize their chances of winning the debate and gaining access to needed resources.

What's more, the disagreements that arise are frequently fractious and even antagonistic. Personalities and egos come into play, and differences are normally resolved through battles of wills and behind-the-scenes maneuvering. The implicit assumption is that a superior solution will emerge from a test of strength among

Idea in Practice

Constructive Conflict

Conflict during decision making takes two forms: *cognitive* (relating to the substance of the work) and *affective* (stemming from interpersonal friction). The first is crucial to effective decision making; the second, destructive. To increase cognitive conflict while decreasing affective:

- **Require vigorous debate.** As a rule, ask tough questions and expect well-framed responses. Pose unexpected theoretical questions that stimulate productive thinking.
- **Prohibit language that triggers defensiveness.** Preface contradictory remarks or questions with phrases that remove blame and fault. ("Your arguments make good sense, but let me play devil's advocate for a moment.")
- **Break up natural coalitions.** Assign people to tasks without consideration of traditional loyalties. Require people with different interests to work together.
- **Shift individuals out of well-worn grooves.** During decision making, ask people to play functional or managerial roles different from their own; for example, lower-level employees assume a CEO's perspective.
- **Challenge stalemated participants to revisit key information.** Ask them to examine underlying assumptions and gather more facts.

Consideration

To gain your team's acceptance and support of a decision-making outcome—even if you've rejected their recommendations—ensure that they perceive the decision-making process as fair. How? Demonstrate consideration throughout the process:

- At the outset, **convey openness** to new ideas and willingness

competing positions. But in fact this approach typically suppresses innovation and encourages participants to go along with the dominant view to avoid further conflict.

By contrast, an inquiry-focused group carefully considers a variety of options and works together to discover the best solution. While people naturally continue to have their own interests, the goal is not to persuade the group to adopt a given point of view but instead to come to agreement on the best course of action. People share information widely, preferably in raw form, to allow participants to draw their own

to accept different views. Avoid indicating you've already made up your mind.

- During the discussion, **listen attentively**. Make eye contact and show patience while others explain their positions. Take notes, ask questions, and probe for deeper explanations.
- Afterward, **explain the rationale behind your decision**. Detail the criteria you used to select a course of action. Spell out how each participant's arguments affected the final decision.

Closure

In addition to stimulating constructive conflict and showing consideration, bring the decision process to closure at the appropriate time. Watch for two problems:

- **Deciding too early**. Worried about being dissenters, decision participants may readily accept the first plausible option rather than thoughtfully analyzing options. Unstated objections surface later—preventing cooperative action during the crucial implementation stage.

  Watch for latent discontent in body language—furrowed brows, crossed arms, the curled-up posture of defiance. Call for a break, encourage each dissenter to speak up, then reconvene. Seek input from people known for raising hard questions and offering fresh perspectives.

- **Deciding too late.** Warring factions face off, restating their positions repeatedly. Or, striving for fairness, people insist on hearing every view and resolving every question before reaching closure.

To escape these endless loops, announce a decision. Accept that the decision-making process is ambiguous and that you'll never have complete, unequivocal data.

conclusions. Rather than suppressing dissension, an inquiry process encourages critical thinking. All participants feel comfortable raising alternative solutions and asking hard questions about the possibilities already on the table.

People engaged in an inquiry process rigorously question proposals and the assumptions they rest on, so conflict may be intense—but it is seldom personal. In fact, because disagreements revolve around ideas and interpretations rather than entrenched positions, conflict is generally healthy, and team members resolve their differ-

Two approaches to decision making

	Advocacy	Inquiry
Concept of decision making	a contest	collaborative problem solving
Purpose of discussion	persuasion and lobbying	testing and evaluation
Participants' role	spokespeople	critical thinkers
Patterns of behavior	strive to persuade others defend your position downplay weaknesses	present balanced arguments remain open to alternatives accept constructive criticism
Minority views	discouraged or dismissed	cultivated and valued
Outcome	winners and losers	collective ownership

ences by applying rules of reason. The implicit assumption is that a consummate solution will emerge from a test of strength among competing ideas rather than dueling positions. Recent accounts of GE's succession process describe board members pursuing just such an open-minded approach. All members met repeatedly with the major candidates and gathered regularly to review their strengths and weaknesses—frequently without Jack Welch in attendance—with little or no attempt to lobby early for a particular choice.

A process characterized by inquiry rather than advocacy tends to produce decisions of higher quality—decisions that not only advance the company's objectives but also are reached in a timely manner and can be implemented effectively. Therefore, we believe that leaders seeking to improve their organizations' decision-making capabilities need to begin with a single goal: moving as quickly as possible from a process of advocacy to one of inquiry.

That requires careful attention to three critical factors, the "three C's" of effective decision making: *conflict, consideration,* and *closure*. Each entails a delicate balancing act.

Constructive Conflict

Critical thinking and rigorous debate invariably lead to conflict. The good news is that conflict brings issues into focus, allowing leaders to make more informed choices. The bad news is that the wrong kind of conflict can derail the decision-making process altogether.

Indeed, conflict comes in two forms—*cognitive* and *affective*. Cognitive, or substantive, conflict relates to the work at hand. It involves disagreements over ideas and assumptions and differing views on the best way to proceed. Not only is such conflict healthy, it's crucial to effective inquiry. When people express differences openly and challenge underlying assumptions, they can flag real weaknesses and introduce new ideas. Affective, or interpersonal, conflict is emotional. It involves personal friction, rivalries, and clashing personalities, and it tends to diminish people's willingness to cooperate during implementation, rendering the decision-making process less effective. Not surprisingly, it is a common feature of advocacy processes.

On examination, the two are easy to distinguish. When a team member recalls "tough debates about the strategic, financial, and operating merits of the three acquisition candidates," she is referring to cognitive conflict. When a team member comments on "heated arguments that degenerated into personal attacks," he means affective conflict. But in practice the two types of conflict are surprisingly hard to separate. People tend to take any criticism personally and react defensively. The atmosphere quickly becomes charged, and even if a high-quality decision emerges, the emotional fallout tends to linger, making it hard for team members to work together during implementation.

The challenge for leaders is to increase cognitive conflict while keeping affective conflict low—no mean feat. One technique is to establish norms that make vigorous debate the rule rather than the exception. Chuck Knight, for 27 years the CEO of Emerson Electric, accomplished this by relentlessly grilling managers during planning reviews, no matter what he actually thought of the proposal on the table, asking tough, combative questions and expecting well-framed responses. The process—which Knight called the "logic of illogic" because of his willingness to test even well-crafted arguments by raising unexpected, and occasionally fanciful, concerns—was undoubtedly intimidating. But during his tenure it produced a steady stream of smart investment decisions and an unbroken string of quarterly increases in net income.

Bob Galvin, when he was CEO of Motorola in the 1980s, took a slightly different approach. He habitually asked unexpected hypothetical questions that stimulated creative thinking. Subsequently, as chairman of the board of overseers for the Malcolm Baldrige National Quality Program, Galvin took his colleagues by surprise when, in response to pressure from constituents to broaden the criteria for the award, he proposed narrowing them instead. In the end, the board did in fact broaden the criteria, but his seemingly out-of-the-blue suggestion sparked a creative and highly productive debate.

Another technique is to structure the conversation so that the process, by its very nature, fosters debate. This can be done by dividing people into groups with different, and often competing, responsibilities. For example, one group may be asked to develop a proposal while the other generates alternative recommendations. Then the groups would exchange proposals and discuss the various options. Such techniques virtually guarantee high levels of cognitive conflict. (The exhibit "Structuring the debate" outlines two approaches for using different groups to stimulate creative thinking.)

But even if you've structured the process with an eye toward encouraging cognitive conflict, there's always a risk that it will become personal. Beyond cooling the debate with "time-outs," skilled leaders use a number of creative techniques to elevate cognitive debate while minimizing affective conflict.

Structuring the debate

By breaking a decision-making body into two subgroups, leaders can often create an environment in which people feel more comfortable engaging in debate. Scholars recommend two techniques in particular, which we call the "point-counterpoint" and "intellectual watchdog" approaches. The first three steps are the same for both techniques:

Point-counterpoint	Intellectual watchdog
The team divides into two subgroups.	The team divides into two subgroups.
Subgroup A develops a proposal, fleshing out the recommendation, the key assumptions, and the critical supporting data.	Subgroup A develops a proposal, fleshing out the recommendation, the key assumptions, and the critical supporting data.
Subgroup A presents the proposal to Subgroup B in written and oral forms.	Subgroup A presents the proposal to Subgroup B in written and oral forms.
Subgroup B generates one or more alternative plans of action.	Subgroup B develops a detailed critique of these assumptions and recommendations. It presents this critique in written and oral forms. Subgroup A revises its proposal based on this feedback.
The subgroups come together to debate the proposals and seek agreement on a common set of assumptions.	The subgroups continue in this revision-critique-revision cycle until they converge on a common set of assumptions.
Based on those assumptions, the subgroups continue to debate various options and strive to agree on a common set of recommendations.	Then, the subgroups work together to develop a common set of recommendations.

First, adroit leaders pay careful attention to the way issues are framed, as well as to the language used during discussions. They preface contradictory remarks or questions with phrases that remove some of the personal sting ("Your arguments make good sense, but let me play devil's advocate for a moment"). They also set ground rules about language, insisting that team members avoid words and behavior that trigger defensiveness. For instance, in the U.S. Army's after-action reviews, conducted immediately after missions to identify mistakes so they can be avoided next time, facilitators make a point of saying, "We don't use the 'b' word, and we don't use the 'f' word. We don't place blame, and we don't find fault."

Second, leaders can help people step back from their preestablished positions by breaking up natural coalitions and assigning people to tasks on some basis other than traditional loyalties. At a leading aerospace company, one business unit president had to deal with two powerful coalitions within his organization during a critical decision about entering into a strategic alliance. When he set up two groups to consider alternative alliance partners, he interspersed the groups with members of each coalition, forcing people with different interests to work with one another. He then asked both groups to evaluate the same wide range of options using different criteria (such as technological capability, manufacturing prowess, or project management skills). The two groups then shared their evaluations and worked together to select the best partner. Because nobody had complete information, they were forced to listen closely to one another.

Third, leaders can shift individuals out of well-grooved patterns, where vested interests are highest. They can, for example, ask team members to research and argue for a position they did not endorse during initial discussions. Similarly, they can assign team members to play functional or managerial roles different from their own, such as asking an operations executive to take the marketing view or asking a lower-level employee to assume the CEO's strategic perspective.

Finally, leaders can ask participants locked in debate to revisit key facts and assumptions and gather more information. Often, people become so focused on the differences between opposing positions that they reach a stalemate. Emotional conflict soon follows. Asking people to examine underlying presumptions can defuse the tension and set the team back on track. For instance, at Enron, when people disagree strongly about whether or not to apply their trading skills to a new commodity or market, senior executives quickly refocus the discussion on characteristics of industry structure and assumptions about market size and customer preferences. People quickly recognize areas of agreement, discover precisely how and why they disagree, and then focus their debate on specific issues.

Consideration

Once a decision's been made and the alternatives dismissed, some people will have to surrender the solution they preferred. At times, those who are overruled resist the outcome; at other times, they display grudging acceptance. What accounts for the difference? The critical factor appears to be the perception of fairness—what scholars call "procedural justice." The reality is that the leader will make the ultimate decision, but the people participating in the process must believe that their views were considered and that they had a genuine opportunity to influence the final decision. Researchers have found that if participants believe the process was fair, they are far more willing to commit themselves to the resulting decision even if their views did not prevail. (For a detailed discussion of this phenomenon, see W. Chan Kim and Renée Mauborgne, "Fair Process: Managing in the Knowledge Economy," HBR July–August 1997).

Many managers equate fairness with *voice*—with giving everyone a chance to express his or her own views. They doggedly work their way around the table, getting everyone's input. However, voice is not nearly as important as *consideration*—people's belief that the leader actively listened to them during the discussions and weighed their views carefully before reaching a decision. In his 1999 book, *Only the Paranoid Survive*, Intel's chairman Andy Grove describes how he explains the distinction to his middle managers: "Your criterion for involvement should be that you're heard and understood. . . . All sides cannot prevail in the debate, but all opinions have value in shaping the right answer."

In fact, voice without consideration is often damaging; it leads to resentment and frustration rather than to acceptance. When the time comes to implement the decision, people are likely to drag their feet if

Advocacy Versus Inquiry in Action: The Bay of Pigs and the Cuban Missile Crisis

PERHAPS THE BEST DEMONSTRATION OF advocacy versus inquiry comes from the administration of President John F. Kennedy. During his first two years in office, Kennedy wrestled with two critical foreign policy decisions: the Bay of Pigs invasion and the Cuban Missile Crisis. Both were assigned to cabinet-level task forces, involving many of the same players, the same political interests, and extremely high stakes. But the results were extraordinarily different, largely because the two groups operated in different modes.

The first group, charged with deciding whether to support an invasion of Cuba by a small army of U.S.-trained Cuban exiles, worked in advocacy mode, and the outcome is widely regarded as an example of flawed decision making. Shortly after taking office, President Kennedy learned of the planned attack on Cuba developed by the CIA during the Eisenhower administration. Backed by the Joint Chiefs of Staff, the CIA argued forcefully for the invasion and minimized the risks, filtering the information presented to the president to reinforce the agency's position. Knowledgeable individuals on the State Department's Latin America desk were excluded from deliberations because of their likely opposition.

Some members of Kennedy's staff opposed the plan but held their tongues for fear of appearing weak in the face of strong advocacy by the CIA. As a result, there was little debate, and the group failed to test some critical underlying assumptions. For example, they didn't question whether the landing would in fact lead to a rapid domestic uprising against Castro, and they failed to find out whether the exiles could fade into the mountains (which were 80 miles from the landing site) should they meet with strong resistance. The resulting invasion is generally considered to be one of the low points of the Cold War. About 100 lives were lost, and the rest of the exiles were taken hostage. The incident was a major embarrassment to the Kennedy administration and dealt a blow to America's global standing.

After the botched invasion, Kennedy conducted a review of the foreign policy decision-making process and introduced five major changes, essentially transforming the process into one of inquiry. First, people were urged to participate in discussions as "skeptical generalists"—that is, as disinterested

they sense that the decision-making process had been a sham—an exercise in going through the motions designed to validate the leader's preferred solution. This appears to have been true of the Daimler-Chrysler merger. Daimler CEO Jurgen Schrempp asked for

critical thinkers rather than as representatives of particular departments. Second, Robert Kennedy and Theodore Sorensen were assigned the role of intellectual watchdog, expected to pursue every possible point of contention, uncovering weaknesses and untested assumptions. Third, task forces were urged to abandon the rules of protocol, eliminating formal agendas and deference to rank. Fourth, participants were expected to split occasionally into subgroups to develop a broad range of options. And finally, President Kennedy decided to absent himself from some of the early task force meetings to avoid influencing other participants and slanting the debate.

The inquiry mode was used to great effect when in October 1962 President Kennedy learned that the Soviet Union had placed nuclear missiles on Cuban soil, despite repeated assurances from the Soviet ambassador that this would not occur. Kennedy immediately convened a high-level task force, which contained many of the same men responsible for the Bay of Pigs invasion, and asked them to frame a response. The group met night and day for two weeks, often inviting additional members to join in their deliberations to broaden their perspective. Occasionally, to encourage the free flow of ideas, they met without the president. Robert Kennedy played his new role thoughtfully, critiquing options frequently and encouraging the group to develop additional alternatives. In particular, he urged the group to move beyond a simple go-no-go decision on a military air strike.

Ultimately, subgroups developed two positions, one favoring a blockade and the other an air strike. These groups gathered information from a broad range of sources, viewed and interpreted the same intelligence photos, and took great care to identify and test underlying assumptions, such as whether the Tactical Air Command was indeed capable of eliminating all Soviet missiles in a surgical air strike. The subgroups exchanged position papers, critiqued each other's proposals, and came together to debate the alternatives. They presented Kennedy with both options, leaving him to make the final choice. The result was a carefully framed response, leading to a successful blockade and a peaceful end to the crisis.

extensive analysis and assessment of potential merger candidates but had long before settled on Chrysler as his choice. In fact, when consultants told him that his strategy was unlikely to create shareholder value, he dismissed the data and went ahead with his plans.

Schrempp may have solicited views from many parties, but he clearly failed to give them much weight.

Leaders can demonstrate consideration throughout the decision-making process. At the outset, they need to convey openness to new ideas and a willingness to accept views that differ from their own. In particular, they must avoid suggesting that their minds are already made up. They should avoid disclosing their personal preferences early in the process, or they should clearly state that any initial opinions are provisional and subject to change. Or they can absent themselves from early deliberations.

During the discussions, leaders must take care to show that they are listening actively and attentively. How? By asking questions, probing for deeper explanations, echoing comments, making eye contact, and showing patience when participants explain their positions. Taking notes is an especially powerful signal, since it suggests that the leader is making a real effort to capture, understand, and evaluate people's thoughts.

And after they make the final choice, leaders should explain their logic. They must describe the rationale for their decision, detailing the criteria they used to select a course of action. Perhaps more important, they need to convey how each participant's arguments affected the final decision or explain clearly why they chose to differ with those views.

Closure

Knowing when to end deliberations is tricky; all too often decision-making bodies rush to a conclusion or else dither endlessly and decide too late. Deciding too early is as damaging as deciding too late, and both problems can usually be traced to unchecked advocacy.

Deciding too early

Sometimes people's desire to be considered team players overrides their willingness to engage in critical thinking and thoughtful analysis, so the group readily accepts the first remotely plausible option. Popularly known as "groupthink," this mind-set is prevalent in the presence of strong advocates, especially in new teams, whose members are still learning the rules and may be less willing to stand out as dissenters.

The danger of groupthink is not only that it suppresses the full range of options but also that unstated objections will come to the surface at some critical moment—usually at a time when aligned, cooperative action is essential to implementation. The leader of a large division of a fast-growing retailer learned this the hard way. He liked to work with a small subset of his senior team to generate options, evaluate the alternatives, and develop a plan of action, and then bring the proposal back to the full team for validation. At that point, his managers would feel they had been presented with a fait accompli and so would be reluctant to raise their concerns. As one of them put it: "Because the meeting is the wrong place to object, we don't walk out of the room as a unified group." Instead, they would reopen the debate during implementation, delaying important initiatives by many months.

As their first line of defense against group-think, leaders need to learn to recognize latent discontent, paying special attention to body language: furrowed brows, crossed arms, or curled-up defiance. To bring disaffected people back into the discussion, it may be best to call for a break, approach dissenters one by one, encourage them to speak up, and then reconvene. GM's Alfred Sloan was famous for this approach, which he would introduce with the following speech: "I take it we are all in complete agreement on the decision here. Then I propose we postpone further discussion of the matter until our next meeting to give ourselves time to develop disagreement and perhaps gain some understanding of what the decision is all about."

Another way to avoid early closure is to cultivate minority views either through norms or through explicit rules. Minority views broaden and deepen debate; they stretch a group's thinking, even though they are seldom adopted intact. It is for this reason that Andy Grove routinely seeks input from "helpful Cassandras," people who are known for raising hard questions and offering fresh perspectives about the dangers of proposed policies.

Deciding too late

Here, too, unchecked advocacy is frequently the source of the problem, and in these instances it takes two main forms. At times, a team hits gridlock: Warring factions refuse to yield, restating their positions over and over again. Without a mechanism for breaking the deadlock, discussions become an endless loop. At other times, people bend over backward to ensure evenhanded participation. Striving for fairness, team members insist on hearing every view and resolving every question before reaching a conclusion. This demand for certainty—for complete arguments backed by unassailable data—is its own peculiar form of advocacy. Once again, the result is usually an endless loop, replaying the same alternatives, objections, and requests for further information. Any member of the group can unilaterally derail the discussion by voicing doubts. Meanwhile, competitive pressures may be demanding an immediate response, or participants may have tuned out long ago, as the same arguments are repeated ad nauseam.

At this point, it's the leader's job to "call the question." Jamie Houghton, the longtime CEO of Corning, invented a vivid metaphor to describe this role. He spoke of wearing two hats when working with his senior team: He figuratively put on his cowboy hat when he wanted to debate with members as an equal, and he donned a bowler when, as CEO, he called the question and announced a decision. The former role allowed for challenges and continued discussion; the latter signaled an end to the debate.

The message here is that leaders—and their teams—need to become more comfortable with ambiguity and be willing to make speedy decisions in the absence of complete, unequivocal data or support. As Dean Stanley Teele of Harvard Business School was fond of telling students: "The art of management is the art of making meaningful generalizations out of inadequate facts."

A Litmus Test

Unfortunately, superior decision making is distressingly difficult to assess in real time. Successful outcomes—decisions of high quality, made in a timely manner and implemented effectively—can be evaluated only after the fact. But by the time the results are in, it's normally too late to take corrective action. Is there any way to find out earlier whether you're on the right track?

There is indeed. The trick, we believe, is to periodically assess the decision-making process, even as it is under way. Scholars now have considerable evidence showing that a small set of process traits is closely linked with superior outcomes. While they are no guarantee of success, their combined presence sharply improves the odds that you'll make a good decision.

Multiple alternatives

When groups consider many alternatives, they engage in more thoughtful analysis and usually avoid settling too quickly on the easy, obvious answer. This is one reason techniques like point-counterpoint, which requires groups to generate at least two alternatives, are so often associated with superior decision making. Usually, keeping track of the number of options being considered will tell if this test has been met. But take care not to double count. Go-no-go choices involve only one option and don't qualify as two alternatives.

Assumption testing

"Facts" come in two varieties: those that have been carefully tested and those that have been merely asserted or assumed. Effective decision-making groups do not confuse the two. They periodically step back from their arguments and try to confirm their assumptions by examining them critically. If they find that some still lack hard evidence, they may elect to proceed, but they will at least know they're venturing into uncertain territory. Alternatively, the group may designate "intellectual watchdogs" who are assigned the task of scrutinizing the process for unchecked assumptions and challenging them on the spot.

Well-defined criteria

Without crisp, clear goals, it's easy to fall into the trap of comparing apples with oranges. Competing arguments become difficult to judge, since advocates will suggest using those measures (net income, return on capital, market presence, share of mind, and so on) that favor their preferred alternative. Fuzzy thinking and long delays are the likely result.

To avoid the problem, the team should specify goals up front and revisit them repeatedly during the decision-making process. These goals can be complex and multifaceted, quantitative and qualitative, but whatever form they take, they must remain at the fore. Studies of merger decisions have found that as the process reaches its final stages and managers feel the pressure of deadlines and the rush to close, they often compromise or adjust the criteria they originally created for judging the appropriateness of the deal.

Dissent and debate

David Hume, the great Scottish philosopher, argued persuasively for the merits of debate when he observed that the "truth springs from arguments amongst friends." There are two ways to measure the health of a debate: the kinds of questions being asked and the level of listening.

Some questions open up discussion; others narrow it and end deliberations. Contrarian hypothetical questions usually trigger healthy debate. A manager who worked for former American Express CEO Harvey Golub points to a time when the company was committed to lowering credit card fees, and Golub unexpectedly proposed raising fees instead. "I don't think he meant it seriously," says the manager. "But he certainly taught us how to think about fees."

The level of listening is an equally important indicator of a healthy decision-making process. Poor listening produces flawed analysis as well as personal friction. If participants routinely interrupt one another or pile on rebuttals before digesting the preceding comment, affective conflict is likely to materialize. Civilized discussions quickly become impossible, for collegiality and group harmony usually disappear in the absence of active listening.

Perceived fairness

A real-time measure of perceived fairness is the level of participation that's maintained after a key midpoint or milestone has been reached. Often, a drop in participation is an early warning of problems with implementation since some members of the group are already showing their displeasure by voting with their feet.

In fact, keeping people involved in the process is, in the end, perhaps the most crucial factor in making a decision—and making it stick. It's a job that lies at the heart of leadership and one that uniquely combines the leader's numerous talents. It requires the fortitude to promote conflict while accepting ambiguity, the wisdom to know when to bring conversations to a close, the patience to help others understand the reasoning behind your choice, and, not least, a genius for balance—the ability to embrace both the divergence that may characterize early discussions and the unity needed for effective implementation. Cyrus the Great, the founder of the Persian Empire and a renowned military leader, understood the true hallmark of leadership in the sixth century BC, when he attributed his success to "diversity in counsel, unity in command."

Originally published in August 2001. Reprint R0108G

Who Has the D?

How Clear Decision Roles Enhance Organizational Performance.

by Paul Rogers and Marcia Blenko

DECISIONS ARE THE COIN OF the realm in business. Every success, every mishap, every opportunity seized or missed is the result of a decision that someone made or failed to make. At many companies, decisions routinely get stuck inside the organization like loose change. But it's more than loose change that's at stake, of course; it's the performance of the entire organization. Never mind what industry you're in, how big and well known your company may be, or how clever your strategy is. If you can't make the right decisions quickly and effectively, and execute those decisions consistently, your business will lose ground.

Indeed, making good decisions and making them happen quickly are the hallmarks of high-performing organizations. When we surveyed executives at 350 global companies about their organizational effectiveness, only 15% said that they have an organization that helps the business outperform competitors. What sets those top performers apart is the quality, speed, and execution of their decision making. The most effective organizations score well on the major strategic decisions—which markets to enter or exit, which businesses to buy or sell, where to allocate capital and talent. But they truly shine when it comes to the critical operating decisions requiring consistency and speed—how to drive product innovation, the best way to position brands, how to manage channel partners.

Even in companies respected for their decisiveness, however, there can be ambiguity over who is accountable for which decisions. As a result, the entire decision-making process can stall, usually at one of four bottlenecks: global versus local, center versus business unit, function versus function, and inside versus outside partners.

The first of these bottlenecks, *global versus local* decision making, can occur in nearly every major business process and function. Decisions about brand building and product development frequently get snared here, when companies wrestle over how much authority local businesses should have to tailor products for their markets. Marketing is another classic global versus local issue—should local markets have the power to determine pricing and advertising?

The second bottleneck, *center versus business unit* decision making, tends to afflict parent companies and their subsidiaries. Business units are on the front line, close to the customer; the center sees the big picture, sets broad goals, and keeps the organization focused on winning. Where should the decision-making power lie? Should a major capital investment, for example, depend on the approval of the business unit that will own it, or should headquarters make the final call?

Function versus function decision making is perhaps the most common bottleneck. Every manufacturer, for instance, faces a balancing act between product development and marketing during the design of a new product. Who should decide what? Cross-functional decisions too often result in ineffective compromise solutions, which frequently need to be revisited because the right people were not involved at the outset.

The fourth decision-making bottleneck, *inside versus outside partners,* has become familiar with the rise of outsourcing, joint ventures, strategic alliances, and franchising. In such arrangements, companies need to be absolutely clear about which decisions can be owned by the external partner (usually those about the execution of strategy) and which must continue to be made internally (decisions about the strategy itself). In the case of outsourcing, for instance, brand-name apparel and footwear marketers once assumed that overseas suppliers could be responsible for decisions about plant employees' wages and working conditions. Big mistake.

Idea in Brief

Decisions are the coin of the realm in business. Every success, every mishap, every opportunity seized or missed stems from a decision someone made—or failed to make. Yet in many firms, decisions routinely stall inside the organization—hurting the entire company's performance.

The culprit? Ambiguity over who's accountable for which decisions. In one auto manufacturer that was missing milestones for rolling out new models, marketers *and* product developers each thought they were responsible for deciding new models' standard features and colors. Result? Conflict over who had final say, endless revisiting of decisions—and missed deadlines that led to lost sales.

How to clarify decision accountability? Assign clear roles for the decisions that most affect your firm's performance—such as which markets to enter, where to allocate capital, and how to drive product innovation. Think "RAPID": Who should recommend a course of action on a key decision? Who must agree to a recommendation before it can move forward? Who will perform the actions needed to implement the decision? Whose input is needed to determine the proposal's feasibility? Who decides—brings the decision to closure and commits the organization to implement it?

When you clarify decision roles, you make the *right* choices—swiftly and effectively.

Clearing the Bottlenecks

The most important step in unclogging decision-making bottlenecks is assigning clear roles and responsibilities. Good decision makers recognize which decisions really matter to performance. They think through who should recommend a particular path, who needs to agree, who should have input, who has ultimate responsibility for making the decision, and who is accountable for follow-through. They make the process routine. The result: better coordination and quicker response times.

Companies have devised a number of methods to clarify decision roles and assign responsibilities. We have used an approach called RAPID, which has evolved over the years, to help hundreds of companies develop clear decision-making guidelines. It is, for sure, not a panacea (an indecisive decision maker, for example, can ruin any good system), but it's an important start. The letters in RAPID stand for the

Idea in Practice

The RAPID Decision Model

For every strategic decision, assign the following roles and responsibilities:

People who . . .	Are responsible for . . .
Recommend	• Making a proposal on a key decision, gathering input, and providing data and analysis to make a sensible choice in a timely fashion • Consulting with input providers—hearing and incorporating their views, and winning their buy-in
Agree	• Negotiating a modified proposal with the recommender if they have concerns about the original proposal • Escalating unresolved issues to the decider if the "A" and "R" can't resolve differences • If necessary, exercising veto power over the recommendation
Perform	• Executing a decision once it's made • Seeing that the decision is implemented promptly and effectively
Input	• Providing relevant facts to the recommender that shed light on the proposal's feasibility and practical implications
Decide	• Serving as the single point of accountability • Bringing the decision to closure by resolving any impasse in the decision-making process • Committing the organization to implementing the decision

primary roles in any decision-making process, although these roles are not performed exactly in this order: recommend, agree, perform, input, and decide—the "D." (See the sidebar "A Decision-Making Primer.")

The people who *recommend* a course of action are responsible for making a proposal or offering alternatives. They need data and analysis to support their recommendations, as well as common sense about what's reasonable, practical, and effective.

The people who *agree* to a recommendation are those who need to sign off on it before it can move forward. If they veto a proposal,

Decision-Role Pitfalls

In assigning decision roles:

- Ensure that only one person "has the D." If two or more people think they're in charge of a particular decision, a tug-of-war results.
- Watch for a proliferation of "A's." Too many people with veto power can paralyze recommenders. If many people must agree, you probably haven't pushed decisions down far enough in your organization.
- Avoid assigning too many "I's." When many people give input, at least some of them aren't making meaningful contributions.

The RAPID Model in Action

Example: At British department-store chain John Lewis, company buyers wanted to increase sales and reduce complexity by offering fewer salt and pepper mill models. The company launched the streamlined product set without involving the sales staff. And sales fell. Upon visiting the stores, buyers saw that salespeople (not understanding the strategy behind the recommendation) had halved shelf space to match the reduction in product range, rather than maintaining the same space but stocking more of the products.

To fix the problem, the company "gave buyers the D" on how much space product categories would have. Sales staff "had the A": If space allocations didn't make sense to them, they could force additional negotiations. They also "had the P," implementing product layouts in stores.

Once decision roles were clarified, sales of salt and pepper mills exceeded original levels.

they must either work with the recommender to come up with an alternative or elevate the issue to the person with the D. For decision making to function smoothly, only a few people should have such veto power. They may be executives responsible for legal or regulatory compliance or the heads of units whose operations will be significantly affected by the decision.

People with *input* responsibilities are consulted about the recommendation. Their role is to provide the relevant facts that are the basis of any good decision: How practical is the proposal? Can manufacturing accommodate the design change? Where there's dissent or

A Decision-Making Primer

GOOD DECISION MAKING DEPENDS ON assigning clear and specific roles. This sounds simple enough, but many companies struggle to make decisions because lots of people feel accountable—or no one does. RAPID and other tools used to analyze decision making give senior management teams a method for assigning roles and involving the relevant people. The key is to be clear who has input, who gets to decide, and who gets it done.

The five letters in RAPID correspond to the five critical decision-making roles: recommend, agree, perform, input, and decide. As you'll see, the roles are not carried out lockstep in this order—we took some liberties for the sake of creating a useful acronym.

Recommend

People in this role are responsible for making a proposal, gathering input, and providing the right data and analysis to make a sensible decision in a timely fashion. In the course of developing a proposal, recommenders consult with the people who provide input, not just hearing and incorporating their views but also building buy in along the way. Recommenders must have analytical skills, common sense, and organizational smarts.

Agree

Individuals in this role have veto power—yes or no—over the recommendation. Exercising the veto triggers a debate between themselves and the recommenders, which should lead to a modified proposal. If that takes too long, or if the two parties simply can't agree, they can escalate the issue to the person who has the D.

Input

These people are consulted on the decision. Because the people who provide input are typically involved in implementation, recommenders have a strong

---

contrasting views, it's important to get these people to the table at the right time. The recommender has no obligation to act on the input he or she receives but is expected to take it into account—particularly since the people who provide input are generally among those who must implement a decision. Consensus is a worthy goal, but as a decision-making standard, it can be an obstacle to action or a recipe for lowest-common-denominator compromise. A more practical objective is to get everyone involved to buy in to the decision.

interest in taking their advice seriously. No input is binding, but this shouldn't undermine its importance. If the right people are not involved and motivated, the decision is far more likely to falter during execution.

Decide

The person with the D is the formal decision maker. He or she is ultimately accountable for the decision, for better or worse, and has the authority to resolve any impasse in the decision-making process and to commit the organization to action.

Perform

Once a decision is made, a person or group of people will be responsible for executing it. In some instances, the people responsible for implementing a decision are the same people who recommended it.

Writing down the roles and assigning accountability are essential steps, but good decision making also requires the right process. Too many rules can cause the process to collapse under its own weight. The most effective process is grounded in specifics but simple enough to adapt if necessary.

When the process gets slowed down, the problem can often be traced back to one of three trouble spots. First is a lack of clarity about who has the D. If more than one person think they have it for a particular decision, that decision will get caught up in a tug-of-war. The flip side can be equally damaging: No one is accountable for crucial decisions, and the business suffers. Second, a proliferation of people who have veto power can make life tough for recommenders. If a company has too many people in the "agree" role, it usually means that decisions are not pushed down far enough in the organization. Third, if there are a lot of people giving input, it's a signal that at least some of them aren't making a meaningful contribution.

Eventually, one person will *decide*. The decision maker is the single point of accountability who must bring the decision to closure and commit the organization to act on it. To be strong and effective, the person with the D needs good business judgment, a grasp of the relevant trade-offs, a bias for action, and a keen awareness of the organization that will execute the decision.

The final role in the process involves the people who will *perform* the decision. They see to it that the decision is implemented promptly and effectively. It's a crucial role. Very often, a good decision executed quickly beats a brilliant decision implemented slowly or poorly.

RAPID can be used to help redesign the way an organization works or to target a single bottleneck. Some companies use the approach for the top ten to 20 decisions, or just for the CEO and his or her direct reports. Other companies use it throughout the organization—to improve customer service by clarifying decision roles on the front line, for instance. When people see an effective process for making decisions, they spread the word. For example, after senior managers at a major U.S. retailer used RAPID to sort out a particularly thorny set of corporate decisions, they promptly built the process into their own functional organizations.

To see the process in action, let's look at the way four companies have worked through their decision-making bottlenecks.

Global Versus Local

Every major company today operates in global markets, buying raw materials in one place, shipping them somewhere else, and selling finished products all over the world. Most are trying simultaneously to build local presence and expertise, and to achieve economies of scale. Decision making in this environment is far from straightforward. Frequently, decisions cut across the boundaries between global and local managers, and sometimes across a regional layer in between: What investments will streamline our supply chain? How far should we go in standardizing products or tailoring them for local markets?

The trick in decision making is to avoid becoming either mindlessly global or hopelessly local. If decision-making authority tilts too far toward global executives, local customers' preferences can easily be overlooked, undermining the efficiency and agility of local operations. But with too much local authority, a company is likely to miss out on crucial economies of scale or opportunities with global clients.

To strike the right balance, a company must recognize its most important sources of value and make sure that decision roles line up with them. This was the challenge facing Martin Broughton, the former CEO and chairman of British American Tobacco, the second-largest tobacco company in the world. In 1993, when Broughton was appointed chief executive, BAT was losing ground to its nearest competitor. Broughton knew that the company needed to take better advantage of its global scale, but decision roles and responsibilities were at odds with this goal. Four geographic operating units ran themselves autonomously, rarely collaborating and sometimes even competing. Achieving consistency across global brands proved difficult, and cost synergies across the operating units were elusive. Industry insiders joked that "there are seven major tobacco companies in the world—and four of them are British American Tobacco." Broughton vowed to change the punch line.

The chief executive envisioned an organization that could take advantage of the opportunities a global business offers—global brands that could compete with established winners such as Altria Group's Marlboro; global purchasing of important raw materials, including tobacco; and more consistency in innovation and customer management. But Broughton didn't want the company to lose its nimbleness and competitive hunger in local markets by shifting too much decision-making power to global executives.

The first step was to clarify roles for the most important decisions. Procurement became a proving ground. Previously, each operating unit had identified its own suppliers and negotiated contracts for all materials. Under Broughton, a global procurement team was set up in headquarters and given authority to choose suppliers and negotiate pricing and quality for global materials, including bulk tobacco and certain types of packaging. Regional procurement teams were now given input into global materials strategies but ultimately had to implement the team's decision. As soon as the global team signed contracts with suppliers, responsibility shifted to the regional teams, who worked out the details of delivery and service with the suppliers in their regions. For materials that did not offer global economies of scale (mentholated filters for the North American market, for example), the regional teams retained their decision-making authority.

As the effort to revamp decision making in procurement gained momentum, the company set out to clarify roles in all its major decisions. The process wasn't easy. A company the size of British American Tobacco has a huge number of moving parts, and developing a practical system for making decisions requires sweating lots of details. What's more, decision-making authority is power, and people are often reluctant to give it up.

It's crucial for the people who will live with the new system to help design it. At BAT, Broughton created working groups led by people earmarked, implicitly or explicitly, for leadership roles in the future. For example, Paul Adams, who ultimately succeeded Broughton as chief executive, was asked to lead the group charged with redesigning decision making for brand and customer management. At the time, Adams was a regional head within one of the operating units. With other senior executives, including some of his own direct reports, Broughton specified that their role was to provide input, not to veto recommendations. Broughton didn't make the common mistake of seeking consensus, which is often an obstacle to action. Instead, he made it clear that the objective was not deciding whether to change the decision-making process but achieving buy in about how to do so as effectively as possible.

The new decision roles provided the foundation the company needed to operate successfully on a global basis while retaining flexibility at the local level. The focus and efficiency of its decision making were reflected in the company's results: After the decision-making overhaul, British American Tobacco experienced nearly ten years of growth well above the levels of its competitors in sales, profits, and market value. The company has gone on to have one of the best-performing stocks on the UK market and has reemerged as a major global player in the tobacco industry.

Center Versus Business Unit

The first rule for making good decisions is to involve the right people at the right level of the organization. For BAT, capturing economies of scale required its global team to appropriate some decision-making powers from regional divisions. For many companies, a similar balancing act takes place between executives at the center and managers in the business units. If too many decisions flow to the center, decision making can grind to a halt. The problem is different but no less critical if the decisions that are elevated to senior executives are the wrong ones.

Companies often grow into this type of problem. In small and midsize organizations, a single management team—sometimes a single leader—effectively handles every major decision. As a company grows and its operations become more complex, however, senior executives can no longer master the details required to make decisions in every business.

A change in management style, often triggered by the arrival of a new CEO, can create similar tensions. At a large British retailer, for example, the senior team was accustomed to the founder making all critical decisions. When his successor began seeking consensus on important issues, the team was suddenly unsure of its role, and many decisions stalled. It's a common scenario, yet most management teams and boards of directors don't specify how decision-making authority should change as the company does.

A growth opportunity highlighted that issue for Wyeth (then known as American Home Products) in late 2000. Through organic growth, acquisitions, and partnerships, Wyeth's pharmaceutical division had developed three sizable businesses: biotech, vaccines, and traditional pharmaceutical products. Even though each business had its own market dynamics, operating requirements, and research focus, most important decisions were pushed up to one group of senior executives. "We were using generalists across all issues," said Joseph M. Mahady, president of North American and global businesses for Wyeth Pharmaceuticals. "It was a signal that we weren't getting our best decision making."

The problem crystallized for Wyeth when managers in the biotech business saw a vital—but perishable—opportunity to establish a leading position with Enbrel, a promising rheumatoid arthritis drug. Competitors were working on the same class of drug, so Wyeth needed to move quickly. This meant expanding production capacity by building a new plant, which would be located at the Grange Castle Business Park in Dublin, Ireland.

The decision, by any standard, was a complex one. Once approved by regulators, the facility would be the biggest biotech plant in the world—and the largest capital investment Wyeth had ever undertaken. Yet peak demand for the drug was not easy to determine. What's more, Wyeth planned to market Enbrel in partnership with Immunex (now a part of Amgen). In its deliberations about the plant, therefore, Wyeth needed to factor in the requirements of building up its technical expertise, technology transfer issues, and an uncertain competitive environment.

Input on the decision filtered up slowly through a gauze of overlapping committees, leaving senior executives hungry for a more detailed grasp of the issues. Given the narrow window of opportunity, Wyeth acted quickly, moving from a first look at the Grange Castle project to implementation in six months. But in the midst of this process, Wyeth Pharmaceuticals' executives saw the larger issue: The company needed a system that would push more decisions down to the business units, where operational knowledge was greatest, and elevate the decisions that required the senior team's input, such as marketing strategy and manufacturing capacity.

In short order, Wyeth gave authority for many decisions to business unit managers, leaving senior executives with veto power over some of the more sensitive issues related to Grange Castle. But after that investment decision was made, the D for many subsequent decisions about the Enbrel business lay with Cavan Redmond, the executive vice president and general manager of Wyeth's biotech division, and his new management team. Redmond gathered input from managers in biotech manufacturing, marketing, forecasting, finance, and R&D, and quickly set up the complex schedules needed to collaborate with Immunex. Responsibility for execution rested firmly with the business unit, as always. But now Redmond, supported by his team, also had authority to make important decisions.

Grange Castle is paying off so far. Enbrel is among the leading brands for rheumatoid arthritis, with sales of $1.7 billion through the first half of 2005. And Wyeth's metabolism for making decisions has increased. Recently, when the U.S. Food and Drug Administration granted priority review status to another new drug, Tygacil, because of the antibiotic's efficacy against drug-resistant infections, Wyeth displayed its new reflexes. To keep Tygacil on a fast track, the company had to orchestrate a host of critical steps—refining the process technology, lining up supplies, ensuring quality control, allocating manufacturing capacity. The vital decisions were made one or two levels down in the biotech organization, where the expertise resided. "Instead of debating whether you can move your product into my shop, we had the decision systems in place to run it up and down the business units and move ahead rapidly with Tygacil," said Mahady. The drug was approved by the FDA in June 2005 and moved into volume production a mere three days later.

Function Versus Function

Decisions that cut across functions are some of the most important a company faces. Indeed, cross-functional collaboration has become an axiom of business, essential for arriving at the best answers for the company and its customers. But fluid decision making across functional teams remains a constant challenge, even for companies known for doing it well, like Toyota and Dell. For instance, a team that thinks it's more efficient to make a decision without consulting other functions may wind up missing out on relevant input or being overruled by another team that believes—rightly or wrongly—it should have been included in the process. Many of the most important cross-functional decisions are, by their very nature, the most difficult to orchestrate, and that can string out the process and lead to sparring between fiefdoms and costly indecision.

The theme here is a lack of clarity about who has the D. For example, at a global auto manufacturer that was missing its milestones for rolling out new models—and was paying the price in falling sales—it turned out that marketers and product developers were confused about which function was responsible for making decisions about standard features and color ranges for new models. When we asked the marketing team who had the D about which features should be standard, 83% said the marketers did. When we

A recipe for a decision-making bottleneck

At one automaker we studied, marketers and product developers were confused about who was responsible for making decisions about new models.

When we asked, "Who has the right to decide which features will be standard?"

- 64% of product developers said, "We do."
- 83% of marketers said, "We do."

When we asked, "Who has the right to decide which colors will be offered?"

- 77% of product developers said, "We do."
- 61% of marketers said, "We do."

Not surprisingly, the new models were delayed.

posed the same question to product developers, 64% said the responsibility rested with them. (See the exhibit "A recipe for a decision-making bottleneck.")

The practical difficulty of connecting functions through smooth decision making crops up frequently at retailers. John Lewis, the leading department store chain in the United Kingdom, might reasonably expect to overcome this sort of challenge more readily than other retailers. Spedan Lewis, who built the business in the early twentieth century, was a pioneer in employee ownership. A strong connection between managers and employees permeated every aspect of the store's operations and remained vital to the company as it grew into the largest employee-owned business in the United Kingdom, with 59,600 employees and more than £5 billion in revenues in 2004.

Even at John Lewis, however, with its heritage of cooperation and teamwork, cross-functional decision making can be hard to sustain. Take salt and pepper mills, for instance. John Lewis, which prides itself on having great selection, stocked nearly 50 SKUs of salt and pepper mills, while most competitors stocked around 20. The company's buyers saw an opportunity to increase sales and reduce complexity by offering a smaller number of popular and well-chosen products in each price point and style.

When John Lewis launched the new range, sales fell. This made no sense to the buyers until they visited the stores and saw how the merchandise was displayed. The buyers had made their decision without fully involving the sales staff, who therefore did not understand the strategy behind the new selection. As a result, the sellers had cut shelf space in half to match the reduction in range, rather than devoting the same amount of shelf space to stocking more of each product.

To fix the communication problem, John Lewis needed to clarify decision roles. The buyers were given the D on how much space to allocate to each product category. If the space allocation didn't make sense to the sales staff, however, they had the authority to raise their concerns and force a new round of negotiations. They also had responsibility for implementing product layouts in the stores. When the communication was sorted out and shelf space was restored, sales of the salt and pepper mills climbed well above original levels.

Crafting a decision-making process that connected the buying and selling functions for salt and pepper mills was relatively easy; rolling it out across the entire business was more challenging. Salt and pepper mills are just one of several hundred product categories for John Lewis. This element of scale is one reason why cross-functional bottlenecks are not easy to unclog. Different functions have different incentives and goals, which are often in conflict. When it comes down to a struggle between two functions, there may be good reasons to locate the D in either place—buying or selling, marketing or product development.

Here, as elsewhere, someone needs to think objectively about where value is created and assign decision roles accordingly. Eliminating cross-functional bottlenecks actually has less to do with shifting decision-making responsibilities between departments and more to do with ensuring that the people with relevant information are allowed to share it. The decision maker is important, of course, but more important is designing a system that aligns decision making and makes it routine.

Inside Versus Outside Partners

Decision making within an organization is hard enough. Trying to make decisions between separate organizations on different continents adds

The Decision-Driven Organization

THE DEFINING CHARACTERISTIC OF HIGH-PERFORMING organizations is their ability to make good decisions and to make them happen quickly. The companies that succeed tend to follow a few clear principles.

Some Decisions Matter More Than Others

The decisions that are crucial to building value in the business are the ones that matter most. Some of them will be the big strategic decisions, but just as important are the critical operating decisions that drive the business day to day and are vital to effective execution.

Action Is the Goal

Good decision making doesn't end with a decision; it ends with implementation. The objective shouldn't be consensus, which often becomes an obstacle to action, but buy in.

Ambiguity Is the Enemy

Clear accountability is essential: Who contributes input, who makes the decision, and who carries it out? Without clarity, gridlock and delay are the most likely outcomes. Clarity doesn't necessarily mean concentrating authority in a few people; it means defining who has responsibility to make decisions, who has input, and who is charged with putting them into action.

layers of complexity that can scuttle the best strategy. Companies that outsource capabilities in pursuit of cost and quality advantages face this very challenge. Which decisions should be made internally? Which can be delegated to outsourcing partners?

These questions are also relevant for strategic partners—a global bank working with an IT contractor on a systems development project, for example, or a media company that acquires content from a studio—and for companies conducting part of their business through franchisees. There is no right answer to who should have the power to decide what. But the wrong approach is to assume that contractual arrangements can provide the answer.

An outdoor-equipment company based in the United States discovered this recently when it decided to scale up production of gas patio heaters for the lower end of the market. The company had some success manufacturing high-end products in China. But with

Speed and Adaptability Are Crucial

A company that makes good decisions quickly has a higher metabolism, which allows it to act on opportunities and overcome obstacles. The best decision makers create an environment where people can come together quickly and efficiently to make the most important decisions.

Decision Roles Trump the Organizational Chart

No decision-making structure will be perfect for every decision. The key is to involve the right people at the right level in the right part of the organization at the right time.

A Well-Aligned Organization Reinforces Roles

Clear decision roles are critical, but they are not enough. If an organization does not reinforce the right approach to decision making through its measures and incentives, information flows, and culture, the behavior won't become routine.

Practicing Beats Preaching

Involve the people who will live with the new decision roles in designing them. The very process of thinking about new decision behaviors motivates people to adopt them.

the advent of superdiscounters like Wal-Mart, Target, and Home Depot, the company realized it needed to move more of its production overseas to feed these retailers with lower-cost offerings. The timetable left little margin for error: The company started tooling up factories in April and June of 2004, hoping to be ready for the Christmas season.

Right away, there were problems. Although the Chinese manufacturing partners understood costs, they had little idea what American consumers wanted. When expensive designs arrived from the head office in the United States, Chinese plant managers made compromises to meet contracted cost targets. They used a lower grade material, which discolored. They placed the power switch in a spot that was inconvenient for the user but easier to build. Instead of making certain parts from a single casting, they welded materials together, which looked terrible.

A Decision Diagnostic

CONSIDER THE LAST THREE MEANINGFUL decisions you've been involved in and ask yourself the following questions.

1. Were the decisions right?
2. Were they made with appropriate speed?
3. Were they executed well?
4. Were the right people involved, in the right way?
5. Was it clear for each decision
   - who would recommend a solution?
   - who would provide input?
   - who had the final say?
   - who would be responsible for following through?
6. Were the decision roles, process, and time frame respected?
7. Were the decisions based on appropriate facts?
8. To the extent that there were divergent facts or opinions, was it clear who had the D?
9. Were the decision makers at the appropriate level in the company?
10. Did the organization's measures and incentives encourage the people involved to make the right decisions?

To fix these problems, the U.S. executives had to draw clear lines around which decisions should be made on which side of the ocean. The company broke down the design and manufacturing process into five steps and analyzed how decisions were made at each step. The company was also much more explicit about what the manufacturing specs would include and what the manufacturer was expected to do with them. The objective was not simply to clarify decision roles but to make sure those roles corresponded directly to the sources of value in the business. If a decision would affect the look and feel of the finished product, headquarters would have to sign off on it. But if a decision would not affect the customer's experience, it could be made in China. If, for example, Chinese engineers found a less expensive material that didn't compromise the product's look, feel, and functionality, they could make that change on their own.

To help with the transition to this system, the company put a team of engineers on-site in China to ensure a smooth handoff of the specs and to make decisions on issues that would become complex and time-consuming if elevated to the home office. Marketing executives in the home office insisted that it should take a customer ten minutes and no more than six steps to assemble the product at home. The company's engineers in China, along with the Chinese manufacturing team, had input into this assembly requirement and were responsible for execution. But the D resided with headquarters, and the requirement became a major design factor. Decisions about logistics, however, became the province of the engineering team in China: It would figure out how to package the heaters so that one-third more boxes would fit into a container, which reduced shipping costs substantially.

If managers suddenly realize that they're spending less time sitting through meetings wondering why they are there, that's an early signal that companies have become better at making decisions. When meetings start with a common understanding about who is responsible for providing valuable input and who has the D, an organization's decision-making metabolism will get a boost.

No single lever turns a decision-challenged organization into a decision-driven one, of course, and no blueprint can provide for all the contingencies and business shifts a company is bound to encounter. The most successful companies use simple tools that help them recognize potential bottlenecks and think through decision roles and responsibilities with each change in the business environment. That's difficult to do—and even more difficult for competitors to copy. But by taking some very practical steps, any company can become more effective, beginning with its next decision.

Originally published in January 2006. Reprint R0601D

How (Un)ethical Are You?

by Mahzarin R. Banaji, Max H. Bazerman, and Dolly Chugh

ANSWER TRUE OR FALSE: "I am an ethical manager."

If you answered "true," here's an uncomfortable fact: You're probably not. Most of us believe that we are ethical and unbiased. We imagine we're good decision makers, able to objectively size up a job candidate or a venture deal and reach a fair and rational conclusion that's in our, and our organization's, best interests. But more than two decades of research confirms that, in reality, most of us fall woefully short of our inflated self-perception. We're deluded by what Yale psychologist David Armor calls the illusion of objectivity, the notion that we're free of the very biases we're so quick to recognize in others. What's more, these unconscious, or implicit, biases can be contrary to our consciously held, explicit beliefs. We may believe with confidence and conviction that a job candidate's race has no bearing on our hiring decisions or that we're immune to conflicts of interest. But psychological research routinely exposes counterintentional, unconscious biases. The prevalence of these biases suggests that even the most well-meaning person unwittingly allows unconscious thoughts and feelings to influence seemingly objective decisions. These flawed judgments are ethically problematic and undermine managers' fundamental work—to recruit and retain superior talent, boost the performance of individuals and teams, and collaborate effectively with partners.

This article explores four related sources of unintentional unethical decision making: implicit forms of prejudice, bias that favors one's own group, conflict of interest, and a tendency to overclaim credit. Because we are not consciously aware of these sources of bias, they often cannot be addressed by penalizing people for their bad decisions. Nor are they likely to be corrected through conventional ethics training. Rather, managers must bring a new type of vigilance to bear. To begin, this requires letting go of the notion that our conscious attitudes always represent what we think they do. It also demands that we abandon our faith in our own objectivity and our ability to be fair. In the following pages, we will offer strategies that can help managers recognize these pervasive, corrosive, unconscious biases and reduce their impact.

Implicit Prejudice: Bias That Emerges from Unconscious Beliefs

Most fair-minded people strive to judge others according to their merits, but our research shows how often people instead judge according to unconscious stereotypes and attitudes, or "implicit prejudice." What makes implicit prejudice so common and persistent is that it is rooted in the fundamental mechanics of thought. Early on, we learn to associate things that commonly go together and expect them to inevitably coexist: thunder and rain, for instance, or gray hair and old age. This skill—to perceive and learn from associations—often serves us well.

But, of course, our associations only reflect approximations of the truth; they are rarely applicable to every encounter. Rain doesn't always accompany thunder, and the young can also go gray. Nonetheless, because we automatically make such associations to help us organize our world, we grow to trust them, and they can blind us to those instances in which the associations are not accurate—when they don't align with our expectations.

Because implicit prejudice arises from the ordinary and unconscious tendency to make associations, it is distinct from conscious forms of prejudice, such as overt racism or sexism. This distinction

Idea in Brief

Are you an ethical manager? Most would probably say, "Of course!" The truth is, most of us are not.

Most of us believe that we're ethical and unbiased. We assume that we objectively size up job candidates or venture deals and reach fair and rational conclusions that are in our organization's best interests.

But the truth is, we harbor many unconscious—and unethical—biases that derail our decisions and undermine our work as managers. Hidden biases prevent us from recognizing high-potential workers and retaining talented managers. They stop us from collaborating effectively with partners. They erode our teams' performance. They can also lead to costly lawsuits.

But how can we root out these biases if they're unconscious? Fortunately, as a manager, you can take deliberate actions to counteract their pull. **Regularly audit your decisions.** Have you, for example, hired a disproportionate number of people of your own race? **Expose yourself to non-stereotypical environments** that challenge your biases. If your department is led by men, spend time in one with women in leadership positions. And **consider counterintuitive options** when making decisions. Don't rely on a mental short-list of candidates for a new assignment; consider every employee with relevant qualifications.

explains why people who are free from conscious prejudice may still harbor biases and act accordingly. Exposed to images that juxtapose black men and violence, portray women as sex objects, imply that the physically disabled are mentally weak and the poor are lazy, even the most consciously unbiased person is bound to make biased associations. These associations play out in the workplace just as they do anywhere else.

In the mid-1990s, Tony Greenwald, a professor of psychology at the University of Washington, developed an experimental tool called the Implicit Association Test (IAT) to study unconscious bias. A computerized version of the test requires subjects to rapidly classify words and images as "good" or "bad." Using a keyboard, test takers must make split-second "good/bad" distinctions between words like "love," "joy," "pain," and "sorrow" and at the same time sort images of faces that are (depending on the bias in question)

Idea in Practice

Unconscious Biases

Are the following unconscious biases levying what amounts to a "stereotype tax" on your company?

Implicit prejudice. Judging according to unconscious stereotypes rather than merit exacts a high business cost. Exposed to images that juxtapose physical disabilities with mental weakness or portray poor people as lazy, even the most consciously unbiased person is bound to make biased associations. As a result, we routinely overlook highly qualified candidates for assignments.

In-group favoritism. Granting favors to people with your same background—your nationality or alma mater—effectively discriminates against those who are different from you. Consider the potential cost of offering bonuses to employees who refer their friends for job openings: hires who may not have made the grade *without* in-group favoritism.

Overclaiming credit. Most of us consider ourselves above average. But when every member of a team thinks he's making the biggest contribution, each starts to think the others aren't pulling their weight. That jeopardizes future collaborations. It also frustrates talented workers who may resign because they feel underappreciated.

Counteract Biases

To keep yourself from making similarly skewed calls, consider these guidelines:

black or white, young or old, fat or thin, and so on. The test exposes implicit biases by detecting subtle shifts in reaction time that can occur when test takers are required to pair different sets of words and faces. Subjects who consciously believe that they have no negative feelings toward, say, black Americans or the elderly are nevertheless likely to be slower to associate elderly or black faces with the "good" words than they are to associate youthful or white faces with "good" words.

Since 1998, when Greenwald, Brian Nosek, and Mahzarin Banaji put the IAT online, people from around the world have taken over 2.5 million tests, confirming and extending the findings of more traditional laboratory experiments. Both show implicit biases to

Gather better data. Expose your own implicit biases. Take the Implicit Association Test (at http://implicit.harvard. edu). If you discover gender or racial biases, examine your hiring and promotion decisions in that new light. When working with others, have team members estimate their colleagues' contributions *before* they claim their own credit.

Rid your workplace of stereotypical cues. Think about the biased associations your workplace may foster. Do your company's advertising and marketing materials frequently include sports metaphors or high-tech jargon? Make a conscious effort to curb such "insider" language—making your products more appealing to a diverse customer base. And if your department invariably promotes the same type of manager—highly analytic, for instance—shadow a department that values a different—perhaps more conceptual—skill-set.

Broaden your mind-set when making decisions. Apply the "veil of ignorance" to your next managerial decision. Suppose you're considering a new policy that would give more vacation time to all employees but eliminate the flextime that has allowed new parents to keep working. How would your opinion differ if you were a parent or childless? Male or female? Healthy or unhealthy? You'll learn how strongly implicit biases influence you.

be strong and pervasive. (For more information on the IAT, see the sidebar "Are You Biased?").

Biases are also likely to be costly. In controlled experiments, psychologists Laurie Rudman at Rutgers and Peter Glick at Lawrence University have studied how implicit biases may work to exclude qualified people from certain roles. One set of experiments examined the relationship between participants' implicit gender stereotypes and their hiring decisions. Those holding stronger implicit biases were less likely to select a qualified woman who exhibited stereotypically "masculine" personality qualities, such as ambition or independence, for a job requiring stereotypically "feminine" qualities, such as interpersonal skills. Yet they would select a qualified man

Are You Biased?

ARE YOU WILLING TO BET that you feel the same way toward European-Americans as you do toward African-Americans? How about women versus men? Or older people versus younger ones? Think twice before you take that bet. Visit implicit.harvard.edu or www.tolerance.org/hidden_bias to examine your unconscious attitudes.

The Implicit Association Tests available on these sites reveal unconscious beliefs by asking takers to make split-second associations between words with positive or negative connotations and images representing different types of people. The various tests on these sites expose the differences—or the alignment—between test takers' conscious and unconscious attitudes toward people of different races, sexual orientation, or physical characteristics. Data gathered from over 2.5 million online tests and further research tells us that unconscious biases are:

- **widely prevalent.** At least 75% of test takers show an implicit bias favoring the young, the rich, and whites.
- **robust.** The mere conscious desire not to be biased does not eliminate implicit bias.
- **contrary to conscious intention.** Although people tend to report little or no *conscious* bias against African-Americans, Arabs, Arab-Americans, Jews, gay men, lesbians, or the poor, they show substantial biases on implicit measures.
- **different in degree depending on group status.** Minority group members tend to show less implicit preference for their own group than majority group members show for theirs. For example, African-Americans report strong preference for their group on explicit measures but show relatively less implicit preference in the tests. Conversely, white Americans report a low explicit bias for their group but a higher implicit bias.
- **consequential.** Those who show higher levels of bias on the IAT are also likely to behave in ways that are more biased in face-to-face interactions with members of the group they are biased against and in the choices they make, such as hiring decisions.
- **costly.** Research currently under way in our lab suggests that implicit bias generates a "stereotype tax"—negotiators leave money on the table because biases cause them to miss opportunities to learn about their opponent and thus create additional value through mutually beneficial trade-offs.

exhibiting these same qualities. The hirers' biased perception was that the woman was less likely to be socially skilled than the man, though their qualifications were in fact the same. These results suggest that implicit biases may exact costs by subtly excluding qualified people from the very organizations that seek their talents.

Legal cases also reveal the real costs of implicit biases, both economic and social. Consider *Price Waterhouse v. Hopkins*. Despite logging more billable hours than her peers, bringing in $25 million to the company, and earning the praise of her clients, Ann Hopkins was turned down for partner, and she sued. The details of the case reveal that her evaluators were explicitly prejudiced in their attitudes. For example, they had commented that Ann "overcompensated for being a woman" and needed a "course at charm school." But perhaps more damning from a legal standpoint was blunt testimony from experimental research. Testifying as an expert witness for the defense, psychology professor Susan Fiske, now at Princeton University, argued that the potential for biased decision making is *inherent* in a system in which a person has "solo" status—that is, a system in which the person is the only one of a kind (the only woman, the only African-American, the only person with a disability, and the like). Judge Gerhard Gesell concluded that "a far more subtle process [than the usual discriminatory intent] is involved" in the assessments made of Ann Hopkins, and she won both in a lower court and in the Supreme Court in what is now a landmark case in discrimination law.

Likewise, the 1999 case of *Thomas v. Kodak* demonstrates that implicit biases can be the basis for rulings. Here, the court posed the question of "whether the employer consciously intended to base the evaluations on race or simply did so because of unthinking stereotypes or bias." The court concluded that plaintiffs can indeed challenge "subjective evaluations which could easily mask covert or unconscious race discrimination." Although courts are careful not to assign responsibility easily for unintentional biases, these cases demonstrate the potential for corporate liability that such patterns of behavior could unwittingly create.

In-Group Favoritism: Bias That Favors Your Group

Think about some of the favors you have done in recent years, whether for a friend, a relative, or a colleague. Have you helped someone get a useful introduction, admission to a school, or a job? Most of us are glad to help out with such favors. Not surprisingly, we tend to do more favors for those we know, and those we know tend to be like ourselves: people who share our nationality, social class, and perhaps religion, race, employer, or alma mater. This all sounds rather innocent. What's wrong with asking your neighbor, the university dean, to meet with a coworker's son? Isn't it just being helpful to recommend a former sorority sister for a job or to talk to your banker cousin when a friend from church gets turned down for a home loan?

Few people set out to exclude anyone through such acts of kindness. But when those in the majority or those in power allocate scarce resources (such as jobs, promotions, and mortgages) to people just like them, they effectively discriminate against those who are different from them. Such "in-group favoritism" amounts to giving extra credit for group membership. Yet while discriminating against those who are different is considered unethical, helping people close to us is often viewed favorably. Think about the number of companies that explicitly encourage this by offering hiring bonuses to employees who refer their friends for job opportunities.

But consider the finding that banks in the United States are more likely to deny a mortgage application from a black person than from a white person, even when the applicants are equally qualified. The common view has been that banks are hostile to African-Americans. While this may be true of some banks and some loan officers, social psychologist David Messick has argued that in-group favoritism is more likely to be at the root of such discriminatory lending. A white loan officer may feel hopeful or lenient toward an unqualified white applicant while following the bank's lending standards strictly with an unqualified black applicant. In denying the black applicant's mortgage, the loan officer may not be expressing hostility toward blacks so much as favoritism toward whites. It's a subtle but crucial distinction.

The ethical cost is clear and should be reason enough to address the problem. But such inadvertent bias produces an additional effect: It erodes the bottom line. Lenders who discriminate in this way, for example, incur bad-debt costs they could have avoided if their lending decisions were more objective. They also may find themselves exposed to damaging publicity or discrimination lawsuits if the skewed lending pattern is publicly revealed. In a different context, companies may pay a real cost for marginal hires who wouldn't have made the grade but for the sympathetic hiring manager swayed by in-group favoritism.

In-group favoritism is tenacious when membership confers clear advantages, as it does, for instance, among whites and other dominant social groups. (It may be weaker or absent among people whose group membership offers little societal advantage.) Thus for a wide array of managerial tasks—from hiring, firing, and promoting to contracting services and forming partnerships—qualified minority candidates are subtly and unconsciously discriminated against, sometimes simply because they are in the minority: There are not enough of them to counter the propensity for in-group favoritism in the majority.

Overclaiming Credit: Bias That Favors You

It's only natural for successful people to hold positive views about themselves. But many studies show that the majority of people consider themselves above average on a host of measures, from intelligence to driving ability. Business executives are no exception. We tend to overrate our individual contribution to groups, which, bluntly put, tends to lead to an overblown sense of entitlement. We become the unabashed, repeated beneficiaries of this unconscious bias, and the more we think only of our own contributions, the less fairly we judge others with whom we work.

Lab research demonstrates this most personal of biases. At Harvard, Eugene Caruso, Nick Epley, and Max Bazerman recently asked MBA students in study groups to estimate what portion of their group's work each had done. The sum of the contribution by all members, of course, must add up to 100%. But the researchers found that the totals for each study group averaged 139%. In a related study, Caruso and his colleagues uncovered rampant overestimates by academic authors of their contribution to shared research projects. Sadly, but not surprisingly, the more the sum of the total estimated group effort exceeded 100% (in other words, the more credit each person claimed), the less the parties wanted to collaborate in the future.

Likewise in business, claiming too much credit can destabilize alliances. When each party in a strategic partnership claims too much credit for its own contribution and becomes skeptical about whether the other is doing its fair share, they both tend to reduce their contributions to compensate. This has obvious repercussions for the joint venture's performance.

Unconscious overclaiming can be expected to reduce the performance and longevity of groups within organizations, just as it diminished the academic authors' willingness to collaborate. It can also take a toll on employee commitment. Think about how employees perceive raises. Most are not so different from the children at Lake Wobegon, believing that they, too, rank in the upper half of their peer group. But many necessarily get pay increases that are below the average. If an employee learns of a colleague's greater compensation—while honestly believing that he himself is more deserving—resentment may be natural. At best, his resentment might translate into reduced commitment and performance. At worst, he may leave the organization that, it seems, doesn't appreciate his contribution.

Conflict of Interest: Bias That Favors Those Who Can Benefit You

Everyone knows that conflict of interest can lead to intentionally corrupt behavior. But numerous psychological experiments show how powerfully such conflicts can unintentionally skew decision making. (For an examination of the evidence in one business arena, see Max Bazerman, George Loewenstein, and Don Moore's November 2002

HBR article, "Why Good Accountants Do Bad Audits.") These experiments suggest that the work world is rife with situations in which such conflicts lead honest, ethical professionals to unconsciously make unsound and unethical recommendations.

Physicians, for instance, face conflicts of interest when they accept payment for referring patients into clinical trials. While, surely, most physicians consciously believe that their referrals are the patient's best clinical option, how do they know that the promise of payment did not skew their decisions? Similarly, many lawyers earn fees based on their clients' awards or settlements. Since going to trial is expensive and uncertain, settling out of court is often an attractive option for the lawyer. Attorneys may consciously believe that settling is in their clients' best interests. But how can they be objective, unbiased judges under these circumstances?

Research done with brokerage house analysts demonstrates how conflict of interest can unconsciously distort decision making. A survey of analysts conducted by the financial research service First Call showed that during a period in 2000 when the Nasdaq dropped 60%, fully 99% of brokerage analysts' client recommendations remained "strong buy," "buy," or "hold." What accounts for this discrepancy between what was happening and what was recommended? The answer may lie in a system that fosters conflicts of interest. A portion of analysts' pay is based on brokerage firm revenues. Some firms even tie analysts' compensation to the amount of business the analysts bring in from clients, giving analysts an obvious incentive to prolong and extend their relationships with clients. But to assume that during this Nasdaq free fall all brokerage house analysts were consciously corrupt, milking their clients to exploit this incentive system, defies common sense. Surely there were some bad apples. But how much more likely it is that most of these analysts believed their recommendations were sound and in their clients' best interests. What many didn't appreciate was that the built-in conflict of interest in their compensation incentives made it impossible for them to see the implicit bias in their own flawed recommendations.

Trying Harder Isn't Enough

As companies keep collapsing into financial scandal and ruin, corporations are responding with ethics-training programs for managers, and many of the world's leading business schools have created new courses and chaired professorships in ethics. Many of these efforts focus on teaching broad principles of moral philosophy to help managers understand the ethical challenges they face.

We applaud these efforts, but we doubt that a well-intentioned, just-try-harder approach will fundamentally improve the quality of executives' decision making. To do that, ethics training must be broadened to include what is now known about how our minds work and must expose managers directly to the unconscious mechanisms that underlie biased decision making. And it must provide managers with exercises and interventions that can root out the biases that lead to bad decisions.

Managers can make wiser, more ethical decisions if they become mindful of their unconscious biases. But how can we get at something outside our conscious awareness? By bringing the conscious mind to bear. Just as the driver of a misaligned car deliberately counteracts its pull, so can managers develop conscious strategies to counteract the pull of their unconscious biases. What's required is vigilance—continual awareness of the forces that can cause decision making to veer from its intended course and continual adjustments to counteract them. Those adjustments fall into three general categories: collecting data, shaping the environment, and broadening the decision-making process.

Collect data

The first step to reducing unconscious bias is to collect data to reveal its presence. Often, the data will be counterintuitive. Consider many people's surprise to learn of their own gender and racial biases on the IAT. Why the surprise? Because most of us trust the "statistics" our intuition provides. Better data are easily, but rarely, collected. One way to get those data is to examine our decisions in a systematic way.

Remember the MBA study groups whose participants overestimated their individual contributions to the group effort so that the totals averaged 139%? When the researchers asked group members to estimate what each of the other members' contributions were *before* claiming their own, the total fell to 121%. The tendency to claim too much credit still persisted, but this strategy of "unpacking" the work reduced the magnitude of the bias. In environments characterized by "I deserve more than you're giving me" claims, merely asking team members to unpack the contributions of others before claiming their own share of the pot usually aligns claims more closely with what's actually deserved. As this example demonstrates, such systematic audits of both individual and group decision-making processes can occur even as the decisions are being made.

Unpacking is a simple strategy that managers should routinely use to evaluate the fairness of their own claims within the organization. But they can also apply it in any situation where team members or subordinates may be overclaiming. For example, in explaining a raise that an employee feels is inadequate, a manager should ask the subordinate not what he thinks he alone deserves but what he considers an appropriate raise after taking into account each coworker's contribution and the pool available for pay increases. Similarly, when an individual feels she's doing more than her fair share of a team's work, asking her to consider other people's efforts before estimating her own can help align her perception with reality, restore her commitment, and reduce a skewed sense of entitlement.

Taking the IAT is another valuable strategy for collecting data. We recommend that you and others in your organization use the test to expose your own implicit biases. But one word of warning: Because the test is an educational and research tool, not a selection or evaluation tool, it is critical that you consider your results and others' to be private information. Simply knowing the magnitude and pervasiveness of your own biases can help direct your attention to areas of decision making that are in need of careful examination and reconsideration. For example, a manager whose testing reveals a bias toward certain groups ought to examine her hiring practices to see if she has indeed been disproportionately favoring those groups. But because so many people harbor such biases, they can also be generally acknowledged, and that knowledge can be used as the basis for changing the way decisions are made. It is important to guard against using pervasiveness to justify complacency and inaction: Pervasiveness of bias is not a mark of its appropriateness any more than poor eyesight is considered so ordinary a condition that it does not require corrective lenses.

Shape your environment

Research shows that implicit attitudes can be shaped by external cues in the environment. For example, Curtis Hardin and colleagues at UCLA used the IAT to study whether subjects' implicit race bias would be affected if the test was administered by a black investigator. One group of students took the test under the guidance of a white experimenter; another group took the test with a black experimenter. The mere presence of a black experimenter, Hardin found, reduced the level of subjects' implicit antiblack bias on the IAT. Numerous similar studies have shown similar effects with other social groups. What accounts for such shifts? We can speculate that experimenters in classrooms are assumed to be competent, in charge, and authoritative. Subjects guided by a black experimenter attribute these positive characteristics to that person, and then perhaps to the group as a whole. These findings suggest that one remedy for implicit bias is to expose oneself to images and social environments that challenge stereotypes.

We know of a judge whose court is located in a predominantly African-American neighborhood. Because of the crime and arrest patterns in the community, most people the judge sentences are black. The judge confronted a paradox. On the one hand, she took a judicial oath to be objective and egalitarian, and indeed she consciously believed that her decisions were unbiased. On the other hand, every day she was exposed to an environment that reinforced the association between black men and crime. Although she consciously rejected racial stereotypes, she suspected that she harbored unconscious prejudices merely from working in a segregated world.

Immersed in this environment each day, she wondered if it was possible to give the defendants a fair hearing.

Rather than allow her environment to reinforce a bias, the judge created an alternative environment. She spent a vacation week sitting in a fellow judge's court in a neighborhood where the criminals being tried were predominantly white. Case after case challenged the stereotype of blacks as criminal and whites as law abiding and so challenged any bias against blacks that she might have harbored.

Think about the possibly biased associations your workplace fosters. Is there, perhaps, a "wall of fame" with pictures of high achievers all cast from the same mold? Are certain types of managers invariably promoted? Do people overuse certain analogies drawn from stereotypical or narrow domains of knowledge (sports metaphors, for instance, or cooking terms)? Managers can audit their organization to uncover such patterns or cues that unwittingly lead to stereotypical associations.

If an audit reveals that the environment may be promoting unconscious biased or unethical behavior, consider creating countervailing experiences, as the judge did. For example, if your department reinforces the stereotype of men as naturally dominant in a hierarchy (most managers are male, and most assistants are female), find a department with women in leadership positions and set up a shadow program. Both groups will benefit from the exchange of best practices, and your group will be quietly exposed to counterstereotypical cues. Managers sending people out to spend time in clients' organizations as a way to improve service should take care to select organizations likely to counter stereotypes reinforced in your own company.

Broaden your decision making

Imagine that you are making a decision in a meeting about an important company policy that will benefit some groups of employees more than others. A policy might, for example, provide extra vacation time for all employees but eliminate the flex time that has allowed many new parents to balance work with their family responsibilities. Another policy might lower the mandatory retirement age, eliminating some older workers but creating advancement opportunities for younger ones. Now pretend that, as you make your decisions, you don't know which group you belong to. That is, you don't know whether you are senior or junior, married or single, gay or straight, a parent or childless, male or female, healthy or unhealthy. You will eventually find out, but not until after the decision has been made. In this hypothetical scenario, what decision would you make? Would you be willing to risk being in the group disadvantaged by your own decision? How would your decisions differ if you could make them wearing various identities not your own?

This thought experiment is a version of philosopher John Rawls's concept of the "veil of ignorance," which posits that only a person ignorant of his own identity is capable of a truly ethical decision. Few of us can assume the veil completely, which is precisely why hidden biases, even when identified, are so difficult to correct. Still, applying the veil of ignorance to your next important managerial decision may offer some insight into how strongly implicit biases influence you.

Just as managers can expose bias by collecting data before acting on intuition, they can take other preemptive steps. What list of names do you start with when considering whom to send to a training program, recommend for a new assignment, or nominate for a fast-track position? Most of us can quickly and with little concentration come up with such a list. But keep in mind that your intuition is prone to implicit prejudice (which will strongly favor dominant and well-liked groups), in-group favoritism (which will favor people in your own group), overclaiming (which will favor you), and conflict of interest (which will favor people whose interests affect your own). Instead of relying on a mental short list when making personnel decisions, start with a full list of names of employees who have relevant qualifications.

Using a broad list of names has several advantages. The most obvious is that talent may surface that might otherwise be overlooked. Less obvious but equally important, the very act of considering a counterstereotypical choice at the conscious level can reduce implicit bias. In fact, merely thinking about hypothetical, counterstereotypical scenarios—such as what it would be like to trust a complex presentation to a female colleague or to receive a promotion from an African-American boss—can prompt less-biased and more ethical decision making. Similarly, consciously considering counterintuitive options in the face of conflicts of interest, or when there's an opportunity to overclaim, can promote more objective and ethical decisions.

The Vigilant Manager

If you answered "true" to the question at the start of this article, you felt with some confidence that you are an ethical decision maker. How would you answer it now? It's clear that neither simple conviction nor sincere intention is enough to ensure that you are the ethical practitioner you imagine yourself to be. Managers who aspire to be ethical must challenge the assumption that they're always unbiased and acknowledge that vigilance, even more than good intention, is a defining characteristic of an ethical manager. They must actively collect data, shape their environments, and broaden their decision making. What's more, an obvious redress is available. Managers should seek every opportunity to implement affirmative action policies—not because of past wrongs done to one group or another but because of the everyday wrongs that we can now document are inherent in the ordinary, everyday behavior of good, well-intentioned people. Ironically, only those who understand their own potential for unethical behavior can become the ethical decision makers that they aspire to be.

Originally published in December 2003. Reprint R0312D

Make Better Decisions

by Thomas H. Davenport

IN RECENT YEARS DECISION MAKERS in both the public and private sectors have made an astounding number of poor calls. For example, the decisions to invade Iraq, not to comply with global warming treaties, to ignore Darfur, are all likely to be recorded as injudicious in history books. And how about the decisions to invest in and securitize subprime mortgage loans, or to hedge risk with credit default swaps? Those were spread across a number of companies, but single organizations, too, made bad decisions. Tenneco, once a large conglomerate, chose poorly when buying businesses and now consists of only one auto parts business. General Motors made terrible decisions about which cars to bring to market. Time Warner erred in buying AOL, and Yahoo in deciding not to sell itself to Microsoft.

Why this decision-making disorder? First, because decisions have generally been viewed as the prerogative of individuals—usually senior executives. The process employed, the information used, the logic relied on, have been left up to them, in something of a black box. Information goes in, decisions come out—and who knows what happens in between? Second, unlike other business processes, decision making has rarely been the focus of systematic analysis inside the firm. Very few organizations have "reengineered" their decisions. Yet there are just as many opportunities to improve decision making as to improve any other process.

Selected Reading

Blink
by Malcolm Gladwell, is a paean to intuitive decision making.

The Wisdom of Crowds
by James Surowiecki, argues for large-group participation in decisions.

How We Decide
by Jonah Lehrer, addresses the psychobiology of decision making and the limits of rationality.

Predictably Irrational
by Dan Ariely, considers behavioral economics and its implications for decision making.

Nudge
by Richard Thaler and Cass Sunstein, is influencing discussions about behavior-oriented policy in Washington, DC.

Two books on analytical and automated decision making:

Competing on Analytics
by Thomas H. Davenport and Jeanne G. Harris

Super Crunchers
by Ian Ayres

Useful insights have been available for a long time. For example, academics defined "groupthink," the forced manufacture of consent, more than half a century ago—yet it still bedevils decision makers from the White House to company boardrooms. In the sixteenth century the Catholic Church established the devil's advocate to criticize canonization decisions—yet few organizations today formalize the advocacy of decision alternatives. Recent popular business books address a host of decision-making alternatives (see "Selected Reading").

However, although businesspeople are clearly buying and reading these books, few companies have actually adopted their recommendations. The consequences of this inattention are becoming

Idea in Brief

Traditionally, decision making in organizations has rarely been the focus of systematic analysis. That may account for the astounding number of recent poor calls, such as decisions to invest in and securitize subprime mortgage loans or to hedge risk with credit default swaps. Business books are rich with insights about the decision process, but organizations have been slow to adopt their recommendations. It's time to focus on decision making, Davenport says, and he proposes four steps: (1) List and prioritize the decisions that must be made; (2) assess the factors that go into each, such as who plays what role, how often the decision must be made, and what information is available to support it; (3) design the roles, processes, systems, and behaviors your organization needs; and (4) institutionalize decision tools and assistance. The Educational Testing Service and The Stanley Works, among others, have succeeded in improving their decisions. ETS established a centralized deliberative body to make evidence-based decisions about new-product offerings, and Stanley has a Pricing Center of Excellence with internal consultants dedicated to its various business units. Leaders should bring multiple perspectives to their decision making, beware of analytical models that managers don't understand, be clear about their assumptions, practice "model management," and—because only people can revise decision criteria over time—cultivate human backups.

ever more severe. It is time to take decision making out of the realm of the purely individual and idiosyncratic; organizations must help their managers employ better decision-making processes. Better processes won't guarantee better decisions, of course, but they can make them more likely.

A Framework for Improving Decisions

Focusing on decisions doesn't necessarily require a strict focus on the mental processes of managers. (Though, admittedly, the black box deserves some unpacking.) It can mean examining the accessible components of decision making—which decisions need to be made, what information is supplied, key roles in the process, and so forth. Smart organizations make multifaceted interventions—addressing technology, information, organizational structure, methods, and personnel. They can improve decision making in four steps:

1. Identification

Managers should begin by listing the decisions that must be made and deciding which are most important—for example, "the top 10 decisions required to execute our strategy" or "the top 10 decisions that have to go well if we are to meet our financial goals." Some decisions will be rare and highly strategic ("What acquisitions will allow us to gain the necessary market share?") while others will be frequent and on the front lines ("How should we decide how much to pay on claims?"). Without some prioritization, all decisions will be treated as equal—which probably means that the important ones won't be analyzed with sufficient care.

2. Inventory

In addition to identifying key decisions, you should assess the factors that go into each of them. Who plays what role in the decision? How often does it occur? What information is available to support it? How well is the decision typically made? Such an examination helps an organization understand which decisions need improvement and what processes might make them more effective, while establishing a common language for discussing decision making.

3. Intervention

Having narrowed down your list of decisions and examined what's involved in making each, you can design the roles, processes, systems, and behaviors your organization should be using to make them. The key to effective decision interventions is a broad, inclusive approach that considers all methods of improvement and addresses all aspects of the decision process—including execution of the decision, which is often overlooked.

4. Institutionalization

Organizations need to give managers the tools and assistance to "decide how to decide" on an ongoing basis. At Air Products and

Chemicals, for example, managers are trained to determine whether a particular decision should be made unilaterally by one manager, unilaterally after consultation with a group, by a group through a majority vote, or by group consensus. In addition, they determine who will be responsible for making the decision, who will be held accountable for results, and who needs to be consulted or informed.

Companies that are serious about institutionalizing better decision making often enlist decision experts to work with executives on improving the process. Chevron, for example, has a decision-analysis group whose members facilitate decision-framing workshops; coordinate data gathering for analysis; build and refine economic and analytical models; help project managers and decision makers interpret analyses; point out when additional information and analysis would improve a decision; conduct an assessment of decision quality; and coach decision makers. The group has trained more than 2,500 decision makers in two-day workshops and has certified 10,000 through an online training module. At Chevron all major capital projects (which are common at large oil companies) have the benefit of systematic decision analysis.

An organization that has adopted these four steps should also assess the quality of decisions after the fact. The assessment should address not only actual business results—which can involve both politics and luck—but also the decision-making process and whatever information the manager relied on. Chevron regularly performs "lookbacks" on major decisions, and assesses not only outcomes but also how the decision might have employed a better process or addressed uncertainty better.

Let's look at how two companies have improved their decision making.

Better New-Product Decisions at ETS

The Educational Testing Service develops and administers such widely recognized tests as the SAT, the GRE, the TOEFL, and the AP. In 2007 Kurt Landgraf, ETS's CEO, concluded that the organization needed to accelerate and improve decisions about new products and services if it was to continue competing effectively. ETS had previously employed a stage-gate approval process for new offerings, but the organization's matrixed structure and diffuse decision-making responsibility made the process ineffective.

Landgraf asked T.J. Elliott, ETS's vice president of strategic workforce solutions, and Marisa Farnum, the associate vice president for technology transfer, to lead a team that would examine the decision process. The team found several fundamental problems. First, decision makers often lacked information about the intellectual property, partners, cycle times, and likely market for new offerings. Second, it was unclear who played what roles when a decision was being made. Third, the structure of the process was vague.

Elliott and Farnum's team created a new process intended to lead to more evidence-based decisions. It introduced a centralized deliberative body to make decisions about new offerings, developed forms that required new metrics for and information about each proposal, and established standards for what constituted strong evidence that the offering fit with ETS strategy and likely market demand. The process has been in operation for 20 months and is widely regarded as a major improvement. It has clearly resulted in fewer bad product-launch decisions. However, the deliberative body has realized that proposals must be nurtured from an earlier stage to create more good offerings. The scope of its governance was expanded recently to evaluate and prioritize all product-adaptation and new-product opportunities.

Better Pricing Decisions at The Stanley Works

The Stanley Works, a maker of tools and other products for construction, industry, and security, has been operating its Pricing Center of Excellence since 2003. Under the banner of the Stanley Fulfillment System, a broad initiative for continual improvement in operations, Stanley had identified several decision domains that were critical to its success, including pricing, sales and operational planning, fulfillment processes, and lean manufacturing. Because all of them had a strong information component, a center of excellence was formed for each. The pricing center brings deep knowledge of pricing, data and analysis tools, and relationships with pricing experts at consulting and software firms to Stanley's business units. It is staffed by a director, internal consultants dedicated to the business units, and IT and data-mining specialists.

The center has made a variety of interventions in how the business units reach and execute pricing decisions. Over time it has developed several pricing methodologies and is now focusing on pricing optimization approaches. It has recommended assigning pricing responsibilities to the business unit managers. It holds regular "gross margin calls" with the units to share successes and review failures. (Stanley's CEO, John Lundgren, and its COO, Jim Loree, frequently participate.) Pricing outcomes have been added to personnel evaluations and compensation reviews. An offshore supplier has been engaged to gather and analyze competitors' prices. The center has helped to develop automated decision making, such as a process for authorizing promotional events. It uses "white space analysis" to analyze customer sales data and identify opportunities for additional sales or margin. It also trains the business units on pricing methods, participates in project start-ups, does coaching and mentoring, and disseminates innovations and best practices in pricing.

The results of the center's work speak for themselves: Gross margin at Stanley grew from 33.9% to more than 40% in six years. The changes have delivered more than $200 million in incremental value to the firm. Bert Davis, Stanley's head of business transformation and information systems, says, "We tried to improve pricing decisions with data and analysis tools alone, but it didn't work. It was only when we established the center that we began to see real improvement in pricing decisions."

Multiple Perspectives Yield Better Results

Analytics and decision automation are among the most powerful tools for improving decision making. A growing number of firms are embracing the former both strategically and tactically, building competitive strategies around their analytical capabilities and making decisions on the basis of data and analytics. (See my article "Competing on Analytics," HBR January 2006.) Analytics are even more effective when they have been embedded in automated systems, which can make many decisions virtually in real time. (Few mortgages or insurance policies in the United States are drawn up without decision automation.)

But if one of these approaches goes awry, it can do serious damage to your business. If you're making poor decisions on loans or insurance policies with an automated system, for example, you can lose money in a torrent—just ask those bankers who issued so many low-quality subprime loans. Therefore, it's critical to balance and augment these decision tools with human intuition and judgment. Organizations should:

- Warn managers not to build into their businesses analytical models they don't understand. This means, of course, that to be effective, managers must increasingly be numerate with analytics. As the Yale economist Robert Shiller told the *McKinsey Quarterly* in April 2009, "You have to be a quantitative person if you're managing a company. The quantitative details really matter."

- Make assumptions clear. Every model has assumptions behind it, such as "Housing prices will continue to rise for the foreseeable future" or "Loan charge-off levels will remain similar to those of the past 10 years." (Both these assumptions, of course, have recently been discredited.) Knowing what the assumptions are makes it possible to anticipate when models are no longer a guide to effective decisions.

- Practice "model management," which keeps track of the models being used within an organization and monitors how well they are working to analyze and predict selected variables. Capital One, an early adopter, has many analytical models in place to support marketing and operations.

The new landscape of decision making

Ancient approaches to decision making have recently been augmented by improvements in technology and new research. But every approach has both benefits and drawbacks.

	Small-group process	Analytics	Automation	Neuroscience
	making effective decisions with just a few people	using data and quantitative analysis to support decision making	using decision rules and algorithms to automate decision processes	learning from brain research that illuminates decision making
Benefits	premature convergence on decisions is unlikely clear responsibilities can be assigned multiple alternatives can be examined	decisions are more likely to be correct the scientific method adds rigor	speed and accuracy criteria for decisions are clear	decision makers know when to use the emotional brain trains the rational brain to perform more effectively individual decision making may be overvalued
Cautionary messages	norms for debate must be rational, not emotional everyone must get on board with the decision after debate	gathering enough data may be difficult and time-consuming correct assumptions are crucial	difficult to develop decision criteria may change	the brain is still poorly understood

(*continued*)

	Behavioral economics	Intuition	Wisdom of crowds
Benefits	incorporating research on economic behavior and thinking into decisions	relying on one's gut and experience to make decisions	using surveys or markets to allow decisions or inputs by large groups
Cautionary messages	illuminates biases and areas of irrationality can nudge decisions in a particular direction findings in the field are still sketchy context and wording can be used to manipulate decisions	easy and requires no data the subconscious can be effective at weighing options typically the least accurate of decision approaches decision makers are easily swayed by context	those close to the issue are well positioned to know the truth crowd-based decisions can be very accurate members of the crowd must not influence one another ongoing participation is difficult to maintain

- Cultivate human backups. Automated decision systems are often used to replace human decision makers—but you lose those people at your peril. It takes an expert human being to revise decision criteria over time or know when an automated algorithm no longer works well.

It's also important to know when a particular decision approach doesn't apply. For example, analytics isn't a good fit in situations when you have to make a really fast decision. And almost all quantitative models—even predictive ones—are based on past data, so if your experience or intuition tells you that the past is no longer a good guide to the present and future, you'll want to employ other decision tools, or at least to create some new data and analyses. (For a quick look at the strengths and weaknesses of various approaches, see the exhibit "The new landscape of decision making.")

Decisions, like any other business activity, won't get better without systematic review. If you don't know which of your decisions are most important, you won't be able to prioritize improvements. If you don't know how decisions are made in your company, you can't change the process for making them. If you don't assess the results of your changes, you're unlikely to achieve better decisions. The way to begin is simply to give decisions the attention they deserve. Without it, any success your organization achieves in decision making will be largely a matter of luck.

Originally published in November 2009. Reprint R0911L

Why Good Leaders Make Bad Decisions

by Andrew Campbell, Jo Whitehead, and Sydney Finkelstein

DECISION MAKING LIES AT THE heart of our personal and professional lives. Every day we make decisions. Some are small, domestic, and innocuous. Others are more important, affecting people's lives, livelihoods, and well-being. Inevitably, we make mistakes along the way. The daunting reality is that enormously important decisions made by intelligent, responsible people with the best information and intentions are sometimes hopelessly flawed.

Consider Jürgen Schrempp, CEO of Daimler-Benz. He led the merger of Chrysler and Daimler against internal opposition. Nine years later, Daimler was forced to virtually give Chrysler away in a private equity deal. Steve Russell, chief executive of Boots, the UK drugstore chain, launched a health care strategy designed to differentiate the stores from competitors and grow through new health care services such as dentistry. It turned out, though, that Boots managers did not have the skills needed to succeed in health care services, and many of these markets offered little profit potential. The strategy contributed to Russell's early departure from the top job. Brigadier General Matthew Broderick, chief of the Homeland Security Operations Center, who was responsible for alerting President Bush and other senior government officials if Hurricane Katrina breached the levees in New Orleans, went home on Monday,

August 29, 2005, after reporting that they seemed to be holding, despite multiple reports of breaches.

All these executives were highly qualified for their jobs, and yet they made decisions that soon seemed clearly wrong. Why? And more important, how can we avoid making similar mistakes? This is the topic we've been exploring for the past four years, and the journey has taken us deep into a field called decision neuroscience. We began by assembling a database of 83 decisions that we felt were flawed at the time they were made. From our analysis of these cases, we concluded that flawed decisions start with errors of judgment made by influential individuals. Hence we needed to understand how these errors of judgment occur.

In the following pages, we will describe the conditions that promote errors of judgment and explore ways organizations can build protections into the decision-making process to reduce the risk of mistakes. We'll conclude by showing how two leading companies applied the approach we describe. To put all this in context, however, we first need to understand just how the human brain forms its judgments.

How the Brain Trips Up

We depend primarily on two hardwired processes for decision making. Our brains assess what's going on using pattern recognition, and we react to that information—or ignore it—because of emotional tags that are stored in our memories. Both of these processes are normally reliable; they are part of our evolutionary advantage. But in certain circumstances, both can let us down.

Pattern recognition is a complex process that integrates information from as many as 30 different parts of the brain. Faced with a new situation, we make assumptions based on prior experiences and judgments. Thus a chess master can assess a chess game and choose a high-quality move in as little as six seconds by drawing on patterns he or she has seen before. But pattern recognition can also mislead us. When we're dealing with seemingly familiar situations, our brains can cause us to think we understand them when we don't.

Idea in Brief

Decision making lies at the heart of our personal and professional lives. Yet the daunting reality is that enormously important decisions made by intelligent, responsible people with the best information and intentions are nevertheless hopelessly flawed at times. In part, that's due to the way our brains work. Modern neuroscience teaches us that two hard-wired processes in the brain—pattern recognition and emotional tagging—are critical to decision making. Both are normally reliable; indeed, they provide us with an evolutionary advantage. But in certain circumstances, either one can trip us up and skew our judgment. In this article, Campbell and Whitehead, directors at the Ashridge Strategic Management Centre, together with Finkelstein, of Dartmouth's Tuck School, describe the conditions that promote errors of judgment and explore how organizations can build safeguards against them into the decision-making process. In their analysis, the authors delineate three "red-flag conditions" that are responsible either for distorting emotional tagging or for encouraging people to see false patterns: conflicts of interest; attachments to people, places, or things; and the presence of misleading memories, which seem, but really are not, relevant and comparable to the current situation. Using a global chemical company as an example, the authors describe the steps leaders can take to counteract those biases: inject fresh experience or analysis, introduce further debate and more challenges to their thinking, and impose stronger governance. Rather than rely on the wisdom of experienced chairmen, the humility of CEOs, or the standard organizational checks and balances, the authors urge, everyone involved in important decisions should explicitly consider whether red flags exist and, if they do, lobby for appropriate safeguards.

What happened to Matthew Broderick during Hurricane Katrina is instructive. Broderick had been involved in operations centers in Vietnam and in other military engagements, and he had led the Homeland Security Operations Center during previous hurricanes. These experiences had taught him that early reports surrounding a major event are often false: It's better to wait for the "ground truth" from a reliable source before acting. Unfortunately, he had no experience with a hurricane hitting a city built below sea level.

By late on August 29, some 12 hours after Katrina hit New Orleans, Broderick had received 17 reports of major flooding and levee breaches. But he also had gotten conflicting information. The Army Corps of Engineers had reported that it had no evidence of levee breaches, and a late afternoon CNN report from Bourbon Street in the French Quarter had shown city dwellers partying and claiming they had dodged the bullet. Broderick's pattern-recognition process told him that these contrary reports were the ground truth he was looking for. So before going home for the night, he issued a situation report stating that the levees had not been breached, although he did add that further assessment would be needed the next day.

Emotional tagging is the process by which emotional information attaches itself to the thoughts and experiences stored in our memories. This emotional information tells us whether to pay attention to something or not, and it tells us what sort of action we should be contemplating (immediate or postponed, fight or flight). When the parts of our brains controlling emotions are damaged, we can see how important emotional tagging is: Neurological research shows that we become slow and incompetent decision makers even though we can retain the capacity for objective analysis.

Like pattern recognition, emotional tagging helps us reach sensible decisions most of the time. But it, too, can mislead us. Take the case of Wang Laboratories, the top company in the word-processing industry in the early 1980s. Recognizing that his company's future was threatened by the rise of the personal computer, founder An Wang built a machine to compete in this sector. Unfortunately, he chose to create a proprietary operating system despite the fact that the IBM PC was clearly becoming the dominant standard in the industry. This blunder, which contributed to Wang's demise a few years later, was heavily influenced by An Wang's dislike of IBM. He believed he had been cheated by IBM over a new technology he had invented early in his career. These feelings made him reject a software platform linked to an IBM product even though the platform was provided by a third party, Microsoft.

Why doesn't the brain pick up on such errors and correct them? The most obvious reason is that much of the mental work we do is unconscious. This makes it hard to check the data and logic we use when we make a decision. Typically, we spot bugs in our personal software only when we see the results of our errors in judgment. Matthew Broderick found out that his ground-truth rule of thumb was an inappropriate response to Hurricane Katrina only after it was too late. An Wang found out that his preference for proprietary software was flawed only after Wang's personal computer failed in the market.

Compounding the problem of high levels of unconscious thinking is the lack of checks and balances in our decision making. Our brains do not naturally follow the classical textbook model: Lay out the options, define the objectives, and assess each option against each objective. Instead, we analyze the situation using pattern recognition and arrive at a decision to act or not by using emotional tags. The two processes happen almost instantaneously. Indeed, as the research of psychologist Gary Klein shows, our brains leap to conclusions and are reluctant to consider alternatives. Moreover, we are particularly bad at revisiting our initial assessment of a situation—our initial frame.

An exercise we frequently run at Ashridge Business School shows how hard it is to challenge the initial frame. We give students a case that presents a new technology as a good business opportunity. Often, a team works many hours before it challenges this frame and starts, correctly, to see the new technology as a major threat to the company's dominant market position. Even though the financial model consistently calculates negative returns from launching the new technology, some teams never challenge their original frame and end up proposing aggressive investments.

Raising the Red Flag

In analyzing how it is that good leaders made bad judgments, we found they were affected in all cases by three factors that either distorted their emotional tags or encouraged them to see a false pattern. We call these factors "red flag conditions."

The first and most familiar red flag condition, *the presence of inappropriate self-interest*, typically biases the emotional importance we place on information, which in turn makes us readier to perceive the patterns we want to see. Research has shown that even well-intentioned professionals, such as doctors and auditors, are unable to prevent self-interest from biasing their judgments of which medicine to prescribe or opinion to give during an audit.

The second, somewhat less familiar condition is *the presence of distorting attachments*. We can become attached to people, places, and things, and these bonds can affect the judgments we form about both the situation we face and the appropriate actions to take. The reluctance executives often feel to sell a unit they've worked in nicely captures the power of inappropriate attachments.

The final red flag condition is *the presence of misleading memories*. These are memories that seem relevant and comparable to the current situation but lead our thinking down the wrong path. They can cause us to overlook or undervalue some important differentiating factors, as Matthew Broderick did when he gave too little thought to the implications of a hurricane hitting a city below sea level. The chance of being misled by memories is intensified by any emotional tags we have attached to the past experience. If our decisions in the previous similar experience worked well, we'll be all the more likely to overlook key differences.

That's what happened to William Smithburg, former chairman of Quaker Oats. He acquired Snapple because of his vivid memories of Gatorade, Quaker's most successful deal. Snapple, like Gatorade, appeared to be a new drinks company that could be improved with Quaker's marketing and management skills. Unfortunately, the similarities between Snapple and Gatorade proved to be superficial, which meant that Quaker ended up destroying rather than creating value. In fact, Snapple was Smithburg's worst deal.

Of course, part of what we are saying is common knowledge: People have biases, and it's important to manage decisions so that these biases balance out. Many experienced leaders do this already. But we're arguing here that, given the way the brain works, we cannot rely on leaders to spot and safeguard against their own errors in judgment. For important decisions, we need a deliberate, structured way to identify likely sources of bias—those red flag conditions—and we need to strengthen the group decision-making process.

Consider the situation faced by Rita Chakra, head of the cosmetics business of Choudry Holdings (the names of the companies and people cited in this and the following examples have been disguised). She was promoted head of the consumer products division and needed to decide whether to promote her number two into her cosmetics job or recruit someone from outside. Can we anticipate any potential red flags in this decision? Yes, her emotional tags could be unreliable because of a distorting attachment she may have to her colleague or an inappropriate self-interest she could have in keeping her workload down while changing jobs. Of course we don't know for certain whether Rita feels this attachment or holds that vested interest. And since the greater part of decision making is unconscious, Rita would not know either. What we do know is that there is a risk. So how should Rita protect herself, or how should her boss help her protect herself?

The simple answer is to involve someone else—someone who has no inappropriate attachments or self-interest. This could be Rita's boss, the head of human resources, a headhunter, or a trusted colleague. That person could challenge her thinking, force her to review her logic, encourage her to consider options, and possibly even champion a solution she would find uncomfortable. Fortunately, in this situation, Rita was already aware of some red flag conditions, and so she involved a headhunter to help her evaluate her colleague and external candidates. In the end, Rita did appoint her colleague but only after checking to see if her judgment was biased.

We've found many leaders who intuitively understand that their thinking or their colleagues' thinking can be distorted. But few leaders do so in a structured way, and as a result many fail to provide sufficient safeguards against bad decisions. Let's look now at a couple of companies that approached the problem of decision bias systematically by recognizing and reducing the risk posed by red flag conditions.

Safeguarding Against Your Biases

A European multinational we'll call Global Chemicals had an underperforming division. The management team in charge of the division had twice promised a turnaround and twice failed to deliver. The CEO, Mark Thaysen, was weighing his options.

This division was part of Thaysen's growth strategy. It had been assembled over the previous five years through two large and four smaller acquisitions. Thaysen had led the two larger acquisitions and appointed the managers who were struggling to perform. The chairman of the supervisory board, Olaf Grunweld, decided to consider whether Thaysen's judgment about the underperforming division might be biased and, if so, how he might help. Grunweld was not second-guessing Thaysen's thinking. He was merely alert to the possibility that the CEO's views might be distorted.

Grunweld started by looking for red flag conditions. (For a description of a process for identifying red flags, see the sidebar, "Identifying Red Flags.") Thaysen built the underperforming division, and his attachment to it might have made him reluctant to abandon the strategy or the team he had put in place. What's more, because in the past he had successfully supported the local managers during a tough turnaround in another division, Thaysen ran the risk of seeing the wrong pattern and unconsciously favoring the view that continued support was needed in this situation, too. Thus alerted to Thaysen's possible distorting attachments and potential misleading memories, Grunweld considered three types of safeguards to strengthen the decision process.

Injecting fresh experience or analysis

You can often counteract biases by exposing the decision maker to new information and a different take on the problem. In this instance, Grunweld asked an investment bank to tell Thaysen what value the company might get from selling the underperforming division. Grunweld felt this would encourage Thaysen to at least consider that radical option—a step Thaysen might too quickly dismiss if he had become overly attached to the unit or its management team.

Identifying Red Flags

RED FLAGS ARE USEFUL ONLY if they can be spotted before a decision is made. How can you recognize them in complex situations? We have developed the following seven-step process:

1. **Lay out the range of options.** It's never possible to list them all. But it's normally helpful to note the extremes. These provide boundaries for the decision.
2. **List the main decision makers.** Who is going to be influential in making the judgment calls and the final choice? There may be only one or two people involved. But there could also be 10 or more.
3. **Choose one decision maker to focus on.** It's usually best to start with the most influential person. Then identify red flag conditions that might distort that individual's thinking.
4. **Check for inappropriate self-interest or distorting attachments.** Is any option likely to be particularly attractive or unattractive to the decision maker because of personal interests or attachments to people, places, or things? Do any of these interests or attachments conflict with the objectives of the main stakeholders?
5. **Check for misleading memories.** What are the uncertainties in this decision? For each area of uncertainty, consider whether the decision maker might draw on potentially misleading memories. Think about past experiences that could mislead, especially ones with strong emotional associations. Think also about previous judgments that could now be unsound, given the current situation.
6. **Repeat the analysis with the next most influential person.** In a complex case, it may be necessary to consider many more people, and the process may bring to light a long list of possible red flags.
7. **Review the list of red flags you have identified** and determine whether the brain's normally efficient pattern-recognition and emotional-tagging processes might be biased in favor of or against some options. If so, put one or more safeguards in place.

Introducing further debate and challenge

This safeguard can ensure that biases are confronted explicitly. It works best when the power structure of the group debating the issue is balanced. While Thaysen's chief financial officer was a strong individual, Grunweld felt that the other members of the executive group would be likely to follow Thaysen's lead without challenging him. Moreover, the head of the underperforming division was a member of the executive group, making it hard for open debate to occur. So Grunweld proposed a steering committee consisting of himself, Thaysen, and the CFO. Even if Thaysen strongly pushed for a particular solution, Grunweld and the CFO would make sure his reasoning was properly challenged and debated. Grunweld also suggested that Thaysen set up a small project team, led by the head of strategy, to analyze all the options and present them to the steering committee.

Imposing stronger governance

The requirement that a decision be ratified at a higher level provides a final safeguard. Stronger governance does not eliminate distorted thinking, but it can prevent distortions from leading to a bad outcome. At Global Chemicals, the governance layer was the supervisory board. Grunweld realized, however, that its objectivity could be compromised because he was a member of both the board and the steering committee. So he asked two of his board colleagues to be ready to argue against the proposal emanating from the steering committee if they felt uncomfortable.

In the end, the steering committee proposed an outright sale of the division, a decision the board approved. The price received was well above expectations, convincing all that they had chosen the best option.

The chairman of Global Chemicals took the lead role in designing the decision process. That was appropriate given the importance of the decision. But many decisions are made at the operating level, where direct CEO involvement is neither feasible nor desirable. That was the case at Southern Electricity, a division of a larger U.S. utility. Southern consisted of three operating units and two powerful functions. Recent regulatory changes meant that prices could not be raised and might even fall. So managers were looking for ways to cut back on capital expenditures.

Division head Jack Williams recognized that the managers were also risk averse, preferring to replace equipment early with the best upgrades available. This, he realized, was a result of some high-profile breakdowns in the past, which had exposed individuals both to complaints from customers and to criticism from colleagues. Williams believed the emotional tags associated with these experiences might be distorting their judgment.

What could he do to counteract these effects? Williams rejected the idea of stronger governance; he felt that neither his management team nor the parent company's executives knew enough to do the job credibly. He also rejected additional analysis, because Southern's analysis was already rigorous. He concluded that he had to find a way to inject more debate into the decision process and enable people who understood the details to challenge the thinking.

His first thought was to involve himself and his head of finance in the debates, but he didn't have time to consider the merits of hundreds of projects, and he didn't understand the details well enough to effectively challenge decisions earlier in the process than he currently was doing, at the final approval stage. Williams finally decided to get the unit and function heads to challenge one another, facilitated by a consultant. Rather than impose this process on his managers, Williams chose to share his thinking with them. Using the language of red flags, he was able to get them to see the problem without their feeling threatened. The new approach was very successful. The reduced capital-expenditure target was met with room to spare and without Williams having to make any of the tough judgment calls himself.

Because we now understand more about how the brain works, we can anticipate the circumstances in which errors of judgment may occur and guard against them. So rather than rely on the wisdom of experienced chairmen, the humility of CEOs, or the standard organizational checks and balances, we urge all involved in important decisions to explicitly consider whether red flags exist and, if they do, to lobby for appropriate safeguards. Decisions that involve no red flags need many fewer checks and balances and thus less bureaucracy. Some of those resources could then be devoted to protecting the decisions most at risk with more intrusive and robust protections.

Originally published in February 2009. Reprint R0902D

Stop Making Plans; Start Making Decisions

by Michael C. Mankins and Richard Steele

IS STRATEGIC PLANNING COMPLETELY USELESS? That was the question the CEO of a global manufacturer recently asked himself. Two years earlier, he had launched an ambitious overhaul of the company's planning process. The old approach, which required business-unit heads to make regular presentations to the firm's executive committee, had broken down entirely. The ExCom members—the CEO, COO, CFO, CTO, and head of HR—had grown tired of sitting through endless PowerPoint presentations that provided them few opportunities to challenge the business units' assumptions or influence their strategies. And the unit heads had complained that the ExCom reviews were long on exhortation but short on executable advice. Worse, the reviews led to very few worthwhile decisions.

The revamped process incorporated state-of-the-art thinking about strategic planning. To avoid information overload, it limited each business to 15 "high-impact" exhibits describing the unit's strategy. To ensure thoughtful discussions, it required that all presentations and supporting materials be distributed to the ExCom at least a week in advance. The review sessions themselves were restructured to allow ample time for give-and-take between the corporate team and the business-unit executives. And rather than force the unit heads to traipse off to headquarters for meetings, the ExCom agreed to spend an unprecedented six weeks each spring visiting all 22 units for daylong sessions. The intent was to make the strategy reviews longer, more focused, and more consequential.

It didn't work. After using the new process for two planning cycles, the CEO gathered feedback from the participants through an anonymous survey. To his dismay, the report contained a litany of complaints: "It takes too much time." "It's at too high a level." "It's disconnected from the way we run the business." And so on. Most damning of all, however, was the respondents' near-universal view that the new approach produced very few real decisions. The CEO was dumbfounded. How could the company's cutting-edge planning process still be so badly broken? More important, what should he do to make strategic planning drive more, better, and faster decisions?

Like this CEO, many executives have grown skeptical of strategic planning. Is it any wonder? Despite all the time and energy most companies put into strategic planning, the process is most often a barrier to good decision making, our research indicates. As a result, strategic planning doesn't really influence most companies' strategy.

In the following pages, we will demonstrate that the failure of most strategic planning is due to two factors: It is typically an annual process, and it is most often focused on individual business units. As such, the process is completely at odds with the way executives actually make important strategy decisions, which are neither constrained by the calendar nor defined by unit boundaries. Not surprisingly, then, senior executives routinely sidestep the planning process. They make the decisions that really shape their company's strategy and determine its future—decisions about mergers and acquisitions, product launches, corporate restructurings, and the like—outside the planning process, typically in an ad hoc fashion, without rigorous analysis or productive debate. Critical decisions are made incorrectly or not at all. More than anything else, this disconnect—between the way planning works and the way decision

Idea in Brief

Most executives view traditional strategic planning as worthless. Why? The process contains serious flaws. First, it's conducted annually, so it doesn't help executives respond swiftly to threats and opportunities (a new competitor, a possible acquisition) that crop up throughout the year.

Second, it unfolds unit by unit—with executive committee members visiting one unit at a time to review their strategic plans. Executives lack sufficient information to provide worthwhile guidance during these "business tours." And the visits take them away from urgent companywide issues, such as whether to enter a new market, outsource a function, or restructure the organization.

Frustrated by these constraints, executives routinely sidestep their company's formal strategic planning process—making ad hoc decisions based on scanty analysis and meager debate. Result? Decisions made incorrectly, too slowly, or not at all.

How to improve the quality *and* quantity of your strategic decisions? Use **continuous issues-focused strategic planning**. Throughout the year, identify the issues you must resolve to enhance your company's performance—particularly those spanning multiple business units. Debate one issue at a time until you've reached a decision. And add issues to your agenda as business realities change.

Your reward? More rigorous debate and more significant strategic decisions each year—made precisely when they're needed.

making happens—explains the frustration, if not outright antipathy, most executives feel toward strategic planning.

But companies can fix the process if they attack its root problems. A small number of forward-looking companies have thrown out their calendar-driven, business-unit-focused planning processes and replaced them with continuous, issues-focused decision making. By changing the timing and focus of strategic planning, they've also changed the nature of top management's discussions about strategy—from "review and approve" to "debate and decide," meaning that senior executives seriously think through every major decision and its implications for the company's performance and value. Indeed, these companies use the strategy development process to drive decision making. As a consequence, they make more

Idea in Practice

To create an effective strategic-planning process:

Link Decision Making and Planning. Create a mechanism that helps you identify the decisions you *must* make to create more shareholder value. Once you've made those decisions, use your traditional planning process to develop an implementation road map.

Example: At Boeing Commercial Airplanes, executives meet regularly to uncover the company's most pressing, long-term strategic issues (such as evolving product strategy, or fueling growth in services). Upon selecting a course of action, they update their long-range business plan with an implementation strategy for that decision. (By separating—but linking—planning and execution, Boeing makes faster and better decisions.)

Focus on Companywide Issues. During strategy discussions, focus on issues spanning multiple business units.

Example: Facing a shortage of investment ideas, Microsoft's leaders began defining issues—such as PC market growth and security—that are critical throughout the company. Dialogues between unit leaders and the executive committee now focus on what Microsoft as a whole can do to address each issue—not which strategies individual units should formulate. Countless new growth opportunities have surfaced.

Develop Strategy Continuously. Spread strategy reviews throughout the year rather than squeezing

than twice as many important strategic decisions each year as companies that follow the traditional planning model. (See the sidebar "Who Makes More Decisions?") These companies have stopped making plans and started making decisions.

Where Planning Goes Wrong

In the fall of 2005, Marakon Associates, in collaboration with the Economist Intelligence Unit, surveyed senior executives from 156 large companies worldwide, all with sales of $1 billion or more (40% of them had revenues over $10 billion). We asked these executives how their companies developed long-range plans and how

them into a two- or three-month window. You'll be able to focus on—and resolve—one issue at a time. And you'll have the flexibility to add issues as soon as business conditions change.

Example: Executives at multi-industry giant Textron review two to three units' strategy per quarter rather than compressing all unit reviews into one quarter annually. They also hold continuous reviews designed to address each strategic issue on the company's agenda. Once an also-ran among its peers, Textron was a top-quartile performer during 2004–2005.

Structure Strategy Reviews to Produce Results. Design and conduct strategy sessions so that participants agree on facts related to each issue before proposing solutions.

Example: At Textron, each strategic issue is resolved through a disciplined process: In one session, the management committee debates the issue at hand and reaches agreement on the relevant facts (e.g., customers' purchase behaviors, a key market's profitability figures). The group then generates several viable strategy alternatives. In a second session, the committee evaluates the alternatives from a strategic and financial perspective and selects a course of action. By moving from facts to alternatives to choices, the group reaches many more decisions than before.

effectively they thought their planning processes drove strategic decisions.

The results of the survey confirmed what we have observed over many years of consulting: The timing and structure of strategic planning are obstacles to good decision making. Specifically, we found that companies with standard planning processes and practices make only 2.5 major strategic decisions each year, on average (by "major," we mean they have the potential to increase company profits by 10% or more over the long term). It's hard to imagine that with so few strategic decisions driving growth, these companies can keep moving forward and deliver the financial performance that investors expect.

Who Makes More Decisions?

COMPANIES SEE A DRAMATIC INCREASE in the quality of their decision making once they abandon the traditional planning model, which is calendar driven and focused on the business units. In our survey, the companies that broke most completely with the past made more than twice as many strategic decisions each year as companies wedded to tradition. What's more, the new structure of the planning process ensures that the decisions are probably the best that could have been made, given the information available to managers at the time.

Here are the average numbers of major strategic decisions reached per year in companies that take the following approaches to strategic planning:

Annual review focused on business units

2.5 decisions per year

Annual review focused on issues

3.5 decisions per year

Continuous review focused on business units

4.1 decisions per year

Continuous review focused on issues

6.1 decisions per year

Source: Marakon Associates and the Economist Intelligence Unit

Even worse, we suspect that the few decisions companies do reach are made in spite of the strategic planning process, not because of it. Indeed, the traditional planning model is so cumbersome and out of sync with the way executives want and need to make decisions that top managers all too often sidestep the process when making their biggest strategic choices.

With the big decisions being made outside the planning process, strategic planning becomes merely a codification of judgments top management has already made, rather than a vehicle for identifying and debating the critical decisions that the company needs to make to produce superior performance. Over time, managers begin to question the value of strategic planning, withdraw from it, and come to rely on other processes for setting company strategy.

The calendar effect

At 66% of the companies in our survey, planning is a periodic event, often conducted as a precursor to the yearly budgeting and capital-approval processes. In fact, linking strategic planning to these other management processes is often cited as a best practice. But forcing strategic planning into an annual cycle risks making it irrelevant to executives, who must make many important decisions throughout the year.

There are two major drawbacks to such a rigid schedule. The first might be called the *time* problem. A once-a-year planning schedule simply does not give executives sufficient time to address the issues that most affect performance. According to our survey, companies that follow an annual planning calendar devote less than nine weeks per year to strategy development. That's barely two months to collect relevant facts, set strategic priorities, weigh competing alternatives, and make important strategic choices. Many issues—particularly those spanning multiple businesses, crossing geographic boundaries, or involving entire value chains—cannot be resolved effectively in such a short time. It took Boeing, for example, almost two years to decide to outsource major activities such as wing manufacturing.

Constrained by the planning calendar, corporate executives face two choices: They can either not address these complex issues—in effect, throwing them in the "too-hard" bucket—or they can address them through some process other than strategic planning. In both cases, strategic planning is marginalized and separated from strategic decision making.

Then there's the *timing* problem. Even when executives allot sufficient time in strategy development to address tough issues, the timing of the process can create problems. At most companies, strategic planning is a batch process in which managers analyze market and competitor information, identify threats and opportunities, and then define a multiyear plan. But in the real world, managers make strategic decisions continuously, often motivated by an immediate need for action (or reaction). When a new competitor enters a market, for instance, or a rival introduces a new technology, executives must act quickly and decisively to safeguard the company's performance. But very few companies (less than 10%, according to our survey) have any sort of rigorous or disciplined process for responding to changes in the external environment. Instead, managers rely on ad hoc processes to correct course or make opportunistic moves. Once again, strategic planning is sidelined, and executives risk making poor decisions that have not been carefully thought through.

M&A decisions provide a particularly egregious example of the timing problem. Acquisition opportunities tend to emerge spontaneously, the result of changes in management at a target company, the actions of a competitor, or some other unpredictable event. Faced with a promising opportunity and limited time in which to act, executives can't wait until the opportunity is evaluated as part of the next annual planning cycle, so they assess the deal and make a quick decision. But because there's often no proper review process, the softer customer- and people-related issues so critical to effective integration of an acquired company can get shortchanged. It is no coincidence that failure to plan for integration is often cited as the primary cause of deal failure.

The business-unit effect

The organizational focus of the typical planning process compounds its calendar effects—or, perhaps more aptly, defects. Two-thirds of the executives we surveyed indicated that strategic planning at their companies is conducted business by business—that is, it is focused on units or groups of units. But 70% of the senior executives who responded to our survey stated they make decisions issue by issue. For example, should we enter China? Should we outsource manufacturing? Should we acquire our distributor? Given this mismatch between the way planning is organized and the way big decisions are made, it's hardly surprising that, once again, corporate leaders look elsewhere for guidance and inspiration. In fact, only 11% of the executives we surveyed believed strongly that planning was worth the effort.

The organizational focus of traditional strategic planning also creates distance, even antagonism, between corporate executives

Traditional Planning

COMPANIES THAT FOLLOW THE TRADITIONAL strategic planning model develop a strategy plan for each business unit at some point during the year. A cross-functional team dedicates less than nine weeks to developing the unit's plan. The executive committee reviews each plan—typically in daylong, on-site meetings—and rubber-stamps the results. The plans are consolidated to produce a companywide strategic plan for review by the board of directors.

Once the strategic-planning cycle is complete, the units dedicate another eight to nine weeks to budgeting and capital planning (in most companies, these processes are not explicitly linked to strategic planning).

The executive committee then holds another round of meetings with each of the business units to negotiate performance targets, resource commitments, and (in many cases) compensation for managers.

The results: an approved but potentially unrealistic strategic plan for each business unit and a separate budget for each unit that is decoupled from the unit's strategic plan.

and business-unit managers. Consider, for example, the way most companies conduct strategy reviews—as formal meetings between senior managers and the heads of each business unit. While these reviews are intended to produce a fact-based dialogue, they often amount to little more than business tourism. The executive committee flies in for a day, sees the sights, meets the natives, and flies out. The business unit, for its part, puts in a lot of work preparing for this royal visit and is keen to make it smooth and trouble free. The unit hopes to escape with few unanswered questions and an approved plan. Accordingly, local managers control the flow of information upward, and senior managers are presented only with information that shows each unit in the best possible light. Opportunities are highlighted; threats are downplayed or omitted.

Even if there's no subterfuge, senior corporate managers still have trouble engaging in constructive dialogue and debate because of what might be called information asymmetry. They just don't have the information they need to be helpful in guiding business units. So when they're presented with a strategic plan that's too good to be believed, they have only two real options: either reject

Continuous, Decision-Oriented Planning

ONCE THE COMPANY AS A whole has identified its most important strategic priorities (typically in an annual strategy update), executive committee dialogues, spread throughout the year, are set up to reach decisions on as many issues as possible. Since issues frequently span multiple business units, task forces are established to prepare the strategic and financial information that's needed to uncover and evaluate strategy alternatives for each issue. Preparation time may exceed nine weeks. The executive committee engages in two dialogues for each issue at three to four hours each. The first dialogue focuses on reaching agreement on the facts surrounding the issue and on a set of viable alternatives. The second focuses on the evaluation of those alternatives and the selection of the best course of action. Once an issue is resolved, a new one is added to the agenda. Critical issues can be inserted into the planning process at any time as market and competitive conditions change.

Once a decision has been reached, the budgets and capital plans for the affected business units are updated to reflect the selected option. Consequently, the strategic-planning process and the capital and budgeting processes are integrated. This significantly reduces the need for lengthy negotiations between the executive committee and unit management over the budget and capital plan.

---

it—a move that's all but unheard-of at most large companies—or play along and impose stretch targets to secure at least the promise that the unit will improve performance. In both cases, the review does little to drive decisions on issues. It's hardly surprising that only 13% of the executives we surveyed felt that top managers were effectively engaged in all aspects of strategy development at their companies—from target setting to debating alternatives to approving strategies and allocating resources.

Decision-Focused Strategic Planning

Strategic planning can't have impact if it doesn't drive decision making. And it can't drive decision making as long as it remains focused on individual business units and limited by the calendar. Over the past several years, we have observed that many of the best-performing companies have abandoned the traditional approach

The results: a concrete plan for addressing each key issue; for each business unit, a continuously updated budget and capital plan that is linked directly to the resolution of critical strategic issues; and more, faster, better decisions per year.

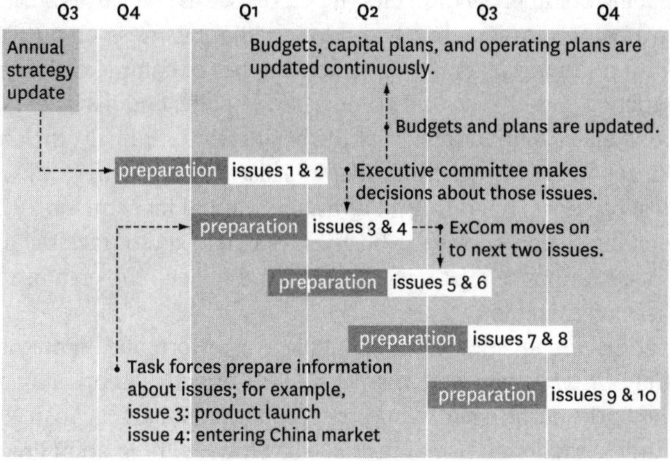

and are focusing explicitly on reaching decisions through the continuous identification and systematic resolution of strategic issues. (The sidebar "Continuous, Decision-Oriented Planning" presents a detailed example of the issues-oriented approach.) Although these companies have found different specific solutions, all have made essentially the same fundamental changes to their planning and strategy development processes in order to produce more, better, and faster decisions.

They separate—but integrate—decision making and plan making

First and most important, a company must take decisions out of the traditional planning process and create a different, parallel process for developing strategy that helps executives identify the decisions they *need to make* to create more shareholder value over time. The output of this new process isn't a plan at all—it's a set of concrete decisions that management can codify into future business plans through the existing planning process, which remains in place. Identifying and making decisions is distinct from creating, monitoring, and updating a strategic plan, and the two sets of tasks require very different, but integrated, processes.

Boeing Commercial Airplanes (BCA) is a case in point. This business unit, Boeing's largest, has had a long-range business plan (LRBP) process for many years. The protracted cycles of commercial aircraft production require the unit's CEO, Alan Mulally, and his leadership team to take a long-term view of the business. Accordingly, the unit's LRBP contains a ten-year financial forecast, including projected revenues, backlogs, operating margins, and capital investments. BCA's leadership team reviews the business plan weekly to track the division's performance relative to the plan and to keep the organization focused on execution.

The weekly reviews were invaluable as a performance-monitoring tool at BCA, but they were not particularly effective at bringing new issues to the surface or driving strategic decision making. So in 2001, the unit's leadership team introduced a Strategy Integration Process focused on uncovering and addressing the business's most important strategic issues (such as determining the best go-to-market strategy for the business, driving the evolution of BCA's product strategy, or fueling growth in services). The team assigned to this process holds strategy integration meetings every Monday to track BCA's progress in resolving these long-term issues. Once a specific course of action is agreed upon and approved by BCA's leadership team, the long-range business plan is updated at the next weekly review to reflect the projected change in financial performance.

The time invested in the new decision-making process is more than compensated for by the time saved in the LRBP process, which is now solely focused on strategy execution. The company gets the best of both worlds—disciplined decision making and superior execution. BCA has maintained the value of the LRBP as an execution tool even as it has increased the quality and quantity of important decisions. Managers believe that the new process is at least partially responsible for the sharp turnaround in Boeing's performance since 2001.

They focus on a few key themes

High-performing companies typically focus their strategy discussions on a limited number of important issues or themes, many of which span multiple businesses. Moving away from a business-by-business planning model in this way has proved particularly helpful for large, complex organizations, where strategy discussions can quickly get bogged down as each division manager attempts to cover every aspect of the unit's strategy. Business-unit managers should remain involved in corporate-level strategy planning that affects their units. But a focus on issues rather than business units better aligns strategy development with decision making and investment.

Consider Microsoft. The world's leading software maker is a highly matrixed organization. No strategy can be effectively executed at the company without careful coordination across multiple functions and across two or more of Microsoft's seven business units, or, as executives refer to them, "P&Ls"—Client; Server and Tools; Information Worker; MSN; Microsoft Business Solutions; Mobile and Embedded Devices; and Home and Entertainment. In late 2004, faced with a perceived shortage of good investment ideas, CEO Steve Ballmer asked Robert Uhlaner, Microsoft's corporate vice president of strategy, planning, and analysis, to devise a new strategic planning process for the company. Uhlaner put in place a Growth and Performance Planning Process that starts with agreement by Ballmer's leadership team on a set of strategic themes—major issues like PC market growth, the entertainment market, and security—that cross business-unit boundaries. These themes not only frame the dialogue for Microsoft's annual strategy review, they also guide the units in fleshing out investment alternatives to fuel the company's growth. Dialogues between the P&L leaders and Ballmer's team focus on what the company can do to address each strategic theme, rather than on individual unit strategies. The early results of this new process are promising. "You have to be careful what you wish for," Uhlaner says. "Our new process has surfaced countless new opportunities for growth. We no longer worry about a dearth of investment ideas, but how best to fund them."

The Disconnect Between Planning and Decision Making

How Executives Plan

66% periodically

Percentage of surveyed executives saying their companies conduct strategic planning only at prescribed times

67% unit by unit

Percentage saying planning is done unit by unit

How Executives Decide

100% continuously

Percentage of executives saying strategic decisions are made without regard to the calendar

70% issue by issue

Percentage saying decisions are made issue by issue

No wonder only 11% of executives are highly satisfied that strategic planning is worth the effort.

Like Microsoft, Diageo North America—a division of the international beer, wine, and spirits marketer—has recently changed the way it conducts strategic planning to allocate resources across its diverse portfolio. Diageo historically focused its planning efforts on individual brands. Brand managers were allowed to make the case for additional investment, no matter what the size of the brand or its strategic role in the portfolio. As a result, resource allocation was bedeviled by endless negotiations between the brands and corporate management. This political wrangling made it extremely difficult for Diageo's senior managers to establish a consistent approach to growth, because a lack of transparency prevented them from discerning, from the many requests for additional funding, which brands really deserved more resources and which did not.

Starting in 2001, Diageo overhauled its approach to strategy development. A crucial change was to focus planning on the factors that the company believed would most drive market growth—for example, an increase in the U.S. Hispanic population. By modeling the impact of these factors on the brand portfolio, Diageo has been better able to match its resources with the brands that have the most growth potential so that it can specify the strategies and investments each brand manager should develop, says Jim Moseley, senior vice president of consumer planning and research for Diageo North America. For example, the division now identifies certain brands for growth and earmarks specific resources for investment in these units. This focused approach has enabled the company to shorten the brand planning process and reduce the time spent on negotiations between the brands and division management. It has also given senior management greater confidence in each brand's ability to contribute to Diageo's growth.

They make strategy development continuous

Effective strategy planners spread strategy reviews throughout the year rather than squeeze them into a two- or three-month window. This allows senior executives to focus on one issue at a time until they reach a decision or set of decisions. Moreover, managers can add issues to the agenda as market and competitive conditions change, so there's no need for ad hoc processes. Senior executives can thus rely on a single strategic planning process—or, perhaps more aptly, a single strategic decision-making model—to drive decision making across the company.

Textron, a $10 billion multi-industry company, has implemented a new, continuous strategy-development process built around a prioritized "decision agenda" comprising the company's most important issues and opportunities. Until 2004, Textron had a fairly traditional strategic planning process. Each spring, the company's operating units—businesses as diverse as Bell Helicopter, E-Z-Go golf cars, and Jacobsen turf maintenance equipment—would develop a five-year strategic plan based on standard templates. Unit managers would then review their strategic plans with Textron's management committee (the company's top five executives) during daylong sessions at each unit. Once the strategy reviews were complete, the units incorporated the results, as best they could, into their annual operating plans and capital budgets.

In June 2004, dissatisfied with the quality and pace of the decision making that resulted from the company's strategy reviews, CEO Lewis Campbell asked Stuart Grief, Textron's vice president for strategy and business development, to rethink the company's strategic planning process. After carefully reviewing the company's practices and gathering feedback from its 30 top executives, Grief and his team designed a new Textron Strategy Process.

There were two important changes. First, rather than concentrate all of the operating-unit strategy reviews in the second quarter of each year, the company now spreads strategy dialogues throughout the year—two to three units are reviewed per quarter. Second, rather than organize the management committee dialogues around business-unit plans, Textron now holds continuous reviews that are designed to address each strategic issue on the company's decision agenda. Both changes have enabled Textron's management committee to be much more effectively engaged in business-unit strategy development. The changes have also ensured that there's a forum in which cross-unit issues can be raised and addressed by top management, with input from relevant business-unit managers. The process has significantly increased the number of strategic decisions the company makes each year. As a result, Textron has gone from being an also-ran among its multi-industrial peers to a top-quartile performer over the past 18 months.

John Cullivan, the director of strategy at Cardinal Health, one of the world's leading health-care products and services companies, reports similar benefits from shifting to a continuous planning model. "Continuous decision making is tough to establish because it requires the reallocation of management time at the top levels of the company," he says. "But the process has enabled us to get sharper focus on the short-term performance of our vertical businesses and make faster progress on our longer-term priorities, some of which are horizontal opportunities that cut across businesses and thus are difficult to manage."

To facilitate continuous strategic decision making, Cardinal has made a series of important changes to its traditional planning process. At the corporate level, for example, the company has put in place a rolling six-month agenda for its executive committee dialogues, a practice that allows everyone inside Cardinal to know what issues management is working on and when decisions will be reached. Similar decision agendas are used at the business-unit and functional levels, ensuring that common standards are applied to all important decisions at the company. And to support continuous decision making at Cardinal, the company has trained "black belts" in new analytical tools and processes and deployed them throughout the organization. This provides each of the company's businesses and functions with the resources needed to address strategic priorities that emerge over time.

They structure strategy reviews to produce real decisions

The most common obstacles to decision making at large companies are disagreements among executives over past decisions, current alternatives, and even the facts presented to support strategic plans. Leading companies structure their strategy review sessions to overcome these problems.

At Textron, for example, strategic-issue reviews are organized around "facts, alternatives, and choices." Each issue is addressed in two half-day sessions with the company's management committee, allowing for eight to ten issues to be resolved throughout the year. In the first session, the management committee debates and reaches agreement on the relevant facts—information on the profitability of key markets, the actions of competitors, the purchase behavior of customers, and so on—and a limited set of viable strategy alternatives. The purpose of this first meeting is not to reach agreement on a specific course of action; rather, the meeting ensures that the group has the best possible information and a robust set of alternatives to consider. The second session is focused on evaluating these alternatives from a strategic and financial perspective and selecting the best course of action. By separating the dialogue around facts and alternatives from the debate over choices, Textron's management committee avoids many of the bottlenecks that plague strategic decision making at most companies and reaches many more decisions than it otherwise would.

Like Textron, Cadbury Schweppes has changed the structure of its strategy dialogues to focus top managers more explicitly on decision making. In 2002, after acquiring and integrating gum-maker Adams—a move that significantly expanded Cadbury's product and geographic reach—the company realized it needed to rethink how it was conducting dialogues about strategy between the corporate center and the businesses. The company made two important changes. First, strategy dialogues were redesigned to incorporate a standard set of facts and metrics about consumers, customers, and competitors. This information helped get critical commercial choices in front of top managers, so that the choices were no longer buried in the business units. Second, senior executives' time was reallocated so they could pay more attention to markets that were crucial to realizing Cadbury's ten-year vision and to making important decisions.

Cadbury's top team now spends one full week per year in each of the countries that are most critical to driving the company's performance, so that important decisions can be informed by direct observation as well as through indirect analysis. Strategy dialogues are now based on a much deeper understanding of the markets. Cadbury's strategic reviews no longer merely consist of reviews of and approval of a strategic plan, and they produce many more important decisions.

Done right, strategic planning can have an enormous impact on a company's performance and long-term value. By creating a planning process that enables managers to discover great numbers of hidden strategic issues and make more decisions, companies will open the door to many more opportunities for long-term growth and profitability. By embracing decision-focused planning, companies will almost certainly find that the quantity and quality of their decisions will improve. And—no coincidence—they will discover an improvement in the quality of the dialogue between senior corporate managers and unit managers. Corporate executives will gain a better understanding of the challenges their companies face, and unit managers will benefit fully from the experience and insights of the company's leaders. As Mark Reckitt, a director of group strategy at Cadbury Schweppes, puts it: "Continuous, decision-focused strategic planning has helped our top management team to streamline its agenda and work with business units and functional management to make far better business-strategy and commercial decisions."

Originally published in January 2006. Reprint R0601F

About the Contributors

MAHZARIN R. BANAJI is the Richard Clarke Cabot Professor of Social Ethics at Harvard University.

MAX H. BAZERMAN is the Jesse Isidor Straus Professor of Business Administration at Harvard Business School.

MARCIA BLENKO is a Bain partner in Boston and leads the firm's global organization practice.

ANDREW CAMPBELL is a director of Ashridge Strategic Management Centre in London.

RAM CHARAN is a business author and adviser. He was on the faculties of Harvard Business School and Northwestern's Kellogg School.

DOLLY CHUGH is an assistant professor of management and organizations at New York University's Stern School of Business.

THOMAS H. DAVENPORT is the President's Distinguished Professor of Information Technology and Management at Babson College.

ROBIN L. DILLON is an associate professor at Georgetown's McDonough School of Business.

SYDNEY FINKELSTEIN is the Steven Roth Professor of Management at the Tuck School of Business at Dartmouth College.

DAVID A. GARVIN is the C. Roland Christensen Professor of Business Administration at Harvard Business School.

JOHN S. HAMMOND is a consultant on decision making and a former professor at Harvard Business School.

DANIEL KAHNEMAN is a senior scholar at the Woodrow Wilson School of Public and International Affairs at Princeton University and a partner at the consultancy The Greatest Good. He was awarded the

Nobel Prize in Economic Sciences in 2002 for his work (with Amos Tversky) on cognitive biases.

RALPH L. KEENEY is a professor emeritus at Duke University's Fuqua School of Business.

DAN LOVALLO is a professor of business strategy at the University of Sydney and a senior adviser to McKinsey & Company.

PETER M. MADSEN is an assistant professor at Brigham Young University's Marriott School of Management.

MICHAEL C. MANKINS is a partner at Bain & Company. He is based in San Francisco and heads the firm's North America organization practice.

HOWARD RAIFFA is the Frank Plumpton Ramsey Professor of Managerial Economics (Emeritus) at Harvard Business School.

MICHAEL A. ROBERTO is the Trustee Professor of Management at Bryant University.

PAUL ROGERS leads Bain & Company's London office.

OLIVIER SIBONY is a director in the Paris office of McKinsey & Company.

RICHARD STEELE is a partner at The Bridgespan Group and heads the firm's New York office.

CATHERINE H. TINSLEY is a professor of management and head of the management group at Georgetown's McDonough School of Business.

JO WHITEHEAD is a director of Ashridge Strategic Management Centre in London.

Index

HBR'S 10 MUST READS

On
Innovation

HBR's 10 Must Reads series is the definitive collection of ideas and best practices for aspiring and experienced leaders alike. These books offer essential reading selected from the pages of *Harvard Business Review* on topics critical to the success of every manager.

Titles include:

HBR's 10 Must Reads on Change Management
HBR's 10 Must Reads on Collaboration
HBR's 10 Must Reads on Communication
HBR's 10 Must Reads on Innovation
HBR's 10 Must Reads on Leadership
HBR's 10 Must Reads on Making Smart Decisions
HBR's 10 Must Reads on Managing People
HBR's 10 Must Reads on Managing Yourself
HBR's 10 Must Reads on Strategic Marketing
HBR's 10 Must Reads on Strategy
HBR's 10 Must Reads on Teams
HBR's 10 Must Reads: The Essentials

HBR'S 10 MUST READS

On Innovation

HARVARD BUSINESS REVIEW PRESS
Boston, Massachusetts

Printed in the United States of America
20 19 18 17 16 15

The web addresses referenced in this book were live and correct at the time of book's publication but may be subject to change.

Library of Congress Cataloging-in-Publication Data

HBR's 10 must reads on innovation.
pages cm
Includes index.
ISBN 978-1-4221-8985-6 (alk. paper)
1. Creative ability in business. 2. Creative thinking. 3. Diffusion of innovations—Management. 4. Technological innovations—Management. 5. New products. I. Harvard business review II. Title: HBR's ten must reads on innovation.
HD53.H394 2013
658.4'063—dc23
2012045970

The paper used in this publication meets the requirements of the American National Standard for Permanence of Paper for Publications and Documents in Libraries and Archives Z39.48-1992.

Contents

HBR'S 10 MUST READS

On Innovation

The Innovation Catalysts

by Roger L. Martin

ONE DAY IN 2007, midway through a five-hour PowerPoint presentation, Scott Cook realized that he wasn't another Steve Jobs. At first it was a bitter disappointment. Like many entrepreneurs, Cook wanted the company he had cofounded to be like Apple—design driven, innovation intensive, wowing consumers year in and year out with fantastic offerings. But that kind of success always seemed to need a powerful visionary at the top.

This article is about how Cook and his colleagues at the software development company Intuit found an alternative to the Steve Jobs model: one that has enabled Intuit to become a design-driven innovation machine. Any corporation—no matter how small or prosaic its business—can make the same grassroots transformation if it really wants to.

The Birth of the Idea

Intuit's transformation arguably began in 2004, with its adoption of the famous Net Promoter Score. Developed by Fred Reichheld, of Bain & Company, NPS depends on one simple question for customers: How likely are you, on a scale of 0 (not at all likely) to 10 (extremely likely), to recommend this product or service to a colleague or friend? "Detractors" answer from 0 to 6, "passives" answer 7 or 8, and "promoters" answer 9 or 10. A company's Net Promoter Score is the percentage of promoters less the percentage of detractors.

For the first couple of years, Intuit saw its NPS rise significantly, owing to a number of marketing initiatives. But by 2007 NPS growth had stalled. It was not hard to see why. Although Intuit had lowered its detractor percentage substantially, it had made little headway with promoters. Customer recommendations of new products were especially disappointing.

Clearly, Intuit needed to figure out how to galvanize its customers. Cook, a member of Procter & Gamble's board of directors, approached Claudia Kotchka, then P&G's vice president of design innovation and strategy, for advice. Following their discussions, Cook and Steve Bennett, then Intuit's CEO, decided to focus on the role of design in innovation at a two-day off-site for the company's top 300 managers. Cook created a one-day program on what he called Design for Delight (D4D)—an event aimed at launching Intuit's reinvention as a design-driven company.

The centerpiece of the day was that five-hour PowerPoint presentation, in which Cook laid out the wonders of design and how it could entice Intuit's customers. The managers listened dutifully and clapped appreciatively at the end, as they were supposed to; Cook was, after all, a company founder. Nevertheless, he was disappointed by his reception. Despite some interest in the ideas presented, there was little energy in the room.

But although the main event fell flat, the one that followed did not. Cook had met a young consulting associate professor at Stanford named Alex Kazaks, whom he'd invited to present for an hour at the off-site. Like Cook, Kazaks began with a PowerPoint presentation, but he ended his after 10 minutes and used the rest of the time for a participatory exercise: The managers worked through a design challenge, creating prototypes, getting feedback, iterating, and refining.

The group was mesmerized. Afterward Cook informally polled the participants, asking what takeaways they'd gotten from the daylong session. Two-thirds of the lessons they reported came from

Idea in Brief

A few years ago the software development company Intuit realized that it needed a new approach to galvanizing customers. The company's Net Promoter Score was faltering, and customer recommendations of new products were especially disappointing. Intuit decided to hold a two-day, off-site meeting for the company's top 300 managers with a focus on the role of design in innovation. One of the days was dedicated to a program called Design for Delight. The centerpiece of the day was a PowerPoint presentation by Intuit founder Scott Cook, who realized midway through that he was no Steve Jobs: The managers listened dutifully, but there was little energy in the room. By contrast, a subsequent exercise in which the participants worked through a design challenge by creating prototypes, getting feedback, iterating, and refining, had them mesmerized. The eventual result was the creation of a team of nine design-thinking coaches—"innovation catalysts"—from across Intuit who were made available to help any work group create prototypes, run experiments, and learn from customers. The process includes a "painstorm" (to determine the customer's greatest pain point), a "sol-jam" (to generate and then winnow possible solutions), and a "code-jam" (to write code "good enough" to take to customers within two weeks). Design for Delight has enabled employees throughout Intuit to move from satisfying customers to delighting them.

the hands-on exercise. This reaction made Cook think: He might not be the next Steve Jobs, but perhaps his company didn't need one. Given a few tools, coaching, and practice, could the grass roots of the company drive success in innovation and customer delight?

From Idea to Initiative

Like most Silicon Valley tech companies, Intuit had user-interface designers, graphic designers, and others buried relatively deep in the organization. Cook turned to a particularly talented young design director, Kaaren Hanson, and asked her what she would do to promote design at Intuit.

Hanson realized that the company needed an organized program for moving from talking about D4D to doing it. She persuaded Cook to let her create a team of design-thinking coaches—"innovation catalysts"—who could help Intuit managers work on initiatives throughout the organization. Hanson selected nine colleagues to join her in this role. Their training and deployment was her central agenda for FY 2009.

In selecting the nine, Hanson looked first for people with a broad perspective on what it meant to be a designer: Beyond creating a graphic user interface that was both appealing and intuitive, it included thinking about whether the software solved the user's problem in a delightful way. She wanted her coaches to be interested in talking to users and solving problems with colleagues rather than depending solely on their own genius. If they were to successfully coach others in design thinking, they'd need an outgoing personality and good people skills.

She invited two direct reports from her own business unit and seven people from other units across the company. The group included six women and four men. They came from a variety of fields within Intuit—design, research, product management—and had titles such as user-interface architect, principal researcher, staff designer, and product manager. Hanson chose people who were influential even though they were all one or two levels below director, meaning closer to the bottom of the organization than the top. All nine signed up enthusiastically.

To begin building design thinking into the DNA of the company, Cook and Hanson organized a series of Design for Delight forums. These were typically attended by more than 1,000 employees and featured a speaker who'd had exemplary success in creating customer delight. Half the featured speakers came from inside Intuit; the other half included the founding CEO of Flip Video, Facebook's top data scientist, and the head of Apple Stores. The forums also showcased D4D successes to date and shared best practices. People who worked together were encouraged to attend together and were asked as a team to identify the one thing they would do differently after the forum.

To ensure that managers who were thinking design didn't become too intimidated to begin the process, or frustrated trying to do something with which they had little experience, or delayed by needing to hire an outside design consultant, Hanson's innovation catalysts were available to help any work group create prototypes, run experiments, and learn from customers. Of course, there was a risk that this would stretch the catalysts too thin, so Hanson placed some constraints on their availability. They were expected to spend 25% of their time on big-payoff projects for Intuit overall. Hanson kept in close contact with general managers who had catalysts working with them to make sure that the catalysts were addressing the managers' biggest problems. She realized that if design momentum was to be maintained, her coaches had to be seen as responsible for three or four visible and high-impact wins a year.

Some enabling came from the very bottom of the organization. In 2008 two employees who had been at Intuit only four months designed an online social network for the D4D initiative, which they rolled out the following year with management's consent but without its direct support. In its first year the new platform, named Brainstorm, generated 32 ideas that made it to market.

From Presentations to Experiments

Traditionally, decisions at Intuit had been made on the basis of PowerPoint presentations. Managers would work to produce both (what they saw as) a great product and a great presentation for selling the concept to their bosses. Under this system Intuit managers voted on ideas and then tried to sell them to customers. A key component of D4D, therefore, was shifting the focus away from managerial presentations. It would be far better, Hanson and Cook realized, to learn directly from customers through experiments.

Today D4D innovations begin with what Intuit calls the painstorm—a process developed by two innovation catalysts, Rachel Evans and Kim McNealy. It is aimed at figuring out customers' greatest pain point for which Intuit can provide relief.

Recruiting the Innovation Catalysts

IN 2008 KAAREN HANSON sent this e-mail to some Intuit colleagues:

Subject: Phase II of Design for Delight—we need YOU

You have been nominated (and your participation has been approved by your manager) to help us drive Phase II of Design for Delight at Intuit. You are a critical leader who can enable Intuit to become one of the principal design-thinking cultures. We have a number of levers at our disposal but we need your help to develop even better ideas to drive design thinking deeper into the organization.

Here's what you'll be committing to:

- **Actively participate in a one-day brainstorm/workshop** in early August to work through what we (as a force of design thinking and as a larger company) might do to take Design for Delight to its next level. Scott will come by and respond to our ideas/plan towards the end of the day
- **Commit to the execution of initiatives** generated through the August workshop
- **Become a more visible Design for Delight leader** across Intuit (e.g., help teach a Design for Delight 101 session/workshop to FastPath or some other such leadership session, contribute to the D4D body of knowledge through existing and future contribution systems, be a sounding board for Intuit execs)
- **Be a D4D coach/facilitator** that the larger company can draw upon (e.g., coach key teams across Intuit in brainstorming, design reviews, etc.)

In total, your commitment will be about 2 days/month—and we'll be able to work around your schedule.

Let me know if you are in for FY09—and I'll get the August date on everyone's calendars. Right now, we're looking at an in-person workshop on August 4th, 5th, or 6th in Mountain View.

In a painstorm, team members talk to and observe customers in their offices or homes rather than sit in Intuit offices and imagine what they want. This exercise often shatters preconceptions. Going into one painstorm for a sales-oriented product, the team was convinced that the product concept should be "Grow your business."

But the painstorm showed that "Grow your business" sounded very ambiguous to customers—it could refer to growing revenues from their existing customers (not a pain point for them) or to acquiring similar small businesses (also not a pain point, but expensive). The true pain point was acquiring entirely new customers through organic sales efforts. "Get customers" was a winning concept that focused laserlike on that.

Next, within two weeks, the group holds a "sol-jam," in which people generate concepts for as many product or service solutions as possible to address the pain points they've identified and then weed the concepts down to a short list for prototyping and testing. In the early days of prototyping, these high-potential solutions were integrated into Intuit's software development process. But the innovation catalysts realized that the best way to maintain momentum would be to get code into users' hands as quickly as possible. This would help determine whether the solution had potential and, if so, what needed to be done to enhance it. So the third step became moving immediately to "code-jam," with the goal of writing code that wasn't airtight but was good enough to take to customers within two weeks of the sol-jam. Thus, proceeding from the painstorm to the first user feedback on a new product usually takes only four weeks.

Let's look at a couple of examples. When Intuit's tax group began to think about mobile apps, Carol Howe, a project manager and innovation catalyst, started with the customer. Her five-person team went "out in the wild," she says, to observe dozens of smartphone users. It quickly narrowed in on millennials, whose income range made them likely candidates for the simplest tax experience. The team created multiple concepts and iterated with customers on a weekly basis. They brought customers in each Friday, distilled what they'd learned on Monday, brainstormed concepts on Tuesday, designed them on Wednesday, and coded them on Thursday, before bringing the customers in again. Through these iterations the team uncovered multiple "delighters." They launched a pilot in California in January 2010 and expanded nationwide in January 2011. The resulting application, SnapTax, has 4.5 stars in both the Apple and Android stores and a Net Promoter Score in the high 80s.

An even better example comes from India. In 2008 members of the India team came up with an idea remote from tax preparation and other core Intuit North America products, none of which were likely to succeed in India. The idea, a service for poor Indian farmers, was interesting enough for Intuit to give Deepa Bachu, a long-time development manager, the green light to explore it. Bachu and an engineer spent weeks following subsistence farmers through their daily lives—in the fields, in their villages, and at the markets where they sold their produce. The two came to appreciate the farmers' greatest pain point—perishable inventory that either went unsold or got a suboptimal price. If Intuit could enable the farmers to consistently sell their produce before spoilage and at a decent price, their pain would be reduced or eliminated.

After the painstorm and the sol-jam, the team went into rapid experimentation. Within seven weeks it was running a test of what was eventually launched as Mobile Bazaar, a simple text-messaging-based marketplace connecting buyers and sellers. To get there so fast, the team had cleverly faked parts of the product that would have been costly and slow to code and build. These came to be known as "fako backends." What the user saw looked real, but behind the user interface was a human being—like the Wizard of Oz behind the curtain—rather than thousands of lines of code that would have taken months to write.

The initial trials showed that half the farmers were able to increase their prices by more than 10%; some of them earned as much as 50% more. Within a year of launch, Mobile Bazaar had 180,000 subscribing farmers, most of them acquired by word of mouth. They report that, on average, the service boosts their prices by 16%.

From Breakthroughs to Culture

Hanson was pleased with the progress of the 10 original innovation catalysts in their first year and with the organization's receptivity, but she knew that Intuit would have to scale up to make the transformation complete. Brad Smith, the new CEO, was raising innovation expectations for the whole company, focusing particularly on new arenas that he described as "mobile, social, and global." Hanson set a goal for FY 2010 to select, train, and deploy another 65 catalysts. This meant sourcing from a broader pool of talent—going deeper into product management and engineering—and creating a small dedicated team to support the catalysts and increase D4D pull from midlevel managers.

She appointed Suzanne Pellican, one of the original 10, to expand the catalysts' number and capabilities. Hanson had learned from the initial work that the strongest design thinkers didn't necessarily make the best catalysts. She says, "We not only needed people who were design thinkers—we also needed people with passion to give D4D away and help others to do great work, versus coming up with a great idea and bringing it to others."

The catalysts also needed mutual support. Hanson's team had found that they did their best work when they worked together. They learned new ideas and techniques from one another and provided moral support in tough situations. So as Pellican scaled up the catalyst corps, she made sure that each catalyst was part of an organized "posse" that typically extended across business units, allowing new methods to travel quickly from one end of the organization to the other.

To increase the catalysts' effectiveness, Hanson established a second small team—led by Joseph O'Sullivan, another of the original 10—to help middle management embrace both design thinking as a concept and the innovation catalysts as enablers. For example, after several catalysts reported encountering resistance at the director level, Hanson and O'Sullivan worked to integrate design thinking into Intuit's leadership training programs, applying it directly to problems that leaders faced. In one training program an IT director was challenged to lead a team tasked with reducing company spending on employees' mobile devices by $500,000. O'Sullivan's group held a one-day session on painstorming and sol-jamming for the team. The IT director achieved the desired saving and won much appreciation from the members of her team for having made their task so much easier than expected. She and the other participants in that leadership training program became fervent D4D advocates.

Encouraging experimentation rather than PowerPoint has enabled employees throughout Intuit to move from satisfying customers to delighting them. Design for Delight has stuck because people see that it is an obviously better and more enjoyable way of innovating.

Innovation activity has increased dramatically in the organization. Take TurboTax, Intuit's single biggest product. In the 2006 tax year the TurboTax unit ran just one customer experiment. In 2010 it ran 600. Experiments in the QuickBooks unit went from a few each year to 40 last year. Intuit now seizes new opportunities more quickly. Brad Smith pushed for D4D-led innovation in the fast-growing arena of mobile apps, and within 24 months the company went from zero to 18, with a number of them, including SnapTax, off to a very successful start. Net Promoter Scores are up across the company, and growth in revenue and income has increased over the past three years.

Scott Cook may not have been another Steve Jobs, but it turned out that Intuit didn't need one.

Originally published in June 2011. Reprint R1106E

Stop the Innovation Wars

by Vijay Govindarajan and Chris Trimble

IT WAS JUST AN INNOCENT COMMENT. While working with a client at a *Fortune* 500 company, we proposed the formation of a special group to execute a new growth strategy. "For now, let's just refer to the group as the innovation team," we suggested.

The client rolled his eyes. "Let's call it anything but that," he said. "What is this so-called innovation team going to do? Brainstorm? Sit around being creative all day? Talk condescendingly about a superior organizational culture? All of this while operating with neither discipline nor accountability? All of this while the rest of us get the real work done?"

Wow. All it took was two words: *innovation team*.

In our experience, innovation teams feel a hostility toward the people responsible for day-to-day operations that is just as biting. The rich vocabulary of disdain includes *bureaucratic, robotic, rigid, ossified, staid, dull, decaying, controlling, patronizing* . . . and just plain *old*. Such animosity explains why most executives believe that any significant innovation initiative requires a team that is separate and isolated from the rest of the company.

But that conventional wisdom is worse than simpleminded. It is flat wrong. Isolation may neutralize infighting, but it also neuters innovation.

The reality is that an innovation initiative must be executed by a partnership that somehow bridges the hostilities—a partnership between a dedicated team and what we call the *performance engine,* the unit responsible for sustaining excellence in ongoing operations. Granted, such an arrangement seems, at first glance, improbable. But to give up on it is to give up on innovation itself. Almost all innovation initiatives build directly upon a company's existing resources and know-how—brands, customer relationships, manufacturing capabilities, technical expertise, and so forth. So when a large corporation asks a group to innovate in isolation, it not only ends up duplicating things it already has but also forfeits its primary advantage over smaller, nimbler rivals—its mammoth asset base.

Over the past decade, we have examined dozens of innovation initiatives and identified some best practices. In the process we built upon foundational management theories such as Jim March's ideas about balancing exploration with exploitation, and Paul Lawrence and Jay Lorsch's argument that firms need to both integrate and differentiate corporate units. We came to the conclusion that the organizational model we prescribe—a partnership between a dedicated team and the performance engine—is surprisingly versatile. It can be adapted to initiatives that span many innovation categories—sustaining and disruptive; incremental and radical; competence enhancing and competence destroying; new processes, new products, new businesses, and high-risk new ventures.

This article will show how to make the unlikeliest partnership work. There are three steps. First, decide which tasks the performance engine can handle and which you'll need to hand off to a dedicated team. Second, assemble the right dedicated team. Third, anticipate and mitigate strains in the partnership. Once you have taken these steps, you'll be in a good position to actually execute on your great ideas.

How One Company Organized for Growth

In most law offices, even in the internet era, you'll find libraries full of weighty and majestic-looking books. The books contain rulings from past cases. With each verdict, judges contribute to a massive body of precedents that shape future decisions. (This is the system,

Idea in Brief

Special teams dedicated to innovation initiatives inevitably run into conflict with the rest of the organization. The people responsible for ongoing operations view the innovators as undisciplined upstarts. The innovators dismiss the operations people as bureaucratic dinosaurs. It's natural to separate the two warring groups. But it's also dead wrong, say Tuck Business School's Govindarajan and Trimble. Nearly all innovation initiatives build on a firm's existing resources and know-how. When a group is asked to innovate in isolation, the corporation forfeits its main advantage over smaller, nimbler rivals—its mammoth asset base. The best approach is to set up a partnership between the dedicated team and the people who maintain excellence in ongoing operations, the company's performance engine. Such partnerships were key to the successful launch of new offerings by legal publisher Westlaw, Lucent Technologies, and WD-40. There are three steps to making the partnership work: First, decide which tasks the performance engine can handle, assigning it only those that flow along the same path as ongoing operations. Next, assemble a dedicated team to carry out the rest, being careful to bring in outside perspectives and create new norms. Last, proactively manage conflicts. The key here is having an innovation leader who can collaborate well with the performance engine and a senior executive who supports the dedicated team, prioritizes the company's long-term interests, and adjudicates contests for resources.

at least, in the United States and many other countries.) Law students spend countless hours mastering the intricacies and subtleties of researching precedents.

West, a 135-year-old business, is one of several publishing houses whose mission is to make legal research easier. After it was acquired by the Thomson Corporation, now Thomson Reuters, in 1996, West experienced five years of double-digit growth, as the industry made a rapid transition from printed books to online databases. But in 2001 a major problem arose. Once nearly all of West's customers had converted to Westlaw, the company's online offering, West's growth plummeted to near zero.

To restart growth, West set its sights on expanding its product line. By studying its customers—law firms, corporate law offices,

Questions to Ask

When Dividing the Labor

1. Does my company already have the needed skills for all aspects of the project?
2. What portions of the innovation initiative are consistent with the existing work relationships in the performance engine?

When Assembling the Dedicated Team

1. What is the right mix of insiders and outsiders?
2. How should the team be structured differently from the performance engine?
3. How should the team be measured and incentivized?

As You Manage the Strains on the Partnership

1. Is there a tone of mutual respect?
2. Are resource conflicts resolved proactively?
3. Is the shared staff giving sufficient attention to the innovation initiative?

---

and law schools, among others—and how they worked, West saw that lawyers had no convenient access to many key sources of information. For example, to examine legal strategies in past cases, law firms were sending runners to courthouses to dig through dusty archives and photocopy old briefs—documents written by lawyers for judges, often to summarize their arguments.

Starting with an online database of briefs, West proceeded to launch a series of new digital products. By 2007, West had restored its organic growth to nearly 7% annually—quite an accomplishment since its customer base was growing much more slowly.

An expansion into databases for different kinds of documents does not seem, at first glance, as if it would have been a stretch for West. But Mike Wilens, then the CEO, and his head of product development, Erv Barbre, immediately saw that the briefs project, because of its size, complexity, and unfamiliarity, was beyond the capabilities of West's performance engine. Some kind of special team was needed. At the same time, Wilens and Barbre were confident that portions of the project could be tackled by West's existing staff. They just had to make sure the two groups worked well together. Ultimately, the new briefs offering succeeded because Wilens and Barbre built an effective partnership between a dedicated team and the performance engine, following the three steps we've outlined.

Divide the Labor

Step one in forming the partnership is to define the responsibilities of each partner. Naturally, you want to assign as much as you can to the performance engine. It already exists and works well. But caution is due. You need to realistically assess what the performance engine can handle while it maintains excellence in ongoing operations.

The proper division of labor can span a wide range—from 10/90, to 50/50, to 90/10 splits. It depends on the nature of the initiative and the performance engine's capabilities. So how do you decide?

The performance engine has two essential limitations. The first is straightforward. Any task that is beyond the capabilities of the individuals within the performance engine must be assigned to the dedicated team. The second limitation is less obvious. It involves work relationships. What Person A and Person B can do together is not just a function of A's skills and B's skills. It is also a function of the way A and B are accustomed to working together. As long as A and B are working inside the performance engine, their work relationship is extremely difficult to change. It is reinforced daily by the demands of ongoing operations. BMW was confronted with this second limitation when it designed its first hybrid vehicle. (See the sidebar "Why BMW Didn't Reinvent the Wheel.")

Therefore, the performance engine should take on only tasks that flow along the same path from person to person that ongoing operations do—at the same pace and with the same people in charge. To ask more of the performance engine is too disruptive. It embeds conflicts between innovation and ongoing operations so deeply within the performance engine that they become impossible to manage.

Case Study: Why BMW Didn't Reinvent the Wheel

AT THE HEART OF EVERY HYBRID automobile lies a regenerative brake. Traditional brakes dissipate the energy produced by a vehicle's motion, generating friction and useless heat. Regenerative brakes, by contrast, capture the energy and put it back to work. An electrical generator built into the brake recharges the hybrid's massive batteries as the car slows.

Chris Bangle, then chief of design at BMW, was discouraged by slow progress early in the company's first effort to design a hybrid vehicle, launched in 2007. The source of the problem, Bangle saw, had nothing to do with engineering prowess; BMW employed the right experts. The problem lay in the company's formal structure and processes. Under its well-established design procedures, there was no reason for battery specialists to speak with brake specialists. There was no routine work flow between them.

Bangle ultimately decided to create a dedicated team to enable the deep collaboration that was necessary among all component specialists involved in the regenerative brake design. He named it the "energy chain" team, and it succeeded in moving the project forward quickly. Although a dedicated team was required for this one aspect of vehicle design, all other aspects of BMW's first hybrid launch—design, engineering, sales, marketing, distribution, and so forth—were handled by its performance engine.

At West, Wilens and Barbre recognized that although product development staffers had deep expertise in judicial decisions—such as *Miranda v. Arizona, Brown v. Board of Education, Roe v. Wade,* and thousands more—they had no experience in gathering briefs, which were scattered throughout countless courthouses and were much harder to track and organize than decisions were. A complicating factor was scale. There can be dozens of briefs for every judicial decision. The dedicated team, at the very least, had to take responsibility for locating and acquiring the briefs—and would need a few outside experts to be effective.

More critically, Wilens and Barbre saw that the briefs project as a whole would be inconsistent with the work relationships within West's product development group. Composed of about 50 legal experts, the group worked on a few dozen small initiatives at a time. The typical project was an improvement to the Westlaw database that involved only two or three people for up to a few weeks. The group was nonhierarchical, and the individuals within it did not depend heavily on one another. In fact, during a given project, a product developer's most important work relationship was likely to be cross-functional, with a peer in the information technology group.

The briefs project was much larger. At its peak, it involved 30 people full-time. The product developers needed to work together in an unfamiliar manner. Each needed to take on a specialized role as part of a tightly structured, close-knit project team. Asking the developers to operate in both modes at once would have been disruptive and confusing for all involved. Therefore Wilens and Barbre assigned nearly the entire product development task to a dedicated team.

However, they assigned the marketing and sales tasks to the performance engine. Marketing and selling briefs was not much different from marketing and selling Westlaw. The buyers were the same, and the value proposition was easy to explain. The work could simply be added to West's existing marketing and sales processes. It would flow along the same path, at the same pace, and with the same people in charge. The sales and marketing teams were a component of the performance engine that could do double duty—a subset we refer to as the *shared staff*.

Assemble the Dedicated Team

Once the labor has been divided and the required skill sets have been identified, the principles for assembling the dedicated team are uncomplicated. First, choose the best people you can get, from any source (internal transfers, external hires, even small acquisitions). Then, organize the team in a way that makes the most sense for the task at hand. Tackle the process as if you were building a new company from the ground up. This was the approach Lucent took in launching a new unit that quickly grew to $2 billion in annual revenues. (See the sidebar "Why Lucent Engineered a Service Business from Scratch.")

Alas, these principles are easy to state but extremely difficult to follow. Companies have a pernicious habit of creating subunits that behave just like the rest of the company, as though a genetic code

Case Study: Why Lucent Engineered a Service Business from Scratch

IN 2006, LUCENT SIGNED a deal to help a major telecommunications company transform its network. Four years earlier, such a huge service deal would have been hard to imagine.

Lucent's historical strength was in products and in making technological breakthroughs in telecommunications hardware. But after the dot-com bust, Lucent needed a new source of growth and looked to services.

While the company had the necessary technical skills for services, it hardly had the organizational DNA. Technologists, not client relationship managers, held most of the power. And the pace of service operations was week to week, a stark departure from telecom hardware purchasing cycles, which lasted years. As such, Lucent recognized that nearly the entire project needed to be executed by a dedicated team.

Lucent assembled that team as if it were building a new company. It hired an outside leader, a veteran of services from EDS, and several experienced service executives. It adopted new HR policies that mimicked those of service companies. And it created a new performance scorecard, one that emphasized workforce utilization, not product line ROI. It even tied compensation for service deliverers directly to their utilization rates. The result? In four years' time, Lucent's service group was generating more than $2 billion in revenues.

---

has been passed from parent to offspring. We think of such subunits as *little performance engines,* and they quickly bring innovation initiatives to a standstill.

The most frequent source of the problem is the instinct to populate dedicated teams entirely with insiders. This is understandable. It's natural to think about who you know before thinking about skills you need. Insiders are easy to find, often cheaper to "hire," and seem less risky because they're known commodities. They also offer a critical benefit: Because of their familiarity with the organization and credibility within it, they can help mitigate conflicts between the dedicated team and the performance engine.

The trouble is that a dedicated team composed entirely of insiders is practically guaranteed to act like a little performance engine. For one thing, everyone has the same biases and instincts, grounded in the history of a single company. Furthermore, work relationships are sticky. As noted earlier, employees who have worked together for years have a hard time altering the way they interact.

Building an effective dedicated team requires breaking down existing work relationships and creating new ones. Including some outsiders, even just one in three, is a powerful expedient. Outsiders have no existing work relationships to break down. They must form new ones from scratch. As a bonus, outsiders naturally challenge assumptions because their biases and instincts are rooted in the experiences of other companies.

Managers can also accelerate the process of breaking down and re-creating work relationships by writing new job descriptions, inventing new and unfamiliar titles, and explicitly shifting the balance of power within the team. Shifting that balance is important because it is rarely the case that a company's traditional power center (say, engineering) should also dominate the dedicated team (if, for example, customers for the innovation initiative will care more about a new product's look than its performance).

Selecting the right people and forming new work relationships are the foundational steps in building an effective dedicated team, but it is also important to pay attention to other forces that shape behaviors. Beyond new work relationships, dedicated teams frequently require performance metrics, incentives, and cultural norms that differ from those of the performance engine.

West built a dedicated team that was distinct from its existing product development staff, choosing a roughly 50/50 mix of insiders and outsiders. The company acquired a small business that had assembled on microfiche a collection of valuable briefs, including the very first brief filed before the U.S. Supreme Court. With it, West brought on board about a dozen people who knew a great deal about briefs and had no work relationships with the West team.

The leader of the briefs effort, Steve Anderson, treated the process of turning the mix of insiders and outsiders into a structured team as a zero-based effort. Rather than drawing on any of West's norms for how work gets done (who's responsible for what, who has what decision rights, and so forth), he simply gathered everyone and said, "Here we are. This is our task. How should we make it happen?"

Of course, the way to organize the effort was not obvious on day one. Innovation initiatives are ambiguous. As Anderson's team gained experience, its structure evolved. It's not essential that the dedicated team's structure be perfectly clear at the outset—only that it be unconstrained by the parent company's past.

Working on Anderson's dedicated team felt much different to the insiders who were part of it. They had less autonomy. They had to collaborate with peers much more closely. And they knew that if they stumbled, they would be letting down not just themselves but their teammates and their company. Some struggled with the transition and chose to return to the performance engine. While this may seem unfortunate, it was actually a mark of Anderson's success. As a general rule, if all the insiders on the dedicated team are comfortable, it must be a little performance engine. (Note that it's also important for insiders to have a clear path to get back to the performance engine. Innovation initiatives frequently fail, and the individuals working on them sometimes don't succeed in their assignments. Companies that create an out for insiders will find that they can more easily motivate people to join a dedicated team.)

To further shape his dedicated team, Anderson drew clear distinctions between its standards and cultural values and those of the performance engine. West had long maintained extremely high quality standards. For judicial decisions—literally, the law itself—customers demanded infallible information. Therefore, West had implemented multistep checks and safeguards in loading documents into its database, a process that often started with scanning a physical document. With briefs, however, West needed to relax, slightly, from being obsessive about quality to being diligent. The dauntingly high number of briefs made exhaustive precautions impractical. Besides, customers cared more about convenience and availability than perfection.

Anticipate and Mitigate the Strains

Make no mistake, nurturing a healthy partnership is challenging. Conflicts between innovation initiatives and ongoing operations are normal and can easily escalate. Tensions become rivalries, rivalries become hostilities, and hostilities become all-out wars in which the company's long-term viability is the clearest loser.

Differences between the two groups run deep. Managers of the performance engine seek to be efficient, accountable, on time, on budget, and on spec. In every company, their basic approach is the same. It is to make every task, process, and activity as repeatable and predictable as possible. An innovation initiative, of course, is exactly the opposite. It is, by nature, nonroutine and uncertain. These incompatibilities create a natural us-versus-them dynamic.

Leaders must counter conflicts by constantly reinforcing a relationship of mutual respect. Dedicated team leaders must remember that profits from the performance engine pay for innovation, and that their success depends on their ability to leverage its assets. They must also remember that pushback from the performance engine does not arise from laziness or from an instinctive resistance to change. Quite the contrary—it arises from the efforts of good people doing good work, trying to run ongoing operations as effectively as possible. For their part, performance engine leaders must recognize that no performance engine lasts forever. To dismiss innovation leaders as reckless rebels intent on undermining discipline in the pursuit of an esoteric dream is to write off the company's future.

For the partnership to work, the leader of the innovation initiative must set the right tone—positive and collaborative. Antagonizing the performance engine is a *really bad* idea. The performance engine always wins in an all-out fight. It is, quite simply, bigger and stronger.

In fact, for precisely that reason, even the best innovation leaders need help from high places. They must be directly supported by an executive senior enough to act in the long-term interests of the company, overriding the performance engine's short-term demands when necessary. This typically means that the innovation leader must report two or more levels higher up than managers with budgets of a similar size. At WD-40, for example, an innovation initiative relied on the direct involvement of the CEO. (See "How WD-40 Minimized Frictions.")

The senior executive to whom the innovation leader reports must be careful not to be a cheerleader only for innovation. He or she

Case Study: How WD-40 Minimized Frictions

TO SPUR ORGANIC GROWTH, Garry Ridge, CEO of WD-40, created a team to develop breakthrough products. He called it Team Tomorrow. It included newly hired research scientists and new outside partners. One of its first endeavors was developing the No-Mess Pen, which made it easy to dispense small quantities of WD-40 in tight spaces. Though it doesn't sound like a radical innovation, the technological challenges were steep, and the product took months to develop.

Historically, WD-40's marketing team had handled product development, which generally entailed routine efforts to improve, renew, or repackage existing products. Now marketing took on the responsibility of partnering with Team Tomorrow to commercialize its offerings.

The sources of conflict in this partnership are not hard to identify. First, some marketing staffers felt that the attractive challenge of developing breakthrough products should have been theirs. Then there was a resource constraint. Would the marketing team expend its limited time and resources on experimental products or proven performers? Finally, marketing worried that Team Tomorrow's new offerings would cannibalize existing products.

Graham Milner and Stephanie Barry, the leaders of Team Tomorrow, overcame these conflicts by taking a collaborative approach, particularly with

must also extol the virtues and importance of the performance engine and emphasize that a long-run victory for the company requires that both sides win.

Together, the innovation leader and the senior executive must anticipate and proactively resolve conflicts. The clashes can be intense, but if the labor is properly divided between the performance engine and the dedicated team, they'll be manageable. The most common conflict is over scarce resources. When the sum of activities, innovation plus ongoing operations, pushes the performance engine beyond its resource constraints, choices must be made.

Sometimes, this competition for scarce resources takes place through formal budgeting processes. Innovation leaders often find themselves seeking explicit commitments from multiple performance

the head of marketing. They shared information, established an open-door policy, and coordinated plans carefully with marketing, anticipating bottlenecks and resource conflicts. Knowing that such conflicts could be resolved only by the CEO, Milner and Barry made sure Ridge was aware of them early, so that he could set priorities. When Ridge saw that it was necessary, he added staff to the marketing team to make sure that it had sufficient bandwidth.

To signal the importance of the long term, Ridge carried a prototype of the pen with him wherever he went. This gave Team Tomorrow the attention it needed, but it also, at least initially, exacerbated feelings among some in the marketing team that they had been left out. Ridge, Milner, and Barry all quickly saw just how important it was to celebrate the accomplishments of the core business's team as well.

Ridge took other steps that contributed to WD-40's success. He made it clear that he would evaluate all involved employees on their effectiveness in collaborating across organizational boundaries. And he was able to lessen the anxiety about cannibalization by collecting data and sharing analyses that showed that the No-Mess Pen generated purely incremental sales.

engine leaders. These negotiations are best resolved through a single plan and budgeting process for the entire innovation initiative, with conflicts directly adjudicated by the senior executive.

In other cases, the competition is for the attention of the shared staff. It's tempting for the innovation leader to think that once the budget for an initiative is approved, the fight for resources is over. It is not. Each shared staff member chooses how much energy to devote to the new initiative every day. The innovation leader's powers of persuasion are critical but may not be adequate. Some companies create special incentives and targets for shared staff members to spur them to keep up with the demands of both innovation and ongoing operations. Others charge the innovation initiative for the shared staff's time. That way, the shared staff treats the innovation leader more like a customer than a distraction.

Emotional conflicts must also be managed. Sometimes resentments are grounded in substantive business conflicts, like the possibility that the innovation initiative may cannibalize the existing business. Senior executives must argue clearly and consistently that the innovation initiative is nonetheless in the company's long-term best interest and do as much as possible to allay fears about job security.

At other times, resentments amount to simple jealousy. The performance engine may feel disenfranchised if the innovation initiative is viewed as the company's most critical project. Or the dedicated team may feel marginalized as pursuers of a quirky experiment. Some companies have countered the effects of envy by making "ability to work productively with internal partners" a key assessment in individual performance reviews.

The briefs project at West faced multiple kinds of conflict but overcame them. Steve Anderson provided the right type of leadership. He viewed the performance engine as his partner, not his enemy. And he received constant support from two senior leaders, Mike Wilens and Erv Barbre.

Wilens and Barbre paid close attention to resource conflicts. When Barbre asked members of the shared staff to make contributions to the briefs effort, he also explicitly discussed what was on their plates and what could be deferred. In some cases, he hired contract labor to help with routine tasks, such as loading documents, to ensure that the priorities of both innovation and ongoing operations could be met.

Meanwhile, Anderson recognized the importance of galvanizing the shared staff. He and his team got people on board by, among other things, creating a skit based on the *Perry Mason* television series. It showed what a lawyer's life was really like and why a product like a briefs database would be enormously valuable. Wilens and Barbre backed up his effort, in part by creating a special incentive for the sales force to push the new offering. All three leaders monitored emotional tensions. As the briefs project started to show signs of success, they saw that some in the performance engine felt as though they had been left out of a real "glamour project." The leaders countered by reinforcing the importance of the core business and by holding events at which they spread credit as widely as possible, within both the dedicated team and the performance engine.

The Unlikeliest Partnership Is Manageable

The reception of West's briefs database exceeded expectations. In fact, the company was deluged with queries about how quickly the database would be expanded to include additional legal specialties and jurisdictions. The company followed with many more initiatives like it, such as new databases of expert testimony and court dockets.

The organizational formula was not always the same for those initiatives. For example, when West pursued a product called PeerMonitor, it assigned almost the entire job—development and commercialization—to the dedicated team. PeerMonitor provided data that enabled law firms to benchmark their business performance against that of rivals. West chose to assign sales and marketing to the dedicated team because selling PeerMonitor required a different skill set and a longer cycle. The target customer was also different: West sold most of its offerings to law librarians, but PeerMonitor was sold directly to managing partners. The PeerMonitor sales force collaborated with the performance engine's sales force to coordinate an overall approach.

West's example is one worthy of study. The company succeeded where others have stumbled because it saw that innovation is not something that happens either inside or outside the existing organization, and that innovation does not require that an upstart fight the establishment. Instead, innovation requires a partnership between a newly formed team and the long-standing one.

While such partnerships are challenging, they are manageable. And they are indispensable. Indeed, without them, innovation goes nowhere.

Originally published in July 2010. Reprint R1007F

How GE Is Disrupting Itself

by Jeffrey R. Immelt, Vijay Govindarajan, and Chris Trimble

IN MAY 2009, General Electric announced that over the next six years it would spend $3 billion to create at least 100 health-care innovations that would substantially lower costs, increase access, and improve quality. Two products it highlighted at the time—a $1,000 handheld electrocardiogram device and a portable, PC-based ultrasound machine that sells for as little as $15,000—are revolutionary, and not just because of their small size and low price. They're also extraordinary because they originally were developed for markets in emerging economies (the ECG device for rural India and the ultrasound machine for rural China) and are now being sold in the United States, where they're pioneering new uses for such machines.

We call the process used to develop the two machines and take them global *reverse innovation,* because it's the opposite of the *glocalization* approach that many industrial-goods manufacturers based in rich countries have employed for decades. With glocalization, companies develop great products at home and then distribute them worldwide, with some adaptations to local conditions. It allows multinationals to make the optimal trade-off between the global scale so crucial to minimizing costs and the local customization required to maximize market share. Glocalization worked fine in an era when rich countries accounted for the vast majority of the market and other countries didn't offer much opportunity. But those days are over—thanks to the rapid development of populous countries like China and India and the slowing growth of wealthy nations.

GE badly needs innovations like the low-cost ECG and ultrasound machines, not only to expand beyond high-end segments in places like China and India but also to preempt local companies in those countries—the emerging giants—from creating similar products and then using them to disrupt GE in rich countries. To put it bluntly: If GE's businesses are to survive and prosper in the next decade, they must become as adept at reverse innovation as they are at glocalization. Success in developing countries is a prerequisite for continued vitality in developed ones.

The problem is that there are deep conflicts between glocalization and reverse innovation. And the company can't simply replace the first with the second, because glocalization will continue to dominate strategy for the foreseeable future. The two models need to do more than coexist; they need to cooperate. This is a heck of a lot easier said than done since the centralized, product-focused structures and practices that have made multinationals so successful at glocalization actually get in the way of reverse innovation, which requires a decentralized, local-market focus.

Almost all the people and resources dedicated to reverse innovation efforts must be based and managed in the local market. These local growth teams need to have P&L responsibility; the power to decide which products to develop for their markets and how to make, sell, and service them; and the right to draw from the company's global resources. Once products have proven themselves in emerging markets, they must be taken global, which may involve pioneering radically new applications, establishing lower price points, and even using the innovations to cannibalize higher-margin products in rich countries. All of those approaches are antithetical to the glocalization model. This article aims to share what GE has learned in trying to overcome that conflict.

Idea in Brief

For decades, General Electric and other industrial-goods manufacturers based in rich countries grew by developing high-end products at home and distributing them globally, with some adaptations to local conditions—an approach known as glocalization. Now they must do an about-face and learn to bring low-end products created specifically for emerging markets into wealthy markets. That process, called reverse innovation, isn't easy to master. It requires a decentralized, local-market focus that clashes with the centralized, product-focused structure that multinationals have evolved for glocalization. In this article, Immelt, GE's CEO, and Govindarajan and Trimble, of Dartmouth's Tuck School of Business, describe how GE has dealt with that challenge. An anomaly within the ultrasound unit of GE Healthcare provided the blueprint. Because China's poorly funded rural clinics couldn't afford the company's sophisticated ultrasound machines, a local team built a cheap, portable ultrasound out of a laptop equipped with special peripherals and software. It not only became a hit in China but jump-started growth in the developed world by pioneering applications for situations where portability is critical, such as at accident sites. The team succeeded because a top executive championed it and gave it unprecedented autonomy. GE has since set up more than a dozen similar operations in an effort to expand beyond the premium segments in developing countries—and to preempt emerging giants from disrupting GE's sales at home

Why Reverse Innovation Is So Important

Glocalization is so dominant today because it has delivered. Largely because of glocalization, GE's revenues outside the United States soared from $4.8 billion, or 19% of total revenues, in 1980, to $97 billion, or more than half of the total, in 2008.

The model came to prominence when opportunities in today's emerging markets were pretty limited—when their economies had yet to take off and their middle or low-end customer segments didn't exist. Therefore, it made sense for multinational manufacturers to simply offer them modifications of products for developed countries. Initially, GE, like other multinationals, was satisfied with the 15% to 20% growth rates its businesses enjoyed in developing countries, thanks to glocalization.

Then in September 2001 one of the coauthors of this piece, Jeff Immelt, who had just become GE's CEO, set a goal: to greatly accelerate organic growth at the company and become less dependent on acquisitions. This made people question many things that had been taken for granted, including the glocalization strategy, which limited the company to skimming the top of emerging markets. A rigorous analysis of GE's health-care, power-generation, and power-distribution businesses showed that if they took full advantage of opportunities that glocalization had ignored in heavily populated places like China and India, they could grow two to three times faster there. But to do that, they'd have to develop innovative new products that met the specific needs and budgets of customers in those markets. That realization, in turn, led GE executives to question two core tenets of glocalization.

Assumption 1: Emerging economies will largely evolve in the same way that wealthy economies did

The reality is, developing countries aren't following the same path and could actually jump ahead of developed countries because of their greater willingness to adopt breakthrough innovations. With far smaller per capita incomes, developing countries are more than happy with high-tech solutions that deliver decent performance at an ultralow cost—a 50% solution at a 15% price. And they lack many of the legacy infrastructures of the developed world, which were built when conditions were very different. They need communications, energy, and transportation products that address today's challenges and opportunities, such as unpredictable oil prices and ubiquitous wireless technologies. Finally, because of their huge populations, sustainability problems are especially urgent for countries like China and India. Because of this, they're likely to tackle many environmental issues years or even decades before the developed world.

All this isn't theory. It's already happening. Emerging markets are becoming centers of innovation in fields like low-cost health-care devices, carbon sequestration, solar and wind power, biofuels, distributed power generation, batteries, water desalination, microfinance, electric cars, and even ultra-low-cost homes.

Assumption 2: Products that address developing countries' special needs can't be sold in developed countries because they're not good enough to compete there

The reality here is, these products can create brand-new markets in the developed world—by establishing dramatically lower price points or pioneering new applications.

Consider GE's health-care business in the United States. It used to make most of its money on premium computed tomography (CT) and magnetic resonance (MR) imaging machines. But to succeed in the era of broader access and reduced reimbursement that President Obama hopes to bring about, the business will probably need to increase by 50% the number of products it offers at lower price points. And that doesn't mean just cheaper versions of high-tech products like imaging machines. The company also must create more offerings like the heated bassinet it developed for India, which has great potential in U.S. inner cities, where infant deaths related to the cold remain high.

And let's not forget that technology often can be improved until it satisfies more demanding customers. The compact ultrasound, which can now handle imaging applications that previously required a conventional machine, is one example. (See the exhibit "Reverse innovation in practice.") Another is an aircraft engine that GE acquired when it bought a Czech aerospace company for $20 million. GE invested an additional $25 million to further develop the engine's technology and now plans to use it to challenge Pratt & Whitney's dominance of the small turboprop market in developed countries. GE's cost position is probably half of what Pratt's is.

Preempting the Emerging Giants

Before the financial crisis plunged the world into a deep recession, GE's leaders had been looking to emerging markets to help achieve their ambitious growth objectives. Now they're counting on these

Reverse innovation in practice

1 Original product

In the 1990s GE served the Chinese ultrasound market with machines developed in the U.S. and Japan.

Conventional ultrasound 2002 price

$100K and up

Typical customers

- Sophisticated hospital imaging centers

Typical uses

- Cardiology (such as measuring the size of passages or blood flow in the heart)
- Obstetrics (monitoring fetal health)
- General radiology (assessing prostate health, for example)

But the expensive, bulky devices sold poorly in China.

2 The emerging market disruption

In 2002 a local team in China leveraged GE's global resources to develop a cheap, portable machine using a laptop computer enhanced with a probe and sophisticated software.

Portable ultrasound 2002 price

$30K–$40K

Typical customers

- China: rural clinics
- U.S.: ambulance squads and emergency rooms

Typical uses

- China: spotting enlarged livers and gallbladder stones
- U.S.: in emergency rooms to identify ectopic pregnancies; at accident sites to check for fluid around the heart; in operating rooms to place catheters for anesthesia

2007 price

$15K

In 2007 the team launched a dramatically cheaper model. Sales in China took off.

3 The new global market

Portable ultrasound global revenues

Thanks to technology advances, higher-priced PC-based models can now perform radiology and obstetrics functions that once required a conventional machine.

Portable ultrasound 2009 price

$15K–$100K

Conventional ultrasound 2009 price

$100K–$350K

markets even more because they think that after the downturn ends, the developed world will suffer a prolonged period of slow growth—1% to 3% a year. In contrast, annual growth in emerging markets could easily reach two to three times that rate.

Ten years ago when GE senior managers discussed the global marketplace, they talked about "the U.S., Europe, Japan, and the rest of the world." Now they talk about "resource-rich regions," such as the Middle East, Brazil, Canada, Australia, and Russia, and "people-rich regions," such as China and India. The "rest of world" means the U.S., Europe, and Japan.

To be honest, the company also is embracing reverse innovation for defensive reasons. If GE doesn't come up with innovations in poor countries and take them global, new competitors from the developing world—like Mindray, Suzlon, Goldwind, and Haier—will.

In GE's markets the Chinese will be bigger players than the Indians will. The Chinese have a real plan to become a major global force in transportation and power generation. GE Power Generation is already regularly running into Chinese enterprises as it competes in Africa, which will be an extremely important region for the company. One day those enterprises may compete with GE in its own backyard.

That's a bracing prospect. GE has tremendous respect for traditional rivals like Siemens, Philips, and Rolls-Royce. But it knows how to compete with them; they will never destroy GE. By introducing products that create a new price-performance paradigm, however, the emerging giants very well could. Reverse innovation isn't optional; it's oxygen.

A Clash of Two Models

Glocalization has defined international strategy for three decades. All the currently dominant ideas—from Christopher A. Bartlett and Sumantra Ghoshal's "transnational" strategy to Pankaj Ghemawat's "adaptation-aggregation" trade-off—fit within the glocalization framework. Since organization follows strategy, it's hardly surprising that glocalization also has molded the way that multinationals are structured and run.

GE is a case in point. For the past 30 years, its organization has evolved to maximize its effectiveness at glocalization. Power and P&L responsibility were concentrated in global business units headquartered in the developed world. The major business functions—including R&D, manufacturing, and marketing—were centralized at headquarters. While some R&D centers and manufacturing operations were moved abroad to tap overseas talent and reduce costs, they focused mainly on products for wealthy countries.

While this approach has enormous advantages, it makes reverse innovation impossible. The experiences of Venkatraman Raja, the head of GE Healthcare's business in India, illustrate why.

GE Healthcare sells an x-ray imaging product called a surgical C-arm, which is used in basic surgeries. A high-quality, high-priced product designed for hospitals in wealthy countries, it has proven tough to sell in India. Raja saw the problem and made a proposal in 2005. He wanted to develop, manufacture, and sell a simpler, easier-to-use, and substantially cheaper product in India. His proposal made sense, and yet, to no one's surprise, it was not approved.

If you were a leader of a GE operation in a developing country, as Raja was, here's what you were up against: Your formal responsibilities included neither general management nor product development. Your responsibility was to sell, distribute, and service GE's global products locally and provide insights into customers' needs to help the company adapt its offerings. You were expected to grow revenues by 15% to 20% a year and make sure that costs increased at a much slower rate, so that margins rose. You were held rigidly accountable for delivering on plan. Just finding the time for an extracurricular activity like creating a proposal for a product tailored to the local market was challenging.

That was nothing, however, compared with the challenge of the next step: selling your proposal internally. Doing so required getting the attention of the general manager at headquarters in the United States, who sat two or more levels above your immediate boss and was far more familiar with a world-renowned medical center in

Boston than a rural clinic outside Bangalore. Even if you got the meeting, you'd have limited time to make your case. (India accounted for just 1% of GE's revenues at the time and occupied roughly the same mindshare of managers with global responsibility.)

If you were extremely persuasive, you might be invited to share the proposal with others. But when you visited the head of global manufacturing, you'd have to counter arguments that a simple, streamlined global product line was much more efficient than custom offerings. When you visited the head of marketing, you'd have to deal with fears that a lower-priced product would weaken the GE brand and cannibalize existing sales. When you met with the head of finance, you'd have to wrestle with concerns that lower-priced products would drag down overall margins. And when you visited the head of global R&D, you'd have to explain why the energies of GE's scientists and engineers—including those in technology centers in emerging markets—should be diverted from projects directed at its most sophisticated customers, who paid top dollar.

Even if you gained support from each of these executives and got the proposal off the ground, you'd still have to compete for capital year after year against more certain projects with shorter-term payoffs. Meanwhile, of course, you'd still have to worry about making your quarterly numbers for your day job.

It was little wonder that successful efforts to develop radically new products for poor countries were extremely rare.

Shifting the Center of Gravity

Obviously, changing long-established structures, practices, and attitudes is an enormous task. As is the case in any major change program, the company's top leaders have to play a major role.

To do so, they must investigate firsthand the size of the opportunity and how it could be exploited and encourage the teams running the corporation's businesses to do the same. As GE's CEO, Jeff goes to China and India two times a year. When he's in, say, China, he'll spend a day at GE's research center in Shanghai and then meet separately with dozens of people in the company's local business operations and just let them talk about what they're working on, what their cost points are, who their competitors are, and so on. On such visits, he has realized that there's a whole realm of technology that the company should be applying faster.

While in China, Jeff will also talk with government leaders, including Premier Wen Jiabao. Wen has told Jeff about his plans to develop China's economy and how making health care affordable for all citizens fits into that. It takes a conversation like that to fully appreciate the opportunities in China.

In India, Jeff will have dinner with the CEOs of Indian companies. At one dinner Anand Mahindra talked about how his company, Mahindra & Mahindra, was making life miserable for John Deere in India with a tractor that cost half the price of Deere's but was still enormously profitable. Such discussions drive home the point that you can make a lot of money in India if you have the right business models.

So the job of the CEO—of any senior business leader, for that matter—is to connect all the dots and then act as a catalyst. It's to give initiatives special status and funding and personally monitor them on a monthly or quarterly basis. And perhaps most important in the case of reverse innovation, it's to push your enterprise to come up with the new organizational form that will allow product and business-model innovation to flourish in emerging markets.

A Homegrown Model

To develop that new organizational form, GE did what it has always done: learn from other companies' experiences but also try to find an internal group that somehow had managed to overcome the hurdles and achieve success. During their annual strategy review, the company's leaders spotted one in the ultrasound unit of GE Healthcare.

GE Healthcare's primary business is high-end medical-imaging equipment. By the late 1980s it had become clear that a new technology—ultrasound—had a bright future. Ultrasound machines, like the other imaging devices, were typically found in sophisticated imaging centers in hospitals. While they delivered lower quality than CT or MR scanners, they did so at much lower cost. The company aimed to be number one in ultrasound.

Over the next decade, GE Healthcare expanded its presence in the market. It built an R&D facility for developing new ultrasound products near its headquarters, in Milwaukee, and made acquisitions and entered into joint ventures around the world. It competed in all three of the primary market segments—obstetrics, cardiology, and general radiology—by launching premium products that employed cutting-edge technologies. By 2000, GE Healthcare had established solid market positions in rich countries around the world.

The results in developing countries, by contrast, were disappointing. By 2000, with the help of a joint venture partner in China, GE saw the problem: In wealthy countries performance mattered most, followed by features; in China price mattered most, followed by portability and ease of use.

The priorities weren't the same because the health-care infrastructure of China was so different from that of rich countries. More than 90% of China's population relied (and still relies) on poorly funded, low-tech hospitals or basic clinics in rural villages. These facilities had no sophisticated imaging centers, and transportation to urban hospitals was difficult, especially for the sick. Patients couldn't come to the ultrasound machines; the ultrasound machines, therefore, had to go to the patients.

There was no way that GE could meet that need by simply scaling down, removing features from, or otherwise adapting its existing ultrasound machines, which were large, bulky, expensive, and complex. It needed a revolutionary product.

In 2002, the company launched its first compact ultrasound, which combined a regular laptop computer with sophisticated software. It sold for as low as $30,000. In late 2007, GE introduced a model that sold for as low as $15,000, less than 15% of the cost of GE's high-end ultrasound machines. Of course, its performance was not as high, but it was nonetheless a hit in rural clinics, where doctors used it for simple applications, such as spotting enlarged livers and gallbladders and stomach irregularities. The software-centric design also made it easy to adjust the machine—for example, to improve the interfaces—after observing how doctors worked with it. Today the portable machine is the growth engine of GE's ultrasound business in China.

Even more exciting, the innovation has generated dramatic growth in the developed world by pioneering new applications where portability is critical or space is constrained, such as at accident sites, where the compacts are used to diagnose problems like pericardial effusions (fluid around the heart); in emergency rooms, where they are employed to identify conditions such as ectopic pregnancies; and in operating rooms, where they aid anesthesiologists in placing needles and catheters.

Six years after their launch, portable ultrasounds were a $278 million global product line for GE, one that was growing at 50% to 60% a year before the worldwide recession hit. Someday every general practitioner may carry both a stethoscope and a compact ultrasound device embedded in his or her PDA.

The products owe their successful development to an organizational anomaly in GE: the existence of multiple ultrasound business units. Although the three primary segments of the ultrasound business are vastly different, GE's initial instinct was to follow the glocalization model when it built the business—that is, to create a single integrated global organization. In 1995, however, Omar Ishrak, a newcomer who had been hired to lead the business, saw that meshing operations would reduce them to a common denominator that served nobody well. He decided to run the business as three independent business units with their own P&L responsibility, all reporting to him.

When the compact ultrasound effort began in China, Ishrak saw that the new business would have little in common with the three units, which were focused on premium products. So instead, he created a fourth independent unit, based in Wuxi, China. It evolved the local growth team (LGT) model, which is based on five critical principles.

1. Shift power to where the growth is

Without autonomy, the LGTs will become pawns of the global business and won't be able to focus on the problems of customers in emerging markets. Specifically, they need the power to develop their own strategies, organizations, and products. Ishrak understood this and gave such broad authority to Diana Tang and J.K. Koo, the leaders of GE's ultrasound effort in China. The pair of GE veterans had deep experience in the ultrasound business, expertise in biomedical engineering and general management, and lengthy careers in Asia.

2. Build new offerings from the ground up

Given the tremendous gulfs between rich countries and poor ones in income, infrastructure, and sustainability needs, reverse innovation must be zero-based. These wide differences cannot be spanned by adapting global products.

The compact ultrasound was built from scratch, although it drew heavily from an existing R&D effort. In the late 1990s, in a product-development center in Israel, GE had started to experiment with a revolutionary new architecture—one that shifted most of the muscle inside an ultrasound machine from the hardware to the software. Instead of a large box full of custom hardware, the scientists and engineers involved in the project envisioned a standard high-performance PC, special peripherals such as an ultrasound probe, and sophisticated software.

The concept generated little excitement in GE Healthcare at the time because it could not come close to matching the performance of the business's premium products. But Ishrak quickly saw the value of the new architecture in developing countries. He encouraged the team in China to pursue the concept further. The resulting compact ultrasound based on a laptop computer hit the mark in China.

3. Build LGTs from the ground up, like new companies

Zero-based innovation doesn't happen without zero-based organizational design. GE's organizational "software"—its hiring practices, reporting structures, titles, job descriptions, norms for working relationships, and power balances between functions—all evolved to support glocalization. LGTs need to rewrite the software.

Tang and Koo constructed a business unit that managed a complete value chain: product development, sourcing, manufacturing, marketing, sales, and service. By recruiting locally, they were able to find most of the expertise they needed—including engineers with deep knowledge of miniaturization and low-power consumption and a commercialization team well versed in health care in rural China.

The LGT also decided that dealers—rather than the direct sales force used by the premium ultrasound units—were the only cost-effective way to reach China's vast and fragmented rural markets and third-tier cities. And instead of relying on GE Healthcare's global customer-support and replacement-parts organizations, it built in-country teams that could provide quicker and less costly service.

4. Customize objectives, targets, and metrics

Innovation endeavors are, by nature, uncertain. It's more important to learn quickly by efficiently testing assumptions than to hit the numbers. So the relevant metrics and standards for LGTs—the ones that resolve the critical unknowns—are rarely the same as those used by the established businesses.

The ultrasound LGT knew that doctors in rural China were less familiar with ultrasounds than doctors in cities. But the team didn't know how much experience rural doctors had with the technology or what features would meet their needs. So it set out to learn how doctors reacted to the machines and what the obstacles to their adoption were. The team discovered that ease of use, especially in primary-care screenings, where doctors test for common local conditions, was even more crucial than anticipated. In response, the new business emphasized training, offered online guides, designed simpler keyboards, created built-in presets for certain tasks, and tracked customer satisfaction to gauge success.

Ishrak was careful to use different criteria to evaluate the performance of the LGT in China. For example, because the government approval process for new product releases is less intricate in China, he set much shorter product-development cycles than were common in wealthy countries. He also agreed to allow the size of the local service organization to deviate from the GE Healthcare's global standards. Since salaries are lower and service is more demanding in

China, a bigger staff relative to the number of installed machines made sense.

5. Have the LGT report to someone high in the organization

LGTs cannot thrive without strong support from the top. The executive overseeing the LGT has three critical roles: mediating conflicts between the team and the global business, connecting the team to resources such as global R&D centers, and helping take the innovations that the team develops into rich countries. Only a senior executive in the global business unit, or even its leader, can accomplish all of that.

Even when it was tiny, the LGT in China reported directly to Ishrak. Because GE Healthcare had an ambitious product-development agenda for rich countries when the compact project was launched, the LGT's engineers might easily have been redirected to other projects if Ishrak hadn't shielded the team. He protected and even expanded the team's resources. By 2007 its number of engineers had grown from 13 to 70 and its total payroll had increased from 132 to 339. Ishrak also personally made sure that the team got the expertise it needed from other parts of GE, such as three highly respected development engineers from Israel, Japan, and South Korea. They worked full-time on the project and got it extra support from GE's R&D centers around the world.

Ishrak included the China LGT in the company's Ultrasound Council, a group of ultrasound executives and market and technology experts who meet for two days three times a year. At the meeting they share knowledge and insights and agree on which major projects to pursue. The council was instrumental in moving knowledge and technology into China.

Finally, Ishrak played a critical role in building a global market for the portable ultrasound. He identified potential new applications in the developed world and saw to it that the three units that sold the premium products aggressively pursued those opportunities.

GE now has more than a dozen local growth teams in China and India. In the midst of a severe global recession, GE's businesses in

China will grow 25% this year—largely because of LGTs. It's way too early to declare victory, however. Progress has been uneven. While some businesses—notably, health care and power generation and distribution—have taken the ball and run with it, others have been less enthusiastic. And though GE's R&D centers in China and India have increased their focus on the problems of developing countries, the vast majority of their resources are still devoted to initiatives for developed ones. So there is still a long way to go.

It's still necessary for the company's top executives to monitor and protect local efforts and make sure they get resources. It's still necessary to experiment with people transfers, organizational structures, and processes to see what works. The biggest experiment is about to come: To speed progress in India, GE is creating a separate P&L that will include all GE businesses in that country and giving the new unit considerable power to tap GE's global R&D resources. It will be headed by a senior vice president who will report to a vice chairman. That's anathema in a company used to a matrix in which product comes first and country second. Nonetheless, the company is going to try it and see if it can create new markets. GE has to learn how to operate on a different axis.

The resistance to giving India its own P&L reflects what is perhaps GE's biggest challenge: changing the mind-set of managers who've spent their careers excelling at glocalization. Even the exemplars have a rich-country bias. In a recent conversation with Jeff, one such manager—the head of a major business that's doing well in India and China—still seemed preoccupied with problems beyond his control in the U.S. "I don't even want to talk to you about your growth plans for the U.S.," Jeff responded. "You've got to triple the size of your Indian business in the next three years. You've got to put more resources, more people, and more products in there, so you're deep in that market and not just skimming the very top. Let's figure out how to do it." That's how senior managers have to think.

Originally published in October 2009. Reprint R0910D

The Customer-Centered Innovation Map

by Lance A. Bettencourt and Anthony W. Ulwick

WE ALL KNOW THAT people "hire" products and services to get a job done. Office workers hire word-processing software to create documents and digital recorders to capture meeting notes. Surgeons hire scalpels to dissect soft tissue and electrocautery devices to control patient bleeding. Janitors hire soap dispensers, paper towels, and cleansing fluid to help remove grime from their hands.

While all this seems obvious, very few companies use the perspective of "getting the job done" to discover opportunities for innovation. In fact, the innovation journey for many companies is little more than hopeful wandering through customer interviews. Such unsystematic inquiry may occasionally turn up interesting tidbits of information, but it rarely uncovers the best ideas or an exhaustive set of opportunities for growth.

We have developed an efficient yet simple system companies can use to find new ways to innovate. Our method, which we call "job mapping," breaks down the task the customer wants done into a series of discrete process steps. By deconstructing a job from beginning to end, a company gains a complete view of all the points at which a customer might desire more help from a product or service—namely, at each step in the job. With a job map in hand, a company can analyze the biggest drawbacks of the products and services customers currently use. Job mapping also gives companies a comprehensive framework with which to identify the metrics customers themselves use to measure success in executing a task. (For a description of these metrics and a discussion about how to gather and prioritize them, see Anthony W. Ulwick's "Turn Customer Input into Innovation" in HBR's January 2002 issue.)

Job mapping differs substantively from process mapping in that the goal is to identify what customers are *trying* to get done at every step, not what they are doing currently. For example, when an anesthesiologist checks a monitor during a surgical procedure, the action taken is just a means to an end. Detecting a change in patient vital signs is the job the anesthesiologist is trying to get done. By mapping out every step of the job and locating opportunities for innovative solutions, companies can discover new ways to differentiate their offerings.

Anatomy of a Customer Job

Over the past 10 years, we have mapped customer jobs in dozens of product and service categories that span professional and consumer services, durable and consumable goods, chemicals, software, and many other industries. Our work has revealed three fundamental principles about customer jobs.

All jobs are processes

Every job, from transplanting a heart to cleaning a floor, has a distinct beginning, middle, and end, and comprises a set of process steps along the way. The starting point for identifying innovation opportunities is to map out—from the customer's perspective—the steps involved in executing a particular job. Once the steps are identified, a company can create value in a number of ways—by improving the execution of specific job steps; eliminating the need for particular inputs or outputs; removing an entire step from the responsibility of the customer; addressing an overlooked step;

Idea in Brief

We all know that people "hire" products to get jobs done. Office workers hire word-processing software to create documents. Surgeons hire scalpels to dissect soft tissue. But few companies keep this in mind while searching for ideas for breakthrough offerings. Instead, they rely on inquiry methods (such as customer interviews) that don't generate the most promising ideas or exhaustive sets of possibilities.

To systematically uncover more—and better—innovative ideas, Bettencourt and Ulwick recommend **job mapping:** Break down a job that customers want done into discrete steps. Then brainstorm ways to make steps easier, faster, or unnecessary.

For example, while cleaning clothes, people don't notice stubborn stains until they've taken the clothes from a dryer and started folding them. If they find a stain, they must repeat the job. A washer that detects persistent stains and takes appropriate action *before* consumers execute the rest of the job would have huge appeal.

resequencing the steps; or enabling steps to be completed in new locations or at different times.

When mapping the job of washing clothes, for example, a company would quickly discover that the step of "verifying that stains have been removed" often comes at the end of the job sequence, after the clothes have been removed from the washing machine, dried, folded, and put away—too late to do much of anything about it. If the washing machine itself could detect the presence of any remaining stains before the wash cycle ended—resequence when verification takes place—it could take the necessary actions at a much more convenient point in the job. If the machine could be designed to remove the need for inputs such as stain removers and bleach, that would be even better.

All jobs have a universal structure

That universal structure, regardless of the customer, has the following process steps: defining what the job requires; identifying and locating needed inputs; preparing the components and the physical environment; confirming that everything is ready; executing the task;

Idea in Practice

All jobs have the same eight steps. To use job mapping, look for opportunities to help customers at every step:

During this step . . .	Customers . . .	Companies can innovate by . . .	Example
1: Define	Determine their goals and plan resources.	Simplifying planning.	Weight Watchers streamlines diet planning by offering a system that doesn't require calorie counting.
2: Locate	Gather items and information needed to do the job.	Making required inputs easier to gather and ensuring they're available when and where needed.	U-Haul provides customers with prepackaged moving kits containing the number and types of boxes required for a move.
3: Prepare	Set up the environment to do the job.	Making set-up less difficult and creating guides to ensure proper set-up of the work area.	Bosch added adjustable levers to its circular saw to accommodate common bevel angles used by roofers to cut wood.
4: Confirm	Verify that they're ready to perform the job.	Giving customers information they need to confirm readiness.	Oracle's ProfitLogic merchandising optimization software confirms optimal timing and level of a store's markdowns for each product.
5: Execute	Carry out the job.	Preventing problems or delays.	Kimberly-Clark's Patient Warning System automatically circulates heated water through thermal pads placed on surgery patients to maintain their normal body temperature during surgery.

During this step . . .	Customers . . .	Companies can innovate by . . .	Example
6: Monitor	Assess whether the job is being successfully executed.	Linking monitoring with improved execution.	Nike makes a running shoe containing a sensor that communicates audio feedback about time, distance, pace, and calories burned to an iPod worn by the runner.
7: Modify	Make alterations to improve execution.	Reducing the need to make alterations and the number of alterations needed.	By automatically downloading and installing updates, Microsoft's operating systems remove hassles for computer users. People don't have to determine which updates are necessary, find the updates, or ensure the updates are compatible with their operating system.
8: Conclude	Finish the job or prepare to repeat it.	Designing products that simplify the process of concluding the job.	3M makes a wound dressing that stretches and adheres only to itself—not to patients' skin or sutures. It thus offers a convenient way for medical personnel to secure dressings at the conclusion of treatment and then remove them after a wound has healed.

monitoring the results and the environment; making modifications; and concluding the job. Because problems can occur at many points in the process, nearly all jobs also require a problem resolution step.

Some steps are more critical than others, depending on the job, but each is necessary to get the job done successfully. For example, when preparing for the task of replacing a hip joint, surgeons sterilize their hands, establish a sterile field between their body and the patient, prep the patient's skin for the incision, and properly position the patient. A janitor about to clean his hands might prepare by simply rolling up his sleeves. Innovation possibilities reside within each of the job steps.

Jobs are separate from solutions

Customers hire different products or services to get the same job done. When preparing income taxes, for example, one person might rely on the services of a CPA, whereas another might use tax preparation software. Others might hire both for different steps in the process.

Many companies are focused on the product or service they're already developing, or on the one the competition is offering, rather than on the help they must give the customer to execute the steps in a job. When the job is the focal point of value creation, companies not only can improve their existing offerings but also can target new, or "blue ocean," market space. While other MP3 manufacturers were concentrating on helping customers listen to music, for example, Apple reconsidered the entire job of music management, enabling customers to acquire, organize, listen to, and share music.

Taken together, these fundamental principles form the foundation of a company's search for opportunities to create customer value.

Creating a Job Map

The goal of creating a job map is not to find out how the customer is executing a job—that only generates maps of existing activities and solutions. Instead the aim is to discover what the customer is trying to get done at different points in executing a job and what must happen at each juncture in order for the job to be carried out successfully. (See the sidebar "Mapping a Customer Job.") Let's look at the steps in detail.

1: Define

What aspects of getting the job done must the customer define up front in order to proceed? This step includes determining objectives; planning the approach; assessing which resources are necessary or available to complete the job; and selecting resources. A financial adviser may label this step "assessing the investment situation," since she must not only gauge investment priorities and risk tolerance but also consider how much money is available and which types of investments to select. An anesthesiologist might call it "formulating the anesthesia plan," since he must choose which type of anesthesia to provide, depending upon case characteristics and the patient's medical history.

In this step, a company can look for ways to help customers understand their objectives, simplify the resource-planning process, and reduce the amount of planning needed. Consider how Weight Watchers assists dieters with the daunting task of losing weight. The company offers a core weight-loss plan that helps the dieter select appropriate foods without the need to count calories, carbohydrates, or anything else. In addition, it provides meal ideas and recipes that fit into its core and points-based diet plans. For dieters desiring more flexibility, Weight Watchers offers instant access to point values for over 27,000 foods and online tools to help dieters gauge the impact of what they eat.

2: Locate

What inputs or items must the customer locate to do the job? Inputs are both tangible (for example, the surgical tools a nurse must locate for an operation) and intangible (say, business or other requirements that a software developer uses when writing code). When tangible

Mapping a Customer Job

TO FIND WAYS TO INNOVATE, deconstruct the job a customer is trying to get done. By working through the questions here, you can map a customer job in just a handful of interviews with customers and internal experts.

Start by understanding the execution step, to establish context and a frame of reference. Next, examine each step before execution and then after, to uncover the role each plays in getting the job done.

To ensure that you are mapping job steps (what the customer is trying to accomplish) rather than process solutions (what is currently being done), ask yourself the validating questions below at each step.

Validating Questions

As defined, does the step specify what the customer is trying to accomplish, or is it only being done to accomplish a more fundamental goal?

> **Valid step:** ascertain patient vital signs
>
> **Invalid step:** check the monitor

Does the step apply universally for any customer executing the job, or does it depend on how a particular customer does the job?

> **Valid step:** place an order
>
> **Invalid step:** call the supplier to place an order

Defining the Execution Step

What are the most central tasks that must be accomplished in getting the job done?

- **Validate the steps**

---

materials are involved, a company might consider streamlining this step by making the required components easier to gather, ensuring that they are available when and where needed, or eliminating the need for some inputs altogether. Consider how U-Haul helps customers locate the inputs necessary to complete the job of moving their physical goods. In addition to being a one-stop shop for moving supplies, U-Haul offers customers prepackaged moving kits that

Defining Pre-Execution Steps

What must happen before the core execution step to ensure the job is successfully carried out?

- What must be defined or planned before the execution step?
- What must be located or gathered?
- What must be prepared or set up?
- What must be confirmed before the execution step?
- **Validate the steps**

Defining Post-Execution Steps

What must happen after the core execution step to ensure the job is successfully carried out?

- What must be monitored or verified after the execution step to ensure the job is successfully performed?
- What must be modified or adjusted after the execution step?
- What must be done to properly conclude the job or to prepare for the next job cycle?
- **Validate the steps**

reduce the time it takes to gather the various boxes and supplies required for a move. In addition, an online partnership with eMove helps customers quickly locate a variety of inputs in the form of human helpers—packers, babysitters, cleaners, and painters. Opportunities abound to help customers assemble intangible materials as well: for instance, retrieve stored data, facilitate the collection of new information, and verify that data are accurate and complete.

3: Prepare

How must the customer prepare the inputs and environment to do the job? Nearly all customer jobs involve an element of setting up and organizing materials. Before cooking french fries, the fast-food operator must open bags, portion, and load fries into baskets; the nurse must set out and organize surgical tools before an operation can begin. It may also be necessary to prepare a working surface or some other aspect of the physical environment. The dentist readies the surface of a molar prior to restoring the tooth; the painter cleans the wall before applying the first coat of paint.

At this stage, companies should consider ways to make setup less difficult. They might invent a means to automate the preparation process; make it easier to organize physical materials; or create guides and safeguards to ensure the proper arrangement of the work area. (For customers dealing with information, companies can help organize, integrate, and examine required data.) Bosch learned of one opportunity to help customers prepare to cut wood when professional roofers told the company that they would like a way to speed the process of setting bevel levels on their saws. Accordingly, Bosch added adjustable levers to its CS20 circular saw to accommodate the most common bevel adjustments such as 30°, 45°, and 60°. This reduced the time needed to cut the wood and increased the accuracy of the adjustments.

4: Confirm

Once preparation is complete, what does the customer need to verify before proceeding with the job to ensure its successful execution? Here, the customer makes sure that materials and the working environment have been properly prepared; validates the quality and functional capacity of material and informational components; and confirms priorities when deciding among execution options. This step is especially critical for jobs in which a delay in execution might risk a customer's money, time, or safety. For example, after preparing a patient for an operation, the surgical nurse must confirm the

Uncovering Opportunities for Innovation

WITH A JOB MAP IN HAND, you can begin to look systematically for opportunities to create value. The questions below can guide you in your search and help you avoid overlooking any possibilities. A great way to begin is to consider the biggest drawbacks of current solutions at each step in the map—in particular, drawbacks related to speed of execution, variability, and the quality of output. To increase the effectiveness of this approach, invite a diverse team of experts—marketing, design, engineering, and even some lead customers—to participate in this discussion.

Opportunities at the job level

- Can the job be executed in a more efficient or effective sequence?
- Do some customers struggle more with executing the job than others (for instance, novices versus experts, older versus younger)?
- What struggles or inconveniences do customers experience because they must rely on multiple solutions to get the job done?
- Is it possible to eliminate the need for particular inputs or outputs from the job?
- Is it necessary that the customers execute all steps for which they are currently responsible? Can the burden be automated or shifted to someone else?
- How may trends affect the way the job is executed in the future?
- In what contexts do customers most struggle with executing the job today? Where else or when else might customers want to execute the job?

Opportunities at the step level

- What causes variability (or unreliability) in executing this step? What causes execution to go off track?
- Do some customers struggle more than others with this step?
- What does this step's ideal output look like (and in what ways is the current output less than ideal)?
- Is this step more difficult to execute successfully in some contexts than others?
- What are the biggest drawbacks of current solutions used to execute this step?
- What makes executing this step time-consuming or inconvenient?

readiness of the patient (jewelry removed, vitals in check); of the equipment and instrumentation (battery power sufficient, scalpels available); and of the operating room (materials in place, sterile field intact).

A company seeking to differentiate itself at this step could help customers gain access to the types of information and feedback they need to confirm readiness and decide among execution alternatives. Another approach is to search for ways to build confirmation into the locating and preparing steps, since this would allow the customer to proceed through the job more quickly and easily. For example, Oracle's ProfitLogic merchandising optimization software removes the responsibility from the merchandiser for confirming the optimal timing and level of markdowns by analyzing thousands of different demand scenarios at the individual product level and recommending the scenario for each product that is likely to yield the highest profit.

5: Execute

What must customers do to execute the job successfully? Whether they're printing a document or administering anesthesia, customers consider the execution step the most important part of the job. Because execution is also the most visible step, customers are especially concerned about avoiding problems and delays, as well as achieving optimal results. An office worker who prints out a document wants to avoid paper jams, running out of toner, and long print queues. She also wants to improve the quality of printed output. An anesthesiologist wants to prevent negative patient reactions and to ensure that the patient is unable to feel pain.

Here, innovating companies can apply their technological knowhow to provide customers with real-time feedback or to automatically correct execution problems. Companies can also think about ways to keep performance consistent in different contexts. Kimberly-Clark's Patient Warming System is a good example of value added in this way. The system relies on a control unit that automatically circulates heated water through thermal pads placed on the patient to avoid temperature spikes during surgery. The system can maintain normal patient temperature with only 20% of the patient body covered, which means the device performs consistently and efficiently in a variety of complex surgical procedures.

6: Monitor

What does the customer need to monitor to ensure that the job is successfully executed? Customers must keep an eye on the results or output during execution, especially to determine whether they have to make adjustments to get the task back on track in the event of a problem. For some jobs, customers must also monitor environmental factors to see whether and when adjustments are necessary. A network administrator, for example, monitors Web traffic to avoid system overload.

While some monitoring activities are passive (like the way a pacemaker monitors heartbeats), others can often be time-consuming and demanding for customers. When the costs of poor execution are significant, as when operating on a patient, solutions that call attention to problems or relevant changes in the environment are especially valuable. Solutions that link monitoring with improved job execution or that provide diagnostic feedback offer considerable value as well. Consider how Nike helps runners monitor their workouts using the Nike+iPod Sport Kit. A sensor placed in Nike shoes communicates with an iPod being worn by the runner, providing ongoing audio feedback about time, distance, pace, and calories burned. When the runner notices he is flagging, he can select his "power song" to reinvigorate himself. The kit also allows runners to track progress against predefined goals.

7: Modify

What might the customer need to alter for the job to be completed successfully? When there are changes in inputs or in the environment, or if the execution is problematic, the customer may need help with updates, adjustments, or maintenance. At this step, customers need help deciding what should be adjusted as well as determining when, how, and where to make changes. Like monitoring, searching for the right adjustment can be both time-consuming and costly. Companies can help by offering ways to get execution back on track when there are problems. They can also provide avenues for reducing the time needed make updates and the number of adjustments the customer has to make to achieve desired results. (In addition, solutions that target the location and preparation steps can be designed to eliminate modifications.) Many software programs perform well at supporting this step. Microsoft, for example, assists customers with the job of modifying their computer to protect against security threats. Automatic updates of its operating system remove the hassle of determining which updates are necessary, finding them, and ensuring that fixes are compatible with various elements of the operating system.

8: Conclude

What must the customer do to finish the job? With some simple jobs such as hand washing, the conclusion is self-evident. Complex jobs, on the other hand, may involve some concluding process steps. The office worker has to retrieve a document from the printer and possibly collate, bind, and store it. An anesthesiologist must document surgery details, as well as wake and oversee transfer of the patient to a postoperative recovery area.

Customers often think of concluding steps as burdensome because the core job has already been completed, so companies need to help them simplify the process. Also, the conclusion of one job cycle is often the start of another or may affect the next one's beginning. When a job is cyclical, companies can help customers make sure that concluding activities are closely connected to the starting point of a new job cycle.

One way to help customers finish the job is to design benefits sought at the conclusion into an earlier step in the process. 3M's Coban Self-Adherent Wrap, for example, offers a convenient way for medical personnel to secure wound dressings at the end of treatment, because it is made of a material that stretches and adheres only to itself. This self-adherence property makes the wrap easy to remove, because it doesn't stick to patient skin or the wound. 3M designed the product in such a way that putting on the wrap anticipates the act of taking it off.

Ancillary Step: Troubleshooting

What problems must the customer troubleshoot and resolve in the course of performing the job? Even in the simplest jobs, things occasionally go wrong—orders are late, printers jam, surgical tools are misplaced, and software test cases fail. When that happens, the customer must disengage from the core job process and enter into a distinct ancillary job of troubleshooting and resolving the problem at hand. What customers want at that point is a speedy resolution—which is a function of how clearly the problem is understood. If the printer jams, for example, how should the office worker remove the damaged paper? If a nurse gets cut when a surgeon hands him a scalpel, what steps must the nurse take to avoid being infected with a blood-borne organism?

When a problem arises, customers need resources, tools, and diagnostics to help them determine a resolution quickly, protect themselves and resources that might be affected, and know when the problem is fixed. They also want solutions that prevent problems at each job step. Consider how MasterCard helps customers with the job of paying for products and services when problems occur. In addition to its zero-liability coverage policy, MasterCard provides downloadable contact numbers so that customers who lose a card while traveling know exactly how to contact the company to report the loss. Then MasterCard can send out emergency cash advances and a replacement card within 48 hours.

To identify opportunities for innovation, some companies focus on product leadership, some on operational excellence, and some on customer intimacy. Some offer services; others offer goods.

Regardless of which business model a company chooses, the fundamental basis for identifying opportunities for growth is the same. When companies understand that customers hire products, services, software, and ideas to get jobs done, they can dissect those jobs to discover the innovation opportunities that are the key to growth.

Originally published in May 2008. Reprint R0805H

Is It Real? Can We Win? Is It Worth Doing?

Managing Risk and Reward in an Innovation Portfolio.

by George S. Day

M

MINOR INNOVATIONS MAKE up 85% to 90% of companies' development portfolios, on average, but they rarely generate the growth companies seek. At a time when companies should be taking bigger—but smart—innovation risks, their bias is in the other direction. From 1990 to 2004 the percentage of major innovations in development portfolios dropped from 20.4 to 11.5—even as the number of growth initiatives rose.[1] The result is internal traffic jams of safe, incremental innovations that delay all projects, stress organizations, and fail to achieve revenue goals.

These small projects, which I call "little i" innovations, are necessary for continuous improvement, but they don't give companies a competitive edge or contribute much to profitability. It's the risky "Big I" projects—new to the company or new to the world—that push the firm into adjacent markets or novel technologies and can generate the profits needed to close the gap between revenue forecasts and growth goals. (According to one study, only 14% of new-product launches were substantial innovations, but they accounted for 61% of all profit from innovations among the companies examined.)[2]

The aversion to Big I projects stems from a belief that they are too risky and their rewards (if any) will accrue too far in the future. Certainly the probability of failure rises sharply when a company ventures beyond incremental initiatives within familiar markets. But avoiding risky projects altogether can strangle growth. The solution is to pursue a disciplined, systematic process that will distribute your innovations more evenly across the spectrum of risk.

Two tools, used in tandem, can help companies do this. The first, the risk matrix, will graphically reveal risk exposure across an entire innovation portfolio. The second, the R-W-W ("real, win, worth it") screen, originated by Dominick ("Don") M. Schrello, of Long Beach, California, can be used to evaluate individual projects. Versions of the screen have been circulating since the 1980s, and since then a growing roster of companies, including General Electric, Honeywell, Novartis, Millipore, and 3M, have used them to assess business potential and risk exposure in their innovation portfolios; 3M has used R-W-W for more than 1,500 projects. I have expanded the screen and used it to evaluate dozens of projects at four global companies, and I have taught executives and Wharton students how to use it as well.

Although both tools, and the steps within them, are presented sequentially here, their actual use is not always linear. The information derived from each one can often be reapplied in later stages of development, and the two tools may inform each other. Usually, development teams quickly discover when and how to improvise on the tools' structured approach in order to maximize learning and value.

The Risk Matrix

To balance its innovation portfolio, a company needs a clear picture of how its projects fall on the spectrum of risk. The risk matrix employs a unique scoring system and calibration of risk to help estimate the probability of success or failure for each project based on how big a stretch it is for the firm: The less familiar the intended market (*x* axis) and the product or technology (*y* axis), the higher the risk. (See the exhibit "Assessing risk across an innovation portfolio.")

Idea in Brief

Incremental innovations (small, safe changes to your firm's offerings) make up 85%–90% of companies' development portfolios. But "little i" projects rarely produce competitive advantage. For that, you need "Big I" innovations—offerings new to your organization or the world. Yes, they're risky. But avoid them, and you may strangle your company's growth.

Day recommends a solution: Increase the proportion of major innovations in your portfolio while carefully managing their risks. Two tools can help:

- A **risk matrix** enables you to estimate each project's probability of success or failure based on how big a stretch it is for your firm. The less familiar the intended market and the product or technology, the higher the risk.
- The **R-W-W ("real," "win," "worth it") screen** helps you evaluate projects' feasibility. The first step in using this tool—asking "Is it real" questions—helps you determine whether customers want your innovation and, if so, whether you can build it.

A project's position on the matrix is determined by its score on a range of factors, such as how closely the behavior of targeted customers will match that of the company's current customers, how relevant the company's brand is to the intended market, and how applicable its technology capabilities are to the new product.

A portfolio review team—typically consisting of senior managers with strategic oversight and authority over development budgets and allocations—conducts the evaluation, with the support of each project's development team. Team members rate each project independently and then explain their rationale. They discuss reasons for any differences of opinion and seek consensus. The resulting scores serve as a project's coordinates on the risk matrix.

The determination of each score requires deep insights. When McDonald's attempted to offer pizza, for example, it assumed that the new offering was closely adjacent to its existing ones, and thus targeted its usual customers. Under that assumption, pizza would be a familiar product for the present market and would appear in the bottom left of the risk matrix. But the project failed, and a post-mortem showed that the launch had been fraught with risk: Because

Idea in Practice

Using the Risk Matrix

Assemble a team to assess each innovation project's potential risk using these criteria:

- How closely target customers' behavior will match current customers'
- How relevant the company's brand is to the intended market
- How applicable your capabilities are to the new product

Neglect to assess risk, and you may make a major misstep.

Example: When McDonald's started offering pizza, it assumed the new product was closely adjacent to existing ones. So it targeted its usual customers. But employees couldn't make and serve a pizza within 30 seconds—which violated McDonald's service-delivery model. And the company's brand didn't give "permission" to offer pizza. The project failed.

Using the R-W-W screen

Used throughout a product's development, the R-W-W screen exposes faulty assumptions, knowledge gaps, sources of risk, and problems suggesting termination. To employ this tool, repeatedly test each project's viability according to these criteria:

Is it real?

A **market** exists for the product if:	The **product** is real if:
• There's a need or desire for the product. • Customers can buy it (for example, they have the money). • There are enough potential buyers. • Consumers will buy (for instance, they're willing to switch to your offering).	• It has precisely described characteristics. • It can be produced with available technology and materials. • It will satisfy the market in its final form.

Can we win?

The **product** will be competitive if:	Your **company** will be competitive if:
• It offers clear advantages over alternatives, such as greater safety or social acceptability (think hybrid cars). • Those advantages can be sustained (for example, through patents). • It can survive competitors' responses (such as a price war).	• It has superior resources (such as engineering or logistics). • Managers have experience in the market and skills appropriate for the project's scale and complexity. • Projects have champions who can energize development teams, sell the vision to senior management, and overcome adversity. • It has mastery of market research tools and shares customers' insights with development-team members.

Is it worth doing?

The product will be **profitable** at an acceptable risk if:	The product makes **strategic sense** if:
• Its forecasted returns are greater than costs—considering matters such as the timing and amount of capital outlays, marketing expenses, breakeven time, and the cost of product extensions needed to keep ahead of competitors.	• It fits with your company's growth strategy; for example, by enhancing customer relationships or creating opportunities for follow-on business.

Assessing risk across an innovation portfolio

The risk matrix*

This tool will reveal the distribution of risk across a company's innovation portfolio. Each innovation can be positioned on the matrix by determining its score on two dimensions—how familiar to the company the intended market is (x axis) and how familiar the product or technology is (y axis)—using the grid "Positioning projects on the matrix." Familiar products aimed at the company's current markets will fall in the bottom left of the matrix, indicating a low probability of failure. New products aimed at unfamiliar markets will fall in the upper right, revealing a high probability of failure.

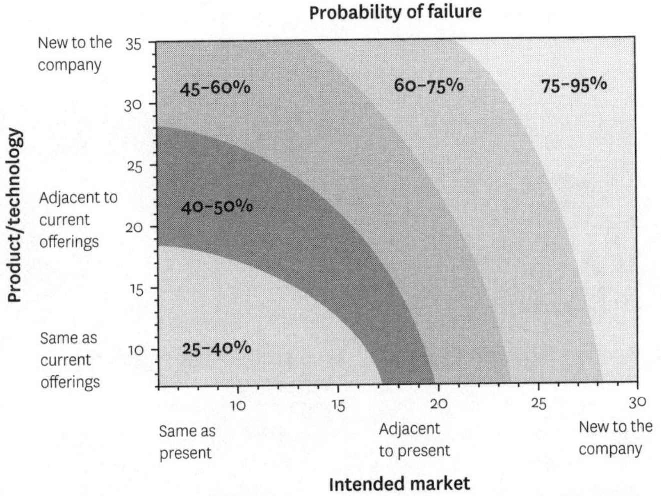

no one could figure out how to make and serve a pizza in 30 seconds or less, orders caused long backups, violating the McDonald's service-delivery model. The postmortem also revealed that the company's brand didn't give "permission" to offer pizza. Even though its core fast-food customers were demographically similar to pizza lovers, their expectations about the McDonald's experience didn't include pizza.

Risk and revenue

Each dot on this risk matrix stands for one innovation in an imaginary company's portfolio. The size of each dot is proportional to the project's estimated revenue. (Companies may choose to illustrate estimated development investment or some other financial measure instead.) This portfolio, dominated by relatively low-risk, low-reward projects, is typical in its distribution.

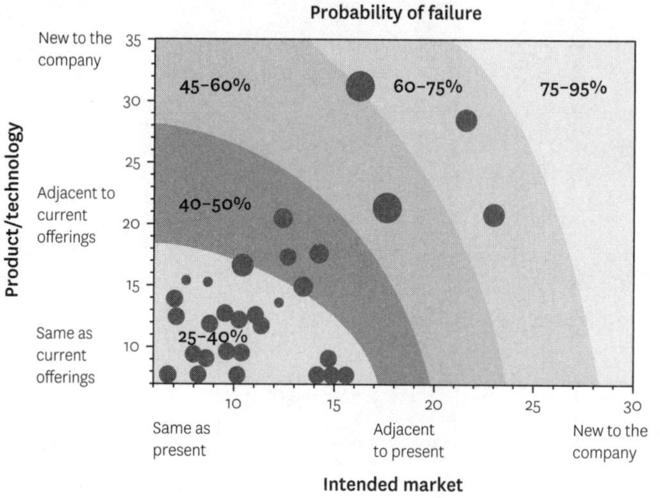

(*continued*)

Once the risk matrix has been completed, it typically reveals two things: that a company has more projects than it can manage well, and that the distribution of Big I and little i innovations is lopsided. Most companies will find that the majority of their projects cluster in the bottom left quadrant of the matrix, and a minority skew toward the upper right.

This imbalance is unhealthy if unsurprising. Discounted cash flow analysis and other financial yardsticks for evaluating development projects are usually biased against the delayed payoffs and uncertainty inherent in Big I innovations. What's more, little i projects tend to drain R&D budgets as companies struggle to keep up

Assessing risk across an innovation portfolio (continued)

Positioning projects on the matrix

Position each innovation product or concept by completing each statement in the left-hand column with one of the options offered across the top to arrive at a score from 1 to 5. Add the six scores in the "Intended market" section to determine the project's x-axis coordinate on the risk matrix. Add the seven scores in the "Product/technology" section to determine its y-axis coordinate.

	Intended market					
	...be the same as in our present market		...partially overlap with our present market		...be entirely different from our present market or are unknown	
Customers' behavior and decision-making processes will...	1	2	3	4	5	
Our distribution and sales activities will...	1	2	3	4	5	
The competitive set (incumbents or potential entrants) will...	1	2	3	4	5	
	...highly relevant		...somewhat relevant		...not at all relevant	
Our brand promise is...	1	2	3	4	5	
Our current customer relationships are...	1	2	3	4	5	
Our knowledge of competitors' behavior and intentions is...	1	2	3	4	5	
					Total (*x*-axis coordinate)	

	Product/technology					
	...is fully applicable		...will require significant adaptation		...is not applicable	
Our current development capability...	1	2	3	4	5	
Our technology competency...	1	2	3	4	5	
Our intellectual property protection...	1	2	3	4	5	
Our manufacturing and service delivery system...	1	2	3	4	5	
	...are identical to those of our current offerings		...overlap somewhat with those of our current offerings		...completely differ from those of our current offerings	
The required knowledge and science bases...	1	2	3	4	5	
The necessary product and service functions...	1	2	3	4	5	
The expected quality standards...	1	2	3	4	5	
					Total (*y*-axis coordinate)	

*This risk matrix was developed from many sources, including long-buried consulting reports by A.T. Kearney and other firms, the extensive literature on the economic performance of acquisitions and alliances, and numerous audits of product and service innovations. It broadly defines "failure" as significantly missing the objectives that were used to justify the investment in the growth initiative. Estimates of the probability of failure have been thoroughly validated in dozens of interviews with consultants and senior managers involved in innovation initiatives and are consistent with recent surveys that place the overall failure rate of new products close to 40%. The ranges in probabilities take into account some of the variability in organizations' definitions of failure and in what constitutes a new market or technology for a given company. The probabilities do not apply to fast-moving consumer goods (where incremental innovations have high long-run failure rates) or ethical pharmaceuticals, and don't distinguish whether "new to the company" is also "new to the world." (Although these are distinct categories, in my experience most major new-to-the-company innovations are also new to the world; for the purposes of this article, they're considered to be broadly overlapping.) "Market" refers to customers, not geographies.

with customers' and salespeople's demands for a continuous flow of incrementally improved products. The risk matrix creates a visual starting point for an ongoing dialogue about the company's mix of projects and their fit with strategy and risk tolerance. The next step is to look closely at each project's prospects in the marketplace.

Screening with R-W-W

The R-W-W screen is a simple but powerful tool built on a series of questions about the innovation concept or product, its potential market, and the company's capabilities and competition (see the exhibit "Screening for success"). It is not an algorithm for making go/no-go decisions but, rather, a disciplined process that can be employed at multiple stages of product development to expose faulty assumptions, gaps in knowledge, and potential sources of risk, and to ensure that every avenue for improvement has been explored. The R-W-W screen can be used to identify and help fix problems that are miring a project, to contain risk, and to expose problems that can't be fixed and therefore should lead to termination.

Innovation is inherently messy, nonlinear, and iterative. For simplicity, this article focuses on using the R-W-W screen in the early stages to test the viability of product concepts. In reality, however, a given product would be screened repeatedly during development—at the concept stage, during prototyping, and early in the launch planning. Repeated assessment allows screeners to incorporate increasingly detailed product, market, and financial analyses into the evaluation, yielding ever more accurate answers to the screening questions.

R-W-W guides a development team to dig deeply for the answers to six fundamental questions: *Is the market real? Is the product real? Can the product be competitive? Can our company be competitive? Will the product be profitable at an acceptable risk? Does launching the product make strategic sense?*

The development team answers these queries by exploring an even deeper set of supporting questions. The team determines where the answer to each question falls on a continuum ranging from definitely yes to definitely no. A definite no to any of the first

Screening for success

Each product concept in your company's innovation portfolio should be assessed by its development team using the R-W-W screen below. A definite yes or no answer to the first-column questions Is it real?, Can we win?, and Is it worth doing? *requires digging deeply for robust answers to the supporting questions in the second and third columns. Often a team will answer maybe; its goal should be to investigate all possible avenues to converting no or maybe into yes. A definite no to any second-column question typically leads to termination of the project, since failure is all but certain. A definite no to any third-column question argues strongly against proceeding with development. (The full set of questions in columns two and three of the screen come from evaluations of more than 50 product failures within two companies I worked with by teams of auditors who asked, "What questions, properly answered, might have prevented the failure?")*

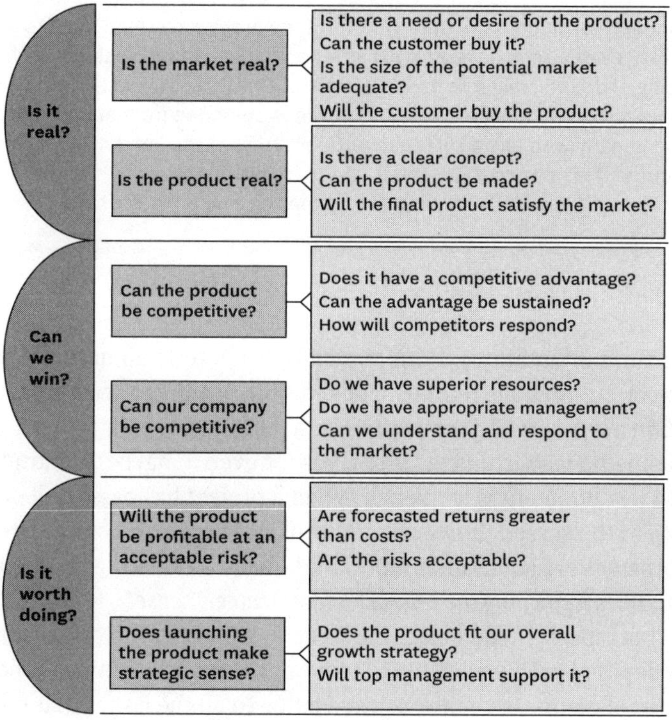

Is it real?
Is the market real?
Is there a need or desire for the product?
Can the customer buy it?
Is the size of the potential market adequate?
Will the customer buy the product?
Is the product real?
Is there a clear concept?
Can the product be made?
Will the final product satisfy the market?
Can we win?
Can the product be competitive?
Does it have a competitive advantage?
Can the advantage be sustained?
How will competitors respond?
Can our company be competitive?
Do we have superior resources?
Do we have appropriate management?
Can we understand and respond to the market?
Is it worth doing?
Will the product be profitable at an acceptable risk?
Are forecasted returns greater than costs?
Are the risks acceptable?
Does launching the product make strategic sense?
Does the product fit our overall growth strategy?
Will top management support it?

DAY

The Screening Team

PROJECT SCREENING TEAMS vary by company, type of initiative, and stage of development. Over the course of R-W-W screening, teams typically involve members from across functions, including R&D, marketing, and manufacturing. They should also work with senior managers who are familiar with the screen and have the expertise and the instincts to push dispassionately for accurate answers, particularly at each decision point during development. At the same time, however, these managers should be sympathetic and willing to provide the team with the resources to fill information gaps.

A critical job in managing the R-W-W process is preventing teams from regarding the screen as an obstacle to be overcome or circumvented. It's also important that the team not regard the screen as simply a go/no-go tool imposed by management—a potential threat to a favorite project. Such a misperception will subvert proper use of the screen as a learning tool for revealing dubious assumptions and identifying problems and solutions.

Because the members of the development team are both evaluators and advocates, the screen is vulnerable to misuse and manipulation. Team members' convictions about the merits of the project may lead them to make cursory evaluations if they fear that a deep assessment, including a frank voicing of doubts, might imperil the project. One way to avoid this pitfall is to enlist a credible outside facilitator, perhaps someone from another part of the company who has a solid new-product track record and no stake in the outcome. This person's job should be to unearth all the key uncertainties, information gaps, and differences of opinion and help resolve them.

five fundamental questions typically leads to termination of the project, for obvious reasons. For example, if the consensus answer to *Can the product be competitive?* is a definite no, and the team can imagine no way to change it to a yes (or even a maybe), continuing with development is irrational. When a project has passed all other tests in the screen, however, and thus is a very good business bet, companies are sometimes more forgiving of a no to the sixth question, *Does launching the product make strategic sense?*

This article will delineate the screening process and demonstrate the depth of probing needed to arrive at valid answers. What follows is not, of course, a comprehensive guide to all the issues that might be raised by each question. Development teams can probe more or less deeply, as needed, at each decision point. (For more on team process, see the sidebar "The Screening Team.")

Is It Real?

Figuring out whether a market exists and whether a product can be made to satisfy that market are the first steps in screening a product concept. Those steps will indicate the degree of opportunity for any firm considering the potential market, so the inquiring company can assess how competitive the environment might be right from the start.

One might think that asking if the envisioned product is even a possibility should come before investigating the potential market. But establishing that the market is real takes precedence for two reasons: First, the robustness of a market is almost always less certain than the technological ability to make something. This is one of the messages of the risk matrix, which shows that the probability of a product failure becomes greater when the *market* is unfamiliar to the company than when the *product or technology* is unfamiliar. A company's ability to crystallize the market concept—the target segment and how the product can do a better job of meeting its needs—is far more important than how well the company fields a fundamentally new product or technology. In fact, research by Procter & Gamble suggests that 70% of product failures across most categories occur because companies misconstrue the market. New Coke is a classic market-concept failure; Netflix got the market concept right. In each case the outcome was determined by the company's understanding of the market, not its facility with the enabling technologies.

Second, establishing the nature of the market can head off a costly "technology push." This syndrome often afflicts companies that emphasize how to solve a problem rather than what problem should be solved or what customer desires need to be satisfied. Segway, with its Personal Transporter, and Motorola, with its Iridium satellite phone, both succumbed to technology push. Segway's PT was an ingenious way to gyroscopically stabilize a two-wheeled platform, but it didn't solve the mobility problems of any target market. The reasons for Iridium's demise are much debated, but one possibility is that mobile satellite services proved less able than terrestrial wireless roaming services to cost-effectively meet the needs of most travelers.

Whether the market and the product are real should dominate the screening dialogue early in the development process, especially for Big I innovations. In the case of little i innovations, a close alternative will already be on the market, which has been proved to be real.

Is the market real?

A market opportunity is real only when four conditions are satisfied: The proposed product will clearly meet a need or solve a problem better than available alternatives; customers are able to buy it; the potential market is big enough to be worth pursuing; and customers are willing to buy the product.

Is there a need or desire for the product? Unmet or poorly satisfied needs must be surfaced through market research using observational, ethnographic, and other tools to explore customers' behaviors, desires, motivations, and frustrations. Segway's poor showing is partly a market-research failure; the company didn't establish at the outset that consumers actually had a need for a self-balancing two-wheeled transporter.

Once a need has been identified, the next question is, *Can the customer buy it?* Even if the proposed product would satisfy a need and offer superior value, the market isn't real when there are objective barriers to purchasing it. Will budgetary constraints prevent customers from buying? (Teachers and school boards, for example, are always eager to invest in educational technologies but often can't find the funding.) Are there regulatory requirements that the new product may not meet? Are customers bound by contracts that would prevent them from switching to a new product? Could manufacturing or distribution problems prevent them from obtaining it?

The team next needs to ask, *Is the size of the potential market adequate?* It's dangerous to venture into a "trombone oil" market, where the product may provide distinctive value that satisfies a need, but the need is minuscule. A market opportunity isn't real unless there are enough potential buyers to warrant developing the product.

Finally, having established customers' need and ability to buy, the team must ask, *Will the customer buy the product?* Are there subjective barriers to purchasing it? If alternatives to the product exist, customers will evaluate them and consider, among other things, whether the new product delivers greater value in terms of features, capabilities, or cost. Improved value doesn't necessarily mean more capabilities, of course. Many Big I innovations, such as the Nintendo Wii, home defibrillators, and Salesforce.com's CRM software as a service, have prevailed by outperforming the incumbents on a few measures while being merely adequate on others. By the same token, some Big I innovations have stumbled because although they had novel capabilities, customers didn't find them superior to the incumbents.

Even when customers have a clear need or desire, old habits, the perception that a switch is too much trouble, or a belief that the purchase is risky can inhibit them. One company encountered just such a problem during the launch of a promising new epoxy for repairing machine parts during routine maintenance. Although the product could prevent costly shutdowns and thus offered unique value, the plant engineers and production managers at whom it was targeted vetoed its use. The engineers wanted more proof of the product's efficacy, while the production managers feared that it would damage equipment. Both groups were risk avoiders. A postmortem of the troubled launch revealed that maintenance people, unlike plant engineers and production managers, like to try new solutions. What's more, they could buy the product independently out of their own budgets, circumventing potential vetoes from higher up. The product was relaunched targeting maintenance and went on to become successful, but the delay was expensive and could have been avoided with better screening.

Customers may also be inhibited by a belief that the product will fail to deliver on its promise or that a better alternative might soon become available. Addressing this reluctance requires foresight into the possibilities of improvement among competitors. The prospects of third-generation (3G) mobile phones were dampened by enhancements in 2.5G phones, such as high-sensitivity antennae that made the incumbent technology perform much better.

Is the product real?

Once a company has established the reality of the market, it should look closely at the product concept and expand its examination of the intended market.

Is there a clear concept? Before development begins, the technology and performance requirements of the concept are usually poorly defined, and team members often have diverging ideas about the product's precise characteristics. This is the time to expose those ideas and identify exactly what is to be developed. As the project progresses and the team becomes immersed in market realities, the requirements should be clarified. This entails not only nailing down technical specifications but also evaluating the concept's legal, social, and environmental acceptability.

Can the product be made? If the concept is solid, the team must next explore whether a viable product is feasible. Could it be created with available technology and materials, or would it require a breakthrough of some sort? If the product can be made, can it be produced and delivered cost-effectively, or would it be so expensive that potential customers would shun it? Feasibility also requires either that a value chain for the proposed product exists or that it can be easily and affordably developed, and that de facto technology standards (such as those ensuring compatibility among products) can be met.

Some years ago the R-W-W screen was used to evaluate a radical proposal to build nuclear power–generating stations on enormous floating platforms moored offshore. Power companies were drawn to the idea, because it solved both cooling and not-in-my-backyard problems. But the team addressing the *Is the product real?* stage of the process found that the inevitable flexing of the giant platforms would lead to metal fatigue and joint wear in pumps and turbines. Since this problem was deemed insurmountable, the team concluded that absent some technological breakthrough, the no answer to the feasibility question could never become even a maybe, and development was halted.

Will the final product satisfy the market? During development, trade-offs are made in performance attributes; unforeseen technical, manufacturing, or systems problems arise; and features are modified. At each such turn in the road, a product designed to meet customer expectations may lose some of its potential appeal. Failure to monitor these shifts can result in the launch of an offering that looked great on the drawing board but falls flat in the marketplace.

Consider the ongoing disappointment of e-books. Even though the newest entrant, the Sony Reader, boasts a huge memory and breakthrough display technology, using it doesn't begin to compare with the experience of reading conventional books. The promised black-on-white effect is closer to dark gray on light gray. Meanwhile, the Reader's unique features, such as the ability to store many volumes and to search text, are for many consumers insufficiently attractive to offset the near $300 price tag. Perhaps most important, consumers are well satisfied with ordinary books. By July of 2007 the entire e-book category had reached only $30 million in sales for the year.

Can We Win?

After determining that the market and the product are both real, the project team must assess the company's ability to gain and hold an adequate share of the market. Simply finding a real opportunity doesn't guarantee success: The more real the opportunity, the more likely it is that hungry competitors are eyeing it. And if the market is already established, incumbents will defend their positions by copying or leapfrogging any innovations.

Two of the top three reasons for new-product failures, as revealed by audits, would have been exposed by the *Can we win?* analysis: Either the new product didn't achieve its market-share goals, or prices dropped much faster than expected. (The third reason is that the market was smaller, or grew more slowly, than expected.)

The questions at this stage of the R-W-W screening carefully distinguish between the offering's ability to succeed in the marketplace and the company's capacity—through resources and management talent—to help it do so.

Can the product be competitive?

Customers will choose one product over alternatives if it's perceived as delivering superior value with some combination of benefits such as better features, lower life-cycle cost, and reduced risk. The team must assess all sources of perceived value for a given product and consider the question *Does it have a competitive advantage?* (Here the customer research that informed the team's evaluation of whether the market and the product were real should be drawn on and extended as needed.) Can someone else's offering provide customers with the same results or benefits? One company's promising laminate technology, for instance, had intrigued technical experts, but the launch failed because the customers' manufacturing people had found other, cheaper ways to achieve the same improvement. The team should also consider whether the product offers additional tangible advantages—such as lifetime cost savings, greater safety, higher quality, and lower maintenance or support needs—or intangible benefits, such as greater social acceptability (think of hybrid cars and synthetic-fur coats) and the promise of reduced risk that is implicit in a trusted brand name.

Can the advantage be sustained? Competitive advantage is only as good as the company's ability to keep imitators at bay. The first line of defense is patents. The project team should evaluate the relevance of its existing patents to the product in development and decide what additional patents may be needed to protect related intellectual property. It should ask whether a competitor could reverse engineer the product or otherwise circumvent patents that are essential to the product's success. If maintaining advantage lies in tacit organizational knowledge, can that knowledge be protected? For example, how can the company ensure that the people who have it will stay? What other barriers to imitation are possible? Can the company lock up scarce resources or enter into exclusive supply contracts?

Consider the case of 3M's computer privacy screen. Although the company's microlouver technology promised unique privacy benefits, its high price threatened to limit sales to a small market niche, making the project's status uncertain. An R-W-W screening, however, revealed that the technology was aggressively patented, so no competitor could imitate its performance. It also clarified an opportunity in adjacent markets for antiglare filters for computers. Armed with these insights, 3M used the technology to launch a full line of privacy and antiglare screens while leveraging its brand equity and sales presence in the office-products market. Five years later the product line formed the basis of one of 3M's fastest-growing businesses.

How will competitors respond? Assuming that patent protection is (or will be) in place, the project team needs to investigate competitive threats that patents can't deflect. A good place to start is a "red team" exercise: If we were going to attack our own product, what vulnerabilities would we find? How can we reduce them? A common error companies make is to assume that competitors will stand still while the new entrant fine-tunes its product prior to launch. Thus the team must consider what competing products will look like when the offering is introduced, how competitors may react after the launch, and how the company could respond. Finally, the team should examine the possible effects of this competitive interplay on prices. Would the product survive a sustained price war?

Can our company be competitive?

After establishing that the offering can win, the team must determine whether or not the company's resources, management, and market insight are better than those of the competition. If not, it may be impossible to sustain advantage, no matter how good the product.

Do we have superior resources? The odds of success increase markedly when a company has or can get resources that both enhance customers' perception of the new product's value and surpass those of competitors. Superior engineering, service delivery, logistics, or brand equity can give a new product an edge by better meeting customers' expectations. The European no-frills airline easyJet, for example, has successfully expanded into cruises and car rentals by leveraging its ability to blend convenience, low cost, and market-appropriate branding to appeal to small-business people and other price-sensitive travelers.

If the company doesn't have superior resources, addressing the deficiency is often straightforward. When the U.S. market leader for high-efficiency lighting products wanted to expand into the local-government market, for example, it recognized two barriers: The company was unknown to the buyers, and it had no experience with the competitive bidding process they used. It overcame these problems by hiring people who were skilled at analyzing competitors, anticipating their likely bids, and writing proposals. Some of these people came from the competition, which put the company's rivals at a disadvantage.

Sometimes, though, deficiencies are more difficult to overcome, as is the case with brand equity. As part of its inquiry into resources, the project team must ask whether the company's brand provides—or denies—permission to enter the market. The 3M name gave a big boost to the privacy screen because it is strongly associated with high-quality, innovative office supplies—whereas the McDonald's name couldn't stretch to include pizza. Had the company's management asked whether its brand equity was both relevant and superior to that of the competition—such as Papa Gino's—the answer would have been equivocal at best.

Do we have appropriate management? Here the team must examine whether the organization has direct or related experience with the market, whether its development-process skills are appropriate for the scale and complexity of the project, and whether the project both fits company culture and has a suitable champion. Success requires a passionate cheerleader who will energize the team, sell the vision to senior management, and overcome skepticism or adversity along the way. But because enthusiasm can blind champions to potentially crippling faults and lead to a biased search for evidence that confirms a project's viability, their advocacy must be constructively challenged throughout the screening process.

Can we understand and respond to the market? Successful product development requires a mastery of market-research tools, an openness to customer insights, and the ability to share them with development-team members. Repeatedly seeking the feedback of potential customers to refine concepts, prototypes, and pricing ensures that products won't have to be recycled through the development process to fix deficiencies.

Most companies wait until after development to figure out how to price the new product—and then sometimes discover that customers won't pay. Procter & Gamble avoids this problem by including pricing research early in the development process. It also asks customers to actually buy products in development. Their answers to *whether* they would buy are not always reliable predictors of future purchasing behavior.

Is It Worth Doing?

Just because a project can pass the tests up to this point doesn't mean it is worth pursuing. The final stage of the screening provides a more rigorous analysis of financial and strategic value.

Will the product be profitable at an acceptable risk?

Few products launch unless top management is persuaded that the answer to *Are forecasted returns greater than costs?* is definitely yes. This requires projecting the timing and amount of capital outlays, marketing expenses, costs, and margins; applying time to breakeven, cash flow, net present value, and other standard financial-performance measures; and estimating the profitability and cash flow from both aggressive and cautious launch plans. Financial projections should also include the cost of product extensions and enhancements needed to keep ahead of the competition.

Forecasts of financial returns from new products are notoriously unreliable. Project managers know they are competing with other worthy projects for scarce resources and don't want theirs to be at a disadvantage. So it is not surprising that project teams' financial reports usually meet upper management's financial-performance requirements. Given the susceptibility of financial forecasts to manipulation, overconfidence, and bias, executives should depend on rigorous answers to the prior questions in the screen for their conclusions about profitability.

Are the risks acceptable? A forecast's riskiness can be initially assessed with a standard sensitivity test: How will small changes in price, market share, and launch timing affect cash flows and breakeven points? A big change in financial results stemming from a small one in input assumptions indicates a high degree of risk. The financial analysis should consider opportunity costs: Committing resources to one project may hamper the development of others.

To understand risk at a deeper level, consider all the potential causes of product failure that have been unearthed by the R-W-W screen and devise ways to mitigate them—such as partnering with a company that has market or technology expertise your firm lacks.

Does launching the product make strategic sense?

Even when a market and a concept are real, the product and the company could win, and the project would be profitable, it may not make strategic sense to launch. To evaluate the strategic rationale for development, the project team should ask two more questions.

Does the product fit our overall growth strategy? In other words, will it enhance the company's capabilities by, for example, driving the expansion of manufacturing, logistics, or other functions? Will it have a positive or a negative impact on brand equity? Will it cannibalize or improve sales of the company's existing products? (If the former, is it better to cannibalize one's own products than to lose sales to competitors?) Will it enhance or harm relationships with stakeholders—dealers, distributors, regulators, and so forth? Does the project create opportunities for follow-on business or new markets that would not be possible otherwise? (Such an opportunity helped 3M decide to launch its privacy screen: The product had only a modest market on its own, but the launch opened up a much bigger market for antiglare filters.) These questions can serve as a starting point for what must be a thorough evaluation of the product's strategic fit. A discouraging answer to just one of them shouldn't kill a project outright, but if the overall results suggest that a project makes little strategic sense, the launch is probably ill-advised.

Will top management support it? It's certainly encouraging for a development team when management commits to the initial concept. But the ultimate success of a project is better assured if management signs on because the project's assumptions can withstand the rigorous challenges of the R-W-W screen.

Notes

1. Robert G. Cooper, "Your NPD Portfolio May Be Harmful to Your Business Health," *PDMA Visions,* April 2005.

2. W. Chan Kim and Renée Mauborgne, "Strategy, Value Innovation, and the Knowledge Economy," *Sloan Management Review,* Spring 1999.

Originally published in December 2007. Reprint R0712S

Six Myths of Product Development

The Fallacies That Cause Delays, Undermine Quality, and Raise Costs.

by Stefan Thomke and Donald Reinertsen

MOST PRODUCT-DEVELOPMENT MANAGERS are always struggling to bring in projects on time and on budget. They never have enough resources to get the job done, and their bosses demand predictable schedules and deliverables. So the managers push their teams to be more parsimonious, to write more-detailed plans, and to minimize schedule variations and waste. But that approach, which may work well in turning around underperforming factories, can actually hurt product-development efforts.

Although many companies treat product development as if it were similar to manufacturing, the two are profoundly different. In the world of manufacturing physical objects, tasks are repetitive, activities are reasonably predictable, and the items being created can be in only one place at a time. In product development many tasks are unique, project requirements constantly change, and the output—thanks, in part, to the widespread use of advanced computer-aided design and simulation and the incorporation of software in physical products—is information, which can reside in multiple places at the same time.

The failure to appreciate those critical differences has given rise to several fallacies that undermine the planning, execution, and evaluation of product-development projects. Together, we have spent more than 50 years studying and advising companies on product-development efforts, and we have encountered these misconceptions—as well as others that arise for different reasons—in a wide range of industries, including semiconductors, autos, consumer electronics, medical devices, software, and financial services. In this article we'll expose them and offer ways to overcome the problems they create.

Fallacy 1: High Utilization of Resources Will Improve Performance

In both our research and our consulting work, we've seen that the vast majority of companies strive to fully employ their product-development resources. (One of us, Donald, through surveys conducted in executive courses at the California Institute of Technology, has found that the average product-development manager keeps capacity utilization above 98%.) The logic seems obvious: Projects take longer when people are not working 100% of the time—and therefore, a busy development organization will be faster and more efficient than one that is not as good at utilizing its people.

But in practice that logic doesn't hold up. We have seen that projects' speed, efficiency, and output quality inevitably decrease when managers completely fill the plates of their product-development employees—no matter how skilled those managers may be. High utilization has serious negative side effects, which managers underestimate for three reasons.

They don't take into full account the intrinsic variability of development work

Many aspects of product development are unpredictable: when projects will arrive, what individual tasks they'll require, and how long it will take workers who've never tackled such tasks before to do them. Companies, however, are most familiar with repetitive

Idea in Brief

Many companies approach product development as if it were manufacturing, trying to control costs and improve quality by applying zero-defect, efficiency-focused techniques. While this tactic can boost the performance of factories, it generally backfires with product development. The process of designing products is profoundly different from the process of making them, and the failure of executives to appreciate the differences leads to several fallacies that actually hurt product-development efforts.

In this article, the authors, an HBS professor and a consultant, expose these misperceptions and others. They look at six dangerous myths:

1. High utilization of resources will make the department more efficient.
2. Processing work in large batches will be more economical.
3. Teams need to faithfully follow their development plan, minimizing any deviations from it.
4. The sooner a project is started, the sooner it will be finished.
5. The more features a product has, the better customers will like it.
6. Projects will be more successful if teams "get them right the first time."

The authors explain the negative effects these "principles" have when applied to product development, offer practical guidelines on overcoming them, and walk readers through a visual tool that will help them keep projects on track.

processes like manufacturing and transaction processing, where the work doesn't change much and surprises are few and far between. Such processes behave in an orderly manner as the utilization of resources increases. Add 5% more work, and it will take 5% more time to complete.

Processes with high variability behave very differently. As utilization increases, delays lengthen dramatically. (See the exhibit "High utilization leads to delays.") Add 5% more work, and completing it may take 100% longer. But few people understand this effect. In our experience with hundreds of product-development teams, we have found that most were significantly overcommitted. To complete all projects on time and on budget, some organizations we worked with would have needed at least 50% more resources than they had.

High utilization leads to delays

The curve below is calculated using Queuing Theory, the mathematical study of waiting lines. It shows that with variable processes, the amount of time projects spend on hold, waiting to be worked on, rises steeply as utilization of resources increases. Though the curve changes slightly depending on the project work, it always turns sharply upward as utilization nears 100%.

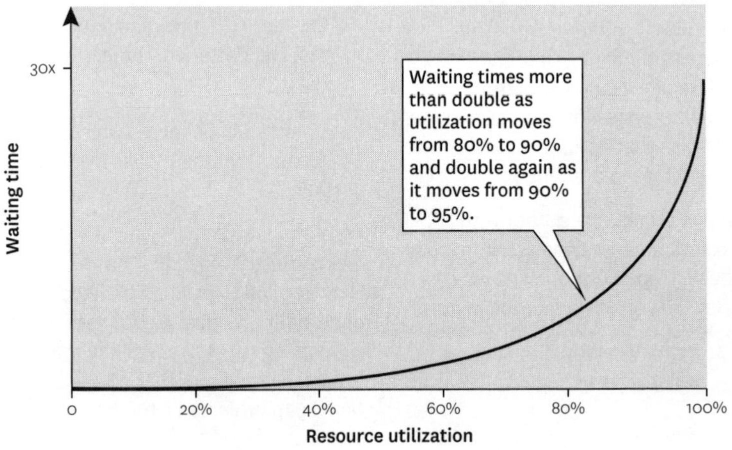

It is true that some variability is the result of a lack of discipline, and that some product-development tasks (like designing components for an airplane prototype or performing clinical trials) include more-repetitive work. But even if some of the work is predictable, when it's combined with other unpredictable work, you will see queuing problems.

They don't understand how queues affect economic performance

High utilization of resources inevitably creates queues of projects. When partially completed work sits idle, waiting for capacity to become available, the duration of the overall project will grow. Queues also delay feedback, causing developers to follow unproductive paths longer. They make it hard for companies to adjust to evolving market needs and to detect weaknesses in their product before it's too late. Ironically, these problems are precisely the ones that managers think high utilization will allow their teams to avoid.

Even when managers know that they're creating queues, they rarely realize the economic cost. Although that cost can be quantified, we've found that the vast majority of companies don't calculate it. Managers need to weigh queue costs against the costs of underutilized capacity in order to strike the right balance.

In product development, work-in-process inventory is predominantly invisible

Manufacturing queues consist of physical things, and when inventory in a factory doubles, it's obvious. That's not the case in product development, where inventory largely consists of information, such as design documentation, test procedures and results, and instructions for building prototypes. When inventory doubles in an engineering process, there are no physical signs. Moreover, because accounting standards require most R&D inventory to be carried at zero value, financial statements give no indication of serious inventory excesses in product development.

It is very difficult to fight a problem that you can't see or measure. Consider the situation at a major pharmaceutical firm. Several years ago its newly appointed head of drug discovery faced a managerial dilemma. Like other senior executives who run large R&D organizations, he was trying to find ways to make his scientists more innovative. He wanted them to experiment more with new chemical compounds that could generate promising new drugs and, at the same time, to eliminate unpromising candidates as early as possible. Experiments with living organisms, however, were the responsibility of animal testing, a department that was not under his control and was run as a cost center. It was evaluated by how efficiently it used testing resources, which naturally led to high utilization. Consequently, the scientists in drug discovery had to wait three to four months for the results of tests that took a little more than a week to perform. The "well-managed" testing organization impeded the discovery unit's progress.

The obvious solution to such problems is to provide a capacity buffer in processes that are highly variable. Some companies have long understood this. For decades, 3M has scheduled product developers at 85% of their capacity. And Google is famous for its "20% time" (allowing engineers to work one day a week on anything they want—a practice that means extra capacity is available if a project falls behind schedule). However, in our experience this kind of solution is quite hard to implement. As we will discuss, few organizations can resist the temptation to use every last bit of available capacity. Managers reflexively start more work whenever they see idle time.

But there are other viable solutions:

Change the management-control systems. For the pharmaceutical company, this might involve taking steps to align the objectives of the animal-testing unit with those of the discovery unit. The company could, for example, reward animal testing for prompt responses (measuring time from request to completion of test) rather than resource utilization.

Selectively increase capacity. Adding extra resources to the areas where the utilization rates are 70% or higher can significantly reduce waiting time. If the pharmaceutical company did this in animal testing, it would obtain feedback on new chemical compounds far faster. In settings where testing is conducted with computer modeling and simulation, increasing capacity is often relatively inexpensive, since it just involves buying additional computer equipment and software licenses.

Limit the number of active projects. If the pharmaceutical firm couldn't increase animal testing's capacity, it could still lower the utilization rate by reducing the number of active projects exploring new chemical compounds. The discipline of putting a hard limit on what goes into a product-development pipeline often results in sharper focus and clearer priorities.

Make the work-in-process inventory easier to see. One method is to use visual control boards. These can take a number of forms, but the key is to have some sort of physical token, such as a Post-it note, represent the development work (see the exhibit "Typical work-in-process control board"). A control board should display all active work and show what state each part of the project is in. It should be at the center of the team's management process. Teams can hold 15-minute daily stand-up meetings around such boards to coordinate efforts and keep work moving.

Fallacy 2: Processing Work in Large Batches Improves the Economics of the Development Process

A second cause of queues in product development is batch size. Let's say a new product is composed of 200 components. You could choose to design and build all 200 parts before you test any of them. If you instead designed and built only 20 components before you began testing, the batch size would be 90% smaller. That would have a profound effect on queue time, because the average queue in a process is directly proportional to batch size.

The reduction of batch sizes is a critical principle of lean manufacturing. Small batches allow manufacturers to slash work in process and accelerate feedback, which, in turn, improves cycle times, quality, and efficiency. Small batches have even greater utility in product development, but few developers realize the power of this method.

One reason is the nature of their work flow. Again, because the information they're producing is mostly invisible to them, the batch sizes are too. Second, developers seem to have an inherent bias to use large batches—possibly because they incorrectly believe that large batches produce economies of scale.

In a well-managed process, the batch size will balance transaction and holding costs (see the exhibit "How to determine optimal batch size"). It's similar to buying eggs at the grocery store. If you buy a 12-month supply on a single trip, your transaction cost is low, but most of the eggs will spoil, increasing your holding cost. If you buy a one-day supply at a time, your spoilage will be low, but your transaction costs will be high. Intuitively, you try to strike a balance between the two.

How to determine optimal batch size

Changes in batch size affect two primary costs: the transaction cost and the holding cost. As batch sizes become larger, average inventory levels rise, which raises holding costs. But at the same time, transaction costs decrease, because it takes fewer transactions to service demand.

The optimal batch size is the point where the total cost (combined holding and transaction cost) is lowest. When a company operates near this point, small deviations have little impact. For example, if a company operates at less than 20% above or below the optimal batch size, total costs increase less than 3%. So even rough estimates permit a company to capture large economic benefits.

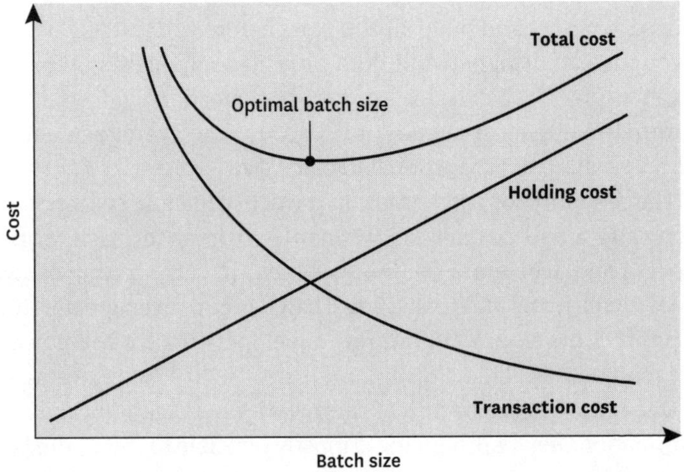

The companies that understand how this works have exploited IT advances to reduce batch sizes, often with astonishing results. Some software companies that used to test large batches of code every 90 days are now testing much smaller batches several times a day. A manufacturer of computer peripherals that used a similar approach with its software group reduced cycle time in software testing by 95% (from 48 months to 2.5 months), improved efficiency by 220%, and decreased defects by 33%. The cost savings were twice as high as the company had expected. Although those results were exceptional, we have found that reducing batch size improves most development projects significantly. Similarly, computerized modeling and simulation tools have dramatically lowered the optimal batch size of experimentation and testing in companies that develop physical products.

Fallacy 3: Our Development Plan Is Great; We Just Need to Stick to It

In all our consulting work and research, we've never come across a single product-development project whose requirements remained stable throughout the design process. Yet many organizations place inordinate faith in their plans. They attribute any deviations to poor management and execution and, to minimize them, carefully track every step against intermediate targets and milestones. Such thinking is fine for highly repetitive activities in established manufacturing processes. But it can lead to poor results in product innovation, where new insights are generated daily and conditions are constantly changing.

A classic study of technical problem solving done by Thomas Allen of MIT highlights the fluid nature of development work. He found that engineers who were developing an aerospace subsystem conceived of and evaluated a number of design alternatives before selecting one that they judged to be the best. Along the way their preferences changed frequently, as they tested and refined competing technical solutions. This is typical in innovation projects: Testing and experimentation reveal what does and doesn't work, and initial assumptions about costs and value may be disproved.

Defining customers' needs can also be hard to do at the outset of a product-development project. When you think about it, that's not surprising: It isn't easy for customers to accurately specify their needs for solutions that don't yet exist. In fact, familiarity with existing product attributes can interfere with an individual's ability to express his or her need for a novel product. Customers' preferences can also shift abruptly during the course of a development project, as competitors introduce new offerings and new trends emerge.

For all those reasons, sticking to the original plan—no matter how excellent its conception and how skillful its execution—can be a recipe for disaster. This is not to suggest that we don't believe in planning. Product development is a set of complex activities that require careful coordination and attention to the smallest detail. However, the plan should be treated as an initial hypothesis that is constantly revised as the evidence unfolds, economic assumptions change, and the opportunity is reassessed. (See "The Value Captor's Process," by Rita Gunther McGrath and Thomas Keil, HBR May 2007.)

Fallacy 4: The Sooner the Project Is Started, the Sooner It Will Be Finished

As we discussed earlier, idle time is anathema to managers. They tend to exploit any downtime by starting a new project. Even if the task cannot be completed because people have to return to another project, managers reason that anything accomplished on the new project is work that won't have to be done later. Such thinking leads companies to start more projects than they can vigorously pursue, diluting resources.

This dilution is dangerous. If a company embarks on a project before it has the resources to move ahead, it will stumble slowly through the development process. That's problematic because product-development work is highly perishable: Assumptions about technologies and the market can quickly become obsolete. The slower a project progresses, the greater the likelihood it will have to be redirected. Indeed, one branch of the military discovered that its cost and schedule overruns were exponentially proportional (to the fourth power) to a project's duration. In other words, when the original schedule of a project doubled, the cost and schedule overruns increased by a factor of 16.

The importance of reducing the amount of work in process is evident when we look at one of the classic formulas of queuing theory: Little's Law. It simply states that, on average, cycle time is proportional to the size of the queue divided by the processing rate. Thus,

Typical work-in-process control board

Control boards make invisible work visible by showing the precise stage that each work item is in. In designing the boards, most teams limit the number of tasks at each stage to prevent delays. This simple board contains features that might be found on a software project that involves a team composed of six to 10 people.

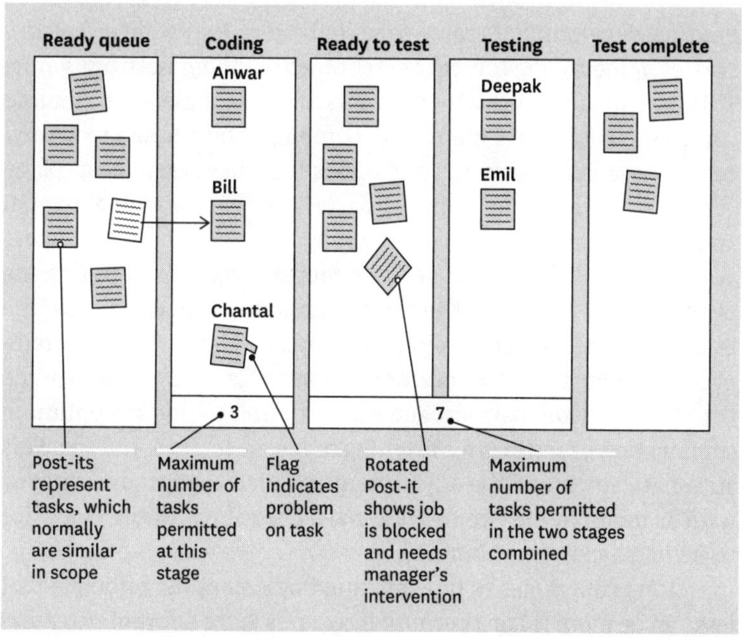

if 20 people are ahead of you in line at Starbucks and the barista is serving five people a minute, you will be served in four minutes. You can shorten the cycle time by raising the processing rate or by reducing the number of jobs under way. In most settings the latter is the only practical choice.

For some product developers the solution has been to rigorously control the rate at which they start work. They match it to the rate at which work is actually completed; carefully manage the number of projects in process; make sure that once a project is launched, it is adequately staffed until it is completed; and resist the temptation to steal resources from an ongoing project to squeeze in new ones.

Fallacy 5: The More Features We Put into a Product, the More Customers Will Like It

Product-development teams seem to believe that adding features creates value for customers and subtracting them destroys value. This attitude explains why products are so complicated: Remote controls seem impossible to use, computers take hours to set up, cars have so many switches and knobs that they resemble airplane cockpits, and even the humble toaster now comes with a manual and LCD displays.

Companies that challenge the belief that more is better create products that are elegant in their simplicity. Bang & Olufsen, the Danish manufacturer of audio products, televisions, and telephones, understands that customers don't necessarily want to fiddle with the equalizer, balance, and other controls to find the optimum combination of settings for listening to music. Its high-end speakers automatically make the adjustments needed to reproduce a song with as much fidelity to the original as possible. All that's left for users to select is the volume.

Getting companies to buy into and implement the principle that less can be more is hard because it requires extra effort in two areas of product development.

Defining the problem

Articulating the problem that developers will try to solve is the most underrated part of the innovation process. Too many companies devote far too little time to it. But this phase is important because it's where teams develop a clear understanding of what their goals are and generate hypotheses that can be tested and refined through experiments. The quality of a problem statement makes all the difference in a team's ability to focus on the few features that really matter.

When Walt Disney was planning Disneyland, he didn't rush to add more features (rides, kinds of food, amount of parking) than other amusement parks had. Rather, he began by asking a much larger question: How could Disneyland provide visitors with a magical customer experience? Surely, the answer didn't come overnight; it required painstakingly detailed research, constant experimentation, and deep insights into what "magical" meant to Disney and its customers. IDEO and other companies have dedicated phases in which they completely immerse themselves in the context in which the envisioned product or service will be used. Their developers read everything of interest about the markets, observe and interview future users, research offerings that will compete with the new product, and synthesize everything that they have learned into pictures, models, and diagrams. The result is deep insights into customers that are tested, improved, or abandoned throughout the iterative development process.

Determining what to hide or omit

Teams are often tempted to show off by producing brilliant technical solutions that amaze their peers and management. But often customers would prefer a product that just works effortlessly. From a customer's point of view, the best solutions solve a problem in the simplest way and hide the work that developers are so proud of.

One company that has understood this is Apple. It is known for many things—innovative products, stylish designs, and savvy marketing—but perhaps its greatest strength is its ability to get to the heart of a problem. (See "The Real Leadership Lessons of Steve Jobs," by Walter Isaacson, in our April issue.) As the late Steve Jobs once explained, "When you start looking at a problem and it seems really simple, you don't really understand the complexity of the problem. And your solutions are way too oversimplified. Then you get into the problem, and you see it's really complicated. And you come up with all these convoluted solutions. . . . That's where most people stop." Not Apple. It keeps on plugging away. "The really great person will keep on going," said Jobs, "and find . . . the key underlying principle of the problem and come up with a beautiful, elegant solution that works."

Determining which features to omit is just as important as—and perhaps more important than—figuring out which ones to include. Unfortunately, many companies, in an effort to be innovative, throw in every possible bell and whistle without fully considering important factors such as the value to customers and ease of use. When such companies do omit some planned functionality, it's typically because they need to cut costs or have fallen behind schedule or because the team has failed in some other way.

Instead, managers should focus on figuring out whether the deletion of any proposed feature might improve a particular product and allow the team to concentrate on things that truly heighten the overall customer experience. This can be determined by treating each alleged requirement as a hypothesis and testing it in small, quick experiments with prospective customers.

Development teams often assume that their products are done when no more features can be added. Perhaps their logic should be the reverse: Products get closer to perfection when no more features can be eliminated. As Leonardo da Vinci once said, "Simplicity is the ultimate sophistication."

Fallacy 6: We Will Be More Successful If We Get It Right the First Time

Many product-development projects fail to meet their objectives for budgets, schedules, and technical performance. Undoubtedly, poor planning, rigid processes, and weak leadership all play a role. But another cause that's often overlooked is managers' demand that their teams "get it right the first time." Requiring success on the first pass biases teams toward the least-risky solutions, even if customers don't consider them much of an improvement over what's already available. Worse yet, teams have little incentive to pursue innovative solutions to customers' problems.

To avoid making mistakes, teams follow a linear process in which each stage (specify, design, build, test, scale, launch) is carefully monitored at review "gates." Work on the next stage cannot

Practical guidelines for overcoming common fallacies

A checklist for today's product-development managers

1. Make queues and information flows visible.
2. Quantify the cost of delays and factor it into your decisions.
3. Introduce resource slack where utilization is highest.
4. Shift the focus of control systems from efficiency to response time.
5. Reduce transaction costs to enable smaller batch sizes and faster feedback.
6. Experiment with smaller batches; you can easily revert to large batches if this doesn't work.
7. Treat the development plan as a hypothesis that will evolve as new information becomes available.
8. Start projects only when you are ready to make a full commitment.
9. Aim for simplicity: Ask what features can be deleted, not just what can be added.
10. Experiment early, rapidly, and frequently, with computer models and physical prototypes, in controlled and real-life customer environments.
11. Emphasize overlapping and iterative—not linear—process designs.
12. Focus on quick feedback instead of first-pass success.

begin until the project passes through the gate. As the project moves down the line, significant commitments are made and the cost of responding to new insights increases by orders of magnitude. Successful tests in late stages are celebrated, and surprises, no matter how valuable they are, are considered setbacks. Unfortunately, such a linear process flow can cause project overruns because test feedback is delayed, teams cling to bad ideas longer than they should, and problems aren't unearthed until it's expensive to solve them.

A tolerance for "getting it wrong the first time" can be the better strategy as long as people iterate rapidly and frequently and learn quickly from their failures. Advances in simulation and rapid-prototyping technologies have made operating in this fashion vastly easier and less expensive.

Consider what we found in a study of 391 teams that designed custom integrated circuits. Teams that followed an iterative approach and conducted early and frequent tests made more errors along the way. But because they used low-cost prototyping technologies, they outperformed (in terms of the time and effort required) teams that tried to get their design right the first time. The teams that faced high prototyping costs invested more effort on specification, development, and verification. And because they did their iterations later in the process—and did far fewer of them—they delayed the discovery of critical problems.

Experimenting with many diverse ideas is crucial to innovation projects. When people experiment rapidly and frequently, many novel concepts will fail, of course. But such early failures can be desirable because they allow teams to eliminate poor options quickly and focus on more-promising alternatives. A crash test that shows that a car design is unsafe, a drug candidate that proves to be toxic, or a software user interface that confuses customers can all be desirable outcomes—provided that they occur early in a process, when few resources have been committed, designs are still very flexible, and other solutions can be tried.

A classic example of the advantages of the "fail early, fail often" approach is Team New Zealand's surprising victory in the 1995 America's Cup. To test ideas for improving the keel design, the team used two nearly identical boats: one boat that was modified during the course of the project and a "control" boat that was not. On a daily basis, the team simulated hypotheses on a local graphics workstation, applied those that looked promising to the one boat, raced it against the control, and analyzed the results. In contrast, its competitor, Team Dennis Conner, which had access to more-powerful computers (supercomputers at Boeing), ran large batches of simulations every few weeks and then tested possible solutions on one boat. The result: Team New Zealand completed many more learning cycles, eliminated unpromising ideas more rapidly, and ended up beating Team Dennis Conner's boat *Young America*.

What we hope is becoming clear by now is that experiments resulting in failures are not necessarily failed experiments. They generate new information that an innovator was unable to foresee. The faster the experimentation cycle, the more feedback can be gathered and incorporated into new rounds of experiments with novel and potentially risky ideas. In such an environment employees tend to persevere when times get tough, engage in more-challenging work, and outperform their risk-averse peers.

But creating this kind of environment isn't easy—a topic that Amy C. Edmondson of Harvard Business School explored in "Strategies for Learning from Failure" (HBR April 2011). Failure can lead to embarrassment and expose gaps in knowledge, which can undermine individuals' self-esteem and standing in an organization. After all, how often are managers promoted and teams rewarded for the early exposure of failures that lead a project to be killed—even though the early redeployment of precious resources benefits the company? This is especially true in organizations that have built a "zero tolerance for failure" or "error-free" (Six Sigma) environment.

Thomas Alva Edison understood all this. He organized his famous laboratories around the concept of rapid experimentation, locating machine shops for building models close to the rooms where experiments were conducted so that machinists could cooperate closely with researchers. The labs had libraries containing a vast number of volumes so that information could be found quickly; nearby storerooms with ample quantities of supplies; and a diverse workforce of craftsmen, scientists, and engineers. Edison wanted to make sure that when he or his people had an idea, it could be immediately turned into a working model or prototype. "The real measure of success is the number of experiments that can be crowded into 24 hours," he said.

Advances in information technology, such as computer-aided design, modeling, and simulation, have already allowed companies to make great strides in developing better products in less time and at a lower cost. Many companies, however, have not tapped the full potential of these tools, because their management thinking has not evolved as quickly as the technology: They still approach the highly variable information-generating work of product development as if it were like manufacturing. As advances in IT continue, the opportunity to improve the product-development process will become even greater. But so will the risks for companies that fail to recognize that product development is profoundly different from manufacturing.

Originally published in May 2012. Reprint R1205E

Innovation: The Classic Traps

by Rosabeth Moss Kanter

INNOVATION IS BACK AT the top of the corporate agenda. Never a fad, but always in or out of fashion, innovation gets rediscovered as a growth enabler every half-dozen years (about the length of a managerial generation). Too often, however, grand declarations about innovation are followed by mediocre execution that produces anemic results, and innovation groups are quietly disbanded in cost-cutting drives. Each generation embarks on the same enthusiastic quest for the next new thing and faces the same challenge of overcoming innovation stiflers. Over the past 25 years, I have conducted research and advised companies during at least four major waves of competitive challenges that led to widespread enthusiasm for innovation.

The first was the dawn of the global information age in the late 1970s and early 1980s, an era that introduced new industries and threatened to topple old ones. Entrepreneurs and foreign competitors imperiled established companies on their own turf. Information technology was beginning to evolve from the clunky mainframe to a consumer and desktop product, and companies such as Apple Computer made Silicon Valley garages the new base for product innovation in the United States. IBM emulated Apple's model by developing its PC in dingy surroundings in Boca Raton, Florida, freed from many corporate constraints. High-quality Japanese products, such as the Sony Walkman and Toyota cars, reflected not just good product design but also innovations in manufacturing processes that forced American giants to create their own programs to generate new ideas faster. "Total quality management" became a passion.

The second wave was the pressure to restructure during the takeover scare of the late 1980s. Buyout groups were attacking traditional companies, seeking to unlock the value of underutilized assets; "shareholder value" became a rallying cry. In Europe, restructuring was associated with the privatization of state-owned enterprises now exposed to the pressures of capital markets. Software was emerging as a major force behind innovation, and the strategic value of IT was touted, with American Airlines' Sabre reservations system widely cited as an example of a process innovation that succeeded as a separate business. Companies created new-venture departments to make sure they captured the value of their own ideas and inventions, rather than allowing a behemoth like Microsoft to arise outside the firm. Financial innovations were the rage: leveraged and management buyouts, derivatives and other forms of financial engineering, or financial supermarkets combining banks and nearly everything else. The restructuring era also favored products that could be instantly global: After defeating a hostile takeover bid in the late 1980s, Gillette boldly and successfully launched Sensor Excel shaving systems in the early 1990s, in identical form worldwide, with a single advertising message.

Third was the digital mania of the 1990s. The promise (and threat) of the World Wide Web drove many established companies to seek radical new business models. Brick-and-mortar companies were at risk for extinction; many rushed to create stand-alone Web ventures, often unconnected to the core business and sometimes in conflict with it. Eyes were on the capital markets rather than on customers, and companies got rich without profits or revenues. AOL bought Time Warner, put its name first, and proceeded to destroy value rather than create innovation.

The current wave of innovation began in a more sober mood, following the dot-com crash and belt-tightening of the global recession. Having recognized the limits of acquisitions and become skeptical about technology hype, companies refocused on organic growth. Surviving giants such as General Electric and IBM have

Idea in Brief

Most companies fuel growth by creating new products and services. Yet too many firms repeat the same growth-sapping mistakes in their efforts to innovate.

For example, some companies adopt the wrong strategy: investing only in ideas they think will become blockbusters. Result? Small ideas that could have generated big profits get rejected. For years, Time, Inc. didn't develop new publications: managers wanted any start-up to succeed on the same scale as the enormously popular *People* magazine. Only after Time decided to gamble on a large number of new publications did revenues rise.

Other companies err on the side of process-strangling innovations by subjecting them to the strict performance criteria their existing businesses must follow. At AlliedSignal, new Internet-based products and services had to satisfy the same financial metrics as established businesses. Budgets contained no funds for investment—so managers working on innovations had to find their own funding. The consequences? Retrofitted versions of old ideas.

To avoid such traps, Kanter advocates applying lessons from past failures to your innovation efforts. For instance, augment potential "big bets" with promising midrange ideas and incremental innovations. And add flexibility to your innovation planning, budgeting, and reviews.

Your reward? Better odds that the new ideas percolating in your company today will score profitable successes in the market tomorrow.

adopted innovation as a corporate theme. GE, for instance, is committed to double-digit growth from within. For its part, IBM is seeking innovation by tackling difficult social problems that require—and showcase—its technology solutions. A good example is World Community Grid, a nonprofit IBM created that aggregates unused computer power from numerous partners to give AIDS researchers and other scientists the ability to work with unusually large data sets. This wave's central focus is on new products designed to offer users new features and functionality to meet emerging needs. Customers and consumer markets have returned to center stage, after having been temporarily crowded out by other obsessions. Companies are seeking new categories to enrich their existing businesses rather than grand new ventures that will take

Idea in Practice

To innovate successfully, replace common mistakes with potent remedies.

Strategy Mistakes

- Rejecting opportunities that at first glance appear too small.
- Assuming that only new products count—not new services or improved processes.
- Launching too many minor product extensions that confuse customers and increase internal complexity.

Remedy: Widen your search and broaden your scope. Support a few big bets at the top that represent clear directions for the future and receive the lion's share of investment. Also create a portfolio of promising midrange ideas. And fund a broad base of early stage ideas or incremental innovations.

Process Mistakes

- Strangling innovation with the same tight planning, budgeting, and reviews applied to existing businesses.
- Rewarding managers for doing only what they committed to do—and discouraging them from making changes as circumstances warrant.

Remedy: Add flexibility to planning and control systems. For instance, reserve special funds for unexpected opportunities.

> ***Example:*** After executives at the struggling UK television network BBC set aside funds in a corporate account to support innovation proposals, a new recruit used money originally allocated for a new BBC training film to make a pilot for *The Office*. The show became the BBC's biggest hit comedy in decades.

Structure Mistakes

- Isolating fledgling and established enterprises in separate silos.

them into totally different realms. Signature innovations in this era include Apple's iPod and Procter & Gamble's Swiffer.

Each wave brought new concepts. For example, the rise of biotechnology, characterized by complicated licensing arrangements, helped legitimize the idea that established firms could outsource R&D and learn from entrepreneurial partners or that consumer products companies could turn to external idea shops, as well as their own labs, to invent new products. Approaches to

- Creating two classes of corporate citizens—those who have all the fun (innovators) and those who must make the money (mainstream business managers).

Remedy: Tighten the human connections between innovators and others throughout your organization. Convene frequent conversations between innovators and mainstream business managers to promote mutual learning and integration of new businesses into the organization. Create overlapping relationships—by having representatives from mainstream businesses rotate through innovation groups or innovation advisory boards. Identify people who lead informal networks that span innovation and mainstream groups, and encourage them to strengthen those connections.

Skills Mistakes

- Allowing innovators to rotate out of teams so quickly that team chemistry can't gel.
- Assuming that innovation teams should be led by the best technical people.

Remedy: Select innovation leaders with strong interpersonal skills. They'll keep the innovation team intact, help innovation teams embrace collective goals, leverage one another's different strengths, and share hard-to-document knowledge while innovations are under development.

> ***Example:*** When Williams-Sonoma launched its ultimately successful e-commerce group, it put a manager in charge who wasn't a technology expert but who could assemble the right team. He chose a mixture of employees from other units who could be ambassadors to their former groups and new hires that brought diverse skills.

innovation also reflected changing economic conditions and geopolitical events. And, of course, innovation has covered a wide spectrum, including technologies, products, processes, and complete business ventures, each with its own requirements.

Still, despite changes to the environment and differences among types of innovation, each wave of enthusiasm has encountered similar dilemmas. Most of these stem from the tensions between protecting revenue streams from existing businesses critical to current success and supporting new concepts that may be crucial to future success. These tensions are exacerbated by the long-known phenomenon that important innovations often arise from outside an industry and beyond the established players, creating extra pressure for companies to find the next big concept quickly. Consequently, a large body of knowledge about innovation dilemmas has arisen.

Books such as Tom Peters and Bob Waterman's *In Search of Excellence,* my own *The Change Masters,* and Gifford Pinchot's *Intrapreneuring* supported the 1980s innovation wave by pointing to the importance of relieving potential innovators of bureaucratic constraints so they could run with their ideas. This was followed by a body of work documenting the difficulty of exploring the new while exploiting the old, reflected in Michael Tushman and Charles O'Reilly's call for more ambidextrous organizations in *Winning Through Innovation;* my work on managing the tensions between the powerful organizational mainstream and fragile new streams produced by innovation groups in *When Giants Learn to Dance;* and Clayton Christensen's more recent finding, in *The Innovator's Dilemma,* that listening to current customers can inhibit breakthrough innovation.

Yet despite all the research and literature, I still observe executives exhibiting the same lack of courage or knowledge that undercut previous waves of innovation. They declare that they want more innovation but then ask, "Who else is doing it?" They claim to seek new ideas but shoot down every one brought to them. And, repeatedly, companies make the same mistakes as their predecessors. For example, a 1983 HBR article by Harvard Business School professor Malcolm Salter, et al., "When Corporate Venture Capital Doesn't Work," provided warnings that companies failed to heed about exactly the same dilemmas they face today: With a few notable exceptions, such as Intel and Reuters, companies' venture-capital departments rarely create significant value for the core business.

It's inevitable that historical memory will fade—but not inevitable that we lose the lessons. Here's a chance to collect some of what is known about innovation traps and how to avoid them.

Strategy Mistakes: Hurdles Too High, Scope Too Narrow

The potential for premium prices and high margins lures executives to seek blockbuster innovations—the next iPod, Viagra, or Toyota Production System. Along the way, they expend enormous resources, though big hits are rare and unpredictable. Meanwhile, in seeking the killer app, managers may reject opportunities that at first glance appear too small, and people who aren't involved in the big projects may feel marginalized.

For years, large consumer products companies typically screened out ideas that couldn't result in revenues of several hundred million dollars within two years. This screen discouraged investments in ideas that couldn't be tested and measured using conventional market research, or that weren't grounded in experience, in favor of ideas that were close to current practice and hardly innovative. In the 1980s and 1990s, Pillsbury, Quaker Oats, and even Procter & Gamble (an innovation powerhouse today) were vulnerable to smaller companies that could quickly roll out new products, thus eroding the giants' market share. P&G, for example, lamented not having introduced a new toilet bowl cleaner before a competitor did, despite P&G labs' having developed similar technology. The rival, of course, gained dominant market share by being a first mover. Likewise, Pillsbury and Quaker lagged the competition in bringing new concepts to market and, as underperformers, were eventually acquired.

Time Incorporated, the magazine wing of Time Warner, for a long time was slow to develop new publications because managers wanted any start-up to have the potential to grow into another *People* or *Sports Illustrated,* two of the company's legendary successes. During the period before Don Logan took the helm in 1992, almost no new magazines were launched. After Logan brought a different innovation strategy to the magazine group, Time developed (or bought) about 100 magazines, which dramatically increased the company's revenues, cash flow, and profits. Not every offering was a blockbuster, but Time had learned what successful innovators know: To get more successes, you have to be willing to risk more failures.

The Lessons of Innovation

INNOVATION GOES IN OR OUT of fashion as a strategic driver of corporate growth, but with every wave of enthusiasm, executives make the same mistakes. Most of the time, they stumble in their R&D efforts because they are engaged in a difficult balancing act: They need to protect existing revenue streams while coaxing along new ones. But "corporate entrepreneurship" doesn't have to be an oxymoron. Innovation can flourish if executives heed business lessons from the past.

Strategy Lessons

- Not every innovation idea has to be a blockbuster. Sufficient numbers of small or incremental innovations can lead to big profits.
- Don't just focus on new product development: Transformative ideas can come from any function—for instance, marketing, production, finance, or distribution.
- Successful innovators use an "innovation pyramid," with several big bets at the top that get most of the investment; a portfolio of promising midrange ideas in test stage; and a broad base of early stage ideas or incremental innovations. Ideas and influence can flow up or down the pyramid.

Process Lessons

- Tight controls strangle innovation. The planning, budgeting, and reviews applied to existing businesses will squeeze the life out of an innovation effort.

A related mistake is to act as if only products count, even though transformative new ideas can come from a range of functions, such as production and marketing. For instance, a fabric company that made complicated woven materials had a long-standing problem: yarn breakage during production, which was reflected in the cost of the company's products and represented a competitive disadvantage. But the top team at the fabric maker continued to talk about the company's search for really big product innovations, such as totally new materials. A new executive, who believed in opening the search for innovation to all employees, joined the company. After a meeting discussing the need for change, a veteran factory worker, who had joined as a young immigrant and still spoke with a heavy

- Companies should expect deviations from plan: If employees are rewarded simply for doing what they committed to do, rather than acting as circumstances would suggest, their employers will stifle and drive out innovation.

Structure Lessons

- While loosening formal controls, companies should tighten interpersonal connections between innovation efforts and the rest of the business.
- Game-changing innovations often cut across established channels or combine elements of existing capacity in new ways.
- If companies create two classes of corporate citizens—supplying the innovators with more perks, privileges, and prestige—those in the existing business will make every effort to crush the innovation.

Skills Lessons

- Even the most technical of innovations requires strong leaders with great relationship and communication skills.
- Members of successful innovation teams stick together through the development of an idea, even if the company's approach to career timing requires faster job rotation.
- Because innovations need connectors—people who know how to find partners in the mainstream business or outside world—they flourish in cultures that encourage collaboration.

accent, tentatively approached the new executive with an idea for ending the breakage. The company tried it, and it worked. When asked how long he had had that idea, the worker replied, "Thirty-two years."

Similarly, because managers at Quaker Oats in the 1990s were too busy tweaking product formulas in minor ways, the company missed numerous opportunities in other arenas, such as distribution—for instance, taking advantage of the smaller, health-oriented outlets used by its Snapple beverage acquisition. And in a packaging coup, Ocean Spray, the cranberry juice company, stole a march on America's largest juice purveyors (then including P&G and Coca-Cola) by getting an 18-month exclusive license for the introduction of Tetra Pak's paper bottles to the U.S. market. Ocean Spray boasted a more eclectic innovation strategy than that of its rivals, including idea forums to explore innovations in any domain and open to any employee. Paper bottles were an instant hit with children (and parents packing their lunches), and Ocean Spray's market share shot way up.

Early in its history, the U.S. auto industry gained a breakthrough innovation from its financial function: Consumer financing opened mass markets for products that previously only the affluent could afford. One Intel breakthrough was in marketing: It treated computer chips like potato chips. As a technology company, Intel could have left innovation to its R&D folks. But by marketing a component directly to consumers, Intel gained enormous power with computer manufacturers, which had little choice but to put an Intel Inside label on every machine.

Similarly, Cemex, the global cement company based in Mexico, has used widespread brainstorming to generate innovations that create other sources of value for a product that could easily become a commodity. Those innovations include branded, bagged cement and technology-enabled delivery methods to get cement to customers as fast as if it were a pizza. And while P&G is getting attention for its product innovations, such as the Swiffer and Crest Whitestrips, its innovations in new media, such as interactive Web sites for the soap operas it sponsors, may prove even more valuable for the company's future.

When a company is both too product centric and too revenue impatient, an additional problem can arise. The organization's innovation energy can dissipate across a raft of tiny me-too projects chasing immediate revenue. Perversely, such projects may raise costs in the long run. While a failure to encourage small wins can mean missed opportunities, too many trivial projects are like seeds sown on stony ground—they might sprout, but they do not take root and grow into anything useful. If new ideas take the form not of distinctive innovations but of modest product variations, the resulting proliferation can dilute the brand, confuse customers, and increase internal complexity—such as offering a dozen sizes and flavors of crackers rather than a new and different snack food, a problem Kraft currently faces.

Process Mistakes: Controls Too Tight

A second set of classic mistakes lies in process; specifically, the impulse to strangle innovation with tight controls—the same planning, budgeting, and reviews applied to existing businesses. The inherent uncertainty of the innovation process makes sidetracks or unexpected turns inevitable. The reason upstart Ocean Spray could grab the paper-bottle opportunity from large U.S. juice makers is that the big companies' funds had already been allocated for the year, and they wanted committees to study the packaging option before making commitments that would deviate from their plans.

AlliedSignal (now Honeywell) in 2000 sought new Internet-based products and services using established strategic-planning and budgeting processes through existing business units. The CEO asked the divisions to bring their best ideas for Internet-related innovations to the quarterly budget reviews. Although designated as a priority, these innovation projects were subjected to the same financial metrics the established businesses were. Budgets contained no additional funds for investment; managers working on innovations had to find their own sources of funding through savings or internal transfers. What emerged were often retrofitted versions of ideas that had been in the pipeline anyway.

Performance reviews, and their associated metrics, are another danger zone for innovations. Established companies don't just want plans; they want managers to stick to those plans. They often reward people for doing what they committed to do and discourage them from making changes as circumstances warrant. At a large defense contractor, for instance, people got low marks for not delivering exactly what they had promised, even if they delivered something better—which led people to underpromise, eventually reducing employees' aspirations and driving out innovation.

In the early 1990s, Bank of Boston (now part of Bank of America) set up an innovative unit called First Community Bank (FCB), the first comprehensive banking initiative to focus on inner-city markets. FCB struggled to convince mainstream managers in Bank of Boston's retail-banking group that the usual performance metrics, such as transaction time and profitability per customer, were not appropriate for this market—which required customer education, among other things—or for a new venture that still needed investment. Mainstream managers argued that "underperforming" branches should be closed. In order to save the innovation, FCB leaders had to invent their own metrics, based on customer satisfaction and loyalty, and find creative ways to show results by clusters of branches. The venture later proved both profitable and important to the parent bank as it embarked on a series of acquisitions.

Structure Mistakes: Connections Too Loose, Separations Too Sharp

While holding fledgling enterprises to the same processes as established businesses is dangerous, companies must be careful how they structure the two entities, to avoid a clash of cultures or conflicting agendas.

The more dramatic approach is to create a unit apart from the mainstream business, which must still serve its embedded base. This was the logic behind the launch of Saturn as an autonomous subsidiary of General Motors. GM's rules were suspended, and the Saturn team was encouraged to innovate in every aspect of vehicle design, production, marketing, sales, and customer service. The hope was that the best ideas would be incorporated back at the parent company, but instead, after a successful launch, Saturn was reintegrated into GM, and many of its innovations disappeared.

In the time it took for Saturn to hit its stride, Toyota—which favored continuous improvement over blockbusters or greenfield initiatives like Saturn—was still ahead of GM in quality, customer satisfaction, and market share growth. Similarly, U.S. charter schools were freed from the rules of public school systems so they could innovate and thus serve as models for improved education. They've employed many innovative practices, including longer school days and focused curricula, but there is little evidence that charter schools have influenced changes in the rest of their school districts.

The problem in both cases can be attributed to poor connections between the greenfield and the mainstream. Indeed, when people operate in silos, companies may miss innovation opportunities altogether. Game-changing innovations often cut across established channels or combine elements of existing capacity in new ways. CBS was once the world's largest broadcaster and owned the world's largest record company, yet it failed to invent music video, losing this opportunity to MTV. In the late 1990s, Gillette had a toothbrush unit (Oral B), an appliance unit (Braun), and a battery unit (Duracell), but lagged in introducing a battery-powered toothbrush.

The likelihood that companies will miss or stifle innovations increases when the potential innovations involve expertise from different industries or knowledge of different technologies. Managers at established organizations may both fail to understand the nature of a new idea and feel threatened by it.

AT&T Worldnet, the Internet access venture of the venerable long-distance telephone company, faced this lethal mix in the mid-1990s. Managers in the traditional consumer services and business services units participated in a series of debates over whether to manage Worldnet as a distinct business unit, with its own P&L, or to include it in the existing business units focused primarily on the consumer sector. While consumer services managers were reluctant to let go of anything, they eventually agreed to a carve-out intended to protect the embryonic venture from being crushed by the bureaucracy and to keep it from being measured against more-mature businesses that were generating significant cash flow rather than requiring investment. They weren't all that concerned, because they believed an Internet service provider would never generate significant revenue and profitability.

But as Worldnet gained momentum, it attracted more attention. The people in consumer services began to view the innovation's possible expansion to provide voice over Internet protocol (VoIP) services as a threat that could cannibalize existing business. Consumer services managers grabbed control of Worldnet and proceeded to starve it. They used it as a platform to sell core land-based long-distance services and started applying the same metrics to the Internet business that were used for consumer long-distance. Pricing was an immediate problem. Worldnet's services had been priced low to fuel growth, to get the scale and network effects of a large group of subscribers, but the mainstream unit did not want to incur losses on any line of business. So it raised prices, and Worldnet's growth stalled. Consumer services managers could then treat Worldnet as a trivial, slow-growing business, not worthy of large investment. They did not allocate sufficient resources to develop Internet access and VoIP technology, restraining important telecom innovations in which AT&T could have been the pioneer.

Cultural clashes exacerbated tensions at AT&T. Mainstream managers had long tenures in the Bell system. The Internet group, however, hired external tech professionals who spoke the language of computers, not telephony.

Even when a new venture is launched within an existing business, culture clashes become class warfare if there are two classes of corporate citizens—those who have all the fun and those who make all the money. The designated innovators, whether an R&D group or a new-venture unit, are identified as creators of the future. They are free of rules or revenue demands and are allowed to play with ideas that don't yet work. Their colleagues are expected to follow rules, meet demands, and make money while feeling like grinds and sometimes being told they are dinosaurs whose business models will soon be obsolete.

In the early 2000s, Arrow Electronics' attempt at an Internet venture, Arrow.com, was given space in the same facility as the traditional sales force. The similarities stopped there. The Internet group was composed of new hires, often young, from a different background, who dressed in a completely different style. It spent money on cushy furniture, including a big expenditure on a new kitchen—justified, it was said, because the Arrow.com team worked 24/7. The traditional sales force, already anxious about the threat Internet-enabled sales posed to its commissions and now aware of its dingier offices, became overtly angry. Relations between the groups grew so acrimonious that a brick wall was erected to separate the two sides of the building. Both teams wasted time battling, endangering customer relationships when the two groups fought over the same customers—after all, Arrow.com was just another distribution channel. The CEO had to intervene and find structures to connect them.

Skills Mistakes: Leadership Too Weak, Communication Too Poor

Undervaluing and underinvesting in the human side of innovation is another common mistake. Top managers frequently put the best technical people in charge, not the best leaders. These technically oriented managers, in turn, mistakenly assume that ideas will speak for themselves if they are any good, so they neglect external communication. Or they emphasize tasks over relationships, missing opportunities to enhance the team chemistry necessary to turn undeveloped concepts into useful innovations.

Groups that are convened without attention to interpersonal skills find it difficult to embrace collective goals, take advantage of the different strengths various members bring, or communicate well enough to share the tacit knowledge that is still unformed and hard to document while an innovation is under development. It takes time to build the trust and interplay among team members that will spark great ideas. MIT researchers have found that for R&D team members to be truly productive, they have to have been on board for at least two years. At one point, Pillsbury realized that the average length of time the company took to go from new product idea to successful commercialization was 24 to 26 months, but the average length of time people spent on product teams was 18 months. No wonder the company was falling behind in innovation.

Changes in team composition that result from companies' preferences for the frequency with which individuals make career moves can make it hard for new ventures to deal with difficult challenges, prompting them to settle for quick, easy, conventional solutions. At Honeywell in the 1980s, leaders of new-venture teams were often promoted out of them before the work had been completed. Because promotions were take-it-or-leave-it offers and pay was tied to size of assets controlled (small by definition in new ventures) rather than difficulty of task, even dedicated innovators saw the virtues of leaving their projects midstream. Honeywell was undermining its own innovation efforts. An executive review of why new ventures failed uncovered this problem, but a technology bias made it hard for old-school managers of that era to increase their appreciation for the value of team bonding and continuity.

Innovation efforts also bog down when communication and relationship building outside the team are neglected. When Gap Incorporated was struggling in the late 1990s, the company mounted several cross-unit projects to find innovations in products, retail concepts, and operations. Some of the project teams quickly became closed environments, and members cut themselves off from their former peers. By failing to tap others' ideas, they produced lackluster recommendations; and by failing to keep peers informed, they missed getting buy-in for even their weak proposals.

Innovators cannot work in isolation if they want their concepts to catch on. They must build coalitions of supporters who will provide air cover for the project, speak up for them in meetings they don't attend, or sponsor the embryonic innovation as it moves into the next stages of diffusion and use. To establish the foundation for successful reception of an innovation, groups must be able to present the radical so it can be understood in familiar terms and to cushion disruptive innovations with assurances that the disruption will be manageable. When technical experts mystify their audiences rather than enlighten them, they lose support—and "no" is always an easier answer than "yes." Groups that work in secret and then present their ideas full-blown at the end face unexpected objections that sometimes kill the project.

Such inattention to relationships and communication with mainstream business managers doomed the launch of Timberland's promising TravelGear line. Developed by an R&D group called the Invention Factory, which was independent of the company's mainstream businesses, TravelGear allowed a user to travel with a single pair of shoes, adding or subtracting components suitable for a range of outdoor activities. The concept won a design award from *BusinessWeek* in 2005. But some existing business teams had not been included in the Invention Factory's developments, and the traditional sales force refused to sell TravelGear products.

By contrast, Dr. Craig Feied's success in developing a state-of-the-art digital network for Washington Hospital Center and its parent, MedStar Health, was a testimony to investment in the human dimension. A small group of programmers designed a user-friendly information system in the emergency department, not the IT department, so they were already close to users. Dr. Feied and his partner, Dr. Mark Smith, made a point of sitting on numerous hospital committees so they would have a wide base of relationships. Their investment in people and their contributions toward shared hospital goals had a positive effect: Feied and Smith's actions helped create good word of mouth and support among other departments for their information system (now called Azyxxi), which resulted in saved time and lives.

The climate for relationships within an innovation group is shaped by the climate outside it. Having a negative instead of a positive culture can cost a company real money. During Seagate Technology's troubled period in the mid-to-late 1990s, the company, a large manufacturer of disk drives for personal computers, had seven different design centers working on innovation, yet it had the lowest R&D productivity in the industry because the centers competed rather than cooperated. Attempts to bring them together merely led people to advocate for their own groups rather than find common ground. Not only did Seagate's engineers and managers lack positive norms for group interaction, but they had the opposite in place: People who yelled in executive meetings received "Dog's Head" awards for the worst conduct. Lack of product and process innovation was reflected in loss of market share, disgruntled customers, and declining sales. Seagate, with its dwindling PC sales and fading customer base, was threatening to become a commodity producer in a changing technology environment.

Under a new CEO and COO, Steve Luczo and Bill Watkins, who operated as partners, Seagate developed new norms for how people should treat one another, starting with the executive group. Their raised consciousness led to a systemic process for forming and running "core teams" (cross-functional innovation groups), and Seagate employees were trained in common methodologies for team building, both in conventional training programs and through participation in difficult outdoor activities in New Zealand and other remote locations. To lead core teams, Seagate promoted people who were known for strong relationship skills above others with greater technical skills. Unlike the antagonistic committees convened during the years of decline, the core teams created dramatic process and product innovations that brought the company back to market leadership. The new Seagate was able to create innovations embedded in a wide range of new electronic devices, such as iPods and cell phones.

Innovation Remedies

The quest for breakthrough ideas, products, and services can get derailed in any or all of the ways described earlier. Fortunately, however, history also shows how innovation succeeds. "Corporate entrepreneurship" need not be an oxymoron. Here are four ways to win.

Strategy remedy: Widen the search, broaden the scope

Companies can develop an innovation strategy that works at the three levels of what I call the "innovation pyramid": a few big bets at the top that represent clear directions for the future and receive the lion's share of investment; a portfolio of promising midrange ideas pursued by designated teams that develop and test them; and a broad base of early stage ideas or incremental innovations permitting continuous improvement. Influence flows down the pyramid, as the big bets encourage small wins heading in the same direction, but it also can flow up, because big innovations sometimes begin life as small bits of tinkering—as in the famously accidental development of 3M's Post-it Notes.

Thinking of innovation in terms of this pyramid gives senior managers a tool for assessing current efforts, making adjustments as ideas prove their value and require further support, and ensuring that there is activity at all levels. A culture of innovation grows because everyone can play. While dedicated groups pursue the big projects and temporary teams develop midrange ideas, everyone else in the company can be invited to contribute ideas. Every employee can be a potential idea scout and project initiator, as IBM is demonstrating. This past July, the company held a three-day InnovationJam on the Web, during which about 140,000 employees and clients—representing 104 countries—contributed about 37,000 ideas and ranked them, giving the company an enormous pool of raw ideas, some of them big, most of them small. Indeed, an organization is more likely to get bigger ideas if it has a wide funnel into which numerous small ideas can be poured. One of the secrets of success for companies that demonstrate high rates of innovation is that they simply try more things.

Gillette adopted the pyramid model as part of its push to accelerate innovation in 2003 and 2004. The result was a stream of innovations in every function and business unit that raised revenues and profits. They included new products such as a battery-powered toothbrush; new concepts in the R&D pipeline, such as the 2006 five-blade, battery-powered Fusion shaving system; innovative marketing campaigns that neutralized the competition, such as the campaign for the Mach3Turbo, which outshone Schick's introduction of its Quattro razor; and new technology in HR. At the first Gillette innovation fair in March 2004, every unit showcased its best ideas of the year in a creative way. The legal department promoted its novel online ethics course with a joke: distributing "get out of jail free" cards like those in *Monopoly*. Having the legal department embrace innovation was a plus for a company in which innovators needed speedy service to file patent applications or help to clear regulatory hurdles.

An innovation strategy that includes incremental innovations and continuous improvement can help to liberate minds throughout the company, making people more receptive to change when big breakthroughs occur.

Process remedy: Add flexibility to planning and control systems

One way to encourage innovation to flourish outside the normal planning cycles is to reserve pools of special funds for unexpected opportunities. That way, promising ideas do not have to wait for the next budget cycle, and innovators do not have to beg for funds from mainstream managers who are measured on current revenues and profits. In the mid-to-late 1990s, autocratic management and rigid controls caused the BBC to slip in program innovation and, consequently, audience share. Budgets were tight, and, once they were set, expenditures were confined to predetermined categories. In 2000, a new CEO and his CFO relaxed the rules and began setting aside funds in a corporate account to support proposals for innovation, making it clear that bureaucratic rules should not stand in the way of creative ideas. The BBC's biggest hit comedy in decades, *The Office,* was an accident, made possible when a new recruit took the initiative to use money originally allocated for a BBC training film to make the pilot.

IBM is building such flexibility directly into its infrastructure. The company established a $100 million innovation fund to support the best ideas arising from its InnovationJam, independent of the normal planning and budgeting processes, to allow bottom-up ideas to flourish. "No one has ever before brought together such a global and diverse set of business thought leaders on this scale to discuss the most pressing issues and opportunities of our age," says Nick Donofrio, IBM's executive vice president of innovation and technology. "We have companies literally knocking at the door and saying, 'Give us your best and brightest ideas, and let's work together to make them a reality.' It's a golden opportunity to create entirely new markets and partnerships."

Besides needing different funding models and development partnerships, the innovation process requires exemption from some corporate requirements; after all, there are numerous differences between established businesses and new ventures. For example, the knowledge that innovations could move forward through rapid prototyping—learning from a series of fast trials—might mean that certain milestones triggering review and additional funding would occur faster than they would for established businesses, following the rhythm of the project rather than a fixed quarterly or annual calendar. For other kinds of projects, greater patience might be required—for instance, when an innovation group encounters unexpected obstacles and needs to rethink its model. The key is flexible, customized treatment.

Structure remedy: Facilitate close connections between innovators and mainstream businesses

While loosening the formal controls that would otherwise stifle innovations, companies should tighten the human connections between those pursuing innovation efforts and others throughout the rest of the business. Productive conversations should take place regularly between innovators and mainstream business managers. Innovation teams should be charged with external communication as part of their responsibility, but senior leaders should also convene discussions to encourage mutual respect rather than tensions and antagonism. Such conversations should be aimed at mutual learning, to minimize cannibalization and to maximize effective reintegration of innovations that become new businesses. In addition to formal meetings, companies can facilitate informal conversations—as Steelcase did by building a design center that would force people to bump into one another—or identify the people who lead informal cross-unit networks and encourage their efforts at making connections.

Innovation groups can be told at the outset that they have a responsibility to serve the mainstream while also seeking bigger innovations to start new businesses. This can be built into their charters and reinforced by overlapping relationships—whether it involves representatives from mainstream businesses rotating through innovation groups or advisory boards overseeing innovation efforts. After its first great idea flopped, Timberland's Invention Factory learned to work closely with mainstream teams to meet their needs for immediate innovations, such as recreational shoes lined with SmartWool, and to seek game-changing breakthroughs. Turner Broadcasting's new-products group mixes project types: stand-alone developments, enhancements for current channels, external partnerships, and venture capital investments. PNC Financial Services Group recently established a new-products group to oversee mainstream developments, such as pricing and product enhancements, as well as growth engines in new capabilities, such as technology-enabled services and back-office services for investment funds. The company's sales of emerging products were up 21% in 2005, accounting for 46% of all sales.

Flexible organizational structures, in which teams across functions or disciplines organize around solutions, can facilitate good connections. Media conglomerate Publicis has "holistic communication" teams, which combine people across its ad agencies (Saatchi & Saatchi, Leo Burnett, Publicis Worldwide, and so on) and technology groups to focus on customers and brands. Novartis has organized around diseases, with R&D more closely connected to markets and customers; this has helped the company introduce pathbreaking innovations faster, such as its cancer drug Gleevec. The success of Seagate's companywide Factory of the Future team at introducing seemingly miraculous process innovations led to widespread use of its core-teams model.

Would-be innovators at AlliedSignal discovered that tackling promising opportunities required outreach across silos. For example, the aerospace division was organized into groups that were dedicated to large commercial airlines, small commercial airlines, and general aviation (private and charter planes), but the best new idea involved differentiating customers by whether they performed their own maintenance or contracted it to others. The division needed to create new connections across previously divided territories in order to begin the innovation process.

The success of Williams-Sonoma as a multichannel retailer innovating in e-commerce can be attributed to the ways its Web pioneers connected their developments to the rest of the company. From the very beginning, CEO Howard Lester refused to consider Internet ventures that were independent of other company operations. The first main Web development was a bridal registry to create new functionality for the mainstream business. When this pilot project proved its value, an e-commerce department was launched and housed in its own building. But rather than standing apart and pursuing its own direction, that department sought to enhance existing channels, not compete with them. It measured its success not only according to e-commerce sales but also according to incremental sales through other channels that the Web had facilitated. To further its close connections with the mainstream business, the department offered free training to the rest of the company.

Skills remedy: Select for leadership and interpersonal skills, and surround innovators with a supportive culture of collaboration

Companies that cultivate leadership skills are more likely to net successful innovations. One reason Williams-Sonoma could succeed in e-commerce quickly and profitably was its careful attention to the human dimension. Shelley Nandkeolyar, the first manager of Williams-Sonoma's e-commerce group, was not the most knowledgeable about the technology, but he was a leader who could assemble the right team. He valued relationships, so he chose a mixture of current employees from other units, who could be ambassadors to their former groups, and new hires that brought new skills. He added cross-company teams to advise and link to the e-commerce team. He invented an integrator role to better connect operations groups and chose Patricia Skerritt, known for being relationship oriented, to fill it.

Similarly, Gail Snowden was able to steer Bank of Boston's First Community Bank through the minefields of middle-manager antagonism toward a successful innovation that produced other innovations (new products and services) because of her leadership skills, not her banking skills. She built a close-knit team of talented people who bonded with one another and felt passion for the mission. Soon her group became one of the parent bank's most desirable places to work. She developed strong relationships with senior executives who helped her deal with tensions in the middle, and she communicated well and often about why her unit needed to be different. Her creativity, vision, teamwork, and persistence helped this group succeed and become a national role model, while other banks' efforts faltered.

IBM's big innovations, such as demonstrating grid computing through World Community Grid, are possible only because the company's culture encourages people to collaborate. CEO Sam

Palmisano has engaged hundreds of thousands of IBMers in a Web-based discussion of company values, and Nick Donofrio, IBM's executive vice president for innovation and technology, works to make 90,000 technical people around the world feel part of one innovation-seeking community. The corporate champion of World Community Grid, IBM vice president Stanley Litow, sought out partners in its business units and geographies to move the innovation forward.

Established companies can avoid falling into the classic traps that stifle innovation by widening the search for new ideas, loosening overly tight controls and rigid structures, forging better connections between innovators and mainstream operations, and cultivating communication and collaboration skills.

Innovation involves ideas that create the future. But the quest for innovation is doomed unless the managers who seek it take time to learn from the past. Getting the balance right between exploiting (getting the highest returns from current activities) and exploring (seeking the new) requires organizational flexibility and a great deal of attention to relationships. It always has, and it always will.

Originally published in November 2006. Reprint R0611C

Discovery-Driven Planning

by Rita Gunther McGrath and Ian C. MacMillan

BUSINESS LORE IS FULL of stories about smart companies that incur huge losses when they enter unknown territory—new alliances, new markets, new products, new technologies. The Walt Disney Company's 1992 foray into Europe with its theme park had accumulated losses of more than $1 billion by 1994. Zapmail, a fax product, cost Federal Express Corporation $600 million before it was dropped. Polaroid lost $200 million when it ventured into instant movies. Why do such efforts often defeat even experienced, smart companies? One obvious answer is that strategic ventures are inherently risky: The probability of failure simply comes with the territory. But many failures could be prevented or their cost contained if senior managers approached innovative ventures with the right planning and control tools.

Discovery-driven planning is a practical tool that acknowledges the difference between planning for a new venture and planning for a more conventional line of business. Conventional planning operates on the premise that managers can extrapolate future results from a well-understood and predictable platform of past experience. One expects predictions to be accurate because they are based on solid knowledge rather than on assumptions. In platform-based planning, a venture's deviations from plan are a bad thing.

The platform-based approach may make sense for ongoing businesses, but it is sheer folly when applied to new ventures. By definition, new ventures call for a company to envision what is unknown, uncertain, and not yet obvious to the competition. The safe, reliable, predictable knowledge of the well-understood business has not yet emerged. Instead, managers must make do with assumptions about the possible futures on which new businesses are based. New ventures are undertaken with a high ratio of assumption to knowledge. With ongoing businesses, one expects the ratio to be the exact opposite. Because assumptions about the unknown generally turn out to be wrong, new ventures inevitably experience deviations—often huge ones—from their original planned targets. Indeed, new ventures frequently require fundamental redirection.

Rather than trying to force startups into the planning methodologies for existing predictable and well-understood businesses, discovery-driven planning acknowledges that at the start of a new venture, little is known and much is assumed. When platform-based planning is used, assumptions underlying a plan are treated as facts—givens to be baked into the plan—rather than as best-guess estimates to be tested and questioned. Companies then forge ahead on the basis of those buried assumptions. In contrast, discovery-driven planning systematically converts assumptions into knowledge as a strategic venture unfolds. When new data are uncovered, they are incorporated into the evolving plan. The real potential of the venture is discovered as it develops—hence the term discovery-driven planning. The approach imposes disciplines different from, but no less precise than, the disciplines used in conventional planning.

Euro Disney and the Platform-Based Approach

Even the best companies can run into serious trouble if they don't recognize the assumptions buried in their plans. The Walt Disney Company, a 49% owner of Euro Disney (now called Disneyland Paris), is known as an astute manager of theme parks. Its success has not been confined to the United States: Tokyo Disneyland has been a financial and public relations success almost from its opening in 1983. Euro Disney is another story, however. By 1993, attendance approached 1 million visitors each month, making the park Europe's most popular paid tourist destination. Then why did it lose so much money?

Idea in Brief

You're weighing a major strategic venture—a first-time alliance, a new market, an innovative product. Beware: business history is littered with stories about smart companies that hemorrhaged multiple millions from ventures gone bad.

Why such massive losses? Too many firms use conventional planning to manage their ventures, say McGrath and MacMillan. They make predictions about a venture's potential based on their established businesses. And they treat the assumptions underlying those predictions—"The product will sell itself," "We'll have no competitors"—as facts. By the time they realize a key assumption was flawed, it's too late to stanch the bleeding.

How to avoid this scenario? As your venture unfolds, use a disciplined process to systematically uncover, test, and (if necessary) revise the assumptions behind your venture's plan. You'll expose the make-or-break uncertainties common to ventures. And you'll address those uncertainties at the lowest possible cost—so you don't set your venture on the path to ruin.

In planning Euro Disney in 1986, Disney made projections that drew on its experience from its other parks. The company expected half of the revenue to come from admissions, the other half from hotels, food, and merchandise. Although by 1993, Euro Disney had succeeded in reaching its target of 11 million admissions, to do so it had been forced to drop adult ticket prices drastically. The average spending per visit was far below plan and added to the red ink.

The point is not to play Monday-morning quarterback with Disney's experience but to demonstrate an approach that could have revealed flawed assumptions and mitigated the resulting losses. The discipline of systematically identifying key assumptions would have highlighted the business plan's vulnerabilities. Let us look at each source of revenue in turn.

Admissions price

In Japan and the United States, Disney found its price by raising it over time, letting early visitors go back home and talk up the park to their neighbors. But the planners of Euro Disney assumed that they could hit their target number of visitors even if they started out with

Idea in Practice

McGrath and MacMillan suggest this five-step process for successful venture planning:

1. Bake Profitability into Your Venture's Plan

Instead of estimating the venture's revenues and then assuming profits will come, create a "reverse income statement" for the project: Determine the profit required to make the venture worthwhile—it should be at least 10%. Then calculate the revenues needed to deliver that profit.

2. Calculate Allowable Costs

Lay out all the activities required to produce, sell, service, and deliver the new product or service to customers. Together, these activities comprise the venture's **allowable costs**. Ask, "If we subtract allowable costs from required revenues, will the venture deliver significant returns?" If not, it may not be worth the risk.

3. Identify Your Assumptions

If you still think the venture *is* worth the risk, work with other managers on the venture team to list all the assumptions behind your profit, revenue, and allowable costs calculations. Use disagreement over assumptions to trigger discussion, and be open to adjusting your list.

an admission price of more than $40 per adult. A major recession in Europe and the determination of the French government to keep the franc strong exacerbated the problem and led to low attendance. Although companies cannot control macroeconomic events, they can highlight and test their pricing assumptions. Euro Disney's prices were very high compared with those of other theme attractions in Europe, such as the aqua palaces, which charged low entry fees and allowed visitors to build their own menus by paying for each attraction individually. By 1993, Euro Disney not only had been forced to make a sharp price reduction to secure its target visitors, it had also lost the benefits of early-stage word of mouth. The talking-up phenomenon is especially important in Europe, as Disney could have gauged from the way word of mouth had benefited Club Med.

Hotel accommodations

Based on its experience in other markets, Disney assumed that people would stay an average of four days in the park's five hotels.

Example: A company has determined that it needs to sell 250 million units of a proposed new product at a particular price to generate the revenue required to meet the venture's profit goal. It decides how many orders it'll need to sell the 250 million units, how many sales calls it'll take to secure those orders, how many salespeople will be required to make those calls, and how much this will cost in sales-force compensation.

4. Determine If the Venture Still Makes Sense

Check your assumptions against your reverse income statement for the venture. Can you still make the required profit, given your latest estimates of revenues and allowable costs? If not, the venture should be scrapped.

5. Test Assumptions at Milestones

If you've decided to move ahead with the venture, use milestone events to test—and, if necessary, further update—your assumptions. Postpone major commitments of resources until evidence from a previous milestone signals that taking the next step is justified.

The average stay in 1993 was only two days. Had the assumption been highlighted, it might have been challenged: Since Euro Disney opened with only 15 rides, compared with 45 at Disney World, people could do them all in a single day.

Food

Park visitors in the United States and Japan "graze" all day. At Euro Disney, the buried assumption was that Europeans would do the same. Euro Disney's restaurants, therefore, were designed for all-day streams of grazers. When floods of visitors tried to follow the European custom of dining at noon, Disney was unable to seat them. Angry visitors left the park to eat, and they conveyed their anger to their friends and neighbors back home.

Merchandise

Although Disney did forecast lower sales per visitor in Europe than in the United States and Japan, the company assumed that Europeans would buy a similar mix of cloth goods and print items. Instead, Euro Disney fell short of plan when visitors bought a far smaller proportion of high-margin items such as T-shirts and hats than expected. Disney could have tested the buried assumption before forecasting sales: Disney's retail stores in European cities sell many fewer of the high-margin cloth items and far more of the low-margin print items.

Disney is not alone. Other companies have paid a significant price for pursuing platform-based ventures built on implicit assumptions that turn out to be faulty. Such ventures are usually undertaken without careful up-front identification and validation of those assumptions, which often are unconscious. We have repeatedly observed that the following four planning errors are characteristic of this approach.

Companies don't have hard data but, once a few key decisions are made, proceed as though their assumptions were facts. Euro Disney's implicit assumptions regarding the way visitors would use hotels and restaurants are good examples.

Companies have all the hard data they need to check assumptions but fail to see the implications. After making assumptions based on a subset of the available data, they proceed without ever testing those assumptions. Federal Express based Zapmail on the assumption that there would be a substantial demand for four-hour delivery of documents faxed from FedEx center to FedEx center. What went unchallenged was the implicit assumption that customers would not be able to afford their own fax machines before long. If that assumption had been unearthed, FedEx would have been more likely to take into account the plunging prices and increasing sales of fax machines for the office and, later, for the home.

Companies possess all the data necessary to determine that a real opportunity exists but make implicit and inappropriate assumptions about their ability to implement their plan. Exxon lost $200 million on its office automation business by implicitly assuming that it could build a direct sales and service support capability to compete head-to-head with IBM and Xerox.

Companies start off with the right data, but they implicitly assume a static environment and thus fail to notice until too late that a key

Some dangerous implicit assumptions

1. Customers will buy our product because we think it's a good product.
2. Customers will buy our product because it's technically superior.
3. Customers will agree with our perception that the product is "great."
4. Customers run no risk in buying from us instead of continuing to buy from their past suppliers.
5. The product will sell itself.
6. Distributors are desperate to stock and service the product.
7. We can develop the product on time and on budget.
8. We will have no trouble attracting the right staff.
9. Competitors will respond rationally.
10. We can insulate our product from competition.
11. We will be able to hold down prices while gaining share rapidly.
12. The rest of our company will gladly support our strategy and provide help as needed.

variable has changed. Polaroid lost $200 million from Polavision instant movies by assuming that a three minute cassette costing $7 would compete effectively against a half-hour videotape costing $20. Polaroid implicitly assumed that the high cost of equipment for videotaping and playback would remain prohibitive for most consumers. Meanwhile, companies pursuing those technologies steadily drove down costs. (See the exhibit "Some dangerous implicit assumptions.")

Discovery-Driven Planning: An Illustrative Case

Discovery-driven planning offers a systematic way to uncover the dangerous implicit assumptions that would otherwise slip unnoticed and thus unchallenged into the plan. The process imposes a strict discipline that is captured in four related documents: a *reverse income statement,* which models the basic economics of the business; *pro forma operations specs,* which lay out the operations needed to run the business; a *key assumptions checklist,* which is used to ensure that assumptions are checked; and a *milestone planning chart,* which specifies the assumptions to be tested at each project milestone. As the venture unfolds and new data are uncovered, each of the documents is updated.

To demonstrate how this tool works, we will apply it retrospectively to Kao Corporation's highly successful entry into the floppy disk business in 1988. We deliberately draw on no inside information about Kao or its planning process but instead use the kind of limited public knowledge that often is all that any company would have at the start of a new venture.

The company

Japan's Kao Corporation was a successful supplier of surfactants to the magnetic-media (floppy disk) industry. In 1981, the company began to study the potential for becoming a player in floppy disks by leveraging the surfactant technology it had developed in its core businesses, soap and cosmetics. Kao's managers realized that they had learned enough process knowledge from their floppy disk customers to supplement their own skills in surface chemistry. They believed they could produce floppy disks at a much lower cost and higher quality than other companies offered at that time. Kao's surfactant competencies were particularly valuable because the quality of the floppy disk's surface is crucial for its reliability. For a company in a mature industry, the opportunity to move current product into a growth industry was highly attractive.

The market

By the end of 1986, the demand for floppy disks was 500 million in the United States, 100 million in Europe, and 50 million in Japan, with growth estimated at 40% per year, compounded. This meant that by 1993, the global market would be approaching 3 billion disks, of which about a third would be in the original equipment manufacturer (OEM) market, namely such big-volume purchasers of disks as IBM, Apple, and Microsoft, which use disks to distribute their software. OEM industry prices were expected to be about 180 yen per disk by 1993. Quality and reliability have always been important product characteristics for OEMs such as software houses because defective disks have a devastating impact on customers' perceptions of the company's overall quality.

The reverse income statement

Discovery-driven planning starts with the bottom line. For Kao, back when it began to consider its options, the question was whether the floppy disk venture had the potential to enhance the company's competitive position and financial performance significantly. If not, why should Kao incur the risk and uncertainty of a major strategic venture?

Here, we impose the first discipline, which is to plan the venture using a reverse income statement, which runs from the bottom line up. (See the exhibit, "First, start with a reverse income statement." The four exhibits referred to in the article are located in the sidebar, "How Kao Might Have Tackled Its New Venture.") Instead of starting with estimates of revenues and working down the income statement to derive profits, we start with *required profits*. We then work our way up the profit and loss to determine how much revenue it will take to deliver the level of profits we require and how much cost can be allowed. The underlying philosophy is to impose revenue and cost disciplines by baking profitability into the plan at the outset: Required profits equal necessary revenues minus allowable costs.

At Kao in 1988, management might have started with these figures: net sales, about 500 billion yen; income before taxes, about 40 billion yen; and return on sales (ROS), 7.5%. Given such figures, how big must the floppy disk opportunity be to justify Kao's attention? Every company will set its own hurdles. We believe that a strategic venture should have the potential to enhance total profits by at least 10%. Moreover, to compensate for the increased risk, it should deliver greater profitability than reinvesting in the existing businesses would. Again, for purposes of illustration, assume that Kao demands a risk premium of 33% greater profitability. Since Kao's return on sales is 7.5%, it will require 10%.

If we use the Kao data, we find that the required profit for the floppy disk venture would be 4 billion yen (10% × 40 billion). To deliver 4 billion yen in profit with a 10% return on sales implies a business with 40 billion yen in sales.

Assuming that, despite its superior quality, Kao will have to price competitively to gain share as a new entrant, it should set a target

How Kao Might Have Tackled Its New Venture: Discovery-Driven Planning in Action

THE GOAL HERE is to determine the value of success quickly. If the venture can't deliver significant returns, it may not be worth the risk.

First, start with a reverse income statement

Total figures

Required profits to add 10% to total profits = 4 billion yen
Necessary revenues to deliver 10% sales margin = 40 billion yen
Allowable costs to deliver 10% sales margin = 36 billion yen

Per unit figures

Required unit sales at 160 yen per unit = 250 million units
Necessary percentage of world market share of OEM unit sales = 25%
Allowable costs per unit for 10% sales margin = 144 yen

Second, lay out all the activities needed to run the venture

Pro forma operations specs

1. Sales

Required disk sales = 250 million disks
Average order size (Assumption 8) = 10,000 disks
Orders required (250 million/10,000) = 25,000

Number of calls to make a sale (Assumption 9) = 4
Sales calls required (4 x 25,000) = 100,000 per year

Calls per day per salesperson (Assumption 10) = 2
Annual salesperson days (100,000/2) = 50,000
Sales force for 250 days per year (Assumption 11)
50,000 salesperson days/250 = 200 people

Salary per salesperson = 10 million yen (Assumption 12)
Total sales-force salary cost (10 million yen x 200) = 2 billion yen

2. Manufacturing

Quality specification of disk surface: 50% fewer flaws than best competitor (Assumption 15)

Annual production capacity per line = 25 per minute x 1440 minutes per day x 348 days (Assumption 16) = 12.5 million disks

Production lines needed (250 million disks/12.5 million disks per line) = 20 lines

Production staffing (30 per line [Assumption 17] x 20 lines) = 600 workers

Salary per worker = 5 million yen (Assumption 18)
Total production salaries (600 x 5 million yen) = 3 billion yen

Materials costs per disk = 20 yen (Assumption 19)
Total materials cost (20 x 250 million disks) = 5 billion yen

Packaging per 10 disks = 40 yen (Assumption 20)
Total packaging costs (40 x 25 million packages) =1 billion yen

3. Shipping

Containers needed per order of 10,000 disks = 1 (Assumption 13)
Shipping cost per container = 100,000 yen (Assumption 14)
Total shipping costs (25,000 orders x 100,000 yen) = 2.5 billion yen

4. Equipment and depreciation

Fixed asset investment to sales = 1:1 (Assumption 5) = 40 billion yen
Equipment life = 3 years (Assumption 7)
Annual depreciation (40 billion yen/3 years) = 13.3 billion yen

---

Keeping a checklist is an important discipline to ensure that each assumption is flagged and tested as a venture unfolds.

Third, track all assumptions

Assumption	Measurement
1. Profit margin	10% of sales
2. Revenues	40 billion yen
3. Unit selling price	160 yen
4. 1993 world OEM market	1 billion disks
5. Fixed asset investment to sales	1:1
6. Effective production capacity per line	25 disks per minute
7. Effective life of equipment	3 years
8. Average OEM order size	10,000 disks
9. Sales calls per OEM order	4 calls per order
10. Sales calls per salesperson per day	2 calls per day
11. Selling days per year	250 days
12. Annual salesperson's salary	10 million yen
13. Containers required per order	1 container

(continued)

How Kao Might Have Tackled Its New Venture: Discovery-Driven Planning in Action (continued)

14. Shipping cost per container	100,000 yen
15. Quality level needed to get customers to switch: % fewer flaws per disk than top competitor	50%
16. Production days per year	348 days
17. Workers per production line per day (10 per line for 3 shifts)	30 per line
18. Annual manufacturing worker's salary	5 million yen
19. Materials costs per disk	20 yen
20. Packaging costs per 10 disks	40 yen
21. Allowable administration costs (See revised reverse income statement, below)	9.2 billion yen

Now, with better data, one can see if the entire business proposition hangs together.

Fourth, revise the reverse income statement

Required margin	10% return on sales
Required profit	4 billion yen
Necessary revenues	40 billion yen
Allowable costs	36 billion yen
Sales-force salaries	2.0 billion yen
Manufacturing salaries	3.0 billion yen
Disk materials	5.0 billion yen
Packaging	1.0 billion yen
Shipping	2.5 billion yen
Depreciation	13.3 billion yen
Allowable administration and overhead costs	9.2 billion yen (Assumption 21)
Per-unit figures	
Selling price	160 yen
Total costs	144 yen
Disk materials costs	20 yen

Finally, plan to test assumptions at milestones

Milestone event—namely, the completion of:	Assumptions to be tested
1. Initial data search and preliminary feasibility analysis	4: 1993 world OEM market 8: Average OEM order size 9: Sales calls per OEM order

	10: Sales calls per salesperson per day 11: Salespeople needed for 250 selling days per year 12: Annual salesperson's salary 13: Containers required per order 14: Shipping cost per container 16: Production days per year 18: Annual manufacturing worker's salary
2. Prototype batches produced	15: Quality to get customers to switch 19: Materials costs per disk
3. Technical testing by customers	3: Unit selling price 15: Quality to get customers to switch
4. Subcontracted production	19: Materials costs per disk
5. Sales of subcontracted production	1: Profit margin 2: Revenues 3: Unit selling price 8: Average OEM order size 9: Sales calls per OEM order 10: Sales calls per salesperson per day 12: Annual salesperson's salary 15: Quality to get customers to switch
6. Purchase of an existing plant	5: Fixed asset investment to sales 7: Effective life of equipment
7. Pilot production at purchased plant	6: Effective production capacity per line 16: Production days per year 17: Workers per production line per day 18: Annual manufacturing worker's salary 19: Materials costs per disk 20: Packaging costs per 10 disks
8. Competitor reaction	1: Profit margin 2: Revenues 3: Unit selling price
9. Product redesign	19: Materials costs per disk 20: Packaging costs per 10 disks
10. Major repricing analysis	1: Profit margin 2: Revenues 3: Unit selling price 4: 1993 world OEM market
11. Plant redesign	5: Fixed asset investment to sales 6: Effective production capacity per line 19: Materials costs per disk

price of 160 yen per disk. That translates into unit sales of 250 million disks (40 billion yen in sales divided by 160 yen per disk). By imposing these simple performance measures at the start (1988), we quickly establish both the scale and scope of the venture: Kao would need to capture 25% of the total world OEM market (25% of 1 billion disks) by 1993. Given what is known about the size of the market, Kao clearly must be prepared to compete globally from the outset, making major commitments not only to manufacturing but also to selling.

Continuing up the profit and loss, we next calculate allowable costs: If Kao is to capture 10% margin on a price of 160 yen per disk, the total cost to manufacture, sell, and distribute the disks worldwide cannot exceed 144 yen per disk. The reverse income statement makes clear immediately that the challenge for the floppy disk venture will be to keep a lid on expenses.

The pro forma operations specs and the assumptions checklist

The second discipline in the process is to construct pro forma operations specs laying out the activities required to produce, sell, service, and deliver the product or service to the customer. Together, those activities comprise the venture's allowable costs. At first, the operations specs can be modeled on a simple spreadsheet without investing in more than a few telephone calls or on-line searches to get basic data. If an idea holds together, it is possible to identify and test underlying assumptions, constantly fleshing out and correcting the model in light of new information. When a company uses this cumulative approach, major flaws in the business concept soon become obvious, and poor concepts can be abandoned long before significant investments are made.

We believe it is essential to use industry standards for building a realistic picture of what the business has to look like to be competitive. Every industry has its own pressures—which determine normal rates of return in that industry—as well as standard performance measures such as asset-to-sales ratios, industry profit margins, plant utilization, and so on. In a globally competitive environment, no sane manager should expect to escape the competitive discipline that is captured and measured in industry standards. These standards are readily available from investment analysts and business information services. In countries with information sources that are less well developed than those in the United States, key industry parameters are still used by investment bankers and, more specifically, by those commercial bankers who specialize in loans to the particular industry. For those getting into a new industry, the best approach is to adapt standards from similar industries.

Note that we do not begin with an elaborate analysis of product or service attributes or an in-depth market study. That comes later. Initially, we are simply trying to capture the venture's embedded assumptions. The basic discipline is to spell out clearly and realistically where the venture will have to match existing industry standards and in what one or two places managers expect to excel and how they expect to do so.

Kao's managers in 1988 might have considered performance standards for the floppy disk industry. Because there would be no reason to believe that Kao could use standard production equipment any better than established competitors could, it would want to plan to match industry performance on measures relating to equipment use. Kao would ascertain, for example, that the effective production capacity per line was 25 disks per minute in the industry; and the effective life of production equipment was three years. Kao's advantage was in surface chemistry and surface physics, which could improve quality and reduce the cost of materials, thus improving margins. When Kao planned its materials cost, it would want to turn that advantage into a specific challenge for manufacturing: Beat the industry standard for materials cost by 25%. The formal framing of operational challenges is an important step in discovery-driven planning. In our experience, people who are good in design and operations can be galvanized by clearly articulated challenges. That was the case at Canon, for example, when Keizo Yamaji challenged the engineers to develop a personal copier that required minimal service and cost less than $1,000, and the Canon engineers rose to the occasion.

A company can test the initial assumptions against experience with similar situations, the advice of experts in the industry, or published information sources. The point is not to demand the highest degree of accuracy but to build a reasonable model of the economics and logistics of the venture and to assess the order of magnitude of the challenges. Later, the company can analyze where the plan is most sensitive to wrong assumptions and do more formal checks. Consultants to the industry—bankers, suppliers, potential customers, and distributors—often can provide low-cost and surprisingly accurate information.

The company must build a picture of the activities that are needed to carry out the business and the costs. Hence in the pro forma operations specs, we ask how many orders are needed to deliver 250 million units in sales; then how many sales calls it will take to secure those orders; then how many salespeople it will take to make the sales calls, given the fact that they are selling to a global OEM market; then how much it will cost in sales-force compensation. (See the exhibit "Second, lay out all the activities needed to run the venture" located on the sidebar "How Kao Might Have Tackled Its New Venture.") Each assumption can be checked, at first somewhat roughly and then with increasing precision. Readers might disagree with our first-cut estimates. That is fine—so might Kao Corporation. Reasonable disagreement triggers discussion and, perhaps, adjustments to the spreadsheet. The evolving document is doing its job if it becomes the catalyst for such discussion.

The third discipline of discovery-driven planning is to compile an assumption checklist to ensure that each assumption is flagged, discussed, and checked as the venture unfolds. (See the exhibit "Third, track all assumptions.")

The entire process is looped back into a revised reverse income statement, in which one can see if the entire business proposition hangs together. (See the exhibit, "Fourth, revise the reverse income statement.") If it doesn't, the process must be repeated until the performance requirements and industry standards can be met; otherwise, the venture should be scrapped.

Milestone planning

Conventional planning approaches tend to focus managers on meeting plan, usually an impossible goal for a venture rife with assumptions. It is also counterproductive—insistence on meeting plan actually prevents learning. Managers can formally plan to learn by using milestone events to test assumptions.

Milestone planning is by now a familiar technique for monitoring the progress of new ventures. The basic idea, as described by Zenas Block and Ian C. MacMillan in the book *Corporate Venturing* (Harvard Business School Press, 1993), is to postpone major commitments of resources until the evidence from the previous milestone event signals that the risk of taking the next step is justified. What we are proposing here is an expanded use of the tool to support the discipline of transforming assumptions into knowledge.

Going back to what Kao might have been thinking in 1988, recall that the floppy disk venture would require a 40-billion-yen investment in fixed assets alone. Before investing such a large sum, Kao would certainly have wanted to find ways to test the most critical assumptions underlying the three major challenges of the venture:

- capturing 25% global market share with a 20-yen-per-disk discount and superior quality;
- maintaining at least the same asset productivity as the average competitor and producing a floppy disk at 90% of the estimated total costs of existing competitors; and
- using superior raw materials and applied surface technology to produce superior-quality disks for 20 yen per unit instead of the industry standard of 27 yen per unit.

For serious challenges like those, it may be worth spending resources to create specific milestone events to test the assumptions before launching a 40-billion-yen venture. For instance, Kao might subcontract prototype production so that sophisticated OEM customers could conduct technical tests on the proposed disk. If the prototypes survive the tests, then, rather than rest on the assumption that it can capture significant business at the target price, Kao might subcontract production of a large batch of floppy disks for resale to customers. It could thus test the appetite of the OEM market for price discounting from a newcomer.

Similarly, for testing its ability to cope with the second and third challenges once the Kao prototype has been developed, it might be worthwhile to buy out a small existing floppy disk manufacturer and apply the technology in an established plant rather than try to start up a greenfield operation. Once Kao can demonstrate its ability to produce disks at the required quality and cost in the small plant, it can move ahead with its own full-scale plants.

Deliberate assumption-testing milestones are depicted in the exhibit "Finally, Plan to Test Assumptions at Milestones," which also shows some of the other typical milestones that occur in most major ventures. The assumptions that should be tested at each milestone are listed with appropriate numbers from the assumption checklist.

In practice, it is wise to designate a *keeper of the assumptions*—someone whose formal task is to ensure that assumptions are checked and updated as each milestone is reached and that the revised assumptions are incorporated into successive iterations of the four discovery-driven planning documents. Without a specific person dedicated to following up, it is highly unlikely that individuals, up to their armpits in project pressures, will be able to coordinate the updating independently.

Discovery-driven planning is a powerful tool for any significant strategic undertaking that is fraught with uncertainty—new-product or market ventures, technology development, joint ventures, strategic alliances, even major systems redevelopment. Unlike platform-based planning, in which much is known, discovery-driven planning forces managers to articulate what they don't know, and it forces a discipline for learning. As a planning tool, it thus raises the visibility of the make-or-break uncertainties common to new ventures and helps managers address them at the lowest possible cost.

Note

The authors wish to thank Shiuchi Matsuda of Waseda University's Entrepreneurial Research Unit for providing case material on Kao's floppy disk venture.

Originally published in July 1995. Reprint 95406

The Discipline of Innovation

by Peter F. Drucker

DESPITE MUCH DISCUSSION THESE days of the "entrepreneurial personality," few of the entrepreneurs with whom I have worked during the past 30 years had such personalities. But I have known many people—salespeople, surgeons, journalists, scholars, even musicians—who did have them without being the least bit entrepreneurial. What all the successful entrepreneurs I have met have in common is not a certain kind of personality but a commitment to the systematic practice of innovation.

Innovation is the specific function of entrepreneurship, whether in an existing business, a public service institution, or a new venture started by a lone individual in the family kitchen. It is the means by which the entrepreneur either creates new wealth-producing resources or endows existing resources with enhanced potential for creating wealth.

Today, much confusion exists about the proper definition of entrepreneurship. Some observers use the term to refer to all small businesses; others, to all new businesses. In practice, however, a great many well-established businesses engage in highly successful entrepreneurship. The term, then, refers not to an enterprise's size or age but to a certain kind of activity. At the heart of that activity is innovation: the effort to create purposeful, focused change in an enterprise's economic or social potential.

Sources of Innovation

There are, of course, innovations that spring from a flash of genius. Most innovations, however, especially the successful ones, result from a conscious, purposeful search for innovation opportunities, which are found only in a few situations. Four such areas of opportunity exist within a company or industry: unexpected occurrences, incongruities, process needs, and industry and market changes.

Three additional sources of opportunity exist outside a company in its social and intellectual environment: demographic changes, changes in perception, and new knowledge.

True, these sources overlap, different as they may be in the nature of their risk, difficulty, and complexity, and the potential for innovation may well lie in more than one area at a time. But together, they account for the great majority of all innovation opportunities.

1. Unexpected occurrences

Consider, first, the easiest and simplest source of innovation opportunity: the unexpected. In the early 1930s, IBM developed the first modern accounting machine, which was designed for banks. But banks in 1933 did not buy new equipment. What saved the company—according to a story that Thomas Watson, Sr., the company's founder and long-term CEO, often told—was its exploitation of an unexpected success: The New York Public Library wanted to buy a machine. Unlike the banks, libraries in those early New Deal days had money, and Watson sold more than a hundred of his otherwise unsalable machines to libraries.

Fifteen years later, when everyone believed that computers were designed for advanced scientific work, business unexpectedly showed an interest in a machine that could do payroll. Univac, which had the most advanced machine, spurned business applications. But IBM immediately realized it faced a possible unexpected success, redesigned what was basically Univac's machine for such mundane applications as payroll, and within five years became a leader in the computer industry, a position it has maintained to this day.

Idea in Brief

In the hypercompetition for breakthrough solutions, managers worry too much about characteristics and personality—"Am I smart enough? Do I have the right temperament?"—and not enough about process. A commitment to the systematic search for imaginative and useful ideas is what successful entrepreneurs share—not some special genius or trait. What's more, entrepreneurship can occur in a business of any size or age because, at heart, it has to do with a certain kind of activity: innovation, the disciplined effort to improve a business's potential.

Most innovations result from a conscious, purposeful search for opportunities—within the company and the industry as well as the larger social and intellectual environment. A successful innovation may come from pulling together different strands of knowledge, recognizing an underlying theme in public perception, or extracting new insights from failure.

The key is to know where to look.

The unexpected failure may be an equally important source of innovation opportunities. Everyone knows about the Ford Edsel as the biggest new-car failure in automotive history. What very few people seem to know, however, is that the Edsel's failure was the foundation for much of the company's later success. Ford planned the Edsel, the most carefully designed car to that point in American automotive history, to give the company a full product line with which to compete with General Motors. When it bombed, despite all the planning, market research, and design that had gone into it, Ford realized that something was happening in the automobile market that ran counter to the basic assumptions on which GM and everyone else had been designing and marketing cars. No longer was the market segmented primarily by income groups; the new principle of segmentation was what we now call "lifestyles." Ford's response was the Mustang, a car that gave the company a distinct personality and reestablished it as an industry leader.

Unexpected successes and failures are such productive sources of innovation opportunities because most businesses dismiss them,

Idea in Practice

Successful entrepreneurs don't wait for innovative ideas to strike like a lightning bolt. They go out looking for innovation opportunities in seven key areas:

1. **Unexpected occurrences.** These often include failures. Few people know, for instance, that the failure of the Edsel led Ford to realize that the auto market was now segmented by lifestyle instead of by income group. Ford's response was the Mustang, and an auto legend was born.
2. **Incongruities.** By the 1960s, cataract removal had become high-tech, except for cutting a ligament, an "old-fashioned" step that was uncomfortable for eye surgeons. Alcon Laboratories responded by modifying an enzyme that dissolved the ligament. Surgeons immediately accepted the new product, giving Alcon a monopoly.
3. **Process needs.** Two process innovations developed around 1890 created "the media" as we know it today: linotype made it possible to produce newspapers quickly, and advertising made it possible to distribute news practically free of charge.
4. **Industry and market changes.** The brokerage firm Donaldson, Lufkin & Jenrette achieved fabulous success because its founders recognized that the emerging market for institutional investors would one day predominate in the industry.

disregard them, and even resent them. The German scientist who around 1905 synthesized novocaine, the first nonaddictive narcotic, had intended it to be used in major surgical procedures like amputation. Surgeons, however, preferred total anesthesia for such procedures; they still do. Instead, novocaine found a ready appeal among dentists. Its inventor spent the remaining years of his life traveling from dental school to dental school making speeches that forbade dentists from "misusing" his noble invention in applications for which he had not intended it.

This is a caricature, to be sure, but it illustrates the attitude managers often take to the unexpected: "It should not have happened." Corporate reporting systems further ingrain this reaction, for they draw attention away from unanticipated possibilities. The typical

5. **Demographic changes.** Why are the Japanese ahead in robotics? Around 1970, everyone knew that there was both a baby bust and an education explosion, such that the number of blue-collar manufacturing workers would decline. Everyone knew—but only the Japanese took action.

6. **Changes in perception.** Such changes don't alter the facts, but can dramatically change their meaning. Americans' health has never been better—yet we're obsessed with preventing disease and staying fit. Innovators who understand our *perception* of health have launched magazines, introduced health foods, and started exercise classes.

7. **New knowledge.** Knowledge-based innovations require long lead times and the convergence of different kinds of knowledge. The computer required knowledge that was available by 1918, but the first operational digital computer did not appear until 1946.

Purposeful innovation begins with looking, asking, and listening. Talent and expert knowledge help, but don't be deluded by all the stories about flashes of insight. The key task is to work out analytically what the innovation has to be in order to satisfy a particular opportunity.

monthly or quarterly report has on its first page a list of problems—that is, the areas where results fall short of expectations. Such information is needed, of course, to help prevent deterioration of performance. But it also suppresses the recognition of new opportunities. The first acknowledgment of a possible opportunity usually applies to an area in which a company does better than budgeted. Thus genuinely entrepreneurial businesses have two "first pages"—a problem page and an opportunity page—and managers spend equal time on both.

2. Incongruities

Alcon Laboratories was one of the success stories of the 1960s because Bill Conner, the company's cofounder, exploited an incongruity in medical technology. The cataract operation is the world's third or fourth most common surgical procedure. During the past 300 years, doctors systematized it to the point that the only "old-fashioned" step left was the cutting of a ligament. Eye surgeons had learned to cut the ligament with complete success, but it was so different a procedure from the rest of the operation, and so incompatible with it, that they often dreaded it. It was incongruous.

Doctors had known for 50 years about an enzyme that could dissolve the ligament without cutting. All Conner did was to add a preservative to this enzyme that gave it a few months' shelf life. Eye surgeons immediately accepted the new compound, and Alcon found itself with a worldwide monopoly. Fifteen years later, Nestlé bought the company for a fancy price.

Such an incongruity within the logic or rhythm of a process is only one possibility out of which innovation opportunities may arise. Another source is incongruity between economic realities. For instance, whenever an industry has a steadily growing market but falling profit margins—as, say, in the steel industries of developed countries between 1950 and 1970—an incongruity exists. The innovative response: minimills.

An incongruity between expectations and results can also open up possibilities for innovation. For 50 years after the turn of the century, shipbuilders and shipping companies worked hard both to make ships faster and to lower their fuel consumption. Even so, the more successful they were in boosting speed and trimming their fuel needs, the worse the economics of ocean freighters became. By 1950 or so, the ocean freighter was dying, if not already dead.

All that was wrong, however, was an incongruity between the industry's assumptions and its realities. The real costs did not come from doing work (that is, being at sea) but from *not* doing work (that is, sitting idle in port). Once managers understood where costs truly lay, the innovations were obvious: the roll-on and roll-off ship and the container ship. These solutions, which involved old technology, simply applied to the ocean freighter what railroads and truckers had been using for 30 years. A shift in viewpoint, not in technology, totally changed the economics of ocean shipping and turned it into one of the major growth industries of the last 20 to 30 years.

3. Process needs

Anyone who has ever driven in Japan knows that the country has no modern highway system. Its roads still follow the paths laid down for—or by—oxcarts in the tenth century. What makes the system work for automobiles and trucks is an adaptation of the reflector used on American highways since the early 1930s. The reflector lets each car see which other cars are approaching from any one of a half-dozen directions. This minor invention, which enables traffic to move smoothly and with a minimum of accidents, exploited a process need.

What we now call the media had its origin in two innovations developed around 1890 in response to process needs. One was Ottmar Mergenthaler's Linotype, which made it possible to produce newspapers quickly and in large volume. The other was a social innovation, modern advertising, invented by the first true newspaper publishers, Adolph Ochs of the *New York Times,* Joseph Pulitzer of the *New York World,* and William Randolph Hearst. Advertising made it possible for them to distribute news practically free of charge, with the profit coming from marketing.

4. Industry and market changes

Managers may believe that industry structures are ordained by the good Lord, but these structures can—and often do—change overnight. Such change creates tremendous opportunity for innovation.

One of American business's great success stories in recent decades is the brokerage firm of Donaldson, Lufkin & Jenrette, recently acquired by the Equitable Life Assurance Society. DL&J was founded in 1960 by three young men, all graduates of the Harvard Business School, who realized that the structure of the financial industry was changing as institutional investors became dominant. These young men had practically no capital and no connections. Still, within a few years, their firm had become a leader in the move to negotiated commissions and one of Wall Street's stellar performers. It was the first to be incorporated and go public.

In a similar fashion, changes in industry structure have created massive innovation opportunities for American health care providers. During the past ten or 15 years, independent surgical and psychiatric clinics, emergency centers, and HMOs have opened throughout the country. Comparable opportunities in telecommunications followed industry upheavals—in transmission (with the emergence of MCI and Sprint in long-distance service) and in equipment (with the emergence of such companies as Rolm in the manufacturing of private branch exchanges).

When an industry grows quickly—the critical figure seems to be in the neighborhood of 40% growth in ten years or less—its structure changes. Established companies, concentrating on defending what they already have, tend not to counterattack when a newcomer challenges them. Indeed, when market or industry structures change, traditional industry leaders again and again neglect the fastest growing market segments. New opportunities rarely fit the way the industry has always approached the market, defined it, or organized to serve it. Innovators therefore have a good chance of being left alone for a long time.

5. Demographic changes

Of the outside sources of innovation opportunities, demographics are the most reliable. Demographic events have known lead times; for instance, every person who will be in the American labor force by the year 2000 has already been born. Yet because policy makers often neglect demographics, those who watch them and exploit them can reap great rewards.

The Japanese are ahead in robotics because they paid attention to demographics. Everyone in the developed countries around 1970 or so knew that there was both a baby bust and an education explosion going on; about half or more of the young people were staying in school beyond high school. Consequently, the number of people available for traditional blue-collar work in manufacturing was bound to decrease and become inadequate by 1990. Everyone knew this, but only the Japanese acted on it, and they now have a ten-year lead in robotics.

Much the same is true of Club Mediterranee's success in the travel and resort business. By 1970, thoughtful observers could have seen the emergence of large numbers of affluent and educated young adults in Europe and the United States. Not comfortable with the kind of vacations their working-class parents had enjoyed—the summer weeks at Brighton or Atlantic City—these young people were ideal customers for a new and exotic version of the "hangout" of their teen years.

Managers have known for a long time that demographics matter, but they have always believed that population statistics change slowly. In this century, however, they don't. Indeed, the innovation opportunities made possible by changes in the numbers of people—and in their age distribution, education, occupations, and geographic location—are among the most rewarding and least risky of entrepreneurial pursuits.

6. Changes in perception

"The glass is half full" and "The glass is half empty" are descriptions of the same phenomenon but have vastly different meanings. Changing a manager's perception of a glass from half full to half empty opens up big innovation opportunities.

All factual evidence indicates, for instance, that in the last 20 years, Americans' health has improved with unprecedented speed—whether measured by mortality rates for the newborn, survival rates for the very old, the incidence of cancers (other than lung cancer), cancer cure rates, or other factors. Even so, collective hypochondria grips the nation. Never before has there been so much concern with or fear about health. Suddenly, everything seems to cause cancer or degenerative heart disease or premature loss of memory. The glass is clearly half empty.

Rather than rejoicing in great improvements in health, Americans seem to be emphasizing how far away they still are from immortality. This view of things has created many opportunities for innovations: markets for new health care magazines, for exercise classes and jogging equipment, and for all kinds of health foods. The fastest growing new U.S. business in 1983 was a company that makes indoor exercise equipment.

A change in perception does not alter facts. It changes their meaning, though—and very quickly. It took less than two years for the computer to change from being perceived as a threat and as something only big businesses would use to something one buys for doing income tax. Economics do not necessarily dictate such a change; in fact, they may be irrelevant. What determines whether people see a glass as half full or half empty is mood rather than fact, and a change in mood often defies quantification. But it is not exotic. It is concrete. It can be defined. It can be tested. And it can be exploited for innovation opportunity.

7. New knowledge

Among history-making innovations, those that are based on new knowledge—whether scientific, technical, or social—rank high. They are the superstars of entrepreneurship; they get the publicity and the money. They are what people usually mean when they talk of innovation, although not all innovations based on knowledge are important.

Knowledge-based innovations differ from all others in the time they take, in their casualty rates, and in their predictability, as well as in the challenges they pose to entrepreneurs. Like most superstars, they can be temperamental, capricious, and hard to direct. They have, for instance, the longest lead time of all innovations. There is a protracted span between the emergence of new knowledge and its distillation into usable technology. Then there is another long period before this new technology appears in the marketplace in products, processes, or services. Overall, the lead time involved is something like 50 years, a figure that has not shortened appreciably throughout history.

To become effective, innovation of this sort usually demands not one kind of knowledge but many. Consider one of the most potent knowledge-based innovations: modern banking. The theory of the entrepreneurial bank—that is, of the purposeful use of capital to generate economic development—was formulated by the Comte de Saint-Simon during the era of Napoleon. Despite Saint-Simon's extraordinary prominence, it was not until 30 years after his death in

1825 that two of his disciples, the brothers Jacob and Isaac Pereire, established the first entrepreneurial bank, the Credit Mobilier, and ushered in what we now call finance capitalism.

The Pereires, however, did not know modern commercial banking, which developed at about the same time across the channel in England. The Credit Mobilier failed ignominiously. A few years later, two young men—one an American, J.P. Morgan, and one a German, Georg Siemens—put together the French theory of entrepreneurial banking and the English theory of commercial banking to create the first successful modern banks: J.P. Morgan & Company in New York, and the Deutsche Bank in Berlin. Ten years later, a young Japanese, Shibusawa Eiichi, adapted Siemens's concept to his country and thereby laid the foundation of Japan's modern economy. This is how knowledge-based innovation always works.

The computer, to cite another example, required no fewer than six separate strands of knowledge:

- binary arithmetic;
- Charles Babbage's conception of a calculating machine, in the first half of the nineteenth century;
- the punch card, invented by Herman Hollerith for the U.S. census of 1890;
- the audion tube, an electronic switch invented in 1906;
- symbolic logic, which was developed between 1910 and 1913 by Bertrand Russell and Alfred North Whitehead;
- and concepts of programming and feedback that came out of abortive attempts during World War I to develop effective anti-aircraft guns.

Although all the necessary knowledge was available by 1918, the first operational digital computer did not appear until 1946.

Long lead times and the need for convergence among different kinds of knowledge explain the peculiar rhythm of knowledge-based innovation, its attractions, and its dangers. During a long gestation period, there is a lot of talk and little action. Then, when all the elements suddenly converge, there is tremendous excitement and activity and an enormous amount of speculation. Between 1880 and 1890, for example, almost 1,000 electric-apparatus companies were founded in developed countries. Then, as always, there was a crash and a shakeout. By 1914, only 25 were still alive. In the early 1920s, 300 to 500 automobile companies existed in the United States; by 1960, only four of them remained.

It may be difficult, but knowledge-based innovation can be managed. Success requires careful analysis of the various kinds of knowledge needed to make an innovation possible. Both J.P. Morgan and Georg Siemens did this when they established their banking ventures. The Wright brothers did this when they developed the first operational airplane.

Careful analysis of the needs—and, above all, the capabilities—of the intended user is also essential. It may seem paradoxical, but knowledge-based innovation is more market dependent than any other kind of innovation. De Havilland, a British company, designed and built the first passenger jet, but it did not analyze what the market needed and therefore did not identify two key factors. One was configuration—that is, the right size with the right payload for the routes on which a jet would give an airline the greatest advantage. The other was equally mundane: How could the airlines finance the purchase of such an expensive plane? Because de Havilland failed to do an adequate user analysis, two American companies, Boeing and Douglas, took over the commercial jet-aircraft industry.

Principles of Innovation

Purposeful, systematic innovation begins with the analysis of the sources of new opportunities. Depending on the context, sources will have different importance at different times. Demographics, for instance, may be of little concern to innovators of fundamental industrial processes like steelmaking, although the Linotype machine became successful primarily because there were not enough skilled typesetters available to satisfy a mass market. By the same token, new knowledge may be of little relevance to someone innovating a social instrument to satisfy a need that changing demographics or tax laws have created. But whatever the situation, innovators must analyze all opportunity sources.

Because innovation is both conceptual and perceptual, would-be innovators must also go out and look, ask, and listen. Successful innovators use both the right and left sides of their brains. They work out analytically what the innovation has to be to satisfy an opportunity. Then they go out and look at potential users to study their expectations, their values, and their needs.

To be effective, an innovation has to be simple, and it has to be focused. It should do only one thing; otherwise it confuses people. Indeed, the greatest praise an innovation can receive is for people to say, "This is obvious! Why didn't I think of it? It's so simple!" Even the innovation that creates new users and new markets should be directed toward a specific, clear, and carefully designed application.

Effective innovations start small. They are not grandiose. It may be to enable a moving vehicle to draw electric power while it runs along rails, the innovation that made possible the electric streetcar. Or it may be the elementary idea of putting the same number of matches into a matchbox (it used to be 50). This simple notion made possible the automatic filling of matchboxes and gave the Swedes a world monopoly on matches for half a century. By contrast, grandiose ideas for things that will "revolutionize an industry" are unlikely to work.

In fact, no one can foretell whether a given innovation will end up a big business or a modest achievement. But even if the results are modest, the successful innovation aims from the beginning to become the standard setter, to determine the direction of a new technology or a new industry, to create the business that is—and remains—ahead of the pack. If an innovation does not aim at leadership from the beginning, it is unlikely to be innovative enough.

Above all, innovation is work rather than genius. It requires knowledge. It often requires ingenuity. And it requires focus. There are clearly people who are more talented innovators than others, but their talents lie in well-defined areas. Indeed, innovators rarely work in more than one area. For all his systematic innovative accomplishments, Thomas Edison worked only in the electrical field. An innovator in financial areas, Citibank for example, is not likely to embark on innovations in health care.

In innovation, as in any other endeavor, there is talent, there is ingenuity, and there is knowledge. But when all is said and done, what innovation requires is hard, focused, purposeful work. If diligence, persistence, and commitment are lacking, talent, ingenuity, and knowledge are of no avail.

There is, of course, far more to entrepreneurship than systematic innovation—distinct entrepreneurial strategies, for example, and the principles of entrepreneurial management, which are needed equally in the established enterprise, the public service organization, and the new venture. But the very foundation of entrepreneurship is the practice of systematic innovation.

Originally published in May 1985. Reprint 3480

Innovation Killers

How Financial Tools Destroy Your Capacity to Do New Things. *by Clayton M. Christensen, Stephen P. Kaufman, and Willy C. Shih*

FOR YEARS WE'VE BEEN puzzling about why so many smart, hardworking managers in well-run companies find it impossible to innovate successfully. Our investigations have uncovered a number of culprits, which we've discussed in earlier books and articles. These include paying too much attention to the company's most profitable customers (thereby leaving less-demanding customers at risk) and creating new products that don't help customers do the jobs they want to do. Now we'd like to name the misguided application of three financial-analysis tools as an accomplice in the conspiracy against successful innovation. We allege crimes against these suspects:

- The use of discounted cash flow (DCF) and net present value (NPV) to evaluate investment opportunities causes managers to underestimate the real returns and benefits of proceeding with investments in innovation.
- The way that fixed and sunk costs are considered when evaluating future investments confers an unfair advantage on challengers and shackles incumbent firms that attempt to respond to an attack.
- The emphasis on earnings per share as the primary driver of share price and hence of shareholder value creation, to the

exclusion of almost everything else, diverts resources away from investments whose payoff lies beyond the immediate horizon.

These are not bad tools and concepts, we hasten to add. But the way they are commonly wielded in evaluating investments creates a systematic bias against innovation. We will recommend alternative methods that, in our experience, can help managers innovate with a much more astute eye for future value. Our primary aim, though, is simply to bring these concerns to light in the hope that others with deeper expertise may be inspired to examine and resolve them.

Misapplying Discounted Cash Flow and Net Present Value

The first of the misleading and misapplied tools of financial analysis is the method of discounting cash flow to calculate the net present value of an initiative. Discounting a future stream of cash flows into a "present value" assumes that a rational investor would be indifferent to having a dollar today or to receiving some years from now a dollar plus the interest or return that could be earned by investing that dollar for those years. With that as an operating principle, it makes perfect sense to assess investments by dividing the money to be received in future years by $(1 + r)^n$, where r is the discount rate—the annual return from investing that money—and n is the number of years during which the investment could be earning that return.

While the mathematics of discounting is logically impeccable, analysts commonly commit two errors that create an anti-innovation bias. The first error is to assume that the base case of not investing in the innovation—the do-nothing scenario against which cash flows from the innovation are compared—is that the present health of the company will persist indefinitely into the future if the investment is not made. As shown in the exhibit "The DCF trap," the mathematics considers the investment in isolation and compares the present value of the innovation's cash stream less project costs with the cash stream in the absence of the investment, which is assumed to be unchanging.

Idea in Brief

Most companies aren't half as innovative as their senior executives want them to be (or as their marketing claims suggest they are). What's stifling innovation? There are plenty of usual suspects, but the authors finger three financial tools as key accomplices. Discounted cash flow and net present value, as commonly used, underestimate the real returns and benefits of proceeding with an investment. Most executives compare the cash flows from innovation against the default scenario of doing nothing, assuming—incorrectly—that the present health of the company will persist indefinitely if the investment is not made. In most situations, however, competitors' sustaining and disruptive investments over time result in deterioration of financial performance. Fixed- and sunk-cost conventional wisdom confers an unfair advantage on challengers and shackles incumbent firms that attempt to respond to an attack. Executives in established companies, bemoaning the expense of building new brands and developing new sales and distribution channels, seek instead to leverage their existing brands and structures. Entrants, in contrast, simply create new ones. The problem for the incumbent isn't that the challenger can spend more; it's that the challenger is spared the dilemma of having to choose between full-cost and marginal-cost options. The emphasis on short-term earnings per share as the primary driver of share price, and hence shareholder value creation, acts to restrict investments in innovative long-term growth opportunities. These are not bad tools and concepts in and of themselves, but the way they are used to evaluate investments creates a systematic bias against successful innovation. The authors recommend alternative methods that can help managers innovate with a much more astute eye for future value.

In most situations, however, competitors' sustaining and disruptive investments over time result in price and margin pressure, technology changes, market share losses, sales volume decreases, and a declining stock price. As Eileen Rudden at Boston Consulting Group pointed out, the most likely stream of cash for the company in the do-nothing scenario is not a continuation of the status quo. It is a nonlinear decline in performance.

It's tempting but wrong to assess the value of a proposed investment by measuring whether it will make us better off than we are

The DCF trap

Most executives compare the cash flows from innovation against the default scenario of doing nothing, assuming—incorrectly—that the present health of the company will persist indefinitely if the investment is not made. For a better assessment of the innovation's value, the comparison should be between its projected discounted cash flow and the more likely scenario of a decline in performance in the absence of innovation investment.

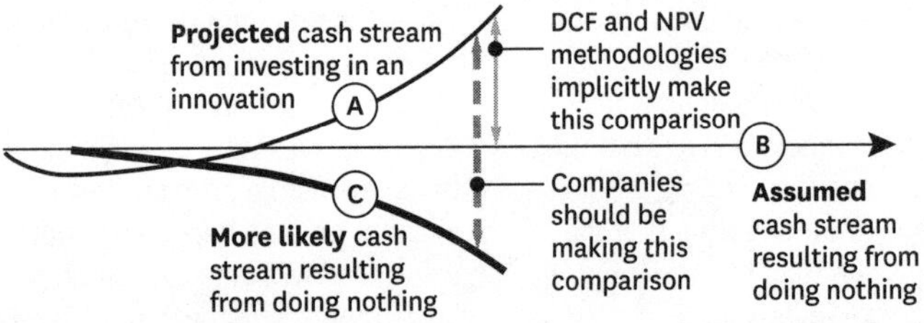

now. It's wrong because, if things are deteriorating on their own, we might be worse off than we are now after we make the proposed investment but better off than we would have been without it. Philip Bobbitt calls this logic Parmenides' Fallacy, after the ancient Greek logician who claimed to have proved that conditions in the real world must necessarily be unchanging. Analysts who attempt to distill the value of an innovation into one simple number that they can compare with other simple numbers are generally trapped by Parmenides' Fallacy.

It's hard to accurately forecast the stream of cash from an investment in innovation. It is even more difficult to forecast the extent to which a firm's financial performance may deteriorate in the absence of the investment. But this analysis must be done. Remember the response that good economists are taught to offer to the question "How are you?" It is "Relative to what?" This is a crucial question. Answering it entails assessing the projected value of the innovation against a range of scenarios, the most realistic of which is often a deteriorating competitive and financial future.

The second set of problems with discounted cash flow calculations relates to errors of estimation. Future cash flows, especially those generated by disruptive investments, are difficult to predict. Numbers for the "out years" can be a complete shot in the dark. To cope with what cannot be known, analysts often project a year-by-year stream of numbers for three to five years and then "punt" by calculating a terminal value to account for everything thereafter. The logic, of course, is that the year-to-year estimates for distant years are so imprecise as to be no more accurate than a terminal value. To calculate a terminal value, analysts divide the cash to be generated in the last year for which they've done a specific estimate by $(r-g)$, the discount rate minus the projected growth rate in cash flows from that time on. They then discount that single number back to the present. In our experience, assumed terminal values often account for more than half of a project's total NPV.

Terminal value numbers, based as they are on estimates for preceding years, tend to amplify errors contained in early-year assumptions. More worrisome still, terminal value doesn't allow for the scenario testing that we described above—contrasting the result of this investment with the deterioration in performance that is the most likely result of doing nothing. And yet, because of market inertia, competitors' development cycles, and the typical pace of disruption, it is often in the fifth year or beyond—the point at which terminal value factors in—that the decline of the enterprise in the do-nothing scenario begins to accelerate.

Arguably, a root cause of companies' persistent underinvestment in the innovations required to sustain long-term success is the indiscriminate and oversimplified use of NPV as an analytical tool. Still, we understand the desire to quantify streams of cash that defy quantification and then to distill those streams into a single number that can be compared with other single numbers: It is an attempt to translate cacophonous articulations of the future into a language—numbers—that everyone can read and compare. We hope to show that numbers are not the only language into which the value of future investments can be translated—and that there are, in fact, other, better languages that all members of a management team can understand.

Using Fixed and Sunk Costs Unwisely

The second widely misapplied paradigm of financial decision making relates to fixed and sunk costs. When evaluating a future course of action, the argument goes, managers should consider only the future or marginal cash outlays (either capital or expense) that are required for an innovation investment, subtract those outlays from the marginal cash that is likely to flow in, and discount the resulting net flow to the present. As with the paradigm of DCF and NPV, there is nothing wrong with the mathematics of this principle—as long as the capabilities required for yesterday's success are adequate for tomorrow's as well. When new capabilities are required for future success, however, this margining on fixed and sunk costs biases managers toward leveraging assets and capabilities that are likely to become obsolete.

For the purposes of this discussion we'll define fixed costs as those whose level is independent of the level of output. Typical fixed costs include general and administrative costs: salaries and benefits, insurance, taxes, and so on. (Variable costs include things like raw materials, commissions, and pay to temporary workers.) Sunk costs are those portions of fixed costs that are irrevocably committed, typically including investments in buildings and capital equipment and R&D costs.

An example from the steel industry illustrates how fixed and sunk costs make it difficult for companies that can and should invest in new capabilities actually to do so. In the late 1960s, steel minimills such as Nucor and Chaparral began disrupting integrated steelmakers such as U.S. Steel (USX), picking off customers in the least-demanding product tiers of each market and then moving relentlessly upmarket, using their 20% cost advantage to capture first the rebar market and then the bar and rod, angle iron, and structural beam markets. By 1988 the minimills had driven the higher-cost integrated mills out of lower-tier products, and Nucor had begun building its first minimill to roll sheet steel in Crawfordsville, Indiana. Nucor estimated that for an investment of $260 million it could sell 800,000 tons of steel annually at a price of $350 per ton. The cash cost to produce a ton of sheet steel in the Crawfordsville mill would be $270. When the timing of cash flows was taken into account, the internal rate of return to Nucor on this investment was over 20%—substantially higher than Nucor's weighted average cost of capital.

Incumbent USX recognized that the minimills constituted a grave threat. Using a new technology called continuous strip production, Nucor had now entered the sheet steel market, albeit with an inferior-quality product, at a significantly lower cost per ton. And Nucor's track record of vigilant improvement meant that the quality of its sheet steel would improve with production experience. Despite this understanding, USX engineers did not even consider building a greenfield minimill like the one Nucor built. The reason? It seemed more profitable to leverage the old technology than to create the new. USX's existing mills, which used traditional technology, had 30% excess capacity, and the marginal cash cost of producing an extra ton of steel by leveraging that excess capacity was less than $50 per ton. When USX's financial analysts contrasted the marginal cash flow of $300 ($350 revenue minus the $50 marginal cost) with the average cash flow of $80 per ton in a greenfield mill, investment in a new low-cost minimill made no sense. What's more, USX's plants were depreciated, so the marginal cash flow of $300 on a low asset base looked very attractive.

And therein lies the rub. Nucor, the attacker, had no fixed or sunk cost investments on which to do a marginal cost calculation. To Nucor, the full cost was the marginal cost. Crawfordsville was the only choice on its menu—and because the IRR was attractive, the decision was simple. USX, in contrast, had two choices on its menu: It could build a greenfield plant like Nucor's with a lower average cost per ton or it could utilize more fully its existing facility.

So what happened? Nucor has continued to improve its process, move upmarket, and gain market share with more efficient continuous strip production capabilities, while USX has relied on the capabilities that had been built to succeed in the past. USX's strategy to maximize marginal profit, in other words, caused the company not to minimize long-term average costs. As a result, the company is locked into an escalating cycle of commitment to a failing strategy.

The attractiveness of any investment can be completely assessed only when it is compared with the attractiveness of the right alternatives on a menu of investments. When a company is looking at adding capacity that is identical to existing capacity, it makes sense to compare the marginal cost of leveraging the old with the full cost of creating the new. But when new technologies or capabilities are required for future competitiveness, margining on the past will send you down the wrong path. The argument that investment decisions should be based on marginal costs is always correct. But when creating new capabilities is the issue, the relevant marginal cost is actually the full cost of creating the new.

When we look at fixed and sunk costs from this perspective, several anomalies we have observed in our studies of innovation are explained. Executives in established companies bemoan how expensive it is to build new brands and develop new sales and distribution channels—so they seek instead to leverage their existing brands and structures. Entrants, in contrast, simply create new ones. The problem for the incumbent isn't that the challenger can outspend it; it's that the challenger is spared the dilemma of having to choose between full-cost and marginal-cost options. We have repeatedly observed leading, established companies misapply fixed-and-sunk-cost doctrine and rely on assets and capabilities that were forged in the past to succeed in the future. In doing so, they fail to make the same investments that entrants and attackers find to be profitable.

A related misused financial practice that biases managers against investment in needed future capabilities is that of using a capital asset's estimated *usable* lifetime as the period over which it should be depreciated. This causes problems when the asset's usable lifetime is longer than its *competitive* lifetime. Managers who depreciate assets according to the more gradual schedule of usable life often face massive write-offs when those assets become competitively obsolete and need to be replaced with newer-technology assets. This was the situation confronting the integrated steelmakers. When building new capabilities entails writing off the old, incumbents face a hit to quarterly earnings that disruptive entrants to the industry do not. Knowing that the equity markets will punish them for a write-off, managers may stall in adopting new technology.

This may be part of the reason for the dramatic increase in private equity buyouts over the past decade and the recent surge of interest in technology-oriented industries. As disruptions continue to shorten the competitive lifetime of major investments made only three to five years ago, more companies find themselves needing to take asset write-downs or to significantly restructure their business models. These are wrenching changes that are often made more easily and comfortably outside the glare of the public markets.

What's the solution to this dilemma? Michael Mauboussin at Legg Mason Capital Management suggests it is to value *strategies,* not projects. When an attacker is gaining ground, executives at the incumbent companies need to do their investment analyses in the same way the attackers do—by focusing on the strategies that will ensure long-term competitiveness. This is the only way they can see the world as the attackers see it and the only way they can predict the consequences of not investing.

No manager would consciously decide to destroy a company by leveraging the competencies of the past while ignoring those required for the future. Yet this is precisely what many of them do. They do it because strategy and finance were taught as separate topics in business school. Their professors of financial modeling alluded to the importance of strategy, and their strategy professors occasionally referred to value creation, but little time was spent on a thoughtful integration of the two. This bifurcation persists in most companies, where responsibilities for strategy and finance reside in the realms of different vice presidents. Because a firm's actual strategy is defined by the stream of projects in which it does or doesn't invest, finance and strategy need to be studied and practiced in an integrated way.

Focusing Myopically on Earnings per Share

A third financial paradigm that leads established companies to underinvest in innovation is the emphasis on earnings per share as the primary driver of share price and hence of shareholder value creation. Managers are under so much pressure, from various directions, to focus on short-term stock performance that they pay less attention to the company's long-term health than they might—to the point where they're reluctant to invest in innovations that don't pay off immediately.

Where's the pressure coming from? To answer that question, we need to look briefly at the principal-agent theory—the doctrine that the interests of shareholders (principals) aren't aligned with those of managers (agents). Without powerful financial incentives to focus the interests of principals and agents on maximizing shareholder value, the thinking goes, agents will pursue other agendas—and in the process, may neglect to pay enough attention to efficiencies or squander capital investments on pet projects—at the expense of profits that ought to accrue to the principals.

That conflict of incentives has been taught so aggressively that the compensation of most senior executives in publicly traded companies is now heavily weighted away from salaries and toward packages that reward improvements in share price. That in turn has led to an almost singular focus on earnings per share and EPS growth as *the* metric for corporate performance. While we all recognize the importance of other indicators such as market position, brands, intellectual capital, and long-term competitiveness, the bias is toward using a simple quantitative indicator that is easily compared period to period and across companies. And because EPS growth is an important driver of near-term share price improvement, managers are biased against investments that will compromise near-term EPS. Many decide instead to use the excess cash on the balance sheet to buy back the company's stock under the guise of "returning money to shareholders." But although contracting the number of shares pumps up earnings per share, sometimes quite dramatically, it does nothing to enhance the underlying value of the enterprise and may even damage it by restricting the flow of cash available for investment in potentially disruptive products and business models. Indeed, some have fingered share-price-based incentive compensation packages as a key driver of the share price manipulation that captured so many business headlines in the early 2000s.

The myopic focus on EPS is not just about the money. CEOs and corporate managers who are more concerned with their reputations than with amassing more wealth also focus on stock price and short-term performance measures such as quarterly earnings. They know that, to a large extent, others' perception of their success is tied up in those numbers, leading to a self-reinforcing cycle of obsession. This behavior cycle is amplified when there is an "earnings surprise." Equity prices over the short term respond positively to upside earnings surprises (and negatively to downside surprises), so investors have no incentive to look at rational measures of long-term performance. To the contrary, they are rewarded for going with the market's short-term model.

The active leveraged buyout market has further reinforced the focus on EPS. Companies that are viewed as having failed to maximize value, as evidenced by a lagging share price, are vulnerable to overtures from outsiders, including corporate raiders or hedge funds that seek to increase their near-term stock price by putting a company into play or by replacing the CEO. Thus, while the past two decades have witnessed a dramatic increase in the proportion of CEO compensation tied to stock price—and a breathtaking increase in CEO compensation overall—they have witnessed a concomitant decrease in the average tenure of CEOs. Whether you believe that CEOs are most motivated by the carrot (major increases in compensation and wealth) or the stick (the threat of the company being sold or of being replaced), you should not be surprised to find so many CEOs focused on current earnings per share as the best predictor of stock price, sometimes to the exclusion of anything else. One study even showed that senior executives were routinely willing to sacrifice long-term shareholder value to meet earnings expectations or to smooth reported earnings.

We suspect that the principal-agent theory is misapplied. Most traditional principals—by which we mean shareholders—don't themselves have incentives to watch out for the long-term health of a company. Over 90% of the shares of publicly traded companies in the United States are held in the portfolios of mutual funds, pension funds, and hedge funds. The average holding period for stocks in these portfolios is less than 10 months—leading us to prefer the term "share owner" as a more accurate description than "shareholder." As for agents, we believe that most executives work tirelessly, throwing their hearts and minds into their jobs, not because they are paid an incentive to do so but because they love what they do. Tying executive compensation to stock prices, therefore, does not affect the intensity or energy or intelligence with which executives perform. But it does direct their efforts toward activities whose impact can be felt within the holding horizon of the typical share owner and within the measurement horizon of the incentive—both of which are less than one year.

Ironically, most so-called principals today are themselves agents—agents of other people's mutual funds, investment portfolios, endowments, and retirement programs. For these agents, the enterprise in which they are investing has no inherent interest or value beyond providing a platform for improving the short-term financial metric by which their fund's performance is measured and their own compensation is determined. And, in a final grand but sad irony, the real principals (the people who put their money into mutual funds and pension plans, sometimes through yet another layer of agents) are frequently the very individuals whose long-term employment is jeopardized when the focus on short-term EPS acts to restrict investments in innovative growth opportunities. We suggest that the principal-agent theory is obsolete in this context. What we really have is an *agent-agent* problem, where the desires and goals of the agent for the share owners compete with the desires and goals of the agents running the company. The incentives are still misaligned, but managers should not capitulate on the basis of an obsolete paradigm.

Processes That Support (or Sabotage) Innovation

As we have seen, managers in established corporations use analytical methods that make innovation investments extremely difficult to justify. As it happens, the most common system for green-lighting investment projects only reinforces the flaws inherent in the tools and dogmas discussed earlier.

Stage-gate innovation

Most established companies start by considering a broad range of possible innovations; they winnow out the less viable ideas, step by step, until only the most promising ones remain. Most such processes include three stages: feasibility, development, and launch. The stages are separated by stage gates: review meetings at which project teams report to senior managers what they've accomplished. On the basis of this progress and the project's potential, the gatekeepers approve the passage of the initiative into the next phase, return it to the previous stage for more work, or kill it.

Many marketers and engineers regard the stage-gate development process with disdain. Why? Because the key decision criteria at each gate are the size of projected revenues and profits from the product and the associated risks. Revenues from products that incrementally improve upon those the company is currently selling can be credibly quantified. But proposals to create growth by exploiting potentially disruptive technologies, products, or business models can't be bolstered by hard numbers. Their markets are initially small, and substantial revenues generally don't materialize for several years. When these projects are pitted against incremental sustaining innovations in the battle for funding, the incremental ones sail through while the seemingly riskier ones get delayed or die.

The process itself has two serious drawbacks. First, project teams generally know how good the projections (such as NPV) need to look in order to win funding, and it takes only nanoseconds to tweak an assumption and run another full scenario to get a faltering project over the hurdle rate. If, as is often the case, there are eight to 10 assumptions underpinning the financial model, changing only a few of them by a mere 2% or 3% each may do the trick. It is then difficult for the senior managers who sit as gatekeepers to even discern which are the salient assumptions, let alone judge whether they are realistic.

The second drawback is that the stage-gate system assumes that the proposed strategy is the right strategy. Once an innovation has been approved, developed, and launched, all that remains is skillful execution. If, after launch, a product falls seriously short of the projections (and 75% of them do), it is canceled. The problem is that, except in the case of incremental innovations, the right strategy—especially which job the customer wants done—cannot be completely known in advance. It must emerge and then be refined.

The stage-gate system is not suited to the task of assessing innovations whose purpose is to build new growth businesses, but most companies continue to follow it simply because they see no alternative.

Discovery-driven planning

Happily, though, there are alternative systems specifically designed to support intelligent investments in future growth. One such process, which Rita Gunther McGrath and Ian MacMillan call *discovery-driven planning,* has the potential to greatly improve the success rate. Discovery-driven planning essentially reverses the sequence of some of the steps in the stage-gate process. Its logic is elegantly simple. If the project teams all know how good the numbers need to look in order to win funding, why go through the charade of making and revising assumptions in order to fabricate an acceptable set of numbers? Why not just put the minimally acceptable revenue, income, and cash flow statement as the standard first page of the gate documents? The second page can then raise the critical issues: "Okay. So we all know this is how good the numbers need to look. What set of assumptions must prove true in order for these numbers to materialize?" The project team creates from that analysis an assumptions checklist—a list of things that need to prove true for the project to succeed. The items on the checklist are rank-ordered, with the deal killers and the assumptions that can be tested with little expense toward the top. McGrath and MacMillan call this a "reverse income statement."

When a project enters a new stage, the assumptions checklist is used as the basis of the project plan for that stage. This is not a plan to execute, however. It is a plan to *learn*—to test as quickly and at as low a cost as possible whether the assumptions upon which success is predicated are actually valid. If a critical assumption proves not to be valid, the project team must revise its strategy until the assumptions upon which it is built are all plausible. If no set of plausible assumptions will support the case for success, the project is killed.

Traditional stage-gate planning obfuscates the assumptions and shines the light on the financial projections. But there is no need to focus the analytical spotlight on the numbers, because the desirability of attractive numbers has never been the question. Discovery-driven planning shines a spotlight on the place where senior management needs illumination—the assumptions that constitute the key uncertainties. More often than not, failure in innovation is rooted in not having asked an important question, rather than in having arrived at an incorrect answer.

Today, processes like discovery-driven planning are more commonly used in entrepreneurial settings than in the large corporations that desperately need them. We hope that by recounting the strengths of one such system we'll persuade established corporations to reassess how they make decisions about investment projects.

We keep rediscovering that the root reason for established companies' failure to innovate is that managers don't have good tools to help them understand markets, build brands, find customers, select employees, organize teams, and develop strategy. Some of the tools typically used for financial analysis, and decision making about investments, distort the value, importance, and likelihood of success of investments in innovation. There's a better way for management teams to grow their companies. But they will need the courage to challenge some of the paradigms of financial analysis and the willingness to develop alternative methodologies.

Originally published in January 2008. Reprint R0801F

About the Contributors

LANCE A. BETTENCOURT is a founding partner at Service 360 Partners.

CLAYTON M. CHRISTENSEN is the Kim B. Clark Professor of Business Administration at Harvard Business School and the world's foremost authority on disruptive innovation.

GEORGE S. DAY is the Geoffrey T. Boisi Professor and a codirector of the Mack Center for Technological Innovation at the University of Pennsylvania's Wharton School.

PETER F. DRUCKER the was the Marie Rankin Clarke Professor of Social Science and Management at Claremont Graduate University.

VIJAY GOVINDARAJAN is the Earl C. Daum 1924 Professor of International Business at the Tuck School of Business at Dartmouth.

JEFFREY R. IMMELT, chairman and CEO of GE, heads President Obama's Council on Jobs and Competitiveness.

ROSABETH MOSS KANTER is the Ernest L. Arbuckle Professor of Business Administration at Harvard Business School.

STEPHEN P. KAUFMAN, a senior lecturer at Harvard Business School, is the retired chairman and CEO of Arrow Electronics.

IAN C. MACMILLAN the Dhirubhai Ambani Professor of Innovation and Entrepreneurship at the University of Pennsylvania's Wharton School.

ROGER L. MARTIN is dean of the University of Toronto's Rotman School of Management.

RITA GUNTHER MCGRATH is a professor at Columbia University's Graduate School of Business.

DONALD REINERTSEN is president of Reinertsen & Associates, a consulting firm in Redondo Beach, California.

WILLY C. SHIH is a professor of management practice at Harvard Business School. He held executive positions at IBM, Silicon Graphics, and Kodak.

STEFAN THOMKE is the William Barclay Harding Professor of Business Administration at Harvard Business School.

CHRIS TRIMBLE is on the faculty at the Tuck School of Business at Dartmouth.

ANTHONY W. ULWICK is the founder and Chief Innovation Officer of Strategyn.

Index

Harvard Business Review
136 Marvel's Blockbuster Machine
94 Digital Doesn't Have to Be Disruptive
116 When a Colleague Is Grieving
The AI-Powered Organization
The main challenge isn't technology. It's culture.
62

VISUAL LIBRARY
The Good-Better-Best Approach to Pricing
Harvard Business Review
Are METRICS Undermining Your Business?
Too many leaders confuse numbers with strategy.
62

HBR'S 10 MUST READS

On Collaboration

HBR's 10 Must Reads series is the definitive collection of ideas and best practices for aspiring and experienced leaders alike. These books offer essential reading selected from the pages of *Harvard Business Review* on topics critical to the success of every manager.

Titles include:

HBR's 10 Must Reads on Change Management
HBR's 10 Must Reads on Collaboration
HBR's 10 Must Reads on Communication
HBR's 10 Must Reads on Innovation
HBR's 10 Must Reads on Leadership
HBR's 10 Must Reads on Making Smart Decisions
HBR's 10 Must Reads on Managing People
HBR's 10 Must Reads on Managing Yourself
HBR's 10 Must Reads on Strategic Marketing
HBR's 10 Must Reads on Strategy
HBR's 10 Must Reads on Teams
HBR's 10 Must Reads: The Essentials

HBR'S 10 MUST READS

On Collaboration

HARVARD BUSINESS REVIEW PRESS
Boston, Massachusetts

Printed in the United States of America
12

The web addresses referenced in this book were live and correct at the time of the book's publication but may be subject to change.

Library of Congress Cataloging-in-Publication Data

HBR's 10 must reads on collaboration.
p. cm.
Includes index.
ISBN 978-1-4221-9012-8 (alk. paper)
1. Business networks. 2. Cooperativeness. 3. Interorganizational relations.
I. Harvard business review. II. Title: HBR's ten must reads on collaboration.
III. Title: Harvard business review's 10 must reads on collaboration.
HD69. S8H39 2013
658'.046—dc23 2012037906

ISBN: 9781422190128
eISBN: 9781422191422

The paper used in this publication meets the requirements of the American National Standard for Permanence of Paper for Publications and Documents in Libraries and Archives z39.48-1992.

Contents

HBR'S 10 MUST READS

On Collaboration

Are You a Collaborative Leader?

by Herminia Ibarra and Morten T. Hansen

WATCHING HIS EMPLOYEES use a new social technology, Marc Benioff, the CEO of Salesforce.com, had an epiphany. His company had developed Chatter, a Facebook-inspired application for companies that allows users to keep track of their colleagues and customers and share information and ideas. The employees had been trying it out internally, not just within their own work groups but across the entire organization. As Benioff read the Chatter posts, he realized that many of the people who had critical customer knowledge and were adding the most value were not even known to the management team.

The view into top management from the rank and file was just as obscure, Benioff knew. For instance, the company's annual management off-site was coming up, and he could tell from talking to employees that they wondered about what went on behind closed doors at that gathering. "They imagined we were dressing up in robes and chanting," he says.

What could he do to bring the top tier of the company closer to the workforce? Benioff asked himself. And then it hit him: Let's use Chatter to blow open the doors of the management off-site.

What greeted the 200 executives who attended that meeting was atypical. All 5,000 Salesforce.com employees had been invited to join them—virtually. Huge TV monitors placed throughout the meeting room displayed the special Chatter forum set up for the off-site. Every manager received an iPod Touch, and every table had an iPad, which attendees could use to post to the forum. A video service broadcast the meeting in real time to all employees, who could beam in and instantaneously express their views on Chatter, too.

The meeting began with the standard presentations. The managers watching them weren't quite sure what to do. Nothing unusual happened at first. Finally, Benioff grabbed the iPad on his table and made a comment on Chatter, noting what he found interesting about what was being said and adding a joke to spice it up. Some in the room followed with a few comments, and then employees watching from their offices launched a few comments back. The snowball started rolling. "Suddenly, the meeting went from a select group participating to the entire company participating," Benioff says.

Comments flew. "We felt the empowerment in the room," recalls Steve Gillmor, the head of technical media strategy.

In the end the dialogue lasted for weeks beyond the actual meeting. More important, by fostering a discussion across the entire organization, Benioff has been able to better align the whole workforce around its mission. The event served as a catalyst for the creation of a more open and empowered culture at the company.

Like Salesforce.com's managers and employees, businesspeople today are working more collaboratively than ever before, not just inside companies but also with suppliers, customers, governments, and universities. Global virtual teams are the norm, not the exception. Facebook, Twitter, LinkedIn, videoconferencing, and a host of other technologies have put connectivity on steroids and enabled new forms of collaboration that would have been impossible a short while ago.

Many executives realize that they need a new playbook for this hyperconnected environment. Those who climbed the corporate ladder in silos while using a "command and control" style can have a difficult time adjusting to the new realities. Conversely, managers who try to lead by consensus can quickly see decision making and execution grind to a halt. Crafting the right leadership style isn't easy.

Idea in Brief

Social media and technologies have put connectivity on steroids and made collaboration more integral to business than ever. But without the right leadership, collaboration can go astray. Employees who try to collaborate on everything may wind up stuck in endless meetings, struggling to reach agreement. On the other side of the coin, executives who came of age during the heyday of "command and control" management can have trouble adjusting their style to fit the new realities.

In their research on top-performing CEOs, Insead professors Ibarra and Hansen have examined what it takes to be a collaborative leader. They've found that it requires connecting people and ideas outside an organization to those inside it, leveraging diverse talent, modeling collaborative behavior at the top, and showing a strong hand to keep teams from getting mired in debate. In this article, they describe tactics that executives from Akamai, GE, Reckitt Benckiser, and other firms use in those four areas and how they foster high-performance collaborative cultures in their organizations.

As part of our research on top-performing CEOs (see "The Best-Performing CEOs in the World," HBR January–February 2010), we've examined what it means to be a collaborative leader. We've discovered that it requires strong skills in four areas: playing the role of connector, attracting diverse talent, modeling collaboration at the top, and showing a strong hand to keep teams from getting mired in debate. The good news is, our research also suggests that these skills can be learned—and can help executives generate exceptional long-term performance.

Play Global Connector

In his best-selling book *The Tipping Point,* Malcolm Gladwell used the term "connector" to describe individuals who have many ties to different social worlds. It's not the number of people they know that makes connectors significant, however; it's their ability to link people, ideas, and resources that wouldn't normally bump into one another. In business, connectors are critical facilitators of collaboration.

Play Global Connector

- Do you attend conferences outside your professional specialty?
- Are you part of a global network like Young Presidents' Organization?
- Do you regularly blog or e-mail employees about trends, ideas, and people you encounter outside your organization?
- How often do you meet with parties outside your company (competitors, consumers, government officials, university contacts, and so on) who are not directly relevant to your immediate job demands or current operations?
- Are you on the board of any outside organizations?

For David Kenny, the president of Akamai Technologies, being a connector is one of the most important ways he adds value. He spends much of his time traveling around the world to meet with employees, partners, and customers. "I spend time with media owners to hear what they think about digital platforms, Facebook, and new pricing models, and with Microsoft leaders to get their views on cloud computing," he says. "I'm interested in hearing how our clients feel about macroeconomic issues, the G20, and how debt will affect future generations." These conversations lead to new strategic insights and relationships, and help Akamai develop critical external partnerships.

Connecting the world outside to people inside the company is crucial to Kenny. He uses a number of tactics to do this. "First, I check in on Foursquare often and post my location to Facebook and Twitter," he says. "It lets employees in different Akamai locations know I'm in town so that anybody at any level can bring me suggestions or concerns. Second, every time I go to one of our locations, I have lunch or coffee with 20 to 40 people. We go around the room, and people ask questions on topics they most want to address. Often my answer is to connect them with others in Akamai or even people at other companies who have expertise on the topic. Third, if I see a big opportunity when meeting with a customer or colleague, I will schedule a follow-up visit and bring along the right experts from

Akamai. Fourth, whenever I travel, I try to make room to meet with two to three people I know in that location. Whenever possible, I bring someone else from Akamai with me to those meetings."

Kenny's networking recently resulted in an important strategic alliance with Ericsson. Akamai is now working with the mobile giant to change consumers' internet experiences on mobile devices. The partnership evolved out of a conversation Kenny had with a midlevel Ericsson executive two years ago at the Monaco Media Forum. "It really changed my idea of what Ericsson could be, and I saw that we were both trying to solve a similar technical problem," Kenny says. "Then I worked through mutual friends to meet their CEO and arranged for the right people on his team to meet with their Akamai counterparts."

Presidents and CEOs aren't the only executives building bridges between their organizations and the outside world nowadays. Take Beth Comstock, the chief marketing officer of General Electric. She is famous for her weekly "BlackBerry Beth" blog, in which she shares what she has learned in her external role for busy (and perhaps more internally focused) GE managers. The pithy and provocative blog goes out to thousands of GE's sales, marketing, and technology leaders. In it, Comstock passes along interesting information that people might have missed, taking care to tie it back to challenges and opportunities GE faces. For example, in a recent post from the World Economic Forum, she reported that a panel of scientists had come to the same conclusion that a GE survey had—that technology alone cannot ensure innovation and that more training in creativity is needed.

"I work hard to curate information that I don't believe many at GE will have heard and to translate information in a way that is relevant to our challenges," says Comstock. "I probably spend half of my time immersed in worlds beyond GE. I hope this encourages my colleagues to be more externally focused. The message is 'If I find it important to spend some of my time this way, maybe you will, too.'"

To connect their organizations to the wider world, collaborative leaders develop contacts not only in the typical areas—local clubs, industry associations, and customer and supplier relations—but beyond them. Networking in adjacent industries, innovation hot spots like Silicon Valley, or emerging economies or with people of different educational or ethnic backgrounds helps open their eyes to new business opportunities and partners. For example, Comstock's external contacts in the innovation space led GE to NASA, with which the corporation has shared insights and best practices. The two organizations have also begun discussions about space technologies that might have applications in health care.

Engage Talent at the Periphery

Research has consistently shown that diverse teams produce better results, provided they are well led. The ability to bring together people from different backgrounds, disciplines, cultures, and generations and leverage all they have to offer, therefore, is a must-have for leaders. Yet many companies spend inordinate amounts of time, money, and energy attracting talented employees only to subject them to homogenizing processes that kill creativity. In a lot of multinational companies, for example, nonnative English speakers are at a disadvantage. To senior management, they don't sound as "leader-like" as the Anglophones, and they end up getting passed over for promotions. At a time when innovations are increasingly originating in emerging markets, companies that allow this to happen lose out.

France's Danone, one of the top performers in our research, makes sure its executives don't encounter such obstacles. When all the managers worldwide get together for the company's annual strategic review, many choose to present in their native tongue. Says CEO Franck Riboud: "We spend a fortune on interpreters so that being less articulate in English is not a barrier. Some of our executives have even presented their business case in native dress. This helps us steal away talent from competitors where those who don't speak perfect English get stuck."

Reckitt Benckiser, the UK-based producer of home, health, and personal care products and another top performer in our research, considers the diversity of its workforce to be one of its competitive advantages—and a key reason it has seen net income grow 17%

Engage Talent at the Periphery

- How diverse is your immediate team in terms of nationality? Gender? Age?
- How much time do you spend outside your home country?
- Have you visited your emerging markets this year?
- Does your network include people in their twenties (who *aren't* your kids)?

annually, on average, from 1999 to 2010. No nationality dominates the company's senior team. Two executives are Dutch, one is German, two are British, one is South African, two are Italian, and one is from India. According to (soon-to-retire) CEO Bart Becht: "It doesn't matter whether I have a Pakistani, a Chinese person, a Brit, or a Turk, man or woman, sitting in the same room, or whether I have people from sales or something else, so long as I have people with different experiences—because the chance for new ideas is much greater when you have people with different backgrounds. The chance for conflict is also higher—and conflict is good per se, as long as it's constructive and gets us to the best idea."

As Becht suggests, nationality isn't the only kind of diversity that matters. Research on creative industries shows that the collaborations that are most successful (whether in terms of patent citation, critical acclaim, or financial return) include both experienced people and newcomers and bring together people who haven't worked with one another before. Leaders need to make a concerted effort to promote this mix: Left to their own devices, people will choose to collaborate with others they know well or who have similar backgrounds. Static groups breed insularity, which can be deadly for innovation. Nokia's former executive team, for example, was 100% Finnish and had worked closely together for more than a decade. Many believe homogeneity explains why the team failed to see the smartphone threat emerging from Silicon Valley.

Collaborative leaders ensure that teams stay fresh via periodic infusions of new players. Including employees from Generation Y—those born from the mid-1970s to the early 2000s, who have grown up sharing knowledge and opinions online—is another obvious way to enliven collaborations. A number of leading companies have begun using technology to harness Gen Y ideas and perspectives. Salesforce.com, as we have seen, brought them in from the periphery by using Chatter to open its management offsite to all staff. At India's HCL, employees throughout the company join virtual conversations on topics that are important to them, and CEO Vineet Nayar reaches out personally through a popular blog that allows him to interact with a broad cross section of employees. In a market where the competition for engineering talent is fierce, the ability to attract the best and brightest helped HCL grow 30% annually from 2008 to 2010.

Collaborate at the Top First

It's not enough for leaders to spot collaborative opportunities and attract the best talent to them. They must also set the tone by being good collaborators themselves. All too often, efforts to collaborate in the middle are sabotaged by political games and turf battles higher up in the organization. Consider that Microsoft, according to a former company executive writing in the *New York Times* last year, developed a viable tablet computer more than a decade ago but failed to preempt Apple's smash hit because competing Microsoft divisions conspired to kill the project.

Part of the problem is that many leadership teams, composed of the CEO and his or her direct reports, actually don't operate as teams. Each member runs his or her own region, function, or product or service category, without much responsibility—or incentive—for aligning the organization's various projects and operations into a coherent whole.

At Brazil's Natura Cosméticos, CEO Alessandro Carlucci has instituted a comprehensive "engagement process" that promotes a collaborative mind-set at all levels and has helped the firm win a top spot on *Fortune*'s list of best companies for leaders. The process was implemented after Natura's highly successful IPO in 2004, when

Collaborate at the Top First

- Do members of your team have any joint responsibilities beyond their individual goals?
- Does the compensation of your direct reports depend on any collective goals or reflect any collective responsibilities?
- What specifically have you done to eradicate power struggles within your team?
- Do your direct reports have both performance and learning goals?

competing agendas among the senior managers began to threaten the company's prospects. Carlucci decided he needed to reorganize the executive committee to unify its members around common goals and stop the power struggles. He asked the members of the top team to make a commitment to self-development as part of their stewardship of the company.

Each executive embarked on a "personal journey" with an external coach, who met with everyone individually and with the team as a group. "It is a different type of coaching," Carlucci explains. "It's not just talking to your boss or subordinates but talking about a person's life history, with their families; it is more holistic, broader, integrating all the different roles of a human being."

Roberto Pedote, Natura's senior vice president for finance, IT, and legal affairs, adds: "I think that the main point is that we are making ourselves vulnerable, showing that we are not supermen, that we have failures; that we are afraid of some things and we don't have all the answers."

Since the engagement process was adopted, Natura's executives have become much better at teaming up on efforts to improve the business, which grew by 21% in 2010. The collaborative mind-set at the top has cascaded down to the rest of the organization, and the process has been rolled out to all the company's managers.

If leaders are to encourage more innovation through partnerships across sectors and with suppliers, customers, and consumers, they need to stop relying heavily on short-term performance indicators. According to the psychologist Carol Dweck, people are driven to do

Collaboration Does Not Equal Consensus

COLLABORATIVE LEADERSHIP IS THE capacity to engage people and groups outside one's formal control and inspire them to work toward common goals—despite differences in convictions, cultural values, and operating norms.

Most people understand intuitively that collaborative leadership is the opposite of the old command-and-control model, but the differences with a consensus-based approach are more nuanced. Following are some helpful distinctions between the three leadership styles.

tasks by either performance or learning goals. When performance goals dominate an environment, people are motivated to show others that they have a valued attribute, such as intelligence or leadership. When learning goals dominate, they are motivated to *develop* the attribute. Performance goals, she finds, induce people to favor tasks that will make them look good over tasks that will help them learn. A shift toward learning goals will make managers more open to exploring opportunities to acquire knowledge from others.

At HCL, CEO Vineet Nayar demonstrated his commitment to collaboration by adopting a radically different 360-degree evaluation for his top managers—one that invited a wide range of employees to weigh in. Although the company had done 360-degree reviews before, each manager had been assessed by a relatively small number of people, mostly within the manager's immediate span of control. As Nayar recalls in his book *Employees First, Customers Second* (Harvard Business Review Press, 2010), "most of the respondents operated within the same area as the person they were evaluating. This reinforced the boundaries between the parts of the pyramid. But we were trying to change all that. We wanted to encourage people to operate across these boundaries." Nayar set the tone by posting his own 360-degree evaluation on the web. Once executives got used to the new transparency, the 360-degree reviews were expanded to a broader group. A new feature, "Happy Feet," was added, allowing all employees whom a manager might affect or influence to evaluate that manager—regardless of their reporting relationship.

Comparing three styles of leadership

	Command and control	Consensus	Collaborative
ORGANIZATIONAL STRUCTURE	Hierarchy	Matrix or small group	Dispersed, cross-organizational network
WHO HAS THE RELEVANT INFORMATION?	Senior management	Formally designated members or representatives of the relevant geographies and disciplines	Employees at all levels and locations and a variety of external stakeholders
WHO HAS THE AUTHORITY TO MAKE FINAL DECISIONS?	The people at the top of the organization have clear authority	All parties have equal authority	The people leading collaborations have clear authority
WHAT IS THE BASIS FOR ACCOUNTABILITY AND CONTROL?	Financial results against plan	Many performance indicators, by function or geography	Performance on achieving shared goals
WHERE DOES IT WORK BEST?	Works well within a defined hierarchy; works poorly for complex organizations and when innovation is important	Works well in small teams; works poorly when speed is important	Works well for diverse groups and cross-unit and cross-company work, and when innovation and creativity are critical

Depoliticizing senior management so that executives are rewarded for collaborating rather than promoting their individual agendas is an absolute essential. At Reckitt Benckiser, there's little tolerance for politics. Says Bart Becht: "We go out of our way to make sure that politics get eradicated, because I think they're very bad for an organization. I think they're poison, to be honest with you." Becht's direct, no-nonsense style and the expectation that people should openly disagree with one another in meetings also help keep politics to a minimum, allowing real teamwork to take hold.

Show a Strong Hand

Once leaders start getting employees to collaborate, they face a different problem: overdoing it. Too often people will try to collaborate on everything and wind up in endless meetings, debating ideas and struggling to find consensus. They can't reach decisions and execute quickly. Collaboration becomes not the oil greasing the wheel but the sand grinding it to a halt.

Effective collaborative leaders assume a strong role directing teams. They maintain agility by forming and disbanding them as opportunities come and go—in much the same way that Hollywood producers, directors, actors, writers, and technicians establish teams for the life of movie projects. Collaborative efforts are highly fluid and not confined to company silos.

Effective leaders also assign clear decision rights and responsibilities, so that at the appropriate point someone can end the discussion and make a final call. Although constructive confrontation and tempered disagreements are encouraged, battles aren't left raging on. This is exactly how things work at Reckitt Benckiser. When teams meet, people know that it is OK—in fact expected—to propose ideas and challenge one another. They debate loudly and furiously until the best idea wins. If no obvious agreement is reached in time, the person chairing the meeting normally makes a decision and the rest of the group falls in line. This ensures vigorous debate but clear decisions and quick action—diversity in counsel, unity in command, as Cyrus the Great once said.

Loosening Control Without Losing Control

In the old world of silos and solo players, leaders had access to everything they needed under one roof, and a command-and-control style served them well. But things have changed: The world has become much more interconnected, and if executives don't know how to tap into the power of those connections, they'll be left behind.

Show a Strong Hand

- Have you killed any collaboration projects in the past six months?
- Do you manage dynamically—forming and disbanding teams quickly as opportunities arise?
- Do the right people in your organization know they can “close” a discussion and make a decision?
- Does your team debate ideas vigorously but then unite behind decisions made?

Leaders today must be able to harness ideas, people, and resources from across boundaries of all kinds. That requires reinventing their talent strategies and building strong connections both inside and outside their organizations. To get all the disparate players to work together effectively, they also need to know when to wield influence rather than authority to move things forward, and when to halt unproductive discussions, squash politicking, and make final calls.

Differences in convictions, cultural values, and operating norms inevitably add complexity to collaborative efforts. But they also make them richer, more innovative, and more valuable. Getting that value is the heart of collaborative leadership.

Originally published in July–August 2011. Reprint R1107D

Social Intelligence and the Biology of Leadership

by Daniel Goleman and Richard Boyatzis

IN 1998, ONE OF US, Daniel Goleman, published in these pages his first article on emotional intelligence and leadership. The response to "What Makes a Leader?" was enthusiastic. People throughout and beyond the business community started talking about the vital role that empathy and self-knowledge play in effective leadership. The concept of emotional intelligence continues to occupy a prominent space in the leadership literature and in everyday coaching practices. But in the past five years, research in the emerging field of social neuroscience—the study of what happens in the brain while people interact—is beginning to reveal subtle new truths about what makes a good leader.

The salient discovery is that certain things leaders do—specifically, exhibit empathy and become attuned to others' moods—literally affect both their own brain chemistry and that of their followers. Indeed, researchers have found that the leader-follower dynamic is not a case of two (or more) independent brains reacting consciously or unconsciously to each other. Rather, the individual minds become, in a sense, fused into a single system. We believe that great leaders are those whose behavior powerfully leverages the system of brain interconnectedness. We place them on the opposite end of the neural continuum from people with serious social disorders, such as autism or Asperger's syndrome, that are characterized by underdevelopment in the areas of the brain associated with social interactions. If we are correct, it follows that a potent way of becoming a better leader is to find authentic contexts in which to learn the kinds of social behavior that reinforce the brain's social circuitry. Leading effectively is, in other words, less about mastering situations—or even mastering social skill sets—than about developing a genuine interest in and talent for fostering positive feelings in the people whose cooperation and support you need.

The notion that effective leadership is about having powerful social circuits in the brain has prompted us to extend our concept of emotional intelligence, which we had grounded in theories of individual psychology. A more relationship-based construct for assessing leadership is *social intelligence,* which we define as a set of interpersonal competencies built on specific neural circuits (and related endocrine systems) that inspire others to be effective.

The idea that leaders need social skills is not new, of course. In 1920, Columbia University psychologist Edward Thorndike pointed out that "the best mechanic in a factory may fail as a foreman for lack of social intelligence." More recently, our colleague Claudio Fernández-Aráoz found in an analysis of new C-level executives that those who had been hired for their self-discipline, drive, and intellect were sometimes later fired for lacking basic social skills. In other words, the people Fernández-Aráoz studied had smarts in spades, but their inability to get along socially on the job was professionally self-defeating.

What's new about our definition of social intelligence is its biological underpinning, which we will explore in the following pages. Drawing on the work of neuroscientists, our own research and consulting endeavors, and the findings of researchers affiliated with the Consortium for Research on Emotional Intelligence in Organizations, we will show you how to translate newly acquired knowledge about mirror neurons, spindle cells, and oscillators into practical, socially intelligent behaviors that can reinforce the neural links between you and your followers.

Idea in Brief

Your behavior can energize—or deflate—your entire organization through **mood contagion**. For example, if you laugh often and set an easygoing tone, you'll trigger similar behaviors among your team members. Shared behaviors unify a team, and bonded groups perform better than fragmented ones.

Mood contagion stems from neurobiology. Positive behaviors—such as exhibiting empathy—create a chemical connection between a leader's and his or her followers' brains. By managing those interconnections adroitly, leaders can deliver measurable business results. For example, after one executive at a *Fortune* 500 company worked with a coach and role model to improve her behavior, employee retention and emotional commitment in her unit soared. And the unit's annual sales jumped 6%.

How to foster the neurobiological changes that create positive behaviors and emotions in your employees? Goleman and Boyatzis advise sharpening your **social intelligence** skills.

Followers Mirror Their Leaders—Literally

Perhaps the most stunning recent discovery in behavioral neuroscience is the identification of *mirror neurons* in widely dispersed areas of the brain. Italian neuroscientists found them by accident while monitoring a particular cell in a monkey's brain that fired only when the monkey raised its arm. One day a lab assistant lifted an ice cream cone to his own mouth and triggered a reaction in the monkey's cell. It was the first evidence that the brain is peppered with neurons that mimic, or mirror, what another being does. This previously unknown class of brain cells operates as neural Wi-Fi, allowing us to navigate our social world. When we consciously or unconsciously detect someone else's emotions through their actions, our mirror neurons reproduce those emotions. Collectively, these neurons create an instant sense of shared experience.

Mirror neurons have particular importance in organizations, because leaders' emotions and actions prompt followers to mirror those feelings and deeds. The effects of activating neural circuitry in followers' brains can be very powerful. In a recent study, our

Idea in Practice

Identify Social Strengths and Weaknesses

Social intelligence skills include the following. Identify which ones you're good at—and which ones need improvement.

Skill	Do you . . .
Empathy	Understand what motivates other people, even those from different backgrounds? Are you sensitive to their needs?
Attunement	Listen attentively and think about how others feel? Are you attuned to others' moods?
Organizational Awareness	Appreciate your group's or organization's culture and values? Understand social networks and know their unspoken norms?
Influence	Persuade others by engaging them in discussion, appealing to their interests, and getting support from key people?
Developing Others	Coach and mentor others with compassion? Do you personally invest time and energy in mentoring and provide feedback that people find helpful for their professional development?
Inspiration	Articulate a compelling vision, build group pride, foster a positive emotional tone, and lead by bringing out the best in people?
Teamwork	Encourage the participation of everyone on your team, support all members, and foster cooperation?

colleague Marie Dasborough observed two groups: One received negative performance feedback accompanied by positive emotional signals—namely, nods and smiles; the other was given positive feedback that was delivered critically, with frowns and narrowed eyes. In subsequent interviews conducted to compare the emotional states of the two groups, the people who had received positive feedback accompanied by negative emotional signals reported feeling worse about their performance than did

Craft a Plan for Change

Now determine how you'll strengthen your social intelligence. Working with a coach—who can debrief you about what she observes—and learning directly from a role model are particularly powerful ways to make needed behavioral changes.

> ***Example:*** Janice was hired as a marketing manager for her business expertise, strategic thinking powers, and ability to deal with obstacles to crucial goals. But within her first six months on the job, she was floundering. Other executives saw her as aggressive and opinionated—as well as careless about what she said and to whom.

Her boss called in a coach, who administered a 360-degree evaluation. Findings revealed that Janice didn't know how to establish rapport with people, notice their reactions to her, read social norms, or recognize others' emotional cues when she violated those norms. Through coaching, Janice learned to express her ideas with conviction (instead of with pit bull–like determination) and to disagree with others without damaging relationships.

By switching to a job where she reported to a socially intelligent mentor, Janice further strengthened her skills, including learning how to critique others' performance in productive ways. She was promoted to a position two levels up where, with additional coaching, she mastered reading cues from direct reports who were still signaling frustration with her. Her company's investment in her (along with her own commitment to change) paid big dividends—in the form of lower turnover and higher sales in Janice's multibillion-dollar unit.

the participants who had received good-natured negative feedback. In effect, the delivery was more important than the message itself. And everybody knows that when people feel better, they perform better. So, if leaders hope to get the best out of their people, they should continue to be demanding but in ways that foster a positive mood in their teams. The old carrot-and-stick approach alone doesn't make neural sense; traditional incentive systems are simply not enough to get the best performance from followers.

Here's an example of what does work. It turns out that there's a subset of mirror neurons whose only job is to detect other people's smiles and laughter, prompting smiles and laughter in return. A boss who is self-controlled and humorless will rarely engage those neurons in his team members, but a boss who laughs and sets an easygoing tone puts those neurons to work, triggering spontaneous laughter and knitting his team together in the process. A bonded group is one that performs well, as our colleague Fabio Sala has shown in his research. He found that top-performing leaders elicited laughter from their subordinates three times as often, on average, as did midperforming leaders. Being in a good mood, other research finds, helps people take in information effectively and respond nimbly and creatively. In other words, laughter is serious business.

It certainly made a difference at one university-based hospital in Boston. Two doctors we'll call Dr. Burke and Dr. Humboldt were in contention for the post of CEO of the corporation that ran this hospital and others. Both of them headed up departments, were superb physicians, and had published many widely cited research articles in prestigious medical journals. But the two had very different personalities. Burke was intense, task focused, and impersonal. He was a relentless perfectionist with a combative tone that kept his staff continually on edge. Humboldt was no less demanding, but he was very approachable, even playful, in relating to staff, colleagues, and patients. Observers noted that people smiled and teased one another—and even spoke their minds—more in Humboldt's department than in Burke's. Prized talent often ended up leaving Burke's department; in contrast, outstanding folks gravitated to Humboldt's warmer working climate. Recognizing Humboldt's socially intelligent leadership style, the hospital corporation's board picked him as the new CEO.

The "Finely Attuned" Leader

Great executives often talk about leading from the gut. Indeed, having good instincts is widely recognized as an advantage for a leader in any context, whether in reading the mood of one's organization or in conducting a delicate negotiation with the competition. Leadership scholars characterize this talent as an ability to recognize patterns, usually born of extensive experience. Their advice: Trust your gut, but get lots of input as you make decisions. That's sound practice, of course, but managers don't always have the time to consult dozens of people.

Findings in neuroscience suggest that this approach is probably too cautious. Intuition, too, is in the brain, produced in part by a class of neurons called *spindle cells* because of their shape. They have a body size about four times that of other brain cells, with an extra-long branch to make attaching to other cells easier and transmitting thoughts and feelings to them quicker. This ultrarapid connection of emotions, beliefs, and judgments creates what behavioral scientists call our social guidance system. Spindle cells trigger neural networks that come into play whenever we have to choose the best response among many—even for a task as routine as prioritizing a to-do list. These cells also help us gauge whether someone is trustworthy and right (or wrong) for a job. Within one-twentieth of a second, our spindle cells fire with information about how we feel about that person; such "thin-slice" judgments can be very accurate, as follow-up metrics reveal. Therefore, leaders should not fear to act on those judgments, provided that they are also attuned to others' moods.

Such attunement is literally physical. Followers of an effective leader experience rapport with her—or what we and our colleague Annie McKee call "resonance." Much of this feeling arises unconsciously, thanks to mirror neurons and spindle-cell circuitry. But another class of neurons is also involved: *Oscillators* coordinate people physically by regulating how and when their bodies move together. You can see oscillators in action when you watch people about to kiss; their movements look like a dance, one body responding to the other seamlessly. The same dynamic occurs when two cellists play together. Not only do they hit their notes in unison, but thanks to oscillators, the two musicians' right brain hemispheres are more closely coordinated than are the left and right sides of their individual brains.

Do Women Have Stronger Social Circuits?

PEOPLE OFTEN ASK WHETHER GENDER differences factor into the social intelligence skills needed for outstanding leadership. The answer is yes and no. It's true that women tend, on average, to be better than men at immediately sensing other people's emotions, whereas men tend to have more social confidence, at least in work settings. However, gender differences in social intelligence that are dramatic in the general population are all but absent among the most successful leaders.

When the University of Toledo's Margaret Hopkins studied several hundred executives from a major bank, she found gender differences in social intelligence in the overall group but not between the most effective men and the most effective women. Ruth Malloy of the Hay Group uncovered a similar pattern in her study of CEOs of international companies. Gender, clearly, is not neural destiny.

Firing Up Your Social Neurons

The firing of social neurons is evident all around us. We once analyzed a video of Herb Kelleher, a cofounder and former CEO of Southwest Airlines, strolling down the corridors of Love Field in Dallas, the airline's hub. We could practically see him activate the mirror neurons, oscillators, and other social circuitry in each person he encountered. He offered beaming smiles, shook hands with customers as he told them how much he appreciated their business, hugged employees as he thanked them for their good work. And he got back exactly what he gave. Typical was the flight attendant whose face lit up when she unexpectedly encountered her boss. "Oh, my honey!" she blurted, brimming with warmth, and gave him a big hug. She later explained, "Everyone just feels like family with him."

Unfortunately, it's not easy to turn yourself into a Herb Kelleher or a Dr. Humboldt if you're not one already. We know of no clear-cut methods to strengthen mirror neurons, spindle cells, and oscillators; they activate by the thousands per second during any encounter, and their precise firing patterns remain elusive. What's more, self-conscious attempts to display social intelligence can often backfire. When you make an intentional effort to coordinate movements with another person, it is not only oscillators that fire. In such situations the brain uses other, less adept circuitry to initiate and guide movements; as a result, the interaction feels forced.

The only way to develop your social circuitry effectively is to undertake the hard work of changing your behavior (see "Primal Leadership: The Hidden Driver of Great Performance," our December 2001 HBR article with Annie McKee). Companies interested in leadership development need to begin by assessing the willingness of individuals to enter a change program. Eager candidates should first develop a personal vision for change and then undergo a thorough diagnostic assessment, akin to a medical workup, to identify areas of social weakness and strength. Armed with the feedback, the aspiring leader can be trained in specific areas where developing better social skills will have the greatest payoff. The training can range from rehearsing better ways of interacting and trying them out at every opportunity, to being shadowed by a coach and then debriefed about what he observes, to learning directly from a role model. The options are many, but the road to success is always tough.

How to Become Socially Smarter

To see what social intelligence training involves, consider the case of a top executive we'll call Janice. She had been hired as a marketing manager by a *Fortune* 500 company because of her business expertise, outstanding track record as a strategic thinker and planner, reputation as a straight talker, and ability to anticipate business issues that were crucial for meeting goals. Within her first six months on the job, however, Janice was floundering; other executives saw her as aggressive and opinionated, lacking in political astuteness, and careless about what she said and to whom, especially higher-ups.

To save this promising leader, Janice's boss called in Kathleen Cavallo, an organizational psychologist and senior consultant with the Hay Group, who immediately put Janice through a 360-degree evaluation. Her direct reports, peers, and managers gave Janice low ratings on empathy, service orientation, adaptability, and managing conflicts. Cavallo learned more by having confidential conversations with the people who worked most closely with Janice. Their complaints focused on her failure to establish rapport with people or even notice their reactions. The bottom line: Janice was adept neither at reading the social norms of a group nor at recognizing people's emotional cues when she violated those norms. Even more dangerous, Janice did not realize she was being too blunt in managing upward. When she had a strong difference of opinion with a manager, she did not sense when to back off. Her "let's get it all on the table and mix it up" approach was threatening her job; top management was getting fed up.

When Cavallo presented this performance feedback as a wake-up call to Janice, she was of course shaken to discover that her job might be in danger. What upset her more, though, was the realization that she was not having her desired impact on other people. Cavallo initiated coaching sessions in which Janice would describe notable successes and failures from her day. The more time Janice spent reviewing these incidents, the better she became at recognizing the difference between expressing an idea with conviction and acting like a pit bull. She began to anticipate how people might react to her in a meeting or during a negative performance review; she rehearsed more-astute ways to present her opinions; and she developed a personal vision for change. Such mental preparation activates the social circuitry of the brain, strengthening the neural connections you need to act effectively; that's why Olympic athletes put hundreds of hours into mental review of their moves.

At one point, Cavallo asked Janice to name a leader in her organization who had excellent social intelligence skills. Janice identified a veteran senior manager who was masterly both in the art of the critique and at expressing disagreement in meetings without damaging relationships. She asked him to help coach her, and she switched to a job where she could work with him—a post she held for two years. Janice was lucky to find a mentor who believed that part of a leader's job is to develop human capital. Many bosses would rather manage around a problem employee than help her get better. Janice's new boss took her on because he recognized her other strengths as invaluable, and his gut told him that Janice could improve with guidance.

Before meetings, Janice's mentor coached her on how to express her viewpoint about contentious issues and how to talk to higher-ups, and he modeled for her the art of performance feedback. By observing him day in and day out, Janice learned to affirm people even as she challenged their positions or critiqued their performance. Spending time with a living, breathing model of effective behavior provides the perfect stimulation for our mirror neurons, which allow us to directly experience, internalize, and ultimately emulate what we observe.

Janice's transformation was genuine and comprehensive. In a sense, she went in one person and came out another. If you think about it, that's an important lesson from neuroscience: Because our behavior creates and develops neural networks, we are not necessarily prisoners of our genes and our early childhood experiences. Leaders can change if, like Janice, they are ready to put in the effort. As she progressed in her training, the social behaviors she was learning became more like second nature to her. In scientific terms, Janice was strengthening her social circuits through practice. And as others responded to her, their brains connected with hers more profoundly and effectively, thereby reinforcing Janice's circuits in a virtuous circle. The upshot: Janice went from being on the verge of dismissal to getting promoted to a position two levels up.

A few years later, some members of Janice's staff left the company because they were not happy—so she asked Cavallo to come back. Cavallo discovered that although Janice had mastered the ability to communicate and connect with management and peers, she still sometimes missed cues from her direct reports when they tried to signal their frustration. With more help from Cavallo, Janice was able to turn the situation around by refocusing her attention on her staff's emotional needs and fine-tuning her communication style. Opinion surveys conducted with Janice's staff before and after Cavallo's second round of coaching documented dramatic increases in their emotional commitment and intention to stay in the organization. Janice and the staff also delivered a 6% increase in annual sales, and after another successful year she was made president of a

Are You a Socially Intelligent Leader?

TO MEASURE AN EXECUTIVE'S SOCIAL intelligence and help him or her develop a plan for improving it, we have a specialist administer our behavioral assessment tool, the Emotional and Social Competency Inventory. It is a 360-degree evaluation instrument by which bosses, peers, direct reports, clients, and sometimes even family members assess a leader according to seven social intelligence qualities.

We came up with these seven by integrating our existing emotional intelligence framework with data assembled by our colleagues at the Hay Group, who used hard metrics to capture the behavior of top-performing leaders at hundreds of corporations over two decades. Listed here are each of the qualities, followed by some of the questions we use to assess them.

Empathy

- Do you understand what motivates other people, even those from different backgrounds?
- Are you sensitive to others' needs?

Attunement

- Do you listen attentively and think about how others feel?
- Are you attuned to others' moods?

Organizational Awareness

- Do you appreciate the culture and values of the group or organization?
- Do you understand social networks and know their unspoken norms?

multibillion-dollar unit. Companies can clearly benefit a lot from putting people through the kind of program Janice completed.

Hard Metrics of Social Intelligence

Our research over the past decade has confirmed that there is a large performance gap between socially intelligent and socially unintelligent leaders. At a major national bank, for example, we found that levels of an executive's social intelligence competencies predicted yearly performance appraisals more powerfully than did the emotional intelligence competencies of self-awareness and

Influence

- Do you persuade others by engaging them in discussion and appealing to their self-interests?
- Do you get support from key people?

Developing Others

- Do you coach and mentor others with compassion and personally invest time and energy in mentoring?
- Do you provide feedback that people find helpful for their professional development?

Inspiration

- Do you articulate a compelling vision, build group pride, and foster a positive emotional tone?
- Do you lead by bringing out the best in people?

Teamwork

- Do you solicit input from everyone on the team?
- Do you support all team members and encourage cooperation?

self-management. (For a brief explanation of our assessment tool, which focuses on seven dimensions, see the sidebar "Are You a Socially Intelligent Leader?")

Social intelligence turns out to be especially important in crisis situations. Consider the experience of workers at a large Canadian provincial health care system that had gone through drastic cutbacks and a reorganization. Internal surveys revealed that the frontline workers had become frustrated that they were no longer able to give their patients a high level of care. Notably, workers whose leaders scored low in social intelligence reported unmet patient-care needs at three times the rate—and emotional exhaustion at four times the

The Chemistry of Stress

WHEN PEOPLE ARE UNDER STRESS, surges in the stress hormones adrenaline and cortisol strongly affect their reasoning and cognition. At low levels, cortisol facilitates thinking and other mental functions, so well-timed pressure to perform and targeted critiques of subordinates certainly have their place. When a leader's demands become too great for a subordinate to handle, however, soaring cortisol levels and an added hard kick of adrenaline can paralyze the mind's critical abilities. Attention fixates on the threat from the boss rather than the work at hand; memory, planning, and creativity go out the window. People fall back on old habits, no matter how unsuitable those are for addressing new challenges.

Poorly delivered criticism and displays of anger by leaders are common triggers of hormonal surges. In fact, when laboratory scientists want to study the highest levels of stress hormones, they simulate a job interview in which an applicant receives intense face-to-face criticism—an analogue of a boss's tearing apart a subordinate's performance. Researchers likewise find that when someone who is very important to a person expresses contempt or disgust toward him, his stress circuitry triggers an explosion by stress hormones and a spike in heart rate of 30 to 40 beats per minute. Then, because of the interpersonal dynamic of mirror neurons and oscillators, the tension spreads to other people. Before you know it, the destructive emotions have infected an entire group and inhibited its performance.

Leaders are themselves not immune to the contagion of stress. All the more reason they should take the time to understand the biology of their emotions.

---

rate—of their colleagues who had supportive leaders. At the same time, nurses with socially intelligent bosses reported good emotional health and an enhanced ability to care for their patients, even during the stress of layoffs (see the sidebar "The Chemistry of Stress"). These results should be compulsory reading for the boards of companies in crisis. Such boards typically favor expertise over social intelligence when selecting someone to guide the institution through tough times. A crisis manager needs both.

As we explore the discoveries of neuroscience, we are struck by how closely the best psychological theories of development map to the newly charted hardwiring of the brain. Back in the 1950s, for example, British pediatrician and psychoanalyst D.W. Winnicott was advocating for play as a way to accelerate children's learning. Similarly, British physician and psychoanalyst John Bowlby emphasized the importance of providing a secure base from which people can strive toward goals, take risks without unwarranted fear, and freely explore new possibilities. Hard-bitten executives may consider it absurdly indulgent and financially untenable to concern themselves with such theories in a world where bottom-line performance is the yardstick of success. But as new ways of scientifically measuring human development start to bear out these theories and link them directly with performance, the so-called soft side of business begins to look not so soft after all.

Originally published in September 2008. Reprint R0809E

Bringing Minds Together

by John Abele

WHEN I WAS invited to submit an article to this spotlight on collaboration, the first question I asked was whether the other contributors and I would have the chance to interact and perhaps integrate our ideas on the topic. I knew that *Harvard Business Review* was deeply rooted in a scholarly tradition—and that worried me. Academic collaboration, I've learned over the years, is something of an oxymoron. More often than not, what is described by that term is really noncollaborative, or worse, pseudo-collaborative work, driven by the long-standing rituals of institutional seniority and the professional and financial incentives to build higher silos with thicker walls. That's a shame since it is our universities that are supposed to have the intellectual force and license to find bold solutions to important problems. On the bright side, there's an extraordinary opportunity for those of us nonacademics who, unconstrained by those customs, see value in getting silos to collide.

The individuals in the stories you are about to read were naturally skillful silo-colliders. Their success in breaking down barriers between and within the scientific, medical, academic, and business communities taught me most of what I know about making progress through collaboration.

My perspective is that of an entrepreneur whose entire career has involved breakthrough innovations, mostly in the scientific and

Community Building

begins with convincing people who don't need to work together that they should. This depends on:

- Inspiring them with a vision of change that is beyond any of their powers to bring about individually
- Convincing them that the other collaborators are vital to the effort and equal to the challenge
- Preventing any one party from benefiting so much that the others feel their contributions are being exploited

medical domains. This wasn't "serial entrepreneurship"—it was long-slog enterprise building in an environment where much of what my colleagues and I did was viewed as politically incorrect. We were developing new approaches that had huge potential value for customers and society but required that well-trained practitioners change their behavior. Despite the clear logic behind the products we invented, markets for them didn't exist. We had to create them in the face of considerable resistance from players invested in the old way and threatened with a loss of power, prestige, and money. Prospects had to be sold on not just our solution but our reframing of the problem, requiring from them a lot of learning—and unlearning of old techniques. Any of the products could have served as the poster child for what Clay Christensen calls "disruptive innovation."

Cash Up Front and Build It Yourself

I got my first glimpse of that kind of collaboration many decades ago, but it continues to teach me lessons to this day. Shortly after I graduated from college (Amherst '59), I went to work for a small company in the Boston area called Advanced Instruments. The lab instruments it made—an osmometer that measured particle concentrations in solutions and a flame photometer that measured ions in solutions—were new to the marketplace, so we regularly invested in booths at the major conferences and trade shows. When traffic in the booth was slow, we'd spend time getting to know folks from

Idea in Brief

Boston Scientific founder John Abele has been party to his share of groundbreaking innovations over the years. But the revolutionary advances in medical science that these breakthroughs brought about were not the efforts of one firm alone, let alone one inventor.

Abele tells two fascinating stories of collaboration—one about Jack Whitehead's upending of hospitals' blood and urine testing procedures and the other about Andreas Gruentzig's success in bringing balloon catheterization into the cardiology mainstream. Both Whitehead and Gruentzig spearheaded the emergence of entirely new fields, bringing together scientist-customers to voluntarily develop standards, training programs, new business models, and even a specialized language to describe their new field.

The process of collaboration, Abele says, is fraught with contradictions and subtlety. It takes consummate leadership skills to persuade others to spend countless hours solving important problems in partnership with people they don't necessarily like. Moreover, managing egos so that each person's commitment, energy, and creativity is unleashed in a way that doesn't disadvantage others requires an impresario personality. Finally, true authenticity—something that few people can project—is critical for earning customers' trust and convincing them that their valuable contributions won't be used for anything other than moving the technology forward.

neighboring exhibits. At one of those conferences, in 1960, I met Jack Whitehead, the CEO of Technicon. I subsequently came to know his company pretty well. Its success is more than just a surprising business story. It's the kind of effort Margaret Mead had in mind when she said, "Never underestimate the power of a small dedicated group of people to change the world. Indeed, it's the only thing that ever has."

Technicon was originally a maker of tissue-processing equipment, and that was a nice business, but slow growing. Jack had been on the lookout for new technologies that would allow him to dramatically expand his business. He made the bold decision to buy the patents and prototypes for a machine that automated the process of analyzing certain chemicals. The doctor who'd invented the machine was a clinical chemist—the person who runs the hospital lab that tests blood, urine, and other body fluids—and his creation was truly amazing. The liquid samples poured into it were transported through transparent tubing made of hydrophobic (water-repelling) materials. Each sample beaded up in the tube rather than spreading out. Air bubbles separated the samples and prevented cross-contamination. Along their journey through the "bubble machine," the samples would pass through a spectrometer, a device that determines the absorption of various wavelengths of light in a liquid sample and thereby indicates what chemicals, and in what quantities, are present.

The inventor was, naturally, proud of his achievement. But when he tried to sell it to the big laboratory supply companies of the time, he was turned down flat. That may seem baffling, given the fact that such instruments now constitute a multibillion-dollar business, with millions of tests being carried out daily. But this was the early 1960s, when physicians were ordering very few tests, and there were plenty of lab technicians to do them. Even the leading instrument makers couldn't see the point of automating the process. More important, the professional societies weren't on board. Not only did they believe that no more tests were needed, they were downright hostile to any outsider who had the temerity to tell them otherwise. To say that this was a new and disruptive technology without a defined market would be an understatement. And although the big companies were pretty good at selling accepted products, they were not (and still are not) up to that kind of challenge. Even if they could envision the change such a machine would usher in, they couldn't manage the culture-changing activities that go with creating new markets. But Jack could.

His outgoing personality and powers of persuasion worked in his favor, but he also came up with a radical sales process. Pointing out that the instrument was new and would remain unique because it was protected by lots of patents, he told all interested buyers that they'd have to spend a week at his factory learning about it—and that payment was required in advance. The training would cover how the instrument worked, what might go wrong, how to fix it, how to use it for different applications, and how to develop new applications. Customers even had to put their own machines together.

Those might sound like terms that would discourage people from buying the machine. A week is a long time for busy scientists, and the factory was nothing fancy. Demanding the money up front seemed pretty aggressive. But every field has its early adopters, and Jack was good at finding them.

The real magic of the approach, however, was in the extraordinary dynamic it created among the participants. Working in Technicon's factory, thinking about applications, they didn't feel like customers, they felt like partners. They got to know Jack and his staff. They worked like the devil during the day and played pretty hard at night—sometimes the reverse. They got to know one another very well. They became a kind of family.

When the week ended, those relationships endured and a vibrant community began to emerge around the innovation. The scientist-customers fixed one another's machines. They developed new applications. They published papers. They came up with new product ideas. They gave talks at scientific meetings. They recruited new customers. In time, they developed standards, training programs, new business models, and even a specialized language to describe their new field.

It wasn't long before Jack's "band of brothers" had become sufficiently large and was producing so many new ideas that he decided to convene what he called the Technicon Symposium. This was pretty heretical since academic societies planned and sponsored all the scientific conferences at the time; companies like Technicon were relegated to the exhibit halls. But the symposium served a clear need, and over the years it grew in size and prestige until it rivaled the professional societies' meetings in quality and reputation. Jack had formed a "user group" long before that strategy had been conceived. He had created a culture in which everyone was both a leader and a follower. It wasn't about money; it was about being a pioneer in a new field.

Watching how this unique strategy helped the field advance and Technicon succeed had a profound effect on me. Most of my colleagues saw what Jack was doing as creative marketing and aggressive business strategy. But I saw it differently, and by now I know that something much bigger was actually going on. He was launching a new field that could be created only by collaboration—and collaboration among people who had previously seen no need to work together. Thanks to Jack's efforts, a group of scientist-customers self-organized to do something he never could have done on his own: advance the responsible development of automated chemical analysis.

As I watched this experiment evolve, and later applied its lessons in my work and philanthropic activities, I came to realize that the kind of collaboration Jack made look simple is in fact a process fraught with contradictions and subtlety. It takes a great collaborative leader. Persuading people to contribute countless hours of effort in partnership with people they don't necessarily like to solve important problems requires consummate leadership skills. Managing egos so that each person's commitment, energy, and creativity is unleashed in a way without disadvantaging others demands an impresario personality. Earning customers' trust and convincing them that their valuable contributions won't be used for anything other than moving the technology forward requires an authenticity few people can project.

The interaction and progress Jack enabled was never heralded as collaboration, though that is what it was. Indeed, I've learned that some of the best collaborative efforts don't look like collaborations. And some projects that are touted as collaborations are Potemkin villages—great-looking facades with no substance behind them.

Two Inventors, One Breakthrough

In 1967 I left Advanced Instruments on friendly terms. Having risen from a sales engineer to general manager of that privately owned company, I was eager to strike out on my own. I soon bought a fledgling start-up called Medi-Tech, which later became Boston Scientific. Its product was a steerable catheter—an amazing integration of chemical, polymeric, metallurgical, mechanical, and processing technologies that allowed users (practitioners in radiology, cardiology, gastroenterology, and urology) to use fluoroscopic imaging to remotely guide a catheter or device to any location in the body. To advance the technology and build a market for it, I turned to Jack Whitehead's strategy of creating a community of users to share applications, education, and research. Although the field wasn't that big, our technology was visibly impressive to brilliant inventor-physicians, and our collaborative strategy differentiated us. We lacked the resources and name recognition that many of our competitors had, but we became known as trustworthy innovators who would listen, share, and ask good questions. Our competitors vied to take opinion leaders out to dinner. Opinion leaders took us out.

Our collaborative outreach led us to a young angiologist by the name of Andreas Gruentzig, who had developed a balloon catheter (a tube with a sausage-shaped balloon at the tip) for the purpose of enlarging narrowed arteries without surgery. He actually built the devices in the kitchen of his apartment, using a razor, tubing, and adhesive.

The basic idea of opening arteries with a catheter, called percutaneous transluminal angioplasty, had been pioneered a decade earlier by a doctor from Oregon, Charles Dotter. But Dotter's technique never took off. Why? In the first place, he used a tapered catheter that simply "snowplowed" the obstructing material to the side or sometimes just pushed it downstream. Gruentzig's balloon was much less traumatic and more effective. Just as important, Dotter's stance toward his potential community pretty much ensured that he would not get the feedback he needed to improve the technology. A classic inventor, he was an exciting speaker but tended to exaggerate claims. He also loved telling surgeons that they'd be out of business in the near future—not a good strategy if he hoped for their help.

Andreas was just as passionate about his ideas, and a magnetic speaker in his own way, but he was understated, careful, and curious. He was an inventor, a technician, an excellent clinician who connected with patients, and a good experimentalist who knew how to design a well-thought-out trial. I should also note that, as a junior

Establishment Bucking

can't be avoided. When a group collaborates on a new solution, there's usually another, bigger, group invested in the way things are done today. Be sure to:

- Recruit some of their respected players into your vanguard
- Create your own center stage to prevent your star project from being pushed into the wings
- Downplay, rather than underscore, the threat your breakthrough poses to their livelihood

physician at the University Hospital in Zurich, he had very little personal or professional authority. Much of his early access and influence was thanks to his friendship with a world-famous cardiac surgeon named Ake Senning, the father of the pacemaker, who had moved from Sweden to Switzerland for tax reasons. Senning's patronage was the reason that Andreas had patients on which to try his new procedure. (Of course, Andreas didn't start with patients; he spent years practicing in the lab on dogs and then cadavers before taking on low-risk patients who could be easily moved to surgery if the procedure was unsuccessful.)

Andreas turned out to be an extraordinary collaborative leader. He presented his ideas in ways that cried out for input from other brilliant minds. Instead of proclaiming that his ideas were revolutionary breakthroughs that would change medicine, Andreas referred to them as incremental advances. He was always the first to point out the deficiencies in the tools he pioneered and was constantly on the lookout for signs that they were flawed. He sought ideas from anyone who might be able to help address problems. He won over surgeons—the very people whose work he was disrupting and thus who were his potential enemies—by presenting all his data in an understated way. People responded in part because of Andreas's unusual willingness to share credit for whatever was achieved. He used the word "we," not "I," when describing the efforts that had made the breakthroughs possible.

Collaboration

is the natural by-product of leaders who are

- Passionately curious—who crave new insights and suspect that others have them
- Modestly confident—who can bounce ideas off brilliant collaborators, without turning it into a competition
- Mildly obsessed—who care more about the collective mission than about how achieving it will benefit their personal fortunes

. . . and may be the only leadership mode that produces breakthrough results.

A Course Becomes a Cause

In the fall of 1976, Andreas presented a poster on his animal work at the American Heart Association's annual meeting, advancing the powerful but controversial idea that balloon catheterization could be used to open coronary arteries. I introduced many of my cardiology and surgeon friends to him at the meeting. Their conversations were so compelling that a number of physicians made plans right then to fly to Switzerland and see firsthand what he was doing. In fact, so many people visited him or invited him to their institutions to demonstrate his procedure that his boss in Zurich put a moratorium on visits and trips.

Undeterred, Andreas found a way around the restrictions. He created a course that would bring all the parties together. He used the then-new capabilities of video to transmit images from the cath lab where he would conduct the procedure to a lecture theatre at the hospital. His innovative approach was a smashing success. It allowed him to share with the audience every detail of how the technology worked, including any problems that arose. To make sure that everyone was engaged, he would periodically ask participants, via video, what they thought he should do next. That willingness to take direction communicated his belief that he and his scientist-customers were equals and this wasn't his project alone. On the last evening of the course, dinner was served on a local hilltop, and a bonfire and torches provided light as the sun went down. At the end of the evening Andreas led his guests in a torchlight parade down the hill. The symbolism was powerful: Everyone was royalty. This group was going to change the world.

What Andreas couldn't have known in that first year was how his idea of a live demonstration course would evolve. Other physicians started their own live demonstration courses on the same principles. When audiences became too large for hospital lecture halls, they began meeting in hotel ballrooms and in convention centers. A moderated panel of contrarian, independent experts would provide play-by-play critical analysis for everyone's benefit. Outside speakers were invited to present slide talks during the downtime between cases. The leading physician educators used audience-response technology to engage participants on difficult issues.

Most strikingly, it proved to be only a short hop hosting on-site meetings to conducting off-site and offshore ones. For example, American medical specialists were eager to learn about technologies not yet approved by the FDA, and the performance and price of video technology made it feasible to view live coverage of cases being performed in other countries. Some courses today assemble many thousands of physicians and involve more than 100 different live cases beamed in from cities around the world.

At that scale, the live demonstration course tends to be thought of as a learning experience, pure and simple, but I would describe it as one of those collaborations that doesn't look like one. All sides of issues and a wide range of perspectives are presented, and controversy is welcomed. As in Andreas's first course, the goal is a collective one: to advance the field through the sharing of research, best practices, trial status, clinical status, and what's coming next.

Creating the Basis for Progress

Perhaps the most important collaborative approach Andreas introduced was the creation of a voluntary registry of the cases he and a few of his U.S. colleagues treated. In contrast to the stultifying record keeping required by "official" bureaucratic entities, this was a way to track results independent of any traditional professional society or academic or government institution. At that time, the FDA had the authority to regulate medical devices, but it was a long way away from figuring out the process details for doing so. That first registry was conceived to generate a body of data that could help the community understand which factors were the most important for success, what needed to be improved, and how the instruments might be modified to safely treat more types of blockages. Cardiologists doing these procedures were pressured by peers to produce careful documentation. Perhaps, as a result, most were a bit less likely to behave recklessly. It is no exaggeration to say that the rapid sharing of experience and techniques enabled by the registry saved many lives and prevented untold complications. There was no long wait, as in a drug trial, for lessons to be extracted; clinical users could take advantage of new information as soon as it came in. Problems were discovered and solutions were offered almost on the fly. And when it came time to publish papers, Andreas and his closest collaborators made sure to spread the intellectual wealth. They developed guidelines for which papers would be published by which authors and when.

By the time the registry was picked up by the National Institutes of Health, several years later, it was well-established as a powerful new methodology in itself. This was the first time that so many physicians had collaborated on a new technique, and it was clear that the collaboration had accelerated both the development of the technique and the learning about it. The approach has since been adopted in many other fields.

A Different Kind of Leadership

One thing that has become clear in the course of this proliferation of registries is how dependent they turn out to be on the capabilities of their leaders. The ability to lead leaders is a rare skill, and Andreas, like Jack Whitehead, was a great role model. In a sense, he was the Linus Torvalds or Jimmy Wales of angioplasty. Just as Torvalds helped spawn the open source movement, and Jimmy Wales spearheaded the Wiki phenomenon, Andreas had created a community of change agents who carried his ideas forward far more efficiently than he could have done on his own.

The key was the dynamic between Andreas and his followers. This was a group of big personalities, full of independent, ego-driven, enormously self-confident men. On top of that, they were rivals. But all of them loved working at the cutting edge of medicine and had dreamed of taking part in a groundbreaking endeavor. When Andreas came along, they saw that possibility. And that's one of the crucial ingredients of collaboration. None of the participants would have said Andreas had the right to give them orders, yet they respected him and were confident he was taking the right steps to ensure that the technology was properly assessed as it was developed. He had earned that confidence, paradoxically, by never presuming to have all the answers. He carefully explained why he did things the way he did, but he always allowed that others might choose alternative methods. Just as Jack Whitehead did with his early band of brothers, Andreas built a corps that prided itself on boldly taking the risks and doing the hard work needed to turn a compelling vision into reality.

With that dynamic established, Andreas didn't need to exert much authority. In fact, he purposely ceded control and applied himself to keeping trust levels high. He role-modeled the investigational discipline that would allay doubts about the process. And he expertly managed the various personalities in the group to keep jealousies or interpersonal friction to a minimum. He encouraged members to continually question and teach one another. He made sure that problems were rooted out, not glossed over, the more quickly to arrive at solutions.

Is It the Tools?

Mention the word "collaboration" to businesspeople today and they immediately think you're going to talk about software. The tech world is boiling over with new tools that enable groups large and small to instantly and easily share complex information and that facilitate and track contributions from many participants. But true collaboration requires more than handy applications—in fact, the same tools can just as easily derail or outright destroy collaboration. The availability of so much software doesn't so much solve our need for collaboration as heighten the difficulty of managing it. To make matters worse, rules and laws that inhibit collaboration continue to shift and clash. The world becomes bumpier in some ways as it becomes flatter in others. In the science domain, the information explosion has led to more silos, not fewer.

For all these reasons, it's more critical than ever to understand the complex soft elements, such as emotional intelligence, that are the makings of a strong collaborative culture. Many people go through the motions, but few know how to really collaborate. I am often struck by the behaviors of otherwise bright people who poison potentially rich collaborations, seemingly without realizing it.

Jack Whitehead and Andreas Gruentzig were true collaborative leaders. There have been people like them in every field throughout history. It may be an exaggeration to compare Jack and Andreas with Gandhi, Mandela, or Martin Luther King, Jr., but let's list the challenges they all faced: Silos with different cultures. Strong egos, messenger killers, and pontificators. Hidden agendas, cynicism, and groupthink. Diverse levels of understanding and a whole range of biases. All these factors make it hard to harness the collective intelligence of great (or even not so great) minds. These leaders overcame the obstacles.

You can be sure that Jack and Andreas didn't get it all right. They had their catastrophes along the way. But their default mind-set was inclusive and questioning, confident and humble. Both had a great sense of theater and used it effectively. They knew how to set the stage for collaboration and employ ritual, symbolism, or humor to disarm and inspire. They recognized that diversity is an antidote to groupthink.

When will these approaches start catching on in boardrooms, mayors' offices, and universities? Look around you. I think you'll see that they already are.

Originally published in July–August 2011. Reprint R1107F

Building a Collaborative Enterprise

by Paul Adler, Charles Heckscher, and Laurence Prusak

A SOFTWARE ENGINEER we'll call James vividly remembers his first day at Computer Sciences Corporation (CSC). The very first message he received: "Here are your Instructions" (yes, with a capital I).

"I thought I was bringing the know-how I'd need to do my job," James recalls. "But sure enough, you open up the Instructions, and it tells you how to do your job: how to lay the code out, where on the form to write a change-request number, and so on. I was shocked."

In this division at CSC, code is no longer developed by individual, freewheeling programmers. They now follow the Capability Maturity Model (CMM), a highly organized process that James initially felt was too bureaucratic: "As a developer, I was pretty allergic to all this paperwork. It's so time-consuming."

Not anymore. "I can see the need for it now," James says. "Now I'm just one of 30 or 40 people who may have to work on this code, so we need a change-request number that everyone can use to identify it. I can see that it makes things much easier."

What James was joining at CSC was neither a code-writing assembly line nor a bunch of autonomous hackers but a new type of organization that excels at combining the knowledge of diverse specialists. We call this kind of enterprise a *collaborative community.*

Collaborative communities encourage people to continually apply their unique talents to group projects—and to become motivated by a collective mission, not just personal gain or the intrinsic pleasures of autonomous creativity. By marrying a sense of common purpose to a supportive structure, these organizations are mobilizing knowledge workers' talents and expertise in flexible, highly manageable group-work efforts. The approach fosters not only innovation and agility but also efficiency and scalability.

A growing number of organizations—including IBM, Citibank, NASA, and Kaiser Permanente—are reaping the rewards of collaborative communities in the form of higher margins on knowledge-intensive work. (The CSC divisions that applied the CMM most rigorously reduced error rates by 75% over six years and achieved a 10% annual increase in productivity, while making products more innovative and technologically sophisticated.) We have found that such clear success requires four new organizational efforts:

- defining and building a shared purpose
- cultivating an ethic of contribution
- developing processes that enable people to work together in flexible but disciplined projects
- creating an infrastructure in which collaboration is valued and rewarded.

Our findings are based on many years of studying institutions that have sustained records of both efficiency and innovation. The writings of great thinkers in sociology—Karl Marx, Max Weber, Émile Durkheim, and Talcott Parsons—also inform our work. These classic figures were trying to make sense of broad economic and social changes during times when capitalism was mutating from small-scale manufacturing to large-scale industry. Our era represents just as momentous a shift, as we make the transition to an economy based on knowledge work and workers.

Idea in Brief

Can large companies be both innovative and efficient? Yes, argue Adler, of the University of Southern California; Heckscher, of Rutgers; and Prusak, an independent consultant. But they must develop new organizational capabilities that will create the atmosphere of trust that knowledge work requires—and the coordinating mechanisms to make it scalable. Specifically, such organizations must learn to:

- Define a shared purpose that guides what people at all levels of the organization are trying to achieve together;
- Cultivate an ethic of contribution in which the highest value is accorded to people who look beyond their specific roles and advance the common purpose;
- Develop scalable procedures for coordinating people's efforts so that process-management activities become truly interdependent; and
- Create an infrastructure in which individuals' spheres of influence overlap and collaboration is both valued and rewarded.

These four goals may sound idealized, but the imperative to achieve them is practical, say the authors. Only the truly collaborative enterprises that can tap into everyone's ideas—in an organized way—will compete imaginatively, quickly, and cost-effectively enough to become the household names of this century.

A Shared Purpose

Sociologist Max Weber famously outlined four bases for social relations, which can be roughly summarized as *tradition, self-interest, affection,* and *shared purpose.* Self-interest underlies what all businesses do, of course. The great industrial corporations of the 20th century also invoked tradition to motivate people. And many of the most innovative companies of the past 30 years—Hewlett-Packard, Microsoft, Apple, Google, and Facebook—have derived strength from strong, broadly felt affection for a charismatic leader.

In focusing on the fourth alternative—a shared purpose—collaborative communities seek a basis for trust and organizational cohesion that is more robust than self-interest, more flexible than tradition, and less ephemeral than the emotional, charismatic appeal of a Steve Jobs, a Larry Page, or a Mark Zuckerberg.

Like a good strategy or vision statement, an effective shared purpose articulates how a group will position itself in relation to competitors and partners—and what key contributions to customers and society will define its success. Kaiser Permanente's Value Compass, for example, succinctly defines the organization's shared purpose this way: "Best quality, best service, most affordable, best place to work."

This shared purpose is not an expression of a company's enduring essence—it's a description of what everyone in the organization is trying to do. It guides efforts at all levels of Kaiser: from top management's business strategy, to joint planning by the company's unique labor-management partnership, right down to unit-based teams' work on process improvement. In that regard, Value Compass is less a vision than a recognition of the challenges that every member of the group has the responsibility to meet every day. (See the sidebar "A Collaborative Dance at Kaiser Permanente.")

Leaders often have trouble articulating such a purpose, falling back on either lofty truisms ("We will delight our customers") or simple financial targets ("We will grow revenues by 20% a year"). Indeed, the development of a common purpose can be a long, complex process.

For instance, IBM, which needed to reorient its employees from a focus on selling "big iron" in the 1990s, spent a decade building a shared understanding of integrated solutions and on-demand customer focus that went beyond simplistic rhetoric. For many years middle managers and technical employees had found it difficult to frame these concepts in practical terms. They didn't understand at an operational level what it meant for the company to offer not just its own products but those of other vendors—and to sell customers not simply what IBM offered but exactly what they needed when they needed it. Today these common purposes have become part of the language shared daily by people from different functions and at various levels of IBM as they face challenges together.

Properly understood, a shared purpose is a powerful organizing principle. Take, for example, e-Solutions, a unit of about 150 people formed in April 2000 within the cash-management division of Citibank to address a competitive threat from AOL, whose customers were already banking, trading stocks, and buying mutual funds online. To meet this challenge, Citibank sought to boost the growth rate of its core cash-management and trade business from 4% to roughly 20%.

But that was just the business goal. The common purpose behind that number was the aspiration to be a leader in creating new and complex online banking products that could be tailored rapidly to customers' needs. To fully grasp this purpose required widespread discussion and a shared understanding of the company's competitive position within the industry, the evolution of customer needs, and the distinctive capabilities of the organization.

A shared purpose is not the verbiage on a poster or in a document, and it doesn't come via charismatic leaders' pronouncements. It is multidimensional, practical, and constantly enriched in debates about concrete problems. Therefore, when we asked managers at e-Solutions why they worked on a given project, they did not answer "Because that's my job" or "That's where the money is." They talked instead about how the project would advance the shared purpose.

An Ethic of Contribution

Collaborative communities share a distinctive set of values, which we call an *ethic of contribution*. It accords the highest value to people who look beyond their specific roles and advance the common purpose.

The collaborative view rejects the notion of merely "doing a good job," unless that actually makes a contribution. We have learned from practically a century of experience with the traditional model that it is quite possible for everyone to work hard as an individual without producing a good collective result. An ethic of contribution means going beyond one's formal responsibilities to solve broader problems, not just applying greater effort. It also rejects the strong individualism of the market model and instead emphasizes working within the group (rather than trying to gain individual control or responsibility) and eliciting the best contributions from each member for the common good.

Consider the way the software engineers at CSC view the aptly named Capability Maturity Model. "A more mature process means you go from freedom to do things your own way to being critiqued," one engineer acknowledges. "It means going from chaos to structure." That structure makes these knowledge workers more conscious of their interdependence, which has in turn encouraged the shift from an ethic of individual creativity to an ethic of contribution. Another engineer uses this analogy:

"It's a bit like street ball versus NBA basketball. Street ball is roughhousing, showing off. You play for yourself rather than the team, and you do it for the love of the game. In professional basketball, you're part of a team, and you practice a lot together, doing drills and playing practice games. You aren't doing it just for yourself or even just for your team: Other people are involved—managers, lawyers, agents, advertisers. It's a business, not just a game."

The type of trust engendered by an ethic of contribution is less of a given than the trust at traditional organizations, which is firmly rooted in a shared set of rules expressed through tokens of the shared culture. (For many years at IBM, for example, all "good" employees wore the same kind of hat.) But it is also less mercurial than trust built upon faith in a charismatic leader and dazzling displays of individual brilliance. Trust in collaborative communities arises from the degree to which each member believes the other members of the group are able and willing to further the shared purpose. (See the sidebar "Three Models of Corporate Community.")

Given this difference in values, people working on collaborative efforts within larger organizations can find themselves at odds with both the loyalists and the free agents in their midst. For instance, contributors at e-Solutions, working within the generally traditional Citibank organization, were suspicious of the tendency to discuss "who you know" rather than focusing on the task at hand.

"Everyone has their own signals that they look for," said one contributor. "If someone comes into the first meeting and starts throwing around names, my hackles go up because that means, rather than focusing on capabilities and market proposition, they're trying to establish credibility in terms of who they know and who they've talked to. . . . That, at the end of the day, doesn't move you an inch down the line."

Instituting Interdependent Processes

Of course, a shared purpose is meaningless if people with different skills and responsibilities can't contribute to it and to one another. Although traditional bureaucracies excel at vertical coordination, they are not good at encouraging horizontal relations. Free-agent communities excel at ad hoc collaboration but are less successful at large-scale interdependent efforts.

The key coordinating mechanism of a collaborative community, which is often made up of overlapping teams, is a process for aligning the shared purpose within and across the projects. We call that type of coordination *interdependent process management,* a family of techniques including *kaizen,* process mapping, and formal protocols for brainstorming, participatory meeting management, and decision making with multiple stakeholders. CMM, with its well-developed methods, for instance, enables CSC's software engineers to quickly tailor proven project-management procedures to the needs of the project at hand.

Interdependent process management is explicit, flexible, and interactive. Processes are carefully worked out and generally written into protocols, but they are revised continually as the demands of the work and of clients change. They are shaped more by people involved in the task than by those at the top. As one CSC project manager put it, "People support what they help create. . . . As a project manager, you're too far away from the technical work to define the [processes] yourself. . . . It's only by involving your key people that you can be confident you have good [procedures] that have credibility in the eyes of their peers."

At e-Solutions, interdependence took shape in the "e-business road map," which was made available online to everyone in the organization, served as a template for emerging projects, and was continually

A Collaborative Dance at Kaiser Permanente

A UNIT OF KAISER PERMANENTE in California developed a new protocol—dubbed the Total Joint Dance—that illustrates how collaborative communities mobilize the knowledge of many diverse contributors to yield scalable business results.

In 2008 Irvine Medical Center wanted to streamline its costliest, most time-intensive surgeries: total-hip and knee-joint replacements. The task was daunting, because the solution required collaboration among specialists who normally fight for resources.

The feat could not have been accomplished by either a traditional or a free-agent type of organization. As Dr. Tadashi Funahashi, the chief of orthopedics, explained, "You have multiple surgeons from multiple different practices, each wanting to do it their own way." What's more, most of Kaiser's employees and insurance customers are unionized. Union cooperation was critical, so neither a top-down administrative mandate nor a surgeon-driven approach was feasible. Kaiser's collaborative community was formalized in the Labor Management Partnership, a joint governance structure involving management and most of Kaiser's employee unions.

In May 2008 a team of OR nurses, surgeons, technicians, and others was assembled. Together this group of union staff, management, and physicians examined every point in the process.

"Usually when we're in the room, we wish it would be done differently," said an OR nurse who was part of the efficiency team. "But this time we actually got a voice in how it's done differently."

Efficiencies were gained by making three types of changes. The first identified parts of the sequential process that could be done simultaneously. Housekeeping staff, for instance, might start the clean-up process when a surgeon begins securing sutures instead of waiting until the patient is out of the operating room.

---

updated and refined. Emerging teams developed their own maps to feed into it as they defined their roles and responsibilities.

In a collaborative community, anyone can initiate changes if his or her work demands it, but considerable discussion is required to figure out the consequences for other participants and to make sure

The second type of change was triggers: cues to a staff member about when to begin a specific task, such as alerting the post-op and transporting departments that a surgery is ending and the patient will be ready for transport in 15 minutes. This matter might sound trivial, but it requires people to think beyond their own jobs to how their roles fit with others'.

The third change was investing in a "floater" nurse who could move between ORs to provide extra help or relieve staff on breaks. That added capacity is costly but pays off in cycle-time reductions—a trade-off that managers miss if they're focused purely on dollars.

The effect of combining better coordination with increased resources was "like night and day," as Dr. Funahashi describes it. "It's the difference between a well-organized, choreographed team and things happening in a default chaotic state."

With these three changes in place, the number of total-hip and knee-joint replacement surgeries increased from one or two up to four a day, and the average turnaround time between procedures dropped from 45 to 20 minutes. Better coordination freed up 188 hours of OR time a year, at an average annual saving of $132,000 per OR.

Patients and employees are also happier with the outcomes. Surveys of OR staff at one Kaiser facility showed an 85% increase in job satisfaction after the new protocol was adopted.

Perhaps most significant from an organizational perspective is that the gains were scalable. For example, the practices have been adopted by general surgery, along with head and neck, urology, vascular, and other surgery specialties at Irvine. And this approach has spread to other Kaiser hospitals.

that everyone understands them. A Citibank e-Solutions manager described it this way:

"Who owns the process map? We all do. All of us have different perspectives, either on particular partners or on the products or on the overall relationship. When we make a change, it gets communicated

Three Models of Corporate Community

TRADITIONAL ENTERPRISES INSPIRE institutional loyalty; free-agent communities foster individualism. Neither type of organization creates the conditions for collaborative trust that business today requires.

Traditional Industrial Model

These densely interconnected communities are bound by strongly shared values and traditions: clear roles, consistent opportunity for advancement, job security, and benefits. The combination of loyalty and bureaucratic structure allows such organizations to reach unprecedented scale but makes them inflexible and slow to innovate.

Free-Agent Model

These organizations are innovative and flexible. They forgo rules, procedures, and deferential relations in favor of individual effort and reward. Loyalties are based on affection for charismatic leaders. This model is effective for modular projects, but weak organizational ties make it difficult to build the extensive team structure that is needed for knowledge-based work.

Collaborative Community Model

These communities are organized around a sense of shared purpose and coordinated through collaboratively developed, carefully documented procedures. They believe that diversity of capability stimulates innovation. Such organizations excel at interdependent knowledge-based work.

to everybody. We've had team meetings to discuss it; everyone understands his role. Originally it was just me and a couple of other people; when we split responsibilities from delivery and execution, we had to redo the exercise."

This kind of process management is tough to maintain. It requires people who are accustomed to more-traditional systems to develop radically new habits. In either bureaucratic or market-oriented organizations, people are given objectives and procedures but are generally left alone to operate within those boundaries. Collaborative process management intrudes on that autonomy—it requires people to continually adapt to others' needs. Accepting the value of this interdependence is often difficult, and the habits of documentation and discussion may require considerable time to take root. A manager at Johnson & Johnson described his group's struggles:

"The team acknowledged problems of poor alignment. As a result, we sat down as a team and put things on a piece of paper. The idea was that I could just go back and refer to something we had decided and say, 'On May 15th we decided x, y, and z.' Within a day, that plan was obsolete. We were making agreements, changing dates, reprioritizing, and not updating the document. The main problem is the informal side conversations between two people. They make a decision without informing the rest of the team. The key is to review this periodically as things change. We need to update and maintain the document as we have conversations."

Creating a Collaborative Infrastructure

If work is organized in teams and workers increasingly serve on more than one team, the need for a new type of authority structure arises—one that involves overlapping spheres of influence. We call it *participative centralization.* It's participative because the collaborative enterprise seeks to mobilize everyone's knowledge; it's centralized because that knowledge must be coordinated so that it can be applied at scale. An e-Solutions contributor described a typical example:

"There are really three heads of the unit. One of them is responsible for my salary, but from a professional perspective they're equally important. One of them tells me more what to do on a tactical level, another more on general direction and vision. The advantage is that there are multiple people who can play multiple roles, so we can get at resources from multiple perspectives. In the e-space it's very useful to be nimble in that way. At the end of the day it is clear who gets to make the decision, but it rarely comes to that. I wouldn't say that decisions are never bumped up; I would say that these flat structures invite more questioning and more discussion, which I think is a good thing because when you have a stricter organizational hierarchy, people are more reluctant to bring things to their superiors."

If what this contributor describes appears to be a matrix, it is. The matrix structure has been tried by many firms during recent decades, and its failure rate is high, so people often assume it's a poor model. But matrix structures actually offer a huge competitive advantage precisely because they are so hard to sustain. They both support and are supported by the other features of the collaborative model: shared purpose, an ethic of collaboration, and interdependent process management. Without those buttresses, the matrix model collapses under the weight of political bickering.

Pay systems are not primary drivers of motivation in collaborative organizations. People will become dissatisfied over time if they feel their pay does not reflect their contributions, but their daily decision making is not guided by the goal of maximizing their compensation. Rather, the operative motivation is what Tracy Kidder, in *The Soul of a New Machine,* memorably labeled the "pinball" theory of management: If you win, you get to play again—to take on a new challenge, to move to a new level. More broadly, people talk about one another's contributions a lot, so collaborative communities foster a relatively accurate reputational system, which becomes the basis for selecting people to participate in new and interesting projects.

That said, pay systems need to be equitable. Given that formal supervisors can't monitor everything that subordinates in different departments are doing on various projects, collaborative organizations rely heavily on some form of multisource, 360-degree feedback.

The Collaborative Revolution

We do not wish to downplay the undeniable challenges of building collaborative communities. Setting and aligning processes that interconnect people on many teams requires constant attention. Not every star player you may wish to attract will want to relinquish autonomy to reap the rewards of a team's effort. Allocating pay fairly according to contribution is tricky.

Indeed, we have found that the patience and skill required to create and maintain a sense of common purpose are rare in corporate hierarchies, particularly given that it is not a set-it-and-forget-it process. The purpose must be continually redefined as markets and clients evolve, and members of the community need to be constantly engaged in shaping and understanding complex collective missions. That kind of participation is costly and time-consuming. And charismatic leaders who believe that they should simply go with their gut often don't relish this way of doing business.

What's more, developing a collaborative community, as IBM's experience attests, is a long-term investment, in tension with many short-term competitive and financial pressures that companies must navigate. So we do not envision a day anytime soon when all companies will be organized entirely into collaborative communities.

Still, few would argue that today's market imperative—to innovate fast enough to keep up with the competition and with customer needs while simultaneously improving cost and efficiency—can be met without the active engagement of employees in different functions and at multiple levels of responsibility. To undertake that endeavor, businesses need a lot more than minimal cooperation and mere compliance. They need everyone's ideas on how to do things better and more cheaply. They need true collaboration.

A century ago a few companies struggled to build organizations reliable enough to take advantage of the emerging mass consumer economy. Those that succeeded became household names: General Motors, DuPont, Standard Oil. Today reliability is no longer a key competitive advantage, and we are at a new turning point. The organizations that will become the household names of this century will be renowned for sustained, large-scale, efficient innovation. The key to that capability is neither company loyalty nor free-agent autonomy but, rather, a strong collaborative community.

Originally published in July–August 2011. Reprint R1107G

Silo Busting

How to Execute on the Promise of Customer Focus.

by Ranjay Gulati

IN 2001, UNDER PRICE pressure from the government and managed health care organizations, GE Medical Systems (now GE Healthcare) created a unit, Performance Solutions, to sell consulting services packaged with imaging equipment as integrated solutions. These solutions, priced at a premium, were intended to enhance productivity by, for instance, reducing patient backlogs. At the time, lots of companies were making the move from selling products to selling solutions in an attempt to differentiate themselves in increasingly commoditized markets.

GE's plan seemed to work well at first. The Performance Solutions unit enjoyed strong initial revenues, in part because most new contracts included additional consulting services valued at $25,000 to $50,000. And the unit had some notable successes. It helped Stanford University Medical Center, for example, make the transition to an all-digital imaging environment at its adult hospital, children's medical center, and an outpatient facility—moves that delivered millions of dollars in new revenues for the medical center and substantial cost savings.

But by 2005, the unit's growth had begun a swift decline. It turned out that equipment salespeople had trouble explaining the value of consulting services, so when they called on customers they couldn't contribute much to the sale of additional services. What's more, these reps were reluctant to allow Performance Solutions salespeople to contact their customers. And by marketing the unit's consulting services with its product portfolio, GE generated solutions that were useful for customers whose problems could clearly be solved using GE's equipment but less compelling for those whose needs were linked only loosely to the imaging products.

In the end, GE refashioned the unit to address customers' needs in a more comprehensive fashion and to better align the sales organization. For instance, the majority of solutions now focus mainly on consulting services and are no longer marketed only with GE equipment. The solutions group secured new contracts valued at more than $500 million in 2006. But in trying to escape the perils of commoditization, the company initially fell into a classic trap: It was seeking to solve customer problems but was viewing those problems through the lens of its own products, rather than from the customer's perspective. It was pulling together what it had on offer in the hope that customers would value the whole more than the sum of its parts.

Over the past five years, I have studied the challenge of top- and bottom-line growth in the face of commoditization, and I have found that many companies make the same mistake. They profess the importance of shifting from products to solutions—in fact, in a survey of senior executives I conducted a few years ago, more than two-thirds of the respondents cited this shift as a strategic priority in the next decade. But their knowledge and expertise are housed within organizational silos, and they have trouble harnessing their resources across those internal boundaries in a way that customers truly value and are willing to pay for.

Some notable exceptions have emerged: companies that, like GE, found ways to transcend those silos in the interest of customer needs. By the late 1990s, for instance, Best Buy had nearly saturated the market with store openings and was facing increased competition not just from other retailers like Wal-Mart but from suppliers such as Dell. It tried to spark growth through various marketing approaches, but the company's efforts didn't take off until it launched a major initiative to restructure around customer solutions. Between 2000 and 2005, Best Buy's stock price grew at an annual rate of almost 30%.

Idea in Brief

For many senior executives, shifting from selling products to selling solutions—packages of products and services—is a priority in today's increasingly commoditized markets. Companies, however, aren't always structured to make that shift. Knowledge and expertise often reside in silos, and many companies have trouble harnessing their resources across those boundaries in a way that customers value and are willing to pay for. Some companies—like GE Healthcare, Best Buy, and commercial real estate provider Jones Lang LaSalle (JLL)—have restructured themselves around customer needs to deliver true solutions. They did so by engaging in four sets of activities. **Coordination**—to deliver customer-focused solutions, three things must occur easily across boundaries: information sharing, division of labor, and decision making. Sometimes this involves replacing traditional silos with customer-focused ones, but more often it entails transcending existing boundaries. JLL has experimented with both approaches. **Cooperation**—customer-centric companies, such as Cisco Systems, develop metrics for customer satisfaction and incentives that reward customer-focused cooperation. Most also shake up the power structure so that people who are closest to customers have the authority to act on their behalf. **Capability**—delivering customer-focused solutions requires some employees to be generalists instead of specialists. They need experience with more than one product or service, a deep knowledge of customer needs, and the ability to traverse internal boundaries. **Connection**—by combining their offerings with those of a partner, companies can cut costs even as they create higher-value solutions, as Starbucks has found through its diverse partnerships. To stand out in a commoditized market, companies must understand what customers value. Ultimately, some customers may be better off purchasing products and services piecemeal.

Commercial real estate provider Jones Lang LaSalle (JLL), under serious price competition, made a similar strategic shift in 2001, when its large customers began demanding integrated real estate services. For instance, corporate customers wanted the same people who found or built property for them to manage it. In response, JLL adopted a solutions-oriented structure that helped attract numerous large and highly profitable new accounts.

For GE Healthcare, Best Buy, and JLL, as well as for other companies I have studied, the journey to understand and unite around customer needs was a multiyear endeavor with major challenges and setbacks along the way. The effort required systematic, ongoing change to help organizations transcend existing product-based or geographic silos and, in some cases, replace them with customer-oriented ones. In particular, I found that successful companies engaged in four sets of activities:

- **Coordination.** Establishing structural mechanisms and processes that allow employees to improve their focus on the customer by harmonizing information and activities across units.
- **Cooperation.** Encouraging people in all parts of the company—through cultural means, incentives, and the allocation of power—to work together in the interest of customer needs.
- **Capability development.** Ensuring that enough people in the organization have the skills to deliver customer-focused solutions and defining a clear career path for employees with those skills.
- **Connection.** Developing relationships with external partners to increase the value of solutions cost effectively.

The first three sets of activities mutually reinforce the effort to put customers at the organization's fore; the fourth dramatically increases the power and reach of solutions by focusing attention beyond the firm's boundaries. All of them help companies transcend internal silos in service of higher-value customer solutions.

Coordination for Customer Focus

As GE Healthcare quickly discovered, it's easy to say that you offer solutions; salespeople may readily seize the concept as their newest product. But I've found that few companies are actually structured to deliver products and services in a synchronized way that's attractive from a customer's perspective. Individual units are historically focused on perfecting their products and processes, and give little thought to how their offerings might be even more valuable to the end user when paired with those of another unit. It's not just that the status quo doesn't reward collaborative behavior—although the right incentives are also critical. It's that the connections literally aren't in place.

One way to forge those connections is to do away with traditional silos altogether and create new ones organized by customer segments or needs. Many companies, however, are understandably reluctant to let go of the economies of scale and depth of knowledge and expertise associated with non-customer-focused silos. A company organized around geographies can customize offerings to suit local preferences, for instance, while a technology-centric firm can be quick to market with technical innovations. In many cases, functional and geographic silos were created precisely to help companies coordinate such activities as designing innovative products or gaining geographic focus. A customer focus requires them to emphasize a different set of activities and coordinate them in a different way.

In their initial attempts to offer customer solutions, companies are likely to create structures and processes that transcend rather than obliterate silos. Such boundary-spanning efforts may be highly informal—even as simple as hoping for or encouraging serendipity and impromptu conversations that lead to unplanned cross-unit solutions. But the casual exchange of information and ideas is generally most effective among senior executives, who have a better understanding than their subordinates of corporate goals and easier access to other leaders in the organization.

One way to achieve more-formal coordination without discarding existing silos is to layer boundary-spanning roles or units over the current structure and charge them with connecting the company's disparate activities to customer needs. JLL, which was created by the 1999 merger of LaSalle Partners and Jones Lang Wootton, had organized the corporate side of its business in the Americas into three units, each offering a particular service: representing tenants who wished to lease or purchase, maintaining

The Four Cs of Customer-Focused Solutions

COMPANIES LOOKING TO GROW in a commoditized marketplace like to say that they offer customer solutions: strategic packages of products and services that are hard to copy and can command premium prices. But most companies aren't set up to deliver solutions that customers truly value. Successful companies make significant changes in four areas to deliver real solutions.

Coordination

In most companies, knowledge and expertise reside in distinct units—organized by product, service, or geography. To deliver customer-focused solutions, companies need mechanisms that allow customer-related information sharing, division of labor, and decision making to occur easily across company boundaries. Sometimes this involves completely obliterating established silos and replacing them with silos organized around the customer, but more often it entails using structures and processes to transcend existing boundaries.

Cooperation

Customer-centric companies use both substance and symbolism to foster a culture of customer-focused cooperation. They develop metrics that measure, for instance, customer satisfaction and incentives that reward customer-focused behavior, even if it sacrifices unit performance. Most also shake up

buildings and properties, and managing real estate development. Each unit had authority over what services to offer, at what price, and to which clients. The units also had profit-and-loss responsibility for their respective businesses.

In 2001 the firm began to hear complaints from such large corporate clients as Bank of America that buying real estate services piecemeal from numerous companies and interacting with relatively junior salespeople were taking up too much executive time. One client explained, "We like him [the ad hoc account manager], but he is too low on the totem pole." At the time, many *Fortune* 500 companies were starting to outsource all real estate management. In response, JLL created an umbrella group, Corporate Solutions, that

the power structure so that people who are closest to customers have the authority to act on their behalf.

Capability

Delivering customer-focused solutions requires at least some employees to have two kinds of generalist skills. The first is experience with more than one product or service, along with a deep knowledge of customer needs (multidomain skills), and the second is an ability to traverse internal boundaries (boundary-spanning skills). In many companies, especially those organized around products, employees aren't rewarded for being generalists. Organizations that succeed in delivering solutions, however, invest significant time and resources in developing generalists. Furthermore, they establish clear career pathways for those who pursue the generalist route.

Connection

By redefining the boundaries of the company in order to connect more tightly with external partners, companies can not only cut costs by outsourcing all but core activities (and perhaps even by finding ways to outsource them) but also create higher-value solutions by combining their offerings with those of a complementary partner. Working with other companies still means crossing boundaries, but in this instance the boundaries are between a company and its partners.

comprised the three service units as well as an account management function, which served as a point of contact for large corporate customers. The account management group was staffed with high-ranking officers who had the authority to negotiate the pricing and delivery of real estate solutions, and the experience to help clients with strategic planning. By approaching Bank of America with a dedicated, senior-level account manager, JLL addressed the customer's complaint and was rewarded with one of just two spots (reduced from five) as a provider of outsourced services for the bank's 65 million square feet of U.S. real estate. Thus began a tremendous run that saw JLL's solutions revenue in the Americas grow more than 50% between 2002 and 2005.

Cisco Systems took a similar, layered approach to customer focus, but with a twist. The company, which had been organized by customer segment from 1997 to 2001, reverted to a technology-focused structure after the Internet bubble burst, forcing the company to address costly redundancies. Under its previous structure, Cisco had been creating the same or similar products for different customer segments, whose needs often overlapped. In fact, in some cases each line of business offered its own technology or solution for the same problem.

However, leaders feared that organizing around technologies, which involved centralizing marketing and R&D, would distance Cisco from customers' requirements. The answer was to retain the company's three sales groups based on customer type but establish a central marketing organization—residing between the technology groups and the customer-facing sales units—responsible for, among other things, facilitating the integration of products and technologies. The marketing group also established a cross-silo solutions-engineering team to bring disparate technologies together in a lab, test them, and create blueprints for end-user solutions. In addition to those structural measures, Cisco implemented several customer-focused processes, such as a customer champion program, which assigned senior executives as advocates for important customers. CEO John Chambers, for instance, was designated Ford's champion in 2002. In 2004 the company supplemented its advocates with cross-functional leadership teams organized by customer type, mimicking the previous structure, at least at the senior management level. Those teams—described by one executive as "the voice of the customer"—oversee six end-to-end processes that cut across functional boundaries such as quote-to-cash (the order cycle) and issue-to-resolution (technical support).

While bridging mechanisms such as cross-silo teams and processes can be very effective, they aren't easy to implement. A history of independence often leads to protectionist behavior. At JLL, for instance, business unit managers were initially reluctant to cede decision-making authority to account managers, particularly ones who lacked experience with that unit's service. Conflicts also arose over pricing and account managers' compensation. What's more, while JLL's Corporate Solutions group had positioned the firm well to meet the increasing demands of corporate real estate customers, single-transaction customers considered the relatively small number of JLL account managers in local markets to be a problem. Those customers wanted professionals who could negotiate the best deal and execute entire transactions. As JLL discovered, the benefits of bundled solutions wear off if customers perceive a weakness in any component. Ultimately, JLL's layered approach to silo busting was still limiting the firm's growth.

To dispense with such tensions, JLL next took the more dramatic and highly formal measure of silo swapping—a wholesale, permanent structural shift to spin internal groups and processes around a customer axis. That is, it swapped its current, service-focused silos for those structured explicitly around the customer to maximize company-customer synergies. As part of that process, it replaced the account management function and the three service silos that had resided within the Corporate Solutions group with two organizations denoted simply Clients and Markets, a restructuring that put more people in the field, closer to clients, and focused all internal groups and processes on customer needs. The Markets organization handled one-off transactions, represented JLL's full range of offerings to those customers, and provided local support for larger clients. As accounts grew, they were assigned an account manager from the Clients organization, which was composed primarily of account teams managing the firm's relationships with large, multiservice customers. These teams were considered profit centers and so had the authority to hire and terminate employees. To preserve its product and service expertise without a product- and service-based structure, JLL embedded service specialists within account teams in both organizations and created a product management team charged with keeping offerings competitive. It's too soon to know how well the customer-focused silos are working, and the firm may face new, unanticipated challenges, but early results look promising: In the past year, revenues have increased by 30% and profits by almost 60%.

Culture of Cooperation

While coordination mechanisms can align tasks and information around customers' needs, they don't necessarily inspire a willingness among members of competing silos to fully cooperate and make sometimes time-consuming and costly adjustments in the interest of customers. Just as important as coordination, then, is a cooperative environment in which people are rewarded for busting through silos to deliver customer solutions. Customer-centric companies live by a set of values that put the customer front and center, and they reinforce those values through cultural elements, power structures, metrics, and incentives that reward customer-focused, solutions-oriented behavior.

Many product-centric companies probably start out with a focus on customers, aiming to design products with broad appeal. But after early successes, they internalize and institutionalize the notion that markets respond primarily to great products and services. Decisions and behaviors, including those related specifically to customers, are then viewed through the lens of the product. Quality, for example, is defined by meeting internal standards rather than customer requirements. Over time, even the sales and marketing departments lose their customer focus, as product successes dominate company lore. In this way, the company develops a pervasive inside-out perspective.

In contrast, customer-focused companies, even those in technology-intensive arenas, build an outside-in perspective into all major elements of their cultures. They hold solving customer problems above all else and celebrate customer-oriented victories. At Cisco, technical innovation is clearly valued. The drive to solve customer problems fuels that innovation no matter where it leads the company, a mind-set that is reflected in the statement on all employee badges, "No Technology Religion." As one manager said, "Being able to listen carefully to create relevancy [for customers] is a more important business value than innovation." In line with this thinking, Cisco puts a relatively large number of employees in direct contact with customers, including groups such as human resources that typically don't interact with customers.

It helped that Cisco had the luxury of an existing culture of customer focus. Cofounder Sandy Lerner, in the company's earliest days, invented a customized multiprotocol router for a customer who initially found no Cisco products that met his needs. From then on, Lerner made it her mission to establish a culture where everybody, even those in units distant from customers, went beyond providing standard customer support to addressing specific problems. Consequently, even when the company reorganized its silos away from the customer in 2001, it was able to maintain enough interaction among units to ensure a customer-centric view.

At least half the battle of promoting cross-silo, customer-focused cooperation lies in the "softer" aspects of culture, including values and the way the company communicates them through images, symbols, and stories. Touting service accomplishments instead of, or at least in addition to, product accomplishments through company lore can begin to shift people's mind-sets. Cisco's employee badges broadcast a focus on customer needs, as does a well-known company legend about how Chambers was 30 minutes late to his first board meeting because he chose to take a call from an irate customer. Linguistic conventions may also be used to signify the value of the customer: Target and Disney refer to customers as "guests."

Another admittedly soft but powerful cultural tool for aligning employees around customer needs is to treat your workers the way you want them to treat customers. The hope is that people will adopt a collaborative orientation and customer focus because they want to, not just because they'll reap a financial reward. Cisco is highly egalitarian, reinforcing the notion that all employees are important, which makes them more likely to cooperate across silos. The company offers equal access to parking spaces, for instance, and designates window-facing cubicles for nonmanagement employees, locating supervisors' offices within the interior of the floor.

Of course, the softer cooperation-promoting measures won't take hold if the harder ones—power structures, metrics, and incentives—don't reinforce them. Power structures are notoriously difficult to change. For example, in a customer-centric environment, people who are close to the customer and adept at building bridges across silos should gain power and prominence; but unit leaders responsible for products or geographies who had clout in the old organization won't hand over their customer relationships and concomitant power bases without a struggle.

That was the case at JLL. Before the company created the Corporate Solutions organization, power resided almost exclusively within the service-based business units. Even after the account manager position was instituted, final pricing authority rested with the units, which made it difficult to compete with multiservice packages. Although solutions ideally carry a premium price, JLL's initial intent was to better serve customers' needs by simplifying the management of real estate and to position the firm as a multiservice provider. However, when JLL created a package of real estate services, the price quickly mounted, resulting in sticker shock among potential customers, many of whom associated buying in bulk with discount pricing. JLL unit heads—who wanted to maximize their own return, not subsidize other units—refused to budge on prices. In some cases, package proposals were delayed, thanks to negotiations that stalled or ended in a stalemate that could be resolved only by those higher in the organization. In other cases, the packages weren't priced competitively, and the firm lost the business.

The issue of autonomy raised concerns as well. JLL's business units were accustomed to a high degree of independence. They protected their client relationships and had always been wary of introducing other services—even before the account management unit was in place—because delivery would be out of their control and they feared damaging the relationships. JLL took several steps to resolve those tensions. For one, it signaled the importance and value of the account manager role by assigning it to only very senior executives, including two who had achieved the title of international director, a distinction earned by less than 2% of employees. The firm also delivered a series of presentations at annual companywide meetings highlighting the significance of the role to the firm's growth.

To ease the pricing standoffs, JLL began in 2003 to allow account managers to provide input into the performance evaluations of business unit employees who touched their clients. At the same time, JLL took steps to retain some power and recognition for the business unit CEOs and, in the process, help them learn more about the services outside their silos and how they might gain personally from cross-unit sales. Unit CEOs, for example, were asked to oversee accounts on which their services were a particularly important component; in this role, unit heads were explicitly responsible for the performance of account managers. Because their bonuses were tied to the account managers' overall performance, the unit heads developed a clearer picture of the value contributed by services outside their silos. They were also required to meet regularly with customers to discuss their needs and the quality of the firm's service.

To support a shifting power landscape, firms must also embrace new metrics and incentives. The product-focused metrics most companies rely on—revenues, growth, and margins—don't reward cross-silo cooperation or customer centricity. Sales commissions in some organizations encourage managers to bring in new customers rather than nurture existing relationships, for example.

Cisco is relentless about measuring and rewarding employees on the basis of customer-related performance indicators. A Web-based survey helps determine the pre- and post-sale satisfaction of customers who buy directly from Cisco or indirectly through resellers. Survey questions focus on a customer's overall experience with and perceptions of Cisco, along with product-specific issues. Follow-up surveys with some customers explore their experiences with certain products more deeply. All bonuses are tied directly to these customer satisfaction data, so employees are encouraged to cooperate across internal boundaries. Moreover, all employees, including interns and part-timers, are eligible for stock options.

Building Capability

Regardless of the incentives and cultural elements in place to enhance customer-focused silo busting, employees will fall back on their old competencies and ways of thinking if they haven't developed new skills. For example, even though one of the companies I studied told product salespeople to include new consulting-based offerings in their pitches to customers, the reps found it easier to give a superficial account of the new offerings or to omit them from their pitches altogether. Old habits die hard.

As a company becomes more adept at inducing coordination and cooperation across units, new skills become valued and desirable. Rather than highly specialized expertise, customer-focused solutions require employees to develop two kinds of skills: multidomain skills (the ability to work with multiple products and services, which requires a deep understanding of customers' needs) and boundary-spanning skills (the ability to forge connections across internal boundaries). Such generalist skills are typically not rewarded or developed in a product-oriented organization, so it's not easy to find customer-facing generalists. The companies that succeed invest significant time and resources in developing generalists. Furthermore, they map clear career paths for those who pursue this route.

At JLL, most of the first account managers had spent the majority of their careers in a single service unit within the firm and remained members of that unit even after becoming account managers. Consequently, they were not always deeply acquainted with the other businesses or able to manage service bundles skillfully. Account managers hired from the outside were generally chosen for their ability to execute real estate transactions, not for the breadth of their service knowledge.

To foster the development of boundary-spanning skills and cultivate a cadre of employees who could grow into the account manager role, JLL began to rotate individuals through the three remaining silos (before swapping the service silos for customer silos), forcing them to acquire greater knowledge of the products, services, and capabilities of each unit, as well as to expand their personal networks across the firm. For those already in account management roles, the company instituted training sessions through regular conference calls and meetings. Early sessions tackled relatively simple tasks, such as the establishment of a common vocabulary. Subsequent sessions focused on improving account managers' knowledge of each unit's offerings and on cross-silo sales skills and new metrics, including the first rudimentary client-based profit-and-loss statements. An unanticipated benefit of the training was that it brought the account managers together regularly, helping them to stop identifying only with their silos and to begin forming a group identity that enhanced their cross-silo networks. As a natural consequence, top management could see that account managers were assuming increased responsibility for a broader range of services.

Best Buy's shift to solutions selling entailed identifying and targeting five large, profitable customer segments: young, tech-savvy adults; busy and affluent professionals; family men; busy, suburban moms; and small-business customers. Each store was designed to suit the needs of its largest customer segment. A "busy mom" store, for instance, features personal shopping assistance and a kid-friendly layout. Stores targeting the tech-savvy offer higher-end consumer electronics and separate showrooms for high-definition home theater systems. When the company rolled out its customer-centric strategy, it conducted extensive training to help employees understand their store's particular customer segment. It also trained sales associates on basic financial metrics to highlight how their efforts on behalf of target customers affect store performance.

At the corporate level, Best Buy created a Customer Centricity University for senior officers who had not been involved with planning the new strategy. For those executives, Best Buy outlined the rationale for the new approach, including detailed financials, and held breakout sessions with the teams responsible for developing and executing the strategy for each customer segment. Over 11 months, all employees and contractors residing at headquarters, as well as many other corporate employees, participated in the program. It was then disbanded, its essential elements incorporated into the company's orientation program for new employees.

Enhancing skill sets is only part of the challenge of capability building. Companies must also develop attractive career paths that give emerging generalist stars a sense of identity and a clear route for advancement. Even specialists whose roles may not change much in the new organization will probably have to develop some generalist skills and learn how these could contribute to their advancement. JLL, for instance, at first had difficulty attracting candidates for account manager positions, largely because the firm had measured success and offered promotions on the basis of achievements within a unit. Job security was a major concern for potential account managers, as one of the first to hold the position explains: "One of the big fears was that these accounts don't last forever. So if a person left his or her specialized area of expertise to run an account and after three years . . . the firm was no longer providing services for that account, employees feared that that person would be out of a job."

JLL addressed the career path issue in part through its customer-focused reorganization—whereby the Clients group housed account managers in a well-defined unit with a clear career trajectory. Other firms have developed "talent marketplaces" to signal the value they place on generalist, cross-silo skills. Modeled after informal marketplaces used within law firms, academia, and R&D units, these forums match employees on a flexible basis with available positions or assignments, thereby allowing generalist and specialist career tracks to coexist.

Connection with External Partners

The three factors we've discussed—coordination, cooperation, and capability building—are silo-busting tactics that align business units around a customer axis. But by redefining the boundaries of the company itself, firms can further fight commoditization in two ways: cutting costs by outsourcing all but core activities (and, in some cases, by finding creative ways to outsource them) and joining forces with companies that have complementary offerings to create even higher-value solutions, which command a larger price premium. Such approaches still require cross-boundary efforts, but the boundaries are between a company and its partners.

Starbucks continues to charge a premium for coffee, previously a commodity product, and exponentially increase the company's sales through intercompany relationships that keep costs low while expanding the firm's offerings. It chooses suppliers very carefully (quality and service take priority over cost) and then shares an unusual amount of financial information, using a two-way, open-book costing model that allows suppliers to see the company's margins and Starbucks to review the vendors' costs. In return, the company expects suppliers to treat it as a preferred customer in terms of pricing, profit percentage, and the resources committed to the partnership.

As for expanding its offerings, Starbucks seeks to enrich the customer experience through alliances with partners in a variety of industries. Its bottled Frappuccino beverage is manufactured, distributed, and marketed through a 50/50 joint venture with PepsiCo; its ice cream is made and distributed by Dreyer's; its supermarket coffees are marketed and distributed by Kraft, one of the company's main competitors in the at-home coffee consumption market. A more recent alliance with Jim Beam Brands brought Starbucks into a new drink category: spirits. In 2005, the two companies launched Starbucks Cream Liqueur, which is sold in liquor stores, restaurants, and bars, but not in coffeehouses.

Starbucks's boundary-expanding moves have extended to nonconsumable items as well. For several years, customers have been able to buy CDs at the stores, and the company recently began to promote movies as part of its ongoing efforts to become, according to the *New York Times,* a "purveyor of premium-blend culture." It sponsors discussion groups (with free coffee) and is considering selling DVDs, publishing new authors, and producing films. To coordinate these promotions and partnerships, Starbucks has formed an entertainment division with offices in Seattle and Los Angeles.

Finally, Starbucks has expanded internationally by leveraging not other companies' products and services but the capabilities of regional partners. Whereas the company owns most of its domestic retail stores, it allows foreign companies to own and operate Starbucks stores in markets where those players are already established. In 1995 Japanese specialty retailer Sazaby opened a Starbucks in Tokyo. In such cases, Starbucks provides operating expertise and control through licensing, while the foreign partners take on financial risk and advise Starbucks on real estate, regulations, suppliers, labor, and culture in the markets they know best. Sharing responsibilities in this way requires Starbucks to apply the principles of coordination, cooperation, and capability building to its external relationships.

Starbucks's relationship-building capability has enabled the company to grow far faster than it could have on its own. What's more, with just about every fast-food company selling premium coffee, and versatile and affordable new coffeemakers lining the shelves at Target, the company has been able to shore up its position by selling not just coffee but a coffeehouse experience, built largely around a series of partnerships and alliances that provide customers with an array of high-quality offerings.

Such relationships can be mutually reinforcing: As one company shrinks operations to cut costs—seeking partners to take on formerly in-house activities—its suppliers must expand their horizons by increasing the range of their offerings or finding their own partners to help them do this. IBM, even while taking over major back-office operations for large companies, has condensed its own core operations by outsourcing activities like repair and server manufacturing to contractors such as Solectron. Solectron, in turn, has expanded its boundaries by acquiring an IBM repair center in the Netherlands, allowing IBM to condense still further.

There are pitfalls to integrating closely with suppliers. Some companies—especially those that are unclear on their core values—give away too much. Others become captive to their key suppliers and lose the motivation to make ongoing investments in new technology. Some also find that they are funding the development expertise and scale that may allow a partner to become a competitor, as when cell phone supplier BenQ moved from making handsets for Motorola to marketing its own brand of handsets in foreign markets where Motorola already had a presence. Integrated partnerships can also be risky if companies put a lot of information into their vendors' hands, as Starbucks does. If trust on either side is eroded, one party could misuse the information.

In managing external relationships to avoid such pitfalls, it makes sense to apply the principles used to manage across internal silos—particularly the principles of coordination and cooperation. The challenges of internal and external execution are not exactly the same, but they share many themes, such as the need to find efficient ways of exchanging information and aligning incentives. So, for instance, Starbucks has a set of formal coordination structures to help information flow between partners. In addition to regular meetings between senior management on both sides, Starbucks has a dedicated training program for employees who will be involved in managing supplier relationships. To ensure that both parties follow clear rules for knowledge sharing, the company has created a handbook for suppliers, which describes the firm's purchasing philosophies and policies, along with the standards vendors must meet on eight criteria.

Cooperation issues may be even more central to external relationships than to internal ones, given the need to apportion value fairly among parties and the omnipresent risk of opportunistic behavior. Cultural fit lays the groundwork for cooperation, and efforts at cultural synchrony may begin even before the partnership does. Starbucks not only conducts a careful assessment of a supplier's brand and operations but also evaluates cultural fit, largely through an event called Discovery Day, when prospective partners come to Seattle to discuss cultural and other commonalities as well as differences between themselves and Starbucks.

In today's ever expanding and shifting business arena, and in light of a growing focus on customer needs, the definitions of what is inside a company and what is outside are no longer clear. But as our sense of firm boundaries evolves, so will our understanding of how best to breach internal and external barriers.

There are few downsides to developing true solutions. The risk is that in the rush to stand out in the crowd, many companies forget that solving customer problems requires a deep knowledge of who their target customers are and what they need. Some customers are better off purchasing products and services piecemeal. Leaders at GE Healthcare originally targeted solutions at large national accounts—which, it turned out, bought largely on price. These clients almost by definition weren't good candidates for the solutions offering. The company consequently refined its target customer profile to focus on multihospital systems—with at least $500 million in annual revenue—that demonstrated a willingness to provide GE with meaningful access to the most-senior executives. Through this targeting, GE Healthcare narrowed its focus to just 150 of the roughly 400 multihospital systems in the U.S. health care market—giving primary attention to 50 accounts that included customers ready to enter into a contractual relationship with GE and those that exhibited many key characteristics and expressed a willingness to work with GE.

The lesson for GE, as for others, is that it doesn't pay to put the solutions cart before the horse of coordinated customer focus. To stand out in a commoditized market, companies must understand what customers truly value. The only way to do that is to break down the traditional, often entrenched, silos and unite resources to focus directly on customer needs.

Originally published in May 2007. Reprint R0705F

Harnessing Your Staff's Informal Networks

by Richard McDermott and Douglas Archibald

IF YOUR SMARTEST EMPLOYEES are getting together to solve problems and develop new ideas on their own, the best thing to do is to stay out of their way, right? Workers can easily share insights electronically, and they often don't want or appreciate executive oversight. Well, think again. Though in-house networks of experts—or "communities of practice"—were once entirely unofficial, today they are increasingly integrated into companies' formal management structures.

Independent, off-the-grid communities have proliferated in recent years, and many companies have counted on them to deliver creative solutions to challenges that bridge functional gaps. But in the past few years, outside forces—technological advances, globalization, increased demands on employees' time—have begun to undermine communities' success. Consider the rise and fall of an informal group of experts at a large water-engineering company located just outside London. Starting in the early 1990s, they began meeting weekly to discuss strategies for designing new water-treatment facilities. The gatherings were so lively and informative that they actually drew crowds of onlookers. (The company can't be named for reasons of confidentiality.)

The community initially thrived because it operated so informally. United by a common professional passion, participants would huddle around conference tables and compare data, trade insights, and argue over which designs would work best with local water systems. And the community achieved results: Participants found ways to significantly cut the time and cost involved in system design by increasing the pool of experience that they could draw upon, tapping insights from different disciplines, and recycling design ideas from other projects.

Too much attention from management, went the thinking, would crush the group's collaborative nature. But the very informality of this community eventually rendered it obsolete. What happened to it was typical: The members gained access to more sophisticated design tools and to vast amounts of data via the internet. Increased global connectivity drew more people into the community and into individual projects. Soon the engineers were spending more time at their desks, gathering and organizing data, sorting through multiple versions of designs, and managing remote contacts. The community started to feel less intimate, and its members, less obligated to their peers. Swamped, the engineers found it difficult to justify time for voluntary meetings. Today the community in effect has dissolved—along with the hopes that it would continue generating high-impact ideas.

Our research has shown that many other communities failed for similar reasons. Nevertheless, communities of practice aren't dead. Many are thriving—you'll find them developing global processes, resolving troubled implementation, and guiding operational efforts. But they differ from their forebears in some important respects. Today they're an actively managed part of the organization, with specific goals, explicit accountability, and clear executive oversight. To get experts to dedicate time to them, companies have to make sure that communities contribute meaningfully to the organization and operate efficiently.

We've observed this shift in our consulting work and in our research. This research was conducted with the Knowledge and Innovation Network at Warwick Business School and funded by the

Idea in Brief

Informal employee networks, or communities of practice, are an inexpensive and efficient way for experts to share knowledge and ideas. But communities work best if they have clear accountability and management oversight.

Effective communities tackle real problems for senior management. At Pfizer, for instance, communities are responsible for helping developers make tough calls on drug-safety issues.

Communities are like teams but focus on the long term. Pfizer's safety communities are assigned organizationwide goals—such as ensuring that safety research uses the latest science—which project teams, focused on specific deliverables, could never meet.

Technology makes global collaboration possible, but successful communities also depend on the human systems—focus, goals, and management attention—that integrate them into the organization.

Warwick Innovative Manufacturing Research Centre and by Schlumberger, an oil-field services company. To examine the health and impact of communities, we did a quantitative study of 52 communities in 10 industries, and a qualitative assessment of more than 140 communities in a dozen organizations, consisting of interviews with support staff, leaders, community members, and senior management.

The communities at construction and engineering giant Fluor illustrate the extent of the change. Global communities have replaced the company's distributed functional structure. While project teams remain the primary organizational unit, 44 discipline- and industry-focused communities, with 24,000 active members, support the teams. The communities provide all functional services—creating guidelines for work practices and procedures; publishing technical documents; and offering career development, access to expert advice, and help with technical questions. They are the first and best source for technical knowledge at Fluor.

Here's one example of how this works: Not long ago, a Fluor nuclear-cleanup project team had to install a soil barrier over a drainage field once used to dispose of radioactive wastewater. But environmental regulators mandated that Fluor first locate and seal a

30-year-old well, now covered over, to prevent contamination of the groundwater table. Poor historical data made it impossible to tell if the well really existed, and ground-penetrating radar also failed to discover it. Simply removing the contaminated soil to find the well would have been costly and risky for workers.

When the team posted a request to Fluor's knowledge communities, one of the experts suggested using an alternative technology from a different industry. The team tried it and found the well. In fact, within two months, Fluor went on to use the same method to locate—or prove the nonexistence of—more than 100 wells and suspected wells. Without the community's help, the project teams may have had to employ expensive, hazardous, and possibly ineffective methods. Any engineer can consult his colleagues, but Fluor's communities offer its engineers a worldwide network of expertise and connections no one person could build or maintain.

Setting Up Communities Strategically

Unlike the independent and self-organizing bodies we saw years ago, today's communities require real structure. Though we once envisioned few rules, we have since identified four principles that govern the design and integration of effective communities.

Focus on issues important to the organization

Sustainable communities tackle real problems that have been defined by senior management. At pharmaceutical firm Pfizer, one such issue is drug safety. The company has about 200 active drug development projects, all in different stages, in different countries, focusing on different disease areas, and using different processes. To advise teams on safety, two types of communities work across these projects—councils and networks. About 20% of Pfizer's safety staff are involved in one or the other.

The nine safety councils focus on major organs of the body, such as the liver or the heart, or on key issues such as pediatric safety. On average, each has a dozen members, representing individual areas of expertise, with deep knowledge of toxicology, clinical development, chemistry, and disease categories. Councils are responsible for helping development project teams make difficult judgment calls on potential safety issues. Their members can be volunteers or appointed by management. They are, as Tim Anderson, Pfizer's head of Drug Safety R&D, told us, "the most elevated form of advice-giving body on safety." Membership in a council is a major recognition of expertise.

The dozen or so networks have voluntary, open membership and focus on disciplines or practices, such as lab functions or techniques; or on emerging technologies, such as nanotechnology. When the demand for advice rises high enough, a network can be elevated to council status.

Because they cross the entire development organization, safety councils and networks can take a "portfolio" approach to potential safety issues—comparing data, tests, and results on similar compounds being developed in different therapeutic areas. Sometimes they use tests and data from one team to support decisions by another, saving months of development time. The Kidney Safety Council, for instance, suggested that new biomarker tests could help assess whether a recent safety finding in an animal model had relevance for humans, which allowed one project to move to initial clinical trials much more quickly. Because the clock on patents starts at the beginning of development, shorter development time has a significant impact on product life span and business results.

In the nonprofit world, the United Nations has established a set of 12 communities that address serious social and economic problems in India. Solution Exchange is composed of people from governmental and development agencies and nongovernmental organizations (NGOs). Addressing issues like nutrition, education, and HIV/AIDS prevention, these practitioner communities now comprise 3,000 to 4,000 members each. They enable grassroots workers to share what they've learned about implementing programs with government agencies, policy makers, and other program implementers. The members' practical insights are increasingly influencing policy design and helping create more effective programs. "We reach more people through Solution Exchange than any other program because it cuts across institutional barriers and allows people to connect regardless of source of funding, organization, or location," notes Maxine Olson, the former resident coordinator of the UN India team.

The communities also function like a research service, collecting and distilling timely suggestions for solutions to important problems. In one instance, members of the Food and Nutrition Security Community helped a midday meal program in the nation's schools by working with local growers to supply a steady stream of vegetables. In the rural south, one NGO created school kitchen gardens, where children were trained to grow vegetables on their own. The community spread these successful ideas to practitioners throughout the country. Since the typical Indian diet provides only 10% of the minimum required vitamins and minerals, the additional vegetables in school lunches led to real improvements in children's health.

Establish community goals and deliverables

Rather than inhibiting the exchange of ideas and information, formal goals and deliverables energize communities. They provide a focus—a reason to meet and participate. More important, they establish the contribution of communities to the organization.

At ConocoPhillips, communities report to functional teams, which are responsible for stewarding improvements in specific areas, such as oil and gas production. The functional teams, typically staffed by eight to 10 senior managers, have aggressive, measurable goals, like reducing the number of unrecovered barrels of oil. Each community owns part of the overall goal and tracks its progress toward achieving it. For example, when the company sought to improve the performance of its well operations globally, the functional team formed a well-optimization community, which then figured out how to reduce unplanned losses related to equipment impairment by 10% a year.

Explicit goals make communities operate more like teams on a day-to-day level, but community goals generally differ from team goals in that they're tied to long-term needs. Pfizer's safety councils assume organizationwide goals, which the project teams, with their focus on specific deliverables, could never meet. Pfizer's kidney council goals include developing a high-level, long-term strategy for research related to kidney toxicity; finding ways to share resources among kidney research projects; and evaluating external opportunities in kidney research, like strategic alliances.

Provide real governance

To be well integrated into the organization, communities, like teams, need strong, formal relationships with the organization's top leadership.

Companies often identify a senior manager to sponsor each community. This can turn out to be a dismal form of governance if those tapped for the role don't understand the purpose and value of the community and don't have the bandwidth to support its leaders. But if senior managers guide communities in a way that matches their long-term perspective, they can be very effective.

Pfizer's communities are sponsored by two senior managers, the heads of Drug Safety R&D and Safety and Risk Management, the two larger organizations the safety councils span. Both executives are highly engaged and meet semiannually with the community leaders to review goals, provide feedback, and understand the communities' impact and needs. For example, when one council proposed developing spreadsheets to mine 10 years of patient data that might reveal patterns of biomarker responses in clinical subpopulations, the sponsors suggested a more rigorous approach: creating an interactive relational database. The sponsors also ensured that the councils had the operational resources they needed, by providing them with two project managers who would help schedule meetings, track action items, maintain a website, and develop communications materials and training programs.

Set high management expectations

However intangible, management's expectations have a strong influence on communities, just as they do on teams. Senior managers' sponsorship is useless if they're not genuinely engaged with the

How Communities Differ from Teams

COMMUNITIES OF PRACTICE ARE different from teams, though less so than we originally thought. Like successful teams, successful communities have goals, deliverables, assigned leadership, accountability for results, and metrics. But they are distinct from teams in four ways:

1. **The long view.** Communities are responsible for the long-term development of a body of knowledge or discipline, even when they have annual goals. Teams, in contrast, focus on a specific deliverable.

2. **Peer collaboration and collective responsibility.** Community leaders establish the direction of the community, connect members, and facilitate discussions, but do not have authority over members.

3. **Intentional network expansion.** Professionals typically consult their peers for help with unusual or difficult technical problems. Communities deliberately seek to expand the internal and external resources and experts available to individuals.

4. **Knowledge management.** Teams typically do not have ongoing responsibility for organizing and documenting what a company has learned in a domain; rather, they focus on a given problem. Communities steward the knowledge in their domain with a view toward solving problems that have not yet been discovered.

communities. In India, where each Solution Exchange community is sponsored by a local UN agency office, participation dropped when engaged agency heads were replaced by less engaged ones. Communities continued to thrive only when new agency heads were committed to them.

In Schlumberger, an oil-field services provider with 77,000 employees in 80 countries, each community has a management sponsor. Most sponsors are highly engaged with their community leaders and activities. The sponsor of a geosciences community, for instance, set six challenges for it based on the division's business goals. One was to publish a series of articles about Schlumberger's research in outside journals, focusing on topics that hadn't been adequately covered in the literature—a major undertaking for the community. At Fluor, management expects communities to be *the* technical resource for the organization and create its standards and procedures. In the words of John McQuary, vice president of knowledge management, "The community leader is the highest technical authority in the company."

Maximizing Communities' Impact

Traditionally, organizations paid little attention to the operations of communities because they saw participation in them as a marginal activity, intended to benefit the members and not necessarily the company. But our research reveals that companies can increase the operational effectiveness of communities in four ways.

Set aside real time for community participation

Community leaders' biggest complaint is that they don't have enough time to execute their duties. When community leadership is a "spare time" activity, it can easily be squeezed out by more pressing priorities. Many companies have now made community leadership a formal component of job descriptions and performance appraisals. In our research we found that community leaders spend one half-day to one day a week on community management, or about 17% of their time on average. In a few organizations, community leadership is a full-time job. The UN's Solution Exchange communities each have a full-time facilitator and research associate.

Some companies link discretionary bonuses to community contributions; others make community leadership a necessary step toward promotion. At Schlumberger, part-time community leadership is one of employees' job objectives, reviewed quarterly with their managers.

Train community leaders in their role

Leading a community is different from leading a team. Communities, our research shows, provide greater value when companies systematically train their leaders. In Schlumberger's communities, leaders are elected by the members annually. New leaders take a one-day course covering the aspects of communities that are different from teams—such as understanding how to find pockets of knowledge and expertise, how to engage volunteers in activities, how to grow membership, how to work with members external to the company, and how to influence operating groups when you don't have direct authority.

ConocoPhillips requires all new community leaders to attend a boot camp that outlines what management expects from them. The training starts by spelling out how community contributions connect to business goals. Then workshops review community governance, support, and expected deliverables and what the company considers critical success factors, such as establishing goals, engaging members, and setting results metrics.

Hold face-to-face events

A decade ago many organizations thought communities were a free way to develop knowledge. All the staff had to do was participate in an occasional meeting. But today most communities of practice include employees in remote locations. While they typically use collaborative software to link remote staff, the most effective communities also hold face-to-face meetings, which usually focus on specific goals. Face-to-face contact fosters the trust and rapport members need to ask for help, admit mistakes, and learn from one another.

Schlumberger enlivens its annual community meetings with competitions for the best examples of how the company's tools improved a customer's performance. Judges are drawn from the community's field, and the criteria for winning are clearly known: technical depth, business relevance, innovativeness of approach, and overall impression. Winners of local competitions participate in regional competitions, and the winners of the regionals compete in a global competition, for which they also write a paper. Last year 36 community representatives presented ideas at this small global event of about 100 people. The winning presenters received a monetary prize and an award from the CEO and chief technology officer.

Use simple IT tools

Most communities don't need complex tools. Typically they use only a few functions, such as discussion forums, document libraries, expertise locators, on-demand teleconferencing, and online meeting spaces where members can edit documents as they discuss them. We found that simplicity, ease of use, and familiarity are far more important than functional sophistication.

When communities of practice first began to appear, we hailed them as a dirt-cheap way to distribute knowledge and share best practices. We thought they would be relatively self-organizing and self-sustaining, flying below the radar of organizational hierarchy. We thought they would flourish with little executive oversight—a notion that seemed to work well at the time. But as life and business have become more complex, we began to see that to make a difference over the long term, communities needed far more structure and oversight.

Despite this, communities remain more efficient and cheaper than other organizational resources and demand less oversight. In times when budgets have shrunk and managers are overwhelmed just dealing with the downturn, communities can be a valuable resource for coordinating work across organizational boundaries, whether across geography, as at Schlumberger and Fluor; across operating groups, as with Pfizer and ConocoPhillips; or down the value stream as at the UN in India. But communities are not as informal as was once thought, nor are they free. Though IT systems make global collaboration possible, successful communities need more. They need the human systems—focus, goals, and management attention—that integrate them into the organization. And they need to operate efficiently enough to respect experts' scarce time.

Originally published in March 2010. Reprint R1003F

Want Collaboration?

Accept—and Actively Manage—Conflict.

by Jeff Weiss and Jonathan Hughes

THE CHALLENGE IS A LONG-STANDING one for senior managers: How do you get people in your organization to work together across internal boundaries? But the question has taken on urgency in today's global and fast-changing business environment. To service multinational accounts, you increasingly need seamless collaboration across geographic boundaries. To improve customer satisfaction, you increasingly need collaboration among functions ranging from R&D to distribution. To offer solutions tailored to customers' needs, you increasingly need collaboration between product and service groups.

Meanwhile, as competitive pressures continually force companies to find ways to do more with less, few managers have the luxury of relying on their own dedicated staffs to accomplish their objectives. Instead, most must work with and through people across the organization, many of whom have different priorities, incentives, and ways of doing things.

Getting collaboration right promises tremendous benefits: a unified face to customers, faster internal decision making, reduced costs through shared resources, and the development of more innovative products. But despite the billions of dollars spent on initiatives to improve collaboration, few companies are happy with the results. Time and again we have seen management teams employ the same few strategies to boost internal cooperation. They restructure their organizations and reengineer their business processes.

They create cross-unit incentives. They offer teamwork training. While such initiatives yield the occasional success story, most of them have only limited impact in dismantling organizational silos and fostering collaboration—and many are total failures. (See the sidebar "The Three Myths of Collaboration.")

So what's the problem? Most companies respond to the challenge of improving collaboration in entirely the wrong way. They focus on the symptoms ("Sales and delivery do not work together as closely as they should") rather than on the root cause of failures in cooperation: conflict. The fact is, you can't improve collaboration until you've addressed the issue of conflict.

This can come as a surprise to even the most experienced executives, who generally don't fully appreciate the inevitability of conflict in complex organizations. And even if they do recognize this, many mistakenly assume that efforts to increase collaboration will significantly reduce that conflict, when in fact some of these efforts—for example, restructuring initiatives—actually produce more of it.

Executives underestimate not only the inevitability of conflict but also—and this is key—its importance to the organization. The disagreements sparked by differences in perspective, competencies, access to information, and strategic focus within a company actually generate much of the value that can come from collaboration across organizational boundaries. Clashes between parties are the crucibles in which creative solutions are developed and wise trade-offs among competing objectives are made. So instead of trying simply to reduce disagreements, senior executives need to embrace conflict and, just as important, institutionalize mechanisms for managing it.

Even though most people lack an innate understanding of how to deal with conflict effectively, there are a number of straightforward ways that executives can help their people—and their organizations—constructively manage it. These can be divided into two main areas: strategies for managing disagreements at the point of conflict and strategies for managing conflict upon escalation up the management chain. These methods can help a company move through the conflict that is a necessary precursor to truly effective collaboration and, more important, extract the value that often lies latent in

Idea in Brief

Companies try all kinds of ways to improve collaboration among different parts of the organization: cross-unit incentive systems, organizational restructuring, teamwork training. While these initiatives produce occasional success stories, most have only limited impact in dismantling organizational silos and fostering collaboration.

The problem? Most companies focus on the symptoms ("Sales and delivery do not work together as closely as they should") rather than on the root cause of failures in cooperation: conflict. The fact is, you can't improve collaboration until you've addressed the issue of conflict. The authors offer six strategies for effectively managing conflict:

- Devise and implement a common method for resolving conflict.
- Provide people with criteria for making trade-offs.
- Use the escalation of conflict as an opportunity for coaching.
- Establish and enforce a requirement of joint escalation.
- Ensure that managers resolve escalated conflicts directly with their counterparts.
- Make the process for escalated conflict-resolution transparent.

The first three strategies focus on the point of conflict; the second three focus on escalation of conflict up the management chain. Together they constitute a framework for effectively managing discord, one that integrates conflict resolution into day-to-day decision-making processes, thereby removing a barrier to cross-organizational collaboration.

intra-organizational differences. When companies are able to do both, conflict is transformed from a major liability into a significant asset.

Strategies for Managing Disagreements at the Point of Conflict

Conflict management works best when the parties involved in a disagreement are equipped to manage it themselves. The aim is to get people to resolve issues on their own through a process that improves—or at least does not damage—their relationships. The

The Three Myths of Collaboration

COMPANIES ATTEMPT TO FOSTER collaboration among different parts of their organizations through a variety of methods, many based on a number of seemingly sensible but ultimately misguided assumptions.

Effective Collaboration Means "Teaming"

Many companies think that teamwork training is the way to promote collaboration across an organization. So they'll get the HR department to run hundreds of managers and their subordinates through intensive two- or three-day training programs. Workshops will offer techniques for getting groups aligned around common goals, for clarifying roles and responsibilities, for operating according to a shared set of behavioral norms, and so on.

Unfortunately, such workshops are usually the right solution to the wrong problems. First, the most critical breakdowns in collaboration typically occur not on actual teams but in the rapid and unstructured interactions between different groups within the organization. For example, someone from R&D will spend weeks unsuccessfully trying to get help from manufacturing to run a few tests on a new prototype. Meanwhile, people in manufacturing begin to complain about arrogant engineers from R&D expecting them to drop everything to help with another one of R&D's pet projects. Clearly, the need for collaboration extends to areas other than a formal team.

The second problem is that breakdowns in collaboration almost always result from fundamental differences among business functions and divisions. Teamwork training offers little guidance on how to work together in the context of competing objectives and limited resources. Indeed, the frequent emphasis on common goals further stigmatizes the idea of conflict in organizations where an emphasis on "polite" behavior regularly prevents effective problem solving. People who need to collaborate more effectively usually don't need to align around and work toward a common goal. They need to quickly and creatively solve problems by managing the inevitable conflict so that it works in their favor.

An Effective Incentive System Will Ensure Collaboration

It's a tantalizing proposition: You can hardwire collaboration into your organization by rewarding collaborative behavior. Salespeople receive bonuses not only for hitting targets for their own division's products but also for hitting cross-selling targets. Staff in corporate support functions like IT and procurement have part of their bonuses determined by positive feedback from their internal clients.

Unfortunately, the results of such programs are usually disappointing. Despite greater financial incentives, for example, salespeople continue to focus on the sales of their own products to the detriment of selling integrated solutions. Employees continue to perceive the IT and procurement departments as difficult to work with, too focused on their own priorities. Why such poor results? To some extent, it's because individuals think—for the most part correctly—that if they perform well in their own operation they will be "taken care of" by their bosses. In addition, many people find that the costs of working with individuals in other parts of the organization—the extra time required, the aggravation—greatly outweigh the rewards for doing so.

Certainly, misaligned incentives can be a tremendous obstacle to cross-boundary collaboration. But even the most carefully constructed incentives won't eliminate tensions between people with competing business objectives. An incentive is too blunt an instrument to enable optimal resolution of the hundreds of different trade-offs that need to be made in a complex organization. What's more, overemphasis on incentives can create a culture in which people say, "If the company wanted me to do that, they would build it into my comp plan." Ironically, focusing on incentives as a means to encourage collaboration can end up undermining it.

Organizations Can Be Structured for Collaboration

Many managers look for structural and procedural solutions—cross-functional task forces, collaborative "groupware," complex webs of dotted reporting lines on the organization chart—to create greater internal collaboration. But bringing people together is very different from getting them to collaborate.

Consider the following scenario. Individual information technology departments have been stripped out of a company's business units and moved to a corporatewide, shared-services IT organization. Senior managers rightly recognize that this kind of change is a recipe for conflict because various groups will now essentially compete with one another for scarce IT resources. So managers try mightily to design conflict out of, and collaboration into, the new organization. For example, to enable collaborative decision making within IT and between IT and the business units, business units are required to enter requests for IT support into a computerized tracking system. The system is designed to enable managers within the IT organization to prioritize projects and optimally deploy resources to meet the various requests.

Despite painstaking process design, results are disappointing. To avoid the inevitable conflicts between business units and IT over project prioritization, managers in the business units quickly learn to bring their requests to those they know in the IT organization rather than entering the requests into the new system. Consequently, IT professionals assume that any project in the system is a lower priority—further discouraging use of the system. People's inability to deal effectively with conflict has undermined a new process specifically designed to foster organizational collaboration.

following strategies help produce decisions that are better informed and more likely to be implemented.

Devise and implement a common method for resolving conflict

Consider for a moment the hypothetical Matrix Corporation, a composite of many organizations we've worked with whose challenges will likely be familiar to managers. Over the past few years, salespeople from nearly a dozen of Matrix's product and service groups have been called on to design and sell integrated solutions to their customers. For any given sale, five or more lead salespeople and their teams have to agree on issues of resource allocation, solution design, pricing, and sales strategy. Not surprisingly, the teams are finding this difficult. Who should contribute the most resources to a particular customer's offering? Who should reduce the scope of their participation or discount their pricing to meet a customer's budget? Who should defer when disagreements arise about account strategy? Who should manage key relationships within the customer account? Indeed, given these thorny questions, Matrix is finding that a single large sale typically generates far more conflict inside the company than it does with the customer. The resulting wasted time and damaged relationships among sales teams are making it increasingly difficult to close sales.

Most companies face similar sorts of problems. And, like Matrix, they leave employees to find their own ways of resolving them. But without a structured method for dealing with these issues, people get bogged down not only in what the right result should be but also in how to arrive at it. Often, they will avoid or work around conflict, thereby forgoing important opportunities to collaborate. And when people do decide to confront their differences, they usually default to the approach they know best: debating about who's right and who's wrong or haggling over small concessions. Among the negative consequences of such approaches are suboptimal, "split-the-difference" resolutions—if not outright deadlock.

Establishing a companywide process for resolving disagreements can alter this familiar scenario. At the very least, a well-defined, well-designed conflict resolution method will reduce transaction costs, such as wasted time and the accumulation of ill will, that often come with the struggle to work though differences. At best, it will yield the innovative outcomes that are likely to emerge from discussions that draw on a multitude of objectives and perspectives. There is an array of conflict resolution methods a company can use. But to be effective, they should offer a clear, step-by-step process for parties to follow. They should also be made an integral part of existing business activities—account planning, sourcing, R&D budgeting, and the like. If conflict resolution is set up as a separate, exception-based process—a kind of organizational appeals court—it will likely wither away once initial managerial enthusiasm wanes.

At Intel, new employees learn a common method and language for decision making and conflict resolution. The company puts them through training in which they learn to use a variety of tools for handling discord. Not only does the training show that top management sees disagreements as an inevitable aspect of doing business, it also provides a common framework that expedites conflict resolution. Little time is wasted in figuring out the best way to handle a disagreement or trading accusations about "not being a team player"; guided by this clearly defined process, people can devote their time and energy to exploring and constructively evaluating a variety of options for how to move forward. Intel's systematic method for working through differences has helped sustain some of the company's hallmark qualities: innovation, operational efficiency, and the ability to make and implement hard decisions in the face of complex strategic choices.

Provide people with criteria for making trade-offs

At our hypothetical Matrix Corporation, senior managers overseeing cross-unit sales teams often admonish those teams to "do what's right for the customer." Unfortunately, this exhortation isn't much help when conflict arises. Given Matrix's ability to offer numerous combinations of products and services, company managers—each with different training and experience and access to different information, not to mention different unit priorities—have, not surprisingly, different opinions about how best to meet customers' needs.

Blue Cross and Blue Shield: build, buy, or ally?

One of the most effective ways senior managers can help resolve cross-unit conflict is by giving people the criteria for making trade-offs when the needs of different parts of the business are at odds with one another. At Blue Cross and Blue Shield of Florida, there are often conflicting perspectives over whether to build new capabilities (for example, a new claims-processing system, as in the hypothetical example below), acquire them, or gain access to them through an alliance. The company uses a grid-like poster (a simplified version of which is shown here) that helps multiple parties analyze the trade-offs associated with these three options. By checking various boxes in the grid using personalized markers, participants indicate how they assess a particular option against a variety of criteria: for example, the date by which the new capability needs to be implemented; the availability of internal resources such as capital and staff needed to develop the capability; and the degree of integration required with existing products and processes. The table format makes criteria and trade-offs easy to compare. The visual depiction of people's "votes" and the ensuing discussion help individuals see how their differences often arise from such factors as access to different data or different prioritizing of objectives. As debate unfolds—and as people move their markers in response to new information—they can see where they are aligned and where and why they separate into significant factions of disagreement. Eventually, the criteria-based dialogue tends to produce a preponderance of markers in one of the three rows, thus yielding operational consensus around a decision.

New claims-processing system

Required implementation time frame	Organizational experience level	Availability of internal resources	Volatility of environment	Complexity of solution	Availability of external resources	Required degree of integration	Required control	
>12 months	High	High	Low	Low	Low	High	High	**Build**
<6 months	Low	High to moderate	Medium	High	High	Medium	Medium	**Buy**
6–12 months	Medium	Moderate to low	High	Moderate	Moderate	Low	Low	**Ally**

Participant 1= Participant 2= Participant 3= Participant 4= Participant 5 =

Source: Blue Cross and Blue Shield of Florida

Similar clashes in perspective result when exasperated senior managers tell squabbling team members to set aside their differences and “put Matrix’s interests first.” That’s because it isn’t always clear what’s best for the company given the complex interplay among Matrix’s objectives for revenue, profitability, market share, and long-term growth.

Even when companies equip people with a common method for resolving conflict, employees often will still need to make zero-sum trade-offs between competing priorities. That task is made much easier and less contentious when top management can clearly articulate the criteria for making such choices. Obviously, it’s not easy to reduce a company’s strategy to clearly defined trade-offs, but it’s worth trying. For example, salespeople who know that five points of market share are more important than a ten-point increase on a customer satisfaction scale are much better equipped to make strategic concessions when the needs and priorities of different parts of the business conflict. And even when the criteria do not lead to a straightforward answer, the guidelines can at least foster productive conversations by providing an objective focus. Establishing such criteria also sends a clear signal from management that it views conflict as an inevitable result of managing a complex business.

At Blue Cross and Blue Shield of Florida, the strategic decision to rely more and more on alliances with other organizations has significantly increased the potential for disagreement in an organization long accustomed to developing capabilities in-house. Decisions about whether to build new capabilities, buy them outright, or gain access to them through alliances are natural flashpoints for conflict among internal groups. The health insurer might have tried to minimize such conflict through a structural solution, giving a particular group the authority to make decisions concerning whether, for instance, to develop a new claims-processing system in-house, to do so jointly with an alliance partner, or to license or acquire an existing system from a third party. Instead, the company established a set of criteria designed to help various groups within the organization—for example, the enterprise alliance group, IT, and marketing—to collectively make such decisions.

The criteria are embodied in a spreadsheet-type tool that guides people in assessing the trade-offs involved—say, between speed in getting a new process up and running versus ensuring its seamless integration with existing ones—when deciding whether to build, buy, or ally. People no longer debate back and forth across a table, advocating their preferred outcomes. Instead, they sit around the table and together apply a common set of trade-off criteria to the decision at hand. The resulting insights into the pros and cons of each approach enable more effective execution, no matter which path is chosen. (For a simplified version of the trade-off tool, see the exhibit "Blue Cross and Blue Shield: build, buy, or ally?")

Use the escalation of conflict as an opportunity for coaching

Managers at Matrix spend much of their time playing the organizational equivalent of hot potato. Even people who are new to the company learn within weeks that the best thing to do with cross-unit conflict is to toss it up the management chain. Immediate supervisors take a quick pass at resolving the dispute but, being busy themselves, usually pass it up to *their* supervisors. Those supervisors do the same, and before long the problem lands in the lap of a senior-level manager, who then spends much of his time resolving disagreements. Clearly, this isn't ideal. Because the senior managers are a number of steps removed from the source of the controversy, they rarely have a good understanding of the situation. Furthermore, the more time they spend resolving internal clashes, the less time they spend engaged in the business, and the more isolated they are from the very information they need to resolve the disputes dumped in their laps. Meanwhile, Matrix employees get so little opportunity to learn about how to deal with conflict that it becomes not only expedient but almost necessary for them to quickly bump conflict up the management chain.

While Matrix's story may sound extreme, we can hardly count the number of companies we've seen that operate this way. And even in the best of situations—for example, where a companywide conflict-management process is in place and where trade-off criteria are well understood—there is still a natural tendency for people to let their

IBM: coaching for conflict

Managers can reduce the repeated escalation of conflict up the management chain by helping employees learn how to resolve disputes themselves. At IBM, executives get training in conflict management and are offered online resources to help them coach others. One tool on the corporate intranet (an edited excerpt of which is shown here) walks managers through a variety of conversations they might have with a direct report who is struggling to resolve a dispute with people from one or more groups in the company—some of whom, by design, will be consulted to get their views but won't be involved in negotiating the final decision.

If you hear from someone reporting to you that . . .	The problem could be that . . .	And you could help your report by saying something like . . .
"Everyone still insists on being a decision maker."	The people your report is dealing with remain concerned that unless they have a formal voice in making the decision—or a key piece of the decision—their needs and interests won't be taken into account.	"You might want to explain why people are being consulted and how this information will be used." "Are there ways to break this decision apart into a series of subissues and assign decision-making roles around those subissues?" "Consider talking to the group about the costs of having everyone involved in the final decision."
"If I consult with this person up front, he might try to force an answer on me or create roadblocks to my efforts to move forward."	The person you are coaching may be overlooking the risks of not asking for input—mainly, that any decision arrived at without input could be sabotaged later on.	"How would you ask someone for input? What would you tell her about your purpose in seeking it? What questions would you ask? What would you say if she put forth a solution and resisted discussing other options?" "Is there a way to manage the risk that she will try to block your efforts other than by not consulting her at all? If you consult with her now, might that in fact lower the risk that she will try to derail your efforts later?"
"I have consulted with all the right parties and have crafted, by all accounts, a good plan. But the decision makers cannot settle on a final decision."	The right people were included in the negotiating group, but the process for negotiating a final decision was not determined.	"What are the ground rules for how decisions will be made? Do all those in the group need to agree? Must the majority agree? Or just those with the greatest competence?" "What interests underlie the objective of having everyone agree? Is there another decision-making process that would meet those interests?"

bosses sort out disputes. Senior managers contribute to this tendency by quickly resolving the problems presented to them. While this may be the fastest and easiest way to fix the problems, it encourages people to punt issues upstairs at the first sign of difficulty. Instead, managers should treat escalations as opportunities to help employees become better at resolving conflict. (For an example of how managers can help their employees improve their conflict resolution skills, see the exhibit "IBM: coaching for conflict.")

At KLA-Tencor, a major manufacturer of semiconductor production equipment, a materials executive in each division oversees a number of buyers who procure the materials and component parts for machines that the division makes. When negotiating a company-wide contract with a supplier, a buyer often must work with the company commodity manager, as well as with buyers from other divisions who deal with the same supplier. There is often conflict, for example, over the delivery terms for components supplied to two or more divisions under the contract. In such cases, the commodity manager and the division materials executive will push the division buyer to consider the needs of the other divisions, alternatives that might best address the collective needs of the different divisions, and the standards to be applied in assessing the trade-offs between alternatives. The aim is to help the buyer see solutions that haven't yet been considered and to resolve the conflict with the buyer in the other division.

Initially, this approach required more time from managers than if they had simply made the decisions themselves. But it has paid off in fewer disputes that senior managers need to resolve, speedier contract negotiation, and improved contract terms both for the company as a whole and for multiple divisions. For example, the buyers from three KLA-Tencor product divisions recently locked horns over a global contract with a key supplier. At issue was the trade-off between two variables: one, the supplier's level of liability for materials it needs to purchase in order to fulfill orders and, two, the flexibility granted the KLA-Tencor divisions in modifying the size of the orders and their required lead times. Each division demanded a different balance between these two factors, and the buyers took the conflict to their managers, wondering if they should try to negotiate each of the different trade-offs into the contract or pick among them. After being coached to consider how each division's business model shaped its preference—and using this understanding to jointly brainstorm alternatives—the buyers and commodity manager arrived at a creative solution that worked for everyone: They would request a clause in the contract that allowed them to increase and decrease flexibility in order volume and lead time, with corresponding changes in supplier liability, as required by changing market conditions.

Strategies for Managing Conflict upon Escalation

Equipped with common conflict resolution methods and trade-off criteria, and supported by systematic coaching, people are better able to resolve conflict on their own. But certain complex disputes will inevitably need to be decided by superiors. Consequently, managers must ensure that, upon escalation, conflict is resolved constructively and efficiently—and in ways that model desired behaviors.

Establish and enforce a requirement of joint escalation

Let's again consider the situation at Matrix. In a typical conflict, three salespeople from different divisions become involved in a dispute over pricing. Frustrated, one of them decides to hand the problem up to his boss, explaining the situation in a short voice-mail message. The message offers little more than bare acknowledgment of the other salespeople's viewpoints. The manager then determines, on the basis of what he knows about the situation, the solution to the problem. The salesperson, armed with his boss's decision, returns to his counterparts and shares with them the verdict—which, given the process, is simply a stronger version of the solution the salesperson had put forward in the first place. But wait! The other two salespeople have also gone to *their* managers and carried back stronger versions of *their* solutions. At this point, each salesperson is locked into what is now "my manager's view" of the right pricing scheme. The problem, already thorny, has become even more intractable.

The best way to avoid this kind of debilitating deadlock is for people to present a disagreement jointly to their boss or bosses. This will reduce or even eliminate the suspicion, surprises, and damaged personal relationships ordinarily associated with unilateral escalation. It will also guarantee that the ultimate decision maker has access to a wide array of perspectives on the conflict, its causes, and the various ways it might be resolved. Furthermore, companies that require people to share responsibility for the escalation of a conflict often see a decrease in the number of problems that are pushed up the management chain. Joint escalation helps create the kind of accountability that is lacking when people know they can provide their side of an issue to their own manager and blame others when things don't work out.

A few years ago, after a merger that resulted in a much larger and more complex organization, senior managers at the Canadian telecommunications company Telus found themselves virtually paralyzed by a daily barrage of unilateral escalations. Just determining who was dealing with what and who should be talking to whom took up huge amounts of senior management's time. So the company made joint escalation a central tenet of its new organizationwide protocols for conflict resolution—a requirement given teeth by managers' refusal to respond to unilateral escalation. When a conflict occurred among managers in different departments concerning, say, the allocation of resources among the departments, the managers were required to jointly describe the problem, what had been done so far to resolve it, and its possible solutions. Then they had to send a joint write-up of the situation to each of their bosses and stand ready to appear together and answer questions when those bosses met to work through a solution. In many cases, the requirement of systematically documenting the conflict and efforts to resolve it—because it forced people to make such efforts—led to a problem being resolved on the spot, without having to be kicked upstairs. Within weeks, this process resulted in the resolution of hundreds of issues that had been stalled for months in the newly merged organization.

Ensure that managers resolve escalated conflicts directly with *their* counterparts

Let's return to the three salespeople at Matrix who took their dispute over pricing to their respective bosses and then met again, only to find themselves further from agreement than before. So what did they do at that point? They sent the problem *back* to their bosses. These three bosses, each of whom thought he'd already resolved the issue, decided the easiest thing to do would be to escalate it themselves. This would save them time and put the conflict before senior managers with the broad view seemingly needed to make a decision. Unfortunately, by doing this, the three bosses simply perpetuated the situation their salespeople had created, putting forward a biased viewpoint and leaving it to their own managers to come up with an answer. In the end, the decision was made unilaterally by the senior manager with the most organizational clout. This result bred resentment back down the management chain. A sense of "we'll win next time" took hold, ensuring that future conflict would be even more difficult to resolve.

It's not unusual to see managers react to escalations from their employees by simply passing conflicts up their own functional or divisional chains until they reach a senior executive involved with all the affected functions or divisions. Besides providing a poor example for others in the organization, this can be disastrous for a company that needs to move quickly. To avoid wasting time, a manager somewhere along the chain might try to resolve the problem swiftly and decisively by herself. But this, too, has its costs. In a complex organization, where many issues have significant implications for numerous parts of the business, unilateral responses to unilateral escalations are a recipe for inefficiency, bad decisions, and ill feelings.

The solution to these problems is a commitment by managers—a commitment codified in a formal policy—to deal with escalated conflict directly with their counterparts. Of course, doing this can feel cumbersome, especially when an issue is time-sensitive. But resolving the problem early on is ultimately more efficient than trying to sort it out later, after a decision becomes known because it has negatively affected some part of the business.

In the 1990s, IBM's sales and delivery organization became increasingly complex as the company reintegrated previously independent divisions and reorganized itself to provide customers with full solutions of bundled products and services. Senior executives soon recognized that managers were not dealing with escalated conflicts and that relationships among them were strained because they failed to consult and coordinate around cross-unit issues. This led to the creation of a forum called the Market Growth Workshop (a name carefully chosen to send a message throughout the company that getting cross-unit conflict resolved was critical to meeting customer needs and, in turn, growing market share). These monthly conference calls brought together managers, salespeople, and frontline product specialists from across the company to discuss and resolve cross-unit conflicts that were hindering important sales—for example, the difficulty salespeople faced in getting needed technical resources from overstretched product groups.

The Market Growth Workshops weren't successful right away. In the beginning, busy senior managers, reluctant to spend time on issues that often hadn't been carefully thought through, began sending their subordinates to the meetings—which made it even more difficult to resolve the problems discussed. So the company developed a simple preparation template that forced people to document and analyze disputes before the conference calls. Senior managers, realizing the problems created by their absence, recommitted themselves to attending the meetings. Over time, as complex conflicts were resolved during these sessions and significant sales were closed, attendees began to see these meetings as an opportunity to be involved in the resolution of high-stakes, high-visibility issues.

Make the process for escalated conflict resolution transparent

When a sales conflict is resolved by a Matrix senior manager, the word comes down the management chain in the form of an action item: Put together an offering with this particular mix of products and services at these prices. The only elaboration may be an admonishment to "get the sales team together, work up a proposal, and get back to the customer as quickly as possible." The problem is solved, at least for the time being. But the salespeople—unless they have been able to divine themes from the patterns of decisions made over time—are left with little guidance on how to resolve similar issues in the future. They may justifiably wonder: How was the decision made? Based on what kinds of assumptions? With what kinds of trade-offs? How might the reasoning change if the situation were different?

In most companies, once managers have resolved a conflict, they announce the decision and move on. The resolution process and rationale behind the decision are left inside a managerial black box. While it's rarely helpful for managers to share all the gory details of their deliberations around contentious issues, failing to take the time to explain how a decision was reached and the factors that went into it squanders a major opportunity. A frank discussion of the trade-offs involved in decisions would provide guidance to people trying to resolve conflicts in the future and would help nip in the bud the kind of speculation—who won and who lost, which managers or units have the most power—that breeds mistrust, sparks turf battles, and otherwise impedes cross-organizational collaboration. In general, clear communication about the resolution of the conflict can increase people's willingness and ability to implement decisions.

During the past two years, IBM's Market Growth Workshops have evolved into a more structured approach to managing escalated conflict, known as Cross-Team Workouts. Designed to make conflict resolution more transparent, the workouts are weekly meetings of people across the organization who work together on sales and delivery issues for specific accounts. The meetings provide a public forum for resolving conflicts over account strategy, solution configuration, pricing, and delivery. Those issues that cannot be resolved at the local level are escalated to regional workout sessions attended by managers from product groups, services, sales, and finance. Attendees then communicate and explain meeting resolutions to their reports. Issues that cannot be resolved at the regional level are escalated to an even higher-level workout meeting attended by cross-unit executives from a larger geographic region—like the Americas or Asia Pacific—and chaired by the general manager of the region presenting the issue. The most complex and strategic issues reach this global forum. The overlapping attendance at these sessions—in which the managers who chair one level of meeting attend sessions at the next level up, thereby observing the decision-making process at that stage—further enhances the transparency of the system among different levels of the company. IBM has further formalized the process for the direct resolution of conflicts between services and product sales on large accounts by designating a managing director in sales and a global relationship partner in IBM global services as the ultimate point of resolution for escalated conflicts. By explicitly making the resolution of complex conflicts part of the job descriptions for both managing director and global relationship partner—and by making that clear to others in the organization—IBM has reduced ambiguity, increased transparency, and increased the efficiency with which conflicts are resolved.

Tapping the Learning Latent in Conflict

The six strategies we have discussed constitute a framework for effectively managing organizational discord, one that integrates conflict resolution into day-to-day decision-making processes, thereby removing a critical barrier to cross-organizational collaboration. But the strategies also hint at something else: that conflict can be more than a necessary antecedent to collaboration.

Let's return briefly to Matrix. More than three-quarters of all cross-unit sales at the company trigger disputes about pricing. Roughly half of the sales lead to clashes over account control. A substantial number of sales also produce disagreements over the design of customer solutions, with the conflict often rooted in divisions' incompatible measurement systems and the concerns of some people about the quality of the solutions being assembled. But managers are so busy trying to resolve these almost daily disputes that they don't see the patterns or sources of conflict. Interestingly, if they ever wanted to identify patterns like these, Matrix managers might find few signs of them. That's because salespeople, who regularly hear their bosses complain about all the disagreements in the organization, have concluded that they'd better start shielding their superiors from discord.

The situation at Matrix is not unusual—most companies view conflict as an unnecessary nuisance—but that view is unfortunate. When a company begins to see conflict as a valuable resource that should be managed and exploited, it is likely to gain insight into problems that senior managers may not have known existed. Because internal friction is often caused by unaddressed strains within an organization or between an organization and its environment, setting up methods to track conflict and examine its causes can provide an interesting new perspective on a variety of issues. In the case of Matrix, taking the time to aggregate the experiences of individual salespeople involved in recurring disputes would likely lead to better approaches to setting prices, establishing incentives for salespeople, and monitoring the company's quality control process.

At Johnson & Johnson, an organization that has a highly decentralized structure, conflict is recognized as a positive aspect of cross-company collaboration. For example, a small internal group charged with facilitating sourcing collaboration among J&J's independent operating companies—particularly their outsourcing of clinical research services—actively works to extract lessons from conflicts. The group tracks and analyzes disagreements about issues such as what to outsource, whether and how to shift spending among suppliers, and what supplier capabilities to invest in. It hosts a council, comprising representatives from the various operating companies, that meets regularly to discuss these differences and explore their strategic implications. As a result, trends in clinical research outsourcing are spotted and information about them is disseminated throughout J&J more quickly. The operating companies benefit from insights about new offshoring opportunities, technologies, and ways of structuring collaboration with suppliers. And J&J, which can now piece together an accurate and global view of its suppliers, is better able to partner with them. Furthermore, the company realizes more value from its relationship with suppliers—yet another example of how the effective management of conflict can ultimately lead to fruitful collaboration.

J&J's approach is unusual but not unique. The benefits it offers provide further evidence that conflict—so often viewed as a liability to be avoided whenever possible—can be valuable to a company that knows how to manage it.

Originally published in March 2005. Reprint R0503F

Shattering the Myths About Enterprise 2.0

by Andrew P. McAfee

DIGITAL COLLABORATION IS ALL the rage in the world of business. Companies in every industry are adopting collaborative software platforms that enable employees to generate more and better output. A May 2009 Forrester Research study found that almost 50% of companies in the U.S. use some kind of social software, and a July 2009 Prescient Digital Media survey revealed that 47% of respondents were using wikis, 45% blogs, and 46% internal discussion forums.

Underpinning this trend is Web 2.0, a term coined in 2004 to describe the internet's capability to allow everyone, even non-techies, to connect with other people and contribute content. Facebook, Twitter, YouTube, and Wikipedia are the best-known examples of this trend, and they have become some of the Web's most popular resources. Three years ago, I coined the term Enterprise 2.0 to highlight the fact that smart companies are embracing Web 2.0 technologies, as well as the underlying approach to collaboration and creation of content.

Enterprise 2.0, which I sometimes call E2.0, refers to how an organization uses *emergent social software platforms,* or ESSPs, to pursue its goals (see the sidebar "What Is Enterprise 2.0?"). This definition emphasizes the most striking feature of the new technologies: They don't impose predetermined workflows, roles and responsibilities, or interdependencies among people, but instead allow them to emerge. This is a profound shift. Most companies use applications like ERP and CRM software, which create cross-functional business processes and specify—in detail and with little flexibility—exactly who does what and when, and who gets to make which decisions. E2.0, in contrast, requires companies to take the opposite approach: to let people create and refine content as equals and with no, or few, preconditions. Using ESSPs enables patterns and structures to take shape over time.

There are several benefits of ESSPs. The tools help people find information and guidance quickly—and reduce duplication of work. They open up innovation processes to more people, which is an advantage because, as open source software advocate Eric Raymond put it, "with enough eyeballs, all bugs are shallow." They harness collective intelligence and the wisdom of crowds to obtain accurate answers to tough questions. They let people build, maintain, and profit from large social networks. They allow executives to realize the dream of creating an up-to-the-minute repository of everything an organization knows. Underlying all these benefits is a style of interaction and collaboration that isn't defined by hierarchy and is relatively unconstrained by it.

However, E2.0 hasn't delivered results or even gotten off the ground everywhere. Many companies refuse to take the plunge because the possible drawbacks—the misuse of blogs or the possibility of information theft, for instance—seem concrete and immediate, whereas the benefits appear nebulous and distant. In addition, many corporations have walked away from their E2.0 initiatives, for three reasons. One, doubts persist about the value of these collaboration tools even when they are being actively used. Two, ESSPs often seem unimpressive initially. Pages in corporate wikis read like documents in a binder; blog posts look like newsletters; and personal pages look like Facebook profiles. Three, many projects simply never took off. Employees didn't flock to use the new technologies, and sponsors wound up with digital wastelands instead of the

Idea in Brief

Web 2.0 technologies are now a staple of social collaboration on the internet. In 2006 Andrew McAfee, of the MIT Center for Digital Business, coined the term Enterprise 2.0 to describe how organizations use emergent social software platforms, or ESSPs, to pursue their goals. However, some organizations don't achieve the many collaboration-related benefits that internal ESSPs can offer. After studying both successful and unsuccessful E2.0 initiatives, McAfee attributes most of the failures to five misconceptions. The first two myths crop up before an E2.0 initiative is launched. One is that the risks of ESSPs, most notably from inappropriate use, will greatly outweigh the rewards. McAfee makes the case that those dangers rarely manifest in practice. The other pre-launch myth is that the ROI of an E2.0 initiative should be calculated in monetary terms. McAfee shows how Enterprise 2.0 can deliver valuable benefits in terms of developing human, organizational, and information capital—without a numerical ROI yield. The final three myths arise after an E2.0 project is deployed. One holds that people will flock to a collaboration platform once it is built. Success actually requires various types of top-down support, including active participation by senior leaders. Another is that E2.0's primary worth is in helping close colleagues work together better. In reality, the value extends to networks of expertise well beyond a user's inner circle. The importance of those far-reaching interpersonal connections also debunks the last myth: that E2.0 should be judged by the information it generates. Information is indeed useful, but E2.0's greatest advantage lies in transforming potential ties between people into actual ones.

rainforests they had expected. In fact, a 2008 McKinsey survey showed that only 21% of companies were entirely satisfied with their E2.0 initiatives and that 22% were entirely dissatisfied.

I have been studying E2.0 projects, both successful and unsuccessful, since companies started deploying these technologies in earnest four years ago. My research shows that, despite the failures, there have been striking successes—and that more big successes are possible if only companies would learn to use these tools well. Most initiatives fail because of five widely held beliefs: reasonable attitudes held by well-meaning people, not the handiwork of saboteurs. Nonetheless, data, research, and case studies show that the

What Is Enterprise 2.0?

ENTERPRISE 2.0 IS THE USE OF EMERGENT social software platforms, or ESSPs, by an organization to pursue its goals. Here's a breakdown of what the term means:

- *Social software,* as a Wikipedia entry roughly characterizes it, enables people to rendezvous, connect, or collaborate through computer-mediated communication and to form online communities.
- *Platforms* are digital environments in which contributions and interactions are visible to everyone and remain until the user deletes them.
- *Emergent* means that the software is "freeform" and contains mechanisms that let the patterns and structure inherent in people's interactions become evident over time.
- *Freeform* software has many or all of the following characteristics: Its use is optional; it does not predefine workflows; it is indifferent to formal hierarchies; and it accepts many types of data.

---

beliefs are wrong; they're the myths of Enterprise 2.0. In the following pages, I'll refute them, starting with two that crop up before an E2.0 initiative is launched and finishing with three that can take hold after deployment.

Myth 1: E2.0's Risks Greatly Outweigh the Rewards

When CEOs first hear about how Enterprise 2.0 works, many become queasy about allowing people to contribute freely to the company's content platforms. They voice a consistent set of concerns: What if someone posts hate speech or pornography? Can't an employee use the forum to denigrate the company, air dirty laundry, or criticize its leadership and strategy? Don't these technologies make it easy for valuable information to seep out of the company and be sold to the highest bidder? If we use these tools, how can we avoid breaking agreements with partners about information sharing? What if rivals use customer-facing websites to air grievances or malign our products and service? Are we liable if people give incorrect information or bad advice on the forums we host? Won't employees use the collaboration software to plan social events instead of work-related activities?

Those risks all exist in theory—but rarely in practice. Over the last four years, I've asked every company I've worked with about the worst things that have happened on their ESSPs. My collection of horror stories is nearly empty. I have yet to come across a single episode that has made me wonder whether companies shouldn't invest in E2.0 technologies. One conversation I had was particularly telling. In late 2007, when I was teaching a group of senior HR executives, one of them said that leaders at her company, which employed many young people, became concerned about how employees represented it online. When her team poked around on Facebook, MySpace, and other sites, it found that employees almost always talked about the company in appropriate ways. The worst thing the team discovered was a photograph of a training session in which some account numbers were dimly visible on a blackboard. When alerted, the employee who posted it immediately apologized and took the photograph down. Even that wasn't necessary; it turned out that the numbers were dummies.

Four factors work together to make E2.0 horror stories so rare. One, although anonymity is the default on the internet, on company intranets attribution is the norm. Users are circumspect and unlikely to "flame" colleagues. If workers do misbehave, companies can identify, counsel, educate, and, if necessary, discipline them. Two, participants usually feel a sense of community and react quickly if they feel that someone is violating the norms. Counterproductive contributions usually meet with a flurry of responses that articulate why the content is out of bounds, reiterate the implicit rules, and offer correction. Three, in addition to an organization's formal leaders, community leaders form a counterbalance. They exert a great deal of influence and shape fellow employees' behavior online. Four, the internet has been in wide use for more than a decade, so most people know how to behave appropriately in online contexts.

If corporations don't believe that these factors provide sufficient protection, they can easily set up a moderation process whereby executives vet contributions before they appear. This precaution is common on customer-facing sites, where spammers and vandals can wreak havoc, but companies can use it internally too. Don't forget, e-mail and text messages are invisible to everyone except senders and receivers, but ESSPs make content visible and thereby turn the entire workforce into compliance monitors. It's a myth that E2.0 is risky; if anything, it lowers companies' risk profiles.

Myth 2: The ROI of E2.0 Must Be Calculated in Monetary Terms

The one aspect of Enterprise 2.0 that I'm asked about more than the risks is the business case for it. E2.0 initiatives, like all IT projects, appear similar to other investment opportunities in that a company spends money to acquire assets (such as, in this case, servers and software CDs). But that's a surface-level matter; the company's deeper goal is to develop its intangible assets—notably its human, organizational, and information capital.

The value of intangible assets can't be measured independently, as several experts have noted; it stems from the assets' ability to help the organization implement its strategy. "Intangible assets, such as knowledge and technology, seldom have a direct impact on financial outcomes such as increased revenues, lowered costs, and higher profits," state HBS professor Robert Kaplan and David Norton unequivocally in their book *Strategy Maps*. Therefore, it's tough to create a business case for E2.0 projects by estimating the monetary return on investment. I have never met leaders of healthy E2.0 initiatives who wished that they had calculated an ROI figure, but I have spoken with many who described ROI exercises as a waste of time and energy.

Companies that are launching Enterprise 2.0 initiatives would do better to focus on three elements other than ROI:

- **Expected cost and timeline.** By now, managers know how to break down the cost of IT projects. They should also estimate how long the E2.0 effort will take, work out the implementation stages, and lay out the milestones.

- **Possible benefits.** The expected benefits from E2.0 must be stated, although descriptions needn't be as detailed as those for the features of a piece of software or as grandiose as the

Enterprise 2.0's Benefits

HERE ARE SIX BENEFITS A COMPANY can get by deploying and using an emergent social software platform:

1. **Group editing** allows multiple people to collaborate on a centrally stored work product such as a document, spreadsheet, presentation, or website.
2. **Authoring** is the ability to generate content and to publish it online for a broad audience. Unlike sending e-mail, authoring is a public act.
3. **Broadcast search** refers to the posting of queries in a public forum in the hope of receiving an answer. People publicize not what they know, but what they don't know.
4. **Network formation and maintenance.** Social network applications keep people in touch with the activities of close and distant contacts. Whenever a user provides an update, it becomes available to the entire network.
5. **Collective intelligence** is the use of technologies, such as prediction markets, to generate answers and forecasts from a dispersed group.
6. **Self-organization** is the ability of users to build communities and information resources without explicit coordination by any central authority. This is the most remarkable benefit of Enterprise 2.0—and the easiest to overlook.

promised results from ERP and CRM implementations such as "organizational transformation" or "customer intimacy." (See the sidebar "Enterprise 2.0's Benefits.")

- **Expected footprint.** Managers should detail the geographic, divisional, and functional reach of the E2.0 projects they are planning.

These three parameters are usually sufficient to allow executives to make decisions about whether it's worth investing in E2.0 projects. Most have little trouble answering questions such as "Is it worth spending $50,000 over the next six months to build a broadcast search system for the company?" The answer won't be an ROI number, but managers can nonetheless address it adeptly. Walking away from the classic business case doesn't mean abandoning clear thinking or planning. However, it's time to replace the myth that E2.0 requires an ROI calculation with the fact that tangible assets can deliver intangible benefits.

Myth 3: If We Build It, They Will Come

Given the popularity of Wikipedia, Facebook, and Twitter, many executives assume that their companies' collaboration platforms will also attract masses of people. They adopt a passive rollout strategy, introduce a few ESSPs, and formally notify people that the forums exist. They then wait for the benefits to accrue—and are shocked when nothing happens.

Popular as large Web 2.0 communities like Facebook are, they still attract only a tiny percentage of internet users. The main task that E2.0 champions face is to draw in a greater fraction of their target audience. That's difficult for two reasons. One, people are busy. Few knowledge workers feel they have the time to take on an additional responsibility, especially one with ill-defined goals and expectations. Two, employees don't know how top management will view their participation in ESSPs. Will senior executives value employees who contribute, or will they assume that those workers aren't interested in their "real" jobs? When the answer isn't clear, an unfortunate sequence of events unfolds. A few people start using the new tools out of curiosity or enthusiasm. They soon perceive that they're talking only to each other or, worse, to no one. Shouting into a void loses its appeal quickly, so they stop. The project is then considered a failure.

To avoid this outcome, I advocate the use of explicit recognition programs, incentives, and other types of top-down support for E2.0 projects. That's how the formal organization can show that it values employees' contributions. Leaders also should use ESSPs themselves. When senior executives allow their blog posts to receive comments and then respond to the feedback, or use social networking software to create a profile and connect with others in the organization, they're demonstrating their belief in E2.0. Similarly, when a company recognizes those who answer others' questions, it asserts that this type of work is valid and valuable. That E2.0 will automatically lure people is a myth; only when people know they're being heard by those who matter will E2.0 become mainstream.

Myth 4: E2.0 Delivers Value Mainly by Helping Close Colleagues Work Better

Most companies currently use ESSPs to support people who are already collaborating. The Prescient Digital Media survey cited earlier, for example, found that E2.0's most popular uses are employee collaboration (77% of respondents) and knowledge management (71%). When those are the goals, a typical scenario is for the organization to establish group-editing environments for all the units—such as labs, workgroups, business units, client teams, and so on—that want them, or to let the entities set them up for themselves. In most cases, these environments are closed: Nobody outside the predefined group can see or edit the content.

However, this approach has shortcomings. Consider the types of interpersonal ties of a typical knowledge worker. She has a small group of close collaborators with whom she has strong professional relationships. There's also a large set of people to whom she has weak ties: coworkers she interacts with periodically, colleagues she knows through coworkers, and other professional acquaintances. Next is another, even larger set of employees who may be valuable to her if only she knew about them. They could keep her from reinventing the wheel on her next project, answer pressing questions, tell her about a good vendor or consultant, let her know that they're working on similar problems, and so on. Finally are the people who wouldn't become colleagues of the knowledge worker even if she had ties to them.

Picture a bull's-eye with four rings; it can represent these four kinds of ties. When an E2.0 initiative consists of closed editing environments, it ignores the benefits that the three outer rings can deliver. Network formation often happens in the second ring. Authoring and broadcast search convert potential ties into actual ones, so they extend to people in the third ring. And collective intelligence works across all four rings; even strangers can trade with one another in prediction markets and generate accurate forecasts.

In short, the benefits of E2.0 technologies manifest themselves in all four rings. It's a myth that companies should focus on group editing among close colleagues; the reality is that Enterprise 2.0 is valuable at every level of interpersonal ties.

Myth 5: E2.0 Should Be Judged by the Information It Generates

It's commonly believed that the value of E2.0 can be assessed by looking at the information it yields. Popular Web 2.0 resources reinforce this idea: Wikipedia is a huge collection of articles, Flickr of pictures, and del.icio.us of web bookmarks. All of them deliver value to users mainly because they're comprehensive and of reasonable quality. It seems logical, then, to judge an organization's collaborative software platforms with one eye on quality and the other on comprehensiveness. This isn't unfair, but it is incomplete. First, ESSPs often capture work in progress rather than polished deliverables. Wiki pages and blog posts will look rough because they're essentially drafts. They're meant to present raw ideas—not refined ones. People should be encouraged to air first-cut concepts in order to show what they're planning to work on, what they're interested in, and what they know. Second, content points to people. Imperfect or incomplete information is valuable when organizations can identify who posted it. The social connection is often the real benefit that E2.0 delivers.

In 2008, for example, Don Burke, one of the evangelists for the U.S. intelligence community's Intellipedia wiki, posted some questions on my behalf on his internal blog. The first was "What, if anything, do Enterprise 2.0 tools let you do that you simply couldn't do before? In other words, have these tools incrementally changed your ability to do your job, or have they more fundamentally changed what your job is and how you do it?" Most respondents stressed the value of the platform's ability to convert potential ties into actual ones. Here are comments from a few of them:

- **From a Defense Intelligence Agency analyst:** "These tools have immensely improved my ability to interact with people that I would never have met otherwise . . . People that would never have been visible before now have a voice."

- **From a National Security Agency analyst:** "Earlier, contacting other agencies was done cautiously and only through official channels. After nearly two years of Intellipedia, this has changed. Using it has become part of my work process, and I have made connections with a variety of analysts outside the intelligence community. I don't know everything, but I do know who I can go to when I need to find out something."
- **From a National Security Agency engineer:** "There's now a place I can go to for answers as opposed to data. By using that data and all the links to people associated with that data, I can find people who are interested in helping me understand the subject matter . . . Their helpful attitude makes me want to help them (and others) in return."
- **From a Central Intelligence Agency analyst:** "The first aspect that comes to mind is the ease of sharing ideas and working collaboratively with intelligence professionals around the world . . . I am actively involved in an early-stage project that would be impossible without these tools."

These responses may not represent the views of the entire intelligence community, but they clearly illustrate that Enterprise 2.0 lets people find new colleagues by converting potential ties into actual ties. The new connections result from content posted on platforms but are invisible in the content itself. E2.0 doesn't only generate information; that's a myth. It also helps connect people.

Nelson Mandela wrote in his autobiography about a leadership lesson he learned from a tribal chief in South Africa: "A leader . . . is like a shepherd. He stays behind the flock, letting the most nimble go out ahead, whereupon the others follow, not realizing that all along they are being directed from behind." Similarly, E2.0 reveals the domains in which people are adept, allows some to show the way, and gets others

How Smart Companies Use Enterprise 2.0

ENTERPRISE 2.0, WHEN IT WORKS, delivers impressive results, as these four examples show:

- Office supply company VistaPrint started a wiki in order to capture what a new engineering hire needed to know. Because this knowledge base often changed quickly, the company suspected that a paper-based solution would become obsolete. Within 18 months, the wiki grew to over 11,000 pages and 600 categories, all generated by employees rather than by a knowledge-management staff.
- Serena Software encouraged its employees to create profiles on Facebook and other social networking sites, both to learn more about one another and to interact with outside parties such as customers and prospective employees. The company eventually attracted twice as many people to its annual user conference—and much better candidates for its job openings.
- The U.S. government has deployed ESSPs across its 16 intelligence agencies, which include the CIA, FBI, National Security Agency, and Defense Intelligence Agency. An internal report concluded that these tools, which include blogs and the Intellipedia wiki, are "already impacting the work practices of analysts. In addition, [they are] challenging deeply held norms about controlling the flow of information between individuals and across organizational boundaries."
- A U.S. gaming company set up an internal prediction market to forecast the sales of a new product. Consumer enthusiasm for new titles is notoriously hard to predict, but the market provided a good crystal ball. The 1,200 employees who traded in the market collectively generated a forecast that turned out to be 61% more accurate than the initial prediction, which had been yielded by conventional means.

---

to follow them when it's in the company's best interest. Enlightened business leaders will use these technologies to lead from behind; the rest will be held back by the fears that stem from believing in myths.

Originally published in November 2009. Reprint W0911A

When Internal Collaboration Is Bad for Your Company

by Morten T. Hansen

INTERNAL COLLABORATION IS ALMOST universally viewed as good for an organization. Leaders routinely challenge employees to tear down silos, transcend boundaries, and work together in cross-unit teams. And although such initiatives often meet with resistance because they place an extra burden on individuals, the potential benefits of collaboration are significant: innovative cross-unit product development, increased sales through cross-selling, the transfer of best practices that reduce costs.

But the conventional wisdom rests on the false assumption that the more employees collaborate, the better off the company will be. In fact, collaboration can just as easily undermine performance. I've seen it happen many times during my 15 years of research in this area. In one instance, Martine Haas, of Wharton, and I studied more than 100 experienced sales teams at a large information technology consulting firm. Facing fierce competition from such rivals as IBM and Accenture for contracts that might be worth $50 million or more, teams putting together sales proposals would often seek advice from other teams with expertise in, say, a technology being implemented by the prospective client. Our research yielded a surprising conclusion about this seemingly sensible practice: The greater the collaboration (measured by hours of help a team received), the worse the result (measured by success in winning contracts). We ultimately determined that experienced teams typically didn't learn as much from their peers as they thought they did. And whatever marginal knowledge they did gain was often outweighed by the time taken away from their work on the proposal.

The problem here wasn't collaboration per se; our statistical analysis found that novice teams at the firm actually benefited from exchanging ideas with their peers. Rather, the problem was determining when it makes sense and, crucially, when it doesn't. Too often a business leader asks, How can we get people to collaborate more? That's the wrong question. It should be, Will collaboration on this project create or destroy value? In fact, to collaborate well is to know when not to do it.

This article offers a simple calculus for differentiating between "good" and "bad" collaboration using the concept of a collaboration premium. My aim is to ensure that groups in your organization are encouraged to work together only when doing so will produce better results than if they worked independently.

How Collaboration Can Go Wrong

In 1996 the British government warned that so-called mad cow disease could be transferred to humans through the consumption of beef. The ensuing panic and disastrous impact on the worldwide beef industry over the next few years drove food companies of all kinds to think about their own vulnerability to unforeseen risks.

The Norwegian risk-management services firm Det Norske Veritas, or DNV, seemed well positioned to take advantage of the business opportunity this represented by helping food companies improve food safety. Founded in 1864 to verify the safety of ships, DNV had expanded over the years to provide an array of risk-management services through some 300 offices in 100 countries.

In the fall of 2002 DNV began to develop a service that would combine the expertise, resources, and customer bases of two of the

Idea in Brief

Are you promoting cross-unit collaboration for collaboration's sake? If so, you may be putting your company at risk. Collaboration can deliver tremendous benefits (innovative offerings, new sales). But it can also backfire if its costs (including delays stemming from turf battles) prove larger than you expected.

To distinguish good collaboration from bad, estimate three factors:

- **Return:** "What cash flow would this collaboration generate if executed effectively?"
- **Opportunity cost:** "What cash flow would we pass up by investing in this project instead of a noncollaborative one?"
- **Collaboration costs:** "What cash flow would we lose owing to problems associated with cross-unit work?"

Would the return exceed the combined opportunity and collaboration costs? If yes, put that collaborative project in motion.

firm's business units: standards certification and risk-management consulting. The certification business had recently created a practice that inspected large food company production chains. The consulting business had also targeted the food industry as a growth area, with the aim of helping companies reduce risks in their supply chains and production processes.

Initial projections for a joint effort were promising: If the two businesses collaborated, cross-marketing their services to customers, they could realize 200% growth from 2004 to 2008, as opposed to 50% if they operated separately. The net cash flow projected for 2004 through 2008 from the joint effort was $40 million. (This and other DNV financial figures are altered here for reasons of confidentiality.)

The initiative was launched in 2003 and run by a cross-unit team charged with cross-selling the two types of services and developing new client relationships with food companies. But the team had trouble capitalizing on what looked like a golden opportunity. Individual business unit revenue from areas where the existing businesses had been strong—Norway for consulting services, for example, and Italy

Idea in Practice

In deciding whether to launch a collaborative effort, managers can fall victim to three common errors. By understanding these errors, you stand a better chance of avoiding them.

Overestimating the Return

Many companies place a mistakenly high economic value on collaboration. Often, the expected results don't materialize.

> ***Example:*** Daimler's $36 billion acquisition of Chrysler in 1998 failed to deliver the promised synergies between the two automakers. In 2007, Daimler sold 80% of Chrysler for a mere $1 billion.

Ignoring Opportunity Costs

Executives often fail to consider opportunities they would forgo by devoting resources to a particular collaborative project. They don't evaluate *non*collaborative activities that might have higher potential.

> ***Example:*** Risk-management services firm DNV decided to combine the expertise, resources, and customer bases of two business units—standards certification and risk-management consulting. The goal? To cross-sell services to help food companies improve food safety. DNV estimated the collaboration's return as $40 million.

But DNV never compared the food-industry opportunity that required cross-unit collaboration with other industry opportunities that wouldn't require collaboration. One opportunity in IT could have been pursued by the

for certification—continued to grow, exceeding projections in 2004. But the two units did little cross-pollination in those markets. Furthermore, the team couldn't get much traction in the United Kingdom and other targeted markets, which was particularly disappointing given that the certification group had established good relations with UK food regulators in the years following the outbreak of mad cow disease.

As new business failed to materialize, the consulting group, which was under pressure from headquarters to improve its overall results in the near term, began shifting its focus from the food industry to other sectors it had earlier targeted for growth, weakening the joint effort. The certification group continued to make the

consulting unit alone, and it had more potential than the food opportunity. But because many of the consulting unit's experts were tied up with the food initiative, progress on the IT opportunity was constrained. The cost of the forgone opportunity was $25 million in revenue.

Underestimating Collaboration Costs

In most companies, it's difficult to get people in different units to work together effectively because:

- People don't want to share resources or customers.
- They resent taking on extra work if it provides little recognition and no financial incentive.
- They have conflicting priorities; for example, some people are dedicated to the initiative full-time, while others aren't.

These tensions create problems that, combined with opportunity costs, can eat into the collaboration's potential—and produce a collaboration *penalty*.

Example: At DNV, competition over customers between the two units caused tensions that ultimately scotched 50% of cross-selling engagements. That amounted to $20 million in collaboration costs. Added to the $25 million opportunity cost for the noncollaborative IT opportunity, total costs were $45 million—$5 million *over* the collaborative food opportunity's expected return of $40 million.

food industry a priority, but with the two groups' combined food industry revenue lagging behind projections in 2005, DNV abandoned the initiative it had launched with such optimism only two years before.

Knowing When (and When Not) to Collaborate

DNV's experience is hardly atypical. All too often plans involving collaboration among different parts of an organization are unveiled with fanfare only to collapse or fizzle out later. The best way to avoid such an outcome is to determine *before* you launch an initiative whether it is likely to yield a *collaboration premium.*

A collaboration premium is the difference between the projected financial return on a project and two often overlooked factors—opportunity cost and collaboration costs. In simple form:

Projected - Opportunity

cost - Collaboration costs

Collaboration premium

The projected return on a project is the cash flow it is expected to generate. The opportunity cost is the cash flow an organization passes up by devoting time, effort, and resources to the collaboration project instead of to something else—particularly something that doesn't require collaboration. Collaboration costs are those arising from the challenges involved in working across organizational boundaries—across business units, functional groups, sales offices, country subsidiaries, manufacturing sites. Cross-company collaboration typically means traveling more, coordinating work, and haggling over objectives and the sharing of information. The resulting tension that can develop between parties often creates significant costs: delays in getting to market, budget overruns, lower quality, limited cost savings, lost sales, damaged customer relationships.

Including collaboration costs makes this analysis different from the usual go/no-go decision making for proposed projects. Obviously, such costs can't be precisely quantified, especially before a project is under way. Still, with some work you can arrive at good approximations. Given how much time managers already spend estimating the return on a project—and, occasionally, the associated opportunity cost—it makes sense to take the additional step of estimating collaboration costs, particularly because they can doom a project.

If, after going through this exercise, you don't foresee a collaboration premium—or if a collaboration *penalty* is likely—the project shouldn't be approved. Indeed, this sort of analysis might have helped DNV steer clear of a promising but ultimately costly business venture.

Avoiding Collaboration That Destroys Value

In calculating the collaboration premium, it's important to avoid several common errors.

Don't overestimate the financial return

Whether because of enthusiasm for collaboration or the natural optimism of managers, many companies place a mistakenly high value on collaboration. Especially when a team's work appears to be a model of collaboration—the parties freely share resources and cooperate in resolving differences while coming up with nifty ideas—it may be easy to overlook the fact that the work is actually generating little value for the company. Never forget that the goal of collaboration is not collaboration but, rather, business results that would be impossible without it.

In numerous well-known instances, collaboration premiums failed to materialize. Daimler's $36 billion acquisition of Chrysler in 1998—with its promise of synergies between the two automakers—and the sale nine years later of 80% of Chrysler for a pitiful $1 billion constitute only the most conspicuous recent example. But collaboration's benefits are usually overvalued in much more mundane settings. Recall how the experienced sales teams at the IT consulting firm that Martine Haas and I studied shared expertise as a matter of course during the preparation of project proposals—never stopping to seriously consider whether they in fact benefited from doing so.

Don't ignore opportunity costs

Executives evaluating any proposed business project should take into account the opportunities they will forgo by devoting resources to that project. If the project requires collaboration, it's important to consider alternative noncollaborative activities with potentially higher returns. The opportunity cost is the estimated cash flow from the most attractive project *not* undertaken.

DNV didn't overestimate the potential financial return of its food initiative, but it did fail to assess the opportunity cost. "There was no consensus at the top level that food was interesting or a priority," said one senior manager. "We had not evaluated the food opportunity against other industry segments." In fact, food was only one of several sectors—including information technology, health care, and government—that DNV's consulting unit had targeted in 2001 as offering growth potential for its risk-management services. The opportunity in IT, which the consulting unit could have pursued on its own, undoubtedly had more potential. The unit made progress in 2004 generating new business in this sector, but it was constrained by a shortage of qualified consultants, some of whom were tied up with the food initiative. To pursue the food initiative, the consulting unit had to forgo additional business from the IT opportunity. I estimate the cost of this forgone opportunity at $25 million or more in lost cash flow.

Don't underestimate collaboration costs

In most companies it's difficult to get people in different units to work together effectively. Issues relating to turf, such as the sharing of resources and customers, often make groups resistant to collaboration. Individuals may resent taking on extra work if they don't get additional recognition or financial incentives. Even when collaboration delivers obvious and immediate benefits to those involved (for example, one unit's software package solves another's current problem), blending the work of two units that usually operate independently creates impediments.

These costs, which should be assessed before committing to a cross-unit project, can be tough to identify and quantify. And they will vary depending on the collaboration culture of an organization. But although they can be reduced over time through companywide efforts to foster collaboration, it's a mistake to underestimate them in the hope that collaboration can be mandated or will naturally improve during the course of a project.

As DNV decided whether to move forward with its food initiative, the project managers failed to consider the substantial collaboration costs the company would incur because it wasn't set up to collaborate. Mistrust between the consulting and certification units

Collaboration During a Recession

INTERNAL COLLABORATION, OFTEN INTENDED to spur new product development or increase revenue, may seem a low priority in a period of profit-focused cost cutting. That's a big mistake. Collaboration ought to be a crucial element of your recession strategy, because it will allow you to generate profits by exploiting existing assets—to do more with what you already have.

Wells Fargo headed into the 2002 recession with an enviable record of cross-selling 3.8 products, on average, per household customer. In 2002 the bank increased this number to an astonishing 4.2—that is, it sold nearly one additional financial product for every two customers in the middle of a recession, squeezing additional profits out of its existing customer base.

Three kinds of collaboration are especially valuable in a recession:

Cross-Selling

Follow the example of Wells Fargo and start programs to sell additional products to existing customers, who are more likely than those who don't know you to buy from you. This can increase your sales and lower the cost of selling, thus raising your profit per customer.

Best-Practice Transfer

Identify units in your company that are particularly efficient at certain activities—for example, the sales office with the lowest personnel costs—and get other units to follow their example. This can improve productivity and lower costs per employee.

Cross-Unit Product Innovation

Find ways of combining existing technologies, products, and brands to create new products, and brands to create new products and services. This is cheaper than developing them from scratch and more likely to succeed because you draw on tested intellectual property. It can increase the number of new products, speed them to market, and lower development costs.

---

escalated as they tried—unsuccessfully, and with much quarreling—to build a common customer database. "All the team members tried to protect their own customers," one manager in the certification group admitted. Because of the reluctance to share customer relationships, the team had to significantly reduce its estimates of the revenue to be generated by cross-selling.

Individual members of the cross-unit team were also pulled by conflicting goals and incentives. Only one team member was dedicated to the initiative full-time; most people had to meet individual targets within their respective units while also working on the joint project. Some people got a dressing down from their managers if their cross-unit work didn't maximize their own unit's revenue.

Even those who saw the benefits of the initiative found it hard to balance their two roles. "We all had personal agendas," said one senior manager in the certification group. "It was difficult to prioritize the food initiative and to pull people out of their daily work to do the cross-area work."

Although assigning a financial number to collaboration costs is difficult, I estimate that the cash flow sacrificed as a result of tension between the two groups, which scotched probably one in two cross-selling opportunities, was roughly $20 million.

Had the likely opportunity and collaboration costs of DNV's food-safety project been estimated, the project would have looked decidedly less attractive. In fact, managers would have seen that, rather than a collaboration premium, it was likely to yield a collaboration penalty of something like $5 million—that is, the projected return of $40 million less an opportunity cost of $25 million and collaboration costs of $20 million.

How Collaboration Can Go Right

That's not the end of DNV's story, however. Several months after the firm abandoned the food-safety initiative, Henrik Madsen was named CEO. He had seen firsthand the poor business results, wasted management effort, and ill will spawned by the initiative, having been head of the certification unit at the time. But he also believed that performance could be enhanced by collaboration at the traditionally decentralized DNV.

Madsen quickly reorganized the firm into four market-oriented business units and began looking for collaboration opportunities. His executive committee systematically evaluated all the possible pairings of units and identified a number of promising opportunities for cross-selling. The unit-by-unit analysis also revealed something else important: pairings that offered no real opportunities for collaboration—an insight that would prevent wasted efforts in the future.

The disciplined process prompted the committee to assess the potential financial return of each opportunity. Estimates totaled roughly 10% of the company's revenue at the time. The projected returns helped the committee prioritize options and assess the opportunity cost of choosing one over another. On the basis of these findings, along with an assessment of likely collaboration costs, the company launched a round of collaboration initiatives.

One of these involved the maritime unit, which provides detailed classification of vessels for companies in the shipping industry, and the IT unit, which specializes in risk-management services for IT systems in many industries. Because ships today operate using sophisticated computer systems, someone needs to help shipping companies manage the risk that those systems will malfunction at sea. There was a clear opportunity to sell IT's services to the maritime unit's customers—if effective collaboration could be achieved between the two units. That opportunity has already borne fruit: The IT unit won a contract to develop information systems for a huge cruise ship being built by a longtime customer of the maritime unit.

The IT unit has also collaborated with the company's energy business to jointly sell services to oil and drilling companies—another opportunity identified in the executive committee's review. That effort enhances the IT unit's service offering with the energy unit's oil and gas industry expertise, a package that most IT competitors can't match. The two units split the revenue, which creates incentives for both.

In pursuing opportunities like these, DNV has worked to reduce some of the typical costs of collaboration. Annie Combelles, the chief operating officer of the IT business, says there was an obvious market for her unit's services among customers of the maritime and energy units. "My concern was that those units understand what we could deliver," she says. "My concern was internal, not external." The IT group appointed a business development manager who had worked at DNV for 12 years, including a stint in the maritime unit, and had a broad personal network within the company. This made him a trusted and knowledgeable liaison to the maritime and other units, reducing potential conflict between them and the IT unit.

What's more, the IT unit has moved cautiously in trying to capitalize on opportunities for internal collaboration. Although the maritime group's longtime relationship with the cruise ship operator provided entrée for the information technology group, maritime didn't want any missteps from IT to jeopardize that valuable relationship. IT therefore initially proposed a risk-assessment project in nonvital areas of the ship such as the "hotel" function, which included the Wi-Fi network, gambling computers, and the 5,000 personal computers to be used by guests. It evaluated each of these systems and identified 30 risks. This success led to a project involving vital areas of the ship, such as the power-management and positioning systems.

DNV's renewed effort to encourage cross-unit collaboration is a work in progress that has nonetheless already produced some hard results: The portion of the IT unit's sales that came from cross-unit collaboration climbed from almost nothing to 5% in 2008, and is projected to be 10% in 2009 and 30% the following year.

Business leaders who trumpet the benefits of working together for the good of the organization are right in seeing collaboration's tremendous potential. But they should temper those exhortations with the kind of analysis I've described here, which provides needed discipline in deciding when collaboration creates—or destroys—value. Ideally, as organizations become better at collaboration, through incentives and shifts in corporate culture, the associated costs will fall and the percentage of projects likely to benefit will rise.

Although the collaboration imperative is a hallmark of today's business environment, the challenge is not to cultivate more collaboration. Rather, it's to cultivate the right collaboration, so that we can achieve the great things not possible when we work alone.

Originally published in April 2009. Reprint R0904G

Which Kind of Collaboration Is Right for You?

by Gary P. Pisano and Roberto Verganti

IN AN ERA WHEN great ideas can sprout from any corner of the world and IT has dramatically reduced the cost of accessing them, it's now conventional wisdom that virtually no company should innovate on its own. The good news is that potential partners and ways to collaborate with them have both expanded enormously in number. The bad news is that greater choice has made the perennial management challenge of selecting the best options much more difficult. Should you open up and share your intellectual property with the community? Should you nurture collaborative relationships with a few carefully selected partners? Should you harness the "wisdom of crowds"? The fervor around open models of collaboration such as crowdsourcing notwithstanding, there is no best approach to leveraging the power of outsiders. Different modes of collaboration involve different strategic trade-offs. Companies that choose the wrong mode risk falling behind in the relentless race to develop new technologies, designs, products, and services.

All too often firms jump into relationships without considering their structure and organizing principles—what we call the *collaborative architecture*. To help senior managers make better decisions about the kinds of collaboration their companies adopt, we have developed a relatively simple framework. The product of our 20 years of research and consulting in this area, it focuses on two basic questions: Given your strategy, how open or closed should your firm's network of collaborators be? And who should decide which problems the network will tackle and which solutions will be adopted?

Collaboration networks differ significantly in the degree to which membership is open to anyone who wants to join. In totally open collaboration, or crowdsourcing, everyone (suppliers, customers, designers, research institutions, inventors, students, hobbyists, and even competitors) can participate. A sponsor makes a problem public and then essentially seeks support from an unlimited number of problem solvers, who may contribute if *they* believe they have capabilities and assets to offer. Open-source software projects such as Linux, Apache, and Mozilla are examples of these networks. Closed networks, in contrast, are like private clubs. Here, you tackle the problem with one or more parties that *you* select because you deem them to have capabilities and assets crucial to the sought-after innovation.

Collaboration networks also differ fundamentally in their form of governance. In some the power to decide which problems are most important, how they'll be solved, what constitutes an acceptable solution, and which solutions should be implemented is completely vested in one firm in the network: the "kingpin." Such networks are hierarchical. Other networks are flat: The players are equal partners in the process and share the power to decide key issues.

Discussions of collaborative innovation in both academic journals and the popular media often wrongly link "openness" only with "flatness"—and even suggest that open, flat approaches are always superior. The notion is deeply flawed, however.

As the exhibit "The four ways to collaborate" shows, there are four basic modes of collaboration: a closed and hierarchical network (an *elite circle*), an open and hierarchical network (an *innovation mall*), an open and flat network (an *innovation community*), and a closed and flat network (a *consortium*).

Idea in Brief

As potential innovation partners and ways to collaborate with them proliferate, it's tough deciding how best to leverage outsiders' power.

To select the right type of collaboration options for your business, Pisano and Verganti recommend understanding the four basic collaboration modes. These modes differ along two dimensions: *openness* (can anyone participate, or just select players?) and *hierarchy* (who makes key decisions—one "kingpin" participant or all players?).

- In the *open, hierarchical* mode, anyone can offer ideas but your company defines the problem and chooses the solution.
- In the *open, flat* mode, anyone can solicit and offer ideas, and no single participant has the authority to decide what is or isn't a valid innovation.
- In the *closed, hierarchical* mode, your company selects certain participants and decides which ideas get developed.
- In the *closed, flat* mode, a select group is invited to offer ideas. But participants share information and intellectual property and make critical decisions together.

Each mode has trade-offs. For example, open networks (whether hierarchical or flat) produce many ideas, but screening them is costly. What to do? Choose modes best suited to your capabilities. For instance, if you can evaluate ideas cheaply but no single participant has all the necessary expertise to shape the innovation, use an open, flat collaboration.

When figuring out which mode is most appropriate for a given innovation initiative, a firm should consider the trade-offs of each, weighing the modes' advantages against the associated challenges and assessing the organizational capabilities, structure, and assets required to manage those challenges. (See the exhibit "How to choose the best mode of collaboration.") Its executives should then choose the mode that best suits the firm's strategy.

Open or Closed Network?

The costs of searching for, screening, and selecting contributors grow as the network becomes larger and can become prohibitive. So understanding when you need a small or a large number of problem

Idea in Practice

Understanding Your Collaboration Options

Dimension	Advantages	Challenges	When to use
Open	• You attract a wide range of possible ideas from domains beyond your experience.	• Screening all the ideas is time-consuming and expensive. • The best idea generators prefer closed networks, where their ideas are more likely implemented.	• You can evaluate proposed solutions cheaply. • You don't know what users want.
Closed	• You receive the best solution from a select knowledge domain.	• You have to know how to identify the right knowledge domain and pick the right parties.	• You need a small number of problem solvers. • You know the correct knowledge domain and parties to draw on.
Hierarchical	• Kingpins control the direction and value of the innovation.	• The right direction may be unclear.	• You have the capabilities and knowledge needed to define the problem and evaluate proposed solutions.
Flat	• Players share the costs, risks, and technical challenges of innovating.	• All parties must arrive at mutually beneficial solutions.	• No single player in the network has the necessary breadth of perspective or capabilities to solve the innovation problem.

Examples of Collaboration Options

Mode	Example
Open, hierarchical	Through InnoCentive.com, sponsor companies post scientific problems that are smaller pieces of their larger R&D program. Anyone can offer solution ideas. The "kingpins" understand the relevant technologies and user needs and can coordinate collaborators' work.
Open, flat	In open-source software community Linux, anyone can participate, define valid innovations, and use any code they deem useful.
Closed, hierarchical	Home-products design company Alessi draws on the talents of 200 independent designers. It decides who participates in its network, which concepts get developed, and which products are launched.
Closed, flat	IBM invited a few select partners to join its Microelectronics Joint Development Alliance for developing semiconductor technologies such as memory and chip-manufacturing processes. Each member has a voice in how technologies are developed.

Choosing Your Collaboration Approach

Select the collaboration mode that best suits your capabilities and strategy.

Example: In developing the iPhone and its applications, Apple initially used closed, hierarchical networks, where it could better control components influencing users' experiences. But once the iPhone was established, Apple defined a growth strategy hinging on adding software functionality and applications. Because it knew it couldn't anticipate all the applications iPhone users might value, it switched to an open, flat network: It introduced a kit allowing third-party developers to create applications based on the iPhone OS platform and to provide them to users directly through the device.

The four ways to collaborate

There are two basic issues that executives should consider when deciding how to collaborate on a given innovation project: Should membership in a network be open or closed? And, should the network's governance structure for selecting problems and solutions be flat or hierarchical? This framework reveals four basic modes of collaboration.

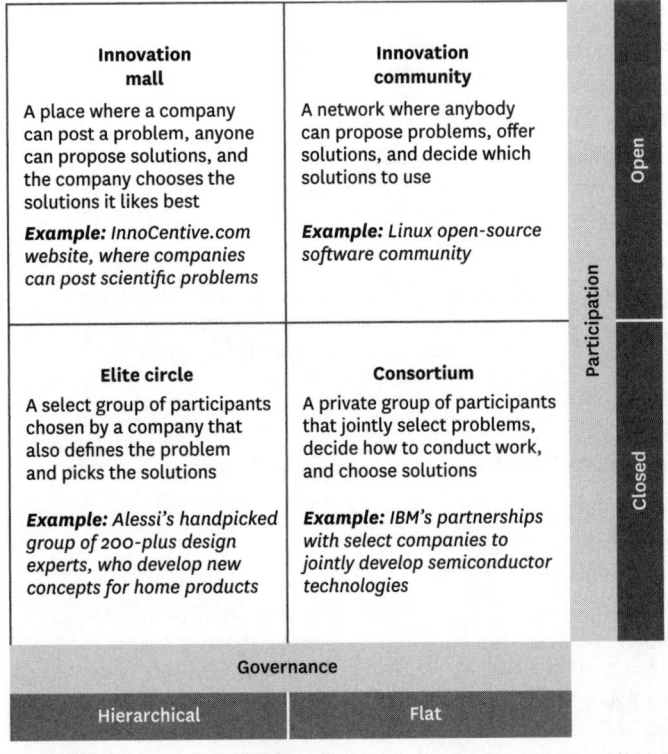

Participation	Governance: Hierarchical	Governance: Flat
Open	**Innovation mall** A place where a company can post a problem, anyone can propose solutions, and the company chooses the solutions it likes best ***Example:*** *InnoCentive.com website, where companies can post scientific problems*	**Innovation community** A network where anybody can propose problems, offer solutions, and decide which solutions to use ***Example:*** *Linux open-source software community*
Closed	**Elite circle** A select group of participants chosen by a company that also defines the problem and picks the solutions ***Example:*** *Alessi's handpicked group of 200-plus design experts, who develop new concepts for home products*	**Consortium** A private group of participants that jointly select problems, decide how to conduct work, and choose solutions ***Example:*** *IBM's partnerships with select companies to jointly develop semiconductor technologies*

solvers is crucial. Closed modes, obviously, tend to be much smaller than open ones.

When you use a closed mode, you are making two implicit bets: that you have identified the knowledge domain from which the best solution to your problem will come, and that you can pick the right collaborators in that field. Alessi, an Italian company famous for the postmodern design of its home products, bet that postmodern architecture would be a fruitful domain for generating interesting product ideas and that it could find the best people in that field to work with. It invited 200-plus collaborators from that domain to propose product designs. If you don't know where to look for solutions or who the key players are (and have no way to find out), a closed mode like Alessi's elite circle is a dangerous shot in the dark.

The big advantage of an open network is its potential to attract an extremely large number of problem solvers and, consequently, a vast number of ideas. You do *not* need to identify either the best knowledge domains or the most appropriate experts in those domains. It's like throwing an open house party: You just make it known you are having a party and provide the right inducements, and (you hope) the right people will show up.

With open participation, you don't need to know your contributors. Indeed, the fact that you *don't* know them can be particularly valuable; interesting innovative solutions can come from people or organizations you might never have imagined had something to contribute. That is the concept behind Threadless.com, a largely online retailer of T-shirts, whose designs come from the masses. By operating an innovation mall where 600,000 members submit proposals for about 800 new designs weekly, Threadless gets a steady flow of unusual and singular ideas. (Mall members and visitors to the website vote on the designs, but the Threadless staff makes the final decision on which ones to produce and rewards their creators.)

Open modes, however, have their disadvantages. Notably, they're not as effective as closed approaches in identifying and attracting the best players. That's because as the number of participants increases, the likelihood that a participant's solution will be selected (especially for an ambiguous problem) decreases. The best parties, therefore, prefer to participate in closed relationships. Open modes work best when the spread between the ideal solution and the average solution is not big and the consequences of missing out on a much better solution from an elite player are small.

How to choose the best mode of collaboration

When selecting a mode of collaborative innovation, executives need to consider the distinct strategic trade-offs of each mode. Below are some important advantages and challenges of the different approaches to collaboration, and examples of capabilities, assets, processes, and kinds of problems that make each easier to carry out.

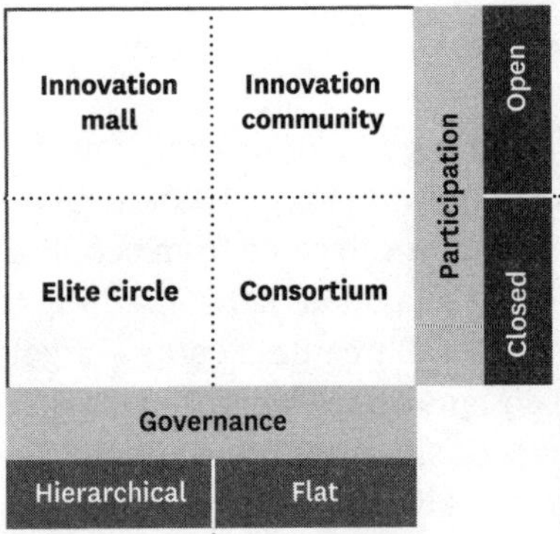

Open

Advantage: You receive a large number of solutions from domains that might be beyond your realm of experience or knowledge, and usually get a broader range of interesting ideas.

Challenge: Attracting several ideas from a variety of domains and screening them.

Enablers: The capability to test and screen solutions at low cost; information platforms that allow parties to contribute easily; small problems that can be solved with simple design tools, or large problems that can be broken into discrete parts that contributors can work on autonomously.

Closed

Advantage: You receive solutions from the best experts in a selected knowledge domain.

Challenge: Identifying the right knowledge domain and the right parties.

Enablers: The capability to find unspotted talent in relevant networks; the capability to develop privileged relationships with the best parties.

Hierarchical

Advantage: You control the direction of innovation and who captures the value from it.

Challenge: Choosing the right direction.

Enablers: The capability to understand user needs; the capability to design systems so that work can be divided among outsiders and then integrated.

Flat

Advantage: You share the burden of innovation.

Challenge: Getting contributors to converge on a solution that will be profitable to you.

Enablers: Processes and rules that drive parties to work in concert to achieve common goals.

Open modes are effective only under certain conditions. First, it must be possible to evaluate proposed solutions at a low cost. Sometimes the screening process is extremely cheap and fast. (For instance, it might be easy to assess whether a particular module of software code works or has bugs.) In other cases, though, the only way to find out whether an idea is worth pursuing is through expensive and time-consuming experiments, and you'll want to consider fewer (but better) ideas. The only way to do that is to invite contributions from the problem solvers that you think will have the best chance of providing good ideas. That is, to opt for a closed mode.

Consider the following simple but scary example. You have a serious illness, and you want to find the best possible treatment. Employing an open mode, you post your problem on the internet, ask for advice, and get 50 ideas that look interesting. But immediately, you face two issues. The first is what statisticians refer to as a sample selection problem: Are these the best 50 ideas out there? Maybe the most knowledgeable doctors are so busy treating patients that they don't participate in these forums, and only the doctors who have time on their hands (a bad sign for sure!) responded. The second issue is that you have to invest a lot of time and resources to evaluate the 50 ideas (visiting doctors and so on). Even worse, you may have only one shot at getting the right treatment. (Are you really going to "try out" more than one surgery?) That is why when confronted with a medical problem, we might do some research to identify elite specialists, pick one, and then seek a second opinion from one or two others.

Alessi is in a similar boat. Given the large population of designers, it could easily launch an open design competition for, say, a corkscrew on its website. With its high standing in the world of design, the firm would probably attract many proposals. However, it is not posing technical problems that have one or a few optimal solutions that can be clearly defined, thereby allowing contributors to screen many of their ideas themselves. Alessi is looking for concepts whose value is based on intangible properties such as aesthetics and emotional and symbolic content. Since there is no clear right or wrong answer, Alessi could receive thousands of proposals, creating a massive evaluation burden for the company. And because the company's strategy is to offer products with radical designs that anticipate market needs, its offerings often initially confuse consumers. Therefore it can't shift the evaluation burden to customers by asking them which designs they prefer, as Threadless does. That's why Alessi has to ensure that it will receive a few good ideas from a relative handful of contributors.

Another requirement of open modes is that participating in them must be easy. This is possible when a problem can be partitioned into small, well-defined chunks that players can work on autonomously at a fairly low cost. Someone creating a potential decoration for a Threadless T-shirt doesn't need sophisticated design infrastructure or knowledge of how the company will knit yarns or tailor shirts. The inherently modular structure of the Linux open-source community allows software developers to create code for new features without touching other parts of the application, which has more than four million lines of code. Over the past decade, such open collaboration has been made easier by information platforms that allow participants to make contributions, share work, and observe the solutions of others.

Of course, not all problems can be partitioned into small, discrete chunks. For example, the development of radically new product concepts or product architectures is an integral task that has to be embraced in its entirety. In such cases, closed modes that provide an environment where collaborators can closely interact must be employed. This is what led IBM to invite a handful of selected partners (including Siemens, Samsung, Freescale, Infineon, and STMicroelectronics) to join its Microelectronics Joint Development Alliance consortia for developing semiconductor technologies such as memory, silicon-on-insulator components, and chip-manufacturing processes.

Flat or Hierarchical Governance?

As discussed earlier, the chief distinction between a hierarchical and a flat form of governance is who gets to define the problem and choose the solution. In the hierarchical form, a specific organization has this authority, which provides it with the advantage of being able to control the direction of the innovation efforts and capture more of the innovation's value. In the flat form, these decisions are either decentralized or made jointly by some or all collaborators; the advantage here is the ability to share with others the costs, risks, and technical challenges of innovating.

Hierarchical governance is desirable when your organization has the capabilities and knowledge needed to define the problem and evaluate proposed solutions. Consider companies that post scientific problems on the innovation mall InnoCentive.com. The problems are generally smaller pieces of the sponsors' much larger R&D programs. These kingpins have a clear understanding of the relevant technologies and markets (user needs and functional requirements) and can define the system configuration and coordinate the work of various collaborators.

Conversely, flat modes work well when no single organization has the necessary breadth of perspective or capabilities. Look again at open-source software projects. These often develop very specific modules of code to address problems that users have encountered (a bug in an existing piece of code or the need for a specific hardware driver). In this case, the users are best positioned to devise and test solutions because they're closest to the problem. Indeed, they usually have discovered the problem in the first place. Or take IBM's microelectronics consortia. Since semiconductor companies other than IBM possessed critical knowledge, skills, and assets needed for microprocessor design, a hierarchical structure would have made no sense.

Flat modes are also appropriate when collaborators all have a vested interest in how a particular problem is solved and will participate only if they get some say in the decisions. For example, all the members of the IBM consortia formed over the years have expected to use in their own factories and product lines the technologies they develop collaboratively. For this reason, IBM and its partners chose a governance structure that provided each a strong voice in how the technology is developed.

Designing incentives—both financial and nonfinancial—that attract external collaborators is crucial with any of the four modes of collaboration. Nonfinancial rewards like high visibility in the job market, an enhanced reputation among a peer group, the psychological fulfillment of pursuing a strong interest, and the chance to use solutions in one's own business can replace or complement monetary rewards. There are no hard rules about which incentives work best with particular forms of collaboration. Although people often associate psychological fulfillment with innovation communities, it can be a powerful incentive in the other modes as well. For example, Alessi not only shares royalties from sales with the designers in its elite circle but also includes their names in product marketing and offers them a high degree of freedom in the design process.

A Matter of Strategy

Choosing a collaboration mode involves more than understanding the trade-offs. A firm must take into account its strategy for building and capturing value. And as the strategy evolves, the right mode of collaboration might change, too.

Consider the approach that Apple used in developing software for the iPhone and how it changed over time. A key part of Apple's business strategy (across all its products) has been to maintain the integrity of its systems. Indeed, one of the joys (and thus differentiators) of an Apple product is that everything—the machine's hardware, software, and peripherals—seems to work together so seamlessly. Historically, this kept Apple more oriented toward closed modes, where it could better control the components that influenced the user's experience. The company took that approach in developing the first generations of the iPhone as well and relied on elite circles to develop early applications for it.

However, once the iPhone was established, Apple faced the challenge of adding software functionality and applications that would fuel more growth. Our framework helps map out the various options Apple had. It could define the applications it thought would be useful (for example, a way to synchronize the iPhone with various mobile banking systems) and then engage the best software designers to develop them (the elite circle mode again). It could partition the development of particular applications into simple chunks and then go to a bazaar like TopCoder.com and tap hordes of software developers to write code for each chunk (the innovation mall mode). It could release a development package to third-party developers and let them define and create applications that would be useful (the innovation community mode). Or Apple could work jointly with a firm like Intuit to create mobile banking software (the consortium mode). Each of these modes could certainly generate new applications, but each would have a very different impact on the iPhone platform.

To stick with the elite circle mode, Apple needed to feel confident that it knew which applications customers would want and could identify the best partners for creating them. Given the huge variety of potential applications, Apple realized that there was no way that, either alone or with a small group of collaborators, it could anticipate all the applications that an iPhone owner might find useful or just fun. So it opted to encourage a thousand flowers to bloom and allow the market to decide which ones should be picked. This reasoning ruled out the elite circle, the consortium, and the innovation mall. Accordingly, Apple introduced a kit in March 2008 that allows a community of third-party developers to create applications based on the iPhone OS platform and provide them to users directly through the iPhone. (If an application is not free, the developers keep 70% of its revenues and Apple gets 30%.)

The rollout of mobile phones using Android, Google's operating system, could prompt Apple to adopt a two-part collaboration strategy. Since Android is open-source software, it may attract an even larger community of developers than the iPhone. So Apple might decide to supplement the applications developed by third parties with proprietary hardware features conceived by its own staff and created with the help of elite circles of hardware manufacturers. That illustrates another important point: Companies can use a combination of collaboration modes simultaneously to support their strategies.

IBM's successful use of *both* an innovation community and consortia to support the strategy of its server and mainframe computer businesses is an excellent real example. IBM's strategy is to compete on the basis of hardware differentiation and service. Toward that end, the company has striven to commoditize operating systems by embracing Linux and participating actively in the open-source community—one of the first major computer makers to do so. But to continue to differentiate its hardware, IBM needs to stay on the leading edge of microprocessor technology. Given the increasing scale required to keep up with the likes of Intel, IBM turned to its consortia of semiconductor companies, which have shared development costs. This combination of innovation approaches has allowed IBM to gain market share in an intensely competitive and dynamic market.

As IBM illustrates, a key component of strategy is exploiting a firm's unique assets and capabilities. In choosing one or more collaborative modes, a firm's senior managers therefore must ask: Which of our unique assets and capabilities are we trying to enhance the value of? And what's the best way to enhance it?

A firm's collaboration capability itself can be exploited for profit. InnoCentive.com, for example, is a spin-off of an innovation mall developed by Eli Lilly for internal purposes. Alessi is now leveraging the value of its connections with more than 200 designers by assisting companies in other businesses with product design. Alessi helps them identify the designers (usually from its own network) who can best address their specific needs. In return, Alessi receives royalties from sales of the resulting products—which now account for almost 30% of its revenues.

A New Source of Advantage

As with any strategic variable, collaborative approaches to innovation offer an array of choices and complex trade-offs. As the examples in this article suggest, each approach can be highly effective under the right conditions. Senior managers need to be wary of the notion that one type of collaboration is superior to others. Open is not always better than closed, and flat is not always better than hierarchical.

Developing an effective approach to collaboration starts with a solid understanding of your company's strategy. What is the business problem you want innovation to solve? Are you (like Alessi) trying to create a distinctive product that breaks boundaries? Are you (like IBM) trying to keep up with larger rivals (like Intel and Taiwan Semiconductor) in an intense technology race? Or are you (like Apple today) looking to broadly expand the applications of your product?

Companies must also ask what unique capabilities they bring to the collaborative process. Firms with deep relationships in a space, for example, are much better positioned to exploit an elite circle mode than a newcomer is.

It's not surprising, then, that differences in strategy and capabilities can lead to different kinds of collaboration networks competing against one another in the same industry. Thus, the task of senior leadership in innovation has broadened and become truly strategic. It is no longer just a matter of hiring the most talented and creative people or establishing the right internal environment for innovation. The new leaders in innovation will be those who can understand how to design collaboration networks and how to tap their potential.

Originally published in December 2008. Reprint R0812F

About the Contributors

HERMINIA IBARRA is a professor of organizational behavior and the Cora Chaired Professor of Leadership and Learning at Insead.

MORTEN T. HANSEN is a management professor at the University of California, Berkeley, School of Information, and at Insead.

DANIEL GOLEMAN is a cochairman of the Consortium for Research on Emotional Intelligence in Organizations at Rutgers University.

RICHARD BOYATZIS is the H. R. Horvitz Professor of Family Business and a professor in the departments of organizational behavior, psychology, and cognitive science at Case Western Reserve University.

JOHN ABELE cofounded Boston Scientific in 1979. Having retired from its board in May 2011, he now serves as director emeritus.

PAUL ADLER is a professor of management and organization at the Marshall School of Business of the University of Southern California, where he holds the Harold Quinton Chair in Business Policy.

CHARLES HECKSCHER is a professor at Rutgers University's School of Management and Labor Relations and director of the Center for Organizational Learning and Transformation.

LAURENCE PRUSAK is an independent consultant who teaches in the Information and Knowledge Strategy program at Columbia University.

RANJAY GULATI is the Jaime and Josefina Chua Tiampo Professor of Business Administration at Harvard Business School.

RICHARD MCDERMOTT is the president of McDermott Consulting and a visiting fellow at Henley Business School.

DOUGLAS ARCHIBALD is the director of Whole Education.

JEFF WEISS is an adjunct professor at the U.S. Military Academy at West Point and a partner at Vantage Partners, a Boston-based consultancy specializing in corporate negotiations and relationship management.

JONATHAN HUGHES is a partner at Vantage Partners.

ANDREW P. MCAFEE is a principal research scientist at the MIT Center for Digital Business.

GARY P. PISANO is the Harry E. Figgie, Jr., Professor of Business Administration at Harvard Business School.

ROBERTO VERGANTI is a professor of innovation management at the Politecnico di Milano, Italy.

Index

Harvard Business Review
136 Marvel's Blockbuster Machine
94 Digital Doesn't Have to Be Disruptive
116 When a Colleague Is Grieving
HBR.ORG
The AI-Powered Organization
The main challenge isn't technology. It's culture.
62

VISUAL LIBRARY
The Good-Better-Best Approach to Pricing
Harvard Business Review
Are METRICS Undermining Your Business?
Too many leaders confuse numbers with strategy.
62

HBR'S 10 MUST READS

On Emotional Intelligence

HBR's 10 Must Reads series is the definitive collection of ideas and best practices for aspiring and experienced leaders alike. These books offer essential reading selected from the pages of *Harvard Business Review* on topics critical to the success of every manager.

Titles include:

HBR's 10 Must Reads 2015
HBR's 10 Must Reads on Change Management
HBR's 10 Must Reads on Collaboration
HBR's 10 Must Reads on Communication
HBR's 10 Must Reads on Emotional Intelligence
HBR's 10 Must Reads on Innovation
HBR's 10 Must Reads on Leadership
HBR's 10 Must Reads on Making Smart Decisions
HBR's 10 Must Reads on Managing People
HBR's 10 Must Reads on Managing Yourself
HBR's 10 Must Reads on Strategic Marketing
HBR's 10 Must Reads on Strategy
HBR's 10 Must Reads on Teams
HBR's 10 Must Reads: The Essentials

HBR'S 10 MUST READS

On Emotional Intelligence

HARVARD BUSINESS REVIEW PRESS
Boston, Massachusetts

Printed in the United States of America
20 19

Library of Congress Cataloging-in-Publication Data

HBR's 10 must reads on emotional intelligence.
pages cm. — (HBR's 10 must reads series)
Includes index.
ISBN 978-1-63369-019-6 (alk. paper) — ISBN 978-1-63369-020-2 (ebook)
1. Emotional intelligence. 2. Work—Psychological aspects. I. Harvard Business Review Press. II. Harvard business review.
BF576.H394 2015
152.4—dc23
2014046481

The paper used in this publication meets the requirements of the American National Standard for Permanence of Paper for Publications and Documents in Libraries and Archives Z39.48-1992.

Contents

HBR'S 10 MUST READS

On Emotional Intelligence

What Makes a Leader?

by Daniel Goleman

EVERY BUSINESSPERSON KNOWS a story about a highly intelligent, highly skilled executive who was promoted into a leadership position only to fail at the job. And they also know a story about someone with solid—but not extraordinary—intellectual abilities and technical skills who was promoted into a similar position and then soared.

Such anecdotes support the widespread belief that identifying individuals with the "right stuff" to be leaders is more art than science. After all, the personal styles of superb leaders vary: Some leaders are subdued and analytical; others shout their manifestos from the mountaintops. And just as important, different situations call for different types of leadership. Most mergers need a sensitive negotiator at the helm, whereas many turnarounds require a more forceful authority.

I have found, however, that the most effective leaders are alike in one crucial way: They all have a high degree of what has come to be known as *emotional intelligence*. It's not that IQ and technical skills are irrelevant. They do matter, but mainly as "threshold capabilities"; that is, they are the entry-level requirements for executive positions. But my research, along with other recent studies, clearly shows that emotional intelligence is the sine qua non of leadership. Without it, a person can have the best training in the world, an incisive, analytical mind, and an endless supply of smart ideas, but he still won't make a great leader.

In the course of the past year, my colleagues and I have focused on how emotional intelligence operates at work. We have examined the relationship between emotional intelligence and effective performance, especially in leaders. And we have observed how emotional intelligence shows itself on the job. How can you tell if someone has high emotional intelligence, for example, and how can you recognize it in yourself? In the following pages, we'll explore these questions, taking each of the components of emotional intelligence—self-awareness, self-regulation, motivation, empathy, and social skill—in turn.

Evaluating Emotional Intelligence

Most large companies today have employed trained psychologists to develop what are known as "competency models" to aid them in identifying, training, and promoting likely stars in the leadership firmament. The psychologists have also developed such models for lower-level positions. And in recent years, I have analyzed competency models from 188 companies, most of which were large and global and included the likes of Lucent Technologies, British Airways, and Credit Suisse.

In carrying out this work, my objective was to determine which personal capabilities drove outstanding performance within these organizations, and to what degree they did so. I grouped capabilities into three categories: purely technical skills like accounting and business planning; cognitive abilities like analytical reasoning; and competencies demonstrating emotional intelligence, such as the ability to work with others and effectiveness in leading change.

To create some of the competency models, psychologists asked senior managers at the companies to identify the capabilities that typified the organization's most outstanding leaders. To create other models, the psychologists used objective criteria, such as a division's profitability, to differentiate the star performers at senior levels within their organizations from the average ones. Those individuals were then extensively interviewed and tested, and their capabilities were compared. This process resulted in the creation

Idea in Brief

What distinguishes great leaders from merely good ones? It isn't IQ or technical skills, says Daniel Goleman. It's **emotional intelligence:** a group of five skills that enable the best leaders to maximize their own *and* their followers' performance. When senior managers at one company had a critical mass of EI capabilities, their divisions outperformed yearly earnings goals by 20%.

The EI skills are:

- *Self-awareness*—knowing one's strengths, weaknesses, drives, values, and impact on others
- *Self-regulation*—controlling or redirecting disruptive impulses and moods
- *Motivation*—relishing achievement for its own sake
- *Empathy*—understanding other people's emotional makeup
- *Social skill*—building rapport with others to move them in desired directions

We're each born with certain levels of EI skills. But we can strengthen these abilities through persistence, practice, and feedback from colleagues or coaches.

of lists of ingredients for highly effective leaders. The lists ranged in length from seven to 15 items and included such ingredients as initiative and strategic vision.

When I analyzed all this data, I found dramatic results. To be sure, intellect was a driver of outstanding performance. Cognitive skills such as big-picture thinking and long-term vision were particularly important. But when I calculated the ratio of technical skills, IQ, and emotional intelligence as ingredients of excellent performance, emotional intelligence proved to be twice as important as the others for jobs at all levels.

Moreover, my analysis showed that emotional intelligence played an increasingly important role at the highest levels of the company, where differences in technical skills are of negligible importance. In other words, the higher the rank of a person considered to be a star performer, the more emotional intelligence capabilities showed up as the reason for his or her effectiveness. When I compared star performers with average ones in senior leadership positions, nearly 90% of the difference in their profiles was attributable to emotional intelligence factors rather than cognitive abilities.

Idea in Practice

Understanding EI's Components

EI Component	Definition	Hallmarks	Example
Self-awareness	Knowing one's emotions, strengths, weaknesses, drives, values, and goals—and their impact on others	• Self-confidence • Realistic self-assessment • Self-deprecating sense of humor • Thirst for constructive criticism	A manager knows tight deadlines bring out the worst in him. So he plans his time to get work done well in advance.
Self-regulation	Controlling or redirecting disruptive emotions and impulses	• Trustworthiness • Integrity • Comfort with ambiguity and change	When a team botches a presentation, its leader resists the urge to scream. Instead, she considers possible reasons for the failure, explains the consequences to her team, and explores solutions with them.
Motivation	Being driven to achieve for the sake of achievement	• A passion for the work itself and for new challenges • Unflagging energy to improve • Optimism in the face of failure	A portfolio manager at an investment company sees his fund tumble for three consecutive quarters. Major clients defect. Instead of blaming external circumstances, she decides to learn from the experience—and engineers a turnaround.

EI Component	Definition	Hallmarks	Example
Empathy	Considering others' feelings, especially when making decisions	• Expertise in attracting and retaining talent • Ability to develop others • Sensitivity to cross-cultural differences	An American consultant and her team pitch a project to a potential client in Japan. Her team interprets the client's silence as disapproval, and prepares to leave. The consultant reads the client's body language and senses interest. She continues the meeting, and her team gets the job.
Social Skill	Managing relationships to move people in desired directions	• Effectiveness in leading change • Persuasiveness • Extensive networking • Expertise in building and leading teams	A manager wants his company to adopt a better Internet strategy. He finds kindred spirits and assembles a de facto team to create a prototype Web site. He persuades allies in other divisions to fund the company's participation in a relevant convention. His company forms an Internet division—and puts him in charge of it.

Strengthening Your EI

Use practice and feedback from others to strengthen specific EI skills.

> ***Example:*** An executive learned from others that she lacked empathy, especially the ability to listen. She wanted to fix the problem, so she asked a coach to tell her when she exhibited poor listening skills. She then role-played incidents to practice giving better responses; for example, not interrupting. She also began observing executives skilled at listening—and imitated their behavior.

The five components of emotional intelligence at work

	Definition	Hallmarks
Self-awareness	The ability to recognize and understand your moods, emotions, and drives, as well as their effect on others	Self-confidence Realistic self-assessment Self-deprecating sense of humor
Self-regulation	The ability to control or redirect disruptive impulses and moods The propensity to suspend judgment—to think before acting	Trustworthiness and integrity Comfort with ambiguity Openness to change
Motivation	A passion to work for reasons that go beyond money or status A propensity to pursue goals with energy and persistence	Strong drive to achieve Optimism, even in the face of failure Organizational commitment
Empathy	The ability to understand the emotional makeup of other people Skill in treating people according to their emotional reactions	Expertise in building and retaining talent Cross-cultural sensitivity Service to clients and customers
Social skill	Proficiency in managing relationships and building networks An ability to find common ground and build rapport	Effectiveness in leading change Persuasiveness Expertise in building and leading teams

Other researchers have confirmed that emotional intelligence not only distinguishes outstanding leaders but can also be linked to strong performance. The findings of the late David McClelland, the renowned researcher in human and organizational behavior, are a good example. In a 1996 study of a global food and beverage company, McClelland found that when senior managers had a critical mass of emotional intelligence capabilities, their divisions outperformed yearly earnings goals by 20%. Meanwhile, division leaders without that critical mass underperformed by almost the same amount. McClelland's findings, interestingly, held as true in the company's U.S. divisions as in its divisions in Asia and Europe.

In short, the numbers are beginning to tell us a persuasive story about the link between a company's success and the emotional intelligence of its leaders. And just as important, research is also demonstrating that people can, if they take the right approach, develop their emotional intelligence. (See the sidebar "Can Emotional Intelligence Be Learned?")

Self-Awareness

Self-awareness is the first component of emotional intelligence—which makes sense when one considers that the Delphic oracle gave the advice to "know thyself" thousands of years ago. Self-awareness means having a deep understanding of one's emotions, strengths, weaknesses, needs, and drives. People with strong self-awareness are neither overly critical nor unrealistically hopeful. Rather, they are honest—with themselves and with others.

People who have a high degree of self-awareness recognize how their feelings affect them, other people, and their job performance. Thus, a self-aware person who knows that tight deadlines bring out the worst in him plans his time carefully and gets his work done well in advance. Another person with high self-awareness will be able to work with a demanding client. She will understand the client's impact on her moods and the deeper reasons for her frustration. "Their trivial demands take us away from the real work that needs

Can Emotional Intelligence Be Learned?

FOR AGES, PEOPLE HAVE DEBATED if leaders are born or made. So too goes the debate about emotional intelligence. Are people born with certain levels of empathy, for example, or do they acquire empathy as a result of life's experiences? The answer is both. Scientific inquiry strongly suggests that there is a genetic component to emotional intelligence. Psychological and developmental research indicates that nurture plays a role as well. How much of each perhaps will never be known, but research and practice clearly demonstrate that emotional intelligence can be learned.

One thing is certain: Emotional intelligence increases with age. There is an old-fashioned word for the phenomenon: maturity. Yet even with maturity, some people still need training to enhance their emotional intelligence. Unfortunately, far too many training programs that intend to build leadership skills—including emotional intelligence—are a waste of time and money. The problem is simple: They focus on the wrong part of the brain.

Emotional intelligence is born largely in the neurotransmitters of the brain's limbic system, which governs feelings, impulses, and drives. Research indicates that the limbic system learns best through motivation, extended practice, and feedback. Compare this with the kind of learning that goes on in the neocortex, which governs analytical and technical ability. The neocortex grasps concepts and logic. It is the part of the brain that figures out how to use a computer or make a sales call by reading a book. Not surprisingly—but mistakenly—it is also the part of the brain targeted by most training programs aimed at enhancing emotional intelligence. When such programs take, in effect, a neocortical approach, my research with the Consortium for Research on Emotional Intelligence in Organizations has shown they can even have a *negative* impact on people's job performance.

To enhance emotional intelligence, organizations must refocus their training to include the limbic system. They must help people break old behavioral habits and establish new ones. That not only takes much more time than conventional training programs, it also requires an individualized approach.

Imagine an executive who is thought to be low on empathy by her colleagues. Part of that deficit shows itself as an inability to listen; she interrupts people and doesn't pay close attention to what they're saying. To fix the problem, the executive needs to be motivated to change, and then she needs practice and feedback from others in the company. A colleague or coach could be tapped to let the executive know when she has been observed failing to listen. She would then have to replay the incident and give a better response; that is, demonstrate her ability to absorb what others are saying. And the executive could be directed to observe certain executives who listen well and to mimic their behavior.

With persistence and practice, such a process can lead to lasting results. I know one Wall Street executive who sought to improve his empathy—specifically his ability to read people's reactions and see their perspectives. Before beginning his quest, the executive's subordinates were terrified of working with him. People even went so far as to hide bad news from him. Naturally, he was shocked when finally confronted with these facts. He went home and told his family—but they only confirmed what he had heard at work. When their opinions on any given subject did not mesh with his, they, too, were frightened of him.

Enlisting the help of a coach, the executive went to work to heighten his empathy through practice and feedback. His first step was to take a vacation to a foreign country where he did not speak the language. While there, he monitored his reactions to the unfamiliar and his openness to people who were different from him. When he returned home, humbled by his week abroad, the executive asked his coach to shadow him for parts of the day, several times a week, to critique how he treated people with new or different perspectives. At the same time, he consciously used on-the-job interactions as opportunities to practice "hearing" ideas that differed from his. Finally, the executive had himself videotaped in meetings and asked those who worked for and with him to critique his ability to acknowledge and understand the feelings of others. It took several months, but the executive's emotional intelligence did ultimately rise, and the improvement was reflected in his overall performance on the job.

It's important to emphasize that building one's emotional intelligence cannot—will not—happen without sincere desire and concerted effort. A brief seminar won't help; nor can one buy a how-to manual. It is much harder to learn to empathize—to internalize empathy as a natural response to people—than it is to become adept at regression analysis. But it can be done. "Nothing great was ever achieved without enthusiasm," wrote Ralph Waldo Emerson. If your goal is to become a real leader, these words can serve as a guidepost in your efforts to develop high emotional intelligence.

to be done," she might explain. And she will go one step further and turn her anger into something constructive.

Self-awareness extends to a person's understanding of his or her values and goals. Someone who is highly self-aware knows where he is headed and why; so, for example, he will be able to be firm in turning down a job offer that is tempting financially but does not fit with his principles or long-term goals. A person who lacks self-awareness is apt to make decisions that bring on inner turmoil by treading on buried values. "The money looked good so I signed on," someone might say two years into a job, "but the work means so little to me that I'm constantly bored." The decisions of self-aware people mesh with their values; consequently, they often find work to be energizing.

How can one recognize self-awareness? First and foremost, it shows itself as candor and an ability to assess oneself realistically. People with high self-awareness are able to speak accurately and openly—although not necessarily effusively or confessionally—about their emotions and the impact they have on their work. For instance, one manager I know of was skeptical about a new personal-shopper service that her company, a major department-store chain, was about to introduce. Without prompting from her team or her boss, she offered them an explanation: "It's hard for me to get behind the rollout of this service," she admitted, "because I really wanted to run the project, but I wasn't selected. Bear with me while I deal with that." The manager did indeed examine her feelings; a week later, she was supporting the project fully.

Such self-knowledge often shows itself in the hiring process. Ask a candidate to describe a time he got carried away by his feelings and did something he later regretted. Self-aware candidates will be frank in admitting to failure—and will often tell their tales with a smile. One of the hallmarks of self-awareness is a self-deprecating sense of humor.

Self-awareness can also be identified during performance reviews. Self-aware people know—and are comfortable talking about—their limitations and strengths, and they often demonstrate a thirst for constructive criticism. By contrast, people with low self-awareness interpret the message that they need to improve as a threat or a sign of failure.

Self-aware people can also be recognized by their self-confidence. They have a firm grasp of their capabilities and are less likely to set themselves up to fail by, for example, overstretching on assignments. They know, too, when to ask for help. And the risks they take on the job are calculated. They won't ask for a challenge that they know they can't handle alone. They'll play to their strengths.

Consider the actions of a midlevel employee who was invited to sit in on a strategy meeting with her company's top executives. Although she was the most junior person in the room, she did not sit there quietly, listening in awestruck or fearful silence. She knew she had a head for clear logic and the skill to present ideas persuasively, and she offered cogent suggestions about the company's strategy. At the same time, her self-awareness stopped her from wandering into territory where she knew she was weak.

Despite the value of having self-aware people in the workplace, my research indicates that senior executives don't often give self-awareness the credit it deserves when they look for potential leaders. Many executives mistake candor about feelings for "wimpiness" and fail to give due respect to employees who openly acknowledge their shortcomings. Such people are too readily dismissed as "not tough enough" to lead others.

In fact, the opposite is true. In the first place, people generally admire and respect candor. Furthermore, leaders are constantly required to make judgment calls that require a candid assessment of capabilities—their own and those of others. Do we have the management expertise to acquire a competitor? Can we launch a new product within six months? People who assess themselves honestly—that is, self-aware people—are well suited to do the same for the organizations they run.

Self-Regulation

Biological impulses drive our emotions. We cannot do away with them—but we can do much to manage them. Self-regulation, which is like an ongoing inner conversation, is the component of emotional intelligence that frees us from being prisoners of our feelings. People engaged in such a conversation feel bad moods and emotional impulses just as everyone else does, but they find ways to control them and even to channel them in useful ways.

Imagine an executive who has just watched a team of his employees present a botched analysis to the company's board of directors. In the gloom that follows, the executive might find himself tempted to pound on the table in anger or kick over a chair. He could leap up and scream at the group. Or he might maintain a grim silence, glaring at everyone before stalking off.

But if he had a gift for self-regulation, he would choose a different approach. He would pick his words carefully, acknowledging the team's poor performance without rushing to any hasty judgment. He would then step back to consider the reasons for the failure. Are they personal—a lack of effort? Are there any mitigating factors? What was his role in the debacle? After considering these questions, he would call the team together, lay out the incident's consequences, and offer his feelings about it. He would then present his analysis of the problem and a well-considered solution.

Why does self-regulation matter so much for leaders? First of all, people who are in control of their feelings and impulses—that is, people who are reasonable—are able to create an environment of trust and fairness. In such an environment, politics and infighting are sharply reduced and productivity is high. Talented people flock to the organization and aren't tempted to leave. And self-regulation has a trickle-down effect. No one wants to be known as a hothead when the boss is known for her calm approach. Fewer bad moods at the top mean fewer throughout the organization.

Second, self-regulation is important for competitive reasons. Everyone knows that business today is rife with ambiguity and change. Companies merge and break apart regularly. Technology transforms work at a dizzying pace. People who have mastered their emotions are able to roll with the changes. When a new program is announced, they don't panic; instead, they are able to suspend judgment, seek out information, and listen to the executives as they explain the new program. As the initiative moves forward, these people are able to move with it.

Sometimes they even lead the way. Consider the case of a manager at a large manufacturing company. Like her colleagues, she had used a certain software program for five years. The program drove how she collected and reported data and how she thought about the company's strategy. One day, senior executives announced that a new program was to be installed that would radically change how information was gathered and assessed within the organization. While many people in the company complained bitterly about how disruptive the change would be, the manager mulled over the reasons for the new program and was convinced of its potential to improve performance. She eagerly attended training sessions—some of her colleagues refused to do so—and was eventually promoted to run several divisions, in part because she used the new technology so effectively.

I want to push the importance of self-regulation to leadership even further and make the case that it enhances integrity, which is not only a personal virtue but also an organizational strength. Many of the bad things that happen in companies are a function of impulsive behavior. People rarely plan to exaggerate profits, pad expense accounts, dip into the till, or abuse power for selfish ends. Instead, an opportunity presents itself, and people with low impulse control just say yes.

By contrast, consider the behavior of the senior executive at a large food company. The executive was scrupulously honest in his negotiations with local distributors. He would routinely lay out his cost structure in detail, thereby giving the distributors a realistic understanding of the company's pricing. This approach meant the executive couldn't always drive a hard bargain. Now, on occasion, he felt the urge to increase profits by withholding information about the company's costs. But he challenged that impulse—he saw that it made more sense in the long run to counteract it. His emotional self-regulation paid off in strong, lasting relationships with distributors that benefited the company more than any short-term financial gains would have.

The signs of emotional self-regulation, therefore, are easy to see: a propensity for reflection and thoughtfulness; comfort with ambiguity and change; and integrity—an ability to say no to impulsive urges.

Like self-awareness, self-regulation often does not get its due. People who can master their emotions are sometimes seen as cold fish—their considered responses are taken as a lack of passion. People with fiery temperaments are frequently thought of as "classic" leaders—their outbursts are considered hallmarks of charisma and power. But when such people make it to the top, their impulsiveness often works against them. In my research, extreme displays of negative emotion have never emerged as a driver of good leadership.

Motivation

If there is one trait that virtually all effective leaders have, it is motivation. They are driven to achieve beyond expectations—their own and everyone else's. The key word here is *achieve*. Plenty of people are motivated by external factors, such as a big salary or the status that comes from having an impressive title or being part of a prestigious company. By contrast, those with leadership potential are motivated by a deeply embedded desire to achieve for the sake of achievement.

If you are looking for leaders, how can you identify people who are motivated by the drive to achieve rather than by external rewards? The first sign is a passion for the work itself—such people seek out creative challenges, love to learn, and take great pride in a job well done. They also display an unflagging energy to do things better. People with such energy often seem restless with the status quo. They are persistent with their questions about why things are done one way rather than another; they are eager to explore new approaches to their work.

A cosmetics company manager, for example, was frustrated that he had to wait two weeks to get sales results from people in the field. He finally tracked down an automated phone system that would beep each of his salespeople at 5 p.m. every day. An automated message then prompted them to punch in their numbers—how many calls and sales they had made that day. The system shortened the feedback time on sales results from weeks to hours.

That story illustrates two other common traits of people who are driven to achieve. They are forever raising the performance bar, and they like to keep score. Take the performance bar first. During performance reviews, people with high levels of motivation might ask to be "stretched" by their superiors. Of course, an employee who combines self-awareness with internal motivation will recognize her limits—but she won't settle for objectives that seem too easy to fulfill.

And it follows naturally that people who are driven to do better also want a way of tracking progress—their own, their team's, and their company's. Whereas people with low achievement motivation are often fuzzy about results, those with high achievement motivation often keep score by tracking such hard measures as profitability or market share. I know of a money manager who starts and ends his day on the Internet, gauging the performance of his stock fund against four industry-set benchmarks.

Interestingly, people with high motivation remain optimistic even when the score is against them. In such cases, self-regulation combines with achievement motivation to overcome the frustration and depression that come after a setback or failure. Take the case of another portfolio manager at a large investment company. After several successful years, her fund tumbled for three consecutive quarters, leading three large institutional clients to shift their business elsewhere.

Some executives would have blamed the nosedive on circumstances outside their control; others might have seen the setback as evidence of personal failure. This portfolio manager, however, saw an opportunity to prove she could lead a turnaround. Two years later, when she was promoted to a very senior level in the company, she described the experience as "the best thing that ever happened to me; I learned so much from it."

Executives trying to recognize high levels of achievement motivation in their people can look for one last piece of evidence: commitment to the organization. When people love their jobs for the work itself, they often feel committed to the organizations that make that work possible. Committed employees are likely to stay with an organization even when they are pursued by headhunters waving money.

It's not difficult to understand how and why a motivation to achieve translates into strong leadership. If you set the performance bar high for yourself, you will do the same for the organization when you are in a position to do so. Likewise, a drive to surpass goals and an interest in keeping score can be contagious. Leaders with these traits can often build a team of managers around them with the same traits. And of course, optimism and organizational commitment are fundamental to leadership—just try to imagine running a company without them.

Empathy

Of all the dimensions of emotional intelligence, empathy is the most easily recognized. We have all felt the empathy of a sensitive teacher or friend; we have all been struck by its absence in an unfeeling coach or boss. But when it comes to business, we rarely hear people praised, let alone rewarded, for their empathy. The very word seems unbusinesslike, out of place amid the tough realities of the marketplace.

But empathy doesn't mean a kind of "I'm OK, you're OK" mushiness. For a leader, that is, it doesn't mean adopting other people's emotions as one's own and trying to please everybody. That would be a nightmare—it would make action impossible. Rather, empathy means thoughtfully considering employees' feelings—along with other factors—in the process of making intelligent decisions.

For an example of empathy in action, consider what happened when two giant brokerage companies merged, creating redundant jobs in all their divisions. One division manager called his people together and gave a gloomy speech that emphasized the number of people who would soon be fired. The manager of another division gave his people a different kind of speech. He was up-front about his own worry and confusion, and he promised to keep people informed and to treat everyone fairly.

The difference between these two managers was empathy. The first manager was too worried about his own fate to consider the feelings of his anxiety-stricken colleagues. The second knew intuitively what his people were feeling, and he acknowledged their fears with his words. Is it any surprise that the first manager saw his division sink as many demoralized people, especially the most talented, departed? By contrast, the second manager continued to be a strong leader, his best people stayed, and his division remained as productive as ever.

Empathy is particularly important today as a component of leadership for at least three reasons: the increasing use of teams; the rapid pace of globalization; and the growing need to retain talent.

Consider the challenge of leading a team. As anyone who has ever been a part of one can attest, teams are cauldrons of bubbling emotions. They are often charged with reaching a consensus—which is hard enough with two people and much more difficult as the numbers increase. Even in groups with as few as four or five members, alliances form and clashing agendas get set. A team's leader must be able to sense and understand the viewpoints of everyone around the table.

That's exactly what a marketing manager at a large information technology company was able to do when she was appointed to lead a troubled team. The group was in turmoil, overloaded by work and missing deadlines. Tensions were high among the members. Tinkering with procedures was not enough to bring the group together and make it an effective part of the company.

So the manager took several steps. In a series of one-on-one sessions, she took the time to listen to everyone in the group—what was frustrating them, how they rated their colleagues, whether they felt they had been ignored. And then she directed the team in a way that brought it together: She encouraged people to speak more openly about their frustrations, and she helped people raise constructive complaints during meetings. In short, her empathy allowed her to understand her team's emotional makeup. The result was not just heightened collaboration among members but also added business, as the team was called on for help by a wider range of internal clients.

Globalization is another reason for the rising importance of empathy for business leaders. Cross-cultural dialogue can easily lead to miscues and misunderstandings. Empathy is an antidote. People who have it are attuned to subtleties in body language; they can hear the message beneath the words being spoken. Beyond that, they have a deep understanding of both the existence and the importance of cultural and ethnic differences.

Consider the case of an American consultant whose team had just pitched a project to a potential Japanese client. In its dealings with Americans, the team was accustomed to being bombarded with questions after such a proposal, but this time it was greeted with a long silence. Other members of the team, taking the silence as disapproval, were ready to pack and leave. The lead consultant gestured them to stop. Although he was not particularly familiar with Japanese culture, he read the client's face and posture and sensed not rejection but interest—even deep consideration. He was right: When the client finally spoke, it was to give the consulting firm the job.

Finally, empathy plays a key role in the retention of talent, particularly in today's information economy. Leaders have always needed empathy to develop and keep good people, but today the stakes are higher. When good people leave, they take the company's knowledge with them.

That's where coaching and mentoring come in. It has repeatedly been shown that coaching and mentoring pay off not just in better performance but also in increased job satisfaction and decreased turnover. But what makes coaching and mentoring work best is the nature of the relationship. Outstanding coaches and mentors get inside the heads of the people they are helping. They sense how to give effective feedback. They know when to push for better performance and when to hold back. In the way they motivate their protégés, they demonstrate empathy in action.

In what is probably sounding like a refrain, let me repeat that empathy doesn't get much respect in business. People wonder how leaders can make hard decisions if they are "feeling" for all the people who will be affected. But leaders with empathy do more than sympathize with people around them: They use their knowledge to improve their companies in subtle but important ways.

Social Skill

The first three components of emotional intelligence are self-management skills. The last two, empathy and social skill, concern a person's ability to manage relationships with others. As a component of emotional intelligence, social skill is not as simple as it sounds. It's not just a matter of friendliness, although people with high levels of social skill are rarely mean-spirited. Social skill, rather, is friendliness with a purpose: moving people in the direction you desire, whether that's agreement on a new marketing strategy or enthusiasm about a new product.

Socially skilled people tend to have a wide circle of acquaintances, and they have a knack for finding common ground with people of all kinds—a knack for building rapport. That doesn't mean they socialize continually; it means they work according to the assumption that nothing important gets done alone. Such people have a network in place when the time for action comes.

Social skill is the culmination of the other dimensions of emotional intelligence. People tend to be very effective at managing relationships when they can understand and control their own emotions and can empathize with the feelings of others. Even motivation contributes to social skill. Remember that people who are driven to achieve tend to be optimistic, even in the face of setbacks or failure. When people are upbeat, their "glow" is cast upon conversations and other social encounters. They are popular, and for good reason.

Because it is the outcome of the other dimensions of emotional intelligence, social skill is recognizable on the job in many ways that will by now sound familiar. Socially skilled people, for instance, are adept at managing teams—that's their empathy at work. Likewise, they are expert persuaders—a manifestation of self-awareness, self-regulation, and empathy combined. Given those skills, good persuaders know when to make an emotional plea, for instance, and when an appeal to reason will work better. And motivation, when publicly visible, makes such people excellent collaborators; their passion for the work spreads to others, and they are driven to find solutions.

But sometimes social skill shows itself in ways the other emotional intelligence components do not. For instance, socially skilled people may at times appear not to be working while at work. They seem to be idly schmoozing—chatting in the hallways with colleagues or joking around with people who are not even connected to their "real" jobs. Socially skilled people, however, don't think it makes sense to arbitrarily limit the scope of their relationships. They build bonds widely because they know that in these fluid times, they may need help someday from people they are just getting to know today.

For example, consider the case of an executive in the strategy department of a global computer manufacturer. By 1993, he was convinced that the company's future lay with the Internet. Over the course of the next year, he found kindred spirits and used his social skill to stitch together a virtual community that cut across levels, divisions, and nations. He then used this de facto team to put up a corporate Web site, among the first by a major company. And, on his own initiative, with no budget or formal status, he signed up the company to participate in an annual Internet industry convention. Calling on his allies and persuading various divisions to donate funds, he recruited more than 50 people from a dozen different units to represent the company at the convention.

Management took notice: Within a year of the conference, the executive's team formed the basis for the company's first Internet division, and he was formally put in charge of it. To get there, the executive had ignored conventional boundaries, forging and maintaining connections with people in every corner of the organization.

Is social skill considered a key leadership capability in most companies? The answer is yes, especially when compared with the other components of emotional intelligence. People seem to know intuitively that leaders need to manage relationships effectively; no leader is an island. After all, the leader's task is to get work done through other people, and social skill makes that possible. A leader who cannot express her empathy may as well not have it at all. And a leader's motivation will be useless if he cannot communicate his passion to the organization. Social skill allows leaders to put their emotional intelligence to work.

It would be foolish to assert that good-old-fashioned IQ and technical ability are not important ingredients in strong leadership. But the recipe would not be complete without emotional intelligence. It was once thought that the components of emotional intelligence were "nice to have" in business leaders. But now we know that, for the sake of performance, these are ingredients that leaders "need to have."

It is fortunate, then, that emotional intelligence can be learned. The process is not easy. It takes time and, most of all, commitment. But the benefits that come from having a well-developed emotional intelligence, both for the individual and for the organization, make it worth the effort.

Originally published in June 1996. Reprint R0401H

Primal Leadership

The Hidden Driver of Great Performance.

by Daniel Goleman, Richard Boyatzis, and Annie McKee

WHEN THE THEORY OF EMOTIONAL intelligence at work began to receive widespread attention, we frequently heard executives say—in the same breath, mind you—"That's incredible," and, "Well, I've known that all along." They were responding to our research that showed an incontrovertible link between an executive's emotional maturity, exemplified by such capabilities as self-awareness and empathy, and his or her financial performance. Simply put, the research showed that "good guys"—that is, emotionally intelligent men and women—finish first.

We've recently compiled two years of new research that, we suspect, will elicit the same kind of reaction. People will first exclaim, "No way," then quickly add, "But of course." We found that of all the elements affecting bottom-line performance, the importance of the leader's mood and its attendant behaviors are most surprising. That powerful pair set off a chain reaction: The leader's mood and behaviors drive the moods and behaviors of everyone else. A cranky and ruthless boss creates a toxic organization filled with negative underachievers who ignore opportunities; an inspirational, inclusive leader spawns acolytes for whom any challenge is surmountable. The final link in the chain is performance: profit or loss.

Our observation about the overwhelming impact of the leader's "emotional style," as we call it, is not a wholesale departure from our research into emotional intelligence. It does, however, represent a deeper analysis of our earlier assertion that a leader's emotional intelligence creates a certain culture or work environment. High levels of emotional intelligence, our research showed, create climates in which information sharing, trust, healthy risk-taking, and learning flourish. Low levels of emotional intelligence create climates rife with fear and anxiety. Because tense or terrified employees can be very productive in the short term, their organizations may post good results, but they never last.

Our investigation was designed in part to look at how emotional intelligence drives performance—in particular, at how it travels from the leader through the organization to bottom-line results. "What mechanism," we asked, "binds the chain together?" To answer that question, we turned to the latest neurological and psychological research. We also drew on our work with business leaders, observations by our colleagues of hundreds of leaders, and Hay Group data on the leadership styles of thousands of executives. From this body of research, we discovered that emotional intelligence is carried through an organization like electricity through wires. To be more specific, the leader's mood is quite literally contagious, spreading quickly and inexorably throughout the business.

We'll discuss the science of mood contagion in more depth later, but first let's turn to the key implications of our finding. If a leader's mood and accompanying behaviors are indeed such potent drivers of business success, then a leader's premier task—we would even say his primal task—is emotional leadership. A leader needs to make sure that not only is he regularly in an optimistic, authentic, high-energy mood, but also that, through his chosen actions, his followers feel and act that way, too. Managing for financial results, then, begins with the leader managing his inner life so that the right emotional and behavioral chain reaction occurs.

Managing one's inner life is not easy, of course. For many of us, it's our most difficult challenge. And accurately gauging how one's emotions affect others can be just as difficult. We know of one CEO, for example, who was certain that everyone saw him as upbeat and reliable; his direct reports told us they found his cheerfulness strained, even fake, and his decisions erratic. (We call this common

Idea in Brief

What *most* influences your company's bottom-line performance? The answer will surprise you—*and* make perfect sense: It's a leader's own mood.

Executives' emotional intelligence—their self-awareness, empathy, rapport with others—has clear links to their own performance. But new research shows that a leader's emotional style also drives everyone *else*'s moods and behaviors—through a neurological process called **mood contagion**. It's akin to "Smile and the whole world smiles with you."

Emotional intelligence travels through an organization like electricity over telephone wires. Depressed, ruthless bosses create toxic organizations filled with negative underachievers. But if you're an upbeat, inspirational leader, you cultivate positive employees who embrace and surmount even the toughest challenges.

Emotional leadership isn't just putting on a game face every day. It means understanding your impact on others—then adjusting your style accordingly. A difficult process of self-discovery—but essential *before* you can tackle your leadership responsibilities.

disconnect "CEO disease.") The implication is that primal leadership demands more than putting on a game face every day. It requires an executive to determine, through reflective analysis, how his emotional leadership drives the moods and actions of the organization, and then, with equal discipline, to adjust his behavior accordingly.

That's not to say that leaders can't have a bad day or week: Life happens. And our research doesn't suggest that good moods have to be high-pitched or nonstop—optimistic, sincere, and realistic will do. But there is no escaping the conclusion that a leader must first attend to the impact of his mood and behaviors before moving on to his wide panoply of other critical responsibilities. In this article, we introduce a process that executives can follow to assess how others experience their leadership, and we discuss ways to calibrate that impact. But first, we'll look at why moods aren't often discussed in the workplace, how the brain works to make moods contagious, and what you need to know about CEO disease.

Idea in Practice

Strengthening Your Emotional Leadership

Since few people have the guts to tell you the truth about your emotional impact, you must discover it on your own. The following process can help. It's based on brain science, as well as years of field research with executives. Use these steps to rewire your brain for greater emotional intelligence.

1. **Who do you want to be?** Imagine yourself as a highly effective leader. What do you see?

   Example: Sofia, a senior manager, often micromanaged others to ensure work was done "right." So she *imagined* herself in the future as an effective leader of her own company, enjoying trusting relationships with coworkers. She saw herself as relaxed, happy, and empowering. The exercise revealed gaps in her current emotional style.

2. **Who are you now?** To see your leadership style as others do, gather 360-degree feedback, especially from peers and subordinates. Identify your weaknesses *and* strengths.

3. **How do you get from here to there?** Devise a plan for closing the gap between who you are and who you want to be.

   Example: Juan, a marketing executive, was intimidating,

No Way! Yes Way

When we said earlier that people will likely respond to our new finding by saying "No way," we weren't joking. The fact is, the emotional impact of a leader is almost never discussed in the workplace, let alone in the literature on leadership and performance. For most people, "mood" feels too personal. Even though Americans can be shockingly candid about personal matters—witness the *Jerry Springer Show* and its ilk—we are also the most legally bound. We can't even ask the age of a job applicant. Thus, a conversation about an executive's mood or the moods he creates in his employees might be construed as an invasion of privacy.

We also might avoid talking about a leader's emotional style and its impact because, frankly, the topic feels soft. When was the last time you evaluated a subordinate's mood as part of her performance

impossible to please—a grouch. Charged with growing his company, he *needed* to be encouraging, optimistic—a coach with a vision. Setting out to understand others, he coached soccer, volunteered at a crisis center, and got to know subordinates by meeting outside of work. These new situations stimulated him to break old habits and try new responses.

4. **How do you make change stick?** Repeatedly rehearse new behaviors—physically *and* mentally—until they're automatic.

   Example: Tom, an executive, wanted to learn how to coach rather than castigate struggling employees. Using his commuting time to visualize a difficult meeting with one employee, he envisioned asking questions and listening, and mentally rehearsed how he'd handle feeling impatient. This exercise prepared him to adopt new behaviors at the actual meeting.

5. **Who can help you?** Don't try to build your emotional skills alone—identify others who can help you navigate this difficult process. Managers at Unilever formed learning groups that helped them strengthen their leadership abilities by exchanging frank feedback and developing strong mutual trust.

appraisal? You may have alluded to it—"Your work is hindered by an often negative perspective," or "Your enthusiasm is terrific"—but it is unlikely you mentioned mood outright, let alone discussed its impact on the organization's results.

And yet our research undoubtedly will elicit a "But of course" reaction, too. Everyone knows how much a leader's emotional state drives performance because everyone has had, at one time or another, the inspirational experience of working for an upbeat manager or the crushing experience of toiling for a sour-spirited boss. The former made everything feel possible, and as a result, stretch goals were achieved, competitors beaten, and new customers won. The latter made work grueling. In the shadow of the boss's dark mood, other parts of the organization became "the enemy," colleagues became suspicious of one another, and customers slipped away.

Our research, and research by other social scientists, confirms the verity of these experiences. (There are, of course, rare cases when a brutal boss produces terrific results. We explore that dynamic in the sidebar "Those Wicked Bosses Who Win.") The studies are too numerous to mention here but, in aggregate, they show that when the leader is in a happy mood, the people around him view everything in a more positive light. That, in turn, makes them optimistic about achieving their goals, enhances their creativity and the efficiency of their decision making, and predisposes them to be helpful. Research conducted by Alice Isen at Cornell in 1999, for example, found that an upbeat environment fosters mental efficiency, making people better at taking in and understanding information, at using decision rules in complex judgments, and at being flexible in their thinking. Other research directly links mood and financial performance. In 1986, for instance, Martin Seligman and Peter Schulman of the University of Pennsylvania demonstrated that insurance agents who had a "glass half-full" outlook were far more able than their more pessimistic peers to persist despite rejections, and thus, they closed more sales. (For more information on these studies and a list of our research base, visit www.eiconsortium.org.)

Many leaders whose emotional styles create a dysfunctional environment are eventually fired. (Of course, that's rarely the stated reason; poor results are.) But it doesn't have to end that way. Just as a bad mood can be turned around, so can the spread of toxic feelings from an emotionally inept leader. A look inside the brain explains both why and how.

The Science of Moods

A growing body of research on the human brain proves that, for better or worse, leaders' moods affect the emotions of the people around them. The reason for that lies in what scientists call the open-loop nature of the brain's limbic system, our emotional center. A closed-loop system is self-regulating, whereas an open-loop system depends on external sources to manage itself. In other words, we rely on connections with other people to determine our moods. The

Those Wicked Bosses Who Win

EVERYONE KNOWS OF a rude and coercive CEO who, by all appearances, epitomizes the antithesis of emotional intelligence yet seems to reap great business results. If a leader's mood matters so much, how can we explain those mean-spirited, successful SOBs?

First, let's take a closer look at them. Just because a particular executive is the most visible, he may not actually lead the company. A CEO who heads a conglomerate may have no followers to speak of; it's his division heads who actively lead people and affect profitability.

Second, sometimes an SOB leader has strengths that counterbalance his caustic behavior, but they don't attract as much attention in the business press. In his early days at GE, Jack Welch exhibited a strong hand at the helm as he undertook a radical company turnaround. At that time and in that situation, Welch's firm, top-down style was appropriate. What got less press was how Welch subsequently settled into a more emotionally intelligent leadership style, especially when he articulated a new vision for the company and mobilized people to follow it.

Those caveats aside, let's get back to those infamous corporate leaders who seem to have achieved sterling business results despite their brutish approaches to leadership. Skeptics cite Bill Gates, for example, as a leader who gets away with a harsh style that should theoretically damage his company.

But our leadership model, which shows the effectiveness of specific leadership styles in specific situations, puts Gates's supposedly negative behaviors in a different light. (Our model is explained in detail in the HBR article "Leadership That Gets Results," which appeared in the March–April 2000 issue.) Gates is the achievement-driven leader par excellence, in an organization that has cherry-picked highly talented and motivated people. His apparently harsh leadership style—baldly challenging employees to surpass their past performance—can be quite effective when employees are competent, motivated, and need little direction—all characteristics of Microsoft's engineers.

In short, it's all too easy for a skeptic to argue against the importance of leaders who manage their moods by citing a "rough and tough" leader who achieved good business results despite his bad behavior. We contend that there are, of course, exceptions to the rule, and that in some specific business cases, an SOB boss resonates just fine. But in general, leaders who are jerks must reform or else their moods and actions will eventually catch up with them.

open-loop limbic system was a winning design in evolution because it let people come to one another's emotional rescue—enabling a mother, for example, to soothe her crying infant.

The open-loop design serves the same purpose today as it did thousands of years ago. Research in intensive care units has shown, for example, that the comforting presence of another person not only lowers the patient's blood pressure but also slows the secretion of fatty acids that block arteries. Another study found that three or more incidents of intense stress within a year (for example, serious financial trouble, being fired, or a divorce) triples the death rate in socially isolated middle-aged men, but it has no impact on the death rate of men with many close relationships.

Scientists describe the open loop as "interpersonal limbic regulation"; one person transmits signals that can alter hormone levels, cardiovascular functions, sleep rhythms, even immune functions, inside the body of another. That's how couples are able to trigger surges of oxytocin in each other's brains, creating a pleasant, affectionate feeling. But in all aspects of social life, our physiologies intermingle. Our limbic system's open-loop design lets other people change our very physiology and hence, our emotions.

Even though the open loop is so much a part of our lives, we usually don't notice the process. Scientists have captured the attunement of emotions in the laboratory by measuring the physiology—such as heart rate—of two people sharing a good conversation. As the interaction begins, their bodies operate at different rhythms. But after 15 minutes, the physiological profiles of their bodies look remarkably similar.

Researchers have seen again and again how emotions spread irresistibly in this way whenever people are near one another. As far back as 1981, psychologists Howard Friedman and Ronald Riggio found that even completely nonverbal expressiveness can affect other people. For example, when three strangers sit facing one another in silence for a minute or two, the most emotionally expressive of the three transmits his or her mood to the other two—without a single word being spoken.

Smile and the World Smiles with You

REMEMBER THAT OLD cliché? It's not too far from the truth. As we've shown, mood contagion is a real neurological phenomenon, but not all emotions spread with the same ease. A 1999 study conducted by Sigal Barsade at the Yale School of Management showed that, among working groups, cheerfulness and warmth spread easily, while irritability caught on less so, and depression least of all.

It should come as no surprise that laughter is the most contagious of all emotions. Hearing laughter, we find it almost impossible not to laugh or smile, too. That's because some of our brain's open-loop circuits are designed to detect smiles and laughter, making us respond in kind. Scientists theorize that this dynamic was hardwired into our brains ages ago because smiles and laughter had a way of cementing alliances, thus helping the species survive.

The main implication here for leaders undertaking the primal task of managing their moods and the moods of others is this: Humor hastens the spread of an upbeat climate. But like the leader's mood in general, humor must resonate with the organization's culture and its reality. Smiles and laughter, we would posit, are only contagious when they're genuine.

The same holds true in the office, boardroom, or shop floor; group members inevitably "catch" feelings from one another. In 2000, Caroline Bartel at New York University and Richard Saavedra at the University of Michigan found that in 70 work teams across diverse industries, people in meetings together ended up sharing moods—both good and bad—within two hours. One study asked teams of nurses and accountants to monitor their moods over weeks; researchers discovered that their emotions tracked together, and they were largely independent of each team's shared hassles. Groups, therefore, like individuals, ride emotional roller coasters, sharing everything from jealousy to angst to euphoria. (A good mood, incidentally, spreads most swiftly by the judicious use of humor. For more on this, see the sidebar "Smile and the World Smiles with You.")

Moods that start at the top tend to move the fastest because everyone watches the boss. They take their emotional cues from him. Even when the boss isn't highly visible—for example, the CEO

Get Happy, Carefully

GOOD MOODS GALVANIZE good performance, but it doesn't make sense for a leader to be as chipper as a blue jay at dawn if sales are tanking or the business is going under. The most effective executives display moods and behaviors that match the situation at hand, with a healthy dose of optimism mixed in. They respect how other people are feeling—even if it is glum or defeated—but they also model what it looks like to move forward with hope and humor.

This kind of performance, which we call resonance, is for all intents and purposes the four components of emotional intelligence in action.

Self-awareness, perhaps the most essential of the emotional intelligence competencies, is the ability to read your own emotions. It allows people to know their strengths and limitations and feel confident about their self-worth. Resonant leaders use self-awareness to gauge their own moods accurately, and they intuitively know how they are affecting others.

Self-management is the ability to control your emotions and act with honesty and integrity in reliable and adaptable ways. Resonant leaders don't let their occasional bad moods seize the day; they use self-management to leave it outside the office or to explain its source to people in a reasonable manner, so they know where it's coming from and how long it might last.

Social awareness includes the key capabilities of empathy and organizational intuition. Socially aware executives do more than sense other people's emotions, they show that they care. Further, they are experts at reading the currents of office politics. Thus, resonant leaders often keenly understand how their words and actions make others feel, and they are sensitive enough to change them when that impact is negative.

Relationship management, the last of the emotional intelligence competencies, includes the abilities to communicate clearly and convincingly,

who works behind closed doors on an upper floor—his attitude affects the moods of his direct reports, and a domino effect ripples throughout the company.

Call That CEO a Doctor

If the leader's mood is so important, then he or she had better get into a good one, right? Yes, but the full answer is more complicated than that. A leader's mood has the greatest impact on performance

disarm conflicts, and build strong personal bonds. Resonant leaders use these skills to spread their enthusiasm and solve disagreements, often with humor and kindness.

As effective as resonant leadership is, it is just as rare. Most people suffer through dissonant leaders whose toxic moods and upsetting behaviors wreak havoc before a hopeful and realistic leader repairs the situation.

Consider what happened recently at an experimental division of the BBC, the British media giant. Even though the group's 200 or so journalists and editors had given their best effort, management decided to close the division.

The shutdown itself was bad enough, but the brusque, contentious mood and manner of the executive sent to deliver the news to the assembled staff incited something beyond the expected frustration. People became enraged—at both the decision and the bearer of the news. The executive's cranky mood and delivery created an atmosphere so threatening that he had to call security to be ushered from the room.

The next day, another executive visited the same staff. His mood was somber and respectful, as was his behavior. He spoke about the importance of journalism to the vibrancy of a society and of the calling that had drawn them all to the field in the first place. He reminded them that no one goes into journalism to get rich—as a profession its finances have always been marginal, job security ebbing and flowing with the larger economic tides. He recalled a time in his own career when he had been let go and how he had struggled to find a new position—but how he had stayed dedicated to the profession. Finally, he wished them well in getting on with their careers.

The reaction from what had been an angry mob the day before? When this resonant leader finished speaking, the staff cheered.

---

when it is upbeat. But it must also be in tune with those around him. We call this dynamic *resonance*. (For more on this, see the sidebar "Get Happy, Carefully.")

We found that an alarming number of leaders do not really know if they have resonance with their organizations. Rather, they suffer from CEO disease; its one unpleasant symptom is the sufferer's near-total ignorance about how his mood and actions appear to the organization. It's not that leaders don't care how they are perceived; most do. But they incorrectly assume that they can decipher this information themselves. Worse, they think that if they are having a negative effect, someone will tell them. They're wrong.

As one CEO in our research explains, "I so often feel I'm not getting the truth. I can never put my finger on it, because no one is actually lying to me. But I can sense that people are hiding information or camouflaging key facts. They aren't lying, but neither are they telling me everything I need to know. I'm always second-guessing."

People don't tell leaders the whole truth about their emotional impact for many reasons. Sometimes they are scared of being the bearer of bad news—and getting shot. Others feel it isn't their place to comment on such a personal topic. Still others don't realize that what they really want to talk about is the effects of the leader's emotional style—that feels too vague. Whatever the reason, the CEO can't rely on his followers to spontaneously give him the full picture.

Taking Stock

The process we recommend for self-discovery and personal reinvention is neither newfangled nor born of pop psychology, like so many self-help programs offered to executives today. Rather, it is based on three streams of research into how executives can improve the emotional intelligence capabilities most closely linked to effective leadership. (Information on these research streams can also be found at www.eiconsortium.org.). In 1989, one of us (Richard Boyatzis) began drawing on this body of research to design the five-step process itself, and since then, thousands of executives have used it successfully.

Unlike more traditional forms of coaching, our process is based on brain science. A person's emotional skills—the attitude and abilities with which someone approaches life and work—are not genetically hardwired, like eye color and skin tone. But in some ways they might as well be, because they are so deeply embedded in our neurology.

A person's emotional skills do, in fact, have a genetic component. Scientists have discovered, for instance, the gene for shyness—which is not a mood, per se, but it can certainly drive a person toward a persistently quiet demeanor, which may be read as a "down" mood.

Other people are preternaturally jolly—that is, their relentless cheerfulness seems preternatural until you meet their peppy parents. As one executive explains, "All I know is that ever since I was a baby, I have always been happy. It drives some people crazy, but I couldn't get blue if I tried. And my brother is the exact same way; he saw the bright side of life, even during his divorce."

Even though emotional skills are partly inborn, experience plays a major role in how the genes are expressed. A happy baby whose parents die or who endures physical abuse may grow into a melancholy adult. A cranky toddler may turn into a cheerful adult after discovering a fulfilling avocation. Still, research suggests that our range of emotional skills is relatively set by our mid-20s and that our accompanying behaviors are, by that time, deep-seated habits. And therein lies the rub: The more we act a certain way—be it happy, depressed, or cranky—the more the behavior becomes ingrained in our brain circuitry, and the more we will continue to feel and act that way.

That's why emotional intelligence matters so much for a leader. An emotionally intelligent leader can monitor his or her moods through self-awareness, change them for the better through self-management, understand their impact through empathy, and act in ways that boost others' moods through relationship management.

The following five-part process is designed to rewire the brain toward more emotionally intelligent behaviors. The process begins with imagining your ideal self and then coming to terms with your real self, as others experience you. The next step is creating a tactical plan to bridge the gap between ideal and real, and after that, to practice those activities. It concludes with creating a community of colleagues and family—call them change enforcers—to keep the process alive. Let's look at the steps in more detail.

"Who do I want to be?"

Sofia, a senior manager at a northern European telecommunications company, knew she needed to understand how her emotional leadership affected others. Whenever she felt stressed, she tended to communicate poorly and take over subordinates' work so that the job would be done "right." Attending leadership seminars hadn't changed her habits, and neither had reading management books or working with mentors.

When Sofia came to us, we asked her to imagine herself eight years from now as an effective leader and to write a description of a typical day. "What would she be doing?" we asked. "Where would she live? Who would be there? How would it feel?" We urged her to consider her deepest values and loftiest dreams and to explain how those ideals had become a part of her everyday life.

Sofia pictured herself leading her own tight-knit company staffed by ten colleagues. She was enjoying an open relationship with her daughter and had trusting relationships with her friends and coworkers. She saw herself as a relaxed and happy leader and parent, and as loving and empowering to all those around her.

In general, Sofia had a low level of self-awareness: She was rarely able to pinpoint why she was struggling at work and at home. All she could say was, "Nothing is working right." This exercise, which prompted her to picture what life would look like if everything were going right, opened her eyes to the missing elements in her emotional style. She was able to see the impact she had on people in her life.

"Who am I now?"

In the next step of the discovery process, you come to see your leadership style as others do. This is both difficult and dangerous. Difficult, because few people have the guts to tell the boss or a colleague what he's really like. And dangerous, because such information can sting or even paralyze. A small bit of ignorance about yourself isn't always a bad thing: Ego-defense mechanisms have their advantages. Research by Martin Seligman shows that high-functioning people generally feel more optimistic about their prospects and possibilities than average performers. Their rose-colored lenses, in fact, fuel the enthusiasm and energy that make the unexpected and the extraordinary achievable. Playwright Henrik Ibsen called such self-delusions "vital lies," soothing mistruths we let ourselves believe in order to face a daunting world.

But self-delusion should come in very small doses. Executives should relentlessly seek the truth about themselves, especially since it is sure to be somewhat diluted when they hear it anyway. One way to get the truth is to keep an extremely open attitude toward critiques. Another is to seek out negative feedback, even cultivating a colleague or two to play devil's advocate.

We also highly recommend gathering feedback from as many people as possible—including bosses, peers, and subordinates. Feedback from subordinates and peers is especially helpful because it most accurately predicts a leader's effectiveness, two, four, and even seven years out, according to research by Glenn McEvoy at Utah State and Richard Beatty at Rutgers University.

Of course, 360-degree feedback doesn't specifically ask people to evaluate your moods, actions, and their impact. But it does reveal how people experience you. For instance, when people rate how well you listen, they are really reporting how well they think you hear them. Similarly, when 360-degree feedback elicits ratings about coaching effectiveness, the answers show whether or not people feel you understand and care about them. When the feedback uncovers low scores on, say, openness to new ideas, it means that people experience you as inaccessible or unapproachable or both. In sum, all you need to know about your emotional impact is in 360-degree feedback, if you look for it.

One last note on this second step. It is, of course, crucial to identify your areas of weakness. But focusing only on your weaknesses can be dispiriting. That's why it is just as important, maybe even more so, to understand your strengths. Knowing where your real self overlaps with your ideal self will give you the positive energy you need to move forward to the next step in the process—bridging the gaps.

"How do I get from here to there?"

Once you know who you want to be and have compared it with how people see you, you need to devise an action plan. For Sofia, this meant planning for a real improvement in her level of self-awareness. So she asked each member of her team at work to give her feedback—weekly, anonymously, and in written form—about her mood and performance and their affect on people. She also committed herself to three tough but achievable tasks: spending an hour each day reflecting on her behavior in a journal, taking a class on group dynamics at a local college, and enlisting the help of a trusted colleague as an informal coach.

Consider, too, how Juan, a marketing executive for the Latin American division of a major integrated energy company, completed this step. Juan was charged with growing the company in his home country of Venezuela as well as in the entire region—a job that would require him to be a coach and a visionary and to have an encouraging, optimistic outlook. Yet 360-degree feedback revealed that Juan was seen as intimidating and internally focused. Many of his direct reports saw him as a grouch—impossible to please at his worst, and emotionally draining at his best.

Identifying this gap allowed Juan to craft a plan with manageable steps toward improvement. He knew he needed to hone his powers of empathy if he wanted to develop a coaching style, so he committed to various activities that would let him practice that skill. For instance, Juan decided to get to know each of his subordinates better; if he understood more about who they were, he thought, he'd be more able to help them reach their goals. He made plans with each employee to meet outside of work, where they might be more comfortable revealing their feelings.

Juan also looked for areas outside of his job to forge his missing links—for example, coaching his daughter's soccer team and volunteering at a local crisis center. Both activities helped him to experiment with how well he understood others and to try out new behaviors.

Again, let's look at the brain science at work. Juan was trying to overcome ingrained behaviors—his approach to work had taken hold over time, without his realizing it. Bringing them into awareness was a crucial step toward changing them. As he paid more attention, the situations that arose—while listening to a colleague, coaching soccer, or talking on the phone to someone who was distraught—all became cues that stimulated him to break old habits and try new responses.

Resonance in Times of Crisis

WHEN TALKING ABOUT LEADERS' moods, the importance of resonance cannot be overstated. While our research suggests that leaders should generally be upbeat, their behavior must be rooted in realism, especially when faced with a crisis.

Consider the response of Bob Mulholland, senior VP and head of the client relations group at Merrill Lynch, to the terrorist attacks in New York. On September 11, 2001, Mulholland and his staff in Two World Financial Center felt the building rock, then watched as smoke poured out of a gaping hole in the building directly across from theirs. People started panicking: Some ran frantically from window to window. Others were paralyzed with fear. Those with relatives working in the World Trade Center were terrified for their safety. Mulholland knew he had to act: "When there's a crisis, you've got to show people the way, step by step, and make sure you're taking care of their concerns."

He started by getting people the information they needed to "unfreeze." He found out, for instance, which floors employees' relatives worked on and assured them that they'd have enough time to escape. Then he calmed the panic-stricken, one at a time. "We're getting out of here now," he said quietly, "and you're coming with me. Not the elevator, take the stairs." He remained calm and decisive, yet he didn't minimize people's emotional responses. Thanks to him, everyone escaped before the towers collapsed.

Mulholland's leadership didn't end there. Recognizing that this event would touch each client personally, he and his team devised a way for financial consultants to connect with their clients on an emotional level. They called every client to ask, "How are you? Are your loved ones okay? How are you feeling?" As Mulholland explains, "There was no way to pick up and do business as usual. The first order of 'business' was letting our clients know we really do care."

Bob Mulholland courageously performed one of the most crucial emotional tasks of leadership: He helped himself and his people find meaning in the face of chaos and madness. To do so, he first attuned to and expressed the shared emotional reality. That's why the direction he eventually articulated resonated at the gut level. His words and his actions reflected what people were feeling in their hearts.

This cueing for habit change is neural as well as perceptual. Researchers at the University of Pittsburgh and Carnegie Mellon University have shown that as we mentally prepare for a task, we activate the prefrontal cortex—the part of the brain that moves us into action. The greater the prior activation, the better we do at the task.

Such mental preparation becomes particularly important when we're trying to replace an old habit with a better one. As neuroscientist Cameron Carter at the University of Pittsburgh found, the prefrontal cortex becomes particularly active when a person prepares to overcome a habitual response. The aroused prefrontal cortex marks the brain's focus on what's about to happen. Without that arousal, a person will reenact tried-and-true but undesirable routines: The executive who just doesn't listen will once again cut off his subordinate, a ruthless leader will launch into yet another critical attack, and so on. That's why a learning agenda is so important. Without one, we literally do not have the brainpower to change.

"How do I make change stick?"

In short, making change last requires practice. The reason, again, lies in the brain. It takes doing and redoing, over and over, to break old neural habits. A leader must rehearse a new behavior until it becomes automatic—that is, until he's mastered it at the level of implicit learning. Only then will the new wiring replace the old.

While it is best to practice new behaviors, as Juan did, sometimes just envisioning them will do. Take the case of Tom, an executive who wanted to close the gap between his real self (perceived by colleagues and subordinates to be cold and hard driving) and his ideal self (a visionary and a coach).

Tom's learning plan involved finding opportunities to step back and coach his employees rather than jumping down their throats when he sensed they were wrong. Tom also began to spend idle moments during his commute thinking through how to handle encounters he would have that day. One morning, while en route to a breakfast meeting with an employee who seemed to be bungling a project, Tom ran through a positive scenario in his mind. He asked questions and listened to be sure he fully understood the situation before trying to solve the problem. He anticipated feeling impatient, and he rehearsed how he would handle these feelings.

Studies on the brain affirm the benefits of Tom's visualization technique: Imagining something in vivid detail can fire the same brain cells actually involved in doing that activity. The new brain circuitry appears to go through its paces, strengthening connections, even when we merely repeat the sequence in our minds. So to alleviate the fears associated with trying out riskier ways of leading, we should first visualize some likely scenarios. Doing so will make us feel less awkward when we actually put the new skills into practice.

Experimenting with new behaviors and seizing opportunities inside and outside of work to practice them—as well as using such methods as mental rehearsal—eventually triggers in our brains the neural connections necessary for genuine change to occur. Even so, lasting change doesn't happen through experimentation and brainpower alone. We need, as the song goes, a little help from our friends.

"Who can help me?"

The fifth step in the self-discovery and reinvention process is creating a community of supporters. Take, for example, managers at Unilever who formed learning groups as part of their executive development process. At first, they gathered to discuss their careers and how to provide leadership. But because they were also charged with discussing their dreams and their learning goals, they soon realized that they were discussing both their work and their personal lives. They developed a strong mutual trust and began relying on one another for frank feedback as they worked on strengthening their leadership abilities. When this happens, the business benefits through stronger performance. Many professionals today have created similar groups, and for good reason. People we trust let us try out unfamiliar parts of our leadership repertoire without risk.

We cannot improve our emotional intelligence or change our leadership style without help from others. We not only practice with other people but also rely on them to create a safe environment in which to experiment. We need to get feedback about how our actions affect others and to assess our progress on our learning agenda.

In fact, perhaps paradoxically, in the self-directed learning process we draw on others every step of the way—from articulating and refining our ideal self and comparing it with the reality to the final assessment that affirms our progress. Our relationships offer us the very context in which we understand our progress and comprehend the usefulness of what we're learning.

Mood over Matter

When we say that managing your mood and the moods of your followers is the task of primal leadership, we certainly don't mean to suggest that mood is all that matters. As we've noted, your actions are critical, and mood and actions together must resonate with the organization and with reality. Similarly, we acknowledge all the other challenges leaders must conquer—from strategy to hiring to new product development. It's all in a long day's work.

But taken as a whole, the message sent by neurological, psychological, and organizational research is startling in its clarity. Emotional leadership is the spark that ignites a company's performance, creating a bonfire of success or a landscape of ashes. Moods matter that much.

Originally published in December 2001. Reprint R0111C

Why It's So Hard to Be Fair

by Joel Brockner

WHEN COMPANY A HAD TO DOWNSIZE, it spent considerable amounts of money providing a safety net for its laid-off workers. The severance package consisted of many weeks of pay, extensive outplacement counseling, and the continuation of health insurance for up to one year. But senior managers never explained to their staff why these layoffs were necessary or how they chose which jobs to eliminate. What's more, the midlevel line managers who delivered the news to terminated employees did so awkwardly, mumbling a few perfunctory words about "not wanting to do this" and then handing them off to the human resources department. Even the people who kept their jobs were less than thrilled about the way things were handled. Many of them heard the news while driving home on Friday and had to wait until Monday to learn that their jobs were secure. Nine months later, the company continued to sputter. Not only did it have to absorb enormous legal costs defending against wrongful termination suits, but it also had to make another round of layoffs, in large part because employee productivity and morale plummeted after the first round was mishandled.

When Company B downsized, by contrast, it didn't offer nearly as generous a severance package. But senior managers there explained the strategic purpose of the layoffs multiple times before they were implemented, and executives and middle managers alike made themselves available to answer questions and express regret both to those who lost their jobs and to those who remained. Line managers worked with HR to tell people that their jobs were being eliminated, and they expressed genuine concern while doing so. As a result, virtually none of the laid-off employees filed a wrongful termination lawsuit. Workers took some time to adjust to the loss of their former colleagues, but they understood why the layoffs had happened. And within nine months, Company B's performance was better than it had been before the layoffs occurred.

Although Company A spent much more money during its restructuring, Company B exhibited much greater *process fairness*. In other words, employees at Company B believed that they had been treated justly. From minimizing costs to strengthening performance, process fairness pays enormous dividends in a wide variety of organizational and people-related challenges. Studies show that when managers practice process fairness, their employees respond in ways that bolster the organization's bottom line both directly and indirectly. Process fairness is more likely to generate support for a new strategy, for instance, and to foster a culture that promotes innovation. What's more, it costs little financially to implement. In short, fair process makes great business sense. So why don't more companies practice it consistently? This article examines that paradox and offers advice on how to promote greater process fairness in your organization.

The Business Case for Fair Process

Ultimately, each employee decides for him or herself whether a decision has been made fairly. But broadly speaking, there are three drivers of process fairness. One is how much input employees believe they have in the decision-making process: Are their opinions requested and given serious consideration? Another is how employees believe decisions are made and implemented: Are they consistent? Are they based on accurate information? Can mistakes be corrected? Are the personal biases of the decision maker minimized? Is ample advance

Idea in Brief

There are myriad ways a company can lose money if it doesn't practice process fairness, including employee theft and turnover, legal costs incurred by defending against wrongful termination suits, and implementing expensive solutions aimed at helping employees cope with the stresses of modern work.

Many executives turn to money first when solving problems, but asking employees for their opinions on a new initiative or explaining to them why you're giving a choice assignment to someone else doesn't cost much money and results in more-satisfied employees. From minimizing costs to strengthening performance, process fairness pays enormous dividends in a wide variety challenges.

Good organizations care not only about the outcomes their managers produce but also about the fairness of the process they use to achieve them. The sooner they minimize the costs of decisions that might threaten employees and maximize the benefits of decisions that may be sources of opportunity for them, the better off they will be.

notice given? Is the decision process transparent? The third factor is how managers behave: Do they explain why a decision was made? Do they treat employees respectfully, actively listening to their concerns and empathizing with their points of view?

It's worth noting that process fairness is distinct from outcome fairness, which refers to employees' judgments of the bottom-line results of their exchanges with their employers. Process fairness doesn't ensure that employees will always get what they want; but it does mean that they will have a chance to be heard. Take the case of an individual who was passed over for a promotion. If he believes that the chosen candidate was qualified, and if his manager has had a candid discussion with him about how he can be better prepared for the next opportunity, chances are he'll be a lot more productive and engaged than if he believes the person who got the job was the boss's pet, or if he received no guidance on how to move forward.

When people feel hurt by their companies, they tend to retaliate. And when they do, it can have grave consequences. A study of nearly 1,000 people in the mid-1990s, led by Duke's Allan Lind and Ohio State's Jerald Greenberg, found that a major determinant of whether employees sue for wrongful termination is their perception of how fairly the termination process was carried out. Only 1% of ex-employees who felt that they were treated with a high degree of process fairness filed a wrongful termination lawsuit versus 17% of those who believed they were treated with a low degree of process fairness. To put that in monetary terms, the expected cost savings of practicing process fairness is $1.28 million for every 100 employees dismissed. That figure—which was calculated using the 1988 rate of $80,000 as the cost of legal defense—is a conservative estimate, since inflation alone has caused legal fees to swell to more than $120,000 today. So, although we can't calculate the precise financial cost of practicing fair process, it's safe to say that expressing genuine concern and treating dismissed employees with dignity is a good deal more affordable than not doing so.

Customers, too, are less likely to file suit against a service provider if they believe they've been treated with process fairness. In 1997, medical researcher Wendy Levinson and her colleagues found that patients typically do not sue their doctors for malpractice simply because they believe that they received poor medical care. A more telling factor is whether the doctor took the time to explain the treatment plan and to answer the patient's questions with consideration—in short, to treat patients with process fairness. Doctors who fail to do so are far more likely to be slapped with malpractice suits when problems arise.

In addition to reducing legal costs, fair process cuts down on employee theft and turnover. A study by management and human resources professor Greenberg examined how pay cuts were handled at two manufacturing plants. At one, a vice president called a meeting at the end of the workweek and announced that the company would implement a 15% pay cut, across the board, for ten weeks. He very briefly explained why, thanked employees, and answered a few questions—the whole thing was over in 15 minutes. The other plant implemented an identical pay cut, but the company president made the announcement to the employees. He told them that other cost-saving options, like layoffs, had been considered but that the pay cuts seemed to be the least unpalatable choice. The president took an hour and a half to address employees' questions and concerns, and he repeatedly expressed regret about having to take this step. Greenberg found that during the ten-week period, employee theft was nearly 80% lower at the second plant than at the first, and employees were 15 times less likely to resign.

Many executives turn to money first to solve problems. But my research shows that companies can reduce expenses by routinely practicing process fairness. Think about it: Asking employees for their opinions on a new initiative or explaining to someone why you're giving a choice assignment to her colleague doesn't cost much money. Of course, companies should continue to offer tangible assistance to employees as well. Using process fairness, however, companies could spend a lot less money and still have more satisfied employees.

Consider the financial fallout that occurs when expatriates leave their overseas assignments prematurely. Conventional wisdom says that expats are more likely to leave early when they or their family members don't adjust well to their new living conditions. So companies often go to great expense to facilitate their adjustment—picking up the tab for housing costs, children's schooling, and the like. In a 2000 study of 128 expatriates, human resources consultant Ron Garonzik, Rutgers Business School professor Phyllis Siegel, and I found that the expats' adjustment to various aspects of their lives outside work had no effect on their intentions to depart prematurely if they believed that their bosses generally treated them fairly. In other words, high process fairness induced expats to stick with an overseas assignment even when they were not particularly enthralled with living abroad.

In a similar vein, some companies have devised expensive solutions to help employees cope with the stress of modern work. They've set up on-site day care centers and sponsored stress management workshops to help reduce absenteeism and burnout. Those efforts are laudable, but process fairness is also an effective strategy. When Phyllis Siegel and I surveyed nearly 300 employees from dozens of organizations, we found that work/life conflict had no measurable effect on employees' commitment—as long as they felt that senior executives provided good reasons for their decisions and treated them with dignity and respect.

Of course, executives should not simply emphasize process fairness over tangible support. Determining exactly how much tangible support to provide is perhaps best captured by the law of diminishing returns. Beyond a moderate level of financial assistance, practicing process fairness proves much more cost effective because, although money does talk, it doesn't say it all.

Fair Process as a Performance Booster

Process fairness can not only minimize costs but can also help to increase value, inspiring operational managers to carry out a well-founded strategic plan eagerly or embrace, rather than sabotage, an organizational change. This form of value is less tangible than direct reduction of expenses, but it affects the bottom line nonetheless.

The fact is, most strategic and organizational change initiatives fail in their implementation, not in their conception. Several years ago, I worked with the CEO of a financial services institution that needed a major restructuring. The bank's operational managers, however, were showing signs of resistance that threatened to stop the process dead in its tracks. I advised the CEO and his senior management team to conduct several town hall–type meetings and to hold informal focus groups with the operational managers. During those talks, it became clear that the managers felt that the CEO and senior executives failed to appreciate the magnitude of the change they were asking for. Interestingly, the managers didn't request additional resources; they simply wanted those at the top to recognize their difficult plight. By expressing authentic interest, senior executives created a trusting environment in which managers felt they could safely voice their true objections to the change effort. That enabled senior managers to respond to the root problem. Moreover, since the operational managers felt respected, they showed a similar level of process fairness with *their* direct reports during the actual restructuring, making the change go more smoothly.

Michael Beer, of Harvard Business School, and Russell Eisenstat, president of the Center for Organizational Fitness, recently provided evidence of how systematically practiced process fairness (embedded in an action-learning methodology known as the strategic fitness process, or SFP) has helped numerous organizations capture value by getting employees to buy in to strategies. A critical element of SFP is the appointment of a task force consisting of eight well-respected managers from one or two levels below senior management. Their job is to interview roughly 100 employees from different parts of the company to learn about the organizational strengths that are apt to facilitate strategy implementation as well as the shortcomings that could hinder it. Task force members distill the information they gain from these interviews into major themes and feed them back to senior management. Then they discuss how the strategy could be rolled out most effectively. SFP is a model for process fairness: More than 25 companies—including Becton, Dickinson; Honeywell; JPMorgan Chase; Hewlett-Packard; and Merck—have used it with great success to hone the substance of their strategic initiatives and, probably more important, to gain employees' commitment to making those initiatives happen.

Most companies say that they want to promote creativity and innovation, but few use process fairness to achieve those ends. They're missing out on a great opportunity to create value. Harvard Business School professor Teresa Amabile has conducted extensive research on employees working in creative endeavors in order to understand how work environments foster or impede creativity and innovation. She has consistently found that work environments in which employees have a high degree of operational autonomy lead to the highest degree of creativity and innovation. Operational autonomy, of course, can be seen as the extreme version of process fairness.

The nature of organizations, though, means that few (if any) employees can have complete operational autonomy—just about everyone has a boss. Creativity and innovation tend to suffer in work environments characterized by low levels of process fairness, such as when employees believe that the organization is strictly controlled by upper management or when they believe that their ideas will be summarily dismissed. When employees believe that their supervisor is open to new ideas and that he or she values their contributions to projects, however, creativity and innovation are more likely to flourish. Two examples illustrate how process fairness creates value by attracting innovative employees or additional customers.

The CEO of a renowned electrical-engineering firm, for instance, wanted to change the corporate culture to be more receptive to new ideas, so he separated a large group of workers into teams of ten, asking each team to come up with ten ideas for improving the business. Then the team leaders were brought into a room where the company's executives were gathered and were asked to "sell" as many of their team's ideas as possible. The executives, for their part, had been instructed to "buy" as many ideas as possible. The team leaders swarmed like bees to honey to the few executives who had reputations for being good listeners and open to new ideas. The other executives stood by idly because team leaders assumed from past experience that they wouldn't listen.

One company that used process fairness to create value is Progressive Casualty Insurance. In 1994, the firm began to give potential customers comparison rates from two competitors along with its own quotes for auto insurance. Even though Progressive's rates weren't always the lowest, the very act of delivering this information created goodwill. Potential customers felt that they were being treated honestly, and the practice drew many new sales.

Why Isn't Everybody Doing It?

With all that process fairness has going for it, one might expect that executives would practice it regularly. Unfortunately, many (if not most) don't. They'd do well to follow the example of Winston Churchill, who keenly understood the cost-effectiveness of process fairness. On the day after the bombing of Pearl Harbor, Churchill wrote a declaration of war to the Japanese, ending it as follows: "I have the honour to be, with high consideration, Sir, Your obedient servant, Winston S. Churchill." After being castigated by his countrymen for the letter's deferential tone, Churchill is said to have retorted, "When you have to kill a man, it costs nothing to be polite."

In a change management seminar I've taught to more than 400 managers, I ask participants to rate themselves on how well they plan and implement organizational change. I also ask the managers' bosses, peers, direct reports, and customers to rate them. The measure contains more than 30 items, and managers consistently give themselves the highest marks on the item that measures process fairness: "When managing change, I make extra efforts to treat people with dignity and respect." Those rating them, however, are not nearly as positive. In fact, this is the only item in which managers' self-assessments are significantly higher than the ratings they receive from each of their groups. It's not entirely clear why this perceptual gap exists. Perhaps managers are tuned in to their intentions to treat others respectfully, but they aren't as good at reading how those intentions come across to others. Or maybe it's just wishful—and self-serving—thinking.

Some managers wrongly believe that tangible resources are always more meaningful to employees than being treated decently. At a cocktail party, the CEO of a major international bank proudly told me about the hefty severance pay his company gave to its laid-off employees. I expressed admiration for his organization's show of concern toward the people who lost their jobs and then asked what had been done for those who remained. Somewhat defensively, he said that it was only necessary to do something for the employees who were "affected" by the layoffs. The others were "lucky enough to still have their jobs." But economically supporting those who lost their jobs doesn't cancel out the need to show process fairness to those affected by the change—which, incidentally, includes everyone. Ironically, the fact that process fairness is relatively inexpensive financially may be why this numbers-oriented executive undervalued it.

Another reason process fairness may be overlooked is because some of its benefits aren't obvious to executives. Social psychologist Marko Elovainio of the University of Helsinki and his colleagues recently conducted a study of more than 31,000 Finnish employees, examining the relationship between employees' negative life events (such as the onset of a severe illness or death of a spouse) and the frequency of sickness-related absences from work for the subsequent 30 months. The study showed that the tendency for negative life events to translate into sickness-related absences depended on how much process fairness employees experienced before the events occurred. That is, *not* being pretreated with process fairness led to absences waiting to happen.

Sometimes corporate policies hinder fair process. The legal department may discourage managers from explaining their decisions, for instance, on the grounds that disclosure of information could make the company vulnerable to lawsuits. Better not to say anything at all, the thinking goes, than to risk having the information come back to haunt the organization in the courtroom. Clearly, legal considerations about what to communicate are important, but they should not be taken to unnecessary extremes. All too often organizations withhold information (such as the alternatives to downsizing that have been considered) when revealing it would have done far more good.

Legal and medical advocates in Hawaii, for instance, are currently drafting a statute that would allow health care professionals to apologize for medical errors without increasing the risk of lawsuits. Doctors often refrain from apologizing for mistakes because they fear that admitting them will anger their patients, who will then be more likely to file malpractice suits. In fact, the opposite is true: Patients who feel they've been treated disrespectfully file *more* malpractice suits than those who feel they have been treated with dignity. By making apologies for medical mistakes inadmissible during a trial, the law would let doctors express regrets without worrying that doing so would hurt them in court.

Managers who unwaveringly believe that knowledge is power may fear that engaging in process fairness will weaken their power. After all, if employees have a voice in deciding how things should be run, who needs a manager? Managers sometimes do run the risk of losing power when they involve others in decision making. But usually the practice of process fairness increases power and influence. When employees feel that they are heard in the decision-making process, they are more likely to support—rather than merely comply with—those decisions, their bosses, and the organization as a whole.

The desire to avoid uncomfortable situations is another reason managers fail to practice process fairness. As Robert Folger of the University of Central Florida has suggested, managers who plan and implement tough decisions often experience conflicting emotions. They might want to approach the affected parties out of sympathy and to explain the thinking behind a decision, but the desire to avoid them is also strong. Andy Molinsky at Brandeis University and Harvard Business School's Joshua Margolis analyzed why managers find it so hard to perform necessary evils (such as laying off employees and delivering other bad news) with interpersonal sensitivity, which is an important element of process fairness. Leaders in this situation have to manage their own internal dramas, including feelings of guilt (for, say, making poor strategic decisions that led to the downsizing) and anxiety (about having sufficient interpersonal sensitivity to accomplish the task gracefully). Instead of wrestling with those uncomfortable emotions, many managers find it easier to sidestep the issue—and the people affected by it—altogether.

"Emotional contagion" also comes into play in these situations. Just as we tend to laugh when we see others laugh, even when we don't know why, we also involuntarily feel anxious or sad when those around us feel that way—and that's uncomfortable. No wonder so many managers avoid people in emotional pain. Unfortunately, such avoidance makes it very unlikely that they will practice process fairness.

I can understand how managers feel. Several years ago, I was working with a telecommunications organization after the first layoffs in the company's history. The CEO and his senior management team wanted me to talk to the midlevel managers about how the layoffs would affect the people who remained and what they could do to help their direct reports "get over it." Feeling betrayed and fearful, however, the midlevel managers were in no mood to help others return to business as usual. They identified me with the problem and implied that I was partly responsible for the decision to downsize. That was a moment of real insight for me: Trying to counsel this unhappy and suspicious group, I completely understood the discomfort that managers experience when they're called on to act compassionately toward people who feel aggrieved. It was much harder than I expected.

The senior managers of the company admitted to me that they were tempted to avoid the rank and file—partly out of guilt and partly because they doubted whether they would be able to keep a cool enough head to practice process fairness. That's a natural response, but ignoring negative emotions only keeps them swirling around longer. When senior managers made themselves more accessible to their workforce, employees reacted positively, and the organization developed a renewed sense of purpose.

Toward Process Fairness

Companies can take several steps to make fair process the norm.

Address the knowledge gaps

Managers need to be warned about the negative emotions they might experience when practicing fair process. Merely acknowledging that it is legitimate to feel like fleeing the scene can help managers withstand the impulse to do so. Studies have shown that people can tolerate negative experiences more easily when they expect them. Just as forewarned surgical patients have been found to experience less postoperative pain, forewarned managers may be better able to cope with (and hence not act on) their negative emotions.

Furthermore, managers are more likely to endure a difficult process when they know that the effort will have a tangible payoff. But it's not enough for managers to be vaguely aware that process fairness is cost effective. Corporate executives should educate them about all the financial benefits, using charts and figures, just as they would when making a business case for other important organizational initiatives.

Invest in training

Study after study has shown that fair-process training can make a big difference. Subordinates of the trained managers, for instance, are not only significantly less likely to steal or to resign from the organization, but they are also more likely to go the extra mile—aiding coworkers who have been absent, helping orient new employees, assisting supervisors with their duties, and working overtime. Several studies by Jerald Greenberg have even found that employees whose managers underwent process fairness training suffered significantly less insomnia when coping with stressful work conditions.

Daniel Skarlicki, of the University of British Columbia's Sauder School of Business, and Gary Latham, of the University of Toronto's Joseph L. Rotman School of Management, have identified some factors of an effective process fairness training program. Participants respond better to active guidance than to a lecture on the benefits of improved process fairness. That's why it's particularly effective to give trainees specific instructions on what they need to do and how they need to do it, such as how to detect resistance to a new strategic initiative. After the participants have practiced these behaviors, give them feedback and let them try again.

When I was working with an executive at a utility company several years ago, for example, I noticed that she made a common mistake: She didn't tell others that she had seriously considered their opinions before making her decisions, even though she had. I advised her to preface her explanations by saying explicitly that she had "given their input some serious thought." Six months later, she told me my advice had been priceless. She learned that it's not enough for executives just to *be* fair, they also have to be *seen* as fair.

Training is most effective when it's delivered in several installments rather than all at once. For example, one successful program consisted of a two-hour session each week for eight weeks, along with assigned role-playing homework. That way, participants could receive feedback from instructors during the formal training sessions and from their peers in between meetings. As with most constructive feedback, referring to behaviors ("You never explained why you made this decision") rather than to traits ("You came across as condescending") proved to be most compelling.

Both the process and the outcome of the training need to be communicated to participants—but not at the same time. Before the sessions begin, focus on the outcome. Participants are likely to be far more engaged if they are told that the program will help them gain their employees' commitment to strategy implementation than if they are told it will help them communicate that they've seriously considered other people's points of view. During the course, however, focus on process. Thinking about expected outcomes (improved strategy implementation, for instance) can distract people from learning the specific practical skills they need (such as how to involve people in decision making) to achieve the desired results.

Finally, it is important for trainees to maintain expectations that are both optimistic and realistic. Once again, the distinction between outcome and process is useful to keep in mind. You can generate optimism by focusing on the outcomes: Touting the improvements that previous trainees have made should help people feel positive about their own chances for growth. And you can inject realism by focusing on the process: Behavioral change is difficult and rarely takes a linear course. Trainees shouldn't expect to get better at process fairness day by day; but, if they keep working at it, they will improve. I suggest trainees ask themselves three months after the program if they are practicing process fairness more on average than they were three months prior to it. Conducting after-action reviews also helps managers continue to hone their skills long after the training sessions are over.

Make process fairness a top priority

Like most managerial behaviors, the practice of process fairness must begin at the top. When senior managers explain why they have made certain strategic decisions, make themselves available for honest two-way communication with the rank and file, involve employees in decision making, provide ample advance notice of change, and treat people's concerns with respect, the practice of process fairness is likely to spread like wildfire throughout the rest of the organization.

By modeling process fairness, senior management does more than communicate organizational values; it also sends a message about "the art of the possible." People are more likely to try to tackle difficult challenges when they see others whom they respect doing so. In one company that was trying to implement a much-needed restructuring, senior executives effectively served as role models not only by describing the mixed feelings they had about practicing process fairness but also by articulating the process they went through that ultimately convinced them to do so. The message they sent was that it was legitimate for operational managers to have mixed emotions, but, at the end of the day, the reasons in favor of practicing process fairness prevailed.

In addition to acting as role models, senior managers may communicate the value they place on process fairness by making its practice a legitimate topic of conversation throughout the organization. I worked with one company, for example, that selected its employee of the month based on process fairness skills as well as bottom-line results. Other organizations have made managers' annual pay raises partly dependent on 360-degree feedback about how they plan and implement decisions, in which perceptions of process fairness figure prominently.

Recent corporate scandals show that giving workforces outcome-only directives ("I don't care how you get there, just get there") can be disastrous. Forward-thinking organizations care not only about the outcomes their managers produce but also about the fairness of the process they use to achieve them. This is not a call for micromanagement. Just as there is usually more than one way to produce financial results, there is more than one way to involve people in decision making, to communicate why certain actions are being undertaken, and to express thoughtfulness and concern.

There is a moral imperative for companies to practice process fairness. It is, simply put, the right thing to do. As such, process fairness is the responsibility of all executives, at all levels, and in all functions; it cannot be delegated to HR. But with that moral responsibility comes business opportunity. An executive must minimize the costs of decisions that might threaten employees and maximize the benefits of decisions that may be sources of opportunity for them. In both instances, practicing process fairness will help get you there. The sooner you realize it, the better off you and your company will be.

Originally published in March 2006. Reprint R0603H

Why Good Leaders Make Bad Decisions

by Andrew Campbell, Jo Whitehead, and Sydney Finkelstein

DECISION MAKING LIES AT THE HEART of our personal and professional lives. Every day we make decisions. Some are small, domestic, and innocuous. Others are more important, affecting people's lives, livelihoods, and well-being. Inevitably, we make mistakes along the way. The daunting reality is that enormously important decisions made by intelligent, responsible people with the best information and intentions are sometimes hopelessly flawed.

Consider Jürgen Schrempp, CEO of Daimler-Benz. He led the merger of Chrysler and Daimler against internal opposition. Nine years later, Daimler was forced to virtually give Chrysler away in a private equity deal. Steve Russell, chief executive of Boots, the UK drugstore chain, launched a health care strategy designed to differentiate the stores from competitors and grow through new health care services such as dentistry. It turned out, though, that Boots managers did not have the skills needed to succeed in health care services, and many of these markets offered little profit potential. The strategy contributed to Russell's early departure from the top job. Brigadier General Matthew Broderick, chief of the Homeland Security Operations Center, who was responsible for alerting

President Bush and other senior government officials if Hurricane Katrina breached the levees in New Orleans, went home on Monday, August 29, 2005, after reporting that they seemed to be holding, despite multiple reports of breaches.

All these executives were highly qualified for their jobs, and yet they made decisions that soon seemed clearly wrong. Why? And more important, how can we avoid making similar mistakes? This is the topic we've been exploring for the past four years, and the journey has taken us deep into a field called decision neuroscience. We began by assembling a database of 83 decisions that we felt were flawed at the time they were made. From our analysis of these cases, we concluded that flawed decisions start with errors of judgment made by influential individuals. Hence we needed to understand how these errors of judgment occur.

In the following pages, we will describe the conditions that promote errors of judgment and explore ways organizations can build protections into the decision-making process to reduce the risk of mistakes. We'll conclude by showing how two leading companies applied the approach we describe. To put all this in context, however, we first need to understand just how the human brain forms its judgments.

How the Brain Trips Up

We depend primarily on two hardwired processes for decision making. Our brains assess what's going on using pattern recognition, and we react to that information—or ignore it—because of emotional tags that are stored in our memories. Both of these processes are normally reliable; they are part of our evolutionary advantage. But in certain circumstances, both can let us down.

Pattern recognition is a complex process that integrates information from as many as 30 different parts of the brain. Faced with a new situation, we make assumptions based on prior experiences and judgments. Thus a chess master can assess a chess game and choose a high-quality move in as little as six seconds by drawing on patterns he or she has seen before. But pattern recognition can also

Idea in Brief

- Leaders make decisions largely through unconscious processes that neuroscientists call pattern recognition and emotional tagging. These processes usually make for quick, effective decisions, but they can be distorted by self-interest, emotional attachments, or misleading memories.
- Managers need to find systematic ways to recognize the sources of bias—what the authors call "red flag conditions"—and then design safeguards that introduce more analysis, greater debate, or stronger governance.
- By using the approach described in this article, companies will avoid many flawed decisions that are caused by the way our brains operate.

mislead us. When we're dealing with seemingly familiar situations, our brains can cause us to think we understand them when we don't.

What happened to Matthew Broderick during Hurricane Katrina is instructive. Broderick had been involved in operations centers in Vietnam and in other military engagements, and he had led the Homeland Security Operations Center during previous hurricanes. These experiences had taught him that early reports surrounding a major event are often false: It's better to wait for the "ground truth" from a reliable source before acting. Unfortunately, he had no experience with a hurricane hitting a city built below sea level.

By late on August 29, some 12 hours after Katrina hit New Orleans, Broderick had received 17 reports of major flooding and levee breaches. But he also had gotten conflicting information. The Army Corps of Engineers had reported that it had no evidence of levee breaches, and a late afternoon CNN report from Bourbon Street in the French Quarter had shown city dwellers partying and claiming they had dodged the bullet. Broderick's pattern-recognition process told him that these contrary reports were the ground truth he was looking for. So before going home for the night, he issued a situation report stating that the levees had not been breached, although he did add that further assessment would be needed the next day.

Idea in Practice

Leaders make quick decisions by recognizing patterns in the situations they encounter, bolstered by emotional associations attached to those patterns. Most of the time, the process works well, but it can result in serious mistakes when judgments are biased.

> ***Example:*** When Wang Laboratories launched its own personal computer, founder An Wang chose to create a proprietary operating system even though the IBM PC was clearly becoming the standard. This blunder was influenced by his belief that IBM had cheated him early in his career, which made him reluctant to consider using a system linked to an IBM product.

To guard against distorted decision making and strengthen the decision process, get the help of an independent person to identify which decision makers are likely to be affected by self-interest, emotional attachments, or misleading memories.

> ***Example:*** The about-to-be-promoted head of the cosmetics business at one Indian company was considering whether to appoint her number two as her successor. She recognized that her judgment might be distorted by her attachment to her colleague and by her vested interest in keeping her workload down during her transition. The executive asked a headhunter to evaluate her colleague and to determine whether better candidates could be found externally.

If the risk of distorted decision making is high, companies need to build safeguards into the decision process: Expose decision makers to additional experience and analysis, design in more debate and opportunities for challenge, and add more oversight.

> ***Example:*** In helping the CEO make an important strategic decision, the chairman of one global chemical company encouraged the chief executive to seek advice from investment bankers, set up a project team to analyze options, and create a steering committee that included the chairman and the CFO to generate the decision.

Emotional tagging is the process by which emotional information attaches itself to the thoughts and experiences stored in our memories. This emotional information tells us whether to pay attention to something or not, and it tells us what sort of action we should be contemplating (immediate or postponed, fight or flight). When the parts of our brains controlling emotions are damaged, we can see how important emotional tagging is: Neurological research shows that we become slow and incompetent decision makers even though we can retain the capacity for objective analysis.

Like pattern recognition, emotional tagging helps us reach sensible decisions most of the time. But it, too, can mislead us. Take the case of Wang Laboratories, the top company in the word-processing industry in the early 1980s. Recognizing that his company's future was threatened by the rise of the personal computer, founder An Wang built a machine to compete in this sector. Unfortunately, he chose to create a proprietary operating system despite the fact that the IBM PC was clearly becoming the dominant standard in the industry. This blunder, which contributed to Wang's demise a few years later, was heavily influenced by An Wang's dislike of IBM. He believed he had been cheated by IBM over a new technology he had invented early in his career. These feelings made him reject a software platform linked to an IBM product even though the platform was provided by a third party, Microsoft.

Why doesn't the brain pick up on such errors and correct them? The most obvious reason is that much of the mental work we do is unconscious. This makes it hard to check the data and logic we use when we make a decision. Typically, we spot bugs in our personal software only when we see the results of our errors in judgment. Matthew Broderick found out that his ground-truth rule of thumb was an inappropriate response to Hurricane Katrina only after it was too late. An Wang found out that his preference for proprietary software was flawed only after Wang's personal computer failed in the market.

Compounding the problem of high levels of unconscious thinking is the lack of checks and balances in our decision making. Our brains do not naturally follow the classical textbook model: Lay out the options, define the objectives, and assess each option against each objective. Instead, we analyze the situation using pattern recognition and arrive at a decision to act or not by using emotional tags. The two processes happen almost instantaneously. Indeed, as the research of psychologist Gary Klein shows, our brains leap to conclusions and are reluctant to consider alternatives. Moreover, we are particularly bad at revisiting our initial assessment of a situation—our initial frame.

An exercise we frequently run at Ashridge Business School shows how hard it is to challenge the initial frame. We give students a case that presents a new technology as a good business opportunity. Often, a team works many hours before it challenges this frame and starts, correctly, to see the new technology as a major threat to the company's dominant market position. Even though the financial model consistently calculates negative returns from launching the new technology, some teams never challenge their original frame and end up proposing aggressive investments.

Raising the Red Flag

In analyzing how it is that good leaders made bad judgments, we found they were affected in all cases by three factors that either distorted their emotional tags or encouraged them to see a false pattern. We call these factors "red flag conditions."

The first and most familiar red flag condition, *the presence of inappropriate self-interest,* typically biases the emotional importance we place on information, which in turn makes us readier to perceive the patterns we want to see. Research has shown that even well-intentioned professionals, such as doctors and auditors, are unable to prevent self-interest from biasing their judgments of which medicine to prescribe or opinion to give during an audit.

The second, somewhat less familiar condition is *the presence of distorting attachments.* We can become attached to people, places, and things, and these bonds can affect the judgments we form about both the situation we face and the appropriate actions to take. The reluctance executives often feel to sell a unit they've worked in nicely captures the power of inappropriate attachments.

The final red flag condition is *the presence of misleading memories.* These are memories that seem relevant and comparable to the current situation but lead our thinking down the wrong path. They can cause us to overlook or undervalue some important differentiating factors, as Matthew Broderick did when he gave too little thought to the implications of a hurricane hitting a city below sea level. The chance of being misled by memories is intensified by any emotional tags we have attached to the past experience. If our decisions in the previous similar experience worked well, we'll be all the more likely to overlook key differences.

That's what happened to William Smithburg, former chairman of Quaker Oats. He acquired Snapple because of his vivid memories of Gatorade, Quaker's most successful deal. Snapple, like Gatorade, appeared to be a new drinks company that could be improved with Quaker's marketing and management skills. Unfortunately, the similarities between Snapple and Gatorade proved to be superficial, which meant that Quaker ended up destroying rather than creating value. In fact, Snapple was Smithburg's worst deal.

Of course, part of what we are saying is common knowledge: People have biases, and it's important to manage decisions so that these biases balance out. Many experienced leaders do this already. But we're arguing here that, given the way the brain works, we cannot rely on leaders to spot and safeguard against their own errors in judgment. For important decisions, we need a deliberate, structured way to identify likely sources of bias—those red flag conditions—and we need to strengthen the group decision-making process.

Consider the situation faced by Rita Chakra, head of the cosmetics business of Choudry Holdings (the names of the companies and people cited in this and the following examples have been disguised). She was promoted head of the consumer products division and needed to decide whether to promote her number two into her cosmetics job or recruit someone from outside. Can we anticipate any potential red flags in this decision? Yes, her emotional tags could be unreliable because of a distorting attachment she may have to her colleague or an inappropriate self-interest she could have in keeping her workload down while changing jobs. Of course we don't know for certain whether Rita feels this attachment or holds that vested interest. And since the greater part of decision making is unconscious, Rita would not know either. What we do know is that there is a risk. So how should Rita protect herself, or how should her boss help her protect herself?

The simple answer is to involve someone else—someone who has no inappropriate attachments or self-interest. This could be Rita's boss, the head of human resources, a headhunter, or a trusted colleague. That person could challenge her thinking, force her to review her logic, encourage her to consider options, and possibly even champion a solution she would find uncomfortable. Fortunately, in this situation, Rita was already aware of some red flag conditions, and so she involved a headhunter to help her evaluate her colleague and external candidates. In the end, Rita did appoint her colleague but only after checking to see if her judgment was biased.

We've found many leaders who intuitively understand that their thinking or their colleagues' thinking can be distorted. But few leaders do so in a structured way, and as a result many fail to provide sufficient safeguards against bad decisions. Let's look now at a couple of companies that approached the problem of decision bias systematically by recognizing and reducing the risk posed by red flag conditions.

Safeguarding Against Your Biases

A European multinational we'll call Global Chemicals had an underperforming division. The management team in charge of the division had twice promised a turnaround and twice failed to deliver. The CEO, Mark Thaysen, was weighing his options.

This division was part of Thaysen's growth strategy. It had been assembled over the previous five years through two large and four smaller acquisitions. Thaysen had led the two larger acquisitions and appointed the managers who were struggling to perform. The chairman of the supervisory board, Olaf Grunweld, decided to consider whether Thaysen's judgment about the underperforming division might be biased and, if so, how he might help. Grunweld was not second-guessing Thaysen's thinking. He was merely alert to the possibility that the CEO's views might be distorted.

Grunweld started by looking for red flag conditions. (For a description of a process for identifying red flags, see the sidebar, "Identifying Red Flags.") Thaysen built the underperforming division, and his attachment to it might have made him reluctant to abandon the strategy or the team he had put in place. What's more, because in the past he had successfully supported the local managers during a tough turnaround in another division, Thaysen ran the risk of seeing the wrong pattern and unconsciously favoring the view that continued support was needed in this situation, too. Thus alerted to Thaysen's possible distorting attachments and potential misleading memories, Grunweld considered three types of safeguards to strengthen the decision process.

Injecting fresh experience or analysis

You can often counteract biases by exposing the decision maker to new information and a different take on the problem. In this instance, Grunweld asked an investment bank to tell Thaysen what value the company might get from selling the underperforming division. Grunweld felt this would encourage Thaysen to at least consider that radical option—a step Thaysen might too quickly dismiss if he had become overly attached to the unit or its management team.

Introducing further debate and challenge

This safeguard can ensure that biases are confronted explicitly. It works best when the power structure of the group debating the issue is balanced. While Thaysen's chief financial officer was a strong individual, Grunweld felt that the other members of the executive group would be likely to follow Thaysen's lead without challenging him. Moreover, the head of the underperforming division was a member of the executive group, making it hard for open debate to occur. So Grunweld proposed a steering committee consisting of himself, Thaysen, and the CFO. Even if Thaysen strongly pushed for a particular solution, Grunweld and the CFO would make sure his reasoning was properly challenged and debated. Grunweld also suggested that Thaysen set up a small project team, led by the head of strategy, to analyze all the options and present them to the steering committee.

Imposing stronger governance

The requirement that a decision be ratified at a higher level provides a final safeguard. Stronger governance does not eliminate distorted thinking, but it can prevent distortions from leading to a bad outcome. At Global Chemicals, the governance layer was the supervisory board. Grunweld realized, however, that its objectivity could be compromised because he was a member of both the board and the steering committee. So he asked two of his board colleagues to be ready to argue against the proposal emanating from the steering committee if they felt uncomfortable.

In the end, the steering committee proposed an outright sale of the division, a decision the board approved. The price received was well above expectations, convincing all that they had chosen the best option.

The chairman of Global Chemicals took the lead role in designing the decision process. That was appropriate given the importance of the decision. But many decisions are made at the operating level, where direct CEO involvement is neither feasible nor desirable. That was the case at Southern Electricity, a division of a larger U.S. utility. Southern consisted of three operating units and two powerful functions. Recent regulatory changes meant that prices could not be raised and might even fall. So managers were looking for ways to cut back on capital expenditures.

Division head Jack Williams recognized that the managers were also risk averse, preferring to replace equipment early with the best upgrades available. This, he realized, was a result of some high-profile breakdowns in the past, which had exposed individuals both to complaints from customers and to criticism from colleagues. Williams believed the emotional tags associated with these experiences might be distorting their judgment.

What could he do to counteract these effects? Williams rejected the idea of stronger governance; he felt that neither his management team nor the parent company's executives knew enough to do the job credibly. He also rejected additional analysis, because Southern's analysis was already rigorous. He concluded that he had to find

Identifying Red Flags

RED FLAGS ARE useful only if they can be spotted before a decision is made. How can you recognize them in complex situations? We have developed the following seven-step process:

1. **Lay out the range of options.** It's never possible to list them all. But it's normally helpful to note the extremes. These provide boundaries for the decision.

2. **List the main decision makers.** Who is going to be influential in making the judgment calls and the final choice? There may be only one or two people involved. But there could also be 10 or more.

3. **Choose one decision maker to focus on.** It's usually best to start with the most influential person. Then identify red flag conditions that might distort that individual's thinking.

4. **Check for inappropriate self-interest or distorting attachments.** Is any option likely to be particularly attractive or unattractive to the decision maker because of personal interests or attachments to people, places, or things? Do any of these interests or attachments conflict with the objectives of the main stakeholders?

5. **Check for misleading memories.** What are the uncertainties in this decision? For each area of uncertainty, consider whether the decision maker might draw on potentially misleading memories. Think about past experiences that could mislead, especially ones with strong emotional associations. Think also about previous judgments that could now be unsound, given the current situation.

6. **Repeat the analysis with the next most influential person.** In a complex case, it may be necessary to consider many more people, and the process may bring to light a long list of possible red flags.

7. **Review the list of red flags you have identified** and determine whether the brain's normally efficient pattern-recognition and emotional-tagging processes might be biased in favor of or against some options. If so, put one or more safeguards in place.

a way to inject more debate into the decision process and enable people who understood the details to challenge the thinking.

His first thought was to involve himself and his head of finance in the debates, but he didn't have time to consider the merits of hundreds of projects, and he didn't understand the details well enough to effectively challenge decisions earlier in the process than he currently was doing, at the final approval stage. Williams finally decided to get the unit and function heads to challenge one another, facilitated by a consultant. Rather than impose this process on his managers, Williams chose to share his thinking with them. Using the language of red flags, he was able to get them to see the problem without their feeling threatened. The new approach was very successful. The reduced capital-expenditure target was met with room to spare and without Williams having to make any of the tough judgment calls himself.

Because we now understand more about how the brain works, we can anticipate the circumstances in which errors of judgment may occur and guard against them. So rather than rely on the wisdom of experienced chairmen, the humility of CEOs, or the standard organizational checks and balances, we urge all involved in important decisions to explicitly consider whether red flags exist and, if they do, to lobby for appropriate safeguards. Decisions that involve no red flags need many fewer checks and balances and thus less bureaucracy. Some of those resources could then be devoted to protecting the decisions most at risk with more intrusive and robust protections.

Originally published in February 2009. Reprint R0902D

Building the Emotional Intelligence of Groups

by Vanessa Urch Druskat and Steven B. Wolff

WHEN MANAGERS FIRST STARTED HEARING ABOUT the concept of emotional intelligence in the 1990s, scales fell from their eyes. The basic message, that effectiveness in organizations is at least as much about EQ as IQ, resonated deeply; it was something that people knew in their guts but that had never before been so well articulated. Most important, the idea held the potential for positive change. Instead of being stuck with the hand they'd been dealt, people could take steps to enhance their emotional intelligence and make themselves more effective in their work and personal lives.

Indeed, the concept of emotional intelligence had real impact. The only problem is that so far emotional intelligence has been viewed only as an individual competency, when the reality is that most work in organizations is done by teams. And if managers have one pressing need today, it's to find ways to make teams work better.

It is with real excitement, therefore, that we share these findings from our research: individual emotional intelligence has a group analog, and it is just as critical to groups' effectiveness. Teams can develop greater emotional intelligence and, in so doing, boost their overall performance.

Why Should Teams Build Their Emotional Intelligence?

No one would dispute the importance of making teams work more effectively. But most research about how to do so has focused on identifying the task processes that distinguish the most successful teams—that is, specifying the need for cooperation, participation, commitment to goals, and so forth. The assumption seems to be that, once identified, these processes can simply be imitated by other teams, with similar effect. It's not true. By analogy, think of it this way: a piano student can be taught to play Minuet in G, but he won't become a modern-day Bach without knowing music theory and being able to play with heart. Similarly, the real source of a great team's success lies in the fundamental conditions that allow effective task processes to emerge—and that cause members to engage in them wholeheartedly.

Our research tells us that three conditions are essential to a group's effectiveness: trust among members, a sense of group identity, and a sense of group efficacy. When these conditions are absent, going through the motions of cooperating and participating is still possible. But the team will not be as effective as it could be, because members will choose to hold back rather than fully engage. To be most effective, the team needs to create emotionally intelligent norms—the attitudes and behaviors that eventually become habits—that support behaviors for building trust, group identity, and group efficacy. The outcome is complete engagement in tasks. (For more on how emotional intelligence influences these conditions, see the sidebar "A Model of Team Effectiveness.")

Three Levels of Emotional Interaction

Make no mistake: a team with emotionally intelligent members does not necessarily make for an emotionally intelligent group. A team, like any social group, takes on its own character. So creating an upward, self-reinforcing spiral of trust, group identity, and group efficacy requires more than a few members who exhibit emotionally intelligent behavior. It requires a team atmosphere in which the norms build emotional capacity (the ability to respond

Idea in Brief

How does IDEO, the celebrated industrial-design firm, ensure that its teams consistently produce the most innovative products under intense deadline and budget pressures? By focusing on its teams' **emotional intelligence**—that powerful combination of self-management skills and ability to relate to others.

Many executives realize that EQ (emotional quotient) is as critical as IQ to an individual's effectiveness. But *groups'* emotional intelligence may be even more important, since most work gets done in teams.

A group's EI isn't simply the sum of its members'. Instead, it comes from norms that support awareness and regulation of emotions within and outside the team. These norms build trust, group identity, and a sense of group efficacy. Members feel that they work better *together* than individually.

Group EI norms build the foundation for true collaboration and cooperation—helping otherwise skilled teams fulfill their highest potential.

constructively in emotionally uncomfortable situations) and influence emotions in constructive ways.

Team emotional intelligence is more complicated than individual emotional intelligence because teams interact at more levels. To understand the differences, let's first look at the concept of individual emotional intelligence as defined by Daniel Goleman. In his definitive book *Emotional Intelligence*, Goleman explains the chief characteristics of someone with high EI; he or she is *aware* of emotions and able to *regulate* them—and this awareness and regulation are directed both *inward*, to one's self, and *outward*, to others. "Personal competence," in Goleman's words, comes from being aware of and regulating one's own emotions. "Social competence" is awareness and regulation of others' emotions.

A group, however, must attend to yet another level of awareness and regulation. It must be mindful of the emotions of its members, its own group emotions or moods, and the emotions of other groups and individuals outside its boundaries.

In this article, we'll explore how emotional incompetence at any of these levels can cause dysfunction. We'll also show how

Idea in Practice

To build a foundation for emotional intelligence, a group must be aware of and constructively regulate the emotions of:

- individual team members
- the whole group
- other key groups with whom it interacts.

How? By establishing EI norms—rules for behavior that are introduced by group leaders, training, or the larger organizational culture. Here are some examples of norms—and what they look like in action—from IDEO:

Emotions of . . .	To Hone Awareness . . .	To Regulate . . .	IDEO Examples
Individual Team Members	Understand the sources of individuals' behavior and take steps to address problematic behavior. Encourage all group members to share their perspectives before making key decisions.	Handle confrontation constructively. If team members fall short, call them on it by letting them know the group needs them. Treat each other in a caring way—acknowledge when someone is upset; show appreciation and respect.	Awareness: A project leader notices a designer's frustration over a marketing decision and initiates negotiations to resolve the issue. Regulation: During brainstorming sessions, participants pelt colleagues with soft toys if they prematurely judge ideas.

establishing specific group norms that create awareness and regulation of emotion at these three levels can lead to better outcomes. First, we'll focus on the individual level—how emotionally intelligent groups work with their individual members' emotions. Next, we'll focus on the group level. And finally, we'll look at the cross-boundary level.

Working with Individuals' Emotions

Jill Kasper, head of her company's customer service department, is naturally tapped to join a new cross-functional team focused on enhancing the customer experience: she has extensive experience in

Emotions of . . .	To Hone Awareness . . .	To Regulate . . .	IDEO Examples
The Whole Group	Regularly assess the group's strengths, weaknesses, and modes of interaction. Invite reality checks from customers, colleagues, suppliers.	Create structures that let the group express its emotions. Cultivate an affirmative environment. Encourage proactive problem solving.	Awareness: Teams work closely with customers to determine what needs improvement. Regulation: "Fingerblaster" toys scattered around the office let people have fun and vent stress.
Other Key Groups	Designate team members as liaisons to key outside constituencies. Identify and support other groups' expectations and needs.	Develop cross-boundary relationships to gain outsiders' confidence. Know the broader social and political context in which your group must succeed. Show your appreciation of other groups.	Regulation: IDEO built such a good relationship with an outside fabricator that it was able to call on it for help during a crisis—on the weekend.

and a real passion for customer service. But her teammates find she brings little more than a bad attitude to the table. At an early brainstorming session, Jill sits silent, arms crossed, rolling her eyes. Whenever the team starts to get energized about an idea, she launches into a detailed account of how a similar idea went nowhere in the past. The group is confused: this is the customer service star they've been hearing about? Little do they realize she feels insulted by the very formation of the team. To her, it implies she hasn't done her job well enough.

When a member is not on the same emotional wavelength as the rest, a team needs to be emotionally intelligent vis-à-vis that individual. In part, that simply means being aware of the problem. Having a

A Model of Team Effectiveness

STUDY AFTER STUDY has shown that teams are more creative and productive when they can achieve high levels of participation, cooperation, and collaboration among members. But interactive behaviors like these aren't easy to legislate. Our work shows that three basic conditions need to be present before such behaviors can occur: mutual trust among members, a sense of group identity (a feeling among members that they belong to a unique and worthwhile group), and a sense of group efficacy (the belief that the team can perform well and that group members are more effective working together than apart).

At the heart of these three conditions are emotions. Trust, a sense of identity, and a feeling of efficacy arise in environments where emotion is well handled, so groups stand to benefit by building their emotional intelligence.

Group emotional intelligence isn't a question of dealing with a necessary evil—catching emotions as they bubble up and promptly suppressing them. Far from it. It's about bringing emotions deliberately to the surface and understanding how they affect the team's work. It's also about behaving in ways that build relationships both inside and outside the team and that strengthen the team's ability to face challenges. Emotional intelligence means exploring, embracing, and ultimately relying on emotion in work that is, at the end of the day, deeply human.

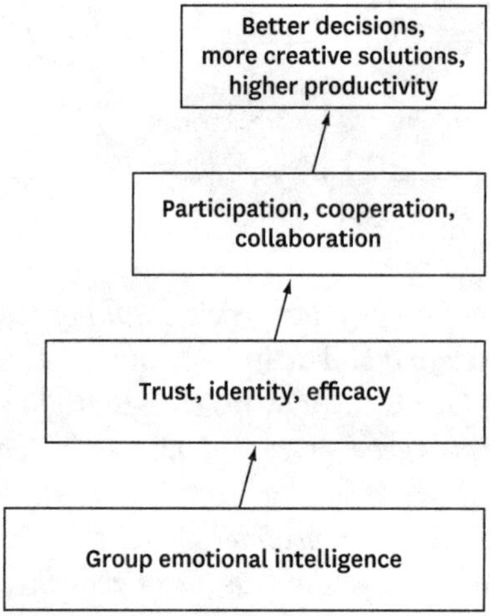

norm that encourages interpersonal understanding might facilitate an awareness that Jill is acting out of defensiveness. And picking up on this defensiveness is necessary if the team wants to make her understand its desire to amplify her good work, not negate it.

Some teams seem to be able to do this naturally. At Hewlett-Packard, for instance, we learned of a team that was attempting to cross-train its members. The idea was that if each member could pinch-hit on everyone else's job, the team could deploy efforts to whatever task required the most attention. But one member seemed very uncomfortable with learning new skills and tasks; accustomed to being a top producer in his own job, he hated not knowing how to do a job perfectly. Luckily, his teammates recognized his discomfort, and rather than being annoyed, they redoubled their efforts to support him. This team benefited from a group norm it had established over time emphasizing interpersonal understanding. The norm had grown out of the group's realization that working to accurately hear and understand one another's feelings and concerns improved member morale and a willingness to cooperate.

Many teams build high emotional intelligence by taking pains to consider matters from an individual member's perspective. Think of a situation where a team of four must reach a decision; three favor one direction and the fourth favors another. In the interest of expedience, many teams in this situation would move directly to a majority vote. But a more emotionally intelligent group would pause first to hear out the objection. It would also ask if everyone were completely behind the decision, even if there appeared to be consensus. Such groups would ask, "Are there any perspectives we haven't heard yet or thought through completely?"

Perspective taking is a team behavior that teamwork experts discuss often—but not in terms of its emotional consequence. Many teams are trained to use perspective-taking techniques to make decisions or solve problems (a common tool is affinity diagramming). But these techniques may or may not improve a group's emotional intelligence. The problem is that many of these techniques consciously attempt to remove emotion from the process by collecting and combining perspectives in a mechanical way. A more effective approach to perspective taking is to ensure that team members see one another making the effort to grapple with perspectives; that way, the team has a better chance of creating the kind of trust that leads to greater participation among members.

An executive team at the Hay Group, a consulting firm, engages in the kind of deep perspective taking we're describing. The team has done role-playing exercises in which members adopt others' opinions and styles of interaction. It has also used a "storyboarding" technique, in which each member creates a small poster representing his or her ideas. As team members will attest, these methods and others have helped the group build trust and increase participation.

Regulating Individuals' Emotions

Interpersonal understanding and perspective taking are two ways that groups can become more aware of their members' perspectives and feelings. But just as important as awareness is the ability to regulate those emotions—to have a positive impact on how they are expressed and even on how individual team members feel. We're not talking about imposing groupthink or some other form of manipulation here—clearly, the goal must be to balance the team's cohesion with members' individuality. We're simply acknowledging that people take their emotional cues from those around them. Something that seems upsetting initially can seem not so bad—or ten times worse—depending on whether one's colleagues are inclined to smooth feathers or fan flames. The most constructive way of regulating team members' emotions is by establishing norms in the group for both confrontation and caring.

It may seem illogical to suggest that an emotionally intelligent group must engage in confrontation, but it's not. Inevitably, a team member will indulge in behavior that crosses the line, and the team must feel comfortable calling the foul. In one manufacturing team we studied, a member told us about the day she selfishly decided to extend her break. Before long, one of her teammates stormed into the break room, saying, "What are you doing in here? Get back out on the floor—your team needs you!" The woman had overstepped the bounds, and she got called on it. There were no hard feelings, because the woman knew the group valued her contributions.

Some teams also find that a little humor helps when pointing out errant behavior. Teasing someone who is habitually late for meetings, for instance, can make that person aware of how important timeliness is to the group. Done right, confrontation can be seen in a positive light; it's a way for the group to say, "We want you in—we need your contribution." And it's especially important when a team must work together on a long-term assignment. Without confrontation, disruptive behavior can fester and erode a sense of trust in a team.

Establishing norms that reinforce caring behavior is often not very difficult and usually a matter of concentrating on little things. When an individual is upset, for example, it may make all the difference to have group members acknowledge that person's feelings. We saw this in a meeting where one team member arrived angry because the time and place of the meeting was very inconvenient for him. When another member announced the sacrifice the man had made to be there, and thanked him, the man's attitude turned around 180 degrees. In general, a caring orientation includes displaying positive regard, appreciation, and respect for group members through behaviors such as support, validation, and compassion.

Interpersonal understanding, perspective taking, confrontation, caring—these norms build trust and a sense of group identity among members. And all of them can be established in teams where they don't arise naturally. You may ask, But is it really worth all the effort? Does it make sense to spend managerial time fostering new norms to accommodate a few prickly personalities? Of course it does. Teams are at the very foundation of an organization, and they won't work effectively without mutual trust and a common commitment to goals.

Working with Group Emotions

Chris couldn't believe it, but he was requesting a reassignment. The team he was on was doing good work, staying on budget, and hitting all its deadlines—though not always elegantly. Its leader, Stan Evans, just got a promotion. So why was being on the team such a downer? At the last major status meeting, they should have been serving champagne—so much had been achieved. Instead, everyone was thoroughly dispirited over a setback they hadn't foreseen, which turned out later to be no big deal. It seemed no matter what happened, the group griped. The team even saw Stan's promotion in a negative light: "Oh, so I guess management wants to keep a closer eye on us" and "I hear Stan's new boss doesn't back this project." Chris had a friend on another team who was happy to put in a good word for him. The work was inherently less interesting—but hey, at least they were having fun.

Some teams suffer because they aren't aware of emotions at the group level. Chris's team, for instance, isn't aware of all it has achieved, and it doesn't acknowledge that it has fallen into a malaise. In our study of effective teams, we've found that having norms for group self-awareness—of emotional states, strengths and weaknesses, modes of interaction, and task processes—is a critical part of group emotional intelligence that facilitates group efficacy. Teams gain it both through self-evaluation and by soliciting feedback from others.

Self-evaluation can take the form of a formal event or a constant activity. At Sherwin Williams, a group of managers was starting a new initiative that would require higher levels of teamwork. Group members hired a consultant, but before the consultant arrived, they met to assess their strengths and weaknesses as a team. They found that merely articulating the issues was an important step toward building their capabilities.

A far less formal method of raising group emotional awareness is through the kind of activity we saw at the Veterans Health Administration's Center for Leadership and Development. Managers there have developed a norm in which they are encouraged to speak up when they feel the group is not being productive. For example, if there's a post-lunch lull and people on the team are low on energy, someone might say, "Don't we look like a bunch of sad sacks?" With attention called to it, the group makes an effort to refocus.

Emotionally competent teams don't wear blinders; they have the emotional capacity to face potentially difficult information and actively seek opinions on their task processes, progress, and performance from the outside. For some teams, feedback may come directly from customers. Others look to colleagues within the company, to suppliers, or to professional peers. A group of designers we studied routinely posts its work in progress on walls throughout the building, with invitations to comment and critique. Similarly, many advertising agencies see annual industry competitions as a valuable source of feedback on their creative teams' work.

Regulating Group Emotions

Many teams make conscious efforts to build team spirit. Team-building outings, whether purely social or Outward Bound–style physical challenges, are popular methods for building this sense of collective enthusiasm. What's going on here is that teams and their leaders recognize they can improve a team's overall attitude—that is, they are regulating group-level emotion. And while the focus of a team-building exercise is often not directly related to a group's actual work, the benefits are highly relevant: teams come away with higher emotional capacity and thus a greater ability to respond to emotional challenges.

The most effective teams we have studied go far beyond the occasional "ropes and rocks" off-site. They have established norms that strengthen their ability to respond effectively to the kind of emotional challenges a group confronts on a daily basis. The norms they favor accomplish three main things: they create resources for working with emotions, foster an affirmative environment, and encourage proactive problem solving.

Teams need resources that all members can draw on to deal with group emotions. One important resource is a common vocabulary. To use an example, a group member at the Veterans Health Administration picked up on another member's bad mood and told him that he was just "cranky" today. The "cranky" term stuck and became the group's gentle way of letting someone know that their negativity was having a bad effect on the group. Other resources may include helpful ways to vent frustrations. One executive team leader we interviewed described his team's practice of making time for a "wailing wall"—a few minutes of whining and moaning about some setback. Releasing and acknowledging those negative emotions, the leader says, allows the group to refocus its attention on the parts of the situation it can control and channel its energy in a positive direction. But sometimes, venting takes more than words. We've seen more than one intense workplace outfitted with toys—like soft projectile shooters—that have been used in games of cube warfare.

Perhaps the most obvious way to build emotional capacity through regulating team-level emotion is simply to create an affirmative environment. Everyone values a team that, when faced with a challenge, responds with a can-do attitude. Again, it's a question of having the right group norms—in this case, favoring optimism, and positive images and interpretations over negative ones. This doesn't always come naturally to a team, as one executive we interviewed at the Hay Group knows. When external conditions create a cycle of negativity among group members, he takes it upon himself to change the atmosphere of the group. He consciously resists the temptation to join the complaining and blaming and instead tries to reverse the cycle with a positive, constructive note.

One of the most powerful norms we have seen for building a group's ability to respond to emotionally challenging situations is an emphasis on proactive problem solving. We saw a lot of this going on in a manufacturing team we observed at AMP Corporation. Much of what this team needed to hit its targets was out of its strict control. But rather than sit back and point fingers, the team worked hard to get what it needed from others, and in some cases, took matters into its own hands. In one instance, an alignment problem in a key machine was creating faulty products. The team studied the problem and approached the engineering group with its own suggested design for a part that might correct the problem. The device worked, and the number of defective products decreased significantly.

This kind of problem solving is valuable for many reasons. It obviously serves the company by removing one more obstacle to profitability. But, to the point of our work, it also shows a team in control of its own emotions. It refused to feel powerless and was eager to take charge.

Working with Emotions Outside the Group

Jim sighed. The "Bugs" team was at it again. Didn't they see that while they were high-fiving one another over their impressive productivity, the rest of the organization was paying for it? This time, in their self-managed wisdom, they'd decided to make a three months' supply of one component. No changeover meant no machine downtime and a record low cost per unit. But now the group downstream was swamped with inventory it didn't need and worried about shortages of something else. Jim braced himself for his visit to the floor. The Bugs didn't take criticism well; they seemed to think they were flawless and that everyone else was just trying to take them down a notch. And what was with that name, anyway? Some kind of inside joke, Jim guessed. Too bad nobody else got it.

The last kind of emotional intelligence any high-performing team should have relates to cross-boundary relationships. Just as individuals should be mindful of their own emotions and others', groups should look both inward and outward emotionally. In the case of the Bugs, the team is acting like a clique—creating close emotional ties within but ignoring the feelings, needs, and concerns of important individuals and teams in the broader organization.

Some teams have developed norms that are particularly helpful in making them aware of the broader organizational context. One practice is to have various team members act as liaisons to important constituencies. Many teams are already made up of members drawn from different parts of an organization, so a cross-boundary perspective comes naturally. Others need to work a little harder. One team we studied realized it would be important to understand the perspective of its labor union. Consequently, a team member from HR went to some lengths to discover the right channels for having a union member appointed to the group. A cross-boundary perspective is especially important in situations where a team's work will have significant impact on others in the organization—for example, where a team is asked to design an intranet to serve everyone's needs. We've seen many situations in which a team is so enamored of its solution that it is caught completely by surprise when others in the company don't share its enthusiasm.

Some of the most emotionally intelligent teams we have seen are so attuned to their broader organizational context that it affects how they frame and communicate their own needs and accomplishments. A team at the chemical-processing company KoSa, for example, felt it needed a new piece of manufacturing equipment, but senior management wasn't so sure the purchase was a priority. Aware that the decision makers were still on the fence, the team decided to emphasize the employee safety benefits of the new machine—just one aspect of its desirability to them, but an issue of paramount importance to management. At a plant safety meeting attended by high-level managers, they made the case that the equipment they were seeking would greatly reduce the risk of injury to workers. A few weeks later they got it.

Sometimes, a team must be particularly aware of the needs and feelings of another group within the organization. We worked with an information technology company where the hardware engineers worked separately from the software engineers to achieve the same goal—faster processing and fewer crashes. Each could achieve only so much independently. When finally a hardware team leader went out of his way to build relationships with the software people, the two teams began to cooperate—and together, they achieved 20% to 40% higher performance than had been targeted.

This kind of positive outcome can be facilitated by norms that encourage a group to recognize the feelings and needs of other groups. We saw effective norms for interteam awareness at a division of AMP, where each manufacturing team is responsible for a step in the manufacturing process and they need one another to complete the product on time. Team leaders there meet in the morning to understand the needs, resources, and schedules of each team. If one team is ahead and another is behind, they reallocate resources. Members of the faster team help the team that's behind and do so in a friendly way that empathizes with their situation and builds the relationship.

Most of the examples we've been citing show teams that are not only aware of but also able to influence outsiders' needs and perspectives. This ability to regulate emotion at the cross-boundary level is a group's version of the "social skills" so critical to individual emotional intelligence. It involves developing external relationships and gaining the confidence of outsiders, adopting an ambassadorial role instead of an isolationist one.

A manufacturing team we saw at KoSa displayed very high social skills in working with its maintenance team. It recognized that, when problems occurred in the plant, the maintenance team often had many activities on its plate. All things being equal, what would make the maintenance team consider this particular manufacturing group a high priority? Knowing a good relationship would be a factor, the manufacturing team worked hard to build good ties with the maintenance people. At one point, for instance, the manufacturing team showed its appreciation by nominating the maintenance team for "Team of the Quarter" recognition—and then doing all the letter writing and behind-the-scenes praising that would ultimately help the maintenance team win. In turn, the manufacturing team's good relationship with maintenance helped it become one of the highest producers in the plant.

A Model for Group Emotional Intelligence

We've been discussing the need for teams to learn to channel emotion effectively at the three levels of human interaction important to them: team to individual member, team to itself, and team to outside entities. Together, the norms we've been exploring help groups work with emotions productively and intelligently. Often, groups with emotionally intelligent members have norms like these in place, but it's unlikely any group would unconsciously come up with *all* the norms we have outlined. In other words, this is a model for group emotional intelligence that any work team could benefit from by applying it deliberately.

What would the ultimate emotionally intelligent team look like? Closest to the ideal are some of the teams we've seen at IDEO, the celebrated industrial design firm. IDEO's creative teams are responsible for the look and feel of products like Apple's first mouse, the Crest toothpaste tube, and the Palm V personal digital assistant. The firm routinely wins competitions for the form and function of its designs and even has a business that teaches creative problem-solving techniques to other companies.

The nature of IDEO's work calls for high group emotional intelligence. Under pressure of client deadlines and budget estimates, the company must deliver innovative, aesthetic solutions that balance human needs with engineering realities. It's a deep philosophical belief at IDEO that great design is best accomplished through the creative friction of diverse teams and not the solitary pursuit of brilliant individuals, so it's imperative that the teams at IDEO click. In our study of those teams, we found group norms supporting emotional intelligence at all three levels of our model.

First, the teams at IDEO are very aware of individual team members' emotions, and they are adept at regulating them. For example, an IDEO designer became very frustrated because someone from marketing was insisting a logo be applied to the designer's product, which he felt would ruin it visually. At a meeting about the product, the team's project leader picked up on the fact that something was wrong. The designer was sitting off by himself, and things "didn't look right." The project leader looked into the situation and then initiated a negotiation that led to a mutual solution.

IDEO team members also confront one another when they break norms. This is common during brainstorming sessions, where the rule is that people must defer judgment and avoid shooting down ideas. If someone breaks that norm, the team comes down on him in a playful yet forceful way (imagine being pelted by foam toys). Or if someone is out of line, the norm is to stand up and call her on it immediately. If a client is in the room, the confrontation is subtler—perhaps a kick under the chair.

Teams at IDEO also demonstrate strengths in group-focused emotional intelligence. To ensure they have a high level of self-awareness, teams constantly seek feedback from both inside and outside the organization. Most important, they work very closely with customers. If a design is not meeting customer expectations, the team finds out quickly and takes steps to modify it.

Regulating group emotion at IDEO often means providing outlets for stress. This is a company that believes in playing and having fun.

Several hundred finger blasters (a toy that shoots soft projectiles) have been placed around the building for employees to pick up and start shooting when they're frustrated. Indeed, the design firm's culture welcomes the expression of emotions, so it's not uncommon for someone—whether happy or angry—to stand up and yell. IDEO has even created fun office projects that people can work on if they need a break. For example, they might have a project to design the company holiday card or to design the "tourist stop" displays seen by visitors.

Finally, IDEO teams also have norms to ensure they are aware of the needs and concerns of people outside their boundaries and that they use that awareness to develop relationships with those individuals and groups. On display at IDEO is a curious model: a toy truck with plastic pieces on springs that pop out of the bed of the truck when a button is pressed. It turns out the model commemorates an incident that taught a variety of lessons. The story centers on a design team that had been working for three weeks on a very complex plastic enclosure for a product. Unfortunately, on the Thursday before a Monday client deadline, when an engineer was taking it to be painted, it slipped from his pickup bed and exploded on the road at 70 mph. The team was willing to work through the weekend to rebuild the part but couldn't finish it without the help of the outside fabricator it had used on the original. Because they had taken the time to build a good relationship with the fabricator, its people were willing to go above and beyond the call of duty. The lighthearted display was a way for teammates to show the engineer that all was forgiven—and a reminder to the rest of the organization of how a team in crisis can get by with a little help from its friends.

Where Do Norms Come From?

Not every company is as dependent on teams and their emotional intelligence as IDEO. But now more than ever, we see companies depending on teams for decisions and tasks that, in another time, would have been the work of individuals. And unfortunately, we also see them discovering that a team can have everything going

Building Norms for Three Levels of Group Emotional Intelligence

GROUP EMOTIONAL INTELLIGENCE IS ABOUT the small acts that make a big difference. It is not about a team member working all night to meet a deadline; it is about saying thank you for doing so. It is not about in-depth discussion of ideas; it is about asking a quiet member for his thoughts. It is not about harmony, lack of tension, and all members liking each other; it is about acknowledging when harmony is false, tension is unexpressed, and treating others with respect. The following table outlines some of the small things that groups can do to establish the norms that build group emotional intelligence.

Individual	Group	Cross-Boundary
Norms that create awareness of emotions		
Interpersonal understanding 1. Take time away from group tasks to get to know one another. 2. Have a "check in" at the beginning of the meeting—that is, ask how everyone is doing. 3. Assume that undesirable behavior takes place for a reason. Find out what that reason is. Ask questions and listen. Avoid negative attributions. 4. Tell your teammates what you're thinking and how you're feeling. ***Perspective taking*** 1. Ask whether everyone agrees with a decision. 2. Ask quiet members what they think. 3. Question decisions that come too quickly. 4. Appoint a devil's advocate.	***Team self-evaluation*** 1. Schedule time to examine team effectiveness. 2. Create measurable task and process objectives and then measure them. 3. Acknowledge and discuss group moods. 4. Communicate your sense of what is transpiring in the team. 5. Allow members to call a "process check." (For instance, a team member might say, "Process check: is this the most effective use of our time right now?") ***Seeking feedback*** 1. Ask your "customers" how you are doing. 2. Post your work and invite comments. 3. Benchmark your processes.	***Organizational understanding*** 1. Find out the concerns and needs of others in the organization. 2. Consider who can influence the team's ability to accomplish its goals. 3. Discuss the culture and politics in the organization. 4. Ask whether proposed team actions are congruent with the organization's culture and politics.

Individual	Group	Cross-Boundary
Norms that help regulate emotions		
Confronting 1. Set ground rules and use them to point out errant behavior. 2. Call members on errant behavior. 3. Create playful devices for pointing out such behavior. These often emerge from the group spontaneously. Reinforce them. ***Caring*** 1. Support members: volunteer to help them if they need it, be flexible, and provide emotional support. 2. Validate members' contributions. Let members know they are valued. 3. Protect members from attack. 4. Respect individuality and differences in perspectives. Listen. 5. Never be derogatory or demeaning.	***Creating resources for working with emotion*** 1. Make time to discuss difficult issues, and address the emotions that surround them. 2. Find creative, shorthand ways to acknowledge and express the emotion in the group. 3. Create fun ways to acknowledge and relieve stress and tension. 4. Express acceptance of members' emotions. ***Creating an affirmative environment*** 1. Reinforce that the team can meet a challenge. Be optimistic. For example, say things like, "We can get through this" or "Nothing will stop us." 2. Focus on what you can control. 3. Remind members of the group's important and positive mission. 4. Remind the group how it solved a similar problem before. 5. Focus on problem solving, not blaming. ***Solving problems proactively*** 1. Anticipate problems and address them before they happen. 2. Take the initiative to understand and get what you need to be effective. 3. Do it yourself if others aren't responding. Rely on yourself, not others.	***Building external relationships*** 1. Create opportunities for networking and interaction. 2. Ask about the needs of other teams. 3. Provide support for other teams. 4. Invite others to team meetings if they might have a stake in what you are doing.

for it—the brightest and most qualified people, access to resources, a clear mission—but still fail because it lacks group emotional intelligence.

Norms that build trust, group identity, and group efficacy are the key to making teams click. They allow an otherwise highly skilled and resourced team to fulfill its potential, and they can help a team faced with substantial challenges achieve surprising victories. So how do norms as powerful as the ones we've described in this article come about? In our research, we saw them being introduced from any of five basic directions: by formal team leaders, by informal team leaders, by courageous followers, through training, or from the larger organizational culture. (For more on how to establish the norms described in this article, see the sidebar "Building Norms for Three Levels of Group Emotional Intelligence.")

At the Hay Group, for example, it was the deliberate action of a team leader that helped one group see the importance of emotions to the group's overall effectiveness. Because this particular group was composed of managers from many different cultures, its leader knew he couldn't assume all the members possessed a high level of interpersonal understanding. To establish that norm, he introduced novelties like having a meeting without a table, using smaller groups, and conducting an inventory of team members' various learning styles.

Interventions like these can probably be done only by a formal team leader. The ways informal leaders or other team members enhance emotional intelligence are typically more subtle, though often just as powerful. Anyone might advance the cause, for example, by speaking up if the group appears to be ignoring an important perspective or feeling—or simply by doing his or her part to create an affirmative environment.

Training courses can also go a long way toward increasing emotional awareness and showing people how to regulate emotions. We know of many companies that now focus on emotional issues in leadership development courses, negotiation and communication workshops, and employee-assistance programs like those for stress management. These training programs can sensitize team members to the importance of establishing emotionally intelligent norms.

Finally, perhaps more than anything, a team can be influenced by a broader organizational culture that recognizes and celebrates employee emotion. This is clearly the case at IDEO and, we believe, at many of the companies creating the greatest value in the new economy. Unfortunately, it's the most difficult piece of the puzzle to put in place at companies that don't already have it. For organizations with long histories of employees checking their emotions at the door, change will occur, if at all, one team at a time.

Becoming Intelligent About Emotion

The research presented in this article arose from one simple imperative: in an era of teamwork, it's essential to figure out what makes teams work. Our research shows that, just like individuals, the most effective teams are emotionally intelligent ones—and that any team can attain emotional intelligence.

In this article, we've attempted to lay out a model for positive change, containing the most important types of norms a group can create to enhance its emotional intelligence. Teams, like all groups, operate according to such norms. By working to establish norms for emotional awareness and regulation at all levels of interaction, teams can build the solid foundation of trust, group identity, and group efficacy they need for true cooperation and collaboration—and high performance overall.

Originally published in March 2001. Reprint R0103E

The Price of Incivility

Lack of Respect Hurts Morale—and the Bottom Line.

by Christine Porath and Christine Pearson

RUDENESS AT WORK IS RAMPANT, and it's on the rise. Over the past 14 years we've polled thousands of workers about how they're treated on the job, and 98% have reported experiencing uncivil behavior. In 2011 half said they were treated rudely at least once a week—up from a quarter in 1998.

The costs chip away at the bottom line. Nearly everybody who experiences workplace incivility responds in a negative way, in some cases overtly retaliating. Employees are less creative when they feel disrespected, and many get fed up and leave. About half deliberately decrease their effort or lower the quality of their work. And incivility damages customer relationships. Our research shows that people are less likely to buy from a company with an employee they perceive as rude, whether the rudeness is directed at them or at other employees. Witnessing just a single unpleasant interaction leads customers to generalize about other employees, the organization, and even the brand.

We've interviewed employees, managers, HR executives, presidents, and CEOs. We've administered questionnaires, run experiments, led workshops, and spoken with doctors, lawyers, judges, law enforcement officers, architects, engineers, consultants, and coaches about how they've faced and handled incivility. And we've collected data from more than 14,000 people throughout the United States and Canada in order to track the prevalence, types, causes, costs, and cures of incivility at work. We know two things for certain: Incivility is expensive, and few organizations recognize or take action to curtail it.

In this article we'll discuss our findings, detail the costs, and propose some interventions. But first, let's look at the various shapes incivility can take.

Forms of Incivility

We've all heard of (or experienced) the "boss from hell." The stress of ongoing hostility from a manager takes a toll, sometimes a big one. We spoke with a man we'll call Matt, who reported to Larry—a volatile bully who insulted his direct reports, belittled their efforts, and blamed them for things over which they had no control. (The names in this article have been changed and the identities disguised.) Larry was rude to customers, too. When he accompanied Matt to one client's store, he told the owner, "I see you're carrying on your father's tradition. This store looked like sh-- then. And it looks like sh-- in your hands."

Matt's stress level skyrocketed. He took a risk and reported Larry to HR. (He wasn't the first to complain.) Called on the carpet, Larry failed to apologize, saying only that perhaps he "used an atomic bomb" when he "could have used a flyswatter." Weeks later Larry was named district manager of the year. Three days after that, Matt had a heart attack.

The conclusion of Matt's story is unusual, but unchecked rudeness is surprisingly common. We heard of one boss who was so routinely abusive that employees and suppliers had a code for alerting one another to his impending arrival ("The eagle has landed!"). The only positive aspect was that their shared dislike helped the employees forge close bonds. After the company died, in the late 1990s, its alums formed a network that thrives to this day.

In some cases an entire department is infected. Jennifer worked in an industry that attracted large numbers of educated young professionals willing to work for a pittance in order to be in a creative

Idea in Brief

Leaders can counter rudeness at work both by monitoring their own actions and by fostering civility in others.

Strategies for managing yourself include modeling good behavior and asking for feedback. Turn off your iPhone during meetings, pay attention to questions, and follow up on promises.

When it comes to managing the organization, you should hire for civility, teach it, create group norms, reward positive behavior, penalize rudeness, and seek out former employees for an honest assessment of your company's culture.

Failure to keep tabs on behavior can allow incivility to creep into everyday interactions—and could cost your organization millions in lost employees, lost customers, and lost productivity.

field. It was widely accepted that they had to pay their dues. The atmosphere included door slamming, side conversations, exclusion, and blatant disregard for people's time. Years later Jennifer still cringes as she remembers her boss screaming, "You made a mistake!" when she'd overlooked a minor typo in an internal memo. There was lots of attrition among low-level employees, but those who did stay seemed to absorb the behaviors they'd been subjected to, and they put newcomers through the same kind of abuse.

Fran was a senior executive in a global consumer products company. After several quarters of outstanding growth despite a down economy, she found herself confronted by a newcomer in the C-suite, Joe. For six months Fran had to jump through hoops to defend the business, even though it had defied stagnation. She never got an explanation for why she was picked on, and eventually she left, not for another job but to escape what she called "a soul-destroying experience."

Incivility can take much more subtle forms, and it is often prompted by thoughtlessness rather than actual malice. Think of the manager who sends e-mails during a presentation, or the boss who "teases" direct reports in ways that sting, or the team leader who takes credit for good news but points a finger at team members when something goes wrong. Such relatively minor acts can be even more insidious than overt bullying, because they are less obvious and easier to overlook—yet they add up, eroding engagement and morale.

The Costs of Incivility

Many managers would say that incivility is wrong, but not all recognize that it has tangible costs. Targets of incivility often punish their offenders and the organization, although most hide or bury their feelings and don't necessarily think of their actions as revenge. Through a poll of 800 managers and employees in 17 industries, we learned just how people's reactions play out. Among workers who've been on the receiving end of incivility:

- 48% intentionally decreased their work effort.
- 47% intentionally decreased the time spent at work.
- 38% intentionally decreased the quality of their work.
- 80% lost work time worrying about the incident.
- 63% lost work time avoiding the offender.
- 66% said that their performance declined.
- 78% said that their commitment to the organization declined.
- 12% said that they left their job because of the uncivil treatment.
- 25% admitted to taking their frustration out on customers.

Experiments and other reports offer additional insights about the effects of incivility. Here are some examples of what can happen.

Creativity suffers

In an experiment we conducted with Amir Erez, a professor of management at the University of Florida, participants who were treated rudely by other subjects were 30% less creative than others in the study. They produced 25% fewer ideas, and the ones they did come up with were less original. For example, when asked what to do with a brick, participants who had been treated badly proposed logical but not particularly imaginative activities, such as "build a house," "build a wall," and "build a school." We saw more sparks from participants who had been treated civilly; their suggestions included "sell the brick on eBay," "use it as a goalpost for a street soccer game," "hang it on a museum wall and call it abstract art," and "decorate it like a pet and give it to a kid as a present."

Performance and team spirit deteriorate

Survey results and interviews indicate that simply witnessing incivility has negative consequences. In one experiment we conducted, people who'd observed poor behavior performed 20% worse on word puzzles than other people did. We also found that witnesses to incivility were less likely than others to help out, even when the person they'd be helping had no apparent connection to the uncivil person: Only 25% of the subjects who'd witnessed incivility volunteered to help, whereas 51% of those who hadn't witnessed it did.

Customers turn away

Public rudeness among employees is common, according to our survey of 244 consumers. Whether it's waiters berating fellow waiters or store clerks criticizing colleagues, disrespectful behavior makes people uncomfortable, and they're quick to walk out without making a purchase.

We studied this phenomenon with the USC marketing professors Debbie MacInnis and Valerie Folkes. In one experiment, half the participants witnessed a supposed bank representative publicly reprimanding another for incorrectly presenting credit card information. Only 20% of those who'd seen the encounter said that they would use the bank's services in the future, compared with 80% of those who hadn't. And nearly two-thirds of those who'd seen the exchange said that they would feel anxious dealing with *any* employee of the bank.

What's more, when we tested various scenarios, we found that it didn't matter whether the targeted employee was incompetent, whether the reprimand had been delivered behind closed doors (but overheard), or whether the employee had done something questionable or illegal, such as park in a handicapped spot. Regardless of the circumstances, people don't like to see others treated badly.

Managing incidents is expensive

HR professionals say that just one incident can soak up weeks of attention and effort. According to a study conducted by Accountemps and reported in *Fortune*, managers and executives at *Fortune* 1,000 firms spend 13% percent of their work time—the equivalent of seven weeks a year—mending employee relationships and otherwise dealing with the aftermath of incivility. And costs soar, of course, when consultants or attorneys must be brought in to help settle a situation.

What's a Leader to Do?

It can take constant vigilance to keep the workplace civil; otherwise, rudeness tends to creep into everyday interactions. Managers can use several strategies to keep their own behavior in check and to foster civility among others.

Managing yourself

Leaders set the tone, so you need to be aware of your actions and of how you come across to others.

Model good behavior. In one of our surveys, 25% of managers who admitted to having behaved badly said they were uncivil because their leaders—their own role models—were rude. If employees see that those who have climbed the corporate ladder tolerate or embrace uncivil behavior, they're likely to follow suit. So turn off your iPhone during meetings, pay attention to questions, and follow up on promises.

One way to help create a culture of respect and bring out your employees' best is to express your appreciation. Personal notes are particularly effective, especially if they emphasize being a role model, treating people well, and living the organization's values. Doug Conant, a former CEO of Campbell Soup, is well aware of the power of personal recognition. During his tenure as president and CEO, he sent more than 30,000 handwritten notes of thanks to employees.

Ask for feedback. You may need a reality check from the people who work for you. A manager at Hanover Insurance decided to ask his employees what they liked and didn't like about his leadership style. He learned that it really bothered them when he glanced at his phone or responded to e-mail during meetings. He now refrains from those activities, and his team appreciates the change.

Employees won't always be honest, but there are tools you can use on your own. For example, keep a journal in which you track instances of civility and incivility and note changes that you'd like to make.

Pay attention to your progress. As Josef, an IT professional, learned more about incivility, he became aware of his tendency to disparage a few nasty colleagues behind their backs. "I hadn't thought about it much until I considered the negative role modeling I was doing," he told us. "I criticized only people who were obnoxious to others and shared my criticisms only with people I trusted and in private, and somehow that made it seem OK. Then I started thinking about how I was just adding to the divide by spreading gossip and creating 'sides.' It was a real eye-opener, and I decided that I wanted to set a better example."

Within a short time Josef noticed that he was logging fewer occasions when he gossiped negatively and that he felt better about himself and his workplace. "I don't know whether anyone else would notice a difference—people already thought I was fair and supportive—but I know that I've changed," he said. "And there's another benefit for all of us: I'm seeing less incivility around me. I think that speaking up when colleagues or subordinates are rude can really make a difference. It puts them on alert that somebody is watching and cares how everyone is treated."

Managing the organization

Monitoring and adjusting your own behavior is an important piece of the puzzle, but you need to take action across the company as well.

Hire for civility. Avoid bringing incivility into the workplace to begin with. Some companies, including Southwest Airlines and Four Seasons, put civility at the fore when they interview applicants.

It's useful to give your team members a say about their prospective colleagues; they may pick up on behavior that would be suppressed in more-formal interviews. Rhapsody, an online subscription music service, conducts group interviews so that employees can evaluate potential teammates. It has been known to turn down applicants who are strong on paper but make the team uncomfortable in some way. In one case, a team considering two applicants felt that the apparently stronger one lacked emotional intelligence: She talked too much and seemed unwilling to listen. So the company hired the other candidate, who has worked out very well.

Only 11% of organizations report considering civility at all during the hiring process, and many of those investigate it in a cursory fashion. But incivility usually leaves a trail of some sort, which can be uncovered if someone's willing to look. One hospital had a near miss when bringing on a new radiologist. It offered the job to Dirk, a talented doctor who came highly recommended by his peers and had aced the interviews. But one assistant in the department had a hunch that something was off. Through a network of personal contacts, she learned that Dirk had left a number of badly treated subordinates in his wake—information that would never have surfaced from his CV. So the department head nixed the hire, telling Dirk that if he accepted the offer, the hospital would let him go right away, which would raise a flag for potential employers.

Teach civility. We're always amazed by how many managers and employees tell us that they don't understand what it means to be civil. One quarter of the offenders we surveyed said that they didn't recognize their behavior as uncivil.

People can learn civility on the job. Role-playing is one technique. At one hospital in Los Angeles, temperamental doctors have to attend "charm school" to decrease their brashness (and reduce the potential for lawsuits). Some organizations offer classes on managing the generation mix, in which they talk about differences in norms of civility and how to improve behavior across generations.

Video can be a good teaching tool, especially when paired with coaching. Film employees during various interactions so that they can observe their own facial expressions, posture, words, and tone of voice. It takes people a while to learn to ignore the camera, but eventually they resume their normal patterns of behavior.

After participating in such an exercise, the CEO of a medical firm told us, "I didn't realize what a jerk I sounded like." To his credit, he used the insight to fashion more-civil communication—and became less of a jerk. Another senior executive reported that he'd always thought he maintained a poker face, but the video revealed obvious "tells." For instance, if he lost interest in a discussion, he'd look away.

We recommend that after being taped, people watch the video in three modes: first, with both sound and image, to get an overall sense of their demeanor; second, without sound, to focus on nonverbal behaviors such as gestures, distancing, and facial expressions; and third, with only sound, to highlight tone of voice, volume and speed of speech, and word choice. People don't take issue just with words; tone can be equally or more potent.

Create group norms. Start a dialogue with your team about expectations. An insurance executive told us that he'd talked with his team about what behaviors worked and what didn't. By the end of the first meeting, the team had produced and taken ownership of concrete norms for civility, such as arriving on time and ignoring e-mail during meetings.

In one of our own workplaces, we've borrowed a practice from sports to take the edge off and to help one another avoid falling into occasional abrasiveness. In our world, incivility can flare up during presentations, because overly zealous professors may vigorously interrogate colleagues and visiting professors in an effort to demonstrate their own intellect. We warn colleagues who are engaging in this behavior by using hand signals to indicate the equivalent of soccer's yellow and red cards. The "yellow card" sign (a fist raised to the side of the head) conveys a warning, letting the interrogator know she needs to think about the phrasing, tone, and intensity of her comments and questions. The "red card" signal (two fingers held up, followed by the classic heave of the thumb) means she's finished for the session—she's been so offensive, repeatedly and after fair warning, that she needs to be "ejected from the game." Faculty members have learned that when they get the red card signal, they have to button it—no more today.

Ochsner Health System, a large Louisiana health care provider, has adopted what it calls "the 10/5 way": If you're within 10 feet of someone, make eye contact and smile. If you're within five feet, say hello. Ochsner has seen greater patient satisfaction and an increase in patient referrals as a result.

Reward good behavior. Collegiality should be a consideration in every performance review, but many companies think only about outcomes and tend to overlook damaging behaviors. What behavior does your review system motivate? All too often we see organizations badly miss the mark. They want collaboration, but you'd never know it from their evaluation forms, which focus entirely on individual assessment, without a single measure of teamwork.

Zappos implemented a "Wow" recognition program designed to capture people in the act of doing the right thing. Any employee at any level who sees a colleague doing something special can award a "Wow," which includes a cash bonus of up to $50. Recipients are automatically eligible for a "Hero" award. Heroes are chosen by top executives; they receive a covered parking spot for a month, a $150 Zappos gift card, and, with full symbolic flair, a hero's cape. Even lighthearted awards like these can be powerful symbols of the importance of civility.

Penalize bad behavior. Even the best companies occasionally make bad hires, and employees from an acquired firm may be accustomed to different norms. The trick is to identify and try to correct any troublesome behavior. Companies often avoid taking action, though, and most incidents go unreported, partly because employees know nothing will come of a report. If you want to foster respect, take complaints seriously and follow up.

Rather than confronting offenders, leaders often opt for an easier solution—moving them to a different location. The result is predictable: The behavior continues in a new setting. One manager told us that his department has been burned so often that it no longer considers internal candidates for managerial positions.

Sometimes the best path is to let someone go. Danny Meyer, the owner of many successful restaurants in Manhattan, will fire talent for uncivil behavior. Gifted but rude chefs don't last at his restaurants because they set off bad vibes. Meyer believes that customers can *taste* employee incivility, even when the behavior occurs in the kitchen.

Many top law firms, hospitals, and businesses we've dealt with have learned the hard way that it simply doesn't pay to harbor habitual offenders, even if they're rainmakers or protégés. Whether offenders have caused multimillion-dollar lawsuits or been responsible for the exit of throngs of employees, often the losses could have been mitigated by early, resolute action. A senior executive of a highly successful company told us recently, "Every mistake we've made in firing a questionable hire was in taking action too late, not too early."

Conduct postdeparture interviews. Organizational memory fades quickly. It's crucial, therefore, to gather information from and reflect on the experiences and reactions of employees who leave because of incivility. If you ask targets during their exit interviews why they're leaving, you'll usually get only vague responses. Interviews conducted six months or so later can yield a truer picture. Talking with former employees after they've distanced themselves from the organization and settled into their new work environments can give you insights about the violations of civility that prompted them to leave.

Companies we've worked with calculate that the tab for incivility can run into the millions. Some years back Cisco put together a detailed estimate of what incivility was costing the company. It factored in its reputation as a consistently great place to work, assumed an extremely low probability of rudeness among its employees, and looked at only three potential costs. Even in this exemplary workplace, it was estimated that incivility cost $12 million a year. That realization led to the creation of Cisco's global workplace civility program.

We close with a warning to those who think consistent civility is an extravagance: Just one habitually offensive employee critically positioned in your organization can cost you dearly in lost employees, lost customers, and lost productivity.

Originally published in January–February 2013. Reprint R1301J

How Resilience Works

by Diane L. Coutu

WHEN I BEGAN MY CAREER IN JOURNALISM—I was a reporter at a national magazine in those days—there was a man I'll call Claus Schmidt. He was in his mid-fifties, and to my impressionable eyes, he was the quintessential newsman: cynical at times, but unrelentingly curious and full of life, and often hilariously funny in a sandpaper-dry kind of way. He churned out hard-hitting cover stories and features with a speed and elegance I could only dream of. It always astounded me that he was never promoted to managing editor.

But people who knew Claus better than I did thought of him not just as a great newsman but as a quintessential survivor, someone who had endured in an environment often hostile to talent. He had lived through at least three major changes in the magazine's leadership, losing most of his best friends and colleagues on the way. At home, two of his children succumbed to incurable illnesses, and a third was killed in a traffic accident. Despite all this—or maybe because of it—he milled around the newsroom day after day, mentoring the cub reporters, talking about the novels he was writing—always looking forward to what the future held for him.

Why do some people suffer real hardships and not falter? Claus Schmidt could have reacted very differently. We've all seen that happen: One person cannot seem to get the confidence back after a layoff; another, persistently depressed, takes a few years off from life after her divorce. The question we would all like answered is, Why? What exactly is that quality of resilience that carries people through life?

It's a question that has fascinated me ever since I first learned of the Holocaust survivors in elementary school. In college, and later in my studies as an affiliate scholar at the Boston Psychoanalytic Society and Institute, I returned to the subject. For the past several months, however, I have looked on it with a new urgency, for it seems to me that the terrorism, war, and recession of recent months have made understanding resilience more important than ever. I have considered both the nature of individual resilience and what makes some organizations as a whole more resilient than others. Why do some people and some companies buckle under pressure? And what makes others bend and ultimately bounce back?

My exploration has taught me much about resilience, although it's a subject none of us will ever understand fully. Indeed, resilience is one of the great puzzles of human nature, like creativity or the religious instinct. But in sifting through psychological research and in reflecting on the many stories of resilience I've heard, I have seen a little more deeply into the hearts and minds of people like Claus Schmidt and, in doing so, looked more deeply into the human psyche as well.

The Buzz About Resilience

Resilience is a hot topic in business these days. Not long ago, I was talking to a senior partner at a respected consulting firm about how to land the very best MBAs—the name of the game in that particular industry. The partner, Daniel Savageau (not his real name), ticked off a long list of qualities his firm sought in its hires: intelligence, ambition, integrity, analytic ability, and so on. "What about resilience?" I asked. "Well, that's very popular right now," he said. "It's the new buzzword. Candidates even tell us they're resilient; they volunteer the information. But frankly, they're just too young to know that about themselves. Resilience is something you realize you have *after* the fact."

Idea in Brief

These are dark days: people are losing jobs, taking pay cuts, suffering foreclosure on their homes. Some of them are snapping—sinking into depression or suffering a permanent loss of confidence.

But others are snapping back; for example, taking advantage of a layoff to build a new career. What carries them through tough times? Resilience.

Resilient people possess three defining characteristics: They coolly accept the harsh realities facing them. They find meaning in terrible times. And they have an uncanny ability to improvise, making do with whatever's at hand.

In deep recessions, resilience becomes more important than ever. Fortunately, you can learn to be resilient.

"But if you could, would you test for it?" I asked. "Does it matter in business?"

Savageau paused. He's a man in his late forties and a success personally and professionally. Yet it hadn't been a smooth ride to the top. He'd started his life as a poor French Canadian in Woonsocket, Rhode Island, and had lost his father at six. He lucked into a football scholarship but was kicked out of Boston University twice for drinking. He turned his life around in his twenties, married, divorced, remarried, and raised five children. Along the way, he made and lost two fortunes before helping to found the consulting firm he now runs. "Yes, it does matter," he said at last. "In fact, it probably matters more than any of the usual things we look for." In the course of reporting this article, I heard the same assertion time and again. As Dean Becker, the president and CEO of Adaptiv Learning Systems, a four-year-old company in King of Prussia, Pennsylvania, that develops and delivers programs about resilience training, puts it: "More than education, more than experience, more than training, a person's level of resilience will determine who succeeds and who fails. That's true in the cancer ward, it's true in the Olympics, and it's true in the boardroom."

Academic research into resilience started about 40 years ago with pioneering studies by Norman Garmezy, now a professor emeritus at the University of Minnesota in Minneapolis. After studying why

Idea in Practice

Resilience can help you survive and recover from even the most brutal experiences. To cultivate resilience, apply these practices.

Face Down Reality

Instead of slipping into denial to cope with hardship, take a sober, down-to-earth view of the reality of your situation. You'll prepare yourself to act in ways that enable you to endure—training yourself to survive before the fact.

> ***Example:*** Admiral Jim Stockdale survived being held prisoner and tortured by the Vietcong in part by accepting he could be held for a long time. (He was held for eight years.) Those who didn't make it out of the camps kept optimistically assuming they'd be released on shorter timetables—by Christmas, by Easter, by the Fourth of July. "I think they all died of broken hearts," Stockdale said.

Search for Meaning

When hard times strike, resist any impulse to view yourself as a victim and to cry, "Why me?" Rather, devise constructs about your suffering to create meaning for yourself and others. You'll build bridges from your present-day ordeal to a fuller, better future. Those bridges will make the present manageable, by removing the sense that the present is overwhelming.

> ***Example:*** Austrian psychiatrist and Auschwitz survivor Viktor Frankl realized that

many children of schizophrenic parents did not suffer psychological illness as a result of growing up with them, he concluded that a certain quality of resilience played a greater role in mental health than anyone had previously suspected.

Today, theories abound about what makes resilience. Looking at Holocaust victims, Maurice Vanderpol, a former president of the Boston Psychoanalytic Society and Institute, found that many of the healthy survivors of concentration camps had what he calls a "plastic shield." The shield was comprised of several factors, including a sense of humor. Often the humor was black, but nonetheless it provided a critical sense of perspective. Other core characteristics that helped included the ability to form attachments to others and the possession of an inner psychological space that protected

to survive the camp, he had to find some purpose. He did so by imagining himself giving a lecture after the war on the psychology of the concentration camp to help outsiders understand what he had been through. By creating concrete goals for himself, he rose above the sufferings of the moment.

Continually Improvise

When disaster hits, be inventive. Make the most of what you have, putting resources to unfamiliar uses and imagining possibilities others don't see.

Example: Mike founded a business with his friend Paul, selling educational materials to schools, businesses, and consulting firms. When a recession hit, they lost many core clients. Paul went through a bitter divorce, suffered a depression, and couldn't work. When Mike offered to buy him out, Paul slapped him with a lawsuit claiming Mike was trying to steal the business.

Mike kept the company going any way he could—going into joint ventures to sell English-language training materials to Russian and Chinese competitors, publishing newsletters for clients, and even writing video scripts for competitors. The lawsuit was eventually settled in his favor, and he had a new and much more solid business than the one he started out with.

the survivors from the intrusions of abusive others. Research about other groups uncovered different qualities associated with resilience. The Search Institute, a Minneapolis-based nonprofit organization that focuses on resilience and youth, found that the more resilient kids have an uncanny ability to get adults to help them out. Still other research showed that resilient inner-city youth often have talents such as athletic abilities that attract others to them.

Many of the early theories about resilience stressed the role of genetics. Some people are just born resilient, so the arguments went. There's some truth to that, of course, but an increasing body of empirical evidence shows that resilience—whether in children, survivors of concentration camps, or businesses back from the brink—can be learned. For example, George Vaillant, the director of the Study of Adult Development at Harvard Medical School in Boston, observes that within various groups studied during a 60-year period, some people became markedly more resilient over their lifetimes. Other psychologists claim that unresilient people more easily develop resiliency skills than those with head starts.

Most of the resilience theories I encountered in my research make good common sense. But I also observed that almost all the theories overlap in three ways. Resilient people, they posit, possess three characteristics: a staunch acceptance of reality; a deep belief, often buttressed by strongly held values, that life is meaningful; and an uncanny ability to improvise. You can bounce back from hardship with just one or two of these qualities, but you will only be truly resilient with all three. These three characteristics hold true for resilient organizations as well. Let's take a look at each of them in turn.

Facing Down Reality

A common belief about resilience is that it stems from an optimistic nature. That's true but only as long as such optimism doesn't distort your sense of reality. In extremely adverse situations, rose-colored thinking can actually spell disaster. This point was made poignantly to me by management researcher and writer Jim Collins, who happened upon this concept while researching *Good to Great*, his book on how companies transform themselves out of mediocrity. Collins had a hunch (an exactly wrong hunch) that resilient companies were filled with optimistic people. He tried out that idea on Admiral Jim Stockdale, who was held prisoner and tortured by the Vietcong for eight years.

Collins recalls: "I asked Stockdale: 'Who didn't make it out of the camps?' And he said, 'Oh, that's easy. It was the optimists. They were the ones who said we were going to be out by Christmas. And then they said we'd be out by Easter and then out by Fourth of July and out by Thanksgiving, and then it was Christmas again.' Then Stockdale turned to me and said, 'You know, I think they all died of broken hearts.'"

In the business world, Collins found the same unblinking attitude shared by executives at all the most successful companies he studied. Like Stockdale, resilient people have very sober and down-to-earth views of those parts of reality that matter for survival. That's not to say that optimism doesn't have its place: In turning around a demoralized sales force, for instance, conjuring a sense of possibility can be a very powerful tool. But for bigger challenges, a cool, almost pessimistic, sense of reality is far more important.

Perhaps you're asking yourself, "Do I truly understand—and accept—the reality of my situation? Does my organization?" Those are good questions, particularly because research suggests most people slip into denial as a coping mechanism. Facing reality, really facing it, is grueling work. Indeed, it can be unpleasant and often emotionally wrenching. Consider the following story of organizational resilience, and see what it means to confront reality.

Prior to September 11, 2001, Morgan Stanley, the famous investment bank, was the largest tenant in the World Trade Center. The company had some 2,700 employees working in the south tower on 22 floors between the 43rd and the 74th. On that horrible day, the first plane hit the north tower at 8:46 a.m., and Morgan Stanley started evacuating just one minute later, at 8:47 a.m. When the second plane crashed into the south tower 15 minutes after that, Morgan Stanley's offices were largely empty. All told, the company lost only seven employees despite receiving an almost direct hit.

Of course, the organization was just plain lucky to be in the second tower. Cantor Fitzgerald, whose offices were hit in the first attack, couldn't have done anything to save its employees. Still, it was Morgan Stanley's hard-nosed realism that enabled the company to benefit from its luck. Soon after the 1993 attack on the World Trade Center, senior management recognized that working in such a symbolic center of U.S. commercial power made the company vulnerable to attention from terrorists and possible attack.

With this grim realization, Morgan Stanley launched a program of preparedness at the micro level. Few companies take their fire drills seriously. Not so Morgan Stanley, whose VP of security for the Individual Investor Group, Rick Rescorla, brought a military discipline to the job. Rescorla, himself a highly resilient, decorated Vietnam vet, made sure that people were fully drilled about what to do in a catastrophe. When disaster struck on September 11, Rescorla was on a bullhorn telling Morgan Stanley employees to stay calm and follow their well-practiced drill, even though some building supervisors were telling occupants that all was well. Sadly, Rescorla himself, whose life story has been widely covered in recent months, was one of the seven who didn't make it out.

"When you're in financial services where so much depends on technology, contingency planning is a major part of your business," says President and COO Robert G. Scott. But Morgan Stanley was prepared for the very toughest reality. It had not just one, but three, recovery sites where employees could congregate and business could take place if work locales were ever disrupted. "Multiple backup sites seemed like an incredible extravagance on September 10," concedes Scott. "But on September 12, they seemed like genius."

Maybe it was genius; it was undoubtedly resilience at work. The fact is, when we truly stare down reality, we prepare ourselves to act in ways that allow us to endure and survive extraordinary hardship. We train ourselves how to survive before the fact.

The Search for Meaning

The ability to see reality is closely linked to the second building block of resilience, the propensity to make meaning of terrible times. We all know people who, under duress, throw up their hands and cry, "How can this be happening to me?" Such people see themselves as victims, and living through hardship carries no lessons for them. But resilient people devise constructs about their suffering to create some sort of meaning for themselves and others.

I have a friend I'll call Jackie Oiseaux who suffered repeated psychoses over a ten-year period due to an undiagnosed bipolar disorder. Today, she holds down a big job in one of the top publishing companies in the country, has a family, and is a prominent member of her church community. When people ask her how she bounced back from her crises, she runs her hands through her hair. "People sometimes say, 'Why me?' But I've always said, 'Why *not* me?' True, I lost many things during my illness," she says, "but I found many more—incredible friends who saw me through the bleakest times and who will give meaning to my life forever."

This dynamic of meaning making is, most researchers agree, the way resilient people build bridges from present-day hardships to a fuller, better constructed future. Those bridges make the present manageable, for lack of a better word, removing the sense that the present is overwhelming. This concept was beautifully articulated by Viktor E. Frankl, an Austrian psychiatrist and an Auschwitz survivor. In the midst of staggering suffering, Frankl invented "meaning therapy," a humanistic therapy technique that helps individuals make the kinds of decisions that will create significance in their lives.

In his book *Man's Search for Meaning*, Frankl described the pivotal moment in the camp when he developed meaning therapy. He was on his way to work one day, worrying whether he should trade his last cigarette for a bowl of soup. He wondered how he was going to work with a new foreman whom he knew to be particularly sadistic. Suddenly, he was disgusted by just how trivial and meaningless his life had become. He realized that to survive, he had to find some purpose. Frankl did so by imagining himself giving a lecture after the war on the psychology of the concentration camp, to help outsiders understand what he had been through. Although he wasn't even sure he would survive, Frankl created some concrete goals for himself. In doing so, he succeeded in rising above the sufferings of the moment. As he put it in his book: "We must never forget that we may also find meaning in life even when confronted with a hopeless situation, when facing a fate that cannot be changed."

Frankl's theory underlies most resilience coaching in business. Indeed, I was struck by how often businesspeople referred to his work. "Resilience training—what we call hardiness—is a way for us to help people construct meaning in their everyday lives," explains Salvatore R. Maddi, a University of California, Irvine psychology professor and the director of the Hardiness Institute in Newport Beach, California. "When people realize the power of resilience training, they often say, 'Doc, is this what psychotherapy is?' But psychotherapy is for people whose lives have fallen apart badly and need repair. We see our work as showing people life skills and attitudes. Maybe those things should be taught at home, maybe they should be taught in schools, but they're not. So we end up doing it in business."

Yet the challenge confronting resilience trainers is often more difficult than we might imagine. Meaning can be elusive, and just because you found it once doesn't mean you'll keep it or find it again. Consider Aleksandr Solzhenitsyn, who survived the war against the Nazis, imprisonment in the gulag, and cancer. Yet when he moved to a farm in peaceful, safe Vermont, he could not cope with the "infantile West." He was unable to discern any real meaning in what he felt to be the destructive and irresponsible freedom of the West. Upset by his critics, he withdrew into his farmhouse, behind a locked fence, seldom to be seen in public. In 1994, a bitter man, Solzhenitsyn moved back to Russia.

Since finding meaning in one's environment is such an important aspect of resilience, it should come as no surprise that the most successful organizations and people possess strong value systems. Strong values infuse an environment with meaning because they offer ways to interpret and shape events. While it's popular these days to ridicule values, it's surely no coincidence that the most resilient organization in the world has been the Catholic Church, which has survived wars, corruption, and schism for more than 2,000 years, thanks largely to its immutable set of values. Businesses that survive also have their creeds, which give them purposes beyond just making money. Strikingly, many companies describe their value systems in religious terms. Pharmaceutical giant Johnson & Johnson, for instance, calls its value system, set out in a document given to every new employee at orientation, the Credo. Parcel company UPS talks constantly about its Noble Purpose.

Value systems at resilient companies change very little over the years and are used as scaffolding in times of trouble. UPS Chairman and CEO Mike Eskew believes that the Noble Purpose helped the company to rally after the agonizing strike in 1997. Says Eskew: "It was a hugely difficult time, like a family feud. Everyone had close friends on both sides of the fence, and it was tough for us to pick sides. But what saved us was our Noble Purpose. Whatever side people were on, they all shared a common set of values. Those values are core to us and never change; they frame most of our important decisions. Our strategy and our mission may change, but our values never do."

The religious connotations of words like "credo," "values," and "noble purpose," however, should not be confused with the actual content of the values. Companies can hold ethically questionable values and still be very resilient. Consider Phillip Morris, which has demonstrated impressive resilience in the face of increasing unpopularity. As Jim Collins points out, Phillip Morris has very strong values, although we might not agree with them—for instance, the value of "adult choice." But there's no doubt that Phillip Morris executives believe strongly in its values, and the strength of their beliefs sets the company apart from most of the other tobacco companies. In this context, it is worth noting that resilience is neither ethically good nor bad. It is merely the skill and the capacity to be robust under conditions of enormous stress and change. As Viktor Frankl wrote: "On the average, only those prisoners could keep alive who, after years of trekking from camp to camp, had lost all scruples in their fight for existence; they were prepared to use every means, honest and otherwise, even brutal . . ., in order to save themselves. We who have come back . . . we know: The best of us did not return."

Values, positive or negative, are actually more important for organizational resilience than having resilient people on the payroll. If resilient employees are all interpreting reality in different ways, their decisions and actions may well conflict, calling into doubt the survival of their organization. And as the weakness of an organization becomes apparent, highly resilient individuals are more likely to jettison the organization than to imperil their own survival.

Ritualized Ingenuity

The third building block of resilience is the ability to make do whatever is at hand. Psychologists follow the lead of French opologist Claude Levi-Strauss in calling this skill bricolage.[1] uingly, the roots of that word are closely tied to the concept of resilience, which literally means "bouncing back." Says Levi-Strauss: "In its old sense, the verb *bricoler* . . . was always used with reference to some extraneous movement: a ball rebounding, a dog straying, or a horse swerving from its direct course to avoid an obstacle."

Bricolage in the modern sense can be defined as a kind of inventiveness, an ability to improvise a solution to a problem without proper or obvious tools or materials. *Bricoleurs* are always tinkering—building radios from household effects or fixing their own cars. They make the most of what they have, putting objects to unfamiliar uses. In the concentration camps, for example, resilient inmates knew to pocket pieces of string or wire whenever they found them. The string or wire might later become useful—to fix a pair of shoes, perhaps, which in freezing conditions might make the difference between life and death.

When situations unravel, bricoleurs muddle through, imagining possibilities where others are confounded. I have two friends, whom I'll call Paul Shields and Mike Andrews, who were roommates throughout their college years. To no one's surprise, when they graduated, they set up a business together, selling educational materials to schools, businesses, and consulting firms. At first, the company was a great success, making both founders paper millionaires. But the recession of the early 1990s hit the company hard, and many core clients fell away. At the same time, Paul experienced a bitter divorce and a depression that made it impossible for him to work. Mike offered to buy Paul out but was instead slapped with a lawsuit claiming that Mike was trying to steal the business. At this point, a less resilient person might have just walked away from the mess. Not Mike. As the case wound through the courts, he kept the company going any way he could—constantly morphing the business until he found a model that worked: going into joint ventures to sell English-language training materials to Russian and Chinese companies. Later, he branched off into publishing newsletters for clients. At one point, he was even writing video scripts for his competitors. Thanks to all this bricolage, by the time the lawsuit was settled in his favor, Mike had an entirely different, and much more solid, business than the one he had started with.

Bricolage can be practiced on a higher level as well. Richard Feynman, winner of the 1965 Nobel Prize in physics, exemplified what

I like to think of as intellectual bricolage. Out of pure curiosity, Feynman made himself an expert on cracking safes, not only looking at the mechanics of safecracking but also cobbling together psychological insights about people who used safes and set the locks. He cracked many of the safes at Los Alamos, for instance, because he guessed that theoretical physicists would not set the locks with random code numbers they might forget but would instead use a sequence with mathematical significance. It turned out that the three safes containing all the secrets to the atomic bomb were set to the same mathematical constant, *e,* whose first six digits are 2.71828.

Resilient organizations are stuffed with bricoleurs, though not all of them, of course, are Richard Feynmans. Indeed, companies that survive regard improvisation as a core skill. Consider UPS, which empowers its drivers to do whatever it takes to deliver packages on time. Says CEO Eskew: "We tell our employees to get the job done. If that means they need to improvise, they improvise. Otherwise we just couldn't do what we do every day. Just think what can go wrong: a busted traffic light, a flat tire, a bridge washed out. If a snowstorm hits Louisville tonight, a group of people will sit together and discuss how to handle the problem. Nobody tells them to do that. They come together because it's our tradition to do so."

That tradition meant that the company was delivering parcels in southeast Florida just one day after Hurricane Andrew devastated the region in 1992, causing billions of dollars in damage. Many people were living in their cars because their homes had been destroyed, yet UPS drivers and managers sorted packages at a diversion site and made deliveries even to those who were stranded in their cars. It was largely UPS's improvisational skills that enabled it to keep functioning after the catastrophic hit. And the fact that the company continued on gave others a sense of purpose or meaning amid the chaos.

Improvisation of the sort practiced by UPS, however, is a far cry from unbridled creativity. Indeed, much like the military, UPS lives on rules and regulations. As Eskew says: "Drivers always put their keys in the same place. They close the doors the same way. They wear their uniforms the same way. We are a company of precision." He believes that although they may seem stifling, UPS's rules were what allowed the company to bounce back immediately after Hurricane Andrew, for they enabled people to focus on the one or two fixes they needed to make in order to keep going.

Eskew's opinion is echoed by Karl E. Weick, a professor of organizational behavior at the University of Michigan Business School in Ann Arbor and one of the most respected thinkers on organizational psychology. "There is good evidence that when people are put under pressure, they regress to their most habituated ways of responding," Weick has written. "What we do not expect under life-threatening pressure is creativity." In other words, the rules and regulations that make some companies appear less creative may actually make them more resilient in times of real turbulence.

Claus Schmidt, the newsman I mentioned earlier, died about five years ago, but I'm not sure I could have interviewed him about his own resilience even if he were alive. It would have felt strange, I think, to ask him, "Claus, did you really face down reality? Did you make meaning out of your hardships? Did you improvise your recovery after each professional and personal disaster?" He may not have been able to answer. In my experience, resilient people don't often describe themselves that way. They shrug off their survival stories and very often assign them to luck.

Obviously, luck does have a lot to do with surviving. It was luck that Morgan Stanley was situated in the south tower and could put its preparedness training to work. But being lucky is not the same as being resilient. Resilience is a reflex, a way of facing and understanding the world, that is deeply etched into a person's mind and soul. Resilient people and companies face reality with staunchness, make meaning of hardship instead of crying out in despair, and improvise solutions from thin air. Others do not. This is the nature of resilience, and we will never completely understand it.

Originally published in May 2002. Reprint R0205B

Note

1. See, e.g., Karl E. Weick, "The Collapse of Sense-making in Organizations: The Mann Gulch Disaster," *Administrative Science Quarterly*, December 1993.

Emotional Agility

How Effective Leaders Manage Their Negative Thoughts and Feelings. *by Susan David and Christina Congleton*

SIXTEEN THOUSAND—that's how many words we speak, on average, each day. So imagine how many unspoken ones course through our minds. Most of them are not facts but evaluations and judgments entwined with emotions—some positive and helpful (*I've worked hard and I can ace this presentation; This issue is worth speaking up about; The new VP seems approachable*), others negative and less so (*He's purposely ignoring me; I'm going to make a fool of myself; I'm a fake*).

The prevailing wisdom says that difficult thoughts and feelings have no place at the office: Executives, and particularly leaders, should be either stoic or cheerful; they must project confidence and damp down any negativity bubbling up inside them. But that goes against basic biology. All healthy human beings have an inner stream of thoughts and feelings that include criticism, doubt, and fear. That's just our minds doing the job they were designed to do: trying to anticipate and solve problems and avoid potential pitfalls.

In our people-strategy consulting practice advising companies around the world, we see leaders stumble not because they *have* undesirable thoughts and feelings—that's inevitable—but because they get *hooked* by them, like fish caught on a line. This happens in one of two ways. They buy into the thoughts, treating them like facts (*It was the same in my last job . . . I've been a failure my whole career*), and avoid situations that evoke them (*I'm not going to take on that new challenge*). Or, usually at the behest of their supporters, they challenge the existence of the thoughts and try to rationalize them away (*I shouldn't have thoughts like this . . . I know I'm not a total failure*), and perhaps force themselves into similar situations, even when those go against their core values and goals (*Take on that new assignment—you've got to get over this*). In either case, they are paying too much attention to their internal chatter and allowing it to sap important cognitive resources that could be put to better use.

This is a common problem, often perpetuated by popular self-management strategies. We regularly see executives with recurring emotional challenges at work—anxiety about priorities, jealousy of others' success, fear of rejection, distress over perceived slights—who have devised techniques to "fix" them: positive affirmations, prioritized to-do lists, immersion in certain tasks. But when we ask how long the challenges have persisted, the answer might be 10 years, 20 years, or since childhood.

Clearly, those techniques don't work—in fact, ample research shows that attempting to minimize or ignore thoughts and emotions serves only to amplify them. In a famous study led by the late Daniel Wegner, a Harvard professor, participants who were told to avoid thinking about white bears had trouble doing so; later, when the ban was lifted, they thought about white bears much more than the control group did. Anyone who has dreamed of chocolate cake and French fries while following a strict diet understands this phenomenon.

Effective leaders don't buy into *or* try to suppress their inner experiences. Instead they approach them in a mindful, values-driven, and productive way—developing what we call *emotional agility*. In our complex, fast-changing knowledge economy, this ability to manage one's thoughts and feelings is essential to business success. Numerous studies, from the University of London professor Frank Bond and others, show that emotional agility can help

Idea in Brief

The prevailing wisdom says that negative thoughts and feelings have no place at the office. But that goes against basic biology. All healthy human beings have an inner stream of thoughts and feelings that include criticism, doubt, and fear. David and Congleton have worked with leaders in various industries to build a critical skill they call emotional agility, which enables people to approach their inner experiences in a mindful, values-driven, and productive way rather than buying into or trying to suppress them. The authors offer four practices (adapted from Acceptance and Commitment Therapy, or ACT) designed to help readers do the same:

- **Recognize your patterns.** You have to realize that you're stuck before you can initiate change.
- **Label your thoughts and emotions.** Labeling allows you to see them as transient sources of data that may or may not prove helpful.
- **Accept them.** Respond to your ideas and emotions with an open attitude, paying attention and letting yourself experience them. They may be signaling that something important is at stake.
- **Act on your values.** Is your response going to serve your organization in the long term and take you toward being the leader you most want to be?

people alleviate stress, reduce errors, become more innovative, and improve job performance.

We've worked with leaders in various industries to build this critical skill, and here we offer four practices—adapted from Acceptance and Commitment Therapy (ACT), originally developed by the University of Nevada psychologist Steven C. Hayes—that are designed to help you do the same: Recognize your patterns; label your thoughts and emotions; accept them; and act on your values.

Fish on a Line

Let's start with two case studies. Cynthia is a senior corporate lawyer with two young children. She used to feel intense guilt about missed opportunities—both at the office, where her peers worked 80 hours a week while she worked 50, and at home, where she was often too

What Are Your Values?

THIS LIST IS DRAWN from the Personal Values Card Sort (2001), developed by W.R. Miller, J. C'de Baca, D.B. Matthews, and P.L. Wilbourne, of the University of New Mexico. You can use it to quickly identify the values you hold that might inform a challenging situation at work. When you next make a decision, ask yourself whether it is consistent with these values.

- Accuracy
- Achievement
- Adventure
- Authority
- Autonomy
- Caring
- Challenge
- Change
- Comfort
- Compassion
- Contribution
- Cooperation
- Courtesy
- Creativity
- Dependability
- Duty
- Family
- Forgiveness
- Friendship
- Fun
- Generosity
- Genuineness
- Growth
- Health
- Helpfulness
- Honesty
- Humility
- Humor
- Justice
- Knowledge
- Leisure
- Mastery
- Moderation
- Nonconformity
- Openness
- Order
- Passion
- Popularity
- Power
- Purpose
- Rationality
- Realism
- Responsibility
- Risk
- Safety
- Self-knowledge
- Service
- Simplicity
- Stability
- Tolerance
- Tradition
- Wealth

distracted or tired to fully engage with her husband and children. One nagging voice in her head told her she'd have to be a better employee or risk career failure; another told her to be a better mother or risk neglecting her family. Cynthia wished that at least one of the voices would shut up. But neither would, and in response she failed to put up her hand for exciting new prospects at the office and compulsively checked messages on her phone during family dinners.

Jeffrey, a rising-star executive at a leading consumer goods company, had a different problem. Intelligent, talented, and ambitious, he was often angry—at bosses who disregarded his views, subordinates who didn't follow orders, or colleagues who didn't pull their weight. He had lost his temper several times at work and been warned to get it under control. But when he tried, he felt that he was shutting off a core part of his personality, and he became even angrier and more upset.

These smart, successful leaders were hooked by their negative thoughts and emotions. Cynthia was absorbed by guilt; Jeffrey was exploding with anger. Cynthia told the voices to go away; Jeffrey bottled his frustration. Both were trying to avoid the discomfort they felt. They were being controlled by their inner experience, attempting to control it, or switching between the two.

Getting Unhooked

Fortunately, both Cynthia and Jeffrey realized that they couldn't go on—at least not successfully and happily—without more-effective inner strategies. We coached them to adopt the four practices.

Recognize your patterns

The first step in developing emotional agility is to notice when you've been hooked by your thoughts and feelings. That's hard to do, but there are certain telltale signs. One is that your thinking becomes rigid and repetitive. For example, Cynthia began to see that her self-recriminations played like a broken record, repeating the same messages over and over again. Another is that the story your mind is telling seems old, like a rerun of some past experience. Jeffrey noticed that his attitude toward certain colleagues (*He's incompetent; There's no way I'm letting anyone speak to me like that*) was quite familiar. In fact, he had experienced something similar in his previous job—and in the one before that. The source of trouble was not just Jeffrey's environment but his own patterns of thought and feeling. You have to realize that you're stuck before you can initiate change.

Label your thoughts and emotions

When you're hooked, the attention you give your thoughts and feelings crowds your mind; there's no room to examine them. One strategy that may help you consider your situation more objectively is the simple act of labeling. Just as you call a spade a spade, call a thought a thought and an emotion an emotion. *I'm not doing enough at work or at home* becomes *I'm having the thought that I'm not doing enough at work or at home.* Similarly, *My coworker is wrong—he makes me so angry* becomes *I'm having the thought that my coworker is wrong, and I'm feeling anger.* Labeling allows you to see your thoughts and feelings for what they are: transient sources of data that may or may not prove helpful. Humans are psychologically able to take this helicopter view of private experiences, and mounting scientific evidence shows that simple, straightforward mindfulness practice like this not only improves behavior and well-being but also promotes beneficial biological changes in the brain and at the cellular level. As Cynthia started to slow down and label her thoughts, the criticisms that had once pressed in on her like a dense fog became more like clouds passing through a blue sky.

Accept them

The opposite of control is acceptance—not acting on every thought or resigning yourself to negativity but responding to your ideas and emotions with an open attitude, paying attention to them and letting yourself experience them. Take 10 deep breaths and notice what's happening in the moment. This can bring relief, but it won't necessarily make you feel good. In fact, you may realize just how upset you really are. The important thing is to show yourself (and others) some compassion and examine the reality of the situation. What's going on—both internally and externally? When Jeffrey acknowledged and made room for his feelings of frustration and anger rather than rejecting them, quashing them, or taking them out on others, he began to notice their energetic quality. They were a signal that something important was at stake and that he needed to take productive action. Instead of yelling at people, he could make a clear request of a colleague or move swiftly on a pressing issue. The more Jeffrey accepted his anger and brought his curiosity to it, the more it seemed to support rather than undermine his leadership.

Evaluate Your Emotional Agility

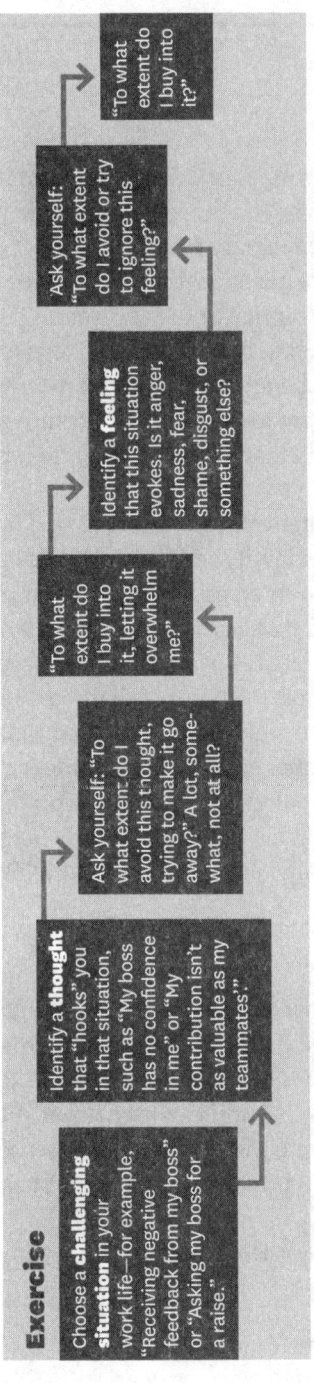

Exercise

Choose a **challenging situation** in your work life—for example, "Receiving negative feedback from my boss" or "Asking my boss for a raise."

Identify a **thought** that "hooks" you in that situation, such as "My boss has no confidence in me" or "My contribution isn't as valuable as my teammates'."

Ask yourself: "To what extent do I avoid this thought, trying to make it go away?" A lot, somewhat, not at all?

"To what extent do I buy into it, letting it overwhelm me?"

Identify a **feeling** that this situation evokes. Is it anger, sadness, fear, shame, disgust, or something else?

Ask yourself: "To what extent do I avoid or try to ignore this feeling?"

"To what extent do I buy into it?"

Advice

If you primarily **avoid** your thoughts and feelings, try to acknowledge them instead. Notice thoughts as they arise and check your emotional state several times a day so that you can identify the useful information your mind is sending you.

If you primarily **buy into** your thoughts and feelings, find your ground. Take 10 deep breaths, notice your environment, and label—rather than being swept up in—them.

If you **alternate,** learn your patterns. Pay attention to which thoughts and feelings you avoid and which you buy into so that you can respond with one of the strategies we describe.

The next step is to take action that aligns with your **values.** (For examples, see the sidebar "What Are Your Values?") Identify which ones you want to apply in the context of the challenging situation you've described.

Act on your values

When you unhook yourself from your difficult thoughts and emotions, you expand your choices. You can decide to act in a way that aligns with your values. We encourage leaders to focus on the concept of *workability*: Is your response going to serve you and your organization in the long term as well as the short term? Will it help you steer others in a direction that furthers your collective purpose? Are you taking a step toward being the leader you most want to be and living the life you most want to live? The mind's thought stream flows endlessly, and emotions change like the weather, but values can be called on at any time, in any situation.

When Cynthia considered her values, she recognized how deeply committed she was to both her family and her work; she loved being with her children, but she also cared passionately about the pursuit of justice. Unhooked from her distracting and discouraging feelings of guilt, she resolved to be guided by her principles. She recognized how important it was to get home for dinner with her family every evening and to resist work interruptions during that time. But she also undertook to make a number of important business trips, some of which coincided with school events that she would have preferred to attend. Confident that her values, not solely her emotions, were guiding her, Cynthia finally found peace and fulfillment.

It's impossible to block out difficult thoughts and emotions. Effective leaders are mindful of their inner experiences but not caught in them. They know how to free up their internal resources and commit to actions that align with their values. Developing emotional agility is no quick fix—even those who, like Cynthia and Jeffrey, regularly practice the steps we've outlined here will often find themselves hooked. But over time, leaders who become increasingly adept at it are the ones most likely to thrive.

Originally published in November 2013. Reprint R1311L

Fear of Feedback

by Jay M. Jackman and Myra H. Strober

NOBODY LIKES PERFORMANCE REVIEWS. Subordinates are terrified they'll hear nothing but criticism. Bosses, for their part, think their direct reports will respond to even the mildest criticism with stonewalling, anger, or tears. The result? Everyone keeps quiet and says as little as possible. That's unfortunate, because most people need help figuring out how they can improve their performance and advance their careers.

This fear of feedback doesn't come into play just during annual reviews. At least half the executives with whom we've worked *never* ask for feedback. Many expect the worst: heated arguments, impossible demands, or even threats of dismissal. So rather than seek feedback, people avoid the truth and instead continue to try to guess what their bosses think.

Fears and assumptions about feedback often manifest themselves in psychologically maladaptive behaviors such as procrastination, denial, brooding, jealousy, and self-sabotage. But there's hope. Those who learn to adapt to feedback can free themselves from old patterns. They can learn to acknowledge negative emotions, constructively reframe fear and criticism, develop realistic goals, create support systems, and reward themselves for achievements along the way.

We'll look closely at a four-step process for doing just that. But before we turn to that process, let's explore why so many people are afraid to hear how they're doing.

Fear Itself

Obviously, some managers have excellent relationships with their bosses. They receive feedback on a regular basis and act on it in ways that improve their performance as well as their prospects for promotion. Sadly, however, such executives are in the minority. In most companies, feedback typically comes via cursory annual performance reviews, during which managers learn little beyond the amount of a forthcoming raise.

People avoid feedback because they hate being criticized, plain and simple. Psychologists have a lot of theories about why people are so sensitive to hearing about their own imperfections. One is that they associate feedback with the critical comments received in their younger years from parents and teachers. Whatever the cause of our discomfort, most of us have to train ourselves to seek feedback and listen carefully when we hear it. Absent that training, the very threat of critical feedback often leads us to practice destructive, maladaptive behaviors that negatively affect not only our work but the overall health of our organizations. The following are some examples of those behaviors.

Procrastination

We procrastinate—usually consciously—when we feel helpless about a situation and are anxious, embarrassed, or otherwise dissatisfied with it. Procrastination commonly contains an element of hostility or anger.

Consider how Joe, a highly accomplished computer scientist in a large technology company, responded to his frustration over not being promoted. (As with all the examples in this article, people's names have been changed.) Although everyone in the company respected his technical competence, he sensed something was wrong. Instead of seriously assessing his performance and asking for feedback, he became preoccupied with inessential details of his projects, played computer solitaire, and consistently failed to meet project deadlines. When Joe asked about his chances for advancement in his annual review, his boss singled out Joe's repeated failure

Idea in Brief

Nobody likes performance reviews. Subordinates are terrified they'll hear nothing but criticism. Bosses, for their part, think their direct reports will respond to even the mildest criticism with stonewalling, anger, or tears. The result? Everyone keeps quiet and says as little as possible. That's unfortunate, because most people need help figuring out how they can improve their performance and advance their careers. This fear of feedback doesn't come into play just during annual reviews. At least half the executives with whom the authors have worked never ask for feedback. People avoid the truth and instead try to guess what their bosses are thinking. Fears and assumptions about feedback often manifest themselves in psychologically maladaptive behaviors such as procrastination, denial, brooding, jealousy, and self-sabotage. But there's hope, say the authors. Those who learn adaptive techniques can free themselves from these destructive responses. They'll be able to deal with feedback better if they acknowledge negative emotions, reframe fear and criticism constructively, develop realistic goals, create support systems, and reward themselves for achievements along the way. The authors take you through four manageable steps for doing just that: self-assessment, external assessment, absorbing the feedback, and taking action toward change.

to finish projects on time or to seek formal extensions when he knew work would be late. In fact, Joe's continued procrastination became a serious performance issue that cost him a promotion.

Denial

We're in denial when we're unable or unwilling to face reality or fail to acknowledge the implications of our situations. Denial is most often an unconscious response.

Angela, a midlevel manager in a consulting firm, drifted into a state of denial when a hoped-for promotion never materialized. Her superiors told her that she hadn't performed as well as they'd expected. Specifically, they told her she'd requested too much time off to spend with her children, she hadn't sufficiently researched a certain industry, she hadn't met her yearly quota of bringing in ten new clients, and so on. Every time she tried to correct these problems, her male superiors put her off with a new series of excuses and challenges. The fact was, they had no intention of promoting her because they were deeply sexist. Accepting that fact would have required Angela to leave, but she chose instead to live in denial. Rather than recognize she was at a dead end, she did nothing about her situation and remained miserable in her job.

Brooding

Brooding is a powerful emotional response, taking the form of morbid preoccupation and a sense of foreboding. Faced with situations they feel they can't master, brooders lapse into passivity, paralysis, and isolation.

Adrian, a training manager, brooded when his boss set forth several stretch goals for him. Believing the goals to be unrealistic, Adrian concluded that he couldn't meet them. Rather than talk with his boss about this, he became desperately unhappy and withdrew from his colleagues. They in turn saw his withdrawal as a snub and began to ignore him. The more they avoided him, the more he brooded. By the end of six months, Adrian's brooding created a self-fulfilling prophecy; because he had met none of his goals, his new projects were assigned to someone else, and his job was in jeopardy.

Jealousy

Comparing ourselves with others is a normal behavior, but it becomes maladaptive when it is based on suspicion, rivalry, envy, or possessiveness. Jealous people may overidealize others whom they perceive to be more talented, competent, and intelligent; in so doing, they debilitate themselves.

Leslie, a talented vice president of a public relations firm, fell into the jealousy trap when her boss noted during a meeting that one of her colleagues had prepared a truly excellent report for a client. Leslie began comparing herself with her colleague, listening carefully to the boss's remarks during meetings and noting his smiles and nods as he spoke. Feeling that she could never rise to her colleague's level, Leslie lost all enthusiasm for her work. Instead of seeking a reality check with her boss, she allowed the green-eyed monster to consume her; ultimately, she quit her job.

Self-sabotage

Examples of self-sabotage, usually an unconscious behavior, are all too common. Even national leaders such as Bill Clinton and Trent Lott have hoisted themselves on their own petards.

Workplaces are full of people who unconsciously undercut themselves. Take, for example, the story of Nancy, a young associate who found herself unable to deal with more than two projects at once. During her review, Nancy resented her boss's feedback that she needed to improve her ability to multitask. But instead of initiating further discussion with him about the remark, she "accidentally" made a nasty comment about him one day within his earshot. As a result, he began looking for ways to get rid of her. When she was eventually fired, her innermost feelings of unworthiness were validated.

These and other maladaptive behaviors are part of a vicious cycle we have seen at play in too many organizations. Indeed, it's not uncommon for employees, faced with negative feedback, to rain private maledictions upon their supervisors. No wonder, then, that supervisors are reluctant to give feedback. But when employees' imagined and real fears go unchecked, the work environment becomes dysfunctional, if not downright poisonous.

Learning to Adapt

Adapting to feedback—which inevitably asks people to change, sometimes significantly—is critical for managers who find themselves in jobs, companies, and industries undergoing frequent transitions. Of course, adaptation is easier said than done, for resistance to change is endemic in human beings. But while most people feel they can't control the negative emotions that are aroused by change, this is not the case. It is possible—and necessary—to think positively about change. Using the following adaptive techniques, you can alter how you respond to feedback and to the changes it demands.

Recognize your emotions and responses

Understanding that you are experiencing fear ("I'm afraid my boss will fire me") and that you are exhibiting a maladaptive response to that fear ("I'll just stay out of his way and keep my mouth shut") are the critical initial steps toward adaptive change. They require ruthless self-honesty and a little detective work, both of which will go a long way toward helping you undo years of disguising your feelings. It's important to understand, too, that a particular maladaptive behavior does not necessarily tell you what emotion underlies it: You may be procrastinating out of anger, frustration, sadness, or other feelings. But persevering in the detective work is important, for the payoff is high. Having named the emotion and response, you can then act—just as someone who fears flying chooses to board a plane anyway. With practice, it gradually becomes easier to respond differently, even though the fear, anger, or sadness may remain.

Maria, a midlevel manager with whom we worked, is a good example of someone who learned to name her emotions and act despite them. Maria was several months overdue on performance reviews for the three people who reported to her. When we suggested that she was procrastinating, we asked her how she felt when she thought about doing the reviews. After some reflection, she said she was extremely resentful that her boss had not yet completed her own performance evaluation; she recognized that her procrastination was an expression of her anger toward him. We helped her realize that she could act despite her anger. Accordingly, Maria completed the performance evaluations for her subordinates and, in so doing, felt as if a huge weight had been lifted from her shoulders. Once she had completed the reviews, she noticed that her relationships with her three subordinates quickly improved, and her boss responded by finishing Maria's performance review.

We should note that Maria's procrastination was not an entrenched habit, so it was relatively easy to fix. Employees who start procrastinating in response to negative emotions early in their work lives won't change that habit quickly—but they can eventually.

Get support

Identifying your emotions is sometimes difficult, and feedback that requires change can leave you feeling inhibited and ashamed. For these reasons, it's critical to ask for help from trusted friends who will listen, encourage, and offer suggestions. Asking for support is often hard, because most corporate cultures expect managers to be self-reliant. Nevertheless, it's nearly impossible to make significant change without such encouragement. Support can come in many forms, but it should begin with at least two people—including, say, a spouse, a minister or spiritual counselor, a former mentor, an old high school classmate—with whom you feel emotionally safe. Ideally, one of these people should have some business experience. It may also help to enlist the assistance of an outside consultant or executive coach.

Reframe the feedback

Another adaptive technique, reframing, allows you to reconstruct the feedback process to your advantage. Specifically, this involves putting the prospect of asking for or reacting to feedback in a positive light so that negative emotions and responses lose their grip.

Take the example of Gary, a junior sales manager for a large manufacturing company. Gary's boss told him that he wasn't sociable enough with customers and prospects. The criticism stung, and Gary could have responded with denial or brooding. Indeed, his first response was to interpret the feedback as shallow. Eventually, though, Gary was able to reframe what he'd heard, first by grudgingly acknowledging it. ("He's right, I'm not very sociable. I tested as an introvert on the Myers-Briggs, and I've always been uncomfortable with small talk.") Then Gary reframed the feedback. Instead of seeing it as painful, he recognized that he could use it to help his career. Avoiding possible maladaptive responses, he was able to ask himself several important questions: "How critical is sociability to my position? How much do I want to keep this job? How much am I willing to change to become more sociable?" In responding, Gary realized two things: that sociability was indeed critical to success

Reframe Your Thinking

ALMOST EVERYONE DREADS performance reviews, which typically take place once a year. But how you respond to the boss's feedback—and how often you request it—will largely affect your performance and chances for career advancement. We've found that getting beyond that sense of dread involves recognizing and naming the emotions and behaviors that are preventing you from initiating feedback discussions. Once you determine those emotional and behavioral barriers, it's a matter of reframing your thoughts and moving toward more adaptive behavior. Below are some examples of how you might turn negative emotions into more positive, productive thoughts.

Possible negative emotion	Maladaptive response	Reframing statement
Anger *(I'm mad at my boss because he won't talk to me directly.)*	Acting out *(stomping around, complaining, being irritable, yelling at subordinates or family)*	It's up to me to get the feedback I need.
Anxiety *(I don't know what will happen.)*	Brooding *(withdrawal, nail biting)* Avoiding *(I'm too busy to ask for feedback.)*	Finding out can open up new opportunities for me.
Fear of confrontation *(I don't want to do this.)*	Denial, procrastination, self-sabotage *(canceling meetings with boss)*	Taking the initiative puts me in charge and gives me some power.

in sales and that he wasn't willing to learn to be more sociable. He requested a transfer and moved to a new position where he became much more successful.

Break up the task

Yet another adaptive technique is to divide up the large task of dealing with feedback into manageable, measurable chunks, and set realistic time frames for each one. Although more than two areas of behavior may need to be modified, it's our experience that most people can't change more than one or two at a time. Taking small

Possible negative emotion	**Maladaptive response**	**Reframing statement**
Fear of reprisal *(If I speak up, will I get a pink slip?)*	Denial *(I don't need any feedback. I'm doing just fine.)*	I really need to know honestly how I'm doing.
Hurt *(Why did he say I wasn't trying hard enough?)*	Irritability, jealousy of others *(silence, plotting to get even)*	I can still pay attention to what he said even though I feel hurt.
Defensiveness *(I'm better than she says.)*	Acting out by not supporting the boss *(You can bet I'm not going to her stupid meeting.)*	Being defensive keeps me from hearing what she has to say.
Sadness *(I thought he liked me!)*	Brooding, withdrawal *(being quieter than usual, feeling demotivated)*	How I'm doing in my job isn't about whether I'm liked.
Fear of change *(How will I ever do all that he wants me to do?)*	Denial *(keep doing things the same way as before)*	I *must* change to keep my job. I need to run the marathon one mile at a time.
Ambivalence *(Should I stay or should I go?)*	Procrastination, passivity *(waiting for somebody else to solve the problem)*	What really serves my interests best? Nobody is as interested in my well-being as I am. *I* need to take some action now.
Resignation *(I have to leave!)*	Resistance to change *(It's just too hard to look for another job. It's not really so bad here.)*	I'll be much happier working somewhere else.

steps and meeting discrete goals reduces your chances of being overwhelmed and makes change much more likely.

Jane, for example, received feedback indicating that the quality of her work was excellent but that her public presentations were boring. A quiet and reserved person, Jane could have felt overwhelmed by what she perceived as the subtext of this criticism: that she was a lousy public speaker and that she'd better transform herself from a wallflower into a writer and actress. Instead, she adapted by breaking down the challenge of "interesting presentations" into its constituent parts (solid and well-constructed content; a commanding delivery; an understanding of the audience; and so on). Then she undertook to teach herself to present more effectively by observing several effective speakers and taking an introductory course in public speaking.

It was important for Jane to start with the easiest task—in this case, observing good speakers. She noted their gestures, the organization of their speeches, their intonation, timing, use of humor, and so forth. Once she felt she understood what good speaking entailed, she was ready to take the introductory speaking course. These endeavors allowed her to improve her presentations. Though she didn't transform herself into a mesmerizing orator, she did learn to command the attention and respect of an audience.

Use incentives

Pat yourself on the back as you make adaptive changes. That may seem like unusual advice, given that feedback situations can rouse us to self-punishment and few of us are in the habit of congratulating ourselves. Nevertheless, nowhere is it written that the feedback process must be a wholly negative experience. Just as a salary raise or a bonus provides incentive to improve performance, rewarding yourself whenever you take an important step in the process will help you to persevere in your efforts. The incentive should be commensurate with the achievement. For example, an appropriate reward for completing a self-assessment might be an uninterrupted afternoon watching ESPN or, for a meeting with the boss, a fine dinner out.

Getting the Feedback You Need

Once you've begun to adapt your responses and behavior, it's time to start seeking regular feedback from your boss rather than wait for the annual performance review to come around. The proactive feedback process we recommend consists of four manageable steps: self-assessment, external feedback, absorbing the feedback, and taking action toward change. The story of Bob, a vice president of human resources, illustrates how one executive used the four-step process to take charge of his work life.

When we first met Bob, he had been on the job for three years and felt he was in a feedback vacuum. Once a year, toward the end of December, Harry—the gruff, evasive CEO to whom he reported—would call Bob in, tell him what a fine job he had been doing, announce his salary for the following year, and give him a small bonus. But this year, Bob had been dealing with thorny issues—including complaints from senior female executives about unfair compensation—and needed some real feedback. Bob wondered how Harry viewed his work. Were there aspects of Bob's performance that Harry wasn't happy with? Did Harry intend to retain Bob in his current position?

Self-assessment

We encouraged Bob to begin by assessing his own performance. Self-assessment can be a tough assignment, particularly if one has never received useful feedback to begin with. The first task in self-assessment was for Bob to determine which elements of his job were most important. The second was to recall informal feedback he had received from coworkers, subordinates, and customers—not only words, but facial expressions, body language, and silences.

Bob took several weeks to do his self-assessment. Once we helped him realize that he was procrastinating with the assessment, he enlisted a support system—his wife and an old college buddy—who encouraged him to finish his tally of recollections. At the end of the process, he recognized that he had received a good deal of positive informal feedback from many of the people with whom he interacted. But he also realized that he was too eager to please and needed to be more assertive in expressing his opinions. We helped him reframe these uncomfortable insights so that he could see them as areas for potential growth.

External feedback

The next phase of the proactive process—asking for feedback—is generally a two-part task: The first involves speaking to a few trusted colleagues to collect information that supports or revises your self-assessment. The second involves directly asking your boss for feedback. Gathering feedback from trusted colleagues shouldn't be confused with 360-degree feedback, which culls a wide variety of perspectives, including those from people who may not know you well. By speaking confidentially with people you genuinely trust, you can keep some of the fear associated with feedback at bay. Trusted colleagues can also help you identify your own emotional and possibly maladaptive responses to criticism, which is particularly beneficial prior to your meeting with your superior. Additionally, feedback conversations with colleagues can often serve as a form of dress rehearsal for the real thing. Sometimes, colleagues point out areas that warrant immediate attention; when they do, it's wise to make those changes before meeting with the boss. On the other hand, if you think you can't trust any of your colleagues, you should bypass such feedback conversations and move directly to setting up a meeting with your boss.

Bob asked for feedback from two trusted colleagues, Sheila and Paul, at meetings that he specifically scheduled for this purpose. He requested both positive and negative feedback and specific examples of areas in which he did well and in which he needed to improve. He listened intently to their comments, interrupting only for clarification. Both told him that he analyzed problems carefully and interacted well with employees. Yet Sheila noted that at particularly busy times of the year, Bob seemed to have difficulty setting his priorities, and Paul pointed out that Bob needed to be more assertive. Armed with his colleagues' feedback, Bob had a clearer notion of his strengths and weaknesses. He realized that some of his difficulties in setting priorities were owing to unclear direction from Harry, and he made a note to raise the matter with him.

The next step in external feedback—the actual meeting with your boss—requires delicate handling, particularly since the request may come as a surprise to him or her. In setting up the meeting, it's important to assure your boss that criticisms and suggestions will be heard, appreciated, and positively acted on. It's vital, too, to set the agenda for the meeting, letting your superior know that you have three or four questions based on your self-assessment and feedback from others. During the meeting, ask for specific examples and suggestions for change while remaining physically and emotionally neutral about the feedback you hear. Watch carefully not only for specific content but also for body language and tone, since feedback can be indirect as well as direct. When the meeting concludes, thank your boss and indicate that you will get back to her with a plan of action after you've had time to absorb what you've heard. Remember, too, that you can terminate the meeting if it becomes counterproductive (for example, if your boss responds to any of your questions with anger).

During his feedback meeting with Harry, Bob inquired about his work priorities. Harry told him that the company's financial situation looked precarious and that Bob should focus on locating and implementing a less costly health benefit plan. Harry warned Bob that a new plan would surely anger some employees, and because of that, Bob needed to develop a tougher skin to withstand the inevitable criticisms.

As Bob learned, feedback meetings can provide more than just a performance assessment; they can also offer some other important and unexpected insights. Bob had been so immersed in HR issues that he had never noted that Harry had been otherwise preoccupied with the company's financial problems.

Absorbing the feedback

Upon hearing critical feedback, you may well experience the negative emotions and maladaptive responses we described earlier. It's important to keep your reactions private until you can replace them with adaptive responses that lead to an appropriate plan of action.

Bob, for example, realized he felt irritated and vaguely hurt at the suggestion that he needed to toughen up. He brooded for a while but then reframed these feelings by recognizing that the negative feedback was as much a commentary on Harry's preoccupations as it was on Bob's performance. Bob didn't use the reframing to negate Harry's feedback; he accepted that he needed to be more assertive and hard-nosed in dealing with employees' issues.

Taking action

The last phase of the proactive feedback process involves coming to conclusions about, and acting on, the information you've received.

Bob, for example, chose to focus on two action strategies: implementing a less costly health care plan—which included preparing himself to tolerate employee complaints—and quietly looking for new employment, since he now understood that the company's future was uncertain. Both of these decisions made Bob uncomfortable, for they evoked his fear of change. But having developed his adaptive responses, he no longer felt trapped by fear. In the months following, he implemented the new health benefits plan without taking his employees' criticisms personally. He also kept an eye on the company's financials and reconnected with his professional network in case it became clear the organization was starting to founder.

The Rewards of Adaptation

Organizations profit when executives seek feedback and are able to deal well with criticism. As executives begin to ask how they are doing relative to management's priorities, their work becomes better aligned with organizational goals. Moreover, as an increasing number of executives in an organization learn to ask for feedback, they begin to transform a feedback-averse environment into a more honest and open one, in turn improving performance throughout the organization.

Equally important, using the adaptive techniques we've mentioned can have a positive effect on executives' private lives. When they free themselves from knee-jerk behaviors in response to emotions, they often find that relationships with family and friends improve. Indeed, they sometimes discover that rather than fear feedback, they look forward to leveraging it.

Originally published in April 2003. Reprint R0304H

The Young and the Clueless

by Kerry A. Bunker, Kathy E. Kram, and Sharon Ting

IN MANY WAYS, 36-year-old Charles Armstrong is a natural leader. He's brilliant, creative, energetic, aggressive—a strategic and financial genius. He's risen quickly through the ranks due to his keen business instincts and proven ability to deliver bottom-line results, at times jumping from one organization to another to leapfrog through the hierarchy. But now his current job is on the line. A division president at an international consumer products company, he's just uncovered a major production setback on a heavily promoted new product. Thousands of orders have been delayed, customers are furious, and the company's stock price has plummeted since the news went public.

Worse, the crisis was utterly preventable. Had Armstrong understood the value of building relationships with his peers and had his subordinates found him approachable, he might have been able to appreciate the cross-functional challenges of developing this particular product. He might have learned of the potential delay months earlier instead of at the eleventh hour. He could have postponed a national advertising campaign and set expectations with investors. He might have even found a way to solve the problems and launch the product on time. But despite his ability to dazzle his superiors with talent and intellect, Armstrong is widely viewed by his peers and subordinates as self-promoting, intolerant, and remote. Perhaps worse, he's only half aware of how others perceive him, and to the extent he does know, he's not terribly concerned. These relationships are not a priority for him. Like so many other talented young managers, Armstrong lacks the emotional competencies that would enable him to work more effectively as part of a team. And now his bosses seem to have unwittingly undermined his career, having promoted him too quickly, before he could develop the relationship skills he needs.

Break the Pattern

What happened with Charles Armstrong is an increasingly common phenomenon. In the past ten years, we've met dozens of managers who have fallen victim to a harmful mix of their own ambition and their bosses' willingness to overlook a lack of people skills. (As with all the examples in these pages, we've changed Armstrong's name and other identifying features to protect our clients' identities.) Indeed, most executives seek out smart, aggressive people, paying more attention to their accomplishments than to their emotional maturity. What's more, they know that their strongest performers have options—if they don't get the job they want at one company, they're bound to get it somewhere else. Why risk losing them to a competitor by delaying a promotion?

The answer is that promoting them can be just as risky. Putting these unseasoned managers into positions of authority too quickly robs them of the opportunity to develop the emotional competencies that come with time and experience—competencies like the ability to negotiate with peers, regulate their emotions in times of crisis, or win support for change. Bosses may be delighted with such managers' intelligence and passion—and may even see younger versions of themselves—but peers and subordinates are more likely to see them as arrogant and inconsiderate, or, at the very least, aloof. And therein lies the problem. At some point in a young manager's career, usually at the vice president level, raw talent and determined ambition become less important than the ability to influence

Idea in Brief

Hell-bent on sabotaging your company? Then promote your brightest young professionals into your most demanding roles—especially when they threaten to leave unless you fast-track them. Nonsense, you say? Hardly.

Promoting talented young managers too quickly prevents them from developing key **emotional competencies**—such as negotiating with peers, regulating negative emotions during crises, and building support for change—skills that come only with time and experience.

Worse, many "young and clueless" managers lack patience, openness, and empathy—qualities more vital than raw intellect at top leadership levels, where business issues grow more complex and stakes are notoriously high.

Aggressive and insensitive, fast-tracked managers may pooh-pooh relationships with peers and subordinates—not realizing they *need* those connections to conquer problems. Issues become crises, defeating managers. Your company, customers, and employees all pay the price.

The solution? **Delay promotions** so managers can mature emotionally. This isn't easy. You must balance confrontation and support, patience and urgency—and risk losing your finest. But premature promoting carries far greater risks.

and persuade. And unless senior executives appreciate this fact and make emotional competence a top priority, these high-potential managers will continue to fail, often at significant cost to the company.

Research has shown that the higher a manager rises in the ranks, the more important soft leadership skills are to his success.[1] Our colleagues at the Center for Creative Leadership have found that about a third of senior executives derail or plateau at some point, most often due to an emotional deficit such as the inability to build a team or regulate their own emotions in times of stress. And in our combined 55 years of coaching and teaching, we've seen firsthand how a young manager risks his career when he fails to develop emotional competencies. But the problem isn't youth per se. The problem is a lack of emotional maturity, which doesn't come easily or automatically and isn't something you learn from a book. It's one thing to understand the importance of relationships at an intellectual level

Idea in Practice

1. **Deepen 360-degree feedback.** Provide broad and deep feedback to help managers see themselves as others do—a must for building self-awareness. Give them verbatim written responses to open-ended questions from a wide variety of peers and subordinates, not just you. Managers may discount your views as biased or uninformed. Allow time for reflection and follow-up conversations.

   Example: Though his business acumen was unmatched in his company, a brilliant 42-year-old VP neglected peer relationships, earning a reputation as detached. Corporate wondered if he could inspire staff to support important new strategies. After an in-depth 360-degree review, he began strengthening interpersonal connections.

2. **Interrupt the ascent.** To help managers learn to move others' hearts and minds, give them special assignments outside their typical career path. They'll *have* to master negotiation and influence skills, rather than relying on rank for authority.

   Example: A quick-tempered regional sales director wasn't ready for promotion to VP. Her boss persuaded her to lead a year-long team investigating cross selling opportunities. She learned to use persuasion to win other division managers' support, building solid relationships. Now a VP, she's perceived as a well-connected manager who can negotiate on her team's behalf.

and to learn techniques like active listening; it's another matter entirely to develop a full range of interpersonal competencies like patience, openness, and empathy. Emotional maturity involves a fundamental shift in self-awareness and behavior, and that change requires practice, diligence, and time.

Armstrong's boss admits that he may have promoted the young manager too soon: "I was just like Charles when I was his age, but I was a director, not a division president. It's easier to make mistakes and learn when you aren't in such a big chair. I want him to succeed, and I think he could make a great CEO one day, but sometimes he puts me at risk. He's just too sure of himself to listen." And so, in many cases, executives do their employees and the company a service by delaying the promotion of a young manager and giving

3. **Act on your commitment.** If you've warned managers that promotion depends on emotional competencies, follow through. These competencies are *not* optional.

   Example: A conflict-averse senior VP managed his own group well but avoided collaborative situations, where the potential for conflict increased. Exploring external alliances, the firm considered collaboration vital. The CEO demoted him, temporarily pulling him from the succession plan. Assigned to a cross-functional team project, he learned to handle disputes and build consensus. He's back on track.

4. **Institutionalize personal development.** Make it clear that success at your company hinges on emotional competence.

   Example: One CEO articulated corporate values emphasizing continual learning, including asking for help. He created incentives encouraging such behaviors and built emotional-skills requirements into the firm's succession planning. Known for learning and growing, the firm attracts and retains talented young executives.

5. **Cultivate informal networks.** Encourage managers to forge mentoring relationships outside the usual hierarchy. They'll encounter diverse leadership styles and viewpoints, gain opportunities for reflection—and mature emotionally.

him the chance to develop his interpersonal skills. Interrupting the manager's ascent long enough to round out his experience will usually yield a much more effective and stable leader.

This article will look at five strategies for boosting emotional competencies and redirecting managers who are paying a price for damaged or nonexistent relationships. The strategies aren't terribly complicated, but implementing them and getting people to change their entrenched behaviors can be very difficult. Many of these managers are accustomed to receiving accolades, and it often isn't easy for them to hear—or act on—difficult messages. You may have to satisfy yourself with small victories and accept occasional slipups. But perhaps the greatest challenge is having the discipline to resist the charm of the young and the clueless—to refrain from promoting them before they are ready and to stay the course even if they threaten to quit.

Deepen 360-Degree Feedback

With its questionnaires and standardized rating scales, 360-degree feedback as it is traditionally implemented may not be sufficiently specific or detailed to get the attention of inexperienced managers who excel at bottom-line measures but struggle with more subtle relationship challenges. These managers will benefit from a deeper and more thorough process that includes time for reflection and follow-up conversations. That means, for example, interviewing a wider range of the manager's peers and subordinates and giving her the opportunity to read verbatim responses to open-ended questions. Such detailed and extensive feedback can help a person see herself more as others do, a must for the young manager lacking the self-awareness to understand where she's falling short.

We witnessed this lack of self-awareness in Bill Miller, a 42-year-old vice president at a software company—an environment where technical ability is highly prized. Miller had gone far on pure intellect, but he never fully appreciated his own strengths. So year after year, in assignment after assignment, he worked doubly hard at learning the complexities of the business, neglecting his relationships with his colleagues as an unintended consequence. His coworkers considered his smarts and business acumen among the finest in the company, but they found him unapproachable and detached. As a result, top management questioned his ability to lead the type of strategic change that would require motivating staff at all levels. Not until Miller went through an in-depth 360-degree developmental review was he able to accept that he no longer needed to prove his intelligence—that he could relax in that respect and instead work on strengthening his personal connections. After months of working hard to cultivate stronger relationships with his employees, Miller began to notice that he felt more included in chance social encounters like hallway conversations.

Art Grainger, a 35-year-old senior manager at a cement and concrete company, was generally considered a champion by his direct reports. He was also known for becoming defensive whenever his peers or superiors questioned or even discussed his unit's performance. Through 360-degree reviews, he discovered that while everyone saw him as committed, results-oriented, and technically brilliant, they also saw him as overly protective, claiming he resisted any action or decision that might affect his department. Even his employees felt that he kept them isolated from the rest of the company, having said he reviewed all memos between departments, didn't invite people from other parts of the company to his department's meetings, and openly criticized other managers. Only when Grainger heard that his staff agreed with what his bosses had been telling him for years did he concede that he needed to change. Since then, he has come to see members of other departments as potential allies and has tried to redefine his team to include people from across the company.

It's worth noting that many of these smart young managers aren't used to hearing criticism. Consequently, they may discount negative feedback, either because the comments don't mesh with what they've heard in previous conversations or because their egos are so strong. Or they may conclude that they can "fix" the problem right away—after all, they've been able to fix most problems they've encountered in the past. But developing emotional competencies requires practice and ongoing personal interactions. The good news is that if you succeed in convincing them that these issues are career threatening, they may apply the same zeal to their emotional development that they bring to their other projects. And that's why 360-degree feedback is so valuable: When it comes from multiple sources and is ongoing, it's difficult to ignore.

Interrupt the Ascent

When people are continually promoted within their areas of expertise, they don't have to stray far from their comfort zones, so they seldom need to ask for help, especially if they're good problem solvers. Accordingly, they may become overly independent and fail to cultivate relationships with people who could be useful to them in the future. What's more, they may rely on the authority that comes with rank rather than learning how to influence people. A command-and-control mentality may work in certain situations, particularly in lower to middle management, but it's usually insufficient in more senior positions, when peer relationships are critical and success depends more on the ability to move hearts and minds than on the ability to develop business solutions.

We sometimes counsel our clients to broaden young managers' skills by assigning them to cross-functional roles outside their expected career paths. This is distinct from traditional job rotation, which has employees spending time in different functional areas to enhance and broaden their knowledge of the business. Rather, the manager is assigned a role in which he doesn't have much direct authority. This will help him focus on developing other skills like negotiation and influencing peers.

Consider the case of Sheila McIntyre, a regional sales director at a technology company. McIntyre had been promoted quickly into the managerial ranks because she consistently outsold her colleagues month after month. In her early thirties, she began angling for another promotion–this time, to vice president—but her boss, Ron Meyer, didn't think she was ready. Meyer felt that McIntyre had a quick temper and little patience for people whom she perceived as less visionary. So he put the promotion on hold, despite McIntyre's stellar performance, and created a yearlong special assignment for her—heading a team investigating cross-selling opportunities. To persuade her to take the job, he not only explained that it would help McIntyre broaden her skills but promised a significant financial reward if she succeeded, also hinting that the hoped-for promotion would follow. It was a stretch for McIntyre. She had to use her underdeveloped powers of persuasion to win support from managers in other divisions. But in the end, her team presented a brilliant cross-selling strategy, which the company implemented over the following year. More important, she developed solid relationships with a number of influential people throughout the organization and learned a lot about the value of others' insights and experiences. McIntyre was eventually promoted to vice president, and to Meyer's satisfaction, her new reports now see her not just as a superstar salesperson but as a well-connected manager who can negotiate on their behalf.

Such cross-functional assignments—with no clear authority or obvious ties to a career path—can be a tough sell. It's not easy to convince young managers that these assignments are valuable, nor is it easy to help them extract relevant knowledge. If the managers feel marginalized, they may not stick around. Remember Bill Miller, the vice president who had neglected his emotional skills in his zeal to learn the business? While he was successful in some of his early informal attempts to build relationships, he was confused and demoralized when his boss, Jerry Schulman, gave him a special assignment to lead a task force reviewing internal processes. Miller had expected a promotion, and the new job didn't feel "real." Schulman made the mistake of not telling Miller that he saw the job as an ideal networking opportunity, so Miller began to question his future at the company. A few months into the new job, Miller gave his notice. He seized an opportunity—a step up—at an arch-rival, taking a tremendous amount of talent and institutional knowledge with him. Had Schulman shared his reasoning with Miller, he might have retained one of his most valuable players—one who had already seen the importance of developing his emotional competence and had begun to make progress.

Act On Your Commitment

One of the reasons employees get stuck in the pattern we've described is that their bosses point out deficits in emotional competencies but don't follow through. They either neglect to articulate the consequences of continuing the destructive behavior or make empty threats but proceed with a promotion anyway. The hard-charging young executive can only conclude that these competencies are optional.

A cautionary tale comes from Mitchell Geller who, at 29, was on the verge of being named partner at a law firm. He had alienated many of his peers and subordinates over the years through his arrogance, a shortcoming duly noted on his yearly performance reviews, yet his keen legal mind had won him promotion after promotion. With Geller's review approaching, his boss, Larry Snow, pointed to heavy attrition among the up-and-coming lawyers who worked for Geller and warned him that further advancement would be contingent on a change in personal style. Geller didn't take the feedback to heart—he was confident that he'd get by, as he always had, on sheer talent. And true to form, Snow didn't stick to his guns. The promotion came through even though Geller's behavior hadn't changed. Two weeks later, Geller, by then a partner responsible for managing client relationships, led meetings with two key accounts. Afterward, the first client approached Snow and asked him to sit in on future meetings. Then the second client withdrew his business altogether, complaining that Geller had refused to listen to alternative points of view.

Contrast Geller's experience with that of 39-year-old Barry Kessler, a senior vice president at an insurance company. For years, Kessler had been heir apparent to the CEO due to his strong financial skills and vast knowledge of the business—that is, until John Mason, his boss and the current CEO, began to question the wisdom of promoting him.

While Kessler managed his own group exceptionally well, he avoided collaboration with other units, which was particularly important as the company began looking for new growth opportunities, including potential alliances with other organizations. The problem wasn't that Kessler was hostile, it was that he was passively disengaged—a flaw that hadn't seemed as important when he was responsible only for his own group. In coaching Kessler, we learned that he was extremely averse to conflict and that he avoided situations where he couldn't be the decision maker. His aversions sharply limited his ability to work with peers.

Mason sent a strong signal, not only to Kessler but to others in the organization, when he essentially demoted Kessler by taking away some of his responsibilities and temporarily pulling him from the succession plan. To give Kessler an opportunity to develop the skills he lacked, Mason asked him to lead a cross-functional team dedicated to finding strategic opportunities for growth. Success would require Kessler to devote more time to developing his interpersonal skills. He had no authority over the other team members, so he had to work through disputes and help the team arrive at a consensus. Two years later, Kessler reports that he is more comfortable with conflict and feedback, and he's worked his way back into the succession plan.

By the way, it's counterproductive to hold managers to a certain standard of behavior without showing that the same standard applies to everyone, right up to top management. In many cases, that means acknowledging your own development goals, which isn't easy. One CEO we worked with, Joe Simons, came to realize during 360-degree feedback and peer coaching that his personal style was interfering with his subordinates' growth. Simons had declared innovation a corporate priority, yet his fear of failure led him to micromanage his employees, stifling their creativity. To stop this pattern and express his newfound commitment to improving his relationship skills, he revealed his personal goals—to seek advice more regularly and to communicate more openly—to his direct reports. He promised to change specific behaviors and asked for the team's feedback and support in this process. Going public with these goals was tough for Simons, a private person raised on traditional command-and-control leadership. Admitting that he needed to change some behaviors felt dangerously weak to him, especially given that the company was going through a difficult time and employees were looking to him for assurance, but his actions made his new priorities clear to employees.

Simons's candor won people's trust and respect, and over the course of many months, others in the company began to reflect more openly on their own emotional skills and engage in similar processes of personal development. Not only did his relationships with his direct reports improve, but Simons became a catalyst and model for others as well. He told us of an encounter with Gwen Marshall, the company's CFO and one of Simons's direct reports. Marshall was concerned about a new hire who wasn't coming up to speed as

Think Before Promoting

IT'S NOT UNUSUAL for a star performer to be promoted into higher management before he's ready. Yes, he may be exceptionally smart and talented, but he may also lack essential people skills. Rather than denying him the promotion altogether, his boss might do well to delay it—and use that time to help develop the candidate's emotional competencies. Here's how.

Deepen 360-Degree Feedback

Go beyond the usual set of questionnaires that make up the traditional 360-degree-feedback process. Interview a wide variety of the manager's peers and subordinates and let him read verbatim responses to open-ended performance questions.

Interrupt the Ascent

Help the inexperienced manager get beyond a command-and-control mentality by pushing him to develop his negotiation and persuasion skills. Instead of promoting him, give him cross-functional assignments where he can't rely on rank to influence people.

Act On Your Commitment

Don't give the inexperienced manager the impression that emotional competencies are optional. Hold him accountable for his interpersonal skills, in some cases taking a tough stance by demoting him or denying him a promotion, but with the promise that changed behaviors will ultimately be rewarded.

Institutionalize Personal Development

Weave interpersonal goals into the fabric of the organization and make emotional competence a performance measure. Also work to institute formal development programs that teach leadership skills and facilitate self-awareness, reflection, and opportunities to practice new emotional competencies.

Cultivate Informal Networks

Encourage the manager to develop informal learning partnerships with peers and mentors in order to expose him to different leadership styles and perspectives. This will provide him with honest and ongoing feedback and continual opportunities to learn.

quickly as she had hoped—he was asking lots of questions and, she felt, not taking enough initiative. She had just snapped at him at the close of a meeting, and he'd looked surprised and angry. In speaking to Simons about the incident, however, she acknowledged that her impatience was perhaps unfair. He was, after all, new to the job. What's more, the nature of finance demanded precise thinking and a thorough knowledge of the business. Marshall ended the conversation by saying she would apologize to the new employee. Simons was surprised at Marshall's comments—he was used to seeing her simply blow off steam and move on to the next task. But possibly due to Simons's example, she had become more attuned to the importance of her own emotional competence. Such reflection has become a habit among Simons's team—a change that has enhanced personal relationships and increased the team's overall performance.

Institutionalize Personal Development

One of the most effective ways to build managers' emotional competencies is to weave interpersonal goals into the fabric of the organization, where everyone is expected to demonstrate a specific set of emotional skills and where criteria for promotion include behaviors as well as technical ability. A built-in process will make it easier to uncover potential problems early and reduce the chances that people identified as needing personal development will feel singled out or unfairly held back. Employees will know exactly what's expected of them and what it takes to advance in their careers.

Here's a case in which institutionalizing personal development was extremely effective: Mark Jones is an executive who was tapped for the CEO job at a major manufacturing company on the condition that he engage a coach because of his reputation for being too blunt and aggressive. A yearlong coaching relationship helped Jones understand the pitfalls associated with his style, and he decided that others could benefit from arriving at such an understanding far earlier in their careers. To that end, he launched several major initiatives to shape the company culture in such a way that personal and professional learning were not only encouraged but expected.

First, he articulated a new set of corporate values and practices that were based on meeting business objectives and developing top-notch leadership skills. One of the values was "Dare to be transparent," which meant that all employees, especially those in senior leadership roles, were expected to be open about their weaknesses, ask for help, and offer honest, constructive feedback to their peers. Knowing that it would be necessary to create incentives and rewards for these new behaviors, Jones took an active role in the review and personal-development goals of the company's top 100 executives, and he mandated that all employees' performance plans incorporate specific actions related to developing their own emotional competencies. Jones also made emotional skills a key qualification in the search for a successor—a requirement that many organizations pay lip service to. Many of them often overvalue raw intellect and depth of knowledge, largely because of the war for talent, which has resulted in a singular focus on hiring and retaining the best and brightest regardless of their emotional competence. Finally, Jones created a new position, corporate learning officer; he and the CLO partnered with a nearby university to create a learning institute where corporate executives could teach in and attend leadership programs. Jones himself is a frequent lecturer and participant in the various courses.

Through all these actions, Jones has made it clear that employees need to make continual learning and emotional development a priority. He's also emphasized that everyone from the CEO on down is expected to set goals for improving personal skills. Since implementing the program, he is finding it easier to attract and retain talented young executives—indeed, his organization has evolved from a recruiter's nightmare to a magnet for young talent. It is becoming known as a place where emerging leaders can find real opportunities to learn and grow.

We worked with another company where the senior management team committed to developing the emotional competencies of the company's leaders. The team first provided extensive education on coaching to the HR department, which in turn supervised a program whereby top managers coached their younger and more inexperienced colleagues. The goal was to have both the experienced and inexperienced benefit: The junior managers provided feedback on the senior people's coaching skills, and the senior people helped foster emotional competencies in their less-experienced colleagues.

The results were encouraging. Wes Burke, an otherwise high-performing manager, had recently been struggling to meet his business targets. After spending time with Burke and conferring with his subordinates and peers, his coach (internal to the organization) came to believe that, in his zest to achieve his goals, Burke was unable to slow down and listen to other people's ideas. Burke wasn't a boor: He had taken courses in communication and knew how to fake listening behaviors such as nodding his head and giving verbal acknowledgments, but he was often distracted and not really paying attention. He never accepted this feedback until one day, while he was walking purposefully through the large operations plant he managed, a floor supervisor stopped him to discuss his ideas for solving an ongoing production problem. Burke flipped on his active-listening mode. After uttering a few acknowledgments and saying, "Thanks, let's talk more about that," he moved on, leaving the supervisor feeling frustrated and at a loss for how to capture his boss's interest. As it happened, Burke's coach was watching. He pulled the young manager aside and said, "You didn't hear a word Karl just said. You weren't really listening." Burke admitted as much to himself and his coach. He then apologized to Karl, much to the supervisor's surprise. Keeping this incident in mind helped Burke remember the importance of his working relationships. His coach had also helped him realize that he shouldn't have assumed his sheer will and drive would somehow motivate his employees. Burke had been wearing people down, physically and psychologically. A year later, Burke's operation was hitting its targets, an accomplishment he partially attributes to the one-on-one coaching he received.

Cultivate Informal Networks

While institutionalized programs to build emotional competencies are critical, some managers will benefit more from an informal network of relationships that fall outside the company hierarchy. Mentoring, for example, can help both junior and senior managers further their emotional development through a new type of relationship. And when the mentoring experience is a positive one, it often acts as a springboard to a rich variety of relationships with others throughout the organization. In particular, it gives junior managers a chance to experience different leadership styles and exposes them to diverse viewpoints.

Sonia Greene, a 32-year-old manager at a consulting firm, was hoping to be promoted to principal, but she hadn't raised the issue with her boss because she assumed he didn't think she was ready, and she didn't want to create tension. She was a talented consultant with strong client relationships, but her internal relationships were weak due to a combination of shyness, an independent nature, and a distaste for conflict, which inhibited her from asking for feedback. When her company launched a mentoring program, Greene signed up, and through a series of lengthy conversations with Jessica Burnham, a partner at the firm, she developed new insights about her strengths and weaknesses. The support of an established player such as Burnham helped Greene become more confident and honest in her development discussions with her boss, who hadn't been aware that Greene was willing to receive and act on feedback. Today, Greene is armed with a precise understanding of what she needs to work on and is well on her way to being promoted. What's more, her relationship with Burnham has prompted her to seek out other connections, including a peer group of up-and-coming managers who meet monthly to share experiences and offer advice to one another.

Peer networking is beneficial to even the most top-level executives. And the relationships needn't be confined within organizational boundaries. Joe Simons, a CEO we mentioned earlier, wanted to continue his own personal development, so he cultivated a relationship with another executive he'd met through our program. The two men have stayed in touch through regular e-mails and phone calls, keeping their discussions confidential so they can feel free to share even the most private concerns. They also get together periodically to discuss their goals for personal development.

Both have found these meetings invaluable, noting that their work relationships have continued to improve and that having a trustworthy confidant has helped each avoid relapsing into old habits during times of stress.

Delaying a promotion can be difficult given the steadfast ambitions of the young executive and the hectic pace of organizational life, which makes personal learning seem like an extravagance. It requires a delicate balance of honesty and support, of patience and goading. It means going against the norm of promoting people almost exclusively on smarts, talent, and business results. It also means contending with the disappointment of an esteemed subordinate.

But taking the time to build people's emotional competencies isn't an extravagance; it's critical to developing effective leaders. Give in to the temptation to promote your finest before they're ready, and you're left with executives who may thrive on change and demonstrate excellent coping and survival skills but who lack the self-awareness, empathy, and social abilities required to foster and nurture those strengths in others. MBA programs and management books can't teach young executives everything they need to know about people skills. Indeed, there's no substitute for experience, reflection, feedback, and, above all, practice.

Originally published in December 2002. Reprint R0212F

Note

1. In his HBR articles "What Makes a Leader?" (November–December 1998) and "Primal Leadership: The Hidden Driver of Great Performance" (with Richard Boyatzis and Annie McKee, December 2001), Daniel Goleman makes the case that emotional competence is the crucial driver of a leader's success.

About the Contributors

RICHARD BOYATZIS chairs the department of organizational behavior at the Weatherhead School of Management at Case Western Reserve University.

JOEL BROCKNER is the Phillip Hettleman Professor of Business at Columbia Business School.

KERRY A. BUNKER is a manager of the Awareness Program for Executive Excellence at the Center for Creative Leadership.

ANDREW CAMPBELL is a director of Ashridge Strategic Management Centre in London.

CHRISTINA CONGLETON, who was formerly a researcher on mindfulness and the brain at Massachusetts General Hospital, is an associate at Evidence Based Psychology and a certified coach.

DIANE L. COUTU is a former senior editor of *Harvard Business Review*.

SUSAN DAVID is the CEO of Evidence Based Psychology, a cofounder of the Institute of Coaching, and an instructor in psychology at Harvard University.

SYDNEY FINKELSTEIN is the Steven Roth Professor of Management at the Tuck School of Business at Dartmouth College.

DANIEL GOLEMAN cochairs the Consortium for Research on Emotional Intelligence in Organizations at Rutgers University.

JAY M. JACKMAN is a psychiatrist and human resources consultant in Stanford, California.

KATHY E. KRAM is a professor of organizational behavior at the Boston University School of Management.

ANNIE McKEE is on the faculty of the University of Pennsylvania's Graduate School of Education.

CHRISTINE PEARSON is a professor of global leadership at Thunderbird School of Global Management.

CHRISTINE PORATH is an associate professor at Georgetown University's McDonough School of Business.

MYRA H. STROBER is a labor economist and professor at Stanford University's School of Education, and by courtesy at the Stanford Graduate School of Business. She is also a human resources consultant.

SHARON TING is a manager of the Awareness Program for Executive Excellence at the Center for Creative Leadership.

VANESSA URCH DRUSKAT is an assistant professor of organizational behavior at the Weatherhead School of Management at Case Western Reserve University.

JO WHITEHEAD is a director of Ashridge Strategic Management Centre in London.

STEVEN B. WOLFF is an assistant professor of management at the School of Management at Marist College.

Index

HBR'S 10 MUST READS

The Essentials

HBR'S 10 MUST READS

The Essentials

HARVARD BUSINESS REVIEW PRESS
Boston, Massachusetts

Printed in the United States of America
45 44 43 42

Library of Congress Cataloging-in-Publication Data
HBR's 10 must reads : the essentials.
p. cm.
Includes index.
ISBN 978-1-4221-3344-6 (pbk. : alk. paper) 1. Management. I. Harvard Business Review. II. Title: HBR's ten must reads. III. Title: Harvard Business Review's 10 must reads.
HD31.H3948 2010
658—dc22
2010030742

The paper used in this publication meets the requirements of the American National Standard for Permanence of Paper for Publications and Documents in Libraries and Archives Z39.48-1992.

Contents

HBR'S 10 MUST READS

The Essentials

Meeting the Challenge of Disruptive Change

by Clayton M. Christensen and Michael Overdorf

THESE ARE SCARY TIMES for managers in big companies. Even before the Internet and globalization, their track record for dealing with major, disruptive change was not good. Out of hundreds of department stores, for example, only one—Dayton Hudson—became a leader in discount retailing. Not one of the minicomputer companies succeeded in the personal computer business. Medical and business schools are struggling—and failing—to change their curricula fast enough to train the types of doctors and managers their markets need. The list could go on.

It's not that managers in big companies can't see disruptive changes coming. Usually they can. Nor do they lack resources to confront them. Most big companies have talented managers and specialists, strong product portfolios, first-rate technological know-how, and deep pockets. What managers lack is a habit of thinking about their organization's capabilities as carefully as they think about individual people's capabilities.

One of the hallmarks of a great manager is the ability to identify the right person for the right job and to train employees to succeed at the jobs they're given. But unfortunately, most managers assume that if each person working on a project is well matched to the job, then the organization in which they work will be, too. Often that is not the case. One could put two sets of identically capable people to work in different organizations, and what they accomplished would be significantly different. That's because organizations themselves—independent of the people and other resources in them—have capabilities. To succeed consistently, good managers need to be skilled not just in assessing people but also in assessing the abilities and disabilities of their organization as a whole.

This article offers managers a framework to help them understand what their organizations are capable of accomplishing. It will show them how their company's disabilities become more sharply defined even as its core capabilities grow. It will give them a way to recognize different kinds of change and make appropriate organizational responses to the opportunities that arise from each. And it will offer some bottom-line advice that runs counter to much that's assumed in our can-do business culture: if an organization faces major change—a disruptive innovation, perhaps—the worst possible approach may be to make drastic adjustments to the existing organization. In trying to transform an enterprise, managers can destroy the very capabilities that sustain it.

Before rushing into the breach, managers must understand precisely what types of change the existing organization is capable and incapable of handling. To help them do that, we'll first take a systematic look at how to recognize a company's core capabilities on an organizational level and then examine how those capabilities migrate as companies grow and mature.

Where Capabilities Reside

Our research suggests that three factors affect what an organization can and cannot do: its resources, its processes, and its values. When thinking about what sorts of innovations their organization will be able to embrace, managers need to assess how each of these factors might affect their organization's capacity to change.

Idea in Brief

Why do so few established companies innovate successfully? Of hundreds of department stores, for instance, only Dayton Hudson became a discount-retailing leader. And not one minicomputer company succeeded in the personal-computer business.

What's going on? After all, most established firms boast deep pockets and talented people. But when a new venture captures their imagination, they get their people working on it within organizational structures (such as functional teams) designed to surmount *old* challenges—not ones that the new venture is facing.

To avoid this mistake, ask:

- **"Does my organization have the right *resources* to support this innovation?"** Resources supporting business-as-usual—people, technologies, product designs, brands, customer and supplier relationships—rarely match those required for new ventures.
- **"Does my organization have the right *processes* to innovate?"** Processes supporting your established business—decision-making protocols, coordination patterns—may hamstring your new venture.
- **"Does my organization have the right *values* to innovate?"** Consider how you decide whether to commit to a new venture. For example, can you tolerate lower profit margins than your established enterprise demands?
- **"What team and structure will best support our innovation effort?"** Should you use a team dedicated to the project within your company? Create a separate spin-off organization?

By selecting the right team and organizational structure for your innovation—and infusing it with the right resources, processes, and values—you heighten your chances of innovating successfully.

Resources

When they ask the question, "What can this company do?" the place most managers look for the answer is in its resources—both the tangible ones like people, equipment, technologies, and cash, and the less tangible ones like product designs, information, brands, and relationships with suppliers, distributors, and customers. Without doubt, access to abundant, high-quality resources increases an organization's

Idea in Practice

Selecting the Right Structure for Your Innovation

If your innovation . . .	Select this type of team . . .	To operate . . .	Because . . .
Fits *well* with your existing values *and* processes	**Functional teams** who work sequentially on issues, or **lightweight teams**—ad hoc cross-functional teams who work simultaneously on multiple issues	Within your existing organization	Owing to the good fit with existing processes and values, no new capabilities or organizational structures are called for.
Fits *well* with existing values but *poorly* with existing processes	**Heavyweight team** dedicated exclusively to the innovation project, with complete responsibility for its success	Within your existing organization	The poor fit with existing processes requires new types of coordination among groups and individuals.
Fits *poorly* with existing values but *well* with existing processes	**Heavyweight team** dedicated exclusively to the innovation project, with complete responsibility for its success	Within your existing organization for development, followed by a spin-off for commercialization	In-house development capitalizes on existing processes. A spin-off for the commercialization phase facilitates new values—such as a different cost structure with lower profit margins.
Fits *poorly* with your existing processes *and* values	**Heavyweight team** dedicated exclusively to the innovation project, with complete responsibility for its success	In a separate spin-off or acquired organization	A spin-off enables the project to be governed by different values *and* ensures that new processes emerge.

chances of coping with change. But resource analysis doesn't come close to telling the whole story.

Processes

The second factor that affects what a company can and cannot do is its processes. By processes, we mean the patterns of interaction, coordination, communication, and decision making employees use to transform resources into products and services of greater worth. Such examples as the processes that govern product development, manufacturing, and budgeting come immediately to mind. Some processes are formal, in the sense that they are explicitly defined and documented. Others are informal: they are routines or ways of working that evolve over time. The former tend to be more visible, the latter less visible.

One of the dilemmas of management is that processes, by their very nature, are set up so that employees perform tasks in a consistent way, time after time. They are *meant* not to change or, if they must change, to change through tightly controlled procedures. When people use a process to do the task it was designed for, it is likely to perform efficiently. But when the same process is used to tackle a very different task, it is likely to perform sluggishly. Companies focused on developing and winning FDA approval for new drug compounds, for example, often prove inept at developing and winning approval for medical devices because the second task entails very different ways of working. In fact, a process that creates the capability to execute one task concurrently defines disabilities in executing other tasks.[1]

The most important capabilities and concurrent disabilities aren't necessarily embodied in the most visible processes, like logistics, development, manufacturing, or customer service. In fact, they are more likely to be in the less visible, background processes that support decisions about where to invest resources—those that define how market research is habitually done, how such analysis is translated into financial projections, how plans and budgets are negotiated internally, and so on. It is in those processes that many organizations' most serious disabilities in coping with change reside.

Values

The third factor that affects what an organization can and cannot do is its values. Sometimes the phrase "corporate values" carries an ethical connotation: one thinks of the principles that ensure patient well-being for Johnson & Johnson or that guide decisions about employee safety at Alcoa. But within our framework, "values" has a broader meaning. We define an organization's values as the standards by which employees set priorities that enable them to judge whether an order is attractive or unattractive, whether a customer is more important or less important, whether an idea for a new product is attractive or marginal, and so on. Prioritization decisions are made by employees at every level. Among salespeople, they consist of on-the-spot, day-to-day decisions about which products to push with customers and which to de-emphasize. At the executive tiers, they often take the form of decisions to invest, or not, in new products, services, and processes.

The larger and more complex a company becomes, the more important it is for senior managers to train employees throughout the organization to make independent decisions about priorities that are consistent with the strategic direction and the business model of the company. A key metric of good management, in fact, is whether such clear, consistent values have permeated the organization.

But consistent, broadly understood values also define what an organization cannot do. A company's values reflect its cost structure or its business model because those define the rules its employees must follow for the company to prosper. If, for example, a company's overhead costs require it to achieve gross profit margins of 40%, then a value or decision rule will have evolved that encourages middle managers to kill ideas that promise gross margins below 40%. Such an organization would be incapable of commercializing projects targeting low-margin markets—such as those in e-commerce—even though another organization's values, driven by a very different cost structure, might facilitate the success of the same project.

Different companies, of course, embody different values. But we want to focus on two sets of values in particular that tend to evolve in most companies in very predictable ways. The inexorable evolution of these two values is what makes companies progressively less capable of addressing disruptive change successfully.

As in the previous example, the first value dictates the way the company judges acceptable gross margins. As companies add features and functions to their products and services, trying to capture more attractive customers in premium tiers of their markets, they often add overhead cost. As a result, gross margins that were once attractive become unattractive. For instance, Toyota entered the North American market with the Corona model, which targeted the lower end of the market. As that segment became crowded with look-alike models from Honda, Mazda, and Nissan, competition drove down profit margins. To improve its margins, Toyota then developed more sophisticated cars targeted at higher tiers. The process of developing cars like the Camry and the Lexus added costs to Toyota's operation. It subsequently decided to exit the lower end of the market; the margins had become unacceptable because the company's cost structure, and consequently its values, had changed.

In a departure from that pattern, Toyota recently introduced the Echo model, hoping to rejoin the entry-level tier with a $10,000 car. It is one thing for Toyota's senior management to decide to launch this new model. It's another for the many people in the Toyota system—including its dealers—to agree that selling more cars at lower margins is a better way to boost profits and equity values than selling more Camrys, Avalons, and Lexuses. Only time will tell whether Toyota can manage this down-market move. To be successful with the Echo, Toyota's management will have to swim against a very strong current—the current of its own corporate values.

The second value relates to how big a business opportunity has to be before it can be interesting. Because a company's stock price represents the discounted present value of its projected earnings stream, most managers feel compelled not just to maintain growth but to maintain a constant rate of growth. For a $40 million company to grow 25%, for instance, it needs to find $10 million in new business the next year. But a $40 billion company needs to find $10 billion in new business the next year to grow at that same rate. It follows that an opportunity that excites a small company isn't big enough to be interesting to a large company. One of the bittersweet results of success, in fact, is that as companies become large, they lose the ability to enter small, emerging markets. This disability is not caused by a change in the resources within the companies—their resources typically are vast. Rather, it's caused by an evolution in values.

The problem is magnified when companies suddenly become much bigger through mergers or acquisitions. Executives and Wall Street financiers who engineer megamergers between already-huge pharmaceutical companies, for example, need to take this effect into account. Although their merged research organizations might have more resources to throw at new product development, their commercial organizations will probably have lost their appetites for all but the biggest blockbuster drugs. This constitutes a very real disability in managing innovation. The same problem crops up in high-tech industries as well. In many ways, Hewlett-Packard's recent decision to split itself into two companies is rooted in its recognition of this problem.

The Migration of Capabilities

In the start-up stages of an organization, much of what gets done is attributable to resources—people, in particular. The addition or departure of a few key people can profoundly influence its success. Over time, however, the locus of the organization's capabilities shifts toward its processes and values. As people address recurrent tasks, processes become defined. And as the business model takes shape and it becomes clear which types of business need to be accorded highest priority, values coalesce. In fact, one reason that many soaring young companies flame out after an IPO based on a single hot product is that their initial success is grounded in resources—often the founding engineers—and they fail to develop processes that can create a sequence of hot products.

Avid Technology, a producer of digital-editing systems for television, is an apt case in point. Avid's well-received technology removed tedium from the video-editing process. On the back of its star product, Avid's stock rose from $16 a share at its 1993 IPO to $49 in mid-1995. However, the strains of being a one-trick pony soon emerged as Avid faced a saturated market, rising inventories and receivables, increased competition, and shareholder lawsuits. Customers loved the product, but Avid's lack of effective processes for consistently developing new products and for controlling quality, delivery, and service ultimately tripped the company and sent its stock back down.

By contrast, at highly successful firms such as McKinsey & Company, the processes and values have become so powerful that it almost doesn't matter which people get assigned to which project teams. Hundreds of MBAs join the firm every year, and almost as many leave. But the company is able to crank out high-quality work year after year because its core capabilities are rooted in its processes and values rather than in its resources.

When a company's processes and values are being formed in its early and middle years, the founder typically has a profound impact. The founder usually has strong opinions about how employees should do their work and what the organization's priorities need to be. If the founder's judgments are flawed, of course, the company will likely fail. But if they're sound, employees will experience for themselves the validity of the founder's problem-solving and decision-making methods. Thus processes become defined. Likewise, if the company becomes financially successful by allocating resources according to criteria that reflect the founder's priorities, the company's values coalesce around those criteria.

As successful companies mature, employees gradually come to assume that the processes and priorities they've used so successfully so often are the right way to do their work. Once that happens and employees begin to follow processes and decide priorities by assumption rather than by conscious choice, those processes and values come to constitute the organization's culture.[2] As companies grow from a few employees to hundreds and thousands of them, the challenge of getting all employees to agree on what needs to be done and how can be daunting for even the best managers. Culture is a powerful management tool in those situations. It enables employees to act autonomously but causes them to act consistently.

Digital's Dilemma

A LOT OF BUSINESS THINKERS have analyzed Digital Equipment Corporation's abrupt fall from grace. Most have concluded that Digital simply read the market very badly. But if we look at the company's fate through the lens of our framework, a different picture emerges.

Digital was a spectacularly successful maker of minicomputers from the 1960s through the 1980s. One might have been tempted to assert, when personal computers first appeared in the market around 1980, that Digital's core capability was in building computers. But if that were the case, why did the company stumble?

Clearly, Digital had the resources to succeed in personal computers. Its engineers routinely designed computers that were far more sophisticated than PCs. The company had plenty of cash, a great brand, good technology, and so on. But it did not have the processes to succeed in the personal computer business. Minicomputer companies designed most of the key components of their computers internally and then integrated those components into proprietary configurations. Designing a new product platform took two to three years. Digital manufactured most of its own components and assembled them in a batch mode. It sold directly to corporate engineering organizations. Those processes worked extremely well in the minicomputer business.

PC makers, by contrast, outsourced most components from the best suppliers around the globe. New computer designs, made up of modular components,

Hence, the factors that define an organization's capabilities and disabilities evolve over time—they start in resources; then move to visible, articulated processes and values; and migrate finally to culture. As long as the organization continues to face the same sorts of problems that its processes and values were designed to address, managing the organization can be straightforward. But because those factors also define what an organization cannot do, they constitute disabilities when the problems facing the company change fundamentally. When the organization's capabilities reside primarily in its people, changing capabilities to address the new problems is relatively simple. But when the capabilities have come to reside in processes and values, and especially when they have become embedded in culture, change can be extraordinarily difficult. (See the sidebar "Digital's Dilemma.")

had to be completed in six to 12 months. The computers were manufactured in high-volume assembly lines and sold through retailers to consumers and businesses. None of these processes existed within Digital. In other words, although the people working at the company had the ability to design, build, and sell personal computers profitably, they were working in an organization that was incapable of doing so because its processes had been designed and had evolved to do other tasks well.

Similarly, because of its overhead costs, Digital had to adopt a set of values that dictated, "If it generates 50% gross margins or more, it's good business. If it generates less than 40% margins, it's not worth doing." Management had to ensure that all employees gave priority to projects according to these criteria or the company couldn't make money. Because PCs generated lower margins, they did not fit with Digital's values. The company's criteria for setting priorities always placed higher-performance minicomputers ahead of personal computers in the resource-allocation process.

Digital could have created a different organization that would have honed the different processes and values required to succeed in PCs—as IBM did. But Digital's mainstream organization simply was incapable of succeeding at the job.

Sustaining Versus Disruptive Innovation

Successful companies, no matter what the source of their capabilities, are pretty good at responding to evolutionary changes in their markets—what in *The Innovator's Dilemma* (Harvard Business School, 1997), Clayton Christensen referred to as *sustaining innovation*. Where they run into trouble is in handling or initiating revolutionary changes in their markets, or dealing with *disruptive innovation*.

Sustaining technologies are innovations that make a product or service perform better in ways that customers in the mainstream market already value. Compaq's early adoption of Intel's 32-bit 386 microprocessor instead of the 16-bit 286 chip was a sustaining innovation. So was Merrill Lynch's introduction of its Cash Management Account, which allowed customers to write checks against their equity accounts. Those were breakthrough innovations that sustained the best customers of these companies by providing something better than had previously been available.

Disruptive innovations create an entirely new market through the introduction of a new kind of product or service, one that's actually worse, initially, as judged by the performance metrics that mainstream customers value. Charles Schwab's initial entry as a bare-bones discount broker was a disruptive innovation relative to the offerings of full-service brokers like Merrill Lynch. Merrill Lynch's best customers wanted more than Schwab-like services. Early personal computers were a disruptive innovation relative to mainframes and minicomputers. PCs were not powerful enough to run the computing applications that existed at the time they were introduced. These innovations were disruptive in that they didn't address the next-generation needs of leading customers in existing markets. They had other attributes, of course, that enabled new market applications to emerge—and the disruptive innovations improved so rapidly that they ultimately could address the needs of customers in the mainstream of the market as well.

Sustaining innovations are nearly always developed and introduced by established industry leaders. But those same companies never introduce—or cope well with—disruptive innovations. Why? Our resources-processes-values framework holds the answer. Industry leaders are organized to develop and introduce sustaining technologies. Month after month, year after year, they launch new and improved products to gain an edge over the competition. They do so by developing processes for evaluating the technological potential of sustaining innovations and for assessing their customers' needs for alternatives. Investment in sustaining technology also fits in with the values of leading companies in that they promise higher margins from better products sold to leading-edge customers.

Disruptive innovations occur so intermittently that no company has a routine process for handling them. Furthermore, because disruptive products nearly always promise lower profit margins per unit sold and are not attractive to the company's best customers, they're inconsistent with the established company's values. Merrill

Lynch had the resources—the people, money, and technology—required to succeed at the sustaining innovations (Cash Management Account) and the disruptive innovations (bare-bones discount brokering) that it has confronted in recent history. But its processes and values supported only the sustaining innovation: they became disabilities when the company needed to understand and confront the discount and on-line brokerage businesses.

The reason, therefore, that large companies often surrender emerging growth markets is that smaller, disruptive companies are actually more capable of pursuing them. Start-ups lack resources, but that doesn't matter. Their values can embrace small markets, and their cost structures can accommodate low margins. Their market research and resource allocation processes allow managers to proceed intuitively; every decision need not be backed by careful research and analysis. All these advantages add up to the ability to embrace and even initiate disruptive change. But how can a large company develop those capabilities?

Creating Capabilities to Cope with Change

Despite beliefs spawned by popular change-management and reengineering programs, processes are not nearly as flexible or adaptable as resources are—and values are even less so. So whether addressing sustaining or disruptive innovations, when an organization needs new processes and values—because it needs new capabilities—managers must create a new organizational space where those capabilities can be developed. There are three possible ways to do that. Managers can

- create new organizational structures within corporate boundaries in which new processes can be developed,
- spin out an independent organization from the existing organization and develop within it the new processes and values required to solve the new problem,
- acquire a different organization whose processes and values closely match the requirements of the new task.

Creating new capabilities internally

When a company's capabilities reside in its processes, and when new challenges require new processes—that is, when they require different people or groups in a company to interact differently and at a different pace than they habitually have done—managers need to pull the relevant people out of the existing organization and draw a new boundary around a new group. Often, organizational boundaries were first drawn to facilitate the operation of existing processes, and they impede the creation of new processes. New team boundaries facilitate new patterns of working together that ultimately can coalesce as new processes. In *Revolutionizing Product Development* (The Free Press, 1992), Steven Wheelwright and Kim Clark referred to these structures as "heavyweight teams."

These teams are entirely dedicated to the new challenge, team members are physically located together, and each member is charged with assuming personal responsibility for the success of the entire project. At Chrysler, for example, the boundaries of the groups within its product development organization historically had been defined by components—power train, electrical systems, and so on. But to accelerate auto development, Chrysler needed to focus not on components but on automobile platforms—the minivan, small car, Jeep, and truck, for example—so it created heavyweight teams. Although these organizational units aren't as good at focusing on component design, they facilitated the definition of new processes that were much faster and more efficient in integrating various subsystems into new car designs. Companies as diverse as Medtronic for its cardiac pacemakers, IBM for its disk drives, and Eli Lilly for its new blockbuster drug Zyprexa have used heavyweight teams as vehicles for creating new processes so they could develop better products faster.

Creating capabilities through a spinout organization

When the mainstream organization's values would render it incapable of allocating resources to an innovation project, the company should spin it out as a new venture. Large organizations cannot be expected to allocate the critical financial and human resources needed to build a strong position in small, emerging markets. And it is very difficult for a company whose cost structure is tailored to compete in high-end markets to be profitable in low-end markets as well. Spinouts are very much in vogue among managers in old-line companies struggling with the question of how to address the Internet. But that's not always appropriate. When a disruptive innovation requires a different cost structure in order to be profitable and competitive, or when the current size of the opportunity is insignificant relative to the growth needs of the mainstream organization, then—and only then—is a spinout organization required.

Hewlett-Packard's laser-printer division in Boise, Idaho, was hugely successful, enjoying high margins and a reputation for superior product quality. Unfortunately, its ink-jet project, which represented a disruptive innovation, languished inside the mainstream HP printer business. Although the processes for developing the two types of printers were basically the same, there was a difference in values. To thrive in the ink-jet market, HP needed to be comfortable with lower gross margins and a smaller market than its laser printers commanded, and it needed to be willing to embrace relatively lower performance standards. It was not until HP's managers decided to transfer the unit to a separate division in Vancouver, British Columbia, with the goal of competing head-to-head with its own laser business, that the ink-jet business finally became successful.

How separate does such an effort need to be? A new physical location isn't always necessary. The primary requirement is that the project not be forced to compete for resources with projects in the mainstream organization. As we have seen, projects that are inconsistent with a company's mainstream values will naturally be accorded lowest priority. Whether the independent organization is physically separate is less important than its independence from the normal decision-making criteria in the resource allocation process. The sidebar "Fitting the Tool to the Task" goes into more detail about what kind of innovation challenge is best met by which organizational structure.

Managers think that developing a new operation necessarily means abandoning the old one, and they're loathe to do that since it

Fitting the Tool to the Task

SUPPOSE THAT AN ORGANIZATION needs to react to or initiate an innovation. The matrix illustrated below can help managers understand what kind of team should work on the project and what organizational structure that team needs to work within. The vertical axis asks the manager to measure the extent to which the organization's existing processes are suited to getting the new job done effectively. The horizontal axis asks managers to assess whether the organization's values will permit the company to allocate the resources the new initiative needs.

In region A, the project is a good fit with the company's processes and values, so no new capabilities are called for. A functional or a lightweight team can tackle the project within the existing organizational structure. A functional team works on function-specific issues, then passes the project on to the next function. A lightweight team is cross-functional, but team members stay under the control of their respective functional managers.

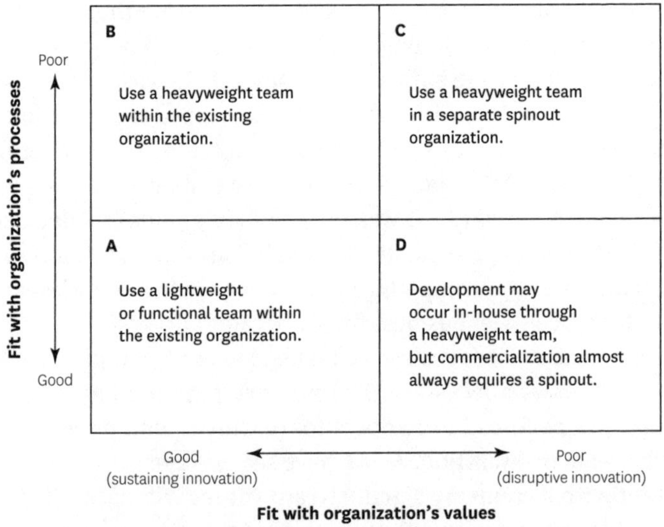

works perfectly well for what it was designed to do. But when disruptive change appears on the horizon, managers need to assemble the capabilities to confront that change before it affects the mainstream business. They actually need to run two businesses in tandem—one whose processes are tuned to the existing business model

In region B, the project is a good fit with the company's values but not with its processes. It presents the organization with new types of problems and therefore requires new types of interactions and coordination among groups and individuals. The team, like the team in region A, is working on a sustaining rather than a disruptive innovation. In this case, a heavyweight team is a good bet, but the project can be executed within the mainstream company. A heavyweight team—whose members work solely on the project and are expected to behave like general managers, shouldering responsibility for the project's success—is designed so that new processes and new ways of working together can emerge.

In region C, the manager faces a disruptive change that doesn't fit the organization's existing processes or values. To ensure success, the manager should create a spinout organization and commission a heavyweight development team to tackle the challenge. The spinout will allow the project to be governed by different values—a different cost structure, for example, with lower profit margins. The heavyweight team (as in region B) will ensure that new processes can emerge.

Similarly, in region D, when a manager faces a disruptive change that fits the organization's current processes but doesn't fit its values, the key to success almost always lies in commissioning a heavyweight development team to work in a spinout. Development may occasionally happen successfully in-house, but successful commercialization will require a spinout.

Unfortunately, most companies employ a one-size-fits-all organizing strategy, using lightweight or functional teams for programs of every size and character. But such teams are tools for exploiting established capabilities. And among those few companies that have accepted the heavyweight gospel, many have attempted to organize *all* of their development teams in a heavyweight fashion. Ideally, each company should tailor the team structure and organizational location to the process and values required by each project.

and another that is geared toward the new model. Merrill Lynch, for example, has accomplished an impressive global expansion of its institutional financial services through careful execution of its existing planning, acquisition, and partnership processes. Now, however, faced with the on-line world, the company is required to plan, acquire, and form partnerships more rapidly. Does that mean Merrill Lynch should change the processes that have worked so well in its traditional investment-banking business? Doing so would be disastrous, if we consider the question through the lens of our framework. Instead, Merrill should retain the old processes when working with the existing business (there are probably a few billion dollars still to be made under the old business model!) and create additional processes to deal with the new class of problems.

One word of warning: in our studies of this challenge, we have never seen a company succeed in addressing a change that disrupts its mainstream values without the personal, attentive oversight of the CEO—precisely because of the power of values in shaping the normal resource allocation process. Only the CEO can ensure that the new organization gets the required resources and is free to create processes and values that are appropriate to the new challenge. CEOs who view spinouts as a tool to get disruptive threats off their personal agendas are almost certain to meet with failure. We have seen no exceptions to this rule.

Creating capabilities through acquisitions

Just as innovating managers need to make separate assessments of the capabilities and disabilities that reside in their company's resources, processes, and values, so must they do the same with acquisitions when seeking to buy capabilities. Companies that successfully gain new capabilities through acquisitions are those that know where those capabilities reside in the acquisition and assimilate them accordingly. Acquiring managers begin by asking, "What created the value that I just paid so dearly for? Did I justify the price because of the acquisition's resources? Or was a substantial portion of its worth created by processes and values?"

If the capabilities being purchased are embedded in an acquired company's processes and values, then the last thing the acquiring manager should do is integrate the acquisition into the parent organization. Integration will vaporize the processes and values of the acquired firm. Once the acquisition's managers are forced to adopt the buyer's way of doing business, its capabilities will disappear.

A better strategy is to let the business stand alone and to infuse the parent's resources into the acquired company's processes and values. This approach truly constitutes the acquisition of new capabilities.

If, however, the acquired company's resources were the reason for its success and the primary rationale for the acquisition, then integrating it into the parent can make a lot of sense. Essentially, that means plugging the acquired people, products, technology, and customers into the parent's processes as a way of leveraging the parent's existing capabilities.

The perils of the ongoing DaimlerChrysler merger can be better understood in this light. Chrysler had few resources that could be considered unique. Its recent success in the market was rooted in its processes—particularly in its processes for designing products and integrating the efforts of its subsystem suppliers. What is the best way for Daimler to leverage Chrysler's capabilities? Wall Street is pressuring management to consolidate the two organizations to cut costs. But if the two companies are integrated, the very processes that made Chrysler such an attractive acquisition will likely be compromised.

The situation is reminiscent of IBM's 1984 acquisition of the telecommunications company Rolm. There wasn't anything in Rolm's pool of resources that IBM didn't already have. Rather, it was Rolm's processes for developing and finding new markets for PBX products that mattered. Initially, IBM recognized the value in preserving the informal and unconventional culture of the Rolm organization, which stood in stark contrast to IBM's methodical style. However, in 1987 IBM terminated Rolm's subsidiary status and decided to fully integrate the company into its own corporate structure. IBM's managers soon learned the folly of that decision. When they tried to push Rolm's resources—its products and its customers—through the processes that had been honed in the large-computer business, the Rolm business stumbled badly. And it was impossible for a computer company whose values had been whetted on profit margins of 18% to get excited about products with much lower profit margins. IBM's integration of Rolm destroyed the very source of the deal's original worth. Daimler-Chrysler, bowing to the investment community's drumbeat for efficiency savings, now stands on the edge of the same precipice. Often, it seems, financial analysts have a better intuition about the value of resources than they do about the value of processes.

By contrast, Cisco Systems' acquisitions process has worked well because, we would argue, it has kept resources, processes, and values in the right perspective. Between 1993 and 1997, it primarily acquired small companies that were less than two years old, early-stage organizations whose market value was built primarily upon their resources, particularly their engineers and products. Cisco plugged those resources into its own effective development, logistics, manufacturing, and marketing processes and threw away whatever nascent processes and values came with the acquisitions because those weren't what it had paid for. On a couple of occasions when the company acquired a larger, more mature organization—notably its 1996 acquisition of StrataCom—Cisco did not integrate. Rather, it let StrataCom stand alone and infused Cisco's substantial resources into StrataCom's organization to help it grow more rapidly.[3]

Managers whose organizations are confronting change must first determine whether they have the resources required to succeed. They then need to ask a separate question: Does the organization have the processes and values it needs to succeed in this new situation? Asking this second question is not as instinctive for most managers because the processes by which work is done and the values by which employees make their decisions have served them well in the past. What we hope this framework introduces into managers' thinking is the idea that the very capabilities that make their organizations effective also define their disabilities. In that regard, a little time spent soul-searching for honest answers to the following questions will pay off handsomely: Are the processes by which work habitually gets done in the organization appropriate for this new problem? And will the values of the organization cause this initiative to get high priority or to languish?

If the answers to those questions are no, it's okay. Understanding a problem is the most crucial step in solving it. Wishful thinking about these issues can set teams that need to innovate on a course fraught with roadblocks, second-guessing, and frustration. The reason that innovation often seems to be so difficult for established companies is that they employ highly capable people and then set them to work within organizational structures whose processes and values weren't designed for the task at hand. Ensuring that capable people are ensconced in capable organizations is a major responsibility of management in a transformational age such as ours.

Originally published in March 2000. Reprint R00202

Notes

1. See Dorothy Leonard-Barton, "Core Capabilities and Core Rigidities: A Paradox in Managing New Product Development," *Strategic Management Journal* (summer, 1992).

2. Our description of the development of an organization's culture draws heavily from Edgar Schein's research, as first laid out in his book *Organizational Culture and Leadership* (Jossey-Bass Publishers, 1985).

3. See Charles A. Holloway, Stephen C. Wheelwright, and Nicole Tempest, "Cisco Systems, Inc.: Post-Acquisition Manufacturing Integration," a case published jointly by the Stanford and Harvard business schools, 1998.

Competing on Analytics

by Thomas H. Davenport

WE ALL KNOW THE POWER of the killer app. Over the years, groundbreaking systems from companies such as American Airlines (electronic reservations), Otis Elevator (predictive maintenance), and American Hospital Supply (online ordering) have dramatically boosted their creators' revenues and reputations. These heralded—and coveted—applications amassed and applied data in ways that upended customer expectations and optimized operations to unprecedented degrees. They transformed technology from a supporting tool into a strategic weapon.

Companies questing for killer apps generally focus all their firepower on the one area that promises to create the greatest competitive advantage. But a new breed of company is upping the stakes. Organizations such as Amazon, Harrah's, Capital One, and the Boston Red Sox have dominated their fields by deploying industrial-strength analytics across a wide variety of activities. In essence, they are transforming their organizations into armies of killer apps and crunching their way to victory.

Organizations are competing on analytics not just because they can—business today is awash in data and data crunchers—but also because they should. At a time when firms in many industries offer similar products and use comparable technologies, business processes are among the last remaining points of differentiation. And analytics competitors wring every last drop of value from those processes. So, like other companies, they know what products their customers want, but they also know what prices those customers will pay, how many items each will buy in a lifetime, and what triggers will make people buy more. Like other companies, they know compensation costs and turnover rates, but they can also calculate how much personnel contribute to or detract from the bottom line and how salary levels relate to individuals' performance. Like other companies, they know when inventories are running low, but they can also predict problems with demand and supply chains, to achieve low rates of inventory and high rates of perfect orders.

And analytics competitors do all those things in a coordinated way, as part of an overarching strategy championed by top leadership and pushed down to decision makers at every level. Employees hired for their expertise with numbers or trained to recognize their importance are armed with the best evidence and the best quantitative tools. As a result, they make the best decisions: big and small, every day, over and over and over.

Although numerous organizations are embracing analytics, only a handful have achieved this level of proficiency. But analytics competitors are the leaders in their varied fields—consumer products, finance, retail, and travel and entertainment among them. Analytics has been instrumental to Capital One, which has exceeded 20% growth in earnings per share every year since it became a public company. It has allowed Amazon to dominate online retailing and turn a profit despite enormous investments in growth and infrastructure. In sports, the real secret weapon isn't steroids, but stats, as dramatic victories by the Boston Red Sox, the New England Patriots, and the Oakland A's attest.

At such organizations, virtuosity with data is often part of the brand. Progressive makes advertising hay from its detailed parsing of individual insurance rates. Amazon customers can watch the company learning about them as its service grows more targeted with frequent purchases. Thanks to Michael Lewis's best-selling book *Moneyball,* which demonstrated the power of statistics in

Idea in Brief

It's virtually impossible to differentiate yourself from competitors based on products alone. Your rivals sell offerings similar to yours. And thanks to cheap offshore labor, you're hard-pressed to beat overseas competitors on product cost.

How to pull ahead of the pack? Become an **analytics competitor:** Use sophisticated data-collection technology and analysis to wring every last drop of value from all your business processes. With analytics, you discern not only what your customers want but also how much they're willing to pay and what keeps them loyal. You look beyond compensation costs to calculate your workforce's exact contribution to your bottom line. And you don't just track existing inventories; you also predict and prevent future inventory problems.

Analytics competitors seize the lead in their fields. Capital One's analytics initiative, for example, has spurred at least 20% growth in earnings per share every year since the company went public.

Make analytics part of *your* overarching competitive strategy, and push it down to decision makers at every level. You'll arm your employees with the best evidence and quantitative tools for making the best decisions—big and small, every day.

professional baseball, the Oakland A's are almost as famous for their geeky number crunching as they are for their athletic prowess.

To identify characteristics shared by analytics competitors, I and two of my colleagues at Babson College's Working Knowledge Research Center studied 32 organizations that have made a commitment to quantitative, fact-based analysis. Eleven of those organizations we classified as full-bore analytics competitors, meaning top management had announced that analytics was key to their strategies; they had multiple initiatives under way involving complex data and statistical analysis, and they managed analytical activity at the enterprise (not departmental) level.

This article lays out the characteristics and practices of these statistical masters and describes some of the very substantial changes other companies must undergo in order to compete on quantitative turf. As one would expect, the transformation requires a significant investment in technology, the accumulation of massive stores of data, and the formulation of companywide strategies for managing

Idea in Practice

To become an analytics competitor:

Champion Analytics from the Top

Acknowledge and endorse the changes in culture, processes, and skills that analytics competition will mean for much of your workforce. And prepare yourself to lead an analytics-focused organization: You will have to understand the theory behind various quantitative methods so you can recognize their limitations. If you lack background in statistical methods, consult experts who understand your business and know how analytics can be applied to it.

Create a Single Analytics Initiative

Place all data-collection and analysis activities under a common leadership, with common technology and tools. You'll facilitate data sharing and avoid the impediments of inconsistent reporting formats, data definitions, and standards.

Example: Procter & Gamble created a centrally managed "überanalytics" group of 100 analysts drawn from many different functions. It applies this critical mass of expertise to pressing cross-functional issues. For instance, sales and marketing analysts supply data on growth opportunities in existing markets to supply-chain analysts, who can then design more responsive supply networks.

Focus Your Analytics Effort

Channel your resources into analytics initiatives that most directly serve your overarching competitive strategy. Harrah's, for

the data. But at least as important, it requires executives' vocal, unswerving commitment and willingness to change the way employees think, work, and are treated. As Gary Loveman, CEO of analytics competitor Harrah's, frequently puts it, "Do we think this is true? Or do we know?"

Anatomy of an Analytics Competitor

One analytics competitor that's at the top of its game is Marriott International. Over the past 20 years, the corporation has honed to a science its system for establishing the optimal price for guest rooms (the key analytics process in hotels, known as revenue management).

instance, aims much of its analytical activity at improving customer loyalty, customer service, and related areas such as pricing and promotions.

Establish an Analytics Culture

Instill a companywide respect for measuring, testing, and evaluating quantitative evidence. Urge employees to base decisions on hard facts. Gauge and reward performance the same way—applying metrics to compensation and rewards.

Hire the Right People

Pursue and hire analysts who possess top-notch quantitative-analysis skills, can express complex ideas in simple terms, and can interact productively with decision makers. This combination may be difficult to find, so start recruiting well before you need to fill analyst positions.

Use the Right Technology

Prepare to spend significant resources on technology such as customer relationship management (CRM) or enterprise resource planning (ERP) systems. Present data in standard formats, integrate it, store it in a data warehouse, and make it easily accessible to everyone. And expect to spend years gathering enough data to conduct meaningful analyses.

Example: It took Dell Computer seven years to create a database that includes 1.5 million records of all its print, radio, broadcast TV, and cable ads. Dell couples the database with data on sales for each region in which the ads appeared (before and after their appearance). The information enables Dell to fine-tune its promotions for every medium—in every region.

Today, its ambitions are far grander. Through its Total Hotel Optimization program, Marriott has expanded its quantitative expertise to areas such as conference facilities and catering, and made related tools available over the Internet to property revenue managers and hotel owners. It has developed systems to optimize offerings to frequent customers and assess the likelihood of those customers' defecting to competitors. It has given local revenue managers the power to override the system's recommendations when certain local factors can't be predicted (like the large number of Hurricane Katrina evacuees arriving in Houston). The company has even created a revenue opportunity model, which computes actual revenues as a percentage of the optimal rates that could have been charged.

That figure has grown from 83% to 91% as Marriott's revenue-management analytics has taken root throughout the enterprise. The word is out among property owners and franchisees: If you want to squeeze the most revenue from your inventory, Marriott's approach is the ticket.

Clearly, organizations such as Marriott don't behave like traditional companies. Customers notice the difference in every interaction; employees and vendors live the difference every day. Our study found three key attributes among analytics competitors:

Widespread use of modeling and optimization

Any company can generate simple descriptive statistics about aspects of its business—average revenue per employee, for example, or average order size. But analytics competitors look well beyond basic statistics. These companies use predictive modeling to identify the most profitable customers—plus those with the greatest profit potential and the ones most likely to cancel their accounts. They pool data generated in-house and data acquired from outside sources (which they analyze more deeply than do their less statistically savvy competitors) for a comprehensive understanding of their customers. They optimize their supply chains and can thus determine the impact of an unexpected constraint, simulate alternatives, and route shipments around problems. They establish prices in real time to get the highest yield possible from each of their customer transactions. They create complex models of how their operational costs relate to their financial performance.

Leaders in analytics also use sophisticated experiments to measure the overall impact or "lift" of intervention strategies and then apply the results to continuously improve subsequent analyses. Capital One, for example, conducts more than 30,000 experiments a year, with different interest rates, incentives, direct-mail packaging, and other variables. Its goal is to maximize the likelihood both that potential customers will sign up for credit cards and that they will pay back Capital One.

Progressive employs similar experiments using widely available insurance industry data. The company defines narrow groups, or cells, of customers: for example, motorcycle riders ages 30 and above, with college educations, credit scores over a certain level, and no accidents. For each cell, the company performs a regression analysis to identify factors that most closely correlate with the losses that group engenders. It then sets prices for the cells, which should enable the company to earn a profit across a portfolio of customer groups, and uses simulation software to test the financial implications of those hypotheses. With this approach, Progressive can profitably insure customers in traditionally high-risk categories. Other insurers reject high-risk customers out of hand, without bothering to delve more deeply into the data (although even traditional competitors, such as Allstate, are starting to embrace analytics as a strategy).

An enterprise approach

Analytics competitors understand that most business functions—even those, like marketing, that have historically depended on art rather than science—can be improved with sophisticated quantitative techniques. These organizations don't gain advantage from one killer app, but rather from multiple applications supporting many parts of the business—and, in a few cases, being rolled out for use by customers and suppliers.

UPS embodies the evolution from targeted analytics user to comprehensive analytics competitor. Although the company is among the world's most rigorous practitioners of operations research and industrial engineering, its capabilities were, until fairly recently, narrowly focused. Today, UPS is wielding its statistical skill to track the movement of packages and to anticipate and influence the actions of people—assessing the likelihood of customer attrition and identifying sources of problems. The UPS Customer Intelligence Group, for example, is able to accurately predict customer defections by examining usage patterns and complaints. When the data point to a potential defector, a salesperson contacts that customer to review and resolve the problem, dramatically reducing the loss of accounts. UPS still lacks the breadth of initiatives of a full-bore analytics competitor, but it is heading in that direction.

Analytics competitors treat all such activities from all provenances as a single, coherent initiative, often massed under one rubric, such as "information-based strategy" at Capital One or "information-based customer management" at Barclays Bank. These programs operate not just under a common label but also under common leadership and with common technology and tools. In traditional companies, "business intelligence" (the term IT people use for analytics and reporting processes and software) is generally managed by departments; number-crunching functions select their own tools, control their own data warehouses, and train their own people. But that way, chaos lies. For one thing, the proliferation of user-developed spreadsheets and databases inevitably leads to multiple versions of key indicators within an organization. Furthermore, research has shown that between 20% and 40% of spreadsheets contain errors; the more spreadsheets floating around a company, therefore, the more fecund the breeding ground for mistakes. Analytics competitors, by contrast, field centralized groups to ensure that critical data and other resources are well managed and that different parts of the organization can share data easily, without the impediments of inconsistent formats, definitions, and standards.

Some analytics competitors apply the same enterprise approach to people as to technology. Procter & Gamble, for example, recently created a kind of überanalytics group consisting of more than 100 analysts from such functions as operations, supply chain, sales, consumer research, and marketing. Although most of the analysts are embedded in business operating units, the group is centrally managed. As a result of this consolidation, P&G can apply a critical mass of expertise to its most pressing issues. So, for example, sales and marketing analysts supply data on opportunities for growth in existing markets to analysts who design corporate supply networks. The supply chain analysts, in turn, apply their expertise in certain decision-analysis techniques to such new areas as competitive intelligence.

The group at P&G also raises the visibility of analytical and data-based decision making within the company. Previously, P&G's crack analysts had improved business processes and saved the firm money; but because they were squirreled away in dispersed domains, many executives didn't know what services they offered or how effective they could be. Now those executives are more likely to tap the company's deep pool of expertise for their projects. Meanwhile, masterful number crunching has become part of the story P&G tells to investors, the press, and the public.

Senior executive advocates

A companywide embrace of analytics impels changes in culture, processes, behavior, and skills for many employees. And so, like any major transition, it requires leadership from executives at the very top who have a passion for the quantitative approach. Ideally, the principal advocate is the CEO. Indeed, we found several chief executives who have driven the shift to analytics at their companies over the past few years, including Loveman of Harrah's, Jeff Bezos of Amazon, and Rich Fairbank of Capital One. Before he retired from the Sara Lee Bakery Group, former CEO Barry Beracha kept a sign on his desk that summed up his personal and organizational philosophy: "In God we trust. All others bring data." We did come across some companies in which a single functional or business unit leader was trying to push analytics throughout the organization, and a few were making some progress. But we found that these lower-level people lacked the clout, the perspective, and the cross-functional scope to change the culture in any meaningful way.

CEOs leading the analytics charge require both an appreciation of and a familiarity with the subject. A background in statistics isn't necessary, but those leaders must understand the theory behind various quantitative methods so that they recognize those methods' limitations—which factors are being weighed and which ones aren't. When the CEOs need help grasping quantitative techniques, they turn to experts who understand the business and how analytics can be applied to it. We interviewed several leaders who had retained such advisers, and these executives stressed the need to find someone who can explain things in plain language and be trusted not to spin the numbers. A few CEOs we spoke with had surrounded themselves with very analytical people—professors, consultants, MIT

Going to Bat for Stats

THE ANALYSIS-VERSUS-INSTINCT DEBATE, a favorite of political commentators during the last two U.S. presidential elections, is raging in professional sports, thanks to several popular books and high-profile victories. For now, analysis seems to hold the lead.

Most notably, statistics are a major part of the selection and deployment of players. *Moneyball*, by Michael Lewis, focuses on the use of analytics in player selection for the Oakland A's—a team that wins on a shoestring. The New England Patriots, a team that devotes an enormous amount of attention to statistics, won three of the last four Super Bowls, and their payroll is currently ranked 24th in the league. The Boston Red Sox have embraced "sabermetrics" (the application of analysis to baseball), even going so far as to hire Bill James, the famous baseball statistician who popularized that term. Analytic HR strategies are taking hold in European soccer as well. One leading team, Italy's A.C. Milan, uses predictive models from its Milan Lab research center to prevent injuries by analyzing physiological, orthopedic, and psychological data from a variety of sources. A fast-rising English soccer team, the Bolton Wanderers, is known for its manager's use of extensive data to evaluate players' performance.

Still, sports managers—like business leaders—are rarely fact-or-feeling purists. St. Louis Cardinals manager Tony La Russa, for example, brilliantly combines analytics with intuition to decide when to substitute a charged-up player in the batting lineup or whether to hire a spark-plug personality to improve morale. In his recent book, *Three Nights in August,* Buzz Bissinger describes that balance: "La Russa appreciated the information generated by computers. He studied the rows and the columns. But he also knew they could take you only so far in baseball, maybe even confuse you with a fog of overanalysis. As far as he knew, there was no way to quantify desire. And those numbers told him exactly what he needed to know when added to twenty-four years of managing experience."

That final sentence is the key. Whether scrutinizing someone's performance record or observing the expression flitting across an employee's face, leaders consult their own experience to understand the "evidence" in all its forms.

---

graduates, and the like. But that was a personal preference rather than a necessary practice.

Of course, not all decisions should be grounded in analytics—at least not wholly so. Personnel matters, in particular, are often well and appropriately informed by instinct and anecdote. More organizations are subjecting recruiting and hiring decisions to statistical analysis (see the sidebar "Going to Bat for Stats"). But research shows that human beings can make quick, surprisingly accurate assessments of personality and character based on simple observations. For analytics-minded leaders, then, the challenge boils down to knowing when to run with the numbers and when to run with their guts.

Their Sources of Strength

Analytics competitors are more than simple number-crunching factories. Certainly, they apply technology—with a mixture of brute force and finesse—to multiple business problems. But they also direct their energies toward finding the right focus, building the right culture, and hiring the right people to make optimal use of the data they constantly churn. In the end, people and strategy, as much as information technology, give such organizations strength.

The right focus

Although analytics competitors encourage universal fact-based decisions, they must choose where to direct resource-intensive efforts. Generally, they pick several functions or initiatives that together serve an overarching strategy. Harrah's, for example, has aimed much of its analytical activity at increasing customer loyalty, customer service, and related areas like pricing and promotions. UPS has broadened its focus from logistics to customers, in the interest of providing superior service. While such multipronged strategies define analytics competitors, executives we interviewed warned companies against becoming too diffuse in their initiatives or losing clear sight of the business purpose behind each.

Another consideration when allocating resources is how amenable certain functions are to deep analysis. There are at least seven common targets for analytical activity, and specific industries may present their own (see "Things You Can Count On"). Statistical models and algorithms that dangle the possibility of performance

Things you can count on

Analytics competitors make expert use of statistics and modeling to improve a wide variety of functions. Here are some common applications:

Function	Description	Exemplars
Supply chain	Simulate and optimize supply chain flows; reduce inventory and stock-outs.	Dell, Wal-Mart, Amazon
Customer selection, loyalty, and service	Identify customers with the greatest profit potential; increase likelihood that they will want the product or service offering; retain their loyalty.	Harrah's, Capital One, Barclays
Pricing	Identify the price that will maximize yield, or profit.	Progressive, Marriott
Human capital	Select the best employees for particular tasks or jobs, at particular compensation levels.	New England Patriots, Oakland A's, Boston Red Sox
Product and service quality	Detect quality problems early and minimize them.	Honda, Intel
Financial performance	Better understand the drivers of financial performance and the effects of nonfinancial factors.	MCI, Verizon
Research and development	Improve quality, efficacy, and, where applicable, safety of products and services.	Novartis, Amazon, Yahoo

breakthroughs make some prospects especially tempting. Marketing, for example, has always been tough to quantify because it is rooted in psychology. But now consumer products companies can hone their market research using multiattribute utility theory—a tool for understanding and predicting consumer behaviors and decisions. Similarly, the advertising industry is adopting econometrics—statistical techniques for measuring the lift provided by different ads and promotions over time.

The most proficient analytics practitioners don't just measure their own navels—they also help customers and vendors measure theirs. Wal-Mart, for example, insists that suppliers use its Retail

Link system to monitor product movement by store, to plan promotions and layouts within stores, and to reduce stock-outs. E.&J. Gallo provides distributors with data and analysis on retailers' costs and pricing so they can calculate the per-bottle profitability for each of Gallo's 95 wines. The distributors, in turn, use that information to help retailers optimize their mixes while persuading them to add shelf space for Gallo products. Procter & Gamble offers data and analysis to its retail customers, as part of a program called Joint Value Creation, and to its suppliers to help improve responsiveness and reduce costs. Hospital supplier Owens & Minor furnishes similar services, enabling customers and suppliers to access and analyze their buying and selling data, track ordering patterns in search of consolidation opportunities, and move off-contract purchases to group contracts that include products distributed by Owens & Minor and its competitors. For example, Owens & Minor might show a hospital chain's executives how much money they could save by consolidating purchases across multiple locations or help them see the trade-offs between increasing delivery frequency and carrying inventory.

The right culture

Culture is a soft concept; analytics is a hard discipline. Nonetheless, analytics competitors must instill a companywide respect for measuring, testing, and evaluating quantitative evidence. Employees are urged to base decisions on hard facts. And they know that their performance is gauged the same way. Human resource organizations within analytics competitors are rigorous about applying metrics to compensation and rewards. Harrah's, for example, has made a dramatic change from a rewards culture based on paternalism and tenure to one based on such meticulously collected performance measurements as financial and customer service results. Senior executives also set a consistent example with their own behavior, exhibiting a hunger for and confidence in fact and analysis. One exemplar of such leadership was Beracha of the Sara Lee Bakery Group, known to his employees as a "data dog" because he hounded them for data to support any assertion or hypothesis.

Not surprisingly, in an analytics culture, there's sometimes tension between innovative or entrepreneurial impulses and the requirement for evidence. Some companies place less emphasis on blue-sky development, in which designers or engineers chase after a gleam in someone's eye. In these organizations, R&D, like other functions, is rigorously metric-driven. At Yahoo, Progressive, and Capital One, process and product changes are tested on a small scale and implemented as they are validated. That approach, well established within various academic and business disciplines (including engineering, quality management, and psychology), can be applied to most corporate processes—even to not-so-obvious candidates, like human resources and customer service. HR, for example, might create profiles of managers' personality traits and leadership styles and then test those managers in different situations. It could then compare data on individuals' performance with data about personalities to determine what traits are most important to managing a project that is behind schedule, say, or helping a new group to assimilate.

There are, however, instances when a decision to change something or try something new must be made too quickly for extensive analysis, or when it's not possible to gather data beforehand. For example, even though Amazon's Jeff Bezos greatly prefers to rigorously quantify users' reactions before rolling out new features, he couldn't test the company's search-inside-the-book offering without applying it to a critical mass of books (120,000, to begin with). It was also expensive to develop, and that increased the risk. In this case, Bezos trusted his instincts and took a flier. And the feature did prove popular when introduced.

The right people

Analytical firms hire analytical people—and like all companies that compete on talent, they pursue the best. When Amazon needed a new head for its global supply chain, for example, it recruited Gang Yu, a professor of management science and software entrepreneur who is one of the world's leading authorities on optimization analytics. Amazon's business model requires the company to manage a constant flow of new products, suppliers, customers, and promotions, as well as deliver orders by promised dates. Since his arrival, Yu and his team have been designing and building sophisticated supply chain systems to optimize those processes. And while he tosses around phrases like "nonstationary stochastic processes," he's also good at explaining the new approaches to Amazon's executives in clear business terms.

Established analytics competitors such as Capital One employ squadrons of analysts to conduct quantitative experiments and, with the results in hand, design credit card and other financial offers. These efforts call for a specialized skill set, as you can see from this job description (typical for a Capital One analyst):

> High conceptual problem-solving and quantitative analytical aptitudes . . . Engineering, financial, consulting, and/or other analytical quantitative educational/work background. Ability to quickly learn how to use software applications. Experience with Excel models. Some graduate work preferred but not required (e.g., MBA). Some experience with project management methodology, process improvement tools (Lean, Six Sigma), or statistics preferred.

Other firms hire similar kinds of people, but analytics competitors have them in much greater numbers. Capital One is currently seeking three times as many analysts as operations people—hardly the common practice for a bank. "We are really a company of analysts," one executive there noted. "It's the primary job in this place."

Good analysts must also have the ability to express complex ideas in simple terms and have the relationship skills to interact well with decision makers. One consumer products company with a 30-person analytics group looks for what it calls "PhDs with personality"—people with expertise in math, statistics, and data analysis who can also speak the language of business and help market their work internally and sometimes externally. The head of a customer analytics group at Wachovia Bank describes the rapport with others his group seeks: "We are trying to build our people as part of the business team," he explains. "We want them sitting at the business table, participating in a discussion of what the key issues are, determining what information needs the businesspeople have, and recommending actions to the business partners. We want this [analytics group] to be not just a general utility, but rather an active and critical part of the business unit's success."

Of course, a combination of analytical, business, and relationship skills may be difficult to find. When the software company SAS (a sponsor of this research, along with Intel) knows it will need an expert in state-of-the-art business applications such as predictive modeling or recursive partitioning (a form of decision tree analysis applied to very complex data sets), it begins recruiting up to 18 months before it expects to fill the position.

In fact, analytical talent may be to the early 2000s what programming talent was to the late 1990s. Unfortunately, the U.S. and European labor markets aren't exactly teeming with analytically sophisticated job candidates. Some organizations cope by contracting work to countries such as India, home to many statistical experts. That strategy may succeed when offshore analysts work on stand-alone problems. But if an iterative discussion with business decision makers is required, the distance can become a major barrier.

The right technology

Competing on analytics means competing on technology. And while the most serious competitors investigate the latest statistical algorithms and decision science approaches, they also constantly monitor and push the IT frontier. The analytics group at one consumer products company went so far as to build its own supercomputer because it felt that commercially available models were inadequate for its demands. Such heroic feats usually aren't necessary, but serious analytics does require the following:

A data strategy. Companies have invested many millions of dollars in systems that snatch data from every conceivable source. Enterprise resource planning, customer relationship management, point-of-sale, and other systems ensure that no transaction or other significant exchange occurs without leaving a mark. But to compete on that information, companies must present it in standard formats, integrate it, store it in a data warehouse, and make it easily accessible to anyone and everyone. And they will need *a lot* of it. For example, a company may spend several years accumulating data on different marketing approaches before it has gathered enough to reliably analyze the effectiveness of an advertising campaign. Dell employed DDB Matrix, a unit of the advertising agency DDB Worldwide, to create (over a period of seven years) a database that includes 1.5 million records on all the computer maker's print, radio, network TV, and cable ads, coupled with data on Dell sales for each region in which the ads appeared (before and after their appearance). That information allows Dell to fine-tune its promotions for every medium in every region.

Business intelligence software. The term "business intelligence," which first popped up in the late 1980s, encompasses a wide array of processes and software used to collect, analyze, and disseminate data, all in the interests of better decision making. Business intelligence tools allow employees to extract, transform, and load (or ETL, as people in the industry would say) data for analysis and then make those analyses available in reports, alerts, and scorecards. The popularity of analytics competition is partly a response to the emergence of integrated packages of these tools.

Computing hardware. The volumes of data required for analytics applications may strain the capacity of low-end computers and servers. Many analytics competitors are converting their hardware to 64-bit processors that churn large amounts of data quickly.

The Long Road Ahead

Most companies in most industries have excellent reasons to pursue strategies shaped by analytics. Virtually all the organizations we identified as aggressive analytics competitors are clear leaders in their fields, and they attribute much of their success to the masterful exploitation of data. Rising global competition intensifies the need for this sort of proficiency. Western companies unable to beat their

You Know You Compete on Analytics When . . .

1. You apply sophisticated information systems and rigorous analysis not only to your core capability but also to a range of functions as varied as marketing and human resources.
2. Your senior executive team not only recognizes the importance of analytics capabilities but also makes their development and maintenance a primary focus.
3. You treat fact-based decision making not only as a best practice but also as a part of the culture that's constantly emphasized and communicated by senior executives.
4. You hire not only people with analytical skills but a lot of people with *the very best* analytical skills—and consider them a key to your success.
5. You not only employ analytics in almost every function and department but also consider it so strategically important that you manage it at the enterprise level.
6. You not only are expert at number crunching but also invent proprietary metrics for use in key business processes.
7. You not only use copious data and in-house analysis but also share them with customers and suppliers.
8. You not only avidly consume data but also seize every opportunity to generate information, creating a "test and learn" culture based on numerous small experiments.
9. You not only have committed to competing on analytics but also have been building your capabilities for several years.
10. You not only emphasize the importance of analytics internally but also make quantitative capabilities part of your company's story, to be shared in the annual report and in discussions with financial analysts.

Indian or Chinese competitors on product cost, for example, can seek the upper hand through optimized business processes.

Companies just now embracing such strategies, however, will find that they take several years to come to fruition. The organizations in our study described a long, sometimes arduous journey. The

UK Consumer Cards and Loans business within Barclays Bank, for example, spent five years executing its plan to apply analytics to the marketing of credit cards and other financial products. The company had to make process changes in virtually every aspect of its consumer business: underwriting risk, setting credit limits, servicing accounts, controlling fraud, cross selling, and so on. On the technical side, it had to integrate data on 10 million Barclaycard customers, improve the quality of the data, and build systems to step up data collection and analysis. In addition, the company embarked on a long series of small tests to begin learning how to attract and retain the best customers at the lowest price. And it had to hire new people with top-drawer quantitative skills.

Much of the time—and corresponding expense—that any company takes to become an analytics competitor will be devoted to technological tasks: refining the systems that produce transaction data, making data available in warehouses, selecting and implementing analytic software, and assembling the hardware and communications environment. And because those who don't record history are doomed not to learn from it, companies that have collected little information—or the wrong kind—will need to amass a sufficient body of data to support reliable forecasting. "We've been collecting data for six or seven years, but it's only become usable in the last two or three, because we needed time and experience to validate conclusions based on the data," remarked a manager of customer data analytics at UPS.

And, of course, new analytics competitors will have to stock their personnel larders with fresh people. (When Gary Loveman became COO, and then CEO, of Harrah's, he brought in a group of statistical experts who could design and implement quantitatively based marketing campaigns and loyalty programs.) Existing employees, meanwhile, will require extensive training. They need to know what data are available and all the ways the information can be analyzed; and they must learn to recognize such peculiarities and shortcomings as missing data, duplication, and quality problems. An analytics-minded executive at Procter & Gamble suggested to me that firms should begin to keep managers in their jobs for longer periods because of the time required to master quantitative approaches to their businesses.

The German pathologist Rudolph Virchow famously called the task of science "to stake out the limits of the knowable." Analytics competitors pursue a similar goal, although the universe they seek to know is a more circumscribed one of customer behavior, product movement, employee performance, and financial reactions. Every day, advances in technology and techniques give companies a better and better handle on the critical minutiae of their operations.

The Oakland A's aren't the only ones playing moneyball. Companies of every stripe want to be part of the game.

Originally published in January 2006. Reprint R0601H

Managing Oneself

by Peter F. Drucker

HISTORY'S GREAT ACHIEVERS—a Napoléon, a da Vinci, a Mozart—have always managed themselves. That, in large measure, is what makes them great achievers. But they are rare exceptions, so unusual both in their talents and their accomplishments as to be considered outside the boundaries of ordinary human existence. Now, most of us, even those of us with modest endowments, will have to learn to manage ourselves. We will have to learn to develop ourselves. We will have to place ourselves where we can make the greatest contribution. And we will have to stay mentally alert and engaged during a 50-year working life, which means knowing how and when to change the work we do.

What Are My Strengths?

Most people think they know what they are good at. They are usually wrong. More often, people know what they are not good at—and even then more people are wrong than right. And yet, a person can perform only from strength. One cannot build performance on weaknesses, let alone on something one cannot do at all.

Throughout history, people had little need to know their strengths. A person was born into a position and a line of work: The peasant's son would also be a peasant; the artisan's daughter, an artisan's wife; and so on. But now people have choices. We need to know our strengths in order to know where we belong.

The only way to discover your strengths is through feedback analysis. Whenever you make a key decision or take a key action, write down what you expect will happen. Nine or 12 months later, compare the actual results with your expectations. I have been practicing this method for 15 to 20 years now, and every time I do it, I am surprised. The feedback analysis showed me, for instance—and to my great surprise—that I have an intuitive understanding of technical people, whether they are engineers or accountants or market researchers. It also showed me that I don't really resonate with generalists.

Feedback analysis is by no means new. It was invented sometime in the fourteenth century by an otherwise totally obscure German theologian and picked up quite independently, some 150 years later, by John Calvin and Ignatius of Loyola, each of whom incorporated it into the practice of his followers. In fact, the steadfast focus on performance and results that this habit produces explains why the institutions these two men founded, the Calvinist church and the Jesuit order, came to dominate Europe within 30 years.

Practiced consistently, this simple method will show you within a fairly short period of time, maybe two or three years, where your strengths lie—and this is the most important thing to know. The method will show you what you are doing or failing to do that deprives you of the full benefits of your strengths. It will show you where you are not particularly competent. And finally, it will show you where you have no strengths and cannot perform.

Several implications for action follow from feedback analysis. First and foremost, concentrate on your strengths. Put yourself where your strengths can produce results.

Second, work on improving your strengths. Analysis will rapidly show where you need to improve skills or acquire new ones. It will also show the gaps in your knowledge—and those can usually be filled. Mathematicians are born, but everyone can learn trigonometry.

Third, discover where your intellectual arrogance is causing disabling ignorance and overcome it. Far too many people—especially

Idea in Brief

We live in an age of unprecedented opportunity: If you've got ambition, drive, and smarts, you can rise to the top of your chosen profession—regardless of where you started out. But with opportunity comes responsibility. Companies today aren't managing their knowledge workers' careers. Rather, we must each be our own chief executive officer.

Simply put, it's up to you to carve out your place in the work world and know when to change course. And it's up to you to keep yourself engaged and productive during a work life that may span some 50 years.

To do all of these things well, you'll need to cultivate a deep understanding of yourself. What are your most valuable strengths and most dangerous weaknesses? Equally important, how do you learn and work with others? What are your most deeply held values? And in what type of work environment can you make the greatest contribution?

The implication is clear: Only when you operate from a combination of your strengths and self-knowledge can you achieve true—and lasting—excellence.

people with great expertise in one area—are contemptuous of knowledge in other areas or believe that being bright is a substitute for knowledge. First-rate engineers, for instance, tend to take pride in not knowing anything about people. Human beings, they believe, are much too disorderly for the good engineering mind. Human resources professionals, by contrast, often pride themselves on their ignorance of elementary accounting or of quantitative methods altogether. But taking pride in such ignorance is self-defeating. Go to work on acquiring the skills and knowledge you need to fully realize your strengths.

It is equally essential to remedy your bad habits—the things you do or fail to do that inhibit your effectiveness and performance. Such habits will quickly show up in the feedback. For example, a planner may find that his beautiful plans fail because he does not follow through on them. Like so many brilliant people, he believes that ideas move mountains. But bulldozers move mountains; ideas show where the bulldozers should go to work. This planner will have to learn that the work does not stop when the plan is completed. He

Idea in Practice

To build a life of excellence, begin by asking yourself these questions:

"What are my strengths?"

To accurately identify your strengths, use **feedback analysis**. Every time you make a key decision, write down the outcome you expect. Several months later, compare the actual results with your expected results. Look for patterns in what you're seeing: What results are you skilled at generating? What abilities do you need to enhance in order to get the results you want? What unproductive habits are preventing you from creating the outcomes you desire? In identifying opportunities for improvement, don't waste time cultivating skill areas where you have little competence. Instead, concentrate on—and build on—your strengths.

"How do I work?"

In what ways do you work best? Do you process information most effectively by reading it, or by hearing others discuss it? Do you accomplish the most by working with other people, or by working alone? Do you perform best while making decisions, or while advising others on key matters? Are you in top form when things get stressful, or do you function optimally in a highly predictable environment?

"What are my values?"

What are your ethics? What do you see as your most important responsibilities for living a worthy, ethical life? Do your organization's ethics resonate with your own values? If not, your career will likely be marked by frustration and poor performance.

"Where do I belong?"

Consider your strengths, preferred work style, and values. Based on these qualities, in what kind of work environment would you fit in best? Find the perfect fit, and you'll transform yourself from a merely acceptable employee into a star performer.

"What can I contribute?"

In earlier eras, companies told businesspeople what their contribution should be. Today, you have choices. To decide how you can best enhance your organization's performance, first ask what the situation requires. Based on your strengths, work style, and values, how might you make the greatest contribution to your organization's efforts?

must find people to carry out the plan and explain it to them. He must adapt and change it as he puts it into action. And finally, he must decide when to stop pushing the plan.

At the same time, feedback will also reveal when the problem is a lack of manners. Manners are the lubricating oil of an organization. It is a law of nature that two moving bodies in contact with each other create friction. This is as true for human beings as it is for inanimate objects. Manners—simple things like saying "please" and "thank you" and knowing a person's name or asking after her family—enable two people to work together whether they like each other or not. Bright people, especially bright young people, often do not understand this. If analysis shows that someone's brilliant work fails again and again as soon as cooperation from others is required, it probably indicates a lack of courtesy—that is, a lack of manners.

Comparing your expectations with your results also indicates what not to do. We all have a vast number of areas in which we have no talent or skill and little chance of becoming even mediocre. In those areas a person—and especially a knowledge worker—should not take on work, jobs, and assignments. One should waste as little effort as possible on improving areas of low competence. It takes far more energy and work to improve from incompetence to mediocrity than it takes to improve from first-rate performance to excellence. And yet most people—especially most teachers and most organizations—concentrate on making incompetent performers into mediocre ones. Energy, resources, and time should go instead to making a competent person into a star performer.

How Do I Perform?

Amazingly few people know how they get things done. Indeed, most of us do not even know that different people work and perform differently. Too many people work in ways that are not their ways, and that almost guarantees nonperformance. For knowledge workers, How do I perform? may be an even more important question than What are my strengths?

Like one's strengths, how one performs is unique. It is a matter of personality. Whether personality be a matter of nature or nurture, it surely is formed long before a person goes to work. And *how* a person performs is a given, just as *what* a person is good at or not good at is a given. A person's way of performing can be slightly modified, but it is unlikely to be completely changed—and certainly not easily. Just as people achieve results by doing what they are good at, they also achieve results by working in ways that they best perform. A few common personality traits usually determine how a person performs.

Am I a reader or a listener?

The first thing to know is whether you are a reader or a listener. Far too few people even know that there are readers and listeners and that people are rarely both. Even fewer know which of the two they themselves are. But some examples will show how damaging such ignorance can be.

When Dwight Eisenhower was Supreme Commander of the Allied forces in Europe, he was the darling of the press. His press conferences were famous for their style—General Eisenhower showed total command of whatever question he was asked, and he was able to describe a situation and explain a policy in two or three beautifully polished and elegant sentences. Ten years later, the same journalists who had been his admirers held President Eisenhower in open contempt. He never addressed the questions, they complained, but rambled on endlessly about something else. And they constantly ridiculed him for butchering the King's English in incoherent and ungrammatical answers.

Eisenhower apparently did not know that he was a reader, not a listener. When he was Supreme Commander in Europe, his aides made sure that every question from the press was presented in writing at least half an hour before a conference was to begin. And then Eisenhower was in total command. When he became president, he succeeded two listeners, Franklin D. Roosevelt and Harry Truman. Both men knew themselves to be listeners and both enjoyed free-for-all press conferences. Eisenhower may have felt that he had to do what his two predecessors had done. As a result, he never even heard the questions journalists asked. And Eisenhower is not even an extreme case of a nonlistener.

A few years later, Lyndon Johnson destroyed his presidency, in large measure, by not knowing that he was a listener. His predecessor, John Kennedy, was a reader who had assembled a brilliant group of writers as his assistants, making sure that they wrote to him before discussing their memos in person. Johnson kept these people on his staff—and they kept on writing. He never, apparently, understood one word of what they wrote. Yet as a senator, Johnson had been superb; for parliamentarians have to be, above all, listeners.

Few listeners can be made, or can make themselves, into competent readers—and vice versa. The listener who tries to be a reader will, therefore, suffer the fate of Lyndon Johnson, whereas the reader who tries to be a listener will suffer the fate of Dwight Eisenhower. They will not perform or achieve.

How do I learn?

The second thing to know about how one performs is to know how one learns. Many first-class writers—Winston Churchill is but one example—do poorly in school. They tend to remember their schooling as pure torture. Yet few of their classmates remember it the same way. They may not have enjoyed the school very much, but the worst they suffered was boredom. The explanation is that writers do not, as a rule, learn by listening and reading. They learn by writing. Because schools do not allow them to learn this way, they get poor grades.

Schools everywhere are organized on the assumption that there is only one right way to learn and that it is the same way for everybody. But to be forced to learn the way a school teaches is sheer hell for students who learn differently. Indeed, there are probably half a dozen different ways to learn.

There are people, like Churchill, who learn by writing. Some people learn by taking copious notes. Beethoven, for example, left behind an enormous number of sketchbooks, yet he said he never actually looked at them when he composed. Asked why he kept them, he is reported to have replied, “If I don’t write it down immediately, I forget it right away. If I put it into a sketchbook, I never forget it and I never have to look it up again." Some people learn by doing. Others learn by hearing themselves talk.

A chief executive I know who converted a small and mediocre family business into the leading company in its industry was one of those people who learn by talking. He was in the habit of calling his entire senior staff into his office once a week and then talking at them for two or three hours. He would raise policy issues and argue three different positions on each one. He rarely asked his associates for comments or questions; he simply needed an audience to hear himself talk. That's how he learned. And although he is a fairly extreme case, learning through talking is by no means an unusual method. Successful trial lawyers learn the same way, as do many medical diagnosticians (and so do I).

Of all the important pieces of self-knowledge, understanding how you learn is the easiest to acquire. When I ask people, "How do you learn?" most of them know the answer. But when I ask, "Do you act on this knowledge?" few answer yes. And yet, acting on this knowledge is the key to performance; or rather, *not* acting on this knowledge condemns one to nonperformance.

Am I a reader or a listener? and How do I learn? are the first questions to ask. But they are by no means the only ones. To manage yourself effectively, you also have to ask, Do I work well with people, or am I a loner? And if you do work well with people, you then must ask, In what relationship?

Some people work best as subordinates. General George Patton, the great American military hero of World War II, is a prime example. Patton was America's top troop commander. Yet when he was proposed for an independent command, General George Marshall, the U.S. chief of staff—and probably the most successful picker of men in U.S. history—said, "Patton is the best subordinate the American army has ever produced, but he would be the worst commander."

Some people work best as team members. Others work best alone. Some are exceptionally talented as coaches and mentors; others are simply incompetent as mentors.

Another crucial question is, Do I produce results as a decision maker or as an adviser? A great many people perform best as advisers but cannot take the burden and pressure of making the decision. A good many other people, by contrast, need an adviser to force themselves to think; then they can make decisions and act on them with speed, self-confidence, and courage.

This is a reason, by the way, that the number two person in an organization often fails when promoted to the number one position. The top spot requires a decision maker. Strong decision makers often put somebody they trust into the number two spot as their adviser—and in that position the person is outstanding. But in the number one spot, the same person fails. He or she knows what the decision should be but cannot accept the responsibility of actually making it.

Other important questions to ask include, Do I perform well under stress, or do I need a highly structured and predictable environment? Do I work best in a big organization or a small one? Few people work well in all kinds of environments. Again and again, I have seen people who were very successful in large organizations flounder miserably when they moved into smaller ones. And the reverse is equally true.

The conclusion bears repeating: Do not try to change yourself—you are unlikely to succeed. But work hard to improve the way you perform. And try not to take on work you cannot perform or will only perform poorly.

What Are My Values?

To be able to manage yourself, you finally have to ask, What are my values? This is not a question of ethics. With respect to ethics, the rules are the same for everybody, and the test is a simple one. I call it the "mirror test."

In the early years of this century, the most highly respected diplomat of all the great powers was the German ambassador in London. He was clearly destined for great things—to become his country's foreign minister, at least, if not its federal chancellor. Yet in 1906 he abruptly resigned rather than preside over a dinner given by the diplomatic corps for Edward VII. The king was a notorious womanizer and made it clear what kind of dinner he wanted. The ambassador is reported to have said, "I refuse to see a pimp in the mirror in the morning when I shave."

That is the mirror test. Ethics requires that you ask yourself, What kind of person do I want to see in the mirror in the morning? What is ethical behavior in one kind of organization or situation is ethical behavior in another. But ethics is only part of a value system—especially of an organization's value system.

To work in an organization whose value system is unacceptable or incompatible with one's own condemns a person both to frustration and to nonperformance.

Consider the experience of a highly successful human resources executive whose company was acquired by a bigger organization. After the acquisition, she was promoted to do the kind of work she did best, which included selecting people for important positions. The executive deeply believed that a company should hire people for such positions from the outside only after exhausting all the inside possibilities. But her new company believed in first looking outside "to bring in fresh blood." There is something to be said for both approaches—in my experience, the proper one is to do some of both. They are, however, fundamentally incompatible—not as policies but as values. They bespeak different views of the relationship between organizations and people; different views of the responsibility of an organization to its people and their development; and different views of a person's most important contribution to an enterprise. After several years of frustration, the executive quit—at considerable financial loss. Her values and the values of the organization simply were not compatible.

Similarly, whether a pharmaceutical company tries to obtain results by making constant, small improvements or by achieving occasional, highly expensive, and risky "breakthroughs" is not primarily an economic question. The results of either strategy may be pretty much the same. At bottom, there is a conflict between a value system that sees the company's contribution in terms of helping physicians do better what they already do and a value system that is oriented toward making scientific discoveries.

Whether a business should be run for short-term results or with a focus on the long term is likewise a question of values. Financial analysts believe that businesses can be run for both simultaneously. Successful businesspeople know better. To be sure, every company has to produce short-term results. But in any conflict between short-term results and long-term growth, each company will determine its own priority. This is not primarily a disagreement about economics. It is fundamentally a value conflict regarding the function of a business and the responsibility of management.

Value conflicts are not limited to business organizations. One of the fastest-growing pastoral churches in the United States measures success by the number of new parishioners. Its leadership believes that what matters is how many newcomers join the congregation. The Good Lord will then minister to their spiritual needs or at least to the needs of a sufficient percentage. Another pastoral, evangelical church believes that what matters is people's spiritual growth. The church eases out newcomers who join but do not enter into its spiritual life.

Again, this is not a matter of numbers. At first glance, it appears that the second church grows more slowly. But it retains a far larger proportion of newcomers than the first one does. Its growth, in other words, is more solid. This is also not a theological problem, or only secondarily so. It is a problem about values. In a public debate, one pastor argued, "Unless you first come to church, you will never find the gate to the Kingdom of Heaven."

"No," answered the other. "Until you first look for the gate to the Kingdom of Heaven, you don't belong in church."

Organizations, like people, have values. To be effective in an organization, a person's values must be compatible with the organization's values. They do not need to be the same, but they must be close enough to coexist. Otherwise, the person will not only be frustrated but also will not produce results.

A person's strengths and the way that person performs rarely conflict; the two are complementary. But there is sometimes a conflict between a person's values and his or her strengths. What one does well—even very well and successfully—may not fit with one's value system. In that case, the work may not appear to be worth devoting one's life to (or even a substantial portion thereof).

If I may, allow me to interject a personal note. Many years ago, I too had to decide between my values and what I was doing successfully. I was doing very well as a young investment banker in London in the mid-1930s, and the work clearly fit my strengths. Yet I did not see myself making a contribution as an asset manager. People, I realized, were what I valued, and I saw no point in being the richest man in the cemetery. I had no money and no other job prospects. Despite the continuing Depression, I quit—and it was the right thing to do. Values, in other words, are and should be the ultimate test.

Where Do I Belong?

A small number of people know very early where they belong. Mathematicians, musicians, and cooks, for instance, are usually mathematicians, musicians, and cooks by the time they are four or five years old. Physicians usually decide on their careers in their teens, if not earlier. But most people, especially highly gifted people, do not really know where they belong until they are well past their mid-twenties. By that time, however, they should know the answers to the three questions: What are my strengths? How do I perform? and, What are my values? And then they can and should decide where they belong.

Or rather, they should be able to decide where they do *not* belong. The person who has learned that he or she does not perform well in a big organization should have learned to say no to a position in one. The person who has learned that he or she is not a decision maker should have learned to say no to a decision-making assignment. A General Patton (who probably never learned this himself) should have learned to say no to an independent command.

Equally important, knowing the answer to these questions enables a person to say to an opportunity, an offer, or an assignment, "Yes, I will do that. But this is the way I should be doing it. This is the way it should be structured. This is the way the relationships should be. These are the kind of results you should expect from me, and in this time frame, because this is who I am."

Successful careers are not planned. They develop when people are prepared for opportunities because they know their strengths, their method of work, and their values. Knowing where one belongs can transform an ordinary person—hardworking and competent but otherwise mediocre—into an outstanding performer.

What Should I Contribute?

Throughout history, the great majority of people never had to ask the question, What should I contribute? They were told what to contribute, and their tasks were dictated either by the work itself—as it was for the peasant or artisan—or by a master or a mistress—as it was for domestic servants. And until very recently, it was taken for granted that most people were subordinates who did as they were told. Even in the 1950s and 1960s, the new knowledge workers (the so-called organization men) looked to their company's personnel department to plan their careers.

Then in the late 1960s, no one wanted to be told what to do any longer. Young men and women began to ask, What do *I* want to do? And what they heard was that the way to contribute was to "do your own thing." But this solution was as wrong as the organization men's had been. Very few of the people who believed that doing one's own thing would lead to contribution, self-fulfillment, and success achieved any of the three.

But still, there is no return to the old answer of doing what you are told or assigned to do. Knowledge workers in particular have to learn to ask a question that has not been asked before: What *should* my contribution be? To answer it, they must address three distinct elements: What does the situation require? Given my strengths, my way of performing, and my values, how can I make the greatest contribution to what needs to be done? And finally, What results have to be achieved to make a difference?

Consider the experience of a newly appointed hospital administrator. The hospital was big and prestigious, but it had been coasting on its reputation for 30 years. The new administrator decided that his contribution should be to establish a standard of excellence in one important area within two years. He chose to focus on the emergency room, which was big, visible, and sloppy. He decided that every patient who came into the ER had to be seen by a qualified nurse within 60 seconds. Within 12 months, the hospital's emergency room had become a model for all hospitals in the United States, and within another two years, the whole hospital had been transformed.

As this example suggests, it is rarely possible—or even particularly fruitful—to look too far ahead. A plan can usually cover no more than 18 months and still be reasonably clear and specific. So the question in most cases should be, Where and how can I achieve results that will make a difference within the next year and a half? The answer must balance several things. First, the results should be hard to achieve—they should require "stretching," to use the current buzzword. But also, they should be within reach. To aim at results that cannot be achieved—or that can be only under the most unlikely circumstances—is not being ambitious; it is being foolish. Second, the results should be meaningful. They should make a difference. Finally, results should be visible and, if at all possible, measurable. From this will come a course of action: what to do, where and how to start, and what goals and deadlines to set.

Responsibility for Relationships

Very few people work by themselves and achieve results by themselves—a few great artists, a few great scientists, a few great athletes. Most people work with others and are effective with other people. That is true whether they are members of an organization or independently employed. Managing yourself requires taking responsibility for relationships. This has two parts.

The first is to accept the fact that other people are as much individuals as you yourself are. They perversely insist on behaving like human beings. This means that they too have their strengths; they too have their ways of getting things done; they too have their values. To be effective, therefore, you have to know the strengths, the performance modes, and the values of your coworkers.

That sounds obvious, but few people pay attention to it. Typical is the person who was trained to write reports in his or her first assignment because that boss was a reader. Even if the next boss is a listener, the person goes on writing reports that, invariably, produce no results. Invariably the boss will think the employee is stupid, incompetent, and lazy, and he or she will fail. But that could have been avoided if the employee had only looked at the new boss and analyzed how *this* boss performs.

Bosses are neither a title on the organization chart nor a "function." They are individuals and are entitled to do their work in the way they do it best. It is incumbent on the people who work with them to observe them, to find out how they work, and to adapt themselves to what makes their bosses most effective. This, in fact, is the secret of "managing" the boss.

The same holds true for all your coworkers. Each works his or her way, not your way. And each is entitled to work in his or her way. What matters is whether they perform and what their values are. As for how they perform—each is likely to do it differently. The first secret of effectiveness is to understand the people you work with and depend on so that you can make use of their strengths, their ways of working, and their values. Working relationships are as much based on the people as they are on the work.

The second part of relationship responsibility is taking responsibility for communication. Whenever I, or any other consultant, start to work with an organization, the first thing I hear about are all the personality conflicts. Most of these arise from the fact that people do not know what other people are doing and how they do their work, or what contribution the other people are concentrating on and what results they expect. And the reason they do not know is that they have not asked and therefore have not been told.

This failure to ask reflects human stupidity less than it reflects human history. Until recently, it was unnecessary to tell any of these things to anybody. In the medieval city, everyone in a district plied the same trade. In the countryside, everyone in a valley planted the same crop as soon as the frost was out of the ground. Even those few people who did things that were not "common" worked alone, so they did not have to tell anyone what they were doing.

Today the great majority of people work with others who have different tasks and responsibilities. The marketing vice president may have come out of sales and know everything about sales, but she knows nothing about the things she has never done—pricing, advertising, packaging, and the like. So the people who do these things must make sure that the marketing vice president understands what they are trying to do, why they are trying to do it, how they are going to do it, and what results to expect.

If the marketing vice president does not understand what these high-grade knowledge specialists are doing, it is primarily their fault, not hers. They have not educated her. Conversely, it is the marketing vice president's responsibility to make sure that all of her coworkers understand how she looks at marketing: what her goals are, how she works, and what she expects of herself and of each one of them.

Even people who understand the importance of taking responsibility for relationships often do not communicate sufficiently with their associates. They are afraid of being thought presumptuous or inquisitive or stupid. They are wrong. Whenever someone goes to his or her associates and says, "This is what I am good at. This is how I work. These are my values. This is the contribution I plan to concentrate on and the results I should be expected to deliver," the response is always, "This is most helpful. But why didn't you tell me earlier?"

And one gets the same reaction—without exception, in my experience—if one continues by asking, "And what do I need to know about your strengths, how you perform, your values, and your proposed contribution?" In fact, knowledge workers should request this of everyone with whom they work, whether as subordinate, superior, colleague, or team member. And again, whenever this is done, the reaction is always, "Thanks for asking me. But why didn't you ask me earlier?"

Organizations are no longer built on force but on trust. The existence of trust between people does not necessarily mean that they like one another. It means that they understand one another. Taking responsibility for relationships is therefore an absolute necessity. It is a duty. Whether one is a member of the organization, a consultant to it, a supplier, or a distributor, one owes that responsibility to all one's coworkers: those whose work one depends on as well as those who depend on one's own work.

The Second Half of Your Life

When work for most people meant manual labor, there was no need to worry about the second half of your life. You simply kept on doing what you had always done. And if you were lucky enough to survive 40 years of hard work in the mill or on the railroad, you were quite happy to spend the rest of your life doing nothing. Today, however, most work is knowledge work, and knowledge workers are not "finished" after 40 years on the job, they are merely bored.

We hear a great deal of talk about the midlife crisis of the executive. It is mostly boredom. At 45, most executives have reached the peak of their business careers, and they know it. After 20 years of doing very much the same kind of work, they are very good at their jobs. But they are not learning or contributing or deriving challenge and satisfaction from the job. And yet they are still likely to face another 20 if not 25 years of work. That is why managing oneself increasingly leads one to begin a second career.

There are three ways to develop a second career. The first is actually to start one. Often this takes nothing more than moving from one kind of organization to another: the divisional controller in a large corporation, for instance, becomes the controller of a medium-sized hospital. But there are also growing numbers of people who move into different lines of work altogether: the business executive or government official who enters the ministry at 45, for instance; or the midlevel manager who leaves corporate life after 20 years to attend law school and become a small-town attorney.

We will see many more second careers undertaken by people who have achieved modest success in their first jobs. Such people have substantial skills, and they know how to work. They need a community—the house is empty with the children gone—and they need income as well. But above all, they need challenge.

The second way to prepare for the second half of your life is to develop a parallel career. Many people who are very successful in their first careers stay in the work they have been doing, either on a full-time or part-time or consulting basis. But in addition, they create a parallel job, usually in a nonprofit organization, that takes another ten hours of work a week. They might take over the administration of their church, for instance, or the presidency of the local Girl Scouts council. They might run the battered women's shelter, work as a children's librarian for the local public library, sit on the school board, and so on.

Finally, there are the social entrepreneurs. These are usually people who have been very successful in their first careers. They love their work, but it no longer challenges them. In many cases they keep on doing what they have been doing all along but spend less and less of their time on it. They also start another activity, usually a nonprofit. My friend Bob Buford, for example, built a very successful television company that he still runs. But he has also founded and built a successful nonprofit organization that works with Protestant churches, and he is building another to teach social entrepreneurs how to manage their own nonprofit ventures while still running their original businesses.

People who manage the second half of their lives may always be a minority. The majority may "retire on the job" and count the years until their actual retirement. But it is this minority, the men and women who see a long working-life expectancy as an opportunity both for themselves and for society, who will become leaders and models.

There is one prerequisite for managing the second half of your life: You must begin long before you enter it. When it first became clear 30 years ago that working-life expectancies were lengthening very fast, many observers (including myself) believed that retired people would increasingly become volunteers for nonprofit institutions. That has not happened. If one does not begin to volunteer before one is 40 or so, one will not volunteer once past 60.

Similarly, all the social entrepreneurs I know began to work in their chosen second enterprise long before they reached their peak in their original business. Consider the example of a successful lawyer, the legal counsel to a large corporation, who has started a venture to establish model schools in his state. He began to do volunteer legal work for the schools when he was around 35. He was elected to the school board at age 40. At age 50, when he had amassed a fortune, he started his own enterprise to build and to run model schools. He is, however, still working nearly full-time as the lead counsel in the company he helped found as a young lawyer.

There is another reason to develop a second major interest, and to develop it early. No one can expect to live very long without experiencing a serious setback in his or her life or work. There is the competent engineer who is passed over for promotion at age 45. There is the competent college professor who realizes at age 42 that she will never get a professorship at a big university, even though she may be fully qualified for it. There are tragedies in one's family life: the breakup of one's marriage or the loss of a child. At such times, a second major interest—not just a hobby—may make all the difference. The engineer, for example, now knows that he has not been very successful in his job. But in his outside activity—as church treasurer, for example—he is a success. One's family may break up, but in that outside activity there is still a community.

In a society in which success has become so terribly important, having options will become increasingly vital. Historically, there was no such thing as "success." The overwhelming majority of people did not expect anything but to stay in their "proper station," as an old English prayer has it. The only mobility was downward mobility.

In a knowledge society, however, we expect everyone to be a success. This is clearly an impossibility. For a great many people, there is at best an absence of failure. Wherever there is success, there has to be failure. And then it is vitally important for the individual, and equally for the individual's family, to have an area in which he or she can contribute, make a difference, and be *somebody*. That means finding a second area—whether in a second career, a parallel career, or a social venture—that offers an opportunity for being a leader, for being respected, for being a success.

The challenges of managing oneself may seem obvious, if not elementary. And the answers may seem self-evident to the point of appearing naïve. But managing oneself requires new and unprecedented things from the individual, and especially from the knowledge worker. In effect, managing oneself demands that each knowledge worker think and behave like a chief executive officer. Further, the shift from manual workers who do as they are told to knowledge workers who have to manage themselves profoundly challenges social structure. Every existing society, even the most individualistic one, takes two things for granted, if only subconsciously: that organizations outlive workers, and that most people stay put.

But today the opposite is true. Knowledge workers outlive organizations, and they are mobile. The need to manage oneself is therefore creating a revolution in human affairs.

Originally published in January 1999. Reprint R0501K

What Makes a Leader?

by Daniel Goleman

EVERY BUSINESSPERSON KNOWS a story about a highly intelligent, highly skilled executive who was promoted into a leadership position only to fail at the job. And they also know a story about someone with solid—but not extraordinary—intellectual abilities and technical skills who was promoted into a similar position and then soared.

Such anecdotes support the widespread belief that identifying individuals with the "right stuff" to be leaders is more art than science. After all, the personal styles of superb leaders vary: Some leaders are subdued and analytical; others shout their manifestos from the mountaintops. And just as important, different situations call for different types of leadership. Most mergers need a sensitive negotiator at the helm, whereas many turnarounds require a more forceful authority.

I have found, however, that the most effective leaders are alike in one crucial way: They all have a high degree of what has come to be known as *emotional intelligence*. It's not that IQ and technical skills are irrelevant. They do matter, but mainly as "threshold capabilities"; that is, they are the entry-level requirements for executive positions. But my research, along with other recent studies, clearly shows that emotional intelligence is the sine qua non of leadership. Without it, a person can have the best training in the world, an incisive, analytical mind, and an endless supply of smart ideas, but he still won't make a great leader.

In the course of the past year, my colleagues and I have focused on how emotional intelligence operates at work. We have examined the relationship between emotional intelligence and effective performance, especially in leaders. And we have observed how emotional intelligence shows itself on the job. How can you tell if someone has high emotional intelligence, for example, and how can you recognize it in yourself? In the following pages, we'll explore these questions, taking each of the components of emotional intelligence—self-awareness, self-regulation, motivation, empathy, and social skill—in turn.

Evaluating Emotional Intelligence

Most large companies today have employed trained psychologists to develop what are known as "competency models" to aid them in identifying, training, and promoting likely stars in the leadership firmament. The psychologists have also developed such models for lower-level positions. And in recent years, I have analyzed competency models from 188 companies, most of which were large and global and included the likes of Lucent Technologies, British Airways, and Credit Suisse.

In carrying out this work, my objective was to determine which personal capabilities drove outstanding performance within these organizations, and to what degree they did so. I grouped capabilities into three categories: purely technical skills like accounting and business planning; cognitive abilities like analytical reasoning; and competencies demonstrating emotional intelligence, such as the ability to work with others and effectiveness in leading change.

To create some of the competency models, psychologists asked senior managers at the companies to identify the capabilities that typified the organization's most outstanding leaders. To create other models, the psychologists used objective criteria, such as a division's profitability, to differentiate the star performers at senior levels within their organizations from the average ones. Those

Idea in Brief

What distinguishes great leaders from merely good ones? It isn't IQ or technical skills, says Daniel Goleman. It's **emotional intelligence:** a group of five skills that enable the best leaders to maximize their own *and* their followers' performance. When senior managers at one company had a critical mass of EI capabilities, their divisions outperformed yearly earnings goals by 20%.

The EI skills are:

- *Self-awareness*—knowing one's strengths, weaknesses, drives, values, and impact on others
- *Self-regulation*—controlling or redirecting disruptive impulses and moods
- *Motivation*—relishing achievement for its own sake
- *Empathy*—understanding other people's emotional makeup
- *Social skill*—building rapport with others to move them in desired directions

We're each born with certain levels of EI skills. But we can strengthen these abilities through persistence, practice, and feedback from colleagues or coaches.

individuals were then extensively interviewed and tested, and their capabilities were compared. This process resulted in the creation of lists of ingredients for highly effective leaders. The lists ranged in length from seven to 15 items and included such ingredients as initiative and strategic vision.

When I analyzed all this data, I found dramatic results. To be sure, intellect was a driver of outstanding performance. Cognitive skills such as big-picture thinking and long-term vision were particularly important. But when I calculated the ratio of technical skills, IQ, and emotional intelligence as ingredients of excellent performance, emotional intelligence proved to be twice as important as the others for jobs at all levels.

Moreover, my analysis showed that emotional intelligence played an increasingly important role at the highest levels of the company, where differences in technical skills are of negligible importance. In other words, the higher the rank of a person considered to be a star performer, the more emotional intelligence capabilities showed up as the reason for his or her effectiveness. When I compared star performers with average ones in senior leadership positions, nearly

Idea in Practice

Understanding EI'S Components

EI Component	Definition	Hallmarks	Example
Self-awareness	Knowing one's emotions, strengths, weaknesses, drives, values, and goals—and their impact on others	• Self-confidence • Realistic self-assessment • Self-deprecating sense of humor • Thirst for constructive criticism	A manager knows tight deadlines bring out the worst in him. So he plans his time to get work done well in advance.
Self-regulation	Controlling or redirecting disruptive emotions and impulses	• Trustworthiness • Integrity • Comfort with ambiguity and change	When a team botches a presentation, its leader resists the urge to scream. Instead, she considers possible reasons for the failure, explains the consequences to her team, and explores solutions with them.
Motivation	Being driven to achieve for the sake of achievement	• A passion for the work itself and for new challenges • Unflagging energy to improve • Optimism in the face of failure	A portfolio manager at an investment company sees his fund tumble for three consecutive quarters. Major clients defect. Instead of blaming external circumstances, she decides to learn from the experience—and engineers a turnaround.

Empathy	Considering others' feelings, especially when making decisions	• Expertise in attracting and retaining talent • Ability to develop others • Sensitivity to cross-cultural differences	An American consultant and her team pitch a project to a potential client in Japan. Her team interprets the client's silence as disapproval, and prepares to leave. The consultant reads the client's body language and senses interest. She continues the meeting, and her team gets the job.
Social Skill	Managing relationships to move people in desired directions	• Effectiveness in leading change • Persuasiveness • Extensive networking • Expertise in building and leading teams	A manager wants his company to adopt a better Internet strategy. He finds kindred spirits and assembles a de facto team to create a prototype Web site. He persuades allies in other divisions to fund the company's participation in a relevant convention. His company forms an Internet division—and puts him in charge of it.

Strengthening Your EI

Use practice and feedback from others to strengthen specific EI skills.

Example: An executive learned from others that she lacked empathy, especially the ability to listen. She wanted to fix the problem, so she asked a coach to tell her when she exhibited poor listening skills. She then role-played incidents to practice giving better responses; for example, not interrupting. She also began observing executives skilled at listening—and imitated their behavior.

The five components of emotional intelligence at work

	Definition	Hallmarks
Self-awareness	The ability to recognize and understand your moods, emotions, and drives, as well as their effect on others	Self-confidence Realistic self-assessment Self-deprecating sense of humor
Self-Regulation	The ability to control or redirect disruptive impulses and moods The propensity to suspend judgment–to think before acting	Trustworthiness and integrity Comfort with ambiguity Openness to change
Motivation	A passion to work for reasons that go beyond money or status A propensity to pursue goals with energy and persistence	Strong drive to achieve Optimism, even in the face of failure Organizational commitment
Empathy	The ability to understand the emotional makeup of other people Skill in treating people according to their emotional reactions	Expertise in building and retaining talent Cross-cultural sensitivity Service to clients and customers
Social Skill	Proficiency in managing relationships and building networks An ability to find common ground and build rapport	Effectiveness in leading change Persuasiveness Expertise in building and leading teams

90% of the difference in their profiles was attributable to emotional intelligence factors rather than cognitive abilities.

Other researchers have confirmed that emotional intelligence not only distinguishes outstanding leaders but can also be linked to strong performance. The findings of the late David McClelland, the renowned researcher in human and organizational behavior, are a good example. In a 1996 study of a global food and beverage company, McClelland found that when senior managers had a critical mass of emotional intelligence capabilities, their divisions outperformed yearly earnings goals by 20%. Meanwhile, division leaders without that critical mass underperformed by almost the same amount. McClelland's findings, interestingly, held as true in the company's U.S. divisions as in its divisions in Asia and Europe.

In short, the numbers are beginning to tell us a persuasive story about the link between a company's success and the emotional intelligence of its leaders. And just as important, research is also demonstrating that people can, if they take the right approach, develop their emotional intelligence. (See the sidebar "Can Emotional Intelligence Be Learned?")

Self-Awareness

Self-awareness is the first component of emotional intelligence—which makes sense when one considers that the Delphic oracle gave the advice to "know thyself" thousands of years ago. Self-awareness means having a deep understanding of one's emotions, strengths, weaknesses, needs, and drives. People with strong self-awareness are neither overly critical nor unrealistically hopeful. Rather, they are honest—with themselves and with others.

People who have a high degree of self-awareness recognize how their feelings affect them, other people, and their job performance. Thus, a self-aware person who knows that tight deadlines bring out the worst in him plans his time carefully and gets his work done well in advance. Another person with high self-awareness will be able to work with a demanding client. She will understand the client's impact on her moods and the deeper reasons for her frustration. "Their

Can Emotional Intelligence Be Learned?

FOR AGES, PEOPLE HAVE DEBATED if leaders are born or made. So too goes the debate about emotional intelligence. Are people born with certain levels of empathy, for example, or do they acquire empathy as a result of life's experiences? The answer is both. Scientific inquiry strongly suggests that there is a genetic component to emotional intelligence. Psychological and developmental research indicates that nurture plays a role as well. How much of each perhaps will never be known, but research and practice clearly demonstrate that emotional intelligence can be learned.

One thing is certain: Emotional intelligence increases with age. There is an old-fashioned word for the phenomenon: maturity. Yet even with maturity, some people still need training to enhance their emotional intelligence. Unfortunately, far too many training programs that intend to build leadership skills—including emotional intelligence—are a waste of time and money. The problem is simple: They focus on the wrong part of the brain.

Emotional intelligence is born largely in the neurotransmitters of the brain's limbic system, which governs feelings, impulses, and drives. Research indicates that the limbic system learns best through motivation, extended practice, and feedback. Compare this with the kind of learning that goes on in the neocortex, which governs analytical and technical ability. The neocortex grasps concepts and logic. It is the part of the brain that figures out how to use a computer or make a sales call by reading a book. Not surprisingly—but mistakenly—it is also the part of the brain targeted by most training programs aimed at enhancing emotional intelligence. When such programs take, in effect, a neocortical approach, my research with the Consortium for Research on Emotional Intelligence in Organizations has shown they can even have a *negative* impact on people's job performance.

To enhance emotional intelligence, organizations must refocus their training to include the limbic system. They must help people break old behavioral habits and establish new ones. That not only takes much more time than conventional training programs, it also requires an individualized approach.

Imagine an executive who is thought to be low on empathy by her colleagues. Part of that deficit shows itself as an inability to listen; she interrupts people and doesn't pay close attention to what they're saying. To fix the problem, the executive needs to be motivated to change, and then she needs practice and feedback from others in the company. A colleague or coach could be tapped to let the executive know when she has been observed failing to listen. She would then have to replay the incident and give a better response; that is, demonstrate her ability to absorb what others are saying. And the executive could be directed to observe certain executives who listen well and to mimic their behavior.

With persistence and practice, such a process can lead to lasting results. I know one Wall Street executive who sought to improve his empathy—specifically his ability to read people's reactions and see their perspectives. Before beginning his quest, the executive's subordinates were terrified of working with him. People even went so far as to hide bad news from him. Naturally, he was shocked when finally confronted with these facts. He went home and told his family—but they only confirmed what he had heard at work. When their opinions on any given subject did not mesh with his, they, too, were frightened of him.

Enlisting the help of a coach, the executive went to work to heighten his empathy through practice and feedback. His first step was to take a vacation to a foreign country where he did not speak the language. While there, he monitored his reactions to the unfamiliar and his openness to people who were different from him. When he returned home, humbled by his week abroad, the executive asked his coach to shadow him for parts of the day, several times a week, to critique how he treated people with new or different perspectives. At the same time, he consciously used on-the-job interactions as opportunities to practice "hearing" ideas that differed from his. Finally, the executive had himself videotaped in meetings and asked those who worked for and with him to critique his ability to acknowledge and understand the feelings of others. It took several months, but the executive's emotional intelligence did ultimately rise, and the improvement was reflected in his overall performance on the job.

It's important to emphasize that building one's emotional intelligence cannot—will not—happen without sincere desire and concerted effort. A brief seminar won't help; nor can one buy a how-to manual. It is much harder to learn to empathize—to internalize empathy as a natural response to people—than it is to become adept at regression analysis. But it can be done. "Nothing great was ever achieved without enthusiasm," wrote Ralph Waldo Emerson. If your goal is to become a real leader, these words can serve as a guidepost in your efforts to develop high emotional intelligence.

trivial demands take us away from the real work that needs to be done," she might explain. And she will go one step further and turn her anger into something constructive.

Self-awareness extends to a person's understanding of his or her values and goals. Someone who is highly self-aware knows where he is headed and why; so, for example, he will be able to be firm in turning down a job offer that is tempting financially but does not fit with his principles or long-term goals. A person who lacks self-awareness is apt to make decisions that bring on inner turmoil by treading on buried values. "The money looked good so I signed on," someone might say two years into a job, "but the work means so little to me that I'm constantly bored." The decisions of self-aware people mesh with their values; consequently, they often find work to be energizing.

How can one recognize self-awareness? First and foremost, it shows itself as candor and an ability to assess oneself realistically. People with high self-awareness are able to speak accurately and openly—although not necessarily effusively or confessionally—about their emotions and the impact they have on their work. For instance, one manager I know of was skeptical about a new personal-shopper service that her company, a major department-store chain, was about to introduce. Without prompting from her team or her boss, she offered them an explanation: "It's hard for me to get behind the rollout of this service," she admitted, "because I really wanted to run the project, but I wasn't selected. Bear with me while I deal with that." The manager did indeed examine her feelings; a week later, she was supporting the project fully.

Such self-knowledge often shows itself in the hiring process. Ask a candidate to describe a time he got carried away by his feelings and did something he later regretted. Self-aware candidates will be frank in admitting to failure—and will often tell their tales with a smile. One of the hallmarks of self-awareness is a self-deprecating sense of humor.

Self-awareness can also be identified during performance reviews. Self-aware people know—and are comfortable talking about—their limitations and strengths, and they often demonstrate a thirst for constructive criticism. By contrast, people with low self-awareness interpret the message that they need to improve as a threat or a sign of failure.

Self-aware people can also be recognized by their self-confidence. They have a firm grasp of their capabilities and are less likely to set themselves up to fail by, for example, overstretching on assignments. They know, too, when to ask for help. And the risks they take on the job are calculated. They won't ask for a challenge that they know they can't handle alone. They'll play to their strengths.

Consider the actions of a midlevel employee who was invited to sit in on a strategy meeting with her company's top executives. Although she was the most junior person in the room, she did not sit there quietly, listening in awestruck or fearful silence. She knew she had a head for clear logic and the skill to present ideas persuasively, and she offered cogent suggestions about the company's strategy. At the same time, her self-awareness stopped her from wandering into territory where she knew she was weak.

Despite the value of having self-aware people in the workplace, my research indicates that senior executives don't often give self-awareness the credit it deserves when they look for potential leaders. Many executives mistake candor about feelings for "wimpiness" and fail to give due respect to employees who openly acknowledge their shortcomings. Such people are too readily dismissed as "not tough enough" to lead others.

In fact, the opposite is true. In the first place, people generally admire and respect candor. Furthermore, leaders are constantly required to make judgment calls that require a candid assessment of capabilities—their own and those of others. Do we have the management expertise to acquire a competitor? Can we launch a new product within six months? People who assess themselves honestly—that is, self-aware people—are well suited to do the same for the organizations they run.

Self-Regulation

Biological impulses drive our emotions. We cannot do away with them—but we can do much to manage them. Self-regulation, which is like an ongoing inner conversation, is the component of emotional intelligence that frees us from being prisoners of our feelings. People engaged in such a conversation feel bad moods and emotional impulses just as everyone else does, but they find ways to control them and even to channel them in useful ways.

Imagine an executive who has just watched a team of his employees present a botched analysis to the company's board of directors. In the gloom that follows, the executive might find himself tempted to pound on the table in anger or kick over a chair. He could leap up and scream at the group. Or he might maintain a grim silence, glaring at everyone before stalking off.

But if he had a gift for self-regulation, he would choose a different approach. He would pick his words carefully, acknowledging the team's poor performance without rushing to any hasty judgment. He would then step back to consider the reasons for the failure. Are they personal—a lack of effort? Are there any mitigating factors? What was his role in the debacle? After considering these questions, he would call the team together, lay out the incident's consequences, and offer his feelings about it. He would then present his analysis of the problem and a well-considered solution.

Why does self-regulation matter so much for leaders? First of all, people who are in control of their feelings and impulses—that is, people who are reasonable—are able to create an environment of trust and fairness. In such an environment, politics and infighting are sharply reduced and productivity is high. Talented people flock to the organization and aren't tempted to leave. And self-regulation has a trickle-down effect. No one wants to be known as a hothead when the boss is known for her calm approach. Fewer bad moods at the top mean fewer throughout the organization.

Second, self-regulation is important for competitive reasons. Everyone knows that business today is rife with ambiguity and change. Companies merge and break apart regularly. Technology transforms work at a dizzying pace. People who have mastered their emotions are able to roll with the changes. When a new program is announced, they don't panic; instead, they are able to suspend judgment, seek out information, and listen to the executives as they explain the new program. As the initiative moves forward, these people are able to move with it.

Sometimes they even lead the way. Consider the case of a manager at a large manufacturing company. Like her colleagues, she had used a certain software program for five years. The program drove how she collected and reported data and how she thought about the company's strategy. One day, senior executives announced that a new program was to be installed that would radically change how information was gathered and assessed within the organization. While many people in the company complained bitterly about how disruptive the change would be, the manager mulled over the reasons for the new program and was convinced of its potential to improve performance. She eagerly attended training sessions—some of her colleagues refused to do so—and was eventually promoted to run several divisions, in part because she used the new technology so effectively.

I want to push the importance of self-regulation to leadership even further and make the case that it enhances integrity, which is not only a personal virtue but also an organizational strength. Many of the bad things that happen in companies are a function of impulsive behavior. People rarely plan to exaggerate profits, pad expense accounts, dip into the till, or abuse power for selfish ends. Instead, an opportunity presents itself, and people with low impulse control just say yes.

By contrast, consider the behavior of the senior executive at a large food company. The executive was scrupulously honest in his negotiations with local distributors. He would routinely lay out his cost structure in detail, thereby giving the distributors a realistic understanding of the company's pricing. This approach meant the executive couldn't always drive a hard bargain. Now, on occasion, he felt the urge to increase profits by withholding information about the company's costs. But he challenged that impulse—he saw that it made more sense in the long run to counteract it. His emotional self-regulation paid off in strong, lasting relationships with distributors that benefited the company more than any short-term financial gains would have.

The signs of emotional self-regulation, therefore, are easy to see: a propensity for reflection and thoughtfulness; comfort with ambiguity and change; and integrity—an ability to say no to impulsive urges.

Like self-awareness, self-regulation often does not get its due. People who can master their emotions are sometimes seen as cold fish—their considered responses are taken as a lack of passion. People with fiery temperaments are frequently thought of as "classic" leaders—their outbursts are considered hallmarks of charisma and power. But when such people make it to the top, their impulsiveness often works against them. In my research, extreme displays of negative emotion have never emerged as a driver of good leadership.

Motivation

If there is one trait that virtually all effective leaders have, it is motivation. They are driven to achieve beyond expectations—their own and everyone else's. The key word here is *achieve*. Plenty of people are motivated by external factors, such as a big salary or the status that comes from having an impressive title or being part of a prestigious company. By contrast, those with leadership potential are motivated by a deeply embedded desire to achieve for the sake of achievement.

If you are looking for leaders, how can you identify people who are motivated by the drive to achieve rather than by external rewards? The first sign is a passion for the work itself—such people seek out creative challenges, love to learn, and take great pride in a job well done. They also display an unflagging energy to do things better. People with such energy often seem restless with the status quo. They are persistent with their questions about why things are done one way rather than another; they are eager to explore new approaches to their work.

A cosmetics company manager, for example, was frustrated that he had to wait two weeks to get sales results from people in the field. He finally tracked down an automated phone system that would beep each of his salespeople at 5 pm every day. An automated message then prompted them to punch in their numbers—how many calls and sales they had made that day. The system shortened the feedback time on sales results from weeks to hours.

That story illustrates two other common traits of people who are driven to achieve. They are forever raising the performance bar, and they like to keep score. Take the performance bar first. During performance reviews, people with high levels of motivation might ask to be "stretched" by their superiors. Of course, an employee who combines self-awareness with internal motivation will recognize her limits—but she won't settle for objectives that seem too easy to fulfill.

And it follows naturally that people who are driven to do better also want a way of tracking progress—their own, their team's, and their company's. Whereas people with low achievement motivation are often fuzzy about results, those with high achievement motivation often keep score by tracking such hard measures as profitability or market share. I know of a money manager who starts and ends his day on the Internet, gauging the performance of his stock fund against four industry-set benchmarks.

Interestingly, people with high motivation remain optimistic even when the score is against them. In such cases, self-regulation combines with achievement motivation to overcome the frustration and depression that come after a setback or failure. Take the case of an another portfolio manager at a large investment company. After several successful years, her fund tumbled for three consecutive quarters, leading three large institutional clients to shift their business elsewhere.

Some executives would have blamed the nosedive on circumstances outside their control; others might have seen the setback as evidence of personal failure. This portfolio manager, however, saw an opportunity to prove she could lead a turnaround. Two years later, when she was promoted to a very senior level in the company, she described the experience as "the best thing that ever happened to me; I learned so much from it."

Executives trying to recognize high levels of achievement motivation in their people can look for one last piece of evidence: commitment to the organization. When people love their jobs for the work itself, they often feel committed to the organizations that make that work possible. Committed employees are likely to stay with an organization even when they are pursued by headhunters waving money.

It's not difficult to understand how and why a motivation to achieve translates into strong leadership. If you set the performance bar high for yourself, you will do the same for the organization when you are in a position to do so. Likewise, a drive to surpass goals and an interest in keeping score can be contagious. Leaders with these traits can often build a team of managers around them with the same traits. And of course, optimism and organizational commitment are fundamental to leadership—just try to imagine running a company without them.

Empathy

Of all the dimensions of emotional intelligence, empathy is the most easily recognized. We have all felt the empathy of a sensitive teacher or friend; we have all been struck by its absence in an unfeeling coach or boss. But when it comes to business, we rarely hear people praised, let alone rewarded, for their empathy. The very word seems unbusinesslike, out of place amid the tough realities of the marketplace.

But empathy doesn't mean a kind of "I'm OK, you're OK" mushiness. For a leader, that is, it doesn't mean adopting other people's emotions as one's own and trying to please everybody. That would be a nightmare—it would make action impossible. Rather, empathy means thoughtfully considering employees' feelings—along with other factors—in the process of making intelligent decisions.

For an example of empathy in action, consider what happened when two giant brokerage companies merged, creating redundant jobs in all their divisions. One division manager called his people together and gave a gloomy speech that emphasized the number of people who would soon be fired. The manager of another division gave his people a different kind of speech. He was up-front about his own worry and confusion, and he promised to keep people informed and to treat everyone fairly.

The difference between these two managers was empathy. The first manager was too worried about his own fate to consider the feelings of his anxiety-stricken colleagues. The second knew intuitively what his people were feeling, and he acknowledged their fears with his words. Is it any surprise that the first manager saw his division sink as many demoralized people, especially the most talented, departed? By contrast, the second manager continued to be a strong leader, his best people stayed, and his division remained as productive as ever.

Empathy is particularly important today as a component of leadership for at least three reasons: the increasing use of teams; the rapid pace of globalization; and the growing need to retain talent.

Consider the challenge of leading a team. As anyone who has ever been a part of one can attest, teams are cauldrons of bubbling emotions. They are often charged with reaching a consensus—which is hard enough with two people and much more difficult as the numbers increase. Even in groups with as few as four or five members, alliances form and clashing agendas get set. A team's leader must be able to sense and understand the viewpoints of everyone around the table.

That's exactly what a marketing manager at a large information technology company was able to do when she was appointed to lead a troubled team. The group was in turmoil, overloaded by work and missing deadlines. Tensions were high among the members. Tinkering with procedures was not enough to bring the group together and make it an effective part of the company.

So the manager took several steps. In a series of one-on-one sessions, she took the time to listen to everyone in the group—what was frustrating them, how they rated their colleagues, whether they felt they had been ignored. And then she directed the team in a way that brought it together: She encouraged people to speak more openly about their frustrations, and she helped people raise constructive complaints during meetings. In short, her empathy allowed her to understand her team's emotional makeup. The result was not just heightened collaboration among members but also added business, as the team was called on for help by a wider range of internal clients.

Globalization is another reason for the rising importance of empathy for business leaders. Cross-cultural dialogue can easily lead to miscues and misunderstandings. Empathy is an antidote. People who have it are attuned to subtleties in body language; they can hear the message beneath the words being spoken. Beyond that, they have a deep understanding of both the existence and the importance of cultural and ethnic differences.

Consider the case of an American consultant whose team had just pitched a project to a potential Japanese client. In its dealings with Americans, the team was accustomed to being bombarded with questions after such a proposal, but this time it was greeted with a long silence. Other members of the team, taking the silence as disapproval, were ready to pack and leave. The lead consultant gestured them to stop. Although he was not particularly familiar with Japanese culture, he read the client's face and posture and sensed not rejection but interest—even deep consideration. He was right: When the client finally spoke, it was to give the consulting firm the job.

Finally, empathy plays a key role in the retention of talent, particularly in today's information economy. Leaders have always needed empathy to develop and keep good people, but today the stakes are higher. When good people leave, they take the company's knowledge with them.

That's where coaching and mentoring come in. It has repeatedly been shown that coaching and mentoring pay off not just in better performance but also in increased job satisfaction and decreased turnover. But what makes coaching and mentoring work best is the nature of the relationship. Outstanding coaches and mentors get inside the heads of the people they are helping. They sense how to give effective feedback. They know when to push for better performance and when to hold back. In the way they motivate their protégés, they demonstrate empathy in action.

In what is probably sounding like a refrain, let me repeat that empathy doesn't get much respect in business. People wonder how leaders can make hard decisions if they are "feeling" for all the people who will be affected. But leaders with empathy do more than sympathize with people around them: They use their knowledge to improve their companies in subtle but important ways.

Social Skill

The first three components of emotional intelligence are self-management skills. The last two, empathy and social skill, concern a person's ability to manage relationships with others. As a component of emotional intelligence, social skill is not as simple as it sounds. It's not just a matter of friendliness, although people with high levels of social skill are rarely mean-spirited. Social skill, rather, is friendliness with a purpose: moving people in the direction you desire, whether that's agreement on a new marketing strategy or enthusiasm about a new product.

Socially skilled people tend to have a wide circle of acquaintances, and they have a knack for finding common ground with people of all kinds—a knack for building rapport. That doesn't mean they socialize continually; it means they work according to the assumption that nothing important gets done alone. Such people have a network in place when the time for action comes.

Social skill is the culmination of the other dimensions of emotional intelligence. People tend to be very effective at managing relationships when they can understand and control their own emotions and can empathize with the feelings of others. Even motivation contributes to social skill. Remember that people who are driven to achieve tend to be optimistic, even in the face of setbacks or failure. When people are upbeat, their "glow" is cast upon conversations and other social encounters. They are popular, and for good reason.

Because it is the outcome of the other dimensions of emotional intelligence, social skill is recognizable on the job in many ways that will by now sound familiar. Socially skilled people, for instance, are adept at managing teams—that's their empathy at work. Likewise, they are expert persuaders—a manifestation of self-awareness, self-regulation, and empathy combined. Given those skills, good persuaders know when to make an emotional plea, for instance, and when an appeal to reason will work better. And motivation, when publicly visible, makes such people excellent collaborators; their passion for the work spreads to others, and they are driven to find solutions.

But sometimes social skill shows itself in ways the other emotional intelligence components do not. For instance, socially skilled people may at times appear not to be working while at work. They seem to be idly schmoozing—chatting in the hallways with colleagues or joking around with people who are not even connected to their "real" jobs. Socially skilled people, however, don't think it makes sense to arbitrarily limit the scope of their relationships. They build bonds widely because they know that in these fluid times, they may need help someday from people they are just getting to know today.

For example, consider the case of an executive in the strategy department of a global computer manufacturer. By 1993, he was convinced that the company's future lay with the Internet. Over the course of the next year, he found kindred spirits and used his social skill to stitch together a virtual community that cut across levels, divisions, and nations. He then used this de facto team to put up a corporate Web site, among the first by a major company. And, on his own initiative, with no budget or formal status, he signed up the company to participate in an annual Internet industry convention. Calling on his allies and persuading various divisions to donate funds, he recruited more than 50 people from a dozen different units to represent the company at the convention.

Management took notice: Within a year of the conference, the executive's team formed the basis for the company's first Internet division, and he was formally put in charge of it. To get there, the executive had ignored conventional boundaries, forging and maintaining connections with people in every corner of the organization.

Is social skill considered a key leadership capability in most companies? The answer is yes, especially when compared with the other components of emotional intelligence. People seem to know intuitively that leaders need to manage relationships effectively; no leader is an island. After all, the leader's task is to get work done through other people, and social skill makes that possible. A leader who cannot express her empathy may as well not have it at all. And a leader's motivation will be useless if he cannot communicate his passion to the organization. Social skill allows leaders to put their emotional intelligence to work.

It would be foolish to assert that good-old-fashioned IQ and technical ability are not important ingredients in strong leadership. But the recipe would not be complete without emotional intelligence. It was once thought that the components of emotional intelligence were "nice to have" in business leaders. But now we know that, for the sake of performance, these are ingredients that leaders "need to have."

It is fortunate, then, that emotional intelligence can be learned. The process is not easy. It takes time and, most of all, commitment. But the benefits that come from having a well-developed emotional intelligence, both for the individual and for the organization, make it worth the effort.

Originally published in June 1996. Reprint R0401H

Putting the Balanced Scorecard to Work

by Robert S. Kaplan and David P. Norton

TODAY'S MANAGERS RECOGNIZE the impact that measures have on performance. But they rarely think of measurement as an essential part of their strategy. For example, executives may introduce new strategies and innovative operating processes intended to achieve breakthrough performance, then continue to use the same short-term financial indicators they have used for decades, measures like return-on-investment, sales growth, and operating income. These managers fail not only to introduce new measures to monitor new goals and processes but also to question whether or not their old measures are relevant to the new initiatives.

Effective measurement, however, must be an integral part of the management process. The balanced scorecard, first proposed in the January–February 1992 issue of HBR ("The Balanced Scorecard—Measures that Drive Performance"), provides executives with a comprehensive framework that translates a company's strategic objectives into a coherent set of performance measures. Much more than a measurement exercise, the balanced scorecard is a management system that can motivate breakthrough improvements in such critical areas as product, process, customer, and market development.

The scorecard presents managers with four different perspectives from which to choose measures. It complements traditional financial indicators with measures of performance for customers, internal processes, and innovation and improvement activities. These measures differ from those traditionally used by companies in a few important ways:

Clearly, many companies already have myriad operational and physical measures for local activities. But these local measures are bottom-up and derived from ad hoc processes. The scorecard's measures, on the other hand, are grounded in an organization's strategic objectives and competitive demands. And, by requiring managers to select a limited number of critical indicators within each of the four perspectives, the scorecard helps focus this strategic vision.

In addition, while traditional financial measures report on what happened last period without indicating how managers can improve performance in the next, the scorecard functions as the cornerstone of a company's current *and* future success.

Moreover, unlike conventional metrics, the information from the four perspectives provides balance between external measures like operating income and internal measures like new product development. This balanced set of measures both reveals the trade-offs that managers have already made among performance measures and encourages them to achieve their goals in the future without making trade-offs among key success factors.

Finally, many companies that are now attempting to implement local improvement programs such as process reengineering, total quality, and employee empowerment lack a sense of integration. The balanced scorecard can serve as the focal point for the organization's efforts, defining and communicating priorities to managers, employees, investors, even customers. As a senior executive at one major company said, "Previously, the one-year budget was our primary management planning device. The balanced scorecard is now used as the language, the benchmark against which all new projects and businesses are evaluated."

The balanced scorecard is not a template that can be applied to businesses in general or even industrywide. Different market situations, product strategies, and competitive environments require different scorecards. Business units devise customized scorecards to fit

Idea in Brief

What makes a balanced scorecard special? Four characteristics stand out:

1. **It is a top-down reflection of the company's mission and strategy.** By contrast, the measures most companies track are bottom-up: deriving from local activities or ad hoc processes, they are often irrelevant to the overall strategy.
2. **It is forward-looking.** It addresses current and future success. Traditional financial measures describe how the company performed during the last reporting period—without indicating how managers can improve performance during the next.
3. **It integrates external and internal measures.** This helps managers see where they have made trade-offs between performance measures in the past and helps ensure that future success on one measure does not come at the expense of another.
4. **It helps you focus.** Many companies track more measures than they can possibly use. But a balanced scorecard requires managers to reach agreement on only those measures that are most critical to the success of the company's strategy. Fifteen to twenty distinct measures are usually enough, each measure custom-designed for the unit to which it applies.

their mission, strategy, technology, and culture. In fact, a critical test of a scorecard's success is its transparency: from the 15 to 20 scorecard measures, an observer should be able to see through to the business unit's competitive strategy. A few examples will illustrate how the scorecard uniquely combines management and measurement in different companies.

Rockwater: Responding to a Changing Industry

Rockwater, a wholly owned subsidiary of Brown & Root/Halliburton, a global engineering and construction company, is a worldwide leader in underwater engineering and construction. Norman

Idea in Practice

Linking measurements to strategy is the heart of a successful scorecard development process. The three key questions to ask here:

1. If we succeed with our vision and strategy, how will we look different
   - to our shareholders and customers?
   - in terms of our internal processes?
   - in terms of our ability to innovate and grow?
2. What are the critical success factors in each of the four scorecard perspectives?
3. What are the key measurements that will tell us whether we're addressing those success factors as planned?

The balanced scorecard also brings an organizational focus to the variety of local change programs under way in a company at any given time. As the benchmark against which all new projects are evaluated, the scorecard functions as more than just a measurement system. In the words of FMC Corp. executive Larry Brady, it becomes "the cornerstone of the way you run the business," that is, "the core of the management system" itself.

Example: Rockwater, an underwater engineering and construction firm, crafted a five-pronged strategy: to provide services that surpassed customers' expectations and needs; to achieve high levels of customer satisfaction; to make continuous improvements in safety, equipment reliability, responsiveness, and cost effectiveness; to recruit and retain high-quality employees; and to realize shareholder expectations. Using the balanced scorecard, Rockwater's senior management translated this strategy into tangible goals and actions.

- The financial measures they chose included return-on-capital employed and cash flow, because shareholders had indicated a preference for short-term results.
- Customer measures focused on those clients most interested in a high value-added relationship.
- The company introduced new benchmarks that emphasized the integration of key internal processes. It also added a safety index as a means of controlling indirect costs associated with accidents.
- Learning and growth targets emphasized the percentage of revenue coming from new services and the rate of improvement of safety and rework measures.

Chambers, hired as CEO in late 1989, knew that the industry's competitive world had changed dramatically. "In the 1970s, we were a bunch of guys in wet suits diving off barges into the North Sea with burning torches," Chambers said. But competition in the subsea contracting business had become keener in the 1980s, and many smaller companies left the industry. In addition, the focus of competition had shifted. Several leading oil companies wanted to develop long-term partnerships with their suppliers rather than choose suppliers based on low-price competition.

With his senior management team, Chambers developed a vision: "As our customers' preferred provider, we shall be the industry leader in providing the highest standards of safety and quality to our clients." He also developed a strategy to implement the vision. The five elements of that strategy were: services that surpass customers' expectations and needs; high levels of customer satisfaction; continuous improvement of safety, equipment reliability, responsiveness, and cost effectiveness; high-quality employees; and realization of shareholder expectations. Those elements were in turn developed into strategic objectives (see the chart "Rockwater's Strategic Objectives"). If, however, the strategic objectives were to create value for the company, they had to be translated into tangible goals and actions.

Rockwater's senior management team transformed its vision and strategy into the balanced scorecard's four sets of performance measures (see the chart "Rockwater's Balanced Scorecard").

Financial measures

The financial perspective included three measures of importance to the shareholder. Return-on-capital-employed and cash flow reflected preferences for short-term results, while forecast reliability signaled the corporate parent's desire to reduce the historical uncertainty caused by unexpected variations in performance. Rockwater management added two financial measures. Project profitability provided focus on the project as the basic unit for planning and control, and sales backlog helped reduce uncertainty of performance.

Rockwater's strategic objectives

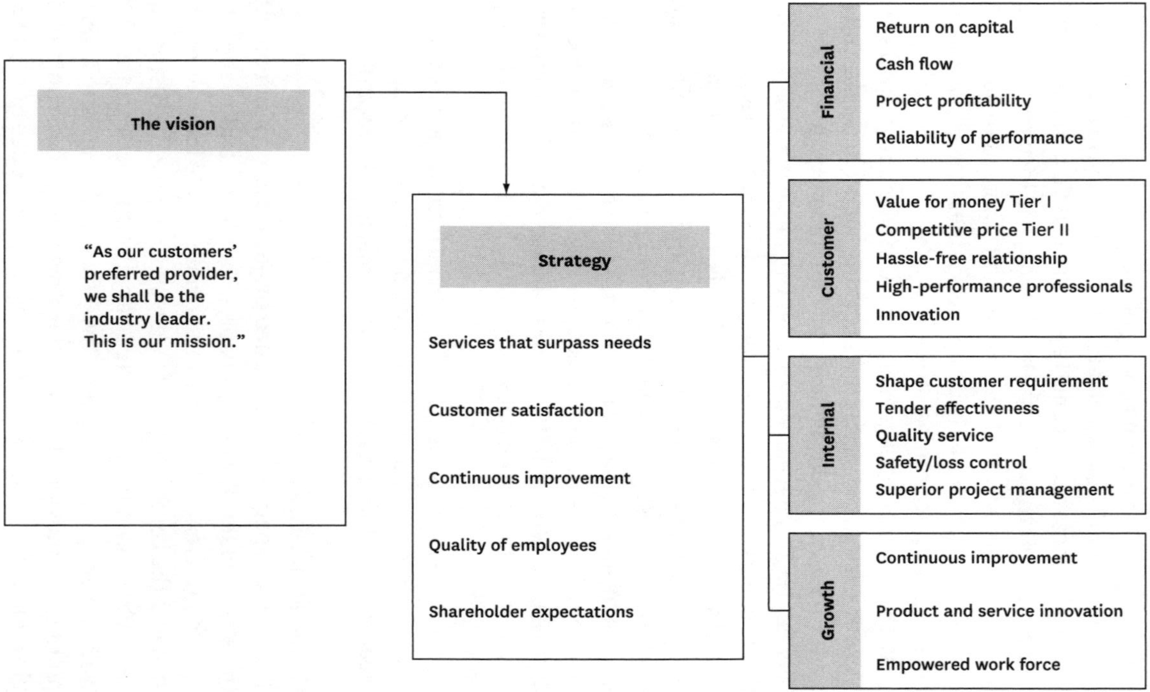
The vision
"As our customers' preferred provider, we shall be the industry leader. This is our mission."
Strategy
Services that surpass needs
Customer satisfaction
Continuous improvement
Quality of employees
Shareholder expectations
Financial
Return on capital
Cash flow
Project profitability
Reliability of performance
Customer
Value for money Tier I
Competitive price Tier II
Hassle-free relationship
High-performance professionals
Innovation
Internal
Shape customer requirement
Tender effectiveness
Quality service
Safety/loss control
Superior project management
Growth
Continuous improvement
Product and service innovation
Empowered work force

Rockwater's balanced scorecard

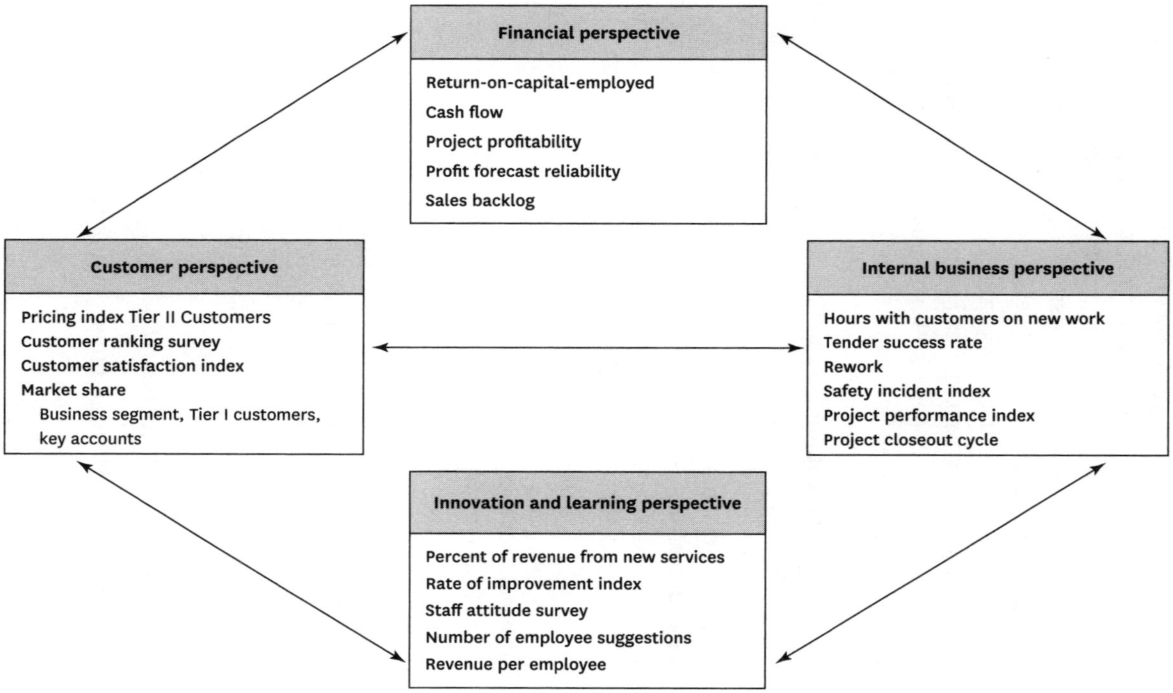

Financial perspective
Return-on-capital-employed
Cash flow
Project profitability
Profit forecast reliability
Sales backlog
Customer perspective
Pricing index Tier II Customers
Customer ranking survey
Customer satisfaction index
Market share
Business segment, Tier I customers, key accounts
Internal business perspective
Hours with customers on new work
Tender success rate
Rework
Safety incident index
Project performance index
Project closeout cycle
Innovation and learning perspective
Percent of revenue from new services
Rate of improvement index
Staff attitude survey
Number of employee suggestions
Revenue per employee

Customer satisfaction

Rockwater wanted to recognize the distinction between its two types of customers: Tier I customers, oil companies that wanted a high value-added relationship, and Tier II customers, those that chose suppliers solely on the basis of price. A price index, incorporating the best available intelligence on competitive position, was included to ensure that Rockwater could still retain Tier II customers' business when required by competitive conditions.

The company's strategy, however, was to emphasize value-based business. An independent organization conducted an annual survey to rank customers' perceptions of Rockwater's services compared to those of its competitors. In addition, Tier I customers were asked to supply monthly satisfaction and performance ratings. Rockwater executives felt that implementing these ratings gave them a direct tie to their customers and a level of market feedback unsurpassed in most industries. Finally, market share by key accounts provided objective evidence that improvements in customer satisfaction were being translated into tangible benefits.

Internal Processes

To develop measures of internal processes, Rockwater executives defined the life cycle of a project from launch (when a customer need was recognized) to completion (when the customer need had been satisfied). Measures were formulated for each of the five business-process phases in this project cycle (see the chart "How Rockwater Fulfills Customer Needs"):

- *Identify:* number of hours spent with prospects discussing new work;
- *Win:* tender success rate;
- *Prepare and Deliver:* project performance effectiveness index, safety/loss control, rework;
- *Closeout*: length of project closeout cycle.

The internal business measures emphasized a major shift in Rockwater's thinking. Formerly, the company stressed performance for each functional department. The new focus emphasized measures that integrated key business processes. The development of a comprehensive and timely index of project performance effectiveness was viewed as a key core competency for the company. Rockwater felt that safety was also a major competitive factor. Internal studies had revealed that the indirect costs from an accident could be 5 to 50 times the direct costs. The scorecard included a safety index, derived from a comprehensive safety measurement system, that could identify and classify all undesired events with the potential for harm to people, property, or process.

The Rockwater team deliberated about the choice of metric for the identification stage. It recognized that hours spent with key prospects discussing new work was an input or process measure rather than an output measure. The management team wanted a metric that would clearly communicate to all members of the organization the importance of building relationships with and satisfying customers. The team believed that spending quality time with key customers was a prerequisite for influencing results. This input measure was deliberately chosen to educate employees about the importance of working closely to identify and satisfy customer needs.

How Rockwater fulfills customer needs

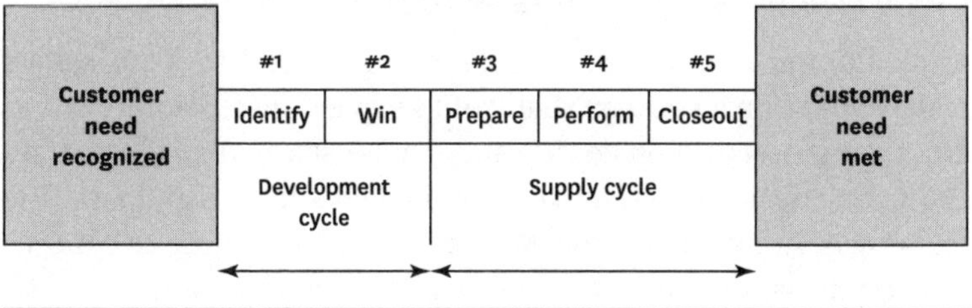

Innovation and improvement

The innovation and learning objectives are intended to drive improvement in financial, customer, and internal process performance. At Rockwater, such improvements came from product and service innovation that would create new sources of revenue and market expansion, as well as from continuous improvement in internal work processes. The first objective was measured by percent revenue from new services and the second objective by a continuous improvement index that represented the rate of improvement of several key operational measures, such as safety and rework. But in order to drive both product/service innovation and operational improvements, a supportive climate of empowered, motivated employees was believed necessary. A staff attitude survey and a metric for the number of employee suggestions measured whether or not such a climate was being created. Finally, revenue per employee measured the outcomes of employee commitment and training programs.

The balanced scorecard has helped Rockwater's management emphasize a process view of operations, motivate its employees, and incorporate client feedback into its operations. It developed a consensus on the necessity of creating partnerships with key customers, the importance of order-of-magnitude reductions in safety-related incidents, and the need for improved management at every phase of multiyear projects. Chambers sees the scorecard as an invaluable tool to help his company ultimately achieve its mission: to be number one in the industry.

Apple Computer: Adjusting Long-Term Performance

Apple Computer developed a balanced scorecard to focus senior management on a strategy that would expand discussions beyond gross margin, return on equity, and market share. A small steering committee, intimately familiar with the deliberations and strategic thinking of Apple's Executive Management Team, chose to concentrate on measurement categories within each of the four perspectives and to select multiple measurements within each category. For the financial perspective, Apple emphasized shareholder value; for the customer perspective, market share and customer satisfaction; for the internal process perspective, core competencies; and, finally, for the innovation and improvement perspective, employee attitudes. Apple's management stressed these categories in the following order.

Customer satisfaction

Historically, Apple had been a technology- and product-focused company that competed by designing better computers. Customer satisfaction metrics are just being introduced to orient employees toward becoming a customer-driven company. J.D. Power & Associates, a customer-survey company, now works for the computer industry. However, because it recognized that its customer base was not homogeneous, Apple felt that it had to go beyond J.D. Power & Associates and develop its own independent surveys in order to track its key market segments around the world.

Core competencies

Company executives wanted employees to be highly focused on a few key competencies: for example, user-friendly interfaces, powerful software architectures, and effective distribution systems. However, senior executives recognized that measuring performance along these competency dimensions could be difficult. As a result, the company is currently experimenting with obtaining quantitative measures of these hard-to-measure competencies.

Employee commitment and alignment

Apple conducts a comprehensive employee survey in each of its organizations every two years; surveys of randomly selected employees are performed more frequently. The survey questions are concerned with how well employees understand the company's strategy as well as whether or not they are asked to deliver results that are consistent with that strategy. The results of the survey are displayed in terms of both the actual level of employee responses and the overall trend of responses.

Market share

Achieving a critical threshold of market share was important to senior management not only for the obvious sales growth benefits but also to attract and retain software developers to Apple platforms.

Shareholder value

Shareholder value is included as a performance indicator, even though this measure is a result—not a driver—of performance. The measure is included to offset the previous emphasis on gross margin and sales growth, measures that ignored the investments required today to generate growth for tomorrow. In contrast, the shareholder value metric quantifies the impact of proposed investments for business creation and development. The majority of Apple's business is organized on a functional basis—sales, product design, and worldwide manufacturing and operations—so shareholder value can be calculated only for the entire company instead of at a decentralized level. The measure, however, helps senior managers in each major organizational unit assess the impact of their activities on the entire company's valuation and evaluate new business ventures.

While these five performance indicators have only recently been developed, they have helped Apple's senior managers focus their strategy in a number of ways. First of all, the balanced scorecard at Apple serves primarily as a planning device, instead of as a control device. To put it another way, Apple uses the measures to adjust the "long wave" of corporate performance, not to drive operating changes. Moreover, the metrics at Apple, with the exception of shareholder value, can be driven both horizontally and vertically into each functional organization. Considered vertically, each individual measure can be broken down into its component parts in order to evaluate how each part contributes to the functioning of the whole. Thought of horizontally, the measures can identify how, for example, design and manufacturing contribute to an area such as customer satisfaction. In addition, Apple has found that its balanced scorecard has helped develop a language of measurable outputs for how to launch and leverage programs.

The five performance indicators at Apple are benchmarked against best-in-class organizations. Today they are used to build business plans and are incorporated into senior executives' compensation plans.

Advanced Micro Devices: Consolidating Strategic Information

Advanced Micro Devices (AMD), a semiconductor company, executed a quick and easy transition to a balanced scorecard. It already had a clearly defined mission, strategy statement, and shared understanding among senior executives about its competitive niche. It also had many performance measures from many different sources and information systems. The balanced scorecard consolidated and focused these diverse measures into a quarterly briefing book that contained seven sections: financial measures; customer-based measures, such as on-time delivery, lead time, and performance-to-schedule; measures of critical business processes in wafer fabrication, assembly and test, new product development, process technology development (e.g., submicron etching precision); and, finally, measures for corporate quality. In addition, organizational learning was measured by imposing targeted rates of improvements for key operating parameters, such as cycle time and yields by process.

At present, AMD sees its scorecard as a systematic repository for strategic information that facilitates long-term trend analysis for planning and performance evaluation.

Driving the Process of Change

The experiences of these companies and others reveal that the balanced scorecard is most successful when it is used to drive the process of change. Rockwater, for instance, came into existence after the merger of two different organizations. Employees came from different cultures, spoke different languages, and had different operating experiences and backgrounds. The balanced scorecard

Building a balanced scorecard

Each organization is unique and so follows its own path for building a balanced scorecard. At Apple and AMD, for instance, a senior finance or business development executive, intimately familiar with the strategic thinking of the top management group, constructed the initial scorecard without extensive deliberations. At Rockwater, however, senior management had yet to define sharply the organization's strategy, much less the key performance levers that drive and measure the strategy's success.

Companies like Rockwater can follow a systematic development plan to create the balanced scorecard and encourage commitment to the scorecard among senior and mid-level managers. What follows is a typical project profile:

1. Preparation

The organization must first define the business unit for which a top-level scorecard is appropriate. In general, a scorecard is appropriate for a business unit that has its own customers, distribution channels, production facilities, and financial performance measures.

2. Interviews: First Round

Each senior manager in the business unit—typically between 6 and 12 executives—receives background material on the balanced scorecard as well as internal documents that describe the company's vision, mission, and strategy.

The balanced scorecard facilitator (either an outside consultant or the company executive who organizes the effort) conducts interviews of approximately 90 minutes each with the senior managers to obtain their input on the company's strategic objectives and tentative proposals for balanced scorecard measures. The facilitator may also interview some principal shareholders to learn about their expectations for the business unit's financial performance, as well as some key customers to learn about their performance expectations for top-ranked suppliers.

3. Executive Workshop: First Round

The top management team is brought together with the facilitator to undergo the process of developing the scorecard (see the chart "Begin by Linking Measurements to Strategy"). During the workshop, the group debates the proposed mission and strategy statements until a consensus is reached. The group then moves from the mission and strategy statement to answer the question, "If I succeed with my vision and strategy, how will my performance differ for shareholders; for customers; for internal business processes; for my ability to innovate, grow, and improve?"

Videotapes of interviews with shareholder and customer representatives can be shown to provide an external perspective to the deliberations. After defining the key success factors, the group formulates a preliminary balanced scorecard containing operational measures for the strategic objectives. Frequently, the group proposes far more than four or five measures for each perspective. At this time, narrowing the choices is not critical, though straw votes can be taken to see whether or not some of the proposed measures are viewed as low priority by the group.

4. Interviews: Second Round

The facilitator reviews, consolidates, and documents the output from the executive workshop and interviews each senior executive about the tentative balanced scorecard. The facilitator also seeks opinions about issues involved in implementing the scorecard.

5. Executive Workshop: Second Round

A second workshop, involving the senior management team, their direct subordinates, and a larger number of middle managers, debates the organization's vision, strategy statements, and the tentative scorecard. The participants, working in groups, comment on the proposed measures, link the various change programs under way to the measures, and start to develop an implementation plan. At the end of the workshop, participants are asked to formulate stretch objectives for each of the proposed measures, including targeted rates of improvement.

6. Executive Workshop: Third Round

The senior executive team meets to come to a final consensus on the vision, objectives, and measurements developed in the first two workshops; to develop stretch targets for each measure on the scorecard; and to identify preliminary action programs to achieve the targets. The team must agree on an implementation program, including communicating the scorecard to employees, integrating the scorecard into a management philosophy, and developing an information system to support the scorecard.

7. Implementation

A newly formed team develops an implementation plan for the scorecard, including linking the measures to databases and information systems, communicating the balanced scorecard throughout the organization, and

(*continued*)

encouraging and facilitating the development of second-level metrics for decentralized units. As a result of this process, for instance, an entirely new executive information system that links top-level business unit metrics down through shop floor and site-specific operational measures could be developed.

8. Periodic Reviews

Each quarter or month, a blue book of information on the balanced scorecard measures is prepared for both top management review and discussion with managers of decentralized divisions and departments. The balanced scorecard metrics are revisited annually as part of the strategic planning, goal setting, and resource allocation processes.

Begin by linking measurements to strategy

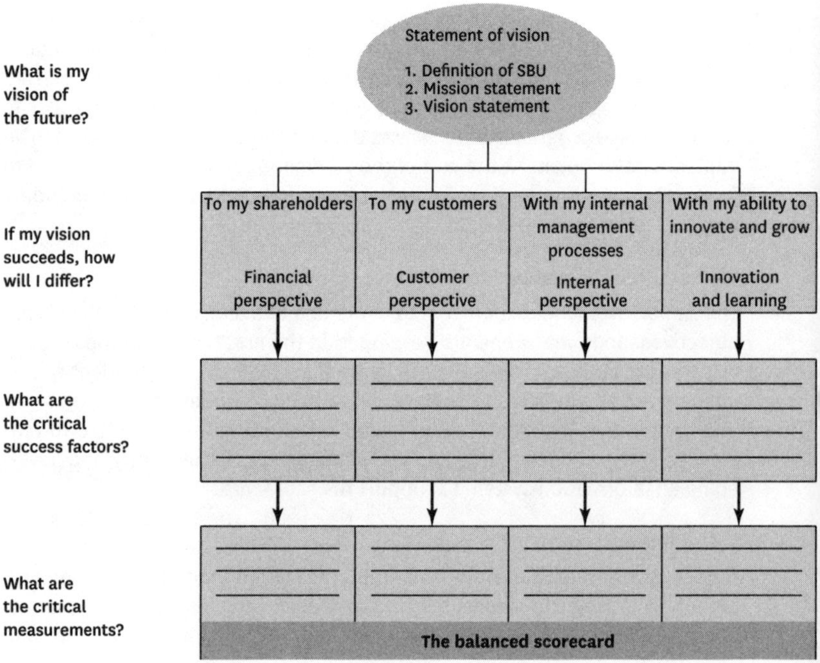

helped the company focus on what it had to do well in order to become the industry leader.

Similarly, Joseph De Feo, chief executive of Service Businesses, one of the three operating divisions of Barclays Bank, had to transform what had been a captive, internal supplier of services into a global competitor. The scorecard highlighted areas where, despite apparent consensus on strategy, there still was considerable disagreement about how to make the strategy operational. With the help of the scorecard, the division eventually achieved consensus concerning the highest priority areas for achievement and improvement and identified additional areas that needed attention, such as quality and productivity. De Feo assessed the impact of the scorecard, saying, “It helped us to drive major change, to become more market oriented, throughout our organization. It provided a shared understanding of our goals and what it took to achieve them.”

Analog Devices, a semiconductor company, served as the prototype for the balanced scorecard and now uses it each year to update the targets and goals for division managers. Jerry Fishman, president of Analog, said, “At the beginning, the scorecard drove significant and considerable change. It still does when we focus attention on particular areas, such as the gross margins on new products. But its main impact today is to help sustain programs that our people have been working on for years.” Recently, the company has been attempting to integrate the scorecard metrics with *hoshin* planning, a procedure that concentrates an entire company on achieving one or two key objectives each year. Analog’s hoshin objectives have included customer service and new product development, for which measures already exist on the company’s scorecard.

But the scorecard isn’t always the impetus for such dramatic change. For example, AMD’s scorecard has yet to have a significant impact because company management didn’t use it to drive the change process. Before turning to the scorecard, senior managers had already formulated and gained consensus for the company’s mission, strategy, and key performance measures. AMD competes in a single industry segment. The top 12 managers are intimately familiar with the markets, engineering, technology, and other key

The Scorecard's Impact on External Reporting

SEVERAL MANAGERS HAVE ASKED whether or not the balanced scorecard is applicable to external reporting. If the scorecard is indeed a driver of long-term performance, shouldn't this information be relevant to the investment community?

In fact, the scorecard does not translate easily to the investment community. A scorecard makes sense primarily for business units and divisions with a well-defined strategy. Most companies have several divisions, each with its own mission and strategy, whose scorecards cannot be aggregated into an overall corporate scorecard. And if the scorecard does indeed provide a transparent vision into a unit's strategy, then the information, even the measures being used, might be highly sensitive data that could reveal much of value to competitors. But most important, as a relatively recent innovation, the scorecard would benefit from several years of experimentation within companies before it becomes a systematic part of reporting to external constituencies.

Even if the scorecard itself were better suited to external reporting, at present the financial community itself shows little interest in making the change from financial to strategic reporting. One company president has found the outside financial community leery of the principles that ground the scorecard: "We use the scorecard more with our customers than with our investors. The financial community is skeptical about long-term indicators and occasionally tells us about some empirical evidence of a negative correlation between stock prices and attention to total quality and internal processes."

However, the investment community has begun to focus on some key metrics of new product performance. Could this be an early sign of a shift to strategic thinking?

levers in this segment. The summary and aggregate information in the scorecard were neither new nor surprising to them. And managers of decentralized production units also already had a significant amount of information about their own operations. The scorecard did enable them to see the breadth and totality of company operations, enhancing their ability to become better managers for the entire company. But, on balance, the scorecard could only encapsulate knowledge that managers in general had already learned.

AMD's limited success with the balanced scorecard demonstrates that the scorecard has its greatest impact when used to drive a change process. Some companies link compensation of senior executives to achieving stretch targets for the scorecard measures. Most are attempting to translate the scorecard into operational measures that become the focus for improvement activities in local units. The scorecard is not just a measurement system; it is a management system to motivate breakthrough competitive performance.

Implementing the Balanced Scorecard at FMC Corporation: An Interview with Larry D. Brady

FMC Corporation is one of the most diversified companies in the United States, producing more than 300 product lines in 21 divisions organized into 5 business segments: industrial chemicals, performance chemicals, precious metals, defense systems, and machinery and equipment. Based in Chicago, FMC has worldwide revenues in excess of $4 billion.

Since 1984, the company has realized annual returns-on-investment of greater than 15%. Coupled with a major recapitalization in 1986, these returns resulted in an increasing shareholder value that significantly exceeded industrial averages. In 1992, the company completed a strategic review to determine the best future course to maximize shareholder value. As a result of that review, FMC adopted a growth strategy to complement its strong operating performance. This strategy required a greater external focus and appreciation of operating trade-offs.

To help make the shift, the company decided to use the balanced scorecard. In this interview conducted by Robert S. Kaplan, Larry D. Brady, executive vice president of FMC, talks about the company's experience implementing the scorecard.

Robert S. Kaplan: ***What's the status of the balanced scorecard at FMC?***

Larry D. Brady: Although we are just completing the pilot phase of implementation, I think that the balanced scorecard is likely to become the cornerstone of the management system at FMC. It enables us to translate business unit strategies into a measurement system that meshes with our entire system of management.

For instance, one manager reported that while his division had measured many operating variables in the past, now, because of the scorecard, it had chosen 12 parameters as the key to its strategy implementation. Seven of these strategic variables were entirely new measurements for the division. The manager interpreted this finding as verifying what many other managers were reporting: the scorecard improved the understanding and consistency of strategy implementation. Another manager reported that, unlike monthly financial statements or even his strategic plan, if a rival were to see his scorecard, he would lose his competitive edge.

It's rare to get that much enthusiasm among divisional managers for a corporate initiative. What led you and them to the balanced scorecard?

FMC had a clearly defined mission: to become our customers' most valued supplier. We had initiated many of the popular improvement programs: total quality, managing by objectives, organizational effectiveness, building a high-performance organization. But these efforts had not been effective. Every time we promoted a new program, people in each division would sit back and ask, "How is that supposed to fit in with the six other things we're supposed to be doing?"

Corporate staff groups were perceived by operating managers as pushing their pet programs on divisions. The diversity of initiatives, each with its own slogan, created confusion and mixed signals about where to concentrate and how the various programs interrelated. At the end of the day, with all these new initiatives, we were still asking division managers to deliver consistent short-term financial performance.

What kinds of measures were you using?

The FMC corporate executive team, like most corporate offices, reviews the financial performance of each operating division monthly. As a highly diversified company that redeploys assets from mature cash generators to divisions with significant growth opportunities, the return-on-capital-employed (ROCE) measure was especially important for us. We were one of the few companies to inflation-adjust our internal financial measures so that we could get a more accurate picture of a division's economic profitability.

At year-end, we rewarded division managers who delivered predictable financial performance. We had run the company tightly for the past 20 years and had been successful. But it was becoming less clear where future growth would come from and where the company should look for breakthroughs into new areas. We had become a high return-on-investment company but had less potential for further growth. It was also not at all clear from our financial reports what progress we were making in implementing long-term initiatives. Questions from the corporate office about spending versus budget also reinforced a focus on the short-term and on internal operations.

But the problem went even deeper than that. Think about it. What is the value added of a corporate office that concentrates on making division managers accountable for financial results that can be added up across divisions? We combine a business that's doing well with a business that's doing poorly and have a total business that performs at an average level. Why not split the company up into independent companies and let the market reallocate capital? If we were going to create value by managing a group of diversified companies, we had to understand and provide strategic focus to their operations. We had to be sure that each division had a strategy that would give it sustainable competitive advantage. In addition, we had to be able to assess, through measurement of their operations, whether or not the divisions were meeting their strategic objectives.

If you're going to ask a division or the corporation to change its strategy, you had better change the system of measurement to be consistent with the new strategy.

How did the balanced scorecard emerge as the remedy to the limitations of measuring only short-term financial results?

In early 1992, we assembled a task force to integrate our various corporate initiatives. We wanted to understand what had to be done differently to achieve dramatic improvements in overall organizational effectiveness. We acknowledged that the company may have become too short-term and too internally focused in its business measures. Defining what should replace the financial focus was more difficult. We wanted managers to sustain their search for continuous improvement, but we also wanted them to identify the opportunities for breakthrough performance.

When divisions missed financial targets, the reasons were generally not internal. Typically, division management had inaccurately estimated market demands or had failed to forecast competitive reactions. A new measurement system was needed to lead operating managers beyond achieving internal goals to searching for competitive breakthroughs in the global marketplace. The system would have to focus on measures of customer service, market position, and new products that could generate long-term value for the business. We used the scorecard as the focal point for the discussion. It forced division managers to answer these questions: How do we become our customers' most valued supplier? How do we become more externally focused? What is my division's competitive advantage? What is its competitive vulnerability?

How did you launch the scorecard effort at FMC?

We decided to try a pilot program. We selected six division managers to develop prototype scorecards for their operations. Each division had to perform a strategic analysis to identify its sources of competitive advantage. The 15 to 20 measures in the balanced scorecard had to be organization-specific and had to communicate clearly what short-term measures of operating performance were consistent with a long-term trajectory of strategic success.

Were the six division managers free to develop their own scorecard?

We definitely wanted the division managers to perform their own strategic analysis and to develop their own measures. That was an essential part of creating a consensus between senior and divisional management on operating objectives. Senior management did, however, place some conditions on the outcomes.

First of all, we wanted the measures to be objective and quantifiable. Division managers were to be just as accountable for improving scorecard measures as they had been for using monthly financial reviews. Second, we wanted output measures not process-oriented measures. Many of the improvement programs under way were emphasizing time, quality, and cost measurements. Focusing on T-Q-C measurements, however, encourages managers to seek narrow process improvements instead of breakthrough output targets. Focusing on achieving outputs forces division managers to understand their industry and strategy and help them to quantify strategic success through specific output targets.

Could you illustrate the distinction between process measures and output measures?

You have to understand your industry well to develop the connection between process improvements and outputs achieved. Take three divisional examples of cycle-time measurement, a common process measure.

For much of our defense business, no premium is earned for early delivery. And the contracts allow for reimbursement of inventory holding costs. Therefore, attempts to reduce inventory or cycle times in this business produce no benefit for which the customer is willing to pay. The only benefits from cycle time or inventory reduction occur when reduction in factory-floor complexity leads to real reductions in product cost. The output performance targets must be real cash savings, not reduced inventory levels or cycle times.

In contrast, significant lead-time reductions could be achieved for our packaging machinery business. This improvement led to lower inventory and an option to access an additional 35% of the market. In this case, the cycle-time improvements could be tied to specific targets for increased sales and market share. It wasn't linear, but output seemed to improve each time we improved throughput times.

And in one of our agricultural machinery businesses, orders come within a narrow time window each year. The current build cycle is longer than the ordering window, so all units must be built to the sales forecast. This process of building to forecast leads to high inventory—more than twice the levels of our other businesses—and frequent overstocking and obsolescence of equipment. Incremental reductions in lead time do little to change the economics of this operation. But if the build cycle time could be reduced to less than the six-week ordering time window for part or all of the build schedule, then a breakthrough occurs. The division can shift to a build-to-order schedule and eliminate the excess inventory caused by building to forecasts. In this case, the benefit from cycle-time reductions is a step-function that comes only when the cycle time drops below a critical level.

So here we have three businesses, three different processes, all of which could have elaborate systems for measuring quality, cost, and time but would feel the impact of improvements in radically different ways. With all the diversity in our business units, senior management really can't have a detailed understanding of the relative impact of time and quality improvements on each unit. All of our senior managers, however, understand output targets, particularly when they are displayed with historical trends and future targets.

Benchmarking has become popular with a lot of companies. Does it tie in to the balanced scorecard measurements?

Unfortunately, benchmarking is one of those initially good ideas that has turned into a fad. About 95% of those companies that have tried benchmarking have spent a lot of money and have gotten very little in return. And the difference between benchmarking and the scorecard helps reinforce the difference between process measures and output measures. It's a lot easier to benchmark a process than to benchmark an output. With the scorecard, we ask each division manager to go outside their organization and determine the approaches that will allow achievement of their long-term output targets. Each of our output measures has an associated long-term target. We have been deliberately vague on specifying when the target is to be accomplished. We want to stimulate a thought process about how to do things differently to achieve the target rather than how to do existing things better. The activity of searching externally for how others have accomplished these breakthrough achievements is called target verification not benchmarking.

Were the division managers able to develop such output-oriented measures?

Well, the division managers did encounter some obstacles. Because of the emphasis on output measures and the previous focus on operations and financial measures, the customer and innovation perspectives proved the most difficult. These were also the two areas where the balanced scorecard process was most helpful in refining and understanding our existing strategies.

But the initial problem was that the management teams ran afoul of both conditions: the measures they proposed tended to be nonquantifiable and input- rather than output-oriented. Several divisions wanted to conduct customer surveys and provide an index of the results. We judged a single index to be of little value and opted instead for harder measures such as price premiums over competitors.

We did conclude, however, that the full customer survey was an excellent vehicle for promoting external focus and, therefore, decided to use survey results to kick-off discussion at our annual operating reviews.

Did you encounter any problems as you launched the six pilot projects?

At first, several divisional managers were less than enthusiastic about the additional freedom they were being given from headquarters. They knew that the heightened visibility and transparency of the scorecard took away the internal trade-offs they had gained experience in making. They initially interpreted the increase in visibility of divisional performance as just the latest attempt by corporate staff to meddle in their internal business processes.

To offset this concern, we designed targets around long-term objectives. We still closely examine the monthly and quarterly statistics, but these statistics now relate to progress in achieving long-term objectives and justify the proper balance between short-term and long-term performance.

We also wanted to transfer quickly the focus from a measurement system to achieving performance results. A measurement orientation reinforces concerns about control and a short-term focus. By emphasizing targets rather than measurements, we could demonstrate our purpose to achieve breakthrough performance.

But the process was not easy. One division manager described his own three-stage implementation process after receiving our directive to build a balanced scorecard: denial—hope it goes away; medicinal—it won't go away, so let's do it quickly and get it over with; ownership—let's do it for ourselves.

In the end, we were successful. We now have six converts who are helping us to spread the message throughout the organization.

I understand that you have started to apply the scorecard not just to operating units but to staff groups as well.

Applying the scorecard approach to staff groups has been even more eye-opening than our initial work with the six operating divisions. We have done very little to define our strategy for corporate staff utilization. I doubt that many companies can respond crisply to the question, "How does staff provide competitive advantage?" Yet we ask that question every day about our line operations. We have just started to ask our staff departments to explain to us whether they are offering low-cost or differentiated services. If they are offering neither, we should probably outsource the function. This area is loaded with real potential for organizational development and improved strategic capability.

My conversations with financial people in organizations reveal some concern about the expanded responsibilities implied by developing and maintaining a balanced scorecard. How does the role of the controller change as a company shifts its primary measurement system from a purely financial one to the balanced scorecard?

Historically, we have had two corporate departments involved in overseeing business unit performance. Corporate development was in charge of strategy, and the controller's office kept the historical records and budgeted and measured short-term performance.

Strategists came up with five- and ten-year plans, controllers one-year budgets and near-term forecasts. Little interplay occurred between the two groups. But the scorecard now bridges the two. The financial perspective builds on the traditional function performed by controllers. The other three perspectives make the division's long-term strategic objectives measurable.

In our old environment, division managers tried to balance short-term profits with long-term growth, while they were receiving different signals depending on whether or not they were reviewing strategic plans or budgets. This structure did not make the balancing of short-term profits and long-term growth an easy trade-off, and, frankly, it let senior management off the hook when it came to sharing responsibility for making the trade-offs.

Perhaps the corporate controller should take responsibility for all measurement and goal setting, including the systems required to implement these processes. The new corporate controller could be an outstanding system administrator, knowledgeable about the various trade-offs and balances, and skillful in reporting and presenting them. This role does not eliminate the need for strategic planning. It just makes the two systems more compatible. The scorecard can serve to motivate and evaluate performance. But I see its primary value as its ability to join together what had been strong but separated capabilities in strategy development and financial control. It's the operating performance bridge that corporations have never had.

How often do you envision reviewing a division's balanced scorecard?

I think we will ask group managers to review a monthly submission from each of their divisions, but the senior corporate team will probably review scorecards quarterly on a rotating basis so that we can review up to seven or eight division scorecards each month.

Isn't it inconsistent to assess a division's strategy on a monthly or quarterly basis? Doesn't such a review emphasize short-term performance?

I see the scorecard as a strategic measurement system, not a measure of our strategy. And I think that's an important distinction.

The monthly or quarterly scorecard measures operations that have been configured to be consistent with our long-term strategy.

Here's an example of the interaction between the short and the long term. We have pushed division managers to choose measures that will require them to create change, for example, penetration of key markets in which we are not currently represented. We can measure that penetration monthly and get valuable short-term information about the ultimate success of our long-term strategy. Of course, some measures, such as annual market share and innovation metrics, don't lend themselves to monthly updates. For the most part, however, the measures are calculated monthly.

Any final thoughts on the scorecard?

I think that it's important for companies not to approach the scorecard as the latest fad. I sense that a number of companies are turning to scorecards in the same way they turned to total quality management, high-performance organization, and so on. You hear about a good idea, several people on corporate staff work on it, probably with some expensive outside consultants, and you put in a system that's a bit different from what existed before. Such systems are only incremental, and you don't gain much additional value from them.

It gets worse if you think of the scorecard as a new measurement system that eventually requires hundreds and thousands of measurements and a big, expensive executive information system. These companies lose sight of the essence of the scorecard: its focus, its simplicity, and its vision. The real benefit comes from making the scorecard the cornerstone of the way you run the business. It should be the core of the management system, not the measurement system. Senior managers alone will determine whether the scorecard becomes a mere record-keeping exercise or the lever to streamline and focus strategy that can lead to breakthrough performance.

Originally published in September 1993. Reprint 93505

Innovation

The Classic Traps. *by Rosabeth Moss Kanter*

INNOVATION IS BACK AT the top of the corporate agenda. Never a fad, but always in or out of fashion, innovation gets rediscovered as a growth enabler every half-dozen years (about the length of a managerial generation). Too often, however, grand declarations about innovation are followed by mediocre execution that produces anemic results, and innovation groups are quietly disbanded in cost-cutting drives. Each generation embarks on the same enthusiastic quest for the next new thing and faces the same challenge of overcoming innovation stiflers. Over the past 25 years, I have conducted research and advised companies during at least four major waves of competitive challenges that led to widespread enthusiasm for innovation.

The first was the dawn of the global information age in the late 1970s and early 1980s, an era that introduced new industries and threatened to topple old ones. Entrepreneurs and foreign competitors imperiled established companies on their own turf. Information technology was beginning to evolve from the clunky mainframe to a consumer and desktop product, and companies such as Apple Computer made Silicon Valley garages the new base for product innovation in the United States. IBM emulated Apple's model by developing its PC in dingy surroundings in Boca Raton, Florida, freed from many corporate constraints. High-quality Japanese products, such as the Sony Walkman and Toyota cars, reflected not just good product design but also innovations in manufacturing processes that forced

American giants to create their own programs to generate new ideas faster. "Total quality management" became a passion.

The second wave was the pressure to restructure during the takeover scare of the late 1980s. Buyout groups were attacking traditional companies, seeking to unlock the value of underutilized assets; "shareholder value" became a rallying cry. In Europe, restructuring was associated with the privatization of state-owned enterprises now exposed to the pressures of capital markets. Software was emerging as a major force behind innovation, and the strategic value of IT was touted, with American Airlines' Sabre reservations system widely cited as an example of a process innovation that succeeded as a separate business. Companies created new-venture departments to make sure they captured the value of their own ideas and inventions, rather than allowing a behemoth like Microsoft to arise outside the firm. Financial innovations were the rage: leveraged and management buyouts, derivatives and other forms of financial engineering, or financial supermarkets combining banks and nearly everything else. The restructuring era also favored products that could be instantly global: After defeating a hostile takeover bid in the late 1980s, Gillette boldly and successfully launched Sensor Excel shaving systems in the early 1990s, in identical form worldwide, with a single advertising message.

Third was the digital mania of the 1990s. The promise (and threat) of the World Wide Web drove many established companies to seek radical new business models. Brick-and-mortar companies were at risk for extinction; many rushed to create stand-alone Web ventures, often unconnected to the core business and sometimes in conflict with it. Eyes were on the capital markets rather than on customers, and companies got rich without profits or revenues. AOL bought Time Warner, put its name first, and proceeded to destroy value rather than create innovation.

The current wave of innovation began in a more sober mood, following the dot-com crash and belt-tightening of the global recession. Having recognized the limits of acquisitions and become skeptical about technology hype, companies refocused on organic growth. Surviving giants such as General Electric and IBM have

Idea in Brief

Most companies fuel growth by creating new products and services. Yet too many firms repeat the same growth-sapping mistakes in their efforts to innovate.

For example, some companies adopt the wrong strategy: investing only in ideas they think will become blockbusters. Result? Small ideas that could have generated big profits get rejected. For years, Time, Inc. didn't develop new publications: managers wanted any start-up to succeed on the same scale as the enormously popular *People* magazine. Only after Time decided to gamble on a large number of new publications did revenues rise.

Other companies err on the side of process-strangling innovations by subjecting them to the strict performance criteria their existing businesses must follow. At AlliedSignal, new Internet-based products and services had to satisfy the same financial metrics as established businesses. Budgets contained no funds for investment—so managers working on innovations had to find their own funding. The consequences? Retrofitted versions of old ideas.

To avoid such traps, Kanter advocates applying lessons from past failures to your innovation efforts. For instance, augment potential "big bets" with promising midrange ideas and incremental innovations. And add flexibility to your innovation planning, budgeting, and reviews.

Your reward? Better odds that the new ideas percolating in your company today will score profitable successes in the market tomorrow.

adopted innovation as a corporate theme. GE, for instance, is committed to double-digit growth from within. For its part, IBM is seeking innovation by tackling difficult social problems that require—and showcase—its technology solutions. A good example is World Community Grid, a nonprofit IBM created that aggregates unused computer power from numerous partners to give AIDS researchers and other scientists the ability to work with unusually large data sets. This wave's central focus is on new products designed to offer users new features and functionality to meet emerging needs. Customers and consumer markets have returned to center stage, after having been temporarily crowded out by other obsessions. Companies are seeking new categories to enrich their existing businesses rather than grand new ventures that will take them into totally different

Idea in Practice

To innovate successfully, replace common mistakes with potent remedies:

Strategy Mistakes

- Rejecting opportunities that at first glance appear too small.
- Assuming that only new products count—not new services or improved processes.
- Launching too many minor product extensions that confuse customers and increase internal complexity.

Remedy: Widen your search and broaden your scope. Support a few big bets at the top that represent clear directions for the future and receive the lion's share of investment. Also create a portfolio of promising midrange ideas. And fund a broad base of early stage ideas or incremental innovations.

Process Mistakes

- Strangling innovation with the same tight planning, budgeting, and reviews applied to existing businesses.
- Rewarding managers for doing only what they committed to do—and discouraging them from making changes as circumstances warrant.

Remedy: Add flexibility to planning and control systems. For instance, reserve special funds for unexpected opportunities.

> ***Example:*** After executives at the struggling UK television network BBC set aside funds in a corporate account to support innovation proposals, a new recruit used money originally allocated for a new BBC training film to make a pilot for *The Office*. The show became the BBC's biggest hit comedy in decades.

Structure Mistakes

- Isolating fledgling and established enterprises in separate silos.

realms. Signature innovations in this era include Apple's iPod and Procter & Gamble's Swiffer.

Each wave brought new concepts. For example, the rise of biotechnology, characterized by complicated licensing arrangements, helped legitimize the idea that established firms could outsource R&D and learn from entrepreneurial partners or that consumer products companies could turn to external idea shops, as well as their own labs, to invent new products. Approaches to

- Creating two classes of corporate citizens—those who have all the fun (innovators) and those who must make the money (mainstream business managers).

Remedy: Tighten the human connections between innovators and others throughout your organization. Convene frequent conversations between innovators and mainstream business managers to promote mutual learning and integration of new businesses into the organization. Create overlapping relationships—by having representatives from mainstream businesses rotate through innovation groups or innovation advisory boards. Identify people who lead informal networks that span innovation and mainstream groups, and encourage them to strengthen those connections.

Skills Mistakes

- Allowing innovators to rotate out of teams so quickly that team chemistry can't gel.
- Assuming that innovation teams should be led by the best technical people.

Remedy: Select innovation leaders with strong interpersonal skills. They'll keep the innovation team intact, help innovation teams embrace collective goals, leverage one another's different strengths, and share hard-to-document knowledge while innovations are under development.

> ***Example:*** When Williams-Sonoma launched its ultimately successful e-commerce group, it put a manager in charge who wasn't a technology expert but who could assemble the right team. He chose a mixture of employees from other units who could be ambassadors to their former groups and new hires that brought diverse skills.

innovation also reflected changing economic conditions and geopolitical events. And, of course, innovation has covered a wide spectrum, including technologies, products, processes, and complete business ventures, each with its own requirements.

Still, despite changes to the environment and differences among types of innovation, each wave of enthusiasm has encountered similar dilemmas. Most of these stem from the tensions between protecting revenue streams from existing businesses critical to

The Lessons of Innovation

INNOVATION GOES IN OR OUT of fashion as a strategic driver of corporate growth, but with every wave of enthusiasm, executives make the same mistakes. Most of the time, they stumble in their R&D efforts because they are engaged in a difficult balancing act: They need to protect existing revenue streams while coaxing along new ones. But "corporate entrepreneurship" doesn't have to be an oxymoron. Innovation can flourish if executives heed business lessons from the past.

Strategy Lessons

- Not every innovation idea has to be a blockbuster. Sufficient numbers of small or incremental innovations can lead to big profits.
- Don't just focus on new product development: Transformative ideas can come from any function—for instance, marketing, production, finance, or distribution.
- Successful innovators use an "innovation pyramid," with several big bets at the top that get most of the investment; a portfolio of promising midrange ideas in test stage; and a broad base of early stage ideas or incremental innovations. Ideas and influence can flow up or down the pyramid.

Process Lessons

- Tight controls strangle innovation. The planning, budgeting, and reviews applied to existing businesses will squeeze the life out of an innovation effort.

current success and supporting new concepts that may be crucial to future success. These tensions are exacerbated by the long-known phenomenon that important innovations often arise from outside an industry and beyond the established players, creating extra pressure for companies to find the next big concept quickly. Consequently, a large body of knowledge about innovation dilemmas has arisen.

Books such as Tom Peters and Bob Waterman's *In Search of Excellence,* my own *The Change Masters,* and Gifford Pinchot's *Intrapreneuring* supported the 1980s innovation wave by pointing to the importance of relieving potential innovators of bureaucratic constraints so they could run with their ideas. This was followed by

- Companies should expect deviations from plan: If employees are rewarded simply for doing what they committed to do, rather than acting as circumstances would suggest, their employers will stifle and drive out innovation.

Structure Lessons

- While loosening formal controls, companies should tighten interpersonal connections between innovation efforts and the rest of the business.
- Game-changing innovations often cut across established channels or combine elements of existing capacity in new ways.
- If companies create two classes of corporate citizens—supplying the innovators with more perks, privileges, and prestige—those in the existing business will make every effort to crush the innovation.

Skills Lessons

- Even the most technical of innovations requires strong leaders with great relationship and communication skills.
- Members of successful innovation teams stick together through the development of an idea, even if the company's approach to career timing requires faster job rotation.
- Because innovations need connectors—people who know how to find partners in the mainstream business or outside world—they flourish in cultures that encourage collaboration.

a body of work documenting the difficulty of exploring the new while exploiting the old, reflected in Michael Tushman and Charles O'Reilly's call for more ambidextrous organizations in *Winning Through Innovation;* my work on managing the tensions between the powerful organizational mainstream and fragile new streams produced by innovation groups in *When Giants Learn to Dance;* and Clayton Christensen's more recent finding, in *The Innovator's Dilemma,* that listening to current customers can inhibit breakthrough innovation.

Yet despite all the research and literature, I still observe executives exhibiting the same lack of courage or knowledge that undercut previous waves of innovation. They declare that they want more innovation but then ask, "Who else is doing it?" They claim to seek new ideas but shoot down every one brought to them. And, repeatedly, companies make the same mistakes as their predecessors. For example, a 1983 HBR article by Harvard Business School professor Malcolm Salter, et al., "When Corporate Venture Capital Doesn't Work," provided warnings that companies failed to heed about exactly the same dilemmas they face today: With a few notable exceptions, such as Intel and Reuters, companies' venture-capital departments rarely create significant value for the core business.

It's inevitable that historical memory will fade—but not inevitable that we lose the lessons. Here's a chance to collect some of what is known about innovation traps and how to avoid them.

Strategy Mistakes: Hurdles Too High, Scope Too Narrow

The potential for premium prices and high margins lures executives to seek blockbuster innovations—the next iPod, Viagra, or Toyota Production System. Along the way, they expend enormous resources, though big hits are rare and unpredictable. Meanwhile, in seeking the killer app, managers may reject opportunities that at first glance appear too small, and people who aren't involved in the big projects may feel marginalized.

For years, large consumer products companies typically screened out ideas that couldn't result in revenues of several hundred million dollars within two years. This screen discouraged investments in ideas that couldn't be tested and measured using conventional market research, or that weren't grounded in experience, in favor of ideas that were close to current practice and hardly innovative. In the 1980s and 1990s, Pillsbury, Quaker Oats, and even Procter & Gamble (an innovation powerhouse today) were vulnerable to smaller companies that could quickly roll out new products, thus eroding the giants' market share. P&G, for example, lamented not having introduced a new toilet bowl cleaner before a competitor did, despite P&G labs' having developed similar technology. The rival, of course, gained dominant market share by being a first mover.

Likewise, Pillsbury and Quaker lagged the competition in bringing new concepts to market and, as underperformers, were eventually acquired.

Time Incorporated, the magazine wing of Time Warner, for a long time was slow to develop new publications because managers wanted any start-up to have the potential to grow into another *People* or *Sports Illustrated,* two of the company's legendary successes. During the period before Don Logan took the helm in 1992, almost no new magazines were launched. After Logan brought a different innovation strategy to the magazine group, Time developed (or bought) about 100 magazines, which dramatically increased the company's revenues, cash flow, and profits. Not every offering was a blockbuster, but Time had learned what successful innovators know: To get more successes, you have to be willing to risk more failures.

A related mistake is to act as if only products count, even though transformative new ideas can come from a range of functions, such as production and marketing. For instance, a fabric company that made complicated woven materials had a long-standing problem: yarn breakage during production, which was reflected in the cost of the company's products and represented a competitive disadvantage. But the top team at the fabric maker continued to talk about the company's search for really big product innovations, such as totally new materials. A new executive, who believed in opening the search for innovation to all employees, joined the company. After a meeting discussing the need for change, a veteran factory worker, who had joined as a young immigrant and still spoke with a heavy accent, tentatively approached the new executive with an idea for ending the breakage. The company tried it, and it worked. When asked how long he had had that idea, the worker replied, "Thirty-two years."

Similarly, because managers at Quaker Oats in the 1990s were too busy tweaking product formulas in minor ways, the company missed numerous opportunities in other arenas, such as distribution—for instance, taking advantage of the smaller, health-oriented outlets used by its Snapple beverage acquisition. And in a packaging coup,

Ocean Spray, the cranberry juice company, stole a march on America's largest juice purveyors (then including P&G and Coca-Cola) by getting an 18-month exclusive license for the introduction of Tetra Pak's paper bottles to the U.S. market. Ocean Spray boasted a more eclectic innovation strategy than that of its rivals, including idea forums to explore innovations in any domain and open to any employee. Paper bottles were an instant hit with children (and parents packing their lunches), and Ocean Spray's market share shot way up.

Early in its history, the U.S. auto industry gained a breakthrough innovation from its financial function: Consumer financing opened mass markets for products that previously only the affluent could afford. One Intel breakthrough was in marketing: It treated computer chips like potato chips. As a technology company, Intel could have left innovation to its R&D folks. But by marketing a component directly to consumers, Intel gained enormous power with computer manufacturers, which had little choice but to put an Intel Inside label on every machine.

Similarly, Cemex, the global cement company based in Mexico, has used widespread brainstorming to generate innovations that create other sources of value for a product that could easily become a commodity. Those innovations include branded, bagged cement and technology-enabled delivery methods to get cement to customers as fast as if it were a pizza. And while P&G is getting attention for its product innovations, such as the Swiffer and Crest Whitestrips, its innovations in new media, such as interactive Web sites for the soap operas it sponsors, may prove even more valuable for the company's future.

When a company is both too product centric and too revenue impatient, an additional problem can arise. The organization's innovation energy can dissipate across a raft of tiny me-too projects chasing immediate revenue. Perversely, such projects may raise costs in the long run. While a failure to encourage small wins can mean missed opportunities, too many trivial projects are like seeds sown on stony ground—they might sprout, but they do not take root and grow into anything useful. If new ideas take the form not of distinctive innovations but of modest product variations, the resulting proliferation can dilute the brand, confuse customers, and increase internal complexity—such as offering a dozen sizes and flavors of crackers rather than a new and different snack food, a problem Kraft currently faces.

Process Mistakes: Controls Too Tight

A second set of classic mistakes lies in process; specifically, the impulse to strangle innovation with tight controls—the same planning, budgeting, and reviews applied to existing businesses. The inherent uncertainty of the innovation process makes sidetracks or unexpected turns inevitable. The reason upstart Ocean Spray could grab the paper-bottle opportunity from large U.S. juice makers is that the big companies' funds had already been allocated for the year, and they wanted committees to study the packaging option before making commitments that would deviate from their plans.

AlliedSignal (now Honeywell) in 2000 sought new Internet-based products and services using established strategic-planning and budgeting processes through existing business units. The CEO asked the divisions to bring their best ideas for Internet-related innovations to the quarterly budget reviews. Although designated as a priority, these innovation projects were subjected to the same financial metrics the established businesses were. Budgets contained no additional funds for investment; managers working on innovations had to find their own sources of funding through savings or internal transfers. What emerged were often retrofitted versions of ideas that had been in the pipeline anyway.

Performance reviews, and their associated metrics, are another danger zone for innovations. Established companies don't just want plans; they want managers to stick to those plans. They often reward people for doing what they committed to do and discourage them from making changes as circumstances warrant. At a large defense contractor, for instance, people got low marks for not delivering exactly what they had promised, even if they delivered something better—which led people to underpromise, eventually reducing employees' aspirations and driving out innovation.

In the early 1990s, Bank of Boston (now part of Bank of America) set up an innovative unit called First Community Bank (FCB), the first comprehensive banking initiative to focus on inner-city markets. FCB struggled to convince mainstream managers in Bank of Boston's retail-banking group that the usual performance metrics, such as transaction time and profitability per customer, were not appropriate for this market—which required customer education, among other things—or for a new venture that still needed investment. Mainstream managers argued that "underperforming" branches should be closed. In order to save the innovation, FCB leaders had to invent their own metrics, based on customer satisfaction and loyalty, and find creative ways to show results by clusters of branches. The venture later proved both profitable and important to the parent bank as it embarked on a series of acquisitions.

Structure Mistakes: Connections Too Loose, Separations Too Sharp

While holding fledgling enterprises to the same processes as established businesses is dangerous, companies must be careful how they structure the two entities to avoid a clash of cultures or conflicting agendas.

The more dramatic approach is to create a unit apart from the mainstream business, which must still serve its embedded base. This was the logic behind the launch of Saturn as an autonomous subsidiary of General Motors. GM's rules were suspended, and the Saturn team was encouraged to innovate in every aspect of vehicle design, production, marketing, sales, and customer service. The hope was that the best ideas would be incorporated back at the parent company, but instead, after a successful launch, Saturn was reintegrated into GM, and many of its innovations disappeared.

In the time it took for Saturn to hit its stride, Toyota—which favored continuous improvement over blockbusters or greenfield initiatives like Saturn—was still ahead of GM in quality, customer satisfaction, and market share growth. Similarly, U.S. charter schools were freed from the rules of public school systems so they could innovate and thus serve as models for improved education. They've employed many innovative practices, including longer school days and focused curricula, but there is little evidence that charter schools have influenced changes in the rest of their school districts.

The problem in both cases can be attributed to poor connections between the greenfield and the mainstream. Indeed, when people operate in silos, companies may miss innovation opportunities altogether. Game-changing innovations often cut across established channels or combine elements of existing capacity in new ways. CBS was once the world's largest broadcaster and owned the world's largest record company, yet it failed to invent music video, losing this opportunity to MTV. In the late 1990s, Gillette had a toothbrush unit (Oral B), an appliance unit (Braun), and a battery unit (Duracell), but lagged in introducing a battery-powered toothbrush.

The likelihood that companies will miss or stifle innovations increases when the potential innovations involve expertise from different industries or knowledge of different technologies. Managers at established organizations may both fail to understand the nature of a new idea and feel threatened by it.

AT&T Worldnet, the Internet access venture of the venerable long-distance telephone company, faced this lethal mix in the mid-1990s. Managers in the traditional consumer services and business services units participated in a series of debates over whether to manage Worldnet as a distinct business unit, with its own P&L, or to include it in the existing business units focused primarily on the consumer sector. While consumer services managers were reluctant to let go of anything, they eventually agreed to a carve-out intended to protect the embryonic venture from being crushed by the bureaucracy and to keep it from being measured against more-mature businesses that were generating significant cash flow rather than requiring investment. They weren't all that concerned, because they believed an Internet service provider would never generate significant revenue and profitability.

But as Worldnet gained momentum, it attracted more attention. The people in consumer services began to view the innovation's possible expansion to provide voice over Internet protocol (VoIP) services as a threat that could cannibalize existing business. Consumer services managers grabbed control of Worldnet and proceeded to starve it. They used it as a platform to sell core land-based long-distance services and started applying the same metrics to the Internet business that were used for consumer long-distance. Pricing was an immediate problem. Worldnet's services had been priced low to fuel growth, to get the scale and network effects of a large group of subscribers, but the mainstream unit did not want to incur losses on any line of business. So it raised prices, and Worldnet's growth stalled. Consumer services managers could then treat Worldnet as a trivial, slow-growing business, not worthy of large investment. They did not allocate sufficient resources to develop Internet access and VoIP technology, restraining important telecom innovations in which AT&T could have been the pioneer.

Cultural clashes exacerbated tensions at AT&T. Mainstream managers had long tenures in the Bell system. The Internet group, however, hired external tech professionals who spoke the language of computers, not telephony.

Even when a new venture is launched within an existing business, culture clashes become class warfare if there are two classes of corporate citizens—those who have all the fun and those who make all the money. The designated innovators, whether an R&D group or a new-venture unit, are identified as creators of the future. They are free of rules or revenue demands and are allowed to play with ideas that don't yet work. Their colleagues are expected to follow rules, meet demands, and make money while feeling like grinds and sometimes being told they are dinosaurs whose business models will soon be obsolete.

In the early 2000s, Arrow Electronics' attempt at an Internet venture, Arrow.com, was given space in the same facility as the traditional sales force. The similarities stopped there. The Internet group was composed of new hires, often young, from a different background, who dressed in a completely different style. It spent money on cushy furniture, including a big expenditure on a new kitchen—justified, it was said, because the Arrow.com team worked 24/7. The traditional sales force, already anxious about the threat

Internet-enabled sales posed to its commissions and now aware of its dingier offices, became overtly angry. Relations between the groups grew so acrimonious that a brick wall was erected to separate the two sides of the building. Both teams wasted time battling, endangering customer relationships when the two groups fought over the same customers—after all, Arrow.com was just another distribution channel. The CEO had to intervene and find structures to connect them.

Skills Mistakes: Leadership Too Weak, Communication Too Poor

Undervaluing and underinvesting in the human side of innovation is another common mistake. Top managers frequently put the best technical people in charge, not the best leaders. These technically oriented managers, in turn, mistakenly assume that ideas will speak for themselves if they are any good, so they neglect external communication. Or they emphasize tasks over relationships, missing opportunities to enhance the team chemistry necessary to turn undeveloped concepts into useful innovations.

Groups that are convened without attention to interpersonal skills find it difficult to embrace collective goals, take advantage of the different strengths various members bring, or communicate well enough to share the tacit knowledge that is still unformed and hard to document while an innovation is under development. It takes time to build the trust and interplay among team members that will spark great ideas. MIT researchers have found that for R&D team members to be truly productive, they have to have been on board for at least two years. At one point, Pillsbury realized that the average length of time the company took to go from new product idea to successful commercialization was 24 to 26 months, but the average length of time people spent on product teams was 18 months. No wonder the company was falling behind in innovation.

Changes in team composition that result from companies' preferences for the frequency with which individuals make career moves can make it hard for new ventures to deal with difficult challenges, prompting them to settle for quick, easy, conventional solutions.

At Honeywell in the 1980s, leaders of new-venture teams were often promoted out of them before the work had been completed. Because promotions were take-it-or-leave-it offers and pay was tied to size of assets controlled (small by definition in new ventures) rather than difficulty of task, even dedicated innovators saw the virtues of leaving their projects midstream. Honeywell was undermining its own innovation efforts. An executive review of why new ventures failed uncovered this problem, but a technology bias made it hard for old-school managers of that era to increase their appreciation for the value of team bonding and continuity.

Innovation efforts also bog down when communication and relationship building outside the team are neglected. When Gap Incorporated was struggling in the late 1990s, the company mounted several cross-unit projects to find innovations in products, retail concepts, and operations. Some of the project teams quickly became closed environments, and members cut themselves off from their former peers. By failing to tap others' ideas, they produced lackluster recommendations; and by failing to keep peers informed, they missed getting buy-in for even their weak proposals.

Innovators cannot work in isolation if they want their concepts to catch on. They must build coalitions of supporters who will provide air cover for the project, speak up for them in meetings they don't attend, or sponsor the embryonic innovation as it moves into the next stages of diffusion and use. To establish the foundation for successful reception of an innovation, groups must be able to present the radical so it can be understood in familiar terms and to cushion disruptive innovations with assurances that the disruption will be manageable. When technical experts mystify their audiences rather than enlighten them, they lose support—and "no" is always an easier answer than "yes." Groups that work in secret and then present their ideas full-blown at the end face unexpected objections that sometimes kill the project.

Such inattention to relationships and communication with mainstream business managers doomed the launch of Timberland's promising TravelGear line. Developed by an R&D group called the Invention Factory, which was independent of the company's mainstream businesses, TravelGear allowed a user to travel with a single pair of shoes, adding or subtracting components suitable for a range of outdoor activities. The concept won a design award from *BusinessWeek* in 2005. But some existing business teams had not been included in the Invention Factory's developments, and the traditional sales force refused to sell TravelGear products.

By contrast, Dr. Craig Feied's success in developing a state-of-the-art digital network for Washington Hospital Center and its parent, MedStar Health, was a testimony to investment in the human dimension. A small group of programmers designed a user-friendly information system in the emergency department, not the IT department, so they were already close to users. Dr. Feied and his partner, Dr. Mark Smith, made a point of sitting on numerous hospital committees so they would have a wide base of relationships. Their investment in people and their contributions toward shared hospital goals had a positive effect: Feied and Smith's actions helped create good word of mouth and support among other departments for their information system (now called Azyxxi), which resulted in saved time and lives.

The climate for relationships within an innovation group is shaped by the climate outside it. Having a negative instead of a positive culture can cost a company real money. During Seagate Technology's troubled period in the mid-to-late 1990s, the company, a large manufacturer of disk drives for personal computers, had seven different design centers working on innovation, yet it had the lowest R&D productivity in the industry because the centers competed rather than cooperated. Attempts to bring them together merely led people to advocate for their own groups rather than find common ground. Not only did Seagate's engineers and managers lack positive norms for group interaction, but they had the opposite in place: People who yelled in executive meetings received "Dog's Head" awards for the worst conduct. Lack of product and process innovation was reflected in loss of market share, disgruntled customers, and declining sales. Seagate, with its dwindling PC sales and fading customer base, was threatening to become a commodity producer in a changing technology environment.

Under a new CEO and COO, Steve Luczo and Bill Watkins, who operated as partners, Seagate developed new norms for how people should treat one another, starting with the executive group. Their raised consciousness led to a systemic process for forming and running "core teams" (cross-functional innovation groups), and Seagate employees were trained in common methodologies for team building, both in conventional training programs and through participation in difficult outdoor activities in New Zealand and other remote locations. To lead core teams, Seagate promoted people who were known for strong relationship skills above others with greater technical skills. Unlike the antagonistic committees convened during the years of decline, the core teams created dramatic process and product innovations that brought the company back to market leadership. The new Seagate was able to create innovations embedded in a wide range of new electronic devices, such as iPods and cell phones.

Innovation Remedies

The quest for breakthrough ideas, products, and services can get derailed in any or all of the ways described earlier. Fortunately, however, history also shows how innovation succeeds. "Corporate entrepreneurship" need not be an oxymoron. Here are four ways to win.

Strategy remedy: widen the search, broaden the scope

Companies can develop an innovation strategy that works at the three levels of what I call the "innovation pyramid": a few big bets at the top that represent clear directions for the future and receive the lion's share of investment; a portfolio of promising midrange ideas pursued by designated teams that develop and test them; and a broad base of early-stage ideas or incremental innovations permitting continuous improvement. Influence flows down the pyramid, as the big bets encourage small wins heading in the same direction, but it also can flow up, because big innovations sometimes begin life as small bits of tinkering—as in the famously accidental development of 3M's Post-it Notes.

Thinking of innovation in terms of this pyramid gives senior managers a tool for assessing current efforts, making adjustments as ideas prove their value and require further support, and ensuring that there is activity at all levels. A culture of innovation grows because everyone can play. While dedicated groups pursue the big projects and temporary teams develop midrange ideas, everyone else in the company can be invited to contribute ideas. Every employee can be a potential idea scout and project initiator, as IBM is demonstrating. This past July, the company held a three-day InnovationJam on the Web, during which about 140,000 employees and clients—representing 104 countries—contributed about 37,000 ideas and ranked them, giving the company an enormous pool of raw ideas, some of them big, most of them small. Indeed, an organization is more likely to get bigger ideas if it has a wide funnel into which numerous small ideas can be poured. One of the secrets of success for companies that demonstrate high rates of innovation is that they simply try more things.

Gillette adopted the pyramid model as part of its push to accelerate innovation in 2003 and 2004. The result was a stream of innovations in every function and business unit that raised revenues and profits. They included new products such as a battery-powered toothbrush; new concepts in the R&D pipeline, such as the 2006 five-blade, battery-powered Fusion shaving system; innovative marketing campaigns that neutralized the competition, such as the campaign for the Mach3Turbo, which outshone Schick's introduction of its Quattro razor; and new technology in HR. At the first Gillette innovation fair in March 2004, every unit showcased its best ideas of the year in a creative way. The legal department promoted its novel online ethics course with a joke: distributing "get out of jail free" cards like those in *Monopoly*. Having the legal department embrace innovation was a plus for a company in which innovators needed speedy service to file patent applications or help to clear regulatory hurdles.

An innovation strategy that includes incremental innovations and continuous improvement can help to liberate minds throughout the company, making people more receptive to change when big breakthroughs occur.

Process remedy: add flexibility to planning and control systems

One way to encourage innovation to flourish outside the normal planning cycles is to reserve pools of special funds for unexpected opportunities. That way, promising ideas do not have to wait for the next budget cycle, and innovators do not have to beg for funds from mainstream managers who are measured on current revenues and profits. In the mid-to-late 1990s, autocratic management and rigid controls caused the BBC to slip in program innovation and, consequently, audience share. Budgets were tight, and, once they were set, expenditures were confined to predetermined categories. In 2000, a new CEO and his CFO relaxed the rules and began setting aside funds in a corporate account to support proposals for innovation, making it clear that bureaucratic rules should not stand in the way of creative ideas. The BBC's biggest hit comedy in decades, *The Office,* was an accident, made possible when a new recruit took the initiative to use money originally allocated for a BBC training film to make the pilot.

IBM is building such flexibility directly into its infrastructure. The company established a $100 million innovation fund to support the best ideas arising from its InnovationJam, independent of the normal planning and budgeting processes, to allow bottom-up ideas to flourish. "No one has ever before brought together such a global and diverse set of business thought leaders on this scale to discuss the most pressing issues and opportunities of our age," says Nick Donofrio, IBM's executive vice president of innovation and technology. "We have companies literally knocking at the door and saying, 'Give us your best and brightest ideas, and let's work together to make them a reality.' It's a golden opportunity to create entirely new markets and partnerships."

Besides needing different funding models and development partnerships, the innovation process requires exemption from some corporate requirements; after all, there are numerous differences between established businesses and new ventures. For example, the knowledge that innovations could move forward through rapid prototyping—learning from a series of fast trials—might mean that certain milestones triggering review and additional funding would occur faster than they would for established businesses, following the rhythm of the project rather than a fixed quarterly or annual calendar. For other kinds of projects, greater patience might be required—for instance, when an innovation group encounters unexpected obstacles and needs to rethink its model. The key is flexible, customized treatment.

Structure remedy: facilitate close connections between innovators and mainstream businesses

While loosening the formal controls that would otherwise stifle innovations, companies should tighten the human connections between those pursuing innovation efforts and others throughout the rest of the business. Productive conversations should take place regularly between innovators and mainstream business managers. Innovation teams should be charged with external communication as part of their responsibility, but senior leaders should also convene discussions to encourage mutual respect rather than tensions and antagonism. Such conversations should be aimed at mutual learning, to minimize cannibalization and to maximize effective reintegration of innovations that become new businesses. In addition to formal meetings, companies can facilitate informal conversations—as Steelcase did by building a design center that would force people to bump into one another—or identify the people who lead informal cross-unit networks and encourage their efforts at making connections.

Innovation groups can be told at the outset that they have a responsibility to serve the mainstream while also seeking bigger innovations to start new businesses. This can be built into their charters and reinforced by overlapping relationships—whether it involves representatives from mainstream businesses rotating through innovation groups or advisory boards overseeing innovation efforts. After its first great idea flopped, Timberland's Invention Factory learned to work closely with mainstream teams to meet their needs for immediate innovations, such as recreational shoes lined with SmartWool, and to seek game-changing breakthroughs. Turner Broadcasting's new-products group mixes project types: standalone developments, enhancements for current channels, external partnerships, and venture capital investments. PNC Financial Services Group recently established a new-products group to oversee mainstream developments, such as pricing and product enhancements, as well as growth engines in new capabilities, such as technology-enabled services and back-office services for investment funds. The company's sales of emerging products were up 21% in 2005, accounting for 46% of all sales.

Flexible organizational structures, in which teams across functions or disciplines organize around solutions, can facilitate good connections. Media conglomerate Publicis has "holistic communication" teams, which combine people across its ad agencies (Saatchi & Saatchi, Leo Burnett, Publicis Worldwide, and so on) and technology groups to focus on customers and brands. Novartis has organized around diseases, with R&D more closely connected to markets and customers; this has helped the company introduce pathbreaking innovations faster, such as its cancer drug Gleevec. The success of Seagate's companywide Factory of the Future team at introducing seemingly miraculous process innovations led to widespread use of its core-teams model.

Would-be innovators at AlliedSignal discovered that tackling promising opportunities required outreach across silos. For example, the aerospace division was organized into groups that were dedicated to large commercial airlines, small commercial airlines, and general aviation (private and charter planes), but the best new idea involved differentiating customers by whether they performed their own maintenance or contracted it to others. The division needed to create new connections across previously divided territories in order to begin the innovation process.

The success of Williams-Sonoma as a multichannel retailer innovating in e-commerce can be attributed to the ways its Web pioneers connected their developments to the rest of the company. From the very beginning, CEO Howard Lester refused to consider Internet ventures that were independent of other company operations. The first main Web development was a bridal registry to create new functionality for the mainstream business. When this pilot project proved its value, an e-commerce department was launched and housed in its own building. But rather than standing apart and pursuing its own direction, that department sought to enhance existing channels, not compete with them. It measured its success not only according to e-commerce sales but also according to incremental sales through other channels that the Web had facilitated. To further its close connections with the mainstream business, the department offered free training to the rest of the company.

Skills remedy: select for leadership and interpersonal skills, and surround innovators with a supportive culture of collaboration

Companies that cultivate leadership skills are more likely to net successful innovations. One reason Williams-Sonoma could succeed in e-commerce quickly and profitably was its careful attention to the human dimension. Shelley Nandkeolyar, the first manager of Williams-Sonoma's e-commerce group, was not the most knowledgeable about the technology, but he was a leader who could assemble the right team. He valued relationships, so he chose a mixture of current employees from other units, who could be ambassadors to their former groups, and new hires that brought new skills. He added cross-company teams to advise and link to the e-commerce team. He invented an integrator role to better connect operations groups and chose Patricia Skerritt, known for being relationship oriented, to fill it.

Similarly, Gail Snowden was able to steer Bank of Boston's First Community Bank through the minefields of middle-manager antagonism toward a successful innovation that produced other innovations (new products and services) because of her leadership skills, not her banking skills. She built a close-knit team of talented people who bonded with one another and felt passion for the mission. Soon her group became one of the parent bank's most desirable places to work. She developed strong relationships with senior executives who helped her deal with tensions in the middle, and she communicated well and often about why her unit needed to be different. Her creativity, vision, teamwork, and persistence helped this group succeed and become a national role model, while other banks' efforts faltered.

IBM's big innovations, such as demonstrating grid computing through World Community Grid, are possible only because the company's culture encourages people to collaborate. CEO Sam Palmisano has engaged hundreds of thousands of IBMers in a Web-based discussion of company values, and Nick Donofrio, IBM's executive vice president for innovation and technology, works to make 90,000 technical people around the world feel part of one innovation-seeking community. The corporate champion of World Community Grid, IBM vice president Stanley Litow, sought out partners in its business units and geographies to move the innovation forward.

Established companies can avoid falling into the classic traps that stifle innovation by widening the search for new ideas, loosening overly tight controls and rigid structures, forging better connections between innovators and mainstream operations, and cultivating communication and collaboration skills.

Innovation involves ideas that create the future. But the quest for innovation is doomed unless the managers who seek it take time to learn from the past. Getting the balance right between exploiting (getting the highest returns from current activities) and exploring (seeking the new) requires organizational flexibility and a great deal of attention to relationships. It always has, and it always will.

Originally published in November 2006. Reprint R0611C

Leading Change

Why Transformation Efforts Fail. *by John P. Kotter*

OVER THE PAST DECADE, I have watched more than 100 companies try to remake themselves into significantly better competitors. They have included large organizations (Ford) and small ones (Landmark Communications), companies based in the United States (General Motors) and elsewhere (British Airways), corporations that were on their knees (Eastern Airlines), and companies that were earning good money (Bristol-Myers Squibb). These efforts have gone under many banners: total quality management, reengineering, rightsizing, restructuring, cultural change, and turnaround. But, in almost every case, the basic goal has been the same: to make fundamental changes in how business is conducted in order to help cope with a new, more challenging market environment.

A few of these corporate change efforts have been very successful. A few have been utter failures. Most fall somewhere in between, with a distinct tilt toward the lower end of the scale. The lessons that can be drawn are interesting and will probably be relevant to even more organizations in the increasingly competitive business environment of the coming decade.

The most general lesson to be learned from the more successful cases is that the change process goes through a series of phases that, in total, usually require a considerable length of time. Skipping steps creates only the illusion of speed and never produces a satisfying result. A second very general lesson is that critical mistakes in any of the phases can have a devastating impact, slowing momentum and

Eight steps to transforming your organization

1 **Establishing a sense of urgency**
- Examining market and competitive realities
- Identifying and discussing crises, potential crises, or major opportunities

2 **Forming a powerful guiding coalition**
- Assembling a group with enough power to lead the change effort
- Encouraging the group to work together as a team

3 **Creating a vision**
- Creating a vision to help direct the change effort
- Developing strategies for achieving that vision

4 **Communicating the vision**
- Using every vehicle possible to communicate the new vision and strategies
- Teaching new behaviors by the example of the guiding coalition

5 **Empowering others to act on the vision**
- Getting rid of obstacles to change
- Changing systems or structures that seriously undermine the vision
- Encouraging risk taking and nontraditional ideas, activities, and actions

6 **Planning for and creating short-term wins**
- Planning for visible performance improvements
- Creating those improvements
- Recognizing and rewarding employees involved in the improvements

7 **Consolidating improvements and producing still more change**
- Using increased credibility to change systems, structures, and policies that don't fit the vision
- Hiring, promoting, and developing employees who can implement the vision
- Reinvigorating the process with new projects, themes, and change agents

8 **Institutionalizing new approaches**
- Articulating the connections between the new behaviors and corporate success
- Developing the means to ensure leadership development and succession

Idea in Brief

Most major change initiatives—whether intended to boost quality, improve culture, or reverse a corporate death spiral—generate only lukewarm results. Many fail miserably.

Why? Kotter maintains that too many managers don't realize transformation is a *process*, not an event. It advances through stages that build on each other. And it takes years. Pressured to accelerate the process, managers skip stages. But shortcuts never work.

Equally troubling, even highly capable managers make critical mistakes—such as declaring victory too soon. Result? Loss of momentum, reversal of hard-won gains, and devastation of the entire transformation effort.

By understanding the stages of change—and the pitfalls unique to each stage—you boost your chances of a successful transformation. The payoff? Your organization flexes with tectonic shifts in competitors, markets, and technologies—leaving rivals far behind.

negating hard-won gains. Perhaps because we have relatively little experience in renewing organizations, even very capable people often make at least one big error.

Error 1: Not Establishing a Great Enough Sense of Urgency

Most successful change efforts begin when some individuals or some groups start to look hard at a company's competitive situation, market position, technological trends, and financial performance. They focus on the potential revenue drop when an important patent expires, the five-year trend in declining margins in a core business, or an emerging market that everyone seems to be ignoring. They then find ways to communicate this information broadly and dramatically, especially with respect to crises, potential crises, or great opportunities that are very timely. This first step is essential because just getting a transformation program started requires the aggressive cooperation of many individuals. Without motivation, people won't help, and the effort goes nowhere.

Compared with other steps in the change process, phase one can sound easy. It is not. Well over 50% of the companies I have watched

Idea in Practice

To give your transformation effort the best chance of succeeding, take the right actions at each stage—and avoid common pitfalls

Stage	Actions needed	Pitfalls
Establish a sense of urgency	• Examine market and competitive realities for potential crises and untapped opportunities. • Convince at least 75% of your managers that the status quo is more dangerous than the unknown.	• Underestimating the difficulty of driving people from their comfort zones • Becoming paralyzed by risks
Form a powerful guiding coalition	• Assemble a group with shared commitment and enough power to lead the change effort. • Encourage them to work as a team outside the normal hierarchy.	• No prior experience in teamwork at the top • Relegating team leadership to an HR, quality, or strategic-planning executive rather than a senior line manager
Create a vision	• Create a vision to direct the change effort. • Develop strategies for realizing that vision.	• Presenting a vision that's too complicated or vague to be communicated in five minutes
Communicate the vision	• Use every vehicle possible to communicate the new vision and strategies for achieving it. • Teach new behaviors by the example of the guiding coalition.	• Undercommunicating the vision • Behaving in ways antithetical to the vision

fail in this first phase. What are the reasons for that failure? Sometimes executives underestimate how hard it can be to drive people out of their comfort zones. Sometimes they grossly overestimate how successful they have already been in increasing urgency. Sometimes they lack patience: "Enough with the preliminaries; let's get on

Empower others to act on the vision	• Remove or alter systems or structures undermining the vision. • Encourage risk taking and nontraditional ideas, activities, and actions.	• Failing to remove powerful individuals who resist the change effort
Plan for and create short-term wins	• Define and engineer visible performance improvements. • Recognize and reward employees contributing to those improvements.	• Leaving short-term successes up to chance • Failing to score successes early enough (12–24 months into the change effort)
Consolidate improvements and produce more change	• Use increased credibility from early wins to change systems, structures, and policies undermining the vision. • Hire, promote, and develop employees who can implement the vision. • Reinvigorate the change process with new projects and change agents.	• Declaring victory too soon—with the first performance improvement • Allowing resistors to convince "troops" that the war has been won
Institutionalize new approaches	• Articulate connections between new behaviors and corporate success. • Create leadership development and succession plans consistent with the new approach.	• Not creating new social norms and shared values consistent with changes • Promoting people into leadership positions who don't personify the new approach

with it." In many cases, executives become paralyzed by the downside possibilities. They worry that employees with seniority will become defensive, that morale will drop, that events will spin out of control, that short-term business results will be jeopardized, that the stock will sink, and that they will be blamed for creating a crisis.

A paralyzed senior management often comes from having too many managers and not enough leaders. Management's mandate is to minimize risk and to keep the current system operating. Change, by definition, requires creating a new system, which in turn always demands leadership. Phase one in a renewal process typically goes nowhere until enough real leaders are promoted or hired into senior-level jobs.

Transformations often begin, and begin well, when an organization has a new head who is a good leader and who sees the need for a major change. If the renewal target is the entire company, the CEO is key. If change is needed in a division, the division general manager is key. When these individuals are not new leaders, great leaders, or change champions, phase one can be a huge challenge.

Bad business results are both a blessing and a curse in the first phase. On the positive side, losing money does catch people's attention. But it also gives less maneuvering room. With good business results, the opposite is true: Convincing people of the need for change is much harder, but you have more resources to help make changes.

But whether the starting point is good performance or bad, in the more successful cases I have witnessed, an individual or a group always facilitates a frank discussion of potentially unpleasant facts about new competition, shrinking margins, decreasing market share, flat earnings, a lack of revenue growth, or other relevant indices of a declining competitive position. Because there seems to be an almost universal human tendency to shoot the bearer of bad news, especially if the head of the organization is not a change champion, executives in these companies often rely on outsiders to bring unwanted information. Wall Street analysts, customers, and consultants can all be helpful in this regard. The purpose of all this activity, in the words of one former CEO of a large European company, is "to make the status quo seem more dangerous than launching into the unknown."

In a few of the most successful cases, a group has manufactured a crisis. One CEO deliberately engineered the largest accounting loss in the company's history, creating huge pressures from Wall Street in the process. One division president commissioned first-ever customer satisfaction surveys, knowing full well that the results would be terrible. He then made these findings public. On the surface, such moves can look unduly risky. But there is also risk in playing it too safe: When the urgency rate is not pumped up enough, the transformation process cannot succeed, and the long-term future of the organization is put in jeopardy.

When is the urgency rate high enough? From what I have seen, the answer is when about 75% of a company's management is honestly convinced that business as usual is totally unacceptable. Anything less can produce very serious problems later on in the process.

Error 2: Not Creating a Powerful Enough Guiding Coalition

Major renewal programs often start with just one or two people. In cases of successful transformation efforts, the leadership coalition grows and grows over time. But whenever some minimum mass is not achieved early in the effort, nothing much worthwhile happens.

It is often said that major change is impossible unless the head of the organization is an active supporter. What I am talking about goes far beyond that. In successful transformations, the chairman or president or division general manager, plus another five or 15 or 50 people, come together and develop a shared commitment to excellent performance through renewal. In my experience, this group never includes all of the company's most senior executives because some people just won't buy in, at least not at first. But in the most successful cases, the coalition is always pretty powerful—in terms of titles, information and expertise, reputations, and relationships.

In both small and large organizations, a successful guiding team may consist of only three to five people during the first year of a renewal effort. But in big companies, the coalition needs to grow to the 20 to 50 range before much progress can be made in phase three and beyond. Senior managers always form the core of the group. But sometimes you find board members, a representative from a key customer, or even a powerful union leader.

Because the guiding coalition includes members who are not part of senior management, it tends to operate outside of the normal hierarchy by definition. This can be awkward, but it is clearly necessary. If the existing hierarchy were working well, there would be no need for a major transformation. But since the current system is not working, reform generally demands activity outside of formal boundaries, expectations, and protocol.

A high sense of urgency within the managerial ranks helps enormously in putting a guiding coalition together. But more is usually required. Someone needs to get these people together, help them develop a shared assessment of their company's problems and opportunities, and create a minimum level of trust and communication. Off-site retreats, for two or three days, are one popular vehicle for accomplishing this task. I have seen many groups of five to 35 executives attend a series of these retreats over a period of months.

Companies that fail in phase two usually underestimate the difficulties of producing change and thus the importance of a powerful guiding coalition. Sometimes they have no history of teamwork at the top and therefore undervalue the importance of this type of coalition. Sometimes they expect the team to be led by a staff executive from human resources, quality, or strategic planning instead of a key line manager. No matter how capable or dedicated the staff head, groups without strong line leadership never achieve the power that is required.

Efforts that don't have a powerful enough guiding coalition can make apparent progress for a while. But, sooner or later, the opposition gathers itself together and stops the change.

Error 3: Lacking a Vision

In every successful transformation effort that I have seen, the guiding coalition develops a picture of the future that is relatively easy to communicate and appeals to customers, stockholders, and employees. A vision always goes beyond the numbers that are typically found in five-year plans. A vision says something that helps clarify the direction in which an organization needs to move. Sometimes the first draft comes mostly from a single individual. It is usually a bit blurry, at least initially. But after the coalition works at it for three or five or even 12 months, something much better emerges through their tough analytical thinking and a little dreaming. Eventually, a strategy for achieving that vision is also developed.

In one midsize European company, the first pass at a vision contained two-thirds of the basic ideas that were in the final product. The concept of global reach was in the initial version from the beginning. So was the idea of becoming preeminent in certain businesses. But one central idea in the final version—getting out of low value-added activities—came only after a series of discussions over a period of several months.

Without a sensible vision, a transformation effort can easily dissolve into a list of confusing and incompatible projects that can take the organization in the wrong direction or nowhere at all. Without a sound vision, the reengineering project in the accounting department, the new 360-degree performance appraisal from the human resources department, the plant's quality program, the cultural change project in the sales force will not add up in a meaningful way.

In failed transformations, you often find plenty of plans, directives, and programs but no vision. In one case, a company gave out four-inch-thick notebooks describing its change effort. In mind-numbing detail, the books spelled out procedures, goals, methods, and deadlines. But nowhere was there a clear and compelling statement of where all this was leading. Not surprisingly, most of the employees with whom I talked were either confused or alienated. The big, thick books did not rally them together or inspire change. In fact, they probably had just the opposite effect.

In a few of the less successful cases that I have seen, management had a sense of direction, but it was too complicated or blurry to be useful. Recently, I asked an executive in a midsize company to describe his vision and received in return a barely comprehensible 30-minute lecture. Buried in his answer were the basic elements of a sound vision. But they were buried—deeply.

A useful rule of thumb: If you can't communicate the vision to someone in five minutes or less and get a reaction that signifies both understanding and interest, you are not yet done with this phase of the transformation process.

Error 4: Undercommunicating the Vision by a Factor of Ten

I've seen three patterns with respect to communication, all very common. In the first, a group actually does develop a pretty good transformation vision and then proceeds to communicate it by holding a single meeting or sending out a single communication. Having used about 0.0001% of the yearly intracompany communication, the group is startled when few people seem to understand the new approach. In the second pattern, the head of the organization spends a considerable amount of time making speeches to employee groups, but most people still don't get it (not surprising, since vision captures only 0.0005% of the total yearly communication). In the third pattern, much more effort goes into newsletters and speeches, but some very visible senior executives still behave in ways that are antithetical to the vision. The net result is that cynicism among the troops goes up, while belief in the communication goes down.

Transformation is impossible unless hundreds or thousands of people are willing to help, often to the point of making short-term sacrifices. Employees will not make sacrifices, even if they are unhappy with the status quo, unless they believe that useful change is possible. Without credible communication, and a lot of it, the hearts and minds of the troops are never captured.

This fourth phase is particularly challenging if the short-term sacrifices include job losses. Gaining understanding and support is tough when downsizing is a part of the vision. For this reason, successful visions usually include new growth possibilities and the commitment to treat fairly anyone who is laid off.

Executives who communicate well incorporate messages into their hour-by-hour activities. In a routine discussion about a business problem, they talk about how proposed solutions fit (or don't fit) into the bigger picture. In a regular performance appraisal, they talk about how the employee's behavior helps or undermines the vision. In a review of a division's quarterly performance, they talk not only about the numbers but also about how the division's executives are contributing to the transformation. In a routine Q&A with employees at a company facility, they tie their answers back to renewal goals.

In more successful transformation efforts, executives use all existing communication channels to broadcast the vision. They turn boring, unread company newsletters into lively articles about the vision. They take ritualistic, tedious quarterly management meetings and turn them into exciting discussions of the transformation. They throw out much of the company's generic management education and replace it with courses that focus on business problems and the new vision. The guiding principle is simple: Use every possible channel, especially those that are being wasted on nonessential information.

Perhaps even more important, most of the executives I have known in successful cases of major change learn to "walk the talk." They consciously attempt to become a living symbol of the new corporate culture. This is often not easy. A 60-year-old plant manager who has spent precious little time over 40 years thinking about customers will not suddenly behave in a customer-oriented way. But I have witnessed just such a person change, and change a great deal. In that case, a high level of urgency helped. The fact that the man was a part of the guiding coalition and the vision-creation team also helped. So did all the communication, which kept reminding him of the desired behavior, and all the feedback from his peers and subordinates, which helped him see when he was not engaging in that behavior.

Communication comes in both words and deeds, and the latter are often the most powerful form. Nothing undermines change more than behavior by important individuals that is inconsistent with their words.

Error 5: Not Removing Obstacles to the New Vision

Successful transformations begin to involve large numbers of people as the process progresses. Employees are emboldened to try new approaches, to develop new ideas, and to provide leadership. The only constraint is that the actions fit within the broad parameters of the overall vision. The more people involved, the better the outcome.

To some degree, a guiding coalition empowers others to take action simply by successfully communicating the new direction. But communication is never sufficient by itself. Renewal also requires the removal of obstacles. Too often, an employee understands the new vision and wants to help make it happen, but an elephant appears to be blocking the path. In some cases, the elephant is in the person's head, and the challenge is to convince the individual that no external obstacle exists. But in most cases, the blockers are very real.

Sometimes the obstacle is the organizational structure: Narrow job categories can seriously undermine efforts to increase productivity or make it very difficult even to think about customers. Sometimes compensation or performance-appraisal systems make people choose between the new vision and their own self-interest. Perhaps worst of all are bosses who refuse to change and who make demands that are inconsistent with the overall effort.

One company began its transformation process with much publicity and actually made good progress through the fourth phase. Then the change effort ground to a halt because the officer in charge of the company's largest division was allowed to undermine most of the new initiatives. He paid lip service to the process but did not change his behavior or encourage his managers to change. He did not reward the unconventional ideas called for in the vision. He allowed human resource systems to remain intact even when they were clearly inconsistent with the new ideals. I think the officer's motives were complex. To some degree, he did not believe the company needed major change. To some degree, he felt personally threatened by all the change. To some degree, he was afraid that he could not produce both change and the expected operating profit. But despite the fact that they backed the renewal effort, the other officers did virtually nothing to stop the one blocker. Again, the reasons were complex. The company had no history of confronting problems like this. Some people were afraid of the officer. The CEO was concerned that he might lose a talented executive. The net result was disastrous. Lower-level managers concluded that senior management had lied to them about their commitment to renewal, cynicism grew, and the whole effort collapsed.

In the first half of a transformation, no organization has the momentum, power, or time to get rid of all obstacles. But the big ones must be confronted and removed. If the blocker is a person, it is important that he or she be treated fairly and in a way that is consistent with the new vision. Action is essential, both to empower others and to maintain the credibility of the change effort as a whole.

Error 6: Not Systematically Planning for, and Creating, Short-Term Wins

Real transformation takes time, and a renewal effort risks losing momentum if there are no short-term goals to meet and celebrate. Most people won't go on the long march unless they see compelling evidence in 12 to 24 months that the journey is producing expected results. Without short-term wins, too many people give up or actively join the ranks of those people who have been resisting change.

One to two years into a successful transformation effort, you find quality beginning to go up on certain indices or the decline in net income stopping. You find some successful new product introductions or an upward shift in market share. You find an impressive productivity improvement or a statistically higher customer satisfaction rating. But whatever the case, the win is unambiguous. The result is not just a judgment call that can be discounted by those opposing change.

Creating short-term wins is different from hoping for short-term wins. The latter is passive, the former active. In a successful transformation, managers actively look for ways to obtain clear performance improvements, establish goals in the yearly planning system, achieve the objectives, and reward the people involved with recognition, promotions, and even money. For example, the guiding coalition at a U.S. manufacturing company produced a highly visible and successful new product introduction about 20 months after the start of its renewal effort. The new product was selected about six months into the effort because it met multiple criteria: It could be designed and launched in a relatively short period, it could be handled by a small team of people who were devoted to the new vision, it had upside potential, and the new product-development team could operate outside the established departmental structure without practical problems. Little was left to chance, and the win boosted the credibility of the renewal process.

Managers often complain about being forced to produce short-term wins, but I've found that pressure can be a useful element in a change effort. When it becomes clear to people that major change will take a long time, urgency levels can drop. Commitments to produce short-term wins help keep the urgency level up and force detailed analytical thinking that can clarify or revise visions.

Error 7: Declaring Victory Too Soon

After a few years of hard work, managers may be tempted to declare victory with the first clear performance improvement. While celebrating a win is fine, declaring the war won can be catastrophic. Until changes sink deeply into a company's culture, a process that can take five to ten years, new approaches are fragile and subject to regression.

In the recent past, I have watched a dozen change efforts operate under the reengineering theme. In all but two cases, victory was declared and the expensive consultants were paid and thanked when the first major project was completed after two to three years. Within two more years, the useful changes that had been introduced slowly disappeared. In two of the ten cases, it's hard to find any trace of the reengineering work today.

Over the past 20 years, I've seen the same sort of thing happen to huge quality projects, organizational development efforts, and more. Typically, the problems start early in the process: The urgency level is not intense enough, the guiding coalition is not powerful enough, and the vision is not clear enough. But it is the premature victory celebration that kills momentum. And then the powerful forces associated with tradition take over.

Ironically, it is often a combination of change initiators and change resistors that creates the premature victory celebration. In their enthusiasm over a clear sign of progress, the initiators go overboard. They are then joined by resistors, who are quick to spot any opportunity to stop change. After the celebration is over, the resistors point to the victory as a sign that the war has been won and the troops should be sent home. Weary troops allow themselves to be convinced that they won. Once home, the foot soldiers are reluctant to climb back on the ships. Soon thereafter, change comes to a halt, and tradition creeps back in.

Instead of declaring victory, leaders of successful efforts use the credibility afforded by short-term wins to tackle even bigger problems. They go after systems and structures that are not consistent with the transformation vision and have not been confronted before. They pay great attention to who is promoted, who is hired, and how people are developed. They include new reengineering projects that are even bigger in scope than the initial ones. They understand that renewal efforts take not months but years. In fact, in one of the most successful transformations that I have ever seen, we quantified the amount of change that occurred each year over a seven-year period. On a scale of one (low) to ten (high), year one received a two, year two a four, year three a three, year four a seven, year five an eight, year six a four, and year seven a two. The peak came in year five, fully 36 months after the first set of visible wins.

Error 8: Not Anchoring Changes in the Corporation's Culture

In the final analysis, change sticks when it becomes "the way we do things around here," when it seeps into the bloodstream of the corporate body. Until new behaviors are rooted in social norms and shared values, they are subject to degradation as soon as the pressure for change is removed.

Two factors are particularly important in institutionalizing change in corporate culture. The first is a conscious attempt to show people how the new approaches, behaviors, and attitudes have helped improve performance. When people are left on their own to make the connections, they sometimes create very inaccurate links. For example, because results improved while charismatic Harry was boss, the troops link his mostly idiosyncratic style with those results instead of seeing how their own improved customer service and productivity were instrumental. Helping people see the right connections requires communication. Indeed, one company was relentless, and it paid off enormously. Time was spent at every major management meeting to discuss why performance was increasing. The company newspaper ran article after article showing how changes had boosted earnings.

The second factor is taking sufficient time to make sure that the next generation of top management really does personify the new approach. If the requirements for promotion don't change, renewal rarely lasts. One bad succession decision at the top of an organization can undermine a decade of hard work. Poor succession decisions are possible when boards of directors are not an integral part of the renewal effort. In at least three instances I have seen, the champion for change was the retiring executive, and although his successor was not a resistor, he was not a change champion. Because the boards did not understand the transformations in any detail, they could not see that their choices were not good fits. The retiring executive in one case tried unsuccessfully to talk his board into a less seasoned candidate who better personified the transformation. In the other two cases, the CEOs did not resist the boards' choices, because they felt the transformation could not be undone by their successors. They were wrong. Within two years, signs of renewal began to disappear at both companies.

There are still more mistakes that people make, but these eight are the big ones. I realize that in a short article everything is made to sound a bit too simplistic. In reality, even successful change efforts are messy and full of surprises. But just as a relatively simple vision is needed to guide people through a major change, so a vision of the change process can reduce the error rate. And fewer errors can spell the difference between success and failure.

Originally published March 1995. Reprint R0701J

Marketing Myopia

by Theodore Levitt

EVERY MAJOR INDUSTRY WAS once a growth industry. But some that are now riding a wave of growth enthusiasm are very much in the shadow of decline. Others that are thought of as seasoned growth industries have actually stopped growing. In every case, the reason growth is threatened, slowed, or stopped is *not* because the market is saturated. It is because there has been a failure of management.

Fateful Purposes

The failure is at the top. The executives responsible for it, in the last analysis, are those who deal with broad aims and policies. Thus:

- The railroads did not stop growing because the need for passenger and freight transportation declined. That grew. The railroads are in trouble today not because that need was filled by others (cars, trucks, airplanes, and even telephones) but because it was *not* filled by the railroads themselves. They let others take customers away from them because they assumed themselves to be in the railroad business rather than in the transportation business. The reason they defined their industry incorrectly was that they were railroad oriented instead of transportation oriented; they were product oriented instead of customer oriented.

- Hollywood barely escaped being totally ravished by television. Actually, all the established film companies went through drastic reorganizations. Some simply disappeared. All of them got into trouble not because of TV's inroads but because of their own myopia. As with the railroads, Hollywood defined its business incorrectly. It thought it was in the movie business when it was actually in the entertainment business. "Movies" implied a specific, limited product. This produced a fatuous contentment that from the beginning led producers to view TV as a threat. Hollywood scorned and rejected TV when it should have welcomed it as an opportunity—an opportunity to expand the entertainment business.

Today, TV is a bigger business than the old narrowly defined movie business ever was. Had Hollywood been customer oriented (providing entertainment) rather than product oriented (making movies), would it have gone through the fiscal purgatory that it did? I doubt it. What ultimately saved Hollywood and accounted for its resurgence was the wave of new young writers, producers, and directors whose previous successes in television had decimated the old movie companies and toppled the big movie moguls.

There are other, less obvious examples of industries that have been and are now endangering their futures by improperly defining their purposes. I shall discuss some of them in detail later and analyze the kind of policies that lead to trouble. Right now, it may help to show what a thoroughly customer-oriented management can do to keep a growth industry growing, even after the obvious opportunities have been exhausted, and here there are two examples that have been around for a long time. They are nylon and glass—specifically, E.I. du Pont de Nemours and Company and Corning Glass Works.

Both companies have great technical competence. Their product orientation is unquestioned. But this alone does not explain their success. After all, who was more pridefully product oriented and product conscious than the erstwhile New England textile companies that have been so thoroughly massacred? The DuPonts and the Cornings have succeeded not primarily because of their product or research

Idea in Brief

What business are you *really* in? A seemingly obvious question—but one we should all ask *before* demand for our companies' products or services dwindles.

The railroads failed to ask this same question—and stopped growing. Why? Not because people no longer needed transportation. And not because other innovations (cars, airplanes) filled transportation needs. Rather, railroads stopped growing because *railroads* didn't move to fill those needs. Their executives incorrectly thought that they were in the railroad business, not the transportation business. They viewed themselves as providing a product instead of serving customers. Too many other industries make the same mistake—putting themselves at risk of obsolescence.

How to ensure continued growth for your company? Concentrate on meeting customers' needs rather than selling products. Chemical powerhouse DuPont kept a close eye on its customers' most pressing concerns—and deployed its technical know-how to create an ever-expanding array of products that appealed to customers and continuously enlarged its market. If DuPont had merely found more uses for its flagship invention, nylon, it might not be around today.

orientation but because they have been thoroughly customer oriented also. It is constant watchfulness for opportunities to apply their technical know-how to the creation of customer-satisfying uses that accounts for their prodigious output of successful new products. Without a very sophisticated eye on the customer, most of their new products might have been wrong, their sales methods useless.

Aluminum has also continued to be a growth industry, thanks to the efforts of two wartime-created companies that deliberately set about inventing new customer-satisfying uses. Without Kaiser Aluminum & Chemical Corporation and Reynolds Metals Company, the total demand for aluminum today would be vastly less.

Error of analysis

Some may argue that it is foolish to set the railroads off against aluminum or the movies off against glass. Are not aluminum and glass naturally so versatile that the industries are bound to have more growth opportunities than the railroads and the movies? This view

Idea in Practice

We put our businesses at risk of obsolescence when we accept any of the following myths:

Myth 1: An ever-expanding and more affluent population will ensure our growth. When markets are expanding, we often assume we don't have to think imaginatively about our businesses. Instead, we seek to outdo rivals simply by improving on what we're already doing. The consequence: We increase the efficiency of *making* our products, rather than boosting the value those products deliver to customers.

Myth 2: There is no competitive substitute for our industry's major product. Believing that our products have no rivals makes our companies vulnerable to dramatic innovations from outside our industries—often by smaller, newer companies that are focusing on customer needs rather than the products themselves.

Myth 3: We can protect ourselves through mass production. Few of us can resist the prospect of the increased profits that come with steeply declining unit costs. But focusing on mass production emphasizes our *company's* needs—when we should be emphasizing our *customers'*.

Myth 4: Technical research and development will ensure our growth. When R&D produces breakthrough products, we may be tempted to organize our companies around the technology rather than the consumer. Instead, we should remain focused on satisfying customer needs.

commits precisely the error I have been talking about. It defines an industry or a product or a cluster of know-how so narrowly as to guarantee its premature senescence. When we mention "railroads," we should make sure we mean "transportation." As transporters, the railroads still have a good chance for very considerable growth. They are not limited to the railroad business as such (though in my opinion, rail transportation is potentially a much stronger transportation medium than is generally believed).

What the railroads lack is not opportunity but some of the managerial imaginativeness and audacity that made them great. Even an amateur like Jacques Barzun can see what is lacking when he says, "I grieve to see the most advanced physical and social organization of the last century go down in shabby disgrace for lack of the same comprehensive imagination that built it up. [What is lacking is] the will of the companies to survive and to satisfy the public by inventiveness and skill."[1]

Shadow of Obsolescence

It is impossible to mention a single major industry that did not at one time qualify for the magic appellation of "growth industry." In each case, the industry's assumed strength lay in the apparently unchallenged superiority of its product. There appeared to be no effective substitute for it. It was itself a runaway substitute for the product it so triumphantly replaced. Yet one after another of these celebrated industries has come under a shadow. Let us look briefly at a few more of them, this time taking examples that have so far received a little less attention.

Dry cleaning

This was once a growth industry with lavish prospects. In an age of wool garments, imagine being finally able to get them clean safely and easily. The boom was on. Yet here we are 30 years after the boom started, and the industry is in trouble. Where has the competition come from? From a better way of cleaning? No. It has come from synthetic fibers and chemical additives that have cut the need for dry cleaning. But this is only the beginning. Lurking in the wings and ready to make chemical dry cleaning totally obsolete is that powerful magician, ultrasonics.

Electric utilities

This is another one of those supposedly "no substitute" products that has been enthroned on a pedestal of invincible growth. When the incandescent lamp came along, kerosene lights were finished. Later, the waterwheel and the steam engine were cut to ribbons by the flexibility, reliability, simplicity, and just plain easy availability of electric motors. The prosperity of electric utilities continues to wax extravagant as the home is converted into a museum of electric gadgetry. How can anybody miss by investing in utilities, with no competition, nothing but growth ahead?

But a second look is not quite so comforting. A score of nonutility companies are well advanced toward developing a powerful chemical fuel cell, which could sit in some hidden closet of every home silently ticking off electric power. The electric lines that vulgarize so many neighborhoods would be eliminated. So would the endless demolition of streets and service interruptions during storms. Also on the horizon is solar energy, again pioneered by nonutility companies.

Who says that the utilities have no competition? They may be natural monopolies now, but tomorrow they may be natural deaths. To avoid this prospect, they too will have to develop fuel cells, solar energy, and other power sources. To survive, they themselves will have to plot the obsolescence of what now produces their livelihood.

Grocery stores

Many people find it hard to realize that there ever was a thriving establishment known as the "corner store." The supermarket took over with a powerful effectiveness. Yet the big food chains of the 1930s narrowly escaped being completely wiped out by the aggressive expansion of independent supermarkets. The first genuine supermarket was opened in 1930, in Jamaica, Long Island. By 1933, supermarkets were thriving in California, Ohio, Pennsylvania, and elsewhere. Yet the established chains pompously ignored them. When they chose to notice them, it was with such derisive descriptions as "cheapy," "horse-and-buggy," "cracker-barrel storekeeping," and "unethical opportunists."

The executive of one big chain announced at the time that he found it "hard to believe that people will drive for miles to shop for foods and sacrifice the personal service chains have perfected and to which [the consumer] is accustomed."[2] As late as 1936, the National Wholesale Grocers convention and the New Jersey Retail Grocers Association said there was nothing to fear. They said that the supers' narrow appeal to the price buyer limited the size of their market. They had to draw from miles around. When imitators came, there would be wholesale liquidations as volume fell. The high sales of the supers were said to be partly due to their novelty. People wanted convenient neighborhood grocers. If the neighborhood stores would "cooperate with their suppliers, pay attention to their costs, and improve their service," they would be able to weather the competition until it blew over.[3]

It never blew over. The chains discovered that survival required going into the supermarket business. This meant the wholesale destruction of their huge investments in corner store sites and in established distribution and merchandising methods. The companies with "the courage of their convictions" resolutely stuck to the corner store philosophy. They kept their pride but lost their shirts.

A self-deceiving cycle

But memories are short. For example, it is hard for people who today confidently hail the twin messiahs of electronics and chemicals to see how things could possibly go wrong with these galloping industries. They probably also cannot see how a reasonably sensible businessperson could have been as myopic as the famous Boston millionaire who early in the twentieth century unintentionally sentenced his heirs to poverty by stipulating that his entire estate be forever invested exclusively in electric streetcar securities. His posthumous declaration, "There will always be a big demand for efficient urban transportation," is no consolation to his heirs, who sustain life by pumping gasoline at automobile filling stations.

Yet, in a casual survey I took among a group of intelligent business executives, nearly half agreed that it would be hard to hurt their heirs by tying their estates forever to the electronics industry. When I then confronted them with the Boston streetcar example, they chorused unanimously, "That's different!" But is it? Is not the basic situation identical?

In truth, *there is no such thing as a growth industry,* I believe. There are only companies organized and operated to create and capitalize on growth opportunities. Industries that assume themselves to be riding some automatic growth escalator invariably descend into stagnation. The history of every dead and dying "growth" industry shows a self-deceiving cycle of bountiful expansion and undetected decay. There are four conditions that usually guarantee this cycle:

1. The belief that growth is assured by an expanding and more affluent population;
2. The belief that there is no competitive substitute for the industry's major product;
3. Too much faith in mass production and in the advantages of rapidly declining unit costs as output rises;
4. Preoccupation with a product that lends itself to carefully controlled scientific experimentation, improvement, and manufacturing cost reduction.

I should like now to examine each of these conditions in some detail. To build my case as boldly as possible, I shall illustrate the points with reference to three industries: petroleum, automobiles, and electronics. I'll focus on petroleum in particular, because it spans more years and more vicissitudes. Not only do these three industries have excellent reputations with the general public and also enjoy the confidence of sophisticated investors, but their managements have become known for progressive thinking in areas like financial control, product research, and management training. If obsolescence can cripple even these industries, it can happen anywhere.

Population Myth

The belief that profits are assured by an expanding and more affluent population is dear to the heart of every industry. It takes the edge off the apprehensions everybody understandably feels about the future. If consumers are multiplying and also buying more of your product or service, you can face the future with considerably more comfort than if the market were shrinking. An expanding market keeps the manufacturer from having to think very hard or imaginatively. If thinking is an intellectual response to a problem, then the absence of a problem leads to the absence of thinking. If your product has an automatically expanding market, then you will not give much thought to how to expand it.

One of the most interesting examples of this is provided by the petroleum industry. Probably our oldest growth industry, it has an enviable record. While there are some current concerns about its growth rate, the industry itself tends to be optimistic.

But I believe it can be demonstrated that it is undergoing a fundamental yet typical change. It is not only ceasing to be a growth industry but may actually be a declining one, relative to other businesses. Although there is widespread unawareness of this fact, it is conceivable that in time, the oil industry may find itself in much the same position of retrospective glory that the railroads are now in. Despite its pioneering work in developing and applying the present-value method of investment evaluation, in employee relations, and in working with developing countries, the petroleum business is a distressing example of how complacency and wrongheadedness can stubbornly convert opportunity into near disaster.

One of the characteristics of this and other industries that have believed very strongly in the beneficial consequences of an expanding population, while at the same time having a generic product for which there has appeared to be no competitive substitute, is that the individual companies have sought to outdo their competitors by improving on what they are already doing. This makes sense, of course, if one assumes that sales are tied to the country's population strings, because the customer can compare products only on a feature-by-feature basis. I believe it is significant, for example, that not since John D. Rockefeller sent free kerosene lamps to China has the oil industry done anything really outstanding to create a demand for its product. Not even in product improvement has it showered itself with eminence. The greatest single improvement—the development of tetraethyl lead—came from outside the industry, specifically from General Motors and DuPont. The big contributions made by the industry itself are confined to the technology of oil exploration, oil production, and oil refining.

Asking for trouble

In other words, the petroleum industry's efforts have focused on improving the *efficiency* of getting and making its product, not really on improving the generic product or its marketing. Moreover, its chief product has continually been defined in the narrowest possible terms—namely, gasoline, not energy, fuel, or transportation. This attitude has helped assure that:

- Major improvements in gasoline quality tend not to originate in the oil industry. The development of superior alternative fuels also comes from outside the oil industry, as will be shown later.
- Major innovations in automobile fuel marketing come from small, new oil companies that are not primarily preoccupied with production or refining. These are the companies that have been responsible for the rapidly expanding multipump gasoline stations, with their successful emphasis on large and clean layouts, rapid and efficient driveway service, and quality gasoline at low prices.

Thus, the oil industry is asking for trouble from outsiders. Sooner or later, in this land of hungry investors and entrepreneurs, a threat is sure to come. The possibility of this will become more apparent when we turn to the next dangerous belief of many managements. For the sake of continuity, because this second belief is tied closely to the first, I shall continue with the same example.

The idea of indispensability

The petroleum industry is pretty much convinced that there is no competitive substitute for its major product, gasoline—or, if there is, that it will continue to be a derivative of crude oil, such as diesel fuel or kerosene jet fuel.

There is a lot of automatic wishful thinking in this assumption. The trouble is that most refining companies own huge amounts of crude oil reserves. These have value only if there is a market for products into which oil can be converted. Hence the tenacious belief in the continuing competitive superiority of automobile fuels made from crude oil.

This idea persists despite all historic evidence against it. The evidence not only shows that oil has never been a superior product for any purpose for very long but also that the oil industry has never really been a growth industry. Rather, it has been a succession of different businesses that have gone through the usual historic cycles of growth, maturity, and decay. The industry's overall survival is owed to a series of miraculous escapes from total obsolescence, of last-minute and unexpected reprieves from total disaster reminiscent of the perils of Pauline.

The perils of petroleum

To illustrate, I shall sketch in only the main episodes. First, crude oil was largely a patent medicine. But even before that fad ran out, demand was greatly expanded by the use of oil in kerosene lamps. The prospect of lighting the world's lamps gave rise to an extravagant promise of growth. The prospects were similar to those the industry now holds for gasoline in other parts of the world. It can hardly wait for the underdeveloped nations to get a car in every garage.

In the days of the kerosene lamp, the oil companies competed with each other and against gaslight by trying to improve the illuminating characteristics of kerosene. Then suddenly the impossible happened. Edison invented a light that was totally nondependent on crude oil. Had it not been for the growing use of kerosene in space heaters, the incandescent lamp would have completely finished oil as a growth industry at that time. Oil would have been good for little else than axle grease.

Then disaster and reprieve struck again. Two great innovations occurred, neither originating in the oil industry. First, the successful development of coal-burning domestic central-heating systems made the space heater obsolete. While the industry reeled, along came its most magnificent boost yet: the internal combustion engine, also invented by outsiders. Then, when the prodigious expansion for gasoline finally began to level off in the 1920s, along came the miraculous escape of the central oil heater. Once again, the escape was provided by an outsider's invention and development. And when that market weakened, wartime demand for aviation fuel came to the rescue. After the war, the expansion of civilian aviation, the dieselization of railroads, and the explosive demand for cars and trucks kept the industry's growth in high gear.

Meanwhile, centralized oil heating—whose boom potential had only recently been proclaimed—ran into severe competition from natural gas. While the oil companies themselves owned the gas that now competed with their oil, the industry did not originate the natural gas revolution, nor has it to this day greatly profited from its gas ownership. The gas revolution was made by newly formed transmission companies that marketed the product with an aggressive ardor. They started a magnificent new industry, first against the advice and then against the resistance of the oil companies.

By all the logic of the situation, the oil companies themselves should have made the gas revolution. They not only owned the gas, they also were the only people experienced in handling, scrubbing, and using it and the only people experienced in pipeline technology and transmission. They also understood heating problems. But, partly because they knew that natural gas would compete with their own sale of heating oil, the oil companies pooh-poohed the potential of gas. The revolution was finally started by oil pipeline executives who, unable to persuade their own companies to go into gas, quit and organized the spectacularly successful gas transmission companies. Even after their success became painfully evident to the oil companies, the latter did not go into gas transmission. The multibillion-dollar business that should have been theirs went to others. As in the past, the industry was blinded by its narrow preoccupation with a specific product and the value of its reserves. It paid little or no attention to its customers' basic needs and preferences.

The postwar years have not witnessed any change. Immediately after World War II, the oil industry was greatly encouraged about its future by the rapid increase in demand for its traditional line of products. In 1950, most companies projected annual rates of domestic expansion of around 6% through at least 1975. Though the ratio of crude oil reserves to demand in the free world was about 20 to 1, with 10 to 1 being usually considered a reasonable working ratio in the United States, booming demand sent oil explorers searching for more without sufficient regard to what the future really promised. In 1952, they "hit" in the Middle East; the ratio skyrocketed to 42 to 1. If gross additions to reserves continue at the average rate of the past five years (37 billion barrels annually), then by 1970, the reserve ratio will be up to 45 to 1. This abundance of oil has weakened crude and product prices all over the world.

An uncertain future

Management cannot find much consolation today in the rapidly expanding petrochemical industry, another oil-using idea that did not originate in the leading firms. The total U.S. production of petrochemicals is equivalent to about 2% (by volume) of the demand for all petroleum products. Although the petrochemical industry is now expected to grow by about 10% per year, this will not offset other drains on the growth of crude oil consumption. Furthermore, while petrochemical products are many and growing, it is important to remember that there are nonpetroleum sources of the basic raw material, such as coal. Besides, a lot of plastics can be produced with relatively little oil. A 50,000-barrel-per-day oil refinery is now considered the absolute minimum size for efficiency. But a 5,000-barrel-per-day chemical plant is a giant operation.

Oil has never been a continuously strong growth industry. It has grown by fits and starts, always miraculously saved by innovations and developments not of its own making. The reason it has not grown in a smooth progression is that each time it thought it had a superior product safe from the possibility of competitive substitutes, the product turned out to be inferior and notoriously subject to obsolescence. Until now, gasoline (for motor fuel, anyhow) has escaped this fate. But, as we shall see later, it too may be on its last legs.

The point of all this is that there is no guarantee against product obsolescence. If a company's own research does not make a product obsolete, another's will. Unless an industry is especially lucky, as oil has been until now, it can easily go down in a sea of red figures—just as the railroads have, as the buggy whip manufacturers have, as the corner grocery chains have, as most of the big movie companies have, and, indeed, as many other industries have.

The best way for a firm to be lucky is to make its own luck. That requires knowing what makes a business successful. One of the greatest enemies of this knowledge is mass production.

Production Pressures

Mass production industries are impelled by a great drive to produce all they can. The prospect of steeply declining unit costs as output rises is more than most companies can usually resist. The profit possibilities look spectacular. All effort focuses on production. The result is that marketing gets neglected.

John Kenneth Galbraith contends that just the opposite occurs.[4] Output is so prodigious that all effort concentrates on trying to get rid of it. He says this accounts for singing commercials, the desecration of the countryside with advertising signs, and other wasteful and vulgar practices. Galbraith has a finger on something real, but he misses the strategic point. Mass production does indeed generate great pressure to "move" the product. But what usually gets emphasized is selling, not marketing. Marketing, a more sophisticated and complex process, gets ignored.

The difference between marketing and selling is more than semantic. Selling focuses on the needs of the seller, marketing on the needs of the buyer. Selling is preoccupied with the seller's need to convert the product into cash, marketing with the idea of satisfying the needs of the customer by means of the product and the whole cluster of things associated with creating, delivering, and, finally, consuming it.

In some industries, the enticements of full mass production have been so powerful that top management in effect has told the sales department, "You get rid of it; we'll worry about profits." By contrast, a truly marketing-minded firm tries to create value-satisfying goods and services that consumers will want to buy. What it offers for sale includes not only the generic product or service but also how it is made available to the customer, in what form, when, under what conditions, and at what terms of trade. Most important, what it offers for sale is determined not by the seller but by the buyer. The seller takes cues from the buyer in such a way that the product becomes a consequence of the marketing effort, not vice versa.

A lag in Detroit

This may sound like an elementary rule of business, but that does not keep it from being violated wholesale. It is certainly more violated than honored. Take the automobile industry.

Here mass production is most famous, most honored, and has the greatest impact on the entire society. The industry has hitched its fortune to the relentless requirements of the annual model change, a policy that makes customer orientation an especially urgent necessity. Consequently, the auto companies annually spend millions of dollars on consumer research. But the fact that the new compact cars are selling so well in their first year indicates that Detroit's vast researches have for a long time failed to reveal what customers really wanted. Detroit was not convinced that people wanted anything different from what they had been getting until it lost millions of customers to other small-car manufacturers.

How could this unbelievable lag behind consumer wants have been perpetuated for so long? Why did not research reveal consumer preferences before consumers' buying decisions themselves revealed the facts? Is that not what consumer research is for—to find out before the fact what is going to happen? The answer is that Detroit never really researched customers' wants. It only researched their preferences between the kinds of things it had already decided to offer them. For Detroit is mainly product oriented, not customer oriented. To the extent that the customer is recognized as having needs that the manufacturer should try to satisfy, Detroit usually acts as if the job can be done entirely by product changes. Occasionally, attention gets paid to financing, too, but that is done more in order to sell than to enable the customer to buy.

As for taking care of other customer needs, there is not enough being done to write about. The areas of the greatest unsatisfied needs are ignored or, at best, get stepchild attention. These are at the point of sale and on the matter of automotive repair and maintenance. Detroit views these problem areas as being of secondary importance. That is underscored by the fact that the retailing and servicing ends of this industry are neither owned and operated nor controlled by the manufacturers. Once the car is produced, things are pretty much in the dealer's inadequate hands. Illustrative of Detroit's arms-length attitude is the fact that, while servicing holds enormous sales-stimulating, profit-building opportunities, only 57 of Chevrolet's 7,000 dealers provide night maintenance service.

Motorists repeatedly express their dissatisfaction with servicing and their apprehensions about buying cars under the present selling setup. The anxieties and problems they encounter during the auto buying and maintenance processes are probably more intense and widespread today than many years ago. Yet the automobile companies do not seem to listen to or take their cues from the anguished consumer. If they do listen, it must be through the filter of their own preoccupation with production. The marketing effort is still viewed as a necessary consequence of the product—not vice versa, as it should be. That is the legacy of mass production, with its parochial view that profit resides essentially in low-cost full production.

What Ford put first

The profit lure of mass production obviously has a place in the plans and strategy of business management, but it must always *follow* hard thinking about the customer. This is one of the most important lessons we can learn from the contradictory behavior of Henry Ford. In a sense, Ford was both the most brilliant and the most senseless marketer in American history. He was senseless because he refused to give the customer anything but a black car. He was brilliant because he fashioned a production system designed to fit market needs. We habitually celebrate him for the wrong reason: for his production genius. His real genius was marketing. We think he was able to cut his selling price and therefore sell millions of $500 cars because his invention of the assembly line had reduced the costs. Actually, he invented the assembly line because he had concluded that at $500 he could sell millions of cars. Mass production was the *result,* not the cause, of his low prices.

Ford emphasized this point repeatedly, but a nation of production-oriented business managers refuses to hear the great lesson he taught. Here is his operating philosophy as he expressed it succinctly:

> Our policy is to reduce the price, extend the operations, and improve the article. You will notice that the reduction of price comes first. We have never considered any costs as fixed. Therefore we first reduce the price to the point where we believe more sales will result. Then we go ahead and try to make the prices. We do not bother about the costs. The new price forces the costs down. The more usual way is to take the costs and then determine the price; and although that method may be scientific in the narrow sense, it is not scientific in the broad sense, because what earthly use is it to know the cost if it tells you that you cannot manufacture at a price at which the article can be sold? But more to the point is the fact that, although one may calculate what a cost is, and of course all of our costs are carefully calculated, no one knows what a cost ought to be. One of the ways of discovering . . . is to name a price so low as to force everybody in the place to the highest point of efficiency. The low price makes everybody dig for profits. We make more discoveries concerning manufacturing and selling under this forced method than by any method of leisurely investigation.[5]

Product provincialism

The tantalizing profit possibilities of low unit production costs may be the most seriously self-deceiving attitude that can afflict a company, particularly a "growth" company, where an apparently assured expansion of demand already tends to undermine a proper concern for the importance of marketing and the customer.

The usual result of this narrow preoccupation with so-called concrete matters is that instead of growing, the industry declines. It usually means that the product fails to adapt to the constantly changing patterns of consumer needs and tastes, to new and modified marketing institutions and practices, or to product developments in competing or complementary industries. The industry has its eyes so firmly on its own specific product that it does not see how it is being made obsolete.

The classic example of this is the buggy whip industry. No amount of product improvement could stave off its death sentence. But had the industry defined itself as being in the transportation business rather than in the buggy whip business, it might have survived. It would have done what survival always entails—that is, change. Even if it had only defined its business as providing a stimulant or catalyst to an energy source, it might have survived by becoming a manufacturer of, say, fan belts or air cleaners.

What may someday be a still more classic example is, again, the oil industry. Having let others steal marvelous opportunities from it (including natural gas, as already mentioned; missile fuels; and jet engine lubricants), one would expect it to have taken steps never to let that happen again. But this is not the case. We are now seeing extraordinary new developments in fuel systems specifically designed to power automobiles. Not only are these developments concentrated in firms outside the petroleum industry, but petroleum is almost systematically ignoring them, securely content in its wedded bliss to oil. It is the story of the kerosene lamp versus the incandescent lamp all over again. Oil is trying to improve hydrocarbon fuels rather than develop *any* fuels best suited to the needs of their users, whether or not made in different ways and with different raw materials from oil.

Here are some things that nonpetroleum companies are working on. More than a dozen such firms now have advanced working models of energy systems which, when perfected, will replace the internal combustion engine and eliminate the demand for gasoline. The superior merit of each of these systems is their elimination of frequent, time-consuming, and irritating refueling stops. Most of these systems are fuel cells designed to create electrical energy directly from chemicals without combustion. Most of them use chemicals that are not derived from oil—generally, hydrogen and oxygen.

Several other companies have advanced models of electric storage batteries designed to power automobiles. One of these is an aircraft producer that is working jointly with several electric utility companies. The latter hope to use off-peak generating capacity to supply overnight plug-in battery regeneration. Another company, also using the battery approach, is a medium-sized electronics firm with extensive small-battery experience that it developed in connection with its work on hearing aids. It is collaborating with an automobile manufacturer. Recent improvements arising from the need for high-powered miniature power storage plants in rockets have put us within reach of a relatively small battery capable of withstanding great overloads or surges of power. Germanium diode applications and batteries using sintered plate and nickel cadmium techniques promise to make a revolution in our energy sources.

Solar energy conversion systems are also getting increasing attention. One usually cautious Detroit auto executive recently ventured that solar-powered cars might be common by 1980.

As for the oil companies, they are more or less "watching developments," as one research director put it to me. A few are doing a bit of research on fuel cells, but this research is almost always confined to developing cells powered by hydrocarbon chemicals. None of them is enthusiastically researching fuel cells, batteries, or solar power plants. None of them is spending a fraction as much on research in these profoundly important areas as it is on the usual run-of-the-mill things like reducing combustion chamber deposits in gasoline engines. One major integrated petroleum company recently took a tentative look at the fuel cell and concluded that although "the companies actively working on it indicate a belief in ultimate success . . . the timing and magnitude of its impact are too remote to warrant recognition in our forecasts."

One might, of course, ask, Why should the oil companies do anything different? Would not chemical fuel cells, batteries, or solar energy kill the present product lines? The answer is that they would indeed, and that is precisely the reason for the oil firms' having to develop these power units before their competitors do, so they will not be companies without an industry.

Management might be more likely to do what is needed for its own preservation if it thought of itself as being in the energy business. But even that will not be enough if it persists in imprisoning itself in the narrow grip of its tight product orientation. It has to think of itself as taking care of customer needs, not finding, refining, or even selling oil. Once it genuinely thinks of its business as taking care of people's transportation needs, nothing can stop it from creating its own extravagantly profitable growth.

Creative destruction

Since words are cheap and deeds are dear, it may be appropriate to indicate what this kind of thinking involves and leads to. Let us start at the beginning: the customer. It can be shown that motorists strongly dislike the bother, delay, and experience of buying gasoline. People actually do not buy gasoline. They cannot see it, taste it, feel it, appreciate it, or really test it. What they buy is the right to continue driving their cars. The gas station is like a tax collector to whom people are compelled to pay a periodic toll as the price of using their cars. This makes the gas station a basically unpopular institution. It can never be made popular or pleasant, only less unpopular, less unpleasant.

Reducing its unpopularity completely means eliminating it. Nobody likes a tax collector, not even a pleasantly cheerful one. Nobody likes to interrupt a trip to buy a phantom product, not even from a handsome Adonis or a seductive Venus. Hence, companies that are working on exotic fuel substitutes that will eliminate the need for frequent refueling are heading directly into the outstretched arms of the irritated motorist. They are riding a wave of inevitability, not because they are creating something that is technologically superior or more sophisticated but because they are satisfying a powerful customer need. They are also eliminating noxious odors and air pollution.

Once the petroleum companies recognize the customer-satisfying logic of what another power system can do, they will see that they have no more choice about working on an efficient, long-lasting fuel (or some way of delivering present fuels without bothering the motorist) than the big food chains had a choice about going into the supermarket business or the vacuum tube companies had a choice about making semiconductors. For their own good, the oil firms will have to destroy their own highly profitable assets. No amount of wishful thinking can save them from the necessity of engaging in this form of "creative destruction."

I phrase the need as strongly as this because I think management must make quite an effort to break itself loose from conventional ways. It is all too easy in this day and age for a company or industry to let its sense of purpose become dominated by the economies of full production and to develop a dangerously lopsided product orientation. In short, if management lets itself drift, it invariably drifts in the direction of thinking of itself as producing goods and services, not customer satisfactions. While it probably will not descend to the depths of telling its salespeople, "You get rid of it; we'll worry about profits," it can, without knowing it, be practicing precisely that formula for withering decay. The historic fate of one growth industry after another has been its suicidal product provincialism.

Dangers of R&D

Another big danger to a firm's continued growth arises when top management is wholly transfixed by the profit possibilities of technical research and development. To illustrate, I shall turn first to a new industry—electronics—and then return once more to the oil companies. By comparing a fresh example with a familiar one, I hope to emphasize the prevalence and insidiousness of a hazardous way of thinking.

Marketing shortchanged

In the case of electronics, the greatest danger that faces the glamorous new companies in this field is not that they do not pay enough attention to research and development but that they pay too much attention to it. And the fact that the fastest-growing electronics firms owe their eminence to their heavy emphasis on technical research is completely beside the point. They have vaulted to affluence on a sudden crest of unusually strong general receptiveness to new technical ideas. Also, their success has been shaped in the virtually guaranteed market of military subsidies and by military orders that in many cases actually preceded the existence of facilities to make the products. Their expansion has, in other words, been almost totally devoid of marketing effort.

Thus, they are growing up under conditions that come dangerously close to creating the illusion that a superior product will sell itself. It is not surprising that, having created a successful company by making a superior product, management continues to be oriented toward the product rather than the people who consume it. It develops the philosophy that continued growth is a matter of continued product innovation and improvement.

A number of other factors tend to strengthen and sustain this belief:

1. Because electronic products are highly complex and sophisticated, managements become top-heavy with engineers and scientists. This creates a selective bias in favor of research and production at the expense of marketing. The organization tends to view itself as making things rather than as satisfying customer needs. Marketing gets treated as a residual activity, "something else" that must be done once the vital job of product creation and production is completed.

2. To this bias in favor of product research, development, and production is added the bias in favor of dealing with controllable variables. Engineers and scientists are at home in the world of concrete things like machines, test tubes, production lines, and even balance sheets. The abstractions to which they feel kindly are those that are testable or manipulatable in the laboratory or, if not testable, then functional, such as Euclid's axioms. In short, the managements of the new glamour-growth companies tend to favor business activities that lend themselves to careful study, experimentation, and control—the hard, practical realities of the lab, the shop, and the books.

What gets shortchanged are the realities of the *market*. Consumers are unpredictable, varied, fickle, stupid, shortsighted, stubborn, and generally bothersome. This is not what the engineer managers say, but deep down in their consciousness, it is what they believe. And this accounts for their concentration on what they know and what they can control—namely, product research, engineering, and production. The emphasis on production becomes particularly attractive when the product can be made at declining unit costs. There is no more inviting way of making money than by running the plant full blast.

The top-heavy science-engineering-production orientation of so many electronics companies works reasonably well today because they are pushing into new frontiers in which the armed services have pioneered virtually assured markets. The companies are in the felicitous position of having to fill, not find, markets, of not having to discover what the customer needs and wants but of having the customer voluntarily come forward with specific new product demands. If a team of consultants had been assigned specifically to design a business situation calculated to prevent the emergence and development of a customer-oriented marketing viewpoint, it could not have produced anything better than the conditions just described.

Stepchild treatment

The oil industry is a stunning example of how science, technology, and mass production can divert an entire group of companies from their main task. To the extent the consumer is studied at all (which is not much), the focus is forever on getting information that is designed to help the oil companies improve what they are now doing. They try to discover more convincing advertising themes, more effective sales promotional drives, what the market shares of the various companies are, what people like or dislike about service station dealers and oil companies, and so forth. Nobody seems as interested in probing deeply into the basic human needs that the industry might be trying to satisfy as in probing into the basic properties of the raw material that the companies work with in trying to deliver customer satisfactions.

Basic questions about customers and markets seldom get asked. The latter occupy a stepchild status. They are recognized as existing, as having to be taken care of, but not worth very much real thought or dedicated attention. No oil company gets as excited about the customers in its own backyard as about the oil in the Sahara Desert. Nothing illustrates better the neglect of marketing than its treatment in the industry press.

The centennial issue of the *American Petroleum Institute Quarterly,* published in 1959 to celebrate the discovery of oil in Titusville, Pennsylvania, contained 21 feature articles proclaiming the industry's greatness. Only one of these talked about its achievements in marketing, and that was only a pictorial record of how service station architecture has changed. The issue also contained a special section on "New Horizons," which was devoted to showing the magnificent role oil would play in America's future. Every reference was ebulliently optimistic, never implying once that oil might have some hard competition. Even the reference to atomic energy was a cheerful catalog of how oil would help make atomic energy a success. There was not a single apprehension that the oil industry's affluence might be threatened or a suggestion that one "new horizon" might include new and better ways of serving oil's present customers.

But the most revealing example of the stepchild treatment that marketing gets is still another special series of short articles on "The Revolutionary Potential of Electronics." Under that heading, this list of articles appeared in the table of contents:

- "In the Search for Oil"
- "In Production Operations"
- "In Refinery Processes"
- "In Pipeline Operations"

Significantly, every one of the industry's major functional areas is listed, *except* marketing. Why? Either it is believed that electronics holds no revolutionary potential for petroleum marketing (which is palpably wrong), or the editors forgot to discuss marketing (which is more likely and illustrates its stepchild status).

The order in which the four functional areas are listed also betrays the alienation of the oil industry from the consumer. The industry is implicitly defined as beginning with the search for oil and ending with its distribution from the refinery. But the truth is, it seems to me, that the industry begins with the needs of the customer for its products. From that primal position its definition moves steadily back stream to areas of progressively lesser importance until it finally comes to rest at the search for oil.

The beginning and end

The view that an industry is a customer-satisfying process, not a goods-producing process, is vital for all businesspeople to understand. An industry begins with the customer and his or her needs, not with a patent, a raw material, or a selling skill. Given the customer's needs, the industry develops backwards, first concerning itself with the physical *delivery* of customer satisfactions. Then it moves back further to *creating* the things by which these satisfactions are in part achieved. How these materials are created is a matter of indifference to the customer, hence the particular form of manufacturing, processing, or what have you cannot be considered as a vital aspect of the industry. Finally, the industry moves back still further to *finding* the raw materials necessary for making its products.

The irony of some industries oriented toward technical research and development is that the scientists who occupy the high executive positions are totally unscientific when it comes to defining their companies' overall needs and purposes. They violate the first two rules of the scientific method: being aware of and defining their companies' problems and then developing testable hypotheses about solving them. They are scientific only about the convenient things, such as laboratory and product experiments.

The customer (and the satisfaction of his or her deepest needs) is not considered to be "the problem"—not because there is any certain belief that no such problem exists but because an organizational lifetime has conditioned management to look in the opposite direction. Marketing is a stepchild.

I do not mean that selling is ignored. Far from it. But selling, again, is not marketing. As already pointed out, selling concerns itself with the tricks and techniques of getting people to exchange their cash for your product. It is not concerned with the values that the exchange is all about. And it does not, as marketing invariably does, view the entire business process as consisting of a tightly integrated effort to discover, create, arouse, and satisfy customer needs. The customer is somebody "out there" who, with proper cunning, can be separated from his or her loose change.

Actually, not even selling gets much attention in some technologically minded firms. Because there is a virtually guaranteed market for the abundant flow of their new products, they do not actually know what a real market is. It is as if they lived in a planned economy, moving their products routinely from factory to retail outlet. Their successful concentration on products tends to convince them of the soundness of what they have been doing, and they fail to see the gathering clouds over the market.

Less than 75 years ago, American railroads enjoyed a fierce loyalty among astute Wall Streeters. European monarchs invested in them heavily. Eternal wealth was thought to be the benediction for anybody who could scrape together a few thousand dollars to put into rail stocks. No other form of transportation could compete with the railroads in speed, flexibility, durability, economy, and growth potentials.

As Jacques Barzun put it, "By the turn of the century it was an institution, an image of man, a tradition, a code of honor, a source of poetry, a nursery of boyhood desires, a sublimest of toys, and the most solemn machine—next to the funeral hearse—that marks the epochs in man's life."[6]

Even after the advent of automobiles, trucks, and airplanes, the railroad tycoons remained imperturbably self-confident. If you had told them 60 years ago that in 30 years they would be flat on their backs, broke, and pleading for government subsidies, they would have thought you totally demented. Such a future was simply not considered possible. It was not even a discussable subject, or an askable question, or a matter that any sane person would consider worth speculating about. Yet a lot of "insane" notions now have matter-of-fact acceptance—for example, the idea of 100-ton tubes of metal moving smoothly through the air 20,000 feet above the earth, loaded with 100 sane and solid citizens casually drinking martinis—and they have dealt cruel blows to the railroads.

What specifically must other companies do to avoid this fate? What does customer orientation involve? These questions have in part been answered by the preceding examples and analysis. It would take another article to show in detail what is required for specific industries. In any case, it should be obvious that building an effective customer-oriented company involves far more than good intentions or promotional tricks; it involves profound matters of human organization and leadership. For the present, let me merely suggest what appear to be some general requirements.

The visceral feel of greatness

Obviously, the company has to do what survival demands. It has to adapt to the requirements of the market, and it has to do it sooner rather than later. But mere survival is a so-so aspiration. Anybody can survive in some way or other, even the skid row bum. The trick is to survive gallantly, to feel the surging impulse of commercial mastery: not just to experience the sweet smell of success but to have the visceral feel of entrepreneurial greatness.

No organization can achieve greatness without a vigorous leader who is driven onward by a pulsating *will to succeed*. A leader has to have a vision of grandeur, a vision that can produce eager followers in vast numbers. In business, the followers are the customers.

In order to produce these customers, the entire corporation must be viewed as a customer-creating and customer-satisfying organism. Management must think of itself not as producing products but as providing customer-creating value satisfactions. It must push this idea (and everything it means and requires) into every nook and cranny of the organization. It has to do this continuously and with the kind of flair that excites and stimulates the people in it. Otherwise, the company will be merely a series of pigeonholed parts, with no consolidating sense of purpose or direction.

In short, the organization must learn to think of itself not as producing goods or services but as *buying customers,* as doing the things that will make people *want* to do business with it. And the chief executive has the inescapable responsibility for creating this environment, this viewpoint, this attitude, this aspiration. The chief executive must set the company's style, its direction, and its goals. This means knowing precisely where he or she wants to go and making sure the whole organization is enthusiastically aware of where that is. This is a first requisite of leadership, for *unless a leader knows where he is going, any road will take him there.*

If any road is okay, the chief executive might as well pack his 179
attaché case and go fishing. If an organization does not know or care where it is going, it does not need to advertise that fact with a ceremonial figurehead. Everybody will notice it soon enough.

Originally published in 1960. Reprint R0407L

Notes

1. Jacques Barzun, "Trains and the Mind of Man," *Holiday,* February 1960.
2. For more details, see M.M. Zimmerman, *The Super Market: A Revolution in Distribution* (McGraw-Hill, 1955).
3. Ibid., pp. 45–47.
4. John Kenneth Galbraith, *The Affluent Society* (Houghton Mifflin, 1958).
5. Henry Ford, *My Life and Work* (Doubleday, 1923).
6. Barzun, "Trains and the Mind of Man."

What Is Strategy?

by Michael E. Porter

I. Operational Effectiveness Is Not Strategy

For almost two decades, managers have been learning to play by a new set of rules. Companies must be flexible to respond rapidly to competitive and market changes. They must benchmark continuously to achieve best practice. They must outsource aggressively to gain efficiencies. And they must nurture a few core competencies in race to stay ahead of rivals.

Positioning—once the heart of strategy—is rejected as too static for today's dynamic markets and changing technologies. According to the new dogma, rivals can quickly copy any market position, and competitive advantage is, at best, temporary.

But those beliefs are dangerous half-truths, and they are leading more and more companies down the path of mutually destructive competition. True, some barriers to competition are falling as regulation eases and markets become global. True, companies have properly invested energy in becoming leaner and more nimble. In many industries, however, what some call *hypercompetition* is a self-inflicted wound, not the inevitable outcome of a changing paradigm of competition.

The root of the problem is the failure to distinguish between operational effectiveness and strategy. The quest for productivity, quality, and speed has spawned a remarkable number of management tools and techniques: total quality management, benchmarking, time-based competition, outsourcing, partnering, reengineering, change management. Although the resulting operational improvements have often been dramatic, many companies have been frustrated by their inability to translate those gains into sustainable profitability. And bit by bit, almost imperceptibly, management tools have taken the place of strategy. As managers push to improve on all fronts, they move farther away from viable competitive positions.

Operational effectiveness: necessary but not sufficient

Operational effectiveness and strategy are both essential to superior performance, which, after all, is the primary goal of any enterprise. But they work in very different ways.

A company can outperform rivals only if it can establish a difference that it can preserve. It must deliver greater value to customers or create comparable value at a lower cost, or do both. The arithmetic of superior profitability then follows: delivering greater value allows a company to charge higher average unit prices; greater efficiency results in lower average unit costs.

Ultimately, all differences between companies in cost or price derive from the hundreds of activities required to create, produce, sell, and deliver their products or services, such as calling on customers, assembling final products, and training employees. Cost is generated by performing activities, and cost advantage arises from performing particular activities more efficiently than competitors. Similarly, differentiation arises from both the choice of activities and how they are performed. Activities, then, are the basic units of competitive advantage. Overall advantage or disadvantage results from all a company's activities, not only a few.[1]

Operational effectiveness (OE) means performing similar activities *better* than rivals perform them. Operational effectiveness includes but is not limited to efficiency. It refers to any number of practices that allow a company to better utilize its inputs by, for example, reducing defects in products or developing better products faster. In contrast, strategic positioning means performing *different* activities from rivals' or performing similar activities in *different* ways.

Differences in operational effectiveness among companies are pervasive. Some companies are able to get more out of their inputs

Idea in Brief

The myriad activities that go into creating, producing, selling, and delivering a product or service are the basic units of competitive advantage. **Operational effectiveness** means performing these activities better—that is, faster, or with fewer inputs and defects—than rivals. Companies can reap enormous advantages from operational effectiveness, as Japanese firms demonstrated in the 1970s and 1980s with such practices as total quality management and continuous improvement. But from a competitive standpoint, the problem with operational effectiveness is that best practices are easily emulated. As all competitors in an industry adopt them, the **productivity frontier**—the maximum value a company can deliver at a given cost, given the best available technology, skills, and management techniques—shifts outward, lowering costs and improving value at the same time. Such competition produces absolute improvement in operational effectiveness, but relative improvement for no one. And the more benchmarking that companies do, the more **competitive convergence** you have—that is, the more indistinguishable companies are from one another.

Strategic positioning attempts to achieve sustainable competitive advantage by preserving what is distinctive about a company. It means performing *different* activities from rivals, or performing *similar* activities in different ways.

than others because they eliminate wasted effort, employ more advanced technology, motivate employees better, or have greater insight into managing particular activities or sets of activities. Such differences in operational effectiveness are an important source of differences in profitability among competitors because they directly affect relative cost positions and levels of differentiation.

Differences in operational effectiveness were at the heart of the Japanese challenge to Western companies in the 1980s. The Japanese were so far ahead of rivals in operational effectiveness that they could offer lower cost and superior quality at the same time. It is worth dwelling on this point, because so much recent thinking about competition depends on it. Imagine for a moment a *productivity frontier* that constitutes the sum of all existing best practices at any given time. Think of it as the maximum value that a

Idea in Practice

Three key principles underlie strategic positioning.

1. **Strategy is the creation of a unique and valuable position, involving a different set of activities.** Strategic position emerges from three distinct sources:
   - serving few needs of many customers (Jiffy Lube provides only auto lubricants)
   - serving broad needs of few customers (Bessemer Trust targets only very high-wealth clients)
   - serving broad needs of many customers in a narrow market (Carmike Cinemas operates only in cities with a population under 200,000)
2. **Strategy requires you to make trade-offs in competing—to choose what *not* to do.** Some competitive activities are incompatible; thus, gains in one area can be achieved only at the expense of another area. For example, Neutrogena soap is positioned more as a medicinal product than as a cleansing agent. The company says "no" to sales based on deodorizing, gives up large volume, and sacrifices manufacturing efficiencies. By contrast, Maytag's decision to extend its product line and acquire other brands represented a failure to make difficult trade-offs: the boost in revenues came at the expense of return on sales.
3. **Strategy involves creating "fit" among a company's activities.** Fit has to do with the ways a company's activities interact and reinforce one another. For example, Vanguard Group aligns all of its activities with a low-cost strategy; it distributes funds directly to consumers and minimizes portfolio turnover. Fit drives both competitive advantage and sustainability: when activities mutually reinforce each other, competitors can't easily imitate them. When Continental Lite tried to match a few of Southwest Airlines' activities, but not the whole interlocking system, the results were disastrous.

Employees need guidance about how to deepen a strategic position rather than broaden or compromise it. About how to extend the company's uniqueness while strengthening the fit among its activities. This work of deciding which target group of customers and needs to serve requires discipline, the ability to set limits, and forthright communication. Clearly, strategy and leadership are inextricably linked.

company delivering a particular product or service can create at a given cost, using the best available technologies, skills, management techniques, and purchased inputs. The productivity frontier can apply to individual activities, to groups of linked activities such as order processing and manufacturing, and to an entire company's activities. When a company improves its operational effectiveness, it moves toward the frontier. Doing so may require capital investment, different personnel, or simply new ways of managing.

The productivity frontier is constantly shifting outward as new technologies and management approaches are developed and as new inputs become available. Laptop computers, mobile communications, the Internet, and software such as Lotus Notes, for example, have redefined the productivity frontier for sales-force operations and created rich possibilities for linking sales with such activities as order processing and after-sales support. Similarly, lean production, which involves a family of activities, has allowed substantial improvements in manufacturing productivity and asset utilization.

Operational effectiveness versus strategic positioning

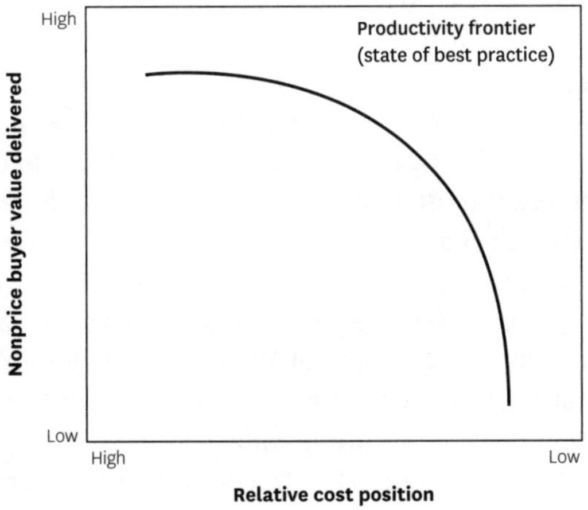

For at least the past decade, managers have been preoccupied with improving operational effectiveness. Through programs such as TQM, time-based competition, and benchmarking, they have changed how they perform activities in order to eliminate inefficiencies, improve customer satisfaction, and achieve best practice. Hoping to keep up with shifts in the productivity frontier, managers have embraced continuous improvement, empowerment, change management, and the so-called learning organization. The popularity of outsourcing and the virtual corporation reflect the growing recognition that it is difficult to perform all activities as productively as specialists.

As companies move to the frontier, they can often improve on multiple dimensions of performance at the same time. For example, manufacturers that adopted the Japanese practice of rapid changeovers in the 1980s were able to lower cost and improve differentiation simultaneously. What were once believed to be real trade-offs—between defects and costs, for example—turned out to be illusions created by poor operational effectiveness. Managers have learned to reject such false trade-offs.

Constant improvement in operational effectiveness is necessary to achieve superior profitability. However, it is not usually sufficient. Few companies have competed successfully on the basis of operational effectiveness over an extended period, and staying ahead of rivals gets harder every day. The most obvious reason for that is the rapid diffusion of best practices. Competitors can quickly imitate management techniques, new technologies, input improvements, and superior ways of meeting customers' needs. The most generic solutions—those that can be used in multiple settings—diffuse the fastest. Witness the proliferation of OE techniques accelerated by support from consultants.

OE competition shifts the productivity frontier outward, effectively raising the bar for everyone. But although such competition produces absolute improvement in operational effectiveness, it leads to relative improvement for no one. Consider the $5 billion-plus U.S. commercial-printing industry. The major players—R.R. Donnelley & Sons Company, Quebecor, World Color Press, and

Big Flower Press—are competing head to head, serving all types of customers, offering the same array of printing technologies (gravure and web offset), investing heavily in the same new equipment, running their presses faster, and reducing crew sizes. But the resulting major productivity gains are being captured by customers and equipment suppliers, not retained in superior profitability. Even industry-leader Donnelley's profit margin, consistently higher than 7% in the 1980s, fell to less than 4.6% in 1995. This pattern is playing itself out in industry after industry. Even the Japanese, pioneers of the new competition, suffer from persistently low profits. (See the sidebar "Japanese Companies Rarely Have Strategies.")

The second reason that improved operational effectiveness is insufficient—competitive convergence—is more subtle and insidious. The more benchmarking companies do, the more they look alike. The more that rivals outsource activities to efficient third parties, often the same ones, the more generic those activities become. As rivals imitate one another's improvements in quality, cycle times, or supplier partnerships, strategies converge and competition becomes a series of races down identical paths that no one can win. Competition based on operational effectiveness alone is mutually destructive, leading to wars of attrition that can be arrested only by limiting competition.

The recent wave of industry consolidation through mergers makes sense in the context of OE competition. Driven by performance pressures but lacking strategic vision, company after company has had no better idea than to buy up its rivals. The competitors left standing are often those that outlasted others, not companies with real advantage.

After a decade of impressive gains in operational effectiveness, many companies are facing diminishing returns. Continuous improvement has been etched on managers' brains. But its tools unwittingly draw companies toward imitation and homogeneity. Gradually, managers have let operational effectiveness supplant strategy. The result is zero-sum competition, static or declining prices, and pressures on costs that compromise companies' ability to invest in the business for the long term.

Japanese Companies Rarely Have Strategies

The Japanese triggered a global revolution in operational effectiveness in the 1970s and 1980s, pioneering practices such as total quality management and continuous improvement. As a result, Japanese manufacturers enjoyed substantial cost and quality advantages for many years.

But Japanese companies rarely developed distinct strategic positions of the kind discussed in this article. Those that did—Sony, Canon, and Sega, for example—were the exception rather than the rule. Most Japanese companies imitate and emulate one another. All rivals offer most if not all product varieties, features, and services; they employ all channels and match one anothers' plant configurations.

The dangers of Japanese-style competition are now becoming easier to recognize. In the 1980s, with rivals operating far from the productivity frontier, it seemed possible to win on both cost and quality indefinitely. Japanese companies were all able to grow in an expanding domestic economy and by penetrating global markets. They appeared unstoppable. But as the gap in operational effectiveness narrows, Japanese companies are increasingly caught in a trap of their own making. If they are to escape the mutually destructive battles now ravaging their performance, Japanese companies will have to learn strategy.

To do so, they may have to overcome strong cultural barriers. Japan is notoriously consensus oriented, and companies have a strong tendency to mediate differences among individuals rather than accentuate them. Strategy, on the other hand, requires hard choices. The Japanese also have a deeply ingrained service tradition that predisposes them to go to great lengths to satisfy any need a customer expresses. Companies that compete in that way end up blurring their distinct positioning, becoming all things to all customers.

This discussion of Japan is drawn from the author's research with Hirotaka Takeuchi, with help from Mariko Sakakibara.

II. Strategy Rests on Unique Activities

Competitive strategy is about being different. It means deliberately choosing a different set of activities to deliver a unique mix of value.

Southwest Airlines Company, for example, offers short-haul, low-cost, point-to-point service between midsize cities and secondary airports in large cities. Southwest avoids large airports and does not fly great distances. Its customers include business travelers, families, and students. Southwest's frequent departures and low fares attract price-sensitive customers who otherwise would travel by bus or car, and convenience-oriented travelers who would choose a full-service airline on other routes.

Most managers describe strategic positioning in terms of their customers: "Southwest Airlines serves price- and convenience-sensitive travelers," for example. But the essence of strategy is in the activities—choosing to perform activities differently or to perform different activities than rivals. Otherwise, a strategy is nothing more than a marketing slogan that will not withstand competition.

A full-service airline is configured to get passengers from almost any point A to any point B. To reach a large number of destinations and serve passengers with connecting flights, full-service airlines employ a hub-and-spoke system centered on major airports. To attract passengers who desire more comfort, they offer first-class or business-class service. To accommodate passengers who must change planes, they coordinate schedules and check and transfer baggage. Because some passengers will be traveling for many hours, full-service airlines serve meals.

Southwest, in contrast, tailors all its activities to deliver low-cost, convenient service on its particular type of route. Through fast turnarounds at the gate of only 15 minutes, Southwest is able to keep planes flying longer hours than rivals and provide frequent departures with fewer aircraft. Southwest does not offer meals, assigned seats, interline baggage checking, or premium classes of service. Automated ticketing at the gate encourages customers to bypass travel agents, allowing Southwest to avoid their commissions. A standardized fleet of 737 aircraft boosts the efficiency of maintenance.

Southwest has staked out a unique and valuable strategic position based on a tailored set of activities. On the routes served by Southwest, a full-service airline could never be as convenient or as low cost.

Ikea, the global furniture retailer based in Sweden, also has a clear strategic positioning. Ikea targets young furniture buyers who want style at low cost. What turns this marketing concept into a strategic

Finding New Positions: The Entrepreneurial Edge

Strategic competition can be thought of as the process of perceiving new positions that woo customers from established positions or draw new customers into the market. For example, superstores offering depth of merchandise in a single product category take market share from broad-line department stores offering a more limited selection in many categories. Mail-order catalogs pick off customers who crave convenience. In principle, incumbents and entrepreneurs face the same challenges in finding new strategic positions. In practice, new entrants often have the edge.

Strategic positionings are often not obvious, and finding them requires creativity and insight. New entrants often discover unique positions that have been available but simply overlooked by established competitors. Ikea, for example, recognized a customer group that had been ignored or served poorly. Circuit City Stores' entry into used cars, CarMax, is based on a new way of performing activities—extensive refurbishing of cars, product guarantees, no-haggle pricing, sophisticated use of in-house customer financing—that has long been open to incumbents.

New entrants can prosper by occupying a position that a competitor once held but has ceded through years of imitation and straddling. And entrants coming from other industries can create new positions because of distinctive activities drawn from their other businesses. CarMax borrows heavily from Circuit City's expertise in inventory management, credit, and other activities in consumer electronics retailing.

Most commonly, however, new positions open up because of change. New customer groups or purchase occasions arise; new needs emerge as societies evolve; new distribution channels appear; new technologies are developed; new machinery or information systems become available. When such changes happen, new entrants, unencumbered by a long history in the industry, can often more easily perceive the potential for a new way of competing. Unlike incumbents, newcomers can be more flexible because they face no trade-offs with their existing activities.

---

positioning is the tailored set of activities that make it work. Like Southwest, Ikea has chosen to perform activities differently from its rivals.

Consider the typical furniture store. Showrooms display samples of the merchandise. One area might contain 25 sofas; another will display five dining tables. But those items represent only a fraction of the choices available to customers. Dozens of books displaying fabric swatches or wood samples or alternate styles offer customers thousands of product varieties to choose from. Salespeople often escort customers through the store, answering questions and helping them navigate this maze of choices. Once a customer makes a selection, the order is relayed to a third-party manufacturer. With luck, the furniture will be delivered to the customer's home within six to eight weeks. This is a value chain that maximizes customization and service but does so at high cost.

In contrast, Ikea serves customers who are happy to trade off service for cost. Instead of having a sales associate trail customers around the store, Ikea uses a self-service model based on clear, in-store displays. Rather than rely solely on third-party manufacturers, Ikea designs its own low-cost, modular, ready-to-assemble furniture to fit its positioning. In huge stores, Ikea displays every product it sells in room-like settings, so customers don't need a decorator to help them imagine how to put the pieces together. Adjacent to the furnished showrooms is a warehouse section with the products in boxes on pallets. Customers are expected to do their own pickup and delivery, and Ikea will even sell you a roof rack for your car that you can return for a refund on your next visit.

Although much of its low-cost position comes from having customers "do it themselves," Ikea offers a number of extra services that its competitors do not. In-store child care is one. Extended hours are another. Those services are uniquely aligned with the needs of its customers, who are young, not wealthy, likely to have children (but no nanny), and, because they work for a living, have a need to shop at odd hours.

The origins of strategic positions

Strategic positions emerge from three distinct sources, which are not mutually exclusive and often overlap. First, positioning can be based on producing a subset of an industry's products or services. I call this *variety-based positioning* because it is based on the choice of product or service varieties rather than customer segments.

Variety-based positioning makes economic sense when a company can best produce particular products or services using distinctive sets of activities.

Jiffy Lube International, for instance, specializes in automotive lubricants and does not offer other car repair or maintenance services. Its value chain produces faster service at a lower cost than broader line repair shops, a combination so attractive that many customers subdivide their purchases, buying oil changes from the focused competitor, Jiffy Lube, and going to rivals for other services.

The Vanguard Group, a leader in the mutual fund industry, is another example of variety-based positioning. Vanguard provides an array of common stock, bond, and money market funds that offer predictable performance and rock-bottom expenses. The company's investment approach deliberately sacrifices the possibility of extraordinary performance in any one year for good relative performance in every year. Vanguard is known, for example, for its index funds. It avoids making bets on interest rates and steers clear of narrow stock groups. Fund managers keep trading levels low, which holds expenses down; in addition, the company discourages customers from rapid buying and selling because doing so drives up costs and can force a fund manager to trade in order to deploy new capital and raise cash for redemptions. Vanguard also takes a consistent low-cost approach to managing distribution, customer service, and marketing. Many investors include one or more Vanguard funds in their portfolio, while buying aggressively managed or specialized funds from competitors.

The people who use Vanguard or Jiffy Lube are responding to a superior value chain for a particular type of service. A variety-based positioning can serve a wide array of customers, but for most it will meet only a subset of their needs.

A second basis for positioning is that of serving most or all the needs of a particular group of customers. I call this *needs-based positioning,* which comes closer to traditional thinking about targeting a segment of customers. It arises when there are groups of customers with differing needs, and when a tailored set of activities can serve those needs best. Some groups of customers are more price sensitive

The Connection with Generic Strategies

In *Competitive Strategy* (The Free Press, 1985), I introduced the concept of generic strategies—cost leadership, differentiation, and focus—to represent the alternative strategic positions in an industry. The generic strategies remain useful to characterize strategic positions at the simplest and broadest level. Vanguard, for instance, is an example of a cost leadership strategy, whereas Ikea, with its narrow customer group, is an example of cost-based focus. Neutrogena is a focused differentiator. The bases for positioning—varieties, needs, and access—carry the understanding of those generic strategies to a greater level of specificity. Ikea and Southwest are both cost-based focusers, for example, but Ikea's focus is based on the needs of a customer group, and Southwest's is based on offering a particular service variety.

The generic strategies framework introduced the need to choose in order to avoid becoming caught between what I then described as the inherent contradictions of different strategies. Trade-offs between the activities of incompatible positions explain those contradictions. Witness Continental Lite, which tried and failed to compete in two ways at once.

than others, demand different product features, and need varying amounts of information, support, and services. Ikea's customers are a good example of such a group. Ikea seeks to meet all the home furnishing needs of its target customers, not just a subset of them.

A variant of needs-based positioning arises when the same customer has different needs on different occasions or for different types of transactions. The same person, for example, may have different needs when traveling on business than when traveling for pleasure with the family. Buyers of cans—beverage companies, for example—will likely have different needs from their primary supplier than from their secondary source.

It is intuitive for most managers to conceive of their business in terms of the customers' needs they are meeting. But a critical element of needs-based positioning is not at all intuitive and is often overlooked. Differences in needs will not translate into meaningful positions unless the best set of activities to satisfy them *also* differs. If that were not the case, every competitor could meet those same needs, and there would be nothing unique or valuable about the positioning.

In private banking, for example, Bessemer Trust Company targets families with a minimum of $5 million in investable assets who want capital preservation combined with wealth accumulation. By assigning one sophisticated account officer for every 14 families, Bessemer has configured its activities for personalized service. Meetings, for example, are more likely to be held at a client's ranch or yacht than in the office. Bessemer offers a wide array of customized services, including investment management and estate administration, oversight of oil and gas investments, and accounting for racehorses and aircraft. Loans, a staple of most private banks, are rarely needed by Bessemer's clients and make up a tiny fraction of its client balances and income. Despite the most generous compensation of account officers and the highest personnel cost as a percentage of operating expenses, Bessemer's differentiation with its target families produces a return on equity estimated to be the highest of any private banking competitor.

Citibank's private bank, on the other hand, serves clients with minimum assets of about $250,000 who, in contrast to Bessemer's clients, want convenient access to loans—from jumbo mortgages to deal financing. Citibank's account managers are primarily lenders. When clients need other services, their account manager refers them to other Citibank specialists, each of whom handles prepackaged products. Citibank's system is less customized than Bessemer's and allows it to have a lower manager-to-client ratio of 1:125. Biannual office meetings are offered only for the largest clients. Both Bessemer and Citibank have tailored their activities to meet the needs of a different group of private banking customers. The same value chain cannot profitably meet the needs of both groups.

The third basis for positioning is that of segmenting customers who are accessible in different ways. Although their needs are similar to those of other customers, the best configuration of activities to reach them is different. I call this *access-based positioning*. Access can be a function of customer geography or customer scale—or of anything that requires a different set of activities to reach customers in the best way.

Segmenting by access is less common and less well understood than the other two bases. Carmike Cinemas, for example, operates movie theaters exclusively in cities and towns with populations under 200,000. How does Carmike make money in markets that are not only small but also won't support big-city ticket prices? It does so through a set of activities that result in a lean cost structure. Carmike's small-town customers can be served through standardized, low-cost theater complexes requiring fewer screens and less sophisticated projection technology than big-city theaters. The company's proprietary information system and management process eliminate the need for local administrative staff beyond a single theater manager. Carmike also reaps advantages from centralized purchasing, lower rent and payroll costs (because of its locations), and rock-bottom corporate overhead of 2% (the industry average is 5%). Operating in small communities also allows Carmike to practice a highly personal form of marketing in which the theater manager knows patrons and promotes attendance through personal contacts. By being the dominant if not the only theater in its markets—the main competition is often the high school football team—Carmike is also able to get its pick of films and negotiate better terms with distributors.

Rural versus urban-based customers are one example of access driving differences in activities. Serving small rather than large customers or densely rather than sparsely situated customers are other examples in which the best way to configure marketing, order processing, logistics, and after-sale service activities to meet the similar needs of distinct groups will often differ.

Positioning is not only about carving out a niche. A position emerging from any of the sources can be broad or narrow. A focused competitor, such as Ikea, targets the special needs of a subset of customers and designs its activities accordingly. Focused competitors thrive on groups of customers who are overserved (and hence overpriced) by more broadly targeted competitors, or underserved (and hence underpriced). A broadly targeted competitor—for example, Vanguard or Delta Air Lines—serves a wide array of customers, performing a set of activities designed to meet their common needs. It ignores or meets only partially the more idiosyncratic needs of particular customer customer groups.

Whatever the basis—variety, needs, access, or some combination of the three—positioning requires a tailored set of activities because it is always a function of differences on the supply side; that is, of differences in activities. However, positioning is not always a function of differences on the demand, or customer, side. Variety and access positionings, in particular, do not rely on *any* customer differences. In practice, however, variety or access differences often accompany needs differences. The tastes—that is, the needs—of Carmike's small-town customers, for instance, run more toward comedies, Westerns, action films, and family entertainment. Carmike does not run any films rated NC-17.

Having defined positioning, we can now begin to answer the question, "What is strategy?" Strategy is the creation of a unique and valuable position, involving a different set of activities. If there were only one ideal position, there would be no need for strategy. Companies would face a simple imperative—win the race to discover and preempt it. The essence of strategic positioning is to choose activities that are different from rivals'. If the same set of activities were best to produce all varieties, meet all needs, and access all customers, companies could easily shift among them and operational effectiveness would determine performance.

III. A Sustainable Strategic Position Requires Trade-offs

Choosing a unique position, however, is not enough to guarantee a sustainable advantage. A valuable position will attract imitation by incumbents, who are likely to copy it in one of two ways.

First, a competitor can reposition itself to match the superior performer. J.C. Penney, for instance, has been repositioning itself from a Sears clone to a more upscale, fashion-oriented, soft-goods retailer. A second and far more common type of imitation is straddling. The straddler seeks to match the benefits of a successful position while maintaining its existing position. It grafts new features, services, or technologies onto the activities it already performs.

For those who argue that competitors can copy any market position, the airline industry is a perfect test case. It would seem that nearly any competitor could imitate any other airline's activities. Any airline can buy the same planes, lease the gates, and match the menus and ticketing and baggage handling services offered by other airlines.

Continental Airlines saw how well Southwest was doing and decided to straddle. While maintaining its position as a full-service airline, Continental also set out to match Southwest on a number of point-to-point routes. The airline dubbed the new service Continental Lite. It eliminated meals and first-class service, increased departure frequency, lowered fares, and shortened turnaround time at the gate. Because Continental remained a full-service airline on other routes, it continued to use travel agents and its mixed fleet of planes and to provide baggage checking and seat assignments.

But a strategic position is not sustainable unless there are trade-offs with other positions. Trade-offs occur when activities are incompatible. Simply put, a trade-off means that more of one thing necessitates less of another. An airline can choose to serve meals—adding cost and slowing turnaround time at the gate—or it can choose not to, but it cannot do both without bearing major inefficiencies.

Trade-offs create the need for choice and protect against repositioners and straddlers. Consider Neutrogena soap. Neutrogena Corporation's variety-based positioning is built on a "kind to the skin," residue-free soap formulated for pH balance. With a large detail force calling on dermatologists, Neutrogena's marketing strategy looks more like a drug company's than a soap maker's. It advertises in medical journals, sends direct mail to doctors, attends medical conferences, and performs research at its own Skincare Institute. To reinforce its positioning, Neutrogena originally focused its distribution on drugstores and avoided price promotions. Neutrogena uses a slow, more expensive manufacturing process to mold its fragile soap.

In choosing this position, Neutrogena said no to the deodorants and skin softeners that many customers desire in their soap. It gave up the large-volume potential of selling through supermarkets and using price promotions. It sacrificed manufacturing efficiencies to achieve the soap's desired attributes. In its original positioning, Neutrogena made a whole raft of trade-offs like those, trade-offs that protected the company from imitators.

Trade-offs arise for three reasons. The first is inconsistencies in image or reputation. A company known for delivering one kind of value may lack credibility and confuse customers—or even undermine its reputation—if it delivers another kind of value or attempts to deliver two inconsistent things at the same time. For example, Ivory soap, with its position as a basic, inexpensive everyday soap, would have a hard time reshaping its image to match Neutrogena's premium "medical" reputation. Efforts to create a new image typically cost tens or even hundreds of millions of dollars in a major industry—a powerful barrier to imitation.

Second, and more important, trade-offs arise from activities themselves. Different positions (with their tailored activities) require different product configurations, different equipment, different employee behavior, different skills, and different management systems. Many trade-offs reflect inflexibilities in machinery, people, or systems. The more Ikea has configured its activities to lower costs by having its customers do their own assembly and delivery, the less able it is to satisfy customers who require higher levels of service.

However, trade-offs can be even more basic. In general, value is destroyed if an activity is overdesigned or underdesigned for its use. For example, even if a given salesperson were capable of providing a high level of assistance to one customer and none to another, the salesperson's talent (and some of his or her cost) would be wasted on the second customer. Moreover, productivity can improve when variation of an activity is limited. By providing a high level of assistance all the time, the salesperson and the entire sales activity can often achieve efficiencies of learning and scale.

Finally, trade-offs arise from limits on internal coordination and control. By clearly choosing to compete in one way and not another, senior management makes organizational priorities clear. Companies that try to be all things to all customers, in contrast, risk confusion in the trenches as employees attempt to make day-to-day operating decisions without a clear framework.

Positioning trade-offs are pervasive in competition and essential to strategy. They create the need for choice and purposefully limit what a company offers. They deter straddling or repositioning, because competitors that engage in those approaches undermine their strategies and degrade the value of their existing activities.

Trade-offs ultimately grounded Continental Lite. The airline lost hundreds of millions of dollars, and the CEO lost his job. Its planes were delayed leaving congested hub cities or slowed at the gate by baggage transfers. Late flights and cancellations generated a thousand complaints a day. Continental Lite could not afford to compete on price and still pay standard travel-agent commissions, but neither could it do without agents for its full-service business. The airline compromised by cutting commissions for all Continental flights across the board. Similarly, it could not afford to offer the same frequent-flier benefits to travelers paying the much lower ticket prices for Lite service. It compromised again by lowering the rewards of Continental's entire frequent-flier program. The results: angry travel agents and full-service customers.

Continental tried to compete in two ways at once. In trying to be low cost on some routes and full service on others, Continental paid an enormous straddling penalty. If there were no trade-offs between the two positions, Continental could have succeeded. But the absence of trade-offs is a dangerous half-truth that managers must unlearn. Quality is not always free. Southwest's convenience, one kind of high quality, happens to be consistent with low costs because its frequent departures are facilitated by a number of low-cost practices—fast gate turnarounds and automated ticketing, for example. However, other dimensions of airline quality—an assigned seat, a meal, or baggage transfer—require costs to provide.

In general, false trade-offs between cost and quality occur primarily when there is redundant or wasted effort, poor control or accuracy, or weak coordination. Simultaneous improvement of cost and differentiation is possible only when a company begins far behind the productivity frontier or when the frontier shifts outward. At the frontier, where companies have achieved current best practice, the trade-off between cost and differentiation is very real indeed.

After a decade of enjoying productivity advantages, Honda Motor Company and Toyota Motor Corporation recently bumped up against the frontier. In 1995, faced with increasing customer resistance to higher automobile prices, Honda found that the only way to produce a less-expensive car was to skimp on features. In the United States, it replaced the rear disk brakes on the Civic with lower-cost drum brakes and used cheaper fabric for the back seat, hoping customers would not notice. Toyota tried to sell a version of its best-selling Corolla in Japan with unpainted bumpers and cheaper seats. In Toyota's case, customers rebelled, and the company quickly dropped the new model.

For the past decade, as managers have improved operational effectiveness greatly, they have internalized the idea that eliminating trade-offs is a good thing. But if there are no trade-offs companies will never achieve a sustainable advantage. They will have to run faster and faster just to stay in place.

As we return to the question, What is strategy? we see that trade-offs add a new dimension to the answer. Strategy is making trade-offs in competing. The essence of strategy is choosing what *not* to do. Without trade-offs, there would be no need for choice and thus no need for strategy. Any good idea could and would be quickly imitated. Again, performance would once again depend wholly on operational effectiveness.

IV. Fit Drives Both Competitive Advantage and Sustainability

Positioning choices determine not only which activities a company will perform and how it will configure individual activities but also how activities relate to one another. While operational effectiveness is about achieving excellence in individual activities, or functions, strategy is about *combining* activities.

Southwest's rapid gate turnaround, which allows frequent departures and greater use of aircraft, is essential to its high-convenience, low-cost positioning. But how does Southwest achieve it? Part of the answer lies in the company's well-paid gate and ground crews, whose productivity in turnarounds is enhanced by flexible union rules. But the bigger part of the answer lies in how Southwest performs other activities. With no meals, no seat assignment, and no interline baggage transfers, Southwest avoids having to perform activities that slow down other airlines. It selects airports and routes to avoid congestion that introduces delays. Southwest's strict limits on the type and length of routes make standardized aircraft possible: every aircraft Southwest turns is a Boeing 737.

What is Southwest's core competence? Its key success factors? The correct answer is that everything matters. Southwest's strategy involves a whole system of activities, not a collection of parts. Its competitive advantage comes from the way its activities fit and reinforce one another.

Fit locks out imitators by creating a chain that is as strong as its *strongest* link. As in most companies with good strategies, Southwest's activities complement one another in ways that create real economic value. One activity's cost, for example, is lowered because of the way other activities are performed. Similarly, one activity's value to customers can be enhanced by a company's other activities. That is the way strategic fit creates competitive advantage and superior profitability.

Types of fit

The importance of fit among functional policies is one of the oldest ideas in strategy. Gradually, however, it has been supplanted on the management agenda. Rather than seeing the company as a whole, managers have turned to "core" competencies, "critical" resources, and "key" success factors. In fact, fit is a far more central component of competitive advantage than most realize.

Fit is important because discrete activities often affect one another. A sophisticated sales force, for example, confers a greater advantage when the company's product embodies premium technology and its marketing approach emphasizes customer assistance and support. A production line with high levels of model variety is more valuable when combined with an inventory and order processing system that minimizes the need for stocking finished goods, a sales process equipped to explain and encourage customization, and an advertising theme that stresses the benefits of product variations that meet a customer's special needs. Such complementarities are pervasive in strategy. Although some fit among activities is generic and applies to many companies, the most valuable fit is strategy-specific because it enhances a position's uniqueness and amplifies trade-offs.[2]

There are three types of fit, although they are not mutually exclusive. First-order fit is *simple consistency* between each activity (function) and the overall strategy. Vanguard, for example, aligns all activities with its low-cost strategy. It minimizes portfolio turnover and does not need highly compensated money managers. The company distributes its funds directly, avoiding commissions to brokers. It also limits advertising, relying instead on public relations and word-of-mouth recommendations. Vanguard ties its employees' bonuses to cost savings.

Consistency ensures that the competitive advantages of activities cumulate and do not erode or cancel themselves out. It makes the strategy easier to communicate to customers, employees, and shareholders, and improves implementation through single-mindedness in the corporation.

Second-order fit occurs when *activities are reinforcing*. Neutrogena, for example, markets to upscale hotels eager to offer their guests a soap recommended by dermatologists. Hotels grant Neutrogena the privilege of using its customary packaging while requiring other soaps to feature the hotel's name. Once guests have tried Neutrogena in a luxury hotel, they are more likely to purchase it at the drugstore or ask their doctor about it. Thus Neutrogena's medical and hotel marketing activities reinforce one another, lowering total marketing costs.

In another example, Bic Corporation sells a narrow line of standard, low-priced pens to virtually all major customer markets (retail, commercial, promotional, and giveaway) through virtually all available channels. As with any variety-based positioning serving a broad group of customers, Bic emphasizes a common need (low price for an acceptable pen) and uses marketing approaches with a broad reach

Mapping activity systems

Activity-system maps, such as this one for Ikea, show how a company's strategic position is contained in a set of tailored activities designed to deliver it. In companies with a clear strategic position, a number of higher-order strategic themes (in dark grey) can be identified and implemented through clusters of tightly linked activities (in light grey).

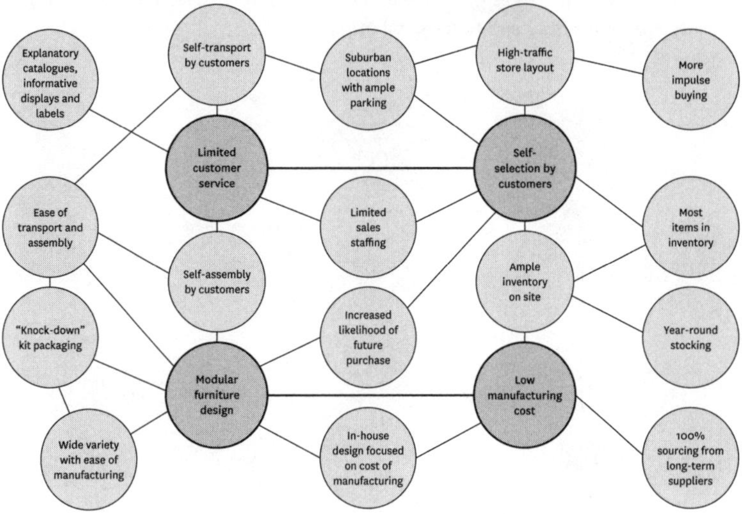

(a large sales force and heavy television advertising). Bic gains the benefits of consistency across nearly all activities, including product design that emphasizes ease of manufacturing, plants configured for low cost, aggressive purchasing to minimize material costs, and in-house parts production whenever the economics dictate.

Yet Bic goes beyond simple consistency because its activities are reinforcing. For example, the company uses point-of-sale displays and frequent packaging changes to stimulate impulse buying. To handle point-of-sale tasks, a company needs a large sales force. Bic's is the largest in its industry, and it handles point-of-sale activities better than its rivals do. Moreover, the combination of point-of-sale

Vanguard's activity system

Activity-system maps can be useful for examining and strengthening strategic fit. A set of basic questions should guide the process. First, is each activity consistent with the overall positioning—the varieties produced, the needs served, and the type of customers accessed? Ask those responsible for each activity to identify how other activities within the company improve or detract from their performance. Second, are there ways to strengthen how activities and groups of activities reinforce one another? Finally, could changes in one activity eliminate the need to perform others?

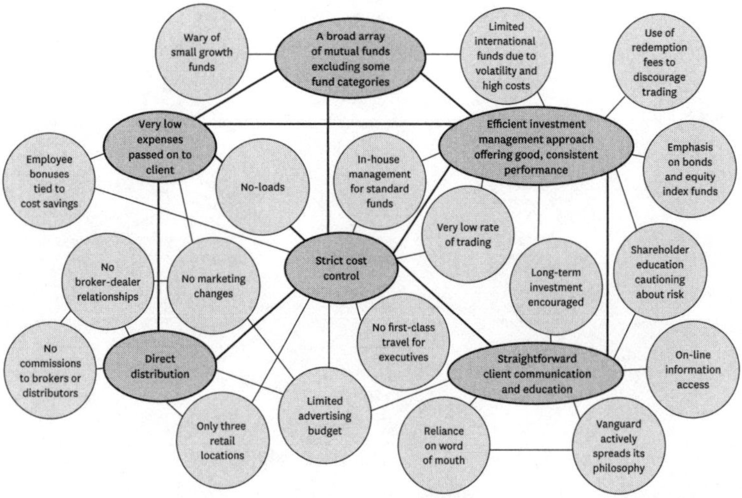

activity, heavy television advertising, and packaging changes yields far more impulse buying than any activity in isolation could.

Third-order fit goes beyond activity reinforcement to what I call *optimization of effort*. The Gap, a retailer of casual clothes, considers product availability in its stores a critical element of its strategy. The Gap could keep products either by holding store inventory or by restocking from warehouses. The Gap has optimized its effort across these activities by restocking its selection of basic clothing almost daily out of three warehouses, thereby minimizing the need to carry

Southwest Airlines' activity system

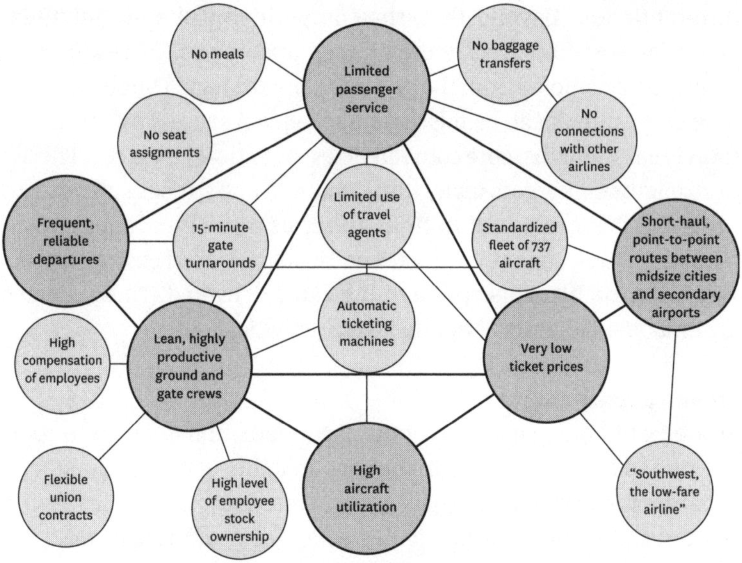

large in-store inventories. The emphasis is on restocking because the Gap's merchandising strategy sticks to basic items in relatively few colors. While comparable retailers achieve turns of three to four times per year, the Gap turns its inventory seven and a half times per year. Rapid restocking, moreover, reduces the cost of implementing the Gap's short model cycle, which is six to eight weeks long.[3]

Coordination and information exchange across activities to eliminate redundancy and minimize wasted effort are the most basic types of effort optimization. But there are higher levels as well. Product design choices, for example, can eliminate the need for after-sale service or make it possible for customers to perform service activities themselves. Similarly, coordination with suppliers or distribution channels can eliminate the need for some in-house activities, such as end-user training.

In all three types of fit, the whole matters more than any individual part. Competitive advantage grows out of the *entire system* of activities. The fit among activities substantially reduces cost or increases differentiation. Beyond that, the competitive value of individual activities—or the associated skills, competencies, or resources—cannot be decoupled from the system or the strategy. Thus in competitive companies it can be misleading to explain success by specifying individual strengths, core competencies, or critical resources. The list of strengths cuts across many functions, and one strength blends into others. It is more useful to think in terms of themes that pervade many activities, such as low cost, a particular notion of customer service, or a particular conception of the value delivered. These themes are embodied in nests of tightly linked activities.

Fit and sustainability

Strategic fit among many activities is fundamental not only to competitive advantage but also to the sustainability of that advantage. It is harder for a rival to match an array of interlocked activities than it is merely to imitate a particular sales-force approach, match a process technology, or replicate a set of product features. Positions built on systems of activities are far more sustainable than those built on individual activities.

Consider this simple exercise. The probability that competitors can match any activity is often less than one. The probabilities then quickly compound to make matching the entire system highly unlikely (.9 x .9 = .81; .9 x .9 x .9 x .9 = .66, and so on). Existing companies that try to reposition or straddle will be forced to reconfigure many activities. And even new entrants, though they do not confront the trade-offs facing established rivals, still face formidable barriers to imitation.

The more a company's positioning rests on activity systems with second- and third-order fit, the more sustainable its advantage will be. Such systems, by their very nature, are usually difficult to untangle from outside the company and therefore hard to imitate. And even if rivals can identify the relevant interconnections, they will have difficulty replicating them. Achieving fit is difficult because it requires the integration of decisions and actions across many independent subunits.

A competitor seeking to match an activity system gains little by imitating only some activities and not matching the whole. Performance does not improve; it can decline. Recall Continental Lite's disastrous attempt to imitate Southwest.

Finally, fit among a company's activities creates pressures and incentives to improve operational effectiveness, which makes imitation even harder. Fit means that poor performance in one activity will degrade the performance in others, so that weaknesses are exposed and more prone to get attention. Conversely, improvements in one activity will pay dividends in others. Companies with strong fit among their activities are rarely inviting targets. Their superiority in strategy and in execution only compounds their advantages and raises the hurdle for imitators.

When activities complement one another, rivals will get little benefit from imitation unless they successfully match the whole system. Such situations tend to promote winner-take-all competition. The company that builds the best activity system—Toys R Us, for instance—wins, while rivals with similar strategies—Child World and Lionel Leisure—fall behind. Thus finding a new strategic position is often preferable to being the second or third imitator of an occupied position.

The most viable positions are those whose activity systems are incompatible because of tradeoffs. Strategic positioning sets the trade-off rules that define how individual activities will be configured and integrated. Seeing strategy in terms of activity systems only makes it clearer why organizational structure, systems, and processes need to be strategy-specific. Tailoring organization to strategy, in turn, makes complementarities more achievable and contributes to sustainability.

One implication is that strategic positions should have a horizon of a decade or more, not of a single planning cycle. Continuity fosters improvements in individual activities and the fit across activities, allowing an organization to build unique capabilities and skills tailored to its strategy. Continuity also reinforces a company's identity.

Conversely, frequent shifts in positioning are costly. Not only must a company reconfigure individual activities, but it must also realign entire systems. Some activities may never catch up to the vacillating strategy. The inevitable result of frequent shifts in strategy, or of failure to choose a distinct position in the first place, is "me-too" or hedged activity configurations, inconsistencies across functions, and organizational dissonance.

What is strategy? We can now complete the answer to this question. Strategy is creating fit among a company's activities. The success of a strategy depends on doing many things well—not just a few—and integrating among them. If there is no fit among activities, there is no distinctive strategy and little sustainability. Management reverts to the simpler task of overseeing independent functions, and operational effectiveness determines an organization's relative performance.

V. Rediscovering Strategy

The failure to choose

Why do so many companies fail to have a strategy? Why do managers avoid making strategic choices? Or, having made them in the past, why do managers so often let strategies decay and blur?

Commonly, the threats to strategy are seen to emanate from outside a company because of changes in technology or the behavior of competitors. Although external changes can be the problem, the greater threat to strategy often comes from within. A sound strategy is undermined by a misguided view of competition, by organizational failures, and, especially, by the desire to grow.

Managers have become confused about the necessity of making choices. When many companies operate far from the productivity frontier, trade-offs appear unnecessary. It can seem that a well-run company should be able to beat its ineffective rivals on all dimensions simultaneously. Taught by popular management thinkers that they do not have to make trade-offs, managers have acquired a macho sense that to do so is a sign of weakness.

Unnerved by forecasts of hypercompetition, managers increase its likelihood by imitating everything about their competitors.

Alternative Views of Strategy

The Implicit Strategy Model of the Past Decade

- One ideal competitive position in the industry
- Benchmarking of all activities and achieving best practice
- Aggressive outsourcing and partnering to gain efficiencies
- Advantages rest on a few key success factors, critical resources, core competencies
- Flexibility and rapid responses to all competitive and market changes

Sustainable Competitive Advantage

- Unique competitive position for the company
- Activities tailored to strategy
- Clear trade-offs and choices vis-à-vis competitors
- Competitive advantage arises from fit across activities
- Sustainability comes from the activity system, not the parts
- Operational effectiveness a given

Exhorted to think in terms of revolution, managers chase every new technology for its own sake.

The pursuit of operational effectiveness is seductive because it is concrete and actionable. Over the past decade, managers have been under increasing pressure to deliver tangible, measurable performance improvements. Programs in operational effectiveness produce reassuring progress, although superior profitability may remain elusive. Business publications and consultants flood the market with information about what other companies are doing, reinforcing the best-practice mentality. Caught up in the race for operational effectiveness, many managers simply do not understand the need to have a strategy.

Companies avoid or blur strategic choices for other reasons as well. Conventional wisdom within an industry is often strong,

Reconnecting with Strategy

Most companies owe their initial success to a unique strategic position involving clear trade-offs. Activities once were aligned with that position. The passage of time and the pressures of growth, however, led to compromises that were, at first, almost imperceptible. Through a succession of incremental changes that each seemed sensible at the time, many established companies have compromised their way to homogeneity with their rivals.

The issue here is not with the companies whose historical position is no longer viable; their challenge is to start over, just as a new entrant would. At issue is a far more common phenomenon: the established company achieving mediocre returns and lacking a clear strategy. Through incremental additions of product varieties, incremental efforts to serve new customer groups, and emulation of rivals' activities, the existing company loses its clear competitive position. Typically, the company has matched many of its competitors' offerings and practices and attempts to sell to most customer groups.

A number of approaches can help a company reconnect with strategy. The first is a careful look at what it already does. Within most well-established companies is a core of uniqueness. It is identified by answering questions such as the following:

- Which of our product or service varieties are the most distinctive?
- Which of our product or service varieties are the most profitable?

---

homogenizing competition. Some managers mistake "customer focus" to mean they must serve all customer needs or respond to every request from distribution channels. Others cite the desire to preserve flexibility.

Organizational realities also work against strategy. Trade-offs are frightening, and making no choice is sometimes preferred to risking blame for a bad choice. Companies imitate one another in a type of herd behavior, each assuming rivals know something they do not. Newly empowered employees, who are urged to seek every possible source of improvement, often lack a vision of the whole and the perspective to recognize trade-offs. The failure to choose sometimes comes down to the reluctance to disappoint valued managers or employees.

- Which of our customers are the most satisfied?
- Which customers, channels, or purchase occasions are the most profitable?
- Which of the activities in our value chain are the most different and effective?

Around this core of uniqueness are encrustations added incrementally over time. Like barnacles, they must be removed to reveal the underlying strategic positioning. A small percentage of varieties or customers may well account for most of a company's sales and especially its profits. The challenge, then, is to refocus on the unique core and realign the company's activities with it. Customers and product varieties at the periphery can be sold or allowed through inattention or price increases to fade away.

A company's history can also be instructive. What was the vision of the founder? What were the products and customers that made the company? Looking backward, one can reexamine the original strategy to see if it is still valid. Can the historical positioning be implemented in a modern way, one consistent with today's technologies and practices? This sort of thinking may lead to a commitment to renew the strategy and may challenge the organization to recover its distinctiveness. Such a challenge can be galvanizing and can instill the confidence to make the needed trade-offs.

The growth trap

Among all other influences, the desire to grow has perhaps the most perverse effect on strategy. Trade-offs and limits appear to constrain growth. Serving one group of customers and excluding others, for instance, places a real or imagined limit on revenue growth. Broadly targeted strategies emphasizing low price result in lost sales with customers sensitive to features or service. Differentiators lose sales to price-sensitive customers.

Managers are constantly tempted to take incremental steps that surpass those limits but blur a company's strategic position. Eventually, pressures to grow or apparent saturation of the target market lead managers to broaden the position by extending product lines, adding new features, imitating competitors' popular services, matching processes, and even making acquisitions. For years, Maytag Corporation's success was based on its focus on reliable, durable washers and dryers, later extended to include dishwashers. However, conventional wisdom emerging within the industry supported the notion of selling a full line of products. Concerned with slow industry growth and competition from broad-line appliance makers, Maytag was pressured by dealers and encouraged by customers to extend its line. Maytag expanded into refrigerators and cooking products under the Maytag brand and acquired other brands—Jenn-Air, Hardwick Stove, Hoover, Admiral, and Magic Chef—with disparate positions. Maytag has grown substantially from $684 million in 1985 to a peak of $3.4 billion in 1994, but return on sales has declined from 8% to 12% in the 1970s and 1980s to an average of less than 1% between 1989 and 1995. Cost cutting will improve this performance, but laundry and dishwasher products still anchor Maytag's profitability.

Neutrogena may have fallen into the same trap. In the early 1990s, its U.S. distribution broadened to include mass merchandisers such as Wal-Mart Stores. Under the Neutrogena name, the company expanded into a wide variety of products—eye-makeup remover and shampoo, for example—in which it was not unique and which diluted its image, and it began turning to price promotions.

Compromises and inconsistencies in the pursuit of growth will erode the competitive advantage a company had with its original varieties or target customers. Attempts to compete in several ways at once create confusion and undermine organizational motivation and focus. Profits fall, but more revenue is seen as the answer. Managers are unable to make choices, so the company embarks on a new round of broadening and compromises. Often, rivals continue to match each other until desperation breaks the cycle, resulting in a merger or downsizing to the original positioning.

Profitable growth

Many companies, after a decade of restructuring and cost-cutting, are turning their attention to growth. Too often, efforts to grow blur uniqueness, create compromises, reduce fit, and ultimately

Emerging Industries and Technologies

Developing a strategy in a newly emerging industry or in a business undergoing revolutionary technological changes is a daunting proposition. In such cases, managers face a high level of uncertainty about the needs of customers, the products and services that will prove to be the most desired, and the best configuration of activities and technologies to deliver them. Because of all this uncertainty, imitation and hedging are rampant: unable to risk being wrong or left behind, companies match all features, offer all new services, and explore all technologies.

During such periods in an industry's development, its basic productivity frontier is being established or reestablished. Explosive growth can make such times profitable for many companies, but profits will be temporary because imitation and strategic convergence will ultimately destroy industry profitability. The companies that are enduringly successful will be those that begin as early as possible to define and embody in their activities a unique competitive position. A period of imitation may be inevitable in emerging industries, but that period reflects the level of uncertainty rather than a desired state of affairs.

In high-tech industries, this imitation phase often continues much longer than it should. Enraptured by technological change itself, companies pack more features—most of which are never used—into their products while slashing prices across the board. Rarely are trade-offs even considered. The drive for growth to satisfy market pressures leads companies into every product area. Although a few companies with fundamental advantages prosper, the majority are doomed to a rat race no one can win.

Ironically, the popular business press, focused on hot, emerging industries, is prone to presenting these special cases as proof that we have entered a new era of competition in which none of the old rules are valid. In fact, the opposite is true.

undermine competitive advantage. In fact, the growth imperative is hazardous to strategy.

What approaches to growth preserve and reinforce strategy? Broadly, the prescription is to concentrate on deepening a strategic position rather than broadening and compromising it. One approach is to look for extensions of the strategy that leverage the existing activity system by offering features or services that rivals would find impossible or costly to match on a stand-alone basis. In other words, managers can ask themselves which activities, features, or forms of competition are feasible or less costly to them because of complementary activities that their company performs.

Deepening a position involves making the company's activities more distinctive, strengthening fit, and communicating the strategy better to those customers who should value it. But many companies succumb to the temptation to chase "easy" growth by adding hot features, products, or services without screening them or adapting them to their strategy. Or they target new customers or markets in which the company has little special to offer. A company can often grow faster—and far more profitably—by better penetrating needs and varieties where it is distinctive than by slugging it out in potentially higher growth arenas in which the company lacks uniqueness. Carmike, now the largest theater chain in the United States, owes its rapid growth to its disciplined concentration on small markets. The company quickly sells any big-city theaters that come to it as part of an acquisition.

Globalization often allows growth that is consistent with strategy, opening up larger markets for a focused strategy. Unlike broadening domestically, expanding globally is likely to leverage and reinforce a company's unique position and identity.

Companies seeking growth through broadening within their industry can best contain the risks to strategy by creating stand-alone units, each with its own brand name and tailored activities. Maytag has clearly struggled with this issue. On the one hand, it has organized its premium and value brands into separate units with different strategic positions. On the other, it has created an umbrella appliance company for all its brands to gain critical mass. With shared design, manufacturing, distribution, and customer service, it will be hard to avoid homogenization. If a given business unit attempts to compete with different positions for different products or customers, avoiding compromise is nearly impossible.

The role of leadership

The challenge of developing or reestablishing a clear strategy is often primarily an organizational one and depends on leadership. With so many forces at work against making choices and tradeoffs in organizations, a clear intellectual framework to guide strategy is a necessary counterweight. Moreover, strong leaders willing to make choices are essential.

In many companies, leadership has degenerated into orchestrating operational improvements and making deals. But the leader's role is broader and far more important. General management is more than the stewardship of individual functions. Its core is strategy: defining and communicating the company's unique position, making trade-offs, and forging fit among activities. The leader must provide the discipline to decide which industry changes and customer needs the company will respond to, while avoiding organizational distractions and maintaining the company's distinctiveness. Managers at lower levels lack the perspective and the confidence to maintain a strategy. There will be constant pressures to compromise, relax trade-offs, and emulate rivals. One of the leader's jobs is to teach others in the organization about strategy—and to say no.

Strategy renders choices about what not to do as important as choices about what to do. Indeed, setting limits is another function of leadership. Deciding which target group of customers, varieties, and needs the company should serve is fundamental to developing a strategy. But so is deciding not to serve other customers or needs and not to offer certain features or services. Thus strategy requires constant discipline and clear communication. Indeed, one of the most important functions of an explicit, communicated strategy is to guide employees in making choices that arise because of trade-offs in their individual activities and in day-to-day decisions.

Improving operational effectiveness is a necessary part of management, but it is *not* strategy. In confusing the two, managers have unintentionally backed into a way of thinking about competition that is driving many industries toward competitive convergence, which is in no one's best interest and is not inevitable.

Managers must clearly distinguish operational effectiveness from strategy. Both are essential, but the two agendas are different.

The operational agenda involves continual improvement everywhere there are no trade-offs. Failure to do this creates vulnerability even for companies with a good strategy. The operational agenda is the proper place for constant change, flexibility, and relentless efforts to achieve best practice. In contrast, the strategic agenda is the right place for defining a unique position, making clear trade-offs, and tightening fit. It involves the continual search for ways to reinforce and extend the company's position. The strategic agenda demands discipline and continuity; its enemies are distraction and compromise.

Strategic continuity does not imply a static view of competition. A company must continually improve its operational effectiveness and actively try to shift the productivity frontier; at the same time, there needs to be ongoing effort to extend its uniqueness while strengthening the fit among its activities. Strategic continuity, in fact, should make an organization's continual improvement more effective.

A company may have to change its strategy if there are major structural changes in its industry. In fact, new strategic positions often arise because of industry changes, and new entrants unencumbered by history often can exploit them more easily. However, a company's choice of a new position must be driven by the ability to find new trade-offs and leverage a new system of complementary activities into a sustainable advantage.

Originally published in November 1996. Reprint 96608

Notes

1. I first described the concept of activities and its use in understanding competitive advantage in *Competitive Advantage* (New York: The Free Press, 1985). The ideas in this article build on and extend that thinking.

2. Paul Milgrom and John Roberts have begun to explore the economics of systems of complementary functions, activities, and functions. Their focus is on the emergence of "modern manufacturing" as a new set of complementary activities, on the tendency of companies to react to external changes with coherent bundles of internal responses, and on the need for central coordination—a strategy—to align functional managers. In the latter case, they model what has long been a bedrock principle of strategy. See Paul Milgrom and John Roberts, "The Economics of Modern Manufacturing: Technology, Strategy, and Organization," *American Economic Review* 80 (1990): 511–528; Paul Milgrom, Yingyi Qian, and John Roberts, "Complementarities, Momentum, and Evolution of Modern Manufacturing," *American Economic Review* 81 (1991) 84–88; and Paul Milgrom and John Roberts,

"Complementarities and Fit: Strategy, Structure, and Organizational Changes in Manufacturing," *Journal of Accounting and Economics*, vol. 19 (March–May 1995): 179–208.

3. Material on retail strategies is drawn in part from Jan Rivkin, "The Rise of Retail Category Killers," unpublished working paper, January 1995. Nicolaj Siggelkow prepared the case study on the Gap.

The Core Competence of the Corporation

by C.K. Prahalad and Gary Hamel

THE MOST POWERFUL WAY to prevail in global competition is still invisible to many companies. During the 1980s, top executives were judged on their ability to restructure, declutter, and delayer their corporations. In the 1990s, they'll be judged on their ability to identify, cultivate, and exploit the core competencies that make growth possible—indeed, they'll have to rethink the concept of the corporation itself.

Consider the last ten years of GTE and NEC. In the early 1980s, GTE was well positioned to become a major player in the evolving information technology industry. It was active in telecommunications. Its operations spanned a variety of businesses including telephones, switching and transmission systems, digital PABX, semiconductors, packet switching, satellites, defense systems, and lighting products. And GTE's Entertainment Products Group, which produced Sylvania color TVs, had a position in related display technologies. In 1980, GTE's sales were $9.98 billion, and net cash flow was $1.73 billion. NEC, in contrast, was much smaller, at $3.8 billion in sales. It had a comparable technological base and computer businesses, but it had no experience as an operating telecommunications company.

Yet look at the positions of GTE and NEC in 1988. GTE's 1988 sales were $16.46 billion, and NEC's sales were considerably higher at $21.89 billion. GTE has, in effect, become a telephone operating company with a position in defense and lighting products. GTE's other businesses are small in global terms. GTE has divested Sylvania TV and Telenet, put switching, transmission, and digital PABX into joint ventures, and closed down semiconductors. As a result, the international position of GTE has eroded. Non-U.S. revenue as a percent of total revenue dropped from 20% to 15% between 1980 and 1988.

NEC has emerged as the world leader in semiconductors and as a first-tier player in telecommunications products and computers. It has consolidated its position in mainframe computers. It has moved beyond public switching and transmission to include such lifestyle products as mobile telephones, facsimile machines, and laptop computers—bridging the gap between telecommunications and office automation. NEC is the only company in the world to be in the top five in revenue in telecommunications, semiconductors, and mainframes. Why did these two companies, starting with comparable business portfolios, perform so differently? Largely because NEC conceived of itself in terms of "core competencies," and GTE did not.

Rethinking the Corporation

Once, the diversified corporation could simply point its business units at particular end product markets and admonish them to become world leaders. But with market boundaries changing ever more quickly, targets are elusive and capture is at best temporary. A few companies have proven themselves adept at inventing new markets, quickly entering emerging markets, and dramatically shifting patterns of customer choice in established markets. These are the ones to emulate. The critical task for management is to create an organization capable of infusing products with irresistible functionality or, better yet, creating products that customers need but have not yet even imagined.

This is a deceptively difficult task. Ultimately, it requires radical change in the management of major companies. It means, first of all,

Idea in Brief

Diversified giant NEC competed in seemingly disparate businesses—semiconductors, telecommunications, computing, and consumer electronics—*and* dominated them all.

How? It considered itself *not* a collection of strategic business units, but a portfolio of **core competencies**—the company's collective knowledge about how to coordinate diverse production skills and technologies.

NEC used its core competencies to achieve what most companies only attempt: invent new markets, exploit emerging ones, delight customers with products they hadn't even imagined—but definitely needed.

Think of a diversified company as a tree: the trunk and major limbs as core products, smaller branches as business units, leaves and fruit as end products. Nourishing and stabilizing everything is the root system: core competencies.

Focusing on core competencies creates unique, integrated systems that reinforce fit among your firm's diverse production and technology skills—a systemic advantage your competitors can't copy.

that top managements of Western companies must assume responsibility for competitive decline. Everyone knows about high interest rates, Japanese protectionism, outdated antitrust laws, obstreperous unions, and impatient investors. What is harder to see, or harder to acknowledge, is how little added momentum companies actually get from political or macroeconomic "relief." Both the theory and practice of Western management have created a drag on our forward motion. It is the principles of management that are in need of reform.

NEC versus GTE, again, is instructive and only one of many such comparative cases we analyzed to understand the changing basis for global leadership. Early in the 1970s, NEC articulated a strategic intent to exploit the convergence of computing and communications, what it called "C&C."[1] Success, top management reckoned, would hinge on acquiring *competencies,* particularly in semiconductors. Management adopted an appropriate "strategic architecture," summarized by C&C, and then communicated its intent to the whole organization and the outside world during the mid-1970s.

Idea in Practice

Clarify Core Competencies

When you clarify competencies, your entire organization knows how to support your competitive advantage—and readily allocates resources to build cross-unit technological and production links. Use these steps:

Articulate a strategic intent that defines your company and its markets (e.g., NEC's "exploit the convergence of computing and communications").

Identify core competencies that support that intent. Ask:

- How long could we dominate our business if we didn't control this competency?
- What future opportunities would we lose without it?
- Does it provide access to multiple markets? (Casio's core competence with display systems let it succeed in calculators, laptop monitors, *and* car dashboards.)
- Do customer benefits revolve around it? (Honda's competence with high-revving, lightweight engines offers multiple consumer benefits.)

Build Core Competencies

Once you've identified core competencies, enhance them:

Invest in needed technologies. Citicorp trumped rivals by adopting an operating system that leveraged its competencies—and let it participate in world markets 24 hours a day.

Infuse resources throughout business units to outpace rivals in new business development. 3M and Honda won races for

NEC constituted a "C&C Committee" of top managers to oversee the development of core products and core competencies. NEC put in place coordination groups and committees that cut across the interests of individual businesses. Consistent with its strategic architecture, NEC shifted enormous resources to strengthen its position in components and central processors. By using collaborative arrangements to multiply internal resources, NEC was able to accumulate a broad array of core competencies.

NEC carefully identified three interrelated streams of technological and market evolution. Top management determined that computing would evolve from large mainframes to distributed processing, components from simple ICs to VLSI, and communications

global brand dominance by creating wide varieties of products from their core competencies. Results? They built image, customer loyalty, and access to distribution channels for all their businesses.

Forge strategic alliances. NEC's collaboration with partners like Honeywell gave it access to the mainframe and semiconductor technologies it needed to build core competencies.

Cultivate a Core-Competency Mind-Set

Competency-savvy managers work well across organizational boundaries, willingly share resources, and think long term. To encourage this mind-set:

Stop thinking of business units as sacrosanct. That imprisons resources in units and motivates managers to hide talent as the company pursues hot opportunities.

Identify projects and people who embody the firm's core competencies. This sends a message: Core competencies are corporate—not unit—resources, and those who embody them can be reallocated. (When Canon spotted opportunities in digital laser printers, it let managers raid other units to assemble talent.)

Gather managers to identify next-generation competencies. Decide how much investment each needs, and how much capital and staff each division should contribute.

from mechanical cross-bar exchange to complex digital systems we now call ISDN. As things evolved further, NEC reasoned, the computing, communications, and components businesses would so overlap that it would be very hard to distinguish among them, and that there would be enormous opportunities for any company that had built the competencies needed to serve all three markets.

NEC top management determined that semiconductors would be the company's most important "core product." It entered into myriad strategic alliances—over 100 as of 1987—aimed at building competencies rapidly and at low cost. In mainframe computers, its most noted relationship was with Honeywell and Bull. Almost all the collaborative arrangements in the semiconductor-component field were oriented toward technology access. As they entered collaborative arrangements, NEC's operating managers understood the rationale for these alliances and the goal of internalizing partner skills. NEC's director of research summed up its competence acquisition during the 1970s and 1980s this way: "From an investment standpoint, it was much quicker and cheaper to use foreign technology. There wasn't a need for us to develop new ideas."

No such clarity of strategic intent and strategic architecture appeared to exist at GTE. Although senior executives discussed the implications of the evolving information technology industry, no commonly accepted view of which competencies would be required to compete in that industry were communicated widely. While significant staff work was done to identify key technologies, senior line managers continued to act as if they were managing independent business units. Decentralization made it difficult to focus on core competencies. Instead, individual businesses became increasingly dependent on outsiders for critical skills, and collaboration became a route to staged exits. Today, with a new management team in place, GTE has repositioned itself to apply its competencies to emerging markets in telecommunications services.

The Roots of Competitive Advantage

The distinction we observed in the way NEC and GTE conceived of themselves—a portfolio of competencies versus a portfolio of businesses—was repeated across many industries. From 1980 to 1988, Canon grew by 264%, Honda by 200%. Compare that with Xerox and Chrysler. And if Western managers were once anxious about the low cost and high quality of Japanese imports, they are now overwhelmed by the pace at which Japanese rivals are inventing new markets, creating new products, and enhancing them. Canon has given us personal copiers; Honda has moved from motorcycles to four-wheel off-road buggies. Sony developed the 8mm camcorder, Yamaha, the digital piano. Komatsu developed an underwater remote-controlled bulldozer, while Casio's latest gambit is a small-screen color LCD television. Who would have anticipated the evolution of these vanguard markets?

In more established markets, the Japanese challenge has been just as disquieting. Japanese companies are generating a blizzard of features and functional enhancements that bring technological sophistication to everyday products. Japanese car producers have been pioneering four-wheel steering, four-valve-per-cylinder engines, in-car navigation systems, and sophisticated electronic engine-management systems. On the strength of its product features, Canon is now a player in facsimile transmission machines, desktop laser printers, even semi-conductor manufacturing equipment.

In the short run, a company's competitiveness derives from the price/performance attributes of current products. But the survivors of the first wave of global competition, Western and Japanese alike, are all converging on similar and formidable standards for product cost and quality—minimum hurdles for continued competition, but less and less important as sources of differential advantage. In the long run, competitiveness derives from an ability to build, at lower cost and more speedily than competitors, the core competencies that spawn unanticipated products. The real sources of advantage are to be found in management's ability to consolidate corporatewide technologies and production skills into competencies that empower individual businesses to adapt quickly to changing opportunities.

Senior executives who claim that they cannot build core competencies either because they feel the autonomy of business units is sacrosanct or because their feet are held to the quarterly budget fire should think again. The problem in many Western companies is not that their senior executives are any less capable than those in Japan nor that Japanese companies possess greater technical capabilities. Instead, it is their adherence to a concept of the corporation that unnecessarily limits the ability of individual businesses to fully exploit the deep reservoir of technological capability that many American and European companies possess.

The diversified corporation is a large tree. The trunk and major limbs are core products, the smaller branches are business units; the leaves, flowers, and fruit are end products. The root system that

Competencies: the roots of competitiveness

The corporation, like a tree, grows from its roots. Core products are nourished by competencies and engender business units, whose fruit are end products.

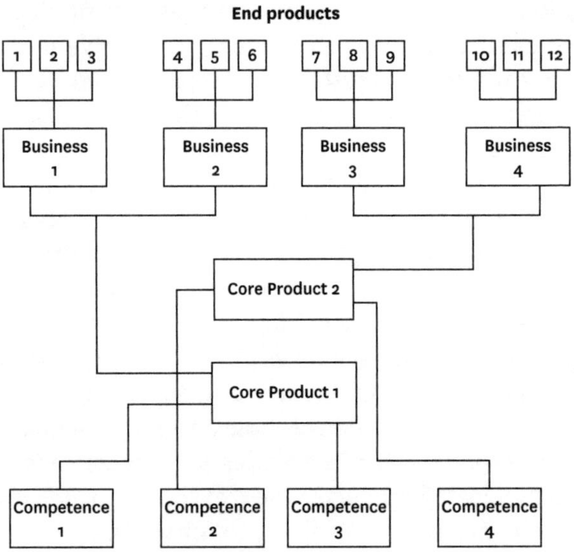

provides nourishment, sustenance, and stability is the core competence. You can miss the strength of competitors by looking only at their end products, in the same way you miss the strength of a tree if you look only at its leaves. (See the chart "Competencies: The Roots of Competitiveness.")

Core competencies are the collective learning in the organization, especially how to coordinate diverse production skills and integrate multiple streams of technologies. Consider Sony's capacity to miniaturize or Philips's optical-media expertise. The theoretical knowledge to put a radio on a chip does not in itself assure a company the skill to produce a miniature radio no bigger than a business card. To bring off this feat, Casio must harmonize know-how in miniaturization, microprocessor design, material science, and ultrathin precision casing—the same skills it applies in its miniature card calculators, pocket TVs, and digital watches.

If core competence is about harmonizing streams of technology, it is also about the organization of work and the delivery of value. Among Sony's competencies is miniaturization. To bring miniaturization to its products, Sony must ensure that technologists, engineers, and marketers have a shared understanding of customer needs and of technological possibilities. The force of core competence is felt as decisively in services as in manufacturing. Citicorp was ahead of others investing in an operating system that allowed it to participate in world markets 24 hours a day. Its competence in systems has provided the company the means to differentiate itself from many financial service institutions.

Core competence is communication, involvement, and a deep commitment to working across organizational boundaries. It involves many levels of people and all functions. World-class research in, for example, lasers or ceramics can take place in corporate laboratories without having an impact on any of the businesses of the company. The skills that together constitute core competence must coalesce around individuals whose efforts are not so narrowly focused that they cannot recognize the opportunities for blending their functional expertise with those of others in new and interesting ways.

Core competence does not diminish with use. Unlike physical assets, which do deteriorate over time, competencies are enhanced as they are applied and shared. But competencies still need to be nurtured and protected; knowledge fades if it is not used. Competencies are the glue that binds existing businesses. They are also the engine for new business development. Patterns of diversification and market entry may be guided by them, not just by the attractiveness of markets.

Consider 3M's competence with sticky tape. In dreaming up businesses as diverse as "Post-it" notes, magnetic tape, photographic film, pressure-sensitive tapes, and coated abrasives, the company has brought to bear widely shared competencies in substrates, coatings, and adhesives and devised various ways to combine them.

Indeed, 3M has invested consistently in them. What seems to be an extremely diversified portfolio of businesses belies a few shared core competencies.

In contrast, there are major companies that have had the potential to build core competencies but failed to do so because top management was unable to conceive of the company as anything other than a collection of discrete businesses. GE sold much of its consumer electronics business to Thomson of France, arguing that it was becoming increasingly difficult to maintain its competitiveness in this sector. That was undoubtedly so, but it is ironic that it sold several key businesses to competitors who were already competence leaders—Black & Decker in small electrical motors, and Thomson, which was eager to build its competence in microelectronics and had learned from the Japanese that a position in consumer electronics was vital to this challenge.

Management trapped in the strategic business unit (SBU) mindset almost inevitably finds its individual businesses dependent on external sources for critical components, such as motors or compressors. But these are not just components. They are core products that contribute to the competitiveness of a wide range of end products. They are the physical embodiments of core competencies.

How Not to Think of Competence

Since companies are in a race to build the competencies that determine global leadership, successful companies have stopped imagining themselves as bundles of businesses making products. Canon, Honda, Casio, or NEC may seem to preside over portfolios of businesses unrelated in terms of customers, distribution channels, and merchandising strategy. Indeed, they have portfolios that may seem idiosyncratic at times: NEC is the only global company to be among leaders in computing, telecommunications, and semiconductors *and* to have a thriving consumer electronics business.

But looks are deceiving. In NEC, digital technology, especially VLSI and systems integration skills, is fundamental. In the core competencies underlying them, disparate businesses become coherent.

It is Honda's core competence in engines and power trains that gives it a distinctive advantage in car, motorcycle, lawn mower, and generator businesses. Canon's core competencies in optics, imaging, and microprocessor controls have enabled it to enter, even dominate, markets as seemingly diverse as copiers, laser printers, cameras, and image scanners. Philips worked for more than 15 years to perfect its optical-media (laser disc) competence, as did JVC in building a leading position in video recording. Other examples of core competencies might include mechantronics (the ability to marry mechanical and electronic engineering), video displays, bioengineering, and microelectronics. In the early stages of its competence building, Philips could not have imagined all the products that would be spawned by its optical-media competence, nor could JVC have anticipated miniature camcorders when it first began exploring videotape technologies.

Unlike the battle for global brand dominance, which is visible in the world's broadcast and print media and is aimed at building global "share of mind," the battle to build world-class competencies is invisible to people who aren't deliberately looking for it. Top management often tracks the cost and quality of competitors' products, yet how many managers untangle the web of alliances their Japanese competitors have constructed to acquire competencies at low cost? In how many Western boardrooms is there an explicit, shared understanding of the competencies the company must build for world leadership? Indeed, how many senior executives discuss the crucial distinction between competitive strategy at the level of a business and competitive strategy at the level of an entire company?

Let us be clear. Cultivating core competence does *not* mean outspending rivals on research and development. In 1983, when Canon surpassed Xerox in worldwide unit market share in the copier business, its R&D budget in reprographics was but a small fraction of Xerox's. Over the past 20 years, NEC has spent less on R&D as a percentage of sales than almost all of its American and European competitors.

Nor does core competence mean shared costs, as when two or more SBUs use a common facility—a plant, service facility, or sales force—or share a common component. The gains of sharing may be substantial, but the search for shared costs is typically a post hoc effort to rationalize production across existing businesses, not a premeditated effort to build the competencies out of which the businesses themselves grow.

Building core competencies is more ambitious and different than integrating vertically, moreover. Managers deciding whether to make or buy will start with end products and look upstream to the efficiencies of the supply chain and downstream toward distribution and customers. They do not take inventory of skills and look forward to applying them in nontraditional ways. (Of course, decisions about competencies *do* provide a logic for vertical integration. Canon is not particularly integrated in its copier business, except in those aspects of the vertical chain that support the competencies it regards as critical.)

Identifying Core Competencies—And Losing Them

At least three tests can be applied to identify core competencies in a company. First, a core competence provides potential access to a wide variety of markets. Competence in display systems, for example, enables a company to participate in such diverse businesses as calculators, miniature TV sets, monitors for laptop computers, and automotive dashboards—which is why Casio's entry into the handheld TV market was predictable. Second, a core competence should make a significant contribution to the perceived customer benefits of the end product. Clearly, Honda's engine expertise fills this bill.

Finally, a core competence should be difficult for competitors to imitate. And it *will* be difficult if it is a complex harmonization of individual technologies and production skills. A rival might acquire some of the technologies that comprise the core competence, but it will find it more difficult to duplicate the more or less comprehensive pattern of internal coordination and learning. JVC's decision in the early 1960s to pursue the development of a videotape competence passed the three tests outlined here. RCA's decision in the late 1970s to develop a stylus-based video turntable system did not.

Few companies are likely to build world leadership in more than five or six fundamental competencies. A company that compiles a list of 20 to 30 capabilities has probably not produced a list of core competencies. Still, it is probably a good discipline to generate a list of this sort and to see aggregate capabilities as building blocks. This tends to prompt the search for licensing deals and alliances through which the company may acquire, at low cost, missing pieces.

Most Western companies hardly think about competitiveness in these terms at all. It is time to take a tough-minded look at the risks they are running. Companies that judge competitiveness, their own and their competitors', primarily in terms of the price/performance of end products are courting the erosion of core competencies—or making too little effort to enhance them. The embedded skills that give rise to the next generation of competitive products cannot be "rented in" by outsourcing and OEM-supply relationships. In our view, too many companies have unwittingly surrendered core competencies when they cut internal investment in what they mistakenly thought were just "cost centers" in favor of outside suppliers.

Consider Chrysler. Unlike Honda, it has tended to view engines and power trains as simply one more component. Chrysler is becoming increasingly dependent on Mitsubishi and Hyundai: between 1985 and 1987, the number of outsourced engines went from 252,000 to 382,000. It is difficult to imagine Honda yielding manufacturing responsibility, much less design, of so critical a part of a car's function to an outside company—which is why Honda has made such an enormous commitment to Formula One auto racing. Honda has been able to pool its engine-related technologies; it has parlayed these into a corporatewide competency from which it develops world-beating products, despite R&D budgets smaller than those of GM and Toyota.

Of course, it is perfectly possible for a company to have a competitive product line-up but be a laggard in developing core competencies—at least for a while. If a company wanted to enter the copier business today, it would find a dozen Japanese companies more than willing to supply copiers on the basis of an OEM private label. But when fundamental technologies changed or if its supplier decided to enter the market directly and become a competitor, that company's product line, along with all of its investments in marketing and distribution, could be vulnerable. Outsourcing can provide a shortcut to a more competitive product, but it typically contributes little to building the people-embodied skills that are needed to sustain product leadership.

Nor is it possible for a company to have an intelligent alliance or sourcing strategy if it has not made a choice about where it will build competence leadership. Clearly, Japanese companies have benefited from alliances. They've used them to learn from Western partners who were not fully committed to preserving core competencies of their own. As we've argued in these pages before, learning within an alliance takes a positive commitment of resources—the travel, a pool of dedicated people, test-bed facilities, time to internalize and test what has been learned.[2] A company may not make this effort if it doesn't have clear goals for competence building.

Another way of losing is forgoing opportunities to establish competencies that are evolving in existing businesses. In the 1970s and 1980s, many American and European companies—like GE, Motorola, GTE, Thorn, and GEC—chose to exit the color television business, which they regarded as mature. If by "mature" they meant that they had run out of new product ideas at precisely the moment global rivals had targeted the TV business for entry, then yes, the industry was mature. But it certainly wasn't mature in the sense that all opportunities to enhance and apply video-based competencies had been exhausted.

In ridding themselves of their television businesses, these companies failed to distinguish between divesting the business and destroying their video media-based competencies. They not only got out of the TV business but they also closed the door on a whole stream of future opportunities reliant on video-based competencies. The television industry, considered by many U.S. companies in the 1970s to be unattractive, is today the focus of a fierce public policy debate about the inability of U.S. corporations to benefit from the $20-billion-a-year opportunity that HDTV will represent in the mid- to late 1990s. Ironically, the U.S. government is being asked to fund a massive research project—in effect, to compensate U.S. companies for their failure to preserve critical core competencies when they had the chance.

In contrast, one can see a company like Sony reducing its emphasis on VCRs (where it has not been very successful and where Korean companies now threaten) without reducing its commitment to video-related competencies. Sony's Betamax led to a debacle. But it emerged with its videotape recording competencies intact and is currently challenging Matsushita in the 8mm camcorder market.

There are two clear lessons here. First, the costs of losing a core competence can be only partly calculated in advance. The baby may be thrown out with the bathwater in divestment decisions. Second, since core competencies are built through a process of continuous improvement and enhancement that may span a decade or longer, a company that has failed to invest in core competence building will find it very difficult to enter an emerging market, unless, of course, it will be content simply to serve as a distribution channel.

American semiconductor companies like Motorola learned this painful lesson when they elected to forgo direct participation in the 256k generation of DRAM chips. Having skipped this round, Motorola, like most of its American competitors, needed a large infusion of technical help from Japanese partners to rejoin the battle in the 1-megabyte generation. When it comes to core competencies, it is difficult to get off the train, walk to the next station, and then reboard.

From Core Competencies to Core Products

The tangible link between identified core competencies and end products is what we call the core products—the physical embodiments of one or more core competencies. Honda's engines, for example, are core products, linchpins between design and development skills that ultimately lead to a proliferation of end products. Core products are the components or subassemblies that actually contribute to the value of the end products. Thinking in terms of core products forces a company to distinguish between the brand share it achieves in end product markets (for example, 40% of the U.S. refrigerator market) and the manufacturing share it achieves in any particular core product (for example, 5% of the world share of compressor output).

Canon is reputed to have an 84% world manufacturing share in desktop laser printer "engines," even though its brand share in the laser printer business is minuscule. Similarly, Matsushita has a world manufacturing share of about 45% in key VCR components, far in excess of its brand share (Panasonic, JVC, and others) of 20%. And Matsushita has a commanding core product share in compressors worldwide, estimated at 40%, even though its brand share in both the air-conditioning and refrigerator businesses is quite small.

It is essential to make this distinction between core competencies, core products, and end products because global competition is played out by different rules and for different stakes at each level. To build or defend leadership over the long term, a corporation will probably be a winner at each level. At the level of core competence, the goal is to build world leadership in the design and development of a particular class of product functionality—be it compact data storage and retrieval, as with Philips's optical-media competence, or compactness and ease of use, as with Sony's micromotors and microprocessor controls.

To sustain leadership in their chosen core competence areas, these companies *seek to maximize their world manufacturing share in core products*. The manufacture of core products for a wide variety of external (and internal) customers yields the revenue and market feedback that, at least partly, determines the pace at which core competencies can be enhanced and extended. This thinking was behind JVC's decision in the mid-1970s to establish VCR supply relationships with leading national consumer electronics companies in Europe and the United States. In supplying Thomson, Thorn, and Telefunken (all independent companies at that time) as well as U.S. partners, JVC was able to gain the cash and the diversity of market experience that ultimately enabled it to outpace Philips and Sony. (Philips developed videotape competencies in parallel with JVC, but it failed to build a worldwide network of OEM relationships that would have allowed it to accelerate the refinement of its videotape competence through the sale of core products.)

JVC's success has not been lost on Korean companies like Goldstar, Sam Sung, Kia, and Daewoo, who are building core product leadership in areas as diverse as displays, semiconductors, and automotive engines through their OEM-supply contracts with Western companies. Their avowed goal is to capture investment initiative away from potential competitors, often U.S. companies. In doing so, they accelerate their competence-building efforts while "hollowing out" their competitors. By focusing on competence and embedding it in core products, Asian competitors have built up advantages in component markets first and have then leveraged off their superior products to move downstream to build brand share. And they are not likely to remain the low-cost suppliers forever. As their reputation for brand leadership is consolidated, they may well gain price leadership. Honda has proven this with its Acura line, and other Japanese car makers are following suit.

Control over core products is critical for other reasons. A dominant position in core products allows a company to shape the evolution of applications and end markets. Such compact audio disc-related core products as data drives and lasers have enabled Sony and Philips to influence the evolution of the computer-peripheral business in optical-media storage. As a company multiplies the number of application arenas for its core products, it can consistently reduce the cost, time, and risk in new product development. In short, well-targeted core products can lead to economies of scale *and* scope.

The Tyranny of the SBU

The new terms of competitive engagement cannot be understood using analytical tools devised to manage the diversified corporation of 20 years ago, when competition was primarily domestic (GE versus Westinghouse, General Motors versus Ford) and all the key players were speaking the language of the same business schools and consultancies. Old prescriptions have potentially toxic side effects.

Two concepts of the corporation: SBU or core competence

	SBU	Core Competence
Basis for competition	Competitiveness of today's products	Interfirm competition to build competencies
Corporate structure	Portfolio of businesses related in product-market terms	Portfolio of competencies, core products, and businesses
Status of the business unit	Autonomy is sacrosanct; the SBU "owns" all resources other than cash	SBU is a potential reservoir of core competencies
Resource allocation	Discrete businesses are the unit of analysis; capital is allocated business by business	Businesses and competencies are the unit of analysis: top management allocates capital and talent
Value added of top management	Optimizing corporate returns through capital allocation trade-offs among businesses	Enunciating strategic architecture and building competencies to secure the future

The need for new principles is most obvious in companies organized exclusively according to the logic of SBUs. The implications of the two alternate concepts of the corporation are summarized in "Two Concepts of the Corporation: SBU or Core Competence."

Obviously, diversified corporations have a portfolio of products and a portfolio of businesses. But we believe in a view of the company as a portfolio of competencies as well. U.S. companies do not lack the technical resources to build competencies, but their top management often lacks the vision to build them and the administrative means for assembling resources spread across multiple businesses. A shift in commitment will inevitably influence patterns of diversification, skill deployment, resource allocation priorities, and approaches to alliances and outsourcing.

We have described the three different planes on which battles for global leadership are waged: core competence, core products, and end products. A corporation has to know whether it is winning or losing on each plane. By sheer weight of investment, a company might be able to beat its rivals to blue-sky technologies yet still lose the race to build core competence leadership. If a company is winning the race to build core competencies (as opposed to building leadership in a few technologies), it will almost certainly outpace rivals in new business development. If a company is winning the race to capture world manufacturing share in core products, it will probably outpace rivals in improving product features and the price/performance ratio.

Determining whether one is winning or losing end-product battles is more difficult because measures of product market share do not necessarily reflect various companies' underlying competitiveness. Indeed, companies that attempt to build market share by relying on the competitiveness of others, rather than investing in core competencies and world core-product leadership, may be treading on quicksand. In the race for global brand dominance, companies like 3M, Black & Decker, Canon, Honda, NEC, and Citicorp have built global brand umbrellas by proliferating products out of their core competencies. This has allowed their individual businesses to build image, customer loyalty, and access to distribution channels.

When you think about this reconceptualization of the corporation, the primacy of the SBU—an organizational dogma for a generation—is now clearly an anachronism. Where the SBU is an article of faith, resistance to the seductions of decentralization can seem heretical. In many companies, the SBU prism means that only one plane of the global competitive battle, the battle to put competitive products on the shelf *today,* is visible to top management. What are the costs of this distortion?

Underinvestment in Developing Core Competencies and Core Products. When the organization is conceived of as a multiplicity of SBUs, no single business may feel responsible for maintaining a viable position in core products nor be able to justify the investment required to build world leadership in some core competence. In the absence of a more comprehensive view imposed by corporate management, SBU managers will tend to underinvest. Recently, companies such as Kodak and Philips have recognized this as a potential problem and have begun searching for new organizational forms that will allow them to develop and manufacture core products for both internal and external customers.

SBU managers have traditionally conceived of competitors in the same way they've seen themselves. On the whole, they've failed to note the emphasis Asian competitors were placing on building leadership in core products or to understand the critical linkage between world manufacturing leadership and the ability to sustain development pace in core competence. They've failed to pursue OEM-supply opportunities or to look across their various product divisions in an attempt to identify opportunities for coordinated initiatives.

Imprisoned Resources. As an SBU evolves, it often develops unique competencies. Typically, the people who embody this competence are seen as the sole property of the business in which they grew up. The manager of another SBU who asks to borrow talented people is likely to get a cold rebuff. SBU managers are not only unwilling to lend their competence carriers but they may actually hide talent to prevent its redeployment in the pursuit of new opportunities. This may be compared to residents of an underdeveloped country hiding most of their cash under their mattresses. The benefits of competencies, like the benefits of the money supply, depend on the velocity of their circulation as well as on the size of the stock the company holds.

Western companies have traditionally had an advantage in the stock of skills they possess. But have they been able to reconfigure them quickly to respond to new opportunities? Canon, NEC, and Honda have had a lesser stock of the people and technologies that compose core competencies but could move them much quicker from one business unit to another. Corporate R&D spending at Canon is not fully indicative of the size of Canon's core competence stock and tells the casual observer nothing about the velocity with which Canon is able to move core competencies to exploit opportunities.

When competencies become imprisoned, the people who carry the competencies do not get assigned to the most exciting opportunities, and their skills begin to atrophy. Only by fully leveraging core competencies can small companies like Canon afford to compete with industry giants like Xerox. How strange that SBU managers, who are perfectly willing to compete for cash in the capital budgeting process, are unwilling to compete for people—the company's most precious asset. We find it ironic that top management devotes so much attention to the capital budgeting process yet typically has no comparable mechanism for allocating the human skills that embody core competencies. Top managers are seldom able to look four or five levels down into the organization, identify the people who embody critical competencies, and move them across organizational boundaries.

Bounded Innovation. If core competencies are not recognized, individual SBUs will pursue only those innovation opportunities that are close at hand—marginal product-line extensions or geographic expansions. Hybrid opportunities like fax machines, laptop computers, hand-held televisions, or portable music keyboards will emerge only when managers take off their SBU blinkers. Remember, Canon appeared to be in the camera business at the time it was preparing to become a world leader in copiers. Conceiving of the corporation in terms of core competencies widens the domain of innovation.

Developing Strategic Architecture

The fragmentation of core competencies becomes inevitable when a diversified company's information systems, patterns of communication, career paths, managerial rewards, and processes of strategy development do not transcend SBU lines. We believe that senior management should spend a significant amount of its time developing a corporatewide strategic architecture that establishes objectives for competence building. A strategic architecture is a road map of the future that identifies which core competencies to build and their constituent technologies.

By providing an impetus for learning from alliances and a focus for internal development efforts, a strategic architecture like NEC's C&C can dramatically reduce the investment needed to secure future market leadership. How can a company make partnerships intelligently without a clear understanding of the core competencies it is trying to build and those it is attempting to prevent from being unintentionally transferred?

Of course, all of this begs the question of what a strategic architecture should look like. The answer will be different for every company. But it is helpful to think again of that tree, of the corporation organized around core products and, ultimately, core competencies. To sink sufficiently strong roots, a company must answer some fundamental questions: How long could we preserve our competitiveness in this business if we did not control this particular core competence? How central is this core competence to perceived customer benefits? What future opportunities would be foreclosed if we were to lose this particular competence?

The architecture provides a logic for product and market diversification, moreover. An SBU manager would be asked: Does the new market opportunity add to the overall goal of becoming the best player in the world? Does it exploit or add to the core competence? At Vickers, for example, diversification options have been judged in the context of becoming the best power and motion control company in the world (see the sidebar "Vickers Learns the Value of Strategic Architecture").

The strategic architecture should make resource allocation priorities transparent to the entire organization. It provides a template for allocation decisions by top management. It helps lower-level managers understand the logic of allocation priorities and disciplines senior management to maintain consistency. In short, it yields a definition of the company and the markets it serves. 3M, Vickers, NEC, Canon, and Honda all qualify on this score. Honda *knew* it was exploiting what it had learned from motorcycles—how to make high-revving, smooth-running, lightweight engines—when it entered the car business. The task of creating a strategic architecture forces the organization to identify and commit to the technical and production linkages across SBUs that will provide a distinct competitive advantage.

It is consistency of resource allocation and the development of an administrative infrastructure appropriate to it that breathes life into a strategic architecture and creates a managerial culture, teamwork, a capacity to change, and a willingness to share resources, to protect proprietary skills, and to think long term. That is also the reason the specific architecture cannot be copied easily or overnight by competitors. Strategic architecture is a tool for communicating with customers

Vickers Learns the Value of Strategic Architecture

The idea that top management should develop a corporate strategy for acquiring and deploying core competencies is relatively new in most U.S. companies. There are a few exceptions. An early convert was Trinova (previously Libbey Owens Ford), a Toledo-based corporation, which enjoys a worldwide position in power and motion controls and engineered plastics. One of its major divisions is Vickers, a premier supplier of hydraulics components like valves, pumps, actuators, and filtration devices to aerospace, marine, defense, automotive, earth-moving, and industrial markets.

Vickers saw the potential for a transformation of its traditional business with the application of electronics disciplines in combination with its traditional technologies. The goal was "to ensure that change in technology does not displace Vickers from its customers." This, to be sure, was initially a defensive move: Vickers recognized that unless it acquired new skills, it could not protect existing markets or capitalize on new growth opportunities. Managers at Vickers attempted to conceptualize the likely evolution of (a) technologies relevant to the power and motion control business, (b) functionalities that would satisfy emerging customer needs, and (c) new competencies needed to creatively manage the marriage of technology and customer needs.

Despite pressure for short-term earnings, top management looked to a 10- to 15-year time horizon in developing a map of emerging customer needs, changing technologies, and the core competencies that would be necessary to bridge the gap between the two. Its slogan was "Into the 21st Century." (A simplified version of the overall architecture developed is shown here.) Vickers is currently in fluid-power components. The architecture identifies two additional competencies, electric-power components and electronic controls. A systems integration capability that would unite hardware, software, and service was also targeted for development.

The strategic architecture, as illustrated by the Vickers example, is not a forecast of specific products or specific technologies but a broad map of the evolving linkages between customer functionality requirements, potential technologies, and core competencies. It assumes that products and systems cannot be defined with certainty for the future but that preempting competitors in the development of new markets requires an early start to building core competencies. The strategic architecture developed by Vickers, while describing the future in competence terms, also provides the basis for making "here and now" decisions about product priorities, acquisitions, alliances, and recruitment.

(continued)

Vickers map of competencies

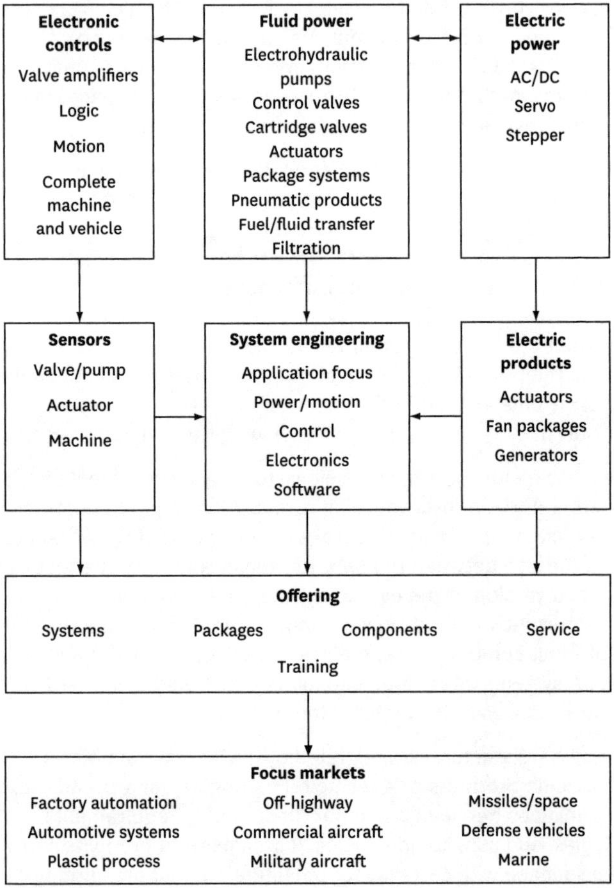

Since 1986, Vickers has made more than ten clearly targeted acquisitions, each one focused on a specific component or technology gap identified in the overall architecture. The architecture is also the basis for internal development of new competencies. Vickers has undertaken, in parallel, a reorganization to enable the integration of electronics and electrical capabilities with mechanical-based competencies. We believe that it will take another two to three years before Vickers reaps the total benefits from developing the strategic architecture, communicating it widely to all its employees, customers, and investors, and building administrative systems consistent with the architecture.

and other external constituents. It reveals the broad direction without giving away every step.

Redeploying to Exploit Competencies

If the company's core competencies are its critical resource and if top management must ensure that competence carriers are not held hostage by some particular business, then it follows that SBUs should bid for core competencies in the same way they bid for capital. We've made this point glancingly. It is important enough to consider more deeply.

Once top management (with the help of divisional and SBU managers) has identified overarching competencies, it must ask businesses to identify the projects and people closely connected with them. Corporate officers should direct an audit of the location, number, and quality of the people who embody competence.

This sends an important signal to middle managers: core competencies are *corporate* resources and may be reallocated by corporate management. An individual business doesn't own anybody. SBUs are entitled to the services of individual employees so long as SBU management can demonstrate that the opportunity it is pursuing yields the highest possible pay-off on the investment in their skills. This message is further underlined if each year in the strategic planning or budgeting process, unit managers must justify their hold on the people who carry the company's core competencies.

Core competencies at Canon

	Precision mechanics	Fine optics	Micro-electronics
Basic camera	■	□	
Compact fashion camera	■	□	
Electronic camera	■	□	
EOS autofocus camera	■	□	■
Video still camera	■	□	■
Laser beam printer	■	□	■
Color video printer	■		■
Bubble jet printer	■		■
Basic fax	■		■
Laser fax	■		■
Calculator			■
Plain paper copier	■	□	■
Battery PPC	■	□	■
Color copier	■	□	■
Laser copier	■	□	■
Color laser copier	■	□	■
NAVI	■	□	■
Still video system	■	□	■
Laser imager	■	□	■
Cell analyzer	■	□	■
Mask aligners	■		■
Stepper aligners	■		■
Excimer laser aligners	■	□	■

Every Canon product is the result of at least one core competency.

Elements of Canon's core competence in optics are spread across businesses as diverse as cameras, copiers, and semiconductor lithographic equipment and are shown in "Core Competencies at Canon." When Canon identified an opportunity in digital laser printers, it gave SBU managers the right to raid other SBUs to pull together the required pool of talent. When Canon's reprographics products division undertook to develop microprocessor-controlled copiers, it turned to the photo products group, which had developed the world's first microprocessor-controlled camera.

Also reward systems that focus only on product-line results and career paths that seldom cross SBU boundaries engender patterns of behavior among unit managers that are destructively competitive. At NEC, divisional managers come together to identify next-generation competencies. Together they decide how much investment needs to be made to build up each future competency and the contribution in capital and staff support that each division will need to make. There is also a sense of equitable exchange. One division may make a disproportionate contribution or may benefit less from the progress made, but such short-term inequalities will balance out over the long term.

Incidentally, the positive contribution of the SBU manager should be made visible across the company. An SBU manager is unlikely to surrender key people if only the other business (or the general manager of that business who may be a competitor for promotion) is going to benefit from the redeployment. Cooperative SBU managers should be celebrated as team players. Where priorities are clear, transfers are less likely to be seen as idiosyncratic and politically motivated.

Transfers for the sake of building core competence must be recorded and appreciated in the corporate memory. It is reasonable to expect a business that has surrendered core skills on behalf of corporate opportunities in other areas to lose, for a time, some of its competitiveness. If these losses in performance bring immediate censure, SBUs will be unlikely to assent to skills transfers next time.

Finally, there are ways to wean key employees off the idea that they belong in perpetuity to any particular business. Early in their careers, people may be exposed to a variety of businesses through a carefully planned rotation program. At Canon, critical people move regularly between the camera business and the copier business and between the copier business and the professional optical-products business. In mid-career, periodic assignments to cross-divisional project teams may be necessary, both for diffusing core competencies and for loosening the bonds that might tie an individual to one business even when brighter opportunities beckon elsewhere. Those who embody critical core competencies should know that their careers are tracked and guided by corporate human resource professionals. In the early 1980s at Canon, all engineers under 30 were invited to apply for membership on a seven-person committee that was to spend two years plotting Canon's future direction, including its strategic architecture.

Competence carriers should be regularly brought together from across the corporation to trade notes and ideas. The goal is to build a strong feeling of community among these people. To a great extent, their loyalty should be to the integrity of the core competence area they represent and not just to particular businesses. In traveling regularly, talking frequently to customers, and meeting with peers, competence carriers may be encouraged to discover new market opportunities.

Core competencies are the wellspring of new business development. They should constitute the focus for strategy at the corporate level. Managers have to win manufacturing leadership in core products and capture global share through brand-building programs aimed at exploiting economies of scope. Only if the company is conceived of as a hierarchy of core competencies, core products, and market-focused business units will it be fit to fight.

Nor can top management be just another layer of accounting consolidation, which it often is in a regime of radical decentralization. Top management must add value by enunciating the strategic architecture that guides the competence acquisition process. We believe an obsession with competence building will characterize the global winners of the 1990s. With the decade under way, the time for rethinking the concept of the corporation is already overdue.

Originally published in May 1990. Reprint 90311

Notes

1. For a fuller discussion, see our article, "Strategic Intent," *HBR,* May–June 1989, p. 63.

2. "Collaborate with Your Competitors and Win," *HBR,* January–February 1989, p. 133, with Yves L. Doz.

About the Contributors

CLAYTON M. CHRISTENSEN is the Robert and Jane Cizik Professor of Business Administration at Harvard Business School.

THOMAS H. DAVENPORT is the President's Distinguished Professor of Information Technology and Management at Babson College.

PETER F. DRUCKER was a writer, teacher, and consultant. His thirty-four books have been published in more than seventy languages. He founded the Peter F. Drucker Foundation for Nonprofit Management.

DANIEL GOLEMAN is Codirector of the Consortium for Research on Emotional Intelligence in Organizations at Rutgers University.

GARY HAMEL is Visiting Professor of Strategic and International Management at the London Business School; cofounder of Strategos, an international consulting company; and director of the Management Innovation Lab.

ROSABETH MOSS KANTER is the Ernest L. Arbuckle Professor of Business Administration at Harvard Business School, specializing in strategy, innovation, and leadership for change

ROBERT S. KAPLAN is the Baker Foundation Professor at Harvard Business School.

JOHN P. KOTTER is the Konosuke Matsushita Professor of Leadership, Emeritus, at Harvard Business School.

THEODORE LEVITT is the Edward W. Carter Professor of Business Administration Emeritus at the Harvard Business School and former editor of the Harvard Business Review.

DAVID P. NORTON is the founder of The Balanced Scorecard Collaborative and a director of The Palladium Group.

MICHAEL OVERDORF is a Dean's research Fellow at Harvard Business School.

MICHAEL E. PORTER is the Bishop William Lawrence University Professor at Harvard Business School. He is the leader of the Institute for Strategy and Competitiveness at Harvard Business School.

C.K. PRAHALAD was the Paul and Ruth McCracken Distinguished University Professor of Corporate Strategy at the University of Michigan's Ross School of Business, until his death in April 2010.

Index

HBR'S 10 MUST READS

On Teams

HBR's 10 Must Reads series is the definitive collection of ideas and best practices for aspiring and experienced leaders alike. These books offer essential reading selected from the pages of *Harvard Business Review* on topics critical to the success of every manager.

Titles include:

HBR's 10 Must Reads on Change Management
HBR's 10 Must Reads on Collaboration
HBR's 10 Must Reads on Communication
HBR's 10 Must Reads on Innovation
HBR's 10 Must Reads on Leadership
HBR's 10 Must Reads on Making Smart Decisions
HBR's 10 Must Reads on Managing People
HBR's 10 Must Reads on Managing Yourself
HBR's 10 Must Reads on Strategic Marketing
HBR's 10 Must Reads on Strategy
HBR's 10 Must Reads on Teams
HBR's 10 Must Reads: The Essentials

HBR'S 10 MUST READS

On Teams

HARVARD BUSINESS REVIEW PRESS
Boston, Massachusetts

Printed in the United States of America
24 23 22 21 20 19 18 17 16

Library of Congress Cataloging-in-Publication Data

HBR's 10 must reads on teams.
pages cm. — (HBR's 10 must reads series)
Includes index.
ISBN 978-1-4221-8987-0 (alk. paper)
1. Teams in the workplace. I. Harvard Business Review Press. II. Title: HBR's ten must reads on teams. III. Title: 10 must reads on teams. IV. Title: Ten must reads on teams.
HD66.H394 2013
658.4'022–dc23 2012046240

The paper used in this publication meets the requirements of the American National Standard for Permanence of Paper for Publications and Documents in Libraries and Archives Z39.48-1992.

Contents

HBR'S 10 MUST READS

On Teams

The New Science of Building Great Teams

The chemistry of high-performing groups is no longer a mystery. ***by Alex "Sandy" Pentland***

IF YOU WERE looking for teams to rig for success, a call center would be a good place to start. The skills required for call center work are easy to identify and hire for. The tasks involved are clear-cut and easy to monitor. Just about every aspect of team performance is easy to measure: number of issues resolved, customer satisfaction, average handling time (AHT, the golden standard of call center efficiency). And the list goes on.

Why, then, did the manager at a major bank's call center have such trouble figuring out why some of his teams got excellent results, while other, seemingly similar, teams struggled? Indeed, none of the metrics that poured in hinted at the reason for the performance gaps. This mystery reinforced his assumption that team building was an art, not a science.

The truth is quite the opposite. At MIT's Human Dynamics Laboratory, we have identified the elusive group dynamics that characterize high-performing teams—those blessed with the energy, creativity, and shared commitment to far surpass other teams. These dynamics are observable, quantifiable, and measurable. And, perhaps most important, teams can be taught how to strengthen them.

Why Do Patterns of Communication Matter So Much?

It seems almost absurd that how we communicate could be so much more important to success than what we communicate.

Yet if we look at our evolutionary history, we can see that language is a relatively recent development and was most likely layered upon older signals that communicated dominance, interest, and emotions among humans. Today these ancient patterns of communication still shape how we make decisions and coordinate work among ourselves.

Consider how early man may have approached problem solving. One can imagine humans sitting around a campfire (as a team) making suggestions, relating observations, and indicating interest or approval with head nods, gestures, or vocal signals. If some people failed to contribute or to signal their level of interest or approval, then the group members had less information and weaker judgment, and so were more likely to go hungry.

Looking for the "It Factor"

When we set out to document the behavior of teams that "click," we noticed we could sense a buzz in a team even if we didn't understand what the members were talking about. That suggested that the key to high performance lay not in the content of a team's discussions but in the manner in which it was communicating. Yet little of the research on team building had focused on communication. Suspecting it might be crucial, we decided to examine it more deeply.

For our studies, we looked across a diverse set of industries to find workplaces that had similar teams with varying performance. Ultimately, our research included innovation teams, post-op wards in hospitals, customer-facing teams in banks, backroom operations teams, and call center teams, among others.

We equipped all the members of those teams with electronic badges that collected data on their individual communication behavior—tone of voice, body language, whom they talked to and how much, and more. With remarkable consistency, the data confirmed that communication indeed plays a critical role in building successful teams. In fact, we've found patterns of communication to be the most

Idea in Brief

Why do some teams consistently deliver high performance while other, seemingly identical teams struggle? Led by Sandy Pentland, researchers at MIT's Human Dynamics Laboratory set out to solve that puzzle. Hoping to decode the "It factor" that made groups click, they equipped teams from a broad variety of projects and industries (comprising 2,500 individuals in total) with wearable electronic sensors that collected data on their social behavior for weeks at a time.

With remarkable consistency, the data showed that the most important predictor of a team's success was its communication patterns. Those patterns were as significant as all other factors—intelligence, personality, talent—combined. In fact, the researchers could foretell which teams would outperform simply by looking at the data on their communication, without even meeting their members.

In this article Pentland shares the secrets of his findings and shows how anyone can engineer a great team. He has identified three key communication dynamics that affect performance: *energy*, *engagement*, and *exploration*. Drawing from the data, he has precisely quantified the ideal team patterns for each. Even more significant, he has seen that when teams map their own communication behavior over time and then make adjustments that move it closer to the ideal, they can dramatically improve their performance.

important predictor of a team's success. Not only that, but they are as significant as all the other factors—individual intelligence, personality, skill, and the substance of discussions—combined.

Patterns of communication, for example, explained why performance varied so widely among the seemingly identical teams in that bank's call center. Several teams there wore our badges for six weeks. When my fellow researchers (my colleagues at Sociometric Solutions—Taemie Kim, Daniel Olguin, and Ben Waber) and I analyzed the data collected, we found that the best predictors of productivity were a team's energy and engagement outside formal meetings. Together those two factors explained one-third of the variations in dollar productivity among groups.

Drawing on that insight, we advised the center's manager to revise the employees' coffee break schedule so that everyone on a team took a break at the same time. That would allow people more time to socialize with their teammates, away from their workstations. Though the suggestion flew in the face of standard efficiency practices, the manager was baffled and desperate, so he tried it. And it worked: AHT fell by more than 20% among lower-performing teams and decreased by 8% overall at the call center. Now the manager is changing the break schedule at all 10 of the bank's call centers (which employ a total of 25,000 people) and is forecasting $15 million a year in productivity increases. He has also seen employee satisfaction at call centers rise, sometimes by more than 10%.

Any company, no matter how large, has the potential to achieve this same kind of transformation. Firms now can obtain the tools and data they need to accurately dissect and engineer high performance. Building great teams has become a science. Here's how it works.

Overcoming the Limits of Observation

When we sense esprit de corps, that perception doesn't come out of the blue; it's the result of our innate ability to process the hundreds of complex communication cues that we constantly send and receive.

But until recently we had never been able to objectively record such cues as data that we could then mine to understand why teams click. Mere observation simply couldn't capture every nuance of human behavior across an entire team. What we had, then, was only a strong sense of the things—good leadership and followership, palpable shared commitment, a terrific brainstorming session—that made a team greater than the sum of its parts.

Recent advances in wireless and sensor technology, though, have helped us overcome those limitations, allowing us to measure that ineffable "It factor." The badges developed at my lab at MIT are in their seventh version. They generate more than 100 data points a minute and work unobtrusively enough that we're confident we're capturing natural behavior. (We've documented a period of adjustment to the badges: Early on, people appear to be aware of them and act unnaturally, but the effect dissipates, usually within an hour.)

We've deployed them in 21 organizations over the past seven years, measuring the communication patterns of about 2,500 people, sometimes for six weeks at a time.

With the data we've collected, we've mapped the communication behaviors of large numbers of people as they go about their lives, at an unprecedented level of detail. The badges produce "sociometrics," or measures of how people interact—such as what tone of voice they use; whether they face one another; how much they gesture; how much they talk, listen, and interrupt; and even their levels of extroversion and empathy. By comparing data gathered from all the individuals on a team with performance data, we can identify the communication patterns that make for successful teamwork.

Those patterns vary little, regardless of the type of team and its goal—be it a call center team striving for efficiency, an innovation team at a pharmaceutical company looking for new product ideas, or a senior management team hoping to improve its leadership. Productive teams have certain data signatures, and they're so consistent that we can predict a team's success simply by looking at the data—without ever meeting its members.

We've been able to foretell, for example, which teams will win a business plan contest, solely on the basis of data collected from team members wearing badges at a cocktail reception. (See "Defend Your Research: We Can Measure the Power of Charisma," HBR January–February 2010.) We've predicted the financial results that teams making investments would achieve, just on the basis of data collected during their negotiations. We can see in the data when team members will report that they've had a "productive" or "creative" day.

The data also reveal, at a higher level, that successful teams share several defining characteristics:

1. Everyone on the team talks and listens in roughly equal measure, keeping contributions short and sweet.
2. Members face one another, and their conversations and gestures are energetic.

3. Members connect directly with one another—not just with the team leader.
4. Members carry on back-channel or side conversations within the team.
5. Members periodically break, go exploring outside the team, and bring information back.

The data also establish another surprising fact: Individual reasoning and talent contribute far less to team success than one might expect. The best way to build a great team is not to select individuals for their smarts or accomplishments but to learn how they communicate and to shape and guide the team so that it follows successful communication patterns.

The Key Elements of Communication

In our research we identified three aspects of communication that affect team performance. The first is *energy,* which we measure by the number and the nature of exchanges among team members. A single exchange is defined as a comment and some acknowledgment—for example, a "yes" or a nod of the head. Normal conversations are often made up of many of these exchanges, and in a team setting more than one exchange may be going on at a time.

The most valuable form of communication is face-to-face. The next most valuable is by phone or videoconference, but with a caveat: Those technologies become less effective as more people participate in the call or conference. The least valuable forms of communication are e-mail and texting. (We collect data on those kinds of communication without using the badges. Still, the number of face-to-face exchanges alone provides a good rough measure of energy.) The number of exchanges engaged in, weighted for their value by type of communication, gives each team member an energy score, which is averaged with other members' results to create a team score.

Energy levels within a team are not static. For instance, in my research group at MIT, we sometimes have meetings at which I update people on upcoming events, rule changes, and other administrative details. These meetings are invariably low energy. But when someone announces a new discovery in the same group, excitement and energy skyrocket as all the members start talking to one another at once.

The second important dimension of communication is *engagement,* which reflects the distribution of energy among team members. In a simple three-person team, engagement is a function of the average amount of energy between A and B, A and C, and B and C. If all members of a team have relatively equal and reasonably high energy with all other members, engagement is extremely strong. Teams that have clusters of members who engage in high-energy communication while other members do not participate don't perform as well. When we observed teams making investment decisions, for instance, the partially engaged teams made worse (less profitable) decisions than the fully engaged teams. This effect was particularly common in far-flung teams that talked mostly by telephone.

The third critical dimension, *exploration,* involves communication that members engage in outside their team. Exploration essentially is the energy between a team and the other teams it interacts with. Higher-performing teams seek more outside connections, we've found. We've also seen that scoring well on exploration is most important for creative teams, such as those responsible for innovation, which need fresh perspectives.

To measure exploration, we have to deploy badges more widely in an organization. We've done so in many settings, including the MIT Media Lab and a multinational company's marketing department, which comprised several teams dedicated to different functions.

Our data also show that exploration and engagement, while both good, don't easily coexist, because they require that the energy of team members be put to two different uses. Energy is a finite resource. The more that people devote to their own team (engagement), the less they have to use outside their team (exploration), and vice versa.

But they must do both. Successful teams, especially successful creative teams, oscillate between exploration for discovery and engagement for integration of the ideas gathered from outside sources. At the MIT Media Lab, this pattern accounted for almost half of the differences in creative output of research groups. And in one industrial research lab we studied, it distinguished teams with high creativity from those with low creativity with almost 90% accuracy.

Beyond Conventional Wisdom

A skeptic would argue that the points about energy, engagement, and exploration are blindingly obvious. But the data from our research improve on conventional wisdom. They add an unprecedented level of precision to our observations, quantify the key dynamics, and make them measurable to an extraordinary degree.

For example, we now know that 35% of the variation in a team's performance can be accounted for simply by the number of face-to-face exchanges among team members. We know as well that the "right" number of exchanges in a team is as many as dozens per working hour, but that going beyond that ideal number decreases performance. We can also state with certainty that in a typical high-performance team, members are listening or speaking to the whole group only about half the time, and when addressing the whole group, each team member speaks for only his or her fair share of time, using brief, to-the-point statements. The other half of the time members are engaging in one-on-one conversations, which are usually quite short. It may seem illogical that all those side exchanges contribute to better performance, rather than distract a team, but the data prove otherwise.

The data we've collected on the importance of socializing not only build on conventional wisdom but sometimes upend it. Social time turns out to be deeply critical to team performance, often accounting for more than 50% of positive changes in communication patterns, even in a setting as efficiency-focused as a call center.

Without the data there's simply no way to understand which dynamics drive successful teams. The managers of one young software company, for instance, thought they could promote better communication among employees by hosting "beer meets" and other events. But the badge data showed that these events had little or no effect. In contrast, the data revealed that making the tables in the company's lunchroom longer, so that strangers sat together, had a huge impact.

A similarly refined view of exploration has emerged in the data. Using fresh perspectives to improve performance is hardly a surprising idea; it's practically management canon. But our research shows that most companies don't do it the right way. Many organizations we've studied seek outside counsel repeatedly from the same sources and only at certain times (when building a business case, say, or doing a postmortem on a project). The best-performing and most creative teams in our study, however, sought fresh perspectives constantly, from all other groups in (and some outside) the organization.

How to Apply the Data

For management tasks that have long defied objective analysis, like team building, data can now provide a foundation on which to build better individual and team performance. This happens in three steps.

Step 1: Visualization

In raw form the data don't mean much to the teams being measured. An energy score of 0.5 may be good for an individual, for example, but descriptions of team dynamics that rely on statistical output are not particularly user-friendly. However, using the formulas we developed to calculate energy, engagement, and exploration, we can create maps of how a team is doing on those dimensions, visualizations that clearly convey the data and are instantly accessible to anyone. The maps starkly highlight weaknesses that teams may not have recognized. They identify low-energy, unengaged team members who, even in the visualization, look as if they're being ignored. (For examples, see the sidebar "Mapping Teamwork.")

When we spot such people, we dig down into their individual badge data. Are they trying to contribute and being ignored or cut off? Do they cut others off and not listen, thereby discouraging colleagues from seeking their opinions? Do they communicate only with one other team member? Do they face other people in meetings or tend to hide from the group physically? Do they speak loudly enough? Perhaps the leader of a team is too dominant; it may be that she is doing most of the talking at meetings and needs to work on

Mapping Teamwork

CONCERNED ABOUT UNEVEN PERFORMANCE across its branches, a bank in Prague outfitted customer-facing teams with electronic sensors for six weeks. The first two maps below display data collected from one team of nine people over the course of different days, and the third illustrates data collected on interactions between management and all the teams.

By looking at the data, we unearthed a divide between teams at the "Soviet era" branches of the bank and teams at more modern facilities. Interestingly, at the Soviet-era branches, where poor team communication was the rule, communication outside teams was much higher, suggesting that those teams were desperately reaching out for answers to their problems. Teams at the modern facilities showed high energy and less need to explore outside. After seeing initial data, the bank's management published these dashboard displays for all the teams to see and also reorganized the teams so that they contained a mix of members from old and new branches. According to the bank, those measures helped improve the working culture within all the teams.

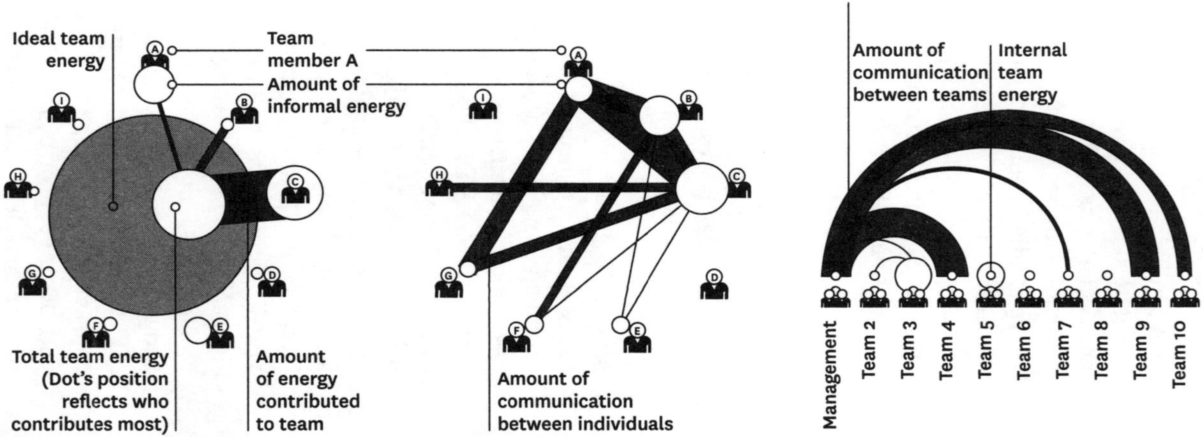

Energy

How team members contribute to a team as a whole

Clearly, these data come from a team at a branch with poor customer service. We can see that A, C, and E give off more informal energy than the rest of the team does. A, B, and C contribute a lot to the team, while the others contribute nothing. The pattern illustrated here is often associated with hierarchical teams in which a boss (C) issues commands while his lieutenants (A and B) reinforce his directions. The three are a "team within a team," and it's likely that the others feel they have no input. Often leaders are shocked and embarrassed to see how much they dominate a team and immediately try to change the pattern. Sharing such a map with the team can make it easier for less energetic individuals to talk about their sense of the team's dysfunction, because data are objective and elevate the discussion beyond attacks or complaints.

Engagement

How team members communicate with one another

This diagram shows that the same team's engagement skews heavily to the same three people (A, B, and C). G is making an effort to reach the decision makers, but the team within the team is where the engagement is. Those three people may be higher up the ladder or simply more extroverted, but that doesn't matter. This pattern is associated with lower performance because the team is not getting ideas or information from many of its members. Leaders can use this map both to assess "invisible" team members (How can they get them more involved? Are they the right people for the project?) and to play the role of a "charismatic connector" by bringing together members who ought to be talking to one another and then helping those members share their thinking with the entire group.

Exploration

How teams communicate with one another

This map shows that management is doing a lot of exploring. Although its internal team energy is relatively low, that is OK. Energy and engagement cannot be high when exploration is, because when you're exploring you have less time to engage with your own team. In a high-functioning organization, however, there would be more exploration among all the teams, and you'd see an arc between, say, Teams 3 and 4, or Teams 5 and 9. A time lapse view of all the teams' exploration would show whether teams were oscillating between communication within their own group (shown by the dots) and exploration with other teams (shown by the arcs). If they're not, it could mean silo busting is needed to encourage proper exploration.

Source: Courtesy of Sociometric Solutions

encouraging others to participate. Energy and engagement maps will make such problems clear. And once we know what they are, we can begin to fix them.

Exploration maps reveal patterns of communication across organizations. They can expose, for instance, whether a department's management is failing to engage with all its teams. Time-lapse views of engagement and exploration will show whether teams are effectively oscillating between those two activities. It's also possible to layer more detail into the visualizations. We can create maps that break out different types of communication among team members, to discover, for example, if teams are falling into counterproductive patterns such as shooting off e-mail when they need more face time. (For an example, see the sidebar "Mapping Communication over Time.")

Mapping Communication over Time

THE MAPS BELOW DEPICT the communication patterns in a German bank's marketing department in the days leading up to and immediately following a major new product launch. The department had teams of four members each in customer service, sales, support, development, and management. Besides collecting data on in-person interactions with sociometric badges, we gathered e-mail data to assess the balance between high-value face-to-face communication and lower-value digital messages.

We did not provide iterative feedback in this project, but if we had, by the end of week one, we would have pointed out three negative trends the group could have corrected: the invisibility of customer service, overreliance on e-mail, and highly uneven communication among groups. If these issues had been addressed, the problems with the product might have surfaced much earlier, and the responses to them would probably have improved.

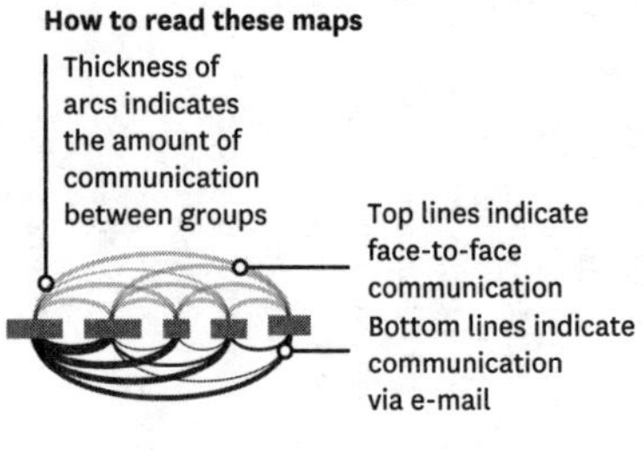
How to read these maps
Thickness of arcs indicates the amount of communication between groups
Top lines indicate face-to-face communication
Bottom lines indicate communication via e-mail

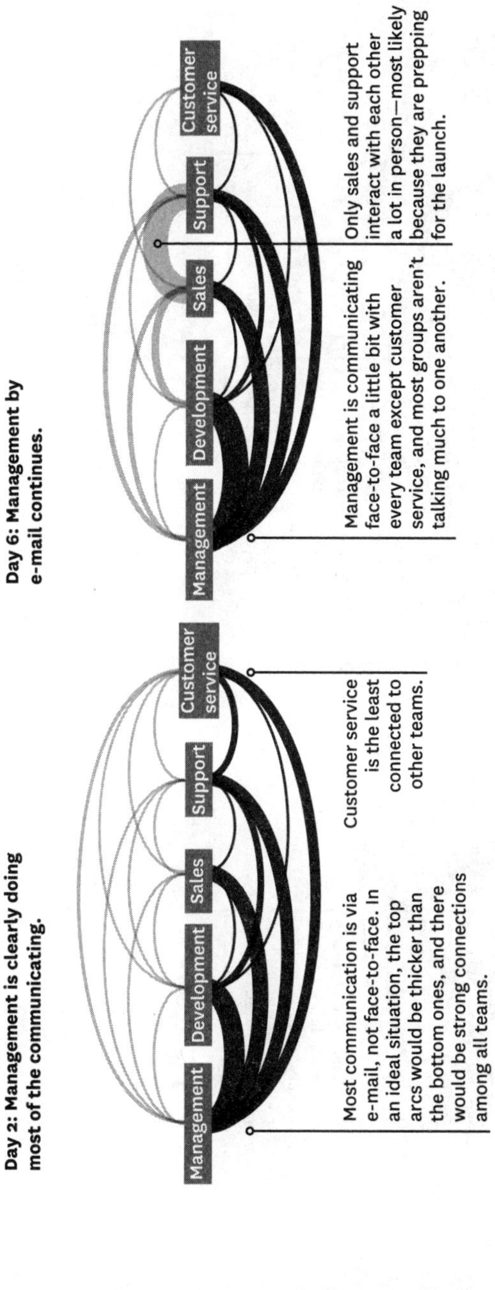
Day 2: Management is clearly doing most of the communicating.
Management
Development
Sales
Support
Customer service
Most communication is via e-mail, not face-to-face. In an ideal situation, the top arcs would be thicker than the bottom ones, and there would be strong connections among all teams.
Customer service is the least connected to other teams.
Day 6: Management by e-mail continues.
Management
Development
Sales
Support
Customer service
Management is communicating face-to-face a little bit with every team except customer service, and most groups aren't talking much to one another.
Only sales and support interact with each other a lot in person—most likely because they are prepping for the launch.

(continued)

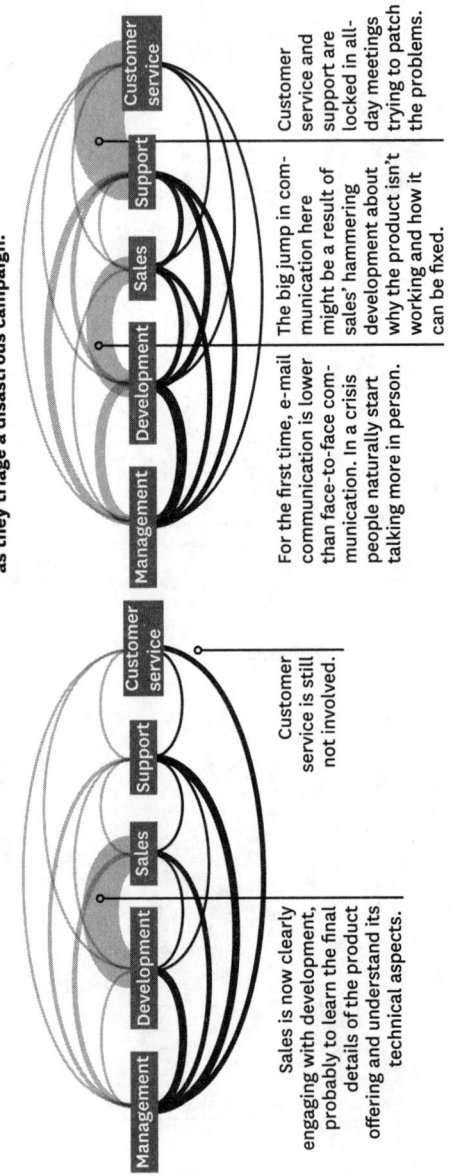

Day 15: As the launch approaches, communication is startlingly low.

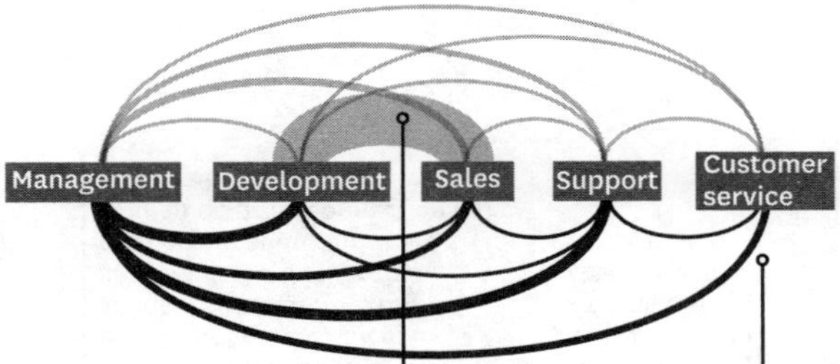

Sales is now clearly engaging with development, probably to learn the final details of the product offering and understand its technical aspects.

Customer service is still not involved.

Day 23: Two days after launch, teams are finally communicating in person, as they triage a disastrous campaign.

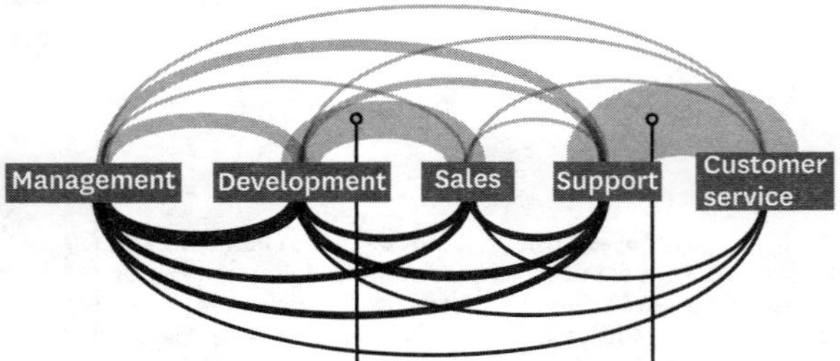

For the first time, e-mail communication is lower than face-to-face communication. In a crisis people naturally start talking more in person.

The big jump in communication here might be a result of sales' hammering development about why the product isn't working and how it can be fixed.

Customer service and support are locked in all-day meetings trying to patch the problems.

Step 2: Training

With maps of the data in hand, we can help teams improve performance through iterative visual feedback.

Work we did with a multicultural design team composed of both Japanese and American members offers a good example. (Visual data are especially effective at helping far-flung and multilingual groups, which face special communication challenges.) The team's maps (see the sidebar "Mapping communication improvement") showed that its communication was far too uneven. They highlighted that the Japanese members were initially reluctant to speak up, leaving the team both low energy and unengaged.

Mapping Communication Improvement

Our data show that far-flung and mixed-language teams often struggle to gel. Distance plays a role: Electronic communication doesn't create the same energy and engagement that face-to-face communication does. Cultural norms play a role too. Visual feedback on communication patterns can help.

For one week we gathered data on a team composed of Japanese and Americans that were brainstorming a new design together in Japan. Each day the team was shown maps of its communication patterns and given simple guidance about what makes good communication (active but equal participation).

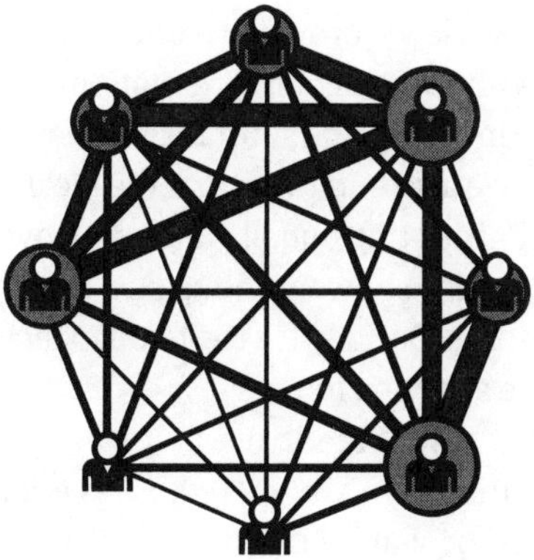

(continued)

Day 1

The two Japanese team members (bottom and lower left) are not engaged, and a team within a team seems to have formed around the member at the top right.

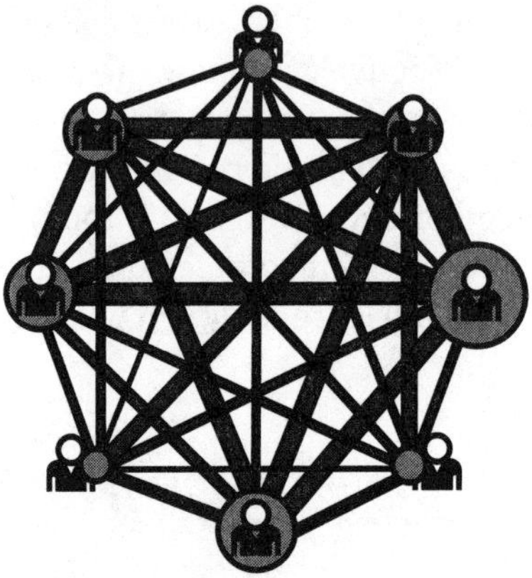

Day 7

The team has improved remarkably. Not only are the Japanese members contributing more to energy and engagement (with the one at the bottom becoming a high-energy, highly engaged team member) but some of the Day 1 "dominators" (on the lower right, for example) have distributed their energy better.

Every day for a week, we provided team members a visualization of that day's work, with some light interpretation of what we saw. (Keep in mind that we didn't know the substance of their work, just how they were interacting.) We also told them that the ideal visualization would show members contributing equally and more overall contributions. By day seven, the maps showed, the team's energy and engagement had improved vastly, especially for the two Japanese members, one of whom had become a driving force.

The notion that visual feedback helps people improve quickly shouldn't be surprising to anyone who has ever had a golf swing analyzed on video or watched himself deliver a speech. Now we have the visual tools to likewise improve teamwork through objective analysis.

Step 3: Fine-tuning performance

We have seen that by using visualizations as a training tool, teams can quickly improve their patterns of communication. But does that translate to improved performance? Yes. The third and final step in using the badge data is to map energy and engagement against performance metrics. In the case of the Japanese-American team, for example, we mapped the improved communication patterns against the team's self-reported daily productivity. The closer the patterns came to those of our high-performance ideal, the higher productivity rose.

We've duplicated this result several times over, running similar feedback loops with teams aiming to be more creative and with executive teams looking for more cohesiveness. In every case the self-reporting on effectiveness mapped to the improved patterns of communication.

Through such maps, we often make important discoveries. One of the best examples comes from the bank's call center. For each team there, we mapped energy and engagement against average handling time (AHT), which we indicated with color. (See the sidebar "Mapping Communication Against Performance.") That map clearly showed that the most efficient work was done by high-energy, high-engagement teams. But surprisingly, it also showed that low-energy, low-engagement teams could outperform teams that were unbalanced—teams that had high energy and low engagement, or low energy and high engagement. The maps revealed that the manager needed to keep energy and engagement in balance as he worked to strengthen them.

If a hard metric like AHT isn't available, we can map patterns against subjective measures. We have asked teams to rate their days on a scale of "creativity" or "frustration," for example, and then seen which patterns are associated with highly creative or frustrating days. Teams often describe this feedback as "a revelation."

Mapping Communication Against Performance

VISUALIZATIONS CAN BE USED to compare energy and engagement with established performance metrics. The map below plots the energy and engagement levels of several teams at a bank call center against the center's metric of efficiency, average handling time (AHT).

The expected team efficiency is based on a statistical analysis of actual team AHT scores over six weeks. Blue indicates high efficiency; red low efficiency. High-energy, high-engagement teams are the most efficient, the map shows. But it also indicates that low-energy, low-engagement teams outperform teams that are out of balance, with high energy and low engagement, or low energy and high engagement. This means the call center manager can pull more than one lever to improve performance. **Points Ⓐ and Ⓑ** are equally efficient, for example, but reflect different combinations of energy and engagement.

The manager wanted to raise energy and engagement in lockstep. We suggested instituting a common coffee break for each team at the call center. This increased the number of interactions, especially informal ones, and raised the teams' energy levels. And because all team members took a break at once, interactions were evenly distributed, increasing engagement. When we mapped energy and engagement against AHT afterward, the results were

Successful tactics

The obvious question at this point is, Once I recognize I need to improve energy and engagement, how do I go about doing it? What are the best techniques for moving those measurements?

Simple approaches such as reorganizing office space and seating are effective. So is setting a personal example—when a manager himself actively encourages even participation and conducts more face-to-face communication. Policy changes can improve teams, too. Eschewing Robert's Rules of Order, for example, is a great way to promote change. In some cases, switching out team members and bringing in new blood may be the best way to improve the energy and engagement of the team, though we've found that this is often unnecessary. Most people, given feedback, can learn to interrupt less, say, or to face other people, or to listen more actively. Leaders should use the data to force change within their teams.

clear: Efficiency in the center increased by 8%, on average, and by as much as 20% for the worst-performing teams.

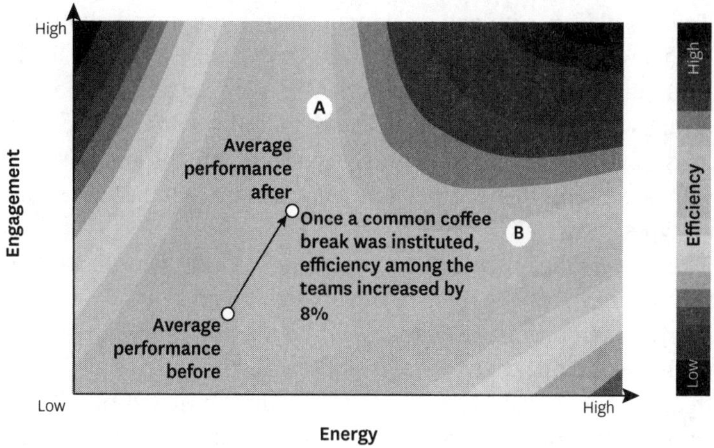

The ideal team player

We can also measure individuals against an ideal. In both productivity-focused and creativity-focused teams, we have discovered the data signature of what we consider the best type of team member. Some might call these individuals "natural leaders." We call them "charismatic connectors." Badge data show that these people circulate actively, engaging people in short, high-energy conversations. They are democratic with their time—communicating with everyone equally and making sure all team members get a chance to contribute. They're not necessarily extroverts, although they feel comfortable approaching other people. They listen as much as or more than they talk and are usually very engaged with whomever they're listening to. We call it "energized but focused listening."

The best team players also connect their teammates with one another and spread ideas around. And they are appropriately exploratory, seeking ideas from outside the group but not at the expense of group engagement. In a study of executives attending an intensive one-week executive education class at MIT, we found that the more of these charismatic connectors a team had, the more successful it was.

Team building is indeed a science, but it's young and evolving. Now that we've established patterns of communication as the single most important thing to measure when gauging the effectiveness of a group, we can begin to refine the data and processes to create more-sophisticated measurements, dig deeper into the analysis, and develop new tools that sharpen our view of team member types and team types.

The sensors that enable this science are evolving as well. As they enter their seventh generation, they're becoming as small and unobtrusive as traditional ID badges, while the amount and types of data they can collect are increasing. We've begun to experiment with apps that present teams and their leaders with real-time feedback on group communications. And the applications for the sensors are expanding beyond the team to include an ever-broader set of situations.

We imagine a company's entire staff wearing badges over an extended period of time, creating "big data" in which we'd find the patterns for everything from team building to leadership to negotiations to performance reviews. We imagine changing the nature of the space we work in, and maybe even the tools we use to communicate, on the basis of the data. We believe we can vastly improve long-distance work and cross-cultural teams, which are so crucial in a global economy, by learning their patterns and adjusting them. We are beginning to create what I call the "God's-eye view" of the organization. But spiritual as that may sound, this view is rooted in evidence and data. It is an amazing view, and it will change how organizations work.

Originally published in April 2012. Reprint R1204C

Why Teams Don't Work

An Interview with J. Richard Hackman. *by Diane Coutu*

OVER THE PAST COUPLE of decades, a cult has grown up around teams. Even in a society as fiercely independent as America, teams are considered almost sacrosanct. The belief that working in teams makes us more creative and productive is so widespread that when faced with a challenging new task, leaders are quick to assume that teams are the best way to get the job done.

Not so fast, says J. Richard Hackman, the Edgar Pierce Professor of Social and Organizational Psychology at Harvard University and a leading expert on teams. Hackman has spent a career exploring—and questioning—the wisdom of teams. To learn from his insights, HBR senior editor Diane Coutu interviewed Hackman in his Harvard office. In the course of their discussion, he revealed just how bad people often are at teamwork. Most of the time, his research shows, team members don't even agree on what the team is supposed to be doing. Getting agreement is the leader's job, and she must be willing to take great personal and professional risks to set the team's direction. And if the leader isn't disciplined about managing who is on the team and how it is set up, the odds are slim that a team will do a good job.

What follows is an edited version of that conversation.

You begin your book* Leading Teams *with a pop quiz: When people work together to build a house, will the job probably (a) get done faster, (b) take longer to finish, or (c) not get done?

That multiple choice question actually appeared on a standardized fourth-grade test in Ohio, and the obvious "answer," of course, is supposed to be *a*—the work gets done faster. I love that anecdote because it illustrates how early we're told that teamwork is good. People tend to think that teams are the democratic—and the efficient—way to get things done. I have no question that when you have a team, the possibility exists that it will generate magic, producing something extraordinary, a collective creation of previously unimagined quality or beauty. But don't count on it. Research consistently shows that teams underperform, despite all the extra resources they have. That's because problems with coordination and motivation typically chip away at the benefits of collaboration. And even when you have a strong and cohesive team, it's often in competition with other teams, and that dynamic can also get in the way of real progress. So you have two strikes against you right from the start, which is one reason why having a team is often worse than having no team at all.

You've said that for a team to be successful, it needs to be real. What does that mean?

At the very least, it means that teams have to be bounded. It may seem silly to say this, but if you're going to lead a team, you ought to first make sure that you know who's on it. In our recent book *Senior Leadership Teams,* Ruth Wageman, Debra Nunes, James Burruss, and I collected and analyzed data on more than 120 top teams around the world. Not surprisingly, we found that almost every senior team we studied thought that it had set unambiguous boundaries. Yet when we asked members to describe their team, fewer than 10% agreed about who was on it. And these were teams of senior executives!

Often the CEO is responsible for the fuzziness of team boundaries. Fearful of seeming exclusionary—or, on the other end of the spectrum, determined to put people on the team for purely political reasons—the chief executive frequently creates a dysfunctional team. In truth, putting together a team involves some ruthless decisions about membership; not everyone who wants to be on the team should be included, and some individuals should be forced off.

Idea in Brief

Contrary to conventional wisdom, teams may be your *worst* option for tackling a challenging task. Problems with coordination, motivation, and competition can badly damage team performance.

Even the best leaders can't *make* a team deliver great results. But you can increase the likelihood of success—by setting the right conditions. For example:

- **Designate a "deviant."** Appoint a naysayer who will challenge the team's desire for too much homogeneity (which stifles creativity).
- **Avoid double digits.** Build teams of no more than nine people. Too many more, and the number of links between members becomes unmanageable.
- **Keep the team together.** Established teams work more effectively than those whose composition changes constantly.

We worked with a large financial services firm where the CFO wasn't allowed on the executive committee because he was clearly a team destroyer. He was disinclined toward teamwork, he was unwilling to work at finding collective solutions, and every team he was on got into trouble. The CEO invited the CFO to stay in his role because he was a truly able executive, but he was not allowed on the senior executive team. Although there were some bruised feelings at first, in the end the CFO was much happier because he didn't have to be in "boring" team meetings, and the team functioned much better without him. The arrangement worked because the CEO communicated extensively with the CFO both before and after every executive committee meeting. And in the CFO's absence, the committee could become a real team.

You also say that a team needs a compelling direction. How does it get one?

There is no one right way to set a direction; the responsibility can fall to the team leader or to someone in the organization outside the team or even to the team itself in the case of partnerships or boards of directors. But however it's done, setting a direction is emotionally demanding because it always involves the exercise of authority, and

Idea in Practice

Additional ideas for getting the best performance from your team.

Be Ruthless About Membership

Putting together a team involves some hard decisions about who will contribute best to accomplishing the team's goals. Not everyone who wants to be on a team should be included, and some individuals should be forced off.

> ***Example:*** In a large financial services firm, the CFO, a brilliant individual contributor, wasn't allowed on the executive committee because he was clearly disinclined toward teamwork and unwilling to work at finding collective solutions. The team functioned much better without him. The arrangement worked because the CEO communicated extensively with the CFO before and after every executive-committee meeting.

Set a Compelling Direction

Make sure your team members know—and agree on—what they're supposed to be doing together. Unless you articulate a clear direction, different members will likely pursue different agendas.

Embrace Your Own Quirkiness

There's no one right style for leading a team, so don't try to ape someone else's leadership approach. You bring your own strengths and weaknesses to the effort. Exploit what you're great at, and get help in the areas where you're not as competent.

that inevitably arouses angst and ambivalence—for both the person exercising it and the people on the receiving end. Leaders who are emotionally mature are willing and able to move toward anxiety-inspiring situations as they establish a clear, challenging team direction. But in doing so, a leader sometimes encounters resistance so intense that it can place his or her job at risk.

That point was dramatically brought home to me a few years ago by a participant in an executive seminar I was teaching. I'd been talking about how leaders who set direction successfully are unafraid to assume personal responsibility for the mission of the team. I mentioned John F. Kennedy and Martin Luther King, Jr., and I got carried away and said that people who read the New Testament knew that Jesus did not convene little team meetings to decide the

Focus Your Coaching on Group Processes

For your team to reap the benefits of any coaching you provide, you'll need to focus that coaching on enhancing group processes, not on guiding and correcting individual behavior. Also, timing is everything. You'll need to know how to:

- **Run a launch meeting,** so members become oriented to and engaged with their tasks.
- **Help the team conduct midpoint reviews** on what's functioning well—and what isn't. This will enable the team to fine-tune its performance strategy.
- **Take a few minutes when the work is finished** to reflect on what went well—and poorly—and to identify ways team members can make the best use of their knowledge and experience the next time around.

Protect Your Deviant

The deviant you designate will say things that nobody else is willing to articulate—such as "Wait a minute, why are we even doing this at all?" or "We've got to stop and maybe change direction."

These observations can open up creative discussion—but they also raise others' anxiety levels. People may feel compelled to crack down on the deviant and try to get him to stop asking difficult questions—maybe even knock him off the team.

Don't let that happen: If you lose your deviant, your team can become mediocre.

goals of the ministry. One of the executives in the class interrupted me and said, "Are you aware that you've just talked about two assassinations and a crucifixion?"

What are some common fallacies about teams?

People generally think that teams that work together harmoniously are better and more productive than teams that don't. But in a study we conducted on symphonies, we actually found that grumpy orchestras played together slightly better than orchestras in which all the musicians were really quite happy.

That's because the cause-and-effect is the reverse of what most people believe: When we're productive and we've done something good together (and are recognized for it), we feel satisfied, not the other way around. In other words, the mood of the orchestra members after a performance says more about how well they did than the mood beforehand.

Another fallacy is that bigger teams are better than small ones because they have more resources to draw upon. A colleague and I once did some research showing that as a team gets bigger, the number of links that need to be managed among members goes up at an accelerating, almost exponential rate. It's managing the links between members that gets teams into trouble. My rule of thumb is no double digits. In my courses, I never allow teams of more than six students. Big teams usually wind up just wasting everybody's time. That's why having a huge senior leadership team—say, one that includes all the CEO's direct reports—may be worse than having no team at all.

Perhaps the most common misperception about teams, though, is that at some point team members become so comfortable and familiar with one another that they start accepting one another's foibles, and as a result performance falls off. Except for one special type of team, I have not been able to find a shred of evidence to support that premise. There is a study that shows that R&D teams do need an influx of new talent to maintain creativity and freshness—but only at the rate of one person every three to four years. The problem almost always is not that a team gets stale but, rather, that it doesn't have the chance to settle in.

So newness is a liability?

Absolutely. The research confirming that is incontrovertible. Consider crews flying commercial airplanes. The National Transportation Safety Board found that 73% of the incidents in its database occurred on a crew's first day of flying together, before people had the chance to learn through experience how best to operate as a team—and 44% of those took place on a crew's very first flight. Also, a NASA study found that fatigued crews who had a history of working together made about half as many errors as crews composed of rested pilots who had not flown together before.

So why don't airlines stick to the same crews?

Because it isn't efficient from a financial perspective. Financially, you get the most from your capital equipment and labor by treating each airplane and each pilot as an individual unit and then using an algorithm to maximize their utilization. That means that pilots often have to dash up and down the concourses just as passengers do, and sometimes you'll have a pilot who will fly two or three different aircraft with two or three different crews in the course of a single day—which is not so wise if you look at the research. I once asked an operations researcher of an airline to estimate how long it would take, if he and I were assigned to work together on a trip, before we could expect to work together again. He calculated that it would be 5.6 years. Clearly, this is not good from a passenger point of view.

The counterexample, by the way, is the Strategic Air Command, or SAC, which would have delivered nuclear bombs had that become necessary during the Cold War years. SAC teams performed better than any other flight crews that we studied. They trained together as a crew, and they became superb at working together because they had to. When you're working together in real time and there can be no mistakes, then you keep your teams together for years and years rather than constantly change their composition.

If teams need to stay together to achieve the best performance, how do you prevent them from becoming complacent?

This is where what I call a deviant comes in. Every team needs a deviant, someone who can help the team by challenging the tendency to want too much homogeneity, which can stifle creativity and learning. Deviants are the ones who stand back and say, "Well, wait a minute, why are we even doing this at all? What if we looked at the thing backwards or turned it inside out?" That's when people say, "Oh, no, no, no, that's ridiculous," and so the discussion about what's ridiculous comes up. Unlike the CFO I mentioned before, who derailed the team by shutting down discussions, the deviant opens up more ideas, and that gets you a lot more originality. In our research, we've looked carefully at both teams that produced something original and those that were merely average, where nothing really sparkled. It turned out that the teams with deviants outperformed teams without them. In many cases, deviant thinking is a source of great innovation.

I would add, though, that often the deviant veers from the norm at great personal cost. Deviants are the individuals who are willing to say the thing that nobody else is willing to articulate. The deviant raises people's level of anxiety, which is a brave thing to do. When the boat is floating with the current, it really is extraordinarily courageous for somebody to stand up and say, "We've got to pause and probably change direction." Nobody on the team wants to hear that, which is precisely why many team leaders crack down on deviants and try to get them to stop asking difficult questions, maybe even knock them off the team. And yet it's when you lose the deviant that the team can become mediocre.

What makes a team effective, and how can a team's leader make it perform better?

A good team will satisfy its internal or external clients, become stronger as a unit as time passes, and foster the learning and growth of its individual members. But even the best leader on the planet can't make a team do well. All anyone can do is increase the likelihood that a team will be great by putting into place five conditions. (See the sidebar "How to Build a Team.") And the leader still will have no guarantees that she will create a magical team. Teams create their own realities and control their own destinies to a greater extent, and far sooner in their existence, than most team leaders realize.

In 1990 I edited a collection of essays by colleagues who had studied teams performing diverse tasks in 27 organizations—everything from a children's theater company to a mental-health-treatment team to a beer-sales-and-delivery team. In those studies, we found that the things that happen the first time a group meets strongly affect how the group operates throughout its entire life. Indeed, the first few minutes of the start of any social system are the most important because they establish not only where the group is going but also what the relationship will be between the team leader and the group, and what basic norms of conduct will be expected and enforced.

How to Build a Team

IN HIS BOOK *LEADING TEAMS*, J. Richard Hackman sets out five basic conditions that leaders of companies and other organizations must fulfill in order to create and maintain effective teams:

1. **Teams must be real.** People have to know who is on the team and who is not. It's the leader's job to make that clear.
2. **Teams need a compelling direction.** Members need to know, and agree on, what they're supposed to be doing together. Unless a leader articulates a clear direction, there is a real risk that different members will pursue different agendas.
3. **Teams need enabling structures.** Teams that have poorly designed tasks, the wrong number or mix of members, or fuzzy and unenforced norms of conduct invariably get into trouble.
4. **Teams need a supportive organization.** The organizational context—including the reward system, the human resource system, and the information system—must facilitate teamwork.
5. **Teams need expert coaching.** Most executive coaches focus on individual performance, which does not significantly improve teamwork. Teams need coaching as a group in team processes—especially at the beginning, midpoint, and end of a team project.

I once asked Christopher Hogwood, the distinguished conductor for many years of the Handel and Haydn Society in Boston, how important the first rehearsal was when he served as an orchestra's guest conductor. "What do you mean, the first *rehearsal*?" he asked. "All I have is the first few minutes." He went on to explain that there's nothing he pays greater attention to than the way he starts the first rehearsal. That's because he knows that the orchestra members will make a very quick assessment about whether or not they're going to make great music together, or whether he is just going to get in their way.

I do think there is one thing leaders such as Hogwood and others can do to improve the chances that a team will become something special, and that is to embrace their own quirkiness. You shouldn't try to lead like Jeff Bezos, because you are not Jeff Bezos. Each leader brings to the task his or her own strengths and weaknesses.

Off and Running: Barack Obama Jump-Starts His Team

by Michael Beschloss

IF THE LAUNCH OF a team is as critical as Professor J. Richard Hackman says, then Barack Obama has done pretty well. He appointed his administration's top officials much faster than most presidents do. Given the monumental crises that faced him the moment he was elected, he had to move quickly. The downside of speed was that some of his choices didn't work out—notably Bill Richardson and Tom Daschle. Obama has certainly brought onto his team people of strong temperaments and contrasting views, starting with Hillary Clinton at the State Department and Jim Jones at the National Security Council. This suggests that we have a president who is unusually sure of his own ability to absorb differing opinions. Appointing people like Clinton also shows his eagerness to harness the talent of his former opponents. Compare that with the record of George W. Bush; his people told many job seekers who had supported John McCain in the 2000 Republican primaries, "Sorry, you backed the wrong horse!"

Of course, Obama is taking a risk by hiring so many strong and contentious personalities. He will inevitably have to spend a lot of time and energy serving as referee. This is what happened with Franklin Roosevelt, who also brought strong-minded figures into his government. One difference with Obama, however, is that FDR temperamentally loved the infighting. He liked to pit people against one another, believing that competition evoked the best performance from everyone. At times FDR actually enjoyed making his underlings suffer. I don't think Obama does.

Most presidents prefer a happy ship, and in some cases their definition of loyalty includes not rocking the boat on major administration programs. Richard Nixon fired his interior secretary, Walter Hickel, for opposing his Vietnam War policies. There was a dissenter (what Hackman calls a deviant) on Lyndon Johnson's team—Undersecretary of State George Ball, who strongly opposed the Vietnam War. Johnson would cite Ball when people complained that he surrounded himself with yes-men, but in fact Ball had little influence when LBJ met with top officials on Vietnam. Everyone in the group knew that Johnson didn't take Ball's antiwar arguments very seriously. If you really want dissenting views, better to use the Roosevelt-Obama model, where they can come from almost any member of the team—and not just from one designated rabble-rouser.

The reappointment of Bush's defense secretary, Robert Gates, also reveals Obama's self-confidence. He's clearly willing to concede that there are things he doesn't know, so he appointed someone with more than three decades of national security experience. This decision has the historical echo of John Kennedy's near-reappointment in 1961 of Dwight Eisenhower's defense secretary, who coincidentally was named Thomas Gates. Like Obama, Kennedy was a young president with little national security background and thought it might reassure people to have the previous defense secretary stay on at the Pentagon. Like Obama, JFK also suspected that a number of things might go wrong with national security during his first year as president. He felt that Americans might be less likely to blame the Democratic president if a Republican secretary of defense was there at his side. In the end Kennedy did not have the stomach for the risk of keeping a Republican appointee at the Pentagon. Obama did.

Obama's first months in office prove the importance of having a president who can convey his view of the country and the world and why he thinks his plans will work. One of Hillary Clinton's biggest criticisms a year ago was that Obama gave great speeches but that it didn't have all that much to do with being a strong president. Obama argued that it did, and he was right. Like Roosevelt's addresses in 1933 and Reagan's in 1981, his public utterances—especially his speech to Congress in February—have done a lot to gain acceptance for his programs from skeptical Americans. However jaded they may be about government, Americans—even those who didn't vote for him—are still inclined to turn to their president to explain foreign and domestic crises. Imagine how much more anxious they might feel now if Obama did not do this so effectively. Unfortunately for us all, it's likely that he'll have to call more on that skill as the crisis mounts in the months ahead.

Michael Beschloss has written nine books about presidential leadership, most recently *Presidential Courage* (Simon & Schuster, 2007).

Exploit the daylights out of the stuff you're great at, and get help in the areas where you're not so good. Don't try to ape any leadership model or team, because there's no one right style for leading a team. There are many different ways to create the conditions for effectiveness, sustain them, and help teams take full advantage of them. The best team leaders are like jazz players, improvising constantly as they go along.

How good are companies at providing a supportive context for teams?

Perversely, the organizations with the best human resource departments often do things that are completely at odds with good team behavior. That's because HR departments tend to put in place systems that are really good at guiding, directing, and correcting individual behavior. Take a personnel system that has been honed by industrial psychologists to identify the skills of a particular job and test individual employees on those skills. In such a system, the HR department will set up training to develop the "right" people in the "right" way. The problem is this is all about the individual. This single-minded focus on the individual employee is one of the main reasons that teams don't do as well as they might in organizations with strong HR departments. Just look at our research on senior executive teams. We found that coaching individual team members did not do all that much to help executive teams perform better.

For the team to reap the benefits of coaching, it must focus on group processes. And timing is everything. The team leader needs to know how to run a launch meeting, so that members become oriented to and engaged with their tasks; how to help the team review at the midpoint what's functioning well—and what isn't—which can correct the team's performance strategy; and how to take a few minutes when the work is finished to reflect on what went well or poorly, which can help members make better use of their knowledge and experience the next time around. Team coaching is about fostering better teamwork on the task, not about enhancing members' social interactions or interpersonal relationships.

There's a lot of talk about virtual teams these days. Can they work, or are they falling victim to what Jo Freeman once called the "tyranny of structurelessness"?

Virtual teams have really come into their own in the past decade, but I don't believe they differ fundamentally from traditional teams. There was a fantasy in the beginning that everyone would be swarming around on the internet, that the wisdom of crowds would automatically prevail, and that structureless groups would come up with new and profound things that face-to-face groups could never have generated. But nirvana never materialized; virtual teams need the basic conditions for effectiveness to be in place just as much as face-to-face teams, if not more so. That said, we are seeing that we can make do with much less face-to-face contact than we ever thought possible. Today's technology, for example, lets you have a chat window open during a web conference so you can type in the word "hand" to signal that you want to talk next. People don't need to see your face to know that you want to speak up. But even well-structured virtual teams need to have a launch meeting with everyone present, a midpoint check-in that's face-to-face, and a live debriefing. I don't think for a minute that we're going to have effective online teams if we don't know who's on the team or what the main work of the team really is, and so far that's still a problem with virtual teams.

Given the difficulty of making teams work, should we be rethinking their importance in organizations?

Perhaps. Many people act as if being a team player is the ultimate measure of one's worth, which it clearly is not. There are many things individuals can do better on their own, and they should not be penalized for it. Go back for a moment to that fourth-grade question about working together to build a house. The answer probably is that teamwork really does take longer or that the house may not get built at all. There are many cases where collaboration, particularly in truly creative endeavors, is a hindrance rather than a help. The challenge for a leader, then, is to find a balance between individual autonomy and collective action. Either extreme is bad, though we are generally more aware of the downside of individualism in organizations, and we forget that teams can be just as destructive by being so strong and controlling that individual voices and contributions and learning are lost.

In one management team we studied, for example, being a team player was so strongly valued that individuals self-censored their contributions for fear of disrupting team harmony. The team, in a spirit of cooperation and goodwill, embarked on a course of action that was bound to fail—for reasons that some members sensed but did not mention as the plans were being laid. One wonders if the crisis in the financial world today would be quite so catastrophic if more people had spoken out in their team meetings about what they knew to be wrongful practices. But again that brings us back to the hazards of courage. You'd like to think that people who do the courageous right thing and speak out will get their reward on earth as well as in heaven. But you don't always get your reward here on earth. While it's true that not being on a team can put your career on hold, being a real and committed team player—whether as a team leader, a deviant, or just a regular member who speaks the truth—can be dangerous business indeed.

Originally published in May 2009. Reprint R0905H

The Discipline of Teams

by Jon R. Katzenbach and Douglas K. Smith

EARLY IN THE 1980S, Bill Greenwood and a small band of rebel railroaders took on most of the top management of Burlington Northern and created a multibillion-dollar business in "piggybacking" rail services despite widespread resistance, even resentment, within the company. The Medical Products Group at Hewlett-Packard owes most of its leading performance to the remarkable efforts of Dean Morton, Lew Platt, Ben Holmes, Dick Alberding, and a handful of their colleagues who revitalized a health care business that most others had written off. At Knight Ridder, Jim Batten's "customer obsession" vision took root at the *Tallahassee Democrat* when 14 frontline enthusiasts turned a charter to eliminate errors into a mission of major change and took the entire paper along with them.

Such are the stories and the work of teams—real teams that perform, not amorphous groups that we call teams because we think that the label is motivating and energizing. The difference between teams that perform and other groups that don't is a subject to which most of us pay far too little attention. Part of the problem is that "team" is a word and concept so familiar to everyone. (See the exhibit "Not all groups are teams: How to tell the difference.")

Or at least that's what we thought when we set out to do research for our book *The Wisdom of Teams* (HarperBusiness, 1993). We wanted to discover what differentiates various levels of team

Not all groups are teams: How to tell the difference

Working group	Team
• Strong, clearly focused leader	• Shared leadership roles
• Individual accountability	• Individual and mutual accountability
• The group's purpose is the same as the broader organizational mission	• Specific team purpose that the team itself delivers
• Individual work products	• Collective work products
• Runs efficient meetings	• Encourages open-ended discussion and active problem-solving meetings
• Measures its effectiveness indirectly by its influence on others (such as financial performance of the business)	• Measures performance directly by assessing collective work products
• Discusses, decides, and delegates	• Discusses, decides, and does real work together

performance, where and how teams work best, and what top management can do to enhance their effectiveness. We talked with hundreds of people on more than 50 different teams in 30 companies and beyond, from Motorola and Hewlett-Packard to Operation Desert Storm and the Girl Scouts.

We found that there is a basic discipline that makes teams work. We also found that teams and good performance are inseparable: You cannot have one without the other. But people use the word "team" so loosely that it gets in the way of learning and applying the discipline that leads to good performance. For managers to make better decisions about whether, when, or how to encourage and use teams, it is important to be more precise about what a team is and what it isn't.

Most executives advocate teamwork. And they should. Teamwork represents a set of values that encourage listening and responding constructively to views expressed by others, giving others the benefit of the doubt, providing support, and recognizing the interests and achievements of others. Such values help teams perform, and they also promote individual performance as well as the performance of

Idea in Brief

The word *team* gets bandied about so loosely that many managers are oblivious to its real meaning—or its true potential. With a run-of-the-mill working group, performance is a function of what the members do as individuals. A team's performance, by contrast, calls for both individual and mutual accountability.

Though it may not seem like anything special, mutual accountability can lead to astonishing results. It enables a team to achieve performance levels that are far greater than the individual bests of the team's members. To achieve these benefits, team members must do more than listen, respond constructively, and provide support to one another. In addition to sharing these team-building values, they must share an essential *discipline*.

an entire organization. But teamwork values by themselves are not exclusive to teams, nor are they enough to ensure team performance. (See the sidebar "Building Team Performance.")

Nor is a team just any group working together. Committees, councils, and task forces are not necessarily teams. Groups do not become teams simply because that is what someone calls them. The entire workforce of any large and complex organization is *never* a team, but think about how often that platitude is offered up.

To understand how teams deliver extra performance, we must distinguish between teams and other forms of working groups. That distinction turns on performance results. A working group's performance is a function of what its members do as individuals. A team's performance includes both individual results and what we call "collective work products." A collective work product is what two or more members must work on together, such as interviews, surveys, or experiments. Whatever it is, a collective work product reflects the joint, real contribution of team members.

Working groups are both prevalent and effective in large organizations where individual accountability is most important. The best working groups come together to share information, perspectives, and insights; to make decisions that help each person do his or her job better; and to reinforce individual performance standards.

Idea in Practice

A team's essential discipline comprises five characteristics:

1. **A meaningful common purpose that the team has helped shape.** Most teams are responding to an initial mandate from outside the team. But to be successful, the team must "own" this purpose, develop its own spin on it.
2. **Specific performance goals that flow from the common purpose.** For example, getting a new product to market in less than half the normal time. Compelling goals inspire and challenge a team, give it a sense of urgency. They also have a leveling effect, requiring members to focus on the collective effort necessary rather than any differences in title or status.
3. **A mix of complementary skills.** These include technical or functional expertise, problem-solving and decision-making skills, and interpersonal skills. Successful teams rarely have all the needed skills at the outset—they develop them as they learn what the challenge requires.
4. **A strong commitment to how the work gets done.** Teams must agree on who will do what jobs, how schedules will be established and honored, and how decisions will be made and modified. On a genuine team, each member does equivalent amounts of real work; all members, the leader included, contribute in concrete ways to the team's collective work-products.

But the focus is always on individual goals and accountabilities. Working-group members don't take responsibility for results other than their own. Nor do they try to develop incremental performance contributions requiring the combined work of two or more members.

Teams differ fundamentally from working groups because they require both individual and mutual accountability. Teams rely on more than group discussion, debate, and decision, on more than sharing information and best-practice performance standards. Teams produce discrete work products through the joint contributions of their members. This is what makes possible performance levels greater than the sum of all the individual bests of team members. Simply stated, a team is more than the sum of its parts.

5. **Mutual accountability.** Trust and commitment cannot be coerced. The process of agreeing upon appropriate goals serves as the crucible in which members forge their accountability to each other—not just to the leader.

Once the essential discipline has been established, a team is free to concentrate on the critical challenges it faces:

- For a team whose purpose is to make recommendations, that means making a fast and constructive start and providing a clean handoff to those who will implement the recommendations.
- For a team that makes or does things, it's keeping the specific performance goals in sharp focus.
- For a team that runs things, the primary task is distinguishing the challenges that require a real team approach from those that don't.

If a task doesn't demand joint work-products, a working group can be the more effective option. Team opportunities are usually those in which hierarchy or organizational boundaries inhibit the skills and perspectives needed for optimal results. Little wonder, then, that teams have become the primary units of productivity in high-performance organizations.

The first step in developing a disciplined approach to team management is to think about teams as discrete units of performance and not just as positive sets of values. Having observed and worked with scores of teams in action, both successes and failures, we offer the following. Think of it as a working definition or, better still, an essential discipline that real teams share: *A team is a small number of people with complementary skills who are committed to a common purpose, set of performance goals, and approach for which they hold themselves mutually accountable.*

The essence of a team is common commitment. Without it, groups perform as individuals; with it, they become a powerful unit of collective performance. This kind of commitment requires a purpose in which team members can believe. Whether the purpose is to

Building Team Performance

ALTHOUGH THERE IS NO guaranteed how-to recipe for building team performance, we observed a number of approaches shared by many successful teams.

Establish urgency, demanding performance standards, and direction. All team members need to believe the team has urgent and worthwhile purposes, and they want to know what the expectations are. Indeed, the more urgent and meaningful the rationale, the more likely it is that the team will live up to its performance potential, as was the case for a customer-service team that was told that further growth for the entire company would be impossible without major improvements in that area. Teams work best in a compelling context. That is why companies with strong performance ethics usually form teams readily.

Select members for skill and skill potential, not personality. No team succeeds without all the skills needed to meet its purpose and performance goals. Yet most teams figure out the skills they will need after they are formed. The wise manager will choose people for their existing skills and their potential to improve existing skills and learn new ones.

Pay particular attention to first meetings and actions. Initial impressions always mean a great deal. When potential teams first gather, everyone monitors the signals given by others to confirm, suspend, or dispel assumptions and concerns. They pay particular attention to those in authority: the team leader and any executives who set up, oversee, or otherwise influence the team. And, as always, what such leaders do is more important than what they say. If a senior executive leaves the team kickoff to take a phone call ten minutes after the session has begun and he never returns, people get the message.

Set some clear rules of behavior. All effective teams develop rules of conduct at the outset to help them achieve their purpose and performance goals. The most critical initial rules pertain to attendance (for example, "no interruptions to take phone calls"), discussion ("no sacred cows"), confidentiality ("the only things to leave this room are what we agree on"), analytic approach ("facts are friendly"), end-product orientation ("everyone gets assignments and does them"), constructive confrontation ("no finger pointing"), and, often the most important, contributions ("everyone does real work").

"transform the contributions of suppliers into the satisfaction of customers," to "make our company one we can be proud of again," or to "prove that all children can learn," credible team purposes have an element related to winning, being first, revolutionizing, or being on the cutting edge.

Set and seize upon a few immediate performance-oriented tasks and goals. Most effective teams trace their advancement to key performance-oriented events. Such events can be set in motion by immediately establishing a few challenging goals that can be reached early on. There is no such thing as a real team without performance results, so the sooner such results occur, the sooner the team congeals.

Challenge the group regularly with fresh facts and information. New information causes a team to redefine and enrich its understanding of the performance challenge, thereby helping the team shape a common purpose, set clearer goals, and improve its common approach. A plant quality improvement team knew the cost of poor quality was high, but it wasn't until they researched the different types of defects and put a price tag on each one that they knew where to go next. Conversely, teams err when they assume that all the information needed exists in the collective experience and knowledge of their members.

Spend lots of time together. Common sense tells us that team members must spend a lot of time together, scheduled and unscheduled, especially in the beginning. Indeed, creative insights as well as personal bonding require impromptu and casual interactions just as much as analyzing spreadsheets and interviewing customers. Busy executives and managers too often intentionally minimize the time they spend together. The successful teams we've observed all gave themselves the time to learn to be a team. This time need not always be spent together physically; electronic, fax, and phone time can also count as time spent together.

Exploit the power of positive feedback, recognition, and reward. Positive reinforcement works as well in a team context as elsewhere. Giving out "gold stars" helps shape new behaviors critical to team performance. If people in the group, for example, are alert to a shy person's initial efforts to speak up and contribute, they can give the honest positive reinforcement that encourages continued contributions. There are many ways to recognize and reward team performance beyond direct compensation, from having a senior executive speak directly to the team about the urgency of its mission to using awards to recognize contributions. Ultimately, however, the satisfaction shared by a team in its own performance becomes the most cherished reward.

Teams develop direction, momentum, and commitment by working to shape a meaningful purpose. Building ownership and commitment to team purpose, however, is not incompatible with taking initial direction from outside the team. The often-asserted assumption that a team cannot "own" its purpose unless management leaves it alone actually confuses more potential teams than it helps. In fact, it is the exceptional case—for example, entrepreneurial situations—when a team creates a purpose entirely on its own.

Most successful teams shape their purposes in response to a demand or opportunity put in their path, usually by higher management. This helps teams get started by broadly framing the company's performance expectation. Management is responsible for clarifying the charter, rationale, and performance challenge for the team, but management must also leave enough flexibility for the team to develop commitment around its own spin on that purpose, set of specific goals, timing, and approach.

The best teams invest a tremendous amount of time and effort exploring, shaping, and agreeing on a purpose that belongs to them both collectively and individually. This "purposing" activity continues throughout the life of the team. By contrast, failed teams rarely develop a common purpose. For whatever reason—an insufficient focus on performance, lack of effort, poor leadership—they do not coalesce around a challenging aspiration.

The best teams also translate their common purpose into specific performance goals, such as reducing the reject rate from suppliers by 50% or increasing the math scores of graduates from 40% to 95%. Indeed, if a team fails to establish specific performance goals or if those goals do not relate directly to the team's overall purpose, team members become confused, pull apart, and revert to mediocre performance. By contrast, when purposes and goals build on one another and are combined with team commitment, they become a powerful engine of performance.

Transforming broad directives into specific and measurable performance goals is the surest first step for a team trying to shape a purpose meaningful to its members. Specific goals, such as getting a new product to market in less than half the normal time, responding to all customers within 24 hours, or achieving a zero-defect rate while simultaneously cutting costs by 40%, all provide firm footholds for teams. There are several reasons:

- Specific team-performance goals help define a set of work products that are different both from an organization-wide mission and from individual job objectives. As a result, such work products require the collective effort of team members to make something specific happen that, in and of itself, adds real value to results. By contrast, simply gathering from time to time to make decisions will not sustain team performance.

- The specificity of performance objectives facilitates clear communication and constructive conflict within the team. When a plant-level team, for example, sets a goal of reducing average machine changeover time to two hours, the clarity of the goal forces the team to concentrate on what it would take either to achieve or to reconsider the goal. When such goals are clear, discussions can focus on how to pursue them or whether to change them; when goals are ambiguous or nonexistent, such discussions are much less productive.
- The attainability of specific goals helps teams maintain their focus on getting results. A product-development team at Eli Lilly's Peripheral Systems Division set definite yardsticks for the market introduction of an ultrasonic probe to help doctors locate deep veins and arteries. The probe had to have an audible signal through a specified depth of tissue, be capable of being manufactured at a rate of 100 per day, and have a unit cost less than a preestablished amount. Because the team could measure its progress against each of these specific objectives, the team knew throughout the development process where it stood. Either it had achieved its goals or not.
- As Outward Bound and other team-building programs illustrate, specific objectives have a leveling effect conducive to team behavior. When a small group of people challenge themselves to get over a wall or to reduce cycle time by 50%, their respective titles, perks, and other stripes fade into the background. The teams that succeed evaluate what and how each individual can best contribute to the team's goal and, more important, do so in terms of the performance objective itself rather than a person's status or personality.

- Specific goals allow a team to achieve small wins as it pursues its broader purpose. These small wins are invaluable to building commitment and overcoming the inevitable obstacles that get in the way of a long-term purpose. For example, the Knight Ridder team mentioned at the outset turned a narrow goal to eliminate errors into a compelling customer service purpose.
- Performance goals are compelling. They are symbols of accomplishment that motivate and energize. They challenge the people on a team to commit themselves, as a team, to make a difference. Drama, urgency, and a healthy fear of failure combine to drive teams that have their collective eye on an attainable, but challenging, goal. Nobody but the team can make it happen. It's their challenge.

The combination of purpose and specific goals is essential to performance. Each depends on the other to remain relevant and vital. Clear performance goals help a team keep track of progress and hold itself accountable; the broader, even nobler, aspirations in a team's purpose supply both meaning and emotional energy.

Virtually all effective teams we have met, read, or heard about, or been members of have ranged between two and 25 people. For example, the Burlington Northern piggybacking team had seven members, and the Knight Ridder newspaper team had 14. The majority of them have numbered less than ten. Small size is admittedly more of a pragmatic guide than an absolute necessity for success. A large number of people, say 50 or more, can theoretically become a team. But groups of such size are more likely to break into subteams rather than function as a single unit.

Why? Large numbers of people have trouble interacting constructively as a group, much less doing real work together. Ten people are far more likely than 50 to work through their individual, functional, and hierarchical differences toward a common plan and to hold themselves jointly accountable for the results.

Large groups also face logistical issues, such as finding enough physical space and time to meet. And they confront more complex constraints, like crowd or herd behaviors, which prevent the intense sharing of viewpoints needed to build a team. As a result, when they try to develop a common purpose, they usually produce only superficial "missions" and well-meaning intentions that cannot be translated into concrete objectives. They tend fairly quickly to reach a point when meetings become a chore, a clear sign that most of the people in the group are uncertain why they have gathered, beyond some notion of getting along better. Anyone who has been through one of these exercises understands how frustrating it can be. This kind of failure tends to foster cynicism, which gets in the way of future team efforts.

In addition to finding the right size, teams must develop the right mix of skills; that is, each of the complementary skills necessary to do the team's job. As obvious as it sounds, it is a common failing in potential teams. Skill requirements fall into three fairly self-evident categories.

Technical or Functional Expertise

It would make little sense for a group of doctors to litigate an employment discrimination case in a court of law. Yet teams of doctors and lawyers often try medical malpractice or personal injury cases. Similarly, product development groups that include only marketers or engineers are less likely to succeed than those with the complementary skills of both.

Problem-Solving and Decision-Making Skills

Teams must be able to identify the problems and opportunities they face, evaluate the options they have for moving forward, and then make necessary trade-offs and decisions about how to proceed. Most teams need some members with these skills to begin with, although many will develop them best on the job.

Interpersonal Skills

Common understanding and purpose cannot arise without effective communication and constructive conflict, which in turn depend on interpersonal skills. These skills include risk taking, helpful criticism, objectivity, active listening, giving the benefit of the doubt, and recognizing the interests and achievements of others.

Obviously, a team cannot get started without some minimum complement of skills, especially technical and functional ones. Still, think about how often you've been part of a team whose members were chosen primarily on the basis of personal compatibility or formal position in the organization, and in which the skill mix of its members wasn't given much thought.

It is equally common to overemphasize skills in team selection. Yet in all the successful teams we've encountered, not one had all the needed skills at the outset. The Burlington Northern team, for example, initially had no members who were skilled marketers despite the fact that their performance challenge was a marketing one. In fact, we discovered that teams are powerful vehicles for developing the skills needed to meet the team's performance challenge. Accordingly, team member selection ought to ride as much on skill potential as on skills already proven.

Effective teams develop strong commitment to a common approach; that is, to how they will work together to accomplish their purpose. Team members must agree on who will do particular jobs, how schedules will be set and adhered to, what skills need to be developed, how continuing membership in the team is to be earned, and how the group will make and modify decisions. This element of commitment is as important to team performance as the team's commitment to its purpose and goals.

Agreeing on the specifics of work and how they fit together to integrate individual skills and advance team performance lies at the heart of shaping a common approach. It is perhaps self-evident that an approach that delegates all the real work to a few members (or staff outsiders) and thus relies on reviews and meetings for its only "work together" aspects, cannot sustain a real team. Every member of a successful team does equivalent amounts of real work; all members, including the team leader, contribute in concrete ways to the team's work product. This is a very important element of the emotional logic that drives team performance.

When individuals approach a team situation, especially in a business setting, each has preexisting job assignments as well as strengths and weaknesses reflecting a variety of talents, backgrounds, personalities, and prejudices. Only through the mutual discovery and understanding of how to apply all its human resources to a common purpose can a team develop and agree on the best approach to achieve its goals. At the heart of such long and, at times, difficult interactions lies a commitment-building process in which the team candidly explores who is best suited to each task as well as how individual roles will come together. In effect, the team establishes a social contract among members that relates to their purpose and guides and obligates how they must work together.

No group ever becomes a team until it can hold itself accountable as a team. Like common purpose and approach, mutual accountability is a stiff test. Think, for example, about the subtle but critical difference between "the boss holds me accountable" and "we hold ourselves accountable." The first case can lead to the second, but without the second, there can be no team.

Companies like Hewlett-Packard and Motorola have an ingrained performance ethic that enables teams to form organically whenever there is a clear performance challenge requiring collective rather than individual effort. In these companies, the factor of mutual accountability is commonplace. "Being in the boat together" is how their performance game is played.

At its core, team accountability is about the sincere promises we make to ourselves and others, promises that underpin two critical aspects of effective teams: commitment and trust. Most of us enter a potential team situation cautiously because ingrained individualism and experience discourage us from putting our fates in the hands of others or accepting responsibility for others. Teams do not succeed by ignoring or wishing away such behavior.

Mutual accountability cannot be coerced any more than people can be made to trust one another. But when a team shares a common purpose, goals, and approach, mutual accountability grows as a natural counterpart. Accountability arises from and reinforces the time, energy, and action invested in figuring out what the team is trying to accomplish and how best to get it done.

When people work together toward a common objective, trust and commitment follow. Consequently, teams enjoying a strong common purpose and approach inevitably hold themselves responsible, both as individuals and as a team, for the team's performance. This sense of mutual accountability also produces the rich rewards of mutual achievement in which all members share. What we heard over and over from members of effective teams is that they found the experience energizing and motivating in ways that their "normal" jobs never could match.

On the other hand, groups established primarily for the sake of becoming a team or for job enhancement, communication, organizational effectiveness, or excellence rarely become effective teams, as demonstrated by the bad feelings left in many companies after experimenting with quality circles that never translated "quality" into specific goals. Only when appropriate performance goals are set does the process of discussing the goals and the approaches to them give team members a clearer and clearer choice: They can disagree with a goal and the path that the team selects and, in effect, opt out, or they can pitch in and become accountable with and to their teammates.

The discipline of teams we've outlined is critical to the success of all teams. Yet it is also useful to go one step further. Most teams can be classified in one of three ways: teams that recommend things, teams that make or do things, and teams that run things. In our experience, each type faces a characteristic set of challenges.

Teams That Recommend Things

These teams include task forces; project groups; and audit, quality, or safety groups asked to study and solve particular problems. Teams that recommend things almost always have predetermined completion dates. Two critical issues are unique to such teams:

getting off to a fast and constructive start and dealing with the ultimate handoff that's required to get recommendations implemented.

The key to the first issue lies in the clarity of the team's charter and the composition of its membership. In addition to wanting to know why and how their efforts are important, task forces need a clear definition of whom management expects to participate and the time commitment required. Management can help by ensuring that the team includes people with the skills and influence necessary for crafting practical recommendations that will carry weight throughout the organization. Moreover, management can help the team get the necessary cooperation by opening doors and dealing with political obstacles.

Missing the handoff is almost always the problem that stymies teams that recommend things. To avoid this, the transfer of responsibility for recommendations to those who must implement them demands top management's time and attention. The more top managers assume that recommendations will "just happen," the less likely it is that they will. The more involvement task force members have in implementing their recommendations, the more likely they are to get implemented.

To the extent that people outside the task force will have to carry the ball, it is critical to involve them in the process early and often, certainly well before recommendations are finalized. Such involvement may take many forms, including participating in interviews, helping with analyses, contributing and critiquing ideas, and conducting experiments and trials. At a minimum, anyone responsible for implementation should receive a briefing on the task force's purpose, approach, and objectives at the beginning of the effort as well as regular reviews of progress.

Teams That Make or Do Things

These teams include people at or near the front lines who are responsible for doing the basic manufacturing, development, operations, marketing, sales, service, and other value-adding activities of a business. With some exceptions, such as new-product development or process design teams, teams that make or do things tend to have no set completion dates because their activities are ongoing.

In deciding where team performance might have the greatest impact, top management should concentrate on what we call the company's "critical delivery points"—that is, places in the organization where the cost and value of the company's products and services are most directly determined. Such critical delivery points might include where accounts get managed, customer service performed, products designed, and productivity determined. If performance at critical delivery points depends on combining multiple skills, perspectives, and judgments in real time, then the team option is the smartest one.

When an organization does require a significant number of teams at these points, the sheer challenge of maximizing the performance of so many groups will demand a carefully constructed and performance-focused set of management processes. The issue here for top management is how to build the necessary systems and process supports without falling into the trap of appearing to promote teams for their own sake.

The imperative here, returning to our earlier discussion of the basic discipline of teams, is a relentless focus on performance. If management fails to pay persistent attention to the link between teams and performance, the organization becomes convinced that "this year, we are doing 'teams'." Top management can help by instituting processes like pay schemes and training for teams responsive to their real time needs, but more than anything else, top management must make clear and compelling demands on the teams themselves and then pay constant attention to their progress with respect to both team basics and performance results. This means focusing on specific teams and specific performance challenges. Otherwise "performance," like "team," will become a cliché.

Teams That Run Things

Despite the fact that many leaders refer to the group reporting to them as a team, few groups really are. And groups that become real teams seldom think of themselves as a team because they are so focused on performance results. Yet the opportunity for such teams includes groups from the top of the enterprise down through the divisional or functional level. Whether it is in charge of thousands of people or just a handful, as long as the group oversees some business, ongoing program, or significant functional activity, it is a team that runs things.

The main issue these teams face is determining whether a real team approach is the right one. Many groups that run things can be more effective as working groups than as teams. The key judgment is whether the sum of individual bests will suffice for the performance challenge at hand or whether the group must deliver substantial incremental performance requiring real joint work products. Although the team option promises greater performance, it also brings more risk, and managers must be brutally honest in assessing the trade-offs.

Members may have to overcome a natural reluctance to trust their fate to others. The price of faking the team approach is high: At best, members get diverted from their individual goals, costs outweigh benefits, and people resent the imposition on their time and priorities. At worst, serious animosities develop that undercut even the potential personal bests of the working-group approach.

Working groups present fewer risks. Effective working groups need little time to shape their purpose, since the leader usually establishes it. Meetings are run against well-prioritized agendas. And decisions are implemented through specific individual assignments and accountabilities. Most of the time, therefore, if performance aspirations can be met through individuals doing their respective jobs well, the working-group approach is more comfortable, less risky, and less disruptive than trying for more elusive team performance levels. Indeed, if there is no performance need for the team approach, efforts spent to improve the effectiveness of the working group make much more sense than floundering around trying to become a team.

Having said that, we believe the extra level of performance teams can achieve is becoming critical for a growing number of companies, especially as they move through major changes during which company performance depends on broad-based behavioral change. When top management uses teams to run things, it should make sure the team succeeds in identifying specific purposes and goals.

This is a second major issue for teams that run things. Too often, such teams confuse the broad mission of the total organization with the specific purpose of their small group at the top. The discipline of teams tells us that for a real team to form, there must be a team purpose that is distinctive and specific to the small group and that requires its members to roll up their sleeves and accomplish something beyond individual end products. If a group of managers looks only at the economic performance of the part of the organization it runs to assess overall effectiveness, the group will not have any team performance goals of its own.

While the basic discipline of teams does not differ for them, teams at the top are certainly the most difficult. The complexities of long-term challenges, heavy demands on executive time, and the deep-seated individualism of senior people conspire against teams at the top. At the same time, teams at the top are the most powerful. At first we thought such teams were nearly impossible. That is because we were looking at the teams as defined by the formal organizational structure; that is, the leader and all his or her direct reports equals the team. Then we discovered that real teams at the top were often smaller and less formalized: Whitehead and Weinberg at Goldman Sachs; Hewlett and Packard at HP; Krasnoff, Pall, and Hardy at Pall Corporation; Kendall, Pearson, and Calloway at Pepsi; Haas and Haas at Levi Strauss; Batten and Ridder at Knight Ridder. They were mostly twos and threes, with an occasional fourth.

Nonetheless, real teams at the top of large, complex organizations are still few and far between. Far too many groups at the top of large corporations needlessly constrain themselves from achieving real team levels of performance because they assume that all direct reports must be on the team, that team goals must be identical to corporate goals, that the team members' positions rather than skills determine their respective roles, that a team must be a team all the time, and that the team leader is above doing real work.

As understandable as these assumptions may be, most of them are unwarranted. They do not apply to the teams at the top we have observed, and when replaced with more realistic and flexible assumptions that permit the team discipline to be applied, real team performance at the top can and does occur. Moreover, as more and more companies are confronted with the need to manage major change across their organizations, we will see more real teams at the top.

We believe that teams will become the primary unit of performance in high-performance organizations. But that does not mean that teams will crowd out individual opportunity or formal hierarchy and process. Rather, teams will enhance existing structures without replacing them. A team opportunity exists anywhere hierarchy or organizational boundaries inhibit the skills and perspectives needed for optimal results. Thus, new-product innovation requires preserving functional excellence through structure while eradicating functional bias through teams. And frontline productivity requires preserving direction and guidance through hierarchy while drawing on energy and flexibility through self-managing teams.

We are convinced that every company faces specific performance challenges for which teams are the most practical and powerful vehicle at top management's disposal. The critical role for senior managers, therefore, is to worry about company performance and the kinds of teams that can deliver it. This means top management must recognize a team's unique potential to deliver results, deploy teams strategically when they are the best tool for the job, and foster the basic discipline of teams that will make them effective. By doing so, top management creates the kind of environment that enables team as well as individual and organizational performance.

Originally published in March 1993. Reprint R0507P

Eight Ways to Build Collaborative Teams

by Lynda Gratton and Tamara J. Erickson

WHEN TACKLING A MAJOR initiative like an acquisition or an overhaul of IT systems, companies rely on large, diverse teams of highly educated specialists to get the job done. These teams often are convened quickly to meet an urgent need and work together virtually, collaborating online and sometimes over long distances.

Appointing such a team is frequently the only way to assemble the knowledge and breadth required to pull off many of the complex tasks businesses face today. When the BBC covers the World Cup or the Olympics, for instance, it gathers a large team of researchers, writers, producers, cameramen, and technicians, many of whom have not met before the project. These specialists work together under the high pressure of a "no retake" environment, with just one chance to record the action. Similarly, when the central IT team at Marriott sets out to develop sophisticated systems to enhance guest experiences, it has to collaborate closely with independent hotel owners, customer-experience experts, global brand managers, and regional heads, each with his or her own agenda and needs.

Our recent research into team behavior at 15 multinational companies, however, reveals an interesting paradox: Although teams that are large, virtual, diverse, and composed of highly educated specialists are increasingly crucial with challenging projects, those same four characteristics make it hard for teams to get anything done. To put it another way, the qualities required for success are the same qualities that undermine success. Members of complex teams are less likely—*absent other influences*—to share knowledge freely, to learn from one another, to shift workloads flexibly to break up unexpected bottlenecks, to help one another complete jobs and meet deadlines, and to share resources—in other words, to collaborate. They are less likely to say that they "sink or swim" together, want one another to succeed, or view their goals as compatible.

Consider the issue of size. Teams have grown considerably over the past ten years. New technologies help companies extend participation on a project to an ever greater number of people, allowing firms to tap into a wide body of knowledge and expertise. A decade or so ago, the common view was that true teams rarely had more than 20 members. Today, according to our research, many complex tasks involve teams of 100 or more. However, as the size of a team increases beyond 20 members, the tendency to collaborate naturally decreases, we have found. Under the right conditions, large teams can achieve high levels of cooperation, but creating those conditions requires thoughtful, and sometimes significant, investments in the capacity for collaboration across the organization.

Working together virtually has a similar impact on teams. The majority of those we studied had members spread among multiple locations—in several cases, in as many as 13 sites around the globe. But as teams became more virtual, we saw, cooperation also declined, unless the company had taken measures to establish a collaborative culture.

As for diversity, the challenging tasks facing businesses today almost always require the input and expertise of people with disparate views and backgrounds to create cross-fertilization that sparks insight and innovation. But diversity also creates problems. Our research shows that team members collaborate more easily and naturally if they perceive themselves as being alike. The differences that inhibit collaboration include not only nationality but also age, educational level, and even tenure. Greater diversity also often

Idea in Brief

To execute major initiatives in your organization—integrating a newly acquired firm, overhauling an IT system—you need **complex** teams. Such teams' defining characteristics—large, virtual, diverse, and specialized—are crucial for handling daunting projects. Yet these very characteristics can also destroy team members' ability to work together, say Gratton and Erickson. For instance, as team size grows, collaboration diminishes.

To maximize your complex teams' effectiveness, construct a basis for collaboration in your company.

Eight practices hinging on relationship building and cultural change can help. For example, create a strong sense of community by sponsoring events and activities that bring people together and help them get to know one another. And use informal mentoring and coaching to encourage employees to view interaction with leaders and colleagues as valuable.

When executives, HR professionals, and team leaders all pitch in to apply these practices, complex teams hit the ground running—the day they're formed.

means that team members are working with people that they know only superficially or have never met before—colleagues drawn from other divisions of the company, perhaps, or even from outside it. We have found that the higher the proportion of strangers on the team and the greater the diversity of background and experience, the less likely the team members are to share knowledge or exhibit other collaborative behaviors.

In the same way, the higher the educational level of the team members is, the more challenging collaboration appears to be for them. We found that the greater the proportion of experts a team had, the more likely it was to disintegrate into nonproductive conflict or stalemate.

So how can executives strengthen an organization's ability to perform complex collaborative tasks—to maximize the effectiveness of large, diverse teams, while minimizing the disadvantages posed by their structure and composition?

To answer that question we looked carefully at 55 large teams and identified those that demonstrated high levels of collaborative behavior despite their complexity. Put differently, they succeeded

Idea in Practice

The authors recommend these practices for encouraging collaboration in complex teams.

What Executives Can Do

- Invest in building and maintaining social relationships throughout your organization.

  Example: Royal Bank of Scotland's CEO commissioned new headquarters built around an indoor atrium and featuring a "Main Street" with shops, picnic spaces, and a leisure club. The design encourages employees to rub shoulders daily, which fuels collaboration in RBS's complex teams.

- Model collaborative behavior.

  Example: At Standard Chartered Bank, top executives frequently fill in for one another, whether leading regional celebrations, representing SCB at key external events, or initiating internal dialogues with employees. They make their collaborative behavior visible through extensive travel and photos of leaders from varied sites working together.

- Use coaching to reinforce a collaborative culture.

  Example: At Nokia, each new hire's manager lists everyone in the organization the newcomer should meet, suggests topics he or she should discuss with each person on the list, and explains why establishing each of these relationships is important.

What HR Can Do

- Train employees in the specific skills required for collaboration: appreciating others, engaging in purposeful conversation,

both because of and despite their composition. Using a range of statistical analyses, we considered how more than 100 factors, such as the design of the task and the company culture, might contribute to collaboration, manifested, for example, in a willingness to share knowledge and workloads. Out of the 100-plus factors, we were able to isolate eight practices that correlated with success—that is, that appeared to help teams overcome substantially the difficulties that were posed by size, long-distance communication, diversity, and specialization. We then interviewed the teams that were very strong in these practices, to find out how they did it. In this article we'll walk through the practices. They fall into four

productively and creatively resolving conflicts, and managing programs.

- Support a sense of community by sponsoring events and activities such as networking groups, cooking weekends, or tennis coaching. Spontaneous, unannounced activities can further foster community spirit.

  Example: Marriott has recognized the anniversary of the company's first hotel opening by rolling back the cafeteria to the 1950s and sponsoring a team twist dance contest.

What Team Leaders Can Do

- Ensure that at least 20%–40% of a new team's members already know one another.

  Example: When Nokia needs to transfer skills across business functions or units, it moves entire small teams intact instead of reshuffling individual people into new positions.

- Change your leadership style as your team develops. At early stages in the project, be task-oriented: articulate the team's goal and accountabilities. As inevitable conflicts start emerging, switch to relationship building.

- Assign distinct roles so team members can do their work independently. They'll spend less time negotiating responsibilities or protecting turf. But leave the *path* to achieving the team's goal somewhat ambiguous. Lacking well-defined tasks, members are more likely to invest time and energy collaborating.

general categories—executive support, HR practices, the strength of the team leader, and the structure of the team itself.

Executive Support

At the most basic level, a team's success or failure at collaborating reflects the philosophy of top executives in the organization. Teams do well when executives invest in supporting social relationships, demonstrate collaborative behavior themselves, and create what we call a "gift culture"—one in which employees experience interactions with leaders and colleagues as something valuable and generously offered, a gift.

Investing in signature relationship practices

When we looked at complex collaborative teams that were performing in a productive and innovative manner, we found that in every case the company's top executives had invested significantly in building and maintaining social relationships throughout the organization. However, the way they did that varied widely. The most collaborative companies had what we call "signature" practices—practices that were memorable, difficult for others to replicate, and particularly well suited to their own business environment.

For example, when Royal Bank of Scotland's CEO, Fred Goodwin, invested £350 million to open a new headquarters building outside Edinburgh in 2005, one of his goals was to foster productive collaboration among employees. Built around an indoor atrium, the new structure allows more than 3,000 people from the firm to rub shoulders daily.

The headquarters is designed to improve communication, increase the exchange of ideas, and create a sense of community among employees. Many of the offices have an open layout and look over the atrium—a vast transparent space. The campus is set up like a small town, with retail shops, restaurants, jogging tracks and cycling trails, spaces for picnics and barbecues—even a leisure club complete with swimming pool, gym, dance studios, tennis courts, and football pitches. The idea is that with a private "Main Street" running through the headquarters, employees will remain on the campus throughout the day—and be out of their offices mingling with colleagues for at least a portion of it.

To ensure that non-headquarters staff members feel they are a part of the action, Goodwin also commissioned an adjoining business school, where employees from other locations meet and learn. The visitors are encouraged to spend time on the headquarters campus and at forums designed to give employees opportunities to build relationships.

Indeed, the RBS teams we studied had very strong social relationships, a solid basis for collaborative activity that allowed them to accomplish tasks quickly. Take the Group Business Improvement (GBI) teams, which work on 30-, 60-, or 90-day projects ranging from back-office fixes to IT updates and are made up of people from across RBS's many businesses, including insurance, retail banking, and private banking in Europe and the United States. When RBS bought NatWest and migrated the new acquisition's technology platform to RBS's, the speed and success of the GBI teams confounded many market analysts.

BP has made another sort of signature investment. Because its employees are located all over the world, with relatively few at headquarters, the company aims to build social networks by moving employees across functions, businesses, and countries as part of their career development. When BP integrates an acquisition (it has grown by buying numerous smaller oil companies), the leadership development committee deliberately rotates employees from the acquired firm through positions across the corporation. Though the easier and cheaper call would be to leave the executives in their own units—where, after all, they know the business—BP instead trains them to take on new roles. As a consequence any senior team today is likely to be made up of people from multiple heritages. Changing roles frequently—it would not be uncommon for a senior leader at BP to have worked in four businesses and three geographic locations over the past decade—forces executives to become very good at meeting new people and building relationships with them.

Modeling collaborative behavior

In companies with many thousands of employees, relatively few have the opportunity to observe the behavior of the senior team on a day-to-day basis. Nonetheless, we found that the perceived behavior of senior executives plays a significant role in determining how cooperative teams are prepared to be.

Executives at Standard Chartered Bank are exceptionally good role models when it comes to cooperation, a strength that many attribute to the firm's global trading heritage. The Chartered Bank received its remit from Queen Victoria in 1853. The bank's traditional business was in cotton from Bombay (now Mumbai), indigo and tea from Calcutta, rice from Burma, sugar from Java, tobacco from Sumatra, hemp from Manila, and silk from Yokohama. The Standard

The Research

OUR WORK IS BASED on a major research initiative conducted jointly by the Concours Institute (a member of BSG Alliance) and the Cooperative Research Project of London Business School, with funding from the Advanced Institute for Management and 15 corporate sponsors. The initiative was created as a way to explore the practicalities of collaborative work in contemporary organizations.

We sent surveys to 2,420 people, including members of 55 teams. A total of 1,543 people replied, a response rate of 64%. Separate surveys were administered to group members, to group leaders, to the executives who evaluated teams, and to HR leaders at the companies involved. The tasks performed by the teams included new-product development, process reengineering, and identifying new solutions to business problems. The companies involved included four telecommunication companies, seven financial services or consulting firms, two media companies, a hospitality firm, and one oil company. The size of the teams ranged from four to 183 people, with an average of 44.

Our objective was to study the levers that executives could pull to improve team performance and innovation in collaborative tasks. We examined scores of possible factors, including the following.

The general culture of the company. We designed a wide range of survey questions to measure the extent to which the firm had a cooperative culture and to uncover employees' attitudes toward knowledge sharing.

Human resources practices and processes. We studied the way staffing took place and the process by which people were promoted. We examined the

Bank was founded in the Cape Province of South Africa in 1863 and was prominent in financing the development of the diamond fields and later gold mines. Standard Chartered was formed in 1969 through a merger of the two banks, and today the firm has 57 operating groups in 57 countries, with no home market.

It's widely accepted at Standard Chartered that members of the general management committee will frequently serve as substitutes for one another. The executives all know and understand the entire business and can fill in for each other easily on almost any task, whether it's leading a regional celebration, representing the company at a key external event, or kicking off an internal dialogue with employees.

extent and type of training, how reward systems were configured, and the extent to which mentoring and coaching took place.

Socialization and network-building practices. We looked at how often people within the team participated in informal socialization, and the type of interaction that was most common. We also asked numerous questions about the extent to which team members were active in informal communities.

The design of the task. We asked team members and team leaders about the task itself. Our interest here was in how they perceived the purpose of the task, how complex it was, the extent to which the task required members of the team to be interdependent, and the extent to which the task required them to engage in boundary-spanning activities with people outside the team.

The leadership of the team. We studied the perceptions team members had of their leaders' style and how the leaders described their own style. In particular, we were interested in the extent to which the leaders practiced relationship-oriented and task-oriented skills and set cooperative or competitive goals.

The behavior of the senior executives. We asked team members and team leaders about their perceptions of the senior executives of their business unit. We focused in particular on whether team members described them as cooperative or competitive.

In total we considered more than 100 factors. Using a range of statistical analyses, we were able to identify eight that correlated with the successful performance of teams handling complex collaborative tasks.

While the behavior of the executive team is crucial to supporting a culture of collaboration, the challenge is to make executives' behavior visible. At Standard Chartered the senior team travels extensively; the norm is to travel even for relatively brief meetings. This investment in face-to-face interaction creates many opportunities for people across the company to see the top executives in action. Internal communication is frequent and open, and, maybe most telling, every site around the world is filled with photos of groups of executives—country and functional leaders—working together.

The senior team's collaborative nature trickles down throughout the organization. Employees quickly learn that the best way to get things done is through informal networks. For example, when a

Collaboration Conundrums

FOUR TRAITS THAT ARE crucial to teams—but also undermine them.

Large Size

Whereas a decade ago, teams rarely had more than 20 members, our findings show that their size has increased significantly, no doubt because of new technologies. Large teams are often formed to ensure the involvement of a wide stakeholder group, the coordination of a diverse set of activities, and the harnessing of multiple skills. As a consequence, many inevitably involve 100 people or more. However, our research shows that as the size of the team increases beyond 20 members, the level of natural cooperation among members of the team decreases.

Virtual Participation

Today most complex collaborative teams have members who are working at a distance from one another. Again, the logic is that the assigned tasks require the insights and knowledge of people from many locations. Team members may be working in offices in the same city or strung across the world. Only

major program was recently launched to introduce a new customer-facing technology, the team responsible had an almost uncanny ability to understand who the key stakeholders at each branch bank were and how best to approach them. The team members' first-name acquaintance with people across the company brought a sense of dynamism to their interactions.

Creating a "gift culture"

A third important role for executives is to ensure that mentoring and coaching become embedded in their own routine behavior—and throughout the company. We looked at both formal mentoring processes, with clear roles and responsibilities, and less formal processes, where mentoring was integrated into everyday activities. It turned out that while both types were important, the latter was more likely to increase collaborative behavior. Daily coaching helps establish a cooperative "gift culture" in place of a more transactional "tit-for-tat culture."

At Nokia informal mentoring begins as soon as someone steps into a new job. Typically, within a few days, the employee's manager will

40% of the teams in our sample had members all in one place. Our research shows that as teams become more virtual, collaboration declines.

Diversity

Often the challenging tasks facing today's businesses require the rapid assembly of people from multiple backgrounds and perspectives, many of whom have rarely, if ever, met. Their diverse knowledge and views can spark insight and innovation. However, our research shows that the higher the proportion of people who don't know anyone else on the team and the greater the diversity, the less likely the team members are to share knowledge.

High Education Levels

Complex collaborative teams often generate huge value by drawing on a variety of deeply specialized skills and knowledge to devise new solutions. Again, however, our research shows that the greater the proportion of highly educated specialists on a team, the more likely the team is to disintegrate into unproductive conflicts.

sit down and list all the people in the organization, no matter in what location, it would be useful for the employee to meet. This is a deeply ingrained cultural norm, which probably originated when Nokia was a smaller and simpler organization. The manager sits with the newcomer, just as her manager sat with her when she joined, and reviews what topics the newcomer should discuss with each person on the list and why establishing a relationship with him or her is important. It is then standard for the newcomer to actively set up meetings with the people on the list, even when it means traveling to other locations. The gift of time—in the form of hours spent on coaching and building networks—is seen as crucial to the collaborative culture at Nokia.

Focused HR Practices

So what about human resources? Is collaboration solely in the hands of the executive team? In our study we looked at the impact of a wide variety of HR practices, including selection, performance management, promotion, rewards, and training, as well as formally sponsored coaching and mentoring programs.

We found some surprises: for example, that the type of reward system—whether based on team or individual achievement, or tied explicitly to collaborative behavior or not—had no discernible effect on complex teams' productivity and innovation. Although most formal HR programs appeared to have limited impact, we found that two practices did improve team performance: training in skills related to collaborative behavior, and support for informal community building. Where collaboration was strong, the HR team had typically made a significant investment in one or both of those practices—often in ways that uniquely represented the company's culture and business strategy.

Ensuring the requisite skills

Many of the factors that support collaboration relate to what we call the "container" of collaboration—the underlying culture and habits of the company or team. However, we found that some teams had a collaborative culture but were not skilled in the practice of collaboration itself. They were encouraged to cooperate, they wanted to cooperate, but they didn't know how to work together very well in teams.

Our study showed that a number of skills were crucial: appreciating others, being able to engage in purposeful conversations, productively and creatively resolving conflicts, and program management. By training employees in those areas, a company's human resources or corporate learning department can make an important difference in team performance.

In the research, PricewaterhouseCoopers emerged as having one of the strongest capabilities in productive collaboration. With responsibility for developing 140,000 employees in nearly 150 countries, PwC's training includes modules that address teamwork, emotional intelligence, networking, holding difficult conversations, coaching, corporate social responsibility, and communicating the firm's strategy and shared values. PwC also teaches employees how to influence others effectively and build healthy partnerships.

A number of other successful teams in our sample came from organizations that had a commitment to teaching employees

Eight Factors That Lead to Success

1. **Investing in signature relationship practices.** Executives can encourage collaborative behavior by making highly visible investments—in facilities with open floor plans to foster communication, for example—that demonstrate their commitment to collaboration.
2. **Modeling collaborative behavior.** At companies where the senior executives demonstrate highly collaborative behavior themselves, teams collaborate well.
3. **Creating a "gift culture."** Mentoring and coaching—especially on an informal basis—help people build the networks they need to work across corporate boundaries.
4. **Ensuring the requisite skills.** Human resources departments that teach employees how to build relationships, communicate well, and resolve conflicts creatively can have a major impact on team collaboration.
5. **Supporting a strong sense of community.** When people feel a sense of community, they are more comfortable reaching out to others and more likely to share knowledge.
6. **Assigning team leaders that are both task- and relationship-oriented.** The debate has traditionally focused on whether a task or a relationship orientation creates better leadership, but in fact both are key to successfully leading a team. Typically, leaning more heavily on a task orientation at the outset of a project and shifting toward a relationship orientation once the work is in full swing works best.
7. **Building on heritage relationships.** When too many team members are strangers, people may be reluctant to share knowledge. The best practice is to put at least a few people who know one another on the team.
8. **Understanding role clarity and task ambiguity.** Cooperation increases when the roles of individual team members are sharply defined yet the team is given latitude on how to achieve the task.

relationship skills. Lehman Brothers' flagship program for its client-facing staff, for instance, is its training in selling and relationship management. The program is not about sales techniques but, rather, focuses on how Lehman values its clients and makes sure that every client has access to all the resources the firm has to offer.

It is essentially a course on strategies for building collaborative partnerships with customers, emphasizing the importance of trust-based personal relationships.

Supporting a sense of community

While a communal spirit can develop spontaneously, we discovered that HR can also play a critical role in cultivating it, by sponsoring group events and activities such as women's networks, cooking weekends, and tennis coaching, or creating policies and practices that encourage them.

At ABN Amro we studied effective change-management teams within the company's enterprise services function. These informal groups were responsible for projects associated with the implementation of new technology throughout the bank; one team, for instance, was charged with expanding online banking services. To succeed, the teams needed the involvement and expertise of different parts of the organization.

The ABN Amro teams rated the company's support for informal communities very positively. The firm makes the technology needed for long-distance collaboration readily available to groups of individuals with shared interests—for instance, in specific technologies or markets—who hold frequent web conferences and communicate actively online. The company also encourages employees that travel to a new location to arrange meetings with as many people as possible. As projects are completed, working groups disband but employees maintain networks of connections. These practices serve to build a strong community over time—one that sets the stage for success with future projects.

Committed investment in informal networks is also a central plank of the HR strategy at Marriott. Despite its size and global reach, Marriott remains a family business, and the chairman, Bill Marriott, makes a point of communicating that idea regularly to employees. He still tells stories of counting sticky nickels at night as a child—proceeds from the root-beer stand founded in downtown Washington, DC, by his mother and father.

How Complex Is the Collaborative Task?

NOT ALL HIGHLY COLLABORATIVE tasks are complex. In assembling and managing a team, consider the project you need to assign and whether the following statements apply:

- The task is unlikely to be accomplished successfully using only the skills within the team.
- The task must be addressed by a new group formed specifically for this purpose.
- The task requires collective input from highly specialized individuals.
- The task requires collective input and agreement from more than 20 people.
- The members of the team working on the task are in more than two locations.
- The success of the task is highly dependent on understanding preferences or needs of individuals outside the group.
- The outcome of the task will be influenced by events that are highly uncertain and difficult to predict.
- The task must be completed under extreme time pressure.

If more than two of these statements are true, the task requires complex collaboration.

Many of the firm's HR investments reinforce a friendly, family-like culture. Almost every communication reflects an element of staff appreciation. A range of "pop-up" events—spontaneous activities—create a sense of fun and community. For example, the cafeteria might roll back to the 1950s, hold a twist dance contest, and in doing so, recognize the anniversary of the company's first hotel opening. Bill Marriott's birthday might be celebrated with parties throughout the company, serving as an occasion to emphasize the firm's culture and values. The chairman recently began his own blog, which is popular with employees, in which he discusses everything from Marriott's efforts to become greener, to his favorite family vacation spots—themes intended to reinforce the idea that the company is a community.

The Right Team Leaders

In the groups that had high levels of collaborative behavior, the team leaders clearly made a significant difference. The question in our minds was how they actually achieved this. The answer, we saw, lay in their flexibility as managers.

Assigning leaders who are both task- and relationship-oriented

There has been much debate among both academics and senior managers about the most appropriate style for leading teams. Some people have suggested that relationship-oriented leadership is most appropriate in complex teams, since people are more likely to share knowledge in an environment of trust and goodwill. Others have argued that a task orientation—the ability to make objectives clear, to create a shared awareness of the dimensions of the task, and to provide monitoring and feedback—is most important.

In the 55 teams we studied, we found that the truth lay somewhere in between. The most productive, innovative teams were typically led by people who were *both* task- and relationship-oriented. What's more, these leaders changed their style during the project. Specifically, at the early stages they exhibited task-oriented leadership: They made the goal clear, engaged in debates about commitments, and clarified the responsibilities of individual team members. However, at a certain point in the development of the project they switched to a relationship orientation. This shift often took place once team members had nailed down the goals and their accountabilities and when the initial tensions around sharing knowledge had begun to emerge. An emphasis throughout a project on one style at the expense of the other inevitably hindered the long-term performance of the team, we found.

Producing ambidextrous team leaders—those with both relationship and task skills—is a core goal of team-leadership development at Marriott. The company's performance-review process emphasizes growth in both kinds of skills. As evidence of their relationship skills, managers are asked to describe their peer network and cite examples of specific ways that network helped them succeed. They also must provide examples of how they've used relationship building to get things done. The development plans that follow these conversations explicitly map out how the managers can improve specific elements of their social relationships and networks. Such a plan might include, for instance, having lunch regularly with people from a particular community of interest.

To improve their task leadership, many people in the teams at Marriott participated in project-management certification programs, taking refresher courses to maintain their skills over time. Evidence of both kinds of capabilities becomes a significant criterion on which people are selected for key leadership roles at the company.

Team Formation and Structure

The final set of lessons for developing and managing complex teams has to do with the makeup and structure of the teams themselves.

Building on heritage relationships

Given how important trust is to successful collaboration, forming teams that capitalize on preexisting, or "heritage," relationships, increases the chances of a project's success. Our research shows that new teams, particularly those with a high proportion of members who were strangers at the time of formation, find it more difficult to collaborate than those with established relationships.

Newly formed teams are forced to invest significant time and effort in building trusting relationships. However, when some team members already know and trust one another, they can become nodes, which over time evolve into networks. Looking closely at our data, we discovered that when 20% to 40% of the team members were already well connected to one another, the team had strong collaboration right from the start.

It helps, of course, if the company leadership has taken other measures to cultivate networks that cross boundaries. The orientation process at Nokia ensures that a large number of people on any team know one another, increasing the odds that even in a company of more than 100,000 people, someone on a companywide team knows someone else and can make introductions.

Nokia has also developed an organizational architecture designed to make good use of heritage relationships. When it needs to transfer skills across business functions or units, Nokia moves entire small teams intact instead of reshuffling individual people into new positions. If, for example, the company needs to bring together a group of market and technology experts to address a new customer need, the group formed would be composed of small pods of colleagues from each area. This ensures that key heritage relationships continue to strengthen over time, even as the organization redirects its resources to meet market needs. Because the entire company has one common platform for logistics, HR, finance, and other transactions, teams can switch in and out of businesses and geographies without learning new systems.

One important caveat about heritage relationships: If not skillfully managed, too many of them can actually disrupt collaboration. When a significant number of people within the team know one another, they tend to form strong subgroups—whether by function, geography, or anything else they have in common. When that happens, the probability of conflict among the subgroups, which we call fault lines, increases.

Understanding role clarity and task ambiguity

Which is more important to promoting collaboration: a clearly defined approach toward achieving the goal, or clearly specified roles for individual team members? The common assumption is that carefully spelling out the approach is essential, but leaving the roles of individuals within the team vague will encourage people to share ideas and contribute in multiple dimensions.

Our research shows that the opposite is true: Collaboration improves when the roles of individual team members are clearly defined and well understood—when individuals feel that they can do a significant portion of their work independently. Without such clarity, team members are likely to waste too much energy negotiating roles or protecting turf, rather than focus on the task. In addition, team members are more likely to want to collaborate if the path to achieving the team's goal is left somewhat ambiguous. If a team perceives the task as one that requires creativity, where the approach is not yet well known or predefined, its members are more likely to invest time and energy in collaboration.

At the BBC we studied the teams responsible for the radio and television broadcasts of the 2006 Proms (a two-month-long musical celebration), the team that televised the 2006 World Cup, and a team responsible for daytime television news. These teams were large—133 people worked on the Proms, 66 on the World Cup, and 72 on the news—and included members with a wide range of skills and from many disciplines. One would imagine, therefore, that there was a strong possibility of confusion among team members.

To the contrary, we found that the BBC's teams scored among the highest in our sample with regard to the clarity with which members viewed their own roles and the roles of others. Every team was composed of specialists who had deep expertise in their given function, and each person had a clearly defined role. There was little overlap between the responsibilities of the sound technician and the camera operator, and so on. Yet the tasks the BBC teams tackle are, by their very nature, uncertain, particularly when they involve breaking news. The trick the BBC has pulled off has been to clarify team members' individual roles with so much precision that it keeps friction to a minimum.

The successful teams we studied at Reuters worked out of far-flung locations, and often the team members didn't speak a common language. (The primary languages were Russian, Chinese, Thai, and English.) These teams, largely composed of software programmers, were responsible for the rapid development of highly complex technical software and network products. Many of the programmers sat at their desks for 12 hours straight developing code, speaking with no one. Ironically, these teams judged cooperative behavior to be high among their members. That may be because each individual was given autonomy over one discrete piece of the project. The rapid pace and demanding project timelines encouraged individual members to work independently to get the job done, but each person's work had to be shaped with an eye toward the overall team goal.

Strengthening your organization's capacity for collaboration requires a combination of long-term investments—in building relationships and trust, in developing a culture in which senior leaders are role models of cooperation—and smart near-term decisions about the ways teams are formed, roles are defined, and challenges and tasks are articulated. Practices and structures that may have worked well with simple teams of people who were all in one location and knew one another are likely to lead to failure when teams grow more complex.

Most of the factors that impede collaboration today would have impeded collaboration at any time in history. Yesterday's teams, however, didn't require the same amount of members, diversity, long-distance cooperation, or expertise that teams now need to solve global business challenges. So the models for teams need to be realigned with the demands of the current business environment. Through careful attention to the factors we've described in this article, companies can assemble the breadth of expertise needed to solve complex business problems—without inducing the destructive behaviors that can accompany it.

Originally published in November 2007. Reprint R0711F

The Power of Small Wins

Want to truly engage your workers? Help them see their own progress. ***by Teresa M. Amabile and Steven J. Kramer***

WHAT IS THE BEST WAY to drive innovative work inside organizations? Important clues hide in the stories of world-renowned creators. It turns out that ordinary scientists, marketers, programmers, and other unsung knowledge workers, whose jobs require creative productivity every day, have more in common with famous innovators than most managers realize. The workday events that ignite their emotions, fuel their motivation, and trigger their perceptions are fundamentally the same.

The Double Helix, James Watson's 1968 memoir about discovering the structure of DNA, describes the roller coaster of emotions he and Francis Crick experienced through the progress and setbacks of the work that eventually earned them the Nobel Prize. After the excitement of their first attempt to build a DNA model, Watson and Crick noticed some serious flaws. According to Watson, "Our first minutes with the models...were not joyous." Later that evening, "a shape began to emerge which brought back our spirits." But when they showed their "breakthrough" to colleagues, they found that their model would not work. Dark days of doubt and ebbing motivation followed. When the duo finally had their bona fide breakthrough, and their colleagues found no fault with it, Watson wrote, "My morale skyrocketed, for I suspected that we now had the answer to the riddle." Watson and Crick were so driven by this success that they practically lived in the lab, trying to complete the work.

Throughout these episodes, Watson and Crick's progress—or lack thereof—ruled their reactions. In our recent research on creative work inside businesses, we stumbled upon a remarkably similar phenomenon. Through exhaustive analysis of diaries kept by knowledge workers, we discovered the *progress principle:* Of all the things that can boost emotions, motivation, and perceptions during a workday, the single most important is making progress in meaningful work. And the more frequently people experience that sense of progress, the more likely they are to be creatively productive in the long run. Whether they are trying to solve a major scientific mystery or simply produce a high-quality product or service, everyday progress—even a small win—can make all the difference in how they feel and perform.

The power of progress is fundamental to human nature, but few managers understand it or know how to leverage progress to boost motivation. In fact, work motivation has been a subject of longstanding debate. In a survey asking about the keys to motivating workers, we found that some managers ranked recognition for good work as most important, while others put more stock in tangible incentives. Some focused on the value of interpersonal support, while still others thought clear goals were the answer. Interestingly, very few of our surveyed managers ranked progress first. (See the sidebar "A Surprise for Managers.")

If you are a manager, the progress principle holds clear implications for where to focus your efforts. It suggests that you have more influence than you may realize over employees' well-being, motivation, and creative output. Knowing what serves to catalyze and nourish progress—and what does the opposite—turns out to be the key to effectively managing people and their work.

In this article, we share what we have learned about the power of progress and how managers can leverage it. We spell out how a focus on progress translates into concrete managerial actions and provide

Idea in Brief

What is the best way to motivate employees to do creative work? Help them take a step forward every day. In an analysis of knowledge workers' diaries, the authors found that nothing contributed more to a positive inner work life (the mix of emotions, motivations, and perceptions that is critical to performance) than making progress in meaningful work. If a person is motivated and happy at the end of the workday, it's a good bet that he or she achieved something, however small. If the person drags out of the office disengaged and joyless, a setback is likely to blame. This progress principle suggests that managers have more influence than they may realize over employees' well-being, motivation, and creative output.

The key is to learn which actions support progress—such as setting clear goals, providing sufficient time and resources, and offering recognition—and which have the opposite effect. Even small wins can boost inner work life tremendously. On the flip side, small losses or setbacks can have an extremely negative effect. And the work doesn't need to involve curing cancer in order to be meaningful. It simply must matter to the person doing it. The actions that set in motion the positive feedback loop between progress and inner work life may sound like Management 101, but it takes discipline to establish new habits. The authors provide a checklist that managers can use on a daily basis to monitor their progress-enhancing behaviors.

a checklist to help make such behaviors habitual. But to clarify why those actions are so potent, we first describe our research and what the knowledge workers' diaries revealed about their *inner work lives.*

Inner Work Life and Performance

For nearly 15 years, we have been studying the psychological experiences and the performance of people doing complex work inside organizations. Early on, we realized that a central driver of creative, productive performance was the quality of a person's inner work life—the mix of emotions, motivations, and perceptions over the course of a workday. How happy workers feel; how motivated they are by an intrinsic interest in the work; how positively they view their organization, their management, their team, their work, and

A Surprise for Managers

IN A 1968 ISSUE OF HBR, Frederick Herzberg published a now-classic article titled "One More Time: How Do You Motivate Employees?" Our findings are consistent with his message: People are most satisfied with their jobs (and therefore most motivated) when those jobs give them the opportunity to experience achievement.

The diary research we describe in this article—in which we microscopically examined the events of thousands of workdays, in real time—uncovered the mechanism underlying the sense of achievement: making consistent, meaningful progress.

But managers seem not to have taken Herzberg's lesson to heart. To assess contemporary awareness of the importance of daily work progress, we recently administered a survey to 669 managers of varying levels from dozens of companies around the world. We asked about the managerial tools that can affect employees' motivation and emotions. The respondents ranked five tools—support for making progress in the work, recognition for good work, incentives, interpersonal support, and clear goals—in order of importance.

Fully 95% of the managers who took our survey would probably be surprised to learn that supporting progress is the primary way to elevate motivation—because that's the percentage that failed to rank progress number one. In fact, only 35 managers ranked progress as the number one motivator—a mere 5%. The vast majority of respondents ranked support for making progress dead last as a motivator and third as an influence on emotion. They ranked "recognition for good work (either public or private)" as the most important factor in motivating workers and making them happy. In our diary study, recognition certainly did boost inner work life. But it wasn't nearly as prominent as progress. Besides, without work achievements, there is little to recognize.

themselves—all these combine either to push them to higher levels of achievement or to drag them down.

To understand such interior dynamics better, we asked members of project teams to respond individually to an end-of-day e-mail survey during the course of the project—just over four months, on average. (For more on this research, see our article "Inner Work Life: Understanding the Subtext of Business Performance," HBR May 2007.) The projects—inventing kitchen gadgets, managing product lines of cleaning tools, and solving complex IT problems for a hotel empire, for example—all involved creativity. The daily survey inquired about participants' emotions and moods, motivation levels, and perceptions of the work environment that day, as well as what work they did and what events stood out in their minds.

Twenty-six project teams from seven companies participated, comprising 238 individuals. This yielded nearly 12,000 diary entries. Naturally, every individual in our population experienced ups and downs. Our goal was to discover the states of inner work life and the workday events that correlated with the highest levels of creative output.

In a dramatic rebuttal to the commonplace claim that high pressure and fear spur achievement, we found that, at least in the realm of knowledge work, people are more creative and productive when their inner work lives are positive—when they feel happy, are intrinsically motivated by the work itself, and have positive perceptions of their colleagues and the organization. Moreover, in those positive states, people are more committed to the work and more collegial toward those around them. Inner work life, we saw, can fluctuate from one day to the next—sometimes wildly—and performance along with it. A person's inner work life on a given day fuels his or her performance for the day and can even affect performance the *next* day.

Once this *inner work life effect* became clear, our inquiry turned to whether and how managerial action could set it in motion. What events could evoke positive or negative emotions, motivations, and perceptions? The answers were tucked within our research participants' diary entries. There are predictable triggers that inflate or deflate inner work life, and, even accounting for variation among individuals, they are pretty much the same for everyone.

The Power of Progress

Our hunt for inner work life triggers led us to the progress principle. When we compared our research participants' best and worst days (based on their overall mood, specific emotions, and motivation levels), we found that the most common event triggering a "best day" was any progress in the work by the individual or the team. The most common event triggering a "worst day" was a setback.

Consider, for example, how progress relates to one component of inner work life: overall mood ratings. Steps forward occurred on 76% of people's best-mood days. By contrast, setbacks occurred on only 13% of those days. (See the exhibit "What happens on a good day?")

Two other types of inner work life triggers also occur frequently on best days: *Catalysts,* actions that directly support work, including help from a person or group, and *nourishers,* events such as shows of respect and words of encouragement. Each has an opposite: *Inhibitors,* actions that fail to support or actively hinder work, and *toxins,* discouraging or undermining events. Whereas catalysts and inhibitors are directed at the project, nourishers and toxins are directed at the person. Like setbacks, inhibitors and toxins are rare on days of great inner work life.

Events on worst-mood days are nearly the mirror image of those on best-mood days (see the exhibit "What happens on a bad day?"). Here, setbacks predominated, occurring on 67% of those days; progress

What happens on a good day?

Progress—even a small step forward—occurs on many of the days people report being in a good mood.

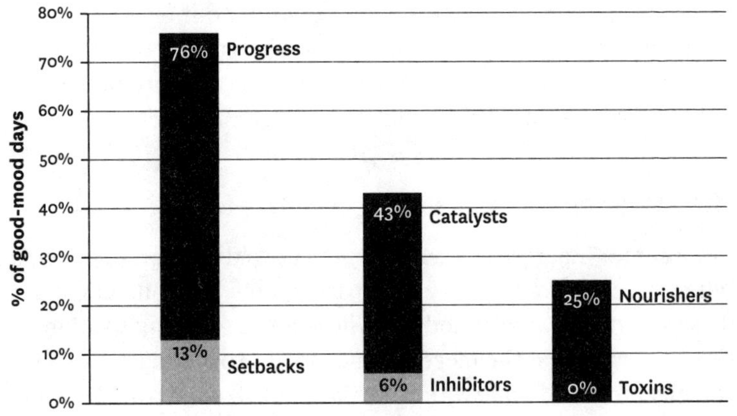

What happens on a bad day?

Events on bad days—setbacks and other hindrances—are nearly the mirror image of those on good days.

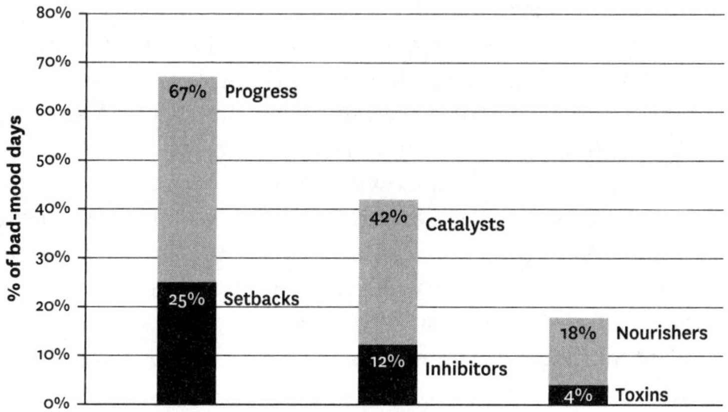

occurred on only 25% of them. Inhibitors and toxins also marked many worst-mood days, and catalysts and nourishers were rare.

This is the progress principle made visible: If a person is motivated and happy at the end of the workday, it's a good bet that he or she made some progress. If the person drags out of the office disengaged and joyless, a setback is most likely to blame.

When we analyzed all 12,000 daily surveys filled out by our participants, we discovered that progress and setbacks influence all three aspects of inner work life. On days when they made progress, our participants reported more positive *emotions*. They not only were in a more upbeat mood in general but also expressed more joy, warmth, and pride. When they suffered setbacks, they experienced more frustration, fear, and sadness.

Motivations were also affected: On progress days, people were more intrinsically motivated—by interest in and enjoyment of the work itself. On setback days, they were not only less intrinsically motivated but also less extrinsically motivated by recognition.

Apparently, setbacks can lead a person to feel generally apathetic and disinclined to do the work at all.

Perceptions differed in many ways, too. On progress days, people perceived significantly more positive challenge in their work. They saw their teams as more mutually supportive and reported more positive interactions between the teams and their supervisors. On a number of dimensions, perceptions suffered when people encountered setbacks. They found less positive challenge in the work, felt that they had less freedom in carrying it out, and reported that they had insufficient resources. On setback days, participants perceived both their teams and their supervisors as less supportive.

To be sure, our analyses establish correlations but do not prove causality. Were these changes in inner work life the result of progress and setbacks, or was the effect the other way around? The numbers alone cannot answer that. However, we do know, from reading thousands of diary entries, that more-positive perceptions, a sense of accomplishment, satisfaction, happiness, and even elation often followed progress. Here's a typical post-progress entry, from a programmer: "I smashed that bug that's been frustrating me for almost a calendar week. That may not be an event to you, but I live a very drab life, so I'm all hyped."

Likewise, we saw that deteriorating perceptions, frustration, sadness, and even disgust often followed setbacks. As another participant, a product marketer, wrote, "We spent a lot of time updating the Cost Reduction project list, and after tallying all the numbers, we are still coming up short of our goal. It is discouraging to not be able to hit it after all the time spent and hard work."

Almost certainly, the causality goes both ways, and managers can use this feedback loop between progress and inner work life to support both.

Minor Milestones

When we think about progress, we often imagine how good it feels to achieve a long-term goal or experience a major breakthrough. These big wins are great—but they are relatively rare. The good news is that even small wins can boost inner work life tremendously. Many of the progress events our research participants reported represented only minor steps forward. Yet they often evoked outsize positive reactions. Consider this diary entry from a programmer in a high-tech company, which was accompanied by very positive self-ratings of her emotions, motivations, and perceptions that day: "I figured out why something was not working correctly. I felt relieved and happy because this was a minor milestone for me."

Even ordinary, incremental progress can increase people's engagement in the work and their happiness during the workday. Across all types of events our participants reported, a notable proportion (28%) of incidents that had a minor impact on the project had a major impact on people's feelings about it. Because inner work life has such a potent effect on creativity and productivity, and because small but consistent steps forward, shared by many people, can accumulate into excellent execution, progress events that often go unnoticed are critical to the overall performance of organizations.

Unfortunately, there is a flip side. Small losses or setbacks can have an extremely negative effect on inner work life. In fact, our study and research by others show that negative events can have a more powerful impact than positive ones. Consequently, it is especially important for managers to minimize daily hassles.

Progress in Meaningful Work

We've shown how gratifying it is for workers when they are able to chip away at a goal, but recall what we said earlier: The key to motivating performance is supporting progress in *meaningful* work. Making headway boosts your inner work life, but only if the work matters to you.

Think of the most boring job you've ever had. Many people nominate their first job as a teenager—washing pots and pans in a restaurant kitchen, for example, or checking coats at a museum. In jobs like those, the power of progress seems elusive. No matter how hard you work, there are always more pots to wash and coats to check; only punching the time clock at the end of the day or getting the paycheck at the end of the week yields a sense of accomplishment.

In jobs with much more challenge and room for creativity, like the ones our research participants had, simply "making progress"—getting tasks done—doesn't guarantee a good inner work life, either. You may have experienced this rude fact in your own job, on days (or in projects) when you felt demotivated, devalued, and frustrated, even though you worked hard and got things done. The likely cause is your perception of the completed tasks as peripheral or irrelevant. For the progress principle to operate, the work must be meaningful to the person doing it.

In 1983, Steve Jobs was trying to entice John Sculley to leave a wildly successful career at PepsiCo to become Apple's new CEO. Jobs reportedly asked him, "Do you want to spend the rest of your life selling sugared water or do you want a chance to change the world?" In making his pitch, Jobs leveraged a potent psychological force: the deep-seated human desire to do meaningful work.

Fortunately, to feel meaningful, work doesn't have to involve putting the first personal computers in the hands of ordinary people, or alleviating poverty, or helping to cure cancer. Work with less profound importance to society can matter if it contributes value to something or someone important to the worker. Meaning can be as simple as making a useful and high-quality product for a customer or providing a genuine service for a community. It can be supporting a colleague or boosting an organization's profits by reducing inefficiencies in a production process. Whether the goals are lofty or modest, as long as they are meaningful to the worker and it is clear how his or her efforts contribute to them, progress toward them can galvanize inner work life.

In principle, managers shouldn't have to go to extraordinary lengths to infuse jobs with meaning. Most jobs in modern organizations are potentially meaningful for the people doing them. However, managers can make sure that employees know just how their work is contributing. And, most important, they can avoid actions that negate its value. (See the sidebar "How Work Gets Stripped of

Its Meaning.") All the participants in our research were doing work that should have been meaningful; no one was washing pots or checking coats. Shockingly often, however, we saw potentially important, challenging work losing its power to inspire.

Supporting Progress: Catalysts and Nourishers

What can managers do to ensure that people are motivated, committed, and happy? How can they support workers' daily progress? They can use catalysts and nourishers, the other kinds of frequent "best day" events we discovered.

Catalysts are actions that support work. They include setting clear goals, allowing autonomy, providing sufficient resources and time, helping with the work, openly learning from problems and successes, and allowing a free exchange of ideas. Their opposites, inhibitors, include failing to provide support and actively interfering with the work. Because of their impact on progress, catalysts and inhibitors ultimately affect inner work life. But they also have a more immediate impact: When people realize that they have clear and meaningful goals, sufficient resources, helpful colleagues, and so on, they get an instant boost to their emotions, their motivation to do a great job, and their perceptions of the work and the organization.

Nourishers are acts of interpersonal support, such as respect and recognition, encouragement, emotional comfort, and opportunities for affiliation. Toxins, their opposites, include disrespect, discouragement, disregard for emotions, and interpersonal conflict. For good and for ill, nourishers and toxins affect inner work life directly and immediately.

Catalysts and nourishers—and their opposites—can alter the meaningfulness of work by shifting people's perceptions of their jobs and even themselves. For instance, when a manager makes sure that people have the resources they need, it signals to them that what they are doing is important and valuable. When managers recognize people for the work they do, it signals that they are important to the organization. In this way, catalysts and nourishers can lend

How Work Gets Stripped of Its Meaning

Diary entries from 238 knowledge workers who were members of creative project teams revealed four primary ways in which managers unwittingly drain work of its meaning.

1. Managers may dismiss the importance of employees' work or ideas. Consider the case of Richard, a senior lab technician at a chemical company, who found meaning in helping his new-product development team solve complex technical problems. However, in team meetings over the course of a three-week period, Richard perceived that his team leader was ignoring his suggestions and those of his teammates. As a result, he felt that his contributions were not meaningful, and his spirits flagged. When at last he believed that he was again making a substantive contribution to the success of the project, his mood improved dramatically:

   > I felt much better at today's team meeting. I felt that my opinions and information were important to the project and that we have made some progress.

2. They may destroy employees' sense of ownership of their work. Frequent and abrupt reassignments often have this effect. This happened repeatedly to the members of a product development team in a giant consumer products company, as described by team member Bruce:

   > As I've been handing over some projects, I do realize that I don't like to give them up. Especially when you have been with them

greater meaning to the work—and amplify the operation of the progress principle.

The managerial actions that constitute catalysts and nourishers are not particularly mysterious; they may sound like Management 101, if not just common sense and common decency. But our diary study reminded us how often they are ignored or forgotten. Even some of the more attentive managers in the companies we studied did not consistently provide catalysts and nourishers. For example, a supply-chain specialist named Michael was, in many ways and on most days, an excellent subteam manager. But he was occasionally so overwhelmed that he became toxic toward his people. When a supplier failed to complete a "hot" order on time and Michael's team had to resort to air shipping to meet the customer's deadline, he realized that the profit margin on the sale would be blown. In irritation, he

> from the start and are nearly to the end. You lose ownership. This happens to us way too often.

3. Managers may send the message that the work employees are doing will never see the light of day. They can signal this—unintentionally—by shifting their priorities or changing their minds about how something should be done. We saw the latter in an internet technology company after user-interface developer Burt had spent weeks designing seamless transitions for non-English-speaking users. Not surprisingly, Burt's mood was seriously marred on the day he reported this incident:

   > Other options for the international [interfaces] were [given] to the team during a team meeting, which could render the work I am doing useless.

4. They may neglect to inform employees about unexpected changes in a customer's priorities. Often, this arises from poor customer management or inadequate communication within the company. For example, Stuart, a data transformation expert at an IT company, reported deep frustration and low motivation on the day he learned that weeks of the team's hard work might have been for naught:

   > Found out that there is a strong possibility that the project may not be going forward, due to a shift in the client's agenda. Therefore, there is a strong possibility that all the time and effort put into the project was a waste of our time.

lashed out at his subordinates, demeaning the solid work they had done and disregarding their own frustration with the supplier. In his diary, he admitted as much:

> As of Friday, we have spent $28,000 in air freight to send 1,500 $30 spray jet mops to our number two customer. Another 2,800 remain on this order, and there is a good probability that they too will gain wings. I have turned from the kindly Supply Chain Manager into the black-masked executioner. All similarity to civility is gone, our backs are against the wall, flight is not possible, therefore fight is probable.

Even when managers don't have their backs against the wall, developing long-term strategy and launching new initiatives can often seem more important—and perhaps sexier—than making sure that subordinates have what they need to make steady progress and feel supported as human beings. But as we saw repeatedly in our research, even the best strategy will fail if managers ignore the people working in the trenches to execute it.

A Model Manager—And a Tool for Emulating Him

We could explain the many (and largely unsurprising) moves that can catalyze progress and nourish spirits, but it may be more useful to give an example of a manager who consistently used those moves—and then to provide a simple tool that can help any manager do so.

Our model manager is Graham, whom we observed leading a small team of chemical engineers within a multinational European firm we'll call Kruger-Bern. The mission of the team's NewPoly project was clear and meaningful enough: develop a safe, biodegradable polymer to replace petrochemicals in cosmetics and, eventually, in a wide range of consumer products. As in many large firms, however, the project was nested in a confusing and sometimes threatening corporate setting of shifting top-management priorities, conflicting signals, and wavering commitments. Resources were uncomfortably tight, and uncertainty loomed over the project's future—and every team member's career. Even worse, an incident early in the project, in which an important customer reacted angrily to a sample, left the team reeling. Yet Graham was able to sustain team members' inner work lives by repeatedly and visibly removing obstacles, materially supporting progress, and emotionally supporting the team.

Graham's management approach excelled in four ways. First, he established a positive climate, one event at a time, which set behavioral norms for the entire team. When the customer complaint stopped the project in its tracks, for example, he engaged immediately with the team to analyze the problem, without recriminations, and develop a plan for repairing the relationship. In doing so, he modeled how to respond to crises in the work: not by panicking or pointing fingers but by identifying problems and their causes, and developing a coordinated action plan. This is both a practical approach and a great way to give subordinates a sense of forward movement even in the face of the missteps and failures inherent in any complex project.

Second, Graham stayed attuned to his team's everyday activities and progress. In fact, the nonjudgmental climate he had established made this happen naturally. Team members updated him frequently—without being asked—on their setbacks, progress, and plans. At one point, one of his hardest-working colleagues, Brady, had to abort a trial of a new material because he couldn't get the parameters right on the equipment. It was bad news, because the NewPoly team had access to the equipment only one day a week, but Brady immediately informed Graham. In his diary entry that evening, Brady noted, "He didn't like the lost week but seemed to understand." That understanding assured Graham's place in the stream of information that would allow him to give his people just what they needed to make progress.

Third, Graham targeted his support according to recent events in the team and the project. Each day, he could anticipate what type of intervention—a catalyst or the removal of an inhibitor; a nourisher or some antidote to a toxin—would have the most impact on team members' inner work lives and progress. And if he could not make that judgment, he asked. Most days it was not hard to figure out, as on the day he received some uplifting news about his bosses' commitment to the project. He knew the team was jittery about a rumored corporate reorganization and could use the encouragement. Even though the clarification came during a well-earned vacation day, he immediately got on the phone to relay the good news to the team.

Finally, Graham established himself as a resource for team members, rather than a micromanager; he was sure to *check in* while never seeming to *check up* on them. Superficially, checking in and checking up seem quite similar, but micromanagers make four kinds of mistakes. First, they fail to allow autonomy in carrying out the work. Unlike Graham, who gave the NewPoly team a clear strategic goal but respected members' ideas about how to meet it, micromanagers dictate every move. Second, they frequently ask subordinates

The Daily Progress Checklist

Near the end of each workday, use this checklist to review the day and plan your managerial actions for the next day. After a few days, you will be able to identify issues by scanning the boldface words. First, focus on progress and setbacks and think about specific events (catalysts, nourishers, inhibitors, and toxins) that contributed to them. Next, consider any clear inner-work-life clues and what further information they provide about progress and other events. Finally, prioritize for action. The action plan for the next day is the most important part of your daily review: What is the one thing you can do to best facilitate progress?

Progress

Which 1 or 2 events today indicated either a small win or a possible breakthrough? (Describe briefly.)

____

____

____

Setbacks

Which 1 or 2 events today indicated either a small setback or a possible crisis? (Describe briefly.)

____

____

____

Catalysts

- ☐ Did the team have clear short- and long-term **goals** for meaningful work?
- ☐ Did team members have sufficient **autonomy** to solve problems and take ownership of the project?
- ☐ Did they have all the **resources** they needed to move forward efficiently?
- ☐ Did they have sufficient **time** to focus on meaningful work?
- ☐ Did I give or get them **help** when they needed or requested it? Did I encourage team members to help one another?
- ☐ Did I discuss **lessons** from today's successes and problems with my team?
- ☐ Did I help **ideas** flow freely within the group?

Inhibitors

- ☐ Was there any confusion regarding long- or short-term **goals** for meaningful work?
- ☐ Were team members overly **constrained** in their ability to solve problems and feel ownership of the project?
- ☐ Did they lack any of the **resources** they needed to move forward effectively?
- ☐ Did they lack sufficient **time** to focus on meaningful work?
- ☐ Did I or others fail to provide needed or requested **help**?
- ☐ Did I "punish" failure or neglect to find **lessons** and/or opportunities in problems and successes?
- ☐ Did I or others cut off the presentation or debate of **ideas** prematurely?

Nourishers

- ☐ Did I show **respect** to team members by recognizing their contributions to progress, attending to their ideas, and treating them as trusted professionals?
- ☐ Did I **encourage** team members who faced difficult challenges?
- ☐ Did I **support** team members who had a personal or professional problem?
- ☐ Is there a sense of personal and professional **affiliation** and camaraderie within the team?

Toxins

- ☐ Did I **disrespect** any team members by failing to recognize their contributions to progress, not attending to their ideas, or not treating them as trusted professionals?
- ☐ Did I **discourage** a member of the team in any way?
- ☐ Did I **neglect** a team member who had a personal or professional problem?
- ☐ Is there tension or **antagonism** among members of the team or between team members and me?

Inner Work Life

Did I see any indications of the quality of my subordinates' inner work lives today? ______

Perceptions of the work, team, management, firm ______

Emotions ______

Motivation ______

What specific events might have affected inner work life today? ______

Action Plan

What can I do tomorrow to start eliminating the inhibitors and toxins identified?

______

______

______

What can I do tomorrow to strengthen the catalysts and nourishers identified and provide the ones that are lacking?

______

______

______

about their work without providing any real help. By contrast, when one of Graham's team members reported problems, Graham helped analyze them—remaining open to alternative interpretations—and often ended up helping to get things back on track. Third, micromanagers are quick to affix personal blame when problems arise, leading subordinates to hide problems rather than honestly discuss how to surmount them, as Graham did with Brady. And fourth, micromanagers tend to hoard information to use as a secret weapon. Few realize how damaging this is to inner work life. When subordinates perceive that a manager is withholding potentially useful information, they feel infantilized, their motivation wanes, and their work is handicapped. Graham was quick to communicate upper management's views of the project, customers' opinions and needs, and possible sources of assistance or resistance within and outside the organization.

In all those ways, Graham sustained his team's positive emotions, intrinsic motivation, and favorable perceptions. His actions serve as a powerful example of how managers at any level can approach each day determined to foster progress.

We know that many managers, however well-intentioned, will find it hard to establish the habits that seemed to come so naturally to Graham. Awareness, of course, is the first step. However, turning an awareness of the importance of inner work life into routine action takes discipline. With that in mind, we developed a checklist for managers to consult on a daily basis (see the sidebar "The Daily Progress Checklist"). The aim of the checklist is managing for meaningful progress, one day at a time.

The Progress Loop

Inner work life drives performance; in turn, good performance, which depends on consistent progress, enhances inner work life. We call this the *progress loop;* it reveals the potential for self-reinforcing benefits.

So, the most important implication of the progress principle is this: By supporting people and their daily progress in meaningful work, managers improve not only the inner work lives of their employees but also the organization's long-term performance, which enhances inner work life even more. Of course, there is a dark side—the possibility of negative feedback loops. If managers fail to support progress and the people trying to make it, inner work life suffers and so does performance; and degraded performance further undermines inner work life.

A second implication of the progress principle is that managers needn't fret about trying to read the psyches of their workers, or manipulate complicated incentive schemes, to ensure that employees are motivated and happy. As long as they show basic respect and consideration, they can focus on supporting the work itself.

To become an effective manager, you must learn to set this positive feedback loop in motion. That may require a significant shift. Business schools, business books, and managers themselves usually focus on managing organizations or people. But if you focus on managing progress, the management of people—and even of entire organizations—becomes much more feasible. You won't have to figure out how to x?ray the inner work lives of subordinates; if you facilitate their steady progress in meaningful work, make that progress salient to them, and treat them well, they will experience the emotions, motivations, and perceptions necessary for great performance. Their superior work will contribute to organizational success. And here's the beauty of it: They will love their jobs.

Originally published in May 2011. Reprint R1105C

Building the Emotional Intelligence of Groups

by Vanessa Urch Druskat and Steven B. Wolff

WHEN MANAGERS FIRST STARTED HEARING ABOUT the concept of emotional intelligence in the 1990s, scales fell from their eyes. The basic message, that effectiveness in organizations is at least as much about EQ as IQ, resonated deeply; it was something that people knew in their guts but that had never before been so well articulated. Most important, the idea held the potential for positive change. Instead of being stuck with the hand they'd been dealt, people could take steps to enhance their emotional intelligence and make themselves more effective in their work and personal lives.

Indeed, the concept of emotional intelligence had real impact. The only problem is that so far emotional intelligence has been viewed only as an individual competency, when the reality is that most work in organizations is done by teams. And if managers have one pressing need today, it's to find ways to make teams work better.

It is with real excitement, therefore, that we share these findings from our research: individual emotional intelligence has a group analog, and it is just as critical to groups' effectiveness. Teams can develop greater emotional intelligence and, in so doing, boost their overall performance.

Why Should Teams Build Their Emotional Intelligence?

No one would dispute the importance of making teams work more effectively. But most research about how to do so has focused on identifying the task processes that distinguish the most successful teams—that is, specifying the need for cooperation, participation, commitment to goals, and so forth. The assumption seems to be that, once identified, these processes can simply be imitated by other teams, with similar effect. It's not true. By analogy, think of it this way: a piano student can be taught to play Minuet in G, but he won't become a modern-day Bach without knowing music theory and being able to play with heart. Similarly, the real source of a great team's success lies in the fundamental conditions that allow effective task processes to emerge—and that cause members to engage in them wholeheartedly.

Our research tells us that three conditions are essential to a group's effectiveness: trust among members, a sense of group identity, and a sense of group efficacy. When these conditions are absent, going through the motions of cooperating and participating is still possible. But the team will not be as effective as it could be, because members will choose to hold back rather than fully engage. To be most effective, the team needs to create emotionally intelligent norms—the attitudes and behaviors that eventually become habits—that support behaviors for building trust, group identity, and group efficacy. The outcome is complete engagement in tasks. (For more on how emotional intelligence influences these conditions, see the sidebar "A Model of Team Effectiveness.")

Three Levels of Emotional Interaction

Make no mistake: a team with emotionally intelligent members does not necessarily make for an emotionally intelligent group. A team, like any social group, takes on its own character. So creating an upward, self-reinforcing spiral of trust, group identity, and group efficacy requires more than a few members who exhibit emotionally

Idea in Brief

How does IDEO, the celebrated industrial-design firm, ensure that its teams consistently produce the most innovative products under intense deadline and budget pressures? By focusing on its teams' **emotional intelligence**—that powerful combination of self-management skills and ability to relate to others.

Many executives realize that EQ (emotional quotient) is as critical as IQ to an individual's effectiveness. But *groups'* emotional intelligence may be even more important, since most work gets done in teams.

A group's EI isn't simply the sum of its members'. Instead, it comes from norms that support awareness and regulation of emotions within and outside the team. These norms build trust, group identity, and a sense of group efficacy. Members feel that they work better *together* than individually.

Group EI norms build the foundation for true collaboration and cooperation—helping otherwise skilled teams fulfill their highest potential.

intelligent behavior. It requires a team atmosphere in which the norms build emotional capacity (the ability to respond constructively in emotionally uncomfortable situations) and influence emotions in constructive ways.

Team emotional intelligence is more complicated than individual emotional intelligence because teams interact at more levels. To understand the differences, let's first look at the concept of individual emotional intelligence as defined by Daniel Goleman. In his definitive book *Emotional Intelligence,* Goleman explains the chief characteristics of someone with high EI; he or she is *aware* of emotions and able to *regulate* them—and this awareness and regulation are directed both *inward,* to one's self, and *outward,* to others. "Personal competence," in Goleman's words, comes from being aware of and regulating one's own emotions. "Social competence" is awareness and regulation of others' emotions.

A group, however, must attend to yet another level of awareness and regulation. It must be mindful of the emotions of its members,

Idea in Practice

To build a foundation for emotional intelligence, a group must be aware of and constructively regulate the emotions of:

- individual team members
- the whole group
- other key groups with whom it interacts.

How? By establishing EI norms—rules for behavior that are introduced by group leaders, training, or the larger organizational culture. Here are some examples of norms—and what they look like in action—from IDEO:

Emotions of . . .	To Hone Awareness . . .	To Regulate . . .	IDEO Examples
Individual team members	• Understand the sources of individuals' behavior and take steps to address problematic behavior. • Encourage all group members to share their perspectives before making key decisions.	• Handle confrontation constructively. If team members fall short, call them on it by letting them know the group needs them. • Treat each other in a caring way—acknowledge when someone is upset; show appreciation and respect.	• Awareness: A project leader notices a designer's frustration over a marketing decision and initiates negotiations to resolve the issue. • Regulation: During brainstorming sessions, participants pelt colleagues with soft toys if they prematurely judge ideas.

its own group emotions or moods, and the emotions of other groups and individuals outside its boundaries.

In this article, we'll explore how emotional incompetence at any of these levels can cause dysfunction. We'll also show how establishing specific group norms that create awareness and regulation

Emotions of . . .	To Hone Awareness . . .	To Regulate . . .	IDEO Examples
The whole group	• Regularly assess the group's strengths, weaknesses, and modes of interaction. • Invite reality checks from customers, colleagues, suppliers.	• Create structures that let the group express its emotions. • Cultivate an affirmative environment. • Encourage proactive problem-solving.	• Awareness: Teams work closely with customers to determine what needs improvement. • Regulation: "Finger-blaster" toys scattered around the office let people have fun and vent stress.
Other key groups	• Designate team members as liaisons to key outside constituencies. • Identify and support other groups' expectations and needs.	• Develop cross-boundary relationships to gain outsiders' confidence. • Know the broader social and political context in which your group must succeed. • Show your appreciation of other groups.	• Regulation: IDEO built such a good relationship with an outside fabricator that it was able to call on it for help during a crisis—on the weekend.

of emotion at these three levels can lead to better outcomes. First, we'll focus on the individual level—how emotionally intelligent groups work with their individual members' emotions. Next, we'll focus on the group level. And finally, we'll look at the cross-boundary level.

A Model of Team Effectiveness

STUDY AFTER STUDY HAS shown that teams are more creative and productive when they can achieve high levels of participation, cooperation, and collaboration among members. But interactive behaviors like these aren't easy to legislate. Our work shows that three basic conditions need to be present before such behaviors can occur: mutual trust among members, a sense of group identity (a feeling among members that they belong to a unique and worthwhile group), and a sense of group efficacy (the belief that the team can perform well and that group members are more effective working together than apart).

At the heart of these three conditions are emotions. Trust, a sense of identity, and a feeling of efficacy arise in environments where emotion is well handled, so groups stand to benefit by building their emotional intelligence.

Group emotional intelligence isn't a question of dealing with a necessary evil—catching emotions as they bubble up and promptly suppressing them. Far from it. It's about bringing emotions deliberately to the surface and understanding how they affect the team's work. It's also about behaving in ways that build relationships both inside and outside the team and that strengthen the team's ability to face challenges. Emotional intelligence means exploring, embracing, and ultimately relying on emotion in work that is, at the end of the day, deeply human.

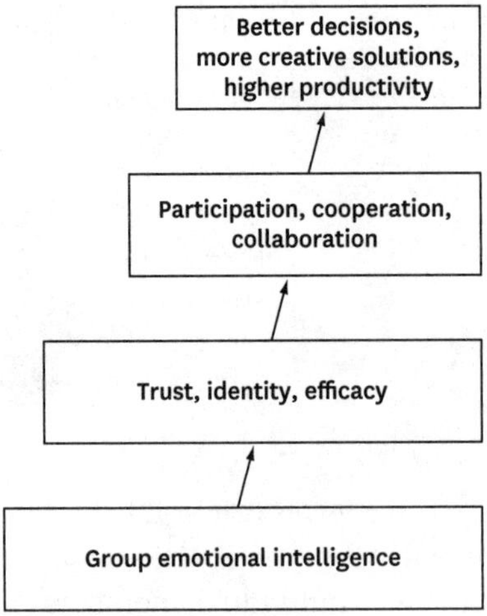

Working with Individuals' Emotions

Jill Kasper, head of her company's customer service department, is naturally tapped to join a new cross-functional team focused on enhancing the customer experience: she has extensive experience in and a real passion for customer service. But her teammates find she brings little more than a bad attitude to the table. At an early brainstorming session, Jill sits silent, arms crossed, rolling her eyes. Whenever the team starts to get energized about an idea, she launches into a detailed account of how a similar idea went nowhere in the past. The group is confused: this is the customer service star they've been hearing about? Little do they realize she feels insulted by the very formation of the team. To her, it implies she hasn't done her job well enough.

When a member is not on the same emotional wave-length as the rest, a team needs to be emotionally intelligent vis-à-vis that individual. In part, that simply means being aware of the problem. Having a norm that encourages interpersonal understanding might facilitate an awareness that Jill is acting out of defensiveness. And picking up on this defensiveness is necessary if the team wants to make her understand its desire to amplify her good work, not negate it.

Some teams seem to be able to do this naturally. At Hewlett-Packard, for instance, we learned of a team that was attempting to cross-train its members. The idea was that if each member could pinch-hit on everyone else's job, the team could deploy efforts to whatever task required the most attention. But one member seemed very uncomfortable with learning new skills and tasks; accustomed to being a top producer in his own job, he hated not knowing how to do a job perfectly. Luckily, his teammates recognized his discomfort, and rather than being annoyed, they redoubled their efforts to support him. This team benefited from a group norm it had established over time emphasizing interpersonal understanding. The norm had grown out of the group's realization that working to accurately hear and understand one another's feelings and concerns improved member morale and a willingness to cooperate.

Many teams build high emotional intelligence by taking pains to consider matters from an individual member's perspective. Think of a situation where a team of four must reach a decision; three favor one direction and the fourth favors another. In the interest of expedience, many teams in this situation would move directly to a majority vote. But a more emotionally intelligent group would pause first to hear out the objection. It would also ask if everyone were completely behind the decision, even if there appeared to be consensus. Such groups would ask, "Are there any perspectives we haven't heard yet or thought through completely?"

Perspective taking is a team behavior that teamwork experts discuss often—but not in terms of its emotional consequence. Many teams are trained to use perspective-taking techniques to make decisions or solve problems (a common tool is affinity diagramming). But these techniques may or may not improve a group's emotional intelligence. The problem is that many of these techniques consciously attempt to remove emotion from the process by collecting and combining perspectives in a mechanical way. A more effective approach to perspective taking is to ensure that team members see one another making the effort to grapple with perspectives; that way, the team has a better chance of creating the kind of trust that leads to greater participation among members.

An executive team at the Hay Group, a consulting firm, engages in the kind of deep perspective taking we're describing. The team has done role-playing exercises in which members adopt others' opinions and styles of interaction. It has also used a "storyboarding" technique, in which each member creates a small poster representing his or her ideas. As team members will attest, these methods and others have helped the group build trust and increase participation.

Regulating Individuals' Emotions

Interpersonal understanding and perspective taking are two ways that groups can become more aware of their members' perspectives and feelings. But just as important as awareness is the ability to regulate those emotions—to have a positive impact on how they are expressed and even on how individual team members feel. We're not talking about imposing groupthink or some other form of manipulation here—clearly, the goal must be to balance the team's cohesion with members' individuality. We're simply acknowledging that people take their emotional cues from those around them. Something that seems upsetting initially can seem not so bad—or ten times worse—depending on whether one's colleagues are inclined to smooth feathers or fan flames. The most constructive way of regulating team members' emotions is by establishing norms in the group for both confrontation and caring.

It may seem illogical to suggest that an emotionally intelligent group must engage in confrontation, but it's not. Inevitably, a team member will indulge in behavior that crosses the line, and the team must feel comfortable calling the foul. In one manufacturing team we studied, a member told us about the day she selfishly decided to extend her break. Before long, one of her teammates stormed into the break room, saying, "What are you doing in here? Get back out on the floor—your team needs you!" The woman had overstepped the bounds, and she got called on it. There were no hard feelings, because the woman knew the group valued her contributions.

Some teams also find that a little humor helps when pointing out errant behavior. Teasing someone who is habitually late for meetings, for instance, can make that person aware of how important timeliness is to the group. Done right, confrontation can be seen in a positive light; it's a way for the group to say, "We want you in—we need your contribution." And it's especially important when a team must work together on a long-term assignment. Without confrontation, disruptive behavior can fester and erode a sense of trust in a team.

Establishing norms that reinforce caring behavior is often not very difficult and usually a matter of concentrating on little things. When an individual is upset, for example, it may make all the difference to have group members acknowledge that person's feelings. We saw this in a meeting where one team member arrived angry because the time and place of the meeting was very inconvenient for him. When another member announced the sacrifice the man had made to be there, and thanked him, the man's attitude turned around 180 degrees. In general, a caring orientation includes displaying positive regard, appreciation, and respect for group members through behaviors such as support, validation, and compassion.

Interpersonal understanding, perspective taking, confrontation, caring—these norms build trust and a sense of group identity among members. And all of them can be established in teams where they don't arise naturally. You may ask, But is it really worth all the effort? Does it make sense to spend managerial time fostering new norms to accommodate a few prickly personalities? Of course it does. Teams are at the very foundation of an organization, and they won't work effectively without mutual trust and a common commitment to goals.

Working with Group Emotions

Chris couldn't believe it, but he was requesting a reassignment. The team he was on was doing good work, staying on budget, and hitting all its deadlines—though not always elegantly. Its leader, Stan Evans, just got a promotion. So why was being on the team such a downer? At the last major status meeting, they should have been serving champagne—so much had been achieved. Instead, everyone was thoroughly dispirited over a setback they hadn't foreseen, which turned out later to be no big deal. It seemed no matter what happened, the group griped. The team even saw Stan's promotion in a negative light: "Oh, so I guess management wants to keep a closer eye on us" and "I hear Stan's new boss doesn't back this project." Chris had a friend on another team who was happy to put in a good word for him. The work was inherently less interesting—but hey, at least they were having fun.

Some teams suffer because they aren't aware of emotions at the group level. Chris's team, for instance, isn't aware of all it has achieved, and it doesn't acknowledge that it has fallen into a malaise. In our study of effective teams, we've found that having norms for group self-awareness—of emotional states, strengths and weaknesses, modes of interaction, and task processes—is a critical part of group emotional intelligence that facilitates group efficacy. Teams gain it both through self-evaluation and by soliciting feedback from others.

Self-evaluation can take the form of a formal event or a constant activity. At Sherwin Williams, a group of managers was starting a new initiative that would require higher levels of teamwork. Group members hired a consultant, but before the consultant arrived, they met to assess their strengths and weaknesses as a team. They found that merely articulating the issues was an important step toward building their capabilities.

A far less formal method of raising group emotional awareness is through the kind of activity we saw at the Veterans Health Administration's Center for Leadership and Development. Managers there have developed a norm in which they are encouraged to speak up when they feel the group is not being productive. For example, if there's a post-lunch lull and people on the team are low on energy, someone might say, "Don't we look like a bunch of sad sacks?" With attention called to it, the group makes an effort to refocus.

Emotionally competent teams don't wear blinders; they have the emotional capacity to face potentially difficult information and actively seek opinions on their task processes, progress, and performance from the outside. For some teams, feedback may come directly from customers. Others look to colleagues within the company, to suppliers, or to professional peers. A group of designers we studied routinely posts its work in progress on walls throughout the building, with invitations to comment and critique. Similarly, many advertising agencies see annual industry competitions as a valuable source of feedback on their creative teams' work.

Regulating Group Emotions

Many teams make conscious efforts to build team spirit. Team-building outings, whether purely social or Outward Bound–style physical challenges, are popular methods for building this sense of collective enthusiasm. What's going on here is that teams and their leaders recognize they can improve a team's overall attitude—that is, they are regulating group-level emotion. And while the focus of a team-building exercise is often not directly related to a group's actual work, the benefits are highly relevant: teams come away with higher emotional capacity and thus a greater ability to respond to emotional challenges.

The most effective teams we have studied go far beyond the occasional "ropes and rocks" off-site. They have established norms that strengthen their ability to respond effectively to the kind of emotional challenges a group confronts on a daily basis. The norms they favor accomplish three main things: they create resources for working with emotions, foster an affirmative environment, and encourage proactive problem solving.

Teams need resources that all members can draw on to deal with group emotions. One important resource is a common vocabulary. To use an example, a group member at the Veterans Health Administration picked up on another member's bad mood and told him that he was just "cranky" today. The "cranky" term stuck and became the group's gentle way of letting someone know that their negativity was having a bad effect on the group. Other resources may include helpful ways to vent frustrations. One executive team leader we interviewed described his team's practice of making time for a "wailing wall"—a few minutes of whining and moaning about some setback. Releasing and acknowledging those negative emotions, the leader says, allows the group to refocus its attention on the parts of the situation it can control and channel its energy in a positive direction. But sometimes, venting takes more than words. We've seen more than one intense workplace outfitted with toys—like soft projectile shooters—that have been used in games of cube warfare.

Perhaps the most obvious way to build emotional capacity through regulating team-level emotion is simply to create an affirmative environment. Everyone values a team that, when faced with a challenge, responds with a can-do attitude. Again, it's a question of having the right group norms—in this case, favoring optimism, and positive images and interpretations over negative ones. This doesn't always come naturally to a team, as one executive we interviewed at the Hay Group knows. When external conditions create a cycle of negativity among group members, he takes it upon himself to change the atmosphere of the group. He consciously resists the temptation to join the complaining and blaming and instead tries to reverse the cycle with a positive, constructive note.

One of the most powerful norms we have seen for building a group's ability to respond to emotionally challenging situations is an emphasis on proactive problem solving. We saw a lot of this going on in a manufacturing team we observed at AMP Corporation. Much of what this team needed to hit its targets was out of its strict control. But rather than sit back and point fingers, the team worked hard to get what it needed from others, and in some cases, took matters into its own hands. In one instance, an alignment problem in a key machine was creating faulty products. The team studied the problem and approached the engineering group with its own suggested design for a part that might correct the problem. The device worked, and the number of defective products decreased significantly.

This kind of problem solving is valuable for many reasons. It obviously serves the company by removing one more obstacle to profitability. But, to the point of our work, it also shows a team in control of its own emotions. It refused to feel powerless and was eager to take charge.

Working with Emotions Outside the Group

Jim sighed. The "Bugs" team was at it again. Didn't they see that while they were high-fiving one another over their impressive productivity, the rest of the organization was paying for it? This time, in their self-managed wisdom, they'd decided to make a three months' supply of one component. No changeover meant no machine downtime and a record low cost per unit. But now the group downstream was swamped with inventory it didn't need and worried about shortages of something else. Jim braced himself for his visit to the floor. The Bugs didn't take criticism well; they seemed to think they were flawless and that everyone else was just trying to take them down a notch. And what was with that name, anyway? Some kind of inside joke, Jim guessed. Too bad nobody else got it.

The last kind of emotional intelligence any high-performing team should have relates to cross-boundary relationships. Just as individuals should be mindful of their own emotions and others', groups should look both inward and outward emotionally. In the case of the Bugs, the team is acting like a clique—creating close emotional ties within but ignoring the feelings, needs, and concerns of important individuals and teams in the broader organization.

Some teams have developed norms that are particularly helpful in making them aware of the broader organizational context. One practice is to have various team members act as liaisons to important constituencies. Many teams are already made up of members drawn from different parts of an organization, so a cross-boundary perspective comes naturally. Others need to work a little harder. One team we studied realized it would be important to understand the perspective of its labor union. Consequently, a team member from HR went to some lengths to discover the right channels for having a union member appointed to the group. A cross-boundary perspective is especially important in situations where a team's work will have significant impact on others in the organization—for example, where a team is asked to design an intranet to serve everyone's needs. We've seen many situations in which a team is so enamored of its solution that it is caught completely by surprise when others in the company don't share its enthusiasm.

Some of the most emotionally intelligent teams we have seen are so attuned to their broader organizational context that it affects how they frame and communicate their own needs and accomplishments. A team at the chemical-processing company KoSa, for example, felt it needed a new piece of manufacturing equipment, but senior management wasn't so sure the purchase was a priority. Aware that the decision makers were still on the fence, the team decided to emphasize the employee safety benefits of the new machine—just one aspect of its desirability to them, but an issue of paramount importance to management. At a plant safety meeting attended by high-level managers, they made the case that the equipment they were seeking would greatly reduce the risk of injury to workers. A few weeks later they got it.

Sometimes, a team must be particularly aware of the needs and feelings of another group within the organization. We worked with an information technology company where the hardware engineers worked separately from the software engineers to achieve the same goal—faster processing and fewer crashes. Each could achieve only so much independently. When finally a hardware team leader went out of his way to build relationships with the software people, the two teams began to cooperate—and together, they achieved 20% to 40% higher performance than had been targeted.

This kind of positive outcome can be facilitated by norms that encourage a group to recognize the feelings and needs of other groups. We saw effective norms for interteam awareness at a division of AMP, where each manufacturing team is responsible for a step in the manufacturing process and they need one another to complete the product on time. Team leaders there meet in the morning to understand the needs, resources, and schedules of each team. If one team is ahead and another is behind, they reallocate resources. Members of the faster

Building Norms for Three Levels of Group Emotional Intelligence

GROUP EMOTIONAL INTELLIGENCE IS about the small acts that make a big difference. It is not about a team member working all night to meet a deadline; it is about saying thank you for doing so. It is not about in-depth discussion of ideas; it is about asking a quiet member for his thoughts. It is not about harmony, lack of tension, and all members liking each other; it is about acknowledging when harmony is false, tension is unexpressed, and treating others with respect. The following table outlines some of the small things that groups can do to establish the norms that build group emotional intelligence.

Individual	*Group*	*Cross-boundary*
Norms that create awareness of emotions		
Interpersonal understanding	***Team self-evaluation***	***Organizational understanding***
1. Take time away from group tasks to get to know one another. 2. Have a "check in" at the beginning of the meeting—that is, ask how everyone is doing. 3. Assume that undesirable behavior takes place for a reason. Find out what that reason is. Ask questions and listen. Avoid negative attributions. 4. Tell your teammates what you're thinking and how you're feeling.	1. Schedule time to examine team effectiveness. 2. Create measurable task and process objectives and then measure them. 3. Acknowledge and discuss group moods. 4. Communicate your sense of what is transpiring in the team. 5. Allow members to call a "process check." (For instance, a team member might say, "Process check: is this the most effective use of our time right now?")	1. Find out the concerns and needs of others in the organization. 2. Consider who can influence the team's ability to accomplish its goals. 3. Discuss the culture and politics in the organization. 4. Ask whether proposed team actions are congruent with the organization's culture and politics.
Perspective taking	***Seeking feedback***	
1. Ask whether everyone agrees with a decision. 2. Ask quiet members what they think. 3. Question decisions that come too quickly. 4. Appoint a devil's advocate.	1. Ask your "customers" how you are doing. 2. Post your work and invite comments. 3. Benchmark your processes.	

Norms that help regulate emotions

Confronting

1. Set ground rules and use them to point out errant behavior.
2. Call members on errant behavior.
3. Create playful devices for pointing out such behavior. These often emerge from the group spontaneously. Reinforce them.

Caring

1. Support members: volunteer to help them if they need it, be flexible, and provide emotional support.
2. Validate members' contributions. Let members know they are valued.
3. Protect members from attack.
4. Respect individuality and differences in perspectives. Listen.
5. Never be derogatory or demeaning.

Creating resources for working with emotion

1. Make time to discuss difficult issues, and address the emotions that surround them.
2. Find creative, shorthand ways to acknowledge and express the emotion in the group.
3. Create fun ways to acknowledge and relieve stress and tension.
4. Express acceptance of members' emotions.

Creating an affirmative environment

1. Reinforce that the team can meet a challenge. Be optimistic. For example, say things like, "We can get through this" or "Nothing will stop us."
2. Focus on what you can control.
3. Remind members of the group's important and positive mission.
4. Remind the group how it solved a similar problem before.
5. Focus on problem solving, not blaming.

Solving problems proactively

1. Anticipate problems and address them before they happen.
2. Take the initiative to understand and get what you need to be effective.
3. Do it yourself if others aren't responding. Rely on yourself, not others.

Building external relationships

1. Create opportunities for networking and interaction.
2. Ask about the needs of other teams.
3. Provide support for other teams.
4. Invite others to team meetings if they might have a stake in what you are doing.

team help the team that's behind and do so in a friendly way that empathizes with their situation and builds the relationship.

Most of the examples we've been citing show teams that are not only aware of but also able to influence outsiders' needs and perspectives. This ability to regulate emotion at the cross-boundary level is a group's version of the "social skills" so critical to individual emotional intelligence. It involves developing external relationships and gaining the confidence of outsiders, adopting an ambassadorial role instead of an isolationist one.

A manufacturing team we saw at KoSa displayed very high social skills in working with its maintenance team. It recognized that, when problems occurred in the plant, the maintenance team often had many activities on its plate. All things being equal, what would make the maintenance team consider this particular manufacturing group a high priority? Knowing a good relationship would be a factor, the manufacturing team worked hard to build good ties with the maintenance people. At one point, for instance, the manufacturing team showed its appreciation by nominating the maintenance team for "Team of the Quarter" recognition—and then doing all the letter writing and behind-the-scenes praising that would ultimately help the maintenance team win. In turn, the manufacturing team's good relationship with maintenance helped it become one of the highest producers in the plant.

A Model for Group Emotional Intelligence

We've been discussing the need for teams to learn to channel emotion effectively at the three levels of human interaction important to them: team to individual member, team to itself, and team to outside entities. Together, the norms we've been exploring help groups work with emotions productively and intelligently. Often, groups with emotionally intelligent members have norms like these in place, but it's unlikely any group would unconsciously come up with *all* the norms we have outlined. In other words, this is a model for group emotional intelligence that any work team could benefit from by applying it deliberately.

What would the ultimate emotionally intelligent team look like? Closest to the ideal are some of the teams we've seen at IDEO, the celebrated industrial design firm. IDEO's creative teams are responsible for the look and feel of products like Apple's first mouse, the Crest toothpaste tube, and the Palm V personal digital assistant. The firm routinely wins competitions for the form and function of its designs and even has a business that teaches creative problem-solving techniques to other companies.

The nature of IDEO's work calls for high group emotional intelligence. Under pressure of client deadlines and budget estimates, the company must deliver innovative, aesthetic solutions that balance human needs with engineering realities. It's a deep philosophical belief at IDEO that great design is best accomplished through the creative friction of diverse teams and not the solitary pursuit of brilliant individuals, so it's imperative that the teams at IDEO click. In our study of those teams, we found group norms supporting emotional intelligence at all three levels of our model.

First, the teams at IDEO are very aware of individual team members' emotions, and they are adept at regulating them. For example, an IDEO designer became very frustrated because someone from marketing was insisting a logo be applied to the designer's product, which he felt would ruin it visually. At a meeting about the product, the team's project leader picked up on the fact that something was wrong. The designer was sitting off by himself, and things "didn't look right." The project leader looked into the situation and then initiated a negotiation that led to a mutual solution.

IDEO team members also confront one another when they break norms. This is common during brainstorming sessions, where the rule is that people must defer judgment and avoid shooting down ideas. If someone breaks that norm, the team comes down on him in a playful yet forceful way (imagine being pelted by foam toys). Or if someone is out of line, the norm is to stand up and call her on it immediately. If a client is in the room, the confrontation is subtler—perhaps a kick under the chair.

Teams at IDEO also demonstrate strengths in group-focused emotional intelligence. To ensure they have a high level of self-awareness, teams constantly seek feedback from both inside and outside the organization. Most important, they work very closely with customers. If a design is not meeting customer expectations, the team finds out quickly and takes steps to modify it.

Regulating group emotion at IDEO often means providing outlets for stress. This is a company that believes in playing and having fun. Several hundred finger blasters (a toy that shoots soft projectiles) have been placed around the building for employees to pick up and start shooting when they're frustrated. Indeed, the design firm's culture welcomes the expression of emotions, so it's not uncommon for someone—whether happy or angry — to stand up and yell. IDEO has even created fun office projects that people can work on if they need a break. For example, they might have a project to design the company holiday card or to design the "tourist stop" displays seen by visitors.

Finally, IDEO teams also have norms to ensure they are aware of the needs and concerns of people outside their boundaries and that they use that awareness to develop relationships with those individuals and groups. On display at IDEO is a curious model: a toy truck with plastic pieces on springs that pop out of the bed of the truck when a button is pressed. It turns out the model commemorates an incident that taught a variety of lessons. The story centers on a design team that had been working for three weeks on a very complex plastic enclosure for a product. Unfortunately, on the Thursday before a Monday client deadline, when an engineer was taking it to be painted, it slipped from his pickup bed and exploded on the road at 70 mph. The team was willing to work through the weekend to rebuild the part but couldn't finish it without the help of the outside fabricator it had used on the original. Because they had taken the time to build a good relationship with the fabricator, its people were willing to go above and beyond the call of duty. The light-hearted display was a way for teammates to show the engineer that all was forgiven—and a reminder to the rest of the organization of how a team in crisis can get by with a little help from its friends.

Where Do Norms Come From?

Not every company is as dependent on teams and their emotional intelligence as IDEO. But now more than ever, we see companies depending on teams for decisions and tasks that, in another time, would have been the work of individuals. And unfortunately, we also see them discovering that a team can have everything going for it—the brightest and most qualified people, access to resources, a clear mission—but still fail because it lacks group emotional intelligence.

Norms that build trust, group identity, and group efficacy are the key to making teams click. They allow an otherwise highly skilled and resourced team to fulfill its potential, and they can help a team faced with substantial challenges achieve surprising victories. So how do norms as powerful as the ones we've described in this article come about? In our research, we saw them being introduced from any of five basic directions: by formal team leaders, by informal team leaders, by courageous followers, through training, or from the larger organizational culture. (For more on how to establish the norms described in this article, see the sidebar "Building Norms for Three Levels of Group Emotional Intelligence.")

At the Hay Group, for example, it was the deliberate action of a team leader that helped one group see the importance of emotions to the group's overall effectiveness. Because this particular group was composed of managers from many different cultures, its leader knew he couldn't assume all the members possessed a high level of interpersonal understanding. To establish that norm, he introduced novelties like having a meeting without a table, using smaller groups, and conducting an inventory of team members' various learning styles.

Interventions like these can probably be done only by a formal team leader. The ways informal leaders or other team members enhance emotional intelligence are typically more subtle, though often just as powerful. Anyone might advance the cause, for example, by speaking up if the group appears to be ignoring an important perspective or feeling—or simply by doing his or her part to create an affirmative environment.

Training courses can also go a long way toward increasing emotional awareness and showing people how to regulate emotions. We know of many companies that now focus on emotional issues in leadership development courses, negotiation and communication workshops, and employee-assistance programs like those for stress management. These training programs can sensitize team members to the importance of establishing emotionally intelligent norms.

Finally, perhaps more than anything, a team can be influenced by a broader organizational culture that recognizes and celebrates employee emotion. This is clearly the case at IDEO and, we believe, at many of the companies creating the greatest value in the new economy. Unfortunately, it's the most difficult piece of the puzzle to put in place at companies that don't already have it. For organizations with long histories of employees checking their emotions at the door, change will occur, if at all, one team at a time.

Becoming Intelligent About Emotion

The research presented in this article arose from one simple imperative: in an era of teamwork, it's essential to figure out what makes teams work. Our research shows that, just like individuals, the most effective teams are emotionally intelligent ones—and that any team can attain emotional intelligence.

In this article, we've attempted to lay out a model for positive change, containing the most important types of norms a group can create to enhance its emotional intelligence. Teams, like all groups, operate according to such norms. By working to establish norms for emotional awareness and regulation at all levels of interaction, teams can build the solid foundation of trust, group identity, and group efficacy they need for true cooperation and collaboration—and high performance overall.

Originally published in March 2001. Reprint 62OX

Managing Multicultural Teams

by Jeanne Brett, Kristin Behfar, and Mary C. Kern

W

WHEN A MAJOR INTERNATIONAL SOFTWARE developer needed to produce a new product quickly, the project manager assembled a team of employees from India and the United States. From the start the team members could not agree on a delivery date for the product. The Americans thought the work could be done in two to three weeks; the Indians predicted it would take two to three months. As time went on, the Indian team members proved reluctant to report setbacks in the production process, which the American team members would find out about only when work was due to be passed to them. Such conflicts, of course, may affect any team, but in this case they arose from cultural differences. As tensions mounted, conflict over delivery dates and feedback became personal, disrupting team members' communication about even mundane issues. The project manager decided he had to intervene—with the result that both the American and the Indian team members came to rely on him for direction regarding minute operational details that the team should have been able to handle itself. The manager became so bogged down by quotidian issues that the project careened hopelessly off even the most pessimistic schedule—and the team never learned to work together effectively.

Multicultural teams often generate frustrating management dilemmas. Cultural differences can create substantial obstacles to effective teamwork—but these may be subtle and difficult to recognize until significant damage has already been done. As in the case above, which the manager involved told us about, managers may create more problems than they resolve by intervening. The challenge in managing multicultural teams effectively is to recognize underlying cultural causes of conflict, and to intervene in ways that both get the team back on track and empower its members to deal with future challenges themselves.

We interviewed managers and members of multicultural teams from all over the world. These interviews, combined with our deep research on dispute resolution and teamwork, led us to conclude that the wrong kind of managerial intervention may sideline valuable members who should be participating or, worse, create resistance, resulting in poor team performance. We're not talking here about respecting differing national standards for doing business, such as accounting practices. We're referring to day-to-day working problems among team members that can keep multicultural teams from realizing the very gains they were set up to harvest, such as knowledge of different product markets, culturally sensitive customer service, and 24-hour work rotations.

The good news is that cultural challenges are manageable if managers and team members choose the right strategy and avoid imposing single-culture-based approaches on multicultural situations.

The Challenges

People tend to assume that challenges on multicultural teams arise from differing styles of communication. But this is only one of the four categories that, according to our research, can create barriers to a team's ultimate success. These categories are direct versus indirect communication; trouble with accents and fluency; differing attitudes toward hierarchy and authority; and conflicting norms for decision making.

Direct versus indirect communication

Communication in Western cultures is typically direct and explicit. The meaning is on the surface, and a listener doesn't have to know

Idea in Brief

If your company does business internationally, you're probably leading teams with members from diverse cultural backgrounds. Those differences can present serious obstacles. For example, some members' lack of fluency in the team's dominant language can lead others to underestimate their competence. When such obstacles arise, your team can stalemate.

To get the team moving again, avoid intervening directly, advise Brett, Behfar, and Kern. Though sometimes necessary, your involvement can prevent team members from solving problems themselves—and learning from that process.

Instead, choose one of three indirect interventions. When possible, encourage team members to **adapt** by acknowledging cultural gaps and working around them. If your team isn't able to be open about their differences, consider **structural intervention** (e.g., reassigning members to reduce interpersonal friction). As a last resort, use an **exit** strategy (e.g., removing a member from the team).

There's no one right way to tackle multicultural problems. But understanding four barriers to team success can help you begin evaluating possible responses.

much about the context or the speaker to interpret it. This is not true in many other cultures, where meaning is embedded in the way the message is presented. For example, Western negotiators get crucial information about the other party's preferences and priorities by asking direct questions, such as "Do you prefer option A or option B?" In cultures that use indirect communication, negotiators may have to infer preferences and priorities from changes—or the lack of them—in the other party's settlement proposal. In cross-cultural negotiations, the non-Westerner can understand the direct communications of the Westerner, but the Westerner has difficulty understanding the indirect communications of the non-Westerner.

An American manager who was leading a project to build an interface for a U.S. and Japanese customer-data system explained the problems her team was having this way: "In Japan, they want to talk and discuss. Then we take a break and they talk within the organization. They want to make sure that there's harmony in the rest of the organization. One of the hardest lessons for me was when I thought they were saying yes but they just meant 'I'm listening to you.'"

Idea in Practice

Four Barriers

The following cultural differences can cause destructive conflicts in a team:

- **Direct versus indirect communication.** Some team members use direct, explicit communication while others are indirect, for example, asking questions instead of pointing out problems with a project. When members see such differences as violations of their culture's communication norms, relationships can suffer.
- **Trouble with accents and fluency.** Members who aren't fluent in the team's dominant language may have difficulty communicating their knowledge. This can prevent the team from using their expertise and create frustration or perceptions of incompetence.
- **Differing attitudes toward hierarchy.** Team members from hierarchical cultures expect to be treated differently according to their status in the organization. Members from egalitarian cultures do not. Failure of some members to honor those expectations can cause humiliation or loss of stature and credibility.
- **Conflicting decision-making norms.** Members vary in how quickly they make decisions and in how much analysis they require beforehand. Someone who prefers making decisions quickly may grow frustrated with those who need more time.

Four Interventions

Your team's unique circumstances can help you determine how to respond to multicultural conflicts. Consider these options:

Intervention Type	When to Use	Example
Adaptation: working with or around differences	Members are willing to acknowledge cultural differences and figure out how to live with them.	An American engineer working on a team that included Israelis was shocked by their in-your-face, argumentative style. Once he noticed they confronted each other and not just

Intervention Type	When to Use	Example
		him—and still worked well together—he realized confrontations weren't personal attacks and accepted their style.
Structural intervention: reorganizing to reduce friction	The team has obvious subgroups, or members cling to negative stereotypes of one another.	An international research team's leader realized that when he led meetings, members "shut down" because they felt intimidated by his executive status. After he hired a consultant to run future meetings, members participated more.
Managerial intervention: making final decisions without team involvement	Rarely; for instance, a new team needs guidance in establishing productive norms.	A software development team's lingua franca was English, but some members spoke with pronounced accents. The manager explained they'd been chosen for their task expertise, not fluency in English. And she directed them to tell customers: "I realize I have an accent. If you don't understand what I'm saying, just stop me and ask questions."
Exit: voluntary or involuntary removal of a team member	Emotions are running high, and too much face has been lost on both sides to salvage the situation.	When two members of a multicultural consulting team couldn't resolve their disagreement over how to approach problems, one member left the firm.

The differences between direct and indirect communication can cause serious damage to relationships when team projects run into problems. When the American manager quoted above discovered that several flaws in the system would significantly disrupt company operations, she pointed this out in an e-mail to her American boss and the Japanese team members. Her boss appreciated the direct warnings; her Japanese colleagues were embarrassed, because she had violated their norms for uncovering and discussing problems. Their reaction was to provide her with less access to the people and information she needed to monitor progress. They would probably have responded better if she had pointed out the problems indirectly—for example, by asking them what would happen if a certain part of the system was not functioning properly, even though she knew full well that it was malfunctioning and also what the implications were.

As our research indicates is so often true, communication challenges create barriers to effective teamwork by reducing information sharing, creating interpersonal conflict, or both. In Japan, a typical response to direct confrontation is to isolate the norm violator. This American manager was isolated not just socially but also physically. She told us, "They literally put my office in a storage room, where I had desks stacked from floor to ceiling and I was the only person there. So they totally isolated me, which was a pretty loud signal to me that I was not a part of the inside circle and that they would communicate with me only as needed."

Her direct approach had been intended to solve a problem, and in one sense, it did, because her project was launched problem-free. But her norm violations exacerbated the challenges of working with her Japanese colleagues and limited her ability to uncover any other problems that might have derailed the project later on.

Trouble with accents and fluency

Although the language of international business is English, misunderstandings or deep frustration may occur because of nonnative speakers' accents, lack of fluency, or problems with translation or usage. These may also influence perceptions of status or competence.

For example, a Latin American member of a multicultural consulting team lamented, "Many times I felt that because of the language difference, I didn't have the words to say some things that I was thinking. I noticed that when I went to these interviews with the U.S. guy, he would tend to lead the interviews, which was understandable but also disappointing, because we are at the same level. I had very good questions, but he would take the lead."

When we interviewed an American member of a U.S.-Japanese team that was assessing the potential expansion of a U.S. retail chain into Japan, she described one American teammate this way: "He was not interested in the Japanese consultants' feedback and felt that because they weren't as fluent as he was, they weren't intelligent enough and, therefore, could add no value." The team member described was responsible for assessing one aspect of the feasibility of expansion into Japan. Without input from the Japanese experts, he risked overestimating opportunities and underestimating challenges.

Nonfluent team members may well be the most expert on the team, but their difficulty communicating knowledge makes it hard for the team to recognize and utilize their expertise. If teammates become frustrated or impatient with a lack of fluency, interpersonal conflicts can arise. Nonnative speakers may become less motivated to contribute, or anxious about their performance evaluations and future career prospects. The organization as a whole pays a greater price: Its investment in a multicultural team fails to pay off.

Some teams, we learned, use language differences to resolve (rather than create) tensions. A team of U.S. and Latin American buyers was negotiating with a team from a Korean supplier. The negotiations took place in Korea, but the discussions were conducted in English. Frequently the Koreans would caucus at the table by speaking Korean. The buyers, frustrated, would respond by appearing to caucus in Spanish—though they discussed only inconsequential current events and sports, in case any of the Koreans spoke Spanish. Members of the team who didn't speak Spanish pretended to participate, to the great amusement of their teammates.

This approach proved effective: It conveyed to the Koreans in an appropriately indirect way that their caucuses in Korean were frustrating and annoying to the other side. As a result, both teams cut back on sidebar conversations.

Differing attitudes toward hierarchy and authority

A challenge inherent in multicultural teammates is that by design, teams have a rather flat structure. But team members from some cultures, in which people are treated differently according to their status in an organization, are uncomfortable on flat teams. If they defer to higher-status team members, their behavior will be seen as appropriate when most of the team comes from a hierarchical culture; but they may damage their stature and credibility—and even face humiliation—if most of the team comes from an egalitarian culture.

One manager of Mexican heritage, who was working on a credit and underwriting team for a bank, told us, "In Mexican culture, you're always supposed to be humble. So whether you understand something or not, you're supposed to put it in the form of a question. You have to keep it open-ended, out of respect. I think that actually worked against me, because the Americans thought I really didn't know what I was talking about. So it made me feel like they thought I was wavering on my answer."

When, as a result of differing cultural norms, team members believe they've been treated disrespectfully, the whole project can blow up. In another Korean-U.S. negotiation, the American members of a due diligence team were having difficulty getting information from their Korean counterparts, so they complained directly to higher-level Korean management, nearly wrecking the deal. The higher-level managers were offended because hierarchy is strictly adhered to in Korean organizations and culture. It should have been their own lower-level people, not the U.S. team members, who came to them with a problem. And the Korean team members were mortified that their bosses had been involved before they themselves could brief them. The crisis was resolved only when high-level U.S. managers made a trip to Korea, conveying appropriate respect for their Korean counterparts.

Conflicting norms for decision making

Cultures differ enormously when it comes to decision making—particularly, how quickly decisions should be made and how much analysis is required beforehand. Not surprisingly, U.S. managers like to make decisions very quickly and with relatively little analysis by comparison with managers from other countries.

A Brazilian manager at an American company who was negotiating to buy Korean products destined for Latin America told us, "On the first day, we agreed on three points, and on the second day, the U.S.-Spanish side wanted to start with point four. But the Korean side wanted to go back and rediscuss points one through three. My boss almost had an attack."

What U.S. team members learn from an experience like this is that the American way simply cannot be imposed on other cultures. Managers from other cultures may, for example, decline to share information until they understand the full scope of a project. But they have learned that they can't simply ignore the desire of their American counterparts to make decisions quickly. What to do? The best solution seems to be to make minor concessions on process—to learn to adjust to and even respect another approach to decision making. For example, American managers have learned to keep their impatient bosses away from team meetings and give them frequent if brief updates. A comparable lesson for managers from other cultures is to be explicit about what they need—saying, for example, "We have to see the big picture before we talk details."

Four Strategies

The most successful teams and managers we interviewed used four strategies for dealing with these challenges: adaptation (acknowledging cultural gaps openly and working around them), structural intervention (changing the shape of the team), managerial intervention (setting norms early or bringing in a higher-level manager), and exit (removing a team member when other options have failed). There is no one right way to deal with a particular kind of multicultural problem; identifying the type of challenge is only the first step. The more crucial step is assessing the circumstances—or "enabling situational conditions"—under which the team is working. For example, does the project allow any flexibility for change, or do deadlines make that impossible? Are there additional resources available that might be tapped? Is the team permanent or temporary? Does the team's manager have the autonomy to make a decision about changing the team in some way? Once the situational conditions have been analyzed, the team's leader can identify an appropriate response (see the exhibit "Identifying the right strategy").

Identifying the right strategy

The most successful teams and managers we interviewed use four strategies for dealing with problems: adaptation (acknowledging cultural gaps openly and working around them), structural intervention (changing the shape of the team), managerial intervention (setting norms early or bringing in a higher-level manager), and exit (removing a team member when other options have failed). Adaptation is the ideal strategy because the team works effectively to solve its own problem with minimal input from management—and, most important, learns from the experience. The guide below can help you identify the right strategy once you have identified both the problem and the "enabling situational conditions" that apply to the team.

Representative problems	Enabling situational conditions	Strategy	Complicating factors
• Conflict arises from decision-making differences • Misunderstanding or stonewalling arises from communication differences	• Team members can attribute a challenge to culture rather than personality • Higher-level managers are not available or the team would be embarrassed to involve them	**Adaptation**	• Team members must be exceptionally aware • Negotiating a common understanding takes time

Representative problems	Enabling situational conditions	Strategy	Complicating factors
• The team is affected by emotional tensions relating to fluency issues or prejudice • Team members are inhibited by perceived status differences among teammates	• The team can be subdivided to mix cultures or expertise • Tasks can be subdivided	**Structural Intervention**	• If team members aren't carefully distributed, subgroups can strengthen preexisting differences • Subgroup solutions have to fit back together
• Violations of hierarchy have resulted in loss of face • An absence of ground rules is causing conflict	• The problem has produced a high level of emotion • The team has reached a stalemate • A higher-level manager is able and willing to intervene	**Managerial Intervention**	• The team becomes overly dependent on the manager • Team members may be sidelined or resistant
• A team member cannot adjust to the challenge at hand and has become unable to contribute to the project	• The team is permanent rather than temporary • Emotions are beyond the point of intervention • Too much face has been lost	**Exit**	• Talent and training costs are lost

Adaptation

Some teams find ways to work with or around the challenges they face, adapting practices or attitudes without making changes to the group's membership or assignments. Adaptation works when team members are willing to acknowledge and name their cultural differences and to assume responsibility for figuring out how to live with them. It's often the best possible approach to a problem, because it typically involves less managerial time than other strategies; and because team members participate in solving the problem themselves, they learn from the process. When team members have this mind-set, they can be creative about protecting their own substantive differences while acceding to the processes of others.

An American software engineer located in Ireland who was working with an Israeli account management team from his own company told us how shocked he was by the Israelis' in-your-face style: "There were definitely different ways of approaching issues and discussing them. There is something pretty common to the Israeli culture: They like to argue. I tend to try to collaborate more, and it got very stressful for me until I figured out how to kind of merge the cultures."

The software engineer adapted. He imposed some structure on the Israelis that helped him maintain his own style of being thoroughly prepared; that accommodation enabled him to accept the Israeli style. He also noticed that team members weren't just confronting him; they confronted one another but were able to work together effectively nevertheless. He realized that the confrontation was not personal but cultural.

In another example, an American member of a postmerger consulting team was frustrated by the hierarchy of the French company his team was working with. He felt that a meeting with certain French managers who were not directly involved in the merger "wouldn't deliver any value to me or for purposes of the project," but said that he had come to understand that "it was very important to really involve all the people there" if the integration was ultimately to work.

A U.S. and UK multicultural team tried to use their differing approaches to decision making to reach a higher-quality decision. This approach, called fusion, is getting serious attention from political scientists and from government officials dealing with multicultural populations that want to protect their cultures rather than integrate or assimilate. If the team had relied exclusively on the Americans' "forge ahead" approach, it might not have recognized the pitfalls that lay ahead and might later have had to back up and start over. Meanwhile, the UK members would have been gritting their teeth and saying "We told you things were moving too fast." If the team had used the "Let's think about this" UK approach, it might have wasted a lot of time trying to identify every pitfall, including the most unlikely, while the U.S. members chomped at the bit and muttered about analysis paralysis. The strength of this team was that some of its members were willing to forge ahead and some were willing to work through pitfalls. To accommodate them all, the team did both—moving not quite as fast as the U.S. members would have on their own and not quite as thoroughly as the UK members would have.

Structural intervention

A structural intervention is a deliberate reorganization or reassignment designed to reduce interpersonal friction or to remove a source of conflict for one or more groups. This approach can be extremely effective when obvious subgroups demarcate the team (for example, headquarters versus national subsidiaries) or if team members are proud, defensive, threatened, or clinging to negative stereotypes of one another.

A member of an investment research team scattered across continental Europe, the UK, and the U.S. described for us how his manager resolved conflicts stemming from status differences and language tensions among the team's three "tribes." The manager started by having the team meet face-to-face twice a year, not to discuss mundane day-to-day problems (of which there were many) but to identify a set of values that the team would use to direct and evaluate its progress. At the first meeting, he realized that when he started to speak, everyone else "shut down," waiting to hear what he had to say. So he hired a consultant to run future meetings. The consultant didn't represent a hierarchical threat and was therefore able to get lots of participation from team members.

Another structural intervention might be to create smaller working groups of mixed cultures or mixed corporate identities in order to get at information that is not forthcoming from the team as a whole. The manager of the team that was evaluating retail opportunities in Japan used this approach. When she realized that the female Japanese consultants would not participate if the group got large, or if their male superior was present, she broke the team up into smaller groups to try to solve problems. She used this technique repeatedly and made a point of changing the subgroups' membership each time so that team members got to know and respect everyone else on the team.

The subgrouping technique involves risks, however. It buffers people who are not working well together or not participating in the larger group for one reason or another. Sooner or later the team will have to assemble the pieces that the subgroups have come up with, so this approach relies on another structural intervention: Someone must become a mediator in order to see that the various pieces fit together.

Managerial intervention

When a manager behaves like an arbitrator or a judge, making a final decision without team involvement, neither the manager nor the team gains much insight into why the team has stalemated. But it is possible for team members to use managerial intervention effectively to sort out problems.

When an American refinery-safety expert with significant experience throughout East Asia got stymied during a project in China, she called in her company's higher-level managers in Beijing to talk to the higher-level managers to whom the Chinese refinery's managers reported. Unlike the Western team members who breached etiquette by approaching the superiors of their Korean counterparts, the safety expert made sure to respect hierarchies in both organizations.

"Trying to resolve the issues," she told us, "the local management at the Chinese refinery would end up having conferences with our Beijing office and also with the upper management within the refinery. Eventually they understood that we weren't trying to insult them or their culture or to tell them they were bad in any way. We were trying to help. They eventually understood that there were significant fire and safety issues. But we actually had to go up some levels of management to get those resolved."

Managerial intervention to set norms early in a team's life can really help the team start out with effective processes. In one instance reported to us, a multicultural software development team's lingua franca was English, but some members, though they spoke grammatically correct English, had a very pronounced accent. In setting the ground rules for the team, the manager addressed the challenge directly, telling the members that they had been chosen for their task expertise, not their fluency in English, and that the team was going to have to work around language problems. As the project moved to the customer-services training stage, the manager advised the team members to acknowledge their accents up front. She said they should tell customers, "I realize I have an accent. If you don't understand what I'm saying, just stop me and ask questions."

Exit

Possibly because many of the teams we studied were project based, we found that leaving the team was an infrequent strategy for managing challenges. In short-term situations, unhappy team members often just waited out the project. When teams were permanent, producing products or services, the exit of one or more members was a strategy of last resort, but it was used—either voluntarily or after a formal request from management. Exit was likely when emotions were running high and too much face had been lost on both sides to salvage the situation.

An American member of a multicultural consulting team described the conflict between two senior consultants, one a Greek woman and the other a Polish man, over how to approach problems: "The woman from Greece would say, 'Here's the way I think we should do it.' It would be something that she was in control of. The guy from Poland would say, 'I think we should actually do it this way instead.' The woman would kind of turn red in the face, upset, and say, 'I just don't think that's the right way of doing it.' It would definitely switch from just professional differences to personal differences.

"The woman from Greece ended up leaving the firm. That was a direct result of probably all the different issues going on between these people. It really just wasn't a good fit. I've found that oftentimes when you're in consulting, you have to adapt to the culture, obviously, but you have to adapt just as much to the style of whoever is leading the project."

Though multicultural teams face challenges that are not directly attributable to cultural differences, such differences underlay whatever problem needed to be addressed in many of the teams we studied. Furthermore, while serious in their own right when they have a negative effect on team functioning, cultural challenges may also unmask fundamental managerial problems. Managers who intervene early and set norms; teams and managers who structure social interaction and work to engage everyone on the team; and teams that can see problems as stemming from culture, not personality, approach challenges with good humor and creativity. Managers who have to intervene when the team has reached a stalemate may be able to get the team moving again, but they seldom empower it to help itself the next time a stalemate occurs.

When frustrated team members take some time to think through challenges and possible solutions themselves, it can make a huge difference. Take, for example, this story about a financial-services call center. The members of the call-center team were all fluent Spanish-speakers, but some were North Americans and some were Latin Americans. Team performance, measured by calls answered per hour, was lagging. One Latin American was taking twice as long with her calls as the rest of the team. She was handling callers' questions appropriately, but she was also engaging in chitchat. When her teammates confronted her for being a free rider (they resented having to make up for her low call rate), she immediately acknowledged the problem, admitting that she did not know how to end the call politely—chitchat being normal in her culture. They rallied to help her: Using their technology, they would break into any of her calls that went overtime, excusing themeselves to the customer, offering to take over the call, and saying that this employee was urgently needed to help out on a different call. The team's solution worked in the short run, and the employee got better at ending her calls in the long run.

In another case, the Indian manager of a multicultural team coordinating a companywide IT project found himself frustrated when he and a teammate from Singapore met with two Japanese members of the coordinating team to try to get the Japan section to deliver its part of the project. The Japanese members seemed to be saying yes, but in the Indian manager's view, their follow-through was insufficient. He considered and rejected the idea of going up the hierarchy to the Japanese team members' boss, and decided instead to try to build consensus with the whole Japanese IT team, not just the two members on the coordinating team. He and his Singapore teammate put together an eBusiness road show, took it to Japan, invited the whole IT team to view it at a lunch meeting, and walked through success stories about other parts of the organization that had aligned with the company's larger business priorities. It was rather subtle, he told us, but it worked. The Japanese IT team wanted to be spotlighted in future eBusiness road shows. In the end, the whole team worked well together—and no higher-level manager had to get involved.

Originally published in November 2006. Reprint R0611D

When Teams Can't Decide

by Bob Frisch

THE EXECUTIVE TEAM IS DELIBERATING about a critical strategic choice, but no matter how much time and effort the team members expend, they cannot reach a satisfactory decision. Then comes that uncomfortable moment when all eyes turn to the CEO. The team waits for the boss to make the final call, yet when it's made, few people like the decision. Blame, though unspoken, is plentiful. The CEO blames the executives for indecisiveness; they resent the CEO for acting like a dictator. If this sounds familiar, you've experienced what I call the *dictator-by-default syndrome*.

For decades this dynamic has been diagnosed as a problem of leadership or teamwork or both. To combat it, companies use team-building and communications exercises that teach executives how to have assertive conversations, give and receive feedback, and establish mutual trust. In doing so, they miss the real problem, which lies not with the people but with the process. This sort of impasse is inherent in the act of arriving at a collective preference on the basis of individual preferences. Once leadership teams understand that voting-system mathematics are the culprit, they can stop wasting time on irrelevant psychological exercises and instead adopt practical measures designed to break the impasse. These measures, proven effective in scores of strategy off-sites for companies of all sizes, enable teams to move beyond the blame cycle to a no-fault style of decision making.

Asking the Impossible

Reaching collective decisions based on individual preferences is an imperfect science. Majority wishes can clash when a group of three or more people attempts to set priorities among three or more items. This "voting paradox," first noted in the eighteenth century by the Marquis de Condorcet, a French mathematician and social theorist, arises because different subsets of the group can generate conflicting majorities for all possible alternatives (see the exhibit "The voting paradox"). A century and a half later, renowned economist Ken Arrow developed his impossibility theorem, which established a series of mathematical proofs based on Condorcet's work.

Suppose a nine-person leadership team that wants to cut costs is weighing three options: (a) closing plants, (b) moving from a direct sales force to distributors, and (c) reducing benefits and pay. While any individual executive may be able to "rack and stack" her preferences,

---

The voting paradox: The boss is always wrong

A management team is attempting to select a fleet vehicle for its company's senior executives. When asked to rank three choices—BMW, Lexus, and Mercedes—the individual team members reach an impasse.

To break it, the CEO intervenes and picks BMW. But as the table shows, two-thirds of the team would have preferred a Lexus. Had he chosen Lexus, however, two-thirds of the team would have preferred Mercedes. And had he chosen Mercedes, two-thirds of the team would have preferred BMW. Instead of being transitive—Lexus beats BMW; Mercedes beats Lexus; therefore Mercedes beats BMW—the choice is circular.

Whatever decision the boss makes, the majority of his team is rooting for a different option. Unjustly, but not surprisingly, he is considered a dictator.

	First choice	Second choice	Third choice
Lou	BMW	Mercedes	Lexus
Sue	Mercedes	Lexus	BMW
Stu	Lexus	BMW	Mercedes

Idea in Brief

When cross-functional teams have trouble making decisions, leaders blame psychological factors like mistrust or poor communication. But the problem isn't the team's people; it's the decision-making process. Each member has constituencies in the organization. So each vies for resources for favored projects—virtually guaranteeing an impasse. To break the impasse, the team leader makes a unilateral decision, leaving a majority of the team disgruntled and resentful of the "dictator."

To improve your team's decision-making process, Frisch recommends several tactics. For example, clearly articulate the outcome your team must achieve. When people understand the goal, they more readily agree on how to get there. And surface members' functional preferences through pre-meeting surveys to identify areas of agreement and disagreement and to gauge the potential for deadlock.

These deceptively simple tactics position your team to prevent stalemates—instead of forcing you to be "dictator-by-default."

it's possible for a majority to be simultaneously found for each alternative. Five members might prefer "closing plants" to "moving sales to distributors" (a > b), and a different set of five might prefer "moving sales" to "reducing benefits and pay" (b > c). By the transitive property, "closing plants" should be preferred to "reducing benefits and pay" (a > c). But the paradox is that five members could rank "reducing benefits and pay" over "closing plants" (c > a). Instead of being transitive, the preferences are circular.

When the CEO is finally forced to choose an option, only a minority of team members will agree with the decision. No matter which option is selected, it's likely that different majorities will prefer alternative outcomes. Moreover, as Arrow demonstrated, no voting method—not allocation of points to alternatives, not rank-ordering of choices, nothing—can solve the problem. It can be circumvented but not cured.

Although the concept is well understood in political science and economics and among some organizational theorists, it hasn't yet crossed over to practical management. Understanding this paradox could greatly alter the way executive teams make decisions.

Idea in Practice

Frisch suggests these tactics for improving your team's decision-making process.

Specify the Desired Outcome

Without clear desired outcomes, team members choose options based on unspoken, differing assumptions. This sets the stage for the dictator-by-default syndrome. To avoid the syndrome, articulate what you want the team to accomplish.

Example: A division of an industrial company was running out of manufacturing capacity for a product made in the U.S. The leadership team assumed the desired outcome was "Achieve the highest possible return on assets." So they discussed shuttering a U.S. plant and building a plant in China, where costs were lower and raw materials closer. But the parent company's desired outcome was "Minimize corporate overhead and maximize earnings." The move to China would mean closing an additional facility that supplied materials to the U.S. plant, significantly lowering earnings. Once the division team understood the desired outcome, it could solve the capacity problem in a way that was consistent with the parent's actual goals.

Provide a Range of Options for Achieving the Desired Outcome

Break alternatives into a broader range of options beyond "Accept the proposed plan," "Reject the plan," and "Defer the decision."

Test Fences and Walls

When team members cite a presumed boundary (for example, a real or imagined corporate policy), ask "Is it a wall (it's

Acknowledging the Problem

To circumvent the dictator-by-default syndrome, CEOs and their teams must first understand the conditions that give rise to it. The syndrome is perhaps most obvious at executive off-sites, but it can crop up in any executive committee meeting of substance.

Most executive teams are, in effect, legislatures. With the exception of the CEO, each member represents a significant constituency in the organization, from marketing to operations to finance. No matter how many times a CEO asks team members to take off their

relatively immovable) or is it a fence (it can be moved)?"

Example: For a division of a global financial services provider, executives never considered expanding their offerings to include banking services. That's because they thought corporate policy prohibited entry into banking. When the division head tested this assumption with her boss, she learned that the real concern was not to do anything that would bring new regulatory requirements (the wall). So the division developed strategic options that included several features of banking that avoided dealing with new regulations.

Surface Preferences Early

Survey members before meetings to identify their preferences and focus the subsequent discussion.

Example: A global credit card company was deciding where to invest in growth. Executive team members conducted a straw poll of countries under consideration. The process enabled them to quickly eliminate countries that attracted no votes. And it focused their subsequent discussion on the two regions where there was most agreement.

Assign Devil's Advocates

Make thorough and dispassionate counterarguments an expected part of strategic deliberations. Assign devil's advocates to make the case against each option. This depersonalizes the discussion and produces more nuanced strategy discussions.

functional hats and view the organization holistically, the executives find it difficult to divorce themselves from their functional responsibilities. Because the team often focuses on assigning resources and setting priorities, members vie for allocations and approval for favored projects. When more than two options are on the table, the scene is set for the CEO to become a dictator by default.

More insidiously, the problem exists even when a team is considering an either/or choice, despite the fact that the voting paradox requires three or more options. Framing strategy considerations as binary choices—"We must either aggressively enter this market or get out of this line of business altogether"—appears to avert the problem. However, such choices always include a third, implied alternative: "Neither of the above." In other words, there could be circular majorities for entering the market, for exiting the business, and for doing neither.

Take, for example, the ubiquitous business case, which usually offers a single, affirmative recommendation: "We should aggressively enter this market now." The only apparent alternative is to forgo the market—but some team members may want to enter it more tentatively, others may want to enter an adjacent market, and still others may want to defer the decision until the market potential becomes clearer.

The use of the business case, which forces decisions into a yes-or-no framework, is a tacit admission that groups are not good at discussing and prioritizing multiple options. Further, when a team of analysts has spent six months working up the business case and only a half hour has been allotted to the item on the agenda, dissenting team members may be reluctant to speak up. Questions from the heads of sales and marketing, who have spent only a day or two with a briefing book and 20 minutes watching a PowerPoint presentation, would most likely be treated as comments tossed from the peanut gallery. So the team remains silent and unwittingly locked in the voting paradox. Ultimately, in order to move on to the next agenda item, either the team appears to reach a majority view or the CEO issues a fiat. In reality, however, there may be competing opinions, alternative majority opinions, and dissatisfaction with the outcome—all of them unstated.

Managing the Impossible

Once CEOs and their teams understand why they have trouble making decisions, they can adopt some straightforward tactics to minimize potential dysfunction.

Articulate clearly what outcome you are seeking

It's surprising how often executives assume that they are talking about the same thing when in fact they are talking past one another. In a discussion of growth, for instance, some may be referring to revenue, others to market share, and others to net income. The discussion should begin with agreement on what outcome the team is trying to achieve. If it's growth, then do all the members agree on which measures are most relevant?

In the absence of clearly articulated goals, participants will choose options based on unspoken, often widely differing, premises, creating a situation that is ripe for the dictator-by-default syndrome. One division of a major industrial company, for example, was running out of manufacturing capacity for a commodity product made in the United States and a specialty product made in Western Europe. Because costs of labor and raw materials were high in both places, the leadership team was considering what seemed like an obvious choice: shutting down the U.S. plant and building a plant in China, where costs were lower and raw materials were closer, to handle the commodity business and any growth in the specialty business. Most members of the team assumed that the desired outcome was to achieve the highest possible return on net assets, which the move to China might well have accomplished.

However, the CEO had been in discussions with corporate managers who were primarily concerned with allocation of overhead throughout the enterprise. The move to China would mean shutting down an additional plant that supplied raw materials to the U.S. plant, with implications for corporate earnings. Once the division team fully understood what outcome the parent company desired—to minimize overhead costs without taking a hit on earnings—it could work on solving the capacity problem in a way that honored the parent's strictures.

It's essential to keep discussion of the desired outcome distinct from discussion about how to achieve it. Sometimes, simply articulating the desired outcome will forestall or dissolve disagreement about solutions because the options can be tested against an accepted premise. It may also help avert the political horse trading that can occur when executives try to protect their interests rather than aiming for a common goal.

Provide a range of options for achieving outcomes

Once the team at the industrial company had articulated the desired outcome, it could break the simplistic "accept," "reject," and "defer" alternatives into a more nuanced range of options: build a specialty plant in China; beef up the plant in Western Europe; or build a commodity plant in China and gradually decommission the U.S. plant.

Test fences and walls

When teams are invited to think about options, they almost immediately focus on what they *can't* do—especially at the divisional level, where they may feel hemmed in by corporate policies, real or imagined. Often the entire team not only assumes that a constraint is real but also shies away when the discussion comes anywhere near it. When team members cite a presumed boundary, my colleagues and I encourage them to ask whether it's a wall, which can't be moved, or a fence, which can.

For example, one division of a global provider of financial services was looking at new avenues for growth. Although expanding the division's offerings to include banking services was a promising possibility, the executive team never considered it, assuming that corporate policy prohibited the company from entering banking. When the division head explicitly tested that assumption with her boss, she found that the real prohibition—the wall—was against doing anything that would bring certain types of new regulatory requirements. With that knowledge, the division's executive team was able to develop strategic options that included some features of banking but avoided any new regulations.

Surface preferences early

Like juries, executive teams can get an initial sense of where they stand by taking nonbinding votes early in the discussion. They can also conduct surveys in advance of meetings in order to identify areas of agreement and disagreement as well as the potential for deadlock.

A global credit card company was deciding where to invest in growth. Ordinarily, executive team members would have embarked on an open-ended discussion in which numerous countries would be under consideration; that tactic would have invited the possibility of multiple majorities. Instead, they conducted a straw poll, quickly eliminating the countries that attracted no votes and focusing their subsequent discussion on the two places where there was the most agreement.

Using weighted preferences is another way to narrow the decision-making field and help prevent the dictator-by-default syndrome. The life and annuities division of a major insurance company had developed a business plan that included a growth in profit of $360 million. The executive team was trying to determine which line of business would deliver that growth. Instead of casting equally weighted votes for various lines of business, each executive was given poker chips representing $360 million and a grid with squares representing the company's products and channels. Team members distributed their chips according to where they thought the projected growth was likely to be found. After discussing the results they repeated the exercise, finding that some agreement emerged.

By the third and final round of the exercise, this weighted voting had helped them narrow their discussion to a handful of businesses and channels, and genuine alignment began to develop among team members. Equally weighted votes might have locked the executive team into the voting paradox, but this technique dissolved the false equality of alternatives that is often at the root of the problem. Proposing options early and allowing people to tailor them reduces the likelihood that executives will be forced into a stalemate that the CEO has to break.

State each option's pros and cons

Rather than engaging in exercises about giving feedback or learning how to have assertive conversations, executives can better spend their time making sure that both sides of every option are forcefully voiced. That may require a devil's advocate.

The concept of a devil's advocate originated in the Roman Catholic Church's canonization process, in which a lawyer is appointed to argue against the canonization of a candidate—even the most apparently saintly. Similarly, in law, each side files its own brief; the defense doesn't simply respond off-the-cuff to the plaintiff's argument.

In business, however, an advocate for a particular option typically delivers a presentation that may contain some discussion of risk but remains entirely the work of someone who is sold on the idea. Members of the executive team are expected to agree with the business case or attack it, although they may have seen it only a few days before the meeting and thus have no way of producing an equally detailed rebuttal or offering solid alternatives. Further, attacking the business case is often perceived as attacking the person who is presenting it. Frequently the only executives with open license to ask tough, probing questions are the CEO and the CFO, but even they lack the detailed knowledge of the team advocating the business case.

By breaking the false binary of a business case into several explicit and implicit alternatives and assigning a devil's advocate to critique each option, you can depersonalize the discussion, making thorough and dispassionate counterarguments an expected part of strategic deliberations. This approach is especially valuable when the preferences of the CEO or other powerful members of the team are well known. If assigning a devil's advocate to each option appears too cumbersome, try a simpler variant: Have the CEO or a meeting facilitator urge each team member to offer two or three suggestions from the perspective of his functional area. Instead of unreasonably asking executives to think like a CEO, which usually elicits silence or perfunctory comments, this tactic puts team members on the solid ground of their expertise and transforms an unsatisfying false binary into far more options for discussion.

A major internet entertainment company adopted a novel version of the devil's advocate approach. The company maintains a council to consider its many potential investments, from upgrading its server farms to adopting new technology to creating special entertainment events on the web. In the past, each opportunity was presented to the council as a business case by an advocate of the investment, and each case was evaluated in isolation.

Frustrated with this haphazard approach, the company established a new system: The council now considers all investment proposals as a portfolio at its monthly strategy meetings. All proposals follow an identical template, allowing for easy comparison and a uniform scoring system. Finally, each one needs sign-off from an independent executive.

This system incorporates the devil's advocate role at two levels. For each proposal the validating executive, not wishing to be accountable for groundless optimism, considers carefully all of the counterarguments, does a reality check, and makes sure the sponsor adjusts the score accordingly. At the portfolio level, the comparative-scoring system reminds the team that the proposals are competing for limited resources, which prompts a more critical assessment.

Devise new options that preserve the best features of existing ones

Despite a team's best efforts, executives can still find themselves at an impasse. That is a measure of both the weightiness of some strategic decisions and the intractability of the voting paradox—it's not necessarily an index of executive dysfunction.

Teams should continue to reframe their options in ways that preserve their original intent, be it a higher return on net assets or greater growth. When they feel the impulse to shoehorn decisions into an either/or framework, they should step back and generate a broader range of options. For instance, the executive team of the property and casualty division of a large insurer wanted to grow either by significantly increasing the company's share with existing agencies or by increasing the total number of agencies that sold its products. Before the leadership team took either path, it needed to decide whether to offer a full line of products or a narrow line. As a result, team members found themselves considering four business models: (1) full product line, existing large agencies; (2) narrow product line, existing large agencies; (3) full product line, more small agencies; and (4) narrow product line, more small agencies. Dissatisfied with those choices, they broke the business down into 16 value attributes, including brand, claim service, agency compensation, price competitiveness, breadth of product offering, and agency-facing technology. Some of these value attributes might apply to all four of the original business models; others to three or fewer. Agent-facing technology, for example, is typical of working with many small agencies, because their sheer numbers preclude high-touch relationships with each one.

The team then graded its company and several competitors on each attribute to find competitive openings that fit with the division's willingness and ability to invest. Instead of four static choices, it now had a much larger number of choices based on different combinations of value attributes. Ultimately, it chose to bring several lagging attributes up to market standard, elevate others to above-market standard, and aggressively emphasize still others. This turned out to be a far less radical redirection than the team had originally assumed was needed.

Two Essential Ground Rules

So far, I have outlined several tactics that leadership teams can use to circumvent the dictator-by-default syndrome. These tactics can be effective whether they are used singly or in tandem. But if teams are to thwart this syndrome, they must adhere to two ground rules.

Deliberate confidentially

A secure climate for the conversation is essential to allow team members to float trial balloons and cut deals. An executive who knows that her speculative remarks about closing plants may be circulated throughout the company will be reluctant to engage in the free play of mind that unfettered strategy discussion demands. Moreover, team members whose priorities don't prevail in the deliberations must be able to save face when the meeting is over. If they are known to have "lost" or to have relinquished something dear to their constituents, their future effectiveness as leaders might be undermined.

Deliberate over an appropriate time frame

All too often the agendas for strategy off-sites contain items like "China market strategy," with 45 minutes allotted for the decision. The result is a discussion that goes nowhere or an arbitrary decision by the CEO that runs roughshod over competing majorities for other options. When new options are devised or existing ones unbundled, team members need time to study them carefully and assess the counterarguments. Breaking up the discussion into several meetings spaced widely apart and interspersed with additional analysis and research gives people a chance to reconsider their preferences. It also gives them time to prepare their constituencies for changes that are likely to emerge as a result of a new strategy.

Leadership and communication exercises have their merits. A team can't make effective decisions if its members don't trust one another or if they fail to listen to one another. The problem I see most often, however, is one that simply cannot be fixed with the psychological tools so often touted in management literature. If executives employ the tactics described here, which are designed to fix the decision-making process, they will have far greater success in achieving real alignment.

Originally published in November 2008. Reprint R0811J

Virtuoso Teams

by Bill Fischer and Andy Boynton

BLOOD ON THE STAGE, RACIAL tensions turned violent, dissonant music, and dancing hoodlums—*West Side Story* was anything but the treacly Broadway musical typical of the late 1950s. It was a high-stakes, radical innovation that fundamentally changed the face of American popular drama. The movie version earned ten Oscars. Not a bad achievement for the team of virtuosos—choreographer Jerome Robbins, writer Arthur Laurents, composer Leonard Bernstein, and lyricist Stephen Sondheim—who created it.

In nearly any area of human achievement—business, the arts, science, athletics, politics—you can find teams that produce outstanding and innovative results. The business world offers a few examples. Think of the Whiz Kids—the team of ten former U.S. Air Force officers recruited en masse in 1946—who brought Ford back from the doldrums. Recall Seymour Cray and his team of "supermen" who, in the early 1960s, developed the very first commercially available supercomputer, far outpacing IBM's most powerful processor. More recently, consider Microsoft's Xbox team, which pulled off the unthinkable by designing a gaming platform that put serious pressure on the top-selling Sony PlayStation 2 in its first few months on the market.

We call such work groups *virtuoso teams,* and they are fundamentally different from the garden-variety groups that most organizations form to pursue more modest goals. Virtuoso teams comprise the elite experts in their particular fields and are specially convened for ambitious projects. Their work style has a frenetic rhythm. They emanate a discernible energy. They are utterly unique in the ambitiousness of their goals, the intensity of their conversations, the degree of their esprit, and the extraordinary results they deliver.

Despite such potential, most companies deliberately avoid virtuoso teams, thinking that the risks are too high. For one thing, it's tough to keep virtuoso teams together once they achieve their goals—burnout and the lure of new challenges rapidly winnow the ranks. For another, most firms consider expert individuals to be too elitist, temperamental, egocentric, and difficult to work with. Force such people to collaborate on a high-stakes project and they just might come to fisticuffs. Even the very notion of managing such a group seems unimaginable. So most organizations fall into default mode, setting up project teams of people who get along nicely. The result is mediocrity. We've seen the pattern often.

For the past six years, we've studied the inner workings of teams charged with important projects in 20 of the world's best-known companies. We've found that some teams with big ambitions and considerable talent systematically fail, sometimes before our very eyes. In interviewing the managers involved, we discovered that virtuoso teams play by a different set of rules than other teams. The several dozen high-performance teams we studied, drawn from diverse fields, fit a few overarching criteria. Not only did they accomplish their enormous goals, but they also changed their businesses, their customers, even their industries.

Unlike traditional teams—which are typically made up of whoever's available, regardless of talent—virtuoso teams consist of star performers who are handpicked to play specific, key roles. These teams are intense and intimate, and they work best when members are forced together in cramped spaces under strict time constraints. They assume that their customers are every bit as smart and sophisticated as they are, so they don't cater to a stereotypical "average." Leaders of virtuoso teams put a premium on great collaboration—and they're not afraid to encourage creative confrontation to get it.

Among the work groups we studied were two from outside the mainstream business world—the creative teams behind *West Side*

Idea in Brief

Imagine these high-stakes scenarios: Your company must enter an untested new market. Or reorganize to take advantage of a new IT platform. Or avert a public relations crisis brought on by product tampering. To manage such feats, you need **virtuoso teams**—groups of top experts in their fields.

But superstars are notorious for being temperamental and egocentric. You worry that forcing a group of them to work together will ignite a fatal explosion. So you're tempted to settle for an ordinary project team instead.

Don't do it. Ordinary teams may play nice, but they produce results as unremarkable as themselves. Assemble your virtuoso team—and manage it with counterintuitive strategies, advise Fischer and Boynton.

For example, instead of emphasizing the collective, celebrate individual egos by creating opportunities for solo performances. Then build *group* ego by encouraging a single-minded focus on the goal. And foster impassioned, direct dialogue that doesn't spare feelings. In the resulting inferno, your team's members will forge their most brilliant ideas.

Story and the 1950s-era television hit *Your Show of Shows* and its successors. Both teams were vivid, unique, and, ultimately, managed to change their very competitive businesses. We also offer a more current business example from Norsk Hydro, the Norwegian energy giant. We intently studied a variety of sources, including diaries, interviews, video archive materials, and the impressions of many of the principals involved. In the following pages, we'll describe in more detail what constitutes a virtuoso team, how these teams work, and what they require in the way of leadership.

Assemble the Stars

Most traditional teams are more concerned with doing than with thinking. In other words, the working assumption is that execution is more important than generating breakthrough ideas. Team assignments, therefore, fall to people who seem to be able to get the work done. A less conventional approach, however, is more likely to produce exceptional results.

Idea in Practice

Fischer and Boynton suggest these principles for leading a virtuoso team.

Assemble the stars. Hire only members with the best skills, even if they have little experience with the problem at hand.

> ***Example:*** After investing heavily in a site promising a big oil find, Norsk Hydro discovered the site was dry. Team leader Kjell Sunde assembled a virtuoso team to avert an investor-relations crisis. The team included the best technical people from across the company. Its goal: Analyze reams of data, pinpoint what went wrong, and convince stakeholders such an outcome wouldn't occur again.

Build the group ego. As your team's project progresses, help stars break through their egocentrism and morph into a powerful, unified team with a shared identity.

> ***Example:*** Sunde initially broke with Norsk Hydro's consensus-driven culture by publicly celebrating his team members and putting them squarely in the spotlight. He established a star mentality by nicknaming them the "A-team." Then he built the team's group ego by protecting members from intrusive scrutiny from above, giving them unlimited access to resources, and treating their conclusions as definitive.

Make work a contact sport. Use face-to-face conversations in designated spaces to foster impassioned dialogue.

> ***Example:*** Sunde established a dedicated team room and filled

In virtuoso teams, thinking is more important than doing: Individual members are hired for their skills and their willingness to dive into big challenges. Instead of assembling a variety of individuals and averaging their talents down to a mean, virtuoso team leaders push each player hard to reach his or her potential within the overall context of the team objective. Virtuoso team members are not shy; they typically want to take on a risky venture that can pull them away from their well-trodden paths. They love daunting challenges, and they accept the risk of exposure and career damage if their projects fail. The risk increases pressure on the team to deliver; accordingly, the individual members give their utmost to assure that radical innovation happens.

it with computer workstations and other scientific and communications equipment. The space functioned as a workroom and meeting place for candid, intense discussions that let members bounce ideas off each other.

Respect the customer's intelligence. Foster the belief that your team's customers want more, not less. You'll encourage them to deliver solutions consistent with this higher perception.

Example: For Norsk Hydro's A-team, "customers" were equity market analysts. The team's job was to manage the market's reaction to news of the dry site. If its explanation was slapdash or incomplete, the company's market value would nosedive. The team provided thoughtful explanations that left market analysts impressed with the firm's ability to respond convincingly and quickly to market concerns. The company received kudos in the press and was spared serious financial erosion.

Herd the cats. Use time management strategies to balance team members' need for individual attention and intellectual freedom with the uncompromising demands and time lines of your high-stakes project.

Example: Sunde forced A-team members to keep presentations to 15 minutes. That encouraged members to use this allotment to maximum effect and discouraged aggressive members from imposing their viewpoints on others. The strong adherence to time "made everyone aware they had to dance to the same rhythm."

If you want great performances of any type, you have to start with great people. In 1949, a young comic named Sid Caesar distanced himself from his competition by relying on a group of virtuoso writers including Neil Simon, Mel Brooks, Carl Reiner, and Woody Allen. *Your Show of Shows* and Caesar's other weekly productions were the biggest commercial successes on TV at the time. Week after week over a period of nine years, Caesar and his cadre of writers created live, consistently award-winning performances in a string of TV comedy hits. Mel Brooks famously likened the group to a World Series ball club, echoing the sentiments of many who acclaimed the team as the greatest writing staff in the history of television.

They may have been the best comedy writers in America—but they weren't the nicest. As is the case with all virtuoso teams, Caesar's staffers engaged daily in high-energy contests. It was as if each writer knew he or she was the best; every day, each tried to top the others for the "best of the best" title. The interpersonal conflict often intensified as the writers jostled aggressively to see whose ideas would be accepted. Mel Brooks frequently irritated Max Liebman, producer of the *Admiral Broadway Revue* and *Your Show of Shows,* and vice versa: Liebman found Brooks arrogant and obnoxious, while Brooks, for his part, declared that he owed no allegiance to Liebman. The tension among team members led Caesar to describe the competitive atmosphere as one filled with "electricity and hate"; two other virtuosos translated Caesar's description into terms of "competition" and "collaboration."

The *West Side Story* group was also famously discordant. To build the team, Jerome Robbins, a young classical ballet choreographer with an impressive résumé, sought out Leonard Bernstein, one of the moving forces in classical music composition and conducting; Arthur Laurents, a highly regarded and successful screenwriter; and budding lyricist Stephen Sondheim. All of these talented players had enormous egos and greedy ambition. In their very first meeting, Laurents refused to play a subordinate role to the famously egotistical Bernstein, insisting vociferously that he was not about to write a libretto for any "goddamned Bernstein opera." All the team members engaged in similarly nasty tugs-of-war with one another. They needed each others' skills, not peace and quiet.

Build the Group Ego

Traditional teams typically operate under the tyranny of the "we"—that is, they put group consensus and constraint above individual freedom. Team harmony is important; conviviality compensates for missing talent. This produces teams with great attitudes and happy members, but, to paraphrase Liebman, "from a polite team comes a polite result."

Traditional teams versus virtuoso teams

Virtuoso teams differ from traditional teams along every dimension, from the way they recruit members to the way they enforce their processes and from the expectations they hold to the results they produce.

Traditional teams	Virtuoso teams
Choose members for availability	**Choose members for skills**
• Assign members according to the individuals' availability and past experience with the problem.	• Insist on hiring only those with the best skills, regardless of the individuals' familiarity with the problem.
• Fill in the team as needed.	• Recruit specialists for each position on the team.
Emphasize the collective	**Emphasize the individual**
• Repress individual egos.	• Celebrate individual egos and elicit the best from each team member.
• Encourage members to get along.	• Encourage members to compete, and create opportunities for solo performances.
• Choose a solution based on consensus.	• Choose a solution based on merit.
• Assure that efficiency trumps creativity.	• Assure that creativity trumps efficiency.
Focus on tasks	**Focus on ideas**
• Complete critical tasks on time.	• Generate a frequent and rich flow of ideas among team members.
• Get the project done on time.	• Find and express the breakthrough idea on time.
Work individually and remotely	**Work together and intensively**
• Require individual members to complete tasks on their own.	• Force members into close physical proximity.
• Allow communication via e-mail, phone, and weekly meetings.	• Force members to work together at a fast pace.
• Encourage polite conversations.	• Force direct dialogue without sparing feelings.
Address the average customer	**Address the sophisticated customer**
• Attempt to reach the broadest possible customer base; appeal to the average.	• Attempt to surprise customers by stretching their expectations; appeal to the sophisticate.
• Base decisions on established market knowledge.	• Defy established market knowledge.
• Affirm common stereotypes.	• Reject common stereotypes.

When virtuoso teams begin their work, individuals are in and group consensus is out. As the project progresses, however, the individual stars harness themselves to the product of the group. Sooner or later, the members break through their own egocentrism and become a plurality with a single-minded focus on the goal. In short, they morph into a powerful team with a shared identity.

Consider how Norsk Hydro used a virtuoso team to handle a looming investor relations crisis. In 2002, Bloc 34, the potential site for a big oil find in Angola, turned out to be dry. Hydro had made a serious investment in the site. Somehow, senior management would have to convincingly explain the company's failure to the financial markets or Hydro's stock could plummet.

The senior managers understood that this problem was too critical to leave to conventional approaches, but Hydro was certainly not a natural environment for a virtuoso team. Rich in heritage, unwieldy, and traditional, with a strong engineering culture and a decidedly Nordic consensus-driven approach to decisions, the company never singled out or recognized individual performers. In fact, most of Hydro's business activities were specialized and separated. Teamwork was satisfactory but unexceptional, and tension among employees was firmly discouraged.

Defying precedent, team leader Kjell Sunde assembled a high-powered group comprising the very best technical people from across the company. Their task? To review a massive stream of data—one that had occupied the minds of some of the best professionals for more than four years. Their goal? To understand what had gone wrong in the original analysis of Bloc 34 and to assure key stakeholders that the company would prevent such an outcome from occurring again. Their deadline? A completely unreasonable six weeks.

Sunde's challenge was to strike a delicate balance between stroking the egos of the elites and focusing them on the task at hand. Each of the brilliant technologists was supremely confident in his abilities. Each had a reputation for being egocentric and difficult. Each had a tendency to dominate and aggressively seek the limelight. In a consensus-driven company like Hydro, the typical modus operandi would have been to exhort the individuals to surrender their egos and play nicely together.

But Sunde went in the opposite direction, completely breaking with corporate culture by publicly celebrating the selected members and putting them squarely in the spotlight. The Bloc 34 Task Force, nicknamed the "A-team," established a star mentality from its very inception. Selection for the project was clearly a sign of trust in each member's ability to perform outstanding work on a seemingly impossible task. For the most part, the members knew one another already, which eliminated the need for them to build polite relationships and helped them jump in right away.

Sunde then set about building the A-team's group ego. He guaranteed the members the respect they craved by assuring them that they would work autonomously—there would be no micromanagement or intrusive scrutiny from above. Team members would have absolute top priority and access to any resources they required, their conclusions would be definitive, and there would be no second-guessing. All this set a positive tone and bolstered group morale.

Still, there were plenty of early clashes. To control the friction, Sunde introduced an overall pattern to the teamwork. First, he paired off individual team members in accordance with their expertise and his sense of their psychological fit. Each half of the couple worked on a separate but related problem, and each pair's problem set fit together with the other sets to form the overall puzzle, which team members had to keep in mind as they worked.

Eventually, each team member understood that if the team failed, he would fail too. This kept any of the members from developing an entrenched sense of idea ownership. As it worked, the team transformed itself from a collection of egocentric individuals into one great totality. Had the group started out as a cohesive whole, individual talents might never have been realized and harnessed to the goal.

Make Work a Contact Sport

Typical teams are all too often spatially dispersed—they are managed remotely and get together only occasionally for debate and discussion. Most of the time, such a scenario works quite well. But when big change and high performance are required, these standard working conditions fall short of the mark. In virtuoso teams, individual players energize each other and stimulate ideas with frequent, intense, face-to-face conversations, often held in cramped spaces over long periods of time. The usual rounds of e-mails, phone calls, and occasional meetings just don't cut it.

When virtuoso teams are in action, impassioned dialogue becomes the critical driver of performance, not the work itself. The inescapable physical proximity of team members ensures that the right messages get to the right people—fast. As a result, virtuoso teams operate at a pace that is many times the speed of normal project teams.

Your Show of Shows and Caesar's other TV programs were developed each week in a small, chaotic suite of rooms on the sixth floor of 130 West 56th Street in Manhattan. Experimentation and rapid prototyping were the name of the game; only the best ideas survived. One team member compared the daily atmosphere to a Marx Brothers movie: People shouted at the top of their lungs; piles of food and cigarette butts lay everywhere. The pace was dizzying, yet everyone stayed focused. The pressure-cooker environment resulted in fierce interpersonal clashes, but there wasn't time to sulk or stay angry. The tight work space and relentless deadlines created a cauldron of energy and a frenzy of ideas.

Members of Norsk Hydro's A-team joked that they were not a task force; rather, they were "forced to task." Sunde established a dedicated room for the team and filled it with computer workstations and other necessary scientific and communications equipment. The space functioned both as a workroom and as a common meeting place (members of the team spent as much as 90 hours per week together). The atmosphere was relaxed and informal, and the discussions that took place there were open, honest, and passionate. Team members "would continually interact," Sunde said, "bouncing ideas off each other and to a degree competing, or at least keeping their eyes on each other."

The intense pressure on virtuoso teams affects project duration as well. These work groups usually break up for one of two reasons: Either the sheer physical, intellectual, and emotional demands take their toll (though *Your Show of Shows* and the team's other comedy hits lasted for nine years, there was high turnover within the writing group) or the stars, who are always in high demand, find themselves drawn to other new and challenging projects. Still, as long as the team members remain passionately interested and feel they have the opportunity to leave a significant mark on their company or their industry, they will work long and hard.

Challenge the Customer

Virtuoso teams believe that customers want more, not less, and that they can appreciate the richness of an aggrandized proposition. Virtuoso teams deliver solutions that are consistent with this higher perception. The vision of the demanding customer becomes a self-fulfilling prophecy, for while competitors create diminished offerings for their clients, virtuoso teams redefine taste and expectations and raise the level of market acceptability.

Before *West Side Story,* Broadway musicals were typically limited to a conventional formula of nostalgia, comedy, and feel-good endings. They were easily marketable entertainment. A typical hit of the day was *Damn Yankees,* a musical about a baseball fan who makes a pact with the devil. There was no room for tragedy, social critique, or even art on the Great White Way.

Robbins, Bernstein, Laurents, and Sondheim believed otherwise, but few agreed with them. Getting *West Side Story* to the stage was a huge challenge because most producers thought the project too risky, dealing as it did with themes of social consciousness and racial violence. How could it possibly make money? As venture capital dried up, Robbins and the others persisted, laying their careers on the line to bring audiences something totally new, daring, and different from anything they had experienced before. The enormous success of their project vindicated them.

Sid Caesar similarly believed that nothing was too much for his audience. At a time when American TV was beginning its long slide into programming mediocrity, Caesar wanted to get away from the crude, pie-in-the-face, seltzer-bottle slapstick that he found degrading. In a turnabout from convention, he and his team regularly presented audiences with challenging material. Liebman put it this way: "We take for granted . . . that the mass audience we're trying to reach isn't a dumb one. It has a high quota of intelligence, and there's no need to play down to it. . . . We strive for adult entertainment, without compromise, and believe that the audience will understand it."

For Norsk Hydro, the "customers" were the equity market analysts. The team members' job was to manage the market's reaction; if their explanation was slapdash or incomplete, the company's market value would nosedive. Faced with a similar situation, most businesses would have tried to downplay the fact that a gigantic project had failed, offering a pallid apology and then weathering the ensuing storm. Some companies, however, are able to turn these incidents to their advantage. (In 1988, for instance, an Ashland Oil storage tank ruptured while being filled. Diesel fuel damaged ecosystems and contaminated drinking water. The company's full disclosure and aggressive cleanup efforts restored its good name.) Likewise, Norsk Hydro turned the Bloc 34 incident to its advantage. The thoughtful explanations the virtuoso team provided left market analysts impressed with the firm's ability to respond convincingly and quickly to market concerns. The company received kudos in the press and was spared from any serious financial erosion.

Herd the Cats

Most leaders of traditional teams—even those working on big projects—emphasize consensus and compromise. Their goal is to keep stress levels low, meet deadlines, and produce acceptable results. By contrast, leaders of virtuoso teams must be far more deft and forceful. Their goal is to help individual performers, and the group as a whole, achieve their utmost potential.

The worst thing you can do to highly talented, independent people is to constrain their expressiveness; you have to trust and encourage their talents. At the same time, however, a team made up of these individuals must meet strict goals and deadlines. Balancing the virtuosos' needs for individual attention and intellectual freedom with the uncompromising demands and time lines of a high-stakes project requires unusual skill. For this reason, leaders of virtuoso teams assume different kinds of roles, and use different management tools, than do leaders of traditional teams.

One way to manage a virtuoso team is to be a rigid—even villainous—perfectionist. Jerome Robbins was a perfect example of this. He combined the unforgiving discipline of a boot camp sergeant with an artist's attention to detail. He pushed, prodded, embarrassed, and demanded excellence from his people; he overlooked no detail in an effort to capture the cast's total attention. For example, he posted articles about interracial gang warfare on the theater walls and encouraged others to find and share similar reports. Each gang-member character had a biography—for the first time on Broadway, there was to be no anonymous chorus—and actors were forbidden to use any other names in the theater. Robbins segregated the cast into their respective gangs. "This stage is the only piece of territory you really own in this theater," he barked. "Nothing else belongs to you. You've got to fight for it." This sparked genuine antagonism between the groups, which imbued the final production with verisimilitude.

Needless to say, tensions ran high, and the stress on individual players was enormous. In the end, many cast members hated Robbins (one thespian observed, "If I go to Hell, I will not be afraid of the devil. Because I have worked with Jerome Robbins."). Still, his hard-nosed leadership won him great respect. Chita Rivera, who starred as Anita in the Broadway version of *West Side Story,* noted that "...if [Robbins] hadn't been the way he was, none of those people would have danced the way they did. None of them would have had the careers that they had...because people give up, we all give up, and we give up a lot of times too soon. He made you do what you were really capable of doing, something you never even dreamed you could possibly do."

Other leaders of virtuoso teams take the opposite tack: They strive for excellence by fostering a galloping sense of intellectual and creative freedom in individuals and in the group as a whole. Sid Caesar let his team members express themselves as freely as possible and encouraged creative pandemonium. Though the process might have looked chaotic to an outside observer—and to NBC's management—Caesar kept the group focused on the goal: to produce the very best comedy possible for each show. His team members would work shoulder to shoulder to write and rewrite the same scene many times in the same week—sometimes in the same day—in a frantic effort to perfect it through repeated testing. Ideas, situations, and lines would be tossed back and forth, and, though most would be rejected, a choice few would be accepted and pursued. In the brainstorming maelstrom, ownership of the ideas was difficult to pinpoint. This created a sense of mutual respect and unity in the group; the writers felt they belonged to something bigger than themselves. "He had total control, but we had total freedom," writer Larry Gelbart, a contributor to *Your Show of Shows,* said of Caesar's management style. This statement goes to the very heart of what it means to lead a virtuoso team.

Regardless of their personal approaches, all leaders of virtuoso teams exploit time as a management tool. At Norsk Hydro, Sunde used time in a very specific way. Because presentations were kept to a strict limit of 15 minutes, members used their allotment to maximum effect. And the time limit prevented the more aggressive members from imposing their points of view on others. The deadline pressure was so great that the team had no choice but to maintain its focus on the task at hand. As one technologist put it, the strong adherence to time "made everyone aware that they had to dance to the same rhythm."

Companies in every industry pursue ambitious projects all the time, tackling big product changes, new market entries, and large reorganizations. But when breakthrough performance is called for, it's clear that business as usual won't suffice.

If you want to stamp out mediocrity, remember the instructive lessons from Sid Caesar's writers' group, the *West Side Story* team, and Norsk Hydro's A-team: Don't hesitate to assemble the very best and let their egos soar. Encourage intense dialogue—and then watch as the sparks fly. If you allow the most brilliant minds in your organization to collide and create, the result will be true excellence.

Originally published in July 2005. Reprint R0507K

How Management Teams Can Have a Good Fight

by Kathleen M. Eisenhardt, Jean L. Kahwajy, and L.J. Bourgeois III

TOP MANAGERS ARE OFTEN STYMIED by the difficulties of managing conflict. They know that conflict over issues is natural and even necessary. Reasonable people, making decisions under conditions of uncertainty, are likely to have honest disagreements over the best path for their company's future. Management teams whose members challenge one another's thinking develop a more complete understanding of the choices, create a richer range of options, and ultimately make the kinds of effective decisions necessary in today's competitive environments.

But, unfortunately, healthy conflict can quickly turn unproductive. A comment meant as a substantive remark can be interpreted as a personal attack. Anxiety and frustration over difficult choices can evolve into anger directed at colleagues. Personalities frequently become intertwined with issues. Because most executives pride themselves on being rational decision makers, they find it difficult even to acknowledge—let alone manage—this emotional, irrational dimension of their behavior.

The challenge—familiar to anyone who has ever been part of a management team—is to keep constructive conflict over issues from degenerating into dysfunctional interpersonal conflict, to encourage managers to argue without destroying their ability to work as a team.

We have been researching the interplay of conflict, politics, and speed in strategic decision making by top-management teams for the past ten years. In one study, we had the opportunity to observe closely the work of a dozen top-management teams in technology-based companies. All the companies competed in fast changing, competitive global markets. Thus all the teams had to make high-stakes decisions in the face of considerable uncertainty and under pressure to move quickly. Each team consisted of between five and nine executives; we were allowed to question them individually and also to observe their interactions firsthand as we tracked specific strategic decisions in the making. The study's design gives us a window on conflict as top-management teams actually experience it and highlights the role of emotion in business decision making.

In 4 of the 12 companies, there was little or no substantive disagreement over major issues and therefore little conflict to observe. But the other 8 companies experienced considerable conflict. In 4 of them, the top-management teams handled conflict in a way that avoided interpersonal hostility or discord. We've called those companies Bravo Microsystems, Premier Technologies, Star Electronics, and Triumph Computers. Executives in those companies referred to their colleagues as "smart," "team player," and "best in the business." They described the way they work as a team as "open," "fun," and "productive." The executives vigorously debated the issues, but they wasted little time on politicking and posturing. As one put it, "I really don't have time." Another said, "We don't gloss over the issues; we hit them straight on. But we're not political." Still another observed of her company's management team, "We scream a lot, then laugh, and then resolve the issue."

The other four companies in which issues were contested were less successful at avoiding interpersonal conflict. We've called those companies Andromeda Processing, Mega Software, Mercury Microdevices, and Solo Systems. Their top teams were plagued by intense animosity. Executives often failed to cooperate, rarely talking with one another,

Idea in Brief

Think "conflict" is a dirty word, especially for top-management teams? It's actually *valuable* for team members to roll up their sleeves and spar (figuratively, that is)—if they do it right. Constructive conflict helps teams make high-stakes decisions under considerable uncertainty *and* move quickly in the face of intense pressure—essential capacities in today's fast-paced markets.

The key? Mitigate *interpersonal* conflict. Most conflicts take a personal turn all too soon. Here's how your team can detach the personal from the professional—and dramatically improve its collective effectiveness.

tending to fragment into cliques, and openly displaying their frustration and anger. When executives described their colleagues to us, they used words such as "manipulative," "secretive," "burned out," and "political."

The teams with minimal interpersonal conflict were able to separate substantive issues from those based on personalities. They managed to disagree over questions of strategic significance and still get along with one another. How did they do that? After analyzing our observations of the teams' behavior, we found that their companies used the same six tactics for managing interpersonal conflict. Team members

- worked with more, rather than less, information and debated on the basis of facts;
- developed multiple alternatives to enrich the level of debate;
- shared commonly agreed-upon goals;
- injected humor into the decision process;
- maintained a balanced power structure;
- resolved issues without forcing consensus.

Those tactics were usually more implicit than explicit in the decision-making work of the management teams, and if the tactics were given names, the names varied from one organization to the next.

Idea in Practice

The best teams use these six tactics to separate substantive issues from personalities:

- **Focus on the facts.** Arm yourselves with a wealth of data about your business *and* your competitors. This encourages you to debate critical *issues*, not argue out of ignorance.

  Example: Star Electronics'* top team "measured everything": bookings, backlogs, margins, engineering milestones, cash, scrap, work-in-process. They also tracked competitors' moves, including product introductions, price changes, and ad campaigns.

- **Multiply the alternatives.** In weighing decisions, consider four or five options at once—even some you don't support. This diffuses conflict, preventing teams from polarizing around just two possibilities.

  Example: To improve Triumph Computer's* lackluster performance, managers gathered facts and then brainstormed a range of alternatives, including radically redirecting strategy with entry into a new market, and even selling the company. The team combined elements of several options to arrive at a creative, robust solution.

- **Create common goals.** Unite a team with common goals. This rallies everyone to work on decisions as collaborations, making it in *everyone's* interest to achieve the best solution.

Nonetheless, the consistency with which all four companies employed all six tactics is testimony to their effectiveness. Perhaps most surprising was the fact that the tactics did not delay—and often accelerated—the pace at which the teams were able to make decisions.

Focus on the Facts

Some managers believe that working with too much data will increase interpersonal conflict by expanding the range of issues for debate. We found that more information is better—if the data are objective and up-to-date—because it encourages people to focus on issues, not personalities. At Star Electronics, for example, the members of the top-management team typically examined a wide variety of operating

Example: Star Electronic's* rallying cry was the goal of creating "*the* computer firm of the decade." Premier Technologies' was to "build the best damn machine on the market."

- **Use humor.** Humor—even if it seems contrived at times—relieves tension and promotes collaborative esprit within a team. Practical jokes, Halloween and April Fool's Day celebrations, and "dessert pig-outs" relax everyone—increasing tactfulness, effective listening, and creativity.
- **Balance the power structure.** The CEO is more powerful than other executives, but the others wield substantial power as well—especially in their own areas of responsibility. This lets the whole team participate in strategic decisions, establishing fairness and equity.
- **Seek consensus with qualification.** If the team can't reach consensus, the most relevant senior manager makes the decision, guided by input from the others. Like balancing the power structure, this tactic also builds fairness and equity.

Example: At Premier Technologies*, managers couldn't agree on a response to a competitor's new-product launch. Ultimately, the CEO and his marketing VP madethe decision. Quipped the CEO: "The function heads do the talking; I pull the trigger."

*All company names have been changed.

measures on a monthly, weekly, and even daily basis. They claimed to "measure everything." In particular, every week they fixed their attention on indicators such as bookings, backlogs, margins, engineering milestones, cash, scrap, and work-in-process. Every month, they reviewed an even more comprehensive set of measures that gave them extensive knowledge of what was actually happening in the corporation. As one executive noted, "We have very strong controls."

Star's team also relied on facts about the external environment. One senior executive was charged with tracking such moves by competitors as product introductions, price changes, and ad campaigns. A second followed the latest technical developments through his network of contacts in universities and other companies. "We over-M.B.A. it," said the CEO, characterizing Star's zealous pursuit of data. Armed with the facts, Star's executives had an extraordinary grasp of the details of their business, allowing them to focus debate on critical issues and avoid useless arguments rooted in ignorance.

At Triumph Computer, we found a similar dedication to current facts. The first person the new CEO hired was an individual to track the progress of engineering-development projects, the new-product lifeblood of the company. Such knowledge allowed the top-management team to work from a common base of facts.

In the absence of good data, executives waste time in pointless debate over opinions. Some resort to self-aggrandizement and ill-formed guesses about how the world might be. People—and not issues—become the focus of disagreement. The result is interpersonal conflict. In such companies, top managers are often poorly informed both about internal operations, such as bookings and engineering milestones, and about external issues, such as competing products. They collect data narrowly and infrequently. In these companies, the vice presidents of finance, who oversee internal data collection, are usually weak. They were often described by people in the companies we studied as "inexperienced" or "detached." In contrast, the vice president of finance at Premier Technologies, a company with little interpersonal conflict, was described as being central to taking "the constant pulse of how the firm is doing."

Management teams troubled by interpersonal conflict rely more on hunches and guesses than on current data. When they consider facts, they are more likely to examine a past measure, such as profitability, which is both historical and highly refined. These teams favor planning based on extrapolation and intuitive attempts to predict the future, neither of which yields current or factual results. Their conversations are more subjective. The CEO of one of the four high-conflict teams told us his interest in operating numbers was "minimal," and he described his goals as "subjective." At another such company, senior managers saw the CEO as "visionary" and "a little detached from the day-to-day operations." Compare those executives with the CEO of Bravo Microsystems, who had a reputation for being a "pragmatic numbers guy."

There is a direct link between reliance on facts and low levels of interpersonal conflict. Facts let people move quickly to the central issues surrounding a strategic choice. Decision makers don't become bogged down in arguments over what the facts *might* be. More important, reliance on current data grounds strategic discussions in reality. Facts (such as current sales, market share, R&D expenses, competitors' behavior, and manufacturing yields) depersonalize the discussion because they are not someone's fantasies, guesses, or self-serving desires. In the absence of facts, individuals' motives are likely to become suspect. Building decisions on facts creates a culture that emphasizes issues instead of personalities.

Multiply the Alternatives

Some managers believe that they can reduce conflict by focusing on only one or two alternatives, thus minimizing the dimensions over which people can disagree. But, in fact, teams with low incidences of interpersonal conflict do just the opposite. They deliberately develop multiple alternatives, often considering four or five options at once. To promote debate, managers will even introduce options they do not support.

For example, Triumph's new CEO was determined to improve the company's lackluster performance. When he arrived, new products were stuck in development, and investors were getting anxious. He launched a fact-gathering exercise and asked senior executives to develop alternatives. In less than two months, they developed four. The first was to sell some of the company's technology. The second was to undertake a major strategic redirection, using the base technology to enter a new market. The third was to redeploy engineering resources and adjust the marketing approach. The final option was to sell the company.

Working together to shape those options enhanced the group's sense of teamwork while promoting a more creative view of Triumph's competitive situation and its technical competencies. As a result, the team ended up combining elements of several options in a way that was more robust than any of the options were individually.

The other teams we observed with low levels of interpersonal conflict also tended to develop multiple options to make major decisions. Star, for example, faced a cash flow crisis caused by explosive growth. Its executives considered, among other choices, arranging for lines of credit from banks, selling additional stock, and forming strategic alliances with several partners. At Bravo, managers explicitly relied on three kinds of alternatives: sincere proposals that the proponent actually backed; support for someone else's proposal, even if only for the sake of argument; and insincere alternatives proposed just to expand the number of options.

There are several reasons why considering multiple alternatives may lower interpersonal conflict. For one, it diffuses conflict: choices become less black and white, and individuals gain more room to vary the degree of their support over a range of choices. Managers can more easily shift positions without losing face.

Generating options is also a way to bring managers together in a common and inherently stimulating task. It concentrates their energy on solving problems, and it increases the likelihood of obtaining integrative solutions—alternatives that incorporate the views of a greater number of the decision makers. In generating multiple alternatives, managers do not stop at obvious solutions; rather, they continue generating further—usually more original—options. The process in itself is creative and fun, setting a positive tone for substantive, instead of interpersonal, conflict.

By contrast, in teams that vigorously debate just one or two options, conflict often does turn personal. At Solo Systems, for instance, the top-management team considered entering a new business area as a way to boost the company's performance. They debated this alternative versus the status quo but failed to consider other options. Individual executives became increasingly entrenched on one side of the debate or the other. As positions hardened, the conflict became more pointed and personal. The animosity grew so great that a major proponent of change quit the company in disgust while the rest of the team either disengaged or slipped into intense and dysfunctional politicking.

Create Common Goals

A third tactic for minimizing destructive conflict involves framing strategic choices as collaborative, rather than competitive, exercises. Elements of collaboration and competition coexist within any management team: executives share a stake in the company's performance, yet their personal ambitions may make them rivals for power. The successful groups we studied consistently framed their decisions as collaborations in which it was in everyone's interest to achieve the best possible solution for the collective.

They did so by creating a common goal around which the team could rally. Such goals do not imply homogeneous thinking, but they do require everyone to share a vision. As Steve Jobs, who is associated with three high-profile Silicon Valley companies—Apple, NeXT, and Pixar—has advised, "It's okay to spend a lot of time arguing about which route to take to San Francisco when everyone wants to end up there, but a lot of time gets wasted in such arguments if one person wants to go to San Francisco and another secretly wants to go to San Diego."

Teams hobbled by conflict lack common goals. Team members perceive themselves to be in competition with one another and, surprisingly, tend to frame decisions negatively, as reactions to threats. At Andromeda Processing, for instance, the team focused on responding to a particular instance of poor performance, and team members tried to pin the blame on one another. That negative framing contrasts with the positive approach taken by Star Electronics executives, who, sharing a common goal, viewed a cash crisis not as a threat but as an opportunity to "build the biggest war chest" for an impending competitive battle. At a broad level, Star's executives shared the goal of creating "*the* computer firm of the decade." As one Star executive told us, "We take a corporate, not a functional, viewpoint most of the time."

Likewise, all the management team members we interviewed at Premier Technologies agreed that their common goal—their rallying cry—was to build "the best damn machine on the market." Thus in their debates they could disagree about critical technical alternatives—in-house versus offshore manufacturing options, for example, or alternative distribution channels—without letting the conflict turn personal.

Many studies of group decision making and intergroup conflict demonstrate that common goals build team cohesion by stressing the shared interest of all team members in the outcome of the debate. When team members are working toward a common goal, they are less likely to see themselves as individual winners and losers and are far more likely to perceive the opinions of others correctly and to learn from them. We observed that when executives lacked common goals, they tended to be closed-minded and more likely to misinterpret and blame one another.

Use Humor

Teams that handle conflict well make explicit—and often even contrived—attempts to relieve tension and at the same time promote a collaborative esprit by making their business fun. They emphasize the excitement of fast-paced competition, not the stress of competing in brutally tough and uncertain markets.

All the teams with low interpersonal conflict described ways in which they used humor on the job. Executives at Bravo Microsystems enjoyed playing gags around the office. For example, pink plastic flamingos—souvenirs from a customer—graced Bravo's otherwise impeccably decorated headquarters. Similarly, Triumph Computers' top managers held a monthly "dessert pig-out," followed by group weight watching. Those seemingly trivial activities were part of the CEO's deliberate plan to make work more fun, despite the pressures of the industry. At Star Electronics, making the company "a fun place" was an explicit goal for the top-management team. Laughter was common during management meetings. Practical jokes were popular at Star, where executives—along with other employees—always celebrated Halloween and April Fools' Day.

At each of these companies, executives acknowledged that at least some of the attempts at humor were contrived—even forced. Even so, they helped to release tension and promote collaboration.

Humor was strikingly absent in the teams marked by high interpersonal conflict. Although pairs of individuals were sometimes friends, team members shared no group social activities beyond a standard holiday party or two, and there were no conscious attempts to create humor. Indeed, the climate in which decisions were made was often just the opposite—hostile and stressful.

Humor works as a defense mechanism to protect people from the stressful and threatening situations that commonly arise in the course of making strategic decisions. It helps people distance themselves psychologically by putting those situations into a broader life context, often through the use of irony. Humor—with its ambiguity—can also blunt the threatening edge of negative information. Speakers can say in jest things that might otherwise give offense because the message is simultaneously serious and not serious. The recipient is allowed to save face by receiving the serious message while appearing not to do so. The result is communication of difficult information in a more tactful and less personally threatening way.

Humor can also move decision making into a collaborative rather than competitive frame through its powerful effect on mood. According to a large body of research, people in a positive mood tend to be not only more optimistic but also more forgiving of others and creative in seeking solutions. A positive mood triggers a more accurate perception of others' arguments because people in a good mood tend to relax their defensive barriers and so can listen more effectively.

Balance the Power Structure

We found that managers who believe that their team's decision-making process is fair are more likely to accept decisions without resentment, even when they do not agree with them. But when they believe the process is unfair, ill will easily grows into interpersonal conflict. A fifth tactic for taming interpersonal conflict, then, is to create a sense of fairness by balancing power within the management team.

Our research suggests that autocratic leaders who manage through highly centralized power structures often generate high levels of interpersonal friction. At the other extreme, weak leaders also engender interpersonal conflict because the power vacuum at the top encourages managers to jockey for position. Interpersonal conflict is lowest in what we call *balanced power structures,* those in which the CEO is more powerful than the other members of the top-management team, but the members do wield substantial power, especially in their own well-defined areas of responsibility. In balanced power structures, all executives participate in strategic decisions.

At Premier Technologies, for example, the CEO—described by others as a "team player"—was definitely the most powerful figure. But each executive was the most powerful decision maker in some clearly defined area. In addition, the entire team participated in all significant decisions. The CEO, one executive observed, "depends on picking good people and letting them operate."

The CEO of Bravo Microsystems, another company with a balanced power structure, summarized his philosophy as "making quick decisions involving as many people as possible." We watched the Bravo team over several months as it grappled with a major

How teams argue but still get along

Tactic →	Strategy
Base discussion on current, factual information. Develop multiple alternatives to enrich the debate.	Focus on issues, not personalities.
Rally around goals. Inject humor into the decision-making process.	Frame decisions as collaborations aimed at achieving the best possible solution for the company.
Maintain a balanced power structure. Resolve issues without forcing consensus.	Establish a sense of fairness and equity in the process.

strategic redirection. After many group discussions, the final decision was made at a multiday retreat involving the whole team.

In contrast, the leaders of the teams marked by extensive interpersonal conflict were either highly autocratic or weak. The CEO at Mercury Microdevices, for example, was the principal decision maker. There was a substantial gap in power between him and the rest of the team. In the decision we tracked, the CEO dominated the process from start to finish, identifying the problem, defining the analysis, and making the choice. Team members described the CEO as "strong" and "dogmatic." As one of them put it, "When Bruce makes a decision, it's like God!"

At Andromeda, the CEO exercised only modest power, and areas of responsibility were blurred within the top-management team, where power was diffuse and ambiguous. Senior executives had to politick amongst themselves to get anything accomplished, and they reported intense frustration with the confusion that existed at the top.

Most executives expected to control some significant aspect of their business but not the entirety. When they lacked power—because of either an autocrat or a power vacuum—they became frustrated by their inability to make significant decisions. Instead of team members, they became politicians. As one executive explained, "We're all jockeying for our spot in the pecking order." Another described "maneuvering for the CEO's ear."

The situations we observed are consistent with classic social-psychology studies of leadership. For example, in a study from the 1960s, Ralph White and Ronald Lippitt examined the effects of different leadership styles on boys in social clubs. They found that boys with democratic leaders—the situation closest to our balanced power structure—showed spontaneous interest in their activities. The boys were highly satisfied, and within their groups there were many friendly remarks, much praise, and significant collaboration. Under weak leaders, the boys were disorganized, inefficient, and dissatisfied. But the worst case was autocratic rule, under which the boys were hostile and aggressive, occasionally directing physical violence against innocent scapegoats. In imbalanced power situations, we observed adult displays of verbal aggression that colleagues described as violent. One executive talked about being "caught in the cross fire." Another described a colleague as "a gun about to go off." A third spoke about "being beat up" by the CEO.

Seek Consensus with Qualification

Balancing power is one tactic for building a sense of fairness. Finding an appropriate way to resolve conflict over issues is another—and, perhaps, the more crucial. In our research, the teams that managed conflict effectively all used the same approach to resolving substantive conflict. It is a two-step process that some executives call *consensus with qualification*. It works like this: executives talk over an issue and try to reach consensus. If they can, the decision is made. If they can't, the most relevant senior manager makes the decision, guided by input from the rest of the group.

When a competitor launched a new product attacking Premier Technologies in its biggest market, for example, there was sharp disagreement about how to respond. Some executives wanted to shift R&D resources to counter this competitive move, even at the risk of diverting engineering talent from a more innovative product then in design. Others argued that Premier should simply repackage an existing product, adding a few novel features. A third group felt that the threat was not serious enough to warrant a major response.

After a series of meetings over several weeks, the group failed to reach consensus. So the CEO and his marketing vice president made the decision. As the CEO explained, "The functional heads do the talking. I pull the trigger." Premier's executives were comfortable with this arrangement—even those who did not agree with the outcome—because everyone had had a voice in the process.

People usually associate consensus with harmony, but we found the opposite: teams that insisted on resolving substantive conflict by forcing consensus tended to display the most interpersonal conflict. Executives sometimes have the unrealistic view that consensus is always possible, but such a naïve insistence on consensus can lead to endless haggling. As the vice president of engineering at Mega Software put it, "Consensus means that everyone has veto power. Our products were too late, and they were too expensive." At Andromeda, the CEO wanted his executives to reach consensus, but persistent differences of opinion remained. The debate dragged on for months, and the frustration mounted until some top managers simply gave up. They just wanted a decision, any decision. One was finally made when several executives who favored one point of view left the company. The price of consensus was a decimated team.

In a team that insists on consensus, deadlines can cause executives to sacrifice fairness and thus weaken the team's support for the final decision. At Andromeda, executives spent months analyzing their industry and developing a shared perspective on important trends for the future, but they could never focus on making the decision. The decision-making process dragged on. Finally, as the deadline of a board meeting drew imminent, the CEO formulated and announced a choice—one that had never even been mentioned in the earlier discussions. Not surprisingly, his team was angry and upset. Had he been less insistent on reaching a consensus, the CEO would not have felt forced by the deadline to act so arbitrarily.

How does consensus with qualification create a sense of fairness? A body of research on procedural justice shows that process fairness, which involves significant participation and influence by all concerned, is enormously important to most people. Individuals are willing to accept outcomes they dislike if they believe that the process by which those results came about was fair. Most people want their opinions to be considered seriously but are willing to accept that those opinions cannot always prevail. That is precisely what occurs in consensus with qualification. As one executive at Star said, "I'm happy just to bring up my opinions."

Apart from fairness, there are several other reasons why consensus with qualification is an important deterrent to interpersonal conflict. It assumes that conflict is natural and not a sign of interpersonal dysfunction. It gives managers added influence when the decision affects their part of the organization in particular, thus

Building a Fighting Team

HOW CAN MANAGERS ENCOURAGE the kind of substantive debate over issues that leads to better decision making? We found five approaches that help generate constructive disagreement within a team:

1. **Assemble a heterogeneous team, including diverse ages, genders, functional backgrounds, and industry experience.** If everyone in the executive meetings looks alike and sounds alike, then the chances are excellent that they probably think alike, too.
2. **Meet together as a team regularly and often.** Team members that don't know one another well don't know one another's positions on issues, impairing their ability to argue effectively. Frequent interaction builds the mutual confidence and familiarity team members require to express dissent.
3. **Encourage team members to assume roles beyond their obvious product, geographic, or functional responsibilities.** Devil's advocates, sky-gazing visionaries, and action-oriented executives can work together to ensure that all sides of an issue are considered.
4. **Apply multiple mind-sets to any issue.** Try role-playing, putting yourself in your competitors' shoes, or conducting war games. Such techniques create fresh perspectives and engage team members, spurring interest in problem solving.
5. **Actively manage conflict.** Don't let the team acquiesce too soon or too easily. Identify and treat apathy early, and don't confuse a lack of conflict with agreement. Often, what passes for consensus is really disengagement.

---

balancing managers' desires to be heard with the need to make a choice. It is an equitable and egalitarian process of decision making that encourages everyone to bring ideas to the table but clearly delineates how the decision will be made.

Finally, consensus with qualification is fast. Processes that require consensus tend to drag on endlessly, frustrating managers with what they see as time-consuming and useless debate. It's not surprising that the managers end up blaming their frustration on the shortcomings of their colleagues and not on the poor conflict-resolution process.

Linking Conflict, Speed, and Performance

A considerable body of academic research has demonstrated that conflict over issues is not only likely within top-management teams but also valuable. Such conflict provides executives with a more inclusive range of information, a deeper understanding of the issues, and a richer set of possible solutions. That was certainly the case in the companies we studied. The evidence also overwhelmingly indicates that where there is little conflict over issues, there is also likely to be poor decision making. "Groupthink" has been a primary cause of major corporate- and public-policy debacles. And although it may seem counterintuitive, we found that the teams that engaged in healthy conflict over issues not only made better decisions but moved more quickly as well. Without conflict, groups lose their effectiveness. Managers often become withdrawn and only superficially harmonious. Indeed, we found that the alternative to conflict is usually not agreement but apathy and disengagement. Teams unable to foster substantive conflict ultimately achieve, on average, lower performance. Among the companies that we observed, low-conflict teams tended to forget to consider key issues or were simply unaware of important aspects of their strategic situation. They missed opportunities to question falsely limiting assumptions or to generate significantly different alternatives. Not surprisingly, their actions were often easy for competitors to anticipate.

In fast-paced markets, successful strategic decisions are most likely to be made by teams that promote active and broad conflict over issues without sacrificing speed. The key to doing so is to mitigate interpersonal conflict.

Originally published in July 1997. Reprint 97402

About the Contributors

TERESA M. AMABILE is the Edsel Bryant Ford Professor of Business Administration at Harvard Business School.

KRISTIN BEHFAR is an assistant professor of organization and management at the University of California, Irvine.

L.J. BOURGEOIS III is a professor of business administration at the University of Virginia's Darden Graduate School of Business.

ANDY BOYNTON is the dean of Boston College's Carroll School of Management.

JEANNE BRETT is the DeWitt W. Buchanan, Jr., Distinguished Professor of Dispute Resolution and Organizations and the director of the Dispute Resolution Research Center at Northwestern University's Kellogg School of Management.

DIANE COUTU is the director of client communications at Banyan Family Business Advisors. She was formerly a senior editor at HBR.

KATHLEEN M. EISENHARDT is a professor of strategy and organization at Stanford University.

TAMARA J. ERICKSON is the CEO and founder of Tammy Erickson Associates, a firm that helps leaders build intelligent organizations.

BILL FISCHER is a professor of technology management at IMD in Lausanne, Switzerland.

BOB FRISCH is the managing partner of the Strategic Offsites Group in Boston.

LYNDA GRATTON is a professor of management practice at London Business School.

JEAN L. KAHWAJY is the founder of Effective Interactions, a communication and leadership consulting firm in Los Altos, California.

JON R. KATZENBACH is a senior partner in the New York office of Booz & Company.

MARY C. KERN is an associate professor of management at Baruch College.

STEVEN J. KRAMER is an independent researcher, writer, and consultant in Wayland, Massachusetts.

ALEX "SANDY" PENTLAND is a professor at MIT, the director of MIT's Human Dynamics Laboratory and the MIT Media Lab Entrepreneurship Program, and the chairman of Sociometric Solutions.

DOUGLAS K. SMITH is chairman of the board of The Rapid Results Institute.

VANESSA URCH DRUSKAT is an associate professor of organizational behavior and management at the University of New Hampshire and a principal at the consulting firm GEI Partners.

STEVEN B. WOLFF is a principal at the consulting firm GEI Partners.

Index

HBR'S 10 MUST READS

On **Managing Across Cultures**

HBR's 10 Must Reads series is the definitive collection of ideas and best practices for aspiring and experienced leaders alike. These books offer essential reading selected from the pages of *Harvard Business Review* on topics critical to the success of every manager.

Titles include:

HBR's 10 Must Reads 2015
HBR's 10 Must Reads 2016
HBR's 10 Must Reads on Change Management
HBR's 10 Must Reads on Collaboration
HBR's 10 Must Reads on Communication
HBR's 10 Must Reads on Emotional Intelligence
HBR's 10 Must Reads on Innovation
HBR's 10 Must Reads on Leadership
HBR's 10 Must Reads on Making Smart Decisions
HBR's 10 Must Reads on Managing Across Cultures
HBR's 10 Must Reads on Managing People
HBR's 10 Must Reads on Managing Yourself
HBR's 10 Must Reads on Strategic Marketing
HBR's 10 Must Reads on Strategy
HBR's 10 Must Reads on Teams
HBR's 10 Must Reads: The Essentials

HBR'S 10 MUST READS

On Managing Across Cultures

HARVARD BUSINESS REVIEW PRESS
Boston, Massachusetts

Printed in the United States of America

10 9 8 7

The web addresses referenced in this book were live and correct at the time of the book's publication but may be subject to change.

Library of Congress Cataloging-in-Publication Data

Names: Harvard Business Review Press, issuing body.
Title: HBR's 10 must reads on managing across cultures / Harvard Business Review Press.
Description: Boston, Massachusetts : Harvard Business Review Press, [2016] | Includes index.
Identifiers: LCCN 2015047174 (print) | LCCN 2016003334 (ebook) | ISBN 9781633691629 (pbk. : alk. paper) | ISBN 9781633691636 ()
Subjects: LCSH: International business enterprises—Personnel management. | Management—Cross-cultural studies. | Corporate culture—Cross-cultural studies. | Diversity in the workplace—Management.
Classification: LCC HF5549.5.E45 H423 2016 (print) | LCC HF5549.5.E45 (ebook) | DDC 658.3008—dc23
LC record available at http://lccn.loc.gov/2015047174

ISBN: 978-1-63369-162-9
eISBN: 978-1-63369-163-6

The paper used in this publication meets the requirements of the American National Standard for Permanence of Paper for Publications and Documents in Libraries and Archives Z39.48-1992.

Contents

HBR'S 10 MUST READS

On Managing Across Cultures

Cultural Intelligence

by P. Christopher Earley and Elaine Mosakowski

YOU SEE THEM AT INTERNATIONAL airports like Heathrow: posters advertising the global bank HSBC that show a grasshopper and the message "USA—Pest. China—Pet. Northern Thailand—Appetizer."

Taxonomists pinned down the scientific definition of the family Acrididae more than two centuries ago. But culture is so powerful it can affect how even a lowly insect is perceived. So it should come as no surprise that the human actions, gestures, and speech patterns a person encounters in a foreign business setting are subject to an even wider range of interpretations, including ones that can make misunderstandings likely and cooperation impossible. But occasionally an outsider has a seemingly natural ability to interpret someone's unfamiliar and ambiguous gestures in just the way that person's compatriots and colleagues would, even to mirror them. We call that *cultural intelligence* or CQ. In a world where crossing boundaries is routine, CQ becomes a vitally important aptitude and skill, and not just for international bankers and borrowers.

Companies, too, have cultures, often very distinctive; anyone who joins a new company spends the first few weeks deciphering its cultural code. Within any large company there are sparring subcultures as well: The sales force can't talk to the engineers, and the PR people lose patience with the lawyers. Departments, divisions, professions, geographical regions—each has a constellation of manners, meanings, histories, and values that will confuse the interloper and cause him or her to stumble. Unless, that is, he or she has a high CQ.

Cultural intelligence is related to emotional intelligence, but it picks up where emotional intelligence leaves off. A person with high emotional intelligence grasps what makes us human and at the same time what makes each of us different from one another. A person with high cultural intelligence can somehow tease out of a person's or group's behavior those features that would be true of all people and all groups, those peculiar to this person or this group, and those that are neither universal nor idiosyncratic. The vast realm that lies between those two poles is culture.

An American expatriate manager we know had his cultural intelligence tested while serving on a design team that included two German engineers. As other team members floated their ideas, the engineers condemned them repeatedly as stunted or immature or worse. The manager concluded that Germans in general are rude and aggressive.

A modicum of cultural intelligence would have helped the American realize he was mistakenly equating the merit of an idea with the merit of the person presenting it and that the Germans were able to make a sharp distinction between the two. A manager with even subtler powers of discernment might have tried to determine how much of the two Germans' behavior was arguably German and how much was explained by the fact that they were engineers.

An expatriate manager who was merely emotionally intelligent would probably have empathized with the team members whose ideas were being criticized, modulated his or her spontaneous reaction to the engineers' conduct, and proposed a new style of discussion that preserved candor but spared feelings, if indeed anyone's feelings had been hurt. But without being able to tell how much of the engineers' behavior was idiosyncratic and how much was culturally determined, he or she would not have known how to influence their actions or how easy it would be to do that.

One critical element that cultural intelligence and emotional intelligence do share is, in psychologist Daniel Goleman's words, "a propensity to suspend judgment—to think before acting." For someone richly endowed with CQ, the suspension might take hours or days, while someone with low CQ might have to take weeks or months. In either case, it involves using your senses to register all

Idea in Brief

In an increasingly diverse business environment, managers must be able to navigate through the thicket of habits, gestures, and assumptions that define their coworkers' differences. Foreign cultures are everywhere—in other countries, certainly, but also in corporations, vocations, and regions. Interacting with individuals within them demands perceptiveness and adaptability. And the people who have those traits in abundance aren't necessarily the ones who enjoy the greatest social success in familiar settings. Cultural intelligence, or CQ, is the ability to make sense of unfamiliar contexts and then blend in. It has three components—the cognitive, the physical, and the emotional/motivational. While it shares many of the properties of emotional intelligence, CQ goes one step further by equipping a person to distinguish behaviors produced by the culture in question from behaviors that are peculiar to particular individuals and those found in all human beings. In their surveys of 2,000 managers in 60 countries, the authors found that most managers are not equally strong in all three of these areas of cultural intelligence. The authors have devised tools that show how to identify one's strengths, and they have developed training techniques to help people overcome weaknesses. They conclude that anyone reasonably alert, motivated, and poised can attain an acceptable CQ.

the ways that the personalities interacting in front of you are different from those in your home culture yet similar to one another. Only when conduct you have actually observed begins to settle into patterns can you safely begin to anticipate how these people will react in the next situation. The inferences you draw in this manner will be free of the hazards of stereotyping.

The people who are socially the most successful among their peers often have the greatest difficulty making sense of, and then being accepted by, cultural strangers. Those who fully embody the habits and norms of their native culture may be the most alien when they enter a culture not their own. Sometimes, people who are somewhat detached from their own culture can more easily adopt the mores and even the body language of an unfamiliar host. They're used to being observers and making a conscious effort to fit in.

Although some aspects of cultural intelligence are innate, anyone reasonably alert, motivated, and poised can attain an acceptable level of cultural intelligence, as we have learned from surveying 2,000 managers in 60 countries and training many others. Given the number of cross-functional assignments, job transfers, new employers, and distant postings most corporate managers are likely to experience in the course of a career, low CQ can turn out to be an inherent disadvantage.

The Three Sources of Cultural Intelligence

Can it really be that some managers are socially intelligent in their own settings but ineffective in culturally novel ones? The experience of Peter, a sales manager at a California medical devices group acquired by Eli Lilly Pharmaceuticals, is not unusual. At the devices company, the atmosphere had been mercenary and competitive; the best-performing employees could make as much in performance bonuses as in salary. Senior managers hounded unproductive salespeople to perform better.

At Lilly's Indianapolis headquarters, to which Peter was transferred, the sales staff received bonuses that accounted for only a small percentage of total compensation. Furthermore, criticism was restrained and confrontation kept to a minimum. To motivate people, Lilly management encouraged them. Peter commented, "Back in L.A., I knew how to handle myself and how to manage my sales team. I'd push them and confront them if they weren't performing, and they'd respond. If you look at my evaluations, you'll see that I was very successful and people respected me. Here in Indianapolis, they don't like my style, and they seem to avoid the challenges that I put to them. I just can't seem to get things done as well here as I did in California."

Peter's problem was threefold. First, he didn't comprehend how much the landscape had changed. Second, he was unable to make his behavior consistent with that of everyone around him. And third, when he recognized that the arrangement wasn't working, he became disheartened.

Peter's three difficulties correspond to the three components of cultural intelligence: the cognitive; the physical; and the emotional/motivational. Cultural intelligence resides in the body and the heart, as well as the head. Although most managers are not equally strong in all three areas, each faculty is seriously hampered without the other two.

Head

Rote learning about the beliefs, customs, and taboos of foreign cultures, the approach corporate training programs tend to favor, will never prepare a person for every situation that arises, nor will it prevent terrible gaffes. However, inquiring about the meaning of some custom will often prove unavailing because natives may be reticent about explaining themselves to strangers, or they may have little practice looking at their own culture analytically.

Instead, a newcomer needs to devise what we call learning strategies. Although most people find it difficult to discover a point of entry into alien cultures, whose very coherence can make them seem like separate, parallel worlds, an individual with high cognitive CQ notices clues to a culture's shared understandings. These can appear in any form and any context but somehow indicate a line of interpretation worth pursuing.

An Irish manager at an international advertising firm was working with a new client, a German construction and engineering company. Devin's experience with executives in the German retail clothing industry was that they were reasonably flexible about deadlines and receptive to highly imaginative proposals for an advertising campaign. He had also worked with executives of a British construction and engineering company, whom he found to be strict about deadlines and intent on a media campaign that stressed the firm's technical expertise and the cost savings it offered.

Devin was unsure how to proceed. Should he assume that the German construction company would take after the German clothing retailer or, instead, the British construction company? He resolved to observe the new client's representative closely and draw general conclusions about the firm and its culture from his behavior, just as he had done in the other two cases. Unfortunately, the client sent a new representative to every meeting. Many came from different business units and had grown up in different countries. Instead of equating the first representative's behavior with the client's corporate culture, Devin looked for consistencies in the various individuals' traits. Eventually he determined that they were all punctual, deadline-oriented, and tolerant of unconventional advertising messages. From that, he was able to infer much about the character of their employer.

Body

You will not disarm your foreign hosts, guests, or colleagues simply by showing you understand their culture; your actions and demeanor must prove that you have already to some extent entered their world. Whether it's the way you shake hands or order a coffee, evidence of an ability to mirror the customs and gestures of the people around you will prove that you esteem them well enough to want to be like them. By adopting people's habits and mannerisms, you eventually come to understand in the most elemental way what it is like to be them. They, in turn, become more trusting and open. University of Michigan professor Jeffrey Sanchez-Burks's research on cultural barriers in business found that job candidates who adopted some of the mannerisms of recruiters with cultural backgrounds different from their own were more likely to be made an offer.

This won't happen if a person suffers from a deep-seated reservation about the called-for behavior or lacks the physical poise to pull it off. Henri, a French manager at Aegis, a media corporation, followed the national custom of greeting his female clients with a hug and a kiss on both cheeks. Although Melanie, a British aerospace manager, understood that in France such familiarity was de rigueur in a professional setting, she couldn't suppress her discomfort when it happened to her, and she recoiled. Inability to receive and reciprocate gestures that are culturally characteristic reflects a low level of cultural intelligence's physical component.

In another instance, a Hispanic community leader in Los Angeles and an Anglo-American businessman fell into conversation at a charity event. As the former moved closer, the latter backed away. It took nearly 30 minutes of waltzing around the room for the community leader to realize that "Anglos" were not comfortable standing in such close physical proximity.

Heart

Adapting to a new culture involves overcoming obstacles and setbacks. People can do that only if they believe in their own efficacy. If they persevered in the face of challenging situations in the past, their confidence grew. Confidence is always rooted in mastery of a particular task or set of circumstances.

A person who doesn't believe herself capable of understanding people from unfamiliar cultures will often give up after her efforts meet with hostility or incomprehension. By contrast, a person with high motivation will, upon confronting obstacles, setbacks, or even failure, reengage with greater vigor. To stay motivated, highly efficacious people do not depend on obtaining rewards, which may be unconventional or long delayed.

Hyong Moon had experience leading racially mixed teams of designers at GM, but when he headed up a product design and development team that included representatives from the sales, production, marketing, R&D, engineering, and finance departments, things did not go smoothly. The sales manager, for example, objected to the safety engineer's attempt to add features such as side-impact air bags because they would boost the car's price excessively. The conflict became so intense and so public that a senior manager had to intervene. Although many managers would have felt chastened after that, Moon struggled even harder to gain control, which he eventually did by convincing the sales manager that the air bags could make the car more marketable. Although he had no experience with cross-functional teams, his successes with single-function teams had given him the confidence to persevere. He commented, "I'd seen these types of disagreements in other teams, and I'd been able to help team members overcome their differences, so I knew I could do it again."

How Head, Body, and Heart Work Together

At the end of 1997, U.S.-based Merrill Lynch acquired UK-based Mercury Asset Management. At the time of the merger, Mercury was a decorous, understated, hierarchical company known for doing business in the manner of an earlier generation. Merrill, by contrast, was informal, fast-paced, aggressive, and entrepreneurial. Both companies had employees of many nationalities. Visiting Mercury about six months after the merger announcement, we were greeted by Chris, a Mercury personnel manager dressed in khakis and a knit shirt. Surprised by the deviation from his usual uniform of gray or navy pinstripes, we asked him what had happened. He told

Diagnosing Your Cultural Intelligence

THESE STATEMENTS REFLECT DIFFERENT facets of cultural intelligence. For each set, add up your scores and divide by four to produce an average. Our work with large groups of managers shows that for purposes of your own development, it is most useful to think about your three scores in comparison to one another. Generally, an average of less than 3 would indicate an area calling for improvement, while an average of greater than 4.5 reflects a true CQ strength.

Rate the extent to which you agree with each statement, using the scale:

1 = strongly disagree, 2 = disagree, 3 = neutral, 4 = agree, 5 = strongly agree.

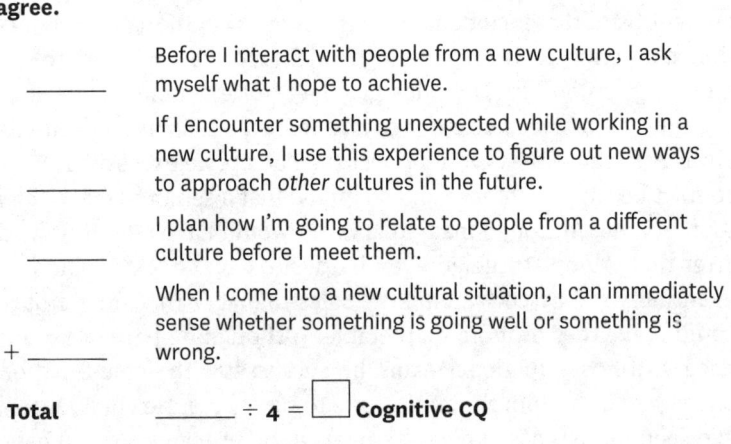

______	Before I interact with people from a new culture, I ask myself what I hope to achieve.
______	If I encounter something unexpected while working in a new culture, I use this experience to figure out new ways to approach *other* cultures in the future.
______	I plan how I'm going to relate to people from a different culture before I meet them.
+ ______	When I come into a new cultural situation, I can immediately sense whether something is going well or something is wrong.
Total	______ ÷ **4** = ☐ **Cognitive CQ**

us that Merrill had instituted casual Fridays in its own offices and then extended the policy on a volunteer basis to its UK sites.

Chris understood the policy as Merrill's attempt to reduce hierarchical distinctions both within and between the companies. The intention, he thought, was to draw the two enterprises closer together. Chris also identified a liking for casual dress as probably an American cultural trait.

Not all Mercury managers were receptive to the change, however. Some went along with casual Fridays for a few weeks, then gave up. Others never doffed their more formal attire, viewing the new policy as a victory of carelessness over prudence and an attempt by Merrill to impose its identity on Mercury, whose professional

______	It's easy for me to change my body language (for example, eye contact or posture) to suit people from a different culture.
______	I can alter my expression when a cultural encounter requires it.
______	I modify my speech style (for example, accent or tone) to suit people from a different culture.
+ ______	I easily change the way I act when a cross-cultural encounter seems to require it.
Total	______ ÷ **4** = ☐ **Physical CQ**

______	I have confidence that I can deal well with people from a different culture.
______	I am certain that I can befriend people whose cultural backgrounds are different from mine.
______	I can adapt to the lifestyle of a different culture with relative ease.
+ ______	I am confident that I can deal with a cultural situation that's unfamiliar.
Total	______ ÷ **4** = ☐ **Emotional/motivational CQ**

dignity would suffer as a result. In short, the Mercury resisters did not understand the impulse behind the change (head); they could not bring themselves to alter their appearance (body); and they had been in the Mercury environment for so long that they lacked the motivation (heart) to see the experiment through. To put it even more simply, they dreaded being mistaken for Merrill executives.

How would you behave in a similar situation? The sidebar "Diagnosing Your Cultural Intelligence" allows you to assess the three facets of your own cultural intelligence and learn where your relative strengths and weaknesses lie. Attaining a high absolute score is not the objective.

Cultural Intelligence Profiles

Most managers fit at least one of the following six profiles. By answering the questions in the exhibit, you can decide which one describes you best.

The provincial can be quite effective when working with people of similar background but runs into trouble when venturing farther afield. A young engineer at Chevrolet's truck division received positive evaluations of his technical abilities as well as his interpersonal skills. Soon he was asked to lead a team at Saturn, an autonomous division of GM. He was not able to adjust to Saturn's highly participative approach to teamwork—he mistakenly assumed it would be as orderly and deferential as Chevy's. Eventually, he was sent back to Chevy's truck division.

The analyst methodically deciphers a foreign culture's rules and expectations by resorting to a variety of elaborate learning strategies. The most common form of analyst realizes pretty quickly he is in alien territory but then ascertains, usually in stages, the nature of the patterns at work and how he should interact with them. Deirdre, for example, works as a broadcast director for a London-based company. Her principal responsibility is negotiating contracts with broadcast media owners. In June 2002, her company decided that all units should adopt a single negotiating strategy, and it was Deirdre's job to make sure this happened. Instead of forcing a showdown with the managers who resisted, she held one-on-one meetings in which she probed their reasons for resisting, got them together to share ideas, and revised the negotiating strategy to incorporate approaches they had found successful. The revised strategy was more culturally flexible than the original proposal—and the managers chose to cooperate.

The natural relies entirely on his intuition rather than on a systematic learning style. He is rarely steered wrong by first impressions. Donald, a brand manager for Unilever, commented, "As part of my job, I need to judge people from a wide variety of cultural backgrounds and understand their needs quickly. When I come into a new situation, I watch everyone for a few minutes and then I get a general sense of what is going on and how I need to act. I'm not really sure how I do it, but it seems to work." When facing ambiguous multicultural situations that he must take control of, the natural may falter because he has never had to improvise learning strategies or cope with feelings of disorientation.

The ambassador, like many political appointees, may not know much about the culture he has just entered, but he convincingly communicates his certainty that he belongs there. Among the managers of multinational companies we have studied, the ambassador is the most common type. His confidence is a very powerful component of his cultural intelligence. Some of it may be derived from watching how other managers have succeeded in comparable situations. The ambassador must have the humility to know what he doesn't know—that is, to know how to avoid underestimating cultural differences, even though doing so will inflict a degree of discomfort.

The mimic has a high degree of control over his actions and behavior, if not a great deal of insight into the significance of the cultural cues he picks up. Mimicry definitely puts hosts and guests at ease, facilitates communication, and builds trust. Mimicry is not, however, the same as pure imitation, which can be interpreted as mocking. Ming, a manager at the Shanghai regional power authority, relates, "When I deal with foreigners, I try to adopt their style of speaking and interacting. I find that simple things like keeping the right distance from the other person or making eye contact or speaking English at a speed that matches the other person's puts them at ease and makes it easier to make a connection. This really makes a difference to newcomers to China because they often are a bit threatened by the place."

The chameleon possesses high levels of all three CQ components and is a very uncommon managerial type. He or she even may be mistaken for a native of the country. More important, chameleons don't generate any of the ripples that unassimilated foreigners inevitably do. Some are able to achieve results that natives cannot, due to their insider's skills and outsider's perspective. We found that only about 5% of the managers we surveyed belonged in this remarkable category.

One of them is Nigel, a British entrepreneur who has started businesses in Australia, France, and Germany. The son of diplomats, Nigel grew up all over the world. Most of his childhood, however, was spent in Saudi Arabia. After several successes of his own, some venture capitalists asked him to represent them in dealings with the founder of a money-losing Pakistani start-up.

To the founder, his company existed chiefly to employ members of his extended family and, secondarily, the citizens of Lahore. The VCs, naturally, had a different idea. They were tired of losses and wanted Nigel to persuade the founder to close down the business.

Upon relocating to Lahore, Nigel realized that the interests of family and community were not aligned. So he called in several community leaders, who agreed to meet with managers and try to convince them that the larger community of Lahore would be hurt if potential investors came to view it as full of businesspeople unconcerned with a company's solvency. Nigel's Saudi upbringing had made him aware of Islamic principles of personal responsibility to the wider community, while his British origins tempered what in another person's hands might have been the mechanical application of those tenets. Throughout the negotiations, he displayed an authoritative style appropriate to the Pakistani setting. In relatively short order, the managers and the family agreed to terminate operations.

Many managers, of course, are a hybrid of two or more of the types. We discovered in our survey of more than 2,000 managers that even more prevalent than the ambassador was a hybrid of that type and the analyst. One example was a female African-American manager in Cairo named Brenda, who was insulted when a small group of young, well-meaning Egyptian males greeted her with a phrase they'd learned from rap music.

"I turned on my heel, went right up to the group and began upbraiding them as strongly as my Arabic would allow," she said. "When I'd had my say, I stormed off to meet a friend."

"After I had walked about half a block, I registered the shocked look on their faces as they listened to my words. I then realized they must have thought they were greeting me in a friendly way. So I went back to talk to the group. They asked me why I was so angry, I explained, they apologized profusely, and we all sat down and had tea and an interesting talk about how the wrong words can easily cause trouble. During our conversation, I brought up a number of examples of how Arabic expressions uttered in the wrong way or by the wrong person could spark an equivalent reaction in them. After spending about an hour with them, I had some new friends."

Brenda's narrative illustrates the complexities and the perils of cross-cultural interactions. The young men had provoked her by trying, ineptly, to ingratiate themselves by using a bit of current slang from her native land. Forgetting in her anger that she was the stranger, she berated them for what was an act of cultural ignorance, not malice. Culturally uninformed mimicry got the young men in trouble; Brenda's—and the men's—cognitive flexibility and willingness to reengage got them out of it.

Cultivating Your Cultural Intelligence

Unlike other aspects of personality, cultural intelligence can be developed in psychologically healthy and professionally competent people. In our work with Deutsche Bank, we introduced a program to improve managers' work relationships with outsourcing partners in India. We developed a two-and-a-half day program that first identified a participant's strengths and weaknesses and then provided a series of steps, which we outline below, to enhance their CQ.

Step 1

The individual examines his CQ strengths and weaknesses in order to establish a starting point for subsequent development efforts. Our self-assessment instrument is one approach, but there are others, such as an assessment of a person's behavior in a simulated business encounter and 360-degree feedback on a person's past behavior in an actual situation. Hughes Electronics, for example, staged a cocktail party to evaluate an expatriate manager's grasp of South Korean social etiquette. Ideally, a manager will undergo a variety of assessments.

Step 2

The person selects training that focuses on her weaknesses. For example, someone lacking physical CQ might enroll in acting classes. Someone lacking cognitive CQ might work on developing his analogical and inductive reasoning—by, for example, reading several business case studies and distilling their common principles.

Step 3

The general training set out above is applied. If motivational CQ is low, a person might be given a series of simple exercises to perform, such as finding out where to buy a newspaper or greeting someone who has arrived to be interviewed. Mastering simple activities such as greetings or transactions with local shopkeepers establishes a solid base from which to move into more demanding activities, such as giving an employee a performance appraisal.

Step 4

The individual organizes her personal resources to support the approach she has chosen. Are there people at her organization with the skills to conduct this training, and does her work unit provide support for it? A realistic assessment of her workload and the time available for CQ enhancement is important.

Step 5

The person enters the cultural setting he needs to master. He coordinates his plans with others, basing them on his CQ strengths and remaining weaknesses. If his strength is mimicry, for example, he would be among the first in his training group to venture forth. If his strength is analysis, he would first want to observe events unfold and then explain to the others why they followed the pattern they did.

Step 6

The individual reevaluates her newly developed skills and how effective they have been in the new setting, perhaps after collecting

Confidence Training

HELMUT WAS A MANAGER at a Berlin-based high-tech company who participated in our cultural-intelligence training program at London Business School. Three months earlier, he had been assigned to a large manufacturing facility in southern Germany to supervise the completion of a new plant and guide the local staff through the launch. Helmut came from northern Germany and had never worked in southern Germany; his direct reports had been raised in southern Germany and had worked for the local business unit for an average of seven years.

Helmut was good at developing new learning strategies, and he wasn't bad at adapting his behavior to his surroundings. But he had low confidence in his ability to cope with his new colleagues. To him, southern Germans were essentially foreigners; he found them "loud, brash, and cliquish."

To capitalize on his resourcefulness and build his confidence, we placed Helmut in heterogeneous groups of people, whom we encouraged to engage in freewheeling discussions. We also encouraged him to express his emotions more openly, in the manner of his southern compatriots, and to make more direct eye contact in the course of role-playing exercises.

Helmut's resourcefulness might have impelled him to take on more ambitious tasks than he could quite handle. It was important he get his footing first, so that some subsequent reversal would not paralyze him. To enhance his motivational CQ, we asked him to list ten activities he thought would be part of his daily or weekly routine when he returned to Munich.

By the time Helmut returned to London for his second training session, he had proved to himself he could manage simple encounters like getting a coffee, shopping, and having a drink with colleagues. So we suggested he might be ready for more challenging tasks, such as providing face-to-face personnel appraisals. Even though Helmut was skilled at analyzing people's behavior, he doubted he was equal to this next set of hurdles. We encouraged him to view his analytic skills as giving him an important advantage. For example, Helmut had noticed that Bavarians were extroverted only with people familiar to them. With strangers they could be as formal as any Prussian. Realizing this allowed him to respond flexibly to either situation instead of being put off balance.

By the time he was asked to lead a quality-improvement team, he had concluded that his leadership style must unfold in two stages—commanding at the outset, then more personal and inclusive. On his third visit to London, Helmut reported good relations with the quality improvement team, and the members corroborated his assessment.

360-degree feedback from colleagues individually or eavesdropping on a casual focus group that was formed to discuss her progress. She may decide to undergo further training in specific areas.

In the sidebar "Confidence Training," we describe how we applied these six steps to the case of Helmut, one of five German managers we helped at their employer's behest as they coped with new assignments within and outside of Germany.

Why can some people act appropriately and effectively in new cultures or among people with unfamiliar backgrounds while others flounder? Our anecdotal and empirical evidence suggests that the answer doesn't lie in tacit knowledge or in emotional or social intelligence. But a person with high CQ, whether cultivated or innate, can understand and master such situations, persevere, and do the right thing when needed.

Originally published in October 2004. Reprint R0410J

Managing Multicultural Teams

by Jeanne Brett, Kristin Behfar, and Mary C. Kern

WHEN A MAJOR INTERNATIONAL SOFTWARE developer needed to produce a new product quickly, the project manager assembled a team of employees from India and the United States. From the start the team members could not agree on a delivery date for the product. The Americans thought the work could be done in two to three weeks; the Indians predicted it would take two to three months. As time went on, the Indian team members proved reluctant to report setbacks in the production process, which the American team members would find out about only when work was due to be passed to them. Such conflicts, of course, may affect any team, but in this case they arose from cultural differences. As tensions mounted, conflict over delivery dates and feedback became personal, disrupting team members' communication about even mundane issues. The project manager decided he had to intervene—with the result that both the American and the Indian team members came to rely on him for direction regarding minute operational details that the team should have been able to handle itself. The manager became so bogged down by quotidian issues that the project careened hopelessly off even the most pessimistic schedule—and the team never learned to work together effectively.

Multicultural teams often generate frustrating management dilemmas. Cultural differences can create substantial obstacles to effective teamwork—but these may be subtle and difficult to recognize until significant damage has already been done. As in the case above, which the manager involved told us about, managers may create more problems than they resolve by intervening. The challenge in managing multicultural teams effectively is to recognize underlying cultural causes of conflict, and to intervene in ways that both get the team back on track and empower its members to deal with future challenges themselves.

We interviewed managers and members of multicultural teams from all over the world. These interviews, combined with our deep research on dispute resolution and teamwork, led us to conclude that the wrong kind of managerial intervention may sideline valuable members who should be participating or, worse, create resistance, resulting in poor team performance. We're not talking here about respecting differing national standards for doing business, such as accounting practices. We're referring to day-to-day working problems among team members that can keep multicultural teams from realizing the very gains they were set up to harvest, such as knowledge of different product markets, culturally sensitive customer service, and 24-hour work rotations.

The good news is that cultural challenges are manageable if managers and team members choose the right strategy and avoid imposing single-culture-based approaches on multicultural situations.

The Challenges

People tend to assume that challenges on multicultural teams arise from differing styles of communication. But this is only one of the four categories that, according to our research, can create barriers to a team's ultimate success. These categories are direct versus indirect communication; trouble with accents and fluency; differing attitudes toward hierarchy and authority; and conflicting norms for decision making.

Direct versus indirect communication

Communication in Western cultures is typically direct and explicit. The meaning is on the surface, and a listener doesn't have to know

Idea in Brief

If your company does business internationally, you're probably leading teams with members from diverse cultural backgrounds. Those differences can present serious obstacles. For example, some members' lack of fluency in the team's dominant language can lead others to underestimate their competence. When such obstacles arise, your team can stalemate.

To get the team moving again, avoid intervening directly, advise Brett, Behfar, and Kern. Though sometimes necessary, your involvement can prevent team members from solving problems themselves—and learning from that process.

Instead, choose one of three indirect interventions. When possible, encourage team members to **adapt** by acknowledging cultural gaps and working around them. If your team isn't able to be open about their differences, consider **structural intervention** (e.g., reassigning members to reduce interpersonal friction). As a last resort, use an **exit** strategy (e.g., removing a member from the team).

There's no one right way to tackle multicultural problems. But understanding four barriers to team success can help you begin evaluating possible responses.

much about the context or the speaker to interpret it. This is not true in many other cultures, where meaning is embedded in the way the message is presented. For example, Western negotiators get crucial information about the other party's preferences and priorities by asking direct questions, such as "Do you prefer option A or option B?" In cultures that use indirect communication, negotiators may have to infer preferences and priorities from changes—or the lack of them—in the other party's settlement proposal. In cross-cultural negotiations, the non-Westerner can understand the direct communications of the Westerner, but the Westerner has difficulty understanding the indirect communications of the non-Westerner.

An American manager who was leading a project to build an interface for a U.S. and Japanese customer-data system explained the problems her team was having this way: "In Japan, they want to talk and discuss. Then we take a break and they talk within the organization. They want to make sure that there's harmony in the rest of the organization. One of the hardest lessons for me was when I thought they were saying yes but they just meant 'I'm listening to you.'"

Idea in Practice

Four Barriers

The following cultural differences can cause destructive conflicts in a team:

- **Direct versus indirect communication.** Some team members use direct, explicit communication while others are indirect, for example, asking questions instead of pointing out problems with a project. When members see such differences as violations of their culture's communication norms, relationships can suffer.
- **Trouble with accents and fluency.** Members who aren't fluent in the team's dominant language may have difficulty communicating their knowledge. This can prevent the team from using their expertise and create frustration or perceptions of incompetence.
- **Differing attitudes toward hierarchy.** Team members from hierarchical cultures expect to be treated differently according to their status in the organization. Members from egalitarian cultures do not. Failure of some members to honor those expectations can cause humiliation or loss of stature and credibility.
- **Conflicting decision-making norms.** Members vary in how quickly they make decisions and in how much analysis they require beforehand. Someone who prefers making decisions quickly may grow frustrated with those who need more time.

Four Interventions

Your team's unique circumstances can help you determine how to respond to multicultural conflicts. Consider these options:

Intervention type	When to use	Example
Adaptation: working with or around differences	Members are willing to acknowledge cultural differences and figure out how to live with them.	An American engineer working on a team that included Israelis was shocked by their in-your-face, argumentative style. Once he noticed they confronted each other and not just him—and still worked well together—he realized confrontations weren't personal attacks and accepted their style.

Intervention type	When to use	Example
Structural intervention: reorganizing to reduce friction	The team has obvious subgroups, or members cling to negative stereotypes of one another.	An international research team's leader realized that when he led meetings, members "shut down" because they felt intimidated by his executive status. After he hired a consultant to run future meetings, members participated more.
Managerial intervention: making final decisions without team involvement	Rarely; for instance, a new team needs guidance in establishing productive norms.	A software development team's lingua franca was English, but some members spoke with pronounced accents. The manager explained they'd been chosen for their task expertise, not fluency in English. And she directed them to tell customers: "I realize I have an accent. If you don't understand what I'm saying, just stop me and ask questions."
Exit: voluntary or involuntary removal of a team member	Emotions are running high, and too much face has been lost on both sides to salvage the situation.	When two members of a multicultural consulting team couldn't resolve their disagreement over how to approach problems, one member left the firm.

The differences between direct and indirect communication can cause serious damage to relationships when team projects run into problems. When the American manager quoted above discovered that several flaws in the system would significantly disrupt company operations, she pointed this out in an e-mail to her American boss and the Japanese team members. Her boss appreciated the direct warnings; her Japanese colleagues were embarrassed, because she had violated their norms for uncovering and discussing problems. Their reaction was to provide her with less access to the people and information she needed to monitor progress. They would probably have responded better if she had pointed out the problems indirectly—for example, by asking them what would happen if a certain part of the system was not functioning properly, even though she knew full well that it was malfunctioning and also what the implications were.

As our research indicates is so often true, communication challenges create barriers to effective teamwork by reducing information sharing, creating interpersonal conflict, or both. In Japan, a typical response to direct confrontation is to isolate the norm violator. This American manager was isolated not just socially but also physically. She told us, "They literally put my office in a storage room, where I had desks stacked from floor to ceiling and I was the only person there. So they totally isolated me, which was a pretty loud signal to me that I was not a part of the inside circle and that they would communicate with me only as needed."

Her direct approach had been intended to solve a problem, and in one sense, it did, because her project was launched problem-free. But her norm violations exacerbated the challenges of working with her Japanese colleagues and limited her ability to uncover any other problems that might have derailed the project later on.

Trouble with accents and fluency

Although the language of international business is English, misunderstandings or deep frustration may occur because of nonnative speakers' accents, lack of fluency, or problems with translation or usage. These may also influence perceptions of status or competence.

For example, a Latin American member of a multicultural consulting team lamented, "Many times I felt that because of the language difference, I didn't have the words to say some things that I was thinking. I noticed that when I went to these interviews with the U.S. guy, he would tend to lead the interviews, which was understandable but also disappointing, because we are at the same level. I had very good questions, but he would take the lead."

When we interviewed an American member of a U.S.-Japanese team that was assessing the potential expansion of a U.S. retail chain into Japan, she described one American teammate this way: "He was not interested in the Japanese consultants' feedback and felt that because they weren't as fluent as he was, they weren't intelligent enough and, therefore, could add no value." The team member described was responsible for assessing one aspect of the feasibility of expansion into Japan. Without input from the Japanese experts, he risked overestimating opportunities and underestimating challenges.

Nonfluent team members may well be the most expert on the team, but their difficulty communicating knowledge makes it hard for the team to recognize and utilize their expertise. If teammates become frustrated or impatient with a lack of fluency, interpersonal conflicts can arise. Nonnative speakers may become less motivated to contribute, or anxious about their performance evaluations and future career prospects. The organization as a whole pays a greater price: Its investment in a multicultural team fails to pay off.

Some teams, we learned, use language differences to resolve (rather than create) tensions. A team of U.S. and Latin American buyers was negotiating with a team from a Korean supplier. The negotiations took place in Korea, but the discussions were conducted in English. Frequently the Koreans would caucus at the table by speaking Korean. The buyers, frustrated, would respond by appearing to caucus in Spanish—though they discussed only inconsequential current events and sports, in case any of the Koreans spoke Spanish. Members of the team who didn't speak Spanish pretended to participate, to the great amusement of their teammates. This approach proved effective: It conveyed to the Koreans in an appropriately indirect way that their caucuses in Korean were frustrating and annoying to the other side. As a result, both teams cut back on sidebar conversations.

Differing attitudes toward hierarchy and authority

A challenge inherent in multicultural teamwork is that by design, teams have a rather flat structure. But team members from some cultures, in which people are treated differently according to their status in an organization, are uncomfortable on flat teams. If they defer to higher-status team members, their behavior will be seen as appropriate when most of the team comes from a hierarchical culture; but they may damage their stature and credibility—and even face humiliation—if most of the team comes from an egalitarian culture.

One manager of Mexican heritage, who was working on a credit and underwriting team for a bank, told us, "In Mexican culture, you're always supposed to be humble. So whether you understand something or not, you're supposed to put it in the form of a question. You have to keep it open-ended, out of respect. I think that actually worked against me, because the Americans thought I really didn't know what I was talking about. So it made me feel like they thought I was wavering on my answer."

When, as a result of differing cultural norms, team members believe they've been treated disrespectfully, the whole project can blow up. In another Korean-U.S. negotiation, the American members of a due diligence team were having difficulty getting information from their Korean counterparts, so they complained directly to higher-level Korean management, nearly wrecking the deal. The higher-level managers were offended because hierarchy is strictly adhered to in Korean organizations and culture. It should have been their own lower-level people, not the U.S. team members, who came to them with a problem. And the Korean team members were mortified that their bosses had been involved before they themselves could brief them. The crisis was resolved only when high-level U.S. managers made a trip to Korea, conveying appropriate respect for their Korean counterparts.

Conflicting norms for decision making

Cultures differ enormously when it comes to decision making—particularly, how quickly decisions should be made and how much analysis is required beforehand. Not surprisingly, U.S. managers like to make decisions very quickly and with relatively little analysis by comparison with managers from other countries.

A Brazilian manager at an American company who was negotiating to buy Korean products destined for Latin America told us, "On the first day, we agreed on three points, and on the second day, the U.S.-Spanish side wanted to start with point four. But the Korean side wanted to go back and rediscuss points one through three. My boss almost had an attack."

What U.S. team members learn from an experience like this is that the American way simply cannot be imposed on other cultures. Managers from other cultures may, for example, decline to share information until they understand the full scope of a project. But they have learned that they can't simply ignore the desire of their American counterparts to make decisions quickly. What to do? The best solution seems to be to make minor concessions on process—to learn to adjust to and even respect another approach to decision making. For example, American managers have learned to keep their impatient bosses away from team meetings and give them frequent if brief updates. A comparable lesson for managers from other cultures is to be explicit about what they need—saying, for example, "We have to see the big picture before we talk details."

Four Strategies

The most successful teams and managers we interviewed used four strategies for dealing with these challenges: adaptation (acknowledging cultural gaps openly and working around them), structural intervention (changing the shape of the team), managerial intervention (setting norms early or bringing in a higher-level manager), and exit (removing a team member when other options have failed). There is no one right way to deal with a particular kind of multicultural problem; identifying the type of challenge is only the first step. The more crucial step is assessing the circumstances—or "enabling situational conditions"—under which the team is working. For example, does the project allow any flexibility for change, or do deadlines make that impossible? Are there additional resources available that might be tapped? Is the team permanent or temporary? Does the team's manager have the autonomy to make a decision about changing the team in some way? Once the situational conditions have been analyzed, the team's leader can identify an appropriate response (see the table "Identifying the right strategy").

Identifying the right strategy

The most successful teams and managers we interviewed use four strategies for dealing with problems: adaptation (acknowledging cultural gaps openly and working around them), structural intervention (changing the shape of the team), managerial intervention (setting norms early or bringing in a higher-level manager), and exit (removing a team member when other options have failed). Adaptation is the ideal strategy because the team works effectively to solve its own problem with minimal input from management—and, most important, learns from the experience. The guide below can help you identify the right strategy once you have identified both the problem and the "enabling situational conditions" that apply to the team.

Representative problems	Enabling situational conditions	Strategy	Complicating factors
• Conflict arises from decision-making differences • Misunderstanding or stonewalling arises from communication differences	• Team members can attribute a challenge to culture rather than personality • Higher-level managers are not available or the team would be embarrassed to involve them	**Adaptation**	• Team members must be exceptionally aware • Negotiating a common understanding takes time
• The team is affected by emotional tensions relating to fluency issues or prejudice • Team members are inhibited by perceived status differences among teammates	• The team can be subdivided to mix cultures or expertise • Tasks can be subdivided	**Structural intervention**	• If team members aren't carefully distributed, subgroups can strengthen preexisting differences • Subgroup solutions have to fit back together

Representative problems	Enabling situational conditions	Strategy	Complicating factors
• Violations of hierarchy have resulted in loss of face • An absence of ground rules is causing conflict	• The problem has produced a high level of emotion • The team has reached a stalemate • A higher-level manager is able and willing to intervene	**Managerial intervention**	• The team becomes overly dependent on the manager • Team members may be sidelined or resistant
• A team member cannot adjust to the challenge at hand and has become unable to contribute to the project	• The team is permanent rather than temporary • Emotions are beyond the point of intervention • Too much face has been lost	**Exit**	• Talent and training costs are lost

Adaptation

Some teams find ways to work with or around the challenges they face, adapting practices or attitudes without making changes to the group's membership or assignments. Adaptation works when team members are willing to acknowledge and name their cultural differences and to assume responsibility for figuring out how to live with them. It's often the best possible approach to a problem, because it typically involves less managerial time than other strategies; and because team members participate in solving the problem themselves, they learn from the process. When team members have this mind-set, they can be creative about protecting their own substantive differences while acceding to the processes of others.

An American software engineer located in Ireland who was working with an Israeli account management team from his own company told us how shocked he was by the Israelis' in-your-face style: "There were definitely different ways of approaching issues and discussing them. There is something pretty common to the Israeli culture: They like to argue. I tend to try to collaborate more, and it got very stressful for me until I figured out how to kind of merge the cultures."

The software engineer adapted. He imposed some structure on the Israelis that helped him maintain his own style of being thoroughly prepared; that accommodation enabled him to accept the Israeli style. He also noticed that team members weren't just confronting him; they confronted one another but were able to work together effectively nevertheless. He realized that the confrontation was not personal but cultural.

In another example, an American member of a postmerger consulting team was frustrated by the hierarchy of the French company his team was working with. He felt that a meeting with certain French managers who were not directly involved in the merger "wouldn't deliver any value to me or for purposes of the project," but said that he had come to understand that "it was very important to really involve all the people there" if the integration was ultimately to work.

A U.S. and UK multicultural team tried to use their differing approaches to decision making to reach a higher-quality decision. This approach, called fusion, is getting serious attention from political scientists and from government officials dealing with multicultural populations that want to protect their cultures rather than integrate or assimilate. If the team had relied exclusively on the Americans' "forge ahead" approach, it might not have recognized the pitfalls that lay ahead and might later have had to back up and start over. Meanwhile, the UK members would have been gritting their teeth and saying "We told you things were moving too fast." If the team had used the "Let's think about this" UK approach, it might have wasted a lot of time trying to identify every pitfall, including the most unlikely, while the U.S. members chomped at the bit and muttered about analysis paralysis. The strength of this team was that some of its members were willing to forge ahead and some were willing to work through pitfalls. To accommodate them all, the team did both—moving not quite as fast as the U.S. members would have on their own and not quite as thoroughly as the UK members would have.

Structural intervention

A structural intervention is a deliberate reorganization or reassignment designed to reduce interpersonal friction or to remove a source of conflict for one or more groups. This approach can be extremely effective when obvious subgroups demarcate the team (for example, headquarters versus national subsidiaries) or if team members are proud, defensive, threatened, or clinging to negative stereotypes of one another.

A member of an investment research team scattered across continental Europe, the UK, and the U.S. described for us how his manager resolved conflicts stemming from status differences and language tensions among the team's three "tribes." The manager started by having the team meet face-to-face twice a year, not to discuss mundane day-to-day problems (of which there were many) but to identify a set of values that the team would use to direct and evaluate its progress. At the first meeting, he realized that when he started to speak, everyone else "shut down," waiting to hear what he had to say. So he hired a consultant to run future meetings. The consultant didn't represent a hierarchical threat and was therefore able to get lots of participation from team members.

Another structural intervention might be to create smaller working groups of mixed cultures or mixed corporate identities in order to get at information that is not forthcoming from the team as a whole. The manager of the team that was evaluating retail opportunities in Japan used this approach. When she realized that the female Japanese consultants would not participate if the group got large, or if their male superior was present, she broke the team up into smaller groups to try to solve problems. She used this technique repeatedly and made a point of changing the subgroups' membership each time so that team members got to know and respect everyone else on the team.

The subgrouping technique involves risks, however. It buffers people who are not working well together or not participating in the larger group for one reason or another. Sooner or later the team will have to assemble the pieces that the subgroups have come up with, so this approach relies on another structural intervention: Someone must become a mediator in order to see that the various pieces fit together.

Managerial intervention

When a manager behaves like an arbitrator or a judge, making a final decision without team involvement, neither the manager nor the team gains much insight into why the team has stalemated. But it is possible for team members to use managerial intervention effectively to sort out problems.

When an American refinery-safety expert with significant experience throughout East Asia got stymied during a project in China, she called in her company's higher-level managers in Beijing to talk to the higher-level managers to whom the Chinese refinery's managers reported. Unlike the Western team members who breached etiquette by approaching the superiors of their Korean counterparts, the safety expert made sure to respect hierarchies in both organizations.

"Trying to resolve the issues," she told us, "the local management at the Chinese refinery would end up having conferences with our Beijing office and also with the upper management within the refinery. Eventually they understood that we weren't trying to insult them or their culture or to tell them they were bad in any way. We were trying to help. They eventually understood that there were significant fire and safety issues. But we actually had to go up some levels of management to get those resolved."

Managerial intervention to set norms early in a team's life can really help the team start out with effective processes. In one instance reported to us, a multicultural software development team's lingua franca was English, but some members, though they spoke grammatically correct English, had a very pronounced accent. In setting the ground rules for the team, the manager addressed the challenge directly, telling the members that they had been chosen for their task expertise, not their fluency in English, and that the team was going to have to work around language problems. As the project moved to the customer-services training stage, the manager advised the team members to acknowledge their accents up front.

She said they should tell customers, "I realize I have an accent. If you don't understand what I'm saying, just stop me and ask questions."

Exit

Possibly because many of the teams we studied were project based, we found that leaving the team was an infrequent strategy for managing challenges. In short-term situations, unhappy team members often just waited out the project. When teams were permanent, producing products or services, the exit of one or more members was a strategy of last resort, but it was used—either voluntarily or after a formal request from management. Exit was likely when emotions were running high and too much face had been lost on both sides to salvage the situation.

An American member of a multicultural consulting team described the conflict between two senior consultants, one a Greek woman and the other a Polish man, over how to approach problems: "The woman from Greece would say, 'Here's the way I think we should do it.' It would be something that she was in control of. The guy from Poland would say, 'I think we should actually do it this way instead.' The woman would kind of turn red in the face, upset, and say, 'I just don't think that's the right way of doing it.' It would definitely switch from just professional differences to personal differences.

"The woman from Greece ended up leaving the firm. That was a direct result of probably all the different issues going on between these people. It really just wasn't a good fit. I've found that oftentimes when you're in consulting, you have to adapt to the culture, obviously, but you have to adapt just as much to the style of whoever is leading the project."

Though multicultural teams face challenges that are not directly attributable to cultural differences, such differences underlay whatever problem needed to be addressed in many of the teams we studied. Furthermore, while serious in their own right when they have a negative effect on team functioning, cultural challenges may also unmask fundamental managerial problems. Managers who intervene early and set norms; teams and managers who structure social interaction and work to engage everyone on the team; and teams that can see problems as stemming from culture, not personality, approach challenges with good humor and creativity. Managers who have to intervene when the team has reached a stalemate may be able to get the team moving again, but they seldom empower it to help itself the next time a stalemate occurs.

When frustrated team members take some time to think through challenges and possible solutions themselves, it can make a huge difference. Take, for example, this story about a financial-services call center. The members of the call-center team were all fluent Spanish-speakers, but some were North Americans and some were Latin Americans. Team performance, measured by calls answered per hour, was lagging. One Latin American was taking twice as long with her calls as the rest of the team. She was handling callers' questions appropriately, but she was also engaging in chitchat. When her teammates confronted her for being a free rider (they resented having to make up for her low call rate), she immediately acknowledged the problem, admitting that she did not know how to end the call politely—chitchat being normal in her culture. They rallied to help her: Using their technology, they would break into any of her calls that went overtime, excusing themselves to the customer, offering to take over the call, and saying that this employee was urgently needed to help out on a different call. The team's solution worked in the short run, and the employee got better at ending her calls in the long run.

In another case, the Indian manager of a multicultural team coordinating a companywide IT project found himself frustrated when he and a teammate from Singapore met with two Japanese members of the coordinating team to try to get the Japan section to deliver its part of the project. The Japanese members seemed to be saying yes, but in the Indian manager's view, their follow-through was insufficient. He considered and rejected the idea of going up the hierarchy to the Japanese team members' boss, and decided instead to try to build consensus with the whole Japanese IT team, not just the two members on the coordinating team. He and his Singapore teammate put together an eBusiness road show, took it to Japan, invited the whole IT team to view it at a lunch meeting, and walked through success stories about other parts of the organization that had aligned with the company's larger business priorities. It was rather subtle, he told us, but it worked. The Japanese IT team wanted to be spotlighted in future eBusiness road shows. In the end, the whole team worked well together—and no higher-level manager had to get involved.

Originally published in November 2006. Reprint R0611D

L'Oréal Masters Multiculturalism

by Hae-Jung Hong and Yves L. Doz

AT THE HEART OF EVERY global business lies a tension that is never fully resolved: Achieving economies of scale and scope demands some uniformity and integration of activities across markets. However, serving regional and national markets requires the adaptation of products, services, and business models to local conditions. As U.S. and European companies increasingly look for customers in emerging economies, both the advantages of global scale and the need for local differentiation will only increase.

It's easy to get the balance wrong. Some offerings may feel like commodities—think refrigerators and washing machines—yet there are often important variations in the way people use them. An Italian washing machine, for instance, has to be made to rather different specs than a Swedish one. Others, such as restaurants and cafés, come across as intrinsically local, yet global formulas and brands do succeed—think Benihana, Wagamama, and Starbucks.

The tension between global integration and local responsiveness is especially high when product development and marketing require complex knowledge. This kind of knowledge—usually tacit and collective, revealed only in action and interaction—is often the mainspring of a company's competitive advantage. The trouble is that tacit knowledge functions best within national boundaries, where workers share a language and cultural and institutional norms and can draw on strong interpersonal networks. Without close, face-to-face interaction between knowledge creators and users, an understanding of how bits of information fit together may be lost and the knowledge may become unusable. Further, when tacit knowledge must cross borders, it is often reduced to information that moves easily (words and numbers, for instance) but may then fall prey to local misinterpretations that are difficult to detect from afar.

The French cosmetics giant L'Oréal exemplifies this global-local tension. It has built a portfolio of brands from many cultures—French, of course (L'Oréal Paris, Garnier, Lancôme), but also American (Maybelline, Kiehl's, SoftSheen-Carson), British (The Body Shop), Italian (Giorgio Armani), and Japanese (Shu Uemura). The company now has offices in more than 130 countries, and in 2012 over half its sales came from new markets outside Europe and North America, mostly in emerging economies, up from only a third as recently as 2009.

In 2012, sales grew in the Asia Pacific region by 18.4% and in Africa and the Middle East by 17.6%, without significant acquisitions. Despite the financial crises in Europe and North America, L'Oréal has been growing and gaining market share, mostly at the expense of its competitors. It is the uncontested world leader in skin care, makeup, and hair color and a close second to P&G in hair care worldwide. Since 2004 L'Oréal's revenue has increased by half and its profits have almost doubled, with an increase in net profits of 17.6% in 2012 alone.

Yet this remarkable global success was built largely by a management team strongly rooted in its home culture. Traditionally employees became part of management over many years, weaving a dense network of relationships through which knowledge about products, cultures, and how to work together was internalized. Since its inception, more than a century ago, L'Oréal has had only five CEOs (including the founder), all but one with long tenures and all promoted from within. Only a few foreigners have become senior executives. Lindsay Owen-Jones, who was CEO from 1988 to 2006, was one of them. Although an Englishman, he was described

Idea in Brief

As the cosmetics company L'Oréal has transformed itself from a very French business into a global leader, it has grappled with the tension that's at the heart of every global enterprise: Achieving economies of scale and scope requires some uniformity and integration of activities across markets. However, serving regional and national markets requires the adaptation of products, services, and business models to local conditions.

Since the late 1990s, the L'Oréal Paris brand—which accounts for half the sales of the consumer products division—has dealt with that tension by nurturing a pool of managers with mixed cultural backgrounds, placing them at the center of knowledge-based interactions in the company's most critical activity: new-product development. L'Oréal Paris builds product development teams around these managers, who, by virtue of their upbringing and experiences, have gained familiarity with the norms and behaviors of multiple cultures and can switch easily among them.

They are uniquely qualified to play several crucial roles: spotting new-product opportunities, facilitating communication across cultural boundaries, assimilating newcomers, and serving as a cultural buffer between executives and their direct reports and between subsidiaries and headquarters.

by members of L'Oréal's founding family as *Français dans l'âme* ("French in his soul"). For decades, L'Oréal recruited few senior executives from outside. After several years the exceptions took pains to explain that they had worked for L'Oréal for a long time and prided themselves on their perfect French.

As its global-local tensions have mounted, L'Oréal has managed them by deploying professionals with multicultural backgrounds in new-product development, the company's most critical source of competitive advantage. That strategy, according to top management, is the main reason for L'Oréal's impressive success in emerging markets. As the company has transformed itself from a very French beauty products business to a global leader, multicultural executives have come to play a critical role in product development not just in Paris but also in New York, Tokyo, Shanghai, Rio, and Mumbai.

Achieving Global-Local Balance

L'Oréal's main consumer-products categories are all highly sensitive to global economies of scale and scope, yet to win customers they must also be responsive to local preferences. This tension is perhaps most critical in the L'Oréal Paris brand, which is sold in mass markets worldwide and accounts for half the sales of the consumer products division.

L'Oréal also has to maintain a steady stream of new products (every year, roughly 20% are new) in order to extend market share in the face of stiff competition from rivals such as Estée Lauder and Revlon and units of global giants such as Unilever and P&G. L'Oréal, which invests 3.5% of its revenue in R&D, outspends all its major competitors: Revlon, for instance, spends 1.7% on R&D, and Estée Lauder about 1%.

As L'Oréal managers confront those challenges, they must be mindful that their products are much more than chemical mixes. They are global symbols of fashion and sophistication, appealing to the idealized self-image of customers. Technical innovation and responsiveness to local tastes must not undermine the brand.

Traditional approaches to internationalization probably would not have resolved L'Oréal's global-local tensions. Structural solutions, such as setting up largely autonomous subsidiaries and regional entities (which might have compromised economies of scale) or global business units (which might have ignored the richness of cultural differences across markets), would not have worked for most L'Oréal products, given their need for both local responsiveness and global integration. Refocusing the company on either a more local or a more global portfolio would have been tantamount to letting the tail wag the dog, forfeiting L'Oréal's many marketing and distribution advantages.

The only alternative to internationalizing the structure was to internationalize the management team. That is what L'Oréal did, but with a twist. The rapid infusion of foreign executives would have disrupted the tightly knit community of senior managers so critical to L'Oréal's success. Relying on global teams—whether function- or project-based—would have been equally difficult. Culturally diverse teams often experience the so-called Tower of Babel syndrome: Their members talk past one another, and teamwork breaks down. Companies quickly realize that little knowledge is actually shared; even seemingly universal and explicit knowledge, such as mathematics, is open to interpretation.

L'Oréal has dealt with these shortcomings by recruiting and building teams around individual managers, who by virtue of their upbringing and experience have gained familiarity with the norms and behaviors of multiple cultures and can switch easily among them.

International Talent

Since the late 1990s, when L'Oréal started to recruit internationally for positions at headquarters, L'Oréal Paris—the unit where we conducted our research—has placed executives from mixed cultural backgrounds in its most critical activity: new-product development. These managers account for a small proportion of L'Oréal Paris employees but for more than a third of the unit's product development team managers—a balance the unit has maintained for more than 10 years.

L'Oréal Paris generally has about 40 product development teams, each working on a different concept. A team consists of three or four people, two of whom may be multicultural. For example, in a team we spoke with that is working on women's hair-care products for Latin America, a Lebanese-Spanish-American manager was in charge of hair color while a French-Irish-Cambodian was in charge of hair care. They shared an office so that they could exchange ideas.

Developing a new product takes at least a year of knowledge exchanges among the product development team, regional subsidiaries, and functional units in France, such as R&D. In addition to interacting with their peers, who may come from different cultures, team managers must discuss their work with top management, formally and informally, as it progresses.

Once a new-product concept is ready, the team presents it at Réunion Internationale, the consumer products division's annual event, held at the Paris headquarters. The teams pitch their launch action plans to regional directors from around the globe, who come looking for ideas that might be ready to hit the market in one or two years.

The multicultural managers are drawn from three pools. The most seasoned come from the company's international subsidiaries and have at least five years of experience in sales and marketing. A few are recruited from other global companies. The third and youngest group consists of graduates of leading international business schools. The recruits undergo a 12-month training program in Paris, New York, Singapore, or Rio, followed by management development programs at Cedep, an executive education consortium in France.

After spending two or three years in global product development at headquarters, the more experienced managers usually return to their home regions as directors, responsible for managing a brand or function. Most of those recruited from business schools remain for another few years in product development at headquarters. After this second tour they, too, usually go to a regional office at the director level, though some remain in Paris. Their promotion prospects, like those of all employees, depend on performance.

An increasing number of multiculturals are starting to find their way into senior management in the company—a sign of the success of the approach. Among the people we met, one Hong Kong–British–French project manager (recruited at headquarters) was subsequently promoted to lead the team developing all facial products for the East Asian market, and an Indian-American-French project manager (recruited from the Indian subsidiary) moved to another division with a significant promotion.

In sum—and there is an important message here for other multinational companies—L'Oréal nurtures a pool of multicultural managers, placing them at the center of knowledge-based interactions among brands, regions, and functions. Let's look at what these young men and women offer the company in return.

The Advantages of Multiculturals

A person rooted in more than one culture is usually able to spot and reconcile differences in understanding and communication, serving as a buffer both within teams and more broadly in the organization. In addition, he or she will probably be more open to adapting to multiple mind-sets and communication modes; it's well known that people find it easier to learn new languages if they have grown up speaking more than one. These skills equip L'Oréal's multiculturals to play five critical roles.

Recognizing new-product opportunities

L'Oréal Paris finds that multiculturals are better placed than others to draw analogies among cultural groups. According to a director who worked with multiculturals for five years, "Their background is a kind of master class in holding more than one idea at the same time. They think as if they were French, American, or Chinese, and all of these together at once."

This very flexible perspective can lead to unexpected opportunities for product innovation. For instance, a French-Irish-Cambodian manager working on skin care noticed that many tinted face creams in Asia had a lifting effect, which minimizes wrinkles. In Europe, creams tended to be either tinted (and considered as makeup) or lifting (and considered as skin care). Drawing on his knowledge of Asian beauty trends and their increasing popularity in Europe, he and his team developed a tinted cream with lifting effects for the French market, which proved to be a success.

Although people rooted in one culture can also uncover such opportunities, multiculturals are more likely to do so—and to do so faster—because they have been dealing with cultural complexities since childhood. As an Indian-American-French manager in a team that launched a men's skin care line in Southeast Asia explained, "I am able to do this because I have a stock of references in different languages: English, Hindi, and French. I read books in three different languages, meet people from different countries, eat food from different countries, and so on. I cannot think about things in one way."

Preventing losses in translation

Even when there's a common syntax or language, as in mathematical and chemical formulas, cross-cultural semantic differences can cause confusion. What the person initiating a communication means is not necessarily what the person receiving the communication hears. The problem thus shifts to who interprets what, and how accurately—a critical issue in the design of new products.

For instance, a French manager's product test failed because he asked a German colleague in the laboratory to translate the characterization of some hair features. Through conversations with an English-French-German manager, the French manager discovered that there had been a gap between what he meant and what the German heard. It was a nuanced difference: The words were the same, but their meaning was not. He had to run the test again, at significant cost. Since then, the multicultural manager who spotted the difference has been called on frequently to decode communications between headquarters and the German office.

Integrating outsiders

Teams staffed with people who are not multicultural find it hard to assimilate newcomers with different behaviors and modes of communication, particularly when the team has developed its own norms or its members belong predominantly to one culture. Given the intensity of a team's internal interactions, incumbent team members can quickly resort to stereotypes about a newcomer, and the situation can become toxic. The presence of a multicultural member can help prevent this dynamic from taking hold.

Consider the experience of a Hong Kong–British–French director: "After a new person joined my team from the Shanghai office, a member complained that she was 'very rude.' I said, 'Let's give her more time to adjust. Maybe she's not being rude and that's just how she expresses herself. Why don't you also try to adapt to her?' When I went to Shanghai, I had a meeting with my new team member and found she was not being rude. The way she expressed herself was direct, without bad intention. I didn't tell her about the complaints but gave some advice on how to better work with people whose cultures are different. When I returned to HQ, I told my group about my experience with the new member. Things became much better."

Emulating multicultural managers

Managers rooted in more than one culture have many skills that allow them to fill five crucial roles. Other managers can learn to play the first two roles through training and management development programs. But the final three roles are based on skills acquired through early life experiences and are therefore more difficult for others to learn. The careful management of international assignments can help. Be cautious about short-term rotations: Without deep exposure to national contexts, managers concentrate on what's common across cultures instead of what's different. As a result, their cultural sensitivity is dulled rather than sharpened.

Role	How multiculturals do it	How others can learn
1. Recognizing new-product opportunities	Sensitivity to one's own and others' cultures	Training with multiculturals and repatriates
2. Preventing losses in translation	Cultural awareness and curiosity	One-on-one coaching by multiculturals
3. Integrating outsiders	Cultural empathy	Regular evaluation by an HR specialist knowledgeable about multiculturals' competence and skills
4. Mediating with bosses	Multilingual skills	Foreign language and semantics training
5. Bridging differences between subsidiaries and headquarters	Contextual understanding and sensitivity	Enhanced promotion prospects for foreign language speakers
	Semantic awareness	Opportunities to carry out leadership responsibilities in a foreign language
	Ability to switch among cultural frames of reference and communication modes	

If a newcomer is disruptive because of personal style or personality, there may be little anyone can do. But if the issue originates in cultural differences, which it often does, multiculturals can help integrate the outsider. They can perform this function because they are adept at moving from one mode of interaction to another. They grew up doing so—switching from one parent to another, or from school to home.

Mediating with bosses

The role of cultural buffer is important at L'Oréal Paris, especially for reducing the potential for conflicts between the multicultural product-development teams and the people they report to, who are, for the most part, French. Here's how a multicultural manager explained one aspect of his role as team leader: "My French boss never starts meetings on time. So whenever we have a meeting planned with him, we can get frustrated if we are not flexible. If I am running behind myself, I make sure to tell my team members in advance why I am behind and ask them for their next availabilities. Conflicts may still exist in my team, but we handle them more tolerantly."

Bridging differences between subsidiaries and headquarters

Multicultural managers have frequently defused acrimonious communications between a subsidiary and L'Oréal Paris. For example, on a project to develop an organic shampoo for the European market, the product development team in Paris asked the Indian unit to find a rare local plant that would provide a key ingredient. The Indians told the team that they would "do their best" but sat on the request. As the team's Indian-American-French leader told us, "Eventually the Indian manager said, 'We need confirmation that this ingredient can really please consumers.'"

At this point, the team leader understood that the initial "We'll do our best" (which the French interpreted as a clear yes) was actually a polite way of saying that they wouldn't do anything. The "We need confirmation" follow-up signaled that the request was too difficult—but the Indians did not want to come out and say that and thus fail to honor a commitment. The leader realized that if he told headquarters that India wouldn't come up with the goods, he risked triggering open conflict between the two parties. Instead, he worked with both to explore other ingredients that would not be so challenging to source.

The team leader grasped that there had not yet been enough collaboration or social interaction between the two teams to allow them to decode each other's expressions of expectations. He could also see that this particular misunderstanding might undermine trust and make more-important tasks harder. (Ultimately he found a substitute ingredient and dropped the matter.) This manager could play a bridging role because he had deep knowledge about both Indian and French ways of expressing commitment, strong communication skills, intense cultural sensitivity, and high flexibility—a bundle of qualities seldom found among managers rooted in just one culture.

For a global company to deploy multiculturals strategically, HR should appoint a manager to lead a program for developing and nurturing them. This manager should obviously be knowledgeable about the competence and skills of these individuals and how they differ from those of other employees. Because of considerable variation among multiculturals themselves, the manager needs to tailor a training system to each one. With this support, commitment to the program from top managers, and the granting of some autonomy in their work, multicultural managers can make a huge difference in whether a company is able to balance global and local imperatives by learning from cultural differences—or instead suffers from them.

As markets and competencies have become more dispersed and differentiated with the strategic thrust into emerging regions, companies need to reverse the old knowledge flows (from their home country to far-flung subsidiaries) and instead learn how to learn from their peripheries. Culturally this is difficult. It calls for a shift from an ethnocentric approach to a truly global network. L'Oréal's strategic use of multicultural managers provides a shortcut: These managers can integrate knowledge from many locations to develop successful new products and minimize conflict between home-country and international executives. It's an approach that can transfer easily to other industry and functional contexts in which complex knowledge from multiple cultures must be coordinated and shared.

Originally published in June 2013. Reprint R1306J

Making Differences Matter

A New Paradigm for Managing Diversity. *by David A. Thomas and Robin J. Ely*

WHY SHOULD COMPANIES CONCERN THEMSELVES with diversity? Until recently, many managers answered this question with the assertion that discrimination is wrong, both legally and morally. But today managers are voicing a second notion as well. A more diverse workforce, they say, will increase organizational effectiveness. It will lift morale, bring greater access to new segments of the marketplace, and enhance productivity. In short, they claim, diversity will be good for business.

Yet if this is true—and we believe it is—where are the positive impacts of diversity? Numerous and varied initiatives to increase diversity in corporate America have been under way for more than two decades. Rarely, however, have those efforts spurred leaps in organizational effectiveness. Instead, many attempts to increase diversity in the workplace have backfired, sometimes even heightening tensions among employees and hindering a company's performance.

This article offers an explanation for why diversity efforts are not fulfilling their promise and presents a new paradigm for understanding—and leveraging—diversity. It is our belief that there is a distinct way to unleash the powerful benefits of a diverse workforce. Although these benefits include increased profitability, they go beyond financial measures to encompass learning, creativity, flexibility, organizational and individual growth, and the ability of a company to adjust rapidly and successfully to market changes. The desired transformation, however, requires a fundamental change in the attitudes and behaviors of an organization's leadership. And that will come only when senior managers abandon an underlying and flawed assumption about diversity and replace it with a broader understanding.

Most people assume that workplace diversity is about increasing racial, national, gender, or class representation—in other words, recruiting and retaining more people from traditionally underrepresented "identity groups." Taking this commonly held assumption as a starting point, we set out six years ago to investigate its link to organizational effectiveness. We soon found that thinking of diversity simply in terms of identity-group representation inhibited effectiveness.

Organizations usually take one of two paths in managing diversity. In the name of equality and fairness, they encourage (and expect) women and people of color to blend in. Or they set them apart in jobs that relate specifically to their backgrounds, assigning them, for example, to areas that require them to interface with clients or customers of the same identity group. African American M.B.A.'s often find themselves marketing products to inner-city communities; Hispanics frequently market to Hispanics or work for Latin American subsidiaries. In those kinds of cases, companies are operating on the assumption that the main virtue identity groups have to offer is a knowledge of their own people. This assumption is limited—and limiting—and detrimental to diversity efforts.

What we suggest here is that diversity goes beyond increasing the number of different identity-group affiliations on the payroll to recognizing that such an effort is merely the first step in managing a diverse workforce for the organization's utmost benefit. Diversity should be understood as *the varied perspectives and approaches to work* that members of different identity groups bring.

Idea in Brief

You know that workforce diversity is smart business: It opens markets, lifts morale, and enhances productivity. So why do most diversity initiatives backfire—heightening tensions and *hindering* corporate performance?

Many of us simply hire employees with diverse backgrounds—then await the payoff. We don't enable employees' differences to transform *how our organization does work*.

When employees use their differences to shape new goals, processes, leadership approaches, and teams, they bring more of themselves to work. They feel more committed to their jobs—and their companies grow.

How to activate this virtuous cycle? Transcend two existing diversity paradigms: **assimilation** ("we're all the same") or **differentiation** ("we celebrate differences"). Adopt a new paradigm—**integration**—that enables employees' differences to matter.

Women, Hispanics, Asian Americans, African Americans, Native Americans—these groups and others outside the mainstream of corporate America don't bring with them just their "insider information." They bring different, important, and competitively relevant knowledge and perspectives about how to actually *do work*—how to design processes, reach goals, frame tasks, create effective teams, communicate ideas, and lead. When allowed to, members of these groups can help companies grow and improve by challenging basic assumptions about an organization's functions, strategies, operations, practices, and procedures. And in doing so, they are able to bring more of their whole selves to the workplace and identify more fully with the work they do, setting in motion a virtuous circle. Certainly, individvuals can be expected to contribute to a company their firsthand familiarity with niche markets. But only when companies start thinking about diversity more holistically—as providing fresh and meaningful approaches to work—and stop assuming that diversity relates simply to how a person looks or where he or she comes from, will they be able to reap its full rewards.

Two perspectives have guided most diversity initiatives to date: the *discrimination-and-fairness paradigm* and the *access-and-legitimacy paradigm*. But we have identified a new, emerging

Idea in Practice

	Assimilation paradigm	Differentiation paradigm
Premise	"We're all the same."	"We celebrate differences."
Strategy	Hire diverse employees; encourage uniform behavior.	Match diverse employees to niche markets.
Advantage	Promotes fair hiring.	Expands markets.
Disadvantages	Subverting differences to encourage harmony, companies miss out on new ideas. Feeling detached from their work, employees' underperform.	Pigeonholed, staff can't influence mainstream work. Employees feel exploited and excluded from other opportunities.
Example	At a consulting company emphasizing quantitative analysis, minority managers encounter skepticism when they suggest interviewing clients. Labeling the incident as racial discord, the firm doesn't explore the potentially valuable new consulting approach.	To improve oversees operations, a U.S. bank assigns Europeans to its foreign offices. They excel—but the company doesn't know why. Not integrating diversity into its culture and practices, it becomes vulnerable: "If the French team resigns, what will we do?!"

approach to this complex management issue. This approach, which we call the *learning-and-effectiveness paradigm,* incorporates aspects of the first two paradigms but goes beyond them by concretely connecting diversity to approaches to work. Our goal is to help business leaders see what their own approach to diversity currently is and how it may already have influenced their companies' diversity efforts. Managers can learn to assess whether they need to

The Integration Paradigm

The **integration paradigm** *transcends* assimilation and differentiation—promoting equal opportunity *and* valuing cultural differences. Result? Employees' diverse perspectives positively impact companies' work.

> *Example*: A public-interest law firm's all-white staff's clients are exclusively white. It hires female attorneys of color, who encourage it to pursue litigation challenging English-only policies. Since such cases didn't fall under traditional affirmative-action work, the firm had ignored them. By taking them, it begins serving more women—immigrants—and enhances the quality of its work. The attorneys of color feel valued, and the firm attracts competent, diverse staff.

Additional suggestions for achieving integration:

1. **Encourage open discussion of cultural backgrounds.**

   Example: A food company's Chinese chemist draws on her cooking—not her scientific—experience to solve a soup-flavoring problem. But to fit in, she avoids sharing the real source of her inspiration with her colleagues—all white men. Open discussion of cultural differences would engage her more fully in work and workplace relationships.

2. **Eliminate all forms of dominance (by hierarchy, function, race, gender, etc.) that inhibit full contribution.** When one firm opened its annual strategy conference to people from all hierarchy levels, everyone knew their contributions were valued.

3. **Secure organizational trust.** In diverse workforces, people share more feelings and ideas. Tensions naturally arise. Demonstrate your commitment to diversity by acknowledging tensions—and resolving them swiftly.

change their diversity initiatives and, if so, how to accomplish that change.

The following discussion will also cite several examples of how connecting the new definition of diversity to the actual *doing* of work has led some organizations to markedly better performance. The organizations differ in many ways—none are in the same industry, for instance—but they are united by one similarity: Their leaders realize that increasing demographic variation does not in itself increase organizational effectiveness. They realize that it is *how* a company defines diversity—and *what it does* with the experiences of being a diverse organization—that delivers on the promise.

The Discrimination-and-Fairness Paradigm

Using the discrimination-and-fairness paradigm is perhaps thus far the dominant way of understanding diversity. Leaders who look at diversity through this lens usually focus on equal opportunity, fair treatment, recruitment, and compliance with federal Equal Employment Opportunity requirements. The paradigm's underlying logic can be expressed as follows:

> Prejudice has kept members of certain demographic groups out of organizations such as ours. As a matter of fairness and to comply with federal mandates, we need to work toward restructuring the makeup of our organization to let it more closely reflect that of society. We need managerial processes that ensure that all our employees are treated equally and with respect and that some are not given unfair advantage over others.

Although it resembles the thinking behind traditional affirmative-action efforts, the discrimination-and-fairness paradigm does go beyond a simple concern with numbers. Companies that operate with this philosophical orientation often institute mentoring and career-development programs specifically for the women and people of color in their ranks and train other employees to respect cultural differences. Under this paradigm, nevertheless, progress in diversity is measured by how well the company achieves its recruitment and retention goals rather than by the degree to which conditions in the company allow employees to draw on their personal assets and perspectives to do their work more effectively. The staff, one might say, gets diversified, but the work does not.

What are some of the common characteristics of companies that have used the discrimination-and-fairness paradigm successfully to increase their demographic diversity? Our research indicates that they are usually run by leaders who value due process and equal treatment of all employees and who have the authority to use top-down directives to enforce initiatives based on those attitudes. Such companies are often bureaucratic in structure, with control processes in place for monitoring, measuring, and rewarding individual performance. And finally, they are often organizations with entrenched, easily observable cultures, in which values like fairness are widespread and deeply inculcated and codes of conduct are clear and unambiguous. (Perhaps the most extreme example of an organization in which all these factors are at work is the United States Army.)

Without doubt, there are benefits to this paradigm: it does tend to increase demographic diversity in an organization, and it often succeeds in promoting fair treatment. But it also has significant limitations. The first of these is that its color-blind, gender-blind ideal is to some degree built on the implicit assumption that "we are all the same" or "we aspire to being all the same." Under this paradigm, it is not desirable for diversification of the workforce to influence the organization's work or culture. The company should operate as if every person were of the same race, gender, and nationality. It is unlikely that leaders who manage diversity under this paradigm will explore how people's differences generate a potential diversity of effective ways of working, leading, viewing the market, managing people, and learning.

Not only does the discrimination-and-fairness paradigm insist that everyone is the same, but, with its emphasis on equal treatment, it puts pressure on employees to make sure that important differences among them do not count. Genuine disagreements about work definition, therefore, are sometimes wrongly interpreted through this paradigm's fairness-unfairness lens—especially when honest disagreements are accompanied by tense debate. A female employee who insists, for example, that a company's advertising strategy is not appropriate for all ethnic segments in the marketplace might feel she is violating the code of assimilation upon which the paradigm is built. Moreover, if she were then to defend her opinion by citing, let us say, her personal knowledge of the ethnic group the company wanted to reach, she might risk being perceived as importing inappropriate attitudes into an organization that prides itself on being blind to cultural differences.

Workplace paradigms channel organizational thinking in powerful ways. By limiting the ability of employees to acknowledge openly their work-related but culturally based differences, the paradigm actually undermines the organization's capacity to learn about and improve its own strategies, processes, and practices. And it also keeps people from identifying strongly and personally with their work—a critical source of motivation and self-regulation in any business environment.

As an illustration of the paradigm's weaknesses, consider the case of Iversen Dunham, an international consulting firm that focuses on foreign and domestic economic-development policy. (Like all the examples in this article, the company is real, but its name is disguised.) Not long ago, the firm's managers asked us to help them understand why race relations had become a divisive issue precisely at a time when Iversen was receiving accolades for its diversity efforts. Indeed, other organizations had even begun to use the firm to benchmark their own diversity programs.

Iversen's diversity efforts had begun in the early 1970s, when senior managers decided to pursue greater racial and gender diversity in the firm's higher ranks. (The firm's leaders were strongly committed to the cause of social justice.) Women and people of color were hired and charted on career paths toward becoming project leaders. High performers among those who had left the firm were persuaded to return in senior roles. By 1989, about 50% of Iversen's project leaders and professionals were women, and 30% were people of color. The 13-member management committee, once exclusively white and male, included five women and four people of color. Additionally, Iversen had developed a strong contingent of foreign nationals.

It was at about this time, however, that tensions began to surface. Senior managers found it hard to believe that, after all the effort to create a fair and mutually respectful work community, some staff members could still be claiming that Iversen had racial discrimination problems. The management invited us to study the firm and deliver an outsider's assessment of its problem.

We had been inside the firm for only a short time when it became clear that Iversen's leaders viewed the dynamics of diversity through the lens of the discrimination-and-fairness paradigm. But where they saw racial discord, we discerned clashing approaches to the actual work of consulting. Why? Our research showed that tensions were strongest among midlevel project leaders. Surveys and interviews indicated that white project leaders welcomed demographic diversity as a general sign of progress but that they also thought the new employees were somehow changing the company, pulling it away from its original culture and its mission. Common criticisms were that African American and Hispanic staff made problems too complex by linking issues the organization had traditionally regarded as unrelated and that they brought on projects that seemed to require greater cultural sensitivity. White male project leaders also complained that their peers who were women and people of color were undermining one of Iversen's traditional strengths: its hard-core quantitative orientation. For instance, minority project leaders had suggested that Iversen consultants collect information and seek input from others in the client company besides senior managers—that is, from the rank and file and from middle managers. Some had urged Iversen to expand its consulting approach to include the gathering and analysis of qualitative data through interviewing and observation. Indeed, these project leaders had even challenged one of Iversen's longstanding, core assumptions: that the firm's reports were objective. They urged Iversen Dunham to recognize and address the subjective aspect of its analyses; the firm could, for example, include in its reports to clients dissenting Iversen views, if any existed.

For their part, project leaders who were women and people of color felt that they were not accorded the same level of authority to carry out that work as their white male peers. Moreover, they sensed that those peers were skeptical of their opinions, and they resented that doubts were not voiced openly.

Meanwhile, there also was some concern expressed about tension between white managers and nonwhite subordinates, who claimed they were being treated unfairly. But our analysis suggested that the manager-subordinate conflicts were not numerous enough

The Research

THIS ARTICLE IS BASED ON a three-part research effort that began in 1990. Our subject was diversity; but, more specifically, we sought to understand three management challenges under that heading. First, how do organizations successfully achieve and sustain racial and gender diversity in their executive and middle-management ranks? Second, what is the impact of diversity on an organization's practices, processes, and performance? And, finally, how do leaders influence whether diversity becomes an enhancing or detracting element in the organization?

Over the following six years, we worked particularly closely with three organizations that had attained a high degree of demographic diversity: a small urban law firm, a community bank, and a 200-person consulting firm. In addition, we studied nine other companies in varying stages of diversifying their workforces. The group included two financial-services firms, three *Fortune* 500 manufacturing companies, two midsize high-technology companies, a private foundation, and a university medical center. In each case, we based our analysis on interviews, surveys, archival data, and observation. It is from this work that the third paradigm for managing diversity emerged and with it our belief that old and limiting assumptions about the meaning of diversity must be abandoned before its true potential can be realized as a powerful way to increase organizational effectiveness.

to warrant the attention they were drawing from top management. We believed it was significant that senior managers found it easier to focus on this second type of conflict than on midlevel conflicts about project choice and project definition. Indeed, Iversen Dunham's focus seemed to be a result of the firm's reliance on its particular diversity paradigm and the emphasis on fairness and equality. It was relatively easy to diagnose problems in light of those concepts and to devise a solution: just get managers to treat their subordinates more fairly.

In contrast, it was difficult to diagnose peer-to-peer tensions in the framework of this model. Such conflicts were about the very nature of Iversen's work, not simply unfair treatment. Yes, they were related to identity-group affiliations, but they were not symptomatic of classic racism. It was Iversen's paradigm that led managers to interpret them as such. Remember, we were asked to assess what was supposed to be a racial discrimination problem. Iversen's discrimination-and-fairness paradigm had created a kind of cognitive blind spot; and, as a result, the company's leadership could not frame the problem accurately or solve it effectively. Instead, the company needed a cultural shift—it needed to grasp what to do with its diversity once it had achieved the numbers. If all Iversen Dunham employees were to contribute to the fullest extent, the company would need a paradigm that would encourage open and explicit discussion of what identity-group differences really mean and how they can be used as sources of individual and organizational effectiveness.

Today, mainly because of senior managers' resistance to such a cultural transformation, Iversen continues to struggle with the tensions arising from the diversity of its workforce.

The Access-and-Legitimacy Paradigm

In the competitive climate of the 1980s and 1990s, a new rhetoric and rationale for managing diversity emerged. If the discrimination-and-fairness paradigm can be said to have idealized assimilation and color- and gender-blind conformism, the access-and-legitimacy paradigm was predicated on the acceptance and celebration of differences. The underlying motivation of the access-and-legitimacy paradigm can be expressed this way:

> We are living in an increasingly multicultural country, and new ethnic groups are quickly gaining consumer power. Our company needs a demographically more diverse workforce to help us gain access to these differentiated segments. We need employees with multilingual skills in order to understand and serve our customers better and to gain legitimacy with them. Diversity isn't just fair; it makes business sense.

Where this paradigm has taken hold, organizations have pushed for access to—and legitimacy with—a more diverse clientele by matching the demographics of the organization to those of critical consumer or constituent groups. In some cases, the effort has led to substantial increases in organizational diversity. In investment banks, for example, municipal finance departments have long led corporate finance departments in pursuing demographic diversity because of the typical makeup of the administration of city halls and county boards. Many consumer-products companies that have used market segmentation based on gender, racial, and other demographic differences have also frequently created dedicated marketing positions for each segment. The paradigm has therefore led to new professional and managerial opportunities for women and people of color.

What are the common characteristics of organizations that have successfully used the access-and-legitimacy paradigm to increase their demographic diversity? There is but one: such companies almost always operate in a business environment in which there is increased diversity among customers, clients, or the labor pool—and therefore a clear opportunity or an imminent threat to the company.

Again, the paradigm has its strengths. Its market-based motivation and the potential for competitive advantage that it suggests are often qualities an entire company can understand and therefore support. But the paradigm is perhaps more notable for its limitations. In their pursuit of niche markets, access-and-legitimacy organizations tend to emphasize the role of cultural differences in a company without really analyzing those differences to see how they actually affect the work that is done. Whereas discrimination-and-fairness leaders are too quick to subvert differences in the interest of preserving harmony, access-and-legitimacy leaders are too quick to push staff with niche capabilities into differentiated pigeonholes without trying to understand what those capabilities really are and how they could be integrated into the company's mainstream work. To illustrate our point, we present the case of Access Capital.

Access Capital International is a U.S. investment bank that in the early 1980s launched an aggressive plan to expand into Europe. Initially, however, Access encountered serious problems opening offices in international markets; the people from the United States who were installed abroad lacked credibility, were ignorant of local cultural norms and market conditions, and simply couldn't seem to connect with native clients. Access responded by hiring Europeans who had attended North American business schools and by assigning them in teams to the foreign offices. This strategy was a marked success. Before long, the leaders of Access could take enormous pride in the fact that their European operations were highly profitable and staffed by a truly international corps of professionals. They took to calling the company "the best investment bank in the world."

Several years passed. Access's foreign offices continued to thrive, but some leaders were beginning to sense that the company was not fully benefiting from its diversity efforts. Indeed, some even suspected that the bank had made itself vulnerable because of how it had chosen to manage diversity. A senior executive from the United States explains:

> If the French team all resigned tomorrow, what would we do? I'm not sure what we *could* do! We've never attempted to learn what these differences and cultural competencies really are, how they change the process of doing business. What is the German country team actually doing? We don't know. We know they're good, but we don't know the subtleties of how they do what they do. We assumed—and I think correctly—that culture makes a difference, but that's about as far as we went. We hired Europeans with American M.B.A.'s because we didn't know why we couldn't do business in Europe—we just assumed there was something cultural about why we couldn't connect. And ten years later, we still don't know what it is. If we knew, then perhaps we could take it and teach it. Which part of the investment banking process is universal and which part of it draws upon particular cultural competencies? What are the commonalities and differences? I may not be German, but maybe I could do better at understanding what it means to be an American doing business in Germany. Our company's biggest failing is that the department heads in London and the directors of the various country teams have never talked about these cultural identity issues openly. We knew enough to *use* people's cultural strengths, as it were, but we never seemed to learn from them.

Access's story makes an important point about the main limitation of the access-and-legitimacy paradigm: under its influence, the motivation for diversity usually emerges from very immediate and often crisis-oriented needs for access and legitimacy—in this case, the need to broker deals in European markets. However, once the organization appears to be achieving its goal, the leaders seldom go on to identify and analyze the culturally based skills, beliefs, and practices that worked so well. Nor do they consider how the organization can incorporate and learn from those skills, beliefs, or practices in order to capitalize on diversity in the long run.

Under the access-and-legitimacy paradigm, it was as if the bank's country teams had become little spin-off companies in their own right, doing their own exotic, slightly mysterious cultural-diversity thing in a niche market of their own, using competencies that for some reason could not become more fully integrated into the larger organization's understanding of itself. Difference was valued within Access Capital—hence the development of country teams in the first place—but not valued enough that the organization would try to integrate it into the very core of its culture and into its business practices.

Finally, the access-and-legitimacy paradigm can leave some employees feeling exploited. Many organizations using this paradigm have diversified only in those areas in which they interact with particular niche-market segments. In time, many individuals recruited for this function have come to feel devalued and used as they begin to sense that opportunities in other parts of the organization are closed to them. Often the larger organization regards the experience of these employees as more limited or specialized, even though many of them in fact started their careers in the mainstream market before moving to special markets where their cultural backgrounds were a recognized asset. Also, many of these people say that when companies have needed to downsize or narrow their marketing focus, it is the special departments that are often the first to go. That situation creates tenuous and ultimately untenable career paths for employees in the special departments.

The Emerging Paradigm: Connecting Diversity to Work Perspectives

Recently, in the course of our research, we have encountered a small number of organizations that, having relied initially on one of the above paradigms to guide their diversity efforts, have come to believe that they are not making the most of their own pluralism. These organizations, like Access Capital, recognize that employees frequently make decisions and choices at work that draw upon their cultural background—choices made because of their identity-group affiliations. The companies have also developed an outlook on diversity that enables them to *incorporate* employees' perspectives into the main work of the organization and to enhance work by rethinking primary tasks and redefining markets, products, strategies, missions, business practices, and even cultures. Such companies are using the learning-and-effectiveness paradigm for managing diversity and, by doing so, are tapping diversity's true benefits.

A case in point is Dewey & Levin, a small public-interest law firm located in a northeastern U.S. city. Although Dewey & Levin had long been a profitable practice, by the mid-1980s its all-white legal staff had become concerned that the women they represented in employment-related disputes were exclusively white. The firm's attorneys viewed that fact as a deficiency in light of their mandate to advocate on behalf of all women. Using the thinking behind the access-and-legitimacy paradigm, they also saw it as bad for business.

Shortly thereafter, the firm hired a Hispanic female attorney. The partners' hope, simply put, was that she would bring in clients from her own community and also demonstrate the firm's commitment to representing all women. But something even bigger than that happened. The new attorney introduced ideas to Dewey & Levin about what kinds of cases it should take on. Senior managers were open to those ideas and pursued them with great success. More women of color were hired, and they, too, brought fresh perspectives. The firm now pursues cases that its previously all-white legal staff would not have thought relevant or appropriate because the link between the firm's mission and the employment issues involved in the cases would not have been obvious to them. For example, the firm has pursued precedent-setting litigation that challenges English-only policies—an area that it once would have ignored because such policies did not fall under the purview of traditional affirmative-action work. Yet it now sees a link between English-only policies and employment issues for a large group of women—primarily recent immigrants—whom it had previously failed to serve adequately. As one of the white principals explains, the demographic composition of Dewey & Levin "has affected the work in terms of expanding notions of what are [relevant] issues and taking on issues and framing them in creative ways that would have never been done [with an all-white staff]. It's really changed the substance—and in that sense enhanced the quality—of our work."

Dewey & Levin's increased business success has reinforced its commitment to diversity. In addition, people of color at the firm uniformly report feeling respected, not simply "brought along as window dressing." Many of the new attorneys say their perspectives are heard with a kind of openness and interest they have never experienced before in a work setting. Not surprisingly, the firm has had little difficulty attracting and retaining a competent and diverse professional staff.

If the discrimination-and-fairness paradigm is organized around the theme of assimilation—in which the aim is to achieve a demographically representative workforce whose members treat one another exactly the same—then the access-and-legitimacy paradigm can be regarded as coalescing around an almost opposite concept: differentiation, in which the objective is to place different people where their demographic characteristics match those of important constituents and markets.

The emerging paradigm, in contrast to both, organizes itself around the overarching theme of integration. Assimilation goes too far in pursuing sameness. Differentiation, as we have shown, overshoots in the other direction. The new model for managing diversity transcends both. Like the fairness paradigm, it promotes equal opportunity for all individuals. And like the access paradigm, it acknowledges cultural differences among people and recognizes the value in those differences. Yet this new model for managing diversity lets the organization internalize differences among employees so that it learns and grows because of them. Indeed, with the model fully in place, members of the organization can say, We are all on the same team, *with* our differences—not *despite* them.

Eight Preconditions for Making the Paradigm Shift

Dewey & Levin may be atypical in its eagerness to open itself up to change and engage in a long-term transformation process. We remain convinced, however, that unless organizations that are currently in the grip of the other two paradigms can revise their view of diversity so as to avoid cognitive blind spots, opportunities will be missed, tensions will most likely be misdiagnosed, and companies will continue to find the potential benefits of diversity elusive.

Hence the question arises: What is it about the law firm of Dewey & Levin and other emerging third-paradigm companies that enables them to make the most of their diversity? Our research suggests that there are eight preconditions that help to position organizations to use identity-group differences in the service of organizational learning, growth, and renewal.

1. The leadership must understand that a diverse workforce will embody different perspectives and approaches to work, and must truly value variety of opinion and insight. We know of a financial services company that once assumed that the only successful sales model was one that utilized aggressive, rapid-fire cold calls. (Indeed, its incentive system rewarded salespeople in large part for the number of calls made.) An internal review of the company's diversity initiatives, however, showed that the company's first- and third-most-profitable employees were women who were most likely to use a sales technique based on the slow but sure building of relationships. The company's top management has now made the link between different identity groups and different approaches to how work gets done and has come to see that there is more than one right way to get positive results.

2. The leadership must recognize both the learning opportunities and the challenges that the expression of different perspectives presents for an organization. In other words, the second precondition is a leadership that is committed to persevering during the long process of learning and relearning that the new paradigm requires.

3. The organizational culture must create an expectation of high standards of performance from everyone. Such a culture isn't one that expects less from some employees than from others. Some organizations expect women and people of color to underperform—a negative assumption that too often becomes a self-fulfilling prophecy. To move to the third paradigm, a company must believe that all its members can and should contribute fully.

4. The organizational culture must stimulate personal development. Such a culture brings out people's full range of useful knowledge and skills—usually through the careful design of jobs that allow people to grow and develop but also through training and education programs.

5. The organizational culture must encourage openness. Such a culture instills a high tolerance for debate and supports constructive conflict on work-related matters.

6. The culture must make workers feel valued. If this precondition is met, workers feel committed to—and empowered within—the organization and therefore feel comfortable taking the initiative to apply their skills and experiences in new ways to enhance their job performance.

7. The organization must have a well-articulated and widely understood mission. Such a mission enables people to be clear about what the company is trying to accomplish. It grounds and guides discussions about work-related changes that staff members might suggest. Being clear about the company's mission helps keep discussions about work differences from degenerating into debates about the validity of people's perspectives. A clear mission provides a focal point that keeps the discussion centered on accomplishment of goals.

8. The organization must have a relatively egalitarian, nonbureaucratic structure. It's important to have a structure that promotes the exchange of ideas and welcomes constructive challenges to the usual way of doing things—from any employee with valuable experience. Forward-thinking leaders in bureaucratic organizations must retain the organization's efficiency-promoting control systems and chains of command while finding ways to reshape the change-resisting mind-set of the classic bureaucratic model. They need to separate the enabling elements of bureaucracy (the ability to get things done) from the disabling elements of bureaucracy (those that create resistance to experimentation).

First Interstate Bank: A Paradigm Shift in Progress

All eight preconditions do not have to be in place in order to begin a shift from the first or second diversity orientations toward the learning-and-effectiveness paradigm. But most should be. First Interstate Bank, a midsize bank operating in a midwestern city, illustrates this point.

First Interstate, admittedly, is not a typical bank. Its client base is a minority community, and its mission is expressly to serve that base through "the development of a highly talented workforce." The bank is unique in other ways: its leadership welcomes constructive criticism; its structure is relatively egalitarian and nonbureaucratic; and its culture is open-minded. Nevertheless, First Interstate had long enforced a policy that loan officers had to hold college degrees. Those without were hired only for support-staff jobs and were never promoted beyond or outside support functions.

Two years ago, however, the support staff began to challenge the policy. Many of them had been with First Interstate for many years and, with the company's active support, had improved their skills through training. Others had expanded their skills on the job, again with the bank's encouragement, learning to run credit checks, prepare presentations for clients, and even calculate the algorithms necessary for many loan decisions. As a result, some people on the support staff were doing many of the same tasks as loan officers. Why, then, they wondered, couldn't they receive commensurate rewards in title and compensation?

This questioning led to a series of contentious meetings between the support staff and the bank's senior managers. It soon became clear that the problem called for managing diversity—diversity based not on race or gender but on class. The support personnel were uniformly from lower socioeconomic communities than were the college-educated loan officers. Regardless, the principle was the same as for race-or gender-based diversity problems. The support staff had different ideas about how the work of the bank should be done. They argued that those among them with the requisite skills should be allowed to rise through the ranks to professional positions, and they believed their ideas were not being heard or accepted.

Their beliefs challenged assumptions that the company's leadership had long held about which employees should have the authority to deal with customers and about how much responsibility administrative employees should ultimately receive. In order to take up this challenge, the bank would have to be open to exploring the requirements that a new perspective would impose on it. It would need to consider the possibility of mapping out an educational and career path for people without degrees—a path that could put such workers on the road to becoming loan officers. In other words, the leadership would have to transform itself willingly and embrace fluidity in policies that in times past had been clearly stated and unquestioningly held.

Today the bank's leadership is undergoing just such a transformation. The going, however, is far from easy. The bank's senior managers now must look beyond the tensions and acrimony sparked by the debate over differing work perspectives and consider the bank's new direction an important learning and growth opportunity.

Shift Complete: Third-Paradigm Companies in Action

First Interstate is a shift in progress; but, in addition to Dewey & Levin, there are several organizations we know of for which the shift is complete. In these cases, company leaders have played a critical role as facilitators and tone setters. We have observed in particular that in organizations that have adopted the new perspective, leaders and managers—and, following in their tracks, employees in general—are taking four kinds of action.

They are making the mental connection

First, in organizations that have adopted the new perspective, the leaders are actively seeking opportunities to explore how identity-group differences affect relationships among workers and affect the way work gets done. They are investing considerable time and energy in understanding how identity-group memberships take on social meanings in the organization and how those meanings manifest themselves in the way work is defined, assigned, and accomplished. When there is no proactive search to understand, then learning from diversity, if it happens at all, can occur only reactively—that is, in response to diversity-related crises.

The situation at Iversen Dunham illustrates the missed opportunities resulting from that scenario. Rather than seeing differences in the way project leaders defined and approached their work as an opportunity to gain new insights and develop new approaches to achieving its mission, the firm remained entrenched in its traditional ways, able to arbitrate such differences only by thinking about what was fair and what was racist. With this quite limited view of the role race can play in an organization, discussions about the topic become fraught with fear and defensiveness, and everyone misses out on insights about how race might influence work in positive ways.

A second case, however, illustrates how some leaders using the new paradigm have been able to envision—and make—the connection between cultural diversity and the company's work. A vice president of Mastiff, a large national insurance company, received a complaint from one of the managers in her unit, an African American man. The manager wanted to demote an African American woman he had hired for a leadership position from another Mastiff division just three months before. He told the vice president he was profoundly disappointed with the performance of his new hire.

"I hired her because I was pretty certain she had tremendous leadership skill," he said. "I knew she had a management style that was very open and empowering. I was also sure she'd have a great impact on the rest of the management team. But she hasn't done any of that."

Surprised, the vice president tried to find out from him what he thought the problem was, but she was not getting any answers that she felt really defined or illuminated the root of the problem. Privately, it puzzled her that someone would decide to demote a 15-year veteran of the company—and a minority woman at that—so soon after bringing her to his unit.

The vice president probed further. In the course of the conversation, the manager happened to mention that he knew the new employee from church and was familiar with the way she handled leadership there and in other community settings. In those less formal situations, he had seen her perform as an extremely effective, sensitive, and influential leader.

That is when the vice president made an interpretive leap. "If that's what you know about her," the vice president said to the manager, "then the question for us is, why can't she bring those skills to work here?" The vice president decided to arrange a meeting with all three present to ask this very question directly. In the meeting, the African American woman explained, "I didn't think I would last long if I acted that way here. My personal style of leadership—that particular style—works well if you have the permission to do it fully; then you can just do it and not have to look over your shoulder."

Pointing to the manager who had planned to fire her, she added, "He's right. The style of leadership I use outside this company can definitely be effective. But I've been at Mastiff for 15 years. I know this organization, and I know if I brought that piece of myself—if I became that authentic—I just wouldn't survive here."

What this example illustrates is that the vice president's learning-and-effectiveness paradigm led her to explore and then make the link between cultural diversity and work style. What was occurring, she realized, was a mismatch between the cultural background of the recently promoted woman and the cultural environment of her work setting. It had little to do with private attitudes or feelings, or gender issues, or some inherent lack of leadership ability. The source of the underperformance was that the newly promoted woman had a certain style and the organization's culture did not support her in expressing it comfortably. The vice president's paradigm led her to ask new questions and to seek out new information, but, more important, it also led her to interpret existing information differently.

The two senior managers began to realize that part of the African American woman's inability to see herself as a leader at work was that she had for so long been undervalued in the organization. And, in a sense, she had become used to splitting herself off from who she was in her own community. In the 15 years she had been at Mastiff, she had done her job well as an individual contributor, but she had never received any signals that her bosses wanted her to draw on her cultural competencies in order to lead effectively.

They are legitimating open discussion

Leaders and managers who have adopted the new paradigm are taking the initiative to "green light" open discussion about how identity-group memberships inform and influence an employee's experience and the organization's behavior. They are encouraging people to make *explicit* use of background cultural experience and the pools of knowledge gained outside the organization to inform and enhance their work. Individuals often do use their cultural competencies at work, but in a closeted, almost embarrassed, way. The unfortunate result is that the opportunity for collective and organizational learning and improvement is lost.

The case of a Chinese woman who worked as a chemist at Torinno Food Company illustrates this point. Linda was part of a product development group at Torinno when a problem arose with the flavoring of a new soup. After the group had made a number of scientific attempts to correct the problem, Linda came up with the solution by "setting aside my chemistry and drawing on my understanding of Chinese cooking." She did not, however, share with her colleagues—all of them white males—the real source of her inspiration for the solution for fear that it would set her apart or that they might consider her unprofessional. Overlaid on the cultural issue, of course, was a gender issue (women cooking) as well as a work-family issue (women doing *home* cooking in a chemistry lab). All of these themes had erected unspoken boundaries that Linda knew could be career-damaging for her to cross. After solving the problem, she simply went back to the so-called scientific way of doing things.

Senior managers at Torinno Foods in fact had made a substantial commitment to diversifying the workforce through a program designed to teach employees to value the contributions of all its members. Yet Linda's perceptions indicate that, in the actual day-to-day context of work, the program had failed—and in precisely one of those areas where it would have been important for it to have worked. It had failed to affirm someone's identity-group experiences as a legitimate source of insight into her work. It is likely that this organization will miss future opportunities to take full advantage of the talent of employees such as Linda. When people believe that they must suggest and apply their ideas covertly, the organization also misses opportunities to discuss, debate, refine, and build on those ideas fully. In addition, because individuals like Linda will continue to think that they must hide parts of themselves in order to fit in, they will find it difficult to engage fully not only in their work but also in their workplace relationships. That kind of situation can breed resentment and misunderstanding, fueling tensions that can further obstruct productive work relationships.

They actively work against forms of dominance and subordination that inhibit full contribution

Companies in which the third paradigm is emerging have leaders and managers who take responsibility for removing the barriers that block employees from using the full range of their competencies, cultural or otherwise. Racism, homophobia, sexism, and sexual harassment are the most obvious forms of dominance that decrease individual and organizational effectiveness—and third-paradigm leaders have zero tolerance for them. In addition, the leaders are aware that organizations can create their own unique patterns of dominance and subordination based on the presumed superiority and entitlement of some groups over others. It is not uncommon, for instance, to find organizations in which one functional area considers itself better than another. Members of the presumed inferior group frequently describe the organization in the very terms used by those who experience identity-group discrimination. Regardless of the source of the oppression, the result is diminished performance and commitment from employees.

What can leaders do to prevent those kinds of behaviors beyond explicitly forbidding any forms of dominance? They can and should test their own assumptions about the competencies of all members of the workforce because negative assumptions are often unconsciously communicated in powerful—albeit nonverbal—ways. For example, senior managers at Delta Manufacturing had for years allowed productivity and quality at their inner-city plants to lag well behind the levels of other plants. When the company's chief executive officer began to question why the problem was never addressed, he came to realize that, in his heart, he had believed that inner-city workers, most of whom were African American or Hispanic, were not capable of doing better than subpar. In the end, the CEO and his senior management team were able to reverse their reasoning and take responsibility for improving the situation. The result was a sharp increase in the performance of the inner-city plants and a message to the entire organization about the capabilities of its entire workforce.

At Mastiff, the insurance company discussed earlier, the vice president and her manager decided to work with the recently promoted African American woman rather than demote her. They realized that their unit was really a pocket inside the larger organization: they did not have to wait for the rest of the organization to make a paradigm shift in order for their particular unit to change. So they met again to think about how to create conditions within their unit that would move the woman toward seeing her leadership position as encompassing all her skills. They assured her that her authentic style of leadership was precisely what they wanted her to bring to the job. They wanted her to be able to use whatever aspects of herself she thought would make her more effective in her work because the whole purpose was to do the job effectively, not to fit some preset traditional formula of how to behave. They let her know that, as a management team, they would try to adjust and change and support her. And they would deal with whatever consequences resulted from her exercising her decision rights in new ways.

Another example of this line of action—working against forms of dominance and subordination to enable full contribution—is the way the CEO of a major chemical company modified the attendance rules for his company's annual strategy conference. In the past, the conference had been attended only by senior executives, a relatively homogeneous group of white men. The company had been working hard on increasing the representation of women and people of color in its ranks, and the CEO could have left it at that. But he reckoned that, unless steps were taken, it would be ten years before the conferences tapped into the insights and perspectives of his newly diverse workforce. So he took the bold step of opening the conference to people from across all levels of the hierarchy, bringing together a diagonal slice of the organization. He also asked the conference organizers to come up with specific interventions, such as small group meetings before the larger session, to ensure that the new attendees would be comfortable enough to enter discussions. The result was that strategy-conference participants heard a much broader, richer, and livelier discussion about future scenarios for the company.

They are making sure that organizational trust stays intact

Few things are faster at killing a shift to a new way of thinking about diversity than feelings of broken trust. Therefore, managers of organizations that are successfully shifting to the learning-and-effectiveness paradigm take one more step: they make sure their organizations remain "safe" places for employees to be themselves. These managers recognize that tensions naturally arise as an organization begins to make room for diversity, starts to experiment with process and product ideas, and learns to reappraise its mission in light of suggestions from newly empowered constituents in the company. But as people put more of themselves out and open up about new feelings and ideas, the dynamics of the learning-and-effectiveness paradigm can produce temporary vulnerabilities. Managers who have helped their organizations make the change successfully have consistently demonstrated their commitment to the process and to all employees by setting a tone of honest discourse, by acknowledging tensions, and by resolving them sensitively and swiftly.

Our research over the past six years indicates that one cardinal limitation is at the root of companies' inability to attain the expected performance benefits of higher levels of diversity: the leadership's vision of the purpose of a diversified workforce. We have described the two most dominant orientations toward diversity and some of their consequences and limitations, together with a new framework for understanding and managing diversity. The learning-and-effectiveness paradigm we have outlined here is, undoubtedly, still in an emergent phase in those few organizations that embody it. We expect that as more organizations take on the challenge of truly engaging their diversity, new and unforeseen dilemmas will arise. Thus, perhaps more than anything else, a shift toward this paradigm requires a high-level commitment to learning more about the environment, structure, and tasks of one's organization, and giving improvement-generating change greater priority than the security of what is familiar. This is not an easy challenge, but we remain convinced that unless organizations take this step, any diversity initiative will fall short of fulfilling its rich promise.

Originally published in September–October 1996. Reprint 96510

Navigating the Cultural Minefield

by Erin Meyer

WHEN AARON ARRIVED IN MOSCOW to take charge of the manufacturing plant his Israeli-owned company had just purchased, he expected to settle in quickly. Although he'd grown up in Tel Aviv, his parents were Russian-born, so he knew the culture and spoke the language well. He'd been highly successful managing Israeli teams and had led a large organization in Canada. Yet six months into his new job, he was still struggling to supervise his team in Moscow. What, specifically, was he doing wrong?

Answering such questions isn't easy, as I've learned from 16 years studying the effects of cultural differences on business success. Although there's been a great deal of research and writing on the subject, much of it fails to present a sufficiently nuanced picture that can be of real use to managers working internationally or with foreign colleagues. As a result, it's all too common to rely on clichés, stereotyping people from different cultures on just one or two dimensions—the Japanese are hierarchical, for example, or the French communicate in subtle ways. This can lead to oversimplified and erroneous assumptions—the Japanese always make top-down decisions, or the French are indirect when giving negative feedback. It then comes as a surprise when your French colleague bluntly criticizes your shortcomings, or when your Japanese clients want buy-in from the cook and the cleaner before reaching a decision.

Time and again, I find that even experienced and cosmopolitan managers have faulty expectations about how people from other cultures operate. The truth is that culture is too complex to be measured meaningfully along just one or two dimensions.

To help managers like Aaron negotiate this complexity, I have built on the work of many in my field to develop a tool called the Culture Map. It is made up of eight scales representing the management behaviors where cultural gaps are most common. By comparing the position of one nationality relative to another on each scale, the user can decode how culture influences day-to-day collaboration. In the following pages, I present the tool, show how it can help you, and discuss the challenges in applying it.

The Culture Map

The eight scales on the map are based on decades of academic research into culture from multiple perspectives. To this foundation I have added my own work, which has been validated by extensive interviews with thousands of executives who have confirmed or corrected my findings. The scales and their metrics are:

Communicating

When we say that someone is a good communicator, what do we actually mean? The responses differ wildly from society to society. I compare cultures along the Communicating scale by measuring the degree to which they are high- or low-context, a metric developed by the American anthropologist Edward Hall. In low-context cultures, good communication is precise, simple, explicit, and clear. Messages are understood at face value. Repetition is appreciated for purposes of clarification, as is putting messages in writing. In high-context cultures, communication is sophisticated, nuanced, and layered. Messages are often implied but not plainly stated. Less is put in writing, more is left open to interpretation, and understanding may depend on reading between the lines.

Idea in Brief

As we increasingly work with colleagues and clients who come from all parts of the world, it is vital to understand how cultural differences affect business. Yet too often we rely on clichés and stereotypes that lead us to false assumptions. To help managers negotiate the complexity of an international work team, INSEAD professor Erin Meyer has developed a tool called the Culture Map, which plots the positions of numerous nationalities along eight behavior scales: Communicating, Evaluating, Persuading, Leading, Deciding, Trusting, Disagreeing, and Scheduling. Meyer suggests that comparing the relative positions of different nationalities along these scales can help us decode how culture influences workplace dynamics. She adds four important rules: Don't underestimate the challenge. Management and work styles stem from lifelong habits that can be hard to change. Apply multiple perspectives. Be aware of your own expectations and behaviors, but also consider how members of other cultures perceive you and fellow teammates. Find the positive in other approaches. The differences that people of varied backgrounds bring to a work group can be great assets. Continually adjust your position. Be prepared to keep adapting your behavior to meld with the styles of your colleagues.

Evaluating

All cultures believe that criticism should be given constructively, but the definition of "constructive" varies greatly. This scale measures a preference for frank versus diplomatic negative feedback. Evaluating is often confused with Communicating, but many countries have different positions on the two scales. The French, for example, are high-context (implicit) communicators relative to Americans, yet they are more direct in their criticism. Spaniards and Mexicans are at the same context level, but the Spanish are much more frank when providing negative feedback. This scale is my own work.

Persuading

The ways in which you persuade others and the kinds of arguments you find convincing are deeply rooted in your culture's philosophical, religious, and educational assumptions and attitudes. The traditional way to compare countries along this scale is to assess how they balance holistic and specific thought patterns. Typically, a Western executive will break down an argument into a sequence of distinct components (specific thinking), while Asian managers tend to show how the components all fit together (holistic thinking). Beyond that, people from southern European and Germanic cultures tend to find deductive arguments (what I refer to as principles-first arguments) most persuasive, whereas American and British managers are more likely to be influenced by inductive logic (what I call applications-first logic). The research into specific and holistic cognitive patterns was conducted by Richard Nisbett, an American professor of social psychology, and the deductive/inductive element is my own work.

Leading

This scale measures the degree of respect and deference shown to authority figures, placing countries on a spectrum from egalitarian to hierarchical. The Leading scale is based partly on the concept of power distance, first researched by the Dutch social psychologist Geert Hofstede, who conducted 100,000 management surveys at IBM in the 1970s. It also draws on the work of Wharton School professor Robert House and his colleagues in their GLOBE (global leadership and organizational behavior effectiveness) study of 62 societies.

Deciding

This scale, based on my own work, measures the degree to which a culture is consensus-minded. We often assume that the most egalitarian cultures will also be the most democratic, while the most hierarchical ones will allow the boss to make unilateral decisions. This isn't always the case. Germans are more hierarchical than Americans, but more likely than their U.S. colleagues to build group agreement before making decisions. The Japanese are both strongly hierarchical and strongly consensus-minded.

Trusting

Cognitive trust (from the head) can be contrasted with affective trust (from the heart). In task-based cultures, trust is built cognitively through work. If we collaborate well, prove ourselves reliable, and respect one another's contributions, we come to feel mutual trust. In a relationship-based society, trust is a result of weaving a strong affective connection. If we spend time laughing and relaxing together, get to know one another on a personal level, and feel a mutual liking, then we establish trust. Many people have researched this topic; Roy Chua and Michael Morris, for example, wrote a landmark paper on the different approaches to trust in the United States and China. I have drawn on this work in developing my metric.

Disagreeing

Everyone believes that a little open disagreement is healthy, right? The recent American business literature certainly confirms this viewpoint. But different cultures actually have very different ideas about how productive confrontation is for a team or an organization. This scale measures tolerance for open disagreement and inclination to see it as either helpful or harmful to collegial relationships. This is my own work.

Scheduling

All businesses follow agendas and timetables, but in some cultures people strictly adhere to the schedule, whereas in others, they treat it as a suggestion. This scale assesses how much value is placed on operating in a structured, linear fashion versus being flexible and reactive. It is based on the "monochronic" and "polychronic" distinction formalized by Edward Hall.

The Culture Map shows positions along these eight scales for a large number of countries, based on surveys and interviews. These profiles reflect, of course, the value systems of a society at large, not those of all the individuals in it, so if you plot yourself on the map, you might find that some of your preferences differ from those of your culture.

Let's go back to my friend Aaron (who, like other managers profiled later, is not identified by his real name). Aaron used the map to uncover the roots of his difficulties managing his Moscow team. As you can see from the exhibit "Comparing management cultures: Israel vs. Russia," there are plenty of cultural similarities between

Israelis and Russians. For example, both value flexible rather than linear scheduling, both accept and appreciate open disagreement, and both approach issues of trust through a relationship lens. But there are also big gaps. For instance, Russians strongly value hierarchy, whereas Israelis are more egalitarian. This suggests that some of Aaron's management practices, developed through his experiences in Israel and Canada, may have been misunderstood by—and demotivating to—his Russian team.

As Aaron considered the large gap on the Leading scale, he began to think about how he'd been encouraged as a child to disagree openly with authority figures in his family and community—a stark

Comparing management cultures: Israel vs. Russia

This Culture Map plots the Israeli and Russian business cultures on eight behavior scales. The profiles are drawn from surveys and interviews of managers from the two countries. While there are many points of similarity, Russians and Israelis diverge with respect to the ways in which they persuade, lead, and decide.

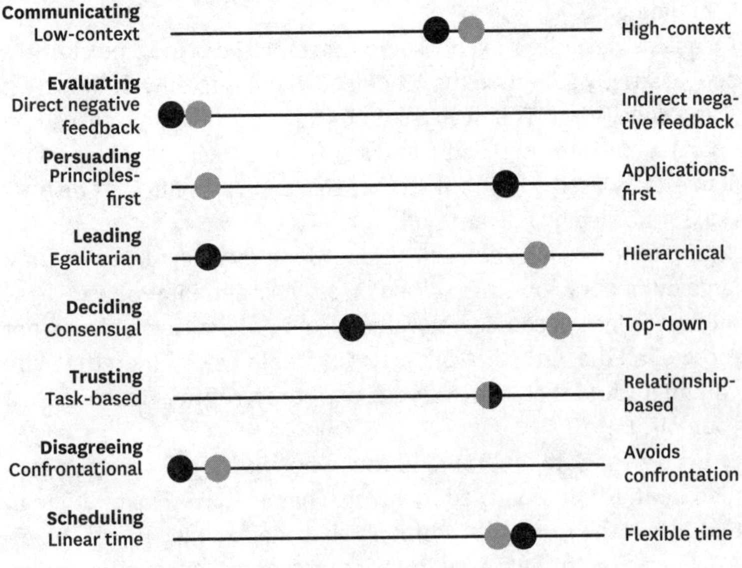

contrast to the Russian tradition of expecting young people to show deep respect and deference to their elders. "In Israel, the boss is just one of the guys," he reflected. "But in Russia, when I try to push decision making down and insist that someone on my team is better positioned to make a decision than I am, it often suggests weak leadership." One of the specific practices getting him into trouble was his tendency to e-mail employees at lower levels of the company without passing through the hierarchical chain or cc'ing their direct bosses; he now understood why the practice made his middle managers so angry.

Sometimes it's fairly easy to bridge the cultural gaps revealed by the mapping process. Aaron found that simply stopping the direct e-mails and going through official channels had a big impact. But some differences are more difficult to overcome, and as you manage across them, it's important to respect the four rules I discuss next. They apply to all the scales, but I'll continue to focus on Leading.

Rule 1: Don't Underestimate the Challenge

Management styles stem from habits developed over a lifetime, which makes them hard to change. Here's a good example: In 2010 Heineken, the Dutch brewing company, purchased a big operation in Monterrey, Mexico, and a large number of Mexican employees are now based at its Amsterdam headquarters. One of these is Carlos, the director of marketing for the Dos Equis brand, who admits that he struggled during his first year in the position:

"It is incredible to manage Dutch people, and nothing like my experience leading Mexican teams. I'll schedule a meeting to roll out a new process, and during it, my team starts challenging the process, taking us in various unexpected directions, ignoring my process altogether, and paying no attention to the fact that they work for me. Sometimes I just watch them astounded. Where is the respect?

"I know this treating everyone as pure equals is the Dutch way, so I keep quiet and try to be patient. But often I just feel like getting down on my knees and pleading, 'Dear colleagues, in case you have forgotten: I-am-the-boss.'"

It didn't take long for Carlos to realize that the leadership skills he had built over the previous decade in Mexico, where more deference to authority is the norm, were not going to transfer easily to the Netherlands. Succeeding would depend on taking an entirely different approach and making ongoing adjustments over the long term. "I realized I was going to need to unlearn many of the techniques that had made me so successful in Mexico and develop others from the ground up," he said.

Rule 2: Apply Multiple Perspectives

If you are leading a global team with, say, Brazilian, Korean, and Indian members, it isn't enough to recognize how your culture perceives each of the others. You need to understand how the Koreans perceive the Indians, how the Indians perceive the Brazilians, and so on, and manage across the map. As you learn to look through multiple lenses, you may see that on some scales the Brazilians, for example, view the Indians in a very different way than the Koreans do.

Let's return to the case of Heineken. A manager from China who had recently moved to Monterrey assessed the Mexicans this way: "They really think everyone is equal. No matter your age, rank, or title, everyone gets a voice here. They want us to call them by their first name and disagree with them in public. For a Chinese person, this is not at all comfortable." His take on Mexican culture, of course, was nothing like Carlos's and actually sounded like Carlos's view of Dutch culture.

The point is that where a culture falls on a scale doesn't in itself mean anything. What matters is the position of one country relative to another. On the Leading scale, Mexico falls somewhere between the Netherlands (one of the most egalitarian countries in the world) and China (strongly hierarchical), and the distances separating them led to these completely contradictory perceptions.

Rule 3: Find the Positive in Other Approaches

When looking at how other cultures work, people tend to see the negative. Steve, an Australian running the business unit of a textile company in China, admits that when he first arrived in the country, he was deeply critical of local leadership practices. The prevailing view, he found, was that "the boss is always right, and even when the boss is very wrong, he is still right." Having been raised to regard a fixed social hierarchy as an inhumane system, subverting individual freedom, he was uncomfortable in his new environment.

Yet Steve gradually came to understand and respect the Chinese system of reciprocal obligation. "In the Confucian concept of hierarchy," he says, "it's important to think not just about the lower-level person's responsibility to follow, but also about the responsibility of the higher person to protect and care for those under him. And there is great beauty in giving a clear instruction and watching your competent and enthusiastic team willingly attack the project without pushing back."

Carlos at Heineken underwent a similar transformation. He developed an appreciation for his Dutch colleagues' more egalitarian work style when he started to focus on the creative ideas generated and the problems averted because his employees felt so comfortable openly challenging his views.

Sometimes cultural diversity can cause inefficiency and confusion. But if the team leader clearly understands how people from varied backgrounds behave, he or she can turn differences into the team's greatest assets. As Steve explains, "Now that I run a Chinese-Australian operation, I think carefully about how to take advantage of the various styles on the team. Sometimes I really need a couple of experts on my staff to tear my ideas apart to ensure that we get the best solution. Sometimes we are under time pressure and I need streamlined reactivity. My overriding goal is to have a complex enough understanding of the various strengths on the team so I can choose the best subteam for each task."

Rule 4: Adjust, and Readjust, Your Position

More and more teams are made up of diverse and globally dispersed members. So as a leader, you'll frequently have to tweak or adapt your own style to better mesh with your working partners. It's not enough to shift to a new position on a single scale; you'll need to widen your comfort zone so that you can move more fluidly back and forth along all eight.

During his first year in Russia, Aaron invested significant time in watching how the most successful local leaders motivated their staff members. He learned step-by-step to be more of a director and less of a facilitator. "It worked," he said, "but when I returned to Israel, I was then accused of centralizing too much. Without realizing it, I had brought what I had developed in Russia back home." Gradually Aaron got better at adapting his behavior to the individuals and context at hand.

As Aaron, Carlos, and Steve all learned, to navigate cultural differences, you might need to go back to square one. Consider which leadership styles are most effective in disparate localities and with people of diverse nationalities. Check your knee-jerk tendencies—and learn to laugh at them. Then practice leading in a wide variety of ways to better motivate and mobilize groups who follow in different ways from the folks back home.

Whether we work in Düsseldorf or Dubai, Brasília or Beijing, New York or New Delhi, we are all part of a global network. This is true in the office or at a meeting, and it is true virtually, when we connect via e-mail, videoconference, Skype, or phone. Today success depends on the ability to navigate the wild variations in the ways people from different societies think, lead, and get things done. By sidestepping common stereotypes and learning to decode the behavior of other cultures along all the scales, we can avoid giving (and taking!) offense and better capitalize on the strengths of increased diversity.

Originally published in May 2014. Reprint R1405K

Values in Tension

Ethics Away from Home. *by Thomas Donaldson*

WHEN WE LEAVE HOME and cross our nation's boundaries, moral clarity often blurs. Without a backdrop of shared attitudes, and without familiar laws and judicial procedures that define standards of ethical conduct, certainty is elusive. Should a company invest in a foreign country where civil and political rights are violated? Should a company go along with a host country's discriminatory employment practices? If companies in developed countries shift facilities to developing nations that lack strict environmental and health regulations, or if those companies choose to fill management and other top-level positions in a host nation with people from the home country, whose standards should prevail?

Even the best-informed, best-intentioned executives must rethink their assumptions about business practice in foreign settings. What works in a company's home country can fail in a country with different standards of ethical conduct. Such difficulties are unavoidable for businesspeople who live and work abroad.

But how can managers resolve the problems? What are the principles that can help them work through the maze of cultural differences and establish codes of conduct for globally ethical business practice? How can companies answer the toughest question in global business ethics: What happens when a host country's ethical standards seem lower than the home country's?

Competing Answers

One answer is as old as philosophical discourse. According to cultural relativism, no culture's ethics are better than any other's; therefore there are no international rights and wrongs. If the people of Indonesia tolerate the bribery of their public officials, so what? Their attitude is no better or worse than that of people in Denmark or Singapore who refuse to offer or accept bribes. Likewise, if Belgians fail to find insider trading morally repugnant, who cares? Not enforcing insider-trading laws is no more or less ethical than enforcing such laws.

The cultural relativist's creed—When in Rome, do as the Romans do—is tempting, especially when failing to do as the locals do means forfeiting business opportunities. The inadequacy of cultural relativism, however, becomes apparent when the practices in question are more damaging than petty bribery or insider trading.

In the late 1980s, some European tanneries and pharmaceutical companies were looking for cheap waste-dumping sites. They approached virtually every country on Africa's west coast from Morocco to the Congo. Nigeria agreed to take highly toxic polychlorinated biphenyls. Unprotected local workers, wearing thongs and shorts, unloaded barrels of PCBs and placed them near a residential area. Neither the residents nor the workers knew that the barrels contained toxic waste.

We may denounce governments that permit such abuses, but many countries are unable to police transnational corporations adequately even if they want to. And in many countries, the combination of ineffective enforcement and inadequate regulations leads to behavior by unscrupulous companies that is clearly wrong. A few years ago, for example, a group of investors became interested in restoring the SS *United States*, once a luxurious ocean liner. Before the actual restoration could begin, the ship had to be stripped of its asbestos lining. A bid from a U.S. company, based on U.S. standards for asbestos removal, priced the job at more than $100 million. A company in the Ukranian city of Sevastopol offered to do the work for less than $2 million. In October 1993, the ship was towed to Sevastopol.

Idea in Brief

What should managers working abroad do when they encounter business practices that seem unethical? Should they, in the spirit of cultural relativism, tell themselves to do in Rome as the Romans do? Or should they take an absolutist approach, using the ethical standards they use at home no matter where they are? Many business practices are neither black nor white but exist in a gray zone, a moral free space through which managers must navigate.

Levi Strauss and Motorola have helped managers by treating company values as absolutes and insisting that suppliers and customers do the same. And, perhaps even more important, both companies have developed detailed codes of conduct that provide clear direction on ethical behavior but also leave room for managers to use the moral imagination that will allow them to resolve ethical tensions responsibly and creatively.

A cultural relativist would have no problem with that outcome, but I do. A country has the right to establish its own health and safety regulations, but in the case described above, the standards and the terms of the contract could not possibly have protected workers in Sevastopol from known health risks. Even if the contract met Ukranian standards, ethical businesspeople must object. Cultural relativism is morally blind. There are fundamental values that cross cultures, and companies must uphold them.

At the other end of the spectrum from cultural relativism is ethical imperialism, which directs people to do everywhere exactly as they do at home. Again, an understandably appealing approach but one that is clearly inadequate. Consider the large U.S. computer-products company that in 1993 introduced a course on sexual harassment in its Saudi Arabian facility. Under the banner of global consistency, instructors used the same approach to train Saudi Arabian managers that they had used with U.S. managers: the participants were asked to discuss a case in which a manager makes sexually explicit remarks to a new female employee over drinks in a bar. The instructors failed to consider how the exercise would work in a culture with strict conventions governing relationships between men and women. As a result, the training sessions were ludicrous.

They baffled and offended the Saudi participants, and the message to avoid coercion and sexual discrimination was lost.

The theory behind ethical imperialism is absolutism, which is based on three problematic principles. Absolutists believe that there is a single list of truths, that they can be expressed only with one set of concepts, and that they call for exactly the same behavior around the world.

The first claim clashes with many people's belief that different cultural traditions must be respected. In some cultures, loyalty to a community—family, organization, or society—is the foundation of all ethical behavior. The Japanese, for example, define business ethics in terms of loyalty to their companies, their business networks, and their nation. Americans place a higher value on liberty than on loyalty; the U.S. tradition of rights emphasizes equality, fairness, and individual freedom. It is hard to conclude that truth lies on one side or the other, but an absolutist would have us select just one.

The second problem with absolutism is the presumption that people must express moral truth using only one set of concepts. For instance, some absolutists insist that the language of basic rights provide the framework for any discussion of ethics. That means, though, that entire cultural traditions must be ignored. The notion of a right evolved with the rise of democracy in post-Renaissance Europe and the United States, but the term is not found in either Confucian or Buddhist traditions. We all learn ethics in the context of our particular cultures, and the power in the principles is deeply tied to the way in which they are expressed. Internationally accepted lists of moral principles, such as the United Nations' Universal Declaration of Human Rights, draw on many cultural and religious traditions. As philosopher Michael Walzer has noted, "There is no Esperanto of global ethics."

The third problem with absolutism is the belief in a global standard of ethical behavior. Context must shape ethical practice. Very low wages, for example, may be considered unethical in rich, advanced countries, but developing nations may be acting ethically if they encourage investment and improve living standards by accepting low wages. Likewise, when people are malnourished or starving, a government may be wise to use more fertilizer in order to improve crop yields, even though that means settling for relatively high levels of thermal water pollution.

When cultures have different standards of ethical behavior—and different ways of handling unethical behavior—a company that takes an absolutist approach may find itself making a disastrous mistake. When a manager at a large U.S. specialty-products company in China caught an employee stealing, she followed the company's practice and turned the employee over to the provincial authorities, who executed him. Managers cannot operate in another culture without being aware of that culture's attitudes toward ethics.

If companies can neither adopt a host country's ethics nor extend the home country's standards, what is the answer? Even the traditional litmus test—What would people think of your actions if they were written up on the front page of the newspaper?—is an unreliable guide, for there is no international consensus on standards of business conduct.

Balancing the Extremes: Three Guiding Principles

Companies must help managers distinguish between practices that are merely different and those that are wrong. For relativists, nothing is sacred and nothing is wrong. For absolutists, many things that are different are wrong. Neither extreme illuminates the real world of business decision making. The answer lies somewhere in between.

When it comes to shaping ethical behavior, companies must be guided by three principles.

- Respect for core human values, which determine the absolute moral threshold for all business activities.
- Respect for local traditions.
- The belief that context matters when deciding what is right and what is wrong.

Consider those principles in action. In Japan, people doing business together often exchange gifts—sometimes expensive ones—in keeping with long-standing Japanese tradition. When U.S. and European companies started doing a lot of business in Japan, many Western businesspeople thought that the practice of gift giving might be wrong rather than simply different. To them, accepting a gift felt like accepting a bribe. As Western companies have become more familiar with Japanese traditions, however, most have come to tolerate the practice and to set different limits on gift giving in Japan than they do elsewhere.

Respecting differences is a crucial ethical practice. Research shows that management ethics differ among cultures; respecting those differences means recognizing that some cultures have obvious weaknesses—as well as hidden strengths. Managers in Hong Kong, for example, have a higher tolerance for some forms of bribery than their Western counterparts, but they have a much lower tolerance for the failure to acknowledge a subordinate's work. In some parts of the Far East, stealing credit from a subordinate is nearly an unpardonable sin.

People often equate respect for local traditions with cultural relativism. That is incorrect. Some practices are clearly wrong. Union Carbide's tragic experience in Bhopal, India, provides one example. The company's executives seriously underestimated how much on-site management involvement was needed at the Bhopal plant to compensate for the country's poor infrastructure and regulatory capabilities. In the aftermath of the disastrous gas leak, the lesson is clear: companies using sophisticated technology in a developing country must evaluate that country's ability to oversee its safe use. Since the incident at Bhopal, Union Carbide has become a leader in advising companies on using hazardous technologies safely in developing countries.

Some activities are wrong no matter where they take place. But some practices that are unethical in one setting may be acceptable in another. For instance, the chemical EDB, a soil fungicide, is banned for use in the United States. In hot climates, however, it quickly becomes harmless through exposure to intense solar radiation and high soil temperatures. As long as the chemical is monitored, companies may be able to use EDB ethically in certain parts of the world.

Defining the Ethical Threshold: Core Values

Few ethical questions are easy for managers to answer. But there are some hard truths that must guide managers' actions, a set of what I call *core human values*, which define minimum ethical standards for all companies.[1] The right to good health and the right to economic advancement and an improved standard of living are two core human values. Another is what Westerners call the Golden Rule, which is recognizable in every major religious and ethical tradition around the world. In Book 15 of his *Analects*, for instance, Confucius counsels people to maintain reciprocity, or not to do to others what they do not want done to themselves.

Although no single list would satisfy every scholar, I believe it is possible to articulate three core values that incorporate the work of scores of theologians and philosophers around the world. To be broadly relevant, these values must include elements found in both Western and non-Western cultural and religious traditions. Consider the examples of values in the table "What do these values have in common?"

At first glance, the values expressed in the two lists seem quite different. Nonetheless, in the spirit of what philosopher John Rawls calls *overlapping consensus*, one can see that the seemingly divergent values converge at key points. Despite important differences between Western and non-Western cultural and religious traditions, both express shared attitudes about what it means to be human. First, individuals must not treat others simply as tools; in other words, they must recognize a person's value as a human being. Next, individuals and communities must treat people in ways that respect people's basic rights. Finally, members of a community must work together to support and improve the institutions on which the community depends. I call those three values *respect for human dignity*, *respect for basic rights*, and *good citizenship*.

Those values must be the starting point for all companies as they formulate and evaluate standards of ethical conduct at home and abroad. But they are only a starting point. Companies need much more specific guidelines, and the first step to developing those is to

What do these values have in common?

Non-Western	Western
Kyosei (Japanese): Living and working together for the common good.	Individual liberty
Dharma (Hindu): The fulfillment of inherited duty.	Egalitarianism
Santutthi (Buddhist): The importance of limited desires.	Political participation
Zakat (Muslim): The duty to give alms to the Muslim poor.	Human rights

translate the core human values into core values for business. What does it mean, for example, for a company to respect human dignity? How can a company be a good citizen?

I believe that companies can respect human dignity by creating and sustaining a corporate culture in which employees, customers, and suppliers are treated not as means to an end but as people whose intrinsic value must be acknowledged, and by producing safe products and services in a safe workplace. Companies can respect basic rights by acting in ways that support and protect the individual rights of employees, customers, and surrounding communities, and by avoiding relationships that violate human beings' rights to health, education, safety, and an adequate standard of living. And companies can be good citizens by supporting essential social institutions, such as the economic system and the education system, and by working with host governments and other organizations to protect the environment.

The core values establish a moral compass for business practice. They can help companies identify practices that are acceptable and those that are intolerable—even if the practices are compatible with a host country's norms and laws. Dumping pollutants near people's homes and accepting inadequate standards for handling hazardous materials are two examples of actions that violate core values.

Similarly, if employing children prevents them from receiving a basic education, the practice is intolerable. Lying about product specifications in the act of selling may not affect human lives directly, but it too is intolerable because it violates the trust that is needed to sustain a corporate culture in which customers are respected.

Sometimes it is not a company's actions but those of a supplier or customer that pose problems. Take the case of the Tan family, a large supplier for Levi Strauss. The Tans were allegedly forcing 1,200 Chinese and Filipino women to work 74 hours per week in guarded compounds on the Mariana Islands. In 1992, after repeated warnings to the Tans, Levi Strauss broke off business relations with them.

Creating an Ethical Corporate Culture

The core values for business that I have enumerated can help companies begin to exercise ethical judgment and think about how to operate ethically in foreign cultures, but they are not specific enough to guide managers through actual ethical dilemmas. Levi Strauss relied on a written code of conduct when figuring out how to deal with the Tan family. The company's Global Sourcing and Operating Guidelines, formerly called the Business Partner Terms of Engagement, state that Levi Strauss will "seek to identify and utilize business partners who aspire as individuals and in the conduct of all their businesses to a set of ethical standards not incompatible with our own." Whenever intolerable business situations arise, managers should be guided by precise statements that spell out the behavior and operating practices that the company demands.

Ninety percent of all *Fortune* 500 companies have codes of conduct, and 70% have statements of vision and values. In Europe and the Far East, the percentages are lower but are increasing rapidly. Does that mean that most companies have what they need? Hardly. Even though most large U.S. companies have both statements of values and codes of conduct, many might be better off if they didn't. Too many companies don't do anything with the documents; they simply paste them on the wall to impress employees, customers, suppliers, and the public. As a result, the senior managers who drafted the statements lose credibility by proclaiming values and not living up to them. Companies such as Johnson & Johnson, Levi Strauss, Motorola, Texas Instruments, and Lockheed Martin, however, do a great deal to make the words meaningful. Johnson & Johnson, for example, has become well known for its Credo Challenge sessions, in which managers discuss ethics in the context of their current business problems and are invited to criticize the company's credo and make suggestions for changes. The participants' ideas are passed on to the company's senior managers. Lockheed Martin has created an innovative site on the World Wide Web and on its local network that gives employees, customers, and suppliers access to the company's ethical code and the chance to voice complaints.

Codes of conduct must provide clear direction about ethical behavior when the temptation to behave unethically is strongest. The pronouncement in a code of conduct that bribery is unacceptable is useless unless accompanied by guidelines for gift giving, payments to get goods through customs, and "requests" from intermediaries who are hired to ask for bribes.

Motorola's values are stated very simply as "How we will always act: [with] constant respect for people [and] uncompromising integrity." The company's code of conduct, however, is explicit about actual business practice. With respect to bribery, for example, the code states that the "funds and assets of Motorola shall not be used, directly or indirectly, for illegal payments of any kind." It is unambiguous about what sort of payment is illegal: "the payment of a bribe to a public official or the kickback of funds to an employee of a customer...." The code goes on to prescribe specific procedures for handling commissions to intermediaries, issuing sales invoices, and disclosing confidential information in a sales transaction—all situations in which employees might have an opportunity to accept or offer bribes.

Codes of conduct must be explicit to be useful, but they must also leave room for a manager to use his or her judgment in situations requiring cultural sensitivity. Host-country employees shouldn't be forced to adopt all home-country values and renounce their own. Again, Motorola's code is exemplary. First, it gives clear direction: "Employees of Motorola will respect the laws, customs, and traditions of each country in which they operate, but will, at the same time, engage in no course of conduct which, even if legal, customary, and accepted in any such country, could be deemed to be in violation of the accepted business ethics of Motorola or the laws of the United States relating to business ethics." After laying down such absolutes, Motorola's code then makes clear when individual judgment will be necessary. For example, employees may sometimes accept certain kinds of small gifts "in rare circumstances, where the refusal to accept a gift" would injure Motorola's "legitimate business interests." Under certain circumstances, such gifts "may be accepted so long as the gift inures to the benefit of Motorola" and not "to the benefit of the Motorola employee."

Striking the appropriate balance between providing clear direction and leaving room for individual judgment makes crafting corporate values statements and ethics codes one of the hardest tasks that executives confront. The words are only a start. A company's leaders need to refer often to their organization's credo and code and must themselves be credible, committed, and consistent. If senior managers act as though ethics don't matter, the rest of the company's employees won't think they do, either.

Conflicts of Development and Conflicts of Tradition

Managers living and working abroad who are not prepared to grapple with moral ambiguity and tension should pack their bags and come home. The view that all business practices can be categorized as either ethical or unethical is too simple. As Einstein is reported to have said, "Things should be as simple as possible—but no simpler." Many business practices that are considered unethical in one setting may be ethical in another. Such activities are neither black nor white but exist in what Thomas Dunfee and I have called *moral free space*.[2] In this gray zone, there are no tight prescriptions for a company's behavior. Managers must chart their own courses—as long as they do not violate core human values.

Consider the following example. Some successful Indian companies offer employees the opportunity for one of their children to gain a job with the company once the child has completed a certain level in school. The companies honor this commitment even when other applicants are more qualified than an employee's child. The perk is extremely valuable in a country where jobs are hard to find, and it reflects the Indian culture's belief that the West has gone too far in allowing economic opportunities to break up families. Not surprisingly, the perk is among the most cherished by employees, but in most Western countries, it would be branded unacceptable nepotism. In the United States, for example, the ethical principle of equal opportunity holds that jobs should go to the applicants with the best qualifications. If a U.S. company made such promises to its employees, it would violate regulations established by the Equal Employment Opportunity Commission. Given this difference in ethical attitudes, how should U.S. managers react to Indian nepotism? Should they condemn the Indian companies, refusing to accept them as partners or suppliers until they agree to clean up their act?

Despite the obvious tension between nepotism and principles of equal opportunity, I cannot condemn the practice for Indians. In a country, such as India, that emphasizes clan and family relationships and has catastrophic levels of unemployment, the practice must be viewed in moral free space. The decision to allow a special perk for employees and their children is not necessarily wrong—at least for members of that country.

How can managers discover the limits of moral free space? That is, how can they learn to distinguish a value in tension with their own from one that is intolerable? Helping managers develop good ethical judgment requires companies to be clear about their core values and codes of conduct. But even the most explicit set of guidelines cannot always provide answers. That is especially true in the thorniest ethical dilemmas, in which the host country's ethical standards not only are different but also seem lower than the home country's. Managers must recognize that when countries have different ethical standards, there are two types of conflict that commonly arise. Each type requires its own line of reasoning.

In the first type of conflict, which I call a *conflict of relative development*, ethical standards conflict because of the countries' different levels of economic development. As mentioned before, developing countries may accept wage rates that seem inhumane to more advanced countries in order to attract investment. As economic conditions in a developing country improve, the incidence of that sort of conflict usually decreases. The second type of conflict is a *conflict of cultural tradition*. For example, Saudi Arabia, unlike most other countries, does not allow women to serve as corporate managers. Instead, women may work in only a few professions, such as education and health care. The prohibition stems from strongly held religious and cultural beliefs; any increase in the country's level of economic development, which is already quite high, is not likely to change the rules.

To resolve a conflict of relative development, a manager must ask the following question: Would the practice be acceptable at home if my country were in a similar stage of economic development? Consider the difference between wage and safety standards in the United States and in Angola, where citizens accept lower standards on both counts. If a U.S. oil company is hiring Angolans to work on an offshore Angolan oil rig, can the company pay them lower wages than it pays U.S. workers in the Gulf of Mexico? Reasonable people have to answer yes if the alternative for Angola is the loss of both the foreign investment and the jobs.

Consider, too, differences in regulatory environments. In the 1980s, the government of India fought hard to be able to import Ciba-Geigy's Entero Vioform, a drug known to be enormously effective in fighting dysentery but one that had been banned in the United States because some users experienced side effects. Although dysentery was not a big problem in the United States, in India, poor public sanitation was contributing to epidemic levels of the disease. Was it unethical to make the drug available in India after it had been banned in the United States? On the contrary, rational people should consider it unethical not to do so. Apply our test: Would the United States, at an earlier stage of development, have used this drug despite its side effects? The answer is clearly yes.

But there are many instances when the answer to similar questions is no. Sometimes a host country's standards are inadequate at any level of economic development. If a country's pollution standards are so low that working on an oil rig would considerably increase a person's risk of developing cancer, foreign oil companies must refuse to do business there. Likewise, if the dangerous side effects of a drug treatment outweigh its benefits, managers should not accept health standards that ignore the risks.

When relative economic conditions do not drive tensions, there is a more objective test for resolving ethical problems. Managers should deem a practice permissible only if they can answer no to both of the following questions: Is it possible to conduct business successfully in the host country without undertaking the practice? and Is the practice a violation of a core human value? Japanese gift giving is a perfect example of a conflict of cultural tradition. Most experienced businesspeople, Japanese and non-Japanese alike, would agree that doing business in Japan would be virtually impossible without adopting the practice. Does gift giving violate a core human value? I cannot identify one that it violates. As a result, gift giving may be permissible for foreign companies in Japan even if it conflicts with ethical attitudes at home. In fact, that conclusion is widely accepted, even by companies such as Texas Instruments and IBM, which are outspoken against bribery.

Does it follow that all nonmonetary gifts are acceptable or that bribes are generally acceptable in countries where they are common? Not at all. (See the sidebar "The Problem with Bribery.") What makes the routine practice of gift giving acceptable in Japan are the limits in its scope and intention. When gift giving moves outside those limits, it soon collides with core human values. For example, when Carl Kotchian, president of Lockheed in the 1970s, carried suitcases full of cash to Japanese politicians, he went beyond the norms established by Japanese tradition. That incident galvanized opinion in the United States Congress and helped lead to passage of the Foreign Corrupt Practices Act. Likewise, Roh Tae Woo went beyond the norms established by Korean cultural tradition when he accepted $635.4 million in bribes as president of the Republic of Korea between 1988 and 1993.

The Problem with Bribery

BRIBERY IS WIDESPREAD AND INSIDIOUS. Managers in transnational companies routinely confront bribery even though most countries have laws against it. The fact is that officials in many developing countries wink at the practice, and the salaries of local bureaucrats are so low that many consider bribes a form of remuneration. The U.S. Foreign Corrupt Practices Act defines allowable limits on petty bribery in the form of routine payments required to move goods through customs. But demands for bribes often exceed those limits, and there is seldom a good solution.

Bribery disrupts distribution channels when goods languish on docks until local handlers are paid off, and it destroys incentives to compete on quality and cost when purchasing decisions are based on who pays what under the table. Refusing to acquiesce is often tantamount to giving business to unscrupulous companies.

I believe that even routine bribery is intolerable. Bribery undermines market efficiency and predictability, thus ultimately denying people their right to a minimal standard of living. Some degree of ethical commitment—some sense that everyone will play by the rules—is necessary for a sound economy. Without an ability to predict outcomes, who would be willing to invest?

There was a U.S. company whose shipping crates were regularly pilfered by handlers on the docks of Rio de Janeiro. The handlers would take about 10% of the contents of the crates, but the company was never sure which 10% it would be. In a partial solution, the company began sending two crates—the first with 90% of the merchandise, the second with 10%. The handlers learned to take the second crate and leave the first untouched. From the company's perspective, at least knowing which goods it would lose was an improvement.

Bribery does more than destroy predictability; it undermines essential social and economic systems. That truth is not lost on businesspeople in countries where the practice is woven into the social fabric. CEOs in India admit that their companies engage constantly in bribery, and they say that they have considerable disgust for the practice. They blame government policies in part, but Indian executives also know that their country's business practices perpetuate corrupt behavior. Anyone walking the streets of Calcutta, where it is clear that even a dramatic redistribution of wealth would still leave most of India's inhabitants in dire poverty, comes face-to-face with the devastating effects of corruption.

Guidelines for Ethical Leadership

Learning to spot intolerable practices and to exercise good judgment when ethical conflicts arise requires practice. Creating a company culture that rewards ethical behavior is essential. The following guidelines for developing a global ethical perspective among managers can help.

Treat corporate values and formal standards of conduct as absolutes

Whatever ethical standards a company chooses, it cannot waver on its principles either at home or abroad. Consider what has become part of company lore at Motorola. Around 1950, a senior executive was negotiating with officials of a South American government on a $10 million sale that would have increased the company's annual net profits by nearly 25%. As the negotiations neared completion, however, the executive walked away from the deal because the officials were asking for $1 million for "fees." CEO Robert Galvin not only supported the executive's decision but also made it clear that Motorola would neither accept the sale on any terms nor do business with those government officials again. Retold over the decades, this story demonstrating Galvin's resolve has helped cement a culture of ethics for thousands of employees at Motorola.

Design and implement conditions of engagement for suppliers and customers

Will your company do business with any customer or supplier? What if a customer or supplier uses child labor? What if it has strong links with organized crime? What if it pressures your company to break a host country's laws? Such issues are best not left for spur-of-the-moment decisions. Some companies have realized that. Sears, for instance, has developed a policy of not contracting production to companies that use prison labor or infringe on workers' rights to health and safety. And BankAmerica has specified as a condition for many of its loans to developing countries that environmental standards and human rights must be observed.

Allow foreign business units to help formulate ethical standards and interpret ethical issues

The French pharmaceutical company Rhône-Poulenc Rorer has allowed foreign subsidiaries to augment lists of corporate ethical principles with their own suggestions. Texas Instruments has paid special attention to issues of international business ethics by creating the Global Business Practices Council, which is made up of managers from countries in which the company operates. With the overarching intent to create a "global ethics strategy, locally deployed," the council's mandate is to provide ethics education and create local processes that will help managers in the company's foreign business units resolve ethical conflicts.

In host countries, support efforts to decrease institutional corruption

Individual managers will not be able to wipe out corruption in a host country, no matter how many bribes they turn down. When a host country's tax system, import and export procedures, and procurement practices favor unethical players, companies must take action.

Many companies have begun to participate in reforming host-country institutions. General Electric, for example, has taken a strong stand in India, using the media to make repeated condemnations of bribery in business and government. General Electric and others have found, however, that a single company usually cannot drive out entrenched corruption. Transparency International, an organization based in Germany, has been effective in helping coalitions of companies, government officials, and others work to reform bribery-ridden bureaucracies in Russia, Bangladesh, and elsewhere.

Exercise moral imagination

Using moral imagination means resolving tensions responsibly and creatively. Coca-Cola, for instance, has consistently turned down requests for bribes from Egyptian officials but has managed to gain political support and public trust by sponsoring a project to plant fruit trees. And take the example of Levi Strauss, which discovered in the early 1990s that two of its suppliers in Bangladesh were employing children under the age of 14—a practice that violated the company's principles but was tolerated in Bangladesh. Forcing the suppliers to fire the children would not have ensured that the children received an education, and it would have caused serious hardship for the families depending on the children's wages. In a creative arrangement, the suppliers agreed to pay the children's regular wages while they attended school and to offer each child a job at age 14. Levi Strauss, in turn, agreed to pay the children's tuition and provide books and uniforms. That arrangement allowed Levi Strauss to uphold its principles and provide long-term benefits to its host country.

Many people think of values as soft; to some they are usually unspoken. A South Seas island society uses the word *mokita*, which means, "the truth that everybody knows but nobody speaks." However difficult they are to articulate, values affect how we all behave. In a global business environment, values in tension are the rule rather than the exception. Without a company's commitment, statements of values and codes of ethics end up as empty platitudes that provide managers with no foundation for behaving ethically. Employees need and deserve more, and responsible members of the global business community can set examples for others to follow. The dark consequences of incidents such as Union Carbide's disaster in Bhopal remind us how high the stakes can be.

Originally published in September–October 1996. Reprint 96502

Notes

1. In other writings, Thomas W. Dunfee and I have used the term *hypernorm* instead of *core human value.*
2. Thomas Donaldson and Thomas W. Dunfee, "Toward a Unified Conception of Business Ethics: Integrative Social Contracts Theory," *Academy of Management Review*, April 1994; and "Integrative Social Contracts Theory: A Communitarian Conception of Economic Ethics," *Economics and Philosophy*, spring 1995.

Global Business Speaks English

by Tsedal Neeley

READY OR NOT, English is now the global language of business. More and more multinational companies are mandating English as the common corporate language—Airbus, Daimler-Chrysler, Fast Retailing, Nokia, Renault, Samsung, SAP, Technicolor, and Microsoft in Beijing, to name a few—in an attempt to facilitate communication and performance across geographically diverse functions and business endeavors.

Adopting a common mode of speech isn't just a good idea; it's a must, even for an American company with operations overseas, for instance, or a French company focused on domestic customers. Imagine that a group of salespeople from a company's Paris headquarters get together for a meeting. Why would you care whether they all could speak English? Now consider that the same group goes on a sales call to a company also based in Paris, not realizing that the potential customer would be bringing in employees from other locations who didn't speak French. This happened at one company I worked with. Sitting together in Paris, employees of those two French companies couldn't close a deal because the people in the room couldn't communicate. It was a shocking wake-up call, and the company soon adopted an English corporate language strategy.

Similar concerns drove Hiroshi Mikitani, the CEO of Rakuten—Japan's largest online marketplace—to mandate in March 2010 that

English would be the company's official language of business. The company's goal was to become the number one internet services company in the world, and Mikitani believed that the new policy—which would affect some 7,100 Japanese employees—was vital to achieving that end, especially as expansion plans were concentrated outside Japan. He also felt responsible for contributing to an expanded worldview for his country, a conservative island nation.

The multibillion-dollar company—a cross between Amazon.com and eBay—was on a growth spree: It had acquired PriceMinister.com in France, Buy.com and FreeCause in the U.S., Play.com in the UK, Tradoria in Germany, Kobo eBooks in Canada, and established joint ventures with major companies in China, Indonesia, Taiwan, Thailand, and Brazil. Serious about the language change, Mikitani announced the plan to employees not in Japanese but in English. Overnight, the Japanese language cafeteria menus were replaced, as were elevator directories. And he stated that employees would have to demonstrate competence on an international English scoring system within two years—or risk demotion or even dismissal.

The media instantly picked up the story, and corporate Japan reacted with fascination and disdain. Honda's CEO, Takanobu Ito, publicly asserted, "It's stupid for a Japanese company to only use English in Japan when the workforce is mainly Japanese." But Mikitani was confident that it was the right move, and the policy is bearing fruit. The English mandate has allowed Mikitani to create a remarkably diverse and powerful organization. Today, three out of six senior executives in his engineering organization aren't Japanese; they don't even speak Japanese. The company continues to aggressively seek the best talent from around the globe. Half of Rakuten's Japanese employees now can adequately engage in internal communication in English, and 25% communicate in English with partners and coworkers in foreign subsidiaries on a regular basis.

Adopting a global language policy is not easy, and companies invariably stumble along the way. It's radical, and it's almost certain to meet with staunch resistance from employees. Many may feel at a disadvantage if their English isn't as good as others', team dynamics and performance can suffer, and national pride can get in the way.

Idea in Brief

Companies are increasingly adopting English as the common corporate language, no matter where they're based. Unrestricted multilingualism is inefficient and gets in the way of accomplishing business goals. If people can't communicate effectively, sales get lost, merger integration drags, productivity slows, and so on. Single-language policies help companies avoid these problems, and English is the natural choice because it is already the dominant language of business.

Implementing an English-only policy is difficult and messy. People may view it as an affront to their cultural identity, or fear that they won't be able to learn enough English to keep up.

However, there's a lot that companies can do to help people along—including providing training, modeling the right behaviors themselves, and keeping the reasons for change front and center at all times.

And in fact, the challenge of getting up to speed may be less daunting than people think. You don't have to reach native fluency to be effective at work. For most people, 3,000 to 5,000 words will do it.

But to survive and thrive in a global economy, companies must overcome language barriers—and English will almost always be the common ground, at least for now.

The fastest-spreading language in human history, English is spoken at a useful level by some 1.75 billion people worldwide—that's one in every four of us. There are close to 385 million native speakers in countries like the U.S. and Australia, about a billion fluent speakers in formerly colonized nations such as India and Nigeria, and millions of people around the world who've studied it as a second language. An estimated 565 million people use it on the internet.

The benefits of "Englishnization," as Mikitani calls it, are significant; however, relatively few companies have systematically implemented an English-language policy with sustained results. Through my research and work over the past decade with companies, I've developed an adoption framework to guide companies in their language efforts. There's still a lot to learn, but success stories do exist. Adopters will find significant advantages.

Why English Only?

There's no question that unrestricted multilingualism is inefficient and can prevent important interactions from taking place and get in the way of achieving key goals. The need to tightly coordinate tasks and work with customers and partners worldwide has accelerated the move toward English as the official language of business no matter where companies are headquartered.

Three primary reasons are driving the move toward English as a corporate standard.

Competitive pressure

If you want to buy or sell, you have to be able to communicate with a diverse range of customers, suppliers, and other business partners. If you're lucky, they'll share your native language—but you can't count on it. Companies that fail to devise a language strategy are essentially limiting their growth opportunities to the markets where their language is spoken, clearly putting themselves at a disadvantage to competitors that have adopted English-only policies.

Globalization of tasks and resources

Language differences can cause a bottleneck—a Tower of Babel, as it were—when geographically dispersed employees have to work together to meet corporate goals. An employee from Belgium may need input from an enterprise in Beirut or Mexico. Without common ground, communication will suffer. Better language comprehension gives employees more firsthand information, which is vital to good decision making. Swiss food giant Nestlé saw great efficiency improvements in purchasing and hiring thanks to its enforcement of English as a company standard.

M&A integration across national boundaries

Negotiations regarding a merger or acquisition are complicated enough when everybody speaks the same language. But when they don't, nuances are easily lost, even in simple e-mail exchanges. Also,

Will Mandarin Be Next?

GIVEN THE SIZE AND GROWTH of the Chinese economy, why move to an English-only policy? Isn't it possible that Mandarin could overtake English as the global language of business? It's possible, but unlikely. There are two reasons for this.

First, English has a giant head start. China can't replicate Britain's colonial history. The British Empire began embedding the English language in many parts of the world as early as the 16th century. Philanthropic work by American and British organizations further spread English, long before corporations began to adopt it at the workplace.

Second, for much of the world, Mandarin is extremely difficult to learn. It's easier to pick up "broken English" than "broken Mandarin." Knowing Mandarin—or any language spoken by huge numbers of people—is an advantage, clearly. But for now, Mandarin is not a realistic option for a one-language policy.

cross-cultural integration is notoriously tricky; that's why when Germany's Hoechst and France's Rhône-Poulenc merged in 1998 to create Aventis, the fifth largest worldwide pharmaceutical company, the new firm chose English as its operating language over French or German to avoid playing favorites. A branding element can also come into play. In the 1990s, a relatively unknown, midsize Italian appliance maker, Merloni, adopted English to further its international image, which gave it an edge when acquiring Russian and British companies.

Obstacles to Successful English-Language Policies

To be sure, one-language policies can have repercussions that decrease efficiency. Evidence from my research at Rakuten—along with a study I conducted with Pamela Hinds of Stanford University and Catherine Cramton of George Mason University at a company I'll call GlobalTech and a study I conducted at a firm I'll call FrenchCo—reveals costs that global English-language rules can create. Proper rollout mitigates the risks, but even well-considered plans can encounter pitfalls. Here are some of the most common.

Change always comes as a shock

No amount of warning and preparation can entirely prevent the psychological blow to employees when proposed change becomes reality. When Marie (all names in this article are disguised, with the exception of Mikitani and Ito) first learned of FrenchCo's English-only policy, she was excited. She had been communicating in English with non-French partners for some time, and she saw the proposed policy as a positive sign that the company was becoming more international. That is, until she attended a routine meeting that was normally held in French. "I didn't realize that the very first meeting after the rule came out was really going to be in English. It was a shock," Marie says. She recalls walking into the meeting with a lot of energy—until she noticed the translator headsets.

"They're humiliating," she says. "I felt like an observer rather than a participant at my own company."

Compliance is spotty

An English mandate created a different problem for a service representative at GlobalTech. Based in Germany, the technology firm had subsidiaries worldwide. Hans, a service representative, received a frantic call from his boss when a key customer's multimillion-dollar financial services operation ground to a halt as a result of a software glitch. Hundreds of thousands of dollars were at stake for both the customer and GlobalTech. Hans quickly placed a call to the technical department in India, but the software team was unable to jump on the problem because all communications about it were in German—despite the English-only policy instituted two years earlier requiring that all internal communications (meetings, e-mails, documents, and phone calls) be carried out in English. As Hans waited for documents to be translated, the crisis continued to escalate. Two years into the implementation, adoption was dragging.

Self-confidence erodes

When nonnative speakers are forced to communicate in English, they can feel that their worth to the company has been diminished, regardless of their fluency level. "The most difficult thing is to have to admit that one's value as an English speaker overshadows one's real value," a FrenchCo employee says. "For the past 30 years the company did not ask us to develop our foreign-language skills or offer us the opportunity to do so," he points out. "Now, it is difficult to accept the fact that we are disqualified." Employees facing one-language policies often worry that the best jobs will be offered only to those with strong English skills, regardless of content expertise.

When my colleagues and I interviewed 164 employees at GlobalTech two years after the company's English-only policy had been implemented, we found that nearly 70% of employees continued to experience frustration with it. At FrenchCo, 56% of medium-fluency English speakers and 42% of low-fluency speakers reported worrying about job advancement because of their relatively limited English skills. Such feelings are common when companies merely announce the new policy and offer language classes rather than implement the shift in a systematic way. It's worth noting that employees often underestimate their own abilities or overestimate the challenge of developing sufficient fluency. (See the exhibit "Gauging fluency.")

Gauging fluency

Progressing from beginner level to advanced—which greatly improves an employee's ability to communicate—involves mastering around 3,500 words. That's a far less daunting task than adding the 10,000 words necessary to move from advanced to native speaker, for which the payoff may be lower.

1,500	3,000	5,000	15,000 words
Beginner	**Intermediate**	**Advanced**	**Native speakers**
These employees are able to cope with basic situations.	At this level, employees can function productively in business settings. They can understand verbal and written communications and express themselves; however, fine shades of meaning may escape them.	These speakers are comfortable with technical terms and nuanced discussion. They may begin to experience diminishing returns on their language efforts.	These employees speak fluently and idiomatically and have all means at their disposal to communicate effectively.

Job security falters

Even though achieving sufficient fluency is possible for most, the reality is that with adoption of an English-only policy, employees' job requirements change—sometimes overnight. That can be a bitter pill to swallow, especially among top performers. Rakuten's Mikitani didn't mince words with his employees: He was clear that he would demote people who didn't develop their English proficiency.

Employees resist

It's not unusual to hear nonnative speakers revert to their own language at the expense of their English-speaking colleagues, often because it's faster and easier to conduct meetings in their mother tongue. Others may take more aggressive measures to avoid speaking English, such as holding meetings at inopportune times. Employees in Asia might schedule a global meeting that falls during the middle of the night in England, for instance. In doing so, nonnative speakers shift their anxiety and loss of power to native speakers.

Many FrenchCo employees said that when they felt that their relatively poor language skills could become conspicuous and have career-related consequences, they simply stopped contributing to common discourse. "They're afraid to make mistakes," an HR manager at the firm explains, "so they will just not speak at all."

In other cases, documents that are supposed to be composed in English may be written in the mother tongue—as experienced by Hans at GlobalTech—or not written at all. "It's too hard to write in English, so I don't do it!" one GlobalTech employee notes. "And then there's no documentation at all."

Performance suffers

The bottom line takes a hit when employees stop participating in group settings. Once participation ebbs, processes fall apart. Companies miss out on new ideas that might have been generated in meetings. People don't report costly errors or offer observations about mistakes or questionable decisions. One of the engineers at GlobalTech's Indian office explained that when meetings reverted into German his ability to contribute was cut off. He lost important

Implementation Tips

EVEN WHEN LANGUAGE MANDATES are implemented with care and forethought, negative emotional and organizational dynamics can still arise. But their power to derail careers and company work can be significantly mitigated by adequately preparing people and systems for the change. Here are steps that companies can take to manage English-only policies.

1. Involve All Employees

Before a company introduces a global English policy, leaders should make a persuasive case for why it matters to employees and the organization. Employees must be assured that they will be supported in building their language skills. Companywide cultural-awareness training will help nonnative speakers feel heard and valued. Leaders should rally workers behind using English to accomplish goals, rather than learn it to meet proficiency standards.

2. Managers Are Referees and Enforcers

Managers must take responsibility for ensuring compliance, and they'll need training in how to productively address sensitive issues arising from the radical change. Groups should set norms prescribing how members will interact, and managers should monitor behavior accordingly. For instance, managers should correct employees who switch into their mother tongue.

3. Native Speakers Must Level the Playing Field

Native speakers can learn to speak more slowly and simplify their vocabularies. They should refrain from dominating conversations and encourage nonnative speakers to contribute. Native speakers may need coaching on how to bring along less proficient colleagues who are working at a disadvantage.

4. Nonnative Speakers Must Comply

Nonnative speakers have a responsibility to comply with the global English policy and to refrain from reverting to their mother tongue, even in informal meetings or communications. More-aggressive actions that exclude or ostracize native speakers, such as scheduling meetings at inopportune times, should be strongly discouraged.

information—particularly in side exchanges—despite receiving meeting notes afterward. Often those quick asides contained important contextual information, background analyses, or hypotheses about the root cause of a particular problem. He neither participated in the meetings nor learned from the problem-solving discussions.

An Adoption Framework

Converting the primary language of a business is no small task. In my work I've developed a framework for assessing readiness and guidelines for adopting the shift. Adoption depends on two key factors: employee buy-in and belief in capacity. Buy-in is the degree to which employees believe that a single language will produce benefits for them or the organization. Belief in their own capacity is the extent to which they are confident that they can gain enough fluency to pass muster.

The two dimensions combine to produce four categories of response to the change, as shown in the exhibit "Four types of employee response." Ideally, employees would fall in what I call the "inspired" category—those who are excited about the move and confident that they can make the shift. They're optimistic and likely to embrace the challenge. But undoubtedly, some employees will feel "oppressed." Those people don't think the change is a good idea, and they don't think they'll cut it.

Four types of employee response

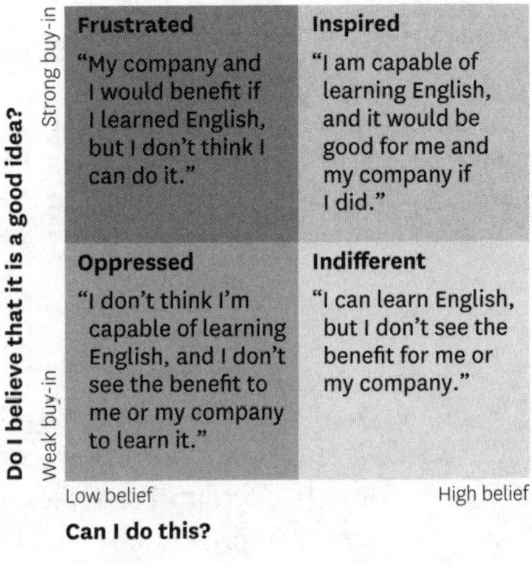

The reality is that without buy-in, employees won't bother to brush up their language; without belief, they'll lose hope. I've identified some guidelines managers can follow to help people along. Rakuten's Mikitani has successfully implemented a version of this framework.

Leaders and managers can help employees move from one box to another more easily than you might expect. There are fairly simple strategies that aid the shift, typically involving some combination of a strong psychological boost and practical training. To shift employees from "frustrated" to "inspired," for instance, managers must offer constant encouragement and an array of language-development opportunities. To shift employees from "indifferent" to "inspired," managers must work on improving buy-in—once these employees feel invested in the change, their skills will follow.

Improving belief in capacity

Managers can use four strategies to help people boost their belief in their ability to develop language proficiency.

Offer opportunities to gain experience with language. Whether through education, employment, or living abroad, experience tends to give people the confidence they need to succeed in this task. You can't change past experience, but you can provide opportunities, such as overseas language training and job rotations, that open new doors and allow employees to stretch their skills. Rakuten has sent senior executives to English-speaking Countries like the UK and the U.S. for full language immersion training. Employees have also been offered weekslong language-training programs in the Philippines. Although not easily scalable to 7,100 Japanese employees, the programs successfully produced individuals with functional English skills. Rakuten also plans to send more than 1,000 engineers to technology conferences outside Japan.

Foster positive attitudes. Attitudes are contagious: People's faith in their own capabilities grows when they see others around them—peers, managers, friends—having positive experiences with the radical change. The reverse is also true, unfortunately. Managers can model good risk-taking behaviors by showing that they too are trying new things, making mistakes, and learning from those mistakes.

Mikitani focused his personal attention on middle managers because he knew that collectively they could influence thousands of employees. He encouraged them to constantly improve their own language skills and even offered to teach them English himself if need be. (Nobody took him up on the offer.) He also encouraged managers to support their subordinates in their efforts to develop their language proficiency.

Use verbal persuasion. Encouragement and positive reinforcement from managers and executives—simple statements like "You can do it" or "I believe in you"—make all the difference. To mitigate turnover threats at Rakuten, managers identified talent that the company wanted to retain and tailored special programs for them, all the while cheering them on. Also, Mikitani repeatedly assured his entire workforce that he would do everything in his power to help every employee meet his or her English-proficiency goals. He made it clear that he believes that with effort everyone can adequately learn the language of business and that he did not want to see anyone leave the company because of the English-only policy.

Encourage good study habits. Companies need to contract with language vendors who specialize in helping employees at various levels of proficiency. The vendors need to be intimately familiar with the company context so that they can guide employees' learning, from how best to allocate their time in improving skills to strategies for composing e-mails in English. Rakuten considers language development to be part of every job and grants people time during the workday to devote to it. Every morning, employees can be seen flipping through their study books in the company's cafeteria or navigating their e-learning portals.

What About Cultural Identity?

MANY GLOBAL EMPLOYEES fear that an English-only policy will strip them of their cultural heritage. I propose an alternative point of view. The more people you can communicate with, the better positioned you are to spread your culture and your message. If people can't understand what you're saying, they can't engage with your company or your brand.

Improving employee buy-in

Shifts in buy-in call for different measures. But they don't operate in isolation: Buy-in and belief go together. Strategies that can help people feel more confident include:

Messaging, messaging, and more messaging. Continual communication from the CEO, executives, and managers is critical. Leaders should stress the importance of globalization in achieving the company's mission and strategy and demonstrate how language supports that. At Rakuten, Mikitani signaled the importance of the English-language policy to his entire organization relentlessly. For instance, each week some 120 managers would submit their business reports, and he would reply to each of them pushing them to develop their language skills. I surveyed employees before and after Rakuten implemented the adoption framework. Results indicated a dramatic increase in buy-in after Mikitani showed his employees that he was "obsessed and committed to Englishnization," as he put it. The vast majority of the employees surveyed said that the policy was a "necessary" move.

Internal marketing. Because a language transformation is a multiyear process whose complexity far exceeds most other change efforts, it is crucial to maintain employee buy-in over time. At Rakuten, the now-English intranet regularly features employee success stories with emphasis on best practices for increasing language competence. Companywide meetings are also held monthly to discuss the English-language policy.

Branding. Managers should encourage people to self-identify as global rather than local employees. It's difficult to develop a global identity with limited exposure to an international environment, of course. Rakuten tackled this challenge by instituting an enterprise-wide social network to promote cross-national interactions. Employees now interact and engage with colleagues worldwide through the company's social networking site.

Adopting a universal English policy is not the end of leadership challenges posed by global communication. Using English as a business language can damage employee morale, create unhealthy divides between native and nonnative speakers, and decrease the overall productivity of team members. Leaders must avoid and soften these potential pitfalls by building an environment in which employees can embrace a global English policy with relative ease. In this way, companies can improve communication and collaboration.

When I asked Mikitani what advice he'd give other CEOs when it comes to enforcing a one-language mandate, he was emphatic about discipline. CEOs need to be role models: If they don't stick to the program, nobody else will. Mikitani even holds one-on-one performance reviews with his top Japanese executives in English. "If you forgive a little," he says, "you'll give up everything."

Mikitani doesn't fear resistance. He believes, as I do, that you can counteract it—and ultimately bring about significant transformation in employees' beliefs and buy-in. A global language change takes perseverance and time, but if you want to surpass your rivals, it's no longer a matter of choice.

Originally published in May 2012. Reprint R1205H

10 Rules for Managing Global Innovation

by Keeley Wilson and Yves L. Doz

COMPANIES ARE WELL AWARE that hidden in their dispersed, global operations is a treasure trove of ideas and capabilities for innovation. But it's proving harder than expected to unearth those ideas or exploit those capabilities in global innovation projects. Some of the challenges of global projects are familiar: figuring out the right role for top executives, for example, or finding a good balance between formal and informal project management processes.

But although the challenges may be familiar, the solutions are not; what works for an innovation project conducted in a single location doesn't necessarily work for one dispersed across many sites around the world. That's partly because many important enablers of innovation happen naturally in colocation. Single location projects draw on large reservoirs of shared tacit knowledge and trust, and when issues arise, senior management is on hand to make decisions and provide direction and support. Team members share the same language, culture, and norms, enabling flexibility and iterative learning as the project unfolds.

When a project spans multiple locations, many of those natural benefits—often taken for granted—are lost. Part of the challenge of dispersed innovation thus becomes how to replicate the positive aspects of colocation while harnessing the unique benefits of a global initiative. To explore this challenge, we spent more than a decade doing field research at 47 companies around the world, including Citibank, HP, Hitachi, Infosys, Intel, LG Electronics, Novartis, Philips, Samsung, Siemens, Vodafone, and Xerox. In 2004 we teamed up with Booz & Company to conduct a global survey that was completed by 186 companies from 19 countries and 17 sectors, with a combined innovation spend of more than US$78 billion. We draw on that work to present a set of guidelines for successfully managing global innovation projects.

1. Start Small

One of the chief enablers of dispersed innovation is the experience of the participating sites in working on global projects. No matter how strong technical capabilities or customer knowledge may be at a particular site, employees will struggle to make a contribution to a global project commensurate with their skills if they have had experience only in colocated development. That's because on single location projects, team members benefit from collective tacit knowledge and a shared context, both of which support rich communication and help build trust and confidence among coworkers. Projects that span multiple sites and time zones are often hobbled by differences in workplace practices, communication patterns, and cultural norms. In the absence of everyday interactions and encounters, people struggle to signal trustworthiness and demonstrate competencies. Making matters worse, many teams are used to competing for resources with teams at other sites, and this creates yet another barrier to trust and collaboration between sites.

To be effective, dispersed teams have to develop a new set of collaboration competencies and establish a collaborative mind-set. This can be done by running small, dispersed projects involving just two or three sites before a project launch. Schneider Electric and Toshiba, two global electronics manufacturers, took this approach when they formed a joint venture, STI, to develop electrical drives and inverters. Although management was enthusiastic about the

Idea in Brief

Many firms struggle to exploit the innovation potential of their global networks. That's partly because they manage global projects like traditional ones. But single-location projects draw on a reservoir of shared tacit knowledge and trust that global projects lack. To get the most from dispersed innovation, managers need a different playbook.

Enabling Conditions

Global teams need collaboration competencies. These can be developed by running projects with just two or three sites before a project launch. Firms also must foster a climate of organizational stability and keep disruptions to a minimum.

Management Structures

Senior executives must have an explicit oversight role in global projects, and one site should be designated as the lead, to avoid time-consuming negotiations.

Resourcing

Companies should invest resources up front in defining the project, and must fight the urge to allocate resources on the basis of availability rather than skills and capabilities. Some knowledge overlap among sites is desirable. Firms should limit the number of external partners, as they add complexity.

Communication

The success of a global project remains dependent upon communication channels that mimic the richness of colocation.

new partnership, engineers at the two companies were not. To build trust between sites, STI organized a series of small, noncritical joint projects under the close scrutiny of senior managers. By the end of the first project, the teams had already begun to feel comfortable collaborating with colleagues at other sites. They quickly established consensus on working practices and protocols, reinforcing trust and providing a good foundation for the more complex global initiatives to come.

2. Provide a Stable Organizational Context

During periods of major organizational change, such as restructurings or acquisitions integration, the complexity of dispersed innovation escalates. Top managers are likely to be focused elsewhere within the organization, leaving their global projects orphaned. Critical decisions are frequently left hanging, and problems often go unaddressed. In a climate of organizational uncertainty, turf battles can flare up, and project team members may become concerned about job security and lose focus.

Consider a global electronics firm we'll call Elecompt. It launched a global innovation project at a time when new acquisitions were being integrated and a major reorganization of R&D was under way. Although the project was of strategic importance, management focus was understandably elsewhere. Problems came to a head when, prompted by fear of job losses, large numbers of highly skilled engineers at one site left the company, causing significant delays.

Of course, it's not possible to undertake global innovation projects only in times of sustained stability, so managers need to anticipate the possible toxic side effects of reorganization on global innovation and shelter teams as much as possible from disruptions. They should focus on creating an atmosphere of stability and bolster employees' sense of self-worth and loyalty to the firm. This will be particularly important for firms that are expanding R&D in China, where competition for talent is so intense that loyalty to employers rarely has time to develop.

3. Assign Oversight and Support Responsibility to a Senior Manager

When the knowledge base underlying a project is fragmented and project teams are scattered over multiple locations, miscommunication, conflict, and stalemates over crucial decision making are much more likely. Project teams often struggle to handle these problems constructively over a distance, especially when disagreements become personal, and so senior managers have to take on a formal role as arbiter, risk manager, support provider, and ultimate decision maker.

Contrast this with the more familiar world of single location projects, where senior managers can give the go-ahead to an innovation project and then step back and let the team get on with it. This hands-off approach works because on-site executives can rely on informal communication and feedback mechanisms to maintain oversight. Being on the spot, they're more likely to become aware of difficulties early on and can intervene when necessary to resolve them.

Companies that are smart about global innovation create an explicit role for senior executives in their projects. For example, at Essilor, a global corrective lens manufacturer, an executive team member is assigned to head up every international project. He or she monitors project progress and is responsible for making key decisions and ensuring that the project meets the firm's strategic objectives.

Essilor undertook a project to develop photochromic lenses with partners PPG and Transitions Optical. The project involved more than 20 sites around the world. To ensure first mover advantage, the schedule was extremely aggressive. Once the project was under way, it became clear that to hit the launch date, the production ramp-up phase would have to be reduced. This could be achieved only by taking shortcuts in the production validation and evaluation processes. None of the managers of the 18 production facilities were comfortable with that kind of risk.

With loose executive oversight and unclear decision rights, the project might have stalled or derailed before the issue came to the attention of senior management. But the executive responsible for the project saw the dilemma immediately and took it to the executive committee. Because time to market was critical, the committee agreed to the shortcuts and made it clear that the risk belonged to the project, not to the production sites. The problem was resolved without any disruption to the work flow, and the product was launched on schedule.

4. Use Rigorous Project Management and Seasoned Project Leaders

In addition to a fully engaged senior manager, a global innovation project requires a strong project management team to drive the project on a day-to-day basis and strong team leaders supported by robust tools and processes. These are necessary to impose discipline, structure, and a shared sense of purpose across the locations.

Firms can approach these challenges in a number of ways. Some adopt rigorous quality programs to provide formal project management for global projects. Siemens uses Design for Six Sigma to define common analytical tools, provide coaching, and set targets and timetables for feedback meetings. Those processes are then adopted across all sites.

Alternatively, firms can build a corporate project-management capability. Essilor, the lens manufacturer, has a corporate unit that runs global projects. The unit includes staff members from all functions and geographies—many of whom spend several years as project managers of global innovation efforts before returning to their area of specialty. These positions are desirable ones: Project managers value the opportunity to work closely with the senior executives assigned to their projects. And because the roles involve extensive travel and exposure to different parts of the firm, project managers leave the unit having built strong cross-cultural skills and robust relationships and networks all over the world.

It's important to note that global innovation projects are so complex that standard tools and processes don't always work well. At the joint venture STI, a project manager realized that misunderstandings resulting from e-mail communication between teams were causing the schedule to slip. With senior management support, he successfully introduced a protocol requiring that all initial communication on a topic be voice-to-voice. At the software firm Synopsys, the global development of a new product ran in parallel to the incremental development of an existing product, a traditional approach at many firms. Concerned that this would lead to an "us versus them" culture, the project manager organized work spaces to mix up the two teams.

5. Appoint a Lead Site

Each site involved in global innovation will see the project through the prism of its own contribution and context, rather than putting the bigger picture first. That's why all sites can't carry equal weight, even if their experience and expertise are equivalent; one has to be designated the lead. That site takes responsibility for delivering the project on time and on budget.

Let's compare the approaches taken by Elecompt on its global project and by Schneider on its STI joint venture with Toshiba. Each site involved in the STI project was a global leader in its field. However, the French site, which had been heavily involved in defining the new product requirements, was given responsibility for the project: coordinating the project management team, integrating the work of the other sites, and making final decisions. Having a clear lead site ensured prompt decision making and a project successfully delivered on time and on budget.

At Elecompt, each site had equal weight in making decisions and managing the project. That meant that every decision and aspect of cooperation had to be negotiated among multiple sites, at best a slow and cumbersome process. With each site defending its own corner, stalemates were common. One engineer noted that "there was an escalation of problems without corresponding solutions." Two years into the project and with renewed senior management focus, the necessary management structures were finally put in place to enable the project to progress.

6. Invest Time Defining the Innovation

Anyone who has worked on a single location project knows that the product or service delivered isn't always what was anticipated at the outset. This is actually one of the great benefits of colocation innovation. Because everyone involved is under the same roof and in frequent communication, continuous learning and adaptation can take place, allowing the design of the product or service to improve over the course of the project.

When a project is split over time zones, cultures, and languages, there is very little latitude for iterative learning. Instead, everything must be defined up front: the product or service architecture, the functionality of individual modules, and the interdependencies and interfaces between modules. In addition, process flows, timelines, and knowledge requirements need to be thoroughly understood so that everyone working on the project has the same understanding of the goals and their individual contributions to them.

Although there is a natural temptation to dive into development as soon as possible, studies show a positive correlation between investment in defining goals and technical specifications and the successful outcome of projects. In the case of Essilor's photochromic lens, despite having less than two years to deliver the new product, the project team invested nine months in defining the modules and multiple interfaces that would be handled by specialist teams from around the world, thereby building a solid foundation for success.

During the definition process, representatives from each project team were colocated for short periods of time. In addition, the constantly globe-trotting project managers held frequent on-site meetings and spent time conferring face-to-face with team members. We believe that a global project can't be effectively defined without some degree of colocation between the different functions and sites involved. Colocation builds relationships and trust up front and supports the sharing of complex ideas and concepts.

7. Allocate Resources on the Basis of Capability, Not Availability

The question of how best to staff a project rarely arises when only one location is involved: That location has presumably been chosen because the teams there have the requisite skills and experience. The effective staffing of a global project, however, requires a great deal of attention in order to select and integrate the best possible knowledge and capabilities.

But all too often, firms see global projects as an opportunity to make the most efficient use of human resources. Teams are selected not because they are the best qualified but because they are available at the time. The consequences of this approach can be seen in the Elecompt project. One of the sites, a U.S. team, was asked to develop a critical piece of software because it had the most staff availability, even though it lacked the required experience, and it struggled as a result. Eventually, when resources became available elsewhere, this module was moved to a team that had the necessary capabilities—but by then, morale had been dented, time wasted, and costs increased.

This availability approach to staffing projects completely undermines the basic rationale for global innovation—to bring together distinctive and differentiated knowledge and capabilities from around the world to create unique innovations. If teams are selected merely because they aren't doing anything else at the time rather than for their distinct capabilities, the project will take on a lot of risk for little benefit.

8. Build Enough Knowledge Overlap for Collaboration

Although sites involved in a project should be selected on the basis of the unique capabilities and knowledge they can bring, there also has to be a small degree of knowledge overlap between sites. Without this, critical interdependencies between modules may not be apparent until the integration phase, when problems are costly to rectify. This doesn't mean replicating the other sites' knowledge, but understanding enough of what they do to anticipate potential interdependencies and interfaces in the development process.

At Siemens, virtual cross-functional teams provide knowledge overlaps to help avoid such problems. Each module is developed by a specialist team and overseen by a virtual team comprising representatives from each of the other modules. This allows potential problems to be flagged and resolved as they arise.

9. Limit the Number of Subcontractors and Partners

In most innovation projects today, part of the work is outsourced or undertaken by development partners in order to access specific competencies, reduce development time, or cut costs. The final consideration in staffing global projects is selecting these external collaborators.

Managing relationships with external parties takes time and energy. So it makes sense in global projects to limit the additional complexity and management burden by keeping the number of subcontractors or partners to a minimum. And just as it's essential to use internal sites that have experience working together, it's easier and less risky to turn to external firms that are trusted and familiar. Choosing partners or subcontractors located close to one of the internal project sites will likewise reduce the potential for cross-cultural misunderstandings and will support face-to-face communication.

An example of the problems that can be caused by involving too many distant external partners in an innovation project can be clearly seen in Boeing's 787 Dreamliner project. This ambitious effort aimed to develop a new plane with significantly reduced operating costs by using innovative composite materials. The project involved over 50 main partners across the U.S., Europe, and East Asia, each charged with developing different subsections.

Coordinating that many partners was difficult, and Boeing had little insight into what was happening at each site. Integration proved extremely complex and constant modifications were required—for example, the new materials initially made it impossible to attach the wings to the fuselage. To get the project back on track, Boeing resorted to collocating its partners for six months. Although the final product was a success, it was delivered almost three years late, during which time Boeing lost orders to the Airbus A350.

10. Don't Rely Solely on Technology for Communication

In the end, the successful execution of a global project remains dependent upon communication channels that go as far as possible to replicate the richness of colocated communication. In single locations, a shared context—cultural, organizational, functional, and technological—makes it easier to discuss complex ideas and resolve problems informally. Because communication in this environment is second nature, managers tend to underestimate the challenge of scaling communication globally.

Information and communications technologies, or ICTs, including e-mail, web meetings, social media platforms, online forums, and video conferencing certainly have a role to play, but those tools shouldn't be overrelied on, because they tend to mask differences between locations, leading to misunderstandings and tension. In addition to ICTs, the communication armory for a global innovation project should include a generous travel budget for face-to-face site visits, project team meetings, and temporary transfers for key people. Also, to encourage team members to feel an allegiance and sense of belonging to a global project rather than their local site, a web of cross-site reporting lines can be put in place. This has the added advantage of forcing communication and knowledge sharing.

Successful globally integrated firms understand the importance of an extensive communications approach. Tata Communications, for example, has a highly dispersed structure that enables it to access the best competencies and market knowledge around the world. Even its top management team is dispersed across the globe. The company has invested in a raft of ICTs to support everyday collaboration, but this is in addition to hefty travel budgets for vital, regular face-to-face communication to drive projects forward, share knowledge, and reinforce trust.

Together, the 10 steps we have outlined represent the foundation for successful global innovation projects. Adopting only one or two may result in fleeting success in some projects but will not produce a stream of positive outcomes. These best practices all need to be put in place and honed over time. It's not easy to build a global innovation capability, but for companies that don't have the skills and processes in place to manage global innovation projects, the future offers a stark choice: Continue with only colocated projects, in the hope that they will fill the innovation pipeline for a few more years until global competition intensifies and makes local innovation a niche activity. Or begin building a capability in global innovation now to take advantage of lower development costs, faster time to market, and, most important, the ability to leverage dispersed knowledge to gain competitive advantage.

Originally published in October 2012. Reprint R1210F

Lost in Translation

by Fons Trompenaars and Peter Woolliams

IT DOESN'T TAKE MUCH experience of life to realize that we vary enormously in how we perceive and respond to failure, and that a great many of those perceptions and responses are shaped by the cultures in which we grew up or now work. Of course, stories about cultural differences and stereotypes have long been a staple of dinner-table conversations and the source of much amusement. But Western multinationals are sinking a huge amount of money into India, China, and Brazil, and emerging giants in those countries are setting up operations both in developed world markets and in other emerging markets. Any business with global aspirations must take seriously cultural differences in general and around failure in particular.

Those differences are a central theme in our research. Drawing on the findings of an ongoing global survey that THT Consulting has conducted over the past 30 years (the results were first published and discussed in *Riding the Waves of Culture*), we have identified the dimensions along which people from various cultures differ regarding failure. Here we discuss in detail the five most important of those dimensions and describe how some forward-looking companies are managing to reconcile cultural differences to create a powerful platform for innovation.

1. Do We Control Our Environment or Does It Control Us?

This dimension determines whether you manage failure with prevention or with response. Cultures that view the environment as *internally* controlled—by an individual or a company—believe that good design and planning can help to avoid most failures. Cultures that view the environment as *externally* controlled accept failure as inevitable and believe that survival depends on developing the skills to respond to it quickly.

We assessed the degree to which respondents in our global survey felt they had control over their lives and found considerable variation. Almost 90% of Israeli respondents and about 80% of those from the United States, Britain, Australia, and Canada felt that they had a strong degree of control over their environment. Predictably, perhaps, only 40% of the Chinese and 50% of the Russians felt they had such control. But the stereotypes don't always hold. Some 70% of people in both South Korea and Indonesia felt they had control. Clearly, there are advantages and disadvantages to both views. People who feel that control is internal see failure as a personal threat and may become authoritarian or manipulative to increase their comfort level. They may write lengthy contracts that cover every conceivable contingency and hedge every clause. But they are less wasteful, because they tend not to repeat mistakes. Cultures that are more fatalistic are also more adaptable. They respond quickly and efficiently to failure. But they tend to leave the causes of failure untreated, so they have to pick up the same pieces again and again, which can be very expensive.

Obviously, a company that combined prevention with adaptability would be a formidable competitor. Emirates, the national airline of Dubai, is a good example. During training exercises, Western pilots try to avoid failure, even though "crashing" in a simulator costs nothing. They propose changes in cockpit design and procedures and change routes to minimize the likelihood of disaster. By contrast, Arab pilots who are given a chance to "fail" without consequences will take risks and respond to them. They want to experience a crisis situation—such as how the controls feel seconds before going into a stall. They'll pass through a virtual cloud rather than around or over it. Emirates learns from pilots of both kinds to prevent failures and improve responses to them, making it one of the safest airlines in the world.

Idea in Brief

People vary enormously in how they perceive and respond to failure, and those perceptions and responses are shaped by the cultures in which they grew up or now work. Western multinationals are sinking a huge amount of money into India, China, and Brazil, and emerging giants in those countries are setting up operations in world markets as well. Any business with global aspirations must take seriously cultural differences in general and around failure in particular. Drawing on the findings of a global survey that has been ongoing for 30 years, Trompenaars and Woolliams have identified the dimensions along which people from various cultures differ regarding failure. They discuss the five most important of those dimensions: (1) Do we view our environment as internally or externally controlled? (2) Which is more important—rules or relationships? (3) Are failures the responsibility of the individual or of the team? (4) How much do we identify with our failures? (5) Do we grant status according to performance or to position? The authors describe how some forward-looking companies are managing to reconcile cultural differences to create a powerful platform for innovation.

2. What's More Important, Rules or Relationships?

How strictly we adhere to rules and how eagerly we make them vary greatly from culture to culture. *Rule-centered* societies like the United States and Britain feel that general rules should have global application and that all comers should compete on a level playing field. *Relationship-centered* countries like China, Russia, and India value bonds with family and friends above abstract rules: Particular circumstances and the people involved may dictate the response to a situation.

Countries in the former category probably better satisfy the desire for distributive justice, but they may become obsessed with rules and regulations—which explains in part why the United States has so many more lawyers than Japan does. Countries in the latter category tend to resolve failure privately, through relationships. The Swiss, North Americans, and Australians are the most rule-oriented, with 70% to 80% of respondents believing that exceptions to rules should not be made to help friends. In the BRIC countries, by contrast, only 25% to 40% would put the rule above the person.

We often see these approaches collide in global organizations, usually in interactions between a headquarters focused on rules and principles and local offices that are highly sensitive to their relationship networks. Typically the local offices appear to conform to rules and principles while actually following local customs. As long as broad financial expectations are met, no one asks questions. But that means the organization as a whole cannot learn from local successes and failures.

A relationship-centered organization, with its tolerance of failure, can encourage innovation and learning. But it may also be wasteful, and its employees may be reluctant to compete with friends, curtailing entrepreneurial opportunities. A rules-centered organization provides clarity and, often, greater cost efficiency. But it also breeds inflexibility and mountains of red tape.

Companies can combine the virtues of both by recognizing that rules and exceptions are mutually sustaining. An exception to a rule may contain the seed of a new rule or illuminate the limits of the old one. Using a technique called "management by exception," which draws attention to any surprise event falling outside existing rules and expectations, managers can strengthen some rules and obviate others. And the existence of rules helps to make exceptional relationships meaningful.

A case in point was provided by a global financial services firm we advised. The company, which was based in Germany, stated that its main value was integrity. But its employees' interpretation of "integrity" varied enormously. Americans saw it as sticking to principles even if that meant being hard on friends. Koreans and many other relationship-centered employees believed that it was best expressed by helping friends even if that meant bending a principle or two.

In the course of several workshops, we uncovered ways of reconciling these two views. It was a Brazilian employee of the firm who pointed out that bending a rule for a friend can be used to motivate that friend. Suppose your friend has been performing badly.

You can say you will fudge his assessment, but only this one time. Indeed, the performance criteria at his next review will actually be tougher—though you are prepared to mentor him if he's willing to try to improve and meet them. In this way you demonstrate both loyalty to your friend and commitment to the rules. Meanwhile, he is motivated to perform better—which is essentially what you hoped to achieve in the first place.

3. Are Failures the Responsibility of the Individual or the Team?

In *individualistic* societies like the United States, workers are very independent and even compete with their colleagues. Although internal competition can be organizationally toxic, it can also be highly productive, especially in businesses that compete on their ability to sell. Naming a Best Salesperson of the Quarter at company award ceremonies helps to boost sales targets.

At the other end of the spectrum are *communitarian* countries, in which people take responsibility for errors as a group, even when only one member is involved. At the Indonesian subsidiary of a U.S. multinational we studied, a local worker had made a serious error that forced the company to redo an entire production batch. The expatriate unit manager asked the Indonesian plant director who had made the error and what action was being taken against her. The manager was amazed when the plant director claimed not to know, saying, "The whole work group has accepted responsibility."

"But if everyone is responsible, then in effect no one is," the manager argued. "They are simply protecting one another's bad work."

"That is not how we see it," the plant manager replied. "The woman concerned was so upset that she went home. She tried to resign. Two of her coworkers had to coax her back again. The group knows she was responsible, and she feels shame. The group also knows that she was new and they did not help her enough or look out for her or see that she was properly trained. That is why the whole group has apologized. They are willing to apologize to you publicly."

A Failure Culture Survey

ASKING EMPLOYEES THE FOLLOWING simple questions can help you assess how failure is viewed across your organization.

1. Are failures a fact of life or can they be avoided by planning?
2. What would you do if a friend made a professional mistake on which you needed to report publicly?
3. Is it individual creativity or team consensus that is most important for avoiding mistakes?
4. Do you address criticism to the task or to the person?
5. Is the seriousness of a mistake affected by the person who made it or not?
6. Are failures attributed to the person or team involved or to the department head?

As the story illustrates, communitarianism can provide a nurturing learning environment. Through team membership we support people to become better individual workers. At the same time, someone who "lets the group down" will experience shame in a communitarian culture. The downside, of course, is that companies dominated by a sense of the group can choke off individual creativity and the striving for personal excellence.

For communitarianism to work well, a group's interests and values must strongly align with the company's objectives—as they clearly did in the Indonesian example. But it is also important that a group's learning spreads, which may mean assigning responsibility for a failure to an individual. In such a case it may be possible to remove the stigma by redefining the failure as a learning opportunity.

What we call "co-opetition" can bring some communitarianism to an individualistic company. At IBM, for example, in addition to receiving bonuses based on their volume, salespeople are rewarded for making good presentations to colleagues on lessons learned from client interactions. The group's performance has risen by 30% since this program was introduced.

We asked our survey respondents whether mistakes like the one made by the Indonesian worker should be borne by the individual or by the group. Russians turned out to be the most individualistic: Almost 70% would blame the individual. Australians (58%) and Americans (54%) came in second and third. Danes were significantly more individualistic (53%) than either the British (48%) or the Dutch (43%). Among the most group-oriented countries, China was slightly more individualistic (36%) than India (35%), Japan, and Brazil (both below 35%), which was unexpected.

4. How Much Do We Identify with Our Failures?

People in *non-identifying* cultures are not afraid of failure. They compartmentalize, viewing a failure as simply an idea that didn't work. Furthermore, they celebrate failure as a learning opportunity. They are, however, more likely to jump to conclusions too quickly, and may waste a lot of energy. For people in *identifying* cultures, failure is a bigger deal. When we asked our survey respondents whether they blamed the person or the idea, we found that 72% of the Dutch and 66% of the Americans blamed the idea, whereas only 31% of the Indians, 29% of the Germans, 24% of the Chinese, and 12% of the Japanese did.

Consider the dynamic we observed between American and German engineers at the semiconductor giant AMD, which we advised shortly after it had set up operations in Germany. The U.S. semiconductor industry can attribute much of its success to the integration of individual creativity with teamwork and to the successful use of failures. When AMD arrived in Dresden, programs were executed in a stereotypical American manner: Videos, workshops, and pep talks were done the "Silicon way" and combined with brainstorming sessions in the so-called war room.

When we interviewed American employees, we heard many complaints about the slowness, lack of creativity, and risk-averseness of their German counterparts when it came to exploratory ideas. The Germans, in turn, claimed that the Americans were too hasty in their behavior, throwing clearly underdeveloped ideas into brainstorming sessions. The reason for this tension quickly emerged in our workshops. Because the Americans separated the ideas from the people, they readily accepted criticism during a brainstorming session: "My idea was hacked into pieces. No problem. On with the next idea." But to the Germans, this approach was misguided: "All that exaggerated business about the importance of effective meetings and brainstorming. Let's just do our homework and everything will work out."

AMD found a way to reconcile these views. In hindsight the solution seems simple. Time-outs were built into each meeting, which allowed the Germans to swap and criticize ideas in private and in German. Failures in the smaller, familiar group were acceptable. Their ideas were then collated on Post-it notes and shared with the Americans. The Americans were astonished at the resultant German creativity.

5. Do We Grant Status According to Performance or Position?

In *achieving* cultures, people value others according to their performance, whereas *ascribing* cultures emphasize a person's position in the organization and the society. This difference plays a role in determining the extent to which people are willing to show initiative and risk failure.

In achieving cultures, people take a lot of personal initiative—but they are often very protective of their achievements, which can play out in the broader culture as a strong sense of property rights and much litigiousness. And if achievement is valued too highly, people may exaggerate their own successes, take credit for those of others, or even game the system. (One of us was at a leading business school recently and came upon an MBA student leaving the library with eight books. When asked why he had so many, the student explained that he was more interested in making sure no one else read them than in reading them himself.) In an overachieving culture, innovation may be stifled when the willingness to risk failure is moderated by a fear of not achieving. To prevent abuse, managers have to be very careful and visibly impartial in assigning credit for successes and failures.

In ascribing cultures, people avoid taking responsibility for actions when their superiors are around, because they gain little—and may actually incite hostility—for successes, whereas they are vulnerable if they make mistakes. Employees first discuss their actions with the boss; once they get the go-ahead, the boss takes responsibility for success or failure. In an achieving culture, if the goal demands it, people will take action and inform the boss later. If things go wrong, the boss will judge whether the risk was reasonably assessed and the action had the potential to achieve the goal.

We heard the following story from the head of process control at a British dairy company. A man we'll call Malcolm, one of the plant's best process operators, knew—like his colleagues— how to read the meters and intervene when necessary. What made him special was his well-developed intuition. If he stopped the production process straightaway when he sensed something was odd, his prompt action saved the company money in 99 out of 100 cases. On night shifts, when his boss wasn't around, he would take the initiative, but on day shifts he would go to his boss for direction. Telling him that he was causing a lot of unnecessary loss by delaying a shutdown for even five minutes didn't change his behavior. The company was able to overcome Malcolm's hesitation by giving him the title of supervisor, empowering him to decide when to shut production down whether his boss was there or not.

A similar gambit worked for an achievement-oriented U.S. bank operating in highly ascribing Argentina. When the American manager of the Argentinean subsidiary complained about the low motivation of his administrative staffers, we advised him to take a look at their job titles, which had been imported from the United States: Departmental Secretary I, II, and III. After the highest-ranking secretary was promoted to Personal Assistant and the others were given titles that made clear the positions of those for whom they worked, a more positive atmosphere quickly developed. The manager told us, "Not only was it in line with their culture, but best of all, it did not affect my budget."

Of course, countries—and even industries—are not the only units of cultural comparison, and they may conceal a wide variation across some of the dimensions. The failure culture of a Japanese car company, for example, may resemble GM's more than Sony's. Variations within companies may arise from people's functional affiliations or hierarchical status. To manage failure as part of a learning strategy, therefore, you must understand just where the variations are most salient in your company. You'll need to conduct research at many levels across your business units, distinguishing by function, business line, hierarchical status, and geography. But at any organizational level, the cultural dimensions we have described here will give you a strong framework for your enquiry.

Originally published in April 2011. Reprint W1104A

The Right Way to Manage Expats

by J. Stewart Black and Hal B. Gregersen

IN TODAY'S GLOBAL ECONOMY, having a workforce that is fluent in the ways of the world isn't a luxury. It's a competitive necessity. No wonder nearly 80% of midsize and large companies currently send professionals abroad—and 45% plan to increase the number they have on assignment.

But international assignments don't come cheap. On average, expatriates cost two to three times what they would in an equivalent position back home. A fully loaded expatriate package including benefits and cost-of-living adjustments costs anywhere from $300,000 to $1 million annually, probably the single largest expenditure most companies make on any one individual except for the CEO.

The fact is, however, that most companies get anemic returns on their expat investments. Over the past decade, we have studied the management of expatriates at about 750 U.S., European, and Japanese companies. We asked both the expatriates themselves and the executives who sent them abroad to evaluate their experiences. In addition, we looked at what happened after expatriates returned home. Was their tenure worthwhile from a personal and organizational standpoint?

Overall, the results of our research were alarming. We found that between 10% and 20% of all U.S. managers sent abroad returned early because of job dissatisfaction or difficulties in adjusting to a foreign country. Of those who stayed for the duration, nearly one-third did not perform up to the expectations of their superiors. And perhaps most problematic, one-fourth of those who completed an assignment left their company, often to join a competitor, within one year after repatriation. That's a turnover rate double that of managers who did not go abroad.

If getting the most out of your expats is so important, why do so many companies get it so wrong? The main reason seems to be that many executives assume that the rules of good business are the same everywhere. In other words, they don't believe they need to—or should have to—engage in special efforts for their expats.

Take the expat assignment process. Executives know that negotiation tactics and marketing strategies can vary from culture to culture. Most do not believe, however, that the variance is sufficient to warrant the expense of programs designed to select or train candidates for international assignments.

Further, once expats are in place, executives back home usually are not inclined to coddle their well-paid representatives. When people are issued first-class tickets on a luxury liner, they're not supposed to complain about being at sea.

Finally, people at the home office find it difficult to imagine that returning expats need help readjusting after just a few years away. They don't see why people who've been given an extended period to explore the Left Bank or the Forbidden City should get a hero's welcome. As a result of such thinking, the only time companies pay special attention to their expats is when something goes spectacularly wrong. And by then, it's too little, too late.

Of course, some companies do engage in serious efforts to make foreign assignments beneficial both for the employees and the organization. Very often, however, such companies consign the responsibility of expat selection, training, and support to the human resources department. Few HR managers—only 11%, according to our research—have ever worked abroad themselves; most have little understanding of a global assignment's unique personal and professional challenges. As a result, they often get bogged down in

Idea in Brief

In the global economy, having a workforce that is fluent in the ways of the world is a competitive necessity. That's why more and more companies are sending more and more professionals abroad. But international assignments don't come cheap: On average, expatriates cost a company two to three times what they would cost in equivalent positions back home. Most companies, however, get anemic returns on their expat investments. The authors discovered that an alarming number of assignments fail in one way or another—some expats return home early, others finish but don't perform as well as expected, and many leave their companies within a year of repatriation. To find out why, the authors recently focused on the small number of companies that manage their expats successfully. They found that all those companies follow three general practices: (1) When they send people abroad, the goal is not just to put out fires. Once expats have doused the flames, they are expected to generate new knowledge for the organization or to acquire skills that will help them become leaders. (2) They assign overseas posts to people whose technical skills are matched or exceeded by their cross-cultural skills. (3) They recognize that repatriation is a time of upheaval for most expats, and they use a variety of programs to help their people readjust. Companies that follow these practices share a conviction that sustained growth rests on the shoulders of individuals with international experience. As a result, they are poised to capture tomorrow's global market opportunities by making their investments in international assignments successful today.

the administrative minutiae of international assignments instead of capturing strategic opportunities.

Over the past several years, we have concentrated on examining the small number of companies that have compiled a winning track record in the process of managing their expats. Their people overseas report a high degree of job satisfaction and back that up with strong performance. These companies also hold on to their expats long after they return home. GE Medical Systems, for example, has all but eliminated unwanted turnover after repatriation and has seen its international sales expand from 10% to more than 50% of its total sales during the last ten years.

The companies that manage their expats effectively come in many sizes and from a wide range of industries. Yet we have found that they all follow three general practices:

When making international assignments, they focus on knowledge creation and global leadership development. Many companies send people abroad to reward them, to get them out of the way, or to fill an immediate business need. At companies that manage the international assignment process well, however, people are given foreign posts for two related reasons: to generate and transfer knowledge, to develop their global leadership skills, or to do both.

They assign overseas posts to people whose technical skills are matched or exceeded by their cross-cultural abilities. Companies that manage expats wisely do not assume that people who have succeeded at home will repeat that success abroad. They assign international posts to individuals who not only have the necessary technical skills but also have indicated that they would be likely to live comfortably in different cultures.

They end expatriate assignments with a deliberate repatriation process. Most executives who oversee expat employees view their return home as a nonissue. The truth is, repatriation is a time of major upheaval, professionally and personally, for two-thirds of expats. Companies that recognize this fact help their returning people by providing them with career guidance and enabling them to put their international experience to work.

Let's explore the practices in turn, illustrating them with companies that have put them to good use over the past several years.

Sending People for the Right Reasons

For as long as companies have been sending people abroad, many have been doing so for the wrong reasons—that is, for reasons that make little long-term business sense. Foreign assignments in glamorous locales such as Paris and London have been used to reward favored employees; posts to distant lands have been used as dumping grounds for the mediocre. But in most cases, companies send people abroad to fill a burning business need: to fight a competitor gaining market share in Brazil, to open a factory in China, to keep the computers running in Portugal.

Immediate business demands cannot be ignored. But the companies that manage their expats effectively view foreign assignments with an eye on the long term. Even when people are sent abroad to extinguish fires, they are expected to plant forests when the embers are cool. They are expected to go beyond pressing problems either to generate new knowledge for the organization or to acquire skills that will help them become leaders.

Imagine a large Canadian company that wants to open a telephone-making plant in Vietnam. It would certainly send a manager who knows how to manufacture phones and how to get a greenfield facility up and running quickly. The manager's performance rating and compensation would reflect those objectives, but that's where most companies would stop. Companies that manage their expats effectively, however, would require more of the manager in Vietnam. Once the plant was established, he would be expected to transfer his knowledge to local professionals—and to learn from them, too. Together, they would be expected to generate innovative ideas.

Nokia, the world's second largest manufacturer of mobile phones, is a good example of a company that effectively uses international assignments to generate knowledge. Unlike most large technology companies, Nokia does not rely on a central R&D function. Instead, it operates 36 centers in 11 countries—from Finland to China to the United States. Senior executives scan their global workforce for engineers and designers who are likely to generate new ideas when combined into a team. They bring these people together in an R&D center for assignments of up to two years, with the explicit objective of inventing new products. The approach works well: Nokia continues to grab global market share by rapidly turning new ideas into successful commercial products, such as the Nokia 6100 series mobile telephones that were launched last year in Beijing and have quickly captured a leading position in markets around the world.

Other companies have more need to focus on the second reason for international assignments: to develop global leadership skills. Such companies would concur with a recent observation by GE's CEO: "The Jack Welch of the future cannot be like me. I've spent my entire career in the United States. The next head of GE will be somebody who has spent time in Bombay, in Hong Kong, in Buenos Aires." An executive cannot develop a global perspective on business or become comfortable with foreign cultures by staying at headquarters or taking short business trips abroad. Such intangibles come instead as a result of having spent more than one sustained period working abroad.

Indeed, the only way to change fundamentally how people think about doing business globally is by having them work abroad for several months at a time. Everyone has a mental map of the world—a set of ingrained assumptions about what people are like and how the world works. But our maps may not be able to point us in the right direction when we try to use them in uncharted territory. Consider the case of a tall American businessman who, during a recent trip to Japan, dined at a traditional restaurant. Upon entering, he bumped his head on the doorjamb. The next day, the same thing happened. It was only on the third time that he remembered to duck. People on international assignments hit their heads on doorjambs many times over the years. Eventually, they learn to duck—to expect that the world abroad will be different from the one they had imagined. Hard experience has rearranged their mental maps or, at the very least, expanded the boundaries on their maps.

It is with such a broadened view of the world that global leaders are made. A vice president for Disney, for example, was posted in 1993 to EuroDisney, the company's struggling theme park just outside Paris. Stephen Burke arrived in France with the same mental map of the company as the senior managers at home. He believed, for instance, that families and alcohol do not mix at Disney theme parks. But after living in France for several months, Burke came to see what an affront EuroDisney's no-alcohol policy was to most of its potential local customers. A glass of wine with lunch was as French as a cheeseburger was American. Further, Burke came to see that Disney's lack of focus on tour operators—a more important distribution channel in Europe than in North America—made it inconvenient to book reservations for complete vacation packages, which many Europeans prefer to arrange.

With his new perspective on the local market, Burke pushed hard to persuade Disney's top management to sell wine at its French park and to create complete vacation packages for tour operators. He succeeded. Because of those and other changes, attendance and hotel occupancy soon skyrocketed, and EuroDisney posted its first operational profit. Burke told us afterward, "The assignment to EuroDisney caused me to challenge long-held assumptions that were based on my experiences and career at Disney. After living in France, I came to look at the world quite differently."

The two principal goals of international assignments—generation of knowledge and development of global leaders—are not mutually exclusive. But it is unlikely that an international posting will allow a company to achieve both goals in every case or to an equal degree. Not every employee going abroad has abundant knowledge to share or the right stuff to be the company's future CEO. What matters, however, is that executives explicitly know beforehand why they are sending a person overseas—and that the reason goes beyond an immediate business problem.

Just as important, it is critical that expats themselves know the rationale for their assignments. Are they being sent abroad to generate knowledge or to develop their leadership skills? At the effective companies we studied, this kind of information helps expats focus on the right objectives in the right measure. For example, a communications company recently transferred one of its top lean-manufacturing experts from Asia to the United States. His task was to help managers understand and implement the practices that had been perfected in Singapore and Japan. The company's senior executives did not expect him to hone his leadership capabilities because they did not believe that he would ascend the corporate ranks. Knowing the main purpose of his posting, the expert was able to focus his energy on downloading his knowledge to other managers. Moreover, he did not build up unrealistic expectations that he would be promoted after returning home.

Companies with foreign operations will always face unexpected crises from time to time. But the companies that reap the most from sending their people abroad recognize that international assignments can't just be about sending in the medics. They must also be about ensuring the organization's health over the long term.

Sending the Right People

Just as managers often send people abroad for the wrong reasons, they frequently send the wrong people. Not because they send people who don't have the necessary technical skills. Indeed, technical skill is frequently the main reason that people are selected for open posts. But managers often send people who lack the ability to adjust to different customs, perspectives, and business practices. In other words, they send people who are capable but culturally illiterate.

Companies that have a strong track record with expats put a candidate's openness to new cultures on an equal footing with the person's technical know-how. After all, successfully navigating within your own business environment and culture does not guarantee that you can maneuver successfully in another one. We know, for instance, of a senior manager at a U.S. carmaker who was an expert at negotiating contracts with his company's steel suppliers. When transferred to Korea to conduct similar deals, the man's confrontational style did nothing but offend the consensus-minded Koreans—to the point where suppliers would not even speak to him directly. What was worse, the man was unwilling to change his way of doing business. He was soon called back to the company's home office, and his replacement spent a year undoing the damage he left in his wake.

How do you weed out people like the man who failed in Korea? The companies that manage expats successfully use a variety of tools to assess cultural sensitivity, from casual observation to formal testing. Interestingly, however, almost all evaluate people early in their careers in order to eliminate some from the potential pool of expats and help others build cross-cultural skills.

Although the companies differ in how they conduct their assessments, our research shows that they seek the following similar characteristics in their expats:

A drive to communicate

Most expats will try to communicate with local people in their new country, but people who end up being successful in their jobs are those that don't give up after early attempts either fail or embarrass them. To identify such people, the most effective companies in our research scanned their ranks for employees who were both enthusiastic and extroverted in conversation, and not afraid to try out their fractured French or talk with someone whose English was weak.

Broad-based sociability

The tendency for many people posted overseas is to stick with a small circle of fellow expats. By contrast, successful global managers establish social ties to the local residents, from shopkeepers to government officials. There is no better source for insights into a local market and no better way to adjust to strange surroundings.

Cultural flexibility

It is human nature to gravitate toward the familiar—that's why many Americans overseas find themselves eating lunch at McDonald's. But the expats who add the most value to their companies—by staying for the duration and being open to local market trends—are those who willingly experiment with different customs. In India, such people eat dal and chapatis for lunch; in Brazil, they follow the fortunes of the local jai alai team.

Cosmopolitan orientation

Expats with a cosmopolitan mind-set intuitively understand that different cultural norms have value and meaning to those who practice them. Companies that send the right people abroad have identified individuals who respect diverse viewpoints; they live and let live.

A collaborative negotiation style

When expats negotiate with foreigners, the potential for conflict is much higher than it is when they are dealing with compatriots. Different cultures can hold radically different expectations about the way negotiations should be conducted. Thus a collaborative negotiation style, which can be important enough in business at home, becomes absolutely critical abroad.

Consider the approach taken by the vice chairman of Huntsman Corporation, a private chemicals company based in Salt Lake City with sales of $4.75 billion. Over the last five years, Jon Huntsman, Jr., has developed an informal but highly successful method for assessing cultural aptitudes in his employees. He regularly asks managers that he thinks have global leadership potential to accompany him on international trips, even if immediate business needs don't justify the expense. During such trips, he takes the managers to local restaurants, shopping areas, and side streets and observes their behavior. Do they approach the strange and unusual sights, sounds, smells, and tastes with curiosity or do they look for the nearest Pizza Hut? Do they try to communicate with local shopkeepers or do they hustle back to the Hilton?

Huntsman also observes how managers act among foreigners at home. In social settings, he watches to see if they seek out the foreign guests or talk only with people they already know. During negotiations with foreigners, he gauges his managers' ability to take a collaborative rather than a combative approach.

Although time consuming and sometimes costly, Huntsman's approach to screening potential expats is actually remarkably efficient. He is able to assess candidates before the pressures of an impending international problem make a quick decision necessary. Consequently, he makes fewer expensive mistakes when choosing whom to send abroad.

Other companies, such as LG Group, a $70 billion Korean conglomerate, take a more formal approach to assessing candidates for foreign assignments. Early in their careers, candidates complete a survey of about 100 questions designed to rate their preparation for global assignments and their cross-cultural skills. Afterward,

LG employees and their managers discuss how specific training courses or future on-the-job experiences could help them enhance their strengths and overcome their weaknesses. From this discussion, a personalized development plan and timetable are generated. Because LG's potential expats are given time to develop their skills, about 97% of them succeed in meeting the company's expectations when they are eventually sent on international assignments.

The surveys used by LG were purchased from an outside company and cost from $300 to $500 per person. Other organizations develop them in-house, with the help of their training or HR departments. In either case, the survey questions generally ask people not to evaluate their own characteristics but to describe their past behavior. For example, they might be asked when they had last eaten a meal from a cuisine that was unfamiliar to them.

A third approach to identifying potential expats is used by Colgate-Palmolive, which has about 70% of its sales outside the United States and decades of international experience. To fill its entry-level marketing positions, the company recruits students from universities or business schools who can demonstrate an ability to handle cross-cultural situations. They may have already worked or lived abroad and will at the very least have traveled extensively; they will often be able to speak a foreign language. In this way, Colgate-Palmolive leverages the investment that other companies have made in an employee's first experience abroad.

Colgate-Palmolive takes a similarly cautious approach once such promising young people are on staff. Instead of sending them on long assignments abroad, it sends them on a series of training stints lasting 6 to 18 months. These assignments do not come with the costly benefits that are provided to high-level expats, such as allowances for housing and a car. This strategy means the company can provide young managers with a broad range of overseas experience. One manager hired in the United States, for example, spent time in the Czech Republic and the Baltic states and recently became country manager in Ukraine—all before celebrating his thirtieth birthday.

Companies face a trade-off between the accuracy and the cost of expat assessment. Although Colgate-Palmolive's approach is probably the most accurate way to assess an individual's potential to succeed on international assignments, it comes with a substantial price tag. That approach is probably most appropriate for a multinational that needs a large cadre of global managers. For companies with lesser workforce requirements, the less costly approaches of Huntsman and LG may make more sense. In any case, the key to success is having a systematic way of assessing the cross-cultural aptitudes of people you may want to send abroad.

Finishing the Right Way

Virtually every effective company we studied took the matter of repatriation seriously. Most companies, however, do not. Consider the findings of our research: about one-third of the expats we surveyed were still filling temporary assignments three months after coming home. More than three-quarters felt that their permanent position upon returning home was a demotion from their posting abroad, and 61% said that they lacked opportunities to put their foreign experience to work. No wonder the average turnover rate of returning professionals reaches 25%. We know of one company that over a two-year period lost all the managers it sent on international assignments within a year of their return—25 people in all. It might just as well have written a check for $50 million and tossed it to the winds.

The story of a senior engineer from a European electronics company is typical. The man was sent to Saudi Arabia on a four-year assignment, at a cost to his employers of about $4 million. During those four years, he learned fluent Arabic, gained new technical skills, and made friends with important businesspeople in the Saudi community. But upon returning home, the man was shocked to find himself frequently scolded that "the way things were done in Saudi Arabia has nothing to do with the way we do things at headquarters." Worse, he was kept waiting almost nine months for a permanent assignment which, when it came, gave him less authority than he had had abroad. Not surprisingly, the engineer left to join a direct competitor a few months later and ended up using the knowledge and skills he had acquired in Saudi Arabia against his former employer.

International assignments end badly for several reasons. First, although employers give little thought to their return, expats believe that a successful overseas assignment is an achievement that deserves recognition. They want to put their new skills and knowledge to use and are often disappointed both by the blasé attitude at headquarters toward their return and by their new jobs. That disappointment can be particularly strong for senior expats who have gotten used to the independence of running a foreign operation. As one U.K. expatriate recently observed, "If you have been the orchestra conductor overseas, it is very difficult to accept a position as second fiddle back home."

Changes in and out of the office can also make homecoming difficult. The company may have reshuffled its top management, reorganized its reporting structure, or even reshaped its culture. Old mentors may have moved on, leaving the returning employee to deal with new decision makers and power brokers. Things change in people's personal lives, too. Friends may have moved away, figuratively or literally. Children may find it hard to settle back into school or relate to old playmates.

The effective companies in our research used straightforward processes to solve these problems. At Monsanto, for example, the head office starts thinking about the next assignments for returning expats three to six months before they will return. As a first step, an HR officer and a line manager who is senior to the expat—both with international experience—assess the skills that the expat has gained during her experience overseas. They also review potential job openings within Monsanto. At the same time, the expat herself writes a report that includes a self-assessment and describes career goals. The three then meet and decide which of the available jobs best fits the expat's capabilities and the organization's needs.

In the six years since it introduced the system, Monsanto has dramatically reduced the turnover rate of its returning expatriates. And because returning employees participate in the process, they feel valued and treated fairly—even if they don't get their job of first choice.

Along with finding their returning expats suitable jobs, effective companies also prepare them for changes in their personal and professional landscapes. For example, the oil and gas company Unocal offers all expats and their families a daylong debriefing program upon their return. The program focuses on common repatriation difficulties, from communicating with colleagues who have not worked abroad to helping children fit in again with their peers. The participants watch videos of past expats and their families discussing their experiences. That sets the stage for a live discussion. In many cases, participants end up sharing tips for coping with repatriation, such as keeping a journal. The journal is useful, many returning expats say, because it helps them examine the sources of their frustrations and anxieties, which in turn helps them think about what they might do to deal with them better.

Although participants find repatriation programs useful, it is seldom cost effective for a company to provide them in-house unless its volume of international assignments is heavy. Most companies that offer such programs outsource them to professional training companies or form consortiums with other companies to share the costs. Effective companies have realized that the money they spend on these programs is a small price to pay for retaining people with global insight and experience.

Companies that manage their expats successfully follow the three practices that make the assignments work from beginning to end. They focus on creating knowledge and developing global leadership skills; they make sure that candidates have cross-cultural skills to match their technical abilities; and they prepare people to make the transition back to their home offices.

Given the poor record that most companies have when it comes to managing expats, it's probably no surprise that we often encounter organizations in which none of the three practices are at work. Some companies, however, are committed to one or two of the practices, and so the question arises, Do you have to follow all three to see a payback on your expat investment? The answer, our research would suggest, is yes. The practices not only reinforce one another, they also cover the entire expat experience, from assignment to return home.

Consider the dividends reaped by Honda of America Manufacturing, perhaps one of the best examples of a company that implements all three practices. Honda starts expat assignments with clear strategic objectives such as the development of a new car model or improved supplier relations. Assignees then complete a survey to identify personal strengths and weaknesses related to the upcoming assignment. Six months before an expat is scheduled to return home, the company initiates an active matchmaking process to locate a suitable job for that person; a debriefing interview is conducted upon repatriation to capture lessons learned from the assignment.

As a result of Honda's integrated approach, nearly all of its expats consistently perform at or above expectations, and the turnover rate for returning employees is less than 5%. Most important, its expats consistently attain the key strategic objectives established at the beginning of each assignment.

Companies like Honda, GE, and Nokia have learned how to reap the full value of international assignments. Their CEOs share a conviction that sustained global growth rests on the shoulders of key individuals, particularly those with international experience. As a result, those companies are poised to capture tomorrow's global market opportunities by making their international assignments—the largest single investments in executive development that they will make—financially successful today.

Originally published in March–April 1999. Reprint 99201

About the Contributors

KRISTIN BEHFAR is an assistant professor at the Paul Merage School of Business at the University of California, Irvine.

J. STEWART BLACK is managing director at the Center for Global Assignments, a research institute and consulting firm in San Diego, California. He is the coauthor, with Hal B. Gregersen, of *So You're Going Overseas* and *So You're Coming Home*, handbooks for expatriates (Global Business Publishers, 1998 and 1999).

JEANNE BRETT is the DeWitt W. Buchanan, Jr., Distinguished Professor of Dispute Resolution and Organizations and the director of the Dispute Resolution Research Center at Northwestern University's Kellogg School of Management in Evanston, Illinois.

THOMAS DONALDSON is a professor at the Wharton School of the University of Pennsylvania in Philadelphia, where he teaches business ethics. He wrote *The Ethics of International Business* (Oxford University Press, 1989) and is the coauthor, with Thomas W. Dunfee, of *The Ties That Bind* (Harvard Business School Press, 1997).

YVES L. DOZ is the Solvay Chaired Professor of Technological Innovation at INSEAD. He is the coauthor (with Keeley Wilson) of *Managing Global Innovation* (Harvard Business Review Press, 2012).

P. CHRISTOPHER EARLEY is a professor and the chair of the Department of Organizational Behavior at the London Business School.

ROBIN J. ELY is an associate professor at Columbia University's School of International and Public Affairs in New York City. Her research and teaching focuses on the influence of race, gender, and ethnicity on career dynamics and organizational effectiveness.

HAL B. GREGERSEN is an associate professor of international management at Brigham Young University's Marriott School of Management in Provo, Utah. He is the coauthor, with J. Stewart Black, of *So*

You're Going Overseas and *So You're Coming Home*, handbooks for expatriates (Global Business Publishers, 1998 and 1999).

HAE-JUNG HONG is an assistant professor at Rouen Business School in France.

MARY C. KERN is an assistant professor at the Zicklin School of Business at Baruch College in New York.

ERIN MEYER is an affiliate professor in organizational behavior, specializing in cross-cultural management, at INSEAD in Fontainebleau, France. She is the author of *The Culture Map: Breaking Through the Invisible Boundaries of Global Business* (PublicAffairs, 2014).

ELAINE MOSAKOWSKI is a professor of management at the University of Colorado at Boulder.

TSEDAL NEELEY is an assistant professor in the organizational behavior unit at Harvard Business School.

DAVID A. THOMAS is an associate professor at the Harvard Business School in Boston, Massachusetts. His research and teaching focus on the influence of race, gender, and ethnicity on career dynamics and organizational effectiveness.

FONS TROMPENAARS is a cofounder of Trompenaars Hampden-Turner Consulting, based in Amsterdam and London, and a coauthor, with Charles Hampden-Turner, of *Riding the Waves of Culture* (McGraw-Hill, 1993).

KEELEY WILSON is a senior research fellow at INSEAD in Fontainebleau, France. She is the coauthor (with Yves L. Doz) of *Managing Global Innovation* (Harvard Business Review Press, 2012).

PETER WOOLLIAMS is a partner with Trompenaars Hampden-Turner Consulting, based in Amsterdam and London, and an emeritus professor at Anglia Ruskin University in the UK.

Index

HBR'S 10 MUST READS

On Managing People

HBR'S 10 MUST READS

On Managing People

HARVARD BUSINESS REVIEW PRESS
Boston, Massachusetts

Printed in the United States of America
40

Library of Congress Cataloging-in-Publication Data
HBR's 10 must reads on managing people.
p. cm.
Includes index.
ISBN 978-1-4221-5801-2 (pbk. : alk. paper) 1. Supervision of employees. 2. Management. 3. Personnel management. I. Harvard business review. II. Title: HBR's ten must reads on managing people. III. Title: Harvard Business review's 10 must reads on managing people.
HF5549.12.H395 2010
658.3—dc22
2010031618

The paper used in this publication meets the requirements of the American National Standard for Permanence of Paper for Publications and Documents in Libraries and Archives Z39.48-1992.

Contents

HBR'S 10 MUST READS

On
Managing People

Leadership That Gets Results

by Daniel Goleman

A

ASK ANY GROUP OF businesspeople the question "What do effective leaders do?" and you'll hear a sweep of answers. Leaders set strategy; they motivate; they create a mission; they build a culture. Then ask "What *should* leaders do?" If the group is seasoned, you'll likely hear one response: the leader's singular job is to get results.

But how? The mystery of what leaders can and ought to do in order to spark the best performance from their people is age-old. In recent years, that mystery has spawned an entire cottage industry: literally thousands of "leadership experts" have made careers of testing and coaching executives, all in pursuit of creating businesspeople who can turn bold objectives—be they strategic, financial, organizational, or all three—into reality.

Still, effective leadership eludes many people and organizations. One reason is that until recently, virtually no quantitative research has demonstrated which precise leadership behaviors yield positive results. Leadership experts proffer advice based on inference, experience, and instinct. Sometimes that advice is which precise leadership behaviors yield positive results. Sometimes that advice is right on target; sometimes it's not.

But new research by the consulting firm Hay/McBer, which draws on a random sample of 3,871 executives selected from a database of more than 20,000 executives worldwide, takes much of the mystery out of effective leadership. The research found six distinct leadership styles, each springing from different components of emotional intelligence. The styles, taken individually, appear to have a direct and unique impact on the working atmosphere of a company, division, or team, and in turn, on its financial performance. And perhaps most important, the research indicates that leaders with the best results do not rely on only one leadership style; they use most of them in a given week—seamlessly and in different measure—depending on the business situation. Imagine the styles, then, as the array of clubs in a golf pro's bag. Over the course of a game, the pro picks and chooses clubs based on the demands of the shot. Sometimes he has to ponder his selection, but usually it is automatic. The pro senses the challenge ahead, swiftly pulls out the right tool, and elegantly puts it to work. That's how high-impact leaders operate, too.

What are the six styles of leadership? None will shock workplace veterans. Indeed, each style, by name and brief description alone, will likely resonate with anyone who leads, is led, or as is the case with most of us, does both. *Coercive leaders* demand immediate compliance. *Authoritative leaders* mobilize people toward a vision. *Affiliative leaders* create emotional bonds and harmony. *Democratic leaders* build consensus through participation. *Pacesetting leaders* expect excellence and self-direction. And *coaching leaders* develop people for the future.

Close your eyes and you can surely imagine a colleague who uses any one of these styles. You most likely use at least one yourself. What is new in this research, then, is its implications for action. First, it offers a fine-grained understanding of how different leadership styles affect performance and results. Second, it offers clear guidance on when a manager should switch between them. It also strongly suggests that switching flexibly is well advised. New, too, is the research's finding that each leadership style springs from different components of emotional intelligence.

Idea in Brief

Many managers mistakenly assume that leadership style is a function of personality rather than strategic choice. Instead of choosing the one style that suits their temperament, they should ask which style best addresses the demands of a particular situation.

Research has shown that the most successful leaders have strengths in the following emotional intelligence competencies: **self-awareness, self-regulation, motivation, empathy, and social skill**. There are six basic styles of leadership; each makes use of the key components of emotional intelligence in different combinations. The best leaders don't know just one style of leadership—they're skilled at several, and have the flexibility to switch between styles as the circumstances dictate.

Measuring Leadership's Impact

It has been more than a decade since research first linked aspects of emotional intelligence to business results. The late David McClelland, a noted Harvard University psychologist, found that leaders with strengths in a critical mass of six or more emotional intelligence competencies were far more effective than peers who lacked such strengths. For instance, when he analyzed the performance of division heads at a global food and beverage company, he found that among leaders with this critical mass of competence, 87% placed in the top third for annual salary bonuses based on their business performance. More telling, their divisions on average outperformed yearly revenue targets by 15% to 20%. Those executives who lacked emotional intelligence were rarely rated as outstanding in their annual performance reviews, and their divisions underperformed by an average of almost 20%.

Our research set out to gain a more molecular view of the links among leadership and emotional intelligence, and climate and performance. A team of McClelland's colleagues headed by Mary Fontaine and Ruth Jacobs from Hay/McBer studied data about or observed thousands of executives, noting specific behaviors and their impact on climate.[1] How did each individual motivate direct reports? Manage change initiatives? Handle crises? It was in a later phase of

Idea in Practice

Managers often fail to appreciate how profoundly the organizational climate can influence financial results. It can account for nearly a third of financial performance. Organizational climate, in turn, is influenced by leadership style—by the way that managers motivate direct reports, gather and use information, make decisions, manage change initiatives, and handle crises. There are six basic leadership styles. Each derives from different emotional intelligence competencies, works best in particular situations, and affects the organizational climate in different ways.

1. **The coercive style.** This "Do what I say" approach can be very effective in a turnaround situation, a natural disaster, or when working with problem employees. But in most situations, coercive leadership inhibits the organization's flexibility and dampens employees' motivation.
2. **The authoritative style.** An authoritative leader takes a "Come with me" approach: she states the overall goal but gives people the freedom to choose their own means of achieving it. This style works especially well when a business is adrift. It is less effective when the leader is working with a team of experts who are more experienced than he is.
3. **The affiliative style.** The hallmark of the affiliative leader is a "People come first" attitude. This style is particularly useful for building team harmony or increasing morale. But its exclusive focus on praise can

the research that we identified which emotional intelligence capabilities drive the six leadership styles. How does he rate in terms of self-control and social skill? Does a leader show high or low levels of empathy?

The team tested each executive's immediate sphere of influence for its climate. "Climate" is not an amorphous term. First defined by psychologists George Litwin and Richard Stringer and later refined by McClelland and his colleagues, it refers to six key factors that influence an organization's working environment: its *flexibility*—that is, how free employees feel to innovate unencumbered by red tape; their sense of *responsibility* to the organization; the level of *standards* that people set; the sense of accuracy about performance

allow poor performance to go uncorrected. Also, affiliative leaders rarely offer advice, which often leaves employees in a quandary.

4. **The democratic style.** This style's impact on organizational climate is not as high as you might imagine. By giving workers a voice in decisions, democratic leaders build organizational flexibility and responsibility and help generate fresh ideas. But sometimes the price is endless meetings and confused employees who feel leaderless.
5. **The pacesetting style.** A leader who sets high performance standards and exemplifies them himself has a very positive impact on employees who are self-motivated and highly competent. But other employees tend to feel overwhelmed by such a leader's demands for excellence—and to resent his tendency to take over a situation.
6. **The coaching style.** This style focuses more on personal development than on immediate work-related tasks. It works well when employees are already aware of their weaknesses and want to improve, but not when they are resistant to changing their ways.

The more styles a leader has mastered, the better. In particular, being able to switch among the authoritative, affiliative, democratic, and coaching styles as conditions dictate creates the best organizational climate and optimizes business performance.

feedback and aptness of *rewards*; the *clarity* people have about mission and values; and finally, the level of *commitment* to a common purpose.

We found that all six leadership styles have a measurable effect on each aspect of climate. (For details, see "Getting Molecular: The Impact of Leadership Styles on Drivers of Climate.") Further, when we looked at the impact of climate on financial results—such as return on sales, revenue growth, efficiency, and profitability—we found a direct correlation between the two. Leaders who used styles that positively affected the climate had decidedly better financial results than those who did not. That is not to say that organizational climate is the only driver of performance. Economic conditions and competitive dynamics matter enormously. But our analysis strongly suggests that climate accounts for nearly a third of results. And that's simply too much of an impact to ignore.

The Styles in Detail

Executives use six leadership styles, but only four of the six consistently have a positive effect on climate and results. Let's look then at each style of leadership in detail. (For a summary of the material that follows, see the chart "The Six Leadership Styles at a Glance.")

The coercive style

The computer company was in crisis mode—its sales and profits were falling, its stock was losing value precipitously, and its shareholders were in an uproar. The board brought in a new CEO with a reputation as a turnaround artist. He set to work chopping jobs, selling off divisions, and making the tough decisions that should have been executed years before. The company was saved, at least in the short-term.

From the start, though, the CEO created a reign of terror, bullying and demeaning his executives, roaring his displeasure at the slightest misstep. The company's top echelons were decimated not just by his erratic firings but also by defections. The CEO's direct reports, frightened by his tendency to blame the bearer of bad news, stopped bringing him any news at all. Morale was at an all-time low—a fact reflected in another downturn in the business after the short-term recovery. The CEO was eventually fired by the board of directors.

It's easy to understand why of all the leadership styles, the coercive one is the least effective in most situations. Consider what the style does to an organization's climate. Flexibility is the hardest hit. The leader's extreme top-down decision making kills new ideas on the vine. People feel so disrespected that they think, "I won't even bring my ideas up—they'll only be shot down." Likewise, people's sense of responsibility evaporates: unable to act on their own initiative, they lose their sense of ownership and feel little accountability for their performance. Some become so resentful they adopt the attitude, "I'm not going to help this bastard."

Coercive leadership also has a damaging effect on the rewards system. Most high-performing workers are motivated by more than money—they seek the satisfaction of work well done. The coercive style erodes such pride. And finally, the style undermines one of the leader's prime tools—motivating people by showing them how their job fits into a grand, shared mission. Such a loss, measured in terms of diminished clarity and commitment, leaves people alienated from their own jobs, wondering, "How does any of this matter?"

Given the impact of the coercive style, you might assume it should never be applied. Our research, however, uncovered a few occasions when it worked masterfully. Take the case of a division president who was brought in to change the direction of a food company that was losing money. His first act was to have the executive conference room demolished. To him, the room—with its long marble table that looked like "the deck of the Starship Enterprise"—symbolized the tradition-bound formality that was paralyzing the company. The destruction of the room, and the subsequent move to a smaller, more informal setting, sent a message no one could miss, and the division's culture changed quickly in its wake.

That said, the coercive style should be used only with extreme caution and in the few situations when it is absolutely imperative, such as during a turnaround or when a hostile takeover is looming. In those cases, the coercive style can break failed business habits and shock people into new ways of working. It is always appropriate during a genuine emergency, like in the aftermath of an earthquake or a fire. And it can work with problem employees with whom all else has failed. But if a leader relies solely on this style or continues to use it once the emergency passes, the long-term impact of his insensitivity to the morale and feelings of those he leads will be ruinous.

The authoritative style

Tom was the vice president of marketing at a floundering national restaurant chain that specialized in pizza. Needless to say, the company's poor performance troubled the senior managers, but they were at a loss for what to do. Every Monday, they met to review

Emotional Intelligence: A Primer

Emotional intelligence—the ability to manage ourselves and our relationships effectively—consists of four fundamental capabilities: self-awareness, self-management, social awareness, and social skill. Each capability, in turn, is composed of specific sets of competencies. Below is a list of the capabilities and their corresponding traits.

Self-Awareness

- *Emotional self-awareness:* the ability to read and understand your emotions as well as recognize their impact on work performance, relationships, and the like.
- *Accurate self-assessment:* a realistic evaluation of your strengths and limitations.
- *Self-confidence:* a strong and positive sense of self-worth.

Self-Management

- *Self-control:* the ability to keep disruptive emotions and impulses under control.
- *Trustworthiness:* a consistent display of honesty and integrity.
- *Conscientiousness:* the ability to manage yourself and your responsibilities.
- *Adaptability:* skill at adjusting to changing situations and overcoming obstacles.
- *Achievement orientation:* the drive to meet an internal standard of excellence.
- *Initiative:* a readiness to seize opportunities.

---

recent sales, struggling to come up with fixes. To Tom, the approach didn't make sense. "We were always trying to figure out why our sales were down last week. We had the whole company looking backward instead of figuring out what we had to do tomorrow."

Tom saw an opportunity to change people's way of thinking at an off-site strategy meeting. There, the conversation began with stale truisms: the company had to drive up shareholder wealth and increase return on assets. Tom believed those concepts didn't have the

Social Awareness

- *Empathy:* skill at sensing other people's emotions, understanding their perspective, and taking an active interest in their concerns.
- *Organizational awareness:* the ability to read the currents of organizational life, build decision networks, and navigate politics.
- *Service orientation:* the ability to recognize and meet customers' needs.

Social Skill

- *Visionary leadership:* the ability to take charge and inspire with a compelling vision.
- *Influence:* the ability to wield a range of persuasive tactics.
- *Developing others:* the propensity to bolster the abilities of others through feedback and guidance.
- *Communication:* skill at listening and at sending clear, convincing, and well-tuned messages.
- *Change catalyst:* proficiency in initiating new ideas and leading people in a new direction.
- *Conflict management:* the ability to de-escalate disagreements and orchestrate resolutions.
- *Building bonds:* proficiency at cultivating and maintaining a web of relationships.
- *Teamwork and collaboration:* competence at promoting cooperation and building teams.

power to inspire a restaurant manager to be innovative or to do better than a good-enough job.

So Tom made a bold move. In the middle of a meeting, he made an impassioned plea for his colleagues to think from the customer's perspective. Customers want convenience, he said. The company was not in the restaurant business, it was in the business of distributing high-quality, convenient-to-get pizza. That notion—and nothing else—should drive everything the company did.

Getting Molecular: The Impact of Leadership Styles on Drivers of Climate

Our research investigated how each leadership style affected the six drivers of climate, or working atmosphere. The figures below show the correlation between each leadership style and each aspect of climate. So, for instance, if we look at the climate driver of flexibility, we see that the coercive style has a −.28 correlation while the democratic style has a .28 correlation, equally strong in the opposite direction. Focusing on the authoritative leadership style, we find that it has a .54 correlation with rewards—strongly positive—and a .21 correlation with responsibility—positive, but not as strong. In other words, the style's correlation with rewards was more than twice that with responsibility.

According to the data, the authoritative leadership style has the most positive effect on climate, but three others—affiliative, democratic, and coaching—follow close behind. That said, the research indicates that no style should be relied on exclusively, and all have at least short-term uses.

	Coercive	Authoritative	Affiliative	Democratic	Pacesetting	Coaching
Flexibility	−.28	.32	.27	.28	−.07	.17
Responsibility	−.37	.21	.16	.23	.04	.08
Standards	.02	.38	.31	.22	−.27	.39
Rewards	−.18	.54	.48	.42	−.29	.43
Clarity	−.11	.44	.37	.35	−.28	.38
Commitment	−.13	.35	.34	.26	−.20	.27
Overall impact on climate	−.26	.54	.46	.43	−.25	.42

With his vibrant enthusiasm and clear vision—the hallmarks of the authoritative style—Tom filled a leadership vacuum at the company. Indeed, his concept became the core of the new mission statement. But this conceptual breakthrough was just the beginning. Tom made sure that the mission statement was built into the company's strategic planning process as the designated driver of growth. And he ensured that the vision was articulated so that local restaurant managers understood they were the key to the company's success and were free to find new ways to distribute pizza.

Changes came quickly. Within weeks, many local managers started guaranteeing fast, new delivery times. Even better, they started to act like entrepreneurs, finding ingenious locations to open new branches: kiosks on busy street corners and in bus and train stations, even from carts in airports and hotel lobbies.

Tom's success was no fluke. Our research indicates that of the six leadership styles, the authoritative one is most effective, driving up every aspect of climate. Take clarity. The authoritative leader is a visionary; he motivates people by making clear to them how their work fits into a larger vision for the organization. People who work for such leaders understand that what they do matters and why. Authoritative leadership also maximizes commitment to the organization's goals and strategy. By framing the individual tasks within a grand vision, the authoritative leader defines standards that revolve around that vision. When he gives performance feedback—whether positive or negative—the singular criterion is whether or not that performance furthers the vision. The standards for success are clear to all, as are the rewards. Finally, consider the style's impact on flexibility. An authoritative leader states the end but generally gives people plenty of leeway to devise their own means. Authoritative leaders give people the freedom to innovate, experiment, and take calculated risks.

Because of its positive impact, the authoritative style works well in almost any business situation. But it is particularly effective when a business is adrift. An authoritative leader charts a new course and sells his people on a fresh long-term vision.

The authoritative style, powerful though it may be, will not work in every situation. The approach fails, for instance, when a leader is working with a team of experts or peers who are more experienced than he is; they may see the leader as pompous or out-of-touch. Another limitation: if a manager trying to be authoritative becomes overbearing, he can undermine the egalitarian spirit of an effective team. Yet even with such caveats, leaders would be wise to grab for the authoritative "club" more often than not. It may not guarantee a hole in one, but it certainly helps with the long drive.

The affiliative style

If the coercive leader demands, "Do what I say," and the authoritative urges, "Come with me," the affiliative leader says, "People come first." This leadership style revolves around people—its proponents value individuals and their emotions more than tasks and goals. The affiliative leader strives to keep employees happy and to create harmony among them. He manages by building strong emotional bonds and then reaping the benefits of such an approach, namely fierce loyalty. The style also has a markedly positive effect on communication. People who like one another a lot talk a lot. They share ideas; they share inspiration. And the style drives up flexibility; friends trust one another, allowing habitual innovation and risk taking. Flexibility also rises because the affiliative leader, like a parent who adjusts household rules for a maturing adolescent, doesn't impose unnecessary strictures on how employees get their work done. They give people the freedom to do their job in the way they think is most effective.

As for a sense of recognition and reward for work well done, the affiliative leader offers ample positive feedback. Such feedback has special potency in the workplace because it is all too rare: outside of an annual review, most people usually get no feedback on their day-to-day efforts—or only negative feedback. That makes the affiliative leader's positive words all the more motivating. Finally, affiliative leaders are masters at building a sense of belonging. They are, for instance, likely to take their direct reports out for a meal or a drink, one-on-one, to see how they're doing. They will bring in a cake to celebrate a group accomplishment. They are natural relationship builders.

Joe Torre, the heart and soul of the New York Yankees, is a classic affiliative leader. During the 1999 World Series, Torre tended ably to the psyches of his players as they endured the emotional pressure cooker of a pennant race. All season long, he made a special point to praise Scott Brosius, whose father had died during the season, for staying committed even as he mourned. At the celebration party after the team's final game, Torre specifically sought out right fielder Paul O'Neill. Although he had received the news of his father's death that morning, O'Neill chose to play in the decisive game—and he burst into tears the moment it ended. Torre made a point of acknowledging O'Neill's personal struggle, calling him a "warrior." Torre also used the spotlight of the victory celebration to praise two players whose return the following year was threatened by contract disputes. In doing so, he sent a clear message to the team and to the club's owner that he valued the players immensely—too much to lose them.

Along with ministering to the emotions of his people, an affiliative leader may also tend to his own emotions openly. The year Torre's brother was near death awaiting a heart transplant, he shared his worries with his players. He also spoke candidly with the team about his treatment for prostate cancer.

The affiliative style's generally positive impact makes it a good all-weather approach, but leaders should employ it particularly when trying to build team harmony, increase morale, improve communication, or repair broken trust. For instance, one executive in our study was hired to replace a ruthless team leader. The former leader had taken credit for his employees' work and had attempted to pit them against one another. His efforts ultimately failed, but the team he left behind was suspicious and weary. The new executive managed to mend the situation by unstintingly showing emotional honesty and rebuilding ties. Several months in, her leadership had created a renewed sense of commitment and energy.

Despite its benefits, the affiliative style should not be used alone. Its exclusive focus on praise can allow poor performance to go uncorrected; employees may perceive that mediocrity is tolerated. And because affiliative leaders rarely offer constructive advice on how to improve, employees must figure out how to do so on their own. When people need clear directives to navigate through complex challenges, the affiliative style leaves them rudderless. Indeed, if overly relied on, this style can actually steer a group to failure. Perhaps that is why many affiliative leaders, including Torre, use this style in close conjunction with the authoritative style. Authoritative leaders state a vision, set standards, and let people know how their

The Six Leadership Styles at a Glance

Our research found that leaders use six styles, each springing from different components of emotional intelligence. Here is a summary of the styles, their origin, when they work best, and their impact on an organization's climate and thus its performance.

	Coercive	Authoritative
The leader's modus operandi	Demands immediate compliance	Mobilizes people toward a vision
The style in a phrase	"Do what I tell you."	"Come with me."
Underlying emotional intelligence competencies	Drive to achieve, initiative, self-control	Self-confidence, empathy, change catalyst
When the style works best	In a crisis, to kick start a turnaround, or with problem employees	When changes require a new vision, or when a clear direction is needed
Overall impact on climate	Negative	Most strongly positive

work is furthering the group's goals. Alternate that with the caring, nurturing approach of the affiliative leader, and you have a potent combination.

The democratic style

Sister Mary ran a Catholic school system in a large metropolitan area. One of the schools—the only private school in an impoverished neighborhood—had been losing money for years, and the archdiocese could no longer afford to keep it open. When Sister Mary eventually got the order to shut it down, she didn't just lock the doors. She called a meeting of all the teachers and staff at the school and explained to them the details of the financial crisis—the first time anyone working at the school had been included in the business side of the institution. She asked for their ideas on ways to keep the school open and on how to handle the closing, should it come to that. Sister Mary spent much of her time at the meeting just listening.

She did the same at later meetings for school parents and for the community and during a successive series of meetings for the school's teachers and staff. After two months of meetings, the consensus was

Affiliative	**Democratic**	**Pacesetting**	**Coaching**
Creates harmony and builds emotional bonds	Forges consensus through participation	Sets high standards for performance	Develops people for the future
"People come first."	"What do you think?"	"Do as I do, now."	"Try this."
Empathy, building relationships, communication	Collaboration, team leadership, communication	Conscientiousness, drive to achieve, initiative	Developing others, empathy, self-awareness
To heal rifts in a team or to motivate people during stressful circumstances	To build buy-in or consensus, or to get input from valuable employees	To get quick results from a highly motivated and competent team	To help an employee improve performance or develop long-term strengths
Positive	Positive	Negative	Positive

clear: the school would have to close. A plan was made to transfer students to other schools in the Catholic system.

The final outcome was no different than if Sister Mary had gone ahead and closed the school the day she was told to. But by allowing the school's constituents to reach that decision collectively, Sister Mary received none of the backlash that would have accompanied such a move. People mourned the loss of the school, but they understood its inevitability. Virtually no one objected.

Compare that with the experiences of a priest in our research who headed another Catholic school. He, too, was told to shut it down. And he did—by fiat. The result was disastrous: parents filed lawsuits, teachers and parents picketed, and local newspapers ran editorials attacking his decision. It took a year to resolve the disputes before he could finally go ahead and close the school.

Sister Mary exemplifies the democratic style in action—and its benefits. By spending time getting people's ideas and buy-in, a leader builds trust, respect, and commitment. By letting workers themselves have a say in decisions that affect their goals and how they do their work, the democratic leader drives up flexibility and responsibility. And by listening to employees' concerns, the democratic leader learns what to do to keep morale high. Finally, because they have a say in setting their goals and the standards for evaluating success, people operating in a democratic system tend to be very realistic about what can and cannot be accomplished.

However, the democratic style has its drawbacks, which is why its impact on climate is not as high as some of the other styles. One of its more exasperating consequences can be endless meetings where ideas are mulled over, consensus remains elusive, and the only visible result is scheduling more meetings. Some democratic leaders use the style to put off making crucial decisions, hoping that enough thrashing things out will eventually yield a blinding insight. In reality, their people end up feeling confused and leaderless. Such an approach can even escalate conflicts.

When does the style work best? This approach is ideal when a leader is himself uncertain about the best direction to take and needs ideas and guidance from able employees. And even if a leader has a strong vision, the democratic style works well to generate fresh ideas for executing that vision.

The democratic style, of course, makes much less sense when employees are not competent or informed enough to offer sound advice. And it almost goes without saying that building consensus is wrongheaded in times of crisis. Take the case of a CEO whose computer company was severely threatened by changes in the market. He always sought consensus about what to do. As competitors stole customers and customers' needs changed, he kept appointing committees to consider the situation. When the market made a sudden shift because of a new technology, the CEO froze in his tracks. The board replaced him before he could appoint yet another task force to consider the situation. The new CEO, while occasionally democratic and affiliative, relied heavily on the authoritative style, especially in his first months.

The pacesetting style

Like the coercive style, the pacesetting style has its place in the leader's repertory, but it should be used sparingly. That's not what we expected to find. After all, the hallmarks of the pacesetting style sound admirable. The leader sets extremely high performance standards and exemplifies them himself. He is obsessive about doing things better and faster, and he asks the same of everyone around him. He quickly pinpoints poor performers and demands more from them. If they don't rise to the occasion, he replaces them with people who can. You would think such an approach would improve results, but it doesn't.

In fact, the pacesetting style destroys climate. Many employees feel overwhelmed by the pacesetter's demands for excellence, and their morale drops. Guidelines for working may be clear in the leader's head, but she does not state them clearly; she expects people to know what to do and even thinks, "If I have to tell you, you're the wrong person for the job." Work becomes not a matter of doing one's best along a clear course so much as second-guessing what the leader wants. At the same time, people often feel that the pacesetter doesn't trust them to work in their own way or to take initiative. Flexibility and responsibility evaporate; work becomes so task focused and routinized it's boring.

As for rewards, the pacesetter either gives no feedback on how people are doing or jumps in to take over when he thinks they're lagging. And if the leader should leave, people feel directionless—they're so used to "the expert" setting the rules. Finally, commitment dwindles under the regime of a pacesetting leader because people have no sense of how their personal efforts fit into the big picture.

For an example of the pacesetting style, take the case of Sam, a biochemist in R&D at a large pharmaceutical company. Sam's superb technical expertise made him an early star: he was the one everyone turned to when they needed help. Soon he was promoted to head of a team developing a new product. The other scientists on the team were as competent and self-motivated as Sam; his métier as team leader became offering himself as a model of how to do first-class scientific work under tremendous deadline pressure, pitching in when needed. His team completed its task in record time.

But then came a new assignment: Sam was put in charge of R&D for his entire division. As his tasks expanded and he had to articulate a vision, coordinate projects, delegate responsibility, and help develop others, Sam began to slip. Not trusting that his subordinates were as capable as he was, he became a micromanager, obsessed with details and taking over for others when their performance slackened. Instead of trusting them to improve with guidance and development, Sam found himself working nights and weekends after stepping in to take over for the head of a floundering research team. Finally, his own boss suggested, to his relief, that he return to his old job as head of a product development team.

Although Sam faltered, the pacesetting style isn't always a disaster. The approach works well when all employees are self-motivated, highly competent, and need little direction or coordination—for example, it can work for leaders of highly skilled and self-motivated professionals, like R&D groups or legal teams. And, given a talented team to lead, pacesetting does exactly that: gets work done on time or even ahead of schedule. Yet like any leadership style, pacesetting should never be used by itself.

The coaching style

A product unit at a global computer company had seen sales plummet from twice as much as its competitors to only half as much. So Lawrence, the president of the manufacturing division, decided to close the unit and reassign its people and products. Upon hearing the news, James, the head of the doomed unit, decided to go over his boss's head and plead his case to the CEO.

What did Lawrence do? Instead of blowing up at James, he sat down with his rebellious direct report and talked over not just the decision to close the division but also James's future. He explained to James how moving to another division would help him develop new skills. It would make him a better leader and teach him more about the company's business.

Lawrence acted more like a counselor than a traditional boss. He listened to James's concerns and hopes, and he shared his own. He said he believed James had grown stale in his current job; it was, after all, the only place he'd worked in the company. He predicted that James would blossom in a new role.

The conversation then took a practical turn. James had not yet had his meeting with the CEO—the one he had impetuously demanded when he heard of his division's closing. Knowing this—and also knowing that the CEO unwaveringly supported the closing—Lawrence took the time to coach James on how to present his case in that meeting. "You don't get an audience with the CEO very often," he noted, "let's make sure you impress him with your thoughtfulness." He advised James not to plead his personal case but to focus on the business unit: "If he thinks you're in there for your own glory, he'll throw you out faster than you walked through the door." And he urged him to put his ideas in writing; the CEO always appreciated that.

Lawrence's reason for coaching instead of scolding? "James is a good guy, very talented and promising," the executive explained to us, "and I don't want this to derail his career. I want him to stay with the company, I want him to work out, I want him to learn, I want him to benefit and grow. Just because he screwed up doesn't mean he's terrible."

Lawrence's actions illustrate the coaching style par excellence. Coaching leaders help employees identify their unique strengths and weaknesses and tie them to their personal and career aspirations. They encourage employees to establish long-term development goals and help them conceptualize a plan for attaining them. They make agreements with their employees about their role and responsibilities in enacting development plans, and they give plentiful instruction and feedback. Coaching leaders excel at delegating; they give employees challenging assignments, even if that means the tasks won't be accomplished quickly. In other words, these leaders are willing to put up with short-term failure if it furthers long-term learning.

Of the six styles, our research found that the coaching style is used least often. Many leaders told us they don't have the time in this high-pressure economy for the slow and tedious work of teaching people and helping them grow. But after a first session, it takes little or no extra time. Leaders who ignore this style are passing up a powerful tool: its impact on climate and performance are markedly positive.

Admittedly, there is a paradox in coaching's positive effect on business performance because coaching focuses primarily on personal development, not on immediate work-related tasks. Even so, coaching improves results. The reason: it requires constant dialogue, and that dialogue has a way of pushing up every driver of climate. Take flexibility. When an employee knows his boss watches him and cares about what he does, he feels free to experiment. After all, he's sure to get quick and constructive feedback. Similarly, the ongoing dialogue of coaching guarantees that people know what is expected of them and how their work fits into a larger vision or strategy. That affects responsibility and clarity. As for commitment, coaching helps there, too, because the style's implicit message is, "I believe in you, I'm investing in you, and I expect your best efforts." Employees very often rise to that challenge with their heart, mind, and soul.

The coaching style works well in many business situations, but it is perhaps most effective when people on the receiving end are "up for it." For instance, the coaching style works particularly well when employees are already aware of their weaknesses and would like to improve their performance. Similarly, the style works well when employees realize how cultivating new abilities can help them advance. In short, it works best with employees who want to be coached.

By contrast, the coaching style makes little sense when employees, for whatever reason, are resistant to learning or changing their ways. And it flops if the leader lacks the expertise to help the employee along. The fact is, many managers are unfamiliar with or simply inept at coaching, particularly when it comes to giving ongoing performance feedback that motivates rather than creates fear or apathy. Some companies have realized the positive impact of the style and are trying to make it a core competence. At some companies, a significant portion of annual bonuses are tied to an executive's development of his or her direct reports. But many organizations have yet to take full advantage of this leadership style. Although the coaching style may not scream "bottom-line results," it delivers them.

Leaders Need Many Styles

Many studies, including this one, have shown that the more styles a leader exhibits, the better. Leaders who have mastered four or more—especially the authoritative, democratic, affiliative, and coaching styles—have the very best climate and business performance. And the most effective leaders switch flexibly among the leadership styles as needed. Although that may sound daunting, we witnessed it more often than you might guess, at both large corporations and tiny start-ups, by seasoned veterans who could explain exactly how and why they lead and by entrepreneurs who claim to lead by gut alone.

Such leaders don't mechanically match their style to fit a checklist of situations—they are far more fluid. They are exquisitely sensitive to the impact they are having on others and seamlessly adjust their style to get the best results. These are leaders, for example, who can read in the first minutes of conversation that a talented but underperforming employee has been demoralized by an unsympathetic, do-it-the-way-I-tell-you manager and needs to be inspired through a reminder of why her work matters. Or that leader might choose to reenergize the employee by asking her about her dreams and aspirations and finding ways to make her job more challenging. Or that initial conversation might signal that the employee needs an ultimatum: improve or leave.

For an example of fluid leadership in action, consider Joan, the general manager of a major division at a global food and beverage company. Joan was appointed to her job while the division was in a deep crisis. It had not made its profit targets for six years; in the most recent year, it had missed by $50 million. Morale among the top management team was miserable; mistrust and resentments were rampant. Joan's directive from above was clear: turn the division around.

Joan did so with a nimbleness in switching among leadership styles that is rare. From the start, she realized she had a short window to demonstrate effective leadership and to establish rapport and trust. She also knew that she urgently needed to be informed about what was not working, so her first task was to listen to key people.

Her first week on the job she had lunch and dinner meetings with each member of the management team. Joan sought to get each person's understanding of the current situation. But her focus was not so much on learning how each person diagnosed the problem as on getting to know each manager as a person. Here Joan employed the affiliative style: she explored their lives, dreams, and aspirations.

She also stepped into the coaching role, looking for ways she could help the team members achieve what they wanted in their careers. For instance, one manager who had been getting feedback that he was a poor team player confided his worries to her. He thought he was a good team member, but he was plagued by persistent complaints. Recognizing that he was a talented executive and a valuable asset to the company, Joan made an agreement with him to point out (in private) when his actions undermined his goal of being seen as a team player.

She followed the one-on-one conversations with a three-day off-site meeting. Her goal here was team building, so that everyone would own whatever solution for the business problems emerged. Her initial stance at the off-site meeting was that of a democratic leader. She encouraged everyone to express freely their frustrations and complaints.

The next day, Joan had the group focus on solutions: each person made three specific proposals about what needed to be done. As Joan clustered the suggestions, a natural consensus emerged about priorities for the business, such as cutting costs. As the group came up with specific action plans, Joan got the commitment and buy-in she sought.

With that vision in place, Joan shifted into the authoritative style, assigning accountability for each follow-up step to specific executives and holding them responsible for their accomplishment. For example, the division had been dropping prices on products without increasing its volume. One obvious solution was to raise prices, but the previous VP of sales had dithered and had let the problem fester. The new VP of sales now had responsibility to adjust the price points to fix the problem.

Over the following months, Joan's main stance was authoritative. She continually articulated the group's new vision in a way that reminded each member of how his or her role was crucial to achieving these goals. And, especially during the first few weeks of the plan's implementation, Joan felt that the urgency of the business crisis justified an occasional shift into the coercive style should someone fail to meet his or her responsibility. As she put it, "I had to be brutal about this follow-up and make sure this stuff happened. It was going to take discipline and focus."

The results? Every aspect of climate improved. People were innovating. They were talking about the division's vision and crowing about their commitment to new, clear goals. The ultimate proof of Joan's fluid leadership style is written in black ink: after only seven months, her division exceeded its yearly profit target by $5 million.

Expanding Your Repertory

Few leaders, of course, have all six styles in their repertory, and even fewer know when and how to use them. In fact, as we have brought the findings of our research into many organizations, the most common responses have been, "But I have only two of those!" and, "I can't use all those styles. It wouldn't be natural."

Such feelings are understandable, and in some cases, the antidote is relatively simple. The leader can build a team with members who employ styles she lacks. Take the case of a VP for manufacturing. She successfully ran a global factory system largely by using the affiliative style. She was on the road constantly, meeting with plant managers, attending to their pressing concerns, and letting them know how much she cared about them personally. She left the division's strategy—extreme efficiency—to a trusted lieutenant with a keen understanding of technology, and she delegated its performance standards to a colleague who was adept at the authoritative approach. She also had a pacesetter on her team who always visited the plants with her.

An alternative approach, and one I would recommend more, is for leaders to expand their own style repertories. To do so, leaders must

Growing Your Emotional Intelligence

Unlike IQ, which is largely genetic—it changes little from childhood—the skills of emotional intelligence can be learned at any age. It's not easy, however. Growing your emotional intelligence takes practice and commitment. But the payoffs are well worth the investment.

Consider the case of a marketing director for a division of a global food company. Jack, as I'll call him, was a classic pacesetter: high-energy, always striving to find better ways to get things done, and too eager to step in and take over when, say, someone seemed about to miss a deadline. Worse, Jack was prone to pounce on anyone who didn't seem to meet his standards, flying off the handle if a person merely deviated from completing a job in the order Jack thought best.

Jack's leadership style had a predictably disastrous impact on climate and business results. After two years of stagnant performance, Jack's boss suggested he seek out a coach. Jack wasn't pleased but, realizing his own job was on the line, he complied.

The coach, an expert in teaching people how to increase their emotional intelligence, began with a 360-degree evaluation of Jack. A diagnosis from multiple viewpoints is essential in improving emotional intelligence because those who need the most help usually have blind spots. In fact, our research found that top-performing leaders overestimate their strengths on, at most, one emotional intelligence ability, whereas poor performers overrate themselves on four or more. Jack was not that far off, but he did rate himself more glowingly than his direct reports, who gave him especially low grades on emotional self-control and empathy.

Initially, Jack had some trouble accepting the feedback data. But when his coach showed him how those weaknesses were tied to his inability to display leadership styles dependent on those competencies—especially the authoritative, affiliative, and coaching styles—Jack realized he had to improve if he wanted to advance in the company. Making such a connection is essential. The reason: improving emotional intelligence isn't done in a weekend or during a seminar—it takes diligent practice on the job, over several months. If people do not see the value of the change, they will not make that effort.

Once Jack zeroed in on areas for improvement and committed himself to making the effort, he and his coach worked up a plan to turn his day-to-day job into a learning laboratory. For instance, Jack discovered he was empathetic when things were calm, but in a crisis, he tuned out others. This tendency hampered his ability to listen to what people were telling him in the very moments he most needed to do so. Jack's plan required him to focus on his behavior during tough situations. As soon as he felt himself tensing up, his job was to immediately step back, let the other person speak, and then ask clarifying questions. The point was to not act judgmental or hostile under pressure.

The change didn't come easily, but with practice Jack learned to defuse his flare-ups by entering into a dialogue instead of launching a harangue. Although he didn't always agree with them, at least he gave people a chance to make their case. At the same time, Jack also practiced giving his direct reports more positive feedback and reminding them of how their work contributed to the group's mission. And he restrained himself from micromanaging them.

Jack met with his coach every week or two to review his progress and get advice on specific problems. For instance, occasionally Jack would find himself falling back on his old pacesetting tactics—cutting people off, jumping in to take over, and blowing up in a rage. Almost immediately, he would regret it. So he and his coach dissected those relapses to figure out what triggered the old ways and what to do the next time a similar moment arose. Such "relapse prevention" measures inoculate people against future lapses or just giving up. Over a six-month period, Jack made real improvement. His own records showed he had reduced the number of flare-ups from one or more a day at the beginning to just one or two a month. The climate had improved sharply, and the division's numbers were starting to creep upward.

Why does improving an emotional intelligence competence take months rather than days? Because the emotional centers of the brain, not just the neocortex, are involved. The neocortex, the thinking brain that learns technical skills and purely cognitive abilities, gains knowledge very quickly, but the emotional brain does not. To master a new behavior, the emotional centers need repetition and practice. Improving your emotional intelligence, then, is akin to changing your habits. Brain circuits that carry leadership habits have to unlearn the old ones and replace them with the new. The more often a behavioral sequence is repeated, the stronger the underlying brain circuits become. At some point, the new neural pathways become the brain's default option. When that happened, Jack was able to go through the paces of leadership effortlessly, using styles that worked for him—and the whole company.

first understand which emotional intelligence competencies underlie the leadership styles they are lacking. They can then work assiduously to increase their quotient of them.

For instance, an affiliative leader has strengths in three emotional intelligence competencies: in empathy, in building relationships, and in communication. Empathy—sensing how people are feeling in the moment—allows the affiliative leader to respond to employees in a way that is highly congruent with that person's emotions, thus building rapport. The affiliative leader also displays a natural ease in forming new relationships, getting to know someone as a person, and cultivating a bond. Finally, the outstanding affiliative leader has mastered the art of interpersonal communication, particularly in saying just the right thing or making the apt symbolic gesture at just the right moment.

So if you are primarily a pacesetting leader who wants to be able to use the affiliative style more often, you would need to improve your level of empathy and, perhaps, your skills at building relationships or communicating effectively. As another example, an authoritative leader who wants to add the democratic style to his repertory might need to work on the capabilities of collaboration and communication. Such advice about adding capabilities may seem simplistic—"Go change yourself"—but enhancing emotional intelligence is entirely possible with practice. (For more on how to improve emotional intelligence, see the sidebar "Growing Your Emotional Intelligence.")

More Science, Less Art

Like parenthood, leadership will never be an exact science. But neither should it be a complete mystery to those who practice it. In recent years, research has helped parents understand the genetic, psychological, and behavioral components that affect their "job performance." With our new research, leaders, too, can get a clearer picture of what it takes to lead effectively. And perhaps as important, they can see how they can make that happen.

The business environment is continually changing, and a leader must respond in kind. Hour to hour, day to day, week to week, executives must play their leadership styles like a pro—using the right one at just the right time and in the right measure. The payoff is in the results.

Originally published in March 2000. Reprint R00204.

Notes

1. Daniel Goleman consults with Hay/McBer on leadership development.

One More Time

How Do You Motivate Employees?

by Frederick Herzberg

HOW MANY ARTICLES, BOOKS, speeches, and workshops have pleaded plaintively, "How do I get an employee to do what I want?"

The psychology of motivation is tremendously complex, and what has been unraveled with any degree of assurance is small indeed. But the dismal ratio of knowledge to speculation has not dampened the enthusiasm for new forms of snake oil that are constantly coming on the market, many of them with academic testimonials. Doubtless this article will have no depressing impact on the market for snake oil, but since the ideas expressed in it have been tested in many corporations and other organizations, it will help—I hope—to redress the imbalance in the aforementioned ratio.

"Motivating" with KITA

In lectures to industry on the problem, I have found that the audiences are usually anxious for quick and practical answers, so I will begin with a straightforward, practical formula for moving people.

What is the simplest, surest, and most direct way of getting someone to do something? Ask? But if the person responds that he or she does not want to do it, then that calls for psychological consultation to determine the reason for such obstinacy. Tell the person? The response shows that he or she does not understand you, and now an expert in communication methods has to be brought in to show you how to get through. Give the person a monetary incentive? I do not need to remind the reader of the complexity and difficulty involved in setting up and administering an incentive system. Show the person? This means a costly training program. We need a simple way.

Every audience contains the "direct action" manager who shouts, "Kick the person!" And this type of manager is right. The surest and least circumlocuted way of getting someone to do something is to administer a kick in the pants—to give what might be called the KITA.

There are various forms of KITA, and here are some of them:

Negative physical KITA

This is a literal application of the term and was frequently used in the past. It has, however, three major drawbacks: 1) It is inelegant; 2) it contradicts the precious image of benevolence that most organizations cherish; and 3) since it is a physical attack, it directly stimulates the autonomic nervous system, and this often results in negative feedback—the employee may just kick you in return. These factors give rise to certain taboos against negative physical KITA.

In uncovering infinite sources of psychological vulnerabilities and the appropriate methods to play tunes on them, psychologists have come to the rescue of those who are no longer permitted to use negative physical KITA. "He took my rug away"; "I wonder what she meant by that"; "The boss is always going around me"—these symptomatic expressions of ego sores that have been rubbed raw are the result of application of:

Negative psychological KITA

This has several advantages over negative physical KITA. First, the cruelty is not visible; the bleeding is internal and comes much later. Second, since it affects the higher cortical centers of the brain with its inhibitory powers, it reduces the possibility of physical backlash. Third, since the number of psychological pains that a person can feel

Idea in Brief

Imagine your workforce so motivated that employees relish *more* hours of work, not fewer, initiate increased responsibility themselves, and boast about their challenging work, not their paychecks or bonuses.

An impossible dream? Not if you understand the counterintuitive force behind motivation—and the ineffectiveness of most performance incentives. Despite media attention to the contrary, motivation does *not* come from perks, plush offices, or even promotions or pay. These **extrinsic incentives** may stimulate people to put their noses to the grindstone—but they'll likely perform only as long as it takes to get that next raise or promotion.

The truth? You and your organization have only limited power to motivate employees. Yes, unfair salaries may damage morale. But when you *do* offer fat paychecks and other extrinsic incentives, people *won't* necessarily work harder or smarter.

Why? Most of us are motivated by **intrinsic rewards**: interesting, challenging work, and the opportunity to achieve and grow into greater responsibility.

Of course, you have to provide some extrinsic incentives. After all, few of us can afford to work for *no* salary. But the *real* key to motivating your employees is enabling them to activate their own *internal* generators. Otherwise, you'll be stuck trying to recharge their batteries yourself—again and again.

is almost infinite, the direction and site possibilities of the KITA are increased many times. Fourth, the person administering the kick can manage to be above it all and let the system accomplish the dirty work. Fifth, those who practice it receive some ego satisfaction (one-upmanship), whereas they would find drawing blood abhorrent. Finally, if the employee does complain, he or she can always be accused of being paranoid; there is no tangible evidence of an actual attack.

Now, what does negative KITA accomplish? If I kick you in the rear (physically or psychologically), who is motivated? *I* am motivated; *you* move! Negative KITA does not lead to motivation, but to movement. So:

Idea in Practice

How do you help employees charge themselves up? **Enrich their jobs** by applying these principles:

- Increase individuals' accountability for their work by removing some controls.
- Give people responsibility for a *complete* process or unit of work.
- Make information available directly to employees rather than sending it through their managers first.
- Enable people to take on new, more difficult tasks they haven't handled before.
- Assign individuals specialized tasks that allow them to become experts.

The payoff? Employees gain an enhanced sense of responsibility and achievement, along with new opportunities to learn and grow—continually.

Example: A large firm began enriching stockholder correspondents' jobs by appointing subject-matter experts within each unit—then encouraging other unit members to consult with them before seeking supervisory help. It also held correspondents personally responsible for their communications' quality and quantity. Supervisors who had proofread and signed *all* letters now checked only 10% of them. And rather than harping on production quotas, supervisors no longer discussed daily quantities.

These deceptively modest changes paid big dividends: Within six months, the correspondents' motivation soared—as measured by their answers to questions such as "How many opportunities do you feel you have in your job for making worthwhile contributions?" Equally valuable, their performance noticeably improved, as measured by their communications' quality and accuracy, and their speed of response to stockholders.

Job enrichment isn't easy. Managers may initially fear that they'll no longer be needed once their direct reports take on more responsibility. Employees will likely require time to master new tasks and challenges.

But managers will eventually rediscover their real functions, for example, *developing* staff rather than simply checking their work. And employees' enthusiasm and commitment will ultimately rise—along with your company's overall performance.

Positive KITA

Let us consider motivation. If I say to you, "Do this for me or the company, and in return I will give you a reward, an incentive, more status, a promotion, all the quid pro quos that exist in the industrial organization," am I motivating you? The overwhelming opinion I receive from management people is, "Yes, this is motivation."

I have a year-old schnauzer. When it was a small puppy and I wanted it to move, I kicked it in the rear and it moved. Now that I have finished its obedience training, I hold up a dog biscuit when I want the schnauzer to move. In this instance, who is motivated—I or the dog? The dog wants the biscuit, but it is I who want it to move. Again, I am the one who is motivated, and the dog is the one who moves. In this instance all I did was apply KITA frontally; I exerted a pull instead of a push. When industry wishes to use such positive KITAs, it has available an incredible number and variety of dog biscuits (jelly beans for humans) to wave in front of employees to get them to jump.

Myths About Motivation

Why is KITA not motivation? If I kick my dog (from the front or the back), he will move. And when I want him to move again, what must I do? I must kick him again. Similarly, I can charge a person's battery, and then recharge it, and recharge it again. But it is only when one has a generator of one's own that we can talk about motivation. One then needs no outside stimulation. One *wants* to do it.

With this in mind, we can review some positive KITA personnel practices that were developed as attempts to instill "motivation":

1. Reducing time spent at work

This represents a marvelous way of motivating people to work—getting them off the job! We have reduced (formally and informally) the time spent on the job over the last 50 or 60 years until we are finally on the way to the "6-day weekend." An interesting variant of this approach is the development of off-hour recreation programs. The philosophy here seems to be that those who play together, work together. The fact is that motivated people seek more hours of work, not fewer.

2. Spiraling wages

Have these motivated people? Yes, to seek the next wage increase. Some medievalists still can be heard to say that a good depression will get employees moving. They feel that if rising wages don't or won't do the job, reducing them will.

3. Fringe benefits

Industry has outdone the most welfare-minded of welfare states in dispensing cradle-to-the-grave succor. One company I know of had an informal "fringe benefit of the month club" going for a while. The cost of fringe benefits in this country has reached approximately 25% of the wage dollar, and we still cry for motivation.

People spend less time working for more money and more security than ever before, and the trend cannot be reversed. These benefits are no longer rewards; they are rights. A 6-day week is inhuman, a 10-hour day is exploitation, extended medical coverage is a basic decency, and stock options are the salvation of American initiative. Unless the ante is continuously raised, the psychological reaction of employees is that the company is turning back the clock.

When industry began to realize that both the economic nerve and the lazy nerve of their employees had insatiable appetites, it started to listen to the behavioral scientists who, more out of a humanist tradition than from scientific study, criticized management for not knowing how to deal with people. The next KITA easily followed.

4. Human relations training

More than 30 years of teaching and, in many instances, of practicing psychological approaches to handling people have resulted in costly human relations programs and, in the end, the same question: How do you motivate workers? Here, too, escalations have taken place. Thirty years ago it was necessary to request, "Please don't spit on the floor." Today the same admonition requires three "pleases" before the employee feels that a superior has demonstrated the psychologically proper attitude.

The failure of human relations training to produce motivation led to the conclusion that supervisors or managers themselves were not psychologically true to themselves in their practice of interpersonal decency. So an advanced form of human relations KITA, sensitivity training, was unfolded.

5. Sensitivity training

Do you really, really understand yourself? Do you really, really, really trust other people? Do you really, really, really, really cooperate? The failure of sensitivity training is now being explained, by those who have become opportunistic exploiters of the technique, as a failure to really (five times) conduct proper sensitivity training courses.

With the realization that there are only temporary gains from comfort and economic and interpersonal KITA, personnel managers concluded that the fault lay not in what they were doing, but in the employee's failure to appreciate what they were doing. This opened up the field of communications, a new area of "scientifically" sanctioned KITA.

6. Communications

The professor of communications was invited to join the faculty of management training programs and help in making employees understand what management was doing for them. House organs, briefing sessions, supervisory instruction on the importance of communication, and all sorts of propaganda have proliferated until today there is even an International Council of Industrial Editors. But no motivation resulted, and the obvious thought occurred that perhaps management was not hearing what the employees were saying. That led to the next KITA.

7. Two-way communication

Management ordered morale surveys, suggestion plans, and group participation programs. Then both management and employees were communicating and listening to each other more than ever, but without much improvement in motivation.

The behavioral scientists began to take another look at their conceptions and their data, and they took human relations one step further. A glimmer of truth was beginning to show through in the writings of the so-called higher-order-need psychologists. People, so they said, want to actualize themselves. Unfortunately, the "actualizing" psychologists got mixed up with the human relations psychologists, and a new KITA emerged.

8. Job participation

Though it may not have been the theoretical intention, job participation often became a "give them the big picture" approach. For example, if a man is tightening 10,000 nuts a day on an assembly line with a torque wrench, tell him he is building a Chevrolet. Another approach had the goal of giving employees a "feeling" that they are determining, in some measure, what they do on the job. The goal was to provide a *sense* of achievement rather than a substantive achievement in the task. Real achievement, of course, requires a task that makes it possible.

But still there was no motivation. This led to the inevitable conclusion that the employees must be sick, and therefore to the next KITA.

9. Employee counseling

The initial use of this form of KITA in a systematic fashion can be credited to the Hawthorne experiment of the Western Electric Company during the early 1930s. At that time, it was found that the employees harbored irrational feelings that were interfering with the rational operation of the factory. Counseling in this instance was a means of letting the employees unburden themselves by talking to someone about their problems. Although the counseling techniques were primitive, the program was large indeed.

The counseling approach suffered as a result of experiences during World War II, when the programs themselves were found to be interfering with the operation of the organizations; the counselors had forgotten their role of benevolent listeners and were attempting to do something about the problems that they heard about. Psychological counseling, however, has managed to survive the negative impact of World War II experiences and today is beginning to flourish with renewed sophistication. But, alas, many of these programs, like all the others, do not seem to have lessened the pressure of demands to find out how to motivate workers.

Since KITA results only in short-term movement, it is safe to predict that the cost of these programs will increase steadily and new varieties will be developed as old positive KITAs reach their satiation points.

Hygiene vs. Motivators

Let me rephrase the perennial question this way: How do you install a generator in an employee? A brief review of my motivation-hygiene theory of job attitudes is required before theoretical and practical suggestions can be offered. The theory was first drawn from an examination of events in the lives of engineers and accountants. At least 16 other investigations, using a wide variety of populations (including some in the Communist countries), have since been completed, making the original research one of the most replicated studies in the field of job attitudes.

The findings of these studies, along with corroboration from many other investigations using different procedures, suggest that the factors involved in producing job satisfaction (and motivation) are separate and distinct from the factors that lead to job dissatisfaction. (See "Factors affecting job attitudes as reported in 12 investigations," which is further explained below.) Since separate factors need to be considered, depending on whether job satisfaction or job dissatisfaction is being examined, it follows that these two feelings are not opposites of each other. The opposite of job satisfaction is not job dissatisfaction but, rather, *no* job satisfaction; and similarly, the opposite of job dissatisfaction is not job satisfaction, but *no* job dissatisfaction.

Factors affecting job attitudes as reported in 12 investigations

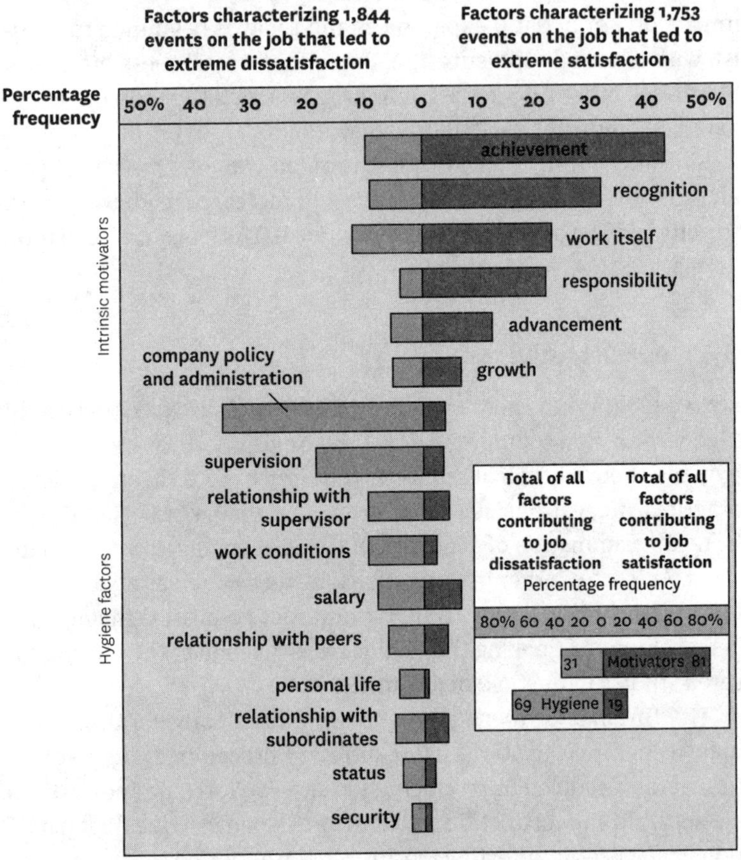

Stating the concept presents a problem in semantics, for we normally think of satisfaction and dissatisfaction as opposites; i.e., what is not satisfying must be dissatisfying, and vice versa. But when it comes to understanding the behavior of people in their jobs, more than a play on words is involved.

Two different needs of human beings are involved here. One set of needs can be thought of as stemming from humankind's animal nature—the built-in drive to avoid pain from the environment, plus all the learned drives that become conditioned to the basic biological needs. For example, hunger, a basic biological drive, makes it necessary to earn money, and then money becomes a specific drive. The other set of needs relates to that unique human characteristic, the ability to achieve and, through achievement, to experience psychological growth. The stimuli for the growth needs are tasks that induce growth; in the industrial setting, they are the job content. Contrariwise, the stimuli inducing pain-avoidance behavior are found in the job environment.

The growth or *motivator* factors that are intrinsic to the job are: achievement, recognition for achievement, the work itself, responsibility, and growth or advancement. The dissatisfaction-avoidance or hygiene (KITA) factors that are extrinsic to the job include: company policy and administration, supervision, interpersonal relationships, working conditions, salary, status, and security.

A composite of the factors that are involved in causing job satisfaction and job dissatisfaction, drawn from samples of 1,685 employees, is shown in "Factors affecting job attitudes as reported in 12 investigations." The results indicate that motivators were the primary cause of satisfaction, and hygiene factors the primary cause of unhappiness on the job. The employees, studied in 12 different investigations, included lower level supervisors, professional women, agricultural administrators, men about to retire from management positions, hospital maintenance personnel, manufacturing supervisors, nurses, food handlers, military officers, engineers, scientists, housekeepers, teachers, technicians, female assemblers, accountants, Finnish foremen, and Hungarian engineers.

They were asked what job events had occurred in their work that had led to extreme satisfaction or extreme dissatisfaction on their part. Their responses are broken down in the figure into percentages of total "positive" job events and of total "negative" job events. (The figures total more than 100% on both the "hygiene" and "motivators" sides because often at least two factors can be attributed to a single event; advancement, for instance, often accompanies assumption of responsibility.)

To illustrate, a typical response involving achievement that had a negative effect for the employee was, "I was unhappy because I didn't do the job successfully." A typical response in the small number of positive job events in the company policy and administration grouping was, "I was happy because the company reorganized the section so that I didn't report any longer to the guy I didn't get along with."

As the lower right-hand part of the figure shows, of all the factors contributing to job satisfaction, 81% were motivators. And of all the factors contributing to the employees' dissatisfaction over their work, 69% involved hygiene elements.

Eternal triangle

There are three general philosophies of personnel management. The first is based on organizational theory, the second on industrial engineering, and the third on behavioral science.

Organizational theorists believe that human needs are either so irrational or so varied and adjustable to specific situations that the major function of personnel management is to be as pragmatic as the occasion demands. If jobs are organized in a proper manner, they reason, the result will be the most efficient job structure, and the most favorable job attitudes will follow as a matter of course.

Industrial engineers hold that humankind is mechanistically oriented and economically motivated and that human needs are best met by attuning the individual to the most efficient work process. The goal of personnel management therefore should be to concoct the most appropriate incentive system and to design the specific working conditions in a way that facilitates the most efficient use of the human machine. By structuring jobs in a manner that leads to the most efficient operation, engineers believe that they can obtain the optimal organization of work and the proper work attitudes.

Behavioral scientists focus on group sentiments, attitudes of individual employees, and the organization's social and psychological climate. This persuasion emphasizes one or more of the various hygiene and motivator needs. Its approach to personnel management is generally to emphasize some form of human relations education, in the hope of instilling healthy employee attitudes and an organizational climate that is considered to be felicitous to human values. The belief is that proper attitudes will lead to efficient job and organizational structure.

There is always a lively debate concerning the overall effectiveness of the approaches of organizational theorists and industrial engineers. Manifestly, both have achieved much. But the nagging question for behavioral scientists has been: What is the cost in human problems that eventually cause more expense to the organization—for instance, turnover, absenteeism, errors, violation of safety rules, strikes, restriction of output, higher wages, and greater fringe benefits? On the other hand, behavioral scientists are hard put to document much manifest improvement in personnel management, using their approach.

The motivation-hygiene theory suggests that work be *enriched* to bring about effective utilization of personnel. Such a systematic attempt to motivate employees by manipulating the motivator factors is just beginning. The term *job enrichment* describes this embryonic movement. An older term, job enlargement, should be avoided because it is associated with past failures stemming from a misunderstanding of the problem. Job enrichment provides the opportunity for the employee's psychological growth, while job enlargement merely makes a job structurally bigger. Since scientific job enrichment is very new, this article only suggests the principles and practical steps that have recently emerged from several successful experiments in industry.

Job loading

In attempting to enrich certain jobs, management often reduces the personal contribution of employees rather than giving them opportunities for growth in their accustomed jobs. Such endeavors, which I shall call horizontal job loading (as opposed to vertical loading, or providing motivator factors), have been the problem of earlier job enlargement programs. Job loading merely enlarges the meaninglessness of the job. Some examples of this approach, and their effect, are:

- Challenging the employee by increasing the amount of production expected. If each tightens 10,000 bolts a day, see if each can tighten 20,000 bolts a day. The arithmetic involved shows that multiplying zero by zero still equals zero.
- Adding another meaningless task to the existing one, usually some routine clerical activity. The arithmetic here is adding zero to zero.
- Rotating the assignments of a number of jobs that need to be enriched. This means washing dishes for a while, then washing silverware. The arithmetic is substituting one zero for another zero.
- Removing the most difficult parts of the assignment in order to free the worker to accomplish more of the less challenging assignments. This traditional industrial engineering approach amounts to subtraction in the hope of accomplishing addition.

These are common forms of horizontal loading that frequently come up in preliminary brainstorming sessions of job enrichment. The principles of vertical loading have not all been worked out as yet, and they remain rather general, but I have furnished seven useful starting points for consideration in "Principles of vertical job loading."

A successful application

An example from a highly successful job enrichment experiment can illustrate the distinction between horizontal and vertical loading of a job. The subjects of this study were the stockholder correspondents employed by a very large corporation. Seemingly, the task required of these carefully selected and highly trained correspondents was quite complex and challenging. But almost all indexes of performance and job attitudes were low, and exit interviewing confirmed that the challenge of the job existed merely as words.

Principles of vertical job loading

Principle	Motivators involved
A. Removing some controls while retaining accountability	Responsibility and personal achievement
B. Increasing the accountability of individuals for own work	Responsibility and recognition
C. Giving a person a complete natural unit of work (module, division, area, and so on)	Responsibility, achievement, and recognition
D. Granting additional authority to employees in their activity; job freedom	Responsibility, achievement, and recognition
E. Making periodic reports directly available to the workers themselves rather than to supervisors	Internal recognition
F. Introducing new and more difficult tasks not previously handled	Growth and learning
G. Assigning individuals specific or specialized tasks, enabling them to become experts	Responsibility, growth, and advancement

A job enrichment project was initiated in the form of an experiment with one group, designated as an achieving unit, having its job enriched by the principles described in "Principles of vertical job loading." A control group continued to do its job in the traditional way. (There were also two "uncommitted" groups of correspondents formed to measure the so-called Hawthorne effect—that is, to gauge whether productivity and attitudes toward the job changed artificially merely because employees sensed that the company was paying more attention to them in doing something different or novel. The results for these groups were substantially the same as for the control group, and for the sake of simplicity I do not deal with them in this summary.) No changes in hygiene were introduced for either group other than those that would have been made anyway, such as normal pay increases.

Employee performance in company experiment

Three-month cumulative average

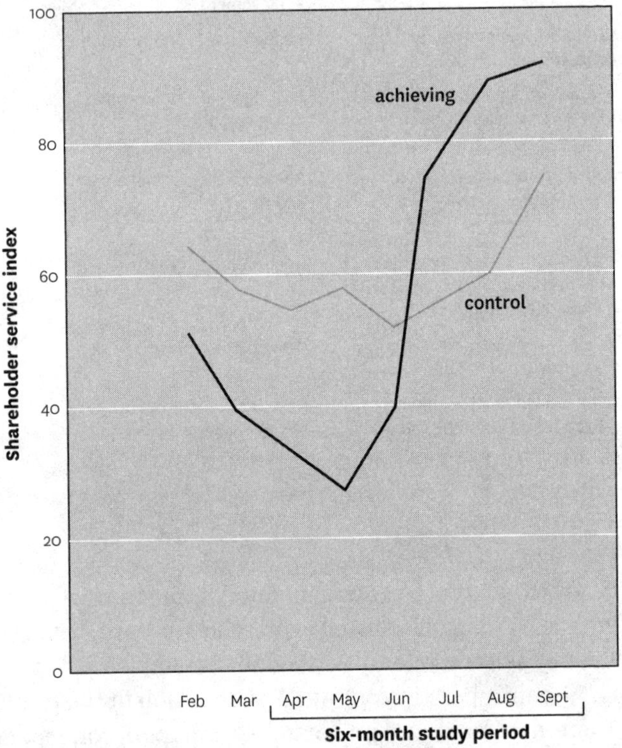

The changes for the achieving unit were introduced in the first two months, averaging one per week of the seven motivators listed in "Principles of vertical job loading." At the end of six months the members of the achieving unit were found to be outperforming their counterparts in the control group and, in addition, indicated a marked increase in their liking for their jobs. Other results showed that the achieving group had lower absenteeism and, subsequently, a much higher rate of promotion.

"Employee performance in company experiment" illustrates the changes in performance, measured in February and March, before the study period began, and at the end of each month of the study period. The shareholder service index represents quality of letters, including accuracy of information, and speed of response to stockholders' letters of inquiry. The index of a current month was averaged into the average of the two prior months, which means that improvement was harder to obtain if the indexes of the previous months were low. The "achievers" were performing less well before the six-month period started, and their performance service index continued to decline after the introduction of the motivators, evidently because of uncertainty after their newly granted responsibilities. In the third month, however, performance improved, and soon the members of this group had reached a high level of accomplishment.

"Change in attitudes toward tasks in company experiment" shows the two groups' attitudes toward their job, measured at the end of March, just before the first motivator was introduced, and again at the end of September. The correspondents were asked 16 questions, all involving motivation. A typical one was, "As you see it, how many opportunities do you feel that you have in your job for making worthwhile contributions?" The answers were scaled from 1 to 5, with 80 as the maximum possible score. The achievers became much more positive about their job, while the attitude of the control unit remained about the same (the drop is not statistically significant).

How was the job of these correspondents restructured? "Enlargement versus enrichment of correspondents' tasks in company experiment" lists the suggestions made that were deemed to be horizontal loading, and the actual vertical loading changes that were incorporated in the job of the achieving unit. The capital letters under "Principle" after "Vertical Loading" refer to the corresponding letters in "Principles of vertical job loading." The reader will note that the rejected forms of horizontal loading correspond closely to the list of common manifestations I mentioned earlier.

Steps for Job Enrichment

Now that the motivator idea has been described in practice, here are the steps that managers should take in instituting the principle with their employees:

1. Select those jobs in which a) the investment in industrial engineering does not make changes too costly, b) attitudes are poor, c) hygiene is becoming very costly, and d) motivation will make a difference in performance.

2. Approach these jobs with the conviction that they can be changed. Years of tradition have led managers to believe that job content is sacrosanct and the only scope of action that they have is in ways of stimulating people.

3. Brainstorm a list of changes that may enrich the jobs, without concern for their practicality.

4. Screen the list to eliminate suggestions that involve hygiene, rather than actual motivation.

5. Screen the list for generalities, such as "give them more responsibility," that are rarely followed in practice. This might seem obvious, but the motivator words have never left industry; the substance has just been rationalized and organized out. Words like "responsibility," "growth," "achievement," and "challenge," for example, have been elevated to the lyrics of the patriotic anthem for all organizations. It is the old problem typified by the pledge of allegiance to the flag being more important than contributions to the country—of following the form, rather than the substance.

6. Screen the list to eliminate any *horizontal* loading suggestions.

7. Avoid direct participation by the employees whose jobs are to be enriched. Ideas they have expressed previously certainly constitute a valuable source for recommended changes, but their direct involvement contaminates the process with human relations *hygiene* and, more specifically, gives them

Change in attitudes toward tasks in company experiment

Mean scores at beginning and end of six-month period

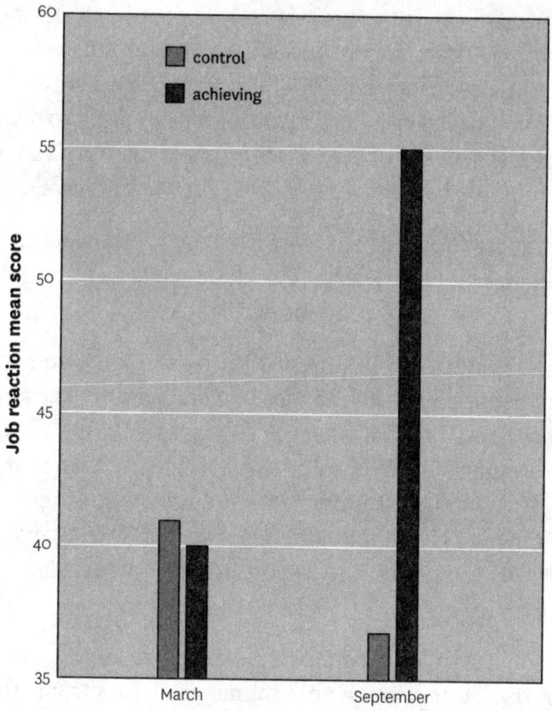

only a *sense* of making a contribution. The job is to be changed, and it is the content that will produce the motivation, not attitudes about being involved or the challenge inherent in setting up a job. That process will be over shortly, and it is what the employees will be doing from then on that will determine their motivation. A sense of participation will result only in short-term movement.

8. In the initial attempts at job enrichment, set up a controlled experiment. At least two equivalent groups should be chosen,

one an experimental unit in which the motivators are systematically introduced over a period of time, and the other one a control group in which no changes are made. For both groups, hygiene should be allowed to follow its natural course for the duration of the experiment. Pre- and post-installation tests of performance and job attitudes are necessary to evaluate the effectiveness of the job enrichment program. The attitude test must be limited to motivator items in order to divorce employees' views of the jobs they are given from all the surrounding hygiene feelings that they might have.

9. Be prepared for a drop in performance in the experimental group the first few weeks. The changeover to a new job may lead to a temporary reduction in efficiency.

10. Expect your first-line supervisors to experience some anxiety and hostility over the changes you are making. The anxiety comes from their fear that the changes will result in poorer performance for their unit. Hostility will arise when the employees start assuming what the supervisors regard as their own responsibility for performance. The supervisor without checking duties to perform may then be left with little to do.

After successful experiment, however, the supervisors usually discover the supervisory and managerial functions they have neglected, or which were never theirs because all their time was given over to checking the work of their subordinates. For example, in the R&D division of one large chemical company I know of, the supervisors of the laboratory assistants were theoretically responsible for their training and evaluation. These functions, however, had come to be performed in a routine, unsubstantial fashion. After the job enrichment program, during which the supervisors were not merely passive observers of the assistants' performance, the supervisors actually were devoting their time to reviewing performance and administering thorough training.

Enlargement versus enrichment of correspondents' tasks in company experiment

Horizontal loading suggestions rejected

Firm quotas could be set for letters to be answered each day, using a rate that would be hard to reach.

The secretaries could type the letters themselves, as well as compose them, or take on any other clerical functions.

All difficult or complex inquiries could be channeled to a few secretaries so that the remainder could achieve high rates of output. These jobs could be exchanged from time to time.

The secretaries could be rotated through units handling different customers and then sent back to their own units.

Vertical loading suggestions adopted	Principle
Subject matter experts were appointed within each unit for other members of the unit to consult before seeking supervisory help. (The supervisor had been answering all specialized and difficult questions.)	G
Correspondents signed their own names on letters. (The supervisor had been signing all letters.)	B
The work of the more experienced correspondents was proofread less frequently by supervisors and was done at the correspondents' desks, dropping verification from 100% to 10%. (Previously, all correspondents' letters had been checked by the supervisor.)	A
Production was discussed, but only in terms such as "a full day's work is expected." As time went on, this was no longer mentioned. (Before, the group had been constantly reminded of the number of letters that needed to be answered.)	D
Outgoing mail went directly to the mailroom without going over supervisor's desks. (The letters had always been routed through the supervisors.)	A
Correspondents were encouraged to answer letters in a more personalized way. (Reliance on the form-letter approach had been standard practice.)	C
Each correspondent was held personally responsible for the quality and accuracy of letters. (This responsibility had been the province of the supervisor and the verifier.)	B, E

What has been called an employee-centered style of supervision will come about not through education of supervisors, but by changing the jobs that they do.

Job enrichment will not be a one-time proposition, but a continuous management function. The initial changes should last for a very long period of time. There are a number of reasons for this:

- The changes should bring the job up to the level of challenge commensurate with the skill that was hired.
- Those who have still more ability eventually will be able to demonstrate it better and win promotion to higher level jobs.
- The very nature of motivators, as opposed to hygiene factors, is that they have a much longer-term effect on employees' attitudes. It is possible that the job will have to be enriched again, but this will not occur as frequently as the need for hygiene.

Not all jobs can be enriched, nor do all jobs need to be enriched. If only a small percentage of the time and money that is now devoted to hygiene, however, were given to job enrichment efforts, the return in human satisfaction and economic gain would be one of the largest dividends that industry and society have ever reaped through their efforts at better personnel management.

The argument for job enrichment can be summed up quite simply: If you have employees on a job, use them. If you can't use them on the job, get rid of them, either via automation or by selecting someone with lesser ability. If you can't use them and you can't get rid of them, you will have a motivation problem.

Originally published in September 1987. Reprint R0301F.

The Set-Up-to-Fail Syndrome

by Jean-François Manzoni and Jean-Louis Barsoux

WHEN AN EMPLOYEE FAILS—or even just performs poorly—managers typically do not blame themselves. The employee doesn't understand the work, a manager might contend. Or the employee isn't driven to succeed, can't set priorities, or won't take direction. Whatever the reason, the problem is assumed to be the employee's fault—and the employee's responsibility.

But is it? Sometimes, of course, the answer is yes. Some employees are not up to their assigned tasks and never will be, for lack of knowledge, skill, or simple desire. But sometimes—and we would venture to say often—an employee's poor performance can be blamed largely on his boss.

Perhaps "blamed" is too strong a word, but it is directionally correct. In fact, our research strongly suggests that bosses—albeit accidentally and usually with the best intentions—are often complicit in an employee's lack of success. (See the sidebar "About the Research.") How? By creating and reinforcing a dynamic that essentially sets up perceived underperformers to fail. If the Pygmalion effect describes the dynamic in which an individual lives up to great expectations, the set-up-to-fail syndrome explains the opposite. It describes a dynamic in which employees perceived to be mediocre or weak performers live down to the low expectations their managers have for them. The result is that they often end up leaving the organization—either of their own volition or not.

The syndrome usually begins surreptitiously. The initial impetus can be performance related, such as when an employee loses a client, undershoots a target, or misses a deadline. Often, however, the trigger is less specific. An employee is transferred into a division with a lukewarm recommendation from a previous boss. Or perhaps the boss and the employee don't really get along on a personal basis—several studies have indeed shown that compatibility between boss and subordinate, based on similarity of attitudes, values, or social characteristics, can have a significant impact on a boss's impressions. In any case, the syndrome is set in motion when the boss begins to worry that the employee's performance is not up to par.

The boss then takes what seems like the obvious action in light of the subordinate's perceived shortcomings: he increases the time and attention he focuses on the employee. He requires the employee to get approval before making decisions, asks to see more paperwork documenting those decisions, or watches the employee at meetings more closely and critiques his comments more intensely.

These actions are intended to boost performance and prevent the subordinate from making errors. Unfortunately, however, subordinates often interpret the heightened supervision as a lack of trust and confidence. In time, because of low expectations, they come to doubt their own thinking and ability, and they lose the motivation to make autonomous decisions or to take any action at all. The boss, they figure, will just question everything they do—or do it himself anyway.

Ironically, the boss sees the subordinate's withdrawal as proof that the subordinate is indeed a poor performer. The subordinate, after all, isn't contributing his ideas or energy to the organization. So what does the boss do? He increases his pressure and supervision again—watching, questioning, and double-checking everything the subordinate does. Eventually, the subordinate gives up on his dreams of making a meaningful contribution. Boss and subordinate typically settle into a routine that is not really satisfactory but, aside from periodic clashes, is otherwise bearable for them. In the

Idea in Brief

That darned employee! His performance keeps deteriorating—*despite* your close monitoring. What's going on?

Brace yourself: *You* may be at fault, by unknowingly triggering the **set-up-to-fail syndrome**. Employees whom you (perhaps falsely) view as weak performers live *down* to your expectations. Here's how:

1. You start with a positive relationship.
2. Something—a missed deadline, a lost client—makes you question the employee's performance. You begin micromanaging him.
3. Suspecting your reduced confidence, the employee starts doubting *himself*. He stops giving his best, responds mechanically to your controls, and avoids decisions.
4. You view his new behavior as additional proof of mediocrity—and tighten the screws further.

Why not just fire him? Because you're likely to repeat the pattern with others. Better to *reverse* the dynamic instead. Unwinding the set-up-to-fail spiral actually pays big dividends: Your company gets the best from your employees—and from you.

worst-case scenario, the boss's intense intervention and scrutiny end up paralyzing the employee into inaction and consume so much of the boss's time that the employee quits or is fired. (See "The set-up-to-fail syndrome: No harm intended: A relationship spirals from bad to worse.")

Perhaps the most daunting aspect of the set-up-to-fail syndrome is that it is self-fulfilling and self-reinforcing—it is the quintessential vicious circle. The process is self-fulfilling because the boss's actions contribute to the very behavior that is expected from weak performers. It is self-reinforcing because the boss's low expectations, in being fulfilled by his subordinates, trigger more of the same behavior on his part, which in turn triggers more of the same behavior on the part of subordinates. And on and on, unintentionally, the relationship spirals downward.

A case in point is the story of Steve, a manufacturing supervisor for a *Fortune* 100 company. When we first met Steve, he came across

Idea in Practice

How Set-Up-to-Fail Starts

A manager categorizes employees as "in" or "out," based on:

- early *perceptions* of employees' motivation, initiative, creativity, strategic perspectives;
- previous bosses' impressions;
- an early mishap; and
- boss-subordinate incompatibility.

The manager then notices *only* evidence supporting his categorization, while dismissing contradictory evidence. The boss also treats the groups differently:

- "In" groups get autonomy, feedback, and expressions of confidence.
- "Out" groups get controlling, formal management emphasizing rules.

The Costs of Set-Up-to-Fail

This syndrome hurts everyone:

- *Employees* stop volunteering ideas and information and asking for help, avoid contact with bosses, or grow defensive.
- The *organization* fails to get the most from employees.
- The *boss* loses energy to attend to other activities. His reputation suffers as other employees deem him unfair.
- *Team spirit* wilts as targeted performers are alienated and strong performers are overburdened.

How to Reverse Set-Up-to-Fail

If the syndrome hasn't started, prevent it:

- Establish expectations with new employees early. Loosen

as highly motivated, energetic, and enterprising. He was on top of his operation, monitoring problems and addressing them quickly. His boss expressed great confidence in him and gave him an excellent performance rating. Because of his high performance, Steve was chosen to lead a new production line considered essential to the plant's future.

In his new job, Steve reported to Jeff, who had just been promoted to a senior management position at the plant. In the first few weeks of the relationship, Jeff periodically asked Steve to write up short analyses of significant quality-control rejections. Although Jeff didn't really explain this to Steve at the time, his request had

the reins as they master their jobs.

- Regularly challenge your own assumptions. Ask: "What are the *facts* regarding this employee's performance?" "Is he really that bad?"
- Convey openness, letting employees challenge your opinions. They'll feel comfortable discussing their performance and relationship with you.

If the syndrome has already erupted, discuss the dynamic with the employee:

1. Choose a neutral, nonthreatening location; use affirming language ("Let's discuss our relationship and roles"); and acknowledge your part in the tension.
2. Agree on the employee's weaknesses and strengths. Support assessments with facts, not feelings.
3. Unearth causes of the weaknesses. Do you disagree on priorities? Does your employee lack specific knowledge or skills? Ask: "How is my behavior making things worse for you?"
4. Identify ways to boost performance. Training? New experiences? Decide the quantity and type of supervision you'll provide. Affirm your desire to improve matters.
5. Agree to communicate more openly: "Next time I do something that communicates low expectations, can you let me know immediately?"

two major objectives: to generate information that would help both of them learn the new production process, and to help Steve develop the habit of systematically performing root cause analysis of quality-related problems. Also, being new on the job himself, Jeff wanted to show his own boss that he was on top of the operation.

Unaware of Jeff's motives, Steve balked. Why, he wondered, should he submit reports on information he understood and monitored himself? Partly due to lack of time, partly in response to what he considered interference from his boss, Steve invested little energy in the reports. Their tardiness and below-average quality annoyed Jeff, who began to suspect that Steve was not a particularly proactive manager. When he asked for the reports again, he was more forceful. For Steve, this merely confirmed that Jeff did not trust him. He withdrew more and more from interaction with him, meeting his demands with increased passive resistance. Before long, Jeff became convinced that Steve was not effective enough and couldn't handle his job without help. He started to supervise Steve's every move—to Steve's predictable dismay. One year after excitedly taking on the new production line, Steve was so dispirited he was thinking of quitting.

How can managers break the set-up-to-fail syndrome? Before answering that question, let's take a closer look at the dynamics that set the syndrome in motion and keep it going.

Deconstructing the Syndrome

We said earlier that the set-up-to-fail syndrome usually starts surreptitiously—that is, it is a dynamic that usually creeps up on the boss and the subordinate until suddenly both of them realize that the relationship has gone sour. But underlying the syndrome are several assumptions about weaker performers that bosses appear to accept uniformly. Our research shows, in fact, that executives typically compare weaker performers with stronger performers using the following descriptors:

- less motivated, less energetic, and less likely to go beyond the call of duty;
- more passive when it comes to taking charge of problems or projects;
- less aggressive about anticipating problems;
- less innovative and less likely to suggest ideas;
- more parochial in their vision and strategic perspective;
- more prone to hoard information and assert their authority, making them poor bosses to their own subordinates.

It is not surprising that on the basis of these assumptions, bosses tend to treat weaker and stronger performers very differently. Indeed, numerous studies have shown that up to 90% of all managers treat some subordinates as though they were members of an in-group, while they consign others to membership in an out-group. Members of the in-group are considered the trusted collaborators and therefore receive more autonomy, feedback, and expressions of confidence from their bosses. The boss-subordinate relationship for this group is one of mutual trust and reciprocal influence. Members of the out-group, on the other hand, are regarded more as hired hands and are managed in a more formal, less personal way, with more emphasis on rules, policies, and authority. (For more on how bosses treat weaker and stronger performers differently, see the chart "In with the In Crowd, Out with the Out.")

Why do managers categorize subordinates into either in-groups or out-groups? For the same reason that we tend to typecast our family, friends, and acquaintances: it makes life easier. Labeling is something we all do, because it allows us to function more efficiently. It saves time by providing rough-and-ready guides for interpreting events and interacting with others. Managers, for instance, use categorical thinking to figure out quickly who should get what tasks. That's the good news.

The downside of categorical thinking is that in organizations it leads to premature closure. Having made up his mind about a subordinate's limited ability and poor motivation, a manager is likely to notice supporting evidence while selectively dismissing contrary evidence. (For example, a manager might interpret a terrific new product idea from an out-group subordinate as a lucky onetime event.) Unfortunately for some subordinates, several studies show that bosses tend to make decisions about in-groups and out-groups even as early as five days into their relationships with employees.

Are bosses aware of this sorting process and of their different approaches to "in" and "out" employees? Definitely. In fact, the bosses we have studied, regardless of nationality, company, or personal background, were usually quite conscious of behaving in a more controlling way with perceived weaker performers. Some of them

About the Research

This article is based on two studies designed to understand better the causal relationship between leadership style and subordinate performance—in other words, to explore how bosses and subordinates mutually influence each other's behavior. The first study, which comprised surveys, interviews, and observations, involved 50 boss-subordinate pairs in four manufacturing operations in *Fortune* 100 companies. The second study, involving an informal survey of about 850 senior managers attending INSEAD executive-development programs over the last three years, was done to test and refine the findings generated by the first study. The executives in the second study represented a wide diversity of nationalities, industries, and personal backgrounds.

preferred to label this approach as "supportive and helpful." Many of them also acknowledged that—although they tried not to—they tended to become impatient with weaker performers more easily than with stronger performers. By and large, however, managers are aware of the controlling nature of their behavior toward perceived weaker performers. For them, this behavior is not an error in implementation; it is intentional.

What bosses typically do *not* realize is that their tight controls end up hurting subordinates' performance by undermining their motivation in two ways: first, by depriving subordinates of autonomy on the job and, second, by making them feel undervalued. Tight controls are an indication that the boss assumes the subordinate can't perform well without strict guidelines. When the subordinate senses these low expectations, it can undermine his self-confidence. This is particularly problematic because numerous studies confirm that people perform up or down to the levels their bosses expect from them or, indeed, to the levels they expect from themselves.[1]

Of course, executives often tell us, "Oh, but I'm very careful about this issue of expectations. I exert more control over my underperformers, but I make sure that it does not come across as a lack of trust or confidence in their ability." We believe what these executives tell us. That is, we believe that they do try hard to disguise their intentions. When we talk to their subordinates, however, we find

The Set-Up-to-Fail Syndrome

No harm intended: A relationship spirals from bad to worse

1. Before the set-up-to-fail syndrome begins, the boss and the subordinate are typically engaged in a positive, or at least neutral, relationship.
2. The triggering event in the set-up-to-fail syndrome is often minor or surreptitious. The subordinate may miss a deadline, lose a client, or submit a subpar report. In other cases, the syndrome's genesis is the boss, who distances himself from the subordinate for personal or social reasons unrelated to performance.
3. Reacting to the triggering event, the boss increases his supervision of the subordinate, gives more specific instructions, and wrangles longer over courses of action.
4. The subordinate responds by beginning to suspect a lack of confidence and senses he's not part of the boss's in-group anymore.

   He starts to withdraw emotionally from the boss and from work. He may also fight to change the boss's image of him, reaching too high or running too fast to be effective.
5. The boss interprets this problem-hoarding, overreaching, or tentativeness as signs that the subordinate has poor judgment and weak capabilities. If the subordinate does perform well, the boss does not acknowledge it or considers it a lucky "one off."

   He limits the subordinate's discretion, withholds social contact, and shows, with increasing openness, his lack of confidence in and frustration with the subordinate.
6. The subordinate feels boxed in and underappreciated. He increasingly withdraws from his boss and from work. He may even resort to ignoring instructions, openly disputing the boss, and occasionally lashing out because of feelings of rejection.

   In general, he performs his job mechanically and devotes more energy to self-protection. Moreover, he refers all nonroutine decisions to the boss or avoids contact with him.
7. The boss feels increasingly frustrated and is now convinced that the subordinate cannot perform without intense oversight. He makes this known by his words and deeds, further undermining the subordinate's confidence and prompting inaction.
8. When the set-up-to-fail syndrome is in full swing, the boss pressures and controls the subordinate during interactions. Otherwise, he avoids contact and gives the subordinate routine assignments only.

   For his part, the subordinate shuts down or leaves, either in dismay, frustration, or anger.

that these efforts are for the most part futile. In fact, our research shows that most employees can—and do—"read their boss's mind." In particular, they know full well whether they fit into their boss's in-group or out-group. All they have to do is compare how they are treated with how their more highly regarded colleagues are treated.

Just as the boss's assumptions about weaker performers and the right way to manage them explains his complicity in the set-up-to-fail syndrome, the subordinate's assumptions about what the boss is thinking explain his own complicity. The reason? When people perceive disapproval, criticism, or simply a lack of confidence and appreciation, they tend to shut down—a behavioral phenomenon that manifests itself in several ways.

Primarily, shutting down means disconnecting intellectually and emotionally. Subordinates simply stop giving their best. They grow

In with the In Crowd, Out with the Out

Boss's behavior toward perceived stronger performers	Boss's behavior toward perceived weaker performers
Discusses project objectives, with a limited focus on project implementation. Gives subordinate the freedom to choose his own approach to solving problems or reaching goals.	Is directive when discussing tasks and goals. Focuses on what needs get done as well as how it should get done.
Treats unfavorable variances, mistakes, or incorrect judgments as learning opportunities.	Pays close attention to unfavorable variances, mistakes, or incorrect judgments.
Makes himself available, as in "let me know if I can help." Initiates casual and personal conversations.	Makes himself available to subordinate on a need-to-see basis. Bases conversations primarily on work-related topics.
Is open to subordinate's suggestions and discusses them with interest.	Pays little interest to subordinate's comments or suggestions about how and why work is done.
Gives subordinate interesting and challenging stretch assignments. Often allows subordinate to choose his own assignments.	Reluctantly gives subordinate anything but routine assignments. When handing out assignments, gives subordinate little choice. Monitors subordinate heavily.
Solicits opinions from subordinate on organizational strategy, execution, policy, and procedures.	Rarely asks subordinate for input about organizational or work-related matters.
Often defers to subordinate's opinion in disagreements.	Usually imposes own views in disagreements.
Praises subordinate for work well done.	Emphasizes what the subordinate is doing poorly.

tired of being overruled, and they lose the will to fight for their ideas. As one subordinate put it, "My boss tells me how to execute every detail. Rather than arguing with him, I've ended up wanting to say, 'Come on, just tell me what you want me to do, and I'll go do it.' You become a robot." Another perceived weak performer explained, "When my boss tells me to do something, I just do it mechanically."

Shutting down also involves disengaging personally—essentially reducing contact with the boss. Partly, this disengagement is motivated by the nature of previous exchanges that have tended to be negative in tone. As one subordinate admitted, "I used to initiate much more contact with my boss until the only thing I received was negative feedback; then I started shying away."

Besides the risk of a negative reaction, perceived weaker performers are concerned with not tainting their images further. Following the often-heard aphorism "Better to keep quiet and look like a fool than to open your mouth and prove it," they avoid asking for help for fear of further exposing their limitations. They also tend to volunteer less information—a simple "heads up" from a perceived underperformer can cause the boss to overreact and jump into action when none is required. As one perceived weak performer recalled, "I just wanted to let my boss know about a small matter, only slightly out of the routine, but as soon as I mentioned it, he was all over my case. I should have kept my mouth closed. I do now."

Finally, shutting down can mean becoming defensive. Many perceived underperformers start devoting more energy to self-justification. Anticipating that they will be personally blamed for failures, they seek to find excuses early. They end up spending a lot of time looking in the rearview mirror and less time looking at the road ahead. In some cases—as in the case of Steve, the manufacturing supervisor described earlier—this defensiveness can lead to noncompliance or even systematic opposition to the boss's views. While this idea of a weak subordinate going head to head with his boss may seem irrational, it may reflect what Albert Camus once observed: "When deprived of choice, the only freedom left is the freedom to say no."

The Syndrome Is Costly

There are two obvious costs of the set-up-to-fail syndrome: the emotional cost paid by the subordinate and the organizational cost associated with the company's failure to get the best out of an employee. Yet there are other costs to consider, some of them indirect and long term.

The boss pays for the syndrome in several ways. First, uneasy relationships with perceived low performers often sap the boss's emotional and physical energy. It can be quite a strain to keep up a facade of courtesy and pretend everything is fine when both parties know it is not. In addition, the energy devoted to trying to fix these relationships or improve the subordinate's performance through increased supervision prevents the boss from attending to other activities—which often frustrates or even angers the boss.

Furthermore, the syndrome can take its toll on the boss's reputation, as other employees in the organization observe his behavior toward weaker performers. If the boss's treatment of a subordinate is deemed unfair or unsupportive, observers will be quick to draw their lessons. One outstanding performer commented on his boss's controlling and hypercritical behavior toward another subordinate: "It made us all feel like we're expendable." As organizations increasingly espouse the virtues of learning and empowerment, managers must cultivate their reputations as coaches, as well as get results.

The set-up-to-fail syndrome also has serious consequences for any team. A lack of faith in perceived weaker performers can tempt bosses to overload those whom they consider superior performers; bosses want to entrust critical assignments to those who can be counted on to deliver reliably and quickly and to those who will go beyond the call of duty because of their strong sense of shared fate. As one boss half-jokingly said, "Rule number one: if you want something done, give it to someone who's busy—there's a reason why that person is busy."

An increased workload may help perceived superior performers learn to manage their time better, especially as they start to delegate to their own subordinates more effectively. In many cases, however, these performers simply absorb the greater load and higher stress which, over time, takes a personal toll and decreases the attention they can devote to other dimensions of their jobs, particularly those yielding longer-term benefits. In the worst-case scenario, overburdening strong performers can lead to burnout.

Team spirit can also suffer from the progressive alienation of one or more perceived low performers. Great teams share a sense of enthusiasm and commitment to a common mission. Even when members of the boss's out-group try to keep their pain to themselves, other team members feel the strain. One manager recalled the discomfort experienced by the whole team as they watched their boss grill one of their peers every week. As he explained, "A team is like a functioning organism. If one member is suffering, the whole team feels that pain."

In addition, alienated subordinates often do not keep their suffering to themselves. In the corridors or over lunch, they seek out sympathetic ears to vent their recriminations and complaints, not only wasting their own time but also pulling their colleagues away from productive work. Instead of focusing on the team's mission, valuable time and energy is diverted to the discussion of internal politics and dynamics.

Finally, the set-up-to-fail syndrome has consequences for the subordinates of the perceived weak performers. Consider the weakest kid in the school yard who gets pummeled by a bully. The abused child often goes home and pummels his smaller, weaker siblings. So it is with the people who are in the boss's out-group. When they have to manage their own employees, they frequently replicate the behavior that their bosses show to them. They fail to recognize good results or, more often, supervise their employees excessively.

Breaking Out Is Hard to Do

The set-up-to-fail syndrome is not irreversible. Subordinates can break out of it, but we have found that to be rare. The subordinate must consistently deliver such superior results that the boss is forced to change the employee from out-group to in-group status—a phenomenon made difficult by the context in which these subordinates operate. It is hard for subordinates to impress their bosses when they must work on unchallenging tasks, with no autonomy and limited resources; it is also hard for them to persist and maintain high standards when they receive little encouragement from their bosses.

Furthermore, even if the subordinate achieves better results, it may take some time for them to register with the boss because of his selective observation and recall. Indeed, research shows that bosses tend to attribute the good things that happen to weaker performers to external factors rather than to their efforts and ability (while the opposite is true for perceived high performers: successes tend to be seen as theirs, and failures tend to be attributed to external uncontrollable factors). The subordinate will therefore need to achieve a string of successes in order to have the boss even contemplate revising the initial categorization. Clearly, it takes a special kind of courage, self-confidence, competence, and persistence on the part of the subordinate to break out of the syndrome.

Instead, what often happens is that members of the out-group set excessively ambitious goals for themselves to impress the boss quickly and powerfully—promising to hit a deadline three weeks early, for instance, or attacking six projects at the same time, or simply attempting to handle a large problem without help. Sadly, such superhuman efforts are usually just that. And in setting goals so high that they are bound to fail, the subordinates also come across as having had very poor judgment in the first place.

The set-up-to-fail syndrome is not restricted to incompetent bosses. We have seen it happen to people perceived within their organizations to be excellent bosses. Their mismanagement of some subordinates need not prevent them from achieving success, particularly when they and the perceived superior performers achieve high levels of individual performance. However, those bosses could be even more successful to the team, the organization, and themselves if they could break the syndrome.

Getting It Right

As a general rule, the first step in solving a problem is recognizing that one exists. This observation is especially relevant to the set-up-to-fail syndrome because of its self-fulfilling and self-reinforcing nature. Interrupting the syndrome requires that a manager understand the dynamic and, particularly, that he accept the possibility that his own behavior may be contributing to a subordinate's underperformance. The next step toward cracking the syndrome, however, is more difficult: it requires a carefully planned and structured intervention that takes the form of one (or several) candid conversations meant to bring to the surface and untangle the unhealthy dynamics that define the boss and the subordinate's relationship. The goal of such an intervention is to bring about a sustainable increase in the subordinate's performance while progressively reducing the boss's involvement.

It would be difficult—and indeed, detrimental—to provide a detailed script of what this kind of conversation should sound like. A boss who rigidly plans for this conversation with a subordinate will not be able to engage in real dialogue with him, because real dialogue requires flexibility. As a guiding framework, however, we offer five components that characterize effective interventions. Although they are not strictly sequential steps, all five components should be part of these interventions.

First, the boss must create the right context for the discussion

He must, for instance, select a time and place to conduct the meeting so that it presents as little threat as possible to the subordinate. A neutral location may be more conducive to open dialogue than an office where previous and perhaps unpleasant conversations have taken place. The boss must also use affirming language when asking the subordinate to meet with him. The session should not be billed as "feedback," because such terms may suggest baggage from the past. "Feedback" could also be taken to mean that the conversation will be one-directional, a monologue delivered by the boss to the subordinate. Instead, the intervention should be described as a meeting to discuss the performance of the subordinate, the role of the boss, and the relationship between the subordinate and the boss. The boss might even acknowledge that he feels tension in the relationship and wants to use the conversation as a way to decrease it.

Finally, in setting the context, the boss should tell the perceived weaker performer that he would genuinely like the interaction to be an open dialogue. In particular, he should acknowledge that he may be partially responsible for the situation and that his own behavior toward the subordinate is fair game for discussion.

Second, the boss and the subordinate must use the intervention process to come to an agreement on the symptoms of the problem

Few employees are ineffective in all aspects of their performance. And few—if any—employees desire to do poorly on the job. Therefore, it is critical that the intervention result in a mutual understanding of the specific job responsibilities in which the subordinate is weak. In the case of Steve and Jeff, for instance, an exhaustive sorting of the evidence might have led to an agreement that Steve's underperformance was not universal but instead largely confined to the quality of the reports he submitted (or failed to submit). In another situation, it might be agreed that a purchasing manager was weak when it came to finding off-shore suppliers and to voicing his ideas in meetings. Or a new investment professional and his boss might come to agree that his performance was subpar when it came to timing the sales and purchase of stocks, but they might also agree that his financial analysis of stocks was quite strong. The idea here is that before working to improve performance or reduce tension in a relationship, an agreement must be reached about what areas of performance contribute to the contentiousness.

We used the word "evidence" above in discussing the case of Steve and Jeff. That is because a boss needs to back up his performance assessments with facts and data—that is, if the intervention is to be useful. They cannot be based on feelings—as in Jeff telling

Steve, "I just have the feeling you're not putting enough energy into the reports." Instead, Jeff needs to describe what a good report should look like and the ways in which Steve's reports fall short. Likewise, the subordinate must be allowed—indeed, encouraged—to defend his performance, compare it with colleagues' work, and point out areas in which he is strong. After all, just because it is the boss's opinion does not make it a fact.

Third, the boss and the subordinate should arrive at a common understanding of what might be causing the weak performance in certain areas

Once the areas of weak performance have been identified, it is time to unearth the reasons for those weaknesses. Does the subordinate have limited skills in organizing work, managing his time, or working with others? Is he lacking knowledge or capabilities? Do the boss and the subordinate agree on their priorities? Maybe the subordinate has been paying less attention to a particular dimension of his work because he does not realize its importance to the boss. Does the subordinate become less effective under pressure? Does he have lower standards for performance than the boss does?

It is also critical in the intervention that the boss bring up the subject of his own behavior toward the subordinate and how this affects the subordinate's performance. The boss might even try to describe the dynamics of the set-up-to-fail syndrome. "Does my behavior toward you make things worse for you?" he might ask, or, "What am I doing that is leading you to feel that I am putting too much pressure on you?"

This component of the discussion also needs to make explicit the assumptions that the boss and the subordinate have thus far been making about each other's intentions. Many misunderstandings start with untested assumptions. For example, Jeff might have said, "When you did not supply me with the reports I asked for, I came to the conclusion that you were not very proactive." That would have allowed Steve to bring his buried assumptions into the open. "No," he might have answered, "I just reacted negatively because you asked for the reports in writing, which I took as a sign of excessive control."

Fourth, the boss and the subordinate should arrive at an agreement about their performance objectives and on their desire to have the relationship move forward

In medicine, a course of treatment follows the diagnosis of an illness. Things are a bit more complex when repairing organizational dysfunction, since modifying behavior and developing complex skills can be more difficult than taking a few pills. Still, the principle that applies to medicine also applies to business: boss and subordinate must use the intervention to plot a course of treatment regarding the root problems they have jointly identified.

The contract between boss and subordinate should identify the ways they can improve on their skills, knowledge, experience, or personal relationship. It should also include an explicit discussion of how much and what type of future supervision the boss will have. No boss, of course, should suddenly abdicate his involvement; it is legitimate for bosses to monitor subordinates' work, particularly when a subordinate has shown limited abilities in one or more facets of his job. From the subordinate's point of view, however, such involvement by the boss is more likely to be accepted, and possibly even welcomed, if the goal is to help the subordinate develop and improve over time. Most subordinates can accept temporary involvement that is meant to decrease as their performance improves. The problem is intense monitoring that never seems to go away.

Fifth, the boss and the subordinate should agree to communicate more openly in the future

The boss could say, "Next time I do something that communicates low expectations, can you let me know immediately?" And the subordinate might say, or be encouraged to say, "Next time I do something that aggravates you or that you do not understand, can you also let me know right away?" Those simple requests can open the door to a more honest relationship almost instantly.

No Easy Answer

Our research suggests that interventions of this type do not take place very often. Face-to-face discussions about a subordinate's performance tend to come high on the list of workplace situations people would rather avoid, because such conversations have the potential to make both parties feel threatened or embarrassed. Subordinates are reluctant to trigger the discussion because they are worried about coming across as thin-skinned or whiny. Bosses tend to avoid initiating these talks because they are concerned about the way the subordinate might react; the discussion could force the boss to make explicit his lack of confidence in the subordinate, in turn putting the subordinate on the defensive and making the situation worse.[2]

As a result, bosses who observe the dynamics of the set-up-to-fail syndrome being played out may be tempted to avoid an explicit discussion. Instead, they will proceed tacitly by trying to encourage their perceived weak performers. That approach has the short-term benefit of bypassing the discomfort of an open discussion, but it has three major disadvantages.

First, a one-sided approach on the part of the boss is less likely to lead to lasting improvement because it focuses on only one symptom of the problem—the boss's behavior. It does not address the subordinate's role in the underperformance.

Second, even if the boss's encouragement were successful in improving the employee's performance, a unilateral approach would limit what both he and the subordinate could otherwise learn from a more up-front handling of the problem. The subordinate, in particular, would not have the benefit of observing and learning from how his boss handled the difficulties in their relationship—problems the subordinate may come across someday with the people he manages.

Finally, bosses trying to modify their behavior in a unilateral way often end up going overboard; they suddenly give the subordinate more autonomy and responsibility than he can handle productively. Predictably, the subordinate fails to deliver to the boss's satisfaction, which leaves the boss even more frustrated and convinced that the subordinate cannot function without intense supervision.

We are not saying that intervention is always the best course of action. Sometimes, intervention is not possible or desirable. There may be, for instance, overwhelming evidence that the subordinate is not capable of doing his job. He was a hiring or promotion mistake, which is best handled by removing him from the position. In other cases, the relationship between the boss and the subordinate is too far gone—too much damage has occurred to repair it. And finally, sometimes bosses are too busy and under too much pressure to invest the kind of resources that intervention involves.

Yet often the biggest obstacle to effective intervention is the boss's mind-set. When a boss believes that a subordinate is a weak performer and, on top of everything else, that person also aggravates him, he is not going to be able to cover up his feelings with words; his underlying convictions will come out in the meeting. That is why preparation for the intervention is crucial. Before even deciding to have a meeting, the boss must separate emotion from reality. Was the situation always as bad as it is now? Is the subordinate really as bad as I think he is? What is the hard evidence I have for that belief? Could there be other factors, aside from performance, that have led me to label this subordinate a weak performer? Aren't there a few things that he does well? He must have displayed above-average qualifications when we decided to hire him. Did these qualifications evaporate all of a sudden?

The boss might even want to mentally play out part of the conversation beforehand. If I say this to the subordinate, what might he answer? Yes, sure, he would say that it was not his fault and that the customer was unreasonable. Those excuses—are they really without merit? Could he have a point? Could it be that, under other circumstances, I might have looked more favorably upon them? And if I still believe I'm right, how can I help the subordinate see things more clearly?

The boss must also mentally prepare himself to be open to the subordinate's views, even if the subordinate challenges him about any evidence regarding his poor performance. It will be easier for the boss to be open if, when preparing for the meeting, he has already challenged his own preconceptions.

Even when well prepared, bosses typically experience some degree of discomfort during intervention meetings. That is not all bad.

The subordinate will probably be somewhat uncomfortable as well, and it is reassuring for him to see that his boss is a human being, too.

Calculating Costs and Benefits

As we've said, an intervention is not always advisable. But when it is, it results in a range of outcomes that are uniformly better than the alternative—that is, continued underperformance and tension. After all, bosses who systematically choose either to ignore their subordinates' underperformance or to opt for the more expedient solution of simply removing perceived weak performers are condemned to keep repeating the same mistakes. Finding and training replacements for perceived weak performers is a costly and recurrent expense. So is monitoring and controlling the deteriorating performance of a disenchanted subordinate. Getting results *in spite of* one's staff is not a sustainable solution. In other words, it makes sense to think of the intervention as an investment, not an expense—with the payback likely to be high.

How high that payback will be and what form it will take obviously depend on the outcome of the intervention, which will itself depend not only on the quality of the intervention but also on several key contextual factors: How long has that relationship been spiraling downward? Does the subordinate have the intellectual and emotional resources to make the effort that will be required? Does the boss have enough time and energy to do his part?

We have observed outcomes that can be clustered into three categories. In the best-case scenario, the intervention leads to a mixture of coaching, training, job redesign, and a clearing of the air; as a result, the relationship and the subordinate's performance improve, and the costs associated with the syndrome go away or, at least, decrease measurably.

In the second-best scenario, the subordinate's performance improves only marginally, but because the subordinate received an honest and open hearing from the boss, the relationship between the two becomes more productive. Boss and subordinate develop a better understanding of those job dimensions the subordinate can do well and those he struggles with. This improved understanding leads the boss and the subordinate to explore *together* how they can develop a better fit between the job and the subordinate's strengths and weaknesses. That improved fit can be achieved by significantly modifying the subordinate's existing job or by transferring the subordinate to another job within the company. It may even result in the subordinate's choosing to leave the company.

While that outcome is not as successful as the first one, it is still productive; a more honest relationship eases the strain on both the boss and the subordinate, and in turn on the subordinate's subordinates. If the subordinate moves to a new job within the organization that better suits him, he will likely become a stronger performer. His relocation may also open up a spot in his old job for a better performer. The key point is that, having been treated fairly, the subordinate is much more likely to accept the outcome of the process. Indeed, recent studies show that the perceived fairness of a process has a major impact on employees' reactions to its outcomes. (See "Fair Process: Managing in the Knowledge Economy," by W. Chan Kim and Renée Mauborgne, HBR July–August 1997.)

Such fairness is a benefit even in the cases where, despite the boss's best efforts, neither the subordinate's performance nor his relationship with his boss improves significantly. Sometimes this happens: the subordinate truly lacks the ability to meet the job requirements, he has no interest in making the effort to improve, and the boss and the subordinate have both professional and personal differences that are irreconcilable. In those cases, however, the intervention still yields indirect benefits because, even if termination follows, other employees within the company are less likely to feel expendable or betrayed when they see that the subordinate received fair treatment.

Prevention Is the Best Medicine

The set-up-to-fail syndrome is not an organizational fait accompli. It can be unwound. The first step is for the boss to become aware of its existence and acknowledge the possibility that he might be part of the problem. The second step requires that the boss initiate a clear, focused intervention. Such an intervention demands an open exchange between the boss and the subordinate based on the evidence of poor performance, its underlying causes, and their joint responsibilities—culminating in a joint decision on how to work toward eliminating the syndrome itself.

Reversing the syndrome requires managers to challenge their own assumptions. It also demands that they have the courage to look within themselves for causes and solutions before placing the burden of responsibility where it does not fully belong. Prevention of the syndrome, however, is clearly the best option.

In our current research, we examine prevention directly. Our results are still preliminary, but it appears that bosses who manage to consistently avoid the set-up-to-fail syndrome have several traits in common. They do not, interestingly, behave the same way with all subordinates. They are more involved with some subordinates than others—they even monitor some subordinates more than others. However, they do so without disempowering and discouraging subordinates.

How? One answer is that those managers begin by being actively involved with all their employees, gradually reducing their involvement based on improved performance. Early guidance is not threatening to subordinates, because it is not triggered by performance shortcomings; it is systematic and meant to help set the conditions for future success. Frequent contact in the beginning of the relationship gives the boss ample opportunity to communicate with subordinates about priorities, performance measures, time allocation, and even expectations of the type and frequency of communication. That kind of clarity goes a long way toward preventing the dynamic of the set-up-to-fail syndrome, which is so often fueled by unstated expectations and a lack of clarity about priorities.

For example, in the case of Steve and Jeff, Jeff could have made explicit very early on that he wanted Steve to set up a system that would analyze the root causes of quality control rejections systematically. He could have explained the benefits of establishing such a system during the initial stages of setting up the new production line, and he might have expressed his intention to be actively involved in the system's design and early operation. His future involvement might then have decreased in such a way that could have been jointly agreed on at that stage.

Another way managers appear to avoid the set-up-to-fail syndrome is by challenging their own assumptions and attitudes about employees on an ongoing basis. They work hard at resisting the temptation to categorize employees in simplistic ways. They also monitor their own reasoning. For example, when feeling frustrated about a subordinate's performance, they ask themselves, "What are the facts?" They examine whether they are expecting things from the employee that have not been articulated, and they try to be objective about how often and to what extent the employee has really failed. In other words, these bosses delve into their own assumptions and behavior before they initiate a full-blown intervention.

Finally, managers avoid the set-up-to-fail syndrome by creating an environment in which employees feel comfortable discussing their performance and their relationships with the boss. Such an environment is a function of several factors: the boss's openness, his comfort level with having his own opinions challenged, even his sense of humor. The net result is that the boss and the subordinate feel free to communicate frequently and to ask one another questions about their respective behaviors before problems mushroom or ossify.

The methods used to head off the set-up-to-fail syndrome do, admittedly, involve a great deal of emotional investment from bosses—just as interventions do. We believe, however, that this higher emotional involvement is the key to getting subordinates to work to their full potential. As with most things in life, you can only expect to get a lot back if you put a lot in. As a senior executive once said to us, "The respect you give is the respect you get." We concur. If you want—indeed, need—the people in your organization to devote their whole hearts and minds to their work, then you must, too.

Originally published in March 1998. Reprint 98209.

Notes

1. *The influence of expectations on performance has been observed in numerous experiments by Dov Eden and his colleagues. See Dov Eden, "Leadership and Expectations: Pygmalion Effects and Other Self-fulfilling Prophecies in Organizations,"* Leadership Quarterly, *Winter 1992, vol. 3, no. 4, pp. 271–305.*

2. *Chris Argyris has written extensively on how and why people tend to behave unproductively in situations they see as threatening or embarrassing. See, for example,* Knowledge for Action: A Guide to Overcoming Barriers to Organizational Change *(San Francisco: Jossey-Bass, 1993).*

Saving Your Rookie Managers from Themselves

by Carol A. Walker

TOM EDELMAN, LIKE A million freshly minted managers before him, had done a marvelous job as an individual contributor. He was smart, confident, forward thinking, and resourceful. His clients liked him, as did his boss and coworkers. Consequently, no one in the department was surprised when his boss offered him a managerial position. Tom accepted with some ambivalence—he loved working directly with clients and was loath to give that up—but on balance, he was thrilled.

Six months later, when I was called into coach Tom (I've disguised his name), I had trouble even picturing the confident insider he once had been. He looked like a deer caught in the headlights. Tom seemed overwhelmed and indeed even used that word several times to describe how he felt. He had started to doubt his abilities. His direct reports, once close colleagues, no longer seemed to respect or even like him. What's more, his department had been beset by a series of small crises, and Tom spent most of his time putting out these fires. He knew this wasn't the most effective use of his time, but he didn't know how to stop. These problems hadn't yet translated into poor business results, but he was in trouble nonetheless.

His boss realized that he was in danger of failing and brought me in to assist. With support and coaching, Tom got the help he needed and eventually became an effective manager. Indeed, he has been promoted twice since I worked with him, and he now runs a small division within the same company. But his near failure—and the path that brought him to that point—is surprisingly typical. Most organizations promote employees into managerial positions based on their technical competence. Very often, however, those people fail to grasp how their roles have changed—that their jobs are no longer about personal achievement but instead about enabling others to achieve, that sometimes driving the bus means taking a backseat, and that building a team is often more important than cutting a deal. Even the best employees can have trouble adjusting to these new realities. That trouble may be exacerbated by normal insecurities that make rookie managers hesitant to ask for help, even when they find themselves in thoroughly unfamiliar territory. As these new managers internalize their stress, their focus becomes internal as well. They become insecure and self-focused and cannot properly support their teams. Inevitably, trust breaks down, staff members are alienated, and productivity suffers.

Many companies unwittingly support this downward spiral by assuming that their rookie managers will somehow learn critical management skills by osmosis. Some rookies do, to be sure, but in my experience they're the exceptions. Most need more help. In the absence of comprehensive training and intensive coaching—which most companies don't offer—the rookie manager's boss plays a key role. Of course, it's not possible for most senior managers to spend hours and hours every week overseeing a new manager's work, but if you know what typical challenges a rookie manager faces, you'll be able to anticipate some problems before they arise and nip others in the bud.

Delegating

Effective delegation may be one of the most difficult tasks for rookie managers. Senior managers bestow on them big responsibilities and tight deadlines, and they put a lot of pressure on them to produce

Idea in Brief

You've wisely promoted a top performer into management. Six months later, this rising star has fallen hard: He's overwhelmed, fearful, not respected by his staff. Why?

You probably promoted him based on his technical competence—then expected him to learn management skills by osmosis.

But he didn't grasp the real challenges of management—for example, empowering others versus striving for personal achievement. Insecure about asking for help, he turned inward. His team's morale plummeted; productivity faltered.

How to save your erstwhile star? Help him master delegating, thinking strategically, and communicating—basic skills that trip up *most* new managers.

results. The natural response of rookies when faced with such challenges is to "just do it," thinking that's what got them promoted in the first place. But their reluctance to delegate assignments also has its roots in some very real fears. First is the fear of losing stature: If I assign high-profile projects to my staff members, they'll get the credit. What kind of visibility will I be left with? Will it be clear to my boss and my staff what value I'm adding? Second is the fear of abdicating control: If I allow Frank to do this, how can I be sure that he will do it correctly? In the face of this fear, the rookie manager may delegate tasks but supervise Frank so closely that he will never feel accountable. Finally, the rookie may be hesitant to delegate work because he's afraid of overburdening his staff. He may be uncomfortable assigning work to former peers for fear that they'll resent him. But the real resentment usually comes when staff members feel that lack of opportunity is blocking their advancement.

Signs that these fears may be playing out include new managers who work excessively long hours, are hesitant to take on new responsibilities, have staff members who seem unengaged, or have a tendency to answer on behalf of employees instead of encouraging them to communicate with you directly.

The first step toward helping young managers delegate effectively is to get them to understand their new role. Acknowledge that

Idea in Practice

Essential management skills for rookie managers:

Delegating. Under pressure to produce, rookies often "just do it" themselves because they fear losing control or overburdening others. But failure to delegate blocks their staffs' advancement, making them resentful, and then disengaged.

How to help:

- Explain that developing staff is *as* essential as financial achievements.
- Lead by example. Trust and empower your rookie; he'll engage his *own* team.
- Encourage him to take small risks in playing to his staff's strengths. Early successes will build his confidence.
- Help him break complex projects into manageable chunks with clear milestones.

Getting support from above. Many rookie managers believe they're in servitude to bosses, not in partnership. To avoid seeming vulnerable, they don't ask for help. But if they don't see you as a critical support source, they won't see *themselves* as one for their team.

How to help:

- Emphasize that open communication is essential to your rookie's success. Discourage covering up problems.
- Introduce him to other managers as resources.
- Have *him* prepare agendas for your regular meetings. The process will help him organize his thoughts.

Projecting confidence. Rookies who don't project confidence won't energize their teams. Frantic, arrogant, or insecure demeanors may repel others in the company.

How to help:

- Encourage "conscious comportment": constant

their job fundamentally differs from an individual contributor's. Clarify what you and the organization value in leaders. Developing talented, promotable staff is critical in any company. Let new managers know that they will be rewarded for these less tangible efforts in addition to hitting numerical goals. Understanding this new role is half the battle for rookie managers, and one that many companies mistakenly assume is evident from the start.

awareness of the image your rookie is projecting.

- Let him express his feelings—but in your office, behind closed doors.
- Keep him from undermining his own authority; e.g., by pushing an initiative only because top management requested it. Walk through the process of presenting an initiative persuasively, ensuring he can *own* the message—not just deliver it.

Focusing on the big picture. Many rookie managers let fire fighting eclipse strategic initiatives. Fire fighting *feels* productive—but it doesn't teach teams to handle challenges themselves or think strategically.

How to help:

- Explain that strategic thinking will constitute more of your rookie's work as his career advances.
- Help him focus on the long-term, big picture. Ask strategic questions; e.g., "What marketplace trends are you seeing that could affect you in six months?"
- Request written plans documenting strategic goals as well as concrete, supporting actions.

Giving constructive feedback. Most rookies dread correcting staffers' inadequate performance. But avoidance costs managers their credibility.

How to help:

- Explain that constructive feedback strengthens staffers' skills.
- Role-play giving feedback about behaviors, not personalities.

After clarifying how your rookie manager's role has changed, you can move on to tactics. Perhaps it goes without saying, but you should lead by example. You have the responsibility to empower the rookie who works for you and do what you can to help him overcome his insecurities about his value to the organization. You can then assist him in looking for opportunities to empower and engage his team.

One young manager I worked with desperately needed to find time to train and supervise new employees. His firm had been recently acquired, and he had to deal with high staff turnover and new industrywide rules and regulations. The most senior person on his staff—a woman who had worked for the acquiring company—was about to return from an extended family leave, and he was convinced that he couldn't ask her for help. After all, she had a part-time schedule, and she'd asked to be assigned to the company's largest client. To complicate matters, he suspected that she resented his promotion. As we evaluated the situation, the manager was able to see that the senior staffer's number one priority was reestablishing herself as an important part of the team. Once he realized this, he asked her to take on critical supervisory responsibilities, balanced with a smaller client load, and she eagerly agreed. Indeed, she returned from leave excited about partnering with her manager to develop the team.

When a new manager grumbles about mounting workloads, seize the opportunity to discuss delegation. Encourage him to take small risks initially, playing to the obvious strengths of his staff members. Asking his super-organized, reliable assistant to take the lead in handling the logistics of a new product launch, for example, is much less risky than asking a star salesperson, unaccustomed to this sort of detailed work, to do it. Early successes will build the manager's confidence and willingness to take progressively larger risks in stretching each team member's capabilities. Reinforce to him that delegation does not mean abdication. Breaking a complex project into manageable chunks, each with clearly defined milestones, makes effective follow-up easier. It's also important to schedule regular meetings before the project even begins in order to ensure that the manager stays abreast of progress and that staff members feel accountable.

Getting Support from Above

Most first-time managers see their relationship with their boss more as one of servitude than of partnership. They will wait for you to initiate meetings, ask for reports, and question results. You may welcome this restraint, but generally it's a bad sign. For one thing, it puts undue pressure on you to keep the flow of communication going. Even more important, it prevents new managers from looking to you as a critical source of support. If they don't see you that way, it's unlikely that they will see themselves that way for their own people. The problem isn't only that your position intimidates them; it's also that they fear being vulnerable. A newly promoted manager doesn't want you to see weaknesses, lest you think you made a mistake in promoting her. When I ask rookie managers about their relationships with their bosses, they often admit that they are trying to "stay under the boss's radar" and are "careful about what [they] say to the boss."

Some inexperienced managers will not seek your help even when they start to founder. Seemingly capable rookie managers often try to cover up a failing project or relationship—just until they can get it back under control. For example, one manager I worked with at a technology company hired a professional 20 years her senior. The transition was rocky, and, despite her best efforts, the individual wasn't acclimating to the organization. (The company, like many in the technology sector, was very youth oriented.) Rather than reaching out to her boss for help, the manager continued to grapple with the situation alone. The staff member ultimately resigned at the busiest time of the year, and the young manager suffered the dual punishment of being understaffed at the worst possible moment and having it known that she had lost a potentially important contributor.

What's the boss of a rookie manager to do? You can begin by clarifying expectations. Explain the connection between the rookie's success and your success, so that she understands that open communication is necessary for you to achieve your goals. Explain that you don't expect her to have all the answers. Introduce her to other managers within the company who may be helpful, and encourage her to contact them as needed. Let her know that mistakes happen but that the cover-up is always worse than the crime. Let her know that you like to receive occasional lunch invitations as much as you like to extend them.

Lunch and drop-by meetings are important, but they usually aren't enough. Consider meeting regularly with a new manager—perhaps weekly in the early stages of a new assignment, moving to biweekly or monthly as her confidence builds. These meetings will develop rapport, provide you with insight into how the person is approaching the job, and make the new manager organize her thoughts on a regular basis. Be clear that the meetings are her time and that it's up to her to plan the agenda. You're there to ask and answer questions and to offer advice. The message you send is that the individual's work is important to you and that you're a committed business partner. More subtly, you're modeling how to simultaneously empower and guide direct reports.

Projecting Confidence

Looking confident when you don't feel confident—it's a challenge we all face, and as senior managers we're usually conscious of the need when it arises. Rookie managers are often so internally focused that they are unaware of this need or the image they project. They are so focused on substance that they forget that form counts, too. The first weeks and months on the job are a critical time for new leaders to reach out to staff. If they don't project confidence, they are unlikely to inspire and energize their teams.

I routinely work with new managers who are unaware that their everyday demeanor is hurting their organizations. In one rapidly growing technology company, the service manager, Linda, faced high levels of stress. Service outages were all too common, and they were beyond her control. Customers were exacting, and they too were under great pressure. Her rapidly growing staff was generally inexperienced. Distraught customers and employees had her tied up in knots almost daily. She consistently appeared breathless, rushed, and fearful that the other shoe was about to drop. The challenge was perhaps too big for a first-time manager, but that's what happens in rapidly growing companies. On one level, Linda was doing an excellent job keeping the operation going. The client base was growing and retention was certainly high—largely as a result of her energy and resourcefulness. But on another level, she was doing a lot of damage.

Linda's frantic demeanor had two critical repercussions. First, she had unwittingly defined the standard for acceptable conduct in her department, and her inexperienced staff began to display the same behaviors. Before long, other departments were reluctant to communicate with Linda or her team, for fear of bothering them or eliciting an emotional reaction. But for the company to arrive at real solutions to the service problems, departments needed to openly exchange information, and that wasn't happening. Second, Linda was not portraying herself to senior managers as promotion material. They were pleased with her troubleshooting abilities, but they did not see a confident, thoughtful senior manager in the making. The image Linda was projecting would ultimately hold back both her career and her department.

Not all rookie managers display the problems that Linda did. Some appear excessively arrogant. Others wear their self-doubt on their sleeves. Whether your managers appear overwhelmed, arrogant, or insecure, honest feedback is your best tool. You can help rookie managers by telling them that it's always safe to let out their feelings—in your office, behind closed doors. Reinforce just how long a shadow they cast once they assume leadership positions. Their staff members watch them closely, and if they see professionalism and optimism, they are likely to demonstrate those characteristics as well. Preach the gospel of conscious comportment—a constant awareness of the image one is projecting to the world. If you observe a manager projecting a less-than-positive image, tell that person right away.

You should also be alert to new managers who undermine their own authority. Linda made another classic rookie mistake when she attempted to get her staff members to implement an initiative that her boss had come up with. In presenting the initiative, she let her team know it was important to implement because it had come from the division's senior vice president. While her intentions were good—rallying the team to perform—her words encouraged the group to focus attention above her rather than on her. There is no quicker way for a rookie manager to lose credibility with her staff than to appear to be a mouthpiece for senior management. Pointing out that senior management will be checking up on the initiative certainly won't hurt, but the rookie manager must take care never to be perceived simply as the messenger.

Just-in-time coaching is often the most effective method for showing rookie managers how to project confidence. For instance, the first time you ask a new manager to carry out an initiative, take a little extra time to walk her through the process. Impress upon her the cardinal rule of management: Your staff members don't necessarily have to like you, but they do need to trust you. Ensure that the new manager owns the message she's delivering.

Layoffs are a classic example of a message the rookie manager will struggle with. Don't allow a rookie to proceed half-prepared. Share as much information as you can. Make sure she's ready for all the likely questions and reactions by asking her to do an informal dry run with you. You might be surprised by how poorly she conveys the message in her first few attempts. A little practice may preserve the image of your manager and your company.

Focusing on the Big Picture

Rookie managers have a real knack for allowing immediate tasks to overshadow overarching initiatives. This is particularly true for those promoted from within, because they've just come from the front lines where they're accustomed to constant fire fighting. As a recent individual contributor armed with plenty of technical know-how, the rookie manager instinctively runs to the immediate rescue of any client or staff member in need. The sense of accomplishment rookies get from such rescues is seductive and far more exhilarating than rooting out the cause of all the fire fighting. And what could be better for team spirit than having the boss jump into the trenches and fight the good fight?

Of course, a leader shows great team spirit if he joins the troops in emergencies. But are all those emergencies true emergencies? Are newer staff members being empowered to handle complex challenges? And if the rookie manager is busy fighting fires, who is thinking strategically for the department? If you're the senior manager and these questions are popping into your head, you may well have a rookie manager who doesn't fully understand his role or is afraid to seize it.

I recently worked with a young manager who had become so accustomed to responding to a steady flow of problems that he was reluctant to block off any time to work on the strategic initiatives we had identified. When I probed, he revealed that he felt a critical part of his role was to wait for crises to arise. "What if I schedule this time and something urgent comes up and I disappoint someone?" he asked. When I pointed out that he could always postpone his strategy sessions if a true emergency arose, he seemed relieved. But he saw the concept of making time to think about the business as self-indulgent—this, despite the fact that his group was going to be asked to raise productivity significantly in the following fiscal year, and he'd done nothing to prepare for that reality.

Senior managers can help rookies by explaining to them that strategic thinking is a necessary skill for career advancement: For first-time managers, 10% of the work might be strategic and 90% tactical. As executives climb the corporate ladder, however, those percentages will flip-flop. To be successful at the next level, managers must demonstrate that they can think and act strategically. You can use your regularly scheduled meetings to help your managers focus on the big picture. Don't allow them to simply review the latest results and move on. Ask probing questions about those results. For example, "What trends are you seeing in the marketplace that could affect you in two quarters? Tell me how your competition is responding to those same trends." Don't let them regale you with the wonderful training their staffs have been getting without asking, "What additional skills do we need to build in the staff to increase productivity by 25% next year?" If you aren't satisfied with your managers' responses, let them know that you expect them to think this way—not to have all the answers, but to be fully engaged in the strategic thought process.

Rookie managers commonly focus on activities rather than on goals. That's because activities can be accomplished quickly (for example, conducting a seminar to improve the sales staff's presentation skills), whereas achieving goals generally takes more time (for example, actually enhancing the sales staff's effectiveness). The senior manager can help the rookie manager think strategically by asking for written goals that clearly distinguish between the goals and their supporting activities. Insisting on a goal-setting discipline will help your new (and not-so-new) managers to organize their strategic game plans. Critical but soft goals, such as staff development, are often overlooked because they are difficult to measure. Putting such goals in print with clear action steps makes them concrete, rendering a sense of accomplishment when they are achieved and a greater likelihood that they will be rewarded. Managers with clear goals will be less tempted to become full-time tacticians. Just as important, the process will help you ensure that they are thinking about the right issues and deploying their teams effectively.

Giving Constructive Feedback

It's human nature to avoid confrontations, and most people feel awkward when they have to correct others' behavior or actions. Rookie managers are no exception, and they often avoid addressing important issues with their staff. The typical scenario goes something like this: A staff member is struggling to meet performance goals or is acting inappropriately in meetings. The manager sits back, watches, and hopes that things will magically improve. Other staff members observe the situation and become frustrated by the manager's inaction. The manager's own frustration builds, as she can't believe the subordinate doesn't get it. The straightforward performance issue has now evolved into a credibility problem. When the manager finally addresses the problem, she personalizes it, lets her frustration seep into the discussion with her staff member, and finds the recipient rushing to defend himself from attack.

Most inexperienced managers wait far too long to talk with staff about performance problems. The senior manager can help by creating an environment in which constructive feedback is perceived not as criticism but as a source of empowerment. This begins with the feedback you offer to your managers about their own development. It can be as simple as getting them to tell you where their weaknesses are before they become problematic. After a good performance review, for example, you might say to your new manager, "By all accounts, you have a bright future here, so it's important that we talk about what you *don't* want me to know. What are you feeling least confident about? How can we address those areas so that you're ready for any opportunity that arises?" You'll probably be surprised by how attuned most high performers are to their own development needs. But they are not likely to do much about them unless you put those needs on the table.

More than likely, the feedback your managers have to offer their staffs will not always be so positive or easy to deliver. The key is to foster in them the desire to help their reports achieve their goals. Under those circumstances, even loathsome personal issues become approachable.

One of my clients managed a high-performing senior staff member who was notably unhelpful to others in the department and who resented her own lack of advancement. Instead of avoiding the issue because he didn't want to tell the staff member that she had a bad attitude, the senior manager took a more productive approach. He leveraged his knowledge of her personal goals to introduce the feedback. "I know that you're anxious for your first management role, and one of my goals is to help you attain that. I can't do that unless I'm completely honest with you. A big part of management is developing stronger skills in your staff. You aren't demonstrating that you enjoy that role. How can we can work together on that?" No guilt, no admonishment—just an offer to help her get what she wanted. Yet the message was received loud and clear.

A brainstorming session this client and I had about ways to offer critical feedback led to that approach. Often, brainstorming sessions can help rookie managers see that sticky personal issues can be broken down into straightforward business issues. In the case of the unhelpful senior staff member, her attitude didn't really need to enter the discussion; her actions did. Recommending a change in action is much easier than recommending a change in attitude. Never forget the old saw: You can't ask people to change their personalities, but you can ask them to change their behaviors.

Indeed, senior managers should share their own techniques for dealing with difficult conversations. One manager I worked with became defensive whenever a staff member questioned her judgment. She didn't really need me to tell her that her behavior was undermining her image and effectiveness. She did need me to offer her some techniques that would enable her to respond differently in the heat of the moment. She trained herself to respond quickly and earnestly with a small repertoire of questions like, "Can you tell me more about what you mean by that?" This simple technique bought her the time she needed to gather her thoughts and engage in an interchange that was productive rather than defensive. She was too close to the situation to come up with the technique herself.

Delegating, thinking strategically, communicating—you may think this all sounds like Management 101. And you're right. The most basic elements of management are often what trip up managers early in their careers. And because they are the basics, the bosses of rookie managers often take them for granted. They shouldn't—an extraordinary number of people fail to develop these skills. I've maintained an illusion throughout this article—that only rookie managers suffer because they haven't mastered these core skills. But the truth is, managers at all levels make these mistakes. An organization that supports its new managers by helping them to develop these skills will have surprising advantages over the competition.

Originally published in April 2002. Reprint R0204H.

What Great Managers Do

by Marcus Buckingham

"THE BEST BOSS I EVER HAD." That's a phrase most of us have said or heard at some point, but what does it mean? What sets the great boss apart from the average boss? The literature is rife with provocative writing about the qualities of managers and leaders and whether the two differ, but little has been said about what happens in the thousands of daily interactions and decisions that allows managers to get the best out of their people and win their devotion. What do great managers actually *do*?

In my research, beginning with a survey of 80,000 managers conducted by the Gallup Organization and continuing during the past two years with in-depth studies of a few top performers, I've found that while there are as many styles of management as there are managers, there is one quality that sets truly great managers apart from the rest: They discover what is unique about each person and then capitalize on it. Average managers play checkers, while great managers play chess. The difference? In checkers, all the pieces are uniform and move in the same way; they are interchangeable. You need to plan and coordinate their movements, certainly, but they all move at the same pace, on parallel paths. In chess, each type of piece moves in a different way, and you can't play if you don't know how each piece moves. More important, you won't win if you don't think carefully about how you move the pieces. Great managers know and value the unique abilities and even the eccentricities of their employees, and they learn how best to integrate them into a coordinated plan of attack.

This is the exact opposite of what great leaders do. Great leaders discover what is universal and capitalize on it. Their job is to rally people toward a better future. Leaders can succeed in this only when they can cut through differences of race, sex, age, nationality, and personality and, using stories and celebrating heroes, tap into those very few needs we all share. The job of a manager, meanwhile, is to turn one person's particular talent into performance. Managers will succeed only when they can identify and deploy the differences among people, challenging each employee to excel in his or her own way. This doesn't mean a leader can't be a manager or vice versa. But to excel at one or both, you must be aware of the very different skills each role requires.

The Game of Chess

What does the chess game look like in action? When I visited Michelle Miller, the manager who opened Walgreens' 4,000th store, I found the wall of her back office papered with work schedules. Michelle's store in Redondo Beach, California, employs people with sharply different skills and potentially disruptive differences in personality. A critical part of her job, therefore, is to put people into roles and shifts that will allow them to shine—and to avoid putting clashing personalities together. At the same time, she needs to find ways for individuals to grow.

There's Jeffrey, for example, a "goth rocker" whose hair is shaved on one side and long enough on the other side to cover his face. Michelle almost didn't hire him because he couldn't quite look her in the eye during his interview, but he wanted the hard-to-cover night shift, so she decided to give him a chance. After a couple of months, she noticed that when she gave Jeffrey a vague assignment, such as "Straighten up the merchandise in every aisle," what should have been a two-hour job would take him all night—and wouldn't be done very well. But if she gave him a more specific task, such as "Put up all

Idea in Brief

You've spent months coaching that employee to treat customers better, work more independently, or get organized—all to no avail.

How to make better use of your precious time? Do what great managers do: Instead of trying to change your employees, identify their unique abilities (and even their eccentricities)—then help them use those qualities to excel in their own way.

You'll need these three tactics:

- **Continuously tweak roles to capitalize on individual strengths.** One Walgreens store manager put a laconic but highly organized employee in charge of restocking aisles—freeing up more sociable employees to serve customers.
- **Pull the triggers that activate employees' strengths.** Offer incentives such as time spent with you, opportunities to work independently, and recognition in forms each employee values most.
- **Tailor coaching to unique learning styles.** Give "analyzers" the information they need before starting a task. Start "doers" off with simple tasks, then gradually raise the bar. Let "watchers" ride shotgun with your most experienced performers.

The payoff for capitalizing on employees' unique strengths? You save time. Your people take ownership for improving their skills. And you teach employees to value differences—building a powerful sense of team.

the risers for Christmas," all the risers would be symmetrical, with the right merchandise on each one, perfectly priced, labeled, and "faced" (turned toward the customer). Give Jeffrey a generic task, and he would struggle. Give him one that forced him to be accurate and analytical, and he would excel. This, Michelle concluded, was Jeffrey's forte. So, as any good manager would do, she told him what she had deduced about him and praised him for his good work.

And a good manager would have left it at that. But Michelle knew she could get more out Jeffrey. So she devised a scheme to reassign responsibilities across the entire store to capitalize on his unique strengths. In every Walgreens, there is a responsibility called "resets and revisions." A reset involves stocking an aisle with new merchandise, a task that usually coincides with a predictable change in

Idea in Practice

A closer look at the three tactics:

Capitalize on Employees' Strengths

First identify each employee's unique strengths: Walk around, observing people's reactions to events. Note activities each employee is drawn to. Ask "What was the best day at work you've had in the past three months?" Listen for activities people find intrinsically satisfying.

Watch for weaknesses, too, but downplay them in your communications with employees. Offer training to help employees overcome shortcomings stemming from lack of skills or knowledge. Otherwise, apply these strategies:

- **Find the employee a partner with complementary talents.** A merchandising manager who couldn't start tasks without exhaustive information performed superbly once her supervisor (the VP) began acting as her "information partner." The VP committed to leaving the manager a brief voicemail update daily and arranging two "touch base" conversations weekly.
- **Reconfigure work to neutralize weaknesses.** Use your creativity to envision more effective work arrangements, and be courageous about adopting unconventional job designs.

Activate Employees' Strengths

The ultimate trigger for activating an employee's strengths is recognition. But each employee plays to a different audience. So tailor your praise accordingly.

customer buying patterns (at the end of summer, for example, the stores will replace sun creams and lip balms with allergy medicines). A revision is a less time-consuming but more frequent version of the same thing: Replace these cartons of toothpaste with this new and improved variety. Display this new line of detergent at this end of the row. Each aisle requires some form of revision at least once a week.

In most Walgreens stores, each employee "owns" one aisle, where she is responsible not only for serving customers but also for

If an employee values recognition from. . .	Praise him by. . .
His peers	• Publicly celebrating his achievement in front of coworkers
You	• Telling him privately but vividly why he's such a valuable team member
Others with similar expertise	• Giving him a professional or technical award
Customers	• Posting a photo of him and his best customer in the office

Tailor Coaching to Learning Style

Adapt your coaching efforts to each employee's unique learning style:

If an employee is . . .	Coach him by. . .
An "**analyzer**"—he requires extensive information before taking on a task, and he hates making mistakes	• Giving him ample classroom time • Role-playing with him • Giving him time to prepare for challenges
A "**doer**"—he uses trial and error to enhance his skills while grappling with tasks	• Assigning him a simple task, explaining the desired outcomes, and getting out of his way • Gradually increasing a task's complexity until he masters his role
A "**watcher**"—he hones his skills by watching other people in action	• Having him "shadow" top performers.

facing the merchandise, keeping the aisle clean and orderly, tagging items with a Telxon gun, and conducting all resets and revisions. This arrangement is simple and efficient, and it affords each employee a sense of personal responsibility. But Michelle decided that since Jeffrey was so good at resets and revisions—and didn't enjoy interacting with customers—this should be his full-time job, in every single aisle.

It was a challenge. One week's worth of revisions requires a binder three inches thick. But Michelle reasoned that not only would

Jeffrey be excited by the challenge and get better and better with practice, but other employees would be freed from what they considered a chore and have more time to greet and serve customers. The store's performance proved her right. After the reorganization, Michelle saw not only increases in sales and profit but also in that most critical performance metric, customer satisfaction. In the subsequent four months, her store netted perfect scores in Walgreens' mystery shopper program.

So far, so very good. Sadly, it didn't last. This "perfect" arrangement depended on Jeffrey remaining content, and he didn't. With his success at doing resets and revisions, his confidence grew, and six months into the job, he wanted to move into management. Michelle wasn't disappointed by this, however; she was intrigued. She had watched Jeffrey's progress closely and had already decided that he might do well as a manager, though he wouldn't be a particularly emotive one. Besides, like any good chess player, she had been thinking a couple of moves ahead.

Over in the cosmetics aisle worked an employee named Genoa. Michelle saw Genoa as something of a double threat. Not only was she adept at putting customers at ease—she remembered their names, asked good questions, was welcoming yet professional when answering the phone—but she was also a neatnik. The cosmetics department was always perfectly faced, every product remained aligned, and everything was arranged just so. Her aisle was sexy: It made you want to reach out and touch the merchandise.

To capitalize on these twin talents, and to accommodate Jeffrey's desire for promotion, Michelle shuffled the roles within the store once again. She split Jeffrey's reset and revision job in two and gave the "revision" part of it to Genoa so that the whole store could now benefit from her ability to arrange merchandise attractively. But Michelle didn't want the store to miss out on Genoa's gift for customer service, so Michelle asked her to focus on the revision role only between 8:30 AM and 11 AM, and after that, when the store began to fill with customers on their lunch breaks, Genoa should shift her focus over to them.

She kept the reset role with Jeffrey. Assistant managers don't usually have an ongoing responsibility in the store, but, Michelle reasoned, he was now so good and so fast at tearing an aisle apart and rebuilding it that he could easily finish a major reset during a five-hour stint, so he could handle resets along with his managerial responsibilities.

By the time you read this, the Jeffrey–Genoa configuration has probably outlived its usefulness, and Michelle has moved on to design other effective and inventive configurations. The ability to keep tweaking roles to capitalize on the uniqueness of each person is the essence of great management.

A manager's approach to capitalizing on differences can vary tremendously from place to place. Walk into the back office at another Walgreens, this one in San Jose, California, managed by Jim Kawashima, and you won't see a single work schedule. Instead, the walls are covered with sales figures and statistics, the best of them circled with red felt-tip pen, and dozens of photographs of sales contest winners, most featuring a customer service representative named Manjit.

Manjit outperforms her peers consistently. When I first heard about her, she had just won a competition in Walgreens' suggestive selling program to sell the most units of Gillette deodorant in a month. The national average was 300; Manjit had sold 1,600. Disposable cameras, toothpaste, batteries—you name it, she could sell it. And Manjit won contest after contest despite working the graveyard shift, from 12:30 AM to 8:30 AM, during which she met significantly fewer customers than did her peers.

Manjit hadn't always been such an exceptional performer. She became stunningly successful only when Jim, who has made a habit of resuscitating troubled stores, came on board. What did Jim do to initiate the change in Manjit? He quickly picked up on her idiosyncrasies and figured out how to translate them into outstanding performance. For example, back in India, Manjit was an athlete—a runner and a weight lifter—and had always thrilled to the challenge of measured performance. When I interviewed her, one of the first

The Research

TO GATHER THE RAW MATERIAL for my book *The One Thing You Need to Know: About Great Managing, Great Leading, and Sustained Individual Success*, from which this article has been adapted, I chose an approach that is rather different from the one I used for my previous books. For 17 years, I had the good fortune to work with the Gallup Organization, one of the most respected research firms in the world. During that time, I was given the opportunity to interview some of the world's best leaders, managers, teachers, salespeople, stockbrokers, lawyers, and public servants. These interviews were a part of large-scale studies that involved surveying groups of people in the hopes of finding broad patterns in the data. For my book, I used this foundation as the jumping-off point for deeper, more individualized research.

In each of the three areas targeted in the book—managing, leading, and sustained individual success—I first identified one or two people in various roles and fields who had measurably, consistently, and dramatically outperformed their peers. These individuals included Myrtle Potter, president of commercial operations for Genentech, who transformed a failing drug into the highest selling prescription drug in the world; Sir Terry Leahy, the president of the European retailing giant Tesco; Manjit, the customer service representative

things out of her mouth was, "On Saturday, I sold 343 low-carb candy bars. On Sunday, I sold 367. Yesterday, 110, and today, 105." I asked if she always knows how well she's doing. "Oh yes," she replied. "Every day I check Mr. K's charts. Even on my day off, I make a point to come in and check my numbers."

Manjit loves to win and revels in public recognition. Hence, Jim's walls are covered with charts and figures, Manjit's scores are always highlighted in red, and there are photos documenting her success. Another manager might have asked Manjit to curb her enthusiasm for the limelight and give someone else a chance. Jim found a way to capitalize on it.

But what about Jim's other staff members? Instead of being resentful of Manjit's public recognition, the other employees came to understand that Jim took the time to see them as individuals and evaluate them based on their personal strengths. They also knew that Manjit's success spoke well of the entire store, so her success galvanized the team. In fact, before long, the pictures of Manjit from Jim Kawashima's top-performing Walgreens store in San Jose, California, who sold more than 1,600 units of Gillette deodorant in one month; and David Koepp, the prolific screenwriter who penned such blockbusters as *Jurassic Park*, *Mission: Impossible*, and *Spider-Man*.

What interested me about these high achievers was the practical, seemingly banal details of their actions and their choices. Why did Myrtle Potter repeatedly turn down promotions before taking on the challenge of turning around that failing drug? Why did Terry Leahy rely more on the memories of his working-class upbringing to define his company's strategy than on the results of customer surveys or focus groups? Manjit works the night shift, and one of her hobbies is weight lifting. Are those factors relevant to her performance? What were these special people doing that made them so very good at their roles?

Once these many details were duly noted and recorded, they slowly came together to reveal the "one thing" at the core of great managing, great leading, and sustained individual success.

began to include other employees from the store, too. After a few months, the San Jose location was ranked number one out of 4,000 in Walgreens' suggestive selling program.

Great Managers Are Romantics

Think back to Michelle. Her creative choreography may sound like a last resort, an attempt to make the best of a bad hire. It's not. Jeffrey and Genoa are not mediocre employees, and capitalizing on each person's uniqueness is a tremendously powerful tool.

First, identifying and capitalizing on each person's uniqueness saves time. No employee, however talented, is perfectly well-rounded. Michelle could have spent untold hours coaching Jeffrey and cajoling him into smiling at, making friends with, and remembering the names of customers, but she probably would have seen little result for her efforts. Her time was much better spent carving out a role that took advantage of Jeffrey's natural abilities.

The Elusive "One Thing"

IT'S BOLD TO CHARACTERIZE ANYTHING as *the* explanation or solution, so it's a risky move to make such definitive assertions as "this is the one thing all great managers do." But with enough research and focus, it is possible to identify that elusive "one thing."

I like to think of the concept of "one thing" as a "controlling insight." Controlling insights don't explain all outcomes or events; they serve as the best explanation of the greatest number of events. Such insights help you know which of your actions will have the most far-reaching influence in virtually every situation.

For a concept to emerge as the single controlling insight, it must pass three tests. First, it must be applicable across a wide range of situations. Take leadership as an example. Lately, much has been made of the notion that there is no one best way to lead and that instead, the most effective leadership style depends on the circumstance. While there is no doubt that different situations require different actions from a leader, that doesn't mean the most insightful thing you can say about leadership is that it's situational. With

Second, capitalizing on uniqueness makes each person more accountable. Michelle didn't just praise Jeffrey for his ability to execute specific assignments. She challenged him to make this ability the cornerstone of his contribution to the store, to take ownership for this ability, to practice it, and to refine it.

Third, capitalizing on what is unique about each person builds a stronger sense of team, because it creates interdependency. It helps people appreciate one anothers' particular skills and learn that their coworkers can fill in where they are lacking. In short, it makes people need one another. The old cliché is that there's no "I" in "team." But as Michael Jordan once said, "There may be no 'I' in 'team,' but there is in 'win.'"

Finally, when you capitalize on what is unique about each person, you introduce a healthy degree of disruption into your world. You shuffle existing hierarchies: If Jeffrey is in charge of all resets and revisions in the store, should he now command more or less respect than an assistant manager? You also shuffle existing assumptions about who is allowed to do what: If Jeffrey devises new methods of resetting

enough focus, you can identify the one thing that underpins successful leadership across all situations and all styles.

Second, a controlling insight must serve as a multiplier. In any equation, some factors will have only an additive value: When you focus your actions on these factors, you see some incremental improvement. The controlling insight should be more powerful. It should show you how to get exponential improvement. For example, good managing is the result of a combination of many actions—selecting talented employees, setting clear expectations, catching people doing things right, and so on—but none of these factors qualifies as the "one thing" that great managers do, because even when done well, these actions merely prevent managers from chasing their best employees away.

Finally, the controlling insight must guide action. It must point to precise things that can be done to create better outcomes more consistently. Insights that managers can act on—rather than simply ruminate over—are the ones that can make all the difference.

an aisle, does he have to ask permission to try these out, or can he experiment on his own? And you shuffle existing beliefs about where the true expertise lies: If Genoa comes up with a way of arranging new merchandise that she thinks is more appealing than the method suggested by the "planogram" sent down from Walgreens headquarters, does her expertise trump the planners back at corporate? These questions will challenge Walgreens' orthodoxies and thus will help the company become more inquisitive, more intelligent, more vital, and, despite its size, more able to duck and weave into the future.

All that said, the reason great managers focus on uniqueness isn't just because it makes good business sense. They do it because they can't help it. Like Shelley and Keats, the nineteenth-century Romantic poets, great managers are fascinated with individuality for its own sake. Fine shadings of personality, though they may be invisible to some and frustrating to others, are crystal clear to and highly valued by great managers. They could no more ignore these subtleties than ignore their own needs and desires. Figuring out what makes people tick is simply in their nature.

The Three Levers

Although the Romantics were mesmerized by differences, at some point, managers need to rein in their inquisitiveness, gather up what they know about a person, and put the employee's idiosyncrasies to use. To that end, there are three things you must know about someone to manage her well: her strengths, the triggers that activate those strengths, and how she learns.

Make the most of strengths

It takes time and effort to gain a full appreciation of an employee's strengths and weaknesses. The great manager spends a good deal of time outside the office walking around, watching each person's reactions to events, listening, and taking mental notes about what each individual is drawn to and what each person struggles with. There's no substitute for this kind of observation, but you can obtain a lot of information about a person by asking a few simple, open-ended questions and listening carefully to the answers. Two queries in particular have proven most revealing when it comes to identifying strengths and weaknesses, and I recommend asking them of all new hires—and revisiting the questions periodically.

To identify a person's strengths, first ask, "What was the best day at work you've had in the past three months?" Find out what the person was doing and why he enjoyed it so much. Remember: A strength is not merely something you are good at. In fact, it might be something you aren't good at yet. It might be just a predilection, something you find so intrinsically satisfying that you look forward to doing it again and again and getting better at it over time. This question will prompt your employee to start thinking about his interests and abilities from this perspective.

To identify a person's weaknesses, just invert the question: "What was the worst day you've had at work in the past three months?" And then probe for details about what he was doing and why it grated on him so much. As with a strength, a weakness is not merely something you are bad at (in fact, you might be quite competent at it). It is something that drains you of energy, an activity that

What You Need to Know About Each of Your Direct Reports

- ☐ What are his or her strengths?
- ☐ What are the triggers that activate those strengths?
- ☐ What is his or her learning style?

you never look forward to doing and that when you are doing it, all you can think about is stopping.

Although you're keeping an eye out for both the strengths and weaknesses of your employees, your focus should be on their strengths. Conventional wisdom holds that self-awareness is a good thing and that it's the job of the manager to identify weaknesses and create a plan for overcoming them. But research by Albert Bandura, the father of social learning theory, has shown that self-assurance (labeled "self-efficacy" by cognitive psychologists), not self-awareness, is the strongest predictor of a person's ability to set high goals, to persist in the face of obstacles, to bounce back when reversals occur, and, ultimately, to achieve the goals they set. By contrast, self-awareness has not been shown to be a predictor of any of these outcomes, and in some cases, it appears to retard them.

Great managers seem to understand this instinctively. They know that their job is not to arm each employee with a dispassionately accurate understanding of the limits of her strengths and the liabilities of her weaknesses but to reinforce her self-assurance. That's why great managers focus on strengths. When a person succeeds, the great manager doesn't praise her hard work. Even if there's some exaggeration in the statement, he tells her that she succeeded because she has become so good at deploying her specific strengths. This, the manager knows, will strengthen the employee's self-assurance and make her more optimistic and more resilient in the face of challenges to come.

The focus-on-strengths approach might create in the employee a modicum of overconfidence, but great managers mitigate this by emphasizing the size and the difficulty of the employee's goals.

They know that their primary objective is to create in each employee a specific state of mind: one that includes a realistic assessment of the difficulty of the obstacle ahead but an unrealistically optimistic belief in her ability to overcome it.

And what if the employee fails? Assuming the failure is not attributable to factors beyond her control, always explain failure as a lack of effort, even if this is only partially accurate. This will obscure self-doubt and give her something to work on as she faces up to the next challenge.

Repeated failure, of course, may indicate weakness where a role requires strength. In such cases, there are four approaches for overcoming weaknesses. If the problem amounts to a lack of skill or knowledge, that's easy to solve: Simply offer the relevant training, allow some time for the employee to incorporate the new skills, and look for signs of improvement. If her performance doesn't get better, you'll know that the reason she's struggling is because she is missing certain talents, a deficit no amount of skill or knowledge training is likely to fix. You'll have to find a way to manage around this weakness and neutralize it.

Which brings us to the second strategy for overcoming an employee weakness. Can you find her a partner, someone whose talents are strong in precisely the areas where hers are weak? Here's how this strategy can look in action. As vice president of merchandising for the women's clothing retailer Ann Taylor, Judi Langley found that tensions were rising between her and one of her merchandising managers, Claudia (not her real name), whose analytical mind and intense nature created an overpowering "need to know." If Claudia learned of something before Judi had a chance to review it with her, she would become deeply frustrated. Given the speed with which decisions were made, and given Judi's busy schedule, this happened frequently. Judi was concerned that Claudia's irritation was unsettling the whole product team, not to mention earning the employee a reputation as a malcontent.

An average manager might have identified this behavior as a weakness and lectured Claudia on how to control her need for information.

Judi, however, realized that this "weakness" was an aspect of Claudia's greatest strength: her analytical mind. Claudia would never be able to rein it in, at least not for long. So Judi looked for a strategy that would honor and support Claudia's need to know, while channeling it more productively. Judi decided to act as Claudia's information partner, and she committed to leaving Claudia a voice mail at the end of each day with a brief update. To make sure nothing fell through the cracks, they set up two live "touch base" conversations per week. This solution managed Claudia's expectations and assured her that she would get the information she needed, if not exactly when she wanted it, then at least at frequent and predictable intervals. Giving Claudia a partner neutralized the negative manifestations of her strength, allowing her to focus her analytical mind on her work. (Of course, in most cases, the partner would need to be someone other than a manager.)

Should the perfect partner prove hard to find, try this third strategy: Insert into the employee's world a technique that helps accomplish through discipline what the person can't accomplish through instinct. I met one very successful screenwriter and director who had struggled with telling other professionals, such as composers and directors of photography, that their work was not up to snuff. So he devised a mental trick: He now imagines what the "god of art" would want and uses this imaginary entity as a source of strength. In his mind, he no longer imposes his own opinion on his colleagues but rather tells himself (and them) that an authoritative third party has weighed in.

If training produces no improvement, if complementary partnering proves impractical, and if no nifty discipline technique can be found, you are going to have to try the fourth and final strategy, which is to rearrange the employee's working world to render his weakness irrelevant, as Michelle Miller did with Jeffrey. This strategy will require of you, first, the creativity to envision a more effective arrangement and, second, the courage to make that arrangement work. But as Michelle's experience revealed, the payoff that may come in the form of increased employee productivity and engagement is well worth it.

Trigger good performance

A person's strengths aren't always on display. Sometimes they require precise triggering to turn them on. Squeeze the right trigger, and a person will push himself harder and persevere in the face of resistance. Squeeze the wrong one, and the person may well shut down. This can be tricky because triggers come in myriad and mysterious forms. One employee's trigger might be tied to the time of day (he is a night owl, and his strengths only kick in after 3 PM). Another employee's trigger might be tied to time with you, the boss (even though he's worked with you for more than five years, he still needs you to check in with him every day, or he feels he's being ignored). Another worker's trigger might be just the opposite—independence (she's only worked for you for six months, but if you check in with her even once a week, she feels micromanaged).

The most powerful trigger by far is recognition, not money. If you're not convinced of this, start ignoring one of your highly paid stars, and watch what happens. Most managers are aware that employees respond well to recognition. Great managers refine and extend this insight. They realize that each employee plays to a slightly different audience. To excel as a manager, you must be able to match the employee to the audience he values most. One employee's audience might be his peers; the best way to praise him would be to stand him up in front of his coworkers and publicly celebrate his achievement. Another's favorite audience might be you; the most powerful recognition would be a one-on-one conversation where you tell him quietly but vividly why he is such a valuable member of the team. Still another employee might define himself by his expertise; his most prized form of recognition would be some type of professional or technical award. Yet another might value feedback only from customers, in which case a picture of the employee with her best customer or a letter to her from the customer would be the best form of recognition.

Given how much personal attention it requires, tailoring praise to fit the person is mostly a manager's responsibility. But organizations can take a cue from this, too. There's no reason why a large company can't take this individualized approach to recognition and apply it to every employee. Of all the companies I've encountered, the North American division of HSBC, a London-based bank, has done the best job of this. Each year it presents its top individual consumer-lending performers with its Dream Awards. Each winner receives a unique prize. During the year, managers ask employees to identify what they would like to receive should they win. The prize value is capped at $10,000, and it cannot be redeemed as cash, but beyond those two restrictions, each employee is free to pick the prize he wants. At the end of the year, the company holds a Dream Awards gala, during which it shows a video about the winning employee and why he selected his particular prize.

You can imagine the impact these personalized prizes have on HSBC employees. It's one thing to be brought up on stage and given yet another plaque. It's another thing when, in addition to public recognition of your performance, you receive a college tuition fund for your child, or the Harley-Davidson motorcycle you've always dreamed of, or—the prize everyone at the company still talks about—the airline tickets to fly you and your family back to Mexico to visit the grandmother you haven't seen in ten years.

Tailor to learning styles

Although there are many learning styles, a careful review of adult learning theory reveals that three styles predominate. These three are not mutually exclusive; certain employees may rely on a combination of two or perhaps all three. Nonetheless, staying attuned to each employee's style or styles will help focus your coaching.

First, there's analyzing. Claudia from Ann Taylor is an analyzer. She understands a task by taking it apart, examining its elements, and reconstructing it piece by piece. Because every single component of a task is important in her eyes, she craves information. She needs to absorb all there is to know about a subject before she can begin to feel comfortable with it. If she doesn't feel she has enough information, she will dig and push until she gets it. She will read the assigned reading. She will attend the required classes. She will take good notes. She will study. And she will still want more.

The best way to teach an analyzer is to give her ample time in the classroom. Role-play with her. Do postmortem exercises with her. Break her performance down into its component parts so she can carefully build it back up. Always allow her time to prepare. The analyzer hates mistakes. A commonly held view is that mistakes fuel learning, but for the analyzer, this just isn't true. In fact, the reason she prepares so diligently is to minimize the possibility of mistakes. So don't expect to teach her much by throwing her into a new situation and telling her to wing it.

The opposite is true for the second dominant learning style, doing. While the most powerful learning moments for the analyzer occur prior to the performance, the doer's most powerful moments occur *during* the performance. Trial and error are integral to this learning process. Jeffrey, from Michelle Miller's store, is a doer. He learns the most while he's in the act of figuring things out for himself. For him, preparation is a dry, uninspiring activity. So rather than role-play with someone like Jeffrey, pick a specific task within his role that is simple but real, give him a brief overview of the outcomes you want, and get out of his way. Then gradually increase the degree of each task's complexity until he has mastered every aspect of his role. He may make a few mistakes along the way, but for the doer, mistakes are the raw material for learning.

Finally, there's watching. Watchers won't learn much through role-playing. They won't learn by doing, either. Since most formal training programs incorporate both of these elements, watchers are often viewed as rather poor students. That may be true, but they aren't necessarily poor learners.

Watchers can learn a great deal when they are given the chance to see the total performance. Studying the individual parts of a task is about as meaningful for them as studying the individual pixels of a digital photograph. What's important for this type of learner is the content of each pixel, its position relative to all the others. Watchers are only able to see this when they view the complete picture.

As it happens, this is the way I learn. Years ago, when I first began interviewing, I struggled to learn the skill of creating a report on a person after I had interviewed him. I understood all the required steps, but I couldn't seem to put them together. Some of my colleagues could knock out a report in an hour; for me, it would take the better part of a day. Then one afternoon, as I was staring morosely into my Dictaphone, I overheard the voice of the analyst next door. He was talking so rapidly that I initially thought he was on the phone. Only after a few minutes did I realize that he was dictating a report. This was the first time I had heard someone "in the act." I'd seen the finished results countless times, since reading the reports of others was the way we were supposed to learn, but I'd never actually heard another analyst in the act of creation. It was a revelation. I finally saw how everything should come together into a coherent whole. I remember picking up my Dictaphone, mimicking the cadence and even the accent of my neighbor, and feeling the words begin to flow.

If you're trying to teach a watcher, by far the most effective technique is to get her out of the classroom. Take her away from the manuals, and make her ride shotgun with one of your most experienced performers.

We've seen, in the stories of great managers like Michelle Miller and Judi Langley, that at the very heart of their success lies an appreciation for individuality. This is not to say that managers don't need other skills. They need to be able to hire well, to set expectations, and to interact productively with their own bosses, just to name a few. But what they do—instinctively—is play chess. Mediocre managers assume (or hope) that their employees will all be motivated by the same things and driven by the same goals, that they will desire the same kinds of relationships and learn in roughly the same way. They define the behaviors they expect from people and tell them to work on behaviors that don't come naturally. They praise those who can overcome their natural styles to conform to preset ideas. In short, they believe the manager's job is to mold, or transform, each employee into the perfect version of the role.

Great managers don't try to change a person's style. They never try to push a knight to move in the same way as a bishop. They know that their employees will differ in how they think, how they build relationships, how altruistic they are, how patient they can be, how much of an expert they need to be, how prepared they need to feel, what drives them, what challenges them, and what their goals are. These differences of trait and talent are like blood types: They cut across the superficial variations of race, sex, and age and capture the essential uniqueness of each individual.

Like blood types, the majority of these differences are enduring and resistant to change. A manager's most precious resource is time, and great managers know that the most effective way to invest their time is to identify exactly how each employee is different and then to figure out how best to incorporate those enduring idiosyncrasies into the overall plan.

To excel at managing others, you must bring that insight to your actions and interactions. Always remember that great managing is about release, not transformation. It's about constantly tweaking your environment so that the unique contribution, the unique needs, and the unique style of each employee can be given free rein. Your success as a manager will depend almost entirely on your ability to do this.

Originally published in March 2005. Reprint R0503D.

Fair Process

Managing in the Knowledge Economy. ***by W. Chan Kim and Renée Mauborgne***

A

A LONDON POLICEMAN GAVE a woman a ticket for making an illegal turn. When the woman protested that there was no sign prohibiting the turn, the policeman pointed to one that was bent out of shape and difficult to see from the road. Furious, the woman decided to appeal by going to court. Finally, the day of her hearing arrived, and she could hardly wait to speak her piece. But she had just begun to tell her side of the story when the magistrate stopped her and summarily ruled in her favor.

How did the woman feel? Vindicated? Victorious? Satisfied?

No, she was frustrated and deeply unhappy. "I came for justice," she complained, "but the magistrate never let me explain what happened." In other words, although she liked the outcome, she didn't like the process that had created it.

For the purposes of their theories, economists assume that people are maximizers of utility, driven mainly by rational calculations of their own self-interest. That is, economists assume people focus solely on outcomes. That assumption has migrated into much of management theory and practice. It has, for instance, become embedded in the tools managers traditionally use to control and motivate employees' behavior—from incentive systems to organizational structures. But it is an assumption that managers would do well to reexamine because we all know that in real life it doesn't always hold true. People do care about outcomes, but—like the woman in London—they also care about the processes that produce those outcomes. They want to know that they had their say—that their point of view was considered even if it was rejected. Outcomes matter, but no more than the fairness of the processes that produce them.

Never has the idea of fair process been more important for managers than it is today. Fair process turns out to be a powerful management tool for companies struggling to make the transition from a production-based to a knowledge-based economy, in which value creation depends increasingly on ideas and innovation. Fair process profoundly influences attitudes and behaviors critical to high performance. It builds trust and unlocks ideas. With it, managers can achieve even the most painful and difficult goals while gaining the voluntary cooperation of the employees affected. Without fair process, even outcomes that employees might favor can be difficult to achieve—as the experience of an elevator manufacturer we'll call Elco illustrates.

Good Outcome, Unfair Process

In the late 1980s, sales in the elevator industry headed south as overconstruction of office space left some large U.S. cities with vacancy rates as high as 20%. Faced with diminished domestic demand for its product, Elco knew it had to improve its operations. The company made the decision to replace its batch-manufacturing system with a cellular approach that would allow self-directed teams to achieve superior performance. Given the industry's collapse, top management felt the transformation had to be made in record time.

Lacking expertise in cellular manufacturing, Elco retained a consulting firm to design a master plan for the conversion. Elco asked the consultants to work quickly and with minimal disturbance to employees. The new manufacturing system would be installed first at Elco's Chester plant, where employee relations were so good that in 1983 workers had decertified their own union. Subsequently, Elco would roll the process out to its High Park plant, where a strong union would probably resist that, or any other, change.

Idea in Brief

In just months, a model workforce degenerated into a cauldron of mistrust, resistance, and plummeting performance. Why? Management launched a major change effort without inviting employees' input, without explaining the reasons for the change, and without clarifying new performance expectations.

In other words, the company ignored **fair process**—a decision-making approach that addresses our basic human need to be valued and respected. When people feel a decision affecting them was made fairly, they trust and cooperate with managers. They share ideas and willingly go beyond the call of duty. Corporate performance soars.

In knowledge-based organizations—whose lifeblood consists of employees' trust, commitment, and ideas—fair process is essential. It enables companies to channel people's energy and creativity toward organizational goals.

The benefits of fair process may seem obvious—yet most organizations don't practice it. Why? Some managers find it threatening, assuming it will diminish their power. They keep employees at arm's length to avoid challenges to their authority. Others believe employees are concerned only with what's best for themselves. But evidence shows that most people will accept outcomes not wholly in their favor—*if* they believe the process for arriving at those outcomes was fair.

Under the leadership of a much beloved plant manager, Chester was in all respects a model operation. Visiting customers were always impressed by the knowledge and enthusiasm of Chester's employees, so much so that the vice president of marketing saw the plant as one of Elco's best marketing tools. "Just let customers talk with Chester employees," he observed, "and they walk away convinced that buying an Elco elevator is the smart choice."

But one day in January of 1991, Chester's employees arrived at work to discover strangers at the plant. Who were these people wearing dark suits, white dress shirts, and ties? They weren't customers. They showed up daily and spoke in low tones to one another. They didn't interact with employees. They hovered behind people's backs, taking notes and drawing fancy diagrams. The rumor

Idea in Practice

Fair process isn't decision by consensus or democracy in the workplace. Its goal is to pursue the best ideas, not create harmony. Fair process consists of three principles:

- ***Engagement*—involving individuals in decisions by inviting their input and encouraging them to challenge one another's ideas.** Engagement communicates management's respect for individuals and their ideas and builds collective wisdom. It generates better decisions and greater commitment from those involved in executing those decisions.
- ***Explanation*—clarifying the thinking behind a final decision.** Explanation reassures people that managers have considered their opinions and made the decision with the company's overall interests at heart. Employees trust managers' intentions—even if their own ideas were rejected.
- ***Expectation clarity*—stating the new rules of the game, including performance standards, penalties for failure, and new responsibilities.** By minimizing political jockeying and favoritism, expectation clarity enables employees to focus on the job at hand.

Example: Facing decreasing demand, an elevator manufacturer we'll call Elco decided to design a more efficient manufacturing system. It would introduce the system at its Chester plant, a model operation with such positive employee relations that it decertified its own union. Then it would incorporate the new system at High Park, a strongly unionized plant highly resistant to change.

Seeking minimal workforce disturbance, managers didn't involve the Chester employees in the system design process, explain why change was necessary, or clarify new performance expectations. Soon rumors about layoffs proliferated, trust and commitment deteriorated, and fights erupted on the shop floor. Quality sank.

Rattled but wiser, Elco took a different tack at their High Park site. Managers held ongoing plantwide meetings to explain the need for the new system, encouraged employees to help design the new process, and laid out new expectations. The anticipated resistance never came—and trusting employees embraced the new system.

circulated that after employees went home in the afternoon, these people would swarm across the plant floor, snoop around people's workstations, and have heated discussions.

During this period, the plant manager was increasingly absent. He was spending more time at Elco's head office in meetings with the consultants—sessions deliberately scheduled away from the plant so as not to distract the employees. But the plant manager's absence produced the opposite effect. As people grew anxious, wondering why the captain of their ship seemed to be deserting them, the rumor mill moved into high gear. Everyone became convinced that the consultants would downsize the plant. They were sure they were about to lose their jobs. The fact that the plant manager was always gone—obviously, he was avoiding them—and that no explanation was given, could only mean that management was, they thought, "trying to pull one over on us." Trust and commitment at the Chester plant quickly deteriorated. Soon, people were bringing in newspaper clippings about other plants around the country that had been shut down with the help of consultants. Employees saw themselves as imminent victims of yet another management fad and resented it.

In fact, Elco managers had no intention of closing the plant. They wanted to cut out waste, freeing people to enhance quality and produce elevators for new international markets. But plant employees could not have known that.

The master plan

In March 1991, management gathered the Chester employees in a large room. Three months after the consultants had first appeared, they were formally introduced. At the same time, management unveiled to employees the master plan for change at the Chester plant. In a meeting that lasted only 30 minutes, employees heard how their time-honored way of working would be abolished and replaced by something called "cellular manufacturing." No one explained why the change was needed, nor did anyone say exactly what would be expected of employees under the new approach. The managers didn't mean to skirt the issues; they just didn't feel they had the time to go into details.

The employees sat in stunned silence, which the managers mistook for acceptance, forgetting how many months it had taken them as leaders to get comfortable with the idea of cellular manufacturing and the changes it entailed. The managers felt good when the meeting was over, believing the employees were on board. With such a terrific staff, they thought, implementation of the new system was bound to go well.

Master plan in hand, management quickly began rearranging the plant. When employees asked what the new layout aimed to achieve, the response was "efficiency gains." The managers didn't have time to explain why efficiency needed to be improved and didn't want to worry employees. But lacking an intellectual understanding of what was happening to them, some employees literally began feeling sick when they came to work.

Managers informed employees that they would no longer be judged on individual performance but rather on the performance of the cell. They said quicker or more experienced employees would have to pick up the slack for slower or less experienced colleagues. But they didn't elaborate. How the new system was supposed to work, management didn't make clear.

In fact, the new cell design offered tremendous benefits to employees, making vacations easier to schedule, for example, and giving them the opportunity to broaden their skills and engage in a greater variety of work. But lacking trust in the change process, employees could see only its negative side. They began taking out their fears and anger on one another. Fights erupted on the plant floor as employees refused to help those they called "lazy people who can't finish their own jobs" or interpreted offers of help as meddling, responding with, "This is my job. You keep to your own workstation."

Chester's model workforce was falling apart. For the first time in the plant manager's career, employees refused to do as they were asked, turning down assignments "even if you fire me." They felt they could no longer trust the once popular plant manager, so they began to go around him, taking their complaints directly to his boss at the head office.

The plant manager then announced that the new cell design would allow employees to act as self-directed teams and that the role of the supervisor would be abolished. He expected people to react with excitement to his vision of Chester as the epitome of the factory of the future, where employees are empowered as entrepreneurial agents. Instead, they were simply confused. They had no idea how to succeed in this new environment. Without supervisors, what would they do if stock ran short or machines broke down? Did empowerment mean that the teams could self-authorize overtime, address quality problems such as rework, or purchase new machine tools? Unclear about how to succeed, employees felt set up to fail.

Time out

By the summer of 1991, both cost and quality performance were in a free fall. Employees were talking about bringing the union back. Finally, in despair, the plant manager phoned Elco's industrial psychologist. "I need your help," he said. "I have lost control."

The psychologist conducted an employee opinion survey to learn what had gone wrong. Employees complained, "Management doesn't care about our ideas or our input." They felt that the company had scant respect for them as individuals, treating them as if they were not worthy of knowing about business conditions: "They don't bother to tell us where we are going and what this means to us." And they were deeply confused and mistrustful: "We don't know exactly what management expects of us in this new cell."

What Is Fair Process?

The theme of justice has preoccupied writers and philosophers throughout the ages, but the systematic study of fair process emerged only in the mid-1970s, when two social scientists, John W. Thibaut and Laurens Walker, combined their interest in the psychology of justice with the study of process. Focusing their attention on legal settings, they sought to understand what makes people trust a legal system so that they will comply with laws without being coerced into doing so. Their research established that people care as

Making Sense of Irrational Behavior at VW and Siemens-Nixdorf

Economic theories do a good job of explaining the rational side of human behavior, but they fall short in explaining why people can act negatively in the face of positive outcomes. Fair process offers managers a theory of behavior that explains—or might help predict—what would otherwise appear to be bewilderingly noneconomic, or irrational, behavior.

Consider what happened to Volkswagen. In 1992, the German carmaker was in the midst of expanding its manufacturing facility in Puebla, Mexico, its only production site in North America. The appreciation of the deutsche mark against the U.S. dollar was pricing Volkswagen out of the U.S. market. But after the North American Free Trade Agreement (NAFTA) became law in 1992, Volkswagen's cost-efficient Mexican facility was well positioned to reconquer the large North American market.

In the summer of 1992, a new labor agreement had to be hammered out. The accord VW signed with the union's secretary-general included a generous 20% pay raise for employees. VW thought the workers would be pleased.

But the union's leaders had not involved the employees in discussions about the contract's terms; they did a poor job of communicating what the new agreement would mean to employees and why a number of work-rule changes were necessary. Workers did not understand the basis for the decisions their leaders had taken. They felt betrayed.

VW's management was completely caught off guard when, on July 21, the employees started a massive walkout that cost the company as much as an estimated $10 million per day. On August 21, about 300 protesters were attacked by police dogs. The government was forced to step in to end the violence. Volkswagen's plans for the U.S. market were in disarray, and its performance was devastated.

In contrast, consider the turnaround of Siemens-Nixdorf Informationssysteme (SNI), the largest European supplier of information technology. Created in 1990 when Siemens acquired the troubled Nixdorf Computer Company, SNI had cut head count from 52,000 to 35,000 by 1994. Anxiety and fear were rampant at the company.

In 1994, Gerhard Schulmeyer, the newly appointed CEO, went out to talk to as many employees as he could. In a series of meetings large and small with a total of more than 11,000 people, Schulmeyer shared his crusading mission to engage everyone in turning the company around. He began by painting a bleakly honest picture of SNI's situation: The company was losing money despite recent efforts to slash costs. Deeper cuts were needed, and every business would have to demonstrate its viability or be eliminated. Schulmeyer set clear but tough rules about how decisions would be made. He then asked for volunteers to come up with ideas.

Within three months, the initial group of 30 volunteers grew to encompass an additional 75 SNI executives and 300 employees. These 405 change agents soon turned into 1,000, then 3,000, then 9,000, as they progressively recruited others to help save the company. Throughout the process, ideas were solicited from managers and employees alike concerning decisions that affected them, and they all understood how decisions would be made. Ideas would be auctioned off to executives willing to champion and finance them. If no executive bought a proposal on its merits, the idea would not be pursued. Although 20% to 30% of their proposals were rejected, employees thought the process was fair.

People voluntarily pitched in—mostly after business hours, often until midnight. In just over two years, SNI has achieved a transformation notable in European corporate history. Despite accumulated losses of DM 2 billion, by 1995 SNI was already operating in the black. In the same period, employee satisfaction almost doubled, despite the radical and difficult changes under way.

Why did employees of Volkswagen revolt, despite their upbeat economic circumstances? How, in the face of such demoralizing economic conditions, could SNI turn around its performance? What is at issue is not *what* the two companies did but *how* they did it. The cases illustrate the tremendous power of fair process—fairness in the process of making and executing decisions. Fair process profoundly influences attitudes and behavior critical to high performance.

much about the fairness of the process through which an outcome is produced as they do about the outcome itself. Subsequent researchers such as Tom R. Tyler and E. Allan Lind demonstrated the power of fair process across diverse cultures and social settings.

We discovered the managerial relevance of fair process more than a decade ago, during a study of strategic decision making in multinational corporations. Many top executives in those corporations were frustrated—and baffled—by the way the senior managers of their local subsidiaries behaved. Why did those managers so often fail to share information and ideas with the executives? Why did they sabotage the execution of plans they had agreed to carry out? In the 19 companies we studied, we found a direct link between processes, attitudes, and behavior. Managers who believed the company's processes were fair displayed a high level of trust and commitment, which, in turn, engendered active cooperation. Conversely, when managers felt fair process was absent, they hoarded ideas and dragged their feet.

In subsequent field research, we explored the relevance of fair process in other business contexts—for example, in companies in the midst of transformations, in teams engaged in product innovation, and in company-supplier partnerships. (See the sidebar "Making Sense of Irrational Behavior at VW and Siemens-Nixdorf.") For companies seeking to harness the energy and creativity of committed managers and employees, the central idea that emerges from our fair-process research is this: Individuals are most likely to trust and cooperate freely with systems—whether they themselves win or lose by those systems—when fair process is observed.

Fair process responds to a basic human need. All of us, whatever our role in a company, want to be valued as human beings and not as "personnel" or "human assets." We want others to respect our intelligence. We want our ideas to be taken seriously. And we want to understand the rationale behind specific decisions. People are sensitive to the signals conveyed through a company's decision-making processes. Such processes can reveal a company's willingness to trust people and seek their ideas—or they can signal the opposite.

The three principles

In all the diverse management contexts we have studied, we have asked people to identify the bedrock elements of fair process. And whether we were working with senior executives or shop floor employees, the same three mutually reinforcing principles consistently emerged: engagement, explanation, and expectation clarity.

Engagement means involving individuals in the decisions that affect them by asking for their input and allowing them to refute the merits of one another's ideas and assumptions. Engagement communicates management's respect for individuals and their ideas. Encouraging refutation sharpens everyone's thinking and builds collective wisdom. Engagement results in better decisions by management and greater commitment from all involved in executing those decisions.

Explanation means that everyone involved and affected should understand why final decisions are made as they are. An explanation of the thinking that underlies decisions makes people confident that managers have considered their opinions and have made those decisions impartially in the overall interests of the company. An explanation allows employees to trust managers' intentions even if their own ideas have been rejected. It also serves as a powerful feedback loop that enhances learning.

Expectation clarity requires that once a decision is made, managers state clearly the new rules of the game. Although the expectations may be demanding, employees should know up front by what standards they will be judged and the penalties for failure. What are the new targets and milestones? Who is responsible for what? To achieve fair process, it matters less what the new rules and policies are and more that they are clearly understood. When people clearly understand what is expected of them, political jockeying and favoritism are minimized, and they can focus on the job at hand.

Notice that fair process is not decision by consensus. Fair process does not set out to achieve harmony or to win people's support through compromises that accommodate every individual's opinions, needs, or interests. While fair process gives every idea a chance, the merit of the ideas—and not consensus—is what drives the decision making.

Nor is fair process the same as democracy in the workplace. Achieving fair process does not mean that managers forfeit their prerogative to make decisions and establish policies and procedures. Fair process pursues the best ideas whether they are put forth by one or many.

"We really screwed up"

Elco managers violated all three basic principles of fair process at the Chester plant. They failed to engage employees in decisions that directly affected them. They didn't explain why decisions were being made the way they were and what those decisions meant to employees' careers and work methods. And they neglected to make clear what would be expected of employees under cellular manufacturing. In the absence of fair process, the employees at Chester rejected the transformation.

A week after the psychologist's survey was completed, management invited employees to meetings in groups of 20. Employees surmised that management was either going to pretend that the survey had never happened or accuse employees of disloyalty for having voiced their complaints. But to their amazement, managers kicked off the meeting by presenting the undiluted survey results and declaring, "We were wrong. We really screwed up. In our haste and ignorance, we did not go through the proper process." Employees couldn't believe their ears. There were whispers in the back of the room, "What the devil did they say?" At more than 20 meetings over the next few weeks, managers repeated their confession. "No one was prepared to believe us at first," one manager said. "We had screwed up too badly."

At subsequent meetings, management shared with employees the company's dismal business forecast and the limited options available. Without cost reduction, Elco would have to raise its prices, and higher prices would further depress sales. That would mean cutting production even more, perhaps even moving manufacturing offshore. Heads nodded. Employees saw the bind the company was in. The business problem was becoming theirs, not just management's.

But still there were concerns: "If we help to cut costs and learn to produce elevators that are twice as good in half the time, will we work ourselves out of a job?" In response, the managers described their strategy to increase sales outside the United States. They also announced a new policy called *proaction time:* No one would be laid off because of any improvements made by an employee. Instead, employees could use their newly free time to attend cross-training programs designed to give them the skills they would need to work in any area of operations. Or employees could act as consultants addressing quality issues. In addition, management agreed not to replace any departing employees with new hires until business conditions improved. At the same time, however, management made it clear that it retained the right to let people go if business conditions grew worse.

Employees may not have liked what they heard, but they understood it. They began to see that they shared responsibility with management for Elco's success. If they could improve quality and productivity, Elco could bring more value to the market and prevent further sales erosion. To give employees confidence that they were not being misled, management pledged to regularly share data on sales, costs, and market trends—a first step toward rebuilding trust and commitment.

Elco's managers could not undo past mistakes, but they could involve employees in making future decisions. Managers asked employees why they thought the new manufacturing cells weren't working and how to fix them. Employees suggested making changes in the location of materials, in the placement of machines, and in the way tasks were performed. They began to share their knowledge; as they did so, the cells were redesigned and performance steadily improved, often far exceeding the expectations originally set by the consultants. As trust and commitment were restored, talk of bringing the union back died out.

High Park's turn

Meanwhile, management worried about introducing the new work methods at Elco's High Park plant, which, unlike the Chester plant, had a history of resisting change. The union was strong at High Park, and some employees there had as much as 25 years' service. Moreover, the plant manager, a young engineer new to High Park, had never run a plant before. The odds seemed to be against him. If change had created animosity at Chester, one could only imagine how much worse the situation could become at High Park.

But management's fears went unrealized. When the consultants came to the plant, the young manager introduced them to all employees. At a series of plantwide meetings, corporate executives openly discussed business conditions and the company's declining sales and profits. They explained that they had visited other companies' plants and had seen the productivity improvements that cellular manufacturing could bring. They announced the proaction-time policy to calm employees' justifiable fears of layoffs. At the High Park plant, managers encouraged employees to help the consultants design the new manufacturing cells, and they encouraged active debate. Then, as the old performance measures were discarded, managers worked with employees to develop new ones and to establish the cell teams' new responsibilities.

Every day, the High Park plant manager waited for the anticipated meltdown, but it never came. Of course, there were some gripes, but even when people didn't like the decisions, they felt they had been treated fairly and, so, willingly participated in the plant's eventual performance turnaround.

Three years later, we revisited a popular local eatery to talk with people from both plants. Employees from both Chester and High Park now believe that the cellular approach is a better way to work. High Park employees spoke about their plant manager with admiration, and they commiserated with the difficulties Elco's managers had in making the changeover to cellular manufacturing. They concluded that it had been a necessary, worthwhile, and positive experience. But Chester employees spoke with anger and indignation as they described their treatment by Elco's managers. (See "The Price of Unfairness.") For them, as for the London woman who had been unfairly ticketed, fair process was as important as—if not more important than—the outcome.

Fair Process in the Knowledge Economy

Fair process may sound like a soft issue, but understanding its value is crucial for managers trying to adapt their companies to the demands of the knowledge-based economy. Unlike the traditional factors of production—land, labor, and capital—knowledge is a resource locked in the human mind. Creating and sharing knowledge are intangible activities that can neither be supervised nor forced out of people. They happen only when people cooperate voluntarily. As the Nobel laureate economist Friedrich Hayek has argued, "Practically every individual . . . possesses unique information" that can be put to use only with "his active cooperation." Getting that cooperation may well turn out to be one of the key managerial issues of the next few decades. (See "Fair Process Is Critical in Knowledge Work.")

Voluntary cooperation was not what Frederick Winslow Taylor had in mind when at the turn of the century he began to develop an arsenal of tools to promote efficiency and consistency by controlling individuals' behavior and compelling employees to comply with management dictates. Traditional management science, which is rooted in Taylor's time-and-motion studies, encouraged a managerial preoccupation with allocating resources, creating economic incentives and rewards, monitoring and measuring performance, and manipulating organizational structures to set lines of authority. These conventional management levers still have their role to play, but they have little to do with encouraging active cooperation. Instead, they operate in the realm of outcome fairness or what social scientists call *distributive justice,* where the psychology works like this: When people get the compensation (or the resources, or the place in the organizational hierarchy) they deserve, they feel satisfied with that outcome. They will reciprocate by fulfilling to the letter their obligation to the company. The psychology of fair process, or *procedural justice,* is quite different. Fair process builds trust and commitment, trust and commitment produce voluntary cooperation, and voluntary cooperation drives performance, leading people to go beyond the call of duty by sharing their knowledge

The Price of Unfairness

Historically, policies designed to establish fair process in organizations arise mainly in reaction to employees' complaints and uprisings. But by then it is too late. When individuals have been so angered by the violation of fair process that they have been driven to organized protest, their demands often stretch well beyond the reasonable to a desire for what theorists call *retributive justice:* Not only do they want fair process restored, they also seek to visit punishment and vengeance upon those who have violated it in compensation for the disrespect the unfair process signals.

Lacking trust in management, employees push for policies that are laboriously detailed, inflexible, and often administratively constricting. They want to ensure that managers will never have the discretion to act unjustly again. In their indignation, they may try to roll back decisions imposed unfairly even when the decisions themselves were good ones—even when they were critical to the company's competitiveness or beneficial to the workers themselves. Such is the emotional power that unfair process can provoke.

Managers who view fair process as a nuisance or as a limit on their freedom to manage must understand that it is the violation of fair process that will wreak the most serious damage on corporate performance. Retribution can be very expensive.

---

and applying their creativity. In all the management contexts we've studied, whatever the task, we have consistently observed this dynamic at work. (See the exhibit "Two complementary paths to performance.")

Consider the transformation of Bethlehem Steel Corporation's Sparrows Point, Maryland, division, a business unit responsible for marketing, sales, production, and financial performance. Until 1993, the 106-year-old division was managed in the classic command-and-control style. People were expected to do what they were told to do—no more and no less—and management and employees saw themselves as adversaries.

That year, Bethlehem Steel introduced a management model so different at Sparrows Point that Taylor—who was, in fact, the company's consulting engineer about 100 years ago—wouldn't have recognized it. The new model was designed to invoke in employees an active sense of responsibility for sharing their knowledge and ideas with one another and with management. It was also meant to encourage them to take the initiative for getting things done. In the words of Joe Rosel, the president of one of the division's five unions, "It's all about involvement, justification for decisions, and a clear set of expectations."

At Sparrows Point, employees are involved in making and executing decisions at three levels. At the top is a joint-leadership team, composed of senior managers and five employee representatives, that deals with companywide issues when they arise. At the department level are area teams, consisting of managers like superintendents and of employees from the different areas of the plant, such as zone committee people. Those teams deal with day-to-day operational issues such as customer service, quality, and logistics. Ad hoc problem-solving teams of employees address opportunities and obstacles as they arise on the shop floor. At each level, teammates share and debate their ideas. Thus, employees are assured a fair hearing for their points of view on decisions likely to affect them. With the exception of decisions involving major changes or resource commitments, the teams make and execute the decisions themselves.

Sparrows Point uses numerous processes and devices to ensure that all employees can understand why decisions have been made and how such decisions need to be executed. There is, for example, a bulletin board where decisions are posted and explained, allowing employees who haven't been directly involved in those decisions to understand what's going on and why. In addition, in more than 70 four-hour seminars, groups ranging in size from 50 to 250 employees have met to discuss changes occurring at the division, learn about new ideas under consideration, and find out how changes might affect employees' roles and responsibilities. A quarterly newsletter and a monthly "report card" of the division's strategic, marketing, operational, and financial performance keeps each of the unit's 5,300 employees informed. And the teams report back to their colleagues about the changes they are making, seeking help in making the ideas work.

Fair Process Is Critical in Knowledge Work

It is easy to see fair process at work on the plant floor, where its violation can produce such highly visible manifestations as strikes, slowdowns, and high defect rates. But fair process can have an even greater impact on the quality of professional and managerial work. That is because innovation is the key challenge of the knowledge-based economy, and innovation requires the exchange of ideas, which in turn depends on trust.

Executives and professionals rarely walk the picket line, but when their trust has not been won, they frequently withhold their full cooperation—and their ideas. In knowledge work, then, ignoring fair process creates high opportunity costs in the form of ideas that never see daylight and initiatives that are never seized. For example:

A multifunctional team is created to develop an important new product. Because it contains representatives from every major functional area of the company, the team *should* produce more innovative products, with less internal fighting, shortened lead times, and lower costs. The team meets, but people drag their feet. Executives at a computer maker developing a new workstation, for example, thoughtfully deploy the traditional management levers. They hammer out a good incentive scheme. They define the project scope and structure. And they allocate the right resources. Yet the trust, idea sharing, and commitment that everyone wants never materialize. Why? Early in the project, manufacturing and marketing representatives on the team propose building a prototype, but the strong design-engineering group driving the project ignores them. Subsequently, problems surface because the design is difficult to manufacture and the application software is inadequate. The team members from manufacturing and marketing are aware of these issues all along but remain passive in sharing their concerns with the powerful

---

Fair process has produced significant changes in people's attitudes and behavior. Consider, for example, the tin mill unit at Sparrows Point. In 1992, the unit's performance was among the worst in the industry. But then, as one employee explains, "People started coming forward and sharing their ideas. They started caring about doing great work, not just getting by. Take the success we've had in light-gauge cable sheathing. We had let this high value-added product slip because the long throughput time required for production held up the other mills in the unit. But after we started getting everyone involved and explained why we needed to improve

design engineers. Instead, they wait until the problems reveal themselves—at which time they are very expensive to fix.

Two companies create a joint venture that offers clear benefits to both parties. But they then hold their cards so close to their chests that they ensure the alliance will create limited value for either partner. The Chinese joint-venture partner of a European engineering group, for example, withholds critical information from the field, failing to report that customers are having problems installing the partner's products and sitting on requests for new product features. Why do the Chinese fail to cooperate fully, even if it means hurting their own business?

Early in the partnership, the Chinese felt they had been shut out of key product and operating decisions. To make matters worse, the Europeans never explained the logic guiding their decisions. As the Chinese withhold critical information, the increasingly frustrated European partner responds in kind by slowing the transfer of managerial know-how, which the Chinese need badly.

Two companies create a supplier partnership to achieve improved value at lower cost. They agree to act in a seamless fashion, as one company. But the supplier seems to spend more energy on developing other customers than on deepening the partnership. One consumer goods manufacturer, for example, keeps delaying the installation of a joint electronic consumer-response data system with a major food retailer. The system will substantially improve inventory management for both partners. But the supplier remains too wary to invest. Why? The retailer has a history of dropping some of the supplier's products without explanation. And the consumer company can't understand the retailer's ambiguous criteria for designating "preferred suppliers."

throughput, ideas started to flow. At first, the company was doubtful: If the product had created a bottleneck before, why should it be different now? But people came up with the idea of using two sequential mills instead of one to eliminate the bottleneck. Did people suddenly get smarter? No. I'd say they started to care."

The object in creating this new way of working at Sparrows Point was to improve the intellectual buy-in and emotional commitment of employees. It has apparently been successful. Since 1993, Sparrows Point has turned a profit three years in a row, the first time that has happened since the late 1970s. The division is becoming a showcase

Two complementary paths to performance

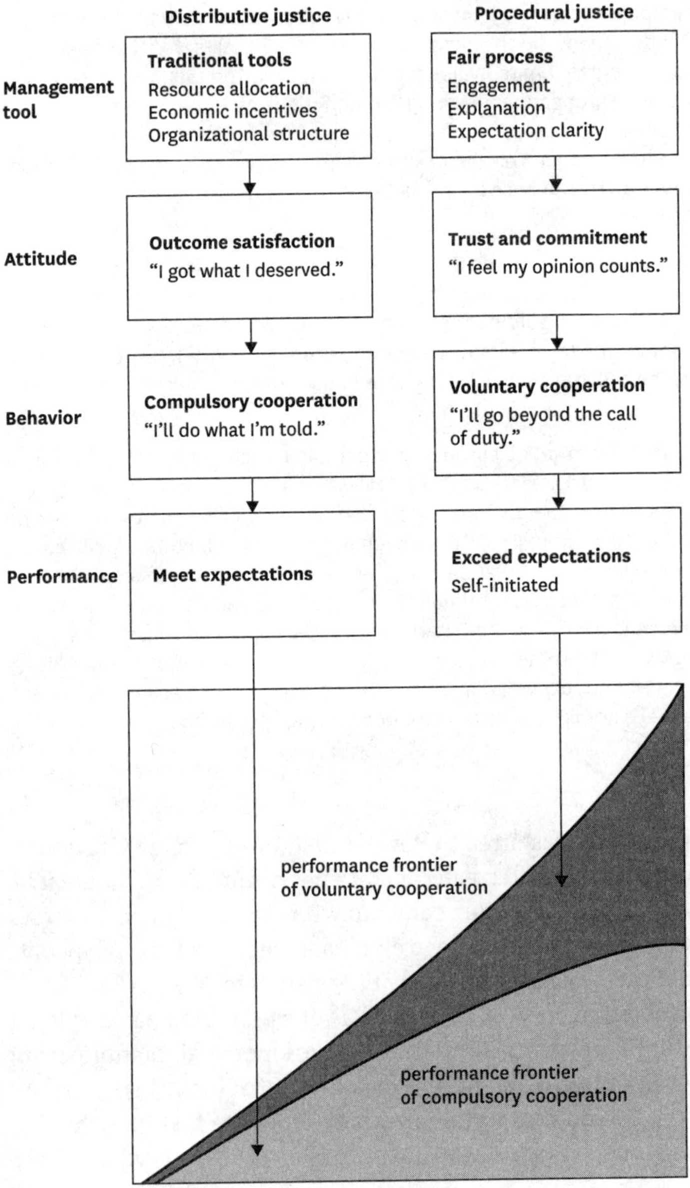
Distributive justice
Procedural justice
Management tool
Traditional tools
Resource allocation
Economic incentives
Organizational structure
Fair process
Engagement
Explanation
Expectation clarity
Attitude
Outcome satisfaction
"I got what I deserved."
Trust and commitment
"I feel my opinion counts."
Behavior
Compulsory cooperation
"I'll do what I'm told."
Voluntary cooperation
"I'll go beyond the call of duty."
Performance
Meet expectations
Exceed expectations
Self-initiated
performance frontier of voluntary cooperation
performance frontier of compulsory cooperation

demonstrating how a declining industry can be revitalized in today's knowledge economy. In the words of one Sparrows Point employee, "Since we know now everything that's going on in the company, we have more trust in management and are more committed to making things happen. People have started doing things beyond the normal call of duty."

Overcoming Mental Barriers

If fair process is such a simple idea and yet so powerful, why do so few companies practice it? Most people think of themselves as fair, and managers are no exception. But if you ask them what it means to be a fair manager, most will describe how they give people the authority they deserve, or the resources they need, or the rewards they have earned. In other words, they will confuse fair process with fair outcomes. The few managers who focus on process might identify only one of the three fair-process principles (the most widely understood is engagement), and they would stop there.

But there are two more fundamental reasons, beyond this simple lack of understanding, that explain why fair process is so rare. The first involves power. Some managers continue to believe that knowledge is power and that they retain power only by keeping what they know to themselves. Their implicit strategy is to preserve their managerial discretion by deliberately leaving the rules for success and failure vague. Other managers maintain control by keeping employees at arm's length, substituting memos and forms for direct, two-way communication, thus avoiding challenges to their ideas or authority. Such styles can reflect deeply ingrained patterns of behavior, and rarely are managers conscious of how they exercise power. For them, fair process would represent a threat.

The second reason is also largely unconscious because it resides in an economic assumption that most of us have grown up taking at face value: the belief that people are concerned only with what's best for themselves. But, as we have seen, there is ample evidence to show that when the process is perceived to be fair, most people will accept outcomes that are not wholly in their favor. People realize that compromises and sacrifices are necessary on the job. They accept the need for short-term personal sacrifices in order to advance the long-term interests of the corporation. Acceptance is conditional, however, hinged as it is on fair process.

Fair process reaches into a dimension of human psychology that hasn't been fully explored in conventional management practice. Yet every company can tap into the voluntary cooperation of its people by building trust through fair processes.

Originally published in July 1997. Reprint R0301K.

Teaching Smart People How to Learn

by Chris Argyris

A**NY COMPANY THAT ASPIRES** to succeed in the tougher business environment of the 1990s must first resolve a basic dilemma: success in the marketplace increasingly depends on learning, yet most people don't know how to learn. What's more, those members of the organization that many assume to be the best at learning are, in fact, not very good at it. I am talking about the well-educated, high-powered, high-commitment professionals who occupy key leadership positions in the modern corporation.

Most companies not only have tremendous difficulty addressing this learning dilemma; they aren't even aware that it exists. The reason: they misunderstand what learning is and how to bring it about. As a result, they tend to make two mistakes in their efforts to become a learning organization.

First, most people define learning too narrowly as mere "problem solving," so they focus on identifying and correcting errors in the external environment. Solving problems is important. But if learning is to persist, managers and employees must also look inward. They need to reflect critically on their own behavior, identify the ways they often inadvertently contribute to the organization's problems, and then change how they act. In particular, they must learn how the very way they go about defining and solving problems can be a source of problems in its own right.

I have coined the terms "single loop" and "double loop" learning to capture this crucial distinction. To give a simple analogy: a thermostat that automatically turns on the heat whenever the temperature in a room drops below 68 degrees is a good example of single-loop learning. A thermostat that could ask, "Why am I set at 68 degrees?" and then explore whether or not some other temperature might more economically achieve the goal of heating the room would be engaging in double-loop learning.

Highly skilled professionals are frequently very good at single-loop learning. After all, they have spent much of their lives acquiring academic credentials, mastering one or a number of intellectual disciplines, and applying those disciplines to solve real-world problems. But ironically, this very fact helps explain why professionals are often so bad at double-loop learning.

Put simply, because many professionals are almost always successful at what they do, they rarely experience failure. And because they have rarely failed, they have never learned how to learn from failure. So whenever their single-loop learning strategies go wrong, they become defensive, screen out criticism, and put the "blame" on anyone and everyone but themselves. In short, their ability to learn shuts down precisely at the moment they need it the most.

The propensity among professionals to behave defensively helps shed light on the second mistake that companies make about learning. The common assumption is that getting people to learn is largely a matter of motivation. When people have the right attitudes and commitment, learning automatically follows. So companies focus on creating new organizational structures—compensation programs, performance reviews, corporate cultures, and the like—that are designed to create motivated and committed employees.

But effective double-loop learning is not simply a function of how people feel. It is a reflection of how they think—that is, the cognitive rules or reasoning they use to design and implement their actions. Think of these rules as a kind of "master program" stored in the brain, governing all behavior. Defensive reasoning can block learning even when the individual commitment to it is high, just as a

Idea in Brief

Problem solving is an example of **single-loop learning.** You identify an error and apply a particular remedy to correct it. But genuine learning involves an extra step, in which you reflect on your assumptions and test the validity of your hypotheses. Achieving this **double-loop learning** is more than a matter of motivation—you have to reflect on the *way* you think.

Failure forces you to reflect on your assumptions and inferences.

Which is why an organization's smartest and most successful employees are often such poor learners: they haven't had the opportunity for introspection that failure affords. So when they do fail—or merely underperform—they can be surprisingly defensive. Instead of critically examining their own behavior, they cast blame outward—on anyone or anything they can.

computer program with hidden bugs can produce results exactly the opposite of what its designers had planned.

Companies can learn how to resolve the learning dilemma. What it takes is to make the ways managers and employees reason about their behavior a focus of organizational learning and continuous improvement programs. Teaching people how to reason about their behavior in new and more effective ways breaks down the defenses that block learning.

All of the examples that follow involve a particular kind of professional: fast-track consultants at major management consulting companies. But the implications of my argument go far beyond this specific occupational group. The fact is, more and more jobs—no matter what the title—are taking on the contours of "knowledge work." People at all levels of the organization must combine the mastery of some highly specialized technical expertise with the ability to work effectively in teams, form productive relationships with clients and customers, and critically reflect on and then change their own organizational practices. And the nuts and bolts of management—whether of high-powered consultants or service representatives, senior managers or factory technicians—increasingly

Idea in Practice

People often profess to be open to critique and new learning, but their actions suggest a very different set of governing values or theories-in-use:

- the desire to remain in unilateral control
- the goal of maximizing "winning" while minimizing "losing"
- the belief that negative feelings should be suppressed
- the desire to appear as rational as possible.

Taken together, these values betray a profoundly defensive posture: a need to avoid embarrassment, threat, or feelings of vulnerability and incompetence. This **closed-loop reasoning** explains why the mere encouragement of open inquiry can be intimidating to some. And it's especially relevant to the behavior of many of the most highly skilled and best-trained employees. Behind their high aspirations are an equally high fear of failure and a tendency to be ashamed when they don't live up to their high standards. Consequently, they become brittle and despondent in situations in which they don't excel immediately.

Fortunately, it *is* possible for individuals and organizations to develop more productive patterns of behavior. Two suggestions for how to make this happen:

1. **Apply the same kind of "tough reasoning" you use to conduct strategic analysis.** Collect the

consists of guiding and integrating the autonomous but interconnected work of highly skilled people.

How Professionals Avoid Learning

For 15 years, I have been conducting in-depth studies of management consultants. I decided to study consultants for a few simple reasons. First, they are the epitome of the highly educated professionals who play an increasingly central role in all organizations. Almost all of the consultants I've studied have MBAs from the top three or four U.S. business schools. They are also highly committed to their work. For instance, at one company, more than 90% of the consultants responded in a survey that they were "highly satisfied" with their jobs and with the company.

most objective data you can find. Make your inferences explicit and test them constantly. Submit your conclusions to the toughest tests of all: make sure they aren't self-serving or impossible for others to verify.

2. **Senior managers must model the desired changes first.** When the leadership demonstrates its willingness to examine critically its own theories-in-use, changing them as indicated, everyone will find it easier to do the same.

Example: The CEO of an organizational-development firm created a case study to address real problems caused by the intense competition among his direct reports. In a paragraph, he described a meeting he intended to have with his subordinates. Then he wrote down what he planned to say, how he thought his subordinates would respond, as well any thoughts or feelings he thought he might have but not express for fear of derailing the conversation. Instead of actually holding the meeting, he analyzed the scenario he had developed *with* his direct reports. The result was an illuminating conversation in which the CEO and his subordinates were able to circumvent the closed-loop reasoning that had characterized so many prior discussions.

I also assumed that such professional consultants would be good at learning. After all, the essence of their job is to teach others how to do things differently. I found, however, that these consultants embodied the learning dilemma. The most enthusiastic about continuous improvement in their own organizations, they were also often the biggest obstacle to its complete success.

As long as efforts at learning and change focused on external organizational factors—job redesign, compensation programs, performance reviews, and leadership training—the professionals were enthusiastic participants. Indeed, creating new systems and structures was precisely the kind of challenge that well-educated, highly motivated professionals thrived on.

And yet the moment the quest for continuous improvement turned to the professionals' *own* performance, something went wrong. It wasn't a matter of bad attitude. The professionals' commitment to excellence was genuine, and the vision of the company was clear. Nevertheless, continuous improvement did not persist. And the longer the continuous improvement efforts continued, the greater the likelihood that they would produce ever-diminishing returns.

What happened? The professionals began to feel embarrassed. They were threatened by the prospect of critically examining their own role in the organization. Indeed, because they were so well paid (and generally believed that their employers were supportive and fair), the idea that their performance might not be at its best made them feel guilty.

Far from being a catalyst for real change, such feelings caused most to react defensively. They projected the blame for any problems away from themselves and onto what they said were unclear goals, insensitive and unfair leaders, and stupid clients.

Consider this example. At a premier management consulting company, the manager of a case team called a meeting to examine the team's performance on a recent consulting project. The client was largely satisfied and had given the team relatively high marks, but the manager believed the team had not created the value added that it was capable of and that the consulting company had promised. In the spirit of continuous improvement, he felt that the team could do better. Indeed, so did some of the team members.

The manager knew how difficult it was for people to reflect critically on their own work performance, especially in the presence of their manager, so he took a number of steps to make possible a frank and open discussion. He invited to the meeting an outside consultant whom team members knew and trusted—"just to keep me honest," he said. He also agreed to have the entire meeting tape-recorded. That way, any subsequent confusions or disagreements about what went on at the meeting could be checked against the transcript. Finally, the manager opened the meeting by emphasizing that no subject was off limits—including his own behavior.

"I realize that you may believe you cannot confront me," the manager said. "But I encourage you to challenge me. You have a responsibility to tell me where you think the leadership made mistakes, just as I have the responsibility to identify any I believe you made. And all of us must acknowledge our own mistakes. If we do not have an open dialogue, we will not learn."

The professionals took the manager up on the first half of his invitation but quietly ignored the second. When asked to pinpoint the key problems in the experience with the client, they looked entirely outside themselves. The clients were uncooperative and arrogant. "They didn't think we could help them." The team's own managers were unavailable and poorly prepared. "At times, our managers were not up to speed before they walked into the client meetings." In effect, the professionals asserted that they were helpless to act differently—not because of any limitations of their own but because of the limitations of others.

The manager listened carefully to the team members and tried to respond to their criticisms. He talked about the mistakes that he had made during the consulting process. For example, one professional objected to the way the manager had run the project meetings. "I see that the way I asked questions closed down discussions," responded the manager. "I didn't mean to do that, but I can see how you might have believed that I had already made up my mind." Another team member complained that the manager had caved in to pressure from his superior to produce the project report far too quickly, considering the team's heavy work load. "I think that it was my responsibility to have said no," admitted the manager. "It was clear that we all had an immense amount of work."

Finally, after some three hours of discussion about his own behavior, the manager began to ask the team members if there were any errors *they* might have made. "After all," he said, "this client was not different from many others. How can we be more effective in the future?"

The professionals repeated that it was really the clients' and their own managers' fault. As one put it, "They have to be open to change and want to learn." The more the manager tried to get the team to examine its own responsibility for the outcome, the more the professionals bypassed his concerns. The best one team member could suggest was for the case team to "promise less"—implying that there was really no way for the group to improve its performance.

The case team members were reacting defensively to protect themselves, even though their manager was not acting in ways that an outsider would consider threatening. Even if there were some truth to their charges—the clients may well have been arrogant and closed, their own managers distant—the way they presented these claims was guaranteed to stop learning. With few exceptions, the professionals made attributions about the behavior of the clients and the managers but never publicly tested their claims. For instance, they said that the clients weren't motivated to learn but never really presented any evidence supporting that assertion. When their lack of concrete evidence was pointed out to them, they simply repeated their criticisms more vehemently.

If the professionals had felt so strongly about these issues, why had they never mentioned them during the project? According to the professionals, even this was the fault of others. "We didn't want to alienate the client," argued one. "We didn't want to be seen as whining," said another.

The professionals were using their criticisms of others to protect themselves from the potential embarrassment of having to admit that perhaps they too had contributed to the team's less-than-perfect performance. What's more, the fact that they kept repeating their defensive actions in the face of the manager's efforts to turn the group's attention to its own role shows that this defensiveness had become a reflexive routine. From the professionals' perspective, they weren't resisting; they were focusing on the "real" causes. Indeed, they were to be respected, if not congratulated, for working as well as they did under such difficult conditions.

The end result was an unproductive parallel conversation. Both the manager and the professionals were candid; they expressed their views forcefully. But they talked past each other, never finding a common language to describe what had happened with the client. The professionals kept insisting that the fault lay with others. The manager kept trying, unsuccessfully, to get the professionals to see how they contributed to the state of affairs they were criticizing. The dialogue of this parallel conversation looks like this:

Professionals: "The clients have to be open. They must want to change."

Manager: "It's our task to help them see that change is in their interest."

Professionals: "But the clients didn't agree with our analyses."

Manager: "If they didn't think our ideas were right, how might we have convinced them?"

Professionals: "Maybe we need to have more meetings with the client."

Manager: "If we aren't adequately prepared and if the clients don't think we're credible, how will more meetings help?"

Professionals: "There should be better communication between case team members and management."

Manager: "I agree. But professionals should take the initiative to educate the manager about the problems they are experiencing."

Professionals: "Our leaders are unavailable and distant."

Manager: "How do you expect us to know that if you don't tell us?"

Conversations such as this one dramatically illustrate the learning dilemma. The problem with the professionals' claims is not that they are wrong but that they aren't useful. By constantly turning the focus away from their own behavior to that of others, the professionals bring learning to a grinding halt. The manager understands the trap but does not know how to get out of it. To learn how to do that requires going deeper into the dynamics of defensive reasoning—and into the special causes that make professionals so prone to it.

Defensive Reasoning and the Doom Loop

What explains the professionals' defensiveness? Not their attitudes about change or commitment to continuous improvement; they really wanted to work more effectively. Rather, the key factor is the way they reasoned about their behavior and that of others.

It is impossible to reason anew in every situation. If we had to think through all the possible responses every time someone asked, "How are you?" the world would pass us by. Therefore, everyone develops a theory of action—a set of rules that individuals use to design and implement their own behavior as well as to understand the behavior of others. Usually, these theories of actions become so taken for granted that people don't even realize they are using them.

One of the paradoxes of human behavior, however, is that the master program people actually use is rarely the one they think they use. Ask people in an interview or questionnaire to articulate the rules they use to govern their actions, and they will give you what I call their "espoused" theory of action. But observe these same people's behavior, and you will quickly see that this espoused theory has very little to do with how they actually behave. For example, the professionals on the case team said they believed in continuous improvement, and yet they consistently acted in ways that made improvement impossible.

When you observe people's behavior and try to come up with rules that would make sense of it, you discover a very different theory of action—what I call the individual's "theory-in-use." Put simply, people consistently act inconsistently, unaware of the contradiction between their espoused theory and their theory-in-use, between the way they think they are acting and the way they really act.

What's more, most theories-in-use rest on the same set of governing values. There seems to be a universal human tendency to design one's actions consistently according to four basic values:

1. To remain in unilateral control;
2. To maximize "winning" and minimize "losing";
3. To suppress negative feelings; and

4. To be as "rational" as possible—by which people mean defining clear objectives and evaluating their behavior in terms of whether or not they have achieved them.

The purpose of all these values is to avoid embarrassment or threat, feeling vulnerable or incompetent. In this respect, the master program that most people use is profoundly defensive. Defensive reasoning encourages individuals to keep private the premises, inferences, and conclusions that shape their behavior and to avoid testing them in a truly independent, objective fashion.

Because the attributions that go into defensive reasoning are never really tested, it is a closed loop, remarkably impervious to conflicting points of view. The inevitable response to the observation that somebody is reasoning defensively is yet more defensive reasoning. With the case team, for example, whenever anyone pointed out the professionals' defensive behavior to them, their initial reaction was to look for the cause in somebody else—clients who were so sensitive that they would have been alienated if the consultants had criticized them or a manager so weak that he couldn't have taken it had the consultants raised their concerns with him. In other words, the case team members once again denied their own responsibility by externalizing the problem and putting it on someone else.

In such situations, the simple act of encouraging more open inquiry is often attacked by others as "intimidating." Those who do the attacking deal with their feelings about possibly being wrong by blaming the more open individual for arousing these feelings and upsetting them.

Needless to say, such a master program inevitably short-circuits learning. And for a number of reasons unique to their psychology, well-educated professionals are especially susceptible to this.

Nearly all the consultants I have studied have stellar academic records. Ironically, their very success at education helps explain the problems they have with learning. Before they enter the world of work, their lives are primarily full of successes, so they have rarely experienced the embarrassment and sense of threat that comes with failure. As a result, their defensive reasoning has rarely been activated. People who rarely experience failure, however, end up not knowing how to deal with it effectively. And this serves to reinforce the normal human tendency to reason defensively.

In a survey of several hundred young consultants at the organizations I have been studying, these professionals describe themselves as driven internally by an unrealistically high ideal of performance: "Pressure on the job is self-imposed." "I must not only do a good job; I must also be the best." "People around here are very bright and hardworking; they are highly motivated to do an outstanding job." "Most of us want not only to succeed but also to do so at maximum speed."

These consultants are always comparing themselves with the best around them and constantly trying to better their own performance. And yet they do not appreciate being required to compete openly with each other. They feel it is somehow inhumane. They prefer to be the individual contributor—what might be termed a "productive loner."

Behind this high aspiration for success is an equally high fear of failure and a propensity to feel shame and guilt when they do fail to meet their high standards. "You must avoid mistakes," said one. "I hate making them. Many of us fear failure, whether we admit it or not."

To the extent that these consultants have experienced success in their lives, they have not had to be concerned about failure and the attendant feelings of shame and guilt. But to exactly the same extent, they also have never developed the tolerance for feelings of failure or the skills to deal with these feelings. This in turn has led them not only to fear failure but also to fear the fear of failure itself. For they know that they will not cope with it superlatively—their usual level of aspiration.

The consultants use two intriguing metaphors to describe this phenomenon. They talk about the "doom loop" and "doom zoom." Often, consultants will perform well on the case team, but because they don't do the jobs perfectly or receive accolades from their managers, they go into a doom loop of despair. And they don't ease into the doom loop, they zoom into it.

As a result, many professionals have extremely "brittle" personalities. When suddenly faced with a situation they cannot immediately handle, they tend to fall apart. They cover up their distress in front of the client. They talk about it constantly with their fellow case team members. Interestingly, these conversations commonly take the form of bad-mouthing clients.

Such brittleness leads to an inappropriately high sense of despondency or even despair when people don't achieve the high levels of performance they aspire to. Such despondency is rarely psychologically devastating, but when combined with defensive reasoning, it can result in a formidable predisposition against learning.

There is no better example of how this brittleness can disrupt an organization than performance evaluations. Because it represents the one moment when a professional must measure his or her own behavior against some formal standard, a performance evaluation is almost tailor-made to push a professional into the doom loop. Indeed, a poor evaluation can reverberate far beyond the particular individual involved to spark defensive reasoning throughout an entire organization.

At one consulting company, management established a new performance-evaluation process that was designed to make evaluations both more objective and more useful to those being evaluated. The consultants participated in the design of the new system and in general were enthusiastic because it corresponded to their espoused values of objectivity and fairness. A brief two years into the new process, however, it had become the object of dissatisfaction. The catalyst for this about-face was the first unsatisfactory rating.

Senior managers had identified six consultants whose performance they considered below standard. In keeping with the new evaluation process, they did all they could to communicate their concerns to the six and to help them improve. Managers met with each individual separately for as long and as often as the professional requested to explain the reasons behind the rating and to discuss what needed to be done to improve—but to no avail. Performance continued at the same low level and, eventually, the six were let go.

When word of the dismissal spread through the company, people responded with confusion and anxiety. After about a dozen consultants angrily complained to management, the CEO held two lengthy meetings where employees could air their concerns.

At the meetings, the professionals made a variety of claims. Some said the performance-evaluation process was unfair because judgments were subjective and biased and the criteria for minimum performance unclear. Others suspected that the real cause for the dismissals was economic and that the performance-evaluation procedure was just a fig leaf to hide the fact that the company was in trouble. Still others argued that the evaluation process was antilearning. If the company were truly a learning organization, as it claimed, then people performing below the minimum standard should be taught how to reach it. As one professional put it: "We were told that the company did not have an up-or-out policy. Up-or-out is inconsistent with learning. You misled us."

The CEO tried to explain the logic behind management's decision by grounding it in the facts of the case and by asking the professionals for any evidence that might contradict these facts.

Is there subjectivity and bias in the evaluation process? Yes, responded the CEO, but "we strive hard to reduce them. We are constantly trying to improve the process. If you have any ideas, please tell us. If you know of someone treated unfairly, please bring it up. If any of you feel that you have been treated unfairly, let's discuss it now or, if you wish, privately."

Is the level of minimum competence too vague? "We are working to define minimum competence more clearly," he answered. "In the case of the six, however, their performance was so poor that it wasn't difficult to reach a decision." Most of the six had received timely feedback about their problems. And in the two cases where people had not, the reason was that they had never taken the responsibility to seek out evaluations—and, indeed, had actively avoided them. "If you have any data to the contrary," the CEO added, "let's talk about it."

Were the six asked to leave for economic reasons? No, said the CEO. "We have more work than we can do, and letting professionals go is extremely costly for us. Do any of you have any information to the contrary?"

As to the company being antilearning, in fact, the entire evaluation process was designed to encourage learning. When a professional is performing below the minimum level, the CEO explained, "we jointly design remedial experiences with the individual. Then we look for signs of improvement. In these cases, either the professionals were reluctant to take on such assignments or they repeatedly failed when they did. Again, if you have information or evidence to the contrary, I'd like to hear about it."

The CEO concluded: "It's regrettable, but sometimes we make mistakes and hire the wrong people. If individuals don't produce and repeatedly prove themselves unable to improve, we don't know what else to do except dismiss them. It's just not fair to keep poorly performing individuals in the company. They earn an unfair share of the financial rewards."

Instead of responding with data of their own, the professionals simply repeated their accusations but in ways that consistently contradicted their claims. They said that a genuinely fair evaluation process would contain clear and documentable data about performance—but they were unable to provide firsthand examples of the unfairness that they implied colored the evaluation of the six dismissed employees. They argued that people shouldn't be judged by inferences unconnected to their actual performance—but they judged management in precisely this way. They insisted that management define clear, objective, and unambiguous performance standards—but they argued that any humane system would take into account that the performance of a professional cannot be precisely measured. Finally, they presented themselves as champions of learning—but they never proposed any criteria for assessing whether an individual might be unable to learn.

In short, the professionals seemed to hold management to a different level of performance than they held themselves. In their conversation at the meetings, they used many of the features of ineffective evaluation that they condemned—the absence of concrete data, for example, and the dependence on a circular logic of "heads we win, tails you lose." It is as if they were saying, "Here are the features of a fair performance-evaluation system. You should abide by them. But we don't have to when we are evaluating you."

Indeed, if we were to explain the professionals' behavior by articulating rules that would have to be in their heads in order for them to act the way they did, the rules would look something like this:

1. When criticizing the company, state your criticism in ways that you believe are valid—but also in ways that prevent others from deciding for themselves whether your claim to validity is correct.
2. When asked to illustrate your criticisms, don't include any data that others could use to decide for themselves whether the illustrations are valid.
3. State your conclusions in ways that disguise their logical implications. If others point out those implications to you, deny them.

Of course, when such rules were described to the professionals, they found them abhorrent. It was inconceivable that these rules might explain their actions. And yet in defending themselves against this observation, they almost always inadvertently confirmed the rules.

Learning How to Reason Productively

If defensive reasoning is as widespread as I believe, then focusing on an individual's attitudes or commitment is never enough to produce real change. And as the previous example illustrates, neither is creating new organizational structures or systems. The problem is that even when people are genuinely committed to improving their performance and management has changed its structures in order to encourage the "right" kind of behavior, people still remain locked in defensive reasoning. Either they remain unaware of this fact, or if they do become aware of it, they blame others.

There is, however, reason to believe that organizations can break out of this vicious circle. Despite the strength of defensive reasoning, people genuinely strive to produce what they intend. They value acting competently. Their self-esteem is intimately tied up with behaving consistently and performing effectively. Companies can use these universal human tendencies to teach people how to reason in a new way—in effect, to change the master programs in their heads and thus reshape their behavior.

People can be taught how to recognize the reasoning they use when they design and implement their actions. They can begin to identify the inconsistencies between their espoused and actual theories of action. They can face up to the fact that they unconsciously design and implement actions that they do not intend. Finally, people can learn how to identify what individuals and groups do to create organizational defenses and how these defenses contribute to an organization's problems.

Once companies embark on this learning process, they will discover that the kind of reasoning necessary to reduce and overcome organizational defenses is the same kind of "tough reasoning" that underlies the effective use of ideas in strategy, finance, marketing, manufacturing, and other management disciplines. Any sophisticated strategic analysis, for example, depends on collecting valid data, analyzing it carefully, and constantly testing the inferences drawn from the data. The toughest tests are reserved for the conclusions. Good strategists make sure that their conclusions can withstand all kinds of critical questioning.

So too with productive reasoning about human behavior. The standard of analysis is just as high. Human resource programs no longer need to be based on "soft" reasoning but should be as analytical and as data-driven as any other management discipline.

Of course, that is not the kind of reasoning the consultants used when they encountered problems that were embarrassing or threatening. The data they collected was hardly objective. The inferences they made rarely became explicit. The conclusions they reached were largely self-serving, impossible for others to test, and as a result, "self-sealing," impervious to change.

How can an organization begin to turn this situation around, to teach its members how to reason productively? The first step is for managers at the top to examine critically and change their own theories-in-use. Until senior managers become aware of how they reason defensively and the counterproductive consequences that result, there will be little real progress. Any change activity is likely to be just a fad.

Change has to start at the top because otherwise defensive senior managers are likely to disown any transformation in reasoning patterns coming from below. If professionals or middle managers begin to change the way they reason and act, such changes are likely to appear strange—if not actually dangerous—to those at the top. The result is an unstable situation where senior managers still believe that it is a sign of caring and sensitivity to bypass and cover up difficult issues, while their subordinates see the very same actions as defensive.

The key to any educational experience designed to teach senior managers how to reason productively is to connect the program to real business problems. The best demonstration of the usefulness of productive reasoning is for busy managers to see how it can make a direct difference in their own performance and in that of the organization. This will not happen overnight. Managers need plenty of opportunity to practice the new skills. But once they grasp the powerful impact that productive reasoning can have on actual performance, they will have a strong incentive to reason productively not just in a training session but in all their work relationships.

One simple approach I have used to get this process started is to have participants produce a kind of rudimentary case study. The subject is a real business problem that the manager either wants to deal with or has tried unsuccessfully to address in the past. Writing the actual case usually takes less than an hour. But then the case becomes the focal point of an extended analysis.

For example, a CEO at a large organizational-development consulting company was preoccupied with the problems caused by the intense competition among the various business functions represented by his four direct reports. Not only was he tired of having the problems dumped in his lap, but he was also worried about the impact the interfunctional conflicts were having on the organization's flexibility. He had even calculated that the money being spent to iron out disagreements amounted to hundreds of thousands of dollars every year. And the more fights there were, the more defensive people became, which only increased the costs to the organization.

In a paragraph or so, the CEO described a meeting he intended to have with his direct reports to address the problem. Next, he divided the paper in half, and on the right-hand side of the page, he wrote a scenario for the meeting—much like the script for a movie or play—describing what he would say and how his subordinates would likely respond. On the left-hand side of the page, he wrote down any thoughts and feelings that he would be likely to have during the meeting but that he wouldn't express for fear they would derail the discussion.

But instead of holding the meeting, the CEO analyzed this scenario *with* his direct reports. The case became the catalyst for a discussion in which the CEO learned several things about the way he acted with his management team.

He discovered that his four direct reports often perceived his conversations as counterproductive. In the guise of being "diplomatic," he would pretend that a consensus about the problem existed, when in fact none existed. The unintended result: instead of feeling reassured, his subordinates felt wary and tried to figure out "what is he *really* getting at."

The CEO also realized that the way he dealt with the competitiveness among department heads was completely contradictory. On the one hand, he kept urging them to "think of the organization as a whole." On the other, he kept calling for actions—department budget cuts, for example—that placed them directly in competition with each other.

Finally, the CEO discovered that many of the tacit evaluations and attributions he had listed turned out to be wrong. Since he had never expressed these assumptions, he had never found out just how wrong they were. What's more, he learned that much of what he thought he was hiding came through to his subordinates anyway—but with the added message that the boss was covering up.

The CEO's colleagues also learned about their own ineffective behavior. They learned by examining their own behavior as they tried to help the CEO analyze his case. They also learned by writing and analyzing cases of their own. They began to see that they too tended to bypass and cover up the real issues and that the CEO was often aware of it but did not say so. They too made inaccurate attributions and evaluations that they did not express. Moreover, the belief that they had to hide important ideas and feelings from the CEO and from each other in order not to upset anyone turned out to be mistaken. In the context of the case discussions, the entire senior management team was quite willing to discuss what had always been undiscussable.

In effect, the case study exercise legitimizes talking about issues that people have never been able to address before. Such a discussion can be emotional—even painful. But for managers with the courage to persist, the payoff is great: management teams and entire organizations work more openly and more effectively and have greater options for behaving flexibly and adapting to particular situations.

When senior managers are trained in new reasoning skills, they can have a big impact on the performance of the entire organization—even when other employees are still reasoning defensively. The CEO who led the meetings on the performance-evaluation procedure was able to defuse dissatisfaction because he didn't respond to professionals' criticisms in kind but instead gave a clear presentation of relevant data. Indeed, most participants took the CEO's behavior to be a sign that the company really acted on the values of participation and employee involvement that it espoused.

Of course, the ideal is for all the members of an organization to learn how to reason productively. This has happened at the company where the case team meeting took place. Consultants and their managers are now able to confront some of the most difficult issues of the consultant-client relationship. To get a sense of the difference productive reasoning can make, imagine how the original conversation between the manager and case team might have gone had everyone engaged in effective reasoning. (The following dialogue is based on actual sessions I have attended with other case teams at the same company since the training has been completed.)

First, the consultants would have demonstrated their commitment to continuous improvement by being willing to examine their own role in the difficulties that arose during the consulting project. No doubt they would have identified their managers and the clients as part of the problem, but they would have gone on to admit that they had contributed to it as well. More important, they would have agreed with the manager that as they explored the various roles of clients, managers, and professionals, they would make sure to test any evaluations or attributions they might make against the data. Each individual would have encouraged the others to question his or her reasoning. Indeed, they would have insisted on it. And in turn, everyone would have understood that act of questioning not as a sign of mistrust or an invasion of privacy but as a valuable opportunity for learning.

The conversation about the manager's unwillingness to say no might look something like this:

Professional #1: "One of the biggest problems I had with the way you managed this case was that you seemed to be unable to say no when either the client or your superior made unfair demands." [Gives an example.]

Professional #2: "I have another example to add. [Describes a second example.] But I'd also like to say that we never really told you how we felt about this. Behind your back we were bad-mouthing you—you know, 'he's being such a wimp'—but we never came right out and said it."

Manager: "It certainly would have been helpful if you had said something. Was there anything I said or did that gave you the idea that you had better not raise this with me?"

Professional #3: "Not really. I think we didn't want to sound like we were whining."

Manager: "Well, I certainly don't think you sound like you're whining. But two thoughts come to mind. If I understand you correctly, you *were* complaining, but the complaining about me and my inability to say no was covered up. Second, if we had discussed this, I might have gotten the data I needed to be able to say no."

Notice that when the second professional describes how the consultants had covered up their complaints, the manager doesn't criticize her. Rather, he rewards her for being open by responding in kind. He focuses on the ways that he too may have contributed to the cover-up. Reflecting undefensively about his own role in the problem then makes it possible for the professionals to talk about their fears of appearing to be whining. The manager then agrees with the professionals that they shouldn't become complainers. At the same time, he points out the counterproductive consequences of covering up their complaints.

Another unresolved issue in the case team meeting concerned the supposed arrogance of the clients. A more productive conversation about that problem might go like this:

Manager: "You said that the clients were arrogant and uncooperative. What did they say and do?"

Professional #1: "One asked me if I had ever met a payroll. Another asked how long I've been out of school."

Professional #2: "One even asked me how old I was!"

Professional #3: "That's nothing. The worst is when they say that all we do is interview people, write a report based on what they tell us, and then collect our fees."

Manager: "The fact that we tend to be so young is a real problem for many of our clients. They get very defensive about it. But I'd like to explore whether there is a way for them to freely express their views without our getting defensive..."

"What troubled me about your original responses was that you assumed you were right in calling the clients stupid. One thing I've noticed about consultants—in this company and others—is that we tend to defend ourselves by bad-mouthing the client."

Professional #1: "Right. After all, if they are genuinely stupid, then it's obviously not our fault that they aren't getting it!"

Professional #2: "Of course, that stance is antilearning and overprotective. By assuming that they can't learn, we absolve ourselves from having to."

Professional #3: "And the more we all go along with the bad-mouthing, the more we reinforce each other's defensiveness."

Manager: "So what's the alternative? How can we encourage our clients to express their defensiveness and at the same time constructively build on it?"

Professional #1: "We all know that the real issue isn't our age; it's whether or not we are able to add value to the client's organization. They should judge us by what we produce. And if we aren't adding value, they should get rid of us—no matter how young or old we happen to be."

Manager: "Perhaps that is exactly what we should tell them."

In both these examples, the consultants and their manager are doing real work. They are learning about their own group dynamics and addressing some generic problems in client-consultant relationships. The insights they gain will allow them to act more effectively in the future—both as individuals and as a team. They are not just solving problems but developing a far deeper and more textured understanding of their role as members of the organization. They are laying the groundwork for continuous improvement that is truly continuous. They are learning how to learn.

Originally published in May 1991. Reprint 4304.

How (Un)ethical Are You?

by Mahzarin R. Banaji, Max H. Bazerman, and Dolly Chugh

ANSWER TRUE OR FALSE: "I am an ethical manager."

If you answered "true," here's an uncomfortable fact: You're probably not. Most of us believe that we are ethical and unbiased. We imagine we're good decision makers, able to objectively size up a job candidate or a venture deal and reach a fair and rational conclusion that's in our, and our organization's, best interests. But more than two decades of research confirms that, in reality, most of us fall woefully short of our inflated self-perception. We're deluded by what Yale psychologist David Armor calls the illusion of objectivity, the notion that we're free of the very biases we're so quick to recognize in others. What's more, these unconscious, or implicit, biases can be contrary to our consciously held, explicit beliefs. We may believe with confidence and conviction that a job candidate's race has no bearing on our hiring decisions or that we're immune to conflicts of interest. But psychological research routinely exposes counterintentional, unconscious biases. The prevalence of these biases suggests that even the most well-meaning person unwittingly allows unconscious thoughts and feelings to influence seemingly objective decisions. These flawed judgments are ethically problematic and undermine managers' fundamental work—to recruit and retain superior talent, boost the performance of individuals and teams, and collaborate effectively with partners.

This article explores four related sources of unintentional unethical decision making: implicit forms of prejudice, bias that favors one's own group, conflict of interest, and a tendency to overclaim credit. Because we are not consciously aware of these sources of bias, they often cannot be addressed by penalizing people for their bad decisions. Nor are they likely to be corrected through conventional ethics training. Rather, managers must bring a new type of vigilance to bear. To begin, this requires letting go of the notion that our conscious attitudes always represent what we think they do. It also demands that we abandon our faith in our own objectivity and our ability to be fair. In the following pages, we will offer strategies that can help managers recognize these pervasive, corrosive, unconscious biases and reduce their impact.

Implicit Prejudice: Bias That Emerges from Unconscious Beliefs

Most fair-minded people strive to judge others according to their merits, but our research shows how often people instead judge according to unconscious stereotypes and attitudes, or "implicit prejudice." What makes implicit prejudice so common and persistent is that it is rooted in the fundamental mechanics of thought. Early on, we learn to associate things that commonly go together and expect them to inevitably coexist: thunder and rain, for instance, or gray hair and old age. This skill—to perceive and learn from associations—often serves us well.

But, of course, our associations only reflect approximations of the truth; they are rarely applicable to every encounter. Rain doesn't always accompany thunder, and the young can also go gray. Nonetheless, because we automatically make such associations to help us organize our world, we grow to trust them, and they can blind us to those instances in which the associations are not accurate—when they don't align with our expectations.

Because implicit prejudice arises from the ordinary and unconscious tendency to make associations, it is distinct from conscious forms of prejudice, such as overt racism or sexism. This distinction

Idea in Brief

Are you an ethical manager? Most would probably say, "Of course!" The truth is, most of us are not.

Most of us believe that we're ethical and unbiased. We assume that we objectively size up job candidates or venture deals and reach fair and rational conclusions that are in our organization's best interests.

But the truth is, we harbor many unconscious—and unethical—biases that derail our decisions and undermine our work as managers. Hidden biases prevent us from recognizing high-potential workers and retaining talented managers. They stop us from collaborating effectively with partners. They erode our teams' performance. They can also lead to costly lawsuits.

But how can we root out these biases if they're unconscious? Fortunately, as a manager, you can take deliberate actions to counteract their pull. **Regularly audit your decisions.** Have you, for example, hired a disproportionate number of people of your own race? **Expose yourself to non-stereotypical environments** that challenge your biases. If your department is led by men, spend time in one with women in leadership positions. And **consider counterintuitive options** when making decisions. Don't rely on a mental short-list of candidates for a new assignment; consider every employee with relevant qualifications.

explains why people who are free from conscious prejudice may still harbor biases and act accordingly. Exposed to images that juxtapose black men and violence, portray women as sex objects, imply that the physically disabled are mentally weak and the poor are lazy, even the most consciously unbiased person is bound to make biased associations. These associations play out in the workplace just as they do anywhere else.

In the mid-1990s, Tony Greenwald, a professor of psychology at the University of Washington, developed an experimental tool called the Implicit Association Test (IAT) to study unconscious bias. A computerized version of the test requires subjects to rapidly classify words and images as "good" or "bad." Using a keyboard, test takers must make split-second "good/bad" distinctions between words like "love," "joy," "pain," and "sorrow" and at the same time sort images of faces that are (depending on the bias in question) black or white,

Idea in Practice

Unconscious Biases

Are the following unconscious biases levying what amounts to a "stereotype tax" on your company?

Implicit prejudice Judging according to unconscious stereotypes rather than merit exacts a high business cost. Exposed to images that juxtapose physical disabilities with mental weakness or portray poor people as lazy, even the most consciously unbiased person is bound to make biased associations. As a result, we routinely overlook highly qualified candidates for assignments.

In-group favoritism Granting favors to people with your same background—your nationality or alma mater—effectively discriminates against those who are different from you. Consider the potential cost of offering bonuses to employees who refer their friends for job openings: hires who may not have made the grade *without* in-group favoritism.

Overclaiming credit Most of us consider ourselves above average. But when every member of a team thinks he's making the biggest contribution, each starts to think the others aren't pulling their weight. That jeopardizes future collaborations. It also frustrates talented workers who may resign because they feel underappreciated.

young or old, fat or thin, and so on. The test exposes implicit biases by detecting subtle shifts in reaction time that can occur when test takers are required to pair different sets of words and faces. Subjects who consciously believe that they have no negative feelings toward, say, black Americans or the elderly are nevertheless likely to be slower to associate elderly or black faces with the "good" words than they are to associate youthful or white faces with "good" words.

Since 1998, when Greenwald, Brian Nosek, and Mahzarin Banaji put the IAT online, people from around the world have taken over 2.5 million tests, confirming and extending the findings of more traditional laboratory experiments. Both show implicit biases to be strong and pervasive. (For more information on the IAT, see "Are You Biased?".)

Counteract Biases

To keep yourself from making similarly skewed calls, consider these guidelines:

Gather better data Expose your own implicit biases. Take the Implicit Association Test (at http://implicit.harvard.edu). If you discover gender or racial biases, examine your hiring and promotion decisions in that new light. When working with others, have team members estimate their colleagues' contributions *before* they claim their own credit.

Rid your workplace of stereotypical cues Think about the biased associations your workplace may foster. Do your company's advertising and marketing materials frequently include sports metaphors or high-tech jargon? Make a conscious effort to curb such "insider" language—making your products more appealing to a diverse customer base. And if your department invariably promotes the same type of manager—highly analytic, for instance—shadow a department that values a different—perhaps more conceptual—skill-set.

Broaden your mind-set when making decisions Apply the "veil of ignorance" to your next managerial decision. Suppose you're considering a new policy that would give more vacation time to all employees but eliminate the flextime that has allowed new parents to keep working. How would your opinion differ if you were a parent or childless? Male or female? Healthy or unhealthy? You'll learn how strongly implicit biases influence you.

Biases are also likely to be costly. In controlled experiments, psychologists Laurie Rudman at Rutgers and Peter Glick at Lawrence University have studied how implicit biases may work to exclude qualified people from certain roles. One set of experiments examined the relationship between participants' implicit gender stereotypes and their hiring decisions. Those holding stronger implicit biases were less likely to select a qualified woman who exhibited stereotypically "masculine" personality qualities, such as ambition or independence, for a job requiring stereotypically "feminine" qualities, such as interpersonal skills. Yet they would select a qualified man exhibiting these same qualities. The hirers' biased perception was that the woman was less likely to be socially skilled than the man, though their qualifications were in fact the same. These results suggest that implicit biases may exact costs by subtly excluding qualified people from the very organizations that seek their talents.

Legal cases also reveal the real costs of implicit biases, both economic and social. Consider *Price Waterhouse v. Hopkins*. Despite logging more billable hours than her peers, bringing in $25 million to the company, and earning the praise of her clients, Ann Hopkins was turned down for partner, and she sued. The details of the case reveal that her evaluators were explicitly prejudiced in their attitudes. For example, they had commented that Ann "overcompensated for being a woman" and needed a "course at charm school." But perhaps more damning from a legal standpoint was blunt testimony from experimental research. Testifying as an expert witness for the defense, psychology professor Susan Fiske, now at Princeton University, argued that the potential for biased decision making is *inherent* in a system in which a person has "solo" status—that is, a system in which the person is the only one of a kind (the only woman, the only African-American, the only person with a disability, and the like). Judge Gerhard Gesell concluded that "a far more subtle process [than the usual discriminatory intent] is involved" in the assessments made of Ann Hopkins, and she won both in a lower court and in the Supreme Court in what is now a landmark case in discrimination law.

Likewise, the 1999 case of *Thomas v. Kodak* demonstrates that implicit biases can be the basis for rulings. Here, the court posed the question of "whether the employer consciously intended to base the evaluations on race or simply did so because of unthinking stereotypes or bias." The court concluded that plaintiffs can indeed challenge "subjective evaluations which could easily mask covert or unconscious race discrimination." Although courts are careful not to assign responsibility easily for unintentional biases, these cases demonstrate the potential for corporate liability that such patterns of behavior could unwittingly create.

In-Group Favoritism: Bias That Favors Your Group

Think about some of the favors you have done in recent years, whether for a friend, a relative, or a colleague. Have you helped someone get a useful introduction, admission to a school, or a job? Most of us are glad to help out with such favors. Not surprisingly, we tend to do more favors for those we know, and those we know tend to be like ourselves: people who share our nationality, social class, and perhaps religion, race, employer, or alma mater. This all sounds rather innocent. What's wrong with asking your neighbor, the university dean, to meet with a coworker's son? Isn't it just being helpful to recommend a former sorority sister for a job or to talk to your banker cousin when a friend from church gets turned down for a home loan?

Few people set out to exclude anyone through such acts of kindness. But when those in the majority or those in power allocate scarce resources (such as jobs, promotions, and mortgages) to people just like them, they effectively discriminate against those who are different from them. Such "in-group favoritism" amounts to giving extra credit for group membership. Yet while discriminating against those who are different is considered unethical, helping people close to us is often viewed favorably. Think about the number of companies that explicitly encourage this by offering hiring bonuses to employees who refer their friends for job opportunities.

But consider the finding that banks in the United States are more likely to deny a mortgage application from a black person than from a white person, even when the applicants are equally qualified. The common view has been that banks are hostile to African-Americans. While this may be true of some banks and some loan officers, social psychologist David Messick has argued that in-group favoritism is more likely to be at the root of such discriminatory lending. A white loan officer may feel hopeful or lenient toward an unqualified white applicant while following the bank's lending standards strictly with an unqualified black applicant. In denying the black applicant's mortgage, the loan officer may not be expressing hostility toward blacks so much as favoritism toward whites. It's a subtle but crucial distinction.

The ethical cost is clear and should be reason enough to address the problem. But such inadvertent bias produces an additional effect: It erodes the bottom line. Lenders who discriminate in this way,

Are You Biased?

ARE YOU WILLING TO bet that you feel the same way toward European-Americans as you do toward African-Americans? How about women versus men? Or older people versus younger ones? Think twice before you take that bet. Visit implicit.harvard.edu or www.tolerance.org/hidden_bias to examine your unconscious attitudes.

The Implicit Association Tests available on these sites reveal unconscious beliefs by asking takers to make split-second associations between words with positive or negative connotations and images representing different types of people. The various tests on these sites expose the differences—or the alignment—between test takers' conscious and unconscious attitudes toward people of different races, sexual orientation, or physical characteristics. Data gathered from over 2.5 million online tests and further research tells us that unconscious biases are:

- **widely prevalent.** At least 75% of test takers show an implicit bias favoring the young, the rich, and whites.
- **robust.** The mere conscious desire not to be biased does not eliminate implicit bias.
- **contrary to conscious intention.** Although people tend to report little or no *conscious* bias against African-Americans, Arabs, Arab-Americans, Jews, gay men, lesbians, or the poor, they show substantial biases on implicit measures.
- **different in degree depending on group status.** Minority group members tend to show less implicit preference for their own group than majority group members show for theirs. For example, African-Americans report strong preference for their group on explicit measures but show relatively less implicit preference in the tests. Conversely, white Americans report a low explicit bias for their group but a higher implicit bias.
- **consequential.** Those who show higher levels of bias on the IAT are also likely to behave in ways that are more biased in face-to-face interactions with members of the group they are biased against and in the choices they make, such as hiring decisions.
- **costly.** Research currently under way in our lab suggests that implicit bias generates a "stereotype tax"—negotiators leave money on the table because biases cause them to miss opportunities to learn about their opponent and thus create additional value through mutually beneficial trade-offs.

for example, incur bad-debt costs they could have avoided if their lending decisions were more objective. They also may find themselves exposed to damaging publicity or discrimination lawsuits if the skewed lending pattern is publicly revealed. In a different context, companies may pay a real cost for marginal hires who wouldn't have made the grade but for the sympathetic hiring manager swayed by in-group favoritism.

In-group favoritism is tenacious when membership confers clear advantages, as it does, for instance, among whites and other dominant social groups. (It may be weaker or absent among people whose group membership offers little societal advantage.) Thus for a wide array of managerial tasks—from hiring, firing, and promoting to contracting services and forming partnerships—qualified minority candidates are subtly and unconsciously discriminated against, sometimes simply because they are in the minority: There are not enough of them to counter the propensity for in-group favoritism in the majority.

Overclaiming Credit: Bias That Favors You

It's only natural for successful people to hold positive views about themselves. But many studies show that the majority of people consider themselves above average on a host of measures, from intelligence to driving ability. Business executives are no exception. We tend to overrate our individual contribution to groups, which, bluntly put, tends to lead to an overblown sense of entitlement. We become the unabashed, repeated beneficiaries of this unconscious bias, and the more we think only of our own contributions, the less fairly we judge others with whom we work.

Lab research demonstrates this most personal of biases. At Harvard, Eugene Caruso, Nick Epley, and Max Bazerman recently asked MBA students in study groups to estimate what portion of their group's work each had done. The sum of the contribution by all members, of course, must add up to 100%. But the researchers found that the totals for each study group averaged 139%. In a related study, Caruso and his colleagues uncovered rampant overestimates by academic authors of their contribution to shared research projects. Sadly, but not surprisingly, the more the sum of the total estimated group effort exceeded 100% (in other words, the more credit each person claimed), the less the parties wanted to collaborate in the future.

Likewise in business, claiming too much credit can destabilize alliances. When each party in a strategic partnership claims too much credit for its own contribution and becomes skeptical about whether the other is doing its fair share, they both tend to reduce their contributions to compensate. This has obvious repercussions for the joint venture's performance.

Unconscious overclaiming can be expected to reduce the performance and longevity of groups within organizations, just as it diminished the academic authors' willingness to collaborate. It can also take a toll on employee commitment. Think about how employees perceive raises. Most are not so different from the children at Lake Wobegon, believing that they, too, rank in the upper half of their peer group. But many necessarily get pay increases that are below the average. If an employee learns of a colleague's greater compensation—while honestly believing that he himself is more deserving—resentment may be natural. At best, his resentment might translate into reduced commitment and performance. At worst, he may leave the organization that, it seems, doesn't appreciate his contribution.

Conflict of Interest: Bias That Favors Those Who Can Benefit You

Everyone knows that conflict of interest can lead to intentionally corrupt behavior. But numerous psychological experiments show how powerfully such conflicts can unintentionally skew decision making. (For an examination of the evidence in one business arena, see Max Bazerman, George Loewenstein, and Don Moore's November 2002 HBR article, "Why Good Accountants Do Bad Audits.") These experiments suggest that the work world is rife with situations in which such conflicts lead honest, ethical professionals to unconsciously make unsound and unethical recommendations.

Physicians, for instance, face conflicts of interest when they accept payment for referring patients into clinical trials. While, surely, most physicians consciously believe that their referrals are the patient's best clinical option, how do they know that the promise of payment did not skew their decisions? Similarly, many lawyers earn fees based on their clients' awards or settlements. Since going to trial is expensive and uncertain, settling out of court is often an attractive option for the lawyer. Attorneys may consciously believe that settling is in their clients' best interests. But how can they be objective, unbiased judges under these circumstances?

Research done with brokerage house analysts demonstrates how conflict of interest can unconsciously distort decision making. A survey of analysts conducted by the financial research service First Call showed that during a period in 2000 when the Nasdaq dropped 60%, fully 99% of brokerage analysts' client recommendations remained "strong buy," "buy," or "hold." What accounts for this discrepancy between what was happening and what was recommended? The answer may lie in a system that fosters conflicts of interest. A portion of analysts' pay is based on brokerage firm revenues. Some firms even tie analysts' compensation to the amount of business the analysts bring in from clients, giving analysts an obvious incentive to prolong and extend their relationships with clients. But to assume that during this Nasdaq free fall all brokerage house analysts were consciously corrupt, milking their clients to exploit this incentive system, defies common sense. Surely there were some bad apples. But how much more likely it is that most of these analysts believed their recommendations were sound and in their clients' best interests. What many didn't appreciate was that the built-in conflict of interest in their compensation incentives made it impossible for them to see the implicit bias in their own flawed recommendations.

Trying Harder Isn't Enough

As companies keep collapsing into financial scandal and ruin, corporations are responding with ethics-training programs for managers, and many of the world's leading business schools have created new courses and chaired professorships in ethics. Many of these efforts focus on teaching broad principles of moral philosophy to help managers understand the ethical challenges they face.

We applaud these efforts, but we doubt that a well-intentioned, just-try-harder approach will fundamentally improve the quality of executives' decision making. To do that, ethics training must be broadened to include what is now known about how our minds work and must expose managers directly to the unconscious mechanisms that underlie biased decision making. And it must provide managers with exercises and interventions that can root out the biases that lead to bad decisions.

Managers can make wiser, more ethical decisions if they become mindful of their unconscious biases. But how can we get at something outside our conscious awareness? By bringing the conscious mind to bear. Just as the driver of a misaligned car deliberately counteracts its pull, so can managers develop conscious strategies to counteract the pull of their unconscious biases. What's required is vigilance—continual awareness of the forces that can cause decision making to veer from its intended course and continual adjustments to counteract them. Those adjustments fall into three general categories: collecting data, shaping the environment, and broadening the decision-making process.

Collect data

The first step to reducing unconscious bias is to collect data to reveal its presence. Often, the data will be counterintuitive. Consider many people's surprise to learn of their own gender and racial biases on the IAT. Why the surprise? Because most of us trust the "statistics" our intuition provides. Better data are easily, but rarely, collected. One way to get those data is to examine our decisions in a systematic way.

Remember the MBA study groups whose participants overestimated their individual contributions to the group effort so that the totals averaged 139%? When the researchers asked group members to estimate what each of the other members' contributions were *before* claiming their own, the total fell to 121%. The tendency to claim too much credit still persisted, but this strategy of "unpacking" the work reduced the magnitude of the bias. In environments characterized by "I deserve more than you're giving me" claims, merely asking team members to unpack the contributions of others before claiming their own share of the pot usually aligns claims more closely with what's actually deserved. As this example demonstrates, such systematic audits of both individual and group decision-making processes can occur even as the decisions are being made.

Unpacking is a simple strategy that managers should routinely use to evaluate the fairness of their own claims within the organization. But they can also apply it in any situation where team members or subordinates may be overclaiming. For example, in explaining a raise that an employee feels is inadequate, a manager should ask the subordinate not what he thinks he alone deserves but what he considers an appropriate raise after taking into account each coworker's contribution and the pool available for pay increases. Similarly, when an individual feels she's doing more than her fair share of a team's work, asking her to consider other people's efforts before estimating her own can help align her perception with reality, restore her commitment, and reduce a skewed sense of entitlement.

Taking the IAT is another valuable strategy for collecting data. We recommend that you and others in your organization use the test to expose your own implicit biases. But one word of warning: Because the test is an educational and research tool, not a selection or evaluation tool, it is critical that you consider your results and others' to be private information. Simply knowing the magnitude and pervasiveness of your own biases can help direct your attention to areas of decision making that are in need of careful examination and reconsideration. For example, a manager whose testing reveals a bias toward certain groups ought to examine her hiring practices to see if she has indeed been disproportionately favoring those groups. But because so many people harbor such biases, they can also be generally acknowledged, and that knowledge can be used as the basis for changing the way decisions are made. It is important to guard against using pervasiveness to justify complacency and inaction: Pervasiveness of bias is not a mark of its appropriateness any more than poor eyesight is considered so ordinary a condition that it does not require corrective lenses.

Shape your environment

Research shows that implicit attitudes can be shaped by external cues in the environment. For example, Curtis Hardin and colleagues at UCLA used the IAT to study whether subjects' implicit race bias would be affected if the test was administered by a black investigator. One group of students took the test under the guidance of a white experimenter; another group took the test with a black experimenter. The mere presence of a black experimenter, Hardin found, reduced the level of subjects' implicit antiblack bias on the IAT. Numerous similar studies have shown similar effects with other social groups. What accounts for such shifts? We can speculate that experimenters in classrooms are assumed to be competent, in charge, and authoritative. Subjects guided by a black experimenter attribute these positive characteristics to that person, and then perhaps to the group as a whole. These findings suggest that one remedy for implicit bias is to expose oneself to images and social environments that challenge stereotypes.

We know of a judge whose court is located in a predominantly African-American neighborhood. Because of the crime and arrest patterns in the community, most people the judge sentences are black. The judge confronted a paradox. On the one hand, she took a judicial oath to be objective and egalitarian, and indeed she consciously believed that her decisions were unbiased. On the other hand, every day she was exposed to an environment that reinforced the association between black men and crime. Although she consciously rejected racial stereotypes, she suspected that she harbored unconscious prejudices merely from working in a segregated world. Immersed in this environment each day, she wondered if it was possible to give the defendants a fair hearing.

Rather than allow her environment to reinforce a bias, the judge created an alternative environment. She spent a vacation week sitting in a fellow judge's court in a neighborhood where the criminals being tried were predominantly white. Case after case challenged the stereotype of blacks as criminal and whites as law abiding and so challenged any bias against blacks that she might have harbored.

Think about the possibly biased associations your workplace fosters. Is there, perhaps, a "wall of fame" with pictures of high achievers all cast from the same mold? Are certain types of managers invariably promoted? Do people overuse certain analogies drawn from stereotypical or narrow domains of knowledge (sports metaphors, for instance, or cooking terms)? Managers can audit their organization to uncover such patterns or cues that unwittingly lead to stereotypical associations.

If an audit reveals that the environment may be promoting unconscious biased or unethical behavior, consider creating countervailing experiences, as the judge did. For example, if your department reinforces the stereotype of men as naturally dominant in a hierarchy (most managers are male, and most assistants are female), find a department with women in leadership positions and set up a shadow program. Both groups will benefit from the exchange of best practices, and your group will be quietly exposed to counterstereotypical cues. Managers sending people out to spend time in clients' organizations as a way to improve service should take care to select organizations likely to counter stereotypes reinforced in your own company.

Broaden your decision making

Imagine that you are making a decision in a meeting about an important company policy that will benefit some groups of employees more than others. A policy might, for example, provide extra vacation time for all employees but eliminate the flex time that has allowed many new parents to balance work with their family responsibilities. Another policy might lower the mandatory retirement age, eliminating some older workers but creating advancement opportunities for younger ones. Now pretend that, as you make your decisions, you don't know which group you belong to. That is, you don't know whether you are senior or junior, married or single, gay or straight, a parent or childless, male or female, healthy or unhealthy. You will eventually find out, but not until after the decision has been made. In this hypothetical scenario, what decision would you make? Would you be willing to risk being in the group disadvantaged by your own decision? How would your decisions differ if you could make them wearing various identities not your own?

This thought experiment is a version of philosopher John Rawls's concept of the "veil of ignorance," which posits that only a person ignorant of his own identity is capable of a truly ethical decision. Few of us can assume the veil completely, which is precisely why hidden biases, even when identified, are so difficult to correct. Still, applying the veil of ignorance to your next important managerial decision may offer some insight into how strongly implicit biases influence you.

Just as managers can expose bias by collecting data before acting on intuition, they can take other preemptive steps. What list of names do you start with when considering whom to send to a training program, recommend for a new assignment, or nominate for a fast-track position? Most of us can quickly and with little concentration come up with such a list. But keep in mind that your intuition is prone to implicit prejudice (which will strongly favor dominant and well-liked groups), in-group favoritism (which will favor people in your own group), overclaiming (which will favor you), and conflict of interest (which will favor people whose interests affect your own). Instead of relying on a mental short list when making personnel decisions, start with a full list of names of employees who have relevant qualifications.

Using a broad list of names has several advantages. The most obvious is that talent may surface that might otherwise be overlooked. Less obvious but equally important, the very act of considering a counterstereotypical choice at the conscious level can reduce implicit bias. In fact, merely thinking about hypothetical, counterstereotypical scenarios—such as what it would be like to trust a complex presentation to a female colleague or to receive a promotion from an African-American boss—can prompt less-biased and more ethical decision making. Similarly, consciously considering counterintuitive options in the face of conflicts of interest, or when there's an opportunity to overclaim, can promote more objective and ethical decisions.

The Vigilant Manager

If you answered "true" to the question at the start of this article, you felt with some confidence that you are an ethical decision maker. How would you answer it now? It's clear that neither simple conviction nor sincere intention is enough to ensure that you are the ethical practitioner you imagine yourself to be. Managers who aspire to be ethical must challenge the assumption that they're always unbiased and acknowledge that vigilance, even more than good intention, is a defining characteristic of an ethical manager. They must actively collect data, shape their environments, and broaden their decision making. What's more, an obvious redress is available. Managers should seek every opportunity to implement affirmative action policies—not because of past wrongs done to one group or another but because of the everyday wrongs that we can now document are inherent in the ordinary, everyday behavior of good, well-intentioned people. Ironically, only those who understand their own potential for unethical behavior can become the ethical decision makers that they aspire to be.

Originally published in December 2003. Reprint 5526.

The Discipline of Teams

by Jon R. Katzenbach and Douglas K. Smith

EARLY IN THE 1980S, Bill Greenwood and a small band of rebel railroaders took on most of the top management of Burlington Northern and created a multibillion-dollar business in "piggybacking" rail services despite widespread resistance, even resentment, within the company. The Medical Products Group at Hewlett-Packard owes most of its leading performance to the remarkable efforts of Dean Morton, Lew Platt, Ben Holmes, Dick Alberding, and a handful of their colleagues who revitalized a health care business that most others had written off. At Knight Ridder, Jim Batten's "customer obsession" vision took root at the *Tallahassee Democrat* when 14 frontline enthusiasts turned a charter to eliminate errors into a mission of major change and took the entire paper along with them.

Such are the stories and the work of teams—real teams that perform, not amorphous groups that we call teams because we think that the label is motivating and energizing. The difference between teams that perform and other groups that don't is a subject to which most of us pay far too little attention. Part of the problem is that "team" is a word and concept so familiar to everyone. (See "Not All Groups Are Teams: How to Tell the Difference.")

Or at least that's what we thought when we set out to do research for our book *The Wisdom of Teams* (HarperBusiness, 1993). We wanted to discover what differentiates various levels of team performance, where and how teams work best, and what top management can do to enhance their effectiveness. We talked with hundreds of people on more than 50 different teams in 30 companies and beyond, from Motorola and Hewlett-Packard to Operation Desert Storm and the Girl Scouts.

We found that there is a basic discipline that makes teams work. We also found that teams and good performance are inseparable: You cannot have one without the other. But people use the word "team" so loosely that it gets in the way of learning and applying the discipline that leads to good performance. For managers to make better decisions about whether, when, or how to encourage and use teams, it is important to be more precise about what a team is and what it isn't.

Most executives advocate teamwork. And they should. Teamwork represents a set of values that encourage listening and responding constructively to views expressed by others, giving others the benefit of the doubt, providing support, and recognizing the interests and achievements of others. Such values help teams perform, and they also promote individual performance as well as the performance of an entire organization. But teamwork values by themselves are not exclusive to teams, nor are they enough to ensure team performance. (See "Building Team Performance.")

Nor is a team just any group working together. Committees, councils, and task forces are not necessarily teams. Groups do not become teams simply because that is what someone calls them. The entire workforce of any large and complex organization is *never* a team, but think about how often that platitude is offered up.

To understand how teams deliver extra performance, we must distinguish between teams and other forms of working groups. That distinction turns on performance results. A working group's performance is a function of what its members do as individuals. A team's performance includes both individual results and what we call "collective work products." A collective work product is what two or more members must work on together, such as interviews, surveys, or experiments. Whatever it is, a collective work product reflects the joint, real contribution of team members.

Idea in Brief

The word *team* gets bandied about so loosely that many managers are oblivious to its real meaning—or its true potential. With a run-of-the-mill working group, performance is a function of what the members do as individuals. A team's performance, by contrast, calls for both individual and mutual accountability.

Though it may not seem like anything special, mutual accountability can lead to astonishing results. It enables a team to achieve performance levels that are far greater than the individual bests of the team's members. To achieve these benefits, team members must do more than listen, respond constructively, and provide support to one another. In addition to sharing these team-building values, they must share an essential *discipline*.

Working groups are both prevalent and effective in large organizations where individual accountability is most important. The best working groups come together to share information, perspectives, and insights; to make decisions that help each person do his or her job better; and to reinforce individual performance standards. But the focus is always on individual goals and accountabilities. Working-group members don't take responsibility for results other than their own. Nor do they try to develop incremental performance contributions requiring the combined work of two or more members.

Teams differ fundamentally from working groups because they require both individual and mutual accountability. Teams rely on more than group discussion, debate, and decision, on more than sharing information and best-practice performance standards. Teams produce discrete work products through the joint contributions of their members. This is what makes possible performance levels greater than the sum of all the individual bests of team members. Simply stated, a team is more than the sum of its parts.

The first step in developing a disciplined approach to team management is to think about teams as discrete units of performance and not just as positive sets of values. Having observed and worked with scores of teams in action, both successes and failures, we offer the following. Think of it as a working definition or, better still, an

Idea in Practice

A team's essential discipline comprises five characteristics:

1. **A meaningful common purpose that the team has helped shape.** Most teams are responding to an initial mandate from outside the team. But to be successful, the team must "own" this purpose, develop its own spin on it.
2. **Specific performance goals that flow from the common purpose.** For example, getting a new product to market in less than half the normal time. Compelling goals inspire and challenge a team, give it a sense of urgency. They also have a leveling effect, requiring members to focus on the collective effort necessary rather than any differences in title or status.
3. **A mix of complementary skills.** These include technical or functional expertise, problem-solving and decision-making skills, and interpersonal skills. Successful teams rarely have all the needed skills at the outset—they develop them as they learn what the challenge requires.
4. **A strong commitment to how the work gets done.** Teams must agree on who will do what jobs, how schedules will be established and honored, and how decisions will be made and modified. On a genuine team, each member does equivalent amounts of real work; all members, the leader included, contribute in concrete ways to the team's collective work-products.

essential discipline that real teams share: *A team is a small number of people with complementary skills who are committed to a common purpose, set of performance goals, and approach for which they hold themselves mutually accountable.*

The essence of a team is common commitment. Without it, groups perform as individuals; with it, they become a powerful unit of collective performance. This kind of commitment requires a purpose in which team members can believe. Whether the purpose is to "transform the contributions of suppliers into the satisfaction of customers," to "make our company one we can be proud of again," or to "prove that all children can learn," credible team purposes have an element related to winning, being first, revolutionizing, or being on the cutting edge.

5. **Mutual accountability.** Trust and commitment cannot be coerced. The process of agreeing upon appropriate goals serves as the crucible in which members forge their accountability to each other—not just to the leader.

Once the essential discipline has been established, a team is free to concentrate on the critical challenges it faces:

- For a team whose purpose is to make recommendations, that means making a fast and constructive start and providing a clean handoff to those who will implement the recommendations.
- For a team that makes or does things, it's keeping the specific performance goals in sharp focus.
- For a team that runs things, the primary task is distinguishing the challenges that require a real team approach from those that don't.

If a task doesn't demand joint work-products, a working group can be the more effective option. Team opportunities are usually those in which hierarchy or organizational boundaries inhibit the skills and perspectives needed for optimal results. Little wonder, then, that teams have become the primary units of productivity in high-performance organizations.

Teams develop direction, momentum, and commitment by working to shape a meaningful purpose. Building ownership and commitment to team purpose, however, is not incompatible with taking initial direction from outside the team. The often-asserted assumption that a team cannot "own" its purpose unless management leaves it alone actually confuses more potential teams than it helps. In fact, it is the exceptional case—for example, entrepreneurial situations—when a team creates a purpose entirely on its own.

Most successful teams shape their purposes in response to a demand or opportunity put in their path, usually by higher management. This helps teams get started by broadly framing the company's performance expectation. Management is responsible for clarifying the charter, rationale, and performance challenge for the team, but management must also leave enough flexibility for the team to develop commitment around its own spin on that purpose, set of specific goals, timing, and approach.

The best teams invest a tremendous amount of time and effort exploring, shaping, and agreeing on a purpose that belongs to them both collectively and individually. This "purposing" activity continues throughout the life of the team. By contrast, failed teams rarely develop a common purpose. For whatever reason—an insufficient focus on performance, lack of effort, poor leadership—they do not coalesce around a challenging aspiration.

The best teams also translate their common purpose into specific performance goals, such as reducing the reject rate from suppliers by 50% or increasing the math scores of graduates from 40% to 95%. Indeed, if a team fails to establish specific performance goals or if those goals do not relate directly to the team's overall purpose, team members become confused, pull apart, and revert to mediocre performance. By contrast, when purposes and goals build on one another and are combined with team commitment, they become a powerful engine of performance.

Transforming broad directives into specific and measurable performance goals is the surest first step for a team trying to shape a purpose meaningful to its members. Specific goals, such as getting a new product to market in less than half the normal time, responding to all customers within 24 hours, or achieving a zero-defect rate while simultaneously cutting costs by 40%, all provide firm footholds for teams. There are several reasons:

- Specific team-performance goals help define a set of work products that are different both from an organization-wide mission and from individual job objectives. As a result, such work products require the collective effort of team members to make something specific happen that, in and of itself, adds real value to results. By contrast, simply gathering from time to time to make decisions will not sustain team performance.
- The specificity of performance objectives facilitates clear communication and constructive conflict within the team.

When a plant-level team, for example, sets a goal of reducing average machine changeover time to two hours, the clarity of the goal forces the team to concentrate on what it would take either to achieve or to reconsider the goal. When such goals are clear, discussions can focus on how to pursue them or whether to change them; when goals are ambiguous or nonexistent, such discussions are much less productive.

- The attainability of specific goals helps teams maintain their focus on getting results. A product-development team at Eli Lilly's Peripheral Systems Division set definite yardsticks for the market introduction of an ultrasonic probe to help doctors locate deep veins and arteries.

  The probe had to have an audible signal through a specified depth of tissue, be capable of being manufactured at a rate of 100 per day, and have a unit cost less than a preestablished amount. Because the team could measure its progress against each of these specific objectives, the team knew throughout the development process where it stood. Either it had achieved its goals or not.

- As Outward Bound and other team-building programs illustrate, specific objectives have a leveling effect conducive to team behavior. When a small group of people challenge themselves to get over a wall or to reduce cycle time by 50%, their respective titles, perks, and other stripes fade into the background. The teams that succeed evaluate what and how each individual can best contribute to the team's goal and, more important, do so in terms of the performance objective itself rather than a person's status or personality.

- Specific goals allow a team to achieve small wins as it pursues its broader purpose. These small wins are invaluable to building commitment and overcoming the inevitable obstacles that get in the way of a long-term purpose. For example, the Knight Ridder team mentioned at the outset turned a narrow goal to eliminate errors into a compelling customer service purpose.

- Performance goals are compelling. They are symbols of accomplishment that motivate and energize. They challenge the people on a team to commit themselves, as a team, to make a difference. Drama, urgency, and a healthy fear of failure combine to drive teams that have their collective eye on an attainable, but challenging, goal. Nobody but the team can make it happen. It's their challenge.

The combination of purpose and specific goals is essential to performance. Each depends on the other to remain relevant and vital. Clear performance goals help a team keep track of progress and hold itself accountable; the broader, even nobler, aspirations in a team's purpose supply both meaning and emotional energy.

Virtually all effective teams we have met, read or heard about, or been members of have ranged between two and 25 people. For example, the Burlington Northern piggybacking team had seven members, and the Knight Ridder newspaper team had 14. The majority of them have numbered less than ten. Small size is admittedly more of a pragmatic guide than an absolute necessity for success. A large number of people, say 50 or more, can theoretically become a team. But groups of such size are more likely to break into subteams rather than function as a single unit.

Why? Large numbers of people have trouble interacting constructively as a group, much less doing real work together. Ten people are far more likely than 50 to work through their individual, functional, and hierarchical differences toward a common plan and to hold themselves jointly accountable for the results.

Large groups also face logistical issues, such as finding enough physical space and time to meet. And they confront more complex constraints, like crowd or herd behaviors, which prevent the intense sharing of viewpoints needed to build a team. As a result, when they try to develop a common purpose, they usually produce only superficial "missions" and well-meaning intentions that cannot be translated into concrete objectives. They tend fairly quickly to reach a point when meetings become a chore, a clear sign that most of the people in the group are uncertain why they have gathered, beyond some notion of getting along better. Anyone who has been through one of these exercises understands how frustrating it can be. This kind of failure tends to foster cynicism, which gets in the way of future team efforts.

In addition to finding the right size, teams must develop the right mix of skills; that is, each of the complementary skills necessary to do the team's job. As obvious as it sounds, it is a common failing in potential teams. Skill requirements fall into three fairly self-evident categories.

Technical or functional expertise

It would make little sense for a group of doctors to litigate an employment discrimination case in a court of law. Yet teams of doctors and lawyers often try medical malpractice or personal injury cases. Similarly, product development groups that include only marketers or engineers are less likely to succeed than those with the complementary skills of both.

Problem-solving and decision-making skills

Teams must be able to identify the problems and opportunities they face, evaluate the options they have for moving forward, and then make necessary trade-offs and decisions about how to proceed. Most teams need some members with these skills to begin with, although many will develop them best on the job.

Interpersonal skills

Common understanding and purpose cannot arise without effective communication and constructive conflict, which in turn depend on interpersonal skills. These skills include risk taking, helpful criticism, objectivity, active listening, giving the benefit of the doubt, and recognizing the interests and achievements of others.

Obviously, a team cannot get started without some minimum complement of skills, especially technical and functional ones. Still, think about how often you've been part of a team whose members were chosen primarily on the basis of personal compatibility or

Not All Groups Are Teams: How to Tell the Difference

Working Group

- Strong, clearly focused leader
- Individual accountability
- The group's purpose is the same as the broader organizational mission
- Individual work products
- Runs efficient meetings
- Measures its effectiveness indirectly by its influence on others (such as financial performance of the business)
- Discusses, decides, and delegates

Team

- Shared leadership roles
- Individual and mutual accountability
- Specific team purpose that the team itself delivers
- Collective work products
- Encourages open-ended discussion and active problem-solving meetings
- Measures performance directly by assessing collective work products
- Discusses, decides, and does real work together

formal position in the organization, and in which the skill mix of its members wasn't given much thought.

It is equally common to overemphasize skills in team selection. Yet in all the successful teams we've encountered, not one had all the needed skills at the outset. The Burlington Northern team, for example, initially had no members who were skilled marketers despite the fact that their performance challenge was a marketing one. In fact, we discovered that teams are powerful vehicles for developing the skills needed to meet the team's performance challenge.

Accordingly, team member selection ought to ride as much on skill potential as on skills already proven.

Effective teams develop strong commitment to a common approach; that is, to how they will work together to accomplish their purpose. Team members must agree on who will do particular jobs, how schedules will be set and adhered to, what skills need to be developed, how continuing membership in the team is to be earned, and how the group will make and modify decisions. This element of commitment is as important to team performance as the team's commitment to its purpose and goals.

Agreeing on the specifics of work and how they fit together to integrate individual skills and advance team performance lies at the heart of shaping a common approach. It is perhaps self-evident that an approach that delegates all the real work to a few members (or staff outsiders) and thus relies on reviews and meetings for its only "work together" aspects, cannot sustain a real team. Every member of a successful team does equivalent amounts of real work; all members, including the team leader, contribute in concrete ways to the team's work product. This is a very important element of the emotional logic that drives team performance.

When individuals approach a team situation, especially in a business setting, each has preexisting job assignments as well as strengths and weaknesses reflecting a variety of talents, backgrounds, personalities, and prejudices. Only through the mutual discovery and understanding of how to apply all its human resources to a common purpose can a team develop and agree on the best approach to achieve its goals. At the heart of such long and, at times, difficult interactions lies a commitment-building process in which the team candidly explores who is best suited to each task as well as how individual roles will come together. In effect, the team establishes a social contract among members that relates to their purpose and guides and obligates how they must work together.

No group ever becomes a team until it can hold itself accountable as a team. Like common purpose and approach, mutual accountability is a stiff test. Think, for example, about the subtle but critical difference between "the boss holds me accountable" and "we hold ourselves accountable." The first case can lead to the second, but without the second, there can be no team.

Companies like Hewlett-Packard and Motorola have an ingrained performance ethic that enables teams to form organically whenever there is a clear performance challenge requiring collective rather than individual effort. In these companies, the factor of mutual accountability is commonplace. "Being in the boat together" is how their performance game is played.

At its core, team accountability is about the sincere promises we make to ourselves and others, promises that underpin two critical aspects of effective teams: commitment and trust. Most of us enter a potential team situation cautiously because ingrained individualism and experience discourage us from putting our fates in the hands of others or accepting responsibility for others. Teams do not succeed by ignoring or wishing away such behavior.

Mutual accountability cannot be coerced any more than people can be made to trust one another. But when a team shares a common purpose, goals, and approach, mutual accountability grows as a natural counterpart. Accountability arises from and reinforces the time, energy, and action invested in figuring out what the team is trying to accomplish and how best to get it done.

When people work together toward a common objective, trust and commitment follow. Consequently, teams enjoying a strong common purpose and approach inevitably hold themselves responsible, both as individuals and as a team, for the team's performance. This sense of mutual accountability also produces the rich rewards of mutual achievement in which all members share. What we heard over and over from members of effective teams is that they found the experience energizing and motivating in ways that their "normal" jobs never could match.

On the other hand, groups established primarily for the sake of becoming a team or for job enhancement, communication, organizational effectiveness, or excellence rarely become effective teams, as demonstrated by the bad feelings left in many companies after experimenting with quality circles that never translated "quality" into specific goals. Only when appropriate performance goals are set does the process of discussing the goals and the approaches to them give team members a clearer and clearer choice: They can disagree with a goal and the path that the team selects and, in effect, opt out, or they can pitch in and become accountable with and to their teammates.

The discipline of teams we've outlined is critical to the success of all teams. Yet it is also useful to go one step further. Most teams can be classified in one of three ways: teams that recommend things, teams that make or do things, and teams that run things. In our experience, each type faces a characteristic set of challenges.

Teams that recommend things

These teams include task forces; project groups; and audit, quality, or safety groups asked to study and solve particular problems. Teams that recommend things almost always have predetermined completion dates. Two critical issues are unique to such teams: getting off to a fast and constructive start and dealing with the ultimate handoff that's required to get recommendations implemented.

The key to the first issue lies in the clarity of the team's charter and the composition of its membership. In addition to wanting to know why and how their efforts are important, task forces need a clear definition of whom management expects to participate and the time commitment required. Management can help by ensuring that the team includes people with the skills and influence necessary for crafting practical recommendations that will carry weight throughout the organization. Moreover, management can help the team get the necessary cooperation by opening doors and dealing with political obstacles.

Missing the handoff is almost always the problem that stymies teams that recommend things. To avoid this, the transfer of responsibility for recommendations to those who must implement them demands top management's time and attention. The more top managers assume that recommendations will "just happen," the less likely it is that they will. The more involvement task force members have in implementing their recommendations, the more likely they are to get implemented.

To the extent that people outside the task force will have to carry the ball, it is critical to involve them in the process early and often, certainly well before recommendations are finalized. Such involvement may take many forms, including participating in interviews, helping with analyses, contributing and critiquing ideas, and conducting experiments and trials. At a minimum, anyone responsible for implementation should receive a briefing on the task force's purpose, approach, and objectives at the beginning of the effort as well as regular reviews of progress.

Teams that make or do things

These teams include people at or near the front lines who are responsible for doing the basic manufacturing, development, operations, marketing, sales, service, and other value-adding activities of a business. With some exceptions, such as new-product development or process design teams, teams that make or do things tend to have no set completion dates because their activities are ongoing.

In deciding where team performance might have the greatest impact, top management should concentrate on what we call the company's "critical delivery points"—that is, places in the organization where the cost and value of the company's products and services are most directly determined. Such critical delivery points might include where accounts get managed, customer service performed, products designed, and productivity determined. If performance at critical delivery points depends on combining multiple skills, perspectives, and judgments in real time, then the team option is the smartest one.

When an organization does require a significant number of teams at these points, the sheer challenge of maximizing the performance of so many groups will demand a carefully constructed and performance-focused set of management processes. The issue here for top management is how to build the necessary systems and process supports without falling into the trap of appearing to promote teams for their own sake.

The imperative here, returning to our earlier discussion of the basic discipline of teams, is a relentless focus on performance. If management fails to pay persistent attention to the link between teams and performance, the organization becomes convinced that "this year, we are doing 'teams'." Top management can help by instituting processes like pay schemes and training for teams responsive to their real time needs, but more than anything else, top management must make clear and compelling demands on the teams themselves and then pay constant attention to their progress with respect to both team basics and performance results. This means focusing on specific teams and specific performance challenges. Otherwise "performance," like "team," will become a cliché.

Teams that run things

Despite the fact that many leaders refer to the group reporting to them as a team, few groups really are. And groups that become real teams seldom think of themselves as a team because they are so focused on performance results. Yet the opportunity for such teams includes groups from the top of the enterprise down through the divisional or functional level. Whether it is in charge of thousands of people or just a handful, as long as the group oversees some business, ongoing program, or significant functional activity, it is a team that runs things.

The main issue these teams face is determining whether a real team approach is the right one. Many groups that run things can be more effective as working groups than as teams. The key judgment is whether the sum of individual bests will suffice for the performance challenge at hand or whether the group must deliver substantial incremental performance requiring real joint work products. Although the team option promises greater performance, it also brings more risk, and managers must be brutally honest in assessing the trade-offs.

Members may have to overcome a natural reluctance to trust their fate to others. The price of faking the team approach is high: At best, members get diverted from their individual goals, costs outweigh benefits, and people resent the imposition on their time and priorities. At worst, serious animosities develop that undercut even the potential personal bests of the working-group approach.

Working groups present fewer risks. Effective working groups need little time to shape their purpose, since the leader usually establishes it. Meetings are run against well-prioritized agendas. And decisions are implemented through specific individual assignments and accountabilities. Most of the time, therefore, if performance aspirations can be met through individuals doing their respective jobs well, the working-group approach is more comfortable, less risky, and less disruptive than trying for more elusive team performance levels. Indeed, if there is no performance need for the team approach, efforts spent to improve the effectiveness of the working group make much more sense than floundering around trying to become a team.

Having said that, we believe the extra level of performance teams can achieve is becoming critical for a growing number of companies, especially as they move through major changes during which company performance depends on broad-based behavioral change. When top management uses teams to run things, it should make sure the team succeeds in identifying specific purposes and goals.

This is a second major issue for teams that run things. Too often, such teams confuse the broad mission of the total organization with the specific purpose of their small group at the top. The discipline of teams tells us that for a real team to form, there must be a team purpose that is distinctive and specific to the small group and that requires its members to roll up their sleeves and accomplish something beyond individual end products. If a group of managers looks only at the economic performance of the part of the organization it runs to assess overall effectiveness, the group will not have any team performance goals of its own.

While the basic discipline of teams does not differ for them, teams at the top are certainly the most difficult. The complexities of long-term challenges, heavy demands on executive time, and the deep-seated individualism of senior people conspire against teams at the top. At the same time, teams at the top are the most powerful. At first we thought such teams were nearly impossible. That is because we were looking at the teams as defined by the formal organizational structure; that is, the leader and all his or her direct reports equals the team. Then we discovered that real teams at the top were often smaller and less formalized: Whitehead and Weinberg at Goldman Sachs; Hewlett and Packard at HP; Krasnoff, Pall, and Hardy at Pall Corporation; Kendall, Pearson, and Calloway at Pepsi; Haas and Haas at Levi Strauss; Batten and Ridder at Knight Ridder. They were mostly twos and threes, with an occasional fourth.

Nonetheless, real teams at the top of large, complex organizations are still few and far between. Far too many groups at the top of large corporations needlessly constrain themselves from achieving real team levels of performance because they assume that all direct reports must be on the team, that team goals must be identical to corporate goals, that the team members' positions rather than skills determine their respective roles, that a team must be a team all the time, and that the team leader is above doing real work.

As understandable as these assumptions may be, most of them are unwarranted. They do not apply to the teams at the top we have observed, and when replaced with more realistic and flexible assumptions that permit the team discipline to be applied, real team performance at the top can and does occur. Moreover, as more and more companies are confronted with the need to manage major change across their organizations, we will see more real teams at the top.

We believe that teams will become the primary unit of performance in high-performance organizations. But that does not mean that teams will crowd out individual opportunity or formal hierarchy and process. Rather, teams will enhance existing structures without replacing them. A team opportunity exists anywhere hierarchy or organizational boundaries inhibit the skills and perspectives needed for optimal results. Thus, new-product innovation requires preserving functional excellence through structure while eradicating functional bias through teams. And frontline productivity requires preserving direction and guidance through hierarchy while drawing on energy and flexibility through self-managing teams.

We are convinced that every company faces specific performance challenges for which teams are the most practical and powerful vehicle at top management's disposal. The critical role for senior

Building Team Performance

Although there is no guaranteed how-to recipe for building team performance, we observed a number of approaches shared by many successful teams.

Establish urgency, demanding performance standards, and direction

All team members need to believe the team has urgent and worthwhile purposes, and they want to know what the expectations are. Indeed, the more urgent and meaningful the rationale, the more likely it is that the team will live up to its performance potential, as was the case for a customer-service team that was told that further growth for the entire company would be impossible without major improvements in that area. Teams work best in a compelling context. That is why companies with strong performance ethics usually form teams readily.

Select members for skill and skill potential, not personality

No team succeeds without all the skills needed to meet its purpose and performance goals. Yet most teams figure out the skills they will need after they are formed. The wise manager will choose people for their existing skills and their potential to improve existing skills and learn new ones.

Pay particular attention to first meetings and actions. Initial impressions always mean a great deal

When potential teams first gather, everyone monitors the signals given by others to confirm, suspend, or dispel assumptions and concerns. They pay particular attention to those in authority: the team leader and any executives who set up, oversee, or otherwise influence the team. And, as always, what such leaders do is more important than what they say. If a senior executive leaves the team kickoff to take a phone call ten minutes after the session has begun and he never returns, people get the message.

Set some clear rules of behavior

All effective teams develop rules of conduct at the outset to help them achieve their purpose and performance goals. The most critical initial rules pertain to attendance (for example, "no interruptions to take phone calls"), discussion ("no sacred cows"), confidentiality ("the only things to leave this room are what we agree on"), analytic approach ("facts are friendly"), end-product orientation ("everyone gets assignments and does them"), constructive confrontation ("no finger pointing"), and, often the most important, contributions ("everyone does real work").

Set and seize upon a few immediate performance-oriented tasks and goals

Most effective teams trace their advancement to key performance-oriented events. Such events can be set in motion by immediately establishing a few challenging goals that can be reached early on. There is no such thing as a real team without performance results, so the sooner such results occur, the sooner the team congeals.

Challenge the group regularly with fresh facts and information

New information causes a team to redefine and enrich its understanding of the performance challenge, thereby helping the team shape a common purpose, set clearer goals, and improve its common approach. A plant quality improvement team knew the cost of poor quality was high, but it wasn't until they researched the different types of defects and put a price tag on each one that they knew where to go next. Conversely, teams err when they assume that all the information needed exists in the collective experience and knowledge of their members.

Spend lots of time together

Common sense tells us that team members must spend a lot of time together, scheduled and unscheduled, especially in the beginning. Indeed, creative insights as well as personal bonding require impromptu and casual interactions just as much as analyzing spreadsheets and interviewing customers. Busy executives and managers too often intentionally minimize the time they spend together. The successful teams we've observed all gave themselves the time to learn to be a team. This time need not always be spent together physically; electronic, fax, and phone time can also count as time spent together.

Exploit the power of positive feedback, recognition, and reward

Positive reinforcement works as well in a team context as elsewhere. Giving out "gold stars" helps shape new behaviors critical to team performance. If people in the group, for example, are alert to a shy person's initial efforts to speak up and contribute, they can give the honest positive reinforcement that encourages continued contributions. There are many ways to recognize and reward team performance beyond direct compensation, from having a senior executive speak directly to the team about the urgency of its mission to using awards to recognize contributions. Ultimately, however, the satisfaction shared by a team in its own performance becomes the most cherished reward.

managers, therefore, is to worry about company performance and the kinds of teams that can deliver it. This means top management must recognize a team's unique potential to deliver results, deploy teams strategically when they are the best tool for the job, and foster the basic discipline of teams that will make them effective. By doing so, top management creates the kind of environment that enables team as well as individual and organizational performance.

Originally published in March 1993. Reprint R0507P.

Managing Your Boss

by John J. Gabarro and John P. Kotter

TO MANY PEOPLE, THE PHRASE "managing your boss" may sound unusual or suspicious. Because of the traditional top-down emphasis in most organizations, it is not obvious why you need to manage relationships upward—unless, of course, you would do so for personal or political reasons. But we are not referring to political maneuvering or to apple polishing. We are using the term to mean the process of consciously working with your superior to obtain the best possible results for you, your boss, and the company.

Recent studies suggest that effective managers take time and effort to manage not only relationships with their subordinates but also those with their bosses. These studies also show that this essential aspect of management is sometimes ignored by otherwise talented and aggressive managers. Indeed, some managers who actively and effectively supervise subordinates, products, markets, and technologies assume an almost passively reactive stance vis-à-vis their bosses. Such a stance almost always hurts them and their companies.

If you doubt the importance of managing your relationship with your boss or how difficult it is to do so effectively, consider for a moment the following sad but telling story:

Frank Gibbons was an acknowledged manufacturing genius in his industry and, by any profitability standard, a very effective executive. In 1973, his strengths propelled him into the position of vice president of manufacturing for the second largest and most profitable company in its industry. Gibbons was not, however, a good manager of people. He knew this, as did others in his company and his industry. Recognizing this weakness, the president made sure that those who reported to Gibbons were good at working with people and could compensate for his limitations. The arrangement worked well.

In 1975, Philip Bonnevie was promoted into a position reporting to Gibbons. In keeping with the previous pattern, the president selected Bonnevie because he had an excellent track record and a reputation for being good with people. In making that selection, however, the president neglected to notice that, in his rapid rise through the organization, Bonnevie had always had good-to-excellent bosses. He had never been forced to manage a relationship with a difficult boss. In retrospect, Bonnevie admits he had never thought that managing his boss was a part of his job.

Fourteen months after he started working for Gibbons, Bonnevie was fired. During that same quarter, the company reported a net loss for the first time in seven years. Many of those who were close to these events say that they don't really understand what happened. This much is known, however: While the company was bringing out a major new product—a process that required sales, engineering, and manufacturing groups to coordinate decisions very carefully—a whole series of misunderstandings and bad feelings developed between Gibbons and Bonnevie.

For example, Bonnevie claims Gibbons was aware of and had accepted Bonnevie's decision to use a new type of machinery to make the new product; Gibbons swears he did not. Furthermore, Gibbons claims he made it clear to Bonnevie that the introduction of the product was too important to the company in the short run to take any major risks.

As a result of such misunderstandings, planning went awry: A new manufacturing plant was built that could not produce the new product designed by engineering, in the volume desired by sales, at a cost agreed on by the executive committee. Gibbons blamed Bonnevie for the mistake. Bonnevie blamed Gibbons.

Idea in Brief

Managing our *bosses*? Isn't that merely manipulation? Corporate cozying up? Out-and-out apple polishing? In fact, we manage our bosses for very good reasons: to get resources to do the best job, not only for ourselves, but for our bosses and our companies as well. We actively pursue a healthy and productive working relationship based on mutual respect and understanding—understanding our own and our bosses' strengths, weaknesses, goals, work styles, and needs. Here's what can happen when we don't:

Example: A new president with a formal work style replaced someone who'd been looser, more intuitive. The new president preferred written reports and structured meetings. One of his managers found this too controlling. He seldom sent background information, and was often blindsided by unanticipated questions. His boss found their meetings inefficient and frustrating. The manager had to resign.

In contrast, here's how another manager's sensitivity to this same boss's style really paid off:

Example: This manager identified the kinds and frequency of information the president wanted. He sent ahead background reports and discussion agendas. The result? Highly productive meetings and even more innovative problem solving than with his previous boss.

Managers often don't realize how much their bosses depend on them. They need cooperation, reliability, and honesty from their direct reports. Many managers also don't realize how much *they* depend on their bosses—for links to the rest of the organization, for setting priorities, and for obtaining critical resources.

Recognizing this mutual dependence, effective managers seek out information about the boss's concerns and are sensitive to his work style. They also understand how their own attitudes toward authority can sabotage the relationship. Some see the boss as the enemy and fight him at every turn; others are overly compliant, viewing the boss as an all-wise parent.

Of course, one could argue that the problem here was caused by Gibbons's inability to manage his subordinates. But one can make just as strong a case that the problem was related to Bonnevie's inability to manage his boss. Remember, Gibbons was not having difficulty with any other subordinates. Moreover, given the personal

Idea in Practice

You can benefit from this mutual dependence and develop a very productive relationship with your boss by focusing on:

- **compatible work styles.** Bosses process information differently. "Listeners" prefer to be briefed in person so they can ask questions. "Readers" want to process written information first, and then meet to discuss.

Decision-making styles also vary. Some bosses are highly involved. Touch base with them frequently. Others prefer to delegate. Inform them about important decisions you've already made.

- **mutual expectations.** Don't passively assume you know what the boss expects. Find out. With some bosses, write detailed outlines of your work for their approval. With others, carefully planned discussions are key.

Also, communicate *your* expectations to find out if they are realistic. Persuade the boss to accept the most important ones.

- **information flow.** Managers typically underestimate what their bosses need to know—and what they *do* know. Keep the boss informed through processes that fit his style. Be forthright about both good and bad news.
- **dependability and honesty.** Trustworthy subordinates only make promises they can keep and don't shade the truth or play down difficult issues.
- **good use of time and resources.** Don't waste your boss's time with trivial issues. Selectively draw on his time and resources to meet the most important goals—yours, his, and the company's.

price paid by Bonnevie (being fired and having his reputation within the industry severely tarnished), there was little consolation in saying the problem was that Gibbons was poor at managing subordinates. Everyone already knew that.

We believe that the situation could have turned out differently had Bonnevie been more adept at understanding Gibbons and at managing his relationship with him. In this case, an inability to manage upward was unusually costly. The company lost $2 million to $5 million, and Bonnevie's career was, at least temporarily, disrupted. Many less costly cases similar to this probably occur regularly in all major corporations, and the cumulative effect can be very destructive.

Misreading the Boss–Subordinate Relationship

People often dismiss stories like the one we just related as being merely cases of personality conflict. Because two people can on occasion be psychologically or temperamentally incapable of working together, this can be an apt description. But more often, we have found, a personality conflict is only a part of the problem—sometimes a very small part.

Bonnevie did not just have a different personality from Gibbons, he also made or had unrealistic assumptions and expectations about the very nature of boss-subordinate relationships. Specifically, he did not recognize that his relationship to Gibbons involved *mutual dependence* between two *fallible* human beings. Failing to recognize this, a manager typically either avoids trying to manage his or her relationship with a boss or manages it ineffectively.

Some people behave as if their bosses were not very dependent on them. They fail to see how much the boss needs their help and cooperation to do his or her job effectively. These people refuse to acknowledge that the boss can be severely hurt by their actions and needs cooperation, dependability, and honesty from them.

Some people see themselves as not very dependent on their bosses. They gloss over how much help and information they need from the boss in order to perform their own jobs well. This superficial view is particularly damaging when a manager's job and decisions affect other parts of the organization, as was the case in Bonnevie's situation. A manager's immediate boss can play a critical role in linking the manager to the rest of the organization, making sure the manager's priorities are consistent with organizational needs, and in securing the resources the manager needs to perform well. Yet some managers need to see themselves as practically self-sufficient, as not needing the critical information and resources a boss can supply.

Many managers, like Bonnevie, assume that the boss will magically know what information or help their subordinates need and provide it to them. Certainly, some bosses do an excellent job of caring for their subordinates in this way, but for a manager to expect that from all bosses is dangerously unrealistic. A more reasonable expectation for managers to have is that modest help will be forthcoming. After all, bosses are only human. Most really effective managers accept this fact and assume primary responsibility for their own careers and development. They make a point of seeking the information and help they need to do a job instead of waiting for their bosses to provide it.

In light of the foregoing, it seems to us that managing a situation of mutual dependence among fallible human beings requires the following:

1. You have a good understanding of the other person and yourself, especially regarding strengths, weaknesses, work styles, and needs.
2. You use this information to develop and manage a healthy working relationship—one that is compatible with both people's work styles and assets, is characterized by mutual expectations, and meets the most critical needs of the other person.

This combination is essentially what we have found highly effective managers doing.

Understanding the Boss

Managing your boss requires that you gain an understanding of the boss and his or her context, as well as your own situation. All managers do this to some degree, but many are not thorough enough.

At a minimum, you need to appreciate your boss's goals and pressures, his or her strengths and weaknesses. What are your boss's organizational and personal objectives, and what are his or her pressures, especially those from his or her own boss and others at the same level? What are your boss's long suits and blind spots?

What is the preferred style of working? Does your boss like to get information through memos, formal meetings, or phone calls? Does he or she thrive on conflict or try to minimize it? Without this information, a manager is flying blind when dealing with the boss, and unnecessary conflicts, misunderstandings, and problems are inevitable.

In one situation we studied, a top-notch marketing manager with a superior performance record was hired into a company as a vice president "to straighten out the marketing and sales problems." The company, which was having financial difficulties, had recently been acquired by a larger corporation. The president was eager to turn it around and gave the new marketing vice president free rein—at least initially. Based on his previous experience, the new vice president correctly diagnosed that greater market share was needed for the company and that strong product management was required to bring that about. Following that logic, he made a number of pricing decisions aimed at increasing high-volume business.

When margins declined and the financial situation did not improve, however, the president increased pressure on the new vice president. Believing that the situation would eventually correct itself as the company gained back market share, the vice president resisted the pressure.

When by the second quarter, margins and profits had still failed to improve, the president took direct control over all pricing decisions and put all items on a set level of margin, regardless of volume. The new vice president began to find himself shut out by the president, and their relationship deteriorated. In fact, the vice president found the president's behavior bizarre. Unfortunately, the president's new pricing scheme also failed to increase margins, and by the fourth quarter, both the president and the vice president were fired.

What the new vice president had not known until it was too late was that improving marketing and sales had been only *one* of the president's goals. His most immediate goal had been to make the company more profitable—quickly.

Nor had the new vice president known that his boss was invested in this short-term priority for personal as well as business reasons.

The president had been a strong advocate of the acquisition within the parent company, and his personal credibility was at stake.

The vice president made three basic errors. He took information supplied to him at face value, he made assumptions in areas where he had no information, and—what was most damaging—he never actively tried to clarify what his boss's objectives were. As a result, he ended up taking actions that were actually at odds with the president's priorities and objectives.

Managers who work effectively with their bosses do not behave this way. They seek out information about the boss's goals and problems and pressures. They are alert for opportunities to question the boss and others around him or her to test their assumptions. They pay attention to clues in the boss's behavior. Although it is imperative that they do this especially when they begin working with a new boss, effective managers also do this on an ongoing basis because they recognize that priorities and concerns change.

Being sensitive to a boss's work style can be crucial, especially when the boss is new. For example, a new president who was organized and formal in his approach replaced a man who was informal and intuitive. The new president worked best when he had written reports. He also preferred formal meetings with set agendas.

One of his division managers realized this need and worked with the new president to identify the kinds and frequency of information and reports that the president wanted. This manager also made a point of sending background information and brief agendas ahead of time for their discussions. He found that with this type of preparation their meetings were very useful. Another interesting result was, he found that with adequate preparation his new boss was even more effective at brainstorming problems than his more informal and intuitive predecessor had been.

In contrast, another division manager never fully understood how the new boss's work style differed from that of his predecessor. To the degree that he did sense it, he experienced it as too much control. As a result, he seldom sent the new president the background information he needed, and the president never felt fully prepared for meetings with the manager. In fact, the president spent much of the time when they met trying to get information that he felt he should have had earlier. The boss experienced these meetings as frustrating and inefficient, and the subordinate often found himself thrown off guard by the questions that the president asked. Ultimately, this division manager resigned.

The difference between the two division managers just described was not so much one of ability or even adaptability. Rather, one of the men was more sensitive to his boss's work style and to the implications of his boss's needs than the other was.

Understanding Yourself

The boss is only one-half of the relationship. You are the other half, as well as the part over which you have more direct control. Developing an effective working relationship requires, then, that you know your own needs, strengths and weaknesses, and personal style.

You are not going to change either your basic personality structure or that of your boss. But you can become aware of what it is about you that impedes or facilitates working with your boss and, with that awareness, take actions that make the relationship more effective.

For example, in one case we observed, a manager and his superior ran into problems whenever they disagreed. The boss's typical response was to harden his position and overstate it. The manager's reaction was then to raise the ante and intensify the forcefulness of his argument. In doing this, he channeled his anger into sharpening his attacks on the logical fallacies he saw in his boss's assumptions. His boss in turn would become even more adamant about holding his original position. Predictably, this escalating cycle resulted in the subordinate avoiding whenever possible any topic of potential conflict with his boss.

In discussing this problem with his peers, the manager discovered that his reaction to the boss was typical of how he generally reacted to counterarguments—but with a difference. His response would overwhelm his peers but not his boss. Because his attempts to discuss this problem with his boss were unsuccessful, he concluded that the only way to change the situation was to deal with his own instinctive reactions. Whenever the two reached an impasse, he would check his own impatience and suggest that they break up and think about it before getting together again. Usually when they renewed their discussion, they had digested their differences and were more able to work them through.

Gaining this level of self-awareness and acting on it are difficult but not impossible. For example, by reflecting over his past experiences, a young manager learned that he was not very good at dealing with difficult and emotional issues where people were involved. Because he disliked those issues and realized that his instinctive responses to them were seldom very good, he developed a habit of touching base with his boss whenever such a problem arose. Their discussions always surfaced ideas and approaches the manager had not considered. In many cases, they also identified specific actions the boss could take to help.

Although a superior–subordinate relationship is one of mutual dependence, it is also one in which the subordinate is typically more dependent on the boss than the other way around. This dependence inevitably results in the subordinate feeling a certain degree of frustration, sometimes anger, when his actions or options are constrained by his boss's decisions. This is a normal part of life and occurs in the best of relationships. The way in which a manager handles these frustrations largely depends on his or her predisposition toward dependence on authority figures.

Some people's instinctive reaction under these circumstances is to resent the boss's authority and to rebel against the boss's decisions. Sometimes a person will escalate a conflict beyond what is appropriate. Seeing the boss almost as an institutional enemy, this type of manager will often, without being conscious of it, fight with the boss just for the sake of fighting. The subordinate's reactions to being constrained are usually strong and sometimes impulsive. He or she sees the boss as someone who, by virtue of the role, is a hindrance to progress, an obstacle to be circumvented or at best tolerated.

Psychologists call this pattern of reactions counterdependent behavior. Although a counterdependent person is difficult for most superiors to manage and usually has a history of strained relationships with superiors, this sort of manager is apt to have even more trouble with a boss who tends to be directive or authoritarian. When the manager acts on his or her negative feelings, often in subtle and nonverbal ways, the boss sometimes does become the enemy. Sensing the subordinate's latent hostility, the boss will lose trust in the subordinate or his or her judgment and then behave even less openly.

Paradoxically, a manager with this type of predisposition is often a good manager of his or her own people. He or she will many times go out of the way to get support for them and will not hesitate to go to bat for them.

At the other extreme are managers who swallow their anger and behave in a very compliant fashion when the boss makes what they know to be a poor decision. These managers will agree with the boss even when a disagreement might be welcome or when the boss would easily alter a decision if given more information. Because they bear no relationship to the specific situation at hand, their responses are as much an overreaction as those of counterdependent managers. Instead of seeing the boss as an enemy, these people deny their anger—the other extreme—and tend to see the boss as if he or she were an all-wise parent who should know best, should take responsibility for their careers, train them in all they need to know, and protect them from overly ambitious peers.

Both counterdependence and overdependence lead managers to hold unrealistic views of what a boss is. Both views ignore that bosses, like everyone else, are imperfect and fallible. They don't have unlimited time, encyclopedic knowledge, or extrasensory perception; nor are they evil enemies. They have their own pressures and concerns that are sometimes at odds with the wishes of the subordinate—and often for good reason.

Altering predispositions toward authority, especially at the extremes, is almost impossible without intensive psychotherapy (psychoanalytic theory and research suggest that such predispositions are deeply rooted in a person's personality and upbringing).

However, an awareness of these extremes and the range between them can be very useful in understanding where your own predispositions fall and what the implications are for how you tend to behave in relation to your boss.

If you believe, on the one hand, that you have some tendencies toward counterdependence, you can understand and even predict what your reactions and overreactions are likely to be. If, on the other hand, you believe you have some tendencies toward overdependence, you might question the extent to which your overcompliance or inability to confront real differences may be making both you and your boss less effective.

Developing and Managing the Relationship

With a clear understanding of both your boss and yourself, you can *usually* establish a way of working together that fits both of you, that is characterized by unambiguous mutual expectations, and that

---

Checklist for Managing Your Boss

Make sure you understand your boss and his or her context, including:

- ☐ Goals and objectives
- ☐ Pressures
- ☐ Strengths, weaknesses, blind spots
- ☐ Preferred work style

Assess yourself and your needs, including:

- ☐ Strengths and weaknesses
- ☐ Personal style
- ☐ Predisposition toward dependence on authority figures

Develop and maintain a relationship that:

- ☐ Fits both your needs and styles
- ☐ Is characterized by mutual expectations
- ☐ Keeps your boss informed
- ☐ Is based on dependability and honesty
- ☐ Selectively uses your boss's time and resources

---

helps you both be more productive and effective. The "Checklist for managing your boss" summarizes some things such a relationship consists of. Following are a few more.

Compatible work styles

Above all else, a good working relationship with a boss accommodates differences in work style. For example, in one situation we studied, a manager (who had a relatively good relationship with his superior) realized that during meetings his boss would often become inattentive and sometimes brusque. The subordinate's own style tended to be discursive and exploratory. He would often digress from the topic at hand to deal with background factors, alternative approaches, and so forth. His boss preferred to discuss problems with a minimum of background detail and became impatient and distracted whenever his subordinate digressed from the immediate issue.

Recognizing this difference in style, the manager became terser and more direct during meetings with his boss. To help himself do this, before meetings, he would develop brief agendas that he used as a guide. Whenever he felt that a digression was needed, he explained why. This small shift in his own style made these meetings more effective and far less frustrating for both of them.

Subordinates can adjust their styles in response to their bosses' preferred method for receiving information. Peter Drucker divides bosses into "listeners" and "readers." Some bosses like to get information in report form so they can read and study it. Others work better with information and reports presented in person so they can ask questions. As Drucker points out, the implications are obvious. If your boss is a listener, you brief him or her in person, *then* follow it up with a memo. If your boss is a reader, you cover important items or proposals in a memo or report, *then* discuss them.

Other adjustments can be made according to a boss's decision-making style. Some bosses prefer to be involved in decisions and problems as they arise. These are high-involvement managers who like to keep their hands on the pulse of the operation. Usually their needs (and your own) are best satisfied if you touch base with them on an ad hoc basis. A boss who has a need to be involved will become involved one way or another, so there are advantages to including him or her at your initiative. Other bosses prefer to delegate—they don't want to be involved. They expect you to come to them with major problems and inform them about any important changes.

Creating a compatible relationship also involves drawing on each other's strengths and making up for each other's weaknesses. Because he knew that the boss—the vice president of engineering—was not very good at monitoring his employees' problems, one manager we studied made a point of doing it himself. The stakes were high: The engineers and technicians were all union members, the company worked on a customer-contract basis, and the company had recently experienced a serious strike.

The manager worked closely with his boss, along with people in the scheduling department and the personnel office, to make sure that potential problems were avoided. He also developed an informal arrangement through which his boss would review with him any proposed changes in personnel or assignment policies before taking action. The boss valued his advice and credited his subordinate for improving both the performance of the division and the labor-management climate.

Mutual expectations

The subordinate who passively assumes that he or she knows what the boss expects is in for trouble. Of course, some superiors will spell out their expectations very explicitly and in great detail. But most do not. And although many corporations have systems that provide a basis for communicating expectations (such as formal planning processes, career planning reviews, and performance appraisal reviews), these systems never work perfectly. Also, between these formal reviews, expectations invariably change.

Ultimately, the burden falls on the subordinate to find out what the boss's expectations are. They can be both broad (such as what kinds of problems the boss wishes to be informed about and when) as well as very specific (such things as when a particular project should be completed and what kinds of information the boss needs in the interim).

Getting a boss who tends to be vague or not explicit to express expectations can be difficult. But effective managers find ways to get that information. Some will draft a detailed memo covering key aspects of their work and then send it to their boss for approval. They then follow this up with a face-to-face discussion in which they go over each item in the memo. A discussion like this will often surface virtually all of the boss's expectations.

Other effective managers will deal with an inexplicit boss by initiating an ongoing series of informal discussions about "good management" and "our objectives." Still others find useful information more indirectly through those who used to work for the boss and through the formal planning systems in which the boss makes commitments to his or her own superior. Which approach you choose, of course, should depend on your understanding of your boss's style.

Developing a workable set of mutual expectations also requires that you communicate your own expectations to the boss, find out if they are realistic, and influence the boss to accept the ones that are important to you. Being able to influence the boss to value your expectations can be particularly important if the boss is an overachiever. Such a boss will often set unrealistically high standards that need to be brought into line with reality.

A flow of information

How much information a boss needs about what a subordinate is doing will vary significantly depending on the boss's style, the situation he or she is in, and the confidence the boss has in the subordinate. But it is not uncommon for a boss to need more information than the subordinate would naturally supply or for the subordinate to think the boss knows more than he or she really does. Effective managers recognize that they probably underestimate what their bosses need to know and make sure they find ways to keep them informed through processes that fit their styles.

Managing the flow of information upward is particularly difficult if the boss does not like to hear about problems. Although many people would deny it, bosses often give off signals that they want to hear only good news. They show great displeasure—usually nonverbally—when someone tells them about a problem. Ignoring individual achievement, they may even evaluate more favorably subordinates who do not bring problems to them.

Nevertheless, for the good of the organization, the boss, and the subordinate, a superior needs to hear about failures as well as successes. Some subordinates deal with a good-news-only boss by finding indirect ways to get the necessary information to him or her, such as a management information system. Others see to it that potential problems, whether in the form of good surprises or bad news, are communicated immediately.

Dependability and honesty

Few things are more disabling to a boss than a subordinate on whom he cannot depend, whose work he cannot trust. Almost no one is intentionally undependable, but many managers are inadvertently so because of oversight or uncertainty about the boss's priorities. A commitment to an optimistic delivery date may please a superior in the short term but become a source of displeasure if not honored. It's difficult for a boss to rely on a subordinate who repeatedly slips deadlines. As one president (describing a subordinate) put it: "I'd rather he be more consistent even if he delivered fewer peak successes—at least I could rely on him."

Nor are many managers intentionally dishonest with their bosses. But it is easy to shade the truth and play down issues. Current concerns often become future surprise problems. It's almost impossible for bosses to work effectively if they cannot rely on a fairly accurate reading from their subordinates. Because it undermines credibility, dishonesty is perhaps the most troubling trait a subordinate can have. Without a basic level of trust, a boss feels compelled to check all of a subordinate's decisions, which makes it difficult to delegate.

Good use of time and resources

Your boss is probably as limited in his or her store of time, energy, and influence as you are. Every request you make of your boss uses up some of these resources, so it's wise to draw on these resources selectively. This may sound obvious, but many managers use up their boss's time (and some of their own credibility) over relatively trivial issues.

One vice president went to great lengths to get his boss to fire a meddlesome secretary in another department. His boss had to use considerable influence to do it. Understandably, the head of the other department was not pleased. Later, when the vice president wanted to tackle more important problems, he ran into trouble. By using up blue chips on a relatively trivial issue, he had made it difficult for him and his boss to meet more important goals.

No doubt, some subordinates will resent that on top of all their other duties, they also need to take time and energy to manage their relationships with their bosses. Such managers fail to realize the importance of this activity and how it can simplify their jobs by eliminating potentially severe problems. Effective managers recognize that this part of their work is legitimate. Seeing themselves as ultimately responsible for what they achieve in an organization, they know they need to establish and manage relationships with everyone on whom they depend—and that includes the boss.

Originally published in January 1980. Reprint R0501J.

About the Contributors

DANIEL GOLEMAN cochairs the Consortium for Research on Emotional Intelligence in Organizations at Rutgers University.

FREDERICK HERZBERG was a professor of management at the University of Utah.

JEAN-FRANÇOIS MANZONI is a professor of leadership and organizational development at IMD in Switzerland.

JEAN-LOUIS BARSOUX is a senior research fellow at Insead in France.

CAROL A. WALKER is the president of Prepared to Lead, a management consulting firm in Weston, Massachusetts.

MARCUS BUCKINGHAM is a consultant and speaker on leadership and management practices.

W. CHAN KIM is the Boston Consulting Group Bruce D. Henderson Chaired Professor of Strategy and International Management at Insead in France.

RENÉE MAUBORGNE is the Insead Distinguished Fellow and a professor of strategy at Insead in France.

CHRIS ARGYRIS is a professor emeritus at Harvard's Graduate School of Education.

MAHZARIN R. BANAJI is the Richard Clarke Cabot Professor of Social Ethics at Harvard University.

MAX H. BAZERMAN is the Jesse Isidor Straus Professor of Business Administration at Harvard Business School.

DOLLY CHUGH is an assistant professor of management and organizations at New York University's Stern School of Business.

JON R. KATZENBACH is a senior partner at Booz & Company, a global management consulting firm.

DOUGLAS K. SMITH is an organizational consultant and a former McKinsey & Company partner.

JOHN J. GABARRO is the UPS Foundation Professor of Human Resource Management, Emeritus, at Harvard Business School.

JOHN P. KOTTER is the Konosuke Matsushita Professor of Leadership, Emeritus, at Harvard Business School.

Index

Harvard
Business
Review
COLLABORATIVE
OVERLOAD
PAGE 57
The Ultima
Marketing
Subscriber Exclusives

HBR'S 10 MUST READS

On Leadership

HBR'S 10 MUST READS

On Leadership

HARVARD BUSINESS REVIEW PRESS
Boston, Massachusetts

Printed in the United States of America

45 44

Library of Congress Cataloging-in-Publication Data

HBR's 10 must reads on leadership

p. cm.

Includes index.

ISBN 978-1-4221-5797-8 (pbk. : alk. paper) 1. Leadership. I. Harvard business review. II. Title: HBR's ten must reads on leadership. III. Title: Harvard business review's 10 must reads on leadership.

HD57.7.H3914 2010

658.4'092—dc22

2010031617

The paper used in this publication meets the requirements of the American National Standard for Permanence of Paper for Publications and Documents in Libraries and Archives Z39.48-1992.

Contents

HBR'S 10 MUST READ

On Leadership

What Makes a Leader?

by Daniel Goleman

EVERY BUSINESSPERSON KNOWS a story about a highly intelligent, highly skilled executive who was promoted into a leadership position only to fail at the job. And they also know a story about someone with solid—but not extraordinary—intellectual abilities and technical skills who was promoted into a similar position and then soared.

Such anecdotes support the widespread belief that identifying individuals with the "right stuff" to be leaders is more art than science. After all, the personal styles of superb leaders vary: Some leaders are subdued and analytical; others shout their manifestos from the mountaintops. And just as important, different situations call for different types of leadership. Most mergers need a sensitive negotiator at the helm, whereas many turnarounds require a more forceful authority.

I have found, however, that the most effective leaders are alike in one crucial way: They all have a high degree of what has come to be known as *emotional intelligence*. It's not that IQ and technical skills are irrelevant. They do matter, but mainly as "threshold capabilities"; that is, they are the entry-level requirements for executive positions. But my research, along with other recent studies, clearly shows that emotional intelligence is the sine qua non of leadership. Without it, a person can have the best training in the world, an incisive, analytical mind, and an endless supply of smart ideas, but he still won't make a great leader.

In the course of the past year, my colleagues and I have focused on how emotional intelligence operates at work. We have examined the relationship between emotional intelligence and effective performance, especially in leaders. And we have observed how emotional intelligence shows itself on the job. How can you tell if someone has high emotional intelligence, for example, and how can you recognize it in yourself? In the following pages, we'll explore these questions, taking each of the components of emotional intelligence—self-awareness, self-regulation, motivation, empathy, and social skill—in turn.

Evaluating Emotional Intelligence

Most large companies today have employed trained psychologists to develop what are known as "competency models" to aid them in identifying, training, and promoting likely stars in the leadership firmament. The psychologists have also developed such models for lower-level positions. And in recent years, I have analyzed competency models from 188 companies, most of which were large and global and included the likes of Lucent Technologies, British Airways, and Credit Suisse.

In carrying out this work, my objective was to determine which personal capabilities drove outstanding performance within these organizations, and to what degree they did so. I grouped capabilities into three categories: purely technical skills like accounting and business planning; cognitive abilities like analytical reasoning; and competencies demonstrating emotional intelligence, such as the ability to work with others and effectiveness in leading change.

To create some of the competency models, psychologists asked senior managers at the companies to identify the capabilities that typified the organization's most outstanding leaders. To create other models, the psychologists used objective criteria, such as a division's profitability, to differentiate the star performers at senior levels within their organizations from the average ones. Those

Idea in Brief

What distinguishes great leaders from merely good ones? It isn't IQ or technical skills, says Daniel Goleman. It's **emotional intelligence:** a group of five skills that enable the best leaders to maximize their own *and* their followers' performance. When senior managers at one company had a critical mass of EI capabilities, their divisions outperformed yearly earnings goals by 20%.

The EI skills are:

- *Self-awareness*—knowing one's strengths, weaknesses, drives, values, and impact on others
- *Self-regulation*—controlling or redirecting disruptive impulses and moods
- *Motivation*—relishing achievement for its own sake
- *Empathy*—understanding other people's emotional makeup
- *Social skill*—building rapport with others to move them in desired directions

We're each born with certain levels of EI skills. But we can strengthen these abilities through persistence, practice, and feedback from colleagues or coaches.

individuals were then extensively interviewed and tested, and their capabilities were compared. This process resulted in the creation of lists of ingredients for highly effective leaders. The lists ranged in length from seven to 15 items and included such ingredients as initiative and strategic vision.

When I analyzed all this data, I found dramatic results. To be sure, intellect was a driver of outstanding performance. Cognitive skills such as big-picture thinking and long-term vision were particularly important. But when I calculated the ratio of technical skills, IQ, and emotional intelligence as ingredients of excellent performance, emotional intelligence proved to be twice as important as the others for jobs at all levels.

Moreover, my analysis showed that emotional intelligence played an increasingly important role at the highest levels of the company, where differences in technical skills are of negligible importance. In other words, the higher the rank of a person considered to be a star performer, the more emotional intelligence capabilities showed up as the reason for his or her effectiveness. When I compared star performers with average ones in senior leadership positions, nearly

Idea in Practice

Understanding EI'S Components

EI Component	Definition	Hallmarks	Example
Self-awareness	Knowing one's emotions, strengths, weaknesses, drives, values, and goals—and their impact on others	• Self-confidence • Realistic self-assessment • Self-deprecating sense of humor • Thirst for constructive criticism	A manager knows tight deadlines bring out the worst in him. So he plans his time to get work done well in advance.
Self-regulation	Controlling or redirecting disruptive emotions and impulses	• Trustworthiness • Integrity • Comfort with ambiguity and change	When a team botches a presentation, its leader resists the urge to scream. Instead, she considers possible reasons for the failure, explains the consequences to her team, and explores solutions with them.
Motivation	Being driven to achieve for the sake of achievement	• A passion for the work itself and for new challenges • Unflagging energy to improve • Optimism in the face of failure	A portfolio manager at an investment company sees his fund tumble for three consecutive quarters. Major clients defect. Instead of blaming external circumstances, she decides to learn from the experience—and engineers a turnaround.

Empathy	Considering others' feelings, especially when making decisions	• Expertise in attracting and retaining talent • Ability to develop others • Sensitivity to cross-cultural differences	An American consultant and her team pitch a project to a potential client in Japan. Her team interprets the client's silence as disapproval, and prepares to leave. The consultant reads the client's body language and senses interest. She continues the meeting, and her team gets the job.
Social Skill	Managing relationships to move people in desired directions	• Effectiveness in leading change • Persuasiveness • Extensive networking • Expertise in building and leading teams	A manager wants his company to adopt a better Internet strategy. He finds kindred spirits and assembles a de facto team to create a prototype Web site. He persuades allies in other divisions to fund the company's participation in a relevant convention. His company forms an Internet division—and puts him in charge of it.

Strengthening Your EI

Use practice and feedback from others to strengthen specific EI skills.

Example: An executive learned from others that she lacked empathy, especially the ability to listen. She wanted to fix the problem, so she asked a coach to tell her when she exhibited poor listening skills. She then role-played incidents to practice giving better responses; for example, not interrupting. She also began observing executives skilled at listening—and imitated their behavior.

The five components of emotional intelligence at work

	Definition	Hallmarks
Self-awareness	The ability to recognize and understand your moods, emotions, and drives, as well as their effect on others	Self-confidence Realistic self-assessment Self-deprecating sense of humor
Self-Regulation	The ability to control or redirect disruptive impulses and moods The propensity to suspend judgment—to think before acting	Trustworthiness and integrity Comfort with ambiguity Openness to change
Motivation	A passion to work for reasons that go beyond money or status A propensity to pursue goals with energy and persistence	Strong drive to achieve Optimism, even in the face of failure Organizational commitment
Empathy	The ability to understand the emotional makeup of other people Skill in treating people according to their emotional reactions	Expertise in building and retaining talent Cross-cultural sensitivity Service to clients and customers
Social Skill	Proficiency in managing relationships and building networks An ability to find common ground and build rapport	Effectiveness in leading change Persuasiveness Expertise in building and leading teams

90% of the difference in their profiles was attributable to emotional intelligence factors rather than cognitive abilities.

Other researchers have confirmed that emotional intelligence not only distinguishes outstanding leaders but can also be linked to strong performance. The findings of the late David McClelland, the renowned researcher in human and organizational behavior, are a good example. In a 1996 study of a global food and beverage company, McClelland found that when senior managers had a critical mass of emotional intelligence capabilities, their divisions outperformed yearly earnings goals by 20%. Meanwhile, division leaders without that critical mass underperformed by almost the same amount. McClelland's findings, interestingly, held as true in the company's U.S. divisions as in its divisions in Asia and Europe.

In short, the numbers are beginning to tell us a persuasive story about the link between a company's success and the emotional intelligence of its leaders. And just as important, research is also demonstrating that people can, if they take the right approach, develop their emotional intelligence. (See the sidebar "Can Emotional Intelligence Be Learned?")

Self-Awareness

Self-awareness is the first component of emotional intelligence—which makes sense when one considers that the Delphic oracle gave the advice to "know thyself" thousands of years ago. Self-awareness means having a deep understanding of one's emotions, strengths, weaknesses, needs, and drives. People with strong self-awareness are neither overly critical nor unrealistically hopeful. Rather, they are honest—with themselves and with others.

People who have a high degree of self-awareness recognize how their feelings affect them, other people, and their job performance. Thus, a self-aware person who knows that tight deadlines bring out the worst in him plans his time carefully and gets his work done well in advance. Another person with high self-awareness will be able to work with a demanding client. She will understand the client's impact on her moods and the deeper reasons for her frustration. "Their

Can Emotional Intelligence Be Learned?

FOR AGES, PEOPLE HAVE DEBATED if leaders are born or made. So too goes the debate about emotional intelligence. Are people born with certain levels of empathy, for example, or do they acquire empathy as a result of life's experiences? The answer is both. Scientific inquiry strongly suggests that there is a genetic component to emotional intelligence. Psychological and developmental research indicates that nurture plays a role as well. How much of each perhaps will never be known, but research and practice clearly demonstrate that emotional intelligence can be learned.

One thing is certain: Emotional intelligence increases with age. There is an old-fashioned word for the phenomenon: maturity. Yet even with maturity, some people still need training to enhance their emotional intelligence. Unfortunately, far too many training programs that intend to build leadership skills—including emotional intelligence—are a waste of time and money. The problem is simple: They focus on the wrong part of the brain.

Emotional intelligence is born largely in the neurotransmitters of the brain's limbic system, which governs feelings, impulses, and drives. Research indicates that the limbic system learns best through motivation, extended practice, and feedback. Compare this with the kind of learning that goes on in the neocortex, which governs analytical and technical ability. The neocortex grasps concepts and logic. It is the part of the brain that figures out how to use a computer or make a sales call by reading a book. Not surprisingly—but mistakenly—it is also the part of the brain targeted by most training programs aimed at enhancing emotional intelligence. When such programs take, in effect, a neocortical approach, my research with the Consortium for Research on Emotional Intelligence in Organizations has shown they can even have a *negative* impact on people's job performance.

To enhance emotional intelligence, organizations must refocus their training to include the limbic system. They must help people break old behavioral habits and establish new ones. That not only takes much more time than conventional training programs, it also requires an individualized approach.

Imagine an executive who is thought to be low on empathy by her colleagues. Part of that deficit shows itself as an inability to listen; she interrupts people and doesn't pay close attention to what they're saying. To fix the problem, the executive needs to be motivated to change, and then she needs practice and feedback from others in the company. A colleague or coach could be tapped to let the executive know when she has been observed failing to listen. She would then have to replay the incident and give a better response; that is, demonstrate her ability to absorb what others are saying. And the executive could be directed to observe certain executives who listen well and to mimic their behavior.

With persistence and practice, such a process can lead to lasting results. I know one Wall Street executive who sought to improve his empathy—specifically his ability to read people's reactions and see their perspectives. Before beginning his quest, the executive's subordinates were terrified of working with him. People even went so far as to hide bad news from him. Naturally, he was shocked when finally confronted with these facts. He went home and told his family—but they only confirmed what he had heard at work. When their opinions on any given subject did not mesh with his, they, too, were frightened of him.

Enlisting the help of a coach, the executive went to work to heighten his empathy through practice and feedback. His first step was to take a vacation to a foreign country where he did not speak the language. While there, he monitored his reactions to the unfamiliar and his openness to people who were different from him. When he returned home, humbled by his week abroad, the executive asked his coach to shadow him for parts of the day, several times a week, to critique how he treated people with new or different perspectives. At the same time, he consciously used on-the-job interactions as opportunities to practice "hearing" ideas that differed from his. Finally, the executive had himself videotaped in meetings and asked those who worked for and with him to critique his ability to acknowledge and understand the feelings of others. It took several months, but the executive's emotional intelligence did ultimately rise, and the improvement was reflected in his overall performance on the job.

It's important to emphasize that building one's emotional intelligence cannot—will not—happen without sincere desire and concerted effort. A brief seminar won't help; nor can one buy a how-to manual. It is much harder to learn to empathize—to internalize empathy as a natural response to people—than it is to become adept at regression analysis. But it can be done. "Nothing great was ever achieved without enthusiasm," wrote Ralph Waldo Emerson. If your goal is to become a real leader, these words can serve as a guidepost in your efforts to develop high emotional intelligence.

trivial demands take us away from the real work that needs to be done," she might explain. And she will go one step further and turn her anger into something constructive.

Self-awareness extends to a person's understanding of his or her values and goals. Someone who is highly self-aware knows where he is headed and why; so, for example, he will be able to be firm in turning down a job offer that is tempting financially but does not fit with his principles or long-term goals. A person who lacks self-awareness is apt to make decisions that bring on inner turmoil by treading on buried values. "The money looked good so I signed on," someone might say two years into a job, "but the work means so little to me that I'm constantly bored." The decisions of self-aware people mesh with their values; consequently, they often find work to be energizing.

How can one recognize self-awareness? First and foremost, it shows itself as candor and an ability to assess oneself realistically. People with high self-awareness are able to speak accurately and openly—although not necessarily effusively or confessionally—about their emotions and the impact they have on their work. For instance, one manager I know of was skeptical about a new personal-shopper service that her company, a major department-store chain, was about to introduce. Without prompting from her team or her boss, she offered them an explanation: "It's hard for me to get behind the rollout of this service," she admitted, "because I really wanted to run the project, but I wasn't selected. Bear with me while I deal with that." The manager did indeed examine her feelings; a week later, she was supporting the project fully.

Such self-knowledge often shows itself in the hiring process. Ask a candidate to describe a time he got carried away by his feelings and did something he later regretted. Self-aware candidates will be frank in admitting to failure—and will often tell their tales with a smile. One of the hallmarks of self-awareness is a self-deprecating sense of humor.

Self-awareness can also be identified during performance reviews. Self-aware people know—and are comfortable talking about—their limitations and strengths, and they often demonstrate a thirst for constructive criticism. By contrast, people with low self-awareness interpret the message that they need to improve as a threat or a sign of failure.

Self-aware people can also be recognized by their self-confidence. They have a firm grasp of their capabilities and are less likely to set themselves up to fail by, for example, overstretching on assignments. They know, too, when to ask for help. And the risks they take on the job are calculated. They won't ask for a challenge that they know they can't handle alone. They'll play to their strengths.

Consider the actions of a midlevel employee who was invited to sit in on a strategy meeting with her company's top executives. Although she was the most junior person in the room, she did not sit there quietly, listening in awestruck or fearful silence. She knew she had a head for clear logic and the skill to present ideas persuasively, and she offered cogent suggestions about the company's strategy. At the same time, her self-awareness stopped her from wandering into territory where she knew she was weak.

Despite the value of having self-aware people in the workplace, my research indicates that senior executives don't often give self-awareness the credit it deserves when they look for potential leaders. Many executives mistake candor about feelings for "wimpiness" and fail to give due respect to employees who openly acknowledge their shortcomings. Such people are too readily dismissed as "not tough enough" to lead others.

In fact, the opposite is true. In the first place, people generally admire and respect candor. Furthermore, leaders are constantly required to make judgment calls that require a candid assessment of capabilities—their own and those of others. Do we have the management expertise to acquire a competitor? Can we launch a new product within six months? People who assess themselves honestly—that is, self-aware people—are well suited to do the same for the organizations they run.

Self-Regulation

Biological impulses drive our emotions. We cannot do away with them—but we can do much to manage them. Self-regulation, which is like an ongoing inner conversation, is the component of emotional intelligence that frees us from being prisoners of our feelings. People engaged in such a conversation feel bad moods and emotional impulses just as everyone else does, but they find ways to control them and even to channel them in useful ways.

Imagine an executive who has just watched a team of his employees present a botched analysis to the company's board of directors. In the gloom that follows, the executive might find himself tempted to pound on the table in anger or kick over a chair. He could leap up and scream at the group. Or he might maintain a grim silence, glaring at everyone before stalking off.

But if he had a gift for self-regulation, he would choose a different approach. He would pick his words carefully, acknowledging the team's poor performance without rushing to any hasty judgment. He would then step back to consider the reasons for the failure. Are they personal—a lack of effort? Are there any mitigating factors? What was his role in the debacle? After considering these questions, he would call the team together, lay out the incident's consequences, and offer his feelings about it. He would then present his analysis of the problem and a well-considered solution.

Why does self-regulation matter so much for leaders? First of all, people who are in control of their feelings and impulses—that is, people who are reasonable—are able to create an environment of trust and fairness. In such an environment, politics and infighting are sharply reduced and productivity is high. Talented people flock to the organization and aren't tempted to leave. And self-regulation has a trickle-down effect. No one wants to be known as a hothead when the boss is known for her calm approach. Fewer bad moods at the top mean fewer throughout the organization.

Second, self-regulation is important for competitive reasons. Everyone knows that business today is rife with ambiguity and change. Companies merge and break apart regularly. Technology transforms work at a dizzying pace. People who have mastered their emotions are able to roll with the changes. When a new program is announced, they don't panic; instead, they are able to suspend judgment, seek out information, and listen to the executives as they explain the new program. As the initiative moves forward, these people are able to move with it.

Sometimes they even lead the way. Consider the case of a manager at a large manufacturing company. Like her colleagues, she had used a certain software program for five years. The program drove how she collected and reported data and how she thought about the company's strategy. One day, senior executives announced that a new program was to be installed that would radically change how information was gathered and assessed within the organization. While many people in the company complained bitterly about how disruptive the change would be, the manager mulled over the reasons for the new program and was convinced of its potential to improve performance. She eagerly attended training sessions—some of her colleagues refused to do so—and was eventually promoted to run several divisions, in part because she used the new technology so effectively.

I want to push the importance of self-regulation to leadership even further and make the case that it enhances integrity, which is not only a personal virtue but also an organizational strength. Many of the bad things that happen in companies are a function of impulsive behavior. People rarely plan to exaggerate profits, pad expense accounts, dip into the till, or abuse power for selfish ends. Instead, an opportunity presents itself, and people with low impulse control just say yes.

By contrast, consider the behavior of the senior executive at a large food company. The executive was scrupulously honest in his negotiations with local distributors. He would routinely lay out his cost structure in detail, thereby giving the distributors a realistic understanding of the company's pricing. This approach meant the executive couldn't always drive a hard bargain. Now, on occasion, he felt the urge to increase profits by withholding information about the company's costs. But he challenged that impulse—he saw that it made more sense in the long run to counteract it. His emotional self-regulation paid off in strong, lasting relationships with distributors that benefited the company more than any short-term financial gains would have.

The signs of emotional self-regulation, therefore, are easy to see: a propensity for reflection and thoughtfulness; comfort with ambiguity and change; and integrity—an ability to say no to impulsive urges.

Like self-awareness, self-regulation often does not get its due. People who can master their emotions are sometimes seen as cold fish—their considered responses are taken as a lack of passion. People with fiery temperaments are frequently thought of as "classic" leaders—their outbursts are considered hallmarks of charisma and power. But when such people make it to the top, their impulsiveness often works against them. In my research, extreme displays of negative emotion have never emerged as a driver of good leadership.

Motivation

If there is one trait that virtually all effective leaders have, it is motivation. They are driven to achieve beyond expectations—their own and everyone else's. The key word here is *achieve*. Plenty of people are motivated by external factors, such as a big salary or the status that comes from having an impressive title or being part of a prestigious company. By contrast, those with leadership potential are motivated by a deeply embedded desire to achieve for the sake of achievement.

If you are looking for leaders, how can you identify people who are motivated by the drive to achieve rather than by external rewards? The first sign is a passion for the work itself—such people seek out creative challenges, love to learn, and take great pride in a job well done. They also display an unflagging energy to do things better. People with such energy often seem restless with the status quo. They are persistent with their questions about why things are done one way rather than another; they are eager to explore new approaches to their work.

A cosmetics company manager, for example, was frustrated that he had to wait two weeks to get sales results from people in the field. He finally tracked down an automated phone system that would beep each of his salespeople at 5 pm every day. An automated message then prompted them to punch in their numbers—how many calls and sales they had made that day. The system shortened the feedback time on sales results from weeks to hours.

That story illustrates two other common traits of people who are driven to achieve. They are forever raising the performance bar, and they like to keep score. Take the performance bar first. During performance reviews, people with high levels of motivation might ask to be "stretched" by their superiors. Of course, an employee who combines self-awareness with internal motivation will recognize her limits—but she won't settle for objectives that seem too easy to fulfill.

And it follows naturally that people who are driven to do better also want a way of tracking progress—their own, their team's, and their company's. Whereas people with low achievement motivation are often fuzzy about results, those with high achievement motivation often keep score by tracking such hard measures as profitability or market share. I know of a money manager who starts and ends his day on the Internet, gauging the performance of his stock fund against four industry-set benchmarks.

Interestingly, people with high motivation remain optimistic even when the score is against them. In such cases, self-regulation combines with achievement motivation to overcome the frustration and depression that come after a setback or failure. Take the case of another portfolio manager at a large investment company. After several successful years, her fund tumbled for three consecutive quarters, leading three large institutional clients to shift their business elsewhere.

Some executives would have blamed the nosedive on circumstances outside their control; others might have seen the setback as evidence of personal failure. This portfolio manager, however, saw an opportunity to prove she could lead a turnaround. Two years later, when she was promoted to a very senior level in the company, she described the experience as "the best thing that ever happened to me; I learned so much from it."

Executives trying to recognize high levels of achievement motivation in their people can look for one last piece of evidence: commitment to the organization. When people love their jobs for the work itself, they often feel committed to the organizations that make that work possible. Committed employees are likely to stay with an organization even when they are pursued by headhunters waving money.

It's not difficult to understand how and why a motivation to achieve translates into strong leadership. If you set the performance bar high for yourself, you will do the same for the organization when you are in a position to do so. Likewise, a drive to surpass goals and an interest in keeping score can be contagious. Leaders with these traits can often build a team of managers around them with the same traits. And of course, optimism and organizational commitment are fundamental to leadership—just try to imagine running a company without them.

Empathy

Of all the dimensions of emotional intelligence, empathy is the most easily recognized. We have all felt the empathy of a sensitive teacher or friend; we have all been struck by its absence in an unfeeling coach or boss. But when it comes to business, we rarely hear people praised, let alone rewarded, for their empathy. The very word seems unbusinesslike, out of place amid the tough realities of the marketplace.

But empathy doesn't mean a kind of "I'm OK, you're OK" mushiness. For a leader, that is, it doesn't mean adopting other people's emotions as one's own and trying to please everybody. That would be a nightmare—it would make action impossible. Rather, empathy means thoughtfully considering employees' feelings—along with other factors—in the process of making intelligent decisions.

For an example of empathy in action, consider what happened when two giant brokerage companies merged, creating redundant jobs in all their divisions. One division manager called his people together and gave a gloomy speech that emphasized the number of people who would soon be fired. The manager of another division gave his people a different kind of speech. He was up-front about his own worry and confusion, and he promised to keep people informed and to treat everyone fairly.

The difference between these two managers was empathy. The first manager was too worried about his own fate to consider the feelings of his anxiety-stricken colleagues. The second knew intuitively what his people were feeling, and he acknowledged their fears with his words. Is it any surprise that the first manager saw his division sink as many demoralized people, especially the most talented, departed? By contrast, the second manager continued to be a strong leader, his best people stayed, and his division remained as productive as ever.

Empathy is particularly important today as a component of leadership for at least three reasons: the increasing use of teams; the rapid pace of globalization; and the growing need to retain talent.

Consider the challenge of leading a team. As anyone who has ever been a part of one can attest, teams are cauldrons of bubbling emotions. They are often charged with reaching a consensus—which is hard enough with two people and much more difficult as the numbers increase. Even in groups with as few as four or five members, alliances form and clashing agendas get set. A team's leader must be able to sense and understand the viewpoints of everyone around the table.

That's exactly what a marketing manager at a large information technology company was able to do when she was appointed to lead a troubled team. The group was in turmoil, overloaded by work and missing deadlines. Tensions were high among the members. Tinkering with procedures was not enough to bring the group together and make it an effective part of the company.

So the manager took several steps. In a series of one-on-one sessions, she took the time to listen to everyone in the group—what was frustrating them, how they rated their colleagues, whether they felt they had been ignored. And then she directed the team in a way that brought it together: She encouraged people to speak more openly about their frustrations, and she helped people raise constructive complaints during meetings. In short, her empathy allowed her to understand her team's emotional makeup. The result was not just heightened collaboration among members but also added business, as the team was called on for help by a wider range of internal clients.

Globalization is another reason for the rising importance of empathy for business leaders. Cross-cultural dialogue can easily lead to miscues and misunderstandings. Empathy is an antidote. People who have it are attuned to subtleties in body language; they can hear the message beneath the words being spoken. Beyond that, they have a deep understanding of both the existence and the importance of cultural and ethnic differences.

Consider the case of an American consultant whose team had just pitched a project to a potential Japanese client. In its dealings with Americans, the team was accustomed to being bombarded with questions after such a proposal, but this time it was greeted with a long silence. Other members of the team, taking the silence as disapproval, were ready to pack and leave. The lead consultant gestured them to stop. Although he was not particularly familiar with Japanese culture, he read the client's face and posture and sensed not rejection but interest—even deep consideration. He was right: When the client finally spoke, it was to give the consulting firm the job.

Finally, empathy plays a key role in the retention of talent, particularly in today's information economy. Leaders have always needed empathy to develop and keep good people, but today the stakes are higher. When good people leave, they take the company's knowledge with them.

That's where coaching and mentoring come in. It has repeatedly been shown that coaching and mentoring pay off not just in better performance but also in increased job satisfaction and decreased turnover. But what makes coaching and mentoring work best is the nature of the relationship. Outstanding coaches and mentors get inside the heads of the people they are helping. They sense how to give effective feedback. They know when to push for better performance and when to hold back. In the way they motivate their protégés, they demonstrate empathy in action.

In what is probably sounding like a refrain, let me repeat that empathy doesn't get much respect in business. People wonder how leaders can make hard decisions if they are "feeling" for all the people who will be affected. But leaders with empathy do more than sympathize with people around them: They use their knowledge to improve their companies in subtle but important ways.

Social Skill

The first three components of emotional intelligence are self-management skills. The last two, empathy and social skill, concern a person's ability to manage relationships with others. As a component of emotional intelligence, social skill is not as simple as it sounds. It's not just a matter of friendliness, although people with high levels of social skill are rarely mean-spirited. Social skill, rather, is friendliness with a purpose: moving people in the direction you desire, whether that's agreement on a new marketing strategy or enthusiasm about a new product.

Socially skilled people tend to have a wide circle of acquaintances, and they have a knack for finding common ground with people of all kinds—a knack for building rapport. That doesn't mean they socialize continually; it means they work according to the assumption that nothing important gets done alone. Such people have a network in place when the time for action comes.

Social skill is the culmination of the other dimensions of emotional intelligence. People tend to be very effective at managing relationships when they can understand and control their own emotions and can empathize with the feelings of others. Even motivation contributes to social skill. Remember that people who are driven to achieve tend to be optimistic, even in the face of setbacks or failure. When people are upbeat, their "glow" is cast upon conversations and other social encounters. They are popular, and for good reason.

Because it is the outcome of the other dimensions of emotional intelligence, social skill is recognizable on the job in many ways that will by now sound familiar. Socially skilled people, for instance, are adept at managing teams—that's their empathy at work. Likewise, they are expert persuaders—a manifestation of self-awareness, self-regulation, and empathy combined. Given those skills, good persuaders know when to make an emotional plea, for instance, and when an appeal to reason will work better. And motivation, when publicly visible, makes such people excellent collaborators; their passion for the work spreads to others, and they are driven to find solutions.

But sometimes social skill shows itself in ways the other emotional intelligence components do not. For instance, socially skilled people may at times appear not to be working while at work. They seem to be idly schmoozing—chatting in the hallways with colleagues or joking around with people who are not even connected to their "real" jobs. Socially skilled people, however, don't think it makes sense to arbitrarily limit the scope of their relationships. They build bonds widely because they know that in these fluid times, they may need help someday from people they are just getting to know today.

For example, consider the case of an executive in the strategy department of a global computer manufacturer. By 1993, he was convinced that the company's future lay with the Internet. Over the course of the next year, he found kindred spirits and used his social skill to stitch together a virtual community that cut across levels, divisions, and nations. He then used this de facto team to put up a corporate Web site, among the first by a major company. And, on his own initiative, with no budget or formal status, he signed up the company to participate in an annual Internet industry convention. Calling on his allies and persuading various divisions to donate funds, he recruited more than 50 people from a dozen different units to represent the company at the convention.

Management took notice: Within a year of the conference, the executive's team formed the basis for the company's first Internet division, and he was formally put in charge of it. To get there, the executive had ignored conventional boundaries, forging and maintaining connections with people in every corner of the organization.

Is social skill considered a key leadership capability in most companies? The answer is yes, especially when compared with the other components of emotional intelligence. People seem to know intuitively that leaders need to manage relationships effectively; no leader is an island. After all, the leader's task is to get work done through other people, and social skill makes that possible. A leader who cannot express her empathy may as well not have it at all. And a leader's motivation will be useless if he cannot communicate his passion to the organization. Social skill allows leaders to put their emotional intelligence to work.

It would be foolish to assert that good-old-fashioned IQ and technical ability are not important ingredients in strong leadership. But the recipe would not be complete without emotional intelligence. It was once thought that the components of emotional intelligence were "nice to have" in business leaders. But now we know that, for the sake of performance, these are ingredients that leaders "need to have."

It is fortunate, then, that emotional intelligence can be learned. The process is not easy. It takes time and, most of all, commitment. But the benefits that come from having a well-developed emotional intelligence, both for the individual and for the organization, make it worth the effort.

Originally published in June 1996. Reprint R0401H

What Makes an Effective Executive

by Peter F. Drucker

AN EFFECTIVE EXECUTIVE DOES NOT need to be a leader in the sense that the term is now most commonly used. Harry Truman did not have one ounce of charisma, for example, yet he was among the most effective chief executives in U.S. history. Similarly, some of the best business and nonprofit CEOs I've worked with over a 65-year consulting career were not stereotypical leaders. They were all over the map in terms of their personalities, attitudes, values, strengths, and weaknesses. They ranged from extroverted to nearly reclusive, from easygoing to controlling, from generous to parsimonious.

What made them all effective is that they followed the same eight practices:

- They asked, "What needs to be done?"
- They asked, "What is right for the enterprise?"
- They developed action plans.
- They took responsibility for decisions.
- They took responsibility for communicating.
- They were focused on opportunities rather than problems.

- They ran productive meetings.
- They thought and said "we" rather than "I."

The first two practices gave them the knowledge they needed. The next four helped them convert this knowledge into effective action. The last two ensured that the whole organization felt responsible and accountable.

Get the Knowledge You Need

The first practice is to ask what needs to be done. Note that the question is not "What do I want to do?" Asking what has to be done, and taking the question seriously, is crucial for managerial success. Failure to ask this question will render even the ablest executive ineffectual.

When Truman became president in 1945, he knew exactly what he wanted to do: complete the economic and social reforms of Roosevelt's New Deal, which had been deferred by World War II. As soon as he asked what needed to be done, though, Truman realized that foreign affairs had absolute priority. He organized his working day so that it began with tutorials on foreign policy by the secretaries of state and defense. As a result, he became the most effective president in foreign affairs the United States has ever known. He contained Communism in both Europe and Asia and, with the Marshall Plan, triggered 50 years of worldwide economic growth.

Similarly, Jack Welch realized that what needed to be done at General Electric when he took over as chief executive was not the overseas expansion he wanted to launch. It was getting rid of GE businesses that, no matter how profitable, could not be number one or number two in their industries.

The answer to the question "What needs to be done?" almost always contains more than one urgent task. But effective executives do not splinter themselves. They concentrate on one task if at all possible. If they are among those people—a sizable minority—who work best with a change of pace in their working day, they pick two tasks. I have never encountered an executive who remains effective while tackling more than two tasks at a time. Hence, after asking what

Idea in Brief

Worried that you're not a born leader? That you lack charisma, the right talents, or some other secret ingredient? No need: leadership isn't about personality or talent. In fact, the best leaders exhibit wildly different personalities, attitudes, values, and strengths—they're extroverted or reclusive, easygoing or controlling, generous or parsimonious, numbers or vision oriented.

So what do effective leaders have in common? They get the right things done, in the right ways—by following eight simple rules:

- Ask what needs to be done.
- Ask what's right for the enterprise.
- Develop action plans.
- Take responsibility for decisions.
- Take responsibility for communicating.
- Focus on opportunities, not problems.
- Run productive meetings.
- Think and say "We," not "I."

Using discipline to apply these rules, you gain the knowledge you need to make smart decisions, convert that knowledge into effective action, and ensure accountability throughout your organization.

needs to be done, the effective executive sets priorities and sticks to them. For a CEO, the priority task might be redefining the company's mission. For a unit head, it might be redefining the unit's relationship with headquarters. Other tasks, no matter how important or appealing, are postponed. However, after completing the original top-priority task, the executive resets priorities rather than moving on to number two from the original list. He asks, "What must be done now?" This generally results in new and different priorities.

To refer again to America's best-known CEO: Every five years, according to his autobiography, Jack Welch asked himself, "What needs to be done *now?*" And every time, he came up with a new and different priority.

But Welch also thought through another issue before deciding where to concentrate his efforts for the next five years. He asked himself which of the two or three tasks at the top of the list he himself was best suited to undertake. Then he concentrated on that

Idea in Practice

Get the Knowledge You Need

Ask what needs to be done. When Jack Welch asked this question while taking over as CEO at General Electric, he realized that dropping GE businesses that couldn't be first or second in their industries was essential—not the overseas expansion he had wanted to launch. Once you know what must be done, identify tasks you're best at, concentrating on one at a time. After completing a task, reset priorities based on new realities.

Ask what's right for the enterprise. Don't agonize over what's best for owners, investors, employees, or customers. Decisions that are right for your *enterprise* are ultimately right for all stakeholders.

Convert Your Knowledge into Action

Develop action plans. Devise plans that specify *desired results* and *constraints* (Is the course of action legal and compatible with the company's mission, values, and policies?). Include *check-in points* and *implications for how you'll spend your time*. And *revise* plans to reflect new opportunities.

Take responsibility for decisions. Ensure that each decision specifies who's accountable for carrying it out, when it must be implemented, who'll be affected by it, and who must be informed. Regularly review decisions, especially hires and promotions. This enables you to correct poor decisions before doing real damage.

Take responsibility for communicating. Get input from superiors, subordinates, and peers on your action plans. Let each know what information you need to get the

task; the others he delegated. Effective executives try to focus on jobs they'll do especially well. They know that enterprises perform if top management performs—and don't if it doesn't.

Effective executives' second practice—fully as important as the first—is to ask, "Is this the right thing for the enterprise?" They do not ask if it's right for the owners, the stock price, the employees, or the executives. Of course they know that shareholders, employees, and executives are important constituencies who have to support a decision, or at least acquiesce in it, if the choice is to be effective. They know that the share price is important not only for the shareholders but also for the enterprise, since the price/earnings ratio sets the cost

job done. Pay equal attention to peers' and superiors' information needs.

Focus on opportunities, not problems. You get results by exploiting opportunities, not solving problems. Identify changes inside and outside your organization (new technologies, product innovations, new market structures), asking "How can we exploit this change to benefit our enterprise?" Then match your best people with the best opportunities.

Ensure Companywide Accountability

Run productive meetings. Articulate each meeting's purpose (Making an announcement? Delivering a report?). Terminate the meeting once the purpose is accomplished. Follow up with short communications summarizing the discussion, spelling out new work assignments and deadlines for completing them. General Motors CEO Alfred Sloan's legendary mastery of meeting follow-up helped secure GM's industry dominance in the mid-twentieth century.

Think and say "We," not "I." Your authority comes from your organization's trust in you. To get the best results, always consider your organization's needs and opportunities before your own.

of capital. But they also know that a decision that isn't right for the enterprise will ultimately not be right for any of the stakeholders.

This second practice is especially important for executives at family owned or family run businesses—the majority of businesses in every country—particularly when they're making decisions about people. In the successful family company, a relative is promoted only if he or she is measurably superior to all nonrelatives on the same level. At DuPont, for instance, all top managers (except the controller and lawyer) were family members in the early years when the firm was run as a family business. All male descendants of the founders were entitled to entry-level jobs at the company. Beyond the entrance level, a family member got a promotion only if a panel composed primarily of nonfamily managers judged the person to be superior in ability and performance to all other employees at the same level. The same rule was observed for a century in the highly successful British family business J. Lyons & Company (now part of a major conglomerate) when it dominated the British food-service and hotel industries.

Asking "What is right for the enterprise?" does not guarantee that the right decision will be made. Even the most brilliant executive is human and thus prone to mistakes and prejudices. But failure to ask the question virtually guarantees the *wrong* decision.

Write an Action Plan

Executives are doers; they execute. Knowledge is useless to executives until it has been translated into deeds. But before springing into action, the executive needs to plan his course. He needs to think about desired results, probable restraints, future revisions, check-in points, and implications for how he'll spend his time.

First, the executive defines desired results by asking: "What contributions should the enterprise expect from me over the next 18 months to two years? What results will I commit to? With what deadlines?" Then he considers the restraints on action: "Is this course of action ethical? Is it acceptable within the organization? Is it legal? Is it compatible with the mission, values, and policies of the organization?" Affirmative answers don't guarantee that the action will be effective. But violating these restraints is certain to make it both wrong and ineffectual.

The action plan is a statement of intentions rather than a commitment. It must not become a straitjacket. It should be revised often, because every success creates new opportunities. So does every failure. The same is true for changes in the business environment, in the market, and especially in people within the enterprise—all these changes demand that the plan be revised. A written plan should anticipate the need for flexibility.

In addition, the action plan needs to create a system for checking the results against the expectations. Effective executives usually build two such checks into their action plans. The first check comes halfway through the plan's time period; for example, at nine months. The second occurs at the end, before the next action plan is drawn up.

Finally, the action plan has to become the basis for the executive's time management. Time is an executive's scarcest and most precious resource. And organizations—whether government agencies, businesses, or nonprofits—are inherently time wasters. The action plan will prove useless unless it's allowed to determine how the executive spends his or her time.

Napoleon allegedly said that no successful battle ever followed its plan. Yet Napoleon also planned every one of his battles, far more meticulously than any earlier general had done. Without an action plan, the executive becomes a prisoner of events. And without check-ins to reexamine the plan as events unfold, the executive has no way of knowing which events really matter and which are only noise.

Act

When they translate plans into action, executives need to pay particular attention to decision making, communication, opportunities (as opposed to problems), and meetings. I'll consider these one at a time.

Take responsibility for decisions

A decision has not been made until people know:

- the name of the person accountable for carrying it out;
- the deadline;
- the names of the people who will be affected by the decision and therefore have to know about, understand, and approve it—or at least not be strongly opposed to it—and
- the names of the people who have to be informed of the decision, even if they are not directly affected by it.

An extraordinary number of organizational decisions run into trouble because these bases aren't covered. One of my clients,

30 years ago, lost its leadership position in the fast-growing Japanese market because the company, after deciding to enter into a joint venture with a new Japanese partner, never made clear who was to inform the purchasing agents that the partner defined its specifications in meters and kilograms rather than feet and pounds—and nobody ever did relay that information.

It's just as important to review decisions periodically—at a time that's been agreed on in advance—as it is to make them carefully in the first place. That way, a poor decision can be corrected before it does real damage. These reviews can cover anything from the results to the assumptions underlying the decision.

Such a review is especially important for the most crucial and most difficult of all decisions, the ones about hiring or promoting people. Studies of decisions about people show that only one-third of such choices turn out to be truly successful. One-third are likely to be draws—neither successes nor outright failures. And one-third are failures, pure and simple. Effective executives know this and check up (six to nine months later) on the results of their people decisions. If they find that a decision has not had the desired results, they don't conclude that the person has not performed. They conclude, instead, that they themselves made a mistake. In a well-managed enterprise, it is understood that people who fail in a new job, especially after a promotion, may not be the ones to blame.

Executives also owe it to the organization and to their fellow workers not to tolerate nonperforming individuals in important jobs. It may not be the employees' fault that they are underperforming, but even so, they have to be removed. People who have failed in a new job should be given the choice to go back to a job at their former level and salary. This option is rarely exercised; such people, as a rule, leave voluntarily, at least when their employers are U.S. firms. But the very existence of the option can have a powerful effect, encouraging people to leave safe, comfortable jobs and take risky new assignments. The organization's performance depends on employees' willingness to take such chances.

A systematic decision review can be a powerful tool for self-development, too. Checking the results of a decision against its expectations shows executives what their strengths are, where they need to improve, and where they lack knowledge or information. It shows them their biases. Very often it shows them that their decisions didn't produce results because they didn't put the right people on the job. Allocating the best people to the right positions is a crucial, tough job that many executives slight, in part because the best people are already too busy. Systematic decision review also shows executives their own weaknesses, particularly the areas in which they are simply incompetent. In these areas, smart executives don't make decisions or take actions. They delegate. Everyone has such areas; there's no such thing as a universal executive genius.

Most discussions of decision making assume that only senior executives make decisions or that only senior executives' decisions matter. This is a dangerous mistake. Decisions are made at every level of the organization, beginning with individual professional contributors and frontline supervisors. These apparently low-level decisions are extremely important in a knowledge-based organization. Knowledge workers are supposed to know more about their areas of specialization—for example, tax accounting—than anybody else, so their decisions are likely to have an impact throughout the company. Making good decisions is a crucial skill at every level. It needs to be taught explicitly to everyone in organizations that are based on knowledge.

Take responsibility for communicating

Effective executives make sure that both their action plans and their information needs are understood. Specifically, this means that they share their plans with and ask for comments from all their colleagues—superiors, subordinates, and peers. At the same time, they let each person know what information they'll need to get the job done. The information flow from subordinate to boss is usually what gets the most attention. But executives need to pay equal attention to peers' and superiors' information needs.

We all know, thanks to Chester Barnard's 1938 classic *The Functions of the Executive,* that organizations are held together by information rather than by ownership or command. Still, far too many executives behave as if information and its flow were the job of the information specialist—for example, the accountant. As a result, they get an enormous amount of data they do not need and cannot use, but little of the information they do need. The best way around this problem is for each executive to identify the information he needs, ask for it, and keep pushing until he gets it.

Focus on opportunities

Good executives focus on opportunities rather than problems. Problems have to be taken care of, of course; they must not be swept under the rug. But problem solving, however necessary, does not produce results. It prevents damage. Exploiting opportunities produces results.

Above all, effective executives treat change as an opportunity rather than a threat. They systematically look at changes, inside and outside the corporation, and ask, "How can we exploit this change as an opportunity for our enterprise?" Specifically, executives scan these seven situations for opportunities:

- an unexpected success or failure in their own enterprise, in a competing enterprise, or in the industry;
- a gap between what is and what could be in a market, process, product, or service (for example, in the nineteenth century, the paper industry concentrated on the 10% of each tree that became wood pulp and totally neglected the possibilities in the remaining 90%, which became waste);
- innovation in a process, product, or service, whether inside or outside the enterprise or its industry;
- changes in industry structure and market structure;
- demographics;
- changes in mind-set, values, perception, mood, or meaning; and
- new knowledge or a new technology.

Effective executives also make sure that problems do not overwhelm opportunities. In most companies, the first page of the monthly management report lists key problems. It's far wiser to list opportunities on the first page and leave problems for the second page. Unless there is a true catastrophe, problems are not discussed in management meetings until opportunities have been analyzed and properly dealt with.

Staffing is another important aspect of being opportunity focused. Effective executives put their best people on opportunities rather than on problems. One way to staff for opportunities is to ask each member of the management group to prepare two lists every six months—a list of opportunities for the entire enterprise and a list of the best-performing people throughout the enterprise. These are discussed, then melded into two master lists, and the best people are matched with the best opportunities. In Japan, by the way, this matchup is considered a major HR task in a big corporation or government department; that practice is one of the key strengths of Japanese business.

Make meetings productive

The most visible, powerful, and, arguably, effective nongovernmental executive in the America of World War II and the years thereafter was not a businessman. It was Francis Cardinal Spellman, the head of the Roman Catholic Archdiocese of New York and adviser to several U.S. presidents. When Spellman took over, the diocese was bankrupt and totally demoralized. His successor inherited the leadership position in the American Catholic church. Spellman often said that during his waking hours he was alone only twice each day, for 25 minutes each time: when he said Mass in his private chapel after getting up in the morning and when he said his evening prayers before going to bed. Otherwise he was always with people in a meeting, starting at breakfast with one Catholic organization and ending at dinner with another.

Top executives aren't quite as imprisoned as the archbishop of a major Catholic diocese. But every study of the executive workday has found that even junior executives and professionals are with other people—that is, in a meeting of some sort—more than half of every business day. The only exceptions are a few senior researchers. Even a conversation with only one other person is a meeting. Hence, if they are to be effective, executives must make meetings productive. They must make sure that meetings are work sessions rather than bull sessions.

The key to running an effective meeting is to decide in advance what kind of meeting it will be. Different kinds of meetings require different forms of preparation and different results.

A meeting to prepare a statement, an announcement, or a press release. For this to be productive, one member has to prepare a draft beforehand. At the meeting's end, a preappointed member has to take responsibility for disseminating the final text.

A meeting to make an announcement—for example, an organizational change. This meeting should be confined to the announcement and a discussion about it.

A meeting in which one member reports. Nothing but the report should be discussed.

A meeting in which several or all members report. Either there should be no discussion at all or the discussion should be limited to questions for clarification. Alternatively, for each report there could be a short discussion in which all participants may ask questions. If this is the format, the reports should be distributed to all participants well before the meeting. At this kind of meeting, each report should be limited to a preset time—for example, 15 minutes.

A meeting to inform the convening executive. The executive should listen and ask questions. He or she should sum up but not make a presentation.

A meeting whose only function is to allow the participants to be in the executive's presence. Cardinal Spellman's breakfast and dinner meetings were of that kind. There is no way to make these meetings productive. They are the penalties of rank. Senior executives are effective to the extent to which they can prevent such meetings from encroaching on their workdays. Spellman, for instance, was effective in large part because he confined such meetings to breakfast and dinner and kept the rest of his working day free of them.

Making a meeting productive takes a good deal of self-discipline. It requires that executives determine what kind of meeting is appropriate and then stick to that format. It's also necessary to terminate the meeting as soon as its specific purpose has been accomplished. Good executives don't raise another matter for discussion. They sum up and adjourn.

Good follow-up is just as important as the meeting itself. The great master of follow-up was Alfred Sloan, the most effective business executive I have ever known. Sloan, who headed General Motors from the 1920s until the 1950s, spent most of his six working days a week in meetings—three days a week in formal committee meetings with a set membership, the other three days in ad hoc meetings with individual GM executives or with a small group of executives. At the beginning of a formal meeting, Sloan announced the meeting's purpose. He then listened. He never took notes and he rarely spoke except to clarify a confusing point. At the end he summed up, thanked the participants, and left. Then he immediately wrote a short memo addressed to one attendee of the meeting. In that note, he summarized the discussion and its conclusions and spelled out any work assignment decided upon in the meeting (including a decision to hold another meeting on the subject or to study an issue). He specified the deadline and the executive who was to be accountable for the assignment. He sent a copy of the memo to everyone who'd been present at the meeting. It was through these memos—each a small masterpiece—that Sloan made himself into an outstandingly effective executive.

Effective executives know that any given meeting is either productive or a total waste of time.

Think and Say "We"

The final practice is this: Don't think or say "I." Think and say "we." Effective executives know that they have ultimate responsibility, which can be neither shared nor delegated. But they have authority only because they have the trust of the organization. This means that they think of the needs and the opportunities of the organization before they think of their own needs and opportunities. This one may sound simple; it isn't, but it needs to be strictly observed.

We've just reviewed eight practices of effective executives. I'm going to throw in one final, bonus practice. This one's so important that I'll elevate it to the level of a rule: *Listen first, speak last.*

Effective executives differ widely in their personalities, strengths, weaknesses, values, and beliefs. All they have in common is that they get the right things done. Some are born effective. But the demand is much too great to be satisfied by extraordinary talent. Effectiveness is a discipline. And, like every discipline, effectiveness *can* be learned and *must* be earned.

Originally published in June 2004. Reprint R0406C

What Leaders Really Do

by John P. Kotter

LEADERSHIP IS DIFFERENT FROM MANAGEMENT, but not for the reasons most people think. Leadership isn't mystical and mysterious. It has nothing to do with having "charisma" or other exotic personality traits. It is not the province of a chosen few. Nor is leadership necessarily better than management or a replacement for it.

Rather, leadership and management are two distinctive and complementary systems of action. Each has its own function and characteristic activities. Both are necessary for success in an increasingly complex and volatile business environment.

Most U.S. corporations today are over-managed and underled. They need to develop their capacity to exercise leadership. Successful corporations don't wait for leaders to come along. They actively seek out people with leadership potential and expose them to career experiences designed to develop that potential. Indeed, with careful selection, nurturing, and encouragement, dozens of people can play important leadership roles in a business organization.

But while improving their ability to lead, companies should remember that strong leadership with weak management is no better, and is sometimes actually worse, than the reverse. The real challenge is to combine strong leadership and strong management and use each to balance the other.

Of course, not everyone can be good at both leading and managing. Some people have the capacity to become excellent managers but not strong leaders. Others have great leadership potential but, for a variety of reasons, have great difficulty becoming strong managers. Smart companies value both kinds of people and work hard to make them a part of the team.

But when it comes to preparing people for executive jobs, such companies rightly ignore the recent literature that says people cannot manage *and* lead. They try to develop leader-managers. Once companies understand the fundamental difference between leadership and management, they can begin to groom their top people to provide both.

The Difference Between Management and Leadership

Management is about coping with complexity. Its practices and procedures are largely a response to one of the most significant developments of the twentieth century: the emergence of large organizations. Without good management, complex enterprises tend to become chaotic in ways that threaten their very existence. Good management brings a degree of order and consistency to key dimensions like the quality and profitability of products.

Leadership, by contrast, is about coping with change. Part of the reason it has become so important in recent years is that the business world has become more competitive and more volatile. Faster technological change, greater international competition, the deregulation of markets, overcapacity in capital-intensive industries, an unstable oil cartel, raiders with junk bonds, and the changing demographics of the work-force are among the many factors that have contributed to this shift. The net result is that doing what was done yesterday, or doing it 5% better, is no longer a formula for success. Major changes are more and more necessary to survive and compete effectively in this new environment. More change always demands more leadership.

Consider a simple military analogy: A peacetime army can usually survive with good administration and management up and down

Idea in Brief

The most pernicious half-truth about leadership is that it's just a matter of charisma and vision—you either have it or you don't. The fact of the matter is that leadership skills are not innate. They can be acquired, and honed. But first you have to appreciate how they differ from management skills.

Management is about coping with *complexity*; it brings order and predictability to a situation. But that's no longer enough—to succeed, companies must be able to adapt to change. Leadership, then, is about learning how to cope with rapid *change*.

How does this distinction play out?

- Management involves planning and budgeting. Leadership involves setting direction.
- Management involves organizing and staffing. Leadership involves aligning people.
- Management provides control and solves problems. Leadership provides motivation.

the hierarchy, coupled with good leadership concentrated at the very top. A wartime army, however, needs competent leadership at all levels. No one yet has figured out how to manage people effectively into battle; they must be led.

These two different functions—coping with complexity and coping with change—shape the characteristic activities of management and leadership. Each system of action involves deciding what needs to be done, creating networks of people and relationships that can accomplish an agenda, and then trying to ensure that those people actually do the job. But each accomplishes these three tasks in different ways.

Companies manage complexity first by *planning and budgeting*—setting targets or goals for the future (typically for the next month or year), establishing detailed steps for achieving those targets, and then allocating resources to accomplish those plans. By contrast, leading an organization to constructive change begins by *setting a direction*—developing a vision of the future (often the distant future) along with strategies for producing the changes needed to achieve that vision.

Management develops the capacity to achieve its plan by *organizing and staffing*—creating an organizational structure and set of jobs for accomplishing plan requirements, staffing the jobs

Idea in Practice

Management and leadership both involve deciding what needs to be done, creating networks of people to accomplish the agenda, and ensuring that the work actually gets done. Their work is complementary, but each system of action goes about the tasks in different ways.

1. Planning and budgeting versus setting direction. The aim of management is predictability—orderly results. Leadership's function is to produce change. Setting the direction of that change, therefore, is essential work. There's nothing mystical about this work, but it is more inductive than planning and budgeting. It involves the search for patterns and relationships. And it doesn't produce detailed plans; instead, direction-setting results in visions and the overarching strategies for realizing them.

> ***Example:*** In mature industries, increased competition usually dampens growth. But at American Express, Lou Gerstner bucked this trend, successfully crafting a vision of a dynamic enterprise.
>
> The new direction he set wasn't a mere attention-grabbing scheme—it was the result of asking fundamental questions about market and competitive forces.

2. Organizing and staffing versus aligning people. Managers look for the right fit between people and jobs. This is essentially a design problem: setting up systems to ensure that plans are implemented precisely and efficiently. Leaders, however, look for the right fit between people and the vision. This is more of a communication problem. It involves getting a large number of people, inside and outside the company, first to believe in an alternative future—and then to take initiative based on that shared vision.

3. Controlling activities and solving problems versus motivating and inspiring. Management strives to make it easy for people to complete routine jobs day after day. But since high energy is essential to overcoming the barriers to change, leaders attempt to touch people at their deepest levels—by stirring in them a sense of belonging, idealism, and self-esteem.

> ***Example:*** At Procter & Gamble's paper products division, Richard Nicolosi underscored the message that "each of us is a leader" by pushing responsibility down to newly formed teams. An entrepreneurial attitude took root, and profits rebounded.

with qualified individuals, communicating the plan to those people, delegating responsibility for carrying out the plan, and devising systems to monitor implementation. The equivalent leadership activity, however, is *aligning people*. This means communicating the new direction to those who can create coalitions that understand the vision and are committed to its achievement.

Finally, management ensures plan accomplishment by *controlling and problem solving*—monitoring results versus the plan in some detail, both formally and informally, by means of reports, meetings, and other tools; identifying deviations; and then planning and organizing to solve the problems. But for leadership, achieving a vision requires *motivating and inspiring*—keeping people moving in the right direction, despite major obstacles to change, by appealing to basic but often untapped human needs, values, and emotions.

A closer examination of each of these activities will help clarify the skills leaders need.

Setting a Direction Versus Planning and Budgeting

Since the function of leadership is to produce change, setting the direction of that change is fundamental to leadership. Setting direction is never the same as planning or even long-term planning, although people often confuse the two. Planning is a management process, deductive in nature and designed to produce orderly results, not change. Setting a direction is more inductive. Leaders gather a broad range of data and look for patterns, relationships, and linkages that help explain things. What's more, the direction-setting aspect of leadership does not produce plans; it creates vision and strategies. These describe a business, technology, or corporate culture in terms of what it should become over the long term and articulate a feasible way of achieving this goal.

Most discussions of vision have a tendency to degenerate into the mystical. The implication is that a vision is something mysterious that mere mortals, even talented ones, could never hope to have. But developing good business direction isn't magic. It is a tough, sometimes exhausting process of gathering and analyzing information.

Aligning People: Chuck Trowbridge and Bob Crandall at Eastman Kodak

EASTMAN KODAK ENTERED THE copy business in the early 1970s, concentrating on technically sophisticated machines that sold, on average, for about $60,000 each. Over the next decade, this business grew to nearly $1 billion in revenues. But costs were high, profits were hard to find, and problems were nearly everywhere. In 1984, Kodak had to write off $40 million in inventory. Most people at the company knew there were problems, but they couldn't agree on how to solve them. So in his first two months as general manager of the new copy products group, established in 1984, Chuck Trowbridge met with nearly every key person inside his group, as well as with people elsewhere at Kodak who could be important to the copier business. An especially crucial area was the engineering and manufacturing organization, headed by Bob Crandall.

Trowbridge and Crandall's vision for engineering and manufacturing was simple: to become a world-class manufacturing operation and to create a less bureaucratic and more decentralized organization. Still, this message was difficult to convey because it was such a radical departure from previous communications, not only in the copy products group but throughout most of Kodak. So Crandall set up dozens of vehicles to emphasize the new direction and align people to it: weekly meetings with his own 12 direct reports; monthly "copy product forums" in which a different employee from each of his departments would meet with him as a group; discussions of recent improvements and new projects to achieve still better results; and quarterly "State of the Department" meetings, where his managers met with everybody in their own departments.

Once a month, Crandall and all those who reported to him would also meet with 80 to 100 people from some area of his organization to discuss anything they wanted. To align his biggest supplier—the Kodak Apparatus Division,

---

People who articulate such visions aren't magicians but broad-based strategic thinkers who are willing to take risks.

Nor do visions and strategies have to be brilliantly innovative; in fact, some of the best are not. Effective business visions regularly have an almost mundane quality, usually consisting of ideas that are already well known. The particular combination or patterning of the ideas may be new, but sometimes even that is not the case.

which supplied one-third of the parts used in design and manufacturing—he and his managers met with the top management of that group over lunch every Thursday. Later, he created a format called "business meetings," where his managers meet with 12 to 20 people on a specific topic, such as inventory or master scheduling. The goal: to get all of his 1,500 employees in at least one of these focused business meetings each year.

Trowbridge and Crandall also enlisted written communication in their cause. A four- to eight-page "Copy Products Journal" was sent to employees once a month. A program called "Dialog Letters" gave employees the opportunity to anonymously ask questions of Crandall and his top managers and be guaranteed a reply. But the most visible and powerful written communications were the charts. In a main hallway near the cafeteria, these huge charts vividly reported the quality, cost, and delivery results for each product, measured against difficult targets. A hundred smaller versions of these charts were scattered throughout the manufacturing area, reporting quality levels and costs for specific work groups.

Results of this intensive alignment process began to appear within six months, and still more surfaced after a year. These successes made the message more credible and helped get more people on board. Between 1984 and 1988, quality on one of the main product lines increased nearly 100-fold. Defects per unit went from 30 to 0.3. Over a three-year period, costs on another product line went down nearly 24%. Deliveries on schedule increased from 82% in 1985 to 95% in 1987. Inventory levels dropped by over 50% between 1984 and 1988, even though the volume of products was increasing. And productivity, measured in units per manufacturing employee, more than doubled between 1985 and 1988.

For example, when CEO Jan Carlzon articulated his vision to make Scandinavian Airlines System (SAS) the best airline in the world for the frequent business traveler, he was not saying anything that everyone in the airline industry didn't already know. Business travelers fly more consistently than other market segments and are generally willing to pay higher fares. Thus, focusing on business customers offers an airline the possibility of high margins, steady business, and

Setting a Direction: Lou Gerstner at American Express

WHEN LOU GERSTNER BECAME PRESIDENT of the Travel Related Services (TRS) arm at American Express in 1979, the unit was facing one of its biggest challenges in AmEx's 130-year history. Hundreds of banks offering or planning to introduce credit cards through Visa and MasterCard that would compete with the American Express card. And more than two dozen financial service firms were coming into the traveler's checks business. In a mature marketplace, this increase in competition usually reduces margins and prohibits growth.

But that was not how Gerstner saw the business. Before joining American Express, he had spent five years as a consultant to TRS, analyzing the money-losing travel division and the increasingly competitive card operation. Gerstner and his team asked fundamental questions about the economics, market, and competition and developed a deep understanding of the business. In the process, he began to craft a vision of TRS that looked nothing like a 130-year-old company in a mature industry.

Gerstner thought TRS had the potential to become a dynamic and growing enterprise, despite the onslaught of Visa and MasterCard competition from thousands of banks. The key was to focus on the global marketplace and, specifically, on the relatively affluent customer American Express had been traditionally serving with top-of-the-line products. By further segmenting this market, aggressively developing a broad range of new products and services, and investing to increase productivity and to lower costs, TRS could provide the best service possible to customers who had enough discretionary income to buy many more services from TRS than they had in the past.

Within a week of his appointment, Gerstner brought together the people running the card organization and questioned all the principles by which they conducted their business. In particular, he challenged two widely shared beliefs—that the division should have only one product, the green card, and that this product was limited in potential for growth and innovation.

---

considerable growth. But in an industry known more for bureaucracy than vision, no company had ever put these simple ideas together and dedicated itself to implementing them. SAS did, and it worked.

What's crucial about a vision is not its originality but how well it serves the interests of important constituencies—customers,

Gerstner also moved quickly to develop a more entrepreneurial culture, to hire and train people who would thrive in it, and to clearly communicate to them the overall direction. He and other top managers rewarded intelligent risk taking. To make entrepreneurship easier, they discouraged unnecessary bureaucracy. They also upgraded hiring standards and created the TRS Graduate Management Program, which offered high-potential young people special training, an enriched set of experiences, and an unusual degree of exposure to people in top management. To encourage risk taking among all TRS employees, Gerstner also established something called the Great Performers program to recognize and reward truly exceptional customer service, a central tenet in the organization's vision.

These incentives led quickly to new markets, products, and services. TRS expanded its overseas presence dramatically. By 1988, AmEx cards were issued in 29 currencies (as opposed to only 11 a decade earlier). The unit also focused aggressively on two market segments that had historically received little attention: college students and women. In 1981, TRS combined its card and travel-service capabilities to offer corporate clients a unified system to monitor and control travel expenses. And by 1988, AmEx had grown to become the fifth largest direct-mail merchant in the United States.

Other new products and services included 90-day insurance on all purchases made with the AmEx card, a Platinum American Express card, and a revolving credit card known as Optima. In 1988, the company also switched to image-processing technology for billing, producing a more convenient monthly statement for customers and reducing billing costs by 25%.

As a result of these innovations, TRS's net income increased a phenomenal 500% between 1978 and 1987—a compounded annual rate of about 18%. The business outperformed many so-called high-tech/high-growth companies. With a 1988 return on equity of 28%, it also outperformed most low-growth but high-profit businesses.

stockholders, employees—and how easily it can be translated into a realistic competitive strategy. Bad visions tend to ignore the legitimate needs and rights of important constituencies—favoring, say, employees over customers or stockholders. Or they are strategically unsound. When a company that has never been better than a weak competitor in an industry suddenly starts talking about becoming number one, that is a pipe dream, not a vision.

One of the most frequent mistakes that overmanaged and underled corporations make is to embrace long-term planning as a panacea for their lack of direction and inability to adapt to an increasingly competitive and dynamic business environment. But such an approach misinterprets the nature of direction setting and can never work.

Long-term planning is always time consuming. Whenever something unexpected happens, plans have to be redone. In a dynamic business environment, the unexpected often becomes the norm, and long-term planning can become an extraordinarily burdensome activity. That is why most successful corporations limit the time frame of their planning activities. Indeed, some even consider "long-term planning" a contradiction in terms.

In a company without direction, even short-term planning can become a black hole capable of absorbing an infinite amount of time and energy. With no vision and strategy to provide constraints around the planning process or to guide it, every eventuality deserves a plan. Under these circumstances, contingency planning can go on forever, draining time and attention from far more essential activities, yet without ever providing the clear sense of direction that a company desperately needs. After awhile, managers inevitably become cynical, and the planning process can degenerate into a highly politicized game.

Planning works best not as a substitute for direction setting but as a complement to it. A competent planning process serves as a useful reality check on direction-setting activities. Likewise, a competent direction-setting process provides a focus in which planning can then be realistically carried out. It helps clarify what kind of planning is essential and what kind is irrelevant.

Aligning People Versus Organizing and Staffing

A central feature of modern organizations is interdependence, where no one has complete autonomy, where most employees are tied to many others by their work, technology, management systems, and hierarchy. These linkages present a special challenge when organizations attempt to change. Unless many individuals line up and move together in the same direction, people will tend to fall all over one another. To executives who are overeducated in management and undereducated in leadership, the idea of getting people moving in the same direction appears to be an organizational problem. What executives need to do, however, is not organize people but align them.

Managers "organize" to create human systems that can implement plans as precisely and efficiently as possible. Typically, this requires a number of potentially complex decisions. A company must choose a structure of jobs and reporting relationships, staff it with individuals suited to the jobs, provide training for those who need it, communicate plans to the workforce, and decide how much authority to delegate and to whom. Economic incentives also need to be constructed to accomplish the plan, as well as systems to monitor its implementation. These organizational judgments are much like architectural decisions. It's a question of fit within a particular context.

Aligning is different. It is more of a communications challenge than a design problem. Aligning invariably involves talking to many more individuals than organizing does. The target population can involve not only a manager's subordinates but also bosses, peers, staff in other parts of the organization, as well as suppliers, government officials, and even customers. Anyone who can help implement the vision and strategies or who can block implementation is relevant.

Trying to get people to comprehend a vision of an alternative future is also a communications challenge of a completely different magnitude from organizing them to fulfill a short-term plan. It's much like the difference between a football quarterback attempting to describe to his team the next two or three plays versus his trying to explain to them a totally new approach to the game to be used in the second half of the season.

Whether delivered with many words or a few carefully chosen symbols, such messages are not necessarily accepted just because they are understood. Another big challenge in leadership efforts is credibility—getting people to believe the message. Many things contribute to credibility: the track record of the person delivering the message, the content of the message itself, the communicator's reputation for integrity and trustworthiness, and the consistency between words and deeds.

Finally, aligning leads to empowerment in a way that organizing rarely does. One of the reasons some organizations have difficulty adjusting to rapid changes in markets or technology is that so many people in those companies feel relatively powerless. They have learned from experience that even if they correctly perceive important external changes and then initiate appropriate actions, they are vulnerable to someone higher up who does not like what they have done. Reprimands can take many different forms: "That's against policy," or "We can't afford it," or "Shut up and do as you're told."

Alignment helps overcome this problem by empowering people in at least two ways. First, when a clear sense of direction has been communicated throughout an organization, lower-level employees can initiate actions without the same degree of vulnerability. As long as their behavior is consistent with the vision, superiors will have more difficulty reprimanding them. Second, because everyone is aiming at the same target, the probability is less that one person's initiative will be stalled when it comes into conflict with someone else's.

Motivating People Versus Controlling and Problem Solving

Since change is the function of leadership, being able to generate highly energized behavior is important for coping with the inevitable barriers to change. Just as direction setting identifies an appropriate path for movement and just as effective alignment gets people moving down that path, successful motivation ensures that they will have the energy to overcome obstacles.

According to the logic of management, control mechanisms compare system behavior with the plan and take action when a deviation is detected. In a well-managed factory, for example, this means the planning process establishes sensible quality targets, the organizing process builds an organization that can achieve those targets, and a control process makes sure that quality lapses are spotted immediately, not in 30 or 60 days, and corrected.

For some of the same reasons that control is so central to management, highly motivated or inspired behavior is almost irrelevant. Managerial processes must be as close as possible to fail-safe and risk free. That means they cannot be dependent on the unusual or hard to obtain. The whole purpose of systems and structures is to help normal people who behave in normal ways to complete routine jobs successfully, day after day. It's not exciting or glamorous. But that's management.

Leadership is different. Achieving grand visions always requires a burst of energy. Motivation and inspiration energize people, not by pushing them in the right direction as control mechanisms do but by satisfying basic human needs for achievement, a sense of belonging, recognition, self-esteem, a feeling of control over one's life, and the ability to live up to one's ideals. Such feelings touch us deeply and elicit a powerful response.

Good leaders motivate people in a variety of ways. First, they always articulate the organization's vision in a manner that stresses the values of the audience they are addressing. This makes the work important to those individuals. Leaders also regularly involve people in deciding how to achieve the organization's vision (or the part most relevant to a particular individual). This gives people a sense of control. Another important motivational technique is to support employee efforts to realize the vision by providing coaching, feedback, and role modeling, thereby helping people grow professionally and enhancing their self-esteem. Finally, good leaders recognize and reward success, which not only gives people a sense of accomplishment but also makes them feel like they belong to an organization that cares about them. When all this is done, the work itself becomes intrinsically motivating.

The more that change characterizes the business environment, the more that leaders must motivate people to provide leadership as well. When this works, it tends to reproduce leadership across the

Motivating People: Richard Nicolosi at Procter and Gamble

FOR ABOUT 20 YEARS AFTER ITS FOUNDING in 1956, Procter & Gamble's paper products division had experienced little competition for its high-quality, reasonably priced, and well-marketed consumer goods. By the late 1970s, however, the market position of the division had changed. New competitive thrusts hurt P&G badly. For example, industry analysts estimate that the company's market share for disposable diapers fell from 75% in the mid-1970s to 52% in 1984.

That year, Richard Nicolosi came to paper products as the associate general manager, after three years in P&G's smaller and faster moving soft-drink business. He found a heavily bureaucratic and centralized organization that was overly preoccupied with internal functional goals and projects. Almost all information about customers came through highly quantitative market research. The technical people were rewarded for cost savings, the commercial people focused on volume and share, and the two groups were nearly at war with each other.

During the late summer of 1984, top management announced that Nicolosi would become the head of paper products in October, and by August he was unofficially running the division. Immediately he began to stress the need for the division to become more creative and market driven, instead of just trying to be a low-cost producer. "I had to make it very clear," Nicolosi later reported, "that the rules of the game had changed."

The new direction included a much greater stress on teamwork and multiple leadership roles. Nicolosi pushed a strategy of using groups to manage the division and its specific products. In October, he and his team designated themselves as the paper division "board" and began meeting first monthly and then weekly. In November, they established "category teams" to manage their major brand groups (like diapers, tissues, towels) and started pushing responsibility down to these teams. "Shun the incremental," Nicolosi stressed, "and go for the leap."

In December, Nicolosi selectively involved himself in more detail in certain activities. He met with the advertising agency and got to know key creative people. He asked the marketing manager of diapers to report directly to him, eliminating a layer in the hierarchy. He talked more to the people who were working on new product development projects.

In January 1985, the board announced a new organizational structure that included not only category teams but also new-brand business teams. By the spring, the board was ready to plan an important motivational event to communicate the new paper products vision to as many people as possible. On June 4, 1985, all the Cincinnati-based personnel in paper plus sales district managers and paper plant managers—several thousand people in all—met in the local Masonic Temple. Nicolosi and other board members described their vision of an organization where "each of us is a leader." The event was videotaped, and an edited version was sent to all sales offices and plants for everyone to see.

All these activities helped create an entrepreneurial environment where large numbers of people were motivated to realize the new vision. Most innovations came from people dealing with new products. Ultra Pampers, first introduced in February 1985, took the market share of the entire Pampers product line from 40% to 58% and profitability from break-even to positive. And within only a few months of the introduction of Luvs Delux in May 1987, market share for the overall brand grew by 150%.

Other employee initiatives were oriented more toward a functional area, and some came from the bottom of the hierarchy. In the spring of 1986, a few of the division's secretaries, feeling empowered by the new culture, developed a secretaries network. This association established subcommittees on training, on rewards and recognition, and on the "secretary of the future." Echoing the sentiments of many of her peers, one paper products secretary said: "I don't see why we, too, can't contribute to the division's new direction."

By the end of 1988, revenues at the paper products division were up 40% over a four-year period. Profits were up 68%. And this happened despite the fact that the competition continued to get tougher.

entire organization, with people occupying multiple leadership roles throughout the hierarchy. This is highly valuable, because coping with change in any complex business demands initiatives from a multitude of people. Nothing less will work.

Of course, leadership from many sources does not necessarily converge. To the contrary, it can easily conflict. For multiple leadership roles to work together, people's actions must be carefully coordinated by mechanisms that differ from those coordinating traditional management roles.

Strong networks of informal relationships—the kind found in companies with healthy cultures—help coordinate leadership activities in much the same way that formal structure coordinates managerial activities. The key difference is that informal networks can deal with the greater demands for coordination associated with nonroutine activities and change. The multitude of communication channels and the trust among the individuals connected by those channels allow for an ongoing process of accommodation and adaptation. When conflicts arise among roles, those same relationships help resolve the conflicts. Perhaps most important, this process of dialogue and accommodation can produce visions that are linked and compatible instead of remote and competitive. All this requires a great deal more communication than is needed to coordinate managerial roles, but unlike formal structure, strong informal networks can handle it.

Informal relations of some sort exist in all corporations. But too often these networks are either very weak—some people are well connected but most are not—or they are highly fragmented—a strong network exists inside the marketing group and inside R&D but not across the two departments. Such networks do not support multiple leadership initiatives well. In fact, extensive informal networks are so important that if they do not exist, creating them has to be the focus of activity early in a major leadership initiative.

Creating a Culture of Leadership

Despite the increasing importance of leadership to business success, the on-the-job experiences of most people actually seem to undermine the development of the attributes needed for leadership. Nevertheless, some companies have consistently demonstrated an ability to develop people into outstanding leader-managers. Recruiting people with leadership potential is only the first step. Equally important is managing their career patterns. Individuals who are effective in large leadership roles often share a number of career experiences.

Perhaps the most typical and most important is significant challenge early in a career. Leaders almost always have had opportunities during their twenties and thirties to actually try to lead, to take a risk, and to learn from both triumphs and failures. Such learning seems essential in developing a wide range of leadership skills and perspectives. These opportunities also teach people something about both the difficulty of leadership and its potential for producing change.

Later in their careers, something equally important happens that has to do with broadening. People who provide effective leadership in important jobs always have a chance, before they get into those jobs, to grow beyond the narrow base that characterizes most managerial careers. This is usually the result of lateral career moves or of early promotions to unusually broad job assignments. Sometimes other vehicles help, like special task-force assignments or a lengthy general management course. Whatever the case, the breadth of knowledge developed in this way seems to be helpful in all aspects of leadership. So does the network of relationships that is often acquired both inside and outside the company. When enough people get opportunities like this, the relationships that are built also help create the strong informal networks needed to support multiple leadership initiatives.

Corporations that do a better-than-average job of developing leaders put an emphasis on creating challenging opportunities for relatively young employees. In many businesses, decentralization is the key. By definition, it pushes responsibility lower in an organization and in the process creates more challenging jobs at lower levels. Johnson & Johnson, 3M, Hewlett-Packard, General Electric, and many other well-known companies have used that approach quite successfully. Some of those same companies also create as many small units as possible so there are a lot of challenging lower-level general management jobs available.

Sometimes these businesses develop additional challenging opportunities by stressing growth through new products or services. Over the years, 3M has had a policy that at least 25% of its revenue should come from products introduced within the last five years. That encourages small new ventures, which in turn offer hundreds of opportunities to test and stretch young people with leadership potential.

Such practices can, almost by themselves, prepare people for small- and medium-sized leadership jobs. But developing people for important leadership positions requires more work on the part of senior executives, often over a long period of time. That work begins with efforts to spot people with great leadership potential early in their careers and to identify what will be needed to stretch and develop them.

Again, there is nothing magic about this process. The methods successful companies use are surprisingly straightforward. They go out of their way to make young employees and people at lower levels in their organizations visible to senior management. Senior managers then judge for themselves who has potential and what the development needs of those people are. Executives also discuss their tentative conclusions among themselves to draw more accurate judgments.

Armed with a clear sense of who has considerable leadership potential and what skills they need to develop, executives in these companies then spend time planning for that development. Sometimes that is done as part of a formal succession planning or high-potential development process; often it is more informal. In either case, the key ingredient appears to be an intelligent assessment of what feasible development opportunities fit each candidate's needs.

To encourage managers to participate in these activities, well-led businesses tend to recognize and reward people who successfully develop leaders. This is rarely done as part of a formal compensation or bonus formula, simply because it is so difficult to measure such achievements with precision. But it does become a factor in decisions about promotion, especially to the most senior levels, and that seems to make a big difference. When told that future promotions will depend to some degree on their ability to nurture leaders, even people who say that leadership cannot be developed somehow find ways to do it.

Such strategies help create a corporate culture where people value strong leadership and strive to create it. Just as we need more people to provide leadership in the complex organizations that dominate our world today, we also need more people to develop the cultures that will create that leadership. Institutionalizing a leadership-centered culture is the ultimate act of leadership.

Originally published May 1990. Reprint R0111F

The Work of Leadership

by Ronald A. Heifetz and Donald L. Laurie

TO STAY ALIVE, JACK PRITCHARD had to change his life. Triple bypass surgery and medication could help, the heart surgeon told him, but no technical fix could release Pritchard from his own responsibility for changing the habits of a lifetime. He had to stop smoking, improve his diet, get some exercise, and take time to relax, remembering to breathe more deeply each day. Pritchard's doctor could provide sustaining technical expertise and take supportive action, but only Pritchard could adapt his ingrained habits to improve his long-term health. The doctor faced the leadership task of mobilizing the patient to make critical behavioral changes; Jack Pritchard faced the adaptive work of figuring out which specific changes to make and how to incorporate them into his daily life.

Companies today face challenges similar to the ones that confronted Pritchard and his doctor. They face adaptive challenges. Changes in societies, markets, customers, competition, and technology around the globe are forcing organizations to clarify their values, develop new strategies, and learn new ways of operating. Often the toughest task for leaders in effecting change is mobilizing people throughout the organization to do adaptive work.

Adaptive work is required when our deeply held beliefs are challenged, when the values that made us successful become less relevant, and when legitimate yet competing perspectives emerge. We see adaptive challenges every day at every level of the workplace—when companies restructure or reengineer, develop or implement strategy, or merge businesses. We see adaptive challenges when marketing has difficulty working with operations, when cross-functional teams don't work well, or when senior executives complain, "We don't seem to be able to execute effectively." Adaptive problems are often systemic problems with no ready answers.

Mobilizing an organization to adapt its behaviors in order to thrive in new business environments is critical. Without such change, any company today would falter. Indeed, getting people to do adaptive work is the mark of leadership in a competitive world. Yet for most senior executives, providing leadership and not just authoritative expertise is extremely difficult. Why? We see two reasons. First, in order to make change happen, executives have to break a longstanding behavior pattern of their own: providing leadership in the form of solutions. This tendency is quite natural because many executives reach their positions of authority by virtue of their competence in taking responsibility and solving problems. But the locus of responsibility for problem solving when a company faces an adaptive challenge must shift to its people. Solutions to adaptive challenges reside not in the executive suite but in the collective intelligence of employees at all levels, who need to use one another as resources, often across boundaries, and learn their way to those solutions.

Second, adaptive change is distressing for the people going through it. They need to take on new roles, new relationships, new values, new behaviors, and new approaches to work. Many employees are ambivalent about the efforts and sacrifices required of them. They often look to the senior executive to take problems off their shoulders. But those expectations have to be unlearned. Rather than fulfilling the expectation that they will provide answers, leaders have to ask tough questions. Rather than protecting people from outside threats, leaders should allow them to feel the pinch of reality in order to stimulate them to adapt. Instead of orienting people to their current roles, leaders must disorient them so that new relationships can develop. Instead of quelling conflict, leaders have to draw

Idea in Brief

What presents your company with its toughest challenges? Shifting markets? Stiffening competition? Emerging technologies? When such challenges intensify, you may need to reclarify corporate values, redesign strategies, merge or dissolve businesses, or manage cross-functional strife.

These **adaptive challenges** are murky, systemic problems with no easy answers. Perhaps even more vexing, the solutions to adaptive challenges *don't* reside in the executive suite. Solving them requires the involvement of people *throughout* your organization.

Adaptive work is tough on everyone. For *leaders*, it's counterintuitive. Rather than providing solutions, you must ask tough questions and leverage employees' collective intelligence. Instead of maintaining norms, you must challenge the "way we do business." And rather than quelling conflict, you need to draw issues out and let people feel the sting of reality.

For your *employees*, adaptive work is painful—requiring unfamiliar roles, responsibilities, values, and ways of working. No wonder employees often try to lob adaptive work back to their leaders.

How to ensure that you *and* your employees embrace the challenges of adaptive work? Applying the following six principles will help.

the issues out. Instead of maintaining norms, leaders have to challenge "the way we do business" and help others distinguish immutable values from historical practices that must go.

Drawing on our experience with managers from around the world, we offer six principles for leading adaptive work: "getting on the balcony," identifying the adaptive challenge, regulating distress, maintaining disciplined attention, giving the work back to people, and protecting voices of leadership from below. We illustrate those principles with an example of adaptive change at KPMG Netherlands, a professional-services firm.

Get on the Balcony

Earvin "Magic" Johnson's greatness in leading his basketball team came in part from his ability to play hard while keeping the whole game situation in mind, as if he stood in a press box or on a balcony

Idea in Practice

1. Get on the balcony. Don't get swept up in the field of play. Instead, move back and forth between the "action" and the "balcony." You'll spot emerging patterns, such as power struggles or work avoidance. This high-level perspective helps you mobilize people to do adaptive work.

2. Identify your adaptive challenge.

> ***Example:*** When British Airways' passengers nicknamed it "Bloody Awful," CEO Colin Marshall knew he had to infuse the company with a dedication to customers. He identified the adaptive challenge as "creating trust throughout British Airways." To diagnose the challenge further, Marshall's team mingled with employees and customers in baggage areas, reservation centers, and planes, asking which beliefs, values, and behaviors needed overhauling. They exposed value-based conflicts underlying surface-level disputes, and resolved the team's own dysfunctional conflicts that impaired companywide collaboration. By understanding themselves, their people, and the company's conflicts, the team strengthened British Airways' bid to become "the World's Favourite Airline."

3. Regulate distress. To inspire change—without disabling people—pace adaptive work:

above the field of play. Bobby Orr played hockey in the same way. Other players might fail to recognize the larger patterns of play that performers like Johnson and Orr quickly understand, because they are so engaged in the game that they get carried away by it. Their attention is captured by the rapid motion, the physical contact, the roar of the crowd, and the pressure to execute. In sports, most players simply may not see who is open for a pass, who is missing a block, or how the offense and defense work together. Players like Johnson and Orr watch these things and allow their observations to guide their actions.

Business leaders have to be able to view patterns as if they were on a balcony. It does them no good to be swept up in the field of action. Leaders have to see a context for change or create one. They should give employees a strong sense of the history of the enterprise

- First, let employees debate issues and clarify assumptions behind competing views—safely.
- Then provide direction. Define *key* issues and values. Control the rate of change: Don't start too many initiatives simultaneously without stopping others.
- Maintain just enough tension, resisting pressure to restore the status quo. Raise tough questions without succumbing to anxiety yourself. Communicate presence and poise.

4. Maintain disciplined attention. Encourage managers to grapple with divisive issues, rather than indulging in scapegoating or denial. Deepen the debate to unlock polarized, superficial conflict. Demonstrate collaboration to solve problems.

5. Give the work back to employees. To instill collective self-confidence—versus dependence on you—support rather than control people. Encourage risk-taking and responsibility—then back people up if they err. Help them recognize they contain the solutions.

6. Protect leadership voices from below. Don't silence whistle-blowers, creative deviants, and others exposing contradictions within your company. Their perspectives can provoke fresh thinking. Ask, "What is this guy *really* talking about? Have we missed something?"

and what's good about its past, as well as an idea of the market forces at work today and the responsibility people must take in shaping the future. Leaders must be able to identify struggles over values and power, recognize patterns of work avoidance, and watch for the many other functional and dysfunctional reactions to change.

Without the capacity to move back and forth between the field of action and the balcony, to reflect day to day, moment to moment, on the many ways in which an organization's habits can sabotage adaptive work, a leader easily and unwittingly becomes a prisoner of the system. The dynamics of adaptive change are far too complex to keep track of, let alone influence, if leaders stay only on the field of play.

We have encountered several leaders, some of whom we discuss in this article, who manage to spend much of their precious time on the balcony as they guide their organizations through change.

Without that perspective, they probably would have been unable to mobilize people to do adaptive work. Getting on the balcony is thus a prerequisite for following the next five principles.

Identify the Adaptive Challenge

When a leopard threatens a band of chimpanzees, the leopard rarely succeeds in picking off a stray. Chimps know how to respond to this kind of threat. But when a man with an automatic rifle comes near, the routine responses fail. Chimps risk extinction in a world of poachers unless they figure out how to disarm the new threat. Similarly, when businesses cannot learn quickly to adapt to new challenges, they are likely to face their own form of extinction.

Consider the well-known case of British Airways. Having observed the revolutionary changes in the airline industry during the 1980s, then chief executive Colin Marshall clearly recognized the need to transform an airline nicknamed Bloody Awful by its own passengers into an exemplar of customer service. He also understood that this ambition would require more than anything else changes in values, practices, and relationships throughout the company. An organization whose people clung to functional silos and valued pleasing their bosses more than pleasing customers could not become "the world's favorite airline." Marshall needed an organization dedicated to serving people, acting on trust, respecting the individual, and making teamwork happen across boundaries. Values had to change throughout British Airways. People had to learn to collaborate and to develop a collective sense of responsibility for the direction and performance of the airline. Marshall identified the essential adaptive challenge: creating trust throughout the organization. He is one of the first executives we have known to make "creating trust" a priority.

To lead British Airways, Marshall had to get his executive team to understand the nature of the threat created by dissatisfied customers: Did it represent a technical challenge or an adaptive challenge? Would expert advice and technical adjustments within basic routines suffice, or would people throughout the company have to learn different ways of doing business, develop new competencies, and begin to work collectively?

Marshall and his team set out to diagnose in more detail the organization's challenges. They looked in three places. First, they listened to the ideas and concerns of people inside and outside the organization—meeting with crews on flights, showing up in the 350-person reservations center in New York, wandering around the baggage-handling area in Tokyo, or visiting the passenger lounge in whatever airport they happened to be in. Their primary questions were, Whose values, beliefs, attitudes, or behaviors would have to change in order for progress to take place? What shifts in priorities, resources, and power were necessary? What sacrifices would have to be made and by whom?

Second, Marshall and his team saw conflicts as clues—symptoms of adaptive challenges. The way conflicts across functions were being expressed were mere surface phenomena; the underlying conflicts had to be diagnosed. Disputes over seemingly technical issues such as procedures, schedules, and lines of authority were in fact proxies for underlying conflicts about values and norms.

Third, Marshall and his team held a mirror up to themselves, recognizing that they embodied the adaptive challenges facing the organization. Early in the transformation of British Airways, competing values and norms were played out on the executive team in dysfunctional ways that impaired the capacity of the rest of the company to collaborate across functions and units and make the necessary trade-offs. No executive can hide from the fact that his or her team reflects the best and the worst of the company's values and norms, and therefore provides a case in point for insight into the nature of the adaptive work ahead.

Thus, identifying its adaptive challenge was crucial in British Airways' bid to become the world's favorite airline. For the strategy to succeed, the company's leaders needed to understand themselves, their people, and the potential sources of conflict. Marshall recognized that strategy development itself requires adaptive work.

Regulate Distress

Adaptive work generates distress. Before putting people to work on challenges for which there are no ready solutions, a leader must realize that people can learn only so much so fast. At the same time, they must feel the need to change as reality brings new challenges. They cannot learn new ways when they are overwhelmed, but eliminating stress altogether removes the impetus for doing adaptive work. Because a leader must strike a delicate balance between having people feel the need to change and having them feel overwhelmed by change, leadership is a razor's edge.

A leader must attend to three fundamental tasks in order to help maintain a productive level of tension. Adhering to these tasks will allow him or her to motivate people without disabling them. First, a leader must create what can be called a *holding environment*. To use the analogy of a pressure cooker, a leader needs to regulate the pressure by turning up the heat while also allowing some steam to escape. If the pressure exceeds the cooker's capacity, the cooker can blow up. However, nothing cooks without some heat.

In the early stages of a corporate change, the holding environment can be a temporary "place" in which a leader creates the conditions for diverse groups to talk to one another about the challenges facing them, to frame and debate issues, and to clarify the assumptions behind competing perspectives and values. Over time, more issues can be phased in as they become ripe. At British Airways, for example, the shift from an internal focus to a customer focus took place over four or five years and dealt with important issues in succession: building a credible executive team, communicating with a highly fragmented organization, defining new measures of performance and compensation, and developing sophisticated information systems. During that time, employees at all levels learned to identify what and how they needed to change.

Thus, a leader must sequence and pace the work. Too often, senior managers convey that everything is important. They start new initiatives without stopping other activities, or they start too many initiatives at the same time. They overwhelm and disorient the very people who need to take responsibility for the work.

Second, a leader is responsible for direction, protection, orientation, managing conflict, and shaping norms. (See the exhibit "Adaptive Work Calls for Leadership.") Fulfilling these responsibilities is also important for a manager in technical or routine situations. But a leader engaged in adaptive work uses his authority to fulfill them differently. A leader provides direction by identifying the organization's adaptive challenge and framing the key questions and issues. A leader protects people by managing the rate of change. A leader orients people to new roles and responsibilities by clarifying business realities and key values. A leader helps expose conflict, viewing it as the engine of creativity and learning. Finally, a leader helps the organization maintain those norms that must endure and challenge those that need to change.

Adaptive work calls for leadership

In the course of regulating people's distress, a leader faces several key responsibilities and may have to use his or her authority differently depending on the type of work situation.

Leader's responsibilities	***Type of situation***	
	Technical or routine	***Adaptive***
Direction	Define problems and provide solutions	Identify the adaptive challenge and frame key questions and issues
Protection	Shield the organization from external threats	Let the organization feel external pressures within a range it can stand
Orientation	Clarify roles and responsibilities	Challenge current roles and resist pressure to define new roles quickly
Managing conflict	Restore order	Expose conflict or let it emerge
Shaping norms	Maintain norms	Challenge unproductive norms

Third, a leader must have presence and poise; regulating distress is perhaps a leader's most difficult job. The pressures to restore equilibrium are enormous. Just as molecules bang hard against the walls of a pressure cooker, people bang up against leaders who are trying to sustain the pressures of tough, conflict-filled work. Although leadership demands a deep understanding of the pain of change—the fears and sacrifices associated with major readjustment—it also requires the ability to hold steady and maintain the tension. Otherwise, the pressure escapes and the stimulus for learning and change is lost.

A leader has to have the emotional capacity to tolerate uncertainty, frustration, and pain. He has to be able to raise tough questions without getting too anxious himself. Employees as well as colleagues and customers will carefully observe verbal and nonverbal cues to a leader's ability to hold steady. He needs to communicate confidence that he and they can tackle the tasks ahead.

Maintain Disciplined Attention

Different people within the same organization bring different experiences, assumptions, values, beliefs, and habits to their work. This diversity is valuable because innovation and learning are the products of differences. No one learns anything without being open to contrasting points of view. Yet managers at all levels are often unwilling—or unable—to address their competing perspectives collectively. They frequently avoid paying attention to issues that disturb them. They restore equilibrium quickly, often with work avoidance maneuvers. A leader must get employees to confront tough tradeoffs in values, procedures, operating styles, and power.

That is as true at the top of the organization as it is in the middle or on the front line. Indeed, if the executive team cannot model adaptive work, the organization will languish. If senior managers can't draw out and deal with divisive issues, how will people elsewhere in the organization change their behaviors and rework their relationships? As Jan Carlzon, the legendary CEO of Scandinavian Airlines System (SAS), told us, "One of the most interesting missions of leadership is getting people on the executive team to listen to and learn from one another. Held in debate, people can learn their way to collective solutions when they understand one another's assumptions. The work of the leader is to get conflict out into the open and use it as a source of creativity."

Because work avoidance is rampant in organizations, a leader has to counteract distractions that prevent people from dealing with adaptive issues. Scapegoating, denial, focusing only on today's technical issues, or attacking individuals rather than the perspectives they represent—all forms of work avoidance—are to be expected when an organization undertakes adaptive work. Distractions have to be identified when they occur so that people will regain focus.

When sterile conflict takes the place of dialogue, a leader has to step in and put the team to work on reframing the issues. She has to deepen the debate with questions, unbundling the issues into their parts rather than letting conflict remain polarized and superficial. When people preoccupy themselves with blaming external forces, higher management, or a heavy workload, a leader has to sharpen the team's sense of responsibility for carving out the time to press forward. When the team fragments and individuals resort to protecting their own turf, leaders have to demonstrate the need for collaboration. People have to discover the value of consulting with one another and using one another as resources in the problem-solving process. For example, one CEO we know uses executive meetings, even those that focus on operational and technical issues, as opportunities to teach the team how to work collectively on adaptive problems.

Of course, only the rare manager intends to avoid adaptive work. In general, people feel ambivalent about it. Although they want to make progress on hard problems or live up to their renewed and clarified values, people also want to avoid the associated distress. Just as millions of U.S. citizens want to reduce the federal budget deficit, but not by giving up their tax dollars or benefits or jobs, so, too, managers may consider adaptive work a priority but have difficulty sacrificing their familiar ways of doing business. People need leadership to help them maintain their focus on the tough questions. Disciplined attention is the currency of leadership.

Give the Work Back to People

Everyone in the organization has special access to information that comes from his or her particular vantage point. Everyone may see different needs and opportunities. People who sense early changes in the marketplace are often at the periphery, but the organization will thrive if it can bring that information to bear on tactical and strategic decisions. When people do not act on their special knowledge, businesses fail to adapt.

All too often, people look up the chain of command, expecting senior management to meet market challenges for which they themselves are responsible. Indeed, the greater and more persistent distresses that accompany adaptive work make such dependence worse. People tend to become passive, and senior managers who pride themselves on being problem solvers take decisive action. That behavior restores equilibrium in the short term but ultimately leads to complacency and habits of work avoidance that shield people from responsibility, pain, and the need to change.

Getting people to assume greater responsibility is not easy. Not only are many lower-level employees comfortable being told what to do, but many managers are accustomed to treating subordinates like machinery that requires control. Letting people take the initiative in defining and solving problems means that management needs to learn to support rather than control. Workers, for their part, need to learn to take responsibility.

Jan Carlzon encouraged responsibility taking at SAS by trusting others and decentralizing authority. A leader has to let people bear the weight of responsibility. "The key is to let them discover the problem," he said. "You won't be successful if people aren't carrying the recognition of the problem and the solution within themselves." To that end, Carlzon sought widespread engagement.

For example, in his first two years at SAS, Carlzon spent up to 50% of his time communicating directly in large meetings and indirectly in a host of innovative ways: through workshops, brainstorming sessions, learning exercises, newsletters, brochures, and exposure in the public media. He demonstrated through a variety of symbolic acts—for example, by eliminating the pretentious executive dining room and burning thousands of pages of manuals and handbooks—the extent to which rules had come to dominate the company. He made himself a pervasive presence, meeting with and listening to people both inside and outside the organization. He even wrote a book, *Moments of Truth* (HarperCollins, 1989), to explain his values, philosophy, and strategy. As Carlzon noted, "If no one else read it, at least my people would."

A leader also must develop collective self-confidence. Again, Carlzon said it well: "People aren't born with self-confidence. Even the most self-confident people can be broken. Self-confidence comes from success, experience, and the organization's environment. The leader's most important role is to instill confidence in people. They must dare to take risks and responsibility. You must back them up if they make mistakes."

Protect Voices of Leadership from Below

Giving a voice to all people is the foundation of an organization that is willing to experiment and learn. But, in fact, whistle-blowers, creative deviants, and other such original voices routinely get smashed and silenced in organizational life. They generate disequilibrium, and the easiest way for an organization to restore equilibrium is to neutralize those voices, sometimes in the name of teamwork and "alignment."

The voices from below are usually not as articulate as one would wish. People speaking beyond their authority usually feel self-conscious and sometimes have to generate "too much" passion to get themselves geared up for speaking out. Of course, that often makes it harder for them to communicate effectively. They pick the wrong time and place, and often bypass proper channels of communication and lines of authority. But buried inside a poorly packaged interjection may lie an important intuition that needs to be teased out and considered. To toss it out for its bad timing, lack of clarity, or seeming unreasonableness is to lose potentially valuable information and discourage a potential leader in the organization.

That is what happened to David, a manager in a large manufacturing company. He had listened when his superiors encouraged people to look for problems, speak openly, and take responsibility. So he raised an issue about one of the CEO's pet projects—an issue that was deemed "too hot to handle" and had been swept under the carpet for years. Everyone understood that it was not open to discussion, but David knew that proceeding with the project could damage or derail key elements of the company's overall strategy. He raised the issue directly in a meeting with his boss and the CEO. He provided a clear description of the problem, a rundown of competing perspectives, and a summary of the consequences of continuing to pursue the project.

The CEO angrily squelched the discussion and reinforced the positive aspects of his pet project. When David and his boss left the room, his boss exploded: "Who do you think you are, with your holier-than-thou attitude?" He insinuated that David had never liked the CEO's pet project because David hadn't come up with the idea himself. The subject was closed.

David had greater expertise in the area of the project than either his boss or the CEO. But his two superiors demonstrated no curiosity, no effort to investigate David's reasoning, no awareness that he was behaving responsibly with the interests of the company at heart. It rapidly became clear to David that it was more important to understand what mattered to the boss than to focus on real issues. The CEO and David's boss together squashed the viewpoint of a leader from below and thereby killed his potential for leadership in the organization. He would either leave the company or never go against the grain again.

Leaders must rely on others within the business to raise questions that may indicate an impending adaptive challenge. They have to provide cover to people who point to the internal contradictions of the enterprise. Those individuals often have the perspective to provoke rethinking that people in authority do not. Thus, as a rule of thumb, when authority figures feel the reflexive urge to glare at or otherwise silence someone, they should resist. The urge to restore social equilibrium is quite powerful, and it comes on fast. One has to get accustomed to getting on the balcony, delaying the impulse, and asking, What is this guy really talking about? Is there something we're missing?

Doing Adaptive Work at KPMG Netherlands

The highly successful KPMG Netherlands provides a good example of how a company can engage in adaptive work. In 1994, Ruud Koedijk, the firm's chairman, recognized a strategic challenge. Although the auditing, consulting, and tax-preparation partnership was the industry leader in the Netherlands and was highly profitable, growth opportunities in the segments it served were limited. Margins in the auditing business were being squeezed as the market became more saturated, and competition in the consulting business was increasing as well. Koedijk knew that the firm needed to move into more profitable growth areas, but he didn't know what they were or how KPMG might identify them.

Koedijk and his board were confident that they had the tools to do the analytical strategy work: analyze trends and discontinuities, understand core competencies, assess their competitive position, and map potential opportunities. They were considerably less certain that they could commit to implementing the strategy that would emerge from their work. Historically, the partnership had resisted attempts to change, basically because the partners were content with the way things were. They had been successful for a long time, so they saw no reason to learn new ways of doing business, either from their fellow partners or from anyone lower down in the organization. Overturning the partners' attitude and its deep impact on the organization's culture posed an enormous adaptive challenge for KPMG.

Koedijk could see from the balcony that the very structure of KPMG inhibited change. In truth, KPMG was less a partnership than a collection of small fiefdoms in which each partner was a lord. The firm's success was the cumulative accomplishment of each of the individual partners, not the unified result of 300 colleagues pulling together toward a shared ambition. Success was measured solely in terms of the profitability of individual units. As one partner described it, "If the bottom line was correct, you were a 'good fellow.'" As a result, one partner would not trespass on another's turf, and learning from others was a rare event. Because independence was so highly valued, confrontations were rare and conflict was camouflaged. If partners wanted to resist firmwide change, they did not kill the issue directly. "Say yes, do no" was the operative phrase.

Koedijk also knew that this sense of autonomy got in the way of developing new talent at KPMG. Directors rewarded their subordinates for two things: not making mistakes and delivering a high number of billable hours per week. The emphasis was not on creativity or innovation. Partners were looking for errors when they reviewed their subordinates' work, not for new understanding or fresh insight. Although Koedijk could see the broad outlines of the adaptive challenges facing his organization, he knew that he could not mandate behavioral change. What he could do was create the conditions for people to discover for themselves how they needed to change. He set a process in motion to make that happen.

To start, Koedijk held a meeting of all 300 partners and focused their attention on the history of KPMG, the current business reality, and the business issues they could expect to face. He then raised the question of how they would go about changing as a firm and asked for their perspectives on the issues. By launching the strategic initiative through dialogue rather than edict, he built trust within the partner ranks. Based on this emerging trust and his own credibility, Koedijk persuaded the partners to release 100 partners and nonpartners from their day-to-day responsibilities to work on the strategic challenges. They would devote 60% of their time for nearly four months to that work.

Koedijk and his colleagues established a strategic integration team of 12 senior partners to work with the 100 professionals (called "the 100") from different levels and disciplines. Engaging people below the rank of partner in a major strategic initiative was unheard of and signaled a new approach from the start: Many of these people's opinions had never before been valued or sought by authority figures in the firm. Divided into 14 task forces, the 100 were to work in three areas: gauging future trends and discontinuities, defining core competencies, and grappling with the adaptive challenges facing the organization. They were housed on a separate floor with their own support staff, and they were unfettered by traditional rules and regulations. Hennie Both, KPMG's director of marketing and communications, signed on as project manager.

As the strategy work got under way, the task forces had to confront the existing KPMG culture. Why? Because they literally could not do their new work within the old rules. They could not work when strong respect for the individual came at the expense of effective teamwork, when deeply held individual beliefs got in the way of genuine discussion, and when unit loyalties formed a barrier to cross-functional problem solving. Worst of all, task force members found themselves avoiding conflict and unable to discuss those problems. A number of the task forces became dysfunctional and unable to do their strategy work.

To focus their attention on what needed to change, Both helped the task forces map the culture they desired against the current culture. They discovered very little overlap. The top descriptors of the current culture were: develop opposing views, demand perfection, and avoid conflict. The top characteristics of the desired culture were: create the opportunity for self-fulfillment, develop a caring environment, and maintain trusting relations with colleagues. Articulating this gap made tangible for the group the adaptive challenge that Koedijk saw facing KPMG. In other words, the people who needed to do the changing had finally framed the adaptive challenge for themselves: How could KPMG succeed at a competence-based strategy that depended on cooperation across multiple units and layers if its people couldn't succeed in these task forces? Armed with that understanding, the task force members could become emissaries to the rest of the firm.

On a more personal level, each member was asked to identify his or her individual adaptive challenge. What attitudes, behaviors, or habits did each one need to change, and what specific actions would he or she take? Who else needed to be involved for individual change to take root? Acting as coaches and consultants, the task force members gave one another supportive feedback and suggestions. They had learned to confide, to listen, and to advise with genuine care.

Progress on these issues raised the level of trust dramatically, and task force members began to understand what adapting their behavior meant in everyday terms. They understood how to identify an adaptive issue and developed a language with which to discuss what they needed to do to improve their collective ability to solve problems. They talked about dialogue, work avoidance, and using the collective intelligence of the group. They knew how to call one another on dysfunctional behavior. They had begun to develop the culture required to implement the new business strategy.

Despite the critical breakthroughs toward developing a collective understanding of the adaptive challenge, regulating the level of distress was a constant preoccupation for Koedijk, the board, and Both. The nature of the work was distressing. Strategy work means broad assignments with limited instructions; at KPMG, people were accustomed to highly structured assignments. Strategy work also means being creative. At one breakfast meeting, a board member stood on a table to challenge the group to be more creative and toss aside old rules. This radical and unexpected behavior further raised the distress level: No one had ever seen a partner behave this way before. People realized that their work experience had prepared them only for performing routine tasks with people "like them" from their own units.

The process allowed for conflict and focused people's attention on the hot issues in order to help them learn how to work with conflict in a constructive manner. But the heat was kept within a tolerable range in some of the following ways:

- On one occasion when tensions were unusually high, the 100 were brought together to voice their concerns to the board in an Oprah Winfrey–style meeting. The board sat in the center of an auditorium and took pointed questions from the surrounding group.
- The group devised sanctions to discourage unwanted behavior. In the soccer-crazy Netherlands, all participants in the process were issued the yellow cards that soccer referees use to indicate "foul" to offending players. They used the cards to

stop the action when someone started arguing his or her point without listening to or understanding the assumptions and competing perspectives of other participants.

- The group created symbols. They compared the old KPMG to a hippopotamus that was large and cumbersome, liked to sleep a lot, and became aggressive when its normal habits were disturbed. They aspired to be dolphins, which they characterized as playful, eager to learn, and happily willing to go the extra mile for the team. They even paid attention to the statement that clothes make: It surprised some clients to see managers wandering through the KPMG offices that summer in Bermuda shorts and T-shirts.
- The group made a deliberate point of having fun. "Playtime" could mean long bicycle rides or laser-gun games at a local amusement center. In one spontaneous moment at the KPMG offices, a discussion of the power of people mobilized toward a common goal led the group to go outside and use their collective leverage to move a seemingly immovable concrete block.
- The group attended frequent two- and three-day off-site meetings to help bring closure to parts of the work.

These actions, taken as a whole, altered attitudes and behaviors. Curiosity became more valued than obedience to rules. People no longer deferred to the senior authority figure in the room; genuine dialogue neutralized hierarchical power in the battle over ideas. The tendency for each individual to promote his or her pet solution gave way to understanding other perspectives. A confidence in the ability of people in different units to work together and work things out emerged. The people with the most curious minds and interesting questions soon became the most respected.

As a result of confronting strategic and adaptive challenges, KPMG as a whole will move from auditing to assurance, from operations consulting to shaping corporate vision, from business-process reengineering to developing organizational capabilities, and from teaching traditional skills to its own clients to creating learning organizations. The task forces identified $50 million to $60 million worth of new business opportunities.

Many senior partners who had believed that a firm dominated by the auditing mentality could not contain creative people were surprised when the process unlocked creativity, passion, imagination, and a willingness to take risks. Two stories illustrate the fundamental changes that took place in the firm's mind-set.

We saw one middle manager develop the confidence to create a new business. He spotted the opportunity to provide KPMG services to virtual organizations and strategic alliances. He traveled the world, visiting the leaders of 65 virtual organizations. The results of his innovative research served as a resource to KPMG in entering this growing market. Moreover, he represented the new KPMG by giving a keynote address discussing his findings at a world forum. We also saw a 28-year-old female auditor skillfully guide a group of older, male senior partners through a complex day of looking at opportunities associated with implementing the firm's new strategies. That could not have occurred the year before. The senior partners never would have listened to such a voice from below.

Leadership as Learning

Many efforts to transform organizations through mergers and acquisitions, restructuring, reengineering, and strategy work falter because managers fail to grasp the requirements of adaptive work. They make the classic error of treating adaptive challenges like technical problems that can be solved by tough-minded senior executives.

The implications of that error go to the heart of the work of leaders in organizations today. Leaders crafting strategy have access to the technical expertise and the tools they need to calculate the benefits of a merger or restructuring, understand future trends and discontinuities, identify opportunities, map existing competencies, and identify the steering mechanisms to support their strategic direction. These tools and techniques are readily available both within organizations and from a variety of consulting firms, and they are very useful. In many cases, however, seemingly good strategies fail to be implemented. And often the failure is misdiagnosed: "We had a good strategy, but we couldn't execute it effectively."

In fact, the strategy itself is often deficient because too many perspectives were ignored during its formulation. The failure to do the necessary adaptive work during the strategy development process is a symptom of senior managers' technical orientation. Managers frequently derive their solution to a problem and then try to sell it to some colleagues and bypass or sandbag others in the commitment-building process. Too often, leaders, their team, and consultants fail to identify and tackle the adaptive dimensions of the challenge and to ask themselves, Who needs to learn what in order to develop, understand, commit to, and implement the strategy?

The same technical orientation entraps business-process-reengineering and restructuring initiatives, in which consultants and managers have the know-how to do the technical work of framing the objectives, designing a new work flow, documenting and communicating results, and identifying the activities to be performed by people in the organization. In many instances, reengineering falls short of the mark because it treats process redesign as a technical problem: Managers neglect to identify the adaptive work and involve the people who have to do the changing. Senior executives fail to invest their time and their souls in understanding these issues and guiding people through the transition. Indeed, engineering is itself the wrong metaphor.

In short, the prevailing notion that leadership consists of having a vision and aligning people with that vision is bankrupt because it continues to treat adaptive situations as if they were technical: The authority figure is supposed to divine where the company is going, and people are supposed to follow. Leadership is reduced to a combination of grand knowing and salesmanship. Such a perspective reveals a basic misconception about the way businesses succeed in addressing adaptive challenges. Adaptive situations are hard to define and resolve precisely because they demand the work and responsibility of managers and people throughout the organization. They are not amenable to solutions provided by leaders; adaptive solutions require members of the organization to take responsibility for the problematic situations that face them.

Leadership has to take place every day. It cannot be the responsibility of the few, a rare event, or a once-in-a-lifetime opportunity. In our world, in our businesses, we face adaptive challenges all the time. When an executive is asked to square conflicting aspirations, he and his people face an adaptive challenge. When a manager sees a solution to a problem—technical in many respects except that it requires a change in the attitudes and habits of subordinates—he faces an adaptive challenge. When an employee close to the front line sees a gap between the organization's purpose and the objectives he is asked to achieve, he faces both an adaptive challenge and the risks and opportunity of leading from below.

Leadership, as seen in this light, requires a learning strategy. A leader, from above or below, with or without authority, has to engage people in confronting the challenge, adjusting their values, changing perspectives, and learning new habits. To an authoritative person who prides himself on his ability to tackle hard problems, this shift may come as a rude awakening. But it also should ease the burden of having to know all the answers and bear all the load. To the person who waits to receive either the coach's call or "the vision" to lead, this change may also seem a mixture of good news and bad news. The adaptive demands of our time require leaders who take responsibility without waiting for revelation or request. One can lead with no more than a question in hand.

Originally published in January 1997. Reprint R0111K

Why Should Anyone Be Led by You?

by Robert Goffee and Gareth Jones

IF YOU WANT TO SILENCE a room of executives, try this small trick. Ask them, "Why would anyone want to be led by you?" We've asked just that question for the past ten years while consulting for dozens of companies in Europe and the United States. Without fail, the response is a sudden, stunned hush. All you can hear are knees knocking.

Executives have good reason to be scared. You can't do anything in business without followers, and followers in these "empowered" times are hard to find. So executives had better know what it takes to lead effectively—they must find ways to engage people and rouse their commitment to company goals. But most don't know how, and who can blame them? There's simply too much advice out there. Last year alone, more than 2,000 books on leadership were published, some of them even repackaging Moses and Shakespeare as leadership gurus.

We've yet to hear advice that tells the whole truth about leadership. Yes, everyone agrees that leaders need vision, energy, authority, and strategic direction. That goes without saying. But we've discovered that inspirational leaders also share four unexpected qualities:

- **They selectively show their weaknesses.** By exposing some vulnerability, they reveal their approachability and humanity.

- **They rely heavily on intuition to gauge the appropriate timing and course of their actions.** Their ability to collect and interpret soft data helps them know just when and how to act.
- **They manage employees with something we call tough empathy.** Inspirational leaders empathize passionately—and realistically—with people, and they care intensely about the work employees do.
- **They reveal their differences.** They capitalize on what's unique about themselves. You may find yourself in a top position without these qualities, but few people will want to be led by you.

Our theory about the four essential qualities of leadership, it should be noted, is not about results per se. While many of the leaders we have studied and use as examples do in fact post superior financial returns, the focus of our research has been on leaders who excel at inspiring people—in capturing hearts, minds, and souls. This ability is not everything in business, but any experienced leader will tell you it is worth quite a lot. Indeed, great results may be impossible without it.

Our research into leadership began some 25 years ago and has followed three streams since then. First, as academics, we ransacked the prominent leadership theories of the past century to develop our own working model of effective leadership. (For more on the history of leadership thinking, see the sidebar "Leadership: A Small History of a Big Topic.") Second, as consultants, we have tested our theory with thousands of executives in workshops worldwide and through observations with dozens of clients. And third, as executives ourselves, we have vetted our theories in our own organizations.

Reveal Your Weaknesses

When leaders reveal their weaknesses, they show us who they are—warts and all. This may mean admitting that they're irritable on Monday mornings, that they are somewhat disorganized, or even

Idea in Brief

The question "Why should anyone be led by you?" strikes fear in the hearts of most executives. With good reason. You can't get anything done without followers, and in these "empowered" times, followers are hard to find—*except* by leaders who excel at capturing people's hearts, minds, and spirits.

How do you do that? Of course, you need vision, energy, authority, and strategic direction—*and* these four additional qualities:

- Show you're human, selectively revealing weaknesses.
- Be a "sensor," collecting soft people data that lets you rely on intuition.
- Manage employees with "tough empathy." Care passionately about them and their work, while giving them only what they *need* to achieve their best.
- Dare to be different, capitalizing on your uniqueness.

Mix and match these qualities to find the right style for the right moment.

Without all four qualities, you might climb to the top. But few people will want to follow you, and your company won't achieve its best results.

rather shy. Such admissions work because people need to see leaders own up to some flaw before they participate willingly in an endeavor. Exposing a weakness establishes trust and thus helps get folks on board. Indeed, if executives try to communicate that they're perfect at everything, there will be no need for anyone to help them with anything. They won't need followers. They'll signal that they can do it all themselves.

Beyond creating trust and a collaborative atmosphere, communicating a weakness also builds solidarity between followers and leaders. Consider a senior executive we know at a global management consultancy. He agreed to give a major presentation despite being badly afflicted by physical shaking caused by a medical condition. The otherwise highly critical audience greeted this courageous display of weakness with a standing ovation. By giving the talk, he had dared to say, "I am just like you—imperfect." Sharing an

Idea in Practice

Reveal Your Weaknesses

Nobody wants to work with a perfect leader—he doesn't appear to need help. So show you're human—warts and all. You'll build collaboration and solidarity between you and your followers, and underscore your approachability.

Tips:

- Don't expose a weakness that others see as fatal. (A new finance director shouldn't reveal his ignorance of discounted cash flow!) Choose a tangential weakness instead.
- Pick a flaw that others consider a strength, e.g., workaholism.

Become a Sensor

Hone your ability to collect and interpret subtle interpersonal cues, detecting what's going on without others' spelling it out.

> ***Example:*** Franz Humer, highly successful CEO of Roche, a health-care research company, senses underlying currents of opinion, gauges unexpressed feelings, and accurately judges relationships' quality.

Tip:

- Test your perceptions: Validate them with a trusted advisor or inner-team member.

Practice Tough Empathy

Real leaders empathize fiercely with their followers and care intensely about their people's work. They're also empathetically "tough." This means giving people not necessarily what they *want*, but what they *need* to achieve their best.

> ***Example:*** BBC CEO Greg Dyke knew that to survive in a digital world, the company had to spend more on programs and less on people. He restructured the organization, but only after explaining this openly and directly to the staff. Though many employees lost jobs, Dyke kept people's commitment.

Dare to Be Different

Capitalizing on what's unique about yourself lets you signal your separateness as a leader, and motivates others to perform better. Followers push themselves more if their leader is just a little aloof.

Tips:

- Don't *over*differentiate yourself—you could lose contact with followers. Robert Horton, former CEO of British Petroleum, conspicuously displayed his formidable intelligence. Followers saw him as arrogant, and detached themselves from him. He was dismissed after three years.
- Distinguish yourself through qualities like imagination, expertise, and adventuresomeness.

imperfection is so effective because it underscores a human being's authenticity. Richard Branson, the founder of Virgin, is a brilliant businessman and a hero in the United Kingdom. (Indeed, the Virgin brand is so linked to him personally that succession is a significant issue.) Branson is particularly effective at communicating his vulnerability. He is ill at ease and fumbles incessantly when interviewed in public. It's a weakness, but it's Richard Branson. That's what revealing a weakness is all about: showing your followers that you are genuine and approachable—human and humane.

Another advantage to exposing a weakness is that it offers a leader valuable protection. Human nature being what it is, if you don't show some weakness, then observers may invent one for you. Celebrities and politicians have always known this. Often, they deliberately give the public something to talk about, knowing full well that if they don't, the newspapers will invent something even worse. Princess Diana may have aired her eating disorder in public, but she died with her reputation intact, indeed even enhanced.

That said, the most effective leaders know that exposing a weakness must be done carefully. They own up to *selective* weaknesses. Knowing which weakness to disclose is a highly honed art. The golden rule is never to expose a weakness that will be seen as a fatal flaw—by which we mean a flaw that jeopardizes central aspects of your professional role. Consider the new finance director of a major corporation. He can't suddenly confess that he's never understood discounted cash flow. A leader should reveal only a tangential flaw—and perhaps even several of them. Paradoxically, this admission will help divert attention away from major weaknesses.

Another well-known strategy is to pick a weakness that can in some ways be considered a strength, such as being a workaholic. When leaders expose these limited flaws, people won't see much of anything and little harm will come to them. There is an important caveat, however: if the leader's vulnerability is not perceived to be genuine, he won't gain anyone's support. Instead he will open himself up to derision and scorn. One scenario we saw repeatedly in our research was one in which a CEO feigns absentmindedness to conceal his

Leadership: A Small History of a Big Topic

PEOPLE HAVE BEEN TALKING about leadership since the time of Plato. But in organizations all over the world—in dinosaur conglomerates and new-economy startups alike—the same complaint emerges: we don't have enough leadership. We have to ask ourselves, Why are we so obsessed with leadership?

One answer is that there is a crisis of belief in the modern world that has its roots in the rationalist revolution of the eighteenth century. During the Enlightenment, philosophers such as Voltaire claimed that through the application of reason alone, people could control their destiny. This marked an incredibly optimistic turn in world history. In the nineteenth century, two beliefs stemmed from this rationalist notion: a belief in progress and a belief in the perfectibility of man. This produced an even rosier world view than before. It wasn't until the end of the nineteenth century, with the writings first of Sigmund Freud and later of Max Weber, that the chinks in the armor appeared. These two thinkers destroyed Western man's belief in rationality and progress. The current quest for leadership is a direct consequence of their work.

The founder of psychoanalysis, Freud theorized that beneath the surface of the rational mind was the unconscious. He supposed that the unconscious was responsible for a fair proportion of human behavior. Weber, the leading critic of Marx and a brilliant sociologist, also explored the limits of reason. Indeed, for him, the most destructive force operating in institutions was something he called technical rationality—that is, rationality without morality.

For Weber, technical rationality was embodied in one particular organizational form—the bureaucracy. Bureaucracies, he said, were frightening not for their inefficiencies but for their efficiencies and their capacity to dehumanize people. The tragic novels of Franz Kafka bear stark testimony to the

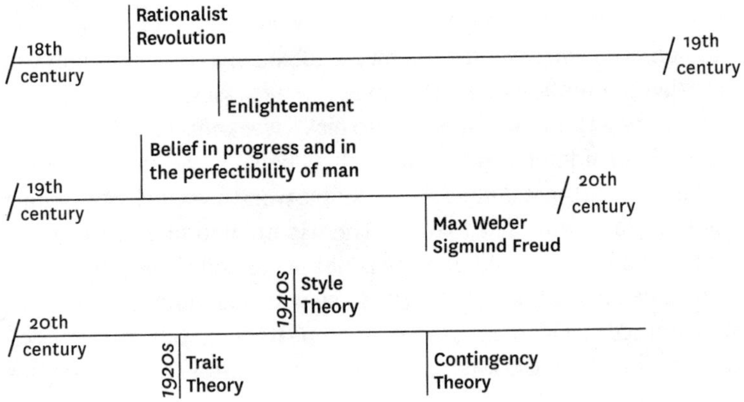

debilitating effects of bureaucracy. Even more chilling was the testimony of Hitler's lieutenant Adolf Eichmann that "I was just a good bureaucrat." Weber believed that the only power that could resist bureaucratization was charismatic leadership. But even this has a very mixed record in the twentieth century. Although there have been inspirational and transformational wartime leaders, there have also been charismatic leaders like Hitler, Stalin, and Mao Tse-tung who committed horrendous atrocities.

By the twentieth century, there was much skepticism about the power of reason and man's ability to progress continuously. Thus, for both pragmatic and philosophic reasons, an intense interest in the concept of leadership began to develop. And indeed, in the 1920s, the first serious research started. The first leadership theory—trait theory—attempted to identify the common characteristics of effective leaders. To that end, leaders were weighed and measured and subjected to a battery of psychological tests. But no one could identify what effective leaders had in common. Trait theory fell into disfavor soon after expensive studies concluded that effective leaders were either above-average height or below.

Trait theory was replaced by style theory in the 1940s, primarily in the United States. One particular style of leadership was singled out as having the most potential. It was a hail-fellow-well-met democratic style of leadership, and thousands of American executives were sent to training courses to learn how to behave this way. There was only one drawback. The theory was essentially capturing the spirit of FDR's America—open, democratic, and meritocratic. And so when McCarthyism and the Cold War surpassed the New Deal, a completely new style was required. Suddenly, everyone was encouraged to behave like a Cold War warrior! The poor executive was completely confused.

Recent leadership thinking is dominated by contingency theory, which says that leadership is dependent on a particular situation. That's fundamentally true, but given that there are endless contingencies in life, there are endless varieties of leadership. Once again, the beleaguered executive looking for a model to help him is hopelessly lost.

For this article, we ransacked all the leadership theories to come up with the four essential leadership qualities. Like Weber, we look at leadership that is primarily antibureaucratic and charismatic. From trait theory, we derived the qualities of weaknesses and differences. Unlike the original trait theorists, however, we do not believe that all leaders have the same weaknesses; our research only showed that all leaders expose some flaws. Tough empathy grew out of style theory, which looked at different kinds of relationships between leaders and their followers. Finally, context theory set the stage for needing to know what skills to use in various circumstances.

inconsistency or even dishonesty. This is a sure way to alienate followers who will remember accurately what happened or what was said.

Become a Sensor

Inspirational leaders rely heavily on their instincts to know when to reveal a weakness or a difference. We call them good situation sensors, and by that we mean that they can collect and interpret soft data. They can sniff out the signals in the environment and sense what's going on without having anything spelled out for them.

Franz Humer, the CEO of Roche, is a classic sensor. He is highly accomplished in detecting shifts in climate and ambience; he can read subtle cues and sense underlying currents of opinion that elude less perceptive people. Humer says he developed this skill as a tour guide in his mid-twenties when he was responsible for groups of 100 or more. "There was no salary, only tips," he explains. "Pretty soon, I knew how to hone in on particular groups. Eventually, I could predict within 10% how much I could earn from any particular group." Indeed, great sensors can easily gauge unexpressed feelings; they can very accurately judge whether relationships are working or not. The process is complex, and as anyone who has ever encountered it knows, the results are impressive.

Consider a human resources executive we worked with in a multinational entertainment company. One day he got news of a distribution problem in Italy that had the potential to affect the company's worldwide operations. As he was thinking about how to hide the information temporarily from the Paris-based CEO while he worked on a solution, the phone rang. It was the CEO saying, "Tell me, Roberto, what the hell's going on in Milan?" The CEO was already aware that something was wrong. How? He had his networks, of course. But in large part, he was gifted at detecting information that wasn't aimed at him. He could read the silences and pick up on nonverbal cues in the organization.

Not surprisingly, the most impressive business leaders we have worked with are all very refined sensors. Ray van Schaik, the chairman of Heineken in the early 1990s, is a good example. Conservative and urbane, van Schaik's genius lay in his ability to read signals he received from colleagues and from Freddie Heineken, the third-generation family member who was "always there without being there." While some senior managers spent a lot of time second-guessing the major shareholder, van Schaik developed an ability to "just know" what Heineken wanted. This ability was based on many years of working with him on the Heineken board, but it was more than that—van Schaik could read Heineken even though they had very different personalities and didn't work together directly.

Success stories like van Schaik's come with a word of warning. While leaders must be great sensors, sensing can create problems. That's because in making fine judgments about how far they can go, leaders risk losing their followers. The political situation in Northern Ireland is a powerful example. Over the past two years, several leaders—David Trimble, Gerry Adams, and Tony Blair, together with George Mitchell—have taken unprecedented initiatives toward peace. At every step of the way, these leaders had to sense how far they could go without losing their electorates. In business, think of mergers and acquisitions. Unless organizational leaders and negotiators can convince their followers in a timely way that the move is positive, value and goodwill quickly erode. This is the situation recently faced by Vodafone and France Telecom in the sale and purchase of Orange.

There is another danger associated with sensing skills. By definition, sensing a situation involves projection—that state of mind whereby you attribute your own ideas to other people and things. When a person "projects," his thoughts may interfere with the truth. Imagine a radio that picks up any number of signals, many of which are weak and distorted. Situation sensing is like that; you can't always be sure what you're hearing because of all the static. The employee who sees her boss distracted and leaps to the conclusion that she is going to be fired is a classic example. Most skills become heightened under threat, but particularly during situation sensing. Such oversensitivity in a leader can be a recipe for disaster. For this reason, sensing capability must always be framed by reality testing. Even the most gifted sensor may need to validate his perceptions with a trusted adviser or a member of his inner team.

Practice Tough Empathy

Unfortunately, there's altogether too much hype nowadays about the idea that leaders *must* show concern for their teams. There's nothing worse than seeing a manager return from the latest interpersonal-skills training program with "concern" for others. Real leaders don't need a training program to convince their employees that they care. Real leaders empathize fiercely with the people they lead. They also care intensely about the work their employees do.

Consider Alain Levy, the former CEO of Polygram. Although he often comes across as a rather aloof intellectual, Levy is well able to close the distance between himself and his followers. On one occasion, he helped some junior record executives in Australia choose singles off albums. Picking singles is a critical task in the music business: the selection of a song can make or break the album. Levy sat down with the young people and took on the work with passion. "You bloody idiots," he added his voice to the melee, "you don't know what the hell you're talking about; we always have a dance track first!" Within 24 hours, the story spread throughout the company; it was the best PR Levy ever got. "Levy really knows how to pick singles," people said. In fact, he knew how to identify with the work, and he knew how to enter his followers' world—one where strong, colorful language is the norm—to show them that he cared.

Clearly, as the above example illustrates, we do not believe that the empathy of inspirational leaders is the soft kind described in so much of the management literature. On the contrary, we feel that real leaders manage through a unique approach we call tough empathy. Tough empathy means giving people what they need, not what they want. Organizations like the Marine Corps and consulting firms specialize in tough empathy. Recruits are pushed to be the best that they can be; "grow or go" is the motto. Chris Satterwaite, the CEO of ell Pottinger Communications and a former chief executive of several ad agencies, understands what tough empathy is all about. He adeptly handles the challenges of managing creative people while making tough decisions. "If I have to, I can be ruthless," he says. "But while they're with me, I promise my people that they'll learn."

Four Popular Myths About Leadership

IN BOTH OUR RESEARCH AND consulting work, we have seen executives who profoundly misunderstand what makes an inspirational leader. Here are four of the most common myths:

Everyone can be a leader.

Not true. Many executives don't have the self-knowledge or the authenticity necessary for leadership. And self-knowledge and authenticity are only part of the equation. Individuals must also want to be leaders, and many talented employees are not interested in shouldering that responsibility. Others prefer to devote more time to their private lives than to their work. After all, there is more to life than work, and more to work than being the boss.

Leaders deliver business results.

Not always. If results were always a matter of good leadership, picking leaders would be easy. In every case, the best strategy would be to go after people in companies with the best results. But clearly, things are not that simple. Businesses in quasi-monopolistic industries can often do very well with competent management rather than great leadership. Equally, some well-led businesses do not necessarily produce results, particularly in the short term.

People who get to the top are leaders.

Not necessarily. One of the most persistent misperceptions is that people in leadership positions are leaders. But people who make it to the top may have done so because of political acumen, not necessarily because of true leadership quality. What's more, real leaders are found all over the organization, from the executive suite to the shop floor. By definition, leaders are simply people who have followers, and rank doesn't have much to do with that. Effective military organizations like the U.S. Navy have long realized the importance of developing leaders throughout the organization.

Leaders are great coaches.

Rarely. A whole cottage industry has grown up around the teaching that good leaders ought to be good coaches. But that thinking assumes that a single person can both inspire the troops and impart technical skills. Of course, it's possible that great leaders may also be great coaches, but we see that only occasionally. More typical are leaders like Steve Jobs whose distinctive strengths lie in their ability to excite others through their vision rather than through their coaching talents.

At its best, tough empathy balances respect for the individual and for the task at hand. Attending to both, however, isn't easy, especially when the business is in survival mode. At such times, caring leaders have to give selflessly to the people around them and know when to pull back. Consider a situation at Unilever at a time when it was developing Persil Power, a detergent that eventually had to be removed from the market because it destroyed clothes that were laundered in it. Even though the product was showing early signs of trouble, CEO Niall FitzGerald stood by his troops. "That was the popular place to be, but I should not have been there," he says now. "I should have stood back, cool and detached, looked at the whole field, watched out for the customer." But caring with detachment is not easy, especially since, when done right, tough empathy is harder on you than on your employees. "Some theories of leadership make caring look effortless. It isn't," says Paulanne Mancuso, president and CEO of Calvin Klein Cosmetics. "You have to do things you don't want to do, and that's hard." It's tough to be tough.

Tough empathy also has the benefit of impelling leaders to take risks. When Greg Dyke took over at the BBC, his commercial competitors were able to spend substantially more on programs than the BBC could. Dyke quickly realized that in order to thrive in a digital world, the BBC needed to increase its expenditures. He explained this openly and directly to the staff. Once he had secured their buy-in, he began thoroughly restructuring the organization. Although many employees were let go, he was able to maintain people's commitment. Dyke attributed his success to his tough empathy with employees: "Once you have the people with you, you can make the difficult decisions that need to be made."

One final point about tough empathy: those more apt to use it are people who really care about something. And when people care deeply about something—anything—they're more likely to show their true selves. They will not only communicate authenticity, which is the precondition for leadership, but they will show that they are doing more than just playing a role. People do not commit to executives who merely live up to the obligations of their jobs.

Can Female Leaders Be True to Themselves?

GENDER DIFFERENCES CAN BE used to either positive or negative effect. Women, in particular, are prone to being stereotyped according to differences—albeit usually not the ones that they would choose. Partly this is because there are fewer women than men in management positions. According to research in social psychology, if a group's representation falls below 20% in a given society, then it's going to be subjected to stereotyping whether it likes it or not. For women, this may mean being typecast as a "helper," "nurturer," or "seductress"—labels that may prevent them from defining their own differences.

In earlier research, we discovered that many women—particularly women in their fifties—try to avoid this dynamic by disappearing. They try to make themselves invisible. They wear clothes that disguise their bodies; they try to blend in with men by talking tough. That's certainly one way to avoid negative stereotyping, but the problem is that it reduces a woman's chances of being seen as a potential leader. She's not promoting her real self and differences.

Another response to negative stereotyping is to collectively resist it—for example, by mounting a campaign that promotes the rights, opportunities, and even the number of women in the workplace. But on a day-to-day basis, survival is often all women have time for, therefore making it impossible for them to organize themselves formally.

A third response that emerged in our research was that women play into stereotyping to personal advantage. Some women, for example, knowingly play the role of "nurturer" at work, but they do it with such wit and skill that they are able to benefit from it. The cost of such a strategy?

It furthers harmful stereotypes and continues to limit opportunities for other women to communicate their genuine personal differences.

They want more. They want someone who cares passionately about the people and the work—just as they do.

Dare to Be Different

Another quality of inspirational leaders is that they capitalize on what's unique about themselves. In fact, using these differences to great advantage is the most important quality of the four we've mentioned. The most effective leaders deliberately use differences to keep a social distance. Even as they are drawing their followers close to them, inspirational leaders signal their separateness.

Often, a leader will show his differences by having a distinctly different dress style or physical appearance, but typically he will move on to distinguish himself through qualities like imagination, loyalty, expertise, or even a handshake. Anything can be a difference, but it is important to communicate it. Most people, however, are hesitant to communicate what's unique about themselves, and it can take years for them to be fully aware of what sets them apart. This is a serious disadvantage in a world where networking is so critical and where teams need to be formed overnight.

Some leaders know exactly how to take advantage of their differences. Take Sir John Harvey-Jones, the former CEO of ICI—what was once the largest manufacturing company in the United Kingdom. When he wrote his autobiography a few years ago, a British newspaper advertised the book with a sketch of Harvey-Jones. The profile had a moustache, long hair, and a loud tie. The drawing was in black and white, but everyone knew who it was. Of course, John Harvey-Jones didn't get to the top of ICI because of eye-catching ties and long hair. But he was very clever in developing differences that he exploited to show that he was adventurous, entrepreneurial, and unique—he was John Harvey-Jones.

There are other people who aren't as aware of their differences but still use them to great effect. For instance, Richard Surface, former managing director of the UK-based Pearl Insurance, always walked the floor and overtook people, using his own pace as a means of communicating urgency. Still other leaders are fortunate enough to have colleagues point out their differences for them. As the BBC's Greg Dyke puts it, "My partner tells me, 'You do things instinctively that you don't understand. What I worry about is that in the process of understanding them you could lose them!'" Indeed, what emerged in our interviews is that most leaders start off not knowing what their differences are but eventually come to know—and use—them more effectively over time. Franz Humer at Roche, for instance, now realizes that he uses his emotions to evoke reactions in others.

Most of the differences we've described are those that tend to be apparent, either to the leader himself or to the colleagues around him. But there are differences that are more subtle but still have very powerful effects. For instance, David Prosser, the CEO of Legal and General, one of Europe's largest and most successful insurance companies, is an outsider. He is not a smooth city type; in fact, he comes from industrial South Wales. And though generally approachable, Prosser has a hard edge, which he uses in an understated but highly effective way. At a recent cocktail party, a rather excitable sales manager had been claiming how good the company was at cross-selling products. In a low voice, Prosser intervened: "We may be good, but we're not good enough." A chill swept through the room. What was Prosser's point? Don't feel so close you can relax! I'm the leader, and I make that call. Don't you forget it. He even uses this edge to good effect with the top team—it keeps everyone on their toes.

Inspirational leaders use separateness to motivate others to perform better. It is not that they are being Machiavellian but that they recognize instinctively that followers will push themselves if their leader is just a little aloof. Leadership, after all, is not a popularity contest.

One danger, of course, is that executives can overdifferentiate themselves in their determination to express their separateness. Indeed, some leaders lose contact with their followers, and doing so is fatal. Once they create too much distance, they stop being good sensors, and they lose the ability to identify and care. That's what appeared to happen during Robert Horton's tenure as chairman and CEO of BP during the early 1990s. Horton's conspicuous display of his considerable—indeed, daunting—intelligence sometimes led others to see him as arrogant and self-aggrandizing. That resulted in overdifferentiation, and it eventually contributed to Horton's dismissal just three years after he was appointed to the position.

Leadership in Action

All four of the qualities described here are necessary for inspirational leadership, but they cannot be used mechanically. They must become or must already be part of an executive's personality. That's why the "recipe" business books—those that prescribe to the Lee Iaccoca or Bill Gates way—often fail. No one can just ape another leader. So the challenge facing prospective leaders is for them to be themselves, but with more skill. That can be done by making yourself increasingly aware of the four leadership qualities we describe and by manipulating these qualities to come up with a personal style that works for you. Remember, there is no universal formula, and what's needed will vary from context to context. What's more, the results are often subtle, as the following story about Sir Richard Sykes, the highly successful chairman and CEO of Glaxo Wellcome, one of the world's leading pharmaceutical companies, illustrates.

When he was running the R&D division at Glaxo, Sykes gave a year-end review to the company's top scientists. At the end of the presentation, a researcher asked him about one of the company's new compounds, and the two men engaged in a short heated debate. The question-answer session continued for another 20 minutes, at the end of which the researcher broached the subject again. "Dr. Sykes," he began in a loud voice, "you have still failed to understand the structure of the new compound." You could feel Sykes's temper rise through the soles of his feet. He marched to the back of the room and displayed his anger before the intellectual brainpower of the entire company. "All right, lad," he yelled, "let us have a look at your notes!"

The Sykes story provides the ideal framework for discussing the four leadership qualities. To some people, Sykes's irritability could have seemed like inappropriate weakness. But in this context, his show of temper demonstrated Sykes's deep belief in the discussion about basic science—a company value. Therefore, his willingness to get angry actually cemented his credibility as a leader. He also showed that he was a very good sensor. If Sykes had exploded earlier in the meeting, he would have quashed the debate. Instead, his anger was perceived as defending the faith. The story also reveals

Sykes's ability to identify with his colleagues and their work. By talking to the researcher as a fellow scientist, he was able to create an empathic bond with his audience. He really cared, though his caring was clearly tough empathy. Finally, the story indicates Sykes's own willingness to show his differences. Despite being one of the United Kingdom's most successful businessmen, he has not conformed to "standard" English. On the contrary, Sykes proudly retains his distinctive northern accent. He also doesn't show the typical British reserve and decorum; he radiates passion. Like other real leaders, he acts and communicates naturally. Indeed, if we were to sum up the entire year-end review at Glaxo Wellcome, we'd say that Sykes was being himself—with great skill.

Unraveling the Mystery

As long as business is around, we will continue to pick apart the underlying ingredients of true leadership. And there will always be as many theories as there are questions. But of all the facets of leadership that one might investigate, there are few so difficult as understanding what it takes to develop leaders. The four leadership qualities are a necessary first step. Taken together, they tell executives to be authentic. As we counsel the executives we coach: "Be yourselves—more—with skill." There can be no advice more difficult to follow than that.

Originally published in September 2000. Reprint R00506

Crucibles of Leadership

by Warren G. Bennis and Robert J. Thomas

A

AS LIFELONG STUDENTS OF LEADERSHIP, we are fascinated with the notion of what makes a leader. Why is it that certain people seem to naturally inspire confidence, loyalty, and hard work, while others (who may have just as much vision and smarts) stumble, again and again? It's a timeless question, and there's no simple answer. But we have come to believe it has something to do with the different ways that people deal with adversity. Indeed, our recent research has led us to conclude that one of the most reliable indicators and predictors of true leadership is an individual's ability to find meaning in negative events and to learn from even the most trying circumstances. Put another way, the skills required to conquer adversity and emerge stronger and more committed than ever are the same ones that make for extraordinary leaders.

Take Sidney Harman. Thirty-four years ago, the then-48-year-old businessman was holding down two executive positions. He was the chief executive of Harman Kardon (now Harman International), the audio components company he had cofounded, and he was serving as president of Friends World College, now Friends World Program, an experimental Quaker school on Long Island whose essential philosophy is that students, not their teachers, are responsible for their education. Juggling the two jobs, Harman was living what he calls a "bifurcated life," changing clothes in his car and eating lunch as he drove between Harman Kardon offices and plants and the Friends World campus. One day while at the college, he was told his company's factory in Bolivar, Tennessee, was having a crisis.

He immediately rushed to the Bolivar factory, a facility that was, as Harman now recalls, "raw, ugly, and, in many ways, demeaning." The problem, he found, had erupted in the polish and buff department, where a crew of a dozen workers, mostly African-Americans, did the dull, hard work of polishing mirrors and other parts, often under unhealthy conditions. The men on the night shift were supposed to get a coffee break at 10 PM. When the buzzer that announced the workers' break went on the fritz, management arbitrarily decided to postpone the break for ten minutes, when another buzzer was scheduled to sound. But one worker, "an old black man with an almost biblical name, Noah B. Cross," had "an epiphany," as Harman describes it. "He said, literally, to his fellow workers, 'I don't work for no buzzer. The buzzer works for me. It's my job to tell me when it's ten o'clock. I got me a watch. I'm not waiting another ten minutes. I'm going on my coffee break.' And all 12 guys took their coffee break, and, of course, all hell broke loose."

The worker's principled rebellion—his refusal to be cowed by management's senseless rule—was, in turn, a revelation to Harman: "The technology is there to serve the men, not the reverse," he remembers realizing. "I suddenly had this awakening that everything I was doing at the college had appropriate applications in business." In the ensuing years, Harman revamped the factory and its workings, turning it into a kind of campus—offering classes on the premises, including piano lessons, and encouraging the workers to take most of the responsibility for running their workplace. Further, he created an environment where dissent was not only tolerated but also encouraged. The plant's lively independent newspaper, the *Bolivar Mirror,* gave workers a creative and emotional outlet—and they enthusiastically skewered Harman in its pages.

Harman had, unexpectedly, become a pioneer of participative management, a movement that continues to influence the shape of workplaces around the world. The concept wasn't a grand idea conceived in the CEO's office and imposed on the plant, Harman says. It

Idea in Brief

What enables one leader to inspire confidence, loyalty, and hard work, while others—with equal vision and intelligence—stumble? How individuals deal with adversity provides a clue.

Extraordinary leaders find meaning in—and learn from—the most negative events. Like phoenixes rising from the ashes, they emerge from adversity stronger, more confident in themselves and their purpose, and more committed to their work.

Such transformative events are called **crucibles**—a severe test or trial. Crucibles are intense, often traumatic—and always unplanned.

grew organically out of his going down to Bolivar to, in his words, "put out this fire." Harman's transformation was, above all, a creative one. He had connected two seemingly unrelated ideas and created a radically different approach to management that recognized both the economic and humane benefits of a more collegial workplace. Harman went on to accomplish far more during his career. In addition to founding Harman International, he served as the deputy secretary of commerce under Jimmy Carter. But he always looked back on the incident in Bolivar as the formative event in his professional life, the moment he came into his own as a leader.

The details of Harman's story are unique, but their significance is not. In interviewing more than 40 top leaders in business and the public sector over the past three years, we were surprised to find that all of them—young and old—were able to point to intense, often traumatic, always unplanned experiences that had transformed them and had become the sources of their distinctive leadership abilities.

We came to call the experiences that shape leaders "crucibles," after the vessels medieval alchemists used in their attempts to turn base metals into gold. For the leaders we interviewed, the crucible experience was a trial and a test, a point of deep self-reflection that forced them to question who they were and what mattered to them. It required them to examine their values, question their assumptions, hone their judgment. And, invariably, they emerged from the crucible stronger and more sure of themselves and their purpose—changed in some fundamental way.

Idea in Practice

The Crucible Experience

Crucibles force leaders into deep self-reflection, where they examine their values, question their assumptions, and hone their judgment.

Example: Sidney Harman—co-founder of audio components company Harman Kardon and president of an experimental college encouraging student-driven education—encountered his crucible when "all hell broke loose" in one of his factories. After managers postponed a scheduled break because the buzzer didn't sound, workers rebelled. "I don't work for no buzzer," one proclaimed.

To Harman, this refusal to bow to management's senseless rule suggested a surprising link between student-driven education and business. Pioneering participative management, Harman transformed his plant into a kind of campus, offering classes and encouraging dissent. He considers the rebellion the formative event in his career—the moment he became a true leader.

The Many Shapes of Crucibles

Some crucibles are violent and life-threatening (encounters with prejudice, illness); others are more positive, yet profoundly challenging (such as demanding bosses or mentors). Whatever the shape, leaders create a narrative telling how they met the challenge and became better for it.

Example: While working for former Atlanta mayor Robert F. Maddox, Vernon Jordan endured repeated racial heckling from Maddox. Rather than letting Maddox's sadism destroy him, Jordan interpreted the behavior as a desperate lashing out by someone who

Leadership crucibles can take many forms. Some are violent, life-threatening events. Others are more prosaic episodes of self-doubt. But whatever the crucible's nature, the people we spoke with were able, like Harman, to create a narrative around it, a story of how they were challenged, met the challenge, and became better leaders. As we studied these stories, we found that they not only told us how individual leaders are shaped but also pointed to some characteristics that seem common to all leaders—characteristics that were formed, or at least exposed, in the crucible.

knew the era of the Old South was ending. Jordan's response empowered him to become an esteemed lawyer and presidential advisor.

Essential Leadership Skills

Four skills enable leaders to learn from adversity:

1. **Engage others in shared meaning.** For example, Sidney Harman mobilized employees around a radical new management approach—amid a factory crisis.
2. **A distinctive, compelling voice.** With words alone, college president Jack Coleman preempted a violent clash between the football team and anti-Vietnam War demonstrators threatening to burn the American flag. Coleman's suggestion to the protestors? Lower the flag, wash it, then put it back up.
3. **Integrity.** Coleman's values prevailed during the emotionally charged face-off between antiwar demonstrators and irate football players.
4. **Adaptive capacity.** This most critical skill includes the *ability to grasp context,* and *hardiness*. Grasping context requires weighing many factors (e.g., how different people will interpret a gesture). Without this quality, leaders can't connect with constituents.

Hardiness provides the perseverance and toughness needed to remain hopeful despite disaster. For instance, Michael Klein made millions in real estate during his teens, lost it all by age 20—then built several more businesses, including transforming a tiny software company into a Hewlett-Packard acquisition.

Learning from Difference

A crucible is, by definition, a transformative experience through which an individual comes to a new or an altered sense of identity. It is perhaps not surprising then that one of the most common types of crucibles we documented involves the experience of prejudice. Being a victim of prejudice is particularly traumatic because it forces an individual to confront a distorted picture of him- or herself, and it often unleashes profound feelings of anger, bewilderment, and even withdrawal. For all its trauma, however, the experience of prejudice is for some a clarifying event. Through it, they gain a clearer vision of who they are, the role they play, and their place in the world.

Consider, for example, Liz Altman, now a Motorola vice president, who was transformed by the year she spent at a Sony camcorder factory in rural Japan, where she faced both estrangement and sexism. It was, says Altman, "by far, the hardest thing I've ever done." The foreign culture—particularly its emphasis on groups over individuals—was both a shock and a challenge to a young American woman. It wasn't just that she felt lonely in an alien world. She had to face the daunting prospect of carving out a place for herself as the only woman engineer in a plant, and nation, where women usually serve as low-level assistants and clerks known as "office ladies."

Another woman who had come to Japan under similar circumstances had warned Altman that the only way to win the men's respect was to avoid becoming allied with the office ladies. But on her very first morning, when the bell rang for a coffee break, the men headed in one direction and the women in another—and the women saved her a place at their table, while the men ignored her. Instinct told Altman to ignore the warning rather than insult the women by rebuffing their invitation.

Over the next few days, she continued to join the women during breaks, a choice that gave her a comfortable haven from which to observe the unfamiliar office culture. But it didn't take her long to notice that some of the men spent the break at their desks reading magazines, and Altman determined that she could do the same on occasion. Finally, after paying close attention to the conversations around her, she learned that several of the men were interested in mountain biking. Because Altman wanted to buy a mountain bike, she approached them for advice. Thus, over time, she established herself as something of a free agent, sometimes sitting with the women and other times engaging with the men.

And as it happened, one of the women she'd sat with on her very first day, the department secretary, was married to one of the engineers. The secretary took it upon herself to include Altman in social gatherings, a turn of events that probably wouldn't have occurred if Altman had alienated her female coworkers on that first day. "Had I just gone to try to break in with [the men] and not had her as an ally, it would never have happened," she says.

Looking back, Altman believes the experience greatly helped her gain a clearer sense of her personal strengths and capabilities, preparing her for other difficult situations. Her tenure in Japan taught her to observe closely and to avoid jumping to conclusions based on cultural assumptions—invaluable skills in her current position at Motorola, where she leads efforts to smooth alliances with other corporate cultures, including those of Motorola's different regional operations.

Altman has come to believe that she wouldn't have been as able to do the Motorola job if she hadn't lived in a foreign country and experienced the dissonance of cultures: ". . . even if you're sitting in the same room, ostensibly agreeing . . . unless you understand the frame of reference, you're probably missing a bunch of what's going on." Altman also credits her crucible with building her confidence—she feels that she can cope with just about anything that comes her way.

People can feel the stigma of cultural differences much closer to home, as well. Muriel ("Mickie") Siebert, the first woman to own a seat on the New York Stock Exchange, found her crucible on the Wall Street of the 1950s and 1960s, an arena so sexist that she couldn't get a job as a stockbroker until she took her first name off her résumé and substituted a genderless initial. Other than the secretaries and the occasional analyst, women were few and far between. That she was Jewish was another strike against her at a time, she points out, when most of big business was "not nice" to either women or Jews. But Siebert wasn't broken or defeated. Instead, she emerged stronger, more focused, and more determined to change the status quo that excluded her.

When we interviewed Siebert, she described her way of addressing anti-Semitism—a technique that quieted the offensive comments of her peers without destroying the relationships she needed to do her job effectively. According to Siebert, at the time it was part of doing business to have a few drinks at lunch. She remembers, "Give somebody a couple of drinks, and they would talk about the Jews." She had a greeting card she used for those occasions that went like this:

Roses are reddish,
Violets are bluish,
In case you don't know,
I am Jewish.

Siebert would have the card hand-delivered to the person who had made the anti-Semitic remarks, and on the card she had written, "Enjoyed lunch." As she recounts, "They got that card in the afternoon, and I never had to take any of that nonsense again. And I never embarrassed anyone, either." It was because she was unable to get credit for the business she was bringing in at any of the large Wall Street firms that she bought a seat on the New York Stock Exchange and started working for herself.

In subsequent years, she went on to found Muriel Siebert & Company (now Siebert Financial Corporation) and has dedicated herself to helping other people avoid some of the difficulties she faced as a young professional. A prominent advocate for women in business and a leader in developing financial products directed at women, she's also devoted to educating children about financial opportunities and responsibility.

We didn't interview lawyer and presidential adviser Vernon Jordan for this article, but he, too, offers a powerful reminder of how prejudice can prove transformational rather than debilitating. In *Vernon Can Read! A Memoir* (Public Affairs, 2001), Jordan describes the vicious baiting he was subjected to as a young man. The man who treated him in this offensive way was his employer, Robert F. Maddox. Jordan served the racist former mayor of Atlanta at dinner, in a white jacket, with a napkin over his arm. He also functioned as Maddox's chauffeur. Whenever Maddox could, he would derisively announce, "Vernon can read!" as if the literacy of a young African-American were a source of wonderment.

Geeks and Geezers

WE DIDN'T SET OUT TO LEARN about crucibles. Our research for this article and for our new book, *Geeks and Geezers,* was actually designed to uncover the ways that *era* influences a leader's motivation and aspirations. We interviewed 43 of today's top leaders in business and the public sector, limiting our subjects to people born in or before 1925, or in or after 1970. To our delight, we learned a lot about how age and era affect leadership style.

Our geeks and geezers (the affectionate shorthand we eventually used to describe the two groups) had very different ideas about paying your dues, work-life balance, the role of heroes, and more. But they also shared some striking similarities—among them a love of learning and strong sense of values. Most intriguing, though, both our geeks and our geezers told us again and again how certain experiences inspired them, shaped them, and, indeed, taught them to lead. And so, as the best research often does, our work turned out to be even more interesting than we thought it would be. We continued to explore the influences of era—our findings are described in our book—but at the same time we probed for stories of these crucible experiences. These are the stories we share with you here.

Subjected to this type of abuse, a lesser man might have allowed Maddox to destroy him. But in his memoir, Jordan gives his own interpretation of Maddox's sadistic heckling, a tale that empowered Jordan instead of embittering him. When he looked at Maddox through the rearview mirror, Jordan did not see a powerful member of Georgia's ruling class. He saw a desperate anachronism, a person who lashed out because he knew his time was up. As Jordan writes about Maddox, "His half-mocking, half-serious comments about my education were the death rattle of his culture. When he saw that I was . . . crafting a life for myself that would make me a man in . . . ways he thought of as being a man, he was deeply unnerved."

Maddox's cruelty was the crucible that, consciously or not, Jordan imbued with redemptive meaning. Instead of lashing out or being paralyzed with hatred, Jordan saw the fall of the Old South and imagined his own future freed of the historical shackles of racism. His ability to organize meaning around a potential crisis turned it into the crucible around which his leadership was forged.

Reinvention in the Extreme: The Power of Neoteny

ALL OF OUR INTERVIEW SUBJECTS described their crucibles as opportunities for reinvention—for taking stock of their lives and finding meaning in circumstances many people would see as daunting and potentially incapacitating. In the extreme, this capacity for reinvention comes to resemble eternal youth—a kind of vigor, openness, and an enduring capacity for wonder that is the antithesis of stereotyped old age.

We borrowed a term from biology—"neoteny," which, according to the *American Heritage Dictionary,* means "retention of juvenile characteristics in the adults of a species"—to describe this quality, this delight in lifelong learning, which every leader we interviewed displayed, regardless of age. To a person, they were full of energy, curiosity, and confidence that the world is a place of wonders spread before them like an endless feast.

Robert Galvin, former Motorola chairman now in his late 70s, spends his weekends windsurfing. Arthur Levitt, Jr., former SEC chairman who turned 71 this year, is an avid Outward Bound trekker. And architect Frank Gehry is now a 72-year-old ice hockey player. But it's not only an affinity for physical activity that characterizes neoteny—it's an appetite for learning and self-development, a curiosity and passion for life.

To understand why this quality is so powerful in a leader, it might help to take a quick look at the scientific principle behind it—neoteny as an evolutionary engine. It is the winning, puppyish quality of certain ancient wolves that allowed them to evolve into dogs. Over thousands of years, humans favored wolves that were the friendliest, most approachable, and most curious. Naturally, people were most drawn to the wolves least likely to attack without warning, that readily locked eyes with them, and that seemed almost human in their eager response to people; the ones, in short, that stayed the most like puppies. Like human infants, they have certain physical qualities that elicit a nurturing response in human adults.

Prevailing over Darkness

Some crucible experiences illuminate a hidden and suppressed area of the soul. These are often among the harshest of crucibles, involving, for instance, episodes of illness or violence. In the case of Sidney Rittenberg, now 79, the crucible took the form of 16 years of unjust imprisonment, in solitary confinement, in Communist China. In 1949

When infants see an adult, they often respond with a smile that begins small and slowly grows into a radiant grin that makes the adult feel at center of the universe. Recent studies of bonding indicate that nursing and other intimate interactions with an infant cause the mother's system to be flooded with oxytocin, a calming, feel-good hormone that is a powerful antidote to cortisol, the hormone produced by stress. Oxytocin appears to be the glue that produces bonding. And the baby's distinctive look and behaviors cause oxytocin to be released in the fortunate adult. That appearance—the one that pulls an involuntary "aaah" out of us whenever we see a baby—and those oxytocin-inducing behaviors allow infants to recruit adults to be their nurturers, essential if such vulnerable and incompletely developed creatures are to survive.

The power of neoteny to recruit protectors and nurturers was vividly illustrated in the former Soviet Union. Forty years ago, a Soviet scientist decided to start breeding silver foxes for neoteny at a Siberian fur farm. The goal was to create a tamer fox that would go with less fuss to slaughter than the typical silver fox. Only the least aggressive, most approachable animals were bred.

The experiment continued for 40 years, and today, after 35 generations, the farm is home to a breed of tame foxes that look and act more like juvenile foxes and even dogs than like their wild forebears. The physical changes in the animals are remarkable (some have floppy, dog-like ears), but what is truly stunning is the change neoteny has wrought in the human response to them. Instead of taking advantage of the fact that these neotenic animals don't snap and snarl on the way to their deaths, their human keepers appear to have been recruited by their newly cute and endearing charges. The keepers and the foxes appear to have formed close bonds, so close that the keepers are trying to find ways to save the animals from slaughter.

Rittenberg was initially jailed, without explanation, by former friends in Chairman Mao Zedong's government and spent his first year in total darkness when he wasn't being interrogated. (Rittenberg later learned that his arrest came at the behest of Communist Party officials in Moscow, who had wrongly identified him as a CIA agent.) Thrown into jail, confined to a tiny, pitch-dark cell, Rittenberg did not rail or panic. Instead, within minutes, he remembered a stanza of verse, four lines recited to him when he was a small child:

They drew a circle that shut me out,
Heretic, rebel, a thing to flout.
But love and I had the wit to win,
We drew a circle that took them in!

That bit of verse (adapted from "Outwitted," a poem by Edwin Markham) was the key to Rittenberg's survival. "My God," he thought, "there's my strategy." He drew the prison guards into his circle, developing relationships that would help him adapt to his confinement. Fluent in Chinese, he persuaded the guards to deliver him books and, eventually, provide a candle so that he could read. He also decided, after his first year, to devote himself to improving his mind—making it more scientific, more pure, and more dedicated to socialism. He believed that if he raised his consciousness, his captors would understand him better. And when, over time, the years in the dark began to take an intellectual toll on him and he found his reason faltering, he could still summon fairy tales and childhood stories such as *The Little Engine That Could* and take comfort from their simple messages.

By contrast, many of Rittenberg's fellow prisoners either lashed out in anger or withdrew. "They tended to go up the wall . . . They couldn't make it. And I think the reason was that they didn't understand . . . that happiness . . . is not a function of your circumstances; it's a function of your outlook on life."

Rittenberg's commitment to his ideals continued upon his release. His cell door opened suddenly in 1955, after his first six-year term in prison. He recounts, "Here was a representative of the central government telling me that I had been wronged, that the government was making a formal apology to me . . . and that they would do everything possible to make restitution." When his captors offered him money to start a new life in the United States or to travel in Europe, Rittenberg declined, choosing instead to stay in China and continue his work for the Communist Party.

And even after a second arrest, which put him into solitary confinement for ten years as retaliation for his support of open democracy during the Cultural Revolution, Rittenberg did not allow his spirit to be broken. Instead, he used his time in prison as an opportunity to question his belief system—in particular, his commitment to Marxism and Chairman Mao. "In that sense, prison emancipated me," he says.

Rittenberg studied, read, wrote, and thought, and he learned something about himself in the process: "I realized I had this great fear of being a turncoat, which . . . was so powerful that it prevented me from even looking at [my assumptions] . . . Even to question was an act of betrayal. After I got out . . . the scales fell away from my eyes and I understood that . . . the basic doctrine of arriving at democracy through dictatorship was wrong."

What's more, Rittenberg emerged from prison certain that absolutely nothing in his professional life could break him and went on to start a company with his wife. Rittenberg Associates is a consulting firm dedicated to developing business ties between the United States and China. Today, Rittenberg is as committed to his ideals—if not to his view of the best way to get there—as he was 50 years ago, when he was so severely tested.

Meeting Great Expectations

Fortunately, not all crucible experiences are traumatic. In fact, they can involve a positive, if deeply challenging, experience such as having a demanding boss or mentor. Judge Nathaniel R. Jones of the U.S. Court of Appeals for the Sixth Circuit, for instance, attributes much of his success to his interaction with a splendid mentor. That mentor was J. Maynard Dickerson, a successful attorney—the first black city prosecutor in the United States—and editor of a local African-American newspaper.

Dickerson influenced Jones at many levels. For instance, the older man brought Jones behind the scenes to witness firsthand the great civil rights struggle of the 1950s, inviting him to sit in on conversations with activists like Thurgood Marshall, Walter White, Roy

Wilkins, and Robert C. Weaver. Says Jones, "I was struck by their resolve, their humor . . . and their determination not to let the system define them. Rather than just feel beaten down, they turned it around." The experience no doubt influenced the many important opinions Judge Jones has written in regard to civil rights.

Dickerson was both model and coach. His lessons covered every aspect of Jones's intellectual growth and presentation of self, including schooling in what we now call "emotional intelligence." Dickerson set the highest standards for Jones, especially in the area of communication skills—a facility we've found essential to leadership. Dickerson edited Jones's early attempts at writing a sports column with respectful ruthlessness, in red ink, as Jones remembers to this day—marking up the copy so that it looked, as Jones says, "like something chickens had a fight over." But Dickerson also took the time to explain every single mistake and why it mattered.

His mentor also expected the teenage Jones to speak correctly at all times and would hiss discreetly in his direction if he stumbled. Great expectations are evidence of great respect, and as Jones learned all the complex, often subtle lessons of how to succeed, he was motivated in no small measure by his desire not to disappoint the man he still calls "Mr. Dickerson." Dickerson gave Jones the kind of intensive mentoring that was tantamount to grooming him for a kind of professional and moral succession—and Jones has indeed become an instrument for the profound societal change for which Dickerson fought so courageously as well. Jones found life-changing meaning in the attention Dickerson paid to him—attention fueled by a conviction that he, too, though only a teenager, had a vital role to play in society and an important destiny.

Another story of a powerful mentor came to us from Michael Klein, a young man who made millions in Southern California real estate while still in his teens, only to lose it by the time he turned 20 and then go on to start several other businesses. His mentor was his grandfather Max S. Klein, who created the paint-by-numbers fad that swept the United States in the 1950s and 1960s. Klein was only four or five years old when his grandfather approached him and offered to share his business expertise. Over the years, Michael Klein's grandfather taught him to learn from and to cope with change, and the two spoke by phone for an hour every day until shortly before Max Klein's death.

The Essentials of Leadership

In our interviews, we heard many other stories of crucible experiences. Take Jack Coleman, 78-year-old former president of Haverford College in Pennsylvania. He told us of one day, during the Vietnam War, when he heard that a group of students was planning to pull down the American flag and burn it—and that former members of the school's football team were going to make sure the students didn't succeed. Seemingly out of nowhere, Coleman had the idea to preempt the violence by suggesting that the protesting students take down the flag, wash it, and then put it back up—a crucible moment that even now elicits tremendous emotion in Coleman as he describes that day.

There's also Common Cause founder John W. Gardner, who died earlier this year at 89. He identified his arduous training as a Marine during World War II as the crucible in which his leadership abilities emerged. Architect Frank Gehry spoke of the biases he experienced as a Jew in college. Jeff Wilke, a general manager at a major manufacturer, told us of the day he learned that an employee had been killed in his plant—an experience that taught him that leadership was about much more than making quarterly numbers.

So, what allowed these people to not only cope with these difficult situations but also learn from them? We believe that great leaders possess four essential skills, and, we were surprised to learn, these happen to be the same skills that allow a person to find meaning in what could be a debilitating experience. First is the ability to engage others in shared meaning. Consider Sidney Harman, who dived into a chaotic work environment to mobilize employees around an entirely new approach to management. Second is a distinctive and compelling voice. Look at Jack Coleman's ability to defuse a potentially violent situation with only his words. Third is a sense of integrity (including a strong set of values). Here, we point again to Coleman, whose values prevailed even during the emotionally charged clash between peace demonstrators and the angry (and strong) former football team members.

But by far the most critical skill of the four is what we call "adaptive capacity." This is, in essence, applied creativity—an almost magical ability to transcend adversity, with all its attendant stresses, and to emerge stronger than before. It's composed of two primary qualities: the ability to grasp context, and hardiness. The ability to grasp context implies an ability to weigh a welter of factors, ranging from how very different groups of people will interpret a gesture to being able to put a situation in perspective. Without this, leaders are utterly lost, because they cannot connect with their constituents. M. Douglas Ivester, who succeeded Roberto Goizueta at Coca-Cola, exhibited a woeful inability to grasp context, lasting just 28 months on the job. For example, he demoted his highest-ranked African-American employee even as the company was losing a $200 million class-action suit brought by black employees—and this in Atlanta, a city with a powerful African-American majority. Contrast Ivester with Vernon Jordan. Jordan realized his boss's time was up—not just his time in power, but the era that formed him. And so Jordan was able to see past the insults and recognize his boss's bitterness for what it was—desperate lashing out.

Hardiness is just what it sounds like—the perseverance and toughness that enable people to emerge from devastating circumstances without losing hope. Look at Michael Klein, who experienced failure but didn't let it defeat him. He found himself with a single asset—a tiny software company he'd acquired. Klein built it into Transoft Networks, which Hewlett-Packard acquired in 1999. Consider, too, Mickie Siebert, who used her sense of humor to curtail offensive conversations. Or Sidney Rittenberg's strength during his imprisonment. He drew on his personal memories and inner strength to emerge from his lengthy prison term without bitterness.

It is the combination of hardiness and ability to grasp context that, above all, allows a person to not only survive an ordeal, but to learn from it, and to emerge stronger, more engaged, and more committed than ever. These attributes allow leaders to grow from their crucibles, instead of being destroyed by them—to find opportunity where others might find only despair. This is the stuff of true leadership.

Originally published in September 2002. Reprint R0209B

Level 5 Leadership

The Triumph of Humility and Fierce Resolve. *by Jim Collins*

IN 1971, A SEEMINGLY ordinary man named Darwin E. Smith was named chief executive of Kimberly-Clark, a stodgy old paper company whose stock had fallen 36% behind the general market during the previous 20 years. Smith, the company's mild-mannered in-house lawyer, wasn't so sure the board had made the right choice—a feeling that was reinforced when a Kimberly-Clark director pulled him aside and reminded him that he lacked some of the qualifications for the position. But CEO he was, and CEO he remained for 20 years.

What a 20 years it was. In that period, Smith created a stunning transformation at Kimberly-Clark, turning it into the leading consumer paper products company in the world. Under his stewardship, the company beat its rivals Scott Paper and Procter & Gamble. And in doing so, Kimberly-Clark generated cumulative stock returns that were 4.1 times greater than those of the general market, outperforming venerable companies such as Hewlett-Packard, 3M, Coca-Cola, and General Electric.

Smith's turnaround of Kimberly-Clark is one the best examples in the twentieth century of a leader taking a company from merely good to truly great. And yet few people—even ardent students of business history—have heard of Darwin Smith. He probably would have liked it that way. Smith is a classic example of a Level 5 leader—an individual who blends extreme personal humility with intense professional will. According to our five-year research study, executives who possess this paradoxical combination of traits are catalysts for the statistically rare event of transforming a good company into a great one. (The research is described in the sidebar "One Question, Five Years, 11 Companies.")

"Level 5" refers to the highest level in a hierarchy of executive capabilities that we identified during our research. Leaders at the other four levels in the hierarchy can produce high degrees of success but not enough to elevate companies from mediocrity to sustained excellence. (For more details about this concept, see the exhibit "The Level 5 Hierarchy.") And while Level 5 leadership is not the only

The Level 5 hierarchy

The Level 5 leader sits on top of a hierarchy of capabilities and is, according to our research, a necessary requirement for transforming an organization from good to great. But what lies beneath? Four other layers, each one appropriate in its own right but none with the power of Level 5. Individuals do not need to proceed sequentially through each level of the hierarchy to reach the top, but to be a full-fledged Level 5 requires the capabilities of all the lower levels, plus the special characteristics of Level 5.

Level 5

Executive: Builds enduring greatness through a paradoxical combination of personal humility plus professional will.

Level 4

Effective leader: Catalyzes commitment to and vigorous pursuit of a clear and compelling vision; stimulates the group to high performance standards.

Level 3

Competent manager: Organizes people and resources toward the effective and efficient pursuit of predetermined objectives.

Level 2

Contributing team member: Contributes to the achievement of group objectives; works effectively with others in a group setting.

Level 1

Highly capable individual: Makes productive contributions through talent, knowledge, skills, and good work habits.

Idea in Brief

Out of 1,435 *Fortune* 500 companies that renowned management researcher Jim Collins studied, only 11 achieved and sustained greatness—garnering stock returns at least three times the market's—for 15 years after a major transition period.

What did these 11 companies have in common? Each had a "Level 5" leader at the helm.

Level 5 leaders blend the paradoxical combination of **deep personal humility** with **intense professional will.** This rare combination also defies our assumptions about what makes a great leader.

Celebrities like Lee Iacocca may make headlines. But mild-mannered, steely leaders like Darwin Smith of Kimberly-Clark boost their companies to greatness—and keep them there.

Example: Darwin Smith—CEO at paper-products maker Kimberly-Clark from 1971 to 1991—epitomizes Level 5 leadership. Shy, awkward, shunning attention, he also showed iron will, determinedly redefining the firm's core business despite Wall Street's skepticism. The formerly lackluster Kimberly-Clark became the worldwide leader in its industry, generating stock returns 4.1 times greater than the general market's.

requirement for transforming a good company into a great one—other factors include getting the right people on the bus (and the wrong people off the bus) and creating a culture of discipline—our research shows it to be essential. Good-to-great transformations don't happen without Level 5 leaders at the helm. They just don't.

Not What You Would Expect

Our discovery of Level 5 leadership is counterintuitive. Indeed, it is countercultural. People generally assume that transforming companies from good to great requires larger-than-life leaders—big personalities like Lee Iacocca, Al Dunlap, Jack Welch, and Stanley Gault, who make headlines and become celebrities.

Compared with those CEOs, Darwin Smith seems to have come from Mars. Shy, unpretentious, even awkward, Smith shunned

Idea in Practice

Humility + Will = Level 5

How do Level 5 leaders manifest humility? They routinely credit others, external factors, and good luck for their companies' success. But when results are poor, they blame themselves. They also act quietly, calmly, and determinedly—relying on inspired standards, not inspiring charisma, to motivate.

Inspired standards demonstrate Level 5 leaders' unwavering will. Utterly intolerant of mediocrity, they are stoic in their resolve to do whatever it takes to produce great results—terminating everything else. And they select superb successors, wanting their companies to become even more successful in the future.

Can You Develop Level 5 Leadership?

Level 5 leaders sit atop a hierarchy of four more common leadership levels—and possess the skills of all four. For example, Level 4 leaders catalyze commitment to and vigorous pursuit of a clear, compelling vision. Can you move from Level 4 to Level 5? Perhaps, *if* you have the Level 5 "seed" within you.

Leaders *without* the seed tend to have monumental egos they can't subjugate to something larger and

attention. When a journalist asked him to describe his management style, Smith just stared back at the scribe from the other side of his thick black-rimmed glasses. He was dressed unfashionably, like a farm boy wearing his first J.C. Penney suit. Finally, after a long and uncomfortable silence, he said, "Eccentric." Needless to say, the *Wall Street Journal* did not publish a splashy feature on Darwin Smith.

But if you were to consider Smith soft or meek, you would be terribly mistaken. His lack of pretense was coupled with a fierce, even stoic, resolve toward life. Smith grew up on an Indiana farm and put himself through night school at Indiana University by working the day shift at International Harvester. One day, he lost a finger on the job. The story goes that he went to class that evening and returned to work the very next day. Eventually, this poor but determined Indiana farm boy earned admission to Harvard Law School.

more sustaining than themselves, i.e., their companies. But for leaders *with* the seed, the right conditions—such as self-reflection or a profoundly transformative event, such as a life-threatening illness—can stimulate the seed to sprout.

Growing to Level 5

Grow Level 5 seeds by practicing these good-to-great disciplines of Level 5 leaders.

First who

Attend to people first, strategy second. Get the right people on the bus and the wrong people off—*then* figure out where to drive it.

Stockdale paradox

Deal with the brutal facts of your current reality—while maintaining absolute faith that you'll prevail.

Buildup-breakthrough flywheel

Keep pushing your organizational "flywheel." With consistent effort, momentum increases until—bang!—the wheel hits the breakthrough point.

The hedgehog concept

Think of your company as three intersecting circles: what it can be best at, how its economics work best, and what ignites its people's passions. Eliminate *everything* else.

He showed the same iron will when he was at the helm of Kimberly-Clark. Indeed, two months after Smith became CEO, doctors diagnosed him with nose and throat cancer and told him he had less than a year to live. He duly informed the board of his illness but said he had no plans to die anytime soon. Smith held to his demanding work schedule while commuting weekly from Wisconsin to Houston for radiation therapy. He lived 25 more years, 20 of them as CEO.

Smith's ferocious resolve was crucial to the rebuilding of Kimberly-Clark, especially when he made the most dramatic decision in the company's history: selling the mills.

To explain: Shortly after he took over, Smith and his team had concluded that the company's traditional core business—coated paper—was doomed to mediocrity. Its economics were bad and the competition weak. But, they reasoned, if Kimberly-Clark were thrust into the fire of the consumer paper products business, better

One Question, Five Years, 11 Companies

THE LEVEL 5 DISCOVERY DERIVES from a research project that began in 1996, when my research teams and I set out to answer one question: Can a good company become a great company and, if so, how? Most great companies grew up with superb parents—people like George Merck, David Packard, and Walt Disney—who instilled greatness early on. But what about the vast majority of companies that wake up partway through life and realize that they're good but not great?

To answer that question, we looked for companies that had shifted from good performance to great performance—and sustained it. We identified comparison companies that had failed to make that sustained shift. We then studied the contrast between the two groups to discover common variables that distinguished those who made and sustained a shift from those who could have but didn't.

More precisely, we searched for a specific pattern: cumulative stock returns at or below the general stock market for 15 years, punctuated by a transition point, then cumulative returns at least three times the market over the next 15 years. (See the accompanying exhibit.) We used data from the University of Chicago Center for Research in Security Prices and adjusted for stock splits and all dividends reinvested. The shift had to be distinct from the industry; if the whole industry showed the same shift, we'd drop the company. We began with 1,435 companies that appeared on the *Fortune* 500 from 1965 to 1995; we found 11 good-to-great examples. That's not a sample; that's the total number that jumped all our hurdles and passed into the study.

Those that made the cut averaged cumulative stock returns 6.9 times the general stock market for the 15 years after the point of transition. To put that in perspective, General Electric under Jack Welch outperformed the general stock market by 2.8:1 during his tenure from 1986 to 2000. One dollar invested in a mutual fund of the good-to-great companies in 1965 grew to $470 by 2000 compared with $56 in the general stock market. These are remarkable numbers, made all the more so by the fact that they came from previously unremarkable companies.

For each good-to-great example, we selected the best direct comparison, based on similarity of business, size, age, customers, and performance leading up to the transition. We also constructed a set of six "unsustained" comparisons (companies that showed a short-lived shift but then fell off) to address the question of sustainability. To be conservative, we consistently picked comparison companies that, if anything, were in better shape than the good-to-great companies were in the years just before the transition.

With 22 research associates working in groups of four to six at a time from 1996 to 2000, our study involved a wide range of both qualitative and quantitative analyses. On the qualitative front, we collected nearly 6,000 articles, conducted 87 interviews with key executives, analyzed companies' internal strategy documents, and culled through analysts' reports. On the quantitative front, we ran financial metrics, examined executive compensation, compared patterns of management turnover, quantified company layoffs and restructurings, and calculated the effect of acquisitions and divestitures on companies' stocks. We then synthesized the results to identify the drivers of good-to-great transformations. One was Level 5 leadership. (The others are described in the sidebar "Not by Level 5 Alone.")

Since only 11 companies qualified as good-to-great, a research finding had to meet a stiff standard before we would deem it significant. Every component in the final framework showed up in all 11 good-to-great companies during the transition era, regardless of industry (from steel to banking), transition decade (from the 1950s to the 1990s), circumstances (from plodding along to dire crisis), or size (from tens of millions to tens of billions). Additionally, every component had to show up in less than 30% of the comparison companies during the relevant years. Level 5 easily made it into the framework as one of the strongest, most consistent contrasts between the good-to-great and the comparison companies.

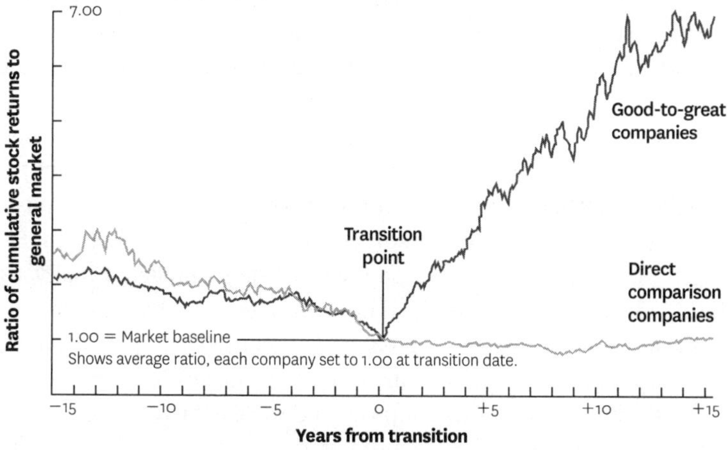

Source: Copyright © 2005 Jim Collins. All rights reserved.

economics and world-class competition like Procter & Gamble would force it to achieve greatness or perish.

And so, like the general who burned the boats upon landing on enemy soil, leaving his troops to succeed or die, Smith announced that Kimberly-Clark would sell its mills—even the namesake mill in Kimberly, Wisconsin. All proceeds would be thrown into the consumer business, with investments in brands like Huggies diapers and Kleenex tissues. The business media called the move stupid, and Wall Street analysts downgraded the stock. But Smith never wavered. Twenty-five years later, Kimberly-Clark owned Scott Paper and beat Procter & Gamble in six of eight product categories. In retirement, Smith reflected on his exceptional performance, saying simply, "I never stopped trying to become qualified for the job."

Not What We Expected, Either

We'll look in depth at Level 5 leadership, but first let's set an important context for our findings. We were not looking for Level 5 or anything like it. Our original question was, Can a good company become a great one and, if so, how? In fact, I gave the research teams explicit instructions to downplay the role of top executives in their analyses of this question so we wouldn't slip into the simplistic "credit the leader" or "blame the leader" thinking that is so common today.

But Level 5 found us. Over the course of the study, research teams kept saying, "We can't ignore the top executives even if we want to. There is something consistently unusual about them." I would push back, arguing, "The comparison companies also had leaders. So what's different here?" Back and forth the debate raged. Finally, as should always be the case, the data won. The executives at companies that went from good to great and sustained that performance for 15 years or more were all cut from the same cloth—one remarkably different from that which produced the executives at the comparison companies in our study. It didn't matter whether the company was in crisis or steady state, consumer or industrial, offering services or products. It didn't matter when the transition took place or how big the company. The successful organizations all had a Level 5 leader at the time of transition.

Furthermore, the absence of Level 5 leadership showed up consistently across the comparison companies. The point: Level 5 is an empirical finding, not an ideological one. And that's important to note, given how much the Level 5 finding contradicts not only conventional wisdom but much of management theory to date. (For more about our findings on good-to-great transformations, see the sidebar "Not by Level 5 Alone.")

Humility + Will = Level 5

Level 5 leaders are a study in duality: modest and willful, shy and fearless. To grasp this concept, consider Abraham Lincoln, who never let his ego get in the way of his ambition to create an enduring great nation. Author Henry Adams called him "a quiet, peaceful, shy figure." But those who thought Lincoln's understated manner signaled weakness in the man found themselves terribly mistaken—to the scale of 250,000 Confederate and 360,000 Union lives, including Lincoln's own.

It might be a stretch to compare the 11 Level 5 CEOs in our research to Lincoln, but they did display the same kind of duality. Take Colman M. Mockler, CEO of Gillette from 1975 to 1991. Mockler, who faced down three takeover attempts, was a reserved, gracious man with a gentle, almost patrician manner. Despite epic battles with raiders—he took on Ronald Perelman twice and the former Coniston Partners once—he never lost his shy, courteous style. At the height of crisis, he maintained a calm business-as-usual demeanor, dispensing first with ongoing business before turning to the takeover.

And yet, those who mistook Mockler's outward modesty as a sign of inner weakness were beaten in the end. In one proxy battle, Mockler and other senior executives called thousands of investors, one by one, to win their votes. Mockler simply would not give in. He chose to fight for the future greatness of Gillette even though he could have pocketed millions by flipping his stock.

Not by Level 5 Alone

Level 5 leadership is an essential factor for taking a company from good to great, but it's not the only one. Our research uncovered multiple factors that deliver companies to greatness. And it is the combined package—Level 5 plus these other drivers—that takes companies beyond unremarkable. There is a symbiotic relationship between Level 5 and the rest of our findings: Level 5 enables implementation of the other findings, and practicing the other findings may help you get to Level 5. We've already talked about who Level 5 leaders are; the rest of our findings describe what they do. Here is a brief look at some of the other key findings.

First Who

We expected that good-to-great leaders would start with the vision and strategy. Instead, they attended to people first, strategy second. They got the right people on the bus, moved the wrong people off, ushered the right people to the right seats—and then they figured out where to drive it.

Stockdale Paradox

This finding is named after Admiral James Stockdale, winner of the Medal of Honor, who survived seven years in a Vietcong POW camp by hanging on to two contradictory beliefs:

His life couldn't be worse at the moment, and his life would someday be better than ever. Like Stockdale, people at the good-to-great companies in our research confronted the most brutal facts of their current reality, yet simultaneously maintained absolute faith that they would prevail in the end. And they held both disciplines—faith and facts—at the same time, all the time.

Buildup-Breakthrough Flywheel

Good-to-great transformations do not happen overnight or in one big leap. Rather, the process resembles relentlessly pushing a giant, heavy flywheel in one direction. At first, pushing it gets the flywheel to turn once. With consistent effort, it goes two turns, then five, then ten, building increasing momentum until—bang!—the wheel hits the breakthrough point, and the momentum

Consider the consequences had Mockler capitulated. If a share flipper had accepted the full 44% price premium offered by Perelman and then invested those shares in the general market for ten years, he still would have come out 64% behind a shareholder who stayed with Mockler and Gillette. If Mockler had given up the fight,

really kicks in. Our comparison companies never sustained the kind of breakthrough momentum that the good-to-great companies did; instead, they lurched back and forth with radical change programs, reactionary moves, and restructurings.

The Hedgehog Concept

In a famous essay, philosopher and scholar Isaiah Berlin described two approaches to thought and life using a simple parable: The fox knows a little about many things, but the hedgehog knows only one big thing very well. The fox is complex; the hedgehog simple. And the hedgehog wins. Our research shows that breakthroughs require a simple, hedgehog-like understanding of three intersecting circles: what a company can be the best in the world at, how its economics work best, and what best ignites the passions of its people. Breakthroughs happen when you get the hedgehog concept and become systematic and consistent with it, eliminating virtually anything that does not fit in the three circles.

Technology Accelerators

The good-to-great companies had a paradoxical relationship with technology. On the one hand, they assiduously avoided jumping on new technology bandwagons. On the other, they were pioneers in the application of carefully selected technologies, making bold, farsighted investments in those that directly linked to their hedgehog concept. Like turbochargers, these technology accelerators create an explosion in flywheel momentum.

A Culture of Discipline

When you look across the good-to-great transformations, they consistently display three forms of discipline: disciplined people, disciplined thought, and disciplined action. When you have disciplined people, you don't need hierarchy. When you have disciplined thought, you don't need bureaucracy. When you have disciplined action, you don't need excessive controls. When you combine a culture of discipline with an ethic of entrepreneurship, you get the magical alchemy of great performance.

---

it's likely that none of us would be shaving with Sensor, Lady Sensor, or the Mach III—and hundreds of millions of people would have a more painful battle with daily stubble.

Sadly, Mockler never had the chance to enjoy the full fruits of his efforts. In January 1991, Gillette received an advance copy of *Forbes*.

The cover featured an artist's rendition of the publicity-shy Mockler standing on a mountaintop, holding a giant razor above his head in a triumphant pose. Walking back to his office just minutes after seeing this public acknowledgment of his 16 years of struggle, Mockler crumpled to the floor and died of a massive heart attack.

Even if Mockler had known he would die in office, he could not have changed his approach. His placid persona hid an inner intensity, a dedication to making anything he touched the best—not just because of what he would get but because he couldn't imagine doing it any other way. Mockler could not give up the company to those who would destroy it, any more than Lincoln would risk losing the chance to build an enduring great nation.

A Compelling Modesty

The Mockler story illustrates the modesty typical of Level 5 leaders. (For a summary of Level 5 traits, see the exhibit "The Yin and Yang of Level 5.") Indeed, throughout our interviews with such executives, we were struck by the way they talked about themselves—or rather, didn't talk about themselves. They'd go on and on about the company and the contributions of other executives, but they would instinctively deflect discussion about their own role. When pressed to talk about themselves, they'd say things like, "I hope I'm not sounding like a big shot," or "I don't think I can take much credit for what happened. We were blessed with marvelous people." One Level 5 leader even asserted, "There are a lot of people in this company who could do my job better than I do."

By contrast, consider the courtship of personal celebrity by the comparison CEOs. Scott Paper, the comparison company to Kimberly-Clark, hired Al Dunlap as CEO—a man who would tell anyone who would listen (and many who would have preferred not to) about his accomplishments. After 19 months atop Scott Paper, Dunlap said in *BusinessWeek,* "The Scott story will go down in the annals of American business history as one of the most successful, quickest turnarounds ever. It makes other turnarounds pale by comparison." He personally accrued $100 million for 603 days of work at Scott

The Yin and Yang of Level 5

Personal humility

Demonstrates a compelling modesty, shunning public adulation; never boastful.

Acts with quiet, calm determination; relies principally on inspired standards, not inspiring charisma, to motivate.

Channels ambition into the company, not the self; sets up successors for even more greatness in the next generation.

Looks in the mirror, not out the window, to apportion responsibility for poor results, never blaming other people, external factors, or bad luck.

Professional will

Creates superb results, a clear catalyst in the transition from good to great.

Demonstrates an unwavering resolve to do whatever must be done to produce the best long-term results, no matter how difficult.

Sets the standard of building an enduring great company; will settle for nothing less.

Looks out the window, not in the mirror, to apportion credit for the success of the company—to other people, external factors, and good luck.

Paper—about $165,000 per day—largely by slashing the workforce, halving the R&D budget, and putting the company on growth steroids in preparation for sale. After selling off the company and pocketing his quick millions, Dunlap wrote an autobiography in which he boastfully dubbed himself "Rambo in pinstripes." It's hard to imagine Darwin Smith thinking, "Hey, that Rambo character reminds me of me," let alone stating it publicly.

Granted, the Scott Paper story is one of the more dramatic in our study, but it's not an isolated case. In more than two-thirds of the comparison companies, we noted the presence of a gargantuan ego that contributed to the demise or continued mediocrity of the company. We found this pattern particularly strong in the unsustained comparison companies—the companies that would show a shift in performance under a talented yet egocentric Level 4 leader, only to decline in later years.

Lee Iacocca, for example, saved Chrysler from the brink of catastrophe, performing one of the most celebrated (and deservedly so) turnarounds in U.S. business history. The automaker's stock rose 2.9 times higher than the general market about halfway through his tenure. But then Iacocca diverted his attention to transforming himself. He appeared regularly on talk shows like the *Today Show* and *Larry King Live,* starred in more than 80 commercials, entertained the idea of running for president of the United States, and promoted his autobiography, which sold 7 million copies worldwide. Iacocca's personal stock soared, but Chrysler's stock fell 31% below the market in the second half of his tenure.

And once Iacocca had accumulated all the fame and perks, he found it difficult to leave center stage. He postponed his retirement so many times that Chrysler's insiders began to joke that Iacocca stood for "I Am Chairman of Chrysler Corporation Always." When he finally retired, he demanded that the board continue to provide a private jet and stock options. Later, he joined forces with noted takeover artist Kirk Kerkorian to launch a hostile bid for Chrysler. (It failed.) Iacocca did make one final brilliant decision: He picked a modest yet determined man—perhaps even a Level 5—as his successor. Bob Eaton rescued Chrysler from its second near-death crisis in a decade and set the foundation for a more enduring corporate transition.

An Unwavering Resolve

Besides extreme humility, Level 5 leaders also display tremendous professional will. When George Cain became CEO of Abbott Laboratories, it was a drowsy, family-controlled business sitting at the bottom quartile of the pharmaceutical industry, living off its cash cow, erythromycin. Cain was a typical Level 5 leader in his lack of pretense; he didn't have the kind of inspiring personality that would galvanize the company. But he had something much more powerful: inspired standards. He could not stand mediocrity in any form and was utterly intolerant of anyone who would accept the idea that good is good enough. For the next 14 years, he relentlessly imposed his will for greatness on Abbott Labs.

Among Cain's first tasks was to destroy one of the root causes of Abbott's middling performance: nepotism. By systematically rebuilding both the board and the executive team with the best people he could find, Cain made his statement. Family ties no longer mattered. If you couldn't become the best executive in the industry within your span of responsibility, you would lose your paycheck.

Such near-ruthless rebuilding might be expected from an outsider brought in to turn the company around, but Cain was an 18-year insider—and a part of the family, the son of a previous president. Holiday gatherings were probably tense for a few years in the Cain clan—"Sorry I had to fire you. Want another slice of turkey?"—but in the end, family members were pleased with the performance of their stock. Cain had set in motion a profitable growth machine. From its transition in 1974 to 2000, Abbott created shareholder returns that beat the market 4.5:1, outperforming industry superstars Merck and Pfizer by a factor of two.

Another good example of iron-willed Level 5 leadership comes from Charles R. "Cork" Walgreen III, who transformed dowdy Walgreens into a company that outperformed the stock market 16:1 from its transition in 1975 to 2000. After years of dialogue and debate within his executive team about what to do with Walgreens' food-service operations, this CEO sensed the team had finally reached a watershed: The company's brightest future lay in convenient drugstores, not in food service. Dan Jorndt, who succeeded Walgreen in 1988, describes what happened next:

> Cork said at one of our planning committee meetings, "Okay, now I am going to draw the line in the sand. We are going to be out of the restaurant business completely in five years." At the time we had more than 500 restaurants. You could have heard a pin drop. He said, "I want to let everybody know the clock is ticking." Six months later we were at our next planning committee meeting and someone mentioned just in passing that we had only five years to be out of the restaurant business. Cork was not a real vociferous fellow. He sort of tapped on the table and said, "Listen, you now have four-and-a-half years. I said you had five years six months ago. Now you've got four-and-a-half years." Well, that next day things really clicked into gear for winding down our restaurant business. Cork never wavered. He never doubted. He never second-guessed.

Like Darwin Smith selling the mills at Kimberly-Clark, Cork Walgreen required stoic resolve to make his decisions. Food service was not the largest part of the business, although it did add substantial profits to the bottom line. The real problem was more emotional than financial. Walgreens had, after all, invented the malted milk shake, and food service had been a long-standing family tradition dating back to Cork's grandfather. Not only that, some food-service outlets were even named after the CEO—for example, a restaurant chain named Corky's. But no matter; if Walgreen had to fly in the face of family tradition in order to refocus on the one arena in which Walgreens could be the best in the world—convenient drugstores—and terminate everything else that would not produce great results, then Cork would do it. Quietly, doggedly, simply.

One final, yet compelling, note on our findings about Level 5: Because Level 5 leaders have ambition not for themselves but for their companies, they routinely select superb successors. Level 5 leaders want to see their companies become even more successful in the next generation and are comfortable with the idea that most people won't even know that the roots of that success trace back to them. As one Level 5 CEO said, "I want to look from my porch, see the company as one of the great companies in the world someday, and be able to say, 'I used to work there.'" By contrast, Level 4 leaders often fail to set up the company for enduring success. After all, what better testament to your own personal greatness than that the place falls apart after you leave?

In more than three-quarters of the comparison companies, we found executives who set up their successors for failure, chose weak successors, or both. Consider the case of Rubbermaid, which grew from obscurity to become one of *Fortune*'s most admired companies—and then, just as quickly, disintegrated into such sorry shape that it had to be acquired by Newell.

The architect of this remarkable story was a charismatic and brilliant leader named Stanley C. Gault, whose name became synonymous in the late 1980s with Rubbermaid's success. Across the 312 articles collected by our research team about the company, Gault comes through as a hard-driving, egocentric executive. In one article, he responds to the accusation of being a tyrant with the statement, "Yes, but I'm a sincere tyrant." In another, drawn directly from his own comments on leading change, the word "I" appears 44 times, while the word "we" appears 16 times. Of course, Gault had every reason to be proud of his executive success: Rubbermaid generated 40 consecutive quarters of earnings growth under his leadership—an impressive performance, to be sure, and one that deserves respect.

But Gault did not leave behind a company that would be great without him. His chosen successor lasted a year on the job and the next in line faced a management team so shallow that he had to temporarily shoulder four jobs while scrambling to identify a new number-two executive. Gault's successors struggled not only with a management void but also with strategic voids that would eventually bring the company to its knees.

Of course, you might say—as one *Fortune* article did—that the fact that Rubbermaid fell apart after Gault left proves his greatness as a leader. Gault was a tremendous Level 4 leader, perhaps one of the best in the last 50 years. But he was not at Level 5, and that is one crucial reason why Rubbermaid went from good to great for a brief, shining moment and then just as quickly went from great to irrelevant.

The Window and the Mirror

As part of our research, we interviewed Alan L. Wurtzel, the Level 5 leader responsible for turning Circuit City from a ramshackle company on the edge of bankruptcy into one of America's most successful electronics retailers. In the 15 years after its transition date in 1982, Circuit City outperformed the market 18.5:1.

We asked Wurtzel to list the top five factors in his company's transformation, ranked by importance. His number one factor? Luck. "We were in a great industry, with the wind at our backs," he said. But wait a minute, we retorted, Silo—your comparison company—was in the same industry, with the same wind and bigger sails. The conversation went back and forth, with Wurtzel refusing to take much credit for the transition, preferring to attribute it largely to just being in the right place at the right time. Later, when we asked him to discuss the factors that would sustain a good-to-great transformation, he said, “The first thing that comes to mind is luck. I was lucky to find the right successor.”

Luck. What an odd factor to talk about. Yet the Level 5 leaders we identified invoked it frequently. We asked an executive at steel company Nucor why it had such a remarkable track record for making good decisions. His response? “I guess we were just lucky.” Joseph F. Cullman III, the Level 5 CEO of Philip Morris, flat out refused to take credit for his company’s success, citing his good fortune to have great colleagues, successors, and predecessors. Even the book he wrote about his career—which he penned at the urging of his colleagues and which he never intended to distribute widely outside the company—had the unusual title *I’m a Lucky Guy*.

At first, we were puzzled by the Level 5 leaders’ emphasis on good luck. After all, there is no evidence that the companies that had progressed from good to great were blessed with more good luck (or more bad luck, for that matter) than the comparison companies. But then we began to notice an interesting pattern in the executives at the comparison companies: They often blamed their situations on bad luck, bemoaning the difficulties of the environment they faced.

Compare Bethlehem Steel and Nucor, for example. Both steel companies operated with products that are hard to differentiate, and both faced a competitive challenge from cheap imported steel. Both companies paid significantly higher wages than most of their foreign competitors. And yet executives at the two companies held completely different views of the same environment.

Bethlehem Steel’s CEO summed up the company’s problems in 1983 by blaming the imports: “Our first, second, and third problems are imports.” Meanwhile, Ken Iverson and his crew at Nucor saw the imports as a blessing: “Aren’t we lucky; steel is heavy, and they have to ship it all the way across the ocean, giving us a huge advantage.” Indeed, Iverson saw the first, second, and third problems facing the U.S. steel industry not in imports but in management. He even went so far as to speak out publicly against government protection against imports, telling a gathering of stunned steel executives in 1977 that the real problems facing the industry lay in the fact that management had failed to keep pace with technology.

The emphasis on luck turns out to be part of a broader pattern that we have come to call "the window and the mirror." Level 5 leaders, inherently humble, look out the window to apportion credit—even undue credit—to factors outside themselves. If they can't find a specific person or event to give credit to, they credit good luck. At the same time, they look in the mirror to assign responsibility, never citing bad luck or external factors when things go poorly. Conversely, the comparison executives frequently looked out the window for factors to blame but preened in the mirror to credit themselves when things went well.

The funny thing about the window-and-mirror concept is that it does not reflect reality. According to our research, the Level 5 leaders were responsible for their companies' transformations. But they would never admit that. We can't climb inside their heads and assess whether they deeply believed what they saw through the window and in the mirror. But it doesn't really matter, because they acted as if they believed it, and they acted with such consistency that it produced exceptional results.

Born or Bred?

Not long ago, I shared the Level 5 finding with a gathering of senior executives. A woman who had recently become chief executive of her company raised her hand. "I believe what you've told us about Level 5 leadership," she said, "but I'm disturbed because I know I'm not there yet, and maybe I never will be. Part of the reason I got this job is because of my strong ego. Are you telling me that I can't make my company great if I'm not Level 5?"

"Let me return to the data," I responded. "Of 1,435 companies that appeared on the *Fortune* 500 since 1965, only 11 made it into our study. In those 11, all of them had Level 5 leaders in key positions, including the CEO role, at the pivotal time of transition. Now, to reiterate, we're not saying that Level 5 is the only element required for the move from good to great, but it appears to be essential."

She sat there, quiet for a moment, and you could guess what many people in the room were thinking. Finally, she raised her hand again. "Can you learn to become Level 5?" I still do not know the answer to that question. Our research, frankly, did not delve into how Level 5 leaders come to be, nor did we attempt to explain or codify the nature of their emotional lives. We speculated on the unique psychology of Level 5 leaders. Were they "guilty" of displacement—shifting their own raw ambition onto something other than themselves? Were they sublimating their egos for dark and complex reasons rooted in childhood trauma? Who knows? And perhaps more important, do the psychological roots of Level 5 leadership matter any more than do the roots of charisma or intelligence? The question remains: Can Level 5 be developed?

My preliminary hypothesis is that there are two categories of people: those who don't have the Level 5 seed within them and those who do. The first category consists of people who could never in a million years bring themselves to subjugate their own needs to the greater ambition of something larger and more lasting than themselves. For those people, work will always be first and foremost about what they get—the fame, fortune, power, adulation, and so on. Work will never be about what they build, create, and contribute. The great irony is that the animus and personal ambition that often drives people to become a Level 4 leader stands at odds with the humility required to rise to Level 5.

When you combine that irony with the fact that boards of directors frequently operate under the false belief that a larger-than-life, egocentric leader is required to make a company great, you can quickly see why Level 5 leaders rarely appear at the top of our institutions. We keep putting people in positions of power who lack the seed to become a Level 5 leader, and that is one major reason why there are so few companies that make a sustained and verifiable shift from good to great.

The second category consists of people who could evolve to Level 5; the capability resides within them, perhaps buried or ignored or simply nascent. Under the right circumstances—with self-reflection, a mentor, loving parents, a significant life experience, or other factors—the seed can begin to develop. Some of the Level 5 leaders in our study had significant life experiences that might have sparked development of the seed. Darwin Smith fully blossomed as a Level 5 after his near-death experience with cancer. Joe Cullman was profoundly affected by his World War II experiences, particularly the last-minute change of orders that took him off a doomed ship on which he surely would have died; he considered the next 60-odd years a great gift. A strong religious belief or conversion might also nurture the seed. Colman Mockler, for example, converted to evangelical Christianity while getting his MBA at Harvard, and later, according to the book *Cutting Edge* by Gordon McKibben, he became a prime mover in a group of Boston business executives that met frequently over breakfast to discuss the carryover of religious values to corporate life.

We would love to be able to give you a list of steps for getting to Level 5—other than contracting cancer, going through a religious conversion, or getting different parents—but we have no solid research data that would support a credible list. Our research exposed Level 5 as a key component inside the black box of what it takes to shift a company from good to great. Yet inside that black box is another—the inner development of a person to Level 5 leadership. We could speculate on what that inner box might hold, but it would mostly be just that: speculation.

In short, Level 5 is a very satisfying idea, a truthful idea, a powerful idea, and, to make the move from good to great, very likely an essential idea. But to provide "ten steps to Level 5 leadership" would trivialize the concept.

My best advice, based on the research, is to practice the other good-to-great disciplines that we discovered. Since we found a tight symbiotic relationship between each of the other findings and Level 5, we suspect that conscientiously trying to lead using the other disciplines can help you move in the right direction. There is no guarantee that doing so will turn executives into full-fledged Level 5 leaders, but it gives them a tangible place to begin, especially if they have the seed within.

We cannot say for sure what percentage of people have the seed within, nor how many of those can nurture it enough to become

Level 5. Even those of us on the research team who identified Level 5 do not know whether we will succeed in evolving to its heights. And yet all of us who worked on the finding have been inspired by the idea of trying to move toward Level 5. Darwin Smith, Colman Mockler, Alan Wurtzel, and all the other Level 5 leaders we learned about have become role models for us. Whether or not we make it to Level 5, it is worth trying. For like all basic truths about what is best in human beings, when we catch a glimpse of that truth, we know that our own lives and all that we touch will be the better for making the effort to get there.

Originally published in January 2001. Reprint R0507M

Seven Transformations of Leadership

by David Rooke and William R. Torbert

MOST DEVELOPMENTAL PSYCHOLOGISTS agree that what differentiates leaders is not so much their philosophy of leadership, their personality, or their style of management. Rather, it's their internal "action logic"—how they interpret their surroundings and react when their power or safety is challenged. Relatively few leaders, however, try to understand their own action logic, and fewer still have explored the possibility of changing it.

They should, because we've found that leaders who do undertake a voyage of personal understanding and development can transform not only their own capabilities but also those of their companies. In our close collaboration with psychologist Susanne Cook-Greuter—and our 25 years of extensive survey-based consulting at companies such as Deutsche Bank, Harvard Pilgrim Health Care, Hewlett-Packard, NSA, Trillium Asset Management, Aviva, and Volvo—we've worked with thousands of executives as they've tried to develop their leadership skills. The good news is that leaders who make an effort to understand their own action logic can improve their ability to lead. But to do that, it's important first to understand what kind of leader you already are.

The Seven Action Logics

Our research is based on a sentence-completion survey tool called the Leadership Development Profile. Using this tool, participants are asked to complete 36 sentences that begin with phrases such as "A good leader . . . ," to which responses vary widely:

". . . cracks the whip."

". . . realizes that it's important to achieve good performance from subordinates."

". . . juggles competing forces and takes responsibility for her decisions."

By asking participants to complete sentences of this type, it's possible for highly trained evaluators to paint a picture of how participants interpret their own actions and the world around them; these "pictures" show which one of seven developmental action logics—Opportunist, Diplomat, Expert, Achiever, Individualist, Strategist, or Alchemist—currently functions as a leader's dominant way of thinking. Leaders can move through these categories as their abilities grow, so taking the Leadership Development Profile again several years later can reveal whether a leader's action logic has evolved.

Over the past 25 years, we and other researchers have administered the sentence-completion survey to thousands of managers and professionals, most between the ages of 25 and 55, at hundreds of American and European companies (as well as nonprofits and governmental agencies) in diverse industries. What we found is that the levels of corporate and individual performance vary according to action logic. Notably, we found that the three types of leaders associated with below-average corporate performance (Opportunists, Diplomats, and Experts) accounted for 55% of our sample. They were significantly less effective at implementing organizational strategies than the 30% of the sample who measured as Achievers. Moreover, only the final 15% of managers in the sample (Individualists, Strategists, and Alchemists) showed the consistent capacity to innovate and to successfully transform their organizations.

Idea in Brief

Every company needs transformational leaders—those who spearhead changes that elevate profitability, expand market share, and change the rules of the game in their industry. But few executives understand the unique strengths needed to become such a leader. Result? They miss the opportunity to develop those strengths. They and their firms lose out.

How to avoid this scenario? Recognize that great leaders are differentiated not by their personality or philosophy but by their **action logic**—how they interpret their own and others' behavior and how they maintain power or protect against threats.

Some leaders rely on action logics that hinder organizational performance. Opportunists, for example, believe in winning any way possible, and often exploit others to score personal gains. Few people follow them for long. Other types prove potent change agents. In particular, Strategists believe that every aspect of their organization is open to discussion and transformation. Their action logic enables them to challenge perceptions that constrain their organizations and to overcome resistance to change. They create compelling, shared visions and lead the pragmatic initiatives needed to realize those visions.

Though Strategists are rare, you *can* develop their defining strengths. How? Diagnose your current action logic and work to upgrade it. The payoff? You help your company execute the changes it needs to excel.

To understand how leaders fall into such distinct categories and corporate performance, let's look in more detail at each leadership style in turn, starting with the least productive (and least complex).

The Opportunist

Our most comforting finding was that only 5% of the leaders in our sample were characterized by mistrust, egocentrism, and manipulativeness. We call these leaders Opportunists, a title that reflects their tendency to focus on personal wins and see the world and other

Idea in Practice

Seven Types of Action Logic

Type	Characteristics	Strengths	Weaknesses
Opportunist	*Wins any way possible.* Self-oriented; manipulative; "might makes right."	Good in emergencies and in pursuing sales.	Few people want to follow them for the long term.
Diplomat	*Avoids conflict.* Wants to belong; obeys group norms; doesn't rock the boat.	Supportive glue on teams.	Can't provide painful feedback or make the hard decisions needed to improve performance.
Expert	*Rules by logic and expertise.* Uses hard data to gain consensus and buy-in.	Good individual contributor.	Lacks emotional intelligence; lacks respect for those with less expertise.
Achiever	*Meets strategic goals.* Promotes teamwork; juggles managerial duties and responds to market demands to achieve goals.	Well suited to managerial work.	Inhibits thinking outside the box.
Individualist	*Operates in unconventional ways.* Ignores rules he/she regards as irrelevant.	Effective in venture and consulting roles.	Irritates colleagues and bosses by ignoring key organizational processes and people.
Strategist	*Generates organizational and personal change.* Highly collaborative; weaves visions with pragmatic, timely initiatives; challenges existing assumptions.	Generates transformations over the short and long term.	None
Alchemist	*Generates social transformations (e.g., Nelson Mandela).* Reinvents organizations in historically significant ways.	Leads societywide change.	None

Changing Your Action Logic Type

To change your action logic type, experiment with new interpersonal behaviors, forge new kinds of relationships, and seize advantage of work opportunities. For example:

To advance from. . .	Take these steps
Expert to Achiever	Focus more on delivering results than on perfecting your knowledge: • Become aware of differences between your assumptions and those of others. For example, practice new conversational strategies such as "You may be right, but I'd like to understand what leads you to believe that." • Participate in training programs on topics such as effective delegation and leading high-performing teams
Achiever to Individualist	Instead of accepting goals as givens to be achieved: • Reflect on the worth of the goals themselves, with the aim of improving future goals • Use annual leadership development planning to thoughtfully set the highest-impact goals
Individualist to Strategist	Engage in peer-to-peer development: • Establish mutual mentoring with members of your professional network (board members, top managers, industry leaders) who can challenge your assumptions and practices, as well as those of your company and industry. ***Example:*** One CEO of a dental hygiene company envisioned introducing affordable dental hygiene in developing countries. He explored the idea with colleagues across the country, eventually proposing an educational and charitable venture that his parent company agreed to fund. He was promoted to a new vice presidency for international ventures within the parent company.

people as opportunities to be exploited. Their approach to the outside world is largely determined by their perception of control—in other words, how they will react to an event depends primarily on whether or not they think they can direct the outcome. They treat other people as objects or as competitors who are also out for themselves.

Opportunists tend to regard their bad behavior as legitimate in the cut and thrust of an eye-for-an-eye world. They reject feedback, externalize blame, and retaliate harshly. One can see this action logic in the early work of Larry Ellison (now CEO of Oracle). Ellison describes his managerial style at the start of his career as "management by ridicule." "You've got to be good at intellectual intimidation and rhetorical bullying," he once told Matthew Symonds of the *Economist*. "I'd excuse my behavior by telling myself I was just having 'an open and honest debate.' The fact is, I just didn't know any better."

Few Opportunists remain managers for long, unless they transform to more effective action logics (as Ellison has done). Their constant firefighting, their style of self-aggrandizement, and their frequent rule breaking is the antithesis of the kind of leader people want to work with for the long term. If you have worked for an Opportunist, you will almost certainly remember it as a difficult time. By the same token, corporate environments that breed opportunism seldom endure, although Opportunists often survive longer than they should because they provide an exciting environment in which younger executives, especially, can take risks. As one ex-Enron senior staffer said, "Before the fall, those were such exciting years. We felt we could do anything, pull off everything, write our own rules. The pace was wild, and we all just rode it." Of course, Enron's shareholders and pensioners would reasonably feel that they were paying too heavily for that staffer's adventure.

The Diplomat

The Diplomat makes sense of the world around him in a more benign way than the Opportunist does, but this action logic can also have extremely negative repercussions if the leader is a senior manager.

Loyally serving the group, the Diplomat seeks to please higher-status colleagues while avoiding conflict. This action logic is focused on gaining control of one's own behavior—more than on gaining control of external events or other people. According to the Diplomat's action logic, a leader gains more enduring acceptance and influence by cooperating with group norms and by performing his daily roles well.

In a support role or a team context, this type of executive has much to offer. Diplomats provide social glue to their colleagues and ensure that attention is paid to the needs of others, which is probably why the great majority of Diplomats work at the most junior rungs of management, in jobs such as frontline supervisor, customer service representative, or nurse practitioner. Indeed, research into 497 managers in different industries showed that 80% of all Diplomats were at junior levels. By contrast, 80% of all Strategists were at senior levels, suggesting that managers who grow into more effective action logics—like that of the Strategist—have a greater chance of being promoted.

Diplomats are much more problematic in top leadership roles because they try to ignore conflict. They tend to be overly polite and friendly and find it virtually impossible to give challenging feedback to others. Initiating change, with its inevitable conflicts, represents a grave threat to the Diplomat, and he will avoid it if at all possible, even to the point of self-destruction.

Consider one Diplomat who became the interim CEO of an organization when his predecessor died suddenly from an aneurysm. When the board split on the selection of a permanent successor, it asked the Diplomat to carry on. Our Diplomat relished his role as a ceremonial figurehead and was a sought-after speaker at public events. Unfortunately, he found the more conflictual requirements of the job less to his liking. He failed, for instance, to replace a number of senior managers who had serious ongoing performance issues and were resisting the change program his predecessor had initiated. Because the changes were controversial, the Diplomat avoided meetings, even planning business trips for the times when the senior team would meet. The team members were so frustrated by the Diplomat's attitude that they eventually resigned en masse. He "resolved" this

Seven Ways of Leading

DIFFERENT LEADERS exhibit different kinds of action logic—ways in which they interpret their surroundings and react when their power or safety is challenged. In our research of thousands of leaders, we observed seven types of action logics. The least effective for organizational leadership are the Opportunist and Diplomat; the most effective, the Strategist and Alchemist. Knowing your own action logic can be the first step toward developing a more effective leadership style. If you recognize yourself as an Individualist, for example, you can work, through both formal and informal measures, to develop the strengths and characteristics of a Strategist.

Action Logic	Characteristics	Strengths	% of research sample profiling at this action logic
Opportunist	*Wins any way possible.* Self-oriented; manipulative; "might makes right."	Good in emergencies and in sales opportunities.	5%
Diplomat	*Avoids overt conflict.* Wants to belong; obeys group norms; rarely rocks the boat.	Good as supportive glue within an office; helps bring people together.	12%
Expert	*Rules by logic and expertise.* Seeks rational efficiency.	Good as an individual contributor.	38%

crisis by thanking the team publicly for its contribution and appointing new team members. Eventually, in the face of mounting losses arising from this poor management, the board decided to demote the Diplomat to his former role as vice president.

The Expert

The largest category of leader is that of Experts, who account for 38% of all professionals in our sample. In contrast to Opportunists,

Achiever	*Meets strategic goals.* Effectively achieves goals through teams; juggles managerial duties and market demands.	Well suited to managerial roles; action and goal oriented.	30%
Individualist	*Interweaves competing personal and company action logics.* Creates unique structures to resolve gaps between strategy and performance.	Effective in venture and consulting roles.	10%
Strategist	*Generates organizational and personal transformations.* Exercises the power of mutual inquiry, vigilance, and vulnerability for both the short and long term.	Effective as a transformational leader.	4%
Alchemist	*Generates social transformations.* Integrates material, spiritual, and societal transformation.	Good at leading society-wide transformations.	1%

who focus on trying to control the world around them, and Diplomats, who concentrate on controlling their own behavior, Experts try to exercise control by perfecting their knowledge, both in their professional and personal lives. Exercising watertight thinking is extremely important to Experts. Not surprisingly, many accountants, investment analysts, marketing researchers, software engineers, and consultants operate from the Expert action logic. Secure in their expertise, they present hard data and logic in their efforts to gain consensus and buy-in for their proposals.

Experts are great individual contributors because of their pursuit of continuous improvement, efficiency, and perfection. But as managers, they can be problematic because they are so completely sure they are right. When subordinates talk about a my-way-or-the-highway type of boss, they are probably talking about someone operating from an Expert action logic. Experts tend to view collaboration as a waste of time ("Not all meetings are a waste of time—some are canceled!"), and they will frequently treat the opinions of people less expert than themselves with contempt. Emotional intelligence is neither desired nor appreciated. As Sun Microsystems' CEO Scott McNealy put it: "I don't do feelings; I'll leave that to Barry Manilow."

It comes as no surprise, then, that after unsuccessfully pleading with him to scale back in the face of growing losses during the dot-com debacle of 2001 and 2002, nearly a dozen members of McNealy's senior management team left.

The Achiever

For those who hope someday to work for a manager who both challenges and supports them and creates a positive team and interdepartmental atmosphere, the good news is that a large proportion, 30%, of the managers in our research measured as Achievers. While these leaders create a positive work environment and focus their efforts on deliverables, the downside is that their style often inhibits thinking outside the box.

Achievers have a more complex and integrated understanding of the world than do managers who display the three previous action logics we've described. They're open to feedback and realize that many of the ambiguities and conflicts of everyday life are due to differences in interpretation and ways of relating. They know that creatively transforming or resolving clashes requires sensitivity to relationships and the ability to influence others in positive ways. Achievers can also reliably lead a team to implement new strategies over a one- to three-year period, balancing immediate and long-term objectives. One study of ophthalmologists in private practice showed that those who scored as Achievers had lower staff turnover, delegated more responsibility, and had practices that earned at least twice the gross annual revenues of those run by Experts.

Achievers often find themselves clashing with Experts. The Expert subordinate, in particular, finds the Achiever leader hard to take because he cannot deny the reality of the Achiever's success even though he feels superior. Consider Hewlett-Packard, where the research engineers tend to score as Experts and the lab managers as higher-level Achievers. At one project meeting, a lab manager—a decided Achiever—slammed her coffee cup on the table and exclaimed, "I *know* we can get 18 features into this, but the customers want delivery some time this century, and the main eight features will do." "Philistine!" snorted one engineer, an Expert. But this kind of conflict isn't always destructive. In fact, it provides much of the fuel that has ignited—and sustained—the competitiveness of many of the country's most successful corporations.

The Individualist

The Individualist action logic recognizes that neither it nor any of the other action logics are "natural"; all are constructions of oneself and the world. This seemingly abstract idea enables the 10% of Individualist leaders to contribute unique practical value to their organizations; they put personalities and ways of relating into perspective and communicate well with people who have other action logics.

What sets Individualists apart from Achievers is their awareness of a possible conflict between their principles and their actions, or between the organization's values and its implementation of those values. This conflict becomes the source of tension, creativity, and a growing desire for further development.

Individualists also tend to ignore rules they regard as irrelevant, which often makes them a source of irritation to both colleagues and bosses. "So, what do you think?" one of our clients asked us as he was debating whether to let go of one of his star performers, a woman who had been measured as an Individualist. Sharon (not her real name) had been asked to set up an offshore shared service function in the Czech Republic in order to provide IT support to two separate and internally competitive divisions operating there. She formed a highly cohesive team within budget and so far ahead of schedule that she quipped that she was "delivering services before Group Business Risk had delivered its report saying it can't be done."

The trouble was that Sharon had a reputation within the wider organization as a wild card. Although she showed great political savvy when it came to her individual projects, she put many people's noses out of joint in the larger organization because of her unique, unconventional ways of operating. Eventually, the CEO was called in (not for the first time) to resolve a problem created by her failure to acknowledge key organizational processes and people who weren't on her team.

Many of the dynamics created by different action logics are illustrated by this story and its outcome. The CEO, whose own action logic was that of an Achiever, did not see how he could challenge Sharon to develop and move beyond creating such problems. Although ambivalent about her, he decided to retain her because she was delivering and because the organization had recently lost several capable, if unconventional, managers.

So Sharon stayed, but only for a while. Eventually, she left the company to set up an offshoring consultancy. When we examine in the second half of this article how to help executives transform their leadership action logics, we'll return to this story to see how both Sharon and the CEO might have succeeded in transforming theirs.

The Strategist

Strategists account for just 4% of leaders. What sets them apart from Individualists is their focus on organizational constraints and perceptions, which they treat as discussable and transformable. Whereas the Individualist masters communication with colleagues who have different action logics, the Strategist masters the second-order organizational impact of actions and agreements. The Strategist is also adept at creating shared visions across different action logics—visions that encourage both personal and organizational transformations. According to the Strategist's action logic, organizational and social change is an iterative developmental process that requires awareness and close leadership attention.

Strategists deal with conflict more comfortably than do those with other action logics, and they're better at handling people's instinctive resistance to change. As a result, Strategists are highly effective change agents. We found confirmation of this in our recent study of ten CEOs in six different industries. All of their organizations had the stated objective of transforming themselves and had engaged consultants to help with the process. Each CEO filled out a Leadership Development Profile, which showed that five of them were Strategists and the other five fell into other action logics. The Strategists succeeded in generating one or more organizational transformations over a four-year period; their companies' profitability, market share, and reputation all improved. By contrast, only two of the other five CEOs succeeded in transforming their organizations—despite help from consultants, who themselves profiled as Strategists.

Strategists are fascinated with three distinct levels of social interplay: personal relationships, organizational relations, and national and international developments. Consider Joan Bavaria, a CEO who, back in 1985, measured as a Strategist. Bavaria created one of the first socially responsible investment funds, a new subdivision of the investments industry, which by the end of 2001 managed more than $3 trillion in funds. In 1982, Bavaria founded Trillium Asset Management, a worker-owned company, which she still heads. She also cowrote the CERES Environmental Principles, which dozens of major companies have signed. In the late 1990s, CERES, working with the United Nations, created the Global Reporting Initiative, which supports financial, social, and environmental transparency and accountability worldwide.

Here we see the Strategist action logic at work. Bavaria saw a unique moment in which to make ethical investing a viable business, then established Trillium to execute her plan. Strategists typically have socially conscious business ideas that are carried out in a highly collaborative manner. They seek to weave together idealist visions with pragmatic, timely initiatives and principled actions. Bavaria worked beyond the boundaries of her own organization to influence the socially responsible investment industry as a whole and later made the development of social and environmental accountability standards an international endeavor by involving the United Nations. Many Achievers will use their influence to successfully promote their own companies. The Strategist works to create ethical principles and practices beyond the interests of herself or her organization.

The Alchemist

The final leadership action logic for which we have data and experience is the Alchemist. Our studies of the few leaders we have identified as Alchemists suggest that what sets them apart from Strategists is their ability to renew or even reinvent themselves and their organizations in historically significant ways. Whereas the Strategist will move from one engagement to another, the Alchemist has an extraordinary capacity to deal simultaneously with many situations at multiple levels. The Alchemist can talk with both kings and commoners. He can deal with immediate priorities yet never lose sight of long-term goals.

Alchemists constitute 1% of our sample, which indicates how rare it is to find them in business or anywhere else. Through an extensive search process, we found six Alchemists who were willing to participate in an up-close study of their daily actions. Though this is obviously a very small number that cannot statistically justify generalization, it's worth noting that all six Alchemists shared certain characteristics. On a daily basis, all were engaged in multiple organizations and found time to deal with issues raised by each. However, they were not in a constant rush—nor did they devote hours on end to a single activity. Alchemists are typically charismatic and extremely aware individuals who live by high moral standards. They focus intensely on the truth. Perhaps most important, they're able to catch unique moments in the history of their organizations, creating symbols and metaphors that speak to people's hearts and minds. In one conservative financial services company in the UK, a recently appointed CEO turned up for work in a tracksuit instead of his usual pinstripes but said nothing about it to anyone. People wondered whether this was a new dress code. Weeks later, the CEO spoke publicly about his attire and the need to be unconventional and to move with greater agility and speed.

A more celebrated example of an Alchemist is Nelson Mandela. Although we never formally profiled Mandela, he exemplifies the Alchemist action logic. In 1995, Mandela symbolized the unity of a new South Africa when he attended the Rugby World Cup game in which the Springboks, the South African national team, were playing. Rugby had been the bastion of white supremacy, but Mandela attended the game. He walked on to the pitch wearing the Springboks' jersey so hated by black South Africans, at the same time giving the clenched fist salute of the ANC, thereby appealing, almost impossibly, both to black and white South Africans. As Tokyo Sexwale, ANC activist and premier of South Africa's Gauteng province, said of him: "Only Mandela could wear an enemy jersey. Only Mandela would go down there and be associated with the Springboks . . . All the years in the underground, in the trenches, denial, self-denial, away from home, prison, it was worth it. That's all we wanted to see."

Evolving as a Leader

The most remarkable—and encouraging—finding from our research is that leaders can transform from one action logic to another. We have, in fact, documented a number of leaders who have succeeded in transforming themselves from Experts into Achievers, from Achievers into Individualists, and from Individualists into Strategists.

Take the case of Jenny, one of our clients, who initially measured as an Expert. She became disillusioned with her role in her company's PR department and resigned in order to, as she said, "sort out what I really want to do." Six months later, she joined a different company in a similar role, and two years after that we profiled her again and she still measured as an Expert. Her decision to resign from the first company, take a "sabbatical," and then join the second company had made no difference to her action logic. At that point, Jenny chose to join a group of peer leaders committed to examining their current leadership patterns and to experimenting with new ways of acting. This group favored the Strategist perspective (and the founder of the group was profiled as an Alchemist), which in the end helped Jenny's development. She learned that her habit of consistently taking a critical position, which she considered "usefully objective," isolated her and generated distrust. As a result of the peer group's feedback, she started a series of small and private experiments, such as asking questions rather than criticizing. She realized that instead of seeing the faults in others, she had to be clear about what *she* could contribute and, in doing so, started the move from an Expert to an Achiever. Spiritually, Jenny learned that she needed an ongoing community of inquiry at the center of her life and found a spiritual home for continuing reflection in Quaker meetings, which later supported (and indeed signaled) her transition from an Achiever to an Individualist.

Two years later, Jenny left the second job to start her own company, at which point she began profiling as a Strategist. This was a highly unusual movement of three action logics in such a short time. We have had only two other instances in which a leader has transformed twice in less than four years.

As Jenny's case illustrates, there are a number of personal changes that can support leadership transformation. Jenny experienced loss of faith in the system and feelings of boredom, irritability, burnout, depression, and even anger. She began to ask herself existential questions. But another indication of a leader's readiness to transform is an increasing attraction to the qualities she begins to intuit in people with more effective action logics. Jenny, as we saw, was drawn to and benefited hugely from her Strategist peer group as well as from a mentor who exhibited the Alchemist action logic. This search for new perspectives often manifests itself in personal transformations: The ready-to-transform leader starts developing new relationships. She may also explore new forms of spiritual practice or new forms of centering and self-expression, such as playing a musical instrument or doing tai chi.

External events can also trigger and support transformation. A promotion, for example, may give a leader the opportunity to expand his or her range of capabilities. Earlier, we cited the frustration of Expert research engineers at Hewlett-Packard with the product and delivery attitude of Achiever lab managers. Within a year of one engineer's promotion to lab manager, a role that required coordination of others and cooperation across departments, the former Expert was profiling as an Achiever. Although he initially took some heat ("Sellout!") from his former buddies, his new Achiever awareness meant that he was more focused on customers' needs and clearer about delivery schedules. For the first time, he understood the dance between engineers trying to perfect the technology and managers trying to deliver on budget and on schedule.

Changes to a manager's work practices and environment can also facilitate transformation. At one company we studied, leaders changed from Achievers to Individualists partly because of simple organizational and process changes. At the company's senior manager meetings, for example, executives other than the CEO had the chance to lead the meetings; these opportunities, which were supported by new spirit of openness, feedback, and frank debate, fostered professional growth among many of the company's leaders.

Planned and structured development interventions are another means of supporting leadership transformation. We worked with a leading oil and gas exploration company on developing the already high-level capabilities of a pool of future senior managers; the managers were profiled and then interviewed by two consultants who explored each manager's action logic and how it constrained and enabled him or her to perform current and recent roles. Challenges were discussed as well as a view of the individual's potential and a possible developmental plan. After the exercise, several managers, whose Individualist and Strategist capabilities had not been fully understood by the company, were appreciated and engaged differently in their roles. What's more, the organization's own definition of leadership talent was reframed to include the capabilities of the Individualist and Strategist action logics. This in turn demanded that the company radically revisit its competency framework to incorporate such expectations as "sees issues from multiple perspectives" and "creates deep change without formal power."

Now that we've looked generally at some of the changes and interventions that can support leadership development, let's turn to some specifics about how the most common transformations are apt to take place.

From Expert to Achiever

This transformation is the most commonly observed and practiced among businesspeople and by those in management and executive education. For the past generation or more, the training departments of large companies have been supporting the development of managers from Experts into Achievers by running programs with titles like "Management by Objectives," "Effective Delegation," and "Managing People for Results." These programs typically emphasize getting results through flexible strategies rather than through one right method used in one right way.

Observant leaders and executive coaches can also formulate well-structured exercises and questions related to everyday work to help Experts become aware of the different assumptions they and others may be making. These efforts can help Experts practice new conversational strategies such as, "You may be right, but I'd like to understand what leads you to believe that." In addition, those wishing to push Experts to the next level should consider rewarding Achiever competencies like timely delivery of results, the ability to manage for performance, and the ability to implement strategic priorities.

Within business education, MBA programs are apt to encourage the development of the more pragmatic Achievers by frustrating the perfectionist Experts. The heavy workloads, use of multidisciplinary and ambiguous case studies, and teamwork requirements all promote the development of Achievers. By contrast, MSc programs, in particular disciplines such as finance or marketing research, tend to reinforce the Expert perspective.

Still, the transition from Expert to Achiever remains one of the most painful bottlenecks in most organizations. We've all heard the eternal lament of engineers, lawyers, and other professionals whose Expert success has saddled them with managerial duties, only to estrange them from the work they love. Their challenge becomes working as highly effective Achievers who can continue to use their in-depth expertise to succeed as leaders and managers.

From Achiever to Individualist

Although organizations and business schools have been relatively successful in developing leaders to the Achiever action logic, they have, with few exceptions, a dismal record in recognizing, supporting, and *actively* developing leaders to the Individualist and Strategist action logics, let alone to the Alchemist logic. This is not surprising. In many organizations, the Achiever, with his drive and focus on the endgame, is seen as the finish line for development: "This is a competitive industry—we need to keep a sharp focus on the bottom line."

The development of leaders beyond the Achiever action logic requires a very different tack from that necessary to bring about the Expert-to-Achiever transformation. Interventions must encourage self-awareness on the part of the evolving leader as well as a greater awareness of other worldviews. In both business and personal relationships, speaking and listening must come to be experienced not as necessary, taken-for-granted ways of communicating predetermined ideas but as intrinsically forward-thinking, creative actions. Achievers use inquiry to determine whether they (and the teams and organization to which they belong) are accomplishing their goals and how they might accomplish them more effectively. The developing Individualist, however, begins to inquire about and reflect on the goals themselves—with the aim of improving future goals. Annual development plans that set new goals, are generated through probing and trusting conversation, are actively supported through executive coaching, and are carefully reviewed at the end of the cycle can be critical enablers at this point. Yet few boards and CEOs appreciate how valuable this time investment can be, and it is all too easily sacrificed in the face of short-term objectives, which can seem more pressing to leaders whose action logics are less developed.

Let's go back to the case of Sharon, the Individualist we described earlier whose Achiever CEO wasn't able to manage her. How might a coach or consultant have helped the CEO feel less threatened by Sharon and more capable of supporting her development while also being more open to his own needs and potential? One way would have been to try role-playing, asking the CEO to play Sharon while the coach or consultant enacts the CEO role. The role-playing might have gone as follows:

"Sharon, I want to talk with you about your future here at our company. Your completion of the Czech project under budget and ahead of time is one more sign that you have the initiative, creativity, and determination to make the senior team here. At the same time, I've had to pick up a number of pieces after you that I shouldn't have had to. I'd like to brainstorm together about how you can approach future projects in a way that eliminates this hassle and gets key players on your side. Then, we can chat several times over the next year as you begin to apply whatever new principles we come up with. Does this seem like a good use of our time, or do you have a different perspective on the issue?"

Note that the consultant in the CEO's role offers clear praise, a clear description of a limitation, a proposed path forward, and an inquiry that empowers the CEO (playing Sharon) to reframe the dilemma if he wishes. Thus, instead of giving the CEO one-way advice about what he should do, the coach enacts a dialogic scenario with him, illustrating a new kind of practice and letting the CEO judge whether the enacted relationship is a positive one. The point is not so much to teach the CEO a new conversational repertoire but to make him more comfortable with how the Individualist sees and makes sense of the world around her and what feedback may motivate her to commit to further learning. Such specific experiments with new ways of listening and talking can gradually dissolve the fears associated with transformational learning.

To Strategist and Beyond

Leaders who are moving toward the Strategist and Alchemist action logics are no longer primarily seeking personal skills that will make them more effective within existing organizational systems. They will already have mastered many of those skills. Rather, they are exploring the disciplines and commitments entailed in creating projects, teams, networks, strategic alliances, and whole organizations on the basis of collaborative inquiry. It is this ongoing practice of reframing inquiry that makes them and their corporations so successful.

The path toward the Strategist and Alchemist action logics is qualitatively different from other leadership development processes. For a start, emergent Strategists and Alchemists are no longer seeking mentors to help them sharpen existing skills and to guide them toward influential networks (although they may seek spiritual and ethical guidance from mentors). Instead, they are seeking to engage in mutual mentoring with peers who are already part of their networks (such as board members, top managers, or leaders within a scientific discipline). The objective of this senior-peer mentoring is not, in conventional terms, to increase the chances of success but to create a sustainable community of people who can challenge the emergent leader's assumptions and practices and those of his company, industry, or other area of activity.

We witnessed just this kind of peer-to-peer development when one senior client became concerned that he, his company, and the industry as a whole were operating at the Achiever level. This concern, of course, was itself a sign of his readiness to transform beyond that logic. This executive—the CEO of a dental hygiene company—and his company were among the most successful of the parent company's subsidiaries. However, realizing that he and those around him had been keeping their heads down, he chose to initiate a research project—on introducing affordable dental hygiene in developing countries—that was decidedly out of the box for him and for the corporation.

The CEO's timing was right for such an initiative, and he used the opportunity to engage in collaborative inquiry with colleagues across the country. Eventually, he proposed an educational and charitable venture, which the parent company funded. The executive was promoted to a new vice presidency for international ventures within the parent company—a role he exercised with an increased sense of collaboration and a greater feeling of social responsibility for his company in emerging markets.

Formal education and development processes can also guide individuals toward a Strategist action logic. Programs in which participants act as leaders and challenge their conventional assumptions about leading and organizing are very effective. Such programs will be either long term (one or two years) or repeated, intense experiences that nurture the moment-to-moment awareness of participants, always providing the shock of dissonance that stimulates them to reexamine their worldviews. Path-breaking programs of this type can be found at a few universities and consultancies around the globe. Bath University in the UK, for instance, sponsors a two-year master's degree in responsibility and business practice in which students work together during six one-week get-togethers. These programs involve small-learning teams, autobiographical writing, psychodrama, deep experiences in nature, and a yearlong business project that involves action and reflection. Interestingly, many people who attend these programs report that these experiences have had the transformative power of a life-altering event, such as a career or existential crisis or a new marriage.

Leadership Teams and Leadership Cultures Within Organizations

So far, our discussion has focused on the leadership styles of individuals. But we have found that our categories of leadership styles can be used to describe teams and organizations as well. Here we will talk briefly about the action logics of teams.

Over the long term, the most effective teams are those with a Strategist culture, in which the group sees business challenges as opportunities for growth and learning on the part of both individuals and the organization. A leadership team at one of the companies we worked with decided to invite managers from across departments to participate in time-to-market new product teams. Seen as a risky distraction, few managers volunteered, except for some Individualists and budding Strategists. However, senior management provided sufficient support and feedback to ensure the teams' early success. Soon, the first participants were promoted and leading their own cross-departmental teams. The Achievers in the organization, seeing that others were being promoted, started volunteering for these teams. Gradually, more people within the organization were experiencing shared leadership, mutual testing of one another's assumptions and practices, and individual challenges that contributed to their development as leaders.

Sadly, few companies use teams in this way. Most senior manager teams operate at the Achiever action logic—they prefer unambiguous targets and deadlines, and working with clear strategies, tactics, and plans, often against tight deadlines. They thrive in a climate of adversity ("When the going gets tough, the tough get going") and derive great pleasure from pulling together and delivering. Typically, the team's leaders and several other members will be Achievers, with several Experts and perhaps one or two Individualists or Strategists (who typically feel ignored). Such Achiever teams are often impatient at slowing down to reflect, are apt to dismiss questions about goals and assumptions as "endless philosophizing," and typically respond with hostile humor to creative exercises, calling them "off-the-wall" diversions. These behaviors will ultimately limit an Achiever team's success.

The situation is worse at large, mature companies where senior management teams operate as Experts. Here, vice presidents see themselves as chiefs and their "teams" as an information-reporting formality. Team life is bereft of shared problem-solving, decision-making, or strategy-formulating efforts. Senior teams limited by the Diplomat action logic are even less functional. They are characterized by strong status differences, undiscussable norms, and ritual "court" ceremonies that are carefully stage-managed.

Individualist teams, which are more likely to be found in creative, consulting, and nonprofit organizations, are relatively rare and very different from Achiever, Expert, and Diplomat teams. In contrast to Achiever teams, they may be strongly reflective; in fact, excessive time may be spent reviewing goals, assumptions, and work practices. Because individual concerns and input are very important to these teams, rapid decision making may be difficult.

But like individual people, teams can change their style. For instance, we've seen Strategist CEOs help Individualist senior teams balance action and inquiry and so transform into Strategist teams. Another example is an Achiever senior team in a financial services company we worked with that was emerging from two years of harsh cost cutting during a market downturn. To adapt to a changing and growing financial services market, the company needed to become significantly more visionary and innovative and learn how to engage its workforce. To lead this transformation, the team had to start with itself. We worked with it to help team members understand the constraints of the Achiever orientation, which required a number of interventions over time. We began by working to improve the way the team discussed issues and by coaching individual members, including the CEO. As the team evolved, it became apparent that its composition needed to change: Two senior executives, who had initially seemed ideally suited to the group because of their achievements, had to be replaced when it became clear that they were unwilling to engage and experiment with the new approach.

During this reorientation, which lasted slightly more than two years, the team became an Individualist group with emergent Strategist capabilities. The CEO, who had profiled at Achiever/Individualist, now profiled as a Strategist, and most other team members showed one developmental move forward. The impact of this was also felt in the team's and organization's ethos: Once functionally divided, the team learned to accept and integrate the diverse opinions of its members. Employee surveys reported increased engagement across the company. Outsiders began seeing the company as ahead of the curve, which meant the organization was better able to attract top talent. In the third year, bottom- and top-line results were well ahead of industry competitors.

The leader's voyage of development is not an easy one. Some people change little in their lifetimes; some change substantially. Despite the undeniably crucial role of genetics, human nature is not fixed. Those who are willing to work at developing themselves and becoming more self-aware can almost certainly evolve over time into truly transformational leaders. Few may become Alchemists, but many will have the desire and potential to become Individualists and Strategists. Corporations that help their executives and leadership teams examine their action logics can reap rich rewards.

Originally published in April 2005. Reprint R0504D

Discovering Your Authentic Leadership

by Bill George, Peter Sims, Andrew N. McLean, and Diana Mayer

DURING THE PAST 50 YEARS, leadership scholars have conducted more than 1,000 studies in an attempt to determine the definitive styles, characteristics, or personality traits of great leaders. None of these studies has produced a clear profile of the ideal leader. Thank goodness. If scholars had produced a cookie-cutter leadership style, individuals would be forever trying to imitate it. They would make themselves into personae, not people, and others would see through them immediately.

No one can be authentic by trying to imitate someone else. You can learn from others' experiences, but there is no way you can be successful when you are trying to be like them. People trust you when you are genuine and authentic, not a replica of someone else. Amgen CEO and president Kevin Sharer, who gained priceless experience working as Jack Welch's assistant in the 1980s, saw the downside of GE's cult of personality in those days. "Everyone wanted to be like Jack," he explains. "Leadership has many voices. You need to be who you are, not try to emulate somebody else."

Over the past five years, people have developed a deep distrust of leaders. It is increasingly evident that we need a new kind of business leader in the twenty-first century. In 2003, Bill George's book, *Authentic Leadership: Rediscovering the Secrets to Creating Lasting Value,* challenged a new generation to lead authentically. Authentic leaders demonstrate a passion for their purpose, practice their values consistently, and lead with their hearts as well as their heads. They establish long-term, meaningful relationships and have the self-discipline to get results. They know who they are.

Many readers of *Authentic Leadership,* including several CEOs, indicated that they had a tremendous desire to become authentic leaders and wanted to know how. As a result, our research team set out to answer the question, "How can people become and remain authentic leaders?" We interviewed 125 leaders to learn how they developed their leadership abilities. These interviews constitute the largest in-depth study of leadership development ever undertaken. Our interviewees discussed openly and honestly how they realized their potential and candidly shared their life stories, personal struggles, failures, and triumphs.

The people we talked with ranged in age from 23 to 93, with no fewer than 15 per decade. They were chosen based on their reputations for authenticity and effectiveness as leaders, as well as our personal knowledge of them. We also solicited recommendations from other leaders and academics. The resulting group includes women and men from a diverse array of racial, religious, and socioeconomic backgrounds and nationalities. Half of them are CEOs, and the other half comprises a range of profit and nonprofit leaders, midcareer leaders, and young leaders just starting on their journeys.

After interviewing these individuals, we believe we understand why more than 1,000 studies have not produced a profile of an ideal leader. Analyzing 3,000 pages of transcripts, our team was startled to see that these people did not identify any universal characteristics, traits, skills, or styles that led to their success. Rather, their leadership emerged from their life stories. Consciously and subconsciously, they were constantly testing themselves through real-world experiences and reframing their life stories to understand who they were at their core. In doing so, they discovered the purpose of their leadership and learned that being authentic made them more effective.

These findings are extremely encouraging: You do not have to be born with specific characteristics or traits of a leader. You do not have to wait for a tap on the shoulder. You do not have to be at the top of your organization. Instead, you can discover your potential right now. As one of our interviewees, Young & Rubicam chairman and CEO Ann Fudge, said, "All of us have the spark of leadership in us, whether it is in business, in government, or as a nonprofit volunteer. The challenge is to understand ourselves well enough to discover where we can use our leadership gifts to serve others."

Discovering your authentic leadership requires a commitment to developing yourself. Like musicians and athletes, you must devote yourself to a lifetime of realizing your potential. Most people Kroger CEO David Dillon has seen become good leaders were self-taught. Dillon said, "The advice I give to individuals in our company is not to expect the company to hand you a development plan. You need to take responsibility for developing yourself."

In the following pages, we draw upon lessons from our interviews to describe how people become authentic leaders. First and most important, they frame their life stories in ways that allow them to see themselves not as passive observers of their lives but rather as individuals who can develop self-awareness from their experiences. Authentic leaders act on that awareness by practicing their values and principles, sometimes at substantial risk to themselves. They are careful to balance their motivations so that they are driven by these inner values as much as by a desire for external rewards or recognition. Authentic leaders also keep a strong support team around them, ensuring that they live integrated, grounded lives.

Learning from Your Life Story

The journey to authentic leadership begins with understanding the story of your life. Your life story provides the context for your experiences, and through it, you can find the inspiration to make an impact in the world. As the novelist John Barth once wrote, "The story of your life is not your life. It is your story." In other words, it is your personal narrative that matters, not the mere facts of your life. Your life narrative is like a permanent recording playing in your head. Over and over, you replay the events and personal interactions that are important to your life, attempting to make sense of them to find your place in the world.

While the life stories of authentic leaders cover the full spectrum of experiences—including the positive impact of parents, athletic coaches, teachers, and mentors—many leaders reported that their motivation came from a difficult experience in their lives. They described the transformative effects of the loss of a job; personal illness; the untimely death of a close friend or relative; and feelings of being excluded, discriminated against, and rejected by peers. Rather than seeing themselves as victims, though, authentic leaders used these formative experiences to give meaning to their lives. They reframed these events to rise above their challenges and to discover their passion to lead.

Let's focus now on one leader in particular, Novartis chairman and CEO Daniel Vasella, whose life story was one of the most difficult of all the people we interviewed. He emerged from extreme challenges in his youth to reach the pinnacle of the global pharmaceutical industry, a trajectory that illustrates the trials many leaders have to go through on their journeys to authentic leadership.

Vasella was born in 1953 to a modest family in Fribourg, Switzerland. His early years were filled with medical problems that stoked his passion to become a physician. His first recollections were of a hospital where he was admitted at age four when he suffered from food poisoning. Falling ill with asthma at age five, he was sent alone to the mountains of eastern Switzerland for two summers. He found the four-month separations from his parents especially difficult because his caretaker had an alcohol problem and was unresponsive to his needs.

At age eight, Vasella had tuberculosis, followed by meningitis, and was sent to a sanatorium for a year. Lonely and homesick, he suffered a great deal that year, as his parents rarely visited him. He still remembers the pain and fear when the nurses held him down during the lumbar punctures so that he would not move. One day, a new physician arrived and took time to explain each step of the procedure.

Vasella asked the doctor if he could hold a nurse's hand rather than being held down. "The amazing thing is that this time the procedure didn't hurt," Vasella recalls. "Afterward, the doctor asked me, 'How was that?' I reached up and gave him a big hug. These human gestures of forgiveness, caring, and compassion made a deep impression on me and on the kind of person I wanted to become."

Throughout his early years, Vasella's life continued to be unsettled. When he was ten, his 18-year-old sister passed away after suffering from cancer for two years. Three years later, his father died in surgery. To support the family, his mother went to work in a distant town and came home only once every three weeks. Left to himself, he and his friends held beer parties and got into frequent fights. This lasted for three years until he met his first girlfriend, whose affection changed his life.

At 20, Vasella entered medical school, later graduating with honors. During medical school, he sought out psychotherapy so he could come to terms with his early experiences and not feel like a victim. Through analysis, he reframed his life story and realized that he wanted to help a wider range of people than he could as an individual practitioner. Upon completion of his residency, he applied to become chief physician at the University of Zurich; however, the search committee considered him too young for the position.

Disappointed but not surprised, Vasella decided to use his abilities to increase his impact on medicine. At that time, he had a growing fascination with finance and business. He talked with the head of the pharmaceutical division of Sandoz, who offered him the opportunity to join the company's U.S. affiliate. In his five years in the United States, Vasella flourished in the stimulating environment, first as a sales representative and later as a product manager, and advanced rapidly through the Sandoz marketing organization.

When Sandoz merged with Ciba-Geigy in 1996, Vasella was named CEO of the combined companies, now called Novartis, despite his young age and limited experience. Once in the CEO's role, Vasella blossomed as a leader. He envisioned the opportunity to build a great global health care company that could help people through lifesaving new drugs, such as Gleevec, which has proved to be highly effective for patients with chronic myeloid leukemia. Drawing on the physician role models of his youth, he built an entirely new Novartis culture centered on compassion, competence, and competition. These moves established Novartis as a giant in the industry and Vasella as a compassionate leader.

Vasella's experience is just one of dozens provided by authentic leaders who traced their inspiration directly from their life stories. Asked what empowered them to lead, these leaders consistently replied that they found their strength through transformative experiences. Those experiences enabled them to understand the deeper purpose of their leadership.

Knowing Your Authentic Self

When the 75 members of Stanford Graduate School of Business's Advisory Council were asked to recommend the most important capability for leaders to develop, their answer was nearly unanimous: self-awareness. Yet many leaders, especially those early in their careers, are trying so hard to establish themselves in the world that they leave little time for self-exploration. They strive to achieve success in tangible ways that are recognized in the external world—money, fame, power, status, or a rising stock price. Often their drive enables them to be professionally successful for a while, but they are unable to sustain that success. As they age, they may find something is missing in their lives and realize they are holding back from being the person they want to be. Knowing their authentic selves requires the courage and honesty to open up and examine their experiences. As they do so, leaders become more humane and willing to be vulnerable.

Of all the leaders we interviewed, David Pottruck, former CEO of Charles Schwab, had one of the most persistent journeys to self-awareness. An all-league football player in high school, Pottruck became MVP of his college team at the University of Pennsylvania. After completing his MBA at Wharton and a stint with Citigroup, he joined Charles Schwab as head of marketing, moving from New York to San Francisco. An extremely hard worker, Pottruck could not understand why his new colleagues resented the long hours he put in and his aggressiveness in pushing for results. "I thought my accomplishments would speak for themselves," he said. "It never occurred to me that my level of energy would intimidate and offend other people, because in my mind I was trying to help the company."

Pottruck was shocked when his boss told him, "Dave, your colleagues do not trust you." As he recalled, "That feedback was like a dagger to my heart. I was in denial, as I didn't see myself as others saw me. I became a lightning rod for friction, but I had no idea how self-serving I looked to other people. Still, somewhere in my inner core the feedback resonated as true." Pottruck realized that he could not succeed unless he identified and overcame his blind spots.

Denial can be the greatest hurdle that leaders face in becoming self-aware. They all have egos that need to be stroked, insecurities that need to be smoothed, fears that need to be allayed. Authentic leaders realize that they have to be willing to listen to feedback—especially the kind they don't want to hear. It was only after his second divorce that Pottruck finally was able to acknowledge that he still had large blind spots: "After my second marriage fell apart, I thought I had a wife-selection problem." Then he worked with a counselor who delivered some hard truths: "The good news is you do not have a wife-selection problem; the bad news is you have a husband-behavior problem." Pottruck then made a determined effort to change. As he described it, "I was like a guy who has had three heart attacks and finally realizes he has to quit smoking and lose some weight."

These days Pottruck is happily remarried and listens carefully when his wife offers constructive feedback. He acknowledges that he falls back on his old habits at times, particularly in high stress situations, but now he has developed ways of coping with stress. "I have had enough success in life to have that foundation of self-respect, so I can take the criticism and not deny it. I have finally learned to tolerate my failures and disappointments and not beat myself up."

Practicing Your Values and Principles

The values that form the basis for authentic leadership are derived from your beliefs and convictions, but you will not know what your true values are until they are tested under pressure. It is relatively easy to list your values and to live by them when things are going well. When your success, your career, or even your life hangs in the balance, you learn what is most important, what you are prepared to sacrifice, and what trade-offs you are willing to make.

Leadership principles are values translated into action. Having a solid base of values and testing them under fire enables you to develop the principles you will use in leading. For example, a value such as "concern for others" might be translated into a leadership principle such as "create a work environment where people are respected for their contributions, provided job security, and allowed to fulfill their potential."

Consider Jon Huntsman, the founder and chairman of Huntsman Corporation. His moral values were deeply challenged when he worked for the Nixon administration in 1972, shortly before Watergate. After a brief stint in the U.S. Department of Health, Education, and Welfare (HEW), he took a job under H.R. Haldeman, President Nixon's powerful chief of staff. Huntsman said he found the experience of taking orders from Haldeman "very mixed. I wasn't geared to take orders, irrespective of whether they were ethically or morally right." He explained, "We had a few clashes, as plenty of things that Haldeman wanted to do were questionable. An amoral atmosphere permeated the White House."

One day, Haldeman directed Huntsman to help him entrap a California congressman who had been opposing a White House initiative. The congressman was part owner of a plant that reportedly employed undocumented workers. To gather information to embarrass the congressman, Haldeman told Huntsman to get the plant manager of a company Huntsman owned to place some undocumented workers at the congressman's plant in an undercover operation.

"There are times when we react too quickly and fail to realize immediately what is right and wrong," Huntsman recalled. "This was one of those times when I didn't think it through. I knew instinctively it was wrong, but it took a few minutes for the notion to percolate. After 15 minutes, my inner moral compass made itself noticed and enabled me to recognize this wasn't the right thing to do. Values that had accompanied me since childhood kicked in. Halfway through my conversation with our plant manager, I said to him, 'Let's not do this. I don't want to play this game. Forget that I called.'"

Huntsman told Haldeman that he would not use his employees in this way. "Here I was saying no to the second most powerful person in the country. He didn't appreciate responses like that, as he viewed them as signs of disloyalty. I might as well have been saying farewell. So be it. I left within the next six months."

Balancing Your Extrinsic and Intrinsic Motivations

Because authentic leaders need to sustain high levels of motivation and keep their lives in balance, it is critically important for them to understand what drives them. There are two types of motivations—extrinsic and intrinsic. Although they are reluctant to admit it, many leaders are propelled to achieve by measuring their success against the outside world's parameters. They enjoy the recognition and status that come with promotions and financial rewards. Intrinsic motivations, on the other hand, are derived from their sense of the meaning of their life. They are closely linked to one's life story and the way one frames it. Examples include personal growth, helping other people develop, taking on social causes, and making a difference in the world. The key is to find a balance between your desires for external validation and the intrinsic motivations that provide fulfillment in your work.

Many interviewees advised aspiring leaders to be wary of getting caught up in social, peer, or parental expectations. Debra Dunn, who has worked in Silicon Valley for decades as a Hewlett-Packard executive, acknowledged the constant pressures from external sources: "The path of accumulating material possessions is clearly laid out. You know how to measure it. If you don't pursue that path, people wonder what is wrong with you. The only way to avoid getting caught up in materialism is to understand where you find happiness and fulfillment."

Moving away from the external validation of personal achievement is not always easy. Achievement-oriented leaders grow so

Your Development as an Authentic Leader

As you read this article, think about the basis for your leadership development and the path you need to follow to become an authentic leader. Then ask yourself these questions:

1. **Which people and experiences in your early life had the greatest impact on you?**
2. **What tools do you use to become self-aware?** What is your authentic self? What are the moments when you say to yourself, this is the real me?
3. **What are your most deeply held values?** Where did they come from? Have your values changed significantly since your childhood? How do your values inform your actions?
4. **What motivates you extrinsically?** What are your intrinsic motivations? How do you balance extrinsic and intrinsic motivation in your life?
5. **What kind of support team do you have?** How can your support team make you a more authentic leader? How should you diversify your team to broaden your perspective?
6. **Is your life integrated?** Are you able to be the same person in all aspects of your life—personal, work, family, and community? If not, what is holding you back?
7. **What does being authentic mean in your life?** Are you more effective as a leader when you behave authentically? Have you ever paid a price for your authenticity as a leader? Was it worth it?
8. **What steps can you take today, tomorrow, and over the next year to develop your authentic leadership?**

---

accustomed to successive accomplishments throughout their early years that it takes courage to pursue their intrinsic motivations. But at some point, most leaders recognize that they need to address more difficult questions in order to pursue truly meaningful success. McKinsey's Alice Woodwark, who at 29 has already achieved notable success, reflected: "My version of achievement was pretty naive, born of things I learned early in life about praise and being valued. But if you're just chasing the rabbit around the course, you're not running toward anything meaningful."

Intrinsic motivations are congruent with your values and are more fulfilling than extrinsic motivations. John Thain, CEO of the New York Stock Exchange, said, "I am motivated by doing a really good job at whatever I am doing, but I prefer to multiply my impact on society through a group of people." Or as Ann Moore, chairman and CEO of Time, put it, "I came here 25 years ago solely because I loved magazines and the publishing world." Moore had a dozen job offers after business school but took the lowest-paying one with Time because of her passion for publishing.

Building Your Support Team

Leaders cannot succeed on their own; even the most outwardly confident executives need support and advice. Without strong relationships to provide perspective, it is very easy to lose your way.

Authentic leaders build extraordinary support teams to help them stay on course. Those teams counsel them in times of uncertainty, help them in times of difficulty, and celebrate with them in times of success. After their hardest days, leaders find comfort in being with people on whom they can rely so they can be open and vulnerable. During the low points, they cherish the friends who appreciate them for who they are, not what they are. Authentic leaders find that their support teams provide affirmation, advice, perspective, and calls for course corrections when needed.

How do you go about building your support team? Most authentic leaders have a multifaceted support structure that includes their spouses or significant others, families, mentors, close friends, and colleagues. They build their networks over time, as the experiences, shared histories, and openness with people close to them create the trust and confidence they need in times of trial and uncertainty. Leaders must give as much to their supporters as they get from them so that mutually beneficial relationships can develop.

It starts with having at least one person in your life with whom you can be completely yourself, warts and all, and still be accepted unconditionally. Often that person is the only one who can tell you the honest truth. Most leaders have their closest relationships with their spouses, although some develop these bonds with another family member, a close friend, or a trusted mentor. When leaders can rely on unconditional support, they are more likely to accept themselves for who they really are.

Many relationships grow over time through an expression of shared values and a common purpose. Randy Komisar of venture capital firm Kleiner Perkins Caufield & Byers said his marriage to Hewlett-Packard's Debra Dunn is lasting because it is rooted in similar values. "Debra and I are very independent but extremely harmonious in terms of our personal aspirations, values, and principles. We have a strong resonance around questions like, 'What is your legacy in this world?' It is important to be in sync about what we do with our lives."

Many leaders have had a mentor who changed their lives. The best mentoring interactions spark mutual learning, exploration of similar values, and shared enjoyment. If people are only looking for a leg up from their mentors, instead of being interested in their mentors' lives as well, the relationships will not last for long. It is the two-way nature of the connection that sustains it.

Personal and professional support groups can take many forms. Piper Jaffray's Tad Piper is a member of an Alcoholics Anonymous group. He noted, "These are not CEOs. They are just a group of nice, hard-working people who are trying to stay sober, lead good lives, and work with each other about being open, honest, and vulnerable. We reinforce each other's behavior by talking about our chemical dependency in a disciplined way as we go through the 12 steps. I feel blessed to be surrounded by people who are thinking about those kinds of issues and actually doing something, not just talking about them."

Bill George's experiences echo Piper's: In 1974, he joined a men's group that formed after a weekend retreat. More than 30 years later, the group is still meeting every Wednesday morning. After an opening period of catching up on each other's lives and dealing with any particular difficulty someone may be facing, one of the group's eight members leads a discussion on a topic he has selected. These discussions are open, probing, and often profound. The key to their success is that people say what they really believe without fear of judgment, criticism, or reprisal. All the members consider the group to be one of the most important aspects of their lives, enabling them to clarify their beliefs, values, and understanding of vital issues, as well as serving as a source of honest feedback when they need it most.

Integrating Your Life by Staying Grounded

Integrating their lives is one of the greatest challenges leaders face. To lead a balanced life, you need to bring together all of its constituent elements—work, family, community, and friends—so that you can be the same person in each environment. Think of your life as a house, with a bedroom for your personal life, a study for your professional life, a family room for your family, and a living room to share with your friends. Can you knock down the walls between these rooms and be the same person in each of them?

As John Donahoe, president of eBay Marketplaces and former worldwide managing director of Bain, stressed, being authentic means maintaining a sense of self no matter where you are. He warned, "The world can shape you if you let it. To have a sense of yourself as you live, you must make conscious choices. Sometimes the choices are really hard, and you make a lot of mistakes."

Authentic leaders have a steady and confident presence. They do not show up as one person one day and another person the next. Integration takes discipline, particularly during stressful times when it is easy to become reactive and slip back into bad habits. Donahoe feels strongly that integrating his life has enabled him to become a more effective leader. "There is no nirvana," he said. "The struggle is constant, as the trade-offs don't get any easier as you get older." But for authentic leaders, personal and professional lives are not a zero-sum game. As Donahoe said, "I have no doubt today that my children have made me a far more effective leader in the workplace. Having a strong personal life has made the difference."

Leading is high-stress work. There is no way to avoid stress when you are responsible for people, organizations, outcomes, and managing the constant uncertainties of the environment. The higher you go, the greater your freedom to control your destiny but also the higher the degree of stress. The question is not whether you can avoid stress but how you can control it to maintain your own sense of equilibrium.

Authentic leaders are constantly aware of the importance of staying grounded. Besides spending time with their families and close friends, authentic leaders get physical exercise, engage in spiritual practices, do community service, and return to the places where they grew up. All are essential to their effectiveness as leaders, enabling them to sustain their authenticity.

Empowering People to Lead

Now that we have discussed the process of discovering your authentic leadership, let's look at how authentic leaders empower people in their organizations to achieve superior long-term results, which is the bottom line for all leaders.

Authentic leaders recognize that leadership is not about their success or about getting loyal subordinates to follow them. They know the key to a successful organization is having empowered leaders at all levels, including those who have no direct reports. They not only inspire those around them, they empower those individuals to step up and lead.

A reputation for building relationships and empowering people was instrumental in chairman and CEO Anne Mulcahy's stunning turnaround of Xerox. When Mulcahy was asked to take the company's reins from her failed predecessor, Xerox had $18 billion in debt, and all credit lines were exhausted. With the share price in free fall, morale was at an all-time low. To make matters worse, the SEC was investigating the company's revenue recognition practices.

Mulcahy's appointment came as a surprise to everyone—including Mulcahy herself. A Xerox veteran, she had worked in field sales and on the corporate staff for 25 years, but not in finance, R&D, or manufacturing. How could Mulcahy cope with this crisis when she had had no financial experience? She brought to the CEO role the relationships she had built over 25 years, an impeccable understanding of the organization, and, above all, her credibility as an authentic leader. She bled for Xerox, and everyone knew it. Because of that, they were willing to go the extra mile for her.

After her appointment, Mulcahy met personally with the company's top 100 executives to ask them if they would stay with the company despite the challenges ahead. "I knew there were people who weren't supportive of me," she said. "So I confronted a couple of them and said, 'This is about the company.'" The first two people Mulcahy talked with, both of whom ran big operating units, decided to leave, but the remaining 98 committed to stay.

Throughout the crisis, people in Xerox were empowered by Mulcahy to step up and lead in order to restore the company to its former greatness. In the end, her leadership enabled Xerox to avoid bankruptcy as she paid back $10 billion in debt and restored revenue growth and profitability with a combination of cost savings and innovative new products. The stock price tripled as a result.

Like Mulcahy, all leaders have to deliver bottom-line results. By creating a virtuous circle in which the results reinforce the effectiveness of their leadership, authentic leaders are able to sustain those results through good times and bad. Their success enables them to attract talented people and align employees' activities with shared goals, as they empower others on their team to lead by taking on greater challenges. Indeed, superior results over a sustained period of time are the ultimate mark of an authentic leader. It may be possible to drive short-term outcomes without being authentic, but authentic leadership is the only way we know to create sustainable long-term results.

For authentic leaders, there are special rewards. No individual achievement can equal the pleasure of leading a group of people to achieve a worthy goal. When you cross the finish line together, all the pain and suffering you may have experienced quickly vanishes. It is replaced by a deep inner satisfaction that you have empowered others and thus made the world a better place. That's the challenge and the fulfillment of authentic leadership.

Originally published in February 2007. Reprint R0702H

In Praise of the Incomplete Leader

by Deborah Ancona, Thomas W. Malone, Wanda J. Orlikowski, and Peter M. Senge

W

WE'VE COME TO EXPECT A LOT OF OUR LEADERS. Top executives, the thinking goes, should have the intellectual capacity to make sense of unfathomably complex issues, the imaginative powers to paint a vision of the future that generates everyone's enthusiasm, the operational know-how to translate strategy into concrete plans, and the interpersonal skills to foster commitment to undertakings that could cost people's jobs should they fail. Unfortunately, no single person can possibly live up to those standards.

It's time to end the myth of the complete leader: the flawless person at the top who's got it all figured out. In fact, the sooner leaders stop trying to be all things to all people, the better off their organizations will be. In today's world, the executive's job is no longer to command and control but to cultivate and coordinate the actions of others at all levels of the organization. Only when leaders come to see themselves as incomplete—as having both strengths and weaknesses—will they be able to make up for their missing skills by relying on others.

Corporations have been becoming less hierarchical and more collaborative for decades, of course, as globalization and the growing importance of knowledge work have required that responsibility and initiative be distributed more widely. Moreover, it is now possible for large groups of people to coordinate their actions, not just by bringing lots of information to a few centralized places but also by bringing lots of information to lots of places through ever-growing networks within and beyond the firm. The sheer complexity and ambiguity of problems is humbling. More and more decisions are made in the context of global markets and rapidly—sometimes radically—changing financial, social, political, technological, and environmental forces. Stakeholders such as activists, regulators, and employees all have claims on organizations.

No one person could possibly stay on top of everything. But the myth of the complete leader (and the attendant fear of appearing incompetent) makes many executives try to do just that, exhausting themselves and damaging their organizations in the process. The incomplete leader, by contrast, knows when to let go: when to let those who know the local market do the advertising plan or when to let the engineering team run with its idea of what the customer needs. The incomplete leader also knows that leadership exists throughout the organizational hierarchy—wherever expertise, vision, new ideas, and commitment are found.

We've worked with hundreds of people who have struggled under the weight of the myth of the complete leader. Over the past six years, our work at the MIT Leadership Center has included studying leadership in many organizations and teaching the topic to senior executives, middle managers, and MBA students. In our practice-based programs, we have analyzed numerous accounts of organizational change and watched leaders struggle to meld top-down strategic initiatives with vibrant ideas from the rest of the organization.

All this work has led us to develop a model of distributed leadership. This framework, which synthesizes our own research with ideas from other leadership scholars, views leadership as a set of four capabilities: *sensemaking* (understanding the context in which a company and its people operate), *relating* (building relationships within and across organizations), *visioning* (creating a compelling picture of the future), and *inventing* (developing new ways to achieve the vision).

Idea in Brief

Have you ever feigned confidence to superiors or reports? Hidden the fact you were confused by the latest business results or blindsided by a competitor's move? If so, you've bought into the **myth of the complete leader:** the flawless being at the top who's got it all figured out.

It's an alluring myth. But in today's world of increasingly complex problems, no human being can meet this standard. Leaders who try only exhaust themselves, endangering their organizations.

Ancona and her coauthors suggest a better way to lead: Accept that you're human, with strengths and weaknesses. Understand the four leadership capabilities all organizations need:

- Sensemaking—interpreting developments in the business environment
- Relating—building trusting relationships
- Visioning—communicating a compelling image of the future
- Inventing—coming up with new ways of doing things

Then find and work with others who can provide the capabilities you're missing.

Take this approach, and you promote leadership throughout your organization, unleashing the expertise, vision, and new ideas your company needs to excel.

While somewhat simplified, these capabilities span the intellectual and interpersonal, the rational and intuitive, and the conceptual and creative capacities required in today's business environment. Rarely, if ever, will someone be equally skilled in all four domains. Thus, incomplete leaders differ from incompetent leaders in that they understand what they're good at and what they're not and have good judgment about how they can work with others to build on their strengths and offset their limitations.

Sometimes, leaders need to further develop the capabilities they are weakest in. The exhibits throughout this article provide some suggestions for when and how to do that. Other times, however, it's more important for leaders to find and work with others to compensate for their weaknesses. Teams and organizations—not just individuals—can use this framework to diagnose their strengths and weaknesses and find ways to balance their skill sets.

Idea in Practice

Incomplete leaders find people throughout their company who can complement their strengths and offset their weaknesses. To do this, understand the four leadership capabilities organizations need. Then diagnose your strength in each:

Capability	What it means	Example	Look for help in this capability if you ...
Sensemaking	Constantly understanding changes in the business environment and interpreting their ramifications for your industry and company	A CEO asks, "How will new technologies reshape our industry?" "How does globalization of labor markets affect our recruitment strategy?"	• Feel strongly that you're always right. • Frequently get blindsided by changes in your company or industry. • Feel resentful when things change.
Relating	Building trusting relationships, balancing advocacy (explaining your viewpoints) with inquiry (listening to understand others' viewpoints), and cultivating networks of supportive confidants	Former Southwest Airlines CEO Herb Kelleher excels at building trusting relationships. He wasn't afraid to tell employees he loved them, and reinforced those emotional bonds with equitable compensation and profit sharing.	• Blame others for failed projects. • Feel others are constantly letting you down or that they can't be trusted. • Frequently experience unpleasant, frustrating, or argumentative interactions with others.

Sensemaking

The term "sensemaking" was coined by organizational psychologist Karl Weick, and it means just what it sounds like: making sense of the world around us. Leaders are constantly trying to understand the contexts they are operating in. How will new technologies reshape the industry? How will changing cultural expectations shift the role of business in society? How does the globalization of labor markets affect recruitment and expansion plans?

Visioning	Creating credible and compelling images of a desired future that people in the organization want to create together	eBay founder Pierre Omidyar envisioned a new way of doing large-scale retailing: an online community where users took responsibility for what happened and had equal access to information.	• Often wonder, "Why are we doing this?" or "Does it really matter?" • Can't remember the last time you felt excited about your work. • Feel you're lacking sense of larger purpose.
Inventing	Creating new ways of approaching tasks or overcoming seemingly insurmountable problems to turn visions into reality	eBay CEO Meg Whitman helped bring Omidyar's vision of online retailing to life by inventing ways to deal with security, vendor reliability, and product diversification.	• Have difficulty relating the company's vision to what you're doing today. • Notice gaps between your firm's aspirations and the way work is organized. • Find that things tend to revert to business as usual.

Weick likened the process of sensemaking to cartography. What we map depends on where we look, what factors we choose to focus on, and what aspects of the terrain we decide to represent. Since these choices will shape the kind of map we produce, there is no perfect map of a terrain. Therefore, making sense is more than an act of analysis; it's an act of creativity. (See the exhibit "Engage in Sensemaking.")

The key for leaders is to determine what would be a useful map given their particular goals and then to draw one that adequately

Engage in sensemaking

1. Get data from multiple sources: customers, suppliers, employees, competitors, other departments, and investors.
2. Involve others in your sensemaking. Say what you think you are seeing, and check with people who have different perspectives from yours.
3. Use early observations to shape small experiments in order to test your conclusions. Look for new ways to articulate alternatives and better ways to understand options.
4. Do not simply apply existing frameworks but instead be open to new possibilities. Try not to describe the world in stereotypical ways, such as good guys and bad guys, victims and oppressors, or marketers and engineers.

represents the situation the organization is facing at that moment. Executives who are strong in this capability know how to quickly capture the complexities of their environment and explain them to others in simple terms. This helps ensure that everyone is working from the same map, which makes it far easier to discuss and plan for the journey ahead. Leaders need to have the courage to present a map that highlights features they believe to be critical, even if their map doesn't conform to the dominant perspective.

When John Reed was CEO of Citibank, the company found itself in a real estate crisis. At the time, common wisdom said that Citibank would need to take a $2 billion write-off, but Reed wasn't sure. He wanted a better understanding of the situation, so to map the problem, he met with federal regulators as well as his managers, the board, potential investors, economists, and real estate experts. He kept asking, "What am I missing here?" After those meetings, he had a much stronger grasp of the problem, and he recalibrated the write-off to $5 billion—which turned out to be a far more accurate estimate. Later, three quarters into the bank's eight-quarter program to deal with the crisis, Reed realized that progress had stopped. He began talking to other CEOs known for their change management skills. This informal benchmarking process led him to devise an organizational redesign.

Throughout the crisis, real estate valuations, investors' requirements, board demands, and management team expectations were all changing and constantly needed to be reassessed. Good leaders understand that sensemaking is a continuous process; they let the map emerge from a melding of observations, data, experiences, conversations, and analyses. In healthy organizations, this sort of sensemaking goes on all the time. People have ongoing dialogues about their interpretations of markets and organizational realities.

At IDEO, a product design firm, sensemaking is step one for all design teams. According to founder David Kelley, team members must act as anthropologists studying an alien culture to understand the potential product from all points of view. When brainstorming a new design, IDEO's teams consider multiple perspectives—that is, they build multiple maps to inform their creative process. One IDEO team was charged with creating a new design for an emergency room. To better understand the experience of a key stakeholder—the patient—team members attached a camera to a patient's head and captured his experience in the ER. The result: nearly ten full hours of film of the ceiling. The sensemaking provoked by this perspective led to a redesign of the ceiling that made it more aesthetically pleasing and able to display important information for patients.

Relating

Many executives who attempt to foster trust, optimism, and consensus often reap anger, cynicism, and conflict instead. That's because they have difficulty relating to others, especially those who don't make sense of the world the way they do. Traditional images of leadership didn't assign much value to relating. Flawless leaders shouldn't need to seek counsel from anyone outside their tight inner circle, the thinking went, and they were expected to issue edicts rather than connect on an emotional level. Times have changed, of course, and in this era of networks, being able to build trusting relationships is a requirement of effective leadership.

Three key ways to do this are *inquiring, advocating,* and *connecting*. The concepts of inquiring and advocating stem from the work of organizational development specialists Chris Argyris and Don Schon. Inquiring means listening with the intention of genuinely understanding the thoughts and feelings of the speaker. Here, the listener suspends judgment and tries to comprehend how and why the speaker has moved from the data of his or her experiences to particular interpretations and conclusions.

Advocating, as the term implies, means explaining one's own point of view. It is the flip side of inquiring, and it's how leaders make clear to others how they reached their interpretations and conclusions. Good leaders distinguish their observations from their opinions and judgments and explain their reasoning without aggression or defensiveness. People with strong relating skills are typically those who've found a healthy balance between inquiring and advocating: They actively try to understand others' views but are able to stand up for their own. (See the exhibit "Build Relationships.")

We've seen countless relationships undermined because people disproportionately emphasized advocating over inquiring. Even though managers pay lip service to the importance of mutual understanding and shared commitment to a course of action, often their real focus is on winning the argument rather than strengthening the connection. Worse, in many organizations, the imbalance goes so far that having one's point of view prevail is what is understood as leadership.

Effective relating does not mean avoiding interpersonal conflict altogether. Argyris and Schon found that "maintaining a smooth

Build relationships

1. Spend time trying to understand others' perspectives, listening with an open mind and without judgment.
2. Encourage others to voice their opinions. What do they care about? How do they interpret what's going on? Why?
3. Before expressing your ideas, try to anticipate how others will react to them and how you might best explain them.
4. When expressing your ideas, don't just give a bottom line; explain your reasoning process.
5. Assess the strengths of your current connections: How well do you relate to others when receiving advice? When giving advice? When thinking through difficult problems? When asking for help?

surface" of conviviality and apparent agreement is one of the most common defensive routines that limits team effectiveness. Balancing inquiring and advocating is ultimately about showing respect, challenging opinions, asking tough questions, and taking a stand.

Consider Twynstra Gudde (TG), one of the largest independent consulting companies in the Netherlands. A few years ago, it replaced the role of CEO with a team of four managing directors who share leadership responsibilities. Given this unique structure, it's vital that these directors effectively relate to one another. They've adopted simple rules, such as a requirement that each leader give his opinion on every issue, majority-rules voting, and veto power for each director.

Clearly, for TG's senior team model to work, members must be skilled at engaging in dialogue together. They continually practice both inquiring and advocating, and because each director can veto a decision, each must thoroughly explain his reasoning to convince the others' that his perspective has merit. It's not easy to reach this level of mutual respect and trust, but over time, the team members' willingness to create honest connections with one another has paid off handsomely. Although they don't always reach consensus, they are able to settle on a course of action. Since this new form of leadership was introduced, TG has thrived: The company's profits have doubled, and employee satisfaction levels have improved. What's more, TG's leadership structure has served as a model for cooperation throughout the organization as well as in the firm's relations with its clients.

The third aspect of relating, connecting, involves cultivating a network of confidants who can help a leader accomplish a wide range of goals. Leaders who are strong in this capability have many people they can turn to who can help them think through difficult problems or support them in their initiatives. They understand that the time spent building and maintaining these connections is time spent investing in their leadership skills. Because no one person can possibly have all the answers, or indeed, know all the right questions to ask, it's crucial that leaders be able to tap into a network of people who can fill in the gaps.

Visioning

Sensemaking and relating can be called the enabling capabilities of leadership. They help set the conditions that motivate and sustain change. The next two leadership capabilities—what we call "visioning" and inventing—are creative and action oriented: They produce the focus and energy needed to make change happen.

Visioning involves creating compelling images of the future. While sensemaking charts a map of what is, visioning produces a map of what could be and, more important, what a leader wants the future to be. It consists of far more than pinning a vision statement to the wall. Indeed, a shared vision is not a static thing—it's an ongoing process. Like sensemaking, visioning is dynamic and collaborative, a process of articulating what the members of an organization want to create together.

Fundamentally, visioning gives people a sense of meaning in their work. Leaders who are skilled in this capability are able to get people excited about their view of the future while inviting others to help crystallize that image. (See the exhibit "Create a Vision.") If they realize other people aren't joining in or buying into the vision, they don't just turn up the volume; they engage in a dialogue about the reality they hope to produce. They use stories and metaphors to paint a vivid picture of what the vision will accomplish, even if they don't have a comprehensive plan for getting there. They know that if the vision is credible and compelling enough, others will generate ideas to advance it.

In South Africa in the early 1990s, a joke was making the rounds: Given the country's daunting challenges, people had two options, one practical and the other miraculous. The practical option was for everyone to pray for a band of angels to come down from heaven and fix things. The miraculous option was for people to talk with one another until they could find a way forward. In F.W. de Klerk's famous speech in 1990—his first after assuming leadership—he called for a nonracist South Africa and suggested that negotiation was the only way to achieve a peaceful transition. That speech sparked a set of changes that led to Nelson Mandela's release from Robben Island

Create a vision

1. Practice creating a vision in many arenas, including your work life, your home life, and in community groups. Ask yourself, "What do I want to create?"
2. Develop a vision about something that inspires you. Your enthusiasm will motivate you and others. Listen to what they find exciting and important.
3. Expect that not all people will share your passion. Be prepared to explain why people should care about your vision and what can be achieved through it. If people don't get it, don't just turn up the volume. Try to construct a shared vision.
4. Don't worry if you don't know how to accomplish the vision. If it is compelling and credible, other people will discover all sorts of ways to make it real—ways you never could have imagined on your own.
5. Use images, metaphors, and stories to convey complex situations that will enable others to act.

prison and the return to the country of previously banned political leaders.

Few of South Africa's leaders agreed on much of anything regarding the country's future. It seemed like a long shot, at best, that a scenario-planning process convened by a black professor from the University of the Western Cape and facilitated by a white Canadian from Royal Dutch Shell would be able to bring about any sort of change. But they, together with members of the African National Congress (ANC), the radical Pan Africanist Congress (PAC), and the white business community, were charged with forging a new path for South Africa.

When the team members first met, they focused on collective sensemaking. Their discussions then evolved into a yearlong visioning process. In his book, *Solving Tough Problems,* Adam Kahane, the facilitator, says the group started by telling stories of "left-wing revolution, right-wing revolts, and free market utopias." Eventually, the leadership team drafted a set of scenarios that described the many paths toward disaster and the one toward sustainable development.

They used metaphors and clear imagery to convey the various paths in language that was easy to understand. One negative scenario, for instance, was dubbed "Ostrich": A nonrepresentative white government sticks its head in the sand, trying to avoid a negotiated settlement with the black majority. Another negative scenario was labeled “Icarus”: A constitutionally unconstrained black government comes to power with noble intentions and embarks on a huge, unsustainable public-spending spree that crashes the economy. This scenario contradicted the popular belief that the country was rich and could simply redistribute wealth from whites to blacks. The Icarus scenario set the stage for a fundamental (and controversial) shift in economic thinking in the ANC and other left-wing parties—a shift that led the ANC government to “strict and consistent fiscal discipline,” according to Kahane.

The group’s one positive scenario involved the government adopting a set of sustainable policies that would put the country on a path of inclusive growth to successfully rebuild the economy and establish democracy. This option was called “Flamingo,” invoking the image of a flock of beautiful birds all taking flight together.

This process of visioning unearthed an extraordinary collective sense of possibility in South Africa. Instead of talking about what other people should do to advance some agenda, the leaders spoke about what they could do to create a better future for everyone. They didn’t have an exact implementation plan at the ready, but by creating a credible vision, they paved the way for others to join in and help make their vision a reality.

Leaders who excel in visioning walk the walk; they work to embody the core values and ideas contained in the vision. Darcy Winslow, Nike’s global director for women’s footwear, is a good example. A 14-year veteran at Nike, Winslow previously held the position of general manager of sustainable business opportunities at the shoe and apparel giant. Her work in that role reflected her own core values, including her passion for the environment. “We had come to see that our customers’ health and our own ability to compete were inseparable from the health of the environment,” she says. So she initiated the concept of ecologically intelligent product design. Winslow’s team worked at determining the chemical composition and environmental effects of every material and process Nike used. They visited factories in China and collected samples of rubber, leather, nylon, polyester, and foams to determine their chemical makeup. This led Winslow and her team to develop a list of "positive" materials—those that weren't harmful to the environment—that they hoped to use in more Nike products. "Environmental sustainability" was no longer just an abstract term on a vision statement; the team now felt a mandate to realize the vision.

Inventing

Even the most compelling vision will lose its power if it floats, unconnected, above the everyday reality of organizational life. To transform a vision of the future into a present-day reality, leaders need to devise processes that will give it life. This inventing is what moves a business from the abstract world of ideas to the concrete world of implementation. In fact, inventing is similar to execution, but the label "inventing" emphasizes that this process often requires creativity to help people figure out new ways of working together.

To realize a new vision, people usually can't keep doing the same things they've been doing. They need to conceive, design, and put into practice new ways of interacting and organizing. Some of the most famous examples of large-scale organizational innovation come from the automotive industry: Henry Ford's conception of the assembly-line factory and Toyota's famed integrated production system.

More recently, Pierre Omidyar, the founder of eBay, invented through his company a new way of doing large-scale retailing. His vision was of an online community where users would take responsibility for what happened. In a 2001 BusinessWeek Online interview, Omidyar explained, "I had the idea that I wanted to create an efficient market and a level playing field where everyone had equal access to information. I wanted to give the power of the market back to individuals, not just large corporations. That was the driving motivation for creating eBay at the start."

Consequently, eBay outsources most of the functions of traditional retailing—purchasing, order fulfillment, and customer service, for example—to independent sellers worldwide. The company estimates that more than 430,000 people make their primary living from selling wares on eBay. If those individuals were all employees of eBay, it would be the second largest private employer in the United States after Wal-Mart.

The people who work through eBay are essentially independent store owners, and, as such, they have a huge amount of autonomy in how they do their work. They decide what to sell, when to sell it, how to price, and how to advertise. Coupled with this individual freedom is global scale. EBay's infrastructure enables them to sell their goods all over the world. What makes eBay's inventing so radical is that it represents a new relationship between an organization and its parts. Unlike typical outsourcing, eBay doesn't pay its retailers—they pay the company.

Inventing doesn't have to occur on such a grand scale. It happens every time a person creates a way of approaching a task or figures out how to overcome a previously insurmountable obstacle. In their book *Car Launch,* George Roth and Art Kleiner describe a highly successful product development team in the automobile industry that struggled with completing its designs on time. Much of the source of the problem, the team members concluded, came from the stovepipe organizational structure found in the product development division. Even though they were a "colocated" team dedicated to designing a common new car, members were divided by their different technical expertise, experience, jargon, and norms of working.

When the team invented a mechanical prototyping device that complemented its computer-aided design tools, the group members found that it facilitated a whole new way of collaborating. Multiple groups within the team could quickly create physical mock-ups of design ideas to be tested by the various engineers from different specialties in the team. The group called the device "the harmony buck," because it helped people break out of their comfortable engineering specialties and solve interdependent design problems together. Development of a "full body" physical mock-up of the new car allowed engineers to hang around the prototype, providing a central focal point for their interactions. It enabled them to more easily identify and raise cross-functional issues, and it facilitated mutual problem solving and coordination.

Cultivate inventiveness

1. Don't assume that the way things have always been done is the best way to do them.
2. When a new task or change effort emerges, encourage creative ways of getting it done.
3. Experiment with different ways of organizing work. Find alternative methods for grouping and linking people.
4. When working to understand your current environment, ask yourself, "What other options are possible?"

In sum, leaders must be able to succeed at inventing, and this requires both attention to detail and creativity. (See the exhibit "Cultivate Inventiveness.")

Balancing the Four Capabilities

Sensemaking, relating, visioning, and inventing are interdependent. Without sensemaking, there's no common view of reality from which to start. Without relating, people work in isolation or, worse, strive toward different aims. Without visioning, there's no shared direction. And without inventing, a vision remains illusory. No one leader, however, will excel at all four capabilities in equal measure.

Typically, leaders are strong in one or two capabilities. Intel chairman Andy Grove is the quintessential sensemaker, for instance, with a gift for recognizing strategic inflection points that can be exploited for competitive advantage. Herb Kelleher, the former CEO of Southwest Airlines, excels at relating. He remarked in the journal *Leader to Leader* that "We are not afraid to talk to our people with emotion. We're not afraid to tell them, 'We love you.' Because we do." With this emotional connection comes equitable compensation and profit sharing.

Apple CEO Steve Jobs is a visionary whose ambitious dreams and persuasiveness have catalyzed remarkable successes for Apple, Next, and Pixar. Meg Whitman, the CEO of eBay, helped bring Pierre Omidyar's vision of online retailing to life by inventing ways to deal with security, vendor reliability, and product diversification.

Once leaders diagnose their own capabilities, identifying their unique set of strengths and weaknesses, they must search for others

Examining Your Leadership Capabilities

Few people wake up in the morning and say, "I'm a poor sensemaker" or "I just can't relate to others." They tend to experience their own weaknesses more as chronic or inexplicable failures in the organization or in those around them. The following descriptions will help you recognize opportunities to develop your leadership capabilities and identify openings for working with others.

Signs of Weak Sensemaking

1. You feel strongly that you are usually right and others are often wrong.
2. You feel your views describe reality correctly, but others' views do not.
3. You find you are often blindsided by changes in your organization or industry.
4. When things change, you typically feel resentful. (That's not the way it should be!)

Signs of Weak Relating

1. You blame others for failed projects.
2. You feel others are constantly letting you down or failing to live up to your expectations.

---

who can provide the things they're missing. (See the sidebar "Examining Your Leadership Capabilities.") Leaders who choose only people who mirror themselves are likely to find their organizations tilting in one direction, missing one or more essential capabilities needed to survive in a changing, complex world. That's why it's important to examine the whole organization to make sure it is appropriately balanced as well. It's the leader's responsibility to create an environment that lets people complement one another's strengths and offset one another's weaknesses. In this way, leadership is distributed across multiple people throughout the organization.

Years ago, one of us attended a three-day meeting on leadership with 15 top managers from different companies. At the close of it,

3. You find that many of your interactions at work are unpleasant, frustrating, or argumentative.
4. You find many of the people you work with untrustworthy.

Signs of Weak Visioning

1. You feel your work involves managing an endless series of crises.
2. You feel like you're bouncing from pillar to post with no sense of larger purpose.
3. You often wonder, "Why are we doing this?" or "Does it really matter?"
4. You can't remember the last time you talked to your family or a friend with excitement about your work.

Signs of Weak Inventing

1. Your organization's vision seems abstract to you.
2. You have difficulty relating your company's vision to what you are doing today.
3. You notice dysfunctional gaps between your organization's aspirations and the way work is organized.
4. You find that things tend to revert to business as usual.

participants were asked to reflect on their experience as leaders. One executive, responsible for more than 50,000 people in his division of a manufacturing corporation, drew two pictures on a flip chart. The image on the left was what he projected to the outside world: It was a large, intimidating face holding up a huge fist. The image on the right represented how he saw himself: a small face with wide eyes, hair standing on end, and an expression of sheer terror.

We believe that most leaders experience that profound dichotomy every day, and it's a heavy burden. How many times have you feigned confidence to superiors or reports when you were really unsure? Have you ever felt comfortable conceding that you were confused by the latest business results or caught off guard by a competitor's move? Would you ever admit to feeling inadequate to cope with the complex issues your firm was facing? Anyone who can identify with these situations knows firsthand what it's like to be trapped in the myth of the complete leader—the person at the top without flaws. It's time to put that myth to rest, not only for the sake of frustrated leaders but also for the health of organizations. Even the most talented leaders require the input and leadership of others, constructively solicited and creatively applied. It's time to celebrate the incomplete—that is, the human—leader.

Originally published in February 2007. Reprint R0702E

About the Contributors

DEBORAH ANCONA is the Seley Distinguished Professor of Management at MIT's Sloan School of Management.

WARREN G. BENNIS is University Professor at the University of Southern California.

JIM COLLINS operates a management research laboratory in Boulder, Colorado.

PETER F. DRUCKER was a professor of social science and management at Claremont Graduate University in California.

BILL GEORGE is a professor of management practice at Harvard Business School.

DANIEL GOLEMAN cochairs the Consortium for Research on Emotional Intelligence in Organizations at Rutgers University.

ROBERT GOFFEE is a professor of organizational behavior at London Business School.

RONALD A. HEIFETZ codirects the Center for Public Leadership at Harvard University's Kennedy School of Government.

GARETH JONES is a fellow of the Centre for Management Development at London Business School.

JOHN P. KOTTER is the Konosuke Matsushita Professor of Leadership, Emeritus, at Harvard Business School.

DONALD L. LAURIE is a founder and managing partner at Oyster International, a Boston-based consulting firm.

THOMAS W. MALONE is the Patrick J. McGovern Professor of Management at MIT's Sloan School of Management.

DIANA MAYER is a former Citigroup executive in New York.

ANDREW N. McLEAN is a research associate at Harvard Business School.

WANDA J. ORLIKOWSKI is the Eaton-Peabody Professor of Communication Sciences at MIT's Sloan School of Management.

DAVID ROOKE is a director at Harthill Consulting in Hewelsfield, England.

PETER M. SENGE is a senior lecturer at MIT's Sloan School of Management.

PETER SIMS established "Leadership Perspectives," a class at the Stanford Graduate School of Business in California.

ROBERT J. THOMAS is a visiting professor of leadership at the Fletcher School of Law and Diplomacy at Tufts University.

WILLIAM R. TORBERT is a professor emeritus of leadership at the Carroll School of Management at Boston College.

Index

HBR'S 10 MUST READS

On Strategic Marketing

HBR's 10 Must Reads series is the definitive collection of ideas and best practices for aspiring and experienced leaders alike. These books offer essential reading selected from the pages of *Harvard Business Review* on topics critical to the success of every manager.

Titles include:

HBR's 10 Must Reads on Change Management
HBR's 10 Must Reads on Collaboration
HBR's 10 Must Reads on Communication
HBR's 10 Must Reads on Innovation
HBR's 10 Must Reads on Leadership
HBR's 10 Must Reads on Making Smart Decisions
HBR's 10 Must Reads on Managing People
HBR's 10 Must Reads on Managing Yourself
HBR's 10 Must Reads on Strategic Marketing
HBR's 10 Must Reads on Strategy
HBR's 10 Must Reads on Teams
HBR's 10 Must Reads: The Essentials

HBR'S 10 MUST READS

On Strategic Marketing

HARVARD BUSINESS REVIEW PRESS
Boston, Massachusetts

Printed in the United States of America
20 19 18 17 16 15 14

Library of Congress Cataloging-in-Publication Data

HBR's 10 must reads on strategic marketing.
p. cm. — (HBR's 10 must read series)
Includes index.
ISBN 978-1-4221-8988-7
1. Marketing—Management. 2. Strategic planning. I. Harvard business review. II. Title: HBR's ten must reads on strategic marketing. III. Title: Harvard business review's 10 must reads on strategic marketing.
HF5415.13.H368 2013
658.8'02—dc23 2012037855

ISBN: 9781422189887
eISBN: 9781422191521

The paper used in this publication meets the requirements of the American National Standard for Permanence of Paper for Publications and Documents in Libraries and Archives z39.48-1992.

Contents

HBR'S 10 MUST READS

On Strategic Marketing

Rethinking Marketing

by Roland T. Rust, Christine Moorman, and Gaurav Bhalla

IMAGINE A BRAND MANAGER sitting in his office developing a marketing strategy for his company's new sports drink. He identifies which broad market segments to target, sets prices and promotions, and plans mass media communications. The brand's performance will be measured by aggregate sales and profitability, and his pay and future prospects will hinge on those numbers.

What's wrong with this picture? This firm—like too many—is still managed as if it were stuck in the 1960s, an era of mass markets, mass media, and impersonal transactions. Yet never before have companies had such powerful technologies for interacting directly with customers, collecting and mining information about them, and tailoring their offerings accordingly. And never before have customers expected to interact so deeply with companies, and each other, to shape the products and services they use. To be sure, most companies use customer relationship management and other technologies to get a handle on customers, but no amount of technology can really improve the situation as long as companies are set up to market products rather than cultivate customers. To compete in this aggressively interactive environment, companies must shift their focus from driving transactions to maximizing customer lifetime value. That means making products and brands subservient to long-term customer relationships. And that means changing strategy and structure across the organization—and reinventing the marketing department altogether.

Cultivating Customers

Not long ago, companies looking to get a message out to a large population had only one real option: blanket a huge swath of customers simultaneously, mostly using one-way mass communication. Information about customers consisted primarily of aggregate sales statistics augmented by marketing research data. There was little, if any, direct communication between individual customers and the firm. Today, companies have a host of options at their disposal, making such mass marketing far too crude.

The exhibit "Building relationships" shows where many companies are headed, and all must inevitably go if they hope to remain competitive. The key distinction between a traditional and a customer-cultivating company is that one is organized to push products and brands whereas the other is designed to serve customers and customer segments. In the latter, communication is two-way and individualized, or at least tightly targeted at thinly sliced segments. This strategy may be more challenging for firms whose distribution channels own or control customer information—as is the case for many packaged-goods companies. But more and more firms now have access to the rich data they need to make a customer-cultivating strategy work.

B2B companies, for instance, use key account managers and global account directors to focus on meeting customers' evolving needs, rather than selling specific products. IBM organizes according to customer needs, such as energy efficiency or server consolidation, and coordinates its marketing efforts across products for a particular customer. IBM's Insurance Process Acceleration Framework is one example of this service-oriented architecture. Customer and industry specialists in IBM's insurance practice work with lead customers to build fast and flexible processes in areas like claims, new business processing, and underwriting. Instead of focusing on

Idea in Brief

Companies have never before had such powerful technologies for understanding and interacting with customers. Yet too many firms operate as if they're stuck in the 1960s, an era of mass marketing, mass media, and impersonal transactions.

To compete in an aggressively interactive environment, companies must shift their focus from driving transactions to maximizing customer lifetime value. That means products and brands must be made subservient to customer relationships. And that means transforming the marketing department—traditionally focused on current sales—into a "customer department" by: replacing the CMO with a chief customer officer, cultivating customers rather than pushing products, adopting new performance metrics, and bringing under the marketing umbrella all customer-focused departments, including R&D and customer service.

Building relationships

Product-Manager Driven
Many companies still depend on product managers and one-way mass marketing to push a product to many customers.

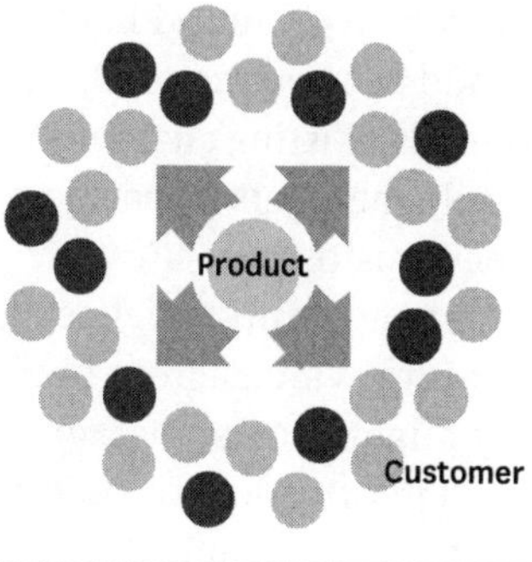

Customer-Manager Driven
What's needed is customer managers who engage individual customers or narrow segments in two-way communications, building long-term relationships by promoting whichever of the company's products the customer would value most at any given time.

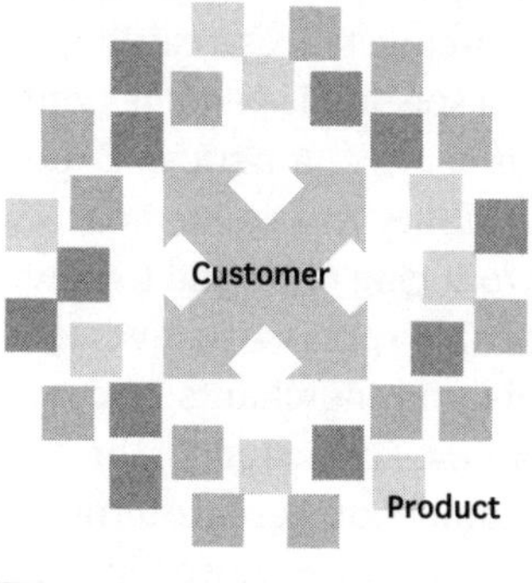

short-term product sales, IBM measures the practice's performance according to long-term customer metrics.

Large B2B firms are often advanced in their customer orientation, and some B2C companies are making notable progress. Increasingly, they view their customer relationships as evolving over time, and they may hand off customers to different parts of the organization selling different brands as their needs change. For instance, Tesco, a leading UK retailer, has recently made significant investments in analytics that have improved customer retention. Tesco uses its data-collecting loyalty card (the Clubcard) to track which stores customers visit, what they buy, and how they pay. This information has helped Tesco tailor merchandise to local tastes and customize offerings at the individual level across a variety of store formats—from sprawling hypermarts to neighborhood shops. Shoppers who buy diapers for the first time at a Tesco store, for example, receive coupons by mail not only for baby wipes and toys but also for beer, according to a *Wall Street Journal* report. Data analysis revealed that new fathers tend to buy more beer because they can't spend as much time at the pub.

On the services side, American Express actively monitors customers' behavior and responds to changes by offering different products. The firm uses consumer data analysis and algorithms to determine customers' "next best product" according to their changing profiles and to manage risk across cardholders. For example, the first purchase of an upper-class airline ticket on a Gold Card may trigger an invitation to upgrade to a Platinum Card. Or, because of changing circumstances a cardholder may want to give an additional card with a specified spending limit to a child or a contractor. By offering this service, American Express extends existing customers' spending ability to a trusted circle of family members or partners while introducing the brand to potential new customers.

American Express also leverages its strategic position between customers and merchants to create long-term value across both relationships. For instance, the company might use demographic data, customer purchase patterns, and credit information to observe that a cardholder has moved into a new home. AmEx capitalizes on that life event by offering special Membership Rewards on purchases from merchants in its network in the home-furnishings retail category.

One insurance and financial services company we know of also proved adept at tailoring products to customers' life events. Customers who lose a spouse, for example, are flagged for special attention from a team that offers them customized products. When a checking account or credit-card customer gets married, she's a good cross-selling prospect for an auto or home insurance policy and a mortgage. Likewise, the firm targets new empty nesters with home equity loans or investment products and offers renter's insurance to graduating seniors.

Reinventing Marketing

These shining examples aside, boards and C-suites still mostly pay lip service to customer relationships while focusing intently on selling goods and services. Directors and management need to spearhead the strategy shift from transactions to relationships and create the culture, structure, and incentives necessary to execute the strategy.

What does a customer-cultivating organization look like? Although no company has a fully realized customer-focused structure, we can see the features of one in a variety of companies making the transition. The most dramatic change will be the marketing department's reinvention as a "customer department." The first order of business is to replace the traditional CMO with a new type of leader—a chief customer officer.

The CCO

Chief customer officers are increasingly common in companies worldwide—there are more than 300 today, up from 30 in 2003. Companies as diverse as Chrysler, Hershey's, Oracle, Samsung, Sears, United Airlines, Sun Microsystems, and Wachovia now have CCOs. But too often the CCO is merely trying to make a conventional organization more customer-centric. In general, it's a poorly defined role—which may account for CCOs' dubious distinction as having the shortest tenure of all C-suite executives.

To be effective, the CCO role as we conceive it must be a powerful operational position, reporting to the CEO. This executive is responsible for designing and executing the firm's customer relationship strategy and overseeing all customer-facing functions.

A successful CCO promotes a customer-centric culture and removes obstacles to the flow of customer information throughout the organization. This includes getting leaders to regularly engage with customers. At USAA, top managers spend two or three hours a week on the call-center phones with customers. This not only shows employees how serious management is about customer interaction but helps managers understand customers' concerns. Likewise, Tesco managers spend one week a year working in stores and interacting with customers as part of the Tesco Week in Store (TWIST) program.

As managers shift their focus to customers, and customer information increasingly drives decisions, organizational structures that block information flow must be torn down. The reality is that despite large investments in acquiring customer data, most firms underutilize what they know. Information is tightly held, often because of a lack of trust, competition for promotions or resources, and the silo mentality. The CCO must create incentives that eliminate these counterproductive mind-sets.

Ultimately, the CCO is accountable for increasing the profitability of the firm's customers, as measured by metrics such as customer lifetime value (CLV) and customer equity as well as by intermediate indicators, such as word of mouth (or mouse).

Customer managers

In the new customer department, customer and segment managers identify customers' product needs. Brand managers, under the customer managers' direction, then supply the products that fulfill those needs. This requires shifting resources—principally people and budgets—and authority from product managers to customer managers. (See the sidebar "What Makes a Customer Manager?")

What Makes a Customer Manager?

IN A SENSE, THE ROLE of customer manager is the ultimate expression of marketing (find out what the customer wants and fulfill the need) while the product manager is more aligned with the traditional selling mind-set (have product, find customer).

Jim Spohrer, the director of Global University Programs at IBM, hires what UCal Berkeley professor Morten Hansen calls "T-shaped" people, who have broad expertise with depth in some areas. Customer managers will be most effective when they're T-shaped, combining deep knowledge of particular customers or segments with broad knowledge of the firm and its products. These managers must also be sophisticated data interpreters, able to extract insights from the increasing amount of information about customers' attitudes and activities acquired by mining blogs and other customer forums, monitoring online purchasing behavior, tracking retail sales, and using other types of analytics. While brand managers may be satisfied with examining the media usage statistics associated with their product, brand usage behavior, and brand chat in communities, customer managers will take a broader and more integrative view of the customer. For instance, when P&G managers responsible for the Max Factor and Cover Girl brands spent a week living on the budget of a low-end consumer, they were acting like customer managers. The experience gave these managers important insights into what P&G, not just the specific brands, could do to improve the lives of these customers.

We'd expect the most effective customer managers to have broad training in the social sciences—psychology, anthropology, sociology, and economics—in addition to an understanding of marketing. They'd approach the customer as behavioral scientists rather than as marketing specialists, observing and collecting information about them, interacting with and learning from them, and synthesizing and disseminating what they learned. For business schools to stay relevant in training customer managers, the curriculum needs to shift its emphasis from marketing products to cultivating customers.

This structure is common in the B2B world. In its B2B activities, Procter & Gamble, for instance, has key account managers for major retailers like Wal-Mart. They are less interested in selling, say, Swiffers than in maximizing the value of the customer relationship over the long term. Some B2C companies use this structure as well, foremost among them retail financial institutions that put managers in charge of segments—wealthy customers, college kids, retirees, and so forth—rather than products.

In a customer-cultivating company, a consumer-goods segment manager might offer customers incentives to switch from less-profitable Brand A to more-profitable Brand B. This wouldn't happen in the conventional system, where brand and product managers call the shots. Brand A's manager isn't going to encourage customers to defect—even if that would benefit the company—because he's rewarded for brand performance, not for improving CLV or some other long-term customer metric. This is no small change: It means that product managers must stop focusing on maximizing their products' or brands' profits and become responsible for helping customer and segment managers maximize theirs.

Customer-facing functions

As the nexus of customer-facing activity, the customer department assumes responsibility for some of the customer-focused functions that have left the marketing department in recent years and some that have not traditionally been part of it.

CRM. Customer relationship management has been increasingly taken on by companies' IT groups because of the technical capability CRM systems require, according to a Harte-Hanks survey of 300 companies in North America: 42% of companies report that CRM is managed by the IT group, 31% by sales, and only 9% by marketing. Yet CRM is, ultimately, a tool for gauging customer needs and behaviors—the new customer department's central role. It makes little sense for the very data required to execute a customer-cultivation strategy to be collected and analyzed outside the customer department. Of course, bringing CRM into the customer department means bringing IT and analytic skills in as well.

Market research. The emphasis of market research changes in a customer-centric company. First, the internal users of market research extend beyond the marketing department to all areas of the organization that touch customers—including finance (the source of

Reimagining the marketing department

The traditional marketing department must be reconfigured as a customer department that puts building customer relationships ahead of pushing specific products.

To this end, product managers and customer-focused departments report to a chief customer officer instead of a CMO, and support the strategies of customer or segment managers.

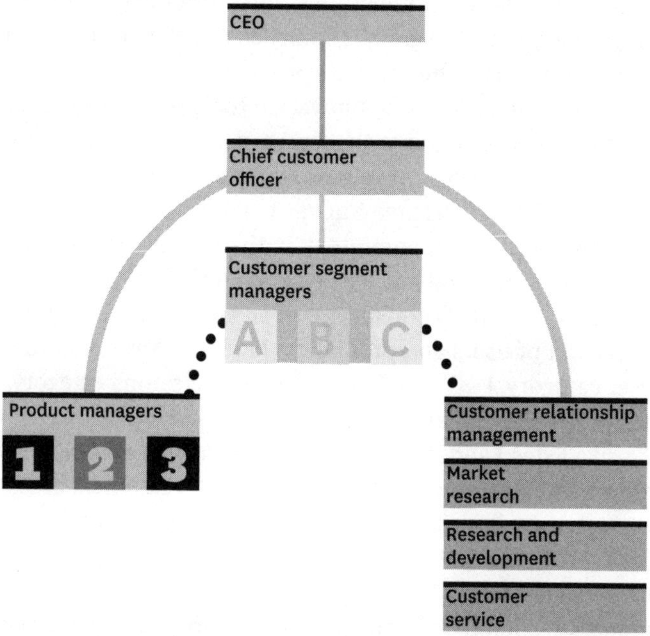

customer payment options) and distribution (the source of delivery timing and service). Second, the scope of analysis shifts from an aggregate view to an individual view of customer activities and value. Third, market research shifts its attention to acquiring the customer input that will drive improvements in customer-focused metrics such as CLV and customer equity.

Research and development. When a product is more about clever engineering than customer needs, sales can suffer. For example, engineers like to pack lots of features into products, but we know that customers can suffer from feature fatigue, which hurts future sales.

To make sure that product decisions reflect real-world needs, the customer must be brought into the design process. Integrating R&D and marketing is a good way to do that. Few companies have done this better than Nokia in Asia, where its market share exceeds 60%. In an industry where manufacturers must introduce scores of new offerings every year, the group's ability to translate customer input about features and value into hit product offerings is legendary. Among its customer-focused innovation tools is Nokia Beta Labs, a virtual developer community that brings users and developer teams together to virtually prototype new features and products, inviting even "wacky ideas" that may never make it to the marketplace. (Nokia adopted a different strategy in the United States, using far less customer input, and has seen its market share slide.)

Examples abound of companies that create new value through the collaboration of users and producers: Mozilla's Firefox in the web browser category, P&G's Swiffer in the home cleaning category, and International Flavors and Fragrances' partnership with B2B customers like Estée Lauder in the perfume market. In a world in which the old R&D-driven models for new product development are giving way to creative collaborations like these, R&D must report to the CCO.

Customer service

This function should be handled in-house, under the customer department's wing—not only to ensure that the quality of service is high but also to help cultivate long-term relationships. Delta Airlines, for example, recently pulled out of its call centers overseas because cultural differences damaged the airline's ability to interact with North American customers. Delta concluded that the negative impact on the quality of customer relationships wasn't worth the cost savings. Now, when customer service gets a call, a representative immediately identifies the caller's segment and routes her to a customer-service specialist trained to work with that segment.

The interaction is captured in the customer information system and used, in turn, by the customer department to divine new customers' needs and create solutions.

If customer service must be outsourced, the function should report in to a high-level internal customer manager, and its IT infrastructure and customer data must be seamlessly integrated with the company's customer databases.

A New Focus on Customer Metrics

Once companies make the shift from marketing products to cultivating customers, they will need new metrics to gauge the strategy's effectiveness. First, companies need to focus less on product profitability and more on customer profitability. Retailers have applied this concept for some time in their use of loss leaders—products that may be unprofitable but strengthen customer relationships.

Second, companies need to pay less attention to current sales and more to CLV. A company in decline may have good current sales but poor prospects. The customer lifetime value metric evaluates the future profits generated from a customer, properly discounted to reflect the time value of money. Lifetime value focuses the company on long-term health—an emphasis that most shareholders and investors should share. Although too often the markets reward short-term earnings at the expense of future performance, that unfortunate tendency will change as future-oriented customer metrics become a routine part of financial reporting. An international movement is under way to require companies to report intangible assets in financial statements. As leading indicators such as customer-centered metrics increasingly appear on financial statements, stock prices will begin to reflect them. Even now, savvy analysts are pushing firms to understand customer retention rates and the value of customer and brand assets.

Third, companies need to shift their focus from brand equity (the value of a brand) to customer equity (the sum of the lifetime values of their customers). Increasing brand equity is best seen as a means to an end, one way to build customer equity (see "Customer-Centered

New metrics for a new model

The shift from marketing products to cultivating customers demands a shift in metrics as well.

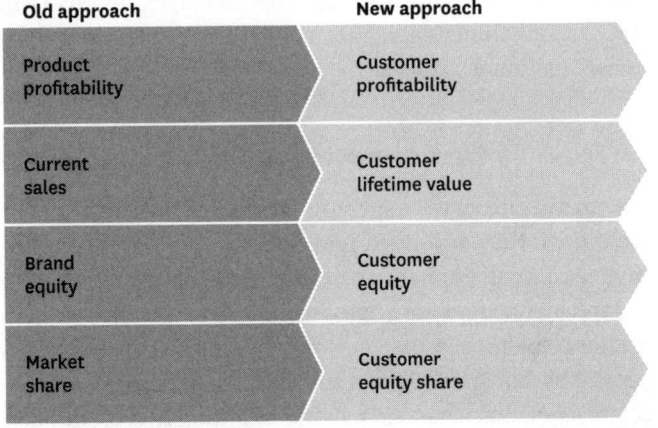

Old approach	New approach
Product profitability	Customer profitability
Current sales	Customer lifetime value
Brand equity	Customer equity
Market share	Customer equity share

Brand Management," HBR September 2004). Customer equity has the added benefit of being a good proxy for the value of the firm, thereby making marketing more relevant to shareholder value.

Fourth, companies need to pay less attention to current market share and more attention to customer equity share (the value of a company's customer base divided by the total value of the customers in the market). Market share offers a snapshot of the company's competitive sales position at the moment, but customer equity share is a measure of the firm's long-term competitiveness with respect to profitability.

Given the increasing importance of customer-level information, companies must become adept at tracking information at several levels—individual, segment, and aggregate. Different strategic decisions require different levels of information, so companies typically need multiple information sources to meet their needs.

At the individual customer level the key metric is customer lifetime value; the marketing activities tracked most closely are direct marketing activities; and the key sources of data are customer databases that the firm compiles. At the segment level the key metric is the lifetime value of the segment (the lifetime value of the average customer times the number of customers in the segment); the marketing activities tracked most closely are marketing efforts targeted at specific customer segments, sometimes using niche media; and the key sources of information are customer panels and survey data. At the aggregate market level, the key metric is customer equity; the marketing activities tracked most closely are mass marketing efforts, often through mass media; and the key sources of information are aggregate sales data and survey data. We see that firms will typically have a portfolio of information sources.

Clearly, companies need metrics for evaluating progress in collecting and using customer information. How frequently managers contribute to and access customer information archives is a good general measure, although it doesn't reveal much about the quality of the information. To get at that, some firms create markets for new customer information in which employees rate the value of contributions.

Like any other organizational transformation, making a product-focused company fully customer-centric will be difficult. The IT group will want to hang on to CRM; R&D is going to fight hard to keep its relative autonomy; and most important, traditional marketing executives will battle for their jobs. Because the change requires overcoming entrenched interests, it won't happen organically. Transformation must be driven from the top down. But however daunting, the shift is inevitable. It will soon be the only competitive way to serve customers.

Originally published in January 2010. Reprint R1001F

Branding in the Digital Age

You're Spending Your Money in All the Wrong Places.

by David C. Edelman

THE INTERNET HAS upended how consumers engage with brands. It is transforming the economics of marketing and making obsolete many of the function's traditional strategies and structures. For marketers, the old way of doing business is unsustainable.

Consider this: Not long ago, a car buyer would methodically pare down the available choices until he arrived at the one that best met his criteria. A dealer would reel him in and make the sale. The buyer's relationship with both the dealer and the manufacturer would typically dissipate after the purchase. But today, consumers are promiscuous in their brand relationships: They connect with myriad brands—through new media channels beyond the manufacturer's and the retailer's control or even knowledge—and evaluate a shifting array of them, often expanding the pool before narrowing it. After a purchase these consumers may remain aggressively engaged, publicly promoting or assailing the products they've bought, collaborating in the brands' development, and challenging and shaping their meaning.

Consumers still want a clear brand promise and offerings they value. What has changed is when—at what touch points—they are most open to influence, and how you can interact with them at those points. In the past, marketing strategies that put the lion's share of resources into building brand awareness and then opening wallets at the point of purchase worked pretty well. But touch points have changed in both number and nature, requiring a major adjustment to realign marketers' strategy and budgets with where consumers are actually spending their time.

Block That Metaphor

Marketers have long used the famous funnel metaphor to think about touch points: Consumers would start at the wide end of the funnel with many brands in mind and narrow them down to a final choice. Companies have traditionally used paid-media push marketing at a few well-defined points along the funnel to build awareness, drive consideration, and ultimately inspire purchase. But the metaphor fails to capture the shifting nature of consumer engagement.

In the June 2009 issue of *McKinsey Quarterly,* my colleague David Court and three coauthors introduced a more nuanced view of how consumers engage with brands: the "consumer decision journey" (CDJ). They developed their model from a study of the purchase decisions of nearly 20,000 consumers across five industries—automobiles, skin care, insurance, consumer electronics, and mobile telecom—and three continents. Their research revealed that far from systematically narrowing their choices, today's consumers take a much more iterative and less reductive journey of four stages: *consider, evaluate, buy,* and *enjoy, advocate, bond.*

Consider

The journey begins with the consumer's top-of-mind consideration set: products or brands assembled from exposure to ads or store displays, an encounter at a friend's house, or other stimuli. In the funnel model, the consider stage contains the largest number of brands; but today's consumers, assaulted by media and awash in choices, often *reduce* the number of products they consider at the outset.

Idea in Brief

Consumers today connect with brands in fundamentally new ways, often through media channels that are beyond manufacturers' and retailers' control. That means traditional marketing strategies must be redesigned to accord with how brand relationships have changed.

In the famous funnel metaphor, a shopper would start with several brands in mind and systematically narrow them down to a final choice. His relationship with both the manufacturer and the retailer ended there. But now, relying heavily on digital interactions, he evaluates a shifting array of options and often engages with the brand through social media after a purchase. Though marketing strategies that focused on building brand awareness and the point of purchase worked pretty well in the past, consumer touch points have changed in nature. For example, in many categories today the single most powerful influence to buy is someone else's advocacy.

The author describes a "consumer decision journey" of four stages: *consider* a selection of brands; *evaluate* by seeking input from peers, reviewers, and others; *buy*; and *enjoy, advocate, bond*. If the consumer's bond with the brand becomes strong enough, she'll enter a buy-enjoy-advocate-buy loop that skips the first two stages entirely.

Smart marketers will study the decision journey for their products and use the insights they gain to revise strategy, media spend, and organizational roles.

Evaluate

The initial consideration set frequently expands as consumers seek input from peers, reviewers, retailers, and the brand and its competitors. Typically, they'll add new brands to the set and discard some of the originals as they learn more and their selection criteria shift. Their outreach to marketers and other sources of information is much more likely to shape their ensuing choices than marketers' push to persuade them.

Buy

Increasingly, consumers put off a purchase decision until they're actually in a store—and, as we'll see, they may be easily dissuaded at that point. Thus point of purchase—which exploits placement, packaging, availability, pricing, and sales interactions—is an ever more powerful touch point.

Enjoy, advocate, bond

After purchase, a deeper connection begins as the consumer interacts with the product and with new online touch points. More than 60% of consumers of facial skin care products, my McKinsey colleagues found, conduct online research about the products *after* purchase—a touch point entirely missing from the funnel. When consumers are pleased with a purchase, they'll advocate for it by word of mouth, creating fodder for the evaluations of others and invigorating a brand's potential. Of course, if a consumer is disappointed by the brand, she may sever ties with it—or worse. But if the bond becomes strong enough, she'll enter an enjoy-advocate-buy loop that skips the consider and evaluate stages entirely.

The Journey in Practice

Although the basic premise of the consumer decision journey may not seem radical, its implications for marketing are profound. Two in particular stand out.

First, instead of focusing on how to allocate spending across media—television, radio, online, and so forth—marketers should target stages in the decision journey. The research my colleagues and I have done shows a mismatch between most marketing allocations and the touch points at which consumers are best influenced. Our analysis of dozens of marketing budgets reveals that 70% to 90% of spend goes to advertising and retail promotions that hit consumers at the consider and buy stages. Yet consumers are often influenced more during the evaluate and enjoy-advocate-bond stages. In many categories the single most powerful impetus to buy is someone else's advocacy. Yet many marketers focus on media spend (principally advertising) rather than on driving advocacy. The coolest banner ads, best search buys, and hottest viral videos may win consideration for a brand, but if the product gets weak reviews—or, worse, isn't even discussed online—it's unlikely to survive the winnowing process.

The second implication is that marketers' budgets are constructed to meet the needs of a strategy that is outdated. When the funnel metaphor reigned, communication was oneway, and every interaction with consumers had a variable media cost that typically outweighed creative's fixed costs. Management focused on "working media spend"—the portion of a marketing budget devoted to what are today known as paid media.

This no longer makes sense. Now marketers must also consider *owned* media (that is, the channels a brand controls, such as websites) and *earned* media (customer-created channels, such as communities of brand enthusiasts). And an increasing portion of the budget must go to "nonworking" spend—the people and technology required to create and manage content for a profusion of channels and to monitor or participate in them.

Launching a Pilot

The shift to a CDJ-driven strategy has three parts: understanding your consumers' decision journey; determining which touch points are priorities and how to leverage them; and allocating resources accordingly—an undertaking that may require redefining organizational relationships and roles.

One of McKinsey's clients, a global consumer electronics company, embarked on a CDJ analysis after research revealed that although consumers were highly familiar with the brand, they tended to drop it from their consideration set as they got closer to purchase. It wasn't clear exactly where the company was losing consumers or what should be done. What *was* clear was that the media-mix models the company had been using to allocate marketing spend at a gross level (like the vast majority of all such models) could not take the distinct goals of different touch points into account and strategically direct marketing investments to them.

The company decided to pilot a CDJ-based approach in one business unit in a single market, to launch a major new TV model. The

Block That Metaphor

Then: The Funnel Metaphor

For years, marketers assumed that consumers started with a large number of potential brands in mind and methodically winnowed their choices until they'd decided which one to buy. After purchase, their relationship with the brand typically focused on the use of the product or service itself.

Now: The Consumer Decision Journey

New research shows that rather than systematically narrowing their choices, consumers add and subtract brands from a group under consideration during an extended evaluation phase. After purchase, they often enter into an open-ended relationship with the brand, sharing their experience with it online.

Consider & buy. Marketers often overemphasize the "consider" and "buy" stages of the journey, allocating more resources than they should to building awareness through advertising and encouraging purchase with retail promotions.

Evaluate & advocate. New media make the "evaluate" and "advocate" stages increasingly relevant. Marketing investments that help consumers navigate the evaluation process and then spread positive word of mouth about the brands they choose can be as important as building awareness and driving purchase.

Bond. If consumers' bond with a brand is strong enough, they repurchase it without cycling through the earlier decision-journey stages.

chief marketing officer drove the effort, engaging senior managers at the start to facilitate coordination and ensure buy-in. The corporate VP for digital marketing shifted most of his time to the pilot, assembling a team with representatives from functions across the organization, including marketing, market research, IT, and, crucially, finance. The team began with an intensive three-month market research project to develop a detailed picture of how TV consumers navigate the decision journey: what they do, what they see, and what they say.

What they do

Partnering with a supplier of online-consumer-panel data, the company identified a set of TV shoppers and drilled down into their

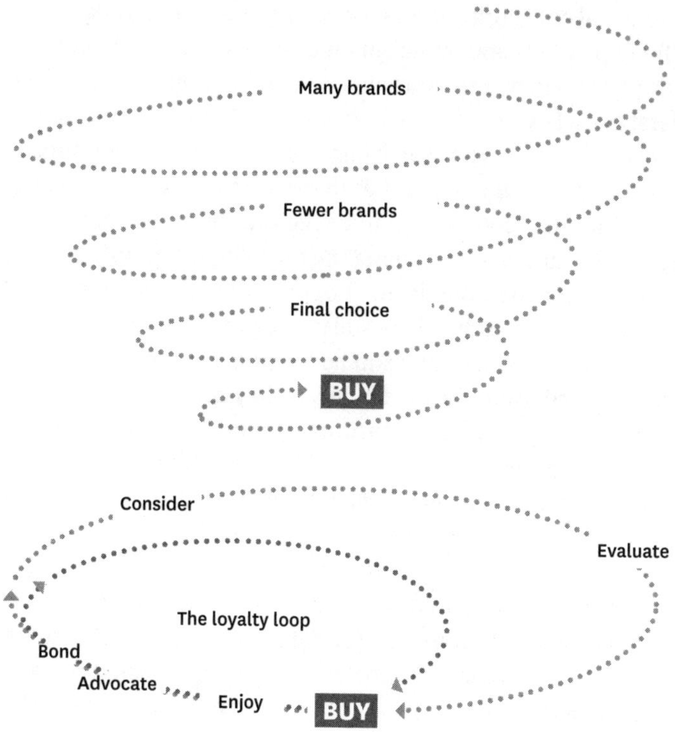

behavior: How did they search? Did they show a preference for manufacturers' or retailers' sites? How did they participate in online communities? Next the team selected a sample of the shoppers for in-depth, one-on-one discussions: How would they describe the stages of their journey, online and off? Which resources were most valuable to them, and which were disappointing? How did brands enter and leave their decision sets, and what drove their purchases in the end?

The research confirmed some conventional wisdom about how consumers shop, but it also overturned some of the company's long-standing assumptions. It revealed that off-line channels such as television advertising, in-store browsing, and direct word of mouth were influential only during the consider stage. Consumers might have a handful of products and brands in mind at this stage, with opinions about them shaped by previous experience, but their attitudes and consideration sets were extremely malleable. At the evaluate stage, consumers didn't start with search engines; rather, they went directly to Amazon.com and other retail sites that, with their rich and expanding array of product-comparison information, consumer and expert ratings, and visuals, were becoming the most important influencers. Meanwhile, fewer than one in 10 shoppers visited manufacturers' sites, where most companies were still putting the bulk of their digital spend. Display ads, which the team had assumed were important at the consider stage, were clicked on only if they contained a discount offer, and then only when the consumer was close to the buy stage. And although most consumers were still making their purchases in stores, a growing number were buying through retail sites and choosing either direct shipping or in-store pickup.

The research also illuminated consumers' lively relationships with many brands after purchase—the enjoy-and-advocate stage so conspicuously absent from the funnel. These consumers often talked about their purchases in social networks and posted reviews online, particularly when they were stimulated by retailers' postpurchase e-mails. And they tended to turn to review sites for troubleshooting advice.

What they see

To better understand consumers' experience, the team unleashed a battery of hired shoppers who were given individual assignments, such as to look for a TV for a new home; replace a small TV in a bedroom; or, after seeing a TV at a friend's house, go online to learn more about it. The shoppers reported what their experience was like and how the company's brand stacked up against competitors'. How did its TVs appear on search engines? How visible were they on retail sites? What did consumer reviews reveal about them? How thorough and accurate was the available information about them?

The results were alarming but not unexpected. Shoppers trying to engage with any of the brands—whether the company's or its competitors'—had a highly fractured experience. Links constantly failed, because page designs and model numbers had changed but the references to them had not. Product reviews, though they were often positive, were scarce on retail sites. And the company's TVs rarely turned up on the first page of a search within the category, in part because of the profusion of broken links. The same story had emerged during the one-on-one surveys. Consumers reported that every brand's model numbers, product descriptions, promotion availability, and even pictures seemed to change as they moved across sites and into stores. About a third of the shoppers who had considered a specific TV brand online during the evaluate stage walked out of a store during the buy stage, confused and frustrated by inconsistencies.

This costly disruption of the journey across the category made clear that the company's new marketing strategy had to deliver an integrated experience from consider to buy and beyond. In fact, because the problem was common to the entire category, addressing it might create competitive advantage. At any rate, there was little point in winning on the other touch-point battlegrounds if this problem was left unaddressed.

What they say

Finally, the team focused on what people were saying online about the brand. With social media monitoring tools, it uncovered the key words consumers used to discuss the company's products—and found deep confusion. Discussion-group participants frequently gave wrong answers because they misunderstood TV terminology. Product ratings and consumer recommendations sometimes triggered useful and extensive discussions, but when the ratings were negative, the conversation would often enter a self-reinforcing spiral. The company's promotions got some positive response, but people mostly said little about the brand. This was a serious problem, because online advocacy is potent in the evaluate stage.

Taking Action

The company's analysis made clear where its marketing emphasis needed to be. For the pilot launch, spending was significantly shifted away from paid media. Marketing inserted links from its own site to retail sites that carried the brand, working with the retailers to make sure the links connected seamlessly. Most important, click-stream analysis revealed that of all the online retailers, Amazon was probably the most influential touch point for the company's products during the evaluate stage. In collaboration with sales, which managed the relationship with Amazon, marketing created content and links to engage traffic there. To encourage buzz, it aggressively distributed positive third-party reviews online and had its traditional media direct consumers to online environments that included promotions and social experiences. To build ongoing postpurchase relationships and encourage advocacy, it developed programs that included online community initiatives, contests, and e-mail promotions. Finally, to address the inconsistent descriptions and other messaging that was dissuading potential customers at the point of purchase, the team built a new content-development and -management system to ensure rigorous consistency across all platforms.

How did the CDJ strategy work? The new TV became the top seller on Amazon.com and the company's best performer in retail stores, far exceeding the marketers' expectations.

A Customer Experience Plan

As our case company found, a deep investigation of the decision journey often reveals the need for a plan that will make the customer's experience coherent—and may extend the boundaries of the brand itself. The details of a customer experience plan will vary according to the company's products, target segments, campaign strategy, and media mix. But when the plan is well executed, consumers' perception of the brand will include everything from discussions in social media to the in-store shopping experience to continued interactions with the company and the retailer.

For instance, Apple has eliminated jargon, aligned product descriptions, created a rich library of explanatory videos, and instituted off-line Genius Bars, all of which ensure absolute consistency, accuracy, and integration across touch points. Similarly, Nike has moved from exhorting consumers to "Just Do It" to actually helping them act on its motto—with Nike+ gear that records and transmits their workout data; global fundraising races; and customized online training programs. Thus its customers' engagement with the brand doesn't necessarily begin or end with a purchase. And millions of consumers in Japan have signed up to receive mobile alerts from McDonald's, which provide tailored messages that include discount coupons, contest opportunities, special-event invitations, and other unique, brand-specific content.

These companies are not indiscriminate in their use of the tactics available for connecting with customers. Instead they customize their approaches according to their category, brand position, and channel relationships. Apple has not yet done much mining of its customer data to offer more-personalized messaging. Nike's presence on search engines shows little distinctiveness. McDonald's hasn't focused on leveraging a core company website. But their decisions are deliberate, grounded in a clear sense of priorities.

New Roles for Marketing

Developing and executing a CDJ-centric strategy that drives an integrated customer experience requires marketing to take on new or expanded roles. Though we know of no company that has fully developed them, many, including the consumer electronics firm we advised, have begun to do so. Here are three roles that we believe will become increasingly important:

Orchestrator

Many consumer touch points are owned-media channels, such as the company's website, product packaging, and customer service and sales functions. Usually they are run by parts of the organization other than marketing. Recognizing the need to coordinate these channels, one of our clients, a consumer durables company, has moved its owned-media functions into the sphere of the chief marketing officer, giving him responsibility for orchestrating them. Along with traditional and digital marketing communications, he now manages customer service and market research, product literature design, and the product registration and warranty program.

Publisher and "content supply chain" manager

Marketers are generating ever-escalating amounts of content, often becoming publishers—sometimes real-time multimedia publishers—on a global scale. They create videos for marketing, selling, and servicing every product; coupons and other promotions delivered through social media; applications and decision support such as tools to help customers "build" and price a car online. One of our clients, a consumer marketer, realized that every new product release required it to create more than 160 pieces of content involving more than 20 different parties and reaching 30 different touch points. Without careful coordination, producing this volume of material was guaranteed to be inefficient and invited inconsistent messaging that would undermine the brand. As we sought best practices, we discovered that few companies have created the roles and systems needed to manage their content supply chain and create a coherent consumer experience.

Uncoordinated publishing can stall the decision journey, as the consumer electronics firm found. Our research shows that in companies where the marketing function takes on the role of publisher in chief—rationalizing the creation and flow of product related content—consumers develop a clearer sense of the brand and are better able to articulate the attributes of specific products. These marketers also become more agile with their content, readily adapting it to sales training videos and other new uses that ultimately enhance consumers' decision journey.

Marketplace intelligence leader

As more touch points become digital, opportunities to collect and use customer information to understand the consumer decision journey and knit together the customer experience are increasing.

But in many companies IT controls the collection and management of data and the relevant budgets; and with its traditional focus on driving operational efficiency, it often lacks the strategic or financial perspective that would incline it to steer resources toward marketing goals.

More than ever, marketing data should be under marketing's control. One global bank offers a model: It created a Digital Governance Council with representatives from all customer-facing functions. The council is led by the CMO, who articulates the strategy, and attended by the CIO, who lays out options for executing it and receives direction and funding from the council.

We believe that marketing will increasingly take a lead role in distributing customer insights across the organization. For example, discoveries about "what the customer says" as she navigates the CDJ may be highly relevant to product development or service programs. Marketing should convene the right people in the organization to act on its consumer insights and should manage the follow-up to ensure that the enterprise takes action.

Starting the Journey

The firms we advise that are taking this path tend to begin with a narrow line of business or geography (or both) where they can develop a clear understanding of one consumer decision journey and then adjust strategy and resources accordingly. As their pilots get under way, companies inevitably encounter challenges they can't fully address at the local level—such as a need for new enterprisewide infrastructure to support a content management system. Or they may have to adapt the design of a social media program to better suit the narrow initiative. In the more successful initiatives we've seen, the CMO has championed the pilot before the executive leadership team. The best results come when a bottom-up pilot is paralleled by a top-down CMO initiative to address cross-functional, infrastructure, and organizational challenges.

Finally, a company must capture processes, successes, and failures when it launches a pilot so that the pilot can be effectively adapted and scaled. A key consideration is that although the basic architecture of a CDJ strategy may remain intact as it is expanded, specific tactics will probably vary from one market and product to another. When the consumer electronics firm discussed here took its CDJ strategy to East Asia, for example, its touch-point analysis revealed that consumers in that part of the world put more stock in blogs and third-party review sites than Western consumers do, and less in manufacturers' or retailers' sites, which they didn't fully trust. They were also less likely to buy online. However, they relied more on mobile apps such as bar-code readers to pull up detailed product information at the point of purchase.

The changes buffeting marketers in the digital era are not incremental—they are fundamental. Consumers' perception of a brand during the decision journey has always been important, but the phenomenal reach, speed, and interactivity of digital touch points makes close attention to the brand experience essential—and requires an executive-level steward. At many start-ups the founder brings to this role the needed vision and the power to enforce it. Established enterprises should have a steward as well. Now is the time for CMOs to seize this opportunity to take on a leadership role, establishing a stronger position in the executive suite and making consumers' brand experience central to enterprise strategy.

Originally published in December 2010. Reprint R1012C

Marketing Myopia

by Theodore Levitt

EVERY MAJOR INDUSTRY was once a growth industry. But some that are now riding a wave of growth enthusiasm are very much in the shadow of decline. Others that are thought of as seasoned growth industries have actually stopped growing. In every case, the reason growth is threatened, slowed, or stopped is *not* because the market is saturated. It is because there has been a failure of management.

Fateful Purposes

The failure is at the top. The executives responsible for it, in the last analysis, are those who deal with broad aims and policies. Thus:

- The railroads did not stop growing because the need for passenger and freight transportation declined. That grew. The railroads are in trouble today not because that need was filled by others (cars, trucks, airplanes, and even telephones) but because it was *not* filled by the railroads themselves. They let others take customers away from them because they assumed themselves to be in the railroad business rather than in the transportation business. The reason they defined their industry incorrectly was that they were railroad oriented instead of transportation oriented; they were product oriented instead of customer oriented.
- Hollywood barely escaped being totally ravished by television. Actually, all the established film companies went through

> drastic reorganizations. Some simply disappeared. All of them got into trouble not because of TV's inroads but because of their own myopia. As with the railroads, Hollywood defined its business incorrectly. It thought it was in the movie business when it was actually in the entertainment business. "Movies" implied a specific, limited product. This produced a fatuous contentment that from the beginning led producers to view TV as a threat. Hollywood scorned and rejected TV when it should have welcomed it as an opportunity—an opportunity to expand the entertainment business.

Today, TV is a bigger business than the old narrowly defined movie business ever was. Had Hollywood been customer oriented (providing entertainment) rather than product oriented (making movies), would it have gone through the fiscal purgatory that it did? I doubt it. What ultimately saved Hollywood and accounted for its resurgence was the wave of new young writers, producers, and directors whose previous successes in television had decimated the old movie companies and toppled the big movie moguls.

There are other, less obvious examples of industries that have been and are now endangering their futures by improperly defining their purposes. I shall discuss some of them in detail later and analyze the kind of policies that lead to trouble. Right now, it may help to show what a thoroughly customer-oriented management can do to keep a growth industry growing, even after the obvious opportunities have been exhausted, and here there are two examples that have been around for a long time. They are nylon and glass—specifically, E.I. du Pont de Nemours and Company and Corning Glass Works.

Both companies have great technical competence. Their product orientation is unquestioned. But this alone does not explain their success. After all, who was more pridefully product oriented and product conscious than the erstwhile New England textile companies that have been so thoroughly massacred? The DuPonts and the Cornings have succeeded not primarily because of their product or research orientation but because they have been thoroughly customer oriented also. It is constant watchfulness for

Idea in Brief

What business are you *really* in? A seemingly obvious question—but one we should all ask *before* demand for our companies' products or services dwindles.

The railroads failed to ask this same question—and stopped growing. Why? Not because people no longer needed transportation. And not because other innovations (cars, airplanes) filled transportation needs. Rather, railroads stopped growing because *railroads* didn't move to fill those needs. Their executives incorrectly thought that they were in the railroad business, not the transportation business. They viewed themselves as providing a product instead of serving customers. Too many other industries make the same mistake—putting themselves at risk of obsolescence.

How to ensure continued growth for your company? Concentrate on meeting customers' needs rather than selling products. Chemical powerhouse DuPont kept a close eye on its customers' most pressing concerns—and deployed its technical know-how to create an ever-expanding array of products that appealed to customers and continuously enlarged its market. If DuPont had merely found more uses for its flagship invention, nylon, it might not be around today.

opportunities to apply their technical know-how to the creation of customer-satisfying uses that accounts for their prodigious output of successful new products. Without a very sophisticated eye on the customer, most of their new products might have been wrong, their sales methods useless.

Aluminum has also continued to be a growth industry, thanks to the efforts of two wartime-created companies that deliberately set about inventing new customer-satisfying uses. Without Kaiser Aluminum & Chemical Corporation and Reynolds Metals Company, the total demand for aluminum today would be vastly less.

Error of analysis

Some may argue that it is foolish to set the railroads off against aluminum or the movies off against glass. Are not aluminum and glass naturally so versatile that the industries are bound to have more growth opportunities than the railroads and the movies? This view commits precisely the error I have been talking about. It defines an

Idea in Practice

We put our businesses at risk of obsolescence when we accept any of the following myths:

Myth 1: An ever-expanding and more affluent population will ensure our growth.

When markets are expanding, we often assume we don't have to think imaginatively about our businesses. Instead, we seek to outdo rivals simply by improving on what we're already doing. The consequence: We increase the efficiency of making our products, rather than boosting the value those products deliver to customers.

Myth 2: There is no competitive substitute for our industry's major product.

Believing that our products have no rivals makes our companies vulnerable to dramatic innovations from outside our industries—often by smaller, newer companies that are focusing on customer needs rather than the products themselves.

Myth 3: We can protect ourselves through mass production.

Few of us can resist the prospect of the increased profits that come with steeply declining unit costs. But focusing on mass production emphasizes our *company's* needs—when we should be emphasizing our *customers'*.

Myth 4: Technical research and development will ensure our growth.

When R&D produces breakthrough products, we may be tempted to organize our companies around the technology rather than the consumer. Instead, we should remain focused on satisfying customer needs.

industry or a product or a cluster of know-how so narrowly as to guarantee its premature senescence. When we mention "railroads," we should make sure we mean "transportation." As transporters, the railroads still have a good chance for very considerable growth. They are not limited to the railroad business as such (though in my opinion, rail transportation is potentially a much stronger transportation medium than is generally believed).

What the railroads lack is not opportunity but some of the managerial imaginativeness and audacity that made them great. Even an amateur like Jacques Barzun can see what is lacking when he says, "I grieve to see the most advanced physical and social organization of the last century go down in shabby disgrace for lack of the same comprehensive imagination that built it up. [What is lacking is] the will of the companies to survive and to satisfy the public by inventiveness and skill."[1]

Shadow of Obsolescence

It is impossible to mention a single major industry that did not at one time qualify for the magic appellation of "growth industry." In each case, the industry's assumed strength lay in the apparently unchallenged superiority of its product. There appeared to be no effective substitute for it. It was itself a runaway substitute for the product it so triumphantly replaced. Yet one after another of these celebrated industries has come under a shadow. Let us look briefly at a few more of them, this time taking examples that have so far received a little less attention.

Dry cleaning

This was once a growth industry with lavish prospects. In an age of wool garments, imagine being finally able to get them clean safely and easily. The boom was on. Yet here we are 30 years after the boom started, and the industry is in trouble. Where has the competition come from? From a better way of cleaning? No. It has come from synthetic fibers and chemical additives that have cut the need for dry cleaning. But this is only the beginning. Lurking in the wings and ready to make chemical dry cleaning totally obsolete is that powerful magician, ultrasonics.

Electric utilities

This is another one of those supposedly "no substitute" products that has been enthroned on a pedestal of invincible growth. When the incandescent lamp came along, kerosene lights were finished. Later, the waterwheel and the steam engine were cut to ribbons by the flexibility, reliability, simplicity, and just plain easy availability of electric motors. The prosperity of electric utilities continues to wax extravagant as the home is converted into a museum of electric gadgetry. How can anybody miss by investing in utilities, with no competition, nothing but growth ahead?

But a second look is not quite so comforting. A score of nonutility companies are well advanced toward developing a powerful chemical fuel cell, which could sit in some hidden closet of every home silently ticking off electric power. The electric lines that vulgarize so many neighborhoods would be eliminated. So would the endless demolition of streets and service interruptions during storms. Also on the horizon is solar energy, again pioneered by nonutility companies.

Who says that the utilities have no competition? They may be natural monopolies now, but tomorrow they may be natural deaths. To avoid this prospect, they too will have to develop fuel cells, solar energy, and other power sources. To survive, they themselves will have to plot the obsolescence of what now produces their livelihood.

Grocery stores

Many people find it hard to realize that there ever was a thriving establishment known as the "corner store." The supermarket took over with a powerful effectiveness. Yet the big food chains of the 1930s narrowly escaped being completely wiped out by the aggressive expansion of independent supermarkets. The first genuine supermarket was opened in 1930, in Jamaica, Long Island. By 1933, supermarkets were thriving in California, Ohio, Pennsylvania, and elsewhere. Yet the established chains pompously ignored them. When they chose to notice them, it was with such derisive descriptions as "cheapy," "horse-and-buggy," "cracker-barrel storekeeping," and "unethical opportunists."

The executive of one big chain announced at the time that he found it "hard to believe that people will drive for miles to shop for foods and sacrifice the personal service chains have perfected and to which [the consumer] is accustomed."[2] As late as 1936, the National Wholesale Grocers convention and the New Jersey Retail Grocers Association said there was nothing to fear. They said that the supers' narrow appeal to the price buyer limited the size of their market. They had to draw from miles around. When imitators came, there would be wholesale liquidations as volume fell. The high sales of the supers were said to be partly due to their novelty. People wanted convenient neighborhood grocers. If the neighborhood stores would "cooperate with their suppliers, pay attention to their costs, and improve their service," they would be able to weather the competition until it blew over.[3]

It never blew over. The chains discovered that survival required going into the supermarket business. This meant the wholesale destruction of their huge investments in corner store sites and in established distribution and merchandising methods. The companies with "the courage of their convictions" resolutely stuck to the corner store philosophy. They kept their pride but lost their shirts.

A self-deceiving cycle

But memories are short. For example, it is hard for people who today confidently hail the twin messiahs of electronics and chemicals to see how things could possibly go wrong with these galloping industries. They probably also cannot see how a reasonably sensible businessperson could have been as myopic as the famous Boston millionaire who early in the twentieth century unintentionally sentenced his heirs to poverty by stipulating that his entire estate be forever invested exclusively in electric streetcar securities. His posthumous declaration, "There will always be a big demand for efficient urban transportation," is no consolation to his heirs, who sustain life by pumping gasoline at automobile filling stations.

Yet, in a casual survey I took among a group of intelligent business executives, nearly half agreed that it would be hard to hurt their heirs by tying their estates forever to the electronics industry. When I then confronted them with the Boston streetcar example, they chorused unanimously, "That's different!" But is it? Is not the basic situation identical?

In truth, *there is no such thing as a growth industry,* I believe. There are only companies organized and operated to create and capitalize on growth opportunities. Industries that assume themselves to be riding some automatic growth escalator invariably descend into stagnation. The history of every dead and dying "growth" industry shows a self-deceiving cycle of bountiful expansion and undetected decay. There are four conditions that usually guarantee this cycle:

1. The belief that growth is assured by an expanding and more affluent population;
2. The belief that there is no competitive substitute for the industry's major product;
3. Too much faith in mass production and in the advantages of rapidly declining unit costs as output rises;
4. Preoccupation with a product that lends itself to carefully controlled scientific experimentation, improvement, and manufacturing cost reduction.

I should like now to examine each of these conditions in some detail. To build my case as boldly as possible, I shall illustrate the points with reference to three industries: petroleum, automobiles, and electronics. I'll focus on petroleum in particular, because it spans more years and more vicissitudes. Not only do these three industries have excellent reputations with the general public and also enjoy the confidence of sophisticated investors, but their managements have become known for progressive thinking in areas like financial control, product research, and management training. If obsolescence can cripple even these industries, it can happen anywhere.

Population Myth

The belief that profits are assured by an expanding and more affluent population is dear to the heart of every industry. It takes the edge off the apprehensions everybody understandably feels about the future. If consumers are multiplying and also buying more of your product or service, you can face the future with considerably more comfort than if the market were shrinking. An expanding market keeps the manufacturer from having to think very hard or imaginatively. If thinking is an intellectual response to a problem, then the absence of a problem leads to the absence of thinking. If your product has an automatically expanding market, then you will not give much thought to how to expand it.

One of the most interesting examples of this is provided by the petroleum industry. Probably our oldest growth industry, it has an enviable record. While there are some current concerns about its growth rate, the industry itself tends to be optimistic.

But I believe it can be demonstrated that it is undergoing a fundamental yet typical change. It is not only ceasing to be a growth industry but may actually be a declining one, relative to other businesses. Although there is widespread unawareness of this fact, it is conceivable that in time, the oil industry may find itself in much the same position of retrospective glory that the railroads are now in. Despite its pioneering work in developing and applying the present-value method of investment evaluation, in employee relations, and in working with developing countries, the petroleum business is a distressing example of how complacency and wrong-headedness can stubbornly convert opportunity into near disaster.

One of the characteristics of this and other industries that have believed very strongly in the beneficial consequences of an expanding population, while at the same time having a generic product for which there has appeared to be no competitive substitute, is that the individual companies have sought to outdo their competitors by improving on what they are already doing. This makes sense, of course, if one assumes that sales are tied to the country's population strings, because the customer can compare products only on a feature-by-feature basis. I believe it is significant, for example, that not since John D. Rockefeller sent free kerosene lamps to China has the oil industry done anything really outstanding to create a demand for its product. Not even in product improvement has it showered itself with eminence. The greatest single improvement—the development of tetraethyl lead—came from outside the industry, specifically from General Motors and DuPont. The big contributions made by the industry itself are confined to the technology of oil exploration, oil production, and oil refining.

Asking for trouble

In other words, the petroleum industry's efforts have focused on improving the *efficiency* of getting and making its product, not really on improving the generic product or its marketing. Moreover, its chief product has continually been defined in the narrowest possible terms—namely, gasoline, not energy, fuel, or transportation. This attitude has helped assure that:

- Major improvements in gasoline quality tend not to originate in the oil industry. The development of superior alternative fuels also comes from outside the oil industry, as will be shown later.
- Major innovations in automobile fuel marketing come from small, new oil companies that are not primarily preoccupied with production or refining. These are the companies that have been responsible for the rapidly expanding multipump gasoline stations, with their successful emphasis on large and clean layouts, rapid and efficient driveway service, and quality gasoline at low prices.

Thus, the oil industry is asking for trouble from outsiders. Sooner or later, in this land of hungry investors and entrepreneurs, a threat is sure to come. The possibility of this will become more apparent when we turn to the next dangerous belief of many managements. For the sake of continuity, because this second belief is tied closely to the first, I shall continue with the same example.

The idea of indispensability

The petroleum industry is pretty much convinced that there is no competitive substitute for its major product, gasoline—or, if there is, that it will continue to be a derivative of crude oil, such as diesel fuel or kerosene jet fuel.

There is a lot of automatic wishful thinking in this assumption. The trouble is that most refining companies own huge amounts of crude oil reserves. These have value only if there is a market for products into which oil can be converted. Hence the tenacious belief in the continuing competitive superiority of automobile fuels made from crude oil.

This idea persists despite all historic evidence against it. The evidence not only shows that oil has never been a superior product for any purpose for very long but also that the oil industry has never really been a growth industry. Rather, it has been a succession of different businesses that have gone through the usual historic cycles of growth, maturity, and decay. The industry's overall survival is owed to a series of miraculous escapes from total obsolescence, of last-minute and unexpected reprieves from total disaster reminiscent of the perils of Pauline.

The perils of petroleum

To illustrate, I shall sketch in only the main episodes. First, crude oil was largely a patent medicine. But even before that fad ran out, demand was greatly expanded by the use of oil in kerosene lamps. The prospect of lighting the world's lamps gave rise to an extravagant promise of growth. The prospects were similar to those the industry now holds for gasoline in other parts of the world. It can hardly wait for the underdeveloped nations to get a car in every garage.

In the days of the kerosene lamp, the oil companies competed with each other and against gaslight by trying to improve the illuminating characteristics of kerosene. Then suddenly the impossible happened. Edison invented a light that was totally nondependent on crude oil. Had it not been for the growing use of kerosene in space heaters, the incandescent lamp would have completely finished oil as a growth industry at that time. Oil would have been good for little else than axle grease.

Then disaster and reprieve struck again. Two great innovations occurred, neither originating in the oil industry. First, the successful development of coal-burning domestic central-heating systems made the space heater obsolete. While the industry reeled, along came its most magnificent boost yet: the internal combustion engine, also invented by outsiders. Then, when the prodigious expansion for gasoline finally began to level off in the 1920s, along came the miraculous escape of the central oil heater. Once again, the escape was provided by an outsider's invention and development. And when that market weakened, wartime demand for aviation fuel came to the rescue. After the war, the expansion of civilian aviation, the dieselization of railroads, and the explosive demand for cars and trucks kept the industry's growth in high gear.

Meanwhile, centralized oil heating—whose boom potential had only recently been proclaimed—ran into severe competition from natural gas. While the oil companies themselves owned the gas that now competed with their oil, the industry did not originate the natural gas revolution, nor has it to this day greatly profited from its gas ownership. The gas revolution was made by newly formed transmission companies that marketed the product with an aggressive ardor. They started a magnificent new industry, first against the advice and then against the resistance of the oil companies.

By all the logic of the situation, the oil companies themselves should have made the gas revolution. They not only owned the gas, they also were the only people experienced in handling, scrubbing, and using it and the only people experienced in pipeline technology and transmission. They also understood heating problems. But, partly because they knew that natural gas would compete with their own sale of heating oil, the oil companies pooh-poohed the potential of gas. The revolution was finally started by oil pipeline executives who, unable to persuade their own companies to go into gas, quit and organized the spectacularly successful gas transmission companies. Even after their success became painfully evident to the oil companies, the latter did not go into gas transmission. The multibillion-dollar business that should have been theirs went to others. As in the past, the industry was blinded by its narrow preoccupation with a specific product and the value of its reserves. It paid little or no attention to its customers' basic needs and preferences.

The postwar years have not witnessed any change. Immediately after World War II, the oil industry was greatly encouraged about its future by the rapid increase in demand for its traditional line of products. In 1950, most companies projected annual rates of domestic expansion of around 6% through at least 1975. Though the ratio of crude oil reserves to demand in the free world was about 20 to 1, with 10 to 1 being usually considered a reasonable working ratio in the United States, booming demand sent oil explorers searching for more without sufficient regard to what the future really promised. In 1952, they "hit" in the Middle East; the ratio skyrocketed to 42 to 1. If gross additions to reserves continue at the average rate of the past five years (37 billion barrels annually), then by 1970, the reserve ratio will be up to 45 to 1. This abundance of oil has weakened crude and product prices all over the world.

An uncertain future

Management cannot find much consolation today in the rapidly expanding petrochemical industry, another oil-using idea that did not originate in the leading firms. The total U.S. production of petrochemicals is equivalent to about 2% (by volume) of the demand for all petroleum products. Although the petrochemical industry is now expected to grow by about 10% per year, this will not offset other drains on the growth of crude oil consumption. Furthermore, while petrochemical products are many and growing, it is important to remember that there are nonpetroleum sources of the basic raw material, such as coal. Besides, a lot of plastics can be produced with relatively little oil. A 50,000-barrel-per-day oil refinery is now considered the absolute minimum size for efficiency. But a 5,000-barrel-per-day chemical plant is a giant operation.

Oil has never been a continuously strong growth industry. It has grown by fits and starts, always miraculously saved by innovations and developments not of its own making. The reason it has not grown in a smooth progression is that each time it thought it had a superior product safe from the possibility of competitive substitutes, the product turned out to be inferior and notoriously subject to obsolescence. Until now, gasoline (for motor fuel, anyhow) has escaped this fate. But, as we shall see later, it too may be on its last legs.

The point of all this is that there is no guarantee against product obsolescence. If a company's own research does not make a product obsolete, another's will. Unless an industry is especially lucky, as oil has been until now, it can easily go down in a sea of red figures—just as the railroads have, as the buggy whip manufacturers have, as the corner grocery chains have, as most of the big movie companies have, and, indeed, as many other industries have.

The best way for a firm to be lucky is to make its own luck. That requires knowing what makes a business successful. One of the greatest enemies of this knowledge is mass production.

Production Pressures

Mass production industries are impelled by a great drive to produce all they can. The prospect of steeply declining unit costs as output rises is more than most companies can usually resist. The profit possibilities look spectacular. All effort focuses on production. The result is that marketing gets neglected.

John Kenneth Galbraith contends that just the opposite occurs.[4] Output is so prodigious that all effort concentrates on trying to get rid of it. He says this accounts for singing commercials, the desecration of the countryside with advertising signs, and other wasteful and vulgar practices. Galbraith has a finger on something real, but he misses the strategic point. Mass production does indeed generate great pressure to "move" the product. But what usually gets emphasized is selling, not marketing. Marketing, a more sophisticated and complex process, gets ignored.

The difference between marketing and selling is more than semantic. Selling focuses on the needs of the seller, marketing on the needs of the buyer. Selling is preoccupied with the seller's need to convert the product into cash, marketing with the idea of satisfying the needs of the customer by means of the product and the whole cluster of things associated with creating, delivering, and, finally, consuming it.

In some industries, the enticements of full mass production have been so powerful that top management in effect has told the sales department, "You get rid of it; we'll worry about profits." By contrast, a truly marketing-minded firm tries to create value-satisfying goods and services that consumers will want to buy. What it offers for sale includes not only the generic product or service but also how it is made available to the customer, in what form, when, under what conditions, and at what terms of trade. Most important, what it offers for sale is determined not by the seller but by the buyer. The seller takes cues from the buyer in such a way that the product becomes a consequence of the marketing effort, not vice versa.

A lag in Detroit

This may sound like an elementary rule of business, but that does not keep it from being violated wholesale. It is certainly more violated than honored. Take the automobile industry.

Here mass production is most famous, most honored, and has the greatest impact on the entire society. The industry has hitched its fortune to the relentless requirements of the annual model change, a policy that makes customer orientation an especially urgent necessity. Consequently, the auto companies annually spend millions of dollars on consumer research. But the fact that the new compact cars are selling so well in their first year indicates that Detroit's vast researches have for a long time failed to reveal what customers really wanted. Detroit was not convinced that people wanted anything different from what they had been getting until it lost millions of customers to other small-car manufacturers.

How could this unbelievable lag behind consumer wants have been perpetuated for so long? Why did not research reveal consumer preferences before consumers' buying decisions themselves revealed the facts? Is that not what consumer research is for—to find out before the fact what is going to happen? The answer is that Detroit never really researched customers' wants. It only researched their preferences between the kinds of things it had already decided to offer them. For Detroit is mainly product oriented, not customer oriented. To the extent that the customer is recognized as having needs that the manufacturer should try to satisfy, Detroit usually acts as if the job can be done entirely by product changes. Occasionally, attention gets paid to financing, too, but that is done more in order to sell than to enable the customer to buy.

As for taking care of other customer needs, there is not enough being done to write about. The areas of the greatest unsatisfied needs are ignored or, at best, get stepchild attention. These are at the point of sale and on the matter of automotive repair and maintenance.

Detroit views these problem areas as being of secondary importance. That is underscored by the fact that the retailing and servicing ends of this industry are neither owned and operated nor controlled by the manufacturers. Once the car is produced, things are pretty much in the dealer's inadequate hands. Illustrative of Detroit's arms-length attitude is the fact that, while servicing holds enormous sales-stimulating, profit-building opportunities, only 57 of Chevrolet's 7,000 dealers provide night maintenance service.

Motorists repeatedly express their dissatisfaction with servicing and their apprehensions about buying cars under the present selling setup. The anxieties and problems they encounter during the auto buying and maintenance processes are probably more intense and widespread today than many years ago. Yet the automobile companies do not seem to listen to or take their cues from the anguished consumer. If they do listen, it must be through the filter of their own preoccupation with production. The marketing effort is still viewed as a necessary consequence of the product—not vice versa, as it should be. That is the legacy of mass production, with its parochial view that profit resides essentially in low-cost full production.

What Ford put first

The profit lure of mass production obviously has a place in the plans and strategy of business management, but it must always *follow* hard thinking about the customer. This is one of the most important lessons we can learn from the contradictory behavior of Henry Ford. In a sense, Ford was both the most brilliant and the most senseless marketer in American history. He was senseless because he refused to give the customer anything but a black car. He was brilliant because he fashioned a production system designed to fit market needs. We habitually celebrate him for the wrong reason: for his production genius. His real genius was marketing. We think he was able to cut his selling price and therefore sell millions of $500 cars because his invention of the assembly line had reduced the costs. Actually, he invented the assembly line because he had concluded that at $500 he could sell millions of cars. Mass production was the *result,* not the cause, of his low prices.

Ford emphasized this point repeatedly, but a nation of production-oriented business managers refuses to hear the great lesson he taught. Here is his operating philosophy as he expressed it succinctly:

> Our policy is to reduce the price, extend the operations, and improve the article. You will notice that the reduction of price comes first. We have never considered any costs as fixed. Therefore we first reduce the price to the point where we believe more sales will result. Then we go ahead and try to make the prices. We do not bother about the costs. The new price forces the costs down. The more usual way is to take the costs and then determine the price; and although that method may be scientific in the narrow sense, it is not scientific in the broad sense, because what earthly use is it to know the cost if it tells you that you cannot manufacture at a price at which the article can be sold? But more to the point is the fact that, although one may calculate what a cost is, and of course all of our costs are carefully calculated, no one knows what a cost ought to be. One of the ways of discovering . . . is to name a price so low as to force everybody in the place to the highest point of efficiency. The low price makes everybody dig for profits. We make more discoveries concerning manufacturing and selling under this forced method than by any method of leisurely investigation.[5]

Product provincialism

The tantalizing profit possibilities of low unit production costs may be the most seriously self-deceiving attitude that can afflict a company, particularly a "growth" company, where an apparently assured expansion of demand already tends to undermine a proper concern for the importance of marketing and the customer.

The usual result of this narrow preoccupation with so-called concrete matters is that instead of growing, the industry declines. It usually means that the product fails to adapt to the constantly changing patterns of consumer needs and tastes, to new and modified marketing institutions and practices, or to product developments in competing or complementary industries. The industry has its eyes so firmly on its own specific product that it does not see how it is being made obsolete.

The classic example of this is the buggy whip industry. No amount of product improvement could stave off its death sentence. But had the industry defined itself as being in the transportation business rather than in the buggy whip business, it might have survived. It would have done what survival always entails—that is, change. Even if it had only defined its business as providing a stimulant or catalyst to an energy source, it might have survived by becoming a manufacturer of, say, fan belts or air cleaners.

What may someday be a still more classic example is, again, the oil industry. Having let others steal marvelous opportunities from it (including natural gas, as already mentioned; missile fuels; and jet engine lubricants), one would expect it to have taken steps never to let that happen again. But this is not the case. We are now seeing extraordinary new developments in fuel systems specifically designed to power automobiles. Not only are these developments concentrated in firms outside the petroleum industry, but petroleum is almost systematically ignoring them, securely content in its wedded bliss to oil. It is the story of the kerosene lamp versus the incandescent lamp all over again. Oil is trying to improve hydrocarbon fuels rather than develop *any* fuels best suited to the needs of their users, whether or not made in different ways and with different raw materials from oil.

Here are some things that nonpetroleum companies are working on. More than a dozen such firms now have advanced working models of energy systems which, when perfected, will replace the internal combustion engine and eliminate the demand for gasoline. The superior merit of each of these systems is their elimination of frequent, time-consuming, and irritating refueling stops. Most of these systems are fuel cells designed to create electrical energy directly from chemicals without combustion. Most of them use chemicals that are not derived from oil—generally, hydrogen and oxygen.

Several other companies have advanced models of electric storage batteries designed to power automobiles. One of these is an aircraft producer that is working jointly with several electric utility companies. The latter hope to use off-peak generating capacity to supply overnight plug-in battery regeneration. Another company, also using the battery approach, is a medium-sized electronics firm with extensive small-battery experience that it developed in connection with its work on hearing aids. It is collaborating with an automobile manufacturer. Recent improvements arising from the need for high-powered miniature power storage plants in rockets have put us within reach of a relatively small battery capable of withstanding great overloads or surges of power. Germanium diode applications and batteries using sintered plate and nickel cadmium techniques promise to make a revolution in our energy sources.

Solar energy conversion systems are also getting increasing attention. One usually cautious Detroit auto executive recently ventured that solar-powered cars might be common by 1980.

As for the oil companies, they are more or less "watching developments," as one research director put it to me. A few are doing a bit of research on fuel cells, but this research is almost always confined to developing cells powered by hydrocarbon chemicals. None of them is enthusiastically researching fuel cells, batteries, or solar power plants. None of them is spending a fraction as much on research in these profoundly important areas as it is on the usual run-of-the-mill things like reducing combustion chamber deposits in gasoline engines. One major integrated petroleum company recently took a tentative look at the fuel cell and concluded that although "the companies actively working on it indicate a belief in ultimate success . . . the timing and magnitude of its impact are too remote to warrant recognition in our forecasts."

One might, of course, ask, Why should the oil companies do anything different? Would not chemical fuel cells, batteries, or solar energy kill the present product lines? The answer is that they would indeed, and that is precisely the reason for the oil firms' having to develop these power units before their competitors do, so they will not be companies without an industry.

Management might be more likely to do what is needed for its own preservation if it thought of itself as being in the energy business. But even that will not be enough if it persists in imprisoning itself in the narrow grip of its tight product orientation. It has to think of itself as taking care of customer needs, not finding, refining, or even selling oil. Once it genuinely thinks of its business as taking care of people's transportation needs, nothing can stop it from creating its own extravagantly profitable growth.

Creative destruction

Since words are cheap and deeds are dear, it may be appropriate to indicate what this kind of thinking involves and leads to. Let us start at the beginning: the customer. It can be shown that motorists strongly dislike the bother, delay, and experience of buying gasoline. People actually do not buy gasoline. They cannot see it, taste it, feel it, appreciate it, or really test it. What they buy is the right to continue driving their cars. The gas station is like a tax collector to whom people are compelled to pay a periodic toll as the price of using their cars. This makes the gas station a basically unpopular institution. It can never be made popular or pleasant, only less unpopular, less unpleasant.

Reducing its unpopularity completely means eliminating it. Nobody likes a tax collector, not even a pleasantly cheerful one. Nobody likes to interrupt a trip to buy a phantom product, not even from a handsome Adonis or a seductive Venus. Hence, companies that are working on exotic fuel substitutes that will eliminate the need for frequent refueling are heading directly into the outstretched arms of the irritated motorist. They are riding a wave of inevitability, not because they are creating something that is technologically superior or more sophisticated but because they are satisfying a powerful customer need. They are also eliminating noxious odors and air pollution.

Once the petroleum companies recognize the customer-satisfying logic of what another power system can do, they will see that they have no more choice about working on an efficient, long-lasting fuel (or some way of delivering present fuels without bothering the motorist) than the big food chains had a choice about going into the supermarket business or the vacuum tube companies had a choice about making semiconductors. For their own good, the oil firms will have to destroy their own highly profitable assets. No amount of wishful thinking can save them from the necessity of engaging in this form of "creative destruction."

I phrase the need as strongly as this because I think management must make quite an effort to break itself loose from conventional ways. It is all too easy in this day and age for a company or industry to let its sense of purpose become dominated by the economies of full production and to develop a dangerously lopsided product orientation. In short, if management lets itself drift, it invariably drifts in the direction of thinking of itself as producing goods and services, not customer satisfactions. While it probably will not descend to the depths of telling its salespeople, "You get rid of it; we'll worry about profits," it can, without knowing it, be practicing precisely that formula for withering decay. The historic fate of one growth industry after another has been its suicidal product provincialism.

Dangers of R&D

Another big danger to a firm's continued growth arises when top management is wholly transfixed by the profit possibilities of technical research and development. To illustrate, I shall turn first to a new industry—electronics—and then return once more to the oil companies. By comparing a fresh example with a familiar one, I hope to emphasize the prevalence and insidiousness of a hazardous way of thinking.

Marketing shortchanged

In the case of electronics, the greatest danger that faces the glamorous new companies in this field is not that they do not pay enough attention to research and development but that they pay too much attention to it. And the fact that the fastest-growing electronics firms owe their eminence to their heavy emphasis on technical research is completely beside the point. They have vaulted to affluence on a sudden crest of unusually strong general receptiveness to new technical ideas. Also, their success has been shaped in the virtually guaranteed market of military subsidies and by military orders that in many cases actually preceded the existence of facilities to make the products. Their expansion has, in other words, been almost totally devoid of marketing effort.

Thus, they are growing up under conditions that come dangerously close to creating the illusion that a superior product will sell itself. It is not surprising that, having created a successful company by making a superior product, management continues to be oriented toward the product rather than the people who consume it. It develops the philosophy that continued growth is a matter of continued product innovation and improvement.

A number of other factors tend to strengthen and sustain this belief:

1. Because electronic products are highly complex and sophisticated, managements become top-heavy with engineers and scientists. This creates a selective bias in favor of research and production at the expense of marketing. The organization tends to view itself as making things rather than as satisfying customer needs. Marketing gets treated as a residual activity, "something else" that must be done once the vital job of product creation and production is completed.

2. To this bias in favor of product research, development, and production is added the bias in favor of dealing with controllable variables. Engineers and scientists are at home in the world of concrete things like machines, test tubes, production lines, and even balance sheets. The abstractions to which they feel kindly are those that are testable or manipulatable in the laboratory or, if not testable, then functional, such as Euclid's axioms. In short, the managements of the new glamour-growth companies tend to favor business activities that lend themselves to careful study, experimentation, and control—the hard, practical realities of the lab, the shop, and the books.

What gets shortchanged are the realities of the *market*. Consumers are unpredictable, varied, fickle, stupid, shortsighted, stubborn, and generally bothersome. This is not what the engineer managers say, but deep down in their consciousness, it is what they believe. And this accounts for their concentration on what they know and what they can control—namely, product research, engineering, and production. The emphasis on production becomes particularly attractive when the product can be made at declining unit costs. There is no more inviting way of making money than by running the plant full blast.

The top-heavy science-engineering-production orientation of so many electronics companies works reasonably well today because they are pushing into new frontiers in which the armed services have pioneered virtually assured markets. The companies are in the felicitous position of having to fill, not find, markets, of not having to discover what the customer needs and wants but of having the customer voluntarily come forward with specific new product demands. If a team of consultants had been assigned specifically to design a business situation calculated to prevent the emergence and development of a customer-oriented marketing viewpoint, it could not have produced anything better than the conditions just described.

Stepchild treatment

The oil industry is a stunning example of how science, technology, and mass production can divert an entire group of companies from their main task. To the extent the consumer is studied at all (which is not much), the focus is forever on getting information that is designed to help the oil companies improve what they are now doing. They try to discover more convincing advertising themes, more effective sales promotional drives, what the market shares of the various companies are, what people like or dislike about service station dealers and oil companies, and so forth. Nobody seems as interested in probing deeply into the basic human needs that the industry might be trying to satisfy as in probing into the basic properties of the raw material that the companies work with in trying to deliver customer satisfactions.

Basic questions about customers and markets seldom get asked. The latter occupy a stepchild status. They are recognized as existing, as having to be taken care of, but not worth very much real thought or dedicated attention. No oil company gets as excited about the customers in its own backyard as about the oil in the Sahara Desert. Nothing illustrates better the neglect of marketing than its treatment in the industry press.

The centennial issue of the *American Petroleum Institute Quarterly,* published in 1959 to celebrate the discovery of oil in Titusville, Pennsylvania, contained 21 feature articles proclaiming the industry's greatness. Only one of these talked about its achievements in marketing, and that was only a pictorial record of how service station architecture has changed. The issue also contained a special section on "New Horizons," which was devoted to showing the magnificent role oil would play in America's future. Every reference was ebulliently optimistic, never implying once that oil might have some hard competition. Even the reference to atomic energy was a cheerful catalog of how oil would help make atomic energy a success. There was not a single apprehension that the oil industry's affluence might be threatened or a suggestion that one "new horizon" might include new and better ways of serving oil's present customers.

But the most revealing example of the stepchild treatment that marketing gets is still another special series of short articles on "The Revolutionary Potential of Electronics." Under that heading, this list of articles appeared in the table of contents:

- "In the Search for Oil"
- "In Production Operations"
- "In Refinery Processes"
- "In Pipeline Operations"

Significantly, every one of the industry's major functional areas is listed, *except* marketing. Why? Either it is believed that electronics holds no revolutionary potential for petroleum marketing (which is palpably wrong), or the editors forgot to discuss marketing (which is more likely and illustrates its stepchild status).

The order in which the four functional areas are listed also betrays the alienation of the oil industry from the consumer. The industry is implicitly defined as beginning with the search for oil and ending with its distribution from the refinery. But the truth is, it seems to me, that the industry begins with the needs of the customer for its products. From that primal position its definition moves steadily back stream to areas of progressively lesser importance until it finally comes to rest at the search for oil.

The beginning and end

The view that an industry is a customer-satisfying process, not a goods-producing process, is vital for all businesspeople to understand. An industry begins with the customer and his or her needs, not with a patent, a raw material, or a selling skill. Given the customer's needs, the industry develops backwards, first concerning itself with the physical *delivery* of customer satisfactions. Then it moves back further to *creating* the things by which these satisfactions are in part achieved. How these materials are created is a matter of indifference to the customer, hence the particular form of manufacturing, processing, or what have you cannot be considered as a vital aspect of the industry. Finally, the industry moves back still further to *finding* the raw materials necessary for making its products.

The irony of some industries oriented toward technical research and development is that the scientists who occupy the high executive positions are totally unscientific when it comes to defining their companies' overall needs and purposes. They violate the first two rules of the scientific method: being aware of and defining their companies' problems and then developing testable hypotheses about solving them. They are scientific only about the convenient things, such as laboratory and product experiments.

The customer (and the satisfaction of his or her deepest needs) is not considered to be "the problem"—not because there is any certain belief that no such problem exists but because an organizational lifetime has conditioned management to look in the opposite direction. Marketing is a stepchild.

I do not mean that selling is ignored. Far from it. But selling, again, is not marketing. As already pointed out, selling concerns itself with the tricks and techniques of getting people to exchange their cash for your product. It is not concerned with the values that the exchange is all about. And it does not, as marketing invariably does, view the entire business process as consisting of a tightly integrated effort to discover, create, arouse, and satisfy customer needs. The customer is somebody "out there" who, with proper cunning, can be separated from his or her loose change.

Actually, not even selling gets much attention in some technologically minded firms. Because there is a virtually guaranteed market for the abundant flow of their new products, they do not actually know what a real market is. It is as if they lived in a planned economy, moving their products routinely from factory to retail outlet. Their successful concentration on products tends to convince them of the soundness of what they have been doing, and they fail to see the gathering clouds over the market.

Less than 75 years ago, American railroads enjoyed a fierce loyalty among astute Wall Streeters. European monarchs invested in them heavily. Eternal wealth was thought to be the benediction for anybody who could scrape together a few thousand dollars to put into rail stocks. No other form of transportation could compete with the railroads in speed, flexibility, durability, economy, and growth potentials.

As Jacques Barzun put it, "By the turn of the century it was an institution, an image of man, a tradition, a code of honor, a source of poetry, a nursery of boyhood desires, a sublimest of toys, and the most solemn machine—next to the funeral hearse—that marks the epochs in man's life."[6]

Even after the advent of automobiles, trucks, and airplanes, the railroad tycoons remained imperturbably self-confident. If you had told them 60 years ago that in 30 years they would be flat on their backs, broke, and pleading for government subsidies, they would have thought you totally demented. Such a future was simply not considered possible. It was not even a discussable subject, or an askable question, or a matter that any sane person would consider worth speculating about. Yet a lot of "insane" notions now have matter-of-fact acceptance—for example, the idea of 100-ton tubes of metal moving smoothly through the air 20,000 feet above the earth, loaded with 100 sane and solid citizens casually drinking martinis—and they have dealt cruel blows to the railroads.

What specifically must other companies do to avoid this fate? What does customer orientation involve? These questions have in part been answered by the preceding examples and analysis. It would take another article to show in detail what is required for specific industries. In any case, it should be obvious that building an effective customer-oriented company involves far more than good intentions or promotional tricks; it involves profound matters of human organization and leadership. For the present, let me merely suggest what appear to be some general requirements.

The visceral feel of greatness

Obviously, the company has to do what survival demands. It has to adapt to the requirements of the market, and it has to do it sooner rather than later. But mere survival is a so-so aspiration. Anybody can survive in some way or other, even the skid row bum. The trick is to survive gallantly, to feel the surging impulse of commercial mastery: not just to experience the sweet smell of success but to have the visceral feel of entrepreneurial greatness.

No organization can achieve greatness without a vigorous leader who is driven onward by a pulsating *will to succeed*. A leader has to have a vision of grandeur, a vision that can produce eager followers in vast numbers. In business, the followers are the customers.

In order to produce these customers, the entire corporation must be viewed as a customer-creating and customer-satisfying organism. Management must think of itself not as producing products but as providing customer-creating value satisfactions. It must push this idea (and everything it means and requires) into every nook and cranny of the organization. It has to do this continuously and with the kind of flair that excites and stimulates the people in it.

Otherwise, the company will be merely a series of pigeonholed parts, with no consolidating sense of purpose or direction.

In short, the organization must learn to think of itself not as producing goods or services but as *buying customers,* as doing the things that will make people *want* to do business with it. And the chief executive has the inescapable responsibility for creating this environment, this viewpoint, this attitude, this aspiration. The chief executive must set the company's style, its direction, and its goals. This means knowing precisely where he or she wants to go and making sure the whole organization is enthusiastically aware of where that is. This is a first requisite of leadership, for *unless a leader knows where he is going, any road will take him there.*

If any road is okay, the chief executive might as well pack his attaché case and go fishing. If an organization does not know or care where it is going, it does not need to advertise that fact with a ceremonial figurehead. Everybody will notice it soon enough.

Originally published in 1960. Reprint R0407L

Notes

1. Jacques Barzun, "Trains and the Mind of Man," *Holiday*, February 1960.

2. For more details, see M.M. Zimmerman, *The Super Market: A Revolution in Distribution* (McGraw-Hill, 1955).

3. Ibid., pp. 45–47.

4. John Kenneth Galbraith, *The Affluent Society* (Houghton Mifflin, 1958).

5. Henry Ford, *My Life and Work* (Doubleday, 1923).

6. Barzun, "Trains and the Mind of Man."

Marketing Malpractice

The Cause and the Cure.

by Clayton M. Christensen, Scott Cook, and Taddy Hall

THIRTY THOUSAND NEW CONSUMER products are launched each year. But over 90% of them fail—and that's after marketing professionals have spent massive amounts of money trying to understand what their customers want. What's wrong with this picture? Is it that market researchers aren't smart enough? That advertising agencies aren't creative enough? That consumers have become too difficult to understand? We don't think so. We believe, instead, that some of the fundamental paradigms of marketing—the methods that most of us learned to segment markets, build brands, and understand customers—are broken. We're not alone in that judgment. Even Procter & Gamble CEO A.G. Lafley, arguably the best-positioned person in the world to make this call, says, "We need to reinvent the way we market to consumers. We need a new model."

To build brands that mean something to customers, you need to attach them to products that mean something to customers. And to do that, you need to segment markets in ways that reflect how customers actually live their lives. In this article, we will propose a way to reconfigure the principles of market segmentation. We'll describe how to create products that customers will consistently value.

And finally, we will describe how new, valuable brands can be built to truly deliver sustained, profitable growth.

Broken Paradigms of Market Segmentation

The great Harvard marketing professor Theodore Levitt used to tell his students, "People don't want to buy a quarter-inch drill. They want a quarter-inch hole!" Every marketer we know agrees with Levitt's insight. Yet these same people segment their markets by type of drill and by price point; they measure market share of drills, not holes; and they benchmark the features and functions of their drill, not their hole, against those of rivals. They then set to work offering more features and functions in the belief that these will translate into better pricing and market share. When marketers do this, they often solve the wrong problems, improving their products in ways that are irrelevant to their customers' needs.

Segmenting markets by type of customer is no better. Having sliced business clients into small, medium, and large enterprises—or having shoehorned consumers into age, gender, or lifestyle brackets—marketers busy themselves with trying to understand the needs of representative customers in those segments and then create products that address those needs. The problem is that customers don't conform their desires to match those of the average consumer in their demographic segment. When marketers design a product to address the needs of a typical customer in a demographically defined segment, therefore, they cannot know whether any specific individual will buy the product—they can only express a likelihood of purchase in probabilistic terms.

Thus the prevailing methods of segmentation that budding managers learn in business schools and then practice in the marketing departments of good companies are actually a key reason that new product innovation has become a gamble in which the odds of winning are horrifyingly low.

There is a better way to think about market segmentation and new product innovation. The structure of a market, seen from the customers' point of view, is very simple: They just need to get things

Idea in Brief

Thirty thousand new consumer products hit store shelves each year. Ninety percent of them fail. Why? We're using misguided market-segmentation practices. For instance, we slice markets based on customer type and define the needs of representative customers in those segments. But actual human beings don't behave like statistically average customers. The consequences? We develop new and enhanced products that don't meet real people's needs.

Here's a better way: Instead of trying to understand the "typical" customer, find out what jobs people want to get done. Then develop **purpose brands:** products or services consumers can "hire" to perform those jobs. FedEx, for example, designed its service to perform the "I-need-to-send-this-from-here-to-there-with-perfect-certainty-as-fast-as-possible" job. FedEx was so much more convenient, reliable, and reasonably priced than the alternatives—the U.S. Postal Service or couriers paid to sit on airlines—that businesspeople around the globe started using "FedEx" as a verb.

A clear purpose brand acts as a two-sided compass: One side guides customers to the right products. The other guides your designers, marketers, and advertisers as they develop and market new and improved products. The payoff? Products your customers consistently value—and brands that deliver sustained profitable growth to your company.

done, as Ted Levitt said. When people find themselves needing to get a job done, they essentially hire products to do that job for them. The marketer's task is therefore to understand what jobs periodically arise in customers' lives for which they might hire products the company could make. If a marketer can understand the job, design a product and associated experiences in purchase and use to do that job, and deliver it in a way that reinforces its intended use, then when customers find themselves needing to get that job done, they will hire that product.

Since most new-product developers don't think in those terms, they've become much too good at creating products that don't help customers do the jobs they need to get done. Here's an all-too-typical example. In the mid-1990s, Scott Cook presided over the launch of a software product called the Quicken Financial Planner, which helped

Idea in Practice

To establish, sustain, and extend your purpose brands.

Observe Consumers in Action

By observing and interviewing people as they're using products, identify jobs they want to get done. Then think of new or enhanced offerings that could do the job better.

> ***Example:*** A fast-food restaurant wanted to improve milk shake sales. A researcher watched customers buying shakes, noting that 40% of shakes were purchased by hurried customers early in the morning and carried out to customers' cars. Interviews revealed that most customers bought shakes to do a similar job: make their commute more interesting, stave off hunger until lunchtime, and give them something they could consume cleanly with one hand. Understanding this job inspired several product-improvement ideas. One example: Move the shake-dispensing machine to the front of the counter and sell customers a prepaid swipe card, so they could dispense shakes themselves and avoid the slow drive-through lane.

Link Products to Jobs Through Advertising

Use advertising to clarify the nature of the job your product performs and to give the product a name that reinforces awareness of its purpose. Savvy ads can even help consumers identify needs they weren't consciously aware of before.

> ***Example:*** Unilever's Asian operations designed a microwavable soup tailored to the job of

customers create a retirement plan. It flopped. Though it captured over 90% of retail sales in its product category, annual revenue never surpassed $2 million, and it was eventually pulled from the market.

What happened? Was the $49 price too high? Did the product need to be easier to use? Maybe. A more likely explanation, however, is that while the demographics suggested that lots of families needed a financial plan, constructing one actually wasn't a job that most people were looking to do. The fact that they should have a financial plan, or even that they said they should have a plan, didn't matter. In hindsight, the fact that the design team had had trouble finding enough "planners" to fill a focus group should have tipped

helping office workers boost their energy and productivity in the late afternoon. Called Soupy Snax, the product generated mediocre results. When Unilever renamed it Soupy Snax—4:00 and created ads showing lethargic workers perking up after using the product, ad viewers remarked, "That's what happens to me at 4:00!" Soupy Snax sales soared.

Extend Your Purpose Brand

If you extend your purpose brand onto products that do different jobs—for example, a toothpaste that freshens breath *and* whitens teeth *and* reduces plaque—customers may become confused and lose trust in your brand.

To extend your brand without destroying it:

- **Develop different products that address a common job.** Sony did this with its various generations of Walkman that helped consumers "escape the chaos in my world."
- **Identify new, related jobs and create purpose brands for them.** Marriott International extended its hotel brand, originally built around full-service facilities designed for large meetings, to other types of hotels. Each new purpose brand had a name indicating the job it was designed to do. For instance, Courtyard Marriott was "hired" by individual business travelers seeking a clean, quiet place to get work done in the evening. Residence Inn was hired by longer-term travelers.

Cook off. Making it easier and cheaper for customers to do things that they are not trying to do rarely leads to success.

Designing Products That Do the Job

With few exceptions, every job people need or want to do has a social, a functional, and an emotional dimension. If marketers understand each of these dimensions, then they can design a product that's precisely targeted to the job. In other words, the job, not the customer, is the fundamental unit of analysis for a marketer who hopes to develop products that customers will buy.

To see why, consider one fast-food restaurant's effort to improve sales of its milk shakes. (In this example, both the company and the product have been disguised.) Its marketers first defined the market segment by product—milk shakes—and then segmented it further by profiling the demographic and personality characteristics of those customers who frequently bought milk shakes. Next, they invited people who fit this profile to evaluate whether making the shakes thicker, more chocolaty, cheaper, or chunkier would satisfy them better. The panelists gave clear feedback, but the consequent improvements to the product had no impact on sales.

A new researcher then spent a long day in a restaurant seeking to understand the jobs that customers were trying to get done when they hired a milk shake. He chronicled when each milk shake was bought, what other products the customers purchased, whether these consumers were alone or with a group, whether they consumed the shake on the premises or drove off with it, and so on. He was surprised to find that 40% of all milk shakes were purchased in the early morning. Most often, these early-morning customers were alone; they did not buy anything else; and they consumed their shakes in their cars.

The researcher then returned to interview the morning customers as they left the restaurant, shake in hand, in an effort to understand what caused them to hire a milk shake. Most bought it to do a similar job: They faced a long, boring commute and needed something to make the drive more interesting. They weren't yet hungry but knew that they would be by 10 AM; they wanted to consume something now that would stave off hunger until noon. And they faced constraints: They were in a hurry, they were wearing work clothes, and they had (at most) one free hand.

The researcher inquired further: "Tell me about a time when you were in the same situation but you didn't buy a milk shake. What did you buy instead?" Sometimes, he learned, they bought a bagel. But bagels were too dry. Bagels with cream cheese or jam resulted in sticky fingers and gooey steering wheels. Sometimes these commuters bought a banana, but it didn't last long enough to solve the boring-commute problem. Doughnuts didn't carry people past the

10 AM hunger attack. The milk shake, it turned out, did the job better than any of these competitors. It took people 20 minutes to suck the viscous milk shake through the thin straw, addressing the boring-commute problem. They could consume it cleanly with one hand. By 10:00, they felt less hungry than when they tried the alternatives. It didn't matter much that it wasn't a healthy food, because becoming healthy wasn't essential to the job they were hiring the milk shake to do.

The researcher observed that at other times of the day parents often bought milk shakes, in addition to complete meals, for their children. What job were the parents trying to do? They were exhausted from repeatedly having to say "no" to their kids. They hired milk shakes as an innocuous way to placate their children and feel like loving parents. The researcher observed that the milk shakes didn't do this job very well, though. He saw parents waiting impatiently after they had finished their own meals while their children struggled to suck the thick shakes up through the thin straws.

Customers were hiring milk shakes for two very different jobs. But when marketers had originally asked individual customers who hired a milk shake for either or both jobs which of its attributes they should improve—and when these responses were averaged with those of other customers in the targeted demographic segment—it led to a one-size-fits-none product.

Once they understood the jobs the customers were trying to do, however, it became very clear which improvements to the milk shake would get those jobs done even better and which were irrelevant. How could they tackle the boring-commute job? Make the milk shake even thicker, so it would last longer. And swirl in tiny chunks of fruit, adding a dimension of unpredictability and anticipation to the monotonous morning routine. Just as important, the restaurant chain could deliver the product more effectively by moving the dispensing machine in front of the counter and selling customers a prepaid swipe card so they could dash in, "gas up," and go without getting stuck in the drive-through lane. Addressing the midday and evening job to be done would entail a very different product, of course.

By understanding the job and improving the product's social, functional, and emotional dimensions so that it did the job better, the company's milk shakes would gain share against the real competition—not just competing chains' milk shakes but bananas, boredom, and bagels. This would grow the category, which brings us to an important point: Job-defined markets are generally much larger than product category-defined markets. Marketers who are stuck in the mental trap that equates market size with product categories don't understand whom they are competing against from the customer's point of view.

Notice that knowing how to improve the product did not come from understanding the "typical" customer. It came from understanding the job. Need more evidence?

Pierre Omidyar did not design eBay for the "auction psychographic." He founded it to help people sell personal items. Google was designed for the job of finding information, not for a "search demographic." The unit of analysis in the work that led to Procter & Gamble's stunningly successful Swiffer was the job of cleaning floors, not a demographic or psychographic study of people who mop.

Why do so many marketers try to understand the consumer rather than the job? One reason may be purely historical: In some of the markets in which the tools of modern market research were formulated and tested, such as feminine hygiene or baby care, the job was so closely aligned with the customer demographic that if you understood the customer, you would also understand the job. This coincidence is rare, however. All too frequently, marketers' focus on the customer causes them to target phantom needs.

How a Job Focus Can Grow Product Categories

New growth markets are created when innovating companies design a product and position its brand on a job for which no optimal product yet exists. In fact, companies that historically have segmented and measured the size of their markets by product category generally find that when they instead segment by job, their market is much larger (and their current share of the job is much smaller) than they had thought. This is great news for smart companies hungry for growth.

Understanding and targeting jobs was the key to Sony founder Akio Morita's approach to disruptive innovation. Morita never did conventional market research. Instead, he and his associates spent much of their time watching what people were trying to get done in their lives, then asking themselves whether Sony's electronics miniaturization technology could help them do these things better, easier, and cheaper. Morita would have badly misjudged the size of his market had he simply analyzed trends in the number of tape players being sold before he launched his Walkman. This should trigger an action item on every marketer's to-do list: Turn off the computer, get out of the office, and observe.

Consider how Church & Dwight used this strategy to grow its baking soda business. The company has produced Arm & Hammer baking soda since the 1860s; its iconic yellow box and Vulcan's hammer-hefting arm have become enduring visual cues for "the standard of purity." In the late 1960s, market research director Barry Goldblatt tells us, management began observational research to understand the diverse circumstances in which consumers found themselves with a job to do where Arm & Hammer could be hired to help. They found a few consumers adding the product to laundry detergent, a few others mixing it into toothpaste, some sprinkling it on the carpet, and still others placing open boxes in the refrigerator. There was a plethora of jobs out there needing to get done, but most customers did not know that they could hire Arm & Hammer baking soda for these cleaning and freshening jobs. The single product just wasn't giving customers the guidance they needed, given the many jobs it could be hired to do.

Today, a family of job-focused Arm & Hammer products has greatly grown the baking soda product category. These jobs include:

- Help my mouth feel fresh and clean (Arm & Hammer Complete Care toothpaste)
- Deodorize my refrigerator (Arm & Hammer Fridge-n-Freezer baking soda)

- Help my underarms stay clean and fresh (Arm & Hammer Ultra Max deodorant)
- Clean and freshen my carpets (Arm & Hammer Vacuum Free carpet deodorizer)
- Deodorize kitty litter (Arm & Hammer Super Scoop cat litter)
- Make my clothes smell fresh (Arm & Hammer Laundry Detergent).

The yellow-box baking soda business is now less than 10% of Arm & Hammer's consumer revenue. The company's share price has appreciated at nearly four times the average rate of its nearest rivals, P&G, Unilever, and Colgate-Palmolive. Although the overall Arm & Hammer brand is valuable in each instance, the key to this extraordinary growth is a set of job-focused products and a communication strategy that help people realize that when they find themselves needing to get one of these jobs done, here is a product that they can trust to do it well.

Building Brands That Customers Will Hire

Sometimes, the discovery that one needs to get a job done is conscious, rational, and explicit. At other times, the job is so much a part of a routine that customers aren't really consciously aware of it. Either way, if consumers are lucky, when they discover the job they need to do, a branded product will exist that is perfectly and unambiguously suited to do it. We call the brand of a product that is tightly associated with the job for which it is meant to be hired a *purpose brand*.

The history of Federal Express illustrates how successful purpose brands are built. A job had existed practically forever: the I-need-to-send-this-from-here-to-there-with-perfect-certainty-as-fast-as-possible job. Some U.S. customers hired the U.S. Postal Service's airmail to do this job; a few desperate souls paid couriers to sit on airplanes. Others even went so far as to plan ahead so they could ship via UPS trucks. But each of these alternatives was kludgy, expensive, uncertain, or inconvenient. Because nobody had yet designed a service to do this job well, the brands of the unsatisfactory alternative services became tarnished when they were hired for this purpose. But after Federal Express designed its service to do that exact job, and did it wonderfully again and again, the FedEx brand began popping into people's minds whenever they needed to get that job done. FedEx became a purpose brand—in fact, it became a verb in the international language of business that is inextricably linked with that specific job. It is a very valuable brand as a result.

Most of today's great brands—Crest, Starbucks, Kleenex, eBay, and Kodak, to name a few—started out as just this kind of purpose brand. The product did the job, and customers talked about it. This is how brand equity is built.

Brand equity can be destroyed when marketers don't tie the brand to a purpose. When they seek to build a general brand that does not signal to customers when they should and should not buy the product, marketers run the risk that people might hire their product to do a job it was not designed to do. This causes customers to distrust the brand—as was the case for years with the post office.

A clear purpose brand is like a two-sided compass. One side guides customers to the right products. The other side guides the company's product designers, marketers, and advertisers as they develop and market improved and new versions of their products. A good purpose brand clarifies which features and functions are relevant to the job and which potential improvements will prove irrelevant. The price premium that the brand commands is the wage that customers are willing to pay the brand for providing this guidance on both sides of the compass.

The need to feel a certain way—to feel macho, sassy, pampered, or prestigious—is a job that arises in many of our lives on occasion. When we find ourselves needing to do one of these jobs, we can hire a branded product whose purpose is to provide such feelings. Gucci, Absolut, Montblanc, and Virgin, for example, are purpose brands. They link customers who have one of these jobs to do with experiences in purchase and use that do those jobs well. These might be called aspirational jobs. In some aspirational situations, it is the brand itself, more than the functional dimensions of the product, that gets the job done.

Purpose Brands and Disruptive Innovations

WE HAVE WRITTEN ELSEWHERE about how to harness the potential of disruptive innovations to create growth. Because disruptive innovations are products or services whose performance is not as good as mainstream products, executives of leading companies often hesitate to introduce them for fear of destroying the value of their brands. This fear is generally unfounded, provided that companies attach a unique purpose brand to their disruptive innovations.

Purpose branding has been the key, for example, to Kodak's success with two disruptions. The first was its single-use camera, a classic disruptive technology. Because of its inexpensive plastic lenses, the new camera couldn't take the quality of photographs that a good 35-millimeter camera could produce on Kodak film. The proposition to launch a single-use camera encountered vigorous opposition within Kodak's film division. The corporation finally gave responsibility for the opportunity to a completely different organizational unit, which launched single-use cameras with a purpose brand—the Kodak FunSaver. This was a product customers could hire when they needed to save memories of a fun time but had forgotten to bring a camera or didn't want to risk harming their expensive one. Creating a purpose brand for a disruptive job differentiated the product, clarified its intended use, delighted the

The Role of Advertising

Much advertising is wasted in the mistaken belief that it alone can build brands. Advertising cannot build brands, but it can tell people about an existing branded product's ability to do a job well. That's what the managers at Unilever's Asian operations found out when they identified an important job that arose in the lives of many office workers at around 4:00 in the afternoon. Drained of physical and emotional energy, people still had to get a lot done before their workday ended. They needed something to boost their productivity, and they were hiring a range of caffeinated drinks, candy bars, stretch breaks, and conversation to do this job, with mixed results.

Unilever designed a microwavable soup whose properties were tailored to that job—quick to fix, nutritious but not too filling, it can be consumed at your desk but gives you a bit of a break when you go

customers, and thereby strengthened the endorsing power of the Kodak brand. Quality, after all, can only be measured relative to the job that needs to be done and the alternatives that can be hired to do it. (Sadly, a few years ago, Kodak pushed aside the FunSaver purpose brand in favor of the word "Max," which now appears on its single-use cameras, perhaps to focus on selling film rather than the job the film is for.)

Kodak scored another purpose-branding victory with its disruptive EasyShare digital camera. The company initially had struggled for differentiation and market share in the head-on megapixel and megazoom race against Japanese digital camera makers (all of whom aggressively advertised their corporate brands but had no purpose brands). Kodak then adopted a disruptive strategy that was focused on a job—sharing fun. It made an inexpensive digital camera that customers could slip into a cradle, click "attach" in their computer's e-mail program, and share photos effortlessly with friends and relatives. Sharing fun, not preserving the highest resolution images for posterity, is the job—and Kodak's EasyShare purpose brand guides customers to a product tailored to do that job. Kodak is now the market share leader in digital cameras in the United States.

to heat it up. It was launched into the workplace under the descriptive brand Soupy Snax. The results were mediocre. On a hunch, the brand's managers then relaunched the product with advertisements showing lethargic workers perking up after using the product and renamed the brand Soupy Snax—4:00. The reaction of people who saw the advertisements was, "That's exactly what happens to me at 4:00!" They needed something to help them consciously discover both the job and the product they could hire to do it. The tagline and ads transformed a brand that had been a simple description of a product into a purpose brand that clarified the nature of the job and the product that was designed to do it, and the product has become very successful.

Note the role that advertising played in this process. Advertising clarified the nature of the job and helped more people realize that they had the job to do. It informed people that there was a product designed to do that job and gave the product a name people could remember. Advertising is not a substitute for designing products that do specific jobs and ensuring that improvements in their features and functions are relevant to that job. The fact is that most great brands were built before their owners started advertising. Think of Disney, Harley-Davidson, eBay, and Google. Each brand developed a sterling reputation before much was spent on advertising.

Advertising that attempts to short-circuit this process and build, as if from scratch, a brand that people will trust is a fool's errand. Ford, Nissan, Macy's, and many other companies invest hundreds of millions to keep the corporate name or their products' names in the general consciousness of the buying public. Most of these companies' products aren't designed to do specific jobs and therefore aren't usually differentiated from the competition. These firms have few purpose brands in their portfolios and no apparent strategies to create them. Their managers are unintentionally transferring billions in profits to branding agencies in the vain hope that they can buy their way to glory. What is worse, many companies have decided that building new brands is so expensive they will no longer do so. Brand building by advertising is indeed prohibitively expensive. But that's because it's the wrong way to build a brand.

Marketing mavens are fond of saying that brands are hollow words into which meaning gets stuffed. Beware. Executives who think that brand advertising is an effective mechanism for stuffing meaning into some word they have chosen to be their brand generally succeed in stuffing it full of vagueness. The ad agencies and media companies win big in this game, but the companies whose brands are getting stuffed generally find themselves trapped in an expensive, endless arms race with competitors whose brands are comparably vague.

The exceptions to this brand-building rule are the purpose brands for aspirational jobs, where the brand must be built through images in advertising. The method for brand building that is appropriate for these jobs, however, has been wantonly and wastefully misapplied to the rest of the world of branding.

Extending—or Destroying—Brand Equity

Once a strong purpose brand has been created, people within the company inevitably want to leverage it by applying it to other products. Executives should consider these proposals carefully. There are rules about the types of extensions that will reinforce the brand—and the types that will erode it.

If a company chooses to extend a brand onto other products that can be hired to do the same job, it can do so without concern that the extension will compromise what the brand does. For example, Sony's portable CD player, although a different product than its original Walkman-branded radio and cassette players, was positioned on the same job (the help-me-escape-the-chaos-in-my-world job). So the new product caused the Walkman brand to pop even more instinctively into customers' minds when they needed to get that job done. Had Sony not been asleep at the switch, a Walkman-branded MP3 player would have further enhanced this purpose brand. It might even have kept Apple's iPod purpose brand from preempting that job.

The fact that purpose brands are job specific means that when a purpose brand is extended onto products that target different jobs, it will lose its clear meaning as a purpose brand and develop a different character instead—an *endorser brand*. An endorser brand can impart a general sense of quality, and it thereby creates some value in a marketing equation. But general endorser brands lose their ability to guide people who have a particular job to do to products that were designed to do it. Without appropriate guidance, customers will begin using endorser-branded products to do jobs they weren't designed to do. The resulting bad experience will cause customers to distrust the brand. Hence, the value of an endorser brand will erode unless the company adds a second word to its brand architecture—a purpose brand alongside the endorser brand. Different jobs demand different purpose brands.

Marriott International's executives followed this principle when they sought to leverage the Marriott brand to address different jobs for which a hotel might be hired. Marriott had built its hotel brand around full-service facilities that were good to hire for large meetings. When it decided to extend its brand to other types of hotels, it adopted a two-word brand architecture that appended to the Marriott endorsement a purpose brand for each of the different jobs its new hotel chains were intended to do. Hence, individual business travelers who need to hire a clean, quiet place to get work done in the evening can hire Courtyard by Marriott—the hotel designed by business travelers for business travelers. Longer-term travelers can hire Residence Inn by Marriott, and so on. Even though these hotels were not constructed and decorated to the same premium standard as full-service Marriott hotels, the new chains actually reinforce the endorser qualities of the Marriott brand because they do the jobs well that they are hired to do.

Milwaukee Electric Tool has built purpose brands with two—and only two—of the products in its line of power tools. The Milwaukee Sawzall is a reciprocating saw that tradesmen hire when they need to cut through a wall quickly and aren't sure what's under the surface. Plumbers hire Milwaukee's Hole Hawg, a right-angle drill, when they need to drill a hole in a tight space. Competitors like Black & Decker, Bosch, and Makita offer reciprocating saws and right-angle drills with comparable performance and price, but none of them has a purpose brand that pops into a tradesman's mind when he has one of these jobs to do. Milwaukee has owned more than 80% of these two job markets for decades.

Interestingly, Milwaukee offers under its endorser brand a full range of power tools, including circular saws, pistol-grip drills, sanders, and jigsaws. While the durability and relative price of these products are comparable to those of the Sawzall and Hole Hawg, Milwaukee has not built purpose brands for any of these other products. The market share of each is in the low single digits—a testament to the clarifying value of purpose brands versus the general connotation of quality that endorser brands confer. Indeed, a clear purpose brand is usually a more formidable competitive barrier than superior product performance—because competitors can copy performance much more easily than they can copy purpose brands.

The tribulations and successes of P&G's Crest brand is a story of products that ace the customer job, lose their focus, and then bounce back to become strong purpose brands again. Introduced in the mid-1950s, Crest was a classic disruptive technology. Its Fluoristan-reinforced toothpaste made cavity-preventing fluoride treatments cheap and easy to apply at home, replacing an expensive and inconvenient trip to the dentist. Although P&G could have positioned the new product under its existing toothpaste brand, Gleem, its managers chose instead to build a new purpose brand, Crest, which was uniquely positioned on a job. Mothers who wanted to prevent cavities in their children's teeth knew when they saw or heard the word "Crest" that this product was designed to do that job. Because it did the job so well, mothers grew to trust the product and in fact became suspicious of the ability of products without the Crest brand to do that job. This unambiguous association made it a very valuable brand, and Crest passed all its U.S. rivals to become the clear market leader in toothpaste for a generation.

But one cannot sustain victory by standing still. Competitors eventually copied Crest's cavity prevention abilities, turning cavity prevention into a commodity. Crest lost share as competitors innovated in other areas, including flavor, mouthfeel, and commonsense ingredients like baking soda. P&G began copying and advertising these attributes. But unlike Marriott, P&G did not append purpose brands to the general endorsement of Crest, and the brand began losing its distinctiveness.

At the end of the 1990s, new Crest executives brought two disruptions to market, each with its own clear purpose brand. They acquired a start-up named Dr. John's and rebranded its flagship electric toothbrush as the Crest SpinBrush, which they sold for $5—far below the price of competitors' models of the time. They also launched Crest Whitestrips, which allowed people to whiten their teeth at home for a mere $25, far less than dentists charged. With these purpose-branded innovations, Crest generated substantial new growth and regained share leadership in the entire tooth care category.

Extending brands without destroying them

There are only two ways: Marketers can develop different products that address a common job, as Sony did with its various generations of Walkman. Or, like Marriott and Milwaukee, they can identify new, related jobs and create new purpose brands that benefit from the "endorser" quality of the original brand.

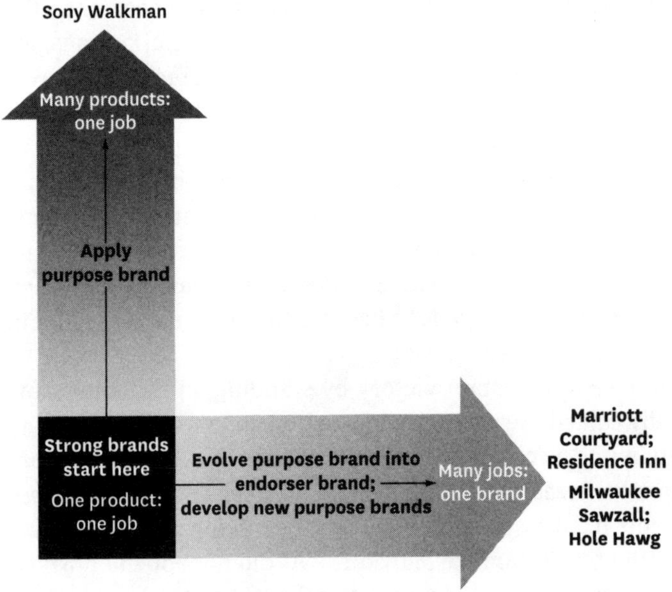

The exhibit "Extending brands without destroying them" diagrams the two ways marketers can extend a purpose brand without eroding its value. The first option is to move up the vertical axis by developing different products that address a common job. This is what Sony did with its Walkman portable CD player. When Crest was still a clear purpose brand, P&G could have gone this route by, say, introducing a Crest-brand fluoride mouth rinse. The brand would have retained its clarity of purpose. But P&G did not, allowing Johnson & Johnson to insert yet another brand, ACT (its own fluoride mouth rinse), into the cavity-prevention job space. Because

P&G pursued the second option, extending its brand along the horizontal axis to other jobs (whitening, breath freshening, and so on), the purpose brand morphed into an endorser brand.

Why Strong Purpose Brands Are So Rare

Given the power that purpose brands have in creating opportunities for differentiation, premium pricing, and growth, isn't it odd that so few companies have a deliberate strategy for creating them?

Consider the automobile industry. There are a significant number of different jobs that people who purchase cars need to get done, but only a few companies have staked out any of these job markets with purpose brands. Range Rover (until recently, at least) was a clear and valuable purpose brand (the take-me-anywhere-with-total-dependability job). The Volvo brand is positioned on the safety job. Porsche, BMW, Mercedes, Bentley, and Rolls-Royce are associated with various aspirational jobs. The Toyota endorser brand has earned the connotation of reliability. But for so much of the rest? It's hard to know what they mean.

To illustrate: Clayton Christensen recently needed to deliver on a long-promised commitment to buy a car as a college graduation gift for his daughter Annie. There were functional and emotional dimensions to the job. The car needed to be stylish and fun to drive, to be sure. But even more important, as his beloved daughter was venturing off into the cold, cruel world, the big job Clay needed to get done was to know that she was safe and for his sweet Annie to be reminded frequently, as she owned, drove, and serviced the car, that her dad loves and cares for her. A hands-free telephone in the car would be a must, not an option. A version of GM's On-Star service, which called not just the police but Clay in the event of an accident, would be important. A system that reminded the occasionally absentminded Annie when she needed to have the car serviced would take a load off her dad's mind. If that service were delivered as a prepaid gift from her father, it would take another load off Clay's mind because he, too, is occasionally absentminded. Should Clay have hired a Taurus, Escape, Cavalier, Neon, Prizm, Corolla, Camry, Avalon, Sentra, Civic,

Accord, Senator, Sonata, or something else? The billions of dollars that automakers spent advertising these brands, seeking somehow to create subtle differentiations in image, helped Clay not at all. Finding the best package to hire was very time-consuming and inconvenient, and the resulting product did the job about as unsatisfactorily as the milk shake had done, a few years earlier.

Focusing a product and its brand on a job creates differentiation. The rub, however, is that when a company communicates the job a branded product was designed to do perfectly, it is also communicating what jobs the product should not be hired to do. Focus is scary—at least the carmakers seem to think so. They deliberately create words as brands that have no meaning in any language, with no tie to any job, in the myopic hope that each individual model will be hired by every customer for every job. The results of this strategy speak for themselves. In the face of compelling evidence that purpose-branded products that do specific jobs well command premium pricing and compete in markets that are much larger than those defined by product categories, the automakers' products are substantially undifferentiated, the average subbrand commands less than a 1% market share, and most automakers are losing money. Somebody gave these folks the wrong recipe for prosperity.

Executives everywhere are charged with generating profitable growth. Rightly, they believe that brands are the vehicles for meeting their growth and profit targets. But success in brand building remains rare. Why? Not for lack of effort or resources. Nor for lack of opportunity in the marketplace. The root problem is that the theories in practice for market segmentation and brand building are riddled with flawed assumptions. Lafley is right. The model is broken. We've tried to illustrate a way out of the death spiral of serial product failure, missed opportunity, and squandered wealth. Marketers who choose to break with the broken past will be rewarded not only with successful brands but with profitably growing businesses as well.

Originally published in December 2005. Reprint R0512D

The Brand Report Card

by Kevin Lane Keller

BUILDING AND PROPERLY MANAGING BRAND equity has become a priority for companies of all sizes, in all types of industries, in all types of markets. After all, from strong brand equity flow customer loyalty and profits. The rewards of having a strong brand are clear.

The problem is, few managers are able to step back and assess their brand's particular strengths and weaknesses objectively. Most have a good sense of one or two areas in which their brand may excel or may need help. But if pressed, many (understandably) would find it difficult even to identify all of the factors they should be considering. When you're immersed in the day-to-day management of a brand, it's not easy to keep in perspective all the parts that affect the whole.

In this article, I'll identify the ten characteristics that the world's strongest brands share and construct a brand report card—a systematic way for managers to think about how to grade their brand's performance for each of those characteristics. The report card can help you identify areas that need improvement, recognize areas in which your brand is strong, and learn more about how your particular brand is configured. Constructing similar report cards for your competitors can give you a clearer picture of their strengths and weaknesses. One caveat: Identifying weak spots for your brand doesn't necessarily mean identifying areas that need more attention. Decisions that might seem straightforward—"We haven't paid much attention to innovation: let's direct more resources toward R&D"—can sometimes prove to be serious mistakes if they undermine another characteristic that customers value more.

The Top Ten Traits

The world's strongest brands share these ten attributes.

The brand excels at delivering the benefits customers truly desire
Why do customers really buy a product? Not because the product is a collection of attributes but because those attributes, together with the brand's image, the service, and many other tangible and intangible factors, create an attractive whole. In some cases, the whole isn't even something that customers know or can say they want.

Consider Starbucks. It's not just a cup of coffee. In 1983, Starbucks was a small Seattle-area coffee retailer. Then while on vacation in Italy, Howard Schultz, now Starbucks chairman, was inspired by the romance and the sense of community he felt in Italian coffee bars and coffee houses. The culture grabbed him, and he saw an opportunity.

"It seemed so obvious," Schultz says in the 1997 book he wrote with Dori Jones Yang, *Pour Your Heart Into It*. "Starbucks sold great coffee beans, but we didn't serve coffee by the cup. We treated coffee as produce, something to be bagged and sent home with the groceries. We stayed one big step away from the heart and soul of what coffee has meant throughout centuries."

And so Starbucks began to focus its efforts on building a coffee bar culture, opening coffee houses like those in Italy. Just as important, the company maintained control over the coffee from start to finish—from the selection and procurement of the beans to their roasting and blending to their ultimate consumption. The extreme vertical integration has paid off. Starbucks locations thus far have successfully delivered superior benefits to customers by appealing to all five senses—through the enticing aroma of the beans, the rich taste of the coffee, the product displays and attractive artwork adorning the walls, the contemporary music playing in the background, and even

Idea in Brief

It sounds simple: boost your brand equity, and watch profits soar. But many companies stumble in trying to manage their brands' performance.

Consider Levi-Strauss. In the mid-1990s, it launched a brand-equity measurement system that suggested the appeal of its flagship 501 jeans was slipping. But its response to that data was flawed: the company took too long, and spent too little, to mount a marketing campaign that would restore its brand equity. Worse, Levi-Strauss's advertising messages to its target youth market missed their mark. Its market share shriveled.

To strengthen your brand, Keller suggests using a **brand report card**—a tool showing how your brand stacks up on the 10 traits shared by the world's strongest brands. For example, how well does your brand deliver benefits consumers truly desire? How strongly have you positioned it against rivals? How consistent are your marketing messages about your brand?

Use the brand report card, and you identify the actions needed to maximize your brand equity. Your reward? Customers' enduring devotion—and the profits that come with it.

the cozy, clean feel of the tables and chairs. The company's startling success is evident: The average Starbucks customer visits a store 18 times a month and spends $3.50 a visit. The company's sales and profits have each grown more than 50% annually through much of the 1990s.

The brand stays relevant

In strong brands, brand equity is tied both to the actual quality of the product or service and to various intangible factors. Those intangibles include "user imagery" (the type of person who uses the brand); "usage imagery" (the type of situations in which the brand is used); the type of personality the brand portrays (sincere, exciting, competent, rugged); the feeling that the brand tries to elicit in customers (purposeful, warm); and the type of relationship it seeks to build with its customers (committed, casual, seasonal). Without losing sight of their core strengths, the strongest brands stay on the leading edge in the product arena and tweak their intangibles to fit the times.

Idea in Practice

Grade Your Brand

Keller recommends assessing your brand on the following attributes:

Your brand	Which means . . .	Example . . .
1. Delivers benefits customers desire.	It creates an engaging customer experience.	Starbucks delivers the romance and sense of community defining Italian coffee bars and appeals to all senses—not just taste.
2. Stays relevant.	Elements of the brand, such as the type of person who uses the brand, are modified to fit the times.	In marketing its razor blades, Gillette tweaks images of men at work and play to reflect contemporary trends.
3. Is priced based on consumers' perceptions of the brand's value.	The nature of the product—for example, premium versus household staple—should influence price.	Through "everyday low pricing," Procter & Gamble aligned its prices with consumer perceptions of its products as household staples.
4. Is properly positioned.	It clearly communicates its similarities to and differences from competing brands.	Visa labels its cards "Gold" and "Platinum" to equate its status with American Express cards. But it also showcases its cards' superiority through ads featuring desirable locations that don't accept American Express.
5. Is consistent.	Marketing communications don't send conflicting messages over time.	Michelob's market share shriveled over an 18-year period characterized by inconsistent advertising about when customers should drink their beer.

6. Fits sensibly into your brand portfolio.	Brands work logically together.	Clothing retailer Gap Inc.'s Old Navy brand targets the broad mass market, the Gap brand covers basic style-and-quality terrain, and the Banana Republic brand anchors the high-end market.
7. Has an integrated marketing strategy.	All marketing activities and channels communicate the same messages about the brand, solidifying the brand's identity.	Coca-Cola's logo, promotions, corporate sponsorship, and interactive Web site all reinforce the company's key values, such as "originality" and "classic refreshment."
8. Has meanings that managers understand.	Managers know consumers' different perceptions of the brand.	Gillette protects the brand identity for its traditional manual razors by marketing its electric razors under the separate Braun name.
9. Receives sustained support.	Companies consistently invest in building and maintaining brand awareness.	A consumer products company continues its advertising and marketing efforts even after building a positive image in consumers' minds.
10. Is constantly monitored	Companies use a formal brand-equity-management system.	After Disney's brand audit revealed that consumers resented excessive exposure of the Disney characters, the company decided not to co-brand a mutual fund.

Gillette, for example, pours millions of dollars into R&D to ensure that its razor blades are as technologically advanced as possible, calling attention to major advances through subbrands (Trac II, Atra, Sensor, Mach3) and signaling minor improvements with modifiers (AtraPlus, SensorExcel). At the same time, Gillette has created a consistent, intangible sense of product superiority with its long-running ads, "The best a man can be," which are tweaked through images of men at work and at play that have evolved over time to reflect contemporary trends.

These days, images can be tweaked in many ways other than through traditional advertising, logos, or slogans. "Relevance" has a deeper, broader meaning in today's market. Increasingly, consumers' perceptions of a company as a whole and its role in society affect a brand's strength as well. Witness corporate brands that very visibly support breast cancer research or current educational programs of one sort or another.

The pricing strategy is based on consumers' perceptions of value

The right blend of product quality, design, features, costs, and prices is very difficult to achieve but well worth the effort. Many managers are woefully unaware of how price can and should relate to what customers think of a product, and they therefore charge too little or too much.

For example, in implementing its value-pricing strategy for the Cascade automatic-dishwashing detergent brand, Procter & Gamble made a cost-cutting change in its formulation that had an adverse effect on the product's performance under certain—albeit somewhat atypical—water conditions. Lever Brothers quickly countered, attacking Cascade's core equity of producing "virtually spotless" dishes out of the dishwasher. In response, P&G immediately returned to the brand's old formulation. The lesson to P&G and others is that value pricing should not be adopted at the expense of essential brand-building activities.

By contrast, with its well-known shift to an "everyday low pricing" (EDLP) strategy, Procter & Gamble did successfully align its prices with consumer perceptions of its products' value while maintaining acceptable profit levels. In fact, in the fiscal year after Procter & Gamble switched to EDLP (during which it also worked very hard to streamline operations and lower costs), the company reported its highest profit margins in 21 years.

The brand is properly positioned

Brands that are well positioned occupy particular niches in consumers' minds. They are similar to and different from competing brands in certain reliably identifiable ways. The most successful brands in this regard keep up with competitors by creating *points of parity* in those areas where competitors are trying to find an advantage while at the same time creating *points of difference* to achieve advantages over competitors in some other areas.

The Mercedes-Benz and Sony brands, for example, hold clear advantages in product superiority and match competitors' level of service. Saturn and Nordstrom lead their respective packs in service and hold their own in quality. Calvin Klein and Harley-Davidson excel at providing compelling user and usage imagery while offering adequate or even strong performance.

Visa is a particularly good example of a brand whose managers understand the positioning game. In the 1970s and 1980s, American Express maintained the high-profile brand in the credit card market through a series of highly effective marketing programs. Trumpeting that "membership has its privileges," American Express came to signify status, prestige, and quality.

In response, Visa introduced the Gold and the Platinum cards and launched an aggressive marketing campaign to build up the status of its cards to match the American Express cards. It also developed an extensive merchant delivery system to differentiate itself on the basis of superior convenience and accessibility. Its ad campaigns showcased desirable locations such as famous restaurants, resorts, and events that did not accept American Express while proclaiming, "Visa. It's everywhere you want to be." The aspirational message cleverly reinforced both accessibility and prestige and helped Visa

Rating Your Brand

RATE YOUR BRAND ON a scale of one to ten (one being extremely poor and ten being extremely good) for each characteristic below. Then create a bar chart that reflects the scores. Use the bar chart to generate discussion among all those individuals who participate in the management of your brands. Looking at the results in that manner should help you identify areas that need improvement, recognize areas in which you excel, and learn more about how your particular brand is configured.

It can also be helpful to create a report card and chart for competitors' brands simply by rating those brands based on your own perceptions, both as a competitor and as a consumer. As an outsider, you may know more about how their brands are received in the marketplace than they do.

Keep that in mind as you evaluate your own brand. Try to look at it through the eyes of consumers' rather than through your own knowledge of budgets, teams, and time spent on various initiatives.

- **The brand excels at delivering the benefits customers truly desire.** Have you attempted to uncover unmet consumer needs and wants? By what methods? Do you focus relentlessly on maximizing your customers' product and service experiences? Do you have a system in place for getting comments from customers to the people who can effect change?
- **The brand stays relevant.** Have you invested in product improvements that provide better value for your customers? Are you in touch with your customers' tastes? With the current market conditions? With new trends as they apply to your offering? Are your marketing decisions based on your knowledge of the above?
- **The pricing strategy is based on consumers' perceptions of value.** Have you optimized price, cost, and quality to meet or exceed customers' expectations? Do you have a system in place to monitor customers' perceptions of your brand's value? Have you estimated how much value your customers believe the brand adds to your product?
- **The brand is properly positioned.** Have you established necessary and competitive points of parity with competitors? Have you established desirable and deliverable points of difference?
- **The brand is consistent.** Are you sure that your marketing programs are not sending conflicting messages and that they haven't done so over time? Conversely, are you adjusting your programs to keep current?

- **The brand portfolio and hierarchy make sense.** Can the corporate brand create a seamless umbrella for all the brands in the portfolio? Do the brands in that portfolio hold individual niches? How extensively do the brands overlap? In what areas? Conversely, do the brands maximize market coverage? Do you have a brand hierarchy that is well thought out and well understood?

- **The brand makes use of and coordinates a full repertoire of marketing activities to build equity.** Have you chosen or designed your brand name, logo, symbol, slogan, packaging, signage, and so forth to maximize brand awareness? Have you implemented integrated push and pull marketing activities that target both distributors and customers? Are you aware of all the marketing activities that involve your brand? Are the people managing each activity aware of one another? Have you capitalized on the unique capabilities of each communication option while ensuring that the meaning of the brand is consistently represented?

- **The brand's managers understand what the brand means to consumers.** Do you know what customers like and don't like about a brand? Are you aware of all the core associations people make with your brand, whether intentionally created by your company or not? Have you created detailed, research-driven portraits of your target customers? Have you outlined customer-driven boundaries for brand extensions and guidelines for marketing programs?

- **The brand is given proper support, and that support is sustained over the long run.** Are the successes or failures of marketing programs fully understood before they are changed? Is the brand given sufficient R&D support? Have you avoided the temptation to cut back marketing support for the brand in reaction to a downturn in the market or a slump in sales?

- **The company monitors sources of brand equity.** Have you created a brand charter that defines the meaning and equity of the brand and how it should be treated? Do you conduct periodic brand audits to assess the health of your brand and to set strategic direction? Do you conduct routine tracking studies to evaluate current market performance? Do you regularly distribute brand equity reports that summarize all relevant research and information to assist marketers in making decisions? Have you assigned explicit responsibility for monitoring and preserving brand equity?

stake out a formidable position for its brand. Visa became the consumer card of choice for family and personal shopping, for personal travel and entertainment, and even for international travel, a former American Express stronghold.

Of course, branding isn't static, and the game is even more difficult when a brand spans many product categories. The mix of points of parity and point of difference that works for a brand in one category may not be quite right for the same brand in another.

The brand is consistent

Maintaining a strong brand means striking the right balance between continuity in marketing activities and the kind of change needed to stay relevant. By continuity, I mean that the brand's image doesn't get muddled or lost in a cacophony of marketing efforts that confuse customers by sending conflicting messages.

Just such a fate befell the Michelob brand. In the 1970s, Michelob ran ads featuring successful young professionals that confidently proclaimed, "Where you're going, it's Michelob." The company's next ad campaign trumpeted, "Weekends were made for Michelob." Later, in an attempt to bolster sagging sales, the theme was switched to "Put a little weekend in your week." In the mid-1980s, managers launched a campaign telling consumers that "The night belongs to Michelob." Then in 1994 we were told, "Some days are better than others," which went on to explain that "A special day requires a special beer." That slogan was subsequently changed to "Some days were made for Michelob."

Pity the poor consumers. Previous advertising campaigns simply required that they look at their calendars or out a window to decide whether it was the right time to drink Michelob; by the mid-1990s, they had to figure out exactly what kind of day they were having as well. After receiving so many different messages, consumers could hardly be blamed if they had no idea when they were supposed to drink the beer. Predictably, sales suffered. From a high in 1980 of 8.1 million barrels, sales dropped to just 1.8 million barrels by 1998.

The brand portfolio and hierarchy make sense

Most companies do not have only one brand; they create and maintain different brands for different market segments. Single product lines are often sold under different brand names, and different brands within a company hold different powers. The corporate, or companywide, brand acts as an umbrella. A second brand name under that umbrella might be targeted at the family market. A third brand name might nest one level below the family brand and appeal to boys, for example, or be used for one type of product.

Brands at each level of the hierarchy contribute to the overall equity of the portfolio through their individual ability to make consumers aware of the various products and foster favorable associations with them. At the same time, though, each brand should have its own boundaries; it can be dangerous to try to cover too much ground with one brand or to overlap two brands in the same portfolio.

The Gap's brand portfolio provides maximum market coverage with minimal overlap. Banana Republic anchors the high end, the Gap covers the basic style-and-quality terrain, and Old Navy taps into the broader mass market. Each brand has a distinct image and its own sources of equity.

BMW has a particularly well-designed and implemented hierarchy. At the corporate brand level, BMW pioneered the luxury sports sedan category by combining seemingly incongruent style and performance considerations. BMW's clever advertising slogan, "The ultimate driving machine," reinforces the dual aspects of this image and is applicable to all cars sold under the BMW name. At the same time, BMW created well-differentiated subbrands through its 3, 5, and 7 series, which suggest a logical order and hierarchy of quality and price.

General Motors, by contrast, still struggles with its brand portfolio and hierarchy. In the early 1920s, Alfred P. Sloan decreed that his company would offer "a car for every purse and purpose." This philosophy led to the creation of the Cadillac, Oldsmobile, Buick, Pontiac, and Chevrolet divisions. The idea was that each division would appeal to a unique market segment on the basis of price, product design, user imagery, and so forth. Through the years, however, the marketing overlap among the five main GM divisions increased, and the divisions' distinctiveness diminished. In the mid-1980s, for example, the company sold a single body type (the J-body) modified only slightly for the five different brand names. In fact, advertisements for Cadillac in the 1980s actually stated that "motors for a Cadillac may come from other divisions, including Buick and Oldsmobile."

In the last ten years, the company has attempted to sharpen the divisions' blurry images by repositioning each brand. Chevrolet has been positioned as the value-priced, entry-level brand. Saturn represents no-haggle customer-oriented service. Pontiac is meant to be the sporty, performance-oriented brand for young people. Oldsmobile is the brand for larger, medium-priced cars. Buick is the premium, "near luxury" brand. And Cadillac, of course, is still the top of the line. Yet the goal remains challenging. The financial performance of Pontiac and Saturn has improved. But the top and bottom lines have never regained the momentum they had years ago. Consumers remain confused about what the brands stand for, in sharp contrast to the clearly focused images of competitors like Honda and Toyota.

The brand makes use of and coordinates a full repertoire of marketing activities to build equity

At its most basic level, a brand is made up of all the marketing elements that can be trademarked—logos, symbols, slogans, packaging, signage, and so on. Strong brands mix and match these elements to perform a number of brand-related functions, such as enhancing or reinforcing consumer awareness of the brand or its image and helping to protect the brand both competitively and legally.

Managers of the strongest brands also appreciate the specific roles that different marketing activities can play in building brand equity. They can, for example provide detailed product information. They can show consumers how and why a product is used, by whom, where, and when. They can associate a brand with a person, place, or thing to enhance or refine its image.

Some activities, such as traditional advertising, lend themselves best to "pull" functions—those meant to create consumer demand for a given product. Others, like trade promotions, work best as "push" programs—those designed to help push the product through distributors. When a brand makes good use of all its resources and also takes particular care to ensure that the essence of the brand is the same in all activities, it is hard to beat.

Coca-Cola is one of the best examples. The brand makes excellent use of many kinds of marketing activities. These include media advertising (such as the global "Always Coca-Cola" campaign); promotions (the recent effort focused on the return of the popular contour bottle, for example); and sponsorship (its extensive involvement with the Olympics). They also include direct response (the Coca-Cola catalog, which sells licensed Coke merchandise) and interactive media (the company's Web site, which offers, among other things, games, a trading post for collectors of Coke memorabilia, and a virtual look at the World of Coca-Cola museum in Atlanta). Through it all, the company always reinforces its key values of "originality," "classic refreshment," and so on. The brand is always the hero in Coca-Cola advertising.

The brand's managers understand what the brand means to consumers

Managers of strong brands appreciate the totality of their brand's image—that is, all the different perceptions, beliefs, attitudes, and behaviors customers associate with their brand, whether created intentionally by the company or not. As a result, managers are able to make decisions regarding the brand with confidence. If it's clear what customers like and don't like about a brand, and what core associations are linked to the brand, then it should also be clear whether any given action will dovetail nicely with the brand or create friction.

The Bic brand illustrates the kinds of problems that can arise when managers don't fully understand their brand's meaning. By emphasizing the convenience of inexpensive, disposable products, the French company Société Bic was able to create a market for nonrefillable ballpoint pens in the late 1950s, disposable cigarette lighters in the early 1970s, and disposable razors in the early 1980s. But in 1989, when Bic tried the same strategy with perfumes in the United States and Europe, the effort bombed.

The perfumes—two for women ("Nuit" and "Jour") and two for men ("Bic for Men" and "Bic Sport for Men")—were packaged in quarter-ounce glass spray bottles that looked like fat cigarette lighters and sold for about $5 each. They were displayed in plastic packages on racks at checkout counters throughout Bic's extensive distribution channels, which included 100,000 or so drugstores, supermarkets, and other mass merchandisers. At the time of the launch, a Bic spokesperson described the products as logical extensions of the Bic heritage: "High quality at affordable prices, convenient to purchase and convenient to use." The company spent $20 million on an advertising and promotion blitz that featured images of stylish people enjoying the perfumes and used the tag line "Paris in your pocket."

What went wrong? Although their other products did stand for convenience and for good quality at low prices, Bic's managers didn't understand that the overall brand image lacked a certain cachet with customers—a critical element when marketing something as tied to emotions as perfume. The marketers knew that customers understood the message they were sending with their earlier products. But they didn't have a handle on the associations that the customers had added to the brand image—a utilitarian, impersonal essence—which didn't at all lend itself to perfume.

By contrast, Gillette has been careful not to fall into the Bic trap. While all of its products benefit from a similarly extensive distribution system, it is very protective of the name carried by its razors, blades, and associated toiletries. The company's electric razors, for example, use the entirely separate Braun name, and its oral care products are marketed under the Oral B name.

The brand is given proper support, and that support is sustained over the long run

Brand equity must be carefully constructed. A firm foundation for brand equity requires that consumers have the proper depth and breadth of awareness and strong, favorable, and unique associations with the brand in their memory. Too often, managers want to take shortcuts and bypass more basic branding considerations—such as achieving the necessary level of brand awareness—in favor of concentrating on flashier aspects of brand building related to image.

A good example of lack of support comes from the oil and gas industry in the 1980s. In the late 1970s, consumers had an extremely positive image of Shell Oil and, according to market research, saw clear differences between that brand and its major competitors. In the early 1980s, however, for a variety of reasons, Shell cut back considerably on its advertising and marketing. Shell has yet to regain the ground it lost. The brand no longer enjoys the same special status in the eyes of consumers, who now view it as similar to other oil companies.

Another example is Coors Brewing. As Coors devoted increasing attention to growing the equity of its less-established brands like Coors Light, and introduced new products like Zima, ad support for the flagship beer plummeted from a peak of about $43 million in 1985 to just $4 million in 1993. What's more, the focus of the ads for Coors beer shifted from promoting an iconoclastic, independent, western image to reflecting more contemporary themes. Perhaps not surprisingly, sales of Coors beer dropped by half between 1989 and 1993. Finally in 1994, Coors began to address the problem, launching a campaign to prop up sales that returned to its original focus. Marketers at Coors admit that they did not consistently give the brand the attention it needed. As one commented: "We've not marketed Coors as aggressively as we should have in the past ten to 15 years."

The company monitors sources of brand equity

Strong brands generally make good and frequent use of in-depth brand audits and ongoing brand-tracking studies. A brand audit is an exercise designed to assess the health of a given brand. Typically, it consists of a detailed internal description of exactly how the brand has been marketed (called a "brand inventory") and a thorough external investigation, through focus groups and other consumer research, of exactly what the brand does and could mean to consumers (called a "brand exploratory"). Brand audits are particularly useful when they are scheduled on a periodic basis. It's critical for managers holding the reins of a brand portfolio to get a clear picture of the products and services being offered and how they are being marketed and branded. It's also important to see how that same picture looks to customers. Tapping customers' perceptions and beliefs often uncovers the true meaning of a brand, or group of brands, revealing where corporate and consumer views conflict and thus showing managers exactly where they have to refine or redirect their branding efforts or their marketing goals.

Tracking studies can build on brand audits by employing quantitative measures to provide current information about how a brand is performing for any given dimension. Generally, a tracking study will collect information on consumers' perceptions, attitudes, and behaviors on a routine basis over time; a thorough study can yield valuable tactical insights into the short-term effectiveness of marketing programs and activities. Whereas brand audits measure where the brand has been, tracking studies measure where the brand is now and whether marketing programs are having their intended effects.

The strongest brands, however, are also supported by formal brand-equity-management systems. Managers of these brands have a written document—a "brand equity charter"—that spells out the company's general philosophy with respect to brands and brand equity as concepts (what a brand is, why brands matter, why brand management is relevant to the company, and so on). It also summarizes the activities that make up brand audits, brand tracking, and other brand research; specifies the outcomes expected of them; and includes the latest findings gathered from such research. The charter then lays out guidelines for implementing brand strategies and tactics and documents proper treatment of the brand's trademark—the rules for how the logo can appear and be used on packaging, in ads, and so forth. These managers also assemble the results of their various tracking surveys and other relevant measures into a brand equity report, which is distributed to management on a monthly, quarterly, or annual basis. The brand equity report not only describes what is happening within a brand but also why.

Even a market leader can benefit by carefully monitoring its brand, as Disney aptly demonstrates. In the late 1980s, Disney became concerned that some of its characters (among them Mickey Mouse and Donald Duck) were being used inappropriately and becoming overexposed. To determine the severity of the problem, Disney undertook an extensive brand audit. First, as part of the brand inventory, managers compiled a list of all available Disney products (manufactured by the company and licensed) and all third-party promotions (complete with point-of-purchase displays and relevant merchandising) in stores worldwide. At the same time, as part of a brand exploratory, Disney launched its first major consumer research study to investigate how consumers felt about the Disney brand.

The results of the brand inventory were a revelation to senior managers. The Disney characters were on so many products and marketed in so many ways that it was difficult to understand how or why many of the decisions had been made in the first place. The consumer study only reinforced their concerns. The study indicated that people lumped all the product endorsements together. Disney was Disney to consumers, whether they saw the characters in films, or heard them in recordings, or associated them with theme parks or products.

Consequently, all products and services that used the Disney name or characters had an impact on Disney's brand equity. And because of the characters' broad exposure in the marketplace, many consumers had begun to feel that Disney was exploiting its name. Disney characters were used in a promotion of Johnson Wax, for instance, a product that would seemingly leverage almost nothing of value from the Disney name. Consumers were even upset when Disney characters were linked to well-regarded premium brands like Tide laundry detergent. In that case, consumers felt the characters added little value to the product. Worse yet, they were annoyed that the characters involved children in a purchasing decision that they otherwise would probably have ignored.

If consumers reacted so negatively to associating Disney with a strong brand like Tide, imagine how they reacted when they saw the hundreds of other Disney-licensed products and joint promotions. Disney's characters were hawking everything from diapers to cars to

McDonald's hamburgers. Consumers reported that they resented all the endorsements because they felt they had a special, personal relationship with the characters and with Disney that should not be handled so carelessly.

As a result of the brand inventory and exploratory, Disney moved quickly to establish a brand equity team to better manage the brand franchise and more selectively evaluate licensing and other third-party promotional opportunities. One of the mandates of this team was to ensure that a consistent image for Disney—reinforcing its key association with fun family entertainment—was conveyed by all third-party products and services. Subsequently, Disney declined an offer to cobrand a mutual fund designed to help parents save for their children's college expenses. Although there was a family association, managers felt that a connection with the financial community suggested associations that were inconsistent with other aspects of the brand's image.

The Value of Balance

Building a strong brand involves maximizing all ten characteristics. And that is, clearly, a worthy goal. But in practice, it is tremendously difficult because in many cases when a company focuses on improving one, others may suffer.

Consider a premium brand facing a new market entrant with comparable features at a lower price. The brand's managers might be tempted to rethink their pricing strategy. Lowering prices might successfully block the new entrant from gaining market share in the short term. But what effect would that have in the long term? Will stepping outside its definition of "premium" change the brand in the minds of its target customers? Will it create the impression that the brand is no longer top of the line or that the innovation is no longer solid? Will the brand's message become cloudy? The price change may in fact attract customers from a different market segment to try the brand, producing a short-term blip in sales. But will those customers be the true target? Will their purchases put off the brand's original market?

The trick is to get a handle on how a brand performs on all ten attributes and then to evaluate any move from all possible perspectives. How will this new ad campaign affect customers' perception of price? How will this new product line affect the brand hierarchy in our portfolio? Does this tweak in positioning gain enough ground to offset any potential damage caused if customers feel we've been inconsistent?

One would think that monitoring brand performance wouldn't necessarily be included in the equation. But even effectively monitoring brand performance can have negative repercussions if you just go through the motions or don't follow through decisively on what you've learned.

Levi-Strauss's experiences are telling. In the mid-1990s, the company put together a comprehensive brand-equity-measurement system. Practically from the time the system was installed, it indicated that the brand image was beginning to slip, both in terms of the appeal of Levi's tight-fitting flagship 501 brand of jeans and how contemporary and cutting edge the overall Levi's brand was. The youth market was going for a much baggier look; competitors were rushing in to fill the gap. Distracted in part by an internal reengineering effort, however, Levi's was slow to respond and when it did, it came up with underfunded, transparently trendy ad campaigns that failed to resonate with its young target market. Its market share in the jeans category plummeted in the latter half of the 1990s. The result? Levi's has terminated its decades-long relationship with ad agency Foote, Cone & Belding and is now attempting to launch new products and new ad campaigns. For Levi's, putting in the system was not enough; perhaps if it had adhered more closely to other branding principles, concentrating on innovating and staying relevant to its customers, it could have better leveraged its market research data.

Negative examples and cautionary words abound, of course. But it is important to recognize that in strong brands the top ten traits have a positive, synergistic effect on one another; excelling at one characteristic makes it easier to excel at another. A deep understanding of a brand's meaning and a well-defined brand position, for example, guide development of an optimal marketing program.

That, in turn, might lead to a more appropriate value-pricing strategy. Similarly, instituting an effective brand-equity-measurement system can help clarify a brand's meaning, capture consumers' reactions to pricing changes and other strategic shifts, and monitor the brand's ability to stay relevant to consumers through innovation.

Brand Equity as a Bridge

Ultimately, the power of a brand lies in the minds of consumers or customers, in what they have experienced and learned about the brand over time. Consumer knowledge is really at the heart of brand equity. This realization has important managerial implications.

In an abstract sense, brand equity provides marketers with a strategic bridge from their past to their future. That is, all the dollars spent each year on marketing can be thought of not so much as expenses but as investments—investments in what consumers know, feel, recall, believe, and think about the brand. And that knowledge dictates appropriate and inappropriate future directions for the brand—for it is consumers who will decide, based on their beliefs and attitudes about a given brand, where they think that brand should go and grant permission (or not) to any marketing tactic or program. If not properly designed and implemented, those expenditures may not be good investments—the right knowledge structures may not have been created in consumers' minds—but they are investments nonetheless.

Ultimately, the value to marketers of brand equity as a concept depends on how they use it. Brand equity can help marketers focus, giving them a way to interpret their past marketing performance and design their future marketing programs. Everything the company does can help enhance or detract from brand equity. Marketers who build strong brands have embraced the concept and use it to its fullest to clarify, implement, and communicate their marketing strategy.

Originally published in January 2000. Reprint R00104

The Female Economy

by Michael J. Silverstein and Kate Sayre

W

WOMEN NOW DRIVE THE WORLD economy.

Globally, they control about $20 trillion in annual consumer spending, and that figure could climb as high as $28 trillion in the next five years. Their $13 trillion in total yearly earnings could reach $18 trillion in the same period. In aggregate, women represent a growth market bigger than China and India combined—more than twice as big, in fact. Given those numbers, it would be foolish to ignore or underestimate the female consumer. And yet many companies do just that, even ones that are confident they have a winning strategy when it comes to women.

Consider Dell's short-lived effort to market laptops specifically to women. The company fell into the classic "make it pink" mind-set with the May 2009 launch of its Della website. The site emphasized colors, computer accessories, and tips for counting calories and finding recipes. It created an uproar among women, who described it as "slick but disconcerting" and "condescending." The blogosphere reacted quickly to the company's "very special site for women." Austin Modine of the online tech publication *The Register* responded acidly, "If you thought computer shopping was a gender-neutral affair, then you've obviously been struck down by an acute case of female hysteria. (Nine out of ten Victorian-age doctors agree.)" The *New York Times* said that Dell had to go to the "school of marketing hard knocks." Within weeks of the launch, the company altered the site's name and focus. "You spoke, we listened," Dell told users. Kudos to Dell for correcting course promptly, but why didn't its marketers catch the potentially awkward positioning before the launch?

Most companies have much to learn about selling to women. In 2008 the Boston Consulting Group fielded a comprehensive study of how women felt about their work and their lives, and how they were being served by businesses. It turned out there was lots of room for improvement. More than 12,000 women, from more than 40 geographies and a variety of income levels and walks of life, responded to our survey. They answered—often with disarming candor—120 questions about their education and finances, homes and possessions, jobs and careers, activities and interests, relationships, and hopes and fears, along with their shopping behavior and spending patterns in some three dozen categories of goods and services. (You can learn more about the survey and take an abridged version of it at www.womenspeakworldwide.com.) We also conducted hundreds of interviews and studied women working in 50 organizations in 13 fields of endeavor.

Here's what we found, in brief: Women feel vastly underserved. Despite the remarkable strides in market power and social position that they have made in the past century, they still appear to be undervalued in the marketplace and underestimated in the workplace. They have too many demands on their time and constantly juggle conflicting priorities—work, home, and family. Few companies have responded to their need for time-saving solutions or for products and services designed specifically for them.

It's still tough for women to find a pair of pants, buy a healthful meal, get financial advice without feeling patronized, or make the time to stay in shape. Although women control spending in most categories of consumer goods, too many businesses behave as if they had no say over purchasing decisions. Companies continue to offer them poorly conceived products and services and outdated marketing narratives that promote female stereotypes. Look at the automotive industry. Cars are designed for speed—not utility, which

Idea in Brief

As a market, women represent an opportunity bigger than China and India combined. They control $20 trillion in consumer spending, and that figure could reach $28 trillion in the next five years. Women drive the world economy, in fact. Yet most companies do a remarkably poor job of serving them, a new study by the Boston Consulting Group reveals.

BCG surveyed more than 12,000 women from a variety of geographies, income levels, and walks of life about their education, finances, homes, jobs, activities, interests, relationships, hopes, and fears, as well as their shopping behaviors and spending patterns. In this article, Silverstein and Sayre, two of the firm's partners, review highlights of the findings and explain the biggest opportunities. While any business would be wise to target female consumers, they say, the greatest potential lies in six industries: food, fitness, beauty, apparel, health care, and financial services.

Address women's concerns effectively, and your company could see the kind of rapid growth that fitness chain Curves enjoyed. Most health clubs are expensive and designed for men, with lots of complicated body-building equipment. Curves, however, understood that time-pressed women needed quick, affordable workouts, and came up with the concept of simple, 30-minute exercise routines geared to women and offered in no-frills spaces. Companies that likewise successfully tailor their offerings to women will be positioned to win when the economy begins to recover.

is what really matters to women. No SUV is built to accommodate a mother who needs to load two small children into it. Or consider a recent ad for Bounty paper towels, in which a husband and son stand by watching a spill cross the room, until Mom comes along and cheerfully cleans up the mess.

Meanwhile, women are increasingly gaining influence in the work world. As we write, the number of working women in the United States is about to surpass the number of working men. Three-quarters of the people who have lost jobs in the current recession are men. To be fair, women are still paid less, on average, than men, and are more likely to work part-time—factors that have helped insulate them somewhat from the crisis. Nevertheless, we believe that as this

The world's largest opportunity

A growth forecast (in trillions)

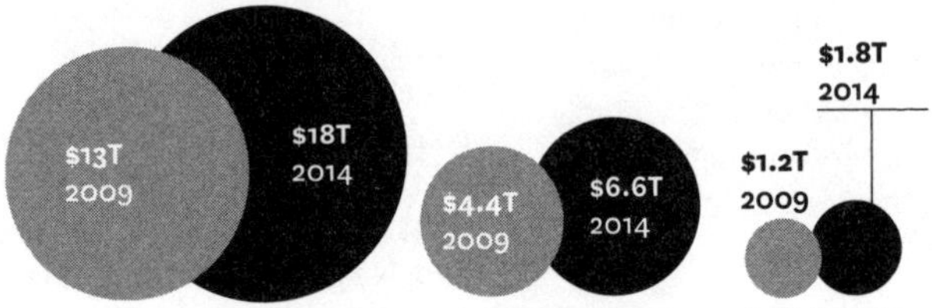

recession abates, women not only will represent one of the largest market opportunities in our lifetimes but also will be an important force in spurring a recovery and generating new prosperity.

Where the Opportunities Lie

Each person's story is different, but when we looked for patterns in our findings, we identified six basic archetypes among our respondents. These types, which are primarily defined by income, age, and stage of life, are *fast-tracker, pressure cooker, relationship focused, managing on her own, fulfilled empty nester,* and *making ends meet*. Few women fall into just one type. Married fast-trackers with children, for instance, are likely at some point in their lives to also fall into the pressure cooker category. (See the exhibit "Six key female consumer segments.")

Despite its limitations, such segmentation is useful in informing the development and marketing of companies' offerings. Knowing whom you're targeting and what she looks for in the marketplace can be a tremendous source of advantage.

Any company would be wise to target female customers, but the greatest potential lies in six industries. Four are businesses where women are most likely to spend more or trade up: food, fitness, beauty, and apparel. The other two are businesses with which women have made their dissatisfaction very clear: financial services and health care.

Food represents one of the largest opportunities. Women are responsible for the lion's share of grocery shopping and meal preparation. Food is also one of consumers' most important budget items, one that can be adjusted but never eliminated.

Favorite grocery stores among the women we surveyed included Whole Foods and Tesco. Though they appeal to different segments, the two chains have each developed a loyal following. Whole Foods has succeeded despite its high prices by targeting the demanding (but well-to-do) fast-trackers, who want high-quality meats and produce and a knowledgeable staff. Tesco stores, which offer one-stop shopping for a wide range of household items, including books, furniture, and financial services, appeal to the time-strapped pressure cookers, who desire convenience.

Fitness is also a big business. In the United States alone the market for diet food has been growing 6% to 9% a year and is worth approximately $10 billion, while the worldwide market is worth about $20 billion. The U.S. health club industry generates revenues of about $14 billion annually.

About two-thirds of our survey respondents described themselves as overweight; what was until recently an American issue has become a global phenomenon. But while women say that their fitness is a priority, in reality it tends to take a backseat. When asked to prioritize the needs of spouses, children, parents, and themselves, nearly all women ranked their own needs second or third—which means they have trouble finding time to work out.

The challenge for companies is to make fitness more accessible to women. For instance, most health clubs are expensive and designed for men. They can feel more like nightclubs than fitness centers and are geared to bodybuilders. Generally, women are less interested in pumping themselves up than in shedding a few pounds, improving their cardiovascular health, and getting toned. Bright lights, electronic music, sweaty men, and complicated equipment are often a turnoff.

Six key female consumer segments

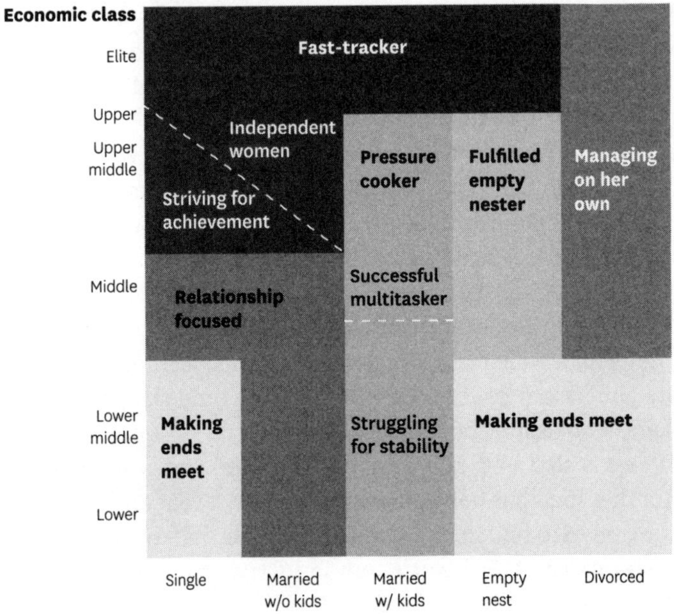

The fitness chain Curves recognized and responded to women's concerns—and grew quickly as a result. Curves has a very simple concept: cheap, fast exercise for women only, with no-frills spaces suited to middle-aged clients of average build. Helpers stand by to usher them through a simple 30-minute circuit, so there's no need to hire a trainer.

Beauty products and services promote a sense of emotional well-being in women. Those we talked with who spent a higher portion of their income on cosmetics felt more satisfied, successful, and

Fast-tracker
24% of population
34% of earned income
- Economic and educational elite
- Seeks adventure and learning

Subsegments:
- Striving for achievement – 15% of population, 19% of earned income; job and recognition are priorities
- Independent women – 9% of population, 15% of earned income; works the most; prizes autonomy

Pressure cooker
22% of population
23% of earned income
- Married with children
- Feels ignored and stereotyped

Subsegments:
- Successful multitasker – 10% of population, 14% of earned income; feels in control
- Struggling for stability – 12% of population, 9% of earned income; constantly battles chaos

Relationship focused
16% of population
13% of earned income
- Content and optimistic
- Isn't pressed for time
- Has ample discretionary income
- Focuses on experiences, not products

Managing on her own
10% of population
9% of earned income
- Single again – divorced or widowed
- Seeks ways to form connections

Fulfilled empty nester
15% of population
16% of earned income
- Largely ignored by marketers
- Concerned about health and aging gracefully
- Focused on travel, exercise, and leisure

Making ends meet
12% of population
5% of earned income
- No money for beauty or exercise
- Majority lack college education
- Seeks credit, value, and small luxuries

powerful; they also reported lower levels of stress even if they worked longer hours.

But even so, women are fundamentally dissatisfied with beauty offerings, and the way the industry is evolving keeps them from spending as much as they might. For one thing, there are too many choices; it's a male-dominated industry in which men make hit-or-miss guesses about what women want, and products come and go at a rapid pace. Women are passionate about the industry and well represented in jobs at the entry level, but female employment drops off at the executive and senior leadership levels. A good first step toward gaining market share might be to put more women at the top—where they can help make key decisions and provide input about what does and doesn't resonate with customers.

Many companies that do well in beauty have made creative use of new technologies to address women's desire to look younger. Facial skin-care products, for instance, have grown into a $20 billion category worldwide. Whereas shelves used to be lined with products whose sole purpose was to moisturize the skin, now there are formulas containing a variety of benefits, such as sun protection, skin plumping, and capillary strengthening—all designed to prevent, or at the very least disguise, aging.

At the top of the range is Switzerland-based La Prairie's Cellular Cream Platinum Rare antiaging moisturizer, which goes for $1,000 for 1.7 ounces. The cream contains a trace of platinum, which, the company claims, "recharges the skin's electrical balance and protects the skin's DNA." Despite the price, customers lined up at luxury retail stores to purchase a jar when the cream was introduced in 2008.

At the other end of the range, Procter & Gamble's Olay brand is available in drugstores. It has morphed from one low-end product with a simple purpose (moisturizing), which about 2% of the population used, into an array of higher-end products with numerous applications and a 40% household penetration. One of the most successful new Olay products is its Regenerist Daily Regenerating Serum, advertised as the next-best thing to cosmetic surgery.

Apparel—including accessories and shoes—is a $47 billion global industry with plenty of room for improvement, primarily when it comes to fit and affordability.

Most women are not a perfect size 6, and they don't like to be reminded of it every time they shop. Trying on clothes is often an exercise in frustration that just reinforces women's negative body images. Banana Republic, a favorite retailer of the women in our survey, has won a loyal following by taking steps to solve the problem of fit, particularly for pants. It offers a variety of cuts to suit different figures, and sizes are consistent across the board. Once you discover your "fit block" (the chain's technical term for body type), you can

Women control the lion's share of consumer spending

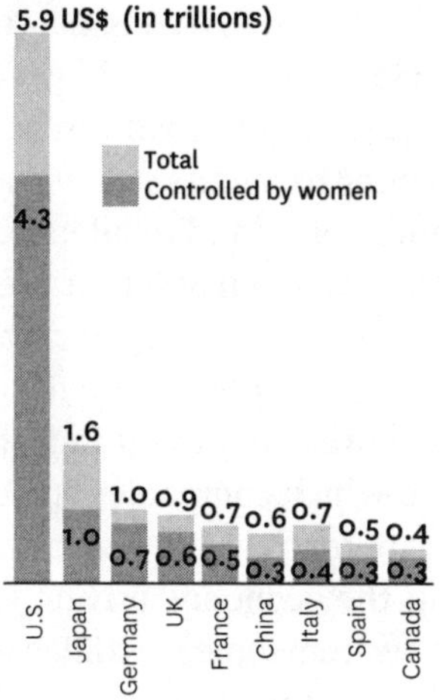

buy multiple pairs of pants, even online, quickly and dependably. Banana Republic has become Gap's most profitable brand, the only one that's grown over the past five years.

By contrast, Express stores focused on style and color but failed to deliver a consistent fit. Women might try on four garments marked "size 8" that actually varied in size from 6 to 12. The chain's sales began to lag so much that its parent company, Limited Brands, ended up exiting the fashion apparel business; it sold Express to a private equity group in 2007.

The costliness of clothing was another sore point for the women in our survey. That explains why respondents also favored Sweden-based H&M. Its stores offer inexpensive, fun, trendy clothes and, with a rapid turnover of stock, an element of surprise each time shoppers visit. Women value the ability to buy a new outfit without breaking the bank. Perhaps contributing to H&M's success is the fact that nearly 80% of the company's employees, 77% of store managers, and 44% of country managers are women. So are seven of the 11 board members.

Few of the women we talked to during the course of our research actually needed new clothing. Most could get away with shopping once or twice a year just to replenish the basics. But given that women say they are willing to spend extra to find clothing that really works for them, manufacturers and retailers can find plenty of untapped potential in the apparel market—if they listen carefully to what women want, seek new technologies that offer superior fabrication and color, and improve comfort and fit.

Financial services wins the prize as the industry least sympathetic to women—and one in which companies stand to gain the most if they can change their approach.

Despite setbacks in the economy, private wealth in the United States is expected to grow from some $14 trillion today to $22 trillion by 2020, and 50% of it will be in the hands of women. Yet women are still continually let down by the level of quality and service they get from financial companies, which presume men to be their target customers.

Our survey respondents were scathing in their comments about financial institutions. They cited a lack of respect, poor advice, contradictory policies, one-size-fits-all forms, and a seemingly endless tangle of red tape that leaves them exhausted and annoyed. Consider just a few quotations from our interviews:

- "I hate being stereotyped because of my gender and age, and I don't appreciate being treated like an infant."
- "As a single woman, I often feel that financial services institutions aren't looking for my business."
- "Financial service reps talk down to women as if we cannot understand more than just the basics."
- "I'm earning close to $1 million a year and should retire with $20 million plus in assets, so I'm not right for a cookie cutter discount broker, nor qualified for high-end wealth management services."

Financial categories where untapped sales to women are worth trillions

Extraordinary amounts of money are up for grabs in the financial services business. The most lucrative opportunities for companies arise at transition points like marriage, divorce, childbirth, and a job change, because women are most likely to make investment decisions around such events.

	Investments & financial advisory	Life insurance	Payments
Unmet needs	• Financial education • Advisers that understand and cater to female life events • Equal treatment with men	• Education about insuring entire household versus just the primary earner • Equitable coverage for working women and men • Valuations for "at-home" work	• Reward programs and payment plans that cater to women
Potential value in U.S.	• About $2.1 trillion in wealth held by high-net-worth divorced or widowed women	• About $2 trillion in incremental coverage	• About $1.4 trillion in credit card purchases
Goals	• Win market share • Grow market	• Grow market • Create new market	• Win market share • Grow market
Key inflection points to target	• Divorce • Death of a spouse	• Marriage • First home purchase • Promotion • Birth of first child	• First credit card • College commencement • First job

An unhappy customer with $20 million plus to invest represents a golden opportunity. Overall, the markets for investment services and life insurance for women are wide open. (For three of the largest opportunities, see the exhibit "Financial categories where untapped sales to women are worth trillions.")

Health care was a source of frustration for women in our survey—and for middle-aged respondents in particular. Women resoundingly reported dissatisfaction with their hospitals and doctors. When polled about the service provided by their general practitioners and specialists, more than 60% of them said those doctors could do "somewhat better" or "significantly better." Seventy-one percent of women aged 30 to 49 were dissatisfied with general practitioners, and 68% of that group were dissatisfied with specialists. More specifically, they were irritated by the amount of time they spent waiting for doctors and lab results, and scheduling and keeping appointments for themselves and their families. Making matters worse, women generally pay significantly more than men do for health insurance.

Again, the opportunities for companies that do cater to women are enormous. Johnson & Johnson, though not a health care services provider, was almost invariably represented (in the form of oral contraception, baby care, bandages, and other products) when we peeked into our respondents' medicine cabinets. The company spends 4% of its sales on consumer research and development—more than twice the industry average—and thus in all likelihood has a better understanding of its female customers than most companies in its space do. For instance, because mothers of young children are one of its important customer groups, the company conducted a clinical study in partnership with a pediatric sleep expert at the Children's Hospital of Philadelphia. Together, they developed a three-step routine to help babies sleep better, consisting of bath, massage, and quiet time. J&J then launched a line of products to complement the routine—with the results of the clinical study to boost their credibility.

Overburdened and Overwhelmed

Considering how often the issue of time—and not enough of it—came up in our survey and our interviews, offering easier and more convenient ways to make purchases would create a clear advantage in all the industries we've discussed. We've seen that women don't make enough time for themselves. They are still far more burdened than men by household tasks; according to our survey, about one-third of men don't help their spouse or partner with chores. In Japan women receive the least support, with 74% getting little or no help from their spouses. At the opposite extreme, 71% of Indian husbands pitch in on household chores.

Our research also showed that pressures change over time. Women are happiest in their early and later years and experience their lowest point in their early and mid forties. That's when they face the greatest challenges in managing work and home, and must deal with caring for both children and aging parents. So this group is especially receptive to products and services that can help them better control their lives and balance their priorities.

A Future of Parity, Power, and Influence

When the dust from the economic crisis settles, we predict, women will occupy an even more important position in the economy and the world order than they now do. What might that economy look like? In some ways it will be characterized by the same trends we've seen over the past five decades. For one thing, women will represent an ever-larger proportion of the workforce. The number of working women has been increasing by about 2.2% a year. We expect an additional 90 million or so women to enter the workforce by 2013, perhaps even more as employment becomes a necessity. At nearly every major consumer company, most middle managers are women. It's only a matter of time before they rise to more-senior positions. Already, women own 40% of the businesses in the United States, and their businesses are growing at twice the rate of U.S. firms as a whole. (Admittedly, the numbers are being skewed as small businesses position themselves for government contracts that favor female-owned companies.) Women will also continue to struggle with work/life balance, conflicting demands, and too little time.

Once companies wake up to the potential of the female economy, they will find a whole new range of commercial opportunities in

How often does your spouse or partner help with household chores?

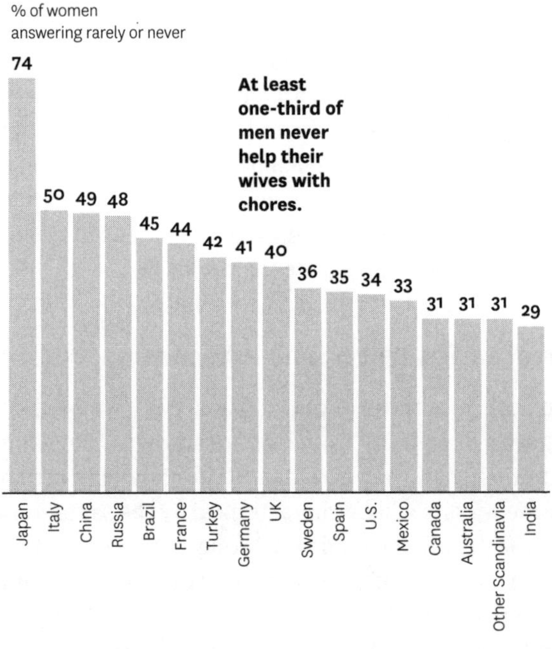

women's social concerns. Women seek to buy products and services from companies that do good for the world, especially for other women. Brands that—directly or indirectly—promote physical and emotional well-being, protect and preserve the environment, provide education and care for the needy, and encourage love and connection will benefit.

And women are the customer. There's no reason they should settle for products that ignore or fail to fully meet their needs, or that do so cynically or superficially. Women will increasingly resist being stereotyped, segmented only by age or income, lumped together into an "all women" characterization, or, worse, undifferentiated from men.

The financial crisis will come to an end, and now is the time to lay the foundation for postrecession growth. A focus on women as a target market—instead of on any geographical market—will up a company's odds of success when the recovery begins. Understanding and meeting women's needs will be essential to rebuilding the economy; therein lies the key to breakout growth, loyalty, and market share.

Originally published in September 2009. Reprint R0909D

Customer Value Propositions in Business Markets

by James C. Anderson, James A. Narus, and Wouter van Rossum

"CUSTOMER VALUE PROPOSITION" has become one of the most widely used terms in business markets in recent years. Yet our management-practice research reveals that there is no agreement as to what constitutes a customer value proposition—or what makes one persuasive. Moreover, we find that most value propositions make claims of savings and benefits to the customer without backing them up. An offering may actually provide superior value—but if the supplier doesn't demonstrate and document that claim, a customer manager will likely dismiss it as marketing puffery. Customer managers, increasingly held accountable for reducing costs, don't have the luxury of simply believing suppliers' assertions.

Take the case of a company that makes integrated circuits (ICs). It hoped to supply 5 million units to an electronic device manufacturer for its next-generation product. In the course of negotiations, the supplier's salesperson learned that he was competing against a company whose price was 10 cents lower per unit. The customer asked each salesperson why his company's offering was superior. This salesperson based his value proposition on the service that he, personally, would provide.

Unbeknownst to the salesperson, the customer had built a customer value model, which found that the company's offering, though 10 cents higher in price per IC, was actually worth 15.9 cents more. The electronics engineer who was leading the development project had recommended that the purchasing manager buy those ICs, even at the higher price. The service was, indeed, worth something in the model—but just 0.2 cents! Unfortunately, the salesperson had overlooked the two elements of his company's IC offering that were most valuable to the customer, evidently unaware how much they were worth to that customer and, objectively, how superior they made his company's offering to that of the competitor. Not surprisingly, when push came to shove, perhaps suspecting that his service was not worth the difference in price, the salesperson offered a 10-cent price concession to win the business—consequently leaving at least a half million dollars on the table.

Some managers view the customer value proposition as a form of spin their marketing departments develop for advertising and promotional copy. This shortsighted view neglects the very real contribution of value propositions to superior business performance. Properly constructed, they force companies to rigorously focus on what their offerings are really worth to their customers. Once companies become disciplined about understanding customers, they can make smarter choices about where to allocate scarce company resources in developing new offerings.

We conducted management-practice research over the past two years in Europe and the United States to understand what constitutes a customer value proposition and what makes one persuasive to customers. One striking discovery is that it is exceptionally difficult to find examples of value propositions that resonate with customers. Here, drawing on the best practices of a handful of suppliers in business markets, we present a systematic approach for developing value propositions that are meaningful to target customers and that focus suppliers' efforts on creating superior value.

Idea in Brief

If you sell products to other companies, you know how hard it's become to win their business. Your customers—pressured to control costs—seem to care only about price. But if you lower prices to stimulate sales, your profits shrink.

So how *can* you persuade your business customers to pay the premium prices your offerings deserve? Craft a compelling **customer value proposition**. Research potential customers' enterprises, identifying their unique requirements. Then explain how your offerings outmatch your rivals' on the criteria that matter most to customers. Document the cost savings and profits your products deliver to existing customers—and will deliver to new customers.

The payoff? You help your customers slash costs—while generating profitable growth for yourself. One company that manufactured resins used in exterior paints discovered this firsthand. By researching the needs of commercial painting contractors—a key customer segment—the company learned that labor constituted the lion's share of contractors' costs, while paint made up just 15% of costs. Armed with this insight, the resin maker emphasized that its product dried so fast that contractors could apply two coats in one day—substantially lowering labor costs. Customers snapped up the product—and happily shelled out a 40% price premium for it.

Three Kinds of Value Propositions

We have classified the ways that suppliers use the term "value proposition" into three types: all benefits, favorable points of difference, and resonating focus. (See the exhibit "Which alternative conveys value to customers?")

All benefits

Our research indicates that most managers, when asked to construct a customer value proposition, simply list all the benefits they believe that their offering might deliver to target customers. The more they can think of, the better. This approach requires the least knowledge about customers and competitors and, thus, the least amount of work to construct. However, its relative simplicity has a major

Idea in Practice

To craft compelling customer value propositions:

Understand Customers' Businesses

Invest time and effort to understand your customers' businesses and identify their unique requirements and preferences.

> ***Example:*** The resin manufacturer deepened its understanding of key customers in several ways. It enrolled managers in courses on how painting contractors estimate jobs. It conducted focus groups and field tests to study products' performance on crucial criteria. It also asked customers to identify performance trade-offs they were willing to make and to indicate their willingness to pay for paints that delivered enhanced performance. And it stayed current on customer needs by joining industry associations composed of key customer segments.

Substantiate Your Value Claims

"We can save you money!" won't cut it as a customer value proposition. Back up this claim in accessible, persuasive language that describes the differences between your offerings and rivals'. And explain how those differences translate into monetary worth for customers.

> ***Example:*** Rockwell Automation precisely calculated cost savings from reduced power usage that customers would gain by purchasing Rockwell's pump solution instead of a competitor's comparable offering. Rockwell used industry-specific metrics to communicate about functionality and performance—including kilowatt-hours spent, number of

potential drawback: *benefit assertion*. Managers may claim advantages for features that actually provide no benefit to target customers.

Such was the case with a company that sold high-performance gas chromatographs to R&D laboratories in large companies, universities, and government agencies in the Benelux countries. One feature of a particular chromatograph allowed R&D lab customers to maintain a high degree of sample integrity. Seeking growth, the company began to market the most basic model of this chromatograph to a new segment: commercial laboratories. In initial meetings with prospective customers, the firm's salespeople touted the benefits of

operating hours per year, and dollars per kilowatt-hour.

significantly lowered energy and maintenance costs.

Document Value Delivered

Create written accounts of cost savings or added value that existing customers have actually captured by using your offerings. And conduct on-site pilots at prospective customer locations to gather data on your products' performance.

Example: Chemical manufacturer Akzo Nobel conducted a two-week pilot on a production reactor at a prospective customer's facility. AN's goal? To study the performance of its high-purity metal organics product relative to the next best alternative in producing compound semiconductor wafers. The study proved that AN's product was as good as or better than rivals' and that it

Make Customer Value Proposition a Central Business Skill

Improve and reward managers' ability to craft compelling customer value propositions.

Example: Quaker Chemical conducts a value-proposition training program annually for chemical program managers. The managers review case studies from industries Quaker serves and participate in simulated customer interviews to gather information needed to devise proposals. The team with the best proposal earns "bragging rights"—highly valued in Quaker's competitive culture. Managers who develop proposals that their director deems viable win gift certificates.

maintaining sample integrity. Their prospects scoffed at this benefit assertion, stating that they routinely tested soil and water samples, for which maintaining sample integrity was not a concern. The supplier was taken aback and forced to rethink its value proposition.

Another pitfall of the all benefits value proposition is that many, even most, of the benefits may be points of parity with those of the next best alternative, diluting the effect of the few genuine points of difference. Managers need to clearly identify in their customer value propositions which elements are points of parity and which are points of difference. (See the sidebar "The Building Blocks of a Successful Customer Value Proposition.") For example, an

Which alternative conveys value to customers?

Suppliers use the term "value proposition" three different ways. Most managers simply list all the benefits they believe that their offering might deliver to target customers. The more they can think of, the better. Some managers do recognize that the customer has an alternative, but they often make the mistake of assuming that favorable points of difference must be valuable for the customer. Best-practice suppliers base their value proposition on the few elements that matter most to target customers, demonstrate the value of this superior performance, and communicate it in a way that conveys a sophisticated understanding of the customer's business priorities.

Value proposition:	**All benefits**	**Favorable points of difference**	**Resonating focus**
Consists of:	All benefits customers receive from a market offering	All favorable points of difference a market offering has relative to the next best alternative	The one or two points of difference (and, perhaps, a point of parity) whose improvement will deliver the greatest value to the customer for the foreseeable future
Answers the customer question:	"Why should our firm purchase your offering?"	"Why should our firm purchase your offering instead of your competitor's?"	"What is *most* worthwhile for our firm to keep in mind about your offering?"
Requires:	Knowledge of own market offering	Knowledge of own market offering and next best alternative	Knowledge of how own market offering delivers superior value to customers, compared with next best alternative
Has the potential pitfall:	Benefit assertion	Value presumption	Requires customer value research

The Building Blocks of a Successful Customer Value Proposition

A SUPPLIER'S OFFERING MAY HAVE many technical, economic, service, or social benefits that deliver value to customers—but in all probability, so do competitors' offerings. Thus, the essential question is, "How do these value elements compare with those of the next best alternative?" We've found that it's useful to sort value elements into three types.

Points of parity are elements with essentially the same performance or functionality as those of the next best alternative.

Points of difference are elements that make the supplier's offering either superior or inferior to the next best alternative.

Points of contention are elements about which the supplier and its customers disagree regarding how their performance or functionality compares with those of the next best alternative. Either the supplier regards a value element as a point of difference in its favor, while the customer regards that element as a point of parity with the next best alternative, or the supplier regards a value element as a point of parity, while the customer regards it as a point of difference in favor of the next best alternative.

---

international engineering consultancy was bidding for a light-rail project. The last chart of the company's presentation listed ten reasons why the municipality should award the project to the firm. But the chart had little persuasive power because the other two finalists could make most of the same claims.

Put yourself, for a moment, in the place of the prospective client. Suppose each firm, at the end of its presentation, gives ten reasons why you ought to award it the project, and the lists from all the firms are almost the same. If each firm is saying essentially the same thing, how do you make a choice? You ask each of the firms to give a final, best price, and then you award the project to the firm that gives the largest price concession. Any distinctions that do exist have been overshadowed by the firms' greater sameness.

Favorable points of difference

The second type of value proposition explicitly recognizes that the customer has an alternative. The recent experience of a leading industrial gas supplier illustrates this perspective. A customer sent the company a request for proposal stating that the two or three suppliers that could demonstrate the most persuasive value propositions would be invited to visit the customer to discuss and refine their proposals. After this meeting, the customer would select a sole supplier for this business. As this example shows, "Why should our firm purchase your offering instead of your competitor's?" is a more pertinent question than "Why should our firm purchase your offering?" The first question focuses suppliers on differentiating their offerings from the next best alternative, a process that requires detailed knowledge of that alternative, whether it be buying a competitor's offering or solving the customer's problem in a different way.

Knowing that an element of an offering is a point of difference relative to the next best alternative does not, however, convey the value of this difference to target customers. Furthermore, a product or service may have several points of difference, complicating the supplier's understanding of which ones deliver the greatest value. Without a detailed understanding of the customer's requirements and preferences, and what it is worth to fulfill them, suppliers may stress points of difference that deliver relatively little value to the target customer. Each of these can lead to the pitfall of *value presumption:* assuming that favorable points of difference must be valuable for the customer. Our opening anecdote about the IC supplier that unnecessarily discounted its price exemplifies this pitfall.

Resonating focus

Although the favorable points of difference value proposition is preferable to an all benefits proposition for companies crafting a consumer value proposition, the resonating focus value proposition should be the gold standard. This approach acknowledges that the managers who make purchase decisions have major, ever-increasing levels of responsibility and often are pressed for time. They want to do business with suppliers that fully grasp critical issues in their business and deliver a customer value proposition that's simple yet powerfully captivating. Suppliers can provide such a customer value proposition by making their offerings superior on the few elements that matter most to target customers, demonstrating and documenting the value of this superior performance, and communicating it in a way that conveys a sophisticated understanding of the customer's business priorities.

This type of proposition differs from favorable points of difference in two significant respects. First, more is not better. Although a supplier's offering may possess several favorable points of difference, the resonating focus proposition steadfastly concentrates on the one or two points of difference that deliver, and whose improvement will continue to deliver, the greatest value to target customers. To better leverage limited resources, a supplier might even cede to the next best alternative the favorable points of difference that customers value least, so that the supplier can concentrate its resources on improving the one or two points of difference customers value most. Second, the resonating focus proposition may contain a point of parity. This occurs either when the point of parity is required for target customers even to consider the supplier's offering or when a supplier wants to counter customers' mistaken perceptions that a particular value element is a point of difference in favor of a competitor's offering. This latter case arises when customers believe that the competitor's offering is superior but the supplier believes its offerings are comparable—customer value research provides empirical support for the supplier's assertion.

To give practical meaning to resonating focus, consider the following example. Sonoco, a global packaging supplier headquartered in Hartsville, South Carolina, approached a large European customer, a maker of consumer packaged goods, about redesigning the packaging for one of its product lines. Sonoco believed that the customer would profit from updated packaging, and, by proposing the initiative itself, Sonoco reinforced its reputation as an innovator. Although the redesigned packaging provided six favorable points of difference relative to the next best alternative, Sonoco chose to emphasize one point of parity and two points of difference in what it called its distinctive value proposition (DVP). The value proposition was that the redesigned packaging would deliver significantly greater manufacturing efficiency in the customer's fill lines, through higher-speed closing, and provide a distinctive look that consumers would find more appealing—all for the same price as the present packaging.

Sonoco chose to include a point of parity in its value proposition because, in this case, the customer would not even consider a packaging redesign if the price went up. The first point of difference in the value proposition (increased efficiency) delivered cost savings to the customer, allowing it to move from a seven-day, three-shift production schedule during peak times to a five-day, two-shift operation. The second point of difference delivered an advantage at the consumer level, helping the customer to grow its revenues and profits incrementally. In persuading the customer to change to the redesigned packaging, Sonoco did not neglect to mention the other favorable points of difference. Rather, it chose to place much greater emphasis on the two points of difference and the one point of parity that mattered most to the customer, thereby delivering a value proposition with resonating focus.

Stressing as a point of parity what customers may mistakenly presume to be a point of difference favoring a competitor's offering can be one of the most important parts of constructing an effective value proposition. Take the case of Intergraph, an Alabama-based provider of engineering software to engineering, procurement, and construction firms. One software product that Intergraph offers, SmartPlant P&ID, enables customers to define flow processes for valves, pumps, and piping within plants they are designing and generate piping and instrumentation diagrams (P&ID). Some prospective customers wrongly presume that SmartPlant's drafting performance would not be as good as that of the next best alternative, because the alternative is built on computer-aided design (CAD), a better-known drafting tool than the relational database platform on which SmartPlant is built. So Intergraph tackled the perception head on, gathering data from reference customers to substantiate that this point of contention was actually a point of parity.

Here's how the company played it. Intergraph's resonating focus value proposition for this software consisted of one point of parity (which the customer initially thought was a point of contention), followed by three points of difference:

Point of parity: Using this software, customers can create P&ID graphics (either drawings or reports) as fast, if not faster, as they can using CAD, the next best alternative.

Point of difference: This software checks all of the customer's upstream and downstream data related to plant assets and procedures, using universally accepted engineering practices, company-specific rules, and project- or process-specific rules at each stage of the design process, so that the customer avoids costly mistakes such as missing design change interdependencies or, worse, ordering the wrong equipment.

Point of difference: This software is integrated with upstream and downstream tasks, such as process simulation and instrumentation design, thus requiring no reentry of data (and reducing the margin for error).

Point of difference: With this software, the customer is able to link remote offices to execute the project and then merge the pieces into a single deliverable database to hand to its customer, the facility owner.

Resonating focus value propositions are very effective, but they're not easy to craft: Suppliers must undertake customer value research to gain the insights to construct them. Despite all of the talk about customer value, few suppliers have actually done customer value research, which requires time, effort, persistence, and some creativity. But as the best practices we studied highlight, thinking through a resonating focus value proposition disciplines a company to research its customers' businesses enough to help solve their problems. As the experience of a leading resins supplier amply illustrates, doing customer value research pays off. (See the sidebar "Case in Point: Transforming a Weak Value Proposition.")

Case in Point: Transforming a Weak Value Proposition

A LEADING SUPPLIER OF specialty resins used in architectural coatings—such as paint for buildings—recognized that its customers were coming under pressure to comply with increasingly strict environmental regulations. At the same time, the supplier reasoned, no coating manufacturer would want to sacrifice performance. So the resins supplier developed a new type of high-performance resins that would enable its customers to comply with stricter environmental standards—albeit at a higher price but with no reduction in performance.

In its initial discussions with customers who were using the product on a trial basis, the resins supplier was surprised by the tepid reaction it received, particularly from commercial managers. They were not enthusiastic about the sales prospects for higher-priced coatings with commercial painting contractors, the primary target market. They would not, they said, move to the new resin until regulation mandated it.

Taken aback, the resins supplier decided to conduct customer value research to better understand the requirements and preferences of its customers' customers and how the performance of the new resin would affect their total cost of doing business. The resins supplier went so far as to study the requirements and preferences of the commercial painting contractors' customers—building owners. The supplier conducted a series of focus groups and field tests with painting contractors to gather data. The performance on primary customer requirements—such as coverage, dry time, and durability—was

Substantiate Customer Value Propositions

In a series of business roundtable discussions we conducted in Europe and the United States, customer managers reported that "We can save you money!" has become almost a generic value proposition from prospective suppliers. But, as one participant in Rotterdam wryly observed, most of the suppliers were telling "fairy tales." After he heard a pitch from a prospective supplier, he would follow up with a series of questions to determine whether the supplier had the people, processes, tools, and experience to actually save his firm money. As often as not, they could not really back up the claims.

studied, and customers were asked to make performance trade-offs and indicate their willingness to pay for coatings that delivered enhanced performance. The resins supplier also joined a commercial painting contractor industry association, enrolled managers in courses on how contractors are taught to estimate jobs, and trained the staff to work with the job-estimation software used by painting contractors.

Several insights emerged from this customer value research. Most notable was the realization that only 15% of a painting contractor's costs are the coatings; labor is by far the largest cost component. If a coating could provide greater productivity—for example, a faster drying time that allowed two coats to be applied during a single eight-hour shift—contractors would likely accept a higher price.

The resins supplier retooled its value proposition from a single dimension, environmental regulation compliance, to a resonating focus value proposition where environmental compliance played a significant but minor part. The new value proposition was "The new resin enables coatings producers to make architectural coatings with higher film build and gives the painting contractors the ability to put on two coats within a single shift, thus increasing painter productivity while also being environmentally compliant." Coatings customers enthusiastically accepted this value proposition, and the resins supplier was able to get a 40% price premium for its new offering over the traditional resin product.

Simply put, to make customer value propositions persuasive, suppliers must be able to demonstrate and document them.

Value word equations enable a supplier to show points of difference and points of contention relative to the next best alternative, so that customer managers can easily grasp them and find them persuasive. A value word equation expresses in words and simple mathematical operators (for example, + and ÷) how to assess the differences in functionality or performance between a supplier's offering and the next best alternative and how to convert those differences into dollars.

Best-practice firms like Intergraph and, in Milwaukee, Rockwell Automation use value word equations to make it clear to customers how their offerings will lower costs or add value relative to the next best alternatives. The data needed to provide the value estimates are most often collected from the customer's business operations by supplier and customer managers working together, but, at times, data may come from outside sources, such as industry association studies. Consider a value word equation that Rockwell Automation used to calculate the cost savings from reduced power usage that a customer would gain by using a Rockwell Automation motor solution instead of a competitor's comparable offering:

$$\begin{aligned}&\text{Power Reduction Cost Savings}\\&\quad= [\text{kW spent} \times \text{number of operating hours per year} \times\\&\quad\text{\$ per kW hour} \times \text{number of years system}\\&\quad\text{solution in operation}]_{\text{Competitor Solution}}\\&\quad-[\text{kW spent} \times \text{number of operating hours per year} \times\\&\quad\text{\$ per kW hour} \times \text{number of years system}\\&\quad\text{solution in operation}]_{\text{Rockwell Automation Solution}}\end{aligned}$$

This value word equation uses industry-specific terminology that suppliers and customers in business markets rely on to communicate precisely and efficiently about functionality and performance.

Demonstrate Customer Value in Advance

Prospective customers must see convincingly the cost savings or added value they can expect from using the supplier's offering instead of the next best alternative. Best-practice suppliers, such as Rockwell Automation and precision-engineering and manufacturing firm Nijdra Groep in the Netherlands, use *value case histories* to demonstrate this. Value case histories document the cost savings or added value that reference customers have actually received from their use of the supplier's market offering. Another way that best-practice firms, such as Pennsylvania-based GE Infrastructure Water & Process Technologies (GEIW&PT) and SKF USA, show the value of their offerings to prospective customers in advance is through *value calculators*. These customer value assessment tools typically are spreadsheet software applications that salespeople or value specialists use on laptops as part of a consultative selling approach to demonstrate the value that customers likely would receive from the suppliers' offerings.

When necessary, best-practice suppliers go to extraordinary lengths to demonstrate the value of their offerings relative to the next best alternatives. The polymer chemicals unit of Akzo Nobel in Chicago recently conducted an on-site two-week pilot on a production reactor at a prospective customer's facility to gather data firsthand on the performance of its high-purity metal organics offering relative to the next best alternative in producing compound semiconductor wafers. Akzo Nobel paid this prospective customer for these two weeks, in which each day was a trial because of daily considerations such as output and maintenance. Akzo Nobel now has data from an actual production machine to substantiate assertions about its product and anticipated cost savings, and evidence that the compound semiconductor wafers produced are as good as or better than those the customer currently grows using the next best alternative. To let its prospective clients' customers verify this for themselves, Akzo Nobel brought them sample wafers it had produced for testing. Akzo Nobel combines this point of parity with two points of difference: significantly lower energy costs for conversion and significantly lower maintenance costs.

Document Customer Value

Demonstrating superior value is necessary, but this is no longer enough for a firm to be considered a best-practice company. Suppliers also must document the cost savings and incremental profits (from additional revenue generated) their offerings deliver to the companies that have purchased them. Thus, suppliers work with their customers to define how cost savings or incremental profits will be tracked and then, after a suitable period of time, work with customer managers to document the results. They use value documenters to further refine their customer value models, create value case histories, enable customer managers to get credit for the cost savings and incremental profits produced, and (because customer managers know that the supplier is willing to return later to document the value received) enhance the credibility of the offering's value.

A pioneer in substantiating value propositions over the past decade, GEIW&PT documents the results provided to customers through its value generation planning (VGP) process and tools, which enable its field personnel to understand customers' businesses and to plan, execute, and document projects that have the highest value impact for its customers. An online tracking tool allows GEIW&PT and customer managers to easily monitor the execution and documented results of each project the company undertakes. Since it began using VGP in 1992, GEIW&PT has documented more than 1,000 case histories, accounting for $1.3 billion in customer cost savings, 24 billion gallons of water conserved, 5.5 million tons of waste eliminated, and 4.8 million tons of air emissions removed.

As suppliers gain experience documenting the value provided to customers, they become knowledgeable about how their offerings deliver superior value to customers and even how the value delivered varies across kinds of customers. Because of this extensive and detailed knowledge, they become confident in predicting the cost savings and added value that prospective customers likely will receive. Some best-practice suppliers are even willing to guarantee a certain amount of savings before a customer signs on.

A global automotive engine manufacturer turned to Quaker Chemical, a Pennsylvania-based specialty chemical and management services firm, for help in significantly reducing its operating costs. Quaker's team of chemical, mechanical, and environmental engineers, which has been meticulously documenting cost savings to customers for years, identified potential savings for this customer through process and productivity improvements. Then Quaker implemented its proposed solution—with a guarantee that savings would be five times more than what the engine manufacturer spent annually just to purchase coolant. In real numbers, that meant savings of $1.4 million a year. What customer wouldn't find such a guarantee persuasive?

Superior Business Performance

We contend that customer value propositions, properly constructed and delivered, make a significant contribution to business strategy and performance. GE Infrastructure Water & Process Technologies' recent development of a new service offering to refinery customers illustrates how general manager John Panichella allocates limited resources to initiatives that will generate the greatest incremental value for his company and its customers. For example, a few years ago, a field rep had a creative idea for a new product, based on his comprehensive understanding of refinery processes and how refineries make money. The field rep submitted a new product introduction (NPI) request to the hydrocarbon industry marketing manager for further study. Field reps or anyone else in the organization can submit NPI requests whenever they have an inventive idea for a customer solution that they believe would have a large value impact but that GEIW&PT presently does not offer. Industry marketing managers, who have extensive industry expertise, then perform scoping studies to understand the potential of the proposed products to deliver significant value to segment customers. They create business cases for the proposed product, which are "racked and stacked" for review. The senior management team of GEIW&PT sort through a large number of potential initiatives competing for limited resources. The team approved Panichella's initiative, which led to the development of a new offering that provided refinery customers with documented cost savings amounting to five to ten times the price they paid for the offering, thus realizing a compelling value proposition.

Sonoco, at the corporate level, has made customer value propositions fundamental to its business strategy. Since 2003, its CEO, Harris DeLoach, Jr., and the executive committee have set an ambitious growth goal for the firm: sustainable, double-digit, profitable growth every year. They believe that distinctive value propositions are crucial to support the growth initiative. At Sonoco, each value proposition must be:

- *Distinctive.* It must be superior to those of Sonoco's competition.
- *Measurable.* All value propositions should be based on tangible points of difference that can be quantified in monetary terms.
- *Sustainable.* Sonoco must be able to execute this value proposition for a significant period of time.

Unit managers know how critical DVPs are to business unit performance because they are one of the ten key metrics on the managers' performance scorecard. In senior management reviews, each unit manager presents proposed value propositions for each target market segment or key customer, or both. The managers then receive summary feedback on the value proposition metric (as well as on each of the nine other performance metrics) in terms of whether their proposals can lead to profitable growth.

In addition, Sonoco senior management tracks the relationship between business unit value propositions and business unit performance—and, year after year, has concluded that the emphasis on DVPs has made a significant contribution toward sustainable, double-digit, profitable growth.

Best-practice suppliers recognize that constructing and substantiating resonating focus value propositions is not a onetime undertaking, so they make sure their people know how to identify what the next value propositions ought to be. Quaker Chemical, for example, conducts a value-proposition training program each year for its chemical program managers, who work on-site with customers and have responsibility for formulating and executing customer value propositions. These managers first review case studies from a variety of industries Quaker serves, where their peers have executed savings projects and quantified the monetary savings produced.

Competing in teams, the managers then participate in a simulation where they interview "customer managers" to gather information needed to devise a proposal for a customer value proposition. The team that is judged to have the best proposal earns "bragging rights," which are highly valued in Quaker's competitive culture. The training program, Quaker believes, helps sharpen the skills of chemical program managers to identify savings projects when they return to the customers they are serving.

As the final part of the training program, Quaker stages an annual real-world contest where the chemical program managers have 90 days to submit a proposal for a savings project that they plan to present to their customers. The director of chemical management judges these proposals and provides feedback. If he deems a proposed project to be viable, he awards the manager with a gift certificate. Implementing these projects goes toward fulfilling Quaker's guaranteed annual savings commitments of, on average, $5 million to $6 million a year per customer.

Each of these businesses has made customer value propositions a fundamental part of its business strategy. Drawing on best practices, we have presented an approach to customer value propositions that businesses can implement to communicate, with resonating focus, the superior value their offerings provide to target market segments and customers. Customer value propositions can be a guiding beacon as well as the cornerstone for superior business performance. Thus, it is the responsibility of senior management and general management, not just marketing management, to ensure that their customer value propositions are just that.

Originally published in March 2006. Reprint R0603F

Getting Brand Communities Right

by Susan Fournier and Lara Lee

IN 1983, HARLEY-DAVIDSON FACED extinction. Twenty-five years later, the company boasted a top-50 global brand valued at $7.8 billion. Central to the company's turnaround, and to its subsequent success, was Harley's commitment to building a brand community: a group of ardent consumers organized around the lifestyle, activities, and ethos of the brand.

Inspired by Harley's results and enabled by Web 2.0 technologies, marketers in industries from packaged goods to industrial equipment are busy trying to build communities around their own brands. Their timing is right. In today's turbulent world, people are hungry for a sense of connection; and in lean economic times, every company needs new ways to do more with what it already has. Unfortunately, although many firms aspire to the customer loyalty, marketing efficiency, and brand authenticity that strong communities deliver, few understand what it takes to achieve such benefits. Worse, most subscribe to serious misconceptions about what brand communities are and how they work.

On the basis of our combined 30 years of researching, building, and leveraging brand communities, we identify and dispel seven commonly held myths about maximizing their value for a firm. For companies considering a community strategy, we offer cautionary tales and design principles. For those with existing brand communities, we provide new approaches for increasing their impact. And as you'll see from our discussion and the online "Community Readiness Audit" at brandcommunity.hbr.org, your decision is not whether a community is right for your brand. It's whether you're willing to do what's needed to get a brand community right.

Myth #1

A brand community is a marketing strategy.

The Reality

A brand community is a business strategy.

Too often, companies isolate their community-building efforts within the marketing function. That is a mistake. For a brand community to yield maximum benefit, it must be framed as a high-level strategy supporting businesswide goals.

Harley-Davidson provides a quintessential example. Following the 1985 leveraged buy-back that saved the company, management completely reformulated the competitive strategy and business model around a brand community philosophy. Beyond just changing its marketing programs, Harley-Davidson re-tooled every aspect of its organization—from its culture to its operating procedures and governance structure—to drive its community strategy.

Harley management recognized that the brand had developed as a community-based phenomenon. The "brotherhood" of riders, united by a shared ethos, offered Harley the basis for a strategic repositioning as the one motorcycle manufacturer that understood bikers on their own terms. To reinforce this community-centric positioning and solidify the connection between the company and its customers, Harley staffed all community-outreach events with employees rather than hired hands. For employees, this regular, close contact with the people they served added such meaning to their work that the weekend out-reach assignments routinely attracted more volunteers than were needed. Many employees

Idea in Brief

Hooray for brand communities—those groups of ardent consumers organized around a brand's lifestyle (think Harley-Davidson devotees and Playstation gamers). Brand-community members buy more, remain loyal, and reduce marketing costs through grassroots evangelism.

But many companies mismanage their brand communities because executives hold false beliefs about how to use these communities to create value. For example, they believe companies should tightly control such communities.

In truth, brand communities generate more value when *members* control them—and when companies create conditions in which communities can thrive. For instance, Vans—a skateboarding shoe manufacturer—had long invited lead users to co-design products, fostering a strong brand community as a result. When privately owned skateboarding parks began closing, Vans supported its community by opening its own park.

became riders, and many riders joined the company. Executives were required to spend time in the field with customers and bring their insights back to the firm. This close-to-the-customer strategy was codified in Harley-Davidson's operating philosophy and reinforced during new-employee orientations. Decisions at all levels were grounded in the community perspective, and the company acknowledged the community as the rightful owner of the brand.

Harley's community strategy was also supported by a radical organizational redesign. Functional silos were replaced with senior leadership teams sharing decision-making responsibility across three imperatives: Create Demand, Produce Product, and Provide Support. Further, the company established a stand-alone organization reporting directly to the president to formalize and nurture the company-community relationship through the Harley Owners Group (H.O.G.) membership club. As a result of this organizational structure, community-building activities were treated not solely as marketing expenses but as companywide, COO-backed investments in the success of the business model.

Idea in Practice

Additional truths about brand communities:

Brand community is a business—not a marketing—strategy.

Don't isolate your community-building efforts within your marketing function. Instead, ensure these efforts support businesswide goals by integrating them into your company's overall strategy.

> ***Example:*** Harley-Davidson reformulated its competitive strategy around brand community. For instance, all community-outreach events are staffed by employees, not freelance contractors. Many employees become riders; many riders join the company.

Brand communities exist to serve their member's needs—not your business.

Members have many community-related needs—including cultivating interests, expanding networks, and relaxing in a safe haven. Discern these needs, then help community members fulfill them.

> ***Example:*** "Third Place" brands like Gold's Gym and Starbucks tap into the need for social links by providing venues that foster personal interaction.

Strong brands arise from the right community structure—not vice versa.

The strongest, most stable structure for a brand community is a "web" whose affiliations are based on close one-to-one connections. To cultivate webs, provide opportunities for members to forge many interpersonal links.

Example: The Harley-Davidson Museum fosters personal connections through programs like the Rivet Wall, where people order custom-engraved rivets that are installed on decorative walls around the museum campus. Visitors viewing their own and others' rivets start chatting, often forging friendships.

Myth #2

A brand community exists to serve the business.

The Reality

A brand community exists to serve the people in it.

Managers often forget that consumers are actually people, with many different needs, interests, and responsibilities. A

Brand communities thrive on conflict and contrast—not love.

Communities are inherently political: "In-groups" need "out-groups" against which to define themselves. To strengthen group unity, create a sense of contrast, conflict, and boundaries.

Example: Dove's Campaign for Real Beauty brought "real women" (less-than-pretty, older, large, skinny) together worldwide to fight industry-imposed beauty ideals. The women formed in camaraderie around this mission.

Communities are strongest when all members—not just opinion leaders—have roles.

In strong communities, everyone plays a value-adding role. Roles include the Mentor (shares expertise with other members), Greeter (welcomes new members), and Storyteller (disseminates the community's history throughout the group).

To cultivate an enduring community, ensure that members can adopt new roles or switch roles as their lives change.

Example: Saddleback Church in Orange County, California, constantly monitors members' needs and creates new subgroups (such as personal financial planning) to keep people engaged.

Online social networks are only a tool—not your community strategy.

Many online interactions are shallow and transient, diluting the community overall. So use online tools selectively to support your brand community's needs.

Example: L'Oréal uses online tools (such as blogs) only with certain brands, such as mainstream Garnier, whose brand-community members value social interaction and view themselves as fighting for a better world.

community-based brand builds loyalty not by driving sales transactions but by helping people meet their needs. Contrary to marketers' assumptions, however, the needs that brand communities can satisfy are not just about gaining status or trying on a new identity through brand affiliation. People participate in communities for a wide variety of reasons—to find emotional support and encouragement, to explore ways to contribute to the greater good, and to cultivate interests and skills, to name a few. For members, brand communities are a means to an end, not an end in themselves.

Outdoorseiten offers an extreme example of how the needs of a community can actually give rise to a brand. The European website outdoorseiten.net originated as a venue where hiking and camping enthusiasts could exchange information about their shared lifestyle: Where is a good place to hike with children? Which shoes are best for rocky terrain? Members collaborated in order to gain access to the resources and skills they needed to accomplish their goals. Eventually, the community created its own Outdoorseiten brand of tents and backpacks. The community's brand grew not from a need to express a shared identity but from a desire to meet members' specialized needs.

Often, people are more interested in the social links that come from brand affiliations than they are in the brands themselves. They join communities to build new relationships. Facebook provides a straightforward example, but country clubs and churches reveal similar dynamics. "Third place" brands such as Gold's Gym and Starbucks tap into this by providing bricks-and-mortar venues that foster interaction. In such instances, brand loyalty is the reward for meeting people's needs for community, not the impetus for the community to form.

Robust communities are built not on brand reputation but on an understanding of members' lives. Pepperidge Farm learned this lesson when its initial community effort—a website stocked with Goldfish-branded kids games—met with little success. Taking a step back from its brand-centric execution to identify areas where kids and parents really needed help, the Goldfish team uncovered alarming statistics about depression and low self-esteem among children. Partnering with psychologist Karen Reivich of the Positive Psychology Center at the University of Pennsylvania, managers recently launched an online community, fishfulthinking.com, that repackages academic research about failure, frustration, hopefulness, and emotional awareness into learning activities and discussion tools designed to help parents develop resiliency in their kids. Putting the brand second is tough for a marketer to do, but it's essential if a strong community is the goal.

Myth #3

Build the brand, and the community will follow.

The Reality

Engineer the community, and the brand will be strong.

Strategy consultancy Jump Associates has identified three basic forms of community affiliation: pools, webs, and hubs (see the exhibit "Three forms of community affiliation"). Effective community strategies combine all three in a mutually reinforcing system.

Members of *pools* are united by shared goals or values (think Republicans, Democrats, or Apple devotees). Decades of brand management theory have schooled managers in a pool-based approach to brand building: Identify and consistently communicate a clear set of values that emotionally connect consumers with the brand. Unfortunately, pools deliver only limited community benefits—people share a set of abstract beliefs but build few interpersonal relationships. Further, the common meaning that holds members together often becomes diluted if the brand attempts to grow. Unless the affiliation to a brand idea is supplemented with human connections, community members are at risk of dropping out. The solution lies in using webs and hubs to strengthen and expand the community.

Web affiliations are based on strong one-to-one connections (think social networking sites or the Cancer Survivors Network). Webs are the strongest and most stable form of community because the people in them are bound by many and varied relationships. The Harley-Davidson Museum, for example, builds webs of interpersonal connections through features such as walls around the campus decorated with large, custom-inscribed stainless-steel rivets commissioned by individuals or groups. As museum visitors read the inscriptions on the rivets, they reflect on the stories and people

Three forms of community affiliation

People have strong associations with a shared activity or goal, or shared values, and loose associations with one another.

The shared activity, goal, or values are the key to this community affiliation.

Examples:

- Apple enthusiasts
- Republicans or Democrats
- Ironman triathletes

People have strong one-to-one relationships with others who have similar or complementary needs.

Personal relationships are the key to this community affiliation.

Examples:

- Facebook
- Cancer Survivors Network
- Hash House Harriers

People have strong connections to a central figure and weaker associations with one another

A charismatic figure is the key to this community affiliation.

Examples:

- Deepak Chopra
- Hannah Montana
- Oprah

behind them. People who meet at the rivet walls soon find themselves comparing interesting inscriptions, and before long they're engaged in conversation, planning to stay in touch and perhaps even share a ride someday. Through rivet walls and other means of fostering interpersonal connections, the museum strengthens the Harley-Davidson brand pool by building webs within it.

Members of *hubs* are united by their admiration of an individual (think Deepak Chopra or Hannah Montana). The hub is a strong albeit unstable form of community that often breaks apart once the central figure is no longer present. But hubs can help communities acquire new members who hold similar values. Harley Davidson, for instance, built a bridge to a younger audience through its association with professional skateboarder and Harley enthusiast Heath Kirchart. Hubs can also be used to create or strengthen a brand pool, a strategy Nike has used since its inception by associating with stars such as Michael Jordan and Tiger Woods. To build stable communities, hub connections must be bonded to the community through webs. With its Nike+ online community, which cultivates peer-to-peer support and interaction by encouraging members to challenge and trash-talk one another, Nike has found a brand-appropriate way of creating webs to strengthen its pool and hubs.

Myth #4

Brand communities should be love-fests for faithful brand advocates.

The Reality

Smart companies embrace the conflicts that make communities thrive.

Most companies prefer to avoid conflict. But communities are inherently political, and conflict is the norm. "In" groups need "out" groups against which to define themselves. PlayStation gamers dismiss Xbox. Apple enthusiasts hate Microsoft and Dell. Dunkin'

Donuts coffee drinkers shun Starbucks. Dividing lines are fundamental even within communities, where perceived degrees of passion and loyalty separate the hard-core fans from the poseurs. Community is all about rivalries and lines drawn in the sand.

Dove's much-lauded "Campaign for Real Beauty" offers a vivid example of how companies can use conflict to their advantage. The campaign brought "real women" together worldwide to stand up against industry-imposed beauty ideals. Older women, large women, skinny women, and less-than-pretty women united in camaraderie against a common foe. Dove identified a latent "out" group and claimed it for its brand.

Firms can reinforce rivalries directly or engage others to fan the flames. Pepsi, renowned for taking on rival Coca-Cola in the orginal Pepsi Challenge, is now running advertising starring lackluster Coke drinkers in dingy retirement homes. Apple's PC-versus-Mac ads sparked not only Microsoft's "I am a PC" countercampaign but also a host of You Tube parodies from both camps. A group's unity is strengthened when such conflicts and contrasts are brought to the fore.

Some companies make the mistake of attempting to smooth things over. Porsche's 2002 launch of the Cayenne SUV provides an instructive case in point. Owners of 911 models refused to accept the Cayenne as a "real" Porsche. They argued that it did not have the requisite racing heritage and painted Cayenne drivers as soccer moms who did not and could not understand the brand. Die-hard Porsche owners even banned Cayenne owners from rennlist.com, a site that started as a discussion board for Porsche enthusiasts and has grown to include pages devoted to Audi, BMW, and Lamborghini. The company attempted to mend the rift through a television campaign, complete with roaring engines at a metaphorical starting gate, aimed at demonstrating that the Cayenne was a genuine member of the Porsche family. The entrenched community was not convinced. Positioning the Cayenne as a race car was "a stretch that only delusional Porsche marketers could possibly attempt—and a flat-out insult to every great Porsche sports car that has come before it," one person wrote on autoextremist.com. Smart managers know that singing around the campfire will not force warring tribes to unite. Communities become stronger by highlighting, not erasing, the boundaries that define them.

Myth #5

Opinion leaders build strong communities.

The Reality

Communities are strongest when everyone plays a role.

Opinion leaders and evangelists play important and well-documented roles in social networks. They spread information, influence decisions, and help new ideas gain traction. But whereas focusing on opinion leaders may be sage advice for buzz campaigns, it is a misguided approach to community building. Robust communities establish cultural bedrock by enabling every-one to play a valuable role.

From our examination of research on communities including the Red Hat Society, Burning Man, Trekkies, and MGB car clubs, we have identified 18 social and cultural roles critical to community function, preservation, and evolution (see the exhibit "Common community roles"). These include performers, supporters, mentors, learners, heroes, talent scouts, and historians, to name a few. In complementary research, Hope Schau of the University of Arizona and Eric Arnould of the University of Wyoming have documented 11 value-creation practices among community members, including evangelizing, customizing, welcoming, badging, competing, and empathizing. Companies with existing communities can evaluate the roles and behaviors currently being demonstrated and identify gaps that could be filled to improve community function. Those designing new communities can create structures and support systems to ensure the availability of a wide range of roles.

Recognizing that life changes often prompt people to reevaluate their affiliations, successful communities give members opportunities to take on new roles, alternate between roles, and negotiate

Common community roles

Members of strong brand communities stay involved and add value by playing a wide variety of roles. In designing a new community or strengthening an existing one, companies should incorporate an assortment of roles into the community structure and help members take on new roles as their needs change. Below are 18 roles critical to a community's function, preservation, and evolution.

Mentor: Teaches others and shares expertise
Learner: Enjoys learning and seeks self-improvement
Back-up: Acts as a safety net for others when they try new things
Partner: Encourages, shares, and motivates
Storyteller: Spreads the community's story throughout the group
Historian: Preserves community memory; codifies rituals and rites
Hero: Acts as a role model within the community
Celebrity: Serves as a figurehead or icon of what the community represents
Decision Maker: Makes choices affecting the community's structure and function
Provider: Hosts and takes care of other members
Greeter: Welcomes new members into the community
Guide: Helps new members navigate the culture
Catalyst: Introduces members to new people and ideas
Performer: Takes the spotlight
Supporter: Participates passively as an audience for others
Ambassador: Promotes the community to outsiders
Accountant: Keeps track of people's participation
Talent Scout: Recruits new members

tensions across roles in conflict—without ever leaving the fold. Nonprofit communities are particularly good in this respect. Saddleback Church of Orange County, California, maintains a cohesive community despite membership of over 20,000 by constantly monitoring individuals' needs and creating subgroups and roles to keep people engaged. Groups are organized not only by age, gender, and interests, but also by shared challenges, social commitments, and family situations. People are offered many types of roles, from active to passive, in small groups and large, and can participate in person, by phone, or online. Assorted print and digital tools help people identify options and map opportunities, so they can easily change roles or try on new ones.

Myth #6

Online social networks are the key to a community strategy.

The Reality

Online networks are just one tool, not a community strategy.

Forming an online community is often a knee-jerk reaction to the CEO's demand for a Web 2.0 strategy. Online social networks get lots of buzz, and given today's enabling technologies it seems silly to pass up opportunities in the virtual world. Unfortunately, most company-sponsored online "communities" are nothing more than far-flung focus groups established in the hope that consumers will bond around the virtual suggestion box. There's nothing wrong with listening to customers, but this isn't a community strategy.

Online social networks can serve valuable community functions. They help people find rich solutions to ambiguous problems and serendipitous connections to people and ideas. Yet even a well-crafted networking site has limitations. The anonymity of web encounters often emboldens antisocial behavior, and the shallow, transient nature of many online interactions results in weak social bonds. And, lest we forget, a huge chunk of life still takes place offline. Physical spaces play important roles in fostering community connections. According to Mark Rosenbaum of Northern Illinois University, communities that are developed in third places like gyms and coffee shops often provide social and emotional support equal to or stronger than family ties—a benefit that delivers price premiums of up to 20%.

Smart marketers use online tools selectively to support community needs. L'Oréal strikes the right balance with its methodical approach. The company maps its brands along two dimensions: (1)

brands of authority versus brands of conversation, and (2) mainstream versus niche brands. Each cell in the grid suggests a different community approach. Brands of authority offer expert affiliation and advice. L'Oréal (the company's mainstream brand of authority) builds community through heavy TV advertising featuring celebrity spokespeople to inspire hub affiliations. La Roche-Posay (a niche brand of authority) nurtures a worldwide community of dermatologists, both online and face-to-face, to expertly represent the brand. Brands of conversation thrive on social interaction and engagement. L'Oréal's Garnier (the company's mainstream brand of conversation) enlists well-known bloggers to share what they're doing to make the world a better place, using these hub figures to strengthen the brand's pool. Kiehl's (a niche brand of conversation) uses a grassroots focus on local charity sponsorships, in-store customer bulletin boards, and required employee volunteerism in the surrounding community to create the social glue. Although the tactics vary, the goal of L'Oréal's community-building strategies is always to connect with the people who make up the community in ways that reaffirm the essence of the brand.

Myth #7

Successful brand communities are tightly managed and controlled.

The Reality

Of and by the people, communities defy managerial control.

Excessive control has been the norm when it comes to community management. From Coca-Cola's pulling of its beloved soda off the shelves in 1985, to Microsoft's stifling of internal blogger Robert Scoble, to Hasbro's suing of fans for publishing content based on its brands, community managers tend to put corporate interests over those of their customers.

Such efforts have led to vigorous debate about how much control to assert over brand communities. That is the wrong question. Brand communities are not corporate assets, so control is an illusion. But relinquishing control does not mean abdicating responsibility. Effective brand stewards participate as community cocreators—nurturing and facilitating communities by creating the conditions in which they can thrive.

Vans, the famed maker of skateboarding shoes, has proved adept at building community through support rather than control. From the beginning, the company recognized its fan base of customers as the owners of its brand. Its self-appointed role was to stay close enough to the fans to understand where they were headed and then pursue the directions that would strengthen the community. From its earliest days, Vans worked with lead users within each of its sports communities to codesign new products. When privately owned skate parks began closing, Vans took care of enthusiasts by opening its own. Vans originally sponsored the Warped Tour, a traveling music festival appealing to young adults, as a way to support its customers' love of music. Later, realizing that amateur skateboarders were lacking a national championship event, Vans persuaded Warped Tour organizers to add one to their lineup and then acquired the Tour outright once it became a major celebration of skateboarding and bicycle motocross (BMX) culture. Warped Tour innovations now include air-conditioned "parental day care" lounges at tour stops to make it easier for young fans to attend, and an online community that supports year-round connections among fans and helps far-flung friends coordinate tour attendance.

Companies build effective communities through a design philosophy that replaces control with a balance of structure and flexibility. Jump Associates has identified nine archetypal community scripts that can be used as a framework for such design (see the exhibit "A sampling of community scripts"). A script is a set of expected behaviors in a particular social situation. Think, for example, of the script you'd follow for a date at a fancy restaurant or a job interview in a CEO's office. Harley-Davidson offers a leading example of how to use scripts to build and enhance community. The Harley-Davidson brand ethos of the "brotherhood" is grounded in the script of the Tribe, in which deep social connections form through shared experiences and traditions. Management first reinforced this script

A sampling of community scripts

A script suggests a set of behaviors that are appropriate for a particular situation. Companies can design brand communities by establishing and reinforcing a base script and then layering on new scripts over time. Vans, a maker of skateboarding shoes, initially sold its products to tight-knit surfer and skateboarding communities. Building direct relationships with these groups and cultivating lead users within them reinforced an implicit Tribe script. By sponsoring competitions and skate parks, Vans introduced the Performance Space script. And through skateboarding clinics and demonstrations, the company added features of the Sewing Circle.

The Tribe
A group with deep interpersonal connections built through shared experiences, rituals, and traditions.

The Fort
An exclusive place for insiders to be safe and feel protected.

The Sewing Circle
A gathering at which people with common interests share experiences, provide support, and socialize.

The Patio
A semiprivate place that facilitates in-depth, meaningful connections.

The Bar
A public space that grants reliable although shallow connections.

The Tour Group
A way to participate in new experiences while staying inside a comfort zone.

The Performance Space
A place where members can be sure of finding an audience for their talents.

The Barn Raising
An effective way to accomplish tasks while socializing.

The Summer Camp
A periodic experience that reaffirms connections.

to strengthen community identity and then gradually introduced elements of new scripts to enrich the experience over time. The Harley Owners Group introduced elements of the Fort (an exclusive place where insiders feel protected) through members-only events and special perks. Rallies and other recurring customer gatherings added the Summer Camp (a periodic experience that reaffirms connections). Both the Harley-Davidson Museum and dealerships were designed to leverage elements of the Patio (a semiprivate place that facilitates in-depth, meaningful connections) and the Bar (a public space that grants reliable but shallow connections) to foster different types of interpersonal connections. By layering those additional scripts over the Tribe foundation, Harley-Davidson was able to build multiple community experiences that appealed to different audiences while retaining a cohesive core.

Whether through constructive engagement, script-based design, or other means, smart companies define the terms of their community participation but discard their illusions of control.

Are You Ready?

Although any brand can benefit from a community strategy, not every company can pull it off. Executing community requires an organization-wide commitment and a willingness to work across functional boundaries. It takes the boldness to reexamine everything from company values to organizational design. And it takes the fortitude to meet people on their own terms, cede control, and accept conflict as part of the package. Is your organization up to the task? To find out, take our online "Community Readiness Audit" by visiting http://hbr.org/2009/04/getting-brand-communities-right/ar/1#.

Community is a potent strategy if it is approached with the right mind-set and skills. A strong brand community increases customer loyalty, lowers marketing costs, authenticates brand meanings, and yields an influx of ideas to grow the business. Through commitment, engagement, and support, companies can cultivate brand communities that deliver powerful returns. When you get community right, the benefits are irrefutable.

Originally published in April 2009. Reprint R0904K

The One Number You Need to Grow

by Frederick F. Reichheld

THE CEOS IN THE room knew all about the power of loyalty. They had already transformed their companies into industry leaders, largely by building intensely loyal relationships with customers and employees. Now the chief executives—from Vanguard, Chick-fil-A, State Farm, and a half-dozen other leading companies—had gathered at a daylong forum to swap insights that would help them further enhance their loyalty efforts. And what they were hearing from Andy Taylor, the CEO of Enterprise Rent-A-Car, was riveting.

Taylor and his senior team had figured out a way to measure and manage customer loyalty without the complexity of traditional customer surveys. Every month, Enterprise polled its customers using just two simple questions, one about the quality of their rental experience and the other about the likelihood that they would rent from the company again. Because the process was so simple, it was fast. That allowed the company to publish ranked results for its 5,000 U.S. branches within days, giving the offices real-time feedback on how they were doing and the opportunity to learn from successful peers.

The survey was different in another important way. In ranking the branches, the company counted only the customers who gave the experience the highest possible rating. That narrow focus on enthusiastic customers surprised the CEOs in the room. Hands shot up. What about the rest of Enterprise's customers, the marginally satisfied who continued to rent from Enterprise and were necessary to its business? Wouldn't it be better to track, in a more sophisticated way, mean or median statistics? No, Taylor said. By concentrating solely on those most enthusiastic about their rental experience, the company could focus on a key driver of profitable growth: customers who not only return to rent again but also recommend Enterprise to their friends.

Enterprise's approach surprised me, too. Most customer satisfaction surveys aren't very useful. They tend to be long and complicated, yielding low response rates and ambiguous implications that are difficult for operating managers to act on. Furthermore, they are rarely challenged or audited because most senior executives, board members, and investors don't take them very seriously. That's because their results don't correlate tightly with profits or growth.

But Enterprise's method—and its ability to generate profitable growth through what appeared to be quite a simple tool—got me thinking that the company might be on to something. Could you get similar results in other industries—including those seemingly more complex than car rentals—by focusing only on customers who provided the most enthusiastic responses to a short list of questions designed to assess their loyalty to a company? Could the list be reduced to a single question? If so, what would that question be?

It took me two years of research to figure that out, research that linked survey responses with actual customer behavior—purchasing patterns and referrals—and ultimately with company growth. The results were clear yet counterintuitive. It turned out that a single survey question can, in fact, serve as a useful predictor of growth. But that question isn't about customer satisfaction or even loyalty—at least in so many words. Rather, it's about customers' willingness to recommend a product or service to someone else. In fact, in most of the industries that I studied, the percentage of customers who were enthusiastic enough to refer a friend or colleague—perhaps the strongest sign of customer loyalty—correlated directly with differences in growth rates among competitors.

The Idea in Brief

Many companies—striving for unprecedented growth by cultivating intensely loyal customers—invest lots of time and money measuring customer satisfaction. But most of the yardsticks they use are complex, yield ambiguous results, and don't necessarily correlate to profits or growth.

The good news is: you don't need expensive surveys and complex statistical models. You only have to ask your customers one question: "How likely is it that you would recommend our company to a friend or colleague?" The more "promoters" your company has, the bigger its growth.

Why is willingness to promote your company such a strong indicator of loyalty—and growth? Because when customers recommend you, they're putting *their* reputations on the line. And they'll take that risk only if they're intensely loyal.

By asking this one question, you collect simple and timely data that correlate with growth. You also get responses you can easily interpret and communicate. Your message to employees—"Get more promoters and fewer detractors"—becomes clear-cut, actionable, and motivating, especially when tied to incentives.

Certainly, other factors besides customer loyalty play a role in driving a company's growth—economic or industry expansion, innovation, and so on. And I don't want to overstate the findings: Although the "would recommend" question generally proved to be the most effective in determining loyalty and predicting growth, that wasn't the case in every single industry. But evangelistic customer loyalty is clearly one of the most important drivers of growth. While it doesn't guarantee growth, in general profitable growth can't be achieved without it.

Furthermore, these findings point to an entirely new approach to customer surveys, one based on simplicity that directly links to a company's results. By substituting a single question—blunt tool though it may appear to be—for the complex black box of the typical customer satisfaction survey, companies can actually put consumer survey results to use and focus employees on the task of stimulating growth.

The Idea in Practice

Calculating Your Net-promoter Score

Asking a statistically valid sample of customers "How likely is it that you would recommend our company to a friend or colleague?" enables you to calculate your **Net-Promoter Score:** the ratio of promoters to detractors.

Based on their responses on a 0 to 10 rating scale, group your customers into "promoters" (9–10 rating—extremely likely to recommend), "passively satisfied" (7–8 rating), and "detractors" (0–6 rating—extremely unlikely to recommend). Then subtract the percentage of detractors from the percentage of promoters. Companies that garner world-class loyalty receive net-promoter scores of 75% to more than 80%.

Using Your Net-promoter Score

Your net-promoter score provides valuable insights into how to get more promoters and fewer detractors. For example, compare your company's scores region to region, branch to branch, sales rep to sales rep, and customer segment to customer segment. Uncover root causes of differences and share best practices from your highest-scoring groups. Also survey your *competitors'* customers using the same method. How does your company stack up against the very high bar of 75% to 80% net-promoter score?

Motivating Change

Use your score to send a clear message to managers and employees about the importance

Loyalty and Growth

Before I describe my research and the results from a number of industries, let's briefly look at the concept of loyalty and some of the mistakes companies make when trying to measure it. First, a definition. Loyalty is the willingness of someone—a customer, an employee, a friend—to make an investment or personal sacrifice in order to strengthen a relationship. For a customer, that can mean sticking with a supplier who treats him well and gives him good value in the long term even if the supplier does not offer the best price in a particular transaction.

Consequently, customer loyalty is about much more than repeat purchases. Indeed, even someone who buys again and again from the same company may not necessarily be loyal to that company but

of promoters—and the dangers of detractors. Consider these guidelines:

- Be sure that everyone in the company knows which customers they're responsible for. Then ensure that all business functions—not just market research—own and accept the survey process and results.
- Make your scores transparent throughout your organization. Present employees with numbers from a previous week (or day) showing the percentages (and names) of customers who are promoters, passively satisfied, and detractors.

  Then issue the managerial charge: "We need more promoters and fewer detractors in order to grow." Explain the dangers of detractors: if your new-customer flow can't keep up with leaks in your customer bucket, marketing costs will mount and cash flow decline.
- Create a sense of urgency by tying rewards to score improvement—giving customers, in essence, veto power over raises and promotions.

  Example: By making field managers ineligible for promotion unless their branch or group of branches matches or exceeds the company's average net-promoter scores, Enterprise Rent-A-Car has seen its survey scores rise—and its growth increase relative to its rivals.

instead may be trapped by inertia, indifference, or exit barriers erected by the company or circumstance. (Someone may regularly take the same airline to a city only because it offers the most flights there.) Conversely, a loyal customer may not make frequent repeat purchases because of a reduced need for a product or service. (Someone may buy a new car less often as he gets older and drives less.)

True loyalty clearly affects profitability. While regular customers aren't always profitable, their choice to stick with a product or service typically reduces a company's customer acquisition costs. Loyalty also drives top-line growth. Obviously, no company can grow if its customer bucket is leaky, and loyalty helps eliminate this outflow. Indeed, loyal customers can raise the water level in the bucket: Customers who are truly loyal tend to buy more over time, as their incomes grow or they devote a larger share of their wallets to a company they feel good about.

And loyal customers talk up a company to their friends, family, and colleagues. In fact, such a recommendation is one of the best indicators of loyalty because of the customer's sacrifice, if you will, in making the recommendation. When customers act as references, they do more than indicate that they've received good economic value from a company; they put their own reputations on the line. And they will risk their reputations only if they feel intense loyalty. (Note that here, too, loyalty may have little to do with repeat purchases. As someone's income increases, she may move up the automotive ladder from the Hondas she has bought for years. But if she is loyal to the company, she will enthusiastically recommend a Honda to, say, a nephew who is buying his first car.)

The tendency of loyal customers to bring in new customers—at no charge to the company—is particularly beneficial as a company grows, especially if it operates in a mature industry. In such a case, the tremendous marketing costs of acquiring each new customer through advertising and other promotions make it hard to grow profitably. In fact, the only path to profitable growth may lie in a company's ability to get its loyal customers to become, in effect, its marketing department.

The Wrong Yardsticks

Because loyalty is so important to profitable growth, measuring and managing it make good sense. Unfortunately, existing approaches haven't proved very effective. Not only does their complexity make them practically useless to line managers, but they also often yield flawed results.

The best companies have tended to focus on customer retention rates, but that measurement is merely the best of a mediocre lot. Retention rates provide, in many industries, a valuable link to profitability, but their relationship to growth is tenuous. That's because they basically track customer defections—the degree to which a bucket is emptying rather filling up. Furthermore, as I have noted, retention rates are a poor indication of customer loyalty in situations where customers are held hostage by high switching costs or other barriers, or where customers naturally outgrow a product because of their aging, increased income, or other factors. You'd want a stronger connection between retention and growth before you went ahead and invested significant money based only on data about retention.

An even less reliable means of gauging loyalty is through conventional customer-satisfaction measures. Our research indicates that satisfaction lacks a consistently demonstrable connection to actual customer behavior and growth. This finding is borne out by the short shrift that investors give to such reports as the American Consumer Satisfaction Index. The ACSI, published quarterly in the *Wall Street Journal,* reflects the customer satisfaction ratings of some 200 U.S. companies. In general, it is difficult to discern a strong correlation between high customer satisfaction scores and outstanding sales growth. Indeed, in some cases, there is an inverse relationship; at Kmart, for example, a significant increase in the company's ACSI rating was accompanied by a sharp decrease in sales as it slid into bankruptcy.

Even the most sophisticated satisfaction measurement systems have serious flaws. I saw this firsthand at one of the Big Three car manufacturers. The marketing executive at the company wanted to understand why, after the firm had spent millions of dollars on customer satisfaction surveys, satisfaction ratings for individual dealers did not relate very closely to dealer profits or growth. When I interviewed dealers, they agreed that customer satisfaction seemed like a reasonable goal. But they also pointed out that other factors were far more important to their profits and growth, such as keeping pressure on salespeople to close a high percentage of leads, filling showrooms with prospects through aggressive advertising, and charging customers the highest possible price for a car.

In most cases, dealers told me, the satisfaction survey is a charade that they play along with to remain in the good graces of the manufacturer and to ensure generous allocations of the hottest-selling models. The pressure they put on salespeople to boost scores often results in postsale pleading with customers to provide top ratings—even if they must offer something like free floor mats or oil changes in return. Dealers are usually complicit with salespeople in this process, a circumstance that further degrades the integrity of these scores. Indeed, some savvy customers negotiate a low price—and then offer to sell the dealer a set of top satisfaction survey ratings for another $500 off the price.

Figuring out a way to accurately measure customer loyalty and satisfaction is extremely important. Companies won't realize the fruits of loyalty until usable measurement systems enable firms to measure their performance against clear loyalty goals—just as they now do in the case of profitability and quality goals. For a while, it seemed as though information technology would provide a means to accurately measure loyalty. Sophisticated customer-relationship-management systems promised to help firms track customer behavior in real time. But the successes thus far have been limited to select industries, such as credit cards or grocery stores, where purchases are so frequent that changes in customer loyalty can be quickly spotted and acted on.

Getting the Facts

So what would be a useful metric for gauging customer loyalty? To find out, I needed to do something rarely undertaken with customer surveys: Match survey responses from individual customers to their actual behavior—repeat purchases and referral patterns—over time. I sought the assistance of Satmetrix, a company that develops software to gather and analyze real-time customer feedback—and on whose board of directors I serve. Teams from Bain also helped with the project.

We started with the roughly 20 questions on the Loyalty Acid Test, a survey that I designed four years ago with Bain colleagues, which does a pretty good job of establishing the state of relations between a company and its customers. (The complete test can be found at http://www.loyaltyrules.com/loyaltyrules/acid_test_customer.html.) We administered the test to thousands of customers recruited from public lists in six industries: financial services, cable and telephony, personal computers, e-commerce, auto insurance, and Internet service providers.

We then obtained a purchase history for each person surveyed and asked those people to name specific instances in which they had referred someone else to the company in question. When this information wasn't immediately available, we waited six to 12 months and gathered information on subsequent purchases and referrals from those individuals. With information from more than 4,000 customers, we were able to build 14 case studies—that is, cases in which we had sufficient sample sizes to measure the link between survey responses of individual customers of a company and those individuals' actual referral and purchase behavior.

The data allowed us to determine which survey questions had the strongest statistical correlation with repeat purchases or referrals. We hoped that we would find at least one question for each industry that effectively predicted such behaviors, which can drive growth. We found something more: One question was best for *most* industries. "How likely is it that you would recommend [company X] to a friend or colleague?" ranked first or second in 11 of the 14 cases studies. And in two of the three other cases, "would recommend" ranked so close behind the top two predictors that the surveys would be nearly as accurate by relying on results of this single question. (For a ranking of the best-scoring questions, see the sidebar "Ask the Right Question.")

These findings surprised me. My personal bet for the top question (probably reflecting the focus of my research on employee loyalty in recent years) would have been "How strongly do you agree that [company X] deserves your loyalty?" Clearly, though, the abstract concept of loyalty was less compelling to customers than what may be the ultimate act of loyalty, a recommendation to a friend. I also expected that "How strongly do you agree that [company X] sets the standard for excellence in its industry?"—with its implications of offering customers both economic benefit and fair treatment—would prove more predictive than it did. One result did not startle me at all. The question "How satisfied are you with [company X's] overall

Ask the Right Question

AS PART OF OUR RESEARCH into customer loyalty and growth, my colleagues and I looked for a correlation between survey responses and actual behavior—repeat purchases, or recommendations to friends and peers—that would ultimately lead to profitable growth. Based on information from 4,000 consumers, we ranked a variety of survey questions according to their ability to predict this desirable behavior. (Interestingly, creating a weighted index—based on the responses to multiple questions and taking into account the relative effectiveness of those questions—provided insignificant predictive advantage.)

The top-ranking question was far and away the most effective across industries:

- How likely is it that you would recommend [company X] to a friend or colleague?

Two questions were effective predictors in certain industries:

- How strongly do you agree that [company X] deserves your loyalty?
- How likely is it that you will continue to purchase products/services from [company X]?

Other questions, while useful in a particular industry, had little general applicability:

- How strongly do you agree that [company X] sets the standard for excellence in its industry?
- How strongly do you agree that [company X] makes it easy for you to do business with it?
- If you were selecting a similar provider for the first time, how likely is it that you would you choose [company X]?
- How strongly do you agree that [company X] creates innovative solutions that make your life easier?
- How satisfied are you with [company X's] overall performance?

performance?" while relevant in certain industries, would prove to be a relatively weak predictor of growth.

So my colleagues and I had the right question—"How likely is it that you would recommend [company X] to a friend or colleague?"—and now we needed to develop a scale to score the responses. This may seem somewhat trivial, but, as statisticians know, it's not. Making customer loyalty a strategic goal that managers can work toward requires a scale as simple and unambiguous as the question itself. The right one will effectively divide customers into practical groups deserving different attention and organizational responses. It must be intuitive to customers when they assign grades and to employees and partners responsible for interpreting the results and taking action. Ideally, the scale would be so easy to understand that even outsiders, such as investors, regulators, and journalists, would grasp the basic messages without needing a handbook and a statistical abstract.

For these reasons, we settled on a scale where ten means "extremely likely" to recommend, five means neutral, and zero means "not at all likely." When we examined customer referral and repurchase behaviors along this scale, we found three logical clusters. "Promoters," the customers with the highest rates of repurchase and referral, gave ratings of nine or ten to the question. The "passively satisfied" logged a seven or an eight, and "detractors" scored from zero to six.

By limiting the promoter designation to only the most enthusiastic customers, we avoided the "grade inflation" that often infects traditional customer-satisfaction assessments, in which someone a molecule north of neutral is considered "satisfied." (This was the danger that Enterprise Rent-A-Car avoided when it decided to focus on its most enthusiastic customers.) And not only did clustering customers into three categories—promoters, the passively satisfied, and detractors—turn out to provide the simplest, most intuitive, and best predictor of customer behavior; it also made sense to frontline managers, who could relate to the goal of increasing the number of promoters and reducing the number of detractors more readily than increasing the mean of their satisfaction index by one standard deviation.

The Growth Connection

All of our analysis to this point had focused on customer survey responses and how well those linked to customers' referral and repurchase behavior at 14 companies in six industries. But the real test

Growth by Word of Mouth

RESEARCH SHOWS THAT, in most industries, there is a strong correlation between a company's growth rate and the percentage of its customers who are "promoters"—that is, those who say they are extremely likely to recommend the company to a friend or colleague. (The net-promoter figure is calculated by subtracting the percentage of customers who say they are unlikely to make a recommendation from the percentage who say they are extremely likely to do so.) It's worth noting that the size of companies has no relationship to their net-promoter status.

Airlines

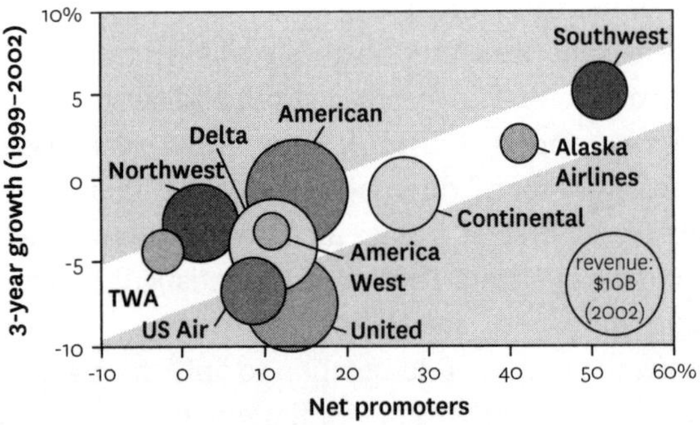

would be how well this approach explained relative growth rates for all competitors in an industry—and across a broader range of industry sectors.

In the first quarter of 2001, Satmetrix began tracking the "would recommend" scores of a new universe of customers, many thousands of them from more than 400 companies in more than a dozen industries. In each subsequent quarter, they then gathered 10,000 to 15,000 responses to a very brief e-mail survey that asked respondents (drawn again from public sources, not Satmetrix's internal client customer lists) to rate one or two companies with which they

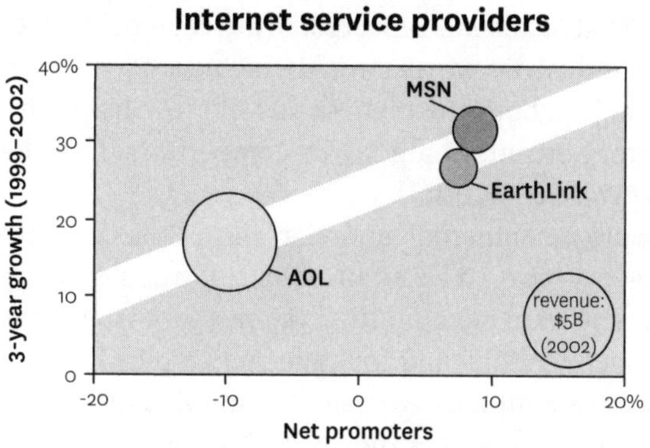

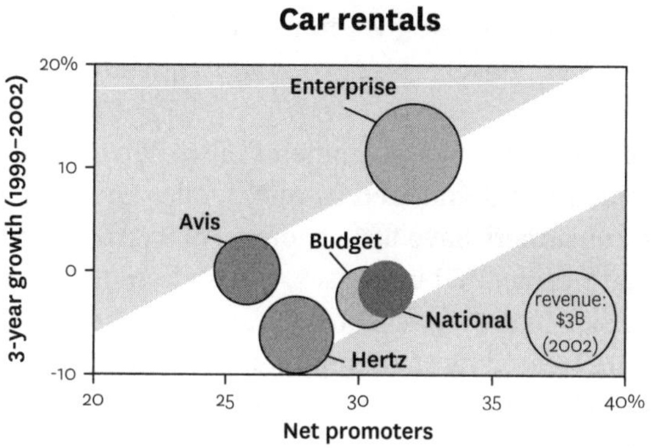

were familiar. Where we could obtain comparable and reliable revenue-growth data for a range of competitors, and where there were sufficient consumer responses, we plotted each firm's net promoters—the percentage of promoters minus the percentage of detractors—against the company's revenue growth rate.

The results were striking. In airlines, for example, a strong correlation existed between net-promoter figures and a company's average growth rate over the three-year period from 1999 to 2002. Remarkably, this one simple statistic seemed to explain the relative growth rates across the entire industry; that is, no airline has found a way to increase growth without improving its ratio of promoters to detractors. That result was reflected, to a greater or lesser degree, in most of the industries we examined—including rental cars, where Enterprise enjoys both the highest rate of growth and the highest net-promoter percentage among its competitors. (See the exhibit "Growth by Word of Mouth.")

The "would recommend" question wasn't the best predictor of growth in every case. In a few situations, it was simply irrelevant. In database software or computer systems, for instance, senior executives select vendors, and top managers typically didn't appear on the public e-mail lists we used to sample customers. Asking users of the system whether they would recommend the system to a friend or colleague seemed a little abstract, as they had no choice in the matter. In these cases, we found that the "sets the standard of excellence" or "deserves your loyalty" questions were more predictive.

Not surprisingly, "would recommend" also didn't predict relative growth in industries dominated by monopolies and near monopolies, where consumers have little choice. For example, in the local telephone and cable TV businesses, population growth and economic expansion in the region determine growth rates, not how well customers are treated by their suppliers. And in certain cases, we found small niche companies that were growing faster than their net-promoter percentages would imply. But for most companies in most industries, getting customers enthusiastic enough to recommend a company appears to be crucial to growth. (To calculate your own net-promoter number, see the sidebar "A Net-Promoter Primer.")

The Dangers of Detractors

The battle for growth among Internet service providers AOL, MSN, and EarthLink brings to life our findings. For years, market leader AOL aggressively focused on new customer acquisition. Through those efforts, AOL more than offset a substantial number of defections. But the company paid much less attention to converting these new customers into intensely loyal promoters. Customer service lapsed, to the point where customers couldn't even find a phone number to contact company representatives to answer questions or resolve problems.

Today, AOL is struggling to grow. Even though AOL's customer count surged to an eventual peak of 35 million, its deteriorating mix of promoters and detractors eventually choked off expansion. The fire hose of new customer flow—filled with people attracted to free trial promotions—couldn't keep up with the leaks in AOL's customer bucket. Defection rates exceeded 200,000 customers per month in 2003. Marketing costs were ratcheted up to stem the tide, and those expenditures, along with the collapse of online advertising, contributed to declines in cash flow of almost 40% between 2001 and 2003.

By 2002, our research found, 42% of the company's customers were detractors, while only 32% were promoters, giving the company a net-promoter percentage of $$$-10%. The current management team is working on the problem, but it's a challenging one because disappointed customers are undoubtedly spreading their opinions about AOL to family, friends, colleagues, and acquaintances.

AOL's dial-up competitors have done a better job in building promoters, and it shows in their relative rates of growth. MSN invested $500 million in R&D to upgrade its service with functional improvements such as improved parental controls and spam filters. By 2003, MSN's promoter population reached 41% of its customer base, compared with a detractor population of 32%, giving the company a net-promoter percentage of 9%. EarthLink managed to nearly match MSN's net-promoter score over this period by continuing to invest in the reliability of its dial-up connections (minimizing the irritation of busy signals and dropped connections) and by making phone support readily available.

AOL's experience vividly illustrates the folly of seeking growth through shortcuts such as massive price cuts or other incentives rather than through building true loyalty. It also illustrates the detrimental effect that detractors' word-of-mouth communications can have on a business—the flip side of customers' recommendations to their friends. Countering a damaged reputation requires a company to create tremendously appealing incentives that will persuade skeptical customers to give a product or service a try, and the incentives drive up already significant customer acquisition costs.

Furthermore, detractors—and even customers who are only passively satisfied but not enthusiastically loyal—typically take a toll on employees and increase service costs. Finally, every detractor represents a missed opportunity to add a promoter to the customer population, one more unpaid salesperson to market your product or service and generate growth.

Keep It Simple

One of the main takeaways from our research is that companies can keep customer surveys simple. The most basic surveys—employing the right questions—can allow companies to report timely data that are easy to act on. Too many of today's satisfaction survey processes yield complex information that's months out of date by the time it reaches frontline managers. Good luck to the branch manager who tries to help an employee interpret a score resulting from a complex weighting algorithm based on feedback from anonymous customers, many of whom were surveyed before the employee had his current job.

Contrast that scenario with one in which a manager presents employees with numbers from the previous week (or day) showing the percentages (and names) of a branch office's customers who are promoters, passively satisfied, and detractors—and then issues the managerial charge, "We need more promoters and fewer detractors in order to grow." The goal is clear-cut, actionable, and motivating.

In short, a customer feedback program should be viewed not as "market research" but as an operating management tool. Again, consider Enterprise Rent-A-Car. The first step in the development of Enterprise's current system was to devise a way to track loyalty by measuring service quality from the customer's perspective. The initial effort yielded a long, unwieldy research questionnaire, one that included the pet questions of everyone involved in drafting the

A Net-Promoter Primer

TRACKING NET PROMOTERS—the percentage of customers who are promoters of a brand or company minus the percentage who are detractors—offers organizations a powerful way to measure and manage customer loyalty. Firms with the highest net-promoter scores consistently garner the lion's share of industry growth. So how can companies get started?

Survey a statistically valid sample of your customers with the following question: "How likely is it that you would recommend [brand or company X] to a friend or colleague?" It's critical to provide a consistent scale for responses that range from zero to ten, where zero means not at all likely, five means neutral, and ten means extremely likely.

Resist the urge to let survey questions multiply; more questions diminish response rates along with the reliability of your sample. You need only one question to determine the status—promoter, passively satisfied, or detractor—of a customer. (Follow-up questions can help unearth the reasons for customers' feelings and point to profitable remedies. But such questions should be tailored to the three categories of customers. Learning how to turn a passively satisfied customer into a promoter requires a very different line of questioning from learning how to resolve the problems of a detractor.)

Calculate the percentage of customers who respond with nine or ten (promoters) and the percentage who respond with zero through six (detractors). Subtract the percentage of detractors from the percentage of promoters to arrive at your net-promoter score. Don't be surprised if your score is lower than you expect. The median net-promoter score of more than 400 companies in 28 industries (based on some 130,000 customer survey responses gathered over the past two-plus years by Satmetrix, a maker of software for managing real-time customer feedback) was just 16%.

Compare net-promoter scores from specific regions, branches, service or sales reps, and customer segments. This often reveals root causes of differences as well as best practices that can be shared. What really counts, of course, is how your company compares with direct competitors. Have your market researchers survey your competitors' customers using the same method. You can then determine how your company stacks up within your industry and whether your current net-promoter number is a competitive asset or a liability.

Improve your score. The companies with the most enthusiastic customer referrals, including eBay, Amazon, and USAA, receive net-promoter scores of 75% to more than 80%. For companies aiming to garner world-class loyalty—and the growth that comes with it—this should be the target.

survey. It only captured average service quality on a regional basis—interesting, but useless, since managers needed to see scores for each individual branch to establish clear accountability. Over time, the sample was expanded to provide this information. And the number of questions on the survey was sharply reduced; this simplified the collating of answers and allowed the company to post monthly branch-level results almost as soon as they were collected.

The company then began examining the relationships between customer responses and actual purchases and referrals. This is when Enterprise learned the value of enthusiasts. Customers who gave the highest rating to their rental experience were three times more likely to rent again than those who gave Enterprise the second-highest grade. When a customer reported a neutral or negative experience, marking him a potential detractor, the interviewer requested permission to immediately forward this information to the branch manager, who was trained how to apologize, identify the root cause of the problem, and resolve it.

The measurement system cost more than $4 million per year, but the company made such significant progress in building customer loyalty that the company's management considers it one of the company's best investments. And the new system had definitely started to get employees' attention. In fact, a few branch managers (perhaps taking a cue from car dealers) attempted to manipulate the system to their benefit. Enterprise responded with a process for spotting—for example, by ensuring that the phone numbers of dissatisfied respondents hadn't been changed, making it difficult to follow up—and punishing "gamers."

Despite the system's success, CEO Andy Taylor felt something was missing. Branch scores were not improving quickly enough, and a big gap continued to separate the worst- and best-performing regions. Taylor's assessment: "We needed a greater sense of urgency." So the management team decided that field managers would not be eligible for promotion unless their branch or group of branches matched or exceeded the company's average scores. That's a pretty radical idea when you think about it: giving customers, in effect, veto power over managerial pay raises and promotions.

The rigorous implementation of this simple customer feedback system had a clear impact on business. As the survey scores rose, so did Enterprise's growth relative to its competition. Taylor cites the linking of customer feedback to employee rewards as one of the most important reasons that Enterprise has continued to grow, even as the business became bigger and, arguably, more mature. (For more on Enterprise's customer survey program, see "Driving Customer Satisfaction," HBR July 2002.)

Converting Customers into Promoters

If collecting and applying customer feedback is this simple, why don't companies already do it this way? I don't want to be too cynical, but perhaps the research firms that administer current customer surveys know there is very little profit margin for them in something as bare-bones as this. Complex loyalty indexes, based on a dozen or more proprietary questions and weighted with a black-box scaling function, simply generate more business for survey firms.

The market research firms have an even deeper fear. With the advent of e-mail and analytical software, leading-edge companies can now bypass the research firms entirely, cutting costs and improving the quality and timeliness of feedback. These new tools enable companies to gather customer feedback and report results in real time, funneling it directly to frontline employees and managers. This can also threaten in-house market research departments, which typically have built their power base through controlling and interpreting customer survey data. Marketing departments understandably focus surveys on the areas they can control, such as brand image, pricing, and product features. But a customer's willingness to recommend to a friend results from how well the customer is treated by frontline employees, which in turn is determined by all the functional areas that contribute to a customer's experience.

For a measure to be practical, operational, and reliable—that is, for it to determine the percentage of net promoters among customers and allow managers to act on it—the process and the results need to be owned and accepted by all of the business functions. And all the people in the organization must know which customers they are responsible for. Overseeing such a process is a more appropriate task for the CFO, or for the general manager of the business unit, than for the marketing department. Indeed, it is too important (and politically charged) to delegate to any one function.

The path to sustainable, profitable growth begins with creating more promoters and fewer detractors and making your net-promoter number transparent throughout your organization. This number is the one number you need to grow. It's that simple and that profound.

Originally published in December 2003. Reprint R0312C

Ending the War Between Sales and Marketing

by Philip Kotler, Neil Rackham, and Suj Krishnaswamy

PRODUCT DESIGNERS LEARNED YEARS ago that they'd save time and money if they consulted with their colleagues in manufacturing rather than just throwing new designs over the wall. The two functions realized it wasn't enough to just coexist—not when they could work together to create value for the company and for customers. You'd think that marketing and sales teams, whose work is also deeply interconnected, would have discovered something similar. As a rule, though, they're separate functions within an organization, and, when they do work together, they don't always get along. When sales are disappointing, Marketing blames the sales force for its poor execution of an otherwise brilliant rollout plan. The sales team, in turn, claims that Marketing sets prices too high and uses too much of the budget, which instead should go toward hiring more salespeople or paying the sales reps higher commissions. More broadly, sales departments tend to believe that marketers are out of touch with what's really going on with customers. Marketing believes the sales force is myopic—too focused on individual customer experiences, insufficiently aware of the larger market, and blind to the future. In short, each group often undervalues the other's contributions.

This lack of alignment ends up hurting corporate performance. Time and again, during research and consulting assignments, we've seen both groups stumble (and the organization suffer) because they were out of sync. Conversely, there is no question that, when Sales and Marketing work well together, companies see substantial improvement on important performance metrics: Sales cycles are shorter, market-entry costs go down, and the cost of sales is lower. That's what happened when IBM integrated its sales and marketing groups to create a new function called Channel Enablement. Before the groups were integrated, IBM senior executives Anil Menon and Dan Pelino told us, Sales and Marketing operated independent of one another. Salespeople worried only about fulfilling product demand, not creating it. Marketers failed to link advertising dollars spent to actual sales made, so Sales obviously couldn't see the value of marketing efforts. And, because the groups were poorly coordinated, Marketing's new product announcements often came at a time when Sales was not prepared to capitalize on them.

Curious about this kind of disconnect between Sales and Marketing, we conducted a study to identify best practices that could help enhance the joint performance and overall contributions of these two functions. We interviewed pairs of chief marketing officers and sales vice presidents to capture their perspectives. We looked in depth at the relationship between Sales and Marketing in a heavy equipment company, a materials company, a financial services firm, a medical systems company, an energy company, an insurance company, two high-tech electronic products companies, and an airline. Among our findings:

- The marketing function takes different forms in different companies at different product life-cycle stages—all of which can deeply affect the relationship between Sales and Marketing.
- The strains between Sales and Marketing fall into two main categories: economic and cultural.
- It's not difficult for companies to assess the quality of the working relationship between Sales and Marketing. (This article includes a diagnostic tool for doing so.)

Idea in Brief

In too many companies, Sales and Marketing feud like Capulets and Montagues. Salespeople accuse marketers of being out of touch with what customers really want or setting prices too high. Marketers insist that salespeople focus too myopically on individual customers and short-term sales at the expense of longer-term profits.

Result? Poor coordination between the two teams—which only raises market-entry costs, lengthens sales cycles, and increases cost of sales.

How to get *your* sales and marketing teams to start working together? Kotler, Rackham, and Krishnaswamy recommend crafting a new relationship between them, one with the right degree of interconnection to tackle your most pressing business challenges.

For example, is your market becoming more commoditized or customized? If so, **align** Sales and Marketing through frequent, disciplined cross-functional communication and joint projects. Is competition becoming more complex than ever? Then fully **integrate** the teams, by having them share performance metrics and rewards and embedding marketers deeply in management of key accounts.

Create the *right* relationship between Sales and Marketing, and you reduce internecine squabbling, enabling these former combatants to boost top- *and* bottom-line growth, together.

- Companies can take practical steps to move the two functions into a more productive relationship, once they've established where the groups are starting from.

Different Roles for Marketing

Before we look closely at the relationship between the two groups, we need to recognize that the nature of the marketing function varies significantly from company to company.

Most small businesses (and most businesses *are* small) don't establish a formal marketing group at all. Their marketing ideas come from managers, the sales force, or an advertising agency. Such businesses equate marketing with selling; they don't conceive of marketing as a broader way to position their firms.

Idea in Practice

How interconnected should *your* Sales and Marketing teams be? The authors recommend determining their existing relationship, then strengthening interconnection if conditions warrant.

What's the Current Relationship?

The relationship is . . .	If sales and marketing . . .
Undefined	• Focus on their own tasks and agendas unless conflict arises between them. • Have developed independently. • Devote meetings between them to conflict resolution, not proactive collaboration.
Defined	• Have rules for preventing disputes. • Share a language for potentially contentious areas (e.g., defining a "lead"). • Use meetings to clarify mutual expectations.
Aligned	• Have clear but flexible boundaries: salespeople use marketing terminology; marketers participate in transactional sales. • Engage in joint planning and training.
Integrated	• Share systems, performance metrics, and rewards. • Behave as if they'll "rise or fall together."

Should You Create More Interconnection?

Strengthening Sales/Marketing interconnection isn't always necessary. For example, if your company is small and the teams operate independently while enjoying positive, informal relationships, don't interfere. The table offers guidelines for companies that *do* need change.

If the current relationship is . . .	**and . . .**	**Then move the relationship to . . .**	**by . . .**
Undefined	• Sales and Marketing have frequent conflicts and compete over resources. • Effort is duplicated, or tasks fall between the cracks.	Defined	• Creating clear rules of engagement, including hand-off points for important tasks (such as lead follow-up).
Defined	• The market is becoming commoditized or customized. • Product life cycles are shortening. • Despite clarified roles, efforts are still duplicated or tasks neglected.	Aligned	• Establishing regular meetings between Sales and Marketing to discuss major opportunities and problems. • Defining who should be consulted on which decisions (e.g., "Involve the brand manager in $2 million+ sales opportunities"). • Creating opportunities for Sales and Marketing to collaborate—for example, planning a conference together or rotating jobs.
Aligned	• The business landscape is marked by complexity and rapid change. • Marketing has split into upstream (strategic) and downstream (tactical) groups.	Integrated	• Having downstream marketers develop sales tools, help salespeople qualify leads, and use feedback from Sales to sell existing offerings to new market segments. • Evaluating and rewarding both teams' performance based on shared important metrics. For instance, establish a sales goal to which both teams commit. And define key sales metrics—such as number of new customers and closings—for salespeople *and* downstream marketers.

Eventually, successful small businesses add a marketing person (or persons) to help relieve the sales force of some chores. These new staff members conduct research to calibrate the size of the market, choose the best markets and channels, and determine potential buyers' motives and influences. They work with outside agencies on advertising and promotions. They develop collateral materials to help the sales force attract customers and close sales. And, finally, they use direct mail, telemarketing, and trade shows to find and qualify leads for the sales force. Both Sales and Marketing see the marketing group as an adjunct to the sales force at this stage, and the relationship between the functions is usually positive.

As companies become larger and more successful, executives recognize that there is more to marketing than setting the four P's: product, pricing, place, and promotion. They determine that effective marketing calls for people skilled in segmentation, targeting, and positioning. Once companies hire marketers with those skills, Marketing becomes an independent player. It also starts to compete with Sales for funding. While the sales mission has not changed, the marketing mission has. Disagreements arise. Each function takes on tasks it believes the other should be doing but isn't. All too often, organizations find that they have a marketing function inside Sales, and a sales function inside Marketing. At this stage, the salespeople wish that the marketers would worry about future opportunities (long-term strategy) and leave the current opportunities (individual and group sales) to them.

Once the marketing group tackles higher-level tasks like segmentation, it starts to work more closely with other departments, particularly Strategic Planning, Product Development, Finance, and Manufacturing. The company starts to think in terms of developing brands rather than products, and brand managers become powerful players in the organization. The marketing group is no longer a humble ancillary to the sales department. It sets its sights much higher: The marketers believe it's essential to transform the organization into a "marketing-led" company. As they introduce this rhetoric, others in the firm—including the sales group—question whether the marketers have the competencies, experience, and understanding to lead the organization.

While Marketing increases its influence within separate business units, it rarely becomes a major force at the corporate level. There are exceptions: Citigroup, Coca-Cola, General Electric, IBM, and Microsoft each have a marketing head at the corporate level. And Marketing is more apt to drive company strategy in major packaged-goods companies such as General Mills, Kraft, and Procter & Gamble. Even then, though, during economic downturns, Marketing is more closely questioned—and its workforce more likely to be cut—than Sales.

Why Can't They Just Get Along?

There are two sources of friction between Sales and Marketing. One is economic, and the other is cultural. The economic friction is generated by the need to divide the total budget granted by senior management to support Sales and Marketing. In fact, the sales force is apt to criticize how Marketing spends money on three of the four P's—pricing, promotion, and product. Take pricing. The marketing group is under pressure to achieve revenue goals and wants the sales force to "sell the price" as opposed to "selling through price." The salespeople usually favor lower prices because they can sell the product more easily and because low prices give them more room to negotiate. In addition, there are organizational tensions around pricing decisions. While Marketing is responsible for setting suggested retail or list prices and establishing promotional pricing, Sales has the final say over transactional pricing. When special low pricing is required, Marketing frequently has no input. The vice president of sales goes directly to the CFO. This does not make the marketing group happy.

Promotion costs, too, are a source of friction. The marketing group needs to spend money to generate customers' awareness of, interest in, preference for, and desire for a product. But the sales force often views the large sums spent on promotion—particularly on television advertising—as a waste of money. The VP of sales tends to think that this money would be better spent increasing the size and quality of the sales force.

When marketers help set the other P, the product being launched, salespeople often complain that it lacks the features, style, or quality their customers want. That's because the sales group's worldview is shaped by the needs of its individual customers. The marketing team, however, is concerned about releasing products whose features have broad appeal.

The budget for both groups also reflects which department wields more power within the organization, a significant factor. CEOs tend to favor the sales group when setting budgets. One chief executive told us, "Why should I invest in more marketing when I can get better results by hiring more salespeople?" CEOs often see sales as more tangible, with more short-run impact. The sales group's contributions to the bottom line are also easier to judge than the marketers' contributions.

The cultural conflict between Sales and Marketing is, if anything, even more entrenched than the economic conflict. This is true in part because the two functions attract different types of people who spend their time in very different ways. Marketers, who until recently had more formal education than salespeople, are highly analytical, data oriented, and project focused. They're all about building competitive advantage for the future. They judge their projects' performance with a cold eye, and they're ruthless with a failed initiative. However, that performance focus doesn't always look like action to their colleagues in Sales because it all happens behind a desk rather than out in the field. Salespeople, in contrast, spend their time talking to existing and potential customers. They're skilled relationship builders; they're not only savvy about customers' willingness to buy but also attuned to which product features will fly and which will die. They want to keep moving. They're used to rejection, and it doesn't depress them. They live for closing a sale. It's hardly surprising that these two groups of people find it difficult to work well together.

If the organization doesn't align incentives carefully, the two groups also run into conflicts about seemingly simple things—for instance, which products to focus on selling. Salespeople may push products with lower margins that satisfy quota goals, while Marketing wants them to sell products with higher profit margins and more promising futures. More broadly speaking, the two groups' performance is judged very differently. Salespeople make a living by closing sales, full stop. It's easy to see who (and what) is successful—almost immediately. But the marketing budget is devoted to programs, not people, and it takes much longer to know whether a program has helped to create long-term competitive advantage for the organization.

Four Types of Relationships

Given the potential economic and cultural conflicts, one would expect some strains to develop between the two groups. And, indeed, some level of dysfunction usually does exist, even in cases where the heads of Sales and Marketing are friendly. The sales and marketing departments in the companies we studied exhibit four types of relationships. The relationships change as the companies' marketing and sales functions mature—the groups move from being unaligned (and often conflicted) to being fully integrated (and usually conflict-free)—though we've seen only a few cases where the two functions are fully integrated.

How well do Sales and Marketing work together?

This instrument (see next page) is intended to help you gauge how well your sales and marketing groups are aligned and integrated. Ask your heads of Sales and Marketing (as well as their staffs) to evaluate each of the following statements on a scale of 1 to 5, where 1 is "strongly disagree" and 5 is "strongly agree." Tally the numbers, and use the scoring key to determine the kind of relationship Sales and Marketing have in your company. The higher the score, the more integrated the relationship. (Several companies have found that their sales forces and their marketing staffs have significantly different perceptions about how well they work together—which in itself is quite interesting.)

(continued)

	Strongly Disagree 1	Disagree 2	Neither 3	Agree 4	Strongly Agree 5
1. Our sales figures are usually close to the sales forecast.	___	___	___	___	___
2. If things go wrong, or results are disappointing, neither function points fingers or blames the other.	___	___	___	___	___
3. Marketing people often meet with key customers during the sales process.	___	___	___	___	___
4. Marketing solicits participation from Sales in drafting the marketing plan.	___	___	___	___	___
5. Our salespeople believe the collateral supplied by Marketing is a valuable tool to help them get more sales.	___	___	___	___	___
6. The sales force willingly cooperates in supplying feedback requested by Marketing.	___	___	___	___	___
7. There is a great deal of common language here between Sales and Marketing.	___	___	___	___	___
8. The heads of Sales and Marketing regularly confer about upstream issues such as idea generation, market sensing, and product development strategy.	___	___	___	___	___
9. Sales and Marketing work closely together to define segment buying behavior.	___	___	___	___	___
10. When Sales and Marketing meet, they do not need to spend much time on dispute resolution and crisis management.	___	___	___	___	___
11. The heads of Sales and Marketing work together on business planning for products and services that will not be launched for two or more years.	___	___	___	___	___

12. We discuss and use common metrics for determining the success of Sales and Marketing.	___	___	___	___	___
13. Marketing actively participates in defining and executing the sales strategy for individual key accounts.	___	___	___	___	___
14. Sales and Marketing manage their activities using jointly developed business funnels, processes, or pipelines that span the business chain—from initial market sensing to customer service.	___	___	___	___	___
15. Marketing makes a significant contribution to analyzing data from the sales funnel and using those data to improve the predictability and effectiveness of the funnel.	___	___	___	___	___
16. Sales and Marketing share a strong "We rise or fall together" culture.	___	___	___	___	___
17. Sales and Marketing report to a single chief customer officer, chief revenue officer, or equivalent C-level executive.	___	___	___	___	___
18. There's significant interchange of people between Sales and Marketing.	___	___	___	___	___
19. Sales and Marketing jointly develop and deploy training programs, events, and learning opportunities for their respective staffs.	___	___	___	___	___
20. Sales and Marketing actively participate in the preparation and presentation of each other's plans to top executives.	___	___	___	___	___

Scoring	
20–39 Undefined	60–79 Aligned
40–59 Defined	80–100 Integrated

___ + ___ + ___ + ___ + ___

= ___ Total

Undefined

When the relationship is undefined, Sales and Marketing have grown independently; each is preoccupied largely with its own tasks and agendas. Each group doesn't know much about what the other is up to—until a conflict arises. Meetings between the two, which are ad hoc, are likely to be devoted to conflict resolution rather than proactive cooperation.

Defined

In a defined relationship, the two groups set up processes—and rules—to prevent disputes. There's a "good fences make good neighbors" orientation; the marketers and salespeople know who is supposed to do what, and they stick to their own tasks for the most part. The groups start to build a common language in potentially contentious areas, such as "How do we define a lead?" Meetings become more reflective; people raise questions like "What do we expect of one another?" The groups work together on large events like customer conferences and trade shows.

Aligned

When Sales and Marketing are aligned, clear boundaries between the two exist, but they're flexible. The groups engage in joint planning and training. The sales group understands and uses marketing terminology such as "value proposition" and "brand image." Marketers confer with salespeople on important accounts. They play a role in transactional, or commodity, sales as well.

Integrated

When Sales and Marketing are fully integrated, boundaries become blurred. Both groups redesign the relationship to share structures, systems, and rewards. Marketing—and to a lesser degree Sales—begins to focus on strategic, forward-thinking types of tasks (market sensing, for instance) and sometimes splits into upstream and downstream groups. Marketers are deeply embedded in the management of key accounts. The two groups develop and implement shared metrics.

Budgeting becomes more flexible and less contentious. A "rise or fall together" culture develops.

We designed an assessment tool that can help organizations gauge the relationship between their sales and marketing departments. (See the exhibit "How well do Sales and Marketing work together?") We originally developed this instrument to help us understand what we were seeing in our research, but the executives we were studying quickly appropriated it for their own use. Without an objective tool of this kind, it's very difficult for managers to judge their cultures and their working environments.

Moving Up

Once an organization understands the nature of the relationship between its marketing and sales groups, senior managers may wish to create a stronger alignment between the two. (It's not always necessary, however. The exhibit "Do we need to be more aligned?" can help organizations decide whether to make a change.)

Moving from undefined to defined

If the business unit or company is small, members of Sales and Marketing may enjoy good, informal relationships that needn't be disturbed. This is especially true if Marketing's role is primarily to support the sales force. However, senior managers should intervene if conflicts arise regularly. As we noted earlier, this generally happens because the groups are competing for scarce resources and because their respective roles haven't been clearly defined. At this stage, managers need to create clear rules of engagement, including handoff points for important tasks like following up on sales leads.

Moving from defined to aligned

The defined state can be comfortable for both parties. "It may not be perfect," one VP of sales told us, "but it's a whole lot better than it was." Staying at this level won't work, though, if your industry is changing in significant ways. If the market is becoming commoditized, for

Do we need to be more aligned?

The nature of relations between Sales and Marketing in your organization can run the gamut—from undefined (the groups act independent of one another) to integrated (the groups share structures, systems, and rewards). Not every company will want to—or should—move from being undefined to being defined or from being defined to being aligned. The following table can help you decide under which circumstances your company should more tightly integrate its sales and marketing functions.

	Undefined	Defined	Aligned
Don't make any changes if . . .	The company is small. The company has good informal relationships. Marketing is still a sales support function.	The company's products and services are fairly cut-and-dried. Traditional marketing and sales roles work in this market. There's no clear and compelling reason to change.	The company lacks a culture of shared responsibility. Sales and Marketing report separately. The sales cycle is fairly short.
Tighten the relationship between Sales and Marketing if . . .	Conflicts are evident between the two functions. There's duplication of effort between the functions; or tasks are falling through the cracks. The functions compete for resources or funding.	Even with careful definition of roles, there's duplication of effort between the functions; or tasks are falling through the cracks. The market is commoditized and makes a traditional sales force costly. Products are developed, or prototyped, or extensively customized during the sales process. Product life cycles are shortening, and technology turnover is accelerating.	A common process or business funnel can be created for managing and measuring revenue-generating activities.
	→ move to Defined	→ move to Aligned	→ move to Integrated

example, a traditional sales force may become costly. Or if the market is moving toward customization, the sales force will need to upgrade its skills. The heads of Sales and Marketing may want to build a more aligned relationship and jointly add new skills. To move from a defined relationship to an aligned one, do the following.

Encourage disciplined communication. When it comes to improving relations between any two functions, the first step inevitably involves improving communication. But it's not as simple as just increasing communication between two groups. More communication is expensive. It eats up time, and it prolongs decision making. We advocate instead for more disciplined communication. Hold regular meetings between Sales and Marketing (at least quarterly, perhaps bimonthly or monthly). Make sure that major opportunities, as well as any problems, are on the agenda. Focus the discussions on action items that will resolve problems, and perhaps even create opportunities, by the next meeting. Salespeople and marketers need to know when and with whom they should communicate. Companies should develop systematic processes and guidelines such as, "You should involve the brand manager whenever the sales opportunity is above $2 million," or "We will not go to print on any marketing collateral until salespeople have reviewed it," or "Marketing will be invited to the top ten critical account reviews." Businesses also need to establish an up-to-date, user-friendly "who to call" database. People get frustrated—and they waste time—searching in the wrong places for help.

Create joint assignments; rotate jobs. As your functions become better aligned, it's important to create opportunities for marketers and salespeople to work together. This will make them more familiar with each other's ways of thinking and acting. It's useful for marketers, particularly brand managers and researchers, to occasionally go along on sales calls. They should get involved with developing alternate solutions for customers, early in the sales process. And they should also sit in on important account-planning sessions. Salespeople, in turn, should help to develop marketing plans and should sit in on product-planning reviews. They should preview ad and sales-promotion campaigns. They should share their deep knowledge about customers' purchasing habits. Jointly, marketers and salespeople should generate a playbook for expanding business with the top ten accounts in each market segment. They should also plan events and conferences together.

Appoint a liaison from Marketing to work with the sales force. The liaison needs to be someone both groups trust. He or she helps to resolve conflicts and shares with each group the tacit knowledge from the other group. It's important not to micromanage the liaison's activities. One of the Marketing respondents in our study described the liaison's role this way: "This is a person who lives with the sales force. He goes to the staff meetings, he goes to the client meetings, and he goes to the client strategy meetings. He doesn't develop product; he comes back and says, 'Here's what this market needs. Here's what's emerging,' and then he works hand in hand with the salesperson and the key customer to develop products."

Colocate marketers and salespeople. It's an old and simple truth that when people are physically close, they will interact more often and are more likely to work well together. One bank we studied located its sales and marketing functions in an empty shopping mall: Different groups and teams within Sales and Marketing were each allocated a storefront. Particularly in the early stages of moving functions toward a more closely aligned relationship, this kind of proximity is a big advantage. Most companies, though, centralize their marketing function, while the members of their sales group remain geographically dispersed. Such organizations need to work harder to facilitate communication between Sales and Marketing and to create shared work.

Improve sales force feedback. Marketers commonly complain that salespeople are too busy to share their experiences, ideas, and insights. Indeed, very few salespeople have an incentive to spend their precious time sharing customer information with Marketing. They have quotas to reach, after all, and limited time in which to meet and sell to customers. To more closely align Sales and Marketing, senior managers need to ensure that the sales force's experience can be tapped with a minimum of disruption. For instance, Marketing can ask the Sales VP to summarize any sales force insights for the month or the quarter. Or Marketing can design shorter information forms, review call reports and CRM data independently, or pay salespeople to make themselves available to interviewers from the marketing group and to summarize what their sales colleagues are thinking about.

Moving from aligned to integrated

Most organizations will function well when Sales and Marketing are aligned. This is especially true if the sales cycle is relatively short, the sales process is fairly straightforward, and the company doesn't have a strong culture of shared responsibility. In complicated or quickly changing situations, there are good reasons to move Sales and Marketing into an integrated relationship. (The exhibit "Sales and Marketing integration checklist" outlines the issues you'll want to think through.) This means integrating such straightforward activities as planning, target setting, customer assessment, and value-proposition development. It's tougher, though, to integrate the two groups' processes and systems; these must be replaced with common processes, metrics, and reward systems. Organizations need to develop shared databases, as well as mechanisms for continuous improvement. Hardest of all is changing the culture to support integration. The best examples of integration we found were in companies that already emphasized shared responsibility and disciplined planning; that were metrics driven; that tied rewards to results; and that were managed through systems and processes. To move from an aligned relationship to an integrated one:

Appoint a chief revenue (or customer) officer. The main rationale for integrating Sales and Marketing is that the two functions have a common goal: the generation of profitable and increasing revenue.

Sales and Marketing integration checklist

To achieve integration between Sales and Marketing, your company needs to focus on the following tasks.

Integrate activities	Integrate processes and systems	Enable the culture	Integrate organizational structures
☐ Jointly involve Sales and Marketing in product planning and in setting sales targets.	☐ Implement systems to track and manage Sales and Marketing's joint activities.	☐ Emphasize shared responsibility for results between the different divisions of the organization.	☐ Split Marketing into upstream and downstream teams.
☐ Jointly involve Sales and Marketing in generating value propositions for different market segments.	☐ Utilize and regularly update shared databases.	☐ Emphasize metrics.	☐ Hire a chief revenue officer.
☐ Jointly involve Sales and Marketing in assessing customer needs.	☐ Establish common metrics for evaluating the overall success of Sales and Marketing efforts.	☐ Tie rewards to results.	
☐ Jointly involve Sales and Marketing in signing off on advertising materials.	☐ Create reward systems to laud successful efforts by Sales and Marketing.	☐ Enforce divisions' conformity to systems and processes.	
☐ Jointly involve Sales and Marketing in analyzing the top opportunities by segment.	☐ Mandate that teams from Sales and Marketing meet periodically to review and improve relations.		
	☐ Require Sales and Marketing heads to attend each other's budget reviews with the CEO.		

The buying funnel

There's a conventional view that Marketing should take responsibility for the first four steps of the typical buying funnel—customer awareness, brand awareness, brand consideration, and brand preference. (The funnel reflects the ways that Marketing and Sales influence customers' purchasing decisions.) Marketing builds brand preference, creates a marketing plan, and generates leads for sales before handing off execution and follow-up tasks to Sales. This division of labor keeps Marketing focused on strategic activities and prevents the group from intruding in individual sales opportunities. But if things do not go well, the blame game begins. Sales criticizes the plan for the brand, and Marketing accuses Sales of not working hard enough or smart enough.

The sales group is responsible for the last four steps of the funnel—purchase intention, purchase, customer loyalty, and customer advocacy. Sales usually develops its own funnel for the selling tasks that happen during the first two steps. (These include prospecting, defining needs, preparing and presenting proposals, negotiating contracts, and implementing the sale.) Apart from some lead generation in the prospecting stage, Marketing all too often plays no role in these tasks.

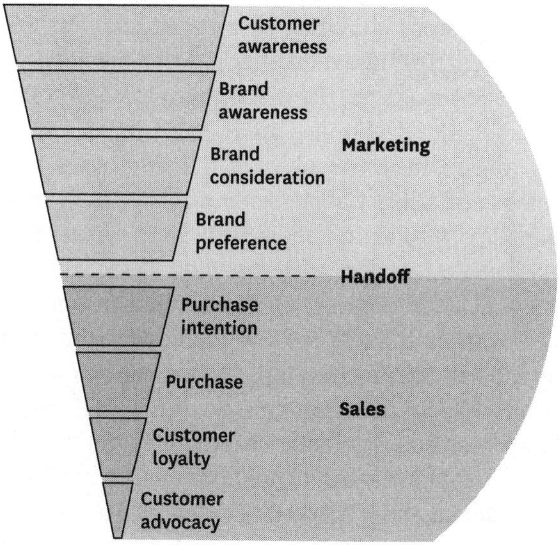

It is logical to put both functions under one C-level executive. Companies such as Campbell's Soup, Coca-Cola, and FedEx have a chief revenue officer (CRO) who is responsible for planning for and delivering the revenue needed to meet corporate objectives. The CRO needs control over the forces affecting revenue—specifically, marketing, sales, service, and pricing. This manager could also be called the chief customer officer (CCO), a title used in such companies as Kellogg; Sears, Roebuck; and United Air Lines. The CCO may be more of a customer ombudsman or customer advocate in some companies; but the title can also signal an executive's broader responsibility for revenue management.

Define the steps in the marketing and sales funnels. Sales and Marketing are responsible for a sequence of activities and events (sometimes called a funnel) that leads customers toward purchases and, hopefully, ongoing relationships. Such funnels can be described from the customer's perspective or from the seller's perspective. (A typical funnel based on the customer's decision sequence is shown in the exhibit "The buying funnel.") Marketing is usually responsible for the first few steps—building customers' brand awareness and brand preference, creating a marketing plan, and generating leads for sales. Then Sales executes the marketing plan and follows up on leads. This division of labor has merit. It is simple, and it prevents Marketing from getting too involved in individual sales opportunities at the expense of more strategic activities. But the handoff brings serious penalties. If things do not go well, Sales can say that the plan was weak, and Marketing can say that the salespeople did not work hard enough or smart enough. And in companies where Marketing makes a handoff, marketers can lose touch with active customers. Meanwhile, Sales usually develops its own funnel describing the sequence of selling tasks. Funnels of this kind—integrated into the CRM system and into sales forecasting and account-review processes—form an increasingly important backbone for sales management. Unfortunately, Marketing often plays no role in these processes. Some companies in our study, however, have integrated Marketing into the sales funnel. During prospecting and qualifying, for instance, Marketing helps Sales to create common standards for leads and opportunities. During the needs-definition stage, Marketing helps Sales develop value propositions. In the solution-development phase, Marketing provides "solution collateral"—organized templates and customizing guides so salespeople can develop solutions for customers without constantly having to reinvent the wheel. When customers are nearing a decision, Marketing contributes case study material, success stories, and site visits to help address customers' concerns. And during contract negotiations, Marketing advises the sales team on planning and pricing. Of course, Marketing's involvement in the sales funnel should be matched by Sales' involvement in the upstream, strategic decisions the marketing group is making. Salespeople should work with the marketing and R&D staffs as they decide how to segment the market, which products to offer to which segments, and how to position those products.

Split Marketing into two groups. There's a strong case for splitting Marketing into upstream (strategic) and downstream (tactical) groups. Downstream marketers develop advertising and promotion campaigns, collateral material, case histories, and sales tools. They help salespeople develop and qualify leads. The downstream team uses market research and feedback from the sales reps to help sell existing products in new market segments, to create new messages, and to design better sales tools. Upstream marketers engage in customer sensing. That is, they monitor the voice of the customer and develop a long view of the company's business opportunities and threats. The upstream team shares its insights with senior managers and product developers—and it participates in product development.

Set shared revenue targets and reward systems. The integrated organization will not succeed unless Sales and Marketing share responsibility for revenue objectives. One marketing manager told us, "I'm going to use whatever tools I need to make sure Sales is effective, because, at the end of the day, I'm judged on that sales target as well." One of the barriers to shared objectives, however, is the thorny issue of shared rewards. Salespeople historically work on commission, and marketers don't. To successfully integrate the two functions, management will need to review the overall compensation policy.

Integrate Sales and Marketing metrics. The need for common metrics becomes critical as Marketing becomes more embedded in the sales process and as Sales plays a more active role in Marketing. "In order to be the customer-intimate company we are," says Larry Norman, president of Financial Markets Group, part of the Aegon USA operating companies, "we need to be metrics driven and have metrics in place that track both sales and marketing performance." On a macro level, companies like General Electric have "the number"—the sales goal to which both Sales and Marketing commit. There is no escaping the fact that, however well integrated Sales and Marketing are, the company will also want to develop metrics to measure and reward each group appropriately.

Sales metrics are easier to define and track. Some of the most common measures are percent of sales quota achieved, number of new customers, number of sales closings, average gross profit per customer, and sales expense to total sales. When downstream marketers become embedded in the sales process—for example, as members of critical account teams—it's only logical to measure and reward their performance using sales metrics. But then how should the company evaluate its upstream marketers? On the basis of the accuracy of their product forecasting, or the number of new market segments they discover? The metrics will vary according to the type of marketing job. Senior managers need to establish different measures for brand managers, market researchers, marketing information systems managers, advertising managers, sales promotion managers, market segment managers, and product managers. It's easier to construct a set of metrics if the marketers' purposes and tasks are clearly outlined. Still, given that upstream marketers are more engaged in sowing the seeds for a better future than in helping to reap the current harvest, the metrics used to judge their performance necessarily become softer and more judgmental.

Obviously, the difference between judging current and future outcomes makes it more complicated for companies to develop common metrics for Sales and Marketing. Upstream marketers in particular need to be assessed according to what they deliver over a longer period. Salespeople, meanwhile, are in the business of converting potential demand into today's sales. As the working relationship between Sales and Marketing becomes more interactive and interdependent, the integrated organization will continue to wrestle with this difficult, but surely not insurmountable, problem.

Senior managers often describe the working relationship between Sales and Marketing as unsatisfactory. The two functions, they say, undercommunicate, underperform, and overcomplain. Not every company will want to—or should—upgrade from defined to aligned relationships or from aligned to integrated relationships. But every company can and should improve the relationship between Sales and Marketing. Carefully planned enhancements will bring salespeople's intimate knowledge of your customers into the company's core. These improvements will also help you serve customers better now and will help you build better products for the future. They will help your company marry softer, relationship-building skills with harder, analytic skills. They will force your organization to closely consider how it rewards people and whether those reward systems apply fairly across functions. Best of all, these improvements will boost both your top-line and bottom-line growth.

Originally published in July 2006. Reprint R0607E

About the Contributors

ROLAND T. RUST is the David Bruce Smith Chair in Marketing at the University of Maryland's Robert H. Smith School of Business.

CHRISTINE MOORMAN is the T. Austin Finch, Sr., Professor of Business Administration at Duke University's Fuqua School of Business.

GAURAV BHALLA is the president of Knowledge Kinetics, based in Reston, Virginia.

DAVID C. EDELMAN is a global coleader of the Digital Marketing and Sales practice at McKinsey & Company.

THEODORE LEVITT was a longtime professor of marketing at Harvard Business School.

CLAYTON M. CHRISTENSEN is the Kim B. Clark Professor of Business Administration at Harvard Business School.

SCOTT COOK is cofounder and chairman of Intuit, based in Mountain View, California.

TADDY HALL is the chief operations officer at Meteor Solutions in Seattle.

KEVIN LANE KELLER is the E. B. Osborn Professor of Marketing at the Tuck School of Business at Dartmouth College.

MICHAEL J. SILVERSTEIN is a senior partner in the Boston Consulting Group's Chicago office.

KATE SAYRE is a partner in the Boston Consulting Group's New York office.

JAMES C. ANDERSON is the William L. Ford Distinguished Professor of Marketing and Wholesale Distribution at Northwestern's Kellogg School of Management.

JAMES A. NARUS is a professor of business marketing at Wake Forest University.

WOUTER VAN ROSSUM is a professor of commercial and strategic management at the University of Twente, The Netherlands.

SUSAN FOURNIER is a professor of marketing at Boston University.

LARA LEE is the president of Outdoor Services.

FREDERICK F. REICHHELD is a director emeritus of the consulting firm Bain & Company and a Bain Fellow.

PHILIP KOTLER is the S. C. Johnson & Son Professor of International Marketing at Northwestern's Kellogg School of Management.

NEIL RACKHAM is a speaker and writer on sales and marketing.

SUJ KRISHNASWAMY is the founder and a principal of Strategic Insights, a Chicago-based business strategy and market research firm specializing in sales-marketing interface.

Index